THE
COLUMBIA
DICTIONARY OF
QUOTATIONS

THE
COLUMBIA
DICTIONARY OF
QUOTATIONS

ROBERT ANDREWS

COLUMBIA UNIVERSITY PRESS   **NEW YORK**

This book is dedicated to

two dimpled lunatics

—Quincy and Evelina—

who prefer books with pictures

COLUMBIA UNIVERSITY PRESS
NEW YORK/CHICHESTER, WEST SUSSEX

Library of Congress Cataloging-in-Publication Data

Andrews, Robert, 1957-

The Columbia book of quotations / Robert Andrews.

p.   cm.

Includes index.

ISBN 0-231-07194-9

1. Quotations, English. 2. Quotations. I. Title.

PN6081.A652   1993

082—dc20   93-27305

                              CIP

Typeface: Times Roman

Designer: Teresa Bonner

Compositor: Columbia University Press

Printer & Binder: Rand McNally

Handlettering on title page by John Stevens

Casebound editions of Columbia University Press books
are printed on permanent and durable acid-free paper.

Printed in the United States of America

c 10 9 8 7 6 5 4 3 2 1

CONTENTS

INTRODUCTION

"Next to the originator of a good sentence is the first quoter of it."—*Ralph Waldo Emerson*

The art of quotation is as old as human speech, and collections of writings and sayings have been with us since the invention of letters. It seems that we have need of a corpus of recognized authorities to bolster our knowledge or confirm our beliefs. Books of quotations are an elemental model of how culture is perpetuated, the wisdom of the tribe passed on to posterity, to be added to, edited, and modified by subsequent generations. But whereas many anthologies remain content to recycle inventories of ancestral wisdom, cataloguing our cultural waymarks according to the gnomic pronouncements of our forebears, *The Columbia Dictionary of Quotations* is a book intended for our own times; its keynote is not familiarity, but aptness. It embraces the past in order to illustrate the present.

Arranged under topics which reflect the gamut of human experience, the quotations in this book have been chosen because they matter, because they were spoken or written by people who matter, and because they address issues as important now as they were for Ben Jonson or Benjamin Franklin. Thus, alongside the established sources I have included others, many previously unanthologized, or at best under-represented, in other collections—figures modern as well as old—who collectively constitute the shapers of our modern cultural landscape.

This format has allowed me to venture far beyond the confines of the conventional quotation anthology, bringing to light all but forgotten sources as well as deeper insights into those icons whom we have always presumed to know. In the welter of unfiltered information unleashed by the media age, it is easy to lose sight of the authentic wellsprings that have fertilized our thought and shaped our consciousness. Fashions change, and increasingly there is a need for us to take stock, to remind ourselves of these formative influences both past and present, to help us understand who we are, where we have come from, where we might end. If, in perusing this mosaic of aperçus and opinions, you find yourself stimulated, subverted, or enlightened, it may well be the challenge of confronting your own image that has aroused you.

The inescapable impression that strikes the reader of these clashing perspectives is how the same topics absorbed the minds of different generations and how "modern" so many of the discussions of them appear to us today: on EQUALITY, for example; on LITERATURE AND SOCIETY; on BUSINESS AND COMMERCE; and on CHILDREN. In assembling all this material, I have been impressed, as I hope the reader will be, not so much by how reactions to these eternal themes have differed through the centuries, but by the degree to which they varied within the same generation and converged across the gulf of years. "Elegant juxtapositions are one of the delights of any anthology," wrote the author A. S. Byatt: here they are accidental, but no less pleasurable. To sift through these quotations is to eavesdrop on an endless argument, a vociferous hubbub of voices that alternately shocks and soothes. Some are, in the words German critic Walter Benjamin, "like wayside robbers who leap out armed and relieve the stroller of his conviction," while others achieve that rate perfection of style summarized by Pope, "What oft was thought, but ne'er so well expressed."

Quotations have been selected on the basis that it is just as important for us to know what Susan Sontag and John Updike said on a certain subject as it is to acquaint ourselves with the views of Jonathan Swift and Henry David Thoreau on the same. Harriet Martineau had an opinion: what was it? Walter Lippmann was a giant in the field of twentieth-century political thought: let us remind ourselves of his argument. Similarly, we need to know what the Marquis de Sade thought about society and moral values, just as we need to be aware of Andrea Dworkin's viewpoint. It is too easy for stereotypes to congeal around certain figures without going to the trouble of listening to what they have to say. The Bible is an important influence on the world, the Qur'an no less so. Dr. Johnson can amuse and entertain us; so can Lenny Bruce. Dr. Martin Luther King, Jr., was a superb speaker: what did he say? And how exactly did his philosophy differ from that of Malcolm X?

Among the voices that have found space in these pages are those of individuals and groups whose contribution to debate has been seriously under-acknowledged in other collections. These include women, dissenters of all persuasions, minorities, homosexuals and lesbians, and a significant sample from non-English-speaking nations—not because there has been any exercise in positive discrimination, but because their literary and polemical engagement in the perennial questions about ourselves and the world we live in is valuable, and we cannot afford to ignore it.

At the same time I make no apology for taking from many habitués of quotation anthologies—such giants of aphorism and wit as Emerson, Wilde, Johnson, and Montaigne, and such stylists as Proust, Thoreau, Woolf, and George Eliot—virtuosi of literature, who invariably seemed to find (in Coleridge's phrase) "the best words in the best order" to describe their experience of life. Readers can expect to encounter plenty of old acquaintances, known or half-known or dredged up from the recesses of memory. Where this anthology differs markedly from most others is in the fact that no quotation has been included simply because it is famous. Rather, the criteria are wit, grace, originality, relevance, usefulness, and meaning. What has been avoided are those stock quotations that have ceased to carry their original resonance, whether through over-use, misapplication, or by a sort of process of petrification whereby the great sayings have been sucked of their life and reduced to triteness, cliché, and parody. This has excluded a lot of Shakespearian and Biblical material that over the years has lost its edge, not to mention much bad poetry, hymns and anthems, and snatches of speeches or songs that, while well known and possibly well composed, have ceased to have much impact for us at the end of the twentieth century.

Once the bland, the dull, and the over familiar have been sifted, what remains inevitably displays a tendency towards the caustic and antagonistic: the devil, we find, has the best tunes. The finest art has always run counter to received opinion. Similarly, the most pointed quotations are those that undermine our prejudices. Quotability, not niceness or correctness, is the prime requirement for inclusion in this book. On the other hand, demagogues and politicians, who specialize in a highly quotable verbal style, are represented far less often here than the flow of their words might seem to warrant. They, more than anyone, have long recognized the power of quotations, knowing that opinions can be sanctified by appealing to precedent. Above all they have seized on and exploited the fact that the power also runs the other way, that every time they themselves are quoted, they assume the influence of an oracle. But their objectives are too limited, their themes too unoriginal, their messages too ephemeral. Thus we live in the epoch of the "soundbite"—a new word for an old trick that has nonetheless attained new heights of artifice and superficiality. The more recent examples of this spurious, manufactured species of quotation have not been included in this collection, although some older exponents such as Winston Churchill and Theodore Roosevelt can be found here by virtue of their combined historical importance and fine oratory. Slogans and refrains, however, do not figure in these pages, since they lack any personal quality.

Indeed it is this vital personal ingredient that more than anything defines a quotation. Without it the words are orphaned, and for this reason these pages include the bare minimum number of contributions by the usually ubiquitous Anon. (although proverbs have been included when they evoke a particular time and mode). A true quotation cannot be divorced from the character who uttered or scribbled it; it should say as much about the person quoted as about the particular subject referred to, and for this reason an anthology of quotations should be a kind of portrait gallery. *The Columbia Dictionary of Quotations* presents as rich a parade of personalities as can be found within the covers of a single book. Here they are, revealed in all their genius and prejudice, goodness and pathos, profundity and absurdity, heroism and evil. Their extracted speeches and writings represent a motley confection of philosophies, ideologies, preoccupations, and temperaments, imprecation, injunction, or insights offering a quotable commentary on the human condition.

Just as an effective quotation is indissolubly bound with the person who created it, so it is inseparable from the spirit and context in which it was originally phrased. A quotation must be authentic or it loses its vigor, and an important feature of this book is the precise citational and contextual information given—more detailed than any previous anthology has provided. It is not enough to quote Jane Austen saying: "Where an opinion is general, it is usually correct." She did not say it, and in all likelihood would have strongly disagreed with the notion. Mary Crawford said it, a character in Austen's *Mansfield Park*, and the statement loses all its poignancy unless one takes this into account. Likewise, such an immortal remark as "A horse is at least human, for God's sake" is imbued with the unique character of Holden Caulfield, the narrator in J. D. Salinger's *Catcher in the Rye*: we are detracting from its energy and humor if we omit to mention this. Such details vitalize a quotation, prompting images and memories that express more than the words on their own ever can. In the same way no one should credit Oliver Stone with believing that "Lunch is for wimps." Stone put the words in the mouth of Gordon Gekko, played by Michael Douglas in the 1987 movie *Wall Street*. This is information we need to know, not only to quote honestly and incisively, but to avoid looking foolish when we learn that the context of the quotation may undermine its message.

It is also instructive to know something of the circumstances in which a quotation first appeared—that, for example, when Oscar Wilde wrote, in *De Profundis*, "What is said of a man is nothing. The point is, who says it," he was writing to his lover Lord Alfred Douglas following the scandal and trial that ruined Wilde. I have also tried to enhance the interest of certain quotations by drawing attention to others by the same or a different author either in agreement or contradiction. The amount of citational information has been a matter of discretion in each case: essays have rarely required much comment, while letters and journal entries, for example, are enriched by one or two words of context. Characters speaking in fiction and drama are named throughout. Dates of first publication have been given in all cases except plays and short poems, where there is often a distracting discrepancy between dates of composition, performance, and publication. On the whole, information has been given as accurately and concisely as space allows, without succumbing to the temptation to swamp the quotation with extraneous facts. Thus where addressees of letters are little know, their names have been omitted, while if they are members of the writer's family, or have some standing in their own right, they are named. For foreign quotations translation dates are appended with more recent works only, where only one translation exists. Translators are named only when they are considered to be of interest in themselves.

As a rule, the information provided should be sufficient not only to place the quotation in context, but to permit anyone interested to locate the words fairly quickly.

Although accuracy has been a paramount consideration in the reproduction of quotations and citational information, the vagaries of publishing and the existence of variant texts mean that there is always scope for confusion. On the whole, the instances are few in this compilation, athough there are a handful of cases in which it is necessary to specify particular editions that have been used. Quotations from Shakespeare have been drawn from the 1987 Oxford University Press edition of the Complete Works, edited by Stanley Wells and Gary Taylor, in which the arrangements of acts and scenes can diverge significantly from those in some other editions, notably in the plays *Pericles*, *Hamlet*, tand *King Lear* (in *King Lear* I have followed the Folio text). In quoting from Oscar Wilde, I have gone to the original, four-act edition of *The Importance of Being Earnest*, later cut to three acts to satisfy theatrical exigencies, in a version which has been subsequently, although unnecessarily, reproduced in many editions. More controversially, quotations from James Joyce's *Ulysses* are from Hans Walter Gabler's "corrected" text, as published by The Bodley Head and Penguin Books in 1986. And lastly, Biblical quotations are taken from the Authorized, or King James, Version.

To quote is to open a form of dialogue, requiring a degree of receptivity on the part of the hearer or reader. There must be an element of recognition of a truth or sentiment, something that sets bells chiming and thoughts racing down newly remembered tracks. Even when it is a strikingly original notion, a fresh formulation, or a felicitous expression, there is always a reference to something in our own experience without which it is merely words. A quotation does not need to be familiar to trigger this response, but it must evoke in us a sense of familiarity. Whether or not the authors quoted in this collection are known to the reader, I hope that browsing through *The Columbia Dictionary of Quotations* will provoke the same thought that recurred to me throughout my research on it: . . . interesting—I would like to know more about this person. My greatest hope is that the selection manages to communicate some of the fun I had in compiling it.

Robert Andrews

ACKNOWLEDGMENTS

A strong thread of family involvement is woven through the history and antecedents of this book. My father, Allen Andrews, set the ball rolling with his *Quotations for Speakers and Writers*, published in 1969. He was at work on a second volume at the time of his death in 1985, a work which I took over and which eventually became *The Concise Columbia Dictionary of Quotations*. A lively interest in this work was taken by my father's twin brother, Andy, and even more by Andy's wife Bim, both of whom contributed to it, as well as to this present collection, for which Andy was sending me original and idiosyncratic suggestions right up to his death in 1992. My mother, Joyce, also read widely and gave considerable time to much of the routine work involved. The presence of all of these family members is strong in these pages, a testimony to the debt I owe them.

Over a period of three and a half years, many other hands were enlisted to bring to fruition *The Columbia Dictionary of Quotations*. First, I should acknowledge the active enthusiasm, encouragement, and—not least—patience of my editor, James Raimes, who in no way deserves the scorn printed on these pages concerning either editors or publishers. The research and drudgery involved in the compilation of the quotations was shared among a number of people, among whom I am particularly grateful to Katie Daniels, Sally Daniels, Perry Guidrey, Joel Hahn, Natasha Hopkins, Angela Jain, Ian Linford, Katia Mele, Susan Plaister, Neil Russell, Julie Rzezniczek, Kerry Satterthwaite, Agata Scamporrino, Gary Seabrook, Tara Swain, Ashly Taggart, and Derek Wall.

In specific areas, Will Ashon was especially helpful in the field of modern American literature, Richard Davoll supplied me with a steady stream of quotations from William Blake and more recondite sources that I would not normally have encountered, while Gill Jackman shared her enthusiasm for and familiarity with the works of George Eliot and Virginia Woolf. To Philip Krynsky, whose formidable powers of research in the currents and eddies of modern European thought were a major contribution to this book, I owe a special note of thanks. His unflagging dedication and generous all-around support were not only of great practical benefit, but he allowed me to share the burdens as well as the excitements generated in the compilation of this book.

Special thanks are also due to Jeffrey Care, of the *Observer* newspaper library, for his permission to make use of the resources under his guardianship and to the staffs of the Bristol University library and the British Library in London, where I was privileged to work under the famous dome before the library's impending transfer to premises that must sadly lack the powerful historical associations of the old building.

At Columbia University Press, Edith Hazen and Frances Kim were particularly helpful with the detailed preparation of the manuscript.

Lastly this dictionary could not have been written without the commitment and stoic forebearance of Jo Morgan, in the multiple roles of researcher, secretary, computer-operator, house-manager, partner, and mother, whose "graceful acts, / Those thousand decencies, that daily flow / From all her words and actions," underpinned the whole enterprise.

THE QUOTATIONS

ABILITY

1 Knowing what you can *not* do is more important than knowing what you can do. In fact, that's good taste.

LUCILLE BALL (1911-89), U.S. actor, producer. Quoted in: Eleanor Harris, *The Real Story of Lucille Ball*, ch. 1 (1954).

2 He is the best sailor who can steer within fewest points of the wind, and exact a motive power out of the greatest obstacles.

HENRY DAVID THOREAU (1817-62), U.S. philosopher, author, naturalist. *A Week on the Concord and Merrimack Rivers*, "Friday" (1849).

ABORTION

1 The one regret I have about my own abortions is that they cost money that might otherwise have been spent on something more pleasurable, like taking the kids to movies and theme parks.

BARBARA EHRENREICH (b. 1941), U.S. author, columnist. *The Worst Years of Our Lives*, "Their Dilemma and Mine" (1991; first published 1989).

2 The emphasis must be not on the right to abortion but on the right to privacy and reproductive control.

RUTH BADER GINSBERG (b. 1933), U.S. educator, Supreme Court justice. Quoted in: *Ms.* (New York, April 1974).

3 The compelled mother loves her child as the caged bird sings. The song does not justify the cage nor the love the enforcement.

GERMAINE GREER (b. 1939), Australian feminist writer. "Abortion," in *Sunday Times* (London, 21 May 1972; repr. in *The Madwoman's Underclothes*, 1986).

4 The cemetery of the victims of human cruelty in our century is extended to include yet another vast cemetery, that of the unborn.

JOHN PAUL II [KAROL WOJTYLA] (b. 1920), Polish ecclesiastic, pope. Quoted in: *Observer* (London, 9 June 1991).

5 The preservation of life seems to be rather a slogan than a genuine goal of the anti-abortion forces; what they want is control. Control over behavior: power over women. Women in the anti-choice movement want to share in male power over women, and do so by denying their own womanhood, their own rights and responsibilities.

URSULA K. LE GUIN (b. 1929), U.S. author. "The Princess," address, Jan. 1982, to National Abortion Rights Action League, Portland, Maine (published in *Dancing at the Edge of the World*, 1989).

6 In the middle-class United States, a veneer of "alternative lifestyles" disguises the reality that, here as everywhere, women's apparent "choices" whether or not to have children are still dependent on the far from neutral will of male legislators, jurists, a male medical and pharmaceutical profession, well-financed lobbies, including the prelates of the Catholic Church, and the political reality that women do not as yet have self-determination over our bodies and still live mostly in ignorance of our authentic physicality, our possible choices, our eroticism itself.

ADRIENNE RICH (b. 1929), U.S. poet. "Motherhood: The Contemporary Emergency and the Quantum Leap," paper, 2 June 1978, read at Future of Mothering Conference, Columbus, Ohio (published in *On Lies, Secrets, and Silence*, 1980).

7 Dread not infanticide; the crime is imaginary: we are always mistress of what we carry in our womb, and we do no more harm in destroying this kind of matter than in evacuating another, by medicines, when we feel the need.

MARQUIS DE SADE (1740-1814), French author. Mme de Saint-Ange, in *Philosophy in the Bedroom*, "Dialogue the Third" (1795).

8 The greatest destroyer of peace is abortion because if a mother can kill her own child, what is left for me to kill you and you to kill me? There is nothing between.

MOTHER TERESA (b. 1910), Albanian-born Roman Catholic missionary in India. Nobel Peace Prize Lecture, 1979.

ABSENCE

1 I was court-martialled in my absence, and sentenced to death in my absence, so I said they could shoot me in my absence.

BRENDAN BEHAN (1923-64), Irish playwright. *The Hostage*, act 1 (1958).

2 Separation penetrates the disappearing person like a pigment and steeps him in gentle radiance.

WALTER BENJAMIN (1892-1940), German critic, philosopher. *One-Way Street*, "Flag. . ." (1928; repr. in *One-Way Street and Other Writings*, 1978).

3 Woman absent is woman dead.

AMBROSE BIERCE (1842-1914), U.S. author. *The Devil's Dictionary* (1881-1906).

4 The heart may think it knows better: the senses know that absence blots people out. We really have no absent friends. The friend becomes a traitor by breaking, however unwillingly or sadly, out of our own zone: a hard judgment is passed on him, for all the pleas of the heart.

ELIZABETH BOWEN (1899-1973), Anglo-Irish novelist. *The Death of the Heart*, pt. 2, ch. 2 (1938).

5 Wives in their husbands' absences grow subtler,
And daughters sometimes run off with the butler.

LORD BYRON (1788-1824), English poet. *Don Juan*, cto. 3, st. 22.

6 It is singular how soon we lose the impression of what ceases to be *constantly* before us; a year impairs; a lustre obliterates. There is little distinct left without an effort of memory. *Then*, indeed, the lights are rekindled for a moment. . . . Let any man try at the end of *ten* years to bring before him the features, or the mind, or the sayings, or the habits, of his best friend.

> LORD BYRON (1788-1824), English poet. *Journal at Ravenna, 1821-22*. Quoted in Doris Langley Moore, *The Late Lord Byron*, ch. 8 (1961; rev. ed., 1976).

7 Our hours in love have wings; in absence, crutches.

> COLLEY CIBBER (1671-1757), English actor-manager, playwright. Tamira, in *Xerxes*, act 4, sc. 3.

8 Separated lovers cheat absence by a thousand fancies which have their own reality. They are prevented from seeing one another and they cannot write; nevertheless they find countless mysterious ways of corresponding, by sending each other the song of birds, the scent of flowers, the laughter of children, the light of the sun, the sighing of the wind, and the gleam of the stars—all the beauties of creation.

> VICTOR HUGO (1802-85), French poet, dramatist, novelist. Marius, in *Les Misérables*, pt. 4, bk. 5, ch. 4 (1862).

9 No man is so perfect, so necessary to his friends, as to give them no cause to miss him less.

> JEAN DE LA BRUYÉRE (1645-96), French writer, moralist. *Characters*, "Of Personal Merit," aph. 35 (1688).

10 Absence lessens the minor passions and increases the great ones, as the wind douses a candle and kindles a fire.

> FRANÇOIS, DUC DE LA ROCHEFOUCAULD (1613-80), French writer, moralist. *Sentences et Maximes Morales*, no. 276 (1678). Comte de Bussy-Rabutin used the same comparison for love: "Absence is to love what wind is to fire; it extinguishes the small, it enkindles the great." (in *Histoire Amoureuse des Gaules*).

11 "Presents," I often say, "endear absents."

> CHARLES LAMB (1775-1834), English essayist, critic. *Essays of Elia*, "A Dissertation Upon Roast Pig" (1820-23).

12 Let me tell you I am better acquainted with you for a long absence, as men are with themselves for a long affliction: absence does but hold off a friend, to make one see him the truer.

> ALEXANDER POPE (1688-1744), English satirical poet. Letter, 14 Dec. 1725, to poet and author Jonathan Swift.

13 How like a winter hath my absence been
From thee, the pleasure of the fleeting year!
What freezings have I felt, what dark days seen,
What old December's bareness everywhere!

> WILLIAM SHAKESPEARE (1564-1616), English dramatist, poet. *Sonnet 97*.

14 When delicate and feeling souls are separated, there is not a feature in the sky, not a movement of the elements, not an aspiration of the breeze, but hints some cause for a lover's apprehension.

> RICHARD BRINSLEY SHERIDAN (1751-1816), Anglo-Irish dramatist. Faulkland, in *The Rivals*, act 2, sc. 1.

ABSTINENCE

1 Renouncement: the heroism of mediocrity.

> NATALIE CLIFFORD BARNEY (1876-1972), U.S.-born French author. Quoted in: "Gods," in *Adam*, no. 299 (London, 1962).

2 With renunciation life begins.

> AMELIA BARR (1831-1919), Anglo-American novelist. *All the Days of My Life*, ch. 9 (1913).

2 Abstainer. A weak man who yields to the temptation of denying himself a pleasure.

> AMBROSE BIERCE (1842-1914), U.S. author. *The Devil's Dictionary* (1881-1906).

4 The best thing to do with the best things in life is to give them up.

> DOROTHY DAY (1897-1980), U.S. religious leader. Quoted in: *Time* (New York, 29 Dec. 1975).

5 Subdue your appetites, my dears, and you've conquered human natur'.

> CHARLES DICKENS (1812-70), English novelist. Mr. Squeers, in *Nicholas Nickleby*, ch. 5 (1838-39).

6 Renunciation remains sorrow, though a sorrow borne willingly.

> GEORGE ELIOT (1819-80), English novelist. *The Mill on the Floss*, bk. 4, ch. 3 (1860).

7 Self-denial is not a virtue: it is only the effect of prudence on rascality.

> GEORGE BERNARD SHAW (1856-1950), Anglo-Irish playwright, critic. *Man and Superman*, "Maxims for Revolutionists: Virtues and Vices" (1903).

8 Self-denial is the shining sore on the leprous body of Christianity.

> OSCAR WILDE (1854-1900), Anglo-Irish playwright, author. Quoted in: Frank Harris, *Oscar Wilde*, ch. 24 (1918).

See also ALCOHOL: ABSTINENCE; ASCETICISM; Blake on LUST; Hugo on SAINTS.

ABSURDITY

1 Absurdity. A statement or belief manifestly inconsistent with one's own opinion.

> AMBROSE BIERCE (1842-1914), U.S. author. *The Devil's Dictionary* (1881-1906).

2 My turn of mind is so given to taking things in the absurd point of view, that it breaks out in spite of me every now and then.

> LORD BYRON (1788-1824), English poet. Remark to the poet Thomas Moore. Quoted in: Doris Langley Moore, *The Late Lord Byron*, ch. 8 (1961; rev. ed., 1976).

3 At any street corner the feeling of absurdity can strike any man in the face.

> ALBERT CAMUS (1913-60), French-Algerian philosopher, author. *The Myth of Sisyphus*, ch. 1, "Absurd Walls" (1942; tr. 1955).

4   It is not funny that anything else should fall down; only that a man should fall down. . . . Why do we laugh? Because it is a gravely religious matter: it is the Fall of Man. Only man can be absurd: for only man can be dignified.

> G. K. CHESTERTON (1874-1936), British author. *All Things Considered,* "Spiritualism" (1908).

5   Modern man must descend the spiral of his own absurdity to the lowest point; only then can he look beyond it. It is obviously impossible to get around it, jump over it, or simply avoid it.

> VÁCLAV HAVEL (b. 1936), Czech playwright, president. *Disturbing the Peace,* ch. 2 (1986; tr. 1990).

6   The privilege of absurdity; to which no living creature is subject, but man only.

> THOMAS HOBBES (1588-1679), English philosopher. *Leviathan,* pt. 1, ch. 5 (1651).

7   It is not in the world of ideas that life is *lived.* Life is lived for better or worse *in* life, and to a man *in* life, his life can be no more absurd than it can be the opposite of absurd, whatever that opposite may be.

> ARCHIBALD MACLEISH (1892-1982), U.S. poet. *Rockefeller University Forum,* "Heaven and Earth and the Cage of Form" (Jan.-Feb. 1968; repr. in *Riders on Earth,* "Return from the Excursion," 1978).

8   We live in a time which has created the art of the absurd. It is our art. It contains happenings, Pop art, camp, a theater of the absurd. . . . Do we have the art because the absurd is the patina of waste. . .? Or are we face to face with a desperate or most rational effort from the deepest resources of the unconscious of us all to rescue civilization from the pit and plague of its bedding?

> NORMAN MAILER (b. 1923), U.S. author. *Cannibals and Christians,* "Introducing our Argument" (1966).

9   There is only one step from the sublime to the ridiculous.

> NAPOLEON BONAPARTE (1769-1821), French general, emperor. Remark, Dec. 1812, to Polish ambassador Abbé de Pradt, on Napoleon's return to Paris by sledge after the failure of his Russian campaign. Quoted in: De Pradt, *Histoire de l'Ambassade dans le Grand-duché de Varsovie en 1812,* p. 215 (1815; also quoted in Comte de Las Cases, *Mémorial de Sainte-Hélène).*

10   In the consciousness of the truth he has perceived, man now sees everywhere only the awfulness or the absurdity of existence. . . and loathing seizes him.

> FRIEDRICH NIETZSCHE (1844-1900), German philosopher. *The Birth of Tragedy,* ch. 7 (1872).

11   The irrationality of a thing is no argument against its existence, rather a condition of it.

> FRIEDRICH NIETZSCHE (1844-1900), German philosopher. *Human, All Too Human,* aph. 332 (1878).

12   Oh, life is a glorious cycle of song,
A medley of extemporanea;
And love is a thing that can never go wrong;
And I am Marie of Roumania.

> DOROTHY PARKER (1893-1967), U.S. humorous writer. *Comment.*

13   People who cannot recognize a palpable absurdity are very much in the way of civilization.

> AGNES REPPLIER (1858-1950), U.S. author, social critic. *In Pursuit of Laughter,* ch. 9 (1936).

14   In the sphere of thought, absurdity and perversity remain the masters of the world, and their dominion is suspended only for brief periods.

> ARTHUR SCHOPENHAUER (1788-1860), German philosopher. "On the Wisdom of Life: Aphorisms." Quoted in: Selected Essays (1851; tr. by T. Bailey Saunders).

See also Knox on DIGNITY.

ABUSE

1   People who treat other people as less than human must not be surprised when the bread they have cast on the waters comes floating back to them, poisoned.

> JAMES BALDWIN (1924-87), U.S. author. *The Price Of The Ticket,* "No Name in the Street" (1985; first published 1972).

2   It's not a slam at *you* when people are rude—it's a slam at the people they've met before.

> F. SCOTT FITZGERALD (1896-1940), U.S. author. Cecilia Brady, in *The Last Tycoon,* ch. 1 (1941).

3   A fly, Sir, may sting a stately horse and make him wince; but one is but an insect, and the other is a horse still.

> SAMUEL JOHNSON (1709-84), English author, lexicographer. Quoted in: James Boswell, *Life of Samuel Johnson,* vol. 1 (1934), note to entry for 20 March 1776.

4   The only cure for contempt is countercontempt.

> H. L. MENCKEN (1880-1956), U.S. journalist. *Minority Report: H. L. Mencken's Notebooks,* no. 99 (1956).

See also INSULTS.

ACADEMIA

1   I realized early on that the academy and the literary world alike—and I don't think there really is a distinction between the two—are always dominated by fools, knaves, charlatans and bureaucrats. And that being the case, any human being, male or female, of whatever status, who has a voice of her or his own, is not going to be liked.

> HAROLD BLOOM (b. 1930), U.S. literary critic, theorist. Interview in *Criticism in Society* (ed. by Imre Salusinski, 1987).

2   There is but one step from the Academy to the Fad.

> SAMUEL BUTLER (1835-1902), English author. *Samuel Butler's Notebooks* (1951, p. 236).

3   If poetry is like an orgasm, an academic can be likened to someone who studies the passion-stains on the bedsheets.

> IRVING LAYTON (b. 1912), Canadian poet. *The Whole Bloody Bird,* "Obs II" (1969).

4   The love of learning, the sequestered nooks,
And all the sweet serenity of books.

> HENRY WADSWORTH LONGFELLOW (1807-82), U.S. poet. *Morituri Salutamus.*

5   A serious problem in America is the gap between academe and the mass media, which *is* our culture. Professors of humanities, with all their leftist fantasies, have little direct knowledge of American life and no impact whatever on public policy.

> CAMILLE PAGLIA (b. 1947), U.S. author, critic, educator. *Sex, Art, and American Culture,* Introduction (1992).

6   Allow me to say that I would long since have committed suicide had desisting made me a professor of Latin.

> EZRA POUND (1885-1972), U.S. poet, critic. Unsent letter, c. 1920, to Professor W. G. Hale of the Univ. of Chicago, in answer to Hale's stinging criticism of Pound's *Homage to Sextus Propertius* in *Poetry* (April 1919). Hale had opined, "If Mr. Pound were a professor of latin, there would be nothing left for him but suicide."

7   Art is not to be taught in Academies. It is what one looks at, not what one listens to, that makes the artist. The real schools should be the streets.

> OSCAR WILDE (1854-1900), Anglo-Irish playwright, author. "The Relation of Dress to Art: A Note in Black and White on Mr. Whistler's Lecture," in *Pall Mall Gazette* (London, 28 Feb. 1885).

8   In universities and intellectual circles, academics can guarantee themselves popularity—or, which is just as satisfying, unpopularity—by being opinionated rather than by being learned.

> A. N. WILSON (b. 1950), British author. *Guardian* book review (London, 30 Sept. 1989).

ACCEPTANCE

1   To *make* oneself an object, to *make* oneself passive, is a very different thing from *being* a passive object.

> SIMONE DE BEAUVOIR (1908-86), French novelist, essayist. *The Second Sex,* bk. 2, pt. 4, ch. 3 (1953).

2   Ah, when to the heart of man
Was it ever less than a treason
To go with the drift of things
To yield with a grace to reason
And bow and accept at the end
Of a love or a season.

> ROBERT FROST (1874-1963), U.S. poet. *Reluctance.*

3   Always fall in with what you're asked to accept. Take what is given, and make it over your way. My aim in life has always been to hold my own with whatever's going. Not against: with.

> ROBERT FROST (1874-1963), U.S. poet. *Vogue* (New York, 14 March 1963).

4   The strongest and most effective [force] in guaranteeing the long-term maintenance of . . . power is not violence in all the forms deployed by the dominant to control the dominated, but consent in all the forms in which the dominated acquiesce in their own domination.

> MAURICE GODELIER (b. 1934), French anthropologist. *The Mental and the Material: Thought, Economy and Society,* Preface (1986).

5   We will have to repent in this generation not merely for the hateful words and actions of the bad people but for the appalling silence of the good people.

> MARTIN LUTHER KING, JR. (1929-1968), U.S. clergyman, civil rights leader. *Why We Can't Wait,* "Letter from Birmingham Jail" (1963).

6   The art of acceptance is the art of making someone who has just done you a small favor wish that he might have done you a greater one.

> RUSSELL LYNES (b. 1910), U.S. editor, critic. *Reader's Digest* (Pleasantville, N.Y., Dec. 1954).

7   Life has no other discipline to impose, if we would but realize it, than to accept life unquestioningly. Everything we shut our eyes to, everything we run away from, everything we deny, denigrate or despise, serves to defeat us in the end. What seems nasty, painful, evil, can become a source of beauty, joy and strength, if faced with an open mind. Every moment is a golden one for him who has the vision to recognize it as such.

> HENRY MILLER (1891-1980), U.S. author. *The World of Sex,* (1940; repr. 1970, p. 101).

8   For the ordinary man is passive. Within a narrow circle (home life, and perhaps the trade unions or local politics) he feels himself master of his fate, but against major events he is as helpless as against the elements. So far from endeavouring to influence the future, he simply lies down and lets things happen to him.

> GEORGE ORWELL (1903-50), British author. *Inside the Whale and Other Essays,* "Inside the Whale" (1940).

9   Some people swallow the universe like a pill; they travel on through the world, like smiling images pushed from behind.

> ROBERT LOUIS STEVENSON (1850-1894), Scottish novelist, essayist, poet. *Virginibus Puerisque,* "Crabbed Age and Youth" (1881).

See also Landor, Shakespeare on DEATH AND DYING.

ACCIDENTS

1   A car crash harnesses elements of eroticism, aggression, desire, speed, drama, kinaesthetic factors, the stylizing of motion, consumer goods, status—all these in one event. I myself see the car crash as a tremenduous sexual event really: a liberation of human and machine libido (if there is such a thing).

> J. G. BALLARD (b. 1930), British author. Interview in *Penthouse* (London, 1970; repr. in *Re/Search,* no. 8/9, San Francisco, 1984).

2   Accidents, try to change them—it's impossible. The accidental reveals man.

> PABLO PICASSO (1881-1973), Spanish artist. Quoted in: *Vogue* (New York, 1 Nov. 1956).

3   I don't believe in accidents. There are only encounters in history. There are no accidents.

> ELIE WIESEL (b. 1928), Rumanian-born U.S. writer. Quoted in:
> *International Herald Tribune* (Paris, 15 Sept. 1992).

ACCOUNTS

1   Keeping accounts, Sir, is of no use when a man is spending his own money, and has nobody to whom he is to account. You won't eat less beef today, because you have written down what it cost yesterday.

> SAMUEL JOHNSON (1709-84), English author, lexicographer.
> Quoted in: James Boswell, *Life of Samuel Johnson*, 1783 (1791).

2   Find myself £43 worse than I was the last month . . . chiefly arisen from my layings-out in clothes for myself and wife; viz., for her, about £12, and for myself, £55 or thereabouts.

> SAMUEL PEPYS (1633-1703), English diarist. Diary entry, 31 Oct. 1663.

3   Counting is the religion of this generation it is its hope and its salvation.

> GERTRUDE STEIN (1874-1946), U.S. author. *Everybody's Autobiography*, ch. 3 (1937).

4   Bourgeois society is infected by monomania: the monomania of accounting. For it, the only thing that has value is what can be counted in francs and centimes. It never hesitates to sacrifice human life to figures which look well on paper, such as national budgets or industrial balance sheets.

> SIMONE WEIL (1909-43), French philosopher, mystic. "La Rationalisation" (written 1937; published in *La Condition Ouvrière*, 1951).

ACCUSATION

1   Accuse. To affirm another's guilt or unworth; most commonly as a justification of ourselves for having wronged him.

> AMBROSE BIERCE (1842-1914), U.S. author. *The Devil's Dictionary* (1881-1906).

2   There are a great many of these accusers, and they have been accusing me now for a great many years, and what is more, they approached you at the most impressionable age, when some of you were children or adolescents; and literally won their case by default, because there was no one to defend me.

> SOCRATES (469-399 B.C.), Greek philosopher. Speech to the jury, during his trial on charges of impiety and corrupting the youth. Quoted in: Plato, *Apology*, sct. 17.

ACHIEVEMENT

1   There are two great rules in life, the one general and the other particular. The first is that every one can in the end get what he wants if he only tries. This is the general rule. The particular rule is that every individual is more or less of an exception to the general rule.

> SAMUEL BUTLER (1835-1902), English author. *Samuel Butler's*

Notebooks (1951), p. 201, quoting Butler's friend and biographer Henry Festing Jones.

2   What in fact have I achieved, however much it may seem? Bits and pieces . . . trivialities. But here they won't tolerate anything else, or anything more. If I wanted to take one step in advance of the current views and opinions of the day, that would put paid to any power I have. Do you know what we are . . . those of us who count as pillars of society? We are society's tools, neither more nor less.

> HENRIK IBSEN (1828-1906), Norwegian dramatist. Bernick, in *Pillars of Society*, act 4.

3   Man can acquire accomplishments or he can become an animal, whichever he wants. God makes the animals, man makes himself.

> G. C. LICHTENBERG (1742-99), German physicist, philosopher. *Aphorisms*, "Notebook F," aph. 49 (written 1765-99; tr. by R. J. Hollingdale, 1990).

4   Man is always more than he can know of himself; consequently, his accomplishments, time and again, will come as a surprise to him.

> GOLO MANN (b. 1909), German historian, son of Thomas Mann. Quoted in: Marcel Reich-Ranicki, *Thomas Mann and His Family*, "Golo Mann—The Liberation of an Unloved One" (1987; tr. 1989).

5   Nothing is as difficult as to achieve results in this world if one is filled full of great tolerance and the milk of human kindness. The person who achieves must generally be a one-ideaed individual, concentrated entirely on that one idea, and ruthless in his aspect toward other men and other ideas.

> CORINNE ROOSEVELT ROBINSON (1861-1933), U.S. poet, sister of Theodore Roosevelt. *My Brother Theodore Roosevelt*, ch. 1 (1921).

6   Man can climb to the highest summits, but he cannot dwell there long.

> GEORGE BERNARD SHAW (1856-1950), Anglo-Irish playwright, critic. Morell, in *Candida*, act 3.

7   When science, art, literature, and philosophy are simply the manifestation of personality they are on a level where glorious and dazzling achievements are possible, which can make a man's name live for thousands of years. But above this level, far above, separated by an abyss, is the level where the highest things are achieved. These things are essentially anonymous.

> SIMONE WEIL (1909-43), French philosopher, mystic. *La Table Ronde*, "Human Personality" (1950; repr. in *Selected Essays*, 1962).

ACQUAINTANCE

1   Acquaintance. A person whom we know well enough to borrow from, but not well enough to lend to.

> AMBROSE BIERCE (1842-1914), U.S. author. *The Devil's Dictionary*, (1881-1906).

2   The beginning of an acquaintance whether with persons or things is to get a definite outline of our ignorance.

> GEORGE ELIOT (1819-80), English novelist. *Daniel Deronda*, bk. 2, ch. 11, epigraph (1874-76).

3   I believe we shall come to care about people less and less. . . . The more people one knows the easier it becomes to replace them. It's one of the curses of London.

> E. M. FORSTER (1879-1970), British novelist, essayist. Margaret Shlegel, in *Howards End*, ch. 15 (1910).

4   I look upon every day to be lost, in which I do not make a new acquaintance.

> SAMUEL JOHNSON (1709-84), English author, lexicographer. Quoted in: James Boswell, *Life of Samuel Johnson*, Nov. 1784 (1791).

5   The mere process of growing old together will make the slightest acquaintance seem a bosom friend.

> LOGAN PEARSALL SMITH (1865-1946), U.S. essayist, aphorist. *All Trivia*, "Last Words" (1933).

6   We need two kinds of acquaintances, one to complain to, while to the others we boast.

> LOGAN PEARSALL SMITH (1865-1946), U.S. essayist, aphorist. *Afterthoughts*, "Other People" (1931).

See also Johnson on FRIENDSHIP; Apocrypha on PRIDE.

ACTING

1   Acting is the expression of a neurotic impulse. It's a bum's life. . . . The principal benefit acting has afforded me is the money to pay for my psychoanalysis.

> MARLON BRANDO (b. 1924), U.S. screen actor. Quoted in: Gary Carey, *Marlon Brando: The Only Contender*, ch. 13 (1985). Brando talked of giving up acting for directing *One-Eyed Jacks* in 1960.

2   I am acquainted with no immaterial sensuality so delightful as good acting.

> LORD BYRON (1788-1824), English poet. Letter, 8 May [?] 1814, to the poet Thomas Moore (published in *Byron's Letters and Journals*, vol. 4, ed. by Leslie A. Marchand, 1975).

3   You don't merely give over your creativity to making a film—you give over your life! In theatre, by contrast, you live these two rather strange lives simultaneously; you have no option but to confront the mould on last night's washing-up.

> DANIEL DAY LEWIS (b. 1957), British stage and screen actor. *City Limits* (London, 7 April 1988).

4   The thing about performance, even if it's only an illusion, is that it is a celebration of the fact that we do contain within ourselves infinite possibilities.

> DANIEL DAY LEWIS (b. 1957), British stage and screen actor. *Rolling Stone* (New York, 8 Feb. 1990).

5   Acting doesn't bring anything to a text. On the contrary, it detracts from it.

> MARGUERITE DURAS (b. 1914), French author, filmmaker. *International Herald Tribune* (Paris, 28 March 1990).

6   You spend all your life trying to do something they put people in asylums for.

> JANE FONDA (b. 1937), U.S. screen actor. Quoted in: Leslie Halliwell, *Filmgoers' Book of Quotes* (1973).

7   More than in any other performing arts the lack of respect for acting seems to spring from the fact that every layman considers himself a valid critic.

> UTA HAGEN (b. 1919), U.S. actor. *Respect for Acting*, pt. 1, Introduction (1973).

8   Abused as we abuse it at present, dramatic art is in no sense cathartic; it is merely a form of emotional masturbation. . . . It is the rarest thing to find a player who has not had his character affected for the worse by the practice of his profession. Nobody can make a habit of self-exhibition, nobody can exploit his personality for the sake of exercising a kind of hypnotic power over others, and remain untouched by the process.

> ALDOUS HUXLEY (1894-1963), British author. *Ends and Means*, ch. 12 (1937).

9   Acting is not about dressing up. Acting is about stripping bare. The whole essence of learning lines is to forget them so you can make them sound like you thought of them that instant.

> GLENDA JACKSON (b. 1937), British actor, Labour politician. Quoted in: *Sunday Telegraph* (London, 26 July 1992).

10   We are born at the rise of the curtain and we die with its fall, and every night in the presence of our patrons we write our new creation, and every night it is blotted out forever; and of what use is it to say to audience or to critic, "Ah, but you should have seen me last Tuesday?"

> MICHEÁL MACLIAMMÓIR (1899-1978), Irish actor. *The Bell*, "Hamlet in Elsinore" (Oct. 1952).

11   It's not a field, I think, for people who need to have success every day: if you can't live with a nightly sort of disaster, you should get out. I wouldn't describe myself as lacking in confidence, but I would just say that . . . the ghosts you chase you never catch.

> JOHN MALKOVICH (b. 1953), U.S. stage and screen actor. *Independent on Sunday* (London, 5 April, 1992), on acting in the theater.

12   I have spent more than half a lifetime trying to express the tragic moment.

> MARCEL MARCEAU (b. 1923), French mime artist. Quoted in: *Guardian* (London, 11 Aug. 1988).

13   Left eyebrow raised, right eyebrow raised.

> ROGER MOORE (b. 1928), British film and television actor. Quoted in: David Brown, *Star Billing*, "Seven Comments on the Art of Acting" (1985). Moore was commenting on his acting range.

14   Acting deals with very delicate emotions. It is not putting up a mask. Each time an actor acts he does not hide; he exposes himself.

> JEANNE MOREAU (b. 1928), French stage and screen actor. *New York Times* (30 June 1976).

15 Acting is a question of absorbing other people's personalities and adding some of your own experience.

PAUL NEWMAN (b. 1925), U.S. screen actor. Quoted in: Leslie Halliwell, *Filmgoers' Companion* (1984).

16 Insecurity, commonly regarded as a weakness in normal people, is the basic tool of the actor's trade.

MIRANDA RICHARDSON (b. 1958), British actor. *Guardian* (London, 5 Dec. 1990).

17 Speak the speach, I pray you, as I pronounced it to you—trippingly on the tongue; but if you mouth it, as many of your players do, I had as lief the town-crier spoke my lines. Nor do not saw the air too much with your hand, thus, but use all gently; for in the very torrent, tempest, and as I may say, the whirlwind of your passion, you must acquire and beget a temperance that may give it smoothness.

WILLIAM SHAKESPEARE (1564-1616), English dramatist, poet. Hamlet, in *Hamlet*, act 3, sc. 2, speaking to the players.

18 An actor who knows his business ought to be able to make the London telephone directory sound enthralling.

DONALD SINDEN (b. 1923), British stage and screen actor. *Observer* (London, 12 Feb. 1989).

19 Imagination, industry, and intelligence—"the three I's"—are all indispensable to the actress, but of these three the greatest is, without doubt, imagination.

ELLEN TERRY (1848-1928), English actor. *The Story of My Life*, ch. 2 (1908).

20 The mere mechanical *technique* of acting can be taught, but the spirit that is to give life to lifeless forms must be born in a man. No dramatic college can teach its pupils to think or to feel. It is Nature who makes our artists for us, though it may be Art who taught them their right mode of expression.

OSCAR WILDE (1854-1900), Anglo-Irish playwright, author. *Court and Society Review* (London, 14 Sept. 1887).

21 Man is least himself when he talks in his own person. Give him a mask, and he will tell you the truth.

OSCAR WILDE (1854-1900), Anglo-Irish playwright, author. Gilbert, in *The Critic as Artist*, pt. 2 (published in *Intentions*, 1891).

See also Griffiths, Hitchcock on CINEMA.

ACTION

1 In this country . . . men seem to live for action as long as they can and sink into apathy when they retire.

CHARLES FRANCIS ADAMS, SR. (1807-86), U.S. statesman, diplomat. Journal entry, 15 April 1836.

2 Action is only coarsened thought—thought becomes concrete, obscure, and unconscious.

HENRI-FRÉDÉRIC AMIEL (1821-81), Swiss philosopher, poet. Journal entry, 30 Dec. 1850.

3 Action without a name, a "who" attached to it, is meaningless.

HANNAH ARENDT (1906-75), German-born U.S. political philosopher. *The Human Condition*, "Action," ch. 24 (1958).

4 What really distinguishes this generation in all countries from earlier generations . . . is its determination to act, its joy in action, the assurance of being able to change things by one's own efforts.

HANNAH ARENDT (1906-75), German-born U.S. political philosopher. *Crises of the Republic*, "Thoughts on Politics and Revolution" (1972).

5 It is vain to say human beings ought to be satisfied with tranquillity: they must have action; and they will make it if they cannot find it.

CHARLOTTE BRONTË (1816-55), English novelist. *Jane Eyre*, ch. 12 (1847).

6 We are born to action; and whatever is capable of suggesting and guiding action has power over us from the first.

CHARLES HORTON COOLEY (1864-1929), U.S. sociologist. *Human Nature and the Social Order*, ch. 9 (1902).

7 Men's actions are too strong for them. Show me a man who has acted, and who has not been the victim and slave of his action.

RALPH WALDO EMERSON (1803-82), U.S. essayist, poet, philosopher. *Representative Men*, "Goethe" (1850).

8 The German intellect wants the French sprightliness, the fine practical understanding of the English, and the American adventure; but it has a certain probity, which never rests in a superficial performance, but asks steadily, *To what end?* A German public asks for a controlling sincerity.

RALPH WALDO EMERSON (1803-82), U.S. essayist, poet, philosopher. *Representative Men*, "Goethe" (1850).

9 An ounce of action is worth a ton of theory.

FRIEDRICH ENGELS (1820-95), German social philosopher. Quoted in: Reg Groves, *The Strange Case of Victor Grayson*, ch. 2 (1975).

10 Action is character.

F. SCOTT FITZGERALD (1896-1940), U.S. author. Notes for *The Last Tycoon*, "Hollywood, ETC." (1941).

11 If you think about it seriously, all the questions about the soul and the immortality of the soul and paradise and hell are at bottom only a way of seeing this very simple fact: that every action of ours is passed on to others according to its value, of good or evil, it passes from father to son, from one generation to the next, in a perpetual movement.

ANTONIO GRAMSCI (1891-1937), Italian political theorist. Letter, 15 June 1931, to his mother (published in *Gramsci: Letters from Prison*, no. 194; tr. by Raymond Rosenthal, 1933).

12 In our era, the road to holiness necessarily passes through the world of action.

DAG HAMMARSKJÖLD (1905-1961), Swedish statesman, secretary-general of U.N. *Markings*, "Night Is Drawing Nigh" (1963).

13 A human action becomes genuinely important when it springs from the soil of a clear-sighted awareness of the temporality and the ephemerality of everything human. It is only this awareness that can breathe any greatness into an action.

> VACLAV HAVEL (b. 1936), Czech playwright, president. *Disturbing the Peace*, ch. 3 (1986; tr. 1990).

14 The first glance at History convinces us that the actions of men proceed from their needs, their passions, their characters and talents; and impresses us with the belief that such needs, passions and interests are the sole spring of actions.

> GEORG HEGEL (1770-1831), German philosopher. *The Philosophy of History*, "Introduction, sct. 3" (1837).

15 Never confuse movement with action.

> ERNEST HEMINGWAY (1899-1961), U.S. author. Quoted by Marlene Dietrich in: A. E. Hotchner, *Papa Hemingway*, pt. 1, ch. 1 (1966 ed.). "In those five words," she added, "he gave me a whole philosophy."

16 Action is at bottom a swinging and flailing of the arms to regain one's balance and keep afloat.

> ERIC HOFFER (1902-83), U.S. philosopher *The Passionate State of Mind*, aph. 25 (1955).

17 One of the marks of a truly vigorous society is the ability to dispense with passion as a midwife of action—the ability to pass directly from thought to action.

> ERIC HOFFER (1902-1983), U.S. philosopher. *Reflections on the Human Condition*, aph. 63 (1973).

18 The sure conviction that we could if we wanted to is the reason so many good minds are idle.

> G. C. LICHTENBERG (1742-99), German physicist, philosopher. *Aphorisms*, "Notebook K," aph. 27 (written 1765-99; tr. by Hollingdale, 1990).

19 Our deeds disguise us. People need endless time to try on their deeds, until each knows the proper deeds for him to do. But every day, every hour, rushes by. There is no time.

> HANIEL LONG (1888-1956), U.S. author, poet, journalist. *Malinche* (1939; ed. 1987, pp. 72-73).

20 Every man feels instinctively that all the beautiful sentiments in the world weigh less than a single lovely action.

> JAMES RUSSELL LOWELL (1819-91), U.S. poet, editor. "Rousseau and the Sentimentalists," in *North American Review* (July 1867; repr. in *Among My Books*, 1870).

21 The curse of me & my nation is that we always think things can be bettered by immediate action of some sort, *any* sort rather than no sort.

> EZRA POUND (1885-1972), U.S. poet, critic. Letter, 7-8 June 1920, to James Joyce (published in *Pound/Joyce: The Letters of Ezra Pound to James Joyce*, ed. by Forrest Read, 1968).

22 The shortest answer is doing.

> ENGLISH PROVERB. Collected in George Herbert, *Jacula Prudentum* (1651).

23 I want to see you shoot the way you shout.

> THEODORE ROOSEVELT (1858-1919), U.S. Republican (later Progressive) politician, president. Address, Oct. 1917, Madison Square Garden, New York.

24 All human actions are equivalent . . . and . . . all are on principle doomed to failure.

> JEAN-PAUL SARTRE (1905-80), French philosopher, author. *Being and Nothingness*, "Conclusion, sct. 2" (1943; tr. 1965).

25 If it were done when 'tis done, then 'twere well
It were done quickly.

> WILLIAM SHAKESPEARE (1564-1616), English dramatist, poet. Macbeth, in *Macbeth*, act 1, sc. 7.

26 There should be less talk; a preaching point is not a meeting point. What do you do then? Take a broom and clean someone's house. That says enough.

> MOTHER TERESA (b. 1910), Albanian-born Roman Catholic missionary. *A Gift for God*, "Carriers of Christ's Love" (1975).

27 I did not wish to take a cabin passage, but rather to go before the mast and on the deck of the world, for there I could best see the moonlight amid the mountains. I do not wish to go below now.

> HENRY DAVID THOREAU (1817-62), U.S. philosopher, author, naturalist. *Walden*, "Conclusion" (1854).

28 The chief difference between words and deeds is that words are always intended for men for their approbation, but deeds can be done only for God.

> LEO TOLSTOY (1828-1910), Russian novelist, philosopher. Letter, 23 Feb. 1903 (published in *Tolstoy's Letters*, vol. 2, 1978).

29 The soul is made for action, and cannot rest till it be employed. Idleness is its rust. Unless it will up and think and taste and see, all is in vain.

> THOMAS TRAHERNE (1636-74), English clergyman, poet, mystic. *Centuries*, "Fourth Century," no. 95 (first published 1908), written c. 1672.

30 No, Ernest, don't talk about action. . . . It is the last resource of those who know not how to dream.

> OSCAR WILDE (1854-1900), Anglo-Irish playwright, author. Gilbert, in *The Critic as Artist*, pt. 1 (published in *Intentions*, 1891).

See also Chesterton on DESTINY; Frederick the Great on KNOWLEDGE; Mansfield on RISK; Bernanos on THOUGHT AND THINKING; Walesa on WORDS.

ACTIVISM

1 It is human agitation, with *all* the vulgarity of needs small and great, with its flagrant disgust for the police who repress it, it is the agitation of *all* men . . . that alone determines revolutionary mental forms, in opposition to bourgeois mental forms.

> GEORGES BATAILLE (1897-1962), French novelist, critic. "'The Old Mole' and the Prefix *Sur* . . ." (1930; published in *Tel Quel*, Paris, no. 34, Summer 1968; repr. in *Visions of Excess: Selected Writings 1927-1939*, ed. Allan Stoekl, 1985).

2 The short lesson that comes out of long experience in political agitation is something like this: *all* the motive power in all of these movements is the instinct of religious feeling. All the obstruction comes from attempting to rely on anything else. Conciliation is the enemy.

> JOHN JAY CHAPMAN (1862-1933), U.S. author. *Practical Agitation*, ch. 1 (1898).

3   I've always had the impression that real militants are like cleaning women, doing a thankless, daily but necessary job.

> FRANÇOIS TRUFFAUT (1932-84), French film director. Letter, May-June 1973, to director Jean-Luc Godard (published in *Letters*, 1989).

4   Agitators are a set of interfering, meddling people, who come down to some perfectly contented class of the community and sow the seeds of discontent amongst them. That is the reason why agitators are so absolutely necessary. Without them, in our incomplete state, there would be no advance towards civilisation.

> OSCAR WILDE (1854-1900), Anglo-Irish playwright, author. "The Soul of Man Under Socialism," in *Fortnightly Review* (London, Feb. 1891; repr. 1895).

See also STRIKES.

ACTORS

1   The actors today really need the whip hand. They're so lazy. They haven't got the sense of pride in their profession that the less socially elevated musical comedy and music hall people or acrobats have. The theater has never been any good since the actors became gentlemen.

> W. H. AUDEN (1907-73), Anglo-American poet. *The Table Talk of W. H. Auden*, "November 16, 1946" (1990; comp. by Alan Ansen, ed. by Nicholas Jenkins).

2   For an actress to be a success, she must have the face of Venus, the brains of a Minerva, the grace of Terpsichore, the memory of a Macaulay, the figure of Juno, and the hide of a rhinoceros.

> ETHEL BARRYMORE (1897-1959), U.S. actor. Quoted in: George Jean Nathan, *The Theatre in the Fifties*, p.30 (1953).

3   The face of Garbo is an Idea, that of Hepburn an Event.

> ROLAND BARTHES (1915-80), French semiologist. *Mythologies*, "The Face of Garbo" (1957; tr. 1972).

4   Directors like Satyajit Ray, Rossellini, Bresson, Buñuel, Forman, Scorsese, and Spike Lee have used non-professional actors precisely in order that the people we see on the screen may be scarcely more *explained* than reality itself. Professionals, except for the greatest, usually play not just the necessary role, but an explanation of the role.

> JOHN BERGER (b. 1926), British author, critic. "Ev'ry Time We Say Goodbye," in *Expressen* (Stockholm, 3 Nov. 1990; repr. in *Keeping a Rendezvous*, 1992).

5   For the theatre one needs long arms; it is better to have them too long than too short. An *artiste* with short arms can never, never make a fine gesture.

> SARAH BERNHARDT (1844-1923), French actor. *Memories of My Life*, ch. 6 (1907).

6   To grasp the full significance of life is the actor's duty, to interpret it is his problem, and to express it his dedication.

> MARLON BRANDO (b. 1924), U.S. screen actor. Quoted in: David Shipman, *Marlon Brando*, ch. 1 (1974; rev. 1989).

7   A man who strains himself on the stage is bound, if he is any good, to strain all the people sitting in the stalls.

> BERTOLT BRECHT (1898-1956), German dramatist, poet. "Emphasis on Sport," in *Berliner Börsen-Courier* (6 Feb. 1926; repr. in *Brecht on Theatre*, pt. 1; ed. and tr. by John Willett, 1964).

8   One forgets too easily the difference between a man and his image, and that there is none between the sound of his voice on the screen and in real life.

> ROBERT BRESSON (b. 1907), French film director. *Notes on the Cinematographer*, "1950-1958: Gestures and Words" (1975).

9   The popularity of that baby-faced boy, who possessed not even the elements of a good actor, was a hallucination in the public mind, and a disgrace to our theatrical history.

> THOMAS CAMPBELL (1777-1844), Scottish poet. *Life of Mrs. Siddons*, ch. 18 (1834). Campell referred to the child actor "Master Betty," William Henry West Betty (1791-1874), who had been taken up by the fashionable world, playing the roles of Romeo and Hamlet at the age of twelve, as well as that of Richard III. The craze lasted two years, to the despair of many, including journalist and poet Leigh Hunt. Hunt was eventually able to write in a contemporary newspaper: "The charm of novelty has at length broken . . . and the town is just now somewhat in the position of the husband who, after passing the honeymoon with a beautiful but childish woman, finds his reason once more returning and is content to sit down and ask why he has been pleased."

10   The basic essential of a great actor is that he loves himself in acting.

> CHARLIE CHAPLIN (1889-1977), British comic actor, filmmaker. *My Autobiography*, ch. 16 (1964).

11   To see him act is like reading Shakespeare by flashes of lightning.

> SAMUEL TAYLOR COLERIDGE (1772-1834), English poet, critic. "Table Talk," in *Specimens of the Table Talk of Samuel Taylor Coleridge*, 27 Apr. 1823 (ed. by Henry Nelson Coleridge, 1835; repr. in *Collected Works*, vol. 14, ed. by Kathleen Coburn, 1990), referring to the actor Edmund Kean.

12   I have often seen an actor laugh off the stage, but I don't remember ever having seen one weep.

> DENIS DIDEROT (1713-84), French philosopher. *Paradox on Acting* (1830; repr. in *Selected Writings*, ed. by Lester G. Crocker, 1966).

13   She represents the unavowed aspiration of the male human being, his potential infidelity—and infidelity of a very special kind, which would lead him to the opposite of his wife, to the "woman of wax" whom he could model at will, make and unmake in any way he wished, even unto death.

MARGUERITE DURAS (b. 1914), French author, filmmaker. "Queen Bardot," in *France-Observateur* (Paris, 1958; repr. in *Outside: Selected Writings*, 1984), referring to Brigitte Bardot.

14   Mr. Clarke played the King all evening as though under constant fear that someone else was about to play the Ace.

EUGENE FIELD (1850-95), U.S. author, critic. Quoted in: Alexander Woollcott, *The Portable Woollcott*, "Capsule Criticism" (1946). Writing for the *Denver Post*, Field was referring to Creston Clarke's performance of King Lear in Denver c. 1880.

15   The great actors are the luminous ones. They are the great conductors of the stage.

MINNIE FISKE (1865-1932), U.S. actor, playwright. Quoted in: Alexander Woollcott, *Mrs. Fiske*, ch. 5 (1917).

16   I was born at the age of twelve on a Metro-Goldwyn-Mayer lot.

JUDY GARLAND (1922-69), U.S. actor. Quoted in: *Observer* (London, 18 Feb. 1951).

17   An actor is a kind of guy who if you ain't talking about him ain't listening.

GEORGE GLASS (1910-84), U.S. film production executive. Quoted in: Bob Thomas, *Brando*, ch. 8 (1973). The quote is frequently attributed to Marlon Brando, who may have heard it from Glass; a similar quip is credited to Michael Wilding: "You can pick out actors by the glazed look that comes into their eyes when the conversation wanders away from themselves."

18   They are, as it were, train-bearers in the pageant of life, and hold a glass up to humanity, frailer than itself. We see ourselves at second-hand in them: they show us all that we are, all that we wish to be, and all that we dread to be. . . . What brings the resemblance nearer is, that, as *they* imitate us, we, in our turn, imitate them. . . . There is no class of society whom so many persons regard with affection as actors.

WILLIAM HAZLITT (1778-1830), English essayist. *The Round Table*, "On Actors and Acting" (1817).

19   Beggars, actors, buffoons, and all that tribe.

HORACE (65-8 B.C.), Roman poet. *Satires*, bk. 1, sct. 2 (c. 35 B.C.).

20   Talk to them about things they don't know. Try to give them an inferiority complex. If the actress is beautiful, screw her. If she isn't, present her with a valuable painting she will not understand. If they insist on being boring, kick their asses or twist their noses. And that's about all there is to it.

JOHN HUSTON (1906-87), U.S. filmmaker. Quoted in: Jean Negulesco, *Things I Did . . . and Things I Think I Did* (1984). Huston was offering advice to a young director on how to handle actors.

21   Players, Sir! I look on them as no better than creatures set upon tables and joint stools to make faces and produce laughter, like dancing dogs.

SAMUEL JOHNSON (1709-84), English author, lexicographer.

Quoted in: James Boswell, *Life of Samuel Johnson*, 1775 entry (1791).

22   Actors are loved because they are unoriginal. Actors stick to their script. The unoriginal man is loved by the mediocrity because this kind of "artistic" expression is something to which the merest five-eighth can climb.

PATRICK KAVANAGH (1905-67), Irish poet, author. *Collected Pruse*, "Signposts" (1967).

23   Some people are addicts. If they don't act, they don't exist.

JEANNE MOREAU (b. 1928), French actor. *International Herald Tribune* (Paris, 15 Nov. 1989).

24   Elizabeth Taylor is pre-feminist woman. This is the source of her continuing greatness and relevance. She wields the sexual power that feminism cannot explain and has tried to destroy. Through stars like Taylor, we sense the world-disordering impact of legendary women like Delilah, Salome, and Helen of Troy. Feminism has tried to dismiss the femme fatale as a misogynist libel, a hoary cliché. But the femme fatale expresses women's ancient and eternal control of the sexual realm. The specter of the femme fatale stalks all men's relations with women.

CAMILLE PAGLIA (b. 1947), U.S. author, critic, educator. "Elizabeth Taylor: Hollywood's Pagan Queen," in *Penthouse* (New York, March 1992; repr. in *Sex, Art, and American Culture*, 1992). Paglia claims to have collected 599 pictures of Taylor during her years at junior high school.

25   She runs the gamut of emotions from A to B.

DOROTHY PARKER (1893-1967), U.S. humorous writer. Quoted in: *Publishers Weekly* (New York, 19 June 1967), referring to Katherine Hepburn.

26   I don't want to read about some of these actresses who are around today. They sound like my niece in Scarsdale. I love my niece in Scarsdale, but I won't buy tickets to see her act.

VINCENT PRICE (b. 1911), U.S. actor. Interview in *UPI* (28 Feb. 1964).

27   In Europe an actor is an artist. In Hollywood, if he isn't working, he's a bum.

ANTHONY QUINN (b. 1915), Mexican-born U.S. actor. Quoted in: Leslie Halliwell, *Filmgoer's Companion* (1984).

28   Oh! it offends me to the soul to hear a robustious periwig-pated fellow, tear a passion to tatters, to very rags, to split the ears of the groundlings.

WILLIAM SHAKESPEARE (1564-1616), English dramatist, poet. Hamlet, in *Hamlet*, act 3, sc. 2, directing the player how to perform the speech he has written.

29   Actors ought to be larger than life. You come across quite enough ordinary, nondescript people in daily life and I don't see why you should be subjected to them on the stage too.

DONALD SINDEN (b. 1923), British stage and screen actor. *Observer* (London, 12 Feb. 1989).

30   Do not try to push your way through to the front ranks of your profession; do not run after distinctions and rewards; but do your utmost to find an entry into the world of beauty.

> KONSTANTIN STANISLAVSKY (1863-1938), Russian theatrical director, actor, theorist. *The Art of the Stage*, "System and Methods of Creative Art," ch. 6 (1950).

31 While we look to the dramatist to give romance to realism, we ask of the actor to give realism to romance.

> OSCAR WILDE (1854-1900), Anglo-Irish playwright, author. Quoted in: *Dramatic Review* (London, 23 May 1885).

See also ACTING; GRETA GARBO; Kael on HAIR; HOLLYWOOD; Hudson on INTERVIEWS; Gordon on KISSING; MARILYN MONROE; STARDOM; Duse on THEATER.

ADDICTION

1 All sin tends to be addictive, and the terminal point of addiction is what is called damnation.

> W. H. AUDEN (1907-73), Anglo-American poet. *A Certain World*, "Hell" (1970).

2 Cocaine habit-forming? Of course not. I ought to know. I've been using it for years.

> TALLULAH BANKHEAD (1903-68), U.S. screen actor. *Tallulah*, ch. 4 (1952). According to Tallulah, this was the riposte she used to shock people when taking throat lozenges. She claimed never to have used cocaine "except medicinally."

3 A junky runs on junk time. When his junk is cut off, the clock runs down and stops. All he can do is hang on and wait for non-junk time to start.

> WILLIAM BURROUGHS (b. 1914), U.S. author. *Junkie*, ch. 10 (1953).

4 I feel that any form of so called psychotherapy is strongly contraindicated for addicts. . . . The question "Why did you start using narcotics in the first place?" should never be asked. It is quite as irrelevant to treatment as it would be to ask a malarial patient why he went to a malarial area.

> WILLIAM BURROUGHS (b. 1914), U.S. author. *The Soft Machine*, Appendix (1961; rev. 1966).

5 It is not heroin or cocaine that makes one an addict, it is the need to escape from a harsh reality. There are more television addicts, more baseball and football addicts, more movie addicts, and certainly more alcohol addicts in this country than there are narcotics addicts.

> SHIRLEY CHISHOLM (b. 1924), U.S. educator, congresswoman. Testimony, 17 Sept. 1969, to House Select Committee on Crime.

6 If an addict who has been completely cured starts smoking again he no longer experiences the discomfort of his first addiction. There exists, therefore, outside alkaloids and habit, a sense for opium, an intangible habit which lives on, despite the recasting of the organism. . . . The dead drug leaves a ghost behind. At certain hours it haunts the house.

> JEAN COCTEAU (1889-1963), French author, filmmaker. *Opium* (1929; tr. 1932; ed. 1957, p. 60).

7 It is not I who become addicted, it is my body.

> JEAN COCTEAU (1889-1963), French author, filmmaker. *Opium* (1929; tr. 1932; repr. 1957, p. 73).

8 My case is a species of madness, only that it is a derangement of the *Volition*, & not of the intellectual faculties.

> SAMUEL TAYLOR COLERIDGE (1772-1834), English poet, critic. Letter, 26 April 1814 (published in *The Collected Letters of Samuel Taylor Coleridge*, vol. 3, 1959), referring to his addiction to laudanum.

9 In this country, don't forget, a habit is no damn private hell. There's no solitary confinement outside of jail. A habit is hell for those you love. And in this country it's the worst kind of hell for those who love you.

> BILLIE HOLIDAY (1915-59), U.S. blues singer. *Lady Sings the Blues*, ch. 24 (1956; rev. 1975), written with William Dufty.

10 Every form of addiction is bad, no matter whether the narcotic be alcohol or morphine or idealism.

> CARL JUNG (1875-1961), Swiss psychiatrist. *Memories, Dreams, Reflections*, ch. 12 (1963).

11 What a vast traffic is drove, what a variety of labour is performed in the world to the maintenance of thousands of families that altogether depend on two silly if not odious customs; the taking of snuff and smoking of tobacco; both of which it is certain do infinitely more hurt than good to those that are addicted to them!

> BERNARD MANDEVILLE (1670-1733), Dutch-born English author, physician. *The Fable of the Bees*, "A Search into the Nature of Society" (1714; rev. 1723).

12 To possess your soul in patience, with all the skin and some of the flesh burnt off your face and hands, is a job for a boy compared with the pains of a man who has lived pretty long in the exhilarating world that drugs or strong waters seem to create and is trying to live now in the first bald desolation created by knocking them off.

> C. E. MONTAGUE (1867-1928), English author, journalist. *Disenchantment*, ch. 15, sct. 1 (1922).

See also Calverley on SMOKING.

ADMIRATION

1 Admiration is a very short-lived passion that immediately decays upon growing familiar with its object, unless it be still fed with fresh discoveries, and kept alive by a new perpetual succession of miracles rising up to its view.

> JOSEPH ADDISON (1672-1719), English essayist. *Spectator*, no. 256 (London, 24 Dec. 1711).

2 Admiration. Our polite recognition of another's resemblance to ourselves.

> AMBROSE BIERCE (1842-1914), U.S. author. *The Devil's Dictionary* (1881-1906).

3 The secret of happiness is to admire without desiring. And that is not happiness.

> F. H. BRADLEY (1846-1924), English philosopher. *Aphorisms*, no. 33 (1930).

4 Oh! death will find me long before I tire
Of watching you.

> RUPERT BROOKE (1887-1915), British poet. *Sonnet*.

5   To cease to admire is a proof of deterioration.

CHARLES HORTON COOLEY (1864-1929), U.S. sociologist. *Human Nature and the Social Order*, ch. 9 (1902).

6   I have always been an admirer. I regard the gift of admiration as indispensable if one is to amount to something; I don't know where I would be without it.

THOMAS MANN (1875-1955), German author, critic. Letter, 1950. Quoted in: Marcel Reich-Ranicki, *Thomas Mann and His Family*, "Thomas Mann—The Birth of Criticism" (1987; tr. 1989).

7   Animals do not admire each other. A horse does not admire its companion.

BLAISE PASCAL (1623-62), French scientist, philosopher. *Pensées* (1670; no. 685 ed. by Krailsheimer, no. 401 ed. by Brunschvicg).

8   You always admire what you really don't understand.

ELEANOR ROOSEVELT (1884-1962), U.S. columnist, lecturer. "Meet the Press," 16 Sept. 1956, NBC TV.

9   Bad artists always admire each other's work. They call it being large-minded and free from prejudice. But a truly great artist cannot conceive of life being shown, or beauty fashioned, under any conditions other than those he has selected.

OSCAR WILDE (1854-1900), Anglo-Irish playwright, author. Gilbert, in *The Critic as Artist*, pt. 2 (published in *Intentions*, 1891).

See also Cocteau on POETS.

ADOLESCENCE

1   What a cunning mixture of sentiment, pity, tenderness, irony surrounds adolescence, what knowing watchfulness! Young birds on their first flight are hardly so hovered around.

GEORGES BERNANOS (1888-1948), French novelist, political writer. *The Diary of a Country Priest*, ch. 4 (1936).

2   So much alarmed that she is quite alarming,
All Giggle, Blush, half Pertness, and half Pout.

LORD BYRON (1788-1824), English poet. *Beppo*, st. 39.

3   The big mistake that men make is that when they turn thirteen or fourteen and all of a sudden they've reached puberty, they believe that they like women. Actually, you're just horny. It doesn't mean you like women any more at twenty-one than you did at ten.

JULES FEIFFER (b. 1929), U.S. cartoonist. *Loose Talk* (ed. by Linda Botts, 1980).

4   They mustn't know my despair, I can't let them see the wounds which they have caused, I couldn't bear their sympathy and their kind-hearted jokes, it would only make me want to scream all the more. If I talk, everyone thinks I'm showing off; when I'm silent they think I'm ridiculous; rude if I answer, sly if I get a good idea, lazy if I'm tired, selfish if I eat a mouthful more than I should, stupid, cowardly, crafty, etc. etc.

ANNE FRANK (1929-45), German Jewish refugee, diarist. *The Diary of a Young Girl* (1947; tr. 1952), entry for 30 Jan. 1943.

5   In the life of children there are two very clear-cut phases, before and after puberty. Before puberty the child's personality has not yet formed and it is easier to guide its life and make it acquire specific habits of order, discipline, and work: after puberty the personality develops impetuously and all extraneous intervention becomes odious, tyrannical, insufferable. Now it so happens that parents feel the responsibility towards their children precisely during this second period, when it is too late: then of course the stick and violence enter the scene and yield very few results indeed. Why not instead take an interest in the child during the first period?

ANTONIO GRAMSCI (1891-1937), Italian political theorist. Letter, 25 Aug. 1930, to his brother (published in *Gramsci: Letters from Prison*, no. 162; tr. by Raymond Rosenthal, 1993).

6   Perhaps a modern society can remain stable only by eliminating adolescence, by giving its young, from the age of ten, the skills, responsibilities, and rewards of grownups, and opportunites for action in all spheres of life. Adolescence should be a time of useful action, while book learning and scholarship should be a preoccupation of adults.

ERIC HOFFER (1902-83), U.S. philosopher. *Reflections on the Human Condition*, aph. 58 (1973).

7   Boys will be boys. And even that wouldn't matter if only we could prevent girls from being girls.

ANTHONY HOPE [SIR ANTHONY HOPE HAWKINS] (1863-1933), British author. *The Dolly Dialogues*, no. 16 (1894).

8   The imagination of a boy is healthy, and the mature imagination of a man is healthy; but there is a space of life between, in which the soul is in a ferment, the character undecided, the way of life uncertain, the ambition thick-sighted: thence proceeds mawkishness.

JOHN KEATS (1795-1821), English poet. *Endymion*, Preface (1818).

9   Remember that as a teenager you are at the last stage in your life when you will be happy to hear that the phone is for you.

FRAN LEBOWITZ (b. 1951), U.S. journalist. *Social Studies*, "Tips for Teens" (1981).

10   Having a thirteen-year-old in the family is like having a general-admission ticket to the movies, radio and TV. You get to understand that the glittering new arts of our civilization are directed to the teen-agers, and by their suffrage they stand or fall.

MAX LERNER (b. 1902), U.S. author, columnist. "Teen-ager," in *New York Post* (4 June 1952; repr. in *The Unfinished Country*, pt. 1, 1959).

11   Teenage boys, goaded by their surging hormones . . . run in packs like the primal horde. They have only a brief season of exhilarating liberty between control by their mothers and control by their wives.

CAMILLE PAGLIA (b. 1947), U.S. author, critic, educator. "Homosexuality at the Fin de Siècle," in *Esquire* (New York, Oct. 1991; repr. in *Sex, Art, and American Culture*, 1992).

12   When you are seventeen you aren't really serious.

ARTHUR RIMBAUD (1854-91), French poet. *Roman*, sct. 1 (repr. in *Collected Poems*, ed. by Oliver Bernard, 1962).

13 I would there were no age between ten and three-and-twenty, or that youth would sleep out the rest; for there is nothing in the between but getting wenches with child, wronging the ancientry, stealing, fighting.

WILLIAM SHAKESPEARE (1564-1616), English dramatist, poet. Shepherd, in *The Winter's Tale*, act 3, sc. 3.

14 Fourteen-year-old, why must you giggle and dote,
Fourteen-year-old, why are you such a goat?
I'm fourteen years old, that is the reason,
I giggle and dote in season.

STEVIE SMITH (1902-1971), British poet. *The Conventionalist.*

ADOPTION

1 Frankly, I adore your catchy slogan, "Adoption, not Abortion," although no one has been able to figure out, even with expert counseling, how to use adoption as a method of birth control, or at what time of the month it is most effective.

BARBARA EHRENREICH (b. 1941), U.S. author, columnist. *The Worst Years of Our Lives*, "My Reply to George" (1991; first published 1989), addressing George Bush.

ADULTERY

1 Can a man take fire in his bosom, and his clothes not be burned? Can one go upon hot coals, and his feet not be burned? So he that goeth in to his neighbor's wife; whosoever toucheth her shall not be innocent.

BIBLE, HEBREW. *Proverbs* 6:27-9.

2 Such is the way of an adulterous woman; she eateth, and wipeth her mouth, and saith, I have done no wickedness.

BIBLE, HEBREW. *Proverbs* 30:20.

3 What men call gallantry, and gods adultery,
Is much more common where the climate's sultry.

LORD BYRON (1788-1824), English poet. *Don Juan*, cto. 1, st. 63.

4 Marriages will survive despite enormous strains. A lover will ask, "Is he happy? Can he still love her?" They don't realise that's not the point, it's all the normal things they do together—going to the supermarket, choosing wallpaper, doing things with the children.

CAROL CLEWLOW (b. 1947), British novelist. Interview in *Observer* (London, 19 Feb. 1989).

5 Life is a game in which the rules are constantly changing; nothing spoils a game more than those who take it seriously. Adultery? Phooey! You should never subjugate yourself to another nor seek the subjugation of someone else to yourself. If you follow that Crispian principle you will be able to say "Phooey," too, instead of reaching for your gun when you fancy yourself betrayed.

QUENTIN CRISP (b. 1908), British author. *Manners from Heaven*, ch. 7 (1984).

6 Adultery is the application of democracy to love.

H. L. MENCKEN (1880-1956), U.S. journalist. *A Book of Burlesques*, "Sententiæ" (1920).

7 One man's folly is often another man's wife.

HELEN ROWLAND (1875-1950), U.S. journalist. *Reflections of a Bachelor Girl* (1903).

8 My libertinage in no wise affects my husband . . . my husband is no more sullied by my debauches than I might be by his. I might fuck with the whole wide world without wounding him in the slightest.

MARQUIS DE SADE (1740-1814), French author. Mme de Saint-Ange, in *Philosophy in the Bedroom*, "Dialogue the Third" (1795).

9 Adultery? Thou shalt not die. Die for adultery!
No, the wren goes to't, and the small gilded fly
Does lecher in my sight. Let copulation thrive.

WILLIAM SHAKESPEARE (1564-1616), English dramatist, poet. Lear, in *King Lear*, act 4, sc. 5.

10 O curse of marriage,
That we can call these delicate creatures ours
And not their appetites!

WILLIAM SHAKESPEARE (1564-1616), English dramatist, poet. Othello, in *Othello*, act 3, sc. 3.

11 Adultery itself in its principle is many times nothing but a curious inquisition after, and envy of another man's enclosed pleasures: and there have been many who refused fairer objects that they might ravish an enclosed woman from her retirement and single possessor.

JEREMY TAYLOR (1613-67), English churchman, devotional writer. *The Rule and Exercises of Holy Living*, ch. 2, sct. 5 (1654, 4th ed.).

12 It is not difficult to deceive the first time, for the deceived possesses no antibodies; unvaccinated by suspicion, she overlooks latenesses, accepts absurd excuses, permits the flimsiest patchings to repair great rents in the quotidian.

JOHN UPDIKE (b. 1932), U.S. author, critic. *Couples*, ch. 2 (1968).

13 The first breath of adultery is the freest; after it, constraints aping marriage develop.

JOHN UPDIKE (b. 1932), U.S. author, critic. *Couples*, ch. 5 (1968).

14 I never had but one intrigue yet: but I confess I long to have another. Pray heaven it end as the first did tho', that we may both grow weary at a time; for 'tis a melancholy thing for lovers to outlive one another.

SIR JOHN VANBRUGH (1663-1726), British playwright. Berinthia, in *The Relapse; or, Virtue in Danger*, act 3, sc. 2 (1708).

15 A mistress should be like a little country retreat near the town, not to dwell in constantly, but only for a night and away.

WILLIAM WYCHERLEY (1640-1716), English dramatist. Dorilant, in *The Country Wife*, act 1.

See also Voltaire on SURPRISE.

ADULTHOOD

1 In my case, adulthood itself was not an advance, although it was a useful waymark.

NICHOLSON BAKER (b. 1957), U.S. author. *The Mezzanine*, ch. 3 (1988).

2 The distinction between children and adults, while probably useful for some purposes, is at bottom a specious one, I feel. There are only individual egos, crazy for love.

DON BARTHELME (1931-89), U.S. author. The narrator (Joseph), in "Me And Miss Mandible" (first published in *Come Back, Dr. Caligari*, 1964; repr. in *Sixty Stories*, 1982).

3 Men are but children of a larger growth,
Our appetites as apt to change as theirs,
And full as craving too, and full as vain.

JOHN DRYDEN (1631-1700), English poet, dramatist, critic. Dollabella, in *All for Love*, act 4, sc. 1 (1678). This speech may have been the origin of Lord Chesterfield's warning to his son in a letter, 5 Sept. 1748, "Women, then, are only children of a larger growth."

4 Grown up, and that is a terribly hard thing to do. It is much easier to skip it and go from one childhood to another.

F. SCOTT FITZGERALD (1896-1940), U.S. author. *The Crack-Up*, "Notebook E" (ed. by Edmund Wilson, 1945).

5 We have not passed that subtle line between childhood and adulthood until we move from the passive voice to the active voice—that is, until we have stopped saying "It got lost," and say, "I lost it."

SYDNEY J. HARRIS (b. 1917), U.S. journalist. *On the Contrary*, ch. 7 (1962).

6 I believe a man is born first unto himself—for the happy developing of himself, while the world is a nursery, and the pretty things are to be snatched for, and pleasant things tasted; some people seem to exist thus right to the end. But most are born again on entering manhood; then they are born to humanity, to a consciousness of all the laughing, and the never-ceasing murmur of pain and sorrow that comes from the terrible multitudes of brothers.

D. H. LAWRENCE (1885-1930), British author. Letter, 3 Dec. 1907 (published in *The Letters of D. H. Lawrence*, vol. 1, ed. by James T. Boulton, 1979).

7 In youth the human body drew me and was the object of my secret and natural dreams. But body after body has taken away from me that sensual phosphorescence which my youth delighted in. Within me is no disturbing interplay now, but only the steady currents of adaptation and of sympathy.

HANIEL LONG (1888-1956), U.S. author, poet, journalist. *Interlinear to Cabeza de Vaca* (1936; repr. 1987, p. 42).

8 Part of the reason for the ugliness of adults, in a child's eyes, is that the child is usually looking upwards, and few faces are at their best when seen from below.

GEORGE ORWELL (1903-50), British author. "Such, Such were the Joys" (1947; repr. in *The Collected Essays, Journalism and Letters of George Orwell*, ed. by Sonia Orwell and Ian Angus, 1968).

9 To be adult is to be alone.

JEAN ROSTAND (1894-1977), French biologist, writer. *Pensées d'un Biologiste* (1939; repr. as *The Substance of Man*, 1962, p. 82).

10 A child becomes an adult when he realizes that he has a right not only to be right but also to be wrong.

THOMAS SZASZ (b. 1920), U.S. psychiatrist. *The Second Sin*, "Childhood" (1973).

11 Adulthood is the ever-shrinking period between childhood and old age. It is the apparent aim of modern industrial societies to reduce this period to a minimum.

THOMAS SZASZ (b. 1920), U.S. psychiatrist. *The Second Sin*, "Social Relations" (1973).

12 We seem but to linger in manhood to tell the dreams of our childhood, and they vanish out of memory ere we learn the language.

HENRY DAVID THOREAU (1817-62), U.S. philosopher, author, naturalist. *Journals* (1906), entry for 19 Feb. 1841.

13 One of the signs of passing youth is the birth of a sense of fellowship with other human beings as we take our place among them.

VIRGINIA WOOLF (1882-1941), British novelist. "Hours in a Library," in *Times Literary Supplement* (London, 30 Nov. 1916).

See also AGE AND AGING; MATURITY; MIDDLE AGE; OLD AGE.

ADVENTURE

1 And yet a little *tumult*, now and then, is an agreeable quickener of sensation; such as a revolution, a battle, or an *adventure* of any lively description.

LORD BYRON (1788-1824), English poet. *Byron's Letters and Journals*, vol. 3 (ed. by Leslie A. Marchand, 1973-81), entry for 22 Nov. 1813.

2 An adventure is only an inconvenience rightly considered. An inconvenience is only an adventure wrongly considered.

G. K. CHESTERTON (1874-1936), British author. *All Things Considered*, "On Running After One's Hat" (1908).

3 The thirst for adventure is the vent which Destiny offers; a war, a crusade, a gold mine, a new country, speak to the imagination and offer swing and play to the confined powers.

RALPH WALDO EMERSON (1803-82), U.S. essayist, poet, philosopher. *Natural History of Intellect*, "Boston" (1893).

4 We are the men of intrinsic value, who can strike our fortunes out of ourselves, whose worth is independent of accidents in life, or revolutions in government: we have heads to get money, and hearts to spend it.

GEORGE FARQUHAR (1678-1707), Irish dramatist. Archer, a "gentleman of broken fortunes," in *The Beaux' Stratagem*, act 1, sc. 1.

5 There are two kinds of adventurers: those who go truly hoping to find adventure and those who go secretly hoping they won't.

WILLIAM LEAST HEAT MOON [WILLIAM TROGDON] (b.

1939), U.S. author. *Blue Highways: A Journey into America*, pt. 2, ch. 4 (1983).

6 A large volume of adventures may be grasped within this little span of life, by him who interests his heart in everything.

LAURENCE STERNE (1713-68), English author. *A Sentimental Journey*, "In the Street—Calais" (1768).

7 I am not an adventurer by choice but by fate.

VINCENT VAN GOGH (1853-90), Dutch painter. Letter, summer 1886 (published in *The Complete Letters of Vincent Van Gogh*, vol. 2, 1958).

8 If we do not find anything very pleasant, at least we shall find something new.

VOLTAIRE (1694-1778), French philosopher, author. Cacambo, in *Candide*, ch. 17 (1759), on journeying downriver into unknown country.

9 The test of an adventure is that when you're in the middle of it, you say to yourself, "Oh, now I've got myself into an awful mess; I wish I were sitting quietly at home." And the sign that something's wrong with you is when you sit quietly at home wishing you were out having lots of adventure.

THORNTON WILDER (1897-1975), U.S. novelist, dramatist. Barnaby, in *The Matchmaker*, act 4.

10 If we didn't live venturously, plucking the wild goat by the beard, and trembling over precipices, we should never be depressed, I've no doubt; but already should be faded, fatalistic and aged.

VIRGINIA WOOLF (1882-1941), British novelist. *A Writer's Diary* (ed. by Leonard Woolf, 1954), entry for 26 May 1924.

ADVERSITY

1 Difficulty, my brethren, is the nurse of greatness— a harsh nurse, who roughly rocks her foster-children into strength and athletic proportion.

WILLIAM CULLEN BRYANT (1794-1878), U.S. poet, editor. Speech, 15 Dec. 1851.

2 It is odd but agitation or contest of any kind gives a rebound to my spirits and sets me up for a time.

LORD BYRON (1788-1824), English poet. Letter, 8 March 1816, to the poet Thomas Moore (published in *Byron's Letters and Journals*, vol. 5, ed. by Leslie A. Marchand, 1973-81).

3 Adversity is sometimes hard upon a man; but for one man who can stand prosperity, there are a hundred that will stand adversity.

THOMAS CARLYLE (1795-1881), Scottish essayist, historian. *On Heroes and Hero-Worship*, "The Hero as Man of Letters," Lecture 5 (1841).

4 I have nothing to offer but blood, toil, tears and sweat.

SIR WINSTON CHURCHILL (1874-1965), British statesman, writer. First speech as prime minister, 13 May 1940, House of Commons.

5 I have often been downcast, but never in despair; I regard our hiding as a dangerous adventure, romantic and interesting at the same time. In my diary I treat all the pri-

vations as amusing. I have made up my mind now to lead a different life from other girls and, later on, different from ordinary housewives. My start has been so very full of interest, and that is the sole reason why I have to laugh at the humorous side of the most dangerous moments.

ANNE FRANK (1929-45), German Jewish refugee, diarist. *The Diary of a Young Girl* (1947; tr. 1952), entry for 3 May 1944.

6 Had there been no difficulties and no thorns in the way, then man would have been in his primitive state and no progress made in civilisation and mental culture.

ANANDABAI JOSHEE (1865-87), Indian physician. Letter, 27 Aug. 1881 (published in Caroline H. Dall, *The Life of Anandabai Joshee*, 1888).

7 Man needs difficulties; they are necessary for health.

CARL JUNG (1875-1961), Swiss psychiatrist. *The Transcendent Function* (1916).

8 Life is truly known only to those who suffer, lose, endure adversity and stumble from defeat to defeat.

RYSZARD KAPUSCINSKI (b. 1932), Polish journalist. *A Warsaw Diary*, in *Granta*, no. 15 (Cambridge, England, 1985).

9 Do you not see how necessary a world of pains and troubles is to school an intelligence and make it a soul?

JOHN KEATS (1795-1821), English poet. Letter, 14 Feb.-3 May 1819, to his brother and sister-in-law, George and Georgiana Keats (published in *Letters of John Keats*, no. 123, ed. by Frederick Page, 1954).

10 Adversity draws men together and produces beauty and harmony in life's relationships, just as the cold of winter produces ice-flowers on the window-panes, which vanish with the warmth.

SØREN KIERKEGAARD (1813-55), Danish philosopher. *The Journals of Søren Kierkegaard: A Selection*, no. 37 (ed. and tr. by Alexander Dru, 1938), entry for Jan. 1836.

11 It is in the gift for employing all the vicissitudes of life to one's own advantage and to that of one's craft that a large part of genius consists.

G. C. LICHTENBERG (1742-99), German physicist, philosopher. *Aphorisms*, "Notebook K," aph. 48 (written 1765-99; tr. by R. J. Hollingdale, 1990).

12 Pleasant it is, when over a great sea the winds trouble the waters, to gaze from shore upon another's great tribulation; not because any man's troubles are a delectable joy, but because to perceive you are free of them yourself is pleasant.

LUCRETIUS (c. 99-C. 55 B.C.), Roman poet, philosopher. *De Rerum Natura*, bk. 2.

13 There is no doubt that life is given us, not to be enjoyed, but to be overcome—to be got over.

ARTHUR SCHOPENHAUER (1788-1860), German philosopher. *Parerga and Paralipomena*, "Counsels and Maxims" (1851).

14 The bravest sight in the world is to see a great man struggling against adversity.

SENECA (c. 5 B.C.-A.D. c. 65), Roman writer, philosopher, statesman. *De Providentia*, sct. 4.

15 Sweet are the uses of adversity
Which, like the toad, ugly and venomous,
Wears yet a precious jewel in his head.

> WILLIAM SHAKESPEARE (1564-1616), English dramatist, poet. Duke Senior, in *As You Like It,* act 2, sc. 1.

16 By trying we can easily learn to endure adversity. Another man's, I mean.

> MARK TWAIN (1835-1910), U.S. author. *Following the Equator,* ch. 39, "Pudd'nhead Wilson's New Calendar" (1897).

17 Misfortunes leave wounds which bleed drop by drop even in sleep; thus little by little they train man by force and dispose him to wisdom in spite of himself. Man must learn to think of himself as a limited and dependent being; and only suffering teaches him this.

> SIMONE WEIL (1909-43), French philosopher, mystic. *La Source Grecque,* pt. 1, ch. 2 (1953).

18 A reasonable amount o' fleas is good fer a dog—keeps him from broodin' over *bein'* a dog, mebbe.

> EDWARD NOYES WESTCOTT (1847-98), U.S. author. *David Harum,* ch. 32 (1898).

19 One likes people much better when they're battered down by a prodigious siege of misfortune than when they triumph.

> VIRGINIA WOOLF (1882-1941), British novelist. *Writer's Diary* (ed. by Leonard Woolf, 1954), entry for 13 Aug. 1921.

See also BIBLE: New Testament on CONTENTMENT; Eric Hoffer on OPPORTUNITY.

ADVERTISING

1 An advertising agency is 85 percent confusion and 15 percent commission.

> FRED ALLEN (1894-1957), U.S. radio comic. *Treadmill to Oblivion,* pt. 2 (1954).

2 If everything on television is, without exception, part of a low-calorie (or even no-calorie) diet, then what good is it complaining about the adverts? By their worthlessness, they at least help to make the programmes around them seem of a higher level.

> JEAN BAUDRILLARD (b. 1929), French semiologist. *America,* "Utopia Achieved" (1986; tr. 1988).

3 Watteau is no less an artist for having painted a fascia board while Sainsbury's is no less effective a business for producing advertisements which entertain and educate instead of condescending and exploiting.

> STEPHEN BAYLEY (b. 1951), British design critic. *Commerce and Culture,* ch. 1 (1989).

4 We read advertisements . . . to discover and enlarge our desires. We are always ready—even eager—to discover, from the announcement of a new product, what we have all along wanted without really knowing it.

> DANIEL J. BOORSTIN (b. 1914), U.S. historian. *The Image,* ch. 5 (1961).

5 It is pretty obvious that the debasement of the human mind caused by a constant flow of fraudulent advertising is no trivial thing. There is more than one way to conquer a country.

> RAYMOND CHANDLER (1888-1959), U.S. author. Letter, 15 Nov. 1951, to his New York literary agent Carl Brandt (published in *Raymond Chandler Speaking,* 1962).

6 You can tell the ideals of a nation by its advertisements.

> NORMAN DOUGLAS (1868-1952), British author. *South Wind,* ch. 7 (1917).

7 Advertising is a racket, like the movies and the brokerage business. You cannot be honest without admitting that its constructive contribution to humanity is exactly minus zero.

> F. SCOTT FITZGERALD (1896-1940), U.S. author. Letter, 24 Aug. 1940, to his daughter Frances Scott Fitzgerald (published in *The Crack-Up,* ed. by Edmund Wilson, 1945).

8 We grew up founding our dreams on the infinite promise of American advertising. I *still* believe that one can learn to play the piano by mail and that mud will give you a perfect complexion.

> ZELDA FITZGERALD (1900-48), U.S. writer. Alabama Beggs, in *Save Me the Waltz,* ch. 4, sct. 3 (1932).

9 That is the kind of ad I like. Facts, facts, facts.

> SAMUEL GOLDWYN (1882-1974), U.S. film producer. Quoted in: Arthur Marx, *Goldwyn: the Man Behind the Myth,* ch. 16 (1976). Goldwyn referred to an advertisement for the film *We Live Again* (1934), which described it as "The greatest motion picture in all history, by the world's most outstanding writer. The directorial genius of Mamoulian, the beauty of Anna Sten and the producing genius of Goldwyn have combined to make the greatest entertainment in the world." The movie flopped.

10 I have discovered the most exciting, the most arduous literary form of all, the most difficult to master, the most pregnant in curious possibilities. I mean the advertisement. . . . It is far easier to write ten passably effective Sonnets, good enough to take in the not too inquiring critic, than one effective advertisement that will take in a few thousand of the uncritical buying public.

> ALDOUS HUXLEY (1894-1963), British author. *On the Margin,* "Advertisement" (1923).

11 Promise, large promise, is the soul of an advertisement.

> SAMUEL JOHNSON (1709-84), English author, lexicographer. *The Idler,* in *Universal Chronicle,* no. 40 (London, 20 Jan. 1759; repr. in *Works of Samuel Johnson,* vol. 2, ed. by W. J. Bate, John M. Bullitt, and L. F. Powell, 1963).

12 The trade of advertising is now so near perfection that it is not easy to propose any improvement. But as every art ought to be exercised in due subordination to the public good, I cannot but propose it as a moral question to these masters of the public ear, whether they do not sometimes play too wantonly with our passions.

> SAMUEL JOHNSON (1709-84), English author, lexicographer. *The Idler,* in *Universal Chronicle,* no. 40 (London, 20 Jan. 1759; repr. in *Works of Samuel Johnson,* vol. 2, ed. by W. J. Bate, John M. Bullitt, and L. F. Powell, 1963).

13 Society drives people crazy with lust and calls it advertising.

> JOHN LAHR (b. 1941), U.S. literary and drama critic. Quoted in: *Guardian* (London, 2 Aug. 1989).

14 The art of advertisement, after the American manner, has introduced into all our life such a lavish use of superlatives, that no standard of value whatever is intact.

> WYNDHAM LEWIS (1882-1957), British author, painter. *The Doom of Youth*, "'Promise' as an Institution," pt. 2 (1932).

15 Ideally, advertising aims at the goal of a programmed harmony among all human impulses and aspirations and endeavors. Using handicraft methods, it stretches out toward the ultimate electronic goal of a collective consciousness.

> MARSHALL MCLUHAN (1911-80), Canadian communications theorist. *Understanding Media*, ch. 23 (1964).

16 Advertising is the greatest art form of the twentieth century.

> MARSHALL MCLUHAN (1911-80), Canadian communications theorist. Quoted in: *Advertising Age* (3 Sept. 1976).

17 Good wine needs no bush,
And perhaps products that people really want need no
hard-sell or soft-sell TV push.
Why not?
Look at pot.

> OGDEN NASH (1902-71), U.S. poet. *Most Doctors Recommend or Yours For Fast Fast Fast Relief*, in *The Old Dog Barks Backwards* (1972).

18 Remove advertising, disable a person or firm from preconising [proclaiming] its wares and their merits, and the whole of society and of the economy is transformed. The enemies of advertising are the enemies of freedom.

> J. ENOCH POWELL (b. 1912), British Conservative politician. Quoted in: *The Listener* (London, 31 July 1969).

19 Advertisers are the interpreters of our dreams—Joseph interpreting for Pharaoh. Like the movies, they infect the routine futility of our days with purposeful adventure. Their weapons are our weaknesses: fear, ambition, illness, pride, selfishness, desire, ignorance. And these weapons must be kept as bright as a sword.

> E. B. WHITE (1899-1985), U.S. author, editor. "Truth in Advertising," in *New Yorker* (11 July 1936; repr. in *Writings from the New Yorker 1927-1976*, ed. by Rebecca M. Dale, 1991).

See also Galbraith on The CONSUMER SOCIETY; McLuhan on ELOQUENCE.

ADVICE

1 Never trust the advice of a man in difficulties.

> AESOP (6TH CENTURY B.C.), Greek fabulist. *Fables*, "The Fox and the Goat."

2 There is as much difference between the counsel that a friend giveth, and that a man giveth himself, as there is between the counsel of a friend and of a flatterer. For there is no such flatterer as is a man's self.

> FRANCIS BACON (1561-1626), English philosopher, essayist, statesman. *Essays*, "Of Friendship" (1597-1625).

3 Counsel woven into the fabric of real life is wisdom.

> WALTER BENJAMIN (1892-1940), German critic, philosopher. *The Storyteller*, sct. 8 (1936; repr. in *Illuminations*, ed. by Hannah Arendt, 1968).

4 Where no counsel is, the people fall; but in the multitude of counsellors there is safety.

> BIBLE, HEBREW. *Proverbs* 11:14.

5 Consult. To seek another's approval of a course already decided on.

> AMBROSE BIERCE (1842-1914), U.S. author. *The Devil's Dictionary* (1881-1906).

6 We hate those who will not take our advice, and despise them who do.

> JOSH BILLINGS [HENRY WHEELER SHAW] (1818-85), U.S. humorist. *Josh Billings, His Sayings*, ch. 28 (1865).

7 Talk that does not end in any kind of action is better suppressed altogether.

> THOMAS CARLYLE (1795-1881), Scottish essayist, historian. Inaugural address, 2 April 1866, on being installed as Rector of the University at Edinburgh (published in *Critical and Miscellaneous Essays*, vol. 7, 1839).

8 In matters of religion and matrimony I never give any advice; because I will not have anybody's torments in this world or the next laid to my charge.

> LORD CHESTERFIELD (1694-1773), English statesman, man of letters. Letter, 12 Oct. 1765 (published in *Lord Chesterfield's Letters to His Godson*, no. 73, Appendix, ed. by Earl of Carnarvon, 1890).

9 There is hardly a man on earth who will take advice unless he is certain that it is positively bad.

> EDWARD DAHLBERG (1900-77), U.S. author, critic. *Alms for Oblivion*, "Moby Dick: A Hamitic Dream" (1964).

10 When we turn to one another for counsel we reduce the number of our enemies.

> KAHLIL GIBRAN (1883-1931), Lebanese poet, novelist. *The Voice of the Master*, pt. 2, ch. 10 (1960; repr. in *A Second Treasury of Kahlil Gibran*, tr. by Anthony Ferris, 1962).

11 The advice of their elders to young men is very apt to be as unreal as a list of the hundred best books.

> OLIVER WENDELL HOLMES, SR. (1841-1935), U.S. jurist. Speech, 8 Jan. 1897, Boston.

12 Advice is what we ask for when we already know the answer but wish we didn't.

> ERICA JONG (b. 1942), U.S. author. *How to Save Your Own Life*, "A day in the life . . .," epigraph (1977).

13 Your friends praise your abilities to the skies, submit to you in argument, and seem to have the greatest deference for you; but, though they may ask it, you never find them following your advice upon their own affairs; nor allowing you to manage your own, without thinking that you should follow theirs. Thus, in fact, they all think themselves wiser than you, whatever they may say.

> LORD MELBOURNE (1779-1848), English statesman, prime minister. Notebook entry. Quoted in: David Cecil, *The Young Melbourne*, ch. 9 (1939).

14 I shall th'effect of this good lesson keep
As watchman to my heart.

> WILLIAM SHAKESPEARE (1564-1616), English dramatist, poet. Ophelia, in *Hamlet*, act 1, sc. 3, in response to the lengthy advice given her by her brother Polonius before his departure for France.

15 I'm not a teacher: only a fellow-traveller of whom you asked the way. I pointed ahead—ahead of myself as well as you.

> GEORGE BERNARD SHAW (1856-1950), Anglo-Irish playwright, critic. Bishop of Chelsea, in *Getting Married*.

16 These words dropped into my childish mind as if you should accidentally drop a ring into a deep well. I did not think of them much at the time, but there came a day in my life when the ring was fished up out of the well, good as new.

> HARRIET BEECHER STOWE (1811-96), U.S. novelist, antislavery campaigner. *Old Town Folks*, ch. 25 (1869).

17 I have lived some thirty-odd years on this planet, and I have yet to hear the first syllable of valuable or even earnest advice from my seniors.

> HENRY DAVID THOREAU (1817-62), U.S. philosopher, author, naturalist. *Journals* (1906), entry for 11 Feb. 1852. The thought was picked up again in Thoreau, *Walden*, "Economy" (1854).

18 I always pass on good advice. It is the only thing to do with it. It is never of any use to oneself.

> OSCAR WILDE (1854-1900), Anglo-Irish playwright, author. Lord Goring, in *An Ideal Husband*, act 1.

19 One cool judgment is worth a thousand hasty counsels. The thing to do is to supply light and not heat.

> WOODROW WILSON (1856-1924), U.S. Democratic politician, president. Speech, 29 Jan. 1916, Pittsburgh, Pa.

20 Some of these people need ten years of therapy—ten sentences of mine do not equal ten years of therapy.

> JEFF ZASLOW (b. 1925), U.S. advice columnist. *International Herald Tribune* (Paris, 24 Jan. 1990), referring to his correspondents.

See also La Rochefoucauld on OLD AGE.

AESTHETICS

1 For aesthetics is the mother of ethics. . . . Were we to choose our leaders on the basis of their reading experience and not their political programs, there would be much less grief on earth. I believe—not empirically, alas, but only theoretically—that for someone who has read a lot of Dickens to shoot his like in the name of an idea is harder than for someone who has read no Dickens.

> JOSEPH BRODSKY (b. 1940), Russian-born U.S. poet, critic. Nobel Prize acceptance speech, 1987.

2 'Tis the perception of the beautiful,
A fine extension of the faculties,
Platonic, universal, wonderful,
Drawn from the stars, and filtered through the skies,
Without which life would be extremely dull.

> LORD BYRON (1788-1824), English poet. *Don Juan*, cto. 2, st. 212.

3 Aesthetic emotion puts man in a state favorable to the reception of erotic emotion. . . . Art is the accomplice of love. Take love away and there is no longer art.

> RÉMY DE GOURMONT (1858-1915), French critic, novelist. *Le Chemin de Velours*," sct. 2, "Success and the Idea of Beauty" (1902; repr. in *Selected Writings*, ed. and tr. by Glen S. Burne, 1966).

4 There are moods in which one feels the impulse to enter a tacit protest against too gross an appetite for pure aesthetics in this starving and sinning world. One turns half away, musingly, from certain beautiful useless things.

> HENRY JAMES (1843-1916), U.S. author. *Italian Hours*, "Florentine Notes," sct. 2 (1909).

5 The beautiful, which is perhaps inseparable from art, is not after all tied to the subject, but to the pictorial representation. In this way and in no other does art overcome the ugly without avoiding it.

> PAUL KLEE (1879-1940), Swiss artist. *The Diaries of Paul Klee 1898-1918*, no. 733 (1957; tr. 1965), Dec. 1905 entry.

6 The esthete stands in the same relation to beauty as the pornographer stands to love, and the politician stands to life.

> KARL KRAUS (1874-1936), Austrian satirist. *Die Fackel*, no. 406/12 (Vienna, 5 Oct. 1915; repr. in Thomas Szasz, *Anti-Freud: Karl Kraus's Criticism of Psychoanalysis and Psychiatry*, 1976).

7 Nothing is beautiful, only man: on this piece of naïvety rests all aesthetics, it is the *first* truth of aesthetics. Let us immediately add its second: nothing is ugly but *degenerate* man—the domain of aesthetic judgment is therewith defined.

> FRIEDRICH NIETZSCHE (1844-1900), German philosopher. *Twilight of the Idols*, "Expeditions of an Untimely Man," aph. 20 (1889).

8 "Art" is an invention of aesthetics, which in turn is an invention of philosophers. . . . What we call art is a game.

> OCTAVIO PAZ (b. 1914), Mexican poet. *Alternating Current*, "André Breton or the Quest of the Beginning" (1967).

9 I hate that aesthetic game of the eye and the mind, played by these connoisseurs, these mandarins who "appreciate" beauty. What *is* beauty, anyway? There's no such thing. I never "appreciate," any more than I "like." I love or I hate.

> PABLO PICASSO (1881-1973), Spanish artist. Quoted in: Françoise Gilot and Carlton Lake, *Life with Picasso*, pt. 6 (1964).

10 "Form follows profit" is the aesthetic principle of our times.

> RICHARD ROGERS (b. 1933), British architect. *Times* (London, 13 Feb. 1991).

See also ART; Waugh on CRIME AND CRIMINALS.

AFFECTATION

1   Let the world know you as you are, not as you think you should be, because sooner or later, if you are posing, you will forget the pose, and then where are you?

> FANNY BRICE (1891-1951), U.S. entertainer. Quoted in: Norman Katkov, *The Fabulous Fanny*, ch. 24 (1952).

2   Our greatest pretenses are built up not to hide the evil and the ugly in us, but our emptiness. The hardest thing to hide is something that is not there.

> ERIC HOFFER (1902-83), U.S. philosopher. *The Passionate State of Mind,* aph. 217 (1955).

3   We are never so ridiculous through what we are as through what we pretend to be.

> FRANÇOIS, DUC DE LA ROCHEFOUCAULD (1613-80), French writer, moralist. *Sentences et Maximes Morales,* no. 134 (1678).

4   Affectation is a very good word when someone does not wish to confess to what he would none the less like to believe of himself.

> G. C. LICHTENBERG (1742-99), German physicist, philosopher. *Aphorisms,* "Notebook F," aph. 149 (written 1765-99; tr. by R. J. Hollingdale, 1990).

AFFECTION

1   It's not till sex has died out between a man and a woman that they can really love. And now I mean affection. Now I mean to be *fond of* (as one is fond of oneself)—to hope, to be disappointed, to live inside the other heart. When I look back on the pain of sex, the love like a wild fox so ready to bite, the antagonism that sits like a twin beside love, and contrast it with affection, so deeply unrepeatable, of two people who have lived a life together (and of whom one must die) it's the affection I find richer. It's that I would have again. Not all those doubtful rainbow colours.

> ENID BAGNOLD (1889-1981), British novelist, playwright. *Autobiography,* ch. 6 (1969).

2   Set your affection on things above, not on things on the earth.

> BIBLE: NEW TESTAMENT. *Colossians* 3:2.

3   The moment we indulge our affections, the earth is metamorphosed; there is no winter and no night; all tragedies, all ennuis, vanish,—all duties even.

> RALPH WALDO EMERSON (1803-82), U.S. essayist, poet, philosopher. *Essays,* "Friendship" (First Series, 1841).

4   If you value a man's regard, *strive* with him. As to *liking,* you like your newspaper—and despise it.

> GEORGE BERNARD SHAW (1856-1950), Anglo-Irish playwright, critic. Letter, 25 Sept. 1896, to actress Ellen Terry (published in *Collected Letters,* vol. 1).

5   One should never direct people towards happiness, because happiness too is an idol of the market-place. One should direct them towards mutual affection. A

beast gnawing at its prey can be happy too, but only human beings can feel affection for each other, and this is the highest achievement they can aspire to.

> ALEXANDER SOLZHENITSYN (b. 1918), Russian novelist. Shulubin, in *Cancer Ward,* pt. 2, ch. 10 (1968).

AFFIRMATIVE ACTION

1   Lots of white people think black people are stupid. They are stupid themselves for thinking so, but regulation will not make them smarter.

> STEPHEN CARTER (b. 1954), U.S. lawyer, author. *Reflections of an Affirmative Action Baby,* ch. 8 (1992).

2   When they kept you out it was because you were black; when they let you in, it is because you are black. That's progress?

> MARILYN FRENCH (b. 1929), U.S. author, critic. Valerie, in *The Women's Room,* ch. 4, sct. 19 (1977).

3   It doesn't do good to open doors for someone who doesn't have the price to get in. If he has the price, he may not need the laws. There is no law saying the Negro has to live in Harlem or Watts.

> RONALD REAGAN (b. 1911), U.S. Republican politician, president. *Chronicle* (San Francisco, 9 Sept. 1967).

AFRICA AND THE AFRICANS

1   While the rest of the world has been improving technology, Ghana has been improving the quality of man's humanity to man.

> MAYA ANGELOU (b. 1928), U.S. author. "Involvement in Black and White," interview, in *Oregonian* (Portland, 17 Feb. 1971; repr. in *Conversations with Maya Angelou,* 1989). Angelou lived and worked in Ghana and Egypt, 1962-66.

2   For Africa to me . . . is more than a glamorous fact. It is a historical truth. No man can know where he is going unless he knows exactly where he has been and exactly how he arrived at his present place.

> MAYA ANGELOU (b. 1928), U.S. author. Quoted in: *New York Times* (16 April 1972).

3   The shadow of a mighty Negro past flits through the tale of Ethiopia the shadowy and of the Egypt the Sphinx. Throughout history, the powers of single blacks flash here and there like falling stars, and die sometimes before the world has rightly gauged their brightness.

> W. E. B. DU BOIS (1868-1963), U.S. civil rights leader, author. *The Souls of Black Folk,* ch. 1 (1903).

4   Is a civilization naturally backward because it is different? Outside of cannibalism, which can be matched in this country, at least, by lynching, there is no vice and no degradation in native African customs which can begin to touch the horrors thrust upon them by white masters. Drunkenness, terrible diseases, immorality, all these things have been gifts of European civilization.

> W. E. B. DU BOIS (1868-1963), U.S. civil rights leader, author. *The Seventh Son,* vol. 2 "Reconstruction and Africa" (1971; first published 1919).

5   Are you there, Africa with the bulging chest and oblong thigh? Sulking Africa, wrought of iron, in the fire,

Africa of the millions of royal slaves, deported Africa, drifting continent, are you there? Slowly you vanish, you withdraw into the past, into the tales of castaways, colonial museums, the works of scholars.

> JEAN GENET (1910-86), French playwright, novelist. Felicity, in *The Blacks* (1958; tr. 1960).

6 Where do whites fit in the New Africa? *Nowhere,* I'm inclined to say . . . and I do believe that it is true that even the gentlest and most westernised Africans would like the emotional idea of the continent entirely without the complication of the presence of the white man for a generation or two. But *nowhere,* as an answer for us whites, is in the same category as remarks like *What's the use of living?* in the face of the threat of atomic radiation. We are living; we are in Africa.

> NADINE GORDIMER (b. 1923), South African author. "Where Do Whites Fit In?," in *Twentieth Century* (April 1959; repr. in *The Essential Gesture*, ed. by Stephen Clingman, 1988).

7 In Africa, there is much confusion. . . . Before, there was no radio, or other forms of communication. . . . Now, in Africa . . . the government talks, people talk, the police talk, the people don't know anymore. They aren't free.

> YOUSSOU N'DOUR (b. 1959), Senegalese musician. Interview in *Africa Beat* (London, Summer 1987).

8 Africa is a paradox which illustrates and highlights neo-colonialism. Her earth is rich, yet the products that come from above and below the soil continue to enrich, not Africans predominantly, but groups and individuals who operate to Africa's impoverishment.

> KWAME NKRUMAH (1900-1972), Ghanaian president. *Neo-Colonialism*, ch. 1 (1965).

9 The African is my brother—but he is my younger brother by several centuries.

> ALBERT SCHWEITZER (1875-1965), French missionary, theologian, musician. Quoted in: *Observer* (London, 23 Oct. 1955).

10 The African race evidently are made to excel in that department which lies between the sensuousness and the intellectual—what we call the elegant arts. These require rich and abundant animal nature, such as they possess; and if ever they become highly civilised, they will excel in music, dancing and elocution.

> HARRIET BEECHER STOWE (1811-96), U.S. novelist, antislavery campaigner. Clayton, in *Dred*, ch. 29 (1856).

See also Macmillan on DECOLONIZATION; Ehrenreich on FAMINE.

AFRICAN AMERICANS

1 The fact that the adult American Negro female emerges a formidable character is often met with amazement, distaste and even belligerence. It is seldom accepted as an inevitable outcome of the struggle won by survivors, and deserves respect if not enthusiastic acceptance.

> MAYA ANGELOU, U.S. author. *I Know Why the Caged Bird Sings*, vol. 1, ch. 34 (1969).

2 When you're called a nigger you look at your father because you think your father can rule the world—every kid thinks that—and then you discover that your father cannot do anything about it. So you begin to despise your father and you realize, oh, that's what a nigger is.

> JAMES BALDWIN (1924-87), U.S. author. *A Dialogue* (1973; with Nikki Giovanni), from a conversation, 4 Nov. 1971, in London.

3 The presence of the blacks is the greatest evil that threatens the United States. They increase, in the Gulf States, faster than do the whites. They cannot be kept for ever in slavery, since the tendencies of the modern world run strongly the other way. They cannot be absorbed into the white population, for the whites will not intermarry with them, not even in the North where they have been free for two generations. Once freed, they would be more dangerous than now, because they would not long submit to be debarred from political rights. A terrible struggle would ensue.

> JAMES BRYCE (1838-1922), British historian, politician and diplomat. *Studies in History and Jurisprudence*, vol. 1, ch. 6 (1901).

4 To be black and an intellectual in America is to live in a box. . . . On the box is a label, not of my own choosing.

> STEPHEN CARTER (b. 1954), U.S. lawyer and author. *Reflections of an Affirmative Action Baby*, Introduction (1992).

5 An American, a Negro . . . two souls, two thoughts, two unreconciled strivings; two warring ideals in one dark body, whose dogged strength alone keeps it from being torn asunder.

> W. E. B. DU BOIS (1868-1963), U.S. civil rights leader, author. *The Souls of Black Folk*, ch. 1 (1903). "The history of the American Negro," wrote Du Bois, "is the history of this strife."

6 We black men seem the sole oasis of simple faith and reverence in a dusty desert of dollars and smartness.

> W. E. B. DU BOIS (1868-1963), U.S. civil rights leader, author. *The Souls of Black Folk*, ch. 1 (1903).

7 To be a Negro is to participate in a culture of poverty and fear that goes far deeper than any law for or against discrimination. . . . After the racist statutes are all struck down, after legal equality has been achieved in the schools and in the courts, there remains the profound institutionalized and abiding wrong that white America has worked on the Negro for so long.

> MICHAEL HARRINGTON (1928-89), U.S. social scientist, author. *The Other America*, ch. 4 (1962).

8 If you wake up in the morning and think you're white, you're bound to meet someone before five o'clock who will let you know you are just another nigger.

> JESSE JACKSON (b. 1941), U.S. clergyman, civil rights leader. *Sun* (London, 20 Sept. 1989).

9 We are the wrong people of the wrong skin in the wrong continent and what in the hell is everybody being reasonable about?

> JUNE JORDAN (b. 1939), U.S. poet, civil rights activist. *Passion.*

10 There is a man who exists as one of the most popular *objects* of leadership, legislation, and quasi-literature in the history of all men. . . . This man, that object of attention, attack, and vast activity, cannot make himself be heard, let alone to understood. *He has never been listened to.* . . . That man is Black and alive in white America where the media of communication do not allow the delivery of his own voice, his own desires, his own rage.

JUNE JORDAN (b. 1939), U.S. poet, civil rights activist. "On Listening: A Good Way to Hear," in *Nation* (New York, 1967; repr. in *Moving Towards Home: Political Essays,* 1989).

11   Body and soul, Black America reveals the extreme questions of contemporary life, questions of freedom and identity: *How can I be who I am?*

JUNE JORDAN (b. 1939), U.S. poet, civil rights activist. "Black Studies: Bringing Back The Person," in *Evergreen Review* (Oct. 1969; repr. in *Moving Towards Home: Political Essays,* 1989).

12   We were here before the mighty words of the Declaration of Independence were etched across the pages of history. Our forebears labored without wages. They made cotton "king." And yet out of a bottomless vitality, they continued to thrive and develop. If the cruelties of slavery could not stop us, the opposition we now face will surely fail. . . . Because the goal of America is freedom, abused and scorned tho' we may be, our destiny is tied up with America's destiny.

MARTIN LUTHER KING, JR. (1929-68), U.S. clergyman, civil rights leader. Letter, April 1963, from Birmingham Jail, Ala. The last sentence of this extract echoes a speech by abolitionist Frederick Douglass, 12 Feb 1862, in Boston: "The destiny of the colored American . . . is the destiny of America."

13   The common goal of 22 million Afro-Americans is respect as *human beings,* the God-given right to be a *human being.* Our common goal is to obtain the *human rights* that America has been denying us. We can never get civil rights in America until our *human rights* are first restored. We will never be recognized as citizens there until we are first recognized as *humans.*

MALCOLM X (1925-65), U.S. black leader. "Racism: the Cancer that is Destroying America," in *Egyptian Gazette* (25 Aug. 1964). See Gregory on CIVIL RIGHTS.

14   The Afro-American experience is the only real culture that America has. Basically, every American tries to walk, talk, dress and behave like African Americans.

HUGH MASAKELA (b. 1939), South African jazz trumpeter. *International Herald Tribune* (Paris, 17 May 1990).

15   The warped, distorted frame we have put around every Negro child from birth is around every white child also. Each is on a different side of the frame but each is pinioned there. And . . . what cruelly shapes and cripples the personality of one is as cruelly shaping and crippling the personality of the other.

LILLIAN SMITH (1897-1966), U.S. author. *Killers of the Dream,* pt. 1, ch. 1 (1949; rev. 1961).

16   If there ever are great revolutions there, they will be caused by the presence of the blacks upon American soil. That is to say, it will not be the equality of social conditions but rather their inequality which may give rise to it.

ALEXIS DE TOCQUEVILLE (1805-59), French social philosopher. *Democracy in America,* vol. 2, pt. 3, ch. 21 (1840).

17   The trouble with our people is as soon as they got out of slavery they didn't want to give the white man nothing else. But the fact is, you got to give 'em something. Either your money, your land, your woman or your ass.

ALICE WALKER (b. 1944), U.S. author, critic. Pa, in *The Color Purple* (1983, p. 155).

See also Carter on CONSERVATIVES; Angelou on GHETTOS; Baldwin on MULTICULTURALISM; García Lorca on NEW YORK; James on SIMPLICITY; Black saying on SUSPICION.

THE AFTERLIFE

1   The chief problem about death, incidentally, is the fear that there may be no afterlife—a depressing thought, particularly for those who have bothered to shave. Also, there is the fear that there is an afterlife but no one will know where it's being held.

WOODY ALLEN (b. 1935), U.S. filmmaker. *Without Feathers,* "The Early Essays" (1976).

2   If a man die, shall he live again? All the days of my appointed time will I wait, till my change come.

BIBLE, HEBREW. *Job* 14:14.

3   Is there any thing beyond?—*who* knows? *He* that can't tell. Who tells there *is?* He who don't know. And when shall he know? Perhaps, when he don't expect it, and generally when he don't wish it. In this last respect, however, all are not alike; it depends a good deal upon education, something upon nerves and habits—but most upon digestion.

LORD BYRON (1788-1824), English poet. *Byron's Letters and Journals,* vol. 3, (ed. by Leslie Marchand, 1973-81), entry for 18 Feb. 1814.

4   Perhaps the only misplaced curiosity is that which persists in trying to find out here, on this side of death, what lies beyond the grave.

COLETTE (1873-1954), French author. *The Pure and the Impure* (1933; repr. in *Earthly Paradise,* pt. 2, "Freedom," ed. by Robert Phelps, 1966).

5   I can imagine myself on my death-bed, spent utterly with lust to touch the next world, like a boy asking for his first kiss from a woman.

ALEISTER CROWLEY (1875-1947), British occultist. *The Confessions of Aleister Crowley,* ch. 54 (1929; rev. 1970).

6   One short sleep past, we wake eternally,
And Death shall be no more; Death, thou shalt die!

JOHN DONNE) (c. 1572-1631), English divine, metaphysical poet. *Death be not Proud.*

7   If I were reincarnated, I'd want to come back a buzzard. Nothing hates him or envies him or wants him or needs him. He is never bothered or in danger, and he can eat anything.

WILLIAM FAULKNER (1897-1962), U.S. novelist. Interview in *Writers at Work* (First Series, ed. by Malcolm Cowley, 1958).

8   At the moment of death I hope to be surprised.

IVAN ILLICH (b. 1926), Austrian-born U.S. theologian, author.

Quoted in: *Sunday Times* (London, 20 Nov. 1988), in reply to a question on his beliefs about the afterlife.

9 All argument is against it; but all belief is for it.

SAMUEL JOHNSON (1709-84), English author, lexicographer. Quoted in: James Boswell, *Life of Samuel Johnson*, vol. 3, 31 March 1778 (ed. by G. B. Hill, 1791).

10 What time has been wasted during man's destiny in the struggle to decide what man's next world will be like! The keener the effort to find out, the less he knew about the present one he lived in.

SEAN O'CASEY (1884-1964), Irish dramatist. *Sunset and Evening Star*, "Shaw's Corner" (1954).

11 There is something very solemn in the thought of a great spirit like hers entering the spiritual world which she did not believe in. If we are right in our faith, what a blessed surprise for her!

MARGARET OLIPHANT (1828-97), English novelist, historian. Letter, 26 Dec. 1880 (published in *Autobiography and Letters of Mrs. Margaret Oliphant*, 1899), referring to novelist George Eliot, whose funeral was shortly to be held.

12 The dread of something after death,
The undiscovered country, from whose bourn
No traveller returns.

WILLIAM SHAKESPEARE (1564-1616), English dramatist, poet. Hamlet, in *Hamlet*, act 3, sc. 1.

13 So, while their bodies moulder here
Their souls with God himself shall dwell,—
But always recollect, my dear,
That wicked people go to hell.

ANN (1782-1866) AND JANE (1783-1824) TAYLOR, English writers of poetry for children. *About Dying*.

14 Oh, one world at a time!

HENRY DAVID THOREAU (1817-62), U.S. philosopher, author, naturalist. Remark made shortly before his death to Parker Pillsbury, when asked whether he believed in an afterlife. Quoted in: F. B. Sanborn, *Henry D. Thoreau* (1882). Brooks Atkinson, in *Walden and Other Writings of Thoreau*, claimed the remark was made to Thoreau's closest friend, William Ellery Channing.

15 I do not think myself to be a worm, and a grub, grass of the field fit only to be burned, a clod, a morsel of putrid atoms that should be thrown to the dungheap, ready for the nethermost pit. Nor if I did should I therefore expect to sit with Angels and Archangels.

ANTHONY TROLLOPE (1815-82), English novelist. Letter, 8 June 1876 (published in *The Letters of Anthony Trollope*, vol. 3, 1983).

16 The yearning for an afterlife is the opposite of selfish: it is love and praise for the world that we are privileged, in this complex interval of light, to witness and experience.

JOHN UPDIKE (b. 1932), U.S. author, critic. *Self-Consciousness: Memoirs*, ch. 6 (1989).

17 Limbo is the place. In Limbo one has natural happiness without the beatific vision; no harps; no communal order; but wine and conversation and imperfect, various humanity. Limbo for the unbaptized, for the pious heathen, the sincere sceptic.

EVELYN WAUGH (1903-66), British novelist. Ambrose, in *Put Out More Flags*, ch. 1, sct. 7 (1942).

18 Eddie did not die. He is no longer on Channel 4, and our sets are tuned to Channel 4; he's on Channel 7, but he's still broadcasting. Physical incarnation is highly overrated; it is one corner of universal possibility.

MARIANNE WILLIAMSON (b. 1953), U.S. benefactor. Quoted in: *Vanity Fair* (New York, June 1991), referring to dancer Edward Stierle, who died of AIDS.

See also Waller on CHRISTIANITY AND THE CHRISTIANS; Donne on DEATH AND DYING.

AGE AND AGING

1 You can only perceive real beauty in a person as they get older.

ANOUK AIMÉE (b. 1932), French actor. Quoted in: *Guardian* (London, 24 Aug. 1988).

2. The class distinctions proper to a democratic society are not those of rank or money, still less, as is apt to happen when these are abandoned, of race, but of age.

W. H. AUDEN (1907-73), Anglo-American poet. *The Dyer's Hand*, pt. 6, "Postscript: Rome v. Monticello" (1962).

3 What's a man's age? He must hurry more, that's all;
Cram in a day, what his youth took a year to hold.

ROBERT BROWNING (1812-89), English poet. *The Flight of the Duchess*, st. 17.

4 A woman's always younger than a man
At equal years.

ELIZABETH BARRETT BROWNING (1806-61), English poet. *Aurora Leigh*, bk. 2 (1857). An explanation follows:
. . . because she is disallowed
Maturing by the outdoor sun and air,
And kept in long-clothes past the age to walk.

5 A lady of a "certain age," which means
Certainly aged.

LORD BYRON (1788-1824), English poet. *Don Juan*, cto. 6, st. 69.

6 It was one of the deadliest and heaviest feelings of my life to feel that I was no longer a boy. From that moment I began to grow old in my own esteem—and in my esteem age is not estimable.

LORD BYRON (1788-1824), English poet. *Detached Thoughts*, no. 72 (1821-22; published in *Byron's Letters and Journals*, vol. 9, ed. by Leslie A. Marchand, 1979).

7 The heart never grows better by age; I fear rather worse; always harder. A young liar will be an old one, and a young knave will only be a greater knave as he grows older.

LORD CHESTERFIELD (1694-1773), English statesman, man of letters. Letter, 17 May 1750 (first published 1774; repr. in *The Letters of the Earl of Chesterfield to His Son*, vol. 2, no. 225, ed. by Charles Strachey, 1901).

8 A man's as old as he's feeling,
A woman as old as she looks.

MORTIMER COLLINS (1827-76), English novelist, poet. *The Unknown Quantity*.

9 Youth is a blunder; Manhood a struggle; Old Age a regret.

> BENJAMIN DISRAELI (1804-81), English statesman, author. *Coningsby*, bk. 3, ch. 1 (1844).

10 I don't believe one grows older. I think that what happens early on in life is that at a certain age one stands still and stagnates.

> T. S. ELIOT (1888-1965), Anglo-American poet, critic. Quoted in: *New York Times* (21 Sept. 1958).

11 The age of a woman doesn't mean a thing. The best tunes are played on the oldest fiddles.

> SIGMUND Z. ENGEL (1869-?). Quoted in: *Newsweek* (New York, 4 July 1949).

12 People between twenty and forty are not sympathetic. The child has the capacity to do but it can't know. It only knows when it is no longer able to do—after forty. Between twenty and forty the will of the child to do gets stronger, more dangerous, but it has not begun to learn to know yet. Since his capacity to do is forced into channels of evil through environment and pressures, man is stong before he is moral. The world's anguish is caused by people between twenty and forty.

> WILLIAM FAULKNER (1897-1962), U.S. novelist. Interview in *Writers at Work* (First Series, ed. by Malcolm Cowley, 1958).

13 A man has every season while a woman only has the right to spring. That disgusts me.

> JANE FONDA (b. 1937), U.S. screen actor. Quoted in: *Daily Mail* (London, 13 Sept. 1989).

14 Among the virtues and vices that make up the British character, we have one vice, at least, that Americans ought to view with sympathy. For they appear to be the only people who share it with us. I mean our worship of the antique. I do not refer to beauty or even historical association. I refer to age, to a quantity of years.

> WILLIAM GOLDING (1911-93), British author. "An Affection for Cathedrals," in *Holiday Magazine* (Indianapolis, Dec. 1965; repr. in *A Moving Target*, 1982).

15 At 20 a man is a peacock, at 30 a lion, at 40 a camel, at 50 a serpent, at 60 a dog, at 70 an ape, and at 80 nothing.

> BALTASAR GRACIÁN (1601-58), Spanish writer, Jesuit priest. *The Art of Worldly Wisdom*, "Know How to Renew Your Character" (1647).

16 The older you get the stronger the wind gets—and it's always in your face.

> JACK NICKLAUS (b. 1940), U.S. golfer. Quoted in: *International Herald Tribune* (Paris, 28 Feb. 1990).

17 Twenty years a child; twenty years running wild; twenty years a mature man—and after that, praying.

> IRISH PROVERB.

18 I have always felt that a woman has the right to treat the subject of her age with ambiguity until, perhaps, she passes into the realm of over ninety. Then it is better she be candid with herself and with the world.

> HELENA RUBINSTEIN (1870-1965), Polish-born U.S. cosmetics manufacturer. *My Life for Beauty*, pt. 1, ch. 1 (1966).

19 When you are younger you get blamed for crimes you never committed and when you're older you begin to get credit for virtues you never possessed. It evens itself out.

> I. F. STONE (1907-89), U.S. author. *International Herald Tribune* (Paris, 16 March 1988).

20 I'm 65 and I guess that puts me in with the geriatrics. But if there were fifteen months in every year, I'd only be 48. That's the trouble with us. We number everything. Take women, for example. I think they deserve to have more than twelve years between the ages of 28 and 40.

> JAMES THURBER (1894-1961), U.S. humorist, illustrator. *Time* (New York, 15 Aug. 1960).

21 For the first fourteen years for a rod they do whine,
For the next as a pearl in the world they do shine,
For the next trim beauty beginneth to swerve,
For the next matrons or drudges they serve,
For the next doth crave a staff for a stay,
For the next a bier to fetch them away.

> THOMAS TUSSER (c. 1520-C. 1580), English writer on agriculture. *Good Husbandry*, pt. 2 (1557; repr. 1812), describing a woman's age.

22 With care, and skill, and cunning art,
She parried Time's malicious dart,
And kept the years at bay,
Till passion entered in her heart
And aged her in a day!

> ELLA WHEELER WILCOX (1850-1919), U.S. poet, journalist. *The Destroyer*.

23 No woman should ever be quite accurate about her age. It looks so calculating.

> OSCAR WILDE (1854-1900), Anglo-Irish playwright, author. Lady Bracknell, in *The Importance of Being Earnest*, act 4.

24 These are the soul's changes. I don't believe in ageing. I believe in forever altering one's aspect to the sun. Hence my optimism.

> VIRGINIA WOOLF (1882-1941), British novelist. *The Diary of Virginia Woolf*, vol. 4 (ed. by Anne O. Bell, 1982), entry for 2 Oct. 1932.

See also Irving on COMPLIMENTS; GENERATIONS; Shakespeare on MATURITY; MIDDLE AGE; YOUTH.

AGE AND AGING: TWENTIES

1 I shall soon be six-and-twenty. Is there anything in the future that can possibly console us for not being always *twenty-five*?

> LORD BYRON (1788-1824), English poet. *Letters and Journals*, vol. 3 (ed. by Leslie A. Marchand, 1974), entry for 1 Dec. 1813.

2 In a few days I'll have lived one score and three days in this vale of tears. On I plod—always bored, often drunk, doing no penance for my faults—rather do I become more tolerant of myself from day to day, hardening my crystal heart with blasphemous humor and shunning only toothpicks, pathos, and poverty as being the three unforgivable things in life.

> F. SCOTT FITZGERALD (1896-1940), U.S. author. Letter, 22 Sept. 1919 (published in *The Letters of F. Scott Fitzgerald,* ed. by Andrew Turnbull, 1963). Fitzgerald in fact would have been 23.

3   One of those men who reach such an acute limited excellence at twenty-one that everything afterward savors of anti-climax.

> F. SCOTT FITZGERALD (1896-1940), U.S. author. The narrator (Nick Carraway) describing Tom Buchanan, in *The Great Gatsby,* ch. 1 (1925).

4   When I was as you are now, towering in the confidence of twenty-one, little did I suspect that I should be at forty-nine, what I now am.

> SAMUEL JOHNSON (1709-84), English author, lexicographer. Letter, 9 Jan. 1758 (published in James Boswell, *Life of Samuel Johnson,* 1791).

5   No gray hairs streak my soul,
no grandfatherly fondness there!
I shake the world with the might of my voice,
and walk—handsome,
twentytwoyearold.

> VLADIMIR MAYAKOVSKY (1893-1930), Russian poet, dramatist. *The cloud in trousers* (tr. by George Reavey).

6   How soon hath Time, the subtle thief of youth,
Stolen on his wing my three-and-twentieth year!

> JOHN MILTON (1608-74), English poet. *On His Having Arrived at the Age of Twenty-three.*

AGE AND AGING: THIRTIES

1   My time has been passed viciously and agreeably; at thirty-one so few years months days hours or minutes remain that *"Carpe Diem"* is not enough. I have been obliged to crop even the seconds—for who can trust to tomorrow?

> LORD BYRON (1788-1824), English poet. Letter, 20 Aug. 1819 (published in *Byron's Letters and Journals,* vol. 6, ed. by Leslie A. Marchand, 1976). The phrase *Carpe diem* ("seize the day") was used by Horace in his *Odes,* bk. 1, ode 11. Byron died at age thirty-six.

2   I always looked to about thirty as the barrier of any real or fierce delight in the passions, and determined to work them out in the younger ore and better veins of the mine—and I flatter myself (perhaps) that I have pretty well done so—and now the dross is coming.

> LORD BYRON (1788-1824), English poet. Letter, 18 Jan. 1823 (published in *Byron's Letters and Journals,* vol. 10, ed. by Leslie A. Marchand, 1973-81). Byron had earlier expressed the same sentiment to poet Thomas Moore, to whom he wrote (2 Feb. 1818): "I will work the mine of my youth to the last vein of the ore, and then—good night. I have lived, and am content."

3   I am thirty-three—the age of the good *Sans-culotte* Jesus; an age fatal to revolutionists.

> CAMILLE DESMOULINS (1760-94), French journalist, revolutionary leader. Answer, 2 April 1784, to the Revolutionary Tribunal, Paris, on the eve of his execution. Quoted in: Thomas Carlyle, *History of the French Revolution,* bk. 6, ch. 2 (1837).

4   Thirty—the promise of a decade of loneliness, a thinning list of single men to know, a thinning brief-case of enthusiasm, thinning hair.

> F. SCOTT FITZGERALD (1896-1940), U.S. author. The narrator (Nick Carraway), in *The Great Gatsby,* ch. 7 (1925).

5   But it's hard to be hip over thirty
When everyone else is nineteen,
When the last dance we learned was the Lindy,
And the last we heard, girls who looked like
  Barbra Streisand
Were trying to do something about it.

> JUDITH VIORST (b. 1935), U.S. poet, journalist. *It's Hard to Be Hip Over Thirty,* in *It's Hard to Be Hip Over Thirty and Other Tragedies of Married Life* (1968).

6   Thirty-five is a very attractive age. London society is full of women of the highest birth who have, of their own free choice, remained thirty-five for years.

> OSCAR WILDE (1854-1900), Anglo-Irish playwright, author. Lady Bracknell, in *The Importance of Being Earnest,* act 4.

See also Byron on BIRTHDAYS; James on CHARACTER; Fitzgerald on FRIENDS.

AGE AND AGING: FORTIES

1   At twenty you have many desires which hide the truth, but beyond forty there are only real and fragile truths—your abilities and your failings.

> GÉRARD DEPARDIEU (b. 1948), French screen actor. *Daily Mail* (London, 4 March 1991).

2   Men who have reached and passed forty-five, have a look as if waiting for the secret of the other world, and as if they were perfectly sure of having found out the secret of this.

> BENJAMIN HAYDON (1786-1846), British artist. *Correspondence and Table Talk,* vol. 2, "Table Talk" (ed. by Frederic Wordsworth Haydon, 1876).

3   Every man over forty is a scoundrel.

> GEORGE BERNARD SHAW (1856-1950), Anglo-Irish playwright, critic. *Man and Superman,* "Maxims for Revolutionists: Stray Sayings" (1903).

4   The man who is a pessimist before 48 knows too much; if he is an optimist after it, he knows too little.

> MARK TWAIN (1835-1910), U.S. author. *Notebook,* ch. 33 (ed. by Albert Bigelow Paine, 1935), entry for Dec. 1902

See also Fitzgerald on FRIENDS.

AGE AND AGING: FIFTIES

1   I think when the full horror of being fifty hits you, you should stay home and have a good cry.

> ALAN BLEASDALE (b. 1946), British playwright, novelist. *Times* (London, 18 June 1992).

2   I'm aiming by the time I'm fifty to stop being an adolescent.

> WENDY COPE (b. 1945), British poet. *Daily Telegraph* (London, 9 Dec. 1992).

3 Women over fifty already form one of the largest groups in the population structure of the western world. As long as they like themselves, they will not be an oppressed minority. In order to like themselves they must reject trivialization by others of who and what they are. A grown woman should not have to masquerade as a girl in order to remain in the land of the living.

> GERMAINE GREER (b. 1939), Australian feminist writer. *The Change: Women, Ageing and the Menopause*, Introduction (1991).

4 Nobody expects to trust his body overmuch after the age of fifty.

> EDWARD HOAGLAND (b. 1932), U.S. novelist, essayist. "Heaven and Nature," in *Harper's* (New York, March 1988; repr. in *Heart's Desire*, 1988).

5 When you get to fifty-two food becomes more important than sex.

> PRUE LEITH (b. 1940), British chef, caterer, writer on cookery. Quoted in: *Guardian* (London, 11 Nov. 1992).

6 The real sadness of fifty is not that you change so much but that you change so little.

> MAX LERNER (b. 1902), U.S. author, columnist. "Fifty," in *New York Post* (18 Dec. 1952; repr. in *The Unfinished Country*, pt. 1, 1959).

7 He was then in his fifty-fourth year, when even in the case of poets reason and passion begin to discuss a peace treaty and usually conclude it not very long afterwards.

> G. C. LICHTENBERG (1742-99), German physicist, philosopher. *Aphorisms*, "Notebook B," aph. 30 (written 1765-99; tr. by R. J. Hollingdale 1990).

8 When you're 50 you start thinking about things you haven't thought about before. I used to think getting old was about vanity—but actually it's about losing people you love. Getting wrinkles is trivial.

> JOYCE CAROL OATES (b. 1938), U.S. author. Interview in *Guardian* (London, 18 Aug. 1989).

9 "Except ye become as little children," except you can wake on your fiftieth birthday with the same forward-looking excitement and interest in life that you enjoyed when you were five, "ye cannot enter the kingdom of God." One must not only die daily, but every day we must be born again.

> DOROTHY L. SAYERS (1893-1957), British author. *Creed or Chaos? and Other Essays in Popular Mythology*, "Strong Meat" (1947).

10 Now, aged 50, I'm just poised to shoot forth quite free straight & undeflected my bolts whatever they are.

> VIRGINIA WOOLF (1882-1941), British novelist. *The Diary of Virginia Woolf*, vol. 4 (ed. by Anne O. Bell, 1982), entry for 2 Oct. 1932.

See also Orwell on FACES.

AGE AND AGING: SIXTIES

1 You must not pity me because my sixtieth year finds me still astonished. To be astonished is one of the surest ways of not growing old too quickly.

> COLETTE (1873-1954), French author. Speech, on being elected to the Belgian Academy (published in *Earthly Paradise*, pt. 4, "Lady of Letters," ed. by Robert Phelps, 1966).

2 One is rarely an impulsive innovator after the age of sixty, but one can still be a very fine orderly and inventive thinker. One rarely procreates children at that age, but one is all the more skilled at educating those who have already been procreated, and education is procreation of another kind.

> G. C. LICHTENBERG (1742-99), German physicist, philosopher. *Aphorisms*, "Notebook K," aph. 51 (written 1765-99; tr. by R. J. Hollingdale, 1990).

3 As life runs on, the road grows strange
With faces new,—and near the end
The milestones into headstones change,
'Neath every one a friend.

> JAMES RUSSELL LOWELL (1819-91), U.S. poet, editor. *Sixty-Eighth Birthday*.

4 With sixty staring me in the face, I have developed inflammation of the sentence structure and definite hardening of the paragraphs.

> JAMES THURBER (1894-1961), U.S. humorist, illustrator. Quoted in: *New York Post* (30 June 1955).

5 Now that I am sixty, I see why the idea of elder wisdom has passed from currency.

> JOHN UPDIKE (b. 1932), U.S. author, critic. *New Yorker* (Nov. 1992).

AGE AND AGING: SEVENTIES

1 There are three classes into which all the women past seventy that ever I knew were to be divided: 1. That dear old soul; 2. That old woman; 3. That old witch.

> SAMUEL TAYLOR COLERIDGE (1772-1834), English poet, critic. *Table Talk* (7 July 1831; published in *Specimens of the Table Talk of Samuel Taylor Coleridge*, ed. by Henry Nelson Coleridge, 1835; repr. in *Collected Works*, vol. 14, ed. by Kathleen Coburn, 1990).

2 To be seventy years young is sometimes far more cheerful and hopeful than to be forty years old.

> OLIVER WENDELL HOLMES, SR. (1809-94), U.S. writer, physician. Letter, 27 May 1889, to poet and reformer Julia Ward Howe on her seventieth birthday.

3 At seventy-seven it is time to be in earnest.

> SAMUEL JOHNSON (1709-84), English author, lexicographer. *Journey to the Western Isles of Scotland*, "Col" (1775; repr. in *Works of Samuel Johnson*, vol. 9, ed. by Mary Lascelles, 1971).

4 To be seventy years old is like climbing the Alps. You reach a snow-crowned summit, and see behind you the deep valley stretching miles and miles away, and before you other summits higher and whiter, which you may have strength to climb, or may not. Then you sit down and meditate and wonder which it will be.

HENRY WADSWORTH LONGFELLOW (1807-82), U.S. poet. Letter, 13 March 1877.

5 It is a bore, I admit, to be past seventy, for you are left for execution, and are daily expecting the death-warrant; but . . . it is not anything very capital we quit. We are, at the close of life, only hurried away from stomach-aches, pains in the joints, from sleepless nights and unamusing days, from weakness, ugliness, and nervous tremors; but we shall all meet again in another planet, cured of all our defects.

SYDNEY SMITH (1771-1845), English writer, clergyman. Letter, 13 Sept. 1842 (published in *The Letters of Sydney Smith,* vol. 2, 1953).

6 Being over seventy is like being engaged in a war. All our friends are going or gone and we survive amongst the dead and the dying as on a battlefield.

MURIEL SPARK (b. 1918), British novelist. Miss Taylor, in *Memento Mori,* ch. 4 (1959).

7 I delight in men over seventy. They always offer one the devotion of a lifetime.

OSCAR WILDE (1854-1900), Anglo-Irish playwright, author. Mrs. Allonby, in *A Woman of No Importance,* act 4.

AGENTS

1 The agent never receipts his bill, puts his hat on and bows himself out. He stays around forever, not only for as long as you can write anything that anyone will buy, but as long as anyone will buy any portion of any right to anything that you ever did write. He just takes ten per cent of your life.

RAYMOND CHANDLER (1888-1959), U.S. author. "Ten Per Cent of Your Life," in *Atlantic Monthly* (Boston, Feb. 1952).

2 Throughout the history of commercial life nobody has ever quite liked the commission man. His function is too vague, his presence always seems one too many, his profit looks too easy, and even when you admit that he has a necessary function, you feel that this function is, as it were, a personification of something that in an ethical society would not need to exist. If people could deal with one another honestly, they would not need agents.

RAYMOND CHANDLER (1888-1959), U.S. author. "Ten Per Cent of Your Life," in *Atlantic Monthly* (Boston, Feb. 1952).

3 It is well-known what a middleman is: he is a man who bamboozles one party and plunders the other.

BENJAMIN DISRAELI (1804-81), English statesman, author. Speech, 11 April 1845.

4 If God had an agent, the world wouldn't be built yet. It'd only be about Thursday.

JERRY REYNOLDS, Sacramento Kings' player personnel director. Quoted in: *Newsweek* (New York, 25 Nov. 1991), remarking on how agents slow down the negotiating process.

5 Let every eye negotiate for itself, And trust no agent.

WILLIAM SHAKESPEARE (1564-1616), English dramatist, poet. Claudio, in *Much Ado About Nothing,* act 2, sc. 1.

6 O world, world! thus is the poor agent despised. O traitors and bawds, how earnestly are you set a-work, and how ill requited! Why should our endeavour be so loved, and the performance so loathed?

WILLIAM SHAKESPEARE (1564-1616), English dramatist, poet. Pandarus, in *Troilus and Cressida,* act 5, sc. 10 (Quarto ed.).

See also Allen on Advertising

AGGRESSION

1 I love to see a young girl go out and grab the world by the lapels. Life's a bitch. You've got to go out and kick ass.

MAYA ANGELOU (b. 1928), U.S. author. "Kicking Ass," interview in *Girl About Town* (13 Oct. 1986; repr. in *Conversations with Maya Angelou,* 1989).

2 Does our ferocity not derive from the fact that our instincts are all too interested in other people? If we attended more to ourselves and became the center, the object of our murderous inclinations, the sum of our intolerances would diminish.

E. M. CIORAN (b. 1911), Rumanian-born French philosopher. *The Temptation to Exist,* title essay (1956).

3 We, the lineal representatives of the successful enactors of one scene of slaughter after another, must, whatever more pacific virtues we may also possess, still carry about with us, ready at any moment to burst into flame, the smoldering and sinister traits of character by means of which they lived through so many massacres, harming others, but themselves unharmed.

WILLIAM JAMES (1842-1910), U.S. psychologist, philosopher. *Principles of Psychology,* vol. 2, ch. 24 (1890).

4 Wolves which batten upon lambs, lambs consumed by wolves, the strong who immolate the weak, the weak victims of the strong: there you have Nature, there you have her intentions, there you have her scheme: a perpetual action and reaction, a host of vices, a host of virtues, in one word, a perfect equilibrium resulting from the equality of good and evil on earth.

MARQUIS DE SADE (1740-1814), French author. Clément, in *Justine, ou les Malheurs de la Vertu* (1791).

5 To knock a thing down, especially if it is cocked at an arrogant angle, is a deep delight to the blood.

GEORGE SANTAYANA (1863-1952), U.S. philosopher, poet. *The Life of Reason,* ch. 3, "Reason in Society" (1905-6).

6 Aggression, the writer's main source of energy.

TED SOLOTAROFF (b. 1928), U.S. editor. "Writing in the Cold," in *Granta,* no. 15 (Cambridge, England, 1985).

AGNOSTICS

1   If only God would give me some clear sign! Like making a large deposit in my name at a Swiss bank.

> WOODY ALLEN (b. 1935), U.S. filmmaker. "Selections from the Allen Notebooks," in *New Yorker* (5 Nov. 1973).

2   There is something Pagan in me that I cannot shake off. In short, I deny nothing, but doubt everything.

> LORD BYRON (1788-1824), English poet. Letter, 4 Dec. 1811 (published in *Byron's Letters and Journals*, vol. 2, ed. by Leslie A. Marchand, 1973-81).

3   I do not pretend to know where many ignorant men are sure—that is all that agnosticism means.

> CLARENCE DARROW (1857-1938), U.S. lawyer, writer. Speech, 13 July 1925, Dayton, Tennessee, defending John T. Scopes on trial for teaching Darwinism.

4   He talks about the Scylla of Atheism and the Charybdis of Christianity—a state of mind which, by the way, is not conducive to bold navigation.

> NORMAN DOUGLAS (1868-1952), British author. Mr. Keith, in *South Wind*, ch. 18 (1917), referring to author Samuel Butler.

5   Lord I disbelieve—help thou my unbelief.

> E. M. FORSTER (1879-1970), British novelist, essayist. *Two Cheers for Democracy*, "What I Believe" (1951), a play on Bible, Mark 9:24, "Lord, I believe, help Thou mine unbelief."

6   Question with boldness even the existence of a God; because, if there be one, he must more approve of the homage of reason, than that of blind-folded fear.

> THOMAS JEFFERSON (1743-1826), U.S. president. Letter, 10 Aug. 1787.

See also Yeats on ENGLAND AND THE ENGLISH.

AGREEMENT

1   You can get assent to almost any proposition so long as you are not going to do anything about it.

> JOHN JAY CHAPMAN (1862-1933), U.S. author. *Practical Agitation*, ch. 7 (1898).

2   Minds do not act together in public; they simply stick together; and when their private activities are resumed, they fly apart again.

> FRANK MOORE COLBY (1865-1925), U.S. editor, essayist. *The Colby Essays*, vol. 1, "Simple Simon" (1926).

3   My idea of an agreeable person is a person who agrees with me.

> BENJAMIN DISRAELI (1804-81), English statesman, author. Hugo Bohun, in *Lothair*, ch. 41 (1870).

4   Thinking isn't agreeing or disagreeing. That's voting.

> ROBERT FROST (1874-1963), U.S. poet. Interview in *Writers at Work* (Second Series, ed. by George Plimpton, 1963).

5   There's nothing is this world more instinctively abhorrent to me than finding myself in agreement with my fellow-humans.

> MALCOLM MUGGERIDGE (1903-90), British broadcaster. "Any

Questions?," radio broadcast, 29 April 1955. Quoted in: *Muggeridge Through the Microphone*, "Mini-Mania" (1967).

6   It may offend us to hear our own thoughts expressed by others: we are not sure enough of their souls.

> JEAN ROSTAND (1894-1977), French biologist, writer. *Pensées d'un Biologiste* (1939; repr. in *The Substance of Man*, "A Biologist's Thoughts," ch. 10, 1962).

See also CONSENSUS; Santayana on MEN AND WOMEN.

AID

1   Fool that I was, upon my eagle's wings
I bore this wren, till I was tired with soaring,
And now he mounts above me.

> JOHN DRYDEN (1631-1700), English poet, dramatist, critic. Antony, in *All for Love*, act 2, sc. 1 (1678).

2   We do not quite forgive a giver. The hand that feeds us is in some danger of being bitten.

> RALPH WALDO EMERSON (1803-82), U.S. essayist, poet, philosopher. *Essays*, "Gifts" (Second Series, 1844).

3   Help a man against his will and you do the same as murder him.

> HORACE (65-8 BC), Roman poet. *Ars Poetica* (c. 13 B.C.).

4   It is not helpful to help a friend by putting coins in his pockets when he has got holes in his pockets.

> DOUGLAS HURD (b. 1930), British Conservative politician. Quoted in: *Observer* (London, 9 June 1991), on aid to Russia.

5   To those people in the huts and villages of half the globe struggling to break the bonds of mass misery, we pledge our best efforts to help them help themselves, for whatever period is required, not because the Communists may be doing it, not because we seek their votes, but because it is right. If a free society cannot help the many who are poor, it cannot save the few who are rich.

> JOHN F. KENNEDY (1917-63), U.S. Democratic politician, president. Inaugural address, 20 Jan. 1961, Washington, D.C.

6   And who is any of us, that without starvation he can go through the kingdoms of starvation?

> HANIEL LONG (1888-1956), U.S. author, poet, journalist. *Interlinear to Cabeza de Vaca* (1936; repr. 1987, p. 50).

7   There is something wrong about the man who wants help. There is somewhere a deep defect, a want, in brief, a need, a crying need, somewhere about that man.

> HERMAN MELVILLE (1819-91), U.S. author. Charlie Noble, in *The Confidence-Man: His Masquerade*, ch. 39 (1857), to Frank Goodman, who had asked Noble for a loan and assistance.

8   Almsgiving tends to perpetuate poverty; aid does away with it once and for all. Almsgiving leaves a man just where he was before. Aid restores him to society as an individual worthy of all respect and not as a man with a grievance. Almsgiving is the generosity of the rich; social aid levels up social inequalities. Charity separates the rich from the poor; aid raises the needy and sets him on the same level with the rich.

> EVA PERÓN (1919-52), Argentinian government official, politician. "My Labour in the Field of Social Aid," address, 5 Dec. 1949, to the American Congress of Industrial Medicine.

9 We are for aiding our allies by sharing some of our material blessings with those nations which share in our fundamental beliefs, but we are against doling out money government to government, creating bureaucracy, if not socialism, all over the world. We set out to help 19 countries. We are helping 107 We spent $146 billion. With that money, we bought a 2-million-dollar yacht for Haile Selassie. We bought dress suits for Greek undertakers, extra wives for Kenya government officials. We bought a thousand TV sets for a place where they have no electricity.

> RONALD REAGAN (b. 1911), U.S. Republican politician, president. "A Time for Choosing," televised address, 27 Oct. 1964 (published in *Speaking My Mind*, 1989).

10 To keep a lamp burning we have to keep putting oil in it.

> MOTHER TERESA (b. 1910), Albanian-born Roman Catholic missionary. Quoted in: *Time* (New York, 29 Dec. 1975).

11 Let us more and more insist on raising funds of love, of kindness, of understanding, of peace. Money will come if we seek first the Kingdom of God—the rest will be given.

> MOTHER TERESA (b. 1910), Albanian-born Roman Catholic missionary. *A Gift for God*, "Carriers of Christ's Love" (1975).

12 The needs of a human being are sacred. Their satisfaction cannot be subordinated either to reasons of state, or to any consideration of money, nationality, race, or color, or to the moral or other value attributed to the human being in question, or to any consideration whatsoever.

> SIMONE WEIL (1909-43), French philosopher, mystic. "Draft for a Statement of Human Obligation" (1943; published in *Selected Essays*, ed. by Richard Rees, 1962).

AIDS

1 Both the Moral Majority, who are recycling medieval language to explain AIDS, and those ultra-leftists who attribute AIDS to some sort of conspiracy, have a clearly political analysis of the epidemic. But even if one attributes its cause to a microorganism rather than the wrath of God, or the workings of the CIA, it is clear that the way in which AIDS has been perceived, conceptualized, imagined, researched and financed makes this the most political of diseases.

> DENNIS ALTMAN (b. 1943), Australian sociologist. *AIDS in the Mind of America*, ch. 2 (1986).

2 Everywhere I go I see increasing evidence of people swirling about in a human cesspit of their own making.

> JAMES ANDERTON (b. 1932), British senior police officer. Quoted in: *City Limits* (London, 18 Dec. 1987), on the AIDS epidemic.

3 It could be said that the AIDS pandemic is a classic own-goal scored by the human race against itself.

> ANNE, PRINCESS ROYAL OF GREAT BRITAIN AND NORTHERN IRELAND (b. 1950). Quoted in: *Daily Telegraph* (London, Feb. 27, 1988).

4 From the point of view of the pharmaceutical industry, the AIDS problem has already been solved. After all, we already have a drug which can be sold at the incredible price of $8,000 an annual dose, and which has the added virtue of not diminishing the market by actually curing anyone.

> BARBARA EHRENREICH (b. 1941), U.S. author, columnist. *The Worst Years of Our Lives*, "Phallic Science" (1991; first published 1988).

5 We are all HIV-positive.

> DIAMANDA GALÁS (b. 1955), U.S. singer. Tattooed on her knuckles. Discussing the tattoo in an interview in *Re/Search*, no. 13, "Angry Women" (San Francisco, 1991), Galás stated, "If I wear the right clothes it will just say 'HIV Positive.' A lot of people already assume I've got AIDS because of my work, just as they assume I'm a lesbian."

6 My thoughts are crowded with death
and it draws so oddly on the sexual
that I am confused
confused to be attracted
by, in effect, my own annihilation.

> THOM GUNN (b. 1929), British poet. *In Time Of Plague*, in *The Man With Night Sweats* (1992).

7 Sometimes I have a terrible feeling that I am dying not from the virus, but from being untouchable.

> AMANDA HEGGS, AIDS sufferer. Quoted in: *Guardian* (London, 12 June 1989).

8 The slow-witted approach to the HIV epidemic was the result of a thousand years of Christian malpractice and the childlike approach of the church to sexuality. If any single man was responsible, it was Augustine of Hippo who murdered his way to sainthood spouting on about the sins located in his genitals.

> DEREK JARMAN (b. 1942), British filmmaker, artist, author. *At Your Own Risk: A Saint's Testament*, "1980's" (1992).

9 We're all going to go crazy, living this epidemic every minute, while the rest of the world goes on out there, all around us, as if nothing is happening, going on with their own lives and not knowing what it's like, what we're going through. We're living through war, but where they're living it's peacetime, and we're all in the same country.

> LARRY KRAMER (b. 1935), U.S. playwright, novelist. Ned, in *The Normal Heart*.

10 . . . strung out and spotty, you wriggle and sigh and kiss all the fellows and make them all die.

> LES MURRAY (b. 1938), Australian poet. *Little Boy Blue*.

11 I have learned more about love, selflessness and human understanding in this great adventure in the world of AIDS than I ever did in the cut-throat, competitive world in which I spent my life.

> ANTHONY PERKINS (1932-92), U.S. screen actor. Statement published posthumously in *Independent on Sunday* (London, Sept. 20, 1992).

12 Any important disease whose causality is murky, and for which treatment is ineffectual, tends to be awash in significance.

> SUSAN SONTAG (b. 1933), U.S. essayist. *Illness As Metaphor,* ch. 8 (1978).

13 AIDS obliges people to think of sex as having, possibly, the direst consequences: suicide. Or murder.

> SUSAN SONTAG (b. 1933), U.S. essayist. *AIDS and Its Metaphors,* ch. 7 (1989).

14 AIDS occupies such a large part in our awareness because of what it has been taken to represent. It seems the very model of all the catastrophes privileged populations feel await them.

> SUSAN SONTAG (b. 1933), U.S. essayist. *AIDS and Its Metaphors,* ch. 8 (1989).

15 The moral immune system of this country has been weakened and attacked, and the AIDS virus is the perfect metaphor for it. The malignant neglect of the last twelve years has led to breakdown of our country's immune system, environmentally, culturally, politically, spiritually and physically.

> BARBRA STREISAND (b. 1942), U.S. singer, actor. "The Way We Were," in *Guardian* (London, 26 Nov. 1992).

16 The AIDS epidemic has rolled back a big rotting log and revealed all the squirming life underneath it, since it involves, all at once, the main themes of our existence: sex, death, power, money, love, hate, disease and panic. No American phenomenon has been so compelling since the Vietnam War.

> EDMUND WHITE (b. 1940), U.S. author. *States of Desire: Travels in Gay America* (1980; "Afterword—AIDS: An American Epidemic," added to 1986 ed.).

See also Jarman on DEATH AND DYING; Updike on SEX.

AIR

1 Wild air, world-mothering air,
Nestling me everywhere,
That each eyelash or hair
Girdles; goes home betwixt
The fleeciest, frailest-fixed
Snowflake; that's fairly mixed
With, riddles, and is rife
In every least thing's life.

> GERARD MANLEY HOPKINS (1844-89), English poet, Jesuit priest. *The Blessed Virgin Compared to the Air We Breathe.*

2 The air is precious to the red man, for all things share the same breath—the beast, the tree, the man, they all share the same breath. The white man does not seem to notice the air he breathes. Like a man dying for many days, he is numb to the stench.

> Attributed to SEATTLE (c. 1784-1866), Chief of the Dwamish, Suquamish, and allied tribes. Letter, 1854, to President Franklin Pierce (published in *Brother Eagle, Sister Sky: A Message from Chief Seattle,* 1990). The letter, in which Seattle pleaded that his name should die with the ceding of the Washington State territories, was shown in 1992 to have been largely a forgery devised by Ted Perry, a television scriptwriter, for a historical epic in 1971.

3 Of all ebriosity, who does not prefer to be intoxicated by the air he breathes?

> HENRY DAVID THOREAU (1817-62), U.S. philosopher, author, naturalist. *Walden,* "Higher Laws" (1854).

AIRPLANES

1 A plane is a bad place for an all-out sleep, but a good place to begin rest and recovery from the trip to the faraway places you've been, a decompression chamber between Here and There. Though a plane is not the ideal place really to think, to reassess or reevaluate things, it is a great place to have the illusion of doing so, and often the illusion will suffice.

> SHANA ALEXANDER (b. 1925), U.S. writer, editor. *The Feminine Eye,* "Overcuddle and Megalull" (1970; first published 1967).

2 Of all the inventions that have helped to unify China perhaps the airplane is the most outstanding. Its ability to annihilate distance has been in direct proportion to its achievements in assisting to annihilate suspicion and misunderstanding among provincial officials far removed from one another or from the officials at the seat of government.

> MADAME CHIANG KAI-SHEK (b. 1898), Chinese educator, reformer. *Shanghai Evening Post* (12 March 1937).

3 I wish I could write well enough to write about aircraft. Faulkner did it very well in *Pylon* but you cannot do something someone else has done though you might have done it if they hadn't.

> ERNEST HEMINGWAY (1899-1961), U.S. author. Letter, July 3, 1956 (published in *Selected Letters,* ed. by Carlos Baker, 1981).

4 I feel about airplanes the way I feel about diets. It seems to me that they are wonderful things for other people to go on.

> JEAN KERR (b. 1923), U.S. author, playwright. *The Snake Has All the Lines,* "Mirror, Mirror on the Wall" (1958).

5 There are no signposts in the sky to show a man has passed that way before. There are no channels marked. The flier breaks each second into new uncharted seas.

> ANNE MORROW LINDBERGH (b. 1906), U.S. author. *North to the Orient,* ch. 1 (1935).

6 The aeroplane has unveiled for us the true face of the earth.

> ANTOINE DE SAINT-EXUPÉRY (1900-1944), French aviator, writer. *Wind, Sand, and Stars,* ch. 5 (published in *Terre des Hommes,* 1939).

7 Success four flights thursday morning all against twenty one mile wind started from Level with engine power alone speed through air thirty one miles longest 57 second inform Press home Christmas.

> ORVILLE WRIGHT (1871-1948), U.S. pioneer aviator. Telegram, 17 Dec. 1903 (published in *The Papers of Wilbur and Orville Wright,* vol. 1, 1953). The telegram was written to Milton Wright—Orville and Wilbur's father—announcing the first successful powered flight, made at Kitty Hawk Sands the same day. The flight time was in fact 59 seconds, not 57.

See also Perot on BUREAUCRACY.

ALCOHOL

1   If all be true that I do think,
There are five reasons we should drink:
Good wine—a friend—or being dry—
Or lest we should be by and by—
Or any other reason why.

> HENRY ALDRICH (1647-1710), English scholar, dean of Christ Church, Oxford. *Reasons For Drinking.*

2   Other countries drink to get drunk, and this is accepted by everyone; in France, drunkenness is a consequence, never an intention. A drink is felt as the spinning out of a pleasure, not as the necessary cause of an effect which is sought: wine is not only a philtre, it is also the leisurely act of drinking.

> ROLAND BARTHES (1915-80), French semiologist. *Mythologies,* "Wine and Milk" (1957; tr. 1972).

3   One drink is too many for me and a thousand not enough.

> BRENDAN BEHAN (1923-64), Irish playwright. Quoted by Rae Jeffs, publicist and assistant to Behan, in: Daniel Farson, *Sacred Monsters,* "Rousting in Dublin" (1988).

4   The decline of the aperitif may well be one of the most depressing phenomena of our time.

> LUIS BUÑUEL (1900-1983), Spanish filmmaker. *My Last Sigh,* ch. 6 (1983).

5   Alcohol is like love. The first kiss is magic, the second is intimate, the third is routine. After that you take the girl's clothes off.

> RAYMOND CHANDLER (1888-1959), U.S. author. Terry Lennox, in *The Long Goodbye,* ch. 4 (1954).

6   Most Americans are born drunk, and really require a little wine or beer to sober them. They have a sort of permanent intoxication from within, a sort of invisible champagne.... Americans do not need to drink to inspire them to do anything, though they do sometimes, I think, need a little for the deeper and more delicate purpose of teaching them how to do nothing.

> G. K. CHESTERTON (1874-1936), British author. *New York Times* (28 June 1931).

7   A sudden violent jolt of it has been known to stop the victim's watch, snap his suspenders and crack his glass eye right across.

> IRVIN S. COBB (1876-1944), U.S. author. Of moonshine corn liquor, as described to the Distillers' Code Authority, N.R.A. (attributed).

8   There is only one really safe, mild, harmless beverage and you can drink as much of that as you like without running the slightest risk, and what you say when you want it is, "Garcon! Un Pernod!"

> ALEISTER CROWLEY (1875-1947), British occultist. *The Confessions of Aleister Crowley,* ch. 63 (1929; rev. 1970), advice to his disciple Victor Neuburg in Paris.

9   Bring in the bottled lightning, a clean tumbler, and a corkscrew.

> CHARLES DICKENS (1812-70), English novelist. "The Gentleman in the Small-clothes," in *Nicholas Nickleby,* ch. 49 (1839).

10   Alcohol is nicissary f'r a man so that now an' thin he can have a good opinion iv himsilf, ondisturbed be th' facts.

> FINLEY PETER DUNNE (1867-1936), U.S. journalist, humorist. "Mr. Dooley on Alcohol," in *Chicago Tribune* (26 April 1914).

11   Alcohol doesn't console, it doesn't fill up anyone's psychological gaps, all it replaces is the lack of God. It doesn't comfort man. On the contrary, it encourages him in his folly, it transports him to the supreme regions where he is master of his own destiny.

> MARGUERITE DURAS (b. 1914), French author. *Practicalities,* "Alcohol" (1987; tr. 1990).

12   No other human being, no woman, no poem or music, book or painting can replace alcohol in its power to give man the illusion of real creation.

> MARGUERITE DURAS (b. 1914), French author. *Practicalities,* "Alcohol" (1987; tr. 1990).

13   There is this to be said in favor of drinking, that it takes the drunkard first out of society, then out of the world.

> RALPH WALDO EMERSON (1803-82), U.S. essayist, poet, philosopher. *The Journals and Miscellaneous Notebooks of Ralph Waldo Emerson,* vol. 16 (ed. by Ronald Bosco and Glen Johnson), 1866 entry.

14   I have fed purely upon ale; I have eat my ale, drank my ale, and I always sleep upon ale.

> GEORGE FARQUHAR (1678-1707), Irish dramatist. The landlord Boniface, in *The Beaux' Stratagem,* act 1, sc. 1.

15   Fill it up. I take as large draughts of liquor as I did of love. I hate a flincher in either.

> JOHN GAY (1685-1732), English dramatist. Mrs. Trapes, in *The Beggar's Opera,* act 3, sc. 6.

16   Don't you drink? I notice you speak slightingly of the bottle. I have drunk since I was fifteen and few things have given me more pleasure. When you work hard all day with your head and know you must work again the next day what else can change your ideas and make them run on a different plane like whisky? When you are cold and wet what else can warm you? Before an attack who can say anything that gives you the momentary well-being that rum does? . . . The only time it isn't good for you is when you write or when you fight. You have to do that cold. But it always helps my shooting. Modern life, too, is often a mechanical oppression and liquor is the only mechanical relief.

> ERNEST HEMINGWAY (1899-1961), U.S. author. Post script to letter, 19 Aug. 1935, to Ivan Kashkin (published in *Selected Letters,* ed. by Carlos Baker, 1981). Kashkin (1899-1963), a critic, poet and translator, was mainly responsible for establishing Hemingway's reputation in the U.S.S.R.

17   Ale, man, ale's the stuff to drink
For fellows whom it hurts to think.

> A. E. HOUSMAN (1859-1936), British poet, classical scholar. *A Shropshire Lad,* no. 62 (1896).

18   Malt does more than Milton can
To justify God's ways to man.

> A. E. HOUSMAN (1859-1936), British poet, classical scholar. *A Shropshire Lad,* no. 62 (1896).

19   They who drink beer will think beer.

WASHINGTON IRVING (1783-1859), U.S. author. *The Sketch Book of Geoffrey Crayon, Gent.*, "Stratford-on-Avon" (1820). This quotation has also been attributed to William Warburton, Bishop of Gloucester (1698-1779).

20   The sway of alcohol over mankind is unquestionably due to its power to stimulate the mystical faculties of human nature, usually crushed to earth by the cold facts and dry criticisms of the sober hour. Sobriety diminishes, discriminates, and says no; drunkenness expands, unites, and says yes.

WILLIAM JAMES (1842-1910), U.S. psychologist, philosopher. *The Varieties of Religious Experience*, Lectures 16-17, "Mysticism" (1902).

21   There are some sluggish men who are improved by drinking; as there are fruits that are not good until they are rotten.

SAMUEL JOHNSON (1709-84), English author, lexicographer. Quoted in: James Boswell, *Life of Samuel Johnson*, 12 April 1776 (1791).

22   Even though a number of people have tried, no one has yet found a way to drink for a living.

JEAN KERR (b. 1923), U.S. author, playwright. Sydney, in *Poor Richard*, act 1.

23   The rapturous, wild, and ineffable pleasure
Of drinking at somebody else's expense.

H. S. LEIGH (1837-83), English author. *Stanzas to an Intoxicated Fly.*

24   Drink! for you know not whence you came
      nor why:
Drink! for you know not why you go,
      nor where.

OMAR KHAYYÁM (11-12TH CENTURY), Persian astronomer, poet. *The Rubáiyát of Omar Khayyám*, st. 74 (tr. by Edward FitzGerald, 1879).

25   Candy,
Is dandy,
But Liquor,
Is quicker.

OGDEN NASH (1902-1971), U.S. poet. *Reflections on Ice-Breaking*, in *Hard Lines* (1931).

26   I only drink to make other people seem more interesting.

GEORGE JEAN NATHAN (1882-1958), U.S. critic. Quoted beneath his picture in Charlie O's bar, New York City.

27   Where does one not find that bland degeneration which beer produces in the spirit!

FRIEDRICH NIETZSCHE (1844-1900), German philosopher. *Twilight of the Idols*, "What the Germans Lack," aph. 2 (1889).

28   A torchlight procession marching down your throat.

JOHN LOUIS O'SULLIVAN (1813-95), U.S. editor. Quoted in: G. W. E. Russell, *Collections and Recollections*, ch. 19 (1898), of whisky.

29   MacDuff: What three things does drink especially provoke?
Porter: Marry, sir, nose-painting, sleep, and urine.

WILLIAM SHAKESPEARE (1564-1616), English dramatist, poet. *Macbeth*, act 2, sc. 3. "Nose-painting" refers to the drunkard's red nose. For the rest of the Porter's speech see Shakespeare on ALCOHOL: DRUNKENNESS.

30   O God, that men should put an enemy in their mouths to steal away their brains! That we should with joy, pleasance, revel, and applause transform ourselves into beasts!

WILLIAM SHAKESPEARE (1564-1616), English dramatist, poet. Cassio, in *Othello*, act 2, sc. 3.

31   At the punch-bowl's brink,
Let the thirsty think,
What they say in Japan:
First the man takes a drink,
Then the drink takes a drink,
Then the drink takes the man!

EDWARD ROWLAND SILL (1841-87), U.S. poet, essayist. *An Adage from the Orient.*

32   No power on earth or above the bottomless pit has such influence to terrorize and make cowards of men as the liquor power. Satan could not have fallen on a more potent instrument with which to thrall the world. Alcohol is king!

ELIZA "MOTHER" STEWART (1816-1908?), U.S. temperance leader. *Memories of the Crusade*, ch. 1 (1888).

33   Better belly burst than good liquor be lost.

JONATHAN SWIFT (1667-1745), Anglo-Irish satirist. Neverout, in *Polite Conversation*, Dialogue 2 (1738), quoting a proverb first collected in James Howell, *Paroimiographia* (1659).

34   There are two things that will be believed of any man whatsoever, and one of them is that he has taken to drink.

BOOTH TARKINGTON (1869-1946), U.S. author. *Penrod*, ch. 10 (1914).

35   You can't be a Real Country unless you have A BEER and an airline—it helps if you have some kind of a football team, or some nuclear weapons, but at the very least you need a BEER.

FRANK ZAPPA (b. 1940), U.S. rock musician. *The Real Frank Zappa Book*, ch. 12 (1989; written with Peter Occhiogrosso)

See also Dryden on The ARMY; Booth on BARS, PUBS, AND CAFÉS; Smith on THE BRITISH; COCKTAILS; Johnson on HEROES; Johnson on MELANCHOLY; WINE; Wilde on WORK.

ALCOHOL: ABSTINENCE

1   He shall separate himself from wine and strong drink, and shall drink no vinegar of wine, or vinegar of strong drink, neither shall he drink any liquor of grapes, nor eat moist grapes, or dried.

BIBLE, HEBREW. *Numbers* 6:3.

2 It's a great advantage not to drink among hard-drinking people. You can hold your tongue and, moreover, you can time any little irregularity of your own so that everybody else is so blind that they don't see or care.

> F. SCOTT FITZGERALD (1896-1940), U.S. author. Jordan Baker, in *The Great Gatsby*, ch. 4 (1925), accounting for Daisy Buchanan's "perfect reputation."

3 I'd hate to be a teetotaller. Imagine getting up in the morning and knowing that's as good as you're going to feel all day.

> DEAN MARTIN (b. 1917), U.S. screen actor, singer. Quoted in: Leslie Halliwell, *Halliwell's Filmgoer's Companion* (1984).

4 I'm only a beer teetotaller, not a champagne teetotaller.

> GEORGE BERNARD SHAW (1856-1950), Anglo-Irish playwright, critic. Proserpine, in *Candida*, act 3.

5 And must I wholly banish hence
These red and golden juices,
And pay my vows to Abstinence,
That pallidest of Muses?

> SIR WILLIAM WATSON (1858-1935), British poet. *To a Fair Maiden Who Bade Me Shun Wine*.

See also ABSTINENCE.

ALCOHOL: DRUNKENNESS

1 An alcoholic has been lightly defined as a man who drinks more than his own doctor.

> ALVAN L. BARACH (1895-1977), U.S. physician. Quoted from *Journal of the American Medical Association* by John Illman in: *Guardian* (London, 29 Dec. 1989).

2 When I played drunks I had to remain sober because I didn't know how to play them when I was drunk.

> RICHARD BURTON (1925-84), British stage and screen actor. Quoted in: Leslie Halliwell, *Halliwell's Filmgoer's Companion* (1984).

3 It is immoral to get drunk because the headache comes after the drinking, but if the headache came first and the drunkenness afterwards, it would be moral to get drunk.

> SAMUEL BUTLER (1835-1902), English author. *Samuel Butler's Notebooks* (1951, p. 101).

4 Man, being reasonable, must get drunk;
The best of life is but intoxication.

> LORD BYRON (1788-1824), English poet. *Don Juan*, cto. 2, st. 179.

5 Drink, and be mad, then; 'tis your country bids!
Gloriously drunk, obey th'important call!

> WILLIAM COWPER (1731-1800), English poet. *The Task*, bk. 4 (1785).

6 Alcohol is barren. The words a man speaks in the night of drunkenness fade like the darkness itself at the coming of day.

> MARGUERITE DURAS (b. 1914), French author. *Practicalities*, "Alcohol" (1987; tr. 1990).

7 When a woman drinks it's as if an animal were drinking, or a child. Alcoholism is scandalous in a woman, and a female alcholic is rare, a serious matter. It's a slur on the divine in our nature.

> MARGUERITE DURAS (b. 1914), French author. *Practicalities*, "Alcohol" (1987; tr. 1990).

8 The hangover became a part of the day as well allowed-for as the Spanish siesta.

> F. SCOTT FITZGERALD (1896-1940), U.S. author. *The Crack-Up*, "My Lost City" (ed. by Edmund Wilson, 1945; first published in *Esquire*, New York, July 1932).

9 The Great Spirit, who made all things, made every thing for some use, and whatever use he designed anything for, that use it should always be put to. Now, when he made rum, he said "*Let this be for the Indians to get drunk with*," and it must be so.

> NATIVE AMERICAN ELDER in Carlisle, Pennsylvania, quoted by Benjamin Franklin in: *Autobiography*, ch. 8 (written 1771-90; published 1868).

10 I can't say whether we had more wit among us now than usual, but I am certain we had more laughing, which answered the end as well.

> OLIVER GOLDSMITH (1728-74), Anglo-Irish author, poet, playwright. The narrator (Dr. Charles Primrose), in *The Vicar of Wakefield*, ch. 32 (1766).

11 I often sit back and think, "I wish I'd done that," and find out later that I already have.

> RICHARD HARRIS (b. 1932), Irish actor. Quoted in: *Sun* (London, 19 May 1988), on his drinking.

12 And he smiled a kind of sickly smile, and curled
up on the floor,
And the subsequent proceedings interested him
no more.

> FRANCIS BRET HARTE (1836-1902), U.S. author, journalist, poet. *The Society Upon the Stanislaus*.

13 Drink not the third glass, which thou canst
not tame,
When once it is within thee.

> GEORGE HERBERT (1593-1633), English clergyman, poet. *The Church-Porch*, st. 5.

14 If merely "feeling good" could decide, drunkenness would be the supremely valid human experience.

> WILLIAM JAMES (1842-1910), U.S. psychologist, philosopher. *The Varieties Of Religious Experience*, Lecture 1, "Religion and Neurology" (1902).

15 A man who exposes himself when he is intoxicated, has not the art of getting drunk.

> SAMUEL JOHNSON (1709-84), English author, lexicographer. Quoted in: James Boswell, *Life of Samuel Johnson*, 24 April 1779 (1791).

16 I believe, if we take habitual drunkards as a class, their heads and their hearts will bear an advantageous comparison with those of any other class. There seems ever to have been a proneness in the brilliant and warm-blooded to fall into this vice.

> ABRAHAM LINCOLN (1809-65), U.S. president. Speech, 22 Feb. 1842, to the Washingtonian Temperance Society, Springfield, Ill.

(published in *The Collected Works of Abraham Lincoln,* vol. 1, ed. by Roy P. Basler, 1953).

17 And when night,
Darkens the streets, then wander forth the sons
Of Belial, flown with insolence and wine.

JOHN MILTON (1608-74), English poet. *Paradise Lost,* bk. 1.

18 For art to exist, for any sort of aesthetic activity or perception to exist, a certain physiological precondition is indispensable: *intoxication.*

FRIEDRICH NIETZSCHE (1844-1900), German philosopher. *Twilight of the Idols,* "Expeditions of an Untimely Man," aph. 8 (1889).

19 The Grape that can with Logic absolute,
The Two-and-Seventy jarring Sects confute.

OMAR KHAYYÁM (11-12TH CENTURY), Persian astronomer, poet. *The Rubáiyát of Omar Khayyám,* st. 43 (tr. by Edward FitzGerald, 1859).

20 I do not live in the world of sobriety.

OLIVER REED (b. 1938), British screen actor. Quoted in: *Sunday Times* (London, 27 Dec. 1987).

21 Drunkenness . . . is temporary suicide.

BERTRAND RUSSELL (1872-1970), British philosopher, mathematician. *The Conquest of Happiness,* ch. 2 (1930).

22 Drunkenness is nothing but voluntary madness.

SENECA (c. 5 B.C.-A.D.65), Roman writer, philosopher, statesman. *Epistulae ad Lucilium,* Epistle 83, sct. 18.

23 It provokes the desire but it takes away the performance. Therefore much drink may be said to be an equivocator with lechery: it makes him and it mars him; it sets him on and it takes him off.

WILLIAM SHAKESPEARE (1564-1616), English dramatist, poet. Porter, in *Macbeth,* act 2, sc. 3.

24 I told you, sir, they were red-hot with drinking;
So full of valour that they smote the air,
For breathing in their faces, beat the ground
For kissing of their feet.

WILLIAM SHAKESPEARE (1564-1616), English dramatist, poet. Ariel, in *The Tempest,* act 4, sc. 1, reporting to Prospero of the drunken state in which he left Trinculo, Stefano and Caliban.

25 It takes that *je ne sais quoi* which we call sophistication for a woman to be magnificent in a drawing-room when her faculties have departed but she herself has not yet gone home.

JAMES THURBER (1894-1961), U.S. humorist, illustrator. *New Yorker* (2 Aug. 1930).

See also Crisp on DINNER PARTIES; Heraclitus on IGNORANCE; Wilde on POETS.

ALIENATION

1 There is only one way left to escape the alienation of present day society: *to retreat ahead of it.*

ROLAND BARTHES (1915-80), French semiologist. *The Pleasure of the Text,* "Modern" (1975).

2 Although the masters make the rules
For the wise men and the fools
I got nothing, Ma, to live up to.

BOB DYLAN (b. 1941), U.S. singer, songwriter. "It's Alright Ma (I'm Only Bleeding)," from the album *Bringing It All Back Home* (1965).

3 By alienation is meant a mode of experience in which the person experiences himself as an alien. He has become, one might say, estranged from himself. He does not experience himself as the center of his world, as the creator of his own acts—but his acts and their consequences have become his masters, whom he obeys, or whom he may even worship. The alienated person is out of touch with himself as he is out of touch with any other person. He, like the others, is experienced as things are experienced; with the senses and with common sense, but at the same time without being related to oneself and to the world outside positively.

ERICH FROMM (1900-80), U.S. psychologist. *The Sane Society,* ch. 5, "Alienation" (1955).

4 Human beings are compelled to live within a lie, but they can be compelled to do so only because they are in fact capable of living in this way. Therefore not only does the system alienate humanity, but at the same time alienated humanity supports this system as its own involuntary masterplan, as a degenerate image of its own degeneration, as a record of people's own failure as individuals.

VÁCLAV HAVEL (b. 1936), Czech playwright, president. *Living in Truth,* pt. 1, sct. 6, "The Power of the Powerless" (1986).

5 There is no religion in which everyday life is not considered a prison; there is no philosophy or ideology that does not think that we live in alienation.

EUGÉNE IONESCO (b. 1912), Rumanian-born French playwright. *Present Past—Past Present,* ch. 5 (1968).

6 We are bemused and crazed creatures, strangers to our true selves, to one another, and to the spiritual and material world—mad, even, from an ideal standpoint we can glimpse but not adopt.

R. D. LAING (1927-89), British psychiatrist. *The Politics of Experience,* Introduction (1967).

7 Alienation as our present destiny is achieved only by outrageous violence perpetrated by human beings on human beings.

R. D. LAING (1927-89), British psychiatrist. *The Politics of Experience,* Introduction (1967).

8 Without alienation, there can be no politics.

ARTHUR MILLER (b. 1915), U.S. dramatist. *Marxism Today* (London, Jan. 1988).

9 The most dangerous aspect of present-day life is the dissolution of the feeling of individual responsibility. Mass solitude has done away with any difference between the internal and the external, between the intellectual and the physical.

EUGENIO MONTALE (1896-1981), Italian poet. *Poet in Our Time* (1972).

ALLIANCES

1 Alliance. In international politics, the union of two thieves who have their hands so deeply inserted in each other's pockets that they cannot separately plunder a third.

> AMBROSE BIERCE (1842-1914), U.S. author. *The Devil's Dictionary* (1881-1906).

2 When bad men combine, the good must associate; else they will fall, one by one, an unpitied sacrifice in a contemptible struggle.

> EDMUND BURKE (1729-97), Irish philosopher, statesman. "Thoughts on the Cause of the Present Discontents," address, 23 April 1770, in which Burke argued the need for political parties.

3 Union may be strength, but it is mere blind brute strength unless wisely directed.

> SAMUEL BUTLER (1835-1902), English author. *Samuel Butler's Notebooks* (1951, p. 197).

4 Coalitions though successful have always found this, that their triumph has been brief.

> BENJAMIN DISRAELI (1804-81), English statesman, author. Address, 16 Dec. 1852, House of Commons.

5 I think that a young state, like a young virgin, should modestly stay at home, and wait the application of suitors for an alliance with her; and not run about offering her amity to all the world; and hazarding their refusal . . . . Our virgin is a jolly one; and tho at present not very rich, will in time be a great fortune, and where she has a favorable predisposition, it seems to me well worth cultivating.

> BENJAMIN FRANKLIN (1706-90), U.S. statesman, writer. Letter, 22 Sept. 1778.

6 All who think cannot but see there is a sanction like that of religion which binds us in partnership in the serious work of the world.

> JOHN HAY (1838-1905), U.S. author, statesman. Address, 21 April 1898, as ambassador in London, on Anglo-American relations.

7 Peace, commerce and honest friendship with all nations; entangling alliances with none.

> THOMAS JEFFERSON (1743-1826), U.S. president. First inaugural address, 4 March 1801.

8 We cannot always assure the future of our friends; we have a better chance of assuring our future if we remember who our friends are.

> HENRY KISSINGER (b. 1923), U.S. Republican politician, secretary of state. *The White House Years*, ch. 29, "A Visit to the Shah of Iran" (1979), said of the changing U.S. policy towards the Shah of Iran.

9 An alliance is like a chain. It is not made stronger by adding weak links to it. A great power like the United States gains no advantage and it loses prestige by offering, indeed peddling, its alliances to all and sundry. An alliance should be hard diplomatic currency, valuable and hard to get, and not inflationary paper from the mimeograph machine in the State Department.

> WALTER LIPPMANN (1889-1974), U.S. journalist. *New York Herald Tribune* (5 Aug. 1952).

10 'Tis our true policy to steer clear of permanent alliances with any portion of the foreign world.

> GEORGE WASHINGTON (1732-99), U.S. general, president. Farewell address, 17 Sept. 1796.

See also Churchill, Gromyko, Roosevelt, Wilson on INTERNATIONAL RELATIONS.

ALTRUISM

1 He who would do good to another must do it in
   Minute Particulars:
General Good is the plea of the scoundrel,
   hypocrite, and flatterer,
For Art and Science cannot exist but in minutely
   organized Particulars.

> WILLIAM BLAKE (1757-1827), English poet, painter, engraver. *Jerusalem*, ch. 3, Plate 55 (1804-20; repr. in *Complete Writings*, ed. by Geoffrey Keynes, 1957).

2 No people do so much harm as those who go about doing good.

> MANDELL CREIGHTON (1843-1901), English prelate, historian. *Life,* vol. 2 (1904).

3 The compulsion to do good is an innate American trait. Only North Americans seem to believe that they always should, may, and actually can choose somebody with whom to share their blessings. Ultimately this attitude leads to bombing people into the acceptance of gifts.

> IVAN ILLICH (b. 1926), Austrian-born U.S. theologian, author. *Celebration of Awareness*, Preface to ch. 2 (1969).

4 That man is good who does good to others; if he suffers on account of the good he does, he is very good; if he suffers at the hands of those to whom he has done good, then his goodness is so great that it could be enhanced only by greater sufferings; and if he should die at their hands, his virtue can go no further: it is heroic, it is perfect.

> JEAN DE LA BRUYÉRE (1645-96), French writer, moralist. *Characters*, "Of Personal Merit," aph. 44 (1688).

5 She is such a good friend that she would throw all her acquaintances into the water for the pleasure of fishing them out again.

> CHARLES, COUNT TALLEYRAND (1754-1838), French statesman. Quoted in: A. Duff Cooper, *Talleyrand*, ch. 3 (1932), speaking to Napoleon of Madame de Staël.

6 As for doing good, that is one of the professions which are full. Moreover, I have tried it fairly, and . . . am satisfied that it does not agree with my constitution.

> HENRY DAVID THOREAU (1817-62), U.S. philosopher, author, naturalist. *Walden*, "Economy" (1854). See Thoreau on GOOD DEEDS.

See also BENEFACTORS; Browning on GOOD DEEDS; PHILANTHROPY.

AMBITION

1 Ambition—it is the last infirmity of noble minds.

> J. M. BARRIE (1860-1937), British playwright. Sir Harry Sims (quoting from his morning paper), in *The Twelve-Pound Look.*

2 Ambition. An overmastering desire to be vilified by enemies while living and made ridiculous by friends when dead.

> AMBROSE BIERCE (1842-1914), U.S. author. *The Devil's Dictionary* (1881-1906).

3 No bird soars too high, if he soars with his own wings.

> WILLIAM BLAKE (1757-1827), English poet, painter, engraver. *The Marriage of Heaven and Hell*, Plate 7, "Proverbs of Hell," (1790-93).

4 What I aspired to be
And was not, comforts me.

> ROBERT BROWNING (1812-89), English poet. *Rabbi Ben Ezra*.

5 'Tis not what man Does which exalts him, but
what man Would do!

> ROBERT BROWNING (1812-89), English poet. *Saul*, st. 18.

6 Ambition can creep as well as soar.

> EDMUND BURKE (1729-97), Irish philosopher, statesman. *Letters on a Regicide Peace*, Letter 3 (1797).

7 All ambitions are lawful except those which climb upward on the miseries or credulities of mankind. All intellectual and artistic ambitions are permissible, up to and even beyond the limit of prudent sanity. They can hurt no one.

> JOSEPH CONRAD (1857-1924), Polish-born English novelist. *A Personal Record*, "A Familiar Preface" (1912).

8 The passion of self-aggrandizement is persistent but plastic; it will never disappear from a vigorous mind, but may become morally higher by attaching itself to a larger conception of what constitutes the self.

> CHARLES HORTON COOLEY (1864-1929), U.S. sociologist. *Human Nature and the Social Order*, ch. 6 (1902).

9 Ambition is a Dead Sea fruit, and the greatest peril to the soul is that one is likely to get precisely what he is seeking.

> EDWARD DAHLBERG (1900-1977), U.S. author, critic. *Alms for Oblivion*, "No Love and No Thanks" (1964).

10 At the age of six I wanted to be a cook. At seven I wanted to be Napoleon. And my ambition has been growing steadily ever since.

> SALVADOR DALI (1904-89), Spanish painter. *The Secret Life of Salvador Dali*, "Prologue" (1948).

11 Hitch your wagon to a star. Let us not fag in paltry works which serve our pot and bag alone.

> RALPH WALDO EMERSON (1803-82), U.S. essayist, poet, philosopher. *Society and Solitude*, "Civilization" (1870).

12 Man is the only creature that strives to surpass himself, and yearns for the impossible.

> ERIC HOFFER (1902-83), U.S. philosopher. *New York Times* (21 July 1969).

13 He that fails in his endeavours after wealth or power will not long retain either honesty or courage.

> SAMUEL JOHNSON (1709-84), English author, lexicographer. *Adventurer*, no. 99 (16 Oct. 1753; repr. in *Works of Samuel Johnson*, vol. 2, ed. by W. J. Bate, John M. Bullitt, and L. F. Powell, 1963).

14 When you go in search of honey you must expect to be stung by bees.

> KENNETH KAUNDA (b. 1924), Zambian politician, president. Quoted in: *Observer* (London, 2 Jan. 1983).

15 He who tip-toes cannot stand; he who strides cannot walk.

> LAO-TZU (6TH CENTURY B.C.), Legendary Chinese philosopher. *Tao-te-ching*, bk. 1, ch. 24 (1963; tr. by T. C. Lau).

16 Nature that fram'd us of four elements,
Warring within our breasts for regiment,
Doth teach us all to have aspiring minds.

> CHRISTOPHER MARLOWE (1564-93), English dramatist, poet. Tamburlaine, in *Tamburlaine the Great*, pt. 1, act 2, sc. 7.

17 If men cease to believe that they will one day become gods then they will surely become worms.

> HENRY MILLER (1891-1980), U.S. author. *The Colossus of Maroussi*, pt. 3 (1941).

18 Men would be angels, angels would be gods.

> ALEXANDER POPE (1688-1744), English satirical poet. *An Essay on Man*, Epistle 1.

19 As he was valiant, I honour him. But as he was ambitious, I slew him.

> WILLIAM SHAKESPEARE (1564-1616), English dramatist, poet. Brutus, in *Julius Caesar*, act 3, sc. 2.

20 Ambition if it feeds at all, does so on the ambition of others.

> SUSAN SONTAG (b. 1933), U.S. essayist. *The Benefactor*, ch. 1 (1963).

21 Ambition often puts Men upon doing the meanest offices; so climbing is performed in the same position with creeping.

> JONATHAN SWIFT (1667-1745), Anglo-Irish satirist. *Thoughts on Various Subjects* (1711).

22 Where there are large powers with little ambition . . . nature may be said to have fallen short of her purposes.

> SIR HENRY TAYLOR (1800-1886), English author. *The Statesman*, ch. 19 (1836).

23 So many worlds, so much to do,
So little done, such things to be.

> LORD TENNYSON (1809-92), English poet. *In Memoriam*, cto. 73, st. 1.

24 Ambition is the last refuge of the failure.

> OSCAR WILDE (1854-1900), Anglo-Irish playwright, author. "Phrases and Philosophies for the Use of the Young," in *Chameleon* (London, Dec. 1894).

See also GETTING AHEAD; Thatcher on OPPORTUNITY; Juvenal on POVERTY AND THE POOR; Wilson on PROMOTION.

THE AMERICAN REVOLUTION

1   The second day of July, 1776, will be the most memorable epoch in the history of America. I am apt to believe that it will be celebrated by succeeding generations as the great anniversary festival. It ought to be commemmorated as the day of deliverance, by solemn acts of devotion to God Almighty. It ought to be solemnized with pomp and parade, with shows, games, sports, guns, bells, bonfires, and illustrations, from one end of this continent to the other, from this time forward forevermore.

> JOHN ADAMS (1735-1826), U.S. statesman, president. Letter, 3 July 1776, to his wife, Abigail Adams.

2   If we apply the term revolution to what happened in North America between 1776 and 1829, it has a special meaning. Normally, the word describes the process by which man transforms himself from one kind of man, living in one kind of society, with one way of looking at the world, into another kind of man, another society, another conception of life. . . . The American case is different: it is not a question of the Old Man transforming himself into the New, but of the New Man becoming alive to the fact that he is new, that he has been transformed already without his having realized it.

> W. H. AUDEN (1907-73), Anglo-American poet. *The Dyer's Hand*, pt. 6, "American Poetry" (1962).

3   I rejoice that America has resisted. Three millions of people, so dead to all the feelings of liberty, as voluntarily to submit to be slaves, would have been fit instruments to make slaves of the rest.

> WILLIAM PITT THE ELDER, LORD CHATHAM (1708-78), English statesman. Address, 14 Jan. 1766, to House of Commons, attacking the Rockingham Ministry.

4   If I were an American, as I am an Englishman, while a foreign troop was landed in my country, I never would lay down my arms—never—never—never!

> WILLIAM PITT THE ELDER, LORD CHATHAM (1708-78), English statesman. Address, 18 Nov. 1777, to House of Lords.

5   The military struggle may frankly be regarded for what it actually was, namely a war for independence, an armed attempt to impose the views of the revolutionists upon the British government and large sections of the colonial population at whatever cost to freedom of opinion or the sanctity of life and property.

> ARTHUR SCHLESINGER (1888-1965), U.S. historian. "The American Revolution Reconsidered," in *Political Science Quarterly* (New York, March 1919; repr. in *The Ambiguity of the American Revolution*, ed. by J. P. Green, 1968).

AMUSEMENT

1   To a man of pleasure every moment appears to be lost, which partakes not of the vivacity of amusement.

> JOSEPH ADDISON (1672-1719), English essayist. *Interesting Anecdotes, Memoirs, Allegories, Essays, and Poetical Fragments*, "The Man of Pleasure" (1794).

2   The intellectual man requires a fine bait; the sots are easily amused. But everybody is drugged with his own frenzy, and the pageant marches at all hours, with music and banner and badge.

> RALPH WALDO EMERSON (1803-82), U.S. essayist, poet, philosopher. *The Conduct of Life*, "Illusions" (1860).

3   Nothing is so perfectly amusing as a total change of ideas.

> LAURENCE STERNE (1713-68), English author. *Tristram Shandy*, Dedication to bk. 9 (1760-67).

ANARCHISM

1   The consistent anarchist . . . should be a socialist, but a socialist of a particular sort. He will not only oppose alienated and specialized labor and look forward to the appropriation of capital by the whole body of workers, but he will also insist that this appropriation be direct, not exercised by some elite force acting in the name of the proletariat. . . . Some sort of council communism is the natural form of revolutionary socialism in an industrial society. It reflects the intuitive understanding that democracy is largely a sham when the industrial system is controlled by any form of autocratic elite, whether of owners, managers, and technocrats, a "vanguard" party, or a State bureaucracy.

> NOAM CHOMSKY (b. 1928), U.S. linguist, political analyst. "Notes on Anarchism," in *New York Review of Books* (21 May 1970).

2   Lady Dynamite, let's dance quickly,
Let's dance and sing and dynamite everything!

> FRENCH ANARCHIST SONG OF THE 1880S.

3   Anarchism is the only philosophy which brings to man the consciousness of himself; which maintains that God, the State, and society are non-existent, that their promises are null and void, since they can be fulfilled only through man's subordination. Anarchism is therefore the teacher of the unity of life; not merely in nature, but in man.

> EMMA GOLDMAN (1869-1940), U.S. anarchist. *Anarchism and Other Essays*, "Anarchism: What It Really Stands For" (1910).

4   The anarchist and the Christian have a common origin.

> FRIEDRICH NIETZSCHE (1844-1900), German philosopher. *The Antichrist*, aph. 57 (1895).

5   My thinking tends to be libertarian. That is, I oppose intrusions of the state into the private realm—as in abortion, sodomy, prostitution, pornography, drug use, or suicide, all of which I would strongly defend as matters of free choice in a representative democracy.

> CAMILLE PAGLIA (b. 1947), U.S. author, critic, educator. *Sex, Art, and American Culture*, Introduction (1992).

6. The ordinary man is an anarchist. He wants to do as he likes. He may want his neighbour to be governed, but he himself doesn't want to be governed. He is mortally afraid of government officials and policemen.

> GEORGE BERNARD SHAW (1856-1950), Anglo-Irish playwright, critic. Speech, 11 April 1933, New York City.

7 People sometimes inquire what form of government is most suitable for an artist to live under. To this question there is only one answer. The form of government that is most suitable to the artist is no government at all.

> OSCAR WILDE (1854-1900), Anglo-Irish playwright, author. "The Soul of Man Under Socialism," in *Fortnightly Review* (London, Feb. 1891; repr. 1895).

See also Aragon on DADA.

ANCESTRY

1 Neither give heed to fables and endless genealogies.

> BIBLE: NEW TESTAMENT. *1 Timothy* 1:4.

2 Genealogy. An account of one's descent from an ancestor who did not particularly care to trace his own.

> AMBROSE BIERCE (1842-1914), U.S. author. *The Devil's Dictionary* (1881-1906).

3 I am, in point of fact, a particularly haughty and exclusive person, of pre-Adamite ancestral descent. You will understand this when I tell you that I can trace my ancestry back to a protoplasmal primordial atomic globule.

> W. S. GILBERT (1836-1911), English librettist. Pooh-Bah, in *The Mikado*, act 1 (1885).

4 There is no king who has not had a slave among his ancestors, and no slave who has not had a king among his.

> HELEN KELLER (1880-1968), U.S. author, lecturer. *The Story of My Life*, pt. 1, ch. 1 (1903).

5 I don't know who my grandfather was; I am much more concerned to know what his grandson will be.

> ABRAHAM LINCOLN (1809-65), U.S. president. Quoted in: Gross, *Lincoln's Own Stories*.

6 They talk about their Pilgrim blood,
Their birthright high and holy!
A mountain-stream that ends in mud
Methinks is melancholy.

> JAMES RUSSELL LOWELL (1819-91), U.S. poet, editor. *An Interview with Miles Standish*, st. 11.

7 It is indeed a desirable thing to be well-descended, but the glory belongs to our ancestors.

> PLUTARCH (46-120), Greek essayist, biographer. *Moralia*, "On the Training of Children" (c. 100 A.D.).

8 There is a certain class of people who prefer to say that their fathers came down in the world through their own follies than to boast that they rose in the world through their own industry and talents. It is the same shabby-genteel sentiment, the same vanity of birth which makes men prefer to believe that they are degenerated angels rather than elevated apes.

> W. WINWOOD READE (1838-75), English traveler, author. *The Martyrdom of Man*, ch. 3, "Materials of Human History" (1872).

9 Englishmen hate Liberty and Equality too much to understand them. But every Englishman loves a pedigree.

> GEORGE BERNARD SHAW (1856-1950), Anglo-Irish playwright, critic. *Man and Superman*, "The Revolutionist's Handbook," sct. 10 (1903).

10 Each has his own tree of ancestors, but at the top of all sits Probably Arboreal.

> ROBERT LOUIS STEVENSON (1850-1894), Scottish novelist, essayist, poet. *Memories and Portraits*, ch. 6, "Pastoral" (1887).

11 In church your grandsire cut his throat;
To do the job too long he tarried:
He should have had my hearty vote
To cut his throat before he married.

> JONATHAN SWIFT (1667-1745), Anglo-Irish satirist. *Verses on an Upright Judge*.

12 I would rather make my name than inherit it.

> WILLIAM MAKEPEACE THACKERAY (1811-63), English author. *The Virginians*, ch. 26 (1857-59)

See also Burton on ARISTOCRACY; Hardy on FACES; Burke, Chesterton on TRADITION.

ANECDOTES

1 An unseasonable tale will always be in the mouth of the unwise.

> APOCRYPHA. *Ecclesiasticus* 20:19.

2 It is not the voice that commands the story: it is the ear.

> ITALO CALVINO (1923-85), Italian author, critic. Marco Polo, in *Invisible Cities* (1972; ed. 1974, p. 135).

3 To have frequent recourse to narrative betrays great want of imagination.

> LORD CHESTERFIELD (1694-1773), English statesman, man of letters. Letter, 19 Oct. 1748 (1774; repr. in *The Letters of the Earl of Chesterfield to His Son*, vol. 1, no. 166, ed. by Charles Strachey, 1901).

4 When a man fell into his anecdotage it was a sign for him to retire from the world.

> BENJAMIN DISRAELI (1804-81), English statesman, author. *Lothair*, ch. 28 (1870).

5 Twenty or thirty years ago, in the army, we had a lot of obscure adventures, and years later we tell them at parties, and suddenly we realize that those two very difficult years of our lives have become lumped together into a few episodes that have lodged in our memory in a standardized form, and are always told in a standardized way, in the same words. But in fact that lump of memories has nothing whatsoever to do with our experience of those two years in the army and what it has made of us.

> VÁCLAV HAVEL (b. 1936), Czech playwright, president. *Disturbing the Peace*, ch. 4 (1986; tr. 1990).

6 How is it that we remember the least triviality that happens to us, and yet not remember how often we have recounted it to the same person?

> FRANÇOIS, DUC DE LA ROCHEFOUCAULD (1613-80), French writer, moralist. *Sentences et Maximes Morales,* no. 313 (1678).

7 Life is too short for a long story.

> LADY MARY WORTLEY MONTAGU (1689-1762), English society figure, letter writer. Letter, 19 July 1759 (published in *Selected Letters,* ed. by Robert Halsband, 1970).

8 Your tale, sir, would cure deafness.

> WILLIAM SHAKESPEARE (1564-1616), English dramatist, poet. Miranda, to Prospero, in *The Tempest,* act 1, sc. 2.

9 With a tale, forsooth, he cometh unto you; with a tale which holdeth children from play, and old men from the chimney corner.

> SIR PHILIP SIDNEY (1554-86), English poet, diplomat, soldier. *Defence of Poesie* (written 1579-80; published 1595).

10 The history of a soldier's wound beguiles the pain of it.

> LAURENCE STERNE (1713-68), English author. *Tristram Shandy,* bk. 1, ch. 25 (1760-67).

11 Faith! he must make his stories shorter
Or change his comrades once a quarter.

> JONATHAN SWIFT (1667-1745), Anglo-Irish satirist. *Verses on the Death of Dr. Swift.*

See also Montagu on TRAVEL.

ANGELS

1 It is not because angels are holier than men or devils that makes them angels, but because they do not expect holiness from one another, but from God only.

> WILLIAM BLAKE (1757-1827), English poet, painter, engraver. *A Vision of the Last Judgement* (1810; repr. in *Complete Writings,* ed. by Geoffrey Keynes, 1957).

2 The Angels were all singing out of tune,
And hoarse with having little else to do,
Excepting to wind up the sun and moon
Or curb a runaway young star or two.

> LORD BYRON (1788-1824), English poet. *The Vision of Judgment,* st. 2.

3 The angels are so enamoured of the language that is spoken in heaven, that they will not distort their lips with the hissing and unmusical dialects of men, but speak their own, whether there be any who understand it or not.

> RALPH WALDO EMERSON (1803-82), U.S. essayist, poet, philosopher. *Essays* "Intellect" (First Series, 1841).

4 Make friends with the angels, who though invisible are always with you. . . . Often invoke them, constantly praise them, and make good use of their help and assistance in all your temporal and spiritual affairs.

> ST. FRANCIS DE SALES (1567-1622), French churchman, devotional writer. *Introduction to the Devout Life,* pt. 2, ch. 16 (1609).

5 There are nine orders of angels, to wit, angels, archangels, virtues, powers, principalities, dominations, thrones, cherubim, and seraphim.

> POPE GREGORY THE GREAT (c. 540-604). *Homilies,* no. 34 (c. 600).

6 Angels may be very excellent sort of folk in their own way, but we, poor mortals in our present state, would probably find them precious slow company.

> JEROME K. JEROME (1859-1927), British author. *Idle Thoughts of an Idle Fellow,* "On Vanity and Vanities" (1889).

7 If an angel were ever to tell us anything of his philosophy I believe many propositions would sound like 2 times 2 equals 13.

> G. C. LICHTENBERG (1742-99), German physicist, philosopher. *Aphorisms,* "Notebook B," aph. 44 (written 1765-99; tr. by R. J. Hollingdale, 1990).

8 In Heaven an angel is nobody in particular.

> GEORGE BERNARD SHAW (1856-1950), Anglo-Irish playwright, critic. *Man and Superman,* "Maxims for Revolutionists: Greatness" (1903).

9 It is not known precisely where angels dwell—whether in the air, the void, or the planets. It has not been God's pleasure that we should be informed of their abode.

> VOLTAIRE (1694-1778), French philosopher, author. *Philosophical Dictionary,* "Angels" (1764).

See also Bible, New Testament on HOSPITALITY.

ANGER

1 It takes two flints to make a fire.

> LOUISA MAY ALCOTT (1832-88), U.S. author. Laurie, in *Little Women,* pt. 2, ch. 16 (1869).

2 We praise a man who feels angry on the right grounds and against the right persons and also in the right manner at the right moment and for the right length of time.

> ARISTOTLE (384-322 B.C.), Greek philosopher. *The Nicomachean Ethics,* ch. 4, sct. 5 subsct. 3 (written c. 340 B.C.).

3 Rage cannot be hidden, it can only be dissembled. This dissembling deludes the thoughtless, and strengthens rage and adds, to rage, contempt.

> JAMES BALDWIN (1924-87), U.S. author. "Stranger in the Village," in *Harper's* (New York, Oct. 1953; repr. in *Notes of a Native Son,* 1955).

4 Be not hasty in thy spirit to be angry: for anger resteth in the bosom of fools.

> BIBLE, HEBREW. *Ecclesiastes* 7:9.

5 Let not the sun go down upon your wrath.

> BIBLE: NEW TESTAMENT. *Ephesians* 4:26. St. Paul speaks.

6 I know of no more disagreeable situation than to be left feeling generally angry without anybody in particular to be angry at.

> FRANK MOORE COLBY (1865-1925), U.S. editor, essayist. *The*

Colby Essays, vol. 1, "The Literature of Malicious Exposure" (1926).

7   Heav'n has no Rage like Love to Hatred turn'd,
Nor Hell a Fury, like a Woman scorn'd.

WILLIAM CONGREVE (1670-1729), English dramatist. Zara, in *The Mourning Bride,* act 3 (1697).

8   Anger is one of the sinews of the soul; he that wants it hath a maimed mind.

THOMAS FULLER (1608-61), English cleric. *The Holy State and the Profane State,* bk. 3, "Of Anger" (1642).

9   Anger is a brief lunacy.

HORACE (65-8 B.C.), Roman poet. *Epistles,* bk. 1, Epistle 2 (22-8 B.C.).

10   When angry, count ten, before you speak; if very angry, an hundred.

THOMAS JEFFERSON (1743-1826), U.S. president. *Decalogue of Canons for observation in practical life,* no. 10. Included in letter, 21 Feb. 1825, to Thomas Jefferson Smith.

11   Indignation is a submission of our thoughts, but not of our desires.

BERTRAND RUSSELL (1872-1970), British philosopher, mathematician. *A Free Man's Worship and Other Essays,* ch. 1 (1976).

12   I am often mad, but I would hate to be nothing but mad: and I think I would lose what little value I may have as a writer if I were to refuse, as a matter of principle, to accept the warming rays of the sun, and to report them, whenever, and if ever, they happen to strike me.

E. B. WHITE (1899-1985), U.S. author, editor. Interview in *Writers at Work* (Eighth Series, ed. by George Plimpton, 1988).

See also Dryden on PATIENCE.

ANIMALS

1   Animals, in their generation, are wiser than the sons of men; but their wisdom is confined to a few particulars, and lies in a very narrow compass.

JOSEPH ADDISON (1672-1719), English essayist. *Spectator* (London, 18 July 1711).

2   A peasant becomes fond of his pig and is glad to salt away its pork. What is significant, and is so difficult for the urban stranger to understand, is that the two statements are connected by an *and* and not by a *but.*

JOHN BERGER (b. 1926), British author, critic. *About Looking,* "Why Look at Animals?" (1980).

3   Bats have no bankers and they do not drink
and cannot be arrested and pay no tax
and, in general, bats have it made.

JOHN BERRYMAN (1914-72), U.S. poet. *Dream Song 63,* in *The Dream Songs* (1969).

4   Man is the only animal that can remain on friendly terms with the victims he intends to eat until he eats them.

SAMUEL BUTLER (1835-1902), English author. *Notebooks,* "Mind and Matter" (1912).

5   Poor little Foal of an oppressed race!
I love the languid patience of thy face.

SAMUEL TAYLOR COLERIDGE (1772-1834), English poet, critic. *To a Young Ass* (1794).

6   Shall we never have done with that cliché, so stupid that it could only be human, about the sympathy of animals for man when he is unhappy? Animals love happiness almost as much as we do. A fit of crying disturbs them, they'll sometimes imitate sobbing, and for a moment they'll reflect our sadness. But they flee unhappiness as they flee fever, and I believe that in the long run they are capable of boycotting it.

COLETTE (1873-1954), French author. *Break of Day* (1961; repr. in *Earthly Paradise,* pt. 4, "The South of France," ed. by Robert Phelps, 1966).

7   Cows are amongst the gentlest of breathing creatures; none show more passionate tenderness to their young when deprived of them; and, in short, I am not ashamed to profess a deep love for these quiet creatures.

THOMAS DE QUINCEY (1785-1859), English author. *Confessions of an English Opium-Eater,* pt. 1 (1822).

8   The following general definition of an animal: a system of different organic molecules that have combined with one another, under the impulsion of a sensation similar to an obtuse and muffled sense of touch given to them by the creator of matter as a whole, until each one of them has found the most suitable position for its shape and comfort.

DENIS DIDEROT (1713-84), French philosopher. *On the Interpretation of Nature,* no. 51 (1753; repr. in *Selected Writings,* ed. by Lester G. Crocker, 1966).

9   Who can . . . guess how much industry and providence and affection we have caught from the pantomime of brutes?

RALPH WALDO EMERSON (1803-82), U.S. essayist, poet, philosopher. *Nature,* "Discipline" (1836).

10   The elephant, not only the largest but the most intelligent of animals, provides us with an excellent example. It is faithful and tenderly loving to the female of its choice, mating only every third year and then for no more than five days, and so secretly as never to be seen, until, on the sixth day, it appears and goes at once to wash its whole body in the river, unwilling to return to the herd until thus purified. Such good and modest habits are an example to husband and wife.

ST. FRANCIS DE SALES (1567-1622), French churchman, devotional writer. *Introduction to the Devout Life,* pt. 3, ch. 39 (1609).

11   Animals are in possession of themselves; their soul is in possession of their body. But they have no right to their life, because they do not will it.

GEORG HEGEL (1770-1831), German philosopher. *The Philosophy of Right,* "Property," Addition 28 (1821; tr. 1942).

12   Animals used to provide a lowlife way to kill and get away with it, as they do still, but, more intriguingly, for some people they are an aperture through which wounds drain. The scapegoat of olden times, driven off for the bystanders' sins, has become a tender thing, a running injury. There, running away . . . is me: hurt it and you are hurting me.

> EDWARD HOAGLAND (b. 1932), U.S. novelist, essayist. "Lament the Red Wolf," in *Sports Illustrated* (New York, 14 Jan. 1974; repr. in *Heart's Desire*, 1988).

13 Animals are stylized characters in a kind of old saga—stylized because even the most acute of them have little leeway as they play out their parts.

> EDWARD HOAGLAND (b. 1932), U.S. novelist, essayist. "Dogs and the Tug of Life," in *Harper's* (New York, Feb. 1975; repr. in *Heart's Desire*, 1988).

14 Nothing to be done really about animals. Anything you do looks foolish. The answer isn't in us. It's almost as if we're put here on earth to show how silly they aren't.

> RUSSELL HOBAN (b. 1925), U.S. author. George Fairbairn, in *Turtle Diary*, ch. 42 (1975).

15 Animals often strike us as passionate machines.

> ERIC HOFFER (1902-83), U.S. philosopher. *Reflections on the Human Condition*, aph. 7 (1973).

16 From the oyster to the eagle, from the swine to the tiger, all animals are to be found in men and each of them exists in some man, sometimes several at the time. Animals are nothing but the portrayal of our virtues and vices made manifest to our eyes, the visible reflections of our souls. God displays them to us to give us food for thought.

> VICTOR HUGO (1802-85), French poet, dramatist, novelist. *Les Misérables*, pt. 1, bk. 5, ch. 5 (1862).

17 The surprise of animals. . . in and out, cats and dogs and a milk goat and chickens and guinea hens, all taken for granted, as if man was intended to live on terms of friendly intercourse with the rest of creation instead of huddling in isolation on the fourteenth floor of an apartment house in a city where animals occurred behind bars in the zoo.

> ELIZABETH JANEWAY (b. 1913), U.S. author. *Accident on Route 37*, "Steven Benedict" (1964).

18 Mankind's true moral test, its fundamental test (which lies deeply buried from view), consists of its attitude towards those who are at its mercy: animals. And in this respect mankind has suffered a fundamental debacle, a debacle so fundamental that all others stem from it.

> MILAN KUNDERA (b. 1929), Czech author, critic. *The Unbearable Lightness of Being*, pt. 7, ch. 2 (1984).

19 Be a good animal, true to your animal instincts.

> D. H. LAWRENCE (1885-1930), British author. The woodkeeper Annable's motto, in *The White Peacock*, pt. 2, ch. 2 (1911).

20 We know what the animals do, what are the needs of the beaver, the bear, the salmon, and other creatures, because long ago men married them and acquired this knowledge from their animal wives. Today the priests say we lie, but we know better.

> NATIVE AMERICANS. Quoted by D. Jenness in: "The Carrier Indians of the Bulkley River," in *Bulletin no. 133, Bureau of American Ethnology* (1943). The quote was picked up by Claude Lévi-Strauss in *The Savage Mind*, ch. 1 (1962).

21 I fear animals regard man as a creature of their own kind which has in a highly dangerous fashion lost its healthy animal reason—as the mad animal, as the laughing animal, as the weeping animal, as the unhappy animal.

> FRIEDRICH NIETZSCHE (1844-1900), German philosopher. *The Gay Science*, aph. 224 (rev. ed. 1887).

22 Four legs good, two legs bad.

> GEORGE ORWELL (1903-50), British author. The animals' revolutionary maxim, in *Animal Farm*, ch. 3 (1945). By the end of the story, the maxim has changed to "Four legs good, two legs *better.*" (ch. 10).

23 In a few generations more, there will probably be no room at all allowed for animals on the earth: no need of them, no toleration of them. An immense agony will have then ceased, but with it there will also have passed away the last smile of the world's youth.

> OUIDA [MARIE LOUISE DE LA RAMÉE] (1839-1908), English novelist. *Critical Studies*, "The Quality of Mercy" (1900).

24 There is something in the unselfish and self-sacrificing love of a brute, which goes directly to the heart of him who has had frequent occasion to test the paltry friendship and gossamer fidelity of mere *Man*.

> EDGAR ALLAN POE (1809-45), U.S. poet, critic, short-story writer. *The Black Cat* (1854).

25 What is man without the beasts? If all the beasts were gone, man would die from a great loneliness of spirit. For whatever happens to the beasts, soon happens to man. All things are connected.

> Attributed to SEATTLE (c. 1784-1866), Chief of the Dwamish, Suquamish, and allied tribes. Letter, 1854, to President Franklin Pierce (published in *Brother Eagle, Sister Sky: A Message from Chief Seattle*, 1990). The letter, in which Seattle pleaded that his name should die with the ceding of the Washington State territories, was shown in 1992 to have been largely a forgery, devised by television scriptwriter Ted Perry for a historical epic in 1971.

26 What is a country without rabbits and partridges? They are among the most simple and indigenous animal products; ancient and venerable families known to antiquity as to modern times; of the very hue and substance of Nature, nearest allied to leaves and to the ground.

> HENRY DAVID THOREAU (1817-62), U.S. philosopher, author, naturalist. *Walden*, "Winter Animals" (1854).

27 The fact that man knows right from wrong proves his *intellectual* superiority to the other creatures; but the fact that he can *do* wrong proves his *moral* inferiority to any creatures that *cannot.*

> MARK TWAIN (1835-1910), U.S. author. Old Man, in "What Is Man?," sct. 6 (1906; repr. in *Complete Essays*, ed. by Charles Neider, 1963).

28 They do not sweat and whine about their condition,
They do not lie awake in the dark and weep for their sins,
They do not make me sick discussing their duty to God,
Not one is dissatisfied, not one is demented with the mania of owning things,

Not one kneels to another, nor to his kind that
lived thousands of years ago.

WALT WHITMAN (1819-92), U.S. poet. *Song of Myself*, sct. 32,
in *Leaves of Grass* (1855).

See also Pascal on ADMIRATION; CATS; DOGS; HORSES; Colette on SCIENTISTS;
ZOOS.

ANNIVERSARIES

1   Let us love nobly, and live, and add again
Years and years unto years, till we attain
To write threescore: this is the second of
   our reign.

JOHN DONNE (c. 1572-1631), English divine, metaphysical
poet. *The Anniversary*.

2   The secret anniversaries of the heart.

HENRY WADSWORTH LONGFELLOW (1807-82), U.S. poet.
Sonnets, "Holidays" (1876).

3   We placed the wreaths upon the splended granite
sarcophagus, and at its feet, and *felt* that *only* the *earthly
robe* we loved so much was there. The pure, tender, loving spirit *which loved us* so tenderly, is above us—loving
us, praying for us, and *free* from *all* suffering and woe—
yes, that *is* a *comfort*, and that *first birthday* in *another*
world must have been a *far* brighter one than *any* in this
poor world below!

VICTORIA (1819-1901), Queen of Great Britain and Ireland. Letter, 20 Aug. 1861 (published in *Letters of Queen Victoria*, vol. 3,
ch. 30, ed. by A. C. Benson and Viscount Esher, 1907). Writing
to Leopold I, King of the Belgians, Queen Victoria was speaking
about the Duchess of Kent.

4   Are there memories left that are safe from the
clutches of phony anniversarists?

W. J. WETHERBY, British journalist. Quoted in: *Guardian* (London, 18 Aug. 1989).

5   The thought of our past years in me doth breed
Perpetual benedictions.

WILLIAM WORDSWORTH (1770-1850), English poet. *Intimations of Immortality*.

See also Adams on THE AMERICAN REVOLUTION.

ANTHOLOGIES

1   Most of those who make collections of verse or epigram are like men eating cherries or oysters: they choose
out the best at first, and end by eating all.

SÉBASTIEN-ROCH NICOLAS DE CHAMFORT (1741-94), French
writer, wit. *Maxims and Considerations*, vol. 1, no. 2 (1796; tr.
1926).

2   As long as mixed grills and combination salads are
popular, anthologies will undoubtedly continue in favor.

ELIZABETH JANEWAY (b. 1913), U.S. author, critic. *The Writer's
Book*, ch. 32 (ed. by Helen Hull, 1950).

3   By some might be said of me that here I have but
gathered a nosegay of strange flowers, and have put nothing of mine unto it but the thread to bind them.

MICHEL DE MONTAIGNE (1533-92), French essayist. *Essays*, bk.
3, ch. 12, "Of Physiognomy" (1588; tr. by John Florio). Montaigne's essays are full of classical quotations.

See also Sontag on QUOTATION.

ANTHROPOLOGY

1   Anthropology is the science which tells us that people are the same the whole world over—except when
they are different.

NANCY BANKS-SMITH, British columnist. Quoted in: *Guardian*
(London, 21 July 1988).

2   Anthropologists are a connecting link between
poets and scientists; though their field-work among
primitive peoples has often made them forget the language of science.

ROBERT GRAVES (1895-1985), British poet, novelist. Speech, 6
Dec. 1963, London School of Economics (published in *Mammon
and the Black Goddess*, "Mammon," 1965).

3   The anthropologists are busy, indeed, and ready to
transport us back into the savage forest where all human
things . . . have their beginnings; but the seed never
explains the flower.

EDITH HAMILTON (1867-1963), U.S. classical scholar, translator. *The Greek Way*, ch. 1 (1930).

4   No contact with savage Indian tribes has ever
daunted me more than the morning I spent with an old
lady swathed in woolies who compared herself to a rotten herring encased in a block of ice.

CLAUDE LÉVI-STRAUSS (b. 1908), French anthropologist. *Tristes
Tropiques*, ch. 1 (1955).

5   Anthropology has always struggled with an
intense, fascinated repulsion towards its subject. . . . [The
anthropologist] submits himself to the exotic to confirm
his own inner alienation as an urban intellectual.

SUSAN SONTAG (b. 1933), U.S. essayist. Quoted in: Neville
Dyson-Hudson, "Structure and Infrastructure in Primitive Society" (published in *The Structuralist Controversy*, ed. by R. Mack-
sey and E. Donato, 1970).

ANTIPATHY

1   Nothing is more common than mutual dislike,
where mutual approbation is particularly expected.

SAMUEL JOHNSON (1709-84), English author, lexicographer.
Letter, 1 May 1780, to Mrs. Thrale. Quoted in: James Boswell,
Life of Samuel Johnson (1791).

2   [They] exchanged the quick, brilliant smile of
women who dislike each other on sight.

MARSHALL PUGH (b. 1925), British journalist, author. *The
Chancer*, ch. 2 (1959).

3   Thou art all ice. Thy kindness freezes.

WILLIAM SHAKESPEARE (1564-1616), English dramatist, poet.
King Richard, in *Richard III*, act 4, sc. 2.

4   Some men there are love not a gaping pig,
Some that are mad if they behold a cat,
And others when the bagpipe sings i'th' nose
Cannot contain their urine.

> WILLIAM SHAKESPEARE (1564-1616), English dramatist, poet. Shylock, in *The Merchant of Venice*, act 4, sc. 1, explaining his behavior toward Antonio, which he ascribes to natural antipathy.

5   Antipathy, dissimilarity of views, hate, contempt, can accompany true love.

> J. AUGUST STRINDBERG (1849-1912), Swedish dramatist, novelist, poet. *The Son of a Servant*, vol. 1 (1886; tr. 1913).

ANTIQUITY

See CLASSICISM AND ANTIQUITY.

APATHY

1   We may have found a cure for most evils; but it has found no remedy for the worst of them all—the apathy of human beings.

> HELEN KELLER (1880-1968), U.S. author, lecturer. *My Religion*, pt. 1, ch. 6 (1927).

2   You see few people here in America who really care very much about living a Christian life in a democratic world.

> CLARE BOOTHE LUCE (1903-87), U.S. diplomat, writer. *Europe in the Spring*, ch. 12 (1940).

3   The difference between our decadence and the Russians' is that while theirs is brutal, ours is apathetic.

> JAMES THURBER (1894-1961), U.S. humorist, illustrator. Quoted in: *Observer* (London, 5 Feb. 1961).

4   Things have dropped from me. I have outlived certain desires; I have lost friends, some by death . . . others through sheer inability to cross the street.

> VIRGINIA WOOLF (1882-1941), British novelist. Bernard, in *The Waves* (1931; repr. 1943, p. 132)

See also INDIFFERENCE.

APHORISMS AND EPIGRAMS

1   An epigram is a flashlight of a truth; a witticism, truth laughing at itself.

> MINNA ANTRIM (1861-?), U.S. epigrammist. *Naked Truth and Veiled Allusions* (1901, p. 37).

2   Our live experiences, fixed in aphorisms, stiffen into cold epigrams. Our heart's blood, as we write it, turns to mere dull ink.

> F. H. BRADLEY (1846-1924), English philosopher. *Aphorisms*, no. 25 (1930).

3   Most maxim-mongers have preferred the prettiness to the justness of a thought, and the turn to the truth; but I have refused myself to everything that my own experience did not justify and confirm.

> LORD CHESTERFIELD (1694-1773), English statesman, man of letters. Letter, 15 Jan. 1753 (1774; repr. in *The Letters of the Earl of Chesterfield to His Son*, vol. 2, no. 297, ed. by Charles Strachey, 1901).

4   Exclusively of the abstract sciences, the largest and worthiest portion of our knowledge consists of aphorisms: and the greatest and best of men is but an aphorism.

> SAMUEL TAYLOR COLERIDGE (1772-1834), English poet, critic. *Aids to Reflection*, "Introductory Aphorisms," aph. 27 (1825; repr. in *Works*, vol. 1, ed. by Professor Shedd, 1853).

5   An aphorism can never be the whole truth; it is either a half-truth or a truth-and-a-half.

> KARL KRAUS (1874-1936), Austrian satirist. *Die Fackel*, no. 270/71 (Vienna, 19 Jan. 1909; repr. in Thomas Szasz, *Anti-Freud: Karl Kraus's Criticism of Psychoanalysis and Psychiatry*, ch. 8, 1976).

6   An aphorism
should be
like a burr:
sting,
. . .
and leave
a little soreness . . .

> IRVING LAYTON (b. 1912), Canadian poet. *The Whole Bloody Bird*, "Aphs" (1969).

7   An epigram is only a wisecrack that's played at Carnegie Hall.

> OSCAR LEVANT (1906-72), U.S. pianist, composer. *Coronet Magazine* (Sept. 1968).

8   He had a wonderful talent for packing thought close, and rendering it portable.

> THOMAS, BABINGTON MACAULAY (1800-59), English historian. "Lord Bacon," in *Edinburgh Review* (July 1837; repr. in *Lord Macaulay's Essays*, 1889), referring to Francis Bacon.

9   Anyone can tell the truth, but only very few of us can make epigrams.

> W. SOMERSET MAUGHAM (1874-1966), British author. *A Writer's Notebook* (1949), 1896 entry. "In the nineties, however," Maugham added, "we all tried to."

10   They are the guiding oracles which man has found out for himself in that great business of ours, of learning how to be, to do, to do without, and to depart.

> JOHN, LORD MORLEY (1838-1923), English writer, Liberal politician. "Address on Aphorisms," 1887, Edinburgh (published in *Studies in Literature*, "Aphorisms," 1890).

11   There are aphorisms that, like airplanes, stay up only while they are in motion.

> VLADIMIR NABOKOV (1899-1977), Russian-born U.S. novelist, poet. Koncheyev, in *The Gift*, ch. 1 (1937; tr. 1963).

12   In the mountains the shortest route is from peak to peak, but for that you must have long legs. Aphorisms should be peaks: and those to whom they are spoken should be big and tall of stature.

> FRIEDRICH NIETZSCHE (1844-1900), German philosopher. *Thus Spoke Zarathustra*, pt. 1, "Of Reading and Writing" (1883-92; tr. 1961).

13 The aphorism, the apophthegm, in which I am the first master among Germans, are the forms of "eternity"; my ambition is to say in ten sentences what everyone else says in a book—what everyone else *does not* say in a book.

> FRIEDRICH NIETZSCHE (1844-1900), German philosopher. *Twilight of the Idols,* "Expeditions of an Untimely Man," aph. 51 (1889).

14 Epigrams succeed where epics fail.

> PERSIAN PROVERB.

15 Certain brief sentences are peerless in their ability to give one the feeling that nothing remains to be said.

> JEAN ROSTAND (1894-1977), French biologist, writer. *Carnets d'un Biologiste,* repr. in *The Substance of Man* (1962).

16 An aphorism ought to be entirely isolated from the surrounding world like a little work of art and complete in itself like a hedgehog.

> FRIEDRICH SCHLEGEL (1772-1829), German philosopher, critic, writer. *Dialogue on Poetry and Literary Aphorisms,* "Selected Aphorisms from *The Athenaeum,*" aph. 206 (1968; first published 1798).

17 It is the nature of aphoristic thinking to be always in a state of concluding; a bid to have the final word is inherent in all powerful phrase-making.

> SUSAN SONTAG (b. 1933), U.S. essayist. *Barthes: Selected Writings,* "Writing Itself: On Roland Barthes," Introduction (1982).

18 He would stab his best friend for the sake of writing an epigram on his tombstone.

> OSCAR WILDE (1854-1900), Anglo-Irish playwright, author. The Czarevitch, in *Vera, or the Nihilists,* act 2, referring to Prince Paul.

See also Wilde on PLATITUDES; Parker on OSCAR WILDE.

APOLOGIES

1 To apologize is to lay the foundation for a future offense.

> AMBROSE BIERCE (1842-1914), U.S. author. *The Devil's Dictionary* (1881-1906).

2 Never make a defence or apology before you be accused.

> CHARLES I (1600-1649), King of England (1625-49). Letter, 3 Sept. 1636, to Lord Wentworth, later Earl of Strafford and Charles's chief Counselor.

3 A stiff apology is a second insult. . . . The injured party does not want to be compensated because he has been wronged; he wants to be healed because he has been hurt.

> G. K. CHESTERTON (1874-1936), British author. *The Common Man,s* "The Real Dr. Johnson" (1950).

4 Never explain—your friends do not need it and your enemies will not believe it anyhow.

> ELBERT HUBBARD (1856-1915), U.S. author. *Selected Writings,* vol. 1, "Index" (1921).

5 An apology? Bah! Disgusting! Cowardly! Beneath the dignity of any gentleman, however wrong he might be.

> BARONESS ORCZY (1865-1947), Hungarian-born British novelist, playwright. *I Will Repay,* Prologue no. 1 (1906).

APPEARANCE

1 Everybody has that thing where they need to look one way but they come out looking another way and that's what people observe. You see someone on the street and essentially what you notice about them is the flaw. It's just extraordinary that we should have been given these peculiarities. . . . Something is ironic in the world and it has to do with the fact that what you intend never comes out like you intend it.

> DIANE ARBUS (1923-71), U.S. photographer. From class lectures given in 1971 (published in *Diane Arbus: An Aperture Monograph,* 1972).

2 He looked about as inconspicuous as a tarantula on a slice of angel food.

> RAYMOND CHANDLER (1888-1959), U.S. author. Philip Marlowe, in *Farewell, My Lovely,* ch. 1 (1940), describing Moose Malloy.

3 The most winning woman I ever knew was hanged for poisoning three little children for their insurance-money, and the most repellent man of my acquaintance is a philanthropist who has spent nearly a quarter of a million upon the London poor.

> SIR ARTHUR CONAN DOYLE (1859-1930), English author. Sherlock Holmes, in *The Sign of Four,* ch. 2 (1890).

4 Great feelings will often take the aspect of error, and great faith the aspect of illusion.

> GEORGE ELIOT (1819-80), English novelist, editor. *Middlemarch,* bk. 8, "Finale" (1871).

5 'Tis very certain that each man carries in his eye the exact indication of his rank in the immense scale of men, and we are always learning to read it. A complete man should need no auxiliaries to his personal presence.

> RALPH WALDO EMERSON (1803-82), U.S. essayist, poet, philosopher. *The Conduct of Life,* "Behavior" (1860).

6 Woman . . . cannot be content with health and agility: she must make exorbitant efforts to appear something that never could exist without a diligent perversion of nature. Is it too much to ask that women be spared the daily struggle for superhuman beauty in order to offer it to the caresses of a subhumanly ugly mate?

> GERMAINE GREER (b. 1939), Australian feminist writer. *The Female Eunuch,* "Loathing and Disgust" (1970).

7 First impressions are often the truest, as we find (not infrequently) to our cost, when we have been wheedled out of them by plausible professions or studied actions. A man's look is the work of years; it is stamped on his countenance by the events of his whole life, nay, more, by the hand of nature, and it is not to be got rid of easily.

> WILLIAM HAZLITT (1778-1830), English essayist. *Table Talk,* vol. 2, "On the Knowledge of Character" (1822).

8   I do not think I had ever seen a nastier-looking man. . . . Under the black hat, when I had first seen them, the eyes had been those of an unsuccessful rapist.

> ERNEST HEMINGWAY (1899-1961), U.S. author. *A Moveable Feast*, ch. 12 (1964), referring to satirical author and painter (Percy) Wyndham Lewis.

9   Nothing so much prevents our being natural as the desire to seem so.

> FRANÇOIS, DUC DE LA ROCHEFOUCAULD (1613-80), French writer, moralist. *Sentences et Maximes Morales*, no. 431 (1678).

10   The most common error made in matters of appearance is the belief that one should disdain the superficial and let the true beauty of one's soul shine through. If there are places on your body where this is a possibility, you are not attractive—you are leaking.

> FRAN LEBOWITZ (b. 1951), U.S. journalist. *Metropolitan Life*, "Manners" (1978).

11   A good man often appears *gauche* simply because he does not take advantage of the myriad mean little chances of making himself look stylish. Preferring truth to form, he is not constantly at work upon the façade of his appearance.

> IRIS MURDOCH (b. 1919), British novelist, philosopher. Bradley Pearson, in *The Black Prince*, pt. 1 (1972).

12   Barring that natural expression of villainy which we all have, the man looked honest enough.

> MARK TWAIN (1835-1910), U.S. author. *A Mysterious Visit* (1870; repr. in *Complete Humourous Sketches and Tales*, ed. by Charles Neider, 1961), referring to a tax assessor.

13   It is only shallow people who do not judge by appearances. The true mystery of the world is the visible, not the invisible.

> OSCAR WILDE (1854-1900), Anglo-Irish playwright, author. Lord Henry, in *The Picture of Dorian Gray*, ch. 1 (1891).

See also Lincoln on The COMMONPLACE; Amies, Ashford, Dickens, Emerson, Johnson, Shakespeare, Shelley, Wodehouse on DRESS; Thoreau on ENTERPRISE; Bacall, Burchill, Euwer, Fielding, Kizer, Schopenhauer on FACES; Unamuno on VANITY.

APPEASEMENT

1   We should seek by all means in our power to avoid war, by analysing possible causes, by trying to remove them, by discussion in a spirit of collaboration and good will. I cannot believe that such a programme would be rejected by the people of this country, even if it does mean the establishment of personal contact with the dictators.

> NEVILLE CHAMBERLAIN (1869-1940), British Conservative politician, prime minister. Speech, 6 Oct. 1938, to the House of Commons, one week after Chamberlain's return from the Munich Conference.

2   An appeaser is one who feeds a crocodile, hoping it will eat him last.

> SIR WINSTON CHURCHILL (1874-1965), British statesman, writer. Quoted in: *The Reader's Digest* (Pleasantville, N.Y., Dec. 1954).

3   There is no calamity which a great nation can invite which equals that which follows a supine submission to wrong and injustice and the consequent loss of national self-respect and honor, beneath which are shielded and defended a people's safety and greatness.

> GROVER CLEVELAND (1837-1908), U.S. Democratic politician, president. Speech, 17 Dec. 1895, to Congress, on the Venezuelan Boundary Dispute with Great Britain.

4   And that is called paying the Dane-geld;
But we've proved it again and again,
That if once you have paid him the Dane-geld
You never get rid of the Dane.

> RUDYARD KIPLING (1865-1936), British author, poet. *The Dane-Geld*.

5   Thus Belial, with words clothed in reason's garb,
Counseled ignoble ease, and peaceful sloth,
Not peace.

> JOHN MILTON (1608-74), English poet. *Paradise Lost*, bk. 2 (1667).

6   I trust that a graduate student some day will write a doctoral essay on the influence of the Munich analogy on the subsequent history of the twentieth century. Perhaps in the end he will conclude that the multitude of errors committed in the name of "Munich" may exceed the original error of 1938.

> ARTHUR M. SCHLESINGER, JR. (b. 1917), U.S. historian. *The Bitter Heritage: Vietnam and American Democracy*, "The Inscrutability of History" (1967).

7   I seem to smell the stench of appeasement in the air.

> MARGARET THATCHER (b. 1925), British Conservative politician, prime minister. *Independent* (London, 31 Oct. 1990), on the Gulf crisis.

See also Jakobovits on ADOLF HITLER; Disraeli on PEACE.

APPETITE

1   The most violent appetites in all creatures are lust and hunger; the first is a perpetual call upon them to propagate their kind, the latter to preserve themselves.

> JOSEPH ADDISON (1672-1719), English essayist. *Spectator* (London, 18 July 1711).

2   I can reason down or deny everything, except this perpetual Belly: feed he must and will, and I cannot make him respectable.

> RALPH WALDO EMERSON (1803-82), U.S. essayist, poet, philosopher. *Representative Men*, "Montaigne, or the Skeptic" (1850).

3   Appetite is essentially insatiable, and where it operates as a criterion of both action and enjoyment (that is, everywhere in the Western world since the sixteenth century) it will infallibly discover congenial agencies (mechanical and political) of expression.

> MARSHALL MCLUHAN (1911-80), Canadian communications theorist. *Horizon* (London, Oct. 1947).

APPLAUSE

1 We must not always judge of the generality of the opinion by the noise of the acclamation.

EDMUND BURKE (1729-97), Irish philosopher, statesman. *First Letter on a Regicide Peace* (1796; published in *The Writings and Speeches of Edmund Burke,* vol. 9, ed. by Paul Langford, 1991).

2 Applause is the spur of noble minds, the end and aim of weak ones.

C. C. COLTON (1780-1832), English author, clergyman. *Lacon,* vol. 1, no. 324 (1820).

3 O, popular applause! what heart of man
Is proof against thy sweet, seducing charms?

WILLIAM COWPER (1731-1800), English poet. *The Task,* bk. 2 (1785).

4 The silence that accepts merit as the most natural thing in the world is the highest applause.

RALPH WALDO EMERSON (1803-82), U.S. essayist, poet, philosopher. "Divinity School Address," 15 July 1838, at Divinity College, Harvard University, Massachusetts (published in *Addresses and Lectures,* 1849).

5 We believe . . . that the applause of silence is the only kind that counts.

ALFRED JARRY (1873-1907), French playwright, author. "Twelve Theatrical Topics," Topic 12 (published in *Dossiers Acénonètes due Collège de 'Pataphysique,* no. 5, 1960; repr. in *The Selected Works of Alfred Jarry,* ed. by Roger Shattuck and Simon Watson Taylor, 1965).

6 To receive applause for works which do not demand all our powers hinders our advance towards a perfecting of our spirit. It usually means that thereafter we stand still.

G. C. LICHTENBERG (1742-99), German physicist, philosopher. *Aphorisms,* "Notebook K," aph. 42 (written 1765-99; tr. by R. J. Hollingdale, 1990).

7 Applause that comes thundering with such force you might think the audience merely suffers the music as an excuse for its ovations.

GREIL MARCUS (b. 1945), U.S. rock journalist. *Mystery Train,* "Elvis: Presliad" (1976).

8 Glorious bouquets and storms of applause . . . are the trimmings which every artist naturally enjoys. But to *move* an audience in such a role, to hear in the applause that unmistakable note which breaks through good theatre manners and comes from the heart, is to feel that you have won through to life itself. Such pleasure does not vanish with the fall of the curtain, but becomes part of one's own life.

DAME ALICE MARKOVA (b. 1910), British ballerina. *Giselle and I,* ch. 18 (1960).

9 They named it Ovation from the Latin *ovis* [a sheep].

PLUTARCH (46-120), Greek essayist, biographer. *Lives,* "Marcellus" (tr. by John Dryden).

10 Applause is a receipt, not a bill.

ARTUR SCHNABEL (1882-1951), German-born U.S. pianist. Quoted in: Irving Kolodin, *The Musical Life,* "Ovation and Triumph" (1958), explaining why he did not render applause the tribute of encores.

ARCHAEOLOGY

1 An archaeologist is the best husband any woman can have: the older she gets, the more interested he is in her.

AGATHA CHRISTIE (1891-1976), British mystery writer. Quoted in: News report (9 March 1954). Christie later denied this remark, attributed to her by her second husband, Sir Max Mallowan.

2 Dug from the tomb of taste-refining time,
Each form is exquisite, each block sublime.
Or good, or bad,—disfigur'd, or deprav'd,—
All art, is at its resurrection sav'd;
All crown'd with glory in the critic's heav'n,
Each merit magnified, each fault forgiven.

SIR MARTIN ARCHER SHEE (1769-1850), Irish portrait painter, president of Royal Academy. *Rhymes on Art, or the Remonstrance of a Painter,* pt. 2 (1805).

ARCHITECTURE

1 A structure becomes architectural, and not sculptural, when its elements no longer have their justification in nature.

GUILLAUME APOLLINAIRE (1880-1918), Italian-born French poet, critic. *The Cubist Painters,* "New Painters" (1913).

2 In my experience, if you have to keep the lavatory door shut by extending your left leg, it's modern architecture.

NANCY BANKS-SMITH, British columnist. *Guardian* (London, 20 Feb. 1979).

3 "Where *do* architects and designers get their ideas?" The answer, of course, is mainly from other architects and designers, so is it mere casuistry to distinguish between tradition and plagiarism?

STEPHEN BAYLEY (b. 1951), British design critic. *Commerce and Culture,* ch. 3 (1989).

4 Architect. One who drafts a plan of your house, and plans a draft of your money.

AMBROSE BIERCE (1842-1914), U.S. author. *The Devil's Dictionary* (1881-1906).

5 You have to give this much to the Luftwaffe: when it knocked down our buildings it did not replace them with anything more offensive than rubble. We did that.

CHARLES, PRINCE OF WALES (b. 1948). Speech, 2 Dec. 1987, at Mansion House, London.

6 A building is akin to dogma; it is insolent, like dogma. Whether or no it is permanent, it claims permanence, like a dogma. People ask why we have no typical architecture of the modern world, like impressionism in painting. Surely it is obviously because we have not enough dogmas; we cannot bear to see anything in the sky that is solid and enduring, anything in the sky that does not change like the clouds of the sky.

G. K. CHESTERTON (1874-1936), British author. *Tremendous Trifles,* "In the Place de la Bastille" (1909).

7 All architecture is great architecture after sunset; perhaps architecture is really a nocturnal art, like the art of fireworks.

> G. K. CHESTERTON (1874-1936), British author. *Tremendous Trifles*, "The Giant" (1909).

8 We shape our buildings: thereafter they shape us.

> SIR WINSTON CHURCHILL (1874-1965), British statesman, writer. *Time* (New York, 12 Sept. 1960).

9 The principle of the Gothic architecture is infinity made imaginable.

> SAMUEL TAYLOR COLERIDGE (1772-1834), English poet, critic. *Table Talk*, in *Specimens of the Table Talk of Samuel Taylor Coleridge* (ed. by Henry Nelson Coleridge, 1835; repr. in *Collected Works*, vol. 14, ed. by Kathleen Coburn, 1990).

10 In short, the building becomes a theatrical demonstration of its functional ideal. In this romanticism, High-Tech architecture is, of course, no different in spirit—if totally different in form—from all the romantic architecture of the past.

> DAN CRUICKSHANK (b. 1949), British architectural critic. *Commerce and Culture*, ch. 4, "Tradition" (ed. by Stephen Bailey, 1989).

11 The terrifying and edible beauty of Art Nouveau architecture.

> SALVADOR DALI (1904-89), Spanish painter. Quoted in: Saranne Alexandrian, *Surrealist Art*, ch. 10 (1969).

12 The job of buildings is to improve human relations: architecture must ease them, not make them worse.

> RALPH ERSKINE (b. 1914), British architect. *Times* (London, 16 Sept. 1992).

13 Light, God's eldest daughter, is a principal beauty in a building.

> THOMAS FULLER (1608-61), English cleric. *The Holy State and the Profane State*, bk. 3, "Of Building" (1642).

14 Architects, painters, and sculptors must recognize anew and learn to grasp the composite character of a building both as an entity and in its separate parts. Only then will their work be imbued with the architectonic spirit which it has lost as "salon art." . . . Together let us desire, conceive, and create the new structure of the future, which will embrace architecture and sculpture and painting in one unity and which will one day rise toward heaven from the hands of a million workers like the crystal symbol of a new faith.

> WALTER GROPIUS (1883-1969), German architect. "The Bauhaus Proclamation" (April 1919; repr. in Hans Wingler, *The Bauhaus*, ch. 2, 1962).

15 The only legitimate artists in England are the architects.

> BENJAMIN HAYDON (1786-1846), British artist. *Correspondence and Table-Talk*, vol. 2, "Table Talk" (ed. by Frederic Wordsworth Haydon, 1876).

16 Architecture is to make us know and remember who we are.

> SIR GEOFFREY JELLICOE (b. 1900), British architect. *International Herald Tribune* (Paris, 6 Nov. 1989).

17 Architecture is the art of how to waste space.

> PHILIP JOHNSON (b. 1906), U.S. architect, historian. *New York Times* (27 Dec. 1964).

18 All architects want to live beyond their deaths.

> PHILIP JOHNSON (b. 1906), U.S. architect, historian. Quoted in: *Observer* (London, 27 Dec. 1987).

19 I don't think of form as a kind of architecture. The architecture is the result of the forming. It is the kinesthetic and visual sense of position and wholeness that puts the thing into the realm of art.

> ROY LICHTENSTEIN (b. 1923), U.S. Pop artist. Interview in Lawrence Alloway, *Lichtenstein*, "Artist's Statements" (1983).

20 Ah, to build, to build!
That is the noblest art of all the arts.
Painting and sculpture are but images,
Are merely shadows cast by outward things
On stone or canvas, having in themselves
No separate existence. Architecture,
Existing in itself, and not in seeming
A something it is not, surpasses them
As substance shadow.

> HENRY WADSWORTH LONGFELLOW (1807-82), U.S. poet. *Michael Angelo*.

21 Nor aught availed him now
To have built in heav'n high tow'rs; nor did
  he scape
By all his engines, but was headlong sent
With his industrious crew to build in hell.

> JOHN MILTON (1608-74), English poet. *Paradise Lost*, bk. 1 (1667). The reference was to the architect Mulciber, who had built Pandemonium, the palace of Satan.

22 The *architect* represents neither a Dionysian nor an Apollinian condition: here it is the mighty act of will, the will which moves mountains, the intoxication of the strong will, which demands artistic expression. The most powerful men have always inspired the architects; the architect has always been influenced by power.

> FRIEDRICH NIETZSCHE (1844-1900), German philosopher. *Twilight of the Idols*, "Expeditions of an Untimely Man," aph. 11 (1889).

23 No person who is not a great sculptor or painter can be an architect. If he is not a sculptor or painter, he can only be a builder.

> JOHN RUSKIN (1819-1900), English art critic, author. *Lectures on Architecture and Painting*, no. 61 (1853).

24 No architecture is so haughty as that which is simple.

> JOHN RUSKIN (1819-1900), English art critic, author. *The Stones of Venice*, vol. 2, ch. 6 (1851-53).

25 We may live without her, and worship without her, but we cannot remember without her. How cold is all history, how lifeless all imagery, compared to that which the living nation writes, and the uncorrupted marble bears!

> JOHN RUSKIN (1819-1900), English art critic, author. *The Seven Lamps of Architecture*, "The Lamp of Memory," sct. 2 (1849), referring to architecture.

26   An architect should live as little in cities as a painter. Send him to our hills, and let him study there what nature understands by a buttress, and what by a dome.

> JOHN RUSKIN (1819-1900), English art critic, author. *The Seven Lamps of Architecture,* "The Lamp of Power," sct. 24 (1849).

27   Believe me, that was a happy age, before the days of architects, before the days of builders.

> SENECA (c. 5 B.C.-A.D. c. 65), Roman writer, philosopher, statesman. *Epistulae ad Lucilium,* Epistle 90.

28   It is the Late city that first defies the land, contradicts Nature in the lines of its silhouette, *denies* all Nature. It wants to be something different from and higher than Nature. These high-pitched gables, these Baroque cupolas, spires, and pinnacles, neither are, nor desire to be, related with anything in Nature. And then begins the gigantic megalopolis, the *city-as-world,* which suffers nothing beside itself and sets about *annihilating* the country picture.

> OSWALD SPENGLER (1880-1936), German historian. *The Decline of the West,* vol. 2, ch. 4, sct. 3 (1926).

29   Form ever follows function.

> LOUIS HENRY SULLIVAN (1856-1924), U.S. architect. "The Tall Office Building Artistically Considered," in *Lippincott's Magazine* (March 1896).

30   True, there are architects so called in this country, and I have heard of one at least possessed with the idea of making architectural ornaments have a core of truth, a necessity, and hence a beauty, as if it were a revelation to him. All very well perhaps from his point of view, but only a little better than the common dilettantism.

> HENRY DAVID THOREAU (1817-62), U.S. philosopher, author, naturalist. *Walden,* "Economy" (1854).

31   Heredity is a strong factor, even in architecture. Necessity first mothered invention. Now invention has little ones of her own, and they look just like grandma.

> E. B. WHITE (1899-1985), U.S. author, editor. "The Old and the New," in *New Yorker* (19 June 1937; repr. in *Writings from the New Yorker 1927-1976,* ed. by Rebecca M. Dale, 1991).

32   Le Corbusier was the sort of relentlessly rational intellectual that only France loves wholeheartedly, the logician who flies higher and higher in ever-decreasing circles until, with one last, utterly inevitable induction, he disappears up his own fundamental aperture and emerges in the fourth dimension as a needle-thin umber bird.

> TOM WOLFE (b. 1931), U.S. journalist, author. *From Bauhaus to Our House,* ch. 1 (1981).

33   *Si monumentum requiris, circumspice.* (If you would see his monument, look around.).

> SIR CHRISTOPHER WREN'S epitaph, by his son, inscribed on his tomb in St. Paul's Cathedral, London.

34   The physician can bury his mistakes, but the architect can only advise his clients to plant vines.

> FRANK LLOYD WRIGHT (1869-1959), U.S. architect. *New York Times Magazine* (4 Oct. 1953).

35   All fine architectural values are human vales, else not valuable.

> FRANK LLOYD WRIGHT (1869-1959), U.S. architect. *The Living City,* pt. 3, "Recapitulation" (1958).

ARGUMENT

1   There are two things which cannot be attacked in front: ignorance and narrow-mindedness. They can only be shaken by the simple development of the contrary qualities. They will not bear discussion.

> LORD ACTON (1834-1902), English historian. Letter, 23 Jan. 1861 (published in *Lord Acton and his Circle,* Letter 74, ed. by Abbot Gasquet, 1906).

2   Argument is conclusive . . . but . . . it does not remove doubt, so that the mind may rest in the sure knowledge of the truth, unless it finds it by the method of experiment. . . . For if any man who never saw fire proved by satisfactory arguments that fire burns . . . his hearer's mind would never be satisfied, nor would he avoid the fire until he put his hand in it . . . that he might learn by experiment what argument taught.

> ROGER BACON (c. 1214–c. 1294), English philosopher, scientist. *Opus Maius,* pt. 4, ch. 1 (1267).

3   Arguments are like fire-arms which a man may keep at home but should not carry about with him.

> SAMUEL BUTLER (1835-1902), English author. *Samuel Butler's Notebooks* (1951, p. 65).

4   Those disputing, contradicting, and confuting people are generally unfortunate in their affairs. They get victory, sometimes, but they never get good will, which would be of more use to them.

> BENJAMIN FRANKLIN (1706-90), U.S. statesman, writer. *Autobiography,* ch. 9 (1868), written 1771-90. Earlier in his autobiography (ch. 1), describing his own "disputatious turn" when younger, a habit he had picked up from reading his father's books, Franklin observed, "Persons of good sense . . . seldom fall into it, except lawyers, university men, and, generally, men of all sorts who have been bred at Edinburgh."

5   An association of men who will not quarrel with one another is a thing which has never yet existed, from the greatest confederacy of nations down to a town meeting or a vestry.

> THOMAS JEFFERSON (1743-1826), U.S. president. Letter, 1 June 1798.

6   When you argue with your inferiors,
you convince them of only one thing:
they are as clever as you.

> IRVING LAYTON (b. 1912), Canadian poet. *The Whole Bloody Bird,* "Aphs" (1969).

7   There is no good in arguing with the inevitable. The only argument available with an east wind is to put on your overcoat.

> JAMES RUSSELL LOWELL (1819-91), U.S. poet, editor. "Democracy," address, 6 Oct. 1884, Birmingham, England (published in *Democracy and Other Addresses,* 1887).

8 The difficult part in an argument is not to defend one's opinion, but rather to know it.

ANDRÉ MAUROIS (1885-1967), French author, critic. Quoted in: Frederic B. Wilcox, *A Little Book of Aphorisms* (1947).

9 You have not converted a man because you have silenced him.

JOHN, LORD MORLEY (1838-1923), English writer, Liberal politician. *On Compromise*, ch. 5 (1874).

10 One often contradicts an opinion when what is uncongenial is really the tone in which it was conveyed.

FRIEDRICH NIETZSCHE (1844-1900), German philosopher. *Human, All Too Human*, aph. 303 (1878).

11 Myself when young did eagerly frequent
Doctor and Saint, and heard great Argument
About it and about: but evermore
Came out by the same Door as in I went.

OMAR KHAYYÁM (c. 11-12th century), Persian astronomer, poet. *The Rubáiyát of Omar Khayyám*, st. 27 (first ed., tr. by Edward FitzGerald, 1859).

12 I will name you the degrees. The first, the Retort Courteous; the second, the Quip Modest; the third, the Reply Churlish; the fourth, the Reproof Valiant; the fifth, the Countercheck Quarrelsome; the sixth, the Lie with Circumstance; the seventh, the Lie Direct.

WILLIAM SHAKESPEARE (1564-1616), English dramatist, poet. Touchstone, in *As You Like It*, act 5, sc. 4.

13 The devil can cite Scripture for his purpose.

WILLIAM SHAKESPEARE (1564-1616), English dramatist, poet. Antonio, in *The Merchant of Venice*, act 1, sc. 3, referring to Shylock.

14 Concerning God, freewill and destiny:
Of all that earth has been or yet may be,
All that vain men imagine or believe,
Or hope can paint or suffering may achieve,
We descanted.

PERCY BYSSHE SHELLEY (1792-1822), English poet. *Julian and Maddalo*. In the poem, Shelley re-created a night spent arguing with Byron in Venice, 23 Aug. 1818.

15 When a thing is said to be not worth refuting you may be sure that either it is flagrantly stupid—in which case all comment is superfluous—or it is something formidable, the very crux of the problem.

MIGUEL DE UNAMUNO (1864-1936), Spanish philosophical writer. *The Tragic Sense of Life*, ch. 5 (1913).

16 How beggarly appear arguments before a defiant deed!

WALT WHITMAN (1819-92), U.S. poet. *Song of the Broad Axe*, sct. 6.

17 I dislike arguments of any kind. They are always vulgar, and often convincing.

OSCAR WILDE (1854-1900), Anglo-Irish playwright, author. Lady Bracknell, in *The Importance of Being Ernest*, act 4. Wilde also wrote, "Arguments are extremely vulgar, for everybody in good society holds exactly the same opinions," in "The Remarkable Rocket," in *The Happy Prince and Other Tales* (1888).

See also Eliot on ELOQUENCE; Gay on INTERVENTION; Butler, Conrad, Frame, James on PERSUASION; Johnson on UNDERSTANDING.

ARISTOCRACY

1 Nobility is a graceful ornament to the civil order. It is the Corinthian capital of polished society.

EDMUND BURKE (1729-97), Irish philosopher, statesman. *Reflections on the Revolution in France* (1790).

2 Almost in every kingdom the most ancient families have been at first princes' bastards.

ROBERT BURTON (1577-1640), English clergyman, author. *Anatomy of Melancholy*, pt. 2, sct. 2, member 1, subsct. 1 (1621).

3 For what were all these country patriots born?
To hunt, and vote, and raise the price of corn?

LORD BYRON (1788-1824), English poet. *The Age of Bronze*, st. 14.

4 Democracy means government by the uneducated, while aristocracy means government by the badly educated.

G. K. CHESTERTON (1874-1936), British author. *New York Times* (1 Feb. 1931).

5 The Pedigree of Honey
Does not concern the Bee—
A Clover, any time, to him,
Is Aristocracy—

EMILY DICKINSON (1830-86), U.S. poet. *The Complete Poems*, no. 1627, version 2 (1955).

6 The aristocrat is the democrat ripe, and gone to seed.

RALPH WALDO EMERSON (1803-82), U.S. essayist, poet, philosopher. *Representative Men*, "Napoleon, the Man of the World" (1850).

7 I have known a German Prince with more titles than subjects, and a Spanish nobleman with more names than shirts.

OLIVER GOLDSMITH (1728-74), Anglo-Irish playwright, author. *The Citizen of the World*, Letter 120 (1762).

8 There is a natural aristocracy among men. The grounds of this are virtue and talents.

THOMAS JEFFERSON (1743-1826), U.S. president. Letter, 28 Oct. 1813, to former president John Adams.

9 What is the use of your pedigrees?

JUVENAL (40-125), Roman satiric poet. *Satires*, Satire 8.

10 Actual aristocracy cannot be abolished by any law: all the law can do is decree how it is to be imparted and who is to acquire it.

G. C. LICHTENBERG (1742-99), German physicist, philosopher. *Aphorisms*, "Notebook L," aph. 44 (written 1765-99; tr. by R. J. Hollingdale, 1990).

11 A fully equipped duke costs as much to keep up as two Dreadnoughts, and dukes are just as great a terror—and they last longer.

DAVID LLOYD GEORGE (1863-1945), British Liberal politician, prime minister. Speech, 9 Oct. 1909, Newcastle upon Tyne, England.

12 Lords are lordliest in their wine.

JOHN MILTON (1608-74), English poet. *Samson Agonistes* (1671).

13 I hate the noise and hurry inseparable from great Estates and Titles, and look upon both as blessings that ought only to be given to fools, for 'tis only to them that they are blessings.

LADY MARY WORTLEY MONTAGU (1689-1762), English society figure, letter writer. Letter, 28 March 1710, to her future husband (published in *The Complete Letters of Lady Mary Wortley Montagu*, 1967).

14 A degenerate nobleman is like a turnip. There is nothing good of him but that which is underground.

ENGLISH SAYING (17th century).

15 If, in looking at the lives of princes, courtiers, men of rank and fashion, we must perforce depict them as idle, profligate, and criminal, we must make allowances for the rich men's failings, and recollect that we, too, were very likely indolent and voluptuous, had we no motive for work, a mortal's natural taste for pleasure, and the daily temptation of a large income. What could a great peer, with a great castle and park, and a great fortune, do but be splendid and idle?

WILLIAM MAKEPEACE THACKERAY (1811-63), English author. *The Four Georges*, "George the Third" (1855).

16 Nothing is quite so wretchedly corrupt as an aristocracy which has lost its power but kept its wealth and which still has endless leisure to devote to nothing but banal enjoyments. All its great thoughts and passionate energy are things of the past, and nothing but a host of petty, gnawing vices now cling to it like worms to a corpse.

ALEXIS DE TOCQUEVILLE (1805-59), French social philosopher. *Democracy in America*, vol. 2, pt. 3, ch. 11 (1840).

17 You should study the Peerage, Gerald. It is the one book a young man about town should know thoroughly, and it is the best thing in fiction the English have ever done.

OSCAR WILDE (1854-1900), Anglo-Irish playwright, author. Lord Illingworth, in *A Woman of No Importance*, act 3.

18 Those comfortably padded lunatic asylums which are known, euphemistically, as the stately homes of England.

VIRGINIA WOOLF (1882-1941), British novelist. *The Common Reader*, "Lady Dorothy Nevill" (1925).

THE ARMS RACE

1 Weapons are like money; no one knows the meaning of *enough*.

MARTIN AMIS (b. 1949), British author. *Einstein's Monsters*, Introduction (1987).

2 If this phrase of the "balance of power" is to be always an argument for war, the pretext for war will never be wanting, and peace can never be secure.

JOHN BRIGHT (1811-89), English radical politician. Speech, 31 March 1854, to House of Commons.

3 Next week Reagan will probably announce that American scientists have discovered that the entire U.S. agricultural surplus can be compacted into a giant tomato one thousand miles across, which will be suspended

above the Kremlin from a cluster of U.S. satellites flying in geosynchronous orbit. At the first sign of trouble the satellites will drop the tomato on the Kremlin, drowning the fractious Muscovites in ketchup.

ALEXANDER COCKBURN (b. 1941), Anglo-Irish journalist. "Reagan's Mousetrap," in *Village Voice* (New York, 5 April 1983; repr. in *Corruptions of Empire*, pt. 2, 1988).

4 At the rate science proceeds, rockets and missiles will one day seem like buffalo—slow, endangered grazers in the black pasture of outer space.

BERNARD COOPER (b. 1936), U.S. physicist. *Gettysburg Review* (Summer 1989; repr. in *Harper's*, New York, Jan. 1990).

5 The ability to get to the verge without getting into the war is the necessary art. . . . If you try to run away from it, if you are scared to go to the brink, you are lost.

JOHN FOSTER DULLES (1888-1959), U.S. Republican politician. Quoted in: *Life* (New York, 16 Jan. 1956). Adlai Stevenson characterized the Dulles-Eisenhower foreign policy as "the power of positive brinking."

6 Every gun that is fired, every warship launched, every rocket fired, signifies, in the final sense, a theft from those who hunger and are not fed, those who are cold and are not clothed. The world in arms is not spending money alone. It is spending the sweat of its labourers, the genius of its scientists, the hopes of its children.

DWIGHT D. EISENHOWER (1890-1969), U.S. general, Republican politician, president. Speech, April 1953, Washington, D.C.

7 Guns will make us powerful; butter will only make us fat.

HERMANN GOERING (1893-1946), German Nazi leader, air marshal. Alleged radio broadcast, Summer 1936, on the Four-Year Plan.

8 We dare not tempt them with weakness. For only when our arms are sufficient beyond doubt can we be certain beyond doubt that they will never be employed.

JOHN F. KENNEDY (1917-63), U.S. Democratic politician, president. Inaugural address, 20 Jan. 1961, Washington, D.C. Quoted in: Theodore C. Sorenson, *Kennedy*, pt. 3, ch. 9 (1965).

9 I would die for my country, but I could never let my country die for me.

NEIL KINNOCK (b. 1942), British Labour politician. Speech, 30 Sept. 1986, to Labour Party Conference on nuclear disarmament. Quoted in: *Guardian* (London, 1 Oct. 1986).

10 The superpowers often behave like two heavily armed blind men feeling their way around a room, each believing himself in mortal peril from the other, whom he assumes to have perfect vision.

HENRY KISSINGER (b. 1923), U.S. Republican politician, secretary of state. Quoted in: *Observer* (London, 30 Sept. 1979).

11 The emotional security and political stability in this country entitle us to be a nuclear power.

SIR RONALD MASON (b. 1930), British scientist, consultant on defense. Quoted in: *Observer* (London, 20 March 1983).

12 So in your discussions of the nuclear freeze proposals, I urge you to beware the temptation of pride—the temptation blithely to declare yourselves above it all and label both sides equally at fault, to ignore the facts of history and the aggressive impulses of an evil empire, to simply call the arms race a giant misunderstanding and thereby remove yourself from the struggle between right and wrong, good and evil.

> RONALD REAGAN (b. 1911), U.S. Republican politician, president. Statement, 8 March 1983, Orlando, Florida. Quoted in: *Reagan's Reign of Error*, "Temptation of Pride" (ed. by Mark Green and Gail MacColl, 1987). Reagan later denied having spoken of "an evil empire."

13 Let him who desires peace prepare for war.

> VEGETIUS (4th century), Roman military strategist. *De Rei Militari*, Prologue, bk. 3

See also Kennedy on PEACE; Rogers on PROGRESS; Shaw on SCIENCE.

THE ARMY

1 If I should die, think only this of me:
That there's some corner of a foreign field
That is for ever England.

> RUPERT BROOKE (1887-1915), British poet. *The Soldier*. Brooke, who died of blood poisoning while serving during World War I, is buried on the island of Skyros, Greece.

2 In the weakness of one kind of authority, and in the fluctuation of all, the officers of an army will remain for some time mutinous and full of faction, until some popular general, who understands the art of conciliating the soldiery, and who possesses the true spirit of command, shall draw the eyes of all men upon himself. Armies will obey him on his personal account. There is no other way of securing military obedience in this state of things.

> EDMUND BURKE (1729-97), Irish philosopher, statesman. *Reflections on the Revolution in France* (1790). Burke's words prefigure the rise of Napoleon in France.

3 He learned the arts of riding, fencing, gunnery,
And how to scale a fortress—or a nunnery.

> LORD BYRON (1788-1824), English poet. *Don Juan*, cto. 1, st. 38.

4 What makes a regiment of soldiers a more noble object of view than the same mass of mob? Their arms, their dresses, their banners, and the *art* and artificial symmetry of their position and movements.

> LORD BYRON (1788-1824), English poet. Letter, 7 Feb. 1821, to publisher John Murray.

5 The General Order is always to manoeuver in a body and on the attack; to maintain strict but not pettifogging discipline; to keep the troops constantly at the ready; to employ the utmost vigilance on sentry go; to use the bayonet on every possible occasion; and to follow up the enemy remorselessly until he is utterly destroyed.

> LAZARE CARNOT (1753-1823), French revolutionary, military strategist. First Order of the Day, 2 Feb. 1794, to army commanders.

6 Soldiers have many faults, but they have one redeeming merit; they are never worshippers of force. Soldiers more than any other men are taught severely and systematically that might is not right. The fact is obvious. The might is in the hundred men who obey. The

right (or what is held to be right) is in the one man who commands them.

> G. K. CHESTERTON (1874-1936), British author. *All Things Considered*, "Thoughts Around Koepenick" (1908).

7 War is too important a matter to be left to the military.

> GEORGES CLEMENCEAU (1841-1929), French statesman. Quoted in: G. Suarez, *Soixante Années d'Histoire Française*, "Clemenceau" (1886).

8 The nation which forgets its defenders will be itself forgotten.

> CALVIN COOLIDGE (1872-1933), U.S. Republican politician, president. Speech, 27 July 1920, Northampton, Massachusetts, accepting the Republican vice-presidential nomination.

9 I had rather have a plain, russet-coated Captain, that knows what he fights for, and loves what he knows, than that which you call a Gentle-man and is nothing else.

> OLIVER CROMWELL (1599-1658), Parliamentarian general, Lord Protector of England. Letter, Sept. 1643. Quoted in: Thomas Carlyle, *Letters and Speeches of Oliver Cromwell* (1845).

10 Come on, you sons of bitches! Do you want to live forever?

> ATTRIBUTED TO DANIEL DALY (1874-1937), Gunnery sergeant, U.S. Marines. Spoken at Belleau Wood, 4 June 1918.

11 Drinking is the soldier's pleasure.

> JOHN DRYDEN (1631-1700), English poet, dramatist, critic. *Alexander's Feast*.

12 Rogues, would you live forever?

> FREDERICK THE GREAT (1712-86), King of Prussia. Alleged cry, 18 June 1757, when rallying his troops at Kolin, Bohemia. below. See Daniel Daly's echo of this above.

13 The courage of a soldier is found to be the cheapest and most common quality of human nature.

> EDWARD GIBBON (1737-94), English historian. *The Decline and Fall of the Roman Empire*, vol. 3, ch. 26 (1776-88).

14 Conscription may have been good for the country, but it damn near killed the army.

> SIR RICHARD HULL (b. 1907), British general. Quoted in: Anthony Sampson, *Anatomy of Britain Today*, ch. 19 (1965).

15 On becoming soldiers we have not ceased to be citizens.

> ADDRESS, "Humble Representation," 1647, to the English Parliament by Oliver Cromwell's soldiers.

16 Every man thinks meanly of himself for not having been a soldier, or not having been at sea.

> SAMUEL JOHNSON (1709-84), English author, lexicographer. Quoted in: James Boswell, *Life of Samuel Johnson*, 10 April 1776 (1791).

17 Now, you mummy's darlings, get a rift on them boots. Definitely shine 'em, my little curly-headed lambs, for in our mob, war or no war, you die with clean boots on.

> GERALD KERSH (1911-68), British author, journalist. *They Die With Their Boots Clean*, Prologue (1941).

18 We aren't no thin red 'eroes, nor we aren't no
blackguards too,
But single men in barricks, most remarkable like
you;
And if sometimes our conduck isn't all your fancy
paints,
Why, single men in barricks don't grow into
plaster saints.

RUDYARD KIPLING (1865-1936), British author, poet. *Tommy.*

19 When you're wounded and left on Afghanistan's
plains,
And the women come out to cut up what remains,
Jest roll to your rifle an' blow out your brains
An' go to your Gawd like a soldier.

RUDYARD KIPLING (1865-1936), British author, poet. *The Young British Soldier.*

20 Children play soldier. That makes sense. But why
do soldiers play children?

KARL KRAUS (1874-1936), Austrian satirist. *Sprüche und Widersprüche,* ch. 4 (1909; repr. in *Half-Truths and One-And-A Half-Truths: Selected Aphorisms,* "In this War we are Dealing . . .," ed. by Harry Zohn, 1976).

21 An army without culture is a dull-witted army, and
a dull-witted army cannot defeat the enemy.

MAO ZEDONG (1893-1976), Founder of the People's Republic of China. "The United Front in Cultural Work" (30 Oct. 1944; published in *Selected Works,* vol. 3).

22 Do you know what a soldier is, young man? He's
the chap who makes it possible for civilised folk to
despise war.

ALLAN MASSIE (b. 1938), British author. Colonel Fernie, in *A Question of Loyalties,* pt. 2, ch. 1 (1989).

23 No profession or occupation is more pleasing than
the military; a profession or exercise both noble in execution (for the strongest, most generous and proudest of
all virtues is true valour) and noble in its cause. No utility either more just or universal than the protection of the
repose or defence of the greatness of one's country. The
company and daily conversation of so many noble,
young and active men cannot but be well-pleasing to you.

MICHEL DE MONTAIGNE (1533-92), French essayist. *Essays,* bk. 3, ch. 13, "Of Experience" (1588; tr. by John Florio).

24 The army is the true nobility of our country.

NAPOLEON III (1808-73), French emperor. Speech, 20 March 1855, at a review of the Imperial Guard, Paris.

25 The military mind is indeed a menace. Old-fashioned futurity that sees only men fighting and dying in
smoke and fire; hears nothing more civilized than a can-
nonade; scents nothing but the stink of battle-wounds and
blood.

SEAN O'CASEY (1884-1964), Irish dramatist. *Sunset and Evening Star,* "And Evening Star" (1954).

26 Soldiers are citizens of death's grey land. . . .
Soldiers are sworn to action; they must win
Some flaming, fatal climax with their lives.

Soldiers are dreamers; when the guns begin
They think of firelit homes, clean beds and wives.

SIEGFRIED SASSOON (1886-1967), British poet. *Dreamers,* st. 1, in *Counter-Attack and Other Poems* (1918).

27 We few, we happy few, we band of brothers.
For he today that sheds his blood with me
Shall be my brother; be ne'er so vile,
This day shall gentle his condition.
And gentlemen in England now abed
Shall think themselves accursed they were not
here,
And hold their manhoods cheap whiles any speaks
That fought with us upon Saint Crispin's day.

WILLIAM SHAKESPEARE (1564-1616), English dramatist, poet. King Henry, in *King Henry V,* act 4, sc. 3.

28 Horribly stuffed with epithets of war.

WILLIAM SHAKESPEARE (1564-1616), English dramatist, poet. Iago, in *Othello,* act 1, sc. 1, describing Othello.

29 'Tis the soldier's life
To have their balmy slumbers waked with strife.

WILLIAM SHAKESPEARE (1564-1616), English dramatist, poet. Othello, in *Othello,* act 2, sc. 3.

30 History shows that there are no invincible armies.

JOSEF STALIN (1879-1953), Soviet leader. Radio broadcast, 3 July 1941, declaring war on Germany, three weeks before Hitler invaded Russia.

31 There are few men more superstitious than soldiers.
They are, after all, the men who live closest to death.

MARY STEWART (b. 1916), British novelist. *The Last Enchantment,* bk. 2, ch. 3 (1979).

32 If our soldiers are not overburdened with money, it
is not because they have a distaste for riches; if their lives
are not unduly long, it is not because they are disinclined
to longevity.

SUN TZU (6th-5th century B.C.), Chinese general. *The Art of War,* ch. 11, axiom 27 (c. 490 B.C., ed. by James Clavell, 1981).

33 Theirs not to make reply,
Theirs not to reason why,
Theirs but to do and die.

LORD TENNYSON (1809-92), English poet. *The Charge of the Light Brigade* (1854).

34 That's what an army is—a mob; they don't fight
with courage that's born in them, but with courage that's
borrowed from their mass, and from their officers.

MARK TWAIN (1835-1910), U.S. author. Colonel Sherburn, in *Huckleberry Finn,* ch. 22 (1884).

35 The feeling about a soldier is, when all is said and
done, he wasn't really going to do very much with his life
anyway. The example usually is: "he wasn't going to
compose Beethoven's Fifth."

KURT VONNEGUT, JR. (b. 1922), U.S. novelist. *City Limits* (London, 11 March 1983).

36 When we assumed the Soldier, we did not lay aside
the Citizen.

GEORGE WASHINGTON (1732-99), U.S. general, president. Address, 26 June 1775, to the New York legislature.

37 I don't know what effect these men will have upon the enemy, but, by God, they terrify me.

> DUKE OF WELLINGTON (1769-1852), English soldier, prime minister. Dispatch, Aug. 1810, speaking of his generals—though commonly thought to refer to the rank-and-file soldiers. A similar remark is attributed to English prime minister Lord North, 1776-77.

38 We have in the service the scum of the earth as common soldiers.

> DUKE OF WELLINGTON (1769-1852), English soldier, prime minister. Dispatch, 2 July 1813, from Vitoria, Spain to Lord Bathurst, War Minister. Quoted in: Stanhope, *Notes of Conversations with the Duke of Wellington* (4 Nov. 1831).

39 O the joy of the strong-brawn'd fighter, towering in the arena in perfect condition, conscious of power, thirsting to meet his opponent.

> WALT WHITMAN (1819-92), U.S. poet. *Leaves of Grass*, "Calamus: A Song of Joys" (1855).

40 Making the world safe for hypocrisy.

> THOMAS WOLFE (1900-38), U.S. author. Luke, in *Look Homeward, Angel*, pt. 3, ch. 36 (1929).

41 Standing armies can never consist of resolute robust men; they may be well-disciplined machines, but they will seldom contain men under the influence of strong passions, or with very vigorous faculties.

> MARY WOLLSTONECRAFT (1759-97), English feminist writer. *A Vindication of the Rights of Women*, ch. 2 (1792).

42 Those that I fight I do not hate,
Those that I guard I do not love.

> W. B. YEATS (1865-1939), Irish poet, playwright. *An Irish Airman Forsees His Death*

See also GENERALS; Roosevelt on PATRIOTISM; UNIFORMS.

ARROGANCE

1 If I cannot brag of knowing something, then I brag of not knowing it; at any rate, brag.

> RALPH WALDO EMERSON (1803-82), U.S. essayist, poet, philosopher. *Journals* (1909-14), 1866 entry.

2 How haughtily he cocks his nose,
To tell what every schoolboy knows.

> JONATHAN SWIFT (1667-1745), Anglo-Irish satirist. *The Country Life.*

See also Burke on YOUTH AND AGE.

ART

1 Art is permitted to survive only if it renounces the right to be different, and integrates itself into the omnipotent realm of the profane.

> THEODOR W. ADORNO (1903-69), German philosopher, sociologist, music critic. *Prisms*, "Perennial Fashion—Jazz" (1967)

2 Twentieth-century art may start with nothing, but it flourishes by virtue of its belief in itself, in the possibility of control over what seems essentially uncontrollable, in the coherence of the inchoate, and in its ability to create its own values.

> A. ALVAREZ (b. 1929), British critic, poet, novelist. *The Savage God*, pt. 4, "Dada: Suicide as an Art" (1971).

3 Art is an experience, not the formulation of a problem.

> LINDSAY ANDERSON (b. 1923), British film director. *Times* (London, 29 March 1989).

4 Without poets, without artists, men would soon weary of nature's monotony. The sublime idea men have of the universe would collapse with dizzying speed. The order which we find in nature, and which is only an effect of art, would at once vanish. Everything would break up in chaos. There would be no seasons, no civilization, no thought, no humanity; even life would give way, and the impotent void would reign everywhere.

> GUILLAUME APOLLINAIRE (1880-1918), Italian-born French poet, critic. *The Cubist Painters*, "On Painting" (1913).

5 Art is a fruit that grows in man, like a fruit on a plant, or a child in its mother's womb.

> JEAN ARP (1887-1948), French-German artist, poet. *Cahiers d'Art*, vol. 22, "Art is a Fruit" (1947; repr. in *On My Way*, ed. by Robert Motherwell, 1948).

6 Pop artists deal with the lowly trivia of possessions and equipment that the present generation is lugging along with it on its safari into the future.

> J. G. BALLARD (b. 1930), British author. Interview in *Books and Bookmen* (London, April 1971; repr. in *Re/Search*, no. 8/9, San Francisco, 1984).

7 The first mistake of Art is to assume that it's serious.

> LESTER BANGS (1948-82), U.S. rock journalist. *Who Put the Bomp* (Winter/Spring 1971; repr. in *Psychotic Reactions & Carburetor Dung*, "James Taylor Marked for Death," 1987).

8 Every great work of art has two faces, one toward its own time and one toward the future, toward eternity.

> DANIEL BARENBOIM (b. 1942), Argentinian-born Israeli pianist, conductor. *International Herald Tribune* (Paris, 20 Jan. 1989).

9 A frenzied passion for art is a canker that devours everything else.

> CHARLES BAUDELAIRE (1821-67), French poet. *L'Ecole Païenne* (1852; repr. in *Complete Works*, vol. 2, ed. by Yves-Gérard le Dantec, rev. by Claude Pichois, 1976).

10 As the twentieth century ends, commerce and culture are comming closer together. The distinction between life and art has been eroded by fifty years of enhanced communications, ever-improving reproduction technologies and increasing wealth.

> STEPHEN BAYLEY (b. 1951), British design critic. *Commerce and Culture*, ch. 1 (1989).

11 In order for the artist to have a world to express he must first be situated in this world, oppressed or oppressing, resigned or rebellious, a man among men.

> SIMONE DE BEAUVOIR (1908-86), French novelist, essayist. *The Ethics of Ambiguity*, ch. 1 (1948).

12 Art! Who comprehends her? With whom can one consult concerning this great goddess?

LUDWIG VAN BEETHOVEN (1770-1827), German composer. Letter, 11 Aug. 1810, to author Bettina von Arnim.

13 The greater the decrease in the social significance of an art form, the sharper the distinction between criticism and enjoyment by the public. The conventional is uncritically enjoyed, and the truly new is criticized with aversion.

WALTER BENJAMIN (1892-1940), German critic, philosopher. *The Work of Art in the Age of Mechanical Reproduction,* sct. 12 (1936; repr. in *Illuminations,* ed. by Hannah Arendt, 1968).

14 I can't tell you what art does and how it does it, but I know that often art has judged the judges, pleaded revenge to the innocent and shown to the future what the past suffered, so that it has never been forgotten. . . . Art, when it functions like this, becomes a meeting-place of the invisible, the irreducible, the enduring, guts, and honour.

JOHN BERGER (b. 1926), British author, critic. *Miners,* exhibition catalogue (1989; repr. in *Keeping a Rendezvous,* 1992).

15 The work of art, just like any fragment of human life considered in its deepest meaning, seems to me devoid of value if it does not offer the hardness, the rigidity, the regularity, the luster on every interior and exterior facet, of the crystal.

ANDRÉ BRETON (1896-1966), French Surrealist. *Mad Love,* ch. 1 (1937; tr. 1987).

16 What is art,
But life upon the larger scale, the higher,
When, graduating up in a spiral line
Of still expanding and ascending gyres,
It pushes toward the intense significance
Of all things, hungry for the Infinite?
Art's life,—and where we live, we suffer and toil.

ELIZABETH BARRETT BROWNING (1806-61), English poet. *Aurora Leigh,* bk. 4 (1857).

17 Art is dangerous. It is one of the attractions: when it ceases to be dangerous you don't want it.

ANTHONY BURGESS (b. 1917), British author, critic. *Face* (London, Dec. 1984).

18 The youth of an art is, like the youth of anything else, its most interesting period. When it has come to the knowledge of good and evil it is stronger, but we care less about it.

SAMUEL BUTLER (1835-1902), English author. *Samuel Butler's Notebooks* (1951, p. 275).

19 It is impossible to give a clear account of the world, but art can teach us to reproduce it—just as the world reproduces itself in the course of its eternal gyrations. The primordial sea indefatigably repeats the same words and casts up the same astonished beings on the same seashore.

ALBERT CAMUS (1913-60), French-Algerian philosopher, author. *The Rebel,* pt. 2, "Absolute Affirmation" (1951; tr. 1953).

20 Art for art's sake is a philosophy of the well-fed.

CAO YU (b. 1910), Chinese dramatist. *Observer* (London, 13 April 1980).

21 A product of the untalented, sold by the unprincipled to the utterly bewildered.

AL CAPP (1909-79), U.S. cartoonist. Quoted in: *National Observer* (Silver Spring, Md., 1 July 1963), referring to abstract art.

22 Fine art, that exists for itself alone, is art in a final state of impotence. If nobody, including the artist, acknowledges art as a means of knowing the world, then art is relegated to a kind of rumpus room of the mind and the irresponsibility of the artist and the irrelevance of art to actual living becomes part and parcel of the practice of art.

ANGELA CARTER (1940-92), British author. *The Sadeian Woman,* "Polemical Preface" (1979).

23 Art is good when it springs from necessity. This kind of origin is the guarantee of its value; there is no other.

NEAL CASSADY (1926-68), U.S. beat hero. Letter, 7-8 Jan. 1948, to Jack Kerouac. Quoted in: Gerald Nicosia, *Memory Babe,* ch. 5, sct. 5 (1983).

25 Religion and art spring from the same root and are close kin. Economics and art are strangers.

WILLA CATHER (1876-1947), U.S. author. *On Writing,* "Four Letters: Escapism" (1949).

26 When I am finishing a picture I hold some God-made object up to it—a rock, a flower, the branch of a tree or my hand—as a kind of final test. If the painting stands up beside a thing man cannot make, the painting is authentic. If there's a clash between the two, it is bad art.

MARC CHAGALL (1889-1985), French artist. *Saturday Evening Post* (New York, 2 Dec. 1962).

27 Art consists of limitation. . . . The most beautiful part of every picture is the frame.

G. K. CHESTERTON (1874-1936), British author. *Tremendous Trifles,* "The Toy Theatre" (1909).

28 Without tradition, art is a flock of sheep without a shepherd. Without innovation, it is a corpse.

SIR WINSTON CHURCHILL (1874-1965), British statesman, author. Address to Royal Academy of Arts. Quoted in: *Time* (New York, 11 May 1954).

29 Art is science made clear.

JEAN COCTEAU (1889-1963), French author, filmmaker. *Le Rappel à l'Ordre,* "Le Coq et l'Arlequin" (1926; repr. in *Collected Works,* vol. 9, 1950).

30 Any work that aspires, however humbly, to the condition of art should carry its justification in every line.

JOSEPH CONRAD (1857-1924), Polish-born English novelist. *The Nigger of the Narcissus,* Preface (1897). Conrad continued, "Art itself may be defined as a single-minded attempt to render the highest kind of justice to the visible universe, by bringing to light the truth, manifold and one, underlying its every aspect."

31 Art is an absolute mistress; she will not be coquetted with or slighted; she requires the most entire self-devotion, and she repays with grand triumphs.

CHARLOTTE SAUNDERS CUSHMAN (1816-76), U.S. actor. Quoted in: Emma Stebbins, *Charlotte Cushman* (1879).

32   Those who write for lucre or fame are grosser Iscariots than the cartel robbers, for they steal the genius of the people, which is its will to resist evil.

> EDWARD DAHLBERG (1900-1977), U.S. author, critic. *Alms for Oblivion,* "For Sale" (1964).

33   This grandiose tragedy that we call modern art.

> SALVADOR DALI (1904-89), Spanish painter. *Dali by Dali,* "The Futuristic Dali" (1970).

34   Progressive art can assist people to learn not only about the objective forces at work in the society in which they live, but also about the intensely social character of their interior lives.   Ultimately, it can propel people toward social emancipation.

> ANGELA DAVIS (b. 1944), U.S. political activist. *Women, Culture, and Politics,* "Art on the Frontline" (written 1984; first published 1985).

35   In art, one idea is as good as another.   If one takes the idea of trembling, for instance, all of a sudden most art starts to tremble.   Michelangelo starts to tremble.   El Greco starts to tremble.   All the Impressionists start to tremble.

> WILLEM DE KOONING (b. 1904), Dutch-born U.S. artist. "A Desperate View," paper, 18 Feb. 1949, delivered to friends (published in Thomas B. Hess, *William de Kooning,* 1968).

36   Art need no longer be an account of past sensations. It can become the direct organization of more highly evolved sensations.   It is a question of producing ourselves, not things that enslave us.

> GUY DEBORD (b. 1931), French Situationist philosopher. *Internationale Situationist,* no. 1 (Paris, June 1958).

37   Art is the most passionate orgy within man's grasp.

> JEAN DUBUFFET (1901-85), French sculptor, painter. "Notes for the Well-Read" (1946; repr. in *Jean Dubuffet: Towards an Alternative Reality,* ed. by Marc Glimcher, 1987).

38   Feminist art is not some tiny creek running off the great river of real art. It is not some crack in an otherwise flawless stone. It is, quite spectacularly I think, art which is not based on the subjugation of one half of the species. It is art which will take the great human themes—love, death, heroism, suffering, history itself—and render them fully human. It may also, though perhaps our imaginations are so mutilated now that we are incapable even of the ambition, introduce a new theme, one as great and as rich as those others—should we call it "joy"?

> ANDREA DWORKIN (b. 1946), U.S. feminist critic. "Feminism, Art, and My Mother Sylvia," speech, 16 April 1974, at Smith College, Northampton, Mass. (published in *Our Blood,* ch. 1, 1976).

39   Art never improves, but . . . the material of art is never quite the same.

> T. S. ELIOT (1888-1965), Anglo-American poet, critic. "Tradition and the Individual Talent," in *Egoist,* sct. 1 (London, Sept. and Dec. 1919; repr. in *Selected Prose of T. S. Eliot,* ed. by Frank Kermode, 1975).

40   Each work of art excludes the world, concentrates attention on itself. For the time it is the only thing worth doing—to do just that; be it a sonnet, a statue, a landscape, an outline head of Caesar, or an oration. Presently we return to the sight of another that globes itself into a whole as did the first, for example, a beautiful garden; and nothing seems worth doing in life but laying out a garden.

> RALPH WALDO EMERSON (1803-82), U.S. essayist, poet, philosopher. *Journals,* vol. 8, "A Self On Trial" (1909-14), entry for 22 March 1839.

41   Perpetual modernness is the measure of merit in every work of art.

> RALPH WALDO EMERSON (1803-82), U.S. essayist, poet, philosopher. *Representative Men,* "Plato" (1850).

42   The aim of every artist is to arrest motion, which is life, by artificial means and hold it fixed so that a hundred years later, when a stranger looks at it, it moves again since it is life. Since man is mortal, the only immortality possible for him is to leave something behind him that is immortal since it will always move. This is the artist's way of scribbling "Kilroy was here" on the wall of the final and irrevocable oblivion through which he must someday pass.

> WILLIAM FAULKNER (1897-1962), U.S. novelist. Interview in *Writers at Work* (First Series, ed. by Malcolm Cowley, 1958).

43   In a decaying society, art, if it is truthful, must also reflect decay. And unless it wants to break faith with its social function, art must show the world as changeable. And help to change it.

> ERNST FISCHER (1899-1972), Austrian editor, poet, critic. *The Necessity of Art,* ch. 2 (1959; tr. 1963).

44   Great art is the contempt of a great man for small art.

> F. SCOTT FITZGERALD (1896-1940), U.S. author. *The Crack-Up,* "Notebook L" (ed. by Edmund Wilson, 1945).

45   Art for art's sake? I should think so, and more so than ever at the present time. It is the one orderly product which our middling race has produced. It is the cry of a thousand sentinels, the echo from a thousand labyrinths, it is the lighthouse which cannot be hidden . . . it is the best evidence we can have of our dignity.

> E. M. FORSTER (1879-1970), British novelist, essayist. Address to PEN Club Congress. Quoted in: Huw Weldon, *Monitor* (1962).

46   One thing that makes art different from life is that in art things have a shape . . . it allows us to fix our emotions on events at the moment they occur, it permits a union of heart and mind and tongue and tear.

> MARILYN FRENCH (b. 1929), U.S. author, critic. *The Women's Room,* ch. 3, sct. 1 (1977).

47   Nature is inside art as its content, not outside as its model.

> NORTHROP FRYE (1912–91), Canadian literary critic. *Fables of Identity* (1963). Quoted in: Stephen Vizinczey, *Truth and Lies in Literature,* "Rules of the Game" (1986).

48   Art is either plagiarism or revolution.

> PAUL GAUGUIN (1848-1903), French artist. Quoted in: Huneker, *Pathos of Distance,* p. 128.

49 The history of modern art is also the history of the progressive loss of art's audience. Art has increasingly become the concern of the artist and the bafflement of the public.

HENRY GELDZAHLER (b. 1935), Belgium-born U.S. curator, art critic. "The Art Audience and the Critic," in *Hudson Review* (New York; Spring 1965; repr. in *The New Art: A Critical Anthology*, ed. by Gregory Battcock, 1966; rev. 1973).

50 The sole art that suits me is that which, rising from unrest, tends toward serenity.

ANDRÉ GIDE (1869-1951), French author. *Journals 1889-1949* (ed. by Justin O'Brien, 1951), entry for 23 Nov. 1940.

51 Art is skill, that is the first meaning of the word.

ERIC GILL (1882-1940), British sculptor, engraver, writer, typographer. *Art,* ch. 1 (1934).

52 Fortunately art is a community effort—a small but select community living in a spiritualized world endeavoring to interpret the wars and the solitudes of the flesh.

ALLEN GINSBERG (b. 1926), U.S. poet. *Journals: Early Fifties Early Sixties,* "Mexico and Return to U.S." (ed. by Gordon Ball, 1977), entry for 11 July 1954.

53 Art attracts us only by what it reveals of our most secret self.

JEAN-LUC GODARD (b. 1930), French filmmaker, author. "What Is Cinema?" in *Les Amis du Cinéma* (Paris, 1 Oct. 1952; repr. in *Godard, on Godard,* ed. and tr. by Tom Milne, 1968).

54 As a general truth, it is safe to say that any picture that produces a moral impression is a bad picture.

EDMOND (1822-96) AND JULES DE GONCOURT (1830-70), French writers. *The Goncourt Journals* (1888-96; repr. in *Pages from the Goncourt Journal,* ed. by Robert Baldick, 1962), entry for 7 Dec. 1860.

55 Art is on the side of the oppressed. Think before you shudder at the simplistic dictum and its heretical definition of the freedom of art. For if art is freedom of the spirit, how can it exist within the oppressors?

NADINE GORDIMER (b. 1923), South African author. "The Essential Gesture," lecture, 12 Oct. 1984, University of Michigan (published in *The Tanner Lectures on Human Values,* ed. by Sterling M. McMurrin, 1985; repr. in *The Essential Gesture,* ed. by Stephen Clingman, 1988).

56 Art is so wonderfully irrational, exuberantly pointless, but necessary all the same. Pointless and yet necessary, that's hard for a puritan to understand.

GÜNTHER GRASS (b. 1927), German author. Interview in *New Statesman & Society* (London, 22 June 1990).

57 There is only one art, whose sole criterion is the power, the authenticity, the revelatory insight, the courage and suggestiveness with which it seeks its truth. ... Thus, from the standpoint of the work and its worth it is irrelevant to which political ideas the artist as a citizen claims allegiance, which ideas he would like to serve with his work or whether he holds any such ideas at all.

VÁCLAV HAVEL (b. 1936), Czech playwright, president. *Living in Truth,* pt. 1, sct. 5, "Six Asides About Culture" (1986).

58 Art is a reality, not a definition; inasmuch as it approaches a reality, it approaches perfection, and inasmuch as it approaches a mere definition, it is imperfect and untrue.

BENJAMIN HAYDON (1786-1846), British artist. *Correspondence and Table Talk,* vol. 2, "Table Talk" (ed. by Frederic Wordsworth Haydon, 1876).

59 If we are to change our world view, images have to change. The artist now has a very important job to do. He's not a little peripheral figure entertaining rich people, he's really needed.

DAVID HOCKNEY (b. 1937), British artist. *Hockney On Photography,* "New York: September 1986" (ed. by Wendy Brown, 1988), from conversations with Paul Joyce.

60 The finest works of art are precious, among other reasons, because they make it possible for us to know, if only imperfectly and for a little while, what it actually feels like to think subtly and feel nobly.

ALDOUS HUXLEY (1894-1963), British author. *Ends and Means,* ch. 12 (1937).

61 A work of art is above all an adventure of the mind.

EUGÈNE IONESCO (b. 1912), Rumanian-born French playwright. *Notes and Counter-Notes,* pt. 2, "An Address Delivered to a Gathering of French and German Writers" (Feb. 1960; published 1962).

62 It is art that *makes* life, makes interest, makes importance . . . and I know of no substitute whatever for the force and beauty of its process.

HENRY JAMES (1843-1916), U.S. author. Letter, 10 July 1915, to author H. G. Wells. Wells wrote in reply (13 July), "I don't clearly understand your concluding phrases. . . . I can only read a sense into it by assuming that you are using `art' for every conscious human activity. I use the word for a research and attainment that is technical and special." Both letters are included in *Letters of Henry James,* vol. 4 (1984).

63 No man but a blockhead ever wrote, except for money.

SAMUEL JOHNSON (1709-84), English author, lexicographer. Quoted in: James Boswell, *Life of Samuel Johnson,* 5 April 1776 (1791).

64 Art is the human disposition of sensible or intelligible matter for an esthetic end.

JAMES JOYCE (1882-1941), Irish author. Stephen Dedalus, in *A Portrait of the Artist as a Young Man,* ch. 5 (1916).

65 Irresponsibility is part of the pleasure of all art; it is the part the schools cannot recognize.

PAULINE KAEL (b. 1919), U.S. film critic. *Going Steady,* "Movies as Opera" (1968).

66 In free society art is not a weapon. . . . Artists are not engineers of the soul.

JOHN F. KENNEDY (1917-63), U.S. Democratic politician, president. Speech, 26 Oct. 1963, Amherst College, Massachusetts.

67 Art, that great undogmatized church.

ELLEN KEY (1849-1926), Swedish author, feminist. *The Renaissance of Motherhood,* pt. 2, ch. 1 (1914).

68 And the first rude sketch that the world had seen
    was joy to his mighty heart,
Till the Devil whispered behind the leaves "It's
    pretty, but is it Art?"

RUDYARD KIPLING (1865-1936), British author, poet. *The Conundrum of the Workshops,* of "Our father Adam," who "sat under the Tree and scratched with a stick in the mould."

69 Art does not reproduce the visible; rather, it makes visible.

PAUL KLEE (1879-1940), Swiss artist. *Creative Credo* (1918; sct. 1 repr. in *The Inward Vision,* 1957).

70 Art is the objectification of feeling.

SUZANNE K. LANGER (1895-1985), U.S. philosopher. *Mind, An Essay on Human Feeling,* vol. 1, pt. 2, ch. 4 (1967).

71 In other countries, art and literature are left to a lot of shabby bums living in attics and feeding on booze and spaghetti, but in America the successful writer or picture-painter is indistinguishable from any other decent businessman.

SINCLAIR LEWIS (1885-1951), U.S. novelist. *Babbitt,* ch. 14, sct. 3 (1922), giving the annual address at the Zenith Real Estate Board.

72 Making social comment is an artificial place for an artist to start from. If an artist is touched by some social condition, what the artist creates will reflect that, but you can't force it.

BELLA LEWITZKY (b. 1916), U.S. dancer. Quoted in: *San Francisco Chronicle* (4 March 1979).

73 Art is the child of Nature; yes,
    Her darling child, in whom we trace
    The features of the mother's face,
    Her aspect and her attitude.

HENRY WADSWORTH LONGFELLOW (1807-82), U.S. poet. *Keramos.*

74 The final purpose of art is to intensify, even, if necessary, to exacerbate, the moral consciousness of people.

NORMAN MAILER (b. 1923), U.S. author. "Hip, Hell, and the Navigator," in *Western Review,* no. 23 (Winter 1959; repr. in *Conversations with Norman Mailer,* ed. by J. Michael Lennon, 1988).

75 There is in fact no such thing as art for art's sake, art that stands above classes, art that is detached from or independent of politics. Proletarian literature and art are part of the whole proletarian revolutionary cause.

MAO ZEDONG (1893-1976), Founder of the People's Republic of China. "Talks at the Yenan Forum on Literature and Art" (May 1942; published in *Selected Works,* vol. 3).

76 We will sing of great crowds excited by work, by pleasure, and by riot; we will sing of the multicolored, polyphonic tides of revolution in the modern capitals; we will sing of the vibrant nightly fervour of arsenals and shipyards blazing with violent electric moons; greedy railway stations that devour smoke-plumed serpents; factories hung on clouds by the crooked lines of their smoke; bridges that stride the rivers like giant gymnasts, flashing in the sun with a glitter of knives; adventurous steamers that sniff the horizons; deep-chested locomotives whose wheels paw the tracks like the hooves of enormous steel horses bridled by tubing; and the sleek flight of planes whose propellers chatter in the wind like banners and seem to cheer like an enthusiastic crowd.

TOMMASO MARINETTI (1876-1944), Italian playwright. "The Founding and Manifesto of Futurism," in *Figaro* (20 Feb. 1909; repr. in *Marinetti: Selected Writings,* ed. by R. W. Flint, 1972).

77 There is nothing more difficult for a truly creative painter than to paint a rose, because before he can do so he has first to forget all the roses that were ever painted.

HENRI MATISSE (1869-1954), French artist. Comment recalled in obituaries reporting his death, 5 Nov. 1954.

78 Experiment is necessary in establishing an academy, but certain principles must apply to this business of art as to any other business which affects the artis tic sense of the community. Great art speaks a language which every intelligent person can understand. The people who call themselves modernists today speak a different language.

ROBERT MENZIES (1894-1978), Australian Liberal politician, prime minister. *Argus* (Sydney, 28 April 1937).

79 The artist is the opposite of the politically minded individual, the opposite of the reformer, the opposite of the idealist. The artist does not tinker with the universe; he recreates it out of his own experience and understanding of life.

HENRY MILLER (1891-1980), U.S. author. *The Cosmological Eye,* "An Open Letter to Surrealists Everywhere" (1939).

80 Art is only a means to life, to the life more abundant. It is not in itself the life more abundant. It merely points the way, something which is overlooked not only by the public, but very often by the artist himself. In becoming an end it defeats itself.

HENRY MILLER (1891-1980), U.S. author. *The Wisdom of the Heart,* "Reflections on Writing" (1947).

81 Art is man's expression of his joy in labour.

WILLIAM MORRIS (1834-96), English artist, writer, printer. "Art under Plutocracy" (1883; repr. in *Collected Works of William Morris,* vol. 23, 1910-15).

82 The public history of modern art is the story of conventional people not knowing what they are dealing with.

ROBERT MOTHERWELL (1915-91), U.S. artist. *The Dada Painters and Poets: An Anthology,* Preface (ed. by Robert Motherwell, 1951).

83 Art is the final cunning of the human soul which would rather do anything than face the gods.

IRIS MURDOCH (b. 1919), British novelist, philosopher. Plato (aged 20), in *Acastos: Two Platonic Dialogues,* "Art and Eros: A Dialogue about Art" (1986). The dialogue was first performed on stage in Feb. 1980.

84 To speak of morals in art is to speak of legislature in sex. Art is the sex of the imagination.

GEORGE JEAN NATHAN (1882-1958), U.S. critic. "Art," in *American Mercury* (July 1929).

85 Art is not merely an imitation of the reality of nature, but in truth a metaphysical supplement to the reality of nature, placed alongside thereof for its conquest.

FRIEDRICH NIETZSCHE (1844-1900), German philosopher. *The Birth of Tragedy,* ch. 24 (1872).

86 Were art to redeem man, it could do so only by saving him from the seriousness of life and restoring him to an unexpected boyishness.

> JOSÉ ORTEGA Y GASSET (1883-1955), Spanish essayist, philosopher. *The Dehumanization of Art*, "Art a Thing of No Consequence" (1925).

87 What distinguishes modern art from the art of other ages is criticism.

> OCTAVIO PAZ (b. 1914), Mexican poet. *Alternating Current*, "Invention, Underdevelopment, Modernity" (1967).

88 Wherever art appears, life disappears.

> FRANCIS PICABIA (1878-1953), French painter, poet. "L'Humour Poetique," in *La Nef*, no. 71-72 (Paris, Dec. 1950/ Jan. 1951; repr. in *Écrits*, vol. 2, "1950-1953," ed. by Olivier Revault d'Allones and Dominique Bouissou, 1978).

89 We all know that Art is not truth. Art is a lie that makes us realize truth, at least the truth that is given us to understand. The artist must know the manner whereby to convince others of the truthfulness of his lies.

> PABLO PICASSO (1881-1973), Spanish artist. "Picasso Speaks," in *The Arts* (New York, May 1923; repr. in Alfred H. Barr, Jr., *Picasso: Fifty Years of His Art*, 1946).

90 Through art we express our conception of what nature is not.

> PABLO PICASSO (1881-1973), Spanish artist. "Picasso Speaks," in *The Arts* (New York, May 1923; repr. in Alfred H. Barr, Jr., *Picasso: Fifty Years of His Art*, 1946).

91 Were I called on to define, *very* briefly, the term Art, I should call it "the reproduction of what the Senses perceive in Nature through the veil of the soul." The mere imitation, however accurate, of what *is* in Nature, entitles no man to the sacred name of "Artist."

> EDGAR ALLAN POE (1809-45), U.S. poet, critic, short-story writer. "Marginalia," in *Southern Literary Messenger* (Richmond, Va., June 1849; repr. in *Essays and Reviews*, 1984).

92 Good art however "immoral" is wholly a thing of virtue . . . Good art can NOT be immoral. By good art I mean art that bears true witness, I mean the art that is most precise.

> EZRA POUND (1885-1972), U.S. poet, critic. *Egoist* (London, 1913). Quoted in: Humphrey Carpenter, *A Serious Character*, pt. 2, ch. 10 (1988).

93 A work of art that contains theories is like an object on which the price tag has been left.

> MARCEL PROUST (1871-1922), French novelist. *Remembrance of Things Past*, vol. 12, ch. 3, "Time Regained" (1927; tr. by Stephen Hudson, 1931).

94 Art is too serious to be taken seriously.

> AD REINHARDT (1913-67), U.S. artist. Notes quoted in Lucy R. Lippard, *Ad Reinhardt*, pt. 1 (1981).

95 There is the falsely mystical view of art that assumes a kind of supernatural inspiration, a possession by universal forces unrelated to questions of power and privilege or the artist's relation to bread and blood. In this view, the channel of art can only become clogged and misdirected by the artist's concern with merely tempo-rary and local disturbances. The song is higher than the struggle.

> ADRIENNE RICH (b. 1929), U.S. poet. *Blood, Bread and Poetry*, title essay (1986).

96 Art, whose honesty must work through artifice, cannot avoid cheating truth.

> LAURA RIDING (1901-91), U.S. poet. *Selected Poems: In Five Sets*, Preface (1975).

97 Surely all art is the result of one's having been in danger, of having gone through an experience all the way to the end, where no one can go any further.

> RAINER MARIA RILKE (1875-1926), German poet. Letter, 24 June 1907, to his wife (published in *Rilke's Letters on Cézanne*, 1952; tr. 1985).

98 Only conservatives believe that subversion is still being carried on in the arts and that society is being shaken by it. . . . Advanced art today is no longer a cause—it contains no moral imperative. There is no virtue in clinging to principles and standards, no vice in selling or in selling out.

> HAROLD ROSENBERG (1906-78), U.S. art critic, author. "The Cultural Situation Today," in *Partisan Review* (New Brunswick, N.J., Summer 1972; repr. as *Discovering the Present*, Introduction, 1973).

99 Not even the visionary or mystical experience ever lasts very long. It is for art to capture that experience, to offer it to, in the case of literature, its readers; to be, for a secular, materialist culture, some sort of replacement for what the love of god offers in the world of faith.

> SALMAN RUSHDIE (b. 1947), Indian-born British author. "Is Nothing Sacred?" Herbert Reade Memorial Lecture, 6 Feb. 1990.

100 I have seen, and heard, much of Cockney impudence before now; but never expected to hear a coxcomb ask two hundred guineas for flinging a pot of paint in the public's face.

> JOHN RUSKIN (1819-1900), English art critic, author. Letter, 18 June 1877 (published in Ruskin's *Fors Clavigera*, 1871-84), referring to Whistler's *Nocturne in Black and Gold: The Falling Rocket*. Oscar Wilde commented that the painting was "worth looking at for about as long as one looks at a real rocket, that is, for somewhat less than a quarter of a minute." Whistler took more seriously Ruskin's remarks, which he made the subject of a lawsuit. See Whistler onVALUE.

101 Art is not a study of positive reality, it is the seeking for ideal truth.

> GEORGE SAND (1804-76), French novelist. *The Haunted Pool*, ch. 1 (1851).

102 The effort of art is to keep what is interesting in existence, to recreate it in the eternal.

> GEORGE SANTAYANA (1863-1952), U.S. philosopher, poet. *The Life of Reason*, "Reason in Art," ch. 8 (1905-6; rev. ed., 1953).

103 As noble Art has survived noble nature, so too she marches ahead of it, fashioning and awakening by her inspiration. Before Truth sends her triumphant light into the depths of the heart, imagination catches its rays, and the peaks of humanity will be glowing when humid night still lingers in the valleys.

> FRIEDRICH VON SCHILLER (1759-1805), German dramatist, poet, essayist. *On the Aesthetic Education of Man,* "Ninth Letter" (1795).

104 Great art is never produced for its own sake. It is too difficult to be worth the effort.

> GEORGE BERNARD SHAW (1856-1950), Anglo-Irish playwright, critic. *Three Plays by Brieux,* Preface (1909).

105 Much of modern art is devoted to lowering the threshold of what is terrible. By getting us used to what, formerly, we could not bear to see or hear, because it was too shocking, painful, or embarrassing, art changes morals.

> SUSAN SONTAG (b. 1933), U.S. essayist. *On Photography,* "America, Seen Through Photographs, Darkly" (1977).

106 The contemporary thing in art and literature is the thing which doesn't make enough difference to the people of that generation so that they can accept it or reject it.

> GERTRUDE STEIN (1874-1946), U.S. author. "How Writing Is Written," in *Choate Literary Magazine* (Feb. 1935; repr. in *How Writing Is Written,* ed. by Robert Bartlett Haas, 1974).

107 Art—the one achievement of Man which has made the long trip up from all fours seem well advised.

> JAMES THURBER (1894-1961), U.S. humorist, illustrator. *Forum and Century* (June 1939; also included in Clifton Fadiman, *I Believe: The Personal Philosophies of Certain Eminent Men and Women of Our Time,* 1939).

108 To say that a work of art is good, but incomprehensible to the majority of men, is the same as saying of some kind of food that it is very good but that most people can't eat it.

> LEO TOLSTOY (1828-1910), Russian novelist, philosopher. *What Is Art?* ch. 10 (1898; published in *Tolstoy on Art,* ed. by Aylmer Maude, 1924).

109 A primary function of art and thought is to liberate the individual from the tyranny of his culture in the environmental sense and to permit him to stand beyond it in an autonomy of perception and judgment.

> LIONEL TRILLING (1905-75), U.S. critic. *Beyond Culture,* Preface (1965).

110 All great art, and today all great artlessness, must appear extreme to the mass of men, as we know them today. It springs from the anguish of great souls. From the souls of men not formed, but deformed in factories whose inspiration is pelf.

> ALEXANDER TROCCHI (1925-83), Italo-Scottish novelist, poet, translator. *Cain's Book* (1960; repr. 1973, p. 145) ["pelf" means money, wealth].

111 If the Revolution has the right to destroy bridges and art monuments whenever necessary, it will stop still less from laying its hand on any tendency in art which, no matter how great its achievement in form, threatens to disintegrate the revolutionary environment or to arouse the internal forces of the Revolution, that is, the proletariat, the peasantry and the intelligentsia, to a hostile opposition to one another. Our standard is, clearly, political, imperative and intolerant.

> LEON TROTSKY (1879-1940), Russian revolutionary. *Literature and Revolution,* ch. 7 (1924).

112 Art is parasitic on life, just as criticism is parasitic on art.

> KENNETH TYNAN (1927-80), British critic. "Ionesco and the Phantom," in *Observer* (London, 6 July 1958; repr. in Eugène Ionesco, *Notes and Counter-Notes,* 1962).

113 Art is a private thing, the artist makes it for himself; a comprehensible work is the product of a journalist. . . . We need works that are strong, straight, precise, and forever beyond understanding.

> TRISTAN TZARA (1896-1963), Rumanian-born French Dadaist. *Dada 3,* "Dada Manifesto 1918" (1918; repr. in *The Dada Painters and Poets,* ed. by Robert Motherwell, 1951).

114 It is not the language of painters but the language of nature which one should listen to. . . . The feeling for the things themselves, for reality, is more important than the feeling for pictures.

> VINCENT VAN GOGH (1853-90), Dutch painter. Letter, 21 July 1882, to his brother Theo (published in *The Complete Letters of Vincent Van Gogh,* vol. 1, 1958).

115 I can't work without a model. I won't say I turn my back on nature ruthlessly in order to turn a study into a picture, arranging the colors, enlarging and simplifying; but in the matter of form I am too afraid of departing from the possible and the true.

> VINCENT VAN GOGH (1853-90), Dutch painter. Letter, Oct. 1888 (published in *The Complete Letters of Vincent Van Gogh,* vol. 3, no. B19, 1958).

116 An artist must be a reactionary. He has to stand out against the tenor of the age and not go flopping along.

> EVELYN WAUGH (1903-66), British novelist. Interview in *Writers at Work* (Third Series, ed. by George Plimpton, 1967).

117 Art is the symbol of the two noblest human efforts: to construct . . . and to refrain from destruction.

> SIMONE WEIL (1909-43), French philosopher, mystic. *The Pre-War Notebook* (1933-39; published in *First and Last Notebooks,* ed. by Richard Rees, 1970).

118 Most works of art, like most wines, ought to be consumed in the district of their fabrication.

> REBECCA WEST (1892-1983), British author. *Ending in Earnest,* "Journey's End Again" (1931).

119 Yes, madam, Nature is creeping up.

> JAMES MCNEILL WHISTLER (1834-1903), U.S. artist. Quoted in: D. C. Seitz, *Whistler Stories* (1913, p. 27), to a woman who said a landscape view reminded her of his work.

120 Art is the imposing of a pattern on experience, and our aesthetic enjoyment is recognition of the pattern.

> ALFRED NORTH WHITEHEAD (1861-1947), British philosopher. *Dialogues,* 10 June 1943 (1954).

121 Art, like Nature, has her monsters, things of bestial shape and with hideous voices.

> OSCAR WILDE (1854-1900), Anglo-Irish playwright, author. *The Picture of Dorian Gray,* ch. 11 (1891).

122 Modern pictures are, no doubt, delightful to look at. At least, some of them are. But they are quite impossible to live with; they are too clever, too assertive, too intellectual. Their meaning is too obvious, and their method too clearly defined. One exhausts what they have to say in a very short time, and then they become as tedious as one's relations.

OSCAR WILDE (1854-1900), Anglo-Irish playwright, author. Gilbert, in *The Critic as Artist*, pt. 2 (published in *Intentions*, 1891).

123 Bad art is a great deal worse than no art at all.

OSCAR WILDE (1854-1900), Anglo-Irish playwright, author. "House Decoration," lecture, 1882 (published in *Aristotle at Afternoon Tea: The Rare Oscar Wilde*, 1991).

124 The moment you think you understand a great work of art, it's dead for you.

ROBERT WILSON (b. 1941), U.S. theater director, designer. Quoted in: *International Herald Tribune* (Paris, 22 May 1990).

125 The notion that the public accepts or rejects anything in modern art . . . is merely romantic fiction. . . . The game is completed and the trophies distributed long before the public knows what has happened.

TOM WOLFE (b. 1931), U.S. journalist, author. *The Painted Word*, ch. 2 (1975).

126 Is there not
An art, a music, and a stream of words
That shalt be life, the acknowledged voice of life?

WILLIAM WORDSWORTH (1770-1850), English poet. *Home at Grasmere* (written 1800; published as *The Recluse*, 1888)

See also AESTHETICS; Warhol on BUSINESS AND COMMERCE; Klee on CARTOONS AND DRAWING; Picasso on CENSORSHIP; Rilke on COLOR; Auden on CREATIVITY; Shaw on CREEDS; Grosz on CULTURE; Hockney on DESIGN; Cather on EDITING; Browning on EFFORT; Martin on ENTERTAINMENT; Woolf on EXCELLENCE; Fischer on HUMANITY; Dali on IMAGE; Reade, Stein on IMITATION; Klee on LIFE AND LIVING; Wolfe on MODERNISM AND POSTMODERNISM; Picasso on MUSEUMS AND GALLERIES; Blake on NUDITY; Wilde on OBSCENITY; OPINION; PAINTING; Gauguin on PHILOSOPHY; Sontag on PHOTOGRAPHY; Sondheim on POPULAR MUSIC; Wilde on POPULARITY; PORTRAITS; Wilde on The PUBLIC; Wilde on REPUBLICANISM; Rosenberg on REVOLUTION; Baudelaire on ROMANTICISM; Klee on SACRIFICE; SCIENCE AND ART; Sontag on SENSATION; Thurber on SPEED; Picasso on STYLE; SURREALISM; Wilde on TASTE; Murdoch on VIRTUE.

ARTISTS

1 Artists are, above all, men who want to become inhuman.

GUILLAUME APOLLINAIRE (1880-1918), Italian-born French poet, critic. *The Cubist Painters*, "On Painting" (1913).

2 The primary distinction of the artist is that he must actively cultivate that state which most men, necessarily, must avoid: the state of being alone.

JAMES BALDWIN (1924-87), U.S. author. "The Creative Process" (1962; repr. in *The Price of the Ticket*, 1985).

3 No one should drive a hard bargain with an artist.

LUDWIG VAN BEETHOVEN (1770-1827), German composer. Letter, 5 June 1822.

4 Any artist should be grateful for a naïve grace which puts him beyond the need to reason elaborately.

SAUL BELLOW (b. 1915), U.S. novelist. Allan Bloom, *The Closing of the American Mind*, Foreword (1987).

5 The artist is extremely lucky who is presented with the worst possible ordeal which will not actually kill him. At that point, he's in business.

JOHN BERRYMAN (1914-72), U.S. poet. Interview in *Writers at Work* (Fourth Series, ed. by George Plimpton, 1976).

6 Artistic growth is, more than it is anything else, a refining of the sense of truthfulness. The stupid believe that to be truthful is easy; only the artist, the great artist, knows how difficult it is.

WILLA CATHER (1873-1947), U.S. author. *The Song of the Lark*, pt. 6, ch. 11 (1915).

7 The creative artist seems to be almost the only kind of man that you could never meet on neutral ground. You can only meet him as an artist. He sees nothing objectively because his own ego is always in the foreground of every picture.

RAYMOND CHANDLER (1888-1959), U.S. author. Letter, 23 June 1950, to publisher Hamish Hamilton (published in *Raymond Chandler Speaking*, 1962).

8 The artistic temperament is a disease that affects amateurs. . . . Artists of a large and wholesome vitality get rid of their art easily, as they breathe easily or perspire easily. But in artists of less force, the thing becomes a pressure, and produces a definite pain, which is called the artistic temperament.

G. K. CHESTERTON (1874-1936), British author. *Heretics*, ch. 17 (1905).

9 The dignity of the artist lies in his duty of keeping awake the sense of wonder in the world. In this long vigil he often has to vary his methods of stimulation; but in this long vigil he is also himself striving against a continual tendency to sleep.

G. K. CHESTERTON (1874-1936), British author. *Generally Speaking*, "On Maltreating Words" (1928).

10 One must be a living man and a posthumous artist.

JEAN COCTEAU (1889-1963), French author, filmmaker. *Le Rappel à l'Ordre*, "Le Coq et l'Arlequin" (1926; repr. in *Collected Works*, vol. 9, 1950).

11 The artist is a member of the leisured classes who cannot pay for his leisure.

CYRIL CONNOLLY (1903-74), British critic. David Pryce-Jones, *Journal and Memoir*, "The Journal of Cyril Connolly 1928-1937" (1983, p. 241).

12 The reward of art is not fame or success but intoxication: that is why so many bad artists are unable to give it up.

CYRIL CONNOLLY (1903-74), British critic. *The Unquiet Grave*, pt. 2 (1944; rev. 1951).

13 An artist is a man of action, whether he creates a personality, invents an expedient, or finds the issue of a complicated situation.

JOSEPH CONRAD (1857-1924), Polish-born English novelist. *The Mirror of the Sea*, ch. 9 (1906).

14 There is only one difference between a madman and me. I am not mad.

SALVADOR DALI (1904-89), Spanish painter. *Diary of a Genius* (1966), entry for May 1952.

15 An artist is forced by others to paint out of his own free will.

> WILLEM DE KOONING (b. 1904), Dutch-born U.S. artist. "A Desperate View," paper, delivered to friends, 18 Feb. 1949 (published in Thomas B. Hess, *William de Kooning*, 1968).

16 Whatever an artist's personal feelings are, as soon as an artist fills a certain area on the canvas or circumscribes it, he becomes historical. He acts from or upon other artists.

> WILLEM DE KOONING (b. 1904), Dutch-born U.S. artist. "A Desperate View," paper, delivered to friends, 18 Feb. 1949 (published in Thomas B. Hess, *William de Kooning*, 1968).

17 For us artists there waits the joyous compromise through art with all that wounded or defeated us in daily life; in this way, not to evade destiny, as the ordinary people try to do, but to fulfil it in its true potential—the imagination.

> LAWRENCE DURRELL (1912-90), British author. *Justine*, pt. 1 (1957).

18 The progress of an artist is a continual self-sacrifice, a continual extinction of personality.

> T. S. ELIOT (1888-1965), Anglo-American poet, critic. "Tradition and the Individual Talent," sct. 1, in *Egoist* (London, Sept. and Dec. 1919; repr. in *Selected Prose of T. S. Eliot*, ed. by Frank Kermode, 1975).

19 Every artist writes his own autobiography.

> HAVELOCK ELLIS (1859-1939), British psychologist. *The New Spirit*, "Tolstoi" (1890).

20 Art is a jealous mistress, and, if a man have a genius for painting, poetry, music, architecture or philosophy, he makes a bad husband and an ill provider.

> RALPH WALDO EMERSON (1803-82), U.S. essayist, poet, philosopher. *The Conduct of Life*, "Wealth" (1860).

21 Artists must be sacrificed to their art. Like bees, they must put their lives into the sting they give.

> RALPH WALDO EMERSON (1803-82), U.S. essayist, poet, philosopher. *Letters and Social Aims*, "Inspiration" (1876).

22 An artist is a creature driven by demons. He don't know why they choose him and he's usually too busy to wonder why. He is completely amoral in that he will rob, borrow, beg, or steal from anybody and everybody to get the work done.

> WILLIAM FAULKNER (1897-1962), U.S. novelist. Interview in *Writers at Work* (First Series, ed. by Malcolm Cowley, 1958).

23 What is an artist? A provincial who finds himself somewhere between a physical reality and a metaphysical one. . . . It's this in-between that I'm calling a province, this frontier country between the tangible world and the intangible one—which is really the realm of the artist.

> FREDERICO FELLINI (b. 1920), Italian filmmaker. Quoted by John Berger in: "Every Time We Say Goodbye," in *Sight and Sound* (London, June 1991).

24 Beware the artist who's an intellectual also. The artist who doesn't fit.

> F. SCOTT FITZGERALD (1896-1940), U.S. author. Amory Blaine, in *This Side of Paradise*, bk. 2, ch. 5 (1920).

25 The true, prescriptive artist strives after artistic truth; the lawless artist, following blind instinct, after an appearance of naturalness. The one leads to the highest peaks of art, the other to its lowest depths.

> JOHANN WOLFGANG VON GOETHE (1749-1832), German poet, dramatist. *Propyläen*, Introduction (1798), a periodical founded by Goethe, taking its title from the gateway to the Acropolis of Athens.

26 There really is no such thing as Art. There are only artists.

> E. H. GOMBRICH (b. 1909), Austrian-born British art critic, historian. *The Story of Art*, Introduction (1950).

27 No artist is ahead of his time. He *is* his time; it is just that others are behind the times.

> MARTHA GRAHAM (1894-1991), U.S. dancer. Quoted in: *Observer Magazine* (London, 8 July 1979).

28 It is very important not to become hard. The artist must always have one skin too few in comparison to other people, so you feel the slightest wind.

> SHUSHA GUPPY (b. 1938), Persian singer, author. Interview in *Guardian* (London, 6 April 1988).

29 An artist's originality is balanced by a corresponding conservatism, a superstitiousness, about it; which might be boiled down to "What worked before will work again."

> NANCY HALE (b. 1908), U.S. writer, editor. *Mary Cassatt: A Biography of the Great American Painter*, pt. 2, ch. 6 (1975).

30 The best work of artists in any age is the work of innocence liberated by technical knowledge. The laboratory experiments that led to the theory of pure color equipped the impressionists to paint nature as if it had only just been created.

> NANCY HALE (b. 1908), U.S. writer, editor. *Mary Cassatt: A Biography of the Great American Painter*, pt. 2, ch. 7 (1975).

31 The individual, the great artist when he comes, uses everything that has been discovered or known about his art up to that point, being able to accept or reject in a time so short it seems that the knowledge was born with him, rather than that he takes instantly what it takes the ordinary man a lifetime to know, and then the great artist goes beyond what has been done or known and makes something of his own.

> ERNEST HEMINGWAY (1899-1961), U.S. author. *Death in the Afternoon*, ch. 10 (1932).

32 Fundamentally the male artist approximates more to the psychology of woman, who, biologically speaking, is a purely creative being and whose personality has been as mysterious and unfathomable to the man as the artist has been to the average person.

> BEATRICE HINKLE (1874-1953), U.S. psychiatrist. *Recreating the Individual*, "The Psychology of the Artist" (1923).

33 We live in an age where the artist is forgotten. He is a researcher. I see myself that way.

> DAVID HOCKNEY (b. 1937), British artist. Quoted in: *Observer* (London, 9 June 1991).

34 There are so many intellectual and moral angels battling for rationalism, good citizenship, and pure spirituality; so many and such eminent ones, so very vocal and authoritative! The poor devil in man needs all the support and advocacy he can get. The artist is his natural champion. When an artist deserts to the side of the angels, it is the most odious of treasons.

ALDOUS HUXLEY (1894-1963), British author. *Do What You Will*, "Wordsworth in the Tropics" (1929).

35 If we pretend to respect the artist at all, we must allow him his freedom of choice, in the face, in particular cases, of innumerable presumptions that the choice will not fructify. Art derives a considerable part of its beneficial exercise from flying in the face of presumptions.

HENRY JAMES (1843-1916), U.S. author. *The Art of Fiction*, (1884; repr. in *Partial Portraits*, 1888).

36 We work in the dark—we do what we can—we give what we have. Our doubt is our passion and our passion is our task. The rest is the madness of art.

HENRY JAMES (1843-1916), U.S. author. Dencombe, in *The Middle Years*, in *Scribner's* (May 1893; repr. in *The Complete Tales of Henry James*, vol. 9, ed. by Leon Edel, 1964).

37 There is nothing fiercer than a failed artist. The energy remains, but, having no outlet, it implodes in a great black fart of rage which smokes up all the inner windows of the soul. Horrible as successful artists often are, there is nothing crueler or more vain than a failed artist.

ERICA JONG (b. 1942), U.S. author. The narrator (Isadora Wing), in *Fear of Flying*, ch. 9 (1973).

38 The artist, like the God of creation, remains within or behind or beyond or above his handiwork, invisible, refined out of existence, indifferent, paring his fingernails.

JAMES JOYCE (1882-1941), Irish author. Stephen Dedalus, in *A Portrait of the Artist as a Young Man*, ch. 5 (1916).

39 The first prerogative of an artist in any medium is to make a fool of himself.

PAULINE KAEL (b. 1919), U.S. film critic. *I Lost It at the Movies*, "Is There a Cure for Film Criticism?" (1965).

40 It seems likely that many of the young who don't wait for others to call them artists, but simply announce that they are, don't have the patience to make art.

PAULINE KAEL (b. 1919), U.S. film critic. *Kiss Kiss Bang Bang*, "Movie Brutalists" (1968).

41 Standing at his appointed place, at the trunk of the tree, he does nothing other than gather and pass on what comes to him from the depths. He neither serves nor rules—he transmits. His position is humble. And the beauty at the crown is not his own. He is merely a channel.

PAUL KLEE (1879-1940), Swiss artist. *On Modern Art* (1924).

42 Only he is an artist who can make a riddle out of a solution.

KARL KRAUS (1874-1936), Austrian satirist. *Nachts*, ch. 2 (1918).

43 Artists have a right to be modest and a duty to be vain.

KARL KRAUS (1874-1936), Austrian satirist. Photograph caption. Quoted in: *In These Great Times: A Karl Kraus Reader* (ed. by Harry Zohn, 1976).

44 An artist is only an ordinary man with a greater potentiality—same stuff, same make up, only more force. And the strong driving force usually finds his weak spot, and he goes cranked, or goes under.

D. H. LAWRENCE (1885-1930), British author. Letter, 31 Oct. 1913 (published in *The Letters of D. H. Lawrence*, vol. 2, ed. by George J. Zytaruk and James T. Boulton, 1981).

45 The product of the artist has become less important than the *fact* of the artist. We wish to absorb this person. We wish to devour someone who has experienced the tragic. In our society this person is much more important than anything he might create.

DAVID MAMET (b. 1947), U.S. playwright. *Writing in Restaurants*, "Exuvial Magic: An Essay Concerning Fashion" (1986).

46 Every production of an artist should be the expression of an adventure of his soul.

W. SOMERSET MAUGHAM (1874-1965), British author. *The Summing Up*, ch. 48 (1938).

47 America is no place for an artist: to be an artist is to be a moral leper, an economic misfit, a social liability. A corn-fed hog enjoys a better life than a creative writer, painter, or musician. To be a rabbit is better still.

HENRY MILLER (1891-1980), U.S. author. *The Air-Conditioned Nightmare*, Preface (1945). See also Miller on ART.

48 The worst sin that can be committed against the artist is to take him at his word, to see in his work a fulfillment instead of an horizon.

HENRY MILLER (1891-1980), U.S. author. *The Cosmological Eye*, "An Open Letter to Surrealists Everywhere" (1939).

49 Great artists have no country.

ALFRED DE MUSSET (1810-57), French poet, novelist, playwright. *Lorenzaccio*, "L'Orfèvre" (1834).

50 Everybody's an artist. Everybody's God. It's just that they're inhibited. I believe in people so much that if the whole of civilization is burned so we don't have any memory of it, even then people will start to build their own art. It is a necessity—a function. We don't need history.

YOKO ONO (b. 1933), Japanese-born U.S. artist. Interview with Abram Deswaan for Dutch TV, Oct. 1968.

51 Being an artist means ceasing to take seriously that very serious person we are when we are not an artist.

JOSÉ ORTEGA Y GASSET (1883-1955), Spanish essayist, philosopher. *The Dehumanization of Art*, "Doomed to Irony" (1925).

52 Artists are the monks of the bourgeois state.

CESARE PAVESE (1908-50), Italian poet, novelist, translator. *The Burning Brand: Diaries 1935-1950* (1952; tr. 1961), entry for 25 July 1940.

53 You are always looking for already-felt emotions, just as you like to get an old pair of trousers back from the cleaners, which seem new when you don't look too closely. Artists are cleaners, don't let yourself be taken in by them. True modern works of art are made not by artists but quite simply by men.

> FRANCIS PICABIA (1878-1953), French painter, poet. *Jésus-Christ Rastquouère*, ch. 4 (1920).

54 They ought to put out the eyes of painters as they do goldfinches in order that they can sing better.

> PABLO PICASSO (1881-1973), Spanish artist. Quoted in: *Intransigeant* (Paris, 15 June 1932).

55 We artists are indestructible; even in a prison, or in a concentration camp, I would be almighty in my own world of art, even if I had to paint my pictures with my wet tongue on the dusty floor of my cell.

> PABLO PICASSO (1881-1973), Spanish artist. *Der Monat* (Berlin, Dec. 1949; repr. in Dore Ashton, *Picasso on Art*, 1972).

56 When I say artist I don't mean in the narrow sense of the word—but the man who is building things—creating molding the earth—whether it be the plains of the west—or the iron ore of Penn. Its all a big game of construction—some with a brush—some with a shovel—some choose a pen.

> JACKSON POLLOCK (1912-56), U.S. artist. Letter, 1932, to his father (published in *Jackson Pollock: A Catalogue Raisonné of Paintings, Drawings and Other Works*, vol. 4, ed. by Francis V. O'Connor and Eugene V. Thaw, 1978).

57 Human life itself may be almost pure chaos, but the work of the artist—the only thing he's good for—is to take these handfuls of confusion and disparate things, things that seem to be irreconcilable, and put them together in a frame to give them some kind of shape and meaning. Even if it's only his view of a meaning. That's what he's for—to give his view of life.

> KATHERINE ANNE PORTER (1890-1980), U.S. short-story writer, novelist. Interview in *Writers at Work* (Second Series, ed. by George Plimpton, 1963).

58 Modern civilization has bred a race with brains like those of rabbits and we who are the heirs of the witch-doctor and the voodoo. We artists who have been so long the despised are about to take over control.

> EZRA POUND (1885-1972), U.S. poet, critic. *Egoist* (London, Feb. 1914).

59 The modern artist must live by craft and violence. His gods are violent gods . . . Those artists, so called, whose work does not show this strife, are uninteresting.

> EZRA POUND (1885-1972), U.S. poet, critic. *Egoist* (London, Feb. 1914).

60 The task of the artist at any time is uncompromisingly simple—to discover what has not yet been done, and to do it.

> CRAIG RAINE (b. 1944), British poet, critic. *Guardian* (London, 19 Aug. 1988).

61 Just as the creative artist is not allowed to choose, neither is he permitted to turn his back on anything: a single refusal, and he is cast out of the state of grace and becomes sinful all the way through.

> RAINER MARIA RILKE (1875-1926), German poet. Letter, 23 Oct. 1907, to his wife (published in *Rilke's Letters on Cézanne*, 1952; tr. 1985).

62 Not since Moses has anyone seen a mountain so greatly.

> RAINER MARIA RILKE (1875-1926), German poet. Quoted in: Rilke, *Letters on Cézanne*, Foreword (1952; tr. 1985), remarking on Cézanne's picture of the Montagne Sainte-Victoire to Count Harry Kessler.

63 You say you are incapable of expressing your thought. How then do you explain the lucidity and brilliance with which you are expressing the thought that you are incapable of thought?

> JACQUES RIVIÈRE (1886-1925), French surrealist. Letter, 25 March 1924, to dramatic theorist Antonin Artaud (published in Artaud, *Correspondance Avec Jacques Rivière*, 1924).

64 Today, each artist must undertake to invent himself, a lifelong act of creation that constitutes the essential content of the artist's work. The meaning of art in our time flows from this function of self-creation. Art is the laboratory for making new men.

> HAROLD ROSENBERG (1906-78), U.S. art critic, author. *Discovering the Present*, pt. 4, ch. 24 (1973).

65 All men are somewhat ridiculous and grotesque; just because they are men; and in this respect, artists might well be regarded as man multiplied by two. So it is, was, and shall be.

> FRIEDRICH SCHLEGEL (1772-1829), German philosopher, critic, writer. *Dialogue on Poetry and Literary Aphorisms*, aph. 145, "Ideas" (1968; first published 1799-1800).

66 The true artist will let his wife starve, his children go barefoot, his mother drudge for his living at seventy, sooner than work at anything but his art.

> GEORGE BERNARD SHAW (1856-1950), Anglo-Irish playwright, critic. Tanner, in *Man and Superman*, act 1.

67 The notion of making money by popular work, and then retiring to do good work, is the most familiar of all the devil's traps for artists.

> LOGAN PEARSALL SMITH (1865-1946), U.S. essayist, aphorist. *Afterthoughts*, "Art and Letters" (1931).

68 Somebody once said that I am incapable of drawing a man, but that I draw abstract things like despair, disillusion, despondency, sorrow, lapse of memory, exile, and that these things are sometimes in a shape that might be called Man or Woman.

> JAMES THURBER (1894-1961), U.S. humorist, illustrator. Interview with Jack Sher in *Detroit Free Press* (25 Feb. 1940).

69 I never felt so fervently thankful, so soothed, so tranquil, so filled with the blessed peace, as I did yesterday when I learned that Michael Angelo was dead.

> MARK TWAIN (1835-1910), U.S. author. *The Innocents Abroad*, ch. 27 (1896). "I used to worship the mighty genius of Michael Angelo," Twain wrote of his visit to Rome, "but I do not want Michael Angelo for breakfast—for luncheon—for dinner—for tea—for supper—for between meals. . . . Here—here it is frightful. He designed St. Peter's; he designed the Pope . . . the eternal bore designed the Eternal City, and unless all men and books do lie, he painted everything in it!"

70 If Botticelli were alive today he'd be working for *Vogue*.

> PETER USTINOV (b. 1921), British actor, writer, director. Quoted in: *Observer* (London, 21 Oct. 1968).

71 An artist needn't be a clergyman or a churchwarden, but he certainly must have a warm heart for his fellow men.

> VINCENT VAN GOGH (1853-90), Dutch painter. Letter, 1 Nov. 1882, to his brother Theo (published in *The Complete Letters of Vincent Van Gogh,* vol. 1, 1958).

72 I would venture to warn against too great intimacy with artists as it is very seductive and a little dangerous.

> VICTORIA (1819-1901), Queen of Great Britain and Ireland. Letter, 21 May 1878, to her daughter, the Crown Princess of Prussia (published in *Queen Victoria in Her Letters and Journals,* ed. by Christopher Hibbert, 1984).

73 A good artist should be isolated. If he isn't isolated, something is wrong.

> ORSON WELLES (1915-84), U.S. filmmaker, actor, producer. Interview in *Hollywood Voices* (ed. by Andrews Sarris, 1971).

74 I had rather be called a journalist than an artist.

> H. G. WELLS (1866-1946), British author. Letter, 8 July 1915, to author Henry James.

75 If the man who paints only the tree, or flower, or other surface he sees before him were an artist, the king of artists would be the photographer. It is for the artist to do something beyond this: in portrait painting to put on canvas something more than the face the model wears for that one day; to paint the man, in short, as well as his features.

> JAMES MCNEILL WHISTLER (1834-1903), U.S. artist. *The Gentle Art of Making Enemies,* "Propositions" (1890).

76 Mr. Whistler always spelt art, and we believe still spells it, with a capital "I."

> OSCAR WILDE (1854-1900), Anglo-Irish playwright, author. "The New President," in *Pall Mall Gazette* (London, 26 Jan. 1889; repr. in *Aristotle at Afternoon Tea: The Rare Oscar Wilde,* 1991).

77 If they have not opened the eyes of the blind, they have at least given great encouragement to the short-sighted, and while their leaders may have all the inexperience of old age, their young men are far too wise to be ever sensible.

> OSCAR WILDE (1854-1900), Anglo-Irish playwright, author. Gilbert, in *The Critic as Artist,* pt. 2 (published in *Intentions,* 1891), speaking of the Impressionists. "Yet," he added, "they will insist on treating painting as if it were a mode of autobiography invented for the use of the illiterate."

78 His work was that curious mixture of bad painting and good intentions that always entitles a man to be called a representative British artist.

> OSCAR WILDE (1854-1900), Anglo-Irish playwright, author. Lord Henry, in *The Picture of Dorian Gray,* ch. 19 (1891), referring to Basil Hallward.

79 One of the dangers of the American artist is that he finds himself almost exclusively thrown in with persons more or less in the arts. He lives among them, eats among them, quarrels with them, marries them.

> THORNTON WILDER (1897-1975), U.S. novelist, dramatist. Interview in *Writers at Work* (First Series, ed. by Malcolm Cowley, 1958).

80 Most works of art are effectively treated as commodities and most artists, even when they justly claim quite other intentions, are effectively treated as a category of independent *craftsmen* or *skilled workers* producing a certain kind of marginal commodity.

> RAYMOND WILLIAMS (1921-88), British novelist, critic. *Keywords,* "Art" (1976).

See also Wilde on ADMIRATION; Wilde on ANARCHISM; Wolfe on BOHEMIA; Picasso on CARTOONS AND DRAWING; Klee on COLOR; Thoreau on CRAFTS; Rilke on CREATIVITY; Picasso on DICTATORSHIP; Wilde on ETHICS; Schiller on FASHION; Picasso on GOD; Jong on HOUSEWORK; Cocteau on IMITATION; Bennett, Emerson, Picasso on INSPIRATION; Wilde on INVENTION; Faulkner on LANDLORDS; Pound on MARRIAGE; Wilde on NEWSPAPERS AND MAGAZINES; Lewis on NIHILISM; Berger, Ray on PAINTING; Nietzsche on PARIS; Wilde on POETS; Stevens on REALISM; Lennox on ROCK 'N' ROLL; Hawthorne on SCULPTURE; Wilde on STYLE; VINCENT VAN GOGH.

THE ARTS

1 When we speak, in gestures or signs, we fashion a real object in the world; the gesture is seen, the words and the song are heard. The arts are simply a kind of writing, which, in one way or another, fixes words or gestures, and gives body to the invisible.

> ALAIN [EMILE-AUGUSTE CHARTIER] (1868-1951), French philosopher. *The Gods,* Introduction (1934; tr. 1988).

2 The more a man cultivates the arts the less he fornicates. A more and more apparent cleavage occurs between the spirit and the brute.

> CHARLES BAUDELAIRE (1821-67), French poet. *My Heart Laid Bare* (c. 1865; published in *Intimate Journals,* sct. 91, 1887; tr. by Christopher Isherwood, 1930; rev. by Don Bachardy, 1989).

3 As for types like my own, obscurely motivated by the conviction that our existence was worthless if we didn't make a turning point of it, we were assigned to the humanities, to poetry, philosophy, painting—the nursery games of humankind, which had to be left behind when the age of science began. The humanities would be called upon to choose a wallpaper for the crypt, as the end drew near.

> SAUL BELLOW (b. 1915), U.S. novelist. *The Adventures of Augie Marsh,* ch. 6 (1949).

4 The arts are not just instantaneous pleasure—if you don't like it, the artist is wrong. I belong to the generation which says if you don't like it, you don't understand and you ought to find out.

> JOHN DRUMMOND (b. 1934), British writer, broadcaster. *Guardian* (London, 9 July 1992).

5 Each of the Arts whose office is to refine, purify, adorn, embellish and grace life is under the patronage of a Muse, no god being found worthy to preside over them.

> ELIZA FARNHAM (1815-64), U.S. writer, feminist. *Woman and Her Era,* pt. 2, ch. 1 (1864).

6 One of the most striking signs of the decay of art is when we see its separate forms jumbled together.

> JOHANN WOLFGANG VON GOETHE (1749-1832), German poet, dramatist. *Propyläen,* Introduction (1798), a periodical founded by Goethe which took its title from the gateway to the Acropolis of Athens.

7 As the unity of the modern world becomes increasingly a technological rather than a social affair, the techniques of the arts provide the most valuable means of insight into the real direction of our own collective purposes.

> MARSHALL MCLUHAN (1911-80), Canadian communications theorist. *The Mechanical Bride,* "Magic that Changes Mood" (1951).

8 There is no true expertise in the humanities without knowing *all* of the humanities. Art is a vast, ancient interconnected web-work, a fabricated tradition. Overconcentration on any one point is a distortion.

> CAMILLE PAGLIA (b. 1947), U.S. author, critic, educator. *New York Times Book Review* (5 May 1991).

9 Humanity is the rich effluvium, it is the waste and the manure and the soil, and from it grows the tree of the arts.

> EZRA POUND (1885-1972), U.S. poet, critic. *Poetry* (Chicago, Oct. 1914). Pound was fulminating against the motto on *Poetry's* cover, that, "To have great poets, there must be great audiences too"—a quote by Whitman (see AUDIENCES). Pound preferred to think that the arts were dependent on no one.

10 But the one thing you shd. not do is to suppose that when something is wrong with the arts, it is wrong with the arts ONLY.

> EZRA POUND (1885-1972), U.S. poet, critic. *Guide to Kulchur,* pt. 1, ch. 5, "ZWECK or the AIM" (1938).

11 What better way to prove that you understand a subject than to make money out of it?

> HAROLD ROSENBERG (1906-78), U.S. art critic, author. "The Cultural Situation Today," in *Partisan Review* (New Brunswick, N. J., Summer 1972; repr. as *Discovering the Present,* Introduction, 1973).

12 O, had I but followed the arts!

> WILLIAM SHAKESPEARE (1564-1616), English dramatist, poet. Sir Andrew Aguecheek, in *Twelfth Night,* act 1, sc. 3, bemoaning the time he spent in "fencing, dancing, and bear-baiting."

13 The vitality of a new movement in Art must be gauged by the fury it arouses.

> LOGAN PEARSALL SMITH (1865-1946), U.S. essayist, aphorist. *Afterthoughts,* "Art and Letters" (1931).

14 In a very ugly and sensible age, the arts borrow, not from life, but from each other.

> OSCAR WILDE (1854-1900), Anglo-Irish playwright, author. "Pen, Pencil and Poison," in *Fortnightly Review* (London, Jan. 1889).

See also Yeats on CENSORSHIP; Morris on COMPETITION; CRITICISM AND THE ARTS; Miller on CULTURE; Santayana on THE UNITED STATES.

ASCETICISM

1 The principle of asceticism never was, nor ever can be, consistently pursued by any living creature. Let but one tenth part of the inhabitants of the earth pursue it consistently, and in a day's time they will have turned it into a Hell.

> JEREMY BENTHAM (1748-1832), English philosopher, jurist, political theorist. *The Principles of Morals and Legislation,* ch. 2 (1789).

2 If a hermit lives in a state of ecstasy, his lack of comfort becomes the height of comfort. He must relinquish it.

> JEAN COCTEAU (1889-1963), French author, filmmaker. *Opium* (1929; tr. 1932; repr. 1957, p. 21).

3 To attempt the destruction of our passions is the height of folly. What a noble aim is that of the zealot who tortures himself like a madman in order to desire nothing, love nothing, feel nothing, and who, if he succeeded, would end up a complete monster!

> DENIS DIDEROT (1713-84), French philosopher. *Philosophic Thoughts,* ch. 5 (1746; repr. in *Selected Writings,* ed. by Lester G. Crocker, 1966).

4 The ascetic makes a necessity of virtue.

> FRIEDRICH NIETZSCHE (1844-1900), German philosopher. *Human, All Too Human,* aph. 76 (1878).

5 In every ascetic morality man worships a part of himself as God and for that he needs to diabolize the other part.

> FRIEDRICH NIETZSCHE (1844-1900), German philosopher. *Human, All Too Human,* aph. 137 (1878).

6 The main motive for "nonattachment" is a desire to escape from the pain of living, and above all from love, which, sexual or non-sexual, is hard work.

> GEORGE ORWELL (1903-50), British author. *Shooting an Elephant,* "Reflections on Gandhi" (1950).

See also Russell on RELIGION.

ASIA

1 The delirium and horror of the East. The dusty catastrophe of Asia. Green only on the banner of the Prophet. Nothing grows here except mustaches.

> JOSEPH BRODSKY (b. 1940), Russian-born U.S. poet, critic. *Less Than One: Selected Essays,* sct. 9, "Flight from Byzantium" (1986).

2 I see not much difference between ourselves & the Turks, save that we have foreskins and they none, that they have long dresses and we short, and that we talk much and they little. In England the vices in fashion are whoring & drinking, in Turkey, sodomy and smoking.

> LORD BYRON (1788-1824), English poet. Letter, 3 May 1810 (published in *Byron's Letters and Journals,* vol. 1, ed. by Leslie A. Marchand, 1973).

3 India is a geographical term. It is no more a united nation than the Equator.

> SIR WINSTON CHURCHILL (1874-1965), British statesman, writer. Speech, 18 March 1931, in Royal Albert Hall, London.

4 Be careful about Burma. Most people cannot remember whether it was Siam and has become Thailand, or whether it is now part of Malaysia and should be called Sri Lanka.

> ALEXANDER COCKBURN (b. 1941), Anglo-Irish journalist. "How to be a Foreign Correspondent," in *More* (New York, May 1976; repr. in *Corruptions of Empire,* pt. 1, 1988).

5 A puff of wind, a puff faint and tepid and laden with strange odours of blossoms, of aromatic wood, comes out the still night—the first sigh of the East on my face. That I can never forget. It was impalpable and enslaving, like a charm, like a whispered promise of mysterious delight. . . . The mysterious East faced me, perfumed like a flower, silent like death, dark like a grave.

> JOSEPH CONRAD (1857-1924), Polish-born English novelist. Marlow, in *Youth* (1902). Of the East, Conrad wrote, "I have seen its secret places and have looked into its very soul."

6 Religion itself becomes offensively monotonous. On every point of vantage are pagodas—stupid stalagmites of stagnant piety.

> ALEISTER CROWLEY (1875-1947), British occultist. *The Confessions of Aleister Crowley*, ch. 54 (1929; rev. 1970), on traveling along the river Irrawaddy in Burma.

7 There exists no politician in India daring enough to attempt to explain to the masses that cows can be eaten.

> INDIRA GANDHI (1917-84), Indian politician, prime minister. Quoted by Oriana Fallaci in: "Indira's Coup," in *New York Review of Books* (18 Sept. 1975).

8 This is Malaya. Everything takes a long, a very long time, in Malaya. Things get done, occasionally, but more often they don't, and the more in a hurry you are, the quicker you break down.

> HAN SUYIN (b. 1917), Chinese author. *And the Rain My Drink*, ch. 2 (1956).

9 Asia is rich in people, rich in culture and rich in resources. It is also rich in trouble.

> HUBERT H. HUMPHREY (1911-78), U.S. Democratic politician, vice president. Speech, 23 April 1966, Washington, D.C.

10 Because the European does not know his own unconscious, he does not understand the East and projects into it everything he fears and despises in himself.

> CARL JUNG (1875-1961), Swiss psychiatrist. R. J. Van Helsdingen, *Beelden uit het onbewuste*, Foreword (1957), included in Jung's *Collected Works*, vol. 18 (ed. by William McGuire).

11 Asia is not going to be civilized after the methods of the West. There is too much Asia and she is too old.

> RUDYARD KIPLING (1865-1936), British author, poet. *Life's Handicap*, "The Man Who Was" (1891).

12 The east is not for me—the sensuous spiritual voluptuousness, the curious sensitiveness of the naked people, their black, bottomless, hopeless eyes.

> D. H. LAWRENCE (1885-1930), British author. Letter, 30 April 1922, to Lady Cynthia Asquith (published in *The Letters of D. H. Lawrence*, vol. 4, ed. by James T. Boulton, E. Mansfield, and W. Roberts, 1987).

13 India has 2,000,000 gods, and worships them all. In religion other countries are paupers; India is the only millionaire.

> MARK TWAIN (1835-1910), U.S. author. *Following the Equator*, ch. 43 (1897).

14 Now the long-feared Asiatic colossus takes its turn as world leader, and we—the white race—have become the yellow man's burden. Let us hope that he will treat us more kindly than we treated him.

> GORE VIDAL (b. 1925), U.S. novelist, critic. *Armageddon? Essays 1983-1987*, "The Day the American Empire Ran Out of Gas" (1987).

See also Kipling on EMPIRE.

ASSASSINATION

1 I thought it was a wonderfully conceptual act actually, to fire a replica pistol at a figurehead—the guy could have been working for Andy Warhol!

> J. G. BALLARD (b. 1930), British author. Interview, 30 Oct. 1982, in *Re/Search*, no. 8/9 (San Francisco, 1984). Ballard was referring to an incident involving the Queen of England in 1981.

2 Assassination is the perquisite of princes.

> EUROPEAN COURT CLICHÉ, 19th century.

3 The figure of the gunman in the window was inextricable from the victim and his history. This sustained Oswald in his cell. It gave him what he needed to live. The more time he spent in a cell, the stronger he would get. Everybody knew who he was now.

> DON DELILLO (b. 1926), U.S. author. *Libra*, pt. 2, "In Dallas" (1988), referring to Lee Harvey Oswald.

4 Assassination has never changed the history of the world.

> BENJAMIN DISRAELI (1804-81), English statesman, author. Speech, 1 May 1865, to House of Commons, on Abraham Lincoln's assassination.

5 A desperate disease requires a dangerous remedy.

> GUY FAWKES (1570-1606), English Catholic conspirator. Quoted in: *The Dictionary of National Biography*, vol. 6, referring to the gunpowder plot to blow up the Houses of Parliament, 5 November 1605, following the dictum of Greek physician Hippocrates.

6 My heart burnt within me with indignation and grief; we could think of nothing else. . . . All night long we had only snatches of sleep, waking up perpetually to the sense of a great shock and grief. Every one is feeling the same. I never knew so universal a feeling.

> ELIZABETH GASKELL (1810-65), English novelist. Letter, 28 April 1865, to Harvard professor Charles E. Norton, on the news of Lincoln's assassination reaching England.

7 You never know what's hit you. A gunshot is the perfect way.

> JOHN F. KENNEDY (1917-63), U.S. Democratic politician, president. Quoted in: Peter Collier and David Horowitz, *The Kennedys*, pt. 3, ch. 3 (1984). Kennedy responded with these words when asked how he would choose to die.

8 In Pierre Elliot Trudeau, Canada has at last produced a political leader worthy of assassination.

> IRVING LAYTON (b. 1912), Canadian poet. *The Whole Bloody Bird*, "Obs II" (1969).

9 Assassination's the fastest way.

> MOLIÈRE (1622-73), French dramatist. Don Pedro, in *Le Sicilien*, sc. 13.

10 Honey, I forgot to duck.

> RONALD REAGAN (b. 1911), U.S. Republican politician, president. Remark, 30 March 1981, to Nancy Reagan after John Hinckley III's assassination attempt. Reagan was echoing the celebrated excuse boxer Jack Dempsey made to his wife after losing a title fight in the 1920s.

11 Assassination is the extreme form of censorship.

> GEORGE BERNARD SHAW (1856-1950), Anglo-Irish playwright, critic. *The Shewing-Up of Blanco Posnet,* "The Rejected Statement Pt. 1: The Limits to Toleration," Preface (1911).

12 If you wish to make a man look noble, your best course is to kill him. What superiority he may have inherited from his race, what superiority nature may have personally gifted him with, comes out in death.

> ALEXANDER SMITH (1830-67), Scottish poet. *Dreamthorp,* "On Death and the Fear of Dying" (1863).

13 A shocking crime was committed on the unscupulous initiative of few individuals, with the blessing of more, and amid the passive acquiescence of all.

> TACITUS (c. 55-c. 120), Roman historian. *The Histories,* bk. 1, sct. 28, on the assassination of Emperor Galba.

14 Before I was shot, I always thought that I was more half-there than all-there—I always suspected that I was watching TV instead of living life. . . . Right when I was being shot and ever since, I knew that I was watching television.

> ANDY WARHOL (1928-87), U.S. Pop artist. *From A to B and Back Again,* ch. 6 (1975.)

See also Anonymous on CONSTITUTIONS; DeLillo The KENNEDY FAMILY; Edward VII on ROYALTY.

ASTROLOGY

1 Faithful horoscope-watching, practiced daily, provides just the sort of small but warm and infinitely reassuring fillip that gets matters off to a spirited start.

> SHANA ALEXANDER (b. 1925), U.S. writer, editor. *The Feminine Eye,* "A Delicious Appeal to Unreason" (1970; first published 1966).

2 The stars which shone over Babylon and the stable in Bethlehem still shine as brightly over the Empire State Building and your front yard today. They perform their cycles with the same mathematical precision, and they will continue to affect each thing on earth, including man, as long as the earth exists.

> LINDA GOODMAN (b. 1929), U.S. astrologer. *Linda Goodman's Sun Signs,* Afterword (1968).

3 We need not feel ashamed of flirting with the zodiac. The zodiac is well worth flirting with.

> D. H. LAWRENCE (1885-1930), British author. "Introduction to *The Dragon of the Apocalypse* by Frederick Carter," in *London Mercury* (July 1930; repr. in *Phoenix: The Posthumous Papers of D. H. Lawrence,* pt. 4, ed. by E. McDonald, 1936). Carter's book eventually appeared under a different title and without Lawrence's introduction. Lawrence's approval of astrology, however, excluded "the rather silly modern way of horoscopy and telling your fortune by the stars." His interest lay in the study of the stars as myth and metaphor.

4 You stars that reigned at my nativity,
Whose influence hath allotted death and hell.

> CHRISTOPHER MARLOWE (1564-93), English dramatist, poet. Faustus, in *The Tragical History of Dr. Faustus,* act 5, sc. 2.

5 Look you, Doubloon, your zodiac here is the life of man in one round chapter. . . . To begin: there's Aries, or the Ram—lecherous dog, he begets us; then, Taurus, or the Bull—he bumps us the first thing; then Gemini, or the Twins—that is, Virtue and Vice; we try to reach Virtue, when lo! comes Cancer the Crab, and drags us back; and here, going from Virtue, Leo, a roaring Lion, lies in the path—he gives a few fierce bites and surly dabs with his paw; we escape, and hail Virgo, the virgin! that's our first love; we marry and think to be happy for aye, when pop comes Libra, or the Scales—happiness weighed and found wanting; and while we are very sad about that, Lord! how we suddenly jump, as Scorpio, or the Scorpion, stings us in rear; we are curing the wound, when whang come the arrows all round; Sagittarius, or the Archer, is amusing himself. As we pluck out the shafts, stand aside! here's the battering-ram, Capricornus, or the Goat; full tilt, he comes rushing, and headlong we are tossed; when Aquarius, or the Waterbearer, pours out his whole deluge and drowns us; and, to wind up, with Pisces, or the Fishes, we sleep.

> HERMAN MELVILLE (1819-91), U.S. author. Stubb, in *Moby Dick,* ch. 99 (1851).

6 This is the excellent foppery of the world: that when we are sick in fortune—often the surfeits of our own behaviour—we make guilty of our disasters the sun, the moon, and stars, as if we were villains on necessity, fools by heavenly compulsion, knaves, thieves, and treachers by spherical predominance, drunkards, liars, and adulterers by an enforced obedience of planetary influence. . . . An admirable evasion of whoremaster man, to lay his goatish disposition on the charge of a star!

> WILLIAM SHAKESPEARE (1564-1616), English dramatist, poet. Edmond, in *King Lear,* act 1, sc. 2.

7 About astrology and palmistry: they are good because they make people vivid and full of possibilities. They are communism at its best. Everybody has a birthday and almost everybody has a palm.

> KURT VONNEGUT, JR. (b. 1922), U.S. novelist. *Wampeters, Foma and Granfalloons,* "When I Was Twenty-One" (1974).

ASTRONOMY

1 Astronomy is perhaps the science whose discoveries owe least to chance, in which human understanding appears in its whole magnitude, and through which man can best learn how small he is.

> G. C. LICHTENBERG (1742-99), German physicist, philosopher. *Aphorisms,* "Notebook C," aph. 23 (written 1765-99; tr. by R. J. Hollingdale, 1990).

2 Adam inquires concerning celestial motions, is doubtfully answered, and exhorted to search rather things more worthy of knowledge.

> JOHN MILTON (1608-14), English poet. *Paradise Lost,* heading of bk. 8. For the angel Raphael's "doubtful answer," see Milton on SCIENCE.

3   It is clear to everyone that astronomy at all events compels the soul to look upwards, and draws it from the things of this world to the other.

> PLATO (c. 427-347 B.C.), Greek philosopher. Glaucon, in *The Republic*, bk. 7, sct. 529. Socrates disagreed: "It seems to me that astronomy, as now handled by those who embark on philosophy, positively makes the soul look downwards."

4   These earthly godfathers of Heaven's lights,
That give a name to every fixed star,
Have no more profit of their shining nights
Than those that walk and wot not what they are.

> WILLIAM SHAKESPEARE (1564-1616), English dramatist, poet. Biron, in *Love's Labour's Lost*, act 1, sc. 1.

5   I try to forget what happiness was,
and when that don't work, I study the stars.

> DEREK WALCOTT (b. 1930), West Indian poet, playwright. *The Schooner*, "Flight," sct. 11, in *The Star-Apple Kingdom* (1980).

6   When I, sitting, heard the astronomer, where he lectured with such applause in the lecture room,
How soon, unaccountable, I became tired and sick;
Till rising and gliding out, I wander'd off by myself,
In the mystical moist night-air, and from time to time,
Look'd up in perfect silence at the stars.

> WALT WHITMAN (1819-92), U.S. poet. *When I Heard the Learn'd Astronomer*.

ATHEISM

1   I had rather believe all the Fables in the Legend, and the Talmud, and the Alcoran, than that this universal frame is without a Mind.

> FRANCIS BACON (1561-1626), English philosopher, essayist, statesman. *Essays*, "Of Atheism" (1597-1625).

2   I am a daylight atheist.

> BRENDAN BEHAN (1923-64), Irish playwright. Quoted in: Daniel Farson, *Sacred Monsters*, "Rousting in Dublin" (1988), by Rae Jeffs, publicist and assistant to Behan.

3   We find the most terrible form of atheism, not in the militant and passionate struggle against the idea of God himself, but in the practical atheism of everyday living, in indifference and torpor. We often encounter these forms of atheism among those who are formally Christians.

> NICOLAI A. BERDYAEV (1874-1948), Russian Christian philosopher. *Truth and Revelation* (1953; repr. in *Christian Existentialism*, ch. 5, "Atheism," 1965).

4   Irreligion. The principal one of the great faiths of the world.

> AMBROSE BIERCE (1842-1914), U.S. author. *The Devil's Dictionary* (1881-1906).

5   Those thinkers who cannot believe in any gods often assert that the love of humanity would be in itself sufficient for them; and so, perhaps, it would, if they had it.

> G. K. CHESTERTON (1874-1936), British author. *Tremendous Trifles*, "The Orthodox Barber" (1909).

6   Forth from his dark and lonely hiding-place,
(Portentous sight!) the owlet Atheism,
Sailing on obscene wings athwart the noon,
Drops his blue-fringed lids, and holds them close,
And hooting at the glorious sun in Heaven,
Cries out, "Where is it?"

> SAMUEL TAYLOR COLERIDGE (1772-1834), English poet, critic. *Fears in Solitude* (1798).

7   He must pull out his own eyes, and see no creature, before he can say, he sees no God; He must be no man, and quench his reasonable soul, before he can say to himself, there is no God.

> JOHN DONNE (c. 1572-1631), English divine, metaphysical poet. *Eighty Sermons*, ser. 23 (1640).

8   If therefore my work is negative, irreligious, atheistic, let it be remembered that atheism—at least in the sense of this work—is the secret of religion itself; that religion itself, not indeed on the surface, but fundamentally, not in intention or according to its own supposition, but in its heart, in its essence, believes in nothing else than the truth and divinity of human nature.

> LUDWIG FEUERBACH (1804-72), German philosopher. *The Essence of Christianity*, Preface (1841).

9   I can't believe in the God of my Fathers. If there is one Mind which understands all things, it will comprehend me in my unbelief. I don't know whose hand hung Hesperus in the sky, and fixed the Dog Star, and scattered the shining dust of Heaven, and fired the sun, and froze the darkness between the lonely worlds that spin in space.

> GERALD KERSH (1911-68), British author, journalist. *They Die With Their Boots Clean*, pt. 3, "Old Silence" (1941).

10   If you don't believe in God, all you have to believe in is decency. . . . Decency is very good. Better decent than indecent. But I don't think it's enough.

> HAROLD MACMILLAN (1894-1986), British Conservative politician, prime minister. Quoted in: Alistair Horne, *Macmillan*, vol. 2, ch. 19 (1989). The comment was made to William F. Buckley, Jr. on "Firing Line," recorded in New York, 20 Nov. 1980.

11   He was an embittered atheist (the sort of atheist who does not so much disbelieve in God as personally dislike Him).

> GEORGE ORWELL (1903-50), British author. *Down and Out in Paris and London*, ch. 30 (1933).

12   Here we are, we're alone in the universe, there's no God, it just seems that it all began by something as simple as sunlight striking on a piece of rock. And here we are. We've only got ourselves. Somehow, we've just got to make a go of it. *We've only ourselves.*

> JOHN OSBORNE (b. 1929), British playwright. Jean, in *The Entertainer*, no. 12.

13   What you don't understand is that it is possible to be an atheist, it is possible not to know if God exists or why He should, and yet to believe that man does not live in a state of nature but in history, and that history as we know it now began with Christ, it was founded by Him on the Gospels.

> BORIS PASTERNAK (1890-1960), Russian poet, novelist, translator. Nikolay Nikolayevich, in *Doctor Zhivago,* ch. 1, sct. 5 (1957).

14   And as for the unbelievers,
   their works are as a mirage in a spacious plain
   which the man athirst supposes to be water,
   till, when he comes to it, he finds it is nothing;
      there indeed he finds God,
   and He pays him his account in full; (and God is swift
   at the reckoning).

> QUR'AN. *Light* 24:39 (ed. by Arthur J. Arberry, 1955).

15   The divine is perhaps that quality in man which permits him to endure the lack of God.

> JEAN ROSTAND (1894-1977), French biologist, writer. *Carnets d'un Biologiste* (repr. in *The Substance of Man,* p. 181, 1962).

16   There is no God, Nature sufficeth unto herself; in no wise hath she need of an author.

> MARQUIS DE SADE (1740-1814), French author. Cur-de-fer, in *Justine, ou les Malheurs de la Vertu* (1791).

17   No one can be an unbeliever nowadays. The Christian Apologists have left one nothing to disbelieve.

> SAKI [H. H. MUNRO] (1870-1916), Scottish author. Lady Caroline, in *The Unbearable Bassington,* ch. 13 (1912).

18   Now we have no God. We have had two: the old God that our fathers handed down to us, that we hated, and never liked; the new one that we made for ourselves, that we loved; but now he has flitted away from us, and we see what he was made of—the shadow of our highest ideal, crowned and throned. Now we have no God.

> OLIVE SCHREINER (1855-1920), South African writer, feminist. *The Story of an African Farm,* pt. 2, ch. 1 (1883).

19   During the crusades all were religious mad, and now all are mad for want of it.

> CAPTAIN J. G. STEDMAN (1744-97), British soldier, author, artist. *Journal,* ch. 10, "Politicks for March" (ed. by Stanbury Thompson, 1962), March 1795 entry.

20   First, whenever a man talks loudly against religion, always suspect that it is not his reason, but his passions, which have got the better of his creed. A bad life and a good belief are disagreeable and troublesome neighbours, and where they separate, depend upon it, 'tis for no other cause but quietness' sake.

> LAURENCE STERNE (1713-68), English author. Trim, in *Tristram Shandy,* bk. 2, ch. 17 (1760-67), reading a sermon.

21   The want of belief is a defect that ought to be concealed when it cannot be overcome.

> JONATHAN SWIFT (1667-1745), Anglo-Irish satirist. *Thoughts on Religion* (1768).

22   Among the repulsions of atheism for me has been its drastic uninterestingness as an intellectual position. Where was the ingenuity, the ambiguity, the humanity (in the Harvard sense) of saying that the universe just happened to happen and that when we're dead we're dead?

> JOHN UPDIKE (b. 1932), U.S. author, critic. *Self-Consciousness: Memoirs,* ch. 4 (1989).

23   An atheist may be simply one whose faith and love are concentrated on the impersonal aspects of God.

> SIMONE WEIL (1909-43), French philosopher, mystic. Quoted in: W. H. Auden, *A Certain World,* "God" (1970).

See also Oliphant on The AFTERLIFE; Dickinson on BELIEF; Muggeridge on CREDULITY; Hemingway on PRAYER

AUDIENCES

1   I never let them cough. They wouldn't dare.

> ETHEL BARRYMORE (1879-1959), Anglo-American actor. *New York Post* (7 June 1956).

2   Your audience gives you everything you need. They tell you. There is no director who can direct you like an audience.

> FANNY BRICE (1891-1951), U.S. entertainer. Quoted in: Norman Katkov, *The Fabulous Fanny,* ch. 6 (1952).

3   It was a good thing to have a couple of thousand people all rigid and frozen together, in the palm of one's hand.

> CHARLES DICKENS (1812-70), English novelist. Quoted in: Fred Kaplan, *Dickens: A Biography,* ch. 11 (1988), referring to reading in public.

4   Discourse on virtue and they pass by in droves, whistle and dance the shimmy, and you've got an audience.

> "DIOGENES OF SINOPE [THE CYNIC]" (c. 410-c. 320 B.C.), Greek philosopher, moralist. *Herakleitos and Diogenes,* pt. 2, Fragment 102 (tr. by Guy Davenport, 1976).

5   It is because the public are a mass—inert, obtuse, and passive—that they need to be shaken up from time to time so that we can tell from their bear-like grunts where they are—and also where they stand. They are pretty harmless, in spite of their numbers, because they are fighting against intelligence.

> ALFRED JARRY (1873-1907), French playwright, author. "Theater Questions," in *La Revue Blanche* (Paris, Jan. 1897; repr. in *The Selected Works of Alfred Jarry,* ed. by Roger Shattuck and Simon Watson Taylor, 1965).

6   I'm not here for your amusement. You're here for mine.

> JOHN LYDON [FORMERLY JOHNNY ROTTEN] (b. 1957), British rock musician. Remark, 1978, to audience in Memphis, Tennessee. Quoted in: *Sex Pistols File* (ed. by Ray Stevenson, 1984).

7   We respond to a drama to that extent to which it corresponds to our dreamlife.

> DAVID MAMET (b. 1947), U.S. playwright. *Writing in Restaurants,* "A National Dream-Life" (1986).

8   My conception of the audience is of a public each member of which is carrying about with him what he thinks is an anxiety, or a hope, or a preoccupation which is his alone and isolates him from mankind; and in this respect at least the function of a play is to reveal him to himself so that he may touch others by virtue of the revelation of his mutuality with them. If only for this reason I regard the theater as a serious business, one that makes or should make man more human, which is to say, less alone.

> ARTHUR MILLER (b. 1915), U.S. dramatist. *Collected Plays*, sct. 2, Introduction (1958).

9 I never failed to convince an audience that the best thing they could do was to go away.

> THOMAS LOVE PEACOCK (1785-1866), English author. Mr. Skionar, in *Crotchet Castle*, ch. 18 (1831).

10 The audience is the most revered member of the theater. Without an audience there is no theater. Every technique learned by the actor, every curtain, every flat on the stage, every careful analysis by the director, every coordinated scene, is for the enjoyment of the audience. They are our guests, our evaluators, and the last spoke in the wheel which can then begin to roll. They make the performance meaningful.

> VIOLA SPOLIN (b. 1911), U.S. theatrical director, producer. *Improvisation for the Theater*, ch. 1 (1963).

11 Some writers take to drink, others take to audiences.

> GORE VIDAL (b. 1925), U.S. novelist, critic. *New York Times* (12 March 1981).

12 To have great poets, there must be great audiences too.

> WALT WHITMAN (1819-92), U.S. poet. *Notes Left Over*, "Ventures on an Old Theme" (1881). This motto adorned the front of *Poetry* magazine and was the object of the vitriolic disapproval of Ezra Pound, who, in 1914, wrote in the pages of the magazine: "The artist is not dependent on the multitude of his listeners. . . . This rabble, this multitude—does *not* create the great artist. They are aimless and drifting without him." See Pound on THE ARTS.

13 An audience is never wrong. An individual member of it may be an imbecile, but a thousand imbeciles together in the dark—that is critical genius.

> BILLY WILDER (b. 1906), U.S. film director. "Arena," TV profile, 24 Jan. 1992, BBC2

See also Marcus on APPLAUSE; Twain on BOSTON; Dodd on COMEDY AND COMEDIANS; Bangs on ENTERTAINMENT.

AUSTRALIA AND THE AUSTRALIANS

1 One of the few moments of happiness a man knows in Australia is that moment of meeting the eyes of another man over the tops of two beer glasses.

> ANONYMOUS. Quoted by Bruce Chatwin in: *The Songlines*, ch. 30, "From the Notebooks" (1987). The words were scribbled in the flyleaf of a paperback copy of *Tristram Shandy* bought in the second-hand bookstore in Alice Springs, Australia.

2 We're built, as a nation, on the grounds of a concentration camp. It's like saying "OK, here's Auschwitz. Here's where we'll start our country."

> PETER CAREY (b. 1943), Australian author. *City Limits* (London, 7 April 1988).

3 From what I have said of the natives of New Holland they may appear to some to be the most wretched people upon earth; but in reality they are far happier than we Europeans, being wholly unacquainted not only with the superfluous, but with the necessary conveniences so much sought after in Europe; they are happy in not knowing the use of them.

> CAPTAIN JAMES COOK (1728-79), English seaman, explorer. Journal entry, Aug. 1770, on his landing in Australia (then named New Holland).

4 Where else in the world is a generous man defined as one who would give you his arsehole and shit through his ribs?

> GERMAINE GREER (b. 1939), Australian feminist writer. "The New Maharajahs," in *Sunday Times* (London, 16 Jan. 1972; repr. in *The Madwoman's Underclothes*, 1986).

5 Australia is a huge rest home, where no unwelcome news is ever wafted on to the pages of the worst newspapers in the world.

> GERMAINE GREER (b. 1939), Australian feminist writer. *Observer* (London, 1 Aug. 1982).

6 Earth is here so kind, that just tickle her with a hoe and she laughs with a harvest.

> DOUGLAS JERROLD (1803-57), English playwright, humorist. *The Wit and Opinions of Douglas Jerrold*, "A Land of Plenty" (1859).

7 In a way Australia is like Catholicism. The company is sometimes questionable and the landscape is grotesque. But you always come back.

> THOMAS KENEALLY (b. 1935), Australian novelist. *Woman's Day* (4 July 1983).

8 I like Australia less and less. The hateful newness, the democratic conceit, every man a little pope of perfection.

> D. H. LAWRENCE (1885-1930), British author. Letter, 28 May 1922 (published in *The Letters of D. H. Lawrence*, vol. 4, ed. by James T. Boulton, E. Mansfield, and W. Roberts, 1987). Later, after leaving Australia, Lawrence was to write, "Still I haven't extricated all of me out of Australia. In one part of myself I came to love it—really to love it, Australia."

9 The Australian mind, I can state with authority, is easily boggled.

> CHARLES OSBORNE (b. 1927), British author, critic. *Daily Telegraph* (London, 21 March 1988).

10 Beyond the horizon, or even the knowledge, of the cities along the coast, a great, creative impulse is at work—the only thing, after all, that gives this continent meaning and a guarantee of the future. Every Australian ought to climb up here, once in a way, and glimpse the various, manifold life of which he is a part.

> VANCE PALMER (1885-1959), Australian author, poet. "The Divide" (1925; repr. in *Intimate Portraits*, ed. by H. P. Heseltine, 1969).

11 I have been disappointed in all my expectations of Australia, except as to its wickedness; for it is far more wicked than I have conceived it possible for any place to be, or than it is possible for me to describe to you in England.

> HENRY PARKES (1815-96), English-born Australian statesman. Letter, 1 May 1840 (published in *An Emigrant's Home Letters*, 1896), written a year after Parkes arrived as an immigrant in Australia.

12 With our splendid harbour, our beautifully situated city, our vast territories, all our varied and inexhaustible natural wealth, if we don't convert our colony into a great and prosperous nation, it will be a miracle of error for which we shall have to answer as for a gigantic sin.

> HENRY PARKES (1815-96), English-born Australian statesman. Speech, 16 March 1867, Melbourne, Australia, on the colony of New South Wales.

13 In the weltering hell of the Moorooroo plain
The Yatala Wangary withers and dies,
And the Worrow Wanilla, demented with pain,
To the Woolgoolga woodlands
Despairingly flies.

> MARK TWAIN (1835-1910), U.S. author. From *A Sweltering Din Australia*, consisting of Australian place-names, in *Following the Equator*, ch. 36 (1897).

See also Hughes on EMPIRE; Lawrence on NATIONS.

AUTHORITY

1 No oppression is so heavy or lasting as that which is inflicted by the perversion and exorbitance of legal authority.

> JOSEPH ADDISON (1672-1719), English essayist. *Interesting Anecdotes, Memoirs, Allegories, Essays, and Poetical Fragments*, "The Cruelty of Parental Tyranny" (1794).

2 To say that authority, whether secular or religious, supplies no ground for morality is not to deny the obvious fact that it supplies a sanction.

> A. J. [SIR ALFRED] AYER (1910-89), British philosopher. *The Meaning of Life and Other Essays*, title essay (1990).

3 Does it follow that I reject all authority? Perish the thought. In the matter of boots, I defer to the authority of the bootmaker.

> MIKHAIL BAKUNIN (1814-76), Russian political theorist. *God and the State* (1871; repr. in *Bakunin on Anarchism*, ed. by Sam Dolgoff, 1980).

4 Nothing strengthens authority so much as silence.

> CHARLES DE GAULLE (1890-1970), French general, president. Quoted in: André Maurois, *The Art of Living*, "The Art of Leadership" (1940).

5 Authority is not a quality one person "has," in the sense that he has property or physical qualities. Authority refers to an interpersonal relation in which one person looks upon another as somebody superior to him.

> ERICH FROMM (1900-1980), U.S. psychologist. *The Sane Society*, ch. 5, "Nineteenth-Century Capitalism" (1955).

6 Authority poisons everybody who takes authority on himself.

> VLADIMIR ILYICH LENIN (1870-1924), Russian revolutionary leader. Quoted in: Tamara Deutsche, *Not By Politics Alone*, ch. 2 (1973), to Kropotkin in May 1919.

7 Authority has always attracted the lowest elements in the human race. All through history mankind has been bullied by scum. Those who lord it over their fellows and toss commands in every direction and would boss the grass in the meadow about which way to bend in the wind are the most depraved kind of prostitutes. They will submit to any indignity, perform any vile act, do anything to achieve power. The worst off-sloughings of the planet are the ingredients of sovereignty. Every government is a parliament of whores. The trouble is, in a democracy the whores are us.

> P. J. O'ROURKE (b. 1947), U.S. journalist. *Parliament of Whores*, "At Home in the Parliament of Whores" (1991).

8 To be free in an age like ours, one must be in a position of authority. That in itself would be enough to make me ambitious.

> ERNEST RENAN (1823-92), French writer, critic, scholar. Letter, 1841, to his elder sister Henriette. Quoted in: H. W. Wardman, *Ernest Renan: A Critical Biography*, "Saint Sulpice and the Hidden God" (1964).

9 However sugarcoated and ambiguous, every form of authoritarianism must start with a belief in some group's greater right to power, whether that right is justified by sex, race, class, religion or all four. However far it may expand, the progression inevitably rests on unequal power and airtight roles within the family.

> GLORIA STEINEM (b. 1934), U.S. feminist writer, editor. *Outrageous Acts and Everyday Rebellions*, "If Hitler Were Alive, Whose Side Would He Be On?" (1983; first published in *Ms.*, New York, Oct./Nov. 1980).

AUTOBIOGRAPHY

1 Every autobiography is concerned with two characters, a Don Quixote, the Ego, and a Sancho Panza, the Self.

> W. H. AUDEN (1907-73), Anglo-American poet. *The Dyer's Hand*, pt. 3, "Hic et Ille," sct. b (1962).

2 Anyone who attempts to relate his life loses himself in the immediate. One can only speak of another.

> AUGUSTO ROA BASTOS (b. 1917), Paraguayan novelist. *I The Supreme* (1974; tr. 1986; repr. 1988, p. 57).

3 Reminiscences, even extensive ones, do not always amount to an autobiography. . . . For autobiography has to do with time, with sequence and what makes up the continuous flow of life. Here, I am talking of a space, of moments and discontinuities. For even if months and years appear here, it is in the form they have in the moment of recollection. This strange form—it may be called fleeting or eternal—is in neither case the stuff that life is made of.

> WALTER BENJAMIN (1892-1940), German critic, philosopher. *A Berlin Chronicle* (1970; repr. in *One-Way Street and Other Writings*, 1978).

4 Autobiography begins with a sense of being alone. It is an orphan form.

> JOHN BERGER (b. 1926), British author, critic. "Mother," in *Three Penny Review* (Summer 1986; repr. in *Keeping a Rendezvous,* 1992).

5 A man's memory is bound to be a distortion of his past in accordance with his present interests, and the most faithful autobiography is likely to mirror less what a man was than what he has become.

> FAWN M. BRODIE (1915-81), U.S. biographer. *No Man Knows My History,* ch. 19 (1945).

6 Biographical data, even those recorded in the public registers, are the most private things one has, and to declare them openly is rather like facing a psychoanalyst.

> ITALO CALVINO (1923-85), Italian novelist, critic. *Grand Bazaar* (Milan, Sept.-Oct. 1980; essay collected in *The Literature Machine,* 1987).

7 When you write down your life, every page should contain something no one has ever heard about.

> ELIAS CANETTI (b. 1905), Austrian novelist, philosopher. *The Secret Heart of the Clock: Notes, Aphorisms, Fragments 1973-1985,* "1973" (1991).

8 Such reproductions may not interest the reader; but after all, this is my autobiography, not his; he is under no obligation to read further in it; he was under none to begin. . . . A modest or inhibited autobiography is written without entertainment to the writer and read with distrust by the reader.

> NEVILLE CARDUS (1889-1975), British journalist, critic. *Autobiography,* pt. 1 (1947).

9 There are people who can write their memoirs with a reasonable amount of honesty, and there are people who simply cannot take themselves seriously enough. I think I might be the first to admit that the sort of reticence which prevents a man from exploiting his own personality is really an inverted sort of egotism.

> RAYMOND CHANDLER (1888-1959), U.S. author. Letter, 22 Sept. 1954, to publisher Hamish Hamilton, rejecting a proposal that Chandler write his memoirs (published in *Raymond Chandler Speaking,* 1962).

10 An autobiography is an obituary in serial form with the last instalment missing.

> QUENTIN CRISP (b. 1908), British author. *The Naked Civil Servant,* ch. 29 (1968).

11 We can only write well about our sins because it is too difficult to recall a virtuous act or even whether it was the result of good or evil motives.

> EDWARD DAHLBERG (1900-1977), U.S. author, critic. *Alms for Oblivion,* "Moby-Dick: A Hamitic Dream" (1964).

12 Democratic societies are unfit for the publication of such thunderous revelations as I am in the habit of making.

> SALVADOR DALI (1904-89), Spanish painter. *Diary of a Genius,* Prologue (1966).

13 *My Turn* is the distilled bathwater of Mrs. Reagan's life. It is for the most part sweetish, with a tart edge of rebuke, but disappointingly free of dirt or particulate matter of any kind.

> BARBARA EHRENREICH (b. 1941), U.S. author, columnist. *The Worst Years of Our Lives,* "The Bathtub Tapes" (1991; first published *New Republic,* 1989).

14 It is long ere we discover how rich we are. Our history, we are sure, is quite tame: we have nothing to write, nothing to infer. But our wiser years still run back to the despised recollections of childhood, and always we are fishing up some wonderful article out of that pond; until, by and by, we begin to suspect that the biography of the one foolish person we know is, in reality, nothing less than the miniature paraphrase of the hundred volumes of the Universal History.

> RALPH WALDO EMERSON (1803-82), U.S. essayist, poet, philosopher. *Essays,* "Intellect" (First Series, 1841).

15 That which resembles most living one's life over again, seems to be to recall all the circumstances of it; and, to render this remembrance more durable, to record them in writing.

> BENJAMIN FRANKLIN (1706-90), U.S. statesman, writer. *Autobiography,* ch. 1 (1868).

16 Truth, naked, unblushing truth, the first virtue of all serious history, must be the sole recommendation of this personal narrative.

> EDWARD GIBBON (1737-94), English historian. *Memoirs of My Life,* Introduction (1796; repr. as *Autobiography,* 1971).

17 I don't think anybody should write his autobiography until after he's dead.

> SAMUEL GOLDWYN (1882-1974), U.S. film producer. Quoted in: Arthur Marx, *Goldwyn: the Man Behind the Myth,* Prologue (1976).

18 Autobiography is now as common as adultery and hardly less reprehensible.

> JOHN GRIGG (b. 1924), British author, journalist. *Sunday Times* (London, 28 Feb. 1962).

19 The remarkable thing is that it is the crowded life that is most easily remembered. A life full of turns, achievements, disappointments, surprises, and crises is a life full of landmarks. The empty life has even its few details blurred, and cannot be remembered with certainty.

> ERIC HOFFER (1902-83), U.S. philosopher. *Reflections on the Human Condition,* aph. 174 (1973).

20 The record of one's life must needs prove more interesting to him who writes it than to him who reads what has been written.

> ELIZABETH KENNY (1886-1952), Australian nurse. *And They Shall Walk,* Foreword (1943), written with Martha Ostenso.

21 I am being frank about myself in this book. I tell of my first mistake on page 850.

> HENRY KISSINGER (b. 1923), U.S. Republican politician, secretary of state. Quoted in: *Observer* (London, 2 Jan. 1983), on the second volume of his memoirs, *Years of Upheaval.*

22 The trouble with writing a book about yourself is that you can't fool around. If you write about someone else, you can stretch the truth from here to Finland. If you write about yourself the slightest deviation makes you realize instantly that there may be honor among thieves, but *you* are just a dirty liar.

> GROUCHO MARX (1895-1977), U.S. comic actor. *Groucho and Me*, ch. 1 (1959).

23 Autobiography is only to be trusted when it reveals something disgraceful. A man who gives a good account of himself is probably lying, since any life when viewed from the inside is simply a series of defeats.

> GEORGE ORWELL (1903-50), British author. "Benefit of Clergy: Some Notes on Salvador Dali" (1944; repr. in *The Collected Essays, Journalism and Letters of George Orwell*, vol. 3, ed. by Sonia Orwell and Ian Angus, 1968).

24 All those writers who write about their childhood! Gentle God, if I wrote about mine you wouldn't sit in the same room with me.

> DOROTHY PARKER (1893-1967), U.S. humorous writer. Interview in *Writers at Work* (First Series, ed. by Malcolm Cowley, 1958).

25 When you put down the good things you ought to have done, and leave out the bad ones you did do—well, that's Memoirs.

> WILL ROGERS (1879-1935), U.S. humorist. *The Autobiography of Will Rogers*, ch. 16 (1949).

26 It isn't that you subordinate your ideas to the force of the facts in autobiography but that you construct a sequence of stories to bind up the facts with a persuasive *hypothesis* that unravels your history's meaning.

> PHILIP ROTH (b. 1933), U.S. novelist. *The Facts*, opening letter to Zuckerman (1988).

27 I write fiction and I'm told it's autobiography, I write autobiography and I'm told it's fiction, so since I'm so dim and they're so smart, let *them* decide what it is or it isn't.

> PHILIP ROTH (b. 1933), U.S. novelist. *Deception*, "Philip" (1990).

28 If you really want to hear about it, the first thing you'll probably want to know is where I was born, and what my lousy childhood was like, and how my parents were occupied and all before they had me, and all that David Copperfield kind of crap, but I don't feel like going into it.

> J. D. SALINGER (b. 1919), U.S. author. The narrator (Holden Caulfield), in *Catcher in the Rye* (1951).

29 Members rise from CMG (known sometimes in Whitehall as "Call Me God") to KCMG ("Kindly Call Me God") to GCMG ("God Calls Me God").

> ANTHONY SAMPSON (b. 1926), British journalist, author. *Anatomy of Britain Today*, ch. 18 (1965).

30 Autobiographies ought to begin with Chapter Two.

> ELLERY SEDGWICK (1872-1960), U.S. editor. *The Happy Profession*, ch. 1 (1948).

31 What pursuit is more elegant than that of collecting the ignominies of our nature and transfixing them for show, each on the bright pin of a polished phrase?

> LOGAN PEARSALL SMITH (1865-1946), U.S. essayist, aphorist. *Afterthoughts*, "Myself" (1931).

32 Don't give your opinions about Art and the Purpose of Life. They are of little interest and, anyway, you can't express them. Don't analyse yourself. Give the relevant facts and let your readers make their own judgments. Stick to your story. It is not the most important subject in history but it is one about which you are uniquely qualified to speak.

> EVELYN WAUGH (1903-66), British novelist. *Tablet* (London, 5 May 1951), in review of Stephen Spender's autobiography, *World Within World*.

33 I dislike modern memoirs. They are generally written by people who have either entirely lost their memories, or have never done anything worth remembering.

> OSCAR WILDE (1854-1900), Anglo-Irish playwright, author. Ernest, in *The Critic as Artist*, pt. 1 (published in *Intentions*, 1891). He continued, "which, however, is, no doubt, the true explanation of their popularity, as the English public always feels perfectly at its ease when a mediocrity is talking to it." In reply, Gilbert disagreed with Ernest's view of autobiography: "In literature mere egotism is delightful."

34 Thus when I come to shape here at this table between my hands the story of my life and set it before you as a complete thing, I have to recall things gone far, gone deep, sunk into this life or that and become part of it; dreams, too, things surrounding me, and the inmates, those old half-articulate ghosts who keep up their hauntings by day and night . . . shadows of people one might have been; unborn selves.

> VIRGINIA WOOLF (1882-1941), British novelist. Bernard, in *The Waves* (1931; ed. 1943, p. 205).

See also Ellis on ARTISTS; BIOGRAPHY; Auden on CONFESSION.

AUTONOMY

1 To be one's own master is to be the slave of self.

> NATALIE CLIFFORD BARNEY (1876-1972), U.S.-born French author. Quoted in: "Samples from Almost Illegible Notebooks," in *Adam*, no. 299 (London, 1962).

2 If sex and creativity are often seen by dictators as subversive activities, it's because they lead to the knowledge that you own your own body (and with it your own voice), and that's the most revolutionary insight of all.

> ERICA JONG (b. 1942), U.S. author. "The Artist as Housewife," in *The First Ms. Reader* (ed. by Francine Kragbrun, 1972).

3 Self-determination has to mean that the leader is your individual gut, and heart, and mind or we're talking about power, again, and its rather well-known impurities. Who is really going to care whether you live or die and who is going to know the most intimate motivation for your laughter and your tears is the only person to be trusted to speak for you and to decide what you will or will not do.

> JUNE JORDAN (b. 1939), U.S. poet, civil rights activist. *Moving Towards Home: Political Essays*, "Civil Wars" (1989; first published 1981).

4 Self-determination, the autonomy of the individual, asserts itself in the right to race his automobile, to handle his power tools, to buy a gun, to communicate to mass audiences his opinion, no matter how ignorant, how aggressive, it may be.

> HERBERT MARCUSE (1898-1979), U.S. political philosopher. *An Essay on Liberation,* ch. 1 (1969).

5   We prefer self-government with danger to servitude in tranquility.

> KWAME NKRUMAH (1900-1972), Ghanaian president. Quoted in: *Axioms of Kwame Nkrumah* (1967), motto of the *Accra Evening News,* founded 1948.

See also INDEPENDENCE.

AUTUMN

1   Autumn wins you best by this its mute
Appeal to sympathy for its decay.

> ROBERT BROWNING (1812-89), English poet. *Paracelsus,* pt. 1.

2   My Sorrow, when she's here with me,
Thinks these dark days of autumn rain
Are beautiful as days can be;
She loves the bare, the withered tree;
She walks the sodden pasture lane.

> ROBERT FROST (1874-1963), U.S. poet. *My November Guest.*

3   O suns and skies and clouds of June,
And flowers of June together,
Ye cannot rival for one hour
October's bright blue weather.

> HELEN HUNT JACKSON (1830-85), U.S. writer, poet. *October's Bright Blue Weather,* st. 1.

4   The teeming Autumn big with rich increase,
Bearing the wanton burden of the prime
Like widowed wombs after their lords' decease.

> WILLIAM SHAKESPEARE (1564-1616), English dramatist, poet. *Sonnet* 97.

5   There is a harmony
In autumn, and a lustre in its sky,
Which through the summer is not heard or seen,
As if it could not be, as if it had not been!

> PERCY BYSSHE SHELLEY (1792-1822), English poet. *Hymn to Intellectual Beauty* (1816).

THE AVANT-GARDE

1   There is a certain kind of person who is so dominated by the desire to be loved for himself alone that he has constantly to test those around him by tiresome behavior; what he says and does must be admired, not because it is intrinsically admirable, but because it is *his* remark, *his* act. Does not this explain a good deal of avant-garde art?

> W. H. AUDEN (1907-73), Anglo-American poet. *The Dyer's Hand,* pt. 1, "Writing" (1962).

2   The difficult and risky task of meeting and mastering the new—whether it be the settlement of new lands or the initiation of new ways of life—is not undertaken by the vanguard of society but by its rear. It is the misfits, failures, fugitives, outcasts and their like who are among the first to grapple with the new.

> ERIC HOFFER (1902-83), U.S. philosopher. *The Passionate State of Mind,* aph. 51 (1955).

3   An avant-garde man is like an enemy inside a city he is bent on destroying, against which he rebels; for like any system of government, an established form of expression is also a form of oppression. The avant-garde man is the opponent of an existing system.

> EUGÈNE IONESCO (b. 1912), Rumanian-born French playwright. "A Talk about the Avant-Garde," lecture, June 1959, Helsinki (repr. in *Notes and Counter Notes,* 1962).

4   *We are the first men of a Future that has not materialized.* We belong to a "great age" that has not "come off." We moved too quickly for the world. We set too sharp a pace.

> WYNDHAM LEWIS (1882-1957), British author, painter. *Blasting and Bombardiering,* pt. 5, "The Period of `Ulysses', `Blast', `The Waste Land'" (1937).

5   Avant-gardism is an addiction that can be appeased only by a revolution in permanence.

> HAROLD ROSENBERG (1906-78), U.S. art critic, author. *Quality: Its Image,* "The Avant-Garde" (ed. by Louis Kronenberger, 1969; repr. in *Discovering the Present,* 1973).

6   After Stéphane Mallarmé, after Paul Verlaine, after Gustave Moreau, after Puvis de Chavannes, after our own verse, after all our subtle colour and nervous rhythm, after the faint mixed tints of Conder, what more is possible? After us the Savage God.

> W. B. YEATS (1865-1939), Irish poet, playwright. *Autobiographies,* bk. 4, sct. 20, "The Trembling of the Veil" (1926).

AWARDS

1   A new kind of award has been added—the deathbed award. It is not an award of any kind. Either the recipient has not acted at all, or was not nominated, or did not win the award the last few times around. It is intended to relieve the guilty conscience of the Academy members and save face in front of the public. The Academy has the horrible taste to have a star, choking with emotion, present this deathbed award so that there can be no doubt in anybody's mind why the award is so hurriedly given. Lucky is the actor who is too sick to watch the proceedings on television.

> MARLENE DIETRICH (1904-92), German-born U.S. film actor. *Marlene Dietrich's ABC,* "Academy Award" (1962).

2   Everyone in our culture wants to win a prize. Perhaps that is the grand lesson we have taken with us from kindergarten in the age of perversions of Dewey-style education: everyone gets a ribbon, and praise becomes a meaningless narcotic to soothe egoistic distemper.

> GERALD EARLY (b. 1952), U.S. author. "Life with Daughters: Watching the Miss America Pageant," in *Kenyon Review* (1991; repr. in *The Best America Essays, 1991,* ed. by Joyce Carol Oates, 1991).

3　The award of a pure gold medal for poetry would flatter the recipient unduly: no poem ever attains such carat purity.

> ROBERT GRAVES (1895-1985), British poet, novelist. Address, Jan. 1960, to the Oxford University Philological Society (published in *Oxford Addresses on Poetry*, "Poetic Gold," 1962). Graves had been awarded a gold medal for services to poetry by the National Poetry Society of America.

4　Like Olympic medals and tennis trophies, all they signified was that the owner had done something of no benefit to anyone more capably than everyone else.

> JOSEPH HELLER (b. 1923), U.S. novelist. Yossarian, in *Catch-22*, ch. 8 (1961), on his view of pennants given as prizes in parades.

5　Lots of people who complained about us receiving the MBE received theirs for heroism in the war—for killing people. We received ours for entertaining other people. I'd say we deserve ours more.

> JOHN LENNON (1940-80), British rock musician. Quoted in: *Beatles Illustrated Lyrics*, vol. 1.

6　The Oscars demonstrate the will of the people to control and judge those they have elected to stand above them (much, perhaps, as in bygone days, an election celebrated the same).

> DAVID MAMET (b. 1947), U.S. playwright. *Writing in Restaurants*, "Oscars" (1986).

7　The cross of the Legion of Honor has been conferred on me. However, few escape that distinction.

> MARK TWAIN (1835-1910), U.S. author. *A Tramp Abroad*, ch. 8 (1880).

8　To refuse awards . . . is another way of accepting them with more noise than is normal.

> PETER USTINOV (b. 1921), British actor, writer, director. Quoted in: David Shipman, *Marlon Brando*, ch. 13 (1989; first published 1974), on the refusal of Oscars by Marlon Brando and George C. Scott.

See also Sampson on AUTOBIOGRAPHY.

AWARENESS

1　To be happy is to be able to become aware of oneself without fright.

> WALTER BENJAMIN (1892-1940), German critic, philosopher. *One-Way Street*, "Fancy Goods" (1928; repr. in *One-Way Street and Other Writings*, 1978).

2　To see, to hear, means nothing. To recognize (or not to recognize) means everything. Between what I do recognize and what I do not recognize there stands myself. And what I do not recognize I shall continue not to recognize.

> ANDRÉ BRETON (1896-1966), French Surrealist. *Surrealism and Painting* (1928).

3　The aim of life is to live, and to live means to be aware, joyously, drunkenly, serenely, divinely aware.

> HENRY MILLER (1891-1980), U.S. author. *The Wisdom of the Heart*, "Creative Death" (1947).

4　Openmindedness should not be fostered because, as Scripture teaches, Truth is great and will prevail, nor because, as Milton suggests, Truth will always win in a free and open encounter. It should be fostered for its own sake.

> RICHARD RORTY (b. 1931), U.S. philosopher. *Contingency, Irony, and Solidarity*, ch. 3, "The Contingency of Community" (1989).

5　Most people grow old within a small circle of ideas, which they have not discovered for themselves. There are perhaps less wrong-minded people than thoughtless.

> LUC, MARQUIS DE VAUVENARGUES (1715-47), French moralist. *Refléxions et Maximes*, no. 238 (1746).

6　The man who is aware of himself is henceforward independent; and he is never bored, and life is only too short, and he is steeped through and through with a profound yet temperate happiness. He alone lives, while other people, slaves of ceremony, let life slip past them in a kind of dream.

> VIRGINIA WOOLF (1882-1941), British novelist. *The Common Reader*, "Montaigne" (First Series, 1925).

BABIES

1　"I have no name:
"I am but two days old."
What shall I call thee?
"I happy am,
"Joy is my name."
Sweet joy befall thee!

> WILLIAM BLAKE (1757-1827), English poet, painter, engraver. *Infant Joy*, st. 1, in *Songs of Innocence* (1789; repr. in *Complete Writings*, ed. by Geoffrey Keynes, 1957).

2　Except that right side up is best, there is not much to learn about holding a baby. There are one hundred and fifty-two distinctly different ways—and all are right! At least all will do.

> HEYWOOD BROUN (1888-1939), U.S. journalist, novelist. *Seeing Things at Night*, "Holding a Baby" (1921).

3　It is a pleasant thing to reflect upon, and furnishes a complete answer to those who contend for the gradual degeneration of the human species, that every baby born into the world is a finer one than the last.

> CHARLES DICKENS (1812-70), English novelist. *Nicholas Nickleby*, ch. 36 (1838-39).

4　Moving between the legs of tables and of chairs,
Rising or falling, grasping at kisses and toys,
Advancing boldly, sudden to take alarm,
Retreating to the corner of arm and knee,
Eager to be reassured, taking pleasure
In the fragrant brilliance of the Christmas tree. . . .

> T. S. ELIOT (1888-1965), Anglo-American poet, critic. *Animula*.

5　Infancy conforms to nobody: all conform to it, so that one babe commonly makes four or five out of the adults who prattle and play to it.

> RALPH WALDO EMERSON (1803-82), U.S. essayist, poet, philosopher. *Essays*, "Self-Reliance" (First Series, 1841).

6　Everyone knows that by far the happiest and universally enjoyable age of man is the first. What is there about babies which makes us hug and kiss and fondle them, so that even an enemy would give them help at that age?

> DESIDERIUS ERASMUS (c. 1466-1536), Dutch humanist. *Praise of Folly,* ch. 13 (1509).

7 No one who has seen a baby sinking back satiated from the breast and falling asleep with flushed cheeks and a blissful smile can escape the reflection that this picture persists as a prototype of the expression of sexual satisfaction in later life.

> SIGMUND FREUD (1856-1939), Austrian psychiatrist. *Three Essays on the Theory of Sexuality,* "Infantile Sexuality," sct. 2 (1905; repr. in *Complete Works,* vol. 7, ed. by James Strachey and Anna Freud, 1953).

8 If you desire to drain to the dregs the fullest cup of scorn and hatred that a fellow human being can pour out for you, let a young mother hear you call dear baby "it."

> JEROME K. JEROME (1859-1927), British author. *Idle Thoughts of an Idle Fellow,* "On Babies" (1889).

9 A loud noise at one end and no sense of responsibility at the other.

> RONALD KNOX (1888-1957), British scholar, priest. Quoted by C. Blackmore in his 1976 Reith lecture.

10 From the moment of birth, when the stone-age baby confronts the twentieth-century mother, the baby is subjected to these forces of violence, called love, as its mother and father have been, and their parents and their parents before them. These forces are mainly concerned with destroying most of its potentialities. This enterprise is on the whole successful.

> R. D. LAING (1927-89), British psychiatrist. *The Politics of Experience,* ch. 3 (1967).

11 Babies are necessary to grown-ups. A new baby is like the beginning of all things—wonder, hope, a dream of possibilities. In a world that is cutting down its trees to build highways, losing its earth to concrete . . . babies are almost the only remaining link with nature, with the natural world of living things from which we spring.

> EDA J. LE SHAN (b. 1922), U.S. educator, author. *The Conspiracy Against Childhood,* ch. 2 (1967).

12 Diaper backward spells repaid. Think about it.

> MARSHALL MCLUHAN (1911-80), Canadian communications theorist. Remark, June 1969, made at American Booksellers Association luncheon, Washington, D.C. Quoted in: *Sun* (Vancouver, 7 June 1969).

13 Every new baby is a blind desperate vote for survival: people who find themselves unable to register an effective political protest against extermination do so by a biological act.

> LEWIS MUMFORD (1895-1990), U.S. social philosopher. *The City in History,* ch. 18 (1961).

14 The tiny madman in his padded cell.

> VLADIMIR NABOKOV (1899-1977), Russian-born U.S. novelist, poet. Humbert Humbert describing an embryo, in *Lolita,* pt. 1, ch. 11 (1955).

15 A baby is God's opinion that life should go on.

> CARL SANDBURG (1878-1967), U.S. poet. *Remembrance Rock,* ch. 2 (1948).

16 We have not all had the good fortune to be ladies. We have not all been generals, or poets, or statesmen; but when the toast works down to the babies, we stand on common ground.

> MARK TWAIN (1835-1910), U.S. author. "The Babies," speech, Nov. 1879 (published in *Mark Twain's Speeches,* ed. by Albert Bigelow Paine, 1923). Twain spoke at a banquet in which the fifteenth toast was, "The babies—as they comfort us in our sorrows, let us not forget them in our festivities."

17 A soiled baby, with a neglected nose, cannot be conscientiously regarded as a thing of beauty.

> MARK TWAIN (1835-1910), U.S. author. *Answers to Correspondents* (1865; published in *Complete Humorous Sketches and Tales,* ed. by Charles Neider, 1961). Twain was replying to a young mother.

18 I don't dislike babies, though I think very young ones rather disgusting.

> VICTORIA (1819-1901), Queen of Great Britain and Ireland. Letter, 8 May 1872, to her daughter, the Crown Princess of Prussia (published in *Queen Victoria in Her Letters and Journals,* ed. by Christopher Hibbert, 1984).

19 Since people are going to be living longer and getting older, they'll just have to learn how to be babies longer.

> ANDY WARHOL (1928-87), U.S. Pop artist. *From A to B and Back Again,* ch. 7 (1975).

20
>   Mark the babe
> Not long accustomed to this breathing world;
> One that hath barely learned to shape a smile,
> Though yet irrational of soul, to grasp
> With tiny finger—to let fall a tear;
> And, as the heavy cloud of sleep dissolves,
> To stretch his limbs, bemocking, as might seem,
> The outward functions of intelligent man.

> WILLIAM WORDSWORTH (1770-1850), English poet. *The Excursion,* bk. 5.

See also Ridler on BIRTH; Churchill on INVESTMENT; Twain on SATIRE.

BALDNESS

1 Bald as the bare mountain tops are bald, with a baldness full of grandeur.

> MATTHEW ARNOLD (1822-88), English poet, critic. *Essays in Criticism,* "Poems of Wordsworth," Preface (Second Series, 1888).

2 The tenderest spot in a man's make-up is sometimes the bald spot on top of his head.

> HELEN ROWLAND (1875-1950), U.S. journalist. *Reflections of a Bachelor Girl* (1903).

3 There is more felicity on the far side of baldness than young men can possibly imagine.

> LOGAN PEARSALL SMITH (1865-1946), U.S. essayist, aphorist. *All Trivia,* "Last Words" (1933).

BANALITY

1   Men are seldom more commonplace than on supreme occasions.

> SAMUEL BUTLER (1835-1902), English author. *Notebooks,* "Material for a Projected Sequel to Alps and Sanctuaries" (1912).

2   A mental disease has swept the planet: banalization. . . . Presented with the alternative of love or a garbage disposal unit, young people of all countries have chosen the garbage disposal unit.

> IVAN CHTCHEGLOV (b. 1934), French political theorist. "Formulary for a New Urbanism" (written Oct. 1953; published in *Internationale Situationiste,* no. 1, Paris, June 1958; repr. in *Situationist International Anthology,* ed. by Ken Knabb, 1981).

3   Banality is a symptom of non-communication. Men hide behind their clichés.

> EUGÈNE IONESCO (b. 1912), Rumanian-born French playwright. *Notes and Counter-Notes,* pt. 4, "Further Notes, 1960" (1962).

4   Banality is a terribly likely consequence of the underuse of a good mind. That is why in particular it is a female affliction.

> CYNTHIA PROPPER-SETON (b. 1926), U.S. author. *The Sea Change of Angela Lewes,* ch. 9 (1971).

5   When the shrivelled skin of the ordinary is stuffed out with meaning, it satisfies the senses amazingly.

> VIRGINIA WOOLF (1882-1941), British novelist. *Orlando,* ch. 6 (1928).

BANKING

1   I hesitate to deposit money in a bank. I am afraid I shall never dare to take it out again. When you go to confession and entrust your sins to the safe-keeping of the priest, do you ever come back for them?

> JEAN BAUDRILLARD (b. 1929), French semiologist. *America,* "Astral America" (1986; tr. 1988).

2   What's breaking into a bank compared with founding a bank?

> BERTOLT BRECHT (1898-1956), German dramatist, poet. Mac, in *The Threepenny Opera,* act 3, sc. 9.

3   Put not your trust in money, but put your money in trust.

> OLIVER WENDELL HOLMES, SR. (1809-94), U.S. writer, physician. *The Autocrat of the Breakfast Table,* ch. 2 (1858).

4   I sincerely believe . . . that banking establishments are more dangerous than standing armies, and that the principle of spending money to be paid by posterity, under the name of funding, is but swindling futurity on a large scale.

> THOMAS JEFFERSON (1743-1826), U.S. president. Letter, 28 May 1816, to political philosopher and senator John Taylor, whose book *An Inquiry into the Principles and Policy of the Government of the United States* (1814) had argued against the harmful effects of finance capitalism.

5   It is no accident that banks resemble temples, preferably Greek, and that the suppliants who come to perform the rites of deposit and withdrawal instinctively lower their voices into the registers of awe. Even the most junior tellers acquire within weeks of their employment the officiousness of hierophants tending an eternal flame. I don't know how they become so quickly inducted into the presiding mysteries, or who instructs them in the finely articulated inflections of contempt for the laity, but somehow they learn to think of themselves as suppliers of the monetarized DNA that is the breath of life.

> LEWIS H. LAPHAM (b. 1935), U.S. essayist, editor. *Money and Class in America,* ch. 8 (1988).

6   With a group of bankers I always had the feeling that success was measured by the extent one gave nothing away.

> LORD LONGFORD (b. 1905), British author, social reformer. Quoted in: Anthony Sampson, *Anatomy of Britain,* ch. 23 (1965).

7   There is too much sour grapes for my taste in the present American attitude. The time to denounce the bankers was when we were all feeding off their gold plate; not now! At present they have not only my sympathy but my preference. They are the last representatives of our native industries.

> EDITH WHARTON (1862-1937), U.S. author. Letter, 11 Feb. 1934 (published in *The Letters of Edith Wharton,* 1988). The letter was written during the economic crisis following the 1929 Wall Street crash.

BANQUETS

1   Feasts must be solemn and rare, or else they cease to be feasts.

> ALDOUS HUXLEY (1894-1963), British author. *Do What You Will,* "Holy Face" (1929).

2   They eat, they drink, and in communion sweet
Quaff immortality and joy.

> JOHN MILTON (1608-74), English poet. The angel Raphael, sharing "the choicest fruits of paradise" with Adam and Eve, in *Paradise Lost,* bk. 5 (1667).

3   There is . . . no glamor at banquets—I mean the large formal banquets of big associations and societies. There is only a kind of dignified confusion that gradually unhinges the mind.

> JAMES THURBER (1894-1961), U.S. humorist, illustrator. *New Yorker* (29 March 1930).

See also Thurber on SPEECHES AND SPEECHMAKING.

BARBARISM

1   And now, what will become of us without
    barbarians?
They were a kind of solution.

> CONSTANTINE CAVAFY (1863-1933), Greek poet. *Waiting for the Barbarians* (1906).

2   The true barbarian is he who thinks everything barbarous but his own tastes and prejudices.

> WILLIAM HAZLITT (1778-1830), English essayist. *Characteristics: In the Manner of Rochefoucault's Maxims,* no. 333 (1823; repr. in *The Complete Works Of William Hazlitt,* vol. 9, ed. by P. P. Howe, 1932).

3 Much reading has brought upon us a learned barbarism.

> G. C. LICHTENBERG (1742-99), German physicist, philosopher. *Aphorisms*, "Notebook F," aph. 144 (written 1765-99; tr. by R. J. Hollingdale, 1990).

4 Barbarism is the absence of standards to which appeal can be made.

> JOSÉ ORTEGA Y GASSET (1883-1955), Spanish essayist, philosopher. *The Revolt of the Masses*, ch. 8 (1930).

5 He is a barbarian, and thinks that the customs of his tribe and island are the laws of nature.

> GEORGE BERNARD SHAW (1856-1950), Anglo-Irish playwright, critic. Caesar, in *Caesar and Cleopatra*, act 2, speaking of Britannus, his secretary, "an islander from the western end of the world, a day's voyage from Gaul."

6 I would suggest that barbarism be considered as a permanent and universal human characteristic which becomes more or less pronounced according to the play of circumstances.

> SIMONE WEIL (1910-43), French philosopher, mystic. "Hitler and Roman Foreign Policy," in *Nouveaux Cahiers* (1 Jan. 1940).

See also PRIMITIVE LIFE.

BARGAINING

1 It is naught, it is naught, saith the buyer: but when he is gone his way, then he boasteth.

> BIBLE, HEBREW. *Proverbs* 20:14.

2 A bargain is in its very essence a *hostile* transaction . . . do not all men try to abate the price of all they buy? I contend that a bargain even between brethren is a declaration of war.

> LORD BYRON (1788-1824), English poet. Letter, 14 July 1821 (published in *Byron's Letters and Journals*, vol. 8, ed. by Leslie A. Marchand, 1973-81).

3 Here's the rule for bargains: "Do other men, for they would do you." That's the true business precept.

> CHARLES DICKENS (1812-70), English novelist. Jonas Chuzzlewit, in *Martin Chuzzlewit*, ch. 11 (1844).

4 Necessity never made a good bargain.

> BENJAMIN FRANKLIN (1706-90), U.S. statesman, writer. *Poor Richard's Almanack*, entry for April 1735 (1758). .

BARS, PUBS, AND CAFÉS

1 After all, it is not where one washes one's neck that counts but where one moistens one's throat.

> DJUNA BARNES (1892-1982), U.S. author, poet, columnist. "Greenwich Village As It Is," in *Pearson's Magazine* (Oct. 1916; repr. in *Djuna Barnes's New York*, 1989).

2 We have to recognise, that the gin-palace, like many other evils, although a poisonous, is still a natural outgrowth of our social conditions. The tap-room in many cases is the poor man's only parlour. Many a man takes to beer, not from the love of beer, but from a natural craving for the light, warmth, company, and comfort which is thrown in along with the beer, and which he can-

not get excepting by buying beer. Reformers will never get rid of the drink shop until they can outbid it in the subsidiary attractions which it offers to its customers.

> WILLIAM BOOTH (1829-1912), English evangelist, founder of the Salvation Army. *In Darkest England, and the Way Out*, pt. 1, ch. 6 (1890).

3 The bar . . . is an exercise in solitude. Above all else, it must be quiet, dark, very comfortable—and, contrary to modern mores, no music of any kind, no matter how faint. In sum, there should be no more than a dozen tables, and a clientele that doesn't like to talk.

> LUIS BUÑUEL (1900-1983), Spanish filmmaker. *My Last Sigh*, ch. 6 (1983), from his autobiography.

4 O City city, I can sometimes hear
Beside a public bar in Lower Thames Street,
The pleasant whining of a mandolin
And a clatter and a chatter from within
Where fishmen lounge at noon.

> T. S. ELIOT (1888-1965), Anglo-American poet, critic. *The Waste Land*, "The Fire Sermon (1922).

5 The bar is the male kingdom. For centuries it was the bastion of male privilege, the gathering place for men away from their women, a place where men could go to freely indulge in The Bull Session . . . the release of the guilty anxiety of the oppressor class.

> SHULAMITH FIRESTONE (b. 1945), Canadian-American author, editor. *Voices from Women's Liberation*, "The Bar as Microcosm" (ed. by Leslie B. Tanner, 1970).

6 Where village statesmen talked with looks profound,
And news much older than their ale went round.

> OLIVER GOLDSMITH (1728-74), Anglo-Irish author, poet, playwright. *The Deserted Village*.

7 There is no private house in which people can enjoy themselves so well as at a capital tavern. . . . No, Sir; there is nothing which has yet been contrived by man by which so much happiness is produced as by a good tavern or inn.

> SAMUEL JOHNSON (1709-84), English author, lexicographer. Quoted in: James Boswell, *Life of Samuel Johnson*, 21 March 1776 (1791).

8 By the time a bartender knows what drink a man will have before he orders, there is little else about him worth knowing.

> DON MARQUIS (1878-1937), U.S. humorist, journalist. Quoted by Franklin P. Adams in: E. Anthony, *O Rare Don Marquis*, ch. 11 (1962).

9 They are universal places, like churches, hallowed meeting places of all mankind.

> IRIS MURDOCH (b. 1919), British novelist, philosopher. Jenkin Riderhood, in *The Book and the Brotherhood*, pt. 2, "Midwinter" (1987).

10 I ask especially that no state shall, by law or otherwise, authorize the return of the saloon, either in its old form or in some modern guise.

> FRANKLIN D. ROOSEVELT (1882-1945), U.S. Democratic politician, president. Speech, 5 Dec. 1933, on the repeal of the Eighteenth Amendment.

BASEBALL

1   Whoever wants to know the heart and mind of America had better learn baseball, the rules and realities of the game.

> JACQUES BARZUN (b. 1907), U.S. scholar. Quoted in: Michael Novak, *The Joy of Sports*, pt. 1 (1976).

2   A ball player's got to be kept hungry to become a big leaguer. That's why no boy from a rich family ever made the big leagues.

> JOE DIMAGGIO (b. 1914), U.S. baseball player. Quoted in: *New York Times* (30 April 1961).

3   In the great department store of life, baseball is the toy department.

> LOS ANGELES SPORTSCASTER. Quoted in: *Independent Magazine* (London, 28 Sept. 1991).

BATTLES

1   All quiet along the Potomac to-night,
No sound save the rush of the river,
While soft falls the dew on the face of the dead,
The picket's off duty forever.

> ETHEL LYNN BEERS (1827-79), U.S. poet. *The Picket Guard*, st. 6.

2   How are the mighty fallen in the midst of the battle! . . . How are the mighty fallen, and the weapons of war perished!

> BIBLE, HEBREW. *2 Samuel* 1:25, 27.

3   For if the trumpet give an uncertain sound, who shall prepare himself to the battle?

> BIBLE: NEW TESTAMENT. *1 Corinthians* 14:8.

4   There can be no reconciliation where there is no open warfare. There must be a battle, a brave boisterous battle, with pennants waving and cannon roaring, before there can be peaceful treaties and enthusiastic shaking of hands.

> MARY ELIZABETH BRADDON (1837-1915), English writer. *Lady Audley's Secret*, ch. 32 (1862).

5   The advantage of time and place in all practical actions is half a victory; which being lost is irrecoverable.

> SIR FRANCIS DRAKE (1540-96), English navigator. Letter, 1588, to Queen Elizabeth I, while awaiting news of the coming of the Spanish Armada.

6   Any coward can fight a battle when he's sure of winning, but give me the man who has pluck to fight when he's sure of losing. That's my way, sir; and there are many victories worse than a defeat.

> GEORGE ELIOT (1819-80), English novelist. Mr. Dempster, in *Janet's Repentance*, ch. 8 (published in *Blackwood's Magazine*, 1857; repr. in *Scenes of Clerical Life*, 1858).

7   My center is giving way, my right is in retreat; situation excellent. I shall attack.

> FERDINAND FOCH (1851-1929), French general. Message allegedly sent to General Joffre during Battle of the Marne, 8 Sept. 1914. Quoted in: B. H. Liddell Hart, *Reputations*, "Ferdi-

nand Foch" (1928). This was in all likelihood apocryphal, originating in Foch's repeated refrain to his troops, Attaquez! According to Liddell Hart, his insistence decimated the companies under his command, and the eventual German withdrawal astonished the exhausted French troops. Other variations of the message include, "Ma droite est enfoncée, ma gauche cède—tout va bien—j'attaque!" ("My right gives way, my left yields, everything's fine—I shall attack!").

8   A battle won is a battle which we will not acknowledge to be lost.

> FERDINAND FOCH (1851-1929), French general. Quoted in: B. H. Liddell Hart, *Reputations*, "Ferdinand Foch" (1928). This saying was a variation of one by French author Joseph de Maistre: "A lost battle is a battle which one believes lost: in a material sense no battle can be lost.".

9   War consisteth not in battle only, or the act of fighting; but in a tract of time, wherein the will to contend by battle is sufficiently known.

> THOMAS HOBBES (1588-1679), English philosopher. *Leviathan*, pt. 1, ch. 13 (1651).

10   When soldiers have been baptized in the fire of a battle-field, they have all one rank in my eyes.

> NAPOLEON BONAPARTE (1769-1821), French general, emperor. Quoted in: Ralph Waldo Emerson, *Representative Men*, "Napoleon" (1850).

11   No battle is worth fighting except the last one.

> J. ENOCH POWELL (b. 1912), British Conservative politician. Quoted in: *Observer* (London, 2 Jan. 1983).

12   In a battle all you need to make you fight is a little hot blood and the knowledge that it's more dangerous to lose than to win.

> GEORGE BERNARD SHAW (1856-1950), Anglo-Irish playwright, critic. The Statue, in *Man and Superman*, act 3.

13   After all the field of battle possesses many advantages over the drawing-room. There at least is no room for pretension or excessive ceremony, no shaking of hands or rubbing of noses, which make one doubt your sincerity, but hearty as well as hard hand-play. It at least exhibits one of the faces of humanity, the former only a mask.

> HENRY DAVID THOREAU (1817-62), U.S. philosopher, author, naturalist. *Journals* (1906), entry for 14 March 1838.

14   Dead battles, like dead generals, hold the military mind in their dead grip.

> BARBARA TUCHMAN (1912-89), U.S. historian. *The Guns of August*, ch. 2 (1962).

BEARDS

1   The hoary head is a crown of glory, if it be found in the way of righteousness.

> BIBLE, HEBREW. *Proverbs* 16:31.

2   There is always a period when a man with a beard shaves it off. This period does not last. He returns headlong to his beard.

> JEAN COCTEAU (1889-1963), French author, filmmaker. *Opium* (1929; tr. 1932; repr. 1957, p. 40).

3   If you teach a poor young man to shave himself, and keep his razor in order, you may contribute more to the happiness of his life than in giving him a thousand guineas. This sum may be soon spent, the regret only remaining of having foolishly consumed it; but in the other case, he escapes the frequent vexation of waiting for barbers, and of their sometimes dirty fingers, offensive breaths, and dull razors.

> BENJAMIN FRANKLIN (1706-90), U.S. statesman, writer. *Autobiography*, ch. 8 (written 1771-90; published 1868).

4   A beard signifies lice, not brains.

> GREEK PROVERB.

5   He that hath a beard is more than a youth, and he that hath no beard is less than a man.

> WILLIAM SHAKESPEARE (1564-1616), English dramatist, poet. Beatrice, in *Much Ado About Nothing*, act 2, sc. 1.

6   In England and America a beard usually means that its owner would rather be considered venerable than virile; on the continent of Europe it often means that its owner makes a special claim to virility.

> REBECCA WEST (1892-1983), British author. *The Thinking Reed*, ch. 10 (1936).

THE BEAT GENERATION

1   Kerouac opened a million coffee bars and sold a million pairs of Levis to both sexes. Woodstock rises from his pages.

> WILLIAM BURROUGHS (b. 1914), U.S. author. *The Adding Machine*, "Remembering Jack Kerouac" (1985).

2   That isn't writing at all, it's typing.

> TRUMAN CAPOTE (b. 1924), U.S. author. Report of a television discussion, referring to the Beat novelists. Quoted in: *New Republic* (Washington, D.C., 9 Feb. 1959).

3   I saw the best minds of my generation destroyed
> by madness, starving hysterical naked,
> dragging themselves through the negro streets at
> dawn looking for an angry fix,
> angelheaded hipsters burning for the ancient
> heavenly connection to the starry dynamo in the
> machinery of night,
> who poverty and tatters and hollow-eyed and high
> sat up smoking in the supernatural darkness of
> cold-water flats floating across the tops of cities
> contemplating jazz.

> ALLEN GINSBERG (b. 1926), U.S. poet. *Howl*.

4   But then they danced down the street like dingledodies, and I shambled after as I've been doing all my life after people who interest me, because the only people for me are the mad ones, the ones who are mad to live, mad to talk, mad to be saved, desirous of everything at the same time, the ones who never yawn or say a commonplace thing, but burn, burn, burn, like fabulous yellow roman candles exploding like spiders across the stars and in the middle you see the blue centerlight pop and everybody goes "Awww!"

> JACK KEROUAC (1922-69), U.S. author. *On the Road*, pt. 1, ch. 1 (1957). In an interview in *Playboy* (June 1959), Kerouac explained the origin of the label "Beat Generation": "John Clel-

lon Holmes . . . and I were sitting around trying to think up the meaning of the Lost Generation and the subsequent Existentialism and I said, `You know, this is really a beat generation,' and he leapt up and said, `That's it, that's right!'"

See also Kerouac on BOHEMIA.

THE BEATLES

1   They sort of Europeanized us all. Before them, our society hadn't been the Great Society as much as it had been the Revlon Society.

> DUSTIN HOFFMAN (b. 1937), U.S. screen actor. *Observer* (London, 19 Feb. 1989).

2   While the music is performed, the cameras linger savagely over the faces of the audience. What a bottomless chasm of vacuity they reveal! Those who flock round the Beatles, who scream themselves into hysteria, whose vacant faces flicker over the TV screen, are the least fortunate of their generation, the dull, the idle, the failures. . .

> PAUL JOHNSON (b. 1928), British journalist. "The Menace of Beatlism," in *New Statesman* (London, 28 Feb. 1964).

3   The trumpets of the Beatles are not the trumpets of Jericho which will cause the walls of socialism to come tumbling down.

> WLADYSLAW KOZDRA (b. 1920), Polish Communist Party official. Speech, at 8th Plenary Session, 16-17 May 1967, of the Central Committee of the Polish Communist Party. Quoted in: Timothy Ryback, *Rock Around the Bloc*, ch. 6 (1990).

4   One has to completely humiliate oneself to be what the Beatles were, and that's what I resent. I didn't know, I didn't foresee. It happened bit by bit, gradually, until this complete craziness is surrounding you, and you're doing exactly what you don't want to do with people you can't stand—the people you hated when you were ten.

> JOHN LENNON (1940-80), British rock musician. Quoted in: *Rolling Stone* (New York, 7 Jan. 1971).

See also Lennon on AWARDS; CHRISTIANITY AND CHRISTIANS; GETTING AHEAD; JOHN LENNON; The TWENTIETH CENTURY; THE 1960s.

BEAUTY

1   Beauty is one of the rare things that do not lead to doubt of God.

> JEAN ANOUILH (1910-87), French playwright. Thomas à Becket, in *Becket*, act 1.

2   Beauty depends on size as well as symmetry. No very small animal can be beautiful, for looking at it takes so small a portion of time that the impression of it will be confused. Nor can any very large one, for a whole view of it cannot be had at once, and so there will be no unity and completeness.

> ARISTOTLE (384 B.C.-322 B.C.), Greek philosopher. *Poetics*, ch. 7, sct. 4.

3   Strange that the vanity which accompanies beauty—excusable, perhaps, when there is such great beauty, or at any rate understandable—should persist after the beauty was gone.

MARY [ELIZABETH, COUNTESS VON] ARNIM (1866-1941), Australian-born British novelist. *Mr. Skeffington,* ch. 6 (1940).

4 I have learnt to love you late, Beauty at once so ancient and so new!

SAINT AUGUSTINE (354-430), Bishop of Hippo, theologian. *Confessions,* bk. 10, sct. 27 (c. 397).

5 Beauty is desired in order that it may be befouled; not for its own sake, but for the joy brought by the certainty of profaning it.

GEORGES BATAILLE (1897-1962), French novelist, critic. *Eroticism,* ch. 13 (1962).

6 There are as many kinds of beauty as there are habitual ways of seeking happiness.

CHARLES BAUDELAIRE (1821-67), French poet. *Curiosités Esthétiques,* "Salon of 1846," sct. 2 (1868; repr. in *The Mirror of Art,* ed. by Jonathan Mayne, 1955). Baudelaire may have been recalling a footnote in ch. 110 of Stendhal's *Histoire de la Peinture en Italie:* "La beauté est l'expression d'une certaine manière habituelle de chercher le bonheur."

7 All forms of beauty, like all possible phenomena, contain an element of the eternal and an element of the transitory—of the absolute and of the particular. Absolute and eternal beauty does not exist, or rather it is only an abstraction creamed from the general surface of different beauties. The particular element in each manifestation comes from the emotions: and just as we have our own particular emotions, so we have our own beauty.

CHARLES BAUDELAIRE (1821-67), French poet. *Curiosités Esthétiques,* "Salon of 1846," sct. 18 (1868; repr. in *The Mirror of Art,* ed. by Jonathan Mayne, 1955).

8 The idea that happiness could have a share in beauty would be too much of a good thing.

WALTER BENJAMIN (1892-1940), German critic, philosopher. *The Image of Proust,* sct. 1 (1929; repr. in *Illuminations,* ed. by Hannah Arendt, 1968).

9 Behold, thou art fair, my love; behold, thou art fair; thou hast doves' eyes within thy locks: thy hair is as a flock of goats, that appear from mount Gilead.

BIBLE, HEBREW. *Song of Solomon* 4:1.

10 Beauty. The power by which a woman charms a lover and terrifies a husband.

AMBROSE BIERCE (1842-1914), U.S. author. *The Devil's Dictionary* (1881-1906).

11 Beauty will be CONVULSIVE or will not be at all.

ANDRÉ BRETON (1896-1966), French surrealist. *Nadja* (1928).

12 Beauty in distress is much the most affecting beauty.

EDMUND BURKE (1729-97), Irish philosopher, statesman. *The Sublime and Beautiful,* Introduction (1756).

13 At the heart of all beauty lies something inhuman, and these hills, the softness of the sky, the outline of these trees at this very minute lose the illusory meaning with which we had clothed them, henceforth more remote than a lost paradise . . . that denseness and that strangeness of the world is absurd.

ALBERT CAMUS (1913-60), French-Algerian philosopher, author. *The Myth of Sisyphus,* ch. 1, "Absurd Walls" (1942; tr. 1955).

14 No; we have been as usual asking the wrong question. It does not matter a hoot what the mockingbird on the chimney is singing. . . . The real and proper question is: Why is it beautiful?

ANNIE DILLARD (b. 1945), U.S. author, poet. *Pilgrim at Tinker Creek,* ch. 7 (1974).

15 There are various orders of beauty, causing men to make fools of themselves in various styles . . . but there is one order of beauty which seems made to turn the heads not only of men, but of all intelligent mammals, even of women. It is a beauty like that of kittens, or very small downy ducks making gentle rippling noises with their soft bills, or babies just beginning to toddle and to engage in conscious mischief—a beauty with which you can never be angry, but that you feel ready to crush for inability to comprehend the state of mind into which it throws you.

GEORGE ELIOT (1819-80), English novelist. *Adam Bede,* bk. 1, ch. 7 (1859), describing the beauty of Hetty Sorrel.

16 It is generally a feminine eye that first detects the moral deficiencies hidden under the "dear deceit" of beauty.

GEORGE ELIOT (1819-80), English novelist. *Adam Bede,* bk. 1, ch. 15 (1859).

17 We ascribe beauty to that which is simple; which has no superfluous parts; which exactly answers its end; which stands related to all things; which is the mean of many extremes.

RALPH WALDO EMERSON (1803-82), U.S. essayist, poet, philosopher. *The Conduct of Life,* "Beauty" (1860).

18 White teeth, white hands, and neck as ivory white,
Black eyes, black brows, black hairs that hide
    delight:
Red lips, red cheeks, and tops of nipples red,
Long legs, long fingers, long locks of her head,
Short feet, short ears, and teeth in measure short,
Broad front, broad breast, broad hips in seemly
    sort,
Straight legs, straight nose and straight her
    pleasures place,
Full thighs, full buttocks, full her belly's space,
Thin lips, thin eyelids, and hair thin and fine,
Small mouth, small waist, small pupils of her
    eyes.

JOHN FLORIO (c. 1553-1625), English author, translator. *Second Frutes,* ch. 8 (1591), James's notion of beauty in a woman.

19 Beauty ought to look a little surprised: it is the emotion that best suits her face. . . . The beauty who does not look surprised, who accepts her position as her due—she reminds us too much of a prima donna.

E. M. FORSTER (1879-1970), British novelist, essayist. *Aspects of the Novel,* ch. 5 (1927).

20   The pursuit of beauty is much more dangerous nonsense than the pursuit of truth or goodness, because it affords a stronger temptation to the ego.

> NORTHROP FRYE (1912-91), Canadian literary critic. *Anatomy of Criticism,* "Mythical Phase: Symbol as Archetype" (1957).

21   There is certainly no absolute standard of beauty. That precisely is what makes its pursuit so interesting.

> JOHN KENNETH GALBRAITH (b. 1908), U.S. economist. Quoted in: *New York Times Magazine* (9 Oct. 1960).

22   Beauty is eternity gazing at itself in a mirror.

> KAHLIL GIBRAN (1883-1931), Lebanese poet, novelist. *The Prophet* (1923).

23   Beauty is composed of an eternal, invariable element whose quantity is extremely difficult to determine, and a relative element which might be, either by turns or all at once, period, fashion, moral, passion.

> JEAN-LUC GODARD (b. 1930), French filmmaker, author. "Defence and Illustration of Classical Construction," in *Cahiers du Cinéma* (Paris, 15 Sept. 1952; repr. in *Godard on Godard,* ed. and tr. by Tom Milne, 1968).

24   There have been many definitions of beauty in art. What is it? Beauty is what the untrained eyes consider abominable.

> EDMOND (1822-96) AND JULES DE GONCOURT (1830-70), French writers. *The Goncourt Journals* (1888-96; repr. in *Pages from the Goncourt Journal,* ed. by Robert Baldick, 1962), entry for 17 Feb. 1859.

25   Beauty for some provides escape,
Who gain a happiness in eyeing
The gorgeous buttocks of the ape
Or Autumn sunsets exquisitely dying.

> ALDOUS HUXLEY (1894-1963), British author. *Ninth Philosopher's Song.*

26   Where beauty is worshipped for beauty's sake as a goddess, independent of and superior to morality and philosophy, the most horrible putrefaction is apt to set in. The lives of the aesthetes are the far from edifying commentary on the religion of beauty.

> ALDOUS HUXLEY (1894-1963), British author. *Proper Studies,* "The Substitutes for Religion" (1927).

27   Beauty is a precious trace that eternity causes to appear to us and that it takes away from us. A manifestation of eternity, and a sign of death as well.

> EUGÈNE IONESCO (b. 1912), Rumanian-born French playwright. *Present Past—Past Present,* ch. 5 (1968).

28   "Beauty is truth, truth beauty,"—that is all
Ye know on earth, and all ye need to know.

> JOHN KEATS (1795-1821), English poet. *Ode on a Grecian Urn.*

29   I'm tired of all this nonsense about beauty being only skin-deep. That's deep enough. What do you want—an adorable pancreas?

> JEAN KERR (b. 1923), U.S. author, playwright. *The Snake Has All the Lines,* "Mirror, Mirror on the Wall" (1958).

30   To emphasize only the beautiful seems to me to be like a mathematical system that only concerns itself with positive numbers.

> PAUL KLEE (1879-1940), Swiss artist. *The Diaries of Paul Klee 1898-1918,* no. 759 (1957; tr. 1965), entry for March 1906.

31   Beauty is as relative as light and dark. Thus, there exists no beautiful woman, none at all, because you are never certain that a still far more beautiful woman will not appear and completely shame the supposed beauty of the first.

> PAUL KLEE (1879-1940), Swiss artist. *The Diaries of Paul Klee 1898-1918,* no. 871 (1957; tr. 1965), 1910 entry.

32   The ideal has many names, and beauty is but one of them.

> W. SOMERSET MAUGHAM (1874-1965), British author. *Cakes and Ale,* ch. 11 (1930).

33   Beauty is an ecstasy; it is as simple as hunger. There is really nothing to be said about it. It is like the perfume of a rose: you can smell it and that is all.

> W. SOMERSET MAUGHAM (1874-1965), British author. Ashenden, contesting the romanticization of beauty, in *Cakes and Ale,* ch. 11 (1930).

34   Beauty is ever to the lonely mind
A shadow fleeting; she is never plain.
She is a visitor who leaves behind
The gift of grief, the souvenir of pain.

> ROBERT NATHAN (1894-1985), U.S. novelist. *Beauty Is Ever to the Lonely Mind.*

35   In the beautiful, man sets himself up as the standard of perfection; in select cases he worships himself in it. . . . Man believes that the world itself is filled with beauty—he *forgets* that it is he who has created it. He alone has bestowed beauty upon the world—alas! only a very human, an all too human, beauty.

> FRIEDRICH NIETZSCHE (1844-1900), German philosopher. *Twilight of the Idols,* "Expeditions of an Untimely Man," aph. 19 (1889).

36   Beauty is our weapon against nature; by it we make objects, giving them limit, symmetry, proportion. Beauty halts and freezes the melting flux of nature.

> CAMILLE PAGLIA (b. 1947), U.S. author, critic, educator. *Sexual Personae,* ch. 2 (1990).

37   The flowers anew, returning seasons bring!
But beauty faded has no second spring.

> AMBROSE PHILIPS (1674-1749), English poet, politician. *Lobbing,* in *The First Pastoral* (1709).

38   I have a horror of people who speak about the beautiful. What is the beautiful? One must speak of problems in painting!

> PABLO PICASSO (1881-1973), Spanish artist. Quoted in: *Vogue* (New York, 1 Nov. 1956).

39   Beauty of whatever kind, in its supreme development, invariably excites the sensitive soul to tears.

> EDGAR ALLAN POE (1809-45), U.S. poet, critic, short-story writer. "The Rationale of Verse," in *The Pioneer* (March 1843).

40 The real sin against life is to abuse and destroy beauty, even one's own—even more, one's own, for that has been put in our care and we are responsible for its well-being.

> KATHERINE ANNE PORTER (1890-1980), U.S. short-story writer, novelist. Herr Freytag, in *Ship of Fools*, pt. 3 (1962).

41 Beauty is the still birth of suffering, every woman knows that.

> EMILY PRAGER (b. 1948), U.S. journalist, author. Lao Bing, in "A Visit from the Footbinder," in *Close Company: Stories of Mothers and Daughters* (ed. by Christine Park and Caroline Heaton, 1987).

42 A poor beauty finds more lovers than husbands.

> ENGLISH PROVERB (17th century), Collected in: George Herbert, *Outlandish Proverbs* (1640).

43 One evening I sat Beauty on my knees—And I found her bitter—And I reviled her.

> ARTHUR RIMBAUD (1854-1891), French poet. *Une Saison en Enfer*, (1874). For a pastiche of this image, see Dali on UGLINESS.

44 Beauty in art is often nothing but ugliness subdued.

> JEAN ROSTAND (1894-1977), French biologist, writer. *Pensées d'un Biologiste* (1939; repr. in *The Substance of Man*, 1962).

45 The beauty that addresses itself to the eyes is only the spell of the moment; the eye of the body is not always that of the soul.

> GEORGE SAND (1804-76), French novelist. *Handsome Lawrence*, ch. 1 (1872).

46 To me, fair friend, you never can be old
For as you were when first your eye I eyed,
Such seems your beauty still.

> WILLIAM SHAKESPEARE (1564-1616), English dramatist, poet. *Sonnet* 104.

47 Beauty is only the promise of happiness.

> STENDHAL (1783-1842), French author. *De l'Amour*, ch. 17, Footnote (1822).

48 Beauty always promises, but never gives anything.

> SIMONE WEIL (1909-43), French philosopher, mystic. "Human Personality" (written 1943; published in *La Table Ronde*, Dec. 1950; repr. in *Selected Essays*, ed. by Richard Rees, 1962).

49 Beauty seen is never lost,
God's colors all are fast.

> JOHN GREENLEAF WHITTIER (1807-92), U.S. poet. *Sunset on the Bearcamp*.

50 I have found that all ugly things are made by those who strive to make something beautiful, and that all beautiful things are made by those who strive to make something useful.

> OSCAR WILDE (1854-1900), Anglo-Irish playwright, author. *The Value of Art in Modern Life* (1884).

51 It is better to be beautiful than to be good. But . . . it is better to be good than to be ugly.

> OSCAR WILDE (1854-1900), Anglo-Irish author. Lord Henry, in *The Picture of Dorian Gray*, ch. 17 (1891).

52 The beauty myth moves for men as a mirage; its power lies in its ever-receding nature. When the gap is closed, the lover embraces only his own disillusion.

> NAOMI WOLF (b. 1962), U.S. author. *The Beauty Myth*, "Sex" (1990).

53 Taught from infancy that beauty is woman's sceptre, the mind shapes itself to the body, and roaming round its gilt cage, only seeks to adorn its prison.

> MARY WOLLSTONECRAFT (1759-97), English feminist writer. *A Vindication of the Rights of Women*, ch. 3 (1792).

See also Picasso on AESTHETICS; Aimée on AGE AND AGING; Greer on APPEARANCE; Meredith on COMMON SENSE; Maugham on HUMOR; Richter on PARTIES; Keats on POETS.

BED

1 My bed shall comfort me, my couch shall ease my complaint.

> BIBLE, HEBREW. Job, in *Job* 7:13.

2 The cool kindliness of sheets, that soon
Smooth away trouble; and the rough male kiss
Of blankets.

> RUPERT BROOKE (1887-1915), British poet. *The Great Lover*.

3 The bed is now as public as the dinner table and governed by the same rules of formal confrontation.

> ANGELA CARTER (1940-92), British author. *The Sadeian Woman*, "Speculative Finale" (1979).

4 Ample make this Bed—
Make this Bed with Awe—
In it wait till Judgment break
Excellent and Fair.

> EMILY DICKINSON (1830-86), U.S. poet. *The Complete Poems*, no. 829 (1955).

5 The happiest part of a man's life is what he passes lying awake in bed in the morning.

> SAMUEL JOHNSON (1709-84), English author, lexicographer. Quoted in: James Boswell, *Journal of a Tour to the Hebrides*, 24 Oct. 1773 (1785).

6 I have thought of a pulley to raise me gradually; but that would give me pain, as it would counteract my natural inclination. I would have something that can dissipate the *vis inertiae* and give elasticity to the muscles. . . . We can heat the body, we can cool it; we can give it tension or relaxation; and surely it is possible to bring it into a state in which rising from bed will not be a pain.

> SAMUEL JOHNSON (1709-84), English author, lexicographer. Quoted in: James Boswell, *Life of Samuel Johnson*, 19 Sept. 1777 (1791).

7 Sleeping in a bed—it is, apparently, of immense importance. Against those who sleep, from choice or necessity, elsewhere society feels righteously hostile. It is not done. It is disorderly, anarchical.

> ROSE MACAULAY (1881-1958), British novelist, essayist. *A Casual Commentary*, "Beds and 'Omes." (1925).

8 How it is I know not; but there is no place like a bed for confidential disclosures between friends. Man and wife, they say, there open the very bottom of their souls to each other; and some old couples often lie and chat over old times till nearly morning. Thus, then, in our hearts' honeymoon, lay I and Queequeg—a cosy, loving pair.

HERMAN MELVILLE (1819-91), U.S. author. *Moby-Dick*, ch. 10 (1851).

9 It is comforting when one has a sorrow to lie in the warmth of one's bed and there, abandoning all effort and all resistance, to bury even one's head under the cover, giving one's self up to it completely, moaning like branches in the autumn wind. But there is still a better bed, full of divine odors. It is our sweet, our profound, our impenetrable friendship.

MARCEL PROUST (1871-1922), French novelist. *Pleasures and Regrets*, "Regrets, Reveries, Changing Skies," no. 11 (1896; tr. 1948).

10 Bed is the poor man's opera.

ITALIAN PROVERB. Quoted in: Aldous Huxley, *Heaven and Hell* (1956).

11 What angel wakes me from my flow'ry bed?

WILLIAM SHAKESPEARE (1564-1616), English dramatist, poet. Titania, woken by Bottom's singing, in *A Midsummer Night's Dream*, act 3, sc. 1.

12 For I've been born and I've been wed—
All of man's peril comes of bed.

C. H. WEBB (1834-1905), U.S. journalist. *Dum Vivimus Vigilamus*.

See also Proverb on LOVERS; Johnson on NIGHT.

BEGGARS

1 All religions have honored the beggar. For he proves that in a matter at the same time as prosaic and holy, banal and regenerative as the giving of alms, intellect and morality, consistency and principles are miserably inadequate.

WALTER BENJAMIN (1892-1940), German critic, philosopher. *One-Way Street*, "No Vagrants!" (1928; repr. in *One-Way Street and Other Writings*, 1978).

2 God ordains that beggars should beg for greatness, as for all else, when greatness shines out of them, and they don't know it.

GEORGES BERNANOS (1888-1948), French novelist, political writer. *The Diary of a Country Priest*, ch. 5 (1936; tr. 1937).

3 Beggars . . . should be entirely abolished! Truly, it is annoying to give to them and annoying not to give to them.

FRIEDRICH NIETZSCHE (1844-1900), German philosopher. *Thus Spoke Zarathustra*, pt. 2, "Of the Compassionate" (1883-92; tr. 1961).

4 If begging should unfortunately be thy lot, knock at the large gates only.

ARAB PROVERB.

5 As for begging, it is safer to beg than to take, but it is finer to take than to beg.

OSCAR WILDE (1854-1900), Anglo-Irish playwright, author. *The Soul of Man under Socialism*, in *Fortnightly Review* (London, Feb. 1891; repr. 1895).

6 Give a beggar a dime and he'll bless you. Give him a dollar and he'll curse you for witholding the rest of your fortune. Poverty is a bag with a hole at the bottom.

ANZIA YEZIERSKA (1881?-1970), Polish author. *Red Ribbon on a White Horse*, ch. 9 (1950).

BEHAVIORISM

1 Of course, Behaviorism "works." So does torture. Give me a no-nonsense, down-to-earth behaviorist, a few drugs, and simple electrical appliances, and in six months I will have him reciting the Athanasian Creed in public.

W. H. AUDEN (1907-73), Anglo-American poet. *A Certain World*, "Behaviorism" (1970).

2 Suppose that humans happen to be so constructed that they desire the opportunity for freely undertaken productive work. Suppose that they want to be free from the meddling of technocrats and commissars, bankers and tycoons, mad bombers who engage in psychological tests of will with peasants defending their homes, behavioral scientists who can't tell a pigeon from a poet, or anyone else who tries to wish freedom and dignity out of existence or beat them into oblivion.

NOAM CHOMSKY (b. 1928), U.S. linguist, political analyst. *For Reasons of State*, "Psychology and Ideology" (1973; first published 1971 as a review of B. F. Skinner, *Beyond Freedom and Dignity*).

3 If we ever do end up acting just like rats or Pavlov's dogs, it will be largely because behaviorism has conditioned us to do so.

RICHARD DEAN ROSEN (b. 1949), U.S. journalist, critic. *Psychobabble: Fast Talk and Quick Cure in the Era of Feeling*, "Psychobabble" (1977).

BELIEF

1 Our systems, perhaps, are nothing more than an unconscious apology for our faults—a gigantic scaffolding whose object is to hide from us our favorite sin.

HENRI-FRÉDÉRIC AMIEL (1821-81), Swiss philosopher, poet. *Journal Intime*, (1882; tr. by Mrs. Humphrey Ward, 1892), entry for 13 Aug. 1865.

2 I started out by believing God for a newer car than the one I was driving. I started out believing God for a nicer apartment than I had. Then I moved up.

JIM BAKKER (b. 1940), U.S. evangelist. Quoted in: *New Yorker* (23 April 1990).

3 Confronted with the impossibility of remaining faithful to one's beliefs, and the equal impossibility of becoming free of them, one can be driven to the most inhuman excesses.

JAMES BALDWIN (1924-87), U.S. author. "Stranger in the Village," in *Harper's* (New York, Oct. 1953; repr. in *Notes of a Native Son*, pt. 2, 1955).

4 We have all had the experience of finding that our reactions and perhaps even our deeds have denied beliefs we thought were ours.

> JAMES BALDWIN (1924-87), U.S. author. "The Crusade of Indignation," in *Nation* (New York, 7 July 1956; repr. in *The Price of the Ticket*, 1985).

5 Every time a child says, "I don't believe in fairies," there is a fairy somewhere that falls down dead.

> J. M. BARRIE (1860-1937), British playwright. Peter, in *Peter Pan*, act 1.

6 Belief like any other moving body follows the path of least resistance.

> SAMUEL BUTLER (1835-1902), English author. *Samuel Butler's Notebooks* (1951, p. 220).

7 All are inclined to believe what they covet, from a lottery-ticket up to a passport to Paradise.

> LORD BYRON (1788-1824), English poet. *Byron's Letters and Journals*, vol. 3 (ed. by Leslie A. Marchand, 1974), entry for 27 Nov. 1813.

8 "One *can't* believe impossible things."
"I daresay you haven't had much practice," said the Queen. "When I was your age, I always did it for half-an-hour a day. Why, sometimes I've believed as many as six impossible things before breakfast."

> LEWIS CARROLL (1832-98), English writer, mathematician. Alice and the White Queen, in *Through the Looking Glass*, ch. 5 (1872).

9 As a first approximation, I define "belief" not as the object of believing (a dogma, a program, etc.) but as the subject's investment in a proposition, the *act* of saying it and considering it as true.

> MICHEL DE CERTEAU (1925-86), French author, critic. *The Practice of Everyday Life*, ch. 13 (1974).

10 Conviction is the conscience of intellect.

> SÉBASTIEN-ROCH NICOLAS DE CHAMFORT (1741-94), French writer, wit. *Maxims and Considerations*, vol. 1, no. 151 (1796; tr. 1926).

11 The abdication of Belief
Makes the Behavior small—
Better an ignis fatuus
Than no illume at all.

> EMILY DICKINSON (1830-86), U.S. poet. *The Complete Poems*, no. 1551 (1955).

12 Belief consists in accepting the affirmations of the soul; unbelief, in denying them.

> RALPH WALDO EMERSON (1803-82), U.S. essayist, poet, philosopher. *Representative Men*, "Montaigne, or The Skeptic" (1850).

13 We are born believing. A man bears beliefs as a tree bears apples.

> RALPH WALDO EMERSON (1803-82), U.S. essayist, poet, philosopher. *The Conduct of Life*, "Worship" (1860).

14 At eighteen our convictions are hills from which we look; at forty-five they are caves in which we hide.

> F. SCOTT FITZGERALD (1896-1940), U.S. author. *Bernice Bobs Her Hair*, sct. 2 (1920).

15 Devout believers are safeguarded in a high degree against the risk of certain neurotic illnesses; their acceptance of the universal neurosis spares them the task of constructing a personal one.

> SIGMUND FREUD (1856-1939), Austrian psychiatrist. *The Future of an Illusion*, ch. 8 (1927; repr. in *Complete Works*, vol. 21, ed. by James Strachey and Anna Freud, 1961).

16 Believing: it means believing in our own lies. And I can say that I am grateful that I got this lesson very early.

> GÜNTHER GRASS (b. 1927), German author. Television broadcast, 3 Nov. 1992, "Omnibus," BBC1.

17 It's an indulgence to sit in a room and discuss your beliefs as if they were a juicy piece of gossip.

> LILLIAN HELLMAN (1907-84), U.S. playwright. Sara Müller, in *Watch on the Rhine*, act 2.

18 As I get older I seem to believe less and less and yet to believe what I do believe more and more.

> DAVID JENKINS (b. 1925), British ecclesiastic, Bishop of Durham. Quoted in: *Daily Telegraph* (London, 2 Nov. 1988).

19 Every man who attacks my belief, diminishes in some degree my confidence in it, and therefore makes me uneasy; and I am angry with him who makes me uneasy.

> SAMUEL JOHNSON (1709-84), English author, lexicographer. Quoted in: James Boswell, *Life of Samuel Johnson*, 3 April 1775 (1791).

20 The word "belief" is a difficult thing for me. I don't *believe*. I must have a reason for a certain hypothesis. Either I *know* a thing, and then I know it—I don't need to believe it.

> CARL JUNG (1875-1961), Swiss psychiatrist. Interview, 1959, in Hugh Burnett, *Face to Face*, p. 51 (1964).

21 A belief is like a guillotine, just as heavy, just as light.

> FRANZ KAFKA (1883-1924), German novelist, short-story writer. *The Collected Aphorisms*, no. 87 (Oct. 1917-Feb. 1918; published in *Shorter Works*, vol. 1, ed. and tr. by Malcolm Pasley, 1973).

22 First we *have* to believe, and then we believe.

> G. C. LICHTENBERG (1742-99), German physicist, philosopher. *Aphorisms*, "Notebook K," aph. 55 (written 1765-99; tr. by R. J. Hollingdale, 1990).

23 With most people disbelief in a thing is founded on a blind belief in some other thing.

> G. C. LICHTENBERG (1742-99), German physicist, philosopher. *Aphorisms*, "Notebook L," aph. 81 (written 1765-99; tr. by R. J. Hollingdale, 1990).

24 What distinguishes the majority of men from the few is their inability to act according to their beliefs.

> HENRY MILLER (1891-1980), U.S. author. *The Cosmological Eye*, "An Open Letter to Surrealists Everywhere" (1939).

25 How many things served us but yesterday as articles of faith, which today we deem but fables?

> MICHEL DE MONTAIGNE (1533-92), French essayist. *Essays*, bk. 1, ch. 26, "It Is Folly to Refer Truth or Falsehood to Our Sufficiency" (1580-88; tr. by John Florio).

26 All beliefs are bald ideas.

> FRANCIS PICABIA (1878-1953), French painter, poet. *Jésus-*

Christ Rastaquoère, ch. 1 (1920; repr. in *Yes No: Poems and Sayings*, "Sayings," ed. by Rémy Hall, 1990).

27 The nobility of a human being is strictly independent of that of his convictions.

JEAN ROSTAND (1894-1977), French biologist, writer. *Carnets d'un Biologiste* (repr. in *The Substance of Man*, 1962).

28 When the intensity of emotional conviction subsides, a man who is in the habit of reasoning will search for logical grounds in favour of the belief which he finds in himself.

BERTRAND RUSSELL (1872-1970), British philosopher, mathematician. *A Free Man's Worship and Other Essays*, ch. 2 (1976).

29 To believe in something not yet proved and to underwrite it with our lives: it is the only way we can leave the future open. Man, surrounded by facts, permitting himself no surmise, no intuitive flash, no great hypothesis, no risk, is in a locked cell. Ignorance cannot seal the mind and imagination more surely.

LILLIAN SMITH (1897-1966), U.S. author. *The Journey*, ch. 15 (1954).

30 Conviction is the conscience of the mind.

MRS. HUMPHREY WARD (1851-1920), British novelist. Elsmere, recalling an axiom of Mr. Gray's, in *Robert Elsmere*, bk. 4, ch. 26 (1888).

See also Swift on ATHEISM; Russell on CREDULITY; CREEDS; Hazlitt on The PRESS.

BENEFACTORS

1 With regard to donations always expect the most from prudent people, who keep their own accounts.

JOSEPH ADDISON (1672-1719), English essayist. *Interesting Anecdotes, Memoirs, Allegories, Essays, and Poetical Fragments*, "Economy and Benevolence" (1794).

2 Because they did not see merit where they should have seen it, people, to express their regret, will go and leave a lot of money to the very people who will be the first to throw stones at the next person who has anything to say and finds a difficulty in getting a hearing.

SAMUEL BUTLER (1835-1902), English author. *Samuel Butler's Notebooks* (1951).

3 Most benefactors are like unskillful generals who take the city and leave the citadel intact.

SÉBASTIEN-ROCH NICOLAS DE CHAMFORT (1741-94), French writer, wit. *Maxims and Considerations*, vol. 2, no. 576 (1796; tr. 1926).

4 In your Salvation shelter I saw poverty, misery, cold and hunger. You gave them bread and treacle and dreams of heaven. I give from thirty shillings a week to twelve thousand a year. They find their own dreams; but I look after the drainage.

GEORGE BERNARD SHAW (1856-1950), Anglo-Irish playwright, critic. Undershaft, in *Major Barbara*, act 3. Undershaft, an armaments manufacturer, here argues with his daughter (Barbara) about the effects on the poor of their differing points of view.

5 Nobody shoots at Santa Claus.

ALFRED E. SMITH (1873-1944), U.S. Democratic politician, governor of New York. Phrase, used repeatedly in campaign speeches in 1936, attacking Franklin D. Roosevelt and the spendthrift policies of the New Deal

See also Thackeray on BOYS; Gilbert on PHILANTHROPY.

BEREAVEMENT

1 Tears are sometimes an inappropriate response to death. When a life has been lived completely honestly, completely successfully, or just completely, the correct response to death's perfect punctuation mark is a smile.

JULIE BURCHILL (b. 1960), British journalist, author. Quoted in: *Independent* (London, 5 Dec. 1989).

2 Never does one feel oneself so utterly helpless as in trying to speak comfort for great bereavement. I will not try it. Time is the only comforter for the loss of a mother.

JANE WELSH CARLYLE (1801-66), Scottish poet. Letter, 27 Dec. 1853, to her husband, Thomas Carlyle (published in *Letters and Memorials*, 1883).

3 It is extraordinary how the house and the simplest possessions of someone who has been left become so quickly sordid.... Even the stain on the coffee cup seems not coffee but the physical manifestation of one's inner stain, the fatal blot that from the beginning had marked one for ultimate aloneness.

COLEMAN DOWELL (1925-1985), U.S. novelist, dramatist, lyricist. *Mrs. October Was Here*, pt. 3, "Tasmania, Now" (1973), entry in Mrs. October's journals.

4 The death of a dear friend, wife, brother, lover, which seemed nothing but privation, somewhat later assumes the aspect of a guide or genius; for it commonly operates revolutions in our way of life, terminates an epoch of infancy or of youth which was waiting to be closed, breaks up a wonted occupation, or a household, or style of living, and allows the formation of new ones more friendly to the growth of character.

RALPH WALDO EMERSON (1803-82), U.S. essayist, poet, philosopher. *Essays*, "Compensation" (First Series, 1841).

5 The sorrow for the dead is the only sorrow from which we refuse to be divorced. Every other wound we seek to heal—every other affliction to forget: but this wound we consider it a duty to keep open—this affliction we cherish and brood over in solitude.

WASHINGTON IRVING (1783-1859), U.S. author. *The Sketch-Book*, "Rural Funerals" (1819-20).

6 Guilt is perhaps the most painful companion of death.

ELISABETH KÜBLER-ROSS (b. 1926), Swiss-born U.S. psychiatrist. *On Death and Dying*, ch. 9 (1969).

7 Grief that is dazed and speechless is out of fashion: the modern woman mourns her husband loudly and tells you the whole story of his death, which distresses her so much that she forgets not the slightest detail about it.

JEAN DE LA BRUYÈRE (1645-96), French writer, moralist. *Characters*, "Of Women," aph. 79 (1688).

8 If, as I can't help suspecting, the dead also feel the pains of separation (and this may be one of their purgatorial sufferings), then for both lovers, and for all pairs of lovers without exception, bereavement is a universal and integral part of our experience of love.

> C. S. LEWIS (1898-1963), British author. *A Grief Observed*, pt. 3 (1961). The book, published under a pseudonym, is an account of mourning for Lewis's dead wife.

9 If we could know
Which of us, darling, would be the first to go,
Who would be first to breast the swelling tide
And step alone upon the other side—
If we could know!

> JULIA HARRIS MAY (1833-1912), U.S. poet. *If We Could Know*.

10 Bereavement is a darkness impenetrable to the imagination of the unbereaved.

> IRIS MURDOCH (b. 1919), British novelist, philosopher. Montague Small, in *The Sacred and Profane Love Machine* (1974).

11 For precious friends hid in death's dateless night.

> WILLIAM SHAKESPEARE (1564-1616), English dramatist, poet. Sonnet 30.

12 Don't order any black things. Rejoice in his memory; and be radiant: leave grief to the children. Wear violet and purple. . . . Be patient with the poor people who will snivel: they don't know; and they think they will live for ever, which makes death a division instead of a bond.

> GEORGE BERNARD SHAW (1856-1950), Anglo-Irish playwright, critic. Letter of condolence, 5 July 1913 (published in *Bernard Shaw: Collected Letters*, vol. 3, 1965). Shaw added: "Let the children cry a little if they want to: it is natural."

13 Peace, peace! he is not dead, he doth not sleep—
He hath awakened from the dream of life—
'Tis we, who lost in stormy visions, keep
With phantoms an unprofitable strife.

> PERCY BYSSHE SHELLEY (1792-1822), English poet. *Adonais*, st. 39. These lines, written for John Keats, were recited by Mick Jagger on the death of fellow Rolling Stone Brian Jones, in London's Hyde Park, 5 July 1969.

14 The bitterest tears shed over graves are for words left unsaid and deeds left undone.

> HARRIET BEECHER STOWE (1811-96), U.S. novelist, anti-slavery campaigner. *Little Foxes*, ch. 3 (1865).

15 On the death of a friend, we should consider that the fates through confidence have devolved on us the task of a double living, that we have henceforth to fulfill the promise of our friend's life also, in our own, to the world.

> HENRY DAVID THOREAU (1817-1862), U.S. philosopher, author, naturalist. *Journals* (1906), entry for 28 Feb. 1840.

16 We feel at first as if some opportunities of kindness and sympathy were lost, but learn afterward that any *pure grief* is ample recompense for all. That is, if we are faithful;—for a spent grief is but sympathy with the soul that disposes events, and is as natural as the resin of Arabian trees.—Only nature has a right to grieve perpetually, for she only is innocent. Soon the ice will melt, and the blackbirds sing along the river which he frequented, as pleasantly as ever. The same everlasting serenity will appear in this face of God, and we will not be sorrowful, if he is not.

> HENRY DAVID THOREAU (1817-62), U.S. philosopher, author, naturalist. Letter, 2 March 1842, to Lucy Brown, sister-in-law of Ralph Waldo Emerson, following the death first of Thoreau's brother, then Emerson's son (published in *The Correspondence of Henry David Thoreau*, 1958).

17 A man's house burns down. The smoking wreckage represents only a ruined home that was dear through years of use and pleasant associations. By and by, as the days and weeks go on, first he misses this, then that, then the other thing. And when he casts about for it he finds that it was in that house. Always it is an *essential*—there was but one of its kind. It cannot be replaced. It was in that house. It is irrevocably lost. . . . It will be years before the tale of lost essentials is complete, and not till then can he truly know the magnitude of his disaster.

> MARK TWAIN (1835-1910), U.S. author. *Autobiography*, ch. 66 (ed. by Charles Neider, 1959). Twain was writing of the death of his daughter Susie Clemens of meningitis, 18 Aug. 1896, explaining how "a man, all unprepared, can receive a thunder-stroke like that and live. . . . It will take mind and memory months and possibly years to gather together the details and thus learn and know the whole extent of the loss."

18 They tell me, Lucy, thou art dead,
That all of thee we loved and cherished
Has with thy summer roses perished;
And left, as its young beauty fled,
An ashen memory in its stead.

> JOHN GREENLEAF WHITTIER (1807-92), U.S. poet. *Lucy Hooper*.

See also Saint-Exupéry on FUNERALS; Phelps on GRIEF; MOURNING; WIDOWHOOD.

BETRAYAL

1 Curse not the king, no not in thy thought; and curse not the rich in thy bedchamber: for a bird of the air shall carry the voice, and that which hath wings shall tell the matter.

> BIBLE, HEBREW. *Ecclesiastes* 10:20.

2 The Son of man goeth as it is written of him: but woe unto that man by whom the Son of man is betrayed! It had been good for that man if he had not been born.

> BIBLE: NEW TESTAMENT. *Matthew* 26:24.

3 They talk of a man betraying his country, his friends, his sweetheart. There must be a moral bond first. All a man can betray is his conscience.

> JOSEPH CONRAD (1857-1924), Polish-born English novelist. Razumov, in *Under Western Eyes*, pt. 1, ch. 2 (1911).

4 Anyone who hasn't experienced the ecstasy of betrayal knows nothing about ecstasy at all.

> JEAN GENET (1910-86), French playwright, novelist. *Prisoner of Love*, pt. 1 (1986; tr. 1989).

5 The most dangerous follower is he whose defection would destroy the whole party: that is to say, the best follower.

> FRIEDRICH NIETZSCHE (1844-1900), German philosopher. *The Wanderer and His Shadow*, aph. 290 (1880).

6
   Under the spreading chestnut tree
I sold you and you sold me:
There lie they, and here lie we
Under the spreading chestnut tree.

GEORGE ORWELL (1903-50), British author. Popular song in *Nineteen Eighty-Four,* pt. 1, ch. 7, and *passim* (1949).

See also TREACHERY.

THE BIBLE

1
   The pencil of the Holy Ghost hath laboured more in describing the afflictions of Job than the felicities of Solomon.

FRANCIS BACON (1561-1626), English philosopher, essayist, statesman. *Essays,* "Of Adversity" (1597-1625).

2
   Prosperity is the blessing of the Old Testament; adversity is the blessing of the New.

FRANCIS BACON (1561-1626), English philosopher, essayist, statesman. *Essays,* "Of Adversity" (1597-1625).

3
   All scripture is given by inspiration of God, and is profitable for doctrine, for reproof, for correction, for instruction in righteousness: that the man of God may be perfect, thoroughly furnished unto all good works.

BIBLE: NEW TESTAMENT. *2 Timothy* 3:16-7.

4
   Both read the Bible day and night,
But thou read'st black where I read white.

WILLIAM BLAKE (1757-1827), English poet, painter, engraver. *The Everlasting Gospel,* sct. A (c. 1818; published in *Complete Writings,* ed. by Geoffrey Keynes, 1957).

5
   Intense study of the Bible will keep any writer from being *vulgar,* in point of style.

SAMUEL TAYLOR COLERIDGE (1772-1834), English poet, critic. *Table Talk* (1835; published in *Specimens of the Table Talk of Samuel Taylor Coleridge,* ed. by Henry Nelson Coleridge; repr. in *Collected Works,* vol. 14, ed. by Kathleen Coburn, 1990).

6
   Immorality, perversion, infidelity, cannibalism, etc., are unassailable by church and civic league if you dress them up in the togas and talliths of the Good Book.

BEN HECHT (1893-1964), U.S. journalist, author, screenwriter. *A Child of the Century,* bk. 5, "Sex in Hollywood" (1954). Hecht was commenting on biblical epics solving "the fornication problem" in Hollywood.

7
   Well, Fitz, I looked all through that bible, it was in very fine print and stumbling on that great book Ecclesiastics, read it aloud to all who would listen. Soon I was alone and began cursing the bloody bible because there were no titles in it—although I found the source of practically every good title you ever heard of. But the boys, principally Kipling, had been there before me and swiped all the good ones so I called the book Men Without Women hoping it would have a large sale among the fairies and old Vassar Girls.

ERNEST HEMINGWAY (1899-1961), U.S. author. Letter, 15 Sept. 1927, to F. Scott Fitzgerald (published in *Selected Letters,* ed. by Carlos Baker, 1981), on searching for a title.

8
   There is much in the Bible against which every instinct of my being rebels, so much that I regret the necessity which has compelled me to read it through from beginning to end. I do not think that the knowledge which I have gained of its history and sources compensates me for the unpleasant details it has forced upon my attention.

HELEN KELLER (1880-1968), U.S. author, lecturer. *The Story of My Life,* pt. 1, ch. 21 (1903).

9
   We have used the Bible as if it were a mere special constable's handbook, an opium dose for keeping beasts of burden patient while they are overloaded.

CHARLES KINGSLEY (1819-75), English author, clergyman. From the second of his Letters to the Chartists by "Parson Lot" (published in the fourth issue of the Christian Socialist paper, *Politics for the People,* 27 May 1848).

10
   Either this is not the Gospel, or we are not Christians.

THOMAS LINACRE (c. 1460-1524), English humanist, physician. Alleged remark, made toward the end of his life, on reading the Gospels for the first time.

11
   The one book necessary to be understood by a divine, is the Bible; any others are to be read, chiefly, in order to understand that.

FRANCIS LOCKIER (1668-1740), English prelate, man of letters. Quoted in: Joseph Spence, *Anecdotes,* pt. 2, "1730-32" (1820).

12
   The English Bible—a book which, if everything else in our language should perish, would alone suffice to show the whole extent of its beauty and power.

THOMAS BABINGTON MACAULAY (1800-1859), English historian. "On John Dryden," in *Edinburgh Review* (Jan. 1828).

13
   Whenever we read the obscene stories, the voluptuous debaucheries, the cruel and torturous executions, the unrelenting vindictiveness, with which more than half the Bible is filled, it would be more consistent that we called it the word of a demon than the Word of God. It is a history of wickedness that has served to corrupt and brutalize mankind.

THOMAS PAINE (1737-1809), Anglo-American political theorist, writer. *The Age of Reason,* pt. 1, "Examination of the Old Testament" (1794).

14
   For eighteen hundred years, though perchance I have no right to say it, the New Testament has been written; yet where is the legislator who has wisdom and practical talent enough to avail himself of the light which it sheds on the science of legislation?

HENRY DAVID THOREAU (1817-62), U.S. philosopher, author, naturalist. *On the Duty of Civil Disobedience* (1849).

15
   My ground is the Bible. Yea, I am a Bible-bigot. I follow it in all things, both great and small.

JOHN WESLEY (1703-91), English preacher, founder of Methodism. *The Journal of John Wesley* (ed. by Nora Ratcliff, 1940), entry for 5 June 1766.

16
   The Bible is for the Government of the People, by the People, and for the People.

GENERAL PROLOGUE TO THE WYCLIFFE TRANSLATION OF THE BIBLE (1384).

See also Shakespeare on ARGUMENT.

BICYCLES

1   Consider a man riding a bicycle. Whoever he is, we can say three things about him. We know he got on the bicycle and started to move. We know that at some point he will stop and get off. Most important of all, we know that if at any point between the beginning and the end of his journey he stops moving and does not get off the bicycle he will fall off it. That is a metaphor for the journey through life of any living thing, and I think of any society of living things.

> WILLIAM GOLDING (1911–93), British author. "Utopias and Antiutopias," address, 13 Feb. 1977, to Les Anglicistes, Lille, France (repr. in *A Moving Target,* 1982).

2   If all feeling for grace and beauty were not extinguished in the mass of mankind at the actual moment, such a method of locomotion as cycling could never have found acceptance; no man or woman with the slightest aesthetic sense could assume the ludicrous position necessary for it.

> OUIDA [MARIE LOUISE DE LA RAMÉE] (1839-1908), English novelist. *Critical Studies,* "The Ugliness of Modern Life" (1900).

3   Let a man find himself, in distinction from others, on top of two wheels with a chain—at least in a poor country like Russia—and his vanity begins to swell out like his tyres. In America it takes an automobile to produce this effect.

> LEON TROTSKY (1879-1940), Russian revolutionary. *The History of the Russian Revolution,* vol. 2, ch. 7 (1933).

4   Cycle tracks will abound in Utopia.

> H. G. WELLS (1866-1946), British author. *A Modern Utopia,* ch. 2, sct. 3 (1905; repr. in *The Works of H. G. Wells,* vol. 9, 1925).

BIGOTRY

1   We call a man a bigot or a slave of dogma because he is a thinker who has thought thoroughly and to a definite end.

> G. K. CHESTERTON (1874-1936), British author. *All Things Considered,* "The Error of Impartiality" (1908).

2   Those who believe in *their* truth—the only ones whose imprint is retained by the memory of men—leave the earth behind them strewn with corpses. Religions number in their ledgers more murders than the bloodiest tyrannies account for, and those whom humanity has called divine far surpass the most conscientious murderers in their thirst for slaughter.

> E. M. CIORAN (b. 1911), Rumanian-born French philosopher. *A Short History of Decay,* ch. 1, "Itinerary of Hate" (1949).

3   Bigotry murders religion, to frighten fools with her ghost.

> C. C. COLTON (1780-1832), English author, clergyman. *Lacon,* vol. 1, no. 101 (1820).

4   Defoe says that there were a hundred thousand country fellows in his time ready to fight to the death against popery, without knowing whether popery was a man or a horse.

> WILLIAM HAZLITT (1778-1830), English essayist. *Sketches and Essays,* "On Prejudice" (1839).

5   When we believe ourselves in possession of the only truth, we are likely to be indifferent to common everyday truths.

> ERIC HOFFER (1902-83), U.S. philosopher. *The Passionate State of Mind,* aph. 83 (1955).

6   You are all fundamentalists with a top dressing of science. That is why you are the stupidest of conservatives and reactionists in politics and the most bigoted of obstructionists in science itself. When it comes to getting a move on you are all of the same opinion: stop it, flog it, hang it, dynamite it, stamp it out.

> GEORGE BERNARD SHAW (1856-1950), Anglo-Irish playwright, critic. A naturalist, addressing other members of the Caravan of the Curious, in *The Adventures of the Black Girl in Her Search for God* (1932),.

7   How it infuriates a bigot, when he is forced to drag out his dark convictions!

> LOGAN PEARSALL SMITH (1865-1946), U.S. essayist, aphorist. *Afterthoughts,* "Other People" (1931).

BILLS

1   Dreading that climax of all human ills
The inflammation of his weekly bills.

> LORD BYRON (1788-1824), English poet. *Don Juan,* cto. 3, st. 35.

2   I did send to you
For certain sums of gold, which you denied me.

> WILLIAM SHAKESPEARE (1564-1616), English dramatist, poet. Brutus to Cassius, in *Julius Caesar,* act 4, sc. 2.

3   It is only by not paying one's bills that one can hope to live in the memory of the commercial classes.

> OSCAR WILDE (1854-1900), Anglo-Irish playwright, author. *Phrases and Philosophies for the Use of the Young,* in *Chameleon* (London, Dec. 1894).

BIOGRAPHY

1   One of the new terrors of death.

> JOHN ARBUTHNOT (1667-1735), Scottish writer, physician. Quoted in: Robert Carruthers, *The Poetical Works of Pope,* vol. 1, ch. 3 (1853). Arbuthnot referred to Edmund Curll, publisher of brief biographies of eminent people following their deaths.

2   Biography should be written by an acute enemy.

> A. J. BALFOUR (1848-1930), British Conservative politician, prime minister. Quoted in: *Observer* (London, 30 Jan. 1927).

3   In writing biography, fact and fiction shouldn't be mixed. And if they are, the fictional points should be printed in red ink, the facts printed in black ink.

> CATHERINE DRINKER BOWEN (1897-1973), U.S. author. Quoted in: *Publisher's Weekly* (New York, 24 March 1958).

4   Show me a character whose life arouses my curiosity, and my flesh begins crawling with suspense.

> FAWN M. BRODIE (1915-81), U.S. biographer. Quoted in: *Los Angeles Times Home Magazine* (20 Feb. 1977).

5   No sooner does a great man depart, and leave his character as public property, than a crowd of little men rushes towards it. There they are gathered together, blinking up to it with such vision as they have, scanning it from afar, hovering round it this way and that, each cunningly endeavouring, by all arts, to catch some reflex of it in the little mirror of himself.

THOMAS CARLYLE (1795-1881), Scottish essayist, historian. *Critical and Miscellaneous Essays,* vol. 1, "Jean Paul Friedrich Richter" (1839; first published 1827).

6 A well-written life is almost as rare as a well-spent one.

THOMAS CARLYLE (1795-1881), Scottish essayist, historian. *Critical and Miscellaneous Essays,* vol. 1, "Jean Paul Friedrich Richter" (1839; first published 1827).

7 If those gentlemen would let me alone I should be much obliged to them. I would say, as Shakespeare would say . . . "Sweet Friend, for Jesus' sake forbear."

THOMAS CARLYLE (1795-1881), Scottish essayist, historian. *A Diary,* ch. 10 (ed. by H. Allingham and D. Radford, 1907). Carlyle, referring to biographers, was quoted by poet and diarist William Allingham in journal entry for 28 Dec. 1868.

8 Read no history: nothing but biography, for that is life without theory.

BENJAMIN DISRAELI (1804-81), English statesman, author. Peter Winter, in *Contarini Fleming,* pt. 1, ch. 23 (1832).

9 The secret of biography resides in finding the link between talent and achievement. A biography seems irrelevant if it doesn't discover the overlap between what the individual did and the life that made this possible. Without discovering that, you have shapeless happenings and gossip.

LEON EDEL (b. 1907), U.S. biographer, critic. Interview in *Writers at Work* (Eighth Series, ed. by George Plimpton, 1988).

10 There is properly no history, only biography.

RALPH WALDO EMERSON (1803-82), U.S. essayist, poet, philosopher. *Essays,* "History" (First Series, 1841). Thomas Carlyle similarly wrote, in his journal, 13 Jan. 1832, "Biography is the only true history."

11 Great geniuses have the shortest biographies.

RALPH WALDO EMERSON (1803-82), U.S. essayist, poet, philosopher. *Representative Men,* "Plato; or, the Philosopher" (1850).

12 There never was a good biography of a good novelist. There couldn't be. He is too many people, if he's any good.

F. SCOTT FITZGERALD (1896-1940), U.S. author. *The Crack-Up,* "Notebook L" (ed. by Edmund Wilson, 1945).

13 Biography is a very definite region bounded on the north by history, on the south by fiction, on the east by obituary, and on the west by tedium.

PHILIP GUEDALLA (1889-1944), British biographer, historian. Quoted in: *Observer* (London, 3 March 1929).

14 I am opposed to writing about the private lives of living authors and psychoanalyzing them while they are alive. Criticism is getting all mixed up with a combination of the Junior F.B.I.-men, discards from Freud and Jung and a sort of Columnist peep-hole and missing laundry list school. . . . Every young English professor sees gold in them dirty sheets now. Imagine what they can do

with the soiled sheets of four legal beds by the same writer and you can see why their tongues are slavering.

ERNEST HEMINGWAY (1899-1961), U.S. author. Letter, 21 Feb. 1952 (published in *Selected Letters,* ed. by Carlos Baker, 1981).

15 If the reviewing of books be . . . "an ungentle craft," the making of them is, for the most part, a dishonest one—and that department of literature which ought to be entrusted to those only who are distinguished for their moral qualities is, not infrequently, in the hands of authors totally devoid of good taste, good feeling, and generous sentiment. The writers of Lives have, in our time, assumed a licence not enjoyed by their more scrupulous predecessors—for they interweave the adventures of the living with the memoirs of the dead; and, pretending to portray the peculiarities which sometimes mark the man of genius, they invade the privacy and disturb the peace of his surviving associates.

JOHN CAM HOBHOUSE (1786-1869), British statesman. Draft for a letter, 7 Nov. 1830. Quoted in: Doris Langley Moore, *The Late Lord Byron,* ch. 11 (1961). Hobhouse was referring to the publication of John Galt's *Life of Lord Byron.*

16 A biography is like a handshake down the years, that can become an arm-wrestle.

RICHARD HOLMES (b. 1945), British biographer. Remark, 16 Oct. 1990, Waterstone's Debate. Quoted in: *Sunday Times* (London, 21 Oct. 1990).

17 Many heroes lived before Agamemnon; but all are unknown and unwept, extinguished in everlasting night, because they have no spirited chronicler.

HORACE (65 B.C.-8 B.C.), Roman poet. *Odes,* bk. 4, ode 9, st. 7.

18 Nobody can write the life of a man but those who have eat and drunk and lived in social intercourse with him.

SAMUEL JOHNSON (1709-84), English author, lexicographer. Quoted in: James Boswell, *Life of Samuel Johnson,* 20 March 1776 (1791). Johnson was referring specifically to Goldsmith's *Life of Parnell.* He later reiterated and qualified this statement: "They only who live with a man can write his life with any genuine exactness and discrimination; and few people who have lived with a man know what to remark about him."

19 A great biography should, like the close of a great drama, leave behind it a feeling of serenity. We collect into a small bunch the flowers, the few flowers, which brought sweetness into a life, and present it as an offering to an accomplished destiny. It is the dying refrain of a completed song, the final verse of a finished poem.

ANDRÉ MAUROIS (1885-1967), French author, critic. *The Art of Writing,* "The Writer's Craft," sct. 5 (1960).

20 The first thing to be done by a biographer in estimating character is to examine the stubs of his victim's cheque-books.

SILAS WEIR MITCHELL (1829-1914), U.S. physician, author. Quoted in: Harvey Cushing, *Life of Sir William Osler,* vol. 1, ch. 21 (1925).

21 Biography is: a system in which the contradictions of a human life are unified.

JOSÉ ORTEGA Y GASSET (1883-1955), Spanish essayist, philosopher. "In Search of Goethe from Within," in *Partisan Review* (New Brunswick, N.J., Dec. 1949; repr. in *The Dehumanization of Art and Other Essays,* 1968).

22 The facts of a person's life will, like murder, come out.

NORMAN SHERRY (b. 1925), British educator, author. Quoted in: *International Herald Tribune* (Paris, 15 Sept. 1989).

23 The immense majority of human biographies are a gray transit between domestic spasm and oblivion.

GEORGE STEINER (b. 1929), French-born U.S. critic, novelist. *In Bluebeard's Castle*, ch. 1 (1971).

24 There was never yet an uninteresting life. Such a thing is an impossibility. Inside of the dullest exterior there is a drama, a comedy, and a tragedy.

MARK TWAIN (1835-1910), U.S. author. The bos'n, in *The Refuge of the Derelicts*, ch. 4 (1905-6; published in *Fables of Man*, ed. by John S. Tuckey, 1972).

25 To write the lives of the great in separating them from their works necessarily ends by above all stressing their pettiness, because it is in their work that they have put the best of themselves.

SIMONE WEIL (1909-43), French philosopher, mystic. "Otto Rühle: Karl Marx," in *La Critique Sociale*, no. 11 (March 1934; reprinted in *Oeuvres Complètes*, vol. 2, no. 1, pt. 5, ch. 4).

26 All good biography, as all good fiction, comes down to the study of original sin, of our inherent disposition to choose death when we ought to choose life.

REBECCA WEST (1892-1983), British author. *Time and Tide* (1941). Quoted as epigraph to Victoria Glendinning, *Rebecca West: A Life* (1987).

27 Just how difficult it is to write biography can be reckoned by anybody who sits down and considers just how many people know the real truth about his or her love affairs.

REBECCA WEST (1892-1983), British author. "The Art of Skepticism," in *Vogue* (New York, 1 Nov. 1952).

28 Formerly we used to canonise our heroes. The modern method is to vulgarise them. Cheap editions of great books may be delightful, but cheap editions of great men are absolutely detestable.

OSCAR WILDE (1854-1900), Anglo-Irish playwright, author. Gilbert, in *The Critic as Artist*, pt. 1 (published in *Intentions*, 1891).

29 Almost any biographer, if he respects facts, can give us much more than another fact to add to our collection. He can give us the creative fact; the fertile fact; the fact that suggests and engenders.

VIRGINIA WOOLF (1882-1941), British novelist. *The Death of the Moth*, "The Art of Biography" (1942).

See also AUTOBIOGRAPHY; Wilde on DISCIPLES.

BIRDS

1 When thou seest an eagle, thou seest a portion of genius; lift up thy head!

WILLIAM BLAKE (1757-1827), English poet, painter, engraver. *The Marriage of Heaven and Hell*, plate 9 (1790-93).

2 A turkey is more occult and awful than all the angels and archangels. In so far as God has partly revealed to us an angelic world, he has partly told us what an angel means. But God has never told us what a turkey means. And if you go and stare at a live turkey for an hour or two, you will find by the end of it that the enigma has rather increased than diminished.

G. K. CHESTERTON (1874-1936), British author. *All Things Considered*, "Christmas" (1908).

3 O fret not after knowledge—I have none,
And yet my song comes native with the warmth.
O fret not after knowledge—I have none,
And yet the Evening listens.

JOHN KEATS (1795-1821), English poet. *What the Thrush Said*, from a letter to John Hamilton Reynolds (published in *Letters of John Keats*, no. 48, ed. by Frederick Page, 1954).

4 She was not quite what you would call refined. She was not quite what you would call unrefined. She was the kind of person that keeps a parrot.

MARK TWAIN (1835-1910), U.S. author. *Following the Equator*, ch. 57, "Pudd'nhead Wilson's New Calendar" (1897).

5 To a man, ornithologists are tall, slender, and bearded so that they can stand motionless for hours, imitating kindly trees, as they watch for birds.

GORE VIDAL (b. 1925), U.S. novelist, critic. *Armageddon? Essays 1983-1987*, "Mongolia!" (1987).

6 Happier of happy though I be, like them
I cannot take possession of the sky,
Mount with a thoughtless impulse, and wheel there,
One of a mighty multitude whose way
And motion is a harmony and dance
Magnificent.

WILLIAM WORDSWORTH (1770-1850), English poet. *Home at Grasmere* (written 1800; published as *The Recluse*, 1888).

BIRTH

1 Birth was the death of him.

SAMUEL BECKETT (1906-89), Irish dramatist, novelist. *Three Occasional Pieces*, "A Piece of Monologue" (1982).

2 Behold, I was shapen in iniquity; and in sin did my mother conceive me.

BIBLE, HEBREW. *Psalms* 51:5.

3 Every morn and every night
Some to misery are born.
Every morn and every night
Some are born to sweet delight.
Some are born to sweet delight,
Some are born to endless night.

WILLIAM BLAKE (1757-1827), English poet, painter, engraver. *Auguries of Innocence*. The last two lines of this passage were picked up by Jim Morrison, of the rock group The Doors, and incorporated in his 1967 song "End of the Night.".

4 My mother groan'd, my father wept,
Into the dangerous world I leapt;
Helpless, naked, piping loud,
Like a fiend hid in a cloud.

WILLIAM BLAKE (1757-1827), English poet, painter, engraver. *Infant Sorrow*, in *Songs of Experience* (1794).

5 The act of birth is the first experience of anxiety, and thus the source and prototype of the affect of anxiety.

> SIGMUND FREUD (1856-1939), Austrian psychiatrist. *The Interpretation of Dreams,* ch. 6, sct. E (1900), footnote added in 1909 (repr. in *Complete Works,* vol. 5, ed. by James Strachey and Anna Freud, 1953).

6 What is this talked-of mystery of birth
But being mounted bareback on the earth?

> ROBERT FROST (1874-1963), U.S. poet. *Riders.*

7 A man may be born, but in order to be born he must first die, and in order to die he must first awake.

> GEORGE GURDJIEFF (c. 1877-1949), Greek-Armenian religious teacher, mystic. Quoted in: P. D. Ouspensky, *In Search of the Miraculous,* ch. 11 (1949). Gurdjieff continued: "If a man dies without having been awakened he cannot be born. If a man is born without having died he may become an 'immortal thing.' Thus the fact that he has not 'died' prevents a man from being 'born'; the fact of his not having awakened prevents him from 'dying'; and should he be born without having died he is prevented from 'being.'"

8 Although it is generally known, I think it's about time to announce that I was born at a very early age.

> GROUCHO MARX (1895-1977), U.S. comic actor. *Groucho and Me,* ch. 1 (1959).

9 The first thing which I can record concerning myself is, that I was born. . . . These are wonderful words. This life, to which neither time nor eternity can bring diminution—this everlasting living soul, *began.* My mind loses itself in these depths.

> MARGARET OLIPHANT (1828-97), English novelist, historian. *Memoirs and Resolutions of Adam Graeme, of Mossgray,* vol. 1, bk. 1, ch. 1 (1852).

10 Compassion and shame come over one who considers how precarious is the origin of the proudest of living beings: often the smell of a lately extinguished lamp is enough to cause a miscarriage. And to think that from such a frail beginning a tyrant or butcher may be born! You who trust in your physical strength, who embrace the gifts of fortune and consider yourself not their ward but their son, you who have a domineering spirit, you who consider yourself a god as soon as success swells your breast, think how little could have destroyed you!

> PLINY THE ELDER (c. 23-79), Roman scholar. *Historia Naturalis,* bk. 7, sct. 7, subsct. 43-44.

11 And when our baby stirs and struggles to be born
It compels humility: what we began
Is now its own.

> ANNE RIDLER (b. 1912), British poet. *For a Child Expected.*

12 We are born, so to speak, twice over; born into existence, and born into life; born a human being, and born a man.

> JEAN-JACQUES ROUSSEAU (1712-78), Swiss-born French philosopher, political theorist. *Émile,* bk. 4 (1762).

13 Being born is like being kidnapped. And then sold into slavery.

> ANDY WARHOL (1928-87), U.S. Pop artist. *From A to B and Back Again,* ch. 6 (1975).

14 Our birth is but a sleep and a forgetting;
The soul that rises with us, our life's star,
Hath had elsewhere its setting,
And cometh from afar:
Not in entire forgetfulness,
And not in utter nakedness,
But trailing clouds of glory do we come
From God, who is our home.

> WILLIAM WORDSWORTH (1770-1850), English poet. *Ode: Intimations of Immortality from Recollections of Early Childhood.*

15 Our birth is nothing but our death begun.

> EDWARD YOUNG (1683-1765), English poet, dramatist. *Night Thoughts,* "The Complaint: Night V" (1742-46).

See also Hebrew Bible, Victoria, on CHILDBIRTH.

BIRTH CONTROL

1 The blind conviction that we have to do something about other people's reproductive behaviour, and that we may have to do it whether they like it or not, derives from the assumption that the world belongs to us, who have so expertly depleted its resources, rather than to them, who have not.

> GERMAINE GREER (b. 1939), Australian feminist writer. *Sex and Destiny,* ch. 14 (1984).

2 If we can get that realistic feminine morality working for us, if we can trust ourselves and so let women think and feel that an unwanted child or an oversize family is wrong—not ethically wrong, not against the rules, but morally wrong, all wrong, wrong like a thalidomide birth, wrong like taking a wrong step that will break your neck—if we can get feminine and human morality out from under the yoke of a dead ethic, then maybe we'll begin to get somewhere on the road that leads to survival.

> URSULA K. LE GUIN (b. 1929), U.S. author. "Moral and Ethical Implications of Family Planning," speech, March 1978, to Planned Parenthood symposium, Portland, Maine (repr. in *Dancing at the Edge of the World,* 1989).

3 It is now quite lawful for a Catholic woman to avoid pregnancy by a resort to mathematics, though she is still forbidden to resort to physics and chemistry.

> H. L. MENCKEN (1880-1956), U.S. journalist. *Notebooks,* "Minority Report" (1956).

4 Contraceptives should be used on all conceivable occasions.

> SPIKE MILLIGAN (b. 1918), British comedian, humorous writer. *The Last Goon Show of All,* 1972; BBC Radio program.

5 No woman can call herself free who does not own and control her body. No woman can call herself free until she can choose consciously whether she will or will not be a mother.

> MARGARET SANGER (1883-1966), U.S. pioneer of birth-control movement. Quoted in: *Parade* (New York, 1 Dec. 1963).

See also Theodore Roosevelt on PROCREATION.

BIRTHDAYS

1 Here lies interred in the eternity of the past, from whence there is no resurrection for the days—whatever there may be for the dust—the thirty-third year of an ill-spent life, which, after a lingering disease of many months sank into a lethargy, and expired, January 22d, 1821, A.D. leaving a successor inconsolable for the very loss which occasioned its existence.

> LORD BYRON (1788-1824), English poet. *Ravenna Journal* (published in *Byron's Letters and Journals*, vol. 8, ed. by Leslie A. Marchand, 1973-81), entry for 22 Jan. 1822.

2 To divide one's life by years is of course to tumble into a trap set by our own arithmetic. The calendar consents to carry on its dull wall-existence by the arbitrary timetables we have drawn up in consultation with those permanent commuters, Earth and Sun. But we, unlike trees, need grow no annual rings.

> CLIFTON FADIMAN (b. 1904), U.S. essayist. "On Being Fifty," in *Holiday* (Indianapolis, Feb. 1955).

3 The return of my birthday, if I remember it, fills me with thoughts which it seems to be the general care of humanity to escape.

> SAMUEL JOHNSON (1709-84), English author, lexicographer. Letter, 21 Sept. 1773, to Hester Thrale (published in *The Letters of Samuel Johnson*, vol. 1, no. 326, ed. by R. W. Chapman, 1952). Johnson added, "I can now look back upon threescore and four years, in which little has been done, and little has been enjoyed, a life diversified by misery, spent part in the sluggishness of penury, and part under the violence of pain, in gloomy discontent, or importunate distress."

4 I'm sorry you are wiser,
I'm sorry you are taller;
I liked you better foolish
And I liked you better smaller.

> ALINE MURRAY KILMER (1888-1944), U.S. poet. *For the Birthday of a Middle-Aged Child.*

5 Our birthdays are feathers in the broad wing of time.

> JEAN PAUL RICHTER (1763-1825), German novelist. *Titan,* ch. 47 (1803).

BLACK CULTURE

1 There is a kind of strength that is almost frightening in black women. It's as if a steel rod runs right through the head down to the feet.

> MAYA ANGELOU (b. 1928), U.S. author. Interview, "A Conversation with Maya Angelou," broadcast 21 Nov. 1973 (published in *Conversations with Maya Angelou*, 1989).

2 It is only in his music, which Americans are able to admire because a protective sentimentality limits their understanding of it, that the Negro in America has been able to tell his story.

> JAMES BALDWIN (1924-87), U.S. author. "Many Thousands Gone," in *Partisan Review* (New Brunswick, N.J., Nov.-Dec. 1951; repr. in *Notes of a Native Son*, pt. 1, 1955).

3 It is a peculiar sensation, this double-consciousness, this sense of always looking at one's self through the eyes of others, of measuring one's soul by the tape of a world that looks on in amused contempt and pity.

> W. E. B. DU BOIS (1868-1963), U.S. civil rights leader, author. *The Souls of Black Folk,* ch. 1 (1903).

4 However painful it may be for me to accept this conclusion, I am obliged to state it: for the black man there is only one destiny. And it is white.

> FRANTZ FANON (1925-61), Martiniquan psychiatrist, philosopher, political activist. *Black Skins, White Masks,* Introduction (1952; tr. 1967).

5 I am black: I am the incarnation of a complete fusion with the world, an intuitive understanding of the earth, an abandonment of my ego in the heart of the cosmos, and no white man, no matter how intelligent he may be, can ever understand Louis Armstrong and the music of the Congo.

> FRANTZ FANON (1925-61), Martiniquan psychiatrist, philosopher, political activist. *Black Skins, White Masks,* "The Woman of Color and the White Man" (1952; tr. 1967). Parody of the "polar" views of Martiniquan author Mayotte Capécia (as illustrated in her 1948 book *Je Suis Martiniquaise*).

6 Besides black art, there is only automation and mechanization.

> FEDERICO GARCÍA LORCA (1898-1936), Spanish poet, playwright. Interview, 1936, published in *Obras Completas*, vol. 3 (1986). Quoted in: *Poet in New York*, Introduction (1940; tr. 1988).

7 I think one of the nicest things that we created as a generation was just the fact that we could say, Hey, I don't like white people.

> NIKKI GIOVANNI (b. 1943), U.S. poet. *A Dialogue* (1973; with James Baldwin), from a conversation in London, 4 Nov. 1971.

8 The burden of being black is that you have to be superior just to be equal. But the glory of it is that, once you achieve, you have achieved, indeed.

> JESSE JACKSON (b. 1941), U.S. clergyman, civil rights leader. Quoted in: *Christian Science Monitor* (Boston, 26 Sept. 1979).

9 In America, the traditional routes to black identity have hardly been normal. Suicide (disappearance by imitation, or willed extinction), violence (hysterical religiosity, crime, armed revolt), and exemplary moral courage; none of these is normal.

> JUNE JORDAN (b. 1939), U.S. poet, civil rights activist. *Black Studies: Bringing Back the Person,* in *Evergreen Review* (Oct. 1969; repr. in *Moving towards Home: Political Essays*, 1989).

10 We do not need to minimize the poverty of the ghetto or the suffering inflicted by whites on blacks in order to see that the increasingly dangerous and unpredictable conditions of middle-class life have given rise to similar strategies for survival. Indeed the attraction of black culture for disaffected whites suggests that black culture now speaks to a general condition.

> CHRISTOPHER LASCH (b. 1932), U.S. historian. *The Culture of Narcissism,* ch. 3, "The Apotheosis of Individualism" (1979).

11 If we became students of Malcolm X, we would not have young black men out there killing each other like they're killing each other now. Young black men would not be impregnating young black women at the rate going on now. We'd not have the drugs we have now, or the alcoholism.

> SPIKE LEE (b. 1956), U.S. film director. Interview in *i-D* (London, Jan. 1993).

12 The Negro revolution is controlled by foxy white liberals, by the Government itself. But the Black Revolution is controlled only by God.

> MALCOLM X (1925-65), U.S. black leader. Speech, 1 Dec. 1963, New York City.

13 What then did you expect when you unbound the gag that muted those black mouths? That they would chant your praises? Did you think that when those heads that our fathers had forcibly bowed down to the ground were raised again, you would find adoration in their eyes?

> JEAN-PAUL SARTRE (1905-80), French philosopher, author. *Anthologie de la Nouvelle Poésie Nègre et Malgache*, Preface, "Orphée Noir" (1948).

14 There are those who believe Black people possess the secret of joy and that it is this that will sustain them through any spiritual or moral or physical devastation.

> ALICE WALKER (b. 1944), U.S. author, critic. *Possessing the Secret of Joy*, Epigraph (1992)

See also AFRICAN AMERICANS; Morrison on MULTICULTURALISM; RACISM.

BLAME

1 There's man all over for you, blaming on his boots the fault of his feet.

> SAMUEL BECKETT (1906-89), Irish dramatist, novelist. Vladimir, in *Waiting for Godot*, act 1.

2 He that rebuketh a man afterwards shall find more favour than he that flattereth with the tongue.

> BIBLE, HEBREW. *Proverbs* 28:23.

3 No one to blame! ... That was why most people led lives they hated, with people they hated. ... How wonderful to have someone to blame! How wonderful to live with one's nemesis! You may be miserable, but you feel forever in the right. You may be fragmented, but you feel absolved of all the blame for it. Take your life in your own hands, and what happens? A terrible thing: no one to blame.

> ERICA JONG (b. 1942), U.S. author. *How to Save Your Own Life*, "Intuition, extuition. . ." (1977).

4 They have a right to censure that have a heart to help.

> WILLIAM PENN (1644-1718), English religious leader, founder of Pennsylvania. *Some Fruits of Solitude*, pt. 1, no. 46 (1693).

5 There is a luxury in self-reproach. When we blame ourselves we feel no one else has a right to blame us.

> OSCAR WILDE (1854-1900), Anglo-Irish playwright, author. *The Picture of Dorian Gray*, ch. 8 (1891).

BLASPHEMY

1 All manner of sin and blasphemy shall be forgiven unto men: but the blasphemy against the Holy Ghost shall not be forgiven unto men.

> BIBLE: NEW TESTAMENT. *Matthew* 12:31.

2 I am very sorry to know and hear how unreverently that most precious jewel, the Word of God, is disputed, rhymed, sung and jangled in every ale-house and tavern, contrary to the true meaning and doctrine of the same.

> HENRY VIII (1491-1547), King of England. Speech to Parliament, 24 Dec. 1545.

3 We cannot assume the injustice of any actions which only create offense, and especially as regards religion and morals. He who utters or does anything to wound the conscience and moral sense of others, may indeed act immorally; but, so long as he is not guilty of being importunate, he violates no right.

> KARL WILHELM VON HUMBOLDT (1767-1835), German statesman, philologist. *The Limits of State Action*, ch. 10 (1792; repr. 1854; tr. and ed. by J. W. Burrow, 1969).

4 I don't think it is given to any of us to be impertinent to great religions with impunity.

> JOHN LE CARRÉ (b. 1931), British thriller writer. Quoted in: *International Herald Tribune* (Paris, 23 May 1989), referring to Salman Rushdie, author of *Satanic Verses*.

5 Where there is no belief, there is no blasphemy.

> SALMAN RUSHDIE (b. 1948), Indian-born British author. *The Satanic Verses*, "Return to Jahilia" (1988).

6 Your blasphemy, Salman, can't be forgiven. . . . To set your words against the Words of God.

> SALMAN RUSHDIE (b. 1948), Indian-born British author. Mahound, in *The Satanic Verses*, "Return to Jahilia" (1988), speaking to Salman the Persian. Despite his crime—of pitting "his Word against mine"—Salman is spared the death-sentence.

BLINDNESS

1 They be blind leaders of the blind. And if the blind lead the blind, both shall fall into the ditch.

> BIBLE: NEW TESTAMENT. *Matthew* 15:14.

2 But who would rush at a benighted man,
And give him two black eyes for being blind?

> THOMAS HOOD (1799-1845), English poet. *Ode to Rae Wilson*.

3 We may remark in passing that to be blind and beloved may, in this world where nothing is perfect, be among the most strangely exquisite forms of happiness. . . . The supreme happiness in life is the assurance of being loved; of being loved for oneself, even in spite of oneself; and this assurance the blind man possesses. In his affliction, to be served is to be caressed. Does he lack anything? no. Possessing love he is not deprived of light. A love, moreover, that is wholly pure. There can be no blindness where there is this certainty.

> VICTOR HUGO (1802-85), French poet, dramatist, novelist. *Les Misérables*, pt. 1, bk. 5, ch. 4 (1862).

4   O loss of sight, of thee I most complain!
Blind among enemies, O worse than chains,
Dungeon, or beggary, or decrepit age!
Light, the prime work of God, to me is extinct,
And all her various objects of delight
Annulled, which might in part my grief have
  eased.
Inferior to the vilest now become
Of man or worm; the vilest here excel me,
They creep, yet see; I, dark in light, exposed
To daily fraud, contempt, abuse and wrong,
Within doors, or without, still as a fool,
In power of others, never in my own;
Scarce half I seem to live, dead more than half.

JOHN MILTON (1608-74), English poet. Samson, in *Samson Agonistes*.

5   To be blind is not miserable; not to be able to bear blindness, that is miserable.

JOHN MILTON (1608-74), English poet. *Second Defence* (1654). Milton's sight was impaired from 1644, his blindness becoming complete in the Winter of 1651-52.

See also Keller on HANDSHAKES; Keller on MUSEUMS AND GALLERIES; VISION.

THE BLUES

1   The music of an unhappy people, of the children of disappointment; they tell of death and suffering and unvoiced longing toward a truer world, of misty wanderings and hidden ways.

W. E. B. DU BOIS (1868-1963), U.S. civil rights leader and author. *The Souls of Black Folk*, ch. 14 (1903).

2   Blues is easy to play, but hard to feel.

JIMI HENDRIX (1942-70), U.S. rock musician. Quoted in: Charles Shaar Murray, *Crosstown Traffic*, ch. 6 (1989).

3   Blues are the songs of despair, but gospel songs are the songs of hope.

MAHALIA JACKSON (1911-72), U.S. gospel singer. *Movin' On Up*, ch. 6 (written with Evan McLoud Wylie, 1966).

4   The blues was like that problem child that you may have had in the family. You was a little bit ashamed to let anybody see him, but you loved him. You just didn't know how other people would take it.

B. B. KING (b. 1925), U.S. blues guitarist. Quoted in: *Sunday Times* (London, 4 Nov. 1984).

5   Blues is to jazz what yeast is to bread—without it, it's flat.

CARMEN MCRAE (b. 1922), U.S. jazz singer. "Blues Is a Woman," speech, 2 July 1980, Newport Jazz Festival, New York City.

6   Who are our true rulers? The Negro poets, to be sure. Do they not set the fashion, and give laws to the public taste? Let one of them, in the swamps of Carolina, compose a new song, and it no sooner reaches the ear of a white amateur, than it is written down, amended (that is, almost spoilt), printed, and then put upon a course of

rapid dissemination, to cease only with the utmost bounds of Anglo-Saxondom, perhaps with the world. Meanwhile, the poor author digs away with his hoe, utterly ignorant of his greatness.

EILEEN SOUTHERN, U.S. author. *The Music of Black Americans* (1971; quoted from *Knickerbocker Magazine*, 1845).

See also JAZZ.

BOATS

See SHIPS AND BOATS.

THE BODY

1   Man consists of two parts, his mind and his body, only the body has more fun.

WOODY ALLEN (b. 1935), U.S. filmmaker. Boris (Allen), in the film *Love and Death* (directed and scripted by Woody Allen, 1975). Quoted in: Graham McCann, *Woody Allen: New Yorker*, ch. 2 (1990).

2   The basic Female body comes with the following accessories: garter belt, panti-girdle, crinoline, camisole, bustle, brassiere, stomacher, chemise, virgin zone, spike heels, nose ring, veil, kid gloves, fishnet stockings, fichu, bandeau, Merry Widow, weepers, chokers, barrettes, bangles, beads, lorgnette, feather boa, basic black, compact, Lycra stretch one-piece with modesty panel, designer peignoir, flannel nightie, lace teddy, bed, head.

MARGARET ATWOOD (b. 1939), Canadian novelist, poet, critic. "The Female Body," in *Michigan Quarterly Review* (1990; repr. in *The Best American Essays, 1991*, ed. by Joyce Carol Oates, 1991).

3   Thy navel is like a round goblet, which wanteth not liquor: thy belly is like an heap of wheat set about with lilies. Thy two breasts are like two young roes that are twins. Thy neck is like a tower of ivory; thine eyes like the fishpools in Heshbon, by the gate of Bath-rabbim: thy nose is as the tower of Lebanon which looketh toward Damascus. Thine head upon thee is like Carmel, and the hair of thine head like purple; the king is held in the galleries. How fair and how pleasant art thou, O love, for delights!

BIBLE, HEBREW. *Song of Solomon* 7:2-6.

4   The human body is not a thing or substance, given, but a continuous creation. The human body is an energy system ... which is never a complete structure; never static; is in perpetual inner self-construction and self-destruction; we destroy in order to make it new.

NORMAN O. BROWN (b. 1913), U.S. philosopher. *Love's Body*, ch. 8 (1967).

5   Why am I so determined to put the shoulder where it belongs? Women have very round shoulders that push forward slightly; this touches me and I say: "One must not hide that!" Then someone tells you: "The shoulder is on the back." I've never seen women with shoulders on their backs.

> COCO CHANEL (1883-1971), French couturiere. Quoted in: Marcel Haedrich, *Coco Chanel: Her Life, Her Secrets,* ch. 21 (1971).

6 A woman watches her body uneasily, as though it were an unreliable ally in the battle for love.

> LEONARD COHEN (b. 1934), Canadian singer, poet, novelist. *The Favourite Game,* bk. 3, ch. 8 (1963)

7 I don't think that the flesh is necessarily treacherous, evil, bad. It is cantankerous, and it is independent. The idea of independence is the key. It really is like colonialism. The colonies suddenly decide that they can and should exist with their own personality and should detach from the control of the mothercountry. At first the colony is perceived as being treacherous. It's a betrayal. Ultimately, it can be seen as the separation of a partner that could be very valuable as an equal rather than as something you dominate.

> DAVID CRONENBERG (b. 1943), Canadian filmmaker. *Cronenberg on Cronenberg,* ch. 5 (ed. by Chris Rodley, 1992).

8 I live in company with a body, a silent companion, exacting and eternal. He it is who notes that individuality which is the seal of the weakness of our race. My soul has wings, but the brutal jailer is strict.

> EUGÈNE DELACROIX (1798-1863), French artist. *The Journal of Eugène Delacroix* (tr. by Walter Pach, 1937), entry for 4 June 1824.

9 Men renounce whatever they have in common with women so as to experience no commonality with women; and what is left, according to men, is one piece of flesh a few inches long, the penis. The penis is sensate; the penis is the man; the man is human; the penis signifies humanity.

> ANDREA DWORKIN (b. 1946), U.S. feminist critic. *Pornography,* ch. 2 (1981).

10 Who has not felt the beauty of a woman's arm?— the unspeakable suggestions of tenderness that lie in the dimpled elbow, and all the varied gently-lessening curves, down to the delicate wrist, with its tiniest, almost imperceptible nicks in the firm softness.

> GEORGE ELIOT (1819-80), English novelist. *The Mill on the Floss,* bk. 6, ch. 10 (1860).

11 It is a sign of a dull nature to occupy oneself deeply in matters that concern the body; for instance, to be over much occupied about exercise, about eating and drinking, about easing oneself, about sexual intercourse.

> EPICTETUS (c. 55-c. 135), Greek Stoic philosopher. *Encheiridion,* no. 41 (tr. by T. W. H. Rolleston, 1881).

12 Our own theological Church, as we know, has scorned and vilified the body till it has seemed almost a reproach and a shame to have one, yet at the same time has credited it with power to drag the soul to perdition.

> ELIZA FARNHAM (1815-64), U.S. writer, feminist. *Woman and Her Era,* pt. 1, ch. 1 (1864).

13 Her body calculated to a millimeter to suggest a bud yet guarantee a flower.

> F. SCOTT FITZGERALD (1896-1940), U.S. author. *Tender Is the Night,* bk. 1, ch. 24 (1934), of Rosemary Hoyt.

14 Why do we spend years using up our bodies to nurture our minds with experience and find our minds turning then to our exhausted bodies for solace?

> ZELDA FITZGERALD (1900-1948), U.S. writer. Alabama Beggs, in *Save Me the Waltz,* ch. 4, sct. 3 (1932).

15 The only bodily organ which is really regarded as inferior is the atrophied penis, a girl's clitoris.

> SIGMUND FREUD (1856-1939), Austrian psychiatrist. *New Introductory Lectures on Psychoanalysis,* Lecture 31, "The Dissection of the Psychical Personality" (1933; repr. in *Complete Works,* vol. 22, ed. by James Strachey and Anna Freud, 1964). Freud was refuting the claims of "Individual Psychologists" that the "inferiority complex" can be traced back to self-perceived organic defects.

16 He had not an ounce of superfluous flesh on his bones, and leanness goes a great way towards gentility.

> ELIZABETH GASKELL (1810-65), English novelist. *Wives and Daughters,* ch. 4 (1866), of Mr. Gibson.

17 Man is a mind betrayed, not served, by his organs.

> EDMOND (1822-96) AND JULES DE GONCOURT (1830-70), French writers. *The Goncourt Journals* (1888-96; repr. in *Pages from the Goncourt Journal,* ed. by Robert Baldick, 1962), entry for 30 July 1861.

18 What we feel and think and are is to a great extent determined by the state of our ductless glands and viscera.

> ALDOUS HUXLEY (1894-1963), British novelist. *Music at Night,* "Meditation on El Greco" (1931).

19 Let me look at the foulness and ugliness of my body. Let me see myself as an ulcerous sore running with every horrible and disgusting poison.

> ST. IGNATIUS OF LOYOLA (1491-1556), Spanish churchman, founder of The Society of Jesus. *Spiritual Exercises,* "First Week," no. 58 (1548).

20 It is so much more difficult to live with one's body than with one's soul. One's body is so much more exacting: what it won't have it won't have, and nothing can make bitter into sweet.

> D. H. LAWRENCE (1885-1930), British author. Letter, 31 Oct. 1913 (published in *The Letters of D. H. Lawrence,* vol. 2, ed. by George J. Zytaruk and James T. Boulton, 1981).

21 The function of muscle is to pull and not to push, except in the case of the genitals and the tongue.

> LEONARDO DA VINCI (1425-1519), Italian artist, scientist. *The Notebooks of Leonardo da Vinci,* vol. 1, ch. 3 (ed. by Edward MacCurdy, 1938).

22 Many things about our bodies would not seem to us so filthy and obscene if we did not have the idea of nobility in our heads.

> G. C. LICHTENBERG (1742-99), German physicist, philosopher. *Aphorisms,* "Notebook D," aph. 6 (written 1765-99; tr. by R. J. Hollingdale, 1990).

23 Our bodies are shaped to bear children, and our lives are a working out of the processes of creation. All our ambitions and intelligence are beside that great elemental point.

PHYLLIS MCGINLEY (1905-78), U.S. poet, author. *The Province of the Heart*, "The Honor of Being a Woman" (1959).

24 When human beings have been fascinated by the contemplation of their own hearts, the more intricate biological pattern of the female has become a model for the artist, the mystic, and the saint. When mankind turns instead to what can be done, altered, built, invented, in the outer world, all natural properties of men, animals, or metals become handicaps to be altered rather than clues to be followed.

MARGARET MEAD (1901-78), U.S. anthropologist. *Male and Female*, ch. 8 (1949).

25 Our own physical body possesses a wisdom which we who inhabit the body lack. We give it orders which make no sense.

HENRY MILLER (1891-1980), U.S. author. *Big Sur and the Oranges of Hieronymous Bosch*, pt. 3, "Paradise Lost" (1957; also published separately as *A Devil in Paradise*, 1956).

26 Wondrous hole! Magical hole! Dazzlingly influential hole! Noble and effulgent hole! From this hole everything follows logically: first the baby, then the placenta, then, for years and years and years until death, a way of life. It is all logic, and she who lives by the hole will live also by its logic. It is, appropriately, logic with a hole in it.

CYNTHIA OZICK (b. 1928), U.S. novelist, short-story writer. "The Hole/Birth Catalog" (published in *The First Ms. Reader*, ed. by Francine Klagsbrun, 1972).

27 In order to live a fully human life we require not only *control* of our bodies (though control is a prerequisite); we must touch the unity and resonance of our physicality, our bond with the natural order, the corporeal grounds of our intelligence.

ADRIENNE RICH (b. 1929), U.S. poet. *Of Woman Born*, ch. 1 (1976).

28 Your body is the church where Nature asks to be reverenced.

MARQUIS DE SADE (1740-1814), French author. Mme Delbène, in *L'Histoire de Juliette, ou les Prospérités du Vice*, pt. 1 (1797).

29 What was my body to me? A kind of flunkey in my service. Let but my anger wax hot, my love grow exalted, my hatred collect in me, and that boasted solidarity between me and my body was gone.

ANTOINE DE SAINT-EXUPÉRY (1900-1944), French aviator, author. *Flight to Arras*, ch. 19 (1942).

30 The body is an instrument, the mind its function, the witness and reward of its operation.

GEORGE SANTAYANA (1863-1952), U.S. philosopher, poet. *The Life of Reason*, "Reason in Common Sense," ch. 9 (1905-6).

31 The brain may be regarded as a kind of parasite of the organism, a pensioner, as it were, who dwells with the body.

ARTHUR SCHOPENHAUER (1788-1860), German philosopher. *Parerga and Paralipomena*, "Aphorisms on the Wisdom of Life" (1851).

32 The authority of any governing institution must stop at its citizen's skin.

GLORIA STEINEM (b. 1934), U.S. feminist writer, editor. "Night Thoughts of a Media-Watcher," in *Ms.* (New York, Nov. 1981).

33 An impersonal and scientific knowledge of the structure of our bodies is the surest safeguard against prurient curiosity and lascivious gloating.

MARIE CARMICHAEL STOPES (1880-1958), British scientist, pioneer of birth control. *Married Love*, ch. 5 (1918).

34 Addiction, obesity, starvation (anorexia nervosa) are political problems, not psychiatric: each condenses and expresses a contest between the individual and some other person or persons in his environment over the control of the individual's body.

THOMAS SZASZ (b. 1920), U.S. psychiatrist. *The Second Sin*, "Control and Self-Control" (1973).

35 Every man is the builder of a temple, called his body, to the god he worships, after a style purely his own, nor can he get off by hammering marble instead. We are all sculptors and painters, and our material is our own flesh and blood and bones.

HENRY DAVID THOREAU (1817-62), U.S. philosopher, author, naturalist. *Walden*, "Higher Laws" (1854).

36 For male and female alike, the bodies of the other sex are messages signaling what we must do—they are glowing signifiers of our own necessities.

JOHN UPDIKE (b. 1932), U.S. author, critic. "The Female Body," in *Michigan Quarterly Review* (1990; repr. in *The Best American Essays, 1991*, ed. by Joyce Carol Oates, 1991).

See also Jong on AUTONOMY; Freud on EXCREMENT AND EXCRETION; Oates on MEN AND WOMEN; Traherne on SELF-KNOWLEDGE; Scruton on SEXUALITY.

BOHEMIA

1 Well, isn't Bohemia a place where everyone is as good as everyone else—and must not a waiter be a little less than a waiter to be a good Bohemian?

DJUNA BARNES (1892-1982), U.S. author, poet, columnist. "Becoming Intimate with the Bohemians," in *New York Morning Telegraph Sunday Magazine* (19 Nov. 1916; repr. in *Djuna Barnes's New York*, 1989).

2 Our affluent society contains those of talent and insight who are driven to prefer poverty, to choose it, rather than to submit to the desolation of an empty abundance. It is a strange part of the other America that one finds in the intellectual slums.

MICHAEL HARRINGTON (1928-89), U.S. social scientist, author. *The Other America*, ch. 5, sct. 1 (1962).

3 Bohemia is nothing more than the little country in which you do not live. If you try to obtain citizenship in it, at once the court and retinue pack the royal archives and treasure and move away beyond the hills.

> O. HENRY (WILLIAM SYDNEY PORTER) (1862-1910), U.S. short-story writer. *The Trimmed Lamp*, "The Country of Elusion" (1907).

4 It is not my fault that certain so-called bohemian elements have found in my writings something to hang their peculiar beatnik theories on.

> JACK KEROUAC (1922-69), U.S. author. Quoted in: *New York Journal-American* (8 Dec. 1960).

5 I could I trust starve like a gentleman. It's listed as part of the poetic training, you know.

> EZRA POUND (1885-1972), U.S. poet, critic. Letter, 1908, to Pound's father. Quoted in: Humphrey Carpenter, *A Serious Character*, pt. 2, ch. 1 (1988).

6 Bohemia has no banner. It survives by discretion.

> TENNESSEE WILLIAMS (1914-83), U.S. dramatist. Marguerite Gautier, in *Camino Real*, Block 7.

7 The modern picture of The Artist began to form: The poor, but free spirit, plebeian but aspiring only to be classless, to cut himself forever free from the bonds of the greedy bourgeoisie, to be whatever the fat burghers feared most, to cross the line wherever they drew it, to look at the world in a way they couldn't *see*, to be high, live low, stay young forever—in short, to be the bohemian.

> TOM WOLFE (b. 1931), U.S. journalist, author. *The Painted Word*, ch. 1 (1975).

BOOKS

1 That is a good book which is opened with expectation and closed with profit.

> A. BRONSON ALCOTT (1799-1888), U.S. educator, social reformer. *Table Talk*, bk. 1, "Books" (1877).

2 Some books are undeservedly forgotten; none are undeservedly remembered.

> W. H. AUDEN (1907-73), Anglo-American poet. *The Dyer's Hand*, pt. 1, "Reading" (1962).

3 Some books are to be tasted, others to be swallowed, and some few to be chewed and digested.

> FRANCIS BACON (1561-1626), English philosopher, essayist, statesman. *Essays*, "Of Studies" (1597-1625).

4 Footnotes are the finer-suckered surfaces that allow tentacular paragraphs to hold fast to the wider reality of the library.

> NICHOLSON BAKER (b. 1957), U.S. author. *The Mezzanine*, footnote to ch. 14 (1988).

5 When the book comes out it may hurt you—but in order for me to do it, it had to hurt me first. I can only tell you about yourself as much as I can face about myself.

> JAMES BALDWIN (1924-87), U.S. author. *A Dialogue* (1973; with Nikki Giovanni), from a conversation in London, 4 Nov. 1971.

6 Of all the ways of acquiring books, writing them oneself is regarded as the most praiseworthy method. . . . Writers are really people who write books not because

they are poor, but because they are dissatisfied with the books which they could buy but do not like.

> WALTER BENJAMIN (1892-1940), German critic, philosopher. *Unpacking My Library* (1931; repr. in *Illuminations*, ed. by Hannah Arendt, 1968).

7 There are worse crimes than burning books. One of them is not reading them.

> JOSEPH BRODSKY (b. 1940), Russian-born U.S. poet, critic. At press conference, Washington, D.C., on acceptance of U.S. poet laureateship. Quoted in: *Independent on Sunday* (London, 19 May 1991).

8 The lessons taught in great books are misleading. The commerce in life is rarely so simple and never so just.

> ANITA BROOKNER (b. 1938), British novelist, art historian. *Novelists in Interview* (ed. by John Haffenden, 1985).

9 Books, books, books!
I had found the secret of a garret-room
Piled high with cases in my father's name;
Piled high, packed large,—where, creeping in and out
Among the giant fossils of my past,
Like some small nimble mouse between the ribs
Of a mastodon, I nibbled here and there
At this or that box, pulling through the gap,
In heats of terror, haste, victorious joy,
The first book first. And how I felt it beat
Under my pillow, in the morning's dark,
An hour before the sun would let me read!
My books!

> ELIZABETH BARRETT BROWNING (1806-61), English poet. *Aurora Leigh*, bk. 1 (1857).

10 The oldest books are still only just out to those who have not read them.

> SAMUEL BUTLER (1835-1902), English author. *Samuel Butler's Notebooks* (1951, p. 266).

11 'Tis pleasant, sure, to see one's name in print;
A book's a book, although there's nothing in't.

> LORD BYRON (1788-1824), English poet. *English Bards and Scotch Reviewers*.

12 Buy good books, and read them; the best books are the commonest, and the last editions are always the best, if the editors are not blockheads.

> LORD CHESTERFIELD (1694-1773), English statesman, man of letters. Letter, 19 March 1750 (repr. in *The Letters of the Earl of Chesterfield to His Son*, vol. 2, no. 220, ed. by Charles Strachey, 1901). Chesterfield also warned, however, "Beware of the *Bibliomanie*."

13 If I had my way books would not be written in English, but in an exceedingly difficult secret language that only skilled professional readers and story-tellers could interpret. Then people like you would have to go to public halls and pay good prices to hear the professionals decode and read the books aloud for you. This plan would have the advantage of scaring off all amateur authors, retired politicians, country doctors and I-Married-a-Midget writers who would not have the patience to learn the secret language.

> ROBERTSON DAVIES (b. 1913), Canadian novelist, journalist. "A Chat with a Great Reader," in *Saturday Night* (Toronto, 11 Sept. 1954; repr. in *The Enthusiasms of Robertson Davies*, 1990).

14 There is no Frigate like a Book
To take us Lands away
Nor any Coursers like a Page
Of prancing Poetry.

> EMILY DICKINSON (1830-86), U.S. poet. *A Book (2)*, in *The Complete Poems*, no. 1263 (1955).

15 Books are fatal: they are the curse of the human race. Nine-tenths of existing books are nonsense, and the clever books are the refutation of that nonsense. The greatest misfortune that ever befell man was the invention of printing.

> BENJAMIN DISRAELI (1804-81), English statesman, author. Mr. Phoebus, in *Lothair*, ch. 29 (1870).

16 The good of a book lies in its being read. A book is made up of signs that speak of other signs, which in their turn speak of things. Without an eye to read them, a book contains signs that produce no concepts; therefore it is dumb.

> UMBERTO ECO (b. 1932), Italian semiologist, novelist. Brother William, in *The Name of the Rose*, "Fifth Day: Vespers" (1980; tr. 1983).

17 We are too civil to books. For a few golden sentences we will turn over and actually read a volume of four or five hundred pages.

> RALPH WALDO EMERSON (1803-82), U.S. essayist, poet, philosopher. *Journals* (1909-1914), entry for 7 June 1841.

18 I wish I could write a beautiful book to break those hearts that are soon to cease to exist: a book of faith and small neat worlds and of people who live by the philosophies of popular songs.

> ZELDA FITZGERALD (1900-1948), U.S. writer. Letter, May 1934, to her psychiatrist. Quoted in: Nancy Milford, *Zelda*, pt. 3, ch. 17 (1970).

19 The only books that influence us are those for which we are ready, and which have gone a little farther down our particular path than we have yet got ourselves.

> E. M. FORSTER (1879-1970), British novelist, essayist. *Two Cheers for Democracy*, "A Book That Influenced Me" (1951).

20 I don't think any good book is based on factual experience. Bad books are about things the writer already knew before he wrote them.

> CARLOS FUENTES (b. 1928), Mexican novelist, short-story writer. Quoted in: *International Herald Tribune* (Paris, 5 Nov. 1991).

21 A book that is shut is but a block.

> THOMAS FULLER (1654-1734), English physician. *Gnomologia*, no. 23 (1732).

22 I know every book of mine by its smell, and I have but to put my nose between the pages to be reminded of all sorts of things.

> GEORGE GISSING (1857-1903), English novelist, critic, essayist. Ryecroft, in *The Private Papers of Henry Ryecroft*, "Spring" (1903).

23 The good parts of a book may be only something a writer is lucky enough to overhear or it may be the wreck of his whole damn life—and one is as good as the other.

> ERNEST HEMINGWAY (1899-1961), U.S. author. Letter, 4 Sept. 1929, to F. Scott Fitzgerald (published in *Selected Letters*, ed. by Carlos Baker, 1981).

24 All good books are alike in that they are truer than if they had really happened and after you are finished reading one you will feel that all that happened to you and afterwards it all belongs to you; the good and the bad, the ecstasy, the remorse, and sorrow, the people and the places and how the weather was.

> ERNEST HEMINGWAY (1899-1961), U.S. author. "Old Newsman Writes: A Letter from Cuba," in *Esquire* (New York, Dec. 1934; repr. in *By-Line Ernest Hemingway*, ed. by William White, 1967).

25 The mortality of all inanimate things is terrible to me, but that of books most of all.

> WILLIAM DEAN HOWELLS (1837-1920), U.S. novelist, critic. Letter, 6 April 1903, to editor Charles Eliot Norton.

26 A bad book is as much of a labour to write as a good one; it comes as sincerely from the author's soul.

> ALDOUS HUXLEY (1894-1963), British author. *Point Counter Point*, ch. 13 (1928).

27 Books are the money of Literature, but only the counters of Science.

> THOMAS HENRY HUXLEY (1825-95), English biologist. "Universities: Actual and Ideal," address, 1874, Aberdeen (published in *Collected Essays*, vol. 3, 1893).

28 Books constitute capital. A library book lasts as long as a house, for hundreds of years. It is not, then, an article of mere consumption but fairly of capital, and often in the case of professional men, setting out in life, it is their only capital.

> THOMAS JEFFERSON (1743-1826), U.S. president. Letter, Sept. 1821, to former President James Madison.

29 *Borrowers of books*—those mutilators of collections, spoilers of the symmetry of shelves, and creators of odd volumes.

> CHARLES LAMB (1775-1834), English essayist, critic. *Essays of Elia*, "The Two Races of Men" (1820-23).

30 One sheds one's sicknesses in books—repeats and presents again one's emotions, to be master of them.

> D. H. LAWRENCE (1885-1930), British author. Letter, 26 Oct. 1913 (published in *The Letters of D. H. Lawrence*, vol. 2, ed. by George J. Zytaruk and James T. Boulton, 1981).

31 I can't bear art that you can walk round and admire. A book should be either a bandit or a rebel or a man in the crowd.

> D. H. LAWRENCE (1885-1930), British author. Letter, 22 Jan. 1925 (published in *The Letters of D. H. Lawrence*, vol. 5, ed. by James T. Boulton, 1987).

32 For a good book has this quality, that it is not merely a petrification of its author, but that once it has been tossed behind, like Deucalion's little stone, it acquires a separate and vivid life of its own.

> CAROLINE LEJEUNE (1897-1973), British film critic. *Chestnuts in Her Lap, 1936-1946*, Introduction (1947).

33 A book is a mirror: if an ape looks into it an apostle is hardly likely to look out.

> G. C. LICHTENBERG (1742-99), German physicist, philosopher. *Aphorisms*, "Notebook E," aph. 49 (written 1765-99; tr. by R. J. Hollingdale, 1990).

34 Do we write books so that they shall merely be read? Don't we also write them for employment in the household? For one that is read from start to finish, thousands are leafed through, other thousands lie motionless, others are jammed against mouseholes, thrown at rats, others are stood on, sat on, drummed on, have gingerbread baked on them or are used to light pipes.

> G. C. LICHTENBERG (1742-99), German physicist, philosopher. *Aphorisms*, "Notebook E," aph. 65 (written 1765-99; tr. by R. J. Hollingdale, 1990).

35 I feel a kind of reverence for the first books of young authors. There is so much aspiration in them, so much audacious hope and trembling fear, so much of the heart's history, that all errors and shortcomings are for a while lost sight of in the amiable self assertion of youth.

> HENRY WADSWORTH LONGFELLOW (1807-82), U.S. poet. *Drift-Wood*, "Table-Talk" (1857; repr. in *Complete Works*, vol. 1, 1886).

36 For books are more than books, they are the life
The very heart and core of ages past,
The reason why men lived and worked and died,
The essence and quintessence of their lives.

> AMY LOWELL (1874-1925), U.S. poet. *The Boston Athenaeum*, in *A Dome of Many-Colored Glass* (1912).

37 Books are the bees which carry the quickening pollen from one to another mind.

> JAMES RUSSELL LOWELL (1819-91), U.S. poet, editor. "Nationality in Literature," in *North American Review* (July 1849), reviewing Longfellow's *Kavanagh*.

38 Everything in the world exists to end up in a book.

> STÉPHANE MALLARMÉ (1842-98), French Symbolist poet. *Variations sur un sujet*, "Quant au Livre: Le Livre, Instrument Spirtuelle" (published in *La Revue Blanche*, Paris, July 1895; repr. in *Mallarmé: The Poems*, ed. and tr. by Keith Bosley, 1977).

39 There are people who read too much: bibliobibuli. I know some who are constantly drunk on books, as other men are drunk on whiskey or religion. They wander through this most diverting and stimulating of worlds in a haze, seeing nothing and hearing nothing.

> H. L. MENCKEN (1880-1956), U.S. journalist. *Minority Report: H. L. Mencken's Notebooks*, no. 71 (1956).

40 This is not a book. This is libel, slander, defamation of character. This is not a book, in the ordinary sense of the word. No, this is a prolonged insult, a gob of spit in the face of Art, a kick in the pants to God, Man, Destiny, Time, Love, Beauty . . . what you will. I am going to sing for you, a little off key perhaps, but I will sing.

> HENRY MILLER (1891-1980), U.S. author. *Tropic of Cancer* (1934). The book was banned in the United States on grounds of obscenity until 1961, when it became a bestseller.

41 A book is a part of life, a manifestation of life, just as much as a tree or a horse or a star. It obeys its own rhythms, its own laws, whether it be a novel, a play, or a diary. The deep, hidden rhythm of life is always there— that of the pulse, the heart beat.

> HENRY MILLER (1891-1980), U.S. author. *The Cosmological Eye*, "Un Etre Etoile" (1939).

42 Until it is kindled by a spirit as flamingly alive as the one which gave it birth a book is dead to us. Words divested of their magic are but dead hieroglyphs.

> HENRY MILLER (1891-1980), U.S. author. *The Books in My Life*, ch. 7 (1951).

43 For books are not absolutely dead things, but do contain a potency of life in them to be as active as that soul was whose progeny they are; nay, they do preserve as in a vial the purest efficacy and extraction of that living intellect that bred them. I know they are as lively, and as vigorously productive, as those fabulous dragon's teeth; and being sown up and down, may chance to spring up armed men.

> JOHN MILTON (1608-74), English poet. *Areopagitica: a Speech for the Liberty of Unlicensed Printing to the Parliament of England* (1644).

44 Books and marriage go ill together.

> MOLIÈRE (1622-73), French dramatist. Martine, in *Les Femmes Savantes*, act 5, sc. 3.

45 Every abridgement of a good book is a fool abridged.

> MICHEL DE MONTAIGNE (1533-92), French essayist. *Essays*, bk. 3, ch. 8, "Of the Art of Conferring" (tr. by John Florio, 1580).

46 A bibliophile of little means is likely to suffer often. Books don't slip from his hands but fly past him through the air, high as birds, high as prices.

> PABLO NERUDA (1904-73), Chilean poet. *Memoirs*, ch. 11 (1974; tr. 1977).

47 The books one reads in childhood, and perhaps most of all the bad and good bad books, create in one's mind a sort of false map of the world, a series of fabulous countries into which one can retreat at odd moments throughout the rest of life, and which in some cases can survive a visit to the real countries which they are supposed to represent.

> GEORGE ORWELL (1903-50), British author. "Riding Down from Bangor" (1946; repr. in *The Collected Essays, Journalism and Letters of George Orwell*, vol. 4, ed. by Sonia Orwell and Ian Angus, 1968).

48 The last thing one discovers in composing a work is what to put first.

> BLAISE PASCAL (1623-62), French scientist, philosopher. *Pensées* (1670; no. 976 ed. by Krailsheimer, no. 19 ed. by Brunschvicg).

49 The books one has written in the past have two surprises in store: one couldn't write them again, and wouldn't want to.

> JEAN ROSTAND (1894-1977), French biologist, writer. *Pensées d'un Biologiste* (1939; repr. in *The Substance of Man*, ch. 8, "A Biologist's Thoughts," 1962).

50 The real risks for any artist are taken . . . in pushing the work to the limits of what is possible, in the attempt to increase the sum of what it is possible to think. Books become good when they go to this edge and risk falling over it—when they endanger the artist by reason of what he has, or has not, *artistically* dared.

> SALMAN RUSHDIE (b. 1947), Indian-born British author. *Imaginary Homelands* (1982).

51   A book is a version of the world. If you do not like it, ignore it; or offer your own version in return.

> SALMAN RUSHDIE (b. 1947), Indian-born British author. Quoted in: *Independent on Sunday* (London, 4 Feb. 1990).

52   How long most people would look at the best book before they would give the price of a large turbot for it?

> JOHN RUSKIN (1819-1900), English art critic, author. *Sesame and Lilies*, Lecture 1, sct. 32 (1865; repr. in *The Works of John Ruskin*, vol. 18, ed. by E. T. Cook and Alexander Weddesburn, 1905).

53   What I like best is a book that's at least funny once in a while . . . . What really knocks me out is a book that, when you're all done reading it, you wish the author that wrote it was a terrific friend of yours and you could call him up on the phone whenever you felt like it. That doesn't happen much, though.

> J.D. SALINGER (b. 1919), U.S. author. The narrator (Holden Caulfield), in *The Catcher in the Rye*, ch. 3 (1951).

54   Buying books would be a good thing if one could also buy the time to read them in: but as a rule the purchase of books is mistaken for the appropriation of their contents.

> ARTHUR SCHOPENHAUER (1788-1860), German philosopher. *Parerga and Paralipomena*, vol. 2, ch. 23, sct. 296a (1851).

55   O, let my books be then the eloquence
And dumb presagers of my speaking breast.

> WILLIAM SHAKESPEARE (1564-1616), English dramatist, poet. *Sonnet* 23.

56   Here, my dear Lucy, hide these books. Quick, quick! Fling "Peregrine Pickle" under the toilette—throw "Roderick Random" into the closet—put "The Innocent Adultery" into "The Whole Duty of Man"; thrust "Lord Aimworth" under the sofa! cram "Ovid" behind the bolster; there—put "The Man of Feeling" into your pocket. Now for them.

> RICHARD BRINSLEY SHERIDAN (1751-1816), Anglo-Irish dramatist. Lydia Languish, in *The Rivals*, act 1, sc. 2.

57   A book is like a man—clever and dull, brave and cowardly, beautiful and ugly. For every flowering thought there will be a page like a wet and mangy mongrel, and for every looping flight a tap on the wing and a reminder that wax cannot hold the feathers firm too near the sun.

> JOHN STEINBECK (1902-68), U.S. author. *Writers at Work*, "On Publishing" (Fourth Series, ed. by George Plimpton, 1977).

58   The age of the book is almost gone.

> GEORGE STEINER (b. 1929), French-born U.S. critic, novelist. Quoted in: *Daily Mail* (London, 27 June 1988).

59   Books are good enough in their own way, but they are a mighty bloodless substitute for life.

> ROBERT LOUIS STEVENSON (1850-94), Scottish novelist, essayist, poet. *Virginibus Puerisque*, "An Apology for Idlers" (1881).

60   Everywhere I have sought rest and not found it, except sitting in a corner by myself with a little book.

> ATTRIBUTED TO THOMAS À KEMPIS (1380-1471), German monk, mystic. *The Imitation of Christ,* Preface to 1617 ed., inscribed on his picture at Zwoll, Holland, where he is buried.

61   Books, not which afford us a cowering enjoyment, but in which each thought is of unusual daring; such as an idle man cannot read, and a timid one would not be entertained by, which even make us dangerous to existing institution—such call I good books.

> HENRY DAVID THOREAU (1817-62), U.S. philosopher, author, naturalist. *A Week on the Concord and Merrimack Rivers,* "Sunday" (1849).

62   How many a man has dated a new era in his life from the reading of a book! The book exists for us, perchance, that will explain our miracles and reveal new ones. The at present unutterable things we may find somewhere uttered.

> HENRY DAVID THOREAU (1817-62), U.S. philosopher, author, naturalist. *Walden,* "Reading" (1854).

63   The Brahmins say that in their books there are many predictions of times in which it will rain. But press those books as strongly as you can, you can not get out of them a drop of water. So you can not get out of all the books that contain the best precepts the smallest good deed.

> LEO TOLSTOY (1828-1910), Russian novelist, philosopher. Letter, 23 Feb. 1903 (published in *Tolstoy's Letters*, vol. 2, 1978).

64   An empty book is like an infant's soul, in which anything may be written. It is capable of all things, but containeth nothing. I have a mind to fill this with profitable wonders.

> THOMAS TRAHERNE (1636-74), English clergyman, poet, mystic. *Centuries,* "First Century," no. 1 (written c. 1672; first published 1908).

65   A good book is the best of friends, the same today and for ever.

> MARTIN TUPPER (1810-89), British author, poet, inventor. *Proverbial Philosophy*, Series 1, "Of Reading" (1838).

66   A big leather-bound volume makes an ideal razorstrap. A thin book is useful to stick under a table with a broken caster to steady it. A large, flat atlas can be used to cover a window with a broken pane. And a thick, old-fashioned heavy book with a clasp is the finest thing in the world to throw at a noisy cat.

> MARK TWAIN (1835-1910), U.S. author. Quoted in: *Greatly Exaggerated,* "Gifts" (ed. by Alex Ayres, 1988). This was Twain's reply to a lady who asked Twain if he thought a book was the most useful gift one could give.

67   Ideally a book would have no order to it, and the reader would have to discover his own.

> RAOUL VANEIGEM (b. 1934), Belgian Situationist philosopher. *The Revolution of Everyday Life,* Introduction (1967; tr. 1983).

68   The books we think we ought to read are poky, dull, and dry;
The books that we would like to read we are ashamed to buy;
The books that people talk about we never can

recall;
And the books that people give us, oh, they're the
worst of all.

CAROLYN WELLS (1870-1942), U.S. author. *On Books*.

69 Camerado! This is no book;
Who touches this touches a man.

WALT WHITMAN (1819-92), U.S. poet. *So Long!*, pt. 4.

70 Old books that have ceased to be of service should
no more be abandoned than should old friends who have
ceased to give pleasure.

SIR PEREGRINE WORSTHORNE (b. 1923), British journalist.
Quoted in: *Independent on Sunday* (London, 5 Aug. 1990).

71 Thy books should, like thy friends, not many be,
Yet such wherein men may thy judgment see.

WILLIAM WYCHERLEY (1640-1716), English dramatist. *Advice
to a Young Friend on the Choice of His Library*.

See also Lamb on BORROWING AND LENDING; Milton on CENSORSHIP; Bierce,
Dahlberg, on CRITICISM AND THE ARTS; Emerson on CRITICS; Ruskin on LIBRARIES;
LITERATURE; Byron on OBSCENITY; READING; Emerson on TRANSLATION.

BOOKS: BESTSELLERS

1 A best-seller is the golden touch of mediocre talent.

CYRIL CONNOLLY (1903-74), British critic. Quoted in: David
Pryce-Jones, *Journal and Memoir*, ch. 11 (1983).

2 No one can write a best seller by trying to. He must
write with complete sincerity; the clichés that make you
laugh, the hackneyed characters, the well-worn situations, the commonplace story that excites your derision,
seem neither hackneyed, well worn nor commonplace to
him. . . . The conclusion is obvious: you cannot write
anything that will convince unless you are yourself convinced. The best seller sells because he writes with his
heart's blood.

W. SOMERSET MAUGHAM (1874-1966), British author. *A
Writer's Notebook* (1949), 1941 entry.

3 The principle of procrastinated rape is said to be the
ruling one in all the great bestsellers.

V. S. PRITCHETT (b. 1901), British author, critic. *The Living
Novel*, "Clarissa" (1946).

4 A best-seller is the gilded tomb of a mediocre talent.

LOGAN PEARSALL SMITH (1865-1946), U.S. essayist, aphorist.
Afterthoughts, "Art and Letters" (1931).

BOOKS: CLASSICS

1 Books that have become classics—books that have
had their day and now get more praise than perusal—
always remind me of retired colonels and majors and
captains who, having reached the age limit, find themselves retired on half pay.

T. B. ALDRICH (1836-1907), U.S. writer, editor. *Ponkapog
Papers*, "Leaves from a Notebook" (1903).

2 Definition of a classic: a book everyone is assumed
to have read and often thinks they have.

ALAN BENNETT (b. 1934), British playwright. *Independent on
Sunday* (London, 27 Jan. 1991).

3 A classic is a book that has never finished saying
what it has to say.

ITALO CALVINO (1923-85), Italian author, critic. "Why Read the
Classics?," in *L'Espresso* (Rome, 28 June 1981; repr. in *The Literature Machine*, 1987). This is one of a series of definitions of "a
classic" in Calvino's essay.

4 A truly great book should be read in youth, again in
maturity and once more in old age, as a fine building
should be seen by morning light, at noon and by moonlight.

ROBERTSON DAVIES (b. 1913), Canadian novelist, journalist.
"Too Much, Too Fast," in *Peterborough Examiner* (Canada, 16
June 1962; repr. in *The Enthusiasms of Robertson Davies*, 1979).

5 There are certain books in the world which every
searcher for truth must know: the Bible, the Critique of
Pure Reason, the Origin of Species, and Karl Marx's
Capital.

W. E. B. DU BOIS (1868-1963), U.S. civil rights leader, author.
The Seventh Son, vol. 2, "Communism, Marxism and the Negro
Problem" (1933; repr. 1971).

6 There are books . . . which take rank in your life
with parents and lovers and passionate experiences, so
medicinal, so stringent, so revolutionary, so authoritative.

RALPH WALDO EMERSON (1803-82), U.S. essayist, poet,
philosopher. *Society and Solitude*, "Books" (1870).

7 A book is never a masterpiece: it becomes one.
Genius is the talent of a dead man.

EDMOND (1822-96) AND JULES DE GONCOURT (1830-70),
French writers, journalists. *The Goncourt Journals* (1956; repr. in
Pages from the Goncourt Journal, ed. by Robert Baldick, 1962),
entry for 23 July 1864.

8 The praise of ancient authors proceeds not from the
reverence of the dead, but from the competition and
mutual envy of the living.

THOMAS HOBBES (1588-1679), English philosopher. *Leviathan*,
"A Review and Conclusion" (1651).

9 The light that radiates from the great novels time
can never dim, for human existence is perpetually being
forgotten by man and thus the novelists' discoveries,
however old they may be, will never cease to astonish.

MILAN KUNDERA (b. 1929), Czech author, critic. Quoted in:
Guardian (London, 3 June 1988).

10 What a sense of security in an old book which Time
has criticized for us!

JAMES RUSSELL LOWELL (1819-91), U.S. poet, editor. *My Study
Windows*, "Library of Old Authors" (1871).

11 Every man with a bellyful of the classics is an
enemy to the human race.

HENRY MILLER (1891-1980), U.S. author. *Tropic of Cancer*
(1934; repr. 1979, p. 276).

12 There is but one way left to save a classic: to give up revering him and use him for our own salvation.

> JOSÉ ORTEGA Y GASSET (1883-1955), Spanish essayist, philosopher. "In Search of Goethe from Within," in *Partisan Review* (New Brunswick, N.J., Dec. 1949; repr. in *The Dehumanization of Art and Other Essays*, 1968).

13 A classic is classic not because it conforms to certain structural rules, or fits certain definitions (of which its author had quite probably never heard). It is classic because of a certain eternal and irrepressible freshness.

> EZRA POUND (1885-1972), U.S. poet, critic. *ABC of Reading*, prefatory "Warning" (1934).

14 For what are the classics but the noblest thoughts of man? They are the only oracles which are not decayed, and there are such answers to the most modern inquiry in them as Delphi and Dodona never gave. We might as well omit to study Nature because she is old.

> HENRY DAVID THOREAU (1817-62), U.S. philosopher, author, naturalist. *Walden*, "Reading" (1854).

15 A classic—something that everybody wants to have read and nobody wants to read.

> MARK TWAIN (1835-1910), U.S. author. Speech, quoting Professor Caleb Winchester, 20 Nov. 1900, Nineteenth Century Club, New York City, (published in *Mark Twain's Speeches*, ed. by Albert Bigelow Paine, 1923). Twain varied the epigram in *Following the Equator*, ch. 25 (1897): "Classic"—a book which people praise and don't read.

16 A classic is a book that doesn't have to be written again.

> CARL VAN DOREN (1885-1950), U.S. man of letters. Quoted by James Thurber in: *Bermudian* (Nov. 1950).

17 The fact is, the public make use of the classics of a country as a means of checking the progress of Art. They degrade the classics into authorities. They use them as bludgeons for preventing the free expression of Beauty in new forms.

> OSCAR WILDE (1854-1900), Anglo-Irish playwright, author. *The Soul of Man under Socialism*, in *Fortnightly Review* (London, Feb. 1891; repr. 1895).

See also Konrád on WRITERS.

BOREDOM

1 Boredom is like a pitiless zooming in on the epidermis of time. Every instant is dilated and magnified like the pores of the face.

> JEAN BAUDRILLARD (b. 1929), French semiologist. *Cool Memories*, ch. 3 (1987; tr. 1990).

2 Boredom is the dream bird that hatches the egg of experience. A rustling in the leaves drives him away.

> WALTER BENJAMIN (1892-1940), German critic, philosopher. *The Storyteller*, sct. 8 (1936; repr. in *Illuminations*, ed. by Hannah Arendt, 1968).

3 Is boredom anything less than the sense of one's faculties slowly dying?

> JOHN BERGER (b. 1926), British author, critic. *A Fortunate Man* (1967; repr. 1976, p. 133).

4 The world is eaten up by boredom. . . . You can't see it all at once. It is like dust. You go about and never notice, you breathe it in, you eat and drink it. It is sifted so fine, it doesn't even grit on your teeth. But stand still for an instant and there it is, coating your face and hands. To shake off this drizzle of ashes you must be for ever on the go. And so people are always "on the go."

> GEORGES BERNANOS (1888-1948), French novelist, political writer. *The Diary of a Country Priest*, ch. 1 (1936; tr. 1937).

5 Life, friends, is boring. We must not say so.
After all, the sky flashes, the great sea yearns,
we ourselves flash and yearn,
and moreover my mother told me as a boy
(repeatedly) "Ever to confess you're bored
means you have no
Inner Resources." I conclude now I have no
inner resources, because I am heavy bored.

> JOHN BERRYMAN (1914-72), U.S. poet. *The Dreamsongs*, no. 14 (1969).

6 Boredom is always counter-revolutionary. Always.

> GUY DEBORD (b. 1931), French Situationist philosopher. *The Incomplete Works of the Situationist International*, "The Bad Old Days Will End" (Nov. 1963; ed. by Christopher Gray, 1974).

7 My mind rebels at stagnation. Give me problems, give me work, give me the most abstruse cryptogram, or the most intricate analysis, and I am in my own proper atmosphere. I can dispense then with artificial stimulants. But I abhor the dull routine of existence. I crave for mental exaltation.

> SIR ARTHUR CONAN DOYLE (1859-1930), English author. Sherlock Holmes, in *The Sign of Four*, ch. 1 (1890).

8 Boredom is not an end-product, is comparatively rather an early stage in life and art. You've got to go by or past or through boredom, as through a filter, before the clear product emerges.

> F. SCOTT FITZGERALD (1896-1940), U.S. author. *The Crack-Up*, "Notebook I" (ed. by Edmund Wilson, 1945).

9 There are moments when, faced with our lack of success, I wonder whether we are failures, proud but impotent. One thing reassures me as to our value: the boredom that afflicts us. It is the hall-mark of quality in modern men.

> EDMOND (1822-96) AND JULES DE GONCOURT (1830-70), French writers. *The Goncourt Journals* (1888-96; repr. in *Pages from the Goncourt Journal*, ed. by Robert Baldick, 1962), entry for 30 July 1861.

10 To do the same thing over and over again is not only boredom: it is to be controlled by rather than to control what you do.

> HERACLITUS (c. 535 B.C.-c. 475 B.C.), Greek philosopher. *Herakleitos and Diogenes*, pt. 1, fragment 89 (tr. by Guy Davenport, 1976).

11 Since boredom advances and boredom is the root of all evil, no wonder, then, that the world goes backwards, that evil spreads. This can be traced back to the very beginning of the world. The gods were bored; therefore they created human beings.

> SØREN KIERKEGAARD (1813-55), Danish philosopher. *Either/Or*, vol. 1, "Rotation of Crops" (1843; tr. 1987).

12 The life of a creator is not the only life nor perhaps the most interesting which a man leads. There is a time for play and a time for work, a time for creation and a time for lying fallow. And there is a time, glorious too in its own way, when one scarcely exists, when one is a complete void. I mean—when boredom seems the very stuff of life.

> HENRY MILLER (1891-1980), U.S. author. *The Books in My Life*, ch. 12 (1951).

13 Only the most acute and active animals are capable of boredom.—A theme for a great poet would be *God's boredom* on the seventh day of creation.

> FRIEDRICH NIETZSCHE (1844-1900), German philosopher. *The Wanderer and His Shadow*, aph. 56 (1880).

14 Against boredom the gods themselves fight in vain.

> FRIEDRICH NIETZSCHE (1844-1900), German philosopher. *The Anti-Christ*, aph. 48 (1895). Nietzsche refers to Schiller's *Maid of Orleans*, act 3, sc. 6: "Against stupidity the gods themselves fight in vain."

15 Man finds nothing so intolerable as to be in a state of complete rest, without passions, without occupation, without diversion, without effort. Then he feels his nullity, loneliness, inadequacy, dependence, helplessness, emptiness.

> BLAISE PASCAL (1623-62), French scientist, philosopher. *Pensées* (1670; no. 622 ed. by Krailsheimer, no. 131 ed. by Brunschvicg).

16 Boredom is . . . a vital problem for the moralist, since at least half the sins of mankind are caused by the fear of it.

> BERTRAND RUSSELL (1872-1970), British philosopher, mathematician. *The Conquest of Happiness*, ch. 4 (1930).

17 Boredom is just the reverse side of fascination: both depend on being outside rather than inside a situation, and one leads to the other.

> SUSAN SONTAG (b. 1933), U.S. essayist. *On Photography*, "America, Seen Through Photographs, Darkly" (1977).

See also ENNUI; Nietzsche on INTROSPECTION.

BORES

1 Bore. A person who talks when you wish him to listen.

> AMBROSE BIERCE (1842-1914), U.S. author. *The Devil's Dictionary* (1881-1906).

2 The pest, in a sense, is a very superior being to us: he knows where to find us and how—usually in the bath or in sexual intercourse or asleep.

> CHARLES BUKOWSKI (b. 1920), U.S. author, poet. *Tales of Ordinary Madness*, "Notes on the Pest" (1967).

3 What's wrong with being a boring kind of guy?

> GEORGE BUSH (b. 1924), U.S. Republican politician, president. Quoted in: *Daily Telegraph* (London, 28 April 1988).

4 Society is now one polished horde,
Formed of two mighty tribes, the *Bores* and *Bored*.

> LORD BYRON (1788-1824), English poet. *Don Juan*, cto. 13, st. 95.

5 I am quite serious when I say that I do not believe there are, on the whole earth besides, so many intensified bores as in these United States. No man can form an adequate idea of the real meaning of the word, without coming here.

> CHARLES DICKENS (1812-70), English novelist. Comment, March 1842, while on an American tour. Quoted in: Hesketh Pearson, *Dickens*, ch. 8 (1949).

6 The age of chivalry is past. Bores have succeeded to dragons.

> BENJAMIN DISRAELI (1804-81), English statesman, author. May Dacre, in *The Young Duke*, bk. 2, ch. 5 (1831).

7 Sir, you have but two topics, yourself and me. I am sick of both.

> SAMUEL JOHNSON (1709-84), English author, lexicographer. Quoted in: James Boswell, *Life of Samuel Johnson*, May 1776 (1791).

8 I . . . begin with the principle that all men are bores. Surely no one will prove himself so great a bore as to contradict me in this.

> SOREN KIERKEGAARD (1813-55), Danish philosopher. *Either/Or*, vol. 1, "Rotation of Crops" (1843; tr. 1944).

9 Bores bore each other too; but it never seems to teach them anything.

> DON MARQUIS (1878-1937), U.S. humorist, journalist. Quoted in: E. Anthony, *The Rare Don Marquis*, ch. 11 (1962).

10 And 'tis remarkable that they
Talk most who have the least to say.

> MATTHEW PRIOR (1664-1721), English poet, diplomat. *Alma*, cto. 2.

11 I don't know about bores. Maybe you shouldn't feel too sorry if you see some swell girl getting married to them. They don't hurt anybody most of them, and maybe they're all terrific whistlers or something. Who the hell knows? Not me.

> J. D. SALINGER (b. 1919), U.S. author. The narrator (Holden Caulfield), in *The Catcher in the Rye*, ch. 17 (1951).

12 For I have neither wit, nor words, nor worth,
Action, nor utterance, nor the power of speech,
To stir men's blood. I only speak right on.
I tell you that which you yourselves do know.

> WILLIAM SHAKESPEARE (1564-1616), English dramatist, poet. Mark Antony, in *Julius Caesar*, act 3, sc. 2.

13 A bore is a man who, when you ask him how he is, tells you.

> BERT LESTON TAYLOR (1866-1921), U.S. humorist, newspaper columnist. *The So-Called Human Race*, (1922, p. 163).

14   A healthy male adult bore consumes each year one and a half times his own weight in other people's patience.

> JOHN UPDIKE (b. 1932), U.S. author, critic. *Assorted Prose*, "Confessions of a Wild Bore" (1965).

See also La Rochefoucauld on ANECDOTES; La Rochefoucauld on CONVERSATION; DULLNESS; Emerson on HEROES.

BORROWING AND LENDING

1   Do not be made a beggar by banqueting upon borrowing, when thou hast nothing in thy purse: for thou shalt lie in wait for thine own life, and be talked on.

> APOCRYPHA. *Ecclesiasticus* 18:33.

2   The book borrower of real stature whom we envisage here proves himself to be an inveterate collector of books not so much by the fervor with which he guards his borrowed treasures and by the deaf ear which he turns to all reminders from the everyday world of legality as by his failure to read these books.

> WALTER BENJAMIN (1892-1940), German critic, philosopher. *Unpacking My Library* (1931; repr. in *Illuminations*, ed. by Hannah Arendt, 1968).

3   The human species, according to the best theory I can form of it, is composed of two distinct races, *the men who borrow* and *the men who lend*.

> CHARLES LAMB (1775-1834), English essayist, critic. *Essays of Elia*, "The Two Races of Men" (1820-23).

4   Neither a borrower nor a lender be,
For loan oft loses both itself and friend,
And borrowing dulls the edge of husbandry.

> WILLIAM SHAKESPEARE (1564-1616), English dramatist, poet. Polonius, giving advice to his son Laertes, departing for France, in *Hamlet*, act 1, sc. 3.

5   The surest way to ruin a man who doesn't know how to handle money is to give him some.

> GEORGE BERNARD SHAW (1856-1950), Anglo-Irish playwright, critic. Boss Mangan, in *Heartbreak House*, act 2.

6   It is difficult to begin without borrowing, but perhaps it is the most generous course thus to permit your fellow-men to have an interest in your enterprise.

> HENRY DAVID THOREAU (1817-62), U.S. philosopher, author, naturalist. *Walden*, "Economy" (1854).

See also Lamb on BOOKS.

BOSTON

1   I have just returned from Boston. It is the only thing to do if you find yourself up there.

> FRED ALLEN (1894-1957), U.S. radio comic. Letter, 12 June 1953, to comedian Groucho Marx.

2   And this is good old Boston,
The home of the bean and the cod,
Where the Lowells talk to the Cabots,
And the Cabots talk only to God.

> JOHN COLLINS BOSSIDY (1860-1928), U.S. oculist. Toast, 1910, at the Holy Cross College alumni dinner at Harvard University.

3   I guess God made Boston on a wet Sunday.

> RAYMOND CHANDLER (1888-1959), U.S. author. Letter, 21 March 1949 (published in *The Selected Letters of Raymond Chandler*, 1981). Chandler was referring to a novel by J. P. Marquand, *Point of No Return*, which he had just finished reading, and which reminded him of "a steel engraving with no color at all."

4   I do not speak with any fondness but the language of coolest history, when I say that Boston commands attention as the town which was appointed in the destiny of nations to lead the civilization of North America.

> RALPH WALDO EMERSON (1803-82), U.S. essayist, poet, philosopher. *The Natural History of the Intellect*, "Boston" (1893).

5   Their hotels are bad. Their pumpkin pies are delicious. Their poetry is not so good.

> EDGAR ALLAN POE (1809-45), U.S. poet, critic, short-story writer. *Broadway Journal* (1845). Quoted in: Julian Symons, *The Tell-Tale Heart: The Life and Works of Edgar Allan Poe*, pt. 1, ch. 12 (1978).

6   The Bostonians are really, as a race, far inferior in point of anything beyond mere intellect to any other set upon the continent of North America. They are decidedly the most servile imitators of the English it is possible to conceive.

> EDGAR ALLAN POE (1809-45), U.S. poet, critic, short-story writer. Letter, 14 Feb. 1849.

7   Tonight I appear for the first time before a Boston audience—4,000 critics.

> MARK TWAIN (1835-1910), U.S. author. Letter, 9 Nov. 1869.

8   The Bostonians take their learning too sadly: culture with them is an accomplishment rather than an atmosphere; their "Hub," as they call it, is the paradise of prigs.

> OSCAR WILDE (1854-1900), Anglo-Irish playwright, author. "The American Invasion," in *Court and Society Review* (London, March 1887).

See also Wilde on CITIES AND CITY LIFE.

THE BOURGEOISIE

1   The petit-bourgeois is a man unable to imagine the Other. If he comes fact to face with him, he blinds himself, ignores and denies him, or else transforms him into himself.

> ROLAND BARTHES (1915-80), French semiologist. *Mythologies*, "Myth on the Right" (1957; tr. 1972).

2   You are the majority—in number and intelligence; therefore you are the force—which is justice. Some are scholars, others are owners; a glorious day will come when the scholars will be owners and the owners scholars. Then your power will be complete, and no man will protest against it.

> CHARLES BAUDELAIRE (1821-67), French poet. "Salon of 1846: To the Bourgeois" (published in *Curiosités Esthétiques*, 1868; repr. in *The Mirror of Art*, ed. by Jonathan Mayne, 1955).

3   It is the corpse of the bourgeoisie that separates us. With us, it is that class that is the carrier of the chromosome of banality.

> JEAN BAUDRILLARD (b. 1929), French semiologist. *America*, "Astral America" (1986; tr. 1988).

4   The bourgeois takes economic power very seriously, and often worships it quite unselfishly.

> NICOLAI A. BERDYAEV (1874-1948), Russian Christian philosopher. *Slavery and Freedom* (1939; repr. in *Christian Existentialism*, ch. 5, "Bourgeosity" ed. by Donald A. Lowrie, 1965).

5   And the wind shall say "Here were decent godless
>   people;
Their only monument the asphalt road
And a thousand lost golf balls."

> T. S. ELIOT (1888-1965), Anglo-American poet, critic. *The Rock*, pt. 1.

6   Never was Catholicism, never were the ideas of chivalry, impressed on men so deeply, so multifariously, as the *bourgeois* ideas.

> ALEXANDER HERZEN (1812-70), Russian journalist, political thinker. *My Past and Thoughts*, vol. 2, pt. 5, ch. 38, "Post Scriptum" (1921; tr. by Constance Garnett, 1924-27).

7   The bourgeois treasures nothing more highly than the self. . . . And so at the cost of intensity he achieves his own preservation and security. His harvest is a quiet mind which he prefers to being possessed by God, as he prefers comfort to pleasure, convenience to liberty, and a pleasant temperature to that deathly inner consuming fire.

> HERMANN HESSE (1877-1962), German novelist, poet. *Steppenwolf*, "Treatise on the Steppenwolf" (1927).

8   How beastly the bourgeois is
especially the male of the species
—presentable, eminently presentable.

> D. H. LAWRENCE (1885-1930), British author. *How Beastly the Bourgeois Is*.

9   The bourgeoisie of the whole world, which looks complacently upon the wholesale massacre after the battle, is convulsed by horror at the desecration of brick and mortar.

> KARL MARX (1818-83), German political theorist, social philosopher. "Address of the General Council of the International Working Men's Association on *The Civil War in France*" (1871; published in *Selected Works*, vol. 2, 1942).

10   The bourgeoisie . . . has been the first to show what man's activity can bring about. It has accomplished wonders far surpassing Egyptian pyramids, Roman aqueducts and Gothic cathedrals. . . . The bourgeoisie . . . draws all, even the most barbarian nations into civilization. . . . It has created enormous cities . . . and has thus rescued a considerable part of the population from the idiocy of rural life. . . . The bourgeoisie, during its rule of scarce one hundred years, has created more massive and more colossal productive forces than have all preceding generations together.

> KARL MARX (1818-83) AND FRIEDRICH ENGELS (1820-95), German social philosophers, revolutionaries. *The Communist Manifesto*, sct. 1, (1848; repr. in *Karl Marx: Selected Works*, vol. 1, 1942).

11   The great disadvantage, and advantage, of the small urban bourgeois is his limited outlook. He sees the world as a middle-class world, and everything outside these limits is either laughable or slightly wicked.

> GEORGE ORWELL (1903-50), British author. *Inside the Whale and Other Essays*, "Charles Dickens" (1940).

12   Our culture is ill-equipped to assert the bourgeois values which would be the salvation of the under-class, because we have lost those values ourselves.

> NORMAN PODHORETZ (b. 1930), U.S. editor, critic, essayist. Quoted in: *Daily Mail* (London, 10 Nov. 1989).

13   The bourgeois are other people.

> JULES RENARD (1864-1910), French novelist, playwright. *Journal 1877-1910* (1977), entry for 28 Jan. 1890.

14   Civilized society is one huge bourgeoisie: no nobleman dares now shock his greengrocer.

> GEORGE BERNARD SHAW (1856-1950), Anglo-Irish playwright, critic. *Man and Superman*, Preface (1903).

15   If one defends the bourgeois, philistine virtues, one does not defend them merely from the demonism or bohemianism of the artist but from the present bourgeoisie itself.

> LIONEL TRILLING (1905-75), U.S. critic. Notebook entry 1951 (published in *Partisan Review 50th Anniversary Edition*, ed. by William Philips, 1985).

See also Weil on ACCOUNTS; Engels on CLASS; Grosz on CULTURE; The MIDDLE CLASS.

BOXING

1   It's just a job. Grass grows, birds fly, waves pound the sand. I beat people up.

> MUHAMMAD ALI (b. 1942), U.S. boxer. Quoted in: *New York Times* (6 April 1977).

2   Boxing is just show business with blood.

> FRANK BRUNO (b. 1961), British boxer. Quoted in: *Guardian* (London, 19 Nov. 1991).

3   I want to keep fighting because it is the only thing that keeps me out of the hamburger joints. If I don't fight, I'll eat this planet.

> GEORGE FOREMAN (b. 1948), U.S. boxer. Quoted in: *Times* (London, 17 Jan. 1990).

4   All fighters are prostitutes and all promotors are pimps.

> LARRY HOLMES (b. 1949), U.S. boxing champion. Quoted in: *Guardian* (London, 24 Dec. 1984).

5 It's the boxers who attract the real women, after all, with their raw primeval strength, beautifully toned bodies and just a touch of vulnerability.

> EAMONN McCABE (b. 1948), British journalist, photographer. Quoted in: *Guardian*, "Elle Supplement" (London, 9 Jan. 1992).

6 That was always the difference between Muhammed Ali and the rest of us. He came, he saw, and if he didn't entirely conquer—he came as close as anybody we are likely to see in the lifetime of this doomed generation.

> HUNTER S. THOMPSON (b. 1939), U.S. journalist. "Last Tango in Vegas: Fear and Loathing in the Far Room," in *Rolling Stone* (18 May 1978; repr. in *The Great Shark Hunt*, pt. 4, 1979).

BOYS

1 Speak roughly to your little boy,
And beat him when he sneezes:
He only does it to annoy,
Because he knows it teases.

> LEWIS CARROLL (1832-98), English author, mathematician. The Duchess, in *Alice's Adventures in Wonderland*, ch. 6 (1865).

2 Boyhood is a most complex and incomprehensible thing. Even when one has been through it, one does not understand what it was. A man can never quite understand a boy, even when he has been the boy.

> G. K. CHESTERTON (1874-1936), British author. *Autobiography*, ch. 3 (1936).

3 I never see any difference in boys. I only know two sorts of boys. Mealy boys and beef-faced boys.

> CHARLES DICKENS (1812-70), English novelist. Mr. Grimwig, in *Oliver Twist*, ch. 14 (1838).

4 A fairly bright boy is far more intelligent and far better company than the average adult.

> J. B. S. HALDANE (1892-1964), British scientist. Quoted in: *New York Times* (13 June 1948).

5 Boys are capital fellows in their own way, among their mates; but they are unwholesome companions for grown people.

> CHARLES LAMB (1775-1834), English essayist, critic. *Essays of Elia*, "The Old and the New Schoolmaster" (1820-23).

6 Every genuine boy is a rebel and an anarch. If he were allowed to develop according to his own instincts, his own inclinations, society would undergo such a radical transformation as to make the adult revolutionary cower and cringe.

> HENRY MILLER (1891-1980), U.S. author. *The Books in My Life*, ch. 4 (1951).

7 What money is better bestowed than that of a schoolboy's tip? How the kindness is recalled by the recipient in after days! It blesses him that gives and him that takes.

> WILLIAM MAKEPEACE THACKERAY (1811-63), English author. *The Newcomes*, bk. 1, ch. 16 (1853-55).

8 There comes a time in every rightly constructed boy's life when he has a raging desire to go somewhere and dig for hidden treasure.

> MARK TWAIN (1835-1910), U.S. author. *Tom Sawyer*, ch. 26 (1876).

See also Hope on ADOLESCENCE; Byron on AGE AND AGING; Miedzian on CONDITIONING.

BRAGGING

1 Mere flim-flam stories, and nothing but shams and lies.

> MIGUEL DE CERVANTES (1547-1616), Spanish writer. Sancho Panza, in *Don Quixote*, pt. 1, bk. 3, ch. 11 (1605; tr. by P. Motteux), remarking on Don Quixote's "bragging and bouncing."

2 There is also this benefit in brag, that the speaker is unconsciously expressing his own ideal. Humor him by all means, draw it all out, and hold him to it.

> RALPH WALDO EMERSON (1803-82), U.S. essayist, poet, philosopher. *English Traits*, "Wealth" (1856).

3 If I cannot brag of knowing something, then I brag of not knowing it; at any rate, brag.

> RALPH WALDO EMERSON (1803-82), U.S. essayist, poet, philosopher. *Journals* (1909-14), entry for Oct.-Nov. 1866.

4 Every other enjoyment malice may destroy; every other panegyric envy may withhold; but no human power can deprive the boaster of his own encomiums.

> SAMUEL JOHNSON (1709-84), English author, lexicographer. *Rambler*, no. 193 (21 Jan. 1752; repr. in *Works of Samuel Johnson*, vol. 5, ed. by W. J. Bate and Albrecht B. Strauss, 1969).

5 If I seem to boast more than is becoming, my excuse is that I brag for humanity rather than for myself.

> HENRY DAVID THOREAU (1817-62), U.S. philosopher, author, naturalist. *Walden*, "Economy" (1854).

See also Emerson on ARROGANCE.

BREAKFAST

1 I suppose the fact is that no friendship can stand the breakfast test. . . . Civilisation has done away with curlpapers, yet at that hour the soul of the *Hausfrau* is as tightly screwed up in them as was ever her grandmother's hair, and though my body comes down mechanically, having been trained that way by punctual parents, my soul never thinks of beginning to wake up for other people till lunch-time, and never does so completely till it has been taken out of doors and aired in the sunshine. Who can begin conventional amiability the first thing in the morning? It is the hour of savage instincts and natural tendencies; it is the triumph of the Disagreeable and the Cross. I am convinced that the Muses and the Graces never thought of having breakfast anywhere but in bed.

> MARY [ELIZABETH, COUNTESS VON] ARNIM (1866-1941), Australian-born British novelist. *Elizabeth and Her German Garden*, "September 15th" (1898).

2 The critical period in matrimony is breakfast-time.

> A. P. HERBERT (1890-1971), British author, politician. *Uncommon Law*, "Is Marriage Lawful?" (1935).

3 The average American's simplest and commonest form of breakfast consists of coffee and beefsteak.

MARK TWAIN (1835-1910), U.S. author. *A Tramp Abroad*, ch. 49 (1879).

4 Only dull people are brilliant at breakfast.

OSCAR WILDE (1854-1900), Anglo-Irish playwright, author. Mrs. Cheveley, in *An Ideal Husband*, act 1.

BREASTS

1 Thy two breasts are like two young roes that are twins, which feed among the lilies.

BIBLE, HEBREW. *Song of Solomon* 4:5.

2 Show me no more those snowy breasts
With azure riverets branched
Where, whilst mine eye with plenty feasts
Yet is my thirst not staunched;
O Tantalus, thy pains ne'er tell
By me thou are prevented
'Tis nothing to be plagued in Hell,
But thus in Heaven tormented.

MICHAEL DRAYTON (1563-1631), English poet. *To His Coy Love*.

3 Uncorseted, her friendly bust
Gives promise of pneumatic bliss.

T. S. ELIOT (1888-1965), Anglo-American poet, critic. *Whispers of Immortality*. "Grishkin"—the character described here—is thought to be a portrayal of Serafima Astafieva (1876-1934), a Russian dancer with the Diaghilev company who opened her own ballet school in London. Ezra Pound also referred to her in his Pisan Cantos 77 and 79 (1945).

4 A full bosom is actually a millstone around a woman's neck: it endears her to the men who want to make their mammet of her, but she is never allowed to think that their popping eyes actually see her. Her breasts . . . are not parts of a person but lures slung around her neck, to be kneaded and twisted like magic putty, or mumbled and mouthed like lolly ices.

GERMAINE GREER (b. 1939), Australian feminist writer. *The Female Eunuch*, "Curves" (1970).

5 The yielding marble of her snowy breast.

EDMUND WALLER (1606-87), English poet. *On a Lady Passing through a Crowd of People*.

See also Gregory on DRESS.

THE BRITISH

1 Britain today is suffering from galloping obsolescence.

TONY BENN (b. 1925), British Labour politician. Speech, 31 Jan. 1963.

2 Think of what our Nation stands for,
Books from Boots' and country lanes,
Free speech, free passes, class distinction,
Democracy and proper drains.

JOHN BETJEMAN (1906-84), British poet. *In Westminster Abbey*, st. 4 (published in *Old Lights for New Chancels*, 1940).

3 There is a marvelous turn and trick to British arrogance; its apparent unconsciousness makes it twice as effectual.

CATHERINE DRINKER BOWEN (1897-1973), U.S. author. *Adventures of a Biographer*, ch. 14 (1946).

4 There's nothing the British like better than a bloke who comes from nowhere, makes it, and then gets clobbered.

MELVYN BRAGG (b. 1939), British broadcaster, author. Quoted in: *Guardian* (London, 23 Sept. 1988), referring to actor Richard Burton.

5 The British do not expect happiness. I had the impression, all the time that I lived there, that they do not want to be happy; they want to be right.

QUENTIN CRISP (b. 1908), British author. "Love Lies Bleeding" (published in *New Statesman and Society*, 9 Aug. 1991; first broadcast 6 Aug. 1991).

6 Oh! what a snug little Island,
A right little, tight little Island!

THOMAS DIBDIN (1771-1841), English actor, playwright. *The Snug Little Island*.

7 Here we have the beautiful British compromise: a man can say anything, he mustn't do anything; a man can listen to anything, but he musn't be roused to do anything. By freedom of speech is meant freedom to talk *about*; speech is not saying-as-an-action.

PAUL GOODMAN (1911-72), U.S. literary author, critic. "Censorship and Pornography on the Stage," lecture, pt. 2 (1959; published in *Creator Spirit Come*, 1977).

8 However British you may be, I am more British still.

HENRY JAMES (1843-1916), U.S. author. Quoted in: H. Montgomery Hyde, *Henry James at Home*, ch. 7, sct. 5 (1969). The remark was made to two English friends at the beginning of August 1914 and reported in a letter written by the poet and critic Edmund Gosse to the *Times* (London, 4 March 1916).

9 What a magnificent land and race is this Britain! Everything about them is of better quality than the corresponding thing in the U.S. . . . Yet I believe (or suspect) that ours is eventually the bigger destiny, if we can only succeed in living up to it.

WILLIAM JAMES (1842-1910), U.S. psychologist, philosopher. Letter, 2 July 1908 (published in *The Letters of William James*, vol. 2, 1920).

10 Only in Britain could it be thought a defect to be "too clever by half." The probability is that too many people are too stupid by three-quarters.

JOHN MAJOR (b. 1943), British Conservative politician, prime minister. Quoted in: *Observer* (London, 7 July 1991).

11 The British tourist is always happy abroad as long as the natives are waiters.

ROBERT MORLEY (b. 1908), British actor. Quoted in: *Observer* (London, 20 April 1958).

12 There is not a more disgusting spectacle under the sun than our subserviency to British criticism. It is disgusting, first, because it is truckling, servile, pusillanimous—secondly, because of its gross irrationality. We *know* the British to bear us little but ill will—we know that, in no case do they utter unbiased opinions of American books . . . we *know* all this, and yet, day after day, submit our necks to the degrading yoke of the crudest opinion that emanates from the fatherland.

> EDGAR ALLAN POE (1809-45), U.S. poet, critic, short-story writer. *Marginalia*, "American Nationality in Literature" (1844-49).

13 The national anthem belongs to the eighteenth century. In it you find us ordering God about to do our political dirty work.

> GEORGE BERNARD SHAW (1856-1950), Anglo-Irish playwright, critic. A member of the Caravan of the Curious, in *The Adventures of the Black Girl in Her Search for God* (1932).

14 What two ideas are more inseparable than beer and Britannia?

> SYDNEY SMITH (1771-1845), English clergyman, writer. Quoted in: Hesketh Pearson, *The Smith of Smiths*, ch. 11 (1934).

15 Of the general inadequacy of intellect in the conduct of life Britain is the most majestic exponent. She is instinctively disliked by such people as French, Persians, Hindus, who are clever by nature, and think that *intellect can rule*. The Italians strayed down this path and disliked us too. But they, and the Greeks, and the Arabs, have a natural perception of other and greater powers and this, I think, is an affinity that binds us. With the others, with the intellectual, it is not our stupidity, but the fact that we prove it possible to live by non-intellectual standards, which makes us disliked.

> FREYA STARK (b. 1893), British travel writer. *Perseus in the Wind*, ch. 4 (1948).

16 Gorgonised me from head to foot,
With a stony British stare.

> LORD TENNYSON (1809-92), English poet. *Maud*, pt. 1, sct. 13, st. 2.

17 The British are a self-distrustful, diffident people, agreeing with alacrity that they are neither successful nor clever, and only modestly claiming that they have a keener sense of humour, more robust common sense, and greater staying power as a nation than all the rest of the world put together.

> Quoted in: *Fourth Leaders from the Times* (1950).

18 To many, no doubt, he will seem to be somewhat blatant and bumptious, but we prefer to regard him as being simply British.

> OSCAR WILDE (1854-1900), Anglo-Irish playwright, author. Book review, *Pall Mall Gazette* (London, 18 Nov. 1886).

See also Football fan on DELINQUENCY; Waugh on EMPIRE; ENGLAND AND THE ENGLISH; Tuchman on GOVERNMENT; Gallico on INSULTS; Macaulay on MORALITY; SCOTLAND AND THE SCOTS; George III on The UNITED STATES; WALES AND THE WELSH.

BROADWAY

1 I'm the end of the line; absurd and appalling as it may seem, serious New York theater has died in my lifetime.

> ARTHUR MILLER (b. 1915), U.S. dramatist. Quoted in: *Times* (London, 11 Jan. 1989).

2 Broadway, such as I see it now and have seen it for twenty-five years, is a ramp that was conceived by St. Thomas Aquinas while he was yet in the womb. It was meant originally to be used only by snakes and lizards, by the horned toad and the red heron, but when the great Spanish Armada was sunk the human kind wriggled out of the ketch and slopped over, creating by a sort of foul, ignominious squirm and wiggle the cunt-like cleft that runs from the Battery south to the golf links north through the dead and wormy center of Manhattan Island.

> HENRY MILLER (1891-1980), U.S. author. *Tropic of Capricorn* (1938; repr. 1966, p. 89).

3 The wide wonder of Broadway is disconsolate in the daytime; but gaudily glorious at night, with a milling crowd filling sidewalk and roadway, silent, going up, going down, between upstanding banks of brilliant lights, each building braided and embossed with glowing, many-coloured bulbs of man-rayed luminance. A glowing valley of the shadow of life. The strolling crowd went slowly by through the kinematically divine thoroughfare of New York.

> SEAN O'CASEY (1884-1964), Irish dramatist. *Rose and Crown*, his autobiography, vol. 5, "In New York Now" (1952).

4 We all know that the theater and every play that comes to Broadway have within themselves, like the human being, the seed of self-destruction and the certainty of death. The thing is to see how long the theater, the play, and the human being can last in spite of themselves.

> JAMES THURBER (1894-1961), U.S. humorist, illustrator. Quoted in: *New York Times* (21 Feb. 1960). On the same subject, Thurber wrote, "Surely no other American institution is so bound around and tightened up by rules, strictures, adages, and superstitions as the Broadway theater."

BUDDHISM

1 They have their belief, these poor Tibet people, that Providence sends down always an Incarnation of Himself into every generation. At bottom some belief in a kind of pope! At bottom still better, a belief that there is a *Greatest* Man; that *he* is discoverable; that, once discovered, we ought to treat him with an obedience which knows no bounds. This is the truth of Grand Lamaism; the "discoverability" is the only error here.

> THOMAS CARLYLE (1795-1881), Scottish essayist, historian. *On Heroes, Hero-Worship and the Heroic in History*, Lecture 1, "The Hero as Divinity" (1841).

2 Buddhism is not a creed, it is a doubt.

> G. K. CHESTERTON (1874-1936), British author. Professor de Worms, in *The Man Who Was Thursday*, ch. 14 (1908).

3 Our civilization, bequeathed to us by fierce adventurers, eaters of meat and hunters, is so full of hurry and combat, so busy about many things which perhaps are of no importance, that it cannot but see something feeble in a civilization which smiles as it refuses to make the battlefield the test of excellence.

> JAMES JOYCE (1882-1941), Irish author. "A Suave Philosophy," in *Daily Express* (Dublin, 6 Feb. 1903; repr. in *Critical Writings*, sct. 12, ed. by Ellsworth Mason and Richard Ellmann, 1959),

reviewing H. Fielding Hall's *The Soul of a People* (on Burmese society and Buddhism).

4   Yoga in Mayfair or Fifth Avenue, or in any other place which is on the telephone, is a spiritual fake.

CARL JUNG (1875-1961), Swiss psychiatrist. *Psychological Commentaries on "The Tibetan Book of the Great Liberation"* (written 1939; published 1954; repr. in *Collected Works*, vol. 11, ed. by William McGuire, 1958).

5   The Buddha, the Godhead, resides quite as comfortably in the circuits of a digital computer or the gears of a cycle transmission as he does at the top of a mountain or in the petals of a flower.

ROBERT M. PIRSIG (b. 1928), U.S. author. *Zen and the Art of Motorcycle Maintenance*, pt. 1, ch. 1 (1974).

6   A religion so cheerless, a philosophy so sorrowful, could never have succeeded with the masses of mankind if presented only as a system of metaphysics. Buddhism owed its success to its catholic spirit and its beautiful morality.

W. WINWOOD READE (1838-75), English traveler, author. *The Martyrdom of Man*, ch. 4, "Summary of Universal History" (1872).

7   Zen . . . does not confuse spirituality with thinking about God while one is peeling potatoes. Zen spirituality is just to peel the potatoes.

ALAN WATTS (1915-73), British-born U.S. philosopher, author. *The Way of Zen*, pt. 2, ch. 2 (1957).

BUREAUCRACY

1   I always get back to the question, is it really necessary that men should consume so much of their bodily and mental energies in the machinery of civilised life? The world seems to me to do much of its toil for that which is not in any sense bread. Again, does not the latent feeling that much of their striving is to no purpose tend to infuse large quantities of *sham* into men's work?"

WILLIAM ALLINGHAM (1824-89), Irish poet, diarist. *A Diary*, ch. 6, 1864 entry (ed. by H. Allingham and D. Radford, 1907). "I have been an 'Official' all my life," Allingham wrote, "without the least turn for it. I never could attain a true *official manner*, which is highly artificial and handles trifles with ludicrously disproportionate gravity."

2   A bureaucracy is sure to think that its duty is to augment official power, official business, or official members, rather than to leave free the energies of mankind; it overdoes the quantity of government, as well as impairs its quality. The truth is, that a skilled bureaucracy . . . is, though it boasts of an appearance of science, quite inconsistent with the true principles of the art of business.

WALTER BAGEHOT (1826-77), English economist, critic. *The English Constitution*, ch. 6 (1867).

3   Poor fellow, he suffers from files.

ANEURIN BEVAN (1897-1960), British Labour politician. Quoted in: Michael Foot, *Aneurin Bevan*, vol. 1, ch. 5 (1962), referring to the administrator and trade unionist Sir Walter Citrine. Citrine, Foot claimed, had a "card-index mind."

4   Nothing can be more contemptible than to suppose Public RECORDS to be true.

WILLIAM BLAKE (1757-1827), English poet, painter, engraver.

Annotations to Bishop Watson, *An Apology for the Bible in a Series of Letters Addressed to Thomas Paine* (1798; published in *Complete Writings*, ed. by Geoffrey Keynes, 1957).

5   A multitude of little superfluous precautions engender here a population of deputies and sub-officials, each of whom acquits himself with an air of importance and a rigorous precision, which seemed to say, though everything is done with much silence, "Make way, I am one of the members of the grand machine of state."

MARQUIS DE CUSTINE (1790-1857), French traveler, author. *Empire of the Czar: A Journey Through Eternal Russia*, ch. 7 (1843; rev. 1989), referring to Russia. De Custine described the Russian officials as "voluntary automata," adding, "In Russian administration, minuteness does not exclude disorder. Much trouble is taken to attain unimportant ends, and those employed believe they can never do enough to show their zeal."

6   It seems to me that there must be an ecological limit to the number of paper pushers the earth can sustain, and that human civilization will collapse when the number of, say, tax lawyers exceeds the world's total population of farmers, weavers, fisherpersons, and pediatric nurses.

BARBARA EHRENREICH (b. 1941), U.S. author, columnist. *The Worst Years of Our Lives*, "Premature Pragmatism" (1991; first published in *Ms.*, 1986).

7   Official dignity tends to increase in inverse ratio to the importance of the country in which the office is held.

ALDOUS HUXLEY (1894-1963), British author. *Beyond the Mexique Bay*, "Puerto Barrios" (1934).

8   The only thing that saves us from the bureaucracy is inefficiency. An efficient bureaucracy is the greatest threat to liberty.

EUGENE J. McCARTHY (b. 1916), U.S. politician. *Time* (New York, 12 Feb. 1979).

9   Bureaucracy, the rule of no one, has become the modern form of despotism.

MARY McCARTHY (1912-89), U.S. author, critic. "The Vita Activa," in *New Yorker* (18 Oct. 1958; repr. in *On the Contrary*, 1961).

10   Government proposes, bureaucracy disposes. And the bureaucracy must dispose of government proposals by dumping them on us.

P. J. O'ROURKE (b. 1947), U.S. journalist. *Parliament of Whores*, "The Bureaucracy" (1991).

11   If we did not have such a thing as an airplane today, we would probably create something the size of N.A.S.A. to make one.

H. ROSS PEROT (b. 1930), U.S. business executive, presidential candidate 1992. Quoted in: *Newsweek* (New York, 1 Dec. 1986).

12   No government ever voluntarily reduces itself in size. Government programs, once launched, never disappear. Actually, a government bureau is the nearest thing to eternal life we'll ever see on this earth!

RONALD REAGAN (b. 1911), U.S. Republican politician, president. "A Time for Choosing," television address, 27 Oct. 1964 (published in *Speaking My Mind*, 1989).

13   If you're going to sin, sin against God, not the bureaucracy; God will forgive you but the bureaucracy won't.

HYMAN G. RICKOVER (1900-1986), U.S. admiral. Quoted in: *New York Times* (3 Nov. 1986).

14 Bureaucracy is not an obstacle to democracy but an inevitable complement to it.

JOSEPH A. SCHUMPETER (1883-1950), Austrian-American economist. *Capitalism, Socialism and Democracy*, ch. 18 (1942).

15 So many signatures for such a small heart.

MOTHER TERESA (b. 1910), Albanian-born Roman Catholic missionary. Quoted in: *Evening Standard* (London, 3 Jan. 1992), on form-filling in a California hospital.

16 There is something about a bureaucrat that does not like a poem.

GORE VIDAL (b. 1925), U.S. novelist, critic. *Sex, Death and Money*, Preface (1968).

BURIAL

1 Just under the surface I shall be, all together at first, then separate and drift, through all the earth and perhaps in the end through a cliff into the sea, something of me. A ton of worms in an acre, that is a wonderful thought, a ton of worms, I believe it.

SAMUEL BECKETT (1906-89), Irish dramatist, novelist. *From an Abandoned Work* (1958).

2 We therefore commit his body to the ground; earth to earth, ashes to ashes, dust to dust; in sure and certain hope of the Resurrection.

BOOK OF COMMON PRAYER (1662). The Burial Service.

3   But
  since he had
The genius to be loved, why let him have
The justice to be honored in his grave.

ELIZABETH BARRETT BROWNING (1806-61), English poet. *Crowned and Buried*, st. 27.

4 Corpses are more fit to be thrown out than is dung.

HERACLITUS c. 535-C.475 B.C.), Greek philosopher. *The Cosmic Fragments*, no. 85 (written c. 480 B.C.).

5 All places are alike,
And every earth is fit for burial.

CHRISTOPHER MARLOWE (1564-93), English dramatist, poet. Edward, in *Edward II*, act 5, sc. 1.

6 I could never bear to be buried with people to whom I had not been introduced.

NORMAN PARKINSON (1913-90), British fashion photographer. Quoted in: *Guardian* (London, 16 Feb. 1990), from his obituary notice.

7 The beautiful uncut hair of graves.

WALT WHITMAN (1819-92), U.S. poet. *Leaves of Grass*, "Song of Myself," sct. 6 (1855).

8 The dreariest spot in all the land
To Death they set apart;
With scanty grace from Nature's hand,
And none from that of Art.

JOHN GREENLEAF WHITTIER (1807-92), U.S. poet. *The Old Burying-Ground*.

See also Saint-Exupéry on FUNERALS.

GEORGE BUSH

1 Consider the vice president, George Bush, a man so bedeviled by bladder problems that he managed, for the last eight years, to be in the men's room whenever an important illegal decision was made.

BARBARA EHRENREICH (b. 1941), U.S. author, columnist. *The Worst Years of Our Lives*, "The Unbearable Being of Whiteness" (1988; repr. 1991).

2 He's nice enough not to want to be associated with a nasty remark but not nice enough not to make it. Lacking the courage of one's nastiness does not make one nice.

MICHAEL KINSLEY (b. 1951), U.S. journalist. Quoted in: *Time* (New York, 16 July 1990).

3 Poor George, he can't help it. He was born with a silver foot in his mouth.

ANN RICHARDS (b. 1933), U.S. Democrat, Texas state official. Quoted in: *Independent* (London, 20 July 1988).

See also Bush on BORES.

BUSINESS AND COMMERCE

1 International business may conduct its operations with scraps of paper, but the ink it uses is human *blood*.

ERIC AMBLER (b. 1909), British novelist. Marukakis, in *A Coffin for Dimitrios*, ch. 5 (1939).

2 For the merchant, even honesty is a financial speculation.

CHARLES BAUDELAIRE (1821-67), French poet. *My Heart Laid Bare* (published in *Intimate Journals*, sct. 97, 1887; tr. by Christopher Isherwood, 1930; rev. by Don Bachardy, 1989).

3 Executives are like joggers. If you stop a jogger, he goes on running on the spot. If you drag an executive away from his business, he goes on running on the spot, pawing the ground, talking business. He never stops hurtling onwards, making decisions and executing them.

JEAN BAUDRILLARD (b. 1929), French semiologist. *Cool Memories*, ch. 5 (1987; tr. 1990).

4 Corporation. An ingenious device for obtaining individual profit without individual responsibility.

AMBROSE BIERCE (1842-1914), U.S. author. *The Devil's Dictionary* (1881-1906).

5 Commerce is so far from being beneficial to arts, or to empire, that it is destructive of both, as all their history shows, for the above reason of individual merit being its great hatred. Empires flourish till they become commercial, and then they are scattered abroad to the four winds.

WILLIAM BLAKE (1757-1827), English poet, painter, engraver. Public address, c. 1810, in Blake's notebook (published in *Complete Writings*, ed. by Geoffrey Keynes, 1957).

6 It is the interest of the commercial world that wealth should be found everywhere.

EDMUND BURKE (1729-97), Irish philosopher, statesman. Letter, 23 April 1778, to Samuel Span, Esq. (published in *Works*, vol. 2).

7 Such is the brutalization of commercial ethics in this country that no one can feel anything more delicate than the velvet touch of a soft buck.

> RAYMOND CHANDLER (1888-1959), U.S. author. Letter, 13 May 1949, to publisher Hamish Hamilton (published in *Raymond Chandler Speaking*, 1962).

8 No man tastes pleasures truly, who does not earn them by previous business; and few people do business well, who do nothing else.

> LORD CHESTERFIELD (1694-1773), English statesman, man of letters. Letter, 7 Aug. 1749 (published 1774; repr. in *The Letters of the Earl of Chesterfield to His Son*, vol. 1, no. 189, ed. by Charles Strachey, 1901).

9 Utility is our national shibboleth: the savior of the American businessman is *fact* and his uterine half-brother, *statistics*.

> EDWARD DAHLBERG (1900-1977), U.S. author, critic. *The Carnal Myth*, Introduction (1968).

10 A client is to me a mere unit, a factor in a problem.

> SIR ARTHUR CONAN DOYLE (1859-1930), English author. Sherlock Holmes, in *The Sign of Four*, ch. 2 (1890).

11 Business? it's quite simple: it's other people's money.

> ALEXANDRE DUMAS (1824-95), French dramatist. Giraud, in *La Question d'Argent*, act 2, sc. 7.

12 The right merchant is one who has the just average of faculties we call *common sense*; a man of a strong affinity for facts, who makes up his decision on what he has seen. He is thoroughly persuaded of the truths of arithmetic. There is always a reason, *in the man,* for his good or bad fortune . . . in making money. Men talk as if there were some magic about this. . . . He knows that all goes on the old road, pound for pound, cent for cent—for every effect a perfect cause—and that good luck is another name for tenacity of purpose.

> RALPH WALDO EMERSON (1803-82), U.S. essayist, poet, philosopher. *The Conduct of Life*, "Wealth" (1860).

13 Honour sinks where commerce long prevails.

> OLIVER GOLDSMITH (1728-74), Anglo-Irish poet, essayist, playwright. *The Traveller*.

14 The most sensible people to be met with in society are men of business and of the world, who argue from what they see and know, instead of spinning cobweb distinctions of what things ought to be.

> WILLIAM HAZLITT (1778-1830), English essayist. "On the Ignorance of the Learned," in *Edinburgh Magazine* (July 1818; repr. in *Table Talk*, 1821).

15 A generation which has passed through the shop has absorbed standards and ambitions which are not of those of spaciousness, and cannot get away from them. Everything with them is done as though for sale, and they naturally have in view the greatest possible benefit, profit and that end of the stuff that will make the best show.

> ALEXANDER HERZEN (1812-70), Russian journalist, political thinker. *My Past and Thoughts*, vol. 3, pt. 8, "Miscellaneous Pieces: Swiss Views" (1921; tr. by Constance Garnett, 1924-27).

16 The selfish spirit of commerce, which knows no country, and feels no passion or principle but that of gain.

> THOMAS JEFFERSON (1743-1826), U.S. president. Letter, 15 April 1809. See Jefferson on TRADE.

17 When you are skinning your customers you should leave some skin on to grow again so that you can skin them again.

> NIKITA KHRUSHCHEV (1894-1971), Soviet premier. Quoted in: *Observer* (London, 28 May 1961), offering advice to British businesspeople.

18 The simple opposition between the people and big business has disappeared because the people themselves have become so deeply involved in big business.

> WALTER LIPPMANN (1889-1974), U.S. journalist. Speech, 25 March 1931, to the Academy of Political Science. Quoted in: Ronald Steel, *Walter Lippmann and the American Century* (1980).

19 If when a businessman speaks of minority employment, or air pollution, or poverty, he speaks in the language of a certified public accountant analyzing a corporate balance sheet, who is to know that he understands the human problems behind the statistical ones? If the businessman would stop talking like a computer printout or a page from the corporate annual report, other people would stop thinking he had a cash register for a heart. It is as simple as that—but that isn't simple.

> LOUIS B. LUNDBORG (1906-81), U.S. banker. *The State of the Language*, "The Voices of Business" (ed. by Christopher Ricks, 1980).

20 The commercial class has always mistrusted verbal brilliancy and wit, deeming such qualities, perhaps with some justice, frivolous and unprofitable.

> DOROTHY NEVILL (1826-1913), English writer, hostess. *The Reminiscences of Lady Dorothy Nevill*, ch. 8 (1907).

21 *Method* goes far to prevent trouble in business: for it makes the task easy, hinders confusion, saves abundance of time, and instructs those that have business depending, both what to do and what to hope.

> WILLIAM PENN (1644-1718), English religious leader, founder of Pennsylvania. *Some Fruits of Solitude*, no. 403 (1693).

22 If we decide to take this level of business creating ability nationwide, we'll all be plucking chickens for a living.

> H. ROSS PEROT (b. 1930), U.S. business executive, presidential candidate 1992. Quoted in: *Time* (New York, 16 Nov. 1992), referring to rival candidate Bill Clinton's initiatives in Arkansas.

23 To business that we love we rise betime,
And go to't with delight.

> WILLIAM SHAKESPEARE (1564-1616), English dramatist, poet. Antony, arming himself before the battle against Octavius Caesar at Alexandria, in *Antony and Cleopatra*, act 4, sc. 4.

24 Commerce has set the mark of selfishness,
The signet of its all-enslaving power,
Upon a shining ore, and called it gold:
Before whose image bow the vulgar great,
The vainly rich, the miserable proud,
The mob of peasants, nobles, priests, and kings,

And with blind feelings reverence the power
That grinds them to the dust of misery.

> PERCY BYSSHE SHELLEY (1792-1822), English poet. *Queen Mab*, pt. 5 (1813).

25 The propensity to truck, barter and exchange one thing for another . . . is common to all men, and to be found in no other race of animals.

> ADAM SMITH (1723-90), Scottish economist. *The Wealth of Nations*, vol. 1, bk. 1, ch. 2 (1776).

26 Perpetual devotion to what a man calls his business is only to be sustained by neglect of many other things.

> ROBERT LOUIS STEVENSON (1850-94), Scottish novelist, essayist, poet. *Virginibus Puerisque*, "An Apology for Idlers" (1881).

27 Everyone lives by selling something, whatever be his right to it.

> ROBERT LOUIS STEVENSON (1850-94), Scottish novelist, essayist, poet. *Across the Plains*, "Beggars," sct. 3 (1892).

28 Great is the hand that holds dominion over
Man by a scribbled name.

> DYLAN THOMAS (1914-53), Welsh poet. *The Hand That Signed the Paper*.

29 Deals are my art form. Other people paint beautifully on canvas or write wonderful poetry. I like making deals, preferably big deals. That's how I get my kicks.

> DONALD TRUMP (b. 1946), U.S. businessman. *Trump: The Art of the Deal*, ch. 1 (1987; written with Tony Schwartz).

30 Being good in business is the most fascinating kind of art. . . . Making money is art and working is art and good business is the best art.

> ANDY WARHOL (1928-87), U.S. Pop artist. *From A to B and Back Again*, ch. 6 (1975).

31 It is very vulgar to talk about one's business. Only people like stockbrokers do that, and then merely at dinner parties.

> OSCAR WILDE (1854-1900), Anglo-Irish playwright, author. Algernon, in *The Importance of Being Earnest*, act 3.

32 What's good for the country is good for General Motors, and *vice versa*.

> CHARLES WILSON (1890-1961), U.S. industrialist, Secretary of Defense. Usual version of statement by Wilson, head of General Motors Corporation, 1941-53, to a U.S. Senate committee, Jan. 1953. The statement as reported by the *New York Times* (24 Feb. 1953) was, "For years I thought what was good for our country was good for General Motors and vice versa. The difference did not exist. Our company is too big. It goes with the welfare of the country." The Democrats on the committee, who were in a majority, focused on the "vice versa" of Wilson's statement, to question his true loyalties.

33 Most men are individuals no longer so far as their business, its activities, or its moralities are concerned. They are not units but fractions.

> WOODROW WILSON (1856-1924), U.S. Democratic politician, president. Speech, 31 Aug. 1910, Chattanooga, Tenn.

See also Dickens on BARGAINING; Bagehot on BUREAUCRACY; Pitt on FINANCE; MANAGEMENT; Wilde on MEETINGS; MONOPOLIES; Carnegie on PARTNERSHIP; Haliburton on PUNCTUALITY; Johnson on RESPECTABILITY; Coolidge on The UNITED STATES.

GEORGE GORDON NOEL BYRON, 6TH BARON BYRON

1 As our actual present world . . . shows itself more clearly—our world of an aristocracy materialised and null, a middle-class purblind and hideous, a lower class crude and brutal—we shall turn our eyes again, and to more purpose, upon this passionate and dauntless soldier of a forlorn hope.

> MATTHEW ARNOLD (1822-88), English poet, critic. *Essays in Criticism*, "Byron" (Second Series, 1888).

2 I have not loved the world, nor the world me;
I have not flatter'd its rank breath, nor bow'd
To its idolatries a patient knee.

> LORD BYRON (1788-1824), English poet. *Childe Harold's Pilgrimage*, cto. 3, st. 113.

3 I really am the meekest and mildest of men since Moses (though the public and mine "excellent wife" cannot find it out).

> LORD BYRON (1788-1824), English poet. Letter, 8 March 1822 (published in *Byron's Letters and Journals*, vol. 9, ed. by Leslie A. Marchand, 1979), referring to *Numbers* 12:3: "Now the man Moses was very meek, above all the men which were upon the face of the earth."

4 If they had said that the sun or the moon had gone out of the heavens, it could not have struck me with the idea of a more awful and dreary blank in creation than the words: "Byron is dead!"

> JANE WELSH CARLYLE (1801-66), Scottish poet. Letter, 20 May 1824, to her future husband, Thomas Carlyle (published in *The Love Letters of Thomas Carlyle and Jane Welsh*, 1908).

5 The genius of Byron, which appeared at the beginning of this century, is like a funeral torch sculptured on our cradles.

> EMILIO CASTELAR Y RIPOLL (1832-99), Spanish statesman, writer. Quoted in: Doris Langley Moore, *The Late Lord Byron*, ch. 15 (1961; rev. 1976). Moore commented: "The reader of our time would be more inclined to compare him to an inexhaustible Roman candle, or one of those rockets that goes on breaking out in varied coruscations and leaves in the air a luminous smoky trail, an acrid tang of gunpowder."

6 Envy has blackened every page of his history. . . . The future, in its justice, will number him among those men whom passions and an excess of activity have condemned to unhappiness, through the gift of genius.

> EUGÈNE DELACROIX (1798-1863), French artist. Note written after the death of Byron, 1825 (published in *The Journal of Eugène Delacroix*, Supplement, tr. by Walter Pach, 1937).

7 The more Byron is known, the better he will be loved.

> CONTESSA TERESA GUICCIOLI (c. 1800-1873), Italian society figure, Byron's mistress. Quoted in: Iris Origo, *The Last Attachment*, Introduction (1949), allegedly said on her death-bed.

8 It is not the passion of a mind struggling with misfortune, or the hopelessness of its desires, but of a mind preying on itself, and disgusted with, or indifferent to all other things.

> WILLIAM HAZLITT (1778-1830), English essayist. *Lectures on the English Poets*, "On the Living Poets" (1818), commenting on Byron's poetry.

9 You speak of Lord Byron and me—there is this great difference between us. He describes what he sees—I describe what I imagine. Mine is the hardest task.

JOHN KEATS (1795-1821), English poet. Letter, 17-27 Sept. 1819, to his brother and sister-in-law George and Georgiana Keats (published in *The Letters of John Keats*, no. 156, ed. by Frederick Page, 1954).

10 Thank God! none of my children have an atom of poetry in their composition!

AUGUSTA LEIGH (1783-1851), Byron's half-sister. Letter, 1 Jan. 1833, to Byron's publisher, John Murray. Quoted in: Doris Langley Moore, *The Late Lord Byron*, ch. 15 (1961; rev. 1976).

11 A few more years will destroy whatever yet remains of that magical potency which once belonged to the name of Byron.

THOMAS, BABINGTON MACAULAY (1800-1859), English historian. "Moore's Life of Lord Byron," in *Edinburgh Review* (June 1831; repr. in *Lord Macaulay's Essays*, 1889).

12 I never heard a single expression of fondness for him fall from the lips of any of those who knew him well.

THOMAS, BABINGTON MACAULAY (1800-1859), English historian, Whig politician. Letter, 7 June 1831, to Hannah and Margaret Macaulay.

13 It is his weakness to be proud: he derives, from a comparison of his own extraordinary mind with the dwarfish intellects that surround him, an intense apprehension of the nothingness of human life.

PERCY BYSSHE SHELLEY (1792-1822), English poet. *Julian and Maddalo*, Preface. The description of Count Maddalo was taken to be a portrait of Byron.

14 Lord Byron is an exceedingly interesting person, and as such is it not to be regretted that he is a slave to the vilest and most vulgar prejudices, and as mad as the winds?

PERCY BYSSHE SHELLEY (1792-1822), English poet. Letter, 17 July 1816, to Thomas Love Peacock (published in *The Letters of Percy Bysshe Shelley*, vol. 1, ed. by Frederick L. Jones, 1964).

See also Byron on ENGLAND AND THE ENGLISH; Byron on GENIUS.

CALIFORNIA AND THE WEST

1 California is a fine place to live—if you happen to be an orange.

FRED ALLEN (1894-1957), U.S. radio comic. *American Magazine* (Dec. 1945).

2 Out where the handclasp's a little stronger,
Out where the smile dwells a little longer,
That's where the West begins.

ARTHUR CHAPMAN (1873-1935), U.S. poet, author. *Out Where the West Begins*, st. 1.

3 It used to be said that you had to know what was happening in America because it gave us a glimpse of our future. Today, the rest of America, and after that Europe, had better heed what happens in California, for it already reveals the type of civilisation that is in store for all of us.

ALISTAIR COOKE (b. 1908), British broadcaster, journalist. *Talk About America*, ch. 38 (1968).

4 California is a place in which a boom mentality and a sense of Chekhovian loss meet in uneasy suspension; in which the mind is troubled by some buried but ineradicable suspicion that things had better work here, because here, beneath that immense bleached sky, is where we run out of continent.

JOAN DIDION (b. 1935), U.S. essayist. *Slouching Towards Bethlehem*, "Notes From a Native Daughter" (1968; first published 1965).

5 The apparent ease of California life is an illusion, and those who believe the illusion will live here in only the most temporary way.

JOAN DIDION (b. 1935), U.S. essayist. *The White Album*, "Holy Water" (1979; first published 1977).

6 The attraction and superiority of California are in its days. It has better days & more of them, than any other country.

RALPH WALDO EMERSON (1803-82), U.S. essayist, poet, philosopher. *The Journals and Miscellaneous Notebooks of Ralph Waldo Emerson*, vol. 16, p. 79 of the original manuscript (ed. by Ronald Bosco and Glen Johnson, 1982), entry for 1871.

7 Only remember—west of the Mississippi it's a little more look, see, act. A little less rationalize, comment, talk.

F. SCOTT FITZGERALD (1896-1940), U.S. author. Letter, summer 1934, to Fitzgerald's biographer and editor of his letters Andrew Turnbull (published in *The Letters of F. Scott Fitzgerald*, ed. by Andrew Turnbull, 1963).

8 I met a Californian who would
Talk California—a state so blessed
He said, in climate, none had ever died there
A natural death, and Vigilance Committees
Had had to organize to stock the graveyards
And vindicate the state's humanity.

ROBERT FROST (1874-1963), U.S. poet. *New Hampshire*.

9 California is a tragic country—like Palestine, like every Promised Land.

CHRISTOPHER ISHERWOOD (1904-86), British author. "Los Angeles," in *Horizon*, (London, 1947; repr. in *Exhumations*, 1966).

10 California is a queer place—in a way, it has turned its back on the world, and looks into the void Pacific. It is absolutely selfish, very empty, but not false, and at least, not full of false effort.

D. H. LAWRENCE (1885-1930), British author. Letter, 24 Sept.1923 (published in *The Letters of D. H. Lawrence*, vol. 4, ed. by James T. Boulton, E. Mansfield and W. Roberts, 1987).

11 Wherever I looked, there was nothing to see but more long streets and thousands of cars going along them, and dried-up country on each side of the streets. It was like the Sahara, only dirty.

MOHAMMED MRABET (b. 1940), Moroccan author. *Look And Move On*, ch. 11 (tr. by Paul Bowles, 1976), of California. "Like the Sahara Only Dirty" was the title of this chapter in Mohammed Mrabet's novelistic autobiography.

12 They are a very decent generous lot of people out here and *they don't expect you to listen*. . . . It's the secret of social ease in this country. They talk entirely for their own pleasure. Nothing they say is designed to be heard.

EVELYN WAUGH (1903-66), British novelist. Sir Francis Hinsley, a British expatriate in California, in *The Loved One* (1948; 1951, p. 8).

13   The almost Oriental politeness of the West Coast is one of its distinctive regional features, in marked contrast to the contentiousness of the East Coast. . . . So few human contacts in Los Angeles go unmediated by glass (either a TV screen or an automobile windshield), that the direct confrontation renders the participants docile, stunned, sweet.

> EDMUND WHITE (b. 1940), U.S. author. *States of Desire: Travels in Gay America*, ch. 1 (1980).

See also LOS ANGELES; SAN FRANCISCO; Didion on WATER.

CANADA AND THE CANADIANS

1   The beginning of Canadian cultural nationalism was not "Am I really that oppressed?" but "Am I really that boring?"

> MARGARET ATWOOD (b. 1939), Canadian novelist, poet, critic. "Dancing On the Edge Of the Precipice," interview with Joyce Carol Oates published in *Ontario Review* (fall-winter 1978; repr. in *Conversations*, ed. by Earl G. Ingersoll, 1990).

2   It is wonderful to feel the grandness of Canada in the raw, not because she is Canada but because she's something sublime that you were born into, some great rugged power that you are a part of.

> EMILY CARR (1871-1945), Canadian artist. *Hundreds and Thousands: The Journals of Emily Carr* (1966), entry for 16 April 1937.

3   Some say that no one ever leaves Montreal, for that city, like Canada itself, is designed to preserve the past, a past that happened somewhere else.

> LEONARD COHEN (b. 1934), Canadian singer, poet, novelist. *The Favourite Game*, bk. 2, sct. 19 (1963).

4   Canada is not really a place where you are encouraged to have large spiritual adventures.

> ROBERTSON DAVIES (b. 1913), Canadian novelist, journalist. *The Enthusiasms of Robertson Davies*, "The Table Talk of Robertson Davies" (1990).

5   I see Canada as a country torn between a very northern, rather extraordinary, mystical spirit which it fears and its desire to present itself to the world as a Scotch banker.

> ROBERTSON DAVIES (b. 1913), Canadian novelist, journalist. *The Enthusiasms of Robertson Davies*, "The Table Talk of Robertson Davies" (1990).

6   Geography has made us neighbors. History has made us friends. Economics has made us partners. And necessity has made us allies. Those whom nature hath so joined together, let no man put asunder.

> JOHN F. KENNEDY (1917-63), U.S. Democratic politician, president. Address, 17 May 1961, to Canadian Parliament, Ottawa.

7   Now I possess and am possessed of the land
  where I would be,
And the curve of half Earth's generous breast shall
  sooth and ravish me!

> RUDYARD KIPLING (1865-1936), British author, poet. *The Prairie (Canada)*.

8   I was so angry to realize I'm a Quebecois, with no past, no history, just two cans of maple syrup.

> JEAN CLAUDE LAUZON (b. 1954), Quebecois film director. Interview in *World Press Review* (New York, Aug. 1992).

9   Canadians look down on the United States and consider it Hell. They are right to do so. Canada is to the United States what, in Dante's scheme, Limbo is to Hell.

> IRVING LAYTON (b. 1912), Canadian poet. *The Whole Bloody Bird*, "Obs II" (1969).

10   The past is still, for us, a place that is not safely settled.

> MICHAEL ONDAATJE (b. 1943), Canadian novelist. *The Faber Book of Contemporary Canadian Short Stories*, Introduction (1990).

See also Layton on ASSASSINATION.

CANCER

1   We "need" cancer because, by the very fact of its incurability, it makes all other diseases, however virulent, *not cancer*.

> GILBERT ADAIR, British author and critic. *Myths and Memories*, "Under the Sign of Cancer" (1986).

2   Nobody knows what the cause is,
Though some pretend they do;
It's like some hidden assassin
Waiting to strike at you.
Childless women get it,
And men when they retire;
It's as if there had to be some outlet
For their foiled creative fire.

> W. H. AUDEN (1907-73), Anglo-American poet. *Dr. Thomas on Cancer in Miss Gee*.

3   My veins are filled, once a week with a Neapolitan carpet cleaner distilled from the Adriatic and I am as bald as an egg. However I still get around and am mean to cats.

> JOHN CHEEVER (1912-82), U.S. author. Letter, 10 May 1982, to Philip Roth (published in *The Letters of John Cheever*, 1989), concerning his cancer and its treatment.

4   I wish I had the voice of Homer
To sing of rectal carcinoma.

> J. B. S. HALDANE (1892-1964), British scientist. *Cancer's a Funny Thing*, in *New Statesman* (London, 21 Feb. 1964). "The main functions of my rhyme," Haldane wrote, "were to induce cancer patients to be operated on early and to be cheerful about it." The poem describes Haldane's colostomy.

5   Cancer patients are lied to, not just because the disease is (or is thought to be) a death sentence, but because it is felt to be obscene—in the original meaning of that word: ill-omened, abominable, repugnant to the senses.

> SUSAN SONTAG (b. 1933), U.S. essayist. *Illness As Metaphor*, ch. 1 (1978).

CANDOR

1 Nakedness is uncomely, as well in mind as body, and it addeth no small reverence to men's manners and actions if they be not altogether open. . . . Therefore set it down: *That a habit of secrecy is both politic and moral.*

> FRANCIS BACON (1561-1626), English philosopher, essayist, statesman. *Essays*, "Of Simulation and Dissimulation" (1597-1625).

2 Always be ready to speak your mind, and a base man will avoid you.

> WILLIAM BLAKE (1757-1827), English poet, painter, engraver. *The Marriage of Heaven and Hell*, "Proverbs of Hell," plate 8 (1790-93; repr. in *Complete Writings*, ed. by Geoffrey Keynes, 1957).

3 Give me the avowed, the erect, the manly foe,
Bold I can meet—perhaps may turn his blow;
But of all plagues, good Heaven, thy wrath can send,
Save, save, oh save me from the Candid Friend.

> GEORGE CANNING (1770-1827), English statesman, prime minister. *New Morality.*

4 Candor is a proof of both a just frame of mind, and of a good tone of breeding. It is a quality that belongs equally to the honest man and to the gentleman.

> JAMES FENIMORE COOPER (1789-1851), U.S. novelist. *The American Democrat*, ch. 23 (1838).

5 "Frank and explicit"—that is the right line to take when you wish to conceal your own mind and to confuse the minds of others.

> BENJAMIN DISRAELI (1804-1881), English statesman, author. *Sybil*, bk. 6, ch. 1, "The Gentleman in Downing Street" (1845).

6 To be candid, in Middlemarch phraseology, meant, to use an early opportunity of letting your friends know that you did not take a cheerful view of their capacity, their conduct, or their position; and a robust candour never waited to be asked for its opinion.

> GEORGE ELIOT (1819-80), English novelist, editor. *Middlemarch*, bk. 8, ch. 74 (1871).

7 If all hearts were open and all desires known—as they would be if people showed their souls—how many gapings, sighings, clenched fists, knotted brows, broad grins, and red eyes should we see in the market-place!

> THOMAS HARDY (1840-1928), English novelist, poet. Note, 18 Aug. 1908 (published in Florence Emily Hardy, *The Later Years of Thomas Hardy*, ch. 10, 1930).

8 There is an unseemly exposure of the mind, as well as of the body.

> WILLIAM HAZLITT (1778-1830), English essayist. *Sketches and Essays*, "On Disagreeable People" (1839). The philosopher and statesman Francis Bacon had expressed a similar idea in his essay "Of Simulation and Dissimulation": "Nakedness is uncomely, as well in mind as in body."

9 You may tell a man thou art a fiend, but not your nose wants blowing; to him alone who can bear a thing of that kind, you may tell all.

> JOHANN KASPAR LAVATER (1741-1801), Swiss divine, poet. *Aphorisms on Man*, no. 84 (1788).

10 It is the weak and confused who worship the pseudosimplicities of brutal directness.

> MARSHALL MCLUHAN (1911-80), Canadian communications theorist. *The Mechanical Bride*, "The Tough as Narcissus" (1951).

11 Let us not be ashamed to speak what we shame not to think.

> MICHEL DE MONTAIGNE (1533-92), French essayist. *Essays*, bk. 3, ch. 5, "Upon some Verses of Virgil" (tr. by John Florio, 1588).

12 Not to expose your true feelings to an adult seems to be instinctive from the age of seven or eight onwards.

> GEORGE ORWELL (1903-50), British author. "Such, Such were the Joys" (1947; repr. in *The Collected Essays, Journalism and Letters of George Orwell*, ed. by Sonia Orwell and Ian Angus, 1968).

CAPITAL PUNISHMENT

1 The killing of a criminal can be moral—but never its legitimation.

> WALTER BENJAMIN (1892-1940), German critic, philosopher. *One-Way Street*, "Hardware" (1928; repr. in *One-Way Street and Other Writings*, 1978).

2 Christ's crucifix shall be made an excuse for executing criminals.

> WILLIAM BLAKE (1757-1827), English poet, painter, engraver. Notes on manuscript of "The Four Zoas" (published in *Complete Writings*, ed. by Geoffrey Keynes, 1957).

3 What will be left of the power of example if it is proved that capital punishment has another power, and a very real one, which degrades men to the point of shame, madness, and murder?

> ALBERT CAMUS (1913-60), French-Algerian philosopher, author. *Resistance, Rebellion and Death*, "Reflections on the Guillotine" (1961).

4 It is a strange, strange fate, and now, as I stand face to face with death, I feel just as if they were going to kill a boy. For I feel like a boy—and my hands are so free from blood and my heart always so compassionate and pitiful that I cannot comprehend that anyone wants to hang me.

> SIR ROGER CASEMENT (1864-1916), Irish colonial administrator, nationalist. Note, Aug. 1916, found in Casement's condemned cell, Pentonville, London. He was executed after attempting to overthrow, with German help, British rule in Ireland.

5 It seems perfectly simple and inevitable, like lying down after a long day's work.

> ROBERT ERSKINE CHILDERS (1870-1922), Irish author, nationalist. Letter, Nov. 1922, to his wife from prison, shortly before his execution.

6 Depend upon it, Sir, when a man knows he is to be hanged in a fortnight, it concentrates his mind wonderfully.

> SAMUEL JOHNSON (1709-84), English author, lexicographer. Quoted in: James Boswell, *Life of Samuel Johnson*, 19 Sept. 1777 (1791).

7 If we are to abolish the death penalty, I should like to see the first step taken by my friends the murderers.

> ALPHONSE KARR (1808-90), French journalist, novelist. *Les*

Guêpes (Paris, 31 Jan. 1849). An alternative source attributes this to a voice from the hall in the French Chamber, during a debate on the death penalty, when a speech proposing abolition was being tumultuously applauded.

8   All grandeur, all power, all subordination to authority rests on the executioner: he is the horror and the bond of human association. Remove this incomprehensible agent from the world and at that very moment order gives way to chaos, thrones topple and society disappears.

JOSEPH DE MAISTRE (1753-1821), French diplomat, philosopher. The Count, in *Les Soirées de Saint-Pétersbourg,* "First Dialogue" (1821; repr. in *The Works of Joseph de Maistre,* ed. Jack Lively, 1965).

9   I went out to Charing Cross to see Major-General Harrison hanged, drawn and quartered—which was done there—he looking as cheerful as any man could do in that condition.

SAMUEL PEPYS (1633-1703), English diarist. Diary entry, 13 Oct. 1660. Thomas Harrison was one of the regicides responsible for Charles I's execution. It was said that he met his death with courage, making a final speech on the scaffold: "By God I have leapt over a wall, by God I have run through a troop, and by God I will go through this death, and he will make it easy."

10   Many a good hanging prevents a bad marriage.

WILLIAM SHAKESPEARE (1564-1616), English dramatist, poet. Feste, in *Twelfth Night,* act 1, sc. 5.

11   There's something dreadfully decisive about a beheading.

ANNE SMEDLEY c. 1894-1950), U.S. author, lecturer. *Battle Hymn of China,* "Farewell!" bk. 9 (1943).

12   The hour of departure has arrived, and we go our ways—I to die and you to live. Which is the better, only God knows.

SOCRATES (469-399 B.C.), Greek philosopher. Quoted in: Plato's *Apology,* sct. 42a. Last words of his speech to the court following the sentence of death imposed on him by the Athenians, who had found him guilty of impiety and the corruption of youth.

13   It is sweet to dance to violins
When Love and Life are fair:
To dance to flutes, to dance to lutes
Is delicate and rare:
But it is not sweet with nimble feet
To dance upon the air!

OSCAR WILDE (1854-1900), Anglo-Irish playwright, author. *The Ballad of Reading Gaol,* sct. 2.

14   It is well for our vanity that we slay the criminal, for if we suffered him to live he might show us what we had gained by his crime.

OSCAR WILDE (1854-1900), Anglo-Irish playwright, author. Gilbert, in *The Critic as Artist,* pt. 1 (published in *Intentions,* 1891).

See also Camus on CRIME AND CRIMINALS; Fouche on ERROR; Camus on LIFE, LUST FOR; Savile, Shakespeare on PUNISHMENT; Pope on TRIALS.

CAPITALISM

1   Fact is Our Lord knew all about the power of money: He gave capitalism a tiny niche in His scheme of things, He gave it a chance, He even provided a first instalment of funds. Can you beat that? It's so magnificent. God despises nothing. After all, if the deal had come off, Judas would probably have endowed sanatoriums, hospitals, public libraries or laboratories.

GEORGES BERNANOS (1888-1948), French novelist, political writer. The Curé de Torcy, in *The Diary of a Country Priest,* ch. 2 (1936).

2   The most eloquent eulogy of capitalism was made by its greatest enemy. Marx is only anti-capitalist in so far as capitalism is out of date.

ALBERT CAMUS (1913-60), French-Algerian philosopher, author. *The Rebel,* pt. 3, "State Terrorism and Rational Terror" (1951; tr. 1953).

3   Predatory capitalism created a complex industrial system and an advanced technology; it permitted a considerable extension of democratic practice and fostered certain liberal values, but within limits that are now being pressed and must be overcome. It is not a fit system for the mid-twentieth century.

NOAM CHOMSKY (b. 1928), U.S. linguist, political analyst. "Language and Freedom," lecture, delivered Jan. 1970, at Loyola University, Chicago (published in *For Reasons of State,* 1973).

4   History suggests that capitalism is a necessary condition for political freedom. Clearly it is not a sufficient condition.

MILTON FRIEDMAN (b. 1912), U.S. economist. *Capitalism and Freedom,* ch. 1 (1962).

5   Capital as such is not evil; it is its wrong use that is evil. Capital in some form or other will always be needed.

MOHANDAS K. GANDHI (1869-1948), Indian political and spiritual leader. *Harijan* (28 July 1940).

6   Capital is a result of labor, and is used by labor to assist it in further production. Labor is the active and initial force, and labor is therefore the employer of capital.

HENRY GEORGE (1839-97), U.S. economist. *Progress and Poverty,* bk. 3, ch. 1 (1879).

7   The unpleasant and unacceptable face of capitalism.

EDWARD HEATH (b. 1916), British Conservative politician, prime minister. Speech, 15 May 1973, to House of Commons, London, on the high emoluments of company directors during a period of recession.

8   Capitalism is at its liberating best in a noncapitalist environment. The crypto-businessman is the true revolutionary in a Communist country.

ERIC HOFFER (1902-83), U.S. philosopher. *Reflections on the Human Condition,* aph. 73 (1973).

9   The decadent international but individualistic capitalism in the hands of which we found ourselves after the war is not a success. It is not intelligent. It is not beautiful. It is not just. It is not virtuous. And it doesn't deliver the goods.

JOHN MAYNARD KEYNES (1883-1946), British economist. *National Self-Sufficiency,* sct. 3 (1933; repr. in *Collected Works,* vol. 9, 1982).

10 The genius of capitalism consists precisely in its lack of morality. Unless he is rich enough to hire his own choir, a capitalist is a fellow who, by definition, can ill afford to believe in anything other than the doctrine of the bottom line. Deprive a capitalist of his God-given right to lie and cheat and steal, and the poor sap stands a better than even chance of becoming one of the abominable wards of the state from whose grimy fingers the Reagan Administration hopes to snatch the ark of democracy.

> LEWIS H. LAPHAM (b. 1935), U.S. essayist and editor. "Moral Dandyism," in *Harper's* (New York, July 1985).

11 Capitalists are no more capable of self-sacrifice than a man is capable of lifting himself up by his own bootstraps.

> VLADIMIR ILYICH LENIN (1870-1924), Russian revolutionary leader. *Letters from Afar*, ch. 4 (1917).

12 In the democratic western countries so-called capitalism leads a saturnalia of "freedom," like a bastard brother of reform.

> WYNDHAM LEWIS (1882-1957), British author, painter. *The Art of Being Ruled*, ch. 2, "Vulgarization and Political Decay" (1926).

13 Capital is money, capital is commodities. . . . By virtue of it being value, it has acquired the occult ability to add value to itself. It brings forth living offspring, or, at the least, lays golden eggs.

> KARL MARX (1818-83), German political theorist, social philosopher. *Capital*, vol. 1, ch. 4 (1867).

14 Capital is dead labor, which, vampire-like, lives only by sucking living labor, and lives the more, the more labor it sucks.

> KARL MARX (1818-83), German political theorist, social philosopher. *Capital*, vol. 1, ch. 10 (1867).

15 Capitalism is an art form, an Apollonian fabrication to rival nature. It is hypocritical for feminists and intellectuals to enjoy the pleasures and conveniences of capitalism while sneering at it. . . . Everyone born into capitalism has incurred a debt to it. Give Caesar his due.

> CAMILLE PAGLIA (b. 1947), U.S. author, critic, educator. *Sexual Personae*, ch. 1 (1990).

16 Advocates of capitalism are very apt to appeal to the sacred principles of liberty, which are embodied in one maxim: *The fortunate must not be restrained in the exercise of tyranny over the unfortunate.*

> BERTRAND RUSSELL (1872-1970), British philosopher, mathematician. *Sceptical Essays*, "Freedom in Society" (1928).

17 The evolution of the capitalist style of life could be easily—and perhaps most tellingly—described in terms of the genesis of the modern Lounge Suit.

> JOSEPH A. SCHUMPETER (1883-1950), Austrian-American economist. *Capitalism, Socialism and Democracy*, ch. 11 (1942).

18 Capitalism inevitably and by virtue of the very logic of its civilization creates, educates and subsidizes a vested interest in social unrest.

> JOSEPH A. SCHUMPETER (1883-1950), Austrian-American economist. *Capitalism, Socialism and Democracy*, ch. 13, sct.2 (1942).

19 The far right seeks to retain the material progress of American capitalism while removing some of its crucial causes and consequences—as though a bridge could be made to change part of its function by blowing up part of its supports and part of its exit.

> RONALD SEGAL (b. 1932), South African author. *America's Receeding Future*, ch. 1 (1968).

20 The ideology of capitalism makes us all into connoisseurs of liberty—of the indefinite expansion of possibility.

> SUSAN SONTAG (b. 1933), U.S. essayist. *Aids and Its Metaphors*, ch. 7 (1989).

21 The first rule of venture capitalism should be Shoot the Inventor.

> SIR RICHARD STOREY (b. 1937), British newspaper publisher. Quoted in: Brian MacArthur, *Eddy Shah: Today and the Newspaper Revolution*, ch. 21 (1988). Sir Richard was one of entrepreneur Eddy Shah's backers.

22 What breaks capitalism, all that will ever break capitalism, is capitalists. The faster they run the more strain on their heart.

> RAYMOND WILLIAMS (1921-88), British novelist, critic. Monkey Pitter, in *Loyalties*, pt. 3, ch. 2 (1985). This was Williams's last novel.

See also Galbraith on ECONOMICS; FREE ENTERPRISE; Lenin on FREEDOM; Keynes on INFLATION; Lincoln on LABOR; Hobsbawm on WAR.

CAPRICE

1 "YES," I answered you last night,
"No," this morning, Sir, I say.
Colours seen by candle-light,
Will not look the same by day.

> ELIZABETH BARRETT BROWNING (1806-61), English Poet. *The Lady's "Yes,"* st. 1.

2 We are the creatures of imagination, passion, and self-will, more than of reason or even of self-interest. . . . Even in the common transactions and daily intercourse of life, we are governed by whim, caprice, prejudice, or accident. The falling of a teacup puts us out of temper for the day; and a quarrel that commenced about the pattern of a gown may end only with our lives.

> WILLIAM HAZLITT (1778-1830), English essayist. "On the Predominant Principles and Excitements in the Human Mind," published in *Examiner* (London, 26 Feb. 1815; repr. in *Collected Works*, ed. by A. R. Waller and Arnold Glover, vol. 11, 1904).

3 She has a whim of iron.

> Attributed to OLIVER HERFORD (1863-1935), U.S. poet, illustrator. Remark referring to his wife. It reappeared in *Excuse it Please*, "Impossible Pudding" (1929): "King Barumph has a whim of iron!"

4 Unpredictability, too, can become monotonous.

> ERIC HOFFER (1902-83), U.S. philosopher. *The Passionate State of Mind*, aph. 224 (1955).

5 "You gave me the key of your heart, my love;
Then why did you make me knock?"
Oh that was yesterday, saints above!
And last night—I changed the lock!

> JOHN BOYLE O'REILLY (1844-90), Irish poet, author. *Constancy.*

6   Never lose sight of the fact that all human felicity lies in man's imagination, and that he cannot think to attain it unless he heeds all his caprices. The most fortunate of persons is he who has the most means to satisfy his vagaries.

MARQUIS DE SADE (1740-1814), French author. Saint-Fond, in *L'Histoire de Juliette, ou les Prospérités du Vice*, pt. 2 (1797).

7   The only difference between a caprice and a life-long passion is that the caprice lasts a little longer.

OSCAR WILDE (1854-1900), Anglo-Irish playwright, author. Lord Henry, in *The Picture of Dorian Gray*, ch. 19 (1891).

CARDS

1   A man's idea in a card game is war—cruel, devastating and pitiless. A lady's idea of it is a combination of larceny, embezzlement and burglary.

FINLEY PETER DUNNE (1867-1936), U.S. journalist, humorist. *Mr. Dooley on Making a Will*, "On the Game of Cards" (1919).

2   When in doubt, win the trick.

EDMOND HOYLE (1672-1769), English writer on cards. *Hoyle's Games*, "Whist, Twenty-Four Short Rules for Learners" (c. 1756).

3   I am sorry I have not learnt to play at cards. It is very useful in life: it generates kindness, and consolidates society.

SAMUEL JOHNSON (1709-84), English author, lexicographer. Quoted in: James Boswell, *Tour of the Hebrides*, 21 Nov. 1773 (1785). Boswell noted that Johnson's remark would be, "a valuable text for many decent old dowagers, and other good company, in various circles, to descant upon."

4   But cards are war, in disguise of a sport.

CHARLES LAMB (1775-1834), English essayist, critic. *Essays of Elia*, "Mrs. Battle's Opinions on Whist" (1820-23).

5   The poker player learns that sometimes both science and common sense are wrong; that the bumblebee *can* fly; that, perhaps, one should never trust an expert; that there are more things in heaven and earth than are dreamt of by those with an academic bent.

DAVID MAMET (b. 1947), U.S. playwright. *Writing in Restaurants*, "Things I Have Learned Playing Poker on the Hill" (1986).

6   The best chess-player in Christendom *may* be little more than the best player of chess; but proficiency in whist implies capacity for success in all these more important undertakings where mind struggles with mind.

EDGAR ALLAN POE (1809-45), U.S. poet, critic, short-story writer. *The Murders in the Rue Morgue* (1841).

7   Because people have no thoughts to deal in, they deal cards, and try and win one another's money. Idiots!

ARTHUR SCHOPENHAUER (1788-1860), German philosopher. *Parerga and Paralipomena*, "Aphorisms on the Wisdom of Life" (1851).

CAREERS

1   People don't choose their careers; they are engulfed by them.

JOHN DOS PASSOS (1896-1970), U.S. novelist. *New York Times* (25 Oct 1959).

2   He was at a starting point which makes many a man's career a fine subject for betting, if there were any gentlemen given to that amusement who could appreciate the complicated probabilities of an arduous purpose, with all the possible thwartings and furtherings of circumstance, all the niceties of inward balance, by which a man swings and makes his point or else is carried headlong.

GEORGE ELIOT (1819-80), English novelist, editor. *Middlemarch*, bk. 2, ch. 15 (1871), said of Lydgate, the new doctor in town.

3   The most successful career must show a waste of strength that might have removed mountains, and the most unsuccessful is not that of the man who is taken unprepared, but of him who has prepared and is never taken. On a tragedy of that kind our national morality is duly silent.

E. M. FORSTER (1879-1970), British novelist, essayist. *Howards End*, ch. 12 (1910).

4   Sometimes you wonder how you got on this mountain. But sometimes you wonder, "How will I get off?"

JOAN MANLEY (b. 1932), U.S. publisher. Quoted in: *Washington Post* (8 April 1979).

5   The life-fate of the modern individual depends not only upon the family into which he was born or which he enters by marriage, but increasingly upon the corporation in which he spends the most alert hours of his best years.

C. WRIGHT MILLS (1916-1962), U.S. sociologist. *The Power Elite*, ch. 1 (1956).

6   Be nice to people on your way up because you'll meet them on your way down.

WILSON MIZNER (1876-1933), U.S. dramatist, wit. Quoted in: Alva Johnson, *The Incredible Mizners* (1953).

7   I have yet to hear a man ask for advice on how to combine marriage and a career.

GLORIA STEINEM (b. 1934), U.S. feminist writer, editor. Radio interview, 2 April 1984, LBC (London).

8   Each of the professions means a prejudice. The necessity for a career forces every one to take sides. We live in the age of the overworked, and the under-educated; the age in which people are so industrious that they become absolutely stupid.

OSCAR WILDE (1854-1900), Anglo-Irish playwright, author. Gilbert, in *The Critic as Artist*, pt. 2 (published in *Intentions*, 1891)

See also Emerson on WORK.

THE CARIBBEAN

1   You know people exaggerate that all is wild in Jamaica. I think that sometimes people fire a shot to try to make you nervous. They are not trying to hurt you.

MICHAEL MANLEY (b. 1924), Jamaican politician, prime minister. *Daily Telegraph* (London, 8 Feb. 1989).

2   I come from a place that likes grandeur; it likes large gestures; it is not inhibited by flourish; it is a rhetor-

ical society; it is a society of physical performance; it is a society of style.

DEREK WALCOTT (b. 1930), West Indian poet, playwright. Interview in *Writers at Work* (Eighth Series; ed. by George Plimpton, 1988).

CARICATURE

1 The most perfect caricature is that which, on a small surface, with the simplest means, most accurately exaggerates, to the highest point, the peculiarities of a human being, at his most characteristic moment in the most beautiful manner.

SIR MAX BEERBOHM (1872-1956), British author. *A Variety of Things*, "The Spirit of Caricature" (1928; essay written 1901).

2 If our caricaturists do not hate their enemies, it is not because they are too big to hate them, but because their enemies are not big enough to hate.

G. K. CHESTERTON (1874-1936), British author. *All Things Considered*, "Conceit and Caricature" (1908).

3 There is hardly any mental misery worse than that of having our own serious phrases, our own rooted beliefs, caricatured by a charlatan or a hireling.

GEORGE ELIOT (1819-80), English novelist, editor. *Felix Holt, The Radical*, ch. 11 (1866).

4 The parody is the last refuge of the frustrated writer. Parodies are what you write when you are associate editor of the Harvard *Lampoon*. The greater the work of literature, the easier the parody. The step up from writing parodies is writing on the wall above the urinal.

ERNEST HEMINGWAY (1899-1961), U.S. author. Quoted in: A. E. Hotchner, *Papa Hemingway*, pt. 1, ch. 4 (1966 ed.).

5 The whole point of Camp is to dethrone the serious. Camp is playful, anti-serious. More precisely, Camp involves a new, more complex relation to "the serious." One can be serious about the frivolous, frivolous about the serious.

SUSAN SONTAG (b. 1933), U.S. essayist. *Against Interpretation*, "Notes on 'Camp'," Note 41 (1966; first published 1964).

THOMAS CARLYLE

1 It was very good of God to let Carlyle and Mrs. Carlyle marry one another and so make only two people miserable instead of four, besides being very amusing.

SAMUEL BUTLER (1835-1902), English author. Letter, 21 Nov. 1984 (published in *Letters Between Samuel Butler and E. M. A. Savage 1871-1885*, 1935). The quote has been erroneously attributed to Tennyson.

2 Thomas Carlyle is incontestably dead at last, by the acknowledgment of all newspapers. I had, however, the pleasure of an intimate intercourse with him when he was an infinitely deader man than he is now.

HENRY JAMES, SR. (1811-82), U.S. philosopher. *Atlantic Monthly* (Boston, May 1881).

3 Carlyle, a man of strong words and attitudes, a rhetorician from necessity, continually agitated by the

desire for a strong faith and the feeling of incapacity for it (— in this a typical Romantic!). . . . Carlyle is an English atheist who wants to be honored for not being one.

FRIEDRICH NIETZSCHE (1844-1900), German philosopher. *Twilight of the Idols*, "Expeditions of an Untimely Man," aph. 12 (1889).

4 I could not help but say that Mr. Carlyle seemed the only virtuous philosopher we had. Upon which his wife answered, "My dear, if Mr. Carlyle's digestion had been stronger, there is no saying what he might have been!"

MARGARET OLIPHANT (1828-97), English novelist, historian. Letter, [?] May 1866, describing conversation between herself and Jane Welsh Carlyle, the wife of historian Thomas Carlyle (published in *Autobiography and Letters of Mrs. Margaret Oliphant*, 1899).

5 The next work of Carlyle will be entitled "Bow-Wow," and the title-page will have a motto from the opening chapter of the Koran: "There is *no* error in this Book."

EDGAR ALLAN POE (1809-45), U.S. poet, critic, short-story writer. *Marginalia* (first published in *Southern Literary Messenger*, Richmond, Va., July 1849; repr. in *Essays and Reviews*, 1984).

6 Rugged, mountainous, volcanic, he was himself more a French revolution than any of his volumes.

WALT WHITMAN (1819-92), U.S. poet. *Specimen Days* (10 Feb. 1881).

CARS

1 What our children have to fear is not the cars on the highways of tomorrow but our own pleasure in calculating the most elegant parameters of their deaths.

J. G. BALLARD (b. 1930), English novelist. *The Atrocity Exhibition*, ch. 8 (1970).

2 The car as we know it is on the way out. To a large extent, I deplore its passing, for as a basically old-fashioned machine, it enshrines a basically old-fashioned idea: freedom. In terms of pollution, noise and human life, the price of that freedom may be high, but perhaps the car, by the very muddle and confusion it causes, may be holding back the remorseless spread of the regimented, electronic society.

J. G. BALLARD (b. 1930), British author. "The Car, The Future" (first published in *Drive*, (London, Autumn 1971; repr. in *Re/Search*, no. 8/9, San Francisco, 1984).

3 I think that cars today are almost the exact equivalent of the great Gothic cathedrals: I mean the supreme creation of an era, conceived with passion by unknown artists, and consumed in image if not in usage by a whole population which appropriates them as a purely magical object.

ROLAND BARTHES (1915-80), French semiologist. *Mythologies*, "The New Citroën" (1957; tr. 1972).

4 Driving is a spectacular form of amnesia. Everything is to be discovered, everything to be obliterated.

JEAN BAUDRILLARD (b. 1929), French semiologist. *America*, "Vanishing Point" (1986; tr. 1988).

5 The improved American highway system . . . isolated the American-in-transit. On his speedway . . . he

had no contact with the towns which he by-passed. If he stopped for food or gas, he was served no local fare or local fuel, but had one of Howard Johnson's nationally branded ice cream flavors, and so many gallons of Exxon. This vast ocean of superhighways was nearly as free of culture as the sea traversed by the *Mayflower* Pilgrims.

> DANIEL J. BOORSTIN (b. 1914), U.S. historian. Reith Lectures, Oct. 1975 (published in *The Exploring Spirit: America and the World Experience*, lecture 4, 1976).

6 A car can massage organs which no masseur can reach. It is the one remedy for the disorders of the great sympathetic nervous system.

> JEAN COCTEAU (1889-1963), French author, filmmaker. *Opium*, (1929; tr. 1932; repr. 1957, p. 20). Cocteau added, "The craving for opium can be endured in a car."

7 Glorious, stirring sight! The poetry of motion! The *real* way to travel! The *only* way to travel! Here today— in next week tomorrow! Villages skipped, towns and cities jumped—always somebody else's horizons! O bliss! O poop-poop! O my! O my!

> KENNETH GRAHAME (1859-1932), British essayist, writer of children's books. Toad, in *The Wind in the Willows*, ch. 2 (1908).

8 The reason American cars don't sell anymore is that they have forgotten how to design the American Dream. What does it matter if you buy a car today or six months from now, because cars are not beautiful. That's why the American auto industry is in trouble: no design, no desire.

> KARL LAGERFELD (b. 1938), German-born French fashion designer. Quoted in: *Vanity Fair* (New York, Feb. 1992).

9 The car has become the carapace, the protective and aggressive shell, of urban and suburban man.

> MARSHALL MCLUHAN (1911-80), Canadian communications theorist. *Understanding Media*, ch. 22 (1964).

10 Automobiles are free of egotism, passion, prejudice and stupid ideas about where to have dinner. They are, literally, selfless. A world designed for automobiles instead of people would have wider streets, larger dining rooms, fewer stairs to climb and no smelly, dangerous subway stations.

> P. J. O'ROURKE (b. 1947), U.S. journalist. *Give War a Chance*, "An Argument in Favor of Automobiles vs Pedestrians" (1992).

11 No other man-made device since the shields and lances of the ancient knights fulfills a man's ego like an automobile.

> SIR WILLIAM (LATER LORD) ROOTES (1894-1964), British automobile manufacturer. Quoted in: "Who Said That?" 14 Jan. 1958, BBC-TV.

12 I don't even like *old* cars . . . I'd rather have a goddam horse. A horse is at least *human*, for God's sake.

> J. D. SALINGER (b. 1919), U.S. author. Holden Caulfield, in *The Catcher in the Rye*, ch. 17 (1951).

13 What I like, or one of the things I like, about motoring is the sense it gives one of lighting accidentally, like a voyager who touches another planet with the tip of his toe, upon scenes which would have gone on, have always gone on, will go on, unrecorded, save for this chance glimpse. Then it seems to me I am allowed to see the heart of the world uncovered for a moment.

> VIRGINIA WOOLF (1882-1941), British novelist. *The Diary of Virginia Woolf*, vol. 3 (ed. by Anne O. Bell, 1980), entry for 21 Aug. 1927.

See also Ballard on ACCIDENTS.

CARTOONS AND DRAWING

1 I could draw *Bloom County* with my nose and pay my cleaning lady to write it, and I'd bet I wouldn't lose 10% of my papers over the next twenty years. Such is the nature of comic-strips. Once established, their half-life is usually more than nuclear waste.

> BERKE BREATHED (b. 1957), U.S. cartoonist and author. *Time* (New York; 25 Dec. 1989).

2 In the final analysis, a drawing simply is no longer a drawing, no matter how self-sufficient its execution may be. It is a symbol, and the more profoundly the imaginary lines of projection meet higher dimensions, the better.

> PAUL KLEE (1879-1940), Swiss artist. *The Diaries of Paul Klee 1898-1918*, no. 681 (1957; tr. 1965), entry July 1905.

3 There is a relationship between cartooning and people like Miró and Picasso which may not be understood by the cartoonist, but it definitely is related even in the early Disney.

> ROY LICHTENSTEIN (b. 1923), U.S. Pop artist. "Talking with Roy Lichtenstein" (published in John Coplan, *Lichtenstein*, 1972). Quoted in: Lawrence Alloway, *Lichtenstein*, ch. 3 (1983).

4 Matisse makes a drawing, then he makes a copy of it. He recopies it five times, ten times, always clarifying the line. He's convinced that the last, the most stripped down, is the best, the purest, the definitive one; and in fact, most of the time, it was the first. In drawing, nothing is better than the first attempt.

> PABLO PICASSO (1881-1973), Spanish artist. Quoted in: Gyula Brassaï, *Picasso and Company*, p. 56 (1964; tr. 1966).

5 A drawing is always dragged down to the level of its caption.

> JAMES THURBER (1894-1961), U.S. humorist, illustrator. *New Yorker* (2 Aug. 1930).

6 My drawings have been described as pre-intentionalist, meaning that they were finished before the ideas for them had occurred to me. I shall not argue the point.

> JAMES THURBER (1894-1961), U.S. humorist, illustrator. *Life* (New York, 14 March 1960).

CATHOLICISM

1 Here is everything which can lay hold of the eye, ear and imagination—everything which can charm and bewitch the simple and ignorant. I wonder how Luther ever broke the spell.

> JOHN ADAMS (1735-1826), U.S. statesman, president. Letter, 9 Oct. 1774, to his wife, Abigail Adams.

2 Coming to Rome, much labour and little profit! The King whom you seek here, unless you bring Him with you you will not find Him.

> ANONYMOUS (9th century Irish). *A Celtic Miscellany,* "Epigram," no. 121 (1951; rev. 1971).

3 Our religion . . . is itself profoundly sad—a religion of universal anguish, and one which, because of its very catholicity, grants full liberty to the individual and asks no better than to be celebrated in each man's own language—so long as he knows anguish and is a painter.

> CHARLES BAUDELAIRE (1821-1867), French poet. "Salon of 1846," sct. 4 (published in *Curiosités Esthétiques,* 1868; repr. in *The Mirror of Art,* ed. by Jonathan Mayne, 1955).

4 Good strong thick stupefying incense-smoke!

> ROBERT BROWNING (1812-89), English poet. *The Bishop Orders His Tomb at Saint Praxed's Church.*

5 The thing with Catholicism, the same as all religions, is that it teaches what *should* be, which seems rather incorrect. This is "what should be." Now, if you're taught to live up to a "what should be" that never existed—only an occult superstition, no proof of this "should be"—then you can sit on a jury and indict easily, you can cast the first stone, you can burn Adolf Eichmann, like that!

> LENNY BRUCE (1925-66), U.S. satirical comedian. *The Essential Lenny Bruce,* "Religions Inc." (ed. by John Cohen, 1967).

6 Anti-Catholicism is the anti-semitism of the intellectual.

> PATRICK BUCHANAN (b. 1938), U.S. journalist, broadcaster, presidential candidate in 1992. *Observer* (London, 15 Dec. 1991).

7 All human life is here, but the Holy Ghost seems to be somewhere else.

> ANTHONY BURGESS (b. 1917), British author and critic. *Observer* (London, 25 May 1986), said of the Vatican in a book review.

8 It is by far the most elegant worship, hardly excepting the Greek mythology. What with incense, pictures, statues, altars, shrines, relics, and the real presence, confession, absolution,—there is something sensible to grasp at. Besides, it leaves no possibility of doubt; for those who swallow their Deity, really and truly, in transubstantiation, can hardly find any thing else otherwise than easy of digestion.

> LORD BYRON (1788-1824), English poet. Letter, 8 March 1822, to poet Thomas Moore (published in *Byron's Letters and Journals,* vol. 9, ed. by Leslie A. Marchand, 1979). Byron explained that he was bringing up one of his own daughters, Allegra, a Catholic, "that she may have her hands full."

9 Look through the whole history of countries professing the Romish religion, and you will uniformly find the leaven of this besetting and accursed principle of action—that the end will sanction any means.

> SAMUEL TAYLOR COLERIDGE (1772-1834), English poet, critic. *Table Talk* (6 Aug. 1831; published in *Specimens of the Table Talk of Samuel Taylor Coleridge,* ed. by Henry Nelson Coleridge, 1835; repr. in *Collected Works,* ed. by Kathleen Coburn, vol. 14, 1990).

10 She had once been a Catholic, but discovering that priests were infinitely more attentive when she was in process of losing or regaining faith in Mother Church, she maintained an enchantingly wavering attitude.

> F. SCOTT FITZGERALD (1896-1940), U.S. author. *This Side of Paradise,* bk. 1, ch. 1 (1920), said of Beatrice Blaine.

11 Today's Catholic church seems to reward authoritarian personalities who are clearly ill, violent, sexually obsessed and unable to remember the past.

> MATTHEW FOX (b. 1940), U.S. clergyman, author. Quoted in: *Independent* (London, 12 Nov. 1988).

12 A little skill in antiquity inclines a man to Popery.

> THOMAS FULLER (1608-61), English cleric. *The Holy State and the Profane State,* bk. 2, ch. 6 (1642). Fuller continues, "But depth in that study brings him about again to our religion.".

13 Catholics are necessarily at war with this age. That we are not more conscious of the fact, that we so often endeavour to make an impossible peace with it—that is the tragedy. You cannot serve God and Mammon.

> ERIC GILL (1882-1940), British sculptor, engraver, writer, typographer. *Essays,* "Idiocy or Ill-Will" (1948).

14 It is the custom of the Roman Church which I unworthily serve with the help of God, to tolerate some things, to turn a blind eye to some, following the spirit of discretion rather than the rigid letter of the law.

> POPE GREGORY VII (?1020-85). Letter, 9 March 1078.

15 I confess that I do not see what good it does to fulminate against the English tyranny while the Roman tyranny occupies the palace of the soul.

> JAMES JOYCE (1882-1941), Irish author. "Ireland, Island of Saints and Sages," lecture, 27 April 1907, Università Popolare Triestina (published in *Critical Writings,* sct. 35, ed. by Ellsworth Mason and Richard Ellmann, 1959).

16 For support, I fall back on my heart. Has a man any fault a woman cannot weave with and try to change into something better, if the god her man prays to is a mother holding a baby?

> HANIEL LONG (1888-1956), U.S. author, poet, journalist. *Malinche* (1939; repr. 1987, p. 73).

17 She thoroughly understands what no other Church has ever understood, how to deal with enthusiasts.

> THOMAS, BABINGTON MACAULAY (1800-1859), English historian and Whig politician. "Ranke's History of the Popes," in *Edinburgh Review* (Oct. 1840; repr. in *Critical and Historical Essays,* 1843), said of the Catholic Church.

18 Catholicism is not a soothing religion. It's a painful religion. We're all gluttons for punishment.

> MADONNA (b. 1959), U.S. singer, actor. Interview in *Rolling Stone* (New York, 23 March 1989).

19 You can't run the Church on Hail Marys.

> ARCHBISHOP PAUL MARCINKUS (b. 1922), U.S. ecclesiastic, Vatican financier. Quoted in: *Observer* (London, 25 May 1986).

20 To care for the quarrels of the past, to identify oneself passionately with a cause that became, politically speaking, a losing cause with the birth of the modern world, is to experience a kind of straining against reality, a rebellious nonconformity that, again, is rare in America, where children are instructed in the virtues of the system they live under, as though history had achieved a happy ending in American civics.

MARY MCCARTHY (1912-1989), U.S. author, critic. *Memories of a Catholic Girlhood,* "To The Reader" (1957).

21 Although every organized patriarchal religion works overtime to contribute its own brand of misogyny to the myth of woman-hate, woman-fear, and woman-evil, the Roman Catholic Church also carries the immense power of very directly affecting women's lives everywhere by its stand against birth control and abortion, and by its use of skillful and wealthy lobbies to prevent legislative change. It is an obscenity—an all-male hierarchy, celibate or not, that presumes to rule on the lives and bodies of millions of women.

ROBIN MORGAN (b. 1941), U.S. feminist author, poet. *Sisterhood Is Powerful,* Introduction (1970).

22 One cannot really be a Catholic and grown up.

GEORGE ORWELL (1903-50), British author. "Manuscript Notebook" (1949; repr. in *The Collected Essays, Journalism and Letters of George Orwell,* vol. 4, ed. by Sonia Orwell and Ian Angus, 1968).

23 If you're going to do a thing, you should do it thoroughly. If you're going to be a Christian, you may as well be a Catholic.

MURIEL SPARK (b. 1918), British novelist. *Independent* (London, 2 Aug. 1989).

24 The Catholic Church has never really come to terms with women. What I object to is being treated either as Madonnas or Mary Magdalenes.

SHIRLEY WILLIAMS (b. 1930), British Liberal-Democrat politician. *Observer* (London, 22 March 1981).

25 It is a dogma of the Roman Church that the existence of God can be proved by natural reason. Now this dogma would make it impossible for me to be a Roman Catholic. If I thought of God as another being like myself, outside myself, only infinitely more powerful, then I would regard it as my duty to defy him.

LUDWIG WITTGENSTEIN (1889-1951), Austrian philosopher. Conversation, 1930 (published in *Personal Recollections,* ch. 6, ed. by Rush Rhees, 1981).

See also Greene on COMMUNISM; The POPE; Pius XI on SOCIALISM.

CATS

1 Your rat tail is all the fashion now. I prefer a bushy plume, carried straight up. You are Siamese and your ancestors lived in trees. Mine lived in palaces. It has been suggested to me that I am a bit of a snob. How true! I prefer to be.

RAYMOND CHANDLER (1888-1959), U.S. author. Letter, Christmas 1948, from Chandler's cat, Taki, to Mike Gibbud, Esq., "a Siamese Cat of imperfect blood line" (published in *Raymond Chandler Speaking,* 1962).

2 I said something which gave you to think I hated cats. But gad, sir, I am one of the most fanatical cat lovers in the business. If you hate them, I may learn to hate you. If your allergies hate them, I will tolerate the situation to the best of my ability.

RAYMOND CHANDLER (1888-1959), U.S. author. Letter, 26 Jan. 1950, to publisher Hamish Hamilton (published in *Raymond Chandler Speaking,* 1962).

3 One cat in a house is a sign of loneliness, two of barrenness, and three of sodomy.

EDWARD DAHLBERG (1900-1977), U.S. author, critic. *Alms for Oblivion,* "Moby-Dick: A Hamitic Dream" (1964).

4 Authors like cats because they are such quiet, lovable, wise creatures, and cats like authors for the same reasons.

ROBERTSON DAVIES (b. 1913), Canadian novelist, journalist. "Mehitabel" (published in *Toronto Daily Star,* 21 Nov. 1959; repr. in *The Enthusiasms of Robertson Davies,* 1990).

5 Cats seem to go on the principle that it never does any harm to ask for what you want.

JOSEPH WOOD KRUTCH (1893-1970), U.S. author, editor. *Twelve Seasons,* "February" (1949).

6 If a fish is the movement of water embodied, given shape, then cat is a diagram and pattern of subtle air.

DORIS LESSING (b. 1919), British novelist. *Particularly Cats,* ch. 2 (1967).

7 persian pussy from over the sea
demure and lazy and smug and fat
none of your ribbons and bells for me
ours is the zest of the alley cat

DON MARQUIS (1878-1937), U.S. humorist, journalist. *archy and mehitabel,* "mehitabels extensive past" (1927).

8 Cats are autocrats of naked self-interest. They are both amoral and immoral, consciously breaking rules. Their "evil" look at such times is no human projection: the cat may be the only animal who savors the perverse or reflects upon it.

CAMILLE PAGLIA (b. 1947), U.S. author, critic, educator. *Sexual Personae,* ch. 2 (1990).

9 Cats exercise . . . a magic influence upon highly developed men of intellect. This is why these long-tailed Graces of the animal kingdom, these adorable, scintillating electric batteries have been the favorite animal of a Mohammed, Cardinal Richlieu, Crebillon, Rousseau, Wieland.

LEOPOLD VON SACHER-MASOCH (1835-95), Austrian novelist. Severin, in *Venus in Furs,* "Confessions of a Supersensual Man" (1870; tr. 1928).

10 Of all God's creatures there is only one that cannot be made the slave of the lash. That one is the cat. If man could be crossed with a cat it would improve man, but it would deteriorate the cat.

MARK TWAIN (1835-1910), U.S. author. *Notebook* (ed. by Albert Bigelow Paine, 1935, pp. 236-37), entry for 1984.

CAUSES

1 No cause is left but the most ancient of all, the one, in fact, that from the beginning of our history has determined the very existence of politics, the cause of freedom versus tyranny.

HANNAH ARENDT (1906-75), German-born U.S. political philosopher. *On Revolution,* Introduction (1963).

2 The power of a movement lies in the fact that it can indeed change the habits of people. This change is not the result of force but of dedication, of moral persuasion.

STEVE BIKO (1946-77), South African political leader. Interview, July 1976. Quoted in: Donald Woods, *Biko,* ch. 2 (1978).

3 A good cause can become bad if we fight for it with means that are indiscriminatingly murderous. A bad cause can become good if enough people fight for it in a spirit of comradeship and self-sacrifice. In the end it is how you fight, as much as why you fight, that makes your cause good or bad.

FREEMAN DYSON (b. 1923), British-born U.S. physicist, author. *Disturbing the Universe,* pt. 1, ch. 4 (1979).

4 Truth never damages a cause that is just.

MOHANDAS K. GANDHI (1869-1948), Indian political and spiritual leader. *Non-Violence in Peace and War,* vol. 2, ch. 162 (1949).

5 The history of progress is written in the blood of men and women who have dared to espouse an unpopular cause, as, for instance, the black man's right to his body, or woman's right to her soul.

EMMA GOLDMAN (1869-1940), U.S. anarchist. "What I Believe" (published in *New York World,* 1908; repr. in *Red Emma Speaks,* pt. 1, ed. by Alix Kates Shulman, 1972).

6 If you would win a man to your cause, first convince him that you are his sincere friend. Therein is a drop of honey that catches his heart, which, say what you will, is the great high-road to his reason, and which, when once gained, you will find but little trouble in convincing his judgment of the justice of your cause.

ABRAHAM LINCOLN (1809-1865), U.S. president. Address, 22 Feb. 1842, to the Washingtonian Temperance Society, Springfield, Ill.

7 To gain that which is worth having, it may be necessary to lose everything else.

BERNADETTE DEVLIN MCALISKEY (b. 1947), Northern Irish politician. *The Price of my Soul,* Preface (1969).

8 The silent majority distrusts people who believe in causes.

BRIAN MOORE (b. 1921), Irish novelist. London *Sunday Times* (15 April 1990).

9 It isn't until you begin to fight in your own cause that you (a) become really committed to winning, and (b) become a genuine ally of other people struggling for their freedom.

ROBIN MORGAN (b. 1941), U.S. feminist author, poet. *Sisterhood Is Powerful,* Introduction (1970).

10 Perhaps misguided moral passion is better than confused indifference.

IRIS MURDOCH (b. 1919), British novelist, philosopher. Jenkin Riderhood, in *The Book and the Brotherhood,* pt. 2, "Midwinter" (1987).

11 You say it is the good cause that hallows even war? I tell you: it is the good war that hallows every cause.

FRIEDRICH NIETZSCHE (1844-1900), German philosopher. *Thus Spoke Zarathustra,* pt. 1, "Of War and Warriors" (1883-92; tr. 1961).

12 A man who has never lost himself in a cause bigger than himself has missed one of life's mountaintop experiences. Only in losing himself does he find himself. Only then does he discover all the latent strengths he never knew he had and which otherwise would have remained dormant.

RICHARD M. NIXON (b. 1913), U.S. Republican politician, president. *Six Crises,* Introduction (1962).

13 Life is not an easy matter. . . . You cannot live through it without falling into frustration and cynicism unless you have before you a great idea which raises you above personal misery, above weakness, above all kinds of perfidy and baseness.

LEON TROTSKY (1879-1940), Russian revolutionary. *Diary in Exile* (1959), entry for 5 April 1935.

See also Weil on VICTORY.

CAUTION

1 Never play cards with a man called Doc. Never eat at a place called Mom's. Never sleep with a woman whose troubles are worse than your own.

NELSON ALGREN (1909-81), U.S. author. Quoted in: *Newsweek* (New York, 2 July 1956).

2 Look twice before you leap.

CHARLOTTE BRONTË (1816-55), English novelist. *Shirley,* ch. 9 (1849).

3 Whenever our neighbour's house is on fire, it cannot be amiss for the engines to play a little on our own.

EDMUND BURKE (1729-97), Irish philosopher, statesman. *Reflections on the Revolution in France* (1790).

4 To withdraw is not to run away, and to stay is no wise action, when there's more reason to fear than to hope.

MIGUEL DE CERVANTES (1547-1616), Spanish writer. Sancho Panza, in *Don Quixote,* pt. 1, bk. 3, ch. 9 (1605; tr. by P. Motteux).

5 Every human being has, like Socrates, an attendant spirit; and wise are they who obey its signals. If it does not always tell us what to do, it always cautions us what not to do.

LYDIA M. CHILD (1802-1880), U.S. abolitionist, writer, editor. *Philothea: A Romance,* ch. 6 (1836).

6 In skating over thin ice, our safety is in our speed.

RALPH WALDO EMERSON (1803-82), U.S. essayist, poet, philosopher. *Essays,* "Prudence" (First Series, 1841).

7 Those who prepared for all the emergencies of life beforehand may equip themselves at the expense of joy.

E. M. FORSTER (1879-70), British novelist, essayist. Margaret Schlegel, in *Howards End,* ch. 7 (1910).

8 Prudence is but experience, which equal time, equally bestows on all men, in those things they equally apply themselves unto.

THOMAS HOBBES (1588-1679), English philosopher. *Leviathan,* pt. 1, ch. 13 (1651).

9 Caution has its place, no doubt, but we cannot refuse our support to a serious venture which challenges the whole of the personality. If we oppose it, we are trying to suppress what is best in man—his daring and his aspirations. And should we succeed, we should only have stood in the way of that invaluable experience which might have given a meaning to life. What would have happened if Paul had allowed himself to be talked out of his journey to Damascus?

CARL JUNG (1875-1961), Swiss psychiatrist. *Collected Works,* vol. 11, "Psychotherapists or the Clergy" (ed. by William McGuire, 1958).

10 Set the foot down with distrust on the crust of the world—it is thin.

EDNA ST. VINCENT MILLAY (1892-1950), U.S. poet. *Huntsman, What Quarry?,* "The Underground System" (1939).

11 Of all the thirty-six alternatives, running away is best.

CHINESE PROVERB.

12 It is the bright day that brings forth the adder,
And that craves wary walking.

WILLIAM SHAKESPEARE (1564-1616), English dramatist, poet. Brutus, in *Julius Caesar,* act 2, sc. 1, contemplating the assassination of Caesar.

13 To fear the worst oft cures the worse.

WILLIAM SHAKESPEARE (1564-1616), English dramatist, poet. Cressida, in *Troilus and Cressida,* act 3, sc. 2. Her answer to Troilus' remark, "Fears make cherubim of angels; they never see truly." She maintains that, "Blind fear, that seeing reason leads, finds safer footing than blind reason, stumbling without fear.".

14 Put all your eggs in the one basket and—WATCH THAT BASKET.

MARK TWAIN (1835-1910), U.S. author. *Pudd'nhead Wilson,* ch. 15, "Pudd'nhead Wilson's Calendar" (1894).

15 Caution is the confidential agent of selfishness.

WOODROW WILSON (1856-1924), U.S. Democratic politician, president. Speech, 12 Feb. 1909, Chicago.

CELIBACY

1 How deep a wound to morals and social purity has that accursed article of the celibacy of the clergy been! Even the best and most enlightened men in Romanist countries attach a notion of impurity to the marriage of a clergyman. And can such a feeling be without its effect on the estimation of the wedded life in general? Impossible! and the morals of both sexes in Spain, Italy, France, &c. prove it abundantly.

SAMUEL TAYLOR COLERIDGE (1772-1834), English poet, critic. *Table Talk* (18 April 1833; published in *Specimens of the Table Talk of Samuel Taylor Coleridge,* ed. by Henry Nelson Coleridge, 1835; repr. in *Collected Works,* ed. by Kathleen Coburn, vol. 14, 1990).

2 Marriage may often be a stormy lake, but celibacy is almost always a muddy horsepond.

THOMAS LOVE PEACOCK (1785-1866), English author. *Melincourt,* ch. 7 (1817).

3 Celibacy is not just a matter of not having sex. It is a way of admiring a person for their humanity, maybe even for their beauty.

TIMOTHY RADCLIFFE (b. 1945), British theologian, Dominican Master General. *Guardian* (London, 3 Aug. 1992).

4 A celibate, like the fly in the heart of an apple, dwells in a perpetual sweetness, but sits alone, and is confined and dies in singularity.

JEREMY TAYLOR (1613-1667), English churchman, devotional writer. *Twenty-Five Sermons,* "The Marriage Ring," sermon 17 (1651)

See also Johnson on MARRIAGE.

CENSORSHIP

1 You can cage the singer but not the song.

HARRY BELAFONTE (b. 1927), U.S. singer, civil rights activist. *International Herald Tribune* (Paris, 3 Oct. 1988), on the arts in South Africa.

2 Tell it not in Gath, publish it not in the streets of Askelon; lest the daughters of the Philistines rejoice, lest the daughters of the uncircumcised triumph.

BIBLE, HEBREW. David, in *2 Samuel* 1:20, of the death of Saul and Jonathan.

3 Those expressions are omitted which can not with propriety be read aloud in the family.

THOMAS BOWDLER (1754-1825), English editor, expurgator. *Family Shakespeare,* Preface (1818).

4 This film is apparently meaningless, but if it has any meaning it is doubtless objectionable.

BRITISH BOARD OF FILM CENSORS. Quoted in: *Halliwell's Filmgoer's Companion* (1984), said of banning Cocteau's *The Seashell and the Clergyman* in 1929.

5 The condition every art requires is, not so much freedom from restriction, as freedom from adulteration and from the intrusion of foreign matter.

WILLA CATHER (1876-1947), U.S. author. *On Writing,* "Four Letters: Escapism" (1949), written 1936.

6 Censors tend to do what only psychotics do: they confuse reality with illusion.

DAVID CRONENBERG (b. 1943), Canadian filmmaker. *Cronenberg on Cronenberg,* ch. 5 (ed. by Chris Rodley, 1992).

7 Don't join the book burners. Don't think you are going to conceal faults by concealing evidence that they ever existed.

DWIGHT D. EISENHOWER (1890-1969), U.S. general, Republican politician, president. Speech, 14 June 1953, Dartmouth College.

8 Every burned book or house enlightens the world; every suppressed or expunged word reverberates through the earth from side to side.

RALPH WALDO EMERSON (1803-82), U.S. essayist, poet, philosopher. *Essays,* "Compensation," (First Series, 1841).

9 Censorship is never over for those who have experienced it. It is a brand on the imagination that affects the individual who has suffered it, forever.

NADINE GORDIMER (b. 1923), South African author. "Censorship and its Aftermath," address, June 1990, to the international Writer's Day conference, London (published in *Index on Censorship,*, Aug 1990).

10 Would you approve of your young sons, young daugters—because girls can read as well as boys—reading this book? Is it a book that you would have lying around in your own house? Is it a book that you would even wish your wife or your servants to read?

MERVYN GRIFFITH-JONES (1909-79), British lawyer. Opening address, 20 Oct. 1961, to jury during the prosecution of Penguin Books, London, for publishing an unexpurgated edition of D. H. Lawrence *Lady Chatterley's Lover.* Quoted in: *The Trial of Lady Chatterley* (1961; ed. by C. H. Rolph). Griffith-Jones was senior prosecuting counsel.

11 We do not fear censorship for we have no wish to offend with improprieties or obscenities, but we do demand, as a right, the liberty to show the dark side of wrong, that we may illuminate the bright side of virtue—the same liberty that is conceded to the art of the written word, that art to which we owe the Bible and the works of Shakespeare.

D. W. GRIFFITHS (1874-1948), U.S. producer, director. "A Plea for the Art of the Motion Picture" (released as *The Birth of a Nation*, Prologue, 1915).

12 It seems not more reasonable to leave the right of printing unrestrained, because writers may be afterwards censured, than it would be to sleep with doors unbolted, because by our laws we can hang a thief.

SAMUEL JOHNSON (1709-84), English author, lexicographer. *Lives of the English Poets*, "Milton" (1779-81), discussing Milton's *Areopagitica.*

13 The upshot was, my paintings must burn
that English artists might finally learn.

D. H. LAWRENCE (1885-1930), British author. *Innocent England*, poem written on the suppression of an exhibition of his paintings in London in 1928 on grounds of obscenity.

14 The crime of book purging is that it involves a rejection of the word. For the word is never absolute truth, but only man's frail and human effort to approach the truth. To reject the word is to reject the human search.

MAX LERNER (b. 1902), U.S. author, columnist. "The Vigilantes and the Chain of Fear" (first published in *New York Post*, 24 June 1953; repr. in *The Unfinished Country*, pt. 4, 1959), said of the McCarthy book burnings.

15 We live in oppressive times. We have, as a nation, become our own thought police; but instead of calling the process by which we limit our expression of dissent and wonder "censorship," we call it "concern for commercial viability."

DAVID MAMET (b. 1947), U.S. playwright. *Writing in Restaurants*, "Radio Drama" (1986).

16 If some books are deemed most baneful and their sale forbid, how, then, with deadlier facts, not dreams of doting men? Those whom books will hurt will not be proof against events. Events, not books, should be forbid.

HERMAN MELVILLE (1819-91), U.S. author. *The Piazza Tales*, "The Encantadas, Or Enchanted Islands—Sketch Eighth: Norfolk Isle and the Chola Widow" (1856).

17 Instead of asking—"How much damage will the work in question bring about?" why not ask—"How much good? How much joy?"

HENRY MILLER (1891-1980), U.S. author. *The Air-Conditioned Nightmare*, "With Edgar Varèse in the Gobi Desert" (1945).

18 As good almost kill a man as kill a good book; who kills a man kills a reasonable creature, God's image; but he who destroys a good book, kills reason itself, kills the image of God, as it were in the eye.

JOHN MILTON (1608-74), English poet. *Areopagitica: a Speech for the Liberty of Unlicensed Printing to the Parliament of England* (1644).

19 Here we have bishops, priests, and deacons, a Censorship Board, vigilant librarians, confraternities and sodalities, Duce Maria, Legions of Mary, Knights of this Christian order and Knights of that one, all surrounding the sinner's free will in an embattled circle.

SEAN O'CASEY (1884-1964), Irish dramatist. Letter, 8 June 1957, to *Irish Times* (Dublin).

20 Art is never chaste. It ought to be forbidden to ignorant innocents, never allowed into contact with those not sufficiently prepared. Yes, art is dangerous. Where it is chaste, it is not art.

PABLO PICASSO (1881-1973), Spanish artist. Quoted in: Antonina Vallentin, *Pablo Picasso*, ch. 11 (1957).

21 When truth is no longer free, freedom is no longer real: the truths of the police are the truths of today.

JACQUES PRÉVERT (1900-1977), French poet. *Spectacle*, "Intermède" (1951).

22 Art made tongue-tied by authority.

WILLIAM SHAKESPEARE (1564-1616), English dramatist, poet. *Sonnet 66.*

23 I am of course confident that I will fulfill my tasks as a writer in all circumstances—from my grave even more successfully and more irrefutably than in my lifetime. No one can bar the road to truth, and to advance its cause I am prepared to accept even death. But may it be that repeated lessons will finally teach us not to stop the writer's pen during his lifetime? At no time has this ennobled our history.

ALEXANDER SOLZHENITSYN (b. 1918), Russian novelist. Open letter, 16 May 1967, to the Fourth Soviet Writers' Congress (published in *Problems of Communism*, July-Aug. 1968; repr. in *Solzhenitsyn: A Documentary Record*, ed. by Leopold Labedz, 1970).

24 Woe to that nation whose literature is cut short by the intrusion of force. This is not merely interference with freedom of the press but the sealing up of a nation's heart, the excision of its memory.

ALEXANDER SOLZHENITSYN (b. 1918), Russian novelist. *Time* (25 Feb. 1974).

25 If we can't stamp out literature in the country, we can at least stop its being brought in from outside.

EVELYN WAUGH (1903-66), British novelist. Customs officer, in *Vile Bodies*, ch. 2 (1930).

26 Right now I think censorship is necessary; the things they're doing and saying in films right now just shouldn't be allowed. There's no dignity anymore and I think that's very important.

> MAE WEST (1892-1980), U.S. screen actor. Interview, *Take One* (Quebec, 22 Jan. 1974).

27 I think you can leave the arts, superior or inferior, to the conscience of mankind.

> W. B. YEATS (1865-1939), Irish poet, playwright. Speech, 7 June 1923, to the Seanad Eireann, the Irish Senate, on the Censorship of Films Bill.

See also Shaw on ASSASSINATION; Hellman on CONSCIENCE; Byron on OBSCENITY; Mill on OPINION.

CEREMONY

1 A funeral is not death, any more than baptism is birth or marriage union. All three are the clumsy devices, coming now too late, now too early, by which Society would register the quick motions of man.

> E. M. FORSTER (1879-1970), British novelist, essayist. *Howards End,* ch. 12 (1910).

2 Ceremony and ritual spring from our heart of hearts: those who govern us know it well, for they would sooner deny us bread than dare alter the observance of tradition.

> F. GONZALEZ-CRUSSI, Mexican professor of pathology, author. *Notes of an Anatomist,* "On Embalming" (1985).

3 Every ceremony or rite has a value if it is performed without alteration. A ceremony is a book in which a great deal is written. Anyone who understands can read it. One rite often contains more than a hundred books.

> GEORGE GURDJIEFF c. 1877-1949), Greek-Armenian religious teacher, mystic. Quoted in: P. D. Ouspensky, *In Search of the Miraculous,* ch. 15 (1949).

4 It is superstitious to put one's hopes in formalities, but arrogant to refuse to submit to them.

> BLAISE PASCAL (1623-62), French scientist and philosopher. *Pensées,* (1670; no. 364 ed. by Krailsheimer, no. 249 ed. by Brunschvicg).

5 Ceremony is the smoke of friendship.

> CHINESE PROVERB.

6 Ceremony was but devised at first
To set a gloss on faint deeds, hollow welcomes,
Recanting goodness, sorry ere 'tis shown;
But where there is true friendship, there needs none.

> WILLIAM SHAKESPEARE (1564-1616), English dramatist, poet. Timon, in *Timon of Athens,* act 1, sc. 2.

7 We must learn which ceremonies may be breached occasionally at our convenience and which ones may never be if we are to live pleasantly with our fellow man.

> AMY VANDERBILT (1908-74), U.S. hostess, author. *New Complete Book of Etiquette,* Introduction to pt. 1 (1963)

See also Waugh on FRIENDLINESS; Lichtenberg on SOLEMNITY.

CERTAINTY

1 If a man will begin with certainties, he shall end in doubts, but if he will be content to begin with doubts, he shall end in certainties.

> FRANCIS BACON (1561-1626), English philosopher, essayist, statesman. *The Advancement of Learning,* bk. 1, ch. 5 (1605).

2 We delight in one knowable thing, which comprehends all that is knowable; in one apprehensible, which draws together all that can be apprehended; in a single being that includes all, above all in the one which is itself the all.

> GIORDANO BRUNO (1548-1600), Italian philosopher. Teofilo, in *Cause, Principle, and Unity,* "Fifth Dialogue" (1588; ed and tr. by Jack Lindsay, 1962).

3 We are not certain, we are never certain. If we were we could reach some conclusions, and we could, at last, make others take us seriously.

> ALBERT CAMUS (1913-60), French-Algerian philosopher, author. Jean-Baptiste Clamence, in *The Fall* (1956).

4 In this world nothing can be said to be certain, except death and taxes.

> BENJAMIN FRANKLIN (1706-90), U.S. statesman, writer. Letter, 13 Nov. 1789 (published in *Complete Works,* vol. 10, ed. by John Bigelow, 1887-88). See Charles Dickens on TRUTH for a similar observation.

5 I am certain of nothing but the holiness of the heart's affections, and the truth of imagination.

> JOHN KEATS (1795-1821), English poet. Letter, 22 Nov. 1817 (published in *Letters of John Keats,* no. 31, ed. by Frederick Page, 1954).

6 It is the dull man who is always sure, and the sure man who is always dull.

> H. L. MENCKEN (1880-1956), U.S. journalist. *Prejudices,* ch. 1 (Second Series, 1920).

7 Ah, what a dusty answer gets the soul
When hot for certainties in this our life!

> GEORGE MEREDITH (1828-1909), English author. *Modern Love,* Sonnet 50 (1862).

8 The only certainty is that nothing is certain.

> PLINY THE ELDER (c. 23-79), Roman scholar. *Historia Naturalis,* bk. 2, ch. 7.

9 If you do know that *here is one hand,* we'll grant you all the rest.

> LUDWIG WITTGENSTEIN (1889-1951), Austrian philosopher. *On Certainty,* sct. 1 (1969). Opening sentence of a response to a lecture by the philosopher G. E. Moore, in which he refuted the premises of skepticism.

10 The best lack all conviction, while the worst
Are full of passionate intensity.

> W. B. YEATS (1865-1939), Irish p.oet, playwright. *The Second Coming*

See also Junius on PERSUASION; Mencken on The PUBLIC; Melbourne on SELF-CONFIDENCE; Fromm on UNCERTAINTY.

CHAMPAGNE

1   It had the taste of an apple peeled with a steel knife.

ALDOUS HUXLEY (1894-1963), British author. Sebastian Barnack, in *Time Must Have a Stop*, ch 12 (1944), assessing a Roederer 1916 champagne.

2   Mr. Edward Carson, QC: Do you drink champagne yourself?
Mr. Oscar Wilde: Yes; iced champagne is a favourite drink of mine—strongly against my doctor's orders.
Mr. Edward Carson, QC: Never mind your doctor's orders, sir!
Mr. Oscar Wilde: I never do.

OSCAR WILDE (1854-1900), Anglo-Irish playwright, author. Exchange, 4 April 1895, during Wilde's prosecution of the Marquess of Queensberry for criminal libel, *Regina (Wilde) v. Queensberry*.

See also Shaw on ALCOHOL; ALCOHOL: ABSTINENCE.

CHANGE

1   Change means movement. Movement means friction. Only in the frictionless vacuum of a nonexistent abstract world can movement or change occur without that abrasive friction of conflict.

SAUL ALINSKY (1909-72), U.S. radical activist. *Rules for Radicals*, "The Purpose" (1971).

2   It is change, continuing change, inevitable change, that is the dominant factor in society today. No sensible decision can be made any longer without taking into account not only the world as it is, but the world as it will be.... This, in turn, means that our statesmen, our businessmen, our everyman must take on a science fictional way of thinking.

ISAAC ASIMOV (1920-92), Russian-born U.S. author. "My Own View" (published in *The Encyclopedia of Science Fiction*, ed. by Robert Holdstock, 1978; repr. in *Asimov on Science Fiction*, 1981).

3   Most of us are about as eager to be changed as we were to be born, and go through our changes in a similar state of shock.

JAMES BALDWIN (1924-87), U.S. author. "Every Good-Bye Ain't Gone" (published in *New York*, 19 Dec 1977; repr. in *The Price Of The Ticket*, 1985).

4   The things that have come into being change continually. The man with a good memory remembers nothing because he forgets nothing.

AUGUSTO ROA BASTOS (b. 1917), Paraguayan novelist. *I the Supreme*, (1974; tr. 1986; Faber rev. ed., 1988, p. 7).

5   The lapse of ages changes all things—time, language, the earth, the bounds of the sea, the stars of the sky, and every thing "about, around, and underneath" man, *except man himself.*

LORD BYRON (1788-1824), English poet. *Byron's Letters and Journals*, vol. 8 (ed. by Leslie A Marchand, 1973-81), journal entry for 9 Jan. 1821.

6   For good and evil, man is a free creative spirit. This produces the very queer world we live in, a world in continuous creation and therefore continuous change and insecurity.

JOYCE CARY (1888-1957), British author. Interview in *Writers at Work* (First Series, ed. by Malcolm Cowley, 1958).

7   If a man like Malcolm X could change and repudiate racism, if I myself and other former Muslims can change, if young whites can change, then there is hope for America.

ELDRIDGE CLEAVER (b. 1935), U.S. black leader, writer. *Soul on Ice*, "The White Race and Its Heroes" (1968).

8   Change begets change. Nothing propagates so fast. If a man habituated to a narrow circle of cares and pleasures, out of which he seldom travels, step beyond it, though for never so brief a space, his departure from the monotonous scene on which he has been an actor of importance would seem to be the signal for instant confusion.... The mine which Time has slowly dug beneath familiar objects is sprung in an instant; and what was rock before, becomes but sand and dust.

CHARLES DICKENS (1812-70), English novelist. *Martin Chuzzlewit*, ch. 18 (1844).

9   Life is measured by the rapidity of change, the succession of influences that modify the being.

GEORGE ELIOT (1819-80), English novelist, editor. *Felix Holt, The Radical*, ch. 48 (1866).

10   When it is not necessary to change, it is necessary not to change.

LUCIUS CARY, LORD FALKLAND (1610-43), English statesman, soldier, patron. Speech, 22 Nov. 1641, to House of Commons. Quoted in: *Discourse on the Infallibility of the Church of Rome* (1660).

11   Most of the change we think we see in life
Is due to truths being in and out of favor.

ROBERT FROST (1874-1963), U.S. poet. *Black Cottage*.

12   You could not step twice into the same rivers; for other waters are ever flowing on to you.

HERACLITUS (c. 535-c. 475 BC), Greek philosopher. Quoted in: Hippocrates, *On The Universe*, aph.41.

13   Change alone is unchanging.

HERACLITUS (c. 535-c. 475 BC), Greek philosopher. *Herakleitos & Diogenes*, pt. 1, fragment 23 (1976; tr. by Guy Davenport).

14   Change is not made without inconvenience, even from worse to better.

RICHARD HOOKER (1554-1600), English theologian. Quoted in: Samuel Johnson, *Dictionary of the English Langauge*, Preface (1755).

15   Only man is not content to leave things as they are but must always be changing them, and when he has done so, is seldom satisfied with the result.

ELSPETH HUXLEY (b. 1907), British author. *The Mottled Lizard*, ch. 4 (1962).

16   There is a certain relief in change, even though it be from bad to worse; as I have found in travelling in a stage-coach, that it is often a comfort to shift one's position and be bruised in a new place.

WASHINGTON IRVING (1783-1859), U.S. author. *Tales of a Traveler*, Preface (1824).

17   Such is the state of life, that none are happy but by the anticipation of change: the change itself is nothing; when we have made it, the next wish is to change again. The world is not yet exhausted; let me see something tomorrow which I never saw before.

SAMUEL JOHNSON (1709-84), English author, lexicographer. Nekayah, in *The History of Rasselas*, ch. 47 (1759).

18   A single day is enough to make us a little larger or, another time, a little smaller.

PAUL KLEE (1879-1940), Swiss artist. *The Diaries of Paul Klee 1898-1918* (1957; tr. 1965), entry for Jan. 1908.

19   The word *change*, so dear to our Europe, has been given a new meaning: it no longer means *a new stage of coherent development* (as it was understood by Vico, Hegel or Marx), but a *shift from one side to another*, from front to back, from the back to the left, from the left to the front (as understood by designers dreaming up the fashion for the next season).

MILAN KUNDERA (b. 1929), Czech author and critic. *Immortality*, pt. 3, "Imagagology" (1991).

20   If we want everything to remain as it is, it will be necessary for everything to change.

GIUSEPPE TOMASI DI LAMPEDUSA (1896-1957), Sicilian author. Prince Tancredi, in *The Leopard*, ch. 1 (1958; tr. 1960).

21   Every moment of one's existence one is growing into more or retreating into less. One is always living a little more or dying a little bit.

NORMAN MAILER (b. 1923), U.S. author. "Hip, Hell, and the Navigator," in *Western Review* (no. 23 winter 1959; repr. in *Conversations with Norman Mailer*, ed. by J. Michael Lennon, 1988).

22   Today the world changes so quickly that in growing up we take leave not just of youth but of the world we were young in. . . . Fear and resentment of what is new is really a lament for the memories of our childhood.

SIR PETER MEDAWAR (1915-87), British immunologist. *Pluto's Republic*, "On `The Effecting of All Things Possible'" (1982).

23   All things change, nothing is extinguished. . . . There is nothing in the whole world which is permanent. Everything flows onward; all things are brought into being with a changing nature; the ages themselves glide by in constant movement.

OVID (43 B.C.-A. D. 17), Roman poet. Pythagoras, in *Metamorphoses*, bk. 15 (c. A.D. 8).

24   Wisdom lies neither in fixity nor in change, but in the dialectic between the two.

OCTAVIO PAZ (b. 1914), Mexican poet. *Times* (London, 8 June 1989).

25   There is nothing exempt from the peril of mutation; the earth, heavens, and whole world is thereunto subject.

SIR WALTER RALEGH (1552-1618), English author, soldier, explorer. *The Cabinet Council*, ch. 24, "Of Civil War" (repr. in *The Works of Sir Walter Raleigh*, vol. 1, 1751).

26   America is the civilization of people engaged in transforming themselves. In the past, the stars of the per-formance were the pioneer and the immigrant. Today, it is youth and the Black.

HAROLD ROSENBERG (1906-78), U.S. art critic, author. *Discovering the Present*, pt. 4, ch. 24 (1973).

27   The primary and most beautiful of Nature's qualities is motion, which agitates her at all times, but this motion is simply a perpetual consequence of crimes, she conserves it by means of crimes only.

MARQUIS DE SADE (1740-1814), French author. Comte de Bressac, in *Justine, ou les Malheurs de la Vertu* (1791; 1991, p. 520).

28   Man's yesterday may ne'er be like his morrow; Nought may endure but Mutability.

PERCY BYSSHE SHELLEY (1792-1822), English poet. *Mutability*.

29   Anything in history or nature that can be described as changing steadily can be seen as heading toward catastrophe.

SUSAN SONTAG (b. 1933), U.S. essayist. *Aids and Its Metaphors*, ch. 8 (1989).

30   A living thing is distinguished from a dead thing by the multiplicity of the changes at any moment taking place in it.

HERBERT SPENCER (1820-1903), English philosopher. *Principles of Biology*, pt. 1, ch. 4 (1865).

31   Let the great world spin for ever down the ringing grooves of change.

LORD TENNYSON (1809-92), English poet. *Locksley Hall* (1842).

32   The changes in our life must come from the impossibility to live otherwise than according to the demands of our conscience . . . not from our mental resolution to try a new form of life.

LEO TOLSTOY (1828-1910), Russian novelist and philosopher. Letter, 23 Feb. 1903 (published in *Tolstoy's Letters*, vol. 2, 1978).

33   Let that which stood in front go behind,
Let that which was behind advance to the front,
Let bigots, fools, unclean persons, offer new
   propositions,
Let the old propositions be postponed.

WALT WHITMAN (1819-1892), U.S. poet. *Reversals*.

See also Calvino on LANGUAGE; Hoffer on REVOLUTION.

CHAOS

1   Chaos often breeds life, when order breeds habit.

HENRY B. ADAMS (1838-1918), U.S. historian. *The Education of Henry Adams*, ch. 16 (1907).

2   To find a form that accommodates the mess, that is the task of the artist now.

SAMUEL BECKETT (1906-89), Irish dramatist, novelist. Conversation with John Driver, 1961. Quoted in: Deirdre Bair, *Samuel Beckett, a Biography*, ch. 21 (1978).

3   Out of chaos God made a world, and out of high passions comes a people.

LORD BYRON (1788-1824), English poet. *Byron's Letters and*

Journals, vol. 8 (1973-81; ed. by Leslie A Marchand), entry in Ravenna journal, 5 Jan. 1821. Byron was describing the nationalist ferment in Italy, in which he himself played an active part. See *Byron on Tyranny.*

4 In all chaos there is a cosmos, in all disorder a secret order.

CARL JUNG (1875-1961), Swiss psychiatrist. *Collected Works,* vol. 9, "Archetypes of the Collective Unconscious," pt. 1 (1959; ed. by William McGuire).

5 There is nothing stable in the world; uproar's your only music.

JOHN KEATS (1795-1821), English poet. Letter, 13-19 Jan. 1818, to his brothers George and Thomas Keats (published in *Letters of John Keats,* no. 37, ed. by Frederick Page, 1954).

6 In order to master the unruly torrent of life the learned man meditates, the poet quivers, and the political hero erects the fortress of his will.

JOSÉ ORTEGA Y GASSET (1883-1955), Spanish essayist, philosopher. *Meditations on Quixote,* "Preliminary Meditation" (1914).

7 Lo! thy dread empire, Chaos! is restor'd;
Light dies before thy uncreating word:
Thy hand, great Anarch! lets the curtain fall;
And universal darkness buries all.

ALEXANDER POPE (1688-1744), English satirical poet. *The Dunciad,* bk. 4.

8 Chaos is a name for any order that produces confusion in our minds.

GEORGE SANTAYANA (1863-1952), U.S. philosopher, poet. *Dominations and Powers,* bk. 1, pt. 1, ch. 1 (1951).

9 Mere anarchy is loosed upon the world,
The blood-dimmed tide is loosed, and everywhere
The ceremony of innocence is drowned.

W. B. YEATS (1865-1939), Irish poet, playwright. *The Second Coming.*

CHARACTER

1 The quality of strength lined with tenderness is an unbeatable combination, as are intelligence and necessity when unblunted by formal education.

MAYA ANGELOU (b. 1928), U.S. author. *I Know Why the Caged Bird Sings,* ch. 29 (1969).

2 Before you advise anyone "Be yourself!" reassess his character.

ANONYMOUS, (20th century).

3 Character contributes to beauty. It fortifies a woman as her youth fades. A mode of conduct, a standard of courage, discipline, fortitude and integrity can do a great deal to make a women beautiful.

JACQUELINE BISSET (b. 1946), U.S. screen actor. Quoted in: *Los Angeles Times* (16 May 1974).

4 Though intelligence is powerless to modify character, it is a dab hand at finding euphemisms for its weaknesses.

QUENTIN CRISP (b. 1908), British author. *The Naked Civil Servant,* ch. 29 (1968).

5 For character too is a process and an unfolding . . . among our valued friends is there not someone or other who is a little too self confident and disdainful; whose distinguished mind is a little spotted with commonness; who is a little pinched here and protruberent there with native prejudices; or whose better energies are liable to lapse down the wrong channel under the influence of transient solicitations?

GEORGE ELIOT (1819-80), English novelist, editor. *Middlemarch,* bk. 2, ch. 15 (1871).

6 A character is like an acrostic or Alexandrian stanza;—read it forward, backward, or across, it still spells the same thing.

RALPH WALDO EMERSON (1803-82), U.S. essayist, poet, philosopher. *Essays,* "Self-Reliance" (First Series, 1841).

7 Gross and obscure natures, however decorated, seem impure shambles; but character gives splendor to youth, and awe to wrinkled skin and gray hairs.

RALPH WALDO EMERSON (1803-82), U.S. essayist, poet, philosopher. *The Conduct of Life,* "Beauty" (1860).

8 I have only got down on to paper, really, three types of people: the person I think I am, the people who irritate me, and the people I'd like to be.

E. M. FORSTER (1879-1970), British novelist, essayist. Address to PEN Club Congress. Quoted in: Huw Weldon, *Monitor* (1962).

9 Deep down, I'm pretty superficial.

AVA GARDNER (1922-90), U.S. screen actor. Quoted in: Roland Flamini, *Ava,* ch. 8 (1983).

10 To keep your character intact you cannot stoop to filthy acts. It makes it easier to stoop the next time.

KATHARINE HEPBURN (b. 1909), U.S. screen actor. Quoted in: *Los Angeles Times* (24 Nov 1974).

11 What is character but the determination of incident? What is incident but the illustration of character?

HENRY JAMES (1843-1916), U.S. author. *The Art of Fiction* (1884; repr. in *Partial Portraits,* 1888).

12 It is well for the world that in most of us, by the age of thirty, the character has set like plaster, and will never soften again.

WILLIAM JAMES (1842-1910), U.S. psychologist, philosopher. *Principles of Psychology,* vol. 1, ch. 4 (1890).

13 It is fortunate to be of high birth, but it is no less so to be of such character that people do not care to know whether you are or are not.

JEAN DE LA BRUYÈRE (1645-96), French writer, moralist. *Characters,* "Of Personal Merit," aph. 21 (1688).

14 Between ourselves and our real natures we interpose that wax figure of idealizations and selections which we call our character.

WALTER LIPPMANN (1889-1974), U.S. journalist. *A Preface to Politics,* ch. 6 (1914).

15 In this world a man must either be anvil or hammer.

HENRY WADSWORTH LONGFELLOW (1807-82), U.S. poet. Berkley, in *Hyperion,* "The Story of Brother Bernardus" (1839).

16 We don't love qualities, we love persons; sometimes by reason of their defects as well as of their qualities.

> JACQUES MARITAIN (1882-1973), French philosopher. *Reflections on America*, ch. 3 (1948).

17 Look, we're all the same; a man is a fourteen-room house—in the bedroom he's asleep with his intelligent wife, in the living-room he's rolling around with some bareass girl, in the library he's paying his taxes, in the yard he's raising tomatoes, and in the cellar he's making a bomb to blow it all up.

> ARTHUR MILLER (b. 1915), U.S. dramatist. Lyman, in *The Ride Down Mount Morgan*, act 2 (1991).

18 Too many lives are needed to make just one.

> EUGENIO MONTALE (1896-1981), Italian poet. *Summer* (published in *Le Occasioni*, 1939). This last line was remembered by author Italo Calvino in a newspaper tribute to Montale after the poet's death.

19 You can tell a lot about a fellow's character by his way of eating jelly beans.

> RONALD REAGAN (b. 1911), U.S. Republican politician, president. *New York Times* (15 Jan. 1981).

20 Character is the basis of happiness and happiness the sanction of character.

> GEORGE SANTAYANA (1863-1952), U.S. philosopher, poet. *The Life of Reason*, ch. 9, "Reason in Common Sense" (1905-6).

21 A man with a so-called character is often a simple piece of mechanism; he has often only one point of view for the extremely complicated relationships of life.

> J. AUGUST STRINDBERG (1849-1912), Swedish dramatist, novelist, poet. *The Son of a Servant*, p. 201 (1886; tr. by Claud Field, 1913).

22 Noble character is best appreciated in those ages in which it can most readily develop.

> TACITUS (c. 55-c. 120), Roman historian. *Agricola*, sct.1.

23 Pity the man who has a character to support—it is worse than a large family—he is silent poor indeed.

> HENRY DAVID THOREAU (1817-1862), U.S. philosopher, author, naturalist. *Journal*, (1906), entry for 28 April 1841.

24 The depth and strength of a human character are defined by its moral reserves. People reveal themselves completely only when they are thrown out of the customary conditions of their life, for only then do they have to fall back on their reserves.

> LEON TROTSKY (1879-1940), Russian revolutionary. *Diary in Exile*, (1959), entry for 5 April 1935.

25 To arrive at a just estimate of a renowned man's character one must judge it by the standards of his time, not ours.

> MARK TWAIN (1835-1910), U.S. author. *Joan of Arc*, Preface (1896).

26 The best index to a person's character is (a) how he treats people who can't do him any good, and (b) how he treats people who can't fight back.

> ABIGAIL VAN BUREN (b. 1918), U.S. columnist. *Dear Abby*, syndicated newspaper column (16 May 1974).

27 It is only the superficial qualities that last. Man's deeper nature is soon found out.

> OSCAR WILDE (1854-1900), Anglo-Irish playwright, author. Cecily, in *The Importance of Being Earnest*, act 3, also in *Phrases and Philosophies for the Use of the Young* (*Chameleon*, London, Dec. 1894).

28 If you will think about what you ought to do for other people, your character will take care of itself. Character is a by-product, and any man who devotes himself to its cultivation in his own case will become a selfish prig.

> WOODROW WILSON (1856-1924), U.S. Democratic politician, president. Speech, 24 Oct. 1914, Pittsburgh, Pa.

See also Beerbohm on GENIUS; Paine on REPUTATION; Emerson on SOCIETY; Stendhal on SOLITUDE.

CHARISMA

1 Let the others have the charisma. I've got the class.

> GEORGE BUSH (b. 1924), U.S. Republican politician, president. Quoted in: *Guardian* (London, 3 Dec. 1988), said in California during presidential campaign.

2 Marvellous is the power which can be exercised, almost unconsciously, over a company, or an individual, or even upon a crowd by one person gifted with good temper, good digestion, good intellects, and good looks.

> ANTHONY TROLLOPE (1815-82), English novelist. *Rachel Ray*, ch. 26 (1863), said of Mrs. Butler Cornbury.

CHARITY

1 In necessary things, unity; in disputed things, liberty; in all things, charity.

> VARIOUSLY ASCRIBED. The formulation was used as a motto by the English Nonconformist clergyman Richard Baxter (1615-91).

2 And though I bestow all my goods to feed the poor, and though I give my body to be burned, and have not charity, it profiteth me nothing. Charity suffereth long, and is kind; charity envieth not; charity vaunteth not itself, is not puffed up.

> BIBLE: NEW TESTAMENT. *1 Corinthians* 13:3-4.

3 God loveth a cheerful giver.

> BIBLE: NEW TESTAMENT. *2 Corinthians* 9:7.

4 Therefore when thou doest thine alms, do not sound a trumpet before thee, as the hypocrites do in the synagogues and in the streets, that they may have glory of men. Verily I say unto you, they have their reward. But when thou doest alms, let not thy left hand know what thy right hand doeth.

> BIBLE: NEW TESTAMENT. *Matthew* 6:2-3, the Sermon on the Mount.

5 A man who sees another man on the street corner with only a stump for an arm will be so shocked the first time he'll give him sixpence. But the second time it'll only be a threepenny bit. And if he sees him a third time, he'll have him cold-bloodedly handed over to the police.

BERTOLT BRECHT (1898-1956), German dramatist, poet. Peachum, in *The Threepenny Opera,* act 1, sc. 1.

6 Having levelled my palace, don't erect a hovel and complacently admire your own charity in giving me that for a home.

EMILY BRONTË (1818-48), English novelist, poet. Catherine, in *Wuthering Heights,* ch. 11 (1847), said to Heathcliff, who had accused her of treating him impersonally.

7 I have always heard, Sancho, that doing good to base fellows is like throwing water into the sea.

MIGUEL DE CERVANTES (1547-1616), Spanish writer. Don Quixote, in *Don Quixote,* pt. 1, ch. 23 (1605).

8 Charity begins at home, and justice begins next door.

CHARLES DICKENS (1812-1870), English novelist. Tigg, in *Martin Chuzzlewit,* ch. 27 (1844).

9 The appalling thing is the degree of charity women are capable of. You see it all the time . . . love lavished on absolute fools. Love's a charity ward, you know.

LAWRENCE DURRELL (1912-90), British author. Interview in *Observer* (London, 11 Nov 1990).

10 Do not tell me . . . of my obligation to put all poor men in good situations. Are they *my* poor? I tell thee, thou foolish philanthropist, that I grudge the dollar, the dime, the cent, I give to such men as do not belong to me and to whom I do not belong.

RALPH WALDO EMERSON (1803-82), U.S. essayist, poet, philosopher. *Essays,* "Self-Reliance" (First Series, 1841).

11 You are much surer that you are doing good when you *pay* money to those who work, as the recompense of their labour, than when you *give* money merely in charity.

SAMUEL JOHNSON (1709-84), English author, lexicographer. Quoted in: James Boswell, *Life of Samuel Johnson,* May 1776 (1791).

12 The giving is the hardest part; what does it cost to add a smile?

JEAN DE LA BRUYÈRE (1645-96), French writer, moralist. *Characters,* "Of the Court," aph. 45 (1688).

13 As for charity, it is a matter in which the immediate effect on the persons directly concerned, and the ultimate consequence to the general good, are apt to be at complete war with one another.

JOHN STUART MILL (1806-73), English philosopher, economist. *The Subjection of Women,* ch. 4 (1869).

14 The organized charity, scrimped and iced,
In the name of a cautious, statistical Christ.

JOHN BOYLE O'REILLY (1844-90), Irish author. *In Bohemia,* st. 5.

15 Charity never humiliated him who profited from it, nor ever bound him by the chains of gratitude, since it was not to him but to God that the gift was made.

ANTOINE DE SAINT-EXUPÉRY (1900-1944), French aviator and author. *Flight to Arras,* ch. 23 (1942).

16 We ourselves feel that what we are doing is just a drop in the ocean. But if that drop was not in the ocean, I think the ocean would be less because of that missing drop. I do not agree with the big way of doing things.

MOTHER TERESA (b. 1910) Albanian-born Roman Catholic missionary. *A Gift for God,* "Carriers of Christ's Love" (1975).

17 Charity. To love human beings in so far as they are nothing. That is to love them as God does.

SIMONE WEIL (1909-43), French philosopher and mystic. "The New York Notebook" (1942; published in *First and Last Notebooks,* ed. by Richard Rees, 1970).

18 Charity creates a multitude of sins.

OSCAR WILDE (1854-1900), Anglo-Irish playwright, author. *The Soul of Man Under Socialism* (published in *Fortnightly Review,* London, Feb. 1890). This dictum was echoed by another by Wilde—"Charity . . . creates a multitude of evils," in *The Critic as Artist,* published in July and September of the same year (1890). Both recall Thoreau's, "This is a charity that hides a multitude of sins," in *Walden,* "Economy" (1854). Thoreau was referring to philanthropists.

See also AID; Blake on ALTRUISM; Nietzsche on BEGGARS; Addison on BENEFACTORS; Thatcher on INTENTIONS; Pollok on LANDLORDS.

CHARM

1 Who will pity a charmer that is bitten with a serpent?

APOCRYPHA. *Ecclesiasticus* 12:13.

2 It's a sort of bloom on a woman. If you have it, you don't need to have anything else; and if you don't have it, it doesn't much matter what else you have.

J. M. BARRIE (1860-1937), British playwright. Maggie Wylie, in *What Every Woman Knows,* act 1.

3 A man of such obvious and exemplary charm must be a liar.

ANITA BROOKNER (b. 1938), British novelist, art historian. Rachel, referring to Michael Sandberg, in *A Friend From England,* ch. 3 (1987).

4 You know what charm is: a way of getting the answer yes without having asked any clear question.

ALBERT CAMUS (1913-60), French-Algerian philosopher, author. Jean-Baptiste Clamence, in *The Fall,* (1956; repr. 1957, p. 43).

5 All charming people have something to conceal, usually their total dependence on the appreciation of others.

CYRIL CONNOLLY (1903-74), British critic. *Enemies of Promise,* ch. 16 (1938).

6 The charms of the passing woman are generally in direct proportion to the swiftness of her passing.

MARCEL PROUST (1871-1922), French novelist. *Remembrance of Things Past,* vol. 4, "Within a Budding Grove," pt. 2, "Place-Names: The Place" (1918; tr. by Ronald and Colette Cortie, 1988).

7 I am bewitched with the rogue's company. If the rascal have not given me medicines to make me love him, I'll be hanged.

WILLIAM SHAKESPEARE (1564-1616), English dramatist, poet. Falstaff, of Prince Hal, in *Henry IV, Pt. 1,* act 2, sc. 2.

8   Charming people live up to the very edge of their charm, and behave as outrageously as the world lets them.

> LOGAN PEARSALL SMITH (1865-1946), U.S. essayist, aphorist. *Afterthoughts*, "Other People" (1931).

9   If most men and women were forced to rely upon physical charm to attract lovers, their sexual lives would be not only meager but in a youth-worshiping country like America painfully brief.

> GORE VIDAL (b. 1925), U.S. novelist, critic. "Notes on Pornography" (published in *New York Review of Books*, 31 March 1966).

10   All charming people, I fancy, are spoiled. It is the secret of their attraction.

> OSCAR WILDE (1854-1900), Anglo-Irish playwright, author. Erskine, in *The Portrait of Mr. W. H.*, ch. 1 (first published in *Blackwood's Edinburgh Magazine*, July 1889).

See also Fitzgerald on MEN AND WOMEN; Wilde on WEAKNESS.

CHASTITY

1   Chastity does not mean abstention from sexual wrong; it means something flaming, like Joan of Arc.

> G. K. CHESTERTON (1874-1936), British author. *Tremendous Trifles*, "A Piece of Chalk" (1909).

2   Chastity is the cement of civilization and progress. Without it there is no stability in society, and without it one cannot attain the Science of Life.

> MARY BAKER EDDY (1821-1910), U.S. founder of the Christian Science movement. *Science and Health*, ch. 3 (1875).

3   It is fatally easy for Western folk, who have discarded chastity as a value for themselves, to suppose that it can have no value for anyone else. At the same time as Californians try to re-invent "celibacy," by which they seem to mean perverse restraint, the rest of us call societies which place a high value on chastity "backward."

> GERMAINE GREER (b. 1939), Australian feminist writer. *Sex and Destiny*, ch. 4 (1984).

4   A woman's chastity consists, like an onion, of a series of coats.

> NATHANIEL HAWTHORNE (1804-64), U.S. author. *English Notebooks* (1870; rev. 1941), journal entry for 16 March 1854.

5   There are no chaste minds. Minds copulate wherever they meet.

> ERIC HOFFER (1902-83), U.S. philosopher. *Reflections on the Human Condition*, aph. 142 (1973).

6   There are few virtuous women who are not bored with their trade.

> FRANÇOIS, DUC DE LA ROCHEFOUCAULD (1613-80), French writer, moralist. *Sentences et Maximes Morales*, no. 367 (1678).

7   Much of the modern resistance to chastity comes from men's belief that they "own" their bodies—those vast and perilous estates, pulsating with the energy that made the worlds, in which they find themselves without their consent and from which they are ejected at the pleasure of Another!

> C. S. LEWIS (1898-1963), British author. Screwtape, in *The Screwtape Letters*, Letter 21 (1942).

8   'Tis chastity, my brother, chastity.
She that has that is clad in complete steel,
And like a quivered nymph with arrows keen
May trace huge forests and unharbored heaths,
Infamous hills and sandy perilous wilds,
Where, through the sacred rays of chastity,
No savage fierce, bandit, or mountaineer
Will dare to soil her virgin purity.

> JOHN MILTON (1608-74), English poet. The Elder Brother, in *Comus*.

9   An unattempted lady could not vaunt of her chastity.

> MICHEL DE MONTAIGNE (1533-92), French essayist. Quoted in: *Essays*, bk. 3, ch. 5, "Upon some Verses of Virgil" (1588; tr. John Florio).

10   These people abstain, it is true: but the bitch Sensuality glares enviously out of all they do.

> FRIEDRICH NIETZSCHE (1844-1900), German philosopher. *Thus Spoke Zarathustra*, pt. 1, "Of Chastity" (1883-92; tr. 1961).

11   How happy is the blameless vestal's lot?
The world forgetting, by the world forgot.

> ALEXANDER POPE (1688-1744), English satirical poet. *Eloisa to Abelard* (1717).

12   Your old virginity is like one of our French withered pears: it looks ill, it eats drily.

> WILLIAM SHAKESPEARE (1564-1616), English dramatist, poet. Paroles, in *All's Well That Ends Well*, act 1, sc. 1.

13   Chastity is a monkish and evangelical superstition, a greater foe to natural temperance even than unintellectual sensuality.

> PERCY BYSSHE SHELLEY (1792-1822), English poet. *Even Love is Sold*, a Note from *Queen Mab* (1813).

14   God hath prepared . . . a little coronet or special reward (extraordinary and beside the great crown of all faithful souls) for those who have not defiled themselves with women.

> JEREMY TAYLOR (1613-67), English churchman, devotional writer. *The Rule and Exercises of Holy Living*, ch. 2, sct. 3 (1650).

15   The generative energy, which, when we are loose, dissipates and makes us unclean, when we are continent invigorates and inspires us. Chastity is the flowering of man; and what are called Genius, Heroism, Holiness, and the like, are but various fruits which succeed it.

> HENRY DAVID THOREAU (1817-62), U.S. philosopher, author, naturalist. *Walden*, "Higher Laws" (1854).

See also Menander on HAIR.

CHEATING

1   A false balance is abomination to the Lord: but a just weight is his delight.

> BIBLE, HEBREW. *Proverbs* 11:1.

2 So cheat your landlord if you can and must, but do not try to shortchange the Muse. It cannot be done. You can't fake quality any more than you can fake a good meal.

WILLIAM BURROUGHS (b. 1914), U.S. author. *The Western Lands,* ch. 2 (1987).

3 Cheat me in the price, but not in the goods.

ENGLISH PROVERB. Collected in Thomas Fuller, *Gnomologia,* no. 1090 (1732).

4 It was beautiful and simple as all truly great swindles are.

O. HENRY [WILLIAM SYDNEY PORTER] (1862-1910), U.S. short-story writer. *The Gentle Grafter,* "The Octopus Marooned" (1908).

5 For nothing can seem foul to those that win.

WILLIAM SHAKESPEARE (1564-1616), English dramatist, poet. King Henry, in *King Henry IV, pt. 1,* act 5, sc. 1.

CHEMISTRY

1 I feel like a white granular mass of amorphous crystals—my formula appears to be isomeric with Spasmotoxin. My aurochloride precipitates into beautiful prismatic needles. My Platinochloride develops octohedron crystals,—with a fine blue florescence. My physiological action is not indifferent. One millionth of a grain injected under the skin of a frog produced instantaneous death accompanied by an orange blossom odor.

LAFCADIO HEARN (1850-1904), U.S. journalist, author. Letter, 1889. Quoted in: Elizabeth Bisland, *The Life and Times of Lafcadio Hearn,* vol. 1 (1906).

2 For me chemistry represented an indefinite cloud of future potentialities which enveloped my life to come in black volutes torn by fiery flashes, like those which had hidden Mount Sinai. Like Moses, from that cloud I expected my law, the principle of order in me, around me, and in the world. . . . I would watch the buds swell in spring, the mica glint in the granite, my own hands, and I would say to myself: "I will understand this, too, I will understand everything."

PRIMO LEVI (1919-87), Italian chemist, author. *The Periodic Table,* "Hydrogen" (1975; tr. 1984).

3 There's nothing colder than chemistry.

ANITA LOOS (1888-1981), U.S. novelist, screenwriter. *Kiss Hollywood Good-by,* ch. 21 (1974).

CHESS

1 Life's too short for chess.

HENRY J. BYRON (1834-84), English dramatist. Talbot Champneys, in *Our Boys,* act 1.

2 I am still a victim of chess. It has all the beauty of art—and much more. It cannot be commercialized. Chess is much purer than art in its social position.

MARCEL DUCHAMP (1887-1968), French artist. *Time* (New York, 10 March 1952). Duchamp had given up painting in favor of chess thirty years before.

3 The chess pieces are the block alphabet which shapes thoughts; and these thoughts, although making a visual design on the chess-board, express their beauty *abstractly,* like a poem. . . . I have come to the personal conclusion that while all artists are not chess players, all chess players are artists.

MARCEL DUCHAMP (1887-1968), French artist. Address, 30 Aug 1952, New York State Chess Association. Quoted in: Kynaston McShine, *Marcel Duchamp,* (ed. by Anne d'Harnoncourt and Kynaston McShine, 1989).

4 Women, by their nature, are not exceptional chess players: they are not great fighters.

GARY KASPAROV (b. 1963), Russian chess player. *Times* (London, 9 Oct. 1990).

5 Chess is ruthless: you've got to be prepared to kill people.

NIGEL SHORT (b. 1965), British chess champion. *Observer* (London, 11 Aug. 1991).

CHICAGO

1 Could anything be more indicative of a slight but general insanity than the aspect of the crowd on the streets of Chicago?

CHARLES HORTON COOLEY (1864-1929), U.S. sociologist. *Human Nature and the Social Order,* ch. 2 (1902).

2 Chicago—is—oh well a façade of skyscrapers facing a lake, and behind the façade every type of dubiousness.

E. M. FORSTER (1879-1970), British novelist and essayist. Letter, 5 June 1947 (published in *Selected Letters of E. M. Forster,* vol. 2, ed. by Mary Lago and P. N. Furbank, 1985).

3 New York is one of the capitals of the world and Los Angeles is a constellation of plastic, San Francisco is a lady, Boston has become Urban Renewal, Philadelphia and Baltimore and Washington blink like dull diamonds in the smog of Eastern Megalopolis, and New Orleans is unremarkable past the French Quarter. Detroit is a one-trade town, Pittsburgh has lost its golden triangle, St. Louis has become the golden arch of the corporation, and nights in Kansas City close early. The oil depletion allowance makes Houston and Dallas naught but checkerboards for this sort of game. But Chicago is a great American city. Perhaps it is the last of the great American cities.

NORMAN MAILER (b. 1923), U.S. author. *Miami and the Siege of Chicago,* "The Siege of Chicago" (1969).

4 Hog Butcher for the World,
Tool Maker, Stacker of Wheat,
Player with Railroads and the Nation's Freight
  Handler;
Stormy, husky, brawling,
City of the Big Shoulders.

CARL SANDBURG (1878-1967), U.S. poet. *Chicago* in *Chicago Poems* (1916).

5 Satan (impatiently) to Newcomer: The trouble with you Chicago people is, that you think you are the best people down here; whereas you are merely the most numerous.

MARK TWAIN (1835-1910), U.S. author. *Following the Equator*, ch. 60, "Pudd'nhead Wilson's New Calendar" (1897).

6 Must we really see Chicago in order to be educated?

OSCAR WILDE (1854-1900), Anglo-Irish playwright, author. Mr. Erskine, in *The Picture of Dorian Gray*, ch. 3 (1891).

See also Wilde on CITIES AND CITY LIFE.

CHILDBIRTH

1 In sorrow thou shalt bring forth children; and thy desire shall be to thy husband, and he shall rule over thee.

BIBLE, HEBREW. *Genesis* 3:16. God's judgment on Eve.

2 A woman when she is in travail hath sorrow, because her hour is come: but as soon as she is delivered of the child, she remembereth no more the anguish, for joy that a man is born into the world.

BIBLE: NEW TESTAMENT. *John* 16:21.

3 It is unheard-of, uncivilized barbarism that any woman should still be forced to bear such monstrous torture. It should be remedied. It should be stopped. It is simply absurd that, with our modern science, painless childbirth does not exist as a matter of course. . . . I tremble with indignation when I think of . . . the unspeakable egotism and blindness of men of science who permit such atrocities when they can be remedied.

ISADORA DUNCAN (1878-1927), U.S. dancer. *My Life*, ch. 19 (1927).

4 No phallic hero, no matter what he does to himself or to another to prove his courage, ever matches the solitary, existential courage of the woman who gives birth.

ANDREA DWORKIN (b. 1946), U.S. feminist critic. "The Sexual Politics of Fear and Courage," speech, first delivered to Queens College, City University of New York, 12 March 1975 (published in *Our Blood*, ch. 5, 1976).

5 Good work, Mary. We all knew you had it in you.

DOROTHY PARKER (1893-1967), U.S. humorous writer. Telegram to a friend who had just become a mother after a prolonged pregnancy. Quoted in: Alexander Woollcott, *While Rome Burns*, "Our Mrs. Parker" (1934).

6 Childbirth is more admirable than conquest, more amazing than self-defense, and as courageous as either one.

GLORIA STEINEM (b. 1934), U.S. feminist writer, editor. "In Praise Of Women's Bodies," in *Ms* (New York, April 1981; repr. in *Outrageous Acts and Everyday Rebellions*, 1983).

7 O! if those selfish men—who are the cause of all one's misery, only knew what their poor slaves go through! What suffering—what humiliation to the delicate feelings of a poor woman, above all a young one—especially with those nasty doctors.

VICTORIA (1819-1901), Queen of Great Britain and Ireland. Letter, 11 July 1860, to her daughter Princess Frederick William (published in *Queen Victoria in Her Letters and Journals*, ed. by Christopher Hibbert, 1984).

CHILD ABUSE

1 The germ of violence is laid bare in the child abuser by the sheer accident of his individual experience . . . in a word, to a greater degree than we like to admit, we are all potential child abusers.

F. GONZALEZ-CRUSSI, Mexican professor of pathology, author. *Notes of an Anatomist*, "Reflections on Child Abuse" (1985).

2 I am not sure how many "sins" I would recognize in the world. Some would surely be defused by changed circumstances. But I can imagine none that is more irredeemably sinful than the betrayal, the exploitation, of the young by those who should care for them.

ELISABETH JANEWAY (b. 1913), U.S. author, critic. "Incest: A Rational Look at the Oldest Taboo," in *Ms.* (New York, Nov. 1981).

3 The farmer takes Jill down the well
and all the king's horses
and all the king's men
can't put that little girl together again
crooked man
crooked man
pumpkin eater
childhood stealer.

SAPPHIRE (b. 1950), U.S. author, poet. *Mickey Mouse Was A Scorpio*, in *Angry Women, Re/Search*, no. 13 (San Francisco, 1991). Sapphire recalled that it was the writing of this poem that first made her suspect she had been abused as a child.

CHILDHOOD

1 *Childhood lasts all through life*. It returns to animate broad sections of adult life. . . . Poets will help us to find this living childhood within us, this permanent, durable immobile world.

GASTON BACHELARD (1884-1962), French scientist, philosopher, literary theorist. *The Poetics of Reverie*, "Introduction," sct.6 (1960; tr. 1969).

2 Nothing fortuitous happens in a child's world. There are no accidents. Everything is connected with everything else and everything can be explained by everything else. . . . For a young child everything that happens is a necessity.

JOHN BERGER (b. 1926), British author, critic. *A Fortunate Man* (1967; repr. 1976, p. 122).

3 Childhood and youth are vanity.

BIBLE, HEBREW. *Ecclesiastes* 11:10.

4 Heaven lies about us in our infancy . . . and the world begins lying about us pretty soon afterward.

AMBROSE BIERCE (1842-1914), U.S. author. *The Devil's Dictionary* (1881-1906), a cynical comment on Wordsworth's famous line (see below).

5 But childhood prolonged, cannot remain a fairyland. It becomes a hell.

LOUISE BOGAN (1897-1970), U.S. poet, critic. "Childhood's False Eden" (1940; published in *Selected Criticism: Poetry and Prose*, 1955). Bogan was referring to Katerine Mansfield.

6 Seven to eleven is a huge chunk of life, full of dulling and forgetting. It is fabled that we slowly lose the gift of speech with animals, that birds no longer visit our windowsills to converse. As our eyes grow accustomed to sight they armour themselves against wonder.

> LEONARD COHEN (b. 1934), Canadian singer, poet, novelist. *The Favourite Game,* bk. 1, ch. 17 (1963).

7   Childhood is a disease—a sickness that you grow out of.

> WILLIAM GOLDING (1911-93), British author. Quoted in: *Guardian* (London, 22 June 1990).

8   Let a man turn to his own childhood—no further— if he will renew his sense of remoteness, and of the mystery of change.

> ALICE MEYNELL (1847-1922), English poet, essayist. *Essays,* "The Illusion of Historic Time" (1914).

9   Childhood is the kingdom where nobody dies. Nobody that matters, that is.

> EDNA ST. VINCENT MILLAY (1892-1950), U.S. poet. "Childhood Is the Kingdom Where Nobody Dies," in *Wine from These Grapes* (1934).

10   The childhood shows the man,
As morning shows the day.

> JOHN MILTON (1608-74), English poet. *Paradise Regained,* bk. 4.

11   What might be taken for a precocious genius is *the genius of childhood.* When the child grows up, it disappears without a trace. It may happen that this boy will become a real painter some day, or even a great painter. But then he will have to begin everything again, from zero.

> PABLO PICASSO (1881-1973), Spanish artist. Quoted in: Gyula Brassaï, *Picasso and Company,* p. 86 (1964; tr. 1966).

12   Come children, let us shut up the box and the puppets, for our play is played out.

> WILLIAM MAKEPEACE THACKERAY (1811-63), English author. *Vanity Fair,* ch. 67 (1848).

13   Is it not strange, that an infant should be heir of the whole world, and see those mysteries which the books of the learned never unfold?

> THOMAS TRAHERNE (1636-74), English clergyman, poet, mystic. *Centuries,* "Third Century," no. 2 (1908), written c. 1672.

14   I am convinced that, except in a few extraordinary cases, one form or another of an unhappy childhood is essential to the formation of exceptional gifts.

> THORNTON WILDER (1897-1975), U.S. novelist, dramatist. Interview in *Writers at Work* (First Series, ed. by Malcolm Cowley, 1958).

15   That great Cathedral space which was childhood.

> VIRGINIA WOOLF (1882-1941), British novelist. *Moments of Being,* "A Sketch of the Past" (written 1939-40; ed. by Jeanne Schulkind, 1976).

16   Heaven lies about us in our infancy!
Shades of the prison-house begin to close
Upon the growing boy.

> WILLIAM WORDSWORTH (1770-1850), English poet. *Intimations of Immortality,* st. 5. See above for Ambrose Bierce's riposte to this.

See also Chesterton on EXPERIENCE; Freud on FATHERS.

CHILDREN

1   Of all the needs (there are none imaginary) a lonely child has, the one that must be satisfied, if there is going to be hope and a hope of wholeness, is the unshaking need for an unshakable God.

> MAYA ANGELOU (b. 1928), U.S. author. *I Know Why the Caged Bird Sings,* ch. 4 (1969).

2   Children's talent to endure stems from their ignorance of alternatives.

> MAYA ANGELOU (b. 1928), U.S. author. *I Know Why the Caged Bird Sings,* ch. 17 (1969).

3   The countenances of children, like those of animals, are masks, not faces, for they have not yet developed a significant profile of their own.

> W. H. AUDEN (1907-73), Anglo-American poet. *A Certain World,* "Face, The Human" (1970).

4   Even a minor event in the life of a child is an event of that child's world and thus a world event.

> GASTON BACHELARD (1884-1962), French scientist, philosopher, literary theorist. *Fragments of a Poetics of Fire,* ch. 1, "The Phoenix, a Linguistic Phenomenon" (1988; tr. 1990).

5   Children have never been very good at listening to their elders, but they have never failed to imitate them.

> JAMES BALDWIN (1924-87), U.S. author. "The Precarious Vogue of Ingmar Bergman" (first published in *Esquire,* New York, April 1960; repr. in *Nobody Knows My Name,* 1961).

6   There is a "sanctity" involved with bringing a child into this world: it is better than bombing one out of it.

> JAMES BALDWIN (1924-1987), U.S. author. *The Price of the Ticket,* "The Devil Finds Work," sct. 1 (1985; first published 1976).

7   There is no sinner like a young saint.

> APHRA BEHN (1640-89), English playwright, poet. Willmore, in *The Rover,* act 1, sc. 2.

8   Foolishness is bound in the heart of a child; but the rod of correction shall drive it far from him.

> BIBLE, HEBREW. *Proverbs* 22:15.

9   It were better for him that a millstone were hanged about his neck, and he cast into the sea, than that he should offend one of these little ones.

> BIBLE: NEW TESTAMENT. *Luke* 17:2.

10   But the child's sob curses deeper in the silence
Than the strong man in his wrath!

> ELIZABETH BARRETT BROWNING (1806-61), English Poet. *The Cry of the Children,* st. 13.

11   What is a neglected child? He is a child not planned for, not wanted. Neglect begins, therefore, before he is born.

> PEARL S. BUCK (1892-1973), U.S. author. *Children for Adoption,* ch. 3 (1964).

12   A society in which adults are estranged from the world of children, and often from their own childhood, tends to hear children's speech only as a foreign language, or as a lie. . . . Children have been treated . . . as congenital fibbers, fakers and fantasisers.

BEATRIX CAMPBELL (b. 1947), British journalist. *Unofficial Secrets*, ch. 2 (1988).

13 Adults find pleasure in deceiving a child. They consider it necessary, but they also enjoy it. The children very quickly figure it out and then practise deception themselves.

ELIAS CANETTI (b. 1905), Austrian novelist, philosopher. *The Secret Heart Of The Clock: Notes, Aphorisms, Fragments 1973-1985*, "1980" (1991).

14 It is not a bad thing that children should occasionally, and politely, put parents in their place.

COLETTE (1873-1954), French novelist. *My Mother's House*, "The Priest on the Wall" (1922).

15 It takes three to make a child.

E. E. CUMMINGS (1894-1962), U.S. poet. *Jottings*, in *Wake*, no. 10, 1951 (repr. in *A Miscellany*, ed. by George J. Firmage, 1958).

16 Discipline is a symbol of caring to a child. He needs guidance. If there is love, there is no such thing as being too tough with a child. A parent must also not be afraid to hang himself. If you have never been hated by your child, you have never been a parent.

BETTE DAVIS (1908-89), U.S. screen actor. *The Lonely Life*, ch. 19 (1962).

17 It might sound a paradoxical thing to say—for surely never has a generation of children occupied more sheer hours of parental time—but the truth is that we neglected you. We allowed you a charade of trivial freedoms in order to avoid making those impositions on you that are in the end both the training ground and proving ground for true independence. We pronounced you strong when you were still weak in order to avoid the struggles with you that would have fed your true strength. We proclaimed you sound when you were foolish in order to avoid taking part in the long, slow, slogging effort that is the only route to genuine maturity of mind and feeling. Thus, it was no small anomaly of your growing up that while you were the most indulged generation, you were also in many ways the most abandoned to your own meager devices by those into whose safekeeping you had been given.

MIDGE DECTER (b. 1927), U.S. author, editor, social critic. *Liberal Parents/Radical Children*, ch. 1 (1975).

18 So long as little children are allowed to suffer, there is no true love in this world.

ISADORA DUNCAN (1878-1927), U.S. dancer. *This Quarter* (Paris, Autumn 1929). From the first chapter of her memoirs, dictated in Berlin in 1924 but never completed.

19 A child is not a salmon mousse. A child is a temporarily disabled and stunted version of a larger person, whom you will someday know. Your job is to help them overcome the disabilities associated with their size and inexperience so that they get on with being that larger person.

BARBARA EHRENREICH (b. 1941), U.S. author and columnist. *The Worst Years of Our Lives*, "Stop Ironing the Diapers" (1991; first published 1989), on the mistake of trying to "mold" children.

20 Ignorance . . . is a painless evil; so, I should think, is dirt, considering the merry faces that go along with it.

GEORGE ELIOT (1819-80), English novelist. *Mr. Gilfil's Love-Story*, ch. 3 (first published in *Blackwood's Magazine*, 1857; repr. in *Scenes of Clerical Life*, 1858).

21 The child with his sweet pranks, the fool of his senses, commanded by every sight and sound, without any power to compare and rank his sensations, abandoned to a whistle or a painted chip, to a lead dragoon, or a gingerbread dog, individualizing everything, generalizing nothing, delighted with every new thing, lies down at night overpowered by the fatigue, which this day of continual pretty madness has incurred. But Nature has answered her purpose with the curly, dimpled lunatic. She has tasked every faculty, and has secured the symmetrical growth of the bodily frame, by all these attitudes and exertions—an end of the first importance, which could not be trusted to any care less perfect than her own.

RALPH WALDO EMERSON (1803-82), U.S. essayist, poet, philosopher. *Essays*, "Nature" (1844; Second Series).

22 When children are doing nothing, they are doing mischief.

HENRY FIELDING (1707-54), English novelist, dramatist. Quoting "a wise old gentleman," in *Tom Jones*, bk. 15, ch. 2 (1749).

23 Strange new problems are being reported in the growing generations of children whose mothers were always there, driving them around, helping them with their homework—an inability to endure pain or discipline or pursue any self-sustained goal of any sort, a devastating boredom with life.

BETTY FRIEDAN (b. 1921), U.S. feminist writer. *The Feminine Mystique*, ch. 1 (1963).

24 She discovered with great delight that one does not love one's children just because they are one's children but because of the friendship formed while raising them.

GABRIEL GARCÍA MÁRQUEZ (b. 1928) Colombian writer. *Love in the Time of Cholera* (1985; repr. 1988, p. 207), said of Fermina Daza.

25 You may give them your love but not your thoughts.
For they have their own thoughts.
You may house their bodies but not their souls,
For their souls dwell in the house of tomorrow,
which you cannot visit, not even in your dreams.

KAHLIL GIBRAN (1883-1931) Lebanese poet, novelist. *The Prophet*, "On Children" (1923).

26 Alas! regardless of their doom,
The little victims play!
No sense have they of ills to come
Nor care beyond today.

THOMAS GRAY (1716-71), English poet. *Ode on a Distant Prospect of Eton College*, st. 6.

27 We in the West do not refrain from childbirth because we are concerned about the population explosion or because we feel we cannot afford children, but because we do not like children.

GERMAINE GREER (b. 1939), Australian feminist writer. *Sex and Destiny*, ch. 1 (1984).

28 A young and vital child knows no limit to his own will, and it is the only reality to him. It is not that he wants at the outset to fight other wills, but that they simply do not exist for him. Like the artist, he goes forth to the work of creation, gloriously alone.

> JANE HARRISON (1850-1928), English classical scholar, author. *Alpha and Omega,* "Darwinism and Religion" (1915).

29 Children . . . seldom have a proper sense of their own tragedy, discounting and keeping hidden the true horrors of their short lives, humbly imagining real calamity to be some prestigious drama of the grown-up world.

> SHIRLEY HAZZARD (b. 1931), Australian-American author. *The Bay of Noon,* ch. 1 (1970).

30 Each child is an adventure into a better life—an opportunity to change the old pattern and make it new.

> HUBERT H. HUMPHREY (1911-78), U.S. Democratic politician, vice president. Speech, 27 July 1965, Detroit, Mich.

31 Our children will not survive our habits of thinking, our failures of the spirit, our wreck of the universe into which we bring new life as blithely as we do. Mostly, our children will resemble our own misery and spite and anger, because we give them no choice about it. In the name of motherhood and fatherhood and education and good manners, we threaten and suffocate and bind and ensnare and bribe and trick children into wholesale emulation of our ways.

> JUNE JORDAN (b. 1939), U.S. poet, civil rights activist. "Old Stories: New Lives," keynote address, 1978, to Child Welfare League of America (published in *Moving Towards Home: Political Essays,* 1989).

32 To rescue our children we will have to let them save us from the power we embody: we will have to trust the very difference that they forever personify. And we will have to allow them the choice, without fear of death: that they may come and do likewise or that they may come and that we will follow them, that a little child will lead us back to the child we will always be, vulnerable and wanting and hurting for love and for beauty.

> JUNE JORDAN (b. 1939), U.S. poet and civil rights activist. "Old Stories: New Lives," keynote address, 1978, to Child Welfare League of America (published in *Moving Towards Home: Political Essays,* 1989).

33 Nothing you do for children is ever wasted. They seem not to notice us, hovering, averting our eyes, and they seldom offer thanks, but what we do for them is never wasted.

> GARRISON KEILLOR (b. 1942), U.S. author. *Leaving Home,* "Easter" (1987).

34 For success in training children the first condition is to become as a child oneself, but this means no assumed childishness, no condescending baby-talk that the child immediately sees through and deeply abhors. What it does mean is to be as entirely and simply taken up with the child as the child himself is absorbed by his life.

> ELLEN KEY (1849-1926), Swedish author, feminist. *The Century of the Child,* ch. 3 (1909).

35 Children also have artistic ability, and there is wisdom in there having it! The more helpless they are, the more instructive are the examples they furnish us; and

they must be preserved free of corruption from an early age.

> PAUL KLEE (1879-1940), Swiss artist. *The Diaries of Paul Klee 1898-1918,* no. 905 (1957; tr. 1965), entry for Jan. 1912.

36 A child learns to discard his ideals, whereas a grown-up never wears out his short pants.

> KARL KRAUS (1874-1936), Austrian satirist. "The Discovery of the North Pole" (first published in *Die Fackel,* Vienna, 1909; repr. in *In These Great Times: A Karl Kraus Reader,* ed. by Harry Zohn, 1976).

37 When I consider how little of a rarity children are— that every street and blind alley swarms with them—that the poorest people commonly have them in most abundance—that there are few marriages that are not blest with at least one of these bargains—how often they turn out ill, and defeat the fond hopes of their parents, taking to vicious courses, which end in poverty, disgrace, the gallows, etc.—I cannot for my life tell what cause for pride there can possibly be in having them.

> CHARLES LAMB (1775-1834), English essayist, critic. *Essays of Elia,* "A Bachelor's Complaint of the Behavior of Married People" (1820-23).

38 What the vast majority of American children needs is to stop being pampered, stop being indulged, stop being chauffeured, stop being catered to. In the final analysis it is not what you do for your children but what you have taught them to do for themselves that will make them successful human beings.

> ANN LANDERS (b. 1918), U.S. columnist. *Ann Landers Says Truth Is Stranger . . . ,* ch. 3 (1968).

39 Above all, though, children are linked to adults by the simple fact that they are in process of turning into them. For this they may be forgiven much. Children are bound to be inferior to adults, or there is no incentive to grow up.

> PHILIP LARKIN (1922-86), British poet. *Required Writing,* "The Savage Seventh" (1984; first published 1959).

40 All God's children are not beautiful. Most of God's children are, in fact, barely presentable.

> FRAN LEBOWITZ (b. 1951), U.S. journalist. *Metropolitan Life,* "Manners" (1978).

41 In all our efforts to provide "advantages" we have actually produced the busiest, most competitive, highly pressured and over-organized generation of youngsters in our history—and possibly the unhappiest. We seem hell-bent on eliminating much of childhood.

> EDA J. LE SHAN (b. 1922), U.S. educator, author. *The Conspiracy against Childhood,* ch. 1 (1967).

42 For little boys are rancorous
When robbed of any myth,
And spiteful and cantankerous
To all their kin and kith.
But little girls can draw conclusions
And profit from their lost illusions.

> PHYLLIS MCGINLEY (1905-1978), U.S. poet, author. *What Every Woman Knows,* in *Times Three* (1960).

43 A child is beset with long traditions. And his infancy is so old, so old, that the mere adding of years in the life to follow will not seem to throw it further back—it is already so far.

> ALICE MEYNELL (1847-1922), English poet, essayist. *Essays,* "The Illusion of Historic Time" (1914).

44 For truly it is to be noted, that children's plays are not sports, and should be deemed as their most serious actions.

> MICHEL DE MONTAIGNE (1533-92), French essayist. *Essays,* bk. 1, ch. 22, "Of Custom," (1580; tr. by John Florio).

45 If help and salvation are to come, they can only come from the children, for the children are the makers of men.

> MARIA MONTESSORI (1870-1952), Italian educator. *The Absorbent Mind,* ch. 1 (1949).

46 One can love a child, perhaps, more deeply than one can love another adult, but it is rash to assume that the child feels any love in return.

> GEORGE ORWELL (1903-50), British author. "Such, Such were the Joys" (1947; repr. in *The Collected Essays, Journalism and Letters of George Orwell* (ed. Sonia Orwell & Ian Angus, 1968). Orwell added: "Looking back on my own childhood, after the infant years were over, I do not believe that I ever felt love for any mature person, except my mother. . . . Love, the spontaneous, unqualified emotion of love was something I could only feel for people who were young."

47 Men are generally more careful of the breed of their horses and dogs than of their children.

> WILLIAM PENN (1644-1718), English religious leader, founder of Pennsylvania. *Some Fruits of Solitude,* pt. 1, no. 85 (1693).

48 Children's liberation is the next item on our civil rights shopping list.

> LETTY COTTIN POGREBIN (b. 1939), U.S. journalist, author. "Down with Sexist Upbringing" (published in *The First Ms. Reader,* ed. by Francine Klagsbrun, 1972).

49 If you have a great passion it seems that the logical thing is to see the fruit of it, and the fruit are children.

> ROMAN POLANSKI (b. 1933), Polish film, director. *Independent on Sunday* (London, 12 May 1991).

50 Better a snotty child than his nose wiped off.

> ENGLISH PROVERB. Collected in George Herbert's *Outlandish Proverbs* (1640).

51 Children suck the mother when they are young and the father when they are old.

> ENGLISH PROVERB. Collected in: J. Ray, *English Proverbs* (1670).

52 Go directly—see what she's doing, and tell her she mustn't.

> *Punch,* vol. 63 (London, 1872).

53 My children cause me the most exquisite suffering of which I have any experience. It is the suffering of ambivalence: the murderous alternation between bitter resentment and raw-edged nerves, and blissful gratification and tenderness. Sometimes I seem to myself, in my feelings toward these tiny guiltless beings, a monster of selfishness and intolerance.

> ADRIENNE RICH (b. 1929), U.S. poet. *Of Woman Born,* ch. 1 (1976).

54 How sharper than a serpent's tooth it is
To have a thankless child.

> WILLIAM SHAKESPEARE (1564-1616), English dramatist, poet. Lear, in *King Lear,* act 1, sc. 4.

55 What's more enchanting than the voices of young people, when you can't hear what they say?

> LOGAN PEARSALL SMITH (1865-1946), U.S. essayist, aphorist. *Afterthoughts,* "Age and Death" (1931).

56 There are few places outside his own play where a child can contribute to the world in which he finds himself. His world: dominated by adults who tell him what to do and when to do it—benevolent tyrants who dispense gifts to their "good" subjects and punishment to their "bad" ones, who are amused at the "cleverness" of children and annoyed by their "stupidities."

> VIOLA SPOLIN (b. 1911), U.S. theatrical director and producer. *Improvisation for the Theater,* ch. 13 (1963).

57 I have been assured by a very knowing American of my acquaintance in London, that a young healthy child, well nursed, is at a year old, a most delicious, nourishing, and wholesome food, whether *stewed, roasted, baked,* or *boiled*; and I make no doubt that it will equally serve in a *fricassee,* or a *ragout.*

> JONATHAN SWIFT (1667-1745), Anglo-Irish satirist. *A Modest Proposal for Preventing the Children of Ireland from Being a Burden to their Parents or the Country* (1729; repr. in *The Prose Works of Jonathan Swift,* ed. by Herbert Davies, vol. 12, 1955). This ironic pamphlet subverted current Whig notions of people being "the wealth of the nation" in the context of the poverty and hunger in Ireland. See Swift on FAMINE, for his comment on the situation there.

58 No man can tell but he that loves his children, how many delicious accents make a man's heart dance in the pretty conversation of those dear pledges; their childishness, their stammering, their little angers, their innocence, their imperfections, their necessities, are so many little emanations of joy and comfort to him that delights in their persons and society.

> JEREMY TAYLOR (1613-67), English churchman, devotional writer. *Twenty-Seven Sermons,* Sermon 18 (1651).

59 Look for me in the nurseries of Heaven.

> FRANCIS THOMPSON (1859-1907), English poet. *To My Godchild.*

60 If men do not keep on speaking terms with children, they cease to be men, and become merely machines for eating and for earning money.

> JOHN UPDIKE (b. 1932), U.S. author, critic. *Assorted Prose,* "A Foreword for Younger Readers" (1965).

61 Americans, indeed, often seem to be so overwhelmed by their children that they'll do anything for them except stay married to the co-producer.

> KATHARINE WHITEHORN (b. 1926), British journalist. *Observations,* "Suffer How Many of the Little Children?" (1970).

62 Once you bring life into the world, you must protect it. We must protect it by changing the world.

> ELIE WIESEL (b. 1928), Rumanian-born U.S. writer. Interview in *Writers at Work* (Eighth Series, ed. by George Plimpton, 1988).

63 Few parents nowadays pay any regard to what their children say to them. The old-fashioned respect for the young is fast dying out.

> OSCAR WILDE (1854-1900), Anglo-Irish playwright, author. Gwendolen, in *The Importance of Being Earnest*, act 1.

64 Winning children (who appear so guileless) are children who have discovered how effective charm and modesty and a delicately calculated spontaneity are in winning what they want.

> THORNTON WILDER (1897-1975), U.S. novelist, dramatist. Interview in *Writers at Work* (First Series, ed. by Malcolm Cowley, 1958).

65 The child is father of the man.

> WILLIAM WORDSWORTH (1770-1850), English poet. *My Heart Leaps Up When I Behold* (1807; written 1802).

See also Coleridge on DANCE; DAUGHTERS; Montagu, Montessori on EDUCATION; Hemingway on FATHERS; Szasz on HAPPINESS; Eliot on HEROES; Byron on HOME AND HOUSES; Tolstoy on HYPOCRISY; Saki on KNOWLEDGE; Aidoo, Montagu, Wilde on PARENTS; SONS; Benchley on TRAVEL; Auden, Szasz on UPBRINGING.

CHINA AND THE CHINESE

1 Nothing and no one can destroy the Chinese people. They are relentless survivors. They are the oldest civilized people on earth. Their civilization passes through phases but its basic characteristics remain the same. They yield, they bend to the wind, but they never break.

> PEARL S. BUCK (1892-1973), U.S. author. *China, Past and Present*, ch. 1 (1972).

2 Chinese civilisation is so systematic that wild animals have been abolished on principle.

> ALEISTER CROWLEY (1875-1947), British occultist. *The Confessions of Aleister Crowley*, ch. 56 (1929; rev. 1970).

3 Histories of the world omitted China; if a Chinaman invented compass or movable type or gunpowder we promptly "forgot it" and named their European inventors. In short, we regarded China as a sort of different and quite inconsequential planet.

> W. E. B. DU BOIS (1868-1963), U.S. civil rights leader, author. *The Seventh Son*, vol. 2, "China" (1971; first published Feb. 1912).

4 Read the Bible. Work hard and honestly. And don't complain.

> BILLY GRAHAM (b. 1918), U.S. evangelist. Message to the Chinese, reported in *International Herald Tribune* (Paris, 18 April 1988).

5 Even one billion Chinese do not a superpower make.

> JOHN LUKACS (b. 1924), Hungarian-born U.S. historian. "The Stirrings of History," *Harper's* (New York, Aug. 1990).

6 Apart from their other characteristics, the outstanding thing about China's 600 million people is that they are "poor and blank." This may seem a bad thing, but in reality it is a good thing. Poverty gives rise to the desire for change, the desire for action and the desire for revolution. On a blank sheet of paper free from any mark, the freshest and most beautiful pictures can be painted.

> MAO ZEDONG (1893-1976), Founder of the People's Republic of China. "Introducing a Co-operative" (15 April 1958). Quoted in: *Quotations from Chairman Mao Tse-Tung* (1967).

7 In a country where misery and want were the foundation of the social structure, famine was periodic, death from starvation common, disease pervasive, thievery normal, and graft and corruption taken for granted, the elimination of these conditions in Communist China is so striking that negative aspects of the new rule fade in relative importance.

> BARBARA TUCHMAN (1912-89), U.S. historian. *Notes from China*, ch. 1 (1972).

8 A black sun has appeared in the sky of my motherland.

> WUER KAIXI, Chinese student leader. Quoted in: *Independent* (London, 29 June 1989), said about the events in Tiananmen Square, Beijing.

See also Madame Chiang Kai-shek on AIRPLANES.

CHIVALRY

1 There is another side to chivalry. If it dispenses leniency, it may with equal justification invoke control.

> FREDA ADLER (b. 1934), U.S. educator and author. *Sisters in Crime*, ch. 4 (1975).

2 The world's male chivalry has perished out,
But women are knights-errant to the last;
And, if Cervantes had been greater still,
He had made his Don a Donna.

> ELIZABETH BARRETT BROWNING (1806-61), English poet. *Aurora Leigh*, bk. 7 (1857).

3 I thought ten thousand swords must have leaped from their scabbards to avenge even a look that threatened her with insult. But the age of chivalry is gone. That of sophisters, economists and calculators has succeeded; and the glory of Europe is gone forever.

> EDMUND BURKE (1729-97), Irish philosopher, statesman. *Reflections on the Revolution in France* (1790), said of Marie Antoinette.

4 Though the practice of chivalry fell even more sadly short of its theoretic standard than practice generally falls below theory, it remains one of the most precious monuments of the moral history of our race, as a remarkable instance of a concerted and organized attempt by a most disorganized and distracted society, to raise up and carry into practice a moral ideal greatly in advance of its social condition and institutions; so much so as to have been completely frustrated in the main object, yet never entirely inefficacious, and which has left a most sensible, and for the most part a highly valuable impress on the ideas and feelings of all subsequent times.

> JOHN STUART MILL (1806-73), English philosopher, economist. *The Subjection of Women*, ch. 4 (1869).

5 When a man opens the car door for his wife, it's either a new car or a new wife.

PRINCE PHILIP, DUKE OF EDINBURGH (b. 1921). *Today* (London, 2 March 1988).

6   He may not shine with courtly graces,
But yet, his kind, respectful air
To woman, whatsoe'er her place is,
It might be well if kings could share.
So, for the chivalric true gentleman,
Give me, I say, our own American.

ELLA WHEELER WILCOX (1855-1919), U.S. poet, journalist. *The True Knight.*

See also Disraeli on BORES.

CHOICE

1   On this narrow planet, we have only the choice between two unknown worlds. One of them tempts us—ah! what a dream, to live in that!—the other stifles us at the first breath.

COLETTE (1873-1954), French author. "The Photographer's Wife," *Gigi* (1945; repr. in *The Collected Stories of Colette,* 1983).

2   I shall be telling this with a sigh
Somewhere ages and ages hence:
Two roads diverged in a wood, and I—
I took the one less travelled by,
And that has made all the difference.

ROBERT FROST (1874-1963), U.S. poet. *The Road Not Taken,* st. 4.

3   Whatever does not spring from a man's free choice, or is only the result of instruction and guidance, does not enter into his very being, but still remains alien to his true nature; he does not perform it with truly human energies, but merely with mechanical exactness.

KARL WILHELM VON HUMBOLDT (1767-1835), German statesman, philologist. *Limits of State Action,* ch. 3 (1792; repr. 1854; tr. and ed. by J. W. Burrow, 1969).

4   I see it all perfectly; there are two possible situations—one can either do this or that. My honest opinion and my friendly advice is this: do it or do not do it—you will regret both.

SØREN KIERKEGAARD (1813-55), Danish philosopher. *Either/Or,* vol. 2, "Balance between Esthetic and Ethical" (1843; tr. 1987).

5   Chief among our gains must be reckoned this possibility of choice, the recognition of many possible ways of life, where other civilizations have recognized only one. Where other civilizations give a satisfactory outlet to only one temperamental type, be he mystic or soldier, business man or artist, a civilization in which there are many standards offers a possibility of satisfactory adjustment to individuals of many different temperamental types, of diverse gifts and varying interests.

MARGARET MEAD (1901-78), U.S. anthropologist. *Coming of Age in Samoa,* ch. 14 (1928).

6   Far too often the choices reality proposes are such as to take away one's taste for choosing.

JEAN ROSTAND (1894-1977), French biologist, writer. *Pensées d'un Biologiste,* ch. 10, "A Biologist's Thoughts" (1939; repr. in *The Substance of Man,* 1962).

7   When the psychiatrist approves of a person's actions, he judges that person to have acted with "free choice"; when he disapproves, he judges him to have acted without "free choice." It is small wonder that people find "free choice" a confusing idea: "free choice" appears to refer to what the person being judged (often called the "patient") *does,* whereas it is actually what the person making the judgment (often a psychiatrist or other mental health worker) *thinks.*

THOMAS SZASZ (b. 1920), U.S. psychiatrist. *The Second Sin,* "Freedom" (1973).

CHRISTIANITY AND THE CHRISTIANS

1   Protestantism has the method of Jesus with His secret too much left out of mind; Catholicism has His secret with His method too much left out of mind; neither has His unerring balance, His intuition, His sweet reasonableness. But both have hold of a great truth, and get from it a great power.

MATTHEW ARNOLD (1822-88), English poet, critic. *Literature and Dogma,* ch. 10 (1873).

2   Christianity has operated with an unmitigated arrogance and cruelty—necessarily, since a religion ordinarily imposes on those who have discovered the true faith the spiritual duty of liberating the infidels.

JAMES BALDWIN (1924-87), U.S. author. "Letter from a Region in My Mind," in *New Yorker* (17 Nov. 1962; repr. in *The Fire Next Time,* 1963).

3   But as it is written, eye hath not seen, nor ear heard, neither have entered into the heart of man, the things which God hath prepared for them that love him.

BIBLE: NEW TESTAMENT. *1 Corinthians* 2:9.

4   Think not that I am come to send peace on earth: I came not to send peace, but a sword.

BIBLE: NEW TESTAMENT. *Matthew* 10:34.

5   Christianity is art & not money. Money is its curse.

WILLIAM BLAKE (1757-1827), English poet, painter, engraver. Notes on *The Laocoön* (engraved c. 1820; repr. in *Complete Writings,* ed. by Geoffrey Keynes, 1957).

6   How natural that the errors of the ancient should be handed down and, mixing with the principles and system which Christ taught, give to us an adulterated Christianity.

OLYMPIA BROWN (1835-1900), U.S. minister (first woman ordained in U.S.). Sermon, c. 13 Jan. 1895, Mukwonago, Wisconsin (published in *Olympia Brown, An Autobiography,* ed. by Gwendolen B. Willis, 1960; repr. in *Annual Journal of the Universalist Historical Society,* vol. 4, 1963).

7   If there is any moral in Christianity, if there is anything to be learned from it, if the whole story is not profitless from first to last, it comes to this: that a man should back his own opinion against the world's.

SAMUEL BUTLER (1835-1902), English author. *Samuel Butler's Notebooks,* (1951, p. 199).

8   People in general are equally horrified at hearing the Christian religion doubted, and at seeing it practised.

> SAMUEL BUTLER (1835-1902), English author. *Samuel Butler's Notebooks* (1951, p. 310). This observation reappeared in Butler's description of a congregation of conservative farmers in *The Way of All Flesh*, ch. 15 (1903): "They would have been equally horrified at hearing the Christian religion doubted, and at seeing it practised."

9   I have a great mind to believe in Christianity for the mere pleasure of fancying I may be damned.

> LORD BYRON (1788-1824), English poet. Quoted in: Benjamin Haydon, "Table Talk" (published in *Correspondence and Table-Talk*, vol. 2, ed. by Frederic Wordsworth Haydon, 1876).

10   The trouble with born-again Christians is that they are an even bigger pain the second time around.

> HERB CAEN (b. 1916), U.S. columnist, author. *San Francisco Chronicle* (20 July 1981).

11   With two thousand years of Christianity behind him . . . a man can't see a regiment of soldiers march past without going off the deep end. It starts off far too many ideas in his head.

> LOUIS-FERDINAND CÉLINE (1894-1961), French author. Ferdinand Bardamu, in *Journey to the End of the Night* (1932; tr. 1934; repr. 1966, p. 123).

12   The Christian ideal has not been tried and found wanting. It has been found difficult; and left untried.

> G. K. CHESTERTON (1874-1936), British author. *What's Wrong With the World*, pt. 1, ch. 5 (1910).

13   He who begins by loving Christianity better than truth, will proceed by loving his own sect or church better than Christianity, and end in loving himself better than all.

> SAMUEL TAYLOR COLERIDGE (1772-1834), English poet, critic. *Aids to Reflection*, "Moral and Religious Aphorisms," aph. 25 (1825; repr. in *Works*, vol. 1, ed. by Professor Shedd, 1853).

14   No one is without Christianity, if we agree on what we mean by that word. It is every individual's individual code of behavior by means of which he makes himself a better human being than his nature wants to be, if he followed his nature only. Whatever its symbol—cross or crescent or whatever—that symbol is man's reminder of his duty inside the human race.

> WILLIAM FAULKNER (1897-1962), U.S. novelist. Interview in *Writers at Work* (First Series, ed. by Malcolm Cowley, 1958).

15   White people really deal more with God and black people with Jesus.

> NIKKI GIOVANNI (b. 1943), U.S. poet. *A Dialogue* (1973; with James Baldwin), a conversation in London, 4 Nov. 1971.

16   Christianity is the highest perfection of humanity.

> SAMUEL JOHNSON (1709-84), English author, lexicographer. Letter, 13 Aug. 1766 (published in *The Letters of Samuel Johnson*, vol. 1, no. 184, ed. by R. W. Chapman, 1952).

17   Any hope that America would finally grow up vanished with the rise of fundamentalist Christianity. Fundamentalism, with its born-again regression, its pink-and-gold concept of heaven, its literal-mindedness, its rambunctious good cheer . . . its anti-intellectualism . . . its puerile hymns . . . and its faith-healing . . . are made to order for King Kid America.

> FLORENCE KING (b. 1936), U.S. author. *Reflections in a Jaundiced Eye*, "Good King Herod" (1989).

18   The Three in One, the One in Three? Not so!
To my own Gods I go.
It may be they shall give me greater ease
Than your cold Christ and tangled Trinities.

> RUDYARD KIPLING (1865-1936), British author, poet. *Plain Tales from the Hills*, chapter heading to "Lispeth" (1888).

19   Christianity will go. It will vanish and shrink. I needn't argue with that; I'm right and I will be proved right. We're more popular than Jesus now; I don't know which will go first—rock and roll or Christianity.

> JOHN LENNON (1940-80), British rock musician. *Evening Standard* (London, 4 March 1966). This remark provoked a storm of reaction, especially in the U.S., causing Lennon to explain himself at a press conference in Chicago, 11 Aug. 1966: "I'm not saying that we're better or greater, or comparing us with Jesus Christ as a person, or God as a thing, or whatever it is. I just said what I said, and it was wrong, or it was taken wrong. And now it's all this."

20   There were honest people long before there were Christians and there are, God be praised, still honest people where there are no Christians. It could therefore easily be possible that people are Christians because true Christianity corresponds to what they would have been even if Christianity did not exist.

> G. C. LICHTENBERG (1742-99), German physicist, philosopher. *Aphorisms*, "Notebook L," aph. 16 (written 1765-99; tr. by R. J. Hollingdale, 1990).

21   The real security of Christianity is to be found in its benevolent morality, in its exquisite adaptation to the human heart, in the facility with which its scheme accommodates itself to the capacity of every human intellect, in the consolation which it bears to the house of mourning, in the light with which it brightens the great mystery of the grave.

> THOMAS, BABINGTON MACAULAY (1800-1859), English historian. "Southey's Colloquies," in *Edinburgh Review* (Jan. 1830; repr. in *Critical and Historical Essays*, 1843).

22   No egoism is so insufferable as that of the Christian with regard to his soul.

> W. SOMERSET MAUGHAM (1874-1965), British author. *A Writer's Notebook* (1949), entry for 1901.

23   Two great European narcotics, alcohol and Christianity.

> FRIEDRICH NIETZSCHE (1844-1900), German philosopher. *Twilight of the Idols*, "What the Germans Lack," aph. 2 (1889).

24   Wherever there are walls I shall inscribe this eternal accusation against Christianity upon them—I can write in letters which make even the blind see . . . I call Christianity the one great curse, the one great intrinsic depravity, the one great instinct for revenge for which no expedient is sufficiently poisonous, secret, subterranean, petty—I call it the one immortal blemish of mankind . . .

> FRIEDRICH NIETZSCHE (1844-1900), German philosopher. *The Anti-Christ*, aph. 62 (1895).

25   What if men take to following where He leads,
Weary of mumbling Athanasian creeds?

> RODEN NOËL (1834-94), English poet. *The Red Flag*.

26 A strong argument for the religion of Christ is this—that offences against *Charity* are about the only ones which men on their death-beds can be made—not to understand—but to *feel*—as *crime*.

> EDGAR ALLAN POE (1809-45), U.S. poet, critic, short-story writer. "Marginalia" in *Southern Literary Messenger* (Richmond, July 1849; repr. in *Essays and Reviews*, 1984).

27 He spends his life explaining from his pulpit that the glory of Christianity consists in the fact that though it is not true it has been found necessary to invent it.

> SAKI [H. H. MUNRO] (1870-1916), Scottish author. The Archdeacon, in *The Unbearable Bassington*, ch. 13 (1912), said of De la Poulett.

28 The early Christian rules of life were not made to last, because the early Christians did not believe that the world itself was going to last.

> GEORGE BERNARD SHAW (1856-1950), Anglo-Irish playwright, critic. Hotchkiss, in *Getting Married*.

29 Here I swear, and as I break my oath may . . . eternity blast me, here I swear that never will I forgive Christianity! It is the only point on which I allow myself to encourage revenge. . . . Oh, how I wish I *were* the Antichrist, that it were *mine* to crush the Demon; to hurl him to his native Hell never to rise again—I expect to gratify some of this insatiable feeling in Poetry.

> PERCY BYSSHE SHELLEY (1792-1822), English poet. Letter, 3 Jan. 1811 (published in *The Letters of Percy Bysshe Shelley*, vol. 1, no. 35, ed. by Frederick L. Jones, 1964).

30 The Bible and the Church have been the greatest stumbling blocks in the way of women's emancipation.

> ELIZABETH CADY STANTON (1815-1902), U.S. campaigner for women's rights. *Free Thought Magazine* (Sept. 1896).

31 Bear the Cross cheerfully and it will bear you.

> THOMAS À KEMPIS (1380-1471), German monk, mystic. *The Imitation of Christ*, pt. 2, ch. 12 (1471).

32 Our brains are no longer conditioned for reverence and awe. We cannot imagine a Second Coming that would not be cut down to size by the televised evening news, or a Last Judgment not subject to pages of holier-than-Thou second-guessing in *The New York Review of Books*.

> JOHN UPDIKE (b. 1932), U.S. author, critic. *Self-Consciousness: Memoirs*, ch. 6 (1989).

33 The fear of hell, or aiming to be blest,
Savours too much of private interest.

> EDMUND WALLER (1606-87), English poet. *Of Divine Love*, cto. 2.

34 I am not a Catholic; but I consider the Christian idea, which has its roots in Greek thought and in the course of the centuries has nourished all of our European civilization, as something that one cannot renounce without becoming degraded.

> SIMONE WEIL (1909-43), French philosopher, mystic. Letter, March 1937 (published in Simone Pétrement, *Vie de Simone Weil*, vol. 2, ch. 3, 1976).

35 Scratch the Christian and you find the pagan—spoiled.

> ISRAEL ZANGWILL (1864-1926), British playwright, novelist. *Sons of the Ghetto*, bk. 2, ch. 6 (1892).

See also CATHOLICISM; The CHURCH; Zhuravlyov on COMMUNISM; De Quincey on FLOWERS; GOD; Tocqueville on ISLAM AND THE MUSLIMS; Lennon, Pound on JESUS CHRIST; Shaw on JUDAISM AND THE JEWS; Farquhar, Hazlitt, O'Brien on SECTS.

CHRISTMAS

1 A woman spent all Christmas Day in a telephone box without ringing anyone. If someone comes to phone, she leaves the box, then resumes her place afterwards. No one calls her either, but from a window in the street, someone watched her all day, no doubt since they had nothing better to do. The Christmas syndrome.

> JEAN BAUDRILLARD (b. 1929), French semiologist. *Cool Memories*, ch. 4 (1987; tr. 1990).

2 Midnight, and the clock strikes. It is Christmas Day, the werewolves' birthday, the door of the solstice still wide enough open to let them all slink through.

> ANGELA CARTER (1940-92), British author. "The Company of Wolves" (published in *Bananas*, ed. by Emma Tenant, 1977).

3 A lovely thing about Christmas is that it's compulsory, like a thunderstorm, and we all go through it together.

> GARRISON KEILLOR (b. 1942), U.S. author. *Leaving Home*, "Exiles" (1987).

4 Call a truce, then, to our labours—let us feast with friends and neighbours,
And be merry as the custom of our caste;
For if "faint and forced the laughter," and if sadness follow after,
We are richer by one mocking Christmas past.

> RUDYARD KIPLING (1865-1936), British author, poet. *Christmas in India*.

5 There are some people who want to throw their arms round you simply because it is Christmas; there are other people who want to strangle you simply because it is Christmas.

> ROBERT LYND (1879-1949), Anglo-Irish essayist, journalist. *The Book of This and That*, "On Christmas" (1915).

6 Please to put a nickel,
Please to put a dime.
How petitions trickle
In at Christmas time!

> PHYLLIS MCGINLEY (1905-78), U.S. poet, author. "Dear Madam: We Know You Will Want to Contribute . . ." published in *Times Three* (1960).

7 This is the month, and this the happy morn,
Wherein the Son of heav'n's eternal King,
Of wedded Maid and Virgin Mother born,
Our great redemption from above did bring.

> JOHN MILTON (1608-74), English poet. *On the Morning of Christ's Nativity*.

8 'Twas Christmas broach'd the mightiest ale;
'Twas Christmas told the merriest tale;

A Christmas gambol oft could cheer
The poor man's heart through half the year.
SIR WALTER SCOTT (1771-1832), Scottish novelist, poet. *Marmion*, Introduction to cto. 6, (1808).

9 So stick up ivy and the bays,
And then restore the heathen ways,
Green will remind you of the Spring,
Though this great day denies the thing,
And mortifies the earth, and all,
But your wild revels, and loose hall.
HENRY VAUGHAN (1622-95), Welsh poet. *The True Christmas.*

10 From a commercial point of view, if Christmas did not exist it would be necessary to invent it.
KATHARINE WHITEHORN (b. 1926), British journalist. *Roundabout*, "The Office Party" (1962).

THE CHURCH

1 It is indolence. . . . Indolence and love of ease; a want of all laudable ambition, of taste for good company, or of inclination to take the trouble of being agreeable, which make men clergymen. A clergyman has nothing to do but be slovenly and selfish; read the newspaper, watch the weather, and quarrel with his wife. His curate does all the work and the business of his own life is to dine.
JANE AUSTEN (1775-1817), English novelist. Mary Crawford, in *Mansfield Park*, ch. 11 (1814).

2 If a man desireth the office of a bishop, he desireth a good work. A bishop then must be blameless, the husband of one wife, vigilant, sober, of good behaviour, given to hospitality, apt to teach; not given to wine, no striker, not greedy of filthy lucre; but patient, not a brawler, not covetous; one that ruleth well his own house, having his children in subjection with all gravity; (for if a man know not how to rule his own house, how shall he take care of the church of God?)
BIBLE: NEW TESTAMENT. *1 Timothy* 3:1-5.

3 People have described me as a "management bishop" but I say to my critics, "Jesus was a management expert too."
GEORGE CAREY (b. 1935), British ecclesiastic, Archbishop of Canterbury. *Daily Telegraph* (London, 26 Feb. 1991).

4 I believe with all my heart that the Church of Jesus Christ should be a Church of blurred edges.
GEORGE CAREY (b. 1935), British ecclesiastic, Archbishop of Canterbury. *Independent* (London, 15 July 1992).

5 A Church which has lost its memory is in a sad state of senility.
HENRY CHADWICK (b. 1920), British educator, historian. *Daily Telegraph* (London, 10 Feb. 1988).

6 The parson knows enough who knows a Duke.
WILLIAM COWPER (1731-1800), English poet. *Tirocinium.*

7 A woman's asking for equality in the church would be comparable to a black person's demanding equality in the Ku Klux Klan.

MARY DALY (b. 1928), U.S. educator, writer, theologian. *The Church and the Second Sex*, New Autobiographical Preface (1975).

8 And of all plagues with which mankind are curst, Ecclesiastic tyranny's the worst.
DANIEL DEFOE (1659-1731), English writer. *The True-Born Englishman*, pt. 2 (1701).

9 His creed no parson ever knew,
For this was still his "simple plan,"
To have with clergymen to do
As little as a Christian can.
SIR FRANCIS DOYLE (1810-88), English poet. *The Unobtrusive Christian.*

10 There is not in the universe a more ridiculous, nor a more contemptible animal, than a proud clergyman.
HENRY FIELDING (1707-54), English novelist, dramatist. *Amelia*, bk. 9, ch. 10 (1751).

11 Those who marry God can become domesticated too—it's just as hum-drum a marriage as all the others. The word "Love" means a formal touch of the lips as in the ceremony of the Mass, and "*Ave Maria*" like "dearest" is a phrase to open a letter. This marriage like the world's marriages was held together by habits and tastes shared in common between God and themselves—it was God's taste to be worshipped and their taste to worship, but only at stated hours like a suburban embrace on a Saturday night.
GRAHAM GREENE (1904-91), British novelist. *A Burnt-Out Case*, pt. 1, ch. 1, sct. 2 (1961).

12 A full-dressed ecclesiastic is a sort of go-cart of divinity; an ethical automaton. A clerical prig is, in general, a very dangerous as well as contemptible character. The utmost that those who thus habitually confound their opinions and sentiments with the outside coverings of their bodies can aspire to, is a negative and neutral character, like wax-work figures, where the dress is done as much to the life as the man, and where both are respectable pieces of pasteboard, or harmless compositions of fleecy hosiery.
WILLIAM HAZLITT (1778-1830), English essayist. "On Clerical Character," published in *Yellow Dwarf* (24/31 Jan. & 7 Feb. 1818; repr. in *Political Essays*, 1819).

13 I'm a priest, not a priestess. . . . "Priestess" implies mumbo jumbo and all sorts of pagan goings-on. Those who oppose us would love to call us priestesses. They can call us all the names in the world—it's better than being invisible.
CARTER HEYWARD (b. 1946), U.S. Episcopal priest. Quoted in: *Ms.* (New York, Dec. 1974).

14 But a priest's life is not supposed to be well-rounded; it is supposed to be one-pointed—a compass, not a weathercock.
ALDOUS HUXLEY (1894-1963), British author. *The Devils of Loudun*, ch. 1 (1952).

15 The Church has always been willing to swap off treasures in heaven for cash down.
ROBERT G. INGERSOLL (1833-99), U.S. lawyer, orator. Speech, 20 Sept. 1880, Chicago.

16 This merriment of parsons is mighty offensive.

SAMUEL JOHNSON (1709-84), English author, lexicographer. Quoted in: James Boswell, *Life of Samuel Johnson*, March 1781 (1791).

17 There is no heresy or no philosophy which is so abhorrent to the church as a human being.

JAMES JOYCE (1882-1941), Irish author. Letter, 22 Nov. 1902, in which Joyce declared his intention of leaving Ireland for good; from a private collection (an inaccurate text, taken from a typescript of this letter, is printed in *Letters of James Joyce*, vol. 1, 1957).

18 Archbishop—A Christian ecclesiastic of a rank superior to that attained by Christ.

H. L. MENCKEN (1880-1956), U.S. journalist. *A Mencken Chrestomathy*, "Sententiæ: Arcana Clestia" (1949).

19 The priesthood is a marriage. People often start by falling in love, and they go on for years without realizing that that love must change into some other love which is so unlike it that it can hardly be recognised as love at all.

IRIS MURDOCH (b. 1919), British novelist, philosopher. Brendan Craddock, in *Henry and Cato*, pt. 2, "The Great Teacher" (1976).

20 Many are called but few are chosen. There are sayings of Christ which suggest that the Church he came to establish will always be a minority affair.

EDWARD NORMAN (b. 1946), British ecclesiastic and educator. *Times* (London, 20 Feb. 1992).

21 If church prelates, past or present, had even an inkling of physiology they'd realise that what they term this inner ugliness creates and nourishes the hearing ear, the seeing eye, the active mind, and energetic body of man and woman, in the same way that dirt and dung at the roots give the plant its delicate leaves and the full-blown rose.

SEAN O'CASEY (1884-1964), Irish dramatist. *Rose And Crown*, "In New York Now" (1952), of the so-called "ugliness under the skin . . . the functioning flesh, blood, bone, muscle," from the 5th volume of O'Casey's autobiography.

22 I do not believe in the creed professed by the Jewish Church, by the Roman Church, by the Greek Church, by the Turkish Church, by the Protestant Church, nor by any church that I know of. My own mind is my own church.

THOMAS PAINE (1737-1809), Anglo-American political theorist, writer. *The Age of Reason*, pt. 1, "The Author's Profession of Faith" (1794).

23 Mass ought to be in Latin, unless you cd. do it in Greek or Chinese. In fact, *any* abracadabra that no bloody member of the public or half-educated ape of a clargimint cd. think he understood.

EZRA POUND (1885-1972), U.S. poet, critic. Letter, 7 March 1940 (published in *The Letters of Ezra Pound 1907-1941*, ed. by D. D. Paige, 1951).

24 Be neither intimate nor distant with the clergy.

IRISH PROVERB.

25 Nearly all the evils in the Church have arisen from bishops desiring *power* more than *light*. They want authority, not outlook.

JOHN RUSKIN (1819-1900), English art critic, author. *Sesame and Lilies*, lecture 1, sct. 22 (repr. in *The Works of John Ruskin*, vol. 18, ed. by E. T. Cook & Alexander Weddesburn, 1905).

26 A glorious Church is like a magnificent feast; there is all the variety that may be, but every one chooses out a dish or two that he likes, and lets the rest alone: how glorious soever the Church is, every one chooses out of it his own religion, by which he governs himself, and lets the rest alone.

JOHN SELDEN (1584-1654), English jurist, statesman. *Table Talk*, "Church" (1686).

27 What is wrong with priests and popes is that instead of being apostles and saints, they are nothing but empirics who say "I know" instead of "I am learning," and pray for credulity and inertia as wise men pray for scepticism and activity.

GEORGE BERNARD SHAW (1856-1950), Anglo-Irish playwright, critic. *The Doctor's Dilemma*, "The Latest Theories," Preface (1911).

28 How can a bishop marry? How can he flirt? The most he can say is "I will see you in the vestry after service."

SYDNEY SMITH (1771-1845), English clergyman, writer. Quoted in: Lady Holland, *Memoir*, vol. 1, ch. 9 (1855). "As the French say," Smith observed, "there are three sexes—men, women and clergymen."

29 I have, alas, only one illusion left, and that is the Archbishop of Canterbury.

SYDNEY SMITH (1771-1845), English clergyman, writer. Quoted in: Lady Holland, *Memoir*, vol. 1, ch. 9 (1855).

30 I never saw, heard, nor read, that the clergy were beloved in any nation where Christianity was the religion of the country. Nothing can render them popular, but some degree of persecution.

JONATHAN SWIFT (1667-1745), Anglo-Irish satirist. *Thoughts on Religion* (published in *Works*, vol. 15, 1765).

31 I think a bishop who doesn't give offence to anyone is probably not a good bishop.

JAMES LAWTON THOMPSON (b. 1936), British cleric. *Daily Telegraph* (London, 30 May 1991).

32 A little, round, fat, oily man of God.

JAMES THOMSON (1700-1748), Scottish poet. *Castle of Indolence*, cto.1, st. 69.

See also Farnham on The BODY; CATHOLICISM; CHRISTIANITY AND THE CHRISTIANS; PROTESTANTISM.

THE CHURCH AND SOCIETY

1 It will, I believe, be everywhere found, that as the clergy are, or are not what they ought to be, so are the rest of the nation.

JANE AUSTEN (1775-1817), English novelist. Edmund, in *Mansfield Park*, ch. 9 (1814).

2 The question confronting the Church today is not any longer whether the man in the street can grasp a religious message, but how to employ the communications media so as to let him have the full impact of the Gospel message.

JOHN PAUL II [KAROL WOJTYLA] (b. 1920), Polish ecclesiastic, Pope. *International Herald Tribune* (Paris, 8 May 1989).

3 Yes, I see the Church as the body of Christ. But, oh! How we have blemished and scarred that body through social neglect and through fear of being nonconformists.

MARTIN LUTHER KING, JR. (1929-68), U.S. clergyman, civil rights leader. "Letter from Birmingham Jail" (published in *Why We Can't Wait*, 1963).

4 Standards of conduct appropriate to civil society or the workings of a democracy cannot be purely and simply applied to the Church.

CARDINAL JOSEPH RATZINGER (b. 1927), German ecclesiastic. *Independent* (London, 27 June 1990).

5 The priesthood in many ways is the ultimate closet in Western civilization, where gay people particularly have hidden for the past two thousand years.

BISHOP JOHN SPONG (b. 1931), U.S. ecclesiastic. *Daily Telegraph* (London, 12 July 1990).

6 In the Church, considered as a social organism, the mysteries inevitably degenerate into beliefs.

SIMONE WEIL (1909-43), French philosopher, mystic. Quoted in: David McLellan, *Simone Weil: Utopian Pessimist*, ch. 9 (1989).

CHURCHES AND CHURCHGOING

1 He was of the faith chiefly in the sense that the church he currently did not attend was Catholic.

KINGSLEY AMIS (b. 1922), British novelist. *One Fat Englishman*, ch. 8 (1963), said of Roger Micheldene.

2 We praise Him, we bless Him, we adore Him, we glorify Him, and we wonder who is that baritone across the aisle and that pretty woman on our right who smells of apple blossoms. Our bowels stir and our cod itches and we amend our prayers for the spiritual life with the hope that it will not be too spiritual.

JOHN CHEEVER (1912-82), U.S. author. *John Cheever: The Journals*, "The Late Forties and the Fifties" (ed. by Robert Gottlieb, 1991), entry for 1956.

3 We enter church, and we have to say, "We have erred and strayed from Thy ways like lost sheep," when what we want to say is, "Why are we made to err and stray like lost sheep?" Then we have to sing, "My soul doth magnify the Lord," when what we want to sing is "O that my soul could find some Lord that it could magnify!"

THOMAS HARDY (1840-1928), English novelist, poet. Note, Jan. 1907 (published in Florence Emily Hardy, *The Later Years of Thomas Hardy*, ch. 9, 1930).

4 Once is orthodox, twice is puritanical.

LORD MELBOURNE (1779-1848), English statesman, prime minister. Reply to the Archbishop of York's invitation to attend evening service. Quoted in: David Cecil, *The Young Melbourne*, ch. 9 (1939).

5 Here, the churches seemed to shrink away into eroding corners. They seem to have ceased to be essential parts of American life. They no longer give life. It is the huge buildings of commerce and trade which now align the people to attention. These in their massive manner of steel and stone say, Come unto me all ye who labour, and we will give you work.

SEAN O'CASEY (1884-1964), Irish dramatist. *Rose And Crown*, vol. 5, "In New York Now" (1952), said of New York.

6 Too hot to go to Church? What about Hell?

Poster in Dayton, Ohio.

7 The act of bellringing is symbolic of all proselytizing religions. It implies the pointless interference with the quiet of other people.

EZRA POUND (1885-1972), U.S. poet, critic. Quoted in: Humphrey Carpenter, *A Serious Character*, pt. 2, ch. 1 (1988).

8 I never weary of great churches. It is my favourite kind of mountain scenery. Mankind was never so happily inspired as when it made a cathedral.

ROBERT LOUIS STEVENSON (1850-94), Scottish novelist, essayist, poet. *An Inland Voyage*, "Noyons Cathedral" (1878).

9 She say, Celie, tell the truth, have you ever found God in church? I never did. I just found a bunch of folks hoping for him to show. Any God I ever felt in church I brought in with me. And I think all the other folks did too. They come to church to *share* God, not find God.

ALICE WALKER (b. 1944), U.S. author, critic. Shug, in *The Color Purple*, p. 165 (ed. by Women's Press, 1983).

10 I don't go to church. Kneeling bags my nylons.

BILLY WILDER (b. 1906), U.S. film director. Jan Sterling, in *Ace in the Hole* (directed and scripted by Billy Wilder, 1951).

SIR WINSTON CHURCHILL

1 His ear is so sensitively attuned to the bugle note of history that he is often deaf to the more raucous clamour of contemporary life.

ANEURIN BEVAN (1897-1960), British Labour politician. Quoted in: Michael Foot, *Aneurin Bevan*, vol. 1, ch. 10 (1962).

2 You seem to have no real purpose in life and won't realize at the age of twenty-two that for a man life means work, and hard work if you mean to succeed.

JENNIE JEROME CHURCHILL (1854-1921), Anglo-American mother of Winston Churchill. Letter, 26 Feb. 1897, to Winston Churchill (published in Ralph G. Martin, *Jennie*, vol. 2, 1971).

3 I am not invested with dictatorial powers. If I were, I should be quite ready to dictate.

SIR WINSTON CHURCHILL (1874-1965), British statesman, writer. Speech, 7 Aug. 1925, to House of Commons, as Chancellor of the Exchequer.

4 Churchill is the very type of a corrupt journalist. There is not a worse prostitute in politics. He himself has written that it's unimaginable what can be done in war with the help of lies. He's an utterly amoral repulsive creature. I'm convinced that he has his place of refuge ready beyond the Atlantic. He obviously won't seek sanctuary in Canada. In Canada he'd be beaten up. He'll go to his friends the Yankees. As soon as this damnable winter is over, we'll remedy all that.

ADOLF HITLER (1889-1945), German dictator. Observation, 18 Feb. 1942, to his guest at dinner, General Rommel (published in *Hitler's Table Talk*, pt. 3, 1953).

5 Old politicians, like old actors, revive in the lime-light. The vacancy which afflicts them in private momentarily lifts when, once more, they feel the eyes of an audience upon them. Their old passion for holding the centre of the stage guides their uncertain footsteps to where the footlights shine, and summons up a wintry smile when the curtain rises.

MALCOLM MUGGERIDGE (1903-90), British broadcaster. *Tread Softly For You Tread on My Jokes,* "Twilight of Greatness" (1966), said of Churchill's last years.

6 It is fun to be in the same decade with you.

FRANKLIN D. ROOSEVELT (1882-1945), U.S. Democratic politician, president. Cable, 30 Jan. 1942, to Churchill, in response to sixtieth birthday greetings.

CINEMA

1 Curiosity doesn't matter any more. These days people don't want to be transported to emotional territories where they don't know how to react.

HECTOR BABENKO (b. 1946), Argentinian film director. *International Herald Tribune* (Paris, 24 Feb. 1992).

2 What is saved in the cinema when it achieves art is a spontaneous continuity with all mankind. It is not an art of the princes or the bourgeoisie. It is popular and vagrant. In the sky of the cinema people learn what they might have been and discover what belongs to them apart from their single lives.

JOHN BERGER (b. 1926), British author, critic. "Ev'ry Time We Say Goodbye" (first published in *Expressen,* Stockholm, 3 Nov. 1990; repr. in *Keeping a Rendezvous,* 1992).

3 Film as dream, film as music. No art passes our conscience in the way film does, and goes directly to our feelings, deep down into the dark rooms of our souls.

INGMAR BERGMAN (b. 1918), Swedish stage and film writer, director. Quoted in: John Berger, "Ev'ry Time We Say Goodbye," in *Sight and Sound* (London, June 1991).

4 My movie is born first in my head, dies on paper; is resuscitated by the living persons and real objects I use, which are killed on film but, placed in a certain order and projected on to a screen, come to life again like flowers in water.

ROBERT BRESSON (B. 1907), French film director. *Notes on the Cinematographer,* "1950-1958: On Looks" (1975).

5 Films can only be made by by-passing the will of those who appear in them, using not what they do, but what they are.

ROBERT BRESSON (b. 1907), French filmmaker. *Times* (London, 1 Nov. 1990).

6 The making of a picture ought surely to be a rather fascinating adventure. It is not; it is an endless contention of tawdry egos, some of them powerful, almost all of them vociferous, and almost none of them capable of anything much more creative than credit-stealing and self-promotion.

RAYMOND CHANDLER (1888-1959), U.S. author. "Writers in Hollywood," in *Atlantic Monthly* (Boston, Nov. 1945).

7 The motion picture is like a picture of a lady in a half-piece bathing suit. If she wore a few more clothes, you might be intrigued. If she wore no clothes at all, you might be shocked. But the way it is, you are occupied with noticing that her knees are too bony and that her toenails are too large. The modern film tries too hard to be real. Its techniques of illusion are so perfect that it requires no contribution form the audience but a mouthful of popcorn.

RAYMOND CHANDLER (1888-1959), U.S. author. *Raymond Chandler Speaking* (1962), extract from notes dated 1950 about the screenplay for *Strangers on a Train.*

8 A film is a petrified fountain of thought.

JEAN COCTEAU (1889-1963), French author, filmmaker. *Esquire* (New York, Feb. 1961).

9 If you can't *believe* a little in what you see on the screen, it's not worth wasting your time on cinema.

SERGE DANEY (1944-92), French film critic. Quoted in: *Sight and Sound* (London, July 1992).

10 Film is more than the twentieth-century art. It's another part of the twentieth-century mind. It's the world seen from inside. We've come to a certain point in the history of film. If a thing can be filmed, the film is implied in the thing itself. This is where we are. The twentieth century is *on film.* . . . You have to ask yourself if there's anything about us more important than the fact that we're constantly on film, constantly watching ourselves.

DON DELILLO (b. 1926), U.S. author. Frank Volterra, in *The Names,* ch. 8 (1982).

11 It struck me that the movies had spent more than half a century saying, "They lived happily ever after" and the following quarter-century warning that they'll be lucky to make it through the weekend. Possibly now we are now entering a third era in which the movies will be sounding a note of cautious optimism: You know it just might work.

NORA EPHRON (B. 1941), U.S. author, journalist. Quoted in: *Los Angeles Times* (27 July 1989), referring to Ephron's screenplay for *When Harry Met Sally* (1989).

12 The cinema is not an art which films life: the cinema is something *between* art and life. Unlike painting and literature, the cinema both gives to life and takes from it, and I try to render this concept in my films. Literature and painting both exist as art from the very start; the cinema doesn't.

JEAN-LUC GODARD (b. 1930), French filmmaker, author. Quoted in: Richard Roud, *Godard,* Introduction (1970; first published 1967).

13 All you need for a movie is a gun and a girl.

JEAN-LUC GODARD (b. 1930), French filmmaker, author. Journal entry 16 May 1991. Quoted in: *Projections* (ed. by John Boorman and Walter Donohue, 1992).

14 As far as the filmmaking process is concerned, stars are essentially worthless—and absolutely essential.

WILLIAM GOLDMAN (b. 1931), U.S. screenwriter, novelist. *Adventures in the Screen Trade,* ch. 1 (1983).

15 Pictures are for entertainment, messages should be delivered by Western Union.

> SAMUEL GOLDWYN (1882-1974), U.S. film producer. Quoted in: Arthur Marx, *Goldwyn*, ch. 15 (1976).

16 We have taken beauty and exchanged it for stilted voices.

> D. W. GRIFFITHS (1874-1948), U.S. producer-director. Quoted in: Leslie Halliwell, *Filmgoer's Companion* (1984), referring in 1928 to the new talking pictures.

17 I discovered early in my movie work that a movie is never any better than the stupidest man connected with it. There are times when this distinction may be given to the writer or director. Most often it belongs to the producer.

> BEN HECHT (1893-1964), U.S. journalist, author, screenwriter. *A Child of the Century*, bk. 5, "Illustrations by Doré (Gustave)" (1954). "The producer," Hecht explained, "is the shadow cast by the studio's owner. It falls across the entire studio product." Hecht's feelings about producers might have been influenced by what he saw as the producer's chief task: "The job of turning good writers into movie hacks. These sinister fellows were always my bosses."

18 Movies are one of the bad habits that corrupted our century. Of their many sins, I offer as the worst their effect on the intellectual side of the nation. It is chiefly from that viewpoint I write of them—as an eruption of trash that has lamed the American mind and retarded Americans from becoming a cultured people.

> BEN HECHT (1893-1964), U.S. journalist, author, screenwriter. *A Child of the Century*, bk. 5, "What the Movies Are" (1954). Hecht—who enjoyed a profitable career as a Hollywood screenwriter (see Hecht on HOLLYWOOD: AND WRITERS)—continued: "They have slapped into the American mind more human misinformation in one evening than the Dark Ages could muster in a decade."

19 You should look straight at a film; that's the only way to see one. Film is not the art of scholars but of illiterates.

> WERNER HERZOG (b. 1942), German film director. *New York Times* (11 Sept. 1977).

20 Dialogue should simply be a sound among other sounds, just something that comes out of the mouths of people whose eyes tell the story in visual terms.

> ALFRED HITCHCOCK (1899-1980), Anglo-American filmmaker. Quoted in: Francois Truffaut, *Hitchcock*, ch. 11 (1967).

21 For me, the cinema is not a slice of life, but a piece of cake.

> ALFRED HITCHCOCK (1899-1980), Anglo-American filmmaker. Quoted in: *Sunday Times* (London, 6 March 1977).

22 All television ever did was shrink the demand for ordinary movies. The demand for extraordinary movies increased. If any one thing is wrong with the movie industry today, it is the unrelenting effort to astonish.

> CLIVE JAMES (b. 1939), Australian writer, critic. *Observer* (London, 16 June 1979).

23 The preserve of ambition and folly in pursuit of illusion, or . . . delusion.

> DEREK JARMAN (b. 1942), British filmmaker, artist, author. *Modern Nature: The Journals of Derek Jarman*, entry for 22 Feb. 1989 (1991), referring to the film industry.

24 The cinema, like the detective story, makes it possible to experience without danger all the excitement, passion and desirousness which must be repressed in a humanitarian ordering of life.

> CARL JUNG (1875-1961), Swiss psychiatrist. Quoted in: Roger Manvell, *Film* (1944).

25 The words "Kiss Kiss Bang Bang," which I saw on an Italian movie poster, are perhaps the briefest statement imaginable of the basic appeal of movies. This appeal is what attracts us, and ultimately what makes us despair when we begin to understand how seldom movies are more than this.

> PAULINE KAEL (B. 1919), U.S. film critic. *Kiss Kiss Bang Bang*, "A Note on the Title" (1968).

26 Life in the movie business is like the beginning of a new love affair: it's full of surprises and you're constantly getting fucked.

> DAVID MAMET (b. 1947), U.S. playwright. Charlie Fox, in *Speed The Plow*, sc. 1 (1988).

27 The movies today are too rich to have any room for genuine artists. They produce a few passable craftsmen, but no artists. Can you imagine a Beethoven making $100,000 a year?

> H. L. MENCKEN (1880-1956), U.S. journalist. *Prejudices*, "Appendix from Moronia" (1937).

28 Cinema is the culmination of the obsessive, mechanistic male drive in western culture. The movie projector is an Apollonian straightshooter, demonstrating the link between aggression and art. Every pictorial framing is a ritual limitation, a barred precinct.

> CAMILLE PAGLIA (b. 1947), U.S. author, critic, educator. *Sexual Personae*, ch. 1 (1990).

29 I guess I think that films have to be made totally by fascists—there's no room for democracy in making film.

> DON PENNEBAKER (b. 1930), U.S. filmmaker. *Independent* (London, 29 July 1988).

30 My belief is that no movie, nothing in life, leaves people neutral. You either leave them up or you leave them down.

> DAVID PUTTNAM (B. 1941), British film producer. *International Herald Tribune* (Paris, 23 Oct. 1989).

31 There's only one thing that can kill the movies, and that's education.

> WILL ROGERS (1879-1935), U.S. humorist. *The Autobiography of Will Rogers*, ch. 6 (1949).

32 Does art reflect life? In movies, yes. Because more than any other art form, films have been a mirror held up to society's porous face.

> MARJORIE ROSEN (b. 1942), U.S. film critic. *Popcorn Venus*, Preface (1973).

33 In good films, there is always a directness that entirely frees us from the itch to interpret.

> SUSAN SONTAG (b. 1933), U.S. essayist. "Against Interpretation," sct. 7, in *Evergreen Review* (Dec. 1964; repr. in *Against Interpretation*, 1966).

34 One of the joys of going to the movies was that it was trashy, and we should never lose that.

OLIVER STONE (b. 1946), U.S. filmmaker. *International Herald Tribune* (Paris, 15 Feb. 1988).

35 Film music should have the same relationship to the film drama that somebody's piano playing in my living room has to the book I am reading.

IGOR STRAVINSKY (1882-1971), Russian-American composer. *Music Digest* (Sept. 1946).

36 All film directors, whether famous or obscure, regard themselves as misunderstood or underrated. Because of that, they all lie. They're obliged to overstate their own importance.

FRANÇOIS TRUFFAUT (1932-84), French film director. Letter, 8 Jan. 1981 (published in *Letters*, 1988).

37 People sometimes say that the way things happen in the movies is unreal, but actually it's the way things happen to you in life that's unreal. The movies make emotions look so strong and real, whereas when things really do happen to you, it's like watching television—you don't feel anything.

ANDY WARHOL (1928-87), U.S. Pop artist. *From A to B and Back Again*, ch. 6 (1975).

38 I rather think the cinema will die. Look at the energy being exerted to revive it—yesterday it was color, today three dimensions. I don't give it forty years more. Witnes the decline of conversation. Only the Irish have remained incomparable conversationalists, maybe because technical progress has passed them by.

ORSON WELLES (1915-84), U.S. filmmaker, actor, producer. *Les Nouvelles Littéraires* (1953). Quoted in: Frank Brady, *Citizen Welles*, ch. 16 (1989).

39 The director is simply the audience. So the terrible burden of the director is to take the place of that yawning vacuum, to *be* the audience and to select from what happens during the day which movement shall be a disaster and which a gala night. His job is to preside over accidents.

ORSON WELLES (1915-84), U.S. filmmaker, actor, producer. Speech, 4 Nov. 1985, at Hollywood Foreign Press Association, broadcast at the memorial service for Welles in Los Angeles (published in Frank Brady, *Citizen Welles*, ch. 21, 1989).

40 A strange thing has happened—while all the other arts were born naked, this, the youngest, has been born fully-clothed. It can say everything before it has anything to say. It is as if the savage tribe, instead of finding two bars of iron to play with, had found scattering the seashore fiddles, flutes, saxophones, trumpets, grand pianos by Erhard and Bechstein, and had begun with incredible energy, but without knowing a note of music, to hammer and thump upon them all at the same time.

VIRGINIA WOOLF (1882-1941), British novelist. *The Captain's Death Bed*, "The Cinema" (1950).

CIRCUMCISION

1 There is no doubt that the practice is a means of suppressing and controlling the sexual behaviour of women. Female circumcision is a physiological chastity belt.

SUE ARMSTRONG, South African journalist. *New Scientist* (London, 2 Feb 1991).

2 Circumcision is startling, all right, particularly when performed by a garlicked old man upon the glory of a newborn body, but then maybe that's what the Jews had in mind and what makes the act seem quintessentially Jewish and the mark of their reality. Circumcision makes it clear as can be that you are here and not there, that you are out and not in—also that you're mine and not theirs. . . . Quite convincingly, circumcision gives the lie to the womb-dream of life in the beautiful state of innocent prehistory, the appealing idyll of living "naturally," unencumbered by man-made ritual. To be born is to lose all that. The heavy hand of human values falls upon you right at the start, marking your genitals as its own.

PHILIP ROTH (b. 1933), U.S. novelist. Nathan Zuckerman writing to Maria, in *The Counterlife*, ch. 5 (1986).

3 They circumcised women, little girls, in Jesus's time. Did he know? Did the subject anger or embarrass him? Did the early church erase the record? Jesus himself was circumcised; perhaps he thought only the cutting done to him was done to women, and therefore, since he survived, it was all right.

ALICE WALKER (b. 1944), U.S. author, critic. *Possessing the Secret of Joy*, pt. 21, "Tashi-Evelyn-Mrs. Johnson" (1992).

CIRCUMSTANCES

1 There are moments when you feel free, moments when you have energy, moments when you have hope, but you can't rely on any of these things to see you through. Circumstances do that.

ANITA BROOKNER (b. 1938), British novelist, art historian. *Novelists in Interview* (ed. by John Haffenden, 1985).

2 It always remains true that if we had been greater, circumstance would have been less strong against us.

GEORGE ELIOT (1819-80), English novelist, editor. *Middlemarch*, bk. 6, ch. 58 (1871).

3 Fortuitous circumstances constitute the moulds that shape the majority of human lives, and the hasty impress of an accident is too often regarded as the relentless decree of all ordaining fate.

AUGUSTA JANE EVANS (1835-1909), U.S. writer. *Unto Death Us Do Part*, ch. 1 (1869).

4 A merciless fate threw me into this maelstrom. I wanted much, I began much, but the gale of the world carried away me and my work.

DRAZA MIHAJLOVIC (1893-1946), Yugoslav soldier, Serbian guerrilla leader. Final defense plea at his trial, 15 July 1946, Belgrade, before his execution by Tito's forces, against whom he had been engaged in civil war.

5 If all our happiness is bound up entirely in our personal circumstances it is difficult not to demand of life more than it has to give.

BERTRAND RUSSELL (1872-1970), British philosopher, mathematician. *The Conquest of Happiness*, ch. 10 (1930).

6 People are always blaming their circumstances for what they are. I don't believe in circumstances. The people who get on in this world are the people who get up and look for the circumstances they want, and, if they can't find them, make them.

> GEORGE BERNARD SHAW (1856-1950), Anglo-Irish playwright, critic. Vivie Warren, in *Mrs. Warren's Profession*, act 2.

7   I don't believe in villains or heroes, only in right or wrong ways that individuals are taken, not by choice, but by necessity or by certain still uncomprehended influences in themselves, their circumstances and their antecedents.

> TENNESSEE WILLIAMS (1914-83), U.S. dramatist. *New York Post* (17 March 1957).

See also Burke on POLITICS.

CITIES AND CITY LIFE

1   One has not great hopes from Birmingham. I always say there is something direful in the sound.

> JANE AUSTEN (1775-1817), English novelist. Mrs. Elton, in *Emma*, ch. 36 (1816).

2   The life of our city is rich in poetic and marvelous subjects. We are enveloped and steeped as though in an atmosphere of the marvelous; but we do not notice it.

> CHARLES BAUDELAIRE (1821-67), French poet. "Salon of 1846," sct.18 (published in *Curiosités Esthétiques*, 1868; repr. in *The Mirror of Art*, ed. by Jonathan Mayne, 1955).

3   Cities are . . . distinguished by the catastrophic forms they presuppose and which are a vital part of their essential charm. New York is King Kong, or the blackout, or vertical bombardment: Towering Inferno. Los Angeles is the horizontal fault, California breaking off and sliding into the Pacific: Earthquake.

> JEAN BAUDRILLARD (b. 1929), French semiologist. *Fatal Strategies*, "Ecstasy And Inertia" (1983; tr. 1990).

4   The cities of the world are concentric, isomorphic, synchronic. Only one exists and you are always in the same one. It's the effect of their permanent revolution, their intense circulation, their instantaneous magnetism.

> JEAN BAUDRILLARD (b. 1929), French semiologist. *Cool Memories*, ch. 3 (1987; tr. 1990).

5   Not to find one's way in a city may well be uninteresting and banal. It requires ignorance—nothing more. But to lose oneself in a city—as one loses oneself in a forest—that calls for a quite different schooling. Then, signboard and street names, passers-by, roofs, kiosks, or bars must speak to the wanderer like a cracking twig under his feet in the forest.

> WALTER BENJAMIN (1892-1940), German critic, philosopher. *A Berlin Chronicle* (written 1932; published 1970; repr. in *One-Way Street and Other Writings*, 1978).

6   Every city has a sex and an age which have nothing to do with demography. Rome is feminine. So is Odessa. London is a teenager, an urchin, and, in this, hasn't changed since the time of Dickens. Paris, I believe, is a man in his twenties in love with an older woman.

> JOHN BERGER (b. 1926), British author, critic. "Imagine Paris,"

in *Harper's* (New York, Jan. 1987; repr. in *Keeping a Rendezvous*, 1992).

7   How doth the city sit solitary, that was full of people! how is she become as a widow! she that was great among the nations, and princess among the provinces, how is she become tributary!

> BIBLE, HEBREW. *Lamentations* 1:1, said of Jerusalem.

8   Cities, like cats, will reveal themselves at night.

> RUPERT BROOKE (1887-1915), British poet. *Letters from America*, ch. 3 (1916).

9   The catalogue of forms is endless: until every shape has found its city, new cities will continue to be born. When the forms exhaust their variety and come apart, the end of cities begins.

> ITALO CALVINO (1923-85), Italian author, critic. *Invisible Cities* (1972; tr. 1974).

10   As a remedy to life in society I would suggest the big city. Nowadays, it is the only desert within our means.

> ALBERT CAMUS (1913-60), French-Algerian philosopher, author. *Notebooks 1935-1942* (1962), entry for March 1940.

11   No city should be too large for a man to walk out of in a morning.

> CYRIL CONNOLLY (1903-74), British critic. *The Unquiet Grave*, pt. 1 (1944; rev. 1951).

12   All that a city will ever allow you is an angle on it—an oblique, indirect sample of what it contains, or what passes through it; a point of view.

> PETER CONRAD (b. 1948), Australian critic, author. *Independent on Sunday* (London, 11 March 1990), said of New York.

13   A great city, whose image dwells in the memory of man, is the type of some great idea. Rome represents conquest; Faith hovers over the towers of Jerusalem; and Athens embodies the pre-eminent quality of the antique world, Art.

> BENJAMIN DISRAELI (1804-81), English statesman, author. *Coningsby*, bk. 4, ch. 1 (1844).

14   Cities give us collision. 'Tis said, London and New York take the nonsense out of a man.

> RALPH WALDO EMERSON (1803-82), U.S. essayist, poet, philosopher. *The Conduct of Life*, "Culture" (1860).

15   Towns are . . . excrescences, grey fluxions, where men, hurrying to find one another, have lost themselves.

> E. M. FORSTER (1879-1970), British novelist, essayist. *The Longest Journey*, ch. 33 (1907).

16   The Metropolis should have been aborted long before it became New York, London or Tokyo.

> JOHN KENNETH GALBRAITH (b. 1908), U.S. economist. *The Age of Uncertainty*, ch. 9 (1977).

17   The two elements the traveler first captures in the big city are extrahuman architecture and furious rhythm. Geometry and anguish. At first glance, the rhythm may be confused with gaiety, but when you look more closely at the mechanism of social life and the painful slavery of both men and machines, you see that it is nothing but a kind of typical, empty anguish that makes even crime and gangs forgivable means of escape.

> FEDERICO GARCÍA LORCA (1898-1936), Spanish poet, playwright. "A Poet in New York," lecture, delivered in Mardrid, March 1932 (published in *Poet in New York,* 1940; tr. 1988).

18 There is a time of life somewhere between the sullen fugues of adolescence and the retrenchments of middle age when human nature becomes so absolutely absorbing one wants to be in the city constantly, even at the height of summer.

> EDWARD HOAGLAND (b. 1932), U.S. novelist, essayist. "City Walking," published in *New York Times Book Review* (1 June 1975; repr. in "Heart's Desire," 1988).

19 In Washington, the first thing people tell you is what their job is. In Los Angeles you learn their star sign. In Houston you're told how rich they are. And in New York they tell you what their rent is.

> SIMON HOGGART (b. 1946), British journalist. *America: A User's Guide,* ch. 1 (1990).

20 We are in danger . . . of making our cities places where business goes on but where life, in its real sense, is lost.

> HUBERT H. HUMPHREY (1911-78), U.S. Democratic politician, vice president. Speech, 13 Sept. 1966, to Urban America Conference, Washington, D.C.

21 A large city cannot be experientially known; its life is too manifold for any individual to be able to participate in it.

> ALDOUS HUXLEY (1894-1963), British author. *Beyond the Mexique Bay,* "Oaxaca" (1934).

22 But look what we have built . . . low-income projects that become worse centers of delinquency, vandalism and general social hopelessness than the slums they were supposed to replace. . . . Cultural centers that are unable to support a good bookstore. Civic centers that are avoided by everyone but bums. . . . Promenades that go from no place to nowhere and have no promenaders. Expressways that eviscerate great cities. This is not the rebuilding of cities. This is the sacking of cities.

> JANE JACOBS (b. 1916), U.S. author. *The Death and Life of Great American Cities,* Introduction (1961).

23 Prepare for death, if here at night you roam,
And sign your will before you sup from home.

> SAMUEL JOHNSON (1709-84), English author, lexicographer. *London.*

24 Towns oftener swamp one than carry one out onto the big ocean of life.

> D. H. LAWRENCE (1885-1930), British author. Letter, 2 Dec. 1908 (published in *The Letters of D. H. Lawrence,* vol. 1, ed. by James T. Boulton, 1979).

25 A city is a place where there is no need to wait for next week to get the answer to a question, to taste the food of any country, to find new voices to listen to and familiar ones to listen to again.

> MARGARET MEAD (1901-78), U.S. anthropologist. *World Enough,* ch. 2 (1975).

26 The city as a center where, any day in any year, there may be a fresh encounter with a new talent, a keen mind or a gifted specialist—this is essential to the life of a country. To play this role in our lives a city must have a soul—a university, a great art or music school, a cathedral or a great mosque or temple, a great laboratory or scientific center, as well as the libraries and museums and galleries that bring past and present together. A city must be a place where groups of women and men are seeking and developing the highest things they know.

> MARGARET MEAD (1901-78), U.S. anthropologist. Quoted in: *Redbook* (New York, Aug. 1978).

27 The city is loveliest when the sweet death racket begins. Her own life lived in defiance of nature, her electricity, her frigidaires, her soundproof walls, the glint of lacquered nails, the plumes that wave across the corrugated sky. Here in the coffin depths grow the everlasting flowers sent by telegraph.

> HENRY MILLER (1891-1980), U.S. author. *Black Spring,* "Megalopolitan Maniac" (1936).

28 America is a nation with no truly national city, no Paris, no Rome, no London, no city which is at once the social center, the political capital, and the financial hub.

> C. WRIGHT MILLS (1916-62), U.S. sociologist. *The Power Elite,* ch. 3 (1956).

29 The city is not a concrete jungle, it is a human zoo.

> DESMOND MORRIS (b. 1928), British anthropologist. *The Human Zoo,* Introduction (1969).

30 The city is a fact in nature, like a cave, a run of mackerel or an ant-heap. But it is also a conscious work of art, and it holds within its communal framework many simpler and more personal forms of art. Mind *takes form* in the city; and in turn, urban forms condition mind.

> LEWIS MUMFORD (1895-1990), U.S. social philosopher. *The Culture of Cities,* Introduction (1938).

31 The chief function of the city is to convert power into form, energy into culture, dead matter into the living symbols of art, biological reproduction into social creativity.

> LEWIS MUMFORD (1895-1990), U.S. social philosopher. *The City in History,* ch. 18 (1961).

32 Today's city is the most vulnerable social structure ever conceived by man.

> MARTIN OPPENHEIMER (b. 1930), German-born U.S. sociologist. *Urban Guerrilla,* ch. 7 (1969).

33 All great art is born of the metropolis.

> EZRA POUND (1885-1972), U.S. poet, critic. Letter, 7 Nov. 1913, to Harriet Monroe (published in *Letters of Ezra Pound 1907-1941,* ed. D. D. Paige, 1951). "The metropolis," Pound explained, "is that which accepts all gifts and all heights of excellence, usually the excellence that is *tabu* in its own village. The metropolis is always accused by the peasant of "being mad after foreign notions." Ten years later, in the *Criterion* (Jan. 1923), Pound wrote, "All civilization has proceeded from cities and cenacles." (Cenacle, supping room, upper chamber).

34 Living in cities is an art, and we need the vocabulary of art, of style, to describe the peculiar relationship between man and material that exists in the continual creative play of urban living. The city as we imagine it, then, soft city of illusion, myth, aspiration, and nightmare, is as real, maybe more real, than the hard city one can locate on maps in statistics, in monographs on urban sociology and demography and architecture.

> JONATHAN RABAN (b. 1942), British author, critic. *Soft City,* ch. 1 (1974).

35 Just as language has no longer anything in common with the thing it names, so the movements of most of the people who live in cities have lost their connexion with the earth; they hang, as it were, in the air, hover in all directions, and find no place where they can settle.

> RAINER MARIA RILKE (1875-1926), German poet. *Worpswede* (1903; repr. in *Rodin and Other Prose Pieces,* 1954).

36 I look upon those pitiful concretions of lime and clay which spring up, in mildewed forwardness, out of the kneaded fields about our capital . . . not merely with the careless disgust of an offended eye, not merely with sorrow for a desecrated landscape, but with a painful foreboding that the roots of our national greatness must be deeply cankered when they are thus loosely struck in their native ground. . . . The crowded tenements of a struggling and restless population differ only from the tents of the Arab or the Gipsy by their less healthy openness to the air of heaven, and less happy choice of their spot of earth; by their sacrifice of liberty without the gain of rest, and of stability without the luxury of change.

> JOHN RUSKIN (1819-1900), English art critic, author. *The Seven Lamps of Architecture,* "The Lamp of Memory," sct. 3 (1849).

37 There is no quiet place in the white man's cities. No place to hear the unfurling of leaves in spring, or the rustle of an insect's wings. But perhaps it is because I am a savage and do not understand. The clatter only seems to insult the ears.

> Attributed to SEATTLE (c. 1784-1866), Chief of the Dwamish, Suquamish & allied Indian tribes. Letter, 1854, to President Franklin Pierce (published in *Brother Eagle, Sister Sky: A Message from Chief Seattle,* 1990). The letter, in which Seattle pleaded that his name should die with the ceding of the Washington State territories, was shown in 1992 to have been largely a forgery, devised by television scriptwriter Ted Perry for a historical epic in 1971.

38 In place of a world, there is a *city*, a *point*, in which the whole life of broad regions is collecting while the rest dries up. In place of a type-true people, born of and grown on the soil, there is a new sort of nomad, cohering unstably in fluid masses, the parasitical city dweller, traditionless, utterly matter-of-fact, religionless, clever, unfruitful, deeply contemptuous of the countryman and especially that highest form of countryman, the country gentleman.

> OSWALD SPENGLER (1880-1936), German historian. *The Decline of the West,* vol. 1, ch. 1, sct. 12 (1926).

39 Commuters give the city its tidal restlessness; natives give it solidity and continuity; but the settlers give it passion.

> E. B. WHITE (1899-1985), U.S. author, editor. "Here is New York," in *Holiday* (Indianapolis, April 1949).

40 The great city is that which has the greatest man or woman:
If it be a few ragged huts, it is still the greatest city

in the whole world.

> WALT WHITMAN (1819-92), U.S. poet. "Song of the Broad Axe," sct.4.

41 Through this broad street, restless ever,
Ebbs and flows a human tide,
Wave on wave a living river;
Wealth and fashion side by side;
Toiler, idler, slave and master, in the same quick current glide.

> JOHN GREENLEAF WHITTIER (1807-92), U.S. poet. *At Washington,* st. 2.

42 The cities of America are inexpressibly tedious. The Bostonians take their learning too sadly; culture with them is an accomplishment rather than an atmosphere; their "Hub," as they call it, is the paradise of prigs. Chicago is a sort of monster-shop, full of bustles and bores. Political life at Washington is like political life in a suburban vestry. Baltimore is amusing for a week, but Philadelphia is dreadfully provincial; and though one can dine in New York one could not dwell there.

> OSCAR WILDE (1854-1900), Anglo-Irish playwright, author. "The American Invasion," in *Court and Society Review* (London, 23 March 1887; repr. in *Aristotle at Afternoon Tea: The Rare Oscar Wilde,* 1991).

43 This city now doth, like a garment, wear
The beauty of the morning; silent bare,
Ships, towers, domes, theatres and temples lie
Open unto the fields and to the sky;
All bright and glittering in the smokeless air.

> WILLIAM WORDSWORTH (1770-1850), English poet. *Composed upon Westminster Bridge* (1807; written 1802).

44 The screech and mechanical uproar of the big city turns the citified head, fills citified ears—as the song of birds, wind in the trees, animal cries, or as the voices and songs of his loved ones once filled his heart. He is sidewalk-happy.

> FRANK LLOYD WRIGHT (1869-1959), U.S. architect. *The Living City,* pt. 1, "Earth" (1958).

45 To look at the cross-section of any plan of a big city is to look at something like the section of a fibrous tumor.

> FRANK LLOYD WRIGHT (1869-1959), U.S. architect. *The Living City,* pt. 2, "Social and Economic Disease" (1958).

See also Cohen on CANADA AND THE CANADIANS; CHICAGO; McGinley on KINDNESS; LONDON; LOS ANGELES; NEW YORK; PARIS; Steinbeck on POLLUTION; Washington on RIOTS; ROME; SAN FRANCISCO; SUBURBIA; TOWN AND COUNTRY; VENICE; WASHINGTON, D.C.

CITIZENSHIP

1 Without free, self-respecting, and autonomous citizens there can be no free and independent nations. Without internal peace, that is, peace among citizens and between the citizens and the state, there can be no guarantee of external peace.

> VÁCLAV HAVEL (b. 1936), Czech playwright, president. *Living in Truth,* pt. 1, sct. 9, "An Anatomy of Reticence" (1986).

2 The true courage of civilized nations is readiness for sacrifice in the service of the state, so that the individual counts as only one amongst many. The important thing here is not personal mettle but aligning oneself with the universal.

GEORG HEGEL (1770-1831), German philosopher. *The Philosophy of Right*, "The State," addition 189 (1821; tr. 1942).

3 It is not the function of our Government to keep the citizen from falling into error; it is the function of the citizen to keep the Government from falling into error.

ROBERT H. JACKSON (1892-1954), U.S. judge. *American Communications Association v. Douds*, May 1950.

4 A strict observance of the written laws is doubtless one of the high virtues of a good citizen, but it is not the highest. The laws of necessity, of self-preservation, of saving our country when in danger, are of higher obligation.

THOMAS JEFFERSON (1743-1826), U.S. president. Letter, 20 Sept. 1810.

5 Our citizenship in the United States is our national character. Our citizenship in any particular state is only our local distinction. By the latter we are known at home, by the former to the world. Our great title is AMERICANS—our inferior one varies with the place.

THOMAS PAINE (1737-1809), Anglo-American political theorist, writer. *The American Crisis*, 19 April 1783 (1776-83).

6 The first requisite of a good citizen in this republic of ours is that he shall be able and willing to pull his weight.

THEODORE ROOSEVELT (1858-1919), U.S. Republican (later Progressive) politician, president. Speech, 11 Nov. 1902, New York City.

7 Whatever makes men good Christians, makes them good citizens.

DANIEL WEBSTER (1782-1852), U.S. lawyer, statesman. Speech, 22 Dec. 1820, Plymouth, Mass.

CIVIL RIGHTS

1 The modern state no longer has anything but rights; it does not recognize duties any more.

GEORGES BERNANOS (1888-1948), French novelist, political writer. *The Last Essays of George Bernanos*, "Why Freedom" (1955).

2 Anglo-Saxon civilization has taught the individual to protect his own rights; American civilization will teach him to respect the rights of others.

WILLIAM JENNINGS BRYAN (1860-1925), U.S. Democratic politician. "America's Mission," speech, 22 Feb. 1899, Washington, D.C.

3 Men are qualified for civil liberty in exact proportion to their disposition to put moral chains upon their own appetites; in proportion as their love to justice is above their rapacity; in proportion as their soundness and sobriety of understanding is above their vanity and presumption; in proportion as they are more disposed to listen to the counsels of the wise and good, in preference to the flattery of knaves.

EDMUND BURKE (1729-97), Irish philosopher, statesman. *A Letter to a Member of the National Assembly*, 19 Jan. 1791.

4 The government of the United States is a device for maintaining in perpetuity the rights of the people, with the ultimate extinction of all privileged classes.

CALVIN COOLIDGE (1872-1933), U.S. Republican politician, president. Speech, 25 Sept. 1924, Philadelphia, Pa.

5 Ignorance, forgetfulness, or contempt of the rights of man are the only causes of public misfortunes and of the corruption of governments.

FRENCH NATIONAL ASSEMBLY. *Declaration of the Rights of Man* (drafted and discussed Aug. 1789; published Sept. 1791).

6 Rights that do not flow from duty well performed are not worth having.

MOHANDAS K. GANDHI (1869-1948), Indian political and spiritual leader. *Non-Violence in Peace and War*, vol. 2, ch. 269 (1949).

7 Civil Rights: What black folks are given in the U.S. on the installment plan, as in civil-rights bills. Not to be confused with *human rights*, which are the dignity, stature, humanity, respect, and freedom belonging to all people by right of their birth.

DICK GREGORY (b. 1932), U.S. comedian, civil rights activist. *Dick Gregory's Political Primer* (1972). See Malcolm X on AFRICAN AMERICANS.

8 We hear about constitutional rights, free speech and the free press. Every time I hear those words I say to myself, "That man is a Red, that man is a Communist." You never heard a real American talk in that manner.

FRANK HAGUE (1876-1956), U.S. mayor of Jersey City, N.J. Speech, 12 Jan. 1938, Jersey City Chamber of Commerce.

9 A state that denies its citizens their basic rights becomes a danger to its neighbors as well: internal arbitrary rule will be reflected in arbitrary external relations. The suppression of public opinion, the abolition of public competition for power and its public exercise opens the way for the state power to arm itself in any way it sees fit. . . . A state that does not hesitate to lie to its own people will not hesitate to lie to other states.

VÁCLAV HAVEL (b. 1936), Czech playwright, president. *Living in Truth*, pt. 1, "An Anatomy of Reticence," sct. 9 (1986).

10 There are those who say to you—we are rushing this issue of civil rights. I say we are 172 years late.

HUBERT H. HUMPHREY (1911-78), U.S. Democratic politician, vice president. Address, 14 July 1948, to Democratic National Convention, Philadelphia, supporting his Civil Rights Amendment to the Party Platform. Humphrey was then mayor of Minneapolis.

11 The theory of *rights* enables us to rise and overthrow obstacles, but not to found a strong and lasting accord between all the elements which compose the nation.

GIUSEPPE MAZZINI (1805-72), Italian nationalist leader. *The Duties of Man*, ch. 1 (1844-58; tr. 1907).

12 To exercise power costs effort and demands courage. That is why so many fail to assert rights to which they are perfectly entitled—because a right is a kind of *power* but they are too lazy or too cowardly to exercise it. The virtues which cloak these faults are called *patience* and *forbearance*.

FRIEDRICH NIETZSCHE (1844-1900), German philosopher. *The Wanderer and His Shadow*, aph. 251 (1880).

See also HUMAN RIGHTS; Mencken on PRIVILEGE.

AMERICAN CIVIL WAR

1 With malice toward none, with charity for all, with firmness in the right, as God gives us to see the right, let us strive on to finish the work we are in, to bind up the nation's wounds, to care for him who shall have borne the battle, and for his widow and his orphan, to do all which may achieve and cherish a just and lasting peace among ourselves, and with all nations.

> ABRAHAM LINCOLN (1809-65), U.S. president. Second Inaugural Address, 4 March 1865.

2 In the South, the war is what A.D. is elsewhere: they date from it.

> MARK TWAIN (1835-1910), U.S. author. *Life on the Mississippi*, ch. 45 (1883).

3 Let's have the Union restored as it was, if we can; but if we can't, *I'm in favor of the Union as it wasn't*.

> ARTEMUS WARD (1834-67), U.S. journalist. *Artemus Ward: His Travels*, "In Canada" (1865).

4 We are constantly thinking of the great war . . . which saved the Union . . . but it was a war that did a great deal more than that. It created in this country what had never existed before—a national consciousness. It was not the salvation of the Union, it was the rebirth of the Union.

> WOODROW WILSON (1856-1924), U.S. Democratic politician, president. Memorial Day address, 31 May 1915, Arlington National Cemetery, Va.

CIVILIZATION

1 Civilization is the lamb's skin in which barbarism masquerades.

> T. B. ALDRICH (1836-1907), U.S. writer, editor. *Ponkapog Papers*, "Leaves from a Notebook" (1903).

2 The skylines lit up at dead of night, the air-conditioning systems cooling empty hotels in the desert and artificial light in the middle of the day all have something both demented and admirable about them. The mindless luxury of a rich civilization, and yet of a civilization perhaps as scared to see the lights go out as was the hunter in his primitive night.

> JEAN BAUDRILLARD (b. 1929), French semiologist. *America*, "Astral America" (1986; tr. 1988).

3 People sometimes tell me that they prefer barbarism to civilisation. I doubt if they have given it a long enough trial. Like the people of Alexandria, they are bored by civilisation; but all the evidence suggests that the boredom of barbarism is infinitely greater.

> KENNETH, LORD CLARK (1903-83), British art historian. *Civilisation*, ch. 1 (1970).

4 Civilization is an active deposit which is formed by the combustion of the Present with the Past. Neither in countries without a Present nor in those without a Past is it to be encountered. Proust in Venice, Matisse's birdcages overlooking the flower market at Nice, Gide on the seventeenth-century quais of Toulon, Lorca in Granada, Picasso by Saint-Germain-des-Prés: there lies civilization and for me it can exist only under those liberal regimes in which the Present is alive and therefore capable of assimilating the Past.

> CYRIL CONNOLLY (1903-74), British critic. *The Unquiet Grave*, pt. 2 (1944; rev. 1951).

5 The civilized are those who get more out of life than the uncivilized, and for this we are not likely to be forgiven.

> CYRIL CONNOLLY (1903-74), British critic. *The Unquiet Grave*, pt. 2 (1944; rev. 1951).

6 Increased means and increased leisure are the two civilizers of man.

> BENJAMIN DISRAELI (1804-81), English statesman, author. Speech, 3 April 1872, Manchester, England.

7 Civilization is a stream with banks. The stream is sometimes filled with blood from people killing, stealing, shouting and doing the things historians usually record, while on the banks, unnoticed, people build homes, make love, raise children, sing songs, write poetry and even whittle statues. The story of civilization is the story of what happened on the banks. Historians are pessimists because they ignore the banks for the river.

> WILL DURANT (1885-1981), U.S. historian. *Life* (New York, 18 Oct. 1963).

8 Is civilization only a higher form of idolatry, that man should bow down to a flesh-brush, to flannels, to baths, diet, exercise, and air?

> MARY BAKER EDDY (1821-1910), U.S. founder of the Christian Science movement. *Science and Health*, ch. 7 (1875).

9 All civilization has from time to time become a thin crust over a volcano of revolution.

> HAVELOCK ELLIS (1859-1939), British psychologist. *Little Essays of Love and Virtue*, ch. 7 (1922).

10 As long as our civilization is essentially one of property, of fences, of exclusiveness, it will be mocked by delusions. Our riches will leave us sick; there will be bitterness in our laughter; and our wine will burn our mouth. Only that good profits, which we can taste with all doors open, and which serves all men.

> RALPH WALDO EMERSON (1803-82), U.S. essayist, poet, philosopher. *Representative Men*, "Napoleon, the Man of the World" (1850).

11 Civilization is a process in the service of Eros, whose purpose is to combine single human individuals, and after that families, then races, peoples and nations, into one great unity, the unity of mankind. Why this has to happen, we do not know; the work of Eros is precisely this.

> SIGMUND FREUD (1856-1939), Austrian psychiatrist. *Civilization and its Discontents*, ch. 6 (1931; repr. in *Complete Works*, Standard Edition, ed. by James Strachey and Anna Freud, vol. 21, 1961).

12 One might enumerate the items of high civilization, as it exists in other countries, which are absent from the texture of American life, until it should become a wonder to know what was left.

> HENRY JAMES (1843-1916), U.S. author. *Hawthorne,* ch. 2 (1879). For some of the things James found to be missing from American life, see James on THE UNITED STATES.

13 Every new stroke of civilization has cost the lives of countless brave men, who have fallen defeated by the "dragon," in their efforts to win the apples of the Hesperides, or the fleece of gold. Fallen in their efforts to overcome the old, half sordid savagery of the lower stages of creation, and win the next stage.

> D. H. LAWRENCE (1885-1930), British author. *St Mawr* (1925; repr. in *The Short Novels,* vol. 2, ed. by George J. Zytaruk & James T. Boulton, 1981). The Dragon in the legend of the Hesperides guarded the golden apples that were thought to have been the symbol of immortality. Hercules, in the eleventh of his twelve labors, slew the dragon and carried away some of the apples.

14 Civilization is drugs, alcohol, engines of war, prostitution, machines and machine slaves, low wages, bad food, bad taste, prisons, reformatories, lunatic asylums, divorce, perversion, brutal sports, suicides, infanticide, cinema, quackery, demagogy, strikes, lockouts, revolutions, putsches, colonization, electric chairs, guillotines, sabotage, floods, famine, disease, gangsters, money barons, horse racing, fashion shows, poodle dogs, chow dogs, Siamese cats, condoms, pessaries, syphilis, gonorrhea, insanity, neuroses, etc., etc.

> HENRY MILLER (1891-1980), U.S. author. *The Cosmological Eye,* "An Open Letter to Surrealists Everywhere" (1939).

15 The word "civilization" to my mind is coupled with death. When I use the word, I see civilization as a crippling, thwarting thing, a stultifying thing. For me it was always so. I don't believe in the golden ages, you see. . . . Civilization is the arteriosclerosis of culture.

> HENRY MILLER (1891-1980), U.S. author. Interview in *Writers at Work* (Second Series, ed. by George Plimpton, 1963).

16 Civilisation—a heap of rubble scavenged by scrawny English Lit. vultures.

> MALCOLM MUGGERIDGE (1903-90), British broadcaster. Quoted in: *New Society* (London, 6 Oct. 1983).

17 Civilization is nothing else than the attempt to reduce force to being the *ultima ratio.*

> JOSÉ ORTEGA Y GASSET (1883-1955), Spanish essayist, philosopher. *The Revolt of the Masses,* ch. 8 (1930).

18 To accept civilisation *as it is* practically means accepting decay.

> GEORGE ORWELL (1903-50), British author. *Inside the Whale and Other Essays,* "Inside the Whale" (1940).

19 A civilized man is one who will give a serious answer to a serious question. Civilization itself is a certain sane balance of values.

> EZRA POUND (1885-1972), U.S. poet, critic. *Guide to Kulchur,* pt. 3, sct. 5, ch. 20 (1938).

20 A civilization is a heritage of beliefs, customs, and knowledge slowly accumulated in the course of centuries, elements difficult at times to justify by logic, but

justifying themselves as paths when they lead somewhere, since they open up for man his inner distance.

> ANTOINE DE SAINT-EXUPÉRY (1900-1944), French aviator, author. *Flight to Arras,* ch. 12 (1942).

21 Civilization must be destroyed. The hairy saints
Of the North have earned this crumb by their complaints.

> WALLACE STEVENS (1879-1955), U.S. poet. *Land of Pine and Marble,* in *New England Verses* (published in *Harmonium,* 1923).

22 Civilization is a movement and not a condition, a voyage and not a harbor.

> A. J. TOYNBEE (1889-1975), British historian. *The Reader's Digest* (Oct. 1958).

23 If Germany, thanks to Hitler and his successors, were to enslave the European nations and destroy most of the treasures of their past, future historians would certainly pronounce that she had civilized Europe.

> SIMONE WEIL (1909-43), French philosopher, mystic. "The Great Beast," pt. 3 (written 1939-40; published in *Selected Essays,* ed. by Richard Rees, 1962).

24 Civilisation is not by any means an easy thing to attain to. There are only two ways by which man can reach it. One is by being cultured, the other by being corrupt.

> OSCAR WILDE (1854-1900), Anglo-Irish playwright, author. Lord Henry, in *The Picture of Dorian Gray,* ch. 19 (1891).

See also Trevelyan on CURIOSITY; Pound on HOPE; Russell on LEISURE; Rogers on PROGRESS; Ellis on SUICIDE; Meredith on WOMEN.

CLASS

1 Have no fellowship with one that is mightier and richer than thyself: for how agree the kettle and the earthen pot together? For if the one be smitten against the other, it shall be broken.

> APOCRYPHA. *Ecclesiasticus* 13:2.

2 If experience has established any one thing in this world, it has established this: that it is well for any great class and description of men in society to be able to say for itself what it wants, and not to have other classes, the so-called educated and intelligent classes, acting for it as its proctors, and supposed to understand its wants and to provide for them. . . . A class of men may often itself not either fully understand its wants, or adequately express them; but it has a nearer interest and a more sure diligence in the matter than any of its proctors, and therefore a better chance of success.

> MATTHEW ARNOLD (1822-88), English poet, critic. *Irish Essays and Others,* "The Future of Liberalism" (1882; repr. in *The Complete Prose Works of Matthew Arnold,* vol. 9, ed. by R. H. Super, 1973).

3 Historically and politically, the petit-bourgeois is the key to the century. . . . The bourgeois and proletariat classes have become abstractions: the petite-bourgeoisie, in contrast, is everywhere, you can see it everywhere, even in the areas of the bourgeois and the proletariat, what's left of them.

> ROLAND BARTHES (1915-80), French semiologist. Interview by

Bernard-Henri Lévy, *Art and Text*, no. 8 (1977; repr. in *Discourses: Conversations in Postmodern Art and Culture*, ed. by Russell Ferguson et al., 1990).

4   Between richer and poorer classes in a free country a mutually respecting antagonism is much healthier than pity on the one hand and dependence on the other, as is, perhaps, the next best thing to fraternal feeling.

> CHARLES HORTON COOLEY (1864-1929), U.S. sociologist. *Human Nature and the Social Order*, ch. 4 (1902).

5   By bourgeoisie is meant the class of modern capitalists, owners of the means of social production and employers of wage labor. By proletariat, the class of modern wage laborers who, having no means of production of their own, are reduced to selling their labor power in order to live.

> FRIEDRICH ENGELS (1820-95), German social philosopher. *Manifesto of the Communist Party*, Footnote (1848), written in collaboration with Karl Marx.

6   When we say a woman is of a certain social class, we really mean her husband or father is.

> ZOË FAIRBAIRNS (b. 1948), British author. Quoted in: *Observer* (London, 9 Jan. 1983).

7   The traveler to the United States will do well . . . to prepare himself for the class-consciousness of the natives. This differs from the already familiar English version in being more extreme and based more firmly on the conviction that the class to which the speaker belongs is inherently superior to all others.

> JOHN KENNETH GALBRAITH (b. 1908), U.S. economist. "The United States," in *New York* (15 Nov. 1971; repr. in *A View from the Stands*, 1986).

8   Each class of society has its own requirements; but it may be said that every class teaches the one immediately below it; and if the highest class be ignorant, uneducated, loving display, luxuriousness, and idle, the same spirit will prevail in humbler life.

> GIRLS' HOME COMPANION. *Girls' Home Companion* (1895). Quoted in: James Walvin, *Victorian Values*, ch. 12 (1987).

9   All the world over, I will back the masses against the classes.

> W. E. GLADSTONE (1809-88), English Liberal prime minister, statesman. Speech, 28 June 1886, Liverpool, England.

10   Classes struggle, some classes triumph, others are eliminated. Such is history; such is the history of civilization for thousands of years.

> MAO ZEDONG (1893-1976), Founder of the People's Republic of China. Quoted in: Stanley Karnow, *Mao and China: From Revolution to Revolution* (1972), said in Aug. 1949.

11   The history of all hitherto existing society is the history of class struggles.

> KARL MARX (1818-83) AND FRIEDRICH ENGELS (1820-95), German social philosophers, revolutionaries. *The Communist Manifesto*, sct.1 (1848; repr. in *Karl Marx: Selected Works*, vol. 1, 1942).

12   Lady Hodmarsh and the duchess immediately assumed the clinging affability that persons of rank assume with their inferiors in order to show them that they are not in the least conscious of any difference in station between them.

> W. SOMERSET MAUGHAM (1874-1965), British author. *Cakes and Ale*, ch. 4 (1930).

13   The want of education and moral training is the only *real* barrier that exists between the different classes of men. Nature, reason, and Christianity recognize no other. Pride may say Nay; but Pride was always a liar, and a great hater of the truth.

> SUSANNA MOODIE (1803-85), Canadian author. *Life in the Clearing*, ch. 3 (1853).

14   The word of the moment is "classless," whether applied to Cockney Society photographers or sprigs of the aristocracy running little bistros round the corner. Mick Jagger, alternately slurring yob and lisping lordling, is classlessness apotheosised.

> PHILIP NORMAN, British author, journalist. *The Life and Good Times of the Rolling Stones*, p. 61 (1989).

15   Throughout recorded time . . . there have been three kinds of people in the world, the High, the Middle, and the Low. They have been subdivided in many ways, they have borne countless different names, and their relative numbers, as well as their attitude towards one another, have varied from age to age: but the essential structure of society has never altered. Even after enormous upheavals and seemingly irrevocable changes, the same pattern has always reasserted itself, just as a gyroscope will always return to equilibrium, however far it is pushed one way or the other. The aims of these three groups are entirely irreconcilable.

> GEORGE ORWELL (1903-50), British author. First words of Goldstein's book, *Nineteen Eighty-Four*, pt. 2, ch. 9 (1949).

16   I am his Highness' dog at Kew;
Pray tell me, sir, whose dog are you?

> ALEXANDER POPE (1688-1744), English satirical poet. *Epigram Engraved on the Collar of a Dog which I Gave to His Royal Highness* [Frederick, Prince of Wales].

17   For the duration of its collective life, or the time during which its identity may be assumed, each class resembles a hotel or an omnibus, always full, but always of different people.

> JOSEPH A. SCHUMPETER (1883-1950), Austrian-American economist. *Social Classes*, ch. 3, no. 7 (1927).

18   Wearing overalls on weekdays, painting somebody else's house to earn money? You're working class. Wearing overalls at weekends, painting your own house to save money? You're middle class.

> LAWRENCE SUTTON. Prizewinner in competition in *Sunday Correspondent* (London) for best definition of class. Quoted in: *New York Times* (31 Oct. 1990).

19   The Americans never use the word *peasant*, because they have no idea of the class which that term denotes; the ignorance of more remote ages, the simplicity of rural life, and the rusticity of the villager have not been preserved among them; and they are alike unacquainted with the virtues, the vices, the coarse habits, and the simple graces of an early stage of civilization.

ALEXIS DE TOCQUEVILLE (1805-59), French social philosopher. *Democracy in America*, vol. 1, ch. 17 (1835).

20   Really, if the lower orders don't set us a good example, what on earth is the use of them? They seem, as a class, to have absolutely no sense of moral responsibility.

OSCAR WILDE (1854-1900), Anglo-Irish playwright, author. Algernon, in *The Importance of Being Earnest*, act 1.

See also Auden on AGE AND AGING; ARISTOCRACY; THE BOURGEOISIE; Bush on CHARISMA; INEQUALITY; Herford on LADIES; Chesterfield on LAUGHTER; Marx on MARXISM; The MIDDLE CLASS; The UPPER CLASS; The WORKING CLASS.

CLASSICISM AND ANTIQUITY

1   It is time for dead languages to be quiet.

NATALIE CLIFFORD BARNEY (1876-1972), U.S.-born French author. Quoted in: *Adam*, no. 299, "On Writing and Writers" (London, 1962; tr. by Ezra Pound).

2   To appreciate present conditions
collate them with those of antiquity.

BASIL BUNTING (1900-1985), British poet. *Chomei at Toyama*.

3   We are really so prejudiced by our educations, that, as the ancients deified their heroes, we deify their madmen.

LORD CHESTERFIELD (1694-1773), English statesman, man of letters. Letter, 22 Feb. 1748 (1774; repr. in *The Letters of the Earl of Chesterfield to His Son*, vol. 1, no. 142, ed. by Charles Strachey, 1901).

4   It is an unscrupulous intellect that does not pay to antiquity its due reverence.

DESIDERIUS ERASMUS (c. 1466-1536), Dutch humanist. *Works of Hilary*, Preface, 5 Jan. 1523.

5   Here is the mistake of the cut-and-dried man of culture. He goes about with the secret of having learned to appreciate the "grand style." He has lived in Homer till he can recall the roll of that many-sounding sea. He has pored over the lofty and pictorial thought of Plato till he begins to pique *himself* upon its grandeur. His fancy has been fed on the quaint old-world genius of Herodotus, his judgment on the melancholy wisdom of Tacitus and the complacent cynicism of Gibbon—and of all this he is conscious and proud.

R. H. HUTTON (1826-97), English editor, critic. "Mr. Grote on the Abuses of Newspaper Criticism," in *Spectator* (London, 29 June 1861; repr. in *A Victorian Spectator: Uncollected Writings of R. H. Hutton*, ed. by Robert H. Tener and Malcolm Woodfield, 1989).

See also Erasmus on GREECE AND THE GREEKS; Connolly on STYLE.

CLICHÉS

1   When the first-rate author wants an exquisite heroine or a lovely morning, he finds that all the superlatives have been worn shoddy by his inferiors. It should be a rule that bad writers must start with plain heroines and ordinary mornings, and, if they are able, work up to something better.

F. SCOTT FITZGERALD (1896-1940), U.S. author. *The Crack-Up*, "Notebook L" (ed. by Edmund Wilson, 1945).

2   The cliché organizes life; it expropriates people's identity; it becomes ruler, defense lawyer, judge, and the law.

VÁCLAV HAVEL (b. 1936), Czech playwright, president. *Disturbing the Peace*, ch. 5 (1986; tr. 1990).

3   We make the oldest stories new when we succeed, and we are trapped by the old stories when we fail.

GREIL MARCUS (b. 1945), U.S. rock journalist. *Mystery Train*, Prologue (1976).

4   Man is a creature who lives not upon bread alone, but principally by catchwords.

ROBERT LOUIS STEVENSON (1850-94), Scottish novelist, essayist, poet. *Virginibus Puerisque*, title essay, pt. 2 (1881).

5   If you want to use a cliché you must take full responsibility for it yourself and not try to fob it off on anon., or on society.

LEWIS THOMAS (b. 1913), U.S. physician, educator. *The Medusa and the Snail*, "Notes on Punctuation" (1979).

6   I seem to have heard that observation before. . . . It has all the vitality of error and all the tediousness of an old friend.

OSCAR WILDE (1854-1900) , Anglo-Irish playwright, author. Gilbert, in *The Critic as Artist*, pt. 1 (published in *Intentions*, 1891).

See also Butler on BANALITY; Gingrich on ELECTIONS; Guedalla on UNIVERSITIES AND COLLEGES.

CLIMATE

1   In the cold of Europe, under prudish northern fogs, except when slaughter is afoot, you only glimpse the crawling cruelty of your fellow men. But their rottenness rises to the surface as soon as they are tickled by the hideous fevers of the tropics.

LOUIS-FERDINAND CÉLINE (1894-1961), French author. Ferdinand Bardamu, in *Journey to the End of the Night* (1932; tr. 1934; repr. 1966, p. 98).

2   The true theater of history is therefore the temperate zone.

GEORG HEGEL (1770-1831), German philosopher. *The Philosophy of History*, Introduction (1832).

3   Warmest climes but nurse the cruelest fangs: the tiger of Bengal crouches in spiced groves of ceaseless verdure. Skies the most effulgent but basket the deadliest thunders: gorgeous Cuba knows tornadoes that never swept tame nothern lands.

HERMAN MELVILLE (1819-91), U.S. author. *Moby-Dick*, ch. 119 (1851).

4   Nobody is so constituted as to be able to live everywhere and anywhere; and he who has great duties to perform, which lay claim to all his strength, has, in this respect, a very limited choice. The influence of climate upon the bodily functions . . . extends so far, that a blunder in the choice of locality and climate is able not only to alienate a man from his actual duty, but also to withhold it from him altogether, so that he never even comes face to face with it.

FRIEDRICH NIETZSCHE (1844-1900), German philosopher. *Ecce Homo,* "Why I Am So Clever," sct. 2 (1888).

CLIQUES

1 The town is divided into various groups, which form so many little states, each with its own laws and customs, its jargon and its jokes. While the association holds and the fashion lasts, they admit nothing well said or well done except by one of themselves, and they are incapable of appreciating anything from another source, to the point of despising those who are not initiated into their mysteries.

JEAN DE LA BRUYÈRE (1645-96), French writer, moralist. *Characters,* "Of the Town," aph. 4 (1688).

2 A fashionable milieu is one in which everybody's opinion is made up of the opinion of all the others. Has everybody a different opinion? Then it is a literary milieu.

MARCEL PROUST (1871-1922), French novelist. *Pleasures and Regrets,* "Fragments From Italian Comedy," no. 10 (1896; tr. 1948).

CLUBS

1 A right rule for a club would be, Admit no man whose presence excludes any one topic. It requires people who are not surprised and shocked, who do and let do, and let be, who sink trifles, and know solid values, and who take a great deal for granted.

RALPH WALDO EMERSON (1803-82), U.S. essayist, poet, philosopher. *Society and Solitude,* "Clubs" (1870).

2 To associate with other like-minded people in small, purposeful groups is for the great majority of men and women a source of profound psychological satisfaction. Exclusiveness will add to the pleasure of being several, but at one; and secrecy will intensify it almost to ecstasy.

ALDOUS HUXLEY (1894-1963), British author. *Beyond the Mexique Bay,* "Chichicastenango" (1934).

3 Please accept my resignation. I don't care to belong to any club that will have me as a member.

GROUCHO MARX (1895-1977), U.S. comic actor. Letter to Hollywood's Friar's Club. Quoted in: Arthur Sheekman, *The Groucho Letters,* Introduction (1967).

4 This happy breed of men, this little world.

WILLIAM SHAKESPEARE (1564-1616), English dramatist, poet. Gaunt, referring to the English in general, in *Richard II,* act 2, sc. 1.

5 Among the laws controlling human societies there is one more precise and clearer, it seems to me, than all the others. If men are to remain civilized or to become civilized, the art of association must develop and improve among them at the same speed as equality of conditions spreads.

ALEXIS DE TOCQUEVILLE (1805-59), French social philosopher. *Democracy in America,* vol. 2, pt. 2, ch. 5 (1840).

See also Thoreau on INSTITUTIONS.

COCKTAILS

1 If you were to ask me if I'd ever had the bad luck to miss my daily cocktail, I'd have to say that I doubt it; where certain things are concerned, I plan ahead.

LUIS BUÑUEL (1900-1983), Spanish filmmaker. *My Last Sigh,* ch. 6 (1983).

2 The only things that the United States has given to the world are skyscrapers, jazz, and cocktails. That is all. And in Cuba, in *our* America, they make much better cocktails.

FEDERICO GARCÍA LORCA (1898-1936), Spanish poet, playwright. Interview, 1933, published in *Obras Completas,* vol. 3 (1986). Quoted in: *Poet in New York,* Introduction (1940; tr. 1988).

3 I misremember who first was cruel enough to nurture the cocktail party into life. But perhaps it would be not too much too say, in fact it would be not enough to say, that it was not worth the trouble.

DOROTHY PARKER (1893-1967), U.S. humorous writer. *Esquire* (New York, Nov. 1964).

COFFEE

1 Coffee in England is just toasted milk.

CHRISTOPHER FRY (b. 1907), British playwright. *New York Post* (29 Nov. 1962).

2 The morning cup of coffee has an exhiliration about it which the cheering influence of the afternoon or evening cup of tea cannot be expected to reproduce.

OLIVER WENDELL HOLMES, SR. (1809-94), U.S. writer, physician. *Over the Teacups,* ch. 1 (1891).

3 If the horseshoe sinks, then drink it.

PLAINS RECIPE FOR COFFEE.

4 Coffee, which makes the politician wise,
And see through all things with his half-shut eyes.

ALEXANDER POPE (1688-1744), English satirical poet. *Rape of the Lock,* cto. 3 (1712).

5 Black as hell, strong as death, sweet as love.

TURKISH PROVERB.

6 After a few months' acquaintance with European "coffee," one's mind weakens, and his faith with it, and he begins to wonder if the rich beverage of home, with its clotted layer of yellow cream on top of it, is not a mere dream after all, and a thing which never existed.

MARK TWAIN (1835-1910), U.S. author. *A Tramp Abroad,* ch. 49 (1880).

THE COLD WAR

1   Let us not be deceived—we are today in the midst of a cold war.

> BERNARD BARUCH (1870-1965), U.S. financier. Speech, 16 April 1947, to South Carolina Legislature, Columbia. A year later, Baruch told the Senate War Investigating Committee, "We are in the midst of a cold war which is getting warmer." Baruch claimed the expression had been suggested to him by his speechwriter and former editor of the *New York World*, Herbert Bayard Swope.

2   The Cold War began with the division of Europe. It can only end when Europe is whole.

> GEORGE BUSH (b. 1924), U.S. Republican politician, president. *Daily Telegraph* (London, 1 June 1989).

3   We walked to the brink and we looked it in the face.

> JOHN FOSTER DULLES (1888-1959), U.S. Republican politician. *Life* (New York, 11 Jan. 1956). The Democrat Adlai Stevenson characterized the Foster Dulles-Eisenhower foreign policy as, "the power of positive brinking."

4   Should the German people lay down their arms, the Soviets . . . would occupy all eastern and south-eastern Europe together with the greater part of the Reich. Over all this territory, which with the Soviet Union included, would be of enormous extent, an iron curtain would at once descend.

> JOSEPH GOEBBELS (1897-1945), German Nazi leader, Minister of Propaganda. *Das Reich* (Nazi propaganda weekly, 23 Feb. 1945). This is thought to be the first use of the phrase "iron curtain" (*ein eiserner Vorhang*) in this context.

5   If we cannot now end our differences, at least we can help make the world safe for diversity.

> JOHN F. KENNEDY (1917-63), U.S. Democratic politician, president. Speech, 10 June 1963, American University, Washington, D.C., on Russo-American relations.

6   Whether you like it or not, history is on our side. We will bury you.

> NIKITA KHRUSHCHEV (1894-1971), Soviet premier. Remark, 18 Nov. 1956, to Western diplomats at the Kremlin, Moscow.

7   They talk about who won and who lost. Human reason won. Mankind won.

> NIKITA KHRUSHCHEV (1894-1971), Soviet premier. Quoted in: *Observer* (London, 11 Nov. 1962), said of the Cuban missile crisis.

8   It was *man* who ended the Cold War in case you didn't notice. It wasn't weaponry, or technology, or armies or campaigns. It was just *man*. Not even Western man either, as it happened, but our sworn enemy in the East, who went into the streets, faced the bullets and the batons and said: we've had enough. It was *their* emperor, not ours, who had the nerve to mount the rostrum and declare he had no clothes. And the ideologies trailed after these impossible events like condemned prisoners, as ideologies do when they've had their day.

> JOHN LE CARRÉ (b. 1931), British novelist. Smiley, in *The Secret Pilgrim*, ch. 12 (1990).

9   The Cold War isn't thawing; it is burning with a deadly heat. Communism isn't sleeping; it is, as always, plotting, scheming, working, fighting.

> RICHARD M. NIXON (b. 1913), U.S. Republican politician, pres-
> ident. "Cuba, Castro and John F. Kennedy," in *The Reader's Digest* (Nov. 1964; repr. in Stephen Ambrose, *Nixon: The Triumph of a Politician*, vol. 2, ch. 2, 1989).

SAMUEL TAYLOR COLERIDGE

1   He has no resolution, he shrinks from pain or labour in any of its shapes. His very attitude bespeaks this: he never straightens his knee joints, he stoops with his fat ill-shapen shoulders, and in walking he does not tread but shovel and slide.

> THOMAS CARLYLE (1795-1881), Scottish essayist and historian. Letter, 24 June 1824, to his brother, following Carlyle's first encounter with Coleridge (published in *Collected Letters*, vol. 3).

2   His thoughts did not seem to come with labour and effort; but as if borne on gusts of genius, and as if the wings of his imagination lifted him off from his feet. . . . His mind was clothed with wings; and raised on them, he lifted philosophy to heaven.

> WILLIAM HAZLITT (1778-1830), English essayist. *Lectures on the English Poets*, "On the Living Poets" (1818). Coleridge, Hazlitt said, was the first poet he had ever known. See Hazlitt on LOQUACITY.

3   You will see Coleridge—he who sits obscure
In the exceeding lustre and the pure
Intense irradiation of a mind,
Which, with its own internal lightning blind,
Flags wearily through darkness and despair—
A cloud-encircled meteor of the air,
A hooded eagle among blinking owls.

> PERCY BYSSHE SHELLEY (1792-1822), English poet. *Letter to Maria Gisborne*.

COLONIALISM

1   A State in the grip of neo-colonialism is not master of its own destiny. It is this factor which makes neo-colonialism such a serious threat to world peace.

> KWAME NKRUMAH (1900-1972), Ghanaian president. *Consciencism*, Introduction (1964).

2   Our business being to colonize the country, there was only one way to do it—by spreading over it all the associations and connections of family life.

> HENRY PARKES (1815-96), English-born Australian statesman. Speech, 14 Aug. 1866, to New South Wales Legislative Assembly.

3   Just as a person who is always asserting that he is too good-natured is the very one from whom to expect, on some occasion, the coldest and most unconcerned cruelty, so when any group sees itself as the bearer of civilization this very belief will betray it into behaving barbarously at the first opportunity.

> SIMONE WEIL (1910-43), French philosopher, mystic. "Hitler and Roman Foreign Policy," in *Nouveaux Cahiers* (1 Jan. 1940).

See also DECOLONIZATION; EMPIRE.

COLOR

1 White . . . is not a mere absence of colour; it is a shining and affirmative thing, as fierce as red, as definite as black. . . . God paints in many colours; but He never paints so gorgeously, I had almost said so gaudily, as when He paints in white.

  G. K. CHESTERTON (1874-1936), British author. *Tremendous Trifles*, "A Piece of Chalk" (1909).

2 Green how I want you green.
Green wind. Green branches.

  FEDERICO GARCÍA LORCA (1898-1936), Spanish poet, playwright. *Romance Sonámbulo*.

3 Blueness doth express trueness.

  BEN JONSON (1573-1637), English dramatist, poet. Amorphus, in *Cynthia's Revels*, act 5, sc. 2.

4 Color possesses me. I don't have to pursue it. It will possess me always, I know it. That is the meaning of this happy hour: Color and I are one. I am a painter.

  PAUL KLEE (1879-1940), Swiss artist. *The Diaries of Paul Klee 1898-1918* (1957: tr. 1965), entry for 16 April 1914, written in Tunisia.

5 The true colour of life is the colour of the body, the colour of the covered red, the implicit and not explicit red of the living heart and the pulses. It is the modest colour of the unpublished blood.

  ALICE MEYNELL (1847-1922), English poet, essayist. *Essays*, "The True Colour of Life" (1914).

6 Color is my day-long obsession, joy and torment. To such an extent indeed that one day, finding myself at the deathbed of a woman who had been and still was very dear to me, I caught myself in the act of focusing on her temples and automatically analyzing the succession of appropriately graded colors which death was imposing on her motionless face.

  CLAUDE MONET (1840-1926), French painter. Remark to Georges Clemenceau. Quoted in: *Claude Monet: Les Nymphéas*, ch. 2 (1926).

7 Colors, like features, follow the changes of the emotions.

  PABLO PICASSO (1881-1973), Spanish artist. *Conversation avec Picasso*, in *Cahiers d'Art*, vol. 10, no. 10 (Paris, 1935; tr. in Alfred H. Barr, Jr., *Picasso: Fifty Years of His Art*, 1946).

8 Why do two colors, put one next to the other, sing? Can one really explain this? no. Just as one can never learn how to paint.

  PABLO PICASSO (1881-1973), Spanish artist. *Arts de France*, no. 6 (Paris; 1946; tr. in Dore Ashton, *Picasso on Art*, 1972).

9 Painting is something that takes place among the colors, and . . . one has to leave them alone completely, so that they can settle the matter among themselves. Their intercourse: this is the whole of painting. Whoever meddles, arranges, injects his human deliberation, his wit, his advocacy, his intellectual agility in any way, is already disturbing and clouding their activity.

  RAINER MARIA RILKE (1875-1926), German poet. Letter to his wife, 21 Oct. 1907 (published in *Rilke's Letters on Cézanne*, 1985; in Germany, 1952).

10 The purest and most thoughtful minds are those which love colour the most.

  JOHN RUSKIN (1819-1900), English art critic and author. *The Stones of Venice*, vol. 2, ch. 5, sct. 30 (1852).

11 There is no blue without yellow and without orange.

  VINCENT VAN GOGH (1853-90), Dutch painter. Letter, June 1888 (published in *The Complete Letters of Vincent Van Gogh*, vol. 3, no. B6, 1958).

12 He had that curious love of green, which in individuals is always the sign of a subtle artistic temperament, and in nations is said to denote a laxity, if not a decadence of morals.

  OSCAR WILDE (1854-1900), Anglo-Irish playwright, author. "Pen, Pencil and Poison," in *Fortnightly Review* (London, Jan. 1889).

13 Mere colour, unspoiled by meaning, and unallied with definite form, can speak to the soul in a thousand different ways.

  OSCAR WILDE (1854-1900), Anglo-Irish playwright, author. Gilbert, in *The Critic as Artist*, pt. 2 (published in *Intentions*, 1891).

See also Van Gogh on The SEA.

COMEDY AND COMEDIANS

1 We are living in the machine age. For the first time in history the comedian has been compelled to supply himself with jokes and comedy material to compete with the machine. Whether he knows it or not, the comedian is on a treadmill to oblivion.

  FRED ALLEN (1894-1957), U.S. comic. *Treadmill to Oblivion*, pt. 4 (1954).

2 Comedy just pokes at problems, rarely confronts them squarely. Drama is like a plate of meat and potatoes, comedy is rather the dessert, a bit like meringue.

  WOODY ALLEN (b. 1935), U.S. filmmaker. Quoted in: Graham McCann, *Woody Allen: New Yorker*, ch. 4 (1990).

3 I think being funny is not anyone's first choice.

  WOODY ALLEN (b. 1935), U.S. filmmaker. *Guardian* (London, 23 March 1992).

4 Humorists can never start to take themselves seriously. It's literary suicide.

  ERMA BOMBECK (b. 1927), U.S. journalist. Quoted in: *Detroit Free Press* (10 Aug. 1978).

5 The only honest art form is laughter, comedy. You can't fake it . . . try to fake three laughs in an hour—ha ha ha ha ha—they'll take you away, man. You can't.

  LENNY BRUCE (1925-66), U.S. satirical comedian. *The Essential Lenny Bruce*, "Performing and the Art of Comedy" (ed. by John Cohen, 1967).

6 Today's comedian has a cross to bear that he built himself. A comedian of the older generation did an "act" and he told the audience, "This is my act." Today's comic is not doing an act. The audience assumes he's telling the truth. What is truth today may be a damn lie next week.

> LENNY BRUCE (1925-66), U.S. satirical comedian. *The Essential Lenny Bruce*, "Performing and the Art of Comedy" (ed. by John Cohen, 1967).

7 Comedy is tragedy that happens to *other* people.

> ANGELA CARTER (1940-92), British author. *Wise Children*, ch. 4 (1991).

8 All I need to make a comedy is a park, a policeman and a pretty girl.

> CHARLIE CHAPLIN (1889-1977), British comic actor, filmmaker. *My Autobiography*, ch. 10 (1964).

9 Life is a tragedy when seen in close-up, but a comedy in long-shot.

> CHARLIE CHAPLIN (1889-1977), British comic actor, filmmaker. Quoted in his obituary: *Guardian* (London, 28 Dec. 1977).

10 Charlie Chaplin's genius was in comedy. He has no sense of humor, particularly about himself.

> LITA GREY CHAPLIN (b. 1908), Second wife of Charlie Chaplin. Radio interview, 1974. Quoted in: Richard Lamparski, *Whatever Became Of . . . ?* (Eighth Series, 1982).

11 If I get a hard audience they are not going to get away until they laugh. Those seven laughs a minute—I've got to have them.

> KEN DODD (b. 1931), British comic. *Daily Telegraph* (London, 20 Sept. 1990).

12 The perception of the comic is a tie of sympathy with other men, a pledge of sanity, and a protection from those perverse tendencies and gloomy insanities in which fine intellects sometimes lose themselves. A rogue alive to the ludicrous is still convertible. If that sense is lost, his fellow-men can do little for him.

> RALPH WALDO EMERSON (1803-82), U.S. essayist, poet, philosopher. *Letters and Social Aims*, "The Comic" (1876).

13 Comedy, like sodomy, is an unnatural act.

> MARTY FELDMAN (1933-82), British comedian. *Times* (London, 9 June 1969).

14 The guy has baggy pants, flat feet, the most miserable, bedraggled-looking little bastard you ever saw; makes itchy gestures as though he's got crabs under his arms—but he's funny.

> STERLING FORD (1883-1939), U.S. comic actor. Quoted in: Charlie Chaplin, *My Autobiography*, ch. 10 (1964), said of Charlie Chaplin.

15 Comedy is an escape, not from truth but from despair; a narrow escape into faith.

> CHRISTOPHER FRY (b. 1907), British playwright. *Time* (New York, 20 Nov. 1950).

16 Comedy deflates the sense precisely so that the underlying lubricity and malice may bubble to the surface.

> PAUL GOODMAN (1911-72), U.S. literary critic, author. "Obsessed by Theatre," in *Nation* (New York, 29 Nov. 1958; repr. in *Creator Spirit Come*, 1977).

17 We mustn't complain too much of being comedians—it's an honourable profession. If only we could be good ones the world might gain at least a sense of style.

We have failed—that's all. We are bad comedians, we aren't bad men.

> GRAHAM GREENE (1904-91), British novelist. The ambassador, in *The Comedians*, pt. 1, ch. 5, sct. 2 (1966).

18 Comedy naturally wears itself out—destroys the very food on which it lives; and by constantly and successfully exposing the follies and weaknesses of mankind to ridicule, in the end leaves itself nothing worth laughing at.

> WILLIAM HAZLITT (1778-1830), English essayist. *The Round Table*, "On Modern Comedy" (1817).

19 A man's got to take a lot of punishment to write a really funny book.

> ERNEST HEMINGWAY (1899-1961), U.S. author. Letter, 6 Dec. 1924 (published in *Selected Letters*, ed. by Carlos Baker, 1981).

20 Comedy comes from conflict, from hatred.

> WARREN MITCHELL (b. 1926), British comedy actor. *Times* (London, 31 Dec. 1990).

21 The test of a real comedian is whether you laugh at him before he opens his mouth.

> GEORGE JEAN NATHAN (1882-1958), U.S. critic. *American Mercury* (Sept. 1929).

22 There is not one female comic who was beautiful as a little girl.

> JOAN RIVERS (b. 1935), U.S. comedienne. Quoted in: *Los Angeles Times* (10 May 1974).

23 My routines come out of total unhappiness. My audiences are my group therapy.

> JOAN RIVERS (b. 1935), U.S. comedienne. Television broadcast, 23 Feb. 1990, BBC 2.

24 In comedy, reconcilement with life comes at the point when to the tragic sense only an inalienable difference or dissension with life appears.

> CONSTANCE ROURKE (1885-1941), U.S. author. *American Humor*, ch. 8 (1931).

25 The reason that there are so few women comics is that so few women can bear being laughed at.

> ANNA RUSSELL (b. 1911), Anglo-American comedienne and singer. *Sunday Times* (London, 25 Aug. 1957).

26 And I did laugh sans intermission
An hour by his dial. O noble fool,
A worthy fool—motley's the only wear.

> WILLIAM SHAKESPEARE (1564-1616), English dramatist, poet. Jaques, in *As You Like It*, act 2, sc. 7. Motley garments were the traditional dress of professional jesters, probably quartered in primary colors, or else woven from different colored threads.

27 Though it make the unskilful laugh, cannot but make the judicious grieve.

> WILLIAM SHAKESPEARE (1564-1616), English dramatist, poet. Hamlet, in *Hamlet* act 3, sc. 2.

28 Comedy has to be done *en clair*. You can't blunt the edge of wit or the point of satire with obscurity. Try to imagine a famous witty saying that is not immediately clear.

> JAMES THURBER (1894-1961), U.S. humorist, illustrator. Letter, 11 March 1954, to critic and poet Malcolm Cowley (repr. in James Thurber, *Collecting Himself*, 1989).

29 The only rules comedy can tolerate are those of taste, and the only limitations those of libel.

> JAMES THURBER (1894-1961), U.S. humorist, illustrator. *Lanterns and Lances*, "The Duchess and the Bugs" (1961).

30 When humor can be made to alternate with melancholy, one has a success, but when the *same* things are funny and melancholic at the same time, it's just wonderful.

> FRANÇOIS TRUFFAUT (1932-84), French film director. Letter, 15 Jan. 1980 (published in *Letters*, 1989; in France, 1988).

31 The comic spirit is given to us in order that we may analyze, weigh, and clarify things in us which nettle us, or which we are outgrowing, or trying to reshape.

> THORNTON WILDER (1897-1975), U.S. novelist, dramatist. Interview, in *Writers at Work* (First Series, ed. by Malcolm Cowley, 1958).

COMMERCE

See BUSINESS AND COMMERCE.

COMMITTEES

1 A technical objection is the first refuge of a scoundrel.

> HEYWOOD BROUN (1888-1939), U.S. journalist, novelist. *New Republic* (Washington, D.C., 15 Dec. 1937).

2 We always carry out by committee anything in which any one of us alone would be too reasonable to persist.

> FRANK MOORE COLBY (1865-1925), U.S. editor, essayist. *The Colby Essays*, vol. 1, "Subsidizing Authors" (1926).

3 The heaping together of paintings by Old Masters in museums is a catastrophe; likewise, a collection of a hundred Great Brains makes one big fathead.

> CARL JUNG (1875-1961), Swiss psychiatrist. Review (1934; repr. in *Collected Works*, vol. 10, "Civilization in Transition," ed. by William McGuire, 1961).

4 A committee is an animal with four back legs.

> JOHN LE CARRÉ (b. 1931), British novelist. Smiley, in *Tinker, Tailor, Soldier, Spy*, pt. 3, ch. 34 (1974).

5 A committee is organic rather than mechanical in its nature: it is not a structure but a plant. It takes root and grows, it flowers, wilts, and dies, scattering the seed from which other committees will bloom in their turn.

> C. NORTHCOTE PARKINSON (1909-93), British historian, political scientist. *Parkinson's Law, or The Pursuit of Progress*, "Directors and Councils" (1958).

6 Muddle is the extra unknown personality in any committee.

> ANTHONY SAMPSON (b. 1926), British journalist, author. *Anatomy of Britain Today*, ch. 15 (1965).

7 When committees gather, each member is necessarily an actor, uncontrollably acting out the part of himself, reading the lines that identify him, asserting his identity. . . . We are designed, coded, it seems, to place the highest priority on being individuals, and we must do this first, at whatever cost, even if it means disability for the group.

> LEWIS THOMAS (b. 1913), U.S. physician, educator. *The Medusa and the Snail*, "On Committees" (1979).

8 Any committee that is the slightest use is composed of people who are too busy to want to sit on it for a second longer than they have to.

> KATHARINE WHITEHORN (b. 1926), British journalist. *Observations*, "Are You Sitting Comfortably?" (1970).

COMMON SENSE

1 Common sense is the measure of the possible; it is composed of experience and prevision; it is calculation applied to life.

> HENRI-FRÉDÉRIC AMIEL (1821-81), Swiss philosopher, poet. *Journal Intime* (1882; tr. by Mrs. Humphry Ward, 1892), entry for 12 Nov. 1852.

2 Common-sense is part of the home-made ideology of those who have been deprived of fundamental learning, of those who have been kept ignorant. This ideology is compounded from different sources: items that have survived from religion, items of empirical knowledge, items of protective scepticism, items culled for comfort from the superficial learning that *is* supplied. But the point is that common-sense can never teach itself, can never advance beyond its own limits, for as soon as the lack of fundamental learning has been made good, all items become questionable and the whole function of common-sense is destroyed. Common-sense can only exist as a category insofar as it can be distinguished from the spirit of enquiry, from philosophy.

> JOHN BERGER (b. 1926), British author, critic. *A Fortunate Man* (1967; repr. 1976, p. 102).

3 Common sense always speaks too late. Common sense is the guy who tells you you ought to have had your brakes relined last week before you smashed a front end this week. Common sense is the Monday morning quarterback who could have won the ball game if he had been on the team. But he never is. He's high up in the stands with a flask on his hip. Common sense is the little man in a grey suit who never makes a mistake in addition. But it's always somebody else's money he's adding up.

> RAYMOND CHANDLER (1888-1959), U.S. author. Philip Marlowe, in *Playback*, ch. 14 (1958).

4 All truth, in the long run, is only common sense clarified.

> THOMAS HENRY HUXLEY (1825-95), English biologist. "On the Study of Biology," lecture, 1876, at South Kensington Museum, London (published in *Collected Essays*, vol. 3, 1893).

5 Common-sense appears to be only another name for the thoughtlessness of the unthinking. It is made of the prejudices of childhood, the idiosyncrasies of individual character and the opinion of the newspapers.

> W. SOMERSET MAUGHAM (1874-1966), British author. *A Writer's Notebook* (1949), entry for 1901.

6 That rarest gift
To Beauty, Common Sense!

> GEORGE MEREDITH (1828-1909), English author. *Modern Love*, sonnet 32 (1862).

7 Why level downward to our dullest perception always, and praise that as common sense? The commonest sense is the sense of men asleep, which they express by snoring.

> HENRY DAVID THOREAU (1817-62), U.S. philosopher, author, naturalist. *Walden*, "Conclusion" (1854).

8 Common sense is judgment without reflection, shared by an entire class, an entire nation, or the entire human race.

> GIAMBATTISTA VICO (1688-1744), Italian philosopher, historian. *The New Science*, bk. 1, para. 142 (ed. 1744; tr. 1984).

9 Nowadays most people die of a sort of creeping common sense, and discover when it is too late that the only things one never regrets are one's mistakes.

> OSCAR WILDE (1854-1900), Anglo-Irish playwright, author. Lord Henry, in *The Picture of Dorian Gray*, ch. 3 (1891).

THE COMMONPLACE

1 Take a commonplace, clean it and polish it, light it so that it produces the same effect of youth and freshness and originality and spontaneity as it did originally, and you have done a poet's job. The rest is literature.

> JEAN COCTEAU (1889-1963), French author, filmmaker. *Le Rappel à l'Ordre*, "Le Secret Professionnel" (1926; 1922; repr. in *Collected Works*, vol. 9, 1950).

2 Nothing is so common-place as to wish to be remarkable.

> OLIVER WENDELL HOLMES, SR. (1809-94), U.S. writer, physician. *The Autocrat of the Breakfast Table*, ch. 12 (1858).

3 Common looking people are the best in the world: that is the reason the Lord makes so many of them.

> ABRAHAM LINCOLN (1809-65), U.S. president. Quoted in: John Hay, *Lincoln and the Civil War in the Diaries and Letters of John Hay* (ed. by Tyler Dennett, 1939), entry for 23 Dec. 1863, said in a dream in reply to one who had called Lincoln "common looking." Lincoln's words on this occasion have also been given as, "The Lord prefers common-looking people. That is the reason He makes so many of them." Quoted in: James Morgan, *Our Presidents*, ch. 6 (1928).

4 The characteristic of the hour is that the commonplace mind, knowing itself to be commonplace, has the assurance to proclaim the rights of the commonplace and to impose them wherever it will.

> JOSÉ ORTEGA Y GASSET (1883-1955), Spanish essayist, philosopher. *The Revolt of the Masses*, ch. 1 (1930). Later in the book (ch. 14), Ortega y Gasset refers to commonplaces as "the tramways of intellectual transportation."

5 If to be interesting is to be uncommonplace, it is becoming a question, with me, if there *are* any commonplace people.

> MARK TWAIN (1835-1910), U.S. author. *Fables of Man*, "The Refuge of the Derelicts," ch. 4 (ed. by John S. Tuckey, 1972), written 1905-6.

6 We can escape the commonplace only by manipulating it, controlling it, thrusting it into our dreams or surrendering it to the free play of our subjectivity.

> RAOUL VANEIGEM (b. 1934), Belgian Situationist philosopher. *The Revolution of Everyday Life*, Introduction (1967; tr. 1983).

7 Thou unassuming common-place
Of Nature, with that homely face.

> WILLIAM WORDSWORTH (1770-1850), English poet. *To the Same Flower [Daisy]*.

See also Butler on BANALITY; Masefield on TRAGEDY.

COMMUNICATION

1 Only connect! That was the whole of her sermon. Only connect the prose and the passion, and both will be exalted, and human love will be seen at its height. Live in fragments no longer. Only connect, and the beast and the monk, robbed of the isolation that is life to either, will die.

> E. M. FORSTER (1879-1970), British novelist, essayist. Margaret Schlegel, in *Howards End*, ch. 22 (1910). "Only connect" also appears as epigraph to the book, of which Goronwy Rees has written, in *A Chapter of Accidents* (1972): "It could be said that these two words, so seductive in their simplicity, so misleading in their ambiguity, had more influence in shaping the emotional attitudes of the English governing class between the two world wars than any other single phrase in the English language.".

2 Something there is that doesn't love a wall,
And wants it down.

> ROBERT FROST (1874-1963), U.S. poet. *Mending Wall*.

3 There is no pleasure to me without communication: there is not so much as a sprightly thought comes into my mind that it does not grieve me to have produced alone, and that I have no one to tell it to.

> MICHEL DE MONTAIGNE (1533-92), French essayist. *Essays*, bk. 3, ch. 9, "Of Vanity" (1588).

4 Transport of the mails, transport of the human voice, transport of flickering pictures—in this century as in others our highest accomplishments still have the single aim of bringing men together.

> ANTOINE DE SAINT-EXUPÉRY (1900-1944), French aviator, writer. *Wind, Sand, and Stars*, ch. 3 (published in *Terre des Hommes*, 1939).

5 Two prisoners whose cells adjoin communicate with each other by knocking on the wall. The wall is the thing which separates them but is also their means of communication. It is the same with us and God. Every separation is a link.

> SIMONE WEIL (1909-43), French philosopher, mystic. *Gravity and Grace*, "Metaxu" (1947; tr. 1952).

See also Bernstein on TECHNIQUE; Rosen on THE TWENTIETH CENTURY: 1970s.

COMMUNISM

1 Our fear that Communism might some day take over most of the world blinds us to the fact that anti-communism already has.

ANONYMOUS U.S. ANALYST (1967). Quoted in: "The Uses of Anticommunism" (published in *The Socialist Register*, vol. 21, 1985).

2   Russian Communism is the illegitimate child of Karl Marx and Catherine the Great.

> CLEMENT ATTLEE (1883-1967), British Labour politician, Prime Minister. Speech, 11 April 1956.

3   Experience has taught me that the shallowest of communist platitudes contains more of a hierarchy of meaning than contemporary bourgeois profundity.

> WALTER BENJAMIN (1892-1940), German critic, philosopher. Letter, 7 March 1931 (published in *Briefe*, Frankfurt, 1966). Quoted in: *One-Way Street and Other Writings*, publisher's note (1978).

4   The terrible thing is that one cannot be a Communist and not let oneself in for the shameful act of recantation. One cannot be a Communist and preserve an iota of one's personal integrity.

> MILOVAN DJILAS (b. 1911), Yugoslav political leader, writer. *Encounter* (London, Dec. 1979). Djilas was a high-ranking member of the Yugoslav Communist Party and member of the government until his dismissal in 1956.

5   What is a Communist? One who has yearnings
For equal division of unequal earnings.

> EBENEZER ELLIOT (1781-1849), English pamphleteer, poet. "Epigram" (1831; published in *Poetical Works*, 1840).

6   You'll see certain Pythagoreans whose belief in communism of property goes to such lengths that they pick up anything lying about unguarded, and make off with it without a qualm of conscience as if it had come to them by law.

> DESIDERIUS ERASMUS (c. 1466-1536), Dutch humanist. *Praise of Folly*, ch. 48 (1509).

7   I have no concern with any economic criticisms of the communist system; I cannot enquire into whether the abolition of private property is expedient or advantageous. But I am able to recognize that the psychological premisses on which the system is based are an untenable illusion. In abolishing private property we deprive the human love of aggression of one of its instruments . . . but we have in no way altered the differences in power and influence which are misused by aggressiveness.

> SIGMUND FREUD (1856-1939), Austrian psychiatrist. *Civilization and its Discontents*, ch. 5 (1930; repr. in *Complete Works*, vol. 21, ed. by James Strachey and Anna Freud, 1961).

8   I am a Communist, a convinced Communist! For some that may be a fantasy. But to me it is my main goal.

> MIKHAIL GORBACHEV (b. 1931), Soviet political leader. Speech, Dec. 1989, to second national Congress of People's Deputies, Moscow. Quoted in: *New York Times* (26 Dec. 1989). A week before, however, *Newsweek* had quoted Gorbachev as confiding to Prime Minister Margaret Thatcher, "I don't even know if I'm a Communist any more." Both pronouncements are discussed in Gail Sheehy, *Gorbachev*, pt. 6, "Sakharov's Warning" (1991).

9   Communism, my friend, is more than Marxism, just as Catholicism . . . is more than the Roman Curia. There is a *mystique* as well as a *politique.* . . . Catholics and Communists have committed great crimes, but at least they have not stood aside, like an established society, and been indifferent. I would rather have blood on my hands than water like Pilate.

> GRAHAM GREENE (1904-91), British novelist. Dr. Magiot's last letter, in *The Comedians*, pt. 2, ch. 4, sct. 4 (1966).

10   Communism has never come to power in a country that was not disrupted by war or corruption, or both.

> JOHN F. KENNEDY (1917-63), U.S. Democratic politician, president. Speech, 3 July 1963, to NATO.

11   Many people feel empty, a world that seemed so strong just collapsed. Forty years have been wasted on stupid strife for the sake of an unsuccessful experiment. The values gathered together have vanished, the strategies for survival have become ridiculous. And so forty years of our lives have become a story, a bad anecdote. But it may be possible to remember these adventures with a kind of irony.

> GEORGE KONRÁD (b. 1933), Hungarian writer, politician. *Sunday Correspondent* (London, 15 April 1990).

12   Communism is Soviet power plus the electrification of the whole country.

> VLADIMIR ILYICH LENIN (1870-1924), Russian revolutionary leader. Report, 1920, to Eighth Congress of the Communist Party (published in *Collected Works*, vol. 42). The words were used as a slogan to promote the plans of the State Committee for the Electrification of Russia.

13   Communism is the opiate of the intellectuals [with] no cure except as a guillotine might be called a cure for dandruff.

> CLARE BOOTHE LUCE (1903-87), U.S. diplomat, writer. *Newsweek* (New York, 24 Jan. 1955).

14   Communists have always played an active role in the fight by colonial countries for their freedom, because the short-term objects of Communism would always correspond with the long-term objects of freedom movements.

> NELSON MANDELA (b. 1918), South African political leader. Statement, April-May 1964, to the court in the Rivonia trial, South Africa. Quoted in Fatima Meer, *Higher than Hope*, pt. 4, ch. 24 (1988-90).

15   Communism is not love. Communism is a hammer which we use to crush the enemy.

> MAO ZEDONG (1893-1976), Founder of the People's Republic of China. Quoted in: *Time* (New York, 18 Dec. 1950).

16   In a higher phase of communist society . . . only then can the narrow horizon of bourgeois right be fully left behind and society inscribe on its banners: from each according to his ability, to each according to his needs.

> KARL MARX (1818-83), German political theorist, social philosopher. *Critique of the Gotha Programme* (1875; repr. in *Selected Works*, vol. 2, 1942).

17   A specter is haunting Europe—the specter of communism.

> KARL MARX (1818-83) AND FRIEDRICH ENGELS (1820-95), German social philosophers, revolutionaries. *The Communist Manifesto*, sct. 2 (1848; repr. in *Karl Marx: Selected Works*, vol. 1, 1942).

18   The theory of the Communists may be summed up in the single sentence: Abolition of private property.

> KARL MARX (1818-83) AND FRIEDRICH ENGELS (1820-95),

German social philosophers, revolutionaries. *The Communist Manifesto*, sct.2 (1848).

19   In the end we beat them with Levi 501 jeans. Seventy-two years of Communist indoctrination and propaganda was drowned out by a three-ounce Sony Walkman. A huge totalitarian system . . . has been brought to its knees because nobody wants to wear Bulgarian shoes. . . . Now they're lunch, and we're number one on the planet.

> P. J. O'ROURKE (b. 1947), U.S. journalist. "The Death of Communism," in *Rolling Stone* (New York, Nov. 1989; repr. in *Give War a Chance*, 1992).

20   The "Communism" of the English intellectual is something explicable enough. It is the patriotism of the deracinated.

> GEORGE ORWELL (1903-50), British author. *Inside the Whale and Other Essays*, "Inside the Whale" (1940).

21   We are the party of all labor.
The whole earth shall be ours to share
And every race and craft our neighbor.
No idle class shall linger there
Like vultures on the wealth we render
From field and factory, mill and mine.
Tomorrow's sun will rise in splendor
And light us till the end of time.

> EUGÈNE POTTIER (1816-87), French poet, communard. *The International* (1871; tr. by Basil Druitt). Set to a marching-tune of Pierre Deygeter, these words have been translated and sung by socialists and communists throughout the world.

22   Communism is inequality, but not as property is. Property is exploitation of the weak by the strong. Communism is exploitation of the strong by the weak.

> PIERRE-JOSEPH PROUDHON (1809-65), French political theorist. *What is Property* (1840).

23   Communism to me is one-third practice and two-thirds explanation.

> WILL ROGERS (1879-1935), U.S. humorist. *Wit and Wisdom*, p. 39 (ed. by Jack Lait, 1936).

24   We must conclude that it is not only a particular political ideology that has failed, but the idea that men and women could ever define themselves in terms that exclude their spiritual needs.

> SALMAN RUSHDIE (b. 1948), Indian-born British author. *Independent* (London, 7 Feb. 1990), said of the changes in Eastern Europe.

25   The final conflict will be between the Communists and the ex-Communists.

> IGNAZIO SILONE (1900-1978), Italian novelist, journalist; U.S. author, columnist. Quoted in: Max Lerner, *The Unfinished Country*, pt. 4, "The Hero as Ex-Communist" (1959), said to Communist leader Palmiro Togliatti. One of the founding members of the Italian Communist Party, Silone left it in 1930, though he continued to align himself with the Left. In 1968, in a symposium with Arthur Koestler, he called himself "a socialist without a party, a Christian without a church."

26   There are only two sorts of people in life you can trust—good Christians and good Communists.

> JOE SLOVO (b. 1926), South African leader of the Communist Party. *Independent* (London, 4 Nov. 1988).

27   Communists are people who fancied that they had an unhappy childhood.

> GERTRUDE STEIN (1874-1946), U.S. author. Quoted by Thornton Wilder in: *Writers at Work* (First Series, ed. by George Plimpton, 1958).

28   The crusade against Communism was even more imaginary than the spectre of Communism.

> A. J. P. TAYLOR (1906-90), British historian. *The Origins of the Second World War*, ch. 2 (1961).

29   Man will become immeasurably stronger, wiser, and subtler; his body will become more harmonious, his movements more rhythmic, his voice more musical. The forms of life will become dynamically dramatic. The average human type will rise to the heights of an Aristotle, a Goethe, or a Marx. And above these heights, new peaks will rise.

> LEON TROTSKY (1879-1940), Russian revolutionary. *Literature and Revolution* (1923; repr. in *The Age of Permanent Revolution: A Trotsky Anthology*, ch. 17, 1964). Trotsky was referring to a Communist society.

30   Let's not talk about Communism. Communism was just an idea, just pie in the sky.

> BORIS YELTSIN (b. 1931), Russian politician, president. Remark during a visit to the U.S. Quoted in: *Independent* (London, 13 Sept. 1989).

31   Communists should be the first to be concerned about other people and country and the last to enjoy themselves.

> ZHAO ZIYANG (b. 1919), Chinese party official. *Financial Times* (London, 21 March 1988).

32   I am a communist because I believe that the Communist idea is a state form of Christianity.

> ALEXANDER ZHURAVLYOV (b. 1924), Byelorussian deputy. Quoted in: *Observer* (London, 8 Sept. 1991).

See also MARXISM; Koestler on RUSSIA AND THE RUSSIANS; SOCIALISM; Khrushchev, Koestler, Solzhenitsyn on The USSR.

COMPANY

1   Two are better than one; because they have a good reward for their labour. For if they fall, the one will lift up his fellow: but woe to him that is alone when he falleth; for he hath not another to help him up. Again, if two lie together, then they have heat: but how can one be warm alone? And if one prevail against him, two shall withstand him; and a threefold cord is not quickly broken.

> BIBLE, HEBREW. *Ecclesiastes* 4:9-12.

2   All who joy would win
Must share it,—Happiness was born a twin.

> LORD BYRON (1788-1824), English poet. *Don Juan*, cto. 2, st. 172.

3   Tell me thy company, and I'll tell thee what thou art.

> MIGUEL DE CERVANTES (1547-1616), Spanish writer. *Don Quixote*, pt. 2, bk. 3, ch. 23 (1615; tr. by P. Motteux and J. Ozell).

4 For my own part, I would rather be in company with a dead man than with an absent one; for if the dead man gives me no pleasure, at least he shows me no contempt; whereas the absent one, silently indeed, but very plainly, tells me that he does not think me worth his attention.

LORD CHESTERFIELD (1694-1773), English statesman, man of letters. Letter, 22 Sept. 1749 (1774; repr. in *The Letters of the Earl of Chesterfield to His Son*, vol. 1, no. 194, ed. by Charles Strachey, 1901).

5 We do not mind our not arriving anywhere nearly so much as our not having any company on the way.

FRANK MOORE COLBY (1865-1925), U.S. editor, essayist. *The Margin of Hesitation*, "Thinking It Through in Haste" (1921).

6 Fan the sinking flame of hilarity with the wing of friendship; and pass the rosy wine.

CHARLES DICKENS (1812-70), English novelist. Dick Swiveller, in *The Old Curiosity Shop*, ch. 7 (1841).

7 A rich rogue now-a-days is fit company for any gentleman; and the world, my dear, hath not such a contempt for roguery as you imagine.

JOHN GAY (1685-1732), English dramatist. Peachum, in *The Beggar's Opera*, act 1, sc. 9.

8 It contributes greatly towards a man's moral and intellectual health, to be brought into habits of companionship with individuals unlike himself, who care little for his pursuits, and whose sphere and abilities he must go out of himself to appreciate.

NATHANIEL HAWTHORNE (1804-64), U.S. author. *The Scarlet Letter*, Introduction, "The Custom-House" (1850).

9 A grave blockhead should always go about with a lively one—they shew one another off to the best advantage.

WILLIAM HAZLITT (1778-1830), English essayist. *Characteristics: In the Manner of Rochefoucault's Maxims*, no. 376 (1823; repr. in *The Complete Works Of William Hazlitt*, vol. 9, ed. by P. P. Howe, 1932).

10 If it were not for the company of fools, a witty man would often be greatly at a loss.

FRANÇOIS, DUC DE LA ROCHEFOUCAULD (1613-80), French writer, moralist. *Sentences et Maximes Morales*, no. 140 (1678).

11 Man loves company, even if it is only that of a smouldering candle.

G. C. LICHTENBERG (1742-99), German physicist, philosopher. *Aphorisms*, aph.40, "Notebook K" (written 1765-99; tr. by R. J. Hollingdale, 1990).

12 Company, villainous company, hath been the spoil of me.

WILLIAM SHAKESPEARE (1564-1616), English dramatist, poet. Oldcastle (Falstaff), in *Henry IV, pt. 1*, act 3, sc. 3.

13 There is a fellowship more quiet even than solitude, and which, rightly understood, is solitude made perfect.

ROBERT LOUIS STEVENSON (1850-94), Scottish novelist, essayist, poet. *Travels With a Donkey*, "A Night Among the Pines" (1879).

14 You could read Kant by yourself, if you wanted; but you must share a joke with some one else.

ROBERT LOUIS STEVENSON (1850-94), Scottish novelist, essayist, poet. *Virginibus Puerisque*, pt. 1 of title essay (1881).

15 I have a great deal of company in my house; especially in the morning, when nobody calls.

HENRY DAVID THOREAU (1817-62), U.S. philosopher, author, naturalist. *Walden*, "Solitude" (1854).

16 More company increases happiness, but does not lighten or diminish misery.

THOMAS TRAHERNE (1636-74), English clergyman, poet, mystic. *Centuries*, "Fourth Century," no. 14 (1908), written c. 1672.

COMPASSION

1 Compassion has no place in the natural order of the world which operates on the basis of necessity. Compassion opposes this order and is therefore best thought of as being in some way supernatural.

JOHN BERGER (b. 1926), British author, critic. *Guardian* (London, 19 Dec. 1991).

2 I know the compassion of others is a relief at first. I don't despise it. But it can't quench pain, it slips through your soul as through a sieve. And when our suffering has been dragged from one pity to another, as from one mouth to another, we can no longer respect or love it.

GEORGES BERNANOS (1888-1948), French novelist, political writer. *The Diary of a Country Priest*, ch. 8 (1936).

3 We hand folks over to God's mercy, and show none ourselves.

GEORGE ELIOT (1819-80), English novelist. *Adam Bede*, ch. 42 (1859).

4 Compassion is the antitoxin of the soul: where there is compassion even the most poisonous impulses remain relatively harmless.

ERIC HOFFER (1902-83), U.S. philosopher. *Reflections on the Human Condition*, aph. 36 (1973).

5 The wretched have no compassion, they can do good only from strong principles of duty.

SAMUEL JOHNSON (1709-84), English author, lexicographer. Letter, 14 April 1781, to Hester Thrale (published in *The Letters of Samuel Johnson*, vol. 2, no. 724; ed. by R. W. Chapman, 1952).

6 There is nothing heavier than compassion. Not even one's own pain weighs so heavy as the pain one feels with someone, for someone, a pain intensified by the imagination and prolonged by a hundred echoes.

MILAN KUNDERA (b. 1929), Czech author, critic. *The Unbearable Lightness of Being*, pt. 1, ch. 15 (1984).

7 Saving lives is not a top priority in the halls of power. Being compassionate and concerned about human life can cause a man to lose his job. It can cause a woman not to get the job to begin with.

MYRIAM MIEDZIAN, U.S. author. *Boys Will Be Boys*, ch. 2 (1991).

8 Minerva save us from the cloying syrup of coercive compassion!

CAMILLE PAGLIA (b. 1947), U.S. author, critic, educator. "The

Big Udder," in *Philadelphia Enquirer* (12 May 1991; repr. in *Sex, Art, and American Culture,* 1992).

9 No deep and strong feeling, such as we may come across here and there in the world, is unmixed with compassion. The more we love, the more the object of our love seems to us to be a victim.

> BORIS PASTERNAK (1890-1960), Russian poet, novelist, translator. *Doctor Zhivago,* ch. 12, sct. 7 (1957).

10 Get it into your head once and for all, my simple and very fainthearted fellow, that what fools call *humaneness* is nothing but a weakness born of fear and egoism; that this chimerical virtue, enslaving only weak men, is unknown to those whose character is formed by stoicism, courage, and philosophy.

> MARQUIS DE SADE (1740-1814), French author. Dolmancé, in *Philosophy in the Bedroom,* "Dialogue the Seventh" (1795).

11 Mercy but murders, pardoning those that kill.

> WILLIAM SHAKESPEARE (1564-1616), English dramatist, poet. Prince Escalus, following Romeo's killing of Tybalt, in *Romeo and Juliet,* act 3, sc. 1.

12 In democratic ages men rarely sacrifice themselves for another, but they show a general compassion for all the human race. One never sees them inflict pointless suffering, and they are glad to relieve the sorrows of others when they can do so without much trouble to themselves. They are not disinterested, but they are gentle.

> ALEXIS DE TOCQUEVILLE (1805-59), French social philosopher. *Democracy in America,* vol. 2, pt. 3, ch. 1 (1840).

See also Desmoulins on REVOLUTIONARIES.

COMPATIBILITY

1 Her name was called Lady Helena Herring and her age was 25 and she mated well with the earl.

> DAISY ASHORD (1881-1972), British writer. *The Young Visiters,* "How It Ended" (1919), written when the author was nine.

2 Her great merit is finding out mine—there is nothing so amiable as discernment.

> LORD BYRON (1788-1824), English poet. Letter, 25 Nov. 1816, to the publisher John Murray (published in *Byron's Letters and Journals,* vol. 5, ed. by Leslie Marchand, 1973-81).

3 Sometimes apparent resemblances of character will bring two men together and for a certain time unite them. But their mistake gradually becomes evident, and they are astonished to find themselves not only far apart, but even repelled, in some sort, at all their points of contact.

> SÉBASTIEN-ROCH NICOLAS DE CHAMFORT (1741-1794), French writer, wit. *Maxims and Considerations,* vol. 1, no. 166 (1796; tr. 1926).

4 Madam your wife and I didn't hit it off the only time I ever saw her. I won't say she was silly, but I think one of us was silly, and it wasn't me.

> ELIZABETH GASKELL (1810-65), English novelist. Squire Hamley, in *Wives and Daughters,* ch. 35 (1866), said to Mr. Gibson.

5 I love her too, but our neuroses just don't match.

> ARTHUR MILLER (b. 1915), U.S. dramatist. Lyman, discussing his wife with his lawyer, in *The Ride Down Mount Morgan,* act 1 (1991).

6 To be happy with a man you must understand him a lot and love him a little. To be happy with a woman you must love her a lot and not try to understand her at all.

> HELEN ROWLAND (1875-1950), U.S. journalist. *A Guide to Men,* "Fourth Interlude" (1922).

7 If we reason, we would be understood; if we imagine, we would that the airy children of our brain were born anew within another's; if we feel, we would that another's nerves should vibrate to our own, that the beams of their eyes should kindle at once and mix and melt into our own, that lips of motionless ice should not reply to lips quivering and burning with the heart's best blood. This is Love.

> PERCY BYSSHE SHELLEY (1792-1822), English poet. *Essay on Love* (1815-19).

8 Madam, I have been looking for a person who disliked gravy all my life; let us swear eternal friendship.

> SYDNEY SMITH (1771-1845), English writer, clergyman. Quoted in: Lady Holland, *Memoir* vol. 1, ch. 9 (1855).

9 You can forgive people who do not follow you through a philosophical disquisition; but to find your wife laughing when you had tears in your eyes, or staring when you were in a fit of laughter, would go some way towards a dissolution of the marriage.

> ROBERT LOUIS STEVENSON (1850-1894), Scottish novelist, essayist, poet. *Virginibus Puerisque,* title essay, pt. 1 (1881).

10 It's true love because
If he said quit drinking martinis but I kept on drinking them
and the next morning I couldn't get out of bed,
He wouldn't tell me he told me.

> JUDITH VIORST (b. 1935), U.S. poet and journalist. *True Love.*

11 Love and sex can go together and sex and unlove can go together and love and unsex can go together. But personal love and personal sex is bad.

> ANDY WARHOL (1928-87), U.S. Pop artist. *From A to B and Back Again,* ch. 3 (1975).

COMPETITION

1 The price which society pays for the law of competition, like the price it pays for cheap comforts and luxuries, is great; but the advantages of this law are also greater still than its cost—for it is to this law that we owe our wonderful material development, which brings improved conditions in its train. But, whether the law be benign or not, we must say of it . . . : It is here; we cannot evade it; no substitutes for it have been found; and while the law may be sometimes hard for the individual, it is best for the race, because it ensures the survival of the fittest in every department.

> ANDREW CARNEGIE (1835-1919), U.S. industrialist, philanthropist. "The Gospel of Wealth," in *North American Review* (Cedar Falls, June 1889). Quoted in: Burton J. Hendrick, *Life of Andrew Carnegie,* vol. 1, ch. 17, 1932).

2   Thou shalt not covet; but tradition
Approves all forms of competition.

>   A. H. CLOUGH (1819-61), English poet. *The Latest Decalogue,* a commentary on the Ten Commandments.

3   The general fact is that the most effective way of utilizing human energy is through an organized rivalry, which by specialization and social control is, at the same time, organized co-operation.

>   CHARLES HORTON COOLEY (1864-1929), U.S. sociologist. *Human Nature and the Social Order,* ch. 8 (1902).

4   It is better for a woman to compete impersonally in society, as men do, than to compete for dominance in her own home with her husband, compete with her neighbors for empty status, and so smother her son that he cannot compete at all.

>   BETTY FRIEDAN (b. 1921), U.S. feminist writer. *The Feminine Mystique,* ch. 18 (1963).

5   Men often compete with one another until the day they die; comradeship consists of rubbing shoulders jocularly with a competitor.

>   EDWARD HOAGLAND (b. 1932), U.S. novelist and essayist. "Heaven and Nature," in *Harper's* (New York, March 1988; repr. in *Heart's Desire,* 1988).

6   So long as the system of competition in the production and exchange of the means of life goes on, the degradation of the arts will go on; and if that system is to last for ever, then art is doomed, and will surely die; that is to say, civilization will die.

>   WILLIAM MORRIS (1834-96), English artist, writer, printer. *Art under Plutocracy* (1883).

COMPLACENCY

1   These are days when no one should rely unduly on his "competence." Strength lies in improvisation. All the decisive blows are struck left-handed.

>   WALTER BENJAMIN (1892-1940), German critic, philosopher. *One-Way Street,* "Chinese Curios" (1928; repr. in *One-Way Street and Other Writings,* 1978).

2   Be not righteous over much; neither make thyself over wise; why shouldest thou destroy thyself?

>   BIBLE, HEBREW. *Ecclesiastes* 7:16.

3   The greatest of faults, I should say, is to be conscious of none.

>   THOMAS CARLYLE (1795-1881), Scottish essayist and historian. *Heroes and Hero-Worship,* "The Hero as Prophet" (1928).

4   Everybody in America is soft, and hates conflict. The cure for this, both in politics and social life, is the same—hardihood. Give them raw truth.

>   JOHN JAY CHAPMAN (1862-1933), U.S. author. *Practical Agitation,* ch. 2 (1898).

5   In all life one should comfort the afflicted, but verily, also, one should afflict the comfortable, and especially when they are comfortably, contentedly, even happily wrong.

>   JOHN KENNETH GALBRAITH (b. 1908), U.S. economist. *Guardian* (London, 28 July 1989).

6   They believe that nothing will happen because they have closed their doors.

>   MAURICE MAETERLINCK (1862-1949) Belgian author. Old Man, in *Interior* (1894). In this play, the old man is looking in on a family who have yet to discover that one of their number has died.

7   America is a hurricane, and the only people who do not hear the sound are those fortunate if incredibly stupid and smug White Protestants who live in the center, in the serene eye of the big wind.

>   NORMAN MAILER (b. 1923), U.S. author. *Advertisements for Myself,* pt. 5, "Advertisement for `Games and Ends'" (1959).

8   They act as if they supposed that to be very sanguine about the general improvement of mankind is a virtue that relieves them from taking trouble about any improvement in particular.

>   JOHN [LORD] MORLEY (1838-1923), English writer, Liberal politician. *On Compromise,* ch. 5 (1874).

9   I cannot help fearing that men may reach a point where they look on every new theory as a danger, every innovation as a toilsome trouble, every social advance as a first step toward revolution, and that they may absolutely refuse to move at all for fear of being carried off their feet. The prospect really does frighten me that they may finally become so engrossed in a cowardly love of immediate pleasures that their interest in their own future and in that of their descendants may vanish, and that they will prefer tamely to follow the course of their destiny rather than make a sudden energetic effort necessary to set things right.

>   ALEXIS DE TOCQUEVILLE (1805-59), French social philosopher. *Democracy in America,* vol. 2, pt. 3, ch. 21 (1840).

10   A Frenchman is self-assured because he regards himself personally both in mind and body as irresistibly attractive to men and women. An Englishman is self-assured as being a citizen of the best-organized state in the world and therefore, as an Englishman, always knows what he should do and knows that all he does as an Englishman is undoubtedly correct. An Italian is self-assured because he is excitable and easily forgets himself and other people. A Russian is self-assured just because he knows nothing and does not want to know anything, since he does not believe that anything can be known. The German's self-assurance is worst of all, stronger and more repulsive than any other, because he imagines that he knows the truth—science—which he himself has invented but which is for him the absolute truth.

>   LEO TOLSTOY (1828-1910), Russian novelist philosopher. *War and Peace,* bk. 9, ch. 10 (1868-69).

COMPLAINT

1   The wheel that squeaks the loudest
Is the one that gets the grease.

>   JOSH BILLINGS (1818-85), U.S. humorist. *The Kicker.*

2   It is a general popular error to suppose the loudest complainers for the public to be the most anxious for its welfare.

EDMUND BURKE (1729-97), Irish philosopher, statesman. *Observations on a Publication,* "The Present State of the Nation" (1769).

3   What annoyances are more painful than those of which we cannot complain?

MARQUIS DE CUSTINE (1790-1857), French traveler, author. *Empire of the Czar: A Journey Through Eternal Russia,* ch. 7 (1843; rev. 1989).

4   There is one topic peremptorily forbidden to all well-bred, to all rational mortals, namely, their distempers. If you have not slept, or if you have slept, or if you have headache, or sciatica, or leprosy, or thunder-stroke, I beseech you, by all angels, to hold your peace, and not pollute the morning.

RALPH WALDO EMERSON (1803-82), U.S. essayist, poet, philosopher. *The Conduct of Life,* "Behavior" (1860).

5   Depend upon it that if a man *talks* of his misfortunes there is something in them that is not disagreeable to him.

SAMUEL JOHNSON (1709-84), English author, lexicographer. Quoted in: James Boswell, *Life of Samuel Johnson,* 1780 entry (1791).

6   When complaints are freely heard, deeply considered and speedily reformed, then is the utmost bound of civil liberty attained that wise men look for.

JOHN MILTON (1608-74), English poet. *Areopagitica: a Speech for the Liberty of Unlicensed Printing to the Parliament of England* (1644).

See also Austen on PITY.

COMPLEXITY

1   The perplexity of life arises from there being too many interesting things in it for us to be interested properly in any of them.

G. K. CHESTERTON (1874-1936), British author. *Tremendous Trifles,* "The Secret of a Train" (1909).

2   I see mysteries and complications wherever I look, and I have never met a steadily logical person.

MARTHA GELLHORN (b. 1908), U.S. journalist, author. *The Face of War,* Introduction (1959).

3   Man is an over-complicated organism. If he is doomed to extinction he will die out for want of simplicity.

EZRA POUND (1885-1972), U.S. poet, critic. *Guide to Kulchur,* pt. 3, sct. 5, ch. 19 (1938).

4   Everything is complicated; if that were not so, life and poetry and everything else would be a bore.

WALLACE STEVENS (1879-1955), U.S. poet. Letter, 19 Dec. 1935 (published in *Letters of Wallace Stevens,* no. 336, ed. by Holly Stevens, 1967).

COMPLIMENTS

1   Pleasant words are as an honeycomb, sweet to the soul, and health to the bones.

BIBLE, HEBREW. *Proverbs* 16:24.

2   No compliment can be eloquent, except as an expression of indifference.

GEORGE ELIOT (1819-1880), English novelist. Maggie Tulliver, responding to Stephen Guest's compliment on their first encounter, in *The Mill on the Floss,* bk. 6, ch. 2 (1860).

3   Compliments cost nothing, yet many pay dear for them.

THOMAS FULLER (1654-1734), English physician. *Gnomologia,* no. 1135 (1732).

4   A compliment is something like a kiss through a veil.

VICTOR HUGO (1802-1885), French poet, dramatist, novelist. *Les Misérables,* "Saint Denis," bk. 8, ch. 1 (1862).

5   Whenever a man's friends begin to compliment him about looking young, he may be sure that they think he is growing old.

WASHINGTON IRVING (1783-1859), U.S. author. *Bracebridge Hall,* "Bachelors" (1822).

6   Hunger is never delicate; they who are seldom gorged to the full with praise may be safely fed with gross compliments, for the appetite must be satisfied before it is disgusted.

SAMUEL JOHNSON (1709-1784), ENGLISH AUTHOR, LEXICOGRAPHER. *Rambler,* no. 193 (London, 21 Jan 1752; repr. in *Works of Samuel Johnson,* vol. 5; ed. by W. J. Bate & Albrecht B. Strauss, 1969).

7   Usually we praise only to be praised.

FRANÇOIS, DUC DE LA ROCHEFOUCAULD (1613-80), French writer, moralist. *Sentences et Maximes Morales,* no. 146 (1678).

8   There is nothing you can say in answer to a compliment. I have been complimented myself a great many times, and they always embarrass me—I always feel that they have not said enough.

MARK TWAIN (1835-1910), U.S. author. "Fulton Day, Jamestown," speech, 23 Sept. 1907 (published in *Mark Twain's Speeches,* ed. by Albert Bigelow Paine, 1923).

9   Women are never disarmed by compliments. Men always are. That is the difference between the two sexes.

OSCAR WILDE (1854-1900), Anglo-Irish playwright, author. Mrs. Cheveley, in *An Ideal Husband,* act 3

See also FLATTERY.

COMPROMISE

1   Compromise. Such an adjustment of conflicting interests as gives each adversary the satisfaction of thinking he has got what he ought not to have, and is deprived of nothing except what was justly his due.

AMBROSE BIERCE (1842-1914), U.S. author. *The Devil's Dictionary* (1881-1906).

2   All government—indeed every human benefit and enjoyment, every virtue and every prudent act—is founded on compromise and barter.

EDMUND BURKE (1729-1797), Irish philosopher, statesman. *Speech on Conciliation with America,* 22 March 1775.

3 Compromise used to mean that half a loaf was better than no bread. Among modern statesmen it really seems to mean that half a loaf is better than a whole loaf.

G. K. CHESTERTON (1874-1936), British author. *What's Wrong With The World*, ch. 3 (1910).

4 The English never draw a line without blurring it.

SIR WINSTON CHURCHILL (1874-1965), British statesman, writer. Speech, 16 Nov. 1948, to House of Commons.

5 Most people hew the battlements of life from compromise, erecting their impregnable keeps from judicious submissions, fabricating their philosophical drawbacks from emotional retractions and scalding marauders in the boiling oil of sour grapes.

ZELDA FITZGERALD (1900-1948), U.S. writer. *Save Me the Waltz*, ch. 1 (1932).

6 Art is uncompromising and life is full of compromises.

GÜNTHER GRASS (b. 1927), German author. Quoted by Arthur Miller in: *Paris Review* (Flushing, N.Y., Summer 1966).

7 If one cannot catch a bird of paradise, better take a wet hen.

NIKITA KHRUSHCHEV (1894-1971), Soviet premier. *Time* (New York, 6 Jan. 1958).

8 Compromise makes a good umbrella but a poor roof.

JAMES RUSSELL LOWELL (1819-1891), U.S. poet, editor. "On Democracy," speech, 6 Oct. 1884, Birmingham, England (published in *Democracy and Other Addresses*, 1886).

9 To be or not to be is not a question of compromise. Either you be or you don't be.

GOLDA MEIR (1898-1978), Israeli politician, prime minister. Quoted in: *New York Times* (12 Dec. 1974), on the question of Israel's future.

10 The worst and best are both inclined
To snap like vixens at the truth.
But, O, beware the middle mind
That purrs and never shows a tooth!

ELINOR WYLIE (1885-1928), U.S. novelist. *Nonsense Rhymes*.

See also Yeats on ENGLAND AND THE ENGLISH; Meir on ISRAEL.

COMPUTERS

1 To err is human, but to really foul things up requires a computer.

ANONYMOUS. Quoted in: "Quote Unquote," 22 Feb. 1982, BBC Radio 4 .

2 Electronic aids, particularly domestic computers, will help the inner migration, the opting out of reality. Reality is no longer going to be the stuff *out there*, but the stuff inside your head. It's going to be commercial and nasty at the same time.

J. G. BALLARD (b. 1930), British author. Interview in *Heavy Metal* (April 1971; repr. in *Re/Search*, no. 8/9, San Francisco, 1984).

3 Computer science only indicates the *retrospective* omnipotence of our technologies. In other words, an

infinite capacity to process data (but only data—i.e. the *already given*) and in no sense a new vision. With that science, we are entering an era of exhaustivity, which is also an era of exhaustion.

JEAN BAUDRILLARD (b. 1929), French semiologist. *Cool Memories*, ch. 4 (1987; tr. 1990).

4 The sad thing about artificial intelligence is that it lacks artifice and therefore intelligence.

JEAN BAUDRILLARD (b. 1929), French semiologist. *Cool Memories*, ch. 4 (1987; tr. 1990).

5 There is never finality in the display terminal's screen, but an irresponsible whimsicality, as words, sentences, and paragraphs are negated at the touch of a key. The significance of the past, as expressed in the manuscript by a deleted word or an inserted correction, is annulled in idle gusts of electronic massacre.

ALEXANDER COCKBURN (b. 1941), Anglo-Irish journalist. "Pull the Plug," in *Mother Jones* (Boulder, 11 Nov. 1986; repr. in *Corruptions of Empire*, pt. 2, 1988), on his preference for typewriters over word processors.

6 It is hardly surprising that children should enthusiastically start their education at an early age with the Absolute Knowledge of computer science; while they are unable to read, for reading demands making judgments at every line. . . . Conversation is almost dead, and soon so too will be those who knew how to speak.

GUY DEBORD (b. 1931), French Situationist philosopher. *Comments on the Society of the Spectacle*, ch. 10 (1988; tr.1990).

7 Man is still the most extraordinary computer of all.

JOHN F. KENNEDY (1917-1963), U.S. Democratic politician, president. Speech, 21 May 1963.

See also Walesa on The WEST.

CONCENTRATION CAMPS

1 Despite the hundreds of attempts, police terror and the concentration camps have proved to be more or less impossible subjects for the artist; since what happened to them was beyond the imagination, it was therefore also beyond art and all those human values on which art is traditionally based.

A. ALVAREZ (b. 1929), British critic, poet and novelist. *The Savage God*, pt. 4, "The Savage God" (1971).

2 The concentration camps, by making death itself anonymous (making it impossible to find out whether a prisoner is dead or alive), robbed death of its meaning as the end of a fulfilled life. In a sense they took away the individual's own death, proving that henceforth nothing belonged to him and he belonged to no one. His death merely set a seal on the fact that he had never existed.

HANNAH ARENDT (1906-1975), German-born U.S. political philosopher. *The Origins of Totalitarianism*, pt. 3, ch. 12, sct. 3 (1951).

3 If you complain of people being shot down in the streets, of the absence of communication or social responsibility, of the rise of everyday violence which people have become accustomed to, and the dehumanization of feelings, then the ultimate development on an organized social level is the concentration camp. . . . The concentration camp is the final expression of human separateness and its ultimate consequence. It is organized abandonment.

> ARTHUR MILLER (b. 1915), U.S. dramatist. *Paris Review* (Flushing, N.Y., Summer 1966). Miller regarded this concept as one of the prime themes of his 1964 play *After the Fall*, which featured a concentration camp in its staging.

4   Here, lads, we live by the law of the *taiga*. But even here people manage to live. D'you know who are the ones the camps finish off? Those who lick other men's left-overs, those who set store by the doctors, and those who peach on their mates.

> ALEXANDER SOLZHENITSYN (b. 1918), Russian novelist. Kuziomin, in *One Day in the Life of Ivan Denisovich,* (1962; tr. 1963).

See also Wiesel on The HOLOCAUST.

CONDITIONING

1   All of childhood's unanswered questions must finally be passed back to the town and answered there. Heroes and bogey men, values and dislikes, are first encountered and labeled in that early environment. In later years they change faces, places and maybe races, tactics, intensities and goals, but beneath those penetrable masks they wear forever the stocking-capped faces of childhood.

> MAYA ANGELOU (b. 1928), U.S. author. *I Know Why the Caged Bird Sings,* ch. 4 (1969), said of one's hometown.

2   Everytime I say "sure" when I mean "no," everytime I smile brightly when I'm exploding with rage, every time I imagine my man's achievement is my own, I know the cheerleader never really died. I feel her shaking her ass inside me and I hear her breathless, girlish voice mutter "T-E-A-M, Yea, Team."

> LOUISE BERNIKOW (b. 1940), U.S. journalist. "Confessons of an Ex-Cheerleader," in *Ms.* (New York, Oct. 1973).

3   Lord, with what care hast Thou begirt us round!
Parents first season us; then schoolmasters
Deliver us to laws; they send us bound
To rules of reason, holy messengers,
Pulpits and Sundays, sorrow dogging sin,
Afflictions sorted, anguish of all sizes,
Fine nets and stratagems to catch us in,
Bibles laid open, millions of surprises,
Blessings beforehand, ties of gratefulness,
The sound of glory ringing in our ears:
Without, our shame; within, our consciences;"
Angels and grace, eternal hopes and fears.
Yet all these fences and their whole array
One cunning bosom-sin blows quite away.

> GEORGE HERBERT (1593-1633), English clergyman, poet. *Sin* in *George Herbert: Poetry and Prose* (ed. by W. H. Auden, 1973).

4   Hardly ever can a youth transferred to the society of his betters unlearn the nasality and other vices of speech bred in him by the associations of his growing years.

Hardly ever, indeed, no matter how much money there be in his pocket, can he ever learn to *dress* like a gentleman-born. The merchants offer their wares as eagerly to him as to the veriest "swell," but he simply *cannot* buy the right things.

> WILLIAM JAMES (1842-1910), U.S. psychologist, philosopher. *Principles of Psychology,* vol. 1, ch. 4 (1890).

5   In schools all over the world, little boys learn that their country is the greatest in the world, and the highest honor that could befall them would be to defend it heroically someday. The fact that empathy has traditionally been conditioned out of boys facilitates their obedience to leaders who order them to kill strangers.

> MYRIAM MIEDZIAN, U.S. author. *Boys Will Be Boys,* ch. 3 (1991).

See also Steinem on FAMILY.

CONFESSION

1   Literary confessors are contemptible, like beggars who exhibit their sores for money, but not so contemptible as the public that buys their books.

> W. H. AUDEN (1907-73), Anglo-American poet. *The Dyer's Hand,* pt. 3, "Hic et Ille" sct. B (1962).

2   We have left undone those things which we ought to have done; and we have done those things which we ought not to have done.

> BOOK OF COMMON PRAYER (1662). *Morning Prayer,* General Confession.

3   No blame should attach to telling the truth. But it does, it does.

> ANITA BROOKNER (b. 1938), British novelist and art historian. Rachel, in *A Friend from England,* ch. 10 (1987).

4   Confession is always weakness. The grave soul keeps its own secrets, and takes its own punishment in silence.

> DOROTHY DIX (1861-1951), U.S. columnist. *Dorothy Dix, Her Book,* ch. 20 (1926).

5   We must not always talk in the market-place of what happens to us in the forest.

> NATHANIEL HAWTHORNE (1804-1864), U.S. author. Hester Prynne, in *The Scarlet Letter,* ch. 22 (1850).

6   The confession of our failings is a thankless office. It savours less of sincerity or modesty than of ostentation. It seems as if we thought our weaknesses as good as other people's virtues.

> WILLIAM HAZLITT (1778-1830), English essayist. *Characteristics: in the Manner of Rochefoucault's Maxims,* no. 43 (1823; repr. in *Collected Works,* vol. 2, ed. by A. R. Waller & Arnold Glover, 1902).

7   We only confess our little faults to persuade people that we have no big ones.

> FRANÇOIS, DUC DE LA ROCHEFOUCAULD (1613-80), French writer, moralist. *Sentences et Maximes Morales,* no. 327 (1678).

8   There are things to confess that enrich the world, and things that need not be said.

JONI MITCHELL (b. 1943), Canadian-born U.S. singer, song-writer. *Independent* (London, 13 May 1988).

9 The worst of my actions or conditions seem not so ugly unto me as I find it both ugly and base not to dare to avouch for them.

MICHEL DE MONTAIGNE (1533-92), French essayist. *Essays*, bk. 3, ch. 5, "Upon some Verses of Virgil" (1588; tr. by John Florio).

10 If any ambitious man have a fancy to revolutionize, at one effort, the universal world of human thought, human opinion, and human sentiment, the opportunity is his own—the road to immortal renown lies straight, open, and unencumbered before him. All that he has to do is to write and publish a very little book. Its title should be simple—a few plain words—"My Heart Laid Bare." But—this little book must be *true to its title*.

EDGAR ALLAN POE (1809-45), U.S. poet, critic, short-story writer. *Marginalia*, "Suggested Title—'Heart Laid Bare'" (1844-49; repr. in *The Centenary Poe*; ed. by Montagu Slater, 1949). *My Heart Laid Bare* was the translation given to Baudelaire's *Intimate Journals* (tr. by Christopher Isherwood, 1930).

11 Confession, alas, is the new handshake.

RICHARD DEAN ROSEN (b. 1949), U.S. journalist and critic. *Psychobabble: Fast Talk and Quick Cure in the Era of Feeling*, "Psychobabble" (1977).

12 Let the trumpet of the day of judgment sound when it will, I shall appear with this book in my hand before the Sovereign Judge, and cry with a loud voice, This is my work, there were my thoughts, and thus was I. I have freely told both the good and the bad, have hid nothing wicked, added nothing good.

JEAN-JACQUES ROUSSEAU (1712-78), Swiss-born French philosopher, political theorist. *The Confessions of Jean-Jacques Rousseau*, vol. 1, pt. 1, bk. 1, Introduction (1781-88, written 1766-70).

13 There is no refuge from confession but suicide, and suicide is confession.

DANIEL WEBSTER (1782-1852), U.S. lawyer, statesman. "Argument on the Murder of Captain White," speech, 6 April 1830, in murder trial, Salem, Massachusetts (repr. in *Writings and Speeches*, vol. 11, 1903). It was during this trial that Webster famously spoke of a "fearful concatenation of circumstances.".

14 It is the confession, not the priest, that gives us absolution.

OSCAR WILDE (1854-1900), Anglo-Irish playwright, author. *The Picture of Dorian Gray*, ch. 8 (1891).

15 A man's very highest moment is, I have no doubt at all, when he kneels in the dust, and beats his breast, and tells all the sins of his life.

OSCAR WILDE (1854-1900), Anglo-Irish playwright, author. *De Profundis* (1905), a letter to Lord Alfred Douglas following Wilde's trial and imprisonment, written in prison.

16 A confession has to be part of your new life.

LUDWIG WITTGENSTEIN (1889-1951), Austrian philosopher. *Culture and Value* (ed. by G. H. von Wright with Heikki Nyman, 1980), journal entry 1931.

CONFORMITY

1 The American ideal, after all, is that everyone should be as much alike as possible.

JAMES BALDWIN (1924-87), U.S. author. "The Harlem Ghetto," in *Commentary* (New York, Feb. 1948; repr. in *Notes of a Native Son*, pt. 2, 1955).

2 For all have not the gift of martyrdom.

JOHN DRYDEN (1631-1700), English poet, dramatist, critic. *The Hind and the Panther*, pt. 2.

3 Society everywhere is in conspiracy against the manhood of every one of its members. . . . The virtue in most request is conformity. Self-reliance is its aversion. It loves not realities and creators, but names and customs.

RALPH WALDO EMERSON (1803-1882), U.S. essayist, poet, philosopher. *Essays*, "Self-Reliance" (First Series, 1841).

4 One lesson we learn early, that in spite of seeming difference, men are all of one pattern. We readily assume this with our mates, and are disappointed and angry if we find that we are premature, and that their watches are slower than ours. In fact, the only sin which we never forgive in each other is difference of opinion.

RALPH WALDO EMERSON (1803-82), U.S. essayist, poet, philosopher. *Society and Solitude*, "Clubs" (1870).

5 Conformity is the jailer of freedom and the enemy of growth.

JOHN F. KENNEDY (1917-63), U.S. Democratic politician, president. Address, 25 Sept. 1961, to the U.N. General Assembly.

6 Every society honors its live conformists and its dead troublemakers.

MIGNON MCLAUGHLIN (b. 1915?), U.S. author, editor. *The Neurotic's Notebook* (1963).

7 The mark of our time is its revulsion against imposed patterns.

MARSHALL MCLUHAN (1911-80), Canadian communications theorist. *Understanding Media*, Introduction (1964).

8 That so few now dare to be eccentric, marks the chief danger of the time.

JOHN STUART MILL (1806-73), English philosopher and economist. *On Liberty*, ch. 3 (1859).

9 To do *exactly as your neighbors* do is the only sensible rule.

EMILY POST (1873-1960), U.S. hostess. *Etiquette*, ch. 33 (1922).

10 We are citizens of an age, as well as of a State; and if it is held to be unseemly, or even inadmissable, for a man to cut himself off from the customs and manners of the circle in which he lives, why should it be less of a duty, in the choice of his activity, to submit his decision to the needs and the taste of his century?

FRIEDRICH VON SCHILLER (1759-1805), German dramatist, poet, essayist. *On the Aesthetic Education of Man*, "Second Letter" (1795).

11 As to conforming outwardly, and living your own life inwardly, I have not a very high opinion of that course.

HENRY DAVID THOREAU (1817-1862), U.S. philosopher, author, naturalist. *Journals* (1906), entry in 1850.

12 I know of no country in which there is so little independence of mind and real freedom of discussion as in America.

ALEXIS DE TOCQUEVILLE (1805-59), French social philosopher. *Democracy in America*, vol. 1, ch. 15 (1835).

13 Fear God, and offend not the Prince nor his laws,
And keep thyself out of the magistrate's claws.

THOMAS TUSSER c. 1520-C. 1580), English writer on agriculture. *Good Husbandry* (1557; repr. 1812).

14 Once conform, once do what other people do because they do it, and a lethargy steals over all the finer nerves and faculties of the soul. She becomes all outer show and inward emptiness; dull, callous, and indifferent.

VIRGINIA WOOLF (1882-1941), British novelist. *The Common Reader*, "Montaigne" (First Series, 1925).

See also CONVENTIONALITY.

CONFUSION

1 In the greatest confusion there is still an open channel to the soul. It may be difficult to find because by midlife it is overgrown, and some of the wildest thickets that surround it grow out of what we describe as our education. But the channel is always there, and it is our business to keep it open, to have access to the deepest part of ourselves.

SAUL BELLOW (b. 1915), U.S. novelist. Allan Bloom, *The Closing of the American Mind*, Foreword (1987).

2 Let nothing be called natural
In an age of bloody confusion,
Ordered disorder, planned caprice,
And dehumanized humanity, lest all things
Be held unalterable!

BERTOLT BRECHT (1898-1956), German dramatist, poet. *The Exception and the Rule*, Prologue (1937).

3 When people are taken out of their depths they lose their heads, no matter how charming a bluff they may put up.

F. SCOTT FITZGERALD (1896-1940), U.S. author. Baby Warren, in *Tender is the Night*, bk. 3, ch. 12 (1934).

4 I'm not confused, I'm just well mixed.

ROBERT FROST (1874-1963), U.S. poet. Quoted in: *Wall Street Journal* (New York, 5 Aug. 1969).

5 Confusion is a word we have invented for an order which is not understood.

HENRY MILLER (1891-1980), U.S. author. *Tropic of Capricorn*, "On the Ovarian Trolley: An Interlude" (1938).

CONGRESS

1 Sure the people are stupid: the human race is stupid. Sure Congress is an inefficient instrument of government. But the people are not stupid enough to abandon representative government for any other kind, including government by the guy who knows.

BERNARD DEVOTO (1897-1955), U.S. historian, critic. *The Easy Chair*, "Sometimes They Vote Right Too" (1955).

2 We have the power to do any damn fool thing we want to do, and we seem to do it about every ten minutes.

J. WILLIAM FULBRIGHT (b. 1905), U.S. Democratic politician. Quoted in: *Time* (New York, 4 Feb. 1952), said of senators.

3 The Few assume to be the *deputies*, but they are often only the *despoilers* of the Many.

GEORG HEGEL (1770-1831), German philosopher. *The Philosophy of History*, pt. 4, sct. 3, ch. 3 (1837).

4 I have seen in the Halls of Congress more idealism, more humaneness, more compassion, more profiles of courage than in any other institution that I have ever known.

HUBERT H. HUMPHREY (1911-78), U.S. Democratic politician, vice president. Speech, 6 June 1965, Syracuse University, New York.

5 I have been up to see the Congress and they do not seem to be able to do anything except to eat peanuts and chew tobacco, while my army is starving.

ROBERT E. LEE (1807-70), U.S. Confederate general. Remark, March 1865, to his son, George Washington Custis Lee, said of the Confederate Congress. Quoted in: *South Atlantic Quarterly* (Durham, N.C., July 1927).

6 The American, if he has a spark of national feeling, will be humiliated by the very prospect of a foreigner's visit to Congress—these, for the most part, illiterate hacks whose fancy vests are spotted with gravy, and whose speeches, hypocritical, unctuous, and slovenly, are spotted also with the gravy of political patronage, these persons are a reflection on the democratic process rather than of it; they expose it in its process rather than of it; they expose it in its underwear.

MARY MCCARTHY (1912-89), U.S. author, critic. "America the Beautiful," in *Commentary* (New York, Sept. 1947; repr. in *On the Contrary*, 1961).

7 It is the duty of the President to propose and it is the privilege of the Congress to dispose.

FRANKLIN D. ROOSEVELT (1882-1945), U.S. Democratic politician, president. Press conference, 23 July 1937.

8 If we were left solely to the wordy wit of legislators in Congress for our guidance, uncorrected by the seasonal experience and the effectual complaints of the people, America would not long retain her rank among the nations.

HENRY DAVID THOREAU (1817-62), U.S. philosopher, author, naturalist. *On the Duty of Civil Disobedience* (1849).

9 The debates of that great assembly are frequently vague and perplexed, seeming to be dragged rather than to march, to the intended goal. Something of this sort must, I think, always happen in public democratic assemblies.

ALEXIS DE TOCQUEVILLE (18-1859), French social philosopher. *Democracy in America*, vol. 2, pt. 1 ch. 21 (1840).

10 It could probably be shown by facts and figures that there is no distinctly native American criminal class except Congress.

MARK TWAIN (1835-1910), U.S. author. *Following the Equator*, ch. 8, "Pudd'nhead Wilson's New Calendar" (1897).

11 This is a Senate of equals, of men of individual honor and personal character, and of absolute independence. We know no masters, we acknowledge no dictators. This is a hall for mutual consultation and discussion; not an arena for the exhibition of champions.

DANIEL WEBSTER (1782-1852), U.S. lawyer, statesman. Speech, 26 Jan 1830, to the U.S. Senate.

12 I believe if we introduced the Lord's Prayer here, senators would propose a large number of amendments to it.

HENRY WILSON (1812-75), U.S. politician. Quoted in: Leon A. Harris *The Fine Art of Political Wit*, ch. 12 (1964).

CONQUEST

1 I have tamed men of iron in my day, shall I not easily crush these men of butter?

FERDINAND ALVAREZ DE TOLEDO, DUKE OF ALBA (1508-82), Spanish general. Quoted in: J. L. Motley, *The Rise of the Dutch Republic*, vol. 2 (1889), alleged reply to the Duchess of Parma on his appointment as Governor-General of the Netherlands, 1567.

2 Conquest is the missionary of valour, and the hard impact of military virtues beats meanness out of the world.

WALTER BAGEHOT (1826-77), English economist, critic. *Physics and Politics*, ch. 2, sct. 3 (1872).

3 We are a conquering race. We must obey our blood and occupy new markets and if necessary new lands.

ALBERT J. BEVERIDGE (1862-1927), U.S. politician, historian. "Grant, the Practical," address, 27 April 1898, to the Middlesex Club of Massachusetts, Boston.

4 In our own time we have seen domination spread over the social landscape to a point where it is beyond all human control. . . . Compared to this stupendous mobilization of materials, of wealth, of human intellect, of human labor for the single goal of domination, all other recent human achievements pale to almost trivial significance. Our art, science, medicine, literature, music and "charitable" acts seem like mere droppings from a table on which gory feasts on the spoils of conquest have engaged the attention of a system whose appetite for rule is utterly unrestrained.

MURRAY BOOKCHIN (b. 1941), U.S. ecologist. *Statecraft as Soulcraft: What Government Does*, Epilogue (1984).

5 Roused by the lash of his own stubborn tail
Our lion now will foreign foes assail.

JOHN DRYDEN (1631-1700), English poet, dramatist, critic. *Astraea Redux*.

6 The desire to conquer is itself a sort of subjection.

GEORGE ELIOT (1819-80), English novelist, editor. *Daniel Deronda*, bk. 1, ch. 10 (1876).

7 Life yields only to the conqueror. Never accept what can be gained by giving in. You will be living off stolen goods, and your muscles will atrophy.

DAG HAMMARSKJÖLD (1905-61), Swedish statesman, Secretary-General of U.N. *Markings*, "Thus It Was" (1876, written 1925-30).

8 If there be one principle more deeply rooted than any other in the mind of every American, it is that we should have nothing to do with conquest.

THOMAS JEFFERSON (1743-1826), U.S. president. Letter, 28 July 1791.

9 If conquerors be regarded as the engine-drivers of History, then the conquerors of thought are perhaps the pointsmen who, less conspicuous to the traveller's eye, determine the direction of the journey.

ARTHUR KOESTLER (1905-83), Hungarian-born British author. *The Sleepwalkers*, pt. 1, ch. 2, sct. 4 (1959).

10 It should be noted that when he seizes a state the new ruler ought to determine all the injuries that he will need to inflict. He should inflict them once and for all, and not have to renew them every day.

NICCOLÒ MACHIAVELLI (1469-1527), Italian political philosopher, statesman. *The Prince*, ch. 8 (1514). "Whoever acts otherwise," Machiavelli added, "either through timidity or bad advice, is always forced to have the knife ready in his hand. . . . Violence should be inflicted once and for all; people will then forget what it tastes like and so be less resentful."

CONSCIENCE

1 The Non-Conformist Conscience makes cowards of us all.

SIR MAX BEERBOHM (1872-1956), British author. *Yellow book*, "King George the Fourth" (1894).

2 Conscience is thoroughly well-bred and soon leaves off talking to those who do not wish to hear it.

SAMUEL BUTLER (1835-1902), English author. *Samuel Butler's Notebooks*, p. 250 (1951).

3 When I contemplate the accumulation of guilt and remorse which, like a garbage-can, I carry through life, and which is fed not only by the lightest action but by the most harmless pleasure, I feel Man to be of all living things the most biologically incompetent and ill-organized. Why has he acquired a seventy years' life-span only to poison it incurably by the mere being of himself? Why has he thrown Conscience, like a dead rat, to putrefy in the well?

CYRIL CONNOLLY (1903-74), British critic. *The Unquiet Grave*, pt. 1 (1944; rev.1951).

4 O conscience, upright and stainless, how bitter a sting to thee is a little fault!

DANTE ALIGHIERI (1265-1321), Italian poet. *The Divine Comedy*, cto. 3, "Purgatory" (completed 1321).

5 In many walks of life, a conscience is a more expensive encumbrance than a wife or a carriage.

THOMAS DE QUINCEY (1785-1859), English author. *Confessions of an English Opium-Eater*, "Preliminary Confessions" (1822).

6 The beginning of compunction is the beginning of a new life.

GEORGE ELIOT (1819-80), English novelist. *Felix Holt, the Radical*, ch. 13 (1866).

7 [A man's] moral conscience is the curse he had to accept from the gods in order to gain from them the right to dream.

> WILLIAM FAULKNER (1897-1962), U.S. novelist. Interview in *Writers at Work* (First Series, ed. by Malcolm Cowley, 1958).

8 Freedom of conscience entails more dangers than authority and despotism.

> MICHEL FOUCAULT (1926-1984), French philosopher. *Madness and Civilization*, ch. 7 (1965).

9 If a superior give any order to one who is under him which is against that man's conscience, although he do not obey it yet he shall not be dismissed.

> ST. FRANCIS OF ASSISI (1182?-1226), Italian friar, founder of the Franciscan Order. Third Admonition of the Order (1221). Quoted in: J. R. H. Moorman, *The Sources for the Life of St. Francis of Assisi* (1940).

10 In the depths of every heart, there is a tomb and a dungeon, though the lights, the music, and revelry above may cause us to forget their existence, and the buried ones, or prisoners whom they hide. But sometimes, and oftenest at midnight, those dark receptacles are flung wide open. In an hour like this, when the mind has a passive sensibility, but no active strength; when the imagination is a mirror, imparting vividness to all ideas, without the power of selecting or controlling them; then pray that your griefs may slumber, and the brotherhood of remorse not break their chain.

> NATHANIEL HAWTHORNE (1804-64), U.S. author. *Twice-Told Tales*, "The Haunted Mind" (1851; repr. in *Works*, vol. 9, 1974).

11 I cannot and will not cut my conscience to fit this year's fashions.

> LILLIAN HELLMAN (1905-84), U.S. playwright. Letter, 19 May 1952, to John S. Wood, Chairman of the House un-American Activities Committee, stating her refusing to testify against colleagues accused of Communist affiliations (published in *Nation*, New York, 31 May 1952).

12 A man's conscience and his judgement is the same thing; and as the judgement, so also the conscience, may be erroneous.

> THOMAS HOBBES (1588-1679), English philosopher. *Leviathan*, pt. 2, ch. 29 (1651).

13 People talk about the conscience, but it seems to me one must just bring it up to a certain point and leave it there. You can let your conscience alone if you're nice to the second housemaid.

> HENRY JAMES (1843-1916), U.S. author. Nanda Brookenham, in *The Awkward Age*, bk. 6, ch. 3 (1899).

14 Conscience was the barmaid of the Victorian soul. Recognizing that human beings were fallible and that their failings, though regrettable, must be humoured, conscience would permit, rather ungraciously perhaps, the indulgence of a number of carefully selected desires.

> C. E. M. JOAD (1891-1953), British author, academic. *The Book of Joad*, ch. 11, "Morals and My Lack of Them" (1899).

15 Conscience: self-esteem with a halo.

> IRVING LAYTON (b. 1912), Canadian poet. *The Whole Bloody Bird*, "Aphs" (1969).

16 The one thing that doesn't abide by majority rule is a person's conscience.

> HARPER LEE (b. 1926), U.S. author. Atticus Finch, in *To Kill a Mockingbird*, pt. 1, ch. 11 (1960).

17 Our conscience is not the vessel of eternal verities. It grows with our social life, and a new social condition means a radical change in conscience.

> WALTER LIPPMANN (1889-1974), U.S. journalist. *A Preface to Politics*, ch. 6 (1914).

18 Conscience is the inner voice which warns us that someone may be looking.

> H. L. MENCKEN (1880-1956), U.S. journalist. *A Mencken Chrestomathy*, "Sententiæ: The Mind of Men" (1914).

19 I think remorse ought to stop biting the consciences that feed it.

> OGDEN NASH (1902-71), U.S. poet. *A Clean Conscience Never Relaxes* (published in *I'm a Stranger Here Myself*, 1938).

20 Again and again I am brought up against it, and again and again I resist it: I don't want to believe it, even though it is almost palpable: *the vast majority lack an intellectual conscience*; indeed, it often seems to me that to demand such a thing is to be in the most populous cities as solitary as in the desert.

> FRIEDRICH NIETZSCHE (1844-1900), German philosopher. *The Gay Science*, aph. 2 (rev. ed. 1887).

21 Men never do evil so fully and cheerfully as when we do it out of conscience.

> BLAISE PASCAL (1623-62), French scientist, philosopher. *Pensées* (1670; no. 813 ed. by Krailsheimer, no. 895 ed. by Brunschvicg).

22 What a man calls his "conscience" is merely the mental action that follows a sentimental reaction after too much wine or love.

> HELEN ROWLAND (1875-1950), U.S. journalist. *A Guide to Men*, "Cymbals and Kettledrums" (1922).

23 My conscience hath a thousand several tongues,
And every tongue brings in a several tale,
And every tale condemns me for a villain.

> WILLIAM SHAKESPEARE (1564-1616), English dramatist, poet. King Richard, in *Richard III*, act 5, sc. 5. Later, before the Battle of Bosworth, Richard rejects conscience with the words, "Conscience is but a word that cowards use, Devised at first to keep the strong in awe" (act 5, sc. 6).

24 Conscience has no more to do with gallantry than it has with politics.

> RICHARD BRINSLEY SHERIDAN (1751-1816), Anglo-Irish dramatist. Isaac Mendoza, in *The Duenna*, act 2, sc. 4.

25 We grow with years more fragile in body, but morally stouter, and can throw off the chill of a bad conscience almost at once.

> LOGAN PEARSALL SMITH (1865-1946), U.S. essayist, aphorist. *Afterthoughts*, "Age and Death" (1931).

26 Conscience is, in most men, an anticipation of the opinions of others.

> SIR HENRY TAYLOR (1800-1886), English author. *The Statesman*, ch. 9 (1836).

27 But that's always the way; it don't make no difference whether you do right or wrong, a person's conscience ain't got no sense, and just goes for him *anyway*. ... It takes up more room than all the rest of a person's insides, and yet ain't no good, nohow. Tom Sawyer thinks the same.

> MARK TWAIN (1835-1910), U.S. author. Huck, in *Huckleberry Finn*, ch. 33 (1884).

28 There are some women ... in whom conscience is so strongly developed that it leaves little room for anything else. Love is scarcely felt before duty rushes to encase it, anger impossible because one must always be calm and see both sides, pity evaporates in expedients, even grief is felt as a sort of bruised sense of injury, a resentment that one should have grief forced upon one when one has always acted for the best.

> SYLVIA TOWNSEND WARNER (1893-1978), British author. *Autumn River*, "Total Loss" (1966).

29 The mere existence of conscience, that faculty of which people prate so much nowadays, and are so ignorantly proud, is a sign of our imperfect development. It must be merged in instinct before we become fine.

> OSCAR WILDE (1854-1900), Anglo-Irish playwright, author. Gilbert, in "The Critic As Artist," pt. 1 (published in *Intentions*, 1891).

30 Conscience makes egotists of us all.

> OSCAR WILDE (1854-1900), Anglo-Irish playwright, author. Lord Henry, in *The Picture of Dorian Gray*, ch. 8 (1891).

See also Eliot on GUILT; Shakespeare on LOVE; Amory on NEW ENGLAND; Smith on The SOUL.

CONSCIOUSNESS AND THE SUBCONSCIOUS

1 The subconscious is ceaselessly murmuring, and it is by listening to these murmurs that one hears the truth.

> GASTON BACHELARD (1884-1962), French scientist, philosopher, literary theorist. *The Poetics of Reverie*, ch. 2, sct. 2 (1960; tr. 1969).

2 The real history of consciousness starts with one's first lie.

> JOSEPH BRODSKY (b. 1940), Russian-born U.S. poet and critic. *Less Than One: Selected Essays*, "Less Than One," sct. 1 (1986; first published 1976).

3 It is our less conscious thoughts and our less conscious actions which mainly mould our lives and the lives of those who spring from us.

> SAMUEL BUTLER (1835-1902), English author. *The Way of All Flesh*, ch. 5 (1903).

4 The unconscious is the ocean of the unsayable, of what has been expelled from the land of language, removed as a result of ancient prohibitions.

> ITALO CALVINO (1923-85), Italian author, critic. "Cybernetics and Ghosts," lecture, delivered in Turin, Nov. 1969 (published in *The Literature Machine*, 1987).

5 A sub-clerk in the post-office is the equal of a conqueror if consciousness is common to them.

> ALBERT CAMUS (1913-60), French-Algerian philosopher and author. *The Myth of Sisyphus*, "The Absurd Man" (1942; tr.1955).

6 Consciousness is much more than the thorn, it is the *dagger* in the flesh.

> E. M. CIORAN (b. 1911), Rumanian-born French philosopher. *The Trouble with Being Born*, ch. 3, (1973).

7 Of Consciousness, her awful Mate
The Soul cannot be rid —
As easy the secreting her
Behind the Eyes of God.

> EMILY DICKINSON (1830-86), U.S. poet. *The Complete Poems*, no. 894 (1955).

8 His was a great sin who first invented consciousness. Let us lose it for a few hours.

> F. SCOTT FITZGERALD (1896-1940), U.S. author. John, in *The Diamond as Big as the Ritz*, ch. 11 (1922), uttered before falling asleep.

9 The ego is not master in its own house.

> SIGMUND FREUD (1856-1939), Austrian psychiatrist. *A Difficulty in the Path of Psycho-Analysis* (1917; repr. in *Complete Works*, vol. 17, ed. by James Strachey & Anna Freud, 1955). This was Freud's conclusion in light of the discoveries made by psychoanalysis that sexual instincts could not be wholly tamed, and that mental processes were unconscious and could "only reach the ego and come under its control through incomplete and untrustworthy perceptions."

10 Our normal waking consciousness, rational consciousness as we call it, is but one special type of consciousness, whilst all about it, parted from it by the filmiest of screens, there lie potential forms of consciousness entirely different.

> WILLIAM JAMES (1842-1910), U.S. psychologist, philosopher. *The Varieties of Religious Experience*, Lectures 16-17, "Mysticism" (1902).

11 The images of the unconscious place a great responsibility upon a man. Failure to understand them, or a shirking of ethical responsibility, deprives him of his wholeness and imposes a painful fragmentariness on his life.

> CARL JUNG (1875-1961), Swiss psychiatrist. *Memories, Dreams, and Reflections*, ch. 6 (1963).

12 My unconscious knows more about the consciousness of the psychologist than his consciousness knows about my unconscious.

> KARL KRAUS (1874-1936), Austrian satirist. *Die Fackel*, no. 445/53 (Vienna, 18 Jan. 1917; repr. in Thomas Szasz, *Anti-Freud: Karl Kraus's Criticism of Psychoanalysis and Psychiatry*, ch. 6, 1976).

13 The human consciousness is really homogeneous. There is no complete forgetting, even in death.

> D. H. LAWRENCE (1885-1930), British author. "Introduction to *The Dragon of the Apocalypse* by Frederick Carter," in *London Mercury* (July 1930; repr. in *Phoenix: The Posthumous Papers of D. H. Lawrence*, pt. 4, ed. by E McDonald, 1936). Carter's book eventually appeared under a different title and without Lawrence's introduction.

14 The waking mind ... is the least serviceable in the arts.

> HENRY MILLER (1891-1980), U.S. author. Interview in *Writers at Work* (Second Series, ed. by George Plimpton, 1963).

15 Man is only a reed, the weakest in nature; but he is a thinking reed. There is no need for the whole universe to take up arms to crush him: a vapor, a drop of water is enough to kill him. But even if the universe were to crush him, man would still be nobler than his slayer, because he knows that he is dying and the advantage the universe has over him. The universe knows nothing of this.

> BLAISE PASCAL (1623-62), French scientist, philosopher. *Pensées* (1670; no. 200 ed. by Krailsheimer, no. 347 ed. by Brunschvicg).

16 The only way to give finality to the world is to give it consciousness.

> MIGUEL DE UNAMUNO (1864-1936), Spanish philosophical writer. *The Tragic Sense of Life*, ch. 7 (1670).

CONSENSUS

1 Consensus is what many people say in chorus but do not believe as individuals.

> ABBA EBAN (b. 1915), Israeli politician. Quoted in: *New Yorker* (23 April 1990).

2 We must indeed all hang together, or, most assuredly, we shall all hang separately.

> BENJAMIN FRANKLIN (1706-90), U.S. statesman, writer. Comment at the signing of the Declaration of Independence, 4 July 1776, in reply to John Hancock's remark that the revolutionaries should be unanimous in their action.

3 Talk about the flag or drugs or crime (never about race or class or justice) and follow the yellow brick road to the wonderful land of "consensus." In place of honest argument among consenting adults the politicians substitute a lullaby for frightened children: the pretense that conflict doesn't really exist, that we have achieved the blessed state in which . . . we no longer need politics.

> LEWIS H. LAPHAM (b. 1935), U.S. essayist and editor. "Democracy in America?," in *Harper's* (New York, Nov. 1990).

4 A consensus politician is someone who does something that he doesn't believe is right because it keeps people quiet when he does it.

> JOHN MAJOR (b. 1943), British Conservative politician, prime minister. *Daily Mail* (London, 4 Jan. 1991).

5 It is not much matter which we say, but mind, we must all say the same.

> LORD MELBOURNE (1779-1848), English statesman, prime minister. Remark, March 1841, at a Cabinet meeting. Quoted in: Walter Bagehot, *The English Constitution*, ch. 1 (1867).

6 To me, consensus seems to be the process of abandoning all beliefs, principles, values and policies. So it is something in which no one believes and to which no one objects.

> MARGARET THATCHER (b. 1925), British Conservative politician, prime minister. Quoted in: Denis Healey, *The Time of My Life*, pt. 4, ch. 23 (1989).

7 Uniform ideas originating among entire peoples unknown to each other must have a common ground of truth.

> GIAMBATTISTA VICO (1688-1744), Italian philosopher and historian. *The New Science*, bk. 1, para. 144 (ed. 1744; tr. 1984).

See also AGREEMENT.

CONSEQUENCES

1 There is not any present moment that is unconnected with some future one. The life of every man is a continued chain of incidents, each link of which hangs upon the former. The transition from cause to effect, from event to event, is often carried on by secret steps, which our foresight cannot divine, and our sagacity is unable to trace. Evil may at some future period bring forth good; and good may bring forth evil, both equally unexpected.

> JOSEPH ADDISON (1672-1719), English essayist. *Interesting Anecdotes, Memoirs, Allegories, Essays, and Poetical Fragments,* "Happiness Not Independent" (1794).

2 Perhaps his might be one of the natures where a wise estimate of consequences is fused in the fires of that passionate belief which determines the consequences it believes in.

> GEORGE ELIOT (1819-80), English novelist, editor. *Daniel Deronda*, bk. 6, ch. 41 (1876), said of Mordecai.

3 For every life and every act
Consequence of good and evil can be shown
And as in time results of many deeds are blended
So good and evil in the end become confounded.

> T. S. ELIOT (1888-1965), Anglo-American poet, critic. Thomas, in *Murder in the Cathedral*, pt. 2.

4 All successful men have agreed in one thing,—they were *causationists*. They believed that things went not by luck, but by law; that there was not a weak or a cracked link in the chain that joins the first and last of things.

> RALPH WALDO EMERSON (1803-1882), U.S. essayist, poet, philosopher. *The Conduct of Life*, ch. 2 (1860).

5 In history an additional result is commonly produced by human actions beyond that which they aim at and obtain—that which they immediately recognize and desire. They gratify their own interest; but something further is thereby accomplished, latent in the actions in question, though not present to their consciousness, and not included in their design.

> GEORG HEGEL (1770-1831), German philosopher. *The Philosophy of History*, "Introduction," sct. 3 (1837). Hegel called this process "the cunning of reason" (*List der Vernunft*).

6 Logical consequences are the scarecrows of fools and the beacons of wise men.

> THOMAS HENRY HUXLEY (1825-95), English biologist. *Science and Culture*, "On the Hypothesis that Animals are Automata" (1881).

7 Results are what you expect, and consequences are what you get.

> Schoolgirl's definition, quoted in: *Ladies' Home Journal* (New York, Jan. 1942).

8 The Devil begat darkness; darkness begat ignorance; ignorance begat error and his brethren; error begat free-will and presumption; free-will begat works; works begat forgetfulness of God; forgetfulness begat transgression; transgression begat superstition; superstition begat satisfaction; satisfaction begat the mass-offering; the mass-offering begat the priest; the priest begat unbelief; unbelief begat hypocrisy; hypocrisy begat traffic in offerings for gain; traffic in offerings for gain begat Purgatory; Purgatory begat the annual solemn vigils; the annual vigils begat church-livings; church-livings begat avarice; avarice begat swelling superfluity; swelling superfluity begat fulness; fulness begat rage; rage begat license; license begat empire and domination; domination begat pomp; pomp begat ambition; ambition begat simony; simony begat the pope and his brethren, about the time of the Babylonish captivity.

MARTIN LUTHER (1483-1546), German leader of the Protestant Reformation. *Table-Talk*, sct. 500 (1569).

9   Nothing is worth doing unless the consequences may be serious.

GEORGE BERNARD SHAW (1856-1950), Anglo-Irish playwright, critic. Hypatia, in *Misalliance*.

CONSERVATIVES

1   When a nation's young men are conservative, its funeral bell is already rung.

HENRY WARD BEECHER (1813-87), U.S. clergyman, editor, writer. *Proverbs from Plymouth Pulpit* (1887).

2   Conservative. A statesman who is enamored of existing evils, as distinguished from a Liberal, who wishes to replace them with others.

AMBROSE BIERCE (1842-1914), U.S. author. *The Devil's Dictionary* (1881-1906).

3   There are no black conservatives. Oh, there are neoconservatives with black skin, but they lack any claim to blackness other than the biological. They have forgotten their roots.

STEPHEN CARTER (b. 1954), U.S. lawyer and author. *Reflections of an Affirmative Action Baby*, ch. 8 (1992).

4   The world is burdened with young fogies. Old men with ossified minds are easily dealt with. But men who look young, act young and everlastingly harp on the fact that they are young, but who nevertheless think and act with a degree of caution that would be excessive in their grandfathers, are the curse of the world. Their very conservatism is secondhand, and they don't know what they are conserving.

ROBERTSON DAVIES (b. 1913), Canadian novelist, journalist. *The Enthusiasms of Robertson Davies*, "The Table Talk of Robertson Davies" (1990).

5   Men are conservatives when they are least vigorous, or when they are most luxurious. They are conservatives after dinner, or before taking their rest; when they are sick or aged. In the morning, or when their intellect or their conscience has been aroused, when they hear music, or when they read poetry, they are radicals.

RALPH WALDO EMERSON (1803-82), U.S. essayist, poet, philosopher. *Essays*, "New England Reformers" (Second Series, 1844).

6   All conservatives are such from personal defects. They have been effeminated by position or nature, born halt and blind, through luxury of their parents, and can only, like invalids, act on the defensive.

RALPH WALDO EMERSON (1803-82), U.S. essayist, poet, philosopher. *The Conduct of Life*, "Fate" (1860).

7   I do not know which makes a man more conservative—to know nothing but the present, or nothing but the past.

JOHN MAYNARD KEYNES (1883-1946), British economist. *The End of Laissez-Faire*, ch. 1 (1926).

8   The appeal of the New Right is simply that it seems to promise that nothing will change in the domestic realm. People are terrified of change there, because it's the last humanizing force left in society, and they think, correctly, that it must be retained.

GERDA LERNER (b. 1920), U.S. educator, author. Quoted in: *Ms.* (New York, Sept. 1981).

9   What is conservatism? Is it not adherence to the old and tried, against the new and untried?

ABRAHAM LINCOLN (1809-65), U.S. president. Speech, 27 Feb. 1860, New York City.

10   Almost always tradition is nothing but a record and a machine-made imitation of the habits that our ancestors created. The average conservative is a slave to the most incidental and trivial part of his forefathers' glory—to the archaic formula which happened to express their genius or the eighteenth-century contrivance by which for a time it was served.

WALTER LIPPMANN (1889-1974), U.S. journalist. *A Preface to Politics*, ch. 1 (1914).

11   The values to which the conservative appeals are inevitably caricatured by the individuals designated to put them into practice.

HAROLD ROSENBERG (1906-78), U.S. art critic, author. "The Cultural Situation Today," in *Partisan Review* (New Brunswick, Summer 1972; repr. as *Discovering the Present*, Introduction, 1973).

12   We hear the haunting presentiment of a dutiful middle age in the current reluctance of young people to select any option except the one they feel will impinge upon them the least.

GAIL SHEEHY (b. 1937), U.S. author and critic. *Passages*, pt. 2, ch. 5 (1976).

13   A little reflection will enable any person to detect in himself that *setness in trifles* which is the result of the unwatched instinct of self-will and to establish over himself a jealous guardianship.

HARRIET BEECHER STOWE (1811-96), U.S. novelist, anti-slavery campaigner. *Little Foxes*, ch. 4 (1865).

14   The word "conservative" is used by the BBC as a portmanteau word of abuse for anyone whose views differ from the insufferable, smug, sanctimonious, naive, guilt-ridden, wet, pink orthodoxy of that sunset home of the third-rate minds of that third-rate decade, the nineteen-sixties.

NORMAN TEBBIT (b. 1931), British Conservative politician. Quoted in: *Independent* (London, 24 Feb. 1990).

15 That man's the true Conservative
Who lops the moulder'd branch away.

> LORD TENNYSON (1809-92), English poet. *Hands All Round.*

16 Loyalty to petrified opinions never yet broke a chain or freed a human soul in this world—and never will.

> MARK TWAIN (1835-1910), U.S. author. "Consistency," paper, read in Hartford, Connecticut, 1884 (published in 1923; repr. in *Complete Essays*, ed. Charles Neider, 1963). The first words of the statement were inscribed beneath Twain's bust in the Hall of Fame, New York University.

17 To be conservative requires no brains whatsoever. Cabbages, cows and conifers are conservatives, and are so stupid they don't even know it. All that is basically required is acceptance of what exists.

> COLIN WELCH (b. 1924), British journalist. *Spectator* (London, 21 July 1967).

See also Tocqueville on COMPLACENCY; White on GENERATIONS; Bagehot on INNOVATION.

CONSISTENCY

1 Consistency, madam, is the first of Christian duties.

> CHARLOTTE BRONTË (1816-55), English novelist. Mr. Brocklehurst, in *Jane Eyre*, ch. 4 (1847), said to Mrs. Reed.

2 A foolish consistency is the hogoblin of little minds, adored by little statesmen and philosophers and divines.

> RALPH WALDO EMERSON (1803-82), U.S. essayist, poet, philosopher. *Essays*, "Self-Reliance" (First Series, 1841).

3 Consistency is contrary to nature, contrary to life. The only completely consistent people are the dead.

> ALDOUS HUXLEY (1894-1963), British author. *Do What You Will*, "Wordsworth in the Tropics" (1929).

4 What, then, is the true Gospel of consistency? Change. Who is the really consistent man? The man who changes. Since change is the law of his being, he cannot be consistent if he stick in a rut.

> MARK TWAIN (1835-1910), U.S. author. "Consistency," paper, read in Hartford, Connecticut, 1884 (published in 1923; repr. in *Complete Essays*, ed. Charles Neider, 1963).

5 Consistency is a virtue for trains: what we want from a philosopher is insights, whether he comes by them consistently or not.

> STEPHEN VIZINCZEY (b. 1933), Hungarian novelist, critic. "Good Faith and Bad," in *Sunday Telegraph* (London, 21 April 1974; repr. in *Truth and Lies in Literature*, 1986), review of Hazel E. Barnes, *Sartre*.

6 Consistency is the last refuge of the unimaginative.

> OSCAR WILDE (1854-1900), Anglo-Irish playwright, author. "The Relation of Dress to Art," in *Pall Mall Gazette* (London, 28 Feb. 1885; repr. in *Aristotle at Afternoon Tea: The Rare Oscar Wilde*, 1991).

CONSPIRACY

1 Civilization is a conspiracy. . . . Modern life is the silent compact of comfortable folk to keep up pretences.

> JOHN BUCHAN (1875-1940), British author, statesman. Andrew Lumley, in *The Power-House*, ch. 3 (1916).

2 If we are on the outside, we assume a conspiracy is the perfect working of a scheme. Silent nameless men with unadorned hearts. A conspiracy is everything that ordinary life is not. It's the inside game, cold, sure, undistracted, forever closed off to us. We are the flawed ones, the innocents, trying to make some rough sense of the daily jostle. Conspirators have a logic and a daring beyond our reach. All conspiracies are the same taut story of men who find coherence in some criminal act.

> DON DELILLO (b. 1926), U.S. author. *Libra*, pt. 2, "In Dallas" (1988).

3 The search for conspiracy only increases the elements of morbidity and paranoia and fantasy in this country. It romanticizes crimes that are terrible because of their lack of purpose. It obscures our necessary understanding, all of us, that in this life there is often tragedy without reason.

> ANTHONY LEWIS (b. 1927), U.S. journalist. *New York Times* (25 Sept. 1975).

4 In countries where associations are free, secret societies are unknown. In America there are factions, but no conspiracies.

> ALEXIS DE TOCQUEVILLE (1805-59), French social philosopher. *Democracy in America*, vol. 1, ch. 12 (1835).

5 Who is that man over there? I don't know him. What is he doing? Is he a conspirator? Have you searched him? Give him till tomorrow to confess, then hang him!—hang him!

> OSCAR WILDE (1854-1900), Anglo-Irish playwright, author. The Czar, in *Vera, or the Nihilists*, act 2. Prince Paul replies, "Sire, you are anticipating history. This is Count Petouchof, your new Ambassador to Berlin."

See also Hardy on INCONSISTENCY.

CONSTITUTIONS

1 Every country has its own constitution; ours is absolutism moderated by assassination.

> ANONYMOUS RUSSIAN. Quoted in: Count Münster, *Political Sketches of the State of Europe 1814-1867* (1868).

2 There is a hearty Puritanism in the view of human nature which pervades the instrument of 1787 It is the work of men who believed in original sin, and were resolved to leave open for transgressors no door which they could possibly shut.

> JAMES BRYCE (1838-1922), British historian, politician, diplomat. *The American Commonwealth*, vol. 1, pt. 1, ch. 26 (1893), said of the U.S. Constitution. Bryce was here agreeing with the opinion of one—unnamed—who said that, "the American Government and Constitution are based on the theology of Calvin and the philosophy of Hobbes."

3 Our constitution works. Our great republic is a government of laws, not of men.

> GERALD R. FORD (b. 1913), U.S. president. Speech, 9 Aug. 1974, on succeeding Richard Nixon as president.

4 The words of the Constitution . . . are so unrestricted by their intrinsic meaning or by their history or by tradition or by prior decisions that they leave the individual Justice free, if indeed they do not compel him, to gather meaning not from reading the Constitution but from reading life.

FELIX FRANKFURTER (1882-1965), U.S. associate justice of the Supreme Court. "The Supreme Court." Quoted in: *Parliamentary Affairs*, vol. 3, no. 1 (London; winter 1949).

5 Our new Constitution is now established, and has an appearance that promises permanency; but in this world nothing can be said to be certain, except death and taxes.

BENJAMIN FRANKLIN (1706-1790), U.S. statesman, writer. Letter, 13 Nov. 1789 (published in *Complete Works*, vol. 10, ed. by John Bigelow, 1887-88).

6 It is the genius of our Constitution that under its shelter of enduring institutions and rooted principles there is ample room for the rich fertility of American political invention.

LYNDON B. JOHNSON (1908-73), U.S. Democratic politician, president. Message, 12 Jan. 1966, to Congress.

7 Your Constitution is all sail and no anchor.

THOMAS BABINGTON MACAULAY (1800-1859), English historian. Letter, 23 May 1857.

8 The proposed Constitution . . . is, in strictness, neither a national nor a federal constitution; but a composition of both.

JAMES MADISON (1751-1836), U.S. president. *Federalist Papers*, no. 39 (Jan. 1788).

9 A constitution that is made for all nations is made for none.

JOSEPH DE MAISTRE (1753-1821), French diplomat, philosopher. *Considerations on France*, ch. 6 (1796; repr. in *The Works of Joseph de Maistre*, ed. by Jack Lively, 1965).

10 A Constitution should be short and obscure.

NAPOLEON BONAPARTE (1769-1821), French general, emperor. Said at Conference of Swiss Deputies, 29 Jan. 1803.

11 The United States Constitution has proved itself the most marvelously elastic compilation of rules of government ever written.

FRANKLIN D. ROOSEVELT (1882-1945), U.S. Democratic politician, president. Radio broadcast, 2 March 1930.

12 There is a higher law than the Constitution.

WILLIAM SEWARD (1801-72), U.S. statesman. Speech, 11 March 1850, to the U.S. Senate, on the issue of slavery. Seward was an active protagonist of emancipation.

13 The American Constitution, one of the few modern political documents drawn up by men who were forced by the sternest circumstances to think out what they really had to face, instead of chopping logic in a university classroom.

GEORGE BERNARD SHAW (1856-1950), Anglo-Irish playwright, critic. *Getting Married*, Preface (1908).

CONSULTANTS

1 In every society some men are born to rule, and some to advise.

RALPH WALDO EMERSON (1803-82), U.S. essayist, poet, philosopher. "The Young American," lecture, 7 Feb. 1844, delivered to Mercantile Library Association, Boston (published in *Addresses and Lectures*, 1849).

2 American couples have gone to such lengths to avoid the interference of in-laws that they have to pay marriage counselors to interfere between them.

FLORENCE KING (b. 1936), U.S. author. *Reflections in a Jaundiced Eye*, "Does Your Child Taste Salty?" (1989).

3 The best servants of the people, like the best valets, must whisper unpleasant truths in the master's ear. It is the court fool, not the foolish courtier, whom the king can least afford to lose.

WALTER LIPPMANN (1889-1974), U.S. journalist. *A Preface to Politics*, ch. 6 (1914).

4 While the doctors consult, the patient dies.

ENGLISH PROVERB.

THE CONSUMER SOCIETY

1 The technological landscape of the present day has enfranchised its own electorates—the inhabitants of marketing zones in the consumer goods society, television audiences and news magazine readerships. . . vote with money at the cash counter rather than with the ballot paper at the polling booth.

J. G. BALLARD (b. 1930), British author. "The Consumer Consumer," in *Ink* (5 June 1971; repr. in *Re/Search*, no. 8/9, San Francisco, San Francisco, 1984).

2 Large department stores, with their luxuriant abundance of canned goods, foods, and clothing, are like the primary landscape and the geometrical locus of affluence. Streets with overcrowded and glittering store windows. . . the displays of delicacies, and all the scenes of alimentary and vestimentary festivity, stimulate a magical salivation. Accumulation is more than the sum of its products: the conspicuousness of surplus, the final and magical negation of scarcity. . .mimic a new-found nature of prodigious fecundity.

JEAN BAUDRILLARD (b. 1929), French semiologist. "Consumer Society," in *La Société de Consommation* (1970; repr. in *Selected Writings*, ed. by Mark Poster, 1988).

3 Living is more a question of what one spends than what one makes.

MARCEL DUCHAMP (1887-1968), French artist. *Dialogues with Marcel Duchamp*, ch. 4 (ed. by Pierre Cabanne, 1967).

4 . . . Everything from toy guns that spark
To flesh-colored Christs that glow in the dark
It's easy to see without looking too far
That not much is really sacred.

BOB DYLAN (b. 1941), U.S. singer, songwriter. "It's Alright Ma (I'm Only Bleeding)," from the album *Bringing it all Back Home* (1965).

5 Every man is a consumer, and ought to be a producer. . . . He is by constitution expensive, and needs to be rich.

> RALPH WALDO EMERSON (1803-82), U.S. essayist, poet, philosopher. *The Conduct of Life*, "Wealth" (1860).

6 Modern man, if he dared to be articulate about his concept of heaven, would describe a vision which would look like the biggest department store in the world, showing new things and gadgets, and himself having plenty of money with which to buy them. He would wander around open-mouthed in this heaven of gadgets and commodities, provided only that there were ever more and newer things to buy, and perhaps that his neighbors were just a little less privileged than he.

> ERICH FROMM (1900-1980), U.S. psychologist. *The Sane Society*, ch. 5, "Alienation" (1955).

7 Consumer wants can have bizarre, frivolous, or even immoral origins, and an admirable case can still be made for a society that seeks to satisfy them. But the case cannot stand if it is the process of satisfying wants that create the wants.

> JOHN KENNETH GALBRAITH (b. 1908), U.S. economist. *The Affluent Society*, ch. 11, sct. 2 (1958).

8 It is hard to contend against one's heart's desire; for whatever it wishes to have it buys at the cost of soul.

> HERACLITUS c. 535-C. 475 B.C.), Greek philosopher. Quoted in: Hippocrates, *On The Universe*, aph. 105.

9 "More!" is as effective a revolutionary slogan as was ever invented by doctrinaires of discontent. The American, who cannot learn to want what he has, is a permanent revolutionary.

> ERIC HOFFER (1902-83), U.S. philosopher. *The Passionate State of Mind*, aph. 22 (1955).

10 The mystical nature of American consumption accounts for its joylessness. We spend a great deal of time in stores, but if we don't seem to take much pleasure in our buying, it's because we're engaged in the acts of sacrifice and self-definition. Abashed in the presence of expensive merchandise, we recognize ourselves. . . as suppliants admitted to a shrine.

> LEWIS H. LAPHAM (b. 1935), U.S. essayist, editor. *Money and Class in America*, ch. 8 (1988).

11 In our rich consumers' civilization we spin cocoons around ourselves and get possessed by our possessions.

> MAX LERNER (b. 1902), U.S. author, columnist. "What Shall I Save?," in *New York Post* (10 Sept. 1952; repr. in *The Unfinished Country*, pt. 1, 1959).

12 The so-called consumer society and the politics of corporate capitalism have created a second nature of man which ties him libidinally and aggressively to the commodity form. The need for possessing, consuming, handling and constantly renewing the gadgets, devices, instruments, engines, offered to and imposed upon the people, for using these wares even at the danger of one's own destruction, has become a "biological" need.

> HERBERT MARCUSE (1898-1979), U.S. political philosopher. *An Essay on Liberation*, ch. 1 (1969).

13 Tomorrow I will discover Sunset Boulevard. Eurhythmic dancing, ball-room dancing, tap dancing, artistic photography, ordinary photography, lousy photography, electro-fever treatment, internal douche treatment, ultra-violet treatment, elocution lessons, psychic readings, institutes of religion, astrological demonstrations, hands read, feet manicured, elbows massaged, faces lifted, warts removed, fat reduced, insteps raised, corsets fitted, busts vibrated, corns removed, hair dyed, glasses fitted, soda jerked, hangovers cured, headaches driven away, flatulence dissipated, limousines rented, the future made clear, the war made comprehensible, octane made higher and butane lower, drive in and get indigestion, flush the kidneys, get a cheap car-wash, stay-awake pills and go-to-sleep pills, Chinese herbs are very good for you and without a Coca-Cola life is unthinkable.

> HENRY MILLER (1891-1980), U.S. author. *The Air-Conditioned Nightmare*, "Soirée in Hollywood" (1945).

14 The power of consumer goods . . . has been engendered by the so-called liberal and progressive demands of freedom, and, by appropriating them, has emptied them of their meaning, and changed their nature.

> PIER PAOLO PASOLINI (1922-75), Italian film director, essayist. "Sono Contro l'Aborto," in *Corriere della Sera* (Milan, 19 Jan. 1975; repr. in *Scritti Corsari*, 1975).

15 With the supermarket as our temple and the singing commercial as our litany, are we likely to fire the world with an irresistible vision of America's exalted purpose and inspiring way of life?

> ADLAI STEVENSON (1900-1965), U.S. Democratic politician. *Wall Street Journal* (New York, 1 June 1960).

16 In the kingdom of consumption the citizen is king. A democratic monarchy: equality before consumption, fraternity in consumption, and freedom through consumption. The dictatorship of consumer goods has finally destroyed the barriers of blood, lineage and race.

> RAOUL VANEIGEM (b. 1934), Belgian Situationist philosopher. *The Revolution of Everyday Life*, ch. 7, sct. 2 (1967; tr. 1983). "The ideology of consumption," Vaneigem wrote, "becomes the consumption of ideology."

17 Conspicuous consumption of valuable goods is a means of reputability to the gentleman of leisure.

> THORSTEIN VEBLEN (1857-1929), U.S. social scientist. *The Theory of the Leisure Class*, ch. 4 (1899).

18 What's great about this country is that America started the tradition where the richest consumers buy essentially the same things as the poorest.

> ANDY WARHOL (1928-87), U.S. Pop artist. *From A to B and Back Again*, ch. 6 (1975).

19 Getting and spending, we lay waste our powers.

> WILLIAM WORDSWORTH (1770-1850), English poet. *Miscellaneous Sonnets*, "The World is Too Much With Us," Sonnet 23 (1827).

See also Boorstin on SALES AND MARKETING; Baudrillard on SHOPPING MALLS.

CONTEMPLATION

1 There exist certain individuals who are, by nature, given purely to contemplation and are utterly unsuited to action, and who, nevertheless, under a mysterious and unknown impulse, sometimes act with a speed which they themselves would have thought beyond them.

CHARLES BAUDELAIRE (1821-67), French poet. "The Bad Glazier," in *La Presse* (Paris, 26 Aug. 1862; repr. in *Complete Works*, vol. 1, "Shorter Prose Poems," ed. by Yves-Gérard le Dantec; rev. by Claude Pichois, 1953).

2 One cannot long remain so absorbed in contemplation of emptiness without being increasingly attracted to it. In vain one bestows on it the name of infinity; this does not change its nature. When one feels such pleasure in non-existence, one's inclination can be completely satisfied only by completely ceasing to exist.

EMILE DURKHEIM (1858-1917), French sociologist. *Suicide*, bk. 2, ch. 6, sct. 1 (1897; tr. 1951).

3 One is not idle because one is absorbed. There is both visible and invisible labor. To contemplate is to toil, to think is to do. The crossed arms work, the clasped hands act. The eyes upturned to Heaven are an act of creation.

VICTOR HUGO (1802-85), French poet, dramatist, novelist. *Les Misérables*, pt. 2, bk. 7, ch. 8 (1862).

4 I admire people who are suited to the contemplative life.... They can sit inside themselves like honey in a jar and just be. It's wonderful to have someone like that around, you always feel you can count on them. You can go away and come back, you can change your mind and your hairdo and your politics, and when you get through doing all these upsetting things, you look around and there they are, just the way they were, just being.

ELIZABETH JANEWAY (b. 1913), U.S. author. *Accident on Route 37*, "Elizabeth Jowett" (1964).

5 The national distrust of the contemplative temperament arises less from an innate Philistinism than from a suspicion of anything that cannot be counted, stuffed, framed or mounted over the fireplace in the den.

LEWIS H. LAPHAM (b. 1935), U.S. essayist, editor. *Money and Class in America*, ch. 8 (1988).

6 With an eye made quiet by the power
Of harmony, and the deep power of joy,
We see into the life of things.

WILLIAM WORDSWORTH (1770-1850), English poet. *Lines Written a Few Miles above Tintern Abbey* (published in Lyrical Ballads, 1798).

CONTENTMENT

1 For I have learned, in whatsoever state I am, therewith to be content.

BIBLE: NEW TESTAMENT. St. Paul in *Philippians* 4:11.

2 People are never free of trying to be content.

MURRAY BOOKCHIN (b. 1941), U.S. ecologist. *Independent* (London, 1 June 1992).

3 There's nought, no doubt, so much the spirit calms
As rum and true religion.

LORD BYRON (1788-1824), English poet. *Don Juan*, cto. 2, st. 34.

4 True contentment is a thing as active as agriculture. It is the power of getting out of any situation all that there is in it. It is arduous and it is rare.

G. K. CHESTERTON (1874-1936), British author. *A Miscellany of Men*, "The Contented Man" (1912).

5 Happy the man, and happy he alone,
He who can call today his own;
He who, secure within, can say,
Tomorrow, do thy worst, for I have lived today.

JOHN DRYDEN (1631-1700), English poet, dramatist, critic. *Imitation of Horace*, bk. 3, ode 29 (1685).

6 If the book is good, is about something that you know, and is truly written, and reading it over you see that this is so, you can let the boys yip and the noise will have that pleasant sound coyotes make on a very cold night when they are out in the snow and you are in your own cabin that you have built or paid for with your work.

ERNEST HEMINGWAY (1899-1961), U.S. author. "Old Newsman Writes: A Letter from Cuba," in *Esquire* (New York, Dec. 1934; repr. in *By-Line Ernest Hemingway*, ed. by William White, 1967).

7 To be content with life—or to live merrily, rather—all that is required is that we bestow on all things only a fleeting, superficial glance; the more thoughtful we become the more earnest we grow.

G. C. LICHTENBERG (1742-1799), German physicist, philosopher. *Aphorisms*, aph. 29, "Notebook K" (written 1765-99; tr. by R. J. Hollingdale, 1990).

8 That blessed mood
In which the burthen of the mystery,
In which the heavy and the weary weight
Of all this unintelligible world
Is lightened.

WILLIAM WORDSWORTH (1770-1850), English poet. *Lines Written a Few Miles above Tintern Abbey* (published in *Lyrical Ballads*, 1798).

CONTRADICTION

1 I happen to feel that the degree of a person's intelligence is directly reflected by the number of conflicting attitudes she can bring to bear on the same topic.

LISA ALTHER (b. 1944), U.S. novelist. Ginny Babcock, in *Kinflicks*, ch. 7 (1976).

2 I believe that truth has only one face: that of a violent contradiction.

GEORGES BATAILLE (1897-1962), French novelist, critic. *The Deadman*, Preface (1967; repr. in *Violent Silence*, ed. by Paul Buck, 1984).

3 What an antithetical mind!—tenderness, roughness—delicacy, coarseness—sentiment, sensuality—soaring and grovelling, dirt and deity—all mixed up in that one compound of inspired clay!

LORD BYRON (1788-1824), English poet. *Byron's Letters and*

Journals, vol. 3, (ed. by Leslie A. Marchand, 1974), entry for 13 Dec. 1813, said of Robert Burns.

4 I have forced myself to contradict myself in order to avoid conforming to my own taste.

MARCEL DUCHAMP (1887-1968), French artist. Quoted in: Harriet Janis and Sidney Janis, "Marcel Duchamp: Anti-Artist," in *View* (New York, 21 March 1945; repr. in Robert Motherwell, *Dada Painters and Poets*, 1951).

5 Let me never fall into the vulgar mistake of dreaming that I am persecuted whenever I am contradicted.

RALPH WALDO EMERSON (1803-82), U.S. essayist, poet, philosopher. *Journals* (1909-14), entry for 8 Nov. 1838.

6 *Doublethink* means the power of holding two contradictory beliefs in one's mind simultaneously, and accepting both of them.

GEORGE ORWELL (1903-50), British author. *Nineteen Eighty-Four*, pt. 2, ch. 9 (1949), extract from Goldstein's book.

See Fitzgerald on INTELLIGENCE.

7 The well-bred contradict other people. The wise contradict themselves.

OSCAR WILDE (1854-1900), Anglo-Irish playwright, author. "Phrases and Philosophies for the Use of the Young," in *Chameleon* (London, Dec. 1894).

See also Whitman on INCONSISTENCY; OPPOSITES; PARADOX.

CONTROVERSY

1 I am continually fascinated at the difficulty intelligent people have in distinguishing what is controversial from what is merely offensive.

NORA EPHRON (b. 1941), U.S. author, journalist. "Barney Collier's Book," in *Esquire* (Jan. 1976).

2 When a thing ceases to be a subject of controversy, it ceases to be a subject of interest.

WILLIAM HAZLITT (1778-1830), English essayist. "The Spirit of Controversy," in *The Atlas* (31 Jan. 1830; repr. in *Complete Works*, vol. 20, ed. by P. P. Howe, 1932).

3 When people generally are aware of a problem, it can be said to have entered the public consciousness. When people get on their hind legs and holler, the problem has not only entered the public consciousness—it has also become a part of the public conscience. At that point, things in our democracy begin to hum.

HUBERT H. HUMPHREY (1911-78), U.S. Democratic politician, vice president. Speech, 11 Oct. 1966, Gannon College, Erie, Pa.

4 When a subject is highly controversial . . . one cannot hope to tell the truth. One can only show how one came to hold whatever opinion one does hold. One can only give one's audience the chance of drawing their own conclusions as they observe the limitations, the prejudices, the idiosyncrasies of the speaker.

VIRGINIA WOOLF (1882-1941), British novelist. *A Room of One's Own*, ch. 1 (1929).

See also Butler on ARGUMENT; DEBATE; Bierce on IMPARTIALITY.

CONVALESCENCE

1 "Healing,"
Papa would tell me,
"is not a science,
but the intuitive art
of wooing Nature."

W. H. AUDEN (1907-73), Anglo-American poet. *The Art of Healing*.

2 With any recovery from morbidity there must go a certain healthy humiliation.

G. K. CHESTERTON (1874-1936), British author. *The Man Who Was Thursday*, ch. 8 (1908).

3 One must not forget that recovery is brought about not by the physician, but by the sick man himself. He heals himself, by his own power, exactly as he walks by means of his own power, or eats, or thinks, breathes or sleeps.

GEORG GRODDECK (1866-1934), German psychoanalyst. *The Book of the It*, Letter 32 (1923).

4 I enjoy convalescence. It is the part that makes the illness worth while.

GEORGE BERNARD SHAW (1856-1950), Anglo-Irish playwright, critic. Lubin, in *Back to Methuselah*, "The Gospel of the Brothers Barnabas."

CONVENTIONALITY

1 What greater reassurance can the weak have than that they are like anyone else?

ERIC HOFFER (1902-83), U.S. philosopher. *The Passionate State of Mind*, aph. 111 (1955).

2 Why can't somebody give us a list of things that everybody thinks and nobody says, and another list of things that everybody says and nobody thinks.

OLIVER WENDELL HOLMES, SR. (1809-94), U.S. writer, physician. *The Professor at the Breakfast-Table*, ch. 6 (1859).

3 Conventional people are roused to fury by departures from convention, largely because they regard such departures as a criticism of themselves.

BERTRAND RUSSELL (1872-1970), British philosopher, mathematician. *The Conquest of Happiness*, ch. 9 (1930).

4 Every generation laughs at the old fashions, but follows religiously the new.

HENRY DAVID THOREAU (1817-62), U.S. philosopher, author, naturalist. *Walden*, "Economy" (1854).

See also CONFORMITY; Diderot on HUMAN NATURE.

CONVERSATION

1 "The time has come," the Walrus said,
"To talk of many things:
Of shoes—and ships—and sealing wax—
Of cabbages—and kings—
And why the sea is boiling hot—
And whether pigs have wings."

LEWIS CARROLL (1832-98), English writer, mathematician. *Through the Looking-Glass*, ch. 4 (1872).

2 There is nothing so dangerous for anyone who has something to hide as conversation! . . . A human being, Hastings, cannot resist the opportunity to reveal himself and express his personality which conversation gives him. Every time he will give himself away.

AGATHA CHRISTIE (1891-1976), British mystery writer. Poirot, in *The ABC Murders*, ch. 31 (1936).

3 A sudden silence in the middle of a conversation suddenly brings us back to essentials: it reveals how dearly we must pay for the invention of speech.

E. M. CIORAN (b. 1911), Rumanian-born French philosopher. *Anathemas and Admirations*, "On the Verge of Existence" (1986).

4 Talk ought always to run obliquely, not nose to nose with no chance of mental escape.

FRANK MOORE COLBY (1865-1925), U.S. editor, essayist. *The Colby Essays*, vol. 1, "Simple Simon" (1926).

5 I find we are growing serious, and then we are in great danger of being dull.

WILLIAM CONGREVE (1670-1729), English dramatist. Araminta, as the conversation turns on the subject of love, in *The Old Bachelor*, act 2, sc. 2.

6 I would rather take hellebore than spend a conversation with a good, little man.

EDWARD DAHLBERG (1900-1977), U.S. author, critic. *Alms for Oblivion*, "The Expatriates: A Memoir" (1964).

7 Mediocre people have an answer for everything and are astonished at nothing. They always want to have the air of knowing better than you what you are going to tell them; when, in their turn, they begin to speak, they repeat to you with the greatest confidence, as if dealing with their own property, the things that they have heard you say yourself at some other place. . . . A capable and superior look is the natural accompaniment of this type of character.

EUGÈNE DELACROIX (1798-1863), French artist. *The Journal of Eugène Delacroix* (tr. by Walter Pach, 1937), entry for 25 Feb. 1852.

8 No collection of people who are all waiting for the same thing are capable of holding a natural conversation. Even if the thing they are waiting for is only a taxi.

BEN ELTON (b. 1959), British author, performer. *Stark*, "Airport Rescue" (1989).

9 In conversation the game is, to say something new with old words. And you shall observe a man of the people picking his way along, step by step, using every time an old boulder, yet never setting his foot on an old place.

RALPH WALDO EMERSON (1803-82), U.S. essayist, poet, philosopher. *The Journals and Miscellaneous Notebooks of Ralph Waldo Emerson*, vol. 11 (ed. by A. W. Plumstead and William H. Gilman, 1975), entry for 1849.

10 Things said for conversation are chalk eggs. Don't *say* things. What you *are* stands over you the while, and thunders so that I cannot hear what you say to the contrary.

RALPH WALDO EMERSON (1803-82), U.S. essayist, poet, philosopher. *Letters and Social Aims*, "Social Aims" (1876).

11 The great secret of succeeding in conversation is to admire little, to hear much; always to distrust our own reason, and sometimes that of our friends; never to pretend to wit, but to make that of others appear as much as possibly we can; to hearken to what is said and to answer to the purpose.

BENJAMIN FRANKLIN (1706-90), U.S. statesman, writer. *Complete Works*, vol. 1, "Miscellaneous Observations" (1728; ed. by John Bigelow, 1887-88).

12 And when you stick on conversation's burrs,
Don't strew your pathway with those dreadful urs.

OLIVER WENDELL HOLMES, SR. (1809-94), U.S. writer, physician. *A Rhymed Lesson*.

13 The happiest conversation is that of which nothing is distinctly remembered but a general effect of pleasing impression.

SAMUEL JOHNSON (1709-84), English author, lexicographer. Quoted in: James Boswell, *Life of Samuel Johnson*, entry for 1781 (1791).

14 We often forgive those who bore us, but we cannot forgive those whom we bore.

FRANÇOIS, DUC DE LA ROCHEFOUCAULD (1613-80), French writer, moralist. *Sentences et Maximes Morales*, no. 304 (1678).

15 The opposite of talking isn't listening. The opposite of talking is waiting.

FRAN LEBOWITZ (b. 1951), U.S. journalist. *Social Studies*, "People" (1981).

16 No one will ever shine in conversation, who thinks of saying fine things: to please, one must say many things indifferent, and many very bad.

FRANCIS LOCKIER (1668-1740), English prelate, man of letters. Quoted in: Joseph Spence, *Anecdotes*, pt. 2, "1730-32" (1820).

17 The Americans. . . have invented so wide a range of pithy and hackneyed phrases that they can carry on an amusing and animated conversation without giving a moment's reflection to what they are saying and so leave their minds free to consider the more important matters of big business and fornication.

W. SOMERSET MAUGHAM (1874-1965), British author. *Cakes and Ale*, ch. 2 (1930).

18 We do not talk—we bludgeon one another with facts and theories gleaned from cursory readings of newspapers, magazines and digests.

HENRY MILLER (1891-1980), U.S. author. *The Air-Conditioned Nightmare*, "The Shadows" (1945).

19 With thee conversing I forget all time.

JOHN MILTON (1608-74), English poet. Eve to Adam, in *Paradise Lost*, bk. 4.

20 Ideal conversation must be an exchange of thought, and not, as many of those who worry most about their shortcomings believe, an eloquent exhibition of wit or oratory.

EMILY POST (1873-1960), U.S. hostess. *Etiquette*, ch. 6 (1922).

21 It is not what we learn in conversation that enriches us. It is the elation that comes of swift contact with tingling currents of thought.

AGNES REPPLIER (1858-1950), U.S. author, social critic. *Compromises*, "The Luxury of Conversation" (1904).

22 It's apparent that we can't proceed any further without a name for this institutionalized garrulousness, this psychological patter, this need to catalogue the ego's condition. Let's call it psychobabble, this spirit which now tyrannizes conversation in the seventies.

RICHARD DEAN ROSEN (b. 1949), U.S. journalist, critic. *Psychobabble: Fast Talk and Quick Cure in the Era of Feeling*, "Psychobabble" (1977). Rosen added, "Psychobabble is difficult to avoid and there is often an embarrassment involved in not using it, somewhat akin to the mild humiliation experienced by American tourists in Paris who cannot speak the native tongue. Psychobabble is now spoken by magazine editors, management consultants, sandal makers, tool and die workers, chiefs of state, Ph.D.s in clinical psychology, and just about everyone else."

23 Say nothing good of yourself, you will be distrusted; say nothing bad of yourself, you will be taken at your word.

JOSEPH ROUX (1834-86), French priest, writer. *Meditations of a Parish Priest*, no. 22, "Joy" (1886).

24 The primary use of conversation is to satisfy the impulse to talk.

GEORGE SANTAYANA (1863-1952), U.S. philosopher, poet. *The Last Puritan*, p. 385 (1935).

25 The techniques of opening conversation are universal. I knew long ago and rediscovered that the best way to attract attention, help, and conversation is to be lost. A man who seeing his mother starving to death on a path kicks her in the stomach to clear the way, will cheerfully devote several hours of his time giving wrong directions to a total stranger who claims to be lost.

JOHN STEINBECK (1902-68), U.S. author. *Travels with Charley: in Search of America*, pt. 1 (1961).

26 An American cannot converse, but he can discuss, and his talk falls into a dissertation. He speaks to you as if he was addressing a meeting; and if he should chance to become warm in the discussion, he will say "Gentlemen" to the person with whom he is conversing.

ALEXIS DE TOCQUEVILLE (1805-59), French social philosopher. *Democracy in America*, vol. 1, ch. 14 (1835). Queen Victoria famously complained that Gladstone addressed her in the same manner, "as if he were addressing a public meeting."

27 War talk by men who have been in a war is always interesting; whereas moon talk by a poet who has not been in the moon is likely to be dull.

MARK TWAIN (1835-1910), U.S. author. *Life on the Mississippi*, ch. 45 (1883).

28 There is no such thing as conversation. It is an illusion. There are intersecting monologues, that is all.

REBECCA WEST (1892-1983), British author. *There Is No Conversation*, "The Harsh Voice," sct. 1 (1935).

29 Talk to every woman as if you loved her, and to every man as if he bored you, and at the end of your first season you will have the reputation of possessing the most perfect social tact.

OSCAR WILDE (1854-1900), Anglo-Irish playwright, author. Lord Illingworth, in *A Woman of No Importance*, act 3.

30 Conversation should touch everything, but should concentrate itself on nothing.

OSCAR WILDE (1854-1900), Anglo-Irish playwright, author. Gilbert, in *The Critic as Artist*, pt. 2 (published in *Intentions*, 1891)

See also Welles on CINEMA; Barrie, Crisp on DINNER PARTIES; English Proverb on GENTLEMEN; Thrale on SAMUEL JOHNSON; Roth on LANGUAGE: ENGLISH; Wilde on LIES AND LYING; Smith on SILENCE; Connolly on SPEECH; Molière on SPEECHES AND SPEECHMAKING; Hazlitt on WIT.

CONVERSION

1 Jesus tapped me on the shoulder and said, Bob, why are you resisting me? I said, I'm not resisting you! He said, You gonna follow me? I said, I've never thought about that before! He said, When you're not following me, you're resisting me.

BOB DYLAN (b. 1941), U.S. singer, songwriter. Quoted in: *Q Magazine* (London, Jan. 1990), said on stage at Syracuse, New York, May 1980.

2 I believe that a man is converted when first he hears the low, vast murmur of life, of human life, troubling his hitherto unconscious self.

D. H. LAWRENCE (1885-1930), British author. Letter, 3 Dec. 1907 (published in *The Letters of D. H. Lawrence*, vol. 1; ed. by James T. Boulton, 1979).

3 I used to say: "there is a God-shaped hole in me." For a long time I stressed the absence, the hole. Now I find it is the shape which has become more important.

SALMAN RUSHDIE (b. 1948), Indian-born British author. *Independent on Sunday* (London, 30 Dec. 1990), said of his conversion to Islam after being branded an "enemy of Islam."

4 Once my heart was captured, reason was shown the door, deliberately and with a sort of frantic joy. I accepted everything, I believed everything, without struggle, without suffering, without regret, without false shame. How can one blush for what one adores?

GEORGE SAND (1804-76), French novelist. *The Story of My Life*, vol. 3, pt. 3, ch. 14 (1856), on her newfound religious faith.

5 The great danger of conversion in all ages has been that when the religion of the high mind is offered to the lower mind, the lower mind, feeling its fascination without understanding it, and being incapable of rising to it, drags it down to its level by degrading it.

GEORGE BERNARD SHAW (1856-1950), Anglo-Irish playwright, critic. *Androcles and the Lion*, Preface (first published in *Prefaces*, 1916).

See also Morley on ARGUMENT.

COOKING

1 Not on morality, but on cookery, let us build our stronghold: there brandishing our frying-pan, as censer, let us offer sweet incense to the Devil, and live at ease on the fat things *he* has provided for his elect!

THOMAS CARLYLE (1795-1881), Scottish essayist, historian. Teufelsdröckh, in *Sartor Resartus*, bk. 2, ch. 7 (1833-34).

2 If cooking becomes an art form rather than a means of providing a reasonable diet, then something is clearly wrong.

> TOM JAINE (b. 1943), British editor of *The Good Food Guide*. *Daily Telegraph* (London, 19 Oct. 1989).

3 I did toy with the idea of doing a cook-book. . . . The recipes were to be the routine ones: how to make dry toast, instant coffee, hearts of lettuce and brownies. But as an added attraction, at no extra charge, my idea was to put a fried egg on the cover. I think a lot of people who hate literature but love fried eggs would buy it if the price was right.

> GROUCHO MARX (1895-1977), U.S. comic actor. *Groucho and Me*, ch. 1 (1959).

4 Kissing don't last: cookery do!

> GEORGE MEREDITH (1828-1909), English author. Mrs. Berry, in *The Ordeal of Richard Feverel*, ch. 28 (1859).

5 We may live without poetry, music and art;
We may live without conscience, and live without
 heart;
We may live without friends; we may live without
 books;
But civilized man cannot live without cooks.

> OWEN MEREDITH (EDWARD R. BULWER, EARL OF LYTTON) (1831-91), English poet, diplomat. *Lucile*, pt. 1, cto.2, st. 19.

6 To the old saying that man built the house but woman made of it a "home" might be added the modern supplement that woman accepted cooking as a chore but man has made of it a recreation.

> EMILY POST (1873-1960), U.S. hostess. *Etiquette*, ch. 34 (1922).

7 'Tis an ill cook that cannot lick his own fingers.

> WILLIAM SHAKESPEARE (1564-1616), English dramatist, poet. Servingman, in *Romeo and Juliet*, act 4, sc. 2.

8 To make a good salad is to be a brilliant diplomatist—the problem is entirely the same in both cases. To know exactly how much oil one must put with one's vinegar.

> OSCAR WILDE (1854-1900), Anglo-Irish playwright, author. Prince Paul, in *Vera, or The Nihilists*, (1880).

9 There is no spectacle on earth more appealing than that of a beautiful woman in the act of cooking dinner for someone she loves.

> THOMAS WOLFE (1900-1938), U.S. author. *The Web and the Rock*, ch. 28 (1939)

CORRESPONDENCE

1 And none will hear the postman's knock
Without a quickening of the heart.
For who can bear to feel himself forgotten?

> W. H. AUDEN (1907-73), Anglo-American poet. *Night Mail*.

2 A person who can write a long letter with ease, cannot write ill.

> JANE AUSTEN (1775-1817), English novelist. Miss Bingley, in *Pride and Prejudice*, ch. 10 (1813).

3 The post-office had a great charm at one period of our lives. When you have lived to my age, you will begin to think letters are never worth going through the rain for.

> JANE AUSTEN (1775-1817), English novelist. Mr. John Knightley, in *Emma*, ch. 34 (1816).

4 As cold waters to a thirsty soul, so is good news from a far country.

> BIBLE, HEBREW. *Proverbs* 25:25.

5 Any relic of the dead is precious, if they were valued living.

> EMILY BRONTË (1818-48), English novelist, poet. Ellen Dean, in *Wuthering Heights*, ch. 13 (1847), said of a letter she has received from Isabella, unhappily married to Heathcliff.

6 Politeness is as much concerned in answering letters within a reasonable time, as it is in returning a bow, immediately.

> LORD CHESTERFIELD (1694-1773), English statesman, man of letters. Letter, 15 Sept. 1768 (published in *Lord Chesterfield's Letters to His Godson*, no. 202, ed. by Earl of Carnarvon, 1889).

7 Sir, more than kisses, letters mingle souls.
For, thus friends absent speak.

> JOHN DONNE (c. 1572-1631), English divine, metaphysical poet. *Verse Letter to Sir Henry Wotton*.

8 How frail and ephemeral . . . is the material substance of letters, which makes their very survival so hazardous. Print has a permanence of its own, though it may not be much worth preserving, but a letter! Conveyed by uncertain transportation, over which the sender has no control; committed to a single individual who may be careless or inappreciative; left to the mercy of future generations, of families maybe anxious to suppress the past, of the accidents of removals and house-cleanings, or of mere ignorance. How often it has been by the veriest chance that they have survived at all.

> ELIZABETH DREW (1887-1965), Anglo-American author, critic. *The Literature of Gossip*, "The Literature of Gossip" (1964).

9 A woman's best love letters are always written to the man she is betraying.

> LAWRENCE DURRELL (1912-90), British author. Justine, in *Clea*, pt. 1, ch. 4 (1960).

10 Life is too precious to be spent in this weaving and unweaving of false impressions, and it is better to live quietly under some degree of misrepresentation than to attempt to remove it by the uncertain process of letter-writing.

> GEORGE ELIOT (1819-80), English novelist. Letter, 8 June 1856 (published in *George Eliot's Life as Related in Her Letters and Journals*, 1885-86).

11 Letters are above all useful as a means of expressing the ideal self; and no other method of communication is quite so good for this purpose. . . . In letters we can reform without practice, beg without humiliation, snip and shape embarrassing experiences to the measure of our own desires. . . .

> ELIZABETH HARDWICK (1916), U.S. author, critic. *A View of My Own*, "Anderson, Millay and Crane in Their Letters" (1962; first published 1953).

12 Or don't you like to write letters. I do because it's such a swell way to keep from working and yet feel you've done something.

> ERNEST HEMINGWAY (1899-1961), U.S. author. Post scriptum to letter, 1 July 1925, to F. Scott Fitzgerald (published in *Ernest Hemingway: Selected Letters*, 1981).

13 A short letter to a distant friend is, in my opinion, an insult like that of a slight bow or cursory salutation—a proof of unwillingness to do much, even where there is a necessity of doing something.

> SAMUEL JOHNSON (1709-84), English author, lexicographer. Letter, 10 June 1761 (published in James Boswell, *Life of Samuel Johnson*, 1791).

14 In a man's letters you know, Madam, his soul lies naked, his letters are only the mirror of his breast, whatever passes within him is shown undisguised in its natural process. Nothing is inverted, nothing distorted, you see systems in their elements, you discover actions in their motives.

> SAMUEL JOHNSON (1709-84), English author, lexicographer. Letter, 27 Oct. 1777, to Hester Thrale (published in *The Letters of Samuel Johnson*, vol. 2, no. 559, ed. by R. W. Chapman, 1952). In his biography, Johnson is reported as saying, "It is now become so much the fashion to publish letters, that in order to avoid it, I put as little into mine as I can." (To which Boswell answered, "Do what you will, Sir, you cannot avoid it. Should you even write as ill as you can, your letters would be published as curiosities.")

15 I hold that the parentheses are by far the most important parts of a non-business letter.

> D. H. LAWRENCE (1885-1930), British author. Letter, 15 April 1908 (published in *The Letters of D. H. Lawrence*, vol. 1, ed. by James T. Boulton, 1979).

16 It does me good to write a letter which is not a response to a demand, a gratuitous letter, so to speak, which has accumulated in me like the waters of a reservoir.

> HENRY MILLER (1891-1980), U.S. author. *The Books in My Life*, ch. 12 (1951).

17 A letter is an unannounced visit, the postman the agent of rude surprises. One ought to reserve an hour a week for receiving letters and afterwards take a bath.

> FRIEDRICH NIETZSCHE (1844-1900), German philosopher. *The Wanderer and His Shadow*, aph. 261 (1880).

18 Correspondences are like smallclothes before the invention of suspenders; it is impossible to keep them up.

> SYDNEY SMITH (1771-1845), English journalist, clergyman, wit. Letter, 31 Jan. 1841.

19 A man who publishes his letters becomes a nudist—nothing shields him from the world's gaze except his bare skin. A writer, writing away, can always fix himself up to make himself more presentable, but a man who has written a letter is stuck with it for all time.

> E. B. WHITE (1899-1985), U.S. author, editor. Letter, 11 June 1975.

See also Waugh on COURTESY; Johnson on EXAMPLE.

CORRUPTION

1 Life is a corrupting process from the time a child learns to play his mother off against his father in the politics of when to go to bed; he who fears corruption fears life.

> SAUL ALINSKY (1909-72), U.S. radical activist. *Rules for Radicals*, "Of Means and Ends" (1971).

2 Among a people generally corrupt, liberty cannot long exist.

> EDMUND BURKE (1729-97), Irish philosopher, statesman. *Letter to the Sheriffs of Bristol*, 3 April 1777 (published in *Works*, vol. 2).

3 Wherever you see a man who gives someone else's corruption, someone else's prejudice as a reason for not taking action himself, you see a cog in The Machine that governs us.

> JOHN JAY CHAPMAN (1862-1933), U.S. author. *Practical Agitation*, ch. 1 (1898).

4 Corruption, the most infallible symptom of constitutional liberty.

> EDWARD GIBBON (1737-94), English historian. *The Decline and Fall of the Roman Empire*, ch. 219 (1776-88).

5 I have often noticed that a bribe. . . has that effect—it changes a relation. The man who offers a bribe gives away a little of his own importance; the bribe once accepted, he becomes the inferior, like a man who has paid for a woman.

> GRAHAM GREENE (1904-91), British novelist. *The Comedians*, pt. 1, ch. 4, sct. 3 (1966).

6 I am against government by crony.

> HAROLD L. ICKES (1874-1952), U.S. Republican politician. Speech, Feb. 1946, on resigning from his post as Secretary of the Interior, referring to President Truman's award of government positions to old friends.

7 Corruption is worse than prostitution. The latter might endanger the morals of an individual, the former invariably endangers the morals of the entire country.

> KARL KRAUS (1874-1936), Austrian satirist. *Morality and Criminal Justice*, title essay (1908; first published in *Die Fackel*, 1902).

8 The sun shineth upon the dunghill, and is not corrupted.

> JOHN LYLY (1554-1606), English author. *Euphues: The Anatomy of Wit*, p. 43 (1578).

9 The accomplice to the crime of corruption is frequently our own indifference.

> BESS MYERSON (b. 1924), U.S. government official, columnist. Quoted in: Claire Safran, "Impeachment?" (published in *Redbook*, New York, April 1974).

10 When rich villains have need of poor ones, poor ones may make what price they will.

> WILLIAM SHAKESPEARE (1564-1616), English dramatist, poet. Borachio, in *Much Ado About Nothing*, act 3, sc. 3.

11 The jingling of the guinea helps the hurt that Honour feels.

> LORD TENNYSON (1809-92), English poet. *Locksley Hall*.

12 There is no odor so bad as that which arises from goodness tainted.

> HENRY DAVID THOREAU (1817-62), U.S. philosopher, author, naturalist. *Walden,* "Economy" (1854).

13 When I want to buy up any politician I always find the anti-monopolists the most purchasable—they don't come so high.

> WILLIAM VANDERBILT (1821-85), U.S. industrialist. *Chicago Daily News* (9 Oct. 1882).

See also French National Assembly on CIVIL RIGHTS; Kennedy on ELECTIONS; Wolfe on JOURNALISM AND JOURNALISTS; Roosevelt on PUBLIC OFFICE; Chesterton on WEALTH.

COSMETICS

1 Isn't that the problem? That women have been swindled for centuries into substituting adornment for love, fashion (as it were) for passion? . . . All the cosmetics names seemed obscenely obvious to me in their promises of sexual bliss. They were all firming or uplifting or invigorating. They made you *tingle.* Or *glow.* Or feel *young.* They were prepared with hormones or placentas or royal jelly. All the juice and joy missing in the lives of these women were to be supplied by the contents of jars and bottles. No wonder they would spend twenty dollars for an ounce of face makeup or thirty for a half-ounce of hormone cream. What price bliss? What price sexual ecstasy?

> ERICA JONG (b. 1942), U.S. author. *How To Save Your Own Life,* "A day in the life . . ." (1977).

2 God hath given you one face, and you make yourselves another.

> WILLIAM SHAKESPEARE (1564-1616), English dramatist, poet. Hamlet to Ophelia, in *Hamlet,* act 3, sc. 1.

3 Women have face-lifts in a society in which women without them appear to vanish from sight.

> NAOMI WOLF (b. 1962), U.S. author. *The Beauty Myth,* "Violence" (1990).

THE COSMOS

1 Why I came here, I know not; where I shall go it is useless to enquire—in the midst of myriads of the living & the dead worlds, stars, systems, infinity, why should I be anxious about an atom?

> LORD BYRON (1788-1824), English poet. Letter, 3 March 1814, to Annabella Milbanke, later Lady Byron (published in *Byron's Letters and Journals,* vol. 4, ed. by Leslie Marchand, 1975).

2 The cosmos is about the smallest hole that a man can hide his head in.

> G. K. CHESTERTON (1874-1936), British author. *Orthodoxy,* ch. 1 (1909).

3 Nothing puzzles me more than time and space; and yet nothing troubles me less, as I never think about them.

> CHARLES LAMB (1775-1834), English essayist, critic. Letter, 2 Jan. 1810, to Thomas Manning.

4 To sum up: 1. The cosmos is a gigantic fly-wheel making 10,000 revolutions a minute. 2. Man is a sick fly taking a dizzy ride on it. 3. Religion is the theory that the wheel was designed and set spinning to give him the ride.

> H. L. MENCKEN (1880-1956), U.S. journalist. "Coda," in *Smart Set* (New York, Dec. 1920; repr. in *A Mencken Chrestomathy,* pt. 1, 1949).

5 How have I been able to live so long outside Nature without identifying myself with it? Everything lives, moves, everything corresponds; the magnetic rays, emanating either from myself or from others, cross the limitless chain of created things unimpeded; it is a transparent network that covers the world, and its slender threads communicate themselves by degrees to the planets and stars. Captive now upon earth, I commune with the chorus of the stars who share in my joys and sorrows.

> GÉRARD DE NERVAL (1808-55), French novelist, poet. *Aurélia,* pt. 2, ch. 6 (1855; repr. in *Selected Writings,* ed. and tr. by Geoffrey Wagner, 1958).

6 All things by immortal power,
Near and Far
Hiddenly
To each other linked are,
That thou canst not stir a flower
Without troubling of a star.

> FRANCIS THOMPSON (1859-1907), English poet. *The Mistress of Vision.*

7 Philosophy offers the rather cold consolation that perhaps we and our planet do not actually exist; religion presents the contradictory and scarcely more comforting thought that we exist but that we cannot hope to get anywhere until we cease to exist. Alcohol, in attempting to resolve the contradiction, produces vivid patterns of Truth which vanish like snow in the morning sun and cannot be recalled; the revelations of poetry are as wonderful as a comet in the skies—and as mysterious. Love, which was once believed to contain the Answer, we now know to be nothing more than an inherited behavior pattern.

> JAMES THURBER (1894-1961), U.S. humorist, illustrator. *Collecting Himself,* "Thinking Ourselves Into Trouble," pt. 1 (1989; first published 1939).

See also Carlyle on the UNIVERSE.

COUNTRY LIFE

1 Cow dung and horse dung, as muck goes, are relatively agreeable. You can even become nostalgic about them. They smell of fermented grain, and on the far side of their smell there is hay and grass.

> JOHN BERGER (b. 1926), British author, critic. *Muck and Its Entanglements,* in *Harper's* (New York, May 1989; repr. in *Keeping a Rendezvous,* as "A Load of Shit," 1992).

2 The country is laid out in a haphazard, sloppy fashion, offensive to the tidy, organized mind.

> ALAN BRIEN (b. 1925), British novelist, humorist. *Punch* (London, 22 March 1979).

3 I live not in myself, but I become
Portion of that around me; and to me
High mountains are a feeling, but the hum
Of human cities torture.

> LORD BYRON (1788-1824), English poet. *Childe Harold's Pilgrimage*, cto. 3, st. 72 (1812).

4 Nothing ages a woman like living in the country.

> COLETTE (1873-1954), French novelist. *Music Hall Sidelights*, "On Tour" (1913).

5 I nauseate walking; 'Tis a country diversion; I loathe the country.

> WILLIAM CONGREVE (1670-1729), English dramatist. Mrs. Millamant, in *The Way of the World*, act 4, sc. 4.

6 It is only in the country that we can get to know a fellow-being or a book.

> CYRIL CONNOLLY (1903-74), British critic. *The Unquiet Grave*, pt. 3 (1944; rev. 1951).

7 The lowest and vilest alleys of London do not present a more dreadful record of sin than does the smiling and beautiful countryside.

> SIR ARTHUR CONAN DOYLE (1859-1930), English author. Sherlock Holmes to Watson, in *The Adventures of Sherlock Holmes*, "Copper Beeches" (1892).

8 The country is not paradise, and can show the vices that grieve a good man everywhere. But there is room in it, and leisure.

> E. M. FORSTER (1879-1970), British novelist, essayist. *The Longest Journey*, ch. 33 (1907).

9 There is nothing good to be had in the country, or if there is, they will not let you have it.

> WILLIAM HAZLITT (1778-1830), English essayist. *Political Essays*, "Observations on Mr. Wordsworth's *Excursion*" (1819).

10 Country people do not behave as if they think life is short; they live on the principle that it is long, and savor variations of the kind best appreciated if most days are the same.

> EDWARD HOAGLAND (b. 1932), U.S. novelist, essayist. "The Ridge-Slope Fox and the Knife Thrower," in *Harper's* (New York, Jan. 1977; repr. in *Heart's Desire*, 1988).

11 In the end, for congenial sympathy, for poetry, for work, for original feeling and expression, for perfect companionship with one's friends—give me the country.

> D. H. LAWRENCE (1885-1930), British author. Letter, 28 Feb. 1909 (published in *The Letters of D. H. Lawrence*, vol. 1, ed. by James T. Boulton, 1979).

12 To put it rather bluntly, I am not the type who wants to go back to the land; I am the type who wants to go back to the hotel.

> FRAN LEBOWITZ (b. 1951), U.S. journalist. *Social Studies*, "Things" (1981).

13 The village had institutionalized all human functions in forms of low intensity. . . . Participation was high and organization was low. This is the formula for stability.

> MARSHALL MCLUHAN (1911-80), Canadian communications theorist. *Understanding Media*, ch. 10 (1964).

14 One day in the country
Is worth a month in town.

> CHRISTINA ROSSETTI (1830-94), English poet, lyricist. *Summer*.

15 And this our life, exempt from public haunt,
Finds tongues in trees, books in the running brooks,
Sermons in stones, and good in everything.

> WILLIAM SHAKESPEARE (1564-1616), English dramatist, poet. Duke Senior, in *As You Like It*, act 2, sc. 1.

16 O Lord! I don't know which is the worst of the country, the walking or the sitting at home with nothing to do.

> GEORGE BERNARD SHAW (1856-1950), Anglo-Irish playwright, critic. Mrs. Warren, in *Mrs. Warren's Profession*, act 2.

17 Anybody can be good in the country. There are no temptations there.

> OSCAR WILDE (1854-1900), Anglo-Irish playwright, author. Lord Henry, in *The Picture of Dorian Gray*, ch. 19 (1891).

See also TOWN AND COUNTRY.

COURAGE

1 Until the day of his death, no man can be sure of his courage.

> JEAN ANOUILH (1910-87), French playwright. Thomas à Becket, in *Becket*, act 1.

2 It is the perpetual dread of fear, *the fear of fear*, that shapes the face of a brave man.

> GEORGES BERNANOS (1888-1948), French novelist, political writer. M. Olivier, in *The Diary of a Country Priest*, ch. 7 (1936).

3 The French courage proceeds from vanity—the German from phlegm—the Turkish from fanaticism & opium—the Spanish from pride—the English from coolness—the Dutch from obstinacy—the Russian from insensibility—but the Italian from anger.

> LORD BYRON (1788-1824), English poet. Letter, 31 Aug. 1820, to publisher John Murray (published in *Byron's Letters and Journals*, vol. 7, ed. by Leslie A. Marchand, 1973-81).

4 "I'm very brave generally," he went on in a low voice: "only today I happen to have a headache."

> LEWIS CARROLL (1832-98), English writer, mathematician. Tweedledum, in *Through the Looking-Glass*, ch. 4 (1872).

5 Brave men are all vertebrates; they have their softness on the surface and their toughness in the middle.

> G. K. CHESTERTON (1874-1936), British author. *Tremendous Trifles*, "The Prehistoric Railway Station" (1909).

6 Courage is almost a contradiction in terms. It means a strong desire to live taking the form of a readiness to die.

> G. K. CHESTERTON (1874-1936), British author. *Orthodoxy*, ch. 6 (1909).

7 Courage is the price that Life exacts for granting peace,
The soul that knows it not, knows no release
From little things.

> AMELIA EARHART (1897-1937), U.S. aviator, author. "Courage" (1927; published in Mary S. Lovell, *The Sound of Wings*, ch. 1, 1989).

8 Nothing gives a fearful man more courage than another's fear.

> UMBERTO ECO (b. 1932), Italian semiologist, novelist. *The Name of the Rose*, "Third Day: After Compline" (1980; tr. 1983).

9 Courage charms us, because it indicates that a man loves an idea better than all things in the world, that he is thinking neither of his bed, nor his dinner, nor his money, but will venture all to put in act the invisible thought of his mind.

> RALPH WALDO EMERSON (1803-82), U.S. essayist, poet, philosopher. *Journals* (1909-1914), entry in 1859.

10 Grace under pressure.

> ERNEST HEMINGWAY (1899-1961), U.S. author. *New Yorker* (30 Nov. 1929). Definition of "guts." The formula was adopted by John F. Kennedy at the start of his collection of essays, *Profiles of Courage* (1956); it possibly originated in the Latin motto, *Fortiter in re, suaviter in modo.*

11 Courage without conscience is a wild beast.

> ROBERT G. INGERSOLL (1833-99), U.S. lawyer, orator. Speech, 29 May 1882, New York City.

12 Courage is a quality so necessary for maintaining virtue, that it is always respected, even when it is associated with vice.

> SAMUEL JOHNSON (1709-1784), English author, lexicographer. Quoted in: James Boswell, *Life of Samuel Johnson,* 11 June 1784 (1791).

13 You take a number of small steps which you believe are right, thinking maybe tomorrow somebody will treat this as a dangerous provocation. And then you wait. If there is no reaction, you take another step: courage is only an accumulation of small steps.

> GEORGE KONRÁD (b. 1933), Hungarian writer, politician. *Sunday Correspondent* (London, 15 April 1990), on surviving as a writer in Communist Hungary.

14 Perfect courage is to do without witnesses what one would be capable of doing with the world looking on.

> FRANÇOIS, DUC DE LA ROCHEFOUCAULD (1613-80), French writer, moralist. *Sentences et Maximes Morales,* no. 216 (1678).

15 Courage is not simply *one* of the virtues but the form of every virtue at the testing point, which means at the point of highest reality.

> C. S. LEWIS (1898-1963), British author. Quoted in: Cyril Connoly, *The Unquiet Grave,* pt. 3 (1944; rev. 1951).

16 Some have been thought brave because they were afraid to run away.

> 18TH-CENTURY ENGLISH PROVERB. Collected in: Thomas Fuller, *Gnomologia* (1732).

17 Valor is common but great souls are rare.

> BERNARD JOSEPH SAURIN (1706-81), French dramatist. Spartacus, in *Spartacus,* act 3, sc. 1.

18 When valour preys on reason,
It eats the sword it fights with.

> WILLIAM SHAKESPEARE (1564-1616), English dramatist, poet. Enobarbus, in *Antony and Cleopatra,* act 3, sc. 13.

19 But screw your courage to the sticking-place
And we'll not fail.

> WILLIAM SHAKESPEARE (1564-1616), English dramatist, poet.

Lady Macbeth to Macbeth, in *Macbeth,* act 1, sc. 7, exhorting him to carry out the murder of Duncan.

20 Valor is of no service, chance rules all, and the bravest often fall by the hands of cowards.

> TACITUS c. 55-C. 120), Roman historian. *The Histories,* bk. 4, sct. 29.

21 Courage is resistance to fear, mastery of fear—not absence of fear. Except a creature be part coward it is not a compliment to say it is brave; it is merely a loose application of the word. Consider the flea!—incomparably the bravest of all the creatures of God, if ignorance of fear were courage.

> MARK TWAIN (1835-1910), U.S. author. *Pudd'nhead Wilson,* ch. 12, "Pudd'nhead Wilson's Calendar" (1894).

COURTESY

1 It is wise to apply the oil of refined politeness to the mechanism of friendship.

> COLETTE (1873-1954), French author. *The Pure and the Impure,* ch. 9 (1933; tr. 1966).

2 We must be as courteous to a man as we are to a picture, which we are willing to give the advantage of a good light.

> RALPH WALDO EMERSON (1803-82), U.S. essayist, poet, philosopher. *The Conduct of Life,* "Behavior" (1860).

3 There can be no defence like elaborate courtesy.

> E. V. LUCAS (1868-1938), British journalist, essayist. *Reading, Writing and Remembering,* ch. 8 (1932).

4 His courtesy was somewhat extravagant. He would write and thank people who wrote to thank him for wedding presents and when he encountered anyone as punctilious as himself the correspondence ended only with death.

> EVELYN WAUGH (1903-66), British novelist. *Life* (New York, 8 April 1946).

See also MANNERS.

COWARDICE

1 He was just a coward and that was the worst luck any man could have.

> ERNEST HEMINGWAY (1899-1961), U.S. author. Robert Jordan, in *For Whom the Bell Tolls,* ch. 30 (1940), said of his father.

2 Cowardice, as distinguished from panic, is almost always simply a lack of ability to suspend the functioning of the imagination.

> ERNEST HEMINGWAY (1899-1961), U.S. author. *Men at War,* Introduction (1942).

3 When cowardice is made respectable, its followers are without number both from among the weak and the strong; it easily becomes a fashion.

> ERIC HOFFER (1902-83), U.S. philosopher. *The Passionate State of Mind,* aph. 203 (1955).

4 I'm a hero with coward's legs.

SPIKE MILLIGAN (b. 1918), British comedian, humorous writer. *Puckoon*, ch. 2 (1963).

5   That man is not truly brave who is afraid either to seem or to be, when it suits him, a coward.

EDGAR ALLAN POE (1809-45), U.S. poet, critic, short-story writer. *Marginalia*, in *Graham's Magazine* (Philadelphia, Dec. 1846; repr. in *Essays and Reviews*, 1984).

6   Cowards die many times before their deaths;
The valiant never taste of death but once.

WILLIAM SHAKESPEARE (1564-1616), English dramatist, poet. Julius Caesar, in *Julius Caesar*, act 2, sc. 2. Caesar disregards objections to his departure on the Ides of March for the Capitol, where he is to be assassinated.

7   Man gives every reason for his conduct save one, every excuse for his crimes save one, every plea for his safety save one; and that one is his cowardice.

GEORGE BERNARD SHAW (1856-1950), Anglo-Irish playwright, critic. Don Juan, in *Man and Superman*, act 3.

8   My valour is certainly going, it is sneaking off! I feel it oozing out as it were, at the palms of my hands!

RICHARD BRINSLEY SHERIDAN (1751-1816), Anglo-Irish dramatist. Acres, in *The Rivals*, act 5, sc. 2.

9   For all men would be cowards if they durst.

JOHN WILMOT, SECOND EARL OF ROCHESTER (1647-80), English poet, courtier. *A Satire against Mankind*.

See also Shaw on HEROES; Twain on TEMPTATION.

CRAFTS

1   A man cannot make a pair of shoes rightly unless he do it in a devout manner.

THOMAS CARLYLE (1795-1881), Scottish essayist, historian. Letter, 22 Oct. 1842.

2   The irregular and intimate quality of things made entirely by the human hand.

WILLA CATHER (1873-1947), U.S. author. *Death Comes for the Archbishop*, bk. 1, ch. 3 (1927).

3   History repeats itself, but the special call of an art which has passed away is never reproduced. It is as utterly gone out of the world as the song of a destroyed wild bird.

JOSEPH CONRAD (1857-1924) , Polish-born English novelist. *The Mirror of the Sea*, ch. 8 (1906).

4   It is the privilege of any human work which is well done to invest the doer with a certain haughtiness. He can well afford not to conciliate, whose faithful work will answer for him.

RALPH WALDO EMERSON (1803-82), U.S. essayist, poet, philosopher. *The Conduct of Life*, "Wealth" (1860).

5   Let a human being throw the energies of his soul into the making of something, and the instinct of workmanship will take care of his honesty.

WALTER LIPPMANN (1889-1974), U.S. journalist. *A Preface to Politics*, ch. 3 (1914).

6   No man who is occupied in doing a very difficult thing, and doing it very well, ever loses his self-respect.

GEORGE BERNARD SHAW (1856-1950), Anglo-Irish playwright, critic. *The Doctor's Dilemma*, Preface, "The Psychology of Self-Respect in Surgeons" (1911).

7   The Artist is he who detects and applies the law from observation of the works of Genius, whether of man or Nature. The Artisan is he who merely applies the rules which others have detected.

HENRY DAVID THOREAU (1817-62), U.S. philosopher, author, naturalist. *A Week on the Concord and Merrimac Rivers*, "Sunday" (1849).

THE CREATION

1   If the Lord Almighty had consulted me before embarking upon Creation, I should have recommended something simpler.

ATTRIBUTED TO ALFONSO X (1221-84), King of Castile and Leon. On hearing an explanation of the Ptolemaic system of astronomy.

2   God's first creature, which was light.

FRANCIS BACON (1561-1626), English philosopher, essayist, statesman. *New Atlantis*, sct. 14 (1627).

3   And the Lord God formed man of the dust of the ground, and breathed into his nostrils the breath of life; and man became a living soul.

BIBLE, HEBREW. *Genesis* 2:7.

4   Man was kreated a little lower than the angells and has bin gittin a little lower ever sinse.

JOSH BILLINGS [HENRY WHEELER SHAW] (1818-85), U.S. humorist. *Josh Billings, His Sayings*, ch. 28 (1865).

5   Every man is as heaven made him, and sometimes a great deal worse.

MIGUEL DE CERVANTES (1547-1616), Spanish writer. Sancho Panza, in *Don Quixote*, pt. 2, bk. 5, ch. 4 (1615; tr. by P. Motteux).

6   when god decided to invent
everything he took one
breath bigger than a circustent
and everything began

E. E. CUMMINGS (1894-1962), U.S. poet. *when god decided to invent*.

7   Imagine spending four billion years stocking the oceans with seafood, filling the ground with fossil fuels, and drilling the bees in honey production—only to produce a race of bed-wetters!

BARBARA EHRENREICH (b. 1941), U.S. author, columnist. *The Worst Years of Our Lives*, "The Great Syringe Tide" (1991; first published as *Mother Jones*, 1988).

8   Thou didst create the night, but I made the lamp.
Thou didst create clay, but I made the cup.
Thou didst create the deserts, mountains and
   forests,
I produced the orchards, gardens and groves.
It is I who made the glass out of stone,
And it is I who turn a poison into an antidote.

SIR MUHAMMAD IQBAL (1873-1938), Indian poet, philosopher. Quoted in: Anita Desai, *The Clear Light of Day*, ch. 2 (1980).

9 There are innumerable questions to which the inquisitive mind can in this state receive no answer: Why do you and I exist? Why was this world created? Since it was to be created, why was it not created sooner?

> SAMUEL JOHNSON (1709-84), English author, lexicographer. Quoted in: James Boswell, *Life of Samuel Johnson*, 9 May 1778 (1791).

10 In the beginning was the Word. Man acts it out. He is the act, not the actor.

> HENRY MILLER (1891-1980), U.S. author. *The World of Sex* (1940; repr. 1970, p. 119).

11 God made man merely to hear some praise
Of what he'd done on those Five Days.

> CHRISTOPHER MORLEY (1890-1957), U.S. novelist, journalist, poet. *Fons et Origo*.

12 Have We not made the earth as a cradle
and the mountains as pegs?
And We created you in pairs,
and We appointed your sleep for a rest;
and We appointed night for a garment,
and We appointed day for a livelihood.
And We have built above you seven strong ones,
and We appointed a blazing lamp
and have sent down out of the rain-clouds water
   cascading
that We may bring forth thereby grain and plants,
   and gardens luxuriant.

> QUR'AN. *The Tiding* 78:6-16 (ed. by Arthur J. Arberry, 1955).

13 We have seen when the earth had to be prepared for the habitation of man, a veil, as it were, of intermediate being was spread between him and its darkness, in which were joined in a subdued measure, the stability and insensibilty of the earth, and the passion and perishing of mankind.

> JOHN RUSKIN (1819-1900), English art critic, author. *Modern Painters*, vol. 5, pt. 7, ch. 1, sct. 1 (1860).

14 None merits the name of Creator but God and the poet.

> TORQUATO TASSO (1544-95), Italian poet. Oft-quoted by Shelley in his letters and essays, this quotation is not found *verbatim* in Tasso's work, but in substance it is in *Discorsi del Poema Eroico*.

15 Why *was* the human race created? Or at least why wasn't something creditable created in place of it? God had His opportunity. He could have made a reputation. But no, He must commit this grotesque folly—a lark which must have cost Him a regret or two when He came to think it over & observe effects.

> MARK TWAIN (1835-1910), U.S. author. Letter, 25 Jan. 1900, to W. D. Howells (published in *The Twain-Howells Letters*, vol. 2, ed. by Henry Nash Smith and William M. Gibson, 1960).

CREATIVITY

1 Whatever creativity is, it is in part a solution to a problem.

> BRIAN ALDISS (b. 1925), British science fiction writer. *Bury My Heart at W. H. Smith's*, "Apéritif" (1990).

2 No one has ever written, painted, sculpted, modeled, built, or invented except literally to get out of hell.

> ANTONIN ARTAUD (1896-1948), French theater producer, actor, theorist. *Van Gogh, the Man Suicided by Society* (1947; repr. in *Selected Writings*, pt. 33, ed. by Susan Sontag, 1976).

3 All works of art are commissioned in the sense that no artist can create one by a simple act of will but must wait until what he believes to be a good idea for a work "comes" to him.

> W. H. AUDEN (1907-73), Anglo-American poet. *The Dyer's Hand*, pt. 1, "Writing" (1962).

4 I must create a system or be enslaved by another man's;
I will not reason and compare: my business is to create.

> WILLIAM BLAKE (1757-1827), English poet, painter, engraver. Los, in *Jerusalem*, ch. 1, plate 10.

5 Make visible what, without you, might perhaps never have been seen.

> ROBERT BRESSON (b. 1907), French film director. *Notes on the Cinematographer*, "1950-1958: The Real" (1975).

6 It's like driving a car at night. You never see further than your headlights, but you can make the whole trip that way.

> E. L. DOCTOROW (b. 1931), U.S. novelist. Interview in *Writers at Work* (Eighth Series, ed. by George Plimpton, 1988), said of his writing technique.

7 All in all, the creative act is not performed by the artist alone; the spectator brings the work in contact with the external world by deciphering and interpreting its inner qualifications and thus adds his contribution to the creative act. This becomes even more obvious when posterity gives its final verdict and sometimes rehabilitates forgotten artists.

> MARCEL DUCHAMP (1887-1968), French artist. "The Creative Act," lecture, April 1957, in Houston, Texas (published in *Art News*, New York, Summer 1957; repr. in Robert Lebel, *Marcel Duchamp*, 1959).

8 I have asked a lot of my emotions—one hundred and twenty stories. The price was high, right up with Kipling, because there was one little drop of something, not blood, not a tear, not my seed, but me more intimately than these, in every story, it was the extra I had. Now it has gone and I am just like you now.

> F. SCOTT FITZGERALD (1896-1940), U.S. author. *The Crack-Up*, "Notebook J: Our April Letter" (ed. by Edmund Wilson, 1945).

9 We try not to have ideas, preferring accidents. To create, you must empty yourself of every artistic thought.

> GILBERT [OF GILBERT AND GEORGE] (b. 1943), Italian-born British artist. *Independent* (London, 17 April 1989).

10 From things that have happened and from things as they exist and from all things that you know and all those you cannot know, you make something through your invention that is not a representation but a whole new thing truer than anything true and alive, and you make it alive, and if you make it well enough, you give it immortality. That is why you write and for no other reason that you know of. But what about all the reasons that no one knows?

ERNEST HEMINGWAY (1899-1961), U.S. author. Interview in *Paris Review* (Flushing, N.Y., Spring 1958; repr. in *Writers at Work*, Second Series, ed. by George Plimpton, 1963).

11 Is not the tremendous strength in men of the impulse to creative work in every field precisely due to their feeling of playing a relatively small part in the creation of living beings, which constantly impels them to an overcompensation in achievement?

KAREN HORNEY (1885-1952), U.S. psychiatrist. *Feminine Psychology*, "The Flight from Womanhood" (1926).

12 Americans worship creativity the way they worship physical beauty—as a way of enjoying elitism without guilt: God did it.

FLORENCE KING (b. 1936), U.S. author. *Reflections in a Jaundiced Eye*, "Democracy" (1989).

13 Everything vanishes around me, and works are born as if out of the void. Ripe, graphic fruits fall off. My hand has become the obedient instrument of a remote will.

PAUL KLEE (1879-1940), Swiss artist. *The Diaries of Paul Klee 1898-1918*, no. 1104 (1957; tr. 1965), entry for Jan./Feb. 1918.

14 True creativity often starts where language ends.

ARTHUR KOESTLER (1905-83), Hungarian-born British novelist, essayist. *The act of Creation*, bk. 1, pt. 2, ch. 7 (1964).

15 All the lies and evasions by which man has nourished himself—*civilization*, in a word—are the fruits of the creative artist. It is the creative nature of man which has refused to let him lapse back into that unconscious unity with life which charactizes the animal world from which he made his escape.

HENRY MILLER (1891-1980), U.S. author. *The Wisdom of the Heart*, "Creative Death" (1947).

16 The desire to create continually is vulgar and betrays jealousy, envy, ambition. If one is something one really does not need to make anything—and one nonetheless does very much. There exists above the "productive" man a yet higher species.

FRIEDRICH NIETZSCHE (1844-1900), German philosopher. *Human, All Too Human*, aph. 210 (1878).

17 We live at a time when man believes himself fabulously capable of creation, but he does not know what to create.

JOSÉ ORTEGA Y GASSET (1883-1955), Spanish essayist, philosopher. *The Revolt of the Masses*, ch. 4 (1930).

18 I understood that all the material of a literary work was in my past life, I understood that I had acquired it in the midst of frivolous amusements, in idleness, in tenderness and in pain, stored up by me without my divining its destination or even its survival, as the seed has in reserve all the ingredients which will nourish the plant.

MARCEL PROUST (1871-1922), French novelist. *Remembrance of Things Past*, vol. 12, "Time Regained," ch. 3 (1927; tr. by Stephen Hudson, 1931).

19 An original is a creation
motivated by desire.

Any reproduction of an original
is motivated be necessity. . .
It is marvelous that we are
the only species that creates
gratuitous forms.
To create is divine, to reproduce
is human.

MAN RAY (1890-1976), U.S. photographer. "Originals Graphic Multiples" (published in *Objets de Mon Affection*, 1983; repr. in Neil Baldwin, *Man Ray*, ch. 24, 1988).

20 Ideally a painter (and, generally, an artist) should not become conscious of his insights: without taking the detour through his reflective processes, and incomprehensibly to himself, all his progress should enter so swiftly into the work that he is unable to recognise them in the moment of transition. Alas, the artist who waits in ambush there, watching, detaining them, will find them transformed like the beautiful gold in the fairy tale which cannot remain gold because some small detail was not taken care of.

RAINER MARIA RILKE (1875-1926), German poet. Letter, 21 Oct. 1907, to Rilke's wife (published in *Rilke's Letters on Cézanne*, 1985).

21 Whoever undertakes to create soon finds himself engaged in creating himself. Self-transformation and the transformation of others have constituted the radical interest of our century, whether in painting, psychiatry, or political action.

HAROLD ROSENBERG (1906-78), U.S. art critic, author. *The Tradition of the New*, Preface (1960).

22 When all is said and done, monotony may after all be the best condition for creation.

MARGARET SACKVILLE (1881-1963), British poet. *The Works of Susan Ferrier*, vol. 1, Introduction (1929).

23 The creative person, the person who moves from an irrational source of power, has to face the fact that this power antagonizes. Under all the superficial praise of the "creative" is the desire to kill. It is the old war between the mystic and the nonmystic, a war to the death.

MAY SARTON (b. 1912), U.S. poet, novelist. *Mrs. Stevens Hears the Mermaids Singing*, pt. 2 (1965).

24 Our current obsession with creativity is the result of our continued striving for immortality in an era when most people no longer believe in an after-life.

ARIANNA STASSINOPOULOS (b. 1950), Greek author. *The Female Woman*, "The Working Woman" (1973).

25 It is almost as if you were frantically constructing another world while the world that you live in dissolves beneath your feet, and that your survival depends on completing this construction at least one second before the old habitation collapses.

TENNESSEE WILLIAMS (1914-83), U.S. dramatist. *Camino Real*, Author's Foreword, written prior to the play's Broadway première and published in *New York Times* (15 March 1953).

26 Some collaboration has to take place in the mind between the woman and the man before the art of creation can be accomplished. Some marriage of opposites has to be consummated. The whole of the mind must lie wide open if we are to get the sense that the writer is communicating his experience with perfect fullness.

VIRGINIA WOOLF (1882-1941), British novelist. *A Room of One's Own*, ch. 6 (1929).

27   A line will take us hours maybe;
Yet if it does not seem a moment's thought,
Our stitching and unstitching has been naught.

W. B. YEATS (1865-1939), Irish poet. *Adam's Curse.*

See also Burgess on DELINQUENCY; Chandler on REASON; Bronte on WRITERS.

CREDIT

1   Creditor.   One of a tribe of savages dwelling beyond the Financial Straits and dreaded for their desolating incursions.

AMBROSE BIERCE (1842-1914), U.S. author. *The Devil's Dictionary* (1881-1906).

2   O Gold! I still prefer thee unto paper,
Which makes bank credit like a bark of vapour.

LORD BYRON (1788-1824), English poet. *Don Juan*, cto. 12, st. 4.

3   A person who can't pay gets another person who can't pay to guarantee that he can pay. Like a person with two wooden legs getting another person with two wooden legs to guarantee that he has got two natural legs. It don't make either of them able to do a walking-match.

CHARLES DICKENS (1812-70), English novelist. Mr. Pancks, in *Little Dorrit*, bk. 1, ch. 23 (1855-57).

4   Blest paper-credit! last and best supply!
That lends corruption lighter wings to fly!

ALEXANDER POPE (1688-1744), English satirical poet. *Epistle to Bathurst.*

5   Beautiful credit! The foundation of modern society. Who shall say that this is not the golden age of mutual trust, of unlimited reliance upon human promises? That is a peculiar condition of society which enables a whole nation to instantly recognize point and meaning in the familiar newspaper anecdote, which puts into the mouth of a distinguished speculator in lands and mines this remark:—"I wasn't worth a cent two years ago, and now I owe two millions of dollars."

MARK TWAIN (1835-1910), U.S. author. *The Gilded Age*, ch. 26 (1873; written with Charles Dudley Warner).

CREDULITY

1   I believe we are still so innocent. The species are still so innocent that a person who is apt to be murdered believes that the murderer, just before he puts the final wrench on his throat, will have enough compassion to give him one sweet cup of water.

MAYA ANGELOU (b. 1928), U.S. author. "Work in Progress," interview (first published June 1973; repr. in *Conversations with Maya Angelou*, 1989).

2   There's a sucker born every minute.

Attributed to PHINEAS T. BARNUM (1810-1891), U.S. show-man. Barnum doubted ever having uttered these words, though he conceded he may have said, "The people like to be humbugged." See the appendix to A. H. Saxon, *P. T. Barnum: The Legend and the Man* (1989), where it is claimed that the phrase: "There's a sucker born every minute, but none of them ever die" originated with a notorious con-man known as "Paper Collar Joe" (real name, Joseph Bessimer), and was later falsely ascribed to Barnum by show-biz rival Adam Forepaugh in a newspaper interview. Barnum never took pains to deny it, and even thanked Forepaugh for the free publicity.

3   A man is his own easiest dupe, for what he wishes to be true he generally believes to be true.

DEMOSTHENES c. 384-322 B.C., Greek orator. *Third Olynthiac*, sct. 19 (349 B.C.).

4   A little credulity helps one on through life very smoothly.

ELIZABETH GASKELL (1810-65), English novelist. Miss Matty, in *Cranford*, ch. 11 (1853).

5   Our credulity is greatest concerning the things we know least about. And since we know least about ourselves, we are ready to believe all that is said about us. Hence the mysterious power of both flattery and calumny.

ERIC HOFFER (1902-1983), U.S. philosopher. *The Passionate State of Mind*, aph. 128 (1955). In the aphorism following, Hoffer added: "It is thus with most of us: we are what other people say we are. We know ourselves chiefly by hearsay."

6   A certain portion of the human race
Has certainly a taste for being diddled.

THOMAS HOOD (1799-1845), English poet. *A Black Job.*

7   I have all my life been on my guard against the information conveyed by the sense of hearing—it being one of my earliest observations, the universal inclination of humankind is to be led by the ears, and I am sometimes apt to imagine that they are given to men as they are to pitchers, purposely that they may be carried about by them.

LADY MARY WORTLEY MONTAGU (1689-1762), English society figure, letter writer. Letter, 1 March 1752, to her daughter Lady Bute (published in *Selected Letters*, ed. by Halsband, 1970).

8   One of the peculiar sins of the twentieth century which we've developed to a very high level is the sin of credulity. It has been said that when human beings stop believing in God they believe in nothing. The truth is much worse: they believe in anything.

MALCOLM MUGGERIDGE (1903-90), British broadcaster. "Woman's Hour," radio broadcast, 23 March 1966. Quoted in: *Muggeridge through the Microphone*, "An Eighth Deadly Sin" (1967).

9   Man is a credulous animal, and must believe *something*; in the absence of good grounds for belief, he will be satisfied with bad ones.

BERTRAND RUSSELL (1872-1970), British philosopher, mathematician. *Unpopular Essays*, "An Outline of Intellectual Rubbish" (1950).

10   The fact that a believer is happier than a sceptic is no more to the point than the fact that a drunken man is happier than a sober one. The happiness of credulity is a cheap and dangerous quality.

GEORGE BERNARD SHAW (1856-1950), Anglo-Irish playwright, critic. *Androcles and the Lion*, Preface (1916).

11 The most positive men are the most credulous.

JONATHAN SWIFT (1667-1745), Anglo-Irish satirist. *Thoughts on Various Subjects* (1711).

12 Man can believe the impossible, but man can never believe the improbable.

OSCAR WILDE (1854-1900), Anglo-Irish playwright, author. Vivian, in *The Decay of Lying* (published in *Intentions*, 1891).

CREEDS

1 Light half-believers of our casual creeds,
Who never deeply felt, nor clearly will'd,
Whose insight never has borne fruit in deeds,
Whose vague resolves never have been fulfill'd.

MATTHEW ARNOLD (1822-88), English poet, critic. *The Scholar-Gipsy* (1853).

2 Vain are the thousand creeds
That move men's hearts, unutterably vain;
Worthless as withered weeds,
Or idlest froth amid the boundless main.

EMILY BRONTË (1818-48), English novelist. *Last Lines*.

3 A man must not swallow more beliefs than he can digest.

HAVELOCK ELLIS (1859-1939), British psychologist. *The Dance of Life*, ch. 5 (1923).

4 As men's prayers are a disease of the will, so are their creeds a disease of the intellect.

RALPH WALDO EMERSON (1803-82), U.S. essayist, poet, philosopher. *Essays*, "Self-Reliance" (First Series, 1841).

5 There lies at the back of every creed something terrible and hard for which the worshipper may one day be required to suffer.

E. M. FORSTER (1879-1970), British novelist, essayist. *Two Cheers for Democracy*, "What I Believe" (1951).

6 I always divide people into two groups. Those who live by what they know to be a lie, and those who live by what they believe, falsely, to be the truth.

CHRISTOPHER HAMPTON (b. 1946), British playwright. Don, in *The Philanthropist*, sc. 6.

7 We hold these truths to be sacred and undeniable; that all men are created equal and independent, that from that equal creation they derive rights inherent and inalienable, among which are the preservation of life, and liberty, and the pursuit of happiness.

THOMAS JEFFERSON (1743-1826), U.S. president. Original draft of the Declaration of Independence (1776), later amended.

8 When suave politeness, tempering bigot zeal,
Corrected "I believe" to "One does feel."

RONALD KNOX (1888-1957), British scholar, priest. *Absolute and Abitofhell*.

9 If you have embraced a creed which appears to be free from the ordinary dirtiness of politics—a creed from which you yourself cannot expect to draw any material advantage—surely that proves that you are in the right?

GEORGE ORWELL (1903-50), British author. *Shooting an Elephant*, "Lear, Tolstoy and the Fool" (1950).

10 I believe in the equality of man; and I believe that religious duties consist in doing justice, loving mercy, and endeavoring to make our fellow-creatures happy.

THOMAS PAINE (1737-1809), Anglo-American political theorist, writer. *The Age of Reason*, pt. 1, "The Author's Profession of Faith" (1794).

11 I believe in Michel Angelo, Velasquez, and Rembrandt; in the might of design, the mystery of color, the redemption of all things by Beauty everlasting, and the message of Art that has made these hands blessed. Amen. Amen.

GEORGE BERNARD SHAW (1856-1950), Anglo-Irish playwright, critic. The dying artist Dubedat, in *The Doctor's Dilemma*, act 4. In a letter to the London *Evening Standard* (22 Nov. 1906), Shaw replied to criticism of this speech, which had been "reprobated on all hands as a sally of which only the bad taste of Bernard Shaw could be capable," with the admission that he had borrowed it from Richard Wagner, "An End in Paris," vol. 7 (1841; tr. by Ashton Ellis), where the dying musician begins his creed with the words, "I believe in God, Mozart, and Beethoven. . . ."

See also BELIEF; Walker on THINGS.

CRIME AND CRIMINALS

1 Stripped of ethical rationalizations and philosophical pretensions, a crime is anything that a group in power chooses to prohibit.

FREDA ADLER (b. 1934), U.S. educator, author. *Sisters in Crime*, ch. 7 (1975).

2 No punishment has ever possessed enough power of deterrence to prevent the commission of crimes. On the contrary, whatever the punishment, once a specific crime has appeared for the first time, its reappearance is more likely than its initial emergence could ever have been.

HANNAH ARENDT (1906-75), German-born U.S. political philosopher. *Eichmann in Jerusalem*, Epilogue (1963).

3 Crime is a fact of the human species, a fact of that species alone, but it is above all the secret aspect, impenetrable and hidden. Crime hides, and by far the most terrifying things are those which elude us.

GEORGES BATAILLE (1897-1962), French novelist, critic. *The Trial of Gilles de Rais*, "The Tragedy of Gilles de Rais: Sacred Monster" (1965; rev. 1991).

4 Abscond. To "move" in a mysterious way, commonly with the property of another.

AMBROSE BIERCE (1842-1914), U.S. author. *The Devil's Dictionary* (1881-1906).

5 Want of money and the distress of a thief can never be alleged as the cause of his thieving, for many honest people endure greater hardships with fortitude. We must therefore seek the cause elsewhere than in want of money, for that is the miser's passion, not the thief's.

WILLIAM BLAKE (1757-1827), English poet, painter, engraver. Letter, 23 Aug. 1799 (published in *The Letters of William Blake*, 1956).

6 The world of crime. . . is a last refuge of the authentic, uncorrupted, spontaneous event.

DANIEL J. BOORSTIN (b. 1914), U.S. historian. *The Image*, ch. 6 (1961).

7 The thief. Once committed beyond a certain point he should not worry himself too much about not being a thief any more. Thieving is God's message to him. Let him try and be a good thief.

SAMUEL BUTLER (1835-1902), English author. *Samuel Butler's Notebooks*, p. 113 (1951).

8 For centuries the death penalty, often accompanied by barbarous refinements, has been trying to hold crime in check; yet crime persists. Why? Because the instincts that are warring in man are not, as the law claims, constant forces in a state of equilibrium.

ALBERT CAMUS (1913-60), French-Algerian philosopher, author. *Resistance, Rebellion and Death*, "Reflections on the Guillotine" (1961).

9 The fear of burglars is not only the fear of being robbed, but also the fear of a sudden and unexpected clutch out of the darkness.

ELIAS CANETTI (b. 1905), Austrian novelist, philosopher. *Crowds and Power*, "The Fear of Being Touched" (1960; tr. 1962).

10 My rackets are run on strictly American lines and they're going to stay that way.

AL CAPONE (1899-1947), U.S. gangster. Interview, c. 1930, with Claud Cockburn (published in *Cockburn Sums Up*, "Mr. Capone, Philosopher," 1981).

11 Crime is terribly revealing. Try and vary your methods as you will, your tastes, your habits, your attitude of mind, and your soul is revealed by your actions.

AGATHA CHRISTIE (1891-1976), British mystery writer. Poirot, in *The ABC Murders*, ch. 17 (1936).

12 Like art and politics, gangsterism is a very important avenue of assimilation into society.

E. L. DOCTOROW (b. 1931), U.S. novelist. *International Herald Tribune* (Paris; 1 Oct. 1990).

13 Successful crimes alone are justified.

JOHN DRYDEN (1631-1700), English poet, dramatist, critic. *The Medal*.

14 There is no society known where a more or less developed criminality is not found under different forms. No people exists whose morality is not daily infringed upon. We must therefore call crime necessary and declare that it cannot be non-existent, that the fundamental conditions of social organization, as they are understood, logically imply it.

EMILE DURKHEIM (1858-1917), French sociologist. *Suicide*, bk. 3, ch. 3, sct. 1 (1897; tr. 1951).

15 Crime seems to change character when it crosses a bridge or a tunnel. In the city, crime is taken as emblematic of class and race. In the suburbs, though, it's intimate and psychological—resistant to generalization, a mystery of the individual soul.

BARBARA EHRENREICH (b. 1941), U.S. author, columnist. *The Worst Years of Our Lives*, "Marginal Men" (1991; first published 1989).

16 We cannot be sure that we ought not to regard the most criminal country as that which in some aspects possesses the highest civilisation.

HAVELOCK ELLIS (1859-1939), British psychologist. *The Dance of Life*, ch. 7 (1923).

17 Commit a crime, and the earth is made of glass.

RALPH WALDO EMERSON (1803-82), U.S. essayist, poet, philosopher. *Essays*, "Compensation" (First Series, 1841).

18 One usually dies because one is alone, or because one has got into something over one's head. One often dies because one does not have the right alliances, because one is not given support. In Sicily the Mafia kills the servants of the State that the State has not been able to protect.

GIOVANNI FALCONE (1939-92), Italian judge. *Men of Honor*, ch. 6 (1992). Falcone, along with his wife and three bodyguards, was blown up on his way into Palermo 23 May 1992.

19 Crimes, like virtues, are their own rewards.

GEORGE FARQUHAR (1678-1707), Irish dramatist. Oriana, in *The Inconstant*, act 4, sc. 2.

20 The lyricism of marginality may find inspiration in the image of the "outlaw," the great social nomad, who prowls on the confines of a docile, frightened order.

MICHEL FOUCAULT (1926-84), French philosopher. *Discipline and Punish: The Birth of the Prison*, pt. 4, ch. 3 (1975).

21 The man who is admired for the ingenuity of his larceny is almost always rediscovering some earlier form of fraud. The basic forms are all known, have all been practised. The manners of capitalism improve. The morals may not.

JOHN KENNETH GALBRAITH (b. 1908), U.S. economist. *The Age of Uncertainty*, ch. 2 (1977).

22 Repudiating the virtues of your world, criminals hopelessly agree to organize a forbidden universe. They agree to live in it. The air there is nauseating: they can breathe it.

JEAN GENET (1910-86), French playwright, novelist. *The Thief's Journal* (1949; tr. 1965).

23 Crimes of which a people is ashamed constitute its real history. The same is true of man.

JEAN GENET (1910-86), French playwright, novelist. Notes for *The Screens*, (1961; tr. 1973).

24 How vainly shall we endeavor to repress crime by our barbarous punishment of the poorer class of criminals so long as children are reared in the brutalizing influences of poverty, so long as the bite of want drives men to crime.

HENRY GEORGE (1839-97), U.S. economist. *Social Problems*, ch. 9 (1883).

25 Crime is naught but misdirected energy.

EMMA GOLDMAN (1869-1940), U.S. anarchist. *Anarchism and Other Essays*, "Anarchism: What It Really Stands For" (1910).

26 There is a heroism in crime as well as in virtue. Vice and infamy have their altars and their religion.

WILLIAM HAZLITT (1778-1830), English essayist. *Characteristics: In the Manner of Rochefoucault's Maxims*, no. 354 (1823; repr. in *The Complete Works of William Hazlitt*, vol. 9, ed. by P. P. Howe, 1932).

27 After all, crime is only a lefthanded form of human endeavor.

> JOHN HUSTON (1906-87), U.S. filmmaker. Emmerich, in *The Asphalt Jungle*, (1950), scripted and directed by Huston; based on a novel by W. R. Burnett.

28 He threatens many that hath injured one.

> BEN JONSON (1573-1637), English dramatist, poet. Silius, in *Fall of Sejanus*, act 2.

29 Squeeze human nature into the straitjacket of criminal justice and crime will appear.

> KARL KRAUS (1874-1936), Austrian satirist. *Morality and Criminal Justice*, "The Riehl Case" (1908).

30 There are crimes which become innocent and even glorious through their splendor, number and excess.

> FRANÇOIS, DUC DE LA ROCHEFOUCAULD (1613-80), French writer, moralist. *Sentences et Maximes Morales*, no. 192 (ed. 1665; no. 35 of first supplement, 1678).

31 The common argument that crime is caused by poverty is a kind of slander on the poor.

> H. L. MENCKEN (1880-1956), U.S. journalist. *Minority Report: H. L. Mencken's Notebooks*, no. 273 (1956).

32 The study of crime begins with the knowledge of oneself. All that you despise, all that you loathe, all that you reject, all that you condemn and seek to convert by punishment springs from you.

> HENRY MILLER (1891-1980), U.S. author. *The Air-Conditioned Nightmare*, "The Soul of Anaesthesia" (1945).

33 A burglar who respects his art always takes his time before taking anything else.

> O. HENRY [WILLIAM SYDNEY PORTER] (1862-1910), U.S. short-story writer. *Sixes and Sevens*, "Makes the Whole World Kin" (1911).

34 It is certain that stealing nourishes courage, strength, skill, tact, in a word, all the virtues useful to a republican system and consequently to our own. Lay partiality aside, and answer me: is theft, whose effect is to distribute wealth more evenly, to be branded as a wrong in our day, under our government which aims at equality? Plainly, the answer is no.

> MARQUIS DE SADE (1740-1814), French author. Dolmancé, in *Philosophy in the Bedroom*, "Dialogue the Fifth: Yet Another Effort, Frenchmen, If You Would Become Republicans" (1795).

35 All, all is theft, all is unceasing and rigorous competition in nature; the desire to make off with the substance of others is the foremost—the most legitimate— passion nature has bred into us . . . and, without doubt, the most agreeable one.

> MARQUIS DE SADE (1740-1814), French author. *Juliette ou les Prospérités du Vice*, vol. 1 (1797).

36 He that is robbed, not wanting what is stol'n, Let him not know't, and he's not robbed at all.

> WILLIAM SHAKESPEARE (1564-1616), English dramatist, poet. Othello, in *Othello*, act 3, sc. 3.

37 The faults of the burglar are the qualities of the financier.

> GEORGE BERNARD SHAW (1856-1950), Anglo-Irish playwright, critic. *Major Barbara*, Preface (1905).

38 A crime persevered in a thousand centuries ceases to be a crime, and becomes a virtue. This is the law of custom, and custom supersedes all other forms of law.

> MARK TWAIN (1835-1910), U.S. author. *Following the Equator*, ch. 63, "Pudd'nhead Wilson's New Calendar (1897).

39 From a single crime know the nation.

> VIRGIL (70-19 B.C.), Roman poet. *Aeneid*, bk. 2.

40 Almost all crime is due to the repressed desire for aesthetic expression.

> EVELYN WAUGH (1903-66), British novelist. Prison Governor Sir Wilfred Lucas-Dockery, in *Decline and Fall*, pt. 3, ch. 1 (1928). Paul Pennyfeather, to whom these words are addressed, has just been informed that he is to be put to work in the Arts and Crafts Workshop.

41 Crime and bad lives are the measure of a State's failure, all crime in the end is the crime of the community.

> H. G. WELLS (1866-1946), British author. *A Modern Utopia*, ch. 5, sct. 2 (1905; repr. in *The Works of H. G. Wells*, vol. 9, 1925).

42 The truth of the matter is that muggers are very interesting people.

> MICHAEL WINNER (b. 1935), British film director. *Daily Express* (London, 11 May 1989).

See also Weil on JUSTICE; Chesterton on PROPERTY; Emerson on VILLAINS.

CRISIS

1 I think it's only in a crisis that Americans see other people. It has to be an American crisis, of course. If two countries fight that do not supply the Americans with some precious commodity, then the education of the public does not take place. But when the dictator falls, when the oil is threatened, then you turn on the television and they tell you where the country is, what the language is, how to pronounce the names of the leaders, what the religion is all about, and maybe you can cut out recipes in the newspaper of Persian dishes.

> DON DELILLO (b. 1926), U.S. author. Andreas Eliades, in *The Names*, ch. 3 (1982).

2 I believe that in the history of art and of thought there has always been at every living moment of culture a "will to renewal." This is not the prerogative of the last decade only. All history is nothing but a succession of "crises"—of rupture, repudiation and resistance. . . . When there is no "crisis," there is stagnation, petrification and death. All thought, all art is aggressive.

> EUGÉNE IONESCO (b. 1912), Rumanian-born French playwright. *Notes and Counter-Notes*, pt. 4, "Have I Written Anti-Theatre?" (1962).

3 When is a crisis reached? When questions arise that can't be answered.

> RYSZARD KAPUSCINSKI (b. 1932), Polish journalist. *A Warsaw Diary* (published in *Granta*, no. 15, Cambridge, England 1985).

4 When written in Chinese the word crisis is composed of two characters. One represents danger and the other represents opportunity.

> JOHN F. KENNEDY (1917-63), U.S. president. Speech, 12 April 1959, Indianapolis, Ind.

5   There can't be a crisis next week. My schedule is already full.

> HENRY KISSINGER (b. 1923), U.S. Republican politician, secretary of state. *New York Times Magazine* (1 June 1969).

6   I am walking over hot coals suspended over a deep pit at the bottom of which are a large number of vipers baring their fangs.

> JOHN MAJOR (b. 1943), British Conservative politician, prime minister. Remark, 24 Oct. 1992, à propos of the disagreements over Britain's membership in Europe. Reported in: *Guardian* (London, 28 Oct. 1992).

7   The easiest period in a crisis situation is actually the battle itself. The most difficult is the period of indecision—whether to fight or run away. And the most dangerous period is the aftermath. It is then, with all his resources spent and his guard down, that an individual must watch out for dulled reactions and faulty judgment.

> RICHARD M. NIXON (b. 1913), U.S. Republican politician, president. *Six Crises*, Introduction (1962). Nixon added, "Crisis can indeed be an agony. But it is the exquisite agony which a man might not want to experience again—yet would not for the world have missed."

8   The time is out of joint. O cursèd spite
That ever I was born to set it right!

> WILLIAM SHAKESPEARE (1564-1616), English dramatist, poet. Hamlet, in *Hamlet,* act 1, sc. 5.

9   We all live in a house on fire, no fire department to call; no way out, just the upstairs window to look out of while the fire burns the house down with us trapped, locked in it.

> TENNESSEE WILLIAMS (1914-83), U.S. dramatist. Chris, in *The Milk Train Doesn't Stop Here Anymore,* sc. 6 (1963).

See also Maritain on The UNITED STATES.

CRITICISM

1   A negative judgment gives you more satisfaction than praise, provided it smacks of jealousy.

> JEAN BAUDRILLARD (b. 1929), French semiologist. *Cool Memories,* ch. 5 (1987; tr.1990).

2   What the public criticizes in you, cultivate. It is you.

> JEAN COCTEAU (1889-1963), French author, filmmaker. *Le Rappel àl'Ordre,* "Le Coq et l'Arlequin" (1926; repr. in *Collected Works,* vol. 9, 1950).

3   In my conscience I believe the baggage loves me, for she never speaks well of me herself, nor suffers any body else to rail at me.

> WILLIAM CONGREVE (1670-1729), English dramatist. Bellmour, in *The Old Bachelor,* act 1, sc. 1, said of Belinda.

4   It is very perplexing how an intrepid frontier people, who fought a wilderness, floods, tornadoes, and the Rockies, cower before criticism, which is regarded as a malignant tumor in the imagination.

> EDWARD DAHLBERG (1900-1977), U.S. author, critic. *Alms for Oblivion,* "No Love and No Thanks" (1964).

5   We might remind ourselves that criticism is as inevitable as breathing, and that we should be none the worse for articulating what passes in our minds when we read a book and feel an emotion about it, for criticizing our own minds in their work of criticism.

> T. S. ELIOT (1888-1965), Anglo-American poet, critic. "Tradition and the Individual Talent," sct. 1, in *Egoist* (London, Sept. and Dec. 1919; repr. in *Selected Prose of T. S. Eliot,* ed. by Frank Kermode, 1975).

6   Praise those of your critics for whom nothing is up to standard.

> DAG HAMMARSKJÖLD (1905-1961), Swedish statesman, Secretary-General of U.N. *Markings,* "Night is Drawing Nigh" (1963), written in 1957.

7   I find the pain of a little censure, even when it is unfounded, is more acute than the pleasure of much praise.

> THOMAS JEFFERSON (1743-1826), U.S. president. Letter, 13 March 1789.

8   Critical remarks are only made by people who love you.

> FEDERICO MAYOR (b. 1934), Spanish biologist, politician, director-general of *UNESCO. Guardian* (London, 24 June 1988).

9   You should never assume contempt for that which it is not very manifest that you have it in your power to possess, nor does a wit ever make a more contemptible figure than when, in attempting satire, he shows that he does not understand that which he would make the subject of his ridicule.

> LORD MELBOURNE (1779-1848), English statesman, prime minister. Notebook entry. Quoted in: David Cecil, *The Young Melbourne,* ch. 9 (1939).

10   Since we cannot attain unto it, let us revenge ourselves with railing against it.

> MICHEL DE MONTAIGNE (1533-92), French essayist. *Essays,* bk. 3, ch. 7, "Of the Incommodity of Greatness" (tr. by John Florio, 1588).

11   In criticism I will be bold, and as sternly, absolutely just with friend and foe. From this purpose nothing shall turn me.

> EDGAR ALLAN POE (1809-45), U.S. poet, critic, short-story writer. Letter, 17 Jan. 1841.

12   Do not use a hatchet to remove a fly from your friend's forehead.

> CHINESE PROVERB.

13   A blind man will not thank you for a looking-glass.

> ENGLISH PROVERB (18th century). Collected in: Thomas Fuller, *Gnomologia* (1732).

14   When a man spends his time giving his wife criticism and advice instead of compliments, he forgets that it was not his good judgment, but his charming manners, that won her heart.

> HELEN ROWLAND (1875-1950), U.S. journalist. *Reflections of a Bachelor Girl* (1903).

15   Of all the cants which are canted in this canting world—though the cant of hypocrites may be the worst—the cant of criticism is the most tormenting!

> LAURENCE STERNE (1713-68), English author. *Tristram Shandy,* bk. 3, ch. 12 (1760-67).

16 I am sorry to think that you do not get a man's most effective criticism until you provoke him. Severe truth is expressed with some bitterness.

> HENRY DAVID THOREAU (1817-62), U.S. philosopher, author, naturalist. *Journals* (1906), entry for 15 March 1854.

17 You should not say it is not good. You should say you do not like it; and then, you know, you're perfectly safe.

> JAMES MCNEILL WHISTLER (1834-1903), U.S. artist. Quoted in: D. C. Seitz, *Whistler Stories* (1913).

18 On an occasion of this kind it becomes more than a moral duty to speak one's mind. It becomes a pleasure.

> OSCAR WILDE (1854-1900), Anglo-Irish playwright, author. Gwendolen, in *The Importance of Being Earnest*, act 3.

Seee also LITERARY CRITICISM.

CRITICISM AND THE ARTS

1 Culture is only true when implicitly critical, and the mind which forgets this revenges itself in the critics it breeds. Criticism is an indispensable element of culture.

> THEODOR W. ADORNO (1903-69), German philosopher, sociologist, music critic. *Prisms,* "Cultural Criticism and Society" (1967).

2 The avocation of assessing the failures of better men can be turned into a comfortable livelihood, providing you back it up with a Ph.D.

> NELSON ALGREN (1909-81), U.S. author. Interview in *Writers at Work* (First Series, ed. by Malcolm Cowley, 1958).

3 Criticism should be a casual conversation.

> W. H. AUDEN (1907-73), Anglo-American poet. *The Table Talk of W. H. Auden,* "November 16, 1946" (comp. by Alan Ansen, ed. by Nicholas Jenkins, 1990).

4 The critical opinions of a writer should always be taken with a large grain of salt. For the most part, they are manifestations of his debate with himself as to what he should do next and what he should avoid.

> W. H. AUDEN (1907-73), Anglo-American poet. *The Dyer's Hand,* pt. 1, "Reading" (1962).

5 To be just, that is to say, to justify its existence, criticism should be partial, passionate and political, that is to say, written from an exclusive point of view, but a point of view that opens up the widest horizons.

> CHARLES BAUDELAIRE (1821-67), French poet. "Salon of 1846," sct. 1 (published in *Curiosités Esthétiques,* 1868; repr. in *The Mirror of Art,* ed. by Jonathan Mayne, 1955).

6 It is from the womb of art that criticism was born.

> CHARLES BAUDELAIRE (1821-67), French poet. "Salon of 1846," sct. 1 (published in *Curiosités Esthétiques,* 1868; repr. in *The Mirror of Art,* ed. by Jonathan Mayne, 1955).

7 Post-modernism has cut off the present from all futures. The daily media add to this by cutting off the past. Which means that critical opinion is often orphaned in the present.

> JOHN BERGER (b. 1926), British author, critic. "Infamy," in *Guardian* (London, 21 Sept. 1990; repr. in *Keeping a Rendezvous,* 1992).

8 The covers of this book are too far apart.

> AMBROSE BIERCE (1842-1914), U.S. author. One-sentence book review, quoted in: C. H. Grattan, *Bitter Bierce* (1929).

9 Writing prejudicial, off-putting reviews is a precise exercise in applied black magic. The reviewer can draw free-floating disagreeable associations to a book by implying that the book is completely unimportant without saying exactly why, and carefully avoiding any clear images that could capture the reader's full attention.

> WILLIAM BURROUGHS (b. 1914), U.S. author. *The Western Lands,* ch. 3 (1987).

10 Reviews and magazines are at best ephemeral & superficial reading. Who thinks of the *grand article* of last year in any given review?

> LORD BYRON (1788-1824), English poet. Letter, 24 Sept. 1821, to the publisher John Murray (published in *Byron's Letters and Journals,* vol. 8, ed. by Leslie A. Marchand, 1973-81). Requesting Murray not to trouble the poet with reviews of his work, Byron added, "My feelings are like the dead, who know nothing and feel nothing of all or aught that is said or done in their regard."

11 Most critical writing is drivel and half of it is dishonest. . . . It is a short cut to oblivion, anyway. Thinking in terms of ideas destroys the power to think in terms of emotions and sensations.

> RAYMOND CHANDLER (1888-1959), U.S. author. Letter, 16 Dec. 1944 (published in *Raymond Chandler Speaking,* 1962).

12 Good critical writing is measured by the perception and evaluation of the subject; bad critical writing by the necessity of maintaining the professional standing of the critic.

> RAYMOND CHANDLER (1888-1959), U.S. author. Letter, 7 May 1948, to *Harper's Magazine* editor Frederick Lewis Allen (published in *Raymond Chandler Speaking,* 1962).

13 Criticism, that fine flower of personal expression in the garden of letters.

> JOSEPH CONRAD (1857-1924) , Polish-born English novelist. *A Personal Record,* "A Familiar Preface" (1912).

14 Hardly a book of human worth, be it heaven's own secret, is honestly placed before the reader; it is either shunned, given a Periclean funeral oration in a hundred and fifty words, or interred in the potter's field of the newspapers' back pages.

> EDWARD DAHLBERG (1900-1977), U.S. author, critic. *Alms for Oblivion,* "For Sale" (1964).

15 The artist doesn't have time to listen to the critics. The ones who want to be writers read the reviews, the ones who want to write don't have the time to read reviews.

> WILLIAM FAULKNER (1897-1962), U.S. novelist. Interview in *Writers at Work* (First Series, ed. by Malcolm Cowley, 1958).

16 Essays, entitled critical, are epistles addressed to the public, through which the mind of the recluse relieves itself of its impressions.

> MARGARET FULLER (1810-50), U.S. writer, lecturer. *Art, Literature and the Drama,* "A Short Essay on Critics" (1858).

17 There are two modes of criticism. One which . . . crushes to earth without mercy all the humble buds of Phantasy, all the plants that, though green and fruitful, are also a prey to insects or have suffered by drouth. It weeds well the garden, and cannot believe the weed in its native soil may be a pretty, graceful plant. There is another mode which enters into the natural history of every thing that breathes and lives, which believes no impulse to be entirely in vain, which scrutinizes circumstances, motive and object before it condemns, and believes there is a beauty in natural form, if its law and purpose be understood.

> MARGARET FULLER (1810-50), U.S. writer, lecturer. *Art, Literature and the Drama*, "Poets of the People" (1858).

18 The author himself is the best judge of his own performance; none has so deeply meditated on the subject; none is so sincerely interested in the event.

> EDWARD GIBBON (1737-94), English historian. *Memoirs of my Life*, (1796; published in Routledge, *Autobiography*, p. 98, 1971).

19 The whole effort of a sincere man is to erect his personal impressions into laws.

> RÉMY DE GOURMONT (1858-1915), French critic, novelist. Quoted in: John Middleton Murry, *Countries of the Mind*, "A Critical Credo" (1922). Murry called this statement, "the motto of a true criticism, conscious of its limitations and its strengths."

20 Nothing would improve newspaper criticism so much as the knowledge that it was to be read by men too hardy to acquiesce in the authoritative statement of the reviewer.

> R. H. HUTTON (1826-97), English editor, critic. "Mr. Grote on the Abuses of Newspaper Criticism," in *Spectator* (London, 29 June 1861; repr. in *A Victorian Spectator: Uncollected Writings of R. H. Hutton*, ed. by Robert H. Tener and Malcolm Woodfield, 1989).

21 As a work of art it has the same status as a long conversation between two not very bright drunks.

> CLIVE JAMES (b. 1939), Australian writer, critic. "A Blizzard of Tiny Kisses," in *London Review of Books* (1980; repr. in *From the Land of Shadows*, 1982), referring to Judith Krantz's *Princess Daisy*, which fetched what was then a record advance of $3,208,875 when the rights were sold at an auction held in New York on 5 Sept. 1979.

22 To criticize is to appreciate, to appropriate, to take intellectual possession, to establish in fine a relation with the criticized thing and to make it one's own.

> HENRY JAMES (1843-1916), U.S. author. *What Maisie Knew*, Preface (1897). The Preface first appeared in the New York Edition of James's work (1907-09) and was later republished in *The Art of the Novel* (ed. by R. P. Blackmur, 1934).

23 Criticism is a study by which men grow important and formidable at very small expense. . . . He whom nature has made weak, and idleness keeps ignorant, may yet support his vanity by the name of a critic.

> SAMUEL JOHNSON (1709-84), English author, lexicographer. *The Idler*, no. 60, in *Universal Chronicle* (London, 9 June 1759; repr. in *Works of Samuel Johnson, Yale Edition*, vol. 2, ed. by W. J. Bate, John M. Bullitt, and L. F. Powell, 1963).

24 I would rather be attacked than unnoticed. For the worst thing you can do to an author is to be silent as to his works. An assault upon a town is a bad thing; but starving it is still worse.

> SAMUEL JOHNSON (1709-84), English author, lexicographer. Quoted in: James Boswell, *Life of Samuel Johnson*, 26 March 1779 (1791).

25 Praise or blame has but a momentary effect on the man whose love of beauty in the abstract makes him a severe critic on his own works.

> JOHN KEATS (1795-1821), English poet. Letter, 9 Oct. 1818 (published in *Letters of John Keats*, no. 90, ed. by Frederick Page, 1954). Despite Shelley's assertion, in his preface to his elegy *Adonais*, that Keats had suffered from the savage criticism of *Endymion* (published April 1818)—which, Shelley claimed, "produced the most violent effect on his susceptible mind," and led to Keats's last, fatal illness, Keats himself described *Endymion*, in the same letter quoted above, as "slip-shod": "Had I been nervous about its being a perfect piece, & with that view asked advice, & trembled over every page, it would not have been written."

26 One does not lash hat lies at a distance. The foibles that we ridicule must at least be a little bit our own. Only then will the work be a part of our own flesh. The garden must be weeded.

> PAUL KLEE (1879-1940), Swiss artist. *The Diaries of Paul Klee 1898-1918*, no. 681 (1957; tr. 1965), entry for July 1905.

27 Without the meditative background that is criticism, works become isolated gestures, ahistorical accidents, soon forgotten.

> MILAN KUNDERA (b. 1929), Czech author, critic. "On Criticism, Aesthetics, and Europe," in *Review of Contemporary Fiction* (Summer 1989; originally from Kundera's introduction to François Ricard, *La Littérature Contre Elle-Même*).

28 Criticism is often not a science; it is a craft, requiring more good health than wit, more hard work than talent, more habit than native genius. In the hands of a man who has read widely but lacks judgment, applied to certain subjects it can corrupt both its readers and the writer himself.

> JEAN DE LA BRUYÈRE (1645-96), French writer, moralist. *Characters*, "Of Books," aph. 63 (1688).

29 Never trust the artist. Trust the tale. The proper function of a critic is to save the tale from the artist who created it.

> D. H. LAWRENCE (1885-1930), British author. *Studies in Classic American Literature*, ch. 1 (1924).

30 It is critical vision alone which can mitigate the unimpeded operation of the automatic.

> MARSHALL MCLUHAN (1911-80), Canadian communications theorist. *The Mechanical Bride*, "Magic that Changes Mood" (1951).

31 Honest criticism means nothing: what one wants is unrestrained passion, fire for fire.

> HENRY MILLER (1891-1980), U.S. author. *Sexus*, ch. 2 (1949).

32 A bad review is even less important than whether it is raining in Patagonia.

> IRIS MURDOCH (b. 1919), British novelist, philosopher. *Times* (London, 6 July 1989).

33 Prolonged, indiscriminate reviewing of books is a quite exceptionally thankless, irritating and exhausting job. It not only involves praising trash but constantly *inventing* reactions towards books about which one has no spontaneous feeling whatever.

> GEORGE ORWELL (1903-50), British author. "Confessions of a Book Reviewer" (1946; repr. in *The Collected Essays, Journalism and Letters of George Orwell*, vol. 4, ed. by Sonia Orwell and Ian Angus, 1968).

34 The greatest honor that can be paid to the work of art, on its pedestal of ritual display, is to *describe* it with sensory completeness. We need a science of description. . . . Criticism is ceremonial revivification.

> CAMILLE PAGLIA (b. 1947), U.S. author, critic, educator. *Sex, Art, and American Culture*, "Sexual Personae: The Cancelled Preface" (1992). "Art," according to Paglia, "is ceremony, and so is criticism."

35 This is not a novel to be tossed aside lightly. It should be thrown with great force.

> DOROTHY PARKER (1893-1967), U.S. humorous writer. Book review. Quoted in: *The Algonquin Wits* (ed. by Robert E. Drennan, 1968).

36 Art is not the application of a canon of beauty but what the instinct and the brain can conceive beyond any canon. When we love a woman we don't start measuring her limbs.

> PABLO PICASSO (1881-1973), Spanish artist. *Conversation avec Picasso*, in *Cahiers d'Art*, vol. 10, no. 10 (Paris, 1935; tr. in Alfred H. Barr, Jr., *Picasso: Fifty Years of His Art*, 1946).

37 I consider criticism merely a preliminary excitement, a statement of things a writer has to clear up in his own head sometime or other, probably antecedent to writing; of no value unless it come to fruit in the created work later.

> EZRA POUND (1885-1972), U.S. poet, critic. *Criterion* (London, Jan. 1923).

38 One of the grotesqueries of present-day American life is the amount of reasoning that goes into displaying the wisdom secreted in bad movies while proving that modern art is meaningless. . . . They have put into practise the notion that a bad art work cleverly interpreted according to some obscure Method is more rewarding than a masterpiece wrapped in silence.

> HAROLD ROSENBERG (1906-78), U.S. art critic, author. *The Tradition of the New*, ch. 18 (1960).

39 For if there is anything to one's praise, it is foolish vanity to be gratified at it, and if it is abuse—why one is always sure to hear of it from one damned good-natured friend or another!

> RICHARD BRINSLEY SHERIDAN (1751-1816), Anglo-Irish dramatist. Sir Fretful Plagiary on not reading the reviewers, in *The Critic*, act 1, sc. 1.

40 I never read a book before reviewing it; it prejudices a man so.

> SYDNEY SMITH (1771-1845), English clergyman, writer. Quoted in: Hesketh Pearson, *The Smith of Smiths*, ch. 3 (1934).

41 In most modern instances, interpretation amounts to the philistine refusal to leave the work of art alone. Real art has the capacity to make us nervous. By reducing the work of art to its content and then interpreting *that*, one tames the work of art. Interpretation makes art manageable, conformable.

> SUSAN SONTAG (b. 1933), U.S. essayist. "Against Interpretation," sct. 5, in *Evergreen Review* (Dec. 1964; repr. in *Against Interpretation*, 1966).

42 The aim of all commentary on art now should be to make works of art—and, by analogy, our own experience—more, rather than less, real to us. The function of

criticism should be to show *how it is what it is*, even *that it is what it is*, rather than to show *what it means*.

> SUSAN SONTAG (b. 1933), U.S. essayist. "Against Interpretation," sct. 9, in *Evergreen Review* (Dec. 1964; repr. in *Against Interpretation*, 1966).

43 Writing criticism is to writing fiction and poetry as hugging the shore is to sailing in the open sea.

> JOHN UPDIKE (b. 1932), U.S. author, critic. *Hugging the Shore*, Foreword (1984).

44 Any authentic work of art must start an argument between the artist and his audience.

> REBECCA WEST (1892-1983), British author. *The Court and the Castle*, pt. 1, ch. 1 (1957).

45 After all, one knows one's weak points so well, that it's rather bewildering to have the critics overlook them & invent others.

> EDITH WHARTON (1862-1937), U.S. author. Letter, 19 Nov. 1907, following the publication of *The Fruit of the Tree* (published in *The Letters of Edith Wharton*, 1988).

46 That is what the highest criticism really is, the record of one's own soul. It is more fascinating than history, as it is concerned simply with oneself. It is more delightful than philosophy, as its subject is concrete and not abstract, real and not vague. It is the only civilised form of autobiography.

> OSCAR WILDE (1854-1900), Anglo-Irish playwright, author. Gilbert, in *The Critic as Artist*, pt. 1 (published in *Intentions*, 1891).

47 Temperament is the primary requisite for the critic—a temperament exquisitely susceptible to beauty, and to the various impressions that beauty gives us.

> OSCAR WILDE (1854-1900), Anglo-Irish playwright, author. Gilbert, in *The Critic as Artist*, pt. 2 (published in *Intentions*, 1891).

48 Not even the most powerful organs of the press, including *Time*, *Newsweek*, and *The New York Times*, can discover a new artist or certify his work and make it stick. . . . They can only bring you the scores.

> TOM WOLFE (b. 1931), U.S. journalist, author. *The Painted Word*, ch. 2 (1975).

49 It is the nature of the artist to mind excessively what is said about him. Literature is strewn with the wreckage of men who have minded beyond reason the opinions of others.

> VIRGINIA WOOLF (1882-1941), British novelist. *A Room of One's Own*, ch. 3 (1929).

See also CRITICISM; LITERARY CRITICISM; Vorster on SOUTH AFRICA; Wilde on TECHNIQUE.

CRITICS

1 The art of the critic in a nutshell: to coin slogans without betraying ideas. The slogans of an inadequate criticism peddle ideas to fashion.

> WALTER BENJAMIN (1892-1940), German critic, philosopher. *One-Way Street*, "Post No Bills: The Critic's Technique in Thirteen Theses" (1928; repr. in *One-Way Street and Other Writings*, 1978).

2 A man must serve his time to every trade
Save censure—critics all are ready made.

LORD BYRON (1788-1824), English poet. *English Bards and Scotch Reviewers.*

3 It is wrong to be harsh with the New York critics, unless one admits in the same breath that it is a condition of their existence that they should write entertainingly about something which is rarely worth writing about at all.

RAYMOND CHANDLER (1888-1959), U.S. author. Letter, 7 May 1948, to *Harper's Magazine* editor Frederick Lewis Allen (published in *Raymond Chandler Speaking*, 1962). In contrast, Chandler declared, "the great critics, of whom there are piteously few, build a home for the truth.".

4 Though by whim, envy, or resentment led,
They damn those authors whom they never read.

CHARLES CHURCHILL (1731-64), English clergyman, poet. *The Candidate.*

5 Unlike other people, our reviewers are powerful because they believe in nothing.

HAROLD CLURMAN (1901-80), U.S. stage director, critic. Quoted in: Robert Brustein, *Who Needs Theatre*, pt. 1, "The Vitality of Harold Clurman" (1987).

6 I review novels to make money, because it is easier for a sluggard to write an article a fortnight than a book a year, because the writer is soothed by the opiate of action, the crank by posing as a good journalist, and having an airhole. I dislike it. I do it and I am always resolving to give it up.

CYRIL CONNOLLY (1903-74), British critic. "The Journal of Cyril Connolly 1928-1937" (published in David Pryce-Jones, *Journal and Memoir*, 1983, p. 156). W. H. Auden, when asked who was the best critic alive, is said to have replied, "Cyril Connolly, alas."

7 Recognise the cunning man not by the corpses he pays homage to but by the living writers he conspires against with the most shameful weapon, Silence, or the briefest review.

EDWARD DAHLBERG (1900-1977), U.S. author, critic. *Alms for Oblivion*, "For Sale" (1964).

8 Men over forty are no judges of a book written in a new spirit.

RALPH WALDO EMERSON (1803-82), U.S. essayist, poet, philosopher. *Lectures and Biographical Sketches*, "The Man of Letters" (1883).

9 In reality, the world have payed too great a compliment to critics, and have imagined them men of much greater profundity than they really are.

HENRY FIELDING (1707-54), English novelist, dramatist. *Tom Jones*, bk. 5, ch. 1 (1749).

10 The good critic is he who relates the adventures of his soul among masterpieces.

ANATOLE FRANCE (1844-1924), French author. Dedicatory letter, (1888), to *The Literary Life.* Somerset Maugham made a similar prescription for artists.

11 Asking a working writer what he thinks about critics is like asking a lamp-post what it feels about dogs.

CHRISTOPHER HAMPTON (b. 1946), British playwright. *Sunday Times Magazine* (London, 16 Oct. 1977).

12 God knows people who are paid to have attitudes toward things, professional critics, make me sick; camp following eunuchs of literature. They won't even whore. They're all virtuous and sterile. And how well meaning and high minded. But they're all camp followers.

ERNEST HEMINGWAY (1899-1961), U.S. author. Letter, 23 May 1925, to Sherwood Anderson (published in *Selected Letters*, ed. by Carlos Baker, 1981).

13 All the critics who could not make their reputations by discovering you are hoping to make them by predicting hopefully your approaching impotence, failure and general drying up of natural juices. Not a one will wish you luck or hope that you will keep on writing unless you have political affiliations in which case these will rally around and speak of you and Homer, Balzac, Zola and Link Steffens.

ERNEST HEMINGWAY (1899-1961), U.S. author. "Old Newsman Writes: A Letter from Cuba," in *Esquire* (New York, Dec. 1934; repr. in *By-Line Ernest Hemingway*, ed. by William White, 1967). A. E. Hotchner, in his portrait, *Papa Hemingway*, quoted Hemingway saying, "One battle doesn't make a campaign but critics treat one book, good or bad, like a whole goddamn war."

14 Nature, when she invented, manufactured, and patented her authors, contrived to make critics out of the chips that were left.

OLIVER WENDELL HOLMES, SR. (1809-94), U.S. writer, physician. *The Professor at the Breakfast-Table*, ch. 1 (1859).

15 In an age of unscrupulous and shameless bookmaking, it is a duty to give notice of the rubbish that cumbers the ground. There is no credit, no real power required for this task. It is the work of an intellectual scavenger, and far from being specially honourable.

R. H. HUTTON (1826-97), English editor, critic. "Mr. Grote on the Abuses of Newspaper Criticism," in *Spectator* (London, 29 June 1861; repr. in *A Victorian Spectator: Uncollected Writings of R. H. Hutton*, ed. by Robert H. Tener and Malcolm Woodfield, 1989). "Still," Hutton added, "if done scrupulously, it is not dishonourable."

16 Of course you're always at liberty to judge the critic. Judge people as critics, however, and you'll condemn them all!

HENRY JAMES (1843-1916), U.S. author. Ralph Touchett to Isabel Archer in *The Portrait of a Lady*, ch. 23 (1881).

17 In the arts, the critic is the only independent source of information. The rest is advertising.

PAULINE KAEL (b. 1919), U.S. film critic. *Newsweek* (New York, 24 Dec. 1973).

18 Let us consider the critic, therefore, as a *discoverer of discoveries.*

MILAN KUNDERA (b. 1929), Czech author, critic. "On Criticism, Aesthetics, and Europe," in *Review of Contemporary Fiction* (summer 1989). Originally from Kundera's Introduction to François Ricard, *La Littérature Contre Elle-Même.*

19 Critics are sentinels in the grand army of letters, stationed at the corners of newspapers and reviews, to challenge every new author.

HENRY WADSWORTH LONGFELLOW (1807-82), U.S. poet. *Kavanagh*, bk. 1, ch. 13 (1849), one of the meditations of Mr. Churchill, inscribed on his pulpit.

20 You know what the critics are. If you tell the truth they only say you're cynical and it does an author no good to get a reputation for cynicism.

> W. SOMERSET MAUGHAM (1874-1965), British author. Alroy Kear, in *Cakes and Ale*, ch. 11 (1930).

21 It is impossible to think of a man of any actual force and originality, universally recognized as having those qualities, who spent his whole life appraising and describing the work of other men.

> H. L. MENCKEN (1880-1956), U.S. journalist. "The Critical Process," in *Smart Set* (New York, Dec. 1921; repr. in *Prejudices*, Third Series, 1922).

22 We have been educated to such a fine—or dull—point that we are incapable of enjoying something new, something different, until we are first told what it's all about. We don't trust our five senses; we rely on our critics and educators, all of whom are failures in the realm of creation. In short, the blind lead the blind. It's the democratic way.

> HENRY MILLER (1891-1980), U.S. author. *The Air-Conditioned Nightmare*, "With Edgar Varèse in the Gobi Desert" (1945).

23 When the critics come around it's always too late.

> SIR SIDNEY NOLAN (1917-92), Australian artist. *Daily Telegraph* (London, 15 Sept. 1992).

24 Did some more sober critic come abroad?
If wrong, I smil'd; if right, I kiss'd the rod.

> ALEXANDER POPE (1688-1744), English satirical poet. *Epistle to Dr. Arbuthnot*.

25 The television critic, whatever his pretensions, does not labour in the same vineyard as those he criticizes; his grapes are all sour.

> FREDERIC RAPHAEL (b. 1931), British author, critic. "The Language of Television" (published in *The State of the Language*, ed. by Christopher Ricks, 1980).

26 Take heed of critics even when they are not fair; resist them even when they are.

> JEAN ROSTAND (1894-1977), French biologist, writer. *Pensées d'un Biologiste* (1939; repr. in *The Substance of Man*, ch. 8, "A Biologist's Thoughts," 1962).

27 A critic is a reader who ruminates. Thus, he should have more than one stomach.

> FRIEDRICH SCHLEGEL (1772-1829), German philosopher, critic, writer. *Dialogue on Poetry and Literary Aphorisms*, aph. 27 from *The Lyceum*, "Selected Aphorisms" (1968; first published 1797).

28 Give me the critic bred in Nature's school,
Who neither talks by rote, nor thinks by rule;
Who feeling's honest dictates still obeys,
And dares, without a precedent, to praise.

> SIR MARTIN ARCHER SHEE (1769-1850), Irish portrait painter, president of Royal Academy. *Rhymes on Art, or the Remonstrance of a Painter*, pt. 2 (1805).

29 Reviewers, with some rare exceptions, are a most stupid and malignant race. As a bankrupt thief turns thief-taker in despair, so an unsuccessful author turns critic.

> PERCY BYSSHE SHELLEY (1792-1822), English poet. *Adonais*, Preface (1821), first draft, later removed.

30 Any critic is entitled to wrong judgments, of course. But certain lapses of judgment indicate the radical failure of an entire sensibility.

> SUSAN SONTAG (b. 1933), U.S. essayist. *Against Interpretation*, "The Literary Criticism of George Lukács" (1966).

31 Give a critic an inch, he'll write a play.

> JOHN STEINBECK (1902-68), U.S. author. *Writers at Work*, "On Critics" (fourth series, ed. by George Plimpton, 1977).

32 Unless a reviewer has the courage to give you unqualified praise, I say ignore the bastard.

> JOHN STEINBECK (1902-68), U.S. author. Quoted in: J. K. Galbraith, *The Affluent Society*, Introduction (1977 ed.), remark describing Galbraith's chance meeting with Steinbeck in an airport lobby, when both were reading a hostile review of Galbraith's book following its first publication in 1958.

33 What we ask of him is, that he should find out for us more than we can find out for ourselves. . . . He must have the passion of a lover.

> ARTHUR SYMONS (1865-1945), British poet, critic. Samuel Taylor's Coleridge, *Biographia Literaria*, Introduction (1906 ed.).

34 A louse in the locks of literature.

> LORD TENNYSON (1809-92), English poet. Quoted in: Evan Charteris, *Life and Letters of Sir Edmund Gosse*, ch. 14 (1931), said of critic J. Churton Collins.

35 A good drama critic is one who perceives what is happening in the theatre of his time. A great drama critic also perceives what is not happening.

> KENNETH TYNAN (1927-80), British critic. *Tynan Right and Left*, Foreword (1967).

36 It is healthier, in any case, to write for the adults one's children will become than for the children one's "mature" critics often are.

> ALICE WALKER (b. 1944), U.S. author, critic. "A Writer Because of, Not in Spite of, Her Children," in *Ms.* (New York, Jan. 1976; repr. in *In Search of our Mothers' Gardens*, 1983).

37 The true critic is he who bears within himself the dreams and ideas and feelings of myriad generations, and to whom no form of thought is alien, no emotional impulse obscure.

> OSCAR WILDE (1854-1900), Anglo-Irish playwright, author. Review of Walter Pater, *Appreciations, with an Essay on Style* (published in *Speaker*, 22 March 1890).

38 The critic has to educate the public; the artist has to educate the critic.

> OSCAR WILDE (1854-1900), Anglo-Irish playwright, author. Letter, 16 Aug 1890, to the editor of the *Scots Observer*, in answer to criticisms levelled at Wilde, *The Picture of Dorian Gray*.

39 Every writer is necessarily a critic—that is, each sentence is a skeleton accompanied by enormous activity of rejection; and each selection is governed by general principles concerning truth, force, beauty, and so on. . . . The critic that is in every fabulist is like the iceberg—nine-tenths of him is under water.

> THORNTON WILDER (1897-1975), U.S. novelist, dramatist. Interview in *Writers at Work* (First Series, ed. by Malcolm Cowley, 1958).

See also CRITICISM AND THE ARTS; Kavanagh on GENERALIZATIONS.

CROWDS

1 If it has to choose who is to be crucified, the crowd will always save Barabbas.

> JEAN COCTEAU (1889-1963), French author, filmmaker. *Le Rappel à l'Ordre*, "Le Coq et l'Arlequin" (1926; repr. in *Collected Works*, vol. 9, 1950).

2 Spiritual superiority only sees the individual. But alas, ordinarily we human beings are sensual and, therefore, as soon as it is a gathering, the impression changes—we see something abstract, the crowd, and we become different. But in the eyes of God, the infinite spirit, all the millions that have lived and now live do not make a crowd, He only sees each individual.

> SØREN KIERKEGAARD (1813-55), Danish philosopher. *The Diary of Søren Kierkegaard*, pt. 5, sct. 3, no. 127 (ed. by Peter Rohde, 1960), entry for 1850.

3 If there is a look of human eyes that tells of perpetual loneliness, so there is also the familiar look that is the sign of perpetual crowds.

> ALICE MEYNELL (1847-1922), English poet, essayist. *Essays*, "Solitude" (1914).

4 Towns are full of people, houses full of tenants, hotels full of guests, trains full of travelers, cafés full of customers, parks full of promenaders, consulting-rooms of famous doctors full of patients, theatres full of spectators, and beaches full of bathers. What previously was, in general, no problem, now begins to be an everyday one, namely, to find room.

> JOSÉ ORTEGA Y GASSET (1883-1955), Spanish essayist, philosopher. *The Revolt of the Masses*, ch. 1 (1930).

5 Great bodies of people are never responsible for what they do.

> VIRGINIA WOOLF (1882-1941), British novelist. *A Room of One's Own*, ch. 2 (1929).

CRUELTY

1 Cruelty is, perhaps, the worst kid of sin. Intellectual cruelty is certainly the worst kind of cruelty.

> G. K. CHESTERTON (1874-1936), British author. *All Things Considered*, "Conceit and Caricature" (1908).

2 Sadism is all right in its place, but it should be directed to proper ends.

> SIGMUND FREUD (1856-1939), Austrian psychiatrist. From Joseph Wortis, *Fragments of an Analysis with Freud*, ch. 3, "22 Jan. 1935" (1954). Freud was discussing the love of hunting, which in modern times seemed "superfluous and sometimes simply barbarous."

3 The impulse to cruelty is, in many people, almost as violent as the impulse to sexual love—almost as violent and much more mischievous.

> ALDOUS HUXLEY (1894-1963), British author. *Beyond the Mexique Bay*, "Chichicastenango" (1934).

4 Almost everything we call "higher culture" is based on the spiritualization and intensification of *cruelty*—this is my proposition. . . . That which constitutes the painful voluptuousness of tragedy is cruelty; that which produces a pleasing effect in so-called tragic pity, indeed fundamentally in everything sublime up to the most highest and most refined thrills of metaphysics, derives its sweetness solely from the ingredient of cruelty mixed in with it.

> FRIEDRICH NIETZSCHE (1844-1900), German philosopher. *Beyond Good and Evil*, aph. 229 (1886).

5 Cruelty, very far from being a vice, is the first sentiment Nature injects in us all. The infant breaks his toy, bites his nurse's breast, strangles his canary long before he is able to reason; cruelty is stamped in animals, in whom, as I think I have said, Nature's laws are more emphatically to be read than in ourselves; cruelty exists amongst savages, so much nearer to Nature than civilized men are; absurd then to maintain cruelty is a consequence of depravity. . . . Cruelty is simply the energy in a man civilization has not yet altogether corrupted: therefore it is a virtue, not a vice.

> MARQUIS DE SADE (1740-1814), French author. Dolmancé, in *Philosophy in the Bedroom*, "Dialogue the Third" (1795).

6 All the cruelty and torment of which the world is full is in fact merely the necessary result of the totality of the forms under which the will to live is objectified.

> ARTHUR SCHOPENHAUER (1788-1860), German philosopher. *Parerga and Paralipomena*, vol. 2, ch. 14, sct. 164 (1851).

7 Cruelty would be delicious if one could only find some sort of cruelty that didn't really hurt.

> GEORGE BERNARD SHAW (1856-1950), Anglo-Irish playwright, critic. Mrs. Hushabye, in *Heartbreak House*, act 2.

8 It is possible that the contemplation of cruelty will not make us humane but cruel; that the reiteration of the badness of our spiritual condition will make us consent to it.

> LIONEL TRILLING (1905-75), U.S. critic. *Partisan Review 50th Anniversary Edition* (ed. by William Philips, 1985), entry in 1948, on Plato's theory of art.

9 All cruel people describe themselves as paragons of frankness!

> TENNESSEE WILLIAMS (1914-83), U.S. dramatist. Mrs. Goforth, in *The Milk Train Doesn't Stop Here Anymore*, sc. 1 (1963).

CRYING

1 The tears of the world are a constant quality. For each one who begins to weep, somewhere else another stops. The same is true of the laugh.

> SAMUEL BECKETT (1906-89), Irish dramatist, novelist. Pozzo, in *Waiting for Godot*, act 1.

2 Oh! too convincing—dangerously dear—
In woman's eye the unanswerable tear!

> LORD BYRON (1788-1824), English poet. *The Corsair*, cto. 2, st. 15.

3 The drying up a single tear has more
Of honest fame, than shedding seas of gore.

> LORD BYRON (1788-1824), English poet. *Don Juan*, cto. 8, st. 3.

4 I wept not, so to stone within I grew.

> DANTE ALIGHIERI (1265-1321), Italian poet. *The Divine Comedy*, "The Inferno," cto. 33 (completed 1321).

5 It opens the lungs, washes the countenance, exercises the eyes, and softens down the temper; so cry away.

CHARLES DICKENS (1812-70), English novelist. Mr. Bumble, in *Oliver Twist*, ch. 37 (1837-39). Mr. Bumble, speaking to Mrs. Bumble, was "pleased and exalted" by tears: "Like washable beaver hats that improve with rain, his nerves were rendered stouter and more vigorous by showers of tears."

6 Whatever tears one may shed, in the end one always blows one's nose.

HEINRICH HEINE (1797-1856), German poet, journalist. Quoted in: Simone de Beauvoir, *Memoirs of a Dutiful Daughter*, bk. 3 (1958; tr. 1959).

7 It is only to the happy that tears are a luxury.

THOMAS MOORE (1779-1852), Irish poet. *Lalla Rookh*, "Prologue No. 2."

8 Shining through tears, like April suns in showers,
That labour to o'ercome the cloud that loads 'em.

THOMAS OTWAY (1652-85), English dramatist. Pierre, in *Venice Preserved*, act 1, sc. 1, said of Belvidera.

9 Only to have a grief
equal to all these tears!

ADRIENNE RICH (b. 1929), U.S. poet. *Peeling Onions* in *Snapshots of a Daughter-in-Law* (1963).

10 There are people who laugh to show their fine teeth; and there are those who cry to show their good hearts.

JOSEPH ROUX (1834-86), French priest, writer. *Meditations of a Parish Priest*, pt. 9, no. 51 (1886).

11 One weeps not save when one is afraid, and that is why kings are tyrants.

MARQUIS DE SADE (1740-1814), French author. Dolmancé, in *Philosophy in the Bedroom*, "Dialogue the Fifth" (1795).

12 I have full cause of weeping, but this heart
Shall break into a hundred thousand flaws
Or ere I'll weep.

WILLIAM SHAKESPEARE (1564-1616), English dramatist, poet. Lear, in *King Lear*, act 2, sc. 2.

13 Laugh, and the world laughs with you;
Weep, and you weep alone;
For the sad old earth must borrow its mirth,
But has trouble enough of its own.

ELLA WHEELER WILCOX (1855-1919), U.S. poet, journalist. *Solitude*, st. 1.

14 Crying is the refuge of plain women but the ruin of pretty ones.

OSCAR WILDE (1854-1900), Anglo-Irish playwright, author. Duchess of Berwick, in *Lady Windermere's Fan*, act 1.

See also Rimbaud on SORROW.

CUBA

1 I had to say something
To strike him very weird,
So I yelled out,
"I like Fidel Castro and his beard."

BOB DYLAN (b. 1941), U.S. singer, songwriter. "Motorpsycho Nightmare," from the album *Another Side of Bob Dylan* (1964).

2 I candidly confess that I have ever looked on Cuba as the most interesting addition which could ever be made to our system of States. The control which, with Florida, this island would give us over the Gulf of Mexico, and the countries and isthmus bordering on it, as well as all those whose waters flow into it, would fill up the measure of our political well-being.

THOMAS JEFFERSON (1743-1826), U.S. president. Letter, 24 Oct. 1823, to President James Monroe.

3 It is my duty to prevent, through the independence of Cuba, the U.S.A. from spreading over the West Indies and falling with added weight upon other lands of Our America. All I have done up to now and shall do hereafter is to that end. . . . I know the Monster, because I have lived in its lair—and my weapon is only the slingshot of David.

JOSÉ MARTÍ (1853-1895), Cuban poet, patriot. Letter, May 1895 (published in *Obras Completas*, vol. 4, "May 1895," 1963).

4 Castro couldn't even go to the bathroom unless the Soviet Union put the nickel in the toilet.

RICHARD M. NIXON (b. 1913), U.S. Republican politician, president. Remark to interviewer, Sept. 1980. Quoted in: Robert Sam Anson, *Exile: The Unquiet Oblivion of Richard M. Nixon*, ch. 17 (1984).

5 Everything was blamed on Castro. Mudslides in California. The fact that you can't buy a decent tomato anymore. Was there an exceptionally high pollen count in Massapequa, Long Island, one day? It was Castro, exporting sneezes.

CALVIN TRILLIN (b. 1935), U.S. journalist, author. "Castro Forgotten, Alas," syndicated column, 18 May 1986.

CULTS

1 The neo-hippie-dips, the sentimentality-crazed iguana anthropomorphizers, the Chicken Littles, the three-bong-hit William Blakes—thank God these people don't actually go outdoors much, or the environment would be even worse than it is already.

P. J. O'ROURKE (b. 1947), U.S. journalist. *Parliament of Whores*, "Dirt of The Earth: The Ecologists" (1991).

2 A cult is a religion with no political power.

TOM WOLFE (b. 1931), U.S. journalist, author. *In Our Time*, ch. 2, "Jonestown" (1980).

CULTURE

1 Culture, then, is a study of perfection, and perfection which insists on becoming something rather than in having something, in an inward condition of the mind and spirit, not in an outward set of circumstances.

MATTHEW ARNOLD (1822-88), English poet, critic. *Culture and Anarchy*, ch. 1 (1869).

2 Culture, the acquainting ourselves with the best that has been known and said in the world, and thus with the history of the human spirit.

MATTHEW ARNOLD (1822-88), English poet, critic. *Literature and Dogma*, Preface (1873).

3 Here in the U.S., culture is not that delicious panacea which we Europeans consume in a sacramental mental space and which has its own special columns in the newspapers—and in people's minds. Culture is space, speed, cinema, technology. This culture is authentic, if anything can be said to be authentic.

JEAN BAUDRILLARD (b. 1929), French semiologist. *America*, "Utopia Achieved" (1986; tr. 1988).

4 We are in the process of creating what deserves to be called the idiot culture. Not an idiot sub-culture, which every society has bubbling beneath the surface and which can provide harmless fun; but the culture itself. For the first time, the weird and the stupid and the coarse are becoming our cultural norm, even our cultural ideal.

CARL BERNSTEIN (b. 1944), U.S. journalist. *Guardian* (London, 3 June 1992).

5 We are like ignorant shepherds living on a site where great civilizations once flourished. The shepherds play with the fragments that pop up to the surface, having no notion of the beautiful structures of which they were once a part.

ALLAN BLOOM (1930-92), U.S. educator, author. *The Closing of the American Mind*, pt. 2, "Our Ignorance" (1987).

6 General jackdaw culture, very little more than a collection of charming miscomprehensions, untargeted enthusiasms, and a general habit of skimming.

WILLIAM BOLITHO (1890-1930), British author. *Twelve against the Gods*, "Isadora Duncan" (1930).

7 Our attitude toward our own culture has recently been characterized by two qualities, braggadocio and petulance. Braggadocio—empty boasting of American power, American virtue, American know-how—has dominated our foreign relations now for some decades. . . . Here at home—within the family, so to speak—our attitude to our culture expresses a superficially different spirit, the spirit of petulance. Never before, perhaps, has a culture been so fragmented into groups, each full of its own virtue, each annoyed and irritated at the others.

DANIEL J. BOORSTIN (b. 1914), U.S. historian. *America and the Image of Europe*, Foreword (1960).

8 A man should be just cultured enough to be able to look with suspicion upon culture at first, not second hand.

SAMUEL BUTLER (1835-1902), English author. *Samuel Butler's Notebooks* (1951, p. 88).

9 Culture: the cry of men in face of their destiny.

ALBERT CAMUS (1913-60), French-Algerian philosopher, author. *Notebooks 1935-1942* (1962), entry for June 1937.

10 Without culture, and the relative freedom it implies, society, even when perfect, is but a jungle. This is why any authentic creation is a gift to the future.

ALBERT CAMUS (1913-60), French-Algerian philosopher, author. *The Myth of Sisyphus & Other Essays*, "The Artist and His Time" (1955).

11 What culture lacks is the taste for anonymous, innumerable germination. Culture is smitten with counting and measuring; it feels out of place and uncomfortable with the innumerable; its efforts tend, on the contrary, to limit the numbers in all domains; it tries to count on its fingers.

JEAN DUBUFFET (1901-85), French sculptor, painter. *Asphyxiating Culture and Other Writings*, "Asphyxiating Culture" (1986; tr. 1988; first published 1968).

12 In the room the women come and go
Talking of Michelangelo.

T. S. ELIOT (1888-1965), Anglo-American poet, critic. *The Love Song of J. Alfred Prufrock*.

13 It is of the essence of imaginative culture that it transcends the limits both of the naturally possible and of the morally acceptable.

NORTHROP FRYE (1912-91), Canadian literary critic. *Anatomy of Criticism*, second essay, "Anagogic Phase: Symbol as Monad" (1957).

14 Culture is a sham if it is only a sort of Gothic front put on an iron building—like Tower Bridge—or a classical front put on a steel frame—like the *Daily Telegraph* building in Fleet Street. Culture, if it is to be a real thing and a holy thing, must be the product of what we actually do for a living—not something added, like sugar on a pill.

ERIC GILL (1882-1940), British sculptor, engraver, writer, typographer. *Essays*, "Education for What" (1948).

15 Whenever I hear the word culture, I reach for my revolver.

ATTRIBUTED TO HERMANN GOERING (1893-1946), German Nazi leader. Whether or not Goering ever said it, the only recorded reference to this remark is from the play *Schlageter* (1933) by Hanns Johst (1890-1978), Nazi playwright and president of the Reich Chamber of Literature. The line was said by a stormtrooper in act 1, sc. 1: *Wenn ich Kultur hore . . . entsichere ich meinen Browning* (literally, "I cock my Browning").

16 One ought, every day at least, to hear a little song, read a good poem, see a fine picture, and, if it were possible, to speak a few reasonable words.

JOHANN WOLFGANG VON GOETHE (1749-1832), German poet, dramatist. *Wilhelm Meister's Apprenticeship*, bk. 5, ch. 1 (1795-96; tr. by Thomas Carlyle).

17 The bourgeoisie and the petty bourgeoisie have armed themselves against the rising proletariat with, among other things, "culture." It's an old ploy of the bourgeoisie. They keep a standing "art" to defend their collapsing culture.

GEORGE GROSZ (1893-1959), German artist. "The Art Scab" (written with John Heartfield) in *Der Gegner*, vol. 1, nos. 10-12 (Berlin, 1920; repr. in *Art Is In Danger*, tr. by Paul Gorrell, 1987).

18 One of the surest signs of the Philistine is his reverence for the superior tastes of those who put him down.

PAULINE KAEL (b. 1919), U.S. film critic. *I Lost It at the Movies*, "Zeitgeist and Poltergeist" (1965).

19 Culture is the tacit agreement to let the means of subsistence disappear behind the purpose of existence. Civilization is the subordination of the latter to the former.

KARL KRAUS (1874-1936), Austrian satirist. "In These Great Times," speech, 19 Nov 1914, in Vienna (first published in *Die Fackel*, Vienna, Dec. 1914; repr. in *In These Great Times: A Karl Kraus Reader*, ed. by Harry Zohn, 1976).

20 High culture is nothing but a child of that European perversion called history, the obsession we have with going forward, with considering the sequence of generations a relay race in which everyone surpasses his predecessor, only to be surpassed by his successor. Without this relay race called history there would be no European art and what characterizes it: a longing for originality, a longing for change. Robespierre, Napoleon, Beethoven, Stalin, Picasso, they're all runners in the relay race, they all belong to the same stadium.

> MILAN KUNDERA (b. 1929), Czech author, critic. Paul, in *Immortality*, pt. 3, "The Brilliant Ally of his Own Gravediggers" (1991).

21 Culture is the name for what people are interested in, their thoughts, their models, the books they read and the speeches they hear, their table-talk, gossip, controversies, historical sense and scientific training, the values they appreciate, the quality of life they admire. All communities have a culture. It is the climate of their civilization.

> WALTER LIPPMANN (1889-1974), U.S. journalist. *A Preface to Politics*, ch. 9 (1914).

22 Eclecticism is the degree zero of contemporary general culture: one listens to reggae, watches a western, eats McDonald's food for lunch and local cuisine for dinner, wears Paris perfume in Tokyo and "retro" clothes in Hong Kong; knowledge is a matter for TV games. It is easy to find a public for eclectic works.

> JEAN FRANÇOIS LYOTARD (b. 1924), French philosopher. "Answering the Question: What is Postmodernism?," in *Critique*, no. 419 (Paris, April 1982; repr. in *The Postmodern Condition: A Report on Knowledge*, 1979; rev. 1986).

23 Letting a hundred flowers blossom and a hundred schools of thought contend is the policy for promoting the progress of the arts and the sciences and a flourishing culture in our land.

> MAO ZEDONG (1893-1976), Founder of the People's Republic of China. Speech, 27 Feb. 1957, Peking. Quoted in: *Quotations of Chairman Mao* (1966).

24 If mass communications blend together harmoniously, and often unnoticeably, art, politics, religion, and philosophy with commercials, they bring these realms of culture to their common denominator—the commodity form. The music of the soul is also the music of salesmanship. Exchange value, not truth value, counts.

> HERBERT MARCUSE (1898-1979), U.S. political philosopher. *One-Dimensional Man*, ch. 3 (1964).

25 The ideas of the ruling class are in every epoch the ruling ideas, i.e., the class which is the ruling *material* force of society, is at the same time its ruling *intellectual* force.

> KARL MARX (1818-83) AND FRIEDRICH ENGELS (1820-95), German social philosophers and revolutionaries. *The German Ideology*, pt. 1, sct. B, "Ruling Class and Ruling Ideas" (1846).

26 A society person who is enthusiastic about modern painting or Truman Capote is already half a traitor to his class. It is middle-class people who, quite mistakenly, imagine that a lively pursuit of the latest in reading and painting will advance their status in the world.

> MARY MCCARTHY (1912-89), U.S. author, critic. *On the Contrary*, pt. 2, "Up the Ladder from *Charm* to *Vogue*" (1961; first published 1950).

27 Our culture has become something that is completely and utterly in love with its parent. It's become a notion of boredom that is bought and sold, where nothing will happen except that people will become more and more terrified of tomorrow, because the new continues to look old, and the old will always look cute.

> MALCOLM MCLAREN (b. 1946), British rock impresario. "Punk and History," transcript of discussion, 24 Sept. 1988, New York City (published in *Discourses: Conversations in Postmodern Art and Culture*, ed. by Russell Ferguson et al., 1990).

28 Men are not suffering from the lack of good literature, good art, good theatre, good music, but from that which has made it impossible for these to become manifest. In short, they are suffering from the silent shameful conspiracy (the more shameful since it is unacknowledged) which has bound them together as enemies of art and artists.

> HENRY MILLER (1891-1980), U.S. author. *Big Sur and the Oranges of Hieronymous Bosch*, pt. 2, ch. 1 (1958).

29 All objects, all phases of culture are alive. They have voices. They speak of their history and interrelatedness. And they are all talking at once!

> CAMILLE PAGLIA (b. 1947), U.S. author, critic, educator. *Sex, Art, and American Culture*, "Sexual Personae: The Cancelled Preface" (1992).

30 If everybody is looking for it, then nobody is finding it. If we were cultured, we would not be conscious of lacking culture. We would regard it as something natural and would not make so much fuss about it. And if we knew the real value of this word we would be cultured enough not to give it so much importance.

> PABLO PICASSO (1881-1973), Spanish artist. Quoted in: Jaime Sabartés, *Picasso: portraits et souvenirs*, ch. 9 (1946).

31 We know that a man can read Goethe or Rilke in the evening, that he can play Bach and Schubert, and go to his day's work at Auschwitz in the morning.

> GEORGE STEINER (b. 1929), French-born U.S. critic, novelist. *Language and Silence*, Preface (1967).

32 For the rest, whatever we have got has been by infinite labour, and search, and ranging through every corner of nature; the difference is that instead of dirt and poison, we have rather chosen to fill our hives with honey and wax, thus furnishing mankind with the two noblest of things, which are sweetness and light.

> JONATHAN SWIFT (1667-1745), Anglo-Irish satirist. Aesop, in *The Battle of the Books*, (1704). Aesop, representing the Ancients, likened them to a bee, as opposed to the spider which stood for the Moderns. The phrase "sweetness and light" was taken up by critic Matthew Arnold in *Culture and Anarchy*, ch. 5 (1869), from which it has passed into general usage.

33 Culture is an instrument wielded by teachers to manufacture teachers, who, in their turn, will manufacture still more teachers.

> SIMONE WEIL (1909-43), French philosopher, mystic. *The Need for Roots*, pt. 2, "Uprootedness in the Towns" (1949).

34 Mrs. Ballinger is one of the ladies who pursue Culture in bands, as though it were dangerous to meet it alone.

> EDITH WHARTON (1862-1937), U.S. author. *Xingu and other Stories*, "Xingu" (1916).

See also Stevens on MUSEUMS AND GALLERIES; Frye on RELIGION.

CUNNING

1 If ye had not plowed with my heifer, ye had not found out my riddle.

> BIBLE, HEBREW. Samson, in *Judges* 14:18, to the men who had answered his riddle, "Out of the eater came forth meat, and out of the strong came forth sweetness."

2 The weak in courage is strong in cunning.

> WILLIAM BLAKE (1757-1827), English poet, painter, engraver. *The Marriage of Heaven and Hell*, Plate 9 (1790-93).

3 With foxes we must play the fox.

> THOMAS FULLER (1654-1734), English physician. *Gnomologia*, no. 5797 (1732).

4 The fly that does not want to be swatted is safest if it sits on the fly-swat.

> G. C. LICHTENBERG (1742-99), German physicist, philosopher. *Aphorisms*, "Notebook J," aph. 70 (tr. by R. J. Hollingdale, 1990), written 1765-99.

5 The greatest cunning is to have none at all.

> CARL SANDBURG (1878-1967), U.S. poet. *The People, Yes*.

6 Simulated disorder postulates perfect discipline; simulated fear postulates courage; simulated weakness postulates strength.

> SUN TZU (6th-5th century B.C.), Chinese general. *The Art of War*, ch. 5, axiom 17 (c. 490 B.C.; ed. by James Clavell, 1981). The translator of this edition, Lionel Giles, added the explanatory note: "If you wish to feign confusion in order to lure the enemy on, you must first have perfect discipline; if you wish to display timidity in order to entrap the enemy, you must have extreme courage; if you wish to parade your weakness in order to make the enemy over-confident, you must have exceeding strength."

See also Disraeli on CANDOR.

CURIOSITY

1 Be not curious in unnecessary matters: for more things are shewed unto thee than men understand.

> APOCRYPHA. *Ecclesiasticus* 3:23.

2 Where the apple reddens
Never pry—
Lest we lose our Edens,
Eve and I.

> ROBERT BROWNING (1812-1889), English poet. *A Woman's Last Word*.

3 All my life I've been harassed by questions: Why is something this way and not another? How do you account for that? This rage to understand, to fill in the blanks, only makes life more banal. If we could only find the courage to leave our destiny to chance, to accept the fundamental mystery of our lives, then we might be closer to the sort of happiness that comes with innocence.

> LUIS BUÑUEL (1900-1983), Spanish filmmaker. *My Last Sigh*, ch. 15 (1983).

4 Curiosity is one of the lowest of the human faculties. You will have noticed in daily life that when people are inquisitive they nearly always have bad memories and are usually stupid at bottom.

> E. M. FORSTER (1879-1970), British novelist, essayist. *Aspects of the Novel*, ch. 5, "The Plot" (1927).

5 Curiosity is one of the most permanent and certain characteristics of a vigorous intellect.

> SAMUEL JOHNSON (1709-84), English author, lexicographer. *Rambler*, no. 103 (London, March 1751; repr. in *Works of Samuel Johnson*, vol. 4, ed. by W. J. Bate & Albrecht B. Strauss, 1969).

6 Curiosity is, in great and generous minds, the first passion and the last.

> SAMUEL JOHNSON (1709-84), English author, lexicographer. *Rambler*, no. 150 (London, 24 Aug. 1751; repr. in *Works of Samuel Johnson*, vol. 5, ed. by W. J. Bate and Albrecht B. Strauss, 1969).

7 Every age has a keyhole to which its eye is pasted.

> MARY McCARTHY (1912-89), U.S. author, critic. *On the Contrary*, pt. 1, "My Confession" (1961; first published 1953).

8 We never stop investigating. We are never satisfied that we know enough to get by. Every question we answer leads on to another question. This has become the greatest survival trick of our species.

> DESMOND MORRIS (b. 1928), British anthropologist. *The Naked Ape*, ch. 5 (1967).

9 I think, at a child's birth, if a mother could ask a fairy godmother to endow it with the most useful gift, that gift would be curiosity.

> ELEANOR ROOSEVELT (1884-1962), U.S. columnist, lecturer. *Today's Health* (Chicago, 2 Oct. 1966).

10 Curiosity is the direct incontinency of the spirit.

> JEREMY TAYLOR (1613-67), English churchman, devotional writer. *The Rule and Exercises of Holy Living*, ch. 2, sct. 5 (4th ed., 1654).

11 Disinterested intellectual curiosity is the life blood of real civilisation.

> G. M. TREVELYAN (1876-1962), British historian. *English Social History*, Introduction (1942).

12 The thirst to know and understand,
A large and liberal discontent.

> SIR WILLIAM WATSON (1858-1935), British poet. *Things That Are More Excellent*.

CUSTOM

1 Of course poets have morals and manners of their own, and custom is no argument with them.

> THOMAS HARDY (1840-1928), English novelist, poet. Faith, in *The Hand of Ethelberta*, ch. 2 (1875).

2   Without the aid of prejudice and custom, I should not be able to find my way across the room.

> WILLIAM HAZLITT (1778-1830), English essayist. *Sketches and Essays*, "On Prejudice" (1839).

3   Custom, then, is the great guide of human life.

> DAVID HUME (1711-76), Scottish philosopher, historian. *An Enquiry Concerning Human Understanding*, sct. 5, pt. 1 (1748). This statement embodied Hume's belief in political obedience arising from habit, as opposed to consent through a "social contract."

4   The despotism of custom is everywhere the standing hindrance to human advancement.

> JOHN STUART MILL (1806-73), English philosopher, economist. *On Liberty*, ch. 3 (1859).

5   Nature is seldom in the wrong, custom always.

> LADY MARY WORTLEY MONTAGU (1689-1762), English society figure, letter writer. Letter, 8 Aug. 1709 (published in *Selected Letters*, ed. by Robert Halsband, 1970).

6   Often, the less there is to justify a traditional custom, the harder it is to get rid of it.

> MARK TWAIN (1835-1910), U.S. author. *Tom Sawyer*, ch. 5 (1876).

7   Customs and convictions change; respectable people are the last to know, or to admit, the change, and the ones most offended by fresh reflections of the facts in the mirror of art.

> JOHN UPDIKE (b. 1932), U.S. author, critic. *New Yorker* (30 July 1990).

CYNICS

1   Cynic. A blackguard whose faulty vision sees things as they are, not as they ought to be.

> AMBROSE BIERCE (1842-1914), U.S. author. *The Devil's Dictionary* (1881-1906). This collection of Bierce's definitions was given the title *The Cynic's Word Book* for its original 1906 publication, though it originally appeared in newspapers under its more famous name, *The Devil's Dictionary*, and was retitled thus for the enlarged 1911 publication.

2   Cynicism is cheap—you can buy it at any Monoprix store—it's built into all poor-quality goods.

> GRAHAM GREENE (1904-91), British novelist. *The Comedians*, pt. 1, ch. 1, sct. 3 (1966).

3   A cynic is not merely one who reads bitter lessons from the past; he is one who is prematurely disappointed in the future.

> SYDNEY J. HARRIS (b. 1917), U.S. journalist. *On the Contrary*, ch. 7 (1962).

4   Cynicism is intellectual dandyism without the coxcomb's feathers.

> GEORGE MEREDITH (1828-1909), English author. Clara Middleton, quoting Mr. Whitford, in *The Egoist*, ch. 7 (1879). Clara added: "It seems to me that cynics are only happy in making the world as barren to others as they have made it for themselves."

5   The cynic, a parasite of civilisation, lives by denying it, for the very reason that he is convinced that it will not fail.

> JOSÉ ORTEGA Y GASSET (1883-1955), Spanish essayist, philosopher. *The Revolt of the Masses*, ch. 11 (1930).

6   Cynicism is the humour of hatred.

> SIR HERBERT BEERBOHM TREE (1853-1917), English actor-manager. Quoted in: Hesketh Pearson, *Beerbohm-Tree*, ch. 12 (1956).

7   Cecil Graham: What is a cynic?
Lord Darlington: A man who knows the price of everything and the value of nothing.

> OSCAR WILDE (1854-1900), Anglo-Irish playwright, author. *Lady Windermere's Fan*, act 3. The same formula was used in *The Picture of Dorian Gray*. See Wilde on VALUE.

See also Oates on LUCK.

DADA

1   No more painters, no more scribblers, no more musicians, no more sculptors, no more religions, no more royalists, no more radicals, no more imperialists, no more anarchists, no more socialists, no more communists, no more proletariat, no more democrats, no more republicans, no more bourgeois, no more aristocrats, no more arms, no more police, no more nations, an end at last to all this stupidity, nothing left, nothing at all, nothing, nothing.

> LOUIS ARAGON (1897-1982), French poet. "Manifesto of the Dada Movement," paper, read at the second Dada event, 5 Feb. 1920, Salon des Indépendents, Paris (first published in *Littérature*, Paris, May 1920; repr. in Maurice Nadeau, *The History of Surrealism*, ch. 3, 1964).

2   . . . a Dada exhibition. Another one! What's the matter with everyone wanting to make a museum piece out of Dada? Dada was a bomb . . . can you imagine anyone, around half a century after a bomb explodes, wanting to collect the pieces, sticking it together and displaying it?

> MAX ERNST (1891-1976), German painter, poet. Quoted in: C. W. E. Bigsby, *Dada and Surrealism*, ch. 1 (1972).

3   Dada hurts. Dada does not jest, for the reason that it was experienced by revolutionary men and not by philistines who demand that art be a decoration for the mendacity of their own emotions. . . . I am firmly convinced that all art will become dadaistic in the course of time, because from Dada proceeds the perpetual urge for its renovation.

> RICHARD HUELSENBECK (1892-1974), German poet, psychoanalyst. "Dada Lives," in *Transition*, no. 25 (Autumn 1936; tr. in *The Dada Painters and Poets: An Anthology*, ed. by Robert Motherwell, 1951).

4   DADA doubts everything. Dada is an armadillo. Everything is Dada, too. Beware of Dada. Anti-dadaism is a disease: selfkleptomania, man's normal condition, is DADA. But the real dadas are against DADA.

> TRISTAN TZARA (1896-1963), Rumanian-born French Dadaist. "Dada Manifesto on Feeble Love and Bitter Love," sct. 7 (first published in *La Vie des Lettres*, no. 4, Paris, 1921; repr. in *The Dada Painters and Poets*, ed. by Robert Motherwell, 1951).

SALVADOR DALI

1   Dali is like a man who hesitates between talent and genius, or, as one might once have said, between vice and virtue.

> ANDRÉ BRETON (1896-1966), French surrealist. "The First Dali Exhibition," preface to an exhibition catalogue (Nov. 1929; repr. in *What is Surrealism? Selected Writings*, ed. by Franklin Rosemont, 1978).

2   Dali was Renaissance man converted to psychoanalysis.

> SALVADOR DALI (1904-89), Spanish painter. Quoted in: Saranne Alexandrian, *Surrealist Art*, ch. 5 (1969).

3   He is like a comedian who for over thirty years has been unable to think of any new jokes.

> EDWARD JAMES (1907-84), British art collector, poet. Quoted by George Melly in: *Observer* (London, 4 Dec. 1988).

4   He is as antisocial as a flea. Clearly, such people are undesirable, and a society in which they can flourish has something wrong with it.

> GEORGE ORWELL (1903-50), British author. "Benefit of Clergy: Some Notes on Salvador Dali" (1944; repr. in *The Collected Essays, Journalism and Letters of George Orwell*, vol. 3, ed. by Sonia Orwell and Ian Angus, 1968).

DAMNATION

1   The damned are in the abyss of Hell, as within a woeful city, where they suffer unspeakable torments, in all their senses and members, because as they have employed all their senses and their members in sinning, so shall they suffer in each of them the punishment due to sin.

> ST. FRANCIS DE SALES (1567-1622), French churchman, devotional writer. *Introduction to the Devout Life*, pt. 2, ch. 15 (1609).

2   Suddenly to realise that one is sitting, damned, among the other damned—it is a most disquieting experience; so disquieting that most of us react to it by immediately plunging more deeply into our particular damnation in the hope, generally realized, that we may be able, at least for a time, to stifle our revolutionary knowledge.

> ALDOUS HUXLEY (1894-1963), British author. *Grey Eminence*, ch. 2 (1941).

3   And this is Hell—and in this smother,
All are damnable and damned;
Each one damning, damns the other;
They are damned by one another.
By none other are they damned.

> PERCY BYSSHE SHELLEY (1792-1822), English poet. *Peter Bell the Third*, pt. 3, "Hell," st. 15.

See also HELL.

DANCE

1   It may be possible to do without dancing entirely. Instances have been known of young people passing many, many months successively without being at any ball of any description, and no material injury accrue either to body or mind; but when a beginning is made—when the felicities of rapid motion have once been, though slightly, felt—it must be a very heavy set that does not ask for more.

> JANE AUSTEN (1775-1817), English novelist. *Emma*, ch. 29 (1816).

2   To shake your rump is to be environmentally aware.

> DAVID BYRNE (b. 1952), U.S. rock musician. Sleeve notes to his compilation of Brazilian Samba music, *O Samba: Brazil Classics 2* (1989).

3   There comes a pause, for human strength
Will not endure to dance without cessation;
And everyone must reach the point at length
Of absolute prostration.

> LEWIS CARROLL (1832-98), English author, mathematician. *Four Riddles*, no. 1 (first published 1869; repr. in *Phantasmagoria and Other Poems*, 1919).

4   Custom has made dancing sometimes necessary for a young man; therefore mind it while you learn it, that you may learn to do it well, and not be ridiculous, though in a ridiculous act.

> LORD CHESTERFIELD (1694-1773), English statesman, man of letters. Letter, 9 Oct. 1746 (first published 1774; repr. in *The Letters of the Earl of Chesterfield to His Son*, vol. 1, no. 113, ed. by Charles Strachey, 1901).

5   The Twist was a guided missile, launched from the ghetto into the very heart of suburbia. The Twist succeeded, as politics, religion, and law could never do, in writing in the heart and soul what the Supreme Court could only write on the books.

> ELDRIDGE CLEAVER (b. 1935), U.S. civil rights leader, writer. *Soul on Ice*, "Convalescence" (1968).

6   How inimitably graceful children are in general before they learn to dance!

> SAMUEL TAYLOR COLERIDGE (1772-1834), English poet, critic. *Table Talk* (1 Jan. 1832; published in *Specimens of the Table Talk of Samuel Taylor Coleridge*, ed. by Henry Nelson Coleridge, 1835; repr. in *Collected Works*, vol. 14, ed. by Kathleen Coburn, 1990).

7   The only dance masters I could have were Jean-Jacques Rousseau, Walt Whitman and Nietzsche.

> ISADORA DUNCAN (1878-1927), U.S. dancer. *My Life*, ch. 8 (1927).

8   The real American type can never be a ballet dancer. The legs are too long, the body too supple and the spirit too free for this school of affected grace and toe walking.

> ISADORA DUNCAN (1878-1927), U.S. dancer. *My Life*, ch. 30 (1927).

9   Dancing begets warmth, which is the parent of wantonness. It is, Sir, the great grandfather of cuckoldom.

> HENRY FIELDING (1707-54), English novelist, dramatist. Sir Positive Trap, in *Love in Several Masques*, act 3, sc. 7.

10   Nothing is more revealing than movement.

> MARTHA GRAHAM (1894-1991), U.S. dancer, choreographer.

"The American Dance" (published in *Modern Dance*, ed. by Virginia Stewart, 1935).

11   We look at the dance to impart the sensation of living in an affirmation of life, to energize the spectator into keener awareness of the vigor, the mystery, the humor, the variety, and the wonder of life. This is the function of the American dance.

MARTHA GRAHAM (1894-1991), U.S. dancer, choreographer. "The American Dance" (published in *Modern Dance*, ed. by Virginia Stewart, 1935).

12   They seldom looked happy. They passed one another without a word in the elevator, like silent shades in hell, hell-bent on their next look from a handsome stranger. Their next rush from a popper. The next song that turned their bones to jelly and left them all on the dance floor with heads back, eyes nearly closed, in the ecstasy of saints receiving the stigmata.

ANDREW HOLLERAN (b. 1943), U.S. journalist, author. *Dancer from the Dance*, ch. 2 (1978), of club regulars.

13   Dancing is a wonderful training for girls, it's the first way you learn to guess what a man is going to do before he does it.

CHRISTOPHER MORLEY (1890-1957), U.S. novelist, journalist, poet. *Kitty Foyle*, ch. 11 (1939).

14   I do not know what the spirit of a philosopher could more wish to be than a good dancer. For the dance is his ideal, also his fine art, finally also the only kind of piety he knows, his "divine service."

FRIEDRICH NIETZSCHE (1844-1900), German philosopher. *The Gay Science*, aph. 381 (1887 ed.).

15   When we were at school we were taught to sing the songs of the Europeans. How many of us were taught the songs of the Wanyamwezi or of the Wahehe? Many of us have learnt to dance the rumba, or the cha cha, to rock and roll and to twist and even to dance the waltz and foxtrot. But how many of us can dance, or have even heard of the gombe sugu, the mangala, nyang'umumi, kiduo, or lele mama?

JULIUS K. NYERERE (b. 1922), Tanzanian president. *Tanzania National Assembly Official Reports* (1962). Quoted in: Chris Stapleton and Chris May, *African All-Stars*, pt. 1 (1987).

16   Dancing with abandon, turning a tango into a fertility rite.

MARSHALL PUGH (b. 1925), British journalist, author. *The Chancer*, ch. 2 (1959).

See also Wilde on CAPITAL PUNISHMENT; Herschel on MUSIC.

DANDIES

1   The dandy should aspire to be uninterruptedly sublime. He should live and sleep in front of a mirror.

CHARLES BAUDELAIRE (1821-67), French poet. "My Heart Laid Bare" (written c. 1865; published in *Intimate Journals*, sct. 27, 1887; tr. by Christopher Isherwood, 1930; rev. by Don Bachardy, 1989).

2   Dandyism is the last flicker of heroism in decadent ages. . . . Dandyism is a setting sun; like the declining star, it is magnificent, without heat and full of melancholy. But alas! the rising tide of democracy, which spreads everywhere and reduces everything to the same level, is daily carrying away these last champions of human pride, and submerging, in the waters of oblivion, the last traces of these remarkable myrmidons.

CHARLES BAUDELAIRE (1821-67), French poet. *L'Art Romantique*, "The Painter of Modern Life," sct. 9 (1869; repr. in *Selected Writings on Art and Artists*, ed. by P. E. Charvet, 1972).

3   I cannot talk with civet in the room,
A fine puss-gentleman that's all perfume.

WILLIAM COWPER (1731-1800), English poet. *Conversation*.

4   Dandyism is . . . a variety of genius.

WILLIAM HAZLITT (1778-1830), English essayist. *The Spirit Of The Age*, "Lord Byron" (1825).

5   The wealthy curlèd darlings of our nation.

WILLIAM SHAKESPEARE (1564-1616), English dramatist, poet. Brabanzio, in *Othello*, act 1, sc. 2.

6   Detachment is the prerogative of an elite; and as the dandy is the nineteenth century's surrogate for the aristocrat in matters of culture, so Camp is the modern dandyism. Camp is the answer to the problem: how to be a dandy in the age of mass culture.

SUSAN SONTAG (b. 1933), U.S. essayist. *Against Interpretation*, "Notes on `Camp'," note 45 (1966; first published 1964).

7   A man who can dominate a London dinner table can dominate the world. The future belongs to the dandy. It is the exquisites who are going to rule.

OSCAR WILDE (1854-1900), Anglo-Irish playwright, author. Lord Illingworth, in *A Woman of No Importance*, act 3.

DANGER

1   To a profound pessimist about life, being in danger is not depressing.

F. SCOTT FITZGERALD (1896-1940), U.S. author. Quoted in: Andrew Turnbull, *Scott Fitzgerald*, ch. 6 (1962).

2   For believe me!—the secret of realizing the greatest fruitfulness and the greatest enjoyment of existence is: to *live dangerously!* Build your cities on the slopes of Vesuvius! Send your ships out into uncharted seas! Live in conflict with your equals and with yourselves! Be robbers and ravagers as long as you cannot be rulers and owners, you men of knowledge! The time will soon be past when you could be content to live concealed in the woods like timid deer!

FRIEDRICH NIETZSCHE (1844-1900), German philosopher. *The Gay Science*, aph. 283 (rev. ed. 1887).

DANTE ALIGHIERI

1   It appears to me that men are hired to run down men of genius under the mask of translators, but Dante gives too much of Caesar: he is not a republican.

WILLIAM BLAKE (1757-1827), English poet, painter, engraver. *Annotations to Boyd's Dante* (written c. 1800; published in *Complete Writings*, ed. by Geoffrey Keynes, 1957).

2   Honor the greatest poet.

DANTE ALIGHIERI (1265-1321), Italian poet. *The Divine Come-dy,* "The Inferno," cto. 4.

3   He stood bewildered, not appalled, on that dark shore which separates the ancient and the modern world. . . . He is power, passion, self-will personified.

WILLIAM HAZLITT (1778-1830), English essayist. *Lectures on the English Poets,* "On Poetry in General" (1818).

4   His very words are instinct with spirit; each is as a spark, a burning atom of inextinguishable thought; and many yet lie covered in the ashes of their birth and preg-nant with a lightning which has yet found no conductor.

PERCY BYSSHE SHELLEY (1792-1822), English poet. *A Defence of Poetry* (written 1821; published 1840).

DAUGHTERS

1   Oh my son's my son till he gets him a wife,
But my daughter's my daughter all her life.

DINAH MULOCK CRAIK (1826-87), English writer, poet. *Young and Old.*

2   How the mother is to be pitied who hath handsome daughters! Locks, bolts, bars, and lectures of morality are nothing to them: they break through them all. They have as much pleasure in cheating a father and mother, as in cheating at cards.

JOHN GAY (1685-1732), English dramatist. Mrs. Peachum, in *The Beggar's Opera,* act 1, sc. 8.

3   I only have two rules for my newly born daughter: she will dress well and never have sex.

JOHN MALKOVICH (b. 1953), U.S. stage and screen actor. *Inde-pendent on Sunday* (London, 5 April 1992).

4   The ultimate end of your education was to make you a good wife.

LADY MARY WORTLEY MONTAGU (1689-1762), English soci-ety figure, letter writer. Letter, 28 Jan. 1753, to her daughter Lady Bute (published in *Selected Letters,* ed. by Robert Halsband, 1970). Lady Montagu advised Lady Bute on bringing up her own daughter "to make her happy in a virgin state."

5   As long as a woman can look ten years younger than her own daughter, she is perfectly satisfied.

OSCAR WILDE (1854-1900), Anglo-Irish playwright, author. Lord Henry, in *The Picture of Dorian Gray,* ch. 4 (1891).

6   A man is free to go up as high as he can reach up to; but I, with all my style and pep, can't get a man my equal because a girl is always judged by her mother.

ANZIA YEZIERSKA (1881?-1970), Polish author. Fanny, in *Hun-gry Hearts and Other Stories,* "The Fat of the Land" (1920), talk-ing of her struggle to escape from the ghetto.

See also Bagnold on FATHERS.

DAY

1   Each morning the day lies like a fresh shirt on our bed; this incomparably fine, incomparably tightly woven tissue of pure prediction fits us perfectly. The happiness of the next twenty-four hours depends on our ability, on waking, to pick it up.

WALTER BENJAMIN (1892-1940), German critic, philosopher. *One-Way Street,* "Madame Ariane—Second Courtyard on the Left" (1928; repr. in *One-Way Street and Other Writings,* 1978).

2   Each time dawn appears, the mystery is there in its entirety.

RENÉ DAUMAL (1908-44), French poet, critic. "Poetry Black, Poetry White," in *Fontaine* no. 19-20 (Paris, March/April 1942; repr. in *The Powers of the Word,* ed. and tr. by Mark Polizzotti, 1991). *Chaque Fois que l'Aube Paraît* was the title given to a posthumous anthology of Daumal's writings.

3   . . . that moment of evening when the light and the darkness are so evenly balanced that the constraint of day and the suspense of night neutralize each other, leaving absolute mental liberty. It is then that the plight of being alive becomes attenuated to its least possible dimensions.

THOMAS HARDY (1840-1928), English novelist, poet. *Tess of the D'Urbervilles,* ch. 13 (1891).

4   What are days for?
Days are where we live.
They come, they wake us
Time and time over.
They are to be happy in:
Where can we live but days?

PHILIP LARKIN (1922-85), British poet. *Days,* st. 1.

5   Here's a new day. O Pendulum move slowly!

HAROLD MUNRO (1879-1932), British poet, critic. *Living.*

6   The arbitrary division of one's life into weeks and days and hours seemed, on the whole, useless. There was but one day for the men, and that was pay day, and one for the women, and that was rent day. As for the children, every day was theirs, just as it should be in every corner of the world.

ALICE CALDWELL RICE (1870-1942), U.S. author. *A Romance of Billy-Goat Hill,* ch. 15 (1912).

7   The genius of American culture and its integrity comes from fidelity to the light. Plain as day, we say. Happy as the day is long. Early to bed, early to rise. American virtues are daylight virtues: honesty, integrity, plain speech. We say yes when we mean yes and no when we mean no, and all else comes from the evil one. Amer-ica presumes innocence and even the right to happiness.

RICHARD RODRIGUEZ (b. 1944), U.S. author, journalist. *Fron-tiers,* "Night and Day" (1990).

8   Each day is a little life: every waking and rising a little birth, every fresh morning a little youth, every going to rest and sleep a little death.

ARTHUR SCHOPENHAUER (1788-1860), German philosopher. *Parerga and Paralipomena,* "Counsels and Maxims" (1851).

9   Little is to be expected of that day, if it can be called a day, to which we are not awakened by our Genius, but by the mechanical nudgings of some servitor, are not awakened by our own newly acquired force and aspira-tions from within, accompanied by the undulations of celestial music, instead of factory bells, and a fragrance filling the air—to a higher life than we fell asleep from; and thus the darkness bear its fruit, and prove itself to be good, no less than the light. That man who does not believe that each day contains an earlier, more sacred, and auroral hour than he has yet profaned, has despaired of life, and is pursuing a descending and darkening way.

HENRY DAVID THOREAU (1817-62), U.S. philosopher, author, naturalist. *Walden*, "Where I Lived, and What I Lived For" (1854).

10 There are more truths in twenty-four hours of a man's life than in all the philosophies.

RAOUL VANEIGEM (b. 1934), Belgian Situationist philosopher. *The Revolution of Everyday Life*, ch. 1, sct. 1 (1967; tr. 1983).

THE DEAD

1 Unquiet souls!
—In the dark fermentation of earth,
In the never idle workshop of nature,
In the eternal movement,
Ye shall find yourselves again.

MATTHEW ARNOLD (1822-88), English poet, critic. *Haworth Churchyard*.

2 The words of a dead man
Are modified in the guts of the living.

W. H. AUDEN (1907-73), Anglo-American poet. *In Memory of W. B. Yeats*, Poem 1, st. 4.

3 A man's death makes everything certain about him. Of course, secrets may die with him. And of course, a hundred years later somebody looking through some papers may discover a fact which throws a totally different light on his life and of which all the people who attended his funeral were ignorant. Death changes the facts qualitatively but not quantitatively. One does not know more facts about a man because he is dead. But what one already knows hardens and becomes definite. We cannot hope for ambiguities to be clarified, we cannot hope for further change, we cannot hope for more. We are now the protagonists and we have to make up our minds.

JOHN BERGER (b. 1926), British author, critic. *A Fortunate Man* (1967; repr. 1976, p. 160).

4 Any relic of the dead is precious, if they were valued living.

EMILY BRONTË (1818-48), English novelist. *Wuthering Heights*, ch. 13 (1847).

5 Man is a noble animal, splendid in ashes, and pompous in the grave.

SIR THOMAS BROWNE (1605-82), English doctor, author. *Urn Burial*, ch. 5 (1658).

6 All that tread,
The globe are but a handful to the tribes,
That slumber in its bosom.

WILLIAM CULLEN BRYANT (1794-1878), U.S. poet, editor. *Thanatopsis*, in *North American Review* (Cedar Falls, Iowa; Sept. 1817).

7 The dead should be judged like criminals, impartially, but they should be allowed the benefit of the doubt.

SAMUEL BUTLER (1835-1902), English author. *Samuel Butler's Notebooks* (1951, p. 223).

8 I have seen a thousand graves opened, and always perceived that whatever was gone, the *teeth and hair* remained of those who had died with them. Is not this odd? They go the very first things in youth & yet last the longest in the dust.

LORD BYRON (1788-1824), English poet. Letter, 18 Nov. 1820, to publisher John Murray (published in *Byron's Letters and Journals*, vol. 7, ed. by Leslie A. Marchand, 1973-81).

9 Woe, woe, woe . . . in a little while we shall all be dead. Therefore let us behave as though we were dead already.

RAYMOND CHANDLER (1888-1959), U.S. author. Letter, 5 Feb. 1951, to publisher Hamish Hamilton (published in *Raymond Chandler Speaking*, 1962).

10 What did it matter where you lay once you were dead? In a dirty sump or in a marble tower on top of a high hill? You were dead, you were sleeping the big sleep, you were not bothered by things like that. Oil and water were the same as wind and air to you.

RAYMOND CHANDLER (1888-1959), U.S. author. Philip Marlowe, in *The Big Sleep*, ch. 32 (1939).

11 I have a piece of great and sad news to tell you: I am dead.

JEAN COCTEAU (1889-1963), French author, filmmaker. *Discours du Grand Sommeil*, "Visite" (1920; repr. in *Collected Works*, vol. 4, 1947).

12 An orphan's curse would drag to hell,
A spirit from on high;
But oh! more horrible than that,
Is a curse in a dead man's eye!

SAMUEL TAYLOR COLERIDGE (1772-1834), English poet, critic. *The Rime of the Ancient Mariner*, pt. 4.

13 And what the dead had no speech for, when living,
They can tell you, being dead: the communication
Of the dead is tongued with fire beyond the language of the living.

T. S. ELIOT (1888-1965), Anglo-American poet, critic. *Little Gidding*, pt. 1, in *Four Quartets*.

14 Each in his narrow cell for ever laid,
The rude forefathers of the hamlet sleep.

THOMAS GRAY (1716-71), English poet. *Elegy in a Country Churchyard*, st. 4.

15 A considerable percentage of the people we meet on the street are people who are empty inside, that is, they are actually *already dead*. It is fortunate for us that we do not see and do not know it. If we knew what a number of people are actually dead and what a number of these dead people govern our lives, we should go mad with horror.

GEORGE GURDJIEFF (c. 1877-1949), Greek-Armenian religious teacher, mystic. Quoted in: P. D. Ouspensky, *In Search of the Miraculous*, ch. 8 (1949).

16 Now, a corpse, poor thing, is an untouchable and the process of decay is, of all pieces of bad manners, the vulgarest imaginable. For a corpse is, by definition, a person absolutely devoid of *savoir vivre*.

ALDOUS HUXLEY (1894-1963), British author. "Vulgarity in Literature" (1930; repr. in *Music at Night and Other Essays*, 1949).

17 I stay a little longer, as one stays,
To cover up the embers that still burn.

HENRY WADSWORTH LONGFELLOW (1807-82), U.S. poet. *Three Friends of Mine.*

18 Either he's dead or my watch has stopped.

GROUCHO MARX (1895-1977), U.S. comic actor. *A Day at the Races* (script by Robert Pirosh, George Seaton and George Oppenheimer, 1937).

19 He has gone over to the majority.

PETRONIUS (1ST CENTURY A.D.), Roman satirist. *Satyricon,* sct. 42.

20 There are few things more difficult than to appraise the work of a man suddenly dead in his youth; to disentangle "promise" from achievement; to save him from that sentimentalizing which confuses the tragedy of the interruption with the merit of the work actually performed.

EZRA POUND (1885-1972), U.S. poet, critic. *Gaudier-Brzeska: a Memoir,* ch. 13 (1916), of the French sculptor (and Vorticist) Henri Gaudier-Brzeska, killed in action in France, 1915.

21 Be the green grass above me,
With showers and dewdrops wet;
And if thou wilt, remember,
And if thou wilt, forget.

CHRISTINA ROSSETTI (1830-94), English poet, lyricist. *Song: "When I Am Dead,"* st. 2.

22 The white man's dead forget the country of their birth when they go to walk among the stars. Our dead never forget this beautiful earth, for it is the mother of the red man.

Attributed to SEATTLE (c. 1784-1866), Chief of the Dwamish, Suquamish, and allied Indian tribes. Letter, 1854, to President Franklin Pierce (published in *Brother Eagle, Sister Sky: A Message from Chief Seattle,* 1990). The letter, in which Seattle pleaded that his name should die with the ceding of the Washington State territories, was shown in 1992 to have been largely a forgery, devised by television scriptwriter Ted Perry for a historical epic in 1971.

23 I come to bury Caesar, not to praise him.
The evil that men do lives after them;
The good is oft interrèd with their bones.

WILLIAM SHAKESPEARE (1564-1616), English dramatist, poet. Mark Antony, in *Julius Caesar,* act 3, sc. 2, delivering Caesar's funeral oration.

24 After life's fitful fever he sleeps well.
Treason has done his worst. Nor steel nor poison,
Malice domestic, foreign levy, nothing
Can touch him further.

WILLIAM SHAKESPEARE (1564-1616), English dramatist, poet. Macbeth, in *Macbeth,* act 3, sc. 2.

25 He has outsoared the shadow of our night;
Envy and calumny and hate and pain,
And that unrest which men miscall delight,
Can touch him not and torture not again;
From the contagion of the world's slow stain,
He is secure.

PERCY BYSSHE SHELLEY (1792-1822), English poet. *Adonais,* st. 40, written for poet John Keats, who died at age 25.

26 We never become really and genuinely our entire and honest selves until we are dead—and not then until we have been dead years and years. People ought to start dead and then they would be honest so much earlier.

MARK TWAIN (1835-1910), U.S. author. *Autobiography,* ch. 55 (ed. by Charles Neider, 1959).

27 To the living we owe respect, but to the dead we owe only the truth.

VOLTAIRE (1694-1778), French philosopher, author. "Première Lettre sur Oedipe" (1719; repr. in *Works,* vol. 1, 1785).

28 No motion has she now, no force;
She neither hears nor sees;
Rolled around in earth's diurnal course,
With rocks, and stones, and trees.

WILLIAM WORDSWORTH (1770-1850), English poet. *A Slumber Did My Spirit Seal,* st. 2. This verse has been the subject of a literary dispute centering on Wordsworth's pantheism: is the death of the girl (Lucy) terrible because she is as inanimate as the earth's inert objects, or consoling because she is one with nature?

See also Wilde on MONUMENTS; Shawcross on WAR CRIMES.

DEAFNESS

1 The very deaf, as I am, hear the most astounding things all round them, which have not, in fact, been said. This enlivens my replies until, through mishearing, a new level of communication is reached.

HENRY GREEN (1905-74), British novelist. Interview in *Writers at Work* (Second Series, ed. by George Plimpton, 1963).

2 The consolation of deaf people is to read, and sometimes to scribble.

VOLTAIRE (1694-1778), French philosopher, author. Letter, 5, Aug. 1761, to Lord Chesterfield, in which Voltaire mentions that the two men share something, "not in point of wit, but in point of ears," in their old age (published in *The Complete Works of Voltaire,* vol. 107, 1972).

DEATH AND DYING

1 See in what peace a Christian can die.

JOSEPH ADDISON 1672-1719), English essayist. Quoted in: Edward Young, *Conjectures on Original Composition* (1759), as Addison's dying words.

2 It's not that I'm afraid to die, I just don't want to be there when it happens.

WOODY ALLEN (b. 1935), U.S. filmmaker. *Without Feathers,* "Death (A Play)" (1976).

3 Like figures on an ancient clock,
Warrior, or saint, or clown
(All's one to the machine) that wake
When each stale hour is done,
And with preliminary whirr
Play their allotted role,
Stiffly advance, engage, retire
Trembling a little still,
So blandly nodding Death and I
Nearer and nearer march,

At the click of night and the click of day,
— Click-clack! We approach, we approach!.

C. D. ANDREWS (1913-92), British poet, scholar. *An Idle Song for the Journey,* in *London Town* (summer 1934).

4   I feel no pain dear mother now,
But oh, I am so dry!
O take me to a brewery,
And leave me there to die.

ANONYMOUS (19th century).

5   Death not merely ends life, it also bestows upon it a silent completeness, snatched from the hazardous flux to which all things human are subject.

HANNAH ARENDT (1906-75), German-born U.S. political philosopher. *The Life of the Mind,* "Thinking," pt. 3, ch. 16 (1978).

6   Truth sits upon the lips of dying men.

MATTHEW ARNOLD (1822-88), English poet, critic. *Sohrab and Rustum.*

7   I do not believe that any man fears to be dead, but only the stroke of death.

FRANCIS BACON (1561-1626), English philosopher, essayist, statesman. *An Essay on Death.*

8   It is as natural to die as to be born; and to a little infant, perhaps, the one is as painful as the other.

FRANCIS BACON (1561-1626), English philosopher, essayist, statesman. *Essays,* "Of Death" (1597-1625).

9   As for death one gets used to it, even if it's only other people's death you get used to.

ENID BAGNOLD (1889-1981), British novelist, playwright. *Autobiography,* ch. 16 (1969).

10   Perhaps the whole root of our trouble, the human trouble, is that we will sacrifice all the beauty of our lives, will imprison ourselves in totems, taboos, crosses, blood sacrifices, steeples, mosques, races, armies, flags, nations, in order to deny the fact of death, which is the only fact we have.

JAMES BALDWIN (1924-87), U.S. author. "Letter from a Region in My Mind," in *New Yorker* (17 Nov. 1962; repr. in *The Fire Next Time,* 1963).

11   When one by one our ties are torn,
And friend from friend is snatched forlorn;
When man is left alone to mourn,
Oh! then how sweet it is to die!

ANNA LETITIA BARBAULD (1743-1825), English author. *A Thought on Death.*

12   To die will be an awfully big adventure.

J. M. BARRIE (1860-1937), British playwright. Peter, in *Peter Pan,* act 3.

13   Personally I have no bone to pick with graveyards, I take the air there willingly, perhaps more willingly than elsewhere, when take the air I must.

SAMUEL BECKETT (1906-89), Irish dramatist, novelist. *First Love* (1970; tr. 1973).

14   As the waters fail from the sea, and the flood decayeth and drieth up: so man lieth down, and riseth not: till the heavens be no more, they shall not awake, nor be raised out of their sleep.

BIBLE, HEBREW. *Job* 14:11-12.

15   Lord, make me to know mine end, and the measure of my days, what it is; that I may know how frail I am.

BIBLE, HEBREW. *Psalms* 39:4.

16   The last enemy that shall be destroyed is death.

BIBLE: NEW TESTAMENT. *1 Corinthians* 15:26.

17   O death, where is thy sting? O grave, where is thy victory?

BIBLE: NEW TESTAMENT. *1 Corinthians* 15:55.

18   And I looked, and behold a pale horse: and his name that sat on him was Death.

BIBLE: NEW TESTAMENT. *Revelation* 6:8.

19   No one's death comes to pass without making some impression, and those close to the deceased inherit part of the liberated soul and become richer in their humaneness.

HERMANN BROCH (1886-1951), Austrian novelist. *The Spell,* ch. 2 (1976; tr. 1987).

20   We all labour against our own cure, for death is the cure of all diseases.

SIR THOMAS BROWNE (1605-82), English doctor, author. *Religio Medici,* pt. 2, ch. 9 (1643).

21   For 'tis not in mere death that men die most.

ELIZABETH BARRETT BROWNING (1806-61), English poet. *Aurora Leigh,* bk. 3 (1857).

22   There is nothing which at once affects a man so much and so little as his own death.

SAMUEL BUTLER (1835-1902), English author. *Samuel Butler's Notebooks,* (1951, p. 241).

23   To die is but to leave off dying and do the thing once for all.

SAMUEL BUTLER (1835-1902), English author. *Samuel Butler's Notebooks* (1951, p. 255).

24   For the sword outwears its sheath,
And the soul wears out the breast.
And the heart must pause to breathe,
And love itself have rest.

LORD BYRON (1788-1824), English poet. *So We'll Go No More A-Roving.*

25   Men are never really willing to die except for the sake of freedom: therefore they do not believe in dying completely.

ALBERT CAMUS (1913-60), French-Algerian philosopher, author. *The Rebel,* pt. 5, "Historic Murder" (1951; tr. 1953).

26   There will be no lasting peace either in the heart of individuals or in social customs until death is outlawed.

ALBERT CAMUS (1913-60), French-Algerian philosopher, author. *Resistance, Rebellion and Death,* "Reflections on the Guillotine," last words (1961).

27   He who is obsessed by death is made guilty by it.

ELIAS CANETTI (b. 1905), Austrian novelist, philosopher. *The Secret Heart of The Clock: Notes, Aphorisms, Fragments 1973-1985,* "1973" (1991).

28 Well, there's a remedy for all things but death, which will be sure to lay us flat one time or other.

> MIGUEL DE CERVANTES (1547-1616), Spanish writer. Sancho Panza, in *Don Quixote*, pt. 2, bk. #5, ch. 10 (1615; tr. by P. Motteux).

29 Death eats up all things, both the young lamb and old sheep; and I have heard our parson say, death values a prince no more than a clown; all's fish that comes to his net; he throws at all, and sweeps stakes; he's no mower that takes a nap at noon-day, but drives on, fair weather or foul, and cuts down the green grass as well as the ripe corn: he's neither squeamish nor queesy-stomach'd, for he swallows without chewing, and crams down all things into his ungracious maw; and tho' you can see no belly he has, he has a confounded dropsy, and thirsts after men's lives, which he guggles down like mother's milk.

> MIGUEL DE CERVANTES (1547-1616), Spanish writer. Sancho Panza, in *Don Quixote*, pt. 2, bk. 5, ch. 20 (1615; tr. by P. Motteux).

30 'Tis the maddest trick a man can ever play in his whole life, to let his breath sneak out of his body without any more ado, and without so much as a rap o'er the pate, or a kick of the guts; to go out like the snuff of a farthing candle, and die merely of the mulligrubs, or the sullens.

> MIGUEL DE CERVANTES (1547-1616), Spanish writer. Sancho Panza, in *Don Quixote*, pt. 2, bk. 6, ch. 41 (1615; tr. by P. Motteux), to the dying Don Quixote.

31 Along with the lazy man . . . the dying man is the immoral man: the former, a subject that does not work; the latter, an object that no longer even makes itself available to be worked on by others.

> MICHEL DE CERTEAU (1925-1986), French author and critic. *The Practice of Everyday Life*, ch. 14, "An Unthinkable Practice" (1974).

32 He had been, he said, an unconscionable time dying; but he hoped that they would excuse it.

> CHARLES II (1630-85), King of England. Quoted in: Macaulay, *History of England*, vol. 1, ch. 4 (1849), on his deathbed.

33 Since the day of my birth, my death began its walk. It is walking toward me, without hurrying.

> JEAN COCTEAU (1889-1963), French author, filmmaker. *La Fin du Potomac*, "Postambule" (1939; repr. in *Collected Works*, vol. 2, 1947).

34 I have wrestled with death. It is the most unexciting contest you can imagine. It takes place in an impalpable greyness, with nothing underfoot, with nothing around, without spectators, without clamour, without glory, without the great desire of victory, without the great fear of defeat.

> JOSEPH CONRAD (1857-1924), Polish-born English novelist. Marlow, in *Heart of Darkness* (1902).

35 Death is a displaced name for a linguistic predicament.

> PAUL DE MAN (1919-83), Belgian-born U.S. literary critic. Quoted in: David Lehman, *Signs of the Times*, ch. 4 (1991). Lehman called this "the ultimate statement of the deconstructive credo."

36 Death is a Dialogue between,
The Spirit and the Dust.

> EMILY DICKINSON (1830-86), U.S. poet. *The Complete Poems*, no. 976 (1955).

37 Let us go in; the fog is rising.

> EMILY DICKINSON (1830-86), U.S. poet. Attributed last words. Quoted in: W. H. Auden, *A Certain World*, "Words, Last" (1970).

38 The infant runs toward it with its eyes closed, the adult is stationary, the old man approaches it with his back turned.

> DENIS DIDEROT (1713-84), French philosopher. *Elements of Physiology*, "Death" (notes written 1774-80, first published 1875; repr. in *Selected Writings*, ed. by Lester G. Crocker, 1966).

39 When I die I want to decompose in a barrel of porter and have it served in all the pubs in Dublin.

> J. P. DONLEAVY (b. 1926), U.S. author. Sebastian Dangerfield, in *The Ginger Man*, ch. 31 (1955).

40 As virtuous men pass mildly away,
And whisper to their souls to go,
Whilst some of their sad friends do say,
The breath goes now, and some say no.

> JOHN DONNE (c. 1572-1631), English divine, metaphysical poet. *Valediction: Forbidden Mourning*.

41 I would not that death should take me asleep. I would not have him meerly seise me, and onely declare me to be dead, but win me, and overcome me. When I must shipwrack, I would do it in a sea, where mine impotencie might have some excuse; not in a sullen weedy lake, where I could not have so much as exercise for my swimming.

> JOHN DONNE (c. 1572-1631), English divine metaphysical poet. Letter, Sept. 1608 (published in *Complete Poetry and Selected Prose*, ed. by John Hayward, 1929).

42 When one man dies, one chapter is not torn out of the book, but translated into a better language.

> JOHN DONNE (c. 1572-1631), English divine, metaphysical poet. *Devotions upon Emergent Occasions*, Meditation 17 (1624).

43 Life is a series of diminishments. Each cessation of an activity either from choice or some other variety of infirmity is a death, a putting to final rest. Each loss, of friend or precious enemy, can be equated with the closing off of a room containing blocks of nerves . . . and soon after the closing off the nerves atrophy and that part of oneself, in essence, drops away. The self is lightened, is held on earth by a gram less of mass and will.

> COLEMAN DOWELL (1925-85), U.S. novelist, dramatist, lyricist. Mrs. October's journal entry in *Mrs. October Was Here*, pt. 3, "Tasmania, Now" (1973).

44 Like pilgrims to th'appointed place we tend;
The world's an inn, and death the journey's end.

> JOHN DRYDEN (1631-1700), English poet, dramatist, critic. *Palamon and Arcite*, bk. 3.

45 I'm trying to die correctly, but it's very difficult, you know.

> LAWRENCE DURRELL (1912-90), British author. *Sunday Times* (London, 20 Nov. 1988).

46 Death is the king of this world: 'tis his park
Where he breeds life to feed him. Cries of pain
Are music for his banquet

> GEORGE ELIOT (1819-80), English novelist. *The Spanish Gypsy*, bk. 2 (1868).

47 Death is the last enemy: once we've got past that I think everything will be alright.

> ALICE THOMAS ELLIS (b. 1932), British author. "In the Psychiatrist's Chair," broadcast, 19 Aug. 1992, BBC Radio 4.

48 It is not death, but dying, which is terrible.

> HENRY FIELDING (1707-54), English novelist, dramatist. *Amelia*, bk. 3, ch. 4 (1751).

49 Death destroys a man: the idea of Death saves him.

> E. M. FORSTER (1879-1970), British novelist, essayist. Helen Schlegel, in *Howards End*, ch. 27 (1927).

50 To die is poignantly bitter, but the idea of having to die without having lived is unbearable.

> ERICH FROMM (1900-80), U.S. psychologist. *Man for Himself*, ch. 4 (1947).

51 A person doesn't die when he should but when he can.

> GABRIEL GARCÍA MÁRQUEZ (b. 1928), Colombian author. Colonel Aureliano Buendia, in *100 Years Of Solitude* (1967; tr. 1970; p. 199 of Picador ed., 1978).

52 We are all of us resigned to death: it's life we aren't resigned to.

> GRAHAM GREENE (1904-91), British novelist. *The Heart of the Matter*, bk. 3, pt. 2, ch. 2, sct. 1 (1948).

53 Your body must become familiar with its death—in all its possible forms and degrees—as a self-evident, imminent, and emotionally neutral step on the way towards the goal you have found worthy of your life.

> DAG HAMMARSKJÖLD (1905-61), Swedish statesman, Secretary-General of U.N. *Markings*, "Night is Drawing Nigh" (1963; written 1957).

54 We sometimes congratulate ourselves at the moment of waking from a troubled dream; it may be so the moment after death.

> NATHANIEL HAWTHORNE (1804-64), U.S. author. *Passages from the American Notebooks* (1868?), entry for 25 Oct. 1836.

55 Death cancels everything but truth; and strips a man of everything but genius and virtue. It is a sort of natural canonization. It makes the meanest of us sacred—it installs the poet in his immortality, and lifts him to the skies. Death is the greatest assayer of the sterling ore of talent. At his touch the drossy particles fall off, the irritable, the personal, the gross, and mingle with the dust—the finer and more ethereal part mounts with winged spirit to watch over our latest memory, and protect our bones from insult. We consign the least worthy qualities to oblivion, and cherish the nobler and imperishable nature with double pride and fondness.

> WILLIAM HAZLITT (1778-1830), English essayist. *The Spirit of the Age*, "Lord Byron" (1825), of the death of Byron.

56 Madam, Life's a piece in bloom
Death goes dogging everywhere:

She's the tenant of the room
He's the ruffian on the stair.

> W. E. HENLEY (1849-1903), English poet, critic, editor. *To W.R.*.

57 The call of death is a call of love. Death can be sweet if we answer it in the affirmative, if we accept it as one of the great eternal forms of life and transformation.

> HERMANN HESSE (1877-1962), German novelist, poet. Letter, 1950 (published in *Hermann Hesse: A Pictorial Biography*, "Montagnola," ed. by Volker Michels, 1973).

58 Ignore death up to the last moment; then, when it can't be ignored any longer, have yourself squirted full of morphia and shuffle off in a coma. Thoroughly sensible, humane and scientific, eh?

> ALDOUS HUXLEY (1894-1963), British author. Bruno Rontini, in *Time Must Have a Stop*, ch. 26 (1944). But in his 1936 novel *Eyeless in Gaza*, ch. 31, Huxley wrote, "Death . . . the only thing we haven't succeeded in completely vulgarizing.".

59 A belief in hell and the knowledge that every ambition is doomed to frustration at the hands of a skeleton have never prevented the majority of human beings from behaving as though death were no more than an unfounded rumour.

> ALDOUS HUXLEY (1894-1963), British author. *Themes and Variations*, "Variations on a Baroque Tomb" (1950).

60 Since the death instinct exists in the heart of everything that lives, since we suffer from trying to repress it, since everything that lives longs for rest, let us unfasten the ties that bind us to life, let us cultivate our death wish, let us develop it, water it like a plant, let it grow unhindered. Suffering and fear are born from the repression of the death wish.

> EUGÈNE IONESCO (b. 1912), Rumanian-born French playwright. *Fragments of a Journal* (1967; repr. 1968, p. 56).

61 The difficulty about all this dying, is that you can't tell a fellow anything about it, so where does the fun come in?

> ALICE JAMES (1848-92), U.S. diarist, sister of Henry and William James. Letter, 11 Dec. 1891, to her brother, psychologist William James (published in *The Diary of Alice James*, ed. by Leon Edel, 1964).

62 I'm not afraid of death but I am afraid of dying. Pain can be alleviated by morphine but the pain of social ostracism cannot be taken away.

> DEREK JARMAN (b. 1942), British filmmaker, artist, author. *At Your Own Risk: A Saint's Testament*, "1980's" (1992), of being HIV positive.

63 It matters not how a man dies, but how he lives. The act of dying is not of importance, it lasts so short a time.

> SAMUEL JOHNSON (1709-84), English author, lexicographer. Quoted in: James Boswell, *Life of Samuel Johnson*, 26 Oct. 1769 (1791).

64 I will be conquered; I will not capitulate.

> SAMUEL JOHNSON (1709-84), English author, lexicographer. Quoted in: James Boswell, *Life of Samuel Johnson*, Nov. 1784 (1791), of his last illness.

65 When I have fears that I may cease to be,
Before my pen has glean'd my teeming brain.

> JOHN KEATS (1795-1821), English poet. First lines of untitled

sonnet, written in letter, 31 Jan. 1818 (published in *Letters of John Keats*, vol. 2, no. 43, ed. by H. E. Rollins, 1958).

66 Land and sea, weakness and decline are great separators, but death is the great divorcer for ever.

JOHN KEATS (1795-1821), English poet. Letter, 30 Sept. 1820 (published in *Letters of John Keats*, no. 239, ed. by Frederick Page, 1954), written shortly after embarking from England on his last journey to Italy, where the poet succumbed to tuberculosis, 23 Feb. 1821.

67 Teach me to live that I may dread,
The grave as little as my bed.

THOMAS KEN (1637-1711), English churchman, hymn-writer. *Morning and Evening Hymn*, st. 3.

68 Because of its tremendous solemnity death is the light in which great passions, both good and bad, become transparent, no longer limited by outward appearences.

SØREN KIERKEGAARD (1813-55), Danish philosopher. *The Journals of Søren Kierkegaard: A Selection*, no. 328 (ed. and tr. by Alexander Dru, 1938), entry for 17 July 1840.

69 It is difficult to accept death in this society *because* it is unfamiliar. In spite of the fact that it happens all the time, we never see it.

ELISABETH KÜBLER-ROSS (b. 1926), Swiss-born U.S. psychiatrist. *Death: The Final Stage of Growth*, ch. 2 (1975).

70 Dying is something we human beings do continuously, not just at the end of our physical lives on this earth.

ELISABETH KÜBLER-ROSS (b. 1926), Swiss-born U.S. psychiatrist. *Death: The Final Stage of Growth*, ch. 6 (1975).

71 Death never takes the wise man by surprise,
He is always ready to go.

JEAN DE LA FONTAINE (1621-95), French poet, fabulist. *Fables*, bk. 8, "La Mort et le Mourant" (1678-79).

72 I warmed both hands before the fire of life;
It sinks, and I am ready to depart.

WALTER SAVAGE LANDOR (1775-1864), English author. *Finis*.

73 We are all dead men on leave.

EUGENE LEVINÉ, Russian Jew, friend of Luxemburg's lover, Jogiches. Quoted in: Hannah Arendt, *Men in Dark Times*, "Rosa Luxemburg: 1871-1919," sct. 3 (1968).

74 It is hard to have patience with people who say "There is no death" or "Death doesn't matter." There is death. And whatever is matters. And whatever happens has consequences, and it and they are irrevocable and irreversible. You might as well say that birth doesn't matter.

C. S. LEWIS (1898-1963), British author. *A Grief Observed*, pt. 1 (1961).

75 The course of my long life hath reached at last
In fragile bark o'er a tempestuous sea
The common harbor, where must rendered be
Account for all the actions of the past.

HENRY WADSWORTH LONGFELLOW (1807-82), U.S. poet. *Old Age*.

76 The grave's a fine and private place,
But none, I think, do there embrace.

ANDREW MARVELL (1621-78), English poet. *To His Coy Mistress*.

77 Some dying men are the most tyrannical; and certainly, since they will shortly trouble us so little for evermore, the poor fellows ought to be indulged.

HERMAN MELVILLE (1819-91), U.S. author. *Moby-Dick*, ch. 110 (1851).

78 At birth man is offered only one choice—the choice of his death. But if this choice is governed by distaste for his own existence, his life will never have been more than meaningless.

JEAN-PIERRE MELVILLE (1917-73), French film director. Prologue to the film, *Le Deuxième Souffle* (1965). Quoted in: Colin McArthur, *Underworld USA*, ch. 13 (1972).

79 Death is someone you see very clearly with eyes in the center of your heart: eyes that see not by reacting to light, but by reacting to a kind of a chill from within the marrow of your own life.

THOMAS MERTON (1915-68), U.S. religious writer, poet. *The Seven Storey Mountain*, pt. 1, ch. 3 (1948).

80 The world is the mirror of myself dying.

HENRY MILLER (1891-1980), U.S. author. *Black Spring*, "Third or Fourth Day of Spring" (1936).

81 In the attempt to defeat death man has been inevitably obliged to defeat life, for the two are inextricably related. Life moves on to death, and to deny one is to deny the other.

HENRY MILLER (1891-1980), U.S. author. *The Wisdom of the Heart*, "Creative Death" (1947).

82 How gladly would I meet,
Mortality, my sentence, and be earth
Insensible! how glad would lay me down,
As in my mother's lap! There I should rest,
And sleep secure.

JOHN MILTON (1608-74), English poet. Adam, in *Paradise Lost*, bk. 10.

83 Yet nightly pitch my moving tent,
A day's march nearer home.

JAMES MONTGOMERY (1771-1854), English poet. *At Home in Heaven*.

84 As death, when we come to consider it closely, is the true goal of our existence, I have formed during the last few years such close relations with this best and truest friend of mankind, that his image is not only no longer terrifying to me, but is indeed very soothing and consoling! And I thank my God for graciously granting me the opportunity . . . of learning that death is the *key* which unlocks the door to our true happiness.

WOLFGANG AMADEUS MOZART (1756-91), Austrian composer. Letter, 4 April 1787, to his father (published in *The Letters of Mozart and His Family*, ed. by Emily Anderson, 2nd ed., 1966).

85 So that he seemed not to relinquish life, but to leave one home for another.

CORNELIUS NEPOS (1ST CENTURY B.C.), Roman historian, biographer. *Lives*, "Atticus."

86 We all of us waited for him to die. The family sent him a cheque every month, and hoped he'd get on with it quietly, without too much vulgar fuss.

JOHN OSBORNE (b. 1929), British playwright. Jimmy, in *Look Back in Anger*, act 2, sc. 1.

87   Die, my dear doctor! That's the last thing I shall do!

> LORD PALMERSTON (1784-1865), English politician, prime minister. Attributed last words.

88   Between my head and my hand, there is always the face of death.

> FRANCIS PICABIA (1878-1953), French painter and poet. "Pithecomorphes," in *Littérature*, Second Series, no. 6 (Paris, 1 Nov. 1922; repr. in *Écrits*, vol. 2, "1922," ed. by Olivier Revault d'Allones and Dominique Bouissou, 1978).

89   Dying
Is an art, like everything else.
I do it exceptionally well.
I do it so it feels like hell.
I do it so it feels real.
I guess you could say I've a call.

> SYLVIA PLATH (1932-63), U.S. poet. *Lady Lazarus*.

90   Thank Heaven! the crisis —
The danger, is past,
And the lingering illness,
Is over at last —,
And the fever called "Living"
Is conquered at last.

> EDGAR ALLAN POE (1809-45), U.S. poet, critic, short-story writer. *For Annie*, st. 1.

91   Good God! how often are we to die before we go quite off this stage? In every friend we lose a part of ourselves, and the best part.

> ALEXANDER POPE (1688-1744), English satirical poet. Letter, 5 Dec. 1732, to poet and author Jonathan Swift, the day after the death of playwright John Gay.

92   We say that the hour of death cannot be forecast, but when we say this we imagine that hour as placed in an obscure and distant future. It never occurs to us that it has any connection with the day already begun or that death could arrive this same afternoon, this afternoon which is so certain and which has every hour filled in advance.

> MARCEL PROUST (1871-1922), French novelist. *Remembrance of Things Past*, vol. 6, "The Guermantes Way," pt. 2, ch. 1 (1921; tr. by Ronald and Odette Cortie, 1988).

93   Death is a shadow that always follows the body.

> ENGLISH PROVERB (14th century).

94   O eloquent, just, and mighty Death! whom none could advise, thou hast persuaded; what none hath dared, thou hast done; and whom all the world hath flattered, thou only hath cast out of the world and despised. Thou hast drawn together all the far-stretched greatness, all the pride, cruelty, and ambition of man, and covered it all over with these two narrow words, *Hic jacet*!

> SIR WALTER RALEGH (1552-1618), English author, soldier, explorer. *History of the World*, bk. 5, pt. 1, ch. 6, sct. 12 (1614).

95   I can die when I wish to: that is my elixir of life.

> ERNEST RENAN (1823-92), French writer, critic, scholar. Quoted in: H. W. Wardman, *Ernest Renan: a Critical Biography*, "The Republic" (1964).

96   So little done, so much to do.

> CECIL RHODES (1853-1902), British imperialist, business mag-
nate. Said on the day of his death. Quoted in: Lewis Michell, *Life of Rhodes*, vol. 2, ch. 39 (1910).

97   And all the winds go sighing,
For sweet things dying.

> CHRISTINA ROSSETTI (1830-94), English poet, lyricist. *A Dirge*.

98   Just like those who are incurably ill, the aged know everything about their dying except exactly when.

> PHILIP ROTH (b. 1933), U.S. novelist. *The Facts*, opening letter to Zuckerman (1988).

99   If Nature denies eternity to beings, it follows that their destruction is one of her laws. Now, once we observe that destruction is so useful to her that she absolutely cannot dispense with it . . . from this moment onward the idea of annihilation which we attach to death ceases to be real . . . what we call the end of the living animal is no longer a true finis, but a simple transformation, a transmutation of matter. According to these irrefutable principles, death is hence no more than a change of form, an imperceptible passage from one existence into another.

> MARQUIS DE SADE (1740-1814), French author. Dolmancé, in *Philosophy in the Bedroom*, "Dialogue the Fifth: Yet Another Effort, Frenchmen, If You Would Become Republicans" (1795).

100   When the body sinks into death, the essense of man is revealed. Man is a knot, a web, a mesh into which relationships are tied. Only those relationships matter. The body is an old crock that nobody will miss. I have never known a man to think of himself when dying. Never.

> ANTOINE DE SAINT-EXUPÉRY (1900-1944), French aviator, author. *Flight to Arras*, ch. 19 (1942).

101   One approaches the journey's end. But the end is a goal, not a catastrophe.

> GEORGE SAND (1804-76), French novelist. "Final Comment by George Sand," closing words (Sept. 1868; published in *The Intimate Journal of George Sand*, 1929).

102   I have a rendezvous with Death,
At some disputed barricade.

> ALAN SEEGER (1888-1916), U.S. poet, soldier. *I Have a Rendezvous with Death*. Seeger was killed in action fighting with the French Foreign Legion during the Somme offensive.

103   The final hour when we cease to exist does not itself bring death; it merely of itself completes the death-process. We reach death at that moment, but we have been a long time on the way.

> SENECA (c. 5 B.C.-A.D. c. 65), Roman writer, philosopher, statesman. *Epistulae ad Lucilium*, Epistle 24.

104   But I will be,
A bridegroom in my death, and run into't
As to a lover's bed.

> WILLIAM SHAKESPEARE (1564-1616), English dramatist, poet. Antony, in *Antony and Cleopatra*, act 4, sc. 15. Defeated and dishonored by Octavius Caesar, Antony longs to join Cleopatra, whom he believes to be dead, but in fact botches his act of suicide.

105   Men must endure,
Their going hence even as their coming hither.
Ripeness is all.

> WILLIAM SHAKESPEARE (1564-1616), English dramatist, poet.

Edgar, in *King Lear*, act 5, sc. 2, to his father Gloucester, who wishes only for death.

106 Nothing in his life,
Became him like the leaving it; he died,
As one that had been studied in his death,
To throw away the dearest thing he owed,
As'twere a careless trifle.

WILLIAM SHAKESPEARE (1564-1616), English dramatist, poet. Malcolm of Cawdor, in *Macbeth*, act 1, sc. 4.

107 The weariest and most loathèd worldly life,
That age, ache, penury and imprisonment
Can lay on nature is a paradise,
To what we fear of death.

WILLIAM SHAKESPEARE (1564-1616), English dramatist, poet. Claudio, in *Measure for Measure*, act 3, sc. 1.

108 He that dies pays all debts.

WILLIAM SHAKESPEARE (1564-1616), English dramatist, poet. Stephano, in *The Tempest*, act 3, sc. 2.

109 Life levels all men. Death reveals the eminent.

GEORGE BERNARD SHAW (1856-1950), Anglo-Irish playwright, critic. *Man and Superman*, "Maxims for Revolutionists: Fame" (1903).

110 Dying is a troublesome business: there is pain to be suffered, and it wrings one's heart; but death is a splendid thing—a warfare accomplished, a beginning all over again, a triumph. You can always see that in their faces.

GEORGE BERNARD SHAW (1856-1950), Anglo-Irish playwright, critic. Letter of condolence, 5 July 1913 (published in *Bernard Shaw: Collected Letters*, vol. 3, 1965). Shaw added: "And come and close my eyes too, when I die; and see me with my mask off as I really was."

111 Life does not cease to be funny when people die any more than it ceases to be serious when people laugh.

GEORGE BERNARD SHAW (1856-1950), Anglo-Irish playwright, critic. Ridgeon, in *The Doctor's Dilemma*, act 5.

112 Death is the veil which those who live call life:
They sleep, and it is lifted.

PERCY BYSSHE SHELLEY (1792-1822), English poet. The Earth, in *Prometheus Unbound*, act 3, sc. 3. In 1818, two years before the publication of this work, Shelley started an untitled sonnet, "Lift not the painted veil which those who live/Call Life . . ."

113 To fear death, my friends, is only to think ourselves wise, without being wise: for it is to think that we know what we do not know. For anything that men can tell, death may be the greatest good that can happen to them: but they fear it as if they knew quite well that it was the greatest of evils. And what is this but that shameful ignorance of thinking that we know what we do not know?

SOCRATES (469-399 B.C.), Greek philosopher. Quoted in: Plato, *Apology*, sct. 29.

114 A fiction about soft or easy deaths . . . is part of the mythology of most diseases that are not considered shameful or demeaning.

SUSAN SONTAG (b. 1933), U.S. essayist. *AIDS and Its Metaphors*, ch. 4 (1989).

115 For those who live neither with religious consolations about death nor with a sense of death (or of anything else) as natural, death is the obsene mystery, the ultimate affront, the thing that cannot be controlled. It can only be denied.

SUSAN SONTAG (b. 1933), U.S. essayist. *Illness As Metaphor*, ch. 7 (1978).

116 If I had my life over again I should form the habit of nightly composing myself to thoughts of death. I would practise, as it were, the remembrance of death. There is no other practice which so intensifies life. Death, when it approaches, ought not to take one by surprise. It should be part of the full expectancy of life. Without an ever-present sense of death life is insipid. You might as well live on the whites of eggs.

MURIEL SPARK (b. 1918), British novelist. Henry Mortimer, in *Memento Mori*, ch. 11 (1959).

117 When it comes to my own turn to lay my weapons down, I shall do so with thankfulness and fatigue, and whatever be my destiny afterward, I shall be glad to lie down with my fathers in honour. It is human at least, if not divine.

ROBERT LOUIS STEVENSON (1850-94), Scottish novelist, essayist, poet. Letter, autumn 1894 (published in *Stevenson's Letters to Charles Baxter*, 1956). Stevenson died in December of that year..

118 In my end is my beginning.

MARY STUART ("MARY QUEEN OF SCOTS") (1542-587), Queen of Scotland. Motto embroidered by herself on her canopy of state, while a prisoner of Elizabeth I of England. Elizabeth eventually ordered Mary's execution after a captivity lasting almost twenty years..

119 It is impossible that anything so natural, so necessary, and so universal as death should ever have been designed by Providence as an evil to mankind.

JONATHAN SWIFT (1667-1745), Anglo-Irish satirist. *Thoughts on Religion* (1768).

120 Authority forgets a dying king.

LORD TENNYSON (1809-92), English poet. *Idylls of the King*, "The Passing of Arthur."

121 Death is an endless night so awful to contemplate that it can make us love life and value it with such passion that it may be the ultimate cause of all joy and all art.

PAUL THEROUX (b. 1941), U.S. novelist, travel writer. "D is for Death," in *Hockney's Alphabet* (ed. by Stephen Spender, 1991), a book published to raise money for AIDS victims.

122 Do not go gentle into that good night,
Old age should burn and rage at close of day;
Rage, rage, against the dying of the light.

DYLAN THOMAS (1914-53), Welsh poet. *Do Not Go Gentle into that Good Night*.

123 Though lovers be lost love shall not;
And death shall have no dominion.

DYLAN THOMAS (1914-53), Welsh poet. *And Death Shall Have No Dominion*. St. Paul used these words in Romans 6:9, "Christ being raised from the dead dieth no more; death hath no more dominion over him."

124 But what is all this fear of and opposition to Oblivion? What is the matter with the soft Darkness, the Dreamless Sleep?

JAMES THURBER (1894-1961), U.S. humorist, illustrator. *Forum and Century* (June 1939). Also included in Clifton Fadiman, *I*

Believe: The Personal Philosophies of Certain Eminent Men and Women of Our Time (1939?).

125 But the peasants—how do the *peasants* die?

> LEO TOLSTOY (1828-1910), Russian novelist, philosopher. Attributed last words. Quoted in: W. H. Auden, *A Certain World,* "Words, Last" (1970).

126 Whoever has lived long enough to find out what life is, knows how deep a debt of gratitude we owe to Adam, the first great benefactor of our race. He brought death into the world.

> MARK TWAIN (1835-1910), U.S. author. *Pudd'nhead Wilson,* ch. 3, "Pudd'nhead Wilson's Calendar" (1894). Twain offered more thanks to Adam in winning for us "the `curse' of labor." See Twain on WORK.

127 Annihilation has no terrors for me, because I have already tried it before I was born—a hundred million years—and I have suffered more in an hour, in this life, than I remember to have suffered in the whole hundred million years put together. There was a peace, a serenity, an absence of all sense of responsibility, an absence of worry, an absence of care, grief, perplexity; and the presence of a deep content and unbroken satisfaction in that hundred million years of holiday which I look back upon with a tender longing and with a grateful desire to resume, when the opportunity comes.

> MARK TWAIN (1835-1910), U.S. author. *Autobiography,* ch. 49 (ed. by Charles Neider, 1959). Twain dictated his memoirs in the last years of his life, after he had lost his second daughter and wife.

128 A man does not die of love or his liver or even of old age; he dies of being a man.

> PERCIVAL ARLAND USSHER (1899-1980), Irish author, critic. *An Alphabet of Aphorisms* (1955).

129 In the twentieth century, death terrifies men less than the absence of real life. All these dead, mechanized, specialized actions, stealing a little bit of life a thousand times a day until the mind and body are exhausted, until that death which is not the end of life but the final saturation with absence.

> RAOUL VANEIGEM (b. 1934), Belgian Situationist philosopher. *The Revolution of Everyday Life,* ch. 4, sct. 2 (1967; tr. 1983).

130 Dear me! I must be turning into a god.

> VESPASIAN (A.D. 9-79), Roman emperor. Last words. Quoted by Suetonius in: *Lives of the Caesars,* "Vespasian," sct. 23 (tr. by Robert Graves).

131 Dying is the most embarrassing thing that can ever happen to you, because someone's got to take care of all your details.

> ANDY WARHOL (1928-87), U.S. Pop artist. Quoted in: Victor Bokris, *Warhol,* "Goodbye 1986-7" (1989).

132 And I will show that nothing can happen more beautiful than death.

> WALT WHITMAN (1819-92), U.S. poet. *Starting from Paumanok,* sct. 13.

133 Against you I will fling myself, unvanquished and unyielding, O Death!

> VIRGINIA WOOLF (1882-1941), British novelist. *The Waves,* final words (1931), chosen by her husband Leonard Woolf as her epitaph at her burial-place and former home, Monk's House,

Rodmell, Sussex, England. Virginia Woolf committed suicide by drowning on 28 March 1941.

134 The good die first,
And they whose hearts are dry as summer dust,
Burn to the socket.

> WILLIAM WORDSWORTH (1770-1850), English poet. The old man, in *The Ruined Cottage,* in *The Excursion,* bk. 1 (1814).

135 I balanced all, brought all to mind,
The years to come seemed waste of breath,
A waste of breath the years behind,
In balance with this life, this death.

> W. B. YEATS (1865-1939), Irish poet, playwright. *An Irish Airman Foresees His Death.*

136 In any man who dies there dies with him,
his first snow and kiss and fight . . .
Not people die but worlds die in them.

> YEVGENY YEVTUSHENKO (b. 1933), Russian poet. *People.*

137 All men think all men mortal, but themselves.

> EDWARD YOUNG (1683-1765), English poet, playwright. *Night Thoughts,* "The Complaint: Night 1" (1742-46).

See also Allen on The AFTERLIFE; Wittgenstein on ETERNITY; LIFE AND DEATH; Bridges on LOVERS; Shaw on SCIENCE; Bright, Kübler-Ross on WAR.

DEBATE

1 Books and harlots have their quarrels in public.

> WALTER BENJAMIN (1892-1940), German critic, philosopher. *One-Way Street,* "no. 13" (1928; repr. in *One-Way Street and Other Writings,* 1978).

2 It is not he who gains the exact point in dispute who scores most in controversy—but he who has shown the better temper.

> SAMUEL BUTLER (1835-1902), English author. *Samuel Butler's Notebooks* (1951, p. 112).

3 Freedom is hammered out on the anvil of discussion, dissent, and debate.

> HUBERT H. HUMPHREY (1911-78), U.S. Democratic politician, vice president. Speech, 6 June 1965, Syracuse University, N.Y.

4 Information, usually seen as the precondition of debate, is better understood as its by-product.

> CHRISTOPHER LASCH (b. 1932), U.S. historian. "The Lost Art of Political Argument" (first published as "Journalism, Publicity, and the Lost Art of Political Argument," in *Gannett Center Journal,* spring 1990; repr. in *Harper's,* New York, Sept. 1990).

5 If I tell you that I would be disobeying the god and on that account it is impossible for me to keep quiet, you won't be persuaded by me, taking it that I am ironizing. And if I tell you that it is the greatest good for a human being to have discussions every day about virtue and the other things you hear me talking about, examining myself and others, and that the unexamined life is not livable for a human being, you will be even less persuaded.

> SOCRATES (469-399 B.C.), Greek philosopher. Speech to the court, while on trial on charges of impiety and corruption. Quoted in: Plato, *Apology,* sct. 38. Socrates was explaining why it would be impossible for him to go into exile and keep his opinions to

himself. The paraphrase of his pronouncement, "The unexamined life is not worth living," has become a "Socratic dictum."

6 A philosopher who is not taking part in discussions is like a boxer who never goes into the ring.

LUDWIG WITTGENSTEIN (1889-1951), Austrian philosopher. Conversation, 1930 (published in *Personal Recollections*, ch. 6, ed. by Rush Rhees, 1981)

See also ARGUMENT; CONTROVERSY.

DEBAUCHERY

1 It is the hour to be drunken! To escape being the martyred slaves of time, be ceaselessly drunk. On wine, on poetry, or on virtue, as you wish.

CHARLES BAUDELAIRE (1821-67), French poet. "Enivrez-vous" (first published in *Figaro*, Paris, 7 Feb. 1864; repr. in *Paris Spleen*, 1869).

2 True debauchery is liberating because it creates no obligations. In it you possess only yourself; hence it remains the favorite pastime of the great lovers of their own person.

ALBERT CAMUS (1913-60), French-Algerian philosopher, author. The narrator (Jean-Baptiste Clamence), in *The Fall* (1956; repr. 1957, p. 77).

3 My problem lies in reconciling my gross habits with my net income.

ERROL FLYNN (1909-59), U.S. screen actor. Quoted in: Jane Mercer, *Great Lovers of the Movies*, "Errol Flynn" (1975).

4 Debauchery is perhaps an act of despair in the face of infinity.

EDMOND (1822-96) AND JULES DE GONCOURT (1830-70), French writers. *The Goncourt Journals* (1888-96; repr. in *Pages from the Goncourt Journal*, ed. by Robert Baldick, 1962), entry for 30 July 1861.

5 How utterly futile debauchery seems once it has been accomplished, and what ashes of disgust it leaves in the soul! The pity of it is that the soul outlives the body, or in other words that impression judges sensation and that one thinks about and finds fault with the pleasure one has taken.

EDMOND (1822-96) AND JULES DE GONCOURT (1830-70), French writers. *The Goncourt Journals* (1888-96; repr. in *Pages from the Goncourt Journal*, ed. by Robert Baldick, 1962), entry for 30 July 1861.

6 My only books,
Were Woman's looks,
And Folly's all they taught me.

THOMAS MOORE (1779-1852), Irish poet. *The Time I've Lost*.

7 You have wished to give her good manners, as if a young girl's happiness were not inseparable from debauchery and immorality, as if the happiest of all women had not incontestably to be she most in filth and libertinage, she who most and best defies every prejudice and who most laughs reputation to scorn.

MARQUIS DE SADE (1740-1814), French author. Dolmancé, in *Philosophy in the Bedroom*, "Dialogue the Seventh" (1795).

See also DISSIPATION.

DEBT

1 A man's indebtedness . . . is not virtue; his repayment is. Virtue begins when he dedicates himself actively to the job of gratitude.

RUTH BENEDICT (1887-1948), U.S. anthropologist. *The Chrysanthemum and the Sword*, ch. 6 (1946).

2 Forgetfulness. A gift of God bestowed upon debtors in compensation for their destitution of conscience.

AMBROSE BIERCE (1842-1914), U.S. author. *The Devil's Dictionary* (1881-1906).

3 It is very iniquitous to make me pay my debts—you have no idea of the pain it gives one.

LORD BYRON (1788-1824), English poet. Letter, 26 Oct. 1819 (published in *Byron's Letters and Journals*, vol. 6, ed. by Leslie A. Marchand, 1973-81).

4 It is said that the world is in a state of bankruptcy, that the world owes the world more than the world can pay.

RALPH WALDO EMERSON (1803-82), U.S. essayist, poet, philosopher. *Essays*, "Gifts" (Second Series, 1844).

5 A creditor is worse than a slave-owner; for the master owns only your person, but a creditor owns your dignity, and can command it.

VICTOR HUGO (1802-85), French poet, dramatist, novelist. Marius, in *Les Misérables*, "Marius," bk. 5, ch. 2.

6 Small debts are like small shot; they are rattling on every side, and can scarcely be escaped without a wound: great debts are like cannon; of loud noise, but little danger.

SAMUEL JOHNSON (1709-84), English author, lexicographer. Letter, 1759, to Joseph Simpson. Quoted in: Boswell, *Life of Samuel Johnson* (1791).

7 In the midst of life we are in debt.

ETHEL WATTS MUMFORD (1878-1940), U.S. novelist, humorous writer. *The Altogether New Cynic's Calendar* (1907; written with Addison Mizner and Oliver Herford). The line is a parody of the First anthem of the service for the Burial of the Dead, in *The Book of Common Prayer* (1662): "In the midst of life we are in death."

8 To John I ow'd great obligation;
But John, unhappily, thought fit
To publish it to all the nation:
Sure John and I are more than quit.

MATTHEW PRIOR (1664-1721), English poet, diplomat. *Epigram—Another*.

9 Speak not of my debts unless you mean to pay them.

ENGLISH PROVERB (17th century). Collected in George Herbert, *Outlandish Proverbs* (1640).

10 Bankruptcy is a sacred state, a condition beyond conditions, as theologians might say, and attempts to investigate it are necessarily obscene, like spiritualism. One knows only that he has passed into it and lives beyond us, in a condition not ours.

JOHN UPDIKE (b. 1932), U.S. author, critic. *Hugging the Shore*, "The Bankrupt Man" (1983).

11 The payment of debts is necessary for social order. The non-payment is quite equally necessary for social order. For centuries humanity has oscillated, serenely unaware, between these two contradictory necessities.

SIMONE WEIL (1909-43), French philosopher, mystic. "On Bankruptcy" (written 1937; published in *Selected Essays,* ed. by Richard Rees, 1962).

DECADENCE

1 The goal of every culture is to decay through over-civilization; the factors of decadence,—luxury, scepticism, weariness and superstition,—are constant. The civilization of one epoch becomes the manure of the next.

CYRIL CONNOLLY (1903-74), British critic. *The Unquiet Grave,* pt. 2 (1944; rev. 1951).

2 Decadence is a difficult word to use since it has become little more than a term of abuse applied by critics to anything they do not yet understand or which seems to differ from their moral concepts.

ERNEST HEMINGWAY (1899-1961), U.S. author. *Death in the Afternoon,* ch. 7 (1932).

3 Every civilization when it loses its inner vision and its cleaner energy, falls into a new sort of sordidness, more vast and more stupendous than the old savage sort. An Augean stable of metallic filth.

D. H. LAWRENCE (1885-1930), British author. *St. Mawr* (1925; repr. in *The Short Novels,* vol. 2, 1979).

4 Men first feel necessity, then look for utility, next attend to comfort, still later amuse themselves with pleasure, thence grow dissolute in luxury, and finally go mad and waste their substance.

GIAMBATTISTA VICO (1688-1744), Italian philosopher, historian. *The New Science,* bk. 1, para. 241 (1744 ed.; tr. 1984).

DECAY

1 Thy decay
Is still impregnate with divinity.

LORD BYRON (1788-1824), English poet. *Childe Harold's Pilgrimage,* cto. 4, st. 55, of Italy.

2 Show me one thing here on earth which has begun well and not ended badly. The proudest palpitations are engulfed in a sewer, where they cease throbbing, as though having reached their natural term: this downfall constitutes the heart's drama and the negative meaning of history.

E. M. CIORAN (b. 1911), Rumanian-born French philosopher. *A Short History of Decay,* ch. 1, "Itinerary of Hate" (1949).

3 Just as the constant increase of entropy is the basic law of the universe, so it is the basic law of life to be ever more highly structured and to struggle against entropy.

VÁCLAV HAVEL (b. 1936), Czech playwright, president. *Living in Truth,* pt. 1, "Letter to Dr. Gustáv Husák" (1986).

4 I have always looked upon decay as being just as wonderful and rich an expression of life as growth.

HENRY MILLER (1891-1980), U.S. author. *The Wisdom of the Heart,* "Reflections on Writing" (1947).

5 'Tis but an hour ago since it was nine,
And after one hour more 'twill be eleven.
And so from hour to hour we ripe and ripe,
And then from hour to hour we rot and rot.
And thereby hangs a tale.

WILLIAM SHAKESPEARE (1564-1616), English dramatist, poet. The "motley fool" Touchstone, reported by Jaques in *As You Like It,* act 2, sc. 7.

6 There are people who, like houses, are beautiful in dilapidation.

LOGAN PEARSALL SMITH (1865-1946), U.S. essayist, aphorist. *Afterthoughts,* "Age and Death" (1931).

7 Old age cannot be cured. An epoch or a civilization cannot be prevented from breathing its last. A natural process that happens to all flesh and all human manifestations cannot be arrested. You can only wring your hands and utter a beautiful swan song.

RENEE WINEGARTEN (b. 1922), British author, critic. "The Idea of Decadence," in *Commentary* (New York, Sept. 1974).

DECEPTION

1 The great advantages of simulation and dissimulation are three. First to lay asleep opposition and to surprise. For where a man's intentions are published, it is an alarum to call up all that are against them. The second is to reserve a man's self a fair retreat: for if a man engage himself, by a manifest declaration, he must go through, or take a fall. The third is, the better to discover the mind of another. For to him that opens himself, men will hardly show themselves adverse; but will fair let him go on, and turn their freedom of speech to freedom of thought.

FRANCIS BACON (1561-1626), English philosopher, essayist, statesman. *Essays,* "Of Simulation and Dissimulation" (1597-1625).

2 Man's mind is so formed that it is far more susceptible to falsehood than to truth.

DESIDERIUS ERASMUS c. 1466-1536), Dutch humanist. *Praise of Folly,* ch. 45 (1509).

3 I became a virtuoso of deceit. It wasn't pleasure I was after, it was knowledge. I consulted the strictest moralists to learn how to appear, philosophers to find out what to think and novelists to see what I could get away with. And, in the end, I distilled everything down to one wonderfully simple principle: win or die.

CHRISTOPHER HAMPTON (b. 1946), British playwright. Merteuil, in *Dangerous Liaisons* (screenplay, 1989).

4 I have always considered it as treason against the great republic of human nature, to make any man's virtues the means of deceiving him.

SAMUEL JOHNSON (1709-84), English author, lexicographer. Rasselas, in *The History of Rasselas,* ch. 46 (1759).

5 To know how to dissimulate is the knowledge of kings.

CARDINAL DE RICHELIEU (1585-1642), French statesman. *Testament Politique,* "Maxims" (1641).

6   It seems to me that there are two kinds of trickery: the "fronts" people assume before one another's eyes, and the "front" a writer puts on the face of reality.

> FRANÇOISE SAGAN (b. 1935), French novelist, playwright. Interview in *Writers at Work* (First Series, ed. by Malcolm Cowley, 1958).

7   For I have sworn thee fair, and thought thee bright,
Who art as black as hell, as dark as night.

> WILLIAM SHAKESPEARE (1564-1616), English dramatist, poet. *Sonnet 147.*

8   Whenever, therefore, people are deceived and form opinions wide of the truth, it is clear that the error has slid into their minds through the medium of certain resemblances to that truth.

> SOCRATES (469-399 B.C.), Greek philosopher. Quoted in: Plato, *Phaedrus*, sct. 262.

9   A deception that elevates us is dearer than a host of low truths.

> MARINA TSVETAEVA (1892-1941), Russian poet. *Pushkin and Pugachev* (1937; repr. in *A Captive Spirit: Selected Prose*, ed. and tr. by J. Marin King, 1980).

See also LIES AND LYING.

DECISIONS

1   Every decision is liberating, even if it leads to disaster. Otherwise, why do so many people walk upright and with open eyes into their misfortune?

> ELIAS CANETTI (b. 1905), Austrian novelist, philosopher. *The Secret Heart Of The Clock: Notes, Aphorisms, Fragments 1973-1985*, "1980" (1991).

2   How could a man be satisfied with a decision between such alternatives and under such circumstances? No more than he can be satisfied with his hat, which he's chosen from among such shapes as the resources of the age offer him, wearing it at best with a resignation which is chiefly supported by comparison.

> GEORGE ELIOT (1819-80), English novelist, editor. *Middlemarch*, bk. 2, ch. 18 (1871), of the Reverend Walter Tyke.

3   The quality of decision is like the well-timed swoop of a falcon which enables it to strike and destroy its victim.

> SUN TZU (6-5TH CENTURY B.C.), Chinese general. *The Art of War*, ch. 5, axiom 13 (c. 490 B.C.; ed. by James Clavell, 1981).

4   When people ask for time, it's always for time to say no. Yes has one more letter in it, but it doesn't take half as long to say.

> EDITH WHARTON (1862-1937), U.S. author. Judith, in *The Children*, ch. 25 (1928).

See also Galbraith on CONFERENCES; Amiel on IMPARTIALITY; INDECISION; Lincoln on RESOLVE.

DECOLONIZATION

1   Many politicians of our time are in the habit of laying it down as a self-evident proposition that no people ought to be free till they are fit to use their freedom. The maxim is worthy of the fool in the old story who resolved not to go into the water until he had learnt to swim. If men are to wait for liberty till they become wise and good in slavery, they may indeed wait forever.

> THOMAS BABINGTON MACAULAY (1800-59), English historian, Whig politician. "Milton," in *Edinburgh Review* (Aug. 1825; repr. in *Critical and Historical Essays*, 1843).

2   The wind of change is blowing through the continent. Whether we like it or not, this growth of national consciousness is a political fact.

> HAROLD MACMILLAN (1894-1986), British Conservative politician, prime minister. Speech, 3 Feb. 1960, to both houses of the South African Parliament, Cape Town.

3   The best way of learning to be an independent sovereign state is to be an independent sovereign state.

> KWAME NKRUMAH (1900-72), Ghanaian president. Speech, 18 May 1956, to Legislative Assembly, Accra.

4   It is far easier for the proverbial camel to pass through the needle's eye, hump and all, than for an erstwhile colonial administration to give sound and honest counsel of a *political* nature to its liberated territory.

> KWAME NKRUMAH (1900-72), Ghanaian president. *Consciencism*, ch. 4 (1964).

5   Everything that is right or natural pleads for separation. The blood of the slain, the weeping voice of nature cries, *'tis time to part.*

> THOMAS PAINE (1737-1809), Anglo-American political theorist, writer. *Common Sense* (1776).

6   I don't think it is always necessary to take up the anti-colonial—or is it post-colonial?—cudgels against English. What seems to me to be happening is that those people who were once colonized by the language are now rapidly remaking it, domesticating it, becoming more and more relaxed about the way they use it—assisted by the English language's enormous flexibility and size, they are carving out large territories for themselves within its frontiers.

> SALMAN RUSHDIE (b. 1948), Indian-born British author. *Imaginary Homelands*, "Commonwealth Literature Does Not Exist" (1991; first published 1983).

DECONSTRUCTION

See STRUCTURALISM AND DECONSTRUCTION.

DECORUM

1   Let them cant about decorum
Who have characters to lose.

> ROBERT BURNS (1759-96), Scottish poet. *Love and Liberty—A Cantata.*

2 One must not make oneself cheap here—that is a cardinal point—or else one is done. Whoever is *most impertinent* has the best chance.

> WOLFGANG AMADEUS MOZART (1756-91), Austrian composer. Letter, 5 Sept. 1781, to his father (published in *The Letters of Mozart and His Family*, 2d ed., ed. by Emily Anderson, 1966). The letter was sent from Vienna, complaining of the coarse linen shirts that Mozart was forced to wear.

DEFEAT

1 I give the fight up: let there be an end,
A privacy, an obscure nook for me.
I want to be forgotten even by God.

> ROBERT BROWNING (1812-89), English poet. *Paracelsus*, pt. 5.

2 Defeat doesn't finish a man—quit does. A man is not finished when he's defeated. He's finished when he quits.

> RICHARD M. NIXON (b. 1913), U.S. Republican politician, president. Note written July, 1969, with reference to Edward Kennedy and the Chappaquiddick Bridge incident. Quoted in: William Safire, *Before the Fall* pt. 3, ch. 4 (1975).

3 To walk through the ruined cities of Germany is to feel an actual doubt about the continuity of civilization.

> GEORGE ORWELL (1903-50), British author. *Observer* (London, 8 April 1945).

4 Commonly, people believe that defeat is characterized by a general bustle and a feverish rush. Bustle and rush are the signs of victory, not of defeat. Victory is a thing of action. It is a house in the act of being built. Every participant in victory sweats and puffs, carrying the stones for the building of the house. But defeat is a thing of weariness, of incoherence, of boredom. And above all of futility.

> ANTOINE DE SAINT-EXUPÉRY (1900-1944), French aviator, author. *Flight to Arras*, ch. 1 (1942).

5 The injustice of defeat lies in the fact that its most innocent victims are made to look like heartless accomplices. It is impossible to see behind defeat, the sacrifices, the austere performance of duty, the self-discipline and the vigilance that are there—those things the god of battle does not take account of.

> ANTOINE DE SAINT-EXUPÉRY (1900-1944), French aviator, author. *Flight to Arras*, ch. 15 (1942).

6 For by superior energies; more strict
Affiance in each other; faith more firm
In their unhallowed principles, the bad
Have fairly earned a victory o'er the weak,
The vacillating, inconsistent good.

> WILLIAM WORDSWORTH (1770-1850), English poet. *The Excursion*, bk. 4.

DEFENSE

1 Our capacity to retaliate must be, and is, massive in order to deter all forms of aggression.

> JOHN FOSTER DULLES (1888-1959), U.S. Republican politician. Speech, 8 Dec. 1955, Chicago.

2 Self-defence is Nature's eldest law.

> JOHN DRYDEN (1631-1700), English poet, dramatist, critic. *Absalom and Achitophel*, pt. 1.

3 There's no telling what might have happened to our defense budget if Saddam Hussein hadn't invaded Kuwait that August and set everyone gearing up for World War II. Can we count on Saddam Hussein to come along every year and resolve our defense-policy debates? Given the history of the Middle East, it's possible.

> P. J. O'ROURKE (b. 1947), U.S. journalist. *Parliament of Whores*, 'Cry Havoc!' and Let Slip the Hogs of Peace" (1991).

4 We're in greater danger today than we were the day after Pearl Harbor. Our military is absolutely incapable of defending this country.

> RONALD REAGAN (b. 1911), U.S. Republican politician, president. *New York Times* (12 April 1980). Quoted in: *Reagan's Reign of Error*, "Temptation of Pride" (ed. by Mark Green and Gail MacColl, 1987).

5 Harsh necessity, and the newness of my kingdom, force me to do such things and to guard my frontiers everywhere.

> VIRGIL (70-19 B.C.), Roman poet. Dido, Queen of Carthage, in *Aeneid*, bk. 1.

DEFIANCE

1 Though I sit down now, the time will come when you will hear me.

> BENJAMIN DISRAELI (1804-81), English statesman, author. Maiden speech, 7 Dec. 1837, to House of Commons.

2 And yet . . . it moves.

> ATTRIBUTED TO GALILEO GALILEI (1564-1642), Italian astronomer, mathematician, physicist. Galileo, referring to the earth, allegedly muttered this remark to his companion in 1633, as he rose from signing a recantation—forced on him by the Inquisition in Rome—of the Copernican theory that the sun, not the earth, was the center of the solar system.

3 Either that wallpaper goes, or I do.

> OSCAR WILDE (1854-1900), Anglo-Irish author. Attributed last words, as he lay dying in a drab Paris hotel room.

DEFINITION

1 Men have defined the parameters of every subject. All feminist arguments, however radical in intent or consequence, are with or against assertions or premises implicit in the male system, which is made credible or authentic by the power of men to name.

> ANDREA DWORKIN (b. 1946), U.S. feminist critic. *Pornography*, ch. 1 (1981).

2 The human mind is so complex and things are so tangled up with each other that, to explain a blade of straw, one would have to take to pieces an entire universe. . . . A definition is a sack of flour compressed into a thimble.

> RÉMY DE GOURMONT (1858-1915), French critic, novelist. "Glory and the Idea of Immortality," sct. 1 (published in *Le Chemin de Velours*, 1902; repr. in *Selected Writings*, ed. and tr. by Glen S. Burne, 1966).

3 By speaking, by thinking, we undertake to clarify things, and that forces us to exacerbate them, dislocate them, schematize them. Every concept is in itself an exaggeration.

JOSÉ ORTEGA Y GASSET (1883-1955), Spanish essayist, philosopher. "In Search of Goethe from Within," in *Partisan Review* (New Brunswick, N.J., Dec. 1949; repr. in *The Dehumanization of Art and Other Essays*, 1968).

4 It is the business of thought to define things, to find the boundaries; thought, indeed, is a ceaseless process of definition. It is the business of Art to give things shape. Anyone who takes no delight in the firm outline of an object, or in its essential character, has no artistic sense. . . . He cannot even be nourished by Art. Like Ephraim, he feeds upon the East wind, which has no boundaries.

VANCE PALMER (1885-1959), Australian author, poet. "On Boundaries" (1921; repr. in *Intimate Portraits*, ed. by H. P. Heseltine, 1969).

5 In the animal kingdom, the rule is, eat or be eaten; in the human kingdom, define or be defined.

THOMAS SZASZ (b. 1920), U.S. psychiatrist. *The Second Sin*, "Language" (1973).

DELIBERATION

1 Deliberation. The act of examining one's bread to determine which side it is buttered on.

AMBROSE BIERCE (1842-1914), U.S. author. *The Devil's Dictionary* (1881-1906).

2 Reflection makes men cowards.

WILLIAM HAZLITT (1778-1830), English essayist. *Characteristics: In the Manner of Rochefoucault's Maxims*, no. 228 (1823; repr. in *The Complete Works Of William Hazlitt*, vol. 9, ed. by P. P. Howe, 1932).

3 Nowadays not even a suicide kills himself in desperation. Before taking the step he deliberates so long and so carefully that he literally chokes with thought. It is even questionable whether he ought to be called a suicide, since it is really thought which takes his life. He does not die *with* deliberation but *from* deliberation.

SØREN KIERKEGAARD (1813-55), Danish philosopher. *The Present Age* (1846; tr. 1940).

DELINQUENCY

1 There are souls that are incurable and lost to the rest of society. Deprive them of one means of folly, they will invent ten thousand others. They will create subtler, wilder methods, methods that are absolutely DESPERATE. Nature herself is fundamentally antisocial, it is only by a usurpation of powers that the organized body of society opposes the *natural* inclination of humanity.

ANTONIN ARTAUD (1896-1948), French theater producer, actor, theorist. *General Security: The Liquidation of Opium* (1925; repr. in *Selected Writings*, pt. 10, ed. by Susan Sontag, 1976), arguing for the free use of opium.

2 Violence among young people . . . is an aspect of their desire to create. They don't know how to use their energy creatively so they do the opposite and destroy.

ANTHONY BURGESS (b. 1917), British author and critic. London *Independent* (London, 31 Jan. 1990).

3 Strange and predatory and truly dangerous, car thieves and muggers—they seem to jeopardize all our cherished concepts, even our self-esteem, our property rights, our powers of love, our laws and pleasures. The only relationship we seem to have with them is scorn or bewilderment, but they belong somewhere on the dark prairies of a country that is in the throes of self-discovery.

JOHN CHEEVER (1912-82), U.S. author. *John Cheever: The Journals*, "The Late Forties and the Fifties" (ed. by Robert Gottlieb, 1991), 1955 entry.

4 We know that their adventures are childish. They themselves are fools. They are ready to kill or be killed over a card-game in which an opponent—or they themselves—was cheating. Yet, thanks to such fellows, tragedies are possible.

JEAN GENET (1910-86), French playwright, novelist. *The Thief's Journal* (1949; tr. 1965), of petty criminals.

5 Gentleman-rankers out on the spree,
Damned from here to Eternity.

RUDYARD KIPLING (1865-1936), British author, poet. *Gentleman-Rankers*.

6 He that seeks trouble never misses.

17TH-CENTURY ENGLISH PROVERB. First collected in George Herbert, *Outlandish Proverbs* (1640).

7 Now, neigbour confines, purge you of your scum!
Have you a ruffian that will swear, drink, dance,
Revel the night, rob, murder, and commit
The oldest sins the newest kind of ways?

WILLIAM SHAKESPEARE (1564-1616), English dramatist, poet. King Henry, in *Henry IV*, pt 2, act 4, sc. 3.

8 If we were doing this in the Falklands they would love it. It's part of our heritage. The British have always been fighting wars.

SOCCER FAN on hooliganism charge. Quoted in: *Independent* (London, 23 Dec. 1988).

See also Burke on MALICE.

DELUSIONS OF GRANDEUR

1 The fly sat upon the axel-tree of the chariot-wheel and said, What a dust do I raise!

AESOP (6th century B.C.), Greek fabulist. *Fables*, "The Fly on the Wheel" (tr. by Francis Bacon in his essay "Of Vain-Glory").

2 The lunatic is the man who lives in a small world but thinks it is a large one; he is the man who lives in a tenth of the truth, and thinks it is the whole. The madman cannot conceive any cosmos outside a certain tale or conspiracy or vision. Hence the more clearly we see the world divided into Saxons and non-Saxons, into our splendid selves and the rest, the more certain we may be that we are slowly and quietly going mad. The more plain and satisfying our state appears, the more we may know that we are living in an unreal world. For the real world is not satisfying. The more clear become the colours and facts of Anglo-Saxon superiority, the more surely we may know we are in a dream.

G. K. CHESTERTON (1874-1936), British author. *Charles Dickens*, "Dickens and America" (1906).

3 I recoil, overcome with the glory of my rosy hue and the knowledge that I, a mere cock, have made the sun rise.

> EDMOND ROSTAND (1868-1918), French poet, playwright. Chanticler, in *The Chanticler*, act 2, sc. 3.

4 When a man says that he is Jesus or Napoleon, or that the Martians are after him, or claims something else that seems outrageous to common sense, he is labeled psychotic and locked up in a madhouse. Freedom of speech is only for normal people.

> THOMAS SZASZ (b. 1920), U.S. psychiatrist. *The Second Sin*, "Schizophrenia" (1973).

DEMAGOGUES

1 In order to move others deeply we must deliberately allow ourselves to be carried away beyond the bounds of our normal sensibility.

> JOSEPH CONRAD (1857-1924), Polish-born English novelist. *A Personal Record*, "A Familiar Preface" (1912).

2 A person of definite character and purpose who comprehends our way of thought is sure to exert power over us. He cannot altogether be resisted; because, if he understands us, he can make us understand him, through the word, the look, or other symbol, which both of us connect with the common sentiment or idea; and thus by communicating an impulse he can move the will.

> CHARLES HORTON COOLEY (1864-1929), U.S. sociologist. *Human Nature and the Social Order*, ch. 4 (1902).

3 The demagogue is usually sly, a detractor of others, a professor of humility and disinterestedness, a great stickler for equality as respects all above him, a man who acts in corners, and avoids open and manly expositions of his course, calls blackguards gentlemen, and gentlemen folks, appeals to passions and prejudices rather than to reason, and is in all respects, a man of intrigue and deception, of sly cunning and management.

> JAMES FENIMORE COOPER (1789-1851), U.S. novelist. *The American Democrat*, "On Demagogues" (1838).

4 The secret of the demagogue is to appear as dumb as his audience so that these people can believe themselves as smart as he is.

> KARL KRAUS (1874-1936), Austrian satirist. *Sprüche und Widersprüche*, ch. 4 (1909); tr. as *Half-Truths and One-And-A Half-Truths*, "Lord, Forgive them . . ." ed. by Harry Zohn, 1976).

5 In every age the vilest specimens of human nature are to be found among demagogues.

> THOMAS BABINGTON MACAULAY (1800-59), English historian, Whig politician. *History of England*, vol. 1, ch. 5 (1849).

6 A demagogue is a person with whom we disagree as to which gang should mismanage the country.

> DON MARQUIS (1878-1937), U.S. humorist, journalist. Quoted in: E. Anthony, *O Rare Don Marquis*, ch. 11 (1962).

See also Wilde on DICTATORS.

DEMOCRACY

1 Remember, democracy never lasts long. It soon wastes, exhausts, and murders itself. There never was a democracy yet that did not commit suicide.

> JOHN ADAMS (1735-1826), U.S. statesman, president. Letter, 15 April 1814 (published in *The Works of John Adams*, vol. 6, 1851).

2 Democracy is the menopause of Western society, the Grand Climacteric of the body social. Fascism is its middle-aged lust.

> JEAN BAUDRILLARD (b. 1929), French semiologist. *Cool Memories*, ch. 1 (1987; tr. 1990).

3 The worst thing I can say about democracy is that it has tolerated the Right Honourable Gentleman for four and a half years.

> ANEURIN BEVAN (1897-1960), British Labour politician. Speech, 23 July 1929, to House of Commons, referring to future prime minister Neville Chamberlain.

4 The tendency of democracies is, in all things, to mediocrity.

> JAMES FENIMORE COOPER (1789-1851), U.S. novelist. *The American Democrat*, "On the Disadvantages of Democracy" (1838).

5 When great changes occur in history, when great principles are involved, as a rule the majority are wrong.

> EUGENE V. DEBS (1855-1926), U.S. trade unionist, co-founder of the U.S. Socialist Party. Speech, 12 Sept. 1918, Cleveland, Ohio, defending himself against charges of sedition. Found guilty, Debs was subsequently jailed for three years..

6 Nor is the people's judgement always true:
The most may err as grossly as the few.

> JOHN DRYDEN (1631-1700), English poet, dramatist, critic. *Absalom and Achitophel*, pt. 1.

7 Democracy don't rule the world,
You'd better get that in your head;
This world is ruled by violence,
But I guess that's better left unsaid.

> BOB DYLAN (b. 1941), U.S. singer, songwriter. "Union Sundown," on the album *Infidels* (1983).

8 Two cheers for Democracy: one because it admits variety and two because it permits criticism.

> E. M. FORSTER (1879-1970), British novelist, essayist. *Two Cheers for Democracy*, "What I Believe" (1951). Forster thought two cheers "quite enough: there is no occasion to give three." The third he reserved for the Republic of Love.

9 When people put their ballots in the boxes, they are, by that act, inoculated against the feeling that the government is not theirs. They then accept, in some measure, that its errors are their errors, its aberrations their aberrations, that any revolt will be against them. It's a remarkably shrewed and rather conservative arrangement when one thinks of it.

> JOHN KENNETH GALBRAITH (b. 1908), U.S. economist. *The Age of Uncertainty*, ch. 12 (1977).

10 Democracy! Bah! When I hear that word I reach for my feather Boa!

> ALLEN GINSBERG (b. 1926), U.S. poet. *Journals: Early Fifties*

Early Sixties, "New York City" (ed. by Gordon Ball, 1977), Oct. 1960 entry, "Subliminal."

11 Democracy is the wholesome and pure air without which a socialist public organization cannot live a full-blooded life.

MIKHAIL GORBACHEV (b. 1931), Soviet president. Speech, 25 Feb. 1986, to 27th Party Congress, Moscow.

12 The freeman, casting with unpurchased hand
The vote that shakes the turrets of the land.

OLIVER WENDELL HOLMES, SR. (1809-94), U.S. writer, physician. *Poetry: a Metrical Essay.*

13 I swear to the Lord,
I still can't see,
Why Democracy means,
Everybody but me.

LANGSTON HUGHES (1902-67), U.S. poet, author. *The Black Man Speaks,* in *Jim Crow's Last Stand* (1943).

14 It is not enough to merely defend democracy. To defend it may be to lose it; to extend it is to strengthen it. Democracy is not property; it is an idea.

HUBERT H. HUMPHREY (1911-78), U.S. Democratic politician, vice president. Address, 1 Oct. 1942, to annual conference of Minnesota Library Association.

15 The majority is never right. Never, I tell you! That's one of these lies in society that no free and intelligent man can help rebelling against. Who are the people that make up the biggest proportion of the population—the intelligent ones or the fools? I think we can agree it's the fools, no matter where you go in this world, it's the fools that form the overwhelming majority.

HENRIK IBSEN (1828-1906), Norwegian dramatist. Dr. Stockmann, in *An Enemy of the People,* act 4.

16 Chinks in America's egalitarian armor are not hard to find. Democracy is the fig leaf of elitism.

FLORENCE KING (b. 1936), U.S. author. *Reflections in a Jaundiced Eye,* "Democracy" (1989).

17 Democracy with its semi-civilization sincerely cherishes junk. The artist's power should be spiritual. But the power of the majority is material. When these worlds meet occasionally, it is pure coincidence.

PAUL KLEE (1879-1940), Swiss artist. *The Diaries of Paul Klee 1898-1918,* no. 747 (1957; tr. 1965), Jan. 1906 entry.

18 Democracy means the opportunity to be everyone's slave.

KARL KRAUS (1874-1936), Austrian satirist. *Die Fackel,* no. 303 (Vienna, 16 Oct. 1911; repr. in Thomas Szasz, *Anti-Freud: Karl Kraus's Criticism of Psychoanalysis and Psychiatry,* ch. 8, 1976).

19 You must drop all your democracy. You must not believe in "the people." One class is no better than another. It must be a case of Wisdom, or Truth. Let the working classes *be* working classes. That is the truth. There must be an aristocracy of people who have wisdom, and there must be a Ruler: a Kaiser: no Presidents and democracies.

D. H. LAWRENCE (1885-1930), British author. Letter, c. 14 July 1915, to philosopher Bertrand Russell (published in *The Letters of D. H. Lawrence,* vol. 2, ed. by George J. Zytaruk and James T. Boulton, 1981).

20 The more I see of democracy the more I dislike it. It just brings everything down to the mere vulgar level of wages and prices, electric light and water closets, and nothing else.

D. H. LAWRENCE (1885-1930), British author. Letter, 13 June 1922, written in Australia (published in *The Letters of D. H. Lawrence,* vol. 4, ed. by James T. Boulton, E. Mansfield, and W. Roberts, 1987).

21 No man is good enough to govern another man without that other's consent.

ABRAHAM LINCOLN (1809-65), U.S. president. Speech, 16 Oct. 1854, Peoria, Ill., in the first of the Lincoln-Douglas debates.

22 As I would not be a *slave,* so I would not be a *master.* This expresses my idea of democracy.

ABRAHAM LINCOLN (1809-65), U.S. president. Autograph fragment, c. 1 Aug. 1858 (published in *The Collected Works of Abraham Lincoln,* vol. 2, ed. by Roy P. Basler, 1953).

23 What we call a democratic society might be defined for certain purposes as one in which the majority is always prepared to put down a revolutionary minority.

WALTER LIPPMANN (1889-1974), U.S. journalist. "Why Should the Majority Rule?," *Harper's* (New York, 1926; repr. in *The Essential Lippman,* pt. 1, sct. 1, 1982).

24 This is one of the paradoxes of the democratic movement—that it loves a crowd and fears the individuals who compose it—that the religion of humanity should have no faith in human beings.

WALTER LIPPMANN (1889-1974), U.S. journalist. *A Preface to Politics,* ch. 1 (1914).

25 A modern democracy is a tyranny whose borders are undefined; one discovers how far one can go only by traveling in a straight line until one is stopped.

NORMAN MAILER (b. 1923), U.S. author. *The Presidential Papers,* Preface (1963).

26 It is a strange fact that freedom and equality, the two basic ideas of democracy, are to some extent contradictory. Logically considered, freedom and equality are mutually exclusive, just as society and the individual are mutually exclusive.

THOMAS MANN (1875-1955), German author, critic. "The War and the Future," speech, 1940 (published in *Order of the Day,* 1942).

27 Democracy is the theory that the common people know what they want, and deserve to get it good and hard.

H. L. MENCKEN (1880-1956), U.S. journalist. *A Book of Burlesques,* "Sententiae" (1920).

28 I confess I enjoy democracy immensely. It is incomparably idiotic, and hence incomparably amusing.

H. L. MENCKEN (1880-1956), U.S. journalist. *Notes on Democracy,* "Last Words" (1926; repr. in *A Mencken Chrestomathy,* pt. 9, 1949).

29 The cure for the evils of democracy is more democracy.

H. L. MENCKEN (1880-1956), U.S. journalist. *Notes on Democracy,* "Its Origins" (1926; repr. in *A Mencken Chrestomathy,* pt. 9, 1949).

30 It is the American vice, the democratic disease which expresses its tyranny by reducing everything unique to the level of the herd.

> HENRY MILLER (1891-1980), U.S. author. *The Wisdom of the Heart*, "Raimu" (1947).

31 Man's capacity for justice makes democracy possible, but man's inclination to injustice makes democracy necessary.

> REINHOLD NIEBUHR (1892-1971), U.S. theologian, historian. *The Children of Light and the Children of Darkness*, Foreword (1944).

32 In a democracy everybody has a right to be represented, including the jerks.

> CHRIS PATTEN (b. 1944), British Conservative politician. *Evening Standard* (London, 2 May 1991).

33 Let the people think they govern and they will be governed.

> WILLIAM PENN (1644-1718), English religious leader, founder of Pennsylvania. *Some Fruits of Solitude* (1693).

34 These, then, will be some of the features of democracy . . . it will be, in all likelihood, an agreeable, lawless, particolored commonwealth, dealing with all alike on a footing of equality, whether they be really equal or not.

> PLATO (c. 427-347 B.C.), Greek philosopher. Socrates, in *The Republic*, bk. 8, sct. 558.

35 Democracy is a political *method*, that is to say, a certain type of institutional arrangement for arriving at political—legislative and administrative—decisions and hence incapable of being an end in itself.

> JOSEPH A. SCHUMPETER (1883-1950), Austrian-American economist. *Capitalism, Socialism and Democracy*, ch. 20, sct. 3 (1942).

36 Democracy substitutes election by the incompetent many for appointment by the corrupt few.

> GEORGE BERNARD SHAW (1856-1950), Anglo-Irish playwright, critic. *Man and Superman*, "Maxims for Revolutionists" (1903).

37 I talk democracy to these men and women. I tell them that they have the vote, and that theirs is the kingdom and the power and the glory. I say to them "You are supreme: exercise your power." They say, "That's right: tell us what to do;" and I tell them. I say "Exercise uour vote intelligently by voting for me." And they do. That's democracy; and a splendid thing it is too for putting the right men in the right place.

> GEORGE BERNARD SHAW (1856-1950), Anglo-Irish playwright, critic. Boanerges, in *The Apple Cart*, act 1.

38 There is a limit to the application of democratic methods. You can inquire of all the passengers as to what type of car they like to ride in, but it is impossible to question them as to whether to apply the brakes when the train is at full speed and accident threatens.

> LEON TROTSKY (1879-1940), Russian revolutionary. *The History of the Russian Revolution*, vol. 3, ch. 6 (1933).

39 I am a democrat only on principle, not by instinct—nobody is *that*. Doubtless some people *say* they are, but this world is grievously given to lying.

> MARK TWAIN (1835-1910), U.S. author. *Notebook*, ch. 31 (ed. by Albert Bigelow Paine, 1935), Feb.-March 1898 entry.

40 Democracy is supposed to give you the feeling of choice, like Painkiller X and Painkiller Y. But they're both just aspirin.

> GORE VIDAL (b. 1925), U.S. novelist, critic. Interview with author Martin Amis, published in *Observer* (London, 7 Feb. 1982).

41 Apparently, a democracy is a place where numerous elections are held at great cost without issues and with interchangeable candidates.

> GORE VIDAL (b. 1925), U.S. novelist, critic. "Gods and Greens," in *Observer* (London, 27 Aug. 1989; repr. in *A View from the Diner's Club*, 1991).

42 Democracy is the recurrent suspicion that more than half of the people are right more than half of the time.

> E. B. WHITE (1899-1985), U.S. author, editor. *New Yorker* (3 July 1944).

43 Democracy means simply the bludgeoning of the people by the people for the people.

> OSCAR WILDE (1854-1900), Anglo-Irish playwright, author. *The Soul of Man Under Socialism* (1895; first published in *The Fortnightly Review*, Feb. 1891).

44 Democracy is not so much a form of government as a set of principles.

> WOODROW WILSON (1856-1924), U.S. Democratic politician, president. *Atlantic Monthly* (Boston, March 1901).

45 That a peasant may become king does not render the kingdom democratic.

> WOODROW WILSON (1856-1924), U.S. Democratic politician, president. Speech, 31 Aug. 1910, Chattanooga, Tenn.

See also Fulbright on DISSENT; ELECTIONS; Bismarck on FORCE; Schumpeter on LIBERTY; Roosevelt on MINORITIES; Baldwin on MULTICULTURALISM; Galbraith on OLD AGE; Chesterton on REVOLUTION; Lincoln, Stoppard on VOTING.

U.S. DEMOCRATIC PARTY

1 The Democratic Party is like a mule. It has neither pride of ancestry nor hope of posterity.

> IGNATIUS DONNELLY (1831-1901), U.S. author, politician. Speech, 13 Sept. 1860, to the Minnesota State Legislature.

2 Our opposition will never understand the Democratic Party. Our Party is—to the unpracticed eyes of the old Republican Tories—a mysterious contraption that usually seems to be moving in a thousand directions. What they don't know is what hurts them. For all that movement in the Democratic Party is caused by the internal combustion of creative ferment, of ideas, of people vigorously committed to the proposition that change and social progress are not only to be desired; they are necessities of twentieth-century America.

> HUBERT H. HUMPHREY (1911-78), U.S. Democratic politician, vice president. Speech, 8 Sept. 1966, to the Democratic State Convention, Buffalo, N.Y.

3 The Republican party makes even its young men seem old; the Democratic Party makes even its old men seem young.

> ADLAI STEVENSON (1900-65), U.S. Democratic politician. Comparing the Republican Party nominee for vice-president

Richard Nixon, to the septuagenarian Democratic vice-president Alben Barkley, during the 1952 presidential race. Quoted in: Earl Mazo, *Richard Nixon: A Political and Personal Portrait*, ch. 7 (1959).

DEPARTURE AND PARTING

1 Parting is all we know of heaven,
And all we need of hell.

EMILY DICKINSON (1830-86), U.S. poet. *The Complete Poems*, no. 1732 (1955).

2 In every parting there is an image of death.

GEORGE ELIOT (1819-80), English novelist. *Amos Barton*, ch. 10 (first published in *Blackwood's Magazine*, 1857; repr. in *Scenes of Clerical Life*, 1858).

3 It's interesting to leave a place, interesting even to think about it. Leaving reminds us of what we can part with and what we can't, then offers us something new to look forward to, to dream about.

RICHARD FORD (b. 1944), U.S. author. "An Urge for Going," in *Harper's* (New York, Feb. 1992).

4 Henceforth I whimper no more, postpone no more, need nothing,
Done with indoor complaints, libraries, querulous criticisms,
Strong and content I travel the open road.

WALT WHITMAN (1819-92), U.S. poet. *Song of the Open Road*, sct. 1 (1856).

See also FAREWELLS.

DEPRESSION

1 Depression moods lead, almost invariably, to accidents. But, when they occur, our mood changes again, since the accident shows we can draw the world in our wake, and that we still retain some degree of power even when our spirits are low. A series of accidents creates a positively light-hearted state, out of consideration for this strange power.

JEAN BAUDRILLARD (b. 1929), French semiologist. *Cool Memories*, ch. 4 (1987; tr. 1990).

2 The term clinical depression finds its way into too many conversations these days. One has a sense that a catastrophe has occurred in the psychic landscape.

LEONARD COHEN (b. 1934), Canadian singer, poet, novelist. *International Herald Tribune* (Paris, 4 Nov. 1988).

3 Geez, if I could get through to you, kiddo, that depression is not sobbing and crying and *giving vent*, it is plain and simple *reduction of feeling*. Reduction, see? Of all feeling. People who keep stiff upper lips find that it's damn hard to smile.

JUDITH GUEST (b. 1936), U.S. author. The psychiatrist Berger to Conrad Jarrett, in *Ordinary People*, ch. 27 (1976).

4 That terrible mood of depression of whether it's any good or not is what is known as The Artist's Reward.

ERNEST HEMINGWAY (1899-1961), U.S. author. Letter, 13 Sept. 1929, to F. Scott Fitzgerald (published in *Selected Letters*, ed. by

Carlos Baker, 1981). Biographer and critic Leon Edel observed, in a 1988 interview, "The greatest enemy of writers is depression, which they can't avoid."

5 The world leans on us. When we sag, the whole world seems to droop.

ERIC HOFFER (1902-83), U.S. philosopher. *The Passionate State of Mind*, aph. 237 (1955).

6 The attitude of unhappiness is not only painful, it is mean and ugly. What can be more base and unworthy than the pining, puling, mumping mood, no matter by what outward ills it may have been engendered? What is more injurious to others? What less helpful as a way out of the difficulty? It but fastens and perpetuates the trouble which occasioned it, and increases the total evil of the situation. At all costs, then, we ought to reduce the sway of that mood; we ought to scout it in ourselves and others, and never show it tolerance.

WILLIAM JAMES (1842-1910), U.S. psychologist, philosopher. *The Varieties of Religious Experience*, lectures 4 and 5 (1977).

7 I am in that temper that if I were under water I would scarcely kick to come to the top.

JOHN KEATS (1795-1821), English poet. Letter, 21-25 May 1818 (published in *Letters of John Keats*, no. 66, ed. by Frederick Page, 1954).

8 In addition to my other numerous acquaintances, I have one more intimate confidant. . . . My depression is the most faithful mistress I have known—no wonder, then, that I return the love.

SOREN KIERKEGAARD (1813-55), Danish philosopher. *Either/Or*, vol. 1, "Diapsalmata" (1843; tr. 1987).

9 Depression is melancholy minus its charms—the animation, the fits.

SUSAN SONTAG (b. 1933), U.S. essayist. *Illness As Metaphor*, ch. 7 (1978).

See also DESPAIR.

THE DESERT

1 The desert is a natural extension of the inner silence of the body. If humanity's language, technology, and buildings are an extension of its constructive faculties, the desert alone is an extension of its capacity for absence, the ideal schema of humanity's disappearance.

JEAN BAUDRILLARD (b. 1929), French semiologist. *America*, "Astral America" (1986; tr. 1988).

2 A desert is a place without expectation.

NADINE GORDIMER (b. 1923), South African author. "Pula!," in *London Magazine* (Feb.-March 1973; repr. in *The Essential Gesture*, ed. by Stephen Clingman, 1988).

3 That undefined and mingled hum,
Voice of the desert never dumb!

JAMES HOGG (1770-1835), Scottish poet. *Verses to Lady Anne Scott*.

4 Only the desert has a fascination—to ride alone—in the sun in the forever unpossessed country—away from man. That is a great temptation . . .

D. H. LAWRENCE (1885-1930), British author. Letter, 29 Sept.

1922, written while in the U.S. (published in *The Letters of D. H. Lawrence,* vol. 4, ed. by James T. Boulton, E. Mansfield, and W. Roberts, 1987).

5   To say nothing is out here is incorrect; to say the desert is stingy with everything except space and light, stone and earth is closer to the truth..

WILLIAM LEAST HEAT MOON [WILLIAM TROGDON] (b. 1939), U.S. author. *Blue Highways: A Journey into America,* pt. 4, ch. 80 (1983).

6   The Mojave is a big desert and a frightening one. It's as though nature tested a man for endurance and constancy to prove whether he was good enough to get to California.

JOHN STEINBECK (1902-1968), U.S. author. *Travels With Charley: in Search of America,* pt. 3 (1962).

See also The WILDERNESS.

DESIGN

1   Interior design is a travesty of the architectural process and a frightening condemnation of the credulity, helplessness and gullibilty of the most formidable consumers—the rich.

STEPHEN BAYLEY (b. 1951), British design critic. *Taste,* pt. 2, "Interiors: Vacuums of Taste" (1991).

2   Perhaps believing in good design is like believing in God, it makes you an optimist.

SIR TERENCE CONRAN (b. 1931), British businessman, designer. *Daily Telegraph* (London, 12 June 1989).

3   Art has to move you and design does not, unless it's a good design for a bus.

DAVID HOCKNEY (b. 1937), British artist. *Guardian* (London, 26 Oct. 1988).

4   Design in art, is a recognition of the relation between various things, various elements in the creative flux. You can't *invent* a design. You recognise it, in the fourth dimension. That is, with your blood and your bones, as well as with your eyes.

D. H. LAWRENCE (1885-1930), British author. *Phoenix: The Posthumous Papers of D. H. Lawrence,* pt. 4, "Art and Morality" (ed. by E. McDonald, 1936).

5   Design is not for philosophy—it's for life.

ISSEY MIYAKE (b. 1939), Japanese fashion designer. *International Herald Tribune* (Paris, 23 March 1992).

6   The complaint . . . about modern steel furniture, modern glass houses, modern red bars and modern streamlined trains and cars is that all these *objets modernes,* while adequate and amusing in themselves, tend to make the people who use them look dated. It is an honest criticism. The human race has done nothing much about changing its own appearance to conform to the form and texture of its appurtenances.

E. B. WHITE (1899-1985), U.S. author, editor. "Fitting In," in *New Yorker* (9 June 1934; repr. in *Writings from the New Yorker 1927-1976,* ed. by Rebecca M. Dale, 1991).

7   Designs in connection with postage stamps and coinage may be described, I think, as the silent ambassadors on national taste.

W. B. YEATS (1865-1939), Irish poet, playwright. Speech, 3 March 1926, to the Seanad Eireann, the Irish Senate, on the Coinage Bill.

DESIRE

1   Man is a creation of desire, not a creation of need.

GASTON BACHELARD (1884-1962), French scientist, philosopher, literary theorist. *The Psychoanalysis of Fire,* ch. 2, "Fire and Reverie" (1938; tr. 1964).

2   And desire shall fail: because man goeth to his long home, and the mourners go about the streets.

BIBLE, HEBREW. *Ecclesiastes* 12:5.

3   He who desires but acts not, breeds pestilence.

WILLIAM BLAKE (1757-1827), English poet, painter, engraver. *The Marriage of Heaven and Hell,* plate 7, "Proverbs of Hell" (1790-93).

4   Almost every desire a poor man has is a punishable offence.

LOUIS-FERDINAND CÉLINE (1894-1961), French author. The narrator (Ferdinand Bardamu), in *Journey to the End of the Night* (1932; tr. 1934; repr. 1966, p. 176).

5   Whenever we confront an unbridled desire we are surely in the presence of a tragedy-in-the-making.

QUENTIN CRISP (b. 1908), British author. *Manners from Heaven,* ch. 8 (1984).

6   It is said that desire is a product of the will, but the converse is in fact true: will is a product of desire.

DENIS DIDEROT (1713-84), French philosopher. *Elements of Physiology,* "Will, Freedom" (notes written 1774-80; first published 1875; repr. in *Selected Writings,* ed. by Lester G. Crocker, 1966).

7   There are confessable agonies, sufferings of which one can positively be proud. Of bereavement, of parting, of the sense of sin and the fear of death the poets have eloquently spoken. They command the world's sympathy. But there are also discreditable anguishes, no less excruciating than the others, but of which the sufferer dare not, cannot speak. The anguish of thwarted desire, for example.

ALDOUS HUXLEY (1894-1963), British author. *Point Counter Point,* ch. 13 (1928).

8   Some desire is necessary to keep life in motion, and he whose real wants are supplied must admit those of fancy.

SAMUEL JOHNSON (1709-84), English author, lexicographer. Imlac, in *The History of Rasselas,* ch. 8 (1759).

9   It belongs to the imperfection of everything human that man can only attain his desire by passing through its opposite.

SØREN KIERKEGAARD (1813-55), Danish philosopher. *The Journals of Søren Kierkegaard: A Selection,* no. 358 (ed. and tr. by Alexander Dru, 1938), 1841 entry.

10   We do not succeed in changing things according to our desire, but gradually our desire changes.

MARCEL PROUST (1871-1922), French novelist. *Remembrance*

of Things Past, vol. 11, "The Sweet Cheat Gone," ch. 1 (1925; tr. by Scott Monkrieff, 1930).

See also Hoffer on TALENT.

DESPAIR

1   I will indulge my sorrows, and give way
To all the pangs and fury of despair.

JOSEPH ADDISON (1672-1719), English essayist. Marcia, in *Cato*, act 4, sc. 3.

2   Despair, in short, seeks its own environment as surely as water finds its own level.

A. ALVAREZ (b. 1929), British critic, poet, novelist. *The Savage God*, pt. 3, "Theories" (1971).

3   So long as we have failed to eliminate any of the causes of human despair, we do not have the right to try to eliminate those means by which man tries to cleanse himself of despair.

ANTONIN ARTAUD (1896-1948), French theater producer, actor, theorist. *General Security: The Liquidation of Opium* (1925; repr. in *Selected Writings*, pt. 10, ed. by Susan Sontag, 1976), arguing for the free use of opium.

4   Intellectual despair results in neither weakness nor dreams, but in violence. . . . It is only a matter of knowing how to give vent to one's rage; whether one only wants to wander like madmen around prisons, or whether one wants to overturn them.

GEORGES BATAILLE (1897-1962), French novelist, critic. "The `Lugubrious Game'," in *Documents*, no. 7 (Paris, Dec 1929; repr. in *Visions of Excess: Selected Writings 1927-1939*, ed. by Allan Stoekl, 1985).

5   Then my verse I dishonour, my pictures despise,
My person degrade & my temper chastise;
And the pen is my terror, the pencil my shame;
And my talents I bury, and dead is my fame.

WILLIAM BLAKE (1757-1827), English poet, painter, engraver. Letter, 16 Aug. 1803 (published in *Complete Writings*, ed. by Geoffrey Keynes, 1957).

6   To those who despair of everything reason cannot provide a faith, but only passion, and in this case it must be the same passion that lay at the root of the despair, namely humiliation and hatred.

ALBERT CAMUS (1913-60), French-Algerian philosopher, author. *The Rebel*, pt. 3, "State Terrorism and Irrational Terror" (1951; tr. 1953).

7   Let judges secretly despair of justice: their verdicts will be more acute. Let generals secretly despair of triumph; killing will be defamed. Let priests secretly despair of faith: their compassion will be true.

LEONARD COHEN (b. 1934), Canadian singer, poet, novelist. *The Spice-Box Of Earth*, "Lines From My Grandfather's Journal" (1961).

8   But what we call our despair is often only the painful eagerness of unfed hope.

GEORGE ELIOT (1819-80), English novelist, editor. *Middlemarch*, bk. 5, ch. 51 (1871).

9   In a real dark night of the soul it is always three o'clock in the morning, day after day.

F. SCOTT FITZGERALD (1896-1940), U.S. author. *Handle With Care* (first published in *Esquire* as second part of Fitzgerald's *Crack-Up* series, March 1936; repr. in *The Crack-Up*, ed. by Edmund Wilson, 1945). "The Dark Night of the Soul" was the title of a poem and commentary by the 16th-century Spanish mystic San Juan de la Cruz (St. John of the Cross).

10   Melancholy has ceased to be an individual phenomenon, an exception. It has become the class privilege of the wage earner, a mass state of mind that finds its cause wherever life is governed by production quotas.

GÜNTHER GRASS (b. 1927), German author. *From the Diary of a Snail*, "On Stasis in Progress" (1972).

11   Despair is the price one pays for setting oneself an impossible aim. It is, one is told, the unforgivable sin, but it is a sin the corrupt or evil man never practises. He always has hope. He never reaches the freezing-point of knowing absolute failure. Only the man of goodwill carries always in his heart this capacity for damnation.

GRAHAM GREENE (1904-91), British novelist. *The Heart of the Matter*, bk. 1, pt. 1, ch. 2, sct. 4 (1948).

12   Despair is typical of those who do not understand the causes of evil, see no way out, and are incapable of struggle. The modern industrial proletariat does not belong to the category of such classes.

VLADIMIR ILYICH LENIN (1870-1924), Russian revolutionary leader. Remark, 1910. Quoted in: Tamara Deutsche, *Not By Politics Alone*, ch. 4 (1973).

13   To be *thoroughly* conversant with a Man's heart, is to take our final lesson in the iron-clasped volume of despair.

EDGAR ALLAN POE (1809-45), U.S. poet, critic, short-story writer. *Marginalia*, in *Southern Literary Messenger* (Richmond, Va., June 1849; repr. in *Essays and Reviews*, 1984).

14   All my life I believed I knew something. But then one strange day came when I realized that I knew nothing, yes, I knew nothing. And so words became void of meaning . . . I have arrived too late at ultimate uncertainty.

EZRA POUND (1885-1972), U.S. poet, critic. *Epoca* (Milan, March 1963).

15   O God, O God,
How weary, stale, flat, and unprofitable
Seem to me all the uses of this world!

WILLIAM SHAKESPEARE (1564-1616), English dramatist, poet. Hamlet, in *Hamlet*, act 1, sc. 2 in his first soliloquy of the play, voicing his unhappiness at his mother's marrying Claudius so soon after his father's death.

16   Despair is perfectly compatible with a good dinner, I promise you.

WILLIAM MAKEPEACE THACKERAY (1811-63), English author. *Lovel the Widower*, ch. 6 (1860).

17   It is a time when one's spirit is subdued and sad, one knows not why; when the past seems a storm-swept desolation, life a vanity and a burden, and the future but a way to death.

MARK TWAIN (1835-1910), U.S. author. *The Gilded Age*, ch. 60 (1873; written with Charles Dudley Warner), of Laura Hawkins's mood.

18 Man dies of cold, not of darkness.

MIGUEL DE UNAMUNO (1864-1936), Spanish philosophical writer. *The Tragic Sense of Life,* ch. 4 (1913).

19 Because I remember, I despair. Because I remember, I have the duty to reject despair.

ELIE WIESEL (b. 1928), Rumanian-born U.S. writer. Nobel lecture, 11 Dec. 1986, Oslo.

20 Through our sunless lanes creeps Poverty with her hungry eyes, and Sin with his sodden face follows close behind her. Misery wakes us in the morning and Shame sits with us at night.

OSCAR WILDE (1854-1900), Anglo-Irish playwright, author. The weaver, in "The Young King," in *A House of Pomegranates* (1891)

See also Keats on DEPRESSION; Kierkegaard on DOUBT.

DESPERATION

1 Desperation is the raw material of drastic change. Only those who can leave behind everything they have ever believed in can hope to escape.

WILLIAM BURROUGHS (b. 1914), U.S. author. *The Western Lands,* ch. 5 (1987).

2 What is most original in a man's nature is often that which is most desperate. Thus new systems are forced on the world by men who simply cannot bear the pain of living with what is. Creators care nothing for their systems except that they be unique. If Hitler had been born in Nazi Germany he wouldn't have been content to enjoy the atmosphere.

LEONARD COHEN (b. 1934), Canadian singer, poet, novelist. The narrator, in *Beautiful Losers* (1970; repr. 1972, p. 61).

3 My interest in desperation lies only in that sometimes I find myself having become desperate. Very seldom do I start out that way. I can see of course that, in the abstract, thinking and all activity is rather desperate.

WILLEM DE KOONING (b. 1904), Dutch-born U.S. artist. "A Desperate View," paper, 18 Feb. 1949, delivered to friends in New York (first published in Thomas B. Hess, *William de Kooning,* 1968).

4 There exists, at the bottom of all abasement and misfortune, a last extreme which rebels and joins battle with the forces of law and respectability in a desperate struggle, waged partly by cunning and partly by violence, at once sick and ferocious, in which it attacks the prevailing social order with the pin-pricks of vice and the hammer-blows of crime.

VICTOR HUGO (1802-85), French poet, dramatist, novelist. *Les Misérables,* pt. 4, bk. 7, ch. 1 (1862).

5 The mass of men lead lives of quiet desperation.

HENRY DAVID THOREAU (1817-62), U.S. philosopher, author, naturalist. *Walden,* "Economy" (1854).

6 She wore far too much rouge last night and not quite enough clothes. That is always a sign of despair in a woman.

OSCAR WILDE (1854-1900), Anglo-Irish playwright, author. Lord Goring, in *An Ideal Husband,* act 2.

DESPOTISM

1 So long as war is the main business of nations, temporary despotism—despotism during the campaign—is indispensable.

WALTER BAGEHOT (1826-77), English economist, critic. *Physics and Politics,* ch. 2, sct. 3 (1872).

2 The arbitrary rule of a just and enlightened prince is always bad. His virtues are the most dangerous and the surest form of seduction: they lull a people imperceptibly into the habit of loving, respecting, and serving his successor, whoever that successor may be, no matter how wicked or stupid.

DENIS DIDEROT (1713-84), French philosopher. *Refutation of Helvétius* (written 1773-76; first published 1875; repr. in *Selected Writings,* ed. by Lester G. Crocker, 1966).

3 Despots play their part in the works of thinkers. Fettered words are terrible words. The writer doubles and trebles the power of his writing when a ruler imposes silence on the people. Something emerges from that enforced silence, a mysterious fullness which filters through and becomes steely in the thought. Repression in history leads to conciseness in the historian, and the rock-like hardness of much celebrated prose is due to the tempering of the tyrant.

VICTOR HUGO (1802-85), French poet, dramatist, novelist. *Les Misérables,* pt. 4, bk. 10 ch. 2 (1862).

4 Man is insatiable for power; he is infantile in his desires and, always discontented with what he has, loves only what he has not. People complain of the despotism of princes; they ought to complain of the despotism of *man.*

JOSEPH DE MAISTRE (1753-1821), French diplomat, philosopher. *Study on Sovereignty,* bk. 2, ch. 2 (1884; repr. in *The Works of Joseph de Maistre,* ed. by Jack Lively, 1965).

5 The French are nice people. I allow them to sing and to write, and they allow me to do whatever I like.

JULES, CARDINAL MAZARIN (1602-61?), Italian-born French statesman. Quoted by Elizabeth Charlotte, Duchess of Orléans, in a letter, 25 Oct. 1715. Mazarin was chief minister during the minority of Louis XIV.

6 The real stumbling-block of totalitarian régimes is not the spiritual need of men for freedom of thought; it is men's inability to stand the physical and nervous strain of a permanent state of excitement, except during a few years of their youth.

SIMONE WEIL (1909-43), French philosopher, mystic. "Cold War Policy in 1939" (written 1939; published in *Selected Essays,* ed. by Richard Rees, 1962).

7 Despotism is unjust to everybody, including the despot, who was probably made for better things.

OSCAR WILDE (1854-1900), Anglo-Irish playwright, author. *The Soul of Man Under Socialism,* in *Fortnightly Review* (London, Feb. 1891; repr. 1895).

8 There are three kinds of despots. There is the despot who tyrannises over the body. There is the despot who tyrannises over the soul. There is the despot who tyrannises over the soul and body alike. The first is called the

Prince. The second is called the Pope. The third is called the People.

> OSCAR WILDE (1854-1900), Anglo-Irish playwright, author. *The Soul of Man Under Socialism,* in *Fortnightly Review* (London, Feb. 1891; repr. 1895).

See also Chamfort on HISTORY; Byron on POLITICS; TYRANNY.

DESTINY

1 What do I know of man's destiny? I could tell you more about radishes.

> SAMUEL BECKETT (1906-89), Irish dramatist, novelist. *Enough,* in *Six Residua* (1978).

2 Destiny. A tyrant's authority for crime and a fool's excuse for failure.

> AMBROSE BIERCE (1842-1914), U.S. author. *The Devil's Dictionary* (1881-1906).

3 I do not believe in a fate that falls on men however they act; but I do believe in a fate that falls on them unless they act.

> G. K. CHESTERTON (1874-1936), British author. *Generally Speaking,* "On Holland" (1928).

4 Destiny is an absolutely definite and inexorable ruler. Physical ability and moral determination count for nothing. It is impossible to perform the simplest act when the gods say "no." I have no idea how they bring pressure to bear on such occasions; I only know that it is irresistible.

> ALEISTER CROWLEY (1875-1947), British occultist. *The Confessions of Aleister Crowley,* ch. 48 (1929; rev. 1970).

5 Fate, then, is a name for facts not yet passed under the fire of thought; for causes which are unpenetrated.

> RALPH WALDO EMERSON (1803-82), U.S. essayist, poet, philosopher. *The Conduct of Life,* "Fate" (1860).

6 Remember that you are an actor in a drama, of such a part as it may please the master to assign you, for a long time or for a little as he may choose. And if he will you to take the part of a poor man, or a cripple, or a ruler, or a private citizen, then may you act that part with grace! For to act well the part that is allotted to us, that indeed is ours to do, but to choose it is another's.

> EPICTETUS c. 55-C. 135 B.C.), Greek Stoic philosopher. *Encheiridion,* no. 17 (tr. by T. W. H. Rolleston, 1881).

7 Failure or success seem to have been allotted to men by their stars. But they retain the power of wriggling, of fighting with their star or against it, and in the whole universe the only really interesting movement is this wriggle.

> E. M. FORSTER (1879-1970), British novelist, essayist. "Our Diversions: The Game of Life" (1919; repr. in *Abinger Harvest,* 1936).

8 *Ça ira.* (It will go its own way.)

> Attributed to BENJAMIN FRANKLIN (1706-90), U.S. statesman, writer. Said about the American Revolution while Franklin was in Paris 1776-77. The remark was popularized and made the refrain of a revolutionary song—the *Carillon National*—by Ladré during the French Revolution of 1789.

9 We are not permitted to choose the frame of our destiny. But what we put into it is ours.

> DAG HAMMARSKJÖLD (1905-61), Swedish statesman, Secretary-General of U.N. *Markings,* "Night Is Drawing Nigh" (1963; written 1950).

10 We are no more free agents than the queen of clubs when she victoriously takes prisoner the knave of hearts.

> LADY MARY WORTLEY MONTAGU (1689-1762), English society figure, letter writer. Letter, 13 Jan. 1759 (published in *Selected Letters,* ed. by Robert Halsband, 1970).

11 The real test of a man is not how well he plays the role he has invented for himself, but how well he plays the role that destiny assigned to him.

> JAN PATOCKA (1907-77), Czech philosopher, activist. Advice given to playwright Václav Havel. Quoted in: Havel, *Disturbing the Peace,* ch. 2, 1990; in Czechoslovakia, 1986).

12 He that is born to be hanged shall never be drowned.

> FRENCH PROVERB (14th century). First recorded in English in A. Barclay, *Gringore's Castle of Labour* (1506).

13 Destiny is something men select; women achieve it only by default or stupendous suffering.

> HARRIET ROSENSTEIN (b. 1932), U.S. author. Quoted in: *Ms.* (New York, July 1974).

14 No cause has he to say his doom is harsh,
Who's made the master of his destiny.

> FRIEDRICH VON SCHILLER (1759-1805), German dramatist, poet, historian. Gessler, in *Wilhelm Tell,* act 3, sc. 3.

15 Nothing can have as its destination anything other than its origin. The contrary idea, the idea of progress, is poison.

> SIMONE WEIL (1909-43), French philosopher, mystic. "The New York Notebook" (1942; published in *First and Last Notebooks,* ed. by Richard Rees, 1970)

See also Omar Khayyám an LIFE AND DEATH; Fiedler on UNITED STATES, PEOPLE OF THE.

DESTRUCTIVENESS

1 The passion for destruction is also a creative passion.

> MIKHAIL BAKUNIN (1814-76), Russian political theorist. *Reaction in Germany* (1842).

2 The destructive character lives from the feeling, not that life is worth living, but that suicide is not worth the trouble.

> WALTER BENJAMIN (1892-1940), German critic, philosopher. "The Destructive Character," in *Frankfurter Zeitung* (20 Nov. 1931; repr. in *One-Way Street and Other Writings,* 1978).

3 We shall not have succeeded in demolishing everything unless we demolish the ruins as well. But the only way I can see of doing that is to use them to put up a lot of fine, well-designed buildings.

> ALFRED JARRY (1873-1907), French playwright, author. *Ubu Enchained,* epigraph (1900).

4 Destruction, hence, like creation, is one of Nature's mandates.

> MARQUIS DE SADE (1740-1814), French author. Dolmancé, in *Philosophy in the Bedroom,* "Dialogue the Fifth" (1795).

DETAIL

1 Men who wish to know about the world must learn about it in its particular details.

> HERACLITUS (c. 535-c. 475 B.C.), Greek philosopher. *Herakleitos and Diogenes*, pt. 1, fragment 3 (tr. by Guy Davenport, 1976).

2 One does a whole painting for one peach and people think just the opposite—that that particular peach is but a detail.

> PABLO PICASSO (1881-1973), Spanish artist. *Vogue* (New York, 1 Nov. 1956).

DETECTIVES

1 Every man at the bottom of his heart believes that he is a born detective.

> JOHN BUCHAN (1875-1940), British author, statesman. Leithen, in *The Power-House* ch. 2 (1916).

2 I'm a very smart guy. I haven't a feeling or a scruple in the world. All I have the itch for is money. I am so money greedy that for twenty-five bucks a day and expenses, mostly gasoline and whisky, I do my thinking myself, what there is of it; I risk my whole future, the hatred of the cops . . . I dodge bullets and eat saps, and say thank you very much, if you have any more trouble, I hope you'll think of me, I'll just leave one of my cards in case anything comes up.

> RAYMOND CHANDLER (1888-1959), U.S. author. Philip Marlowe, in *The Big Sleep*, ch. 32 (1939).

3 The private detective of fiction is a fantastic creation who acts and speaks like a real man. He can be completely realistic in every sense but one, that one sense being that in life as we know it such a man would not be a private detective.

> RAYMOND CHANDLER (1888-1959), U.S. author. Letter, 19 April 1951 (published in *Raymond Chandler Speaking*, 1962).

4 You can always tell a detective on TV. He never takes his hat off.

> RAYMOND CHANDLER (1888-1959), U.S. author. Philip Marlowe, in *Playback*, ch. 14 (1958).

5 "It is of the highest importance in the art of detection to be able to recognise out of a number of facts which are incidental and which are vital. . . . I would call your attention to the curious incident of the dog in the night-time."
"The dog did nothing in the night-time."
"That was the curious incident."

> SIR ARTHUR CONAN DOYLE (1859-1930), English author. Sherlock Holmes and Inspector Gregory, in *The Memoirs of Sherlock Holmes*, "Silver Blaze" (1893).

6 At bottom, I mean profoundly at bottom, the FBI has nothing to do with Communism, it has nothing to do with catching criminals, it has nothing to do with the Mafia, the syndicate, it has nothing to do with trust-busting, it has nothing to do with interstate commerce, it has nothing to do with anything but serving as a church for the mediocre. A high church for the true mediocre.

> NORMAN MAILER (b. 1923), U.S. author. *The Presidential Papers*, "Sixth Presidential Paper—A Kennedy Miscellany: An Impolite Interview" (1963). Mailer called the FBI "the only absolute organization in America."

7 As the strong man exults in his physical ability, delighting in such exercises as call his muscles into action, so glories the analyst in that moral activity which *disentangles*.

> EDGAR ALLAN POE (1809-45), U.S. poet, critic, short-story writer. *The Murders in the Rue Morgue* (1841).

See also Doyle on FICTION: SUSPENSE AND MYSTERY; The POLICE.

THE DEVIL

1 Be sober, be vigilant; because your adversary the devil, as a roaring lion, walketh about, seeking whom he may devour.

> BIBLE: NEW TESTAMENT. *1 Peter* 5:8.

2 An apology for the Devil—it must be remembered that we have only heard one side of the case. God has written all the books.

> SAMUEL BUTLER (1835-1902), English author. *Notebooks*, "Higgledy-Piggledy" (1912).

3 Lucifer also has died with God, and from his ashes has arisen a spiteful demon who does not even understand the object of his venture.

> ALBERT CAMUS (1913-60), French-Algerian philosopher, author. *The Rebel*, pt. 5, "Moderation and Excess" (1951; tr. 1953).

4 And Satan trembles when he sees,
The weakest saint upon his knees.

> WILLIAM COWPER (1731-1800), English poet. *Exhortation to Prayer*, in *Olney Hymns*, bk. 2, no. 60 (1779).

5 I was not content to believe in a personal devil and serve him, in the ordinary sense of the word. I wanted to get hold of him personally and become his chief of staff.

> ALEISTER CROWLEY (1875-1947), British occultist. *The Confessions of Aleister Crowley*, ch. 5 (1929; rev. 1970).

6 This is a puzzling world, and Old Harry's got a finger in it.

> GEORGE ELIOT (1819-80), English novelist. Mr. Tulliver, in *The Mill on the Floss*, bk. 3, ch. 9 (1860). "Old Harry" was the Devil.

7 When the Devil quotes Scriptures, it's not, really, to deceive, but simply that the masses are so ignorant of theology that somebody has to teach them the elementary texts before he can seduce them.

> PAUL GOODMAN (1911-72), U.S. author, poet, critic. *Five Years*, "Spring and Summer 1956," sct. 6 (1966).

8 The world is all the richer for having a devil in it, *so long as we keep our foot upon his neck*.

> WILLIAM JAMES (1842-1910), U.S. psychologist, philosopher. *The Varieties of Religious Experience*, lecture 2, "Circumscription of the Topic" (1902).

9 The devil is an optimist if he thinks he can make people worse than they are.

> KARL KRAUS (1874-1936), Austrian satirist. *Die Fackel*, no. 277/78 (Vienna, 31 March 1909; repr. in Thomas Szasz, *Anti-*

Freud: Karl Kraus's Criticism of Psychoanalysis and Psychiatry, ch. 8, 1976).

10 Those who consider the Devil to be a partisan of Evil and angels to be warriors for Good accept the demagogy of the angels . Things are clearly more complicated.

MILAN KUNDERA (b. 1929), Czech author, critic. *The Book of Laughter and Forgetting,* pt. 2, ch. 4 (1978; tr. 1980).

11 There are two equal and opposite errors into which our race can fall about the devils. One is to disbelieve in their existence. The other is to believe, and to feel an excessive and unhealthy interest in them. They themselves are equally pleased by both errors and hail a materialist or a magician with the same delight.

C. S. LEWIS (1898-1963), British author. *The Screwtape Letters,* Preface (1942).

12 In all systems of theology the devil figures as a male person. . . . Yes, it is women who keep the church going.

DON MARQUIS (1878-1937), U.S. humorist, journalist. Quoted in: E. Anthony, *O Rare Don Marquis,* ch. 11 (1962).

13 Better to reign in Hell than serve in Heaven.

JOHN MILTON (1608-74), English poet. Satan, in *Paradise Lost,* bk. 1.

14 The Prince of Darkness is a gentleman.

WILLIAM SHAKESPEARE (1564-1616), English dramatist, poet. Edgar, in the disguise of Poor Tom, in *King Lear,* act 3, sc. 4.

15 We may not pay Satan reverence, for that would be indiscreet, but we can at least respect his talents. A person who has for untold centuries maintained the imposing position of spiritual head of four-fifths of the human race, and political head of the whole of it, must be granted the possession of executive abilities of the loftiest order.

MARK TWAIN (1835-1910), U.S. author. "Concerning the Jews," in *Harper's* (New York, Sept. 1899; repr. in *Complete Essays,* ed. by Charles Neider, 1963).

DIARIES

1 A man who keeps a diary pays,
   Due toll to many tedious days;
   But life becomes eventful—then,
   His busy hand forgets the pen.
   Most books, indeed, are records less
   Of fulness than of emptiness.

WILLIAM ALLINGHAM (1824-89), Irish poet, diarist. *A Diary,* ch. 6 (ed. by H. Allingham and D. Radford, 1907), entry for 24-28 March 1864.

2 These pages reproduce me very imperfectly, and there are many things in me of which I find no trace in them. I suppose it is because, in the first place, sadness takes up the pen more readily than joy; and, in the next, because I depend so much upon surrounding circumstances. When there is no call upon me, and nothing to put me to the test, I fall back into melancholy; and so the practical man, the cheerful man, the literary man, does not appear in these pages. The portrait is lacking in proportion and breadth; it is one-sided, and wants a center; it has, as it were, been painted from too near.

HENRI-FRÉDÉRIC AMIEL (1821-81), Swiss philosopher, poet. *Journal Intime* (1882; tr. by Mrs. Humphrey Ward, 1892), entry for 23 Dec. 1866.

3 What the Journal posits is not the tragic question, the Madman's question: "Who am I?", but the comic question, the Bewildered Man's question: "Am I?" A comic—a comedian, that's what the Journal keeper is.

ROLAND BARTHES (1915-80), French semiologist. "Deliberation," in *Tel Quel,* no. 82 (Paris, Winter 1979; repr. in *Barthes: Selected Writings,* 1982).

4 The Journal is not essentially a confession, a story about oneself. It is a Memorial. What does the writer have to remember? Himself, who he is when he is not writing, when he is living his daily life, when he is alive and real, and not dying and without truth.

MAURICE BLANCHOT (b. 1907), French literary theorist, author. "The Essential Solitude," in *The Space of Literature* (1955; repr. in *The Gaze of Orpheus, and Other Literary Essays,* ed. by P. Adams Sitney, 1981).

5 This journal is a relief. When I am tired. . .out comes this, and down goes every thing. But I can't read it over—and God knows what contradictions it may contain. If I am sincere with myself (but I fear one lies more to one's self than to any one else) every page should confute, refute, and utterly abjure its predecessor.

LORD BYRON (1788-1824), English poet. *Byron's Letters and Journals,* vol. 3, (ed. by Leslie Marchand, 1974), entry for 6 Dec. 1813.

6 "The horror of that moment," the King went on, "I shall never, *never* forget!" "You will, though," the Queen said, "if you don't make a memorandum of it."

LEWIS CARROLL (1832-98), English writer, mathematician. *Through the Looking-Glass,* ch. 1 (1872).

7 The moment a man sets his thoughts down on paper, however secretly, he is in a sense writing for publication.

RAYMOND CHANDLER (1888-1959), U.S. author. Working notes on the celebrated Julia Wallace murder case (published in *Raymond Chandler Speaking,* 1962).

8 I think this journal will be disadvantageous for me, for I spend my time now like a spider spinning my own entrails.

MARY BOKIN CHESNUT (1823-86), U.S. diarist. *Diary for Dixie* (1949), entry for 14 March 1861.

9 After the writer's death, reading his journal is like receiving a long letter.

JEAN COCTEAU (1889-1963), French author, filmmaker. *Past Tense: Diaries,* vol. 2 (1988), entry for 7 June 1953. Cocteau was writing of Kafka's journal, which he had "read and re-read."

10 The literature of the inner life is very largely a record of struggle with the inordinate passions of the social self.

CHARLES HORTON COOLEY (1864-1929), U.S. sociologist. *Human Nature and the Social Order,* ch. 6 (1902).

11 I am carrying out my plan, so long formulated, of keeping a journal. What I most keenly wish is not to forget that I am writing for myself alone. Thus I shall always tell the truth, I hope, and thus I shall improve myself. These pages will reproach me for my changes of mind.

EUGÉNE DELACROIX (1798-1863), French artist. *The Journal of Eugène Delacroix*, (tr. by Walter Pach, 1937), opening words of first entry, 3 Sept. 1822.

12   Lovers who love truly do not write down their happiness.

ANATOLE FRANCE (1844-1924), French author. *The Crime of Sylvestre Bonnard*, "The Log, November 30 1859" (1881).

13   Bolkenstein, a Minister, was speaking on the Dutch programme from London, and he said that they ought to make a collection of diaries and letters after the war. Of course, they all made a rush at my diary immediately. Just imagine how interesting it would be if I were to publish a romance of the "Secret Annexe." The title alone would be enough to make people think it was a detective story.

ANNE FRANK (1929-45), German Jewish refugee, diarist. *The Diary of a Young Girl* (1947; tr. 1952), entry for 29 March 1944. The original title which Anne Frank gave to her diary was *Het Achterbuis*, which has been translated as "The Secret Annexe."

14   The diary is an art form just as much as the novel or the play. The diary simply requires a greater canvas.

HENRY MILLER (1891-1980), U.S. author. *The Cosmological Eye*, "Un Etre Etoile" (1939).

15   In Hollywood now when people die they don't say, "Did he leave a will?" but "Did he leave a diary?"

LIZA MINNELLI (b. 1946), U.S. actor. *Observer Magazine* (London, 13 Aug. 1989).

16   I do not keep a diary. Never have. To write a diary every day is like returning to one's own vomit.

J. ENOCH POWELL (b. 1912), British Conservative politician. *Sunday Times* (London, 6 Nov. 1977).

17   The palest ink is better than the best memory.

CHINESE PROVERB.

18   How hard it is to make your thoughts look anything but imbecile fools when you paint them with ink on paper.

OLIVE SCHREINER (1855-1920), South African writer, feminist. Lyndall, in *The Story of an African Farm*, pt. 2, ch. 4 (1883).

19   A diary is more or less the work of a man of clay whose hands are clumsy and in whose eyes there is no light.

WALLACE STEVENS (1879-1955), U.S. poet. *Souvenirs and Prophecies: the Young Wallace Stevens*, ch. 3 (ed. by Holly Stevens, 1977), entry for 26 July 1899.

20   What is a diary as a rule? A document useful to the person who keeps it, dull to the contemporary who reads it, invaluable to the student, centuries afterwards, who treasures it!

ELLEN TERRY (1848-1928), English actor. *The Story of My Life*, ch. 14 (1908).

21   I do not know but thoughts written down thus in a journal might be printed in the same form with greater advantage than if the related ones were brought together into separate essays. They are now allied to life, and are

seen by the reader not to be far-fetched. It is more simple, less artful. I feel that in the other case I should have no proper frame for my sketches. Mere facts and names and dates communicate more than we suspect. . . . Perhaps I can never find so good a setting for my thoughts as I shall thus have taken them out of. The crystal never sparkles more brightly than in the cavern.

HENRY DAVID THOREAU (1817-62), U.S. philosopher, author, naturalist. *Journals*, (1906), entry for 27-28 Jan. 1852.

22   Reasons for not keeping a notebook: 1) the ambiguity of the reader—it is never quite oneself. 2) I usually hate the sight of my handwriting—it lives too much and I dislike its life—I mean by "lives," of course, betrays too much!

LIONEL TRILLING (1905-75), U.S. critic. Notebook entry, 1944 (published in *Partisan Review 50th Anniversary Edition*, ed. by William Philips, 1985).

23   Where I would like to discover facts, I find fancy. Where I would like to learn what I did, I learn only what I was thinking. They are loaded with opinion, moral thoughts, quick evaluations, youthful hopes and cares and sorrows. Occasionally, they manage to report something in exquisite honesty and accuracy. That is why I have refrained from burning them.

E. B. WHITE (1899-1985), U.S. author, editor. Interview in *Writers at Work* (Eighth Series, 1988), speaking of his own journals.

24   I never travel without my diary. One should always have something sensational to read in the train.

OSCAR WILDE (1854-1900), Anglo-Irish playwright, author. Gwendolen, in *The Importance of Being Earnest*, act 3.

25   Afraid lest he be caught up in a net of words, tripped up, bewildered and so defeated—thrown aside—a man hesitates to write down his innermost convictions.

WILLIAM CARLOS WILLIAMS (1883-1963), U.S. poet. *The Embodiment Of Knowledge* (1974), journal entry for 7 July 1929.

26   The good diarist writes either for himself alone or for a posterity so distant that it can safely hear every secret and justly weigh every motive. For such an audience there is need neither of affectation nor of restraint. Sincerity is what they ask, detail, and volume; skill with the pen comes in conveniently, but brilliance is not necessary; genius is a hindrance even; and should you know your business and do it manfully, posterity will let you off mixing with great men, reporting famous affairs, or having lain with the first ladies in the land.

VIRGINIA WOOLF (1882-1941), British novelist. *The Common Reader*, "Rambling Round Evelyn" (First Series, 1925; written 1920).

DICTATORSHIP

1   There ought to be an absolute dictatorship . . . a dictatorship of painters . . . a dictatorship of one painter . . . to suppress all those who have betrayed us, to suppress the cheaters, to suppress the tricks, to suppress mannerisms, to suppress charms, to suppress history, to suppress a heap of other things. But common sense always gets away with it. Above all, let's have a revolution against that!

PABLO PICASSO (1881-1973), Spanish artist. "Conversation

avec Picasso," in *Cahiers d'Art*, vol. 10, no. 10 (1935); tr. in Alfred H. Barr, Jr., *Picasso: Fifty Years of His Art*, 1946).

2   In inner-party politics, these methods lead, as we shall yet see, to this: the party organization substitutes itself for the party, the central committee substitutes itself for the organization, and, finally, a "dictator" substitutes himself for the central committee.

> LEON TROTSKY (1879-1940), Russian revolutionary. *Our Political Tasks* (1904), on Lenin's plans for organizing the Bolshevik Party as a highly centralized and authoritarian body prior to the Russian Revolution. Quoted in: Isaac Deutscher, *The Prophet Armed*, ch. 3 (1963). Trotsky was later to join Lenin in the Bolshevik Party, help mastermind the Revolution of 1917 and ultimately be killed by the "dictator" Stalin.

3   Better the rule of One, whom all obey,
Than to let clamorous demagogues betray
Our freedom with the kiss of anarchy.

> OSCAR WILDE (1854-1900), Anglo-Irish playwright, author. *Libertatis Sacra Fames* ["Sacred Hunger for Liberty"].

See also Orwell on POWER.

DICTIONARIES

1   At painful times, when composition is impossible and reading is not *enough*, grammars and dictionaries are excellent for *distraction*.

> ELIZABETH BARRETT BROWNING (1806-61), English poet. Letter, April 1839, to Mary Russell Mitford (published in *Elizabeth Barrett to Miss Mitford*, 1954).

2   Actually if a writer needs a dictionary he should not write. He should have read the dictionary at least three times from beginning to end and then have loaned it to someone who needs it. There are only certain words which are valid and similies (bring me my dictionary) are like defective ammunition (the lowest thing I can think of at this time).

> ERNEST HEMINGWAY (1899-61), U.S. author. Letter, 20 March 1953, to the critic Bernard Berenson (published in *Selected Letters*, ed. by Carlos Baker, 1981). Hemingway's spelling, as shown in his letters, was appalling..

3   Every other author may aspire to praise; the lexicographer can only hope to escape reproach, and even this negative recompense has been yet granted to very few.

> SAMUEL JOHNSON (1709-84), English author, lexicographer. *Dictionary of the English Language*, Preface (1755).

4   Lexicographer: a writer of dictionaries, a harmless drudge, that busies himself in tracing the original, and detailing the signification of words.

> SAMUEL JOHNSON (1709-84), English author, lexicographer. *Dictionary of the English Language* (1755). Under the entry for *Dull*, Johnson gave the following illustration: "To make dictionaries is *dull* work."

5   I am not a literary man. . . . I am a man of science, and I am interested in that branch of Anthropolgy which deals with the history of human speech.

> J. A. H. MURRAY (1837-1915), English lexicographer. Lecture to the Ashmolean History Society, Oxford. Quoted by his granddaughter, K. M. Elisabeth Murray, in: *Caught in the Web of Words* (1977), her biography of him. Murray was editor of the Oxford English Dictionary, on which he worked from 1879 until his death, though it was not published until 1928.

DIET

1   'Tis a superstition to insist on a special diet. All is made at last of the same chemical atoms.

> RALPH WALDO EMERSON (1803-82), U.S. essayist, poet, philosopher. *The Conduct of Life*, "Culture" (1860).

2   To safeguard one's health at the cost of too strict a diet is a tiresome illness indeed.

> FRANÇOIS, DUC DE LA ROCHEFOUCAULD (1613-1680), French writer, moralist. *Sentences et Maximes Morales*, no. 208 (ed. 1665; no. 56 of First Supplement, 1678).

3   If you wish to grow thinner, diminish your dinner,
And take to light claret instead of pale ale;
Look down with an utter contempt upon butter,
And never touch bread till it's toasted—or stale

> H. S. LEIGH (1837-83), English author. *A Day for Wishing*.

4   To ask women to become unnaturally thin is to ask them to relinquish their sexuality.

> NAOMI WOLF (b. 1962), U.S. author. *The Beauty Myth*, "Hunger" (1990).

DIGNITY

1   Every man has his dignity. I'm willing to forget mine, but at my own discretion and not when someone else tells me to.

> DENIS DIDEROT (1713-84), French philosopher. Rameau's nephew, in *Rameau's Nephew* (written 1762; published 1821; repr. in *Selected Writings*, ed. by Lester G. Crocker, 1966).

2   Only man has dignity; only man, therefore, can be funny.

> RONALD KNOX (1888-1957), British scholar, priest. *Essays In Satire*, Introduction (1928).

3   Each of us, face to face with other men, is clothed with some sort of dignity, but we know only too well all the unspeakable things that go on in the heart.

> LUIGI PIRANDELLO (1867-1936), Italian author, playwright. The Father, in *Six Characters in Search of an Author*, act 1 (1921).

4   Perhaps the only true dignity of man is his capacity to despise himself.

> GEORGE SANTAYANA (1863-1952), U.S. philosopher, poet. *Spinoza's Ethics*, Introduction (1910).

5   Human Dignity has gleamed only now and then and here and there, in lonely splendor, throughout the ages, a hope of the better men, never an achievement of the majority.

> JAMES THURBER (1894-1961), U.S. humorist, illustrator. *Collecting Himself*, "Thinking Ourselves Into Trouble," pt. 3 (1989; first published 1939).

DINNER PARTIES

1   In dinner talk it is perhaps allowable to fling any faggot rather than let the fire go out.

> J. M. BARRIE (1860-1937), British playwright. *Tommy and Grizel*, ch. 3 (1900).

2 I had rather munch a crust of brown bread and an onion in a corner, without any more ado or ceremony, than feed upon turkey at another man's table, where one is fain to sit mincing and chewing his meat an hour together, drink little, be always wiping his fingers and his chops, and never dare to cough nor sneeze, though he has never so much a mind to it, nor do a many things which a body may do freely by one's self.

> MIGUEL DE CERVANTES (1547-1616), Spanish writer. Sancho Panza, in *Don Quixote*, pt. 1, bk. 2, ch. 3 (1605; tr. by P. Motteux).

3 Dining-out is a vice, a dissipation of spirit punished by remorse. We eat, drink and talk a little too much, abuse all our friends, belch out our literary preferences and are egged on by accomplices in the audience to acts of mental exhibitionism. Such evenings cannot fail to diminish those who take part in them.

> CYRIL CONNOLLY (1903-1974), British critic. *The Unquiet Grave*, pt. 2 (1944; rev. 1951).

4 Conversation did not flow with the drink; it drowned in it.

> QUENTIN CRISP (b. 1908), British author. *The Naked Civil Servant*, ch. 22 (1968).

5 Hostesses who entertain much must make up their parties as ministers make up their cabinets, on grounds other than personal liking.

> GEORGE ELIOT (1819-80), English novelist, editor. *Daniel Deronda*, bk. 1, ch. 5 (1874-76).

6 The best number for a dinner party is two—myself and a dam' good head waiter.

> NUBAR GULBENKIAN (1896-1972), British oil tycoon, socialite. *Daily Telegraph* (London, 14 Jan. 1965).

7 The formal Washington dinner party has all the spontaneity of a Japanese imperial funeral.

> SIMON HOGGART (b. 1946), British journalist. *Observer* (London, 31 Dec. 1989).

8 A host is like a general: calamities often reveal his genius.

> HORACE (65-8 B.C.), Roman poet. *Satires*, bk. 2, Satire 8 (c. 35 B.C.).

9 She was a woman who, between courses, could be graceful with her elbows on the table.

> HENRY JAMES (1843-1916), U.S. author. *The Ambassadors*, bk. 7, ch. 1 (1903), of Madame de Vionnett.

10 This was a good enough dinner, to be sure; but it was not a dinner to *ask* a man to.

> SAMUEL JOHNSON (1709-84), English author, lexicographer. Quoted in: James Boswell, *Life of Samuel Johnson*, 5 Aug. 1763 (1791).

11 At a dinner party one should eat wisely but not too well, and talk well but not too wisely.

> W. SOMERSET MAUGHAM (1874-1966), British author. *A Writer's Notebook* (1949), 1896 entry.

12 When her guests were awash with champagne and
    with gin,
She was recklessly sober, as sharp as a pin.
An abstemious man would reel at her look,
As she rolled a bright eye and praised his las
    book.

> WILLIAM PLOMER (1903-73), South African author, poet. *Slightly Foxed, or The Widower of Bayswater*, verse 7, in *Collected Poems*, "London Ballads and Poems" (1960).

13 The table kills more people than war does.

> CATALAN PROVERB. Quoted in: Colman Andrews, *Catalan Cuisine*.

14 When at length they rose to go to bed, it struck each man as he followed his neighbour upstairs that the one before him walked very crookedly.

> R. S. SURTEES (1803-64), English novelist. *Mr. Sponge's Sporting Tour*, ch. 35 (1853).

15 He showed me his bill of fare to tempt me to dine with him; said I, I value not your bill of fare, give me your bill of company.

> JONATHAN SWIFT (1667-1745), Anglo-Irish satirist. *Journal to Stella*, 2 Sept. 1711.

16 After a good dinner one can forgive anybody, even one's own relations.

> OSCAR WILDE (1854-1900), Anglo-Irish playwright, author. Lady Caroline, in *A Woman of No Importance*, act 2.

See also BANQUETS; Wilde on DANDIES; Thoreau on GOVERNMENT.

DIPLOMACY

1 An ambassador is not simply an agent; he is also a spectacle.

> WALTER BAGEHOT (1826-77), English economist, critic. *The English Constitution*, ch. 4 (1867).

2 Consul. In American politics, a person who having failed to secure an office from the people is given one by the Administration on condition that he leave the country.

> AMBROSE BIERCE (1842-1914), U.S. author. *The Devil's Dictionary* (1881-1906).

3 If you are to stand up for your Government you must be able to stand up to your Government.

> SIR HAROLD, LATER LORD, CACCIA (1905-90?), British ambassador. Quoted in: *Anatomy of Britain*, ch. 17 (1965), said while British ambassador at Washington.

4 To act with doubleness towards a man whose own conduct was double, was so near an approach to virtue that it deserved to be called by no meaner name than diplomacy.

> GEORGE ELIOT (1819-80), English novelist, editor. *Felix Holt, The Radical*, ch. 29 (1866), on the hypocrisy and corruption present in politics at the time of the first Reform Bill (1832).

5 There are few ironclad rules of diplomacy but to one there is no exception. When an official reports that talks were useful, it can safely be concluded that nothing was accomplished.

> JOHN KENNETH GALBRAITH (b. 1908), U.S. economist. "The American Ambassador," in *Foreign Service Journal* (Washington, D.C., June 1969).

6 Diplomats were invented simply to waste time.

> DAVID LLOYD GEORGE (1863-1945), Welsh Liberal politician,

prime minister. Comment on preparations for the Versailles Peace Conference, Nov. 1918.

7 Diplomacy is to do and say,
The nastiest things in the nicest way.

> ISAAC GOLDBERG (1887-1938), U.S. critic. *The Reflex.*

8 Speak softly and carry a big stick.

> THEODORE ROOSEVELT (1858-1919), U.S. Republican (later Progressive) politician, president. Speech, 2 Sept. 1901, Minnesota State Fair, quoting a favorite adage and referring to military preparation and the Monroe Doctrine.

9 My advice to any diplomat who wants to have a good press is to have two or three kids and a dog.

> CARL ROWAN (b. 1925), U.S. ambassador to Finland. *New Yorker* (7 Dec. 1963).

10 When envoys are sent with compliments in their mouths, it is a sign that the enemy wishes for a truce.

> SUN TZU (6-5TH CENTURY B.C.), Chinese general. *The Art of War*, ch. 9, axiom 38 (c. 490 B.C.; ed. by James Clavell, 1981).

11 Diplomacy means all the wicked devices of the Old World, spheres of influence, balances of power, secret treaties, triple alliances, and, during the interwar period, appeasement of Fascism.

> BARBARA TUCHMAN (1912-89), U.S. historian. "If Mao Had Come to Washington in 1945," in *Foreign Affairs* (New York, Oct. 1972), referring to "the deep-seated American distrust . . . of diplomacy and diplomats."

12 A diplomat these days is nothing but a head-waiter who's allowed to sit down occasionally.

> PETER USTINOV (b. 1921), British actor, writer, director. The General, in *Romanoff and Juliet*, act 1. The part of the General was played by Ustinov himself in the first production of the play.

13 An Ambassador is an honest man sent to lie abroad for the good of his country.

> SIR HENRY WOTTON (1568-1639), English diplomat, poet. Written in the album of Christopher Fleckmore, c. 1612. Quoted in: Izaak Walton, *Life of Sir Henry Wotton* (published in *Reliquiae Wottonianae*, 1651). Wotton wrote the remark while in Germany, en route to Venice where he was serving as James I's envoy. However, he spoiled his pun by writing it in Latin, thus reducing "*to lie*" (*ad mentiendum*) to one meaning only—and thereby ruining his career.

14 Once the Xerox copier was invented, diplomacy died.

> ANDREW YOUNG (b. 1932), U.S. politician, diplomat. *Playboy* (Chicago, July 1977).

See also Wilde on COOKING; TACT; Benn on WAR.

DISABILITY

1 The chief misery of the decline of the faculties, and a main cause of the irritability that often goes with it, is evidently the isolation, the lack of customary appreciation and influence, which only the rarest tact and thoughtfulness on the part of others can alleviate.

> CHARLES HORTON COOLEY (1864-1929), U.S. sociologist. *Human Nature and the Social Order*, ch. 6 (1902).

2 The sense of an entailed disadvantage—the deformed foot doubtfully hidden by the shoe, makes a restlessly active spiritual yeast, and easily turns a self-centred, unloving nature into an Ishmaelite. But in the rarer sort, who presently see their own frustrated claim as one among a myriad, the inexorable sorrow takes the form of fellowship and makes the imagination tender.

> GEORGE ELIOT (1819-80), English novelist, editor. *Daniel Deronda*, bk. 2, ch. 16 (1876).

3 I have often been asked, "Do not people bore you?" I do not understand quite what that means. I suppose the calls of the stupid and curious, especially of newspaper reporters, are always inopportune. I also dislike people who try to talk down to my understanding. They are like people who when walking with you try to shorten their steps to suit yours; the hypocrisy in both cases is equally exasperating.

> HELEN KELLER (1880-1968), U.S. blind/deaf author, lecturer. *The Story of My Life*, pt. 1, ch. 23 (1903).

4 The invalid is a parasite on society. In a certain state it is indecent to go on living. To vegetate on in cowardly dependence on physicians and medicaments after the meaning of life, the right to life, has been lost ought to entail the profound contempt of society.

> FRIEDRICH NIETZSCHE (1844-1900), German philosopher. *Twilight of the Idols*, "Expeditions of an Untimely Man," aph. 36 (1889).

DISAPPOINTMENT

1 When you think of the huge uninterrupted success of a book like *Don Quixote*, you're bound to realize that if humankind have not yet finished being revenged, by sheer laughter, for being let down in their greatest hope, it is because that hope was cherished so long and lay so deep!

> GEORGES BERNANOS (1888-1948), French novelist and political writer. M. Olivier, in *The Diary of a Country Priest*, ch. 7 (1936).

2 It's precisely the disappointing stories, which have no proper ending and therefore no proper meaning, that sound true to life.

> MAX FRISCH (1911-91), Swiss author, architect. Stiller, in *I'm Not Stiller*, "First Notebook" (1954; tr. 1958).

3 Disappointment is a sort of bankruptcy—the bankruptcy of a soul that expends too much in hope and expectation.

> ERIC HOFFER (1902-83), U.S. philosopher. *The Passionate State of Mind*, aph. 264 (1955).

4 Disappointment, when it involves neither shame nor loss, is as good as success; for it supplies as many images to the mind, and as many topics to the tongue.

> SAMUEL JOHNSON (1709-84), English author, lexicographer. Letter, 26 June 1775, to Hester Thrale (published in *The Letters of Samuel Johnson*, vol. 2, no. 411, ed. by R. W. Chapman, 1952).

5 There can be no deep disappointment where there is not deep love.

> MARTIN LUTHER KING, JR. (1929-68), U.S. clergyman, civil

rights leader. "Letter from Birmingham Jail" (published in *Why We Can't Wait*, 1963).

6   "Blessed is the man who expects nothing, for he shall never be disappointed" was the ninth beatitude.

ALEXANDER POPE (1688-1744), English satirical poet. Letter, 6 Oct. 1727, to playwright John Gay. Quoted in: Roscoe, *Life of Pope*, vol. 10.

7   In this world there are two tragedies. One is not getting what one wants, and the other is getting it. The last is much the worst.

OSCAR WILDE (1854-1900), Anglo-Irish playwright, author. Dumby, in *Lady Windermere's Fan*, act 3. George Bernard Shaw expressed a similar idea in *Man and Superman,*, published ten years after *Lady Windermere's Fan*, act 4, when Mendoza says: "There are two tragedies in life. One is to lose your heart's desire. The other is to gain it."

DISASTERS

1   The earth is mankind's ultimate haven, our blessed *terra firma*. When it trembles and gives way beneath our feet, it's as though one of God's cheques has bounced.

GILBERT ADAIR, British author, critic. Quoted in: London *Sunday Correspondent Magazine* (24 Dec. 1989).

2   Calamities are of two kinds: misfortune to ourselves, and good fortune to others.

AMBROSE BIERCE (1842-1914), U.S. author. *The Devil's Dictionary* (1881-1906).

3   What quarrel, what harshness, what unbelief in each other can subsist in the presence of a great calamity, when all the artifical vesture of our life is gone, and we are all one with each other in primitive mortal needs?

GEORGE ELIOT (1819-80), English novelist, editor. *The Mill on the Floss*, bk. 7, ch. 5 (1860).

4   The compensations of calamity are made apparent to the understanding also, after long intervals of time. A fever, a mutilation, a cruel disappointment, a loss of wealth, a loss of friends, seems at the moment unpaid loss, and unpayable. But the sure years reveal the deep remedial force that underlies all facts.

RALPH WALDO EMERSON (1803-82), U.S. essayist, poet, philosopher. *Essays*, "Compensation" (First Series, 1841).

5   The bosses of our mass media, press, radio, film and television, succeed in their aim of taking our minds off disaster. Thus, the distraction they offer demands the antidote of maximum concentration on disaster.

ERNST FISCHER (1899-1972), Austrian editor, poet, critic. *Art Against Ideology*, ch. 1 (1966; tr. 1969).

6   Man's extremity is God's opportunity.

JOHN FLAVEL (1630-91), English evangelist, author. *A Faithful and Ancient Account of Some Late and Wonderful Sea Deliverances* (c. 1680).

7   Our sympathy is cold to the relation of distant misery.

EDWARD GIBBON (1737-94), English historian. *The Decline and Fall of the Roman Empire*, ch. 49 (1776-88).

8   Down went the owners—greedy men whom hope of gain allured:

Oh, dry the starting tear, for they were heavily insured.

W. S. GILBERT (1836-1911), English librettist. *The "Bab" Ballads*, "Etiquette" (1866-71).

9   Perhaps catastrophe is the natural human environment, and even though we spend a good deal of energy trying to get away from it, we are programmed for survival amid catastrophe.

GERMAINE GREER (b. 1939), Australian feminist writer. *Sex and Destiny*, ch. 14 (1984).

10   A great calamity . . . is as old as the trilobites an hour after it has happened.

OLIVER WENDELL HOLMES, SR. (1809-94), U.S. writer, physician. *The Autocrat of the Breakfast Table*, ch. 2 (1858).

11   The popularity of disaster movies . . . expresses a collective perception of a world threatened by irresistible and unforeseen forces which *nevertheless are thwarted at the last moment*. Their thinly veiled symbolic meaning might be translated thus: We are innocent of wrongdoing. We are attacked by unforeseeable forces come to harm us. We are, thus, innocent even of negligence. Though those forces are insuperable, *chance* will come to our aid and we shall emerge victorious.

DAVID MAMET (b. 1947), U.S. playwright. *Writing in Restaurants*, "Decadence" (1986).

12   The stabbing horror of life is not contained in calamities and disasters, because these things wake one up and one gets very familiar and intimate with them and finally they become tame again. . . . No, it is more like being in a hotel room in Hoboken let us say, and just enough money in one's pocket for another meal.

HENRY MILLER (1891-1980), U.S. author. *Tropic of Capricorn* (1939; repr. 1966, p. 278).

DISC JOCKEYS

1   Do they merit vitriol, even a drop of it? Yes, because they corrupt the young, persuading them that the mature world, which produced Beethoven and Schweitzer, sets an even higher value on the transient anodynes of youth than does youth itself . . . . They are the Hollow Men. They are electronic lice.

ANTHONY BURGESS (b. 1917), British author, critic. *Punch* (London, 20 Sept. 1967), referring to disc jockeys.

2   This particularly rapid, unintelligible patter
Isn't generally heard, and if it is it doesn't matter!

W. S. GILBERT (1836-1911), English librettist. Despard, in *Ruddigore*, act 2.

3   Radio news is bearable. This is due to the fact that while the news is being broadcast the disc jockey is not allowed to talk.

FRAN LEBOWITZ (b. 1951), U.S. journalist. *Metropolitan Life*, "No News Is Bearable" (1978).

4   So, too, if, to our surprise, we should meet one of these morons whose remarks are so conspicuous a part of the folklore of the world of the radio—remarks made without using either the tongue or the brain, spouted much like the spoutings of small whales—we should recognize him as below the level of nature but not as below the level of the imagination.

WALLACE STEVENS (1879-1955), U.S. poet. *The Necessary Angel,* "Three Academic Pieces," no. 1 (1947; repr. 1951).

DISCIPLES

1   Ye are the salt of the earth: but if the salt has lost its savour, wherewith shall it be salted?

BIBLE: NEW TESTAMENT. *Matthew* 5:13; from the Sermon on the Mount.

2   Behold, I send you forth as sheep in the midst of wolves: be ye therefore wise as serpents, and harmless as doves.

BIBLE: NEW TESTAMENT. *Matthew* 10:16; Jesus, sending forth the Apostles.

3   Once the good man was dead, one wore his hat and another his sword as he had worn them, a third had himself barbered as he had, a fourth walked as he did, but the honest man that he was—nobody any longer wanted to be that.

G. C. LICHTENBERG (1742-99), German physicist, philosopher. *Aphorisms,* "Notebook C," aph. 36 (written 1765-99; tr. by R. J. Hollingdale, 1990).

4   Disciples be damned. It's not interesting. It's only the masters that matter. Those who create.

PABLO PICASSO (1881-1973), Spanish artist. Quoted in: Michel George-Michel, *De Renoir à Picasso,* (1954, pp. 94-95).

5   Every great man nowadays has his disciples, and it is usually Judas who writes the biography.

OSCAR WILDE (1854-1900), Anglo-Irish playwright, author. "The Butterfly's Boswell," in *Court and Society Review* (London, 20 April 1887). The aphorism reappeared in *The Critic as Artist,* pt. 1 (published in *Intentions,* 1891).

DISCIPLINE

1   The rod and reproof give wisdom: but a child left to himself bringeth his mother to shame.

BIBLE, HEBREW. *Proverbs* 29:15.

2   So far as discipline is concerned, freedom means not its absence but the use of higher and more rational forms as contrasted with those that are lower or less rational.

CHARLES HORTON COOLEY (1864-1929), U.S. sociologist. *Human Nature and the Social Order,* ch. 12 (1902).

3   Blind and unwavering indiscipline at all times constitutes the real strength of all free men.

ALFRED JARRY (1873-1907), French playwright, author. Corporal, in *Ubu Enchained,* act 1, sc. 2.

4   Discipline must come through liberty. . . . We do not consider an individual disciplined only when he has been rendered as artificially silent as a mute and as immovable as a paralytic. He is an individual annihilated, not disciplined.

MARIA MONTESSORI (1870-1952), Italian educationist. *The Montessori Method,* ch. 5 (1912).

5   Reasonable orders are easy enough to obey; it is capricious, bureaucratic or plain idiotic demands that form the habit of discipline.

BARBARA TUCHMAN (1912-89), U.S. historian. *Stilwell and the American Experience in China: 1911-1945,* pt. 1, ch. 1 (1970).

DISCONTENT

1   You will never be happy if you continue to search for what happiness consists of. You will never live if you are looking for the meaning of life.

ALBERT CAMUS (1913-60), French-Algerian philosopher, author. The fool, in "Intuitions" (written Oct. 1932; published in *Youthful Writings,* 1976).

2   The essence of man is, discontent, divine discontent; a sort of love without a beloved, the ache we feel in a member we no longer have.

JOSÉ ORTEGA Y GASSET (1883-1955), Spanish essayist, philosopher. Lecture, 1916, remembered by Ortega in another lecture, "Historical Reason," no. 4, Buenos Aires, Oct. 1940.

3   Man hath still either toys or care:
But hath no root, nor to one place is tied,
But ever restless and irregular,
About this earth doth run and ride.
He knows he hath a home, but scarce knows
  where;
He says it is so far,
That he has quite forgot how to go there.

HENRY VAUGHAN (1622-95), Welsh poet. *Man,* st. 3.

4   Discontent is the first step in the progress of a man or a nation.

OSCAR WILDE (1854-1900), Anglo-Irish playwright, author. Lord Illingworth, in *A Woman of No Importance,* act 2.

See also DISSATISFACTION.

DISCOVERY

1   They are ill discoverers that think there is no land when they see nothing but sea.

FRANCIS BACON (1561-1626), English philosopher, essayist, statesman. *The Advancement of Learning,* bk. 2, ch. 7, sct. 5 (1605).

2   The way a child discovers the world constantly replicates the way science began. You start to notice what's around you, and you get very curious about how things work. How things interrelate. It's as simple as seeing a bug that intrigues you. You want to know where it goes at night; who its friends are; what it eats.

DAVID CRONENBERG (b. 1943), Canadian filmmaker. *Cronenberg On Cronenberg,* ch. 1 (ed. by Chris Rodley, 1992).

3   If a man knew anything, he would sit in a corner and be modest; but he is such an ignorant peacock, that he goes bustling up and down, and hits on extraordinary discoveries.

RALPH WALDO EMERSON (1803-82), U.S. essayist, poet, philosopher. *English Traits,* "Cockayne" (1856).

4 The discovery of the North Pole is one of those realities which could not be avoided. It is the wages which human perseverance pays itself when it thinks that something is taking too long. The world needed a discoverer of the North Pole, and in all areas of social activity, merit was less important here than opportunity.

> KARL KRAUS (1874-1936), Austrian satirist. "The Discovery of the North Pole," in *Die Fackel* (Vienna, 1909; repr. in *In These Great Times: A Karl Kraus Reader*, ed. by Harry Zohn, 1976).

5 If we make a couple of discoveries here and there we need not believe things will go on like this for ever . . . . Just as we hit water when we dig in the earth, so we discover the incomprehensible sooner or later.

> G. C. LICHTENBERG (1742-99), German physicist, philosopher. *Aphorisms*, "Notebook F," aph. 82 (written 1765-99; tr. by R. J. Hollingdale, 1990).

6 What is there that confers the noblest delight? What is that which swells a man's breast with pride above that which any other experience can bring to him? Discovery! To know that you are walking where none others have walked; that you are beholding what human eye has not seen before; that you are breathing a virgin atmosphere. To give birth to an idea, to discover a great thought—an intellectual nugget, right under the dust of a field that many a brain-plough had gone over before. To find a new planet, to invent a new hinge, to find a way to make the lightnings carry your messages. To be the *first*—that is the idea.

> MARK TWAIN (1835-1910), U.S. author. *The Innocents Abroad*, ch. 26 (1869).

See also EXPLORATION.

DISCRETION

1 Discretion of speech is more than eloquence, and to speak agreeably to him with whom we deal is more than to speak in good words, or in good order.

> FRANCIS BACON (1561-1626), English philosopher, essayist, statesman. *Essays*, "Of Discourse" (1597-1625).

2 As a jewel of gold in a swine's snout, so is a fair woman which is without discretion.

> BIBLE, HEBREW. *Proverbs* 11:22.

3 Be wiser than other people, if you can; but do not tell them so.

> LORD CHESTERFIELD (1694-1773), English statesman, man of letters. Letter, 29 Nov. 1745 (first published 1774; repr. in *The Letters of the Earl of Chesterfield to His Son*, vol. 1, no. 104, ed. by Charles Strachey, 1901). Some editions give this letter dated 19 Nov. 1745.

4 Nothing is more dangerous than a friend without discretion; even a prudent enemy is preferable.

> JEAN DE LA FONTAINE (1621-95), French poet, fabulist. The moral of fable, *L'Ours et l'Amateur des Jardins*, in *Fables*, bk. 8, no. 10 (1678-79).

5 A closed mouth catches no flies.,

> ITALIAN PROVERB. *Don Quixote*, bk. 3, ch. 11, pt. 1 (1605). This is one of the "catalogue of musty proverbs" quoted by Sancho Panza..

6 Be advised what thou dost discourse of, and what thou maintainest whether touching religion, state, or vanity; for if thou err in the first, thou shalt be accounted profane; if in the second, dangerous; if in the third, indiscreet and foolish.

> SIR WALTER RALEGH (1552-1618), English author, soldier, explorer. *Instructions to His Son and to Posterity*, ch. 4, "Private Quarrels to be Avoided" (1632; repr. in *The Works of Sir Walter Raleigh*, vol. 2, 1751; also *Advice to a Son*, 1962).

7 I cannot and do not live in the world of discretion, not as a writer, anyway. I would prefer to, I assure you—it would make life easier. But discretion is, unfortunately, not for novelists.

> PHILIP ROTH (b. 1933), U.S. novelist. Phillip, in *Deception* (1990, p. 190 of Jonathan Cape ed.), to his wife.

8 Give every man thine ear but few thy voice.
Take each man's censure, but reserve thy judgement.

> WILLIAM SHAKESPEARE (1564-1616), English dramatist, poet. Polonious, in *Hamlet*, act 1, sc. 3, giving advice to his son Laertes, departing for France.

DISEASE

1 Which came first the intestine or the tapeworm?

> WILLIAM BURROUGHS (b. 1914), U.S. author. Interview, 12 April 1992, on *The South Bank Show*, LWT.

2 Even diseases have lost their prestige, there aren't so many of them left. . . . Think it over . . . no more syphilis, no more clap, no more typhoid . . . antibiotics have taken half the tragedy out of medicine.

> LOUIS-FERDINAND CÉLINE (1894-1961), French author. Interview, 1960, published in *Critical Essays on Louis-Ferdinand Céline* (ed. by William F. Buckley, 1989).

3 A decadent civilization compromises with its disease, cherishes the virus infecting it, loses its self-respect.

> E. M. CIORAN (b. 1911), Rumanian-born French philosopher. *The Temptation to Exist*, "Rages and Resignations: Saint Paul" (1956).

4 Disease is a vital expression of the human organism.

> GEORG GRODDECK (1866-1934), German psychoanalyst. *The Book of the It*, letter 31 (1923).

5 One might say, for example, that a patient has a *kind* of St Vitus's dance; a *kind* of dropsy; a *kind* of nerve fever; a *kind* of ague. One would *never* say, however (to end once and for all the confusion of these names) "He *has* St. Vitus's dance," "He *has* nerve fever," "He *has* dropsy," "He *has* ague," since there simply are not any fixed, unchanging diseases to be known by such names.

> SAMUEL HAHNEMANN (1755-1843), German physician, founder of homeopathy. *Organon of Medicine*, sct. 81 (6th ed., 1842; tr. 1983).

6 Disease generally begins that equality which death completes.

> SAMUEL JOHNSON (1709-84), English author, lexicographer. *Rambler*, no. 48 (London, 1 Sept. 1750).

7   He who considers disease results to be the disease itself, and expects to do away with these as diseases, is insane. It is an insanity in medicine, an insanity that has grown out of the milder forms of mental disorder in science, crazy whims.

JAMES TYLER KENT (1849-1916), U.S. homeopathic teacher, physician. *Lectures on Homeopathic Philosophy*, Lecture 1 (1900).

8   Disease an never be conquered, can never be quelled by emotion's wailful screaming or faith's cymballic prayer. It can only be conquered by the energy of humanity and the cunning in the mind of man. In the patience of a Curie, in the enlightenment of a Faraday, a Rutherford, a Pasteur, a Nightingale, and all other apostles of light and cleanliness, rather than of a woebegone godliness, we shall find final deliverance from plague, pestilence, and famine.

SEAN O'CASEY (1884-1964), Irish dramatist. *Inishfallen, Fare Thee Well*, vol 1., title chapter (1949).

9   With the modern diseases (once TB, now cancer) the romantic idea that the disease expresses the character is invariably extended to assert that the character causes the disease—because it has not expressed itself. Passion moves inward, striking and blighting the deepest cellular recesses.

SUSAN SONTAG (b. 1933), U.S. essayist. *Illness As Metaphor*, ch. 6 (1978).

10   The biggest disease today is not leprosy or tuberculosis, but rather the feeling of being unwanted.

MOTHER TERESA (b. 1910), Albanian-born Roman Catholic missionary in India. Quoted in: *Observer* (London, 3 Oct. 1971).

11   Is not disease the rule of existence? There is not a lily pad floating on the river but has been riddled by insects. Almost every shrub and tree has its gall, oftentimes esteemed its chief ornament and hardly to be distinguished from the fruit. If misery loves company, misery has company enough. Now, at midsummer, find me a perfect leaf or fruit.

HENRY DAVID THOREAU (1817-62), U.S. philosopher, author, naturalist. *Journals* (1906), entry for 1 Sept. 1851.

See also ILLNESS.

DISGRACE

1   Oh! no! we never mention her,
Her name is never heard;
My lips are now forbid to speak,
That once familiar word.

THOMAS H. BAYLY (1797-1839), English writer, poet. *Oh! No! We Never Mention Her.*

2   Let us not speak of them; but look, and pass on.

DANTE ALIGHIERI (1265-1321), Italian poet. *The Divine Comedy*, "The Inferno," cto. 3 (completed 1321).

3   She is absolutely inadmissible into society. Many a woman has a past, but I am told that she has at least a dozen, and that they all fit.

OSCAR WILDE (1854-1900), Anglo-Irish playwright, author. The

Duchess of Berwick, in *Lady Windermere's Fan*, act 1, speaking of Mrs. Erlynne.

DISILLUSION

1   The wise man, knowing how to enjoy achieved results without having constantly to replace them with others, finds in them an attachment to life in the hour of difficulty. But the man who has always pinned all his hopes on the future and lived with his eyes fixed upon it, has nothing in the past as a comfort against the present's afflictions, for the past was nothing to him but a series of hastily experienced stages. What blinded him to himself was his expectation always to find further on the happiness he had so far missed. Now he is stopped in his tracks; from now on nothing remains behind or ahead of him to fix his gaze upon.

EMILE DURKHEIM (1858-1917), French sociologist. *Suicide*, bk. 2, ch. 5, sct. 3 (1897; tr. 1951).

2   We could hardly believe that after so many ordeals, after all the trials of modern skepticism, there was still so much left in our souls to destroy.

ALEXANDER HERZEN (1812-70), Russian journalist, political thinker. *From the Other Shore*, "After the Storm" (1855).

3   I saw that all beings are fated to happiness: action is not life, but a way of wasting some force, an ennervation. Morality is the weakness of the brain.

ARTHUR RIMBAUD (1854-91), French poet. *Une Saison en Enfer*, "Délires II: Alchimie du Verbe" (1874; repr. in *Collected Poems*, ed. by Oliver Bernard, 1962).

WALT DISNEY

1   I must admit that the existence of Disneyland (which I *know* is real) proves that we are not living in Judaea in 50 AD. . . . Saint Paul would never go near Disneyland. Only children, tourists, and visiting Soviet high officials ever go to Disneyland. Saints do not.

PHILIP K. DICK (1928-82), U.S. science fiction writer. Introduction, *I Hope I Shall Arrive Soon*, "How to Build a Universe That Doesn't Fall Apart Two Days Later" (1986).

2   Disney World has acquired by now something of the air of a national shrine. American parents who don't take their children there sense obscurely that they have failed in some fundamental way, like Muslims who never made it to Mecca.

SIMON HOGGART (b. 1946), British journalist. *America: A User's Guide*, ch. 9 (1990).

3   He's the master of the nightmare. He's the Gustave Doré of the world of Henry Ford and Co., Inc.

HENRY MILLER (1891-1980), U.S. author. *The Air-Conditioned Nightmare*, "Good news! God is Love!" (1945).

4   Take the serious side of Disney, the Confucian side of Disney. It's in having taken an ethos . . . where you have the values of courage and tenderness asserted in a way that everybody can understand. You have got an absolute genius there. You have got a greater correlation of nature than you have had since the time of Alexander the Great.

> EZRA POUND (1885-1972), U.S. poet, critic. Interview in *Writers at Work* (Second Series, ed. by George Plimpton, 1963).

DISSATISFACTION

1 In a land which is fully settled, most men must accept their local environment or try to change it by political means; only the exceptionally gifted or adventurous can leave to seek his fortune elsewhere. In America, on the other hand, to move on and make a fresh start somewhere else is still the normal reaction to dissatisfaction and failure.

> W. H. AUDEN (1907-73), Anglo-American poet. *Faber Book of Modern American Verse,* Introduction (1956).

2 Man is the only creature who refuses to be what he is.

> ALBERT CAMUS (1913-60), French-Algerian philosopher, author. *The Rebel,* Introduction (1951; tr. 1953).

3 No sooner is your ocean filled, than he grumbles that it might have been of better vintage. Try him with half of a Universe, of an Omnipotence, he sets to quarrelling with the proprietor of the other half, and declares himself the most maltreated of men. Always there is a black spot in our sunshine: it is even as I said, the *Shadow of Ourselves.*

> THOMAS CARLYLE (1795-1881), Scottish essayist, historian. Teufelsdröckh, in *Sartor Resartus,* bk. 2, ch. 9 (1833-34).

4 There are three wants which never can be satisfied: that of the rich, who wants something more; that of the sick, who wants something different; and that of the traveler, who says, "Anywhere but here."

> RALPH WALDO EMERSON (1803-82), U.S. essayist, poet, philosopher. *The Conduct of Life,* "Considerations by the Way" (1860).

5 The problem lay buried, unspoken for many years in the minds of American women. It was a strange stirring, a sense of dissatisfaction, a yearning that women suffered in the middle of the twentieth century in the United States. Each suburban housewife struggled with it alone. As she made the beds, shopped for groceries, matched slipcover material, ate peanut butter sandwiches with her children, chauffeured Cub Scouts and Brownies, lay beside her husband at night, she was afraid to ask even of herself the silent question: "Is this all?"

> BETTY FRIEDAN (b. 1921), U.S. feminist writer. *The Feminine Mystique,* ch. 1 (1963), opening paragraph.

6 The idiot who praises, with enthusiastic tone, All centuries but this, and every country but his own.

> W. S. GILBERT (1836-1911), English librettist. Ko Ko, in *The Mikado,* act 1.

7 The chemistry of dissatisfaction is as the chemistry of some marvelously potent tar. In it are the building stones of explosives, stimulants, poisons, opiates, perfumes and stenches.

> ERIC HOFFER (1902-83), U.S. philosopher. *The Passionate State of Mind,* aph. 14 (1955).

8 If there is dissatisfaction with the status quo, good. If there is ferment, so much the better. If there is restlessness, I am pleased. Then let there be ideas, and hard thought, and hard work. If man feels small, let man make himself bigger.

> HUBERT H. HUMPHREY (1911-78), U.S. Democratic politician, vice president. Speech, 14 Jan. 1966, University of Chicago.

9 No, no, we are not satisifed, and we will not be satisfied until justice rolls down like waters and righteousness like a mighty stream.

> MARTIN LUTHER KING, JR. (1929-68), U.S. clergyman, civil rights leader. Speech, 28 Aug. 1963, Washington, D.C.

10 A fierce unrest seethes at the core,
Of all existing things:,
It was the eager wish to soar,
That gave the gods their wings.

> DON MARQUIS (1878-1937), U.S. humorist, journalist. *Unrest.*

11 As long as I have a want, I have a reason for living. Satisfaction is death.

> GEORGE BERNARD SHAW (1856-1950), Anglo-Irish playwright, critic. Gregory Lunn, in *Overruled.*

12 If we are suffering illness, poverty, or misfortune, we think we shall be satisfied on the day it ceases. But there too, we know it is false; so soon as one has got used to not suffering one wants something else.

> SIMONE WEIL (1909-43), French philosopher, mystic. "Some Thoughts on the Love of God" (Oct. 1940 - May 1942; published in *On Science, Necessity, and the Love of God,* ed. by Richard Rees, 1968).

See also DISCONTENT.

DISSENT

1 Has there ever been a society which has died of dissent? Several have died of conformity in our lifetime.

> JACOB BRONOWSKI (1908-74), British scientist, author. Lecture, 19 March 1953, given at the Massachusetts Institute of Technology (published in *Science and Human Values,* "The Sense of Human Dignity," sct. 5, 1961).

2 I stood among them, but not of them; in a shroud
Of thoughts which were not their thoughts.

> LORD BYRON (1788-1824), English poet. *Childe Harold's Pilgrimage,* cto. 3, st. 113.

3 Assent—and you are sane—,
Demur—you're straightway dangerous—,
And handled with a Chain—.

> EMILY DICKINSON (1830-86), U.S. poet. *The Complete Poems,* no. 435 (1955).

4 Wild intelligence abhors any narrow world; and the world of women must stay narrow, or the woman is an outlaw. No woman could be Nietzsche or Rimbaud without ending up in a whorehouse or lobotomized.

> ANDREA DWORKIN (b. 1946), U.S. feminist critic. *Right-Wing Women,* ch. 2 (1978).

5 May we never confuse honest dissent with disloyal subversion.

> DWIGHT D. EISENHOWER (1890-1969), U.S. general, Republican politician, president. Speech, 31 May 1954, New York City.

6 In a democracy dissent is an act of faith. Like medicine, the test of its value is not in its taste, but its effects.

J. WILLIAM FULBRIGHT (b. 1905), U.S. Democratic politician. Speech, 21 April 1966, to the U.S. Senate.

7 I would like you to understand completely, also emotionally, that I'm a political detainee and will be a political prisoner, that I have nothing now or in the future to be ashamed of in this situation. That, at bottom, I myself have in a certain sense asked for this detention and this sentence, because I've always refused to change my opinion, for which I would be willing to give my life and not just remain in prison. That therefore I can only be tranquil and content with myself.

ANTONIO GRAMSCI (1891-1937), Italian political theorist. Letter, 10 May 1928, to his mother (published in *Gramsci: Letters from Prison*, no. 99; tr. by Raymond Rosenthal, 1993). Gramsci had been arrested in 1926, when Mussolini outlawed the Communist Party, and spent the rest of his life in prison.

8 You do not become a "dissident" just because you decide one day to take up this most unusual career. You are thown into it by your personal sense of responsibility, combined with a complex set of external circumstances. You are cast out of the existing structures and placed in a position of conflict with them. It begins as an attempt to do your work well, and ends with being branded an enemy of society.

VÁCLAV HAVEL (b. 1936), Czech playwright, president. *Living in Truth*, pt. 1, "The Power of the Powerless," sct. 14 (1986).

9 It is hard for any one to be an honest politician who is not born and bred a Dissenter.

WILLIAM HAZLITT (1778-1830), English essayist. "On Court Influence," in *Yellow Dwarf* (3 and 10 Jan. 1818; repr. in *Political Essays*, 1819).

10 The beginning of thought is in disagreement—not only with others but also with ouselves.

ERIC HOFFER (1902-83), U.S. philosopher. *The Passionate State of Mind*, aph. 266 (1955).

11 Though dissenters seem to question everything in sight, they are actually bundles of dusty answers and never conceived a new question. What offends us most in the literature of dissent is the lack of hesitation and wonder.

ERIC HOFFER (1902-83), U.S. philosopher. *Reflections on the Human Condition*, aph. 49 (1973).

12 The dissenter is every human being at those moments of his life when he resigns momentarily from the herd and thinks for himself.

ARCHIBALD MACLEISH (1892-1982), U.S. poet. "In Praise of Dissent," in *New York Times* (16 Dec. 1956).

13 If all mankind minus one, were of one opinion, and only one person were of the contrary opinion, mankind would be no more justified in silencing that one person, than he, if he had the power, would be justified in silencing mankind.

JOHN STUART MILL (1806-73), English philosopher, economist. *On Liberty*, ch. 2 (1859).

14 To shoot a man because one disagrees with his interpretation of Darwin or Hegel is a sinister tribute to the supremacy of ideas in human affairs—but a tribute nevertheless.

GEORGE STEINER (b. 1929), French-born U.S. critic, novelist. *Language and Silence*, "Marxism and the Literary Critic" (1967).

15 Discussion in America means dissent.

JAMES THURBER (1894-1961), U.S. humorist, illustrator. *Lanterns and Lances*, "The Duchess and the Bugs" (1961).

16 The rule is perfect: *in all matters of opinion our adversaries are insane.*

MARK TWAIN (1835-1910), U.S. author. *Christian Science*, bk. 1, ch. 5 (1907; repr. in *What Is Man?*, ed. by Paul Baender, 1973).

17 The original "crime" of "niggers" and lesbians is that they prefer themselves.

ALICE WALKER (b. 1944), U.S. author, critic. "Breaking Chains and Encouraging Life," in *Ms.* (New York, April 1980; repr. in *In Search of our Mothers' Gardens*, 1983).

See also Dubuffet on NONCONFORMITY; Wilde on OBEDIENCE; Buchwald, Debs, Havel, Kennedy, Pankhurst on PROTEST.

DISSIPATION

1 Voluptuaries, consumed by their senses, always begin by flinging themselves with a great display of frenzy into an abyss. But they survive, they come to the surface again. And they develop a routine of the abyss: "It's four o'clock . . . At five I have my abyss. . . ."

COLETTE (1873-1954), French author. *The Pure and the Impure* (1933; repr. in *Earthly Paradise*, pt. 2, "Freedom," ed. by Robert Phelps, 1966).

2 Dissipation is a form of self-sacrifice.

ERIC HOFFER (1902-83), U.S. philosopher. *The Passionate State of Mind*, aph. 9 (1955). Hoffer adds: "The passage from this to other forms of self-sacrifice is not uncommon. Passionate sinning has not infrequently been an apprenticeship to sainthood."

3 They had both noticed that a life of dissipation sometimes gave to a face the look of gaunt suffering spirituality that a life of asceticism was supposed to give and quite often did not.

KATHERINE ANNE PORTER (1890-1980), U.S. short-story writer and novelist. *Ship of Fools*, pt. 3 (1962), of Herr Freytag and Mrs. Treadwell.

See also DEBAUCHERY.

DIVERSITY

1 We cannot feel strongly toward the totally unlike because it is unimaginable, unrealizable; nor yet toward the wholly like because it is stale—identity must always be dull company. The power of other natures over us lies in a stimulating difference which causes excitement and opens communication, in ideas similar to our own but not identical, in states of mind attainable but not actual.

CHARLES HORTON COOLEY (1864-1929), U.S. sociologist. *Human Nature and the Social Order*, ch. 4 (1902).

2   Our flag is red, white and blue, but our nation is a rainbow—red, yellow, brown, black and white—and we're all precious in God's sight.

> JESSE JACKSON (b. 1941), U.S. clergyman, civil rights leader. Speech, 16 July 1984.

3   Ultimately, America's answer to the intolerant man is diversity, the very diversity which our heritage of religious freedom has inspired.

> ROBERT KENNEDY (1925-68), U.S. Attorney General, Democratic politician. *The Pursuit of Justice*, pt. 3 "Extremism, Left and Right" (1964).

4   The diversity in the faculties of men, from which the rights of property originate, is not less an insuperable obstacle to an uniformity of interests. The protection of these faculties is the first object of government.

> JAMES MADISON (1751-1836), U.S. president. *Federalist Papers*, no. 10 (Nov. 1787).

5   *E pluribus unum.* (Out of many, one.)

> MOTTO FOR THE SEAL OF THE UNITED STATES. Adopted 20 June 1782, recommended by John Adams, Benjamin Franklin and Thomas Jefferson, 10 Aug. 1776, and proposed by Swiss artist Pierre Eugene du Simitière. It had originally appeared on the title page of the *Gentleman's Journal* (Jan. 1692).

6   Order is Heaven's first law; and this confessed,
Some are, and must be, greater than the rest,
More rich, more wise; but who infers from hence
That such are happier, shocks all common sense.
Condition, circumstance, is not the thing;
Bliss is the same in subject or in king.

> ALEXANDER POPE (1688-1744), English satirical poet. *An Essay On Man*, Epistle 1. See Johnson on HAPPINESS.

See also MULTICULTURALISM.

DIVORCE

1   Divorce. A resumption of diplomatic relations and rectification of boundaries.

> AMBROSE BIERCE (1842-1914), U.S. author. *The Devil's Dictionary* (1881-1906).

2   I know one husband and wife who, whatever the official reasons given to the court for the break up of their marriage, were really divorced because the husband believed that nobody ought to read while he was talking and the wife that nobody ought to talk while she was reading.

> VERA BRITTAIN (1893-1970), British author. Quoted in: Jilly Cooper and Tom Hartman, *Violets and Vinegar*, "The Battle Done" (1980).

3   Two lives that once part are as ships that divide.

> EDWARD BULWER-LYTTON (1803-73), English author, politician. *A Lament*.

4   People named John and Mary never divorce. For better or for worse, in madness and in saneness, they seem bound together for eternity by their rudimentary nomenclature. They may loathe and despise one another, quarrel, weep, and commit mayhem, but they are not free to divorce. Tom, Dick, and Harry can go to Reno on a whim, but nothing short of death can separate John and Mary.

> JOHN CHEEVER (1912-82), U.S. author. *John Cheever: The Journals*, "The Sixties" (ed. by Robert Gottlieb, 1991), 1966 entry. Cheever's wife was named Mary.

5   The only solid and lasting peace between a man and his wife is, doubtless, a separation.

> LORD CHESTERFIELD (1694-1773), English statesman, man of letters. Letter, 1 Sept. 1763 (first published 1774; repr. in *The Letters of the Earl of Chesterfield to His Son*, vol. 2, no. 370, ed. by Charles Strachey, 1901).

6   The possibility of divorce renders both marriage partners stricter in their observance of the duties they owe to each other. Divorces help to improve morals and to increase the population.

> DENIS DIDEROT (1713-1784), French philosopher. *Observations on the Drawing Up of Laws* (written 1774 for Catherine the Great; first published 1921; repr. in *Selected Writings*, ed. by Lester G. Crocker, 1966).

7   Many divorces are not really the result of irreparable injury but involve, instead, a desire on the part of the man or woman to shatter the setup, start out from scratch alone, and make life work for them all over again. They want the risk of disaster, want to touch bottom, see where bottom is, and, coming up, to breathe the air with relief and relish again.

> EDWARD HOAGLAND (b. 1932), U.S. novelist, essayist. "Other Lives," in *Harper's* (New York, July 1973; repr. in *Heart's Desire*, 1988).

8   Being divorced is like being hit by a Mack truck. If you live through it, you start looking very carefully to the right and to the left.

> JEAN KERR (b. 1923), U.S. author, playwright. Mary, in *Mary, Mary*, act 1.

9   You know, that's the only good thing about divorce; you get to sleep with your mother.

> CLARE BOOTHE LUCE (1903-87), U.S. diplomat, writer. Little Mary, in *The Women*, act 3 (1936).

10   Gimme the Plaza, the jet and $150 million, too . . .

> Headline, *New York Post*, 13 Feb. 1990, reporting Ivana Trump's divorce settlement demands of husband Donald.

11   A Roman divorced from his wife, being highly blamed by his friends, who demanded, "Was she not chaste? Was she not fair? Was she not fruitful?" holding out his shoe, asked them whether it was not new and well made. "Yet," added he, "none of you can tell where it pinches me.

> PLUTARCH (c. 46-120 A.D.), Greek essayist, biographer. *Parallel Lives: Aemilius Paulus*, sct. 5.

12   A lot of people have asked me how short I am. Since my last divorce, I think I'm about $100,000 short.

> MICKEY ROONEY (b. 1920), U.S. actor, entertainer. *Chicago Sun-Times* (22 June 1978).

13   France may claim the happiest marriages in the world, but the happiest divorces in the world are "made in America."

> HELEN ROWLAND (1875-1950), U.S. journalist. *A Guide to Men*, "What Every Woman Wonders" (1922).

14 When two people decide to get a divorce, it isn't a sign that they "don't understand" one another, but a sign that they have, at last, begun to.

HELEN ROWLAND (1875-1950), U.S. journalist. *A Guide to Men*, "Divorces" (1922).

15 You can't stay married in a situation where you are afraid to go to sleep in case your wife might cut your throat.

MIKE TYSON (b. 1966), U.S. boxer. Quoted in: *Daily Telegraph* (London, 1 Feb. 1989).

16 Divorce is probably of nearly the same date as marriage. I believe, however, that marriage is some weeks the more ancient.

VOLTAIRE (1694-1778), French philosopher, author. *Philosophical Dictionary*, "Divorce" (1764).

17 A New York divorce is in itself a diploma of virtue.

EDITH WHARTON (1862-1937), U.S. author. *The Descent of Man*, ch. 1 (1904).

18 It is he who has broken the bond of marriage—not I. I only break its bondage.

OSCAR WILDE (1854-1900), Anglo-Irish playwright, author. Lady Windermere, in *Lady Windermere's Fan*, act 2.

DOCTORS

1 Honour a physician with the honour due unto him for the uses which ye may have of him: for the Lord hath created him. For of the most High cometh healing, and ye shall receive honour of the king. The skill of the physician shall lift up his head: and in the sight of great men he shall be in admiration.

APOCRYPHA. *Ecclesiasticus* 38:1-3.

2 A doctor, like anyone else who has to deal with human beings, each of them unique, cannot be a scientist; he is either, like the surgeon, a craftsman, or, like the physician and the psychologist, an artist. . . . This means that in order to be a good doctor a man must also have a good character, that is to say, whatever weaknesses and foibles he may have, he must love his fellow human beings in the concrete and desire their good before his own.

W. H. AUDEN (1907-73), Anglo-American poet. *A Certain World*, "Medicine" (1970).

3 When a man goes through six years' training to be a doctor he will never be the same. He knows too much.

ENID BAGNOLD (1889-1981), British novelist and playwright. *Autobiography*, ch. 15 (1969).

4 One of the fundamental reasons why so many doctors become cynical and disillusioned is precisely because, when the abstract idealism has worn thin, they are uncertain about the value of the actual lives of the patients they are treating. This is not because they are callous or personally inhuman: it is because they live in and accept a society which is incapable of knowing what a human life is worth.

JOHN BERGER (b. 1926), British author, critic. *A Fortunate Man* (1967; repr. 1976, pp. 165-66).

5 A skilful leech is better far,
Than half a hundred men of war.

SAMUEL BUTLER (1612-80), English poet. *Hudibras*, pt. 1, cto. 2.

6 Surgeons must be very careful,
When they take the knife!,
Underneath their fine incisions,
Stirs the Culprit—*Life!*

EMILY DICKINSON (1830-86), U.S. poet. *The Complete Poems*, no. 108 (1955).

7 When a doctor does go wrong he is the first of criminals. He has nerve and he has knowledge.

SIR ARTHUR CONAN DOYLE (1859-1930), English author. Sherlock Holmes, in *The Adventures of Sherlock Holmes*, "The Speckled Band" (1892), of Dr. Grimesby Roylott.

8 The more ignorant, reckless and thoughtless a doctor is, the higher his reputation soars even amongst powerful princes.

DESIDERIUS ERASMUS (c. 1466-1536), Dutch humanist. *Praise of Folly*, ch. 33 (1509).

9 The doctor should be opaque to his patients and, like a mirror, should show them nothing but what is shown to him.

SIGMUND FREUD (1856-1939), Austrian psychiatrist. *Recommendations to Physicians Practising Psycho-Analysis*, sct. G (1912; repr. in *Complete Works*, vol. 12, ed. by James Strachey and Anna Freud, 1958), on the ideal practice of psychoanalysis.

10 The doctor found, when she was dead,
Her last disorder mortal.

OLIVER GOLDSMITH (1728-74), Anglo-Irish author, poet, playwright. *Elegy on Mrs. Mary Blaize*.

11 The physician's highest calling, his *only* calling, is to make sick people healthy—to heal, as it is termed.

SAMUEL HAHNEMANN (1755-1843), German physician, founder of homeopathy. *Organon of Medicine* (6th ed., 1842; tr. 1983), opening paragraph.

12 I have noticed that doctors who fail in the practice of medicine have a tendency to seek one another's company and aid in consultation. A doctor who cannot take out your appendix properly will recommend you to a doctor who will be unable to remove your tonsils with success.

ERNEST HEMINGWAY (1899-1961), U.S. author. *A Farewell to Arms*, ch. 15 (1929).

13 Life is short, the art long, opportunity fleeting, experiment treacherous, judgment difficult.

HIPPOCRATES (c. 460-c. 370 B.C.), Greek physician. The first of his *Aphorisms*, sometimes translated into Latin as *Ars longa, vita brevis*, of the art of healing.

14 What I call a good patient is one who, having found a good physician, sticks to him till he dies.

OLIVER WENDELL HOLMES, SR. (1809-94), U.S. writer, physician. Lecture, 2 March 1871, New York.

15 I suppose one has a greater sense of intellectual degradation after an interview with a doctor than from any human experience.

ALICE JAMES (1848-92), U.S. diarist, sister of Henry and William James. Letter, 27 Sept. 1890, to her brother, psychologist William

James (published in *The Diary of Alice James*, ed. by Leon Edel, 1964).

16   My doctor gave me six months to live but when I couldn't pay the bill, he gave me six months more.

WALTER MATTHAU (b. 1920), U.S. screen actor. Quoted in: David Brown, *Star Billing* (1985), said following a heart attack.

17   I wasn't driven into medicine by a social conscience but by rampant curiosity.

JONATHAN MILLER (b. 1936), British doctor, humorist, director. Quoted in: *Observer* (London, 5 Feb. 1983).

18   Instead of wishing to see more doctors made by women joining what there are, I wish to see as few doctors, either male or female, as possible. For, mark you, the women have made no improvement—they have only tried to be "men" and they have only succeeded in being third-rate men.

FLORENCE NIGHTINGALE (1820-1910), English nurse. Letter, 12 Sept. 1860, to the philosopher John Stuart Mill (published in *Forever Yours, Florence Nightingale: Selected Letters*, ch. 3, 1989).

19   Is it not also true that no physician, in so far as he is a physician, considers or enjoins what is for the physician's interest, but that all seek the good of their patients? For we have agreed that a physician strictly so called, is a ruler of bodies, and not a maker of money, have we not?

PLATO (c. 427-347 B.C.), Greek philosopher. Socrates, in *The Republic*, bk. 1, sct. 342.

20   Cured yesterday of my disease,
I died last night of my physician.

MATTHEW PRIOR (1664-1721), English poet, diplomat. *The Remedy Worse than the Disease*.

21   For each illness that doctors cure with medicine, they provoke ten in healthy people by inoculating them with the virus that is a thousand times more powerful than any microbe: the idea that one is ill.

MARCEL PROUST (1871-1922), French novelist. Dr. du Boulbon, in *Remembrance of Things Past*, vol. 5, "The Guermantes Way," pt. 1, ch. 2 (1921; tr. by Ronald and Colette Cortie, 1988).

22   Every doctor will allow a colleague to decimate a whole countryside sooner than violate the bond of professional etiquet by giving him away.

GEORGE BERNARD SHAW (1856-1950), Anglo-Irish playwright, critic. *The Doctor's Dilemma*, Preface, "Recoil of the Dogma of Medical Infallibility on the Doctor" (1911).

23   The doctor learns that if he gets ahead of the superstitions of his patients he is a ruined man; and the result is that he instinctively takes care not to get ahead of them.

GEORGE BERNARD SHAW (1856-1950), Anglo-Irish playwright, critic. *The Doctor's Dilemma*, Preface, "The Reforms Also Come from the Laity" (1911).

24   There are worse occupations in this world than feeling a woman's pulse.

LAURENCE STERNE (1713-1768), English author. *A Sentimental Journey*, "The Pulse, Paris" (1768).

25   The best doctors in the world are Doctor Diet, Doctor Quiet, and Doctor Merryman.

JONATHAN SWIFT (1667-1745), Anglo-Irish satirist. Lord Smart, in *Polite Conversation*, dialogue 2 (1738). Swift was repeating an

adage first recorded by the physician William Bullein in his *Government of Health*, folio 50 (1558).

26   Men who are occupied in the restoration of health to other men, by the joint exertion of skill and humanity, are above all the great of the earth. They even partake of divinity, since to preserve and renew is almost as noble as to create.

VOLTAIRE (1694-1778), French philosopher, author. *Philosophical Dictionary*, "Physicians" (1764).

27   For what Harley Street specialist has time to understand the body, let alone the mind or both in combination, when he is a slave to thirteen thousand a year?

VIRGINIA WOOLF (1882-1941), British novelist. *Three Guineas* (1938, p. 82).

See also Proverb on CONSULTANTS; Piozzi on LIFE AND DEATH; Buñuel on OLD AGE; Plath on SUNDAY.

DOCTRINE

1   A faith is something you die for, a doctrine is something you kill for. There is all the difference in the world.

TONY BENN (b. 1925), British Labour politician. Television broadcast, 11 April 1989, BBC-TV.

2   The American doctrinaire is the converse of the American demagogue, and, in this way, is scarcely less injurious to the public. The first deals in poetry, the last in cant. He is as much a visionary on one side, as the extreme theoretical democrat is a visionary on the other.

JAMES FENIMORE COOPER (1789-1851), U.S. novelist. *The American Democrat*, "On Demagogues" (1838).

3   The greatest horrors in the history of mankind are not due to the ambition of the Napoleons or the vengeance of the Agamemnons, but to the doctrinaire philosophers. The theories of the sentimentalist Rousseau inspired the integrity of the passionless Robespierre. The cold-blooded calculations of Karl Marx led to the judicial and business-like operations of the Cheka.

ALEISTER CROWLEY (1875-1947), British occultist. *The Confessions of Aleister Crowley*, ch. 61 (1929; rev. 1970).

4   It was then that I began to look into the seams of your doctrine. I wanted only to pick at a single knot; but when I had got that undone, the whole thing raveled out. And then I understood that it was all machine-sewn.

HENRIK IBSEN (1828-1906), Norwegian dramatist. Mrs. Alving, in *Ghosts*, act 2.

5   A striking feature of moral and political argument in the modern world is the extent to which it is innovators, radicals, and revolutionaries who revive old doctrines, while their conservative and reactionary opponents are the inventors of new ones.

ALASDAIR CHALMERS MACINTYRE (b. 1929), British philosopher. *A Short History of Ethics*, ch. 17 (1966).

6   A doctrinaire is a fool but an honest man.

LORD MELBOURNE (1779-1848), English statesman, prime minister. Quoted in: David Cecil, *The Young Melbourne*, ch. 9 (1939).

7   A doctrine serves no purpose in itself, but it is indispensable to have one if only to avoid being deceived by false doctrines.

> SIMONE WEIL (1909-43), French philosopher, mystic. *Ecrits de Londres*, ch. 10, "Fragments et Notes" (1957).

DOGMATISM

1   When I read of the vain discussions of the present day about the Virgin Birth and other old dogmas which belong to the past, I feel how great the need is still of a real interest in the religion which builds up character, teaches brotherly love, and opens up to the seeker such a world of usefulness and the beauty of holiness.

> OLYMPIA BROWN (1835-1900), U.S. minister (first woman ordained in U.S.). *Olympia Brown, An Autobiography*, ch. 5 (ed. by Gwendolen B. Willis, 1960; published in *Annual Journal of the Universalist Historical Society*, vol. 4, 1963).

2   Any stigma, as the old saying is, will serve to beat a dogma.

> PHILIP GUEDALLA (1889-1944), British author. *Masters and Men*, "Ministers of State" (1923).

3   We should always be prepared so as never to err to believe that what I see as white is black, if the hierarchic Church defines it thus.

> ST. IGNATIUS OF LOYOLA (1491-1556), Spanish churchman, founder of The Society of Jesus. *Spiritual Exercises*, no. 365 (1548).

4   Dogmatism is puppyism come to its full growth.

> DOUGLAS JERROLD (1803-57), English playwright, humorist. *The Wit and Opinions of Douglas Jerrold*, "Man Made of Money" (1859).

5   The greater the ignorance the greater the dogmatism.

> SIR WILLIAM OSLER (1849-1919), Canadian physician. *Montreal Medical Journal* (Sept. 1902).

See also Newman on RELIGION.

DOGS

1   If a dog doesn't put you first where are you both? In what relation? A dog needs God. It lives by your glances, your wishes. It even shares your humour. This happens about the fifth year. If it doesn't happen you are only keeping an animal.

> ENID BAGNOLD (1889-1981), British novelist, playwright. *Autobiography*, ch. 10 (1969).

2   A dog teaches a boy fidelity, perseverance, and to turn around three times before lying down.

> ROBERT BENCHLEY (1889-1945), U.S. humorous writer. Quoted in: *Artemus Ward, His Book*, Introduction (1964 ed.).

3   Dog. A kind of additional or subsidiary Deity designed to catch the overflow and surplus of the world's worship.

> AMBROSE BIERCE (1842-1914), U.S. author. *The Devil's Dictionary* (1881-1906).

4   The great pleasure of a dog is that you may make a fool of yourself with him and not only will he not scold you, but he will make a fool of himself too.

> SAMUEL BUTLER (1835-1902), English author. *Note-books*, "Higgledy-Piggledy" (1912).

5   In order to really enjoy a dog, one doesn't merely try to train him to be semihuman. The point of it is to open oneself to the possibility of becoming partly a dog.

> EDWARD HOAGLAND (b. 1932), U.S. novelist, essayist. "Dogs and the Tug of Life," in *Harper's* (New York, Feb. 1975; repr. in *Heart's Desire*, 1988).

6   Near this spot are deposited the remains of one who possessed Beauty without Vanity, Strength without Insolence, Courage without Ferocity, and all the Virtues of Man without his Vices. This praise, which would be unmeaning Flattery, if inscribed over human ashes, is but a just Tribute to the Memory of BOATSWAIN, a Dog.

> JOHN CAM HOBHOUSE (1786-1869), British statesman. Inscription on the monument raised for Lord Byron's dog, Boatswain, in the grounds of Newstead Abbey, Byron's seat in Nottinghamshire. These lines have often been attributed to Byron, but a draft of a letter written by Hobhouse in 1830, quoted in: Doris Langley Moore, *The Late Lord Byron*, ch. 10 (1961; rev. 1976), shows that Byron decided to use Hobhouse's epitaph instead of his own: "To mark a friend's remains these stones arise/I never knew but one—and here he lies."

7   You may drive a dog off the King's armchair, and it will climb into the preacher's pulpit; he views the world unmoved, unembarrassed, unabashed.

> JEAN DE LA BRUYÉRE (1645-96), French writer, moralist. *Characters*, "Of Personal Merit," aph. 38 (1688).

8   If you are a dog and your owner suggests that you wear a sweater . . . suggest that he wear a tail.

> FRAN LEBOWITZ (b. 1951), U.S. journalist. *Social Studies*, "Pointers for Pets" (1981).

9   Extraordinary creature! So close a friend, and yet so remote.

> THOMAS MANN (1875-1955), German author, critic. *Stories of Three Decades*, "A Man and his Dog" (1930; first published 1919).

10   The meeting in the open of two dogs, strangers to each other, is one of the most painful, thrilling, and pregnant of all conceivabale encounters; it is surrounded by an atmosphere of the last canniness, presided over by a constraint for which I have no preciser name; they simply cannot pass each other, their mutual embarrassment is frightful to behold.

> THOMAS MANN (1875-1955), German author, critic. *Stories of Three Decades*, "A Man and his Dog" (1930; first published 1919).

11   A door is what a dog is perpetually on the wrong side of.

> OGDEN NASH (1902-71), U.S. poet. *A Dog's Best Friend is his Illiteracy*, in *The Private Dining Room* (1953).

12   I always disliked dogs, those protectors of cowards who lack the courage to fight an assailant themselves.

> J. AUGUST STRINDBERG (1849-1912), Swedish dramatist, novelist, poet. *A Madman's Defense*, pt. 3, ch. 1 (1968).

13 If you pick up a starving dog and make him prosperous, he will not bite you. This is the principal difference between a dog and a man.

MARK TWAIN (1835-1910), U.S. author. *Pudd'nhead Wilson,* ch. 16, "Pudd'nhead Wilson's Calendar" (1894).

14 His friends he loved. His direst earthly foes —
Cats—I believe he did but feign to hate.
My hand will miss the insinuated nose,
Mine eyes the tail that wagg'd contempt at Fate.

SIR WILLIAM WATSON (1858-1935), British poet. *An Epitaph.*

See also Pope on CLASS; Pope on LOYALTY; Auden on THEOLOGY.

DOUBT

1 It is the human condition to question one god after another, one appearance after another, or better, one apparition after another, always pursuing the truth of the imagination, which is not the same as the truth of appearance.

ALAIN [ÉMILE-AUGUSTE CHARTIER] (1868-1951), French philosopher. *The Gods,* Introduction (1934; tr. 1988).

2 The real questions are the ones that obtrude upon your consciousness whether you like it or not, the ones that make your mind start vibrating like a jackhammer, the ones that you "come to terms with" only to discover that they are still there. The real questions refuse to be placated. They barge into your life at the times when it seems most important for them to stay away. They are the questions asked most frequently and answered most inadequately, the ones that reveal their true natures slowly, reluctantly, most often against your will.

INGRID BENGIS (b. 1944), U.S. author. *Combat in the Erogenous Zone,* "Man-Hating" (1973).

3 No, when the fight begins within himself,
A man's worth something.

ROBERT BROWNING (1812-89), English poet. *Bishop Blougram's Apology.*

4 Between the conception,
And the creation,
Between the emotion,
And the response,
Falls the Shadow.

T. S. ELIOT (1888-1965), Anglo-American poet, critic. *The Hollow Men,* sct. 5.

5 Half the failures of this world arise from pulling in one's horse as he is leaping.

JULIUS HARE (1795-1855) AND AUGUSTUS HARE (1792-1834), English clerics, writers. *Guesses at Truth,* Series #1 (1827).

6 Doubt is thought's despair; despair is personality's doubt. . . . Doubt and despair . . . belong to completely different spheres; different sides of the soul are set in motion. . . . Despair is an expression of the total personality, doubt only of thought.

SØREN KIERKEGAARD (1813-55), Danish philosopher. *Either/Or,* vol. 2, "Balance between Esthetic and Ethical" (1843; tr. 1987).

7 Doubt must be no more than vigilance, otherwise it can become dangerous.

G. C. LICHTENBERG (1742-99), German physicist, philosopher. *Aphorisms,* "Notebook F," aph. 53 (written 1765-99; tr. by R. J. Hollingdale, 1990).

8 Doubt, it seems to me, is the central condition of a human being in the twentieth century.

SALMAN RUSHDIE (b. 1947), Indian-born British author. Quoted in: *Observer* (London, 19 Feb. 1989).

9 There is a vulgar incredulity, which in historical matters, as well as in those of religion, finds it easier to doubt than to examine.

SIR WALTER SCOTT (1771-1832), Scottish novelist, poet. *The Fair Maid of Perth,* Introduction (1828).

See also Hebrew Bible on INDECISION; UNCERTAINTY.

DRAWING

See CARTOONS AND DRAWING.

DREAMS

1 Whoso regardeth dreams is like him that catcheth at a shadow, and followeth after the wind.

APOCRYPHA. *Ecclesiasticus* 34:2.

2 A daydream is a meal at which images are eaten. Some of us are gourmets, some gourmands, and a good many take their images precooked out of a can and swallow them down whole, absent-mindedly and with little relish.

W. H. AUDEN (1907-73), Anglo-American poet. *The Dyer's Hand,* pt. 3, "Hic et Ille," sct. C (1962).

3 Reverie is not a mind vacuum. It is rather the gift of an hour which knows the plenitude of the soul.

GASTON BACHELARD (1884-1962), French scientist, philosopher, literary theorist. *The Poetics of Reverie,* ch. 2, sct. 3 (1960; tr. 1969).

4 Dreams have only the pigmentation of fact.

DJUNA BARNES (1892-1982), U.S. author, poet, columnist. Doctor, in *Nightwood,* ch. 5 (1936).

5 America has been a land of dreams. A land where the aspirations of people from countries cluttered with rich, cumbersome, aristocratic, ideological pasts can reach for what once seemed unattainable. Here they have tried to make dreams come true. . . . Yet now . . . we are threatened by a new and particularly American menace. It is not the menace of class war, of ideology, of poverty, of disease, of illiteracy, or demagoguery, or of tyranny, though these now plague most of the world. It is the menace of unreality.

DANIEL J. BOORSTIN (b. 1914), U.S. historian. *The Image,* ch. 6 (1961).

6 There couldn't be a society of people who didn't dream. They'd be dead in two weeks.

WILLIAM BURROUGHS (b. 1914), U.S. author. Taped conversation, 1974, New York City. Quoted in: Victor Bockris, *With*

William Burroughs: A Report from the Bunker, "On Dreams" (1981).

7 I do not understand the capricious lewdness of the sleeping mind.

JOHN CHEEVER (1912-82), U.S. author. *John Cheever: The Journals*, "The Late Forties and the Fifties" (ed. by Robert Gottlieb, 1991), 1955 entry.

8 One of the characteristics of the dream is that nothing surprises us in it. With no regret, we agree to live in it with strangers, completely cut off from our habits and friends.

JEAN COCTEAU (1889-1963), French author, filmmaker. *La Difficulté d'Etre*, "Du Rêve" (1947).

9 A man that is born falls into a dream like a man who falls into the sea. If he tries to climb out into the air as inexperienced people endeavour to do, he drowns.

JOSEPH CONRAD (1857-1924), Polish-born English novelist. Marlow, in *Lord Jim*, ch. 20 (1900).

10 A dream is a scripture, and many scriptures are nothing but dreams.

UMBERTO ECO (b. 1932), Italian semiologist, novelist. Brother William, in *The Name of the Rose*, "Sixth Day: After Terce" (1980; tr. 1983).

11 His life was a sort of dream, as are most lives with the mainspring left out.

F. SCOTT FITZGERALD (1896-1940), U.S. author. *The Crack-Up*, "Notebook C" (ed. by Edmund Wilson, 1945).

12 We do not really feel grateful toward those who make our dreams come true; they ruin our dreams.

ERIC HOFFER (1902-83), U.S. philosopher. *The Passionate State of Mind*, aph. 232 (1955).

13 We've removed the ceiling above our dreams. There are no more impossible dreams.

JESSE JACKSON (b. 1941), U.S. clergyman, civil rights leader. *Independent* (London, 9 June 1988).

14 Dream is not a revelation. If a dream affords the dreamer some light on himself, it is not the person with closed eyes who makes the discovery but the person with open eyes lucid enough to fit thoughts together. Dream— a scintillating mirage surrounded by shadows—is essentially *poetry*.

MICHEL LEIRIS (1901-90), French anthropologist, author. Quoted in: Roger Shattuck, *Nights as Day, Days as Nights* Introduction (1961).

15 But sure there is need of other remedies than dreaming, a weak contention of art against nature.

MICHEL DE MONTAIGNE (1533-92), French essayist. *Essays*, bk. 3, ch. 5, "Upon some Verses of Virgil" (tr. by John Florio, 1588).

16 Our dreams are a second life. I have never been able to penetrate without a shudder those ivory or horned gates which seperate us from the invisible world.

GÉRARD DE NERVAL (1808-55), French novelist, poet. *Aurélia*, pt. 1, ch. 1 (1855).

17 In bed my real love has always been the sleep that rescued me by allowing me to dream.

LUIGI PIRANDELLO (1867-1936), Italian author, playwright. Silia, in *The Rules of the Game*, act 2.

18 If a little dreaming is dangerous, the cure for it is not to dream less but to dream more, to dream all the time.

MARCEL PROUST (1871-1922), French novelist. *Remembrance of Things Past*, vol. 4, "Within a Budding Grove," pt. 2, "Seascape, with Frieze of Girls" (1918; tr. by Scott Monkrieff, 1924).

19 It has never been my object to record my dreams, just the determination to realize them.

MAN RAY (1890-1976), U.S. photographer. Julien Levy exhibition catalogue, April 1945. Quoted in: Neil Baldwin, *Man Ray* Introduction (1988).

20 I have had a most rare vision. I have had a dream past the wit of man to say what dream it was. Man is but an ass if he go about t'expound this dream.

WILLIAM SHAKESPEARE (1564-1616), English dramatist, poet. Bottom, in *A Midsummer Night's Dream*, act 4, sc. 1.

23 How many of our daydreams would darken into nightmares, were there a danger of their coming true!

LOGAN PEARSALL SMITH (1865-1946), U.S. essayist, aphorist. *Afterthoughts*, "Life and Human Nature" (1931).

22 I dream, therefore I exist.

J. AUGUST STRINDBERG (1849-1912), Swedish dramatist, novelist, poet. *A Madman's Defense*, pt. 1, ch. 7 (1968).

23 Dreams come true; without that possibility, nature would not incite us to have them.

JOHN UPDIKE (b. 1932), U.S. author, critic. *Self-Consciousness: Memoirs*, ch. 3 (1989).

24 Unfortunately, the balance of nature decrees that a super-abundance of dreams is paid for by a growing potential for nightmares.

PETER USTINOV (b. 1921), British actor, writer, director. *Independent* (London, 25 Feb. 1989), speaking of the U.S.A.

25 Society often forgives the criminal; it never forgives the dreamer.

OSCAR WILDE (1854-1900), Anglo-Irish playwright, author. Gilbert, in *The Critic as Artist*, pt. 2 (published in *Intentions*, (1891).

26 But I, being poor, have only my dreams;
I have spread my dreams under your feet;
Tread softly because you tread on my dreams.

W. B. YEATS (1865-1939), Irish poet, playwright. *He Wishes for the Cloths of Heaven*.

See also Lawrence on HUMANKIND; Houston on IDEALISM; Dylan on NATURE; Shaw on VISIONARIES.

DRESS

1 There is not so variable a thing in nature as a lady's head-dress.

JOSEPH ADDISON (1672-1719), English essayist. *Spectator* (London, July 1711).

2 The best-dressed woman is one whose clothes wouldn't look too strange in the country.

SIR HARDY AMIES (b. 1909), British tailor, dressmaker to Queen Elizabeth II. *International Herald Tribune* (Paris, 20 June 1989).

3 You look rather rash my dear your colors don't quite match your face.

> DAISY ASHFORD (1881-1972), British writer. Mr. Salteena, in *The Young Visiters*, "Starting Gaily" (written when the author was aged nine; published 1919).

4 Women's sexy underwear is a minor but significant growth industry of late-twentieth-century Britain in the twilight of capitalism.

> ANGELA CARTER (1940-92), British author. *Nothing Sacred*, "The Bridled Sweeties" (1977; repr. 1982).

5 Nothing goes out of fashion sooner than a long dress with a very low neck.

> COCO CHANEL (1883-1971), French couturière. Quoted in: Marcel Haedrich, *Coco Chanel: Her Life, Her Secrets*, ch. 21 (1971).

6 Any affectation whatsoever in dress implies, in my mind, a flaw in the understanding.

> LORD CHESTERFIELD (1694-1773), English statesman, man of letters. Letter, 30 Dec. 1748 (first published 1774; repr. in *The Letters of the Earl of Chesterfield to His Son*, vol. 2, no. 225, ed. by Charles Strachey, 1901).

7 There is no such thing as a moral dress. . . . It's people who are moral or immoral.

> JENNIE JEROME CHURCHILL (1854-1921), Anglo-American mother of Winston Churchill. Quoted in: *Daily Chronicle* (London, 16 Feb. 1921).

8 Great men are seldom over-scrupulous in the arrangement of their attire.

> CHARLES DICKENS (1812-70), English novelist. *The Pickwick Papers*, ch. 2 (1836-37).

9 I have heard with admiring submission the experience of the lady who declared that the sense of being perfectly well dressed gives a feeling of inward tranquility which religion is powerless to bestow.

> RALPH WALDO EMERSON (1803-82), U.S. essayist, poet, philosopher. *Letters and Social Aims*, "Social Aims" (1876).

10 A fine woman shews her charms to most advantage when she seems most to conceal them. The finest bosom in nature is not so fine as what imagination forms.

> DR. GREGORY (18th century), English physician. *A Father's Legacy to his Daughters* (1809, p. 64).

11 They look quite promising in the shop; and not entirely without hope when I get them back into my wardrobe. But then, when I put them on they tend to deteriorate with a very strange rapidity and one feels so sorry for them.

> JOYCE GRENFELL (1910-79), British actor, writer. "Stately as a Galleon," in *English Lit.* (1978), referring to clothes.

12 The origins of clothing are not practical. They are mystical and erotic. The primitive man in the wolf-pelt was not keeping dry; he was saying: "Look what I killed. Aren't I the best?"

> KATHARINE HAMNETT (b. 1948), British fashion designer. *Independent on Sunday* (London, 10 March 1991).

13 Clothes make the poor invisible. . . . America has the best-dressed poverty the world has ever known.

> MICHAEL HARRINGTON (1928-89), U.S. social scientist, author. *The Other America*, ch. 1, sct. 1 (1962).

14 Sir, a man who cannot get to heaven in a green coat, will not find his way thither the sooner in a grey one.

> SAMUEL JOHNSON (1709-84), English author, lexicographer. Quoted in: Hester Piozzi, *Anecdotes of the Late Samuel Johnson* (1786; repr. in *Johnsonian Miscellanies*, vol. 1, ed. by George Birkbeck Hill, 1891, p. 222).

15 Where women are concerned, the rule is never to go out with anyone better dressed than you.

> JOHN MALKOVICH (b. 1953), U.S. stage and screen actor. *Independent on Sunday* (London, 5 April 1992).

16 It is principally for the sake of the leg that a change in the dress of man is so much to be desired. . . . The leg is the best part of the figure . . . and the best leg is the man's. . . . Man should no longer disguise the long lines, the strong forms, in those lengths of piping or tubing that are of all garments the most stupid.

> ALICE MEYNELL (1847-1922), English poet, essayist. *Essays*, "Unstable Equilibrium" (1914).

17 Where's the man could ease a heart,
Like a satin gown?

> DOROTHY PARKER (1893-1967), U.S. humorous writer. *The Satin Dress*, st. 1, in *Enough Rope* (1927).

18 Brevity is the soul of lingerie.

> DOROTHY PARKER (1893-1967), U.S. humorous writer. *Vogue*, caption. Quoted in: Alexander Woollcott, *While Rome Burns*, "Our Mrs. Parker" (1934).

19 An accent mark, perhaps, instead of a whole western accent—a point of punctuation rather than a uniform twang. That is how it should be worn: as a quiet point of character reference, an apt phrase of sartorial allusion—macho, sotto voce.

> PHIL PATTON (b. 1953), U.S. author and journalist. *Esquire* (New York, Feb. 1990), referring to bolo ties.

20 I have often said that I wish I had invented blue jeans: the most spectacular, the most practical, the most relaxed and nonchalant. They have expression, modesty, sex appeal, simplicity—all I hope for in my clothes.

> YVES SAINT LAURENT (b. 1936), French couturier. *Ritz*, no. 85 (London, 1984).

21 Costly thy habit as thy purse can buy,
But not expressed in fancy; rich not gaudy;
For the apparel oft proclaims the man.

> WILLIAM SHAKESPEARE (1564-1616), English dramatist, poet. Polonius, in *Hamlet*, act 1, sc. 3, giving advice to his son Laertes, departing for France.

22 The beauty of the internal nature cannot be so far concealed by its accidental vesture, but that the spirit of its form shall communicate itself to the very disguise and indicate the shape it hides from the manner in which it is worn. A majestic form and graceful motions will express themselves through the most barbarous and tasteless costume.

> PERCY BYSSHE SHELLEY (1792-1822), English poet. *A Defence of Poetry* (written 1821, published 1840).

23 For women . . . bras, panties, bathing suits, and other stereotypical gear are visual reminders of a commercial, idealized feminine image that our real and diverse female bodies can't possibly fit. Without these visual references, each individual woman's body demands to be accepted on its own terms. We stop being comparatives. We begin to be unique.

GLORIA STEINEM (b. 1934), U.S. feminist writer, editor. "In Praise of Women's Bodies," in *Ms.* (New York, April 1981; repr. in *Outrageous Acts and Everyday Rebellions,* 1983).

24   It is an interesting question how far men would retain their relative rank if they were divested of their clothes.

HENRY DAVID THOREAU (1817-62), U.S. philosopher, author, naturalist. *Walden,* "Economy" (1854).

25   I hold that gentleman to be the best-dressed whose dress no one observes.

ANTHONY TROLLOPE (1815-1882), English novelist. *Thackeray,* ch. 9 (1879).

26   One should either be a work of art, or wear a work of art.

OSCAR WILDE (1854-1900), Anglo-Irish playwright, author. "Phrases and Philosophies for the Use of the Young," in *Chameleon* (London, Dec. 1894).

27   [He] was a tubby little chap who looked as if he had been poured into his clothes and had forgotten to say "when!"

P. G. WODEHOUSE (1881-1975), British novelist. *Very Good, Jeeves!,* "Jeeves and the Impending Doom" (1930).

28   There is much to support the view that it is clothes that wear us, and not we, them; we may make them take the mould of arm or breast, but they mould our hearts, our brains, our tongues to their liking.

VIRGINIA WOOLF (1882-1941), British novelist. *Orlando,* ch. 4 (1928).

See also Thoreau on ENTERPRISE; Berger on NUDITY; Eliot on SHOES; UNIFORMS.

DRUGS

1   I don't respond well to mellow, you know what I mean, I-I have a tendency to . . . if I get too mellow, I-I ripen and then rot.

WOODY ALLEN (b. 1935), U.S. filmmaker. Alvy Singer (Allen), in *Annie Hall* (directed by Woody Allen; scripted by Allen with Marshall Brickman, 1977; repr. in *Four Films of Woody Allen,* 1982), explaining to Annie Hall (Diane Keaton) why he is passing on a marijuana party.

2   It is not opium which makes me work but its absence, and in order for me to feel its absence it must from time to time be present.

ANTONIN ARTAUD (1896-1948), French theater producer, actor, theorist. *Appeal to Youth: Intoxication-Disintoxication* (1934; repr. in *Selected Writings,* pt. 24, ed. by Susan Sontag, 1976).

3   Opiate. An unlocked door in the prison of Identity. It leads into the jail yard.

AMBROSE BIERCE (1842-1914), U.S. author. *The Devil's Dictionary* (1881-1906).

4   The whole LSD, STP, marijuana, heroin, hashish, prescription cough medicine crowd suffers from the "Watchtower" itch: you gotta be with us, man, or you're out, you're dead. This pitch is a continual and seeming

MUST with those who use the stuff. It's no wonder they keep getting busted.

CHARLES BUKOWSKI (b. 1920), U.S. author, poet. *Tales of Ordinary Madness,* "The Big Pot Game" (1967).

5   Under the pressure of the cares and sorrows of our mortal condition, men have at all times, and in all countries, called in some physical aid to their moral consolations—wine, beer, opium, brandy, or tobacco.

EDMUND BURKE (1729-97), Irish philosopher, statesman. *Thoughts and Details on Scarcity,* (Nov. 1795; published in *Works,* vol. 5).

6   Junk is the ideal product . . . the ultimate merchandise. No sales talk necessary. The client will crawl through a sewer and beg to buy.

WILLIAM BURROUGHS (b. 1914), U.S. author. *The Naked Lunch,* Introduction (1959).

7   Everything one does in life, even love, occurs in an express train racing toward death. To smoke opium is to get out of the train while it is still moving. It is to concern oneself with something other than life or death.

JEAN COCTEAU (1889-1963), French author, filmmaker. *Opium* (1929; tr. 1932; repr. 1957, p. 25).

8   Take me, I am the drug; take me, I am hallucinogenic.

SALVADOR DALI (1904-89), Spanish painter. *Dali by Dali,* "The Hallucinogenic Dali" (1970).

9   Thou hast the keys of Paradise, oh just, subtle, and mighty opium!

THOMAS DE QUINCEY (1785-1859), English author. *Confessions of an English Opium-Eater,* pt. 2, "The Pleasures of Opium" (1822).

10   Drug misuse is not a disease, it is a decision, like the decision to step out in front of a moving car. You would call that not a disease but an error of judgment.

PHILIP K. DICK (1928-82), U.S. science fiction writer. *A Scanner Darkly,* "Author's Note" (1977).

11   There seems to be no stopping drug frenzy once it takes hold of a nation. What starts with an innocuous HUGS, NOT DRUGS bumper sticker soon leads to wild talk of shooting dealers and making urine tests a condition for employment—anywhere.

BARBARA EHRENREICH (b. 1941), U.S. author, columnist. *The Worst Years of Our Lives,* "Drug Frenzy" (1991; first published 1988).

12   There is held to be no surer test of civilisation than the increase per head of the consumption of alcohol and tobacco. Yet alcohol and tobacco are recognisable poisons, so that their consumption has only to be carried far enough to destroy civilisation altogether.

HAVELOCK ELLIS (1859-1939), British psychologist. *The Dance Of Life,* ch. 7 (1923).

13   Tobacco and opium have broad backs, and will cheerfully carry the load of armies, if you choose to make them pay high for such joy as they give and such harm as they do.

RALPH WALDO EMERSON (1803-82), U.S. essayist, poet, philosopher. *Society and Solitude,* "Civilization" (1870).

14 Woe to you, my Princess, when I come . . . you shall see who is the stronger, a gentle little girl who doesn't eat enough or a big wild man *who has cocaine in his body*.

> SIGMUND FREUD (1856-1939), Austrian psychiatrist. Letter, 2 June 1884, to his fiancée, Martha Bernays. Quoted in: Ernest Jones, *Sigmund Freud: Life and Work,* vol. 1, ch. 6, "The Cocaine Episode" (1953). Freud added, "I am just now collecting the literature for a song of praise to this magical substance," though his interest in cocaine ended with his repudiation of it and a long-lasting sense of reproach.

15 Nobody stopped thinking about those psychedelic experiences. Once you've been to some of those places, you think, "How can I get back there again but make it a little easier on myself?"

> JERRY GARCIA (b. 1942), U.S. rock musician. *Rolling Stone* (New York, 30 Nov. 1989).

16 No monster vibration, no snake universe hallucinations. Many tiny jeweled violet flowers along the path of a living brook that looked like Blake's illustration for a canal in grassy Eden: huge Pacific watery shore, Orlovsky dancing naked like Shiva long-haired before giant green waves, titanic cliffs that Wordsworth mentioned in his own Sublime, great yellow sun veiled with mist hanging over the planet's oceanic horizon. No harm.

> ALLEN GINSBERG (b. 1926), U.S. poet. Letter, 2 June 1966 (published in *Paris Review,* Flushing, N.Y., summer 1966), describing an LSD experience in Big Sur, Calif.

17 Nobody saves America by sniffing cocaine,
Jiggling yr knees blankeyed in the rain,
When it snows in yr nose you catch cold in yr brain.

> ALLEN GINSBERG (b. 1926), U.S. poet. Quoted in: Barry Miles, *Ginsberg: A Biography,* ch. 16 (1989).

18 Thou source of all my bliss and all my woe,
That found'st me poor at first, and keep'st me so.

> OLIVER GOLDSMITH (1728-74), Anglo-Irish author, poet, playwright. *The Deserted Village,* referring specifically to Poetry.

19 Only one thing is certain: if pot is legalized, it won't be for our benefit but for the authorities'. To have it legalized will also be to lose control of it.

> GERMAINE GREER (b. 1939), Australian feminist writer. "Flip-top Legal Pot," in *Oz* (London, Oct. 1968; repr. in *The Madwoman's Underclothes,* 1986).

20 If you think dope is for kicks and for thrills, you're out of your mind. There are more kicks to be had in a good case of paralytic polio or by living in an iron lung. If you think you need stuff to play music or sing, you're crazy. It can fix you so you can't play nothing or sing nothing.

> BILLIE HOLIDAY (1915-59), U.S. blues singer. *Lady Sings the Blues,* ch. 23 (1956; written with William Dufty; rev. 1975).

21 If we could sniff or swallow something that would, for five or six hours each day, abolish our solitude as individuals, atone us with our fellows in a glowing exaltation of affection and make life in all its aspects seem not only worth living, but divinely beautiful and significant, and if this heavenly, world-transfiguring drug were of such a kind that we could wake up next morning with a clear head and an undamaged constitution—then, it seems to me, all our problems (and not merely the one small problem of discovering a novel pleasure) would be wholly solved and earth would become paradise.

> ALDOUS HUXLEY (1894-1963), British author. *Music at Night and Other Essays,* "Wanted, a New Pleasure" (1949). Huxley's earlier writings revealed a different attitude: "I prefer being sober to even the rosiest and most agreeable intoxications," he wrote in his Introduction to *Texts and Pretexts* (1932). "The peyotl-trances of Swinburne, for example, have always left me perfectly *compos mentis*; I do not catch the infection."

22 Which is better: to have Fun with Fungi or to have Idiocy with Ideology, to have Wars because of Words, to have Tomorrow's Misdeeds out of Yesterday's Miscreeds?

> ALDOUS HUXLEY (1894-1963), British author. "Culture and the Individual," in *Moksha: Writings on Psychedelics and the Visionary Experience (1931-1963)* (ed. by Horowitz and Palmer, 1977).

23 To punish drug takers is like a drunk striking the bleary face it sees in the mirror. Drugs will not be brought under control until society itself changes, enabling men to use them as primitive man did: welcoming the visions they provided not as fantasies, but as intimations of a different, and important, level of reality.

> BRIAN INGLIS (1916), British journalist, author. *The Forbidden Game: A Social History of Drugs,* "Postscript" (1975).

24 The basic thing nobody asks is why do people take drugs of any sort? . . . Why do we have these accessories to normal living to live? I mean, is there something wrong with society that's making us so pressurized, that we cannot live without guarding ourselves against it?

> JOHN LENNON (1940-80), British rock musician. "Dick Cavett Show," 24 Sept. 1971. Lennon added, "If people take any notice of what we say, we say we've been through the drug scene, man, and there's nothing like being straight."

25 The worst drugs are as bad as anybody's told you. . . . It's just a dumb trip, which I can't condemn people if they get into it, because one gets into it for one's own personal, social, emotional reasons. It's something to be avoided if one can help it.

> JOHN LENNON (1940-1980), British rock musician. *Dick Cavett Show,* 24 Sept. 1971.

26 They shoulda called me Little Cocaine, I was sniffing so much of the stuff! My nose got big enough to back a diesel truck in, unload it, and drive it right out again.

> LITTLE RICHARD (b. 1932), U.S. rock'n'roll musician. Quoted in: Charles White, *The Life and Times of Little Richard,* pt. 4 (1984).

27 One's condition on marijuana is always existential. One can feel the importance of each moment and how it is changing one. One feels one's being, one becomes aware of the enormous apparatus of nothingness—the hum of a hi-fi set, the emptiness of a pointless interruption, one becomes aware of the war between each of us, how the nothingness in each of us seeks to attack the being of others, how our being in turn is attacked by the nothingness in others.

> NORMAN MAILER (b. 1923), U.S. author. Interview in *Writers at Work* (Third Series, ed. by George Plimpton, 1967).

28 Is marijuana addictive? Yes, in the sense that most of the really pleasant things in life are worth endlessly repeating.

> RICHARD NEVILLE (b. 1941), Australian journalist. *Playpower,* "Johnny Pot Wears Gold Sandals and a Black Derby Hat" (1971).

29 Marijuana is . . . self-punishing. It makes you acutely sensitive, and in this world, what worse punishment could there be?

> P. J. O'ROURKE (b. 1947), U.S. journalist. *Rolling Stone* (New York, 30 Nov. 1989).

30 No drug, not even alcohol, causes the fundamental ills of society. If we're looking for the sources of our troubles, we shouldn't test people for drugs, we should test them for stupidity, ignorance, greed and love of power.

> P. J. O'ROURKE (b. 1947), U.S. journalist. *Give War A Chance,* "Studying For Our Drug Test" (1992).

31 We're talking scum here. Air should be illegal if they breathe it.

> POLICEMAN. Quoted by P. J. O'Rourke in: *Rolling Stone* (New York, 30 Nov. 1989), on drug abusers, Washington, D.C.

32 Let us not forget who we are. Drug abuse is a repudiation of everything America is.

> RONALD REAGAN (b. 1911), U.S. Republican politician, president. Joint television broadcast with Nancy Reagan, fall 1986, announcing a national crusade against the use of drugs. Quoted in: Lewis H. Lapham, *Money and Class in America,* ch. 5, sct. 1 (1988).

33 It's an ordinary day for Brian. Like, he died every day, you know.

> PETE TOWNSHEND (b. 1945), British rock musician. Quoted in: Philip Norman, *The Life and Good Times of the Rolling Stones* (1989), on Brian Jones's death by drowning in July 1969.

34 In my day, we didn't have the cocaine, so we went out and knocked somebody over the head and *took* the money. But today, all this cocaine and crack, it doesn't give kids a chance.

> BARRY WHITE (b. 1944), U.S. singer. *City Limits* (London, 7 April 1988).

35 Of all that Orient lands can vaunt,
Of marvels with our own competing,
The strangest is the Haschish plant,
And what will follow on its eating.

> JOHN GREENLEAF WHITTIER (1807-92), U.S. poet. *The Haschish,* st. 1.

36 The human mind is capable of excitement without the application of gross and violent stimulants; and he must have a very faint perception of its beauty and dignity who does not know this.

> WILLIAM WORDSWORTH (1770-1850), English poet. *Lyrical Ballads,* Preface (2nd ed., 1801).

37 A drug is neither moral nor immoral—it's a chemical compound. The compound itself is not a menace to society until a human being treats it as if consumption bestowed a temporary license to act like an asshole.

> FRANK ZAPPA (b. 1940), U.S. rock musician. *The Real Frank Zappa Book,* ch. 17 (1989; written with Peter Occhiogrosso).

See also ADDICTION; Nietzsche on CHRISTIANITY AND THE CHRISTIANS; Artaud on DESPAIR; Artaud on SUFFERING.

DULLNESS

1 Authors have established it as a kind of rule, that a man ought to be dull sometimes; as the most severe reader makes allowances for many rests and nodding-places in a voluminous writer.

> JOSEPH ADDISON (1672-1719), English essayist. *Spectator,* no. 124 (London, 23 July 1711).

2 There is no such thing on earth as an uninteresting subject; the only thing that can exist is an uninterested person.

> G. K. CHESTERTON (1874-1936), British author. *Heretics,* ch. 3 (1905).

3 Prudent Dulness marked him for a mayor.

> CHARLES CHURCHILL (1731-64), English clergyman, poet. *The Rosciad.*

4 What can he mean by coming among us? He is not only dull himself, but the cause of dullness in others.

> SAMUEL FOOTE (1720-77), English dramatist. Of "a law-lord, who, it seems, once took a fancy to associate with the wits of London." Quoted in: James Boswell, *Life of Samuel Johnson,* 1783 (1791).

5 What a comfort a dull but kindly person is, to be sure, at times! A ground-glass shade over a gas-lamp does not bring more solace to our dazzled eyes than such a one to our minds.

> OLIVER WENDELL HOLMES, SR. (1809-94), U.S. writer, physician. *The Autocrat of the Breakfast-Table,* ch. 1 (1858).

6 Sir, he was dull in company, dull in his closet, dull everywhere. He was dull in a new way, and that made many people think him *great.*

> SAMUEL JOHNSON (1709-84), English author, lexicographer. Quoted in: James Boswell, *Life of Samuel Johnson,* 28 March 1775 (1791), on poet Thomas Gray.

7 It is to be noted that when any part of this paper appears dull there is a design in it.

> SIR RICHARD STEELE (1672-1729), English dramatist, essayist, editor. *Tatler,* no. 38 (London).

8 Dullness is the coming of age of seriousness.

> OSCAR WILDE (1854-1900), Anglo-Irish playwright, author. "Phrases and Philosophies for the Use of the Young," in *Chameleon* (London, Dec. 1894).

See also BORES; Mencken on CERTAINTY; Addison on READING.

DUTY

1 Duty. That which sternly impels us in the direction of profit, along the line of desire.

> AMBROSE BIERCE (1842-1914), U.S. author. *The Devil's Dictionary* (1881-1906).

2 When one has come to accept a certain course as duty he has a pleasant sense of relief and of lifted responsibility, even if the course involves pain and renunciation. It is like obedience to some external authority; any clear way, though it lead to death, is mentally preferable to the tangle of uncertainty.

> CHARLES HORTON COOLEY (1864-1929), U.S. sociologist. *Human Nature and the Social Order*, ch. 10 (1902).

3   The reward of one duty is the power to fulfil another.

> GEORGE ELIOT (1819-80), English novelist. Moredecai, in *Daniel Deronda*, bk. 6, ch. 46 (1874-76), quoting a Hebrew sage.

4   Oh! Duty is an icy shadow. It will freeze you. It cannot fill the heart's sanctuary.

> AUGUSTA JANE EVANS (1835-1909), U.S. writer. *Beulah*, ch. 13 (1859).

5   Duty largely consists of pretending that the trivial is critical.

> JOHN FOWLES (b. 1926), British novelist. *The Magus*, ch. 18 (1965).

6   Pressed into service means pressed out of shape.

> ROBERT FROST (1874-1963), U.S. poet. *The Self-Seeker*.

7   I sighed as a lover, I obeyed as a son.

> EDWARD GIBBON (1737-94), English historian. *Memoirs of My Life* (1796; published by Routledge as *Autobiography*, 1971, p. 55). Gibbon is speaking of his father's refusal to accept his attachment to the pastor's daughter Mademoiselle Susan Curchod.

8   A task becomes a duty from the moment you suspect it to be an essential part of that integrity which alone entitles a man to assume responsibility.

> DAG HAMMARSKJÖLD (1905-61), Swedish statesman, Secretary-General of U.N. *Markings*, "Night is Drawing Nigh" (1963; written 1955).

9   I slept, and dreamed that life was Beauty;
I woke, and found that life was Duty.

> ELLEN STURGIS HOOPER (1816-41), U.S. poet. *Beauty and Duty*.

10   It is not enough for us to prostrate ourselves under the tree which is Creation, and to contemplate its tremendous branches filled with stars. We have a duty to perform, to work upon the human soul, to defend the mystery against the miracle, to worship the incomprehensible while rejecting the absurd; to accept, in the inexplicable, only what is necessary; to dispel the superstitions that surround religion—to rid God of His Maggots.

> VICTOR HUGO (1802-85), French poet, dramatist, novelist. *Les Misérables*, pt. 2, bk. 7, ch. 5 (1862).

11   Where there are no rights, there are no duties.

> HENRI BENJAMIN CONSTANT DE REBECQUE (1767-1830), French writer, orator, statesman. "On Political Reactions," in *France*, pt. 6, no. 1 (1797).

12   A sense of duty is useful in work but offensive in personal relations. People wish to be liked, not to be endured with patient resignation.

> BERTRAND RUSSELL (1872-1970), British philosopher, mathematician. *The Conquest of Happiness*, ch. 9 (1930).

13   When a stupid man is doing something he is ashamed of, he always declares that it is his duty.

> GEORGE BERNARD SHAW (1856-1950), Anglo-Irish playwright, critic. Apollodorus, in *Caesar and Cleopatra*, act 3.

14   There is no duty we so much underrate as the duty of being happy.

> ROBERT LOUIS STEVENSON (1850-94), Scottish novelist, essayist, poet. *Virginibus Puerisque*, "An Apology for Idlers" (1881).

15   It is easier to do one's duty to others than to one's self. If you do your duty to others, you are considered reliable. If you do your duty to yourself, you are considered selfish.

> THOMAS SZASZ (b. 1920), U.S. psychiatrist. *The Second Sin*, "Personal Conduct" (1973).

16   Duties are not performed for duty's *sake*, but because their *neglect* would make the man *uncomfortable*. A man performs but *one* duty—the duty of contenting his spirit, the duty of making himself agreeable to himself.

> MARK TWAIN (1835-1910), U.S. author. Old Man, in "What Is Man?," sct. 2 (1906; repr. in *Complete Essays*, ed. by Charles Neider, 1963).

17   Oh, duty is what one expects from others, it is not what one does oneself.

> OSCAR WILDE (1854-1900), Anglo-Irish playwright, author. Lord Illingworth, in *A Woman of No Importance*, act 2.

18   Stern Daughter of the Voice of God!
O Duty! if that name thou love,
Who art a light to guide, a rod
To check the erring, and reprove.

> WILLIAM WORDSWORTH (1770-1850), English poet. *Ode to Duty*, st. 1.

See also Shaw on ENGLAND AND THE ENGLISH.

BOB DYLAN

1   I'm glad I'm not me!

> BOB DYLAN (b. 1941), U.S. singer, songwriter. From Donn Pennebaker's film *Don't Look Back* (1967), reading newspaper report, 1965.

2   Dylan is to me the perfect symbol of the anti-artist in our society. He is against everything—the last resort of someone who doesn't really want to change the world. . . . Dylan's songs accept the world as it is.

> EWAN MACCOLL (1915-1989), British folk singer and songwriter. Interview in *Melody Maker* (London, Sept. 1965). Quoted in: Robert Shelton, *No Direction Home*, ch. 8 (1986).

3   If it is true that rock stars weather into institutions, then Dylan has started now to resemble the Church of England: the dwindling popularity of his product cannot diminish the intensity of the arguments among his congregation.

> ROBERT SANDALL, British journalist. *Sunday Times* (London, 19 May 1991).

4   Bob freed your mind the way Elvis freed your body. He showed us that just because music was innately physical did not mean that it was anti-intellectual. He had the vision and the talent to make a pop record that contained the whole world.

> BRUCE SPRINGSTEEN (b. 1949), U.S. rock musician. Speech, 20 Jan. 1988, at the Rock-and-Roll Hall of Fame induction dinner,

New York City (published in *The Dylan Companion*, pt. 8, ed. by Elizabeth Thomson and David Gutman, 1990).

5 Dylan used to sound like a lung cancer victim singing Woody Guthrie. Now he sounds like a Rolling Stone singing Immanuel Kant.

Twin City a Go-Go (Minneapolis, 1965). Quoted in: Robert Shelton, *No Direction Home*, ch. 2, "Prophet Without Honor" (1986)

THE EARTH

1 The earth is the very quintessence of the human condition.

HANNAH ARENDT (1906-75), German-born U.S. political philosopher. *The Human Condition*, Prologue (1958).

2 After one look at this planet any visitor from outer space would say "I WANT TO SEE THE MANAGER."

WILLIAM BURROUGHS (b. 1914), U.S. author. *The Adding Machine*, "Women: A Biological Mistake?" (1985).

3 We will look upon the earth and her sister planets as being *with* us, not *for* us. One does not rape a sister.

MARY DALY (b. 1928), U.S. educator, writer, theologian. *Beyond God the Father*, ch. 6 (1973).

4 Some of us still get all weepy when we think about the Gaia Hypothesis, the idea that earth is a big furry goddess-creature who resembles everybody's mom in that she knows what's best for us. But if you look at the historical record—Krakatoa, Mt. Vesuvius, Hurricane Charley, poison ivy, and so forth down the ages—you have to ask yourself: Whose side is she on, anyway?

BARBARA EHRENREICH (b. 1941), U.S. author, columnist. *The Worst Years of Our Lives*, "The Great Syringe Tide" (1991; first published in *Mother Jones*, 1988).

5 The earth only has so much bounty to offer and inventing ever larger and more notional prices for that bounty does not change its real value.

BEN ELTON (b. 1959), British author, performer. *Stark*, "Dinner in Los Angeles" (1989).

6 Let me enjoy the earth no less
Because the all-enacting Might
That fashioned forth its loveliness
Had other aims than my delight.

THOMAS HARDY (1840-1928), English novelist, poet. *Let Me Enjoy the Earth*.

7 As we begin to comprehend that the earth itself is a kind of manned spaceship hurtling through the infinity of space—it will seem increasingly absurd that we have not better organized the life of the human family.

HUBERT H. HUMPHREY (1911-78), U.S. Democratic politician, vice president. Speech, 26 Sept. 1966, San Fernando Valley State College, California.

8 Our roots are in the dark; the earth is our country. Why did we look up for blessing—instead of around, and down? What hope we have lies there. Not in the sky full of orbiting spy-eyes and weaponry, but in the earth we have looked down upon. Not from above, but from below. Not in the light that blinds, but in the dark that nourishes, where human beings grow human souls.

URSULA K. LE GUIN (b. 1929), U.S. author. "A Left-Handed Commencement Address," to Mills College Class of 1983 (published in *Dancing at the Edge of the World*, 1989).

9 To see the earth as we now see it, small and beautiful in that eternal silence where it floats, is to see ourselves as riders on the earth together, brothers on that bright loveliness in the unending night—brothers who *see* now they are truly brothers.

ARCHIBALD MACLEISH (1892-1982), U.S. poet. "Riders on Earth Together, Brothers in Eternal Cold," in *New York Times* (25 Dec. 1968; repr. in *Riders on Earth*, as "Bubble of Blue Air," 1978), commenting on the first pictures of the earth from the moon.

10 You must teach your children that the ground beneath their feet is the ashes of your grandfathers. So that they will respect the land, tell your children that the earth is rich with the lives of our kin. Teach your children what we have taught our children, that the earth is our mother. Whatever befalls the earth befalls the sons of the earth. If men spit upon the ground, they spit upon themselves.

ATTRIBUTED TO SEATTLE (c. 1784-1866), Chief of the Dwamish, Suquamish and allied Indian tribes. Letter, 1854, to President Franklin Pierce (published in *Brother Eagle, Sister Sky: A Message from Chief Seattle*, 1990). The letter, in which Seattle pleaded that his name should die with the ceding of the Washington State territories, was shown in 1992 to have been largely a forgery, devised by television scriptwriter Ted Perry for a historical epic in 1971.

11 God owns heaven
but He craves the earth.

ANNE SEXTON (1928-74), U.S. poet. *The Earth*, st. 2, in *The Awful Rowing Toward God* (1975).

12. The earth is not a mere fragment of dead history, stratum upon stratum like the leaves of a book, to be studied by geologists and antiquaries chiefly, but living poetry like the leaves of a tree, which precede flowers and fruit—not a fossil earth, but a living earth; compared with whose great central life all animal and vegetable life is merely parasitic. Its throes will heave our exuviæ from their graves.

HENRY DAVID THOREAU (1817-62), U.S. philosopher, author, naturalist. *Walden*, "Spring" (1854).

13 Next to reasoning, the greatest handicap to the optimum development of Man lies in the fact that this planet is just barely habitable. Its minimum temperatures are too low, and its maximum temperatures too high. Its day is not long enough, and its night is too long. The disposition of its water and earth is distinctly unfortunate (the existence of the Mediterranean Sea in the place where we find it is perhaps the unhappiest accident in the whole firmament). These factors encourage depression, fear, war, and lack of vitality. They describe a planet, which is by no means perfectly devised for the nurturing or for the perpetuation of a higher intelligence.

JAMES THURBER (1894-1961), U.S. humorist, illustrator. *Collecting Himself*, "Thinking Ourselves Into Trouble," pt. 2 (1989).

14 Is it possible that I am not alone in believing that in the dispute between Galileo and the Church, the Church was right and the centre of man's universe *is* the earth?

STEPHEN VIZINCZEY (b. 1933), Hungarian novelist, critic. "Rules of the Game," in *Times* (London, 12 Nov. 1970; repr. in *Truth and Lies in Literature*, 1986), in review of Northrop Frye's *The Stubborn Structure*.

15 In this broad earth of ours,
Amid the measureless grossness and the slag,
Enclosed and safe within its central heart,
Nestles the seed perfection.

WALT WHITMAN (1819-92), U.S. poet. *Song of the Universal.*

See also Adair on DISASTERS; Seattle on ECOLOGY; Vidal on POPULATION.

EASTER AND GOOD FRIDAY

1 Christmas and Easter can be subjects for poetry, but Good Friday, like Auschwitz, cannot. The reality is so horrible, it is not surprising that people should have found it a stumbling block to faith.

W. H. AUDEN (1907-73), Anglo-American poet. *A Certain World*, "Friday, Good" (1970).

2 The dripping blood our only drink,
The bloody flesh our only food:
In spite of which we like to think
That we are sound, substantial flesh and blood —
Again, in spite of that, we call this Friday good.

T. S. ELIOT (1888-1965), Anglo-American poet, critic. *East Coker*, pt.4, in *Four Quartets.*

3 Unfortunately there is nothing more inane than an Easter carol. It is a religious perversion of the activity of Spring in our blood.

WALLACE STEVENS (1879-1955), U.S. poet. Letter, 23 April 1916 (Easter Sunday), to his future wife Elsie Moll Kachel (published in *Letters of Wallace Stevens*, no. 202, ed. by Holly Stevens, 1967).

EATING

See FOOD AND EATING.

ECCENTRICITY

1 Only the other day I was inquiring of an entire bed of old-fashioned roses, forced to listen to my ramblings on the meaning of the universe as I sat cross-legged in the lotus position in front of them.

CHARLES, PRINCE OF WALES (b. 1948). *Daily Telegraph* (London, 15 Nov. 1988).

2 Thou strange piece of wild nature!

COLLEY CIBBER (1671-1757), English actor-manager, playwright. Lord Wronglove to Lord George, in *The Lady's Last Stake*, act. 1, sc. 1.

3 The English like eccentrics. They just don't like them living next door.

JULIAN CLARY (b. 1959), British comedian, entertainer. *Daily Telegraph* (London, 2 Sept. 1992).

4 The sound principle of a topsy-turvy lifestyle in the framework of an upside-down world order has stood every test.

KARL KRAUS (1874-1936), Austrian satirist. "In Praise of a Topsy-Turvy Lifestyle," in *Simplicissimus* (Munich, 1908; repr. in *In These Great Times: A Karl Kraus Reader*, ed. by Harry Zohn, 1976).

5 Cranks live by theory, not by pure desire. They want votes, peace, nuts, liberty, and spinning-looms not because they love these things, as a child loves jam, but because they think they ought to have them. That is one element which makes the crank.

ROSE MACAULAY (1881-1958), British novelist, essayist. *A Casual Commentary*, "Cranks" (1925).

6 The lunatic fringe wags the underdog.

H. L. MENCKEN (1880-1956), U.S. journalist. *A Mencken Chrestomathy*, "Sententiæ: The Citizen and the State" (1949).

7 Eccentricity has always abounded when and where strength of character has abounded; and the amount of eccentricity in a society has generally been proportional to the amount of genius, mental vigour, and moral courage which it contained.

JOHN STUART MILL (1806-73), English philosopher, economist. *On Liberty*, ch. 3 (1859).

8 Eccentricity is *not*, as dull people would have us believe, a form of madness. It is often a kind of innocent pride, and the man of genius and the aristocrat are frequently regarded as eccentrics because genius and aristocrat are entirely unafraid of and uninfluenced by the opinions and vagaries of the crowd.

EDITH SITWELL (1887-1964), British poet, critic. *Taken Care Of*, ch. 15 (1965).

9 So long as a man rides his Hobby-Horse peaceably and quietly along the King's highway, and neither compels you or me to get up behind him—pray, Sir, what have either you or I to do with it?

LAURENCE STERNE (1713-68), English author. *Tristram Shandy*, bk. 1, ch. 7 (1759-67).

10 You must not blame me if I do talk to the clouds.

HENRY DAVID THOREAU (1817-62), U.S. philosopher, author, naturalist. Letter, 2 March 1842, to Lucy Brown, sister-in-law of essayist and philospher Ralph Waldo Emerson (published in *The Correspondence of Henry David Thoreau*, 1958).

See also Mill on CONFORMITY; Twain on VIRTUE.

ECOLOGY

1 Ecology is rather like sex—every new generation likes to think they were the first to discover it.

MICHAEL ALLABY (b. 1933), British author, ecologist. *Times* (London, 6 Oct 1989).

2 Humanity has passed through a long history of one-sidedness and of a social condition that has always contained the potential of destruction, despite its creative achievements in technology. The great project of our time must be to open the other eye: to see all-sidedly and wholly, to heal and transcend the cleavage between humanity and nature that came with early wisdom.

> MURRAY BOOKCHIN (b. 1941), U.S. ecologist. *The Ecology of Freedom,* ch. 1 (1982).

3 The sun, the moon and the stars would have disappeared long ago . . . had they happened to be within the reach of predatory human hands.

> HAVELOCK ELLIS (1859-1939), British psychologist. *The Dance of Life,* ch. 7 (1923).

4 The question of whether it's God's green earth is not at center stage, except in the sense that if so, one is reminded with some regularity that He may be dying.

> EDWARD HOAGLAND (b. 1932), U.S. novelist and essayist. *Weekend Guardian* (London, 20-21 Jan. 1990).

5 O if we but knew what we do
When we delve or hew—
Hack and rack the growing green!
Since country is so tender
To touch, her being so slender,
That, like this sleek and seeing ball
But a prick will make no eye at all,
Where we, even where we mean
To mend her we end her,
When we hew or delve:
After-comers cannot guess the beauty been.

> GERARD MANLEY HOPKINS (1844-89), English poet, Jesuit priest. *Binsey Poplars,* st. 2.

6 A chain is no stronger than its weakest link, and life is after all a chain.

> WILLIAM JAMES (1842-1910), U.S. psychologist, philosopher. *The Varieties of Religious Experience,* Lectures 6-7, "The Sick Soul" (1902).

7 We, the generation that faces the next century, can add the . . . solemn injunction "If we don't do the impossible, we shall be faced with the unthinkable."

> PETRA KELLY (1947-92), German Green Party founder, spokeswoman. Quoted in: *Vanity Fair* (New York, Jan. 1993).

8 How to be green? Many people have asked us this important question. It's really very simple and requires no expert knowledge or complex skills. Here's the answer. Consume less. Share more. Enjoy life.

> PENNY KEMP (b. 1951) AND DEREK WALL (b. 1965), British ecologists. *A Green Manifesto for the 1990s,* Dedication (1990).

9 We abuse land because we regard it as a commodity belonging to us. When we see land as a community to which we belong, we may begin to use it with love and respect.

> ALDO LEOPOLD (1886-1948), U.S. forester. Quoted in: Stewart L. Udall, *The Quiet Crisis,* ch. 14 (1963).

10 The development of civilization and industry in general has always shown itself so active in the destruction of forests that everything that has been done for their conservation and production is completely insignificant in comparison.

> KARL MARX (1818-83), German political theorist, social philosopher. *Capital,* vol.2, ch. 13 (1867).

11 Green politics at its worst amounts to a sort of Zen fascism; less extreme, it denounces growth and seeks to stop the world so that we can all get off.

> CHRIS PATTEN (b. 1944), British Conservative politician. *Independent* (London, 19 April 1989). Patten was at the time secretary of state for the environment.

12 The nation that destroys its soil destroys itself.

> FRANKLIN D. ROOSEVELT (1882-1945), U.S. Democratic politician, president. Letter, 26 Feb. 1937, to state governors, urging uniform soil conservation laws.

13 This we know: the earth does not belong to man; man belongs to the earth. This we know. All things are connected like the blood which unites one family. All things are connected. Whatever befalls the earth befalls the sons of the earth. Man did not weave the web of life: he is merely a strand in it. Whatever he does to the web, he does to himself.

> Attributed to SEATTLE (c. 1784-1866), Chief of the Dwamish, Suquamish and allied Indian tribes. Letter, 1854, to President Franklin Pierce, (published in *Brother Eagle, Sister Sky: A Message from Chief Seattle,* 1990). The letter, in which Seattle pleaded that his name should die with the ceding of the Washington State territories, was shown in 1992 to have been largely a forgery, devised by television scriptwriter Ted Perry for a historical epic in 1971.

14 Guns have metamorphosed into cameras in this earnest comedy, the ecology safari, because nature has ceased to be what it always had been—what people needed protection from. Now nature tamed, endangered, mortal—needs to be protected from people.

> SUSAN SONTAG (b. 1933), U.S. essayist. *On Photography,* "In Plato's Cave" (1977).

15 And he gave it for his opinion, that whoever could make two ears of corn, or two blades of grass, to grow upon a spot of ground where only one grew before, would deserve better of mankind, and do more essential service to his country, than the whole race of politicians put together.

> JONATHAN SWIFT (1667-1745), Anglo-Irish satirist. The king of Brobdingnag to Gulliver, in *Gullivers Travels,* "A Voyage to Brobdingnag," ch.7 (1726). The physicist Henry Augustus Rowland (1848-1901) is quoted in D. S. Greenberg, *The Politics of Pure Science,* (1967) as saying, "He who makes two blades of grass grow where one grew before is the benefactor of mankind, but he who obscurely worked to find the laws of such growth is the intellectual superior as well as the greater benefactor of mankind."

16 We cannot cheat on DNA. We cannot get round photosynthesis. We cannot say I am not going to give a damn about phytoplankton. All these tiny mechanisms provide the preconditions of our planetary life. To say we do not care is to say in the most literal sense that "we choose death."

> BARBARA WARD (1914-81), British author, educator. "Only One Earth," in *Who Speaks for Earth?* (ed. by Maurice F. Strong, 1973).

See also POLLUTION.

ECONOMICS

1　Economic growth may one day turn out to be a curse rather than a good, and under no conditions can it either lead into freedom or constitute a proof for its existence.

> HANNAH ARENDT (1906-75), German-born U.S. political philosopher. *On Revolution*, ch. 6 (1963).

2　It seems to be a law in American life that whatever enriches us anywhere except in the wallet inevitably becomes uneconomic.

> RUSSELL BAKER (b. 1925), U.S. journalist. *New York Times* (24 March 1968).

3　In the usual (though certainly not in every) public decision on economic policy, the choice is between courses that are almost equally good or equally bad. It is the narrowest decisions that are most ardently debated. If the world is lucky enough to enjoy peace, it may even one day make the discovery, to the horror of doctrinaire free-enterprisers and doctrinaire planners alike, that what is called capitalism and what is called socialism are both capable of working quite well.

> JOHN KENNETH GALBRAITH (b. 1908), U.S. economist. *The American Economy: Its Substance and Myth* (1949; published in *Years of the Modern*, ed. by J. W. Chase).

4　In economics, hope and faith coexist with great scientific pretension and also a deep desire for respectability.

> JOHN KENNETH GALBRAITH (b. 1908), U.S. economist. *New York Times Magazine* (7 June 1970).

5　If economists could manage to get themselves thought of as humble, competent people on a level with dentists, that would be splendid.

> JOHN MAYNARD KEYNES (1883-1946), British economist. *Essays in Persuasion*, ch. 5, "The Future," (1931).

6　The day is not far off when the economic problem will take the back seat where it belongs, and the arena of the heart and the head will be occupied or reoccupied, by our real problems—the problems of life and of human relations, of creation and behaviour and religion.

> JOHN MAYNARD KEYNES (1883-1946), British economist. *First Annual Report of the Arts Council* (1945-46).

7　In our time, the curse is monetary illiteracy, just as inability to read plain print was the curse of earlier centuries.

> EZRA POUND (1885-1972), U.S. poet, critic. *Guide to Kulchur*, pt. 4, sct. 8, ch. 31 (1938).

8　But while they prate of economic laws, men and women are starving. We must lay hold of the fact that economic laws are not made by nature. They are made by human beings.

> FRANKLIN D. ROOSEVELT (1882-1945), U.S. Democratic politician, president. Speech, 2 July 1932, to Democratic national convention, accepting presidential nomination.

9　Call a thing immoral or ugly, soul-destroying or a degradation of man, a peril to the peace of the world or to the well-being of future generations; as long as you have not shown it to be "uneconomic" you have not really questioned its right to exist, grow, and prosper.

> E. F. SCHUMACHER (1911-77), German-born British economist. *Small is Beautiful*, pt. 1, ch. 3 (1973).

10　If all economists were laid end to end, they would not reach a conclusion.

> Attributed to GEORGE BERNARD SHAW (1856-1950), Anglo-Irish playwright, critic.

11　The animals that depend on instinct have an inherent knowledge of the laws of economics and of how to apply them; Man, with his powers of reason, has reduced economics to the level of a farce which is at once funnier and more tragic than Tobacco Road.

> JAMES THURBER (1894-1961), U.S. humorist, illustrator. *Forum and Century* (June 1939) and included in Clifton Fadiman, *I Believe: The Personal Philosophies of Certain Eminent Men and Women of Our Time* (1939).

12　The science hangs like a gathering fog in a valley, a fog which begins nowhere and goes nowhere, an incidental, unmeaning inconvenience to passers-by.

> H. G. WELLS (1866-1946), British author. *A Modern Utopia*, ch.3, sct. 3 (1905; repr. in *The Works of H. G. Wells*, vol. 9, 1925), on the science of economics.

See also Keynes on IDEOLOGY; RECESSION.

ECONOMIZING

1　Mere parsimony is not economy. . . . Expense, and great expense, may be an essential part in true economy.

> EDMUND BURKE (1729-97), Irish philosopher, statesman. *A Letter to a Noble Lord* (1796; published in *Works*, vol. 5).

2　The further through life I drift
The more obvious it becomes that I am lacking in thrift.

> OGDEN NASH (1902-371), U.S. poet. *A Penny Saved Is Impossible*, in *Good Intentions* (1942).

3　The timid man calls himself cautious, the sordid man thrifty.

> PUBLILIUS SYRUS (1st century B.C.), Roman writer of mimes. *Sententiae*, no. 689.

See also MISERLINESS; William of Occam on MOTTOS.

THE ECONOMY

1　Everyone is always in favour of general economy and particular expenditure.

> SIR ANTHONY EDEN (1897-1977), British Conservative politician, prime minister. Quoted in: *Observer* (London, 17 June 1958).

2　The first panacea for a mismanaged nation is inflation of the currency; the second is war. Both bring a temporary prosperity; both bring a permanent ruin. But both are the refuge of political and economic opportunists.

> ERNEST HEMINGWAY (1899-1961), U.S. author. "Notes on the Next War: A Serious Topical Letter," in *Esquire* (New York, Sept.

263 • Editing

1935; repr. in *By-Line Ernest Hemingway*, ed. by William White, 1967).

3   We might come closer to balancing the Budget if all of us lived closer to the Commandments and the Golden Rule.

RONALD REAGAN (b. 1911), U.S. president. Quoted in: *Observer* (London, 5 Feb. 1983).

4   The government's view of the economy could be summed up in a few short phrases: If it moves, tax it. If it keeps moving, regulate it. And if it stops moving, subsidize it.

RONALD REAGAN (b. 1911), U.S. Republican politician, president. Address, 15 Aug. 1986, to the White House Conference on Small Business.

5   Economic progress, in capitalist society, means turmoil.

JOSEPH A. SCHUMPETER (1883-1950), Austrian-American economist. *Capitalism, Socialism and Democracy*, ch. 3 (1942).

See also Weil on WAR.

ECSTASY

1   Life has always taken place in a tumult without apparent cohesion, but it only finds its grandeur and its reality in ecstasy and in ecstatic love.

GEORGES BATAILLE (1897-1962), French novelist, critic. "The Sacred Conspiracy," in *Acéphale*, no. 1 (Paris, 1 June 1936; repr. in *Visions of Excess: Selected Writings 1927-1939*, ed. by Allan Stoekl, 1985).

2   O my God, what must a soul be like when it is in this state! It longs to be all one tongue with which to praise the Lord. It utters a thousand pious follies, in a continuous endeavor to please Him who thus possesses it.

SAINT TERESA OF AVILA (1515-82), Spanish nun, mystic. *Life*, ch. 16 (tr. by Cohen, 1957).

3   Ecstasy is not really part of the scene we can do on celluloid.

ORSON WELLES (1915-84), U.S. filmmaker, actor, producer. Interview in David Frost, *The Americans*, "Can a Martian Survive by Pretending to be a Leading American Actor?" (1970).

EDEN

1   And out of the ground made the Lord God to grow every tree that is pleasant to the sight, and good for food: the tree of life also in the midst of the garden, and the tree of knowledge of good and evil. And a river went out of Eden to water the garden.

BIBLE, HEBREW. *Genesis* 2:9-10.

2   The Expulsion from Eden is an act of vindictive womanish spite; the Fall of Man, as recounted in the Bible, comes nearer to the Fall of God.

CYRIL CONNOLLY (1903-74), British critic. *The Unquiet Grave*, pt. 1 (1944; rev. 1951).

3   Happy a while in Paradise they lay;
But quickly woman longed to go astray:
Some foolish new adventure needs must prove,
And the first devil she saw, she chang'd her love:
To his temptations, lewdly she inclined
Her soul, and, for an apple, damn'd mankind.

THOMAS OTWAY (1652-85), English dramatist. Castalio, in *The Orphan*, act 3, sc. 1.

4   One classic American landscape haunts all of American literature. It is a picture of Eden, perceived at the instant of history when corruption has just begun to set it. The serpent has shown his scaly head in the undergrowth. The apple gleams on the tree. The old drama of the Fall is ready to start all over again.

JONATHAN RABAN (b. 1942), British author, critic. *For Love and Money*, pt. 5 (1987).

EDITING

1   The work was like peeling an onion. The outer skin came off with difficulty . . . but in no time you'd be down to its innards, tears streaming from your eyes as more and more beautiful reductions became possible.

EDWARD BLISHEN (b. 1920), British author. *Donkey Work*, pt. 1, ch. 2 (1983), on his work adapting books for serial reading.

2   Art, it seems to me, should simplify . . . finding what conventions of form and what detail one can do without and yet preserve the spirit of the whole—so that all that one has suppressed and cut away is there to the reader's consciousness as much as if it were in type on the page.

WILLA CATHER (1876-1947), U.S. author. *On Writing*, "On the Art of Fiction" (1949).

3   Would you convey my compliments to the purist who reads your proofs and tell him or her that I write in a sort of broken-down patois which is something like the way a Swiss waiter talks, and that when I split an infinitive, God damn it, I split it so it will stay split, and when I interrupt the velvety smoothness of my more or less literate syntax with a few sudden words of bar-room vernacular, that is done with the eyes wide open and the mind relaxed but attentive.

RAYMOND CHANDLER (1888-1959), U.S. author. Letter, 18 Jan. 1948, to *Atlantic Monthly* editor Edward Weeks (published in *Raymond Chandler Speaking*, 1962).

4   What I have crossed out I didn't like. What I haven't crossed out I'm dissatisfied with.

CECIL B. DE MILLE (1881-1959), U.S. film director-producer. Quoted in: Leslie Halliwell, *Halliwell's Filmgoer's Companion* (1984), in a note attached to rejected manuscript.

5   In art economy is always beauty.

HENRY JAMES (1843-1916), U.S. author. "The Altar of the Dead," Preface (1895). The Preface first appeared in the New York Edition of James's work (1907-09) and was later republished in *The Art of the Novel* (ed. by R. P. Blackmur, 1934).

6   Read your own compositions, and when you meet with a passage which you think is particularly fine, strike it out.

SAMUEL JOHNSON (1709-84), English author, lexicographer.

Quoted in: James Boswell, *Life of Samuel Johnson* (1791), taken from remarks made by a college tutor.

7 A writer is unfair to himself when he is unable to be hard on himself.

MARIANNE MOORE (1887-1972), U.S. poet. Interview in *Writers at Work* (Second Series, ed. by George Plimpton, 1963).

8 Remember the waterfront shack with the sign FRESH FISH SOLD HERE. Of course it's fresh, we're on the ocean. Of course it's for sale, we're not giving it away. Of course it's here, otherwise the sign would be someplace else. The final sign: FISH.

PEGGY NOONAN (b. 1950), U.S. author, presidential speechwriter. *What I Saw at the Revolution*, ch. 4 (1990).

9 I have only made this [letter] longer because I have not had the time to make it shorter.

BLAISE PASCAL (1623-62), French scientist, philosopher. *Lettres Provinciales*, Letter 16 (1657).

10 Editing is the same as quarreling with writers—same thing exactly.

HAROLD ROSS (1892-1951), U.S. editor. *Time* (New York, 6 March 1950).

11 Whether the flower looks better in the nosegay than in the meadow where it grew and we had to wet our feet to get it! Is the scholastic air any advantage?

HENRY DAVID THOREAU (1817-62), U.S. philosopher, author, naturalist. *Journals* (1906), entry for 27 Jan 1852, reflecting on the possible effect of editing his journals into essays.

12 Editing should be, especially in the case of old writers, a counseling rather than a collaborating task. The tendency of the writer-editor to collaborate is natural, but he should say to himself, "How can I help this writer to say it better in his own style?" and avoid "How can I show him how I would write it, if it were my piece?"

JAMES THURBER (1894-1961), U.S. humorist, illustrator. Memo, 1959, to *New Yorker*, in *New York Times Book Review* (4 Dec. 1988).

13 There is a difference between a book of two hundred pages from the very beginning, and a book of two hundred pages which is the result of an original eight hundred pages. The six hundred are there. Only you don't see them.

ELIE WIESEL (b. 1928), Rumanian-born U.S. writer. Interview in *Writers at Work* (Eighth Series, ed. by George Plimpton, 1988).

See also Smith on WRITING.

EDITORS

1 Rides in the whirlwind and directs the storm.

JOSEPH ADDISON (1672-1719), English essayist. *The Campaign*.

2 I trust it will not be giving away professional secrets to say that many readers would be surprised, perhaps shocked, at the questions which some newspaper editors will put to a defenseless woman under the guise of flattery.

KATE CHOPIN (1851-1904), U.S. author. "On Certain Brisk

Days," in *St. Louis Post-Dispatch* (26 Nov. 1899; repr. in *The Complete Works of Kate Chopin*, vol. 2, pt. 4).

3 Will you tell me my fault, frankly as to yourself, for I had rather wince, than die. Men do not call the surgeon to commend the bone, but to set it, Sir.

EMILY DICKINSON (1830-86), U.S. poet. Letter, July 1862, to clergyman and writer T. W. Higginson (published in *The Letters of Emily Dickinson*, vol. 2, 1958).

4 If they have a popular thought they have to go into a darkened room and lie down until it passes.

KELVIN MACKENZIE (b. 1946), British newspaper editor. *Independent* (London, 19 Sept. 1989), on editors of the "quality press."

5 An editor is someone who separates the wheat from the chaff and then prints the chaff.

ADLAI STEVENSON (1900-1965), U.S. Democratic politician. Quoted in: *The Stevenson Wit* (1966). The aphorism has also been attributed to Elbert Hubbard.

EDUCATION

1 What sculpture is to a block of marble, education is to an human soul.

JOSEPH ADDISON (1672-1719), English essayist. *Spectator*, no. 215 (London, 6 Nov. 1711).

2 It is very nearly impossible . . . to become an educated person in a country so distrustful of the independent mind.

JAMES BALDWIN (1924-87), U.S. author. "They Can't Turn Back," in *Mademoiselle* (New York, Aug. 1960; repr. in *The Price of the Ticket*, 1985).

3 The paradox of education is precisely this—that as one begins to become conscious one begins to examine the society in which he is being educated.

JAMES BALDWIN (1924-87), U.S. author. "The Negro Child—His Self-Image," in *Saturday Review* (New York, 21 Dec. 1963; repr. in *The Price of The Ticket* as "A Talk to Teachers," 1985).

4 Train up a child in the way he should go: and when he is old, he will not depart from it.

BIBLE, HEBREW. *Proverbs* 22:6.

5 Education. That which discloses to the wise and disguises from the foolish their lack of understanding.

AMBROSE BIERCE (1842-1914), U.S. author. *The Devil's Dictionary* (1881-1906).

6 Education [is not] a discipline at all. Half vocational, half an emptiness dressed up in garments borrowed from philosophy, psychology, literature.

EDWARD BLISHEN (b. 1920), British author. *Donkey Work*, pt. 3, ch. 6 (1983).

7 The liberally educated person is one who is able to resist the easy and preferred answers, not because he is obstinate but because he knows others worthy of consideration.

ALLAN BLOOM (1930-92), U.S. educator, author. *The Closing of the American Mind*, Preface (1987).

8 Education in our times must try to find whatever there is in students that might yearn for completion, and to reconstruct the learning that would enable them autonomously to seek that completion.

> ALLAN BLOOM (b. 1930), U.S. educator, author. *The Closing of the American Mind*, pt. 1, "Books" (1987).

9   In my early life, and probably even today, it is not sufficiently understood that a child's education should include at least a rudimentary grasp of religion, sex, and money. Without a basic knowledge of these three primary facts in a normal human being's life—subjects which stir the emotions, create events and opportunities, and if they do not wholly decide must greatly influence an individual's personality—no human being's education can have a safe foundation.

> PHYLLIS BOTTOME (1884-1963), Anglo-American novelist. *Search for a Soul*, ch. 9 (1947).

10   Education makes a people easy to lead, but difficult to drive; easy to govern but impossible to enslave.

> LORD BROUGHAM (1778-1868), Scottish Whig politician. Speech, 29 Jan. 1828, to the House of Commons.

11   There's a new tribunal now
Higher than God's—The educated man's!

> ROBERT BROWNING (1812-89), English poet. *The Ring and the Book*, bk. 10.

12   Education must have two foundations—morality as a support for virtue, prudence as a defence for self against the vices of others. By letting the balance incline to the side of morality, you only make dupes or martyrs; by letting it incline to the other, you make calculating egoists.

> SÉBASTIEN-ROCH NICOLAS DE CHAMFORT (1741-94), French writer, wit. *The Cynic's Breviary* (ed. by William G. Hutchison, 1902).

13   It's fairly obvious that American education is a cultural flop. Americans are not a well-educated people culturally, and their vocational education often has to be learned all over again after they leave school and college. On the other hand, they have open quick minds and if their education has little sharp positive value, it has not the stultifying effects of a more rigid training.

> RAYMOND CHANDLER (1888-1959), U.S. author. *The Notebooks of Raymond Chandler*, "Notes on English and American Style" (1976).

14   It is no small mischief to a boy, that many of the best years of his life should be devoted to the learning of what can never be of any real use to any human being. His mind is necessarily rendered frivolous and superficial by the long habit of attaching importance to *words* instead of *things*; to *sound* instead of sense.

> WILLIAM COBBETT (1762-1835), English journalist, reformer. "To Mr. Benbow," in *Political Register* (London, 29 Nov. 1817; repr. in *The Opinions of William Cobbett*, ch. 16, ed. by G. D. H. and Margaret Cole, 1944).

15   Better build schoolrooms for "the boy"
Than cells and gibbets for "the man."

> ELIZA COOK (1818-89), English poet. *A Song for the Ragged Schools*.

16   Philosophy, astronomy, and politics were marked at zero, I remember. Botany variable, geology profound as regards the mud stains from any region within fifty miles of town, chemistry eccentric, anatomy unsystematic, sensational literature and crime records unique, violin player, boxer, swordsman, lawyer, and self-poisoner by cocaine and tobacco.

> SIR ARTHUR CONAN DOYLE (1859-1930), English author. Dr. Watson, in *The Adventures of Sherlock Holmes*, "The Five Orange Pips" (1892), referring to the limits of Holmes's knowledge and character.

17   Respect the child. Be not too much his parent. Trespass not on his solitude.

> RALPH WALDO EMERSON (1803-82), U.S. essayist, poet, philosopher. *Lectures and Biographical Sketches*, "Education" (1883).

18   Spoon feeding in the long run teaches us nothing but the shape of the spoon.

> E. M. FORSTER (1879-1970), British novelist, essayist. Quoted in: *Observer* (London, 7 Oct. 1951).

19   Since every effort in our educational life seems to be directed toward making of the child a being foreign to itself, it must of necessity produce individuals foreign to one another, and in everlasting antagonism with each other.

> EMMA GOLDMAN (1869-1940), U.S. anarchist. "The Child and Its Enemies," in *Mother Earth* (New York, April 1906; repr. in *Red Emma Speaks*, pt. 2, ed. by Alix Kates Shulman, 1972).

20   We live less and less, and we learn more and more. Sensibility is surrendering to intelligence.

> RÉMY DE GOURMONT (1858-1915), French critic, novelist. "The Value of Education," in *Le Chemin de Velours* (1902; repr. in *Selected Writings*, ed. and tr. by Glen S. Burne, 1966).

21   We are commanded to love God with *all our minds*, as well as with all our hearts, and we commit a great sin if we *forbid or prevent* that cultivation of the mind in others which would enable them to perform this duty.

> ANGELINA GRIMKÉ (1805-79), U.S. abolitionist, feminist. "Appeal to the Christian Women of the South," in *Anti-Slavery Examiner* (Sept. 1836; repr. in *The Oven Birds: American Women on Womanhood 1820-1920*, ed. by Gail Parker, 1972).

22   Anyone who has passed through the regular gradations of a classical education, and is not made a fool by it, may consider himself as having had a very narrow escape.

> WILLIAM HAZLITT (1778-1830), English essayist. "On the Ignorance of the Learned," in *Edinburgh Magazine* (July 1818; repr. in *Table Talk*, 1821).

23   Education is the art of making man ethical.

> GEORG HEGEL (1770-1831), German philosopher. *The Philosophy of Right*, no. 58 (1821; tr. 1942).

24   Education at school continues what has been done at home: it crystallizes the optical illusion, consolidates it with book learning, theoretically legitimizes the traditional trash and trains the children to *know without understanding* and to accept *denominations for definitions*. Astray in his conceptions, entangled in words, man loses the flair for truth, the taste for nature. What a powerful intellect must you possess, to be suspicious of this moral carbon dioxide and with your head swimming already, to hurl yourself out of it into the fresh air, with which, into the bargain, everyone round is trying to scare you!

> ALEXANDER HERZEN (1812-70), Russian journalist, political thinker. *My Past and Thoughts*, vol. 3, pt. 6, ch. 10 (1921; tr. by Constance Garnett, 1924-27).

25 It is because the body is a machine that education is possible. Education is the formation of habits, a superinducing of an artificial organisation upon the natural organisation of the body.

> THOMAS HENRY HUXLEY (1825-95), English biologist. "On Descartes' `Discourse Touching the method of Using One's Reason Rightly and of Seeking Scientific Truth'" (1870; published in *Collected Essays*, vol. 1, 1893).

26 I can prove at any time that my education tried to make another person out of me than the one I became. It is for the harm, therefore, that my educators could have done me in accordance with their intentions that I reproach them; I demand from their hands the person I now am, and since they cannot give him to me, I make of my reproach and laughter a drumbeat sounding in the world beyond.

> FRANZ KAFKA (1883-1924), German novelist, short-story writer. *The Diaries of Franz Kafka 1910-1923* (ed. by Max Brod, 1948), 1910 entry.

27 The educator must above all understand how to wait; to reckon all effects in the light of the future, not of the present.

> ELLEN KEY (1849-1926), Swedish author, feminist. *The Morality of Woman and Other Essays*, "The Conventional Woman" (1911).

28 Adults who still derive childlike pleasure from hanging gifts of a ready-made education on the Christmas tree of a child waiting outside the door to life do not realize how unreceptive they are making the children to everything that constitutes the true surprise of life.

> KARL KRAUS (1874-1936), Austrian satirist. "The World of Posters," in *Simplicissimus* (Munich, 1909; repr. in *In These Great Times: A Karl Kraus Reader*, ed. by Harry Zohn, 1976).

29 Education is a crutch with which the foolish attack the wise to prove that they are not idiots.

> KARL KRAUS (1874-1936), Austrian satirist. *Die Fackel* (Vienna, 7 Nov. 1912; repr. in Thomas Szasz, *Anti-Freud: Karl Kraus's Criticism of Psychoanalysis and Psychiatry*, ch. 8, 1976).

30 The only fence against the world is a thorough knowledge of it.

> JOHN LOCKE (1632-1704), English philosopher. *Some Thoughts Concerning Education*, sct. 88 (1693).

31 Our attitude towards ourselves should be "to be satiable in learning" and towards others "to be tireless in teaching."

> MAO ZEDONG (1893-1976), Founder of the People's Republic of China. "The Role of the Chinese Communist Party in the National War" (Oct. 1938; published in *Selected Works*, vol. 2).

32 The system—the American one, at least—is a vast and noble experiment. It has been polestar and exemplar for other nations. But from kindergarten until she graduates from college the girl is treated in it exactly like her brothers. She studies the same subjects, becomes proficient at the same sports. Oh, it is a magnificent lore she learns, education for the mind beyond anything Jane Austen or Saint Theresa or even Mrs. Pankhurst ever dreamed. It is truly Utopian. But Utopia was never meant to exist on this disheveled planet.

> PHYLLIS MCGINLEY (1905-78), U.S. poet, author. *The Province of the Heart*, "The Honor of Being a Woman" (1959).

33 The school system, custodian of print culture, has no place for the rugged individual. It is, indeed, the homogenizing hopper into which we toss our integral tots for processing.

> MARSHALL MCLUHAN (1911-80), Canadian communications theorist. *The Gutenberg Galaxy*, "Cervantes Confronted Typographic Man in the Figure of Don Quixote" (1962).

34 People commonly educate their children as they build their houses, according to some plan they think beautiful, without considering whether it is suited to the purposes for which they are designed.

> LADY MARY WORTLEY MONTAGU (1689-1762), English society figure, letter writer. Letter, 19 Feb. 1750, to her daughter Lady Bute (published in *Selected Letters*, ed. by Robert Halsband, 1970).

35 If an educational act is to be efficacious, it will be only that one which tends to *help* toward the complete unfolding of life. To be thus helpful it is necessary rigorously to avoid the *arrest of spontaneous movements and the imposition of arbitrary tasks*.

> MARIA MONTESSORI (1870-1952), Italian educationist. *The Montessori Method*, ch. 5 (1912).

36 If education is always to be conceived along the same antiquated lines of a mere transmission of knowledge, there is little to be hoped from it in the bettering of man's future. For what is the use of transmitting knowledge if the individual's total development lags behind?

> MARIA MONTESSORI (1870-1952), Italian educationist. *The Absorbent Mind*, ch. 1 (1949).

37 The wretch who digs the mine for bread,
Or ploughs, that others may be fed,
Feels less fatigued than that decreed
To him who cannot think or read.

> HANNAH MORE (1745-1833), English writer, reformer, philanthropist. *Florio*, pt. 1.

38 Education costs money, but then so does ignorance.

> SIR CLAUS MOSER (b. 1922), German-born British academic, Warden of Wadham College, Oxford. *Daily Telegraph* (London, 21 Aug. 1990).

39 Education has become a prisoner of contemporaneity. It is the past, not the dizzy present, that is the best door to the future.

> CAMILLE PAGLIA (b. 1947), U.S. author, critic, educator. *Sex, Art, and American Culture*, Introduction (1992).

40 Let us describe the education of our men. . . . What then is the education to be? Perhaps we could hardly find a better than that which the experience of the past has already discovered, which consists, I believe, in gymnastic, for the body, and music for the mind.

> PLATO (c. 427-347 B.C.), Greek philosopher. Socrates, in *The Republic*, bk. 2, sct. 376.

41 'Tis education forms the common mind,
Just as the twig is bent, the tree's inclined.

ALEXANDER POPE (1688-1744), English satirical poet. *Epistle to Cobham.*

42 The purpose of education is to keep a culture from being drowned in senseless repetitions, each of which claims to offer a new insight.

HAROLD ROSENBERG (1906-78), U.S. art critic, author. "The Cultural Situation Today," in *Partisan Review* (New Brunswick, N.J., Summer 1972; repr. as *Discovering the Present,* Introduction, 1973).

43 We are born weak, we need strength; helpless, we need aid; foolish, we need reason. All that we lack at birth, all that we need when we come to man's estate, is the gift of education.

JEAN-JACQUES ROUSSEAU (1712-78), Swiss-born French philosopher, political theorist. *Emile,* bk. 1 (1762).

44 True education makes for inequality; the inequality of individuality, the inequality of success, the glorious inequality of talent, of genius; for inequality, not mediocrity, individual superiority, not standardization, is the measure of the progress of the world.

FELIX E. SCHELLING (1858-1945), U.S. educator. *Pedagogically Speaking,* ch. 8 (1929).

45 Every uneducated person is a caricature of himself.

FRIEDRICH SCHLEGEL (1772-1829), German philosopher, critic, writer. *Dialogue on Poetry and Literary Aphorisms,* "Selected Aphorisms from *The Athenaeum*," aph. 63 (1968; first published 1798).

46 To me education is a leading out of what is already there in the pupil's soul. To Miss Mackay it is a putting in of something that is not there, and that is not what I call education, I call it intrusion.

MURIEL SPARK (b. 1918), British novelist. Miss Brodie, in *The Prime of Miss Jean Brodie,* ch. 2 (1961).

47 Now, if the principle of toleration were once admitted into classical education—if it were admitted that the great object is to read and enjoy a language, and the stress of the teaching were placed on the few things absolutely essential to this result, if the tortoise were allowed time to creep, and the bird permitted to fly, and the fish to swim, towards the enchanted and divine sources of Helicon—all might in their own way arrive there, and rejoice in its flowers, its beauty, and its coolness.

HARRIET BEECHER STOWE (1811-96), U.S. novelist, anti-slavery campaigner. *Little Foxes,* ch. 5 (1865).

48 I am beginning to suspect all elaborate and special systems of education. They seem to me to be built up on the supposition that every child is a kind of idiot who must be taught to think.

ANNE SULLIVAN (1866-1936), U.S. educator of the deaf and blind. Letter, 8 May 1887 (published in Helen Keller, *The Story of My Life,* pt. 3, ch. 3, 1903). Sullivan was Helen Keller's tutor 1887-94.

49 Every act of conscious learning requires the willingness to suffer an injury to one's self-esteem. That is why young children, before they are aware of their own self-importance, learn so easily; and why older persons, especially if vain or important, cannot learn at all.

THOMAS SZASZ (b. 1920), U.S. psychiatrist. *The Second Sin,* "Education" (1973).

50 It is an axiom in political science that unless a people are educated and enlightened it is idle to expect the continuance of civil liberty or the capacity for self-government.

TEXAS DECLARATION OF INDEPENDENCE, 2 March 1836.

51 What does education often do? It makes a straight-cut ditch of a free, meandering brook.

HENRY DAVID THOREAU (1817-62), U.S. philosopher, author, naturalist. *Journals* (1906), Oct./Nov. 1850 entry.

52 How could youths better learn to live than by at once trying the experiment of living?

HENRY DAVID THOREAU (1817-62), U.S. philosopher, author, naturalist. *Walden,* "Economy" (1854).

53 The most important part of teaching = to teach what it is to *know.*

SIMONE WEIL (1909-43), French philosopher, mystic. *London Notebook* (written 1943, published 1950; repr. in *First and Last Notebooks,* pt. 4, ed. by Richard Rees, 1970).

54 Human history becomes more and more a race between education and catastrophe.

H. G. WELLS (1866-1946), British author. *The Outline of History* (1920; 1951 ed., ch. 40).

55 Education is an admirable thing, but it is well to remember from time to time that nothing that is worth knowing can be taught.

OSCAR WILDE (1854-1900), Anglo-Irish playwright, author. Gilbert, in *The Critic as Artist,* pt. 1 (published in *Intentions,* 1891).

56 The whole theory of modern education is radically unsound. Fortunately in England, at any rate, education produces no effect whatsoever. If it did, it would prove a serious danger to the upper classes, and probably lead to acts of violence in Grosvenor Square.

OSCAR WILDE (1854-1900), Anglo-Irish playwright, author. Lady Bracknell, in *The Importance of Being Earnest,* act 1.

See also Montagu on DAUGHTERS; English Proverb on GENTLEMEN; Hughes on PLAY; Trevelyan on READING; SCHOOL; STUDENTS; TEACHERS; UNIVERSITIES AND COLLEGES; Emerson on UPBRINGING.

EFFORT

1 The human condition is such that pain and effort are not just symptoms which can be removed without changing life itself; they are the modes in which life itself, together with the necessity to which it is bound, makes itself felt. For mortals, the "easy life of the gods" would be a lifeless life.

HANNAH ARENDT (1906-75), German-born U.S. political philosopher. *The Human Condition,* ch. 16, "Labor" (1958).

2   Inscribe all human effort with one word,
   Artistry's haunting curse, the Incomplete!

> ROBERT BROWNING (1812-89), English poet. *The Ring and the Book*, bk. 11.

3   There's no taking trout with dry breeches.

> MIGUEL DE CERVANTES (1547-1616), Spanish writer. Sancho, in *Don Quixote*, pt. 2, ch. 71 (1615).

4   The secret of the truly successful, I believe, is that they learned very early in life how *not* to be busy. They saw through that adage, repeated to me so often in childhood, that anything worth doing is worth doing well. The truth is, many things are worth doing only in the most slovenly, halfhearted fashion possible, and many other things are not worth doing at all.

> BARBARA EHRENREICH (b. 1941), U.S. author, columnist. *The Worst Years of Our Lives*, "The Cult of Busyness" (1991; first published 1985).

5   God gives every bird his worm, but He does not throw it into the nest.

> P. D. JAMES (b. 1920), British mystery writer. Jonah the tramp, in *Devices and Desires*, ch. 40 (1989), quoting a wayside pulpit.

6   But the effort, the effort! And as the marrow is eaten out of a man's bones and the soul out of his belly, contending with the strange rapacity of savage life, the lower stage of creation, he cannot make the effort any more.

> D. H. LAWRENCE (1885-1930), British author. *St. Mawr* (1925; repr. in *The Short Novels*, vol. 2, 1979).

7   I made up my mind long ago that life was too short to do anything for myself that I could pay others to do for me.

> W. SOMERSET MAUGHAM (1874-1966), British author. *A Writer's Notebook* (1949), entry in 1941.

8   There is no limit to what a man can do so long as he does not care a straw who gets the credit for it.

> C. E. MONTAGUE (1867-1928), English author, journalist. *Disenchantment*, ch. 15, sct. 3 (1922).

9   Effort is only effort when it begins to hurt.

> JOSÉ ORTEGA Y GASSET (1883-1955), Spanish essayist, philosopher. "In Search of Goethe from Within," in *Partisan Review* (New Brunswick, N.J., Dec. 1949; repr. in *The Dehumanization of Art and Other Essays*, 1968).

10   Everyone confesses in the abstract that exertion which brings out all the powers of body and mind is the best thing for us all; but practically most people do all they can to get rid of it, and as a general rule nobody does much more than circumstances drive them to do.

> HARRIET BEECHER STOWE (1811-96), U.S. novelist, anti-slavery campaigner. "The Lady Who Does Her Own Work," in *Atlantic Monthly* (Boston, 1864).

EGOTISM

1   Egotist. A person of low taste, more interested in himself than me.

> AMBROSE BIERCE (1842-1914), U.S. author. *The Devil's Dictionary* (1881-1906).

2   The source of our actions resides in an unconscious propensity to regard ourselves as the center, the cause, and the conclusion of time. Our reflexes and our pride transform into a planet the parcel of flesh and consciousness we are.

> E. M. CIORAN (b. 1911), Rumanian-born French philosopher. *A Short History of Decay*, ch. 1, "The Anti-Prophet" (1949).

3   "I" is a militant social tendency, working to hold and enlarge its place in the general current of tendencies. So far as it can it waxes, as all life does. To think of it as apart from society is a palpable absurdity of which no one could be guilty who really *saw* it as a fact of life.

> CHARLES HORTON COOLEY (1864-1929), U.S. sociologist. *Human Nature and the Social Order*, ch. 5 (1902).

4   There is nothing more natural than to consider everything as starting from oneself, chosen as the center of the world; one finds oneself thus capable of condemning the world without even wanting to hear its deceitful chatter.

> GUY DEBORD (b. 1931), French Situationist philosopher. *Panegyric*, pt. 1 (1989).

5   The egoism which enters into our theories does not affect their sincerity; rather, the more our egoism is satisfied, the more robust is our belief.

> GEORGE ELIOT (1819-80), English novelist, editor. *Middlemarch*, bk. 5, ch. 53 (1871).

6   An inflated consciousness is always egocentric and conscious of nothing but its own existence. It is incapable of learning from the past, incapable of understanding contemporary events, and incapable of drawing right conclusions about the future. It is hypnotized by itself and therefore cannot be argued with. It inevitably dooms itself to calamities that must strike it dead.

> CARL JUNG (1875-1961), Swiss psychiatrist. *Psychology and Alchemy* (1944; repr. in *Collected Works*, vol. 12, para. 563, ed. by William McGuire, 1968).

7   If being an egomaniac means I believe in what I do and in my art or my music, then in that respect you can call me that. . . . I believe in what I do, and I'll say it.

> JOHN LENNON (1940-80), British rock musician. "The Tomorrow Show" (April 1975), NBC-TV.

8   Egotism is usually subversive of sagacity.

> MARIANNE MOORE (1887-1972), U.S. poet. "Comment," in *Dial*, no. 82 (New York, March 1927; repr. in *Complete Prose*, 1987).

9   There is nothing in the world so enjoyable as a thorough-going monomania . . .

> AGNES REPPLIER (1858-1950), U.S. author, social critic. *Books and Men*, "The Decay of Sentiment" (1888).

10   If the egotist is weak, his egotism is worthless. If the egotist is strong, acute, full of distinctive character, his egotism is precious, and remains a possession of the race.

> ALEXANDER SMITH (1830-67), Scottish poet. *Dreamthorp*, "On the Writing of Essays" (1863).

11   If some really acute observer made as much of egotism as Freud has made of sex, people would forget a good deal about sex and find the explanation for everything in egotism.

> WALLACE STEVENS (1879-1955), U.S. poet. Letter, 10 Jan.

1936, published in *Letters of Wallace Stevens*, no. 339 (ed. by Holly Stevens, 1967).

12 I should not talk so much about myself if there were anybody else whom I knew as well.

HENRY DAVID THOREAU (1817-62), U.S. philosopher, author, naturalist. *Walden*, "Economy" (1854).

See also SELFISHNESS.

ALBERT EINSTEIN

1 Through the mythology of Einstein, the world blissfully regained the image of knowledge reduced to a formula.

ROLAND BARTHES (1915-80), French semiologist. *Mythologies*, "The Brain of Einstein" (1957; tr. 1972).

2 By an application of the theory of relativity to the taste of readers, to-day in Germany I am called a German man of science, and in England I am represented as a Swiss Jew. If I come to be regarded as a *bête noire* the descriptions will be reversed, and I shall become a Swiss Jew for the Germans and a German man of science for the English!

ALBERT EINSTEIN (1879-1955), German-born U.S. theoretical physicist. "Einstein on His Theory," in *Times* (London, 28 Nov. 1919).

3 If my theory of relativity is proven correct, Germany will claim me as a German and France will declare that I am a citizen of the world. Should my theory prove untrue, France will say that I am a German and Germany will declare that I am a Jew.

ALBERT EINSTEIN (1879-1955), German-born U.S. theoretical physicist. Address, Dec. 1929, at the Sorbonne. Quoted in: *New York Times* (16 Feb. 1930).

4 Einstein is not . . . merely an artist in his moments of leisure and play, as a great statesman may play golf or a great soldier grow orchids. He retains the same attitude in the whole of his work. He traces science to its roots in emotion, which is exactly where art is also rooted.

HAVELOCK ELLIS (1859-1939), British psychologist. *The Dance of Life*, ch. 3 (1923).

5 Einstein is loved because he is gentle, respected because he is wise. Relativity being not for most of us, we elevate its author to a position somewhere between Edison, who gave us a tangible gleam, and God, who gave us the difficult dark and the hope of penetrating it.

E. B. WHITE (1899-1985), U.S. author, editor. "Inimicable Forces," in *New Yorker* (8 April 1933; repr. in *Writings from the New Yorker 1927-1976*, ed. by Rebecca M. Dale, 1991).

See also Picasso on GENIUS.

ELECTIONS

1 When the leaders choose to make themselves bidders at an auction of popularity, their talents, in the construction of the state, will be of no service. They will become flatterers instead of legislators; the instruments, not the guides, of the people.

EDMUND BURKE (1729-97), Irish philosopher, statesman. *Reflections on the Revolution in France* (1790).

2 You campaign in poetry. You govern in prose.

MARIO CUOMO (b. 1932), U.S. Democratic politician. *New Republic* (Washington, D.C., 8 April 1985).

3 I never vote for anyone. I always vote against.

W. C. FIELDS (1879-1946), U.S. screen actor. Quoted in: Leslie Halliwell, *Halliwell's Filmgoer's Companion* (1984).

4 In every election in American history both parties have their clichés. The party that has the clichés that ring true wins.

NEWT GINGRICH (b. 1943), U.S. Republican politician. *International Herald Tribune* (Paris, 1 Aug. 1988).

5 It doesn't matter who you vote for, the government always gets in.

GRAFFITO in London, 1970s.

6 ''Mos anytime you see whitemen spose to fight each other an' you not white, well you know you got trouble, because they blah-blah loud about Democrat or Republican an' they huffin' an' puff about democracy someplace else but relentless, see, the deal come down evil on somebody don' have no shirt an' tie, somebody don' live in no whiteman house no whiteman country.

JUNE JORDAN (b. 1939), U.S. poet, civil rights activist. *Moving towards Home: Political Essays*, "White Tuesday" (1989), on the 1984 U.S. presidential election.

7 I just received the following wire from my generous Daddy—"Dear Jack, Don't buy a single vote more than is necessary. I'll be damned if I'm going to pay for a landslide."

JOHN F. KENNEDY (1917-63), U.S. Democratic politician, president. Speech, 1958, at the Gridiron Dinner, Washington, D.C. Quoted in: Bill Adler, *The Wit of President Kennedy* (1964).

8 Football strategy does not originate in a scrimmage: it is useless to expect solutions in a political compaign.

WALTER LIPPMANN (1889-1974), U.S. journalist. *A Preface to Politics*, ch. 3 (1914).

9 Finishing second in the Olympics gets you silver. Finishing second in politics gets you oblivion.

RICHARD M. NIXON (b. 1913), U.S. Republican politician, president. Quoted in: *Sunday Times* (London, 13 Nov. 1988), referring to the defeat of Michael Dukakis by George Bush in the 1988 presidential election.

10 Maybe a nation that consumes as much booze and dope as we do and has our kind of divorce statistics should pipe down about "character issues." Either that or just go ahead and determine the presidency with three-legged races and pie-eating contests. It would make better TV.

P. J. O'ROURKE (b. 1947), U.S. journalist. *Parliament of Whores*, "Attack of the Midget Vote Suckers" (1991).

11 There is a sort of exotic preposterousness about a lot of elections, the way arguments are made even cruder.

CHRIS PATTEN (b. 1944), British Conservative politician. Quoted in: *Observer* (London, 30 June 1991). Patten was organizer of the electoral campaign of 1992, which led to a fourth successive victory for the Conservative Party though he himself lost his seat.

12 Which one of the three candidates would you want your daughter to marry?

> H. ROSS PEROT (b. 1930), U.S. business executive, presidential candidate 1992. *International Herald Tribune* (Paris, 29 Oct. 1992).

13 Why should I? Someone is bound to do it for me.

> RICKSHAW DRIVER, Bangladesh. Quoted in: *Daily Telegraph* (London, 4 Feb. 1988), on being asked if he had voted in the Bangladesh election.

14 The English people believes itself to be free; it is gravely mistaken; it is free only during election of members of parliament; as soon as the members are elected, the people is enslaved; it is nothing. In the brief moment of its freedom, the English people makes such a use of that freedom that it deserves to lose it.

> JEAN-JACQUES ROUSSEAU (1712-78), Swiss-born French philosopher, political theorist. *The Social Contract*, bk. 3, ch. 15 (1762).

15 The advance planning and sense stimuli employed to capture a $10 million cigarette or soap market are nothing compared to the brainwashing and propaganda blitzes used to ensure control of the largest cash market in the world: the Executive Branch of the United States Government.

> PHYLLIS SCHLAFLY (b. 1924), U.S. author, political activist. *A Choice Not an Echo*, ch. 1 (1964).

16 There's small choice in rotten apples.

> WILLIAM SHAKESPEARE (1564-1616), English dramatist, poet. Hortensio, in *The Taming of the Shrew*, act 1, sc. 1, responding to Gremio's likening of marriage to Katherina—the "shrew"—to being "whipped at the high cross every morning."

17 Everyone was tired with the old style politicians and their flowery rhetoric. I just told them there are tough times ahead, but that they would be less tough with me in charge.

> ANIBAL CAVACO SILVA (b. 1939), Portuguese premier. *Independent* (London, 13 Jan. 1992).

18 Indeed, you won the elections, but I won the count.

> ANASTASIO SOMOZA (1896-1956), Nicaraguan dictator. Quoted in: *Guardian* (London, 17 June 1977), said to an opponent accusing him of rigging the election.

19 The idea that you can merchandise candidates for high office like breakfast cereal—that you can gather votes like box tops—is, I think, the ultimate indignity to the democratic process.

> ADLAI STEVENSON (1900-1965), U.S. Democratic politician. Speech, 18 Aug. 1956, at Democratic National Convention.

See also Pope on GOVERNMENT.

ELEGANCE

1 Elegance does not consist in putting on a new dress.

> COCO CHANEL (1883-1971), French couturière. Quoted in: Marcel Haedrich, *Coco Chanel: Her Life, Her Secrets*, ch. 21 (1971).

2 For me, elegance is not to pass unnoticed but to get to the very soul of what one is.

> CHRISTIAN LACROIX (b. 1951), French fashion designer. *International Herald Tribune* (Paris, 21 Jan. 1992).

3 We must never confuse elegance with snobbery.

> YVES SAINT LAURENT (b. 1936), French couturier. *Ritz*, no. 85 (London, 1984).

4 It is not possible for a man to be elegant without a touch of femininity.

> VIVIENNE WESTWOOD (b. 1941), British fashion designer. *Independent* (London, 12 July 1990).

ELOPEMENT

1 The reasons why I did not foreacquaint you with it (to deal with the same plainness that I have used) were these. I knew my present estate less than fit for her, I knew (yet I know not why) that I stood not right in your opinion. I knew that to have given any intimation of it had been to impossibilitate the whole matter.

> JOHN DONNE (c. 1572-1631), English divine, metaphysical poet. Letter, 2 Feb. 1602, Sir George More (published in *Complete Poetry and Selected Prose*, ed. by John Hayward, 1929), explaining why he had eloped with More's daughter, Anne.

2 You, that are going to be married, think things can never be done too fast: but we that are old, and know what we are about, must elope methodically, madam.

> OLIVER GOLDSMITH (1728-74), Anglo-Irish playwright, author. Jarvis to Olivia, in *The Good Natur'd Man*, act 4.

ELOQUENCE

1 You have such strong words at command, that they make the smallest argument seem formidable.

> GEORGE ELIOT (1819-80), English novelist, editor. Esther to Felix, in *Felix Holt, The Radical*, ch. 5 (1866).

2 He talked on for ever; and you wished him to talk on for ever.

> WILLIAM HAZLITT (1778-1830), English essayist. *Lectures on the English Poets*, "On the Living Poets" (1818), said of Samuel Taylor Coleridge.

3 True eloquence consists in saying all that need be said and no more.

> FRANÇOIS, DUC DE LA ROCHEFOUCAULD (1613-80), French writer, moralist. *Sentences et Maximes Morales*, no. 250 (1678).

4 The finest eloquence is that which gets things done; the worst is that which delays them.

> DAVID LLOYD GEORGE (1863-1945), British Liberal politician, prime minister. Speech, Jan. 1919, Paris Peace Conference.

5 Today it is not the classroom nor the classics which are the repositories of models of eloquence, but the ad agencies.

> MARSHALL MCLUHAN (1911-80), Canadian communications theorist. *The Mechanical Bride*, "Plain Talk" (1951).

6 To acquire immunity to eloquence is of the utmost importance to the citizens of a democracy.

> BERTRAND RUSSELL (1872-1970), British philosopher, mathematician. *Power*, ch. 18, sct. 4 (1938).

See also Molière on SPEECHES AND SPEECHMAKING.

EMBARRASSMENT

1 Girls blush, sometimes, because they are alive,
Half wishing they were dead to save the shame.
The sudden blush devours them, neck and brow;
They have drawn too near the fire of life, like gnats,
And flare up bodily, wings and all. What then?
Who's sorry for a gnat . . . or girl?

> ELIZABETH BARRETT BROWNING (1806-61), English poet. *Aurora Leigh*, bk. 2 (1857).

2 He scratched his ear, the infallible resource
To which embarrassed people have recourse.

> LORD BYRON (1788-1824), English poet. *Don Juan*, cto. 6, st. 100.

3 There's a blush for won't, and a blush for shan't,
And a blush for having done it:
There's a blush for thought and a blush for naught,
And a blush for just begun it.

> JOHN KEATS (1795-1821), English poet. *Sharing Eve's Apple*, st. 2.

4 We never forgive those who make us blush.

> JEAN-FRANÇOIS DE LA HARPE (1739-1803), French poet, playwright. Mélanie, in *Mélanie*, act 3, sc. 1.

5 Man is the only animal that blushes. Or needs to.

> MARK TWAIN (1835-1910), U.S. author. *Following the Equator*, ch. 27, "Pudd'nhead Wilson's New Calendar" (1897).

RALPH WALDO EMERSON

1 What I loved in the man was his health, his unity with himself; all people and all things seemed to find their quite peaceable adjustment with him, not a proud domineering one, as after doubtful *contest*, but a spontaneous-looking peaceable, even humble one.

> THOMAS CARLYLE (1795-1881), Scottish essayist, historian. Letter, 10 Sept. 1833, to John Stuart Mill (published in *Letters of Thomas Carlyle*, 1923). Mill had given Emerson a letter of introduction to Carlyle, which Emerson presented in person.

2 Never in my life have I met anyone who did not agree that Emerson is an inspiring writer. One may not accept his thought in toto, but one comes away from a reading of him purified, so to say, and exalted. He takes you to the heights, he gives you wings. He is daring, very daring. In our day he would be muzzled, I am certain.

> HENRY MILLER (1891-1980), U.S. author. *The Books in My Life*, ch. 11 (1951).

3 Such a man as instinctively feeds on pure ambrosia and leaves alone the indigestible in things.

> FRIEDRICH NIETZSCHE (1844-1900), German philosopher. *Twilight of the Idols*, "Expeditions of an Untimely Man," aph. 13 (1889).

EMIGRANTS AND REFUGEES

1 Emigration, forced or chosen, across national frontiers or from village to metropolis, is the quintessential experience of our time.

> JOHN BERGER (b. 1926), British author, critic. *And Our Faces, My Heart, Brief as Photos*, pt. 2 (1984).

2 To live and die amongst foreigners may seem less absurd than to live persecuted or tortured by one's fellow countrymen . . . But to emigrate is always to dismantle the centre of the world, and so to move into a lost, disoriented one of fragments.

> JOHN BERGER (b. 1926), British author, critic. *And Our Faces, My Heart, Brief as Photos*, pt. 2 (1984).

3 One must apply one's reason to everything here, learning to obey, to shut up, to help, to be good, to give in, and I don't know what else. I'm afraid I shall use up all my brains too quickly, and I haven't got so very many. Then I shall not have any left for when the war is over.

> ANNE FRANK (1929-45), German Jewish refugee, diarist. *The Diary of a Young Girl* (1947; tr. 1952), entry for 22 Dec. 1942.

4 It is not as easy to emigrate with steel mills as it is with the manuscript of a novel.

> GOLO MANN (b. 1909), German historian, son of Thomas Mann. Quoted in: Marcel Reich-Ranicki, *Thomas Mann and His Family*, "Golo Mann: The Liberation of an Unloved One" (1987; tr. 1989), of the industrialists who financed Hitler.

5 As a lone ant from a broken ant-hill
from the wreckage of Europe, ego scriptor.

> EZRA POUND (1885-1972), U.S. poet, critic. *The Pisan Cantos*, cto. 76 (1948).

6 Freedom-loving people around the world must say . . . I am a refugee in a crowded boat foundering off the coast of Vietnam. I am Laotian, a Cambodian, a Cuban, and a Miskito Indian in Nicaragua. I, too, am a potential victim of totalitarianism.

> RONALD REAGAN (b. 1911), U.S. Republican politician, president. Speech, 27 May 1985, at Bergen-Belsen Concentration Camp, Germany (published in *Speaking My Mind*, 1989).

EMOTION

1 The only questions worth asking today are whether humans are going to have any emotions tomorrow, and what the quality of life will be if the answer is no.

> LESTER BANGS (1948-82), U.S. rock journalist. *Gig* (Jan. 1978).

2 It is very difficult to be wholly joyous or wholly sad on this earth. The comic, when it is human, soon takes upon itself a face of pain; and some of our griefs . . . have their source in weaknesses which must be recognized with smiling compassion as the common inheritance of us all.

> JOSEPH CONRAD (1857-1924), Polish-born English novelist. *A Personal Record*, "A Familiar Preface" (1912).

3 There are strings in the human heart that had better not be vibrated.

> CHARLES DICKENS (1812-70), English novelist. Mr. Tappertit, in *Barnaby Rudge*, ch. 22 (1841).

4 You learn to put your emotional luggage where it will do some good, instead of using it to shit on other people, or blow up aeroplanes.

> MARGARET DRABBLE (b. 1939), British novelist. Quoted in: *Observer* (London, 6 Oct. 1991).

5 Our emotions
Are only "incidents"
In the effort to keep day and night together.

> T. S. ELIOT (1888-1965), Anglo-American poet, critic. *A Note on War Poetry*, st. 3-4.

6 We find nothing easier than being wise, patient, superior. We drip with the oil of forbearance and sympathy, we are absurdly just, we forgive everything. For that very reason we ought to discipline ourselves a little; for that very reason we ought to *cultivate* a little emotion, a little emotional vice, from time to time. It may be hard for us; and among ourselves we may perhaps laugh at the appearance we thus present. But what of that! We no longer have any other mode of self-overcoming available to us: this is *our* asceticism, *our* penance.

> FRIEDRICH NIETZSCHE (1844-1900), German philosopher. *Twilight of the Idols*, "Expeditions of an Untimely Man," aph. 28 (1889).

7 He is not affected by the reality of distress touching his heart, but by the showy resemblance of it striking his imagination. He pities the plumage, but forgets the dying bird.

> THOMAS PAINE (1737-1809), Anglo-American political theorist, writer. *The Rights of Man*, "Rights of Man," pt. 1 (1791), of Edmund Burke à propos his essay *Reflections on the Revolution in France* (1790).

8 The young man who has not wept is a savage, and the old man who will not laugh is a fool.

> GEORGE SANTAYANA (1863-1952), U.S. philosopher, poet. *Dialogues in Limbo*, ch. 3 (1925).

9 The advantage of the emotions is that they lead us astray.

> OSCAR WILDE (1854-1900), Anglo-Irish playwright, author. Lord Henry, in *The Picture of Dorian Gray*, ch. 3 (1891)

See also Arnold on RELIGION; Conrad on RESERVE.

EMPIRE

1 Not once or twice in our rough island-story
The path of booty was the way to glory.

> ANONYMOUS.

2 Keep our Empire undismembered
Guide our Forces by Thy Hand,
Gallant blacks from far Jamaica,
Honduras and Togoland;
Protect them Lord in all their fights,
And, even more, protect the whites.

> JOHN BETJEMAN (1906-84), British poet. *In Westminster Abbey*, st. 3 (published in *Old Lights for New Chancels*, 1940).

3 The foundation of empire is art & science. Remove them or degrade them, & the empire is no more. Empire follows art & not vice versa as Englishmen suppose.

> WILLIAM BLAKE (1757-1827), English poet, painter, engraver. Annotations to Sir Joshua Reynolds, *Discourses* (c. 1808; repr. in *Complete Writings*, ed. by Geoffrey Keynes, 1957).

4 The day of small nations has long passed away. The day of Empires has come.

> JOSEPH CHAMBERLAIN (1836-1914), British politician. Speech, 12 May 1904, Birmingham.

5 The conquest of the earth, which mostly means the taking it away from those who have a different complexion or slightly flatter noses than ourselves, is not a pretty thing when you look into it.

> JOSEPH CONRAD (1857-1924), Polish-born English novelist. *The Heart of Darkness*, ch. 1 (1902).

6 An empire is an immense egotism.

> RALPH WALDO EMERSON (1803-82), U.S. essayist, poet, philosopher. "The Young American," lecture, 7 Feb. 1844, delivered to Mercantile Library Association, Boston (published in *Addresses and Lectures*, 1849).

7 How is the Empire?

> GEORGE V (1865-1936), King of Great Britain and Ireland. Attributed last words, as reported to the nation 21 Jan. 1936—the day after the king's death—in a broadcast tribute by Prime Minister Stanley Baldwin, though other accounts deny this was the king's last utterance.

8 If Germany is to become a colonising power, all I say is, "God speed her!" She becomes our ally and partner in the execution of the great purposes of Providence for the advantage of mankind.

> W. E. GLADSTONE (1809-98), English statesman, prime minister. Speech, 12 March 1885, to the House of Commons.

9 Exploitation and oppression is not a matter of *race*. It is the system, the apparatus of world-wide brigandage called imperialism, which made the Powers behave the way they did. I have no illusions on this score, nor do I believe that any Asian nation or African nation, in the same state of dominance, and with the same system of colonial profit-amassing and plunder, would have behaved otherwise.

> HAN SUYIN (b. 1917), Chinese author. *The Crippled Tree*, pt.1, ch. 9 (1965).

10 Without the Empire we should be tossed like a cork in the cross current of world politics. It is at once our sword and our shield.

> WILLIAM MORRIS HUGHES (1864-1952), Australian prime minister. Speech, 1926, Melbourne, Australia.

11 Take up the White Man's burden—
Send forth the best ye breed—
Go, bind your sons to exile
To serve your captives' need.

> RUDYARD KIPLING (1865-1936), British author, poet. *The White Man's Burden*.

12 And the end of the fight is a tombstone white with the name of the late deceased,

And the epitaph drear: "A Fool lies here who tried to hustle the East."

RUDYARD KIPLING (1865-1936), British author, poet. *The Naulahka*, ch. 5, heading (1892).

13 The reluctant obedience of distant provinces generally costs more than it [the territory] is worth. Empires which branch out widely are often more flourishing for a little timely pruning.

THOMAS, BABINGTON MACAULAY (1800-1859), English historian, Whig politician. "War of the Succession in Spain," in *Edinburgh Review* (Jan. 1833; repr. in *Critical and Historical Essays*, 1843).

14 The mission of the United States is one of benevolent assimilation.

WILLIAM MCKINLEY (1843-1901), U.S. Republican politician, president. Letter, 21 Dec. 1898.

15 How marvellous it all is! Built not by saints and angels, but the work of men's hands; cemented with men's honest blood and with a world of tears, welded by the best brains of centuries past; not without the taint and reproach incidental to all human work, but constructed on the whole with pure and splendid purpose. Human, and yet not wholly human—for the most heedless and the most cynical must see the finger of the Divine.

LORD ROSEBERY (1847-1929), English Liberal politician, prime minister. Rectorial Address, 16 Nov. 1900, Glasgow University, said of the British Empire.

16 We seem, as it were, to have conquered and peopled half the world in a fit of absence of mind.

SIR J. R. SEELEY (1834-95), English classicist, historian. *The Expansion of England*, Lecture 1 (1883).

17 To found a great empire for the sole purpose of raising up a people of customers, may at first sight appear a project fit only for a nation of shopkeepers. It is, however, a project altogether unfit for a nation of shopkeepers, but extremely fit for a nation that is governed by shopkeepers.

ADAM SMITH (1723-90), Scottish economist. *The Wealth of Nations*, vol. 2, bk. 4, ch. 7 (1776). *Stevenson's Book of Quotations* cites a similar remark made slightly earlier—by English economist Josiah Tucker in *Four Tracts on Political and Commercial Subjects* (1766)—but Adam Smith's version was probably the source for its wider dissemination, and the origin of Napoleon's more famous utterance, "England is a nation of shopkeepers."

See Napoleon Bonaparte on ENGLAND AND THE ENGLISH.

18 To plunder, to slaughter, to steal, these things they misname empire; and where they make a wilderness, they call it peace.

TACITUS (c. 55-c. 120), Roman historian. Quoting the British chief Calgalus speaking of the Romans in: *Agricola*, sct. 30.

19 We *must* annex those people. We can afflict them with our wise and beneficent government. We can introduce the novelty of thieves, all the way up from street-car pickpockets to municipal robbers and Government defaulters, and show them how amusing it is to arrest them and try them and then turn them loose—some for cash and some for "political influence." We can make them ashamed of their simple and primitive justice. . . .

We can make that little bunch of sleepy islands the hottest corner on earth, and array it in the moral splendor of our high and holy civilization. Annexation is what the poor islanders need. "Shall we to men benighted, the lamp of life deny?"

MARK TWAIN (1835-1910), U.S. author. "The Sandwich Islands," Letter 2 (first published 1866; repr. in *Complete Essays*, ed. by Charles Neider, 1963).

20 Roman, remember that you shall rule the nations by your authority, for this is to be your skill, to make peace the custom, to spare the conquered, and to wage war until the haughty are brought low.

VIRGIL (70-19 B.C.), Roman poet. Anchises, in *Aeneid*, bk. 6, describing the task of the Romans.

21 There is no human failure greater than to launch a profoundly important endeavour and then leave it half done. This is what the West has done with its colonial system. It shook all the societies in the world loose from their old moorings. But it seems indifferent whether or not they reach safe harbour in the end.

BARBARA WARD (1914-81), British author, educator. *The Rich Nations and the Poor Nations*, ch. 2 (1962).

22 Other nations use "force"; we Britons alone use "Might."

EVELYN WAUGH (1903-66), British novelist. Mr. Baldwin, in *Scoop*, bk. 2, ch. 5 sct. 1 (1938).

See also COLONIALISM; DECOLONIZATION; Roosevelt on INTERNATIONAL RELATIONS.

THE END OF THE WORLD

1 The day the world ends, no one will be there, just as no one was there when it began. This is a scandal. Such a scandal for the human race that it is indeed capable collectively, out of spite, of hastening the end of the world by all means just so it can enjoy the show.

JEAN BAUDRILLARD (b. 1929), French semiologist. *Cool Memories*, ch. 5 (1987; tr. 1990).

2 Amen. Even so, come, Lord Jesus.

BIBLE: NEW TESTAMENT. *Revelation* 22:20.

3 The planet's survival has become so uncertain that any effort, any thought that presupposes an assured future amounts to a mad gamble.

ELIAS CANETTI (b. 1905), Austrian novelist, philosopher. *The Secret Heart of the Clock: Notes, Aphorisms, Fragments 1973-1985*, "1979" (1991).

4 In the zone of perdition where my youth went as if to complete its education, one would have said that the portents of an imminent collapse of the whole edifice of civilization had made an appointment.

GUY DEBORD (b. 1931), French Situationist philosopher. *Panegyric*, pt. 2 (1989).

5 This is the way the world ends
This is the way the world ends

This is the way the world ends
Not with a bang but a whimper.

> T. S. ELIOT (1888-1965), Anglo-American poet, critic. *The Hollow Men.*

6 God seems to have left the receiver off the hook, and time is running out.

> ARTHUR KOESTLER (1905-83), Hungarian-born British author. *The Ghost in the Machine,* ch. 18 (1967).

7 The world began without man, and it will end without him.

> CLAUDE LÉVI-STRAUSS (b. 1908), French anthropologist. *Tristes Tropiques,* pt. 9, ch. 40 (1955).

8 We are close to dead. There are faces and bodies like gorged maggots on the dance floor, on the highway, in the city, in the stadium; they are a host of chemical machines who swallow the product of chemical factories, aspirin, preservatives, stimulant, relaxant, and breathe out their chemical wastes into a polluted air. The sense of a long last night over civilization is back again.

> NORMAN MAILER (b. 1923), U.S. author. *Cannibals and Christians,* "Introducing Our Argument" (1966).

9 The world dies over and over again, but the skeleton always gets up and walks.

> HENRY MILLER (1891-1980), U.S. author. *The Wisdom of the Heart,* "Uterine Hunger" (1941).

10 The last man of the world-city no longer *wants* to live—he may cling to life as an individual, but as a type, as an aggregate, no, for it is a characteristic of this collective existence that it eliminates the terror of death.

> OSWALD SPENGLER (1880-1936), German historian. *The Decline of the West,* vol. 2, ch. 4, sct. 5 (1928).

11 It isn't necessary to imagine the world ending in fire or ice—there are two other possibilities: one is paperwork, and the other is nostalgia.

> FRANK ZAPPA (b. 1940), U.S. rock musician. *The Real Frank Zappa Book,* ch. 9 (1989; written with Peter Occhiogrosso).

See also NUCLEAR ARMAGEDDON.

ENDS AND MEANS

1 The first sign of corruption in a society that is still alive is that the end justifies the means.

> GEORGES BERNANOS (1888-1948), French novelist, political writer. *The Last Essays of Georges Bernanos,* "Why Freedom?" (1955).

2 Perfection of means and confusion of goals seem—in my opinion—to characterize our age.

> ALBERT EINSTEIN (1879-1955), German-born U.S. theoretical physicist. *Out of My Later Years,* ch. 14 (1950).

3 We have perhaps a natural fear of ends. We would rather be always on the way than arrive. Given the means, we hang on to them and often forget the ends.

> ERIC HOFFER (1902-83), U.S. philosopher. *Reflections on the Human Condition,* aph. 121 (1973).

4 The end may justify the means as long as there is something that justifies the end.

> LEON TROTSKY (1879-1940), Russian revolutionary. Quoted in: Alberto Pozzolini, *Antonio Gramsci: an Introduction to his Thought,* Preface (1970).

See also Koestler on POLITICS.

ENDURANCE

1 The men who learn endurance, are they who call the whole world, brother.

> CHARLES DICKENS (1812-70), English novelist. Mr. Haredale, in *Barnaby Rudge,* ch. 79 (1841).

2 Since ev'ry man who lives is born to die,
And none can boast sincere felicity,
With equal mind, what happens, let us bear,
Nor joy nor grieve too much for things beyond our care.

> JOHN DRYDEN (1631-1700), English poet, dramatist, critic. *Palamon and Arcite.*

3 Brute force crushes many plants. Yet the plants rise again. The Pyramids will not last a moment compared with the daisy. And before Buddha or Jesus spoke the nightingale sang, and long after the words of Jesus and Buddha are gone into oblivion the nightingale still will sing. Because it is neither preaching nor commanding nor urging. It is just singing. And in the beginning was not a Word, but a chirrup.

> D. H. LAWRENCE (1885-1930), British author. *Etruscan Places,* ch. 2 (1932).

4 An arch never sleeps.

> INDIAN SAYING.

ENEMIES

1 Never trust thine enemy: for like as iron rusteth, so is his wickedness. Though he humble himself and go crouching, yet take good heed and beware of him, and thou shalt be unto him as if thou hadst wiped a looking-glass, and thou shalt know that his rust hath not been altogether wiped away.

> APOCRYPHA. *Ecclesiasticus* 12:10-11.

2 Our greatest foes, and whom we must chiefly combat, are within.

> MIGUEL DE CERVANTES (1547-1616), Spanish writer. Don Quixote, in *Don Quixote,* pt. 2, bk. 5, ch. 8 (1615; tr. by P. Motteux).

3 You shall judge of a man by his foes as well as by his friends.

> JOSEPH CONRAD (1857-1924), Polish-born English novelist. Marlow, in *Lord Jim,* ch. 34 (1900).

4 Abatement in the hostility of one's enemies must never be thought to signify they have been won over. It only means that one has ceased to constitute a threat.

> QUENTIN CRISP (b. 1908), British author. *The Naked Civil Servant,* ch. 24 (1968).

5 I do not approve the extermination of the enemy; the policy of exterminating or, as it is barbarously said, liquidating enemies, is one of the most alarming developments of modern war and peace, from the point of view of those who desire the survival of culture. One needs the enemy.

T. S. ELIOT (1888-1965), Anglo-American poet, critic. *Note Towards the Definition of Culture*, ch. 3 (1948).

6 Much has been written about her enemies. She picked them with care, and God knows they deserved her.

JULES FEIFFER (b. 1929), U.S. cartoonist, writer. Quoted in: Peter Fiebleman, *Lilly: Reminiscences of Lillian Hellman*, Appendix (1988), said of Lillian Hellman in graveside eulogy.

7 You can discover what your enemy fears most by observing the means he uses to frighten you.

ERIC HOFFER (1902-83), U.S. philosopher. *The Passionate State of Mind*, aph. 222 (1955).

8 Treating your adversary with respect is giving him an advantage to which he is not entitled.

SAMUEL JOHNSON (1709-84), English author, lexicographer. Quoted in: James Boswell, *Tour to the Hebrides*, 15 Aug. 1773 (1785).

9 Forgive your enemies, but never forget their names.

ATTRIBUTED TO JOHN F. KENNEDY (1917-63), U.S. Democratic politician, president.

10 At the bottom of enmity between strangers lies indifference.

SØREN KIERKEGAARD (1813-55), Danish philosopher. *The Journals of Søren Kierkegaard: A Selection*, no. 1144 (ed. and tr. by Alexander Dru, 1938), entry for 1850.

11 The real enemy can always be met and conquered, or won over. Real antagonism is based on love, a love which has not recognized itself.

HENRY MILLER (1891-1980), U.S. author. *The Air-Conditioned Nightmare*, "Stieglitz and Marin" (1945).

12 You must not fight too often with one enemy, or you will teach him all your art of war.

NAPOLEON BONAPARTE (1769-1821), French general, emperor. Quoted in: Ralph Waldo Emerson, *Representative Men*, "Uses of Great Men" (1850).

13 You may have enemies whom you hate, but not enemies whom you despise. You must be proud of your enemy: then the success of your enemy shall be your success too.

FRIEDRICH NIETZSCHE (1844-1900), German philosopher. *Thus Spoke Zarathustra*, pt. 1, "Of War and Warriors" (1883-92; tr. 1961).

14 Our enemy is by tradition our savior, in preventing us from superficiality.

JOYCE CAROL OATES (b. 1938), U.S. author. Quoted in: "Master Race," published in *Partisan Review 50th Anniversary Edition* (ed. by William Phillips, 1985).

15 The Catholic and the Communist are alike in assuming that an opponent cannot be both honest and intelligent.

GEORGE ORWELL (1903-50), British author. "The Prevention of Literature" (1946; repr. in *Collected Essays*, 1961).

16 Then if my friendships break and bend,
There's little need to cry
The while I know that every foe
Is faithful till I die.

DOROTHY PARKER (1893-1967), U.S. humorous writer. *The Heel.*

17 Take heed of enemies reconciled, and of meat twice boiled.

ENGLISH PROVERB. Collected in John Ray, *English Proverbs* (1670).

18 I hate admitting that my enemies have a point.

SALMAN RUSHDIE (b. 1948), Indian-born British author. Hamza, in The Satanic Verses, "Mahound" (1988).

19 We can come to look upon the deaths of our enemies with as much regret as we feel for those of our friends, namely, when we miss their existence as witnesses to our success.

ARTHUR SCHOPENHAUER (1788-1860), German philosopher. *Parerga and Paralipomena*, vol. 2, ch. 26, sct. 311a (1851).

20 You have many enemies, that know not
Why they are so, but, like to village curs,
Bark when their fellows do.

WILLIAM SHAKESPEARE (1564-1616), English dramatist, poet. King Henry to Cardinal Wolsey, in *King Henry VIII*, act 2, sc. 4. The play (first known as *All is True*) is thought to have been co-written with poet and playwright John Fletcher (1579-1625).

21 I learned early in life that you get places by having the right enemies.

BISHOP JOHN SPONG (b. 1931), U.S. ecclesiastic. *Guardian* (London, 20 July 1988).

22 If you know the enemy and know yourself, you need not fear the result of a hundred battles. If you know yourself but not the enemy, for every victory gained you will also suffer a defeat. If you know neither the enemy nor yourself, you will succumb in every battle.

SUN TZU (6-5TH CENTURY B.C.), Chinese general. *The Art of War*, ch. 3, Axiom 18 (c. 490 B.C., ed. by James Clavell, 1981).

23 I have only ever made one prayer to God, a very short one: "O Lord, make my enemies ridiculous." And God granted it.

VOLTAIRE (1694-1778), French philosopher, author. Letter, 16 May 1767.

24 One of the most time-consuming things is to have an enemy.

E. B. WHITE (1899-1985), U.S. author, editor. *Essays of E. B. White*, "A Report in January" (1977; first published 1958).

25 For my enemy is dead, a man divine as myself is dead.

WALT WHITMAN (1819-92), U.S. poet. "Reconciliation."

26 I choose my friends for their good looks, my acquaintances for their good characters, and my enemies for their intellects. A man cannot be too careful in the choice of his enemies.

OSCAR WILDE (1854-1900), Anglo-Irish playwright, author. Lord Henry, in *The Picture of Dorian Gray*, ch. 1 (1891).

27   To have friends, you know, one need only be good-natured; but when a man has no enemy left there must be something mean about him.

> OSCAR WILDE (1854-1900), Anglo-Irish playwright, author. Prince Paul, in *Vera, or the Nihilists,* act 2.

See also Canning on CANDOR; Gandhi on FRIENDSHIP; Sterne on JOKES AND JOKERS; Hitler on LEADERSHIP; Barrie on MOTIVES; Twain on WAR.

ENERGY

1   Coal is a portable climate. It carries the heat of the tropics to Labrador and the polar circle; and it is the means of transporting itself whithersoever it is wanted. Watt and Stephenson whispered in the ear of mankind their secret, that *a half-ounce of coal will draw two tons a mile,* and coal carries coal, by rail and by boat, to make Canada as warm as Calcutta, and with its comfort brings its industrial power.

> RALPH WALDO EMERSON (1803-82), U.S. essayist, poet, philosopher. *The Conduct of Life,* "Wealth" (1860).

2   Is it a fact—or have I dreamt it—that, by means of electricity, the world of matter has become a great nerve, vibrating thousands of miles in a breathless point of time?

> NATHANIEL HAWTHORNE (1804-64), U.S. author. Clifford Pyncheon, in *The House of the Seven Gables,* ch. 17 (1851).

See also The NUCLEAR AGE.

ENGAGEMENT

1   An engaged woman is always more agreeable than a disengaged. She is satisfied with herself. Her cares are over, and she feels that she may exert all her powers of pleasing without suspicion. All is safe with a lady engaged; no harm can be done.

> JANE AUSTEN (1775-1817), English novelist. Henry Crawford, in *Mansfield Park,* ch. 5 (1814).

2   I am about to be married, and am of course in all the misery of a man in pursuit of happiness.

> LORD BYRON (1788-1824), English poet. Letter, 15 Oct. 1814 (published in *Byron's Letters and Journals,* vol. 4, ed. by Leslie A. Marchand, 1975).

3   Can you support the expense of a husband, hussy, in gaming, drinking and whoring? Have you money enough to carry on the daily quarrels of man and wife about who shall squander most?

> JOHN GAY (1685-1732), English dramatist. Peachum, in *The Beggar's Opera,* act 1, sc. 8.

4   No sooner met but they looked; no sooner looked but they loved; no sooner loved but they sighed; no sooner sighed but they asked one another the reason; no sooner knew the reason but they sought the remedy; and in these degrees have they made a pair of stairs to marriage, which they will climb incontinent, or else be incontinent before marriage.

> WILLIAM SHAKESPEARE (1564-1616), English dramatst, poet.

Rosalind, disguised as Ganymede, in *As You Like It,* act 5, sc. 2, referring to Oliver and Celia.

5   Pardon me, you are not engaged to any one. When you do become engaged to some one, I, or your father, should his health permit him, will inform you of the fact. An engagement should come on a young girl as a surprise, pleasant or unpleasant, as the case may be. It is hardly a matter that she could be allowed to arrange for herself.

> OSCAR WILDE (1854-1900), Anglo-Irish playwright, author. Lady Bracknell to Gwendolen, in *The Importance of Being Earnest,* act 1.

ENGINEERING

1   A good scientist is a person with original ideas. A good engineer is a person who makes a design that works with as few original ideas as possible. There are no prima donnas in engineering.

> FREEMAN DYSON (b. 1923), British-born U.S. physicist, author. *Disturbing the Universe,* pt. 1, ch. 10 (1979).

2   One has to look out for engineers—they begin with sewing machines and end up with the atomic bomb.

> MARCEL PAGNOL (1895-1974), French dramatist, film director. *Critique des Critiques,* ch. 3 (1949).

3   For 'tis the sport to have the engineer
Hoisted with his own petard.

> WILLIAM SHAKESPEARE (1564-1616), English dramatist, poet. Hamlet, in *Hamlet,* act 3, sc. 4, describing the untrustworthiness of Rosencrantz and Guildenstern. (These lines do not appear in the 1604 quarto ed.).

4   To define it rudely but not inaptly, engineering . . . is the art of doing that well with one dollar, which any bungler can do with two after a fashion.

> ARTHUR MELLEN WELLINGTON (1847-95), U.S. engineer. *The Economic Theory of the Location of Railways,* Introduction (6th ed., 1900).

ENGLAND AND THE ENGLISH

1   Your Englishman, confronted by something abnormal will always pretend that it isn't there. If he can't pretend that, he will look through the object, or round it, or above it or below it, or in any direction except into it. If, however, you *force* him to look into it, he will at once pretend that he sees the object not for what it is but for something that he would like it to be.

> JAMES AGATE (1877-1947), British drama critic. *The Selective Ego,* "Ego 1" (ed. by Tim Beaumont, 1976), entry for 14 Oct. 1932.

2   One has often wondered whether upon the whole earth there is anything so unintelligent, so unapt to perceive how the world is really going, as an ordinary young Englishman of our upper class.

> MATTHEW ARNOLD (1822-88), English poet, critic. *Culture and Anarchy,* ch. 2 (1869).

3   Surely the one thing needful for a Christian and an Englishman to study is Christian and moral and political philosophy, and then we should see our way a little more clearly without falling into Judaism, or Toryism, or Jacobinism, or any other *ism* whatever.

> THOMAS ARNOLD (1795-1842), English educator, scholar. Letter, 9 May 1836 (published in *The Life and Correspondence of Thomas Arnold, D.D.*, vol. 2, 1845).

4 Why doesn't the United States take over the monarchy and unite with England? England does have important assets. Naturally the longer you wait, the more they will dwindle. At least you could use it for a summer resort instead of Maine.

> W. H. AUDEN (1907-73), Anglo-American poet. *The Table Talk of W. H. Auden*, "February 1947" (comp. by Alan Ansen, ed. by Nicholas Jenkins, 1990).

5 I am living in the Midlands
That are sodden and unkind.

> HILAIRE BELLOC (1870-1953), British author. *The South Country.*

6 Since the French Revolution Englishmen are all intermeasurable one by another, certainly a happy state of agreement to which I for one do not agree.

> WILLIAM BLAKE (1757-1827), English poet, painter, engraver. Letter, 24 Oct. 1910, to George Cumberland (repr. in *Complete Writings*, ed. by Geoffrey Keynes, 1957).

7 For Cambridge people rarely smile,
Being urban, squat, and packed with guile.

> RUPERT BROOKE (1887-1915), British poet. *The Old Vicarage, Grantchester.*

8 I've always felt that English women had to be approached in a sisterly manner, rather than an erotic manner.

> ANTHONY BURGESS (b. 1917), British author, critic. *Times* (London, 27 July 1988).

9 England has the most sordid literary scene I've ever seen. They all meet in the same pub. This guy's writing a foreword for this person. They all have to give radio programs, they *have* to do all this just in order to scrape by. They're all scratching each other's backs.

> WILLIAM BURROUGHS (b. 1914), U.S. author. Taped conversation, 1980, New York City (published in Victor Bockris, *With William Burroughs: A Report from the Bunker*, "Burroughs in London," 1981).

10 Cool, and quite English, imperturbable.

> LORD BYRON (1788-1824), English poet. *Don Juan*, cto. 13, st. 14.

11 I am sure my bones would not rest in an English grave, or my clay mix with the earth of that country. I believe the thought would drive me mad on my deathbed could I suppose that any of my friends would be base enough to convey my carcass back to her soil. I would not even feed her worms if I could help it.

> LORD BYRON (1788-1824), English poet. Letter, 7 June 1819, to publisher John Murray (published in *Byron's Letters and Journals*, vol. 6, ed. by Leslie A. Marchand, 1976). After Byron's death from a fever in Greece, his body was brought back to England where it was interred together with his ancestors near his home at Newstead Abbey, having been refused burial at Westminster Abbey.

12 In England there are sixty different religions, and only one sauce.

> Attributed to FRANCESCO CARACCIOLI (1752-99), Neapolitan naval commander.

13 In the past, the English tried to impose a system wherever they went. They destroyed the nation's culture and one of the by-products of their systemisation was that they destroyed their own folk culture.

> MARTIN CARTHY (b. 1941), English folk singer, musician. Interview in *Guardian* (London, 29 Dec. 1988).

14 The English may not always be the best writers in the world, but they are incomparably the best dull writers.

> RAYMOND CHANDLER (1888-1959), U.S. author. *The Simple Art of Murder* (1950; first published in *Atlantic Monthly*, Boston, Dec. 1944).

15 The rolling English drunkard made the rolling English road.
A reeling road, a rolling road, that rambles round the shire.

> G. K. CHESTERTON (1874-1936), British author. *The Rolling English Road.*

16 'Tis a glorious charter, deny it who can,
That's birthed in the words, "I'm an Englishman."

> ELIZA COOK (1818-89), English poet. *An Englishman.*

17 In Bengal to move at all
Is seldom, if ever, done,
But mad dogs and Englishmen
Go out in the midday sun.

> NOËL COWARD (1899-1973), British playwright, actor, composer. "Mad Dogs and Englishmen," from *Collected Sketches and Lyrics* (1931).

18 No people in the world can make you feel so small as the English.

> ROBERTSON DAVIES (b. 1913), Canadian novelist, journalist. *The Enthusiasms of Robertson Davies*, "The Table Talk of Robertson Davies" (1990).

19 Kent, sir—everybody knows Kent—apples, cherries, hops, and women.

> CHARLES DICKENS (1812-70), English novelist. Jingle, in *The Pickwick Papers*, ch. 2 (1836-37).

20 I wish the English still possessed a shred of the old sense of humour which Puritanism, and dyspepsia, and newspaper reading, and tea-drinking have nearly extinguished.

> NORMAN DOUGLAS (1868-1952), British author. *South Wind*, ch. 32 (1917).

21 I find the Englishman to be him of all men who stands firmest in his shoes. They have in themselves what they value in their horses, mettle and bottom.

> RALPH WALDO EMERSON (1803-82), U.S. essayist, poet, philosopher. *English Traits*, "Manners" (1856).

22 England is the paradise of women, the purgatory of men, and the hell of horses.

> JOHN FLORIO (c. 1553-1625), English author, translator. Silvestro, in *Second Frutes*, ch. 12 (1591).

23 It is not that the Englishman can't feel—it is that he is afraid to feel. He has been taught at his public school that feeling is bad form. He must not express great joy or sorrow, or even open his mouth too wide when he talks—his pipe might fall out if he did.

> E. M. FORSTER (1879-1970), British novelist and essayist. "Notes

on the English Character" (first published 1920; repr. in *Abinger Harvest*, 1936).

24 The Germans are called brutal, the Spanish cruel, the Americans superficial, and so on; but we are perfide Albion, the island of hypocrites, the people who have built up an Empire with a Bible in one hand, a pistol in the other, and financial concessions in both pockets. Is the charge true? I think it is.

E. M. FORSTER (1879-1970), British novelist, essayist. *Notes on the English Character* (1920; repr. in *Abinger Harvest*, 1936). Forster defined English hypocrisy as "unconscious deceit" and "muddle-headedness."

25 The English are probably the most tolerant, least religious people on earth.

DAVID GOLDBERG (b. 1939), Senior Rabbi, Liberal Jewish Synagogue, London. Letter to *Times* (London, 17 April 1980), on the furor that followed a controversial production of the documentary "Death of a Princess" on BBC-TV.

26 Even crushed against his brother in the Tube the average Englishman pretends desperately that he is alone.

GERMAINE GREER (b. 1939), Australian feminist writer. *The Female Eunuch*, "Womanpower" (1970).

27 English culture is basically homosexual in the sense that the men only really care about other men.

GERMAINE GREER (b. 1939), Australian feminist writer. *Daily Mail* (London, 18 April 1988).

28 The boneless quality of English conversation, which, so far as I have heard it, is all form and no content. Listening to Britons dining out is like watching people play first-class tennis with imaginary balls.

MARGARET HALSEY (b. 1910), U.S. author. *With Malice Toward Some*, pt. 1, "June 12" (1938).

29 I shall never love England till she sues to us for help; and, in the meantime, the fewer triumphs she obtains, the better for all the parties. An Englishman in adversity is a very respectable character; he does not lose his dignity, but merely comes to a proper conceit of himself. . . . I seem to myself like a spy or a traitor, when I meet their eyes, and am conscious that I neither hope nor fear in sympathy with them, although (unless they detect me for an American by my aspect) they look at me in full confidence of sympathy.

NATHANIEL HAWTHORNE (1804-64), U.S. author. *English Notebooks* (1870; rev. 1941), entry for 6 Oct. 1854.

30 The English (it must be owned) are rather a foul-mouthed nation.

WILLIAM HAZLITT (1778-1830), English essayist. *Table Talk*, "On Criticism" (1821-22).

31 The Englishman never enjoys himself except for a noble purpose.

A. P. HERBERT (1890-1971), British author, politician. Mr. Justice Plush, in *Uncommon Law*, "Is Fox-Hunting Fun?" (1935).

32 It must not be thought that the cowardly feeling of caution and uneasy self-preservation is innate in the English character. It is the consequence of a corpulence derived from wealth and of the training of all thoughts and passions for acquisitiveness.

ALEXANDER HERZEN (1812-70), Russian journalist, political

thinker. *My Past and Thoughts*, vol. 3, pt. 6, "England" (1921; tr. by Constance Garnett, 1924-27).

33 An Englishman's never so natural as when he's holding his tongue.

HENRY JAMES (1843-1916), U.S. author. Isabel Archer, in *The Portrait of a Lady*, ch. 10 (1881).

34 Most English talk is a quadrille in a sentry-box.

HENRY JAMES (1843-1916), U.S. author. The Duchess, in *The Awkward Age* bk. 5, ch. 4 (1899).

35 And what should they know of England who only England know?

RUDYARD KIPLING (1865-1936), British author, poet. *The English Flag*.

36 We do not regard Englishmen as foreigners. We look on them only as rather mad Norwegians.

HALVARD LANGE (b. 1918), Norwegian historian, politician. Quoted in: *Observer* (London, 9 March 1957).

37 Why, why, why was I born an Englishman!—my cursed, rotten-boned, pappy-hearted countrymen, *why* was I sent to *them*?

D. H. LAWRENCE (1885-1930), British author. Letter, 3 July 1912, to writer and critic Edward Garnett (published in *The Letters of D. H. Lawrence*, vol. 1, ed. by James T. Boulton, 1979).

38 An acre in Middlesex is better than a principality in Utopia.

THOMAS, BABINGTON MACAULAY (1800-1859), English historian, Whig politician. "Lord Bacon," in *Edinburgh Review* (July 1837; repr. in *Critical and Historical Essays*, 1843).

39 We love the indomitable bellicose patriotism that sets you apart; we love the national pride that guides your muscularly courageous race; we love the potent individualism that doesn't prevent you from opening your arms to individualists of every land, whether libertarians or anarchists.

TOMMASO MARINETTI (1876-1944), Italian playwright, founder of Futurism. "Futurist Speech to the English," 1910, Lyceum Club, London (published in *Marinetti: Selected Writings*, ed. by R. W. Flint, 1972).

40 The English have all the material requisites for the revolution. What they lack is the spirit of generalization and revolutionary ardour.

KARL MARX (1818-83), German political theorist, social philosopher. Pamphlet, Jan. 1870, against the Bakuninists.

41 This is the only country in the world where the food is more dangerous than sex.

JACKIE MASON (b. 1931), U.S. comic. *Daily Telegraph* (London, 17 Feb. 1989).

42 If an Englishman gets run down by a truck he apologizes to the truck.

JACKIE MASON (b. 1931), U.S. comic. *Independent* (London, 20 Sept. 1990).

43 On the Continent people have good food; in England people have good table manners.

GEORGE MIKES (b. 1912), Hungarian-born British humorist. *How to be an Alien*, ch. 1, sct. 1 (1946).

44 They make other nations seem pale and flighty,
But they do think England is God almighty,
And you must remind them now and then
That other countries breed other men.

ALICE DUER MILLER (1874-1942), U.S. novelist, poet. *The White Cliffs*, a long narrative poem extolling Britain's resistance during World War II.

45 Lords and Commoners of England, consider what nation it is whereof ye are, and whereof ye are the governors; a nation not slow and dull, but of a quick, ingenious and piercing spirit, acute to invent, subtle and sinewy to discourse, not beneath the reach of any point the highest that human capacity can soar to.

JOHN MILTON (1608-74), English poet. *Areopagitica: a Speech for the Liberty of Unlicensed Printing to the Parliament of England* (1644).

46 With its baby rivers and little towns, each with its
abbey or its cathedral,
with voices—one voice perhaps, echoing through
the transept—The
criterion of suitability and convenience.

MARIANNE MOORE (1887-1972), U.S. poet. *England*.

47 This land is a little land; too much shut up within the narrow seas, as it seems, to have much space for swelling into hugeness: there are no great wastes overwhelming in their dreariness, no great solitudes of forests, no terrible untrodden mountain-walls: all is measured, mingled, varied, gliding easily one thing into another: little rivers, little plains, swelling, speedily-changing uplands, all beset with handsome orderly trees; little hills, little mountains, netted over with the walls of sheep-walks: all is little; yet not foolish and blank, but serious rather, and abundant of meaning for such as choose to seek it: it is neither prison nor palace, but a decent home.

WILLIAM MORRIS (1834-96), English artist, writer, printer. *Hopes and Fears for Art*, "The Lesser Arts" (1882; repr. in *Collected Works*, vol. 22). "Some people praise this homeliness overmuch," Morris added.

48 The people of England are never so happy as when you tell them they are ruined.

ARTHUR MURPHY (1727-1805), Irish-born English dramatist. Pamphlet, in *The Upholsterer*, act 2, sc. 1.

49 England is a nation of shopkeepers.

Attributed to NAPOLEON BONAPARTE (1769-1821), French general, emperor. In Paul F. Boller, Jr., and John George, *They Never Said It: A Book of Fake Quotes, Misquotes and Misleading Attributions* (1990), it is claimed that Napoleon overheard the phrase and adopted it from Bernard de Vieuzac Barère, who in turn was quoting economist Adam Smith. See Smith on EMPIRE.

50 The English are the nation of consummate cant.

FRIEDRICH NIETZSCHE (1844-1900), German philosopher. *Twilight of the Idols*, "Expeditions of an Untimely Man," aph. 12 (1889).

51 A family with the wrong members in control—that, perhaps, is as near as one can come to describing England in a phrase.

GEORGE ORWELL (1903-50), British author. *The Lion and the Unicorn*, pt. 1, "England Your England" (1941).

52 As a rule they will refuse even to sample a foreign dish, they regard such things as garlic and olive oil with disgust, life is unliveable to them unless they have tea and puddings.

GEORGE ORWELL (1903-50), British author. "The English People" (1944; repr. in *The Collected Essays, Journalism and Letters of George Orwell*, vol. 3, ed. by Sonia Orwell & Ian Angus, 1968), on the English attitude toward food.

53 The English are probably more capable than most peoples of making revolutionary change without bloodshed. In England, if anywhere, it would be possible to abolish poverty without destroying liberty.

GEORGE ORWELL (1903-50), British author. "The English People" (1944; repr. in *The Collected Essays, Journalism and Letters of George Orwell*, vol. 3, ed. by Sonia Orwell & Ian Angus, 1968).

54 Damn you, England. You're rotting now, and quite soon you'll disappear. My hate will outrun you yet if only for a few seconds. I wish it could be eternal.

JOHN OSBORNE (b. 1929), British playwright. Letter to the left-wing *Tribune* (Aug. 1961).

55 But Lord! to see the absurd nature of Englishmen, that cannot forbear laughing and jeering at everything that looks strange.

SAMUEL PEPYS (1633-1703), English diarist. Diary entry, 27 Nov. 1662.

56 English life, while very pleasant, is rather bland. I expected kindness and gentility and I found it, but there is such a thing as too much couth.

S. J. PERELMAN (1904-79), U.S. humorist. Quoted in: *Observer* (London, 24 Sept. 1971).

57 He carries his English weather in his heart wherever he goes, and it becomes a cool spot in the desert, and a steady and sane oracle amongst all the delirium of mankind.

GEORGE SANTAYANA (1863-1952), U.S. philosopher, poet. *Soliloquies in England*, "The British Character" (1922).

58 This blessèd plot, this earth, this realm, this
England
This nurse, this teeming womb of royal kings,
. . .
This land of such dear souls, this dear dear land.

WILLIAM SHAKESPEARE (1564-1616), English dramatist, poet. John of Gaunt, in *Richard II*, act 2, sc. 1, contrasting England as "This other Eden" with its present state of degeneration, "leased out . . . like to a tenement or pelting farm."

59 Englishmen never will be slaves: they are free to do whatever the Government and public opinion allow them to do.

GEORGE BERNARD SHAW (1856-1950), Anglo-Irish playwright, critic. The Devil, in *Man and Superman*, act 3.

60 There is nothing so bad or so good that you will not find an Englishman doing it; but you will never find an Englishman in the wrong. He does everything on principle. He fights you on patriotic principles; he robs you on business principles; he enslaves you on imperial principles; he bullies you on manly principles; he supports his king on loyal principles and cuts off his king's head on republican principles. His watchword is always Duty;

and he never forgets that the nation which lets its duty get on the opposite side to its interest is lost.

> GEORGE BERNARD SHAW (1856-1950), Anglo-Irish playwright, critic. Napoleon, in *The Man of Destiny.*

61 We are a nation of governesses.

> GEORGE BERNARD SHAW (1856-1950), Anglo-Irish playwright, critic. *New Statesman* (London, 12 April 1913).

62 This Englishwoman is so refined
She has no bosom and no behind.

> STEVIE SMITH (1902-71), British poet. *This Englishwoman.*

63 What a pity it is that we have no amusements in England but vice and religion!

> SYDNEY SMITH (1771-1845), English clergyman, writer. Quoted in: Hesketh Pearson, *The Smith of Smiths*, ch. 10 (1934).

64 I cannot but conclude the bulk of your natives to be the most pernicious race of little, odious vermin that Nature ever suffered to crawl upon the surface of the earth.

> JONATHAN SWIFT (1667-1745), Anglo-Irish satirist. The king of Brobdingnag to Gulliver, in *Gulliver's Travels*, ch. 6, "A Voyage to Brobdingnag" (1726).

65 Who the first inhabitants of Britain were, whether natives or immigrants, remains obscure; one must remember we are dealing with barbarians.

> TACITUS (c. 55-c. 120), Roman historian. *Agricola*, sct. 11.

66 Always in England if you had the type of brain that was capable of understanding T. S. Eliot's poetry or Kant's logic, you could be sure of finding large numbers of people who would hate you violently.

> D. J. TAYLOR (b. 1960), British author. *Guardian* (London, 14 Sept. 1989).

67 England is nothing but the last ward of the European madhouse, and quite possibly it will prove to be the ward for particularly violent cases.

> LEON TROTSKY (1879-1940), Russian revolutionary. *Diary in Exile* (1959), entry for 11 April 1935.

68 How superbly brave is the Englishman in the presence of the awfulest forms of danger & death; & how abject in the presence of any & all forms of hereditary rank.

> MARK TWAIN (1835-1910), U.S. author. *Mark Twain's Notebooks and Journals*, vol. 3 (1979; ed. by Frederick Anderson), entry in Notebook 28.

69 The best sun we have is made of Newcastle coal, and I am determined never to reckon upon any other.

> HORACE WALPOLE (1717-97), English author. Letter, 15 June 1768.

70 You never find an Englishman among the underdogs—except in England, of course.

> EVELYN WAUGH (1903-66), British novelist. Sir Ambrose Abercrombie, in *The Loved One*, (1948; repr. 1951, p. 13).

71 The real weakness of England lies, not in incomplete armaments or unfortified coasts, not in the poverty that creeps through sunless lanes, or the drunkenness that brawls in loathsome courts, but simply in the fact that her ideals are emotional and not intellectual.

> OSCAR WILDE (1854-1900), Anglo-Irish playwright, author.

Gilbert, in *The Critic as Artist*, pt. 2 (published in *Intentions*, 1891).

72 You know what the Englishman's idea of compromise is? He says, Some people say there is a God. Some people say there is no God. The truth probably lies somewhere between these two statements.

> W. B. YEATS (1865-1939), Irish poet. Quoted by Wilfred Whitten in: *John O'London's Weekly* (24 June 1949).

See also Shaw on BARBARISM; The BRITISH; Shakespeare on CLUBS; Clary on ECCENTRICITY; Heine on GERMANY AND THE GERMANS; Shaw on HORSES; Connolly on The MASSES; Thackeray on The MIDDLE CLASS; Shaw on MORALITY; Voltaire on MULTICULTURALISM; Beecham on MUSIC; Mikes on ORDER; Yeats on PHILOSOPHERS; Wells on REFORM; Barrie on SCOTLAND AND THE SCOTS; Mikes, Muggeridge on SEX; Whitehorn on The WEATHER; Byron on WINTER.

ENJOYMENT

1 He has spent his life best who has enjoyed it most. God will take care that we do not enjoy it any more than is good for us.

> SAMUEL BUTLER (1835-1902), English author. *Samuel Butler's Notebooks* (1951).

2 Listen to the cry of a woman in labor at the hour of giving birth—look at the dying man's struggle at his last extremity, and then tell me whether something that begins and ends thus could be intended for enjoyment.

> SØREN KIERKEGAARD (1813-55), Danish philosopher. *The Diary of Søren Kierkegaard*, pt. 1, no. 31 (1854; ed. by Peter Rohde, 1960).

3 The first half of it consists of the capacity to enjoy without the chance; the last half consists of the chance without the capacity.

> MARK TWAIN (1835-1910), U.S. author. Letter, 19 July 1901 (published in *Letters of Mark Twain*, ed. by Albert Bigelow Paine, 1917), of life.

ENLIGHTENMENT

1 No one who has lived even for a fleeting moment for something other than life in its conventional sense and has experienced the exaltation that this feeling produces can then renounce his new freedom so easily.

> ANDRÉ BRETON (1896-1966), French Surrealist. *Surrealism and Painting* (1928).

2 I don't know Who—or what—put the question, I don't know when it was put. I don't even remember answering. But at some moment I did answer *Yes* to Someone—or Something—and from that hour I was certain that existence is meaningful and that, therefore, my life, in self-surrender, had a goal.

> DAG HAMMARSKJÖLD (1905-61), Swedish statesman, Secretary-General of U.N. Note written Whitsunday 1961 (published in *Markings*, 1964).

3 In this world, which is so plainly the antechamber of another, there are no happy men. The true division of humanity is between those who live in light and those who live in darkness. Our aim must be to diminish the number of the latter and increase the number of the former. That is why we demand education and knowledge.

> VICTOR HUGO (1802-85), French poet, dramatist, novelist. *Les Misérables*, pt. 4, bk. 7, ch. 1 (1862).

4 The moment of truth, the sudden emergence of a new insight, is an act of intuition. Such intuitions give the appearance of miraculous flushes, or short-circuits of reasoning. In fact they may be likened to an immersed chain, of which only the beginning and the end are visible above the surface of consciousness. The diver vanishes at one end of the chain and comes up at the other end, guided by invisible links.

> ARTHUR KOESTLER (1905-83), Hungarian-born British novelist, essayist. *The Act of Creation*, pt. 2, ch. 8 (1964).

5 The light which puts out our eyes is darkness to us. Only that day dawns to which we are awake. There is more day to dawn. The sun is but a morning star.

> HENRY DAVID THOREAU (1817-62), U.S. philosopher, author, naturalist. *Walden*, "Conclusion" (1854).

6 A man whose mind feels that it is captive would prefer to blind himself to the fact. But if he hates falsehood, he will not do so; and in that case he will have to suffer a lot. He will beat his head against the wall until he faints. He will come to again and look with terror at the wall, until one day he begins afresh to beat his head against it; and once again he will faint. And so on endlessly and without hope. One day he will wake up on the other side of the wall.

> SIMONE WEIL (1909-43), French philosopher, mystic. "Human Personality," in *La Table Ronde* (Dec. 1950, repr. in *Selected Essays*, ed. by Richard Rees, 1962).

See also INSPIRATION.

ENNUI

1 The real pleasure of being Mick Jagger was in having everything but being tempted by nothing . . . a smouldering ill will which silk clothes, fine food, wine, women, and every conceivable physical pampering somehow aggravated . . . a drained and languorous, exquisitely photogenic ennui.

> ANONYMOUS "CHRONICLER." Quoted in: Philip Norman, *The Life and Good Times of the Rolling Stones* (1989).

2 After having exhausted all the arguments on behalf of evil, one utters the creed's dictums with nostalgia rather than with fervor.

> JOSEPH BRODSKY (b. 1940), Russian-born U.S. poet, critic. *Less Than One: Selected Essays*, "The Power of the Elements" (1986; first published 1980).

3 What'll we do with ourselves this afternoon? And the day after that, and the next thirty years?

> F. SCOTT FITZGERALD (1896-1940), U.S. author. Daisy Buchanan, in *The Great Gatsby*, ch. 7 (1925).

4 I do not care for anything. I do not care to ride, for the exercise is too violent. I do not care to walk, walking is too strenuous. I do not care to lie down, for I should either have to remain lying, and I do not care to do that,

or I should have to get up again, and I do not care to do that either. *Summa summarum*: I do not care at all.

> SØREN KIERKEGAARD (1813-55), Danish philosopher. *Either/Or*, vol. 1, "Diapsalmata" (1843; tr. 1944).

5 What a day-to-day affair life is.

> JULES LAFORGUE (1860-87), French Symbolist poet. *Les Complaintes*, "Complainte sur certains ennuis" (1885).

6 Alas, the flesh is weary, and I've read all the books.

> STÉPHANE MALLARMÉ (1842-98), French Symbolist poet. *Brise Marin*.

7 She, while her lover pants upon her breast,
Can mark the figures on an Indian chest.

> ALEXANDER POPE (1688-1744), English satirical poet. *Epistle to a Lady*.

8 The evil which assails us is not in the localities we inhabit but in ourselves. We lack strength to endure the least task, being incapable of suffering pain, powerless to enjoy pleasure, impatient with everything. How many invoke death when, after having tried every sort of change, they find themselves reverting to the same sensations, unable to discover any new experience.

> SENECA (c. 5 B.C.-A.D. c. 65), Roman writer, philosopher, statesman. *Moral Essays*, "De Tranquillitate Animi" (On Tranquility of Mind), sct. 2, subsct. 15.

9 Life is as tedious as a twice-told tale,
Vexing the dull ear of a drowsy man.

> WILLIAM SHAKESPEARE (1564-1616), English dramatist, poet. Louis the Dauphin, in *King John*, act 3, sc. 4.

10 Don't tell me that you have exhausted Life. When a man says that, one knows that life has exhausted him.

> OSCAR WILDE (1854-1900), Anglo-Irish playwright, author. Lady Narborough, in the *The Picture of Dorian Gray*, ch. 15 (1891).

See also BOREDOM.

ENTERPRISE

1 Much of our American progress has been the product of the individual who had an idea; pursued it; fashioned it; tenaciously clung to it against all odds; and then produced it, sold it, and profited from it.

> HUBERT H. HUMPHREY (1911-78), U.S. Democratic politician, vice president. Address, 29 June 1966, to United States Junior Chamber of Commerce, Detroit, Michigan.

2 An enterprizing foole needs little wit.

> ENGLISH PROVERB. Quoted in: *Cotgrave Dictionary* (1611).

3 I say, beware of all enterprises that require new clothes, and not rather a new wearer of clothes.

> HENRY DAVID THOREAU (1817-62), U.S. philosopher, author, naturalist. *Walden*, "Economy" (1854).

4 In the end, you're measured not by how much you undertake but by what you finally accomplish.

> DONALD TRUMP (b. 1946), U.S. businessman. *Trump: The Art of the Deal*, ch. 14 (1987; written with Tony Schwartz).

ENTERTAINMENT

1   The ultimate sin of any performer is contempt for the audience.

> LESTER BANGS (1948-82), U.S. rock journalist. *Village Voice* (New York, 29 Aug. 1977).

2   Compare . . . the cinema with theatre. Both are dramatic arts. Theatre brings actors before a public and every night during the season they re-enact the same drama. Deep in the nature of theatre is a sense of ritual. The cinema, by contrast, transports its audience individually, singly, *out* of the theatre towards the unknown.

> JOHN BERGER (b. 1926), British author, critic. "Ev'ry Time We Say Goodbye," in *Expressen* (Stockholm, 3 Nov. 1990; repr. in *Keeping a Rendezvous*, 1992).

3   The reason I'm in this business, I assume all performers are—it's "Look at me, Ma!" It's acceptance, you know—"Look at me, Ma, look at me, Ma, look at me, Ma." And if your mother watches, you'll show off till you're exhausted; but if your mother goes, *Ptshew!*

> LENNY BRUCE (1925-66), U.S. satirical comedian. *The Essential Lenny Bruce*, "Performing and the Art of Comedy" (ed. by John Cohen, 1967).

4   The Miss America contest is . . . the most perfectly rendered theater in our culture, for it so perfectly captures what we yearn for: a low-class ritual, a polished restatement of vulgarity, that wants to open the door to high-class respectability by way of plain middle-class anxiety and ambition.

> GERALD EARLY (b. 1952), U.S. author. "Life With Daughters: Watching the Miss America Pageant," in *Kenyon Review* (1991; repr. in *The Best American Essays, 1991*, ed. by Joyce Carol Oates, 1991).

5   Th' only way t' entertain some folks is t' listen t' 'em.

> KIN [F. MCKINNEY] HUBBARD (1868-1930), U.S. humorist, journalist. *Abe Martin's Wisecracks* (ed. by E. V. Lucas, 1930).

6   Every country gets the circus it deserves. Spain gets bullfights. Italy gets the Catholic Church. America gets Hollywood.

> ERICA JONG (b. 1942), U.S. author. *How To Save Your Own Life*, Epigraph, "Take the Red-Eye . . ." (1977).

7   I believe entertainment can aspire to be art, and can become art, but if you set out to make art you're an idiot.

> STEVE MARTIN (b. 1945), U.S. comedian and comic actor. *Today* (London, 17 May 1989).

8   The essential is to excite the spectators. If that means playing *Hamlet* on a flying trapeze or in an aquarium, you do it.

> ORSON WELLES (1915-84), U.S. filmmaker, actor, producer. Quoted in: Frank Brady, *Citizen Welles*, ch. 16 (1989; originally published in *Les Nouvelles Littéraires*, 1953).

ENTHUSIASM

1   Enthusiasms, like stimulants, are often affected by people with small mental ballast.

> MINNA ANTRIM (1861-?), U.S. epigrammist. *Naked Truth and Veiled Allusions* (1901).

2   Enthusiasm. A distemper of youth, curable by small doses of repentance in connection with outward applications of experience.

> AMBROSE BIERCE (1842-1914), U.S. author. *The Devil's Dictionary* (1881-1906).

3   Life is too short to be little. Man is never so manly as when he feels deeply, acts boldly, and expresses himself with frankness and with fervour.

> BENJAMIN DISRAELI (1804-81), English statesman, author. *Coningsby*, bk. 7, ch. 2 (1844).

4   Nothing great was ever achieved without enthusiasm.

> RALPH WALDO EMERSON (1803-82), U.S. essayist, poet, philosopher. *Essays*, "Circles" (First Series, 1841).

5   The figure of the enthusiast who has just discovered jogging or a new way to fix tofu can be said to stand or, more accurately, to tremble on the threshold of conversion, as the representative American.

> LEWIS H. LAPHAM (b. 1935), U.S. essayist, editor. "The Complete American," in *Harper's* (New York, Nov. 1981).

6   There is a small steam engine in his brain which not only sets the cerebral mass in motion, but keeps the owner in hot water.

> *New York Weekly Mirror*, (5 July 1845). Quoted in: Julian Symons, *The Tell-Tale Heart: The Life and Works of Edgar Allan Poe*, pt. 1, ch. 12 (1978).

THE ENVIRONMENT

1   We cannot permit the extreme in the environmental movement to shut down the United States. We cannot shut down the lives of many Americans by going to the extreme on the environment.

> GEORGE BUSH (b. 1924), U.S. Republican politician, president. Speech, 30 May 1992, at campaign rally, California, on the Rio de Janeiro Earth Summit.

2   Conservation must become before recreation.

> CHARLES, PRINCE OF WALES (b. 1948). *Times* (London, 5 July 1989).

3   Is a park any better than a coal mine? What's a mountain got that a slag pile hasn't? What would you rather have in your garden—an almond tree or an oil well?

> JEAN GIRAUDOUX (1882-1944), French diplomat, author. A prospector, in *The Madwoman of Chaillot*, act 1.

4   The poor tread lightest on the earth. The higher our income, the more resources we control and the more havoc we wreak.

> PAUL HARRISON (b. 1936), U.S. playwright, director. *Guardian* (London, 1 May 1992).

5   They're busy making bigger roads,
and better roads and more,

so that people can discover
even faster than before
that everything is everywhere alike.

PIET HEIN (b. 1905), Dutch inventor, poet. *Road Sense*, in *Grooks* (1966).

6 Cities are expanding at an alarming rate. Inter-tidal zones are being polluted as mangroves gives way to marina. Over-consumption is leading to soil erosion and desertification, which in turn cause famine and exert pressure on formally fertile areas. We are pulling out the plugs of the system that keeps us alive. Every indicator is showing red: species diversity, water quality, weather patterns, the number of refugees. . . . We are unravelling nature like an old jumper.

PENNY KEMP (b. 1951) AND DEREK WALL (b. 1965), British ecologists. *A Green Manifesto for the 1990s*, ch. 4 (1990).

7 That which is not good for the bee-hive cannot be good for the bees.

MARCUS AURELIUS (121-80), Roman emperor, philosopher. *Meditations*, bk. 6, sct. 54.

8 What have we achieved in mowing down mountain ranges, harnessing the energy of mighty rivers, or moving whole populations about like chess pieces, if we ourselves remain the same restless, miserable, frustrated creatures we were before? To call such activity progress is utter delusion. We may succeed in altering the face of the earth until it is unrecognizable even to the Creator, but if we are unaffected wherein lies the meaning?

HENRY MILLER (1891-1980), U.S. author. *The World of Sex* (1940; repr. 1970, pp. 118-19).

9 I am I plus my surroundings and if I do not preserve the latter, I do not preserve myself.

JOSÉ ORTEGA Y GASSET (1883-1955), Spanish essayist, philosopher. *Meditations on Quixote*, "To the Reader" (1914).

10 If the federal government had been around when the Creator was putting His hand to this state, Indiana wouldn't be here. It'd still be waiting for an environmental impact statement.

RONALD REAGAN (b. 1911), U.S. Republican politician, president. Speech, 9 Feb. 1982 (published in *Speaking My Mind*, "The Wit and Wisdom of Ronald Reagan," 1989).

11 If I were a Brazilian without land or money or the means to feed my children, I would be burning the rain forest too.

STING [GORDON MATTHEW SUMNER] (b. 1951), British rock musician. *International Herald Tribune* (Paris, 14 April 1989).

12 It hurts the spirit, somehow, to read the word *environments*, when the plural means that there are so many alternatives there to be sorted through, as in a market, and voted on.

LEWIS THOMAS (b. 1913), U.S. physician, educator. *The Lives of a Cell*, "Natural Man" (1974).

13 Modern man's capacity for destruction is quixotic evidence of humanity's capacity for reconstruction. The powerful technological agents we have unleashed against the environment include many of the agents we require for its reconstruction.

GEORGE F. WILL (b. 1941), U.S. political columnist. *Statecraft as Soulcraft: What Government Does*, ch. 7 (1984).

See also ECOLOGY.

ENVY

1 The envied are like bureaucrats; the more impersonal they are, the greater the illusion (for themselves and for others) of their power.

JOHN BERGER (b. 1926), British critic. *Ways of Seeing*, ch. 7 (1972).

2 Some folks rail against other folks, because other folks have what some folks would be glad of.

HENRY FIELDING (1707-54), English novelist, dramatist. Slipshod, in *Joseph Andrews*, bk. 4, ch. 6 (1742).

3 Fools may our scorn, not envy, raise.
For envy is a kind of praise.

JOHN GAY (1685-1732), English dramatist. *Fables*, "The Hound and the Huntsman" (1727).

4 Helpless, unknown, and unremembered, most human beings, however sensitive, idealistic, intelligent, go through life as passengers rather than chauffeurs. Although we may pretend that it is the chauffeur who is the social inferior . . . most of us, like Toad of Toad Hall, would not mind a turn at the wheel ourselves.

RALPH HARPER (b. 1915), U.S. cleric, author. *The World of the Thriller*, pt. 3, "Outside the Law" (1969).

5 Envy among other ingredients has a mixture of the love of justice in it. We are more angry at undeserved than at deserved good-fortune.

WILLIAM HAZLITT (1778-1830), English essayist. *Characteristics*, no. 19 (first published anonymously in 1823; repr. in *Complete Works*, vol. 9. ed. by P. P. Howe, 1932).

6 His scorn of the great is repeated too often to be real; no man thinks much of that which he despises.

SAMUEL JOHNSON (1709-84), English author, lexicographer. *Lives of the English Poets*, "Pope" (1779-81), referring to Alexander Pope.

7 Man will do many things to get himself loved, he will do all things to get himself envied.

MARK TWAIN (1835-1910), U.S. author. *Following the Equator*, ch. 21, "Pudd'nhead Wilson's New Calendar" (1897).

See also Berger on GLAMOR; Beerbohm on GREATNESS.

EPIGRAMS

See APHORISMS AND EPIGRAMS.

EPITAPHS

1 Don't pity me now,
Don't pity me never;

I'm going to do nothing
For ever and ever.

JAMES AGATE (1877-1947), British drama critic. A "char-woman's epitaph," in *Ego* (14 March 1933). She was a "self-deceiver," Agate claimed. "At least I will lay odds that anybody meeting her in Heaven will find her scrubbing marble and dusting porphyry with a new-born gleam in her old eye."

2 Posterity will ne'er survey
A nobler grave than this:
Here lie the bones of Castlereagh:
Stop, traveller, and piss.

LORD BYRON (1788-1824), English poet. *Epitaph for Castlereagh* (1822). Robert Stewart, Viscount Castlereagh, a Tory foreign secretary, was held responsible for many of his government's repressive measures abroad. He committed suicide 12 Aug. 1822.

3 Nor has his death the world deceiv'd
Less than his wondrous life surpriz'd;
For if he like a madman liv'd
At least he like a wise one dy'd.

MIGUEL DE CERVANTES (1547-1616), Spanish writer. Don Quixote's epitaph, in *Don Quixote*, pt. 2, bk. 6, ch. 41 (1615; tr. by P. Motteux).

4 Green leaves on a dead tree is our epitaph—green leaves, dear reader, on a dead tree.

CYRIL CONNOLLY (1903-74), British critic. "The Journal of Cyril Connolly 1928-1937" (published in David Pryce-Jones, *Journal and Memoir*, 1983). Pryce-Jones chose these words for his book's epigraph.

5 Let no man write my epitaph; for as no man who knows my motives dare now vindicate them, let not prejudice or ignorance asperse them. Let them rest in obscurity and peace! Let my memory be left in oblivion, my tomb remain uninscribed, until other times and other men can do justice to my character.

ROBERT EMMET (1778-1803), Irish patriot. Speech, 19 Sept. 1803, from the dock on the eve of his execution, following his abortive uprising against British rule.

6 The body
Of
Benjamin Franklin
Printer
(Like the cover of an old book
Its contents torn out
And stripped of its lettering and gilding)
Lies here, food for worms.
But the work shall not be lost
For it will (as he believed) appear once more
In a new and more elegant edition
Revised and corrected
by
The Author.

BENJAMIN FRANKLIN (1706-90), U.S. statesman, writer. *Epitaph on Himself*, in *Complete Works*, vol. 10 (ed. by John Bigelow, 1887-88). Composed in 1728, when Franklin was 22, it was not used on Franklin's monument. See Franklin on LIFE.

7 And were an epitaph to be my story
I'd have a short one ready for my own.
I would have written of me on my stone:
I had a lover's quarrel with the world.

ROBERT FROST (1874-1963), U.S. poet. *Lesson for Today*.

8 Oh, write of me, not "Died in bitter pains,"
But "Emigrated to another star!"

HELEN HUNT JACKSON (1830-85), U.S. writer, poet. *Emigravit*.

9 In lapidary inscriptions a man is not upon oath.

SAMUEL JOHNSON (1709-84), English author, lexicographer. Quoted in: James Boswell, *Life of Samuel Johnson*, 1775 (1791).

10 At last God caught his eye.

HARRY SECOMBE (b. 1921), Welsh comedian, singer. "Epitaph for a head waiter," in *Punch* (London, 17 May 1962).

11 When I die, my epitaph should read: *She Paid the Bills.* That's the story of my private life.

GLORIA SWANSON (1897-1983), U.S. screen actor. Quoted in: *Saturday Evening Post* (New York, 22 July 1950).

EQUALITY

1 The beginning of reform is not so much to equalize property as to train the noble sort of natures not to desire more, and to prevent the lower from getting more.

ARISTOTLE (384-322 B.C.), Greek philosopher. *Politics*, bk. 2, ch. 7, sct. 1267b (c. 343 B.C.).

2 Equality, in a social sense, may be divided into that of condition and that of rights. Equality of condition is incompatible with civilization, and is found only to exist in those communities that are but slightly removed from the savage state. In practice, it can only mean a common misery.

JAMES FENIMORE COOPER (1789-1851), U.S. novelist. *The American Democrat*, "On the Disadvantages of a Monarchy" (1838).

3 A commitment to sexual equality with males . . . is a commitment to becoming the rich instead of the poor, the rapist instead of the raped, the murderer instead of the murdered.

ANDREA DWORKIN (b. 1946), U.S. feminist critic. "Renouncing Sexual `Equality'," speech, 12 Oct. 1974, at the National Organization for Women Conference on Sexuality, New York City (published in *Our Blood*, ch. 2, 1976).

4 All this talk about equality. The only thing people really have in common is that they are all going to die.

BOB DYLAN (b. 1941), U.S. singer, songwriter. Remark, 1966. Quoted in: Robert Shelton, *No Direction Home*, ch. 1, "Kaddish" (1986).

5 When a bachelor of philosophy from the Antilles refuses to apply for certification as a teacher on the grounds of his color I say that philosophy has never saved anyone. When someone else strives and strains to prove to me that black men are as intelligent as white men I say that intelligence has never saved anyone: and that is true, for, if philosophy and intelligence are invoked to proclaim the equality of men, they have also been employed to justify the extermination of men.

FRANTZ FANON (1925-61), Martiniquan psychiatrist, philosopher, political activist. *Black Skins, White Masks*, Introduction (1952; tr. 1967).

6 Just as modern mass production requires the standardization of commodities, so the social process requires standardization of man, and this standardization is called equality.

> ERICH FROMM (1900-1980), U.S. psychologist. *The Art of Loving*, ch. 2 (1956).

7　That all men are equal is a proposition to which, at ordinary times, no sane human being has ever given his assent.

> ALDOUS HUXLEY (1894-1963), British author. *Proper Studies*, "The Idea of Equality" (1927).

8　Subordination tends greatly to human happiness. Were we all upon an equality, we should have no other enjoyment than mere animal pleasure.

> SAMUEL JOHNSON (1709-84), English author, lexicographer. Quoted in: James Boswell, *Life of Samuel Johnson* (1791).

9　The deadly Hydra now is the hydra of Equality. Liberty, Equality and Fraternity is the three-fanged serpent.

> D. H. LAWRENCE (1885-1930), British author. Letter, 16 July 1915, to philosopher Bertrand Russell (published in *The Letters of D. H. Lawrence*, vol. 2, ed. by George J. Zytaruk & James T. Boulton, 1981).

10　The intelligence suffers today automatically in consequence of the attack on all authority, advantage, or privilege. These things are not done away with, it is needless to say, but numerous scapegoats are made of the less politically powerful, to satisfy the egalitarian rage awakened.

> WYNDHAM LEWIS (1882-1957), British author, painter. *The Art of Being Ruled*, pt. 13, "The Politics of the Intellect" (1926).

11　If the worker and his boss enjoy the same television program and visit the same resort places, if the typist is as attractively made up as the daughter of her employer, if the Negro owns a Cadillac, if they all read the same newspaper, then this assimilation indicates not the disappearance of classes, but the extent to which the needs and satisfactions that serve the preservation of the Establishment are shared by the underlying population.

> HERBERT MARCUSE (1898-1979), U.S. political philosopher. *One-Dimensional Man*, ch. 1 (1964).

12　The doctrine of equality! . . . There exists no more poisonous poison: for it *seems* to be preached by justice itself, while it is the *end* of justice.

> FRIEDRICH NIETZSCHE (1844-1900), German philosopher. *Twilight of the Idols*, "Expeditions of an Untimely Man," aph. 48 (1889).

13　All animals are equal but some animals are more equal than others.

> GEORGE ORWELL (1903-50), British author. *Animal Farm*, ch. 10 (1945), the animals' Commandment at the end. The original version was, "All animals are equal."

14　No advance in wealth, no softening of manners, no reform or revolution has ever brought human equality a millimetre nearer.

> GEORGE ORWELL (1903-50), British author. *1984*, pt. 2, ch. 9 (1949), extract from Goldstein's book.

15　The trauma of the Sixties persuaded me that my generation's egalitarianism was a sentimental error. . . . I now see the hierarchical as both beautiful and necessary.

Efficiency liberates; egalitarianism tangles, delays, blocks, deadens.

> CAMILLE PAGLIA (b. 1947), U.S. author, critic, educator. *Sex, Art, and American Culture*, "Sexual Personae: The Cancelled Preface" (1992).

16　In America everybody is of opinion that he has no social superiors, since all men are equal, but he does not admit that he has no social inferiors.

> BERTRAND RUSSELL (1872-1970), British philosopher, mathematician. *Unpopular Essays*, ch. 10, "Ideas that Have Harmed Mankind" (1950).

17　We were equals once when we lay new-born babes on our nurse's knees. We will be equal again when they tie up our jaws for the last sleep.

> OLIVE SCHREINER (1855-1920), South African writer, feminist. Lyndall to Waldo, in *The Story of an African Farm*, pt. 2, ch. 4 (1883).

18　Between persons of equal income there is no social distinction except the distinction of merit. Money is nothing: character, conduct, and capacity are everything. . . . There would be great people and ordinary people and little people, but the great would always be those who had done great things, and never the idiots whose mothers had spoiled them and whose fathers had left them a hundred thousand a year; and the little would be persons of small minds and mean characters, and not poor persons who had never had a chance. That is why idiots are always in favour of inequality of income (their only chance of eminence), and the really great in favour of equality.

> GEORGE BERNARD SHAW (1856-1950), Anglo-Irish playwright, critic. *The Intelligent Woman's Guide to Socialism and Capitalism*, ch. 22 (1928).

19　Prosperity or egalitarianism—you have to choose. I favor freedom—you never achieve real equality anyway: you simply sacrifice prosperity for an illusion.

> MARIO VARGAS LLOSA (b. 1936), Peruvian novelist. *Independent on Sunday* (London, 5 May 1991).

20　Modern equalitarian societies . . . whether democratic or authoritarian in their political forms, always base themselves on the claim that they are making life happier. . . . Happiness thus becomes the chief political issue—in a sense, the only political issue—and for that reason it can never be treated as an issue at all.

> ROBERT WARSHOW (1917-55), U.S. author. "The Gangster as Tragic Hero," in *Partisan Review* (New Brunswick, N.J., 1948; repr. in *The Immediate Experience*, 1970).

21　Equality is the public recognition, effectively expressed in institutions and manners, of the principle that an equal degree of attention is due to the needs of all human beings.

> SIMONE WEIL (1909-43), French philosopher, mystic. "Draft for a Statement of Human Obligations" (published in *Selected Essays*, ed. by Richard Rees, 1962).

See also France on LAWS AND THE LAW.

EROTICISM

1 Eroticism is assenting to life even in death.

GEORGES BATAILLE (1897-1962), French novelist, critic. *Eroticism,* Introduction (1957).

2 Erotica is simply high-class pornography; better produced, better conceived, better executed, better packaged, designed for a better class of consumer.

ANDREA DWORKIN (b. 1946), U.S. feminist critic. *Pornography,* Preface (1981).

3 A man's eroticism is a woman's sexuality.

KARL KRAUS (1874-1936), Austrian satirist. *Sprüche und Widersprüche,* ch. 1 (1909; repr. in *Half-Truths and One-And-A Half-Truths: Selected Aphorisms,* "Not for Women but Against Men," ed. by Harry Zohn, 1976).

4 Eroticism is like a dance: one always leads the other.

MILAN KUNDERA (b. 1929), Czech author, critic. *Immortality,* pt. 3, "The Cat" (1991).

5 In this loveless everyday life eroticism is a substitute for love.

HENRI LEFEBVRE (b. 1901), French philosopher. *Everyday Life in the Modern World,* ch. 4 (1962).

6 Pornography is about dominance. Erotica is about mutuality.

GLORIA STEINEM (b. 1934), U.S. feminist writer, editor. *Outrageous Acts and Everyday Rebellions,* "Erotica vs Pornography," adapted from articles in *Ms.* (New York, Aug. 1977 and Nov. 1978).

7 The modern erotic ideal: man and woman in loving sexual embrace experiencing simultaneous orgasm through genital intercourse. This is a psychiatric-sexual myth useful for fostering feelings of sexual inadequacy and personal inferiority. It is also a rich source of "psychiatric patients."

THOMAS SZASZ (b. 1920), U.S. psychiatrist. *The Second Sin,* "Sex" (1973).

8 Eroticism has its own moral justification because it says that pleasure is enough for me; it is a statement of the individual's sovereignty.

MARIO VARGAS LLOSA (b. 1936), Peruvian novelist. *International Herald Tribune* (Paris, 23 Oct. 1990).

See also PORNOGRAPHY; SENSUALITY.

ERROR

1 An error is the more dangerous in proportion to the degree of truth which it contains.

HENRI-FRÉDÉRIC AMIEL (1821-81), Swiss philosopher, poet. *Journal Intime* (1882; tr. by Mrs. Humphrey Ward, 1892), entry for 12 Nov. 1852.

2 There exists a black kingdom which the eyes of man avoid because its landscape fails signally to flatter them. This darkness, which he imagines he can dispense with in describing the light, is error with its unknown characteristics. . . . Error is certainty's constant companion. Error is the corollary of evidence. And anything said about truth may equally well be said about error: the delusion will be no greater.

LOUIS ARAGON (1897-1982), French poet. *Paris Peasant,* "Preface to a Modern Mythology" (1926).

3 There is no original truth, only original error.

GASTON BACHELARD (1884-1962), French scientist, philosopher, literary theorist. *Fragments of a Poetics of Fire,* "A Retrospective Glance at the Lifework of a Master of Books" (1988; tr. 1990).

4 Every great mistake has a halfway moment, a split second when it can be recalled and perhaps remedied.

PEARL S. BUCK (1892-1973), U.S. author. *What America Means to Me,* ch. 10 (1942).

5 Mistakes are almost always of a sacred nature. Never try to correct them. On the contrary: rationalise them, understand them thoroughly. After that, it will be possible for you to sublimate them.

SALVADOR DALI (1904-89), Spanish painter. *Diary of a Genius* (1966), entry for 30 June 1952.

6 Truth is one, but error proliferates. Man tracks it down and cuts it up into little pieces hoping to turn it into grains of truth. But the ultimate atom will always essentially be an error, a miscalculation.

RENÉ DAUMAL (1908-44), French poet, critic. "The Lie of the Truth," *Essais et Notes,* vol. 2 (ed. by Claudio Rugafiori, 1972; repr. in *The Lie of The Truth,* tr. by Phil Powrie, 1989).

7 Error is a supposition that pleasure and pain, that intelligence, substance, life, are existent in matter. Error is neither Mind nor one of Mind's faculties. Error is the contradiction of Truth. Error is a belief without understanding. Error is unreal because untrue. It is that which seemeth to be and is not. If error were true, its truth would be error, and we should have a self-evident absurdity—namely, *erroneous truth.* Thus we should continue to lose the standard of Truth.

MARY BAKER EDDY (1821-1910), U.S. founder of the Christian Science movement. *Science and Health,* ch. 14 (1875).

8 Errors look so very ugly in persons of small means—one feels they are taking quite a liberty in going astray; whereas people of fortune may naturally indulge in a few delinquencies.

GEORGE ELIOT (1819-80), English novelist. *Janet's Repentance,* ch. 25 (first published in *Blackwood's Magazine,* 1857; repr. in *Scenes of Clerical Life,* 1858).

9 It is worse than a crime: it is a mistake.

Attributed to JOSEPH FOUCHÉ (1759-1820), French Minister of Police under Napoleon. Remark on the execution of the abducted royalist émigré, the Duc d'Enghien, at Vincennes, 21 March 1804. In his *Mémoires,* Fouché wrote, "Many are mistaken, few are blameworthy."

10 Mistakes are a fact of life
It is the response to error that counts.

NIKKI GIOVANNI (b. 1943), U.S. poet. *Of Liberation,* st. 16, in *Black Feeling/Black Talk/Black Judgement* (1970).

11 The road to wisdom?—Well, it's plain
and simple to express:
Err
and err

and err again
but less
and less
and less.

PIET HEIN (b. 1905), Dutch inventor, poet. *Grooks,* "The Road to Wisdom" (1966).

12 The greatest blunders, like the thickest ropes, are often compounded of a multitude of strands. Take the rope apart, separate it into the small threads that compose it, and you can break them one by one. You think, "That is all there was!" But twist them all together and you have something tremendous.

VICTOR HUGO (1802-85), French poet, dramatist, novelist. *Les Misérables,* pt. 2, bk. 5, ch. 10 (1862).

13 She had an unequalled gift . . . of squeezing big mistakes into small opportunities.

HENRY JAMES (1843-1916), U.S. author. "Greville Fane," in *Illustrated London News* (17 and 24 Sept. 1892; repr. in *The Real Thing and Other Tales,* 1893), of Fane's command of French and Italian.

14 That fellow seems to me to possess but one idea, and that is a wrong one.

SAMUEL JOHNSON (1709-84), English author, lexicographer. Quoted in: James Boswell, *Life of Samuel Johnson,* entry for 1770 (1791).

15 Mistakes are, after all, the foundations of truth, and if a man does not know what a thing *is,* it is at least an increase in knowledge if he knows what it is *not.*

CARL JUNG (1875-1961), Swiss psychiatrist. *Aion* (1951; repr. in *Collected Works,* vol. 9, pt. 2, para. 429, ed. by William McGuire, 1959).

16 People are so busy dreaming the American Dream, fantasizing about what they *could* be or have a *right* to be, that they're all asleep at the switch. Consequently we are living in the Age of Human Error.

FLORENCE KING (b. 1936), U.S. author. *Reflections in a Jaundiced Eye,* "The Age of Human Error" (1989).

17 To err is *human* also in so far as animals seldom or never err, or at least only the cleverest of them do so.

G. C. LICHTENBERG (1742-99), German physicist, philosopher. *Aphorisms,* "Notebook G," aph. 30 (written 1765-99; tr. by R. J. Hollingdale, 1990).

18 The study of error is not only in the highest degree prophylactic, but it serves as a stimulating introduction to the study of truth.

WALTER LIPPMANN (1889-1974), U.S. journalist. *Public Opinion,* ch. 17 (1922).

19 So long as a person who has made mistakes . . . honestly and sincerely wishes to be cured and to mend his ways, we should welcome him and cure his sickness so that he can become a good comrade. We can never succeed if we just let ourselves go and lash at him.

MAO ZEDONG (1893-1976), Founder of the People's Republic of China. Speech, 1965, Peking (published in *Selected Works,* vol. 3, p. 50).

20 What then in the last resort are the truths of mankind?—They are the *irrefutable* errors of mankind.

FRIEDRICH NIETZSCHE (1844-1900), German philosopher. *The Gay Science,* aph. 265 (rev. ed., 1887).

21 Falsity cannot keep an idea from being beautiful; there are certain errors of such ingenuity that one could regret their not ranking among the achievements of the human mind.

JEAN ROSTAND (1894-1977), French biologist, writer. *Pensées d'un Biologiste* (1939; repr. in *The Substance of Man,* "A Biologist's Thoughts," ch. 7, 1962).

22 It is sometimes well for a blatant error to draw attention to overmodest truths.

JEAN ROSTAND (1894-1977), French biologist, writer. *Pensées d'un Biologiste* (1939; repr. in *The Substance of Man,* "A Biologist's Thoughts," ch. 7, 1962).

23 Every epoch, under names more or less specious, has deified its peculiar errors.

PERCY BYSSHE SHELLEY (1792-1822), English poet. *A Defence of Poetry* (1840).

24 We often discover what will do, by finding out what will not do; and probably he who never made a mistake never made a discovery.

SAMUEL SMILES (1812-1904), Scottish author. *Self Help,* ch. 11 (1859).

25 The broadest and most prevalent error requires the most disinterested virtue to sustain it.

HENRY DAVID THOREAU (1817-62), U.S. philosopher, author, naturalist. *On the Duty of Civil Disobedience* (1849).

26 A poet can survive everything but a misprint.

OSCAR WILDE (1854-1900), Anglo-Irish playwright, author. *Pall Mall Gazette* (London, 14 Oct. 1886).

See also Huxley on FALLIBILITY; Eliot on OBSTINACY; Butler on TRUTH.

ESCAPISM

1 Hell is of this world and there are men who are unhappy escapees from hell, escapees destined ETERNALLY to reenact their escape.

ANTONIN ARTAUD (1896-1948), French theater producer, actor, theorist. *General Security: The Liquidation of Opium* (1925; repr. in *Selected Writings,* pt. 10, ed. by Susan Sontag, 1976).

2 The shortest way out of Manchester is notoriously a bottle of Gordon's gin; out of any businessman's life there is the mirage of Paris; out of Paris, or mediocrity of talent and imagination, there are all the drugs, from subtle, all-conquering opium to cheating, cozening cocaine.

WILLIAM BOLITHO (1890-1930), British author. *Twelve Against the Gods,* "Cagliostro (and Seraphina)" (1930).

3 Leave everything. Leave Dada. Leave your wife. Leave your mistress. Leave your hopes and fears. Leave your children in the woods. Leave the substance for the shadow. Leave your easy life, leave what you are given for the future. Set off on the roads.

ANDRÉ BRETON (1896-1966), French surrealist. *Les Pas Perdus,* "Lâchez tout!" (1924).

4 Man seeks to escape himself in myth, and does so by any means at his disposal. Drugs, alcohol, or lies. Unable to withdraw into himself, he disguises himself. Lies and inaccuracy give him a few moments of comfort.

JEAN COCTEAU (1889-1963), French author, filmmaker. *Diary of an Unknown*, "On Invisibility" (1953; tr. 1988).

5 Man staggers through life yapped at by his reason, pulled and shoved by his appetites, whispered to by fears, beckoned by hopes. Small wonder that what he craves most is self-forgetting.

ERIC HOFFER (1902-83), U.S. philosopher. *The Passionate State of Mind*, aph. 219 (1955).

6 There is a cheap literature that speaks to us of the need of escape. It is true that when we travel we are in search of distance. But distance is not to be found. It melts away. And escape has never led anywhere. The moment a man finds that he must play the races, go the Arctic, or make war in order to feel himself alive, that man has begin to spin the strands that bind him to other men and to the world. But what wretched strands! A civilization that is really strong fills man to the brim, though he never stir. What are we worth when motionless, is the question.

ANTOINE DE SAINT-EXUPÉRY (1900-1944), French aviator, author. *Flight to Arras*, ch. 12 (1942).

See also Mead on PROPHETS; Rushdie on STRESS.

THE ESTABLISHMENT

1 The worst enemy of good government is not our ignorant foreign voter, but our educated domestic railroad president, our prominent business man, our leading lawyer.

JOHN JAY CHAPMAN (1862-1933), U.S. author. *Practical Agitation*, ch. 2 (1898).

2 There is nothing more agreeable in life than to make peace with the Establishment—and nothing more corrupting.

A. J. P. TAYLOR (1906-90), British historian. "William Cobbett," in *New Statesman* (29 Aug. 1953).

ETERNITY

1 Eternity—waste of time.

NATALIE CLIFFORD BARNEY (1876-1972), U.S.-born French author. Quoted in: *Adam*, "Gods," no. 299 (London, 1962).

2 Eternity is in love with the productions of time.

WILLIAM BLAKE (1757-1827), English poet, painter, engraver. *The Marriage of Heaven and Hell*, Plate 7, "Proverbs of Hell" (1790-93; repr. in *Complete Writings*, ed. by Geoffrey Keynes, 1957).

3   *. . . L'eternité.*
            C'est la mer mêlée
                Au soleil.
(Eternity. It is the sea mingled with the sun.)

ARTHUR RIMBAUD (1854-91), French poet. *Delires II: Faim*, in *Une Saison en Enfer* (1874).

4 Death is not an event in life: we do not live to experience death. If we take eternity to mean not infinite temporal duration but timelessness, then eternal life belongs to those who live in the present.

LUDWIG WITTGENSTEIN (1889-1951), Austrian philosopher. *Tractatus Logico-Philosophicus*, sct. 6:4311 (1921, tr. 1922).

See also IMMORTALITY.

ETHICS

1 Everywhere, the ethical predicament of our time imposes itself with an urgency which suggests that even the question "Have we anything to eat?" will be answered not in material but in ethical terms.

HUGO BALL (1886-1927), German Dadaist poet. Quoted in: Hans Richter, *Dada: Art and Anti-Art*, ch. 1, "The Language of Paradise" (1964).

2 Ethics is in origin the art of recommending to others the sacrifices required for cooperation with oneself.

BERTRAND RUSSELL (1872-1970), British philosopher, mathematician. *A Free Man's Worship and Other Essays*, ch. 6 (1976).

3 No artist has ethical sympathies. An ethical sympathy in an artist is an unpardonable mannerism of style.

OSCAR WILDE (1854-1900), Anglo-Irish playwright, author. *The Picture of Dorian Gray*, Preface (1891).

ETIQUETTE

1 He who observes etiquette but objects to lying is like someone who dresses fashionably but wears no vest.

WALTER BENJAMIN (1892-1940), German critic, philosopher. *One-Way Street*, "Fancy Goods" (1928; repr. in *One-Way Street and Other Writings*, 1978).

2 Nothing more rapidly inclines a person to go into a monastery than reading a book on etiquette. There are so many trivial ways in which it is possible to commit some social sin.

QUENTIN CRISP (b. 1908), British author. *Manners from Heaven*, ch. 1 (1984).

3 A commercial society whose members are essentially ascetic and indifferent in social ritual has to be provided with blueprints and specifications for evoking the right tone for every occasion.

MARSHALL MCLUHAN (1911-80), Canadian communications theorist. *The Mechanical Bride*, "Emily Post" (1951).

4 Those who have mastered etiquette, who are entirely, impeccably right, would seem to arrive at a point of exquisite dullness.

DOROTHY PARKER (1893-1967), U.S. humorous writer. "Mrs. Post Enlarges on Etiquette," in *The New Yorker* (31 Dec. 1927; repr. in *The Portable Dorothy Parker*, pt. 2, 1944; rev. 1973).

5 Perfect behavior is born of complete indifference.

CESARE PAVESE (1908-50), Italian poet, novelist, translator. *The Burning Brand: Diaries 1935-1950* (1952; tr. 1961), entry for 21 Feb. 1940.

EUROPE

1   Whoever speaks of Europe is wrong: it is a geographical expression.

> OTTO VON BISMARCK (1815-98), Prussian statesman. Marginal comment on a letter, Nov. 1876, from the Russian Chancellor Gorchakov.

2   Whatever else may divide us, Europe is our common home; a common fate has linked us through the centuries, and it continues to link us today.

> LEONID BREZHNEV (1906-82), Soviet leader. Speech, 23 Nov. 1981, Bonn, Germany.

3   There is no freedom in Europe—that's certain—it is besides a worn out portion of the globe.

> LORD BYRON (1788-1824), English poet. Letter, 3 Oct. 1819 (published in *Byron's Letters and Journals,* vol. 6, ed. by Leslie A. Marchand, 1976).

4   Europe has lived on its contradictions, flourished on its differences, and, constantly transcending itself thereby, has created a civilization on which the whole world depends even when rejecting it. This is why I do not believe in a Europe unified under the weight of an ideology or of a technocracy that overlooked these differences.

> ALBERT CAMUS (1913-60), French-Algerian philosopher, author. Interview in *Demain* (Paris, 24 Oct. 1957; repr. as "The Wager of Our Generation," in *Resistance, Rebellion and Death,* 1961).

5   Intimately concerned as we are with the system of Europe, it does not follow that we are therefore called upon to mix ourselves on every occasion, with a restless and meddling activity, in the concerns of the nations which surround us.

> GEORGE CANNING (1770-1827), English statesman, prime minister. Speech, 28 Oct. 1823.

6   We are asking the nations of Europe between whom rivers of blood have flowed to forget the feuds of a thousand years.

> SIR WINSTON CHURCHILL (1874-1965), British statesman, writer. Speech, 14 Feb. 1948.

7   If you live in Europe . . . things change . . . but continuity never seems to break. You don't have to throw the past away.

> NADINE GORDIMER (b. 1923), South African author. Madame Bagnelli, in *Burger's Daughter,* pt. 2 (1979).

8   Their Europeanism is nothing but imperialism with an inferiority complex.

> DENIS HEALEY (b. 1917), British Labour politician. Quoted in: *Observer* (London, 7 Oct. 1962), referring to the Conservative Party.

9   Europe is so well gardened that it resembles a work of art, a scientific theory, a neat metaphysical system. Man has re-created Europe in his own image.

> ALDOUS HUXLEY (1894-1963), British author. *Do What You Will,* "Wordsworth in the Tropics" (1929).

10   I doubt that the evil spirits of the past, under which we in Europe have already suffered more than enough this century, have been banished for ever.

> HELMUT KOHL (b. 1930), German politician, Chancellor. *Independent* (London, 28 Oct. 1992).

11   War and culture, those are the two poles of Europe, her heaven and hell, her glory and shame, and they cannot be separated from one another. When one comes to an end, the other will end also and one cannot end without the other. The fact that no war has broken out in Europe for fifty years is connected in some mysterious way with the fact that for fifty years no new Picasso has appeared either.

> MILAN KUNDERA (b. 1929), Czech author, critic. Paul, in *Immortality,* pt. 3, "The Brilliant Ally of his own Gravediggers" (1991).

12   When an American heiress wants to buy a man, she at once crosses the Atlantic. The only really materialistic people I have ever met have been Europeans.

> MARY MCCARTHY (1912-89), U.S. author, critic. "America the Beautiful" (first published in *Commentary,* Sept. 1947; repr. in *On the Contrary,* 1961).

13   That grand drama in a hundred acts, which is reserved for the next two centuries of Europe—the most terrible, most questionable and perhaps also the most hopeful of all dramas . . .

> FRIEDRICH NIETZSCHE (1844-1900), German philosopher. *The Genealogy of Morals,* Essay 3, aph. 27 (1887; tr. 1899).

14   I am writing to resist the view that Europe and civilization are going to Hell. If I am being "crucified for an idea"—that is, the coherent idea around which my muddles accumulated—it is probably the idea that European culture ought to survive, that the best qualities of it ought to survive along with whatever cultures, in whatever universality. Against the propaganda of terror and the propaganda of luxury, have you a nice simple answer?

> EZRA POUND (1885-1972), U.S. poet, critic. Interview in *Writers at Work* (Second Series, ed. by George Plimpton, 1963).

15   The Federated Republic of Europe—the United States of Europe—that is what must be. National autonomy no longer suffices. Economic evolution demands the abolition of national frontiers. If Europe is to remain split into national groups, then Imperialism will recommence its work. Only a Federated Republic of Europe can give peace to the world.

> LEON TROTSKY (1879-1940), Russian revolutionary. Conversation, 30 Oct. 1917, at Smolny, Petrograd, reported by John Reed in *Ten Days That Shook the World,* ch. 3 (1926)

See also West on BEARDS; Bush on The COLD WAR; Fisher on RACE.

EASTERN EUROPE

1   There is no Soviet domination of Eastern Europe and there never will be under this administration.

> GERALD R. FORD (b. 1913), U.S. president. TV debate, 6 Oct. 1976, with presidential contender Jimmy Carter.

2   We are finding out that what looked like a neglected house a year ago is in fact a ruin.

> VÁCLAV HAVEL (b. 1936), Czech playwright, president. *Daily Telegraph* (London, 3 Jan. 1991), on the state of Czechoslovakia and other ex-Soviet Bloc countries.

3   All free men, wherever they may live, are citizens of Berlin, and therefore, as a free man, I take pride in the words, *Ich bin ein Berliner.*

> JOHN F. KENNEDY (1917-63), U.S. Democratic politician, president. Speech, 26 June 1963, West Berlin, Germany. Quoted in: Theodore C. Sorenson, *Kennedy,* pt. 5, ch. 21 (1965).

4   The era of long parades past an official podium filled with cold faces is gone. Celebrating is now a right, not a duty.

> LOTHAR DE MAIZIÈRE (b. 1940), German lawyer, politician. Speech on May Day, while East German Prime Minister. Quoted in: *Independent* (London, 5 May 1990).

5   Reality has become so absorbing that the streets, the television, and the journals have confiscated the public interest and people are no longer thirsty for culture on a higher level.

> ANDRE PLESU (b. 1948), Romanian culture minister. *International Herald Tribune* (Paris, 14 Nov. 1990).

See also Goebbels on The COLD WAR; Konrád on COMMUNISM; Havel on OPPRESSION.

EUROPE AND AMERICA

1   The heritage of the American Revolution is forgotten, and the American government, for better and for worse, has entered into the heritage of Europe as though it were its patrimony—unaware, alas, of the fact that Europe's declining power was preceded and accompanied by political bankruptcy, the bankruptcy of the nation-state and its concept of sovereignty.

> HANNAH ARENDT (1906-75), German-born U.S. political philosopher. *Crises of the Republic,* "On Violence," sct. 1 (1972).

2   Europe has what we do not have yet, a sense of the mysterious and inexorable limits of life, a sense, in a word, of tragedy. And we have what they sorely need: a sense of life's possibilities.

> JAMES BALDWIN (1924-87), U.S. author. *Nobody Knows My Name,* "The Discovery of What it Means to Be an American" (1961).

3   The confrontation between America and Europe reveals not so much a rapprochement as a distortion, an unbridgeable rift. There isn't just a gap between us, but a whole chasm of modernity.

> JEAN BAUDRILLARD (b. 1929), French semiologist. *America,* "Astral America" (1986; tr. 1988).

4   Until now when we have started to talk about the uniqueness of America we have almost always ended by comparing ourselves to Europe. Toward her we have felt all the attraction and repulsions of Oedipus.

> DANIEL J. BOORSTIN (b. 1914), U.S. historian. *America and The Image Of Europe,* Foreword (1960).

5   I've come to think of Europe as a hardcover book, America as the paperback version.

> DON DELILLO (b. 1926), U.S. author. Owen Brademas, in *The Names,* ch. 1 (1982).

6   Can we never extract the tapeworm of Europe from the brain of our countrymen?

> RALPH WALDO EMERSON (1803-82), U.S. essayist, poet, philosopher. *The Conduct of Life,* "Culture" (1860).

7   We go to Europe to be Americanized.

> RALPH WALDO EMERSON (1803-82), U.S. essayist, poet, philosopher. *The Conduct of Life,* "Culture" (1860).

8   In Europe life is histrionic and dramatized, and . . . in America, except when it is trying to be European, it is direct and sincere.

> WILLIAM DEAN HOWELLS (1837-1920), U.S. novelist, critic. "Their Silver Wedding Journey," in *Harper's* (New York, Sept. 1899).

9   It's a complex fate, being an American, and one of the responsibilities it entails is fighting against a superstitious valuation of Europe.

> HENRY JAMES (1843-1916), U.S. author. Letter, 4 Feb. 1872, to editor Charles Eliot Norton (published in *Henry James Letters,* vol. 1, ed. by Leon Edel, 1974).

10   It seems the natural thing for us to listen whilst the Europeans talk.

> WILLIAM JAMES (1842-1910), U.S. psychologist, philosopher. *The Varieties of Religious Experience,* Lecture 1 (1902).

11   I have ever deemed it fundamental for the United States never to take active part in the quarrels of Europe. Their political interests are entirely distinct from ours. Their mutual jealousies, their balance of power, their complicated alliances, their forms and principles of government, are all foreign to us. They are nations of eternal war.

> THOMAS JEFFERSON (1743-1826), U.S. president. Letter, 11 June 1823, to President James Monroe, six months before the formulation of U.S. foreign policy in the Monroe Doctrine.

12   I should think the American admiration of five-minute tourists has done more to kill the sacredness of old European beauty and aspiration than multitudes of bombs would have done.

> D. H. LAWRENCE (1885-1930), British author. *Studies in Classic American Literature,* ch. 4 (1924).

13   Europe's the mayonnaise, but America supplies the good old lobster.

> D. H. LAWRENCE (1885-1930), British author. *The Lovely Lady,* "Things" (1933).

14   People nowadays have such high hopes of America and the political conditions obtaining there that one might say the desires, at least the secret desires, of all enlightened Europeans are *deflected to the west,* like our magnetic needles.

> G. C. LICHTENBERG (1742-99), German physicist, philosopher. *Aphorisms,* "Notebook G," aph. 2 (written 1765-99; tr. by R. J. Hollingdale, 1990).

15   The immense popularity of American movies abroad demonstrates that Europe is the unfinished negative of which America is the proof.

> MARY MCCARTHY (1912-89), U.S. author, critic. "America the Beautiful" (first published in *Commentary,* Sept. 1947; repr. in *On the Contrary,* 1961).

16 It would be about as easy for an American to become a Chinaman or a Hindoo as for him to acquire an Englishness or a Frenchness or a European-ness that is more than half skin deep.

EZRA POUND (1885-1972), U.S. poet, critic. *New Age* (London, 14 Nov. 1912).

17 In European thought in general, as contrasted with American, vigor, life and originality have a kind of easy, professional utterance. American—on the other hand, is expressed in an eager amateurish way. A European gives a sense of scope, of survey, of consideration. An American is strained, sensational. One is artistic gold; the other is bullion.

WALLACE STEVENS (1879-1955), U.S. poet. *Letters of Wallace Stevens*, no. 112 (ed. by Holly Stevens, 1967), entry for 9 April 1906.

18 As a rule we develop a borrowed European idea forward, and . . . Europe develops a borrowed American idea backwards.

MARK TWAIN (1835-1910), U.S. author. *Complete Essays*, "Some National Stupidities" (ed. by Charles Neider, 1963).

19 Europe has a set of primary interests, which to us have none, or a very remote relation. Hence she must be engaged in frequent controversies, the causes of which are essentially foreign to our concerns. Hence, therefore, it must be unwise in us to implicate ourselves, by artificial ties, in the ordinary vicissitudes of her politics or the ordinary combinations and collisions of her friendships or enmities.

GEORGE WASHINGTON (1732-99), U.S. general, president. Farewell address, 17 Sept. 1796. Europe was at this time embroiled in the Napoleonic Wars.

20 The Yanks have colonized our subconscious.

WIM WENDERS (b. 1945), German filmmaker. Robert Lander (Hans Zischler), in the film *Kings of the Road* (1976).

See also Baudrillard on CULTURE; Auden on FACES; Reston on JOURNALISM AND JOURNALISTS.

EUTHANASIA

1 Euthanasia is a long, smooth-sounding word, and it conceals its danger as long, smooth words do, but the danger is there, nevertheless.

PEARL S. BUCK (1892-1973), U.S. author. *The Child Who Never Grew*, ch. 2 (1950).

2 To die proudly when it is no longer possible to live proudly. Death of one's own free choice, death at the proper time, with a clear head and with joyfulness, consummated in the midst of children and witnesses: so that an actual leave-taking is possible while he who is leaving *is still there*.

FRIEDRICH NIETZSCHE (1844-1900), German philosopher. *Twilight of the Idols*, "Expeditions of an Untimely Man," aph. 36 (1889).

3 Just as I shall select my ship when I am about to go on a voyage, or my house when I propose to take a resi-

dence, so I shall choose my death when I am about to depart from life.

SENECA (c. 5 B.C.-A.D. c. 65), Roman writer, philosopher, statesman. *Epistulae ad Lucilium*, Epistle 70, sct. 11.

4 O, let him pass. He hates him
That would upon the rack of this tough world
Stretch him out longer.

WILLIAM SHAKESPEARE (1564-1616), English dramatist, poet. Kent, in *King Lear*, act 5, sc. 3.

EVANGELISM

1 Why should I apologize because God throws in crystal chandeliers, mahogany floors, and the best construction in the world?

JIM BAKKER (b. 1940), U.S. evangelist. Quoted in: *New Yorker* (23 April 1990), said of his luxury religious center, Heritage U.S.A.

2 For we wrestle not against flesh and blood, but against principalities, against powers, against the rules of the darkness of this world, against spiritual wickedness in high places.

BIBLE: NEW TESTAMENT. St. Paul in *Ephesians 6:12*.

3 In soliciting donations from his flock, a preacher may promise eternal life in a celestial city whose streets are paved with gold, and that's none of the law's business. But if he promises an annual free stay in a luxury hotel on Earth, he'd better have the rooms available.

Charlotte Observer (6 Oct. 1989), commenting on the prosecution of local televangelist Jim Bakker on charges of fraud and conspiracy.

4 There is no arguing with the pretenders to a divine knowledge and to a divine mission. They are possessed with the sin of pride, they have yielded to the perennial temptation.

WALTER LIPPMANN (1889-1974), U.S. journalist. *The Public Philosophy*, ch. 7, sct. 5.

5 In full view of his television audience, he preached a new religion—or a new form of Christianity—based on faith in financial miracles and in a Heaven here on earth with a water slide and luxury hotels. It was a religion of celebrity and showmanship and fun, which made a mockery of all puritanical standards and all canons of good taste. Its standard was excess, and its doctrines were tolerance and freedom from accountability.

New Yorker (23 April 1990), on televangelist Jim Bakker.

6 Nothing makes one so vain as being told that one is a sinner.

OSCAR WILDE (1854-1900), Anglo-Irish playwright, author. Lord Henry, in *The Picture of Dorian Gray*, ch. 8 (1891).

7 God is definitely out of the closet.

MARIANNE WILLIAMSON (b. 1953), U.S. benefactor. Quoted in: *Vanity Fair* (New York, June 1991).

EVENTS

1 A society which allows an abominable event to burgeon from its dungheap and grow on its surface is like a man who lets a fly crawl unheeded across his face or saliva dribble unstemmed from his mouth—either epileptic or dead.

> JEAN BAUDRILLARD (b. 1929), French semiologist. *Cool Memories*, ch. 4 (1987; tr. 1990).

2 In the world we live in . . . everything militates in favor of things that have not yet happened, of things that will never happen again.

> ANDRÉ BRETON (1896-1966), French Surrealist. *Surrealism and Painting* (1928).

3 The enemy of the conventional wisdom is not ideas but the march of events.

> JOHN KENNETH GALBRAITH (b. 1908), U.S. economist. Quoted in: *The Affluent Society* (1958; introduction to 1977 ed.).

4 Like a kick in the butt, the force of events wakes slumberous talents.

> EDWARD HOAGLAND (b. 1932), U.S. novelist, essayist. *Guardian* (London, 11 Aug. 1990).

5 One of the extraordinary things about human events is that the unthinkable becomes thinkable.

> SALMAN RUSHDIE (b. 1948), Indian-born British author. Interview in *Guardian* (London, 8 Nov. 1990).

6 The great events of life often leave one unmoved; they pass out of consciousness, and, when one thinks of them, become unreal. Even the scarlet flowers of passion seem to grow in the same meadow as the poppies of oblivion.

> OSCAR WILDE (1854-1900), Anglo-Irish playwright, author. Erskine, in *The Portrait of Mr. W. H.*, ch. 1 (first published in *Blackwood's Edinburgh Magazine*, July 1889).

EVIL

1 The trouble with Eichmann was precisely that so many were like him, and that the many were neither perverted nor sadistic, that they were, and still are, terribly and terrifyingly normal. From the viewpoint of our legal institutions and of our moral standards of judgment, this normality was much more terrifying than all the atrocities put together.

> HANNAH ARENDT (1906-75), German-born U.S. political philosopher. *Eichmann in Jerusalem*, Epilogue (1963).

2 Evil is unspectacular and always human,
And shares our bed and eats at our own table.

> W. H. AUDEN (1907-73), Anglo-American poet. *Herman Melville*, st. 4.

3 Evil is done without effort, *naturally*, it is the working of fate; good is always the product of an art.

> CHARLES BAUDELAIRE (1821-67), French poet. "The Painter of Modern Life," sct. 11, published in *L'Art Romantique* (1869; repr. in *Selected Writings on Art and Artists*, ed. by P. E. Charvet, 1972).

4 There are evils . . . that have the ability to survive identification and go on for ever . . . money, for instance, or war.

> SAUL BELLOW (b. 1915), U.S. novelist. Albert Corde, in *The Dean's December*, ch. 13 (1982).

5 Nothing in the nature around us is evil. This needs to be repeated since one of the human ways of *talking oneself into* inhuman acts is to cite the supposed cruelty of nature.

> JOHN BERGER (b. 1926), British author, critic. "Muck and Its Entanglements," in *Harper's* (New York, May 1989; repr. as "A Load of Shit," in *Keeping a Rendezvous*, 1992).

6 The surest defense against Evil is extreme individualism, originality of thinking, whimsicality, even—if you will—eccentricity. That is, something that can't be feigned, faked, imitated; something even a seasoned imposter couldn't be happy with.

> JOSEPH BRODSKY (b. 1940), Russian-born U.S. poet, critic. *Less Than One: Selected Essays*, "A Commencement Address" (1986; delivered at Williams College, 1984).

7 Evil is like water, it abounds, is cheap, soon fouls, but runs itself clear of taint.

> SAMUEL BUTLER (1835-1902), English author. *Samuel Butler's Notebooks* (1951, p. 223).

8 We may draw good out of evil; we must not do evil, that good may come.

> MARIA WESTON CHAPMAN (1806-85), U.S. abolitionist. "How Can I Help to Abolish Slavery," speech, New York, 1855.

9 Man must vanquish himself, must do himself violence, in order to perform the slightest action untainted by evil.

> E. M. CIORAN (b. 1911), Rumanian-born French philosopher. *The New Gods*, "The Demiurge" (1969; tr. 1974).

10 The belief in a supernatural source of evil is not necessary; men alone are quite capable of every wickedness.

> JOSEPH CONRAD (1857-1924), Polish-born English novelist. The "dame de compagnie," in *Under Western Eyes*, pt. 2, ch. 4 (1911).

11 The pious pretence that evil does not exist only makes it vague, enormous and menacing.

> ALEISTER CROWLEY (1875-1947), British occultist. *The Confessions of Aleister Crowley*, ch. 33 (1929; rev. 1970).

12 Evil be to him who evil thinks.

> EDWARD III (1312-77), King of England (1327-77). Quoted in: Polydore Vergil, *Anglicae Historiae*. Alleged remark at the falling of the Countess of Salisbury's garter, presumably when the order of Garter was founded in 1344: no contemporary evidence whatsoever, but the traditional tale was current in Henry VIII's reign.

13 No evil dooms us hopelessly except the evil we love, and desire to continue in, and make no effort to escape from.

> GEORGE ELIOT (1819-80), English novelist, editor. *Daniel Deronda*, bk. 7, ch. 57 (1876).

14 So far as we are human, what we do must be either evil or good: so far as we do evil or good, we are human: and it is better, in a paradoxical way, to do evil than to do nothing: at least we exist.

> T. S. ELIOT (1888-1965), Anglo-American poet, critic. *The Inti-*

mate *Journals of Charles Baudelaire,* "Baudelaire," Introduction (tr. by Christopher Isherwood, 1930; repr. in *Selected Prose of T. S. Eliot,* ed. by Frank Kermode, 1975.

15 Nature, more of a stepmother than a mother in several ways, has sown a seed of evil in the hearts of mortals, especially in the more thoughtful men, which makes them dissatisfied with their own lot and envious of another's.

DESIDERIUS ERASMUS (c. 1466-1536), Dutch humanist. *Praise of Folly,* ch. 22 (1509).

16. Must I do all the evil I can before I learn to shun it? Is it not enough to know the evil to shun it? If not, we should be sincere enough to admit that we love evil too well to give it up.

MOHANDAS K. GANDHI (1869-1948), Indian political and spiritual leader. *Non-Violence in Peace and War,* vol. 2, ch. 74 (1949).

17 There surely is in human nature an inherent propensity to extract all the good out of all the evil.

BENJAMIN HAYDON (1786-1846), British artist. "Table Talk," in *Correspondence and Table-Talk,* vol. 2 (ed. by Frederic Wordsworth Haydon, 1876).

18 Some people show evil as a great racehorse shows breeding. They have the dignity of a hard chancre.

ERNEST HEMINGWAY (1899-1961), U.S. author. *A Moveable Feast,* ch. 12 (1964).

19 But evil is wrought by want of Thought
As well as want of Heart!

THOMAS HOOD (1799-1845), English poet. *The Lady's Dream.*

20 There is hardly a man clever enough to recognize the full extent of the evil he does.

FRANÇOIS, DUC DE LA ROCHEFOUCAULD (1613-80), French writer, moralist. *Sentences et Maximes Morales,* no. 269 (1678).

21 It is a power stronger than will. . . . Could a stone escape from the laws of gravity? Impossible. Impossible, for evil to form an alliance with good.

ISIDORE DUCASSE, COMTE DE LAUTRÉAMONT (1846-70), French author, poet. *Maldoror,* bk. 1, ch. 3 (1870; tr. 1978).

22 This is the very worst wickedness, that we refuse to acknowledge the passionate evil that is in us. This makes us secret and rotten.

D. H. LAWRENCE (1885-1930), British author. Letter, 8 April 1915 (published in *The Letters of D. H. Lawrence,* vol. 2, ed. by George J. Zytaruk and James T. Boulton, 1981).

23 We are tainted by modern philosophy which has taught us that *all is good,* whereas evil has polluted everything and in a very real sense *all is evil,* since nothing is in its proper place.

JOSEPH DE MAISTRE (1753-1821), French diplomat, philosopher. *Considerations on France,* ch. 3 (1796; repr. in *The Works of Joseph de Maistre,* ed. by Jack Lively, 1965).

24 If there was no moral evil upon earth, there would be no physical evil.

JOSEPH DE MAISTRE (1753-1821), French diplomat, philosopher. The Count, in *Les Soirées de Saint-Pétersbourg,* "First Dialogue" (1821; repr. in *The Works of Joseph de Maistre,* ed. by Jack Lively, 1965).

25 Evil is something you recognise immediately you see it: it works through charm.

BRIAN MASTERS (b. 1939), British author. *Daily Telegraph* (London, 31 May 1991).

26 There is no explanation for evil. It must be looked upon as a necessary part of the order of the universe. To ignore it is childish, to bewail it senseless.

W. SOMERSET MAUGHAM (1874-1965), British author. *The Summing Up,* ch. 73 (1938).

27 But what is the greatest evil? If you are going to epitomize evil, what is it? Is it the bomb? The greatest evil that one has to fight constantly, every minute of the day until one dies, is the worse part of oneself.

PATRICK MCGOOHAN (b. 1928), Anglo-American actor. Quoted in: Dave Rogers, *The Prisoner and Danger Man,* "I Am Not a Number, I Am a Free Man" (1989).

28 What wisdom can there be to choose, what continence to forbear without the knowledge of evil? He that can apprehend and consider vice with all her baits and seeming pleasures, and yet abstain, and yet distinguish, and yet prefer that which is truly better, he is the true warfaring Christian.

JOHN MILTON (1608-74), English poet. *Areopagitica: a Speech for the Liberty of Unlicensed Printing to the Parliament of England* (1644).

29 I couldn't claim that I have never felt the urge to explore evil, but when you descend into hell you have to be very careful.

KATHLEEN RAINE (b. 1908), British poet. *Times* (London, 18 April 1992).

30 All histories do shew, and wise politicians do hold it necessary that, for the well-governing of every Commonweal, it behoveth man to presuppose that all men are evil, and will declare themselves so to be when occasion is offered.

SIR WALTER RALEGH (1552-1618), English author, soldier, explorer. *The Cabinet Council,* ch. 25, "A Collection of Political Observations," (1751; repr. in *The Works of Sir Walter Raleigh,* vol. 1).

31 *Evil* is . . . a moral entity and not a created one, an eternal and not a perishable entity: it existed before the world; it constituted the monstruous, the execrable being who was also to fashion such a hideous world. It will hence exist after the creatures which people this world.

MARQUIS DE SADE (1740-1814), French author. Saint-Fond, in *L'Histoire de Juliette, ou les Prospérités du Vice,* pt. 2 (1797).

32 Only among people who think no evil can Evil monstrously flourish.

LOGAN PEARSALL SMITH (1865-1946), U.S. essayist, aphorist. *Afterthoughts,* "Other People" (1931).

33 Evil is neither suffering nor sin; it is both at the same time, it is something common to them both. For they are linked together; sin makes us suffer and suffering makes us evil, and this indissoluble complex of suffering and sin is the evil in which we are submerged against our will, and to our horror.

SIMONE WEIL (1909-43), French philosopher, mystic. "Some

Thoughts on the Love of God" (Oct. 1940-May 1942; published in *On Science, Necessity, and the Love of God*, ed. by Richard Rees, 1968).

34 When choosing between two evils, I always like to pick the one I never tried before.

MAE WEST (1892-1980), U.S. screen actor. As Frisco Doll, in the film *Klondike Annie* (1936).

See also WICKEDNESS.

EVOLUTION

1 Man has lost the basic skill of the ape, the ability to scratch its back. Which gave it extraordinary independence, and the liberty to associate for reasons other than the need for mutual back-scratching.

JEAN BAUDRILLARD (b. 1929), French semiologist. *Cool Memories*, ch. 5 (1987; tr. 1990).

2 The question is this—Is man an ape or an angel? My Lord, I am on the side of the angels. I repudiate with indignation and abhorrence these new fangled theories.

BENJAMIN DISRAELI (1804-81), English statesman, author. Speech, 25 Nov. 1864, Diocesan Conference, Oxford.

3 Natural selection, as it has operated in human history, favors not only the clever but the murderous.

BARBARA EHRENREICH (b. 1941), U.S. author, columnist. *The Worst Years of Our Lives*, "Iranscam: Oliver North and the Warrior Caste" (1991).

4 It is curious how there seems to be an instinctive disgust in Man for his nearest ancestors and relations. If only Darwin could conscientiously have traced man back to the Elephant or the Lion or the Antelope, how much ridicule and prejudice would have been spared to the doctrine of Evolution.

HAVELOCK ELLIS (1859-1939), British psychologist. *Impressions and Comments* (1914), entry for 8 May 1913.

5 While Darwinian Man, though well-behaved,
At best is only a monkey shaved!

W. S. GILBERT (1836-1911), English librettist. Lady Psyche, in *Princess Ida*, act 2.

6 God . . . created a number of possibilities in case some of his prototypes failed—that is the meaning of evolution.

GRAHAM GREENE (1904-91), British novelist. Mr. Visconti, in *Travels With My Aunt*, pt. 2, ch. 7 (1969).

7 The prehuman creature from which man evolved was unlike any other living thing in its malicious viciousness toward its own kind. . . . Humanization was not a leap forward but a groping toward survival.

ERIC HOFFER (1902-83), U.S. philosopher. *Reflections on the Human Condition*, aph. 19 (1973).

8 Historians will have to face the fact that natural selection determined the evolution of cultures in the same manner as it did that of species.

KONRAD LORENZ (1903-89), Austrian ethologist. *On Aggression*, "Ecce Homo!," ch. 13 (1963; tr. 1966).

9 We live between two worlds; we soar in the atmosphere; we creep upon the soil; we have the aspirations of creators and the propensities of quadrupeds. There can be but one explanation of this fact. We are passing from the animal into a higher form, and the drama of this planet is in its second act.

W. WINWOOD READE (1838-75), English traveler, author. *The Martyrdom of Man*, ch. 3, "Materials of Human History" (1872).

10. Organic life, we are told, has developed gradually from the protozoon to the philosopher, and this development, we are assured, is indubitably an advance. Unfortunately it is the philosopher, not the protozoon, who gives us this assurance.

BERTRAND RUSSELL (1872-1970), British philosopher, mathematician. *Mysticism and Logic*, ch. 6 (1917).

11 An extra-terrestrial philosopher, who had watched a single youth up to the age of twenty-one and had never come across any other human being, might conclude that it is the nature of human beings to grow continually taller and wiser in an indefinite progress towards perfection; and this generalisation would be just as well founded as the generalisation which evolutionists base upon the previous history of this planet.

BERTRAND RUSSELL (1872-1970), British philosopher, mathematician. *A Free Man's Worship and Other Essays*, ch. 6 (1976).

12 It is disturbing to discover in oneself these curious revelations of the validity of the Darwinian theory. If it is true that we have sprung from the ape, there are occasions when my own spring appears not to have been very far.

CORNELIA OTIS SKINNER (1901-79), U.S. author, actor. *The Ape in Me*, "The Ape in Me" (1959).

13 The more specific idea of Evolution now reached is—a change from an indefinite, incoherent homogeneity to a definite, coherent heterogeneity, accompanying the dissipation of motion and integration of matter.

HERBERT SPENSER (1820-1903), English philosopher. *First Principles*, vol. 1, pt. 2, ch. 16, para. 138 (1862).

14 The historic ascent of humanity, taken as a whole, may be summarized as a succession of victories of consciousness over blind forces—in nature, in society, in man himself.

LEON TROTSKY (1879-1940), Russian revolutionary. *The History of the Russian Revolution*, vol. 3, "Conclusions" (1933).

15 Evolution is the law of policies: Darwin said it, Socrates endorsed it, Cuvier proved it and established it for all time in his paper on "The Survival of the Fittest." These are illustrious names, this is a mighty doctrine: nothing can ever remove it from its firm base, nothing dissolve it, but evolution.

MARK TWAIN (1835-1910), U.S. author. "Three Thousand Years Among the Microbes," ch. 8, in *Which Was the Dream?* (ed. by John S. Tuckey, 1967).

16 We are the products of editing, rather than of authorship.

GEORGE WALD (b. 1906), U.S. biochemist. "The Origin of Optical Activity," in *Annals of the New York Academy of Sciences*, vol. 69 (1957).

17 Biologically the species is the accumulation of the experiments of all its successful individuals since the beginning.

> H. G. WELLS (1866-1946), British author. *A Modern Utopia*, ch. 3, sct. 4 (1905; repr. in *The Works of H. G. Wells*, vol. 9, 1925).

See also Vonnegut on INTELLIGENCE.

EXAGGERATION

1 An element of exaggeration clings to the popular judgment: great vices are made greater, great virtues greater also; interesting incidents are made more interesting, softer legends more soft.

> WALTER BAGEHOT (1826-77), English economist, critic. "The Waverley Novels" (1858; repr. in *Literary Studies,* vol. 2, 1878).

2 It is only a short step from exaggerating what we can find in the world to exaggerating our power to remake the world. Expecting more novelty than there is, more greatness than there is, and more strangeness than there is, we imagine ourselves masters of a plastic universe. But a world we can shape to our will . . . is a shapeless world.

> DANIEL J. BOORSTIN (b. 1914), U.S. historian. *The Image*, ch. 4 (1961).

3 Danger lies in the writer becoming the victim of his own exaggeration, losing the exact notion of sincerity, and in the end coming to despise truth itself as something too cold, too blunt for his purpose—as, in fact, not good enough for his insistent emotion. From laughter and tears the descent is easy to snivelling and giggles.

> JOSEPH CONRAD (1857-1924), Polish-born English novelist. *A Personal Record*, "A Familiar Preface" (1912).

4 'Tis a rule of manners to avoid exaggeration.

> RALPH WALDO EMERSON (1803-82), U.S. essayist, poet, philosopher. *Letters and Social Aims,* "Social Aims" (1876).

5 Eschew the monumental. Shun the Epic. All the guys who can paint great big pictures can paint great small ones.

> ERNEST HEMINGWAY (1899-1961), U.S. author. Letter, 5-6 Jan. 1932 (published in *Selected Letters,* ed. by Carlos Baker, 1981).

6 Thought is a process of exaggeration. The refusal to exaggerate is not infrequently an alibi for the disinclination to think or praise.

> ERIC HOFFER (1902-83), U.S. philosopher. *The Passionate State of Mind,* aph. 186 (1955).

7 It is the essence of truth that it is never excessive. Why should it exaggerate? There is that which should be destroyed and that which should be simply illuminated and studied. How great is the force of benevolent and searching examination! We must not resort to the flame where only light is required.

> VICTOR HUGO (1802-85), French poet, dramatist, novelist. *Les Misérables,* pt. 2, bk. 7, ch. 3 (1862).

8 We always weaken whatever we exaggerate.

> JEAN-FRANÇOIS DE LA HARPE (1739-1803), French poet, playwright. M de Faublas, in *Mélanie,* act 1, sc. 1.

9 Who breaks a butterfly on a wheel?

> ALEXANDER POPE (1688-1744), English satirical poet. Lord Hervey, in *Epistle to Dr. Arbuthnot* (1735). The line has passed into common usage, and was made famous in the 1960s when it was used to head the London *Times* leader (1 July 1967), on Mick Jagger and Keith Richards' arrest on drugs charges—an article which was thought to have contributed to their acquittal.

10 Camp is a vision of the world in terms of style—but a particular kind of style. It is love of the exaggerated.

> SUSAN SONTAG (b. 1933), U.S. essayist. *Against Interpretation,* "Notes on `Camp,' " Note 8 (1966; first published 1964).

11 Where there is no exaggeration there is no love, and where there is no love there is no understanding. It is only about things that do not interest one, that one can give a really unbiased opinion; and this is no doubt the reason why an unbiased opinion is always valueless.

> OSCAR WILDE (1854-1900), Anglo-Irish playwright, author. *Speaker* (London, 22 Mar 1890), review of Walter Pater, *Appreciations, with an Essay on Style*.

EXAMINATIONS

1 As long as learning is connected with earning, as long as certain jobs can only be reached through exams, so long must we take this examination system seriously. If another ladder to employment was contrived, much so-called education would disappear, and no one would be a penny the stupider.

> E. M. FORSTER (1879-1970), British novelist, essayist. *New York Times* (24 Nov. 1963).

2 Do not on any account attempt to write on both sides of the paper at once.

> W. C. SELLAR (1898-1951) AND R. J. YEATMAN (1897-1968), British authors. *1066 and All That,* "Test Paper V" (1930).

3 Examinations, sir, are pure humbug from beginning to end. If a man is a gentleman, he knows quite enough, and if he is not a gentleman, whatever he knows is bad for him.

> OSCAR WILDE (1854-1900), Anglo-Irish playwright, author. Lord Fermor, in *The Picture of Dorian Gray,* ch. 3 (1891). Lord Illingworth made the same pronouncement in *A Woman of No Importance,* act 3, first performed three years after the publication of *Dorian Gray*.

EXAMPLE

1 No rules exist, and examples are simply life-savers answering the appeals of rules making vain attempts to exist.

> ANDRÉ BRETON (1896-1966), French Surrealist. *Surrealism and Painting* (1928).

2 He preaches well that lives well.

> MIGUEL DE CERVANTES (1547-1616), Spanish writer. Sancho Panza, in *Don Quixote,* pt. 2, bk. 5, ch. 20 (1615; tr. P. Motteux).

3 The presence of a noble nature, generous in its wishes, ardent in its charity, changes the lights for us: we begin to see things again in their larger, quieter masses, and to believe that we too can be seen and judged in the wholeness of our character.

GEORGE ELIOT (1819-80), English novelist, editor. *Middle-march*, bk. 8, ch. 76 (1871).

4 The world is upheld by the veracity of good men: they make the earth wholesome. They who lived with them found life glad and nutritious. Life is sweet and tolerable only in our belief in such society.

RALPH WALDO EMERSON (1803-82), U.S. essayist, poet, philosopher. *Representative Men*, ch. 1, "Uses of Great Men" (1850).

5 It is not so much the example of others we imitate as the reflection of ourselves in their eyes and the echo of ourselves in their words.

ERIC HOFFER (1902-83), U.S. philosopher. *The Passionate State of Mind*, aph. 130 (1955).

6 This, then, is the test we must set for ourselves; not to march alone but to march in such a way that others will wish to join us.

HUBERT H. HUMPHREY (1911-78), U.S. Democratic politician, vice president. Speech, 6 Jan 1967, Buffalo, New York.

7 They teach the morals of a whore, and the manners of a dancing master.

SAMUEL JOHNSON (1709-84), English author, lexicographer. Quoted in: James Boswell, *Life of Samuel Johnson*, 1754 entry (1791), referring to Lord Chesterfield's *Letters to His Son*.

8 Folks don't like to have somebody around knowin' more than they do. It aggravates 'em. You're not gonna change any of them by talkin' right, they've got to want to learn themselves, and when they don't want to learn there's nothing you can do but keep your mouth shut or talk their language.

HARPER LEE (b. 1926), U.S. author. Calpurnia, in *To Kill a Mockingbird*, pt. 2, ch. 12 (1960).

9 Example moves the world more than doctrine. The great exemplars are the poets of action, and it makes little difference whether they be forces for good or forces for evil.

HENRY MILLER (1891-1980), U.S. author. *The Cosmological Eye*, "An Open Letter to Surrealists Everywhere" (1939).

10 Example is a bright looking-glass, universal and for all shapes to look into.

MICHEL DE MONTAIGNE (1533-92), French essayist. *Essays*, bk. 3, ch. 13, "Of Experience" (tr. by John Florio, 1588).

11 Few things are harder to put up with than the annoyance of a good example.

MARK TWAIN (1835-1910), U.S. author. *Pudd'nhead Wilson*, ch. 1, "Pudd'nhead Wilson's Calendar" (1894).

12 Illustrious examples *engross, prejudice*, and *intimidate*. They *engross* our attention, and so prevent a due inspection of ourselves; they *prejudice* our judgment in favour of their abilities, and so lessen the sense of our own; and they *intimidate* us with the splendour of their renown, and thus under diffidence bury our strength.

EDWARD YOUNG (1683-1765), English poet, dramatist. *Conjectures on Original Composition* (1759).

See also Cuomo on FATHERS.

EXASPERATION

1 Lord Ronald said nothing; he flung himself from the room, flung himself upon his horse and rode madly off in all directions.

STEPHEN LEACOCK (1869-1944), Canadian humorist, economist. *Nonsense Novels*, "Gertrude the Governess" (1911).

2 Your damned nonsense can I stand twice or once, but sometimes always, by God, never.

HANS RICHTER (1843-1916), German conductor. Quoted in: Leon Harris, *The Fine Art of Political Wit*, ch. 12 (1964), to the second flute in the Covent Garden orchestra, quoted by British MP J.E.S. Simon in the House of Commons, 13 Feb. 1958.

3 Sir, you have tasted two whole worms; you have hissed all my mystery lectures and been caught fighting a liar in the quad; you will leave by the next town drain.

ATTRIBUTED TO REV. W. A. SPOONER (1844-1930), Warden of New College, Oxford. One of many "Spoonerisms" now considered apocryphal.

4 Well, if I called the wrong number, why did you answer the phone?

JAMES THURBER (1894-1961), U.S. humorist, illustrator. Cartoon caption in *New Yorker* (5 June 1937).

EXCELLENCE

1 The sad truth is that excellence makes people nervous.

SHANA ALEXANDER (b. 1925), U.S. writer, editor. *The Feminine Eye*, "Neglected Kids—the Bright Ones" (1970; first published 1966).

2 Excellence encourages one about life generally; it shows the spiritual wealth of the world.

GEORGE ELIOT (1819-80), English novelist, editor. Daniel Deronda, in *Daniel Deronda*, bk. 5, ch. 36 (1876).

3 One shining quality lends a lustre to another, or hides some glaring defect.

WILLIAM HAZLITT (1778-1830), English essayist. *Characteristics*, no. 162 (first published anonymously in 1823; repr. in *Complete Works*, vol. 9, ed. P. P. Howe, 1932).

4 It's enough for you to do it once for a few men to remember you. But if you do it year after year, then many people remember you and they tell it to their children, and their children and grandchildren remember and, if it concerns books, they can read them. And if it's good enough, it will last as long as there are human beings.

ERNEST HEMINGWAY (1899-1961), U.S. author. Quoted in: Malcolm Cowley, "Portrait of Mr. Papa," in *Life* (New York, 10 Jan. 1949).

5 From time to time there appear on the face of the earth men of rare and consummate excellence, who dazzle us by their virtue, and whose outstanding qualities shed a stupendous light. Like those extraordinary stars of whose origins we are ignorant, and of whose fate, once they have vanished, we know even less, such men have neither forebears nor descendants: they are the whole of their race.

JEAN DE LA BRUYÈRE (1645-96), French writer, moralist. *Characters*, "Of Personal Merit," aph. 22 (1688).

6 Always strive to excel, but only on weekends.

RICHARD RORTY (b. 1931), U.S. philosopher. Quoted in: *New York Times Magazine* (12 Feb. 1990).

7 When workmen strive to do better than well,
They do confound their skill in covetousness.

WILLIAM SHAKESPEARE (1564-1616), English dramatist, poet. Pembroke, in *King John,* act 4, sc. 2.

8 Then to Silvia let us sing
That Silvia is excelling.
She excels each mortal thing
Upon the dull earth dwelling.

WILLIAM SHAKESPEARE (1564-1616), English dramatist, poet. Proteus, in *The Two Gentlemen of Verona,* act 4, sc. **2**   Proteus, singing outside Silvia's chamber, was attempting to woo her ostensibly on behalf of Thurio, actually for himself. This is the third and last verse of one of the most famous of Shakespeare's songs, set to music by, among others, Schubert.

9 The best is the enemy of the good.

VOLTAIRE (1694-1778), French philosopher, author. *Philosophical Dictionary,* "Dramatic Art" (1764).

10 A masterpiece is . . . something said once and for all, stated, finished, so that it's there complete in the mind, if only at the back.

VIRGINIA WOOLF (1882-1941), British novelist. Letter, 1 Jan. 1933 (published in *The Sickle Side of the Moon: Letters, vol. 5,* ed. by Nigel Nicolson, 1979).

EXCESS

1 We have almost succeeded in leveling all human activities to the common denominator of securing the necessities of life and providing for their abundance.

HANNAH ARENDT (1906-75), German-born U.S. political philosopher. *The Human Condition,* pt. 3, ch. 17 (1958).

2 Let's not quibble! I'm the foe of moderation, the champion of excess. If I may lift a line from a die-hard whose identity is lost in the shuffle, "I'd rather be strongly wrong than weakly right."

TALLULAH BANKHEAD (1903-68), U.S. screen actor. *Tallulah,* ch. 4 (1952).

3 We are no longer in a state of growth; we are in a state of excess. We are living in a society of excrescence. . . . The boil is growing out of control, recklessly at cross purposes with itself, its impacts multiplying as the causes disintegrate.

JEAN BAUDRILLARD (b. 1929), French semiologist. "The Anorexic Ruins," paper, Autumn 1986, New York (repr. in *Looking Back on the End of the World,* ed. by Dietmar Kamper and Christoph Wulf, 1989).

4 The road of excess leads to the palace of wisdom.

WILLIAM BLAKE (1757-1827), English poet, painter, engraver. *The Marriage of Heaven and Hell,* Plate 7, "Proverbs of Hell" (1790-93; repr. in *Complete Writings,* ed. by Geoffrey Keynes, 1957).

5 Excess on occasion is exhilarating. It prevents moderation from acquiring the deadening effect of habit.

W. SOMERSET MAUGHAM (1874-1965), British author. *The Summing Up,* ch. 15 (1938).

6 Ours is a culture based on excess, on overproduction; the result is a steady loss of sharpness in our sensory experience. All the conditions of modern life—its material plenitude, its sheer crowdedness—conjoin to dull our sensory faculties.

SUSAN SONTAG (b. 1933), U.S. essayist. "Against Interpretation," sct. 9, in *Evergreen Review* (Dec. 1964, repr. in *Against Interpretation,* 1966).

7 Moderation is a fatal thing. . . . Nothing succeeds like excess.

OSCAR WILDE (1854-1900), Anglo-Irish playwright, author. Lord Illingworth, in *A Woman of No Importance,* act 3.

8 Americans are overreaching; overreaching is the most admirable and most American of the many American excesses.

GEORGE F. WILL (b. 1941), U.S. political columnist. *Statecraft as Soulcraft: What Government Does,* ch. 4 (1984).

EXCREMENT AND EXCRETION

1 Where there is a stink of shit
there is a smell of being.

ANTONIN ARTAUD (1896-1948), French theater producer, actor, theorist. "The Pursuit of Fecality," in *To Have Done with the Judgment of God* (1947; repr. in *Selected Writings,* pt. 37, ed. by Susan Sontag, 1976).

2 What makes shit such a universal joke is that it's an unmistakeable reminder of our duality, of our soiled nature and of our will to glory. It is the ultimate *lèse-majesté.*

JOHN BERGER (b. 1926), British author, critic. "Muck and Its Entanglements" in *Harper's* (New York, May 1989; repr. in *Keeping a Rendezvous* as "A Load of Shit", 1992).

3 Since man's highest mission on earth is to spiritualize everything, it is his excrement in particular that needs it most.

SALVADOR DALI (1904-89), Spanish painter. *Diary of a Genius* (1966), entry for 2 Sept. 1952.

4 When he urinated, it sounded like night prayer.

F. SCOTT FITZGERALD (1896-1940), U.S. author. *The Crack-Up,* "Notebook M" (ed. by Edmund Wilson, 1945).

5 The excremental is all too intimately and inseparably bound up with the sexual: the position of the genitals—*inter urinas et faeces*—remains the decisive and unchangeable factor. One might say here, varying a well-known saying of the great Napoleon: "Anatomy is destiny."

SIGMUND FREUD (1856-1939), Austrian psychiatrist. *On the Universal Tendency to Debasement in the Sphere of Love,* sct. 3 (1912; repr. in *Complete Works, Standard Edition,* vol. 11, ed. by James Strachey and Anna Freud, 1957). Napoleon had said, "Politics is destiny" (as reported by German poet Goethe in conversation with him in 1808).

6 The confidence and security of a people can be measured by their attitude toward laxatives. At the high noon of the British sun, soldiers in far-flung outposts of the Empire doctored themselves with "a spoonful o' gunpowder in a cuppa 'ot tea." Purveyors and users of harsh laxatives were not afraid of being thought mean and unfriendly just because their laxatives were. But in America, the need to be nice is so consuming that nobody would dare take a laxative that makes you run up the stairs two at a time, pushing others aside and yelling, "Get out of the way!"

> FLORENCE KING (b. 1936), U.S. author. *Reflections in a Jaundiced Eye,* "Nice Guyism" (1989).

7 It amazes me that organs that piss
Can give human beings such perfect bliss.

> IRVING LAYTON (b. 1912), Canadian poet. *Aphs,* in *The Whole Bloody Bird* (1969).

8 Male urination really *is* a kind of accomplishment, an arc of transcendance. A woman merely waters the ground she stands on.

> CAMILLE PAGLIA (b. 1947), U.S. author, critic, educator. *Sexual Personae,* ch. 1 (1990).

See also Berger on COUNTRY LIFE.

EXCUSES

1 Your letter of excuses has arrived. I receive the letter but do not admit the excuses except in courtesy, as when a man treads on your toes and begs your pardon—the pardon is granted, but the joint aches, especially if there is a corn upon it.

> LORD BYRON (1788-1824), English poet. Letter, 2 Feb. 1821, to the publisher John Murray (published in *Byron's Letters and Journals,* vol. 8, ed. by Leslie A. Marchand, 1973-81).

2 To offer the complexities of life as an excuse for not addressing oneself to the simpler, more manageable (trivial) aspects of daily existence is a perversity often indulged in by artists, husbands, intellectuals—and critics of the Women's Movement.

> BARBARA GRIZZUTI HARRISON (1941), U.S. author, publicist. *Unlearning the Lie: Sexism in School,* Introduction (1973).

3 The girl who can't dance says the band can't play.

> YIDDISH PROVERB.

4 And oftentimes excusing of a fault
Doth make the fault the worser by th'excuse.

> WILLIAM SHAKESPEARE (1564-1616), English dramatist, poet. Pembroke, in *King John,* act 4, sc. 2.

5 Two wrongs don't make a right, but they make a good excuse.

> THOMAS SZASZ (b. 1920), U.S. psychiatrist. *The Second Sin,* "Social Relations" (1973).

See also Addison on LIES AND LYING.

EXERCISE

1 Athletes have studied how to leap and how to survive the leap some of the time and return to the ground. They don't always do it well. But they are our philoso-phers of actual moments and the body and soul in them, and of our manoeuvres in our emergencies and longings.

> HAROLD BRODKEY (b. 1930), U.S. author. "Meditations on an Athlete," in *Cape* (London, July 1992).

2 Exercise is the yuppie version of bulimia.

> BARBARA EHRENREICH (b. 1941), U.S. author, columnist. *The Worst Years of Our Lives,* "Food Worship" (1991; first published 1985).

3 The only athletic sport I ever mastered was backgammon.

> DOUGLAS JERROLD (1803-57), English playwright, humorist. Quoted in: W. Jerrold, *Douglas Jerrold,* vol. 1, ch. 1 (1914).

4 Our growing softness, our increasing lack of physical fitness, is a menace to our security.

> JOHN F. KENNEDY (1917-63), U.S. Democratic politician, president. *The Soft America* (1960; repr. in *Sport and Society: an Anthology,* ed. by John T. Talamini and Charles H. Page, 1973).

5 Modern bodybuilding is ritual, religion, sport, art, and science, awash in Western chemistry and mathematics. Defying nature, it surpasses it.

> CAMILLE PAGLIA (b. 1947), U.S. author, critic, educator. "Alice in Muscle Land," book review, in *Boston Globe* (27 Jan. 1991; repr. in *Sex, Art, and American Culture,* 1992).

6 I wish to preach, not the doctrine of ignoble ease, but the doctrine of the strenuous life.

> THEODORE ROOSEVELT (1858-1919), U.S. Republican (later Progressive) politician, president. Speech, 10 April 1899, Chicago, Ill.

See also Wilde on HUNTING; SPORT.

EXILE

1 By the rivers of Babylon, there we sat down, yea, we wept: when we remembered Zion.

> BIBLE, HEBREW. *Psalms* 137:1.

2 It would be enough for me to have the system of a jury of twelve versus the system of one judge as a basis for preferring the U.S. to the Soviet Union. . . . I would prefer the country you can leave to the country you cannot.

> JOSEPH BRODSKY (b. 1940), Russian-born U.S. poet, critic. *Writers at Work* (Eighth Series, ed. by George Plimpton, 1988). Brodsky was "asked" to leave the U.S.S.R in 1972.

3 An exile, saddest of all prisoners,
Who has the whole world for a dungeon strong,
Seas, mountains, and the horizon's verge for bars.

> LORD BYRON (1788-1824), English poet. *The Prophecy of Dante,* cto. 4.

4 The ideal place for me is the one in which it is most natural to live as a foreigner.

> ITALO CALVINO (1923-85), Italian author, critic. *Grand Bazaar* (Milan, Sept.-Oct. 1980; repr. in *The Literature Machine,* 1987).

5 Excluded by my birth and tastes from the social order, I was not aware of its diversity. . . . Nothing in the world was irrelevant: the stars on a general's sleeve, the stock-market quotations, the olive harvest, the style of the judiciary, the wheat exchange, flower-beds. . . . Nothing. This order, fearful and feared, whose details were all inter-related, had a meaning: my exile.

> JEAN GENET (1910-86), French playwright, novelist. *The Thief's Journal* (1949; repr. 1965, p. 151).

6   Exile as a mode of genius no longer exists; in place of Joyce we have the fragments of work appearing in *Index on Censorship.*

> NADINE GORDIMER (b. 1923), South African author. "The Essential Gesture," lecture, 12 Oct. 1984, University of Michigan (published in *The Tanner Lectures on Human Values,* ed. by Sterling M. McMurrin, 1985; repr. in *The Essential Gesture,* ed. by Stephen Clingman, 1988).

7   I have loved justice and hated iniquity: therefore I die in exile.

> Attributed to POPE GREGORY VII (?1020-85). Last words in Salerno, Italy, where he had taken refuge after being ousted from Rome by the Holy Roman Emperor Henry IV.

8   Let those who desire a secure homeland conquer it. Let those who do not conquer it live under the whip and in exile, watched over like wild animals, cast from one country to another, concealing the death of their souls with a beggar's smile from the scorn of free men.

> JOSÉ MARTÍ (1853-95), Cuban poet, patriot. *Obras Completas,* vol. 3, "April 1894," pt. 1 (tr. by Carlos Ripoll in *José Martí: Thoughts/Pensamientos,* 1980, p. 109).

9   Such is the miraculous nature of the future of exiles: what is first uttered in the impotence of an overheated apartment becomes the fate of nations.

> SALMAN RUSHDIE (b. 1948), Indian-born British author. *The Satanic Verses,* "Ayesha" (1988), of the Imam exiled in London.

10   My first few weeks in America are always miserable, because the tastes I am cursed with are all of a kind that cannot be gratified here, & I am not enough in sympathy with our "gros public" to make up for the lack on the aesthetic side. One's friends are delightful; but *we* are none of us Americans, we don't think or feel as the Americans do, we are the wretched exotics produced in a European glass-house, the most déplacé & useless class on earth!

> EDITH WHARTON (1862-1937), U.S. author. Letter, 5 June 1903, to Sara Norton, daughter of distinguished scholar Charles Eliot Norton (published in *The Letters of Edith Wharton,* 1988). Wharton spent most of her adult life in Europe.

See also Joyce on FAITH; Wilde on YOUTH.

EXISTENCE

1   It is living and ceasing to live that are imaginary solutions. Existence is elsewhere.

> ANDRÉ BRETON (1896-1966), French surrealist. *Manifesto of Surrealism* (1924; repr. in *Manifestoes of Surrealism,* 1969).

2   In order to exist just once in the world, it is necessary never again to exist.

> ALBERT CAMUS (1913-60), French-Algerian philosopher, author. *The Rebel,* pt. 4 (1951; tr. 1953).

3   To exist is equivalent to an act of faith, a protest against the truth, an interminable prayer. . . . As soon as they consent to live, the unbeliever and the man of faith are fundamentally the same, since both have made the only decision that defines a *being.*

> E. M. CIORAN (b. 1911), Rumanian-born French philosopher. *The Temptation to Exist,* title essay (1956).

4   There is no means of *proving* it is preferable to be than not to be.

> E. M. CIORAN (b. 1911), Rumanian-born French philosopher. *The New Gods,* "Strangled Thoughts," sct. 1 (first published 1969; tr. 1974).

5   Being is a fiction invented by those who suffer from becoming.

> COLEMAN DOWELL (1925-85), U.S. novelist, dramatist, lyricist. *Mrs. October Was Here,* pt. 3, "Tasmania, Now" (1973), entry in Mrs. October's journals.

6   Man is the only animal for whom his own existence is a problem which he has to solve.

> ERICH FROMM (1900-1980), U.S. psychologist. *Man for Himself,* ch. 3 (1947).

7   Nothing exists except by virtue of a disequilibrium, an injustice. All existence is a theft paid for by other existences; no life flowers except on a cemetery.

> RÉMY DE GOURMONT (1858-1915), French critic, novelist. "The Dissociation of Ideas" (1899; repr. in *Selected Writings,* ed. and tr. by Glen S. Burne, 1966).

8   The individual who has to justify his existence by his own efforts is in eternal bondage to himself.

> ERIC HOFFER (1902-83), U.S. philosopher. *The Ordeal of Change,* ch. 5 (1964).

9   There's nothing that makes you so aware of the improvisation of human existence as a song unfinished. Or an old address book.

> CARSON MCCULLERS (1917-67), U.S. author. Ferris, in "The Sojourner," in *The Ballad of the Sad Cafe* (1951).

10   The cradle rocks above an abyss, and common sense tells us that our existence is but a brief crack of light between two eternities of darkness.

> VLADIMIR NABOKOV (1899-1977), Russian-born U.S. novelist, poet. *Speak, Memory,* ch. 1, sct. 1 (1955, rev. 1966).

11   Existence really is an imperfect tense that never becomes a present.

> FRIEDRICH NIETZSCHE (1844-1900), German philosopher. *The Use and Abuse of History,* sct. 1 (1874).

12   One is still what one is going to cease to be and already what one is going to become. One lives one's death, one dies one's life.

> JEAN-PAUL SARTRE (1905-80), French philosopher, author. *Saint Genet: Actor and Martyr,* bk. 2, "The Melodious Child Dead in Me . . ." (1952; tr. 1963).

13   There's a time when you have to explain to your children why they're born, and it's a marvelous thing if you know the reason by then.

> HAZEL SCOTT (1920-81), U.S. entertainer. Quoted in: *Ms.* (New York, Nov. 1974).

14 Existence is no more than the precarious attainment of relevance in an intensely mobile flux of past, present, and future.

> SUSAN SONTAG (b. 1933), U.S. essayist. *Styles of Radical Will*, "'Thinking Against Oneself': Reflections on Cioran" (1969).

15 Being is the great explainer.

> HENRY DAVID THOREAU (1817-62), U.S. philosopher, author, naturalist. Journal entry, 26 Feb. 1841.

16 Existence itself does not feel horrible; it feels like an ecstasy, rather, which we have only to be still to experience.

> JOHN UPDIKE (b. 1932), U.S. author, critic. *Self-Consciousness: Memoirs*, ch. 6 (1989).

EXPATRIATES

1 Voyagers discover that the world can never be larger than the person that is in the world; but it is impossible to foresee this, it is impossible to be warned.

> JAMES BALDWIN (1924-87), U.S. author. "The New Lost Generation," in *Esquire* (New York, July 1961; repr. in *The Price of the Ticket*, 1985), on the futility of running from a situation, with particular reference to his own "exile" in Paris.

2 It is a mistake to expect good work from expatriates for it is not what they do that matters but what they are not doing.

> CYRIL CONNOLLY (1903-74), British critic. *Enemies of Promise*, pt. 2, ch. 13 note (1938).

3 You're an expatriate. You've lost touch with the soil. You get precious. Fake European standards have ruined you. You drink yourself to death. You become obsessed by sex. You spend all your time talking, not working. You are an expatriate, see? You hang around cafés.

> ERNEST HEMINGWAY (1899-1961), U.S. author. Bill Gorton to Jake Barnes, in *The Sun Also Rises*, bk. 2, ch. 12 (1926). Jake replies: "It sounds like a swell life."

4 If I were to live my life over again, I would be an American. I would steep myself in America, I would know no other land.

> HENRY JAMES (1843-1916), U.S. author. Remark, 1899, to writer Hamlin Garland. Quoted in: Tony Tanner, *Hawthorne*, Introduction (1879). See James on THE UNITED STATES.

5 When the Irishman is found outside of Ireland in another environment, he very often becomes a respected man. The economic and intellectual conditions that prevail in his own country do not permit the development of individuality. . . . No one who has any self-respect stays in Ireland, but flees afar as though from a country that has undergone the visitation of an angered Jove.

> JAMES JOYCE (1882-1941), Irish author. "Ireland, Island of Saints and Sages," lecture, 27 April 1907, at Università Popolare Triestina (published in *Critical Writings*, sct. 35, ed. by Ellsworth Mason and Richard Ellmann, 1959).

6 We make a mistake forsaking England and moving out into the periphery of life. After all, Taormina, Ceylon, Africa, America — as far as *we* go, they are only the negation of what we ourselves stand for and are: and

we're rather like Jonahs running away from the place we belong.

> D. H. LAWRENCE (1885-1930), British author. Letter, 30 March 1922, written in Ceylon (published in *The Letters of D. H. Lawrence*, vol. 4, ed. by James T. Boulton, E. Mansfield, and W. Roberts, 1987). See the Hebrew Bible, *Jonah* 1:1-3, in which Jonah is instructed by God to preach in Nineveh, but instead boards a ship bound for Tarshish.

7 I dunno what my 23 infantile years in America signify. I left as soon as motion was autarchic—I mean *my* motion.

> EZRA POUND (1885-1972), U.S. poet, critic. Letter, 29 Oct. 1940 (published in *The Letters of Ezra Pound 1907-1941*, ed. by D. D. Paige, 1950).

8 The realization that he is white in a black country, and respected for it, is the turning point in the expatriate's career. He can either forget it, or capitalize on it. Most choose the latter.

> PAUL THEROUX (b. 1941), U.S. novelist, travel writer. "Tarzan Is an Expatriate." Quoted in: Patrick Marnham, *Dispatches from Africa*, ch. 1 (1981).

EXPECTATION

1 Nothing sets a person up more than having something turn out just the way it's supposed to be, like falling into a Swiss snowdrift and seeing a big dog come up with a little cask of brandy round its neck.

> CLAUD COCKBURN (1904-81), British author, journalist. *Cockburn Sums Up*, "Printing House Square" (1981).

2 I know not anything more pleasant, or more instructive, than to compare experience with expectation, or to register from time to time the difference between idea and reality. It is by this kind of observation that we grow daily less liable to be disappointed.

> SAMUEL JOHNSON (1709-84), English author, lexicographer. Letter, 27 June 1758 (published in James Boswell, *Life of Samuel Johnson*, 1791).

EXPERIENCE

1 Experience is a good teacher, but she sends in terrific bills.

> MINNA ANTRIM (1861-?), U.S. epigrammist. *Naked Truth and Veiled Allusions* (1901, p. 99).

2 Experience is a private, and a very largely speechless affair.

> JAMES BALDWIN (1924-87), U.S. author. "A Question of Identity," in *Partisan Review* (New Brunswick, N.J., July/Aug. 1954; repr. in *Notes of a Native Son*, 1955).

3 Only he who can view his own past as an abortion sprung from compulsion and need can use it to full advantage in the present. For what one has lived is at best comparable to a beautiful statue which has had all its limbs knocked off in transit, and now yields nothing but the precious block out of which the image of one's future must be hewn.

> WALTER BENJAMIN (1892-1940), German critic, philosopher. *One-Way Street*, "Antiques" (1928; repr. in *One-Way Street and Other Writings*, 1978).

4 Experience. The wisdom that enables us to recognise in an undesirable old acquaintance the folly that we have already embraced.

> AMBROSE BIERCE (1842-1914), U.S. author. *The Devil's Dictionary* (1881-1906).

5 Experience, like a pale musician, holds
A dulcimer of patience in his hand.

> ELIZABETH BARRETT BROWNING (1806-61), English Poet. *Perplexed Music*.

6 Don't learn to do, but learn in doing. Let your falls not be on a prepared ground, but let them be *bona fide* falls in the rough and tumble of the world.

> SAMUEL BUTLER (1835-1902), English author. *Samuel Butler's Notebooks* (1951, p. 157).

7 The notion of a universality of human experience is a confidence trick and the notion of a universality of female experience is a clever confidence trick.

> ANGELA CARTER (1940-92), British author. *The Sadeian Woman*, "Polemical Preface" (1979).

8 Experience is a dim lamp, which only lights the one who bears it.

> LOUIS-FERDINAND CÉLINE (1894-1961), French author. Interview in *Writers at Work* (Third Series, ed. by George Plimpton, 1967).

9 There is a sort of veteran woman of condition, who, having lived always in the *grand monde*, and having possibly had some gallantries, together with the experience of five and twenty or thirty years, form a young fellow better than all the rules that can be given him. . . . Wherever you go, make some of those women your friends; which a very little matter will do. Ask their advice, tell them your doubts or difficulties as to your behaviour; but take great care not to drop one word of their experience; for experience implies age, and the suspicion of age, no woman, let her be ever so old, ever forgives.

> LORD CHESTERFIELD (1694-1773), English statesman, man of letters. Letter, 11 Jan. 1750 (first published 1774; repr. in *The Letters of the Earl of Chesterfield to His Son*, vol. 2, no. 213, ed. by Charles Strachey, 1901).

10 When you have really exhausted an experience you always reverence and love it. The two things that nearly all of us have thoroughly and really been through are childhood and youth. And though we would not have them back again on any account, we feel that they are both beautiful, because we have drunk them dry.

> G. K. CHESTERTON (1874-1936), British author. *A Miscellany of Men*, "The Contented Man" (1912).

11 To most men, experience is like the stern lights of a ship, which illumine only the track it has passed.

> SAMUEL TAYLOR COLERIDGE (1772-1834), English poet, critic. *Table Talk*, 1820, reported by Thomas Allsop (published in *Letters and Conversations of S. T. Coleridge*, vol. 1, 1836; repr. in *Collected Works*, vol. 14, ed. by Kathleen Coburn, 1990).

12 Common experience is the gold reserve which confers an exchange value on the currency which words are; without this reserve of shared experiences, all our pronouncements are cheques drawn on insufficient funds.

> RENÉ DAUMAL (1908-44), French poet, critic. *A Night of Serious Drinking*, Foreword (1938).

13 I try to avoid experience if I can. Most experience is bad.

> E. L. DOCTOROW (b. 1931), U.S. novelist. Interview in *Writers at Work* (Eighth Series, ed. by George Plimpton, 1967).

14 You learn from a conglomeration of the incredible past—whatever experience gotten in any way whatsoever.

> BOB DYLAN (b. 1941), U.S. singer, songwriter. *Tarantula*, "Subterranean Homesick Blues & the Blond Waltz" (1970).

16 Is it not rather what we expect in men, that they should have numerous strands of experience lying side by side and never compare them with each other?

> GEORGE ELIOT (1819-80), English novelist, editor. *Middlemarch*, bk. 6, ch. 58 (1871-72).

17 But human experience is usually paradoxical, that means incongruous with the phrases of current talk or even current philosophy.

> GEORGE ELIOT (1819-80), English novelist, editor. *Daniel Deronda*, bk. 8, ch. 69 (1876).

18 No matter how vital experience might be while you lived it, no sooner was it ended and dead than it became as lifeless as the piles of dry dust in a school history book.

> ELLEN GLASGOW (1874-1945), U.S. novelist. *In This Our Life*, pt. 3, ch. 9 (1941).

19 In going where you have to go, and doing what you have to do, and seeing what you have to see, you dull and blunt the instrument you write with. But I would rather have it bent and dulled and know I had to put it on the grindstone again and hammer it into shape and put a whetstone to it, and know that I had something to write about, than to have it bright and shining and nothing to say, or smooth and well oiled in the closet, but unused.

> ERNEST HEMINGWAY (1899-1961), U.S. author. *The First Forty-Nine Stories*, Preface (1944).

20 Experience is not a matter of having actually swum the Hellespont, or danced with the dervishes, or slept in a doss-house. It is a matter of sensibility and intuition, of seeing and hearing the significant things, of paying attention at the right moments, of understanding and co-ordinating. Experience is not what happens to a man; it is what a man does with what happens to him.

> ALDOUS HUXLEY (1894-1963), British author. *Texts and Pretexts*, Introduction (1932).

21 Experience is never limited, and it is never complete; it is an immense sensibility, a kind of huge spider-web of the finest silken threads suspended in the chamber of consciousness, and catching every air-borne particle in its tissue.

> HENRY JAMES (1843-1916), U.S. author. *The Art of Fiction* (1884; repr. in *Partial Portraits*, 1888).

22 The power to guess the unseen from the seen, to trace the implications of things, to judge the whole piece by the pattern, the condition of feeling life in general so completely that you are well on your way to knowing any particular corner of it—this cluster of gifts may almost be said to constitute experience.

> HENRY JAMES (1843-1916), U.S. author. *The Art of Fiction* (1884; repr. in *Partial Portraits*, 1888).

23 It is not necessary that you leave the house. Remain at your table and listen. Do not even listen, only wait. Do not even wait, be wholly still and alone. The world will present itself to you for its unmasking, it can do no other, in ecstasy it will writhe at your feet.

FRANZ KAFKA (1883-1924), German novelist, short-story writer. *The Collected Aphorisms*, no. 109 (Oct. 1917-Feb. 1918; published in *Shorter Works*, vol. 1, ed. and tr. by Malcolm Pasley, 1973).

24 What is the good of drawing conclusions from experience? I don't deny we sometimes draw the right conclusions, but don't we just as often draw the wrong ones?

G. C. LICHTENBERG (1742-99), German physicist, philosopher. *Aphorisms*, "Notebook F," aph. 123 (written 1765-99; tr. by R. J. Hollingdale, 1990).

25 Experience is a comb which nature gives to men when they are bald.

EASTERN PROVERB.

26 If a man deceives me once, shame on him; if he deceives me twice, shame on me.

ITALIAN PROVERB.

27 Experience comprises illusions lost, rather than wisdom gained.

JOSEPH ROUX (1834-86), French priest, writer. *Meditations of a Parish Priest*, pt. 4, no. 28 (1886).

28 In the revolt against idealism, the ambiguities of the word "experience" have been perceived, with the result that realists have more and more avoided the word.

BERTRAND RUSSELL (1872-1970), British philosopher, mathematician. "On the Nature of Acquaintance," sct. 1 (1914; repr. in *Logic and Knowledge*, 1956).

29 We learn through experience and experiencing, and no one teaches anyone anything. This is as true for the infant moving from kicking to crawling to walking as it is for the scientist with his equations. If the environment permits it, anyone can learn whatever he chooses to learn; and if the individual permits it, the environment will teach him everything it has to teach.

VIOLA SPOLIN (b. 1911), U.S. theatrical director, producer. *Improvisation for the Theater*, ch. 1 (1963).

30 Men may rise on stepping-stones
Of their dead selves to higher things.

LORD TENNYSON (1809-92), English poet. *In Memoriam*, pt. 1, st. 1.

31 We should be careful to get out of an experience only the wisdom that is in it — and stop there; lest we be like the cat that sits down on a hot stove-lid. She will never sit down on a hot stove-lid again — and that is well; but also she will never sit down on a cold one anymore.

MARK TWAIN (1835-1910), U.S. author. *Following the Equator*, ch. 11, "Pudd'nhead Wilson's New Calendar" (1897).

32 There is no wider gulf in the universe than yawns between those on the hither and thither side of vital experience.

REBECCA WEST (1892-1983), British author. *Black Lamb and Grey Falcon*, vol. 1, "Serbia" (1942).

33 Experience is the name every one gives to their mistakes.

OSCAR WILDE (1854-1900), Anglo-Irish playwright, author. Dumby, in *Lady Windermere's Fan*, act 3. Wilde used the same formulation in *The Picture of Dorian Gray*, ch. 4.

34 We can have in life but one great experience at best, and the secret of life is to reproduce that experience as often as possible.

OSCAR WILDE (1854-1900), Anglo-Irish playwright, author. Lord Henry,.in *The Picture of Dorian Gray*, ch. 17 (1891).

See also Blake on EXCESS; Johnson on EXPECTATION.

EXPERTS

1 America has always been a country of amateurs where the professional, that is to say, the man who claims authority as a member of an élite which knows the law in some field or other, is an object of distrust and resentment.

W. H. AUDEN (1907-73), Anglo-American poet. *Faber Book of Modern American Verse*, Introduction (1956).

2 An expert is a man who has made all the mistakes which can be made in a very narrow field.

NIELS BOHR (1885-1962), Danish physicist. Quoted in: Alan Mackay, *The Harvest of a Quiet Eye* (1977).

3 Too bad that all the people who know how to run the country are busy driving taxicabs and cutting hair.

GEORGE BURNS (b. 1896), U.S. comedian. *Life* (New York, Dec. 1979).

4 It is surely a matter of common observation that a man who knows no one thing intimately has no views worth hearing on things in general. The farmer philosophizes in terms of crops, soils, markets, and implements, the mechanic generalizes his experiences of wood and iron, the seaman reaches similar conclusions by his own special road; and if the scholar keeps pace with these it must be by an equally virile productivity.

CHARLES HORTON COOLEY (1864-1929), U.S. sociologist. *Human Nature and the Social Order*, ch. 4 (New York, 1902).

5 What a delightful thing is the conversation of specialists! One understands absolutely nothing and it's charming.

EDGAR DEGAS (1834-1917), French painter, sculptor. Quoted by Daniel Halévy, 31 Jan. 1892, in *Degas Letters*, Appendix (ed. by Marcel Guerin, 1947).

6 We do not need to be shoemakers to know if our shoes fit, and just as little have we any need to be professionals to acquire knowledge of matters of universal interest.

GEORG HEGEL (1770-1831), German philosopher. *The Philosophy of Right*, no. 58 (1821; tr. 1942).

7 Specialized meaninglessness has come to be regarded, in certain circles, as a kind of hall-mark of true science.

ALDOUS HUXLEY (1894-1963), British author. *Ends and Means*, ch. 14, "Beliefs" (1937).

8 It is, after all, the responsibility of the expert to operate the familiar and that of the leader to transcend it.

HENRY KISSINGER (b. 1923), U.S. Republican politician, Secretary of State. *Years of Upheaval,* ch. 10, "The Foreign Service" (1982).

9   This world is run by people who know how to do things. They know how things work. They are *equipped.* Up there, there's a layer of people who run everything. But we—we're just peasants. We don't understand what's going on, and we can't do anything.

DORIS LESSING (b. 1919), British novelist. Dorothy, in *The Good Terrorist* (1985, p. 330).

10   We have not overthrown the divine right of kings to fall down for the divine right of experts.

HAROLD MACMILLAN (1894-1986), British Conservative politician, prime minister. Speech, 16 Aug. 1950, Strasbourg, France.

11   A specialist is someone who does everything else worse.

RUGGIERO RICCI (b. 1918), U.S. violinist. *Daily Telegraph* (London, 25 May 1990).

12   Only by strict specialization can the scientific worker become fully conscious, for once and perhaps never again in his lifetime, that he has achieved something that will endure. A really definitive and good accomplishment is today always a specialized accomplishment. And whoever lacks the capacity to put on blinders, so to speak, and to come up to the idea that the fate of his soul depends upon whether or not he makes the correct conjecture at this passage of this manuscript may as well stay away from science. He will never have what one may call the "personal experience" of science. Without this strange intoxication, ridiculed by every outsider; without this passion . . . you have *no* calling for science and you should do something else. For nothing is worthy of man as man unless he can pursue it with passionate devotion.

MAX WEBER (1864-1920), German sociologist. *Essays in Sociology,* "Science as a Vocation" (1919; ed. by H. H. Gerth and C. Wright Mills, 1946).

See also Chesterton on JURIES.

EXPLORATION

1   The American experience stirred mankind from *discovery* to *exploration.* From the cautious quest for what they knew (or thought they knew) was out there, into an enthusiastic reaching to the unknown. These are two substantially different kinds of human enterprise.

DANIEL J. BOORSTIN (b. 1914), U.S. historian. Reith Lectures, Oct. 1975 (published in *The Exploring Spirit: America and the World Experience,* Lecture 1 (1976).

2   In my writing I am acting as a map maker, an explorer of psychic areas . . . a cosmonaut of inner space, and I see no point in exploring areas that have already been thoroughly surveyed.

WILLIAM BURROUGHS (b. 1914), U.S. author. Remark, 1964. Quoted in: Eric Mottram, *William Burroughs: The Algebra of Need,* pt. 1, ch. 1 (1977).

3   We shall not cease from exploration
And the end of all our exploring

Will be to arrive where we started
And know the place for the first time.

T. S. ELIOT (1888-1965), Anglo-American poet, critic. *Little Gidding,* pt. 5, in *Four Quartets.*

4   It is easier to sail many thousand miles through cold and storm and cannibals, in a government ship, with five hundred men and boys to assist one, than it is to explore the private sea, the Atlantic and Pacific Ocean of one's being alone. . . . It is not worth the while to go round the world to count the cats in Zanzibar.

HENRY DAVID THOREAU (1817-62), U.S. philosopher, author, naturalist. *Walden,* "Conclusion" (1854).

EXTRAVAGANCE

1   As to the rout that is made about people who are ruined by extravagance, it is no matter to the nation that some individuals suffer. When so much general productive exertion is the consequence of luxury, the nation does not care though there are debtors in gaol; nay, they would not care though their creditors were there too.

SAMUEL JOHNSON (1709-84), English author, lexicographer. Quoted in: James Boswell, *Life of Samuel Johnson,* May 1776 (1791).

2   I get so tired listening to one million dollars here, one million dollars there, it's so petty.

IMELDA MARCOS (b. 1929), Filipino First Lady. Quoted in: *Times* (London, 22 June 1990), complaining of the numerous witnesses called to testify against her during her trial on charges of embezzlement in New York.

3   My candle burns at both ends;
It will not last the night;
But ah, my foes, and oh, my friends—
It gives a lovely light!

EDNA ST. VINCENT MILLAY (1892-1950), U.S. poet. *First Fig.*

4   Where there is no extravagance there is no love, and where there is no love there is no understanding.

OSCAR WILDE (1854-1900), Anglo-Irish playwright, author. "Mr. Pater's Last Volume," in *The Artist as Critic: Critical Writings of Oscar Wilde* (ed. by Richard Ellman, 1982).

EXTREMISM

1   This woman did not fly to extremes; she lived there.

QUENTIN CRISP (b. 1908), British author. *The Naked Civil Servant,* ch. 3 (1968).

2   So over violent, or over civil
That every man with him was God or Devil.

JOHN DRYDEN (1631-1700), English poet, dramatist, critic. *Absalom and Achitophel,* pt. 1.

3   I would remind you that extremism in the defense of liberty is no vice! And let me remind you also that moderation in the pursuit of justice is no virtue!

BARRY GOLDWATER (b. 1909), U.S. Republican politician. Speech, 16 July 1964, accepting presidential nomination, Republican National Convention, San Francisco. The Democratic candidate for the presidency, Lyndon B. Johnson, answered this statement in a speech in New York, 31 Oct. 1964: "Extremism in the pursuit of the Presidency is an unpardonable vice. Moderation in the affairs of the nation is the highest virtue." Three days later Johnson won a sweeping victory against Goldwater in the presidential election.

4 What is objectionable, what is dangerous, about extremists is not that they are extreme, but that they are intolerant. The evil is not what they say about their cause, but what they say about their opponents.

> ROBERT KENNEDY (1925-68), U.S. Attorney General, Democratic politician. *The Pursuit of Justice,* pt. 3, "Extremism, Left and Right" (1964).

5 The question is not whether we will be extremists, but what kind of extremists we will be.

> MARTIN LUTHER KING, JR. (1929-68), U.S. clergyman, civil rights leader. "Letter from Birmingham Jail," in *Why We Can't Wait* (1963).

6 Extreme positions are not succeeded by moderate ones, but by *contrary* extreme positions.

> FRIEDRICH NIETZSCHE (1844-1900), German philosopher. *The Will to Power,* aph. 55 (1888; tr. 1967).

7 It is the nature of men having escaped one extreme, which by force they were constrained long to endure, to run headlong into the other extreme, forgetting that virtue doth always consist in the mean.

> SIR WALTER RALEGH (1552-1618), English author, soldier, explorer. *The Cabinet Council,* ch. 25, "A Collection of Political Observations" (repr. in *The Works of Sir Walter Raleigh,* vol. 1, 1751).

FACES

1 Every European visitor to the United States is struck by the comparative rarity of what he would call a face, by the frequency of men and women who look like elderly babies. If he stays in the States for any length of time, he will learn that this cannot be put down to a lack of sensibility—the American feels the joys and sufferings of human life as keenly as anybody else. The only plausible explanation I can find lies in his different attitude to the past. To have a face, in the European sense of the word, it would seem that one must not only enjoy and suffer but also desire to preserve the memory of even the most humiliating and unpleasant experiences of the past.

> W. H. AUDEN (1907-73), Anglo-American poet. *The Dyer's Hand,* pt. 3, "Hic et Ille," sct. D (1962).

2 My face looks like a wedding-cake left out in the rain.

> W. H. AUDEN (1907-73), Anglo-American poet. Quoted in: Humphrey Carpenter, *W. H. Auden,* pt. 2, ch. 6 (1981).

3 I think your whole life shows in your face and you should be proud of that.

> LAUREN BACALL (b. 1924), U.S. actor. *Daily Telegraph* (London, 2 March 1988).

4 Time engraves our faces with all the tears we have not shed.

> NATALIE CLIFFORD BARNEY (1876-1972), U.S.-born French author. Quoted in: George Wickes, *The Amazon of Letters,* ch. 10 (1976).

5 I have eyes like those of a dead pig.

> MARLON BRANDO (b. 1924), U.S. screen actor. Quoted in: Leslie Halliwell, *Halliwell's Filmgoer's Companion* (1984).

6 People remain what they are even if their faces fall apart.

> BERTOLT BRECHT (1898-1956), German dramatist, poet. Garga, in *In the Jungle of Cities,* sc. 9.

7 It has been said that a pretty face is a passport. But it's not, it's a visa, and it runs out fast.

> JULIE BURCHILL (b. 1960), British journalist, author. "Kiss and Sell," in *Mail on Sunday* (London, 1988; repr. in *Sex and Sensibility,* 1992).

8 A blank helpless sort of face, rather like a rose just before you drench it with D.D.T.

> JOHN CAREY (b. 1934), British author, critic. *Sunday Times* (London, 20 Sept. 1981; repr. in *Original Copy,* pt. 2, "Keeping Up with the Coopers," 1987), of photographs of society figure Lady Diana Cooper.

9 The eyes those silent tongues of love.

> MIGUEL DE CERVANTES (1547-1616), Spanish author. Antonio's Amorous Complaint, in *Don Quixote,* pt. 1, bk. 2, ch. 3 (1605; tr. by P. Motteux).

10 He . . . had a face like a blessing.

> MIGUEL DE CERVANTES (1547-1616), Spanish author. *Don Quixote,* pt. 1, bk. 2, ch. 4 (1605; tr. by P. Motteux), Peter's description of the shepherd and scholar Chrysostome (Grisóstomo).

11 A strange and somewhat impassive physiognomy is often, perhaps, an advantage to an orator, or leader of any sort, because it helps to fix the eye and fascinate the mind.

> CHARLES HORTON COOLEY (1864-1929), U.S. sociologist. *Human Nature and the Social Order,* ch. 9 (1902).

12 A man finds room in the few square inches of the face for the traits of all his ancestors; for the expression of all his history, and his wants.

> RALPH WALDO EMERSON (1803-82), U.S. essayist, poet, philosopher. *The Conduct of Life,* "Behavior" (1860).

13 As a beauty I'm not a great star.
Others are handsomer far;
But my face—I don't mind it
Because I'm behind it;
It's the folks out in front that I jar.

> A. H. EUWER (1877-?), U.S. author, illustrator. *Limeratomy.*

14 The human face is the organic seat of beauty. . . . It is the register of value in development, a record of Experience, whose legitimate office is to perfect the life, a legible language to those who will study it, of the majestic mistress, the soul.

> ELIZA FARNHAM (1815-64), U.S. writer, feminist. *Woman and Her Era,* pt. 1, ch. 1 (1864).

15 It has to be displayed, this face, on a more or less horizontal plane. Imagine a man wearing a mask, and imagine that the elastic which holds the mask on has just broken, so that the man (rather than let the mask slip off) has to tilt his head back and balance the mask on his real face. This is the kind of tyranny which Lawson's face exerts over the rest of his body as he cruises along the corridors. . . . He doesn't look down his nose at you, he looks along his nose.

> JAMES FENTON (b. 1949), British poet, critic. *New Statesman* (London, 23 July 1976), referring to former Chancellor Nigel Lawson.

16 A good face they say, is a letter of recommendation. O Nature, Nature, why art thou so dishonest, as ever to send men with these false recommendations into the World!

> HENRY FIELDING (1707-54), English novelist, dramatist. Dr. Harrison, in *Amelia*, vol. 3, bk. 9, ch. 5 (1751). The proverb referred to was attributed to Aristotle by Diogenes Laertius in *Lives of Eminent Philosophers*, bk. 5, sct. 18: "Beauty he declared to be a greater recommendation than any letter of introduction."

17 The faces of most American women over thirty are relief maps of petulant and bewildered unhappiness.

> F. SCOTT FITZGERALD (1896-1940), U.S. author. Letter, later dated 5 Oct. 1940, to his daughter Frances Scott Fitzgerald (published in *The Crack-Up*, ed. by Edmund Wilson, 1945).

18 I am the family face;
Flesh perishes, I live on,
Projecting trait and trace
Through time to times anon,
And leaping from place to place
Over oblivion.

> THOMAS HARDY (1840-1928), English novelist, poet. *Heredity*.

19 Our masks, always in peril of smearing or
  cracking,
In need of continuous check in the mirror or
  silverware,
Keep us in thrall to ourselves, concerned with our
  surfaces.

> CAROLYN KIZER (b. 1925), U.S. poet, educator. *Pro Femina*, in *Knock upon Silence* (1963).

20 The serial number of a human specimen is the face, that accidental and unrepeatable combination of features. It reflects neither character nor soul, nor what we call the self. The face is only the serial number of a specimen.

> MILAN KUNDERA (b. 1929), Czech author, critic. *Immortality*, pt. 1, ch. 3 (1991).

21 We can see nothing whatever of the soul unless it is visible in the expression of the countenance; one might call the faces at a large assembly of people a history of the human soul written in a kind of Chinese ideograms.

> G. C. LICHTENBERG (1742-99), German physicist, philosopher. *Aphorisms*, "Notebook B," aph. 11 (written 1765-99; tr. by R. J. Hollingdale, 1990).

22 Was this the face that launch'd a thousand ships,
And burnt the topless towers of Ilium?

> CHRISTOPHER MARLOWE (1564-93), English dramatist, poet. Faustus, in *The Tragical History of Dr. Faustus*, act 5, sc. 1.

23 A face is too slight a foundation for happiness.

> LADY MARY WORTLEY MONTAGU (1689-1762), English society figure, letter writer. Letter, 25 April 1710, to her future husband (published in *Selected Letters* (ed. by Robert Halsband, 1970).

24 That the public can grow accustomed to any face is proved by the increasing prevalence of Keith's ruined physiognomy on TV documentaries and chat shows, as familiar and homely a horror as Grandpa in *The Munsters*.

> PHILIP NORMAN , British author, journalist. *The Life and Good Times of the Rolling Stones*, Introduction (1989), of Keith Richards. Richards, Norman wrote, "is as endearing a personality as ever lurked within the aspect of Count Dracula on a bad morning. Who, looking into that grave-hollowed face, would ever suspect quick wit, authentic humour or the boozy, affectionate voice of some old-time theatrical actor-manager?"

26 What is your fortune, my pretty maid?
"My face is my fortune, Sir," she said.

> NURSERY RHYME, *Where Are You Going to My Pretty Maid?*

26 At 50, everyone has the face he deserves.

> GEORGE ORWELL (1903-50), British author. *The Collected Essays, Journalism and Letters of George Orwell*, vol. 4 (ed. by Sonia Orwell and Ian Angus, 1968), last entry. Albert Camus, in *The Fall* (1956), expressed much the same when he wrote: "After a certain age every man is responsible for his face."

27 After a certain number of years our faces become our biographies. We get to be responsible for our faces.

> CYNTHIA OZICK (b. 1928), U.S. novelist, short-story writer. Interview in *Writers at Work* (Eighth Series, ed. by George Plimpton, 1988).

28 What is a face, really? Its own photo? Its makeup? Or is it a face as painted by such or such painter? That which is in front? Inside? Behind? And the rest? Doesn't everyone look at himself in his own particular way? Deformations simply do not exist.

> PABLO PICASSO (1881-1973), Spanish artist. *Arts de France*, no. 6 (Paris, 1946). Quoted in: *Picasso on Art* (ed. by Dore Ashton, 1972).

29 The features of our face are hardly more than gestures which force of habit made permanent. Nature, like the destruction of Pompeii, like the metamorphosis of a nymph into a tree, has arrested us in an accustomed movement.

> MARCEL PROUST (1871-1922), French novelist. *Remembrance of Things Past*, vol. 4, "Within a Budding Grove," pt. 2, "Seascape, with Frieze of Girls" (1918; tr. by Scott Monkrieff, 1924).

30 A man's face as a rule says more, and more interesting things, than his mouth, for it is a compendium of everything his mouth will ever say, in that it is the monogram of all this man's thoughts and aspirations.

> ARTHUR SCHOPENHAUER (1788-1860), German philosopher. *Parerga and Paralipomena*, vol. 2, ch. 29, sct. 377 (1851).

31 The tartness of his face sours ripe grapes.

> WILLIAM SHAKESPEARE (1564-1616), English dramatist, poet. Menenius, in *Coriolanus*, act 5, sc. 4.

32 Thus is his cheek the map of days outworn.

> WILLIAM SHAKESPEARE (1564-1616), English dramatist, poet. *Sonnet* 68.

33 Wrinkles should merely indicate where smiles have been.

> MARK TWAIN (1835-1910), U.S. author. *Following the Equator*, ch. 52, "Pudd'nhead Wilson's New Calendar" (1897).

34 This face is a dog's snout sniffing for garbage,
Snakes nest in that mouth, I hear the sibilant threat.

> WALT WHITMAN (1819-92), U.S. poet. *Faces*, sct. 2.

35 A man's face is his autobiography. A woman's face is her work of fiction.

> OSCAR WILDE (1854-1900), Anglo-Irish playwright, author. Quoted in: H. Montgomery Hyde, *Oscar Wilde,* ch. 9 (1976).

36 The face is the soul of the body.

> LUDWIG WITTGENSTEIN (1889-1951), Austrian philosopher. *Culture and Value* (ed. by G. H. von Wright and Heikki Nyman, 1980), 1932-34 entry.

37 Tom's great yellow bronze mask all draped upon an iron framework. An inhibited, nerve-drawn; dropped face—as if hung on a scaffold of heavy private brooding; & thought.

> VIRGINIA WOOLF (1882-1941), British novelist. *The Diary of Virginia Woolf,* vol. 5 (ed. by Anne O. Bell, 1984), entry for 16 Feb. 1940, describing T. S. Eliot at a dinner party.

See also Twain on APPEARANCE; BEARDS; Auden on CHILDREN; NOSES.

FACTS

1 Facts can't be recounted; much less twice over, and far less still by different persons. I've already drummed that thoroughly into your head. What happens is that your wretched memory remembers the words and forgets what's behind them.

> AUGUSTO ROA BASTOS (b. 1917), Paraguayan novelist. *I the Supreme* (1974; tr. 1986; repr. 1988).

2 The construction of life is at present in the power of facts far more than convictions.

> WALTER BENJAMIN (1892-1940), German critic, philosopher. *One-Way Street,* "Filling Station" (1928; repr. in *One-Way Street and Other Writings,* 1978).

3 It is the nature of all greatness not to be exact.

> EDMUND BURKE (1729-97), Irish philosopher, statesman. "First Speech on Conciliation with America: On American Taxation," speech, 19 April 1774, to House of Commons.

4 What are your historical Facts; still more your biographical? Wilt thou know a Man . . . by stringing-together beadrolls of what thou namest Facts?

> THOMAS CARLYLE (1795-1881), Scottish essayist, historian. Teufelsdröckh, in *Sartor Resartus,* bk. 2, ch. 10 (1833-34).

5 I grow daily to honour facts more and more, and theory less and less. A fact, it seems to me, is a great thing—a sentence printed, if not by God, then at least by the Devil.

> THOMAS CARLYLE (1795-1881), Scottish essayist, historian. Letter, 29 April 1836, to Ralph Waldo Emerson.

6 Now, what I want is, Facts. Teach these boys and girls nothing but Facts. Facts alone are wanted in life. Plant nothing else, and root out everything else. You can only form the minds of reasoning animals upon Facts: nothing else will ever be of any service to them. This is the principle on which I bring up my own children, and this is the principle on which I bring up these children. Stick to Facts, sir!

> CHARLES DICKENS (1812-70), English novelist. Mr. Gradgrind, in *Hard Times,* bk. 1, ch. 1 (1854). Thomas Gradgrind was "a man of realities. A man of facts and calculations."

7 Some facts should be suppressed, or, at least, a just sense of proportion should be observed in treating them.

> SIR ARTHUR CONAN DOYLE (1859-1930), English author. Sherlock Holmes, in *The Sign of Four,* ch. 1 (1890).

8 Time dissipates to shining ether the solid angularity of facts.

> RALPH WALDO EMERSON (1803-82), U.S. essayist, poet, philosopher. *Essays,* "History" (First Series, 1841).

9 Every fact is related on one side to sensation, and, on the other, to morals. The game of thought is, on the appearance of one of these two sides, to find the other; given the upper, to find the under side.

> RALPH WALDO EMERSON (1803-82), U.S. essayist, poet, philosopher. *Representative Men,* ch. 4, "Montaigne" (1850).

10 Anyone who knows a strange fact shares in its singularity.

> JEAN GENET (1910-86), French playwright, novelist. *Prisoner of Love,* pt. 1 (1986; tr. 1989).

11 The facts: nothing matters but the facts: worship of the facts leads to everything, to happiness first of all and then to wealth.

> EDMOND (1822-96) AND JULES DE GONCOURT (1830-70), French writers. *The Goncourt Journals* (1888-96; repr. in *Pages from the Goncourt Journal,* ed. by Robert Baldick, 1962), entry for 30 July 1861.

12 Facts are counterrevolutionary.

> ERIC HOFFER (1902-1983), U.S. philosopher. *The Passionate State of Mind,* aph. 73 (1955).

13 All generous minds have a horror of what are commonly called "facts." They are the brute beasts of the intellectual domain. Who does not know fellows that always have an ill-conditioned fact or two that they lead after them into decent company like so many bull-dogs, ready to let them slip at every ingenious suggestion, or convenient generalization, or pleasant fancy? I allow no "facts" at this table.

> OLIVER WENDELL HOLMES, SR. (1809-94), U.S. writer, physician. *The Autocrat of the Breakfast-Table,* ch. 1 (1858).

14 Facts are ventriloquists' dummies. Sitting on a wise man's knee they may be made to utter words of wisdom; elsewhere, they say nothing, or talk nonsense, or indulge in sheer diabolism.

> ALDOUS HUXLEY (1894-1963), British author. Bruno Rontini's notes, in *Time Must Have a Stop,* ch. 30 (1944).

15 The fatal futility of Fact.

> HENRY JAMES (1843-1916), U.S. author. *The Spoils of Poynton,* Preface (1897). The preface first appeared in the New York edition of James's work (1907-9) and was later republished in *The Art of the Novel* (ed. by R. P. Blackmur, 1934).

16 Our esteem for facts has not neutralized in us all religiousness. It is itself almost religious. Our scientific temper is devout.

> WILLIAM JAMES (1842-1910), U.S. psychologist, philosopher. *Pragmatism,* Lecture 1, "The Present Dilemma in Philosophy" (1907).

17 The ultimate umpire of all things in life is—Fact.

> AGNES C. LAUT (1871-1936), Canadian journalist, author. *The Conquest of the Great Northwest,* ch. 20 (1908).

18 I'm not afraid of facts, I welcome facts *but a congeries of facts is not equivalent to an idea.* This is the essential fallacy of the so-called "scientific" mind. People who mistake facts for ideas are incomplete thinkers; they are gossips.

CYNTHIA OZICK (b. 1928), U.S. novelist, short-story writer. "We Are the Crazy Lady and Other Feisty Feminist Fables," published in *The First Ms. Reader* (ed. by Francine Klagsbrun, 1972).

19 A fact is like a sack—it won't stand up if it's empty. To make it stand up, first you have to put in it all the reasons and feelings that caused it in the first place.

LUIGI PIRANDELLO (1867-1936), Italian author, playwright. The Father, in *Six Characters in Search of an Author*, act 1 (1921).

20 I might show facts as plain as day:
But, since your eyes are blind, you'd say,
"Where? What?" and turn away.

CHRISTINA ROSSETTI (1830-94), English poet, lyricist. *A Sketch*, st. 3.

21 Obviously the facts are never just coming at you but are incorporated by an imagination that is formed by your previous experience. Memories of the past are not memories of facts but memories of your imaginings of the facts.

PHILIP ROTH (b. 1933), U.S. novelist. *The Facts*, opening letter to Zuckerman (1988).

22 Those who forget good and evil and seek only to know the facts are more likely to achieve good than those who view the world through the distorting medium of their own desires.

BERTRAND RUSSELL (1872-1970), British philosopher, mathematician. *A Free Man's Worship and Other Essays*, ch. 2 (1976).

23 She always says, my lord, that facts are like cows. If you look them in the face hard enough they generally run away.

DOROTHY L. SAYERS (1893-1957), British author. Bunter, in *Clouds of Witness*, ch. 4 (1926).

24 Oh, don't tell me of facts—I never believe facts: you know Canning said nothing was so fallacious as facts, except figures.

SYDNEY SMITH (1771-1845), English writer, clergyman. Quoted in: Lady Holland, *Memoir* vol. 1, "Recipe for Salad" (1855).

25 Facts are stubborn things.

TOBIAS SMOLLETT (1721-71), Scottish novelist, surgeon. *Gil Blas de Santillane*, bk. 10, ch. 1 (1715; tr. by Alain René Lesage, 1755).

26 My facts shall be falsehoods to the common sense. I would so state facts that they shall be significant, shall be myths or mythologic. Facts which the mind perceived, thoughts which the body thought—with these I deal.

HENRY DAVID THOREAU (1817-62), U.S. philosopher, author, naturalist. *Journals* (1906), entry for 9 Nov. 1851.

27 Facts are generally overesteemed. For most practical purposes, a thing is what men think it is. When they judged the earth flat, it was flat. As long as men thought slavery tolerable, tolerable it was. We live down here among shadows, shadows among shadows.

JOHN UPDIKE (b. 1932), U.S. author, critic. The Statesman Buchanan, in *Buchanan Dying*, act 1 (1974).

28 It is the spirit of the age to believe that any fact, no matter how suspect, is superior to any imaginative exercise, no matter how true.

GORE VIDAL (b. 1925), U.S. novelist, critic. "French Letters: Theories of the New Novel," in *Encounter* (London, Dec. 1967).

See also Woolf on BIOGRAPHY; Boyd on HAPPINESS; Scott on NEWSPAPERS AND MAGAZINES; Twain on PROPAGANDA.

FAILURE

1 There are few things more dreadful than dealing with a man who knows he is going under, in his own eyes, and in the eyes of others. Nothing can help that man. What is left of that man flees from what is left of human attention.

JAMES BALDWIN (1924-87), U.S. author. *The Price of the Ticket*, Introduction (1985).

2 We are all failures—at least, all the best of us are.

J. M. BARRIE (1860-1937), British playwright. Rectorial address, 3 May 1922, St. Andrew's University, Scotland.

3 Ever tried. Ever failed. No matter. Try Again. Fail again. Fail better.

SAMUEL BECKETT (1906-89), Irish dramatist, novelist. *Worstward Ho* (1984).

4 Everything ultimately fails, for we die, and that is either the penultimate failure or our most enigmatical achievement.

EDWARD DAHLBERG (1900-1977), U.S. author, critic. *Alms for Oblivion*, "Our Vanishing Cooperative Colonies" (1964).

5 Failure after long perseverance is much grander than never to have a striving good enough to be called a failure.

GEORGE ELIOT (1819-80), English novelist. Dorothea, in *Middlemarch*, bk. 2, ch. 22 (1871-72).

6 All of us failed to match our dreams of perfection. So I rate us on the basis of our splendid failure to do the impossible.

WILLIAM FAULKNER (1897-1962), U.S. novelist. Interview in *Writers at Work* (First Series, ed. by Malcolm Cowley, 1958), referring to Faulkner's writing contemporaries.

7 And nothing to look backward to with pride,
And nothing to look forward to with hope.

ROBERT FROST (1874-1963), U.S. poet. *The Death of the Hired Man*.

8 He was a self-made man who owed his lack of success to nobody.

JOSEPH HELLER (b. 1923), U.S. novelist. *Catch-22*, ch. 3 (1961), of Colonel Cargill.

9 There is no loneliness greater than the loneliness of a failure. The failure is a stranger in his own house.

ERIC HOFFER (1902-83), U.S. philosopher. *The Passionate State of Mind*, aph. 223 (1955).

10 Our achievements speak for themselves. What we have to keep track of are our failures, discouragements, and doubts. We tend to forget the past difficulties, the many false starts, and the painful groping. We see our past achievements as the end result of a clean forward thrust, and our present difficulties as signs of decline and decay.

> ERIC HOFFER (1902-83), U.S. philosopher. *Reflections on the Human Condition*, aph. 157 (1973).

11 Failure, then, failure! so the world stamps us at every turn. We strew it with our blunders, our misdeeds, our lost opportunities, with all the memorials of our inadequacy to our vocation. And with what a damning emphasis does it then blot us out! No easy fine, no mere apology or formal expiation, will satisfy the world's demands, but every pound of flesh exacted is soaked with all its blood. The subtlest forms of suffering known to man are connected with the poisonous humiliations incidental to these results.

> WILLIAM JAMES (1842-1910), U.S. psychologist, philosopher. *The Varieties of Religious Experience*, Lectures 6 and 7 (1902).

12 There is not a fiercer hell than the failure in a great object.

> JOHN KEATS (1795-1821), English poet. *Endymion*, Preface (1818).

13 When we can begin to take our failures nonseriously, it means we are ceasing to be afraid of them. It is of immense importance to learn to laugh at ourselves.

> KATHERINE MANSFIELD (1888-1923), New Zealand-born British author. *The Journal of Katherine Mansfield* (1927), Oct. 1922 entry.

14 No failure in America, whether of love or money, is ever simple; it is always a kind of betrayal, of a mass of shadowy, shared hopes.

> GREIL MARCUS (b. 1945), U.S. rock journalist. *Mystery Train*, "Robert Johnson" (1976).

15 He's not the finest character that ever lived. But he's a human being, and a terrible thing is happening to him. So attention must be paid.

> ARTHUR MILLER (b. 1915), U.S. dramatist. Linda, in *Death of a Salesman*, act 1, of her husband Willy Loman.

16 The world itself is pregnant with failure, is the perfect manifestation of imperfection, of the consciousness of failure.

> HENRY MILLER (1891-1980), U.S. author. *The Wisdom of the Heart*, "Reflections of Writing" (1947).

17 It is only possible to succeed at second-rate pursuits—like becoming a millionaire or a prime minister, winning a war, seducing beautiful women, flying thought the stratosphere or landing on the moon. First-rate pursuits—involving, as they must, trying to understand what life is about and trying to convey that understanding—inevitably result in a sense of failure. A Napoleon, a Churchill, a Roosevelt can feel themselves to be successful, but never a Socrates, a Pascal, a Blake. Understanding is for ever unattainable. Therein lies the inevitablility of failure in embarking upon its quest, which is none the less the only one worthy of serious attention.

> MALCOLM MUGGERIDGE (1903-90), British broadcaster. "Woman's Hour," radio broadcast, 5 Aug. 1965. Quoted in: *Muggeridge through the Microphone*, "Failure" (1967).

18 The world is divided into two categories: failures and unknowns.

> FRANCIS PICABIA (1878-1953), French painter, poet. "L'Humour Poetique," in *La Nef*, no. 71-72 (Paris, Dec. 1950-Jan. 1951; repr. in *Yes No: Poems and Sayings*, "Sayings," ed. by Rémy Remy Hall, 1990).

19 Everyone pushes a falling fence.

> CHINESE PROVERB.

20 Our business in this world is not to succeed, but to continue to fail, in good spirits.

> ROBERT LOUIS STEVENSON (1850-94), Scottish novelist, essayist, poet. "Reflections and Remarks on Human Life," sct. 4 (1878; repr. in *Complete Works*, vol. 26, 1924).

21 Why is it so painful to watch a person sink? Because there is something unnatural in it, for nature demands personal progress, evolution, and every backward step means wasted energy.

> J. AUGUST STRINDBERG (1849-1912), Swedish dramatist, novelist, poet. *A Madman's Defense*, pt. 2, ch. 5 (1968).

22 I cannot give you the formula for success, but I can give you the formula for failure—which is: Try to please everybody.

> HERBERT B. SWOPE (1882-1958), U.S. journalist. Speech, 20 Dec. 1950.

See also Marcus on CLICHÉS; Shakespeare on COURAGE; Hare on DOUBT; Eliot on PURPOSE; Maugham on SUCCESS.

FAIRIES

1 Up the airy mountain,
   Down the rushy glen,
   We daren't go a-hunting
   For fear of little men.

> WILLIAM ALLINGHAM (1824-89), Irish poet, diarist. *The Fairies*, in *Day and Night Songs* (1855).

2 When the first baby laughed for the first time, the laugh broke into a thousand pieces and they all went skipping about, and that was the beginning of fairies. And now when every new baby is born its first laugh becomes a fairy. So there ought to be one fairy for every boy or girl.

> J. M. BARRIE (1860-1937), British playwright. Peter, in *Peter Pan*, act 1.

3 God defend me from that Welsh fairy,
   Lest he transform me to a piece of cheese!

> WILLIAM SHAKESPEARE (1564-1616), English dramatist, poet. Sir John Falstaff, in *The Merry Wives of Windsor*, act 5, sc. 5. Falstaff's reference to Sir Hugh Evans (disguised as a satyr) was based on the notion that the Welsh were great eaters of cheese.

4 The land of faery
   Where nobody gets old and godly and grave,
   Where nobody gets old and crafty and wise,
   Where nobody gets old and bitter of tongue.

> W. B. YEATS (1865-1939), Irish poet. *The Land of Heart's Desire*.

FAITH

1   May it not be that, just as we have to have faith in Him, God has to have faith in us and, considering the history of the human race so far, may it not be that "faith" is even more difficult for Him than it is for us?

> W. H. AUDEN (1907-73), Anglo-American poet. *A Certain World*, "God" (1970).

2   You don't decide to build a church because you have money in the bank. You build because God says this is what I should do. Faith is the supplier of things hoped for and the evidence of things not seen.

> JIM BAKKER (b. 1940), U.S. evangelist. Quoted in: *New Yorker* (23 April 1990).

3   Faith is not a thing which one "loses," we merely cease to shape our lives by it.

> GEORGES BERNANOS (1888-1948), French novelist, political writer. *The Diary of a Country Priest*, ch. 4 (1936).

4   Faith is the substance of things hoped for, the evidence of things not seen.

> BIBLE: NEW TESTAMENT. *Hebrews* 11:1.

5   For verily I say unto you, that whosoever shall say unto this mountain, Be thou removed, and be thou cast into the sea; and shall not doubt in his heart, but shall believe that those things which he saith shall come to pass; he shall have whatsoever he saith.

> BIBLE: NEW TESTAMENT. Jesus, in *Mark* 11:23. *Matthew* 21:21 also refers to this speech.

6   If thou canst believe, all things are possible to him that believeth.

> BIBLE: NEW TESTAMENT. Jesus' words to the father of a sick child, in *Mark* 9:23.

7   Faith. Belief without evidence in what is told by one who speaks without knowledge, of things without parallel.

> AMBROSE BIERCE (1842-1914), U.S. author. *The Devil's Dictionary* (1881-1906).

8   What is faith but a kind of betting or speculation after all? It should be, "I bet that my Redeemer liveth."

> SAMUEL BUTLER (1835-1902), English author. *Samuel Butler's Notebooks* (1951; first published 1912).

9   It is useless to tell one *not* to *reason* but to *believe*—you might as well tell a man not to wake but *sleep*.

> LORD BYRON (1788-1824), English poet. *Detached Thoughts*, no. 96 (1821-22; published in *Byron's Letters and Journals*, vol. 9, ed. by Leslie A. Marchand, 1979).

10   Faith—is the Pierless Bridge
Supporting what We see
Unto the Scene that We do not—.

> EMILY DICKINSON (1830-86), U.S. poet. *The Complete Poems*, no. 915 (1955).

11   Reason is our soul's left hand, Faith her right,
By these we reach divinity.

> JOHN DONNE (c. 1572-1631), English divine, metaphysical poet. *Verse Letter to the Countess of Bedford* (c. 1607-8).

12   Faith, to my mind, is a stiffening process, a sort of mental starch, which ought to be applied as sparingly as possible.

> E. M. FORSTER (1879-1970), British novelist, essayist. *Two Cheers for Democracy*, "What I Believe" (1951).

13   If you have abandoned one faith, do not abandon all faith. There is always an alternative to the faith we lose. Or is it the same faith under another mask?

> GRAHAM GREENE (1904-91), British novelist. Closing words of Dr. Magiot's last letter, in *The Comedians*, pt. 2, ch. 4, sct. 4 (1966).

14   In properly organized groups no faith is required; what is required is simply a little trust and even that only for a little while, for the sooner a man begins to verify all he hears the better it is for him.

> GEORGE GURDJIEFF (c. 1877-1949), Greek-Armenian religious teacher, mystic. Quoted in: P. D. Ouspensky, *In Search of the Miraculous*, ch. 11 (1949).

15   Absolute faith corrupts as absolutely as absolute power.

> ERIC HOFFER (1902-83), U.S. philosopher. *Reflections on the Human Condition*, aph. 13 (1973).

16   Our faith is faith in someone else's faith, and in the greatest matters this is most the case.

> WILLIAM JAMES (1842-1910), U.S. psychologist, philosopher. "The Will to Believe," in *New World* (June 1896).

17   All things are inconstant except the faith in the soul, which changes all things and fills their inconstancy with light, but though I seem to be driven out of my country as a misbeliever I have found no man yet with a faith like mine.

> JAMES JOYCE (1882-1941), Irish author. Letter from a private collection, 22 Nov. 1902, in which Joyce declared his intention of leaving Ireland for good. An inaccurate text, taken from a typescript of this letter, is printed in *Letters of James Joyce*, vol. 1 (1957).

18   Faith is the highest passion in a human being. Many in every generation may not come that far, but none comes further.

> SØREN KIERKEGAARD (1813-55), Danish philosopher. *Fear and Trembling*, "Epilogue" (1843; tr. 1985).

19   Every Age has its own peculiar faith. . . . Any attempt to translate into facts the mission of one Age with the machinery of another, can only end in an indefinite series of abortive efforts. Defeated by the utter want of proportion between the means and the end, such attempts might produce martyrs, but never lead to victory.

> GIUSEPPE MAZZINI (1805-72), Italian nationalist leader. *Faith and the Future*, sct. 6 (1835; tr. in *Essays by Joseph Mazzini*, ed. by Bolton King, 1894).

20   Faith, like a jackal, feeds among the tombs, and even from these dead doubts she gathers her most vital hope.

> HERMAN MELVILLE (1819-91), U.S. author. *Moby-Dick*, ch. 7 (1851).

21   Faith may be defined briefly as an illogical belief in the occurrence of the improbable. . . . A man full of faith is simply one who has lost (or never had) the capacity for clear and realistic thought. He is not a mere ass: he is actually ill.

> H. L. MENCKEN (1880-1956), U.S. journalist. *Prejudices*, ch. 14, "The Believer" (Third Series, 1922).

22 My faith is the grand drama of my life. I'm a believer, so I sing words of God to those who have no faith. I give bird songs to those who dwell in cities and have never heard them, make rhythms for those who know only military marches or jazz, and paint colours for those who see none.

> OLIVIER MESSIAEN (1908-92), French composer, organist. *Independent* (London, 9 Dec. 1988).

23 Back of every creation, supporting it like an arch, is faith. Enthusiasm is nothing: it comes and goes. But if one *believes*, then miracles occur.

> HENRY MILLER (1891-1980), U.S. author. *The Air-Conditioned Nightmare*, "With Edgar Varèse in the Gobi Desert" (1945).

24 It is as absurd to argue men, as to torture them, into believing.

> CARDINAL JOHN NEWMAN (1801-90), English churchman, theologian. Sermon, 11 Dec. 1831, Oxford, England.

25 Life is a battle between faith and reason in which each feeds upon the other, drawing sustenance from it and destroying it.

> REINHOLD NIEBUHR (1892-1971), U.S. theologian, historian. *Leaves from the Notebook of a Tamed Cynic* (1930), 1928 entry.

26 Faith certainly tells us what the senses do not, but not the contrary of what they see; it is above, not against them.

> BLAISE PASCAL (1623-62), French scientist, philosopher. *Pensées* (1670; no. 185 ed. by Krailsheimer, no. 265 ed. by Brunschvicg).

27 It is the heart which perceives God and not the reason. That is what faith is: God perceived by the heart, not by the reason.

> BLAISE PASCAL (1623-62), French scientist, philosopher. *Pensées* (1670; no. 424 ed. by Krailsheimer, no. 278 ed. by Brunschvicg).

28 Faith is an excitement and an enthusiasm: it is a condition of intellectual magnificence to which we must cling as to a treasure, and not squander on our way through life in the small coin of empty words, or in exact and priggish argument.

> GEORGE SAND (1804-76), French novelist. Letter, 25 May 1866 (published in *Correspondence*, vol. 4, 1883).

29 The words which express our faith and piety are not definite; yet they are significant and fragrant like frankincense to superior natures.

> HENRY DAVID THOREAU (1817-62), U.S. philosopher, author, naturalist. *Walden*, "Conclusion" (1854).

30 Despotism may govern without faith, but liberty cannot. . . . How is it possible that society should escape destruction if the moral tie is not strengthened in proportion as the political tie is relaxed? And what can be done with a people who are their own masters if they are not submissive to the Deity?

> ALEXIS DE TOCQUEVILLE (1805-59), French social philosopher. *Democracy in America*, vol. 1, ch. 17 (1835).

31 It was the schoolboy who said, "Faith is believing what you know ain't so."

> MARK TWAIN (1835-1910), U.S. author. *Following the Equator*, ch. 12, "Pudd'nhead Wilson's New Calendar" (1897).

32 Philosophic argument, especially that drawn from the vastness of the universe, in comparison with the apparent insignificance of this globe, has sometimes shaken my reason for the faith that is in me; but my heart has always assured and reassured me that the gospel of Jesus Christ must be Divine Reality. The Sermon on the Mount cannot be a mere human production. This belief enters into the very depth of my conscience. The whole history of man proves it.

> DANIEL WEBSTER (1782-1852), U.S. lawyer, statesman. Spoken on the eve of his death and carved as his epitaph.

33 The mysteries of faith are degraded if they are made into an object of affirmation and negation, when in reality they should be an object of contemplation.

> SIMONE WEIL (1909-43), French philosopher, mystic. *Gravity and Grace*, "Intelligence and Grace" (1947; tr. 1952).

See also Johnson on The AFTERLIFE; Benn on DOCTRINE; Hoffer on TECHNOLOGY.

FALLIBILITY

1 Fear of error which everything recalls to me at every moment of the flight of my ideas, this mania for control, makes men prefer reason's imagination to the imagination of the senses. And yet it is always the imagination alone which is at work.

> LOUIS ARAGON (1897-1982), French poet. *Paris Peasant*, "Preface to a Modern Mythology" (1926).

2 To be positive. To be mistaken at the top of one's voice.

> AMBROSE BIERCE (1842-1914), U.S. author. *The Devil's Dictionary* (1881-1906).

3 Both men and women are fallible. The difference is, women know it.

> ELEANOR BRON (b. 1934), British actor, author. *Times* (London, 28 July 1992).

4 We all carry within us our places of exile, our crimes, and our ravages. But our task is not to unleash them on the world; it is to fight them in ourselves and in others.

> ALBERT CAMUS (1913-60), French-Algerian philosopher, author. *The Rebel*, pt. 5, "Moderation and Excess" (1951; tr. 1953).

5 The organizations of men, like men themselves, seem subject to deafness, nearsightedness, lameness, and involuntary cruelty. We seem tragically unable to help one another, to understand one another.

> JOHN CHEEVER (1912-82), U.S. author. *John Cheever: The Journals*, "The Sixties" (ed. by Robert Gottlieb, 1991), 1963 entry.

6 I beseech you, in the bowels of Christ, think it possible you may be mistaken.

> OLIVER CROMWELL (1599-1658), Parliamentarian general, Lord Protector of England. Letter, 3 Aug. 1650, to the General Assembly of the Scottish Kirk.

7   It is well that there is no one without a fault; for he would not have a friend in the world.

> WILLIAM HAZLITT (1778-1830), English essayist. *Characteristics: In the Manner of Rochefoucault's Maxims*, no. 66 (1823; repr. in *The Complete Works of William Hazlitt*, vol. 9, ed. by P. P. Howe, 1932).

8   Man approaches the unattainable truth through a succession of errors.

> ALDOUS HUXLEY (1894-1963), British author. *Do What You Will*, "Wordsworth in the Tropics" (1929).

9   It is in our faults and failings, not in our virtues, that we touch each other, and find sympathy. . . . It is in our follies that we are one.

> JEROME K. JEROME (1859-1927), British author. *Idle Thoughts of an Idle Fellow*, "On Vanity and Vanities" (1889).

10   Once we know our weaknesses they cease to do us any harm.

> G. C. LICHTENBERG (1742-99), German physicist, philosopher. *Aphorisms*, "Notebook D," aph. 5 (written 1765-99; tr. by R. J. Hollingdale, 1990).

11   In the works of man, everything is as poor as its author; vision is confined, means are limited, scope is restricted, movements are labored, and results are humdrum.

> JOSEPH DE MAISTRE (1753-1821), French diplomat, philosopher. *Considerations on France*, ch. 1 (1796; repr. in *The Works of Joseph de Maistre*, ed. by Jack Lively, 1965).

12   It wounds a man less to confess that he has failed in any pursuit through idleness, neglect, the love of pleasure, etc., etc., which are his own faults, than through incapacity and unfitness, which are the faults of his nature.

> LORD MELBOURNE (1779-1848), English statesman, prime minister. Quoted in: David Cecil, *The Young Melbourne*, ch. 9 (1939).

13   If I have any justification for having lived it's simply, I'm nothing but faults, failures and so on, but I have tried to make a good pair of shoes. There's some value in that.

> ARTHUR MILLER (b. 1915), U.S. dramatist. *Marxism Today* (London, Jan. 1988).

14   It says nothing against the ripeness of a spirit that it has a few worms.

> FRIEDRICH NIETZSCHE (1844-1900), German philosopher. *Assorted Opinions and Maxims*, aph. 353 (1879).

15   The first faults are theirs that commit them, the second theirs that permit them.

> ENGLISH PROVERB (18th century).

16   In the stress of modern life, how little room is left for that most comfortable vanity that whispers in our ears that failures are not faults! Now we are taught from infancy that we must rise or fall upon our own merits; that vigilance wins success, and incapacity means ruin.

> AGNES REPPLIER (1858-1950), U.S. author, social critic. *Books and Men*, "On the Benefits of Superstition" (1888).

17   A life spent in making mistakes is not only more honorable but more useful than a life spent doing nothing.

> GEORGE BERNARD SHAW (1856-1950), Anglo-Irish playwright, critic. *The Doctor's Dilemma*, "The Technical Problem," Preface (1911).

18   We are built to make mistakes, coded for error.

> LEWIS THOMAS (b. 1913), U.S. physician, educator. *The Medusa and the Snail*, "To Err is Human" (1979).

19   Our failings sometimes bind us to one another as closely as could virtue itself.

> LUC, MARQUIS DE VAUVENARGUES (1715-47), French moralist. *Refléxions et Maximes*, no. 176 (1746).

See also Wilde on MEN AND WOMEN; Eliot on PROPHECY.

FAME

1   Fame often makes a writer vain, but seldom makes him proud.

> W. H. AUDEN (1907-73), Anglo-American poet. *The Dyer's Hand*, pt. 1, "Writing" (1962).

2   Those who have known the famous are publicly debriefed of their memories, knowing as their own dusk falls that they will only be remembered for remembering someone else.

> ALAN BENNETT (b. 1934), British playwright. Peggy, in *Prick Up Your Ears: The Screenplay* (1987).

3   The strongest poison ever known
Came from Caesar's laurel crown.

> WILLIAM BLAKE (1757-1827), English poet, painter, engraver. *Auguries of Innocence*, in *Poems from the Pickering Manuscript* (c. 1808; repr. in *Complete Writings*, ed. by Geoffrey Keynes, 1957).

4   Celebrity-worship and hero-worship should not be confused. Yet we confuse them every day, and by doing so we come dangerously close to depriving ourselves of all real models. We lose sight of the men and women who do not simply seem great because they are famous but are famous because they are great. We come closer and closer to degrading all fame into notoriety.

> DANIEL J. BOORSTIN (b. 1914), U.S. historian. *The Image*, ch. 2 (1961).

5   But the iniquity of oblivion blindly scattereth her poppy, and deals with the memory of men without distinction to merit of perpetuity.

> SIR THOMAS BROWNE (1605-82), English physician, author. *Urn Burial*, ch. 5 (1658).

6   Happy is the man who hath never known what it is to taste of fame—to have it is a purgatory, to want it is a Hell!

> EDWARD BULWER-LYTTON (1803-73), English author, politician. *The Last of the Barons*, bk. 5, ch. 1 (1843).

7   Fame is no sanctuary from the passing of youth . . . suicide is much easier and more acceptable in Hollywood than growing old gracefully.

> JULIE BURCHILL (b. 1960), British journalist, author. *Girls on Film*, ch. 3 (1986).

8 My great comfort is, that the temporary celebrity I have wrung from the world has been in the very teeth of all opinions and prejudices. I have flattered no ruling powers; I have never concealed a single thought that tempted me.

> LORD BYRON (1788-1824), English poet. Letter, 9 April 1814, to the poet Thomas Moore (published in *Byron's Letters and Journals*, vol. 4, ed. by Leslie A. Marchand, 1975).

9 I would much rather have men ask why I have no statue than why I have one.

> CATO THE ELDER (234-149 B.C.), Roman statesman. Quoted in: Plutarch, *Parallel Lives*, "Marcus Cato," ch. 19, sct. 4.

10 If you are ambitious of climbing up to the difficult, and in a manner inaccessible, summit of the Temple of Fame, your surest way is to leave on one hand the narrow path of Poetry, and follow the narrower track of Knight-Errantry, which in a trice may raise you to an imperial throne.

> MIGUEL DE CERVANTES (1547-1616), Spanish writer. *Don Quixote*, pt. 2, bk. 5, ch. 18 (1615; tr. by P. Motteux). "With these words," Cervantes continues, "Don Quixote seemed to have summed up the whole evidence of his madness."

11 To want fame is to prefer dying scorned than forgotten.

> E. M. CIORAN (b. 1911), Rumanian-born French philosopher. *The New Gods*, "Strangled Thoughts," sct. 1 (1969; tr. 1974).

12 A legend is an old man with a cane known for what he used to do. I'm still doing it.

> MILES DAVIS (1926-91), U.S. jazz musician. *International Herald Tribune* (Paris, 17 July 1991).

13 Fame is a fickle food
Upon a shifting plate.

> EMILY DICKINSON (1830-86), U.S. poet. *The Complete Poems*, no. 1659 (1955).

14 What is popularly called fame is nothing but an empty name and a legacy from paganism.

> DESIDERIUS ERASMUS (c. 1466-1536), Dutch humanist. *A Letter to Martin Dorp* (1515).

15 The love of fame is almost another name for the love of excellence; or it is the ambition to attain the highest excellence, sanctioned by the highest authority, that of time.

> WILLIAM HAZLITT (1778-1830), English essayist. *The Round Table*, "On Different Sorts of Fame" (1817).

16 There are names written in her immortal scroll at which Fame blushes!

> WILLIAM HAZLITT (1778-1830), English essayist. *Characteristics: in the Manner of Rochefoucault's Maxims*, no. 132 (1823; repr. in *Collected Works*, vol. 2, ed. by A. R. Waller and Arnold Glover, 1902).

17 It is a mark of many famous people that they cannot part with their brightest hour.

> LILLIAN HELLMAN (1905-84), U.S. playwright. *Pentimento*, "Theatre" (1973).

18 I'm afraid of losing my obscurity. Genuineness only thrives in the dark. Like celery.

> ALDOUS HUXLEY (1894-1963), British author. Miss Thriplow, in *Those Barren Leaves*, pt. 1, ch. 1 (1925).

19 Who would wish to be among the commonplace crowd of the little famous—who are each individually lost in a throng made up of themselves?

> JOHN KEATS (1795-1821), English poet. Letter, 23 Aug. 1819 (published in *Letters of John Keats*, no. 144, ed. by Frederick Page, 1954).

20 Throughout my life, I have seen narrow-shouldered men, without a single exception, committing innumerable stupid acts, brutalizing their fellows and perverting souls by all means. They call the motive for their actions fame.

> ISIDORE DUCASSE, COMTE DE LAUTRÉAMONT (1846-70), French author, poet. *Maldoror*, bk. 1, ch. 5 (1870; tr. 1978).

21 A celebrity is one who is known to many persons he is glad he doesn't know.

> H. L. MENCKEN (1880-1956), U.S. journalist. *A Mencken Chrestomathy*, "Sententiæ: The Mind of Men" (1949).

22 The professional celebrity, male and female, is the crowning result of the star system of a society that makes a fetish of competition. In America, this system is carried to the point where a man who can knock a small white ball into a series of holes in the ground with more efficiency than anyone else thereby gains social access to the President of the United States.

> C. WRIGHT MILLS (1916-62), U.S. sociologist. *The Power Elite*, ch. 4 (1956).

23 In the world of the celebrity, the hierarchy of publicity has replaced the hierarchy of descent and even of great wealth.

> C. WRIGHT MILLS (1916-62), U.S. sociologist. Quoted in: Studs Terkel, *Talking to Myself* bk. 4, ch. 1 (1977).

24 Not to know me argues yourselves unknown.

> JOHN MILTON (1608-74), English poet. Satan to "two fair angels", in *Paradise Lost*, bk. 4.

25 Fame will go by and, so long, I've had you, fame. If it goes by, I've always known it was fickle. So at least it's something I experienced, but that's not where I live.

> MARILYN MONROE (1926-62), U.S. screen actor. Conclusion of taped conversation published in *Life* (New York, 3 Aug 1962), the day that Monroe died.

26 It is better to be a has-been than a never-was.

> CECIL PARKINSON (b. 1932), British Conservative politician. *Guardian* (London, 29 June 1990). Parkinson was forced to resign from his position as chairman of the Conservative party in 1987, following the exposure of his extramarital affair with his former secretary, Sara Keays, and her resulting pregnancy, though he later returned to the cabinet.

27 Now there is fame! Of all—hunger, misery, the incomprehension by the public—fame is by far the worst. It is the castigation of God by the artist. It is sad. It is true.

> PABLO PICASSO (1881-1973), Spanish artist. Quoted in: David Douglas Duncan, *Picasso's Picassos* (1961, p. 74).

28 'Tis the white stag, Fame, we're a-hunting,
Bid the world's hounds come to horn!

> EZRA POUND (1885-1972), U.S. poet, critic. *The White Stag*.

29 Renown? I've already got more of it than those I respect, and will never have as much as those for whom I feel contempt..

> JEAN ROSTAND (1894-1977), French biologist, writer. *Carnets d'un Biologiste* (repr. in *The Substance of Man*, 1962, p. 197).

30 To become a celebrity is to become a brand name. There is Ivory Soap, Rice Krispies, and Philip Roth. Ivory is the soap that floats; Rice Krispies the breakfast cereal that goes snap-crackle-pop; Philip Roth the Jew who masturbates with a piece of liver.

> PHILIP ROTH (b. 1933), U.S. novelist. *Reading Myself and Others*, "Interview with Le Nouvel Observateur," May 1981 (rev. ed. 1985).

31 Time hath . . .
A wallet at his back, wherein he puts
Alms for oblivion, a great-sized monster
Of ingratitudes.

> WILLIAM SHAKESPEARE (1564-1616), English dramatist, poet. Ulysses, in *Troilus and Cressida*, act 3, sc. 3.

32 Because I have conducted my own operas and love sheep-dogs; because I generally dress in tweeds, and sometimes, at winter afternoon concerts, have even conducted in them; because I was a militant suffragette and seized a chance of beating time to "The March of the Women" from the window of my cell in Holloway Prison with a tooth-brush; because I have written books, spoken speeches, broadcast, and don't always make sure that my hat is on straight; for these and other equally pertinent reasons, in a certain sense I am well known.

> DAME ETHEL SMYTH (1858-1944), British composer, feminist. *As Time Went On*, Epilogue (1936).

33 The love of the famous, like all strong passions, is quite abstract. Its intensity can be measured mathematically, and it is independent of persons.

> SUSAN SONTAG (b. 1933), U.S. essayist. *The Benefactor*, ch. 9 (1963).

34 Celebrity is a mask that eats into the face. As soon as one is aware of being "somebody," to be watched and listened to with extra interest, input ceases, and the performer goes blind and deaf in his overanimation. One can either see or be seen.

> JOHN UPDIKE (b. 1932), U.S. author, critic. *Self-Consciousness: Memoirs*, ch. 6 (1989).

See also Shaw on DEATH; Woolf on PUBLICITY.

FAMILY

1 Man is the head of the family, woman the neck that turns the head.

> CHINESE APHORISM.

2 Love, by reason of its passion, destroys the in-between which relates us to and separates us from others. As long as its spell lasts, the only in-between which can insert itself between two lovers is the child, love's own product. The child, this in-between to which the lovers now are related and which they hold in common, is rep-resentative of the world in that it also separates them; it is an indication that they will insert a new world into the existing world. Through the child, it is as though the lovers return to the world from which their love had expelled them. But this new worldliness, the possible result and the only possibly happy ending of a love affair, is, in a sense, the end of love, which must either overcome the partners anew or be transformed into another mode of belonging together.

> HANNAH ARENDT (1906-75), German-born U.S. political philosopher. *The Human Condition*, pt. 5, ch. 33 (1958).

3 He that hath wife and children hath given hostages to fortune; for they are impediments to great enterprises, either of virtue or mischief.

> FRANCIS BACON (1561-1626), English philosopher, essayist, statesman. *Essays*, "Of Marriage and Single Life" (1597-1625).

4 Family jokes, though rightly cursed by strangers, are the bond that keeps most families alive.

> STELLA BENSON (1892-1933), British author. *Pipers and a Dancer*, ch. 9 (1924).

5 A brother offended is harder to be won than a strong city: and their contentions are like the bars of a castle.

> BIBLE, HEBREW. *Proverbs* 18:19.

6 You hear a lot of dialogue on the death of the American family. Families aren't dying. They're merging into big conglomerates.

> ERMA BOMBECK (b. 1927), U.S. journalist. "Empty Fridge, Empty Nest," in *San Francisco Examiner* (1 Oct. 1978).

7 I think the ideal situation for a family is to be completely incestuous.

> WILLIAM BURROUGHS (b. 1914), U.S. author. Taped conversation, 1980, New York City (published in Victor Bockris, *With William Burroughs: A Report from the Bunker*, "On Dreams," 1981).

8 The family is the test of freedom; because the family is the only thing that the free man makes for himself and by himself.

> G. K. CHESTERTON (1874-1936), British author. *Fancies Versus Fads*, "Dramatic Unities" (1923).

9 If Mr. Vincent Price were to be co-starred with Miss Bette Davis in a story by Mr. Edgar Allan Poe directed by Mr. Roger Corman, it could not fully express the pent-up violence and depravity of a single day in the life of the average family.

> QUENTIN CRISP (b. 1908), British author. *Manners from Heaven*, ch. 2 (1984).

10 Accidents will occur in the best-regulated families; and in families not regulated by that pervading influence which sanctifies while it enhances . . . in short, by the influence of Woman, in the lofty character of Wife, they may be expected with confidence, and must be borne with philosophy.

> CHARLES DICKENS (1812-70), English novelist. Mr. Micawber, in *David Copperfield*, ch. 28 (1850).

11 Family quarrels are bitter things. They don't go according to any rules. They're not like aches or wounds;

they're more like splits in the skin that won't heal because there's not enough material.

> F. SCOTT FITZGERALD (1896-1940), U.S. author. *The Crack-Up*, "Notebook O" (ed. by Edmund Wilson, 1945).

12 The awe and dread with which the untutored savage contemplates his mother-in-law are amongst the most familiar facts of anthropology.

> JAMES G. FRAZER (1854-1941), Scottish classicist, anthropologist. *The Golden Bough*, ch. 18 (1922 ed.).

13 What a man sows, that shall he and his relations reap.

> CLARISSA GRAVES (1892-1985?), British poet, translator. Letter, Feb. 1928. Quoted in: *Robert Graves: The Years with Laura 1926-1940*, bk. 2, ch. 9 (1990), referring to the problems connected with the behavior of her brother, poet Robert Graves.

14 The only perfect love to be found on earth is not sexual love, which is riddled with hostility and insecurity, but the wordless commitment of families, which takes as its model mother-love. This is not to say that fathers have no place, for father-love, with its driving for self-improvement and discipline, is also essential to survival, but that uncorrected father-love, father-love as it were practised by both parents, is a way to annihilation.

> GERMAINE GREER (b. 1939), Australian feminist writer. *The Madwoman's Underclothes*, Introduction (1986).

15 The striking point about our model family is not simply the compete-compete, consume-consume style of life it urges us to follow.... The striking point, in the face of all the propaganda, is how few Americans actually live this way.

> LOUISE KAPP HOWE (b. 1934), U.S. author, editor. *The Future of The Family*, Introduction (1972).

16 Growing up human is uniquely a matter of social relations rather than biology. What we learn from connections within the family takes the place of instincts that program the behavior of animals; which raises the question, how good are these connections?

> ELIZABETH JANEWAY (b. 1913), U.S. author, critic. "Incest: A Rational Look at the Oldest Taboo," in *Ms.* (New York, Nov. 1981).

17 As the family goes, so goes the nation and so goes the whole world in which we live.

> JOHN PAUL II [KAROL WOJTYLA] (b. 1920), Polish ecclesiastic, pope. Quoted in: *Observer* (London, 7 Dec. 1986).

18 The most socially subversive institution of our time is the one-parent family.

> PAUL JOHNSON (b. 1928), British journalist. Quoted in: *Sunday Correspondent Magazine* (London, 24 Dec. 1989).

19 Parents and children seldom act in concert: each child endeavours to appropriate the esteem or fondness of the parents, and the parents, with yet less temptation, betray each other to their children.

> SAMUEL JOHNSON (1709-84), English author, lexicographer. Nekayah, in *The History of Rasselas*, ch. 26 (1759).

20 The roaring of the wind is my wife and the stars through the window pane are my children. The mighty

abstract idea I have of beauty in all things stifles the more divided and minute domestic happiness.

> JOHN KEATS (1795-1821), English poet. Letter, 14-31 Oct. 1818, to his brother and sister-in-law (published in *Letters of John Keats*, no. 94, ed. by Frederick Page, 1954). George and Georgiana Keats, married in June of that year and recently settled in the United States, had urged the poet to think of starting a family.

21 The proliferation of support groups suggests to me that too many Americans are growing up in homes that do not contain a grandmother. A home without a grandmother is like an egg without salt and Helpists know it. They have jumped into the void left by the disappearance of morbid old ladies from the bosom of the American family.

> FLORENCE KING (b. 1936), U.S. author. *Reflections in a Jaundiced Eye*, "Does Your Child Taste Salty?" (1989).

22 A poor relation is the most irrelevant thing in nature, a piece of impertinent correspondency, an odious approximation, a haunting conscience, a preposterous shadow, lengthening in the noon-tide of our prosperity.... He is known by his knock.

> CHARLES LAMB (1775-1834), English essayist, critic. *Last Essays of Elia*, "Poor Relations" (1833).

23 With a new *familiarity* and a flesh-creeping "homeliness" entirely of this unreal, materialistic world, where all "sentiment" is coarsely manufactured and advertised in colossal sickly captions, disguised for the sweet tooth of a monstrous baby called "the Public," the family as it is, broken up on all hands by the agency of feminist and economic propaganda, reconstitutes itself in the image of the state.

> WYNDHAM LEWIS (1882-1957), British author, painter. *The Art of Being Ruled*, "The Family and Feminism," ch. 4 (1926).

24 As to the family, I have never understood how that fits in with the other ideals—or, indeed, why it should be an ideal at all. A group of closely related persons living under one roof; it is a convenience, often a necessity, sometimes a pleasure, sometimes the reverse; but who first exalted it as admirable, an almost religious ideal?

> ROSE MACAULAY (1881-1958), British novelist, essayist. *The World My Wilderness*, ch. 20 (1950).

25 The Family is the Country of the heart. There is an angel in the Family who, by the mysterious influence of grace, of sweetness, and of love, renders the fulfilment of duties less wearisome, sorrows less bitter. The only pure joys unmixed with sadness which it is given to man to taste upon earth are, thanks to this angel, the joys of the Family.

> GIUSEPPE MAZZINI (1805-72), Italian nationalist leader. *The Duties of Man*, ch. 6 (1844-58; tr. 1907).

26 Sisters are always drying their hair.
Locked into rooms, alone,
They pose at the mirror, shoulders bare,
Trying this way and that their hair,
Or fly importunate down the stair
To answer the telephone.

> PHYLLIS MCGINLEY (1905-78), U.S. poet, author. *Girl's-Eye View of Relatives: Triolet against Sisters*, in *Times Three* (1960).

27 Nobody has ever before asked the nuclear family to live all by itself in a box the way we do. With no relatives, no support, we've put it in an impossible situation.

MARGARET MEAD (1901-78), U.S. anthropologist. Quoted in: *New Realities* (June 1978).

28 Every man sees in his relatives, and especially in his cousins, a series of grotesque caricatures of himself.

H. L. MENCKEN (1880-1956), U.S. journalist. *Smart Set* (New York, Aug. 1919; repr. in *Prejudices*, Third Series, "The Relative," 1922).

29 There is not much less vexation in the government of a private family than in the managing of an entire state.

MICHEL DE MONTAIGNE (1533-92), French essayist. *Essays*, bk. 1, ch. 38, "Of Solitariness" (1580; tr. by John Florio).

30 Families are nothing other than the idolatry of duty.

ANN OAKLEY (b. 1944), British sociologist, author. *Taking It like a Woman*, "The War Between Love and The Family II" (1984).

31 The family spirit has rendered man carnivorous.

FRANCIS PICABIA (1878-1953), French painter, poet. "Pithecomorphes," in *Littérature*, Second Series, no. 6 (Paris, 1 Nov. 1922; repr. in *Yes No: Poems and Sayings*, "Sayings," tr. by Rémy Hall, 1990).

32 In our family, as far as we are concerned, we were born and what happened before that is myth.

V. S. PRITCHETT (b. 1900), British author. *A Cab at the Door*, vol. 1 (1968), opening words of his autobiography.

33 One of the oddest features of western Christianized culture is its ready acceptance of the myth of the stable family and the happy marriage. We have been taught to accept the myth not as an heroic ideal, something good, brave, and nearly impossible to fulfil, but as the very fibre of normal life. Given most families and most marriages, the belief seems admirable but foolhardly.

JONATHAN RABAN (b. 1942), British author, critic. *For Love and Money*, pt. 3 (1987).

34 For there is no friend like a sister
In calm or stormy weather;
To cheer one on the tedious way,
To fetch one if one goes astray,
To lift one if one totters down,
To strengthen whilst one stands.

CHRISTINA ROSSETTI (1830-94), English poet, lyricist. *Goblin Market*.

35 The family is an early expedient and in many ways irrational. If the race had developed a special sexless class to be nurses, pedagogues, and slaves, like the workers among ants and bees, then the family would have been unnecessary. Such a division of labor would doubtless have involved evils of its own, but it would have obviated some drags and vexations proper to the family.

GEORGE SANTAYANA (1863-1952), U.S. philosopher, poet. *The Life of Reason*, "Reason in Society," ch. 2 (1905-6, rev. ed. 1953).

36 Big sisters are the crab grass in the lawn of life.

CHARLES SCHULZ (b. 1922), U.S. cartoonist. Linus, in *Peanuts* (1952).

37 [He] didn't dare to, because his father had a weak heart and habitually threatened to drop dead if anybody hurt his feelings. You may have noticed that people with weak hearts are the tyrants of English married life.

GEORGE BERNARD SHAW (1856-1950), Anglo-Irish playwright, critic. The Bishop of Chelsea, in *Getting Married*.

38 When our relatives are at home, we have to think of all their good points or it would be impossible to endure them. But when they are away, we console ourselves for their absence by dwelling on their vices.

GEORGE BERNARD SHAW (1856-1950), Anglo-Irish playwright, critic. Captain Shotover, in *Heartbreak House*, act 1.

39 A family's photograph album is generally about the extended family—and, often, is all that remains of it.

SUSAN SONTAG (b. 1933), U.S. essayist. *On Photography*, "In Plato's Cave" (1977).

40 The family is the basic cell of government: it is where we are trained to believe that we are human beings or that we are chattel, it is where we are trained to see the sex and race divisions and become callous to injustice even if it is done to ourselves, to accept as biological a full system of authoritarian government.

GLORIA STEINEM (b. 1934), U.S. feminist writer, editor. Speech, July 1981, to the National Women's Political Causus Conference, Albuquerque, New Mexico.

41 Happy or unhappy, families are all mysterious. We have only to imagine how differently we would be described—and will be, after our deaths—by each of the family members who believe they know us.

GLORIA STEINEM (b. 1934), U.S. feminist writer, editor. *Outrageous Acts and Everyday Rebellions*, "Ruth's Song" (1984).

42 Family . . . the home of all social evil, a charitable institution for comfortable women, an anchorage for house-fathers, and a hell for children.

J. AUGUST STRINDBERG (1849-1912), Swedish dramatist, novelist, poet. *The Son of a Servant*, vol. 1 (1886; tr. by Claud Field, 1913, p. 12).

43 Lord, confound this surly sister,
Blight her brow with blotch and blister,
Cramp her larynx, lung and liver,
In her guts a galling give her.

JOHN MILLINGTON SYNGE (1871-1909), Irish poet, dramatist. *The Curse*.

44 He that loves not his wife and children feeds a lioness at home, and broods a nest of sorrows.

JEREMY TAYLOR (1613-67), English churchman, devotional writer. *Twenty-Seven Sermons*, Sermon 18 (1651).

45 All happy families resemble one another, but each unhappy family is unhappy in its own way.

LEO TOLSTOY (1828-1910), Russian novelist, philosopher. *Anna Karenina* (1873-76), opening words.

46 Relations are simply a tedious pack of people, who haven't got the remotest knowledge of how to live, nor the smallest instinct about when to die.

OSCAR WILDE (1854-1900), Anglo-Irish playwright, author. Algernon, in *The Importance of Being Earnest*, act 1.

47 I can't help detesting my relations. I suppose it comes from the fact that none of us can stand other people having the same faults as ourselves.

OSCAR WILDE (1854-1900), Anglo-Irish playwright, author. Lord Henry, in *The Picture of Dorian Gray*, ch. 1 (1891).

See also Wilde on DINNER PARTIES; FATHERS; Dickens on GREATNESS; Crisp on LIVING TOGETHER; MOTHERS; PARENTS; Elizabeth II on ROYALTY.

FAMINE

1 Half-starved spiders prey'd on half-starved flies.

CHARLES CHURCHILL (1731-64), English clergyman, poet. *The Prophecy of Famine.*

2 When the Somalians were merely another hungry third world people, we sent them guns. Now that they are falling down dead from starvation, we send them troops. Some may see in this a tidy metaphor for the entire relationship between north and south. But it would make a whole lot more sense nutritionally—as well as providing infinitely more vivid viewing—if the Somalians could be persuaded to eat the troops.

BARBARA EHRENREICH (b. 1941), U.S. author, columnist. *Guardian* (London, 9 Jan. 1993).

3 There are flood and drouth
Over the eyes and in the mouth,
Dead water and dead sand
Contending for the upper hand.
The parched eviscerate soil
Gapes at the vanity of toil,
Laughs without mirth.
This is the death of the earth.

T. S. ELIOT (1888-1965), Anglo-American poet, critic. *Little Gidding*, pt. 2, in *Four Quartets.*

4 There was no corn—in the wide market-place
All loathliest things, even human flesh, was sold;
They weighed it in small scales—and many a face
Was fixt in eager horror then; his gold
The miser brought; the tender maid, grown bold
Through hunger, bared her scornèd charms in
  vain.

PERCY BYSSHE SHELLEY (1792-1822), English poet. *The Revolt of Islam*, cto. 10.

5 I will venture to affirm, that the three seasons wherein our corn has miscarried did no more contribute to our present misery, than one spoonful of water thrown upon a rat already drowned would contribute to his death; and that the present plentiful harvest, although it should be followed by a dozen ensuing, would no more restore us, than it would the rat aforesaid to put him near the fire, which might indeed warm his fur-coat, but never bring him back to life.

JONATHAN SWIFT (1667-1745), Anglo-Irish satirist. *A Proposal that all the Ladies and Women of Ireland Should Appear Constantly in Irish Manactures* (1729; repr. in *The Prose Works of Jonathan Swift*, vol. 12, ed. by Herbert Davies, 1955). Swift argued that the chronic situation in Ireland was principally due to the harsh policies carried out by the English over a prolonged period.

FANATICS

1 Just as every conviction begins as a whim so does every emancipator serve his apprenticeship as a crank. A fanatic is a great leader who is just entering the room.

HEYWOOD BROUN (1888-1939), U.S. journalist, novelist. *New York World* (6 Feb. 1928).

2 A fanatic is one who can't change his mind and won't change the subject.

SIR WINSTON CHURCHILL (1874-1965), British statesman, writer. Quoted in: *New York Times* (5 July 1954).

3 The fanatic is incorruptible: if he kills for an idea, he can just as well get himself killed for one; in either case, tyrant or martyr, he is a monster.

E. M. CIORAN (b. 1911), Rumanian-born French philosopher. *A Short History of Decay*, ch. 1, "Genealogy of Fanaticism" (1949).

4 The most dangerous madmen are those created by religion, and . . . people whose aim is to disrupt society always know how to make good use of them on occasion.

DENIS DIDEROT (1713-84), French philosopher. *Conversations with a Christian Lady* (1777; repr. in *Selected Writings*, ed. by Lester G. Crocker, 1966).

5 A fanatic is a man that does what he thinks the Lord would do if He knew the facts of the case.

FINLEY PETER DUNNE (1867-1936), U.S. journalist, humorist. *Mr. Dooley's Opinions*, "Casual Observations" (1890).

6 Fervor is the weapon of choice of the impotent.

FRANTZ FANON (1925-61), Martiniquan psychiatrist, philosopher, political activist. *Black Skins, White Masks*, Introduction (1952; tr. 1967).

7 Defined in psychological terms, a fanatic is a man who consciously over-compensates a secret doubt.

ALDOUS HUXLEY (1894-1963), British author. *Proper Studies*, "The Substitutes for Religion," "The Religion of Sex" (1927).

8 Mere human beings can't afford to be fanatical about anything. . . . Not even about justice or loyalty. The fanatic for justice ends by murdering a million helpless people to clear a space for his law-courts. If we are to survive on this planet, there must be compromises.

STORM JAMESON (1891-1986), British novelist. Vancura, in *A Cup of Tea for Mr. Thorgill*, ch. 28 (1957).

9 In the fevered state of our country, no good can ever result from any attempt to set one of these fiery zealots to rights, either in fact or principle. They are determined as to the facts they will believe, and the opinions on which they will act. Get by them, therefore, as you would by an angry bull; it is not for a man of sense to dispute the road with such an animal.

THOMAS JEFFERSON (1743-1826), U.S. president. Letter, 24 Nov. 1808, to his grandson, Thomas Jefferson Randolph.

10 If you see one cold and vehement at the same time, set him down for a fanatic.

JOHANN KASPAR LAVATER (1741-1801), Swiss divine, poet. *Aphorisms on Man*, no. 282 (1788).

11 Fanatics are picturesque, mankind would rather see gestures than listen to *reasons*.

> FRIEDRICH NIETZSCHE (1844-1900), German philosopher. *The Anti-Christ*, aph. 54 (1895).

12 The worst of madmen is a saint run mad.

> ALEXANDER POPE (1688-1744), English satirical poet. *Imitations of Horace*, bk. 1, Epistle 6, "To Mr. Murray" (1738).

13 Throughout human history, the apostles of purity, those who have claimed to possess a total explanation, have wrought havoc among mere mixed-up human beings.

> SALMAN RUSHDIE (b. 1948), Indian-born British author. "In Good Faith," in *Independent on Sunday* (London, 4 Feb. 1990).

14 Fanaticism consists in redoubling your effort when you have forgotten your aim.

> GEORGE SANTAYANA (1863-1952), U.S. philosopher, poet. *The Life of Reason*, Introduction, "Reason in Commonsense" (1905-86).

15 I carry from my mother's womb
A fanatic's heart.

> W. B. YEATS (1865-1939), Irish poet, playwright. *Remorse for Intemperate Speech*.

See also Junius on PERSUASION; Keats on SECTS.

FANTASY

1 The whole fauna of human fantasies, their marine vegetation, drifts and luxuriates in the dimly lit zones of human activity, as though plaiting thick tresses of darkness. Here, too, appear the lighthouses of the mind, with their outward resemblance to less pure symbols. The gateway to mystery swings open at the touch of human weakness and we have entered the realms of darkness. One false step, one slurred syllable together reveal a man's thoughts.

> LOUIS ARAGON (1897-1982), French poet. *Paris Peasant*, "The Passage de l'Opéra" (1926).

2 I consider it useless and tedious to represent what *exists*, because nothing that *exists* satisfies me. Nature is ugly, and I prefer the monsters of my fancy to what is positively trivial.

> CHARLES BAUDELAIRE (1821-67), French poet. "Salon of 1859," sct. 3, published in *Curiosités Esthétiques* (1868; repr. in *The Mirror of Art*, ed. by Jonathan Mayne, 1955).

3 A partner evoked by sophisticated electric brain stimulation could be as real and much more satisfying than the boy or girl next door. . . . All the stars in Hollywood living or dead are there for your pleasure. Sated with superstars, you can lay Cleopatra, Helen of Troy, Isis, Madame Pompadour, or Aphrodite. You can get fucked by Pan, Jesus Christ, Apollo or the Devil himself.

> WILLIAM BURROUGHS (b. 1914), U.S. author. *The Adding Machine*, "Civilian Defense" (1985).

4 The mind can make
Substance, and people planets of its own
With beings brighter than have been, and give
A breath to forms which can outlive all flesh.

> LORD BYRON (1788-1824), English poet. *The Dream*, sct. 1.

5 The dream of reason produces monsters. Imagination deserted by reason creates impossible, useless thoughts. United with reason, imagination is the mother of all art and the source of all its beauty.

> FRANCISCO JOSÉ DE GOYA Y LUCIENTES (1746-1828), Spanish painter. Caption to *Caprichos*, no. 43, a series of eighty etchings completed in 1798, satirical and grotesque in form.

6 Fantasies are more than substitutes for unpleasant reality; they are also dress rehearsals, plans. All acts performed in the world begin in the imagination.

> BARBARA GRIZZUTI HARRISON (1941), U.S. author, publicist. "Talking Dirty," in *Ms.* (New York, Oct. 1973).

7 The pleasures of the imagination are as it were only drawings and models which are played with by poor people who cannot afford the real thing.

> G. C. LICHTENBERG (1742-99), German physicist, philosopher. *Aphorisms*, "Notebook C," aph. 38 (written 1765-99; tr. by R. J. Hollingdale, 1990).

8 But fantasy *kills* imagination, pornography is death to art.

> IRIS MURDOCH (b. 1919), British novelist, philosopher. Alfred Ludens, in *The Message to the Planet*, pt. 1 (1989).

9 We live under continual threat of two equally fearful, but seemingly opposed, destinies: unremitting banality and inconceivable terror. It is fantasy, served out in large rations by the popular arts, which allows most people to cope with these twin specters.

> SUSAN SONTAG (b. 1933), U.S. essayist. *Against Interpretation*, "The Imagination of Disaster" (1966).

10 One's real life is so often the life that one does not lead.

> OSCAR WILDE (1854-1900), Anglo-Irish playwright, author. *Rose-Leaf and Apple-Leaf: Envoi*.

FAREWELLS

1 Let us eat and drink; for to morrow we shall die.

> BIBLE, HEBREW. *Isaiah* 22:13. Almost the same words are found in *1 Corinthians* 15:32.

2 All farewells should be sudden, when forever.

> LORD BYRON (1788-1824), English poet. Sardanapalus, in *Sardanapalus*, act 5, sc. 1.

3 When I died last, and, Dear, I die
As often as from thee I go
Though it be but an hour ago,
And lovers' hours be full eternity.

> JOHN DONNE c. 1572-1631), English divine, metaphysical poet. *The Legacy*.

4 I always made an awkward bow.

> JOHN KEATS (1795-1821), English poet. Last words of the last letter sent by Keats, 30 Nov. 1820, following his remark, "I can scarcely bid you goodbye, even in a letter." (published in *Letters of John Keats*, ed. by Frederick Page, no. 242, 1954). Two weeks

earlier, desperately ill with tuberculosis, the poet had arrived in Rome, where he was to die on 23 Feb. 1821.

5   *Partir, c'est mourir un peu.*
(To leave is to die a little.)

FRENCH PROVERB. Also incorporated into Edmond Haraucourt, *Rondel de l'Adieu.*

6   Every parting gives a foretaste of death, every reunion a hint of the resurrection.

ARTHUR SCHOPENHAUER (1788-1860), German philosopher. *Parerga and Paralipomena,* vol. 2, ch. 26, sct. 310 (1851).

7   Come,
Let's have one other gaudy night. Call to me
All my sad captains. Fill our bowls once more.
Let's mock the midnight bell.

WILLIAM SHAKESPEARE (1564-1616), English dramatist, poet. Antony, in *Antony and Cleopatra,* act 3, sc. 13. The poet Thom Gunn took the phrase "my sad captains" for a poem and volume of verse published 1961.

8   Faithless is he that says farewell when the road darkens.

J. R. R. TOLKIEN (1892-1973), British novelist, scholar. The dwarf Gimli, in *The Fellowship of the Ring,* pt. 1, ch. 3, *The Lord of the Rings,* bk. 2 of trilogy (1954).

See also DEPARTURE AND PARTING.

FARMING AND FARMERS

1   How can he get wisdom that holdeth the plough, and that glorieth in the goad, that driveth oxen, and is occupied in their labors, and whose talk is of bullocks?

APOCRYPHA. *Ecclesiasticus* 38:25.

2   There is, of course, a gold mine or a buried treasure on every mortgaged homestead. Whether the farmer ever digs for it or not, it is there, haunting his daydreams when the burden of debt is most unbearable.

FAWN M. BRODIE (1915-81), U.S. biographer. *No Man Knows My History,* ch. 2 (1945).

3   There are only three things that can kill a farmer: lightning, rolling over in a tractor, and old age.

BILL BRYSON (b. 1951), U.S. author, journalist. *The Lost Continent: Travels in Small Town America,* ch. 4 (1989).

4   Our farmers round, well pleased with constant gain,
Like other farmers, flourish and complain.

GEORGE CRABBE (1754-1832), English poet, clergyman. *Baptisms,* in *The Parish Register,* pt. 1 (1807).

5   Farming looks mighty easy when your plow is a pencil, and you're a thousand miles from the corn field.

DWIGHT D. EISENHOWER (1890-1969), U.S. general, Republican politician, president. Speech, 25 Sept. 1956, Peoria, Ill.

6   The first farmer was the first man, and all historic nobility rests on possession and use of land.

RALPH WALDO EMERSON (1803-82), U.S. essayist, poet, philosopher. *Society and Solitude,* "Farming" (1870).

7   There seem to be but three ways for a nation to acquire wealth. The first is by *war,* as the Romans did, in plundering their conquered neighbours. This is *robbery.* The second by *commerce,* which is generally *cheating.* The third by *agriculture,* the only *honest way,* wherein man receives a real increase of the seed thrown into the ground, in a kind of continual miracle, wrought by the hand of God in his favor, as a reward for his innocent life and his virtuous industry.

BENJAMIN FRANKLIN (1706-90), U.S. statesman, writer. *Positions to Be Examined Concerning National Wealth* (written 4 April 1769; published in *Complete Works,* vol. 4, ed. by John Bigelow, 1887-88).

8   There is no gilding of setting sun or glamor of poetry to light up the ferocious and endless toil of the farmers' wives.

HAMLIN GARLAND (1860-1940), U.S. author. *Boy Life on the Prairie,* "Melons and Early Frost" (1899).

9   He felt with the force of a revelation that to throw up the clods of earth manfully is as beneficent as to revolutionise the world. It was not the matter of the work, but the mind that went into it, that counted—and the man who was not content to do small things well would leave great things undone.

ELLEN GLASGOW (1874-1945), U.S. novelist. *The Voice of the People,* bk. 2, ch. 4 (1900).

10   Whenever there are in any country uncultivated lands and unemployed poor, it is clear that the laws of property have been so far extended as to violate natural right. The earth is given as a common stock for man to labor and live on. . . . The small landowners are the most precious part of a state.

THOMAS JEFFERSON (1743-1826), U.S. president. Letter, 28 Oct. 1785, to politician (later president) James Madison.

11   Bowed by the weight of centuries he leans
Upon his hoe and gazes on the ground,
The emptiness of ages in his face,
And on his back the burden of the world.

EDWIN MARKHAM (1852-1940), U.S. poet. *The Man with the Hoe.*

12   No one hates his job so heartily as a farmer.

H. L. MENCKEN (1880-1956), U.S. journalist. "What is Going on in the World," in *American Mercury* (Nov. 1933).

13   Farm policy, although it's complex, can be explained. What it can't be is believed. No cheating spouse, no teen with a wrecked family car, no mayor of Washington, D.C., videotaped in flagrante delicto has ever come up with anything as farfetched as U.S. farm policy.

P. J. O'ROURKE (b. 1947), U.S. journalist. *Parliament of Whores,* "How to Tell Your Ass from This Particular Hole in the Ground" (1991).

14   The master's eye is the best fertilizer.

PLINY THE ELDER (c. 23-79), Roman scholar. *Historia Naturalis,* bk. 18, sct. 24.

15   With the introduction of agriculture mankind entered upon a long period of meanness, misery, and madness, from which they are only now being freed by the beneficent operation of the machine.

> BERTRAND RUSSELL (1872-1970), British philosopher, mathematician. *The Conquest of Happiness*, ch. 10 (1930).

16 I see upon their noble brows the seal of the Lord, for they were born kings of the earth far more truly than those who possess it only from having bought it.

> GEORGE SAND (1804-76), French novelist. *The Haunted Pool*, ch. 2 (1851), speaking of peasants.

17 It is sad, no doubt, to exhaust one's strength and one's days in cleaving the bosom of this jealous earth, which compels us to wring from it the treasures of its fertility, when a bit of the blackest and coarsest bread is, at the end of the day's work, the sole recompense and the sole profit attaching to so arduous a toil.

> GEORGE SAND (1804-76), French novelist. *The Haunted Pool*, ch. 2 (1851).

18 By avarice and selfishness, and a groveling habit, from which none of us is free, of regarding the soil as property, or the means of acquiring property chiefly, the landscape is deformed, husbandry is degraded with us, and the farmer leads the meanest of lives. He knows Nature but as a robber.

> HENRY DAVID THOREAU (1817-62), U.S. philosopher, author, naturalist. *Walden*, "The Bean-Field" (1854).

19 Farmers are respectable and interesting to me in proportion as they are poor.

> HENRY DAVID THOREAU (1817-62), U.S. philosopher, author, naturalist. *Walden*, "The Ponds" (1854).

20 No race can prosper till it learns there is as much dignity in tilling a field as in writing a poem.

> BOOKER T. WASHINGTON (1856-1915), U.S. educator. Address, 18 Sept. 1895, Atlanta Exposition.

21 I know of no pursuit in which more real and important services can be rendered to any country than by improving its agriculture, its breed of useful animals, and other branches of a husbandman's cares.

> GEORGE WASHINGTON (1732-99), U.S. general, president. Letter, 20 July 1794.

22 When *tillage* begins, other arts follow. The farmers, therefore, are the founders of human civilization.

> DANIEL WEBSTER (1782-1852), U.S. lawyer, statesman. "Remarks on the Agriculture of England," speech, 13 Jan. 1840, Boston.

23 A good farmer is nothing more nor less than a handy man with a sense of humus.

> E. B. WHITE (1899-1985), U.S. author, editor. *One Man's Meat*, "The Practical Farmer" (1944).

24 Give fools their gold, and knaves their power;
Let fortune's bubbles rise and fall;
Who sows a field, or trains a flower,
Or plants a tree, is more than all.

> JOHN GREENLEAF WHITTIER (1807-92), U.S. poet. *A Song of Harvest*.

See also Swift on ECOLOGY.

FASCISM

1 Fascism is not in itself a new order of society. It is the future refusing to be born.

> ANEURIN BEVAN (1897-1960), British Labour politician. Quoted in: Michael Foot, *Aneurin Bevan*, vol. 1, ch. 10 (1962).

2 I have often thought that if a rational Fascist dictatorship were to exist, then it would choose the American system.

> NOAM CHOMSKY (b. 1928), U.S. linguist, political analyst. *Language and Responsibility*, pt. 1, ch. 1 (1979, with Mitsou Ronat).

3 The strategic adversary is fascism . . . the fascism in us all, in our heads and in our everyday behavior, the fascism that causes us to love power, to desire the very thing that dominates and exploits us.

> MICHEL FOUCAULT (1926-84), French philosopher. Gilles Deleuze and Félix Guattari, *Anti-Oedipus*, Preface (1972).

4 We enter parliament in order to supply ourselves, in the arsenal of democracy, with its own weapons. . . . If democracy is so stupid as to give us free tickets and salaries for this bear's work, that is its affair. . . . We do not come as friends, nor even as neutrals. We come as enemies. As the wolf bursts into the flock, so we come.

> JOSEPH GOEBBELS (1897-1945), German Nazi leader, minister of propaganda. *Der Angriff* (Berlin, 30 April 1928).

5 Our movement took a grip on cowardly Marxism and from it extracted the meaning of socialism. It also took from the cowardly middle-class parties their nationalism. Throwing both into the cauldron of our way of life there emerged, as clear as a crystal, the synthesis—German National Socialism.

> HERMANN GOERING (1893-1946), German Nazi leader, air marshal. Speech, 9 April 1933, Sports Palast, Berlin.

6 Fascism, the more it considers and observes the future and the development of humanity, quite apart from political considerations of the moment, believes neither in the possibility nor the utility of perpetual peace.

> BENITO MUSSOLINI (1883-1945), Italian dictator. *The Political and Social Doctrine of Fascism* (1932).

7 AS A MIND, who the hell else is there left for me to take an interest IN??

> EZRA POUND (1885-1972), U.S. poet, critic. Letter, 28 Aug. 1934, referring to Mussolini. Quoted in: Humphrey Carpenter, *A Serious Character*, pt. 3, ch. 13 (1988). In the opening lines of canto 74, first of Pound's *Pisan Cantos* (written in 1948 while he was awaiting trial for treason), Pound spoke of "the enormous tragedy of the dream in the peasant's bent shoulders." Interviewed in May 1945, he had described Mussolini as "a very human, imperfect character who lost his head."

8 Fascism is a European inquietude. It is a way of knowing everything—history, the State, the achievement of the proletarianization of public life, a new way of knowing the phenomena of our epoch.

> J. A. PRIMO DE RIVERA (1903-36), Spanish Falangist politician. Quoted in: Hugh Thomas, *The Spanish Civil War*, bk. 1, ch. 8 (1961).

9 Fascism is not defined by the number of its victims, but by the way it kills them.

> JEAN-PAUL SARTRE (1905-80), French philosopher, author. "On

the Execution of Julius and Ethel Rosenberg," in *Libération* (Paris, 22 June 1953).

10 Fascism was a counter-revolution against a revolution that never took place.

IGNAZIO SILONE (1900-1978), Italian novelist, journalist. *The School for Dictators*, ch. 4 (1938)

See also Baudrillard on DEMOCRACY; ADOLF HITLER; NAZISM.

FASHION

1 I never cared for fashion much, amusing little seams and witty little pleats: it was the girls I liked.

DAVID BAILEY (b. 1938), British photographer. *Independent* (London, 5 Nov. 1990).

2 Fashions are born and they die too quickly for anyone to learn to love them.

BETTINA BALLARD (1903-1961), U.S. editor. *In My Fashion*, ch. 1 (1960).

3 All fashions are charming, or rather relatively charming, each one being a new striving, more or less well conceived, after beauty, an approximate statement of an ideal, the desire for which constantly teases the unsatisfied human mind.

CHARLES BAUDELAIRE (1821-67), French poet. "The Painter of Modern Life," sct. 11, in *L'Art Romantique* (1869; repr. in *Selected Writings on Art and Artists*, ed. by P. E. Charvet, 1972).

4 Fashion is the most intense expression of the phenomenon of neomania, which has grown ever since the birth of capitalism. Neomania assumes that purchasing the new is the same as acquiring value. . . . If the purchase of a new garment coincides with the wearing out of an old one, then obviously there is no fashion. If a garment is worn beyond the moment of its natural replacement, there is pauperization. Fashion flourishes on surplus, when someone buys more than he or she needs.

STEPHEN BAYLEY (b. 1951), British design critic. *Taste*, pt. 2, "Fashion: Being and Dressing" (1991).

5 Change of fashion is the tax levied by the industry of the poor on the vanity of the rich.

SÉBASTIEN-ROCH NICOLAS DE CHAMFORT (1741-94), French writer, wit. *Maxims and Considerations*, vol. 1, no. 163 (tr. by E. Powys Mathers, 1926).

6 Fashion is made to become unfashionable.

COCO CHANEL (1883-1971), French couturière. *Life* (New York, 19 Aug. 1957).

7 Fashion is architecture: it is a matter of proportions.

COCO CHANEL (1883-1971), French couturiere. Quoted in: Marcel Haedrich, *Coco Chanel: Her Life, Her Secrets*, ch. 21 (1971).

8 You know, one had as good be out of the world, as out of the fashion.

COLLEY CIBBER (1671-1757), English actor-manager, playwright. Narcissa, in *Love's Last Shift*, act 2, sc. 1. The proverb can be dated back to 1639.

9 "Women's fashion" is a euphemism for fashion created by men for women.

ANDREA DWORKIN (b. 1946), U.S. feminist critic. *Pornography*, ch. 4 (1981).

10 Only the minute and the future are interesting in fashion—it exists to be destroyed. If everybody did everything with respect, you'd go nowhere.

KARL LAGERFELD (b. 1938), German-born French fashion designer. Quoted in: *Vanity Fair* (New York, Feb. 1992).

11 People ask how can a Jewish kid from the Bronx do preppy clothes? Does it have to do with class and money? It has to do with dreams.

RALPH LAUREN (b. 1939), U.S. couturier. *International Herald Tribune* (Paris, 7 April 1992).

12 The same costume will be Indecent 10 years before its time, Shameless 5 years before its time, *Outré* (daring) 1 year before its time, Smart, Dowdy 1 year after its time, Hideous 20 years after its time, Ridiculous 20 years after its time, Amusing 30 years after its time, Quaint 50 years after its time, Charming 70 years after its time, Romantic 100 years after its time, Beautiful 150 years after its time.

JAMES LAVER (1899-1975), British art critic, author. *Taste and Fashion*, ch. 18 (1937). "The erogenous zone," Laver wrote, "is always shifting, and it is the business of fashion to pursue it, without ever catching it up."

13 Even truth needs to be clad in new garments if it is to appeal to a new age.

G. C. LICHTENBERG (1742-99), German physicist, philosopher. *Aphorisms*, "Notebook C," aph. 33 (written 1765-99; tr. by R. J. Hollingdale 1990).

14 The pursuit of Fashion is the attempt of the middle class to co-opt tragedy. In adopting the clothing, speech, and personal habits of those in straitened, dangerous, or pitiful circumstances, the middle class seeks to have what it feels to be the exigent and nonequivocal experiences had by those it emulates.

DAVID MAMET (b. 1947), U.S. playwright. *Writing in Restaurants*, "Exuvial Magic: an Essay Concerning Fashion" (1986).

15 Fashion is like the ashes left behind by the uniquely shaped flames of the fire, the trace alone revealing that a fire actually took place.

PAUL DE MAN (1919-83), Belgian-born U.S. literary critic. "Literary History and Literary Modernity," lecture, Sept. 1969 (repr. in *Blindness and Insight*, 1971; rev. 1983).

16 If one considers how much reason every person has for anxiety and timid self-concealment, and how three-quarters of his energy and goodwill can be paralyzed and made unfruitful by it, one has to be very grateful to fashion, insofar as it sets that three-quarters free and communicates self-confidence and mutual cheerful agreeableness to those who know they are subject to its law.

FRIEDRICH NIETZSCHE (1844-1900), German philosopher. *Assorted Opinions and Maxims*, aph. 209 (published as first supplement to *Human, All Too Human*, 1879).

17 I who have been involved with all styles of painting can assure you that the only things that fluctuate are the waves of fashion which carry the snobs and speculators;

the number of true connoisseurs remains more or less the same.

PABLO PICASSO (1881-1973), Spanish artist. *Mirador* (Barcelona, 9 Aug. 1934).

18 In olden days a glimpse of stocking
Was looked on as something shocking
But now, God knows,
Anything goes.

COLE PORTER (1893-1964), U.S. composer, lyricist. "Anything Goes" (1934).

19 It pains me physically to see a woman victimized, rendered pathetic, by fashion.

YVES SAINT LAURENT (b. 1936), French couturier. *Ritz*, no. 85 (London, 1984). In the same article, Saint Laurent described fashion as a "kind of vitamin for style."

20 Fashion is something barbarous, for it produces innovation without reason and imitation without benefit.

GEORGE SANTAYANA (1863-1952), U.S. philosopher, poet. *The Life of Reason*, "Reason in Religion," ch. 7 (1905-6).

21 Fashion is born by small facts, trends, or even politics, never by trying to make little pleats and furbelows, by trinkets, by clothes easy to copy, or by the shortening or lengthening of a skirt.

ELSA SCHIAPARELLI (1890-1973), Italian fashion designer. *Shocking Life*, ch. 9 (1954).

22 No doubt the artist is the child of his time; but woe to him if he is also its disciple, or even its favorite.

FRIEDRICH VON SCHILLER (1759-1805), German dramatist, poet, essayist. *On the Aesthetic Education of Man*, "Ninth Letter" (1795).

23 He who goes against the fashion is himself its slave.

LOGAN PEARSALL SMITH (1865-1946), U.S. essayist, aphorist. *Afterthoughts*, "Art and Letters" (1931).

24 We worship not the Graces, nor the Parcae, but Fashion. She spins and weaves and cuts with full authority. The head monkey at Paris puts on a traveler's cap, and all the monkeys in America do the same.

HENRY DAVID THOREAU (1817-62), U.S. philosopher, author, naturalist. *Walden*, "Economy" (1854).

25 Fashion, by which what is really fantastic becomes for a moment the universal.

OSCAR WILDE (1854-1900), Anglo-Irish playwright, author. Lord Henry, in *The Picture of Dorian Gray* (1891).

26 The great attraction of fashion is that it diverted attention from the insoluble problems of beauty and provided an easy way—which money could buy . . . to a simply stated, easily reproduced ideal of beauty, however temporary that ideal.

THEODORE ZELDIN (b. 1923), U.S. author. Quoted in: Arthur Marwick, *Beauty in History*, pt. 1, ch. 2 (1988).

See also Butler on ACADEMIA; Hellman on CONSCIENCE; Updike on CUSTOM; Bayley on HAUTE COUTURE; Saint Laurent on MODELS AND MODELING; Oliphant, Saint Laurent on STYLE.

FATHERS

1 That he delights in the misery of others no man will confess, and yet what other motive can make a father cruel?

JOSEPH ADDISON (1672-1719), English essayist. *Interesting Anecdotes, Memoirs, Allegories, Essays, and Poetical Fragments*, "The Cruelty of Parental Tyranny" (1794).

2 A father is always making his baby into a little woman. And when she is a woman he turns her back again.

ENID BAGNOLD (1889-1981), British novelist, playwright. *Autobiography*, ch. 4 (1969).

3 Those who have never had a father can at any rate never know the sweets of losing one. To most men the death of his father is a new lease of life.

SAMUEL BUTLER (1835-1902), English author. *Samuel Butler's Notebooks* (1951, p. 100).

4 As fathers commonly go, it is seldom a misfortune to be fatherless; and considering the general run of sons, as seldom a misfortune to be childless.

LORD CHESTERFIELD (1694-1773), English statesman, man of letters. Letter, 15 July 1751 (1774; repr. in *The Letters of the Earl of Chesterfield to His Son*, vol. 2, no. 264, ed. by Charles Strachey, 1901).

5 Blessed indeed is the man who hears many gentle voices call him father!

LYDIA M. CHILD (1802-80), U.S. abolitionist, writer, editor. *Philothea: A Romance*, ch. 19 (1836).

6 If the new American father feels bewildered and even defeated, let him take comfort from the fact that whatever he does in any fathering situation has a fifty percent chance of being right.

BILL COSBY (b. 1937), U.S. comedian, actor. *Fatherhood*, ch. 5 (1986).

7 Be kind to thy father, for when thou wert young,
Who loved thee so fondly as he?
He caught the first accents that fell from thy tongue,
And joined in thy innocent glee.

MARGARET COURTNEY (1822-62), U.S. poet. *Be Kind*.

8 I watched a small man with thick calluses on both hands work fifteen and sixteen hours a day. I saw him once literally bleed from the bottoms of his feet, a man who came here uneducated, alone, unable to speak the language, who taught me all I needed to know about faith and hard work by the simple eloquence of his example.

MARIO CUOMO (b. 1932), U.S. Democratic politician. Commenting on his father, in address, 16 July 1984, to the Democratic National Convention.

9 What a dreadful thing it must be to have a dull father.

MARY MAPES DODGE (1838?-1905), U.S. writer, editor. *Hans Brinker or the Silver Skates*, "Boys and Girls" (1865).

10 I cannot think of any need in childhood as strong as the need for a father's protection.

SIGMUND FREUD (1856-1939), Austrian psychiatrist. *Civiliza-*

tion and Its Discontents (1931; repr. in *Complete Works*, vol. 21, ed. by James Strachey and Anna Freud, 1961).

11 A man knows when he is growing old because he begins to look like his father.

GABRIEL GARCíA MáRQUEZ (b. 1928), Colombian writer. *Love in the Time of Cholera* (1985; tr. 1988).

12 To be a successful father . . . there's one absolute rule: when you have a kid, don't look at it for the first two years.

ERNEST HEMINGWAY (1899-1961), U.S. author. Quoted in: A. E. Hotchner, *Papa Hemingway*, pt. 2, ch. 5 (1966).

13 The thing to remember about fathers is, they're men.
A girl has to keep it in mind:
They are dragon-seekers, bent on improbable rescues.
Scratch any father, you find
Someone chock-full of qualms and romantic terrors,
Believing change is a threat—
Like your first shoes with heels on, like your first bicycle
It took such months to get.

PHYLLIS MCGINLEY (1905-78), U.S. poet, author. *Girl's-Eye View of Relatives: First Lesson,* in *Times Three* (1960).

14 I stopped loving my father a long time ago. What remained was the slavery to a pattern.

ANAïS NIN (1903-77), Franco-American novelist, diarist. *Under a Glass Bell*, "Birth" (1948).

15 One father is more than a hundred schoolmasters.

ENGLISH PROVERB (17th century). Collected in: George Herbert, *Outlandish Proverbs* (1640).

16 It doesn't matter who my father was; it matters who I remember he was.

ANNE SEXTON (1928-1974), U.S. poet. *The Poet's Story*, "A Small Journal" (ed. by Howard Moss, 1974), entry for 1 Jan. 1972.

17 It is a wise father that knows his own child.

WILLIAM SHAKESPEARE (1564-1616), English dramatist, poet. Launcelot, in *The Merchant of Venice*, act 2, sc. 2, repeating a proverbial saying as he attempts to make his blind father Gobbo understand he is Gobbo's son.

18 An unforgiving eye, and a damned disinheriting countenance!

RICHARD BRINSLEY SHERIDAN (1751-1816), Anglo-Irish dramatist. Careless, in *The School for Scandal*, act 4, sc. 1, describing the portrait of Sir Oliver Surface.

19 That is the thankless position of the father in the family—the provider for all, and the enemy of all.

J. AUGUST STRINDBERG (1849-1912), Swedish dramatist, novelist, poet. *The Son of a Servant* (1886; tr. by Claud Field, 1913).

20 *None* of you can *ever* be proud enough of being the *child* of SUCH a Father who has not his *equal* in this world—so great, so good, so faultless. Try, all of you, to follow in his footsteps and don't be discouraged, for to be *really* in everything like him *none* of you, I am sure, will

ever be. Try, therefore, to be like him in *some* points, and you will have *acquired a great deal*.

VICTORIA (1819-1901), Queen of Great Britain and Ireland. Letter, 26 Aug. 1857, to the Prince of Wales, later King Edward VII.

21 It no longer bothers me that I may be constantly searching for father figures; by this time, I have found several and dearly enjoyed knowing them all.

ALICE WALKER (b. 1944), U.S. author, critic. "In Search of Zora Neale Hurston," in *Ms.* (New York, March 1975; repr. in *In Search of Our Mothers' Gardens*, "Looking for Zora," 1983).

22 Fathers should be neither seen nor heard. That is the only proper basis for family life.

OSCAR WILDE (1854-1900), Anglo-Irish playwright, author. Lord Goring, in *An Ideal Husband*, act 4.

23 The American father . . . is never seen in London. He passes his life entirely in Wall Street and communicates with his family once a month by means of a telegram in cipher.

OSCAR WILDE (1854-1900), Anglo-Irish playwright, author. "The American Invasion," in *Court and Society Review* (London, 23 March 1887).

See also Freud on GOD; PARENTS.

FATHERS AND SONS

1 Sir Walter, being strangely surprised and put out of his countenance at so great a table, gives his son a damned blow over the face. His son, as rude as he was, would not strike his father, but strikes over the face the gentleman that sat next to him and said "Box about:'twill come to my father anon."

JOHN AUBREY (1626-97), English antiquarian, writer. *Brief Lives*, "Sir Walter Raleigh" (1813; rev. ed. 1898).

2 If the relationship of father to son could really be reduced to biology, the whole earth would blaze with the glory of fathers and sons.

JAMES BALDWIN (1924-87), U.S. author. *The Price of the Ticket*, sct. 1, "The Devil Finds Work" (1985; first published 1976).

3 In peace the sons bury their fathers, but in war the fathers bury their sons.

CROESUS (d. c. 560 B.C.), Lydian king. Quoted in: Francis Bacon, *Apophthegms*, no. 149, said to the Persian king Cambyses.

4 Leontine: An only son, sir, might expect more indulgence.
Croaker: An only father, sir, might expect more obedience.

OLIVER GOLDSMITH (1728-74), Anglo-Irish author. *The Good Natur'd Man*, act 1.

5 Sons have always a rebellious wish to be disillusioned by that which charmed their fathers.

ALDOUS HUXLEY (1894-1963), British author. "Vulgarity in Literature" (1930; repr. in *Music at Night and Other Essays*, 1949).

6 His father watched him across the gulf of years and pathos which always must divide a father from his son.

J. P. MARQUAND (1893-1960), U.S. novelist. *The Late George Apley*, ch. 10 (1937).

7   We think our fathers fools, so wise we grow;
Our wiser sons, no doubt will think us so.

ALEXANDER POPE (1688-1744), English satirical poet. *Essay on Criticism.*

8   A man's desire for a son is usually nothing but the wish to duplicate himself in order that such a remarkable pattern may not be lost to the world.

HELEN ROWLAND (1875-1950), U.S. journalist. *Reflections of a Bachelor Girl* (1903).

9   What harsh judges fathers are to all young men!

TERENCE (c. 190-159 B.C.), Roman dramatist. *Heauton Timorumenos.*

FATIGUE

1   Never tire yourself more than necessary, even if you have to found a culture on the fatigue of your bones.

ANTONIN ARTAUD (1896-1948), French theatre producer, actor, theorist. *Ci-Gît* (1947; repr. in *Selected Writings*, pt. 36, *Indian Culture* and *Here Lies*, ed. by Susan Sontag, 1976).

2   I am poured out like water, and all my bones are out of the joint: my heart is like wax; it is melted in the midst of my bowels.

BIBLE, HEBREW. David, in *Psalms* 22:14.

3   There are only the pursued, the pursuing, the busy, and the tired.

F. SCOTT FITZGERALD (1896-1940), U.S. author. The narrator (Nick Carraway), in *The Great Gatsby*, ch. 4 (1925).

4   Men weary as much of not doing the things they want to do as of doing the things they do not want to do.

ERIC HOFFER (1902-83), U.S. philosopher. *The Passionate State of Mind*, aph. 221 (1955).

FAULTS AND FAULT-FINDING

1   A man's personal defects will commonly have with the rest of the world precisely that importance which they have to himself. If he makes light of them, so will other men.

RALPH WALDO EMERSON (1803-82), U.S. essayist, poet, philosopher. *English Traits*, "Cockayne" (1856).

2   A benevolent man should allow a few faults in himself, to keep his friends in countenance.

BENJAMIN FRANKLIN (1706-90), U.S. statesman, writer. *Autobiography*, ch. 6 (written 1771-90, published 1868).

3   People may flatter themselves just as much by thinking that their faults are always present to other people's minds, as if they believe that the world is always contemplating their individual charms and virtues.

ELIZABETH GASKELL (1810-65), English novelist. Lady Cumnor, in *Wives and Daughters*, ch. 50 (1866).

4   There are some faults so nearly allied to excellence that we can scarce weed out the vice without eradicating the virtue.

OLIVER GOLDSMITH (1728-74), Anglo-Irish author. Sir William Honeywood, in *The Good Natur'd Man*, act 1.

5   Humility is not my forté, and whenever I dwell for any length of time on my own shortcomings, they gradually begin to seem mild, harmless, rather engaging little things, not at all like the staring defects in other people's characters.

MARGARET HALSEY (b. 1910), U.S. author. *With Malice toward Some*, pt. 1, "June 15" (1938).

6   It is easier to discover a deficiency in individuals, in states, and in Providence, than to see their real import and value.

GEORG HEGEL (1770-1831), German philosopher. *The Philosophy of History*, "Introduction," sct. 3 (1837).

7   If we had no faults of our own, we should not take so much pleasure in noticing those in others.

FRANÇOIS, DUC DE LA ROCHEFOUCAULD (1613-80), French writer, moralist. *Sentences et Maximes Morales*, no. 31 (1678).

8   It is always well to accept your own shortcomings with candor but to regard those of your friends with polite incredulity.

RUSSELL LYNES (b. 1910), U.S. editor, critic. "The Art of Accepting," in *Vogue* (New York, 1 Sept. 1952).

9   The essence of a man is found in his faults.

FRANCIS PICABIA (1878-1953), French painter, poet. *591* (Paris, 21 Jan. 1952; repr. in *Écrits*, vol. 2, "1950-1953," ed. by Olivier Revault d'Allones and Dominique Bouissou, 1978).

10   A man can become so accustomed to the thought of his own faults that he will begin to cherish them as charming little "personal characteristics."

HELEN ROWLAND (1875-1950), U.S. journalist. *A Guide to Men*, "Brides" (1922).

11   The more defects a man may have, the older he is, the less lovable, the more resounding his success.

MARQUIS DE SADE (1740-1814), French author. Clément, in *Justine, ou les Malheurs de la Vertu* (1791).

See also Carlyle on COMPLACENCY; La Rochefoucauld on CONFESSION; FALLIBILITY; Wilde on MEN AND WOMEN.

FAUX-PAS

1   To slip upon a pavement is better than to slip with the tongue: so the fall of the wicked shall come speedily.

APOCRYPHA. *Ecclesiasticus* 20:18.

2   Nothing dates one so dreadfully as to think someplace is uptown. . . . At our age one must be watchful of these conversational gray hairs.

RUTH GORDON (b. 1896), U.S. playwright, actor. Clyde in *The Leading Lady*, act 1 (1948).

3   A gaffe is when a politician tells the truth.

MICHAEL KINSLEY (b. 1951), U.S. journalist. *Guardian* (London, 14 Jan. 1992).

4   Dentopedalogy is the science of opening your mouth and putting your foot in it. I've been practising it for years.

PRINCE PHILIP, DUKE OF EDINBURGH (b. 1921). Address to Britain's General Dental Council. Quoted in: *Time* (New York, 21 Nov. 1960).

FAVORS

1   Our friends are generally ready to do everything for us, except the very thing we wish them to do.

> WILLIAM HAZLITT (1778-1830), English essayist. *Characteristics*, no. 87 (first published anonymously in 1823; repr. in *Complete Works*, vol. 9, ed. by P. P. Howe, 1932).

2. The person whose doors I enter with most pleasure, and quit with most regret, never did me the smallest favour.

> WILLIAM HAZLITT (1778-1830), English essayist. "On the Spirit of Obligations" (1824; repr. in *The Plain Speaker*, 1826).

3   The pleasure we derive from doing favors is partly in the feeling it gives us that we are not altogether worthless. It is a pleasant surprise to ourselves.

> ERIC HOFFER (1902-83), U.S. philosopher. *The Passionate State of Mind*, aph. 113 (1955).

4   Too great a hurry to discharge an obligation is a kind of ingratitude.

> FRANÇOIS, DUC DE LA ROCHEFOUCAULD (1613-80), French writer, moralist. *Sentences et Maximes Morales*, no. 226 (1678).

5   Benefits should be conferred gradually; and in that way they will taste better.

> NICCOLò MACHIAVELLI (1469-1527), Italian political philosopher, statesman. *The Prince*, ch. 8 (1514).

6   It is kindness to refuse immediately what you intend to deny.

> PUBLILIUS SYRUS (1st century B.C.), Roman writer of mimes. *Sententiae*, no.470.

7   O how wretched
Is that poor man that hangs on princes' favours!
There is betwixt that smile we would aspire to,
That sweet aspect of princes, and their ruin,
More pangs and fears than wars or women have,
And when he falls, he falls like Lucifer,
Never to hope again.

> WILLIAM SHAKESPEARE (1564-1616), English dramatist, poet. Cardinal Wolsey, in *Henry VIII*, act 3, sc. 2.

FEAR

1   An ugly sight, a man who is afraid.

> JEAN ANOUILH (1910-87), French playwright. Antigone, in *Antigone*.

2   At man's core there is a voice that wants him never to give in to fear. But if it is true that in general man cannot give in to fear, at the very least he postpones indefinitely the moment when he will have to confront himself with the object of his fear ... when he will no longer have the assistance of reason as guaranteed by God, or when he will no longer have the assistance of God such as reason guaranteed. It is necessary to recoil, but it is necessary to leap, and perhaps one only recoils in order to leap better.

> GEORGES BATAILLE (1897-1962), French novelist, critic. "Le Mal dans le Platonisme et le Sadisme," lecture, 1947. Quoted in: Jean-Michel Heimont, *On Bataille*, "Two Values of Sade in Bataille's Text" (ed. by Alan Stoekl, 1990).

3   Terror is as much a part of the concept of truth as runniness is of the concept of jam. We wouldn't like jam if it didn't, by its very nature, ooze. We wouldn't like truth if it wasn't sticky, if, from time to time, it didn't ooze blood.

> JEAN BAUDRILLARD (b. 1929), French semiologist. *Cool Memories*, ch. 5 (1987; tr. 1990).

4   The man who has ceased to fear has ceased to care.

> F. H. BRADLEY (1846-1924), English philosopher. *Aphorisms*, no. 63 (1930).

5   No passion so effectually robs the mind of all its powers of acting and reasoning as fear.

> EDMUND BURKE (1729-97), Irish philosopher, statesman. *The Origin of our Ideas of the Sublime and Beautiful*, pt. 2, ch. 2 (1756).

6   The timidity of the child or the savage is entirely reasonable; they are alarmed at this world, because this world is a very alarming place. They dislike being alone because it is verily and indeed an awful idea to be alone. Barbarians fear the unknown for the same reason that Agnostics worship it—because it is a fact.

> G. K. CHESTERTON (1874-1936), British author. *Tremendous Trifles*, "The Red Angel" (1909).

7   Fear can supplant our real problems only to the extent—unwilling either to assimilate or to exhaust it—we perpetuate it within ourselves like a temptation and enthrone it at the very heart of our solitude.

> E. M. CIORAN (b. 1911), Rumanian-born French philosopher. *The Temptation to Exist*, title essay (1956).

8   If hopes were dupes, fears may be liars.

> ARTHUR HUGH CLOUGH (1819-61), English poet. *Say Not the Struggle Nought Availeth*.

9   How does one kill fear, I wonder? How do you shoot a spectre through the heart, slash off its spectral head, take it by its spectral throat?

> JOSEPH CONRAD (1857-1924), Polish-born English novelist. Marlow, in *Lord Jim*, ch. 33 (1900).

10   By the time we are women, fear is as familiar to us as air. It is our element. We live in it, we inhale it, we exhale it, and most of the time we do not even notice it. Instead of "I am afraid," we say, "I don't want to," or "I don't know how," or "I can't."

> ANDREA DWORKIN (b. 1946), U.S. feminist critic. "The Sexual Politics of Fear and Courage," speech, 12 March 1975, Queens College, City University of New York (published in *Our Blood*, ch. 5, 1976).

11   I will show you fear in a handful of dust.

> T. S. ELIOT (1888-1965), Anglo-American poet, critic. *The Burial of the Dead*, in *The Waste Land* (1922).

12   He has not learned the lesson of life who does not every day surmount a fear.

> RALPH WALDO EMERSON (1803-82), U.S. essayist, poet, philosopher. *Society and Solitude*, "Courage" (1870).

13   Those who love to be feared fear to be loved, and they themselves are more afraid than anyone, for whereas other men fear only them, they fear everyone.

> ST. FRANCES DE SALES (1567-1622), French churchman, devo-

tional writer. Quoted by Bishop Jean-Pierre Camus in: *The Spirit of Saint Frances de Sales,* ch. 7, sct. 3 (1952).

14 There is the fear that we shan't prove worthy in the eyes of someone who knows us at least as well as we know ourselves. That is the fear of God. And there is the fear of Man—fear that men won't understand us and we shall be cut of from them.

ROBERT FROST (1874-1963), U.S. poet. Quoted in: *Newsweek* (New York, 11 Feb. 1963).

15 The truth is that there is no terror untempered by some great moral idea.

JEAN-LUC GODARD (b. 1930), French filmmaker, author. "Strangers on a Train," in *Cahiers du Cinéma* (Paris, 10 March 1952; repr. in *Godard on Godard,* ed. and tr. by Tom Milne, 1968).

16 There is no terror in a bang, only in the anticipation of it.

ALFRED HITCHCOCK (1899-1980), Anglo-American filmmaker. Quoted in: Leslie Halliwell, *Halliwell's Filmgoer's Companion* (1984).

17 My "fear" . . . is my substance, and probably the best part of me.

FRANZ KAFKA (1883-1924), German novelist, short-story writer. Letter to Milena Jesenská. Quoted in: Margarete Buber-Neumann, *Milena,* ch. 7 (1989).

18 There is nothing strange about fear: no matter in what guise it presents itself it is something with which we are all so familiar that when a man appears who is without it we are at once enslaved by him.

HENRY MILLER (1891-1980), U.S. author. *The Wisdom of the Heart,* "The Enormous Womb" (1947).

19 People react to fear, not love—they don't teach that in Sunday School, but it's true.

RICHARD M. NIXON (b. 1913), U.S. Republican politician, president. Quoted in: William Safire, *Before The Fall,* Prologue (1975).

20 Let me assert my firm belief that the only thing we have to fear is fear itself.

FRANKLIN D. ROOSEVELT (1882-1945), U.S. Democratic politician, president. Speech, 2 July 1932, repeated in his first inaugural address, 4 March 1933. The expression has numerous precedents, including the Duke of Wellington, Montaigne and the Bible, and was used by Sir Winston Churchill during World War II.

21 That fear first created the gods is perhaps as true as anything so brief could be on so great a subject.

GEORGE SANTAYANA (1863-1952), U.S. philosopher, poet. *The Life of Reason,* "Reason in Religion," ch. 3 (1905-6).

See also Shakespeare on CAUTION; Connolly on HATE; Bible: New Testament on LOVE.

FEELINGS

1 Cowardice and courage are never without a measure of affection. Nor is love. Feelings are never true. They play with their mirrors.

JEAN BAUDRILLARD (b. 1929), French semiologist. *Cool Memories,* ch. 2 (1987; tr. 1990).

2 Feeling without judgement is a washy draught indeed; but judgement untempered by feeling is too bitter and husky a morsel for human deglutition.

CHARLOTTE BRONTË (1816-55), English novelist. *Jane Eyre,* ch. 21 (1847). "Deglutition" means the action of swallowing [Oxford English Dictionary]).

3 To have in general but little feeling, seems to be the only security against feeling too much on any particular occasion.

GEORGE ELIOT (1819-80), English novelist, editor. *Middlemarch,* bk. 1, ch. 7 (1871).

4 Individuality is founded in feeling; and the recesses of feeling, the darker, blinder strata of character, are the only places in the world in which we catch real fact in the making, and directly perceive how events happen, and how work is actually done.

WILLIAM JAMES (1842-1910), U.S. psychologist, philosopher. *The Varieties of Religious Experience,* Lecture 20, "Conclusions" (1902).

See also Orwell on CANDOR; EMOTION.

HUMAN FELLOWSHIP

1 The ideal of brotherhood of man, the building of the Just City, is one that cannot be discarded without lifelong feelings of disappointment and loss. But, if we are to live in the real world, discard it we must. Its very nobility makes the results of its breakdown doubly horrifying, and it breaks down, as it always will, not by some external agency but because it cannot work.

KINGSLEY AMIS (b. 1922), British novelist. *Sunday Telegraph* (London, 2 July 1967).

2 We must love one another or die.

W. H. AUDEN (1907-73), Anglo-American poet. *September 1, 1939,* st. 8. Auden later repudiated the line, insisting that it be altered for a 1955 anthology to "We must love one another and die." He referred to the poem as "the most dishonest poem I have ever written."

3 We must love one another, yes, yes, that's all true enough, but nothing says we have to like each other. It may be the very recognition of all men as our brothers that accounts for the sibling rivalry, and even enmity, we have toward so many of them.

PETER DE VRIES (b. 1910), U.S. author. Opening sentences (spoken by the narrator, Jim Tickler) of *The Glory of the Hummingbird,* ch. 1 (1974).

4 The common erotic project of destroying women makes it possible for men to unite into a brotherhood; this project is the only firm and trustworthy groundwork for cooperation among males and all male bonding is based on it.

ANDREA DWORKIN (b. 1946), U.S. feminist critic. "The Root Cause," speech, 26 Sept. 1975, Massachusetts Institute of Technology, Cambridge (published in *Our Blood,* ch. 9, 1976).

5 The principle of the brotherhood of man is . . . narcissistic . . . for the grounds for that love have always been the assumption that we ought to realize that we are the same the whole world over.

GERMAINE GREER (b. 1939), Australian feminist writer. *The Female Eunuch,* "Love" (1970).

6 There is always a chance that he who sets himself up as his brother's keeper will end up by being his jail-keeper.

ERIC HOFFER (1902-83), U.S. philosopher. *The Passionate State of Mind,* aph. 106 (1955).

7 The brotherhood of men doen not imply their equality. Families have their fools and their men of genius, their black sheep and their saints, their worldly successes and their worldly failures. A man should treat his brothers lovingly and with justice, according to the deserts of each. But the deserts of every brother are not the same.

ALDOUS HUXLEY (1894-1963), British author. *Proper Studies,* "The Idea of Equality: Equality and Christianity" (1927).

8 The world has narrowed to a neighborhood before it has broadened to brotherhood.

LYNDON B. JOHNSON (1908-73), U.S. Democratic politician, president. Speech, 17 Dec. 1963, New York City.

9 I have a dream that one day on the red hills of Georgia the sons of former slaves and the sons of former slave owners will be able to sit down together at the table of brotherhood.

MARTIN LUTHER KING, JR. (1929-68), U.S. clergyman, civil rights leader. Speech, 28 Aug. 1963, Washington, D.C.

10 Nothing is more repugnant to me than brotherly feelings grounded in the common baseness people see in one another.

MILAN KUNDERA (b. 1929), Czech author, critic. Ludvik, in *The Joke,* pt. 3, ch. 9 (1967; tr. 1982).

11 The brotherhood of man is evoked by particular men according to their circumstances. But it seldom extends to all men. In the name of our freedom and our brotherhood we are prepared to blow up the other half of mankind and to be blown up in our turn.

R. D. LAING (1927-89), British psychiatrist. *The Politics of Experience,* ch. 4 (1967).

12 The great universal family of men is a utopia worthy of the most mediocre logic.

ISIDORE DUCASSE, COMTE DE LAUTRÉAMONT (1846-70), French author, poet. *Maldoror,* bk. 1, ch. 9 (1870; tr. 1978).

13 I believe in the brotherhood of man, all men, but I don't believe in brotherhood with anybody who doesn't want brotherhood with me. I believe in treating people right, but I'm not going to waste my time trying to treat somebody right who doesn't know how to return the treatment.

MALCOLM X (1925-65), U.S. radical leader. Speech, 12 Dec. 1964, New York City.

14 I feel that the Godhead is broken up like the bread at the Supper, and that we are the pieces. Hence this infinite fraternity of feeling.

HERMAN MELVILLE (1819-91), U.S. author. Letter, 17 Nov. 1851, to Nathaniel Hawthorne (published in *The Letters of Herman Melville,* ed. by Merrell R. Davis & William H. Gilman, 1960).

15 One can be a brother only *in* something. Where there is no tie that binds men, men are not united but merely lined up.

ANTOINE DE SAINT-EXUPÉRY (1900-1944), French aviator, author. *Flight to Arras,* ch. 23 (1942).

16 The most dangerous word in any human tongue is the word for brother. It's inflammatory.

TENNESSEE WILLIAMS (1914-83), U.S. dramatist. Gutman, in *Camino Real,* block 2.

See also Woolf on ADULTHOOD; Dickens on ENDURANCE; Hoffer on The MASSES.

FEMINISM

1 The sadness of the women's movement is that they don't allow the necessity of love. See, I don't personally trust any revolution where love is not allowed.

MAYA ANGELOU (b. 1928), U.S. author. "Listening to Maya Angelou," in *California Living* (14 May 1975; repr. in *Conversations with Maya Angelou,* 1989).

2 The true Republic: men, their rights and nothing more; women, their rights and nothing less.

SUSAN B. ANTHONY (1820-1906), U.S. suffragette. Motto printed on the front of her newspaper, *Revolution.*

3 Feminism is an entire world view or gestalt, not just a laundry list of women's issues.

CHARLOTTE BUNCH (b. 1944), U.S. editor, author. "Understanding Feminist Theory," in *New Directions for Women* (New York, Sept.-Oct. 1981).

4 The freedom that women were supposed to have found in the Sixties largely boiled down to easy contraception and abortion; things to make life easier for men, in fact.

JULIE BURCHILL (b. 1960), British journalist, author. *Damaged Gods,* "Born Again Cows" (1986).

5 A good part—and definitely the most fun part—of being a feminist is about frightening men.

JULIE BURCHILL (b. 1960), British journalist, author. *Time Out* (London, 16 Nov. 1989).

6 Just because we're sisters under the skin doesn't mean we've got much in common.

ANGELA CARTER (1940-92), British author. *Guardian* (London, 25 Oct. 1990).

7 Let us rise in the moral power of womanhood; and give utterance to the voice of outraged mercy, and insulted justice, and eternal truth, and mighty love and holy freedom.

MARIA WESTON CHAPMAN (1806-85), U.S. abolitionist. Address to Boston Female Anti-Slavery Society (published in *Liberator,* 13 Aug. 1836).

8 One of the reasons for the failure of feminism to dislodge deeply held perceptions of male and female behaviour was its insistence that women were victims, and men powerful patriarchs, which made a travesty of ordinary people's experience of the mutual interdependence of men and women.

ROSALIND COWARD (b. 1953), British author. *Our Treacherous Hearts*, ch. 9 (1992).

9 The fundamental impulse of the movement is neither masturbatory nor concretely lesbian—although it of course offers warm houseroom to both these possibilities; it is an impulse to maidenhood—to that condition in which a woman might pretend to a false fear or loathing of the penis in order to escape from any responsibility for the pleasure and well-being of the man who possesses it.

MIDGE DECTER (b. 1927), U.S. author, editor, social critic. *The New Chastity and Other Arguments against Women's Liberation*, ch. 2 (1972).

10 The embattled gates to equal rights indeed opened up for modern women, but I sometimes think to myself: "That is not what I meant by freedom—it is only `social progress.'"

HELENE DEUTSCH (1884-1982), U.S. psychiatrist. *Confrontations with Myself*, ch. 1 (1973).

11 Men who want to support women in our struggle for freedom and justice should understand that it is not terrifically important to us that they learn to cry; it is important to us that they stop the crimes of violence against us.

ANDREA DWORKIN (b. 1946), U.S. feminist critic. "The Rape Atrocity and the Boy Next Door," speech, 1 March 1975, State University of New York, Stony Brook (published in *Our Blood*, ch. 4, 1976).

12 Women have been taught that, for us, the earth is flat, and that if we venture out, we will fall off the edge. Some of us have ventured out nevertheless, and so far we have not fallen off. It is my faith, my feminist faith, that we will not.

ANDREA DWORKIN (b. 1946), U.S. feminist critic. "Redefining Nonviolence," speech, 5 April 1975, Boston College (published in *Our Blood*, ch. 6, sct. 2, 1976).

13 Feminism is hated because women are hated. Antifeminism is a direct expression of misogyny; it is the political defense of women hating.

ANDREA DWORKIN (b. 1946), U.S. feminist critic. *Right-Wing Women*, ch. 6 (1978).

14 The feminist anti-pornography movement, no less than the feminist movement of a century ago, encourages the assumption that male and female sexuality, and possibly morality, are as unlike as yin and yang.

BARBARA EHRENREICH (b. 1941), U.S. author, columnist. *The Worst Years of Our Lives*, "Why We Lost the E.R.A." (1991; first published in *Atlantic Monthly*, 1986).

15 "I hate discussions of feminism that end up with who does the dishes," she said. So do I. But at the end, there are always the damned dishes.

MARILYN FRENCH (b. 1929), U.S. author, critic. Isolde, in *The Women's Room*, ch. 1, sct. 21 (1977).

16 Surely women's liberation is a most unpromising panacea. But the movement is working politically, because our sexuality is so confused, our masculinity so uncertain, and our families so beleaguered that no one knows what they are for or how they are sustained.

GEORGE GILDER (b. 1939), U.S. editor, speechwriter, author. *Sexual Suicide*, Introduction (1973).

17 Merely external emancipation has made of the modern woman an artificial being. . . . Now, woman is confronted with the necessity of emancipating herself from emancipation, if she really desires to be free.

EMMA GOLDMAN (1869-1940), U.S. anarchist. *Anarchism and Other Essays*, "The Tragedy of Women's Emancipation" (1910).

18 The sight of women talking together has always made men uneasy; nowadays it means rank subversion.

GERMAINE GREER (b. 1939), Australian feminist writer. *The Female Eunuch*, "Summary" (1970).

19 Women's liberation, if it abolishes the patriarchal family, will abolish a necessary substructure of the authoritarian state, and once that withers away Marx will have come true willy-nilly, so let's get on with it.

GERMAINE GREER (b. 1939), Australian feminist writer. *The Female Eunuch*, "Revolution" (1970).

20 There has come into existence, chiefly in America, a breed of men who claim to be feminists. They imagine that they have understood "what women want" and that they are capable of giving it to them. They help with the dishes at home and make their own coffee in the office, basking the while in the refulgent consciousness of virtue. . . . Such men are apt to think of the true male feminists as utterly chauvinistic.

GERMAINE GREER (b. 1939), Australian feminist writer. "Eternal War: Strindberg's View of Sex," in *Spectator* (London, 3 June 1978; repr. in *The Madwoman's Underclothes*, 1986).

21 Thou art blind to the danger of marrying a woman who feels and acts out the principle of equal rights.

ANGELINA GRIMKÉ (1805-79), U.S. abolitionist, feminist. Letter, Feb. 1838, to abolitionist Theodore Dwight Weld (published in *Letters of Theodore Dwight Weld, Angelina Grimké Weld, and Sarah Grimké, 1822-1844*, vol. 2, ed. by Gilbert H. Barnes and Dwight L. Dumond, 1934).

22 Movements born in hatred very quickly take on the characteristics of the thing they oppose.

J. S. HABGOOD (b. 1927), British ecclesiastic, Archbishop of York. Quoted in: *Observer* (London, 4 May 1986), referrring to ultra-feminists.

23 Ah, I fancy it is just the same with most of what you call your "emancipation." You have read yourself into a number of new ideas and opinions. You have got a sort of smattering of recent discoveries in various fields—discoveries that seem to overthrow certain principles which have hitherto been held impregnable and unassailable. But all this has only been a matter of intellect, Miss West—superficial acquisition. It has not passed into your blood.

HENRIK IBSEN (1828-1906), Norwegian dramatist. Rector Kroll, addressing Rebecca West, in *Rosmersholm*, act 3.

24 I am blackly bored when they are at large & at work; but somehow I am still *more* blackly bored when they are shut up in Holloway & we are deprived of them.

HENRY JAMES (1843-1916), U.S. author. Letter, 13 March 1912, to Edith Wharton (published in *Henry James & Edith Wharton:*

Letters 1900-1915, ed. by Lyall Powers, 1990), referring to "the window-smashing women." Holloway is a women's prison in London.

25   I am a feminist, and what that means to me is much the same as the meaning of the fact that I am Black: it means that I must undertake to love myself and to respect myself as though my very life depends upon self-love and self-respect.

JUNE JORDAN (b. 1939), U.S. poet, civil rights activist. "Where Is the Love?," address, 1978, to the Black Writers' Conference, Howard University (published in *Moving Towards Home: Political Essays,* 1989).

26   I became a feminist as an alternative to becoming a masochist.

SALLY KEMPTON (b. 1943), U.S. author. "Cutting Loose," in *Esquire* (New York, July 1970).

27   Women's liberation is the liberation of the feminine in the man and the masculine in the woman.

CORITA KENT (b. 1918), U.S. artist. Quoted in: *Los Angeles Times* (11 July 1974).

28   The emancipation of women is practically the greatest egoistic movement of the nineteenth century, and the most intense affirmation of the right of the self that history has yet seen.

ELLEN KEY (1849-1926), Swedish author, feminist. *The Century of the Child,* ch. 2 (1909).

29   As a result of the feminist revolution, "feminine" becomes an abusive epithet.

WYNDHAM LEWIS (1882-1957), British author, painter. *The Art of Being Ruled,* "The 'Vicious' Circle," ch. 6 (1926).

30   Feminism was recognized by the average man as a conflict in which it was impossible for a man, as a chivalrous *gentleman,* as a respecter of the rights of little nations (like little Belgium), as a highly evolved citizen of a highly civilized community, to refuse the claim of this better half to self-determination.

WYNDHAM LEWIS (1882-1957), British author, painter. *The Art of Being Ruled,* "The Family and Feminism," ch. 8 (1926).

31   The people I'm furious with are the Women's Liberationists. They keep getting up on soapboxes and proclaiming women are brighter than men. That's true, but it should be kept quiet or it ruins the whole racket.

ANITA LOOS (1893-1981), U.S. screenwriter. Quoted in: *Observer* (London, 30 Dec. 1973).

32   The suffering of either sex—of the male who is unable, because of the way in which he was reared, to take the strong initiating or patriarchal role that is still demanded of him, or of the female who has been given too much freedom of movement as a child to stay placidly within the house as an adult—this suffering, this discrepancy, this sense of failure in an enjoined role, is the point of leverage for social change.

MARGARET MEAD (1901-78), U.S. anthropologist. *Male and Female,* ch. 15 (1949).

33   Women's Liberation is just a lot of foolishness. It's the men who are discriminated against. They can't bear children. And no one's likely to do anything about that.

GOLDA MEIR (1898-1978), Israeli politician, prime minister. Quoted in: *Newsweek* (New York, 23 Oct. 1972).

34   We need a new kind of feminism, one that stresses personal responsibility and is open to art and sex in all their dark, unconsoling mysteries. The feminist of the *fin de siècle* will be bawdy, streetwise, and on-the-spot confrontational, in the prankish Sixties way.

CAMILLE PAGLIA (b. 1947), U.S. author, critic, educator. *Sex, Art, and American Culture,* Introduction (1992).

35   The emancipation of today displays itself mainly in cigarettes and shorts. There is even a reaction from the ideal of an intellectual and emancipated womanhood, for which the pioneers toiled and suffered, to be seen in painted lips and nails, and the return of trailing skirts and other absurdities of dress which betoken the slave-woman's intelligent companionship.

SYLVIA PANKHURST (1882-1960), British suffragist, journalist, author. Quoted in: David Mitchell, *The Fighting Pankhursts,* pt. 5, ch. 3 (1967).

36   There must be a world revolution which puts an end to all materialistic conditions hindering woman from performing her natural role in life and driving her to carry out man's duties in order to be equal in rights.

COLONEL MUHAMMAR QADDAFI (b. 1938), Libyan leader. *The Green Book,* pt. 3, "Woman" (1976-79).

37   The connections between and among women are the most feared, the most problematic, and the most potentially transforming force on the planet.

ADRIENNE RICH (b. 1929), U.S. poet. "Disloyal to Civilization: Feminism, Racism, Gynophobia," in *Chrysalis,* no. 7 (1979; repr. in *On Lies, Secrets, and Silence,* 1980).

38   The modern woman is the curse of the universe. A disaster, that's what. She thinks that before her arrival on the scene no woman ever did anything worthwhile before, no woman was ever liberated until her time, no woman really ever amounted to anything.

ADELA ROGERS ST. JOHNS (1894-1988), U.S. journalist. Quoted in: *Los Angeles Herald-Examiner* (13 Oct. 1974).

39   Feminism is a political mistake. Feminism is a mistake made by women's intellect, a mistake which her instinct will recognize.

VALENTINE DE SAINT-POINT (1875-1953), French poet, author. "Manifesto of the Futurist Woman" (1912; repr. in *Futurism and Futurisms,* "Dictionary of Futurism," ed. by Pontus H. Ulten, 1986).

40   Whether we regard the Women's Liberation movement as a serious threat, a passing convulsion, or a fashionable idiocy, it is a movement that mounts an attack on practically everything that women value today and introduces the language and sentiments of political confrontation into the area of personal relationships.

ARIANNA STASSINOPOULOS (b. 1950), Greek author. *The Female Woman,* "The Emancipated Woman" (1973).

41   Liberation is an evershifting horizon, a total ideology that can never fulfill its promises. . . . It has the therapeutic quality of providing emotionally charged rituals of solidarity in hatred—it is the amphetamine of its believers.

> ARIANNA STASSINOPOULOS (b. 1950), Greek author. *The Female Woman*, "The Liberated Woman? . . . and Her Liberators" (1973).

42 I owe nothing to Women's Lib.

> MARGARET THATCHER (b. 1925), British Conservative politician, prime minister. Quoted in: *Observer* (London, 1 Dec. 1974).

43 If I were a woman, I would never trust men who say they are feminists. Either they are acting out of guilt, trying to establish credentials, or they think they might be able to pick up more girls. If I were a woman, I would say, go away and have your first period. Then come back and tell me you are a feminist.

> DAVID THOMAS (b. 1959), British editor. *Guardian/Elle Supplement* (London, 9 Jan. 1992).

44 The Queen is most anxious to enlist everyone who can speak or write to join in checking this mad, wicked folly of "Woman's Rights" with all its attendant horrors on which her poor, feeble sex is bent, forgetting every sense of womanly feeling and propriety.

> VICTORIA (1819-1901), Queen of Great Britain and Ireland. Letter, 29 May 1870.

45 If the abstract rights of man will bear discussion and explanation, those of women, by a parity of reasoning, will not shrink from the same test: though a different opinion prevails in this country.

> MARY WOLLSTONECRAFT (1759-97), English feminist writer. *A Vindication of the Rights of Women*, "Dedication" (1792).

46 The history of men's opposition to women's emancipation is more interesting perhaps than the story of that emancipation itself.

> VIRGINIA WOOLF (1882-1941), British novelist. *A Room of One's Own*, ch. 3 (1929).

See also Lewis on POLITICAL CORRECTNESS; Paglia on MADONNA.

FERTILITY

1 I don't know what it is about fecundity that so appalls. I suppose it is the teeming evidence that birth and growth, which we value, are ubiquitous and blind, that life itself is so astonishingly cheap, that nature is as careless as it is bountiful, and that with extravagance goes a crushing waste that will one day include our own cheap lives.

> ANNIE DILLARD (b. 1945), U.S. author, poet. *Pilgrim at Tinker Creek*, ch. 10 (1974).

2 I'm hurt, hurt and humiliated beyond endurance, seeing the wheat ripening, the fountains never ceasing to give water, the sheep bearing hundreds of lambs, the she-dogs, until it seems the whole country rises to show me its tender sleeping young while I feel two hammer-blows here instead of the mouth of my child.

> FEDERICO GARCÍA LORCA (1898-1936), Spanish poet, playwright. Yerma, in *Yerma*, act 2, sc. 2.

3 The management of fertility is one of the most important functions of adulthood.

> GERMAINE GREER (b. 1939), Australian feminist writer. *Sex and Destiny*, ch. 2 (1984).

4 The disruptive powers of excessive national fecundity may have played a greater part in bursting the bonds of convention than either the power of ideas or the errors of autocracy.

> JOHN MAYNARD KEYNES (1883-1946), British economist. *The Economic Consequences of Peace* (1919; repr. in *Collected Works*, vol. 2, 1971).

5 Virginity is now a mere preamble or waiting room to be got out of as soon as possible; it is without significance. Old age is similarly a waiting room, where you go after life's over and wait for cancer or a stroke. The years before and after the menstrual years are vestigial: the only meaningful condition left to women is that of fruitfulness.

> URSULA LE GUIN (b. 1929), U.S. author. "The Space Crone," in *The Co-Evolution Quarterly* (Summer 1976; repr. in *Dancing at the Edge of the World*, 1989).

See also Jerrold on AUSTRALIA AND THE AUSTRALIANS.

FESTIVALS

1 There is nothing funny about Halloween. This sarcastic festival reflects, rather, an infernal demand for revenge by children on the adult world.

> JEAN BAUDRILLARD (b. 1929), French semiologist. *America*, "Astral America" (1986; tr. 1988).

2 Washington's birthday is as close to a secular Christmas as any Christian country dare come this side of blasphemy.

> ALISTAIR COOKE (b. 1908), British broadcaster, journalist. *Talk About America*, ch. 3 (1968). "When Americans are sorely troubled," Cooke added, "they turn for official inspiration not to the Qur'an or Bible but to the colonial scriptures, to the sayings of the Founding Fathers, most of all to the speeches of Washington."

3 The red-letter days, now become, to all intents and purposes, dead-letter days.

> CHARLES LAMB (1775-1834), English essayist, critic. *Essays of Elia*, "Oxford in the Vacation" (1820-23).

4 It is at a fair that man can be drunk forever on liquor, love, or fights; at a fair that your front pocket can be picked by a trotting horse looking for sugar, and your hind pocket by a thief looking for his fortune.

> E. B. WHITE (1899-1985), U.S. author, editor. *One Man's Meat*, "Fall" (1944).

5 Seasons pursuing each other the indescribable crowd is gathered, it is the fourth of Seventh-month, (what salutes of cannon and small arms!)

> WALT WHITMAN (1819-92), U.S. poet. *Song of Myself*, sct. 15, in *Leaves of Grass* (1855).

6 Ah! on Thanksgiving day, when from East and from West,
From North and from South, come the pilgrim and guest,

When the gray-haired New Englander sees round
  his board
The old broken links of affection restored,
When the care-wearied man seeks his mother once
  more,
And the worn matron smiles where the girl smiled
  before.
What moistens the lip and what brightens the eye?
What calls back the past, like the rich Pumpkin
  pie?

JOHN GREENLEAF WHITTIER (1807-92), U.S. poet. *The Pumpkin*, st. 2.

See also CHRISTMAS; EASTER AND GOOD FRIDAY.

FICTION

1 Although our productions have afforded more extensive and unaffected pleasure than those of any other literary corporation in the world, no species of composition has been so much decried. . . . "And what are you reading, Miss——?" "Oh! it is only a novel!" replies the young lady; while she lays down her book with affected indifference, or momentary shame. "It is only *Cecilia,* or *Camilla,* or *Belinda*"; or, in short, only some work in which the greatest powers of the mind are displayed, in which the most thorough knowledge of human nature, the happiest delineation of its varieties, the liveliest effusions of wit and humour, are conveyed to the world in the best chosen language.

JANE AUSTEN (1775-1817), English novelist. *Northanger Abbey,* ch. 5 (1818).

2 We live in a world ruled by fictions of every kind—mass merchandising, advertising, politics conducted as a branch of advertising, the instant translation of science and technology into popular imagery, the increasing blurring and intermingling of identities within the realm of consumer goods, the preempting of any free or original imaginative response to experience by the television screen. We live inside an enormous novel. For the writer in particular it is less and less necessary for him to invent the fictional content of his novel. The fiction is already there. The writer's task is to invent the reality.

J. G. BALLARD (b. 1930), English novelist. Introduction to the 1974 French edition of *Crash* (1973).

3 Novels are longer than life.

NATALIE CLIFFORD BARNEY (1876-1972), U.S.-born French author. Quoted in: *Adam,* no. 299, "On Writing and Writers" (tr. by Ezra Pound, 1962).

4 Fiction is not imagination. It is what anticipates imagination by giving it the form of reality. This is quite opposite to our own natural tendency which is to anticipate reality by imagining it, or to flee from it by idealizing it. That is why we shall never inhabit true fiction; we are condemned to the imaginary and nostalgia for the future.

JEAN BAUDRILLARD (b. 1929), French semiologist. *America,* "Utopia Achieved" (1986; tr. 1988). Baudrillard is referring specifically to the European experience. The American way of life, he says, is "spontaneously fictional, since it is a transcending of the imaginary in reality."

5 The traditional novel form continues to enlarge our experience in those very areas where the wide-angle lens and the Cinerama screen tend to narrow it.

DANIEL J. BOORSTIN (b. 1914), U.S. historian. *The Image,* ch. 4 (1961).

6 Writing novels preserves you in a state of innocence—a lot passes you by—simply because your attention is otherwise diverted.

ANITA BROOKNER (b. 1938), British novelist, art historian. *Novelists in Interview* (ed. by John Haffenden, 1985).

7 Our interest's on the dangerous edge of things.
The honest thief, the tender murderer,
The superstitious atheist.

ROBERT BROWNING (1812-89), English poet. *Bishop Blougram's Apology.* These lines were suggested by Graham Greene as the epigraph he would choose for all of his novels.

8 If you write fiction you are, in a sense, corrupted. There's a tremendous corruptibility for the fiction writer because you're dealing mainly with sex and violence. These remain the basic themes, they're the basic themes of Shakespeare whether you like it or not.

ANTHONY BURGESS (b. 1917), British author, critic. *Face* (London, Dec. 1984).

9 Novelists are perhaps the last people in the world to be entrusted with opinions. The nature of a novel is that it has no opinions, only the dialectic of contrary views, some of which, all of which, may be untenable and even silly. A novelist should not be too intelligent either, although . . . he may be permitted to be an intellectual.

ANTHONY BURGESS (b. 1917), British author, critic. *You've Had Your Time,* ch. 2 (1990).

10 But I hate things *all fiction* . . . there should always be some foundation of fact for the most airy fabric—and pure invention is but the talent of a liar.

LORD BYRON (1788-1824), English poet. Letter, 2 April 1817, to publisher John Murray (published in *Byron's Letters and Journals,* vol. 5, ed. by Leslie A. Marchand, 1973-81).

11 Romances I ne'er read like those I have seen.

LORD BYRON (1788-1824), English poet. *Don Juan,* cto. 14, st. 80.

12 Novels as dull as dishwater, with the grease of random sentiments floating on top.

ITALO CALVINO (1923-85), Italian author, critic. "The Novel as Spectacle," in *Il Giorno* (Milan, 14 Oct. 1970); repr. in *The Literature Machine,* 1987).

13 A novel is never anything but a philosophy put into images.

ALBERT CAMUS (1913-60), French-Algerian philosopher, author. Review of Jean Paul Sartre, *La Nausée,* in *Alger Républicain* (Algiers, 20 Oct. 1938; repr. in *Selected Essays and Notebooks,* ed. and tr. by Philip Thody, 1970).

14 What is a novel if not a conviction of our fellowmen's existence strong enough to take upon itself a form of imagined life clearer than reality and whose accumulated verisimilitude of selected episodes puts to shame the pride of documentary history?

JOSEPH CONRAD (1857-1924), Polish-born English novelist. *A Personal Record,* ch. 1 (1912).

15 The narrative impulse is always with us; we couldn't imagine ourselves through a day without it.

> ROBERT COOVER (b. 1932), U.S. writer. *Time Out* (London, 7 May 1986).

16 If I were a writer, how I would enjoy being told the novel is dead. How liberating to work in the margins, outside a central perception. You are the ghoul of literature. Lovely.

> DON DELILLO (b. 1926), U.S. author. Owen Brademas, in *The Names*, ch. 4 (1982).

17 There is no longer any such thing as fiction or non-fiction; there's only narrative.

> E. L. DOCTOROW (b. 1931), U.S. novelist. *New York Times Book Review* (27 Jan. 1988).

18 I at least have so much to do in unravelling certain human lots, and seeing how they were woven and inter-woven, that all the light I can command must be concentrated on this particular web, and not dispersed over that tempting range of relevancies called the universe.

> GEORGE ELIOT (1819-80), English novelist, editor. *Middlemarch*, bk. 2, ch. 15 (1871).

19 The purpose of a work of fiction is to appeal to the lingering after-effects in the reader's mind as differing from, say, the purpose of oratory or philosophy which respectively leave people in a fighting or thoughtful mood.

> F. SCOTT FITZGERALD (1896-1940), U.S. author. Letter, 1 June 1934, to Ernest Hemingway (published in *The Letters of F. Scott Fitzgerald*, ed. by Andrew Turnbull, 1963).

20 The final test for a novel will be our affection for it, as it is the test of our friends, and of anything else which we cannot define.

> E. M. FORSTER (1879-1970), British novelist, essayist. *Aspects of the Novel*, "Introductory" (1927).

21 Writing a novel is not merely going on a shopping expedition across the border to an unreal land: it is hours and years spent in the factories, the streets, the cathedrals of the imagination.

> JANET FRAME (b. 1924), New Zealand novelist, poet. *The Envoy from Mirror City*, vol. 1, ch. 20 (1985).

22 By its very nature, the novel indicates that we are becoming. There is no final solution. There is no last word.

> CARLOS FUENTES (b. 1928), Mexican novelist, short-story writer. *Guardian* (London, 24 Feb. 1989).

23 Novelists do not write as birds sing, by the push of nature. It is part of the job that there should be much routine and some daily stuff on the level of carpentry.

> WILLIAM GOLDING (1911–93), British author. "Rough Magic," lecture, 16 Feb. 1977, University of Kent, Canterbury (repr. in *A Moving Target*, 1982).

24 When writing a novel a writer should create living people; people not characters. A *character* is a caricature.

> ERNEST HEMINGWAY (1899-1961), U.S. author. *Death in the Afternoon*, ch. 16 (1932).

25 You know that fiction, prose rather, is possibly the roughest trade of all in writing. You do not have the reference, the old important reference. You have the sheet of blank paper, the pencil, and the obligation to invent truer than things can be true. You have to take what is not palpable and make it completely palpable and also have it seem normal and so that it can become a part of experience of the person who reads it.

> ERNEST HEMINGWAY (1899-1961), U.S. author. Letter, 24 Sept. 1954, to the critic Bernard Berenson (published in *Selected Letters*, ed. by Carlos Baker, 1981).

26 It's with bad sentiments that one makes good novels.

> ALDOUS HUXLEY (1894-1963), British author. Letter, 10 July 1962. Quoted in: *Aldous Huxley: the Critical Heritage* (ed. by Donald Watt, 1975). Huxley believed this to be the explanation for why his novel *Island*—published that year and greatly criticized—was "so inadequate."

27 Writing a novel is actually searching for victims. As I write I keep looking for casualties. The stories uncover the casualties.

> JOHN IRVING (b. 1942), U.S. author. Interview in *Writers at Work* (Eighth Series, ed. by George Plimpton, 1988).

28 The only reason for the existence of a novel is that it does attempt to represent life.

> HENRY JAMES (1843-1916), U.S. author. *The Art of Fiction* (1884; repr. in *Partial Portraits*, 1888).

29 The time-honored bread-sauce of the happy ending.

> HENRY JAMES (1843-1916), U.S. author. *Theatricals: Second Series*, Prefatory Note (1894).

30 When I heard the word "stream" uttered with such a revolting primness, what I think of is urine and not the contemporary novel. And besides, it isn't new, it is far from the *dernier cri*. Shakespeare used it continually, much too much in my opinion, and there's *Tristam Shandy*, not to mention the *Agamemnon*.

> JAMES JOYCE (1882-1941), Irish author. Quoted in: Frederic Prokosch, *Voices: A Memoir*, "At Sylvia's" (1983), referring to "the stream of consciousness." Joyce was replying to the assertion by the young author and poet Prokosch that Molly Bloom's final monologue in *Ulysses* represented this form. "Molly Bloom was a down-to-earth lady," Joyce said. "She would never have indulged in anything so refined as a stream of consciousness."

31 A novel that does not uncover a hitherto unknown segment of existence is immoral. Knowledge is the novel's only morality.

> MILAN KUNDERA (b. 1929), Czech author, critic. *New York Review of Books* (19 July 1984).

32 All great novels, all true novels, are bisexual.

> MILAN KUNDERA (b. 1929), Czech author, critic. *Times* (London, 16 May 1991).

33 Would you not like to try *all* sorts of lives—one is so very small—but that is the satisfaction of writing—one can impersonate so many people.

> KATHERINE MANSFIELD (1888-1923), New Zealand-born British author. Letter, 24 April 1907 (published in *Collected Letters*, vol. 1, ed. by Vincent O'Sullivan and Margaret Scott, 1984).

34 For if the proper study of mankind is man, it is evidently more sensible to occupy yourself with the coherent, substantial and significant creatures of fiction than with the irrational and shadowy figures of real life.

> W. SOMERSET MAUGHAM (1874-1965), British author. Ashenden, in *Cakes and Ale,* ch. 16 (1930).

35 The really great novel . . . tends to be the exact negative of its author's life.

> ANDRÉ MAUROIS (1885-1967), French author, critic. *The Art of Writing,* "The Writer's Craft," sct. 4 (1960).

36 By measuring individual human worth, the novelist reveals the full enormity of the State's crime when it sets out to crush that individuality.

> IAN MCEWAN (b. 1938), British author. *A Move Abroad,* Preface (1989).

37 A novelist is, like all mortals, more fully at home on the surface of the present than in the ooze of the past.

> VLADIMIR NABOKOV (1899-1977), Russian-born U.S. novelist, poet. *Strong Opinions,* ch. 3 (1973).

38 For a Jewish Puritan of the middle class, the novel is serious, the novel is work, the novel is conscientious application—why, the novel is practically the retail business all over again.

> HOWARD NEMEROV (1920-91), U.S. poet, novelist, critic. *Journal of the Fictive Life,* "Reflexions of the Novelist Felix Ledger," sct. C (1965).

39 Jesus of Nazareth could have chosen simply to express Himself in moral precepts; but like a great poet He chose the form of the parable, wonderful short stories that entertained and clothed the moral precept in an eternal form. It is not sufficient to catch man's mind, you must also catch the imaginative faculties of his mind.

> DUDLEY NICHOLS (1895-1960), U.S. screenwriter. "The Writer and the Film," in *Theatre Arts* (Oct. 1943).

40 It seems that the fiction writer has a revolting attachment to the poor, for even when he writes about the rich, he is more concerned with what they lack than with what they have.

> FLANNERY O'CONNOR (1925-64), U.S. author. *Mystery and Manners,* "The Teaching of Literature" (ed. by Sally and Robert Fitzgerald, 1972).

41 The first sentence of every novel should be: "Trust me, this will take time but there is order here, very faint, very human." Meander if you want to get to town.

> MICHAEL ONDAATJE (b. 1943), Canadian novelist. *In the Skin of a Lion,* bk. 2, "Palace of Purification" (1987).

42 When the characters are really alive before their author, the latter does nothing but follow them in their action, in their words, in the situations which they suggest to him.

> LUIGI PIRANDELLO (1867-1936), Italian author, playwright. The Father, in *Six Characters in Search of an Author,* act 3.

43 Undermining experience, embellishing experience, rearranging and enlarging experience into a species of mythology.

> PHILIP ROTH (b. 1933), U.S. novelist. Letter to Zuckerman (published in *The Facts,* 1988), describing the life of a fiction writer.

44 The acceptance that all that is solid has melted into the air, that reality and morality are not givens but imper-

fect human constructs, is the point from which fiction begins.

> SALMAN RUSHDIE (b. 1947), Indian-born British author. "Is Nothing Sacred?" Herbert Reade Memorial Lecture, 6 Feb. 1990.

45 The novel does not seek to establish a privileged language but it insists upon the freedom to portray and analyse the struggle between the different contestants for such privileges.

> SALMAN RUSHDIE (b. 1947), Indian-born British author. "Is Nothing Sacred?" Herbert Reade Memorial Lecture, 6 Feb. 1990.

46 Democritus plucked his eye out because he could not look at a woman without thinking of her as a woman. If he had read a few of our novels, he would have torn himself to pieces.

> WALLACE STEVENS (1879-1955), U.S. poet. *The Necessary Angel,* "The Noble Rider and the Sound of Words" (1951; lecture first published 1942).

47 Educating a son I should allow him no fairy tales and only a very few novels. This is to prevent him from having 1. the sense of romantic solitude (if he is worth anything he will develop a proper and useful solitude) which identification with the *hero* gives. 2. cant ideas of right and wrong, absurd systems of honor and morality which never never will he be able completely to get rid of, 3. the attainment of "ideals," of *a priori* desires, of *a priori* emotions. He should amuse himself with fact only: he will then not learn that if the weak younger son do or do not the magical honorable thing he will win the princess with hair like flax.

> LIONEL TRILLING (1905-75), U.S. critic. *Partisan Review 50th Anniversary Edition* (ed. by William Philips, 1985), 1928 notebook entry.

48 Persons attempting to find a motive in this narrative will be prosecuted; persons attempting to find a moral in it will be banished; persons attempting to find a plot in it will be shot.

> MARK TWAIN (1835-1910), U.S. author. *Huckleberry Finn,* "By Order of the Author," "Notice" (1884).

49 Truth *is* stranger than fiction, but it is because Fiction is obliged to stick to possibilities; Truth isn't.

> MARK TWAIN (1835-1910), U.S. author. *Following the Equator,* ch. 15, "Pudd'nhead Wilson's New Calendar" (1897).

50 No matter how ephemeral it is, a novel is something, while despair is nothing.

> MARIO VARGAS LLOSA (b. 1936), Peruvian novelist. *The Real Life of Alejandro Mayta,* ch. 3 (1984; tr. 1986).

51 Writing fiction has become a priestly business in countries that have lost their faith.

> GORE VIDAL (b. 1925), U.S. novelist, critic. *Independent* (London, 16 Aug. 1989).

52 I find in most novels no imagination at all. They seem to think the highest form of the novel is to write about marriage, because that's the most important thing there is for middle-class people.

> GORE VIDAL (b. 1925), U.S. novelist, critic. *Guardian* (London, 2 Nov. 1989).

53 There is something else which has the power to awaken us to the truth. It is the works of writers of genius. . . . They give us, in the guise of fiction, something equivalent to the actual density of the real, that density which life offers us every day but which we are unable to grasp because we are amusing ourselves with lies.

SIMONE WEIL (1909-43), French philosopher, mystic. "Morality and Literature," in *Cahiers du Sud* (Marseilles, Jan. 1944).

54 One should not be too severe on English novels; they are the only relaxation of the intellectually unemployed.

OSCAR WILDE (1854-1900), Anglo-Irish playwright, author. *Pall Mall Gazette* (London, 4 Aug. 1886).

55 The good ended happily, and the bad unhappily. That is what Fiction means.

OSCAR WILDE (1854-1900), Anglo-Irish playwright, author. Miss Prism, in *The Importance of Being Earnest,* act 2, on her own novel.

56 Fiction is like a spider's web, attached ever so lightly perhaps, but still attached to life at all four corners. Often the attachment is scarcely perceptible.

VIRGINIA WOOLF (1882-1941), British novelist. *A Room Of One's Own,* ch. 3 (1929).

57 Novels so often provide an anodyne and not an antidote, glide one into torpid slumbers instead of rousing one with a burning brand.

VIRGINIA WOOLF (1882-1941), British novelist. *A Room of One's Own,* ch. 5 (1929).

See also Philip Roth on AUTOBIOGRAPHY; Pritchett on BOOKS: BESTSELLERS; Stone on LIFE; Hemingway on LITERATURE AND SOCIETY; O'Connor on MANNERS; Stevens on POETRY; James on READING; SCIENCE FICTION; Chandler on STORYTELLING; Baudrillard on The UNITED STATES.

FICTION: SUSPENSE AND MYSTERY

1 It is just possible that the tensions in a novel of murder are the simplest and yet most complete pattern of the tensions on which we live in this generation.

RAYMOND CHANDLER (1888-1959), U.S. author. Letter, 17 Oct. 1948, to critic James Sandoe (published in *Raymond Chandler Speaking,* 1962).

2 Let us never accept the point of view that mysteries are written by hacks. The poorest of us shed our blood over every chapter. The best of us start from scratch with every new book.

RAYMOND CHANDLER (1888-1959), U.S. author. Letter, Oct. 1955 (published in *Raymond Chandler Speaking,* 1962).

3 The perfect detective story cannot be written. The type of mind which can evolve the perfect problem is not the type of mind that can produce the artistic job of writing.

RAYMOND CHANDLER (1888-1959), U.S. author. *The Notebooks of Raymond Chandler,* "Twelve Notes on the Mystery Story" (1976).

4 Detection is, or ought to be, an exact science, and should be treated in the same cold and unemotional man-

ner. You have attempted to tinge it with romanticism, which produces much the same effect as if you worked a love-story or an elopement into the fifth proposition of Euclid.

SIR ARTHUR CONAN DOYLE (1859-1930), English author. Sherlock Holmes to Dr. Watson, in *The Sign of Four,* ch. 1 (1890). Watson had written what he called "a small brochure, with the somewhat fantastic title of `A Study in Scarlet'"—the name of the tale in which Conan Doyle first introduced Sherlock Holmes.

5 We ignore thriller writers at our peril. Their genre is the political condition. They massage our dreams and magnify our nightmares. If it is true that we always need enemies, then we will always need writers of fiction to encode our fears and fantasies.

DANIEL EASTERMAN (b. 1949), Irish author. *Million Magazine* (London, Sept.-Oct. 1991).

6 The mystery form is like gymnastic equipment: you can grasp hold of it and show off what you can do.

MICKEY FRIEDMAN (b. 1944), U.S. author. *International Herald Tribune* (Paris, 31 Jan. 1990).

7 Thrillers are like life—more like life than you are . . . it's what we've all made of the world.

GRAHAM GREENE (1904-91), British novelist. Arthur Rowe, in *The Ministry of Fear,* bk. 1, ch. 5 (1943).

8 The main question raised by the thriller is not what kind of world we live in, or what reality is like, but what it has done to us.

RALPH HARPER (b. 1915), U.S. cleric, author. *The World of the Thriller,* pt. 3, "The Emotions" (1969).

9 What the detective story is about is not murder but the restoration of order.

P. D. JAMES (b. 1920), British mystery writer. Interview in *Face* (London, Dec. 1986).

10 For decades to come the spy world will continue to be the collective couch where the subconscious of each nation is confessed.

JOHN LE CARRÉ (b. 1931), British thriller writer. Quoted in: *Observer* (London, 19 Nov. 1989).

11 Death seems to provide the minds of the Anglo-Saxon race with a greater fund of amusement than any other single subject.

DOROTHY L. SAYERS (1893-1957), British author. *The Third Omnibus of Crime,* Introduction (1935).

See also Chandler on DETECTIVES.

FIDELITY

1 Fidelity. A virtue peculiar to those who are about to be betrayed.

AMBROSE BIERCE (1842-1914), U.S. author. *The Devil's Dictionary* (1881-1906).

2 Constancy . . . that small change of love, which people exact so rigidly, receive in such conterfeit coin, and repay in baser metal.

LORD BYRON (1788-1824), English poet. Letter, 17 Nov. 1816,

to poet Thomas Moore (published in *Byron's Letters and Journals*, vol. 5, ed. by Leslie A. Marchand, 1973-81).

3 I have been faithful to thee, Cynara, in my fashion.

> ERNEST DOWSON (1867-1900), English poet. *Cynara* (full title: *Non sum qualis eram bonae sub regno Cynarae*), closing line of each stanza.

4 We only part to meet again.
Change, as ye list, ye winds: my heart shall be
The faithful compass that still points to thee.

> JOHN GAY (1685-1732), English dramatist. *Sweet William's Farewell to Black-Eyed Susan.*

5 Matrimonial devotion
Doesn't seem to suit her notion.

> W. S. GILBERT (1836-1911), English librettist. Ko-Ko, in *The Mikado*, act 2.

6 Not observation of a duty but liberty itself is the pledge that assures fidelity.

> ELLEN KEY (1849-1926), Swedish author, feminist. *The Morality of Woman and Other Essays*, "The Morality of Woman" (1911).

7 Constancy has nothing virtuous in itself, independently of the pleasure it confers, and partakes of the temporizing spirit of vice in proportion as it endures tamely moral defects of magnitude in the object of its indiscreet choice.

> PERCY BYSSHE SHELLEY (1792-1822), English poet. *Even Love Is Sold*, a note from *Queen Mab* (1813).

8 What a fuss people make about fidelity! Why, even in love it is purely a question for physiology. It has nothing to do with our own will. Young men want to be faithful, and are not; old men want to be faithless, and cannot: that is all one can say.

> OSCAR WILDE (1854-1900), Anglo-Irish playwright, author. Lord Henry, in *The Picture of Dorian Gray*, ch. 2 (1891).

9 People who love only once in their lives are . . . shallow people. What they call their loyalty, and their fidelity, I call either the lethargy of custom or their lack of imagination. Faithfulness is to the emotional life what consistency is to the life of the intellect—simply a confession of failures.

> OSCAR WILDE (1854-1900), Anglo-Irish playwright, author. Lord Henry, in *The Picture of Dorian Gray*, ch. 4 (1891).

See also Auden on HOMOSEXUALITY; Hebrew Bible, Pope on LOYALTY; Shaw on VIRTUE.

FIGHTING

1 The full value of this life can only be got by fighting; the violent take it by storm. And if we have accepted everything we have missed something—war. This life of ours is a very enjoyable fight, but a very miserable truce.

> G. K. CHESTERTON (1874-1936), British author. *Charles Dickens*, "The Optimism of Dickens" (1906).

2 The world is a fine place and worth fighting for.

> ERNEST HEMINGWAY (1899-1961), U.S. author. Robert Jordan, in *For Whom the Bell Tolls*, ch. 43 (1940).

3 Fighting is like champagne. It goes to the heads of cowards as quickly as of heroes. Any fool can be brave on a battlefield when it's be brave or else be killed.

> MARGARET MITCHELL (1900-1949), U.S. novelist. Ashley Wilkes, in *Gone with the Wind*, vol. 2, pt. 4, ch. 31 (1936).

4 That is the whole secret of successful fighting. Get your enemy at a disadvantage; and never, on any account, fight him on equal terms.

> GEORGE BERNARD SHAW (1856-1950), Anglo-Irish playwright, critic. Sergius, in *Arms and the Man*, act 2.

See also BATTLES.

FINANCE

1 The objects of a financier are, then, to secure an ample revenue; to impose it with judgment and equality; to employ it economically; and, when necessity obliges him to make use of credit, to secure its foundations in that instance, and for ever, by the clearness and candour of his proceedings, the exactness of his calculations, and the solidity of his funds.

> EDMUND BURKE (1729-97), Irish philosopher, statesman. *Reflections on the Revolution in France* (1790).

2 We estimate the wisdom of nations by seeing what they did with their surplus capital.

> RALPH WALDO EMERSON (1803-82), U.S. essayist, poet, philosopher. *English Traits*, "Wealth" (1856).

3 What we now call "finance" is, I hold, an intellectual perversion of what began as warm human love.

> ROBERT GRAVES (1895-1985), British poet, novelist. Speech, 6 Dec. 1963, London School of Economics (published in *Mammon and the Black Goddess*, "Mammon," 1965).

4 Women's battle for financial equality has barely been joined, much less won. Society still traditionally assigns to woman the role of money-handler rather than money-maker, and our assigned specialty is far more likely to be home economics than financial economics.

> PAULA NELSON (b. 1945), U.S. business executive. *The Joy of Money*, ch. 1 (1975).

5 The Law of Triviality . . . briefly stated, it means that the time spent on any item of the agenda will be in inverse proportion to the sum involved.

> C. NORTHCOTE PARKINSON (1909-93), British historian, political scientist. *Parkinson's Law, or The Pursuit of Progress*, "High Finance" (1958).

6 The little I know of it has not served to raise my opinion of what is vulgarly called the "Monied Interest;" I mean, that blood-sucker, that muckworm, that calls itself "the friend of government."

> WILLIAM PITT THE ELDER, LORD CHATHAM (1708-78), English statesman. Speech, 22 Nov. 1770, to the House of Lords, London.

7 When it comes to finances, remember that there are no withholding taxes on the wages of sin.

> MAE WEST (1892-1980), U.S. screen actor. *On Sex, Health and E.S.P.*, "Last Word" (1975).

FIRE

1 The world, an entity out of everything, was created by neither gods nor men, but was, is and will be eternally living fire, regularly becoming ignited and regularly becoming extinguished.

HERACLITUS (c. 535-c. 475 B.C.), Greek philosopher. *The Cosmic Fragments*, no. 20 (c. 480 B.C.).

2 Oh! thou clear spirit of clear fire, whom on these seas I as Persian once did worship, till in the sacramental act so burned by thee, that to this hour I bear the scar; I now know thee, thou clear spirit, and I now know that thy right worship is defiance. To neither love nor reverence wilt thou be kind; and e'en for hate thou canst but kill; and all are killed. No fearless fool now fronts thee.

HERMAN MELVILLE (1819-91), U.S. author. Captain Ahab, in *Moby-Dick*, ch. 119 (1851).

THE FIRST LADY

1 Roughly speaking, the President of the United States knows what his job is. Constitution and custom spell it out, for him as well as for us. His wife has no such luck. The First Lady has no rules; rather each new woman must make her own.

SHANA ALEXANDER (b. 1925), U.S. writer, editor. *The Feminine Eye*, "The Best First Lady" (1970; first published 1968).

2 The first lady is, and always has been, an unpaid public servant elected by one person, her husband.

LADY BIRD JOHNSON (b. 1912), U.S. First Lady. *A White House Diary* (1970), entry for 14 March 1968.

3 I do not think it altogether inappropriate to introduce myself to this audience. I am the man who accompanied Jacqueline Kennedy to Paris, and I have enjoyed it.

JOHN F. KENNEDY (1917-63), U.S. Democratic politician, president. Speech, 2 June 1961, at SHAPE Headquarters, Paris, France.

4 The one thing I do not want to be called is First Lady. It sounds like a saddle horse.

JACQUELINE KENNEDY ONASSIS (b. 1929), U.S. First Lady. Advice to her secretary following the inauguration of John F. Kennedy. Quoted in: Peter Collier and David Horowitz, *The Kennedys*, pt. 3, ch. 2 (1984).

5 I see the first lady as another means to keep a president from becoming isolated.

NANCY REAGAN (b. 1923), U.S. First Lady. *International Herald Tribune* (Paris, 26 May 1988).

6 You will feel that you are no longer clothing yourself, you are dressing a public monument.

ELEANOR ROOSEVELT (1884-1962), U.S. columnist, lecturer. Warning to wives of future presidents, in *New York Herald Tribune* (27 Oct. 1960).

FISHING

1 If fishing is a religion, fly fishing is high church.

TOM BROKAW (b. 1940), U.S. journalist, broadcaster. Quoted in: *International Herald Tribune* (Paris, 10 Sept. 1991).

2 Somebody just back of you while you are fishing is as bad as someone looking over your shoulder while you write a letter to your girl.

ERNEST HEMINGWAY (1899-1961), U.S. author. "Trout Fishing in Europe," in *The Toronto Star Weekly* (17 Nov. 1923; repr. in *By-Line Ernest Hemingway*, ed. by William White, 1967).

3 Some people are under the impression that all that is required to make a good fisherman is the ability to tell lies easily and without blushing; but this is a mistake. Mere bald fabrication is useless; the veriest tyro can manage that. It is in the circumstantial detail, the embellishing touches of probability, the general air of scrupulous—almost of pedantic—veracity, that the experienced angler is seen.

JEROME K. JEROME (1859-1927), British author. *Three Men in a Boat*, ch. 17 (1889).

4 Fly fishing may be a very pleasant amusement; but angling or float fishing I can only compare to a stick and a string, with a worm at one end and a fool at the other.

SAMUEL JOHNSON (1709-1784), English author, lexicographer. Quoted in: Hawker, *On Worm Fishing*.

5 The perch swallows the grub-worm, the pickerel swallows the perch, and the fisherman swallows the pickerel; and so all the chinks in the scale of being are filled.

HENRY DAVID THOREAU (1817-62), U.S. philosopher, author, naturalist. *Walden*, "The Pond in Winter" (1854).

6 We may say of angling, as Dr. Boteler said of strawberries, "Doubtless God could have made a better berry, but doubtless God never did"; and so, if I might be judge, God never did make a more calm, quiet, innocent recreation than angling.

IZAAK WALTON (1593-1683), English author, biographer. *The Compleat Angler*, ch. 5 (1653).

F. SCOTT FITZGERALD

1 What is most appalling in an F. Scott Fitzgerald book is that it is *peopleless* fiction: Fitzgerald writes about spectral, muscled suits; dresses, hats, and sleeves which have some sort of vague, libidinous throb. These are plainly the product of sickness.

EDWARD DAHLBERG (1900-1977), U.S. author, critic. *Alms For Oblivion*, "Peopleless Fiction" (1964).

2 I am not a great man, but sometimes I think the impersonal and objective equality of my talent and the sacrifices of it, in pieces, to preserve its essential value has some sort of epic grandeur.

F. SCOTT FITZGERALD (1896-1940), U.S. author. Letter, 1940, to his daughter Frances Scott Fitzgerald (first published in *The Crack-Up*, ed. by Edmund Wilson, 1945). The words "some sort of epic grandeur" were used by Matthew J. Bruccoli as a title for his 1981 biography of Fitzgerald.

3 I talk with the authority of failure—Ernest with the authority of success. We could never sit across the same table again.

F. SCOTT FITZGERALD (1896-1940), U.S. author. *The Crack-Up*, "Notebook L" (ed. by Edmund Wilson, 1945), referring to his relationship with Ernest Hemingway.

4 Mr. Fitzgerald—I believe that is how he spells his name—seems to believe that plagiarism begins at home.

> ZELDA FITZGERALD (1900-1948), U.S. writer. *Tribune*, review of F. Scott Fitzgerald, *The Beautiful and the Damned* (New York, 2 April 1922). Quoted in: Nancy Milford, *Zelda*, pt. 2, ch. 7 (1970). "On one page," she elaborated, "I recognized a portion of an old diary of mine which mysteriously disappeared shortly after my marriage."

5 His meter was bitter, and ironic and spectacular and inviting: so was life. There wasn't much other life during those times than to what his pen paid the tribute of poetic tragic glamour and offered the reconciliation of the familiarities of tragedy.

> ZELDA FITZGERALD (1900-1948), U.S. writer. *Hemingway/Fitzgerald Annual* (1974; repr. in Matthew J. Bruccoli, *Some Sort of Epic Grandeur*, ch. 61, 1981).

6 Scott took LITERATURE so solemnly. He never understood that it was just writing as well as you can and finishing what you start.

> ERNEST HEMINGWAY (1899-1961), U.S. author. Letter, 12 May 1950, to Arthur Mizener (published in *Selected Letters*, ed. by Carlos Baker, 1981). Mizener wrote a biography of Scott Fitzgerald, and edited his essays and short stories.

7 His talent was as natural as the pattern that was made by the dust on a butterfly's wings. At one time he understood it no more than the butterfly did and he did not know when it was brushed or marred. Later he became conscious of his damaged wings and of their construction and he learned to think and could not fly any more because the love of flight was gone and he could only remember when it had been effortless.

> ERNEST HEMINGWAY (1899-1961), U.S. author. *A Moveable Feast*, ch. 17 (1964).

FLATTERY

1 Between flattery and admiration there often flows a river of contempt.

> MINNA ANTRIM (b. 1861), U.S. epigrammist. *Naked Truth and Veiled Allusions* (1901, p. 106).

2 Flattery corrupts both the receiver and the giver.

> EDMUND BURKE (1729-97), Irish philosopher, statesman. *Reflections on the Revolution in France* (1790).

3 The reason that adulation is not displeasing is that, though untrue, it shows one to be of consequence enough, in one way or other, to induce people to lie.

> LORD BYRON (1788-1824), English poet. *Byron's Letters and Journals*, vol. 3 (ed. by Leslie A. Marchand, 1974), entry for 28 Nov. 1813.

4 Women who are either indisputably beautiful, or indisputably ugly, are best flattered upon the score of their understandings; but those who are in a state of mediocrity are best flattered upon their beauty, or at least their graces: for every woman who is not absolutely ugly, thinks herself handsome.

> LORD CHESTERFIELD (1694-1773), English statesman, man of letters. Letter, 5 Sept. 1748 (first published 1774; repr. in *The Letters of the Earl of Chesterfield to His Son*, vol. 1, no. 161, ed. by Charles Strachey, 1901).

5 Just praise is only a debt, but flattery is a present.

> SAMUEL JOHNSON (1709-84), English author, lexicographer. *Rambler*, no. 155 (London, 10 Sept. 1751; repr. in *Works of Samuel Johnson*, vol. 5, ed. by W. J. Bate & Albrecht B. Strauss, 1969).

6 He who says he hates every kind of flattery, and says it in earnest, certainly does not yet know every kind of flattery.

> G. C. LICHTENBERG (1742-99), German physicist, philosopher. *Aphorisms*, "Notebook K," aph. 41 (written 1765-99; tr. by R. J. Hollingdale, 1990).

7 Flattery makes friends and truth makes enemies.

> SPANISH PROVERB.

8 But it is hard to know them from friends, they are so obsequious and full of protestations; for a wolf resembles a dog, so doth a flatterer a friend.

> SIR WALTER RALEGH (1552-1618), English author, soldier, explorer. *Instructions to His Son and to Posterity*, ch. 3, "Wisest Men Have Been Abused by Flatterers" (1632; repr. in *The Works of Sir Walter Raleigh*, vol. 2, 1751; also in *Advice to a Son*, 1962).

9 To make a man perfectly happy tell him he works too hard, that he spends too much money, that he is "misunderstood" or that he is "different"; none of this is necessarily complimentary, but it will flatter him infinitely more that merely telling him that he is brilliant, or noble, or wise, or good.

> HELEN ROWLAND (1875-1950), U.S. journalist. *A Guide to Men*, "Intermezzo" (1922).

10 What really flatters a man is that you think him worth flattering.

> GEORGE BERNARD SHAW (1856-1950), Anglo-Irish playwright, critic. Broadbent, in *John Bull's Other Island*, act 4.

11 Baloney is flattery laid on so thick it cannot be true, and blarney is flattery so thin we love it.

> FULTON J. SHEEN (1895-1979), U.S. clergyman, author. Speech, 3 Dec. 1938, Boston.

12 The art of pleasing is the art of deceiving.

> LUC, MARQUIS DE VAUVENARGUES (1715-47), French moralist. *Refléxions et Maximes*, no. 329 (1746).

See also COMPLIMENTS; Chinese proverb on HUMILITY; Chesterfield on INGRATIATION; Shakespeare on POLITICIANS; Smith on PRAISE; Disraeli on ROYALTY; Craig on OSCAR WILDE.

FLIRTING

1 The pleasure of one's effect on other people still exists in age—what's called making a hit. But the hit is much rarer and made of different stuff.

> ENID BAGNOLD (1889-1981), British novelist, playwright. *Autobiography*, ch. 5 (1969).

2 We have progressively improved into a less spiritual species of tenderness—but the seal is not yet fixed though the wax is preparing for the impression.

> LORD BYRON (1788-1824), English poet. Letter, 14 Oct. 1813 (published in *Byron's Letters and Journals*, vol. 3, ed. by Leslie A. Marchand, 1974).

3 Is not the whole world a vast house of assignation of which the filing system has been lost?

QUENTIN CRISP (b. 1908), British author. *The Naked Civil Servant*, ch. 11 (1968).

4 O Polly, you might have toyed and kissed,
By keeping men off, you keep them on.

JOHN GAY (1685-1732), English dramatist. Mrs. Peach, in *The Beggar's Opera*, act 1, sc. 8, air 9.

5 There are few things that we so unwillingly give up, even in advanced age, as the supposition that we still have the power of ingratiating ourselves with the fair sex.

SAMUEL JOHNSON (1709-84), English author, lexicographer. Quoted in: "Johnsoniana," in *European Magazine* (Jan. 1785; repr. in *Johnsonian Miscellanies*, vol. 2, "Anecdotes by George Stevens," ed. by George Birkbeck Hill, 1891).

6 No matter how happily a woman may be married, it always pleases her to discover that there is a nice man who wishes that she were not.

H. L. MENCKEN (1880-1956), U.S. journalist. *A Mencken Chrestomathy*, "Sententiæ: Masculum et Feminam Creavit Eos" (1949).

7 The pretty fellows you speak of, I own entertain me sometimes, but is it impossible to be diverted with what one despises? I can laugh at a puppet show, at the same time I know there is nothing in it worth my attention or regard.

LADY MARY WORTLEY MONTAGU (1689-1762), English society figure, letter writer. Letter, 28 March 1710, to her future husband (published in *The Complete Letters of Lady Mary Wortley Montagu*, 1967).

8 To have a man who can flirt is next thing to indispensable to a leader of society.

MARGARET OLIPHANT (1828-97), English novelist, historian. Miss Marjoribanks, in *Chronicles of Carlingford*, no. 4, *Miss Marjoribanks*, ch. 13 (1866).

9 The hardest task of a girl's life, nowadays, is to prove to a man that his intentions are serious.

HELEN ROWLAND (1875-1950), U.S. journalist. *A Guide to Men*, "Intermezzo" (1922).

10 Why does a man take it for granted that a girl who flirts with him wants him to kiss her—when, nine times out of ten, she only wants him to *want* to kiss her?

HELEN ROWLAND (1875-1950), U.S. journalist. *A Guide to Men*, "First Interlude" (1922).

11 Whoever loves above all the approach of love will never know the joy of attaining it.

ANTOINE DE SAINT-EXUPÉRY (1900-1944), French aviator, author. *The Wisdom of the Sands*, ch. 2 (1948).

12 The amount of women in London who flirt with their own husbands is perfectly scandalous. It looks so bad. It is simply washing one's clean linen in public.

OSCAR WILDE (1854-1900), Anglo-Irish playwright, author. Algernon, in *The Importance of Being Earnest*, act 1.

See also Wilde on MARRIAGE.

FLOWERS

1 These flowers, which were splendid and sprightly,
Waking in the dawn of the morning,
In the evening will be a pitiful frivolity,
Sleeping in the cold night's arms.

PEDRO CALDERÓN DE LA BARCA (1600-1681), Spanish playwright. *Éstas, que fueron pompa y alegría*.

2 Flowers have spoken to me more than I can tell in written words. They are the hieroglyphics of angels, loved by all men for the beauty of the character, though few can decypher even fragments of their meaning.

LYDIA M. CHILD (1802-80), U.S. abolitionist, writer, editor. Letter, 1 Sept. 1842 (published in *Letters from New York*, vol. 1, Letter 26, 1843).

3 Flowers . . . that are so pathetic in their beauty, frail as the clouds, and in their colouring as gorgeous as the heavens, had through thousands of years been the heritage of children—honoured as the jewellery of God only by *them*—when suddenly the voice of Christianity, counter-signing the voice of infancy, raised them to a grandeur transcending the Hebrew throne, although founded by God himself, and pronounced Solomon in all his glory not to be arrayed like one of these.

THOMAS DE QUINCEY (1785-1859), English author. *Confessions of an English Opium-Eater*, pt. 1 (1822).

4 Flowers . . . are a proud assertion that a ray of beauty outvalues all the utilities of the world.

RALPH WALDO EMERSON (1803-82), U.S. essayist, poet, philosopher. *Essays*, "Gifts" (Second Series, 1844).

5 'Tis the last rose of summer,
Left blooming alone;
All her lovely companions are faded and gone.

THOMAS MOORE (1779-1852), Irish poet. *'Tis the Last Rose of Summer*.

6 Every flower is a soul blossoming in Nature.

GÉRARD DE NERVAL (1808-55), French novelist, poet. *Vers Dorés*, in *L'Artiste* (Paris, 16 March 1845, under the title "Pensée Antique"; repr. in *Selected Writings*, ed. and tr. by Geoffrey Wagner, 1958).

7 When you take a flower in your hand and really look at it, it's your world for the moment. I want to give that world to someone else. Most people in the city rush around so, they have no time to look at a flower. I want them to see it whether they want to or not.

GEORGIA O'KEEFFE (1887-1986), U.S. artist. Quoted in: *New York Post* (16 May 1946; repr. in Laurie Lisle, *Portrait of an Artist*, 1986).

8 I hate flowers—I paint them because they're cheaper than models and they don't move.

GEORGIA O'KEEFFE (1887-1986), U.S. artist. Quoted in: *New York Herald Tribune* (18 April 1954; repr. in Laurie Lisle, *Portrait Of An Artist*, 1986), in answer to the remark, "How perfect to meet you with flowers in your hands!"

9 Today as in the time of Pliny and Columella, the hyacinth flourishes in Wales, the periwinkle in Illyria, the daisy on the ruins of Numantia; while around them cities have changed their masters and their names, collided and smashed, disappeared into nothingness, their peaceful generations have crossed down the ages as fresh and smiling as on the days of battle.

EDGAR QUINET (1803-75), French poet, historian, politician. Johann Herder, *Philosophy of Human History* Introduction (1825; repr. in *Complete Works*, vol. 2, 1857). This passage was quoted in the original French by James Joyce in *Finnegans Wake.*

10   Keep not your roses for my dead, cold brow
The way is lonely, let me feel them now.

ARABELLA SMITH (1844-1916), U.S. poet. *If I Should Die To-Night.*

11   One of the most attractive things about the flowers is their beautiful reserve.

HENRY DAVID THOREAU (1817-62), U.S. philosopher, author, naturalist. *Journals* (1906), entry for 17 June 1853. The remark comes after a description of a visitor who "pestered" Thoreau "with his benignity. . . . They lick you as a cow her calf. They would fain wrap you about with their bowels."

12   To me the meanest flower that blows can give
Thoughts that do often lie too deep for tears.

WILLIAM WORDSWORTH (1770-1850), English poet. *Intimations of Immortality* (1807).

FOOD AND EATING

1   Sadder than destitution, sadder than a beggar is the man who eats alone in public. Nothing more contradicts the laws of man or beast, for animals always do each other the honor of sharing or disputing each other's food.

JEAN BAUDRILLARD (b. 1929), French semiologist. *America,* "New York" (1986; tr. 1988).

2   Taking food alone tends to make one hard and coarse. Those accustomed to it must lead a Spartan life if they are not to go downhill. Hermits have observed, if for only this reason, a frugal diet. For it is only in company that eating is done justice; food must be divided and distributed if it is to be well received.

WALTER BENJAMIN (1892-1940), German critic, philosopher. *One-Way Street,* "Augeas' Self-Service Restaurant" (1928; repr. in *One-Way Street and Other Writings,* 1978).

3   Edible. Good to eat and wholesome to digest, as a worm to a toad, a toad to a snake, a snake to a pig, a pig to a man, and a man to a worm.

AMBROSE BIERCE (1842-1914), U.S. author. *The Devil's Dictionary* (1881-1906).

4   Clearly, some time ago makers and consumers of American junk food passed jointly through some kind of sensibility barrier in the endless quest for new taste sensations. Now they are a little like those desperate junkies who have tried every known drug and are finally reduced to mainlining toilet bowl cleanser in an effort to get still higher.

BILL BRYSON (b. 1951), U.S. author, journalist. *The Lost Continent: Travels in Small Town America,* ch. 3 (1989).

5   The healthy stomach is nothing if it is not conservative. Few radicals have good digestions.

SAMUEL BUTLER (1835-1902), English author. *Samuel Butler's Notebooks* (1951, p. 90).

6   A woman should never be seen eating or drinking, unless it be lobster salad and Champagne, the only true feminine & becoming viands.

LORD BYRON (1788-1824), English poet. Letter, 25 Sept. 1812 (published in *Byron's Letters and Journals,* vol. 2, ed. by Leslie A. Marchand, 1973-81).

7   The right diet directs sexual energy into the parts that matter.

BARBARA CARTLAND (b. 1901), British novelist. Quoted in: *Observer* (London, 11 Jan. 1981).

8   It has been an unchallengeable American doctrine that cranberry sauce, a pink goo with overtones of sugared tomatoes, is a delectable necessity of the Thanksgiving board and that turkey is uneatable without it. . . . There are some things in every country that you must be born to endure; and another hundred years of general satisfaction with Americans and America could not reconcile this expatriate to cranberry sauce, peanut butter, and drum majorettes.

ALISTAIR COOKE (b. 1908), British broadcaster, journalist. *Talk About America,* ch. 2 (1968).

9   Gluttony is an emotional escape, a sign something is eating us.

PETER DE VRIES (b. 1910), U.S. author. Crystal, in *Comfort Me with Apples,* ch. 15 (1956).

10   Upscale people are fixated with food simply because they are now able to eat so much of it without getting fat, and the reason they don't get fat is that they maintain a profligate level of calorie expenditure. The very same people whose evenings begin with melted goats cheese . . . get up at dawn to run, break for a mid-morning aerobics class, and watch the evening news while racing on a stationary bicycle.

BARBARA EHRENREICH (b. 1941), U.S. author, columnist. *The Worst Years of Our Lives,* "Food Worship" (1991; first published 1985).

11   Let the stoics say what they please, we do not eat for the good of living, but because the meat is savory and the appetite is keen.

RALPH WALDO EMERSON (1803-82), U.S. essayist, poet, philosopher. *Essays,* "Nature" (Second Series, 1844).

12   Roast Beef, Medium, is not only a food. It is a philosophy. Seated at Life's Dining Table, with the menu of Morals before you, your eye wanders a bit over the entrées, the hors d'oeuvres, and the things *à la* though you know that Roast Beef, Medium, is safe and sane, and sure.

EDNA FERBER (1887-1968), U.S. author. *Roast Beef, Medium,* Foreword (1911).

13   Sharing food with another human being is an intimate act that should not be indulged in lightly.

M. F. K. FISHER (b. 1908), U.S. culinary writer. *An Alphabet for Gourmets,* "A Is for Dining Alone" (1949).

14   It is the mark of a mean, vulgar and ignoble spirit to dwell on the thought of food before meal times or worse to dwell on it afterwards, to discuss it and wallow in the remembered pleasures of every mouthful. Those whose minds dwell before dinner on the spit, and after on the dishes, are fit only to be scullions.

ST. FRANCIS DE SALES (1567-1622), French churchman, devotional writer. *Introduction to the Devout Life*, pt. 3, ch. 39 (1609).

15 There is such a thing as food and such a thing as poison. But the damage done by those who pass off poison as food is far less than that done by those who generation after generation convince people that food is poison.

PAUL GOODMAN (1911-72), U.S. author, poet, critic. *Five Years*, "Ireland, Spring 1958," sct. 2 (1966).

16 He who does not mind his belly, will hardly mind anything else.

SAMUEL JOHNSON (1709-84), English author, lexicographer. Quoted in: James Boswell, *Life of Samuel Johnson*, 5 Aug. 1763 (1791). Boswell described Johnson's dedication to eating thus: "I never knew any man who relished good eating more than he did. When at table he was totally absorbed in the business of the moment. . . . To those whose sensations were delicate, this could not but be disgusting; and it was doubtless not very suitable to the character of a philosopher. . . . But it must be owned that Johnson, though he could be rigidly *abstemious*, was not a *temperate* man."

17 A man seldom thinks with more earnestness of anything than he does of his dinner.

SAMUEL JOHNSON (1709-84), English author, lexicographer. Quoted in: Hester Piozzi, *Anecdotes of Samuel Johnson* (1786; repr. in *Johnsonian Miscellanies*, vol. 1, ed. by George Birkbeck Hill, 1897).

18 He who cannot eat horsemeat need not do so. Let him eat pork. But he who cannot eat pork, let him eat horsemeat. It's simply a question of taste.

NIKITA KHRUSHCHEV (1894-1971), Soviet premier. *New York World-Telegram and Sun* (25 Aug. 1964).

19 The act of putting into your mouth what the earth has grown is perhaps your most direct interaction with the earth.

FRANCES MOORE LAPPÉ (b. 1944), U.S. ecologist, author. *Diet For A Small Planet*, pt. 1 (1971).

20 If you're going to America, bring your own food.

FRAN LEBOWITZ (b. 1951), U.S. journalist. *Social Studies*, "Fran Lebowitz's Travel Hints" (1981).

21 Food probably has a very great influence on the condition of men. Wine exercises a more visible influence, food does it more slowly but perhaps just as surely. Who knows if a well-prepared soup was not responsible for the pneumatic pump or a poor one for a war?

G. C. LICHTENBERG (1742-99), German physicist, philosopher. *Aphorisms*, "Notebook A," aph. 14 (written 1765-99; tr. by R. J. Hollingdale, 1990).

22 One should eat to live, not live to eat.

MOLIÈRE (1622-73), French dramatist. Valère, in *The Miser*, act 3, sc. 1.

23 He who eats alone chokes alone.

ARAB PROVERB. Quoted in: *H. L. Mencken's Dictionary of Quotations* (1942).

24 It's better that it should make you sick than that you don't eat it at all.

CATALAN PROVERB. Quoted in: Colman Andrews, *Catalan Cuisine*.

25 Appetite comes with eating.

FRENCH PROVERB.

26 Hors d'oeuvres have always a pathetic interest for me; they remind me of one's childhood that one goes through wondering what the next course is going to be like—and during the rest of the menu one wishes one had eaten more of the hors d'oeuvres.

SAKI [H. H. MUNRO] (1870-1916), Scottish author. Reginald, in *Reginald*, "Reginald at the Carlton," (1904).

27 You needn't tell me that a man who doesn't love oysters and asparagus and good wines has got a soul, or a stomach either. He's simply got the instinct for being unhappy highly developed.

SAKI [H. H. MUNRO] (1870-1916), Scottish author. Clovis, in "The Match-Maker," published in *The Chronicles of Clovis*, (1911).

28 To eat is to appropriate by destruction.

JEAN-PAUL SARTRE (1905-80), French philosopher, author. *Being and Nothingness*, "Doing and Having," sct. 3 (1943; tr. 1965).

29 Eating is not merely a material pleasure. Eating well gives a spectacular joy to life and contributes immensely to goodwill and happy companionship. It is of great importance to the morale.

ELSA SCHIAPARELLI (1890-1973), Italian fashion designer. *Shocking Life*, ch. 21 (1954).

30 There is no love sincerer than the love of food.

GEORGE BERNARD SHAW (1856-1950), Anglo-Irish playwright, critic. Tanner, in *Man and Superman*, act 1.

31 That food has always been, and will continue to be, the basis for one of our greater snobbisms does not explain the fact that the attitude toward the food choice of others is becoming more and more heatedly exclusive until it may well turn into one of those forms of bigotry against which gallant little committees are constantly planning campaigns in the cause of justice and decency.

CORNELIA OTIS SKINNER (1901-79), U.S. author, actor. *Bottoms Up!*, "Your Very Good Health" (1950).

32 For much of the female half of the world, food is the first signal of our inferiority. It lets us know that our own families may consider female bodies to be less deserving, less needy, less valuable.

GLORIA STEINEM (b. 1934), U.S. feminist writer, editor. "The Politics of Food," in *Ms.* (New York, Feb. 1980; repr. in *Outrageous Acts and Everyday Rebellions*, 1983).

33 Lunch is for wimps.

OLIVER STONE (b. 1946), U.S. filmmaker. Gordon Gekko (played by Michael Douglas), in the film *Wall Street* (written by Oliver Stone and Stanley Weiser, directed by Stone, 1987). The character of Gekko was loosely based on convicted securities dealer Ivan Boesky (see Boesky on GREED).

34 I have found it to be the most serious objection to coarse labors long continued, that they compelled me to eat and drink coarsely also.

HENRY DAVID THOREAU (1817-62), U.S. philosopher, author, naturalist. *Walden*, "Higher Laws" (1854).

35   Only dull people are brilliant at breakfast.

> OSCAR WILDE (1854-1900), Anglo-Irish playwright, author. Mrs. Cheveley, in *An Ideal Husband,* act 1.

36   One cannot think well, love well, sleep well, if one has not dined well.

> VIRGINIA WOOLF (1882-1941), British novelist. *A Room of One's Own,* ch. 1 (1929).

See also APPETITE; BREAKFAST; DIET; Cervantes on DINNER PARTIES; Thoreau on GREED; MEAT; Connolly on SOLITUDE.

FOOLS AND FOLLIES

1   In days gone by, we were afraid of dying in dishonor or a state of sin. Nowadays, we are afraid of dying fools. Now the fact is that there is no Extreme Unction to absolve us of foolishness. We endure it here on earth as subjective eternity.

> JEAN BAUDRILLARD (b. 1929), French semiologist. *Cool Memories,* ch. 4 (1987; tr. 1990).

2   As a dog returneth to his vomit, so a fool returneth to his folly.

> BIBLE, HEBREW. *Proverbs* 26:11.

3   But God hath chosen the foolish things of the world to confound the wise; and God hath chosen the weak things of the world to confound the things which are mighty.

> BIBLE: NEW TESTAMENT. *I Corinthians* 1:27.

4   A fool sees not the same tree that a wise man sees.

> WILLIAM BLAKE (1757-1827), English poet, painter, engraver. *The Marriage of Heaven and Hell,* plate 7, "Proverbs of Hell" (1790-93; repr. in *Complete Writings,* ed. by Geoffrey Keynes, 1957).

5   However big the fool, there is always a bigger fool to admire him.

> NICOLAS BOILEAU-DESPRÉAUX (1636-1711), French poet, critic. *L'Art Poétique,* cto. 1 (1674).

6   There are more fools than knaves in the world, else the knaves would not have enough to live upon.

> SAMUEL BUTLER (1612-80), English poet. *Genuine Remains in Verse and Prose,* vol. 2 (1759).

7   He is mad past recovery, but yet he has lucid intervals.

> MIGUEL DE CERVANTES (1547-1616), Spanish author. Don Lorenzo, in *Don Quixote,* pt. 2, bk. 5, ch. 18 (1615; tr. by P. Motteux), describing Don Quixote.

8   When he said we were trying to make a fool of him, I could only murmur that the Creator had beat us to it.

> ILKA CHASE (b. 1905), U.S. author, actor. Quoted in: Jilly Cooper and Tom Hartman, *Violets and Vinegar,* "Mrs. Crankhurst" (1980).

9   In the vain laughter of folly wisdom hears half its applause.

> GEORGE ELIOT (1819-80), English novelist. *Romola,* bk. 1, ch. 12 (1863).

10   In short, no association or alliance can be happy or stable without me. People can't long tolerate a ruler, nor can a master his servant, a maid her mistress, a teacher his pupil, a friend his friend nor a wife her husband, a landlord his tenant, a soldier his comrade nor a partygoer his companion, unless they sometimes have illusions about each other, make use of flattery, and have the sense to turn a blind eye and sweeten life for themselves with the honey of folly.

> DESIDERIUS ERASMUS (c. 1466-1536), Dutch humanist. The Goddess of Folly, in *Praise of Folly,* ch. 21 (1509).

11   The entire world is my temple, and a very fine one too, if I'm not mistaken, and I'll never lack priests to serve it as long as there are men.

> DESIDERIUS ERASMUS (c. 1466-1536), Dutch humanist. The Goddess of Folly, in *Praise of Folly,* ch. 47 (1509).

12   Sometimes one likes foolish people for their folly, better than wise people for their wisdom.

> ELIZABETH GASKELL (1810-65), English novelist. Mr. Gibson, in *Wives and Daughters,* ch. 54 (1866).

13   He who lives without folly isn't so wise as he thinks.

> FRANÇOIS, DUC DE LA ROCHEFOUCAULD (1613-80), French writer, moralist. *Sentences et Maximes Morales,* no. 209 (1678).

14   A clever child brought up with a foolish one can itself become foolish. Man is so perfectable and corruptible he can become a fool through good sense.

> G. C. LICHTENBERG (1742-99), German physicist, philosopher. *Aphorisms,* "Notebook F," aph. 69 (written 1765-99; tr. by R. J. Hollingdale, 1990).

15   A spoon does not know the taste of soup, nor a learned fool the taste of wisdom.

> WELSH PROVERB.

16   They never open their mouths without subtracting from the sum of human knowledge.

> THOMAS B. REED (1839-1902), U.S. lawyer, politician. *The Life of T. B. Reed,* ch. 21 (1914), speaking of two colleagues in the House of Representatives.

17   The great God endows His children variously. To some he gives intellect—and they move the earth. To some he allots heart—and the beating pulse of humanity is theirs. But to some He gives only a soul, without intelligence—and these, who never grow up, but remain always His children, are God's fools, kindly, elemental, simple, as if from His palette the Artist of all had taken one colour instead of many.

> MARY ROBERTS RINEHART (1876-1958), U.S. author. *Love Stories,* "God's Fool" (1920).

18 The dullness of the fool is the whetstone of the wits.

> WILLIAM SHAKESPEARE (1564-1616), English poet, dramatist. Celia, in *As You Like It,* act 1, sc. 2.

19   He uses his folly like a stalking-horse, and under the presentation of that he shoots his wit.

> WILLIAM SHAKESPEARE (1564-1616), English dramatist, poet. Duke Senior of Touchstone, in *As You Like It,* act 5, sc. 4.

20   The ultimate result of shielding men from the effects of folly, is to fill the world with fools.

> HERBERT SPENCER (1820-1903), English philosopher. *Essays,* vol. 3, "State Tamperings with Money and Banks" (1891).

21   That's the penalty we have to pay for our acts of foolishness—someone else always suffers for them.

> ALFRED SUTRO (1863-1933), British dramatist. Susan Lesson, in *The Perfect Lover*, act 2.

22   Let us be thankful for the fools. But for them the rest of us could not succeed.

> MARK TWAIN (1835-1910), U.S. author. *Following the Equator*, ch. 28, "Pudd'nhead Wilson's New Calendar" (1897).

23   Looking foolish does the spirit good. The need not to look foolish is one of youth's many burdens; as we get older we are exempted from more and more, and float upward in our heedlessness, singing *Gratia Dei sum quod sum.*

> JOHN UPDIKE (b. 1932), U.S. author, critic. *Self-Consciousness: Memoirs*, ch. 6 (1989). *Gratia Dei sum quod sum* ("Thanks be to God that I am what I am")—one of the epigraphs of Updike's volume of memoirs—is inscribed on the tomb of Bishop West of Ely in Ely Cathedral, England.

See also La Rochefoucauld on COMPANY; Byron, Johnson on LAUGHTER; Fielding on MARRIAGE; Young on MIDDLE AGE; Pope on SPONTANEITY; Bible: New Testament on TOLERANCE.

FOOTBALL

1   People stress the violence. That's the smallest part of it. Football is brutal only from a distance. In the middle of it there's a calm, a tranquility. The players accept pain. There's a sense of order even at the end of a running play with bodies stewn everywhere. When the systems interlock, there's a satisfaction to the game that can't be duplicated. There's a harmony.

> DON DELILLO (b. 1926), U.S. author. Emmett Creed, in *End Zone*, ch. 28 (1972).

2   Conventional wisdom notwithstanding, there is no reason either in football or in poetry why the two should not meet in a man's life if he has the weight and cares about the words.

> ARCHIBALD MACLEISH (1892-1982), U.S. poet. *Riders on Earth*, "Moonlighting on Yale Field" (1978).

3   There is a progression of understanding *vis-à-vis* pro football that varies drastically with the factor of *distance*—physical, emotional, intellectual and every other way . . . Which is exactly the way it should be, in the eyes of the amazingly small number of people who own and control the game, because it is this finely managed distance factor that accounts for the high-profit *mystique* that blew the sacred institution of baseball off its "national pastime" pedestal in less than fifteen years.

> HUNTER S. THOMPSON (b. 1939), U.S. journalist. "Fear and Loathing at the Superbowl," in *Rolling Stone* (New York, 15 Feb. 1973; repr. in *The Great Shark Hunt*, 1979).

4   Football combines the two worst things about America: it is violence punctuated by committee meetings.

> GEORGE F. WILL (b. 1941), U.S. political columnist. *International Herald Tribune* (Paris, 7 May 1990).

FORCE

1   The great questions of the day will not be settled by means of speeches and majority decisions . . . but by iron and blood.

> OTTO VON BISMARCK (1815-98), Prussian statesman. Speech, 29 Sept. 1862. "Iron and blood" and "blood and iron" were favorite expressions of Bismarck's.

2   The use of force alone is but *temporary*. It may subdue for a moment; but it does not remove the necessity of subduing again: and a nation is not governed, which is perpetually to be conquered.

> EDMUND BURKE (1729-97), Anglo-Irish philosopher, statesman. "Speech on Conciliation with America," 22 March 1775.

3   Coercion may prevent many transgressions; but it robs even actions which are legal of a part of their beauty. Freedom may lead to many transgressions, but it lends even to vices a less ignoble form.

> KARL WILHELM VON HUMBOLDT (1767-1835), German statesman, philologist. *The Limits of State Action*, ch. 8 (1792; repr. 1854; tr. and ed. by J. W. Burrow, 1969).

4   Be careful: they have arms, and no alternatives.

> RYSZARD KAPUSCINSKI (b. 1932), Polish journalist. "A Warsaw Diary," in *Granta*, no. 15 (Cambridge, England, 1985).

5   Some people draw a comforting distinction between "force" and "violence." . . . I refuse to cloud the issue by such word-play. . . . The power which establishes a state is violence; the power which maintains it is violence; the power which eventually overthrows it is violence. . . . Call an elephant a rabbit only if it gives you comfort to feel that you are about to be trampled to death by a rabbit.

> KENNETH KAUNDA (b. 1924), Zambian statesman, President. Quoted in: *Kaunda on Violence*, pt. 1 (1980).

6   Where force is necessary, there it must be applied boldly, decisively and completely. But one must know the limitations of force; one must know when to blend force with a manoeuvre, a blow with an agreement.

> LEON TROTSKY (1879-1940), Russian revolutionary. *What Next?*, ch. 14 (1932).

7   Who were the fools who spread the story that brute force cannot kill ideas? Nothing is easier. And once they are dead they are no more than corpses.

> SIMONE WEIL (1909-43), French philosopher, mystic. "Three Letters on History: Théophile de Viau" (written 1938 or 1939; published in *Selected Essays*, ed. by Richard Rees, 1962).

8   Force is as pitiless to the man who possesses it, or thinks he does, as it is to its victims; the second it crushes, the first it intoxicates. The truth is, nobody really possesses it.

> SIMONE WEIL (1909-43), French philosopher, mystic. "The *Iliad* or the Poem of Force," in *Cahiers du Sud* (Marseilles, Dec. 1940/Jan. 1941; repr. in *Simone Weil: An Anthology*, ed. by Sian Miles, tr. by Mary McCarthy, 1986).

FOREIGN COUNTRIES

1   When Americans look out on the world, they see nothing but dark and menacing strangers who appear to have no sense of rhythm at all, nor any respect or affection for white people; and white Americans really do not know what to make of all this, except to increase the defense budget.

> JAMES BALDWIN (1924-87), U.S. author. *The Price of the Ticket*, "Notes on the House of Bondage" (1985).

2 You can always tell a Midwestern couple in Europe because they will be standing in the middle of a busy intersection looking at a wind-blown map and arguing over which way is west. European cities, with their wandering streets and undisciplined alleys, drive Midwesterners practically insane.

> BILL BRYSON (b. 1951), U.S. author, journalist. *The Lost Continent: Travels in Small Town America*, ch. 2 (1989).

3 What affects men sharply about a foreign nation is not so much finding or not finding familiar things; it is rather not finding them in the familiar place.

> G. K. CHESTERTON (1874-1936), British author. *Generally Speaking*, "On Flags" (1928).

4 Things that we do
'Neath the Red, White and Blue,
Though they can't be called happy or glorious,
Certainly keep us notorious.

> NOËL COWARD (1899-1973), British playwright, actor, composer. *Bright Young People*, in *Collected Sketches and Lyrics* (1931).

5 "Abroad," that large home of ruined reputations.

> GEORGE ELIOT (1819-80), English novelist. *Felix Holt*, Epilogue (1866).

6 Oh, has the foul atmosphere of foreign lands extinguished *all* your self-respect? Do you come back sordid and sycophantic, and the slave of opinions you would once have utterly detested?

> AUGUSTA JANE EVANS (1835-1909), U.S. writer. *Beulah*, ch. 18 (1859).

7 Americans are rather like bad Bulgarian wine: they don't travel well.

> BERNARD FALK (1943-90), British broadcaster, author. Quoted in: *Observer* (London, 27 April 1986).

8 We have already eaten breakfast to the accompaniment, in our morning newspapers, of too many "Yankee Go Home" signs, too many riots, too many denunciations of ourselves, to believe that leadership, even in the cause of peace, can reward us with international laurel wreaths.

> HUBERT H. HUMPHREY (1911-78), U.S. Democratic politician, vice president. Address, 31 May 1966, Huron College, S. Dak.

9 If a foreign country doesn't look like a middle-class suburb of Dallas or Detroit, then obviously the natives must be dangerous as well as badly dressed.

> LEWIS H. LAPHAM (b. 1935), U.S. essayist, editor. *Money and Class in America*, ch. 5, sec. 1 (1988).

10 Being abroad makes you conscious of the whole imitative side of human behavior. The ape in man.

> MARY MCCARTHY (1912-89), U.S. author, critic. *Birds of America*, "Epistle from Mother Carey's Chicken" (1965).

11 I have never been in any country where they did not do something better than we do it, think some thoughts better than we think, catch some inspiration from heights above our own.

> MARIA MITCHELL (1818-89), U.S. astronomer. *Maria Mitchell: Life, Letters, and Journals* (1896), entry for July 1973.

12 Well, I learned a lot. . . . You'd be surprised. They're all individual countries.

> RONALD REAGAN (b. 1911), U.S. Republican politician, president. Quoted in: *Washington Post* (6 Dec. 1982), following Reagan's tour of South America.

13 A man's feet must be planted in his country, but his eyes should survey the world.

> GEORGE SANTAYANA (1863-1952), U.S. philosopher, poet. *The Life of Reason*, "Reason in Society," ch. 7 (1905-6).

14 The gentle reader will never, never know what a consummate ass he can become, until he goes abroad.

> MARK TWAIN (1835-1910), U.S. author. *The Innocents Abroad*, ch. 23 (1869).

FOREIGN POLICY

1 U.S. international and security policy . . . has as its primary goal the preservation of what we might call "the Fifth Freedom," understood crudely but with a fair degree of accuracy as the freedom to rob, to exploit and to dominate, to undertake any course of action to ensure that existing privilege is protected and advanced.

> NOAM CHOMSKY (b. 1928), U.S. linguist, political analyst. *The Culture of Terrorism*, Preface (1988).

2 Americans think of themselves collectively as a huge rescue squad on twenty-four-hour call to any spot on the globe where dispute and conflict may erupt.

> ELDRIDGE CLEAVER (b. 1935), U.S. black leader, writer. *Soul on Ice*, pt. 2, "Rallying Round the Flag" (1968).

3 Foreign policy is really domestic policy with its hat on.

> HUBERT H. HUMPHREY (1911-78), U.S. Democratic politician, vice president. Address, 29 June 1966, to the United States Junior Chamber of Commerce, Detroit, Mich.

4 Domestic policy can only defeat us; foreign policy can kill us.

> JOHN F. KENNEDY (1917-63), U.S. Democratic politician, president. Quoted in: Arthur M. Schlesinger, Jr., *The Imperial Presidency*, ch. 11, sct. 7 (1973).

5 Most foreign policies that history has marked highly, in whatever country, have been originated by leaders who were opposed by experts.

> HENRY KISSINGER (b. 1923), U.S. Republican politician, secretary of state. *Years of Upheaval*, ch. 10, "The Foreign Service" (1982).

6 The American foreign policy trauma of the sixties and seventies was caused by applying valid principles to unsuitable conditions.

> HENRY KISSINGER (b. 1923), U.S. Republican politician, secretary of state. *Guardian* (London, 16 Dec. 1992), arguing against a role for the U.S. as world policeman.

7 Our policy is directed not against any country or doctrine, but against hunger, poverty, desperation and chaos. Its purpose should be the revival of a working economy in the world so as to permit the emergence of political and social conditions in which free institutions can exist.

> GEORGE C. MARSHALL (1880-1959), U.S. general, Democratic politician. Speech, 5 June 1947, Harvard University, describing what became known as the Marshall Plan for recovery in post-war Europe.

8   Maybe it's understandable what a history of failures America's foreign policy has been. We are, after all, a country full of people who came to America to get away from foreigners. Any prolonged examination of the U.S. government reveals foreign policy to be America's miniature schnauzer—a noisy but small and useless part of the national household.

> P. J. O'ROURKE (b. 1947), U.S. journalist. *Parliament of Whores,* "Very Foreign Policy" (1991).

9   Whatever it is that the government does, sensible Americans would prefer that the government do it to somebody else. This is the idea behind foreign policy.

> P. J. O'ROURKE (b. 1947), U.S. journalist. *Parliament of Whores,* "Very Foreign Policy" (1991).

10   We cannot play innocents abroad in a world that is not innocent.

> RONALD REAGAN (b. 1911), U.S. Republican politician, president. Speech, 6 Feb. 1985 (published in *Speaking My Mind,* "The Wit and Wisdom of Ronald Reagan," 1989).

11   In foreign policy you have to wait twenty-five years to see how it comes out.

> JAMES RESTON (b. 1909), U.S. journalist. *International Herald Tribune* (Paris, 18 Nov. 1991).

12   We cannot be any stronger in our foreign policy— for all the bombs and guns we may heap up in our arsenals—than we are in the spirit which rules inside the country. Foreign policy, like a river, cannot rise above its source.

> ADLAI STEVENSON (1900-1965), U.S. Democratic politician. Speech, 4 Dec. 1954, New Orleans (published in *What I Think,* 1956).

13   We are apt to say that a foreign policy is successful only when the country, or at any rate the governing class, is united behind it. In reality, every line of policy is repudiated by a section, often by an influential section, of the country concerned. A foreign minister who waited until everyone agreed with him would have no foreign policy at all.

> A. J. P. TAYLOR (1906-90), British historian. *The Trouble Makers,* ch. 1 (1957).

See also DIPLOMACY; INTERNATIONAL RELATIONS; Cleaver on INTERVENTION; Humphrey on ISOLATION; Humphrey on LEADERSHIP; Buchanan on The NEW WORLD ORDER.

FOREIGNERS

1   The less sophisticated of my forbears avoided foreigners at all costs, for the very good reason that, in their circles, speaking in tongues was commonly a prelude to snake handling. The more tolerant among us regarded foreign languages as a kind of speech impediment that could be overcome by willpower.

> BARBARA EHRENREICH (b. 1941), U.S. author, columnist. *The Worst Years of Our Lives,* "Language Barrier" (1991; first published 1989).

2   I've noticed that the children of other nations always seem precocious. That's because the strange manners of their elders have caught our attention most and the children echo those manners enough to seem like their parents.

> F. SCOTT FITZGERALD (1896-1940), U.S. author. *The Crack-Up,* "Notebook O" (ed. by Edmund Wilson, 1945).

3   Xenophobia looks like becoming the mass ideology of the 20th-century *fin-de-siècle.* What holds humanity together today is the denial of what the human race has in common

> ERIC HOBSBAWM (b. 1917), British historian. Lecture to the American Anthropological Association (repr. in *Anthropology Today,* Feb. 1992).

4   Uncle Matthew's four years in France and Italy between 1914 and 1918 had given him no great opinion of foreigners. "Frogs," he would say, "are slightly better than Huns or Wops, but abroad is unutterably bloody and foreigners are fiends."

> NANCY MITFORD (1904-73), British author. *The Pursuit of Love,* ch. 15 (1945).

5   All people who have reached the point of becoming nations tend to despise foreigners, but there is not much doubt that the English-speaking races are the worst offenders. One can see this from the fact that as soon as they become fully aware of any foreign race they invent an insulting nickname for it.

> GEORGE ORWELL (1903-50), British author. *Inside the Whale and Other Essays,* "Charles Dickens" (1940).

6   Who's 'im, Bill? A stranger! 'Eave 'arf a brick at 'im.

> *PUNCH,* Vol. 26 (London, 1854).

7   They spell it Vinci and pronounce it Vinchy; foreigners always spell better than they pronounce.

> MARK TWAIN (1835-1910), U.S. author. *The Innocents Abroad,* ch. 19 (1869).

See also Cooley on IMMIGRATION.

FORGIVENESS

1   In contrast to revenge, which is the natural, automatic reaction to transgression and which, because of the irreversibility of the action process can be expected and even calculated, the act of forgiving can never be predicted; it is the only reaction that acts in an unexpected way and thus retains, though being a reaction, something of the original character of action.

> HANNAH ARENDT (1906-75), German-born U.S. political philosopher. *The Human Condition,* "Action," ch. 33 (1958).

2   My transgression is sealed up in a bag, and thou sewest up mine iniquity.

> BIBLE, HEBREW. *Job* 14:17.

3   It is a verry delicate job to forgive a man, without lowering him in his own estimashun, and yures too.

JOSH BILLINGS [HENRY WHEELER SHAW] (1818-85), U.S. humorist. *Josh Billings, His Sayings*, ch. 39 (1865).

4   We all like to forgive, and love best not those who offend us least, nor who have done most for us, but those who make it most easy for us to forgive them.

SAMUEL BUTLER (1835-1902), English author. *Samuel Butler's Notebooks* (1951, p.236).

5   Absolute virtue is impossible and the republic of forgiveness leads, with implacable logic, to the republic of the guillotine.

ALBERT CAMUS (1913-60), French-Algerian philosopher, author. *The Rebel*, pt. 3, "The Regicides" (1951; tr. 1953).

6   One can't relive one's life. Forgiveness is not what's difficult; one's always too ready to forgive. And it does no good, that's obvious.

LOUIS-FERDINAND CÉLINE (1894-1961), French author. The narrator (Ferdinand Bardamu), in *Journey to the End of the Night* (1932; tr. 1934; repr. 1966, p. 186).

7   Once a woman has forgiven her man, she must not reheat his sins for breakfast.

MARLENE DIETRICH (1904-92), German-born U.S. film actor. *Marlene Dietrich's ABC*, "Forgiveness" (1962).

8   Would not love see returning penitence afar off, and fall on its neck and kiss it?

GEORGE ELIOT (1819-80), English novelist, editor. *Middlemarch*, bk. 2, ch. 21 (1871).

9   "To forgive oneself"—? No, that doesn't work: we have to *be forgiven*. But we can only believe this is possible if we ourselves can forgive.

DAG HAMMARSKJÖLD (1905-61), Swedish statesman, secretary-general of U.N. *Markings*, "Night is Drawing Nigh" (1963).

10   Of course God will forgive me; that's His job.

HEINRICH HEINE (1797-1856), German poet, journalist. Quoted in: Edmond and Charles Goncourt, *Journal* (23 Feb. 1863), said on his deathbed, in reply to a priest who had told him God would forgive his sins. The psychiatrist Sigmund Freud commented on this: "The force of the joke lies in its purpose. What it means to say is nothing else than: 'Of course he'll forgive me. That's what he's there for, and that's the only reason I've taken him on (as one engages one's doctor or one's lawyer).' So in the dying man, as he lay there powerless, a consciousness stirred that he had created God and equipped him with power so as to make use of him when the occasion arose. What was supposed to be the created being revealed itself just before its annihilation as the creator." (from *Jokes and Their Relation to the Unconscious*, "The Purposes of Jokes," 1905).

11   Forgive you?—Oh, of course, dear,
A dozen times a week!
We women were created
Forgiveness but to speak.

ELLA HIGGINSON (1862-1940), U.S. writer, journalist. *Wearing Out Love*.

12   Nobody ever forgets where he buried a hatchet.

KIN (F. MCKINNEY) HUBBARD (1868-1930), U.S. humorist, journalist. *Indianapolis News* (4 Jan. 1925).

13   The condition of being forgiven is self-abandonment. The proud man prefers self-reproach, however painful—because the reproached self isn't abandoned; it remains intact.

ALDOUS HUXLEY (1894-1963), British author. Bruno Rontini's notes, in *Time Must Have a Stop*, ch. 30 (1944).

14   We pardon to the extent that we love.

FRANÇOIS, DUC DE LA ROCHEFOUCAULD (1613-80), French writer, moralist. *Sentences et Maximes Morales*, no. 330 (1678).

15   How shall I lose the sin, yet keep the sense,
And love th'offender, yet detest th'offence?

ALEXANDER POPE (1688-1744), English satirical poet. *Eloisa to Abelard*.

16   Youth, which is forgiven everything, forgives itself nothing: age, which forgives itself everything, is forgiven nothing.

GEORGE BERNARD SHAW (1856-1950), Anglo-Irish playwright, critic. *Man and Superman*, "Maxims for Revolutionists: Stay Sayings" (1903).

17   Their errors have been weighed and found to have been dust in the balance; if their sins were as scarlet, they are now white as snow: they have been washed in the blood of the mediator and the redeemer, Time.

PERCY BYSSHE SHELLEY (1792-1822), English poet. *A Defence of Poetry* (written 1821; published 1840), referring specifically to the reputations of poets.

18   The stupid neither forgive nor forget; the naïve forgive and forget; the wise forgive but do not forget.

THOMAS SZASZ (b. 1920), U.S. psychiatrist. *The Second Sin*, "Personal Conduct" (1973).

19   Forgive! How many will say, "forgive," and find
A sort of absolution in the sound
To hate a little longer!

LORD TENNYSON (1809-92), English poet. *Sea Dreams*.

See also La Rochefoucauld on CONVERSATION; Wilde on DINNER PARTIES; Bible: New Testament on INJURY; Crisp on KNOWLEDGE; Lavater on THE PUBLIC.

FRANCE AND THE FRENCH

1   Everything ends this way in France. Weddings, christenings, duels, burials, swindlings, affairs of state—everything is a pretext for a good dinner.

JEAN ANOUILH (1910-87), French playwright. Monsieur Orlas, in *Cécile*.

2   France, fam'd in all great arts, in none supreme.

MATTHEW ARNOLD (1822-88), English poet, critic. *To a Republican Friend*.

3   The sickly cultural pathos which the whole of France indulges in, that fetishism of the cultural heritage.

JEAN BAUDRILLARD (b. 1929), French semiologist. *America*, "Utopia Achieved" (1986; tr. 1988).

4   A bad liver is to a Frenchman what a nervous breakdown is to an American. Everyone has had one and everyone wants to talk about it.

ART BUCHWALD (b. 1925), U.S. humorist. *New York Herald Tribune* (16 Jan. 1958).

5 France was long a despotism tempered by epigrams.

> THOMAS CARLYLE (1795-1881), Scottish essayist, historian. *History of the French Revolution*, pt. 1, bk. 1, ch. 1 (1837).

6 France is the only place where you can make love in the afternoon without people hammering on your door.

> BARBARA CARTLAND (b. 1901), British novelist. Quoted in: *Guardian* (London, 24 Dec. 1984).

7 Old France, weighed down with history, prostrated by wars and revolutions, endlessly vacillating from greatness to decline, but revived, century after century, by the genius of renewal!

> CHARLES DE GAULLE (1890-1970), French general, president. *War Memoirs*, vol. 3, ch. 7 (1959).

8 How can anyone govern a nation that has two hundred and forty-six different kinds of cheese?

> CHARLES DE GAULLE (1890-1970), French general, president. Quoted in: *Newsweek* (New York, 1 Oct. 1962).

9 For all of us Frenchmen, the guiding rule of our epoch is to be faithful to France.

> CHARLES DE GAULLE (1890-1970), French general, president. Speech, 28 Sept. 1963, Lyons.

10 The English are crooked as a nation and honest as individuals. The contrary is true of the French, who are honest as a nation and crooked as individuals.

> EDMOND (1822-96) AND JULES DE GONCOURT (1830-70), French writers. *The Goncourt Journals* (1888-96; repr. in *Pages from the Goncourt Journal*, ed. by Robert Baldick, 1962), entry for 29 Oct. 1868.

11 *Liberté! Fraternité! Sexualité!*

> GRAFFITO in the Paris Métro, 1980s.

12 France is a people of the same quality as Greece and Italy. She is Athenian in beauty and Roman in grandeur. Moreover, she is generous. She gives herself. More often than other peoples, she knows the mood of devotion and sacrifice. But it is a mood that comes and goes; and this is the great danger for those who seek to run when she is content to walk, and to walk when she wishes to stay still. France has her relapses into materialism, and at certain moments the ideas which obstruct the working of her splendid mind contain nothing that recalls her greatness but are rather of the dimensions of Missouri or some other southern state. What can be done about it? The giantess plays the dwarf; great France has her fantasies of smallness. That is all.

> VICTOR HUGO (1802-85), French poet, dramatist, novelist. *Les Misérables*, pt. 5, bk. 1, ch. 20 (1862).

13 . . . So damn your food and damn your wines,
Your twisted loaves and twisting vines,
Your *table d'hôte*, your *à la carte*. . . .
From now on you can keep the lot.
Take every single thing you've got,
Your land, your wealth, your men, your dames,
Your dream of independent power,
And dear old Konrad Adenauer,
And stick them up your Eiffel Tower.

> ANTHONY JAY (b. 1930), British writer, journalist. Published in *Time* (New York, 8 Feb. 1963), extract from verse on France's rejection of Britain's entry into the European Economic Community.

14 It's true that the French have a certain obsession with sex, but it's a particularly adult obsession. France is the thriftiest of all nations; to a Frenchman sex provides the most economical way to have fun. The French are a logical race.

> ANITA LOOS (1888-1981), U.S. novelist, screenwriter. *Kiss Hollywood Good-by*, ch. 21 (1974).

15 In France a woman will not go to sleep until she has talked over affairs of state with her lover or her husband.

> JULES, CARDINAL MAZARIN (1602-61), Italian-born French statesman. Attributed remark (c. 1650).

16 The Frenchman is first and foremost a *man*. He is likeable often just because of his weaknesses, which are always thoroughly human, even if despicable.

> HENRY MILLER (1891-1980), U.S. author. *The Wisdom of the Heart*, "Raimu" (1947).

17 One becomes aware in France, after having lived in America, that sex pervades the air. It's there all around you, like a fluid.

> HENRY MILLER (1891-1980), U.S. author. Interview in *Writers at Work* (Second Series, ed. by George Plimpton, 1963).

18 The French are a logical people, which is one reason the English dislike them so intensely. The other is that they own France, a country which we have always judged to be much too good for them.

> ROBERT MORLEY (b. 1908), British actor, wit. *A Musing Morley*, "France and the French" (1974).

19 The moment Germany rises as a great power, France gains a new importance as a *cultural power*.

> FRIEDRICH NIETZSCHE (1844-1900), German philosopher. *Twilight of the Idols*, "What the Germans Lack," aph. 4 (1889).

20 There's something Vichy about the French.

> IVOR NOVELLO (1893-1951), Welsh actor, composer, playwright. Quoted by: Edward Marsh, in letter, March 1941 (published in *Ambrosia and Small Beer*, ch. 4, ed. by Christopher Hassall, 1964).

21 Basically the French are all peasants.

> PABLO PICASSO (1881-1973), Spanish artist. Conversation, 16 Feb. 1935, on French painters (published in *Le Point*, vol. 7, no. 42, Sovillac, France, Oct. 1952).

22 The French bourgeois doesn't dislike shit, provided it is served up to him at the right time.

> JEAN-PAUL SARTRE (1905-80), French philosopher, author. *Saint Genet: Actor and Martyr*, bk. 2, "To Succeed in Being All, Strive to Be Nothing in Anything" (1952; tr. 1963).

23 In France one must adapt oneself to the fragrance of a urinal.

> GERTRUDE STEIN (1874-1946), U.S. author. Said to author and poet Frederic Prokosch. Quoted in: Prokosch, *Voices: A Memoir*, "Style" (1983). Prokosch had paid a visit to Stein in Paris, asking her opinion of the city. "Alice deplores the public urinals," Stein explained. "I keep explaining to Alice that the Parisians are all wine-drinkers and for a gentleman the bladder is more restless than for a lady."

24 France has neither winter nor summer nor morals—apart from these drawbacks it is a fine country.

> MARK TWAIN (1835-1910), U.S. author. *Mark Twain's Notebooks and Journals*, vol. 2 (ed. by Frederick Anderson, 1975), entry in Notebook 18.

25 It is not enough that France should be regarded as a country which enjoys the remains of a freedom acquired long ago. If she is still to count in the world—and if she does not intend to, she may as well perish—she must be seen by her own citizens and by all men as an ever-flowing source of liberty. There must not be a single genuine lover of freedom in the whole world who can have a valid reason for hating France.

> SIMONE WEIL (1909-43), French philosopher, mystic. "Cold War Policy in 1939" (written 1939; published in *Selected Essays*, ed. by Richard Rees, 1962).

26 [France is] a country where the money falls apart but you can't tear the toilet paper.

> BILLY WILDER (b. 1906), U.S. film director. Quoted in: Maurice Zolotow, *Billy Wilder in Hollywood*, ch. 18 (1977).

See also Barthes on ALCHOHOL; PARIS; Saint-Exupéry on WORLD WAR II.

BENJAMIN FRANKLIN

1 Printer, philosopher, scientist, author and patriot, impeccable husband and citizen, why isn't he an archetype? Pioneers, Oh Pioneers! Benjamin was one of the greatest pioneers of the United States. Yet we just can't do with him. What's wrong with him then? Or what's wrong with us?

> D. H. LAWRENCE (1885-1930), British author. *Studies in Classic American Literature*, ch. 2 (1923).

2 If to be venerated for benevolence, if to be admired for talents, if to be esteemed for patriotism, if to be beloved for philanthropy, can gratify the human mind, you must have the pleasing consolation to know that you have not lived in vain. And I flatter myself that it will not be ranked among the least grateful occurrences of your life to be assured that, so long as I retain my memory, you will be thought on with respect, veneration, and affection by your sincere friend.

> GEORGE WASHINGTON (1732-99), U.S. general, president. Letter, 23 Sept. 1789, to Benjamin Franklin.

FREE ENTERPRISE

1 A free-enterprise economy depends only on *markets*, and according to the most advanced mathematical macroeconomic theory, markets depend only on *moods*: specifically, the mood of the men in the pinstripes, also known as the Boys on the Street. When the Boys are in a good mood, the market thrives; when they get scared or sullen, it is time for each one of us to look into the retail apple business.

> BARBARA EHRENREICH (b. 1941), U.S. author, columnist. *The Worst Years of Our Lives*, "How You Can Save Wall Street" (1991; first published 1988).

2 That's free enterprise, friends: freedom to gamble, freedom to lose. And the great thing—the truly democratic thing about it—is that you don't even have to be a player to lose.

> BARBARA EHRENREICH (b. 1941), U.S. author, columnist. *The Worst Years of Our Lives*, "How You Can Save Wall Street" (1991; first published 1988).

3 The great dialectic in our time is not, as anciently and by some still supposed, between capital and labor; it is between economic enterprise and the state.

> JOHN KENNETH GALBRAITH (b. 1908), U.S. economist. *A History of Economics*, ch. 21 (1987).

4 The market came with the dawn of civilization and it is not an invention of capitalism. . . . If it leads to improving the well-being of the people there is no contradiction with socialism.

> MIKHAIL GORBACHEV (b. 1931). Soviet political leader. Quoted in: *Guardian* (London, 21 June 1990).

5 Agriculture, manufactures, commerce, and navigation, the four pillars of our prosperity, are then most thriving when left most free to individual enterprise. Protection from casual embarrassments, however, may sometimes be seasonably interposed.

> THOMAS JEFFERSON (1743-1826), U.S. president. First Annual Message to Congress, 8 Dec. 1801.

6 Freedom of enterprise was from the beginning not altogether a blessing. As the liberty to work or to starve, it spelled toil, insecurity, and fear for the vast majority of the population. If the individual were no longer compelled to prove himself on the market, as a free economic subject, the disappearance of this freedom would be one of the greatest achievements of civilization.

> HERBERT MARCUSE (1898-1979), U.S. political philosopher. *One-Dimensional Man*, ch. 1 (1964).

7 Entrepreneurial profit . . . is the expression of the value of what the entrepreneur contributes to production.

> JOSEPH A. SCHUMPETER (1883-1950), Austrian-American economist. *The Theory of Economic Development*, ch. 4 (1934).

See also Humphrey on ENTERPRISE.

FREE WILL

1 The most intellectual of men are moved quite as much by the circumstances which they are used to as by their own will. The active voluntary part of a man is very small, and if it were not economised by a sleepy kind of habit, its results would be null.

> WALTER BAGEHOT (1826-77), English economist, critic. *The English Constitution*, ch. 1 (1867).

2 The liberated man is not the one who is freed in his ideal reality, his inner truth, or his transparency; he is the man who changes spaces, who circulates, who changes sex, clothes, and habits according to fashion, *rather than morality*, and who changes opinions not as his conscience dictates but in response to opinion polls.

> JEAN BAUDRILLARD (b. 1929), French semiologist. *America*, "Utopia Achieved" (1986; tr. 1988).

3 Whereas the Greeks gave to will the boundaries of reason, we have come to put the will's impulse in the very center of reason, which has, as a result, become deadly.

> ALBERT CAMUS (1913-60), French-Algerian philosopher, author. *The Myth of Sisyphus & Other Essays*, "Helen's Exile" (1955; first published 1948).

4 The will is never free—it is always attached to an object, a purpose. It is simply the engine in the car—it can't steer.

> JOYCE CARY (1888-1957), British author. Interview in *Writers at Work* (First Series, ed. by Malcolm Cowley, 1958).

5 Do what thou wilt shall be the whole of the law.

> ALEISTER CROWLEY (1875-1947), British occultist. *The Confessions of Aleister Crowley*, prelude (1929; rev. 1970). This maxim is repeated throughout Crowley's works, as representing the key to his philosophy.

6 The man who arrives young believes that he exercises his will because his star is shining. The man who only asserts himself at thirty has a balanced idea of what will power and fate have each contributed, the one who gets there at forty is liable to put the emphasis on will alone.

> F. SCOTT FITZGERALD (1896-1940), U.S. author. "Early Success," in *American Cavalcade* (Oct. 1937; repr. in *The Crack-Up*, ed. by Edmund Wilson, 1945).

7 There are no galley-slaves in the royal vessel of divine love—every man works his oar voluntarily!

> ST. FRANCIS DE SALES (1567-1622), French churchman, devotional writer. Quoted in:Bishop Jean-Pierre Camus, *The Spirit of Saint Frances de Sales*, ch. 7, sct. 3 (1952).

8 A man may be a pessimistic determinist before lunch and an optimistic believer in the will's freedom after it.

> ALDOUS HUXLEY (1894-1963), British author. *Do What You Will*, "Pascal," sct. 23 (1929).

9 Fatalism, whose solving word in all crises of behavior is "All striving is vain," will never reign supreme, for the impulse to take life strivingly is indestructible in the race. Moral creeds which speak to that impulse will be widely successful in spite of inconsistency, vagueness, and shadowy determination of expectancy. Man needs a rule for his will, and will invent one if one be not given him.

> WILLIAM JAMES (1842-1910), U.S. psychologist, philosopher. *Principles of Psychology*, vol. 2, ch. 21 (1890), extracted from original article, "Rationality, Activity and Faith," published in *Princeton Review*, July 1882.

10 Man is a masterpiece of creation if for no other reason than that, all the weight of evidence for determinism notwithstanding, he believes he has free will.

> G. C. LICHTENBERG (1742-99), German physicist, philosopher. *Aphorisms*, "Notebook J," aph. 249 (written 1765-99; tr. by R. J. Hollingdale, 1990).

11 We are all bound to the throne of the Supreme Being by a flexible chain which restrains without enslaving us. The most wonderful aspect of the universal scheme of things is the action of free beings under divine guidance.

> JOSEPH DE MAISTRE (1753-1821), French diplomat, philoso-

pher. *Considerations on France*, ch. 1 (1796; repr. in *The Works of Joseph de Maistre*, ed. by Jack Lively, 1965).

12 It can even come about that a created will cancels out, not perhaps the *exertion*, but the result of divine action; for in this sense, *God* himself has told us that God wishes things which do not happen because man does not wish them! Thus the rights of men are immense, and his greatest misfortune is to be unaware of them.

> JOSEPH DE MAISTRE (1753-1821), French diplomat, philosopher. The Senator, in *Les Soirées de Saint-Pétersbourg*, "Fifth Dialogue" (1821; repr. in *The Works of Joseph de Maistre*, ed. by Jack Lively, 1965).

13 The strongest knowledge (that of the total unfreedom of the human will) is nonetheless the poorest in successes: for it always has the strongest opponent, human vanity.

> FRIEDRICH NIETZSCHE (1844-1900), German philosopher. *Assorted Opinions and Maxims*, aph. 50 (1879).

14 I assess the power of a will by how much resistance, pain, torture it endures and knows how to turn to its advantage.

> FRIEDRICH NIETZSCHE (1844-1900), German philosopher. *The Will to Power*, bk. 2, note 362 (1888; tr. 1967).

15 One of the annoying things about believing in free will and individual responsibility is the difficulty of finding somebody to blame your problems on. And when you do find somebody, it's remarkable how often his picture turns up on your driver's license.

> P. J. O'ROURKE (b. 1947), U.S. journalist. *Rolling Stone* (New York, 30 Nov. 1989).

16 Will power is only the tensile strength of one's own disposition. One cannot increase it by a single ounce.

> CESARE PAVESE (1908-50), Italian poet, novelist, translator. *The Burning Brand: Diaries 1935-1950* (1952; tr. 1961), entry for 15 Jan. 1938.

17 We defy augury. There's a special providence in the fall of a sparrow. If it be now, 'tis not to come. If it be not to come, it will be now. If it be not now, yet it will come. The readiness is all.

> WILLIAM SHAKESPEARE (1564-1616), English dramatist, poet. Hamlet, in *Hamlet*, act 5, sc. 2, responding to Horatio's offer to forestall Hamlet's duel with Laertes, of which Hamlet has a premonition that all is not well.

18 We human beings do have some genuine freedom of choice and therefore some effective control over our own destinies. I am not a determinist. But I also believe that the decisive choice is seldom the latest choice in the series. More often than not, it will turn out to be some choice made relatively far back in the past.

> A. J. TOYNBEE (1889-1975), British historian. "Some Great `If's' of History," *New York Times* (5 March 1961).

See also James on RESIGNATION.

FREEDOM

1 When we were told that by freedom we understood free enterprise, we did very little to dispel this monstrous falsehood. . . . Wealth and economic well-being, we have asserted, are the fruits of freedom, while we should have been the first to know that this kind of "happiness" . . . has been an unmixed blessing only in this country, and it is a minor blessing compared with the truly political freedoms, such as freedom of speech and thought, of assembly and association, even under the best conditions.

> HANNAH ARENDT (1906-75), German-born U.S. political philosopher. *On Revolution*, ch. 6 (1963).

2   Any honest examination of the national life proves how far we are from the standard of human freedom with which we began. The recovery of this standard demands of everyone who loves this country a hard look at himself, for the greatest achievments must begin somewhere, and they always begin with the person. If we are not capable of this examination, we may yet become one of the most distinguished and monumental failures in the history of nations.

> JAMES BALDWIN (1924-87), U.S. author. "Nobody Knows My Name," in *Partisan Review* (New Brunswick, N.J., Winter 1959; repr. in *Nobody Knows My Name*, 1961).

3   As for freedom, it will soon cease to exist in any shape or form. Living will depend upon absolute obedience to a strict set of arrangements, which it will no longer be possible to transgress. The air traveler is not free. In the future, life's passengers will be even less so: they will travel through their lives fastened to their (corporate) seats.

> JEAN BAUDRILLARD (b. 1929), French semiologist. *Cool Memories*, ch. 3 (1987; tr. 1990).

4   Freedom is the by-product of economic surplus.

> ANEURIN BEVAN (1897-1960), British Labour politician. Quoted in: Michael Foot, *Aneurin Bevan*, vol. 1, ch. 3 (1962).

5   Freedom is poetry, taking liberties with words, breaking the rules of normal speech, violating common sense. Freedom is violence.

> NORMAN O. BROWN (b. 1913), U.S. philosopher. *Love's Body*, ch. 15 (1966).

6   None who have always been free can understand the terrible fascinating power of the hope of freedom to those who are not free.

> PEARL S. BUCK (1892-1973), U.S. novelist. *What America Means to Me*, ch. 4 (1943).

7   Yet, Freedom! yet thy banner, torn, but flying,
Streams like the thunderstorm *against* the wind.

> LORD BYRON (1788-1824), English poet. *Childe Harold's Pilgrimage*, cto. 4, st. 98.

8   The only conception of freedom I can have is that of the prisoner or the individual in the midst of the State. The only one I know is freedom of thought and action.

> ALBERT CAMUS (1913-60), French-Algerian philosopher, author. *The Myth of Sisyphus*, ch. 1 (1942; tr. 1955).

9   Without freedom, no art; art lives only on the restraints it imposes on itself, and dies of all others. But without freedom, no socialism either, except the socialism of the gallows.

> ALBERT CAMUS (1913-60), French-Algerian philosopher,

author. "Socialism of the Gallows," interview in *Demain* (Paris, 21 Feb. 1957; repr. in *Resistance, Rebellion, and Death,* 1961).

10   For me, the principal fact of life is the free mind. For good and evil, man is a free creative spirit. This produces the very queer world we live in, a world in continuous creation and therefore continuous change and insecurity. A perpetually new and lively world, but a dangerous one, full of tragedy and injustice. A world in everlasting conflict between the new idea and the old allegiances, new arts and new inventions against the old establishment.

> JOYCE CARY (1888-1957), British author. Interview in *Writers at Work* (First Series, ed. by Malcolm Cowley, 1958).

11   What we want is not freedom but its appearances. It is for these simulacra that man has always striven. And since freedom, as has been said, is no more than a *sensation,* what difference is there between being free and believing ourselves free?

> E. M. CIORAN (b. 1911), Rumanian-born French philosopher. *The New Gods*, sct. 3, "Strangled Thoughts" (1969; tr. 1974).

12   The progress of freedom depends more upon the maintenance of peace, the spread of commerce, and the diffusion of education, than upon the labours of cabinets and foreign offices.

> RICHARD COBDEN (1804-65), English radical politician. Speech, 26 June 1850, to the House of Commons.

13   No matter what a man does, he is not fully sane or human unless there is a spirit of freedom in him, a soul unconfined by purpose and larger than the practicable world.

> CHARLES HORTON COOLEY (1864-1929), U.S. sociologist. *Human Nature and the Social Order*, ch. 5 (1902).

14   Every general increase of freedom is accompanied by some degeneracy, attributable to the same causes as the freedom.

> CHARLES HORTON COOLEY (1864-1929), U.S. sociologist. *Human Nature and the Social Order*, ch. 12 (1902).

15   No man has received from nature the right to give orders to others. Freedom is a gift from heaven, and every individual of the same species has the right to enjoy it as soon as he is in enjoyment of his reason.

> DENIS DIDEROT (1713-84), French philosopher. *Encyclopedia*, vol. 1, "Political Authority" (1751; repr. in *Selected Writings*, ed. by Lester G. Crocker, 1966).

16   History does not long entrust the care of freedom to the weak or the timid.

> DWIGHT D. EISENHOWER (1890-1969), U.S. general, Republican politician, president. Inaugural address, 20 Jan. 1953.

17   I gave my life for freedom—this I know:
For those who bade me fight had told me so.

> W. N. EWER (1885-1976), British journalist. *Five Souls.*

18   There should be a sympathy with freedom, a desire to give it scope, founded not upon visionary ideas, but upon the long experience of many generations within the shores of this happy isle, that in freedom you lay the firmest foundations both of loyalty and order.

> W. E. GLADSTONE (1809-88), English Liberal prime minister, statesman. Speech, 27 Nov. 1879, West Calder, Scotland.

19 The history of the world is none other than the progress of the consciousness of freedom.

> GEORG HEGEL (1770-1831), German philosopher. *The Philosophy of History*, "Introduction," sct. 3 (1837).

20 The East knew and to the present day knows only that *One* is Free; the Greek and the Roman world, that *some* are free; the German World knows that *All* are free. The first political form therefore which we observe in History, is *Despotism*, the second *Democracy* and *Aristocracy*, the third, *Monarchy*.

> GEORG HEGEL (1770-1831), German philosopher. *The Philosophy of History*, "Classification of Historic Data" (1837).

21 Only very slowly and late have men come to realize that unless freedom is universal it is only extended privilege.

> CHRISTOPHER HILL (b. 1912), British historian. *The Century of Revolution*, ch. 20 (1961).

22 The basic test of freedom is perhaps less in what we are free to do than in what we are free not to do. It is the freedom to refrain, withdraw and abstain which makes a totalitarian regime impossible.

> ERIC HOFFER (1902-83), U.S. philosopher. *The Passionate State of Mind*, aph. 176 (1955).

23 Freedom is but the possibility of a various and indefinite activity; while government, or the exercise of dominion, is a single, yet real activity. The longing for freedom, therefore, is at first only too frequently suggested by the deep-felt consciousness of its absence.

> KARL WILHELM VON HUMBOLDT (1767-1835), German statesman, philologist. *Limits of State Action*, "Introduction" (1792; repr. 1854; tr. and ed. by J. W. Burrow, 1969).

24 Freedom is the most contagious virus known to man.

> HUBERT H. HUMPHREY (1911-78), U.S. Democratic politician, vice president. Speech, 29 Oct. 1964, New York City.

25 The free way of life proposes ends, but it does not prescribe means.

> ROBERT KENNEDY (1925-68), U.S. attorney general, Democratic politician. *The Pursuit of Justice*, pt. 5, "Berlin East and West" (1964).

26 Freedom is never voluntarily given by the oppressor; it must be demanded by the oppressed.

> MARTIN LUTHER KING, JR. (1929-68), U.S. clergyman, civil rights leader. "Letter from Birmingham Jail," published in *Why We Can't Wait* (1963).

27 Freedom's just another word for nothing left to lose.

> KRIS KRISTOFFERSON (b. 1936), U.S. singer, songwriter. "Me and Bobby McGee," song written with Fred Foster (1969).

28 Men are free when they are in a living homeland, not when they are straying and breaking away. Men are free when they are obeying some deep, inward voice of religious belief. Obeying from within. Men are free when they belong to a living, organic, *believing* community, active in fulfilling some unfulfilled, perhaps unrealized purpose. Not when they are escaping to some wild west. The most unfree souls go west, and shout of freedom.

Men are freest when they are most unconscious of freedom. The shout is a rattling of chains, always was.

> D. H. LAWRENCE (1885-1930), British author. *Studies in Classic American Literature*, ch. 1 (1924). "Men are not free when they are doing just what they like," added Lawrence. "The moment you can do just what you like, there is nothing you care about doing."

29 Freedom in capitalist society always remains about the same as it was in ancient Greek republics: Freedom for slave owners.

> VLADIMIR ILYICH LENIN (1870-1924), Russian revolutionary leader. *The State and Revolution*, ch. 5, sct. 2 (1917).

30 What most clearly characterizes true freedom and its true employment is its misemployment.

> G. C. LICHTENBERG (1742-99), German physicist, philosopher. *Aphorisms*, "Notebook L," aph. 49 (written 1765-99; tr. by R. J. Hollingdale, 1990).

31 Freedom is hunting, feeding, danger;
that, that is freedom—that it is which makes
the veins to swell, the breast to heave and glow
Aye, that is freedom,—that is pleasure—life!

> MARIE LOVELL (1803-77), English actor, playwright. Ingomar, in *Ingomar, the Barbarian*, act 1.

32 Freedom is the only law which genius knows.

> JAMES RUSSELL LOWELL (1819-91), U.S. poet, editor. "Elizabethan Dramatists, Omitting Shakespeare: John Webster" (1843; published in *Lowell's Early Prose Writings*, 1902).

33 Freedom is always and exclusively freedom for the one who thinks differently.

> ROSA LUXEMBURG (1870-1919), German revolutionary. Prison notes, 1918 (published in *The Russian Revolution*, ch. 6, 1922; tr. 1961).

34 Man in general, if reduced to himself, is too wicked to be free.

> JOSEPH DE MAISTRE (1753-1821), French diplomat, philosopher. *Four Chapters on Russia*, ch. 1 (1859). Quoted in: Isaiah Berlin, *The Crooked Timber of Humanity* (1990).

35 You can't separate peace from freedom because no one can be at peace unless he has his freedom.

> MALCOLM X (1925-65), U.S. black leader. "Prospects for Freedom in 1965," speech, 7 Jan. 1965, New York City (published in *Malcolm X Speaks*, ch. 12, 1965).

36 There's something contagious about demanding freedom.

> ROBIN MORGAN (b. 1941), U.S. feminist author, poet. *Sisterhood Is Powerful*, Introduction (1970).

37 How is freedom measured, in individuals as in nations? By the resistance which has to be overcome, by the effort it costs to stay *aloft*. One would have to seek the highest type of free man where the greatest resistance is constantly being overcome: five steps from tyranny, near the threshold of the danger of servitude.

> FRIEDRICH NIETZSCHE (1844-1900), German philosopher. *Twilight of the Idols*, "Expeditions of an Untimely Man," aph. 38 (1889).

38 Freedom is the freedom to say that two plus two make four. If that is granted, all else follows.

> GEORGE ORWELL (1903-50), British author. Winston Smith, in *1984*, pt. 1, ch. 7 (1949), writing in his diary.

39 Freedom prospers when religion is vibrant and the rule of law under God is acknowledged.

> RONALD REAGAN (b. 1911), U.S. Republican politician, president. Speech, 8 March 1983, at the Annual Convention of the National Association of Evangelicals, Orlando, Fla. (published in *Speaking My Mind*, 1989).

40 We look forward to a world founded upon four essential human freedoms. The first is freedom of speech and expression everywhere in the world. The second is freedom of every person to worship God in his own way everywhere in the world. The third is freedom from want . . . everywhere in the world. The fourth is freedom from fear . . . anywhere in the world.

> FRANKLIN D. ROOSEVELT (1882-1945), U.S. Democratic politician, president. Speech, 6 Jan. 1941, to Congress.

41 Man is born free, and everywhere he is in chains.

> JEAN-JACQUES ROUSSEAU (1712-78), Swiss-born French philosopher, political theorist. Opening sentence of *The Social Contract*, ch. 1 (1762). More than a hundred years earlier, John Milton had written in his pamphlet *The Tenure of Kings and Magistrates* (1649): "No man who knows aught, can be so stupid to deny that all men naturally were born free."

42 No human being, however great, or powerful, was ever so free as a fish.

> JOHN RUSKIN (1819-1900), English art critic, author. *The Two Paths*, lecture 5 (1859).

43 Women, like men, ought to have their youth so glutted with freedom they hate the very idea of freedom.

> VITA SACKVILLE-WEST (1892-1962), British novelist, poet. Letter, 1 June 1919, to her husband, diplomat and author Harold Nicolson. Quoted in: Nigel Nicolson, *Portrait of a Marriage* (1973).

44 There's only one free person in this society, and he is white and male.

> HAZEL SCOTT (1920-81), U.S. entertainer. Quoted in: *Ms.* (New York, Nov. 1974).

45 Freedom is not an ideal, it is not even a protection, if it means nothing more than freedom to stagnate, to live without dreams, to have no greater aim than a second car and another television set.

> ADLAI STEVENSON (1900-1965), U.S. Democratic politician. "Putting First Things First," in *Foreign Affairs* (New York, Jan. 1960).

46 It is by the goodness of God that in our country we have those three unspeakably precious things: freedom of speech, freedom of conscience, and the prudence never to practice either of them.

> MARK TWAIN (1835-1910), U.S. author. *Following the Equator*, ch. 20, "Pudd'nhead Wilson's New Calendar" (1897).

See also Humphrey on DEBATE; Cooley on DISCIPLINE; Humboldt on FORCE; Baudrillard on FREE WILL; FREEDOM OF SPEECH; Chamfort on HISTORY; Alinsky on INDIVIDUALITY; LIBERTY; Lenin on The STATE.

FREEDOM OF SPEECH

1 If we don't believe in freedom of expression for people we despise, we don't believe in it at all.

> NOAM CHOMSKY (b. 1928), U.S. linguist, political analyst. Television interview with John Pilger on "The Late Show," 25 Nov. 1992, BBC2, excerpted in *Guardian* (London, 23 Nov. 1992).

2 We who officially value freedom of speech above life itself seem to have nothing to talk about but the weather.

> BARBARA EHRENREICH (b. 1941), U.S. author, columnist. *The Worst Years of Our Lives*, "The Moral Bypass" (1991; first published 1985).

3 We are willing enough to praise freedom when she is safely tucked away in the past and cannot be a nuisance. In the present, amidst dangers whose outcome we cannot foresee, we get nervous about her, and admit censorship.

> E. M. FORSTER (1879-1970), British novelist, essayist. *Two Cheers for Democracy*, "The Tercentenary of the Areopagitica" (1951).

4 The primacy of the word, basis of the human psyche, that has in our age been used for mind-bending persuasion and brain-washing pulp, disgraced by Goebbels and debased by advertising copy, remains a force for freedom that flies out between all bars.

> NADINE GORDIMER (b. 1923), South African author. "The Unkillable Word," address, 17 April 1980 (published as "Censorship and the Word" in *The Bloody Horse*, Sept.-Oct. 1980; repr. in *The Essential Gesture*, ed. by Stephen Clingman, 1988).

5 We hear about constitutional rights, free speech and the free press. Every time I hear those words I say to myself, "That man is a Red, that man is a Communist." You never heard a real American talk in that manner.

> FRANK HAGUE (1876-1956), U.S. politician. Speech, 12 Jan. 1938, to the Jersey City Chamber of Commerce.

6 Every man has a right to utter what he thinks truth, and every other man has a right to knock him down for it. Martyrdom is the test.

> SAMUEL JOHNSON (1709-84), English author, lexicographer. Quoted in: James Boswell, *Life of Samuel Johnson*, 1780 (1791).

7 How absurd men are! They never use the liberties they have, they demand those they do not have. They have freedom of thought, they demand freedom of speech.

> SØREN KIERKEGAARD (1813-55), Danish philosopher. *Either/Or*, vol. 1, "Diapsalmata" (1843; tr. 1987).

8 When one makes a Revolution, one cannot mark time; one must always go forward—or go back. He who now talks about the "freedom of the press" goes backward, and halts our headlong course towards Socialism.

> VLADIMIR ILYICH LENIN (1870-1924), Russian revolutionary leader. Speech, 17 Nov. 1917, Smolny, Petrograd. Quoted in: John Reed, *Ten Days That Shook the World*, ch. 11 (1926).

9 Give me the liberty to know, to utter, and to argue freely according to conscience, above all liberties.

> JOHN MILTON (1608-74), English poet. *Areopagitica: a Speech for the Liberty of Unlicensed Printing to the Parliament of England* (1644).

10 Marks on paper are free—free speech—press—pictures all go together I suppose.

> GEORGIA O'KEEFFE (1887-1986), U.S. artist. Letter, 14 Jan. 1916, to Anita Pollitzer. Quoted in: Laurie Lisle, *Portrait of an Artist*, ch. 3 (1986).

11 Free speech is the whole thing, the whole ball game. Free speech is life itself.

> SALMAN RUSHDIE (b. 1948), Indian-born British author. Interview in *Guardian* (London, 8 Nov. 1990).

12 The first principle of a free society is an untrammeled flow of words in an open forum.

> ADLAI STEVENSON (1900-1965), U.S. Democratic politician. *New York Times* (19 Jan. 1962). But see Stevenson on OPINION for his earlier reservations on the subject of free speech.

13 In America the majority raises formidable barriers around the liberty of opinion; within these barriers an author may write what he pleases, but woe to him if he goes beyond them.

> ALEXIS DE TOCQUEVILLE (1805-59), French social philosopher. *Democracy in America*, vol. 1, ch. 15 (1835).

14 I disapprove of what you say, but I will defend to the death your right to say it.

> VOLTAIRE (1694-1778), French philosopher, author. Paraphrase of Voltaire's sentiments in his *Essay on Tolerance*, as stated in: Evelyn Beatrice Hall, under the pseudonym S. G. Tallentyre, *The Friends of Voltaire* (1907). However, in February 1770, Voltaire wrote to M. le Riche: "Monsieur l'Abbé, I detest what you write, but I would give my life to make it possible for you to continue to write."

See also Szasz on DELUSIONS OF GRANDEUR; FREEDOM; LIBERTY; Junius on The PRESS.

THE FRENCH REVOLUTION

1 Revolutions are celebrated when they are no longer dangerous.

> PIERRE BOULEZ (b. 1925), French composer, conductor. *Guardian* (London, 13 Jan. 1989), on the bicentenary celebrations of the French revolution.

2 The French Revolution gave birth to no artists but only to a great journalist, Desmoulins, and to an under-the-counter writer, Sade. The only poet of the times was the guillotine.

> ALBERT CAMUS (1913-60), French-Algerian philosopher, author. *The Rebel*, pt. 4 (1951; tr. 1953).

3 It was the best of times, it was the worst of times, it was the age of wisdom, it was the age of foolishness, it was the epoch of belief, it was the epoch of incredulity, it was the season of Light, it was the season of Darkness, it was the spring of hope, it was the winter of despair, we had everything before us, we had nothing before us, we were all going direct to Heaven, we were all going direct the other way—in short, the period was so far like the present period, that some of its noisiest authorities insisted on its being received, for good or for evil, in the superlative degree of comparison only.

> CHARLES DICKENS (1812-70), English novelist. Opening lines of *A Tale of Two Cities*, bk. 1, ch. 1 (1859).

4 How much the greatest event it is that ever happened in the world! and how much the best!

> CHARLES JAMES FOX (1749-1806), English Whig politician. Letter, 30 July 1789, on the fall of the Bastille. Fox's support for the French Revolution led to the rupture of his cherished friendship with Edmund Burke over the issue.

5 Justice has its anger, my lord Bishop, and the wrath of justice is an element of progress. Whatever else may be said of it, the French Revolution was the greatest step forward by mankind since the coming of Christ. It was unfinished, I agree, but still it was sublime. It released the untapped springs of society; it softened hearts, appeased, tranquilized, enlightened, and set flowing through the world the tides of civilization. It was good. The French Revolution was the anointing of humanity.

> VICTOR HUGO (1802-85), French poet, dramatist, novelist. The old revolutionary, in *Les Misérables*, pt. 1, bk. 1, ch. 10 (1862).

6 I think perhaps we manage our revolutions much more quietly in this country.

> MARGARET THATCHER (b. 1925), British Conservative politician, prime minister. *Daily Telegraph* (London, 12 July 1989), said in the wake of the bicentenary celebrations of the French Revolution in Paris.

7 Bliss was it in that dawn to be alive,
But to be young was very heaven!

> WILLIAM WORDSWORTH (1770-1850), English poet. *The Prelude*, bk. 11.

See also Burke on REPRESSION.

SIGMUND FREUD

1 For one who lived among enemies so long:
if often he was wrong and at times, absurd,
to us he is no more a person
now but a whole climate of opinion.

> W. H. AUDEN (1907-73), Anglo-American poet. *In Memory of Sigmund Freud.*

2 Science is always discovering odd scraps of magical wisdom and making a tremendous fuss about its cleverness.

> ALEISTER CROWLEY (1875-1947), British occultist. *The Confessions of Aleister Crowley*, ch. 64 (1929; rev. 1970), referring to Freudian theories.

3 Without hesitation, I place Freud among the heroes. He dispossessed the Jewish people of the greatest and most influential of all heroes—Moses.

> SALVADOR DALI (1904-89), Spanish painter. *Diary of a Genius* (1966), entry for 11 May 1957.

4 I am actually not at all a man of science, not an observer, not an experimenter, not a thinker. I am by temperament nothing but a conquistador—an adventurer, if you want it translated—with all the curiosity, daring, and tenacity characteristic of a man of this sort.

> SIGMUND FREUD (1856-1939), Austrian psychiatrist. Letter, 1 Feb. 1900 (published in *The Complete Letters of Sigmund Freud to Wilhelm Fliess 1887-1904*, 1985).

5 I have often felt as though I had inherited all the defiance and all the passions with which our ancestors defended their Temple and could gladly sacrifice my life for one great moment in history. And at the same time I always felt so helpless and incapable of expressing these ardent passions even by a word or a poem.

> SIGMUND FREUD (1856-1939), Austrian psychiatrist. Letter, 2

Feb. 1918, to his fiancée, Martha Bernays (published in *The Letters of Sigmund Freud*, 1961).

6 Incidentally, why was it that none of all the pious ever discovered psycho-analysis? Why did it have to wait for a completely godless Jew?

SIGMUND FREUD (1856-1939), Austrian psychiatrist. Letter, 9 Oct. 1918 (published in *Psycho-Analysis and Faith: The Letters of Sigmund Freud and Oscar Pfister*, 1963).

7 Here was a big constructive imagination; here was a mere doctor laying bare the origins of Greek drama as no classical scholar had ever done, teaching the anthropologist what was really meant by his *totem and taboo*, probing the mysteries of sin, of sanctity, of sacrament— a man who, because he understood, purged the human spirit from fear. I have no confidence in psycho-analysis as a method of therapeutics . . . but I am equally sure that for generations almost every branch of human knowledge will be enriched and illumined by the imagination of Freud.

JANE HARRISON (1850-1928), English classical scholar, writer. *Reminiscences of a Student's Life*, "Conclusion" (1925).

8 Sigmund Freud was a novelist with a scientific background. He just didn't know he was a novelist. All those damn psychiatrists after him, they didn't know he was a novelist either.

JOHN IRVING (b. 1942), U.S. author. Interview in *Writers at Work* (Eighth Series, ed. by George Plimpton, 1988).

9 Freud was a hero. He descended to the "Underworld" and met there stark terrors. He carried with him his theory as a Medusa's head which turned these terrors to stone.

R. D. LAING (b. 1927), British psychiatrist. *The Divided Self*, pt. 1, ch. 1 (1959).

10 The Freudian theory is one of the most important foundation stones for an edifice to be built by future generations, the dwelling of a freer and wiser humanity.

THOMAS MANN (1875-1955), German author, critic. *New York Times* (21 June 1939).

11 Let me say at once that I reject completely the vulgar, shabby, fundamentally medieval world of Freud, with its crankish quest for sexual symbols (something like searching for Baconian acrostics in Shakespeare's works) and its bitter little embryos spying, from their natural nooks, upon the love life of their parents.

VLADIMIR NABOKOV (1899-1977), Russian-born U.S. novelist, poet. *Speak, Memory*, ch. 1, sct. 1 (1955; rev. 1966).

See also PSYCHOANALYSIS.

FRIENDLESSNESS

1 Friendless. Having no favors to bestow. Destitute of fortune. Addicted to utterance of truth and common sense.

AMBROSE BIERCE (1842-1914), U.S. author. *The Devil's Dictionary* (1881-1906).

2 It pays to know who your friends are but it also pays to know you ain't got any friends.

BOB DYLAN (b. 1941), U.S. singer, songwriter. *Tarantula*, "Prelude to the Flatpick" (1970).

See also Shelley on LEADERSHIP.

FRIENDLINESS

1 If a stranger taps you on the ass and says, "How's the little lady today!" you will probably cringe. But if he's an American, he's only being friendly.

MARGARET ATWOOD (b. 1939), Canadian novelist, poet, critic. "A Question of Metamorphosis," interview, in *Malahat Review*, no. 41 (1977; repr. in *Conversations*, ed. by Earl G. Ingersoll, 1990).

2 The social, friendly, honest man,
Whate'er he be,
'Tis he fulfils great Nature's plan,
And none but he!

ROBERT BURNS (1759-96), Scottish poet. *Epistle to John Lapraik*, no. 2.

3 A friend to all is a friend to none.

ENGLISH PROVERB (18th century). Collected in: Thomas Fuller, *Gnomologia* (1732).

4 The American has dwindled into an Odd Fellow— one who may be known by the development of his organ of gregariousness.

HENRY DAVID THOREAU (1817-62), U.S. philosopher, author, naturalist. *On the Duty of Civil Disobedience* (1849).

5 That impersonal insensitive friendliness which takes the place of ceremony in that land of waifs and strays.

EVELYN WAUGH (1903-66), British novelist. *The Loved One* (1948; repr. 1951, p. 71), of Aimée Thanatogenos, an American.

FRIENDS

1 Forsake not an old friend; for the new is not comparable to him: a new friend is as new wine; when it is old, thou shalt drink it with pleasure.

APOCRYPHA. *Ecclesiasticus* 9:10.

2 To the query, "What is a friend?" his reply was "A single soul dwelling in two bodies."

ARISTOTLE (384-322 B.C.), Greek philosopher. Quoted in: Diogenes Laertius, *Lives of Eminent Philosophers*, "Aristotle," bk. 5, sct. 20.

3 Between friends differences in taste or opinion are irritating in direct proportion to their triviality.

W. H. AUDEN (1907-73), Anglo-American poet. *The Dyer's Hand*, pt. 3, "Hic et Ille," sct. D (1962).

4 Friends, both the imaginary ones you build for yourself out of phrases taken from a living writer, or real ones from college, and relatives, despite all the waste of ceremony and fakery and the fact that out of an hour of conversation you may have only five minutes in which the old entente reappears, are the only real means for foreign ideas to enter your brain.

> NICHOLSON BAKER (b. 1957), U.S. author. *U And I: A True Story*, ch. 4 (1991).

5 From quiet homes and first beginning,
Out to the undiscovered ends,
There's nothing worth the wear of winning,
But laughter and the love of friends.

> HILAIRE BELLOC (1870-1953), British author. *Dedicatory Ode*.

6 Thus much for thy assurance know; a hollow friend is but a hellish foe.

> NICHOLAS BRETON (c. 1545-1626), English author, poet. *The Mother's Blessing* (1602-3; repr. in *Works in Verse and Prose of Nicholas Breton*, vol. 2, 1879).

7 I have had, and may have still, a thousand friends, as they are called, in *life*, who are like one's partners in the waltz of this world—not much remembered when the ball is over.

> LORD BYRON (1788-1824), English poet. Letter, 16 Nov. 1822, to Mary Shelley (published in *Byron's Letters and Journals*, vol. 10, ed. by Leslie A. Marchand, 1973-81).

8 A man must eat a peck of salt with his friend, before he knows him.

> MIGUEL DE CERVANTES (1547-1616), Spanish writer. Sancho Panza, in *Don Quixote*, pt. 1, bk. 3, ch. 1 (1605; tr. by P. Motteux).

9 I have three kinds of friends: those who love me, those who pay no attention to me, and those who detest me.

> SÉBASTIEN-ROCH NICOLAS DE CHAMFORT (1741-94), French writer, wit. Quoted in: G. C. Lichtenberg, *Aphorisms*, "Notebook K," aph. 53 (written 1765-99; tr. by R. J. Hollingdale, 1990).

10 Most people enjoy the inferiority of their best friends.

> LORD CHESTERFIELD (1694-1773), English statesman, man of letters. Letter, 9 July 1750 (first published 1774; repr. in *The Letters of the Earl of Chesterfield to His Son*, vol. 2, no. 229, ed. by Charles Strachey, 1901).

11 Treat your friends as you do your pictures, and place them in their best light.

> JENNIE JEROME CHURCHILL (1854-1921), Anglo-American mother of Winston Churchill. *Small Talk on Big Subjects*, "Friendship" (1916).

12 And though thou notest from thy safe recess
Old friends burn dim, like lamps in noisome air
Love them for what they are; nor love them less,
Because to thee they are not what they were.

> SAMUEL TAYLOR COLERIDGE (1772-1834), English poet, critic. *Duty Surviving Self-Love*.

13 My true friends have always given me that supreme proof of devotion, a spontaneous aversion for the man I loved.

> COLETTE (1873-1954), French author. *Break of Day* (1928; repr. 1961, p. 11). Of her younger friends, Colette wrote, "I instinctively like to acquire and store up what promises to outlast me."

14 In America every woman has her set of girl-friends; some are cousins, the rest are gained at school. These form a permanent committee who sit on each other's affairs, who "come out" together, marry and divorce together, and who end as those groups of bustling, heartless well-informed club-women who govern society. Against them the Couple of Ehepaar is helpless and Man in their eyes but a biological interlude.

> CYRIL CONNOLLY (1903-74), British critic. *The Unquiet Grave*, pt. 1 (1944; rev. 1951).

15 The man that hails you Tom or Jack,
And proves by thumps upon your back
How he esteems your merit,
Is such a friend, that one had need
Be very much his friend indeed
To pardon or to bear it.

> WILLIAM COWPER (1731-1800), English poet. *Friendship* (1800).

16 Best friend, my well-spring in the wilderness!

> GEORGE ELIOT (1819-80), English novelist. *The Spanish Gypsy*, bk. 3 (1868).

17 To act the part of a true friend requires more conscientious feeling than to fill with credit and complacency any other station or capacity in social life.

> SARAH ELLIS (1812-72), English missionary, writer. *Pictures of Private Life*, ch. 4 (1834).

18 A friend may well be reckoned the masterpiece of Nature.

> RALPH WALDO EMERSON (1803-82), U.S. essayist, poet, philosopher. *Essays*, "Friendship" (First Series, 1841).

19 I do then with my friends as I do with my books. I would have them where I can find them, but I seldom use them.

> RALPH WALDO EMERSON (1803-82), U.S. essayist, poet, philosopher. *Essays*, "Friendship" (First Series, 1841).

20 It is in the thirties that we want friends. In the forties we know they won't save us any more than love did.

> F. SCOTT FITZGERALD (1896-1940), U.S. author. *The Crack-Up*, "Notebook O" (ed. by Edmund Wilson, 1945).

21 There are few things in which we deceive ourselves more than in the esteem we profess to entertain for our firends. It is little better than a piece of quackery. The truth is, we think of them as we please—that is, as *they* please or displease us.

> WILLIAM HAZLITT (1778-1830), English essayist. *Characteristics*, no. 60 (published anonymously in 1823; repr. in *Complete Works*, vol. 9, ed. by P. P. Howe, 1932).

22 I like a friend the better for having faults that one can talk about.

> WILLIAM HAZLITT (1778-1830), English essayist. *The Plain Speaker*, "On the Pleasure of Hating" (1826).

23 Never, my dear Sir, do you take it into your head that I do not love you; you may settle yourself in full confidence both of my love and my esteem; I love you as a kind man, I value you as a worthy man, and hope in time to reverence you as a man of exemplary piety.

> SAMUEL JOHNSON (1709-84), English author, lexicographer. Letter, 27 Aug. 1775, to James Boswell (published in *The Letters of Samuel Johnson*, vol. 2, no. 431, ed. by R. W. Chapman, 1952).

24 In a bad marriage, friends are the invisible glue. If we have enough friends, we may go on for years, intending to leave, talking about leaving—instead of actually getting up and leaving.

ERICA JONG (b. 1942), U.S. author. *How to Save Your Own Life*, "A Day in the Life . . ." (1977).

25 In the misfortunes of our best friends we always find something not altogether displeasing to us.

FRANÇOIS, DUC DE LA ROCHEFOUCAULD (1613-1680), French writer, moralist. *Sentences et Maximes Morales*, no. 576 of collected maxims (1665; ed. by FitzGibbon, 1957).

26 It is more shameful to distrust one's friends than to be deceived by them.

FRANÇOIS, DUC DE LA ROCHEFOUCAULD (1613-80), French writer, satirist. *Sentences et Maximes Morales*, no. 84 (1678).

27 God gives us our relatives—thank God we can choose our friends.

ETHEL WATTS MUMFORD (1878-1940), U.S. novelist, humor writer. *The Cynic's Calendar*, p. 1 (written with Addison Mizner and Oliver Herford, 1903).

28 Friends are like fiddle strings, they must not be screwed too tight.

ENGLISH PROVERB. Collected in H. G. Bohn, *A Handbook of Proverbs* (1855).

29 Men are more evanescent than pictures, yet one sorrows for lost friends, and pictures *are* my friends. I have none others. I am never long enough with men to attach myself to them; and whatever feelings of attachment I have are to material things.

JOHN RUSKIN (1819-1900), English art critic, author. Letter, 28 Jan. 1852, to his father. Quoted in: *Ruskin Today*, sct. 36 (ed. by Kenneth Clark, 1964).

30 The friends thou hast, and their adoption tried,
Grapple them to thy soul with hoops of steel,
But do not dull thy palm with entertainment
Of each new-hatched unfledged comrade.

WILLIAM SHAKESPEARE (1564-1616), English dramatist, poet. Polonius, in *Hamlet*, act 1, sc. 3, giving advice to his son Laertes, departing for France.

31 I can't forgive my friends for dying; I don't find these vanishing acts of theirs at all amusing.

LOGAN PEARSALL SMITH (1865-1946), U.S. essayist, aphorist. *Afterthoughts*, "Age and Death" (1931).

32 So long as we are loved by others I should say that we are almost indispensable; and no man is useless while he has a friend.

ROBERT LOUIS STEVENSON (1850-94), Scottish novelist, essayist, poet. *Across the Plains*, "Lay Morals" (1892).

33 I am speaking now of the highest duty we owe our friends, the noblest, the most sacred—that of keeping their own nobleness, goodness, pure and incorrupt. . . . If we *let* our friend become cold and selfish and exacting without a remonstrance, we are no true lover, no true friend.

HARRIET BEECHER STOWE (1811-96), U.S. novelist, anti-slavery campaigner. *Little Foxes*, ch. 3 (1865).

34 To say that a man is your Friend, means commonly no more than this, that he is not your enemy. Most contemplate only what would be the accidental and trifling advantages of Friendship, as that the Friend can assist in time of need by his substance, or his influence, or his counsel. . . . Even the utmost goodwill and harmony and practical kindness are not sufficient for Friendship, for Friends do not live in harmony merely, as some say, but in melody.

HENRY DAVID THOREAU (1817-62), U.S. philosopher, author, naturalist. *A Week on the Concord and Merrimack Rivers*, "Wednesday" (1849).

35 We have not so good a right to hate any as our Friend.

HENRY DAVID THOREAU (1817-62), U.S. philosopher, author, naturalist. *A Week on the Concord and Merrimack Rivers*, "Wednesday" (1849).

36 I do not believe that friends are necessarily the people you like best, they are merely the people who got there first.

PETER USTINOV (b. 1921), British actor, writer, director. *Dear Me*, ch. 5 (1977).

37 We shelter children for a time; we live side by side with men; and that is all. We owe them nothing, and are owed nothing. I think we owe our friends more, especially our female friends.

FAY WELDON (b. 1933), British novelist. The narrator (Praxis Duveen), in *Praxis*, ch. 19 (1978).

38 Some people go to priests; others to poetry; I to my friends.

VIRGINIA WOOLF (1882-1941), British novelist. Bernard, in *The Waves* (1931; repr. 1943, p. 189).

See also Bowen, Pope on ABSENCE; ACQUAINTANCE; Talleyrand on ALTRUISM; Shakespeare on BEREAVEMENT; Canning on CANDOR; La Fontaine on DISCRETION; Rossetti on FAMILY; Horace on GREATNESS; Welles on HARD TIMES; Gay, Gray on HYPOCRISY; Milligan on MONEY; Sargent on PORTRAITS; Vidal on SUCCESS.

FRIENDSHIP

1 Friendships, in general, are suddenly contracted; and therefore it is no wonder they are easily dissolved.

JOSEPH ADDISON (1672-1719), English essayist. *Interesting Anecdotes, Memoirs, Allegories, Essays, and Poetical Fragments*, "Of Friendship" (1794).

2 The greatest sweetener of human life is Friendship. To raise this to the highest pitch of enjoyment, is a secret which but few discover.

JOSEPH ADDISON (1672-1719), English essayist. *Interesting Anecdotes, Memoirs, Allegories, Essays, and Poetical Fragments*, "Of Friendship" (1794).

3 Love is blind; friendship closes its eyes.

ANONYMOUS.

4 Thy friendship oft has made my heart to ache:
Do be my enemy for friendship's sake.

WILLIAM BLAKE (1757-1827), English poet, painter, engraver. *Manuscript Notebooks*, no. 39 (c. 1808-1811; repr. in *Complete Writings*, 1957), to William Hayley.

5 Friendship is one of the most tangible things in a world which offers fewer and fewer supports.

KENNETH BRANAGH (b. 1960), British actor, director. *Daily Telegraph* (London, 4 Nov. 1992).

6 Love is like the wild rose-briar;
Friendship like the holly-tree.
The holly is dark when the rose-briar blooms,
But which will bloom most constantly?

EMILY BRONTË (1818-48), English novelist. *Love and Friendship* (1846).

7 Accountability in friendship is the equivalent of love without strategy.

ANITA BROOKNER (b. 1938), British novelist, art historian. *Women Writers Talk* (ed. by Olga Kenyon, 1989).

8 Love is only chatter,
Friends are all that matter.

GELETT BURGESS (1866-1951), U.S. humorist. *Willy and the Lady.*

9 A man's friendships are, like his will, invalidated by marriage—but they are also no less invalidated by the marriage of his friends.

SAMUEL BUTLER (1835-1902), English author. *The Way of All Flesh*, ch. 75 (1903).

10 Friendship is Love without his wings!

LORD BYRON (1788-1824), English poet. *L'Amitié est L'Amour Sans Ailes.*

11 A mistress never is nor can be a friend. While you agree, you are lovers; and when it is over, anything but friends.

LORD BYRON (1788-1824), English poet. *Letters and Journals*, vol. 3 (ed. by Leslie A. Marchand, 1974), entry for 24 Nov. 1813.

12 I have always laid it down as a maxim—and found it justified by experience—that a man and a woman make far better friendships than can exist between two of the same sex—but *then* with the condition that they never have made or are to make love to each other.

LORD BYRON (1788-1824), English poet. Letter, 1 Dec. 1822 (published in *Byron's Letters and Journals*, vol. 10, ed. by Leslie A. Marchand, 1973-81). Byron echoed this notion in *Don Juan*, cto. 14, st. 93: "No friend like to a woman Earth discovers,/So that you have not been nor will be lovers."

13 Friendship is a pretty full-time occupation if you really are friendly with somebody. You can't have too many friends because then you're just not really friends.

TRUMAN CAPOTE (1924-84), U.S. author. *Conversations With Truman Capote*, ch. 3, "Love, Sex, and Fear" (ed. by Lawrence Grobel, 1985).

14 Only solitary men know the full joys of friendship. Others have their family—but to a solitary and an exile his friends are everything.

WILLA CATHER (1876-1947), U.S. author. *Shadows on the Rock*, bk. 3, ch. 5 (1931).

15 But just as delicate fare does not stop you from craving for saveloys, so tried and exquisite friendship does not take away your taste for something new and dubious.

COLETTE (1873-1954), French author. "The Rainy Moon," pub-

lished in *Chambre d'Hôtel*, (1940; repr. in *The Collected Stories of Colette*, 1983).

16 No man can be friends with a woman he finds attractive. He always wants to have sex with her. Sex is always out there. Friendship is ultimately doomed and that is the end of the story.

NORA EPHRON (b. 1941), U.S. author, journalist. Harry (played by Billy Crystal) to Sally (Meg Ryan), in the film *When Harry Met Sally* (screenplay by Ephron, directed by Rob Reiner, 1989).

17 When all is said and done, friendship is the only trustworthy fabric of the affections. So-called love is a delirious inhuman state of mind: when hot it substitutes indulgence for fair play; when cold it is cruel, but friendship is warmth in cold, firm ground in a bog.

MILES FRANKLIN (1879-1954), Australian authoress. *My Career Goes Bung*, ch. 19 (written 1900; published 1946).

18 It is easy enough to be friendly to one's friends. But to befriend the one who regards himself as your enemy is the quintessence of true religion. The other is mere business.

MOHANDAS K. GANDHI (1869-1948), Indian political and spiritual leader. *Non-Violence in Peace and War*, vol. 2, ch. 248 (1948).

19 Friendship is a disinterested commerce between equals; love, an abject intercourse between tyrants and slaves.

OLIVER GOLDSMITH (1728-74), Anglo-Irish author, poet, playwright. Mr. Honeywood, in *The Good Natur'd Man*, act 1.

20 Old friendships are like meats served up repeatedly, cold, comfortless, and distasteful. The stomach turns against them.

WILLIAM HAZLITT (1778-1830), English essayist. *The Plain Speaker*, "On the Pleasure of Hating" (1826).

21 There are persons who cannot make friends. Who are they? Those who cannot be friends. It is not the want of understanding or good nature, of entertaining or useful qualities, that you complain of: on the contrary, they have probably many points of attraction; but they have one that neutralises all these—they care nothing about you, and are neither the better nor worse for what you think of them. They manifest no joy at your approach; and when you leave them, it is with a feeling that they can do just as well without you. This is not sullenness, nor indifference, nor absence of mind; but they are intent solely on their own thoughts, and you are merely one of the subjects they exercise them upon. They live in society as in a solitude.

WILLIAM HAZLITT (1778-1830), English essayist. "On Disagreeable People," in *The Monthly Magazine* (Aug. 1827; repr. in *Sketches and Essays*, 1839).

22 Friendship is but another name for an alliance with the follies and the misfortunes of others. Our own share of miseries is sufficient: why enter then as volonters into those of another?

THOMAS JEFFERSON (1743-1826), U.S. president. Letter, 12 Oct. 1786, to Maria Cosway.

23 The most fatal disease of friendship is gradual

decay, or dislike hourly increased by causes too slender for complaint, and too numerous for removal.

> SAMUEL JOHNSON (1709-84), English author, lexicographer. *The Idler*, no. 23, in *Universal Chronicle* (London, 23 Sept. 1758; repr. in *Works of Samuel Johnson*, vol. 2, ed. by W. J. Bate, John M. Bullitt and L. F. Powell, 1963).

24 If a man does not make new acquaintance as he advances through life, he will soon find himself left alone. A man, Sir, should keep his friendship in constant repair.

> SAMUEL JOHNSON (1709-84), English author, lexicographer. Quoted in: James Boswell, *Life of Samuel Johnson*, 1755 entry (1791), though quoting Johnson's opinion "at a subsequent period of his life."

25 Love between man and man is impossible because there must not be sexual intercourse and friendship between man and woman is impossible because there must be sexual intercourse.

> JAMES JOYCE (1882-1941), Irish author. Mr. Duffy, in *Dubliners*, "A Painful Case" (1914), of his relationship with Mrs. Sinico.

26 If a man urge me to tell wherefore I loved him, I feel it cannot be expressed but by answering: Because it was he, because it was myself.

> MICHEL DE MONTAIGNE (1533-92), French essayist. *Essays*, bk. 1, ch. 27, "Of Friendship" (1580-88; tr. by John Florio), of Etienne de la Boétie.

27 A woman may very well form a friendship with a man, but for this to endure, it must be assisted by a little physical antipathy.

> FRIEDRICH NIETZSCHE (1844-1900), German philosopher. *Human, All Too Human*, ch. 7, aph. 390 (1878).

28 The sacrifices of friendship were beautiful in her eyes as long as she was not asked to make them.

> SAKI [H. H. MUNRO] (1870-1916), Scottish author. *Beasts and Super-Beasts*, "Fur" (1914), said of Suzanne.

29 What men have called friendship is only a social arrangement, a mutual adjustment of interests, an interchange of services given and received; it is, in sum, simply a business from which those involved propose to derive a steady profit for their own self-love.

> FRANÇOIS, DUC DE LA ROCHEFOUCAULD (1613-80), French writer, moralist. *Sentences et Maximes Morales*, no. 83 (1678).

30 The very flexibility and ease which make men's friendships so agreeable while they endure, make them the easier to destroy and forget. And a man who has a few friends, or one who has a dozen (if there be any one so wealthy on this earth), cannot forget on how precarious a base his happiness reposes; and how by a stroke or two of fate—a death, a few light words, a piece of stamped paper, a woman's bright eyes—he may be left, in a month, destitute of all.

> ROBERT LOUIS STEVENSON (1850-94), Scottish novelist, essayist, poet. *Virginibus Puerisque*, title essay, sct. 1 (1881).

31 Friendship can only exist between persons with similar interests and points of view. Man and woman by the conventions of society are born with different interests and different points of view.

> J. AUGUST STRINDBERG (1849-1912), Swedish dramatist, nov-

elist, poet. *The Son of a Servant* (1886; tr. by Claud Field, 1913, p.132).

32 Your notions of friendship are new to me; I believe every man is born with his quantum, and he cannot give to one without robbing another. I very well know to whom I would give the first place in my friendship, but they are not in the way, I am condemned to another scene, and therefore I distribute it in pennyworths to those about me, and who displease me least, and should do the same to my fellow prisoners if I were condemned to a jail.

> JONATHAN SWIFT (1667-1745), Anglo-Irish satirist. Letter, 20 Sept. 1723, to poet Alexander Pope, who had previously written to Swift, "My friendships are increased by new ones, yet no part of the warmth I felt for the old is diminished."

33 The holy passion of friendship is of so sweet and steady and loyal and enduring a nature that it will last through a whole lifetime, if not asked to lend money.

> MARK TWAIN (1835-1910), U.S. author. *Pudd'nhead Wilson*, ch. 8, "Pudd'nhead Wilson's Calendar" (1894).

34 Be courteous to all, but intimate with few, and let those few be well tried before you give them your confidence. True friendship is a plant of slow growth, and must undergo and withstand the shocks of adversity before it is entitled to the appellation.

> GEORGE WASHINGTON (1732-99), U.S. general, president. Letter, 15 Jan. 1783.

35 Learn to reject friendship, or rather the dream of friendship. To want friendship is a great fault. Friendship ought to be a gratuitous joy, like the joys afforded by art, or life (like aesthetic joys). I must refuse it in order to be worthy to receive it.

> SIMONE WEIL (1909-43), French philosopher, mystic. *The Pre-War Notebook* (1933-39; published in *First and Last Notebooks*, ed. by Richard Rees, 1970).

36 Camerado, I give you my hand!
I give you my love more precious than money,
I give you myself before preaching or law;
Will you give me yourself?

> WALT WHITMAN (1819-92), U.S. poet. *Song of the Open Road*, verse 15 (1856).

37 All love that has not friendship for its base,
Is like a mansion built upon the sand.

> ELLA WHEELER WILCOX (1855-1919), U.S. poet, journalist. *Upon the Sand*.

38 Between men and women there is no friendship possible. There is passion, enmity, worship, love, but no friendship.

> OSCAR WILDE (1854-1900), Anglo-Irish playwright, author. Lord Darlington, in *Lady Windermere's Fan*, act 2.

39 Laughter is not at all a bad beginning for a friendship, and it is far the best ending for one.

> OSCAR WILDE (1854-1900), Anglo-Irish playwright, author. Lord Henry, in *The Picture of Dorian Gray*, ch. 1 (1891).

40 I am already kindly disposed towards you. My friendship it is not in my power to give: this is a gift which no man can make, it is not in our own power: a sound and healthy friendship is the growth of time and circumstance, it will spring up and thrive like a wild-flower when these favour, and when they do not, it is in vain to look for it.

> WILLIAM WORDSWORTH (1770-1850), English poet. Letter, 29 July 1803, to author Thomas De Quincey, who had written Wordsworth a letter expressing his admiration. The two had never met.

41   Good fellowship and friendship are lasting, rational and manly pleasures.

> WILLIAM WYCHERLEY (1640-1716), English dramatist. Horner, in *The Country Wife*, act 1.

Se also ACQUAINTANCE; Chinese proverb on CEREMONY; Colette on COURTESY; Pope on DEATH AND DYING; Lessing on HATE; Woolf on INTIMACY; Hazlitt on PUNCTUALITY.

FRIGIDITY

1   Men always fall for frigid women because they put on the best show.

> FANNY BRICE (1891-1951), U.S. entertainer. Quoted in: Ben Hecht, *A Child of the Century*, bk. 5, "Don Juan in Hollywood" (1954). Hecht added, "Don Juan is apt to prefer the hullaballoo of spurious passion to the simpler noises of honest sex."

2   Show me a frigid women and, nine times out of ten, I'll show you a little man.

> JULIE BURCHILL (b. 1960), British journalist, author. "Where's the Beef?" in *Arena*, (London, 1988; repr. in *Sex and Sensibility*, 1992).

3   Frigidity is desire imagined by a woman who doesn't desire the man offering himself to her. It's the desire of a woman for a man who hasn't yet come to her, whom she doesn't yet know. She's faithful to this stranger even before she belongs to him. Frigidity is the non-desire for whatever is not him.

> MARGUERITE DURAS (b. 1914), French author, filmmaker. *Practicalities*, "Men" (1987; tr. 1990).

4   Frigidity is largely nonsense. It is this generation's catchword, one only vaguely understood and constantly misused. Frigid women are few. There is a host of diffident and slow-ripening ones.

> PHYLLIS MCGINLEY (1905-78), U.S. poet, author. *The Province of the Heart*, "The Honor of Being a Woman" (1959).

FRUSTRATION

1   The tragedy of life is not that man loses, but that he almost wins.

> HEYWOOD BROUN (1888-1939), U.S. journalist, novelist. *Pieces of Hate, and Other Enthusiasms*, "Sport for Art's Sake" (1922).

2   Every thought derives from a thwarted sensation.

> E. M. CIORAN (b. 1911), Rumanian-born French philosopher. *The Trouble with Being Born*, ch. 5 (1973).

3   The torment of human frustration, whatever its immediate cause, is the knowledge that the self is in prison, its vital force and "mangled mind" leaking away in lonely, wasteful self-conflict.

> ELIZABETH DREW (1887-1965), Anglo-American author, critic.

Poetry: A Modern Guide to Its Understanding and Enjoyment, pt. 2, ch. 13 (1959).

4   It is the awareness of unfulfilled desires which gives a nation the feeling that it has a mission and a destiny.

> ERIC HOFFER (1902-83), U.S. philosopher. *The Passionate State of Mind*, aph. 24 (1955).

5   I feel as if I were a piece in a game of chess, when my opponent says of it: That piece cannot be moved.

> SØREN KIERKEGAARD (1813-55), Danish philosopher. *Either/Or*, vol. 1, "Diapsalmata" (1843; tr. 1987).

6   It is misery, you know, unspeakable misery for the man who lives alone and who detests sordid, casual affairs; not old enough to do without women, but not young enough to be able to go and look for one without shame!

> LUIGI PIRANDELLO (1867-1936), Italian author, playwright. The Father, in *Six Characters in Search of an Author*, act 1 (1921).

FUN

1   Fun I love, but too much fun is of all things the most loathsome. Mirth is better than fun, and happiness is better than mirth.

> WILLIAM BLAKE (1757-1827), English poet, painter, engraver. Letter, 23 Aug. 1799 (published in *The Letters of William Blake*, 1956).

2   All animals, except man, know that the principal business of life is to enjoy it.

> SAMUEL BUTLER (1835-1902), English author. *The Way of All Flesh*, ch. 19 (1903).

3   Horse-play, romping, frequent and loud fits of laughter, jokes, waggery, and indiscriminate familiarity, will sink both merit and knowledge into a degree of contempt. They compose at most a merry fellow; and a merry fellow was never yet a respectable man.

> LORD CHESTERFIELD (1694-1773), English statesman, man of letters. Letter, 30 Aug. 1749 (first published 1774; repr. in *The Letters of the Earl of Chesterfield to His Son*, vol. 1, no. 190, ed. by Charles Strachey, 1901).

4   For present joys are more to flesh and blood
Than a dull prospect of a distant good.

> JOHN DRYDEN (1631-1700), English poet, dramatist, critic. *The Hind and the Panther*.

5   People must not do things for fun. We are not here for fun. There is no reference to fun in any act of Parliament.

> A. P. HERBERT (1890-1971), British author, politician. Lord Light, in *Uncommon Law*, "Is it a Free Country?" (1935).

6   Fun is a good thing but only when it spoils nothing better.

> GEORGE SANTAYANA (1863-1952), U.S. philosopher, poet. *The Sense of Beauty*, "The Comic" (1896).

7   Every time I hear that word, I cringe. Fun! I think it's disgusting; it's just running around. It's not my idea of pleasure.

> VIVIENNE WESTWOOD (b. 1941), British fashion designer. *Independent on Sunday* (London, 18 Feb. 1990).

FUNCTION

1   He gains everyone's approval who mixes the pleasant with the useful.

> HORACE (65-8 B.C.), Roman poet. *Ars Poetica* (c. 13 B.C.).

2   Form and function are a unity, two sides of one coin. In order to enhance function, appropriate form must exist or be created.

> IDA P. ROLF (1896-1979), U.S. biochemist, physical therapist. *Rolfing: The Integration of Human Structions*, Preface (1977).

3   Remember that the most beautiful things in the world are the most usless; peacocks and lilies for instance.

> JOHN RUSKIN (1819-1900), English art critic, author. *The Stones of Venice*, vol. 1, ch. 2, sct. 17 (1851).

4   Utility is the great idol of the age, to which all powers must do service and all talents swear allegiance.

> FRIEDRICH VON SCHILLER (1759-1805), German dramatist, poet, essayist. *On the Aesthetic Education of Man*, "Second Letter" (1795).

5   We can forgive a man for making a useful thing as long as he does not admire it. The only excuse for making a useless thing is that one admires it intensely.

> OSCAR WILDE (1854-1900), Anglo-Irish playwright, author. *The Picture of Dorian Gray*, Preface (1891).

FUNERALS

1   The only reason I might go to the funeral is to make absolutely sure that he's dead.

> "AN EMINENT EDITOR" of Press Baron Lord Beaverbook. Quoted in: Anthony Sampson, *Anatomy of Britain Today*, ch. 9 (1965).

2   No Life can pompless pass away—
The lowliest career
To the same Pageant wends its way
As that exalted here—

> EMILY DICKINSON (1830-86), U.S. poet. *The Complete Poems*, no. 1626 (1955).

3   As grand
And griefless as a rich man's funeral.

> SIDNEY THOMPSON DOBELL (1824-74), English poet. *A Musing on a Victory*.

4   Worldly faces never look so worldly as at a funeral. They have the same effect of grating incongruity as the sound of a coarse voice breaking the solemn silence of night.

> GEORGE ELIOT (1819-80), English novelist. *Janet's Repentance*, ch. 25, in *Blackwood's Magazine* (1857; repr. in *Scenes of Clerical Life*, 1858).

5   Funeral pomp is more for the vanity of the living than for the honor of the dead.

> FRANÇOIS, DUC DE LA ROCHEFOUCAULD (1613-1680), French writer, moralist. *Sentences et Maximes Morales*, no. 593 (1664; ed. by FitzGibbon, 1957).

6   Memorial services are the cocktail parties of the geriatric set.

> HAROLD MACMILLAN (1894-1986), British Conservative politician, prime minister. Quoted in: Alistair Horne, *Macmillan*, vol. 2, ch. 20 (1989).

7   On a day of burial there is no perspective—for space itself is annihilated. Your dead friend is still a fragmentary being. The day you bury him is a day of chores and crowds, of hands false or true to be shaken, of the immediate cares of mourning. The dead friend will not really die until tomorrow, when silence is round you again. Then he will show himself complete, as he was—to tear himself away, as he was, from the substantial you. Only then will you cry out because of him who is leaving and whom you cannot detain.

> ANTOINE DE SAINT-EXUPÉRY (1900-1944), French aviator, author. *Flight to Arras*, ch. 2 (1942).

8   Where a blood relation sobs, an intimate friend should choke up, a distant acquaintance should sigh, a stranger should merely fumble sympathetically with his handkerchief.

> MARK TWAIN (1835-1910), U.S. author. *Letters from the Earth*, "From an Unfinished Burlesque of Books on Etiquette," pt. 1, "At the Funeral" (ed. by Bernard DeVoto, 1962). Twain added: "Where the occasion is military, the emotions should be graded according to military rank, the highest officer present taking precedence in emotional violence, and the rest modifying their feelings according to their position in the service."

FUTILITY

1   The gods had condemned Sisyphus to ceaselessly rolling a rock to the top of a mountain, whence the stone would fall back of its own weight. They had thought with some reason that there is no more dreadful punishment than futile and hopeless labor.

> ALBERT CAMUS (1913-60), French-Algerian philosopher, author. *The Myth of Sisyphus*, ch. 4 (1942; tr. 1955).

2   A constant smirk upon the face, and a whiffling activity of the body, are strong indications of futility.

> LORD CHESTERFIELD (1694-1773), English statesman, man of letters. Letter, 30 Aug. 1749 (first published 1774; repr. in *The Letters of the Earl of Chesterfield to His Son*, vol. 1, no. 190, ed. by Charles Strachey, 1901).

3   I have measured out my life with coffee spoons.

> T. S. ELIOT (1888-1965), Anglo-American poet, critic. *The Love Song of J. Alfred Prufrock*.

4   No! I am not Prince Hamlet, nor was meant to be:
Am an attendant lord, one that will do
To swell a progress, start a scene or two, advise the prince.

> T. S. ELIOT (1888-1965), Anglo-American poet, critic. *The Love Song of J. Alfred Prufrock*.

5   Life is indeed darkness save when there is urge,
And all urge is blind save when there is knowl
edge,
And all knowledge is vain save when there is work,
And all work is empty save when there is love.

> KAHLIL GIBRAN (1883-1931) Lebanese poet, novelist. *The Prophet* (1923).

6 It is the superfluous things for which men sweat.

SENECA (c. 5 B.C.-A.D. c. 65), Roman writer, philosopher, statesman. *Epistulae ad Lucilium*, Epistle 4.

7 A walking shadow, a poor player,
that struts and frets his hour upon the stage,
And then is heard no more.

WILLIAM SHAKESPEARE (1564-1616), English dramatist, poet. Macbeth, in *Macbeth*, act 5, sc. 5.

8 He is useless on top of the ground; he ought to be be under it, inspiring the cabbages.

MARK TWAIN (1835-1910), U.S. author. *Pudd'nhead Wilson*, ch. 21, "Pudd'nhead Wilson's Calendar" (1894).

THE FUTURE

1 I would sum up my fear about the future in one word: *boring*. And that's my one fear: that everything has happened; nothing exciting or new or interesting is ever going to happen again . . . the future is just going to be a vast, conforming *suburb of the soul*.

J. G. BALLARD (b. 1930), British author. Interview, 30 Oct. 1982, in *Re/Search*, no. 8/9 (San Francisco, 1984).

2 I have a Vision of the Future, chum.
The workers' flats in fields of soya beans
Tower up like silver pencils, score on score.

JOHN BETJEMAN (1906-84), British poet. *The Planster's Vision*, in *New Bats in Old Belfries* (1945).

3 Future. That period of time in which our affairs prosper, our friends are true and our happiness is assured.

AMBROSE BIERCE (1842-1914), U.S. author. *The Devil's Dictionary* (1881-1906).

4 All futurity
Seems teeming with endless destruction never to
be repelled;
Desperate remorse swallows the present in a
quenchless rage.

WILLIAM BLAKE (1757-1827), English poet, painter, engraver. *The Four Zoas*, "Night the Eighth" (1795-1804; published in *Complete Writings*, ed. by Geoffrey Keynes, 1957).

5 I don't try to describe the future. I try to prevent it.

RAY BRADBURY (b. 1920), U.S. writer of science fiction. Quoted by Arthur C. Clarke in: *Independent* (London, 16 July 1992).

6 Real generosity towards the future lies in giving all to the present.

ALBERT CAMUS (1913-60), French-Algerian philosopher, author. *The Rebel*, pt. 5, "Beyond Nihilism" (1951; tr. 1953).

7 The future? Like unwritten books and unborn children, you don't talk about it.

DIETRICH FISCHER-DIESKAU (b. 1925), German baritone singer. *Daily Telegraph* (London, 14 Oct. 1988).

8 The danger of the past was that men became slaves. The danger of the future is that men may become robots. True enough, robots do not rebel. But given man's nature, robots cannot live and remain sane, they become "Golems," they will destroy their world and themselves because they cannot stand any longer the boredom of a meaningless life.

ERICH FROMM (1900-1980), U.S. psychologist. *The Sane Society*, ch. 9 (1955). Fromm was referring to a speech made by Adlai Stevenson at Columbia University in 1954: "We are not in danger of becoming slaves any more, but of becoming robots."

9 We already have the statistics for the future: the growth percentages of pollution, overpopulation, desertification. The future is already in place.

GÜNTHER GRASS (b. 1927), German author. Interview in *New Statesman & Society* (London, 22 June 1990).

10 Tomorrow is an old deceiver, and his cheat never grows stale.

SAMUEL JOHNSON (1709-84), English author, lexicographer. Letter, 24 May 1773, to Hester Thrale (published in *The Letters of Samuel Johnson*, vol. 1, no. 311, ed. by R. W. Chapman, 1952).

11 A fixed image of the future is in the worst sense ahistorical.

JULIET MITCHELL (b. 1940), New Zealand author. "Women—The Longest Revolution," in *New Left Review* (London, Nov./Dec. 1966).

12 There are certain moments when we might wish the future were built by men of the past.

JEAN ROSTAND (1894-1977), French biologist, writer. *Carnets d'un Biologiste* (repr. in *The Substance of Man*, 1962, p. 196).

13 The gigantic shadows which futurity casts upon the present.

PERCY BYSSHE SHELLEY (1792-1822), English poet. *A Defence of Poetry* (written 1821; published 1840).

14 The future is made of the same stuff as the present.

SIMONE WEIL (1909-43), French philosopher, mystic. "Some Thoughts on the Love of God" (Oct. 1940-May 1942; published in *On Science, Necessity, and the Love of God*, ed. by Richard Rees, 1968).

15 It is possible to believe that all the past is but the beginning of a beginning, and that all that is and has been is but the twilight of the dawn. It is possible to believe that all the human mind has ever accomplished is but the dream before the awakening.

H. G. WELLS (1866-1946), British author. "The Discovery of the Future," lecture, 24 Jan. 1902, at the Royal Institute, London (published in *Nature*, no. 65, 1902).

16 The past is of no importance. The present is of no importance. It is with the future that we have to deal. For the past is what man should not have been. The present is what man ought not to be. The future is what artists are.

OSCAR WILDE (1854-1900), Anglo-Irish playwright, author. *The Soul of Man Under Socialism*, published in *Fortnightly Review* (London, Feb 1891; repr. 1895).

See also Orwell on The PAST; Murdoch on The PRESENT.

GALLERIES

See MUSEUMS AND GALLERIES.

GAMBLING

1   I have to confess that I had gambled on my soul and lost it with heroic insouciance and lightness of touch. The soul is so impalpable, so often useless, and sometimes such a nuisance, that I felt no more emotion on losing it than if, on a stroll, I had mislaid my visiting card.

CHARLES BAUDELAIRE (1821–67), French poet. "The Generous Gambler," in *Figaro* (Paris, 7 Feb. 1864; repr. in *Complete Works*, vol. 4,"Shorter Prose Poems," ed. by Yves-Gérard le Dantec; rev. by Claude Pichois, 1953).

2   I have a notion that gamblers are as happy as most people, being always excited; women, wine, fame, the table, even ambition, sate now & then, but every turn of the card & cast of the dice keeps the gambler alive— besides one can game ten times longer than one can do any thing else.

LORD BYRON (1788–1824), English poet. Detached Thoughts, no. 33 (1821–22; published in Byron's Letters and Journals, vol. 9, ed. by Leslie A. Marchand, 1979).

3   The world is the house of the strong. I shall not know until the end what I have lost or won in this place, in this vast gambling den where I have spent more than sixty years, dicebox in hand, shaking the dice.

DENIS DIDEROT (1713–84), French philosopher. *Elements of Physiology* "Conclusion" (written 1774–80; published 1875; repr. in *Selected Writings*, ed. by Lester G. Crocker, 1966).

4   Of all mechanics, of all servile handycrafts-men, a gamester is the vilest. But yet, as many of the quality are of the profession, he is admitted amongst the politest company.

JOHN GAY (1685–1732), English dramatist. Matt of the Mint, in *The Beggar's Opera*, act 3, sc. 4.

5   Sir, I do not call a gamester a dishonest man; but I call him an unsocial man, an unprofitable man. Gaming is a mode of transferring property without producing any intermediate good.

SAMUEL JOHNSON (1709–84), English author, lexicographer. Quoted in: James Boswell, *Life of Samuel Johnson*, 6 April 1772 (1791).

6   There are two great pleasures in gambling: that of winning and that of losing.

FRENCH PROVERB.

7   He was . . . a degenerate gambler. That is, a man who gambled simply to gamble and must lose. As a hero who goes to war must die. Show me a gambler and I'll show you a loser, show me a hero and I'll show you a corpse.

MARIO PUZO (b. 1920), U.S. novelist. *Fools Die*, ch. 2 (1978), referring to Jordan Hawley.

8   Nothing is sacred to a gamester.

BERNARD JOSEPH SAURIN (1706–81), French dramatist. Henriette, in *Beverley*, act 1, sc. 1.

9   Someone once asked me why women don't gamble as much as men do, and I gave the common-sensical reply that we don't have as much money. That was a true but incomplete answer. In fact, women's total instinct for gambling is satisfied by marriage.

GLORIA STEINEM (b. 1934), U.S. feminist writer, editor. "Night Thoughts of a Media Watcher," in *Ms.* (New York, Nov. 1981; repr. in *Outrageous Acts and Everyday Rebellions*, 1983).

10   It is the child of avarice, the brother of iniquity, and the father of mischief.

GEORGE WASHINGTON (1732–99), U.S. general, president. Letter, 15 Jan. 1783.

See also Butler on FAITH; Dostoyevsky on LOSING.

GAMES

1   No human being is innocent, but there is a class of innocent human actions called Games.

W. H. AUDEN (1907–73), Anglo-American poet. *The Dyer's Hand*, pt. 7, "Dingly Dell & The Fleet" (1962).

2   One of life's primal situations; the game of hide and seek. Oh, the delicious thrill of hiding while the others come looking for you, the delicious terror of being discovered, but what panic when, after a long search, the others abandon you! You mustn't hide too well. You mustn't be too good at the game. The player must never be bigger than the game itself.

JEAN BAUDRILLARD (b. 1929), French semiologist. *Cool Memories*, ch. 3 (1987; tr. 1990).

3   Intelligence and war are games, perhaps the only meaningful games left. If any player becomes too proficient, the game is threatened with termination.

WILLIAM BURROUGHS (b. 1914), U.S. author. *The Adding Machine*, "The Hundred Year Plan" (1985).

4   I recently learned something quite interesting about video games. Many young people have developed incredible hand, eye, and brain coordination in playing these games. The air force believes these kids will be our outstanding pilots should they fly our jets.

RONALD REAGAN (b. 1911), U.S. Republican politician, president. Statement, 8 August 1983. Quoted in: *Reagan's Reign of Error*, "Temptation of Pride" (ed. by Mark Green and Gail MacColl, 1987).

See also GAMBLING; PLAY.

MOHANDAS K. GANDHI

1   It is . . . alarming and also nauseating to see Mr. Gandhi, a seditious Middle Temple lawyer, now posing as a fakir of a type well-known in the East, striding half-naked up the steps of the Viceregal Palace, while he is still organising and conducting a defiant campaign of civil disobedience, to parley on equal terms with the representative of the King Emperor.

SIR WINSTON CHURCHILL (1874–1965), British statesman, writer. Speech, 23 Feb. 1931, Epping, England, referring to

Gandhi's release from prison in India to discuss political devolution with the Viceroy.

2 The horror of Gandhi's murder lies not in the political motives behind it or in its consequences for Indian policy or for the future of non-violence; the horror lies simply in the fact that any man could look into the face of this extraordinary person and deliberately pull a trigger.

MARY MCCARTHY (1912–89), U.S. author, critic. *On the Contrary*, pt. 1, "Gandhi" (1961; first published 1949).

GRETA GARBO

1 I want to be alone . . . I just want to be alone.

GRETA GARBO (1905–90), Swedish-born U.S. actor. *Grand Hotel*, film directed by Edmund Goulding from the novel by Vicki Baum (1932).

2 A deer in the body of a woman, living resentfully in the Hollywood zoo.

CLARE BOOTHE LUCE (1903–87), U.S. diplomat, writer. Quoted in: Leslie Halliwell, *Halliwell's Filmgoer's Companion* (1984).

3 What, when drunk, one sees in other women, one sees in Garbo sober.

KENNETH TYNAN (1927–80), British critic. *Curtains*, pt. 2, "The American Theatre" (1961).

4 "The only one who has ever been really mysterious." (Joan Crawford); "Her mystery was as thick as a London fog." (Tallulah Bankhead); "In a quick turn of her head, in a frank look, a boyish pout, in that proud glance from lowered lids, so pitying and yet so distant that in others it would be supercilious, in all those expressions of conscious beauty, which when imitated become clumsy, or arrogant, or ridiculous, there is a manifestation of what Hollywood cannot destroy. In the presence of this mystery all that is second-rate can be forgotten." (Cecil Beaton).

TRIBUTES *paid at Garbo's death, quoted in the newspaper obituaries on her death, 15 April 1990.*

See also Barthes on ACTORS.

GARDENS

1 God Almighty first planted a garden. And indeed, it is the purest of human pleasures.

FRANCIS BACON (1561–1626), English philosopher, essayist, statesman. *Essays*, "Of Gardens" (1597–1625).

2 The kiss of the sun for pardon,
The song of the birds for mirth,
One is nearer God's Heart in a garden
Than anywhere else on earth.

DOROTHY FRANCES GURNEY (1858–1932), U.S. poet. *God's Garden*.

3 Annihilating all that's made
To a green thought in a green shade.

ANDREW MARVELL (1621–78), English metaphysical poet. *The Garden*, st. 6.

4 The true gardener then brushes over the ground with slow and gentle hand, to liberate a space for breath round some favourite; but he is not thinking about destruction except incidentally. It is only the amateur like myself who becomes obsessed and rejoices with a sadistic pleasure in weeds that are big and bad enough to pull, and at last, almost forgetting the flowers altogether, turns into a Reformer.

FREYA STARK (b. 1893–1993), British travel writer. *Perseus in the Wind*, ch. 17 (1948).

5 What a man needs in gardening is a cast-iron back, with a hinge in it.

CHARLES DUDLEY WARNER (1829–1900), U.S. essayist, novelist. *My Summer in a Garden*, "Third Week" (1871).

See also FLOWERS.

GENDER

1 We are all androgynous, not only because we are all born of a woman impregnated by the seed of a man but because each of us, helplessly and forever, contains the other—male in female, female in male, white in black and black in white. We are a part of each other. Many of my countrymen appear to find this fact exceedingly inconvenient and even unfair, and so, very often, do I. But none of us can do anything about it.

JAMES BALDWIN (1924–87), U.S. author. *The Price of the Ticket*, "Here Be Dragons" (1985).

2 In sex we have the source of man's true connection with the cosmos and of his servile dependence. The categories of sex, male and female, are cosmic categories, not merely anthropological categories.

NICOLAI A. BERDYAEV (1874–1948), Russian Christian philosopher. *The Meaning of the Creative Act* (1916; repr. in *Christian Existentialism*, ch. 5, "Love," ed. by Donald A. Lowrie, 1965).

3 There is neither male nor female: for ye are all one in Christ Jesus.

BIBLE: NEW TESTAMENT. *Galatians* 3:28.

4 After centuries of conditioning of the female into the condition of perpetual girlishness called femininity, we cannot remember what femaleness is. Though feminists have been arguing for years that there is a self-defining female energy, and a female libido that is not expressed merely in response to demands by the male, and a female way of being and of experiencing the world, we are still not close to understanding what it might be. Yet every mother who has held a girl child in her arms has known that she was different from a boy child and that she would approach the reality around her in a different way . . . . She is a female and she will die female, and though many centuries should pass, archaeologists would identify her skeleton as the remains of a female creature.

GERMAINE GREER (b. 1939), Australian feminist writer. *The Change: Women, Ageing and the Menopause*, ch. 2 (1991).

5 The multitude will hardly believe the excessive force of education, and in the difference of modesty between men and women, ascribe that to nature, which is altogether owing to early instruction: *Miss* is scarce three years old, but she's spoke to every day to hide her leg, and rebuked in good earnest if she shews it; whilst *little Master* at the same age is bid to take up his coats, and piss like a man.

> BERNARD MANDEVILLE (1670–1733), Dutch-born English author, physician. *The Fable of the Bees*, "Remark (C)" (1714; rev. 1723).

6 The loss of sex polarity is part and parcel of the larger disintegration, the reflex of the soul's death, and coincident with the disappearance of great men, great deeds, great causes, great wars, etc.

> HENRY MILLER (1891–1980), U.S. author. *The Cosmological Eye*, "The Universe of Death" (1939).

7 Perhaps nothing is so depressing an index of the inhumanity of the male-supremacist mentality as the fact that the more genial human traits are assigned to the underclass: affection, response to sympathy, kindness, cheerfulness.

> KATE MILLET (b. 1934), U.S. feminist author. *Sexual Politics*, ch. 4 (1970), of a table of character traits assignable to male and female roles.

8 In the theory of gender I began from zero. There is no masculine power or privilege I did not covet. But slowly, step by step, decade by decade, I was forced to acknowledge that even a woman of abnormal will cannot escape her hormonal identity.

> CAMILLE PAGLIA (b. 1947), U.S. author, critic, educator. *Sex, Art, and American Culture*, "Sexual Personae: The Cancelled Preface" (1992).

9 To be sure he's a "Man," the male must see to it that the female be clearly a "Woman," the opposite of a "Man," that is, the female must act like a faggot.

> VALERIE SOLANAS (b. 1940), U.S. artist, writer. *The SCUM Manifesto* (1968).

10 It would be futile to attempt to fit women into a masculine pattern of attitudes, skills and abilities and disastrous to force them to suppress their specifically female characteristics and abilities by keeping up the pretense that there are no differences between the sexes.

> ARIANNA STASSINOPOULOS (b. 1950), Greek author. *The Female Woman*, "The Natural Woman" (1973).

11 Except for their genitals, I don't know what immutable differences exist between men and women. Perhaps there are some other unchangeable differences; probably there are a number of irrelevant differences. But it is clear that until social expectations for men and women are equal, until we provide equal respect for both sexes, answers to this question will simply reflect our prejudices.

> NAOMI WEISSTEIN (b. 1939), U.S. psychologist, author. "Woman as Nigger," in *Psychology Today* (New York, Oct. 1969).

12 It would be a thousand pities if women wrote like men, or lived like men, or looked like men, for if two sexes are quite inadequate, considering the vastness and variety of the world, how should we manage with one only? Ought not education to bring out and fortify the

differences rather than the similarities? For we have too much likeness as it is, and if an explorer should come back and bring word of other sexes looking through the branches of other trees at other skies, nothing would be of greater service to humanity; and we should have the immense pleasure into the bargain of watching Professor X rush for his measuring-rods to prove himself "superior."

> VIRGINIA WOOLF (1882–1941), British novelist. *A Room of One's Own*, ch. 5 (1929).

13 Different though the sexes are, they inter-mix. In every human being a vacillation from one sex to the other takes place, and often it is only the clothes that keep the male or female likeness, while underneath the sex is very opposite of what it is above.

> VIRGINIA WOOLF (1882–1941), British novelist. *Orlando* (1928; p. 172).

See also MEN AND WOMEN.

GENERALIZATIONS

1 To generalize is to be an idiot. To particularize is the alone distinction of merit. General knowledges are those knowledges that idiots possess.

> WILLIAM BLAKE (1757–1827), English poet, painter, engraver. Annotations to Sir Joshua Reynolds, *Discourses*, "Discourse II" (c. 1808; repr. in *Complete Writings*, ed. by Geoffrey Keynes, 1957).

2 An idea is always a generalization, and generalization is a property of thinking. To generalize means to think.

> GEORG HEGEL (1770–1831), German philosopher. *The Philosophy of Right*, "Introduction," addition 4 (1821; tr. 1942).

3 We are more prone to generalize the bad than the good. We assume that the bad is more potent and contagious.

> ERIC HOFFER (1902–83), U.S. philosopher. *Reflections on the Human Condition*, aph. 162 (1973).

4 A sweeping statement is the only statement worth listening to. The critic without faith gives balanced opinions, usually about second-rate writers.

> PATRICK KAVANAGH (1905–67), Irish poet, author. *Collected Prose*, "Signposts" (1967).

5 Generalisation is necessary to the advancement of knowledge; but particularly is indispensable to the creations of the imagination. In proportion as men know more and think more they look less at individuals and more at classes. They therefore make better theories and worse poems.

> THOMAS, BABINGTON MACAULAY (1800–1859), English historian. "Milton," in *Edinburgh Review* (Aug. 1825; repr. in *Critical and Historical Essays*, 1843).

6 Obvious enough that generalities work to protect the mind from the great outdoors; is it possible that this was in fact their first purpose?

> HOWARD NEMEROV (1920–91), U.S. poet, novelist, critic. *Journal of the Fictive Life*, "Reflexions of the Novelist Felix Ledger," sct. C (1965).

7 Any general statement is like a cheque drawn on a bank. Its value depends on what is there to meet it.

> EZRA POUND (1885–1972), U.S. poet, critic. *ABC of Reading*, ch. 1, sct. 2 (1934).

GENERALS

1 I am convinced that the best service a retired general can perform is to turn in his tongue along with his suit, and to mothball his opinions.

> OMAR NELSON BRADLEY (1893–1981), U.S. general. Armed Forces Day address. Quoted in: *New York Times* (17 May 1959).

2 Humility must always be the portion of any man who receives acclaim earned in the blood of his followers and the sacrifices of his friends.

> DWIGHT D. EISENHOWER (1890–1969), U.S. general, Republican politician, president. Speech, 12 July 1945, Guildhall, London.

3 In enterprise of martial kind,
When there was any fighting,
He led his regiment from behind—
He found it less exciting.

> W. S. GILBERT (1836–1911), English librettist. Duke of Plaza-Toro, in *The Gondoliers*, act 1.

4 I think with the Romans, that the general of today should be a soldier tomorrow if necessary.

> THOMAS JEFFERSON (1743–1826), U.S. president. Letter, 1 Jan. 1797, to James Madison, congressman and later president.

5 The Creator has not thought proper to mark those in the forehead who are of stuff to make good generals. We are first, therefore, to seek them blindfold, and then let them learn the trade at the expense of great losses.

> THOMAS JEFFERSON (1743–1826), U.S. president. Letter, 6 Feb. 1813.

6 Tell me what brand of whiskey that Grant drinks. I would like to send a barrel of it to my other generals.

> Attributed to ABRAHAM LINCOLN (1809–65), U.S. president. Quoted in: *New York Herald* (26 Nov. 1863), in reply to comments about Grant's drinking habits.

7 Like the old soldier of the ballad, I now close my military career and just fade away, an old soldier who tried to do his duty as God gave him the light to see that duty. Goodbye.

> DOUGLAS MACARTHUR (1880–1964), U.S. general. Speech, 19 April 1951, to Congress, on his dismissal from command of UN forces in Korea, for dissenting with the Truman administration's conduct of the war. Truman called the speech "nothing but a bunch of damn bullshit," in Merle Miller, *Plain Speaking: Conversations with Harry S Truman*, ch. 25 (1973). The "ballad" referred to by MacArthur was a popular barrack-room ditty, which originated in a British army World War I song.

8 A general is just as good or just as bad as the troops under his command make him.

> DOUGLAS MACARTHUR (1880–1964), U.S. general. Speech, 16 Aug. 1962, on receiving a Congressional resolution of gratitude.

9 The nearest the modern general or admiral comes to a small-arms encounter of any sort is at a duck hunt in the company of corporation executives at the retreat of Continental Motors, Inc.

> C. WRIGHT MILLS (1916–62), U.S. sociologist. *The Power Elite*, ch. 8 (1956).

10 I made all my generals out of mud.

> NAPOLEON BONAPARTE (1769–1821), French general, emperor. Quoted in: Ralph Waldo Emerson, *Representative Men*, "Napoleon" (1850).

11 To a surprising extent the war-lords in shining armour, the apostles of the martial virtues, tend not to die fighting when the time comes. History is full of ignominious getaways by the great and famous.

> GEORGE ORWELL (1903–50), British author. "Who Are the War Criminals?" (1943; repr. in *The Collected Essays, Journalism and Letters of George Orwell*, vol. 2, ed. by Sonia Orwell and Ian Angus, 1968).

12 One murder made a villain,
Millions a hero.

> BEILBY PORTEUS (1731–1808), English clergyman, writer. *Death*. The remark was revived in Charlie Chaplin's 1947 film *Monsieur Verdoux..*

13 The general who advances without coveting fame and retreats without fearing disgrace, whose only thought is to protect his country and do good service for his sovereign, is the jewel of the kingdom.

> SUN TZU (6th-5th century B.C.), Chinese general. *The Art of War*, ch. 10, axiom 24 (c. 490 B.C.; ed. by James Clavell, 1981).

14 Perfect soldier, perfect gentleman . . . never gave offence to anyone not even the enemy.

> A. J. P. TAYLOR (1906–90), British historian. Letter, 16 March 1973 (published in *Letters to Eva*, ed. by Eva Haraszti Taylor, 1991), referring to Field Marshal Alexander.

15 The best generals I have known were . . . stupid or absent-minded men . . . . Not only does a good army commander not need any special qualities, on the contrary he needs the absence of the highest and best human attributes—love, poetry, tenderness, and philosophic inquiring doubt. He should be limited, firmly convinced that what he is doing is very important (otherwise he will not have sufficient patience), and only then will he be a brave leader. God forbid that he should be humane, should love, or pity, or think of what is just and unjust.

> LEO TOLSTOY (1828–1910), Russian novelist, philosopher. Prince Andrew, in *War and Peace*, bk. 9, ch. 11 (1868–9).

See also The ARMY.

GENERATIONS

1 One generation passeth away, and another generation cometh: but the earth abideth for ever. The sun also ariseth, and the sun goeth down, and hasteth to the place where he arose.

> BIBLE, HEBREW. *Ecclesiastes* 1:4,5. Ernest Hemingway's book title *The Sun Also Rises* (1926) comes from this passage.

2 The generations of men run on in the tide of time,

But leave their destined lineaments permanent for ever & ever.

> WILLIAM BLAKE (1757–1827), English poet, painter, engraver. *Milton*, plate 22 (repr. in *Complete Writings*, ed. by Geoffrey Keynes, 1957).

3 Twenty can't be expected to tolerate sixty in all things, and sixty gets bored stiff with twenty's eternal love affairs.

> EMILY CARR (1871–1945), Canadian artist. *Hundreds and Thousands: The Journals of Emily Carr* (1966), entry for 12 Aug. 1934.

4 The dead might as well try to speak to the living as the old to the young.

> WILLA CATHER (1873–1947), U.S. author. *One of Ours*, bk. 2, ch. 6 (1922).

5 Eighteen might look at thirty-four through a rising mist of adolescence; but twenty-two would see thirty-eight with discerning clarity.

> F. SCOTT FITZGERALD (1896–1940), U.S. author. *Tender Is the Night*, bk. 2, ch. 19 (1934).

6 We may consider each generation as a distinct nation, with a right, by the will of its majority, to bind themselves, but none to bind the succeeding generation, more than the inhabitants of another country.

> THOMAS JEFFERSON (1743–1826), U.S. president. Letter, 24 June 1813, on the incurring of a national debt.

7 Our tastes greatly alter. The lad does not care for the child's rattle, and the old man does not care for the young man's whore.

> SAMUEL JOHNSON (1709–84), English author, lexicographer. Quoted in: James Boswell, *Life of Samuel Johnson*, Spring 1776 (1791).

8 We have to hate our immediate predecessors to get free of their authority.

> D. H. LAWRENCE (1885–1930), British author. Quoted in: Henry Miller, *The Wisdom of the Heart*, "Creative Death" (1941).

9 From the earliest times the old have rubbed it into the young that they are wiser than they, and before the young had discovered what nonsense this was they were old too, and it profited them to carry on the imposture.

> W. SOMERSET MAUGHAM (1874–1965), British author. Ashenden, in *Cakes and Ale*, ch. 11 (1930).

10 It's all that the young can do for the old, to shock them and keep them up to date.

> GEORGE BERNARD SHAW (1856–1950), Anglo-Irish playwright, critic. *Fanny's First Play*, "Induction" (1912).

11 The old know what they want; the young are sad and bewildered.

> LOGAN PEARSALL SMITH (1865–1946), U.S. essayist, aphorist. *All Trivia*, "Last Words" (1933).

12 Nothing so dates a man as to decry the younger generation.

> ADLAI STEVENSON (1900–1965), U.S. Democratic politician. Speech, 8 Oct. 1952, University of Wisconsin.

13 I suppose you think that persons who are as old as your father and myself are always thinking about very grave things, but I know that we are meditating the same old themes that we did when we were ten years old, only we go more gravely about it.

> HENRY DAVID THOREAU (1817–62), U.S. philosopher, author, naturalist. Letter, 31 July 1849, to Ellen Emerson (then 10 years old), eldest child of Ralph Waldo Emerson (published in *The Correspondence of Henry David Thoreau*, 1958).

14 I avoid talking before the youth of the age as I would dancing before them: for if one's tongue don't move in the steps of the day, and thinks to please by its old graces, it is only an object of ridicule.

> HORACE WALPOLE (1717–97), English author. Letter, 15 April 1768.

15 It is fortunate that each generation does not comprehend its own ignorance. We are thus enabled to call our ancestors barbarous.

> CHARLES DUDLEY WARNER (1829–1900), U.S. editor, author. *Backlog Studies*, "Second Study" (1873).

16 A man's liberal and conservative phases seem to follow each other in a succession of waves from the time he is born. Children are radicals. Youths are conservatives, with a dash of criminal negligence. Men in their prime are liberals (as long as their digestion keeps pace with their intellect). The middle aged . . . run to shelter: they insure their life, draft a will, accumulate mementos and occasional tables, and hope for security. And then comes old age, which repeats childhood—a time full of humors and sadness, but often full of courage and even prophecy.

> E. B. WHITE (1899–1985), U.S. author, editor. "Life Phases," in *New Yorker* (20 Feb. 1937; repr. in *Writings from the New Yorker 1927–1976*, ed. by Rebecca M. Dale, 1991).

17 The old believe everything; the middle-aged suspect everything; the young know everything.

> OSCAR WILDE (1854–1900), Anglo-Irish playwright, author. "Phrases and Philosophies for the Use of the Young," in *Chameleon* (London, Dec. 1894).

18 The longer I live the more keenly I feel that whatever was good enough for our fathers is not good enough for us.

> OSCAR WILDE (1854–1900), Anglo-Irish playwright, author. Lord Henry, in the *The Picture of Dorian Gray*, ch. 4 (1891).

See also AGE AND AGING: Addison on INJURY; Burke on YOUTH; Johnson on YOUTH AND AGE.

GENEROSITY

1 It is always so pleasant to be generous, though very vexatious to pay debts.

> RALPH WALDO EMERSON (1803–82), U.S. essayist, poet, philosopher. *Essays*, "Gifts" (Second Series, 1844).

2 People who think they're generous to a fault usually think that's their only fault.

> SYDNEY J. HARRIS (b. 1917), U.S. journalist. *On the Contrary*, ch. 7 (1962).

3 There is sublime thieving in all giving. Someone gives us all he has and we are his.

> ERIC HOFFER (1902–83), U.S. philosopher. *The Passionate State of Mind*, aph. 236 (1955).

4 Sir, he throws away his money without thought and without merit. I do not call a tree generous that sheds its fruit at every breeze.

> SAMUEL JOHNSON (1709–84), English author, lexicographer. Quoted in: James Boswell, *Tour of the Hebrides* (1785), referring to English sailors.

5 Generosity lies less in giving much than in giving at the right moment.

> JEAN DE LA BRUYÈRE (1645–96), French writer, moralist. *Characters*, "Of the Heart," aph. 47 (1688).

6 What is called generosity is usually only the vanity of giving; we enjoy the vanity more than the thing given.

> FRANÇOIS, DUC DE LA ROCHEFOUCAULD (1613–80), French writer, moralist. *Sentences et Maximes Morales*, no. 263 (1678).

7 Generosity is nothing else than a craze to possess. All which I abandon, all which I give, I enjoy in a higher manner through the fact that I give it away . . . . To give is to enjoy possessively the object which one gives.

> JEAN-PAUL SARTRE (1905–80), French philosopher, author. *Being and Nothingness*, "Doing and Having," sct. 2 (1943; tr. 1965).

8 Give all thou canst; high Heaven rejects the lore
Of nicely-calculated less or more.

> WILLIAM WORDSWORTH (1770–1850), English poet. *Tax Not the Royal Saint.*

See also GIFTS AND GIVING; Lever on GOVERNMENT.

GENIUS

1 To do easily what is difficult for others is the mark of talent. To do what is impossible for talent is the mark of genius.

> HENRI-FRÉDÉRIC AMIEL (1821–81), Swiss philosopher, poet. *Journal Intime* (1882; tr. by Mrs. Humphry Ward, 1892), entry for 17 Dec. 1856.

2 We know that the nature of genius is to provide idiots with ideas twenty years later.

> LOUIS ARAGON (1897–1982), French poet. *Treatise on Style*, pt. 1, "The Pen" (1928).

3 There are big men, men of intellect, intellectual men, men of talent and men of action; but the great man is difficult to find, and it needs—apart from discernment—a certain greatness to find him.

> MARGOT ASQUITH (1864–1945), British socialite. *The Autobiography of Margot Asquith*, vol. 1, ch. 8 (1920).

4 Genius is no more than childhood recaptured at will, childhood equipped now with man's physical means to express itself, and with the analytical mind that enables it to bring order into the sum of experience, involuntarily amassed.

> CHARLES BAUDELAIRE (1821–67), French poet. "The Painter of Modern life," sct. 3, in *L'Art Romantique* (1869; repr. in *Selected Writings on Art and Artists*, ed. by P. E. Charvet, 1972).

5 Men of genius are not quick judges of character.

Deep thinking and high imagining blunt that trivial instinct by which you and I size people up.

> SIR MAX BEERBOHM (1872–1956), British author. *And Even Now*, "Quia Imperfectum" (1920).

6 What is genius—but the power of expressing a new individuality?

> ELIZABETH BARRETT BROWNING (1806–61), English poet. Letter, 14 Jan. 1843, to author Mary Russell Mitford (published in *Elizabeth Barrett to Miss Mitford*, 1954).

7 A genius can never expect to have a good time anywhere, if he is a genuine article, but America is about the last place in which life will be endurable at all for an inspired writer of any kind.

> SAMUEL BUTLER (1835–1902), English author. *Samuel Butler's Notebooks* (1951, p. 257).

8 I really cannot know whether I am or am not the Genius you are pleased to call me, but I am very willing to put up with the mistake, if it be one. It is a title dearly enough bought by most men, to render it endurable, even when not quite clearly made out, which it never *can* be till the Posterity, whose decisions are merely dreams to ourselves, has sanctioned or denied it, while it can touch us no further.

> LORD BYRON (1788–1824), English poet. Letter, 10 June 1822, to author Isaac D'Israeli (published in *Byron's Letters and Journals*, vol. 9, ed. by Leslie A. Marchand, 1979).

9 What Romantic terminology called genius or talent or inspiration is nothing other than finding the right road empirically, following one's nose, taking shortcuts.

> ITALO CALVINO (1923–85), Italian author, critic. "Cybernetics and Ghosts," lecture, Nov. 1969, Turin (published in *The Literature Machine*, 1987).

10 The eye of genius has always a plaintive expression, and its natural language is pathos.

> LYDIA M. CHILD (1802–80), U.S. abolitionist, writer, editor. Letter, 27 April 1843 (published in *Letters from New York*, vol. 1, letter 39, 1843).

11 Genius, like truth, has a shabby and neglected mien.

> EDWARD DAHLBERG (1900–1977), U.S. author, critic. *Alms for Oblivion*, "For Sale" (1964).

12 Few people can see genius in someone who has offended them.

> ROBERTSON DAVIES (b. 1913), Canadian novelist, journalist. "Dylan Thomas and Hector Berlioz," in *Saturday Night* (Canada, 9 June 1956; repr. in *The Enthusiasms of Robertson Davies*, 1990).

13 What makes men of genius, or rather, what they make, is not new ideas, it is that idea—possessing them—that what has been said has still not been said enough.

> EUGÈNE DELACROIX (1798–1863), French artist. *The Journal of Eugène Delacroix* (tr. by Walter Pach, 1937), entry for 15 May 1824.

14 Genius is present in every age, but the men carrying it within them remain benumbed unless extraordinary events occur to heat up and melt the mass so that it flows forth.

> DENIS DIDEROT (1713–84), French philosopher. *On Dramatic*

Poetry (1758; repr. in *Selected Writings*, ed. by Lester G. Crocker, 1966).

15 Genius, when young, is divine.

BENJAMIN DISRAELI (1804–81), English statesman, author. Sidonia, in *Coningsby*, bk. 3, ch. 1 (1844).

16 Mediocrity knows nothing higher than itself, but talent instantly recognizes genius.

SIR ARTHUR CONAN DOYLE (1859–1930), English author. *The Valley of Fear*, ch. 1 (1915).

17 Great wits are sure to madness near allied,
And thin partitions do their bounds divide.

JOHN DRYDEN (1631–1700), English poet, dramatist, critic. *Absalom and Achitophel*, pt. 1.

18 Genius at first is little more than a great capacity for receiving discipline.

GEORGE ELIOT (1819–80), English novelist, editor. Kleismer, in *Daniel Deronda*, bk. 3, ch. 23 (1876).

19 In every work of genius we recognize our own rejected thoughts: they come back to us with a certain alienated majesty.

RALPH WALDO EMERSON (1803–82), U.S. essayist, poet, philosopher. *Essays*, "Self-Reliance" (First Series, 1841).

20 The hearing ear is always found close to the speaking tongue; and no genius can long or often utter anything which is not invited and gladly entertained by men around him.

RALPH WALDO EMERSON (1803–82), U.S. essayist, poet, philosopher. *English Traits*, "Race" (1856).

21 Everybody hates a prodigy, detests an old head on young shoulders.

DESIDERIUS ERASMUS (c. 1466–1536), Dutch humanist. *Praise of Folly*, ch. 13 (1509).

22 Genius goes around the world in its youth incessantly apologizing for having large feet. What wonder that later in life it should be inclined to raise those feet too swiftly to fools and bores.

F. SCOTT FITZGERALD (1896–1940), U.S. author. *The Crack-Up*, "Notebook E" (ed. by Edmund Wilson, 1945).

23 It is not because the touch of genius has roused genius to production, but because the admiration of genius has made talent ambitious, that the harvest is still so abundant.

MARGARET FULLER (1810–50), U.S. writer, lecturer. *Art, Literature and the Drama*, "The Modern Drama" (1858).

24 Unpretending mediocrity is good, and genius is glorious; but a weak flavor of genius in an essentially common person is detestable. It spoils the grand neutrality of a commonplace character, as the rinsings of an unwashed wine-glass spoil a draught of fair water.

OLIVER WENDELL HOLMES, SR. (1809–94), U.S. writer, physician. *The Autocrat of the Breakfast-Table*, ch. 1 (1858).

25 Saying that a great genius is mad, while at the same time recognizing his artistic worth, is like saying that he had rheumatism or suffered from diabetes. Madness, in fact, is a medical term that can claim no more notice from the objective critic than he grants the charge of heresy raised by the theologian, or the charge of immorality raised by the police.

JAMES JOYCE (1882–1941), Irish author. "William Blake," lecture, March 1912, Università Popolare Triestina (published in *Critical Writings*, sct. 43, ed. by Ellsworth Mason and Richard Ellmann, 1959).

26 Genius sits in a glass house—but in an unbreakable one—conceiving ideas. After giving birth, it falls into madness. Stretches out its hand through the window toward the first person happening by. The demon's claw rips, the iron fist grips. Before, you were a model, mocks the ironic voice between serrated teeth, for me, you are raw material to work on. I throw you against the glass wall, so that you remain stuck there, projected and stuck . . . . (Then come the lovers of art and contemplate the bleeding work from outside. Then come the photographers. "New art," it says in the newspaper the following day. The learned journals give it a name that ends in "ism.")

PAUL KLEE (1879–1940), Swiss artist.)*The Diaries of Paul Klee 1898–1918*, no. 690 (1957; tr. 1965), Aug. 1905 entry.

27 Who in the same given time can produce more than others has *vigor*; who can produce more and better, has *talents*; who can produce what none else can, has *genius*.

JOHANN KASPAR LAVATER (1741–1801), Swiss divine, poet. *Aphorisms on Man*, no. 23 (1788).

28 What I do not like about our definitions of genius is that there is in them nothing of the day of judgment, nothing of resounding through eternity and nothing of the footsteps of the Almighty.

G. C. LICHTENBERG (1742–99), German physicist, philosopher. *Aphorisms*, "Notebook E," aph. 92 (written 1765–99; tr. by R. J. Hollingdale, 1990).

29 Better beware of notions like genius and inspiration; they are a sort of magic wand and should be used sparingly by anybody who wants to see things clearly.

JOSÉ ORTEGA Y GASSET (1883–1955), Spanish essayist, philosopher. *Notes on the Novel*, "Decline of the Novel" (1925).

30 It is personality with a penny's worth of talent. Error which chances to rise above the commonplace.

PABLO PICASSO (1881–1973), Spanish artist. Quoted in: Jaime Sabartés, *Picasso: portraits et souvenirs*, ch. 9 (1946), commenting on genius.

31 The genius of Einstein leads to Hiroshima.

PABLO PICASSO (1881–1973), Spanish artist. Remark, 1946, to Françoise Gilot. Quoted in: Françoise Gilot and Carlton Lake, pt. 2, *Life with Picasso* (1964).

32 A man of genius has a right to any mode of expression.

EZRA POUND (1885–1972), U.S. poet, critic. Letter, 4 Feb. 1918, to the painter J. B. Yeats (father of W. B. Yeats). Quoted in: Humphrey Carpenter, *A Serious Character*, pt. 2, ch. 10 (1988).

33 One of the satisfactions of a genius is his will-power and obstinacy.

MAN RAY (1890–1976), U.S. photographer. Letter, 18 May 1941 to his sister. Quoted in: Neil Baldwin, *Man Ray* (1988).

34 Genius is, to be sure, not a matter of arbitrariness, but rather of freedom, just as wit, love, and faith, which once shall become arts and disciplines. We should demand genius from everybody, without, however, expecting it.

FRIEDRICH SCHLEGEL (1772–1829), German philosopher, critic, writer. *Dialogue on Poetry and Literary Aphorisms,* "Selected Aphorisms from *The Lyceum,* aph. 16 (1968; first published 1797).

35 Great minds are related to the brief span of time during which they live as great buildings are to a little square in which they stand: you cannot see them in all their magnitude because you are standing too close to them.

ARTHUR SCHOPENHAUER (1788–1860), German philosopher. *Parerga and Paralipomena,* vol. 2, ch. 20, sct. 242 (1851).

36 It takes a lot of time to be a genius, you have to sit around so much doing nothing, really doing nothing.

GERTRUDE STEIN (1874–1946), U.S. author. *Everybody's Autobiography,* ch. 2 (1937).

37 Every man is a potential genius until he does something.

SIR HERBERT BEERBOHM TREE (1853–1917), English actormanager. Quoted in: Hesketh Pearson, *Beerbohm-Tree* ch. 12 (1956).

38 Thousands of geniuses live and die undiscovered—either by themselves or by others.

MARK TWAIN (1835–1910), U.S. author. *Autobiography,* ch. 27 (ed. by Charles Neider, 1959).

39 Real genius is nothing else but the supernatural virtue of humility in the domain of thought.

SIMONE WEIL (1909–43), French philosopher, mystic. "Human Personality," published in *La Table Ronde* (Dec. 1950; repr. in *Selected Essays,* ed. by Richard Rees, 1962).

40 Everybody denies I am a genius—but nobody ever called me one!

ORSON WELLES (1915–85), U.S. filmmaker. Quoted in: Leslie Halliwell, *Halliwell's Filmgoer's Companion* (1984).

41 Genius lasts longer than Beauty. That accounts for the fact that we all take such pains to over-educate ourselves.

OSCAR WILDE (1854–1900), Anglo-Irish playwright, author. Lord Henry, in *The Picture of Dorian Grey,* ch. 1 (1891).

42 I put all my genius into my life; I put only my talent into my works.

OSCAR WILDE (1854–1900), Anglo-Irish playwright, author. Quoted in: André Gide, *Journals 1889–1949* (1951), entry for 29 June 1913.

43 Masterpieces are not single and solitary births; they are the outcome of many years of thinking in common, of thinking by the body of the people, so that the experience of the mass is behind the single voice.

VIRGINIA WOOLF (1882–1941), British novelist. *A Room of One's Own,* ch. 4 (1929).

See also Lichtenberg on ADVERSITY; Picasso on CHILDHOOD; Lichtenberg on GREATNESS; Browning on RESPECTABILITY; Pope on SCIENCE; Wilde on SELF-IMAGE; Hazlitt on SHAKESPEARE; Longfellow on SOCIABILITY; Picasso on SUCCESS.

GENOCIDE

1 Better extirpate the whole breed, root and branch. And this, unless the German people come to their senses, is what we propose to do.

GERTRUDE ATHERTON (1857–1948), U.S. novelist. *New York Times* (18 Aug. 1918), from one of a series of articles Atherton wrote to bolster the war effort. She later admitted in her autobiography, "Virulent was a weak word for those articles."

2 Genocide begins, however improbably, in the conviction that classes of biological distinction indisputably sanction social and political discrimination.

ANDREA DWORKIN (b. 1946), U.S. feminist critic. *Letters from a War-Zone,* "Biological Superiority: The World's Most Dangerous and Deadly Idea," sct. 3 (1987; first published 1978).

3 People are inexterminable—like flies and bedbugs. There will always be some that survive in cracks and crevices—that's us.

ROBERT FROST (1874–1963), U.S. poet. Quoted in: *Observer* (London, 29 March 1959).

See also Herzog on KILLING.

GENTLEMEN

1 I am parshial to ladies if they are nice[.] I suppose it is my nature. I am not quite a gentleman but you would hardly notice it.

DAISY ASHFORD (1881–1972), British writer. Alfred Salteena, in *The Young Visiters,* "Quite a Young Girl" (written when the author was aged nine; published 1919).

2 Whom do we dub as Gentleman? The
Knave, the fool, the brute—
If they but own full tithe of gold, and
Wear a courtly suit.

ELIZA COOK (1818–89), English poet. *Nature's Gentleman,* st. 1.

3 I do not know the American gentleman, God forgive me for putting two such words together.

CHARLES DICKENS (1812–70), English novelist. Quoted in: Hesketh Pearson, *Dickens,* ch. 8 (1949).

4 Gentleman. A man who buys two of the same morning paper from the doorman of his favorite nightclub when he leaves with his girl.

MARLENE DIETRICH (1904–92), German-born U.S. film actor. *Marlene Dietrich's ABC,* "Gentleman" (1962).

5 Repose and cheerfulness are the badge of the gentleman,—repose in energy.

RALPH WALDO EMERSON (1803–82), U.S. essayist, poet, philosopher. *The Conduct of Life,* "Culture" (1860).

6 Being a gentleman is the number one priority, the chief question integral to our national life.

EDWARD FOX (b. 1934), British stage and screen actor. Quoted in: *Daily Telegraph* (London, 14 Feb. 1992).

7 He was the product of an English public school and university. He was, moreover, a modern product of those

seats of athletic exercise. He had little education and highly devloped muscles—that is to say, he was no scholar, but essentially a gentleman.

> H. SETON MERRIMAN (1862–1903), English novelist. *The Sowers,* ch. 1 (1896), of Alexis.

8 For everybody knows that it requires very little to satisfy the gentlemen, if a woman will only give her mind to it.

> MARGARET OLIPHANT (1828–97), English novelist, historian. *Miss Marjoribanks,* ch. 13 (1866), no. 4 of *Chronicles of Carlingford.*

9 Anyone can be heroic from time to time, but a gentleman is something you have to be all the time.

> LUIGI PIRANDELLO (1867–1936), Italian author, playwright. Maurizio, in *The Pleasure of Honesty,* act 1.

10 Believe me, there exists no such dilemma as that in which a gentleman is placed when he is forced to reply to a blackguard.

> EDGAR ALLAN POE (1809–45), U.S. poet, critic, short-story writer. Letter, 4 Jan. 1848 (published in Julian Symons, *The Tell-Tale Heart: The Life and Works of Edgar Allan Poe,* pt. 1, ch. 13, 1978).

11 Education begins a gentleman, conversation completes him.

> ENGLISH PROVERB (18th century). Collected in: Thomas Fuller, *Gnomologia* (1732).

12 He is every other inch a gentleman.

> REBECCA WEST (1892–1983), British author. Quoted in: Victoria Glendinning, *Rebecca West,* pt. 3, ch. 5 (1987), referring to novelist Michael Arlen. Columnist and wit Alexander Woollcott is also credited with this remark about Arlen in *Wit's End* (ed. by Robert E. Drennan, 1968).

See also Cromwell on The ARMY; Wilde on EXAMINATIONS; Macaulay on The NAVY; Congreve on UNIVERSITIES AND COLLEGES; Maugham on WRITERS.

GERMANY AND THE GERMANS

1 A frightful dialect for the stupid, the pedant and dullard sort.

> THOMAS CARLYLE (1795–1881), Scottish essayist, historian. *History of Frederick II,* vol. 1 (1858–65), on the German language. Carlyle's attitude to German was no doubt influenced by his difficulty in mastering it; he qualified his dislike by adding, "in the hands of the gifted does it become supremely good." He later became adept in the language, and greatly influenced by it.

2 The tears I have cried over Germany have dried. I have washed my face.

> MARLENE DIETRICH (1904–92), German-born U.S. film actor. *Marlene Dietrich's ABC,* "Germany" (1962).

3 It's like the Beatles coming together again—let's hope they don't go on a world tour.

> MATT FREI, British journalist. Quoted in: *Listener* (London, 21 June 1990), on German reunification.

4 They came, they saw, they did a little shopping.

> REPORT, *NEWSWEEK* (New York, 4 Dec. 1989). Graffito on the Berlin wall, following the influx of thousands of East Berliners into West Berlin after the lifting of travel restrictions.

5 The German language "speaks Being," while all the others merely "speak of Being."

> MARTIN HEIDEGGER (1889–1976), German philosopher. Quoted in: Frank Kermode, *An Appetite for Poetry: Essays in Literary Interpretation,* Prologue (1989).

6 In action, the English have the advantage enjoyed by free men always entitled to free discussion: of having a ready judgment on every question. We Germans, on the other hand, are always thinking. We think so much that we never form a judgment.

> HEINRICH HEINE (1797–1856), German poet, journalist. *French Affairs,* "The English Freedom" (1832; repr. in *Heinrich Heine: Works of Prose,* ed. by Hermann Kesten, 1943).

7 Germany will either be a world power or will not be at all.

> ADOLF HITLER (1889–1945), German dictator. *Mein Kampf,* vol. 2, ch. 14 (1925).

8 How much atonement is enough? The bombing must be allowed as at least part-payment: those of our young people who are concerned about the moral problem posed by the Allied air offensive should at least consider the moral problem that would have been posed if the German civilian population had not suffered at all.

> CLIVE JAMES (b. 1939), Australian writer, critic. "Postcard from Munich," in *Observer* (13 Feb. 1983; repr in *Flying Visits,* 1984).

9 Everybody should know that Germany will not go it alone: there will be no restless Reich.

> HELMUT KOHL (b. 1930), German politician, Chancellor. Quoted in: *International Herald Tribune* (Paris; 3 Oct. 1990).

10 Germany is a queer country: one can't regard it dispassionately. I alternate between hating it thoroughly, stick stock and stone, and yearning over it fit to break my heart. I can't help feeling it a young and adorable country—adolescent—with the faults of adolescence.

> D. H. LAWRENCE (1885–1930), British author. Letter, 22 Aug. 1914, to poet Amy Lowell (published in *The Letters of D. H. Lawrence,* vol. 2, ed. by George J. Zytaruk and James T. Boulton, 1981). England had declared war on Germany on 4 Aug. 1914.

11 Unhappy German nation, how do you like the Messianic rôle allotted to you, not by God, nor by destiny, but by a handful of perverted and bloody-minded men.

> THOMAS MANN (1875–1955), German author, critic. *Order of the Day,* "This War" (1942; first published 1939).

12 I love Germany so dearly that I hope there will always be two of them.

> FRANÇOIS MAURIAC (1885–1970), French author. Quoted in: *Newsweek* (New York, 20 Nov. 1989).

13 The Teutons have been singing the swan song ever since they entered the ranks of history. They have always confounded truth with death.

> HENRY MILLER (1891–1980), U.S. author. *Plexus,* ch. 17 (1963). Miller was discussing Nietzsche and Spengler.

14 Everything ponderous, viscous, and pompously clumsy, all long-winded and wearying species of style are developed in profuse variety among Germans.

> FRIEDRICH NIETZSCHE (1844–1900), German philosopher. *Beyond Good and Evil,* ch. 2, aph. 28 (1886).

15 The Germans—once they were called the nation of thinkers: do they still think at all? Nowadays the Germans are bored with intellect, the Germans mistrust intellect, politics devours all seriousness for really intellectual things—*Deutschland, Deutschland über alles* was, I fear, the end of German philosophy.

FRIEDRICH NIETZSCHE (1844–1900), German philosopher. *Twilight of the Idols,* "What the Germans Lack," aph. 1 (1889).

16 How much dreary heaviness, lameness, dampness, sloppiness, how much *beer* there is in the German intellect!

FRIEDRICH NIETZSCHE (1844–1900), German philosopher. *Twilight of the Idols,* "What the Germans Lack," aph. 2 (1889).

17 West Germans are tall, pert and orthodontically corrected, with hands, teeth and hair as clean as their clothes and clothes as sharp as their looks. Except for the fact that they all speak English pretty well, they're indistinguishable from Americans.

P. J. O'ROURKE (b. 1947), U.S. journalist. "The Death of Communism," in *Rolling Stone* (Nov. 1989; repr. in *Give War a Chance,* 1992).

18 Germany has reduced savagery to a science, and this great war for the victorious peace of justice must go on until the German cancer is cut clean out of the world body.

THEODORE ROOSEVELT (1858–1919), U.S. Republican (later Progressive) politician, president. Speech, 30 Sept. 1917, Johnstown, Pennsylvania.

19 When they are not at war they do a little hunting, but spend most of their time in idleness, sleeping and eating. The strongest and most warlike do nothing. They vegetate, while the care of hearth and home and fields is left to the women, the old and the weak. Strange inconsistency of temperament, which makes the same men lovers of sloth and haters of tranquility.

TACITUS (c. 55–c. 120), Roman historian. *Germania,* sct. 15 (98).

20 I can *understand* German as well as the maniac that invented it, but I *talk* it best through an interpreter.

MARK TWAIN (1835–1910), U.S. author. Quoted in: *Greatly Exaggerated,* "German" (ed. by Alex Ayres, 1988). Twain described German as "the language which enables a man to travel all day in one sentence without changing cars."

21 Whenever the literary German dives into a sentence, that is the last you are going to see of him till he emerges on the other side of his Atlantic with his verb in his mouth.

MARK TWAIN (1835–1910), U.S. author. *A Connecticut Yankee in King Arthur's Court,* ch. 22 (1889).

See also EMERSON on ACTION Wiesel on The HOLOCAUST; Borrow on SMOKING.

GETTING AHEAD

1 It is commonly supposed that the art of pleasing is a wonderful aid in the pursuit of fortune; but the art of being bored is infinitely more successful.

SÉBASTIEN-ROCH NICOLAS DE CHAMFORT (1741–94), French writer, wit. *Maxims and Considerations,* vol. 1, no. 116 (1796; tr. 1926).

2 No man rises so high as he knows not whither he goes.

OLIVER CROMWELL (1599–1658), Parliamentarian general, Lord Protector of England. Quoted in: A. J. P. Taylor, *Essays in English History,* "Cromwell and the Historians" (1976).

3 It's them as take advantage that get advantage i' this world.

GEORGE ELIOT (1819–80), English novelist. Mrs. Poyser, in *Adam Bede,* bk. 4, ch. 32 (1859).

4 To get it right, be born with luck or else make it. *Never* give up. Get the knack of getting people to help you and also pitch in yourself. A little money helps, but what *really* gets it right is to *never*—I repeat—*never* under any conditions face the facts.

RUTH GORDON (b. 1896), U.S. playwright, actor. *Myself Among Others,* "Myself Among Others" (1970).

5 There are only two ways of getting on in the world: by one's own industry, or by the stupidity of others.

JEAN DE LA BRUYÈRE (1645–96), French writer, moralist. *Characters,* "Of Worldly Goods," aph. 52 (1688).

6 You have to be a bastard to make it, and that's a fact. And the Beatles are the biggest bastards on earth.

JOHN LENNON (1940–80), British rock musician. Quoted in: *Lennon Remembers* (ed. by Jann Wenner, p. 87. 1970).

7 The path of social advancement is, and must be, strewn with broken friendships.

H. G. WELLS (1866–1946), British author. *Kipps,* bk. 2, ch. 5 (1905).

See also AMBITION; Rayburn on MOTTOS; PROMOTION; Barrie on SCOTLAND AND THE SCOTS; SUCCESS; WINNING.

GHETTOS

1 The needs of a society determine its ethics, and in the Black American ghettos the hero is that man who is offered only the crumbs from his country's table but by ingenuity and courage is able to take for himself a Lucullan feast.

MAYA ANGELOU (b. 1928), U.S. author. *I Know Why the Caged Bird Sings,* ch. 29 (1969).

2 All over Harlem, Negro boys and girls are growing into stunted maturity, trying desperately to find a place to stand; and the wonder is not that so many are ruined but that so many survive.

JAMES BALDWIN (1924–87), U.S. author. "The Harlem Ghetto," in *Commentary* (New York, Feb. 1948; repr. in *Notes of a Native Son,* pt. 2, 1955).

3 The trouble with us is that the ghetto of the Middle Ages and the children of the twentieth century have to live under one roof.

ANZIA YEZIERSKA (1881?–1970), Polish author. Benny, in *Hungry Hearts and Other Stories,* "The Fat of the Land" (1920).

See also SLUMS.

GHOSTS

1 The more enlightened our houses are, the more their walls ooze ghosts.

ITALO CALVINO (1923–85), Italian author, critic. "Cybernetics and Ghosts," lecture, Nov. 1969, Turin (published in *The Literature Machine*, 1987).

2 The distance that the dead have gone
Does not at first appear—
Their coming back seems possible
For many an ardent year.

EMILY DICKINSON (1830–86), U.S. poet. *The Complete Poems*, no. 1742 (1955).

3 I almost think we're all of us Ghosts, Pastor Manders. It's not only what we have inherited from our father and mother that "walks" in us. It's all sorts of dead ideas, and lifeless old beliefs, and so forth. They have no vitality, but they cling to us all the same, and we can't get rid of them. Whenever I take up a newspaper, I seem to see Ghosts gliding between the lines. There must be Ghosts all the country over, as thick as the sand of the sea. And then we are, one and all, so pitifully afraid of the light.

HENRIK IBSEN (1828–1906), Norwegian dramatist. Mrs. Alving, in *Ghosts*, act 2.

4 you want to know
whether i believe in ghosts
of course i do not believe in them
if you had known
as many of them as i have
you would not
believe in them either

DON MARQUIS (1878–1937), U.S. humorist, journalist. *ghosts* in *archy and mehitabel* (1927).

GIFTS AND GIVING

1 It is rare indeed that people give. Most people guard and keep; they suppose that it is they themselves and what they identify with themselves that they are guarding and keeping, whereas what they are actually guarding and keeping is their system of reality and what they assume themselves to be.

JAMES BALDWIN (1924–87), U.S. author. "Letter from a Region in My Mind," in *New Yorker* (17 Nov. 1962; repr. in *The Fire Next Time*, 1963).

2 Gifts must affect the receiver to the point of shock.

WALTER BENJAMIN (1892–1940), German critic, philosopher. *One-Way Street*, "Fancy Goods" (1928; repr. in *One-Way Street and Other Writings*, 1978).

3 It is normal to give away a little of one's life in order not to lose it all.

ALBERT CAMUS (1913–60), French-Algerian philosopher, author. *Notebooks 1935–1942* (1962), entry for 22 Nov. 1937.

4 One must be poor to know the luxury of giving!

GEORGE ELIOT (1819–80), English novelist. *Middlemarch*, bk. 2, ch. 17 (1871–72).

5 The only gift is a portion of thyself.

RALPH WALDO EMERSON (1803–82), U.S. essayist, poet, philosopher. *Essays*, "Gifts" (First Series, 1841).

6 Giving presents is a talent; to know what a person wants, to know when and how to get it, to give it lovingly and well. Unless a character possesses this talent there is no moment more annihilating to ease than that in which a present is received and given.

PAMELA GLENCONNER (1871–1928), British author. *Edward Wyndhan Tennant: A Memoir*, ch. 5 (1919).

7 A cheque or credit card, a Gucci bag strap, anything of value will do. Give as you live.

JESSE JACKSON (b. 1941), U.S. clergyman, civil rights leader. Quoted in: *Daily Telegraph* (London, 6 April 1988). Jackson was fund-raising in Aspen, Colo.

8 Why is it no one ever sent me yet
One perfect limousine, do you suppose?
Ah no, it's always just my luck to get
One perfect rose.

DOROTHY PARKER (1893–1967), U.S. humorous writer. *One Perfect Rose*.

9 When people grow gradually rich their requirements and standard of living expand in proportion, while their present-giving instincts often remain in the undeveloped condition of their earlier days. Something showy and not-too-expensive in a shop is their only conception of the ideal gift.

SAKI [H. H. MUNRO] (1870–1916), Scottish author. Eleanor, in "Fur," in *Beasts and Super-Beasts* (1914).

10 Trust not the horse, O Trojans. Be it what it may, I fear the Grecians even when they offer gifts.

VIRGIL (70–19 B.C.), Roman poet. Laocoön, in *Aeneid*, bk. 2.

11 Behold, I do not give lectures or a little charity,
When I give I give myself.

WALT WHITMAN (1819–92), U.S. poet. *Song of Myself*, sct. 40, in *Leaves of Grass* (1855).

See also Lamb on ABSENCE; GENEROSITY; Hebrew Bible on INGRATIATION.

GIRLS

1 Girls are so queer you never know what they mean. They say No when they mean Yes, and drive a man out of his wits for the fun of it.

LOUISA MAY ALCOTT (1832–88), U.S. author. Laurie, in *Little Women*, pt. 2, ch. 12 (1869).

2 We say that a girl with her doll anticipates the mother. It is more true, perhaps, that most mothers are still but children with playthings.

F. H. BRADLEY (1846–1924), English philosopher. *Aphorisms*, no. 23 (1930).

3 There is no need to waste pity on young girls who are having their moments of disillusionment, for in another moment they will recover their illusion.

COLETTE (1873–1954), French author. "Wedding Day," pt. 2, published in *Earthly Paradise* (ed. by Robert Phelps, 1966).

4 A toddling little girl is a centre of common feeling which makes the most dissimilar people understand each other.

GEORGE ELIOT (1819–80), English novelist. *Janet's Repentance*, ch. 8, in *Blackwood's Magazine* (1857; repr. in *Scenes of Clerical Life,* 1858).

5 We know less about the sexual life of little girls than of boys. But we need not feel ashamed of this distinction; after all, the sexual life of adult women is a "dark continent" for psychology.

SIGMUND FREUD (1856–1939), Austrian psychiatrist. *The Question of Lay Analysis,* pt. 4 (1926; repr. in *Complete Works,* vol. 20, ed. by James Strachey and Anna Freud, 1959). The phrase *dark continent* was written in English.

6 Girls like to be played with, and rumpled a little too, sometimes.

OLIVER GOLDSMITH (1728–74), Anglo-Irish playwright, author. Hardcastle, in *She Stoops to Conquer,* act 5, sc. 1.

7 What we ought to see in the agonies of puberty is the result of the conditioning that maims the female personality in creating the feminine.

GERMAINE GREER (b. 1939), Australian feminist writer. *The Female Eunuch,* "Puberty" (1970).

8 The knowingness of little girls
Is hidden underneath their curls.

PHYLLIS MCGINLEY (1905–78), U.S. poet, author. *What Every Woman Knows* in *Times Three* (1960).

9 Even from their infancy we frame them to the sports of love: their instruction, behaviour, attire, grace, learning and all their words aimeth only at love, respects only affection. Their nurses and their keepers imprint no other thing in them.

MICHEL DE MONTAIGNE (1533–92), French essayist. *Essays,* bk. 3, ch. 5, "Upon some Verses of Virgil" (tr. by John Florio, 1588).

10 Between the age limits of nine and fourteen there occur maidens who, to certain bewitched travellers, twice or many times older than they, reveal their true nature which is not human, but nymphic (that is, demoniac); and these chosen creatures I propose to designate as "nymphets."

VLADIMIR NABOKOV (1899–1977), Russian-born U.S. novelist, poet. *Lolita,* pt. 1, ch. 5 (1955). This sequence was cut in the 1962 film directed by Stanley Kubrick..

11 You may chisel a boy into shape, as you would a rock, or hammer him into it, if he be of a better kind, as you would a piece of bronze. But you cannot hammer a girl into anything. She grows as a flower does.

JOHN RUSKIN (1819–1900), English art critic, author. *Sesame and Lilies,* lecture 2, sct. 78 (1865; repr. in *The Works of John Ruskin,* vol. 18, ed. by E. T. Cook and Alexander Weddesburn, 1905).

12 The restlessness that comes upon girls upon summer evenings results in lasting trouble unless it is speedily controlled. The right kind of man does not look for a wife on the streets, and the right kind of girl waits till the man comes to her home for her.

SEDALIA TIMES (1900). Quoted in: Rudi Blesh and Harriet Janis, *They All Played Ragtime,* ch. 1 (1958). This quote appeared in an article arguing that "a curfew law that will include children over sixteen" be imposed.

13 It is easy to see that, even in the freedom of early youth, an American girl never quite loses control of herself; she enjoys all permitted pleasures without losing her head about any of them, and her reason never lets the reins go, though it may often seem to let them flap.

ALEXIS DE TOCQUEVILLE (1805–59), French social philosopher. *Democracy in America,* vol. 2, pt. 3, ch. 9 (1840).

See also Hope on ADOLESCENCE.

GIVE AND TAKE

1 It is by teaching that we teach ourselves, by relating that we observe, by affirming that we examine, by showing that we look, by writing that we think, by pumping that we draw water into the well.

HENRI-FRÉDÉRIC AMIEL (1821–81), Swiss philosopher, poet. *Journal Intime* (1882; tr. by Mrs. Humphry Ward, 1892), entry for 27 Oct. 1853.

2 I do detest everything which is not perfectly mutual.

LORD BYRON (1788–1824), English poet. Letter, 21 Oct. 1813 (published in *Byron's Letters and Journals,* vol. 3, ed. by Leslie Marchand, 1974).

3 While you have a thing it can be taken from you . . . but when you give it, you have given it. No robber can take it from you. It is yours then for ever when you have given it. It will be yours always. That is to give.

JAMES JOYCE (1882–1941), Irish author. Richard Rowan, in *Exiles,* act 2 (1918).

4 Before he left, Aunt William pressed a sovereign into his hand guiltily, as if it were conscience money. He, on his side, took it as though it were a doctor's fee, and both ignored the transaction.

ADA LEVERSON (1862–1933), English novelist. *The Twelfth Hour,* "Aunt William" (1907).

5 Do not do unto others as you would that they should do unto you. Their tastes may not be the same.

GEORGE BERNARD SHAW (1856–1950), Anglo-Irish playwright, critic. *Man and Superman,* "Maxims for Revolutionists: The Golden Rule" (1903).

6 Do unto the other feller the way he'd like to do unto you, an' do it fust.

EDWARD NOYES WESTCOTT (1847–98), U.S. author. *David Harum,* ch. 20 (1898).

See also La Bruyére on CHARITY.

GLAMOR

1 Glamour cannot exist without personal social envy being a common and widespread emotion.

JOHN BERGER (b. 1926), British critic. *Ways of Seeing,* ch. 7 (1972).

2 It was a blonde. A blonde to make a bishop kick a hole in a stained-glass window.

RAYMOND CHANDLER (1888–1959), U.S. author. Philip Marlowe, in *Farewell, My Lovely,* ch. 13 (1940), of Helen Grayle.

3   A blond in a red dress can do without introductions—but not without a bodyguard.

> RONA JAFFE (b. 1932), U.S. novelist. Quoted in: Katharine Whitehorn, *Roundabout*, "Bottled in Blonde" (1962).

GLORY

1   The paths of glory lead but to the grave.

> THOMAS GRAY (1716–71), English poet. *Elegy in a Country Churchyard*, st. 9.

2   The glory of a great man ought always to be estimated by the means used to acquire it.

> FRANÇOIS, DUC DE LA ROCHEFOUCAULD (1613–80), French writer, moralist. *Sentences et Maximes Morales*, no. 157 (1678).

3   Military glory—the attractive rainbow that rises in showers of blood.

> ABRAHAM LINCOLN (1809–65), U.S. president. Speech, 12 Jan. 1848, to the House of Representatives, arguing against the war with Mexico.

4   Is it not passing brave to be a King,
And ride in triumph through Persepolis?

> CHRISTOPHER MARLOWE (1564–93), English dramatist, poet. *Tamburlaine the Great*, pt. 1.

5   The final event to himself has been, that as he rose like a rocket, he fell like the stick.

> THOMAS PAINE (1737–1809), Anglo-American political theorist, writer. *Letter to the Addressers on the Late Proclamation* (1792), referring to Paine's political adversary Edmund Burke.

6   I have touched the highest point of all my greatness,
And from that full meridian of my glory
I haste now to my setting.

> WILLIAM SHAKESPEARE (1564–1616), English dramatist, poet. Wolsey, in *King Henry VIII*, act 3, sc. 2.

7   Avoid shame but do not seek glory—nothing so expensive as glory.

> SYDNEY SMITH (1771–1845), English writer, clergyman. Quoted in: Lady Holland, *Memoir*, vol. 1, ch. 4 (1855).

8   I will not by the noise of bloody wars and the dethroning of kings advance you to glory: but by the gentle ways of peace and love.

> THOMAS TRAHERNE (1636–74), English clergyman, poet, mystic. *Centuries*, "First Century," no. 4 (written c. 1672; first published 1908).

9   No statement about God is simply, literally true. God is far more than can be measured, described, defined in ordinary language, or pinned down to any particular happening.

> DAVID JENKINS (b. 1925), British theologian, bishop of Durham. Quoted in: *Guardian* (London, 24 Dec. 1984).

See also Hugo on POPULARITY.

GOD

1   I find it interesting that the meanest life, the poorest existence, is attributed to God's will, but as human beings become more affluent, as their living standard and style begin to ascend the material scale, God descends the scale of responsibility at a commensurate speed.

> MAYA ANGELOU (b. 1928), U.S. author. *I Know Why the Caged Bird Sings*, vol. 1, ch. 18 (1969).

2   With God, what is terrible is that one never knows whether it's not just a trick of the devil.

> JEAN ANOUILH (1910–87), French playwright. The Archbishop, in *The Lark*.

3   "God is Love," we are taught as children to believe. But when we first begin to get some inkling of how He loves us, we are repelled; it seems so cold, indeed, not love at all as we understand the word.

> W. H. AUDEN (1907–73), Anglo-American poet. *A Certain World*, "God" (1970).

4   To place oneself in the position of God is painful: being God is equivalent to being tortured. For being God means that one is in harmony with all that is, including the worst. The existence of the worst evils is unimaginable unless God willed them.

> GEORGES BATAILLE (1897–1962), French novelist, critic. "Bataille, Feydeau and God," interview with Marguerite Duras in *France-Observateur* (1957; repr. in Duras, *Outside: Selected Writings*, 1984).

5   The bastard! He doesn't exist!

> SAMUEL BECKETT (1906–89), Irish dramatist, novelist. Hamm, in *Endgame*, after attempting to pray. Clov replies, "Not yet."

6   How can one better magnify the Almighty than by sniggering with him at his little jokes, particularly the poorer ones.

> SAMUEL BECKETT (1906–89), Irish dramatist, novelist. Winnie, in *Happy Days*, act 1 (1961).

7   What preoccupies us, then, is not God as a fact of nature, but as a fabrication useful for a God-fearing society. God himself becomes not a power but an image.

> DANIEL J. BOORSTIN (b. 1914), U.S. historian. *The Image*, ch. 5 (1961).

8   To speak of God, to think of God, is in every respect to show what one is made of. . . . *I have always wagered against God* and I regard the little that *I have won* in this world as simply the outcome of this bet. However paltry may have been the stake (my life) I am conscious of having won to the full. Everything that is doddering, squint-eyed, vile, polluted and grotesque is summoned up for me in that one word: God!

> ANDRÉ BRETON (1896–1966), French Surrealist. *Surrealism and Painting*, footnote (1928).

9   If someone were to prove to me—right this minute—that God, in all his luminousness, exists, it wouldn't change a single aspect of my behavior.

> LUIS BUÑUEL (1900–1983), Spanish filmmaker. *My Last Sigh*, ch. 15 (1983).

10   As you know, God is generally on the side of the big squadrons against the small ones.

> COMTE DE BUSSY-RABUTIN (1618–1693), French soldier, writer. Letter, 18 Oct. 1677. This is the earliest known version of the dictum that was later adapted by Anouilh and Voltaire. See also Voltaire below and Anouilh on THE RICH.

11 If God wants us to do a thing, he should make his wishes sufficiently clear. Sensible people will wait till he has done this before paying much attention to him.

> SAMUEL BUTLER (1835–1902), English author. *Samuel Butler's Notebooks* (1951, p. 116).

12 Whether or not God is dead: it is impossible to keep silent about him who was there for so long.

> ELIAS CANETTI (b. 1905), Austrian novelist, philosopher. *The Secret Heart of the Clock: Notes, Aphorisms, Fragments 1973–1985,* "1973" (1991).

13 Man appoints, and God disappoints.

> MIGUEL DE CERVANTES (1547–1616), Spanish writer. Sancho Panza, in *Don Quixote,* pt. 2, bk. 6, ch. 22 (1615; tr. by P. Motteux).

14 God: a disease we imagine we are cured of because no one dies of it nowadays.

> E. M. CIORAN (b. 1911), Rumanian-born French philosopher. *The Trouble with Being Born,* ch. 10 (1973).

15 There cannot be a personal God without a pessimistic religion. As soon as there is a personal God he is a disappointing God.

> CYRIL CONNOLLY (1903–74), British critic. *The Unquiet Grave,* pt. 1 (1944; rev. 1951).

16 If God is male, then male is God. The divine patriarch castrates women as long as he is allowed to live on in the human imagination.

> MARY DALY (b. 1928), U.S. educator, writer, theologian. *Beyond God the Father,* ch. 1 (1973).

17 Why indeed must "God" be a noun? Why not a verb—the most active and dynamic of all.

> MARY DALY (b. 1928), U.S. educator, writer, theologian. *Beyond God the Father,* ch. 2 (1973).

18 God is subtle, but he is not malicious.

> ALBERT EINSTEIN (1879–1955), German-born U.S. theoretical physicist. Remark, April 1921, during his first visit to Princeton University, later carved above the fireplace of the Common Room of Fine Hall in the former Mathematical Institute. In 1946, Einstein gave a freer translation: "God is slick, but he ain't mean."

19 The dice of God are always loaded.

> RALPH WALDO EMERSON (1803–82), U.S. essayist, poet, philosopher. *Essays,* "Compensation" (First Series, 1841).

20 The psychoanalysis of individual human beings, however, teaches us with quite special insistence that the god of each of them is formed in the likeness of his father, that his personal relation to God depends on his relation to his father in the flesh and oscillates and changes along with that relation, and that at bottom God is nothing other than an exalted father.

> SIGMUND FREUD (1856–1939), Austrian psychiatrist. *Totem and Taboo,* pt. 4, sct. 6 (1913; repr. in *Complete Works,* vol. 13, ed. by James Strachey and Anna Freud, 1953).

21 Forgive, O Lord, my little jokes on Thee
And I'll forgive Thy great big one on me.

> ROBERT FROST (1874–1963), U.S. poet. *Cluster of Faith.*

22 Here is God's purpose—
for God, to me, it seems,
is a verb
not a noun,
proper or improper.

> R. BUCKMINSTER FULLER (1895–1983), U.S. architect, engineer. Untitled poem (published in *No More Secondhand God,* 1963).

23 God is day and night, winter and summer, war and peace, surfeit and hunger.

> HERACLITUS (c. 535-c. 475 B.C.), Greek philosopher. *The Cosmic Fragments,* no. 36 (c. 480 B.C.).

24 Throw away thy rod,
Throw away thy wrath;
O my God,
Take the gentle path.

> GEORGE HERBERT (1593–1633), English clergyman, poet. *Discipline.*

25 To the excessively fearful the chief characteristic of power is its arbitrariness. Man had to gain enormously in confidence before he could conceive an all-powerful God who obeys his own laws.

> ERIC HOFFER (1902–83), U.S. philosopher. *Reflections on the Human Condition,* aph. 163 (1973).

26 I admit that the generation which produced Stalin, Auschwitz and Hiroshima will take some beating; but the radical and universal consciousness of the death of God is still ahead of us; perhaps we shall have to colonize the stars before it is finally borne in upon us that God is not out there.

> R. J. HOLLINGDALE (b. 1930), British author, critic, translator. *Thomas Mann: A Critical Study,* ch. 8 (1971).

27 Smitten as we are with the vision of social righteousness, a God indifferent to everything but adulation, and full of partiality for his individual favorites, lacks an essential element of largeness.

> WILLIAM JAMES (1842–1910), U.S. psychologist, philosopher. *The Varieties of Religious Experience,* lectures 14–15, "The Value of Saintliness" (1902).

28 God is the tangential point between zero and infinity.

> ALFRED JARRY (1873–1907), French playwright, author. *Gestes et Opinions du Docteur Faustroll Pataphysicien,* bk. 8, ch. 41 (1911; repr. in *The Selected Works of Alfred Jarry,* ed. by Roger Shattuck and Simon Watson Taylor, 1965).

29 Let none turn over books, or roam the stars in quest of God, who sees him not in man.

> JOHANN KASPAR LAVATER (1741–1801), Swiss divine, poet. *Aphorisms on Man,* no. 398 (1788).

30 I cannot be a materialist—but Oh, how is it possible that a God who speaks to all hearts can let Belgravia go laughing to a vicious luxury, and Whitechapel cursing to a filthy debauchery—such suffering, such dreadful suffering—and shall the short years of Christ's mission atone for it all?

> D. H. LAWRENCE (1885–1930), British author. Letter, 3 Dec. 1907 (published in *The Letters of D. H. Lawrence,* vol. 1, ed. by James T. Boulton, 1979).

31 God is only a great imaginative experience.

> D. H. LAWRENCE (1885–1930), British author. "Introduction to

The Dragon of the Apocalypse by Frederick Carter," in *London Mercury* (July 1930, repr. in *Phoenix: The Posthumous Papers of D. H. Lawrence*, pt. 4, ed. by E. McDonald, 1936). Carter's book eventually appeared under a different title and without Lawrence's introduction.

32   God is indeed dead.
He died of self-horror
when He saw the creature He had made
   in His own image.

IRVING LAYTON (b. 1912), Canadian poet. *The Whole Bloody Bird*, "Aphs" (1969).

33   God is a concept by which we measure our pain.

JOHN LENNON (1940–80), British rock musician. "God," on the album *Plastic Ono Band* (1970).

34   Can a mortal ask questions which God finds unanswerable? Quite easily, I should think. All nonsense questions are unanswerable.

C. S. LEWIS (1898–1963), British author. *A Grief Observed*, pt. 4 (1961).

35   Without doubt God is the universal moving force, but each being is moved according to the nature that God has given it . . . . He directs angels, man, animals, brute matter, in sum all created things, but each *according to its nature*, and man having been created free, he is freely led. This rule is truly *the eternal law* and in it we must believe.

JOSEPH DE MAISTRE (1753–1821), French diplomat, philosopher. The Senator, in *Les Soirées de Saint-Pétersbourg*, "Fifth Dialogue" (1821; repr. in *The Works of Joseph de Maistre*, ed. by Jack Lively, 1965).

36   God is the immemorial refuge of the incompetent, the helpless, the miserable. They find not only sanctuary in His arms, but also a kind of superiority, soothing to their macerated egos: He will set them above their betters.

H. L. MENCKEN (1880–1956), U.S. journalist. *Minority Report: H. L. Mencken's Notebooks*, no. 35 (1956).

37   God, I can push the grass apart
And lay my finger on Thy heart.

EDNA ST. VINCENT MILLAY (1892–1950), U.S. poet. *Renascence*, st. 7.

38   To honor him whom we have made is far from honoring him that hath made us..

MICHEL DE MONTAIGNE (1533–92), French essayist. *Essays*, bk. 2, ch. 12, "An Apology of Raimond Sebond" (1580; tr. by John Florio).

39   If triangles made a god, they would give him three sides.

CHARLES DE MONTESQUIEU (1689–1755), French philosopher, lawyer. *Lettres persanes*, letter 59 (1721).

40   I fear we are not getting rid of God because we still believe in grammar.

FRIEDRICH NIETZSCHE (1844–1900), German philosopher. *Twilight of the Idols*, "'Reason' in Philosophy," aph. 5 (1889).

41   Men have always need of god! A god to defend them against other men..

FRANCIS PICABIA (1878–1953), French painter, poet. "Trompettes de Jericho," in *Comedia* (Paris, 19 Jan. 1922; repr.

in *Écrits*, vol. 2, "1922," ed. by Olivier Revault d'Allones and Dominique Bouissou, 1978).

42   God is really only another artist. He invented the giraffe, the elephant, and the cat. He has no real style. He just keeps on trying other things.

PABLO PICASSO (1881–1973), Spanish artist. Quoted in: Françoise Gilot and Carlton Lake, *Life with Picasso*, pt. 1 (1964).

43   If God lived on earth, people would break his windows.

JEWISH PROVERB. Quoted in: Claud Cockburn, *Cockburn Sums Up*, epigraph (1981).

44   God will provide—ah, if only He would till He does!

YIDDISH PROVERB.

45   If the sea were ink
For the words of my Lord,
the sea would be spent before the Words of my
   Lord are spent.

QUR'AN. *The Cave* 18:109 (ed. by Arthur J. Arberry, 1955).

46   God, that checkroom of our dreams.

JEAN ROSTAND (1894–1977), French biologist, writer. *Carnets d'un Biologiste* (repr. in *The Substance of Man*, 1962). Other translations give "dumping ground" for *dépotoir*.

47   If we really think about it, God exists for any single individual who puts his trust in Him, not for the whole of humanity, with its laws, its organizations, and its violence. Humanity is the demon which God does not succeed in destroying.

SALVATORE SATTA (1902–75), Italian jurist, novelist. *The Day of Judgment*, ch. 15 (1979).

48   To me the sole hope of human salvation lies in teaching Man to regard himself as an experiment in the realization of God, to regard his hands as God's hand, his brain as God's brain, his purpose as God's purpose. He must regard God as a helpless Longing, which *longed* him into existence by its desperate need for an executive organ.

GEORGE BERNARD SHAW (1856–1950), Anglo-Irish playwright, critic. Letter, 19 Aug. 1909 to dramatist and patron Lady Gregory (published in *Collected Letters*, vol. 2, 1972).

49   Those who set out to serve both God and Mammon soon discover that there isn't a God.

LOGAN PEARSALL SMITH (1865–1946), U.S. essayist, aphorist. *Afterthoughts*, "Other People" (1931).

50   I know not what you believe of God, but I believe He gave yearnings and longings to be filled, and that He did not mean all our time should be devoted to feeding and clothing the body.

LUCY STONE (1818–93), U.S. feminist, editor. "Disappointment Is the Lot of Women," speech, 17–18 Oct. 1855. Quoted in: Elizabeth Cady Stanton, Susan B. Antony, and Mathilda Gage, *History of Woman Suffrage*, vol. 1 (1881).

51   It is an insult to God to believe in God. For on the one hand it is to suppose that he has perpetrated acts of incalculable cruelty. On the other hand, it is to suppose that he has perversely given his human creatures an instrument—their intellect—which must inevitably lead them, if they are dispassionate and honest, to deny his existence. It is tempting to conclude that if he exists, it is the atheists and agnostics that he loves best, among those with any pretensions to education. For they are the ones who have taken him most seriously.

GALEN STRAWSON (b. 1952), British philosopher, literary critic. Quoted in: *Independent* (London, 24 June 1990).

52 If you talk to God, you are praying; if God talks to you, you have schizophrenia.

THOMAS SZASZ (b. 1920), U.S. psychiatrist. *The Second Sin,* "Schizophrenia" (1973).

53 It seems to me that the god that is commonly worshipped in civilized countries is not at all divine, though he bears a divine name, but is the overwhelming authority and respectability of mankind combined. Men reverence one another, not yet God.

HENRY DAVID THOREAU (1817–62), U.S. philosopher, author, naturalist. *A Week on the Concord and Merrimac Rivers,* "Sunday" (1849).

54 People are too apt to treat God as if he were a minor royalty.

SIR HERBERT BEERBOHM TREE (1853–1917), English actor-manager. Quoted in: Hesketh Pearson, *Beerbohm-Tree,* ch. 12 (1956).

55 We need God, not in order to understand the *why,* but in order to feel and sustain the ultimate *wherefore,* to give a meaning to the universe.

MIGUEL DE UNAMUNO (1864–1936), Spanish philosophical writer. *The Tragic Sense of Life,* ch. 7 (1913).

56 The guarantee that our self enjoys an intended relation to the outer world is most, if not all, we ask from religion. God is the self projected onto reality by our natural and necessary optimism. He is the not-me personified.

JOHN UPDIKE (b. 1932), U.S. author, critic. *Self-Consciousness: Memoirs,* ch. 6 (1989).

57 God is not on the side of the big battalions, but on the side of those who shoot best.

VOLTAIRE (1694–1778), French philosopher, author. *Notebooks,* vol. 2, "The Piccini Notebooks" (1968 ed.).

58 It is only the impossible that is possible for God. He has given over the possible to the mechanics of matter and the autonomy of his creatures.

SIMONE WEIL (1909–43), French philosopher, mystic. "A War of Religions" (written 1943; published in *Selected Essays,* ed. by Richard Rees, 1962).

59 We can only know one thing about God—that he is what we are not. Our wretchedness alone is an image of this. The more we contemplate it, the more we contemplate him.

SIMONE WEIL (1909–43), French philosopher, mystic. *Gravity and Grace,* "Attention and Will" (1947; tr. 1952).

60 In relation to God, we are like a thief who has burgled the house of a kindly householder and been allowed to keep some of the gold. From the point of view of the lawful owner this gold is a gift; Form the point of view of the burglar it is a theft. He must go and give it back. It is the same with our existence. We have stolen a little of

God's being to make it ours. God has made us a gift of it. But we have stolen it. We must return it.

SIMONE WEIL (1909–43), French philosopher, mystic. *New York Notebook* (1950; repr. in *First and Last Notebooks,* ed. by Richard Rees, 1970).

61 In the faces of men and women I see God, and in
    my own face in the glass,
I find letters from God dropt in the street, and
    every one is sign'd by God's name.
And I leave them where they are, for I know that
    wheresoe'er I go,
Others will punctually come for ever and ever.

WALT WHITMAN (1819–92), U.S. poet. *Song of Myself,* sct. 48, in *Leaves of Grass* (1855).

62 I rarely speak about God. To God, yes. I protest against Him. I shout at Him. But to open a discourse about the qualities of God, about the problems that God imposes, theodicy, no. And yet He is there, in silence, in filigree.

ELIE WIESEL (b. 1928), Rumanian-born U.S. writer. Interview in *Writers at Work* (Eighth Series, ed. by George Plimpton, 1988).

See also Allen on AGNOSTICS; Schreiner on ATHEISM; Shaw on The BRITISH; Angelou on CHILDREN; The CREATION; Grimké on EDUCATION; Pascal on FAITH; Heine on FORGIVENESS; Maistre on FREE WILL; O'Neill on GODS AND GODDESSES; Butler on HUMANKIND; Henry Miller on IMAGINATION; Walker on JESUS CHRIST; Greek Proverb on LUCK; Cary, James on MIRACLES; Bible: New Testament on PRIVILEGE; Anouilh on The RICH; De Vries on SALVATION; Joubert on SPACE; Renan on SPIRITUALITY; Bible: New Testament on THE STATUS QUO.

GODS AND GODDESSES

1 We know all their gods; they ignore ours. What they call our sins are our gods, and what they call their gods, we name otherwise.

NATALIE CLIFFORD BARNEY (1876–1972), U.S.-born French author. Quoted in: "Gods" in *Adam,* no. 299 (1962).

2 A woman clothed with the sun, and the moon under her feet, and upon her head a crown of twelve stars.

BIBLE: NEW TESTAMENT. *Revelation* 12:1.

3 All good fortune is a gift of the gods, and . . . you don't win the favor of the ancient gods by being good, but by being *bold.*

ANITA BROOKNER (b. 1938), British novelist, art historian. *Writers at Work* (Eighth Series, ed. by George Plimpton, 1988).

4 I think there are innumerable gods. What we on earth call God is a little tribal God who has made an awful mess. Certainly forces operating through human consciousness control events.

WILLIAM S. BURROUGHS (b. 1914), U.S. author. Interview in *Writers at Work* (Third Series, ed. by George Plimpton, 1967).

5 Mother goddesses are just as silly a notion as father gods. If a revival of the myths of these cults gives woman emotional satisfaction, it does so at the price of obscuring the real conditions of life. This is why they were invented in the first place.

ANGELA CARTER (1940–92), British author. *The Sadeian Woman,* "Polemical Preface" (1979).

6 A civilization is destroyed only when its gods are destroyed.

> E. M. CIORAN (b. 1911), Rumanian-born French philosopher. *The New Gods* title essay (1969; tr. 1974).

7 All the gods are dead except the god of war.

> ELDRIDGE CLEAVER (b. 1935), U.S. black leader, writer. *Soul on Ice,* pt. 1, "Four Vignettes: 'The Christ' and His Teachings" (1968).

8 'Tis the old secret of the gods that they come in low disguises.

> RALPH WALDO EMERSON (1803–82), U.S. essayist, poet, philosopher. *Society and Solitude,* "Works and Days" (1870).

9 And some to Meccah turn to pray, and I toward thy bed, Yasmin.

> JAMES ELROY FLECKER (1884–1915), British poet. Hassan, in *Hassan,* act 1, sc. 2 (1922).

10 There is in general good reason to suppose that in several respects the gods could all benefit from instruction by us human beings. We humans are—more humane.

> FRIEDRICH NIETZSCHE (1844–1900), German philosopher. *Beyond Good and Evil,* aph. 295 (1886).

11 When men make gods, there is no God!

> EUGENE O'NEILL (1888–1953), U.S. dramatist. Lazarus, in *Lazarus Laughed,* act 2, sc. 2.

12 And again: No more gods! no more gods! Man is King, Man is God!— But the great Faith is Love!

> ARTHUR RIMBAUD (1854–91), French poet. *Soleil et Chair,* sct. 1 (repr. in *Collected Poems,* ed. by Oliver Bernard, 1962).

13 While the womanly god demands our veneration, the godlike woman kindles our love; but while we allow ourslves to melt in the celestial loveliness, the celestial self-sufficiency holds us back in awe.

> FRIEDRICH VON SCHILLER (1759–1805), German dramatist, poet, essayist. *On the Aesthetic Education of Man,* "Fifteenth Letter" (1795), describing the statue Juno Ludvoci.

THE GOLDEN RULE

1 Think in the morning. Act in the noon. Eat in the evening. Sleep in the night.

> WILLIAM BLAKE (1757–1827), English poet, painter, engraver. *The Marriage of Heaven and Hell,* plate 9, "Proverbs of Hell" (1790).

2 Be studious in your profession, and you will be learned. Be industrious and frugal, and you will be rich. Be sober and temperate, and you will be healthy. Be in general virtuous, and you will be happy. At least you will, by such conduct, stand the best chance for such consequences.

> BENJAMIN FRANKLIN (1706–90), U.S. statesman, writer. Letter, 9 Aug. 1768 (published in *Complete Works,* vol. 4, ed. by John Bigelow, 1887–88).

3 There is no more important rule of conduct in the world than this: attach yourself as much as you can to people who are abler than you and yet not so very different that you cannot understand them.

> G. C. LICHTENBERG (1742–99), German physicist, philosopher. *Aphorisms,* "Notebook F," aph. 81 (written 1765–99; tr. by R. J. Hollingdale, 1990).

4 Absolutely speaking, Do unto others as you would that they should do unto you is by no means a golden rule, but the best of current silver. An honest man would have but little occasion for it. It is golden not to have any rule at all in such a case.

> HENRY DAVID THOREAU (1817–62), U.S. philosopher, author, naturalist. *A Week on the Concord and Merrimack Rivers,* "Sunday" (1849).

GOLF

1 If there is any larceny in a man, golf will bring it out.

> PAUL GALLICO (1897–1976), U.S. novelist. *New York Times* (6 March 1977).

2 Elderly gentlemen, gentle in all respects, kind to animals, beloved by children, and fond of music, are found in lonely corners of the downs, hacking at sandpits or tussocks of grass, and muttering in a blind, ungovernable fury elaborate maledictions which could not be extracted from them by robbery or murder. Men who would face torture without a word become blasphemous at the short fourteenth. It is clear that the game of golf may well be included in that category of intolerable provocations which may legally excuse or mitigate behaviour not otherwise excusable.

> A. P. HERBERT (1890–1971), British author, politician. Mr. Justice Trout, in *Uncommon Law,* "Is a Golfer a Gentleman?" (1935), bringing judgment in a case involving ungentlemanly conduct on the course.

3 If you watch a game, it's fun. If you play it, it's recreation. If you work at it, it's golf.

> BOB HOPE (b. 1903), U.S. comedian. Quoted in: *The Reader's Digest* (Oct. 1958).

4 If you think it's hard to meet new people, try picking up the wrong golf ball.

> JACK LEMMON (b. 1925), U.S. actor. *Sports Illustrated* (New York, 9 Dec. 1985) .

5 Golf is a fine relief from the tensions of office, but we are a little tired of holding the bag.

> ADLAI STEVENSON (1900–1965), U.S. Democratic politician. Quoted in: Leon Harris, *The Fine Art of Political Wit,* ch. 10 (1964), referring to President Eisenhower's passion for golf.

6 Golf is a good walk spoiled.

> Attributed to MARK TWAIN (1835–1910), U.S. author. Quoted in: *Greatly Exaggerated,* "Golf" (ed. by Alex Ayres, 1988).

7 A day
Spent in a round of strenuous idleness.

> WILLIAM WORDSWORTH (1770–1850), English poet. *The Prelude,* bk. 4.

GOOD DEEDS

1 What monster have we here?
A great Deed at this hour of day?

A great just Deed—and not for pay?
Absurd,—or insincere.

ELIZABETH BARRETT BROWNING (1806–61), English Poet. *A Tale of Villafrance*, st. 4.

2　In dreams the truth is learned that all good works are done in the absence of a caress.

LEONARD COHEN (b. 1934), Canadian singer, poet, novelist. *The Favourite Game*, bk. 3, ch. 8 (1963).

3　Though language forms the preacher,
'Tis "good works" make the man.

ELIZA COOK (1818–89), English poet. *Good Works.*

4　The last temptation is the greatest treason:
To do the right deed for the wrong reason.

T. S. ELIOT (1888–1965), Anglo-American poet, critic. Thomas, in *Murder in the Cathedral*, pt. 1.

5　Verily the kindness that gazes upon itself in a mirror turns to stone,
And a good deed that calls itself by tender names becomes the parent to a curse.

KAHLIL GIBRAN (1883–1931), Lebanese poet, novelist. *The Prophet*, "The Farewell" (1923).

6　The greatest pleasure I know, is to do a good action by stealth, and to have it found out by accident.

CHARLES LAMB (1775–1834), English essayist, critic. Quoted in: *Athenaeum* (London, 4 Jan. 1834).

7　It is the mark of a good action that it appears inevitable in retrospect.

ROBERT LOUIS STEVENSON (1850–94), Scottish novelist, essayist, poet. "Reflections and Remarks on Human Life," sct. 4 (1878; repr. in *Complete Works*, vol. 26, 1924).

8　If I knew for a certainty that a man was coming to my house with the conscious design of doing me good, I should run for my life.

HENRY DAVID THOREAU (1817–62), U.S. philosopher, author, naturalist. *Walden*, "Economy" (1854).

9　Though it is possible to utter words only with the intention to fulfill the will of God, it is very difficult not to think about the impression which they will produce on men and not to form them accordingly. But deeds you can do quite unknown to men, only for God. And such deeds are the greatest joy that a man can experience.

LEO TOLSTOY (1828–1910), Russian novelist, philosopher. Letter, 23 Feb. 1903 (published in *Tolstoy's Letters*, vol. 2, 1978).

10　Always do right—this will gratify some and astonish the rest.

MARK TWAIN (1835–1910), U.S. author. Message, 16 Feb. 1901, to the Young People's Society, New York City. President Harry S Truman had this remark framed behind his desk in the Oval Office.

11　A good picture is equivalent to a good deed.

VINCENT VAN GOGH (1853–90), Dutch painter. Letter, 1890 (published in *The Complete Letters of Vincent Van Gogh*, vol. 3, no. 626a, 1958).

12　That best portion of a good man's life;

His little, nameless, unremembered acts
Of kindness and of love.

WILLIAM WORDSWORTH (1770–1850), English poet. *Lines Written a Few Miles Above Tintern Abbey.*

See also ALTRUISM; BENEFACTORS; Shaw on INTENTIONS; La Rochefoucauld on MOTIVES; CHARITY.

GOOD FRIDAY

See EASTER AND GOOD FRIDAY.

GOODNESS

1　Freedom, morality, and the human dignity of the individual consists precisely in this; that he does good not because he is forced to do so, but because he freely conceives it, wants it, and loves it.

MIKHAIL BAKUNIN (1814–76), Russian political theorist. *God and the State* (1871; repr. in *Bakunin on Anarchism*, ed. by Sam Dolgoff, 1980).

2　No one can be good for long if goodness is not in demand.

BERTOLT BRECHT (1898–1956), German dramatist, poet. First God, in *The Good Woman of Setzuan*, scene 1a.

3　A good heart will help you to a bonny face, my lad . . . and a bad one will turn the bonniest into something worse than ugly.

EMILY BRONTË (1818–48), English novelist, poet. Nelly, in *Wuthering Heights*, ch. 7 (1847), speaking to Heathcliff.

4　We all have known
Good critics, who have stamped out poet's hopes;
Good statesmen, who pulled ruin on the state;
Good patriots, who, for a theory, risked a cause;
Good kings, who disembowelled for a tax;
Good Popes, who brought all good to jeopardy;
Good Christians, who sat still in easy-chairs;
And damned the general world for standing up.—
Now, may the good God pardon all good men!

ELIZABETH BARRETT BROWNING (1806–61), English poet. *Aurora Leigh*, bk. 4 (1857).

5　As if one could know the good a person is capable of, when one doesn't know the bad he might do.

ELIAS CANETTI (b. 1905), Austrian novelist, philosopher. *The Secret Heart of the Clock: Notes, Aphorisms, Fragments 1973–1985*, "1975" (1991).

6　Every person is responsible for all the good within the scope of his abilities, and for no more, and none can tell whose sphere is the largest.

GAIL HAMILTON (1833–96), U.S. writer, humorist. *Country Living and Country Thinking*, "Men and Women" (1862).

7　If goodness were only a theory, it were a pity it should be lost to the world. There are a number of things, the idea of which is a clear gain to the mind. Let people, for instance, rail at friendship, genius, freedom, as long as they will—the very names of these despised qualities are better than anything else that could be substituted for them, and embalm even the most envenomed satire against them.

> WILLIAM HAZLITT (1778–1830), English essayist. *Sketches and Essays,* "On Cant and Hypocrisy" (1839).

8 Mere goodness can achieve little against the power of nature.

> GEORG HEGEL (1770–1831), German philosopher. *The Philosophy of Right,* addition 58 (1821; tr. 1942).

9 Good is a product of the ethical and spiritual artistry of individuals; it cannot be mass-produced.

> ALDOUS HUXLEY (1894–1963), British author. *Grey Eminence,* ch. 10 (1941).

10 How sick one gets of being "good," how much I should respect myself if I could burst out and make everyone wretched for twenty-four hours; embody selfishness.

> ALICE JAMES (1848–92), U.S. diarist. Letter, 11 Dec 1889, to her brother, psychologist William James (published in *The Diary of Alice James,* ed. by Leon Edel, 1964).

11 True human goodness, in all its purity and freedom, can come to the fore only when its recipient has no power.

> MILAN KUNDERA (b. 1929), Czech author, critic. *The Unbearable Lightness of Being,* pt. 7, ch. 2 (1984).

12 There are few good women who do not tire of their rôle.

> FRANÇOIS, DUC DE LA ROCHEFOUCAULD (1613–80), French writer, moralist. *Sentences et Maximes Morales,* no. 367 (1678).

13 The Crucifixion and other historical precedents notwithstanding, many of us still believe that outstanding goodness is a kind of armor, that virtue, seen plain and bare, gives pause to criminality. But perhaps it is the other way around.

> MARY MCCARTHY (1912–89), U.S. author, critic. *On the Contrary,* pt. 1, "Gandhi" (1961; first published 1949).

14 Being good is just a matter of temperament in the end.

> IRIS MURDOCH (b. 1919), British novelist, philosopher. Kate Gray, in *The Nice and the Good,* ch. 14 (1968).

15 What is good?—All that heightens the feeling of power, the will to power, power itself in man.

> FRIEDRICH NIETZSCHE (1844–1900), German philosopher. *The Anti-Christ,* aph. 2 (1895).

16 The good is, like nature, an immense landscape in which man advances through centuries of exploration.

> JOSÉ ORTEGA Y GASSET (1883–1955), Spanish essayist, philosopher. *Meditations on Quixote,* "To the Reader" (1914).

17 On the whole, human beings want to be good, but not too good, and not quite all the time.

> GEORGE ORWELL (1903–50), British author. "The Art of Donald McGill," in *Horizon* (London, Sept. 1941; repr. in *Collected Essays,* 1961).

18 In the world of knowledge, the essential Form of Good is the limit of our inquiries, and can barely be perceived; but, when perceived, we cannot help concluding that it is in every case the source of all that is bright and beautiful—in the visible world giving birth to light and its master, and in the intellectual world dispensing, immediately and with full authority, truth and reason—and that whosoever would act wisely, either in private or in public, must set this Form of Good before his eyes.

> PLATO (c. 427–347 B.C.), Greek philosopher. Socrates, in *The Republic,* bk. 7, sct. 517.

19 To conceive the good, in fact, is not sufficient; it must be made to succeed among men. To accomplish this less pure paths must be followed.

> ERNEST RENAN (1823–92), French writer, critic, scholar. *The Life of Jesus,* ch. 5 (1863).

20 A man, to be greatly good, must imagine intensely and comprehensively; he must put himself in the place of another and of many others; the pains and pleasures of his species must become his own.

> PERCY BYSSHE SHELLEY (1792–1822), English poet. *A Defence of Poetry* (written 1821; published 1840).

21 Goodness is the only investment that never fails.

> HENRY DAVID THOREAU (1817–62), U.S. philosopher, author, naturalist. *Walden,* "Higher Laws" (1854).

22 To be good is noble, but to teach others how to be good is nobler—and no trouble.

> MARK TWAIN (1835–1910), U.S. author. *Following the Equator,* flyleaf of first edition (1897).

23 At the bottom of the heart of every human being, from earliest infancy until the tomb, there is something that goes on indomitably expecting, in the teeth of all experience of crimes committed, suffered, and witnessed, that good and not evil will be done to him. It is this above all that is sacred in every human being.

> SIMONE WEIL (1909–43), French philosopher, mystic. "Human Personality," in *La Table Ronde* (written 1943; published Dec. 1950; repr. in *Selected Essays,* ed. by Richard Rees, 1962).

24 One of the darkest evils of our world is surely the unteachable wildness of the Good.

> H. G. WELLS (1866–1946), British author. *A Modern Utopia,* ch. 2, sct. 6 (1905; repr. in *The Works of H. G. Wells,* vol. 9, 1925).

25 If you pretend to be good, the world takes you very seriously. If you pretend to be bad, it doesn't. Such is the astounding stupidity of optimism.

> OSCAR WILDE (1854–1900), Anglo-Irish playwright, author. Lord Darlington, in *Lady Windermere's Fan,* act 1.

26 To be good, according to the vulgar standard of goodness, is obviously quite easy. It merely requires a certain amount of sordid terror, a certain lack of imaginative thought, and a certain low passion for middle-class respectability.

> OSCAR WILDE (1854–1900), Anglo-Irish playwright, author. Gilbert, in "The Critic as Artist," pt. 2 (published in *Intentions,* 1891).

See also Byron on HUMANKIND; KINDNESS.

GOSSIP

1 The Athenians and strangers which were there spent their time in nothing else, but either to tell or to hear some new thing.

BIBLE: NEW TESTAMENT. St. Paul in *Acts* 17:21.

2 Not only idle, but tattlers also and busybodies, speaking things which they ought not.

BIBLE: NEW TESTAMENT. St. Paul in *1 Timothy* 5:13.

3 Confidante. One entrusted by A with the secrets of B confided to herself by C.

AMBROSE BIERCE (1842–1914), U.S. author. *The Devil's Dictionary* (1881–1906).

4 Alas! they had been friends in youth;
But whispering tongues can poison truth.

SAMUEL TAYLOR COLERIDGE (1772–1834), English poet, critic. *Christabel*, pt. 2.

5 None are so fond of secrets as those who do not mean to keep them.

C. C. COLTON (1780–1832), English author. *Lacon*, vol. 1, no. 40 (1820).

6 They come together like the Coroner's Inquest, to sit upon the murdered reputations of the week.

WILLIAM CONGREVE (1670–1729), English dramatist. Fainall, in *The Way of the World*, act 1, sc. 1.

7 The inspired scribbler always has the gift for gossip in our common usage . . . he or she can always inspire the commonplace with an uncommon flavor, and transform trivialities by some original grace or sympathy or humor or affection.

ELIZABETH DREW (1887–1965), Anglo-American author, critic. *The Literature of Gossip*, "The Literature of Gossip" (1964).

8 While gossip among women is universally ridiculed as low and trivial, gossip among men, especially if it is about women, is called theory, or idea, or fact.

ANDREA DWORKIN (b. 1946), U.S. feminist critic. *Right-Wing Women*, ch. 1 (1978).

9 Gossip is a sort of smoke that comes from the dirty tobacco-pipes of those who diffuse it: it proves nothing but the bad taste of the smoker.

GEORGE ELIOT (1819–80), English novelist. *Daniel Deronda*, bk. 2, ch. 13 (1876).

10 Young people do not perceive at once that the giver of wounds is the enemy and the quoted tattle merely the arrow.

F. SCOTT FITZGERALD (1896–1940), U.S. author. *The Crack-Up*, "Notebook O" (ed. by Edmund Wilson, 1945).

11 Gossip is the opiate of the oppressed.

ERICA JONG (b. 1942), U.S. author. The narrator (Isadora Wing), in *Fear of Flying*, ch. 6 (1973).

12 Men have always detested women's gossip because they suspect the truth: their measurements are being taken and compared.

ERICA JONG (b. 1942), U.S. author. The narrator (Isadora Wing), in *Fear of Flying*, ch. 6 (1973).

13 Anyone who has obeyed nature by transmitting a piece of gossip experiences the explosive relief that accompanies the satisfying of a primary need.

PRIMO LEVI (1919–87), Italian chemist, author. "About Gossip,"

in *La Stampa* (Turin, Italy, 24 June 1986; repr. in *The Mirror Maker*, 1989).

14 Gossip isn't scandal and it's not merely malicious. It's chatter about the human race by lovers of the same. Gossip is the tool of the poet, the shop-talk of the scientist, and the consolation of the housewife, wit, tycoon and intellectual. It begins in the nursery and ends when speech is past.

PHYLLIS MCGINLEY (1905–78), U.S. poet, author. "A New Year and No Resolutions," in *Woman's Home Companion* (Jan. 1957).

15 Of course we women gossip on occasion. But our appetite for it is not as avid as a man's. It is in the boys' gyms, the college fraternity houses, the club locker rooms, the paneled offices of business that gossip reaches its luxuriant flower.

PHYLLIS MCGINLEY (1905–78), U.S. poet, author. *The Province of the Heart*, "Some of My Best Friends . . ." (1959).

16 A cruel story runs on wheels, and every hand oils the wheels as they run.

OUIDA (1839–1908), English novelist. *Wisdom, Wit and Pathos*, "Moths" (1884).

17 I maintain that, if everyone knew what others said about him, there would not be four friends in the world.

BLAISE PASCAL (1623–62), French scientist, philosopher. *Pensées* (1670; no. 792 ed. by Krailsheimer, no. 101 ed. by Brunschvicg).

18 My arse contemplates those who talk behind my back.

FRANCIS PICABIA (1878–1953), French painter, poet. *391*, no. 15 (10 July 1921; repr. in *Yes No: Poems and Sayings*, "Sayings," ed. by Rémy Hall, 1990).

19 And all who told it added something new,
And all who heard it, made enlargements too.

ALEXANDER POPE (1688–1744), English satirical poet. *The Temple of Fame*.

20 At ev'ry word a reputation dies.

ALEXANDER POPE (1688–1744), English satirical poet. *The Rape of the Lock*, cto. 3.

21 Ah, well, the truth is always one thing, but in a way it's the other thing, the gossip, that counts. It shows where people's hearts lie.

PAUL SCOTT (1920–78), British author. Count Bronowsky, in *The Day of the Scorpion*, bk. 1, pt. 3, ch. 3 (1968).

22 Gossip is news running ahead of itself in a red satin dress.

LIZ SMITH (b. 1923), U.S. journalist, author. *American Way*, syndicated column (3 Sept. 1985). "Most good gossip columnists," Smith wrote in 1991, "have a touch of Savonarola in them."

23 How awful to reflect that what people say of us is true!

LOGAN PEARSALL SMITH (1865–1946), U.S. essayist, aphorist. *Afterthoughts*, "Life and Human Nature" (1931).

24 It takes your enemy and your friend, working together, to hurt you to the heart: the one to slander you and the other to get the news to you.

MARK TWAIN (1835–1910), U.S. author. *Following the Equator,* ch. 9, "Pudd'nhead Wilson's New Calendar" (1897).

25   Everyone realizes that one can believe little of what people say about each other. But it is not so widely realized that even less can one trust what people say about themselves.

REBECCA WEST (1892–1983), British author. Quoted in: *Sunday Telegraph* (London, 1975), as epigraph to Victoria Glendinning, *Rebecca West: A Life* (1987).

26   There is only one thing in the world worse than being talked about, and that is not being talked about.

OSCAR WILDE (1854–1900), Anglo-Irish playwright, author. Lord Henry, in *The Picture of Dorian Gray,* ch. 1 (1891).

See also Wilde on SCANDAL; Wilde on SLANDER; Connolly on SUICIDE.

GOVERNMENT

1   It is often said that men are ruled by their imaginations; but it would be truer to say they are governed by the weakness of their imaginations.

WALTER BAGEHOT (1826–77), English economist, critic. *The English Constitution,* ch. 2 (1867).

2   Government is the great fiction, through which everybody endeavors to live at the expense of everybody else.

FRÉDÉRIC BASTIAT (1801–50), French political economist. *Essays on Political Economy,* pt. 3, "Government" (1872; first published 1846).

3   Governing today means giving acceptable signs of credibility. It is like advertising and it is the same effect that is achieved—commitment to a scenario.

JEAN BAUDRILLARD (b. 1929), French semiologist. *America,* "The End of U.S. Power?" (1986; tr. 1988).

4   The object of government in peace and in war is not the glory of rulers or of races, but the happiness of the common man.

WILLIAM, LORD BEVERIDGE (1879–1963), British economist. *Social Insurance and Allied Services,* pt. 7 (1942).

5   But their determination to banish fools foundered ultimately in the installation of absolute idiots.

BASIL BUNTING (1900–1985), British poet. *The Spoils,* on the decline of government under the Turkish Seljuk dynasty.

6   Nothing turns out to be so oppressive and unjust as a feeble government.

EDMUND BURKE (1729–97), Irish philosopher, statesman. *Reflections on the Revolution in France* (1790).

7   Men are to be guided only by their self-interests. Good government is a good balancing of these; and, except a keen eye and appetite for self-interest, requires no virtue in any quarter. To both parties it is emphatically a machine: to the discontented, a "taxing-machine;" to the contented, a "machine for securing property." Its duties and its faults are not those of a father, but of an active parish-constable.

THOMAS CARLYLE (1795–1881), Scottish essayist, historian.

Signs of the Times (1829; first published in *Edinburgh Review,* no. 98).

8   In the long-run every Government is the exact symbol of its People, with their wisdom and unwisdom; we have to say, Like People like Government.

THOMAS CARLYLE (1795–1881), Scottish essayist, historian. *Past and Present,* bk. 4, ch. 4 (1843).

9   Thou cam'st out of thy mother's belly without government, thou hast liv'd hitherto without government, and thou may'st be carried to thy long home without government, when it shall please the Lord. How many people in this world live without government, yet do well enough, and are well look'd upon?

MIGUEL DE CERVANTES (1547–1616), Spanish writer. Teresa Panza (Sancho's wife), in *Don Quixote,* pt. 2, bk. 5, ch. 37 (1615; tr. by P. Motteux).

10   Good government is the outcome of private virtue.

JOHN JAY CHAPMAN (1862–1933), U.S. author. *Practical Agitation,* ch. 2 (1898).

11   The three great ends which a statesman ought to propose to himself in the government of a nation, are,—
1. Security to possessors;
2. Facility to acquirers; and,
3. Hope to all.

SAMUEL TAYLOR COLERIDGE (1772–1834), English poet, critic. "Table Talk," in *Specimens of the Table Talk of Samuel Taylor Coleridge* (ed. by Henry Nelson Coleridge, 1835; repr. in *Collected Works,* vol. 14, ed. by Kathleen Coburn, 1990).

12   Nations it may be have fashioned their Governments, but the Governments have paid them back in the same coin.

JOSEPH CONRAD (1857–1924), Polish-born English novelist. The narrator, in *Under Western Eyes,* pt. 1, ch. 2 (1911).

13   I say to myself that I mustn't let myself be cut off in there, and yet the moment I enter my bag is taken out of my hand, I'm pushed in, shepherded, nursed and above all cut off, alone. Whitehall envelops me.

RICHARD CROSSMAN (1907–74), British Labour politician. Diary entry, 22 Oct. 1964, after his first week in the Cabinet.

14   Let us treat the men and women well: treat them as if they were real: perhaps they are.

RALPH WALDO EMERSON (1803–82), U.S. essayist, poet, philosopher. *Essays,* "Experience" (Second Series, 1844).

15   Truth is the glue that holds government together.

GERALD R. FORD (b. 1913), U.S. president. Speech, 9 Aug. 1974, on succeeding Richard Nixon as president.

16   Those who govern, having much business on their hands, do not generally like to take the trouble of considering and carrying into execution new projects. The best public measures are therefore seldom adopted from previous wisdom, but forced by the occasion.

BENJAMIN FRANKLIN (1706–90), U.S. statesman, writer. *Autobiography,* ch. 9 (written 1771–90; published 1868).

17   The contented and economically comfortable have a very discriminating view of government. Nobody is ever indignant about bailing out failed banks and failed savings and loans associations . . . . But when taxes must be paid for the lower middle class and poor, the government assumes an aspect of wickedness.

> JOHN KENNETH GALBRAITH (b. 1908), U.S. economist. Quoted in: *Guardian* (London, 23 May 1992).

18 I would not give half a guinea to live under one form of government rather than another. It is of no moment to the happiness of an individual.

> SAMUEL JOHNSON (1709–84), English author, lexicographer. Quoted in: James Boswell, *Life of Samuel Johnson,* 31 March 1772 (1791).

19 Of the best rulers,
The people only know that they exist;
The next best they love and praise
The next they fear;
And the next they revile.
When they do not command the people's faith,
Some will lose faith in them,
And then they resort to oaths!
But of the best when their task is accomplished,
their work done,
The people all remark, "We have done it our
selves."

> LAO-TZU (6th century B.C.), Chinese philosopher. *The Wisdom of Laotse,* ch. 17 (ed. and tr. by Lin Yutang, 1948).

20 To govern is to choose. To appear to be unable to choose is to appear to be unable to govern.

> NIGEL LAWSON (b. 1932), British Conservative politician. Quoted in: *Daily Mail* (London, 26 March 1991).

21 Generosity is a part of my character, and I therefore hasten to assure this Government that I will never make an allegation of dishonesty against it wherever a simple explanation of stupidity will suffice.

> LESLIE (BARON) LEVER (1905–77), British solicitor, Labour politician. Speech, to House of Commons, London. Quoted in: Leon Harris, *The Fine Art of Political Wit,* ch. 12 (1964).

22 Freedom of men under government is to have a standing rule to live by, common to every one of that society, and made by the legislative power vested in it; a liberty to follow my own will in all things, when the rule prescribes not, and not to be subject to the inconstant, unknown, arbitrary will of another man.

> JOHN LOCKE (1632–1704), English philosopher. *Second Treatise on Civil Government* (1690).

23 Nothing is so galling to a people not broken in from the birth as a paternal, or in other words a meddling government, a government which tells them what to read and say and eat and drink and wear.

> THOMAS, BABINGTON MACAULAY (1800–1859), English historian, Whig politician. "Southey's *Colloquies on Society,*" in *Edinburgh Review* (Jan. 1830; repr. in *Critical and Historical Essays,* 1843).

24 What is government itself but the greatest of all reflections on human nature? If men were angels, no government would be necessary. If angels were to govern men, neither external nor internal controls on government would be necessary.

> JAMES MADISON (1751–1836), U.S. president. *Federalist Papers,* no. 47 (Jan. 1788).

25 Every country has the government it deserves.

> JOSEPH DE MAISTRE (1753–1821), French diplomat, philosopher. Letter, Aug. 1811.

26 The whole duty of government is to prevent crime and to preserve contracts.

> LORD MELBOURNE (1779–1848), English statesman, prime minister. Quoted in: David Cecil, *Lord M,* ch. 3 (1954).

27 Government is actually the worst failure of civilized man. There has never been a really good one, and even those that are most tolerable are arbitrary, cruel, grasping and unintelligent.

> H. L. MENCKEN (1880–1956), U.S. journalist. *Minority Report: H. L. Mencken's Notebooks,* no. 68 (1956).

28 Not wishing to be disturbed over moral issues of the political economy, Americans cling to the notion that the government is a sort of automatic machine, regulated by the balancing of competing interests.

> C. WRIGHT MILLS (1916–62), U.S. sociologist. *The Power Elite,* ch. 11 (1956).

29 To administer is to govern: to govern is to reign. That is the essence of the problem.

> HONORÉ, COMTE DE MIRABEAU (1749–91), French statesman, revolutionary. Memorandum, 3 July 1790. Mirabeau believed to the end of his life in monarchy as the only possible form of government, though in a constitutional frame.

30 For its part, Government will listen. We will strive to listen in new ways—to the voices of quiet anguish, to voices that speak without words, the voices of the heart, to the injured voices, and the anxious voices, and the voices that have despaired of being heard.

> RICHARD M. NIXON (b. 1913), U.S. Republican politician, president. First inaugural address, 20 Jan. 1969.

31 If you join government, calmly make your contribution and move on. Don't go along to get along; do your best and when you have to—and you will—leave, and be something else.

> PEGGY NOONAN (b. 1950), U.S. author, presidential speechwriter. *What I Saw at the Revolution,* "Another Epilogue" (1990).

32 Giving money and power to government is like giving whiskey and car keys to teenage boys.

> P. J. O'ROURKE (b. 1947), U.S. journalist. *Parliament of Whores,* Preface, "Why God is a Republican and Santa Claus Is a Democrat" (1991).

33 The government is huge, stupid, greedy and makes nosy, officious and dangerous intrusions into the smallest corners of life—this much we can stand. But the real problem is that government is boring. We could cure or mitigate the other ills Washington visits on us if we could only bring ourselves to pay attention to Washington itself. But we cannot.

> P. J. O'ROURKE (b. 1947), U.S. journalist. *Parliament of Whores,* "The Mystery of Government" (1991).

34 To rule is not so much a question of the heavy hand as the firm seat.

> JOSÉ ORTEGA Y GASSET (1883–1955), Spanish essayist, philosopher. *The Revolt of the Masses,* ch. 14 (1930).

35 Society in every state is a blessing, but Government, even in its best state, is but a necessary evil; in its worst state, an intolerable one.

> THOMAS PAINE (1737–1809), Anglo-American political theorist, writer. *Common Sense*, ch. 1 (1776).

36 The punishment which the wise suffer who refuse to take part in the government, is to live under the government of worse men.

> PLATO (428–347 B.C.), Greek philosopher. Quoted in: Ralph Waldo Emerson, *Society and Solitude*, "Eloquence" (1870).

37 For Forms of Government let fools contest;
Whate'er is best administer'd is best.

> ALEXANDER POPE (1688–1744), English satirical poet. *An Essay on Man*, Epistle 3.

38 Whoso taketh in hand to frame any state or government ought to presuppose that all men are evil, and at occasions will show themselves so to be.

> SIR WALTER RALEGH (1552–1618), English author, soldier, explorer. *The Cabinet Council*, ch. 26, "Maxims of State" (repr. in *The Works of Sir Walter Raleigh*, vol. 1, 1751).

39 Government does not solve problems; it subsidizes them.

> RONALD REAGAN (b. 1911), U.S. Republican politician, president. Speech, 11 Dec. 1972 (published in *Speaking My Mind*, "The Wit and Wisdom of Ronald Reagan," 1989).

40 The government is us; we are the government, you and I.

> THEODORE ROOSEVELT (1858–1919), U.S. Republican (later Progressive) politician, president. Speech, 9 Sept. 1902, Asheville, N.C.

41 There is something to be said for government by a great aristocracy which has furnished leaders to the nation in peace and war for generations; even a democrat like myself must admit this. But there is absolutely nothing to be said for government by a plutocracy, for government by men very powerful in certain lines and gifted with the "money touch," but with ideals which in their essence are merely those of so many glorified pawnbrokers.

> THEODORE ROOSEVELT (1858–1919), U.S. Republican (later Progressive) politician, president. Letter, 15 Nov. 1913.

42 I don't judge a regime by the damning criticism of the opposition, but by the ingenuous praise of the partisan.

> JEAN ROSTAND (1894–1977), French biologist, writer. *Pensées d'un Biologiste* (1939; repr. in *The Substance of Man*, "A Biologist's Thoughts," ch. 10, 1962).

43 The mechanism that directs government cannot be virtuous, because it is impossible to thwart every crime, to protect oneself from every criminal without being criminal too; that which directs corrupt mankind must be corrupt itself; and it will never be by means of virtue, virtue being inert and passive, that you will maintain control over vice, which is ever active: the governor must be more energetic than the governed.

> MARQUIS DE SADE (1740–1814), French author. Saint-Fond, in *L'Histoire de Juliette, ou les Prospérités du Vice*, pt. 3 (1797).

44 Men are not governed by justice, but by law or persuasion. When they refuse to be governed by law or persuasion, they have to be governed by force or fraud, or both.

> GEORGE BERNARD SHAW (1856–1950), Anglo-Irish playwright, critic. Lord Summerhays, in *Misalliance*.

45 The art of government is the organization of idolatry. The bureaucracy consists of functionaries; the aristocracy, of idols; the democracy, of idolaters. The populace cannot understand the bureaucracy: it can only worship the national idols.

> GEORGE BERNARD SHAW (1856–1950), Anglo-Irish playwright, critic. *Man and Superman*, "Maxims for Revolutionists: Idolatry" (1903).

46 Government is an evil; it is only the thoughtlessness and vices of men that make it a necessary evil. When all men are good and wise, government will of itself decay.

> PERCY BYSSHE SHELLEY (1792–1822), English poet. *An Address to the Irish People* (1812). These sentiments reflect those expressed in Thomas Paine's *Common Sense* (1776)..

47 The Athenians govern the Greeks; I govern the Athenians; you, my wife, govern me; your son governs you.

> THEMISTOCLES (c. 528–c. 462 B.C.), Athenian statesman. Quoted in: Plutarch, *Parallel Lives*, "Themistocles," sct. 18. Themistocles was alleging that his son was the most powerful man in Greece.

48 Government is at best but an expedient; but most governments are usually, and all governments are sometimes, inexpedient. The objections which have been brought against a standing army, and they are many and weighty, and deserve to prevail, may also at last be brought against a standing government.

> HENRY DAVID THOREAU (1817–62), U.S. philosopher, author, naturalist. Letter, 31 July 1849, to Ellen Emerson (then 10 years old), eldest child of Ralph Waldo Emerson (published in *The Correspondence of Henry David Thoreau*, 1958).

49 This American government—what is it but a tradition, though a recent one, endeavoring to transmit itself unimpaired to posterity, but each instant losing some of its integrity? It has not the vitality and force of a single living man; for a single man can bend it to his will.

> HENRY DAVID THOREAU (1817–62), U.S. philosopher, author, naturalist. *On the Duty of Civil Disobedience* (1849).

50 The government of the world I live in was not framed, like that of Britain, in after-dinner conversations over the wine.

> HENRY DAVID THOREAU (1817–62), U.S. philosopher, author, naturalist. *Walden*, "Conclusion" (1854).

51 In quiet and untroubled times it seems to every administrator that it is only by his efforts that the whole population under his rule is kept going, and in this consciousness of being indispensable every administrator finds the chief reward of his labor and efforts. While the sea of history remains calm the ruler-administrator in his frail bark, holding on with a boat hook to the ship of the people and himself moving, naturally imagines that his efforts move the ship he is holding on to. But as soon as a storm arises and the sea begins to heave and the ship to move, such a delusion is no longer possible. The ship moves independently with its own enormous motion, the boat hook no longer reaches the moving vessel, and suddenly the administrator, instead of appearing a ruler and a source of power, becomes an insignificant, useless, feeble man.

> LEO TOLSTOY (1828–1910), Russian novelist, philosopher. *War and Peace*, bk. 11, ch. 12 (1868–69).

52 No more distressing moment can ever face a British government than that which requires it to come to a hard, fast and specific decision.

> BARBARA TUCHMAN (1912–89), U.S. historian. *The Guns of August*, ch. 9 (1962).

53 Government is either organized benevolence or organized madness; its peculiar magnitude permits no shading.

> JOHN UPDIKE (b. 1932), U.S. author, critic. The Statesman Buchanan, in *Buchanan Dying*, act 1 (1974).

54 I love my government not least for the extent to which it leaves me alone.

> JOHN UPDIKE (b. 1932), U.S. author, critic. Testimony, 30 Jan. 1978, given before the Subcommittee on Select Education of the House of Representatives Committee on Education and Labor, Boston (published in Updike, *Hugging the Shore*, Appendix, 1983).

55 Governments need to have both shepherds and butchers.

> VOLTAIRE (1694–1778), French philosopher, author. *Notebooks*, vol. 2, "The Piccini Notebooks" (1968 ed.).

56 Mankind, when left to themselves, are unfit for their own government.

> GEORGE WASHINGTON (1732–99), U.S. general, president. Letter, 31 Oct. 1786.

See also Steinem on The BODY; Reagan on BUREAUCRACY; Ickes on CORRUPTION; Caccia on DIPLOMACY; Reagan on The ECONOMY; Graffito on ELECTIONS; Cooper on INEQUALITY; Rogers on JOKES AND JOKERS; Calhoun on The MAJORITY; Phillips on NEWSPAPERS AND MAGAZINES; Disraeli on OPPOSITION; Jefferson on The PRESS; Chesterton on The RICH; Bagehot on ROYALTY; Baudrillard on SCANDAL; Shaw, Voltaire on TAXATION.

GRACE

1 There can be a fundamental gulf of gracelessness in a human heart which neither our love nor our courage can bridge.

> MRS. PATRICK CAMPBELL (1865–1940), British actress. *My Life and Some Letters*, ch. 19 (1922).

2 Grace is always natural, though that does not prevent its being often used to hide a lie. The rude shocks and uncomfortably constraining influences of life disappear among graceful women and poetical men; they are the most deceptive beings in creation; distrust and doubt cannot stand before them; they create what they imagine; if they do not lie to others, they do to their own hearts; for illusion is their element, fiction their vocation, and pleasures in appearance their happiness. Beware of grace in woman, and poetry in man—weapons the more dangerous because the least dreaded!

> MARQUIS DE CUSTINE (1790–1857), French traveler, author. *Empire of the Czar: A Journey Through Eternal Russia*, ch. 7 (1843; rev. 1989).

GRAFFITI

1 In New York—whose subway trains in particular have been "tattooed" with a brio and an energy to put our own rude practitioners to shame—not an inch of free space is spared *except that of advertisements . . . .* Even the most chronically dispossessed appear prepared to endorse the legitimacy of the "haves."

> GILBERT ADAIR, British author, critic. *Myths and Memories*, "Cleaning and Cleansing" (1986).

2 In the dime stores and bus stations,
People talk of situations,
Read books, repeat quotations,
Draw conclusions on the wall.

> BOB DYLAN (b. 1941), U.S. singer, songwriter. "Love Minus Zero/No Limit," on the album *Bringing It All Back Home* (1965).

3 What harm cause not those huge draughts or pictures which wanton youth with chalk or coals draw in each passage, wall or stairs of our great houses, whence a cruel contempt of our natural store is bred in them?

> MICHEL DE MONTAIGNE (1533–92), French essayist. *Essays*, bk. 3, ch. 5, "Upon some Verses of Virgil" (tr. by John Florio, 1588).

GRAMMAR, SPELLING, AND PUNCTUATION

1 Cut out all these exclamation points. An exclamation point is like laughing at your own joke.

> F. SCOTT FITZGERALD (1896–1940), U.S. author. Quoted in: Sheilah Graham and Gerold Frank, *Beloved Infidel*, ch. 18 (1958).

2 You can be a little ungrammatical if you come from the right part of the country.

> ROBERT FROST (1874–1963), U.S. poet. *Atlantic* (Boston, Jan. 1962).

3 What the devil to do with the sentence "Who the devil does he think he's fooling?" You can't write "Whom the devil—"

> PAUL GOODMAN (1911–72), U.S. author, poet, critic. *Five Years*, "September to December 1958," sct. 2 (1966).

4 My attitude toward punctuation is that it ought to be as conventional as *possible*. The game of golf would lose a good deal if croquet mallets and billiard cues were allowed on the putting green. You ought to be able to show that you can do it a good deal better than anyone else with the regular tools before you have a license to bring in your own improvements.

> ERNEST HEMINGWAY (1899–1961), U.S. author. Letter, 15 May 1925 (published in *Selected Letters*, ed. by Carlos Baker, 1981).

5 My spelling is Wobbly. It's good spelling but it Wobbles, and the letters get in the wrong places.

> A. A. MILNE (1882–1958), British author. Winnie-the-Pooh, in *Winnie-the-Pooh*, ch. 6 (1926).

6 Grammar, which can govern even Kings.

> MOLIÈRE (1622–73), French dramatist. Philaminte, in *Les Femmes Savantes*, act 2, sc. 6.

7   The writer who neglects punctuation, or mispunctuates, is liable to be misunderstood. . . . For the want of merely a comma, it often occurs that an axiom appears a paradox, or that a sarcasm is converted into a sermonoid.

> EDGAR ALLAN POE (1809–45), U.S. poet, critic, short-story writer. "Marginalia," in *Graham's Magazine* (Philadelphia, Feb. 1848; repr. in *Essays and Reviews,* 1984).

8   Sometimes you get a glimpse of a semicolon coming, a few lines farther on, and it is like climbing a steep path through woods and seeing a wooden bench just at a bend in the road ahead, a place where you can expect to sit for a moment, catching your breath.

> LEWIS THOMAS (b. 1913), U.S. physician, educator. *The Medusa and the Snail,* "Notes on Punctuation" (1979).

9   When I hear the hypercritical quarreling about grammar and style, the position of the particles, etc., etc., stretching or contracting every speaker to certain rules of theirs . . . I see that they forget that the first requisite and rule is that expression shall be vital and natural, as much as the voice of a brute or an interjection: first of all, mother tongue; and last of all, artificial or father tongue. Essentially your truest poetic sentence is as free and lawless as a lamb's bleat.

> HENRY DAVID THOREAU (1817–62), U.S. philosopher, author, naturalist. *Journals* (1906), entry for 2 Jan. 1859.

10   Any fool can make a rule
And every fool will mind it.

> HENRY DAVID THOREAU (1817–62), U.S. philosopher, author, naturalist. *Journals* (1906), entry for 3 Feb. 1860.

11   From one casual of mine he picked this sentence. "After dinner, the men moved into the living room." I explained to the professor that this was Ross's way of giving the men time to push back their chairs and stand up. There must, as we know, be a comma after every move, made by men, on this earth.

> JAMES THURBER (1894–1961), U.S. humorist, illustrator. Memo, 1959, to *New Yorker* (first published in *New York Times Book Review,* 4 Dec. 1988), in answer to an English professor's query. Harold Ross was editor at the *New Yorker.*

12   Grammar is the logic of speech, even as logic is the grammar of reason.

> RICHARD CHEVENIX TRENCH (1807–86), Irish ecclesiastic, archbishop of Dublin. *On the Study of Words,* Lecture 1 (1858).

13   As far as I'm concerned, "whom" is a word that was invented to make everyone sound like a butler.

> CALVIN TRILLIN (b. 1935), U.S. journalist, author. "Whom Says So?," in *Nation,* (New York, 8 June 1985).

14   Ultimately it's all a matter of style. What it comes down to is this: Do you spell Jennifer with a *J* or *G*? That's a class division. As a populist, I'm all for *G*.

> GORE VIDAL (b. 1925), U.S. novelist, critic. Interview in *Time* (New York, 28 Sept. 1992).

15   Commas in *The New Yorker* fall with the precision of knives in a circus act, outlining the victim.

> E. B. WHITE (1899–1985), U.S. author, editor. Interview in *Writers at Work* (Eighth Series, ed. by George Plimpton, 1988).

16   Like everything metaphysical the harmony between thought and reality is to be found in the grammar of the language.

> LUDWIG WITTGENSTEIN (1889–1951), Austrian philosopher. *Zettel,* sct. 55 (1967).

GRATITUDE

1   This race is never grateful: from the first,
One fills their cup at supper with pure wine,
Which back they give at cross-time on a sponge,
In bitter vinegar.

> ELIZABETH BARRETT BROWNING (1806–61), English poet. *Aurora Leigh,* bk. 8 (1857).

2   Maybe the only thing worse than having to give gratitude constantly . . . is having to accept it.

> WILLIAM FAULKNER (1897–1962), U.S. novelist. Temple Drake, in *Requiem for a Nun,* act 2, sc. 1.

3   There are minds so impatient of inferiority that their gratitude is a species of revenge, and they return benefits, not because recompense is a pleasure, but because obligation is a pain.

> SAMUEL JOHNSON (1709–84), English author, lexicographer. Quoted in: *Rambler,* no. 87 (15 Jan. 1751; repr. in *Works of Samuel Johnson,* Yale Edition, vol. 4, ed. by W. J. Bate and Albrecht B. Strauss, 1969).

4   In most of mankind gratitude is merely a secret hope of further favors.

> FRANÇOIS, DUC DE LA ROCHEFOUCAULD (1613–80), French writer, moralist. *Sentences et Maximes Morales,* no. 298 (1678).

5   One can never pay in gratitude; one can only pay "in kind" somewhere else in life.

> ANNE MORROW LINDBERGH (b. 1906), U.S. author. *North to the Orient,* ch. 19 (1935).

6   Gratitude is the most exquisite form of courtesy.

> JACQUES MARITAIN (1882–1973), French philosopher. *Reflections on America,* ch. 17 (1948).

7   Gratitude—the meanest and most snivelling attribute in the world.

> DOROTHY PARKER (1893–1967), U.S. humorous writer. Interview in *Writers at Work* (First Series, ed. by Malcolm Cowley, 1958).

8   He receives comfort like cold porridge.

> WILLIAM SHAKESPEARE (1564–1616), English dramatist, poet. Sebastian, in *The Tempest,* act 2, sc. 1.

9   Gratitude . . . is a sickness suffered by dogs.

> JOSEF STALIN (1879–1953), Soviet leader. Quoted in: Nikolai Tolstoy, *Stalin's Secret War,* ch. 2 (1981).

GREATNESS

1   The first element of greatness is fundamental humbleness (this should not be confused with servility); the second is freedom from self; the third is intrepid courage, which, taken in its widest interpretation, generally goes with truth; and the fourth—the power to love—although I have put it last, is the rarest.

> MARGOT ASQUITH (1864–1945), British socialite. *The Autobiography of Margot Asquith,* vol. 1, ch. 8 (1920).

2   Everybody comes along at the right time . . . . Leonardo was lucky because he came along at the right time. Oscar Wilde was lucky because he came at the right time—if he hadn't gone to court and been martyred he wouldn't be such a cult hero now. Or Jesus Christ—if he came back now he would really be up the shit because there's no capital punishment.

> DAVID BAILEY (b. 1938), British photographer. Quoted in: *Face* (London, Dec. 1984).

3   We shall never resolve the enigma of the relation between the negative foundations of greatness and that greatness itself.

> JEAN BAUDRILLARD (b. 1929), French semiologist. *America*, "Utopia Achieved" (1986; tr. 1988).

4   The dullard's envy of brilliant men is always assuaged by the suspicion that they will come to a bad end.

> SIR MAX BEERBOHM (1872–1956), British author. *Zuleika Dobson*, ch. 4 (1911).

5   The great must submit to the dominion of prudence and of virtue, or none will long submit to the dominion of the great.

> EDMUND BURKE (1729–97), Irish philosopher, statesman. Letter, 26 May 1795 (published in *The Writings and Speeches of Edmund Burke*, vol. 9, ed. by Paul Langford, 1991).

6   Sighing that Nature formed but one such man,
And broke the die.

> LORD BYRON (1788–1824), English poet. *Monody on the Death of Sheridan*.

7   What millions died that Caesar might be great!

> THOMAS CAMPBELL (1777–1844), Scottish poet. *Pleasures of Hope*, pt. 2.

8   No great man lives in vain. The history of the world is but the biography of great men.

> THOMAS CARLYLE (1795–1881), Scottish essayist, historian. *On Heroes and Hero-Worship*, lecture 1, "The Hero as Divinity" (1841).

9   No sadder proof can be given by a man of his own littleness than disbelief in great men.

> THOMAS CARLYLE (1795–1881), Scottish essayist, historian. *On Heroes and Hero-Worship*, lecture 1, "The Hero as Divinity" (1841).

10   It is a melancholy truth that even great men have their poor relations.

> CHARLES DICKENS (1812–70), English novelist. *Bleak House*, ch. 28 (1852).

11   At most, the greatest persons are but great wens, and excrescences; men of wit and delightfull conversation, but as moales for ornament, except they be so incorporated into the body of the world that they contribute something to the sustentation of the whole.

> JOHN DONNE (c. 1572–1631), English divine, metaphysical poet. Letter, Sept. 1608 (published in *Complete Poetry and Selected Prose*, ed. by John Hayward, 1929).

12   Despite everybody who has been born and has died, the world has just gone on. I mean, look at Napoleon—but we went right on. Look at Harpo Marx—the world went around, it didn't stop for a second. It's sad but true. John Kennedy, right?

> BOB DYLAN (b. 1941), U.S. singer, songwriter. Interview, 1966, with Robert Shelton, published in Shelton, *No Direction Home* (1986).

13   To be great is to be misunderstood.

> RALPH WALDO EMERSON (1803–82), U.S. essayist, poet, philosopher. *Essays*, "Self-Reliance" (First Series, 1841).

14   The search after the great men is the dream of youth, and the most serious occupation of manhood.

> RALPH WALDO EMERSON (1803–82), U.S. essayist, poet, philosopher. *Representative Men*, "Uses of Great Men" (1850).

15   I distrust Great Men. They produce a desert of uniformity around them and often a pool of blood too, and I always feel a little man's pleasure when they come a cropper.

> E. M. FORSTER (1879–1970), British novelist, essayist. *Two Cheers for Democracy*, "What I Believe" (1951).

16   Great men are rarely isolated mountain-peaks; they are the summits of ranges.

> THOMAS WENTWORTH HIGGINSON (1823–1911), U.S. clergyman, writer. *Atlantic Essays*, "A Plea for Culture" (1871).

17   A great man's greatest good luck is to die at the right time.

> ERIC HOFFER (1902–83), U.S. philosopher, *The Passionate State of Mind*, aph. 276 (1955).

18   To have a great man for a friend seems pleasant to those who have never tried it; those who have, fear it.

> HORACE (65–8 B.C.), Roman poet. *Epistles*, bk. 1, Epistle 18 (22–8 B.C.).

19   There is a sacred horror about everything grand. It is easy to admire mediocrity and hills; but whatever is too lofty, a genius as well as a mountain, an assembly as well as a masterpiece, seen too near, is appalling.

> VICTOR HUGO (1802–85), French poet, dramatist, novelist. *Ninety-Three*, pt. 2, bk. 3, ch. 1 (1879).

20   False greatness is unsociable and remote: conscious of its own frailty, it hides, or at least averts its face, and reveals itself only enough to create an illusion and not be recognized as the meanness that it really is. True greatness is free, kind, familiar and popular; it lets itself be touched and handled, it loses nothing by being seen at close quarters; the better one knows it, the more one admires it.

> JEAN DE LA BRUYÈRE (1645–96), French writer, moralist. *Characters*, "Of Personal Merit," aph. 42 (1688).

21   There are people who possess not so much genius as a certain talent for perceiving the desires of the century, or even of the decade, before it has done so itself.

> G. C. LICHTENBERG (1742–99), German physicist, philosopher. *Aphorisms*, "Notebook D," aph. 70 (written 1765–99; tr. by R. J. Hollingdale, 1990).

22   Lives of great men all remind us
We can make our lives sublime,
And departing, leave behind us,
Footprints on the sand of time.

HENRY WADSWORTH LONGFELLOW (1807–82), U.S. poet. *Psalm of Life.*

23 You know, sometimes, when they say you're ahead of your time, it's just a polite way of saying you have a real bad sense of timing.

GEORGE MCGOVERN (b. 1922), U.S. Democratic politician. Quoted in: *Guardian* (London, 14 March 1990).

24 The world isn't kept running because it's a paying proposition. (God doesn't make a cent on the deal.) The world goes on because a few men in every generation believe in it utterly, accept it unquestioningly; they underwrite it with their lives.

HENRY MILLER (1891–1980), U.S. author. *The Air-Conditioned Nightmare,* "With Edgar Varèse in the Gobi Desert" (1945).

25 Let us never forget that the greatest man is never more than an animal disguised as a god.

FRANCIS PICABIA (1878–1953), French painter, poet. "Jésus dit à ces Juifs," in *La Vie Moderne* (Paris, 25 Feb. 1923; repr. in *Écrits,* vol. 2, "1923," ed. by Olivier Revault d'Allones and Dominique Bouissou, 1978).

26 Greatness, in order to gain recognition, must all too often consent to ape greatness.

JEAN ROSTAND (1894–1977), French biologist, writer. *Pensées d'un Biologiste* (1939; repr. in *The Substance of Man,* 1962).

27 Th' abuse of greatness is when it disjoins
Remorse from power.

WILLIAM SHAKESPEARE (1564–1616), English dramatist, poet. Brutus, in *Julius Caesar,* act 2, sc. 1, contemplating the assassination of Caesar.

28 Some are born great, some achieve greatness, and some have greatness thrust upon 'em.

WILLIAM SHAKESPEARE (1564–1616), English dramatist, poet. Malvolio, in *Twelfth Night,* act 2, sc. 5, quoting Maria's letter.

29 Great men hallow a whole people, and lift up all who live in their time.

SYDNEY SMITH (1771–1845), English clergyman, writer. Quoted in: Lady Holland, *Memoir,* vol. 1, ch. 7 (1855).

30 In my opinion, most of the great men of the past were only there for the beer—the wealth, prestige and grandeur that went with the power.

A. J. P. TAYLOR (1906–90), British historian. Quoted in: Peter Vansittart, *Voices 1870–1914,* Introduction (1984).

31 In historic events, the so-called great men are labels giving names to events, and like labels they have but the smallest connection with the event itself. Every act of theirs, which appears to them an act of their own will, is in an historical sense involuntary and is related to the whole course of history and predestined from eternity.

LEO TOLSTOY (1828–1910), Russian novelist, philosopher. *War and Peace,* bk. 9, ch. 1 (1868–69).

32 None think the great unhappy, but the great.

EDWARD YOUNG (1683–1765), English poet, dramatist. *The Love of Fame,* Satire 1 (1725–28).

See also Burke on FACTS; Shakespeare on GLORY; Vauvenargues on IMMORTALITY; Acton on LEADERSHIP; Conrad on MANAGEMENT; La Bruyere on PUBLIC OFFICE; Holmes on SCHOLARSHIP AND SCHOLARS.

GREECE AND THE GREEKS

1 The Cretans are always liars, evil beasts, slow bellies.

BIBLE: NEW TESTAMENT. Quoted in: *Titus* 1:12 (attributed to Epimenides).

2 Ancient of days! august Athena! where,
Where are thy men of might? thy grand in soul?
Gone—glimmering through the dream of things that were.

LORD BYRON (1788–1824), English poet. *Childe Harold's Pilgrimage,* cto. 2, st. 2.

3 The isles of Greece, the isles of Greece!
Where burning Sappho loved and sung.
Where grew the arts of war and peace,
Where Delos rose, and Phoebus sprung!
Eternal summer gilds them yet,
But all, except their sun, is set.

LORD BYRON (1788–1824), English poet. *Don Juan,* cto. 3, st. 86, verse 1.

4 Out of all those centuries the Greeks can count seven sages at the most, and if anyone looks at them more closely I swear he'll not find so much as a half-wise man or even a third of a wise man among them.

DESIDERIUS ERASMUS (c. 1466–1536), Dutch humanist. *Praise of Folly,* ch. 46 (1509).

5 The Greeks possessed a knowledge of human nature we seem hardly able to attain to without passing through the strengthening hibernation of a new barbarism.

G. C. LICHTENBERG (1742–99), German physicist, philosopher. *Aphorisms,* "Notebook F," aph. 44 (written 1765–99; tr. by R. J. Hollingdale, 1990).

6 Greek philosophy seems to have met with something with which a good tragedy is not supposed to meet, namely, a dull ending.

KARL MARX (1818–83), German political theorist, social philosopher. *Doctorial Dissertation* (1840; repr. in *Karl Marx and Friedrich Engels: Collected Works,* vol. 1, 1975).

7 The mention of Greece fills the mind with the most exalted sentiments and arouses in our bosoms the best feelings of which our nature is capable.

JAMES MONROE (1758–1831), U.S. president. Message to Congress, Dec. 1822.

8 It was *modesty* which in Greece invented the word "philosopher" and left the splendid arrogance of calling oneself wise to the actors of the spirit—the modesty of such monsters of pride and self-glorification as Pythagoras, as Plato.

FRIEDRICH NIETZSCHE (1844–1900), German philosopher. *The Gay Science,* aph. 351 (1887).

9 We are only geometricians of matter; the Greeks were, first of all, geometricians in the apprenticeship to virtue.

SIMONE WEIL (1909–43), French philosopher, mystic. "The *Iliad* or the Poem of Force," in *Cahiers du Sud* (Marseilles, Dec. 1940/Jan 1941; repr. in *Simone Weil: An Anthology,* ed. by Sian Miles, tr. by Mary Mcarthy, 1986).

10 Whatever, in fact, is modern in our life we owe to the Greeks. Whatever is an anachronism is due to mediaevalism.

OSCAR WILDE (1854–1900), Anglo-Irish playwright, author. Gilbert, in "The Critic as Artist," pt. 1 (published in *Intentions*, 1891).

GREED

1 Satiety is a mongrel that barks at the heels of plenty.

MINNA ANTRIM (b. 1861), U.S. epigrammist. *Naked Truth and Veiled Allusions* (1901).

2 The love of money is the root of all evil.

BIBLE: NEW TESTAMENT. *1 Timothy* 6:10.

3 Greed is all right, by the way . . . I think greed is healthy. You can be greedy and still feel good about yourself.

IVAN F. BOESKY (b. 1937), U.S. financier. Commencement Address, 18 May 1986, School of Business Administration, University of California, Berkeley. Boesky's words were later picked up in Oliver Stone's film, *Wall Street* (1987), spoken by Gordon Gecko. Boesky himself was later convicted of conspiring to file false documents with the federal government, involving insider trading violations, and agreed to pay $100 million in fines and illicit profits.

4 Nothing retains less of desire in art, in science, than this will to industry, booty, possession.

ANDRÉ BRETON (1896–1966), French Surrealist. *Mad Love*, ch. 3 (1937; tr. 1987).

5 So for a good old-gentlemanly vice,
I think I must take up with avarice.

LORD BYRON (1788–1824), English poet. *Don Juan*, cto. 1, st. 216.

6 Greed, like the love of comfort, is a kind of fear.

CYRIL CONNOLLY (1903–74), British critic. *The Unquiet Grave*, pt. 1 (1944, rev. 1951).

7 From top to bottom of the ladder, greed is aroused without knowing where to find ultimate foothold. Nothing can calm it, since its goal is far beyond all it can attain. Reality seems valueless by comparison with the dreams of fevered imaginations; reality is therefore abandoned.

EMILE DURKHEIM (1858–1917), French sociologist. *Suicide*, bk. 2, ch. 5, sct. 3 (1897; tr. 1951).

8 Greed is a bottomless pit which exhausts the person in an endless effort to satisfy the need without ever reaching satisfaction.

ERICH FROMM (1900–1980), U.S. psychologist. *Escape from Freedom*, ch. 4 (1941).

9 Avarice, sphincter of the heart.

MATTHEW GREEN (1696–1737), English poet. *The Spleen*.

10 Avarice, the spur of industry.

DAVID HUME (1711–76), Scottish philosopher, historian. *Essays Moral, Political, and Literary*, "Of Civil Liberty" (1742).

11 Avarice is generally the last passion of those lives of which the first part has been squandered in pleasure, and the second devoted to ambition. He that sinks under the fatigue of getting wealth, lulls his age with the milder business of saving it.

SAMUEL JOHNSON (1709–84), English author, lexicographer. Quoted in: *Rambler*, no. 151 (London, 31 Aug. 1751; repr. in *Works of Samuel Johnson*, vol. 5, ed. by W. J. Bate and Albrecht B. Strauss, 1969).

12 For at least another hundred years we must pretend to ourselves and to every one that fair is foul and foul is fair; for foul is useful and fair is not. Avarice and usury and precaution must be our gods for a little longer still.

JOHN MAYNARD KEYNES (1883–1946), British economist. *Essays in Persuasion*, ch. 5, "The Future" (1931). Keynes argued that the "detestable . . . love of money" and other vices of greed must continue until the economy has grown enough to satisfy human wants and provide the potential for removing poverty.

13 The wish to acquire more is admittedly a very natural and common thing; and when men succeed in this they are always praised rather than condemned. But when they lack the ability to do so and yet want to acquire more at all costs, they deserve condemnation for their mistakes.

NICCOLÒ MACHIAVELLI (1469–1527), Italian political philosopher, statesman. *The Prince*, ch. 3 (1514).

14 God forgives the sin of gluttony.

CATALAN PROVERB. Quoted in: Colman Andrews, *Catalan Cuisine*.

15 Let me tell you, Cassius, you yourself
Are much condemn'd to have an itching palm.

WILLIAM SHAKESPEARE (1564–1616), English dramatist, poet. Brutus, in *Julius Caesar*, act 4, sc. 2.

16 Wars and revolutions and battles are due simply and solely to the body and its desires. All wars are undertaken for the acquisition of wealth; and the reason why we have to acquire wealth is the body, because we are slaves in its service.

SOCRATES (469–399 B.C.), Greek philosopher. Quoted in: Plato, *Phaedo*, sct. 65c–66e.

17 He who distinguishes the true savor of his food can never be a glutton; he who does not cannot be otherwise.

HENRY DAVID THOREAU (1817–62), U.S. philosopher, author, naturalist. *Walden*, "Higher Laws" (1854).

18 It is of the nobility of man's soul that he is insatiable: for he hath a benefactor so prone to give, that he delighteth in us for asking. Do not your inclinations tell you that the WORLD is yours? Do you not covet all? Do you not long to have it; to enjoy it; to overcome it? To what end do men gather riches, but to multiply more? Do they not like Pyrrhus the King of Epire, add house to house and lands to lands, that they may get it all?

THOMAS TRAHERNE (1636–74), English clergyman, poet, mystic. *Centuries* "First Century," no. 22 (written c. 1672; first published 1908).

19 The point is that you can't be too greedy.

DONALD TRUMP (b. 1946), U.S. businessman. *Trump: The Art of the Deal*, ch. 2 (written with Tony Schwartz, 1987).

20 Men hate the individual whom they call avaricious only because nothing can be gained from him.

VOLTAIRE (1694–1778), French philosopher, author. *Philosophical Dictionary*, "Avarice" (1764).

See also De Vries on FOOD AND EATING; Calvino on LOVE.

GRIEF

1   When we suffer anguish we return to early childhood because that is the period in which we first learnt to suffer the experience of total loss. It was more than that. It was the period in which we suffered more total losses than in all the rest of our life put together.

> JOHN BERGER (b. 1926), British author, critic. *A Fortunate Man* (1967; repr. 1976, p. 122).

2   Weeping may endure for a night, but joy cometh in the morning.

> BIBLE, HEBREW. *Psalms* 30:5.

3   I tell you, hopeless grief is passionless.

> ELIZABETH BARRETT BROWNING (1806–61), English Poet. *Grief.*

4   In deep sadness there is no place for sentimentality.

> WILLIAM BURROUGHS (b. 1914), U.S. author. *Queer*, ch. 8 (1985).

5   Pain hardens, and great pain hardens greatly, whatever the comforters say, and suffering does not ennoble, though it may occasionally lend a certain rigid dignity of manner to the suffering frame.

> A. S. BYATT (b. 1936), British author. Quoted in: *Daily Telegraph* (London, 21 July 1986).

6   There is immunity in reading, immunity in formal society, in office routine, in the company of old friends and in the giving of officious help to strangers, but there is no sanctuary in one bed from the memory of another. The past with its anguish will break through every defence-line of custom and habit; we must sleep and therefore we must dream.

> CYRIL CONNOLLY (1903–74), British critic. *The Unquiet Grave*, pt. 1 (1944; rev. 1951).

7   This is the Hour of Lead—
Remembered, if outlived,
As Freezing persons, recollect the Snow—
First—Chill—then Stupor—then the letting go—.

> EMILY DICKINSON (1830–86), U.S. poet. *The Complete Poems*, no. 341 (1955).

8   She was no longer wrestling with the grief, but could sit down with it as a lasting companion and make it a sharer in her thoughts.

> GEORGE ELIOT (1819–80), English novelist, editor. *Middlemarch*, bk. 8, ch. 80 (1871), of Dorothea Brooke.

9   In all the silent manliness of grief.

> OLIVER GOLDSMITH (1728–74), Anglo-Irish author. *The Deserted Village.*

10   While grief is fresh, every attempt to divert only irritates. You must wait till grief be *digested*, and then amusement will dissipate the remains of it.

> SAMUEL JOHNSON (1709–84), English author, lexicographer.

Quoted in: James Boswell, *Life of Samuel Johnson*, 10 April 1776 (1791).

11   Grief at the absence of a loved one is happiness compared to life with a person one hates.

> JEAN DE LA BRUYÈRE (1645–96), French writer, moralist. *Characters*, "Of the Heart," aph. 40 (1688).

12   No one ever told me that grief felt so like fear.

> C. S. LEWIS (1898–1963), British author. *A Grief Observed* (1961), opening sentence of a book of mourning for his dead wife.

13   Sorrow, the great idealizer.

> JAMES RUSSELL LOWELL (1819–91), U.S. poet, editor. *Among My Books*, "Spenser" (Second Series, 1876).

14   No matter how deep and dark your pit, how dank your shroud,
Their heads are heroically unbloody and unbowed.

> OGDEN NASH (1902–71), U.S. poet. *Look for the Silver Lining*, in *Happy Days* (1933), on "The cheery souls who drop around after every catastrophe and think they are taking the curse off/By telling you about somebody who is even worse off."

15   Who originated that most exquisite of inquisitions, the condolence system?

> ELIZABETH STUART PHELPS (1844–1911), U.S. writer. *The Gates Ajar*, ch. 2 (1869).

16   Nothing becomes so offensive so quickly as grief. When fresh it finds someone to console it, but when it becomes chronic, it is ridiculed, and rightly.

> SENECA (c. 5 B.C.–A.D. c. 65), Roman writer, philosopher, statesman. *Epistulae ad Lucilium*, Epistle 68.

17   The display of grief makes more demands than grief itself. How few men are sad in their own company.

> SENECA (c. 5 B.C.–A.D. c. 65), Roman writer, philosopher, statesman. *Epistulae ad Lucilium*, Epistle 99.

18   Grief fills the room up of my absent child,
Lies in his bed, walks up and down with me,
Puts on his pretty looks, repeats his words.

> WILLIAM SHAKESPEARE (1564–1616), English dramatist, poet. Constance, in *King John*, act 3, sc. 4, of her separation from her son Arthur.

19   The human heart dares not stay away too long from that which hurt it most. There is a return journey to anguish that few of us are released from making.

> LILLIAN SMITH (1897–1966), U.S. author. *Killers of the Dream*, pt. 1, ch. 1 (1949; rev. 1961).

20   What right have I to grieve, who have not ceased to wonder?

> HENRY DAVID THOREAU (1817–62), U.S. philosopher, author, naturalist. Letter, 2 March 1842, to Lucy Brown, sister-in-law of Ralph Waldo Emerson, following death first of Thoreau's brother, then Emerson's son (published in *The Correspondence of Henry David Thoreau*, 1958).

21   In struggling against anguish one never produces serenity; the struggle against anguish only produces new forms of anguish.

> SIMONE WEIL (1909–43), French philosopher, mystic. Draft of letter to André Weil 1940 (published in *Seventy Letters*, pt. 2, no. 39, 1965).

22 But there are other things than dissipation that thicken the features. Tears, for example.

> REBECCA WEST (1892–1983), British author. *Black Lamb and Grey Falcon,* "Serbia" (1941).

See also Shaw, Thoreau on BEREAVEMENT; Smith on MONEY; MOURNING; UNHAPPINESS; WIDOWHOOD.

THE GROTESQUE

1 There's a quality of legend about freaks. Like a person in a fairy tale who stops you and demands that you answer a riddle. Most people go through life dreading they'll have a traumatic experience. Freaks were born with their trauma. They've already passed their test in life. They're aristocrats.

> DIANE ARBUS (1923–71), U.S. photographer. From class lectures given in 1971 (published in *Diane Arbus: An Aperture Monograph,* 1972).

2 Her skin was white as leprosy,
The nightmare Life-in-Death was she,
Who thicks man's blood with cold.

> SAMUEL TAYLOR COLERIDGE (1772–1834), English poet, critic. *The Ancient Mariner,* pt. 3, st. 11.

3 I have found that anything that comes out of the South is going to be called grotesque by the Northern reader, unless it is grotesque, in which case it is going to be called realistic.

> FLANNERY O'CONNOR (1925–64), U.S. author. "Some Aspects of the Grotesque in Southern Fiction," paper, read at Wesleyan College for Women, Macon, Georgia (published in *Cluster Review,* Macon, 1965; repr. in *Mystery and Manners,* ed. by Sally and Robert Fitzgerald, 1972).

4 The freakish is no longer a private zone, difficult of access. People who are bizarre, in sexual disgrace, emotionally violent are seen daily on the newsstands, on TV, in the subways. Hobbesian man roams the streets, quite visible, with glitter in his hair.

> SUSAN SONTAG (b. 1933), U.S. essayist. *On Photography,* "America, Seen Through Photographs, Darkly" (1977).

GROWTH

1 The fatal metaphor of progress, which means leaving things behind us, has utterly obscured the real idea of growth, which means leaving things inside us.

> G. K. CHESTERTON (1874–1936), British author. *Fancies Versus Fads,* "The Romance of Rhyme" (1923).

2 Unlimited economic growth has the marvelous quality of stilling discontent while maintaining privilege, a fact that has not gone unnoticed among liberal economists.

> NOAM CHOMSKY (b. 1928), U.S. linguist, political analyst. *For Reasons of State,* Introduction (1973).

3 A tree that can fill the span of a man's arms
Grows from a downy tip;
A terrace nine stories high
Rises from hodfuls of earth;

A journey of a thousand miles
Starts from beneath one's feet.

> LAO-TZU (6th century B.C.), Chinese philosopher. *Tao-te-ching,* bk. 2, ch. 64 (tr. by T. C. Lau, 1963).

4 All growth is a leap in the dark, a spontaneous unpremeditated act without benefit of experience.

> HENRY MILLER (1891–1980), U.S. author. *The Wisdom of the Heart,* "The Absolute Collective" (1947).

5 What is the most rigorous law of our being? Growth. No smallest atom of our moral, mental, or physical structure can stand still a year. It grows—it must grow; nothing can prevent it.

> MARK TWAIN (1835–1910), U.S. author. "Consistency," paper, read in Hartford, Connecticut, in 1884 (published 1923; repr. in *Complete Essays,* ed. by Charles Neider, 1963).

GUERRILLA WARFARE

1 The conventional army loses if it does not win. The guerrilla wins if he does not lose.

> HENRY KISSINGER (b. 1923), U.S. Republican politician, secretary of state. Quoted in: *Foreign Affairs* (New York, Jan. 1969), on the war in Vietnam.

2 It is necessary to turn political crisis into armed crisis by performing violent actions that will force those in power to transform the military situation into a political situation. That will alienate the masses, who, from then on, will revolt against the army and the police and blame them for this state of things.

> CARLOS MARIGHELLA (d. 1969), Brazilian guerrilla leader. *Minimanual of the Urban Guerrilla* (1969).

3 Insurrection—by means of guerrilla bands—is the true method of warfare for all nations desirous of emancipating themselves from a foreign yoke . . . It is invincible, indestructible.

> GIUSEPPE MAZZINI (1805–72), Italian nationalist leader. *General Instructions for the Members of Young Italy,* sct. 4 (1831).

See also Kirkpatrick on VIETNAM.

GUESTS

1 One might well say that mankind is divisible into two great classes: hosts and guests.

> SIR MAX BEERBOHM (1872–1956), British essayist, caricaturist. *And Even Now,* "Hosts and Guests" (1920; essay written 1918).

2 Whoever is admitted or sought for, in company, upon any other account than that of his merit and manners, is never respected there, but only made use of. We will have such-a-one, for he sings prettily; we will invite such-a-one to a ball, for he dances well; we will have such-a-one at supper, for he is always joking and laughing; we will ask another because he plays deep at all games, or because he can drink a great deal. These are all vilifying distinctions, mortifying preferences, and exclude all ideas of esteem and regard. Whoever *is had* (as it is called) in company for the sake of any one thing singly, is singly that thing, and will never be considered in any other light; consequently never respected, let his merits be what they will.

> LORD CHESTERFIELD (1694–1773), English statesman, man of letters. Letter, 30 Aug. 1749 (published 1774; repr. in *The Letters of the Earl of Chesterfield to His Son*, vol. 1, no. 190, ed. by Charles Strachey, 1901).

3   Some men are like musical glasses; to produce their finest tones, you must keep them wet.

> SAMUEL TAYLOR COLERIDGE (1772–1834), English poet, critic. "Table Talk," in *Specimens of the Table Talk of Samuel Taylor Coleridge* (ed. by Henry Nelson Coleridge, 1835; repr. in *Collected Works*, ed. by Kathleen Coburn, vol. 14, 1990).

4   When any one of our relations was found to be a person of a very bad character, a troublesome guest, or one we desired to get rid of, upon his leaving my house I ever took care to lend him a riding-coat, or a pair of boots, or sometimes a horse of small value, and I always had the satisfaction of finding he never came back to return them.

> OLIVER GOLDSMITH (1728–74), Anglo-Irish author, poet, playwright. The narrator (Dr. Charles Primrose), in *The Vicar of Wakefield*, ch. 1 (1766).

5   Makin' a long stay short is a great aid t' popularity.

> KIN [F. MCKINNEY] HUBBARD (1868–1930), U.S. humorist, journalist. *Abe Martin's Wisecracks* (ed. by E. V. Lucas, 1930).

6   The first day a man is a guest, the second a burden, the third a pest.

> EDOUARD LABOULAYE (1811–83), French writer, satirist. Abdallah, in *Abdallah*, ch. 9 (1871).

7   Frank Harris has been received in all the great houses—once!

> OSCAR WILDE (1854–1900), Anglo-Irish playwright, author. Quoted in: John F. Gallagher's introduction to Harris, *My Life and Loves* (1963 ed.).

See also DINNER PARTIES; HOSPITALITY.

GUILT

1   It is quite gratifying to feel guilty if you haven't done anything wrong: how noble! Whereas it is rather hard and certainly depressing to admit guilt and to repent.

> HANNAH ARENDT (1906–75), German-born U.S. political philosopher. *Eichmann in Jerusalem*, ch. 15 (1963).

2   A poor American feels guilty at being poor, but less guilty than an American *rentier* who has inherited wealth but is doing nothing to increase it; what can the latter do but take to drink and psychoanalysis?

> W. H. AUDEN (1907–73), Anglo-American poet. *The Dyer's Hand*, pt. 6, "Postscript: The Almighty Dollar" (1962).

3   Even upon such a basis hast thou built
A monument, whose cement hath been guilt!

> LORD BYRON (1788–1824), English poet. *Lines on Hearing that Lady Byron Was Ill*.

4   Fancy that thou deservest to be hanged . . . thou wilt feel it happiness to be only shot: fancy that thou deservest to be hanged in a hair halter, it will be a luxury to die in hemp.

> THOMAS CARLYLE (1795–1881), Scottish essayist, historian. Teufelsdröckh, in *Sartor Resartus*, bk. 2, ch. 9 (1833–34).

5   Guilt always hurries towards its complement, punishment; only there does its satisfaction lie.

> LAWRENCE DURRELL (1912–90), British author. *Justine*, pt. 3 (1957).

6   Solomon's Proverbs, I think, have omitted to say, that as the sore palate findeth grit, so an uneasy consciousness heareth innuendos.

> GEORGE ELIOT (1819–80), English novelist, editor. *Middlemarch*, bk. 3, ch. 31 (1871).

7   In the small circle of pain within the skull
You still shall tramp and tread one endless round
Of thought, to justify your action to yourselves,
Weaving a fiction which unravels as you weave,
Pacing forever in the hell of make-believe
Which never is belief: this is your fate on earth
And we must think no further of you.

> T. S. ELIOT (1888–1965), Anglo-American poet, critic. Third Priest, in *Murder in the Cathedral*, pt. 2 (1935).

8   Guilt has very quick ears to an accusation.

> HENRY FIELDING (1707–54), English novelist, dramatist. *Amelia*, bk. 3, ch. 11 (1751).

9   The extent of one man's guilt may be defined by how much of it is experienced by the party he injured.

> RYSZARD KAPUSCINSKI (b. 1932), Polish journalist. "A Warsaw Diary," in *Granta*, no. 15 (Cambridge, England, 1985).

10   True guilt is guilt at the obligation one owes to oneself to be oneself. False guilt is guilt felt at not being what other people feel one ought to be or assume that one is.

> R. D. LAING (1927–89), British psychiatrist. *The Self and Others*, ch. 10 (1961).

11   How extraordinary it is that one feels most guilt about the sins one is unable to commit.

> V. S. PRITCHETT (b. 1900), British author, critic. *Midnight Oil*, vol. 2, ch. 10 (1971).

12   The offender never pardons.

> ENGLISH PROVERB. Collected in George Herbert, *Outlandish Proverbs* (1640).

13   I had most need of blessing, and "Amen"
Stuck in my throat.

> WILLIAM SHAKESPEARE (1564–1616), English dramatist, poet. Macbeth, in *Macbeth*, act 2, sc. 2.

HABIT

1   Certes, they been lyk to houndes, for an hound whan he comth by the roser, or by other bushes, though he may nat pisse, yet wole he heve up his leg and make a contenaunce to pisse.

> GEOFFREY CHAUCER (1340–1400), English poet. *The Canterbury Tales*, "Parson's Tale: Sequitur de Luxuria," sct. 855 (published in *The Works of Geoffrey Chaucer*, ed. by Alfred W. Pollard et. al., 1898).

2   To *exist* is a habit I do not despair of acquiring.

> E. M. CIORAN (b. 1911), Rumanian-born French philosopher. *The Temptation to Exist*, title essay (1956).

3   Habit with him was all the test of truth,
It must be right: I've done it from my youth.

> GEORGE CRABBE (1754–1832), English clergyman, poet. *The Borough,* letter 3, "The Vicar."

4   Wise living consists perhaps less in acquiring good habits than in acquiring as few habits as possible.

> ERIC HOFFER (1902–83), U.S. philosopher. *The Passionate State of Mind,* aph. 264 (1955).

5   Habit is thus the enormous fly-wheel of society, its most precious conservative agent. It alone is what keeps us all within the bounds of ordinance, and saves the children of fortune from the envious uprisings of the poor.

> WILLIAM JAMES (1842–1910), U.S. psychologist, philosopher. *Principles of Psychology,* vol. 1, ch. 4 (1890).

6   One might call habit a moral friction: something that prevents the mind from gliding over things but connects it with them and makes it hard for it to free itself from them.

> G. C. LICHTENBERG (1742–99), German physicist, philosopher. *Aphorisms,* aph. 10, "Notebook A" (written 1765–99; tr. by R. J. Hollingdale, 1990).

7   Habit is a second nature that destroys the first. But what is nature? Why is habit not natural? I am very much afraid that nature itself is only a first habit, just as habit is a second nature.

> BLAISE PASCAL (1623–62), French scientist, philosopher. *Pensées,* (1670; no. 126 ed. by Krailsheimer, no. 93 ed. by Brunschvicg).

8   The regularity of a habit is generally in proportion to its absurdity.

> MARCEL PROUST (1871–1922), French novelist. *Remembrance of Things Past,* vol. 9 "The Captive," pt. 1, ch. 1 (1922; tr. 1929).

9   Habits are the daughters of action, but then they nurse their mother, and produce daughters after her image, but far more beautiful and prosperous.

> JEREMY TAYLOR (1613–67), English churchman, devotional writer. *Twenty-Five Sermons,* Sermon 14, "Of Lukewarmness and Zeal" (1651).

10   Habit is habit, and not to be flung out of the window by any man, but coaxed downstairs a step at a time.

> MARK TWAIN (1835–1910), U.S. author. *Pudd'nhead Wilson,* ch. 6, "Pudd'nhead Wilson's Calendar" (1894).

11   To fall into a habit is to begin to cease to be.

> MIGUEL DE UNAMUNO (1864–1936), Spanish philosophical writer. *The Tragic Sense of Life,* ch. 9 (1913).

12   Rigid, the skeleton of habit alone upholds the human frame.

> VIRGINIA WOOLF (1882–1941), British novelist. *Mrs. Dalloway* (1925, p. 62).

HAIR

1   But if a woman have long hair, it is a glory to her: for *her* hair is given her for a covering.

> BIBLE: NEW TESTAMENT. *I Corinthians* 11:15.

2   People get real comfortable with their features. Nobody gets comfortable with their hair. Hair trauma. It's the universal thing.

> JAMIE LEE CURTIS (b. 1958), U.S. screen actor. *U.S.* (21 Feb. 1991).

3   Robert Redford . . . has turned almost alarmingly blond—he's gone past platinum, he must be into plutonium; his hair is coordinated with his teeth.

> PAULINE KAEL (b. 1919), U.S. film critic. *Reeling,* pt. 2, "The Sting" (1976).

4   Being blond is definitely a different state of mind. I can't really put my finger on it, but the artifice of being blond has some incredible sort of sexual connotation.

> MADONNA (b. 1959), U.S. singer, actor. Interview in *Rolling Stone* (New York, 23 March 1989).

5   In truth, a mature man who uses hair-oil, unless medicinally, that man has probably got a quoggy spot in him somewhere. As a general rule, he can't amount to much in his totality.

> HERMAN MELVILLE (1819–91), U.S. author. *Moby-Dick,* ch. 25 (1851).

6   A chaste woman ought not to die her hair yellow.

> MENANDER (c. 342-c. 291 B.C.), Greek playwright. *Fragments,* no. 610.

7   Fair tresses man's imperial race insnare,
And beauty draws us with a single hair.

> ALEXANDER POPE (1688–1744), English satirical poet. *The Rape of the Lock,* cto. 2.

8   A woman with cut hair is a filthy spectacle, and much like a monster . . . it being natural and comely to women to nourish their hair, which even God and nature have given them for a covering, a token of subjection, and a natural badge to distinguish them from men.

> WILLIAM PRYNNE (1600–1669), English Puritan pamphleteer. *Histriomastix* (1632).

See also BALDNESS; BEARDS; Byron on The DEAD, Juvenal on MEN AND MASCULINITY.

HANDSHAKES

1   The hands of those I meet are dumbly eloquent to me. The touch of some hands is an impertinence. I have met people so empty of joy, that when I clasped their frosty finger-tips, it seemed as if I were shaking hands with a northeast storm. Others there are whose hands have sunbeams in them, so that their grasp warms my heart.

> HELEN KELLER (1880–1968), U.S. blind/deaf author, lecturer. *The Story of My Life,* pt. 1, ch. 23 (1903).

2   If we shake hands with icy fingers, it is because we've burnt them so hatefully before.

> LOGAN PEARSALL SMITH (1865–1946), U.S. essayist, aphorist. *Afterthoughts,* "Age and Death" (1931).

HAPPINESS

1 If happiness is activity in accordance with excellence, it is reasonable that it should be in accordance with the highest excellence.

> ARISTOTLE (384–322 B.C.), Greek philosopher. *Nicomachean Ethics*, bk. 10, ch. 7.

2 The said truth is that it is the greatest happiness of the greatest number that is the measure of right and wrong.

> JEREMY BENTHAM (1748–1832), English philosopher, political theorist, jurist. *Fragment of Government* (1776), repeated with minor variations in later writings. Bentham ascribed the originator of this definition to be either clergyman and scientist Joseph Priestley (1733–1804) or Italian legal reformer Cesare Beccaria (1738–94), though the Scottish philosopher Francis Hutcheson had said much the same in his *Inquiry into the Original of our Ideas of Beauty and Virtue*, pt. 2, sct.3 (1725): "That action is best which procures the greatest happiness for the greatest numbers."

3 We all want to be happy, and we're all going to die. . . . You might say those are the only two unchallengeably true facts that apply to every human being on this planet.

> WILLIAM BOYD (b. 1952), British novelist. Loomis Gage, in *Stars and Bars*, pt. 2, ch. 6 (1984).

4 But the whim we have of happiness is somewhat thus. By certain valuations, and averages, of our own striking, we come upon some sort of average terrestrial lot; this we fancy belongs to us by nature, and of indefeasible rights. It is simple payment of our wages, of our deserts; requires neither thanks nor complaint. . . . Foolish soul! What act of legislature was there that *thou* shouldst be happy? A little while ago thou hadst no right to *be* at all.

> THOMAS CARLYLE (1795–1881), Scottish essayist, historian. Teufelsdröckh, in *Sartor Resartus*, bk. 2, ch. 9 (1833–34).

5 It seldom happens that any felicity comes so pure as not to be tempered and allayed by some mixture of sorrow.

> MIGUEL DE CERVANTES (1547–1616), Spanish writer. The slave, in *Don Quixote*, pt. 1, bk. 4, ch. 14 (1605; tr. by P. Motteux).

6 Happiness is a mystery, like religion, and should never be rationalised.

> G. K. CHESTERTON (1874–1936), British author. *Heretics*, ch. 7 (1905).

7 Happiness is always a by-product. It is probably a matter of temperament, and for anything I know it may be glandular. But it is not something that can be demanded from life, and if you are not happy you had better stop worrying about it and see what treasures you can pluck from your own brand of unhappiness.

> ROBERTSON DAVIES (b. 1913), Canadian novelist, journalist. "The Table Talk of Robertson Davies," in /ital/Maclean's (Toronto, Sept. 1972; repr. in *The Enthusiasms of Robertson Davies*, 1990).

8 Gaiety—a quality of ordinary men. Genius always presupposes some disorder in the machine.

> DENIS DIDEROT (1713–84), French philosopher. *Elements of Physiology*, "Diseases" (notes written 1774–80; first published 1875; repr. in *Selected Writings*, ed. by Lester G. Crocker, 1966).

9 Shall I give you my recipe for happiness? I find everything useful and nothing indispensable. I find everything wonderful and nothing miraculous. I reverence the body. I avoid first causes like the plague.

> NORMAN DOUGLAS (1868–1952), British author. Mr. Keith, in *South Wind*, ch. 18 (1917).

10 One feels inclined to say that the intention that man should be "happy" is not included in the plan of "Creation."

> SIGMUND FREUD (1856–1939), Austrian psychiatrist. *Civilization and its Discontents*, ch. 2 (1930; repr. in *Complete Works*, vol. 21, ed. by James Strachey & Anna Freud, 1961). Freud defined happiness as, in the strictest sense, "the (preferably sudden) satisfaction of needs which have been dammed up to a high degree." It was thus episodic by nature, since "we are so made that we can derive intense enjoyment only from a contrast and very little from a state of things."

11 Happiness makes up in height what it lacks in length.

> ROBERT FROST (1874–1963), U.S. poet. Title of a poem published in *A Witness Tree* (1942).

12 The hardest habit of all to break
Is the terrible habit of happiness.

> THEODOSIA GARRISON (1874–1944), U.S. poet, author. *The Lake.*

13 Point me out the happy man and I will point you out either egotism, selfishness, evil—or else an absolute ignorance.

> GRAHAM GREENE (1904–91), British novelist. *The Heart of the Matter*, bk. 2, pt. 1, ch. 1, sct. 3 (1948).

14 The History of the world is not the theatre of happiness. Periods of happiness are blank pages in it, for they are periods of harmony—periods when the antithesis is in abeyance.

> GEORG HEGEL (1770–1831), German philosopher. *The Philosophy of History*, "Introduction," sct. 3 (1837).

15 The search for happiness is one of the chief sources of unhappiness.

> ERIC HOFFER (1902–83), U.S. philosopher. *The Passionate State of Mind*, aph. 280 (1955).

16 The great end of all human industry is the attainment of happiness. For this were arts invented, sciences cultivated, laws ordained, and societies modelled, by the most profound wisdom of patriots and legislators. Even the lonely savage, who lies exposed to the inclemency of the elements and the fury of wild beasts, forgets not, for a moment, this grand object of his being.

> DAVID HUME (1711–76), Scottish philosopher, historian. *Essays Moral, Political, and Literary*, pt. 1, "The Stoic" (1742; repr. in *The Philosophical Works of David Hume*, vol. 3, 1826).

17 I can sympathise with people's pains, but not with their pleasures. There is something curiously boring about somebody else's happiness.

> ALDOUS HUXLEY (1894–1963), British author. *Limbo*, "Cynthia" (1920).

18 Sir, that all who are happy, are equally happy, is not true. A peasant and a philosopher may be equally *satisfied*, but not equally *happy*. Happiness consists in the multiplicity of agreeable consciousness.

> SAMUEL JOHNSON (1709–84), English author, lexicographer. Quoted in: Boswell, *Life of Samuel Johnson*, Feb. 1766 (1791). Johnson was arguing against the proposition by David Hume (in the essay *The Sceptic*) that "a little miss, dressed in a new gown for a dancing-school ball, receives as complete enjoyment as the greatest orator, who triumphs in the splendor of his eloquence." See also Pope on DIVERSITY.

19 In theory there is a possibility of perfect happiness: To believe in the indestructible element within one, and not to strive towards it.

> FRANZ KAFKA (1883–1924), German novelist, short-story writer. *The Collected Aphorisms*, no. 68 (Oct. 1917–Feb. 1918; published in *Shorter Works*, vol. 1, ed. and tr. by Malcolm Pasley, 1973).

20 Ask yourself whether you are happy, and you cease to be so.

> JOHN STUART MILL (1806–73), English philosopher, economist. *Autobiography*, ch. 5 (1873).

21 There is something ridiculous and even quite indecent in an individual *claiming* to be happy. Still more a people or a nation making such a claim. The pursuit of happiness . . . is without any question the most fatuous which could possibly be undertaken. This lamentable phrase "the pursuit of happiness" is responsible for a good part of the ills and miseries of the modern world.

> MALCOLM MUGGERIDGE (1903–90), British broadcaster. "Woman's Hour," radio broadcast, 5 Oct. 1965. Quoted in: *Muggeridge Through the Microphone* (1967). Muggeridge continued: "The pursuit of happiness in any case soon resolved itself into the pursuit of pleasure—something quite different. Pleasure is but a mirage of happiness—a false vision of shade and refreshment seen across parched sand."

22 Happiness is a matter of one's most ordinary everyday mode of consciousness being busy and lively and unconcerned with self. To be damned is for one's ordinary everyday mode of consciousness to be unremitting agonising preoccupation with self.

> IRIS MURDOCH (b. 1919), British novelist, philosopher. Willy Kost, in *The Nice and the Good*, ch. 22 (1968).

23 The most exciting happiness is the happiness generated by forces beyond your control.

> OGDEN NASH (1902–71), U.S. poet. *The Anatomy of Happiness*, in *I'm a Stranger Here Myself* (1938).

24 Even if happiness forgets you a little bit, never completely forget about it.

> JACQUES PRÉVERT (1900–1977), French poet. *Spectacle*, "Intermede" (1951).

25 Happiness serves hardly any other purpose than to make unhappiness possible.

> MARCEL PROUST (1871–1922), French novelist. *Remembrance of Things Past*, vol. 12, ch. 3, "Time Regained" (1927; tr. by Stephen Hudson, 1931).

26 Let us be grateful to people who make us happy; they are the charming gardeners who make our souls blossom.

> MARCEL PROUST (1871–1922), French novelist. *Pleasures and Regrets*, "Regrets, Reveries, Changing Skies," no. 12 (1896; tr. 1948).

27 Happiness lies neither in vice nor in virtue; but in the manner we appreciate the one and the other, and the choice we make pursuant to our individual organization.

> MARQUIS DE SADE (1740–1814), French author. Saint-Fond, in *L'Histoire de Juliette, ou les Prospérités du Vice*, pt. 2 (1797).

28 Happiness is the only sanction of life; where happiness fails, existence remains a mad and lamentable experiment.

> GEORGE SANTAYANA (1863–1952), U.S. philosopher, poet. *The Life of Reason*, "Reason in Common Sense," ch. 8 (1905–6, rev. ed. 1953).

29 But O, how bitter a thing it is to look into happiness through another man's eyes.

> WILLIAM SHAKESPEARE (1564–1616), English dramatist, poet. Orlando, in *As You Like It*, act 5, sc. 21–42.

30 We have no more right to consume happiness without producing it than to consume wealth without producing it.

> GEORGE BERNARD SHAW (1856–1950), Anglo-Irish playwright, critic. Morell, in *Candida*, act 1.

31 Life at its noblest leaves mere happiness far behind; and indeed cannnot endure it. . . . Happiness is not the object of life: life has no object: it is an end in itself; and courage consists in the readiness to sacrifice happiness for an intenser quality of life.

> GEORGE BERNARD SHAW (1856–1950), Anglo-Irish playwright, critic. Letter, Dec. 1900 (published in *Collected Letters*, vol. 2, 1972).

32 Give a man health and a course to steer; and he'll never stop to trouble about whether he's happy or not.

> GEORGE BERNARD SHAW (1856–1950), Anglo-Irish playwright, critic. Brassbound, in *Captain Brassbound's Conversion*, act 3.

33 Happiness is a wine of the rarest vintage, and seems insipid to a vulgar taste.

> LOGAN PEARSALL SMITH (1865–1946), U.S. essayist, aphorist. *Afterthoughts*, "Life and Human Nature" (1931).

34 We are never happy; we can only remember that we were so once.

> ALEXANDER SMITH (1830–67), Scottish poet. *Dreamthorp*, "On Death and the Fear of Dying" (1863).

35 Let no man be called happy before his death. Till then, he is not happy, only lucky.

> Attributed to SOLON (c. 640–c. 558 B.C.), Greek statesman and poet. In answer to the fabulously wealthy Croesus, who asked him who was the happiest man Solon had encountered on his travels—expecting Solon to name Croesus himself. Croesus dismissed Solon, only to remember his words when sentenced to death following his disastrous invasion of Persia (though the sentence was rescinded when the Persian king, Cyrus, heard the tale). The story is related by Herodotus in his *Histories*, bk. 1, though has no historical basis: Solon died before he could have met Croesus.

36 Happiness consumes itself like a flame. It cannot burn for ever, it must go out, and the presentiment of its end destroys it at its very peak.

> J. AUGUST STRINDBERG (1849–1912), Swedish dramatist, novelist, poet. The Husband, in *A Dream Play*.

37 Happiness is an imaginary condition, formerly

often attributed by the living to the dead, now usually attributed by adults to children, and by children to adults.

THOMAS SZASZ (b. 1920), U.S. psychiatrist. *The Second Sin*, "Emotions" (1973).

38 We are made happy when reason can discover no occasion for it. The memory of some past moments is more persuasive than the experience of present ones. There have been visions of such breadth and brightness that these motes were invisible in their light.

HENRY DAVID THOREAU (1817–62), U.S. philosopher, author, naturalist. Letter of condolence, 2 March 1842, to Lucy Brown, Ralph Waldo Emerson's sister-in-law (published in *The Correspondence of Henry David Thoreau*, 1958).

39 Happiness was not made to be boasted, but enjoyed. Therefore tho' others count me miserable, I will not believe them if I know and feel myself to be happy; nor fear them.

THOMAS TRAHERNE (1636–74), English clergyman, poet, mystic. *Centuries*, "Fourth Century," no. 12 (written c. 1672; first published 1908).

40 You never enjoy the world aright, till the sea itself floweth in your veins, till you are clothed with the heavens and crowned with the stars.

THOMAS TRAHERNE (1636–74), English clergyman, poet, mystic. *Centuries*, "First Century," no. 29 (c. 1672, first published 1908).

41 Happiness ain't a *thing in itself*—it's only a contrast with something that ain't pleasant. . . . And so, as soon as the novelty is over and the force of the contrast dulled, it ain't happiness any longer, and you have to get something fresh.

MARK TWAIN (1835–1910), U.S. author. Sam Bartlett, in *Captain Stormfield's Visit to Heaven*, ch. 1 (written 1907; published in *The Complete Short Stories*, ed. by Charles Neider, 1957).

42 There are people who can do all fine and heroic things but one: keep from telling their happinesses to the unhappy.

MARK TWAIN (1835–1910), U.S. author. *Following the Equator*, ch. 26, "Pudd'nhead Wilson's New Calendar" (1897).

43 There is that in me—I do not know what it is—but I know it is in me . . .
I do not know it—it is without name—it is a word unsaid,
It is not in any dictionary, utterance, symbol . . .
Do you see O my brothers and sisters?
It is not chaos or death—it is form, union, plan—it is eternal life—it is Happiness.

WALT WHITMAN (1819–92), U.S. poet. *Leaves of Grass*, "Song of Myself," sct. 50 (1855).

44 When we are happy we are always good, but when we are good we are not always happy.

OSCAR WILDE (1854–1900), Anglo-Irish playwright, author. Lord Henry, in *The Picture of Dorian Gray*, ch. 6 (1891).

See also Byron on COMPANY; CONTENTMENT; Camus on DISCONTENT; Warshow on EQUALITY; Smith on HOME AND HOUSES; Shaw on UNHAPPINESS.

HARD TIMES

1 Hardship makes the world obscure.

DON DELILLO (b. 1926), U.S. author. James Axton, in *The Names*, ch. 12 (1982).

2 Bad times have a scientific value. These are occasions a good learner would not miss.

RALPH WALDO EMERSON (1803–82), U.S. essayist, poet, philosopher. *The Conduct of Life*, "Considerations by the Way" (1860).

3 As favor and riches forsake a man, we discover in him the foolishness they concealed, and which no one perceived before.

JEAN DE LA BRUYÈRE (1645–96), French writer, moralist. *Characters*, "Of Worldly Goods," aph. 4 (1688).

4 In really hard times the rules of the game are altered. The inchoate mass begins to stir. It becomes potent, and when it strikes, . . . it strikes with incredible emphasis. Those are the rare occasions when a national will emerges from the scattered, specialized, or indifferent blocs of voters who ordinarily elect the politicians. Those are for good or evil the great occasions in a nation's history.

WALTER LIPPMANN (1889–1974), U.S. journalist. "The New Congress," in *New York Herald Tribune* (8 Dec. 1931; repr. in *The Essential Lippman*, pt. 3, sct. 6, 1982).

5 Thy fate is the common fate of all;
Into each life some rain must fall.

HENRY WADSWORTH LONGFELLOW (1807–82), U.S. poet. *The Rainy Day*.

6 every cloud
has its silver
lining but it is
sometimes a little
difficult to get it to
the mint

DON MARQUIS (1878–1937), U.S. humorist, journalist. *archy and mehitabel*, "certain maxims of archy" (1927).

7 Life isn't meant to be easy. It's hard to take being on the top—or on the bottom. I guess I'm something of a fatalist. You have to have a sense of history, I think, to survive some of these things. . . . Life is one crisis after another.

RICHARD M. NIXON (b. 1913), U.S. Republican politician, president. Quoted in: Robert Sam Anson, *Exile: The Unquiet Oblivion of Richard M. Nixon*, ch. 17 (1984), on the Watergate scandal, said to interviewer Sept. 1980.

8 I don't like people who have never fallen or stumbled. Their virtue is lifeless and it isn't of much value. Life hasn't revealed its beauty to them.

BORIS PASTERNAK (1890–1960), Russian poet, novelist, translator. Zhivago, in *Doctor Zhivago*, ch. 13, sct. 12 (1957).

9 When you are down and out something always turns up—and it is usually the noses of your friends.

ORSON WELLES (1915–85), U.S. filmmaker. *New York Times* (1 April 1962).

See also ADVERSITY; Addison on STARDOM.

HASTE

1 Being in a hurry is one of the tributes he pays to life.

ELIZABETH ASQUITH BIBESCO (1897–1945), British author, poet. *Balloons.*

2 Does the devil possess you? You're leaping over the hedge before you come at the stile.

MIGUEL DE CERVANTES (1547–1616), Spanish writer. Sancho Panza to Don Quixote, in *Don Quixote,* pt. 1, bk. 3, ch. 4 (1605; tr. by P. Motteux).

3 Ther nis no werkman, whatsoevere he be,
That may bothe werke wel and hastily.

GEOFFREY CHAUCER (1340–1400), English poet. Januarie, in *The Canterbury Tales,* "The Merchant's Tale" (c. 1387–1400).

4 Whoever is in a hurry, shows that the thing he is about is too big for him.

LORD CHESTERFIELD (1694–1773), English statesman, man of letters. Letter, 30 Aug. 1749 (first published 1774; repr. in *The Letters of the Earl of Chesterfield to His Son,* vol. 1, no. 190, ed. by Charles Strachey, 1901).

5 The feeling of being hurried is not usually the result of living a full life and having no time. It is on the contrary born of a vague fear that we are wasting our life. When we do not do the one thing we ought to do, we have no time for anything else—we are the busiest people in the world.

ERIC HOFFER (1902–83), U.S. philosopher. *Reflections on the Human Condition,* aph. 156 (1973).

6 A nation rushing hastily too and fro, busily employed in idleness.

PHAEDRUS (1st century A.D.), Roman fabulist. *Fables,* bk. 5, fable 2.

7 He sows hurry and reaps indigestion.

ROBERT LOUIS STEVENSON (1850–94), Scottish novelist, essayist, poet. *Virginibus Puerisque,* "An Apology for Idlers" (1881), on "industrious fellows."

See also Browning on AGE AND AGING; Carroll on MODERN TIMES; Thurber on SPEED.

HATE

1 To be loved is to be fortunate, but to be hated is to achieve distinction.

MINNA ANTRIM (b. 1861), U.S. epigrammist. *Naked Truth and Veiled Allusions,* (1901, p. 60).

2 While love ceaselessly strives toward that which lies at the hiddenmost center, hatred only perceives the topmost surface and perceives it so exclusively that the devil of hatred, despite all his terror-inspiring cruelty, never is entirely free of ridicule and of a somewhat dilettantish aspect. One who hates is a man holding a magnifying-glass, and when he hates someone, he knows precisely that person's surface, from the soles of his feet all the way up to each hair on the hated head. Were one merely to seek information, one should inquire of the man who hates, but if one wishes to know what truly is, one better ask the one who loves.

HERMANN BROCH (1886–1951), Austrian novelist. *The Spell,* ch. 9 (1976; tr. 1987).

3 Now hatred is by far the longest pleasure;
Men love in haste, but they detest at leisure.

LORD BYRON (1788–1824), English poet. *Don Juan,* cto. 13, st. 6.

4 But hatred is a much more delightful passion & never cloys; it will make us all happy for the rest of our lives.

LORD BYRON (1788–1824), English poet. Letter, 19 April 1813 (published in *Byron's Letters and Journals,* vol. 3, ed. by Leslie Marchand, 1974).

5 You must embrace the man you hate, if you cannot be justified in knocking him down.

LORD CHESTERFIELD (1694–1773), English statesman, man of letters. Letter, 15 Jan. 1753 (first published 1774; repr. in *The Letters of the Earl of Chesterfield to His Son,* vol. 2, no. 297, ed. by Charles Strachey, 1901).

6 You are done for—a living dead man—not when you stop loving but stop hating. Hatred preserves: in it, in its chemistry, resides the "mystery" of life. Not for nothing is hatred still the best tonic ever discovered, for which any organism, however feeble, has a tolerance.

E. M. CIORAN (b. 1911), Rumanian-born French philosopher. *The New Gods,* "Strangled Thoughts," sct. 1 (1969; tr. 1974).

7 Afflicted with existence, each man endures like an animal the consequences which proceed from it. Thus, in a world where everything is detestable, hatred becomes huger than the world and, having transcended its object, cancels itself out.

E. M. CIORAN (b. 1911), Rumanian-born French philosopher. *A Short History of Decay,* ch. 1, "Itinerary of Hate" (1949).

8 The price of hating other human beings is loving oneself less.

ELDRIDGE CLEAVER (b. 1935), U.S. black leader, writer. *Soul on Ice* (1968), written from Folsom Prison, California, 25 June 1965.

9 There is no hate without fear. Hate is crystallized fear, fear's dividend, fear objectivized. We hate what we fear and so where hate is, fear is lurking. Thus we hate what threatens our person, our liberty, our privacy, our income, our popularity, our vanity and our dreams and plans for ourselves. If we can isolate this element in what we hate we may be able to cease from hating.

CYRIL CONNOLLY (1903–74), British critic. *The Unquiet Grave,* pt. 3 (1944, rev. 1951).

10 When we hate a person, with an intimate, imaginative, human hatred, we enter into his mind, or sympathize—any strong interest will arouse the imagination and create some sort of sympathy.

CHARLES HORTON COOLEY (1864–1929), U.S. sociologist. *Human Nature and the Social Order,* ch. 4 (1902).

11 There are glances of hatred that stab, and raise no cry of murder.

GEORGE ELIOT (1819–80), English novelist. *Felix Holt, the Radical,* Introduction (1866).

12 I never hated a man enough to give him diamonds back.

ZSA ZSA GABOR (b. 1920), Hungarian-born U.S. screen actor. Quoted in: *Observer* (London, 28 Aug. 1957).

13 What we need is hatred. From it our ideas are born.

JEAN GENET (1910–86), French playwright, novelist. *The Blacks*, Epigraph (1959; tr. 1960).

14 Take away hatred from some people, and you have men without faith.

ERIC HOFFER (1902–83), U.S. philosopher. *The Passionate State of Mind*, aph. 225 (1955).

15 Men hate more steadily than they love.

SAMUEL JOHNSON (1709–84), English author, lexicographer. Quoted in: Boswell's *Life of Samuel Johnson*, 15 Sept. 1777 (1791).

16 Hate must make a man productive. Otherwise one might as well love.

KARL KRAUS (1874–1936), Austrian satirist. *Pro Domo et Mundo*, ch. 6 (1912).

17 Hate traps us by binding us too tightly to our adversary.

MILAN KUNDERA (b. 1929), Czech author, critic. *Immortality*, pt. 1, ch. 5 (1991).

18 The most deadly fruit is borne by the hatred which one grafts on an extinguished friendship.

GOTTHOLD EPHRAIM LESSING (1729–81), German philosopher, dramatist. Philotas, in *Philotas*, act 3.

19 The man of knowledge must be able not only to love his enemies but also to hate his friends.

FRIEDRICH NIETZSCHE (1844–1900), German philosopher. *Ecce Homo*, Foreword (1888).

20 Always remember, others may hate you. Those who hate you don't win unless you hate them. And then you destroy yourself.

RICHARD M. NIXON (b. 1913), U.S. Republican politician, president. Speech, 9 Aug. 1974, to members of his administration, on leaving office.

21 Hatred is a feeling which leads to the extinction of values.

JOSÉ ORTEGA Y GASSET (1883–1955), Spanish essayist, philosopher. *Meditations on Quixote*, "To the Reader" (1914).

22 To make oneself hated is more difficult than to make oneself loved.

PABLO PICASSO (1881–1973), Spanish artist. *Vogue* (New York, 1 Nov. 1956).

23 The greatest hatred, like the greatest virtue and the worst dogs, is silent.

JEAN PAUL RICHTER (1763–1825), German novelist. *Hesperus*, ch. 12 (1795).

24 Hatred, for the man who is not engaged in it, is a little like the odor of garlic for one who hasn't eaten any.

JEAN ROSTAND (1894–1977), French biologist, writer. *Pensees d'un Biologiste*, ch. 10 (1939; repr. in *The Substance of Man*, 1962).

25 *Hatred* is an affair of the heart; *contempt* that of the head.

ARTHUR SCHOPENHAUER (1788–1860), German philosopher. *Parerga and Paralipomena*, vol. 2, ch. 26, sct. 324 (1851).

26 It is human nature to hate the man whom you have hurt.

TACITUS (c. 55–c. 120 B.C.), Roman historian. *Agricola*, sct. 42.

27 We hold our hate too choice a thing
For light and careless lavishing.

SIR WILLIAM WATSON (1858–1936), British poet. *Hate*.

See also La Rochefoucauld on LOVE.

HATS

1 The hat is not for the street: it will never be democratized. But there are certain houses that one cannot enter without a hat. And one must always wear a hat when lunching with people whom one does not know well. One appears to one's best advantage.

COCO CHANEL (1883–1971), French couturière. Quoted in: Marcel Haedrich, *Coco Chanel: Her Life, Her Secrets*, ch. 21 (1971).

2 Well, you look so pretty in it
Honey, can I jump on it sometime?
Yes, I just wanna see
If it's really that expensive kind
You know it balances on your head
Just like a mattress balances
On a bottle of wine
Your brand new leopard-skin pill-box hat.

BOB DYLAN (b. 1941), U.S. singer, songwriter. "Leopard-Skin Pill-Box Hat" from the album *Blonde on Blonde* (1968).

3 The hat is the pride of man; for he who cannot keep his hat on before kings and emperors is no free man.

FRIEDRICH VON SCHILLER (1759–1805), German dramatist, poet, historian. Kellermeister, in *Piccolomini*, act 4, sc. 5 (tr. by Samuel Taylor Coleridge).

4 Hats divide generally into three classes: offensive hats, defensive hats, and shrapnel.

KATHARINE WHITEHORN (b. 1926), British journalist. *Shouts and Murmurs*, "Hats" (1963).

HAUTE COUTURE

1 Fashion is primitive in its insistence on exhibitionism, which withers in isolation. The catwalk fashion show with its incandescent hype is its apotheosis. A ritualized gathering of connoiseurs and the spoilt at a spotlit parade of snazzy pulchritude, it is an industrialized version of the pagan festivals of renewal. At the end of each seasonal display, a priesthood is enjoined to carry news of the omens to the masses.

STEPHEN BAYLEY (b. 1951), British design critic. *Taste*, pt. 2, "Fashion: Being and Dressing" (1991).

2 Haute Couture should be fun, foolish and almost unwearable.

CHRISTIAN LACROIX (b. 1951), French fashion designer. Quoted in: *Observer* (London, 27 Dec. 1987).

3 If you want to establish an international presence you can't do so from New York. You need the consecration of Paris.

> OSCAR DE LA RENTA (b. 1932), Dominican fashion designer. *International Herald Tribune* (Paris, 26 Feb. 1991).

4 A designer who is not also a couturier, who hasn't learned the most refined mysteries of physically creating his models, is like a sculptor who gives his drawings to another man, an artisan, to accomplish. For him the truncated process of creating will always be an interrupted act of love, and his style will bear the shame of it, the impoverishment.

> YVES SAINT LAURENT (b. 1936), French *couturier*. *Ritz*, no. 85 (1984).

5 All costumes are caricatures. The basis of Art is not the Fancy Ball.

> OSCAR WILDE (1854–1900), Anglo-Irish playwright, author. "The Relation of Dress to Art: A Note in Black and White on Mr. Whistler's Lecture," in *Pall Mall Gazette* (London, 28 Feb. 1885).

HAWAII

1 Hawaii is not a state of mind, but a state of grace.

> PAUL THEROUX (b. 1941), U.S. author. *Observer* (London, 29 Oct. 1989).

HEALTH

1 People who don't know how to keep themselves healthy ought to have the decency to get themselves buried, and not waste time about it.

> HENRIK IBSEN (1828–1906), Norwegian dramatist. Ulfhejm, in *When We Dead Awaken*, act 1.

2 Health is my expected heaven.

> JOHN KEATS (1795–1821), English poet. Letter, c. 1 March 1820, to his fiancée Fanny Brawne (published in *Letters of John Keats*, no. 194, ed. by Frederick Page, 1954). Keats suffered from, and died of, tuberculosis.

3 The vitamin has been reified. A chemical intangible originally defined as a unit of nutritive value, it was long ago reified into a pill. Now it *is* a pill; no one except a few precise scientists define it as anything else. Once the vitamin became a pill, it became "real" according to the precepts of American Cartesianism: "I swallow it, therefore it is."

> FLORENCE KING (b. 1936), U.S. author. *Reflections in a Jaundiced Eye*, "From Captain Marvel to Captain Valium" (1989).

4 A sound mind in a sound body, is a short, but full description of a happy state in this World: he that has these two, has little more to wish for; and he that wants either of them, will be little the better for anything else.

> JOHN LOCKE (1632–1704), English philosopher. *Some Thoughts Concerning Education*, opening sentences (1693).

5 Of all the anti-social vested interests the worst is the vested interest in ill-health.

> GEORGE BERNARD SHAW (1856–1950), Anglo-Irish playwright and critic. *The Doctor's Dilemma*, "The Latest Theories," Preface (1911).

6 The preservation of health is a *duty*. Few seem conscious that there is such a thing as physical morality.

> HERBERT SPENCER (1820–1903), English philosopher. *Education*, ch. 4 (1861).

7 Measure your health by your sympathy with morning and spring. If there is no response in you to the awakening of nature—if the prospect of an early morning walk does not banish sleep, if the warble of the first bluebird does not thrill you—know that the morning and spring of your life are past. Thus may you feel your pulse.

> HENRY DAVID THOREAU (1817–62), U.S. philosopher, author, naturalist. *Journals* (1906), entry for 25 Feb. 1859.

8 He had had much experience of physicians, and said, "the only way to keep your health is to eat what you don't want, drink what you don't like, and do what you'd druther not."

> MARK TWAIN (1835–1910), U.S. author. *Following the Equator*, ch. 49, "Pudd'nhead Wilson's New Calendar" (1897).

9 Health is a state of complete physical, mental and social well-being, and not merely the absence of disease or infirmity.

> CONSTITUTION. THE WORLD HEALTH ORGANIZATION

See also La Rochefoucauld on DIET; Lebanese proverb on HYGIENE.

HEARTBREAK

1 Had we never lov'd sae kindly,
Had we never lov'd sae blindly,
Never met—or never parted—
We had ne'er been broken-hearted.

> ROBERT BURNS (1759–96), Scottish poet. *Ae Fond Kiss*.

2 It isn't enough for your heart to break because everybody's heart is broken now.

> ALLEN GINSBERG (b. 1926), U.S. poet. *Indian Journals* (1970), entry for 6 Sept. 1962, written in Calcutta.

3 Don't waste time trying to break a man's heart; be satisfied if you can just manage to chip it in a brand new place.

> HELEN ROWLAND (1875–1950), U.S. journalist. *A Guide to Men*, "Syncopations" (1922).

4 It is a curious sensation: the sort of pain that goes mercifully beyond our powers of feeling. When your heart is broken, your boats are burned: nothing matters any more. It is the end of happiness and the beginning of peace.

> GEORGE BERNARD SHAW (1856–1950), Anglo-Irish playwright, critic. Ellie, in *Heartbreak House*, act 2.

5 A broken heart is a very pleasant complaint for a man in London if he has a comfortable income.

> GEORGE BERNARD SHAW (1856–1950), Anglo-Irish playwright, critic. Ann, in *Man and Superman*, act 4.

6 How else but through a broken heart
May Lord Christ enter in?

> OSCAR WILDE (1854–1900), Anglo-Irish playwright, author. *The Ballad of Reading Gaol*, pt. 5, st. 14.

See also LOVE, ENDED.

HEAVEN

1 Heaven is the place where the donkey at last catches up with the carrot.

ANONYMOUS.

2 And I heard a voice from heaven, as the voice of many waters, and as the voice of a great thunder: and I heard the voice of harpers harping with their harps.

BIBLE: NEW TESTAMENT. *Revelation* 14:2.

3 Men are admitted into Heaven not because they have curbed & governed their passions or have no passions, but because they have cultivated their understandings. The treasures of Heaven are not negations of passion, but realities of intellect, from which all the passions emanate uncurbed in their eternal glory. The fool shall not enter into Heaven let him be ever so holy.

WILLIAM BLAKE (1757–1827), English poet, painter, engraver. *A Vision of the Last Judgement* (1810; repr. in *Complete Writings*, ed. by Geoffrey Keynes, 1957).

4 But somewhere, beyond Space and Time,
Is wetter water, slimier slime!
And there (they trust) there swimmeth One
Who swam ere rivers were begun,
Immense, of fishy form and mind,
Squamous, omnipotent, and kind.

RUPERT BROOKE (1887–1915), British poet. *Heaven.*

5 Heaven is so far of the Mind
That were the Mind dissolved—
The Site—of it—by Architect
Could not again be proved—

EMILY DICKINSON (1830–86), U.S. poet. *The Complete Poems*, no. 370, (1955).

6 Well, I don't know, but I've been told
The streets in heaven are lined with gold.
I ask you how things could get much worse
If the Russians happen to get up there first;
Wowee! pretty scary!

BOB DYLAN (b. 1941), U.S. singer, songwriter. "I Shall Be Free No. 10" on the album *Another Side of Bob Dylan* (1964).

7 Heaven gives its glimpses only to those Not in position to look too close.

ROBERT FROST (1874–1963), U.S. poet. *A Passing Glimpse.*

8 Heaven must be an awfully dull place if the poor in spirit live there.

EMMA GOLDMAN (1869–1940), U.S. anarchist. "The Failure of Christianity," in *Mother Earth* (New York; April 1913; repr. in *Red Emma Speaks*, pt. 2, ed. by Alix Kates Shulman, 1972), referring to first beatitude, "Blessed are the poor in spirit for theirs is the kingdom of heaven" (New Testament, *Matthew* 5:3).

9 If people would forget about utopia! When rationalism destroyed heaven and decided to set it up here on earth, that most terrible of all goals entered human ambition. It was clear there'd be no end to what people would be made to suffer for it.

NADINE GORDIMER (b. 1923), South African author. Bernard, in *Burger's Daughter*, pt. 2 (1979).

10 To me heaven would be a big bull ring with me holding two barrera seats and a trout stream outside that no one else was allowed to fish in and two lovely houses in the town; one where I would have my wife and children and be monogamous and love them truly and well and the other where I would have my nine beautiful mistresses on nine different floors.

ERNEST HEMINGWAY (1899–1961), U.S. author. Letter, 1 July 1925, to F. Scott Fitzgerald (published in *Ernest Hemingway: Selected Letters*, 1981).

11 You forget that the kingdom of heaven suffers violence: and the kingdom of heaven is like a woman.

JAMES JOYCE (1882–1941), Irish author. Robert Hand, in *Exiles*, act 2 (1918).

12 Of all the inventions of man I doubt whether any was more easily accomplished than that of a Heaven.

G. C. LICHTENBERG (1742–99), German physicist, philosopher. *Aphorisms*, "Notebook L," aph. 34 (written 1765–99; tr. by R. J. Hollingdale, 1990).

13 The trouble with kingdoms of heaven on earth is that they're liable to come to pass, and then their fraudulence is apparent for all to see. We need a kingdom of heaven in Heaven, if only because it can't be realised.

MALCOLM MUGGERIDGE (1903–90), British broadcaster. *Jesus Rediscovered*, "Me and Myself" (1979).

14 The "kingdom of Heaven" is a condition of the heart—not something that comes "upon the earth" or "after death."

FRIEDRICH NIETZSCHE (1844–1900), German philosopher. *The Anti-Christ*, aph. 34 (1895).

15 As for evildoers, for them awaits a painful chastisement;
but for those who believe, and do deeds
of righteousness, they shall be admitted
to gardens underneath which rivers flow,
therein dwelling forever,
by the leave of their Lord, their greeting
therein: "Peace!"

QUR'AN. *Abraham* 14:28 (ed. by Arthur J. Arberry, 1955).

16 Our remedies oft in ourselves do lie,
Which we ascribe to heaven.

WILLIAM SHAKESPEARE (1564–1616), English dramatist, poet. Helena, in *All's Well That Ends Well*, act 1, sc. 1.

17 The human mind is inspired enough when it comes to inventing horrors; it is when it tries to invent a Heaven that it shows itself cloddish.

EVELYN WAUGH (1903–66), British novelist. Ambrose, in *Put Out More Flags*, ch. 1, sct. 7 (1942).

18 The doctrine of the Kingdom of Heaven, which was the main teaching of Jesus, is certainly one of the most revolutionary doctrines that ever stirred and changed human thought.

H. G. WELLS (1866–1946), British author. *Outline of History*, vol. 1, ch. 28, sct. 2 (1920).

heroes tend to be anonymous. In this life of illusion and quasi-illusion, the person of solid virtues who can be admired for something more substantial than his well-knownness often proves to be the unsung hero: the teacher, the nurse, the mother, the honest cop, the hard worker at lonely, underpaid, unglamorous, unpublicized jobs.

DANIEL J. BOORSTIN (b. 1914), U.S. historian. *The Image*, ch. 2 (1961).

6 Unhappy the land that is in need of heroes.

BERTOLT BRECHT (1898–1956), German dramatist, poet. Galileo, in *Life of Galileo*, sc. 13, responding to Andrea's remark, "Unhappy the land that has no heroes."

7 All men are possible heroes: every age,
Heroic in proportions, double-faced,
Looks backward and before, expects a morn
And claims an epos. Ay, but every age
Appears to souls who live in it (ask Carlyle)
Most unheroic.

ELIZABETH BARRETT BROWNING (1806–61), English poet. *Aurora Leigh*, bk. 5 (1857).

8 One who never turned his back but marched breast
    forward,
Never doubted clouds would break,
Never dreamed, though right were worsted, wrong
    would triumph.
Held we fall to rise, are baffled to fight better,
Sleep to wake.

ROBERT BROWNING (1812–89), English poet. *Asolando*, "Epilogue," st. 3 (1889).

9 The drying up a single tear has more
Of honest fame than shedding seas of gore.

LORD BYRON (1788–1824), English poet. *Don Juan*, cto. 8, st. 3 (1823).

10 The poetry of heroism appeals irresistibly to those who don't go to a war, and even more to those whom the war is making enormously wealthy. It's always so.

LOUIS-FERDINAND CÉLINE (1894–1961), French author. The narrator (Ferdinand Bardamu), in *Journey to the End of the Night*, (1932; tr. 1934; ed. 1966, p. 69).

11 Down these mean streets a man must go who is not himself mean, who is neither tarnished nor afraid. . . . He is the hero, he is everything. He must be a complete man and a common man and yet an unusual man. He must be, to use a rather weathered phrase, a man of honor, by instinct, by inevitability, without thought of it, and certainly without saying it. He must be the best man in his world and a good enough man for any world.

RAYMOND CHANDLER (1888–1959), U.S. author. *The Simple Art of Murder* (1950; first published in *Atlantic Monthly*, Boston, Dec. 1944).

12 I am convinced that a light supper, a good night's sleep, and a fine morning, have sometimes made a hero of the same man, who, by an indigestion, a restless night, and rainy morning, would have proved a coward.

LORD CHESTERFIELD (1694–1773), English statesman, man of letters. Letter, 26 April 1748 (published in 1774; repr. in *The Letters of the Earl of Chesterfield to His Son*, vol. 1, no. 149, ed. by Charles Strachey, 1901).

13 Never in the field of human conflict was so much owed by so many to so few.

SIR WINSTON CHURCHILL (1874–1965), British statesman, writer. Speech, 20 Aug. 1940, House of Commons, on the pilots who fought the Battle of Britain.

14 Let us therefore brace ourselves to our duty, and so bear ourselves that if the British Empire and its Commonwealth last for a thousand years, men will still say, "This was their finest hour."

SIR WINSTON CHURCHILL (1874–1965), British statesman. Speech, 18 June 1940, House of Commons, announcing the fall of France, and the start of the "Battle of Britain. Two days later, a week after the Germans had entered Paris, France concluded an armistice with Germany.

15 The "paper tiger" hero, James Bond, offering the whites a triumphant image of themselves, is saying what many whites want desperately to hear reaffirmed: *I am still the White Man, lord of the land, licensed to kill, and the world is still an empire at my feet.*

ELDRIDGE CLEAVER (b. 1935), U.S. black leader, writer. *Soul on Ice*, "The White Race and Its Heroes" (1968).

16 To have no heroes is to have no aspiration, to live on the momentum of the past, to be thrown back upon routine, sensuality, and the narrow self.

CHARLES HORTON COOLEY (1864–1929), U.S. sociologist. *Human Nature and the Social Order*, ch. 8 (1902).

17 Now stiff on a pillar with a phallic air
Nelson stylites in Trafalgar Square
Reminds the British what once they were.

LAWRENCE DURRELL (1912–90), British author. *A Ballad of the Good Lord Nelson*.

18 A man can be a hero if he is a scientist, or a soldier, or a drug addict, or a disc jockey, or a crummy mediocre politician. A man can be a hero because he suffers and despairs; or because he thinks logically and analytically; or because he is "sensitive;" or because he is cruel. Wealth establishes a man as a hero, and so does poverty. Virtually any circumstance in a man's life will make him a hero to some group of people and has a mythic rendering in the culture—in literature, art, theater, or the daily newspapers.

ANDREA DWORKIN (b. 1946), U.S. feminist critic. "The Sexual Politics of Fear and Courage," speech, 12 March 1975, Queen's College, City University of New York (published in *Our Blood*, ch. 5, 1976).

19 I think of a hero as someone who understands the degree of responsibility that comes with his freedom.

BOB DYLAN (b. 1941), U.S. singer, songwriter. Interview in booklet accompanying the *Biograph* album set (1985).

20 Children demand that their heroes should be fleckless, and easily believe them so: perhaps a first discovery to the contrary is less revolutionary shock to a passionate child than the threatened downfall of habitual beliefs which makes the world seem to totter for us in maturer life.

GEORGE ELIOT (1819–80), English novelist, editor. *Daniel Deronda*, bk. 2, ch. 16 (1876).

21 Heroism feels and never reasons, and therefore is always right.

RALPH WALDO EMERSON (1803–82), U.S. essayist, poet, philosopher. *Essays*, "Heroism" (First Series, 1841).

22 Every hero becomes a bore at last.

RALPH WALDO EMERSON (1803–82), U.S. essayist, poet, philosopher. *Representative Men*, "Uses of Great Men" (1850).

23 Bardot, Byron, Hitler, Hemingway, Monroe, Sade: we do not require our heroes to be subtle, just to be big. Then we can depend on someone to make them subtle.

D. J. ENRIGHT (b. 1920), British poet and critic. *Conspirators and Poets*, "The Marquis and the Madame" (1966; first published 1953).

24 Show me a hero and I will write you a tragedy.

F. SCOTT FITZGERALD (1896–1940), U.S. author. *The Crack-Up*, "Notebook E" (ed. by Edmund Wilson, 1945).

25 A big man has no time really to do anything but just sit and be big.

F. SCOTT FITZGERALD (1896–1940), U.S. author. Amory Blaine, in *This Side of Paradise*, bk. 2, ch. 2, "Restlessness" (1920).

26 I offer neither pay, nor quarters, nor food; I offer only hunger, thirst, forced marches, battles and death. Let him who loves his country with his heart, and not merely with his lips, follow me.

GIUSEPPE GARIBALDI (1807–82), Italian patriot, soldier. Speech, 2 July 1849, to the Garibaldi legion besieged in Rome.

27 The fame of heroes owes little to the extent of their conquests and all to the success of the tributes paid to them.

JEAN GENET (1910–86), French playwright, novelist. *Prisoner of Love*, pt. 1 (1986; tr. 1989).

28 The greatest obstacle to being heroic is the doubt whether one may not be going to prove one's self a fool; the truest heroism is to resist the doubt; and the profoundest wisdom, to know when it ought to be resisted, and when it be obeyed.

NATHANIEL HAWTHORNE (1804–64), U.S. author. *The Blithedale Romance*, ch. 2 (1852).

29 Once the state has been founded, there can no longer be any heroes. They come on the scene only in uncivilized conditions.

GEORG HEGEL (1770–1831), German philosopher. *The Philosophy of Right*, "Wrong," Addition 58 (1821; tr. 1942).

30 What with making their way and enjoying what they have won, heroes have no time to think. But the sons of heroes—ah, they have all the necessary leisure.

ALDOUS HUXLEY (1894–1963), British author. "Vulgarity in Literature" (1930; repr. in *Music at Night and Other Essays*, 1949).

31 Mankind's common instinct for reality . . . has always held the world to be essentially a theatre for heroism. In heroism, we feel, life's supreme mystery is hidden. We tolerate no one who has no capacity whatever for it in any direction. On the other hand, no matter what a man's frailties otherwise may be, if he be willing to risk death, and still more if he suffer it heroically, in the service he has chosen, the fact consecrates him forever.

WILLIAM JAMES (1842–1910), U.S. psychologist, philosopher.

The Varieties of Religious Experience, Lectures 14–15, "The Value of Saintliness" (1902).

32 Claret is the liquor for boys; port for men; but he who aspires to be a hero must drink brandy.

SAMUEL JOHNSON (1709–84), English author, lexicographer. Quoted in: Boswell, *Life of Samuel Johnson*, 7 April 1779 (1791).

33 Heroes are created by popular demand, sometimes out of the scantiest materials.

GERALD W. JOHNSON (1890–1980), U.S. author. *American Heroes and Hero-Worship*, ch. 1 (1943).

34 All our lives we fought against exalting the individual, against the elevation of the single person, and long ago we were over and done with the business of a hero, and here it comes up again: the glorification of one personality. This is not good at all. I am just like everybody else.

VLADIMIR ILYICH LENIN (1870–1924), Russian revolutionary leader. Quoted in: Tamara Deutsche, *Not By Politics Alone*, ch. 2 (1973), remark after being shot in 1918.

35 What is our task? To make Britain a fit country for heroes to live in.

DAVID LLOYD GEORGE (1863–1945), British Liberal politician, Prime Minister. Speech, 24 Nov. 1918, Wolverhampton, England.

36 And how can man die better
Than facing fearful odds,
For the ashes of his fathers,
And the temples of his Gods?

THOMAS BABINGTON MACAULAY (1800–1859), English historian and Whig politician. Horatius, in *Lays of Ancient Rome*, "Horatius," st. 27 (1842).

37 The ordinary man is involved in action, the hero acts. An immense difference.

HENRY MILLER (1891–1980), U.S. author. *The Books in My Life*, ch. 10 (1951).

38 Ultimately a hero is a man who would argue with the gods, and so awakens devils to contest his vision. The more a man can achieve, the more he may be certain that the devil will inhabit a part of his creation.

NORMAN MAILER (b. 1923), U.S. author. *The Presidential Papers*, Preface (1963).

39 Most people aren't appreciated enough, and the bravest things we do in our lives are usually known only to ourselves. No one throws ticker tape on the man who chose to be faithful to his wife, on the lawyer who didn't take the drug money, or the daughter who held her tongue again and again. All this anonymous heroism.

PEGGY NOONAN (b. 1950), U.S. author, presidential speechwriter. *What I Saw at the Revolution*, ch. 13 (1990).

40 The high sentiments always win in the end, the leaders who offer blood, toil, tears and sweat always get more out of their followers than those who offer safety and a good time. When it comes to the pinch, human beings are heroic.

GEORGE ORWELL (1903–50), British author. "The Art of Donald McGill" in *Horizon* (London, Sept. 1941; repr. in *Collected Essays*, 1961).

41   No pain, no palm; no thorns, no throne; no gall, no glory; no cross, no crown.

WILLIAM PENN (1644–1718), English religious leader, founder of Pennsylvania. *No Cross, No Crown*, pamphlet (1669).

42   As a rule, all heroism is due to a lack of reflection, and thus it is necessary to maintain a mass of imbeciles. If they once understand themselves the ruling men will be lost.

ERNEST RENAN (1823–92), French writer, critic, scholar. Orlando, in *Caliban*, act 2, sc. 1.

43   Had we lived I should have had a tale to tell of the hardihood, endurance and courage of my companions which would have stirred the heart of every Englishman. These rough notes and our dead bodies must tell the tale.

ROBERT FALCON SCOTT (1863–1912), British antarctic explorer. "Message to the public," in Scott's journal, shortly before his death on the way back from his expedition to the South Pole. His last entry, written 29 March 1912, read: "It seems a pity but I do not think I can write any more. . . . For God's sake look after our people." Extracts published in *Scott's Last Expedition*, vol. 1, ch. 20 (ed. by Leonard Huxley, 1913).

44   If we are marked to die, we are enough
To do our country loss; and if to live,
The fewer men, the greater share of honour.

WILLIAM SHAKESPEARE (1564–1616), English dramatist, poet. King Henry, in *King Henry V*, act 4, sc. 3., before the Battle of Agincourt.

45   You cannot be a hero without being a coward.

GEORGE BERNARD SHAW (1856–1950), Anglo-Irish playwright, critic. John Bull, *Other Island*, Preface (1907).

46   The more characteristic American hero in the earlier day, and the more beloved type at all times, was not the hustler but the whittler.

MARK SULLIVAN (1874–1952), U.S. journalist and historian. *Our Times: The United States, 1900–1925*, vol. 3, ch. 9 (1930).

47   The opportunities for heroism are limited in this kind of world: the most people can do is sometimes not to be as weak as they've been at other times.

ANGUS WILSON (1913–91), British author. Interview in *Writers at Work* (First Series, ed. by Malcolm Cowley, 1958).

48   It's true that heroes are inspiring, but mustn't they also do some rescuing if they are to be worthy of their name? Would Wonder Woman matter if she only sent commiserating telegrams to the distressed?

JEANETTE WINTERSON (b. 1959), British author. *Independent* (London, 6 Jan. 1990).

See also Porteus on GENERALS; Pirandello on GENTLEMEN; Whitman on PROFESSIONS.

HETEROSEXUALITY

1   Such figures as Boy George do not disturb me nearly so much as do those relentlessly hetero (sexual?) keepers of the keys and seals, those who know what the world needs in the way of order and who are ready and willing to supply that order.

JAMES BALDWIN (1924–87), U.S. author. "Freaks and the Amer-

ican Ideal of Manhood" in *Playboy* (Chicago, Jan. 1985; repr. in *The Price of the Ticket*, "Here Be Dragons," 1985).

2   Heterosexuality is dangerous. It tempts you to aim at a perfect duality of desire.

MARGUERITE DURAS (b. 1914), French author, filmmaker. *Practicalities*, "Men" (1987; tr. 1990).

3   In heterosexual love there's no solution. Man and woman are irreconcilable, and it's the doomed attempt to do the impossible, repeated in each new affair, that lends heterosexual love its grandeur.

MARGUERITE DURAS (b. 1914), French author, filmmaker. *Practicalities*, "Men" (1987; tr. 1990).

4   Competence in heterosexuality, or at least the appearance or pretense of such competence, is as much a public affair as a private one. Thus, going steady is a high school diploma in heterosexuality; engagement a BA; marriage an MA; and children a PhD.

THOMAS SZASZ (b. 1920), U.S. psychiatrist. *The Second Sin*, "Sex" (1973).

See also Mailer on HOMOSEXUALITY; Jarman on MEN; Vidal on SEXUALITY.

HIPPIES

1   Old hippies don't die, they just lie low until the laughter stops and their time comes round again.

JOSEPH GALLIVAN (b. 1964), British journalist. *Independent* (London, 30 Aug. 1990).

2   The hippie is the scion of surplus value. The dropout can only claim sanctity in a society which offers something to be dropped out of—career, ambition, conspicuous consumption. The effects of hippie sanctimony can only be felt in the context of others who plunder his lifestyle for what they find good or profitable, a process known as rip-off by the hippie, who will not see how savagely he has pillaged intricate and demanding civilizations for his own parodic lifestyle.

GERMAINE GREER (b. 1939), Australian feminist writer. "Hippies in Asia," in *Sunday Times* (London, 27 Aug. 1972; repr. in *The Madwoman's Underclothes*, 1986).

3   When we heard about the hippies, the barely more than boys and girls who decided to try something different . . . we laughed at them. Smug in our certain awareness that . . . communal life must be more difficult even than nuclear family life, which we know, to our very nerve endings, is disastrous, we condemned them, our children, for seeking a different future. We hated them for their flowers, for their love, and for their unmistakeable rejection of every hideous, mistaken compromise that we had made throughout our hollow, money-bitten, frightened, adult lives.

JUNE JORDAN (b. 1939), U.S. poet, civil rights activist. "Old Stories: New Lives," keynote address, 1978, Child Welfare League of America (published in *Moving Towards Home: Political Essays*, 1989).

4   His hair has the long jesuschrist look. He is wearing the costume clothes. But most of all, he now has a very tolerant and therefore withering attitude toward all those who are still struggling in the old activist political ways . . . while he, with the help of psychedelic chemicals, is exploring the infinite regions of human consciousness.

TOM WOLFE (b. 1931), U.S. author, journalist. *The Electric Kool-Aid Acid Test*, ch. 26 (1968).

See also McCarthy on The TWENTIETH CENTURY: THE 1960s.

HISTORIANS

1 It is the true office of history to represent the events themselves, together with the counsels, and to leave the observations and conclusions thereupon to the liberty and faculty of every man's judgement.

FRANCIS BACON (1561–1626), English philosopher, essayist, statesman. *Advancement of Learning*, bk. 2 (1605).

2 To give an accurate and exhaustive account of that period would need a far less brilliant pen than mine.

SIR MAX BEERBOHM (1872–1956), British essayist, caricaturist. *The Yellow Book*, vol. 4, "1880" (1895).

3 Historian. A broad–gauge gossip.

AMBROSE BIERCE (1842–1914), U.S. author. *The Devil's Dictionary* (1881–1906).

4 And hiving wisdom with each studious year,
In meditation dwelt, with learning wrought,
And shaped his weapon with an edge severe,
Sapping a solemn creed with solemn sneer.

LORD BYRON (1788–1824), English poet. *Childe Harold's Pilgrimage*, cto. 3, st. 107, written of historian Edward Gibbon.

5 The historian's job is to aggrandize, promoting accident to inevitability and innocuous circumstance to portent.

PETER CONRAD (b. 1948), Australian critic, author. *The Art of the City*, ch. 1 (1984).

6 I can see . . . only one safe rule for the historian: that he should recognize in the development of human destinies the play of the contingent and the unforeseen.

H. A. L. FISHER (1865–1940), British historian, Liberal politician. *History of Europe*, Preface (1935).

7 The historian must have . . . some conception of how men who are not historians behave. Otherwise he will move in a world of the dead. He can only gain that conception through personal experience, and he can only use his personal experiences when he is a genius.

E. M. FORSTER (1879–1970), British novelist, essayist. *Abinger Harvest*, "Captain Edward Gibbon" (1936; essay first published 1931).

8 History repeats itself. Historians repeat each other.

PHILIP GUEDALLA (1889–1944), British author. *Supers and Supermen*, "Some Historians" (1920).

9 You treat world history as a mathematician does mathematics, in which nothing but laws and formulas exist, no reality, no good and evil, no time, no yesterday, no tomorrow, nothing but an eternal, shallow, mathematical present.

HERMANN HESSE (1877–1962), German novelist, poet. Father Jacobus, in *The Glass Bead Game*, ch. 4 (1943; tr. 1960).

10 One cannot be a good historian of the outward, visible world without giving some thought to the hidden, private life of ordinary people; and on the other hand one cannot be a good historian of this inner life without taking into account outward events where these are relevant. They are two orders of fact which reflect each other, which are always linked and which sometimes provoke each other.

VICTOR HUGO (1802–85), French poet, dramatist, novelist. *Les Misérables*, pt. 4, bk. 7, ch. 1 (1862).

11 Great abilites are not requisite for an Historian; for in historical composition, all the greatest powers of the human mind are quiescent. He has facts ready to his hand; so there is no exercise of invention. Imagination is not required in any degree; only about as much as is used in the lowest kinds of poetry. Some penetration, accuracy, and colouring, will fit a man for the task, if he can give the application which is necessary.

SAMUEL JOHNSON (1709–84), English author, lexicographer. Quoted in: Boswell, *Life of Samuel Johnson*, 6 July 1763 (1791).

12 Historian—An unsuccessful novelist.

H. L. MENCKEN (1880–1956), U.S. journalist. *A Mencken Chrestomathy*, "Sententiæ: The Mind of Men" (1949).

13 I love those historians that are either very simple or most excellent. . . . Such as are between both (which is the most common fashion), it is they that spoil all; they will needs chew our meat for us and take upon them a law to judge, and by consequence to square and incline the story according to their fantasy.

MICHEL DE MONTAIGNE (1533–92), French essayist. *Essays*, bk. 2, ch. 10, "Of Books" (tr. by John Florio, 1580).

14 Historians desiring to write the actions of men, ought to set down the simple truth, and not say anything for love or hatred; also to choose such an opportunity for writing as it may be lawful to think what they will, and write what they think, which is a rare happiness of the time.

SIR WALTER RALEGH (1552–1618), English author, soldier, explorer. *The Cabinet Council*, ch. 25, "A Collection of Political Observations" (repr. in *The Works of Sir Walter Raleigh*, vol. 1, 1751).

15 Historians are left forever chasing shadows, painfully aware of their inability ever to reconstruct a dead world in its completeness however thorough or revealing their documentation. . . . We are doomed to be forever hailing someone who has just gone around the corner and out of earshot.

SIMON SCHAMA (b. 1945), British historian. *Dead Certainties*, "Afterword" (1991).

16 Ignorance is the first requisite of the historian—ignorance, which simplifies and clarifies, which selects and omits, with a placid perfection unattainable by the highest art.

LYTTON STRACHEY (1880–1932), British biographer, historian. *Eminent Victorians*, Preface (1918).

17 Study men, not historians.

HARRY S TRUMAN (1884–1972), U.S. democratic politician, president. Quoted in: Robert H. Ferrell, *Off the Record* (1980).

18 Anybody can make history. Only a great man can write it.

OSCAR WILDE (1854–1900), Anglo-Irish playwright, author. Gilbert, in *The Critic as Artist*, pt. 1 (published in *Intentions*, 1891).

19 To give an accurate description of what has never occurred is not merely the proper occupation of the historian, but the inalienable privilege of any man of parts and culture.

OSCAR WILDE (1854–1900), Anglo-Irish playwright, author. Gilbert, in *The Critic as Artist*, pt. 1 (published in *Intentions*, 1891).

See also Durant on CIVILIZATION; Hobsbawm on NATIONALISM.

HISTORY

1 History is a relay of revolutions.

SAUL ALINSKY (1909–72), U.S. radical activist. *Rules for Radicals*, "Of Means and Ends" (1971).

2 Every time history repeats itself the price goes up.

ANONYMOUS.

3 History is, strictly speaking, the study of questions; the study of answers belongs to anthropology and sociology.

W. H. AUDEN (1907–73), Anglo-American poet. *The Dyer's Hand*, pt. 3, "Hic et Ille," sct. B (1962).

4 History, real solemn history, I cannot be interested in. . . . I read it a little as a duty; but it tells me nothing that does not either vex or weary me. The quarrels of popes and kings, with wars and pestilences in every page; the men all so good for nothing, and hardly any women at all.

JANE AUSTEN (1775–1817), English novelist. Catherine Morland, in *Northanger Abbey*, ch. 14 (1818).

5 Histories make men wise; poets witty; the mathematics subtle; natural philosophy deep; moral grave; logic and rhetoric able to contend.

FRANCIS BACON (1561–1626), English philosopher, essayist, statesman. *Essays*, "Of Studies" (1597–1625).

6 The best history is but like the art of Rembrandt; it casts a vivid light on certain selected causes, on those which were best and greatest; it leaves all the rest in shadow and unseen.

WALTER BAGEHOT (1826–77), English economist, critic. *Physics and Politics*, ch. 2, sct. 2 (1872).

7 American history is longer, larger, more various, more beautiful, and more terrible than anything anyone has ever said about it.

JAMES BALDWIN (1924–87), U.S. author. "A Talk To Teachers," 16 Oct. 1963 (published in *The Price of the Ticket*, 1985).

8 History. An account, mostly false, of events, mostly unimportant, which are brought about by rulers, mostly knaves, and soldiers, mostly fools.

AMBROSE BIERCE (1842–1914), U.S. author. *The Devil's Dictionary* (1881–1906).

9 That great dust-heap called "history."

AUGUSTINE BIRRELL (1850–1933), British essayist, Liberal politician. *Obiter Dicta*, "Carlyle" (1884).

10 Acts themselves alone are history. . . . Tell me the acts, O historian, and leave me to reason upon them as I please; away with your reasoning and your rubbish! All that is not action is not worth reading.

WILLIAM BLAKE (1757–1827), English poet, painter, engraver. *A Descriptive Catalogue*, no. 5 (1809; repr. in *Complete Writings*, ed. by Geoffrey Keynes, 1957).

11 Universal history is the history of a few metaphors.

JORGE LUIS BORGES (1899–1986), Argentinian author. *Pascal's Sphere* (1951; repr. in *Other Inquisitions*, 1960; tr. 1964).

12 English history is all about men liking their fathers, and American history is all about men hating their fathers and trying to burn down everything they ever did.

MALCOLM BRADBURY (b. 1932), British author. *Stepping Westward*, bk. 2, ch. 5 (1965).

13 All true histories contain instruction; though, in some, the treasure may be hard to find, and when found, so trivial in quantity that the dry, shrivelled kernel scarcely compensates for the trouble of cracking the nut.

ANNE BRONTË (1820–49), English novelist, poet. *Agnes Grey*, ch. 1 (1847).

14 The history of the world is the record of the weakness, frailty and death of public opinion.

SAMUEL BUTLER (1835–1902), English author. *Notebooks*, "Pictures and Books" (1912).

15 If man is reduced to being nothing but a character in history, he has no other choice but to subside into the sound and fury of a completely irrational history or to endow history with the form of human reason.

ALBERT CAMUS (1913–60), French-Algerian philosopher, author. *The Rebel*, pt. 3, "State Terrorism and Rational Terror" (1951; tr. 1953). Camus was criticizing Hegelian theory.

16 History, as an entirety, could only exist in the eyes of an observer outside it and outside the world. History, only exists, in the final analysis, for God.

ALBERT CAMUS (1913–60), French-Algerian philosopher, author. *The Rebel*, pt. 5, "Historic Murder" (1951; tr. 1953).

17 Happy the people whose annals are vacant.

THOMAS CARLYLE (1795–1881), Scottish essayist, historian. *History of the French Revolution*, pt. 1, bk. 2, ch. 1 (1837), written in reply to an aphorism of Montesquieu, "Happy the people whose annals are tiresome."

18 History, a distillation of Rumour.

THOMAS CARLYLE (1795–1881), Scottish essayist, historian. *History of the French Revolution*, pt. 1, bk. 7, ch. 5 (1837).

19 Only the history of free peoples is worth our attention; the history of men under a despotism is merely a collection of anecdotes.

SÉBASTIEN-ROCH NICOLAS DE CHAMFORT (1741–94), French writer, wit. *Maxims and Considerations,* vol. 2, no. 487 (1796; tr. 1926).

20 The disadvantage of men not knowing the past is that they do not know the present. History is a hill or high point of vantage, from which alone men see the town in which they live or the age in which they are living.

G. K. CHESTERTON (1874–1936), British author. *All I Survey,* "On St. George Revivified" (1933).

21 History is nothing but a procession of false Absolutes, a series of temples raised to pretexts, a degradation of the mind before the Improbable.

E. M. CIORAN (b. 1911), Rumanian-born French philosopher. *A Short History of Decay,* ch. 1, "Genealogy of Fanaticism" (1949).

22 History is a needle
for putting men asleep
anointed with the poison
Of all they want to keep.

LEONARD COHEN (b. 1934), Canadian singer, poet, novelist. *Flowers For Hitler,* "On Hearing A Name Long Unspoken," st. 3 (1964).

23 The bases for historical knowledge are not empirical facts but written texts, even if these texts masquerade in the guise of wars or revolutions.

PAUL DE MAN (1919–83), Belgian-born U.S. literary critic. "Literary History and Literary Modernity," lecture, Sept. 1969 (repr. in *Blindness and Insight,* 1971, rev. 1983).

24 History is the present. That's why every generation writes it anew. But what most people think of as history is its end product, myth.

E. L. DOCTOROW (b. 1931), U.S. novelist. *Writers at Work* (Eighth Series, ed. by George Plimpton, 1988).

25 We as women know that there are no disembodied processes; that all history originates in human flesh; that all oppression is inflicted by the body of one against the body of another; that all social change is built on the bone and muscle, and out of the flesh and blood, of human creators.

ANDREA DWORKIN (b. 1946), U.S. feminist critic. "Our Blood: The Slavery of Women in Amerika," speech, 23 Aug. 1975, to the National Organization for Women, Washington, D.C. (published in *Our Blood,* ch. 8, 1976).

26 A people without history
Is not redeemed from time, for history is a pattern
Of timeless moments.

T. S. ELIOT (1888–1965), Anglo-American poet, critic. *Little Gidding,* pt. 5, in *Four Quartets.*

27 History is more or less bunk. It's tradition. We don't want tradition. We want to live in the present and the only history that is worth a tinker's damn is the history we make today.

HENRY FORD (1863–1947), U.S. industrialist. Interview in *Chicago Tribune* (25 May 1916). Ford later sued the paper for libel after an editorial had described him as an "anarchist" and "ignorant idealist." In the course of the action, the motor magnate was cross-examined for eight days during which he was forced to defend his views of history. The *Tribune* was found guilty and fined 6 cents.

28 There is a sort of myth of History that philosophers have. . . . History for philosophers is some sort of great, vast continuity in which the freedom of individuals and economic or social determinations come and get entangled. When someone lays a finger on one of those great themes—continuity, the effective exercise of human liberty, how individual liberty is articulated with social determinations—when someone touches one of these three myths, these good people start crying out that History is being raped or murdered.

MICHEL FOUCAULT (1926–84), French philosopher. Interview in *La Quinzaine Littéraire* (15 March 1968; repr. in Didier Eribon, *Michel Foucault,* 1989; tr. 1991).

29 History . . . is, indeed, little more than the register of the crimes, follies, and misfortunes of mankind.

EDWARD GIBBON (1737–94), English historian. *The Decline and Fall of the Roman Empire,* ch. 3 (1776).

30 There are only two great currents in the history of mankind: the baseness which makes conservatives and the envy which makes revolutionaries.

EDMOND (1822–96) AND JULES DE GONCOURT (1830–70), French writers. *The Goncourt Journals* (1888–96; repr. in *Pages from the Goncourt Journal,* ed. by Robert Baldick, 1962), entry for 12 July 1867.

31 But what experience and history teach is this—that peoples and governments have never learned anything from history, or acted on principles deduced from it.

GEORG HEGEL (1770–1831), German philosopher. *The Philosophy of History,* Introduction (1807).

32 World history is a court of judgment.

GEORG HEGEL (1770–1831), German philosopher. *The Philosophy of Right,* pt. 3, sct. 3, "World History" (1821). See below, a similar statement on history by Schiller.

33 Regarding History as the slaughter-bench at which the happiness of peoples, the wisdom of States, and the virtue of individuals have been victimized—the question involuntarily arises—to what principle, to what final aim these enormous sacrifices have been offered.

GEORG HEGEL (1770–1831), German philosopher. *The Philosophy of History,* sct. 3, "Introduction" (1837).

34 History is a child building a sand-castle by the sea, and that child is the whole majesty of man's power in the world.

HERACLITUS (c. 535–c.475 B.C.), Greek philosopher. *Herakleitos & Diogenes,* pt. 1, Fragment 24 (tr. by Guy Davenport, 1976).

35 To study history means submitting to chaos and nevertheless retaining faith in order and meaning. It is a very serious task, young man, and possibly a tragic one.

HERMANN HESSE (1877–1962), German novelist, poet. Father Jacobus, in *The Glass Bead Game,* ch. 4 (1943; tr. 1960).

36 History seems to us an arena of instincts and fashions, of appetite, avarice, and craving for power, of blood lust, violence, destruction, and wars, of ambitious ministers, venal generals, bombarded cities, and we too easily forget that this is only one of its many aspects. Above all we forget that we ourselves are a part of history, that we are the product of growth and are condemned to perish if we lose the capacity for further growth and change. We are ourselves history and share the responsibility for world history and our position in it. But we gravely lack awareness of this responsibility.

HERMANN HESSE (1877–1962), German novelist, poet. *The Glass Bead Game*, ch. 11 (1943; tr. 1960).

37 Events in the past may be roughly divided into those which probably never happened and those which do not matter. This is what makes the trade of historian so attractive.

W. R. INGE (1860–1954), Dean of St. Paul's, London. *Assessments and Anticipations*, "Prognostications" (1929).

38 Who has fully realized that history is not contained in thick books but lives in our very blood?

CARL JUNG (1875–1961), Swiss psychiatrist. *Woman in Europe* (1927; repr. in *Collected Works*, vol. 10, para. 26, ed. by William McGuire, 1964).

39 History repeats itself, first as tragedy, second as farce.

KARL MARX (1818–83), German political theorist, social philosopher. Paraphrase of the opening sentences of Marx, *The Eighteenth Brumaire of Louis Bonaparte* (1852; repr. in *Karl Marx: Selected Works*, vol. 2, 1942). The actual words were: "Hegel remarks somewhere that all great, world-historical facts and personages occur, as it were, twice. He has forgotten to add: the first time as tragedy, the second as farce."

40 Men make their own history, but they do not make it just as they please; they do not make it under circumstances chosen by themselves, but under circumstances directly found, given and transmitted from the past. The tradition of all the dead generations weighs like a nightmare on the brain of the living.

KARL MARX (1818–83), German political theorist, social philosopher. *The Eighteenth Brumaire of Louis Bonaparte*, sct. 1 (1852; repr. in *Selected Works*, vol. 2, 1942).

41 We know only a single science, the science of history. One can look at history from two sides and divide it into the history of nature and the history of men. However, the two sides are not to be divided off; as long as men exist the history of nature and the history of men are mutually conditioned.

KARL MARX (1818–83) AND FRIEDRICH ENGELS (1820–95), German social philosophers, revolutionaries. *The German Ideology*, sct. 1, footnote (1845–46; repr. in *Karl Marx and Friedrich Engels: Collected Works*, vol. 5, 1976). This note was crossed out in the finished version.

42 History does nothing; it does not possess immense riches, it does not fight battles. It is men, real, living, who do all this. . . . It is not "history" which uses men as a means of achieving—as if it were an individual person—its own ends. History is nothing but the activity of men in pursuit of their ends.

KARL MARX (1818–83) AND FRIEDRICH ENGELS (1820–95), German social philosophers, revolutionaries. *The Holy Family* (1844–45).

43 All history is the record of man's signal failure to thwart his destiny—the record, in other words, of the few men of destiny who, through the recognition of their symbolic rôle, made history.

HENRY MILLER (1891–1980), U.S. author. *The Wisdom of the Heart*, "Creative Death" (1947).

44 History is the myth, the true myth, of man's fall made manifest in time.

HENRY MILLER (1891–1980), U.S. author. *Plexus*, ch. 12 (1949).

45 Only strong personalities can endure history, the weak ones are extinguished by it.

FRIEDRICH NIETZSCHE (1844–1900), German philosopher. *Thoughts out of Season*, pt. 2, sct. 5 (1874).

46 We have need of history in its entirety, not to fall back into it, but to see if we can escape from it.

JOSÉ ORTEGA Y GASSET (1883–1955), Spanish essayist, philosopher. *The Revolt of the Masses*, ch. 10 (1930).

47 I believe that history has shape, order, and meaning; that exceptional men, as much as economic forces, produce change; and that passé abstractions like beauty, nobility, and greatness have a shifting but continuing validity.

CAMILLE PAGLIA (b. 1947), U.S. author, critic, educator. *Sex, Art, and American Culture*, "Sexual Personae: The Cancelled Preface" (1992).

48 What is history? Its beginning is that of the centuries of systematic work devoted to the solution of the enigma of death, so that death itself may eventually be overcome. That is why people write symphonies, and why they discover mathematical infinity and electromagnetic waves.

BORIS PASTERNAK (1890–1960), Russian poet, novelist, translator. Nikolay Nikolayevich, in *Doctor Zhivago*, ch. 1, sct. 5 (1957).

49 Anyone, however, who has had dealings with dates knows that they are worse than elusive, they are perverse. Events do not happen at the right time, nor in their proper sequence. That sense of harmony with place and season which is so stong in the historian—if he be a readable historian—is lamentably lacking in history, which takes no pains to verify his most convincing statements.

AGNES REPPLIER (1858–1950), U.S. author, social critic. *To Think of Tea!*, ch. 1 (1932).

50 Those who cannot remember the past are condemned to repeat it.

GEORGE SANTAYANA (1863–1952), U.S. philosopher, poet. *Life of Reason*, "Reason in Common Sense," ch. 12 (1905–6). William L. Shirer used this quote as an epigraph in his *Rise and Fall of the Third Reich* (1959).

51 The history of the world is the world's court of justice.

FRIEDRICH VON SCHILLER (1759–1805), German dramatist, poet, historian. Inaugural lecture, 26 May 1789, as Professor of History at the University of Jena, Weimar, Germany. See Hegel on HISTORY above, rendering a similar idea.

52 The subject of history is the gradual realization of all that is practically necessary.

FRIEDRICH SCHLEGEL (1772–1829), German philosopher, critic, writer. *Dialogue on Poetry and Literary Aphorisms*, "Selected Aphorisms from *The Athenaeum*," aph. 90 (1968; first published 1798).

53 Science and Technology revolutionize our lives, but memory, tradition and myth frame our response. Expelled from individual consciousness by the rush of change, history finds its revenge by stamping the collective unconscious with habits, values, expectations, dreams. The dialectic between past and future will continue to form our lives.

> ARTHUR M. SCHLESINGER, JR. (b. 1917), U.S. historian. "The Challenge of Change," in *New York Times Magazine* (27 July 1986).

54 History is not what you thought. *It is what you can remember.* All other history defeats itself.

> W. C. SELLAR (1898–1951) AND R. J. YEATMAN (1897–1968), British authors. *1066 and All That,* Preface (1930).

55 The principle office of history I take to be this: to prevent virtuous actions from being forgotten, and that evil words and deeds should fear an infamous reputation with posterity.

> TACITUS (c. 55-c. 120 A.D.), Roman historian. *The Histories,* bk. 3, sct. 65.

56 History is Philosophy teaching by examples.

> THUCYDIDES (c. 460-c. 400 B.C.), Athenian historian. Quoted by Dionysius of Halicarnassus in: *Ars Rhetorica,* ch. 11, sct. 2.

57 History not used is nothing, for all intellectual life is action, like practical life, and if you don't use the stuff—well, it might as well be dead.

> A. J. TOYNBEE (1889–1975), British historian. Television broadcast, 17 April 1955, NBC-TV.

58 Social history might be defined negatively as the history of a people with the politics left out.

> G. M. TREVELYAN (1876–1962), British historian. *English Social History,* Introduction (1942).

59 There is nothing new in the world except the history you do not know.

> HARRY S TRUMAN (1884–1972), U.S. Democratic politician, president. Quoted in: William Hillman, *Mr. President,* pt. 2, ch. 1 (1952).

60 The very ink in which history is written is merely fluid prejudice.

> MARK TWAIN (1835–1910), U.S. author. *Following the Equator,* ch. 69, "Pudd'nhead Wilson's New Calendar" (1897).

61 History should be written as philosophy.

> VOLTAIRE (1694–1778), French philosopher, author. Letter, 31 Oct. 1738.

62 A country losing touch with its own history is like an old man losing his glasses, a distressing sight, at once vulerable, unsure, and easily disoriented.

> GEORGE WALDEN (b. 1939), British Conservative politician. *Times* (London, 20 Dec. 1986).

63 As soon as histories are properly told there is no more need of romances.

> WALT WHITMAN (1819–92), U.S. poet. *Leaves of Grass,* Preface (1855).

64 The one duty we owe to history is to rewrite it.

> OSCAR WILDE (1854–1900), Anglo-Irish playwright, author. Gilbert, in *The Critic as Artist,* pt. 1 (published in *Intentions,* 1891).

65 Americans, more than most people, believe that history is the result of individual decisions to implement conscious intentions. For Americans, more than most people, history has been that. . . . This sense of openness, of possibility and autonomy, has been a national asset as precious as the topsoil of the Middle West. But like topsoil, it is subject to erosion; it requires tending. And it is not bad for Americans to come to terms with the fact that for them too, history is a story of inertia and the unforeseen.

> GEORGE F. WILL (b. 1941), U.S. political columnist. *Statecraft as Soulcraft: What Government Does,* ch. 7 (1984).

66 What has history to do with me? Mine is the first and only world! I want to report how I find the world. What others have told me about the world is a very small and incidental part of my experience. I have to judge the world, to measure things.

> LUDWIG WITTGENSTEIN (1889–1951), Austrian philosopher. *Notebooks 1914–1916,* entry for 2 Sept. 1915 (ed. by Anscombe 1961; later refomulated in *Tractatus Logico-Philosophicus,* sct. 5:63, 1921, tr. 1922). Wittgenstein paraphrased: "I am my world. (The microcosm)."

67 It would strike me as ridiculous to want to doubt the existence of Napoleon; but if someone doubted the existence of the earth 150 years ago, perhaps I should be more willing to listen, for now he is doubting our whole system of evidence.

> LUDWIG WITTGENSTEIN (1889–1951), Austrian philosopher. *On Certainty,* sct. 185 (ed. by Anscombe and von Wright, 1969).

See also Emerson on BIOGRAPHY; Disraeli, Emerson on MINORITIES; Camus on NOSTALGIA; Johnson on SLANDER; De Gaulle on SOLITUDE; Eliot on WOMEN.

ADOLF HITLER

1 The Führer is always quite cheerful, cheerful with all his heart, when he is having tea with his friends during the night, or when he is training his dogs!

> MARTIN BORMANN (1900–1945), German Nazi leader. Annotations to letter, 25 Dec. 1943, from his wife Gerda (published in *The Bormann Letters,* ed. by Hugh Trevor-Roper, 1954).

2 I thank heaven for a man like Adolf Hitler, who built a front line of defense against the anti-Christ of Communism.

> FRANK BUCHMAN (1878–1961), U.S. evangelist. *New York World-Telegram* (25 Aug. 1936).

3 As for Hitler, his professed religion unhesitatingly juxtaposed the God-Providence and Valhalla. Actually his god was an argument at a political meeting and a manner of reaching an impressive climax at the end of speeches.

> ALBERT CAMUS (1913–60), French-Algerian philosopher, author. *The Rebel,* pt. 3, "State Terrorism and Irrational Terror" (1951; tr. 1953).

4 It is true that this man was nothing but an elemental force in motion, directed and rendered more effective by extreme cunning and by a relentless tactical clairvoyance . . . . Hitler was history in its purest form.

> ALBERT CAMUS (1913–60), French-Algerian philosopher, author. *The Rebel,* pt. 3, "State Terrorism and Irrational Terror" (1951; tr. 1953).

5 If Hitler invaded hell I would make at least a favourable reference to the devil in the House of Commons.

> SIR WINSTON CHURCHILL (1874–1965), British statesman, writer. *The History of the Second World War: The Grand Alliance*, ch. 20 (1950).

6 After fifteen years of work I have achieved, as a common German soldier and merely with my fanatical will-power, the unity of the German nation, and have freed it from the death sentence of Versailles.

> ADOLF HITLER (1889–1945), German dictator. Proclamation, 21 Dec. 1941, to the armed forces after taking over as Commander-in-Chief of the army.

7 Silence, indifference and inaction were Hitler's principal allies.

> LORD JAKOBOVITS (b. 1921), Chief Rabbi of the British Commonwealth. *Independent* (London, 5 Dec. 1989), on the prosecution of alleged war criminals.

8 Hitler is no worse, nay better, in my opinion, than the other lugs. He makes the German mistake of being tactless, that's all.

> HENRY MILLER (1891–1980), U.S. author. Letter, March 1939, to author Lawrence Durrell, shortly after the Nazis had marched into Czechoslovakia (published in *The Durrell-Miller Letters 1935–80*, 1988).

9 Adolf Hitler was a Jeanne d'Arc, a saint. He was a martyr. Like many martyrs, he held extreme views.

> EZRA POUND (1885–1972), U.S. poet, critic. Interview in *Philadelphia Record* and *Chicago Sun* (9 May 1945).

HOBOS

1 Wandering stars, to whom is reserved the blackness of darkness for ever.

> BIBLE, HEBREW. *Jude* verse 13.

2 And meanwhile we have gone on living,
Living and partly living,
Picking together the pieces,
Gathering faggots at nightfall,
Building a partial shelter,
For sleeping and eating and drinking and laughter.

> T. S. ELIOT (1888–1965), Anglo-American poet, critic. The Chorus of Women of Canterbury, in *Murder in the Cathedral*, pt. 1.

3 Those colorful denizens of male despair, the Bowery bum and the rail-riding hobo, have been replaced by the bag lady and the welfare mother. Women have even taken over Skid Row.

> FLORENCE KING (b. 1936), U.S. author. *Reflections in a Jaundiced Eye*, "From Captain Marvel to Captain Valium" (1989).

4 Bums are the well-to-do of this day. They didn't have as far to fall.

> JACKSON POLLOCK (1912–56), U.S. artist. Letter, 3 Feb. 1933, to his father (published in *Jackson Pollock: A Catalogue Raisonné of Paintings, Drawings and Other Works*, vol. 4, ed. by Francis V. O'Connor & Eugene V. Thaw, 1978). "This day" referred to the Great Depression.

5 The hunchback in the park

A solitary mister
Propped between trees and water.

> DYLAN THOMAS (1914–53), Welsh poet. *The Hunchback in the Park*.

6 Like two doomed ships that pass in storm
We had crossed each other's way:
But we made no sign, we said no word,
We had no word to say.

> OSCAR WILDE (1854–1900), Anglo-Irish playwright, author. *The Ballad of Reading Gaol*, pt. 2, st. 12.

See also SOLITUDE.

HOLLAND AND THE DUTCH

1 Holland is a dream, Monsieur, a dream of gold and smoke—smokier by day, more gilded by night. And night and day that dream is peopled with Lohengrins like these, dreamily riding their black bicycles with high handle-bars, funereal swans constantly drifting throughout the whole country, around the seas, along the canals.

> ALBERT CAMUS (1913–60), French-Algerian philosopher, author. The narrator (Jean-Baptiste Clamence), in *The Fall* (1956; repr. 1957, p. 12).

2 Apart from cheese and tulips, the main product of the country is advocaat, a drink made from lawyers.

> ALAN COREN (b. 1938), British editor, humorist. *The Sanity Inspector*, "All You Need to Know about Europe" (1974).

3 Where the broad ocean leans against the land.

> OLIVER GOLDSMITH (1728–74), Anglo-Irish poet, essayist, playwright. *The Traveller*.

4 Those Dutchmen had hardly any imagination or fantasy, but their good taste and their scientific knowledge of composition were enormous.

> VINCENT VAN GOGH (1853–90), Dutch painter. Letter, July 1888 (published in *The Complete Letters of Vincent Van Gogh*, vol. 3, no. B12, 1958).

HOLLYWOOD

1 Hollywood is a place where people from Iowa mistake each other for stars.

> FRED ALLEN (1894–1957), U.S. radio comic. Quoted in: Maurice Zolotow, *No People Like Show People*, ch. 8 (1951).

2 In Beverly Hills . . . they don't throw their garbage away. They make it into television shows.

> WOODY ALLEN (b. 1935), U.S. filmmaker. Alvy Singer (Allen), in the film *Annie Hall*, (directed by Woody Allen, scripted by Allen with Marshall Brickman, 1977; repr. in *Four Films of Woody Allen*, 1982).

3 The sumptuous age of stars and images is reduced to a few artificial tornado effects, pathetic fake buildings, and childish tricks which the crowd pretends to be taken in by to avoid feeling too disappointed. Ghost towns, ghost people. The whole place has the same air of obsolescence about it as Sunset or Hollywood Boulevard.

> JEAN BAUDRILLARD (b. 1929), French semiologist. *America*, "Astral America" (1986; tr. 1988).

4   If New York is the Big Apple, tonight Hollywood is the Big Nipple.

> BERNARDO BERTOLUCCI (b. 1940), Italian filmmaker. Quoted in: *Guardian* (London, 13 April 1988), said at Oscar presentation ceremony.

5   Fame is no sanctuary from the passing of youth . . . suicide is much easier and more acceptable in Hollywood than growing old gracefully.

> JULIE BURCHILL (b. 1960), British journalist, author. *Girls on Film*, ch. 3 (1986).

6   To survive there, you need the ambition of a Latin-American revolutionary, the ego of a grand opera tenor, and the physical stamina of a cow pony.

> BILLIE BURKE (1885–1970), U.S. stage and screen actor. Quoted in: Leslie Halliwell, *Filmgoer's Companion* (1984).

7   Some are able and humane men and some are low-grade individuals with the morals of a goat, the artistic integrity of a slot machine, and the manners of a floor-walker with delusions of grandeur.

> RAYMOND CHANDLER (1888–1959), U.S. author. "Writers in Hollywood," in *Atlantic Monthly* (Nov. 1945), on movie producers.

8   Its idea of "production value" is spending a milion dollars dressing up a story that any good writer would throw away. Its vision of the rewarding movie is a vehicle for some glamour-puss with two expressions and eighteen changes of costume, or for some male idol of the muddled millions with a permanent hangover, six worn-out acting tricks, the build of a lifeguard, and the mentality of a chicken-strangler.

> RAYMOND CHANDLER (1888–1959), U.S. author. "Writers in Hollywood," in *Atlantic Monthly* (Boston, Nov. 1945).

9   The overall picture, as the boys say, is of a degraded community whose idealism even is largely fake. The pretentiousness, the bogus enthusiasm, the constant drinking and drabbing, the incessant squabbling over money, the all-pervasive agent, the strutting of the big shots (and their usually utter incompetence to achieve anything they start out to do), the constant fear of losing all this fairy gold and being the nothing they have never ceased to be, the snide tricks, the whole damn mess is out of this world.

> RAYMOND CHANDLER (1888–1959), U.S. author. Letter, 12 Jan. 1946, to publisher Alfred A. Knopf (published in *Raymond Chandler Speaking*, 1962). Chandler preceded this tirade against Hollywood by stating, "Do not think I completely despise it, because I don't."

10   The motion picture made in Hollywood, if it is to create art at all, must do so within such strangling limitations of subject and treatment that it is a blind wonder it ever achieves any distinction beyond the purely mechanical slickness of a glass and chromium bathroom.

> RAYMOND CHANDLER (1888–1959), U.S. author. "Oscar Night in Hollywood" in *Sight and Sound* (1982).

11   There is in Hollywood, as in all cultures in which gambling is the central activity, a lowered sexual energy, an inability to devote more than token attention to the preoccupations of the society outside. The action is everything, more consuming than sex, more immediate than politics; more important always than the acquisition of money, which is never, for the gambler, the true point of the exercise.

> JOAN DIDION (b. 1934), U.S. essayist. *The White Album*, "In Hollywood" (1979).

12   It's a mining town in lotus land.

> F. SCOTT FITZGERALD (1896–1940), U.S. author. Wylie White, in *The Last Tycoon*, ch. 1 (1941).

13   Isn't Hollywood a dump—in the human sense of the word. A hideous town, pointed up by the insulting gardens of its rich, full of the human spirit at a new low of debasement.

> F. SCOTT FITZGERALD (1896–1940), U.S. author. Letter, 29 July 1940 (published in *The Letters of F. Scott Fitzgerald*, ed. by Andrew Turnbull, 1963).

14   Studio executives are intelligent, brutally overworked men and women who share one thing in common with baseball managers: they wake up every morning of the world with the knowledge that sooner or later they're going to get fired.

> WILLIAM GOLDMAN (b. 1931), U.S. screenwriter, novelist. *Adventures in the Screen Trade*, ch. 1 (1983).

15   "Too caustic?" To hell with the cost. If it's a good picture, we'll make it.

> SAMUEL GOLDWYN (1882–1974), U.S. film producer. Quoted in: Alva Johnston, *The Great Goldwyn*, ch. 1 (1937), to a director who was asked his opinion of a script.

16   In the court of the movie Owner, none criticized, none doubted. And none dared speak of art. In the Owner's mind art was a synonym for bankruptcy. . . . The movie Owners are the only troupe in the history of entertainment that has never been seduced by the adventure of the entertainment world.

> BEN HECHT (1893–1964), U.S. journalist, author, screenwriter. *A Child of the Century*, bk. 5, "The Captive Muse" (1954).

17   The average Hollywood film star's ambition is to be admired by an American, courted by an Italian, married to an Englishman and have a French boyfriend.

> KATHARINE HEPBURN (b. 1909), U.S. actor. *New York Journal-American* (22 Feb. 1954).

18   Hollywood has always been a cage . . . a cage to catch our dreams.

> JOHN HUSTON (1906–87), U.S. filmmaker. Quoted in: London *Sunday Times* (27 Dec. 1987).

19   Where is Hollywood located? Chiefly between the ears. In that part of the American brain lately vacated by God.

> ERICA JONG (b. 1942), U.S. author. *How To Save Your Own Life*, "Hello to Hollywood . . ." epigraph (1977).

20   There rise her timeless capitals of empires daily born,
Whose plinths are laid at midnight and whose streets are packed at morn;
And here come tired youths and maids that feign to love or sin
In tones like rusty razor blades to tunes like smitten tin.

RUDYARD KIPLING (1865–1936), British author, poet. *Naaman's Song,* interpreted as a description of Hollywood.

21 Just like those other black holes from outer space, Hollywood is postmodern to this extent: it has no center, only a spreading dead zone of exhaustion, inertia, and brilliant decay.

ARTHUR KROKER (b. 1945), MARILOUISE KROKER AND DAVID COOK (b. 1946), Canadian sociologists. *Panic Encyclopedia,* "Panic Hollywood" (1989).

22 Strip away the phony tinsel of Hollywood and you find the real tinsel underneath.

OSCAR LEVANT (1906–72), U.S. pianist, composer. Quoted in: *Halliwell's Filmgoer's Companion* (1984).

23 You can fool all the people all the time if the advertising is right and the budget is big enough.

JOSEPH E. LEVINE (b. 1905), U.S. film producer, executive. Quoted in: *Halliwell's Filmgoer's Companion* (1984).

24 If we have to tell Hollywood good-by, it may be with one of those tender, old-fashioned, seven-second kisses exchanged between two people of the *opposite* sex, with all their clothes on.

ANITA LOOS (1893–81), U.S. novelist, screenwriter. *Kiss Hollywood Good-by,* ch. 21 (1974).

25 We Americans have always considered Hollywood, at best, a sinkhole of depraved venality. And, of course, it is. It is not a Protective Monastery of Aesthetic Truth. It is a place where everything is incredibly expensive.

DAVID MAMET (b. 1947), U.S. playwright. *Writing in Restaurants,* "A Playwright in Hollywood" (1986).

26 Hollywood's a place where they'll pay you a thousand dollars for a kiss, and fifty cents for your soul. I know, because I turned down the first offer often enough and held out for the fifty cents.

MARILYN MONROE (1926–62), U.S. screen actor. Quoted in: *Marilyn Monroe In Her Own Words,* "Acting" (1990).

27 Hollywood money isn't money. It's congealed snow, melts in your hand, and there you are.

DOROTHY PARKER (1893–1967), U.S. humorous writer. Interview in *Writers at Work* (First Series, ed. by Malcolm Cowley, 1958).

28 Hollywood is a place that attracts people with massive holes in their souls.

JULIA PHILLIPS (b. 1945), U.S. film producer. *Times* (London, 3 April 1991).

29 Hollywood's like Egypt, full of crumbled pyramids. It'll never come back. It'll just keep on crumbling until finally the wind blows the last studio prop across the sands.

DAVID O. SELZNICK (1902–65), U.S. film producer. Quoted in: Hecht, *A Child of the Century,* bk. 5, "Enter, the Movies" (1954).

30 You don't resign from these jobs, you escape from them.

DAWN STEEL (b. 1946), U.S. film producer and executive. *International Herald Tribune* (Paris, 10 Jan. 1990), said upon quitting as president of Columbia Pictures.

31 If you have a vagina *and* an attitude in this town, then that's a lethal combination.

SHARON STONE (b. 1958), U.S. actor. *Empire* (London, June 1992).

32 Bankers, nepotists, contracts and talkies: on four fingers one may count the leeches which have sucked a young and vigorous industry into paresis.

DALTON TRUMBO (1905–76), U.S. screenwriter. "The Fall of Hollywood" in *North American Review* (Cedar Falls, Aug. 1933).

33 Hollywood is the only industry, even taking in soup companies, which does not have laboratories for the purpose of experimentation.

ORSON WELLES (1915–84), U.S. filmmaker, actor, producer. Quoted in: Frank Brady, *Citizen Welles,* Epilogue (1989).

See also Quinn on ACTORS; CINEMA; Hecht on PROMISCUITY; Hecht on STARDOM.

HOLLYWOOD AND WRITERS

1 I went out there for a thousand a week, and I worked Monday, and I got fired Wednesday. The guy that hired me was out of town Tuesday.

NELSON ALGREN (1909–81), U.S. author. Interview in *Writers at Work* (First Series, ed. by Malcolm Cowley, 1958).

2 If it's a good script I'll do it. And if it's a bad script, and they pay me enough, I'll do it.

GEORGE BURNS (b. 1896), U.S. comedian. *International Herald Tribune* (Paris, 9 Nov. 1988).

3 That's one thing I like about Hollywood. The writer is there revealed in his ultimate corruption. He asks no praise, because his praise comes to him in the form of a salary check. In Hollywood the average writer is not young, not honest, not brave, and a bit overdressed. But he is darn good company, which book writers as a rule are not. He is better than what he writes. Most book writers are not as good.

RAYMOND CHANDLER (1888–1959), U.S. author. Letter, 6 Dec. 1948, to *San Francisco Chronicle* critic Lenore Glen Offord (published in *Raymond Chandler Speaking,* 1962).

4 If my books had been any worse, I should not have been invited to Hollywood, and . . . if they had been any better, I should not have come.

RAYMOND CHANDLER (1888–1959), U.S. author. Letter, 12 Dec. 1945, to *Atlantic Monthly* editor, Charles W. Morton, in response to criticism of his article, *Writers in Hollywood.*

5 They don't want you until you have made a name, and by the time you have made a name, you have developed some kind of talent they can't use. All they will do is spoil it, if you let them.

RAYMOND CHANDLER (1888–1959), U.S. author. Letter, 7 Nov. 1951, to editor Dale Warren (published in *Raymond Chandler Speaking,* 1962).

6 I hate the place like poison with a sincere hatred.

F. SCOTT FITZGERALD (1896–1940), U.S. author. Letter, 10 Jan. 1935, to his agent, replying to a suggestion that Fitzgerald should return to Hollywood to work on a script of *Tender is the Night* (published in *As Ever, Scott Fitz,* ed. by Matthew J. Bruccoli, 1973).

7 Hollywood held this double lure for me, tremendous sums of money for work that required no more effort than a game of pinochle.

> BEN HECHT (1893–1964), U.S. journalist, author, screenwriter. *A Child of the Century*, bk. 5, "Enter, the Movies" (1954). But a few pages further, Hecht maintained that, "Half of the large sum paid me for writing a movie script was in payment for listening to the producer and obeying him. . . . The movies pay as much for obedience as for creative work. An able writer is paid a larger sum than a man of small talent. But he is paid this added money not to use his superior talents."

8   You write a book like that that you're fond of over the years, then you see that happen to it, it's like pissing in your father's beer.

> ERNEST HEMINGWAY (1899–1961), U.S. author. Quoted in: A. E. Hotchner, *Papa Hemingway* (1966 ed.). Hemingway made this remark after seeing David O. Selznick's remake of *A Farewell to Arms* (1957).

9   I devoutly believe it is the writer who has matured the film medium more than anyone else in Hollywood. Even when he knew nothing about his work, he brought at least knowledge of life and a more grown-up mind, a maturer feeling about the human being.

> DUDLEY NICHOLS (1895–1960), U.S. screenwriter. "Film Writing" in *Theatre Arts* (Dec. 1942).

10   Sam Goldwyn said, "How'm I gonna do decent pictures when all my good writers are in jail?" Then he added, the infallible Goldwyn, "Don't misunderstand me, they all ought to be hung." Mr. Goldwyn didn't know about "hanged." That's all there is to say.

> DOROTHY PARKER (1893–1967), U.S. humorous writer. Interview in *Writers at Work*, First Series (ed. by Malcolm Cowley, 1958).

11   I can't talk about Hollywood. It was a horror to me when I was there and it's a horror to look back on. I can't imagine how I did it. When I got away from it I couldn't even refer to the place by name. "Out there," I called it.

> DOROTHY PARKER (1893–1967), U.S. humorous writer. Interview in *Writers at Work* (First Series, ed. by Malcolm Cowley, 1958).

See also Chandler on WRITING: SCRIPTS AND SCREENPLAYS.

THE HOLOCAUST

1   It is painful to recall a past intensity, to estimate your distance from the Belsen heap, to make your peace with numbers. Just to get up each morning is to make a kind of peace.

> LEONARD COHEN (b. 1934), Canadian singer, poet, novelist. *The Spice-Box of Earth*, "Lines From My Grandfather's Journal" (1965).

2   I have not made a study of it, but believe that it is a minor point in the history of the war.

> JEAN-MARIE LE PEN (b. 1928), French nationalist politician. Quoted in: *Sunday Times* (London, 27 Dec. 1987). Said of the Holocaust.

3   Without centuries of Christian antisemitism, Hitler's passionate hatred would never have been so fervently echoed.

> ROBERT RUNCIE (b. 1921), British ecclesiastic, Archbishop of Canterbury. *Daily Telegraph* (London, 10 Nov. 1988).

4   Today, almost forty years later, I grow dizzy when I recall that the number of manufactured tanks seems to have been more important to me than the vanished victims of racism.

> ALBERT SPEER (1905–81), German architect, Nazi official. *The Slave State*, ch. 21 (1981).

5   How do you describe the sorting out on arriving at Auschwitz, the separation of children who see a father or mother going away, never to be seen again? How do you express the dumb grief of a little girl and the endless lines of women, children and rabbis being driven across the Polish or Ukrainian landscapes to their deaths? No, I can't do it. And because I'm a writer and teacher, I don't understand how Europe's most cultured nation could have done that. For these men who killed with submachine-guns in the Ukraine were university graduates. Afterwards they would go home and read a poem by Heine. So what happened?

> ELIE WIESEL (b. 1928), Rumanian-born U.S. writer. Quoted in: *Le Monde* (Paris, 4 June 1987). Wiesel, a survivor of the concentration camps, was testifying at the trial of Klaus Barbie in Lyons, 2 June 1987. In an earlier interview he spoke of the continuing impact of the Holocaust on his life: "There isn't a day, there simply isn't a day without my thinking of death or of looking into death, darkness, or seeing that fire or trying to understand what happened. There isn't a day." (*Writers at Work*, Eighth Series, ed. by George Plimpton, 1988).

See also Wiesel on SURVIVAL.

HOME AND HOUSES

1   If I were asked to name the chief benefit of the house, I should say: the house shelters day-dreaming, the house protects the dreamer, the house allows one to dream in peace.

> GASTON BACHELARD (1884–1962), French scientist, philosopher, literary theorist. *The Poetics of Space*, ch. 1, "The House" (1958; tr. 1964).

2   Houses are built to live in, and not to look on: therefore let use be preferred before uniformity.

> FRANCIS BACON (1561–1626), English philosopher, essayist, statesman. *Essays*, "Of Building" (1597–1625).

3   People's backyards are much more interesting than their front gardens, and houses that back on to railways are public benefactors.

> JOHN BETJEMAN (1906–84), British poet. Quoted in: *Observer* (London, 20 March 1983).

4   There are things you just can't do in life. You can't beat the phone company, you can't make a waiter see you until he's ready to see you, and you can't go home again.

> BILL BRYSON (b. 1951), U.S. author, journalist. *The Lost Continent: Travels in Small Town America*, ch. 2 (1989).

5   An empty house is like a stray dog or a body from which life has departed.

> SAMUEL BUTLER (1835–1902), English author. *The Way of All Flesh*, ch. 72 (1903).

6   The place is very well & quiet & the children only scream in a low voice.

LORD BYRON (1788–1824), English poet. Letter, 21 Sept. 1813 (published in *Byron's Letters and Journals*, vol. 3, ed. by Leslie Marchand, 1974).

7   Never weather-beaten sail more willing bent
to shore.

THOMAS CAMPION (1567–1620), English poet, musician. *Never Weather-beaten Sail*, from *Two Books of Airs*, "Divine and Moral Songs" (c. 1613).

8   You are a king by your own fireside, as much as any monarch in his throne.

MIGUEL DE CERVANTES (1547–1616), Spanish writer. *Don Quixote*, Preface (1605; tr. by P. Motteux).

9   Home—that blessed word, which opens to the human heart the most perfect glimpse of Heaven, and helps to carry it thither, as on an angel's wings.

LYDIA M. CHILD (1802–80), U.S. abolitionist, writer, editor. Letter, Jan. 1843 (published in *Letters from New York*, vol. 1, letter 34, 1843).

10   In the matter of furnishing, I find a certain absence of ugliness far worse than ugliness.

COLETTE (1873–1954), French author. "The Photographer's Wife," in *Gigi* (1945; repr. in *The Collected Stories of Colette*, 1983).

11   Going home must be like going to render an account.

JOSEPH CONRAD (1857–1924), Polish-born English novelist. Marlow, in *Lord Jim*, ch. 21 (1900).

12   When I can no longer bear to think of the victims of broken homes, I begin to think of the victims of intact ones.

PETER DE VRIES (b. 1910), U.S. author. Augie, in *The Tunnel of Love*, ch. 8 (1954).

13   Home is a name, a word, it is a strong one; stronger than magician ever spoke, or spirit ever answered to, in the strongest conjuration.

CHARLES DICKENS (1812–70), English novelist. *Martin Chuzzlewit*, ch. 35 (1844).

14   Drab Habitation of Whom?
Tabernacle or Tomb—
Or Dome of Worm—
Or Porch of Gnome—
Or some Elf's Catacomb?

EMILY DICKINSON (1830–86), U.S. poet. *The Complete Poems*, no. 893 (1955).

15   Many a man who thinks to found a home discovers that he has merely opened a tavern for his friends.

NORMAN DOUGLAS (1868–1952), British author. Mr. Keith, in *South Wind*, ch. 24 (1917).

16   A house means a family house, a place specially meant for putting children and men in so as to restrict their waywardness and distract them from the longing for adventure and escape they've had since time began.

MARGUERITE DURAS (b. 1914), French author, filmmaker. *Practicalities*, "House and Home" (1987; tr. 1990).

17   The house a woman creates is a Utopia. She can't help it—can't help trying to interest her nearest and dearest not in happiness itself but in the search for it.

MARGUERITE DURAS (b. 1914), French author, filmmaker. *Practicalities*, "House and Home" (1987; tr. 1990).

18   Construed . . . as turf, home just seems a provisional claim, a designation you make upon a place, not one it makes on you. A certain set of buildings, a glimpsed, smudged window-view across a schoolyard, a musty aroma sniffed behind a garage when you were a child, all of which come crowding in upon your latter-day senses—those are pungent things and vivid, even consoling. But to me they are also inert and nostalgic and unlikely to connect you to the real, to that essence art can sometimes achieve, which is permanence.

RICHARD FORD (b. 1944), U.S. author. "An Urge for Going" in *Harper's* (New York, Feb. 1992).

19   Home is the place where, when you have to go there,
They have to take you in.

ROBERT FROST (1874–1963), U.S. poet. "Husband," in *The Death of the Hired Man*. "Wife" replies:

I should have called it
Something you somehow haven't to deserve.

20   Estate agents. You can't live with them, you can't live with them. The first sign of these nasty purulent sores appeared round about 1894. With their jangling keys, nasty suits, revolting beards, moustaches and tinted spectacles, estate agents roam the land causing perturbation and despair. If you try and kill them, you're put in prison: if you try and talk to them, you vomit. There's only one thing worse than an estate agent but at least that can be safely lanced, drained and surgically dressed. Estate agents. Love them or loathe them, you'd be mad not to loathe them.

STEPHEN FRY (b. 1957), British comic actor, author. Stephen, in *A Bit of Fry & Laurie*, "Lavatories" (1990).

21   One never reaches home, but wherever friendly paths intersect the whole world looks like home for a time.

HERMANN HESSE (1877–1962), German novelist, poet. Frau Eva, in *Demian*, ch. 5 (1960).

22   I want a house that has got over all its troubles; I don't want to spend the rest of my life bringing up a young and inexperienced house.

JEROME K. JEROME (1859–1927), British author. *They and I*, ch. 11 (1909).

23   It is, indeed, at home that every man must be known by those who would make a just estimate either of his virtue or felicity; for smiles and embroidery are alike occasional, and the mind is often dressed for show in painted honour, and fictitious benevolence.

SAMUEL JOHNSON (1709–84), English author, lexicographer. *Rambler*, no. 68 (London, 10 Nov. 1750; repr. in *Works of Samuel Johnson, Yale Edition*, vol. 3, ed. by W. J. Bate & Albrecht B. Strauss, 1969).

24   No money is better spent than what is laid out for domestic satisfaction.

SAMUEL JOHNSON (1709–84), English author, lexicographer. Quoted in: Boswell, *Life of Samuel Johnson*, 14 April 1776 (1791).

25   Owning your own home is America's unique recipe for avoiding revolution and promoting pseudo-equality at the same time. To keep citizens puttering in their yards instead of sputtering on the barricades, the government has gladly deprived itself of billions in tax revenues by letting home "owners" deduct mortgage interest payments.

> FLORENCE KING (b. 1936), U.S. author. *Reflections in a Jaundiced Eye*, "Democracy" (1989).

26   Were I Diogenes, I would not move out of a kilderkin into a hogshead, though the first had had nothing but small beer in it, and the second reeked claret.

> CHARLES LAMB (1775–1834), English essayist, critic. Letter, 28 March 1809, to Thomas Manning (published in *Complete Works of Charles Lamb*, vol. 2, 1882), on his horror of moving.

27   A house is a machine for living in.

> LE CORBUSIER (1887–1965), Swiss-born French architect. *Toward a New Architecture*, ch. 1, "Eyes Which Do Not See: Airplanes" (1923; tr. 1946).

28   I live in my house as I live inside my skin: I know more beautiful, more ample, more sturdy and more picturesque skins: but it would seem to me unnatural to exchange them for mine.

> PRIMO LEVI (1919–87), Italian chemist, author. *Other People's Trades*, "My House" (1985; tr. 1989).

29   What the Nation must realize is that the home, when both parents work, is non-existent. Once we have honestly faced that fact, we must act accordingly.

> AGNES MEYER (1887–1970), U.S. author, journalist. "Living Conditions of the Woolworker," in *Washington Post* (10 April 1943).

30   If you want a golden rule that will fit everything, this is it: Have nothing in your houses that you do not know to be useful or believe to be beautiful.

> WILLIAM MORRIS (1834–96), English artist, writer, printer. "The Decorative Arts: Their Relation to Modern Life and Progress," lecture (published in *Hopes and Fears for Art*, "The Lesser Arts," 1882).

31   The poorest man may in his cottage bid defiance to all the forces of the Crown. It may be frail—its roof may shake—the wind may blow through it—the storm may enter—the rain may enter—but the King of England cannot enter!—all his forces dare not cross the threshold of the ruined tenement!

> WILLIAM PITT THE ELDER, LORD CHATHAM (1708–78), English statesman. Speech, c. March 1763. Quoted in: Henry Peter Brougham, *Historical Sketches of Statesmen who Flourished in the Time of George III*, vol. 1, p. 52 (1839).

32   Every man likes the smell of his own farts.

> ICELANDIC PROVERB. Collected by W. H. Auden and Louis Kronenberger in *The Viking Book of Aphorisms* (1962). A form of the proverb also existed in ancient Rome, as attested by playwright Terence in *Andria*, act 4, sc. 2: "Every man's ordure well/To his own sense doth smell" (tr. by John Florio).

33   He makes his home where the living is best.

> LATIN PROVERB. Quoted in: Alan L. Mackay, *The Harvest of a Quiet Eye* (1977).

34   "Home" is any four walls that enclose the right person.

> HELEN ROWLAND (1875–1950), U.S. journalist. *Reflections of a Bachelor Girl* (1903), p. 9.

35   If men lived like men indeed, their houses would be temples—temples which we should hardly dare to injure, and in which it would make us holy to be permitted to live; and there must be a strange dissolution of natural affection, a strange unthankfulness for all that homes have given and parents taught, a strange consciousness that we have been unfaithful to our fathers' honour, or that our own lives are not such as would make our dwellings sacred to our children, when each man would fain build to himself, and build for the little revolution of his own life only.

> JOHN RUSKIN (1819–1900), English art critic, author. *The Seven Lamps of Architecture*, "The Lamp of Memory," sct. 3 (1849).

36   It takes patience to appreciate domestic bliss; volatile spirits prefer unhappiness.

> GEORGE SANTAYANA (1863–1952), U.S. philosopher, poet. *The Life of Reason*, "Reason in Society," ch. 2 (1905–6).

37   A comfortable house is a great source of happiness. It ranks immediately after health and a good conscience.

> SYDNEY SMITH (1771–1845), English writer, clergyman. Letter, 29 Sept. 1843.

38   Home is a place not only of strong affections, but of entire unreserve; it is life's undress rehearsal, its backroom, its dressing room, from which we go forth to more careful and guarded intercourse, leaving behind us much ital/debris of cast-off and everyday clothing.

> HARRIET BEECHER STOWE (1811–96), U.S. novelist, anti-slavery campaigner. *Little Foxes*, ch. 1 (1865).

39   I had three chairs in my house; one for solitude, two for friendship, three for society.

> HENRY DAVID THOREAU (1817–62), U.S. philosopher, author, naturalist. *Walden*, "Visitors" (1854).

40   Should not every apartment in which man dwells be lofty enough to create some obscurity overhead, where flickering shadows may play at evening about the rafters?

> HENRY DAVID THOREAU (1817–62), U.S. philosopher, author, naturalist. *Walden*, "House-Warming" (1854).

41   I have been photographing our toilet, that glossy enameled receptacle of extraordinary beauty.... Here was every sensuous curve of the "human figure divine" but minus the imperfections. Never did the Greeks reach a more significant consummation to their culture, and it somehow reminded me, in the glory of its chaste convulsions and in its swelling, sweeping, forward movement of finely progressing contours, of the Victory of Samothrace.

> EDWARD WESTON (1886–1958), U.S. photographer. *The Daybooks of Edward Weston*, vol. 1, pt. 4, ch. 1 (ed. by Nancy Newhall, 1925), entry for 21 Oct. 1925.

42   It is the personality of the mistress that the home expresses. Men are forever guests in our homes, no matter how much happiness they may find there.

> ELSIE DE WOLFE (1865–1950), British actor, hostess. *The House in Good Taste*, ch. 1 (1920).

See also The HOMELESS: HOUSEWORK: Bowen on LONELINESS; Said on POVERTY AND THE POOR; Lebowitz on SNOBBERY.

THE HOMELESS

1 The foxes have holes, and the birds of the air have nests; but the Son of man hath not where to lay his head.

> BIBLE: NEW TESTAMENT. Jesus, in *Matthew* 8:20.

2 To be shelterless and alone in the open country, hearing the wind moan and watching for day through the whole long weary night; to listen to the falling rain, and crouch for warmth beneath the lee of some old barn or rick, or in the hollow of a tree; are dismal things—but not so dismal as the wandering up and down where shelter is, and beds and sleepers are by thousands; a houseless rejected creature.

> CHARLES DICKENS (1812–70), English novelist. *Barnaby Rudge*, ch. 18 (1841).

3 Do not ask the name of the person who seeks a bed for the night. He who is reluctant to give his name is the one who most needs shelter.

> VICTOR HUGO (1802–85), French poet, dramatist, novelist. Bienvenu Myriel, the bishop of Digne, in *Les Misérables*, pt. 1, bk. 1, ch. 6 (1862).

4 Let not him who is houseless pull down the house of another, but let him work diligently and build one for himself, thus by example assuring that his own shall be safe from violence when built.

> ABRAHAM LINCOLN (1809–65), U.S. president. Speech, 21 March 1864, in reply to committee from the New York Workingmen's Association.

5 You scour the Bowery, ransack the Bronx,
Through funeral parlors and honky-tonks.
From river to river you comb the town
For a place to lay your family down.

> OGDEN NASH (1902–71), U.S. poet. *Nature Abhors a Vacancy*, in *Versus* (1949).

6 What we have found in this country, and maybe we're more aware of it now, is one problem that we've had, even in the best of times, and that is the people who are sleeping on the grates, the homeless, you might say, by choice.

> RONALD REAGAN (b. 1911), U.S. Republican politician, president. Quoted in: Mark Green & Gail MacColl, *Reagan's Reign of Error*, "A Deficit of Economics" (1987), from statement made 31 Jan. 1984.

7 I am my brother's keeper, and he's sleeping pretty rough these days.

> ARCHBISHOP DEREK WORLOCK (b. 1920), British Roman Catholic cleric. London *Observer* (London, 16 Dec. 1990).

See also Macaulay on BED; Stevenson on NIGHT.

HOMOSEXUALITY

1 Human beings are distinguished by a capacity for experience as well as by their behavior, and homosexu-
ality is as much a matter of emotion as of genital manipulation. . . . As we each examine our own sense of identity we realize how much more complex is the question of homosexuality than a mere Kinsey-like computation of orgasms.

> DENNIS ALTMAN (b. 1943), Australian sociologist. *Homosexual Oppression and Liberation*, ch. 1 (1971).

2 Sexual fidelity is more important in a homosexual relationship than in any other. In other relationships there are a variety of ties. But here, fidelity is the only bond.

> W. H. AUDEN (1907–73), Anglo-American poet. *The Table Talk of W. H. Auden*, "October 20, 1947" (comp. by Alan Ansen, ed. by Nicholas Jenkins, 1990).

3 I'm always amazed at the American practice of allowing one party to a homosexual act to remain passive—it's so undemocratic. Sex must be mutual.

> W. H. AUDEN (1907–73), Anglo-American poet. *The Table Talk of W. H. Auden*, "10 December, 1947" (comp. by Alan Ansen, ed. by Nicholas Jenkins, 1990).

4 The condition that is now called gay was then called queer. The operative word was *faggot* and, later, pussy, but those epithets really had nothing to do with the question of sexual preference: You were being told simply that you had no balls.

> JAMES BALDWIN (1924–87), U.S. author. "Freaks and the American Ideal of Manhood," in *Playboy* (Chicago, Jan. 1985; repr. in *The Price of the Ticket*, "Here Be Dragons," 1985).

5 He said "Next time can I bring my friend?"
And I thought "Does he mean friend?"
And I thought "Yes he *does* mean friend."
Which was quite bold in those days.
It was the Dark Ages. Men and men.
And they could still put you in prison for it.
And did, dear.

> ALAN BENNETT (b. 1934), British playwright. Peggy, in *Prick up Your Ears: The Screenplay* (1987).

6 If a man also lie with mankind, as he lieth with a woman, both of them have committed an abomination: they shall surely be put to death; their blood shall be upon them.

> BIBLE, HEBREW. *Leviticus* 20:13.

7 This is a celebration of individual freedom, not of homosexuality. No government has the right to tell its citizens when or whom to love. The only queer people are those who don't love anybody.

> RITA MAE BROWN (b. 1944), U.S. feminist writer. Speech, 28 Aug. 1982, at the opening of the Gay Olympics in San Francisco.

8 In homosexual sex you know exactly what the other person is feeling, so you are identifying with the other person completely. In heterosexual sex you have no idea what the other person is feeling.

> WILLIAM BURROUGHS (b. 1914), U.S. author. Quoted in: Victor Bockris, *With William Burroughs: A Report from the Bunker*, "On Men" (1981).

9 At my back I hear the word—"homosexual"—and it seems to split my world in two. . . . It is ignorance, our ignorance of one another, that creates this terrifying erotic chaos. Information, a crumb of information, seems to light the world.

JOHN CHEEVER (1912–82), U.S. author. *John Cheever: The Journals*, "The Sixties" (ed. by Robert Gottlieb, 1991), entry in 1966.

10 I, for one, do not think homosexuality is the latest advance over heterosexuality in the scale of human evolution. Homosexuality is a sickness, just as are baby-rape or wanting to become head of General Motors.

ELDRIDGE CLEAVER (b. 1935), U.S. black leader, writer. *Soul on Ice*, "Notes on a Native Son" (1968).

11 The . . . problem that confronts homosexuals is that they set out to win the love of a "real" man. If they succeed, they fail. A man who "goes with" other men is not what they would call a real man. The conundrum is incapable of resolution, but that does not make homosexuals give it up.

QUENTIN CRISP (b. 1908), British author. *The Naked Civil Servant*, ch. 9 (1968).

12 In homosexual love the passion is homosexuality itself. What a homosexual loves, as if it were his lover, his country, his art, his land, is homosexuality.

MARGUERITE DURAS (b. 1914), French author, filmmaker. *Practicalities*, "Men" (1987; tr. 1990).

13 We think that we live in a heterosexual society because most men are fixated on women as sexual objects; but, in fact, we live in a homosexual society because all credible transactions of power, authority, and authenticity take place among men; all transactions based on equity and individuality take place among men. Men are real; therefore, all real relationship is between men; all real communication is between men; all real reciprocity is between men; all real mutuality is between men.

ANDREA DWORKIN (b. 1946), U.S. feminist critic. "The Root Cause," speech, 26 Sept. 1975, Massachusetts Institute of Technology, Cambridge (published in *Our Blood*, ch. 9, 1976).

14 Sexuality is a part of our behavior. It's part of our world freedom. Sexuality is something that we ourselves create. It is our own creation, and much more than the discovery of a secret side of our desire. We have to understand that with our desires go new forms of relationships, new forms of love, new forms of creation. Sex is not a fatality; it's a possibiity for creative life. It's not enough to affirm that we are gay but we must also create a gay life.

MICHEL FOUCAULT (1926–84), French philosopher. "Sex, Power and the Politics of Identity," interview, Oct. 1982 (published in *Advocate*, Los Angeles, 7 Aug. 1984; repr. in Didier Eribon, *Michel Foucault*, 1989; tr. 1991).

15 Homosexuality is assuredly no advantage, but it is nothing to be ashamed of, no vice, no degradation; it cannot be classified as an illness; we consider it to be a variation of the sexual function, produced by a certain arrest of sexual development. Many highly respectable individuals of ancient and modern times have been homosexuals, several of the greatest men among them (Plato, Michelangelo, Leonardo da Vinci, etc.). It is a great injustice to persecute homosexuality as a crime—and a cruelty, too. If you do not believe me, read the books of Havelock Ellis.

SIGMUND FREUD (1856–1939), Austrian psychiatrist. Letter, 9 April 1935, to a woman requesting treatment for her son (published in *The Letters of Sigmund Freud*, 1961).

16 The modern queer was invented by Tennessee Williams. Brando in blue jeans, sneakers, white T-shirt and leather jacket. When you saw that, you knew they were available.

DEREK JARMAN (b. 1942), British filmmaker, artist, author. *At Your Own Risk: A Saint's Testament*, "1960's" (1992).

17 The queers of the sixties, like those since, have connived with their repression under a veneer of respectability. Good mannered city queens in suits and pinstripes, so busy establishing themselves, were useless at changing anything.

DEREK JARMAN (b. 1942), British filmmaker, artist, author. *At Your Own Risk: A Saint's Testament*, "1960's" (1992).

18 For men who want to flee Family Man America and never come back, there is a guaranteed solution: homosexuality is the new French Foreign Legion.

FLORENCE KING (b. 1936), U.S. author. *Reflections in a Jaundiced Eye*, "From Captain Marvel to Captain Valium" (1989).

19 Bisexuality is almost a necessary factor in artistic production; at any rate, the tinge of masculinity within me helped me in my work.

KÄTHE KOLLWITZ (1867–1945), German artist. *Diaries and Letters*, 1942 (ed. by Hans Kollwitz, 1955).

20 I've spent fifteen years of my life fighting for our right to be free and make love whenever, wherever. . . And you're telling me that all those years of what being gay stood for is wrong. . . and I'm a murderer. We have been so oppressed! Don't you remember how it was? Can't you see how important it is for us to love openly, without hiding and without guilt?

LARRY KRAMER (b. 1935), U.S. playwright, novelist. Mickey, in *The Normal Heart*.

21 The only way we'll have real pride is when we demand recognition of a culture that isn't just sexual. It's all there—all through history we've been there; but we have to claim it, and identify who was in it, and articulate what's in our minds and hearts and all our creative contributions to this earth. And until we do that, and until we organise ourselves block by neighborhood by city by state into a united visible community that fights back, we're doomed.

LARRY KRAMER (b. 1935), U.S. playwright, novelist. Ned, in *The Normal Heart*.

22 There is probably no sensitive heterosexual alive who is not preoccupied with his latent homosexuality.

NORMAN MAILER (b. 1923), U.S. author. *Advertisements for Myself*, "The Homosexual Villain" (1959).

23 One cannot serve this Eros without becoming a stranger in society as it is today; one cannot commit oneself to this form of love without incurring a mortal wound.

KLAUS MANN (1906–49), German author, son of Thomas Mann. Quoted in: Marcel Reich-Ranicki, *Thomas Mann and His Family*, "Klaus Mann" (1987; tr. 1989). Mann was speaking of his homosexuality.

24   I think a lot of gay people who are not dealing with their homosexuality get into right-wing politics.

> ARMISTEAD MAUPIN (b. 1944), U.S. journalist, author. *Guardian* (London, 22 April 1988).

25   This sort of thing may be tolerated by the French—but we are British, thank God.

> VISCOUNT MONTGOMERY (1887–1976), British soldier. Speech, 26 May 1965, to House of Lords in debate on Homosexuality Bill.

26   Gay men are guardians of the masculine impulse. To have anonymous sex in a dark alleyway is to pay homage to the dream of male freedom. The unknown stranger is a wandering pagan god. The altar, as in prehistory, is anywhere you kneel.

> CAMILLE PAGLIA (b. 1947), U.S. author, critic, educator. "Homosexuality at the Fin de Siècle," in *Esquire* (New York, Oct. 1991; repr. in *Sex, Art, and American Culture*, 1992).

27   She never felt much in common with gay men; it was like telling her she ought to feel empathy with child molesters because they were both defined by the law as sexual deviants.

> MARGE PIERCY (b. 1936), U.S. poet, novelist. *The High Cost of Living*, ch. 3 (1978), referring to the character Leslie.

28   O my friends, can there be an extravagance to equal that of imagining that a man must be a monster deserving to lose his life because he has preferred enjoyment of the asshole to that of the cunt, because a young man with whom he finds two pleasures, those of being at once lover and mistress, has appeared to him preferable to a young girl, who promises him but half as much! He shall be a villain, a monster, for having wished to play the role of a sex not his own! Indeed! Why then has Nature created him susceptible of this pleasure?

> MARQUIS DE SADE (1740–1814), French author. Dolmancé, in *Philosophy in the Bedroom*, "Dialogue the Fifth" (1795).

29   A person's sexuality is so much more than one word "gay." No one refers to anyone as just "hetero" because that doesn't say anything. Sexual identity is broader than a label.

> GUS VAN SANT, U.S. gay filmmaker. Quoted in: *Sight and Sound* (London, Aug. 1992).

30   The scorn directed against drags is especially virulent; they have become the outcasts of gay life, the "queers" of homosexuality. In fact, they are classic scapegoats. Our old fears about our sissiness, still with us though masked by the new macho fascism, are now located, isolated, quarantined through our persecution of the transvestite.

> EDMUND WHITE (b. 1940), U.S. author. *States of Desire: Travels in Gay America*, ch. 2 (1980).

31   "The Love that dare not speak its name" in this century is such a great affection of an elder for a younger man as there was between David and Jonathan, such as Plato made the very basis of his philosophy, and such as you find in the sonnets of Michelangelo and Shakespeare. It is that deep, spiritual affection that is as pure as it is perfect . . . . It is in this century misunderstood . . . and on account of it I am placed where I am now.

> OSCAR WILDE (1854–1900), Anglo-Irish playwright, author. Quoted in: H. Montgomery Hyde, *Oscar Wilde*, ch. 6, (1976). Wilde made this statement during his first trial for "indecent acts," *Regina v. Wilde and Taylor* (30 April 1895). "I am the Love that dare not speak its name," was the concluding line of the poem *Two Loves*, contributed by Lord Alfred Douglas to the undergraduate magazine *The Chameleon*.

See also Kramer on AIDS; Spong on The CHURCH AND SOCIETY; Greer on ENGLAND AND THE ENGLISH; LESBIANISM; Jarman on MEN; Sontag on MINORITIES; Jarman on NAMES; Altman on SEXUAL DEVIATION; Jarman, Vidal on SEXUALITY.

HONESTY

1   A few honest men are better than numbers.

> OLIVER CROMWELL (1599–1658), Parliamentarian general, Lord Protector of England. Letter, Sept. 1643.

2   To live outside the law, you must be honest.

> BOB DYLAN (b. 1941), U.S. singer, songwriter. "Absolutely Sweet Marie" on the album *Blonde on Blonde* (1968). A similar observation was made in Don Siegel's 1958 film, *The Line-Up.*.

3   Nothing astonishes men so much as common sense and plain dealing.

> RALPH WALDO EMERSON (1803–82), U.S. essayist, poet, philosopher. *Essays*, "Art" (First Series, 1841).

4   No such thing as a man willing to be honest—that would be like a blind man willing to see.

> F. SCOTT FITZGERALD (1896–1940), U.S. author. *The Crack-Up*, "Notebook E," ed. by Edmund Wilson (1945).

5   Honest men
    are the soft easy cushions on which knaves
    Repose and fatten.

> THOMAS OTWAY (1652–85), English dramatist. Pierre, in *Venice Preserved*, act 1, sc. 1.

6   Though I am not naturally honest, I am so sometimes by chance.

> WILLIAM SHAKESPEARE (1564–1616), English dramatist, poet. Autolycus, in *The Winter's Tale*, act 4, sc. 4.

7   I am afraid we must make the world honest before we can honestly say to our children that honesty is the best policy.

> GEORGE BERNARD SHAW (1856–1950), Anglo-Irish playwright, critic. Broadcast, 11 July 1932

See also CANDOR; Canning on FRIENDS; Shaw on SINCERITY.

HONOR

1   Since an intelligence common to us all makes things known to us and formulates them in our minds, honorable actions are ascribed by us to virtue, and dishonorable actions to vice; and only a madman would conclude that these judgments are matters of opinion, and not fixed by nature.

> CICERO (106–43 B.C.), Roman orator, philosopher. *De Legibus*, bk. 1, ch. 16, sct. 45 (85 A.D.).

2   As to honour—you know—it's a very fine mediaeval inheritance which women never got hold of. It wasn't theirs.

> JOSEPH CONRAD (1857–1924), Polish-born English novelist. Marlow, in *Chance*, ch. 2 (1914).

3 The louder he talked of his honor, the faster we counted our spoons.

> RALPH WALDO EMERSON (1803–82), U.S. essayist, poet, philosopher. *The Conduct of Life*, "Worship" (1870).

4 My honor is my loyalty.

> HEINRICH HIMMLER (1900–1945), German Nazi leader. Formulated as the watchword of the S.S. Nazi élite (tr. by Hannah Arendt in *The Origins of Totalitarianism*, ch. 10, 1951). The U.S. Government Printing Office, *Nazi Conspiracy and Aggression*, vol. 5 (1946–48), gives an alternative translation: "My honor signifies faithfulness."

5 Because there is very little honor left in American life, there is a certain built-in tendency to destroy masculinity in American men.

> NORMAN MAILER (b. 1923), U.S. author. *Cannibals and Christians*, "Petty Notes on Some Sex in America" (1966; first published 1962–63).

6 The only thing of weight that can be said against modern honour is that it is directly opposite to religion. The one bids you bear injuries with patience, the other tells you if you don't resent them, you are not fit to live.

> BERNARD MANDEVILLE (1670–1733), Dutch-born English author, physician. *The Fable of the Bees*, "Remark (R)" (1714; rev. 1723).

7 Without money honor is merely a disease.

> JEAN RACINE (1639–99), French dramatist. Petit Jean, in *Les Plaideurs*, act 1, sc. 1 (1669).

8 Honor has not to be won; it must only not be lost.

> ARTHUR SCHOPENHAUER (1788–1860), German philosopher. *Parerga and Paralipomena*, vol. 1, "Aphorisms on the Wisdom of Life," ch. 4 (1851).

9 It is the dissimilarities and inequalities among men which give rise to the notion of honor; as such differences become less, it grows feeble; and when they disappear, it will vanish too.

> ALEXIS DE TOCQUEVILLE (1805–59), French social philosopher. *Democracy in America*, vol. 2, pt. 3, ch. 18 (1840).

10 There is no question what the roll of honor in America is. The roll of honor consists of the names of men who have squared their conduct by ideals of duty.

> WOODROW WILSON (1856–1924), U.S. Democratic politician, president. Speech, 27 Feb. 1916, Washington, D.C.

HOPE

1 Still bent to make some port he knows not where,
Still standing for some false impossible shore.

> MATTHEW ARNOLD (1822–88), English poet, critic. *A Summer Night*.

2 But what is Hope? Nothing but the paint on the face of Existence; the least touch of truth rubs it off, and then we see what a hollow-cheeked harlot we have got hold of.

> LORD BYRON (1788–1824), English poet. Letter, 28 Oct. 1815, to the poet Thomas Moore (published in *Byron's Letters and Journals*, vol. 4, ed. by Leslie Marchand, 1975).

3 "Hope" is the thing with feathers—
That perches in the soul—
And sings the tunes without the words—
And never stops—at all—.

> EMILY DICKINSON (1830–86), U.S. poet. *The Complete Poems*, no. 254 (1955).

4 Hope is definitely not the same thing as optimism. It is not the conviction that something will turn out well, but the certainty that something makes sense, regardless of how it turns out.

> VÁCLAV HAVEL (b. 1936), Czech playwright, president. *Disturbing the Peace*, ch. 5 (1986; tr. 1990).

5 Hope is the only universal liar who never loses his reputation for veracity.

> ROBERT G. INGERSOLL (1833–99), U.S. lawyer, orator. Speech, Manhattan Liberal Club (published in *Truth-Seeker*, 28 Feb. 1892).

6 The natural flights of the human mind are not from pleasure to pleasure, but from hope to hope.

> SAMUEL JOHNSON (1709–84), English author, lexicographer. *Rambler*, no. 2 (London, 24 March 1750; repr. in *Works of Samuel Johnson*, vol. 3, ed. by W. J. Bate and Albrecht B. Strauss, 1969).

7 Hope is itself a species of happiness, and, perhaps, the chief happiness which this world affords: but, like all other pleasures immoderately enjoyed, the excesses of hope must be expiated by pain; and expectations improperly indulged must end in disappointment.

> SAMUEL JOHNSON (1709–84), English author, lexicographer. Letter, 8 June 1762 (published in Boswell, *Life of Samuel Johnson*, 1791).

8 Hope is the feeling you have that the feeling you have isn't permanent.

> JEAN KERR (b. 1923), U.S. author, playwright. Felicia, in *Finishing Touches*, act 3.

9 Hope is a bad thing. It means that you are not what you want to be. It means that part of you is dead, if not *all* of you. It means that you entertain illusions. It's a sort of spiritual clap, I should say.

> HENRY MILLER (1891–1980), U.S. author. *The Cosmological Eye*, "Peace! It's Wonderful!" (1939).

10 Ah, Hope! what would life be, stripped of thy encouraging smiles, that teach us to look behind the dark clouds of to-day, for the golden beams that are to gild the morrow.

> SUSANNA MOODIE (1803–85), Canadian author. *Life in the Clearing*, ch. 1 (1853).

11 Man is a victim of dope
In the incurable form of hope.

> OGDEN NASH (1902–71), U.S. poet. *Good-by, Old Year, You Oaf or Why Don't They Pay the Bonus?*, in *The Primrose Path* (1935).

12 Take hope from the heart of man and you make him a beast of prey.

> OUIDA (MARIE LOUISE DE LA RAMÉE) (1839–1908), English novelist. "A Village Commune" (1881; published in *Wisdom, Wit and Pathos*, 1884).

13 One measure of a civilization, either of an age or of a single individual, is what that age or person really wishes to *do*. A man's hope measures his civilization. The attainability of the hope measures, or may measure, the civilization of his nation and time.

EZRA POUND (1885–1972), U.S. poet, critic. *Guide to Kulchur*, pt. 3, sct. 6, ch. 22 (1938).

14 Hope, the patent medicine
For disease, disaster, sin.

WALLACE RICE (1859–1939), U.S. poet, editor. *Hope*.

15 Hope is like a harebell trembling from its birth . . .

CHRISTINA ROSSETTI (1830–94), English poet, lyricist. *Hope Is Like a Harebell* [harebell = bluebell].

16 Hope is the most sensitive part of a poor wretch's soul; whoever raises it only to torment him is behaving like the executioners in Hell who, they say, incessantly renew old wounds and concentrate their attention on that area of it that is already lacerated.

MARQUIS DE SADE (1740–1814), French author. Letter, 20 Feb. 1781, to his wife from Vincennes prison (published in *Selected Letters*, no. 7, ed. by Margaret Crosland, 1965).

17 The miserable have no other medicine
But only hope.

WILLIAM SHAKESPEARE (1564–1616), English dramatist, poet. Claudio, in *Measure for Measure*, act 3, sc. 1.

18 Cold hopes swarm like worms within our living clay.

PERCY BYSSHE SHELLEY (1792–1822), English poet. *Adonais*, st. 39.

19 Just as despair can come to one only from other human beings, hope, too, can be given to one only by other human beings.

ELIE WIESEL (b. 1928), Rumanian-born U.S. writer. Nobel lecture, Oslo, 11 Dec. 1986.

HORROR

1 I think of horror films as art, as films of confrontation. Films that make you confront aspects of your own life that are difficult to face. Just because you're making a horror film doesn't mean you can't make an artful film.

DAVID CRONENBERG (b. 1943), Canadian filmmaker. *Cronenberg On Cronenberg*, ch. 4 (ed. by Chris Rodley, 1992).

2 I don't believe in evil, I believe only in horror. In nature there is no evil, only an abundance of horror: the plagues and the blights and the ants and the maggots.

ISAK DINESEN [KAREN BLIXEN] (1885–1962), Danish author. Quoted in: Prokosch, *Voices: A Memoir*, "Phantoms" (1983).

3 Where there is no imagination there is no horror.

SIR ARTHUR CONAN DOYLE (1859–1930), English author. Sherlock Holmes, in *A Study in Scarlet*, ch. 5 (1887).

4 One might say that the true subject of the horror genre is the struggle for recognition of all that our civilization represses and oppresses.

ROBIN WOOD (b. 1931), British film critic, author. *American Nightmare: Essays on the Horror Film*, Introduction (ed. by Britton, Lippe, Williams, & Wood, 1979).

HORSES

1 A horse is dangerous at both ends and uncomfortable in the middle.

IAN FLEMING (1908–64), British author. Quoted in: *Sunday Times* (London, 9 Oct. 1966).

2 They say Princes learn no art truly, but the art of horsemanship. The reason is, the brave beast is no flatterer. He will throw a prince as soon as his groom.

BEN JONSON (1573–1637), English dramatist, poet. *Timber, or Discoveries Made upon Men and Matter*, "Illiteratus Princeps," para.95 (1641). The aphorism is attributed to Carneades by Montaigne in his *Essays*, bk. 3, ch. 7, "Of the Incommodity of Greatness" (1588): "Princes' children learnt nothing aright but to manage and ride horses; forsomuch as in all other exercises every man yieldeth and giveth them the victory; but a horse, who is neither a flatterer nor a courtier, will as soon throw the child of a king as the son of a base porter."

3 The horse, the horse! The symbol of surging potency and power of movement, of action, in man.

D. H. LAWRENCE (1885–1930), British author. *Apocalypse*, ch. 10 (1931).

4 It takes a good deal of physical courage to ride a horse. This, however, I have. I get it at about forty cents a flask, and take it as required.

STEPHEN LEACOCK (1869–1944), Canadian humorist, economist. *Literary Lapses*, "Reflections on Riding" (1910).

5 My beautiful, my beautiful! That standest meekly by,
With thy proudly-arched and glossy neck, and dark and fiery eye!

CAROLINE SHERIDAN NORTON (1808–77), English writer, poet. *The Arab's Farewell to His Steed*.

6 I've often said there's nothing better for the inside of a man than the outside of a horse.

RONALD REAGAN (b. 1911), U.S. Republican politician, president. Remark, 13 Aug. 1987, North Platte, Nebr. The *New York Times* had previously quoted this remark as early as 2 Oct. 1981.

7 Go anywhere in England where there are natural, wholesome, contented, and really nice English people; and what do you always find? That the stables are the real centre of the household.

GEORGE BERNARD SHAW (1856–1950), Anglo-Irish playwright, critic. Lady Utterword, in *Heartbreak House*, act 3.

See also Pascal on ADMIRATION; Salinger on CARS.

HOSPITALITY

1 Be not forgetful to entertain strangers: for thereby some have entertained angels unawares.

BIBLE: NEW TESTAMENT. *Hebrews* 13:2.

2 We'll teach you to drink deep ere you depart.

WILLIAM SHAKESPEARE (1564–1616), English dramatist, poet. Hamlet, in *Hamlet*, act 1, sc. 2.

3 Nowadays the host does not admit you to *his* hearth, but has got the mason to build one for yourself somewhere in his alley, and hospitality is the art of *keeping* you at the greatest distance.

> HENRY DAVID THOREAU (1817–62), U.S. philosopher, author, naturalist. *Walden*, "House-Warming" (1854).

4   I'm sure I don't know half the people who come to my house. Indeed, from all I hear, I shouldn't like to.

> OSCAR WILDE (1854–1900), Anglo-Irish playwright, author. Lady Markby, in *An Ideal Husband*, act 2.

5   I have heard people eat most heartily of another man's meat, that is, what they do not pay for.

> WILLIAM WYCHERLEY (1640–1716), English dramatist. Lady Fidget, in *The Country Wife*, act 5.

See also GUESTS; Douglas on HOME AND HOUSES.

HOSPITALS

1   I would rather be kept alive in the efficient if cold altruism of a large hospital than expire in a gush of warm sympathy in a small one.

> ANEURIN BEVAN (1897–1960), British Labour politician. Speech, 30 April 1946, House of Commons.

2   How many desolate creatures on the earth
Have learnt the simple dues of fellowship
And social comfort, in a hospital.

> ELIZABETH BARRETT BROWNING (1806–61), English poet. *Aurora Leigh*, bk. 3 (1857).

3   The sick man must follow his illness to the place where it is treated. . . . He is set aside in one of the technical and secret zones (hospitals, prisons, refuse dumps) which relieve the living of everything that might hinder the chain of production and consumption, and which . . . repair and select what can be sent back up to the surface of progress.

> MICHEL DE CERTEAU (1925–86), French author, critic. *The Practice of Everyday Life*, ch. 14, "An Unthinkable Practice" (1974).

4   We achieve "active" mastery over illness and death by delegating all responsibility for their management to physicians, and by exiling the sick and the dying to hospitals. But hospitals serve the convenience of staff not patients: we cannot be properly ill in a hospital, nor die in one decently; we can do so only among those who love and value us. The result is the institutionalized dehumanization of the ill, characteristic of our age.

> THOMAS SZASZ (b. 1920), U.S. psychiatrist. *The Second Sin*, "Personal Conduct" (1973).

See also Certeau on ILLNESS.

HOSTAGES

1   People are capable of doing an awful lot when they have no choice and I had no choice. Courage is when you have choices.

> TERRY ANDERSON, U.S. hostage. *International Herald Tribune* (Paris, 6 May 1992).

2   Neither dead nor alive, the hostage is suspended by an incalculable outcome. It is not his destiny that awaits for him, nor his own death, but anonymous chance, which can only seem to him something absolutely arbitrary. . . . He is in a state of radical emergency, of virtual extermination.

> JEAN BAUDRILLARD (b. 1929), French semiologist. *Fatal Strategies*, "Figures of the Transpolitical" (1983; tr. 1990).

3   We are all hostages, and we are all terrorists. This circuit has replaced that other one of masters and slaves, the dominating and the dominated, the exploiters and the exploited. . . . It is worse than the one it replaces, but at least it liberates us from liberal nostalgia and the ruses of history.

> JEAN BAUDRILLARD (b. 1929), French semiologist. *Fatal Strategies*, "Figures of the Transpolitical" (1983; tr. 1990).

4   Hostage is a crucifying aloneness. It is a silent, screaming slide into the bowels of ultimate despair. Hostage is a man hanging by his fingernails over the edge of chaos, feeling his fingers slowly straightening. Hostage is the humiliating stripping away of every sense and fibre of body and mind and spirit that make us what we are. Hostage is a mutant creation filled with fear, self-loathing, guilt and death-wishing. But he is a man, a rare, unique and beautiful creation of which these things are no part.

> BRIAN KEENAN (b. 1950), Irish teacher, hostage in Lebanon. Quoted in: *Independent* (London, 31 Aug. 1990).

5   If I were to be taken hostage, I would not plead for release nor would I want my government to be blackmailed. I think certain government officials, industrialists and celebrated persons should make it clear they are prepared to be sacrificed if taken hostage. If that were done, what gain would there be for terrorists in taking hostages?

> MARGARET MEAD (1901–78), U.S. anthropologist. Quoted in: *Parade* (New York, 20 May 1979).

6   Freeing hostages is like putting up a stage set, which you do with the captors, agreeing on each piece as you slowly put it together; then you leave an exit through which both the captor and the captive can walk with sincerity and dignity.

> TERRY WAITE (b. 1939), British religious adviser. Television broadcast, 3 Nov. 1986, ABC TV, on his trips to Lebanon as emissary of the Archbishop of Canterbury to negotiate the release of hostages held by terrorists. On 20 Jan. 1987, Waite was himself kidnapped, not freed until Nov. 1991.

HOTELS

1   A writer is in danger of allowing his talent to dull who lets more than a year go past without finding himself in his rightful place of composition, the small single unluxurious "retreat" of the twentieth century, the hotel bedroom.

> CYRIL CONNOLLY (1903–74), British critic. *Enemies of Promise*, pt. 2, ch. 14 (1938).

2 Of course great hotels have always been social ideas, flawless mirrors to the particular societies they service.

> JOAN DIDION (b. 1935), U.S. essayist. *The White Album*, "In the Islands" (1979).

3 Doorman—a genius who can open the door of your car with one hand, help you in with the other, and still have one left for the tip.

> DOROTHY KILGALLEN (1913–65), U.S. columnist, television personality. Quoted in: Jilly Cooper & Tom Hartman, *Violets and Vinegar*, "Come Away, Poverty's Catching" (1980).

4 The hotel was once where things coalesced, where you could meet both townspeople and travelers. Not so in a motel. No matter how you build it, the motel remains the haunt of the quick and dirty, where the only locals are Chamber of Commerce boys every fourth Thursday. Who ever heard the returning traveler exclaim over one of the great motels of the world he stayed in? Motels can be big, but never grand.

> WILLIAM LEAST HEAT MOON [WILLIAM TROGDON] (b. 1939), U.S. author. *Blue Highways: A Journey into America*, pt. 5, ch. 2 (1983).

5 I've always thought a hotel ought to offer optional small animals. . . . I mean a cat to sleep on your bed at night, or a dog of some kind to act pleased when you come in. You ever notice how a hotel room feels so lifeless?

> ANNE TYLER (b. 1941), U.S. author. Macon Leary, in *The Accidental Tourist*, ch. 9 (1985)

HOUSEWORK

1 Housekeeping ain't no joke.

> LOUISA MAY ALCOTT (1832–88), U.S. author. The cook Hannah, in *Little Women*, pt. 1, ch. 11 (1868).

2 The works of women are symbolical.
We sew, sew, prick our fingers, dull our sight,
Producing what? A pair of slippers, sir,
To put on when you're weary—or a stool
To stumble over and vex you . . . "curse that stool!"
Or else at best, a cushion, where you lean
And sleep, and dream of something we are not,
But would be for your sake. Alas, alas!
This hurts most, this . . . that, after all, we are paid
The worth of our work, perhaps.

> ELIZABETH BARRETT BROWNING (1806–61), English poet. *Aurora Leigh*, bk. 1 (1857).

3 I make no secret of the fact that I would rather lie on a sofa than sweep beneath it. But you have to be efficient if you're going to be lazy.

> SHIRLEY CONRAN (b. 1932), British designer, journalist. *Superwoman*, "The Reason Why" (1975).

4 Cleaning your house while your kids are still growing is like shoveling the walk before it stops snowing.

> PHYLLIS DILLER (b. 1917), U.S. author, actor. Quoted in: Jilly Cooper & Tom Hartman, *Violets and Vinegar*, "I Liked You Better Smaller" (1980).

5 The suburban housewife—she was the dream image of the young American women and the envy, it was said, of women all over the world. The American housewife—freed by science and labor-saving appliances from the drudgery, the dangers of childbirth, and the illnesses of her grandmother . . . had found true feminine fulfilment.

> BETTY FRIEDAN (b. 1921), U.S. feminist writer. *The Feminine Mystique*, ch. 1 (1963).

6 The labor of women in the house, certainly, enables men to produce more wealth than they otherwise could; and in this way women are economic factors in society. But so are horses.

> CHARLOTTE PERKINS GILMAN (1860–1935), U.S. feminist, writer. *Women and Economics*, ch. 1 (1898).

7 Now, as always, the most automated appliance in a household is the mother.

> BEVERLY JONES (b. 1927), U.S. feminist writer. *The Florida Paper on Women's Liberation*, "The Dynamics of Marriage and Motherhood" (1970).

8 Perhaps all artists were, in a sense, housewives: tenders of the earth household.

> ERICA JONG (b. 1942), U.S. author. "The Artist as Housewife," in *The First Ms Reader* (ed. by Francine Kragbrun, 1972).

9 You all know that even when women have full rights, they still remain fatally downtrodden because all housework is left to them. In most cases housework is the most unproductive, the most barbarous and the most arduous work a woman can do. It is exceptionally petty and does not include anything that would in any way promote the development of the woman.

> VLADIMIR ILYICH LENIN (1870–1924), Russian revolutionary leader. *Collected Works*, "The Tasks of the Working Women's Movement in the Soviet Republic" (1965; first published 1919).

10 The labor of keeping house is labor in its most naked state, for labor is toil that never finishes, toil that has to be begun again the moment it is completed, toil that is destroyed and consumed by the life process.

> MARY MCCARTHY (1912–89), U.S. author, critic. "The Vita Activa," in *New Yorker* (18 Oct. 1958; repr. in *On the Contrary*, 1961).

11 Each home has been reduced to the bare essentials—to barer essentials than most primitive people would consider possible. Only one woman's hands to feed the baby, answer the telephone, turn off the gas under the pot that is boiling over, soothe the older child who has broken a toy, and open both doors at once. She is a nutritionist, a child psychologist, an engineer, a production manager, an expert buyer, all in one. Her husband sees her as free to plan her own time, and envies her; she sees him as having regular hours and envies him.

> MARGARET MEAD (1901–78), U.S. anthropologist. *Male and Female*, ch. 16 (1949).

12 Housework is work directly opposed to the possibility of human self-actualization.

> ANN OAKLEY (b. 1944), British sociologist, author. *Woman's Work: The Housewife, Past and Present*, ch. 9 (1974).

13 I hate housework! You make the beds, you do the

dishes—and six months later you have to start all over again.

> JOAN RIVERS (b. 1935), U.S. comedienne. Quoted in: *Woman Talk*, "Work" (ed. by Michèle Brown & Ann O'Connor, 1984).

14 For a woman to get a rewarding sense of total creation by way of the multiple monotonous chores that are her daily lot would be as irrational as for an assembly line worker to rejoice that he had created an automobile because he tightened a bolt.

> EDITH MENDEL STERN (1901–75), U.S. author, critic. "Women are Household Slaves," in *American Mercury* (Jan. 1949).

15 Untidy is perhaps too mild a word; slut would be a better one. Being a slut is of course partly a matter of bad luck as well as bad management: things just do boil over oftener, fuses blow sooner, front doors bang leaving us outside in our dressing-gowns; but it goes deeper than bad luck. We are not actually incapable of cleaning our homes: but we are liable to reorganize instead of scrub; we do our cleaning in a series of periodic assaults. A mother-in-law has only to appear over the horizon and we act like the murderer in a Ray Bradbury story who kept on wiping the finger prints off the fruit at the bottom of the bowl. We work in a frenzy; but... the frenzy usually subsides before we have got everything back into the cupboards again.

> KATHARINE WHITEHORN (b. 1926), British journalist. *Roundabout*, "Nought for Homework" (1962).

16 When it comes to housework the one thing no book of household management can ever tell you is how to begin. Or maybe I mean *why*.

> KATHARINE WHITEHORN (b. 1926), British journalist. *Roundabout*, "Nought for Homework" (1962).

17 Man is made for something better than disturbing dirt.

> OSCAR WILDE (1854–1900), Anglo-Irish playwright, author. *The Soul of Man Under Socialism*, in *Fortnightly Review* (London, Feb. 1891, repr. 1895).

HUMAN NATURE

1 The principle that human nature, in its psychological aspects, is nothing more than a product of history and given social relations removes all barriers to coercion and manipulation by the powerful.

> NOAM CHOMSKY (b. 1928), U.S. linguist, political analyst. *Reflections on Language*, ch. 3 (1976). Chomsky was arguing against the theory of determinism in psychology.

2 It is not human nature we should accuse but the despicable conventions that pervert it.

> DENIS DIDEROT (1713–84), French philosopher. *On Dramatic Poetry* (1758; repr. in *Selected Writings*, ed. by Lester G. Crocker, 1966).

3 Now I believe I can hear the philosophers protesting that it can only be misery to live in folly, illusion, deception and ignorance, but it isn't—it's human.

> DESIDERIUS ERASMUS (c. 1466–1536), Dutch humanist. *Praise of Folly*, ch. 32 (1509).

4 Poor human nature, what horrible crimes have been committed in thy name!

> EMMA GOLDMAN (1869–1940), U.S. anarchist. *Anarchism and Other Essays*, "Anarchism: What It Really Stands For" (1910).

5 There is an electric fire in human nature tending to purify—so that among these human creatures there is continually some birth of new heroism. The pity is that we must wonder at it, as we should at finding a pearl in rubbish.

> JOHN KEATS (1795–1821), English poet. Letter, 14 Feb.–3 May 1819, to his brother and sister-in-law, George and Georgiana Keats (published in *Letters of John Keats*, no. 123, ed. by Frederick Page, 1954).

6 We are all murderers and prostitutes—no matter to what culture, society, class, nation one belongs, no matter how normal, moral, or mature, one takes oneself to be.

> R. D. LAING (1927–89), British psychiatrist. *The Politics of Experience*, Introduction (1967).

7 What is called an acute knowledge of human nature is mostly nothing but the observer's own weaknesses reflected back from others.

> G. C. LICHTENBERG (1742–99), German physicist, philosopher. *Aphorisms*, "Notebook G," aph. 7 (written 1765–99; tr. by R. J. Hollingdale, 1990).

8 Man has demonstrated that he is master of everything—except his own nature.

> HENRY MILLER (1891–1980), U.S. author. *The Air-Conditioned Nightmare*, "With Edgar Varèse in the Gobi Desert" (1945).

9 I have never, in all my various travels, seen but two sorts of people . . . I mean men and women, who always have been, and ever will be, the same. The same vices and the same follies have been the fruit of all ages, though sometimes under different names.

> LADY MARY WORTLEY MONTAGU (1689–1762), English society figure, letter writer. Letter, 5 Jan. 1748, to her daughter Lady Bute (published in *Selected Letters*, ed. by Robert Halsband, 1970).

10 The nature of peoples is first crude, then severe, then benign, then delicate, finally dissolute.

> GIAMBATTISTA VICO (1688–1744), Italian philosopher, historian. *The New Science*, bk. 1, para. 242 (ed. 1744; tr. 1984).

11 The only thing that one really knows about human nature is that it changes. Change is the one quality we can predicate of it. The systems that fail are those that rely on the permanency of human nature, and not on its growth and development. The error of Louis XIV was that he thought human nature would always be the same. The result of his error was the French Revolution. It was an admirable result.

> OSCAR WILDE (1854–1900), Anglo-Irish playwright, author. *The Soul of Man Under Socialism*, in *Fortnightly Review* (London, Feb. 1891; repr. 1895).

12 Really I don't like human nature unless all candied over with art.

> VIRGINIA WOOLF (1882–1941), British novelist. *The Diary of Virginia Woolf*, vol. 3 (ed. by Anne O. Bell, 1980), entry for 13 May 1926.

See also Begahot on INNOVATION; Melville on LITERATURE; Browne on SELF-DESTRUCTIVENESS.

HUMAN RIGHTS

1 Words like "freedom," "justice," "democracy" are not common concepts; on the contrary, they are rare. People are not born knowing what these are. It takes enormous and, above all, individual effort to arrive at the respect for other people that these words imply.

> JAMES BALDWIN (1924–87), U.S. author. "The Crusade of Indignation," in *Nation* (New York, 7 July 1956; repr. in *The Price of the Ticket*, 1985).

2 America did not invent human rights. In a very real sense . . . human rights invented America.

> JIMMY CARTER (b. 1924), U.S. Democratic politician, president. Farewell address, 14 Jan. 1981.

3 A right is not what someone gives you; it's what no one can take from you.

> RAMSEY CLARK (b. 1927), U.S. attorney general. *New York Times* (2 Oct. 1977).

4 Rights! There are no rights whatever without corresponding duties. Look at the history of the growth of our constitution, and you will see that our ancestors never upon any occasion stated, as a ground for claiming any of their privileges, an abstract right inherent in themselves; you will nowhere in our parliamentary records find the miserable sophism of the Rights of Man.

> SAMUEL TAYLOR COLERIDGE (1772–1834), English poet, critic. *Table Talk*, 20 Nov. 1831 (published in *Specimens of the Table Talk of Samuel Taylor Coleridge*, ed. by Henry Nelson Coleridge, 1835; repr. in *Collected Works*, vol. 14, ed. by Kathleen Coburn, 1990).

5 Men speak of natural rights, but I challenge any one to show where in nature any rights existed or were recognized until there was established for their declaration and protection a duly promulgated body of corresponding laws.

> CALVIN COOLIDGE (1872–1933), U.S. Republican politician, president. Speech, 27 July 1920, Northampton, Mass., accepting the Republican vice presidential nomination.

6 The demand for equal rights in every vocation of life is just and fair; but, after all, the most vital right is the right to love and be loved.

> EMMA GOLDMAN (1869–1940), U.S. anarchist. *Anarchism and Other Essays*, "The Tragedy of Women's Emancipation" (1910).

7 Close by the Rights of Man, at the least set beside them, are the Rights of the Spirit.

> VICTOR HUGO (1802–85), French poet, dramatist, novelist. *Les Misérables*, pt. 2, bk. 7, ch. 5 (1862).

8 Most people, no doubt, when they espouse human rights, make their own mental reservations about the proper application of the word "human."

> SUZANNE LAFOLLETTE (1893–1983), U.S. editor, author. *Concerning Women*, "The Beginnings of Emancipation" (1926).

9 One cannot imagine St. Francis of Assisi talking about rights.

> SIMONE WEIL (1909–43), French philosopher, mystic. "Human Personality," in *La Table Ronde* (written 1943; published Dec. 1950; repr. in *Selected Essays*, ed. by Richard Rees, 1962).

10 In the old times men carried out their rights for themselves as they lived, but nowadays every baby seems born with a social manifesto in its mouth much bigger than itself.

> OSCAR WILDE (1854–1900), Anglo-Irish playwright, author. Prince Paul, in *Vera, or the Nihilists*, act 3.

See also CIVIL RIGHTS.

HUMANISM

1 My law-givers are Erasmus and Montaigne, not Moses and St Paul.

> E. M. FORSTER (1879–1970), British novelist, essayist. *Two Cheers for Democracy*, "What I Believe" (1951). In another essay in the collection, "Gide and George," Forster wrote: "A humanist has four leading characteristics—curiosity, a free mind, belief in good taste, and belief in the human race."

2 When men can no longer be theists, they must, if they are civilized, become humanists.

> WALTER LIPPMANN (1889–1974), U.S. journalist. *A Preface to Morals*, pt. 1, ch. 7, sct. 7 (1929).

3 Humanism was not wrong in thinking that truth, beauty, liberty, and equality are of infinite value, but in thinking that man can get them for himself without grace.

> SIMONE WEIL (1909–43), French philosopher, mystic. "The Romanesque Renaissance," in *Cahiers du Sud* (Marseilles, 1941 or 1942; repr. in *Selected Essays*, ed. by Richard Rees, 1962).

4 Humanism, it seems, is almost impossible in America where material progress is part of the national romance whereas in Europe such progress is relished because it feels nice.

> PAUL WEST (b. 1930), British author, critic. *The Wine of Absurdity*, "George Santayana" (1966).

See also Jefferson on AGNOSTICS; O'Rourke on FREE WILL.

HUMANKIND

1 Man himself is an enigma in motion; his questions never stay asked; whereas the mold, the footprint, and by natural extension, the statue itself, like the vaults, the arches, the temples with which man records his own passing, remain immobile and fix a moment of man's life, upon which one might endlessly meditate.

> ALAIN [ÉMILE-AUGUSTE CHARTIER] (1868–1951), French philosopher. *The Gods*, Introduction (1934; tr. 1988).

2 I love men, not for what unites them, but for what divides them, and I want to know most of all what gnaws at their hearts.

> GUILLAUME APOLLINAIRE (1880–1918), Italian-born French poet, critic. *Mercure de France*, no. 331 (Paris, 1 April 1911; repr. in *Anecdotiques*, 1926).

3 If we consider the superiority of the human species, the size of its brain, its powers of thinking, language and organization, we can say this: were there the slightest possibility that another rival or superior species might appear, on earth or elsewhere, man would use every means at his disposal to destroy it.

> JEAN BAUDRILLARD (b. 1929), French semiologist. *Cool Memories,* ch. 3 (1987; tr. 1990).

4 Drinking when we are not thirsty and making love at any time, madam, is all that distinguishes us from the other animals.

> PIERRE DE BEAUMARCHAIS (1732–99), French dramatist. Antonio, in *Le Mariage de Figaro,* act 2, sc. 21.

5 Ye shall be as gods, knowing good and evil.

> BIBLE, HEBREW. The Serpent, in *Genesis* 3:5, tempting Eve to bite the apple.

6 Cruelty has a Human Heart,
And jealousy a Human Face;
Terror the Human Form Divine,
And secrecy the Human Dress.
The Human Dress is forged Iron,
The Human Form a Fiery Forge,
The Human Face a Furnace seal'd,
The Human Heart its hungry gorge.

> WILLIAM BLAKE (1757–1827), English poet, painter, engraver. *A Divine Image* (1794), a poem etched on a copper plate in Blake's usual manner, but never included in any copy of the *Songs of Experience,* and so probably rejected by him.

7 Man is God's highest present development. He is the latest thing in God.

> SAMUEL BUTLER (1835–1902), English author. *Samuel Butler's Notebooks,* (1951, p. 114).

8 Man is born passionate of body, but with an innate though secret tendency to the love of Good in his mainspring of Mind. But God help us all! It is at present a sad jar of atoms.

> LORD BYRON (1788–1824), English poet. *Detached Thoughts,* no. 96 (1821–22; published in *Byron's Letters and Journals,* vol. 9, ed. by Leslie A. Marchand, 1979).

9 The human race is a zone of living things that should be defined by tracing its confines.

> ITALO CALVINO (1923–85), Italian author, critic. Epitome of Pliny's view in *Natural History,* Preface (Italian tr., 1982; repr. in *The Literature Machine,* 1987).

10 There is no doubt: the study of man is just beginning, at the same time that his end is in sight.

> ELIAS CANETTI (b. 1905), Austrian novelist, philosopher. *The Secret Heart Of The Clock: Notes, Aphorisms, Fragments 1973–1985,* "1980" (1991).

11 Man is an exception, whatever else he is. If he is not the image of God, then he is a disease of the dust. If it is not true that a divine being fell, then we can only say that one of the animals went entirely off its head.

> G. K. CHESTERTON (1874–1936), British author. *All Things Considered,* "Wine When it is Red" (1908).

12 To the eyes of a god, mankind must appear as a species of bacteria which multiply and become progressively virulent whenever they find themselves in a congenial culture, and whose activity diminishes until they disappear completely as soon as proper measures are taken to sterilise them.

> ALEISTER CROWLEY (1875–1947), British occultist. *The Confessions of Aleister Crowley,* ch. 68 (1929; rev. 1970).

13 Humanity i love you because
when you're hard up you pawn your
intelligence to buy a drink

> E E CUMMINGS (1894–1962), U.S. poet. *La Guerre no. 2,* in *XLI Poems* (1925).

14 Though man is the only beast that can write, he has small reason to be proud of it. When he utters something that is wise it is nothing that the river horse does not know, and most of his creations are the result of accident.

> EDWARD DAHLBERG (1900–1977), U.S. author, critic. *The Carnal Myth,* ch. 5 (1968).

15 Consider your breed;
you were not made to live like beasts,
but to follow virtue and knowledge.

> DANTE ALIGHIERI (1265–1321), Italian poet. Ulysses, in *The Divine Comedy,* "The Inferno," cto. 18 (completed 1321), urging his companions to a journey that would prove disastrous.

16 Man is head, chest and stomach. Each of these animals operates, more often than not, individually. I eat, I feel, I even, although rarely, think. . . . This jungle crawls and teems, is hungry, roars, gets angry, devours itself, and its cacophonic concert does not even stop when you are asleep.

> RENÉ DAUMAL (1908–44), French poet, critic. *Essais et Notes,* vol. 2, "The Lie of the Truth" (ed. by Claudio Rugafiori, 1972; repr. in *The Lie of The Truth,* tr. by Phil Powrie, 1989).

17 Man is not only a contributory creature, but a total creature; he does not only make one, but he is all; he is not a piece of the world, but the world itself; and next to the glory of God, the reason why there is a world.

> JOHN DONNE (c. 1572–1631), English divine and metaphysical poet. *Sermons,* no. 35 (1625).

18 Man, became man through work, who stepped out of the animal kingdom as transformer of the natural into the artificial, who became therefore the magician, man the creator of social reality, will always stay the great magician, will always be Prometheus bringing fire from heaven to earth, will always be Orpheus enthralling nature with his music. Not until humanity itself dies will art die.

> ERNST FISCHER (1899–1972), Austrian editor, poet, critic. *The Necessity of Art,* ch. 5 (1959; tr. 1963).

19 As the archeology of our thought easily shows, man is an invention of recent date. And one perhaps nearing its end.

> MICHEL FOUCAULT (1926–84), French essayist, philosopher. *The Order of Things,* ch. 10 (1966; tr. 1970).

20 I have found little that is "good" about human beings on the whole. In my experience most of them are trash, no matter whether they publicly subscribe to this or that ethical doctrine or to none at all. That is something that you cannot say aloud, or perhaps even think.

> SIGMUND FREUD (1856–1939), Austrian psychiatrist. Letter, 9 Oct. 1918 (published in *The International Psycho-Analytical Library no. 59,* "Psycho-Analysis and Faith: The Letters of Sigmund Freud and Oscar Pfister," 1963).

21 Man has, as it were, become a kind of prosthetic God. When he puts on all his auxiliary organs, he is truly magnificent; but those organs have not grown on him and they still give him much trouble at times.

> SIGMUND FREUD (1856–1939), Austrian psychiatrist. *Civilization and its Discontents*, ch. 3 (1931; repr. in *Complete Works, Standard Edition*, vol. 21, ed. by James Strachey & Anna Freud, 1961).

22 Man is more interesting than men. God made *him* and not them in his image. Each one is more precious than all.

> ANDRÉ GIDE (1869–1951), French author. *Journals 1889–1949*, "Literature and Ethics" (ed. by Justin O'Brien, 1951), entry in 1901.

23 Man . . . knows only when he is satisfied and when he suffers, and only his sufferings and his satisfactions instruct him concerning himself, teach him what to seek and what to avoid. For the rest, man is a confused creature; he knows not whence he comes or whither he goes, he knows little of the world, and above all, he knows little of himself.

> JOHANN WOLFGANG VON GOETHE (1749–1832), German poet, dramatist. Quoted in: John Peter Eckermann, *Conversations with Goethe* (1836).

24 Mind and spirit together make up that which separates us from the rest of the animal world, that which enables a man to know the truth and that which enables him to die for the truth.

> EDITH HAMILTON (1867–1963), U.S. classical scholar, translator. *The Greek Way*, ch. 1 (1930).

25 Man is the only animal that laughs and weeps; for he is the only animal that is struck with the difference between what things are and what they ought to be.

> WILLIAM HAZLITT (1778–1830), English essayist. *Lectures on the English Comic Writers*, "Lecture 1" (1819). This passage was copied and inserted in the notebooks of Adlai Stevenson.

26 What constitutes a real, live human being is more of a mystery than ever these days, and men—each one of whom is a valuable, unique experiment on the part of nature—are shot down wholesale.

> HERMANN HESSE (1877–1962), German novelist, poet. The narrator (Sinclair), in *Demian*, Prologue (1960).

27 Man was nature's mistake—she neglected to finish him—and she has never ceased paying for her mistake.

> ERIC HOFFER (1902–83), U.S. philosopher. *Reflections on the Human Condition*, aph. 4 (1973).

28 Mankind is not a circle with a single center but an ellipse with two focal points of which facts are one and ideas the other.

> VICTOR HUGO (1802–85), French poet, dramatist, novelist. *Les Misérables*, pt. 4, bk. 7, ch. 1 (1862).

29 The Goddamn human race deserves itself, and as far as I'm concerned it can have it.

> ELIZABETH JANEWAY (b. 1913), U.S. author. *Accident on Route 37*, "Charles Benedict" (1964).

30 Out of timber so crooked as that from which man is made nothing entirely straight can be carved.

> IMMANUEL KANT (1724–1804), German philosopher. "Idee zu einer Allgemeinen Gesichte in Weltburgerlicher Absicht" (1784). Quoted in: Isaiah Berlin, *Crooked Timber of Humanity*, epigraph (1990).

31 The world of men is dreaming, it has gone mad in its sleep, and a snake is strangling it, but it can't wake up.

> D. H. LAWRENCE (1885–1930), British author. Letter, 14 May 1915 (published in *The Letters of D. H. Lawrence*, vol. 2, ed. by George J. Zytaruk & James T. Boulton, 1981).

32 Humans are amphibians—half spirit and half animal. . . . As spirits they belong to the eternal world, but as animals they inhabit time.

> C. S. LEWIS (1898–1963), British author. Screwtape, in *The Screwtape Letters*, letter 8 (1942).

33 That man is the noblest creature may also be inferred from the fact that no other creature has yet contested this claim.

> G. C. LICHTENBERG (1742–99), German physicist, philosopher. *Aphorisms*, "Notebook D," aph. 58 (written 1765–99; tr. by R. J. Hollingdale, 1990).

34 The decay of decency in the modern age, the rebellion against law and good faith, the treatment of human beings as things, as the mere instruments of power and ambition, is without a doubt the consequence of the decay of the belief in man as something more than an animal animated by highly conditioned reflexes and chemical reactions. For, unless man is something more than that, he has no rights that anyone is bound to respect, and there are no limitations upon his conduct which he is bound to obey.

> WALTER LIPPMANN (1889–1974), U.S. journalist. "The Forgotten Foundation," in *New York Herald Tribune* (17 Dec. 1938; repr. in *The Essential Lippman*, pt. 4, sct. 1, 1982).

35 Let me look into a human eye; it is better than to gaze into sea or sky; better than to gaze upon God.

> HERMAN MELVILLE (1819–91), U.S. author. Captain Ahab, in *Moby-Dick*, ch. 132 (1851).

36 Man is a beautiful machine that works very badly.

> H. L. MENCKEN (1880–1956), U.S. journalist. *Minority Report: H. L. Mencken's Notebooks*, no. 20 (1956).

37 The man who is forever disturbed about the condition of humanity either has no problems of his own or has refused to face them.

> HENRY MILLER (1891–1980), U.S. author. *Sexus*, ch. 9 (1949). Miller emphasized that he was referring to "the great majority, not of the emancipated few who, having thought things through, are privileged to identify themselves with all humanity and thus enjoy that greatest of all luxuries: service."

38 We are, to put it mildly, in a mess, and there is a strong chance that we shall have exterminated ourselves by the end of the century. Our only consolation will have to be that, as a species, we have had an exciting term of office.

> DESMOND MORRIS (b. 1928), British anthropologist. *The Naked Ape*, ch. 5 (1967).

39 Human affairs are not serious, but they have to be taken seriously.

> IRIS MURDOCH (b. 1919), British novelist, philosopher. Bren-

dan Craddock, in *Henry and Cato,* pt. 2, "The Great Teacher" (1976).

40 Man is no longer an artist, he has become a work of art.

FRIEDRICH NIETZSCHE (1844–1900), German philosopher. *The Birth of Tragedy,* ch. 1 (1872).

41 *I teach you the Superman* [*Übermensch*]. Man is something that should be overcome.

FRIEDRICH NIETZSCHE (1844–1900), German philosopher. *Thus Spoke Zarathustra,* pt. 1, "Zarathustra's Prologue," sct. 3 (1883–92).

42 If, presume not to God to scan;
The proper study of Mankind is Man.
Plac'd on this isthmus of a middle state,
A being darkly wise, and rudely great.

ALEXANDER POPE (1688–1744), English satirical poet. *An Essay on Man,* Epistle 2.

43 The law of humanity ought to be composed of the past, the present, and the future, that we bear within us; whoever possesses but one of these terms, has but a fragment of the law of the moral world.

EDGAR QUINET (1803–75), French poet, historian, politician. Lecture, 15 May 1844 (published in *Ultramontanism, or The Roman Church and Modern Society,* "The Roman Church and History—Vico," 1845).

44 I wish I loved the Human Race;
I wish I loved its silly face;
I wish I liked the way it walks;
I wish I liked the way it talks;
And when I'm introduced to one
I wish I thought *What Jolly Fun!*

SIR WALTER RALEGH (1861–1922), English scholar, critic. *The Wishes of an Elderly Man,* in *Laughter from a Cloud* (1923).

45 An effective human being is a whole that is greater than the sum of its parts.

IDA P. ROLF (1896–1979), U.S. biochemist, physical therapist. *Rolfing: The Integration of Human Structions,* Preface (1977).

46 We say nothing essential about the cathedral when we speak of its stones. We say nothing essential about Man when we seek to define him by the qualities of men.

ANTOINE DE SAINT-EXUPÉRY (1900–1944), French aviator, author. *Flight to Arras,* ch. 23 (1942).

47 Man is a useless passion.

JEAN-PAUL SARTRE (1905–80), French philosopher, author. *Being and Nothingness,* "Doing and Having," sct. 3 (1943; tr. 1965).

48 It is peculiar to mankind to transcend mankind.

FRIEDRICH SCHLEGEL (1772–1829), German philosopher, critic, writer. *Dialogue on Poetry and Literary Aphorisms,* "Ideas," aph. 21 (1968; first published 1799–1800).

49 What a piece of work is a man! How noble in reason, how infinite in faculty, in form and moving how express and admirable, in action how like an angel, in apprehension how like a god—the beauty of the world, the paragon of animals!

WILLIAM SHAKESPEARE (1564–1616), English dramatist, poet. Hamlet, in *Hamlet,* act 2, sc. 2.

50 Physically there is nothing to distinguish human society from the farm-yard except that children are more troublesome and costly than chickens and calves and that men and women are not so completely enslaved as farm stock.

GEORGE BERNARD SHAW (1856–1950), Anglo-Irish playwright, critic. *Getting Married,* "The Personal Sentimental Basis of Monogamy," Preface (1908).

51 I am human and let nothing human be alien to me.

TERENCE (c. 190–159 B.C.), Roman dramatist. Chremes, in *The Self-Tormentor* [*Heauton timorumenos*], act 1, sc. 1.

52 One has but to observe a community of beavers at work in a stream to understand the loss in his sagacity, balance, co-operation, competence, and purpose which Man has suffered since he rose up on his hind legs. . . . He began to chatter and he developed Reason, Thought, and Imagination, qualities which would get the smartest group of rabbits or orioles in the world into inextricable trouble overnight.

JAMES THURBER (1894–1961), U.S. humorist, illustrator. *Collecting Himself,* "Thinking Ourselves Into Trouble," pt. 2 (1989).

53 Man lives consciously for himself, but is an unconscious instrument in the attainment of the historic, universal, aims of humanity.

LEO TOLSTOY (1829–1910), Russian novelist, philosopher. *War and Peace,* bk. 9, ch. 1 (1868–69).

54 Such is the human race. Often it does seem such a pity that Noah and his party did not miss the boat.

MARK TWAIN (1835–1910), U.S. author. *Christian Science,* bk. 2, ch. 7, (1907; repr. in *What Is Man?,* ed. by Paul Baender, 1973).

55 I would suggest that barbarism be considered as a permanent and universal human characteristic which becomes more or less pronounced according to the play of circumstances.

SIMONE WEIL (1910–43), French philosopher, mystic. "Hitler and Foreign Policy," in *Nouveux Cahiers* (1 Jan. 1940).

56 Man is the unnatural animal, the rebel child of nature, and more and more does he turn himself against the harsh and fitful hand that reared him.

H. G. WELLS (1866–1946), British author. *A Modern Utopia,* ch. 5, sct. 2, (1905; repr. in *The Works of H. G. Wells,* vol. 9, 1925).

57 It is because Humanity has never known where it was going that it has been able to find its way.

OSCAR WILDE (1854–1900), Anglo-Irish playwright, author. Gilbert, in *The Critic as Artist,* pt. 1 (published in *Intentions,* 1891).

58 We're all of us guinea pigs in the laboratory of God. Humanity is just a work in progress.

TENNESSEE WILLIAMS (1914–83), U.S. dramatist. The Gipsy, in *Camino Real,* block 12 (1953).

See also Nietzsche on AESTHETICS; Butler on ANIMALS; Smith on BUSINESS AND COMMERCE; Huxley on CHANGE; Pascal on CONSCIOUSNESS AND THE SUBCONSCIOUS; Hebrew Bible, Billings, Cervantes, Morley on THE CREATION; Twain on EMBARRASSMENT; Gilbert on EVOLUTION; Butler on FUN; Satta on GOD; Ouida on HOPE; Johnson on IDLENESS; Emerson on INTELLIGENCE; MISANTHROPY; Addison on LAUGHTER; Huxley on MORALITY; Shaw on PARASITES: Miller on POTENTIAL; Gay on SOCIABILITY; Lawrence on THE SOUL; Marvell on SURVIVAL; Carlyle on TOOLS; Chesterton on VIRTUE; Calvino on THE WORLD.

HUMILIATION

1 I was never proud till you sought to make me too base.

ROBERT DEVEREUX, SECOND EARL OF ESSEX (1566–1601), Elizabethan soldier, courtier. Letter, Aug. 1598, to Queen Elizabeth I, after a quarrel in which she had boxed his ears.

2 Humiliation is the beginning of sanctification.

JOHN DONNE (c. 1572–1631), English divine and metaphysical poet. *Eighty Sermons,* ser. 7 (1640).

3 The one thing to do
Is to do nothing. Wait. . . .
You will find that you survive humiliation.
And that's an experience of incalculable value.

T. S. ELIOT (1888–1965), Anglo-American poet, critic. Unidentified Guest (later identified as Sir Henry Harcourt-Reilly), in *The Cocktail Party,* act 1, sc. 1.

4 Avoiding humiliation is the core of tragedy and comedy.

JOHN GUARE (b. 1938), U.S. playwright. *Independent* (London, 17 Oct. 1988).

See also Weil on NATIONS; Havel on SUBMISSION; Weil on TRUTH.

HUMILITY

1 At home I am a nice guy: but I don't want the world to know. Humble people, I've found, don't get very far.

MUHAMMAD ALI (b. 1942), U.S. boxer. *Sunday Express* (London, 13 Jan. 1963).

2 Nothing is more deceitful than the appearance of humility. It is often only carelessness of opinion, and sometimes an indirect boast.

JANE AUSTEN (1775–1817), English novelist. Darcy, in *Pride and Prejudice,* ch. 10 (1813).

3 I've never had a humble opinion in my life. If you're going to have one, why bother to be humble about it?

JOAN BAEZ (b. 1941), U.S. singer. *International Herald Tribune* (Paris, 2 Dec. 1992).

4 I'm a fart in a gale of wind, a humble violet, under a cow pat.

DJUNA BARNES (1892–1982), U.S. author, poet, columnist. Doctor, in *Nightwood,* ch. 5 (1936).

5 Hugo, like a priest, always has his head bowed—bowed so low that he can see nothing except his own navel.

CHARLES BAUDELAIRE (1821–67), French poet. Of Victor Hugo, in "Squibs," published in *Intimate Journals,* sct. 22 (1887; tr. by Christopher Isherwood, 1930; rev. by Don Bachardy, 1989).

6 I really do not see much use in exalting the humble and meek; they do not remain humble and meek long when they are exalted.

SAMUEL BUTLER (1835–1902), English author. *Samuel Butler's Notebooks* (1951, p. 220).

7 Humility has its origin in an awareness of unworthiness, and sometimes too in a dazzled awareness of saintliness.

COLETTE (1873–1954), French author. Speech on being elected to the Belgian Academy (published in *Earthly Paradise,* pt. 4, "Lady of Letters," ed. by Robert Phelps, 1966).

8 To make us feel small in the right way is a function of art; men can only make us feel small in the wrong way.

E. M. FORSTER (1879–1970), British novelist, essayist. *Two Cheers for Democracy,* "A Book That Influenced Me" (1951).

9 Turning the other cheek is a kind of moral jiu-jitsu.

GERALD STANLEY LEE (1862–1944), U.S. clergyman, writer. *Crowds,* bk. 4, ch. 9 (1913).

10 A man who has humility will have acquired in the last reaches of his beliefs the saving doubt of his own certainty.

WALTER LIPPMANN (1889–1974), U.S. journalist. *The Public Philosophy,* ch. 10, sct. 4 (1955).

11 If you bow at all bow low.

CHINESE PROVERB.

12 Humility is a virtue all preach, none practise, and yet everybody is content to hear. The master thinks it good doctrine for his servant, the laity for the clergy, and the clergy for the laity.

JOHN SELDEN (1584–1654), English jurist, statesman. *Table Talk,* "Humility" (1686).

13 Study to do another's will rather than thine own. Choose ever to have less rather than more. Seek ever the lower place and to be subject to all; ever wish and pray that the will of God may be perfectly done in thee and in all. Behold such a man enters the bounds of peace and calm.

THOMAS À KEMPIS (1380–1471), German monk, mystic. *The Imitation of Christ,* pt. 3, ch. 25 (1471).

14 In the intellectual order, the virtue of humility is nothing more nor less than the power of attention."

SIMONE WEIL (1909–43), French philosopher, mystic. *Gravity and Grace,* "Intelligence and Grace" (1947; tr. 1952).

See also Weil on GENIUS; Coleridge on PRIDE.

HUMOR

1 Mirth is like a flash of lightning, that breaks through a gloom of clouds, and glitters for a moment; cheerfulness keeps up a kind of daylight in the mind, and fills it with a steady and perpetual serenity.

JOSEPH ADDISON (1672–1719), English essayist. *Spectator,* no. 381 (London, 17 May 1712).

2 Among those whom I like or admire, I can find no common denominator, but among those whom I love, I can: all of them make me laugh.

W. H. AUDEN (1907–73), Anglo-American poet. *The Dyer's Hand,* pt. 7, "Notes on the Comic" (1962).

3 All my humor is based upon destruction and despair. If the whole world were tranquil, without disease and violence, I'd be standing on the breadline right in back of J. Edgar Hoover.

> LENNY BRUCE (1925–66), U.S. satirical comedian. *The Essential Lenny Bruce*, "Performing and the Art of Comedy" (ed. by John Cohen, 1967).

4   Humour is by far the most significant activity of the human brain.

> EDWARD DE BONO (b. 1933), British writer on thinking processes. *Daily Mail* (London, 29 Jan. 1990).

5   The comic is the perception of the opposite; humor is the feeling of it.

> UMBERTO ECO (b. 1932), Italian semiologist, novelist. "De consolatione Philosophiae" (1980; repr. in *Travels in Hyperreality*, tr. by William Weaver, 1986).

6   A difference of tastes in jokes is a great strain on the affections.

> GEORGE ELIOT (1819–80), English novelist. *Daniel Deronda*, bk. 2, ch. 15 (1874–76).

7   Humor, a good sense of it, is to Americans what manhood is to Spaniards and we will go to great lengths to prove it. Experiments with laboratory rats have shown that, if one psychologist in the room laughs at something a rat does, all of the other psychologists in the room will laugh equally. Nobody wants to be left holding the joke.

> GARRISON KEILLOR (b. 1942), U.S. writer. *We Are Still Married*, Introduction (1989).

8   Any discussion of the problems of being funny in America will not make sense unless we substitute the word *wit* for *humor*. Humor inspires sympathetic good-natured laughter and is favored by the "healing-power" gang. Wit goes for the jugular, not the jocular, and it's the opposite of football; instead of building character, it tears it down.

> FLORENCE KING (b. 1936), U.S. author. *Reflections in a Jaundiced Eye*, "The State of the Funny Bone" (1989).

9   The hall-mark of American humour is its pose of illiteracy.

> RONALD KNOX (1888–1957), British scholar, priest. *Essays In Satire*, Introduction (1928).

10   It is well known that Beauty does not look with a good grace on the timid advances of Humour.

> W. SOMERSET MAUGHAM (1874–1965), British author. *Cakes and Ale*, ch. 11 (1930).

11   Good taste and humour are a contradiction in terms, like a chaste whore.

> MALCOLM MUGGERIDGE (1903–90), British broadcaster. Quoted in: *Time* (New York, 14 Sept. 1953), defending his editorship of the humorous magazine *Punch*.

12   Wit is a weapon. Jokes are a masculine way of inflicting superiority. But humour is the pursuit of a gentle grin, usually in solitude.

> FRANK MUIR (b. 1920), British humorist, writer. *Daily Mail* (London, 26 April 1990).

13   Humor has been a fashioning instrument in America, cleaving its way through the national life, holding tenaciously to the spread elements of that life. Its mode has often been swift and coarse and ruthless, beyond art and beyond established civilization. It has engaged in warfare against the established heritage, against the bonds of pioneer existence. Its objective—the unconscious objective of a disunited people—has seemed to be that of creating fresh bonds, a new unity, the semblance of a society and the rounded completion of an American type.

> CONSTANCE ROURKE (1885–1941), U.S. author. *American Humor*, ch. 9 (1931).

14   The wit makes fun of other persons; the satirist makes fun of the world; the humorist makes fun of himself, but in so doing, he identifies himself with people—that is, people everywhere, not for the purpose of taking them apart, but simply revealing their true nature.

> JAMES THURBER (1894–1961), U.S. humorist, illustrator. *New York Post*, transcript of Ed Murrow's CBS-TV show, "Small World," 25 March 1959.

15   Humor is emotional chaos remembered in tranquility.

> JAMES THURBER (1894–1961), U.S. humorist, illustrator. *New York Post* (29 Feb. 1960). A slightly different version of Thurber's aphorism was recorded as early as 1936, when it was attributed to him in Max Eastman, *Enjoyment of Laughter*: "Humor is a kind of emotional chaos told about calmly and quietly in retrospect. There is always a laugh in the utterly familiar." See Wordsworth on POETRY for the origin of the quip.

16   Never say a humorous thing to a man who does not possess humour. He will always use it in evidence against you.

> SIR HERBERT BEERBOHM TREE (1853–1917), English actor-manager. Quoted in: Hesketh Pearson, *Beerbohm-Tree*, ch. 12 (1956).

17   Probably it is impossible for humor to be ever a revolutionary weapon. Candide can do little more than generate irony.

> LIONEL TRILLING (1905–75), U.S. critic. Notebook entry 1931–32, published in *Partisan Review 50th Anniversary Edition* (ed. by William Philips, 1985).

18   Humor must not professedly teach and it must not professedly preach, but it must do both if it would live forever.

> MARK TWAIN (1835–1910), U.S. author. *Autobiography*, ch. 55 (ed. by Charles Neider, 1959). "By forever," Twain added, "I mean thirty years. With all its preaching it is not likely to outlive so long a term as that."

19   I used to think that everything was just being funny but now I don't know. I mean, how can you tell?

> ANDY WARHOL (1928–87), U.S. Pop artist. Quoted in: *Vogue* (New York, 1 March 1970).

20   Every American, to the last man, lays claim to a "sense" of humor and guards it as his most significant spiritual trait, yet rejects humor as a contaminating element wherever found. America is a nation of comics and comedians; nevertheless, humor has no stature and is accepted only after the death of the perpetrator.

> E. B. WHITE (1899–1985), U.S. author, editor. "The Humor Paradox," in *New Yorker* (27 Sept 1952; repr. in *Writings from the New Yorker 1927–1976*, ed. by Rebecca M. Dale, 1991).

21   Humor is not a mood but a way of looking at the world. So if it is correct to say that humor was stamped out in Nazi Germany, that does not mean that people were not in good spirits, or anything of that sort, but something much deeper and more important.

> LUDWIG WITTGENSTEIN (1889–1951), Austrian philosopher. *Culture and Value* (ed. by G. H. von Wright with Heikki Nyman, 1980), entry in 1948.

See also COMEDY AND COMEDIANS; Knox on DIGNITY; HUMOR, SENSE OF; JOKES AND JOKERS; Thurber on McCARTHYISM; Woolf on TRANSLATION; Coleridge on WIT.

SENSE OF HUMOR

1   To appreciate nonsense requires a serious interest in life.

> GELETT BURGESS (1866–1951), U.S. humorist, illustrator. *The Romance of the Commonplace,* "The Sense of Humor" (1916).

2   Men will confess to treason, murder, arson, false teeth, or a wig. How many of them will own up to a lack of humor?

> FRANK MOORE COLBY (1865–1925), U.S. editor, essayist. *The Colby Essays,* vol. 1, "Satire and Teeth" (1926).

3   Anyone who takes himself too seriously always runs the risk of looking ridiculous; anyone who can consistently laugh at himself does not.

> VÁCLAV HAVEL (b. 1936), Czech playwright, president. *Disturbing the Peace,* ch. 2 (1986; tr. 1990).

4   They say the seeds of what we will do are in all of us, but it always seemed to me that in those who make jokes in life the seeds are covered with better soil and with a higher grade of manure.

> ERNEST HEMINGWAY (1899–1961), U.S. author. *A Moveable Feast,* ch. 11 (1964).

5   An emotional man may possess no humor, but a humorous man usually has deep pockets of emotion, sometimes tucked away or forgotten.

> CONSTANCE ROURKE (1885–1941), U.S. author. *American Humor,* ch. 1 (1931).

6   He was born with a gift of laughter and a sense that the world was mad. And that was all his patrimony.

> RAFAEL SABATINI (1875–1950), Italian-born British author. *Scaramouche,* bk. 1, ch. 1 (1921), opening words, describing the book's hero André-Louis Moreau.

HUNGER

1   Viewed narrowly, all life is universal hunger and an expression of energy associated with it.

> MARY RITTER BEARD (1876–1958), U.S. historian. *Understanding Women,* ch. 1 (1931).

2   A dog starved at his master's gate
Predicts the ruin of the state.

> WILLIAM BLAKE (1757–1827), English poet, painter, engraver. *Auguries of Innocence* in *Poems from the Pickering Manuscript* (c. 1808; published in *Complete Writings,* ed. by Geoffrey Keynes, 1957).

3   There's no sauce in the world like hunger.

> MIGUEL DE CERVANTES (1547–1616), Spanish writer. Teresa Panza (Sancho's wife), in *Don Quixote,* pt. 2, bk. 5, ch. 5 (1615;

tr. P. Motteux). This well-honed proverb was first attributed to Socrates by Cicero in *De Finibus,* bk. 2, sct. 90.

4   Society is composed of two great classes—those who have more dinners than appetite, and those who have more appetite than dinners.

> SÉBASTIEN-ROCH NICOLAS DE CHAMFORT (1741–94), French writer, wit. *Maxims and Considerations,* vol. 1, no. 194 (1796; tr. 1902).

5   The Queen has lands and gold, Mother
The Queen has lands and gold,
While you are forced to your empty breast
A skeleton Babe to hold . . .

> AMELIA EDWARDS (1831–92), English writer, Egyptologist. *Give Me Three Grains of Corn, Mother,* st. 4.

6   Hunger is insolent, and will be fed.

> HOMER (9th century B.C.?). *Odyssey,* bk. 7 (tr. by Alexander Pope).

7   The belly is the reason why man does not mistake himself for a god.

> FRIEDRICH NIETZSCHE (1844–1900), German philosopher. *Beyond Good and Evil,* ch. 4, aph. 141 (1886).

8   A hungry man is an angry man.

> ENGLISH PROVERB. Collected in James Howell, *Proverbs,* no. 13 (1659).

9   You cannot reason with a hungry belly; it has no ears.

> GREEK PROVERB.

10   A hungry man is not a free man.

> ADLAI STEVENSON (1900–1965), U.S. Democratic politician. Speech, 6 Sept. 1952, Kasson, Minn.

11   If sometimes our poor people have had to die of starvation, it is not that God didn't care for them, but because you and I didn't give, were not an instrument of love in the hands of God, to give them that bread, to give them that clothing; because we did not recognize him, when once more Christ came in distressing disguise, in the hungry man, in the lonely man, in the homeless child, and seeking for shelter.

> MOTHER TERESA (b. 1910), Albanian-born Roman Catholic missionary. *A Gift for God,* "Suffering" (1975).

12   Feast, and your halls are crowded;
Fast, and the world goes by.

> ELLA WHEELER WILCOX (1855–1919), U.S. poet, journalist. *Solitude,* st. 3.

13   In the Lord's Prayer, the first petition is for daily bread. No one can worship God or love his neighbor on an empty stomach.

> WOODROW WILSON (1856–1924), U.S. Democratic politician, president. Speech, 23 May 1912, New York City.

See also FAMINE.

HUNTING

1   Each outcry of the hunted hare
A fibre from the brain does tear.

> WILLIAM BLAKE (1757–1827), English poet, painter, engraver. *Auguries of Innocence,* in *Poems from the Pickering Manuscript* (c. 1808; published in *Complete Writings,* ed. by Geoffrey Keynes, 1957).

2   There is a passion *for hunting something* deeply implanted in the human breast.

> CHARLES DICKENS (1812–70), English novelist. *Oliver Twist,* ch. 10 (1838), referring to chasing pickpockets.

3   Courage and grace is a formidable mixture. The only place to see it is the bullring.

> MARLENE DIETRICH (1904–92), German-born U.S. film actor. *Marlene Dietrich's ABC,* "Matador" (1962).

4   They take unbelievable pleasure in the hideous blast of the hunting horn and baying of the hounds. Dogs' dung smells sweet as cinnamon to them.

> DESIDERIUS ERASMUS (c. 1466–1536), Dutch humanist. *Praise of Folly,* ch. 38 (1509), referring to hunters.

5   When you have shot one bird flying you have shot all birds flying. They are all different and they fly in different ways but the sensation is the same and the last one is as good as the first.

> ERNEST HEMINGWAY (1899–1961), U.S. author. Nick Adams, in "Fathers and Sons," in *Winner Take Nothing* (1932).

6   It is very strange, and very melancholy, that the paucity of human pleasures should persuade us ever to call hunting one of them.

> SAMUEL JOHNSON (1709–84), English author, lexicographer. Hester Piozzi, *Anecdotes of Samuel Johnson* (1786; repr. in *Johnsonian Miscellanies,* vol. 1, ed. by George Birkbeck Hill, 1897).

7   The wanton Troopers riding by
Have shot my Fawn and it will die.
Ungentle men! They cannot thrive
To kill thee. Thou ne'er didst alive
Them any harm: alas, nor could
Thy death yet do them any good.

> ANDREW MARVELL (1621–78), English poet. *The Nymph Complaining for the Death of her Fawn.*

8   Though I am an old horse, and have seen and heard a great deal, I never yet could make out why men are so fond of this sport; they often hurt themselves, often spoil good horses, and tear up the fields, and all for a hare, or a fox, or a stag, that they could get more easily some other way; but we are only horses, and don't know.

> ANNA SEWELL (1820–78), English author. Duchess (Black Beauty's mother), in *Black Beauty,* pt. 1, ch. 2 (1877).

9   When a man wants to murder a tiger he calls it sport; when a tiger wants to murder him he calls it ferocity.

> GEORGE BERNARD SHAW (1856–1950), Anglo-Irish playwright, critic. *Man and Superman,* "Maxims for Revolutionists: Crime and Punishment" (1903).

10   One knows so well the popular idea of health. The English country gentleman galloping after a fox—the unspeakable in full pursuit of the uneatable.

> OSCAR WILDE (1854–1900), Anglo-Irish playwright, author. Lord Illingworth, in *A Woman of No Importance,* act 1.

HUSBANDS

1   No man worth his salt, no man of spirit and spine, no man for whom I could have any respect, could rejoice in the identification of Tallulah's husband. It's tough enough to be bogged down in a legend. It would be even tougher to marry one.

> TALLULAH BANKHEAD (1903–68), U.S. screen actor. *Tallulah,* ch. 14 (1952).

2   Every man who is high up likes to think he has done it all himself; and the wife smiles, and lets it go at that. It's our only joke.

> J. M. BARRIE (1860–1937), British playwright. Maggie Shand, in *What Every Woman Knows,* act 4.

3   When a man hath taken a new wife, he shall not go out to war, neither shall he be charged with any business: but he shall be free at home one year, and shall cheer up his wife which he hath taken.

> BIBLE, HEBREW. *Deuteronomy* 24:5.

4   Husbands, love your wives, and be not bitter against them.

> BIBLE: NEW TESTAMENT. *Colossians* 3:19.

5   Menny think tha luv their husbands almost tew deth, when in fack, tha are only jealous ov them.

> JOSH BILLINGS [HENRY WHEELER SHAW] (1818–85), U.S. humorist. *Josh Billings, His Sayings,* ch. 51 (1865).

6   You—poor and obscure, and small and plain as you are—I entreat to accept me as a husband.

> CHARLOTTE BRONTË (1816–55), English novelist. Mr. Rochester, in *Jane Eyre,* ch. 23 (1847).

7   The bitterest creature under heaven is the wife who discovers that her husband's bravery is only bravado, that his strength is only a uniform, that his power is but a gun in the hands of a fool.

> PEARL S. BUCK (1892–1973), U.S. author. *To My Daughters, With Love,* "Love and Marriage" (1967).

8   I've never yet met a man who could look after me. I don't need a husband. What I need is a wife.

> JOAN COLLINS (b. 1933), British screen actor. Quoted in: *Sunday Times* (London, 27 Dec. 1987).

9   I revere the memory of Mr. F. as an estimable man and most indulgent husband, only necessary to mention Asparagus and it appeared or to hint at any little delicate thing to drink and it came like magic in a pint bottle; it was not ecstasy but it was comfort.

> CHARLES DICKENS (1812–70), English novelist. Flora Finching, in *Little Dorrit,* bk. 1, ch. 24.

10   *Do* let him read the papers. But not while you accusingly tiptoe around the room, or perch much like a silent bird of prey on the edge of your most uncomfortable chair. (He will read them anyway, and he *should* read them, so let him choose his own good time.) Don't make a big exit. Just go. But kiss him quickly, before you go, otherwise he might think you are angry; *he is used to suspecting he is doing something wrong.*

> MARLENE DIETRICH (1904–92), German-born U.S. film actor. *Marlene Dietrich's ABC,* "Married Love" (1962).

11 Personally, I can't see why it would be any less romantic to find a husband in a nice four-color catalogue than in the average downtown bar at happy hour.

> BARBARA EHRENREICH (b. 1941), U.S. author, columnist. *The Worst Years of Our Lives,* "Tales of the Man Shortage" (1991; first published in *Mother Jones,* 1986).

12 A good husband makes a good wife.

> JOHN FLORIO (c. 1553–1625), English author, translator. Silvestro, in *Second Frutes,* ch. 12 (1591). The adage is also found in Robert Burton, *Anatomy of Melancholy,* pt. 3, sct. 3 (1621).

13 Though bachelors be the strongest stakes, married men are the best binders, in the hedge of the commonwealth.

> THOMAS FULLER (1608–61), English cleric. *The Holy State and the Profane State,* bk. 4, ch. 20 (1642).

14 Husbands are like fires. They go out when unattended.

> ZSA ZSA GABOR (b. 1919), Hungarian-born U.S. actor. *Newsweek* (New York, 28 March 1960).

15 An early-rising man . . . a good spouse but a bad husband.

> GABRIEL GARCÍA MÁRQUEZ (b. 1928), Colombian author. The widow Monteil, in *In Evil Hour* (1968; tr. 1979).

16 I think there's something degrading about having a husband for a rival. It's humiliating if you fail and commonplace if you succeed.

> CHRISTOPHER HAMPTON (b. 1946), British playwright. Merteuil, in *Dangerous Liaisons* (screenplay, 1989).

17 You know I won't turn over a new leaf I am so obstinate, but then I am no less obstinate in being your affectionate Husband.

> WILLIAM HOGARTH (1697–1764), English painter, engraver. Closing words of a letter to his wife, 6 June 1749, from facsimile in A. M. Broadley, *Chats on Autographs* (1910).

18 Those men are most apt to be obsequious and conciliating abroad, who are under the discipline of shrews at home.

> WASHINGTON IRVING (1783–1859), U.S. author. *The Sketch-Book,* "Rip Van Winkle" (1819–20).

19 I've had the boyhood thing of being Elvis. Now I want to be with my best friend, and my best friend's my wife. Who could ask for anything more?

> JOHN LENNON (1940–80), British rock musician. Interview for KFRC RKO Radio, given 8 Dec. 1980, the day of Lennon's murder.

20 Husbands never become good; they merely become proficient.

> H. L. MENCKEN (1880–1956), U.S. journalist. *A Mencken Chrestomathy,* "Sententiæ: Masculum et Feminam Creavit Eos" (1949).

21 Husbands are chiefly good as lovers when they are betraying their wives.

> MARILYN MONROE (1926–62), U.S. screen actor. Quoted in: *Marilyn Monroe In Her Own Words,* "Weddings & Divorces" (1990).

22 The calmest husbands make the stormiest wives.

> ENGLISH PROVERB (17th century). Quoted in: Isaac d'Israeli, *Curiosities of Literature,* pt. 1 (1834).

23 A good husband is healthy and absent.

> JAPANESE PROVERB. Quoted in: *Sunday Times* (London, 16 Dec. 1990).

24 When you see what some girls marry, you realize how they must hate to work for a living.

> HELEN ROWLAND (1875–1950), U.S. journalist. *Reflections of a Bachelor Girl* (1903).

25 A husband is what is left of a lover, after the nerve has been extracted.

> HELEN ROWLAND (1875–1950), U.S. journalist. *A Guide to Men,* "Prelude" (1922).

26 Before marriage, a man will go home and lie awake all night thinking about something you said; after marriage, he'll go to sleep before you finish saying it.

> HELEN ROWLAND (1875–1950), U.S. journalist. *A Guide to Men,* "First Interlude" (1922).

27 I think every woman's entitled to a middle husband she can forget.

> ADELA ROGERS ST. JOHNS (b. 1893), U.S. journalist. Quoted in: *Los Angeles Times* (13 Oct. 1974).

28 A little in drink, but at all times your faithful husband.

> SIR RICHARD STEELE (1672–1729), English dramatist, essayist, editor. Midnight letter to his wife, 27 Sept. 1708.

29 In marriage, a man becomes slack and selfish, and undergoes a fatty degeneration of his moral being.

> ROBERT LOUIS STEVENSON (1850–94), Scottish novelist, essayist, poet. *Virginibus Puerisque,* title essay sct. 1 (1881).

30 Some pray to marry the man they love,
My prayer will somewhat vary;
I humbly pray to Heaven above
That I love the man I marry.

> ROSE PASTOR STOKES (1879–1933), U.S. social worker. *My Prayer.*

31 From the moment I liberated Brigitte, the moment I showed her how to be truly herself, our marriage was all downhill.

> ROGER VADIM (b. 1927), French filmmaker. *Sunday Express* (London, 2 July 1972). Vadim was speaking of Brigitte Bardot.

32 His purity was too great, his aspiration *too high* for this poor, *miserable* world! His great soul is *now only* enjoying *that* for which it *was* worthy!

> VICTORIA (1819–1901), Queen of Great Britain and Ireland. Letter, 20 Dec. 1861, to Leopold I, King of the Belgians (published in *Letters of Queen Victoria,* vol. 3, ch. 30, ed. by A.C. Benson and Viscount Esher, 1907). Victoria was referring to Albert, the Prince Consort.

33 The husbands of very beautiful women belong to the criminal classes.

> OSCAR WILDE (1854–1900), Anglo-Irish playwright, author. Lord Henry, in the *The Picture of Dorian Gray*, ch. 15 (1891).

34 They are horribly tedious when they are good husbands, and abominably conceited when they are not.

> OSCAR WILDE (1854–1900), Anglo-Irish playwright, author. Mrs. Allonby, in *A Woman of No Importance*, act 2

See also Christie on ARCHAEOLOGY; MARRIAGE; Gay on VILLAINS; WIVES.

HYGIENE

1 Bath twice a day to be really clean, once a day to be passably clean, once a week to avoid being a public menace.

> ANTHONY BURGESS (b. 1917), British author, critic. *Inside Mr. Enderby*, ch. 2, sct. 1 (1963).

2 A Turkish bath—that marble paradise of sherbert and sodomy.

> LORD BYRON (1788–1824), English poet. Letter, 12 Aug. 1819, to publisher John Murray (published in *Byron's Letters and Journals*, vol. 6, ed. by Leslie A. Marchand, 1976).

3 Man does not live by soap alone; and hygiene, or even health, is not much good unless you can take a healthy view of it—or, better still, feel a healthy indifference to it.

> G. K. CHESTERTON (1874–1936), British author. *All I Survey*, "On St. George Revivified" (1933).

4 Henri IV's feet and armpits enjoyed an international reputation.

> ALDOUS HUXLEY (1894–1963), British author. *The Devils of Loudun*, ch. 10 (1952). Huxley was referring to the stories that circulated concerning the "physiological accidents" of the French royal court. "It was precisely because great men tried to seem more than human," he wrote, "that the rest of the world welcomed any reminder that, in part at least, they were still merely animal."

5 Hygiene is the corruption of medicine by morality. It is impossible to find a hygienest who does not debase his theory of the healthful with a theory of the virtuous. . . . The true aim of medicine is not to make men virtuous; it is to safeguard and rescue them from the consequences of their vices.

> H. L. MENCKEN (1880–1956), U.S. journalist. *Prejudices*, "The Physician" (Third Series, 1922).

6 Hygiene is two thirds of health.

> LEBANESE PROVERB.

HYPOCHONDRIA

1 Imaginary pains are by far the most real we suffer, since we feel a constant need for them and invent them because there is no way of doing without them.

> E. M. CIORAN (b. 1911), Rumanian-born French philosopher. *The Trouble with Being Born*, ch. 3 (1973).

2 This is really the common mentality of prisoners: they read with great attention all the articles that deal with illnesses and send away for treatises and "be your own doctor" or "emergency treatments" and end up by discovering that they have at least 300 or 400 illnesses, whose symptoms they are experiencing.

> ANTONIO GRAMSCI (1891–1937), Italian political theorist. Letter, 23 March 1931 (published in *Gramsci: Letters from Prison*, no. 184, tr. by Raymond Rosenthal, 1993).

See also Proust on DOCTORS.

HYPOCRISY

1 What makes it so plausible to assume that hypocrisy is the vice of vices is that integrity can indeed exist under the cover of all other vices except this one. Only crime and the criminal, it is true, confront us with the perplexity of radical evil; but only the hypocrite is really rotten to the core.

> HANNAH ARENDT (1906–75), German-born U.S. political philosopher. *On Revolution*, ch. 2 (1963).

2 Keep thy smooth words and juggling homilies
For those who know thee not.

> LORD BYRON (1788–1824), English poet. Sardanapalus, in *Sardanapalus*, act 2, sc. 1, to Beleses, the soothsayer.

3 The smylere with the knyf under the cloke.

> GEOFFREY CHAUCER (1340–1400), English poet. *The Canterbury Tales*, "The Knight's Tale" (c. 1387–1400).

4 If we divine a discrepancy between a man's words and his character, the whole impression of him becomes broken and painful; he revolts the imagination by his lack of unity, and even the good in him is hardly accepted.

> CHARLES HORTON COOLEY (1864–1929), U.S. sociologist. *Human Nature and the Social Order*, ch. 9 (1902).

5 With affection beaming in one eye, and calculation shining out of the other.

> CHARLES DICKENS (1812–70), English novelist. *Martin Chuzzlewit*, ch. 8 (1844), referring to Mrs. Todgers.

6 An open foe may prove a curse,
But a pretended friend is worse.

> JOHN GAY (1685–1732), English dramatist. *Fables*, "The Shepherd's Dog and the Wolf" (1727).

7 A fav'rite has no friend!

> THOMAS GRAY (1716–71), English poet. *Ode on the Death of a Favourite Cat*.

8 A hypocrite despises those whom he deceives, but has no respect for himself. He would make a dupe of himself too, if he could.

> WILLIAM HAZLITT (1778–1830), English essayist. *Characteristics: In the Manner of Rochefoucault's Maxims*, no. 398 (1823; repr. in *The Complete Works of William Hazlitt*, vol. 9, ed. by P.P. Howe, 1932).

9 No man is a hypocrite in his pleasures.

> SAMUEL JOHNSON (1709–84), English author, lexicographer. Quoted in: Boswell, *Life of Samuel Johnson*, 19 June 1784 (1791).

10 Man is the only animal that learns by being hypocritical. He pretends to be polite and then, eventually, he *becomes* polite.

JEAN KERR (b. 1923), U.S. author, playwright. Jeff, in *Finishing Touches*, act 1.

11 Hypocrisy is a tribute that vice pays to virtue.

FRANÇOIS, DUC DE LA ROCHEFOUCAULD (1613–80), French writer, moralist. *Sentences et Maximes Morales*, no. 218 (1678).

12 No habit or quality is more easily acquired than hypocrisy, nor any thing sooner learned than to deny the sentiments of our hearts and the principle we act from: but the seeds of every passion are innate to us, and nobody comes into the world without them.

BERNARD MANDEVILLE (1670–1733), Dutch-born English author, physician. *The Fable of the Bees*, "An Essay on Charity and Charity-Schools" (1714; rev. 1723).

13 Hypocrisy is the most difficult and nerve-racking vice that any man can pursue; it needs an unceasing vigilance and a rare detachment of spirit. It cannot, like adultery or gluttony, be practised at spare moments; it is a whole-time job.

W. SOMERSET MAUGHAM (1874–1965), British author. *Cakes and Ale*, ch. 1 (1930).

14 For neither man nor angel can discern
Hypocrisy, the only evil that walks
Invisible, except to God alone.

JOHN MILTON (1608–74), English poet. *Paradise Lost*, bk. 3.

15 It is impossible to calculate the moral mischief, if I may so express it, that mental lying has produced in society. When a man has so far corrupted and prostituted the chastity of his mind as to subscribe his professional belief to things he does not believe he has prepared himself for the commission of every other crime.

THOMAS PAINE (1737–1809), Anglo-American political theorist, writer. *The Age of Reason*, pt. 1, "The Author's Profession of Faith" (1794).

16 Hypocrisy in anything whatever may deceive the cleverest and most penetrating man, but the least wide-awake of children recognizes it, and is revolted by it, however ingeniously it may be disguised.

LEO TOLSTOY (1828–1910), Russian novelist, philosopher. *Anna Karenina*, pt. 3, ch. 9 (1873–76).

17 And the wild regrets, and the bloody sweats,
None knew so well as I:
For he who lives more lives than one
More deaths than one must die.

OSCAR WILDE (1854–1900), Anglo-Irish playwright, author. *The Ballad of Reading Gaol*, pt. 3.

18 How clever you are, my dear! You never mean a single word you say.

OSCAR WILDE (1854–1900), Anglo-Irish playwright, author. Lady Hunstanton to Mrs. Allonby, in *A Woman of No Importance*, act 2.

19 The only thing worse than a liar is a liar that's also a hypocrite!

TENNESSEE WILLIAMS (1914–83), U.S. dramatist. Rosa, in *The Rose Tattoo*, act 3.

IDEALISM

1 Idealism is the despot of thought, just as politics is the despot of will.

MIKHAIL BAKUNIN (1814–76), Russian political theorist. *A Circular Letter to My Friends in Italy* (1871).

2 Instead of killing and dying in order to produce the being that we are not, we have to live and let live in order to create what we are.

ALBERT CAMUS (1913–60), French-Algerian philosopher, author. *The Rebel*, pt. 3, "Rebellion and Revolution" (1951; tr. 1953).

3 Nearly all the Escapists in the long past have managed their own budget and their social relations so unsuccessfully that I wouldn't want them for my landlords, or my bankers, or my neighbors. They were valuable, like powerful stimulants, only when they were left out of the social and industrial routine.

WILLA CATHER (1876–1947), U.S. author. *On Writing*, "Four Letters: Escapism" (written 1936; published 1949).

4 The idealist walks on tiptoe, the materialist on his heels.

MALCOLM DE CHAZAL (1902–81), French writer. *Sens Plastique*, vol. 2 (1946).

5 Why should we strive, with cynic frown,
To knock their fairy castles down?

ELIZA COOK (1818–89), English poet. *Oh! Dear to Memory*.

6 The idealist's programme of political or economic reform may be impracticable, absurd, demonstrably ridiculous; but it can never be successfully opposed merely by pointing out that this is the case. A negative opposition cannot be wholly effectual: there must be a competing idealism; something must be offered that is not only less objectionable but more desirable.

CHARLES HORTON COOLEY (1864–1929), U.S. sociologist. *Human Nature and the Social Order*, ch. 9 (1902).

7 There is no force so democratic as the force of an ideal.

CALVIN COOLIDGE (1872–1933), U.S. Republican politician, president. Speech, 27 Nov. 1920, New York City.

8 An idealist is a person who helps other people to be prosperous.

HENRY FORD (1863–1947), U.S. industrialist. Remarks to the court in Mt. Clemens, Michigan, July 1919, during Ford's libel case against the *Chicago Tribune*. An editorial in the paper had described him as an "anarchist" and "ignorant idealist"; the *Tribune* was found guilty and fined 6 cents.

9 It's really a wonder that I haven't dropped all my ideals because they seem so absurd and impossible to carry out. Yet, I keep them, because in spite of everything I still believe that people are really good at heart. I simply can't build up my hopes on a foundation consisting of confusion, misery, and death. I see the world gradually being turned into a wilderness, I hear the ever-approaching thunder, which will destroy us too, I can feel the sufferings of millions and yet, if I look up into the heavens, I think that it will all come right, that this cruelty too will end, and that peace and tranquility will return again.

> ANNE FRANK (1929–45), German Jewish refugee, diarist. *The Diary of a Young Girl* (1947; tr. 1952), entry for 15 July 1944. On 4 Aug. 1944, a little less than three weeks after writing this entry, Anne and the other occupants of the secret annex in which they had been hiding were arrested by the Nazis and sent to concentration camps in Germany.

10 We for a certainty are not the first
Have sat in taverns while the tempest hurled
Their hopeful plans to emptiness, and cursed
Whatever brute and blackguard made the world.

> A. E. HOUSMAN (1859–1936), British poet, classical scholar. *Last Poems*, no. 9 (1922).

11 When your dreams tire, they go underground
and out of kindness that's where they stay.

> LIBBY HOUSTON (b. 1941), British poet. *Gold*, in *Necessity* (1988).

12 You should never have your best trousers on when you turn out to fight for freedom and truth.

> HENRIK IBSEN (1828–1906), Norwegian dramatist. Mrs. Stockmann, in *An Enemy of the People*, act 5.

13 Don't use that foreign word "ideals." We have that excellent native word "lies."

> HENRIK IBSEN (1828–1906), Norwegian dramatist. Reilling, in *The Wild Duck*, act 5.

14 The further limits of our being plunge, it seems to me, into an altogether other dimension of existence from the sensible and merely "understandable" world. Name it the mystical region, or the supernatural region, whichever you choose. So far as our ideal impulses originate in this region (and most of them do originate in it, for we find them possessing us in a way for which we cannot articulately account), we belong to it in a more intimate sense than that in which we belong to the visible world, for we belong in the most intimate sense wherever our ideals belong.

> WILLIAM JAMES (1842–1910), U.S. psychologist, philosopher. *The Varieties of Religious Experience*, Lecture 20 (1902).

15 Our salvation is in striving to achieve what we know we'll never achieve.

> RYSZARD KAPUSCINSKI (b. 1932), Polish journalist. *A Warsaw Diary*, in *Granta*, no. 15 (Cambridge, England, 1985).

16 When one paints an ideal, one does not need to limit one's imagination.

> ELLEN KEY (1849–1926), Swedish author, feminist. *The Morality of Woman and Other Essays*, "The Woman of the Future" (1911).

17 The enemy of idealism is zealotry.

> NEIL KINNOCK (b. 1942), British Labour politician. Quoted in: *Observer* (London, 27 Dec. 1987).

18 It is the style of idealism to console itself for the loss of something old with the ability to gape at something new.

> KARL KRAUS (1874–1936), Austrian satirist. "The Discovery of the North Pole," in *Die Fackel*, no. 287 (Vienna, Sept. 1909; repr. in *In These Great Times: A Karl Kraus Reader*, ed. by Harry Zohn, 1976).

19 Idealist: a cynic in the making.

> IRVING LAYTON (b. 1912), Canadian poet. *The Whole Bloody Bird*, "Aphs" (1969).

20 If you are going to build something in the air it is always better to build castles than houses of cards.

> G. C. LICHTENBERG (1742–99), German physicist, philosopher. *Aphorisms*, "Notebook F," aph. 39 (written 1765–99; tr. by R. J. Hollingdale, 1990).

21 Some day the soft Ideal that we wooed
Confronts us fiercely, foe-beset, pursued,
And cries reproachful: "Was it then my praise,
And not myself was loved? Prove now thy truth;
I claim of thee the promise of thy youth."

> JAMES RUSSELL LOWELL (1819–91), U.S. poet, editor. *Ode Recited at the Harvard Commemmoration*, often known as *Commemmoration Ode*.

22 Many have dreamed up republics and principalities that have never in truth been known to exist; the gulf between how one should live and how one does live is so wide that that a man who neglects what is actually done for what should be done learns the way to self-destruction rather than self-preservation.

> NICCOLÓ MACHIAVELLI (1469–1527), Italian political philosopher, statesman. *The Prince*, ch. 15 (1514).

23 An idealist is one who, on noticing that a rose smells better than a cabbage, concludes that it will also make better soup.

> H. L. MENCKEN (1880–1956), U.S. journalist. *A Book of Burlesques*, "Sententiae" (1920).

24 The idealist is incorrigible: if he is thrown out of his heaven he makes an ideal of his hell.

> FRIEDRICH NIETZSCHE (1844–1900), German philosopher. *Miscellaneous Maxims and Opinions*, no. 23 (1879).

25 The ideal, without doubt, varies, but its enemies, alas, are always the same.

> JEAN ROSTAND (1894–1977), French biologist, writer. *Carnets d'un Biologiste*, "The Substance of Man," p. 196 (1962).

26 Ideals are like stars; you will not succeed in touching them with your hands. But like the seafaring man on the desert of waters, you choose them as your guides, and following them you will reach your destiny.

> CARL SCHURZ (1829–1906), German-born U.S. senator. Speech, 18 April 1859, Boston.

27 A man gazing on the stars is proverbially at the mercy of the puddles in the road.

> ALEXANDER SMITH (1830–67), Scottish poet. *Dreamthorp*, "Men of Letters" (1863).

28 When they come downstairs from their Ivory Towers, idealists are very apt to walk straight into the gutter.

> LOGAN PEARSALL SMITH (1865–1946), U.S. essayist. *Afterthoughts*, "Other People" (1931).

29 If you have built castles in the air, your work need not be lost; that is where they should be. Now put the foundations under them.

> HENRY DAVID THOREAU (1817–62), U.S. philosopher, author, naturalist. *Walden*, "Conclusion" (1854).

30 Saddle your dreams afore you ride 'em.

> MARY WEBB (1881–1927), British author. *Precious Bane*, bk. 1, ch. 6 (1924).

31 Most idealistic people are skint. I have discovered that people with money have no imagination, and people with imagination have no money.

> GEORGE WEISS [CAPTAIN RAINBOW] (b. 1940), British eccentric. *Guardian* (London, 3 Nov. 1984).

32 We are all in the gutter, but some of us are looking at the stars.

> OSCAR WILDE (1854–1900), Anglo-Irish playwright, author. Lord Darlington, in *Lady Windermere's Fan*, act 3.

33 A map of the world that does not include Utopia is not worth even glancing at, for it leaves out the one country at which Humanity is always landing.

> OSCAR WILDE (1854–1900), Anglo-Irish playwright, author. *The Soul of Man under Socialism* (1895; first published in *The Fortnightly Review*, Feb. 1891)

See also Jung on ADDICTION; Douglas on ADVERTISING; Maugham on BEAUTY; Arnold on HOPE; Huxley on POLITICIANS; Wilson on The UNITED STATES; Chesterton on UNITED STATES, PEOPLE OF THE.

IDEAS

1 Ideas are refined and multiplied in the commerce of minds. In their splendor, images effect a very simple communion of souls.

> GASTON BACHELARD (1884–1962), French scientist, philosopher, literary theorist. *The Poetics of Reverie*, sct. 4, "Introduction" (1960; tr. 1969).

2 Ideas are invented only as correctives to the past. Through repeated rectifications of this kind one may hope to disengage an idea that is valid.

> GASTON BACHELARD (1884–1962), French scientist, philosopher, literary theorist. *Fragments of a Poetics of Fire*, "A Retrospective Glance at the Lifework of a Master of Books" (1988; tr. 1990).

3 Such as take lodgings in a head
That's to be let unfurnished.

> SAMUEL BUTLER (1612–80), English poet. *Hudibras*, pt. 1, cto. 1.

4 It doesn't matter how new an idea *is:* what matters is how new it *becomes.*

> ELIAS CANETTI (b. 1905), Austrian novelist, philosopher. *The Secret Heart Of The Clock: Notes, Aphorisms, Fragments 1973-1985*, "1981" (1991).

5 A man is not necessarily intelligent because he has plenty of ideas, any more than he is a good general because he has plenty of soldiers.

> SÉBASTIEN-ROCH NICOLAS DE CHAMFORT (1741–94), French writer, wit. *Maxims and Considerations*, vol. 2, no. 446 (1796).

6 Hang ideas! They are tramps, vagabonds, knocking at the back-door of your mind, each taking a little of your substance, each carrying away some crumb of that belief in a few simple notions you must cling to if you want to live decently and would like to die easy!

> JOSEPH CONRAD (1857–1924), Polish-born English novelist. Marlow, in *Lord Jim*, ch. 5 (1900).

7 Ideas are powerful things, requiring not a studious contemplation but an action, even if it is only an inner action. Their acquisition obligates each man in some way to change his life, even if it is only his inner life. They demand to be stood for. They dictate where a man must concentrate his vision. They determine his moral and intellectual priorities. They provide him with allies and make him enemies. In short, ideas impose an interest in their ultimate fate which goes far beyond the realm of the merely reasonable.

> MIDGE DECTER (b. 1927), U.S. author, editor, social critic. *The Liberated Woman and Other Americans*, pt. 2, ch. 2 (1971).

8 Harold, like the rest of us, had many impressions which saved him the trouble of distinct ideas.

> GEORGE ELIOT (1819–80), English novelist, editor. *Felix Holt, The Radical*, ch. 47 (1866), said of Harold Transome.

9 It's very good for an idea to be commonplace. The important thing is that a new idea should develop out of what is already there so that it soon becomes an old acquaintance. Old acquaintances aren't by any means always welcome, but at least one can't be mistaken as to who or what they are.

> PENELOPE FITZGERALD (b. 1916), British author. Fred Fairly, in *The Gate of Angels*, ch. 20 (1990), lecturing to his students at Cambridge.

10 Ideas are fatal to caste.

> E. M. FORSTER (1879–1970), British novelist, essayist. *A Passage to India*, pt. 1, ch. 7 (1924).

11 There are more ideas on earth than intellectuals imagine. And these ideas are more active, stronger, more resistant, more passionate than "politicians" think. We have to be there at the birth of ideas, the bursting outward of their force: not in books expressing them, but in events manifesting this force, in struggles carried on around ideas, for or against them. Ideas do not rule the world. But it is because the world has ideas . . . that it is not passively ruled by those who are its leaders or those who would like to teach it, once and for all, what it must think.

> MICHEL FOUCAULT (1926–84), French philosopher. "Les Reportages d'Idées," in *Corriere Della Sera* (Milan, 12 Nov. 1978; repr. in Didier Eribon, *Michel Foucault*, 1989; tr. 1991).

12 It is ideas, not vested interests, which are dangerous for good or evil.

> JOHN MAYNARD KEYNES (1883–1946), British economist. *The General Theory of Employment, Interest and Money*, ch. 24, "Concluding Notes" (1936).

13 Concepts, like individuals, have their histories and are just as incapable of withstanding the ravages of time as are individuals. But in and through all this they retain a kind of homesickness for the scenes of their childhood.

> SØREN KIERKEGAARD (1813–55), Danish philosopher. *The Concept of Irony*, pt. 1, Introduction (1841; tr. 1966).

14 Not just in commerce but in the world of ideas too our age is putting on a veritable clearence sale. Everything can be had so dirt cheap that one begins to wander whether in the end anyone will want to make a bid.

> SØREN KIERKEGAARD (1813–55), Danish philosopher. *Fear and Trembling*, Preface (1843; tr. 1985).

15 The ideas of a time are like the clothes of a season: they are as arbitrary, as much imposed by some superior will which is seldom explicit. They are utilitarian and political, the instruments of smooth-running government.

WYNDHAM LEWIS (1882–1957), British author, painter. *The Art of Being Ruled*, ch. 3, "Beyond Action and Reaction" (1926).

16 Ideas too are a life and a world.

G. C. LICHTENBERG (1742–99), German physicist, philosopher. *Aphorisms*, "Notebook F," aph. 70 (written 1765–99; tr. by R. J. Hollingdale, 1990).

17 An idea is a putting truth in check-mate.

JOSÉ ORTEGA Y GASSET (1883–1955), Spanish essayist, philosopher. *The Revolt of the Masses*, ch. 8 (1930).

18 An idea is a point of departure and no more. As soon as you elaborate it, it becomes transformed by thought.

PABLO PICASSO (1881–1973), Spanish artist. Quoted in: Jaime Sabartés, *Picasso: portraits et souvenirs*, ch. 7 (1946).

19 People find ideas a bore because they do not distinguish between live ones and stuffed ones on a shelf.

EZRA POUND (1885–1972), U.S. poet, critic. *Guide to Kulchur*, pt. 1, sct. 1, ch. 5 (1938).

20 A powerful idea communicates some of its strength to him who challenges it.

MARCEL PROUST (1871–1922), French novelist. *Remembrance of Things Past*, vol. 3, "Within a Budding Grove," pt. 1, "Madame Swann at Home" (1918; tr. by Scott Monkrieff, 1924).

21 The difference between people and ideas is . . . only superficial.

RICHARD RORTY (b. 1931), U.S. philosopher. *Contingency, Irony, and Solidarity*, ch. 5, "Self-Creation and Affiliation: Proust, Nietzsche, and Heidegger" (1989).

22 To love an idea is to love it a little more than one should.

JEAN ROSTAND (1894–1977), French biologist, writer. *Carnets d'un Biologiste* (repr. in *The Substance of Man*, 1962; p. 181).

23 Ideas that enter the mind under fire remain there securely and for ever.

LEON TROTSKY (1879–1940), Russian revolutionary. *My Life*, ch. 35 (1930).

24 The value of an idea has nothing whatsoever to do with the sincerity of the man who expresses it. Indeed, the probabilities are that the more insincere the man is, the more purely intellectual will the idea be, as in that case it will not be coloured by either his wants, his desires, or his prejudices.

OSCAR WILDE (1854–1900), Anglo-Irish playwright, author. Lord Henry, in *The Picture of Dorian Gray*, ch. 1 (1891).

See also Sterne on AMUSEMENT; Vauvenargues on AWARENESS; Gilbert on CREATIVITY; Steiner on DISSENT; Bagehot on INNOVATION; Debord on PLAGIARISM; Fuseli on The SENSES.

IDENTITY

1 An identity would seem to be arrived at by the way in which the person faces and uses his experience.

JAMES BALDWIN (1924–87), U.S. author. *The Price of The Ticket*, "No Name in the Street" (1985; first published 1972).

2 An identity is questioned only when it is menaced, as when the mighty begin to fall, or when the wretched begin to rise, or when the stranger enters the gates, never, thereafter, to be a stranger. . . . Identity would seem to be the garment with which one covers the nakedness of the self: in which case, it is best that the garment be loose, a little like the robes of the desert, through which one's nakedness can always be felt, and, sometimes, discerned. This trust in one's nakedness is all that gives one the power to change one's robes.

JAMES BALDWIN (1924–87), U.S. author. *The Price of The Ticket*, sct. 2, "The Devil Finds Work" (1985; first published 1976).

3 It is always the same: once you are liberated, you are forced to ask who you are.

JEAN BAUDRILLARD (b. 1929), French semiologist. *America*, "Astral America" (1986; tr. 1988).

4 Man may be defined as the animal that can say "I," that can be aware of himself as a separate entity.

ERICH FROMM (1900–80), U.S. psychologist. *The Sane Society*, ch. 3, "Sense of Identity" (1955).

5 Sir, a man may be so much of everything, that he is nothing of anything.

SAMUEL JOHNSON (1709–84), English author, lexicographer. Quoted in: James Boswell, *Life of Samuel Johnson*, 1783 entry (1791).

6 I believe that man is in the last resort so free a being that his right *to be* what he believes himself to be cannot be contested.

G. C. LICHTENBERG (1742–99), German physicist, philosopher. *Aphorisms*, "Notebook L," aph. 98 (written 1765–99; tr. by R. J. Hollingdale, 1990).

7 There comes a point in many people's lives when they can no longer play the role they have chosen for themselves. When that happens, we are like actors finding that someone has changed the play.

BRIAN MOORE (b. 1921), Irish novelist. *Sunday Times* (London, 15 April 1990). "What I write about," Moore added, "is the mess that follows."

8 The real meditation is . . . the meditation on one's *identity*. Ah, voilà une chose!! You try it. You try finding out why you're you and not somebody else. And who in the blazes are you anyhow? Ah, voilà une chose!

EZRA POUND (1885–1972), U.S. poet, critic. Letter, 21 April 1913, to Pound's fiancée (later wife) Dorothy Shakespear (published in *Ezra Pound and Dorothy Shakespear: Their Letters 1909–1914*, ed. by Omar Pound and A. Walton Litz, 1985).

9 *I* is another.

ARTHUR RIMBAUD (1854–91), French poet. Letter, 13 May 1871 (published in *Collected Poems*, ed. by Oliver Bernard, 1962).

10 Identity is a bag and a gag. Yet it exists for me with all the force of a fatal disease. Obviously I am here, a mind and a body. To say there's no proof my body exists would be arty and specious and if my mind is more ephemeral, less provable, the solution of being a writer with solid (touchable, tearable, burnable) books is as close as anyone has come to a perfect answer.

JUDITH ROSSNER (b. 1935), U.S. author. *Nine Months in the Life of an Old Maid*, pt. 2 (1969).

11 The minute you or anybody else knows what you are you are not it, you are what you or anybody else knows you are and as everything in living is made up of finding out what you are it is extraordinarily difficult really not to know what you are and yet to be that thing.

GERTRUDE STEIN (1874–1946), U.S. author. *Everybody's Autobiography*, ch. 3 (1937).

12 Trying to define yourself is like trying to bite your own teeth.

ALAN WATTS (1915–73), British-born U.S. philosopher, author. *Life* (New York, 21 April 1961).

IDEOLOGY

1 There are no more ideologies in the authentic sense of false consciousness, only advertisements for the world through its duplication and the provocative lie which does not seek belief but commands silence.

THEODOR W. ADORNO (1903–69), German philosopher, sociologist, music critic. *Prisms*, "Cultural Criticism and Society" (1967).

2 Ideology has very little to do with "consciousness". . . . It is profoundly *unconscious*.

LOUIS ALTHUSSER (b. 1918), Algerian-born French Marxist philosopher. *For Marx*, ch. 7, sct. 4 (1965).

3 Whoever today speaks of human existence in terms of power, efficiency, and "historical tasks" . . . is an actual or potential assassin.

ALBERT CAMUS (1913–60), French-Algerian philosopher, author. Address, 1946, Columbia University, New York City. Quoted in: Paul West, *The Wine of Absurdity*, "Albert Camus" (1966).

4 Methods of thought which claim to give the lead to our world in the name of revolution have become, in reality, ideologies of consent and not of rebellion.

ALBERT CAMUS (1913–60), French-Algerian philosopher, author. *The Rebel*, pt. 3, "Rebellion and Revolution" (1951; tr. 1953).

5 What persuades men and women to mistake each other from time to time for gods or vermin is ideology. One can understand well enough how human beings may struggle and murder for good material reasons—reasons connected, for instance, with their physical survival. It is much harder to grasp how they may come to do so in the name of something as apparently abstract as ideas. Yet ideas are what men and women live by, and will occasionally die for.

TERRY EAGLETON (b. 1943), British critic. *Ideology*, Introduction (1991).

6 It is possible to lead astray an entire generation, to strike it blind, to drive it insane, to direct it towards a false goal. Napoleon proved this.

ALEXANDER HERZEN (1812–70), Russian journalist, political thinker. *From the Other Shore*, "Donoso-Cortes" (1855).

7 There cannot be peaceful coexistence in the ideological realm. Peaceful coexistence corrupts.

JIANG QING (1914–91), Chinese party official, wife of Mao Tse-tung. Remark, April 1967. Quoted in: Stanley Karnow, *Mao and China: From Revolution to Revolution*, ch. 15 (1972).

8 Our blight is ideologies—they are the long-expected Antichrist!

CARL JUNG (1875–1961), Swiss psychiatrist. *The Tibetan Book of the Great Liberation* (1954; repr. in *Collected Works*, vol. 11, para. 778, ed. by William McGuire, 1958).

9 The ideas of economists and political philosophers, both when they are right and when they are wrong, are more powerful than is commonly understood. Indeed the world is ruled by little else. Practical men, who believe themselves to be quite exempt from any intellectual influence, are usually the slaves of some defunct economist.

JOHN MAYNARD KEYNES (1883–1946), British economist. *The General Theory of Employment, Interest and Money*, ch. 24, "Concluding Notes" (1936).

10 Ideologies . . . have no heart of their own. They're the whores and angels of our striving selves.

JOHN LE CARRÉ (b. 1931), British novelist. Smiley, in *The Secret Pilgrim*, ch. 12 (1990).

11 If you take away ideology, you are left with a case by case ethics which in practise ends up as me first, me only, and in rampant greed.

RICHARD NELSON (b. 1950), U.S. playwright. *Independent* (London, 12 July 1989).

12 Under the species of Syndicalism and Fascism there appears for the first time in Europe a type of man who does not want to give reasons or to be right, but simply shows himself resolved to impose his opinions.

JOSÉ ORTEGA Y GASSET (1883–1955), Spanish essayist, philosopher. *The Revolt of the Masses*, ch. 8 (1930).

13 Art and ideology often interact on each other; but the plain fact is that both spring from a common source. Both draw on human experience to explain mankind to itself; both attempt, in very different ways, to assemble coherence from seemingly unrelated phenomena; both stand guard for us against chaos.

KENNETH TYNAN (1927–80), British critic. "Ionesco and the Phantom," in *Observer* (London, 6 July 1958; repr. in Eugène Ionesco, *Notes and Counter-Notes*, 1962).

14 Everything ideological possesses *meaning*: it represents, depicts, or stands for something lying outside itself. In other words, it is a *sign. Without signs there is no ideology.*

V. N. VOLOSINOV (1905–60), Russian linguist. *Marxism and the Philosophy of Language*, ch. 1 (1929).

15 Now different races and nationalities cherish different ideals of society that stink in each other's nostrils with an offensiveness beyond the power of any but the most monstrous private deed.

REBECCA WEST (1892–1983), British author. *Black Lamb and Grey Falcon*, Epilogue (1941)

See also Galbraith on ECONOMICS; Cooley on IDEALISM.

IDLENESS

1 Life is mostly froth and bubble.
Two things stand like stone:
Dodging duty at the double,
Leaving work alone.
ANONYMOUS.

2 You must have been warned against letting the golden hours slip by. Yes, but some of them are golden only because we let them slip.
J. M. BARRIE (1860–1937), British playwright. Rectorial address, 3 May 1922, St. Andrew's University, Scotland.

3 The harvest truly is plenteous, but the labourers are few.
BIBLE: NEW TESTAMENT. *Matthew* 9:37. Jesus refers to the lack of proselytizers among the multitude, shortly before sending forth his apostles endowed with miraculous powers.

4 Idleness is an appendix to nobility.
ROBERT BURTON (1577–1640), English clergyman, author. *Anatomy of Melancholy*, pt. 1, sct. 2, memb. 2, subsct. 6 (1621).

5 Idleness [is] only a coarse name for my infinite capacity for living in the present.
CYRIL CONNOLLY (1903–74), British critic. "The Journal of Cyril Connolly 1928–1937," in David Pryce-Jones, *Journal and Memoir* (1983, p. 228).

6 What is this life if, full of care,
We have no time to stand and stare?
W. H. DAVIES (1871–1940), British poet. *Leisure*.

7 Sometimes I think that idlers seem to be a special class for whom nothing can be planned, plead as one will with them—their only contribution to the human family is to warm a seat at the common table.
F. SCOTT FITZGERALD (1896–1940), U.S. author. Letter, 7 July 1938, to his daughter Frances "Scottie" Fitzgerald (published in *The Letters of F. Scott Fitzgerald*, ed. by Andrew Turnbull, 1963).

8 It is impossible to enjoy idling thoroughly unless one has plenty of work to do. There is no fun in doing nothing when you have nothing to do. Wasting time is merely an occupation then, and a most exhausting one. Idleness, like kisses, to be sweet must be stolen.
JEROME K. JEROME (1859–1927), British author. *Idle Thoughts of an Idle Fellow*, "On Being Idle" (1889).

9 Perhaps man is the only being that can properly be called idle.
SAMUEL JOHNSON (1709–84), English author, lexicographer. *The Idler*, no. 1, published in *Universal Chronicle* (London, 15 April 1758; repr. in *Works of Samuel Johnson*, vol. 2, ed. by W. J. Bate, John M. Bullitt, and L. F. Powell, 1963).

10 As peace is the end of war, so to be idle is the ultimate purpose of the busy.
SAMUEL JOHNSON (1709–84), English author, lexicographer. *The Idler*, no. 1, published in *Universal Chronicle* (London, 15 April 1758; repr. in *Works of Samuel Johnson*, vol. 2, ed. by W. J. Bate, John M. Bullitt, and L. F. Powell, 1963). "Perhaps man," Johnson wrote, "is the only being that can properly be called idle."

11 Far from idleness being the root of all evil, it is rather the only true good.
SØREN KIERKEGAARD (1813–55), Danish philosopher. *Either/Or*, vol. 1, "The Rotation Method" (1843).

12 Democracy divides people into workers and loafers. It makes no provision for those who have no time to work.
KARL KRAUS (1874–1936), Austrian satirist. *Sprüche und Widersprüche*, ch. 4 (1909; tr. in *Half-Truths and One-And-A Half-Truths*, "Lord, Forgive Them . . ." ed. by Harry Zohn, 1976).

13 There is nothing worse than an idle hour, with no occupation offering. People who have many such hours are simply animals waiting docilely for death. We all come to that state soon or late. It is the curse of senility.
H. L. MENCKEN (1880–1956), U.S. journalist. *Minority Report: H. L. Mencken's Notebooks*, no. 87 (1956).

14 The insupportable labour of doing nothing.
SIR RICHARD STEELE (1672–1729), English dramatist, essayist, editor. *The Tatler*, no. 54 (London, Aug. 1709).

15 A faculty for idleness implies a catholic appetite and a strong sense of personal identity.
ROBERT LOUIS STEVENSON (1850–94), Scottish novelist, essayist, poet. *Virginibus Puerisque*, "An Apology for Idlers" (1881).

16 The man who does not betake himself at once and desperately to sawing is called a loafer, though he may be knocking at the doors of heaven all the while.
HENRY DAVID THOREAU (1817–62), U.S. philosopher, author, naturalist. *Journals* (1906), entry for 28 Dec. 1852.

17 It is better to have loafed and lost than never to have loafed at all.
JAMES THURBER (1894–1961), U.S. humorist, illustrator. *Fables for Our Time*, "The Courtship of Arthur and Al" (1940).

18 'Tis the voice of the sluggard; I heard him complain,
You have wak'd me too soon, I must slumber again.
ISAAC WATTS (1674–1748), English hymn-writer. *The Sluggard*.

19 Yet it is in our idleness, in our dreams, that the submerged truth sometimes comes to the top.
VIRGINIA WOOLF (1882–1941), British novelist. *A Room of One's Own*, ch. 2 (1929).

IGNORANCE

1 The ground for taking ignorance to be restrictive of freedom is that it causes people to make choices which they would not have made if they had seen what the realization of their choices involved.
A. J. [SIR ALFRED] AYER (1910–89), British philosopher. *The Meaning of Life and Other Essays*, "The Concept of Freedom" (1990).

2 It is certain, in any case, that ignorance, allied with power, is the most ferocious enemy justice can have.
JAMES BALDWIN (1924–87), U.S. author. *The Price of The Ticket*, "No Name in the Street" (1972; repr. 1985).

3 Ignorance is an evil weed, which dictators may cultivate among their dupes, but which no democracy can afford among its citizens.

SIR WILLIAM BEVERIDGE (LATER LORD BEVERIDGE) (1879–1963), British economist. *Full Employment in a Full Society*, pt. 4 (1944).

4 Only Socrates knew, after a lifetime of unceasing labor, that he was ignorant. Now every high-school student knows that. How did it become so easy?

ALLAN BLOOM (1930–92), U.S. educator, author. *The Closing of the American Mind*, Introduction (1987).

5 Ignorance is not innocence but sin.

ROBERT BROWNING (1812–89), English poet. *The Inn Album*, cto. 5.

6 Ignorance is the mother of devotion.

DEAN HENRY COLE (1500–1580), English prelate. *Disputation with the Papists at Westminster*, 31 March 1559.

7 There can be no more ancient and traditional American value than ignorance. English-only speakers brought it with them to this country three centuries ago, and they quickly imposed it on the Africans—who were not allowed to learn to read and write—and on the Native Americans, who were simply not allowed.

BARBARA EHRENREICH (b. 1941), U.S. author, columnist. *The Worst Years of Our Lives*, "Language Barrier" (1989; repr. 1991).

8 Where ignorance is bliss,
'Tis folly to be wise.

THOMAS GRAY (1716–71), English poet. *Ode on a Distant Prospect of Eton College*, last lines.

9 Hide our ignorance as we will, an evening of wine soon reveals it.

HERACLITUS (c. 535-c. 475 B.C.), Greek philosopher. *Herakleitos and Diogenes*, fragment 53, pt. 1 (tr. by Guy Davenport, 1976).

10 The ignorant are a reservoir of daring. It almost seems that those who have yet to discover the known are particularly equipped for dealing with the unknown. The unlearned have often rushed in where the learned feared to tread, and it is the credulous who are tempted to attempt the impossible. They know not whither they are going, and give chance a chance.

ERIC HOFFER (1902–83), U.S. philosopher. *Reflections on the Human Condition*, aph. 124 (1973).

11 Nothing in the world is more dangerous than sincere ignorance and conscientious stupidity.

MARTIN LUTHER KING, JR. (1929–68), U.S. clergyman, civil rights leader. *Strength to Love*, pt. 4, ch. 3 (1963).

12 In expanding the field of knowledge, we but increase the horizon of ignorance.

HENRY MILLER (1891–1980), U.S. author. *The Wisdom of the Heart*, title essay (1947).

13 There is natural ignorance and there is artificial ignorance. I should say at the present moment the artificial ignorance is about eighty-five per cent.

EZRA POUND (1885–1972), U.S. poet, critic. Interview in *Writers at Work* (Second Series, ed. by George Plimpton, 1963).

14 Better be ignorant of a matter than half know it.

PUBLILIUS SYRUS (1st century B.C.), Roman writer of mimes. *Sententiae*, no. 865.

15 Everybody is ignorant, only on different subjects.

WILL ROGERS (1879–1935), U.S. humorist. *The Illiterate Digest*, "Defending My Soup Plate Position" (1924).

16 One's ignorance is one's chief asset.

WALLACE STEVENS (1879–1955), U.S. poet. *Opus Posthumous*, "Adagia" (1959).

17 The truth is that our race survived ignorance; it is our scientific genius that will do us in.

STEPHEN VIZINCZEY (b. 1933), Hungarian novelist, critic. "Leonardo's Regret," in *Times* (London, 21 Sept. 1970; repr. in *Truth and Lies in Literature*, 1986), review of Richie Calder, *The Age of the Eye*.

18 I do not approve of anything that tampers with natural ignorance. Ignorance is like a delicate exotic fruit; touch it and the bloom is gone.

OSCAR WILDE (1854–1900), Anglo-Irish playwright, author. Lady Bracknell, in *The Importance of Being Earnest*, act 1

Bloom on CULTURE; Buñuel on CURIOSITY; McLaughin on INNOCENCE; Eliot on KNOWLEDGE; Lau-Tzu on KNOWLEDGE; Keillor on PARENTS; Gray on THOUGHT AND THINKING; Montagu on YOUTH.

ILLEGITIMACY

1 There are no illegitimate children, only illegitimate parents—if the term is to be used at all.

BERNADETTE DEVLIN MCALISKEY (b. 1947), Northern Irish politician. Quoted in: *Irish Times* (Dublin, 31 July 1971). The words are not original—the lawyer León Yankwich said the same during a hearing at the State District Court, Southern District of California, in 1928, and he was quoting the journalist O. O. McIntyre.

ILLNESS

1 It's usually the stupid people that develop long illnesses. You need more than indolence and selfishness, you need endurance to make a good patient.

W. H. AUDEN (1907–73), Anglo-American poet. *The Table Talk of W. H. Auden*, "February 1947" (comp. by Alan Ansen, ed. by Nicholas Jenkins, 1990).

2 The sick man is taken away by the institution that takes charge not of the individual, but of his illness, an isolated object transformed or eliminated by technicians devoted to the defense of health the way others are attached to the defense of law and order or tidiness.

MICHEL DE CERTEAU (1925–86), French author, critic. *The Practice of Everyday Life*, ch. 14, "An Unthinkable Practice" (1974).

3 If God causes man to be sick, sickness must be good, and its opposite, health, must be evil, for all that He makes is good and will stand forever. If the transgression of God's law produces sickness, it is right to be sick; and we cannot if we would, and should not if we could, annul the decrees of wisdom. It is the transgression of a belief of mortal mind, not of a law of matter nor of divine Mind, which causes the belief of sickness. The remedy is Truth, not matter,—the truth that disease is *unreal*.

MARY BAKER EDDY (1821–1910), U.S. founder of the Christian Science movement. *Science and Health*, ch. 8 (1875).

4 It occurred to me that there was no difference

between men, in intelligence or race, so profound as the difference between the sick and the well.

> F. SCOTT FITZGERALD (1896–1940), U.S. author. The narrator (Nick Carraway), in *The Great Gatsby*, ch. 7 (1925).

5 A strong egoism is a protection against disease, but in the last resort we must begin to love in order that we may not fall ill, and must fall ill if, in consequence of frustration, we cannot love.

> SIGMUND FREUD (1856–1939), Austrian psychiatrist. *On Narcissism: An Introduction* (1914; repr. in *Collected Papers*, vol. 4, 1948).

6 You aren't ill: it is just that you are made of second-rate materials.

> NATALIA GINZBURG (b. 1916), Italian novelist. Alberto, in *Family Sayings* (1963; tr. 1967; rev. 1984, p. 98), to his wife, Miranda.

7 Sickness sensitizes man for observation, like a photographic plate.

> EDMOND (1822–96) AND JULES DE GONCOURT (1830–70), French writers. *The Goncourt Journals* (1888–96; repr. in *Pages from the Goncourt Journal*, ed. by Robert Baldick, 1962), entry for 27 March 1865.

8 Sickness is mankind's greatest defect.

> G. C. LICHTENBERG (1742–99), German physicist, philosopher. *Aphorisms*, "Notebook F," aph. 100 (written 1765–99; tr. by R. J. Hollingdale, 1990).

9 As a cure for the cold, take your toddy to bed, put one bowler hat at the foot, and drink until you see two.

> SIR ROBERT BRUCE LOCKHART (1886–1970), British author, diplomat, journalist. Quoted in: *Independent* (London, 25 Nov. 1989).

10 And as for sickness: would we not almost be tempted to ask whether we can in any way do without it? Only great pain is, as the teacher of *great suspicion*, the ultimate liberator of the spirit. . . . It is only great pain, that slow protracted pain which takes its time and in which we are as it were burned with green wood, that compels us philosophers to descend into our ultimate depths and to put from us all trust, all that is good-hearted, palliated, gentle, average, wherein perhaps our humanity previously reposed. I doubt whether such pain "improves"—but I do know it *deepens* us.

> FRIEDRICH NIETZSCHE (1844–1900), German philosopher. *The Gay Science*, Preface, aph. 3 (rev. ed., 1887).

11 Illness is the doctor to whom we pay most heed; to kindness, to knowledge, we make promise only; pain we obey.

> MARCEL PROUST (1871–1922), French novelist. *Remembrance of Things Past*, vol. 1, pt. 2, ch. 1, "Cities of the Plain" (1922).

12 Illness is the night-side of life, a more onerous citizenship. Everyone who is born holds dual citizenship, in the kingdom of the well and in the kingdom of the sick. Although we all prefer to use only the good passport, sooner or later each of us is obliged, at least for a spell, to identify ourselves as citizens of that other place.

> SUSAN SONTAG (b. 1933), U.S. essayist. *Illness As Metaphor*, (1978), opening words.

13 Societies need to have one illness which becomes identified with evil, and attaches blame to its "victims."

> SUSAN SONTAG (b. 1933), U.S. essayist. *AIDS and Its Metaphors*, ch. 1 (1989).

14 The fact that illness is associated with the poor—who are, from the perspective of the privileged, aliens in one's midst—reinforces the association of illness with the foreign: with an exotic, often primitive place.

> SUSAN SONTAG (b. 1933), U.S. essayist. *AIDS and Its Metaphors*, ch. 5 (1989).

15 We are so fond of one another, because our ailments are the same.

> JONATHAN SWIFT (1667–1745), Anglo-Irish satirist. *Journal to Stella* (1710–13), entry for 1 Feb 1711.

16 Dearest Lord, may I see you today and every day in the person of your sick, and, whilst nursing them, minister unto you. Though you hide yourself behind the unattractive disguise of the irritable, the exacting, the unreasonable, may I still recognize you, and say: "Jesus, my patient, how sweet it is to serve you."

> MOTHER TERESA (b. 1910), Albanian-born Roman Catholic missionary. *A Gift for God*, "Love to Pray" (1975).

17 We are such docile creatures, normally, that it takes a virus to jolt us out of life's routine. A couple of days in a fever bed are, in a sense, health-giving; the change in body temperature, the change in pulse rate, and the change of scene have a restorative effect on the system equal to the hell they raise.

> E. B. WHITE (1899–1985), U.S. author, editor. "The Cold," in *New Yorker* (10 Nov. 1951; repr. in *Writings from the New Yorker 1927–1976*, ed. by Rebecca M. Dale, 1991).

18 Sickness disgusts us with death, and we wish to get well, which is a way of wishing to live. But weakness and suffering, with manifold bodily woes, soon discourage the invalid from trying to regain ground: he tires of those respites which are but snares, of that faltering strength, those ardors cut short, and that perpetual lying in wait for the next attack.

> MARGUERITE YOURCENAR (1903–87), French novelist. *Memoirs of Hadrian*, "Patientia" (1954)

See also AIDS; CANCER; DISEASE; Proust on DOCTORS; Certeau on HOSPITALS.

ILLUSION

1 What seems to be, is, to those to whom it
It seems to be, and is productive of the most
  dreadful
Consequences to those to whom it seems to be,
  even of
Torments, despair, eternal death.

> WILLIAM BLAKE (1757–1827), English poet, painter, engraver. *Jerusalem*, ch. 2, plate 36 (1804–1820; repr. in *Complete Writings*, ed. by Geoffrey Keynes, 1957).

2 Pray look better, Sir . . . those things yonder are no giants, but windmills.

> MIGUEL DE CERVANTES (1547–1616), Spanish writer. Sancho

Panza, in *Don Quixote*, pt. 1, bk. 1, ch. 8 (1605; tr. by P. Motteux).

3 We must select the Illusion which appeals to our temperament and embrace it with passion, if we want to be happy.

CYRIL CONNOLLY (1903–74), British critic. *The Unquiet Grave*, pt. 3 (1944; rev. 1951).

4 For what we call illusions are often, in truth, a wider vision of past and present realities—a willing movement of a man's soul with the larger sweep of the world's forces—a movement towards a more assured end than the chances of a single life.

GEORGE ELIOT (1819–80), English novelist, editor. *Felix Holt, The Radical*, ch. 16 (1866).

5 What difference is there, do you think, between those in Plato's cave who can only marvel at the shadows and images of various objects, provided they are content and don't know what they miss, and the philosopher who has emerged from the cave and sees the real things?

DESIDERIUS ERASMUS (c. 1466–1536), Dutch humanist. *Praise of Folly*, ch. 45 (1509).

6 People who have realized that this is a dream imagine that it is easy to wake up, and are angry with those who continue sleeping, not considering that the whole world that environs them does not permit them to wake. Life proceeds as a series of optical illusions, artificial needs and imaginary sensations.

ALEXANDER HERZEN (1812–70), Russian journalist, political thinker. *My Past and Thoughts*, vol. 3, pt. 6, "England" (1921; tr. by Constance Garnett, 1924–27), on the power of history.

7 For me, it is as though at every moment the actual world had completely lost its actuality. As though there was nothing there; as though there were no foundations for anything or as though it escaped us. Only one thing, however, is vividly present: the constant tearing of the veil of appearances; the constant destruction of everything in construction. Nothing holds together, everything falls apart.

EUGÈNE IONESCO (b. 1912), Rumanian-born French playwright. *Notes and Counter-Notes*, pt. 2, "Brief Notes for Radio" (1962).

8 It appears to me that almost any man may like the spider spin from his own inwards his own airy citadel.

JOHN KEATS (1795–1821), English poet. Letter, 19 Feb. 1818 (published in *Letters of John Keats*, no. 48, ed. by Frederick Page, 1954).

9 A hallucination is a fact, not an error; what is erroneous is a judgment based upon it.

BERTRAND RUSSELL (1872–1970), British philosopher, mathematician. "On the Nature of Acquaintance: Neutral Monism" (1914; repr. in *Logic and Knowledge*, 1956).

10 Don't part with your illusions. When they are gone you may still exist, but you have ceased to live.

MARK TWAIN (1835–1910), U.S. author. *Following the Equator*, ch. 59, "Pudd'nhead Wilson's New Calendar" (1897).

11 It isn't safe to sit in judgment upon another person's illusion when you are not on the inside. While you are thinking it is a dream, he may be knowing it is a planet.

MARK TWAIN (1835–1910), U.S. author. "Three Thousand Years Among the Microbes," ch. 13 (written 1905; published in *Which Was the Dream?*, ed. by John S. Tuckey, 1967).

12 Artists use frauds to make human beings seem more wonderful than they really are. Dancers show us human beings who move much more gracefully than human beings really move. Films and books and plays show us people talking much more entertainingly than people really talk, make paltry human enterprises seem important. Singers and musicians show us human beings making sounds far more lovely than human beings really make. Architects give us temples in which something marvelous is obviously going on. Actually, practically nothing is going on.

KURT VONNEGUT, JR. (b. 1922), U.S. novelist. *Wampeters, Foma and Granfalloons*, "When I Was Twenty-One" (1974).

IMAGE

1 We are all hungry and thirsty for concrete images. Abstract art will have been good for one thing: to restore its exact virginity to figurative art.

SALVADOR DALI (1904–89), Spanish painter. *Diary of a Genius* (1966), entry for 2 Aug. 1953.

2 Metaphors are much more tenacious than facts.

PAUL DE MAN (1919–83), Belgian-born U.S. literary critic. *Allegories Of Reading*, pt. 1, ch. 1, "Semiology And Rhetoric" (1979).

3 Nowadays people's visual imagination is so much more sophisticated, so much more developed, particularly in young people, that now you can make an image which just slightly suggests something, they can make of it what they will.

ROBERT DOISNEAU (b. 1912), French photographer. *Weekend Guardian* (London, 4 April 1992).

4 For such an advanced civilization as ours to be without images that are adequate to it is as serious a defect as being without memory.

WERNER HERZOG (b. 1942), German film director. *New York Times* (11 Sept. 1977).

5 The reign of imagagology begins where history ends.

MILAN KUNDERA (b. 1929), Czech author, critic. Paul, in *Immortality*, pt. 3, "Imagagology" (1991), on the death of ideology.

6 Logicians may reason about abstractions. But the great mass of men must have images. The strong tendency of the multitude in all ages and nations to idolatry can be explained on no other principle.

THOMAS BABINGTON MACAULAY (1800–59), English historian. "Milton," in *Edinburgh Review* (Aug. 1825; repr. in *Critical and Historical Essays*, 1843).

7 We operate with nothing but things which do not exist, with lines, planes, bodies, atoms, divisible time, divisible space—how should explanation even be possible when we first make everything into an *image*, into our own image!

FRIEDRICH NIETZSCHE (1844–1900), German philosopher. *The Gay Science,* aph. 112 (rev. ed., 1887).

8   The visual is sorely undervalued in modern scholarship. Art history has attained only a fraction of the conceptual sophistication of literary criticism. . . . Drunk with self-love, criticism has hugely overestimated the centrality of language to western culture. It has failed to see the electrifying sign language of images.

CAMILLE PAGLIA (b. 1947), U.S. author, critic, educator. *Sexual Personae,* ch. 1 (1990).

9   The Image is more than an idea. It is a vortex or cluster of fused ideas and is endowed with energy.

EZRA POUND (1885–1972), U.S. poet, critic. *Selected Prose 1909–1965,* pt. 7, "Affirmations—As for Imagisme" (ed. by William Cookson, 1973).

10   Industrial societies turn their citizens into image-junkies; it is the most irresistible form of mental pollution. Poignant longings for beauty, for an end to probing below the surface, for a redemption and celebration of the body of the world. Ultimately, having an experience becomes identical with taking a photograph of it.

SUSAN SONTAG (b. 1933), U.S. essayist. *On Photography,* "In Plato's Cave" (1977).

11   Isn't life a series of images that change as they repeat themselves?

ANDY WARHOL (1928–87), U.S. Pop artist. Quoted in: Victor Bokris, *Warhol,* "Too Much Work 1980–84" (1989).

IMAGINATION

1   Man is an imagining being.

GASTON BACHELARD (1884–1962), French scientist, philosopher, literary theorist. *The Poetics of Reverie,* ch. 2, sct. 10 (1960; tr. 1969).

2   The human imagination . . . has great difficulty in living strictly within the confines of a materialist practice or philosophy. It dreams, like a dog in its basket, of hares in the open.

JOHN BERGER (b. 1926), British author, critic. "The Soul and the Operator," in *Expressen* (Stockholm, 19 March 1990; repr. in *Keeping a Rendezvous,* 1992).

3   To me this world is all one continued vision of fancy or imagination, and I feel flattered when I am told so. What is it sets Homer, Virgil and Milton in so high a rank of art? Why is the Bible more entertaining and instructive than any other book? Is it not because they are addressed to the imagination, which is spiritual sensation, and but mediately to the understanding or reason?

WILLIAM BLAKE (1757–1827), English poet, painter, engraver. Letter, 23 Aug. 1799 (published in *Complete Writings,* ed. by Geoffrey Keynes, 1957).

4   To reduce the imagination to a state of slavery—even though it would mean the elimination of what is commonly called happiness—is to betray all sense of absolute justice within oneself. Imagination alone offers me some intimation of what *can be.*

ANDRÉ BRETON (1896–1966), French surrealist. *Manifesto of Surrealism* (1924; repr. in *Manifestos of Surrealism,* 1969).

5   Fortunately, somewhere between chance and mystery lies imagination, the only thing that protects our freedom, despite the fact that people keep trying to reduce it or kill it off altogether.

LUIS BUÑUEL (1900–83), Spanish filmmaker. *My Last Sigh,* ch. 15 (1983), from his autobiography.

6   Only in men's imagination does every truth find an effective and undeniable existence. Imagination, not invention, is the supreme master of art as of life.

JOSEPH CONRAD (1857–1924), Polish-born English novelist. *A Personal Record,* ch. 1 (1912).

7   The imaginations which people have of one another are the *solid facts* of society.

CHARLES HORTON COOLEY (1864–1929), U.S. sociologist. *Human Nature and the Social Order,* ch. 3 (1902).

8   What is the imagination? Only an arm or weapon of the interior energy; only the precursor of the reason.

RALPH WALDO EMERSON (1803–82), U.S. essayist, poet, philosopher. *Society and Solitude,* "Books" (1870).

9   Imagination is the eye of the soul.

JOSEPH JOUBERT (1754–1824), French essayist, moralist. *Pensées,* no. 42 (1842).

10   My imagination is a monastery and I am its monk.

JOHN KEATS (1795–1821), English poet. Letter, 16 Aug. 1820, to Percy Bysshe Shelley (published in *Letters of John Keats,* no. 227, ed. by Frederick Page, 1954).

11   My imagination makes me human and makes me a fool; it gives me all the world and exiles me from it.

URSULA K. LE GUIN (b. 1929), U.S. author. "Winged: the Creatures on my Mind," in *Harper's* (New York, Aug. 1990).

12   Imagination is the voice of daring. If there is anything Godlike about God it is that. He dared to imagine everything.

HENRY MILLER (1891–1980), U.S. author. *Sexus,* ch. 14 (1949).

13   The genius of Man in our time has gone into jet-propulsion, atom-splitting, penicillin-curing, etc. There is none over for works of imagination; of spiritual insight or mystical enlightenment. I asked for bread and was given a tranquilliser. It is important to recognise that in our time man has not written one word, thought one thought, put two notes or two bricks together, splashed colour on to canvas or concrete into space, in a manner which will be of any conceivable *imaginative* interest to posterity.

MALCOLM MUGGERIDGE (1903–90), British broadcaster. *Tread Softly For You Tread on My Jokes,* "I Like Dwight" (1966).

14   Imagination, the supreme delight of the immortal and the immature, should be limited. In order to enjoy life, we should not enjoy it too much.

VLADIMIR NABOKOV (1899–1977), Russian-born U.S. novelist, poet. *Speak, Memory,* ch. 1, sct. 1 (1955; rev. 1966).

15   It will be found, in fact, that the ingenious are always fanciful, and the *truly* imaginative never otherwise than analytic.

EDGAR ALLAN POE (1809–45), U.S. poet, critic, short-story writer. *The Murders in the Rue Morgue* (1841).

16   It is more than likely that the brain itself is, in origin and development, only a sort of great clot of genital fluid held in suspense or reserved . . . This hypothesis . . . would explain the enormous content of the brain as a maker or presenter of images.

EZRA POUND (1885–1972), U.S. poet, critic. "Translator's Postscript" to Pound's translation of Remy de Gourmont, *Physique de l'Amour* (1922).

17   It is eminently a *weariable* faculty, eminently delicate, and incapable of bearing fatigue; so that if we give it too many objects at a time to employ itself upon, or very grand ones for a long time together, it fails under the effort, becomes jaded, exactly as the limbs do by bodily fatigue, and incapable of answering any farther appeal till it has had rest.

JOHN RUSKIN (1819–1900), English art critic, author. *Modern Painters*, vol. 3, pt. 4, ch. 10, sct. 14–15 (1856), referring to the imagination.

18   The imagination is the spur of delights . . . all depends upon it, it is the mainspring of everything; now, is it not by means of the imagination one knows joy? Is it not of the imagination that the sharpest pleasures arise?

MARQUIS DE SADE (1740–1814), French author. Dolmancé, in *Philosophy in the Bedroom*, "Dialogue the Third" (1795).

19   How delightful are the pleasures of the imagination! In those delectable moments, the whole world is ours; not a single creature resists us, we devastate the world, we repopulate it with new objects which, in turn, we immolate. The means to every crime is ours, and we employ them all, we multiply the horror a hundredfold.

MARQUIS DE SADE (1740–1814), French author. Belmor, in *L'Histoire de Juliette, ou les Prospérités du Vice*, pt. 3 (1797).

20   The great instrument of moral good is the imagination.

PERCY BYSSHE SHELLEY (1792–1822), English poet. *A Defence of Poetry* (written 1821; published 1840). This axiom was the cornerstone of Shelley's philosophy.

21   To regard the imagination as metaphysics is to think of it as part of life, and to think of it as part of life is to realize the extent of artifice. We live in the mind.

WALLACE STEVENS (1879–1955), U.S. poet. *The Necessary Angel*, "Imagination as Value" (1949; repr. 1951).

22   The imagination is man's power over nature.

WALLACE STEVENS (1879–1955), U.S. poet. *Opus Posthumous*, "Adagia" (1959).

23   Perhaps in a book review it is not out of place to note that the safety of the state depends on cultivating the imagination.

STEPHEN VIZINCZEY (b. 1933), Hungarian novelist, critic. "Mind of a Mass Murderer," review of Gitta Sereny, *Into That Darkness*, in *Sunday Telegraph* (London, 8 Sept. 1974; repr. in *Truth and Lies in Literature*, 1986).

24   Imagination is always the fabric of social life and the dynamic of history. The influence of real needs and compulsions, of real interests and materials, is indirect because the crowd is never conscious of it.

SIMONE WEIL (1909–43), French philosopher, mystic. "A Note on Social Democracy" (written 1937; published in *Selected Essays*, ed. by Richard Rees, 1962).

See also Terry on ACTING; FANTASY; Shelley on GOODNESS; George Weiss on IDEALISM; Keats on MUSIC; Blake on NATURE; Spacks on WOMEN.

IMITATION

1   Man is an idiot. He doesn't know how to do anything without copying, without imitating, without plagiarizing, without aping. It might even have been that man invented generation by coitus after seeing the grasshopper copulate.

AUGUSTO ROA BASTOS (b. 1917), Paraguayan novelist. *I The Supreme* (1974; tr. 1986; 1988, p. 133).

2   An original artist is unable to copy. So he has only to copy in order to be original.

JEAN COCTEAU (1889–1963), French author, filmmaker. *Le Rappel à l'Ordre*, "Le Coq et l'Arlequin" (1926; repr. in *Collected Works*, vol. 9, 1950).

3   Those who do not want to imitate anything, produce nothing.

SALVADOR DALI (1904–89), Spanish painter. *Dali by Dali*, "The Futuristic Dali" (1970).

4   Imitation, if it is not forgery, is a fine thing. It stems from a generous impulse, and a realistic sense of what can and cannot be done.

JAMES FENTON (b. 1949), British poet, critic. "Ars Poetica," no. 47, in *Independent on Sunday* (London, 16 Dec. 1990).

5   When people are free to do as they please, they usually imitate each other.

ERIC HOFFER (1902–1983), U.S. philosopher. *The Passionate State of Mind*, aph. 33 (1955). Hoffer adds, "A society which gives unlimited freedom to the individual, more often than not attains a disconcerting sameness. On the other hand, where communal discipline is strict but not ruthless . . . originality is likely to thrive."

6   Almost all absurdity of conduct arises from the imitation of those whom we cannot resemble.

SAMUEL JOHNSON (1709–84), English author, lexicographer. *Rambler*, no. 135 (London, 2 July 1751; repr. in *Works of Samuel Johnson*, vol. 4, ed. by W. J. Bate and Albrecht B. Strauss, 1969).

7   The only good copies are those which make us see the absurdity of bad originals.

FRANÇOIS, DUC DE LA ROCHEFOUCAULD (1613–80), French writer, moralist. *Sentences et Maximes Morales*, no. 133 (1678).

8   To do the opposite of something is also a form of imitation, namely an imitation of its opposite.

G. C. LICHTENBERG (1742–99), German physicist, philosopher. *Aphorisms*, "Notebook D," aph. 96 (written 1765–99; tr. by R. J. Hollingdale, 1990).

9   Men nearly always follow the tracks made by others and proceed in their affairs by imitation, even though they cannot entirely keep to the tracks of others or emulate the prowess of their models. So a prudent man should always follow in the footsteps of great men and imitate those who have been outstanding. If his own prowess fails to compare with theirs, at least it has an air of greatness about it. He should behave like those archers who, if they are skilful, when the target seems too distant, know the capabilities of their bow and aim a good deal higher than their objective, not in order to shoot so high but so that by aiming high they can reach the target.

> NICCOLÒ MACHIAVELLI (1469–1527), Italian political philosopher, statesman. *The Prince*, ch. 6 (1514).

10 Artistic genius is an expansion of monkey imitativeness.

> W. WINWOOD READE (1838–75), English traveler, author. *The Martyrdom of Man*, ch. 3, "Materials of Human History" (1872).

11 Man's natural character is to imitate; that of the sensitive man is to resemble as closely as possible the person whom he loves. It is only by imitating the vices of others that I have earned my misfortunes.

> MARQUIS DE SADE (1740–1814), French author. Letter, 15 Aug. 1781, to his wife from Vincennes prison (published in *Selected Letters*, no. 9, ed. by Margaret Crosland, 1965).

12 Posterity weaves no garlands for imitators.

> FRIEDRICH VON SCHILLER (1759–1805), German dramatist, poet, historian. *Wallenstein's Camp*, Prologue (1798).

13 Nature is commonplace. Imitation is more interesting.

> GERTRUDE STEIN (1874–1946), U.S. author. Quoted in: Charlie Chaplin, *My Autobiography*, ch. 20 (1964).

See also Child on NATURE; Picasso on SUCCESS.

IMMIGRATION

1 The making of an American begins at the point where he himself rejects all other ties, any other history, and himself adopts the vesture of his adopted land.

> JAMES BALDWIN (1924–87), U.S. author. "Many Thousands Gone," in *Partisan Review* (New Brunswick, N.J., Nov.–Dec. 1951; repr. in *Notes of a Native Son*, pt. 1, 1955).

2 Alien. An American sovereign in his probationary state.

> AMBROSE BIERCE (1842–1914), U.S. author. *The Devil's Dictionary* (1881–1906).

3 There is nothing less to our credit than our neglect of the foreigner and his children, unless it be the arrogance most of us betray when we set out to "americanize" him.

> CHARLES HORTON COOLEY (1864–1929), U.S. sociologist. *Human Nature and the Social Order*, ch. 6 (1902).

4 The proposition that Muslims are welcome in Britain if, and only if, they stop behaving like Muslims is a doctrine which is incompatible with the principles that guide a free society.

> ROY HATTERSLEY (b. 1932), British Labour politician. *Independent* (London, 21 July 1989).

5 It almost seems that nobody can hate America as much as native Americans. America needs new immigrants to love and cherish it.

> ERIC HOFFER (1902–83), U.S. philosopher. *Reflections on the Human Condition*, aph. 52 (1973).

6 "Keep, ancient lands, your storied pomp!" cries she

With silent lips. "Give me your tired, your poor,
Your huddled masses yearning to breathe free,
The wretched refuse of your teeming shore.
Send these, the homeless, tempest-tossed, to me;
I lift my lamp beside the golden door."

> EMMA LAZARUS (1849–87), U.S. poet. *The New Colossus*, (1886), written for inscription on the Statue of Liberty.

7 The great social adventure of America is no longer the conquest of the wilderness but the absorption of fifty different peoples.

> WALTER LIPPMANN (1889–1974), U.S. journalist. *A Preface to Politics*, ch. 6 (1914).

8 Every immigrant who comes here should be required within five years to learn English or leave the country.

> THEODORE ROOSEVELT (1858–1919), U.S. Republican (later Progressive) politician, president. *Kansas City Star* (27 April 1918).

9 Without comprehension, the immigrant would forever remain shut—a stranger in America. Until America can release the heart as well as train the hand of the immigrant, he would forever remain driven back upon himself, corroded by the very richness of the unused gifts within his soul.

> ANZIA YEZIERSKA (1881?–1970), Polish-American author. *Hungry Hearts and Other Stories*, pt. 3, "How I Found America" (1920). Anzia Yezierska, born in Russian Poland, emigrated to the USA at age seventeen.

IMMORTALITY

1 I don't want to achieve immortality through my work . . . I want to achieve it through not dying.

> WOODY ALLEN (b. 1935), U.S. filmmaker. Quoted in: Edward Lax, *Woody Allen and his Comedy*, ch. 12 (1975).

2 Immortality is what nature possesses without effort and without anybody's assistance, and immortality is what the mortals must therefore try to achieve if they want to live up to the world into which they were born, to live up to the things which surround them and to whose company they are admitted for a short while.

> HANNAH ARENDT (1906–75), German-born U.S. political philosopher. *Between Past and Future*, ch. 2 (1961).

3 Every idea is endowed of itself with immortal life, like a human being. All created form, even that which is created by man, is immortal. For form is independent of matter: molecules do not constitute form.

> CHARLES BAUDELAIRE (1821–67), French poet. *My Heart Laid Bare*, sct. 102 (written c. 1865; published in *Intimate Journals*, 1887; tr. by Christopher Isherwood, 1930; rev. by Don Bachardy, 1989).

4 Films and gramophone records, music, books and buildings show clearly how vigorously a man's life and work go on after his "death," whether we feel it or not, whether we are aware of the individual names or not. . . . There is no such thing as death according to our view!

> MARTIN BORMANN (1900–1945), German Nazi leader. Memorandum, 17 Feb. 1944 (published in *The Bormann Letters*, ed. by Hugh Trevor-Roper, 1954).

5 To himself every one is an immortal. He may know that he is going to die, but he can never know that he is dead.

SAMUEL BUTLER (1835–1902), English author. *Samuel Butler's Notebooks* (1951, p. 117).

6 It has been said that the immortality of the soul is a "grand peut-être"—but still it is a *grand* one. Everybody clings to it—the stupidest, and dullest, and wickedest of human bipeds is still persuaded that he is immortal.

LORD BYRON (1788–1824), English poet. *Ravenna Journal* (published in *Byron's Letters and Journals*, vol. 8, ed. by Leslie A. Marchand, 1973–81), entry for 25 Jan. 1821.

7 For them that think death's honesty
Won't fall upon them naturally
Life sometimes
Must get lonely.

BOB DYLAN (b. 1941), U.S. singer, songwriter. "It's Alright Ma (I'm Only Bleeding)," on the album *Bringing it all Back Home* (1965).

8 Higher than the question of our duration is the question of our deserving. Immortality will come to such as are fit for it, and he would be a great soul in future must be a great soul now.

RALPH WALDO EMERSON (1803–82), U.S. essayist, poet, philosopher. *The Conduct of Life*, "Worship" (1860).

9 He had decided to live for ever or die in the attempt.

JOSEPH HELLER (b. 1923), U.S. author. *Catch-22*, ch. 3 (1961), of Yossarian.

10 Immortal mortals, mortal immortals, one living the others' death and dying the others' life.

HERACLITUS (c. 535-c. 475 B.C.), Greek philosopher. *The Cosmic Fragments*, no. 67 (c. 480 B.C.).

11 Perhaps nature is our best assurance of immortality.

ELEANOR ROOSEVELT (1884–1962), U.S. columnist, lecturer. "My Day," syndicated newspaper column (24 April 1945).

12 But thy eternal summer shall not fade.

WILLIAM SHAKESPEARE (1564–1616), English dramatist, poet. *Sonnet* 18.

13 The belief in immortality has always seemed cowardly to me. When very young I learned that all things die, and all that we wish of good must be won on this earth or not at all.

ANNE SMEDLEY (c. 1894–1950), U.S. author, lecturer. *Battle Hymn of China*, bk. 1, "The Pattern" (1943).

14 To achieve great things we must live as though we were never going to die.

LUC, MARQUIS DE VAUVENARGUES (1715–47), French moralist. *Refléxions et Maximes*, no. 142 (1746).

15 Deathlessness should be arrived at in a . . . haphazard fashion. Loving fame as much as any man, we shall carve our initials in the shell of a tortoise and turn him loose in a peat bog.

E. B. WHITE (1899–1985), U.S. author, editor. "Immortality," in *New Yorker* (28 March 1936; repr. in *Writings from the New Yorker 1927–1976*, ed. by Rebecca M. Dale, 1991).

16 Man, as long as he lives, is immortal. One minute before his death he shall be immortal. But one minute later, God wins.

ELIE WIESEL (b. 1928), Rumanian-born U.S. writer. Interview in *Writers at Work* (Eighth Series, ed. George Plimpton, 1988), paraphrasing Jewish tradition.

See also Hebrew Bible, Young on DEATH AND DYING; ETERNITY; Byron on the SOUL.

IMPARTIALITY

1 The man who insists upon seeing with perfect clearness before he decides, never decides. Accept life, and you must accept regret.

HENRI-FRÉDÉRIC AMIEL (1821–81), Swiss philosopher, poet. *Journal Intime* (1882; tr. by Mrs. Humphrey Ward, 1892), entry for 17 Dec. 1856.

2 If we keep an open mind, too much is likely to fall into it.

NATALIE CLIFFORD BARNEY (1876–1972), U.S.-born French author. Quoted in: "Samples from Almost Illegible Notebooks," in *Adam*, no 299 (London, 1962).

3 Impartial. Unable to perceive any promise of personal advantage from espousing either side of a controversy.

AMBROSE BIERCE (1842–1914), U.S. author. *The Devil's Dictionary* (1881–1906).

4 What people call impartiality may simply mean indifference, and what people call partiality may simply mean mental activity.

G. K. CHESTERTON (1874–1936), British author. *All Things Considered*, "The Error of Impartiality" (1908).

5 Our impartiality is kept for abstract merit and demerit, which none of us ever saw.

GEORGE ELIOT (1819–80), English novelist, editor. *Middlemarch*, bk. 4, ch. 40 (1871).

6 Balance is the enemy of art.

RICHARD EYRE (b. 1943), British theater, film and TV director. *Independent* (London, 28 Oct. 1992).

7 Man is always partial and is quite right to be. Even impartiality is partial.

G. C. LICHTENBERG (1742–99), German physicist, philosopher. *Aphorisms*, "Notebook F," aph. 78 (written 1765–99; tr. by R. J. Hollingdale, 1990).

8 The man who sees both sides of a question is a man who sees absolutely nothing at all.

OSCAR WILDE (1854–1900), Anglo-Irish playwright, author. Gilbert, in *The Critic as Artist*, pt. 2 (published in *Intentions*, 1891).

IMPOTENCE

1 All it means, if you wilt that way with a lady, is that you haven't yet really met her. You're not trying to make love to a woman, you're trying not to miss an opportunity.

CLIVE JAMES (b. 1939), Australian writer, critic, TV host. *Falling Towards England*, ch. 8 (1985).

2   This is the monstruosity in love, lady—that the will is infinite and the execution confined; that the desire is boundless and the act a slave to limit.

> WILLIAM SHAKESPEARE (1564–1616), English dramatist, poet. Troilus, in *Troilus and Cressida*, act 3, sc. 2, referring to the discrepancy between lovers' aspirations and their desires.

3   Thou treacherous, base deserter of my flame,
False to my passion, fatal to my fame,
Through what mistaken magic dost thou prove
So true to lewdness, so untrue to love?

> JOHN WILMOT, SECOND EARL OF ROCHESTER (1647–80), English poet, courtier. *The Imperfect Enjoyment.*

IMPULSE

1   It will be difficult for me not to make sport for the Philistines by pulling down a house or two, since when I once take pen in hand, I *must* say what comes uppermost, or fling it away.

> LORD BYRON (1788–1824), English poet. Letter, 6 June 1822, to publisher John Murray (published in *Byron's Letters and Journals*, vol. 9, ed. by Leslie A. Marchand, 1979).

2   The awful daring of a moment's surrender
Which an age of prudence can never retract.

> T. S. ELIOT (1888–1965), Anglo-American poet, critic. *The Wasteland*, pt. 5, "What the Thunder Said" (1922).

3   The most decisive actions of our life—I mean those that are most likely to decide the whole course of our future—are, more often than not, unconsidered.

> ANDRÉ GIDE (1869–1951), French author. Hildebrant, in *The Counterfeiters*, pt. 3, ch. 16 (1925).

INCEST

1   Sexual abuse of children now presents society with the ultimate crisis of patriarchy, when children refuse to protect their fathers by keeping secrets.

> BEATRIX CAMPBELL (b. 1947), British journalist. *Unofficial Secrets*, ch. 2 (1988).

2   As long as fathers rule but do not nurture, as long as mothers nurture but do not rule, the conditions favoring the development of father-daughter incest will prevail.

> JUDITH LEWIS HERMAN (b. 1942), U.S. author. *Father-Daughter Incest* (1981).

3   Philosophically, incest asks a fundamental question of our shifting mores: not simply what is normal and what is deviant, but whether such a thing as deviance exists at all in human relationships if they seem satisfactory to those who share them.

> ELISABETH JANEWAY (b. 1913), U.S. author, critic. "Incest: A Rational Look at the Oldest Taboo," in *Ms.* (New York, Nov. 1981).

4   The protection of a ten-year-old girl from her father's advances is a necessary condition of social order, but the protection of the father from temptation is a necessary condition of his continued social adjustment. The protections that are built up in the child against desire for the parent become the essential counterpart to the attitudes in the parent that protect the child.

> MARGARET MEAD (1901–78), U.S. anthropologist. *Male and Female*, ch. 9 (1949).

INCONSISTENCY

1   Wise men are not wise at all hours, and will speak five times from their taste or their humor, to once from their reason.

> RALPH WALDO EMERSON (1803–82), U.S. essayist, poet, philosopher. *The Conduct of Life*, "Wealth" (1860).

2   Like the British Constitution, she owes her success in practice to her inconsistencies in principle.

> THOMAS HARDY (1840–1928), English novelist, poet. Mrs. Napper, in *The Hand of Ethelberta*, ch. 9 (1876), speaking of Ethelberta.

3   People who honestly mean to be true really contradict themselves much more rarely than those who try to be "consistent."

> OLIVER WENDELL HOLMES, SR. (1809–94), U.S. writer, physician. *The Professor at the Breakfast Table*, ch. 2 (1860).

4   Do I contradict myself?
Very well then I contradict myself,
(I am large, I contain multitudes).

> WALT WHITMAN (1819–92), U.S. poet. *Song of Myself*, sct. 51, in *Leaves of Grass* (1855).

INDECISION

1   He has conferred on the practice of vacillation the aura of statesmanship.

> KENNETH BAKER (b. 1934), British Conservative politician. *Daily Telegraph* (London, 11 Oct. 1989), on S.D.P. leader Dr. David Owen.

2   You need an infinite stretch of time ahead of you to start to think, infinite energy to make the smallest decision. The world is getting denser. The immense number of useless projects is bewildering. Too many things have to be put in to balance up an uncertain scale. You can't disappear anymore. You die in a state of total indecision.

> JEAN BAUDRILLARD (b. 1929), French semiologist. *Cool Memories*, ch. 3 (1987; tr. 1990).

3   We know what happens to people who stay in the middle of the road. They get run over.

> ANEURIN BEVAN (1897–1960), British Labour politician. Quoted in: *Observer* (London, 9 Dec. 1935).

4   How long halt ye between two opinions?

> BIBLE, HEBREW. Elijah, speaking to the children of Israel, in *1 Kings* 18:21.

5   Neither have they hearts to stay,
Nor wit enough to run away.

> SAMUEL BUTLER (1612–80), English poet. *Hudibras*, pt. 3, cto. 3.

6   In a minute there is time

For decisions and revisions which a minute will reverse.

T. S. ELIOT (1888–1965), Anglo-American poet, critic. *The Love Song of J. Alfred Prufrock*.

7 There is no more miserable human being than one in whom nothing is habitual but indecision, and for whom the lighting of every cigar, the drinking of every cup, the time of rising and going to bed every day, and the beginning of every bit of work, are subjects of express volitional deliberation.

WILLIAM JAMES (1842–1910), U.S. psychologist, philosopher. *Principles of Psychology*, vol. 1, ch. 4 (1890).

8 The human heart is like a ship on a stormy sea driven about by winds blowing from all four corners of heaven.

MARTIN LUTHER (1483–1546), German leader of the Protestant Reformation. Preface to his translation of the *Psalms* (1534).

9 Perhaps, on the whole, embarrassment and perplexity are a kind of natural accompaniment to life and movement; and it is better to be driven out of your senses with thinking which of two things you ought to do than to do nothing whatever, and be utterly uninteresting to all the world.

MARGARET OLIPHANT (1828–97), English novelist, historian. Miss Marjoribanks, in *Chronicles of Carlingford*, bk. 4, *Miss Marjoribanks*, ch. 38 (1866).

10 Most men ebb and flow in wretchedness between the fear of death and the hardship of life; they are unwilling to live, and yet they do not know how to die.

SENECA (c. 5 B.C.– A.D. c. 65), Roman writer, philosopher, statesman. *Epistulae ad Lucilium*, Epistle 4, sct. 6.

11 He who hesitates is sometimes saved.

JAMES THURBER (1894–1961), U.S. humorist, illustrator. *The Thurber Carnival*, "The Glass in the Field" (1945).

12 I must have a prodigious quantity of mind; it takes me as much as a week, sometimes, to make it up.

MARK TWAIN (1835–1910), U.S. author. *The Innocents Abroad*, ch. 7 (1869).

INDEPENDENCE

1 Nature never said to me: *Do not be poor;* still less did she say: *Be rich;* her cry to me was always: *Be independent.*

SÉBASTIEN-ROCH NICOLAS DE CHAMFORT (1741–94), French writer, wit. *Maxims and Considerations*, vol. 1, no. 281 (1796; tr. 1926).

2 In the word of no master am I bound to believe.

HORACE (65–8 B.C.), Roman poet. *Epistles*, bk. 1, Epistle 1 (22–8 B.C.), hence *nullius in verba*—the motto of the Royal Society of London.

3 The thing is, you see, that the strongest man in the world is the man who stands alone.

HENRIK IBSEN (1828–1906), Norwegian dramatist. Dr. Stockmann, in *An Enemy of the People*, act 5.

4 It's easy to be independent when you've got money. But to be independent when you haven't got a thing—that's the Lord's test.

MAHALIA JACKSON (1911–72), U.S. gospel singer. *Movin' On Up*, ch. 1 (1966; written with Evan McLoud Wylie).

5 I equally dislike the favour of the public with the love of a woman—they are both a cloying treacle to the wings of independence.

JOHN KEATS (1795–1821), English poet. Letter, 23 Aug. 1819 (published in *Letters of John Keats*, no. 144, ed. by Frederick Page, 1954).

6 Our treatment of both older people and children reflects the value we place on independence and autonomy. We do our best to make our children independent from birth. We leave them all alone in rooms with the lights out and tell them, "Go to sleep by yourselves." And the old people we respect most are the ones who will fight for their independence, who would sooner starve to death than ask for help.

MARGARET MEAD (1901–78), U.S. anthropologist. Quoted in: *Family Circle* (New York, 26 July 1977).

7 The man who goes alone can start today; but he who travels with another must wait till that other is ready, and it may be a long time before they get off.

HENRY DAVID THOREAU (1817–62), U.S. philosopher, author, naturalist. *Walden*, "Economy" (1854).

8 The beauty of independence, departure, actions
that rely on themselves.

WALT WHITMAN (1819–92), U.S. poet. *Song of the Broad Axe*, sct. 3.

9 Independence I have long considered as the grand blessing of life, the basis of every virtue; and independence I will ever secure by contracting my wants, though I were to live on a barren heath.

MARY WOLLSTONECRAFT (1759–97), English feminist writer. *A Vindication of the Rights of Women*, "Dedication" (1792).

See also AUTONOMY; Cobbett on POVERTY AND THE POOR.

INDIANS, AMERICAN

See NATIVE AMERICANS.

INDIFFERENCE

1 Lukewarmness I account a sin,
As great in love as in religion.

ABRAHAM COWLEY (1618–67), English essayist, poet. *The Request*.

2 Wherever the citizen becomes indifferent to his fellows, so will the husband be to his wife, and the father of a family toward the members of his household.

KARL WILHELM VON HUMBOLDT (1767–1835), German statesman, philologist. *Limits of State Action*, ch. 3 (1792; repr. 1854; tr. and ed. by J. W. Burrow, 1969).

3 I have protracted my work till most of those whom I wished to please have sunk into the grave, and success and miscarriage are empty sounds: I therefore dismiss it with frigid tranquillity, having little to fear or hope from censure or from praise.

> SAMUEL JOHNSON (1709–84), English author, lexicographer. *Dictionary of the English Language,* Preface (1755).

4 Nothing can contribute more to peace of soul than the lack of any opinion whatever.

> G. C. LICHTENBERG (1742–99), German physicist, philosopher. *Aphorisms,* "Notebook E," aph. 11 (written 1765–99; tr. by R. J. Hollingdale, 1990).

5 Pain has its reasons, pleasure is totally indifferent.

> FRANCIS PICABIA (1878–1953), French painter, poet. *Who Knows: Poems and Aphorisms* (1950; 1986, p. 50).

6 It means nothing to me. I have no opinion about it, and I don't care.

> PABLO PICASSO (1881–1973), Spanish artist. Quoted in: *New York Times* (21 July 1969), reacting to the first moon-landing.

7 The worst sin towards our fellow creatures is not to hate them, but to be indifferent to them; that's the essence of inhumanity.

> GEORGE BERNARD SHAW (1856–1950), Anglo-Irish playwright, critic. Anderson, in *The Devil's Disciple,* act 2.

8 Men are accomplices to that which leaves them indifferent.

> GEORGE STEINER (b. 1929), French-born U.S. critic, novelist. *Language and Silence,* "A Kind of Survivor" (1967).

9 The opposite of love is not hate, it's indifference. The opposite of art is not ugliness, it's indifference. The opposite of faith is not heresy, it's indifference. And the opposite of life is not death, it's indifference.

> ELIE WIESEL (b. 1928), Rumanian-born U.S. writer. *U.S. News and World Report* (New York, 27 Oct. 1986).

See also APATHY.

INDIVIDUALITY

1 The greatest enemy of individual freedom is the individual himself.

> SAUL ALINSKY (1909–72), U.S. radical activist. *Rules for Radicals,* Prologue (1971).

2 More and more, when faced with the world of men, the only reaction is one of individualism. Man alone is an end unto himself. Everything one tries to do for the common good ends in failure.

> ALBERT CAMUS (1913–60), French-Algerian philosopher, author. *Notebooks 1935–1942* (1962), March 1940 entry.

3 Losing faith in your own singularity is the start of wisdom, I suppose; also the first announcement of death.

> PETER CONRAD (b. 1948), Australian critic, author. *Down Under: Revisiting Tasmania,* pt. 6, "In the Family" (1988).

4 Each man must have his "I"; it is more necessary to him than bread; and if he does not find scope for it within the existing institutions he will be likely to make trouble.

> CHARLES HORTON COOLEY (1864–1929), U.S. sociologist. *Human Nature and the Social Order,* ch. 6 (1902).

5 Individuality is the aim of political liberty. By leaving to the citizen as much freedom of action and of being, as comports with order and the rights of others, the institutions render him truly a freeman. He is left to pursue his means of happiness in his own manner.

> JAMES FENIMORE COOPER (1789–1851), U.S. novelist. *The American Democrat,* "Individuality" (1838).

6 The trouble with the sacred Individual is that he has no significance, except as he can acquire it from others, from the social whole.

> BERNARD DEVOTO (1897–1955), U.S. historian, critic. "The Easy Chair," in *Harper's* (New York, May 1941).

7 The individual, man as a man, man as a brain, if you like, interests me more than what he makes, because I've noticed that most artists only repeat themselves.

> MARCEL DUCHAMP (1887–1968), French artist. *Dialogues with Marcel Duchamp,* ch. 5 (ed. by Pierre Cabanne, 1967).

8 Each man must grant himself the emotions that he needs and the morality that suits him.

> RÉMY DE GOURMONT (1858–1915), French critic, novelist. "Success and the Idea of Beauty," sct. 3 (published in *Le Chemin de Velours,* 1902; repr. in *Selected Writings,* ed. and tr. by Glen S. Burne, 1966).

9 *Why runners make lousy communists.* In a word, *individuality.* It's the one characteristic all runners, as different as they are, seem to share . . . Stick with it. Push yourself. Keep running. And you'll never lose that wonderful sense of individuality you now enjoy. Right, comrade?

> ADVERTISEMENT FOR RUNNING SHOES at the 1984 Olympic Games in Los Aangeles. Quoted in: *Guardian* (London, 29 Dec. 1984).

10 In each individual the spirit is made flesh, in each one the whole of creation suffers, in each one a Savior is crucified.

> HERMANN HESSE (1877–1962), German novelist, poet. Narrator (Sinclair), in *Demian,* Prologue (1960).

11 It is the individual only who is timeless. Societies, cultures, and civilizations—past and present—are often incomprehensible to outsiders, but the individual's hungers, anxieties, dreams, and preoccupations have remained unchanged through the millenia.

> ERIC HOFFER (1902–83), U.S. philosopher. *Reflections on the Human Condition,* aph. 183 (1973).

12 The great challenge which faces us is to assure that, in our society of big-ness, we do not strangle the voice of creativity, that the rules of the game do not come to overshadow its purpose, that the grand orchestration of society leaves ample room for the man who marches to the music of another drummer.

> HUBERT H. HUMPHREY (1911–78), U.S. Democratic politician, vice president. Address, 29 June 1966, United States Junior Chamber of Commerce, Detroit, Mich.

13 Resistance to the organized mass can be effected only by the man who is as well organized in his individuality as the mass itself.

> CARL JUNG (1875–1961), Swiss psychiatrist. *The Undiscovered Self,* ch. 4 (1957; repr. in *Collected Works,* vol. 10, para. 540, ed. by William McGuire, 1964).

14　Comrades! We must abolish the cult of the individual decisively, once and for all.

> NIKITA KHRUSHCHEV (1894–1971), Soviet premier. Speech, 25 Feb. 1956, to the secret session of the 20th Congress of the Communist Party. Khrushchev used the occasion to identify Stalin as the chief exponent of the cult of the individual by "the glorification of his own person."

15　The definition of the individual was: a multitude of one million divided by one million.

> ARTHUR KOESTLER (1905–83), Hungarian-born British author. *Darkness at Noon,* "The Grammatical Fiction" (1940), on the teaching of the Party.

16　A gesture cannot be regarded as the expression of an individual, as his creation (because no individual is capable of creating a fully original gesture, belonging to nobody else), nor can it even be regarded as that person's instrument; on the contrary, it is gestures that use us as their instruments, as their bearers and incarnations.

> MILAN KUNDERA (b. 1929), Czech author, critic. *Immortality,* pt. 1, ch. 2 (1991).

17　Except in a few well-publicized instances (enough to lend credence to the iconography painted on the walls of the media), the rigorous practice of rugged individualism usually leads to poverty, ostracism and disgrace. The rugged individualist is too often mistaken for the misfit, the maverick, the spoilsport, the sore thumb.

> LEWIS H. LAPHAM (b. 1935), U.S. essayist, editor. *Money and Class in America,* ch. 9 (1988).

18　In bourgeois society capital is independent and has individuality, while the living person is dependent and has no individuality.

> KARL MARX (1818–83) AND FRIEDRICH ENGELS (1820–95), German social philosophers, revolutionaries. *The Communist Manifesto,* sct. 2 (1848).

19　What is wanted—whether this is admitted or not—is nothing less than a fundamental remoulding, indeed weakening and abolition of the *individual:* one never tires of enumerating and indicating all that is evil and inimical, prodigal, costly, extravagant in the form individual existence has assumed hitherto, one hopes to manage more cheaply, more safely, more equitably, more uniformly if there exist only *large bodies and their members.*

> FRIEDRICH NIETZSCHE (1844–1900), German philosopher. *Daybreak,* aph. 132 (1881).

20　The nail that sticks up will be hammered down.

> JAPANESE PROVERB.

21　Those who talk about individuality the most are the ones who most object to deviation, and in a few years it may be the other way around. Some day everybody will just think what they want to think, and then everybody will probably be thinking alike; that seems to be what is happening.

> ANDY WARHOL (1928–87), U.S. pop artist. *Art News,* vol. 62, no. 7 (Nov. 1963).

22　America is not anything if it consists of each of us. It is something only if it consists of all of us.

> WOODROW WILSON (1856–1924), U.S. Democratic politician, president. Speech, 29 Jan. 1916, Pittsburgh, Pa.

See also Cocteau on CRITICISM.

INDOLENCE

1　I look upon indolence as a sort of *suicide;* for the man is effectually destroyed, though the appetites of the brute may survive.

> LORD CHESTERFIELD (1694–1773), English statesman, man of letters. Letter, 26 Feb. 1754 (first published 1774; repr. in *The Letters of the Earl of Chesterfield to His Son,* vol. 2, no. 308, ed. by Charles Strachey, 1901).

2　There are men here and there to whom the whole of life is like an after-dinner hour with a cigar; easy, pleasant, empty, perhaps enlivened by some fable of strife to be forgotten—before the end is told—even if there happens to be any end to it.

> JOSEPH CONRAD (1857–1924), Polish-born English novelist. Marlow, in *Lord Jim,* ch. 5 (1900).

3　The present generation, wearied by its chimerical efforts, relapses into complete indolence. Its condition is that of a man who has only fallen asleep towards morning: first of all come great dreams, then a feeling of laziness, and finally a witty or clever excuse for remaining in bed.

> SØREN KIERKEGAARD (1813–55), Danish philosopher. *The Present Age* (1846; tr. 1940).

4　Prostration is our natural position. A wormlike movement from a spot of sunlight to a spot of shade, and back, is the type of movement that is natural to men.

> WYNDHAM LEWIS (1882–1957), British author, painter. *The Art of Being Ruled,* "'Call Yourself a Man!'" (1926).

INDUSTRY

1　It is an axiom, enforced by all the experience of the ages, that they who rule industrially will rule politically.

> ANEURIN BEVAN (1897–1960), British Labour politician. Quoted in: Michael Foot, *Aneurin Bevan,* vol. 1, ch. 2 (1962).

2　Industry has operated against the artisan in favor of the idler, and also in favor of capital and against labor. Any mechanical invention whatsoever has been more harmful to humanity than a century of war.

> RÉMY DE GOURMONT (1858–1915), French critic, novelist. "The Value of Education" (published in *Le Chemin de Velours,* 1902; repr. in *Selected Writings,* ed. and tr. by Glen S. Burne, 1966).

3　Colonial system, public debts, heavy taxes, protection, commercial wars, etc., these offshoots of the period of manufacture swell to gigantic proportions during the period of infancy of large-scale industry. The birth of the latter is celebrated by a vast, Herod-like slaughter of the innocents.

> KARL MARX (1818–83), German political theorist, social philosopher. *Capital,* vol. 1, ch. 31 (1867).

4　We have created an industrial order geared to automatism, where feeble-mindedness, native or acquired, is necessary for docile productivity in the factory; and where a pervasive neurosis is the final gift of the meaningless life that issues forth at the other end.

LEWIS MUMFORD (1895–1990), U.S. social philosopher. *The Conduct of Life,* "The Fulfillment of Man" (1951).

5 It has been my fate in a longlife of production to be credited chiefly with the equivocal virtue of industry, a quality so excellent in morals, so little satisfactory in art.

MARGARET OLIPHANT (1828–97), English novelist, historian. *The Heir Presumptive and the Heir Apparent,* Preface (1892).

6 The reality is that zero defects in products plus zero pollution plus zero risk on the job is equivalent to maximum growth of government plus zero economic growth plus runaway inflation.

DIXIE LEE RAY (b. 1924), U.S. Democratic politician, government official. "Scientists and Engineers for Secure Energy," speech, 1980. Quoted in: Esther Stineman, *American Political Women* (1980).

7 The great cry that rises from all our manufacturing cities, louder than the furnace blast, is all in very deed for this—that we manufacture everything there except men.

JOHN RUSKIN (1819–1900), English art critic, author. *The Stones of Venice,* vol. 2, ch. 6, para. 16 (1851–53).

8 In an industrial society which confuses work and productivity, the necessity of producing has always been an enemy of the desire to create.

RAOUL VANEIGEM (b. 1934), Belgian Situationist philosopher. *The Revolution of Everyday Life,* ch. 5 (1967; tr. 1983).

INEQUALITY

1 The rich man in his castle,
The poor man at his gate,
God made them, high or lowly,
And order'd their estate.

CECIL F. ALEXANDER (1818–95), English poet. *All Things Bright and Beautiful.*

2 When Adam delved and Eve span,
Who was then the gentleman?

JOHN BALL (hanged 1381), English priest, agitator. Verse preached to rebels at Blackheath, outside London, 12 June 1381, during the Peasants' Revolt.

3 My old grannum (rest her soul) was wont to say, there were but two families in the world, have-much and have-little.

MIGUEL DE CERVANTES (1547–1616), Spanish writer. Sancho Panza, in *Don Quixote,* pt. 2, bk. 5, ch. 20 (1615; tr. by P. Motteux).

4 We accept and welcome . . . as conditions to which we must accommodate ourselves, great inequality of environment; the concentration of business, industrial and commercial, in the hands of a few; and the law of competition between these, as being not only beneficial, but essential for the future progress of the race.

ANDREW CARNEGIE (1835–1919), U.S. industrialist, philanthropist. "The Gospel of Wealth," in *North American Review* (Cedar Falls, Iowa, June 1889). Quoted in: Burton J. Hendrick, *Life of Andrew Carnegie,* vol. 1, ch. 17 (1932).

5 The very existence of government at all, infers inequality. The citizen who is preferred to office becomes the superior to those who are not, so long as he is the repository of power, and the child inherits the wealth of the parent as a controlling law of society.

JAMES FENIMORE COOPER (1789–1851), U.S. novelist. *The American Democrat,* "On American Equality" (1838).

6 Two nations between whom there is no intercourse and no sympathy; who are as ignorant of each other's habits, thoughts, and feelings, as if they were dwellers in different zones, or inhabitants of different planets. . . . The rich and the poor.

BENJAMIN DISRAELI (1804–81), English statesman, author. Stephen Morley, in *Sybil,* bk. 2, ch. 5 (1845).

7 The only inequalities that matter begin in the mind. It is not income levels but differences in mental equipment that keep people apart, breed feelings of inferiority.

JACQUETTA HAWKES (b. 1910), British archaeologist. *New Statesman* (London, Jan. 1957).

8 So far is it from being true that men are naturally equal, that no two people can be half an hour together, but one shall acquire an evident superiority over the other.

SAMUEL JOHNSON (1709–84), English author, lexicographer. Quoted in: James Boswell, *Life of Samuel Johnson,* 15 Feb. 1766 (1791).

9 There is always inequality in life. Some men are killed in a war and some men are wounded and some men never leave the country. Life is unfair.

JOHN F. KENNEDY (1917–63), U.S. president. Press conference, 21 March 1962.

10 I never could believe that Providence had sent a few men into the world, ready booted and spurred to ride, and millions ready saddled and bridled to be ridden.

RICHARD RUMBOLD (1622–85), English soldier, conspirator. Speech on the scaffold, Edinburgh, 1685. Quoted in: Macaulay, *History of England,* vol. 1, ch. 5 (1849). Rumbold, one of the guards about the scaffold at the execution of Charles I in 1649, was implicated in the failed rebellion of the Duke of Monmouth, for which both men were executed.

11 There is no good . . . in living in a society where you are merely the equal of everybody else. . . . The true pleasure of life is to live with your inferiors.

WILLIAM MAKEPEACE THACKERAY (1811–63), English author. *The Newcomes,* bk. 1, ch. 9 (1855).

12 However energetically society in general may strive to make all the citizens equal and alike, the personal pride of each individual will always make him try to escape from the common level, and he will form some inequality somewhere to his own profit.

ALEXIS DE TOCQUEVILLE (1805–59), French social philosopher. *Democracy in America,* vol. 2, pt. 3, ch. 13 (1840).

See also CLASS; Schelling on EDUCATION; Woolf on SELF-CONFIDENCE.

INERTIA

1 Nothing happens, nobody comes, nobody goes, it's awful.

SAMUEL BECKETT (1906–89), Irish dramatist, novelist. Estragon, in *Waiting for Godot,* act 1.

2 Lest he should wander irretrievably from the right path, he stands still.

WILLIAM HAZLITT (1778–1830), English essayist. *Lectures on the English Poets,* "On the Living Poets" (1818), of the poet Thomas Campbell.

3 Fix'd like a plan on his peculiar spot,
To draw nutrition, propagate, and rot.

ALEXANDER POPE (1688–1744), English satirical poet. *An Essay on Man,* Epistle 2.

INFALLIBILITY

1 From a worldly point of view, there is no mistake so great as that of being always right.

SAMUEL BUTLER (1835–1902), English author. *Samuel Butler's Notebooks,* p. 250 (1951).

2 We like security: we like the pope to be infallible in matters of faith, and grave doctors to be so in moral questions so that we can feel reassured.

BLAISE PASCAL (1623–62), French scientist, philosopher. *Pensées* (1670; no. 516 ed. by Krailsheimer, no. 880 ed. by Brunschvicg).

3 We are none of us infallible—not even the youngest of us.

WILLIAM HEPWORTH THOMPSON (1810–86), English academic, Master of Trinity College, Cambridge. Quoted in: G. W. E. Russell, *Collections and Recollections,* ch. 18 (1898), referring to G. W. Balfour, then a junior fellow at Trinity College, Cambridge, later politician and Secretary for Ireland. A similar aphorism has been attributed to the Master of Balliol, Oxford, Benjamin Jowett (1817–93): "Even the youngest among us is not infallible."

See also Shaw on The CHURCH; Carlyle on COMPLACENCY.

INFATUATION

1 Can it be that chance has made me one of those women so immersed in one man that, whether they are barren or not, they carry with them to the grave the shriveled innocence of an old maid?

COLETTE (1873–1954), French author. *Break of Day* (1961; repr. in *Earthly Paradise,* pt. 4, "The South of France," ed. by Robert Phelps, 1966).

2 Take me to you, imprison me, for I,
Except you enthrall me, never shall be free,
Nor ever chaste, except you ravish me.

JOHN DONNE (c. 1572–1631), English divine and metaphysical poet. Last lines of *Holy Sonnets,* no. 14.

3 Strange, that some of us, with quick alternate vision, see beyond our infatuations, and even while we rave on the heights, behold the wide plain where our persistent self pauses and awaits us.

GEORGE ELIOT (1819–80), English novelist. *Middlemarch,* bk. 2, ch. 15 (1871–72).

4 I understand by this passion the union of desire, friendship, and tenderness, which is inflamed by a single female, which prefers her to the rest of her sex, and which seeks her possession as the supreme or the sole happiness of our being.

EDWARD GIBBON (1737–94), English historian. *Memoirs of my Life* (1796; published in Routledge, *Autobiography,* 1971, pp. 54–55), of Gibbon's youthful attachment to Mademoiselle Susan Curchod, who he claimed was the only woman in his life, and whom he later rejected. See Gibbon on DUTY.

5 There aren't many irritations to match the condescension which a woman metes out to a man who she believes has loved her vainly for the past umpteen years.

EDWARD HOAGLAND (b. 1932), U.S. novelist, essayist. *Heart's Desire,* "The Lapping, Itchy Edge of Love" (1988).

6 I know I am but summer to your heart,
And not the full four seasons of the year.

EDNA ST. VINCENT MILLAY (1892–1950), U.S. poet. *I know I am but summer to your heart.*

7 One does not kill oneself for love of *a* woman, but because love—any love—reveals us in our nakedness, our misery, our vulnerability, our nothingness.

CESARE PAVESE (1908–50), Italian poet, novelist, translator. *The Burning Brand: Diaries 1935–1950* (1952; tr. 1961), entry for 25 March 1950. See Pavese on SUICIDE.

8 I stalk about her door
Like a strange soul upon the Stygian banks
Staying for waftage.

WILLIAM SHAKESPEARE (1564–1616), English dramatist, poet. Troilus, in *Troilus and Cressida,* act 3, sc. 2.

9 Nay, but Jack, such eyes! such eyes! so innocently wild! so bashfully irresolute! Not a glance but speaks and kindles some thought of love! Then, Jack, her cheeks! her cheeks, Jack! so deeply blushing at the insinuations of her tell-tale eyes! Then, Jack, her lips! O, Jack, lips smiling at their own discretion! and, if not smiling, more sweetly pouting—more lovely in sullenness! Then, Jack, her neck! O, Jack, Jack!

RICHARD BRINSLEY SHERIDAN (1751–1816), Anglo-Irish dramatist. Sir Anthony Absolute, describing Lydia Languish, whom he wants his son to marry, in *The Rivals,* act 3, sc. 1.

10 It is best to love wisely, no doubt: but to love foolishly is better than not to be able to love at all.

WILLIAM MAKEPEACE THACKERAY (1811–63), English author. *Pendennis,* ch. 6 (1848–50).

11 Men who care passionately for women attach themselves at least as much to the temple and to the accessories of the cult as to their goddess herself.

MARGUERITE YOURCENAR (1903–87), French novelist. *Memoirs of Hadrian,* "Varius Multiplex Multi Formis" (1954).

INFIDELITY

1 Inconstancy no sin will prove
If we consider that we love

But the same beauty in another face,
Like the same body in another place.

EDWARD HERBERT (1583–1648), English soldier, diplomat, poet (brother of George Herbert). *Inconstancy.*

2   Men and women are not born inconstant: they are made so by their early amorous experiences.

ANDRE MAUROIS (1885–1967), French author, critic. *The Art of Living,* "The Art of Loving" (1940).

3   A woman one loves rarely suffices for all our needs, so we deceive her with another whom we do not love.

MARCEL PROUST (1871–1922), French novelist. *Remembrance of Things Past,* vol. 12, "Time Regained," ch. 1 (1927; tr. by Stephen Hudson, 1931).

4   Every man wants a woman to appeal to his better side, his nobler instincts and his higher nature—and another woman to help him forget them.

HELEN ROWLAND (1875–1950), U.S. journalist. *A Guide to Men,* "Second Interlude" (1922).

5   No lover, if he be of good faith, and sincere, will deny he would prefer to see his mistress dead than unfaithful.

MARQUIS DE SADE (1740–1814), French author. Noirceuil, in *L'Histoire de Juliette, ou les Prospérités du Vice,* pt. 2 (1797).

6   I had been happy, if the general camp,
Pioneers and all, had tasted her sweet body,
So I had nothing known.

WILLIAM SHAKESPEARE (1564–1616), English dramatist, poet. Othello, in *Othello,* act 3, sc. 3.

7   It is better to have a prosaic husband and to take a romantic lover.

STENDHAL (1783–1842), French author. *De l'Amour,* "Various Fragments," sct. 10 (1822).

8   The hood-winked husband shows his anger, and the word jealous is flung in his face. Jealous husband equals betrayed husband. And there are women who look upon jealousy as synonymous with impotence, so that the betrayed husband can only shut his eyes, powerless in the face of such accusations.

J. AUGUST STRINDBERG (1849–1912), Swedish dramatist, novelist, poet. *A Madman's Defense,* pt. 2, ch. 1 (1968).

9   You may build castles in the air, and fume, and fret, and grow thin and lean, and pale and ugly, if you please. But I tell you, no man worth having is true to his wife, or can be true to his wife, or ever was, or will be so.

SIR JOHN VANBRUGH (1663–1726), British playwright. Berinthia, in *The Relapse; or, Virtue in Danger,* act 3, sc. 2 (1708).

10   Those who are faithful know only the trivial side of love: it is the faithless who know love's tragedies.

OSCAR WILDE (1854–1900), Anglo-Irish playwright, author. Lord Henry, in *The Picture of Dorian Gray,* ch. 1 (1891).

See also ADULTERY; Auden on INTELLECT AND INTELLECTUALS.

INFINITY

1   There is no more steely barb than that of the Infinite.

CHARLES BAUDELAIRE (1821–67), French poet. "The Artist's Confiteor," in *La Presse* (Paris, 26 Aug 1862; repr. in *Complete Works,* vol. 1, "Shorter Prose Poems," ed. by Yves-Gérard le Dantec; rev. by Claude Pichois, 1953).

2   The poetic notion of infinity is far greater than that which is sponsored by any creed.

JOSEPH BRODSKY (b. 1940), Russian-born U.S. poet, critic. Interview in *Writers at Work* (Eighth Series, ed. by George Plimpton, 1988), on the "worrying" fact that W. H. Auden was a formal churchgoer in later life.

3   Whenever we encounter the Infinite in man, however imperfectly understood, we treat it with respect. Whether in the synagogue, the mosque, the pagoda, or the wigwam, there is a hideous aspect which we execrate and a sublime aspect which we venerate. So great a subject for spiritual contemplation, such measureless dreaming—the echo of God on the human wall!

VICTOR HUGO (1802–85), French poet, dramatist, novelist. *Les Misérables,* pt. 2, bk. 7, ch. 1 (1862).

4   I mistrust the satisfaction which makes a display of the possession of Infinity; that is called fatuity in philosophic terms.

EDGAR QUINET (1803–75), French poet, historian, politician. *Ultramontanism, or The Roman Church and Modern Society,* "The Roman Church and Science—Galileo" (published 1845; lecture, 7 May 1844).

5   If any philosopher had been asked for a definition of infinity, he might have produced some unintelligible rigmarole, but he would certainly not have been able to give a definition that had any meaning at all.

BERTRAND RUSSELL (1872–1970), British philosopher, mathematician. *A Free Man's Worship and Other Essays,* ch. 5 (1976).

6   This moment exhibits infinite space, but there is a space also wherein all moments are infinitely exhibited, and the everlasting duration of infinite space is another region and room of joys.

THOMAS TRAHERNE (1636–74), English clergyman, poet, mystic. *Centuries,* "Fifth Century," no. 6 (written c. 1672; published 1908).

INFLATION

1   The best way to destroy the capitalist system is to debauch the currency. By a continuing process of inflation governments can confiscate, secetly and unobserved, an important part of the wealth of their citizens.

JOHN MAYNARD KEYNES (1883–1946), British economist. *Essays in Persuasion,* ch. 2 (1931).

2   Inflation is as violent as a mugger, as frightening as an armed robber and as deadly as a hit man.

RONALD REAGAN (b. 1911), U.S. Republican politician, president. Speech to Republican Party fund-raising dinner. Quoted in: *Los Angeles Times* (20 Oct. 1978).

3   Imagine believing in the control of inflation by curbing the money supply! That is like deciding to stop your dog fouling the sidewalk by plugging up its rear end. It is highly unlikely to succeed, but if it does it kills the hound.

MICHAEL D. STEPHENS. "On Sinai, There's No Economics," in *New York Times* (13 Nov. 1981).

INFLUENCE

1 One concept corrupts and confuses the others. I am not speaking of the Evil whose limited sphere is ethics; I am speaking of the infinite.

JORGE LUIS BORGES (1899–1986), Argentinian author. *Avatars Of The Tortoise* (1939; repr. in *Other Inquisitions,* 1960; tr. 1964).

2 The secret of my influence has always been that it remained secret.

SALVADOR DALI (1904–89), Spanish painter. *The Secret Life of Salvador Dali,* ch. 11 (1948).

3 Who shall set a limit to the influence of a human being?

RALPH WALDO EMERSON (1803–82), U.S. essayist, poet, philosopher. *The Conduct of Life,* "Power" (1860).

4 It would be difficult to exaggerate the degree to which we are influenced by those we influence.

ERIC HOFFER (1902–83), U.S. philosopher. *The Passionate State of Mind,* aph. 124 (1955).

5 We live in a world which is full of misery and ignorance, and the plain duty of each and all of us is to try to make the little corner he can influence somewhat less miserable and somewhat less ignorant than it was before he entered it.

THOMAS HENRY HUXLEY (1825–95), English biologist. "On The Physical Basis Of Life" (1868; published in *Collected Essays,* vol. 1, 1893).

6 Power lasts ten years; influence not more than a hundred.

KOREAN PROVERB. Quoted in: Alan L. Mackay, *The Harvest of a Quiet Eye* (1977).

INFORMATION

1 Information can tell us everything. It has all the answers. But they are answers to questions we have not asked, and which doubtless don't even arise.

JEAN BAUDRILLARD (b. 1929), French semiologist. *Cool Memories,* ch. 5 (1987; tr. 1990).

2 Among all the world's races, some obscure Bedouin tribes possibly apart, Americans are the most prone to misinformation. This is not the consequence of any special preference for mendacity, although at the higher levels of their public administration that tendency is impressive. It is rather that so much of what they themselves believe is wrong.

JOHN KENNETH GALBRAITH (b. 1908), U.S. economist. "The United States," in *New York* (15 Nov. 1971; repr. in *A View from the Stands,* 1986).

3 Information networks straddle the world. Nothing remains concealed. But the sheer volume of information dissolves the information. We are unable to take it all in.

GÜNTHER GRASS (b. 1927), German author. Interview in *New Statesman & Society* (London, 22 June 1990).

4 When action grows unprofitable, gather information; when information grows unprofitable, sleep.

URSULA K. LE GUIN (b. 1929), U.S. author. *The Left Hand of Darkness,* ch. 3 (1969).

5 Knowledge in the form of an informational commodity indispensable to productive power is already, and will continue to be, a major—perhaps *the* major—stake in the worldwide competition for power. It is conceivable that the nation-states will one day fight for control of information, just as they battled in the past for control over territory, and afterwards for control over access to and exploitation of raw materials and cheap labor.

JEAN FRANÇOIS LYOTARD (b. 1924), French philosopher. *The Postmodern Condition: A Report on Knowledge,* Introduction (1979).

6 The more the data banks record about each one of us, the less we exist.

MARSHALL MCLUHAN (1911–1980), Canadian communications theorist. *Playboy* (Chicago, March 1969).

7 Information is the oxygen of the modern age. It seeps through the walls topped by barbed wire, it wafts across the electrified borders.

RONALD REAGAN (b. 1911), U.S. Republican politician, president. *Guardian* (London, 14 June 1989).

8 The idea that information can be stored in a changing world without an overwhelming depreciation of its value is false. It is scarcely less false than the more plausible claim that after a war we may take our existing weapons, fill their barrels with cylinder oil, and coat their outsides with sprayed rubber film, and let them statically await the next emergency.

NORBERT WIENER (1894–1964), U.S. mathematician, educator, founder of cybernetics. *The Human Use of Human Beings,* ch. 7 (1950).

9 Private information is practically the source of every large modern fortune.

OSCAR WILDE (1854–1900), Anglo-Irish playwright, author. Sir Robert Chiltern, in *An Ideal Husband,* act 1.

See also Higgins on RESEARCH.

INGRATIATION

1 Many will intreat the favour of the prince: and every man is a friend to him that giveth gifts.

BIBLE, HEBREW. *Proverbs* 19:6.

2 He makes people pleased with him by making them first pleased with themselves.

LORD CHESTERFIELD (1694–1773), English statesman, man of letters. Letter, 18 Jan. 1750 (first published 1774; repr. in *The Letters of the Earl of Chesterfield to His Son,* vol. 2, no. 214, ed. by Charles Strachey, 1901), of the "agreeable, well-bred man".

3 The art of pleasing consists in being pleased.

WILLIAM HAZLITT (1778–1830), English essayist. *The Round Table,* vol. 1, "On Manner" (1817; written with Leigh Hunt).

4 If I have said something to hurt a man once, I shall not get the better of this by saying many things to please him.

SAMUEL JOHNSON (1709–84), English author, lexicographer. Quoted in: James Boswell, *Life of Samuel Johnson*, 15 Sept. 1777 (1791).

5 Call the bald man, "Boy;" make the sage thy toy; Greet the youth with solemn face; praise the fat man for his grace.

HELEN ROWLAND (1875–1950), U.S. journalist. *A Guide to Men*, "Maxims of Cleopatra," no. 10 (1922).

6 Whenever he met a great man he grovelled before him, and my-lorded him as only a free-born Briton can do.

WILLIAM MAKEPEACE THACKERAY (1811–63), English author. *Vanity Fair*, ch. 13 (1848), of Mr. Osborne.

7 You might as well fall flat on your face as lean over too far backward.

JAMES THURBER (1894–1961), U.S. humorist, illustrator. *Fables for Our Time*, "The Bear who Let it Alone" (1940).

See also Swope on FAILURE.

INGRATITUDE

1 That's the trouble with directors. Always biting the hand that lays the golden egg.

SAMUEL GOLDWYN (1882–1974), U.S. film producer. Quoted in: Arthur Marx, *Goldwyn: the Man Behind the Myth*, ch. 17 (1976).

2 People who bite the hand that feeds them usually lick the boot that kicks them.

ERIC HOFFER (1902–83), U.S. philosopher. *Reflections on the Human Condition*, aph. 141 (1973).

3 We seldom find people ungrateful so long as we are in a condition to render them service.

FRANÇOIS, DUC DE LA ROCHEFOUCAULD (1613–1680), French writer, moralist. *Sentences et Maximes Morales*, no. 306 (1678).

INHERITANCE

1 People don't have fortunes left them in that style nowadays; men have to work and women to marry for money. It's a dreadfully unjust world.

LOUISA MAY ALCOTT (1832–88), U.S. author. Meg, in *Little Women*, pt. 1, ch. 15 (1868).

2 One does not jump, and spring, and shout hurrah! at hearing one has got a fortune, one begins to consider responsibilities, and to ponder business; on a base of steady satisfaction rise certain grave cares, and we contain ourselves, and brood over our bliss with a solemn brow.

CHARLOTTE BRONTË (1816–55), English novelist. *Jane Eyre*, ch. 33 (1847).

3 My sword I give to him that shall succeed me in my pilgrimage, and my courage and skill to him that can get it.

JOHN BUNYAN (1628–88), English Baptist preacher, author. Mr. Valiant-for-Truth, in *The Pilgrim's Progress*, pt. 2 (1684), making his farewell.

4 In this choice of inheritance we have given to our frame of polity the image of a relation in blood; binding up the constitution of our country with our dearest domestic ties; adopting our fundamental laws into the bosom of our family affections; keeping inseparable and cherishing with the warmth of all their combined and mutually reflected charities, our state, our hearths, our sepulchres, and our altars.

EDMUND BURKE (1729–97), Irish philosopher, statesman. *Reflections on the Revolution in France* (1790).

5 The way to be immortal (I mean not to die at all) is to have me for your heir. I recommend you to put me in your will and you will see that (as long as *I* live at least) you will never even catch cold.

LORD BYRON (1788–1824), English poet. Letter, 23 March 1821 (published in *Byron's Letters and Journals*, vol. 8, ed. by Leslie A. Marchand, 1973–81).

6 I would as soon leave my son a curse as the almighty dollar.

ANDREW CARNEGIE (1835–1919), U.S. industrialist, philanthropist. Inscription in album. Quoted in: Burton J. Hendrick, *Life of Andrew Carnegie*, vol. 1, ch. 17 (1932). See Carnegie on WEALTH.

7 There is a strange charm in the thoughts of a good legacy, or the hopes of an estate, which wondrously removes or at least alleviates the sorrow that men would otherwise feel for the death of friends.

MIGUEL DE CERVANTES (1547–1616), Spanish writer. *Don Quixote*, pt. 2, bk. 6, ch. 41 (1615; tr. by P. Motteux).

8 All heiresses are beautiful.

JOHN DRYDEN (1631–1700), English poet, dramatist, critic. Albanat, in *King Arthur*, act 1, sc. 1.

9 Of course, money will do after its kind, and will steadily work to unspiritualize and unchurch the people to whom it was bequeathed.

RALPH WALDO EMERSON (1803–82), U.S. essayist, poet, philosopher. *English Traits*, "Religion" (1856).

10 Say not you know another entirely till you have divided an inheritance with him.

JOHANN KASPAR LAVATER (1741–1801), Swiss divine, poet. *Aphorisms on Man*, no. 157 (1788).

11 Men sooner forget the death of their father than the loss of their patrimony.

NICCOLÒ MACHIAVELLI (1469–1527), Italian political philosopher, statesman. *The Prince*, ch. 17 (1514).

12 Lifestyles and sex roles are passed from parents to children as inexorably as blue eyes or small feet.

LETTY COTTIN POGREBIN (b. 1939), U.S. journalist, author. "Down with Sexist Upbringing," in *The First Ms. Reader*, (ed. by Francine Klagsbrun, 1972).

13 But thousands die without or this or that, Die, and endow a college, or a cat: To some, indeed, Heaven grants the happier fate, T'enrich a bastard, or a son they hate.

ALEXANDER POPE (1688–1744), English satirical poet. *Epistle to Lord Bathurst.*

14 The weeping of an heir is laughter in disguise.

PUBLILIUS SYRUS (1st century B.C.), Roman writer of mimes. *Sententiae,* no. 221. Montaigne, in his *Essays,* bk. 1, ch. 37, attributes this aphorism to the second-century Roman grammarian Aulus Gellius in *Noctes Atticae,* bk. 17, ch. 14.

See also Cervantes on WILLS.

INHIBITION

1 How very seldom do you encounter in the world a man of great abilities, acquirements, experience, who will unmask his mind, unbutton his brains, and pour forth in careless and picturesque phrase all the results of his studies and observation; his knowledge of men, books, and nature. On the contrary, if a man has by any chance an original idea, he hoards it as if it were old gold; and rather avoids the subject with which he is most conversant, from fear that you may appropriate his best thoughts.

BENJAMIN DISRAELI (1804–81), English statesman, author. *Coningsby,* bk. 7, ch. 2 (1844).

2 Yet if a woman never lets herself go, how will she ever know how far she might have got? If she never takes off her high-heeled shoes, how will she ever know how far she could walk or how fast she could run?

GERMAINE GREER (b. 1939), Australian feminist writer. *The Change: Women, Ageing and the Menopause,* ch. 2 (1991).

3 My defences were so great. The cocky rock and roll hero who knows all the answers was actually a terrified guy who didn't know how to cry. Simple.

JOHN LENNON (1940–80), British rock musician. *Playboy* (Chicago, Sept. 1980).

INJURY

1 Young men soon give, and soon forget, affronts;
Old age is slow in both.

JOSEPH ADDISON (1672–1719), English essayist. Syphax, in *Cato,* act 2, sc. 5.

2 If thy brother trespass against thee, rebuke him; and if he repent, forgive him. And if he trespass against thee seven times in a day, and seven times in a day turn again to thee, saying, I repent; thou shalt forgive him.

BIBLE: NEW TESTAMENT. *Luke* 17:3–4.

3 To live is to hurt others, and through others, to hurt oneself. Cruel earth! How can we manage not to touch anything? To find what ultimate exile?

ALBERT CAMUS (1913–60), French-Algerian philosopher, author. *American Journals* (1978; tr. 1988), entry for 1 Aug. 1949.

4 No man lives without jostling and being jostled; in all ways he has to elbow himself through the world, giving and receiving offence.

THOMAS CARLYLE (1795–1881), Scottish essayist, historian. *Critical and Miscellaneous Essays,* vol. 4, bk. 1, ch. 4 (1838).

5 There is nothing that people bear more impatiently, or forgive less, than contempt: and an injury is much sooner forgotten than an insult.

LORD CHESTERFIELD (1694–1773), English statesman, man of letters. Letter, 9 Oct. 1746 (first published 1774; repr. in *The Letters of the Earl of Chesterfield to His Son,* vol. 1, no. 113, ed. by Charles Strachey, 1901).

6 Children show scars like medals. Lovers use them as secrets to reveal. A scar is what happens when the word is made flesh.

LEONARD COHEN (b. 1934), Canadian singer, poet, novelist. *The Favourite Game,* bk. 1, ch. 1 (1963).

7 There are some cases . . . in which the sense of injury breeds—not the will to inflict injuries and climb over them as a ladder, but—a hatred of all injury.

GEORGE ELIOT (1819–80), English novelist, editor. *Daniel Deronda,* bk. 2, ch. 16 (1876).

8 An honest man speaks the truth, *though* it may give offence; a vain man, *in order that* it may.

WILLIAM HAZLITT (1778–1830), English essayist. *Characteristics,* no. 387 (first published anonymously in 1823; repr. in *Complete Works,* vol. 9, ed. by P. P. Howe, 1932).

9 The troubles of the young are soon over; they leave no external mark. If you wound the tree in its youth the bark will quickly cover the gash; but when the tree is very old, peeling the bark off, and looking carefully, you will see the scar there still. All that is buried is not dead.

OLIVE SCHREINER (1855–1920), South African writer, feminist. *The Story of an African Farm,* pt. 1, ch. 13 (1883).

10 Kindnesses are easily forgotten; but injuries!—what worthy man does not keep *those* in mind?

WILLIAM MAKEPEACE THACKERAY (1811–63), English author. *Lovel the Widower,* ch. 1 (1860).

11 It's a fact that it is much more comfortable to be in the position of the person who has been offended than to be the unfortunate cause of it.

BARBARA WALTERS (b. 1931), U.S. journalist, broadcaster. *How to Talk With Practically Anybody About Practically Anything,* ch. 6 (1970).

12 No one likes having offended another person; hence everyone feels so much better if the other person doesn't show he's been offended. Nobody likes being confronted by a wounded spaniel. Remember that. It is much easier patiently—and tolerantly—to avoid the person you have injured than to approach him as a friend. You need courage for that.

LUDWIG WITTGENSTEIN (1889–1951), Austrian philosopher. *Culture and Value* (1931; ed. by G. H. von Wright with Heikki Nyman, 1980), 1931 entry

See also ABUSE.

INJUSTICE

1 Justice is my being allowed to do whatever I like. Injustice is whatever prevents my doing so.

SAMUEL BUTLER (1835–1902), English author. *Samuel Butler's Notebooks* (1951, p. 56).

2   Children will still die unjustly even in a perfect society. Even by his greatest effort, man can only propose to diminish, arithmetically, the sufferings of the world.

ALBERT CAMUS (1913–60), French-Algerian philosopher, author. *The Rebel*, pt. 5, "Beyond Nihilism" (1951; tr. 1953).

3   When one has been threatened with a great injustice, one accepts a smaller as a favour.

JANE WELSH CARLYLE (1801–66), Scottish poet. *Letters and Memorials* (1883), entry for 21 Nov. 1855.

4   Progress is the injustice each generation commits with regard to its predecessors.

E. M. CIORAN (b. 1911), Rumanian-born French philosopher. *The Trouble with Being Born*, ch. 8 (1973).

5   I tremble for my country when I reflect that God is just; that his justice cannot sleep forever.

THOMAS JEFFERSON (1743–1826), U.S. president. *Notes on the State of Virginia*, query 18 (written 1781; published 1784).

6   As long as justice and injustice have not terminated their ever renewing fight for ascendancy in the affairs of mankind, human beings must be willing, when need is, to do battle for the one against the other.

JOHN STUART MILL (1806–73), English philosopher, economist. *Dissertations and Discussions*, "The Contest in America" (1859).

7   We have so many people who can't see a fat man standing beside a thin one without coming to the conclusion that the fat man got that way by taking advantage of the thin one!

RONALD REAGAN (b. 1911), U.S. Republican politician, president. "A Time for Choosing," television address, 27 Oct. 1964 (published in *Speaking My Mind*, 1989).

INNOCENCE

1   People who shut their eyes to reality simply invite their own destruction, and anyone who insists on remaining in a state of innocence long after that innocence is dead turns himself into a monster.

JAMES BALDWIN (1924–87), U.S. author. "Stranger in the Village," in *Harper's* (New York, Oct. 1953; repr. in *Notes of a Native Son*, pt. 2, 1955).

2   There is no aphrodisiac like innocence.

JEAN BAUDRILLARD (b. 1929), French semiologist. *Cool Memories*, ch. 5 (1987; tr. 1990).

3   No man ever looks at the world with pristine eyes. He sees it edited by a definite set of customs and institutions and ways of thinking.

RUTH BENEDICT (1887–1948), U.S. anthropologist. *Patterns of Culture*, ch. 1 (1934).

4   Every harlot was a virgin once.

WILLIAM BLAKE (1757–1827), English poet, painter, engraver. *The Gates of Paradise*, Epilogue (1793–1818; ed. by Geoffrey Keynes, 1957).

5   Only the old are innocent. That is what the Victorians understood, and the Christians. Original sin is a prop-

erty of the young. The old grow beyond corruption very quickly.

MALCOLM BRADBURY (b. 1932), British author. Dr. Jochum, in *Stepping Westward,* bk. 1, ch. 1 (1965).

6   The greenhorn is the ultimate victor in everything; it is he that gets the most out of life.

G. K. CHESTERTON (1874–1936), British author. *A Shilling for My Thoughts*, "The Fairy Pickwick" (1916).

7   Innocence always calls mutely for protection when we would be so much wiser to guard ourselves against it: innocence is like a dumb leper who has lost his bell, wandering the world, meaning no harm.

GRAHAM GREENE (1904–91), British novelist. *The Quiet American*, pt. 1, ch. 3, sct. 3 (1955). Later in the book (pt. 3, ch. 2, sct. 1), the narrator describes Pyle—"the quiet American" of the title, a fumbling idealist in cold-war Vietnam—in similar terms: "What's the good? He'll always be innocent, you can't blame the innocent, they are always guiltless. All you can do is control them or eliminate them. Innocence is a kind of insanity."

8   All things truly wicked start from an innocence.

ERNEST HEMINGWAY (1899–1961), U.S. author. *A Moveable Feast*, ch. 17 (1964).

9   Those who are incapable of commiting great crimes will not easily suspect others of doing so.

FRANÇOIS, DUC DE LA ROCHEFOUCAULD (1613–80), French writer, moralist. *Sentences et Maximes Morales* (1665; no. 592 of collected maxims, ed. by FitzGibbon, 1957). Samuel Johnson reiterated the remark in a letter, 6 May 1755, quoted in: James Boswell, *Life of Samuel Johnson* (1791): "Men do not suspect faults which they do not commit."

10   She looked as though butter wouldn't melt in her mouth—or anywhere else.

ELSE LANCHESTER (1902–86), British-born U.S. actor. Attributed, referring to actor Maureen O'Hara.

11   It's innocence when it charms us, ignorance when it doesn't.

MIGNON MCLAUGHLIN (b. 1915?), U.S. author, editor. *The Neurotic's Notebook* (1963).

12   To vice, innocence must always seem only a superior kind of chicanery.

OUIDA (1839–1908), English novelist. *Two Little Wooden Shoes* (1874; published in *Wisdom, Wit and Pathos,* 1884).

13   Prudishness is pretense of innocence without innocence. Women have to remain prudish as long as men are sentimental, dense, and evil enough to demand of them eternal innocence and lack of education. For innocence is the only thing which can ennoble lack of education.

FRIEDRICH SCHLEGEL (1772–1829), German philosopher, critic, writer. *Dialogue on Poetry and Literary Aphorisms*, "Selected Aphorisms from *The Athenaeum*," aph. 31 (1968; first published 1798).

14   I know we're not saints or virgins or lunatics; we know all the lust and lavatory jokes, and most of the dirty people; we can catch buses and count our change and cross the roads and talk real sentences. But our innocence goes awfully deep, and our discreditable secret is that we don't know anything at all, and our horrid inner secret is that we don't care that we don't.

DYLAN THOMAS (1914–53), Welsh poet. Letter, 1936, to

Caitlin, later his wife (published in *The Collected Letters of Dylan Thomas*, 1985).

15 Look for me in the nurseries of heaven.

FRANCIS THOMPSON (1859–1907), English poet. *To My God-child*.

16 Certainly Adam in Paradise had not more sweet and curious apprehensions of the world, than I when I was a child.

THOMAS TRAHERNE (1636–74), English clergyman, poet, mystic. *Centuries*, "Third Century," no. 1 (written c. 1672; published 1908).

17 The essential self is innocent, and when it tastes its own innocence knows that it lives for ever.

JOHN UPDIKE (b. 1932), U.S. author, critic. *Self-Consciousness: Memoirs*, ch. 1 (1989).

18 Nothing looks so like innocence as an indiscretion.

OSCAR WILDE (1854–1900), Anglo-Irish playwright, author. Cecil Graham, in *Lady Windermere's Fan*, act 2.

19 Children, I grant, should be innocent; but when the epithet is applied to men, or women, it is but a civil term for weakness.

MARY WOLLSTONECRAFT (1759–97), English feminist writer. *A Vindication of the Rights of Women*, ch. 2 (1792).

20 I am to be broken. I am to be derided all my life. I am to be cast up and down among these men and women, with their twitching faces, with their lying tongues, like a cork on a rough sea. Like a ribbon of weed I am flung far every time the door opens.

VIRGINIA WOOLF (1882–1941), British novelist. *The Waves* (1931, p. 77).

See also Buñuel on CURIOSITY.

INNOVATION

1 As the births of living creatures, at first, are ill-shapen: so are all *Innovations*, which are the births of time.

FRANCIS BACON (1561–1626), English philosopher, essayist, statesman. *Essays*, "Of Innovations" (1597–1625).

2 One of the greatest pains to human nature is the pain of a new idea.

WALTER BAGEHOT (1826–77), English economist, critic. *Physics and Politics*, ch. 5 (1872).

3 To innovate is not to reform.

EDMUND BURKE (1729–97), Irish philosopher, statesman. *Letter to a Noble Lord* (published in *Works*, vol. 5, 1796).

4 Innovation! One cannot be forever innovating. I want to create classics.

COCO CHANEL (1883–1971), French couturière. Quoted in: Marcel Haedrich, *Coco Chanel: Her Life, Her Secrets*, ch. 21 (1971).

5 Pure innovation is more gross than error.

GEORGE CHAPMAN (1559–1634), English dramatist, poet, translator. King Henry, in *Bussy D'Ambois*, act 1, sc. 2.

6 Anyone who has invented a better mousetrap, or the contemporary equivalent, can expect to be harassed by strangers demanding that you read their unpublished manuscripts or undergo the humiliation of public speaking, usually on remote Midwestern campuses.

BARBARA EHRENREICH (b. 1941), U.S. author and columnist. *The Worst Years of Our Lives*, "The Cult of Busyness" (1991; first published in *New York Times*, 1985).

7 Great innovations should not be forced on slender majorities.

THOMAS JEFFERSON (1743–1826), U.S. president. Letter, 2 May 1808.

8 The difficulty lies, not in the new ideas, but in escaping from the old ones, which ramify, for those brought up as most of us have been, into every corner of our minds.

JOHN MAYNARD KEYNES (1883–1946), British economist. *The General Theory of Employment, Interest and Money*, Preface (1936).

9 No one asks you to throw Mozart out of the window. Keep Mozart. Cherish him. Keep Moses too, and Buddha and Lao tse and Christ. Keep them in your heart. But make room for the others, the coming ones, the ones who are already scratching on the window-panes.

HENRY MILLER (1891–1980), U.S. author. *The Air-Conditioned Nightmare*, "With Edgar Varèse in the Gobi Desert" (1945).

10 You let *me* throw the bricks through the front window. You go in at the back and take the swag.

EZRA POUND (1885–1972), U.S. poet, critic. Remark to poet T. S. Eliot, reported by Pound acolyte and critic Hugh Kenner. Quoted in: Humphrey Carpenter, *A Serious Character*, pt. 2, ch. 13 (1988).

11 Most new things are not good, and die an early death; but those which push themselves forward and by slow degrees force themselves on the attention of mankind are the unconscious productions of human wisdom, and must have honest consideration, and must not be made the subject of unreasoning prejudice.

THOMAS BRACKETT REED (1839–1902), U.S. Republican politician. *North American Review* (Cedar Falls, Iowa, Dec. 1902).

See also Twain on ORIGINALITY.

INSANITY

1 There is in every madman a misunderstood genius whose idea, shining in his head, frightened people, and for whom delirium was the only solution to the strangulation that life had prepared for him.

ANTONIN ARTAUD (1896–1948), French theater producer, actor, theorist. *Van Gogh, the Man Suicided by Society* (1947; repr. in *Selected Writings*, pt. 33, ed. by Susan Sontag, 1976).

2 Man disavows, and Deity disowns me:
Hell might afford my miseries a shelter;
Therefore hell keeps her ever-hungry mouths all
Bolted against me.

WILLIAM COWPER (1731–1800), English poet. *Lines Written*

During a Period of Insanity. The poem, one of Cowper's *Sapph-ics*, was written in 1763, a year in which Cowper made three sui-cide attempts, which were followed by a period of insanity and hospitalization.

3   Where does one go from a world of insanity? Somewhere on the other side of despair.

> T. S. ELIOT (1888–1965), Anglo-American poet, critic. Harry, Lord Monchensey, in *The Family Reunion*, pt. 2, sc. 2.

4   I doubt if a single individual could be found from the whole of mankind free from some form of insanity. The only difference is one of degree. A man who sees a gourd and takes it for his wife is called insane because this happens to very few people.

> DESIDERIUS ERASMUS (c. 1466–1536), Dutch humanist. *Praise of Folly*, ch. 38 (1509).

5   How strange to have failed as a social creature—even criminals do not fail that way—they are the law's "Loyal Opposition," so to speak. But the insane are always mere guests on earth, eternal strangers carrying around broken decalogues that they cannot read.

> F. SCOTT FITZGERALD (1896–1940), U.S. author. Letter, Dec. 1940, to his daughter Frances Scott Fitzgerald (published in *The Letters of F. Scott Fitzgerald*, ed. by Andrew Turnbull, 1963), of his wife Zelda. Zelda was then receiving treatment for her mental illness.

6   Insanity is often the logic of an accurate mind over-tasked.

> OLIVER WENDELL HOLMES, SR. (1809–94), U.S. writer, physi-cian. *The Autocrat of the Breakfast-Table*, ch. 2 (1858).

7   If you commit a big crime then you are crazy, and the more heinous the crime the crazier you must be. Therefore you are not responsible, and nothing is your fault.

> PEGGY NOONAN (b. 1950), U.S. author, presidential speech-writer. On the insanity verdict handed down to John Hinckley, would-be assassin of President Reagan in 1981, as reported by Noonan and Dan Rather. Quoted in: Noonan, *What I Saw at the Revolution*, ch. 2 (1990). "The insane are with us, it is true," con-tinued their report. "But so are the calculating. And what they learn from this verdict is that you can do anything; you can wait like a jackal and shoot a man in the head and leave him for dead and buy your way out with clever laywers and expensive pyschi-atrists."

8   Let us consider that we are all partially insane. It will explain us to each other; it will unriddle many rid-dles; it will make clear and simple many things which are involved in haunting and harassing difficulties and obscurities now.

> MARK TWAIN (1835–1910), U.S. author. *Christian Science*, bk. 1, ch. 5 (1907; repr. in *What Is Man?* ed. by Paul Baender, 1973).

9   You must always be puzzled by mental illness. The thing I would dread most, if I became mentally ill, would be your adopting a common sense attitude; that you could take it for granted that I was deluded.

> LUDWIG WITTGENSTEIN (1889–1951), Austrian philosopher. Conversations 1947–48 (published in *Personal Recollections*, ch. 6, ed. by Rush Rhees, 1981).

See also MADNESS.

INSECTS

1   The mortal enemies of man are not his fellows of another continent or race; they are the aspects of the physical world which limit or challenge his control, the disease germs that attack him and his domesticated plants and animals, and the insects that carry many of these germs as well as working notable direct injury. This is not . . . the age of man, however great his superiority in size and intelligence; it is literally the age of insects.

> W. C. ALLEE (1885–1955), U.S. zoologist. *The Social Life of Insects*, ch. 7 (1939).

2   Now what sort of man or woman or monster would stroke a centipede I have ever seen? "And here is my good big centipede!" If such a man exists, I say kill him without more ado. He is a traitor to the human race.

> WILLIAM BURROUGHS (b. 1914), U.S. author. *The Western Lands*, ch. 4 (1987).

3   His Labor is a Chant—
His Idleness—a Tune—
Oh, for a Bee's experience
Of Clovers, and of Noon!

> EMILY DICKINSON (1830–86), U.S. poet. *The Complete Poems*, no. 916 (1955).

4   Of what use, however, is a general certainty that an insect will not walk with his head hindmost, when what you need to know is the play of inward stimulus that sends him hither and thither in a network of possible paths?

> GEORGE ELIOT (1819–80), English novelist, editor. *Daniel Deronda*, bk. 3, ch. 25 (1876).

5   Butterflies . . . not quite birds, as they were not quite flowers, mysterious and fascinating as are all inde-terminate creatures.

> ELIZABETH GOUDGE (1900–1984), British novelist. *The Child from the Sea*, bk. 1, pt. 2, ch. 1 (1970).

6   Long after the bomb falls and you and your good deeds are gone, cockroaches will still be here, prowling the streets like armored cars.

> TAMA JANOWITZ (b. 1957), U.S. author. *Slaves of New York*, "Modern Saint 271" (1986).

7   That is your trick, your bit of filthy magic:
Invisibility, and the anaesthetic power
To deaden my attention in your direction.

> D. H. LAWRENCE (1885–1930), British author. *The Mosquito*.

8   After the planet becomes theirs, many millions of years will have to pass before a beetle particularly loved by God, at the end of its calculations will find written on a sheet of paper in letters of fire that energy is equal to the mass multiplied by the square of the velocity of light. The new kings of the world will live tranquilly for a long time, confining themselves to devouring each other and being parasites among each other on a cottage industry scale.

> PRIMO LEVI (1919–87), Italian chemist, author. *Other People's Trades*, "Beetles" (1985; tr. 1989).

9   The butterfly's attractiveness derives not only from colors and symmetry: deeper motives contribute to it. We would not think them so beautiful if they did not fly, or if they flew straight and briskly like bees, or if they stung, or above all if they did not enact the perturbing mystery of metamorphosis: the latter assumes in our eyes the value of a badly decoded message, a symbol, a sign.

PRIMO LEVI (1919–87), Italian chemist, author. *Other People's Trades*, "Butterflies" (1985; tr. 1989).

10   a man
thinks he amounts
to a great deal
but to a
flea or a
mosquito a human being is
merely something
good to eat

DON MARQUIS (1878–1937), U.S. humorist, journalist. *archy and mehitabel*, "certain maxims of archy" (1927).

11   As a thinker and planner the ant is the equal of any savage race of men; as a self-educated specialist in several arts she is the superior of any savage race of men; and in one or two high mental qualities she is above the reach of any man, savage or civilized!

MARK TWAIN (1835–1910), U.S. author. Old Man, in "What Is Man?" sct. 6 (1906; repr. in *Complete Essays*, ed. by Charles Neider, 1963).

INSECURITY

1   Don't touch me! Don't question me! Don't speak to me! Stay with me!

SAMUEL BECKETT (1906–89), Irish dramatist, novelist. Estragon, in *Waiting for Godot*, act 2.

2   Probably the only place where a man can feel really secure is in a maximum security prison, except for the imminent threat of release.

GERMAINE GREER (b. 1939), Australian feminist writer. *The Female Eunuch*, "Security" (1970).

3   I'm hostile to men, I'm hostile to women, I'm hostile to cats, to poor cockroaches, I'm afraid of horses.

NORMAN MAILER (b. 1923), U.S. author. *The Presidential Papers*, "The Sixth Presidential Paper—A Kennedy Miscellany: An Impolite Interview" (1963).

4   In a world we find terrifying, we ratify that which doesn't threaten us.

DAVID MAMET (b. 1947), U.S. playwright. *Writing in Restaurants*, "Notes for a Catalogue for Raymond Saunders" (1986).

5   A man who has nothing which he cares about more than he does about his personal safety is a miserable creature who has no chance of being free, unless made and kept so by the existing of better men than himself.

JOHN STUART MILL (1806–73), English philosopher, economist. *Dissertations and Discussions*, "The Contest in America" (1859).

6   The man who looks for security, even in the mind, is like a man who would chop off his limbs in order to have artificial ones which will give him no pain or trouble.

HENRY MILLER (1891–1980), U.S. author. *Sexus*, ch. 14 (1949).

7   Men are afraid to rock the boat in which they hope to drift safely through life's currents, when, actually, the boat is stuck on a sandbar. They would be better off to rock the boat and try to shake it loose, or, better still, jump in the water and swim for the shore.

THOMAS SZASZ (b. 1920), U.S. psychiatrist. *The Second Sin*, "Personal Conduct" (1973).

8   My apprehensions come in crowds;
I dread the rustling of the grass;
The very shadows of the clouds
Have power to shake me as they pass:
I question things and do not find
One that will answer to my mind;
And all the world appears unkind.

WILLIAM WORDSWORTH (1770–1850), English poet. *The Affliction of Margaret*.

INSENSITIVITY

1   It's what you do, unthinking,
That makes the quick tear start;
The tear may be forgotten—
But the hurt stays in the heart.

ELLA HIGGINSON (1862–1940), U.S. writer, journalist. *Wearing Out Love*.

2   We may have civilized bodies and yet barbarous souls. We are blind to the real sights of this world; deaf to its voice; and dead to its death. And not till we know, that one grief outweighs ten thousand joys will we become what Christianity is striving to make us.

HERMAN MELVILLE (1819–91), U.S. author. *Redburn*, ch. 58 (1849).

INSIGNIFICANCE

1   There is hardly any one so insignificant that he does not seem imposing to some one at some time.

CHARLES HORTON COOLEY (1864–1929), U.S. sociologist. *Human Nature and the Social Order*, ch. 9 (1902).

2   No man is much regarded by the rest of the world. He that considers how little he dwells upon the condition of others, will learn how little the attention of others is attracted by himself. While we see multitudes passing before us, of whom perhaps not one appears to deserve our notice or excites our sympathy, we should remember, that we likewise are lost in the same throng, that the eye which happens to glance upon us is turned in a moment on him that follows us, and that the utmost which we can reasonably hope or fear is to fill a vacant hour with prattle, and be forgotten.

SAMUEL JOHNSON (1709–84), English author, lexicographer. *Rambler*, no. 159 (London, 24 Sept. 1751; repr. in *Works of Samuel Johnson*, vol. 5, ed. by W. J. Bate and Albrecht B. Strauss, 1969).

3   It needs more skill than I can tell
To play the second fiddle well.

C. H. SPURGEON (1834–92), English preacher. *Salt-Cellars*.

4   We are merely the stars' tennis-balls, struck and

bandied
Which way please them.

JOHN WEBSTER (1580–1625), English dramatist. Bosola, in *The Duchess of Malfi*, act 5, sc. 4. See Shakespeare on LIFE AND LIVING, expressing a similar idea.

See also THINGS, TRIVIAL.

INSOMNIA

1 When I lie down, I say, When shall I arise, and the night be gone? and I am full of tossings to and fro unto the dawning of the day.

BIBLE, HEBREW. *Job* 7:4.

2 Impossible to spend sleepless nights and accomplish anything: if, in my youth, my parents had not *financed* my insomnias, I should surely have killed myself.

E. M. CIORAN (b. 1911), Rumanian-born French philosopher. *Anathemas and Admirations*, "On the Verge of Existence" (1986).

3 The last refuge of the insomniac is a sense of superiority to the sleeping world.

LEONARD COHEN (b. 1934), Canadian singer, poet, novelist. Lawrence Breavman, in *The Favourite Game*, bk. 4, sct. 12 (1963).

4 O sleep, O gentle sleep,
Nature's soft nurse, how have I frighted thee,
That thou no more wilt weigh my eye-lids down
And steep my senses in forgetfulness?

WILLIAM SHAKESPEARE (1564–1616), English dramatist, poet. King Henry, in *Henry IV, Part 2*, act 3, sc. 1.

5 Not poppy, nor mandragora,
Nor all the drowsy syrups of the world,
Shall ever medicine thee to that sweet sleep
Which thou owed'st yesterday.

WILLIAM SHAKESPEARE (1564–1616), English dramatist, poet. Iago to Othello, in *Othello*, act 3, sc. 3.

INSPIRATION

1 To the artist is sometimes granted a sudden, transient insight which serves in this matter for experience. A flash, and where previously the brain held a dead fact, the soul grasps a living truth! At moments we are all artists.

ARNOLD BENNETT (1867–1931), British novelist. *The Journals of Arnold Bennett* (1932), entry for 18 March 1897.

2 *When you do not know what you are doing* and what you are doing is the best—that is inspiration.

ROBERT BRESSON (b. 1907), French film director. *Notes on the Cinematographer*, "1950–1958: The Real" (1975).

3 Stung by the splendour of a sudden thought.

ROBERT BROWNING (1812–89), English poet. *A Death in the Desert*.

4 Out of the closets and into the museums, libraries, architectural monuments, concert halls, bookstores, recording studios and film studios of the world. Everything belongs to the inspired and dedicated thief. . . . Words, colors, light, sounds, stone, wood, bronze belong to the living artist. They belong to anyone who can use them. Loot the Louvre! *A bas l'originalité*, the sterile and assertive ego that imprisons us as it creates. *Vive le sol*—pure, shameless, total. We are not responsible. Steal anything in sight.

WILLIAM BURROUGHS (b. 1914), U.S. author. *The Adding Machine*, "Les Voleurs" (1985).

5 Invention flags, his brain goes muddy,
And black despair succeeds brown study.

WILLIAM CONGREVE (1670–1729), English dramatist. *An Impossible Thing*.

6 Had it not been for you, I should have remained what I was when we first met, a prejudiced, narrow-minded being, with contracted sympathies and false knowledge, wasting my life on obsolete trifles, and utterly insensible to the privilege of living in this wondrous age of change and progress.

BENJAMIN DISRAELI (1804–81), English statesman, author. Lothair to Theodora, in *Lothair*, ch. 49 (1870).

7 Most of us who turn to any subject we love remember some morning or evening hour when we got on a high stool to reach down an untried volume, or sat with parted lips listening to a new talker, or for very lack of books began to listen to the voices within, as the first traceable beginning of our love.

GEORGE ELIOT (1819–80), English novelist, editor. *Middlemarch*, bk. 2, ch. 15 (1871).

8 The torpid artist seeks inspiration at any cost, by virtue or by vice, by friend or by fiend, by prayer or by wine.

RALPH WALDO EMERSON (1803–82), U.S. essayist, poet, philosopher. *The Conduct of Life*, "Power" (1860).

9 An idea ran back and forward in his head like a blind man, knocking over the solid furniture.

F. SCOTT FITZGERALD (1896–1940), U.S. author. *The Crack-Up*, "Notebook M" (ed. by Edmund Wilson, 1945).

10 I had a monumental idea this morning, but I didn't like it.

SAMUEL GOLDWYN (1882–1974), U.S. film producer. Quoted in: Alva Johnston, *The Great Goldwyn*, ch. 1 (1937).

11 I didn't have to think up so much as a comma or a semicolon; it was all given, straight from the celestial recording room. Weary, I would beg for a break, an intermission, time enough, let's say, to go to the toilet or take a breath of fresh air on the balcony. Nothing doing!

HENRY MILLER (1891–1980), U.S. author. *Big Sur and the Oranges of Hieronymous Bosch*, pt. 2, "A Fortune in Francs" (1957), on the composition of *Tropic of Capricorn*. Miller added, "How could I possibly imagine then that some few years later a judicial triumvirate, eager to prove me a sinner, would accuse me of having written such passages 'for gain'?"

12 The artist is a receptacle for emotions that come from all over the place: from the sky, from the earth, from a scrap of paper, from a passing shape, from a spider's web.

PABLO PICASSO (1881–1973), Spanish artist. *Conversation avec*

Picasso, in *Cahiers d'Art*, vol. 10, no. 10 (1935; tr. in Alfred H. Barr Jr., *Picasso: Fifty Years of His Art*, 1946).

13 You beat your Pate, and fancy Wit will come:
Knock as you please, there's no body at home.
ALEXANDER POPE (1688–1744), English satirical poet. *Another Epigram*, in *Miscellanies*, vol. 3 (1732).

14 My sole inspiration is a telephone call from a director.
COLE PORTER (1893–1964), U.S. composer, lyricist. Press interview, 8 Feb. 1955.

15 Write while the heat is in you. . . . The writer who postpones the recording of his thoughts uses an iron which has cooled to burn a hole with. He cannot inflame the minds of his audience.
HENRY DAVID THOREAU (1817–62), U.S. philosopher, author, naturalist. *Journals* (1906), entry for 10 Feb. 1852.

See also Calvino on GENIUS; Emerson on PASSION.

INSTINCT

1 An absolute can only be given in an *intuition*, while all the rest has to do with *analysis*. We call intuition here the *sympathy* by which one is transported into the interior of an object in order to coincide with what there is unique and consequently inexpressible in it. Analysis, on the contrary, is the operation which reduces the object to elements already known.
HENRI BERGSON (1859–1941), French philosopher. "Introduction to Metaphysics" (1903; repr. in *The Creative Mind*, 1946).

2 If men as individuals surrender to the call of their elementary instincts, avoiding pain and seeking satisfaction only for their own selves, the result for them all taken together must be a state of insecurity, of fear, and of promiscuous misery.
ALBERT EINSTEIN (1879–1955), German-born U.S. theoretical physicist. *Out of My Later Years*, ch. 7 (1950).

3 Intuition and concepts constitute . . . the elements of all our knowledge, so that neither concepts without an intuition in some way corresponding to them, nor intuition without concepts, can yield knowledge.
IMMANUEL KANT (1724–1804), German philosopher. *Critique of Pure Reason*, "Transcendental Doctrine of Elements: Transcendental Logic," sct. 1 (1781).

4 *Instinct.* When the house burns one forgets even lunch. Yes, but one eats it later in the ashes.
FRIEDRICH NIETZSCHE (1844–1900), German philosopher. *Beyond Good and Evil*, ch. 4, aph. 83 (1886).

5 The natural man has only two primal passions, to get and to beget.
SIR WILLIAM OSLER (1849–1919), Canadian physician. *Science and Immortality*, ch. 2 (1904).

6 What is peculiar in the life of a man consists not in his obedience, but his opposition, to his instincts. In one direction or another he strives to live a supernatural life.
HENRY DAVID THOREAU (1817–62), U.S. philosopher, author, naturalist. *Journals* (1906), 1850 entry.

See also Bradley on METAPHYSICS.

INSTITUTIONS

1 The whole history of civilisation is strewn with creeds and institutions which were invaluable at first, and deadly afterwards.
WALTER BAGEHOT (1826–77), English economist, critic. *Physics and Politics*, ch. 2, sct. 3 (1872).

2 If you're treated a certain way you become a certain kind of person. If certain things are described to you as being real they're real for you whether they're real or not.
JAMES BALDWIN (1924–87), U.S. author. *A Dialogue* (1973; with Nikki Giovanni), from a conversation in London, 4 Nov. 1971.

3 What is a wife and what is a harlot? What is a church and what
Is a theatre? are they two and not one? can they exist separate?
Are not religion and politics the same thing?
Brotherhood is religion,
O demonstrations of reason dividing families in cruelty and pride!
WILLIAM BLAKE (1757–1827), English poet, painter, engraver. *Jerusalem*, plate 57 (repr. in *Complete Writings*, ed. by Geoffrey Keynes, 1957).

4 Institutions—government, churches, industries, and the like—have properly no other function than to contribute to human freedom; and in so far as they fail, on the whole, to perform this function, they are wrong and need reconstruction.
CHARLES HORTON COOLEY (1864–1929), U.S. sociologist. *Human Nature and the Social Order*, ch. 12 (1902).

5 An institution is the lengthened shadow of one man.
RALPH WALDO EMERSON (1803–82), U.S. essayist, poet, philosopher. *Essays*, "Self-reliance" (First Series, 1841).

6 In any great organization it is far, far safer to be wrong with the majority than to be right alone.
JOHN KENNETH GALBRAITH (b. 1908), U.S. economist. *Guardian* (London, 28 July 1989).

7 Every institution not only carries within it the seeds of its own dissolution, but prepares the way for its most hated rival.
W. R. INGE (1860–1954), Dean of St. Paul's, London. *Outspoken Essays*, "The Victorian Age" (Second Series, 1922).

8 Whether lawyer, politician or executive, the American who knows what's good for his career seeks an institutional rather than an individual identity. He becomes the man from NBC or IBM. The institutional imprint furnishes him with pension, meaning, proofs of existence. A man without a company name is a man without a country.
LEWIS H. LAPHAM (b. 1935), U.S. essayist, editor. *Money and Class in America*, ch. 9 (1988).

9 Why has mankind had such a craving to be imposed

upon? Why this lust after imposing creeds, imposing deeds, imposing buildings, imposing language, imposing works of art? The thing becomes an imposition and a weariness at last. Give us things that are alive and flexible, which won't last too long and become an obstruction and a weariness. Even Michelangelo becomes at last a lump and a burden and a bore. It is so hard to see past him.

> D. H. LAWRENCE (1885–1930), British author. *Etruscan Places,* ch. 2 (1932).

10 Power is not of a man. Wealth does not center in the person of the wealthy. Celebrity is not inherent in any personality. To be celebrated, to be wealthy, to have power requires access to major institutions.

> C. WRIGHT MILLS (1916–62), U.S. sociologist. *The Power Elite,* ch. 1 (1956).

11 What are all political and social institutions, but always a religion, which in realizing itself, becomes incarnate in the world?

> EDGAR QUINET (1803–75), French poet, historian, politician. *Ultramontanism, or The Roman Church and Modern Society,* "The Roman Church and History—Vico" (1845; lecture, 15 May 1844).

12 The more rational an institution is the less it suffers by making concessions to others.

> GEORGE SANTAYANA (1863–1952), U.S. philosopher, poet. *The Life of Reason,* "Reason in Science," ch. 9 (1905–6).

13 The way in which men cling to old institutions after the life has departed out of them, and out of themselves, reminds me of those monkeys which cling by their tails—aye, whose tails contract about the limbs, even the dead limbs, of the forest, and they hang suspended beyond the hunter's reach long after they are dead. It is of no use to argue with such men. They have not an apprehensive intellect, but merely, as it were a prehensile tail.

> HENRY DAVID THOREAU (1817–62), U.S. philosopher, author, naturalist. *Journals* (1906), entry for 19 Aug. 1851.

14 Wherever a man goes, men will pursue him and paw him with their dirty institutions, and, if they can, constrain him to belong to their desperate odd-fellow society.

> HENRY DAVID THOREAU (1817–62), U.S. philosopher, author, naturalist. *Walden,* "The Village" (1854).

15 Monarchies, aristocracies, and religions are all based upon that large defect in your race—the individual's distrust of his neighbor, and his desire, for safety's or comfort's sake, to stand well in his neighbor's eye. These institutions will always remain, and always flourish, and always oppress you, affront you, and degrade you, because you will always be and remain slaves of minorities. There was never a country where the majority of the people were in their secret hearts loyal to any of these institutions.

> MARK TWAIN (1835–1910), U.S. author. Satan, in "The Mysterious Stranger," ch. 9 (1916; repr. in *The Complete Short Stories,* ed. by Charles Neider, 1957).

INSULTS

1 No one can be as calculatedly rude as the British, which amazes Americans, who do not understand studied insult and can only offer abuse as a substitute.

> PAUL GALLICO (1897–1976), U.S. novelist. *New York Times* (14 Jan. 1962).

2 The only gracious way to accept an insult is to ignore it; if you can't ignore it, top it; if you can't top it, laugh at it; if you can't laugh at it, it's probably deserved.

> RUSSELL LYNES (b. 1910), U.S. editor, critic. *The Reader's Digest* (British ed., Dec. 1961).

3 Daily life is governed by an economic system in which the production and consumption of insults tends to balance out.

> RAOUL VANEIGEM (b. 1934), Belgian Situationist philosopher. *The Revolution of Everyday Life,* ch. 2, sct. 1 (1967; tr. 1983).

See also ABUSE.

INSURANCE

1 Insurance. An ingenious modern game of chance in which the player is permitted to enjoy the comfortable conviction that he is beating the man who keeps the table.

> AMBROSE BIERCE (1842–1914), U.S. author. *The Devil's Dictionary* (1881–1906).

2 You don't need to pray to God any more when there are storms in the sky, but you do have to be insured.

> BERTOLT BRECHT (1898–1956), German dramatist, poet. Pelagea Vlasova, in *The Mother,* sc. 10.

3 For almost seventy years the life insurance industry has been a smug sacred cow feeding the public a steady line of sacred bull.

> RALPH NADER (b. 1934), U.S. consumer rights activist. Testimony to U.S. Senate subcommittee. Quoted in: *New York Times* (19 May 1974).

See also Gilbert on DISASTERS.

INTEGRITY

1 One must live the way one thinks or end up thinking the way one has lived.

> PAUL BOURGET (1852–1935), French novelist. *Le Démon de Midi,* "Conclusion" (1914).

2 You can't, in sound morals, condemn a man for taking care of his own integrity. It is his clear duty. And least of all can you condemn an artist pursuing, however humbly and imperfectly, a creative aim. In that interior world where his thought and his emotions go seeking for the experience of imagined adventures, there are no policemen, no law, no pressure of circumstance or dread of opinion to keep him within bounds. Who then is going to say Nay to his temptations if not his conscience?

> JOSEPH CONRAD (1857–1924), Polish-born English novelist. *A Personal Record,* "A Familiar Preface" (1912).

3 There is nothing more likely to drive a man mad, than the being unable to get rid of the idea of the distinction between right and wrong, and an obstinate, constitutional preference of the true to the agreeable.

> WILLIAM HAZLITT (1778–1830), English essayist. *Lectures on the English Poets*, "On Swift, Young, Gray, Collins &c." (1818), on Jonathan Swift.

4 He who is upright in his way of life and free from sin.

> HORACE (65–8 B.C.), Roman poet. *Odes*, bk. 1, ode 22 (23 B.C.).

5 There is no alleviation for the sufferings of mankind except veracity of thought and of action, and the resolute facing of the world as it is when the garment of make-believe by which pious hands have hidden its uglier features is stripped off.

> THOMAS HENRY HUXLEY (1825–95), English biologist. *Collected Essays*, vol. 1, "Autobiography" (1893).

6 Integrity without knowledge is weak and useless, and knowledge without integrity is dangerous and dreadful.

> SAMUEL JOHNSON (1709–84), English author, lexicographer. The astronomer, in *The History of Rasselas*, ch. 41 (1759).

7 I cannot and will not recant anything, for to go against conscience is neither right nor safe. Here I stand, I can do no other, so help me God. Amen.

> MARTIN LUTHER (1483–1546), German leader of the Protestant Reformation. Speech, 18 April 1521, at the Diet of Worms, Germany, where he was summoned by the Holy Roman Emperor Charles V in an attempt to effect a conciliation between Luther and the established Church. The words, "Here I stand, I can do no other"—added in Luther's handwriting to the original printed version of the speech—were later inscribed on the monument to Luther at Worms: *Hier steh' ich, ich kann nicht anders.*

8 A man should *be* upright, not be *kept* upright.

> MARCUS AURELIUS (121–180 A.D.), Roman emperor, philosopher. *Meditations*, bk. 3, sct. 5.

9 I will never again go to people under false pretenses even if it is to give them the Holy Bible. I will never again sell anything, even if I have to starve. I am going home now and I will sit down and really write about people.

> HENRY MILLER (1891–1980), U.S. author. *Tropic of Capricorn* (1938; 1966, p. 174).

10 It is necessary to the happiness of man that he be mentally faithful to himself. Infidelity does not consist in believing, or in disbelieving; it consists in professing to believe what he does not believe.

> THOMAS PAINE (1737–1809), Anglo-American political theorist, writer. *The Age of Reason*, pt. 1, "The Author's Profession of Faith" (1794).

11 He that doth not as other men do, but endeavoureth that which ought to be done, shall thereby rather incur peril than preservation; for whoso laboureth to be sincerely perfect and good shall necessarily perish, living among men that are generally evil.

> SIR WALTER RALEGH (1552–1618), English author, soldier, explorer. *The Cabinet Council*, ch. 25, "A Collection of Political Observations" (repr. in *The Works of Sir Walter Raleigh*, vol. 1, 1751).

12 I ever will profess myself the greatest friend to those whose actions best correspond with their doctrine; which, I am sorry to say, is too seldom the case amongst those nations who pretend most to civilization.

> CAPTAIN J. G. STEDMAN (1744–97), British soldier, author, artist. *Narrative of a Five Years' Expedition against the Revolted Negroes of Surinam*, ch. 24 (1796; repr. 1971).

13 The laboring man has not leisure for a true integrity day by day.

> HENRY DAVID THOREAU (1817–62), U.S. philosopher, author, naturalist. *Walden*, "Economy" (1854).

14 Few men have virtue to withstand the highest bidder.

> GEORGE WASHINGTON (1732–99), U.S. general, president. Letter, 17 Aug. 1779. Quoted in: *Maxims of Washington*, "Virtue and Vice" (1942).

INTELLECT AND INTELLECTUALS

1 I was asked to-night why I refuse to have truck with intellectuals after business hours. But of course I won't. 1. I am not an intellectual. Two minutes' talk with Aldous Huxley, William Glock, or any of the New Statesman crowd would expose me utterly. 2. I am too tired after my day's work to man the intellectual palisade. 3. When my work is finished I want to eat, drink, smoke, and relax. 4. I don't know very much, but what I do know I know better than anybody, and I don't want to argue about it. I know what I think about an actor or an actress, and am not interested in what anybody else thinks. My mind is not a bed to be made and re-made.

> JAMES AGATE (1877–1947), British drama critic. *The Selective Ego*, "Ego 6" (ed. by Tim Beaumont, 1976), entry for 9 June 1943.

2 I've never been an intellectual but I have this look.

> WOODY ALLEN (b. 1935), U.S. filmmaker. *International Herald Tribune* (Paris, 18 March 1992).

3 To the man-in-the-street, who, I'm sorry to say,
Is a keen observer of life,
The word "Intellectual" suggests straight away
A man who's untrue to his wife.

> W. H. AUDEN (1907–73), Anglo-American poet. *New Year Letter*, Note to l. 1277 (1961).

4 I've been called many things, but never an intellectual.

> TALLULAH BANKHEAD (1903–68), U.S. screen actor. *Tallulah*, ch. 15 (1952).

5 The intellectual is a middle-class product; if he is not born into the class he must soon insert himself into it, in order to exist. He is the fine nervous flower of the bourgeoisie.

> LOUISE BOGAN (1897–1970), U.S. poet, critic. "Some Notes on Popular and Unpopular Art" (1943; published in *Selected Criticism: Poetry and Prose*, 1955).

6 The intellectual tradition is one of servility to power, and if I didn't betray it I'd be ashamed of myself.

> NOAM CHOMSKY (b. 1928), U.S. linguist, political analyst. Television Interview on "The Late Show," BBC2, 25 Nov. 1992.

Excerpted in *Guardian* (London, 23 Nov. 1992), responding to an accusation of betrayal by Arthur Schlesinger, Jr.

7 Clever people seem not to feel the natural pleasure of bewilderment, and are always answering questions when the chief relish of a life is to go on asking them.

FRANK MOORE COLBY (1865–1925), U.S. editor, essayist. *The Colby Essays*, vol. 1, "Simple Simon" (1926).

8 If intellection and knowledge were mere passion from without, or the bare reception of extraneous and adventitious forms, then no reason could be given at all why a mirror or looking-glass should not understand; whereas it cannot so much as sensibly perceive those images which it receives and reflects to us.

RALPH J. CUDWORTH (1617–88), English theologian, philosopher. *Treatise Concerning Eternal and Immutable Morality*, bk. 4, ch. 1, sct. 3 (1731).

9 Intellectual sodomy, which comes from the refusal to be simple about plain matters, is as gross and abundant today as sexual perversion and they are nowise different from one another.

EDWARD DAHLBERG (1900–1977), U.S. author, critic. *Alms for Oblivion*, "Moby-Dick: A Hamitic Dream" (1964).

10 We should take care not to make the intellect our god; it has, of course, powerful muscles, but no personality.

ALBERT EINSTEIN (1879–1955), German-born U.S. scientist. *Out of My Later Life*, ch. 51 (1950).

11 Only those who know the supremacy of the intellectual life . . . can understand the grief of one who falls from that serene activity into the absorbing soul-wasting struggle with worldly annoyances.

GEORGE ELIOT (1819–80), English novelist. *Middlemarch*, bk. 8, ch. 73 (1872).

12 Ask a wise man to dinner and he'll upset everyone by his gloomy silence or tiresome questions. Invite him to a dance and you'll have a camel prancing about. Haul him off to a public entertainment and his face will be enough to spoil the people's entertainment.

DESIDERIUS ERASMUS (c. 1466–1536), Dutch humanist. *Praise of Folly*, ch. 25 (1509).

13 The work of an intellectual is not to mould the political will of others; it is, through the analyses that he does in his own field, to re-examine evidence and assumptions, to shake up habitual ways of working and thinking, to dissipate conventional familiarities, to re-evaluate rules and institutions and . . . to participate in the formation of a political will (where he has his role as citizen to play).

MICHEL FOUCAULT (1926–84), French philosopher. "The Concern for Truth," interview in *Le Magazine Littéraire* (Paris, May 1984; repr. in *Foucault Live*, ed. by Sylvère Lotringer, 1989).

14 And still they gazed, and still the wonder grew,
That one small head could carry all he knew.

OLIVER GOLDSMITH (1728–74), Anglo-Irish poet, essayist, playwright. *The Deserted Village*, of the village schoolmaster.

15 There's always something suspect about an intellectual on the winning side.

16 Intellectuals can tell themselves anything, sell themselves any bill of goods, which is why they were so often patsies for the ruling classes in nineteenth-century France and England, or twentieth-century Russia and America.

LILLIAN HELLMAN (1907–84), U.S. playwright. Hellman, *An Unfinished Woman*, ch. 13 (1969), entry for 30 April 1967.

17 A highbrow is the kind of person who looks at a sausage and thinks of Picasso.

A. P. HERBERT (1890–1971), British author, politician. Mr. Haddock, a witness, in *Uncommon Law*, "Is 'Highbrow' Libellous?" (1935).

18 Science and art are only too often a superior kind of dope, possessing this advantage over booze and morphia: that they can be indulged in with a good conscience and with the conviction that, in the process of indulging, one is leading the "higher life."

ALDOUS HUXLEY (1894–1963), British author. *Ends and Means*, ch. 14 (1937).

19 Nothing mattered except states of mind, chiefly our own.

JOHN MAYNARD KEYNES (1883–1946), British economist. *Essays in Biography*, ch. 39 (1933), of the "Apostles" group at Cambridge University.

20 *I think, therefore I am* is the statement of an intellectual who underrates toothaches.

MILAN KUNDERA (b. 1929), Czech author, critic. *Immortality*, pt. 4, ch. 11 (1991).

21 My great religion is a belief in the blood, the flesh, as being wiser than the intellect. We can go wrong in our minds. But what our blood feels and believes and says, is always true. The intellect is only a bit and a bridle.

D. H. LAWRENCE (1885–1930), British author. Letter, 17 Jan. 1913 (published in *The Letters of D. H. Lawrence*, vol. 1, ed. by James T. Boulton, 1979).

22 A sort of war of revenge on the intellect is what, for some reason, thrives in the contemporary social atmosphere.

WYNDHAM LEWIS (1882–1957), British author, painter. *The Art of Being Ruled*, "The 'Vicious' Circle," ch. 3 (1926).

23 On a level plain, simple mounds look like hills; and the insipid flatness of our present bourgeoisie is to be measured by the altitude of its "great intellects."

KARL MARX (1818–83), German political theorist, social philosopher. *Capital*, vol. 1, ch. 16 (1867).

24 The intellectual *is* different from the ordinary man, but only in certain sections of his personality, and even then not all the time.

GEORGE ORWELL (1903–50), British author. "Rudyard Kipling" (1942; repr. in *Critical Essays*, 1947).

25 The intellect is a very nice whirligig toy, but how people take it seriously is more than I can understand.

EZRA POUND (1885–1972), U.S. poet, critic. Letter (undated) to Pound's mother. Quoted in: Humphrey Carpenter, *A Serious Character*, pt. 5, ch. 6 (1988).

26 Our intellect is not the most subtle, the most pow-

VÁCLAV HAVEL (b. 1936), Czech playwright, president. *Disturbing the Peace*, ch. 5 (1986; tr. 1990).

erful, the most appropriate, instrument for revealing the truth. It is life that, little by little, example by example, permits us to see that what is most important to our heart, or to our mind, is learned not by reasoning but through other agencies. Then it is that the intellect, observing their superiority, abdicates its control to them upon reasoned grounds and agrees to become their collaborator and lackey.

> MARCEL PROUST (1871–1922), French novelist. *Remembrance of Things Past*, vol. 11, "The Sweet Cheat Gone," ch. 1 (1925; tr. by Ronald and Colette Cortie, 1988).

27 If we look into ourselves we discover propensities which declare that our intellects have arisen from a lower form; could our minds be made visible we should find them tailed.

> W. WINWOOD READE (1838–75), English traveler, author. *The Martyrdom of Man*, ch. 3, "Materials of Human History" (1872).

28 To be wholly devoted to some intellectual exercise is to have succeeded in life.

> ROBERT LOUIS STEVENSON (1850–94), Scottish novelist, essayist, poet. *Weir of Hermiston*, ch. 2 (1896).

29 The intellect is not a serious thing, and never has been. It is an instrument on which one plays, that is all.

> OSCAR WILDE (1854–1900), Anglo-Irish playwright, author. Lord Illingworth, in *A Woman of No Importance*, act 1.

30 Never stay up on the barren heights of cleverness, but come down into the green valleys of silliness.

> LUDWIG WITTGENSTEIN (1889–1951), Austrian philosopher. *Culture and Value* (ed. by G. H. von Wright with Heikki Nyman, 1980), entry for 1934.

31 There can be no two opinions as to what a highbrow is. He is the man or woman of thoroughbred intelligence who rides his mind at a gallop across country in pursuit of an idea.

> VIRGINIA WOOLF (1882–1941), British novelist. *The Death of the Moth*, "Middlebrow" (1942).

32 The good are so harsh to the clever,
The clever so rude to the good!

> ELIZABETH WORDSWORTH (1840–1932), British educator. *Good and Clever*.

See also Orwell on COMMUNISM; Pascall on ORIGINALITY; De Quincey on TEA.

INTELLIGENCE

1 Cleverness is serviceable for everything, sufficient for nothing.

> HENRI-FRÉDÉRIC AMIEL (1821–81), Swiss philosopher, poet. Journal entry, 16 Feb. 1868.

2 Undernourished, intelligence becomes like the bloated belly of a starving child: swollen, filled with nothing the body can use.

> ANDREA DWORKIN (b. 1946), U.S. feminist critic. *Right-Wing Women*, ch. 2 (1978).

3 One definition of man is "an intelligence served by organs."

> RALPH WALDO EMERSON (1803–82), U.S. essayist, poet, philosopher. *Society and Solitude*, "Works and Days" (1870). Emerson may have taken this definition from Louis De Bonald, *Théorie de Pouvoir Politique et Religieux* (1796). See Huxley on INTELLIGENCE.

4 The test of a first-rate intelligence is the ability to hold two opposed ideas in the mind at the same time, and still retain the ability to function.

> F. SCOTT FITZGERALD (1896–1940), U.S. author. "The Crack-Up," in *Esquire* (New York, Feb. 1936; repr. in *The Crack-Up*, ed. by Edmund Wilson, 1945). See George Orwell on CONTRADICTION.

5 Reason is man's faculty for *grasping* the world by thought, in contradiction to intelligence, which is man's ability to *manipulate* the world with the help of thought. Reason is man's instrument for arriving at the truth, intelligence is man's instrument for manipulating the world more successfully; the former is essentially human, the latter belongs to the animal part of man.

> ERICH FROMM (1900–1980), U.S. psychologist. *The Sane Society*, ch. 3, "The Need for a Frame of Orientation and Devotion—Reason vs. Irrationality" (1955).

6 Man is an intelligence, not served by, but in servitude to his organs.

> ALDOUS HUXLEY (1894–1963), British author. *Themes and Variations*, "Variations on a Philosopher" (1950).

7 The height of cleverness is being able to conceal it.

> FRANÇOIS, DUC DE LA ROCHEFOUCAULD (1613–80), French writer, moralist. *Sentences et Maximes Morales*, no. 245 (1678).

8 He is far too intelligent to become really cerebral.

> URSULA K. LE GUIN (b. 1929), U.S. author. "Review of *Difficult Loves* by Italo Calvino," in *Washington Post Book World* (18 Nov 1984; repr. in *Dancing at the Edge of the World*, 1989), of Italo Calvino.

9 There are three kinds of intelligence: one kind understands things for itself, the other appreciates what others can understand, the third understands neither for itself nor through others. This first kind is excellent, the second good, and the third kind useless.

> NICCOLÒ MACHIAVELLI (1469–1527), Italian political philosopher, statesman. *The Prince*, ch. 22 (1513).

10 Nature shows that with the growth of intelligence comes increased capacity for pain, and it is only with the highest degree of intelligence that suffering reaches its supreme point.

> ARTHUR SCHOPENHAUER (1788–1860), German philosopher. *Parerga and Paralipomena*, footnote to "Aphorisms on the Wisdom of Life" (1851).

11 Intelligence . . . is really a kind of taste: taste in ideas.

> SUSAN SONTAG (b. 1933), U.S. essayist. *Against Interpretation*, "Notes on 'Camp'" (1966; first published 1964).

12 I was taught that the human brain was the crowning glory of evolution so far, but I think it's a very poor scheme for survival.

> KURT VONNEGUT, JR (b. 1922), U.S. novelist. Quoted in: *Observer* (London, 27 Dec. 1987).

13 Whatever debases the intelligence degrades the entire human being.

SIMONE WEIL (1909–43), French philosopher, mystic. Letter, 30 March 1936 (published in *Seventy Letters,* 1965).

14 The role of the intelligence—that part of us which affirms and denies and formulates opinions—is merely to submit.

SIMONE WEIL (1909–43), French philosopher, mystic. *Gravity and Grace,* "Intelligence and Grace" (1947; tr. 1952).

See also Keats on ADVERSITY; Crisp on CHARACTER; La Rochefoucauld on SELF-DECEPTION.

INTELLIGIBILITY

1 The true knowledge or science which exists nowhere but in the mind itself, has no other entity at all besides intelligibility; and therefore whatsoever is clearly intelligible, is absolutely true.

RALPH J. CUDWORTH (1617–88), English theologian, philosopher. *Treatise Concerning Eternal and Immutable Morality,* bk. 4, ch. 5, sct. 7 (1731).

2 Unless one is a genius, it is best to aim at being intelligible.

ANTHONY HOPE [ANTHONY HOPE HAWKINS] (1863–1933), British author. The narrator (Mr. Carter), in *The Dolly Dialogues,* no. 15 (1894).

3 I strive to be brief but I become obscure.

HORACE (65–8 B.C.), Roman poet. *Ars Poetica* (c. 13 B.C.).

4 The only chance for victory over the brainwash is the right of every man to have his ideas judged one at a time. You never get clarity as long as you have these packaged words, as long as a word is used by twenty-five people in twenty-five different ways. That seems to me to be the first fight, if there is going to be any intellect left.

EZRA POUND (1885–1972), U.S. poet, critic. Interview in *Writers at Work* (Second Series, ed. by George Plimpton, 1963).

5 Never be lucid, never state,
If you would be regarded great.

DYLAN THOMAS (1914–53), Welsh poet. *The Hand That Signed the Paper.*

6 Nowadays to be intelligible is to be found out.

OSCAR WILDE (1854–1900), Anglo-Irish playwright, author. Lord Darlington, in *Lady Windermere's Fan,* act 1.

7 Once something becomes discernible, or understandable, we no longer need to repeat it. We can destroy it.

ROBERT WILSON (b. 1941), U.S. theater director, designer. Quoted in: *Sunday Times* (London, 17 Nov. 1991).

INTENTIONS

1 Would that well-thinking people should be replaced by thinking ones.

NATALIE CLIFFORD BARNEY (1876–1972), U.S.-born French author. Quoted in: "Gods," in *Adam,* no. 299 (London, 1962).

2 I am sure of nothing so little as my own intentions.

LORD BYRON (1788–1824), English poet. Letter, 20 Jan. 1811

(published in *Byron's Letters and Journals,* vol. 2, ed. by Leslie A. Marchand, 1973–81).

3 Moral of the Work. In war: resolution. In defeat: defiance. In victory: magnanimity. In peace: goodwill.

SIR WINSTON CHURCHILL (1874–1965), British statesman, writer. Epigraph to *The Second World War: The Gathering Storm,* vol. 1 (1948).

4 His designs were strictly honourable, as the phrase is; that is, to rob a lady of her fortune by way of marriage.

HENRY FIELDING (1707–54), English novelist, dramatist. Mrs. Fitzpatrick, in *Tom Jones,* bk. 11, ch. 4 (1749), of Mr. Fitzpatrick.

5 The greatest events occur without intention playing any part in them; chance makes good mistakes and undoes the most carefully planned undertaking. The world's greatest events are not produced, they happen.

G. C. LICHTENBERG (1742–99), German physicist, philosopher. *Aphorisms,* "Notebook K," aph. 68 (written 1765–99; tr. R. J. Hollingdale, 1990).

6 With malice toward none; with charity for all; with firmness in the right, as God gives us to see the right—let us strive on to finish the work we are in.

ABRAHAM LINCOLN (1809–65), U.S. president. Second Inaugural Address, 4 March 1865.

7 Hell is paved with good intentions, not with bad ones. All men mean well.

GEORGE BERNARD SHAW (1856–1950), Anglo-Irish playwright, critic. *Man and Superman,* "Maxims for Revolutionists: Good Intentions" (1903). The saying is an old one, traceable at its earliest to St. Francis of Assisi, and picked up by John Wesley and Samuel Johnson, among others.

8 No one would remember the Good Samaritan if he'd only had good intentions—he had money as well.

MARGARET THATCHER (b. 1925), British Conservative politician, prime minister. Television interview, 6 Jan. 1986. Quoted in: *Times* (London, 12 Jan. 1986).

See also Morley on DANCE; Eliot on GOOD DEEDS; Shakespeare on IMPOTENCE; Shaw on MOTIVES; Camus on PRINCIPLES.

INTERNATIONAL RELATIONS

1 We do not covet anything from any nation except their respect.

SIR WINSTON CHURCHILL (1874–1965), British statesman, writer. Broadcast, 21 Oct. 1940, to the French people.

2 There is one safeguard known generally to the wise, which is an advantage and security to all, but especially to democracies as against despots. What is it? Distrust.

DEMOSTHENES (c. 384–322 B.C.), Greek orator. *Second Philippic,* sct. 24 (344 B.C.).

3 Greece is a sort of American vassal; the Netherlands is the country of American bases that grow like tulip bulbs; Cuba is the main sugar plantation of the American monopolies; Turkey is prepared to kow-tow before any United States pro-consul and Canada is the boring second fiddle in the American symphony.

ANDREI ANDREYEVICH GROMYKO (1909–89), Soviet diplomat. *New York Herald Tribune* (30 June 1953).

4 If you live among wolves you have to act like a wolf.

NIKITA KHRUSHCHEV (1894–1971), Soviet premier. Quoted in: *Observer* (London, 26 Sept. 1971).

5 The country that is more developed industrially only shows, to the less developed, the image of its own future.

KARL MARX (1818–83), German political theorist, social philosopher. *Capital*, Preface (first ed., 1867).

6 The United States never lost a war or won a conference.

WILL ROGERS (1879–1935), U.S. humorist. Remark following the Versailles Peace Conference, in which President Woodrow Wilson spurned all suggestions that the U.S. should take territory or payment following its participation in World War I. Quoted in: *Wit and Wisdom* (ed. by Jack Lait, 1936, p. 18).

7 In the field of world policy I would dedicate this nation to the policy of the good neighbor.

FRANKLIN D. ROOSEVELT (1882–1945), U.S. Democratic politician, president. First inaugural address, 4 March 1933.

8 When great nations fear to expand, shrink from expansion, it is because their greatness is coming to an end. Are we, still in the prime of our lusty youth, still at the beginning of our glorious manhood, to sit down among the outworn people, to take our place with the weak and the craven? A thousand times no!

THEODORE ROOSEVELT (1858–1919), U.S. Republican (later Progressive) politician, president. Speech, Sept. 1899, Akron, Ohio, justifying the war against Spain.

9 In April 1917 the illusion of isolation was destroyed, America came to the end of innocence, and of the exuberant freedom of bachelor independence. That the responsibilities of world power have not made us happier is no surprise. To help ourselves manage them, we have replaced the illusion of isolation with a new illusion of omnipotence.

BARBARA TUCHMAN (1912–89), U.S. historian. "How We Entered World War I," in *New York Times Magazine* (5 May 1967).

10 There can be no greater error than to expect, or calculate, upon real favors from nation to nation. It is an illusion which experience must cure, which a just pride ought to discard.

GEORGE WASHINGTON (1732–99), U.S. general, president. Farewell Address, 17 Sept. 1796.

11 Interest does not tie nations together; it sometimes separates them. But sympathy and understanding does unite them.

WOODROW WILSON (1856–1924), U.S. Democratic politician, president. Speech, 27 Oct. 1913.

See also Cleaver, Eden, Rühe on INTERVENTION; Humphrey on ISOLATION.

INTERNATIONALISM

1 A steady patriot of the World alone,
The friend of every country but his own.

GEORGE CANNING (1770–1827), English statesman, prime minister. *The New Morality*, of the Jacobin.

2 All good men are international. Nearly all bad men are cosmopolitan. If we are to be international we must be national.

G. K. CHESTERTON (1874–1936), British author. *All Things Considered*, "French and English" (1908).

3 Nations have lost their old omnipotence; the patriotic tie does not hold. Nations are getting obsolete, we go and live where we will.

RALPH WALDO EMERSON (1803–82), U.S. essayist, poet, philosopher. *English Traits*, "Wealth" (1856).

4 Our country is the world—our countrymen are all mankind.

WILLIAM LLOYD GARRISON (1805–79), U.S. abolitionist. Prospectus of Garrison's anti-slavery newspaper, *The Liberator* (15 Dec. 1837).

5 The individual whose vision encompasses the whole world often feels nowhere so hedged in and out of touch with his surroundings as in his native land.

EMMA GOLDMAN (1869–1940), U.S. anarchist. "The Individual, Society and the State" (first published c. 1940; repr. in *Red Emma Speaks*, pt. 1, ed. by Alix Kates Shulman, 1972).

6 We deny your internationalism, because it is a luxury which only the upper classes can afford; the working people are hopelessly bound to their native shores.

BENITO MUSSOLINI (1883–1945), Italian dictator. Addressed to the Socialists in the Italian Chamber of Deputies, 21 June 1921, in Mussolini's first speech as a member of parliament.

7 My country is the world, and my religion is to do good.

THOMAS PAINE (1737–1809), Anglo-American political theorist, writer. *Rights of Man*, pt. 2, ch. 5 (1792).

8 The man who loves other countries as much as his own stands on a level with the man who loves other women as much as he loves his own wife.

THEODORE ROOSEVELT (1858–1919), U.S. Republican (later Progressive) politician, president. Speech, 6 Sept. 1918, New York City, on the anniversary of the first Battle of the Marne.

INTERVENTION

1 Mutual repect implies discretion and reserve even in love itself; it means preserving as much liberty as possible to those whose life we share. We must distrust our instinct of intervention, for the desire to make one's own will prevail is often disguised under the mask of solicitude.

HENRI-FRÉDÉRIC AMIEL (1821–81), Swiss philosopher, poet. *Journal Intime* (1882; tr. by Mrs. Humphrey Ward, 1892), entry for 7 Nov. 1862.

2 Most of the trouble in this world has been caused by folks who can't mind their own business, because they have no business of their own to mind, any more than a smallpox virus has.

WILLIAM BURROUGHS (b. 1914), U.S. author. *The Adding Machine*, "My Own Business" (1985).

3 "If everybody minded their own business," the Duchess said in a hoarse growl, "the world would go round a deal faster than it does."

LEWIS CARROLL (1832–98), English author, mathematician. *Alice's Adventures in Wonderland*, ch. 6 (1865).

4　Americans think of themselves collectively as a huge rescue squad on twenty-four-hour call to any spot on the globe where dispute and conflict may erupt.

> ELDRIDGE CLEAVER (b. 1935), U.S. civil rights leader, writer. *Soul on Ice,* "Rallying Round the Flag" (1968).

5　We best avoid wars by taking even physical action to stop small ones.

> SIR ANTONY EDEN (1897–1977), British Conservative politician, prime minister. Speech, 1 Nov. 1956, to the House of Commons, on the Anglo-French intervention in the Israeli-Egyptian conflict.

6　Those who in quarrels interpose,
Must often wipe a bloody nose.

> JOHN GAY (1685–1732), English dramatist. *Fables,* "The Mastiff" (1727).

7　All of Western tradition, from the late bloom of the British Empire right through the early doom of Vietnam, dictates that *you do something spectacular and irreversible* whenever you find yourself in or whenever you impose yourself upon a wholly unfamiliar situation belonging to somebody else. Frequently it's your soul or your honor or your manhood, or democracy itself, at stake.

> JUNE JORDAN (b. 1939), U.S. poet, civil rights activist. "Beyond Apocalypse Now," speech, 1980, Lewis and Clark University, Oregon (published in *Moving Towards Home: Political Essays,* 1989).

8　I am not willing to risk the lives of German soldiers for countries whose names we cannot spell properly.

> VOLKER RÜHE (b. 1942), German politician, defense minister. *Independent* (London, 28 Aug. 1992).

INTERVIEWS

1　The best interviews—like the best biographies—should sing the strangeness and variety of the human race.

> LYNN BARBER (b. 1944), British journalist. London *Independent on Sunday* (24 Feb. 1991).

2　The politician being interviewed clearly takes a great deal of trouble to imagine an ending to his sentence: and if he stopped short? His entire policy would be jeopardized!

> ROLAND BARTHES (1915–80), French semiologist. *The Pleasure of the Text,* "Sentence" (1975).

3　I cried, "Come, tell me how you live!"
And thumped him on the head.

> LEWIS CARROLL (1832–98), English author, mathematician. The White Knight's song, in *Through the Looking-Glass,* ch. 8 (1865).

4　The media no longer ask those who know something . . . to share that knowledge with the public. Instead they ask those who know nothing to represent the ignorance of the public and, in so doing, to legitimate it.

> SERGE DANEY (1944–92), French film critic. Quoted in: *Sight and Sound* (London, July 1992).

5　Listening to someone talk isn't at all like listening to their words played over on a machine. What you hear when you have a face before you is never what you hear when you have before you a winding tape.

> ORIANA FALLACI (b. 1930), Italian author. *The Egotists,* Foreword (1963).

6　If, sir, I possessed . . . the power of conveying unlimited sexual attraction through the potency of my voice, I would not be reduced to accepting a miserable pittance from the BBC for interviewing a faded female in a damp basement.

> GILBERT HARDING (1907–60), British broadcaster. Recalled by Wynford Waughan Thomas in: *Gilbert Harding By His Friends* (ed. by Stephen Grenfell, 1961), on being asked to sound more sexy when interviewing Mae West.

7　I'm notorious for giving a bad interview. I'm an actor and I can't help but feel I'm boring when I'm on as myself.

> ROCK HUDSON (1925–85), U.S. screen actor. Quoted in: *TV Times* (London, 19 Oct. 1972).

8　Questioning is not the mode of the conversation among gentlemen.

> SAMUEL JOHNSON (1709–84), English author, lexicographer. Quoted in: James Boswell, *Life of Samuel Johnson,* 25 March 1776 (1791).

9　You mustn't always believe what I say. Questions tempt you to tell lies, particularly when there is no answer.

> PABLO PICASSO (1881–1973), Spanish artist. Quoted in: Roland Penrose, *Picasso: His Life and Work,* ch. 13 (1958).

10　It is not every question that deserves an answer.

> PUBLILIUS SYRUS (1st century B.C.), Roman writer of mimes. *Sententiae,* no. 581.

11　Never try to look into both eyes at the same time. . . . Switch your gaze from one eye to the other. That signals warmth and sincerity.

> DOROTHY SARNOFF (b. 1917), U.S. publicist. *Times* (London, 27 April 1988).

12　My opposition [to interviews] lies in the fact that offhand answers have little value or grace of expression, and that such oral give and take helps to perpetuate the decline of the English language.

> JAMES THURBER (1894–1961), U.S. humorist, illustrator. Letter to Henry Brandon following a lengthy interview with him. Quoted in: Brandon, *As We Are* (1961).

13　It rots a writer's brain, it cretinises you. You say the same thing again and again, and when you do that happily you're well on the way to being a cretin. Or a politician.

> JOHN UPDIKE (b. 1932), U.S. author, critic. Interview by novelist Martin Amis, published in *Observer* (London, 30 Aug. 1987).

14　Questions are never indiscreet. Answers sometimes are.

> OSCAR WILDE (1854–1900), Anglo-Irish playwright, author. Mrs. Cheveley, in *An Ideal Husband,* act 1.

INTIMACY

1   What people don't realize is that intimacy has its conventions as well as ordinary social intercourse. There are three cardinal rules—don't take somebody else's boyfriend unless you've been specifically invited to do so, don't take a drink without being asked, and keep a scrupulous accounting in financial matters.

W. H. AUDEN (1907–73), Anglo-American poet. *The Table Talk of W. H. Auden,* "31 December, 1947" (comp. by Alan Ansen, ed. by Nicholas Jenkins, 1990).

2   Intimacies between women go backwards, beginning with revelations and ending up in small talk without loss of esteem.

ELIZABETH BOWEN (1899–1973), Anglo-Irish novelist. *The Death of the Heart,* pt. 2, ch. 1 (1938).

3   If ever a man and his wife, or a man and his mistress, who pass nights as well as days together, absolutely lay aside all good breeding, their intimacy will soon degenerate into a coarse familiarity, infallibly productive of contempt or disgust.

LORD CHESTERFIELD (1694–1773), English statesman, man of letters. Letter, 3 Nov. 1749 (first published 1774; repr. in *The Letters of the Earl of Chesterfield to His Son,* vol. 1, no. 200, ed. by Charles Strachey, 1901).

4   You don't hold any mystery for me, darling, do you mind? There isn't a particle of you that I don't know, remember, and want.

NOËL COWARD (1899–1973), British playwright, actor, composer. Elyot, in *Private Lives,* act 1.

5   To really know someone is to have loved and hated him in turn.

MARCEL JOUHANDEAU (1888–1979), French writer. *Défense de l'enfer,* "Erotologie" (1935).

6   The many faces of intimacy: the Victorians could experience it through correspondence, but not through cohabitation; contemporary men and women can experience it through fornication, but not through friendship.

THOMAS SZASZ (b. 1920), U.S. psychiatrist. *The Second Sin,* "Social Relations" (1973).

7   If one could be friendly with women, what a pleasure—the relationship so secret and private compared with relations with men. Why not write about it truthfully?

VIRGINIA WOOLF (1882–1941), British novelist. *The Diary of Virginia Woolf,* vol. 2 (ed. by Anne O. Bell, 1978), entry for 1 Nov. 1924.

INTOLERANCE

1   Intolerance is evidence of impotence.

ALEISTER CROWLEY (1875–1947), British occultist. *The Confessions of Aleister Crowley,* ch. 69 (1929; rev. 1970).

2   Intolerance is the "Do Not Touch" sign on something that cannot bear touching. We do not mind having our hair ruffled, but we will not tolerate any familiarity with the toupee which covers our baldness.

ERIC HOFFER (1902–83), U.S. philosopher. *The Passionate State of Mind,* aph. 62 (1955).

3   If Woody Allen were a Muslim, he'd be dead by now.

SALMAN RUSHDIE (b. 1947), Indian-born British author. Quoted in: *Independent* (London, 18 Feb. 1989), of the anger and death threats of Muslim extremists following the publication of Rushdie's novel, *The Satanic Verses* (1988).

4   Some men there are love not a gaping pig,
Some that are mad if they behold a cat,
And others when the bag-pipe sings i'th nose
Cannot contain their urine.

WILLIAM SHAKESPEARE (1564–1616), English dramatist, poet. Shylock, in *The Merchant of Venice,* act. 4, sc. 1 (c. 1597).

5   Intolerance respecting other people's religion is toleration itself in comparison with intolerance respecting other people's art.

WALLACE STEVENS (1879–1955), U.S. poet. *Opus Posthumous,* "Adagia" (1959).

See also Kennedy on DIVERSITY.

INTROSPECTION

1   What is interesting about self-analysis is that it leads nowhere—it is an art form in itself.

ANITA BROOKNER (b. 1938), British novelist, art historian. Interview in *Writers at Work* (Eighth Series, ed. by George Plimpton, 1988).

2   Self-revelation is a cruel process. The real picture, the real "you" never emerges. Looking for it is as bewildering as trying to know how you really look. Ten different mirrors show you ten different faces.

SHASHI DESHPANDE (b. 1938), Indian author. *That Long Silence,* ch. 1 (1988).

3   The man whose whole activity is diverted to inner meditation becomes insensible to all his surroundings. If he loves, it is not to give himself, to blend in fecund union with another being, but to meditate on his love. His passions are mere appearances, being sterile. They are dissipated in futile imaginings, producing nothing external to themselves.

ÉMILE DURKHEIM (1858–1917), French sociologist. *Suicide,* bk. 2, ch. 6, sct. 1 (1897; tr. 1951).

4   The terrible fluidity of self-revelation.

HENRY JAMES (1843–1916), U.S. author. *The Ambassadors,* Preface (1909 ed.).

5   The mind can weave itself warmly in the cocoon of its own thoughts, and dwell a hermit anywhere.

JAMES RUSSELL LOWELL (1819–91), U.S. poet, editor. "On a Certain Condescension in Foreigners," in *Atlantic Monthly* (Boston, Jan. 1869).

6   One receives as reward for much *ennui,* despondency, boredom—such as a solitude without friends, books, duties, passions must bring with it—those quarter-hours of profoundest contemplation within oneself and nature. He who completely entrenches himself against boredom also entrenches himself against himself: he will never get to drink the strongest refreshing draught from his own innermost fountain.

FRIEDRICH NIETZSCHE (1844–1900), German philosopher. *The Wanderer and his Shadow*, aph. 200 (published as second supplement to *Human, All Too Human*, 1880).

7　But when the self speaks to the self, who is speaking?—the entombed soul, the spirit driven in, in, in to the central catacomb; the self that took the veil and left the world—a coward perhaps, yet somehow beautiful, as it flits with its lantern restlessly up and down the dark corridors.

VIRGINIA WOOLF (1882–1941), British novelist. *Monday or Tuesday*, "An Unwritten Novel" (1921).

INVENTION

1　This is the patent age of new inventions
For killing bodies, and for saving souls,
All propagated with the best intentions.

LORD BYRON (1788–1824), English poet. *Don Juan*, cto. 1, st. 132.

2　Man is a shrewd inventor, and is ever taking the hint of a new machine from his own structure, adapting some secret of his own anatomy in iron, wood, and leather, to some required function in the work of the world.

RALPH WALDO EMERSON (1803–82), U.S. essayist, poet, philosopher. *English Traits*, "Wealth" (1856).

3　That is what we are supposed to do when we are at our best—make it all up—but make it up so truly that later it will happen that way.

ERNEST HEMINGWAY (1899–1961), U.S. author. Letter, 28 May 1934, to F. Scott Fitzgerald (published in *Selected Letters*, ed. by Carlos Baker, 1981).

4　A new gadget that lasts only five minutes is worth more than an immortal work that bores everyone.

FRANCIS PICABIA (1878–1953), French painter, poet. "M. Paul Signac, M. Francis Picabia et Dada," in *Figaro* (Paris, 20 Jan. 1922; repr. in *Écrits*, vol. 2, "1922," ed. by Olivier Revault d'Allones and Dominique Bouissou, 1978).

5　In my own time there have been inventions of this sort, transparent windows . . . tubes for diffusing warmth equally through all parts of a building . . . short-hand, which has been carried to such a perfection that a writer can keep pace with the most rapid speaker. But the inventing of such things is drudgery for the lowest slaves; philosophy lies deeper. It is not her office to teach men how to use their hands. The object of her lessons is to form the soul.

SENECA (c. 5 B.C.– A.D. c. 65), Roman writer, philosopher, statesman. *Epistulae ad Lucilium*, Epistle 90, sct. 25.

6　It is only the unimaginative who ever invents. The true artist is known by the use he makes of what he annexes.

OSCAR WILDE (1854–1900), Anglo-Irish playwright, author. Art review, 30 May 1885.

INVESTMENT

1　There is no finer investment for any community than putting milk into babies.

SIR WINSTON CHURCHILL (1874–1965), British statesman, writer. Radio broadcast, 21 March 1943 (published in *Complete Speeches*, vol. 7, 1974).

2　The social object of skilled investment should be to defeat the dark forces of time and ignorance which envelope our future.

JOHN MAYNARD KEYNES (1883–1946), British economist. *General Theory of Employment, Interest and Money*, bk. 4, ch. 12, sct. 5 (1936).

3　'Tis money that begets money.

ENGLISH PROVERB. Collected in Thomas Fuller, *Gnomologia* (1732). The first recorded version of this adage, possibly of Italian origin, is in T. Wilson, *Discourse upon Usury* (1572): "Money getteth money."

4　Money itself isn't lost or made, it's simply transferred from one perception to another. This painting here. I bought it 10 years ago for 60 thousand dollars. I could sell it today for 600. The illusion has become real and the more real it becomes, the more desperately they want it.

OLIVER STONE (b. 1946), U.S. filmmaker. Gordon Gekko (played by Michael Douglas), in the film *Wall Street* (written by Oliver Stone and Stanley Weiser, directed by Stone, 1987). The character of Gekko was loosely based on financier Ivan Boesky (see Boesky on GREED).

5　Sometimes your best investments are the ones you don't make.

DONALD TRUMP (b. 1946), U.S. businessman. *Trump: The Art of the Deal*, ch. 1 (1987; written with Tony Schwartz).

INVOLVEMENT

1　To say yes, you have to sweat and roll up your sleeves and plunge both hands into life up to the elbows. It's easy to say no, even if it means dying.

JEAN ANOUILH (1910–87), French playwright. Creon, in *Antigone*.

2　None of us liveth to himself, and no man dieth to himself.

BIBLE: NEW TESTAMENT. *Romans* 14:7.

3　I ask you to join in a re-United States. We need to empower our people so they can take more responsibility for their own lives in a world that is ever smaller, where everyone counts. . . . We need a new spirit of community, a sense that we are all in this together, or the American Dream will continue to wither. Our destiny is bound up with the destiny of every other American.

BILL CLINTON (b. 1946), U.S. Democratic politician, president. Speech to supporters, 4 Nov. 1992, Little Rock, Arkansas. Quoted in: *Guardian* (London, 5 Nov. 1992).

4　I recommend limiting one's involvement in other people's lives to a pleasantly scant minimum. This may seem too stoical a position in these madly passionate times, but madly passionate people rarely make good on their madly passionate promises.

QUENTIN CRISP (b. 1908), British author. *Manners from Heaven*, ch. 8 (1984).

5　No man is an island entire of itself; every man is a piece of the Continent, a part of the main. . . . Any man's death diminishes me because I am involved in Mankind; and therefore never send to know for whom the bell tolls; it tolls for thee.

JOHN DONNE (c. 1572–1631), English divine and metaphysical poet. *Devotions Upon Emergent Occasions*, Meditation 17 (1624).

6 The kind of relatedness to the world may be noble or trivial, but even being related to the basest kind of pattern is immensely preferable to being alone.

ERICH FROMM (1900–1980), U.S. psychologist. *Escape from Freedom,* ch. 1 (1941).

7 America I'm putting my queer shoulder to the wheel.

ALLEN GINSBERG (b. 1926), U.S. poet. *America.*

8 The gap between the committed and the indifferent is a Sahara whose faint trails, followed by the mind's eye only, fade out in sand.

NADINE GORDIMER (b. 1923), South African author. "Great Problems in the Street" (first published in *I Will Still Be Moved,* ed. by Marion Friedmann, 1963; repr. in *The Essential Gesture,* ed. by Stephen Clingman, 1988).

9 It is easy to talk of sitting at home contented, when others are seeing or making shows. But not to have been where it is supposed, and seldom supposed falsely, that all would go if they could; to be able to say nothing when everyone is talking; to have no opinion when everyone is judging; to hear exclamations of rapture without power to depress; to listen to falsehoods without right to contradict, is, after all, a state of temporary inferiority, in which the mind is rather hardened by stubbornness, than supported by fortitude. If the world be worth winning let us enjoy it, if it is to be despised let us despise it by conviction. But the world is not to be despised but as it is compared with something better.

SAMUEL JOHNSON (1709–84), English author, lexicographer. Letter, 21 June 1775, to Hester Thrale (published in *The Letters of Samuel Johnson,* vol. 2, no. 409, ed. by R. W. Chapman, 1952).

10 One must either take an interest in the human situation or else parade before the void.

JEAN ROSTAND (1894–1977), French biologist, writer. *Pensées d'un Biologiste* (1939; repr. in *The Substance of Man,* 1962, p. 82).

See also Debs on PROTEST.

IRAQ AND THE GULF WAR

1 According to U.S. strategy, if you never *see* the other, his destruction will be more acceptable . . . so that when Iraqi soldiers surrendered, sooner than expected, it was as if they emerged from a dream, a flash-back, a lost epoch—an epoch when the enemy still had a body and was still "like us."

SERGE DANEY (1944–92), French film critic. Quoted in: *Sight and Sound* (London, July 1992).

2 The Gulf War was like teenage sex. We got in too soon and out too soon.

TOM HARKIN (b. 1939), U.S. Democratic politician, Senator. Quoted in: *Independent on Sunday* (London, 29 Sept. 1991).

3 We have proved we are not modern. We have proved we are not religious in the real sense of the word. We have proved that we cannot afford democracy.

MUHAMMAD HEIKAL (b. 1923), Egyptian journalist. *Independent* (London, 11 March 1992), on the Arab world after the Gulf War.

4 If Kuwait grew carrots we wouldn't give a damn.

LAWRENCE KORB (b. 1939), Former U.S. assistant defense secretary. *International Herald Tribune* (Paris, 21 Aug. 1990), on the motives for "Operation Desert Storm."

5 Experts are saying that President Bush's goal now is to politically humiliate Saddam Hussein. Why don't we just make him the next Democratic presidential nominee?

JAY LENO (b. 1950), U.S. comedian, actor. *International Herald Tribune* (Paris, 18 March 1991).

6 We spend all day broadcasting on the radio and TV telling people back home what's happening here. And we learn what's happening here by spending all day monitoring the radio and TV broadcasts from back home.

P. J. O'ROURKE (b. 1947), U.S. journalist. *Give War A Chance,* "Gulf Diary" (1992; first published in *Rolling Stone*), entry for 31 January 1991.

IRELAND AND THE IRISH

1 Poor Paddy of all Christian men I think
On basest food pours down the vilest drink.

WILLIAM ALLINGHAM (1824–89), Irish poet, diarist. *Lawrence Bloomfield,* ch. 12 (1864). These two lines, as Allingham proudly noted in his diary, were quoted by Liberal politician William Gladstone—an advocate of Irish Home Rule—in the House of Commons, 30 May 1864, with reference to a proposed alteration of spirit duties.

2 History of Ireland—lawlessness and turbulency, robbery and oppression, hatred and revenge, blind selfishness everywhere—no principle, no heroism. What can be done with it?

WILLIAM ALLINGHAM (1824–89), Irish poet, diarist. *A Diary,* ch. 8 (ed. by H. Allingham and D. Radford, 1907), entry for 11 Nov. 1866.

3 Yet dearer still that Irish hill than all the world beside;
It's home, sweet home, where'er I roam, through lands and waters wide.

WILLIAM ALLINGHAM (1824–89), Irish poet, diarist. *Adieu to Belashanny.*

4 I came here for one thing only, to try to help national Ireland—and if there is no such thing in existence then the sooner I pay for my illusions the better.

SIR ROGER CASEMENT (1864–1916), Irish colonial administrator, nationalist. Letter, 29 April 1915, written from Germany, where he was trying to form an Irish Brigade of Irish prisoners of war with the aim of freeing Ireland from British rule. Landing in Ireland, 21 April 1916, he was arrested three days later and executed in August of that year. See Casement on CAPITAL PUNISHMENT.

5 For the great Gaels of Ireland
Are the men that God made mad,

For all their wars are merry
And all their songs are sad.

> G. K. CHESTERTON (1874–1936), British author. *Ballad of the White Horse.*

6   Not in vain is Ireland pouring itself all over the earth. Divine Providence has a mission for her children to fulfill; though a mission unrecognized by political economists. There is ever a moral balance preserved in the universe, like the vibrations of the pendulum. The Irish, with their glowing hearts and reverent credulity, are needed in this cold age of intellect and skepticism.

> LYDIA M. CHILD (1802–80), U.S. abolitionist, writer, editor. Letter, 8 Dec. 1842 (published in *Letters from New York*, vol. 1, letter 33, 1843).

7   The Irishman in English literature may be said to have been born with an apology in his mouth.

> JAMES CONNOLLY (1870–1916), Irish syndicalist, Republican leader. *Labour in Irish History*, Foreword (1910).

8   Ireland, as distinct from her people, is nothing to me; and the man who is bubbling over with love and enthusiasm for "Ireland," and can yet pass unmoved through our streets and witness all the wrong and the suffering, the shame and the degradation wrought upon the people of Ireland—yea, wrought by Irishmen upon Irish men and women, without burning to end it, is, in my opinion, a fraud and a liar in his heart, no matter how he loves that combination of chemical elements he is pleased to call Ireland.

> JAMES CONNOLLY (1870–1916), Irish syndicalist, Republican leader. Epigraph to *Labour in Ireland* (1916).

9   Consider Ireland. . . . You have a starving population, an absentee aristocracy, and an alien Church, and in addition the weakest executive in the world. That is the Irish Question.

> BENJAMIN DISRAELI (1804–81), English statesman, author. Speech, 16 Feb. 1844, to House of Commons.

10   To marry the Irish is to look for poverty.

> J. P. DONLEAVY (b. 1926), U.S. author. *The Ginger Man*, ch. 2 (1955).

11   No people can more exactly interpret the inmost meaning of the present situation in Ireland than the American Negro. The scheme is simple. You knock a man down and then have him arrested for assault. You kill a man and then hang the corpse.

> W. E. B. DU BOIS (1868–1963), U.S. civil rights leader, author. *The Seventh Son*, "Bleeding Ireland" (1971; first published 1921).

12   Ireland still remains the Holy Isle whose aspirations must on no account be mixed with the profane class-struggles of the rest of the sinful world . . . the Irish peasant must not on any account know that the Socialist workers are his sole allies in Europe.

> FRIEDRICH ENGELS (1820–95), German social philosopher. Letter, 9 Dec. 1869, to Karl Marx (published in *Marx and Engels: Collected Works*, vol. 43, 1988).

13   Irish Americans are about as Irish as black Americans are African.

> BOB GELDOF (b. 1954), Irish rock singer. Quoted in: *Observer* (London, 22 June 1986).

14   Ireland is where strange tales begin and happy endings are possible.

> CHARLES HAUGHEY (b. 1925), Irish Fianna Fáil politician, prime minister. *Daily Telegraph* (London, 14 July 1988).

15   This is our fate: eight hundred years' disaster,
crazily tangled like the Book of Kells:
the dream's distortion and the land's division,
the midnight raiders and the prison cells.

> JOHN HEWITT (b. 1907), Irish author, poet, playwright. *An Irishman in Coventry.*

16   Our day will come.

> SLOGAN OF THE I.R.A.

17   The Irish are a fair people; they never speak well of one another.

> SAMUEL JOHNSON (1709–84), English author, lexicographer. Quoted in: James Boswell, *Life of Samuel Johnson,* Feb. 1775 (1791).

18   Ireland is the old sow that eats her farrow.

> JAMES JOYCE (1882–1941), Irish author. Stephen Dedalus, in *A Portrait of the Artist as a Young Man*, ch. 5 (1916).

19   When the soul of a man is born in this country there are nets flung at it to hold it back from flight. You talk to me of nationality, language, religion. I shall try to fly by those nets.

> JAMES JOYCE (1882–1941), Irish author. Stephen Dedalus, in *A Portrait of the Artist as a Young Man*, ch. 5 (1916).

20   It seems to me you do not care what banality a man expresses so long as he expresses it in Irish.

> JAMES JOYCE (1882–1941), Irish author. Stephen Daedalus, in *Stephen Hero*, ch. 17 (1944; rev. 1975), in answer to Madden's attempts to convert him to Irish nationalism.

21   If I did not know that I am a genuine Dane, I could almost be tempted to explain my self-contradictions by supposing that I am an Irishman. For the Irish do not have the heart to immerse their children totally when they have them baptized; they want to keep a little paganism in reserve; generally the child is totally immersed under water but with the right arm free, so that he will be able to wield a sword with it, embrace the girls.

> SØREN KIERKEGAARD (1813–55), Danish philosopher. *Journals and Papers*, vol. 5 (ed. by Howard V. Hong and Edna H. Hong, 1978), entry no. 5556, 1840–42.

22   Och, Dublin City, there is no doubtin',
Bates every city upon the say;
'Tis there you'll see O'Connell spoutin',
An' Lady Morgan makin' tay;
For 'tis the capital of the finest nation,
Wid charmin' pisintry on a fruitful sod,
Fightin' like divils for conciliation
An' hatin' each other for the love of God.

> Attributed to CHARLES JAMES LEVER (1809–72), Irish novelist. *Dublin City.* Lady Morgan in her *Memoirs*, vol. 2, 30 Oct. 1826, mentions this compliment paid to her by a street ballad singer.

23   The Irish . . . are the damnedest race. They put so much emphasis on so many wrong things.

> MARGARET MITCHELL (1900–1949), U.S. novelist. Rhett Butler, in *Gone with the Wind*, vol. 2, pt. 4, ch. 34 (1936).

24   My one claim to originality among Irishmen is that I have never made a speech.

> GEORGE MOORE (1852–1933), Irish author. *Ave*, ch. 4 (1911).

25   The Irish are often nervous about having the appropriate face for the occasion. They have to be happy at weddings, which is a strain, so they get depressed; they have to be sad at funerals, which is easy, so they get happy.

> PEGGY NOONAN (b. 1950), U.S. author, presidential speechwriter. *What I Saw at the Revolution*, ch. 13 (1990).

26   Irishness is not primarily a question of birth or blood or language; it is the condition of being involved in the Irish situation, and usually of being mauled by it.

> CONOR CRUISE O'BRIEN (b. 1917), Irish historian, critic, diplomat. "Irishness," in *New Statesman* (London, Jan. 1959).

27   Life springs from death and from the graves of patriot men and women spring living nations. . . . They think that they have pacified Ireland. They think that they have purchased half of us and intimidated the other half. They think that they have foreseen everything, think they have provided against everything; but the fools, the fools, the fools, they have left us our Fenian dead, and while Ireland holds these graves Ireland unfree shall never be at peace.

> PATRICK HENRY PEARSE (1879–1916), Irish nationalist leader. Graveside oration, 1 Aug. 1915. The last part of this speech was later incorporated into Sean O'Casey, *The Plough and the Stars*, act 2 (1926).

28   There is no topic . . . more soporific and generally boring than the topic of Ireland *as Ireland, as a nation.*

> EZRA POUND (1885–1972), U.S. poet, critic. *New Age* (London, 8 Jan. 1920).

29   It is often said that in Ireland there is an excess of genius unsustained by talent; but there is talent in the tongues.

> V. S. PRITCHETT (b. 1900), British author and critic. *Midnight Oil*, vol. 2, ch. 6 (1971).

30   An Irishman's heart is nothing but his imagination.

> GEORGE BERNARD SHAW (1856–1950), Anglo-Irish playwright, critic. Larry Doyle, in *John Bull's Other Island*, act 1.

31   Your wits can't thicken in that soft moist air, on those white springy roads, in those misty rushes and brown bogs, on those hillsides of granite rocks and magenta heather. You've no such colours in the sky, no such lure in the distances, no such sadness in the evenings. Oh the dreaming! the dreaming! the torturing, heart-scalding, never satisfying dreaming, dreaming, dreaming, dreaming!

> GEORGE BERNARD SHAW (1856–1950), Anglo-Irish playwright, critic. Larry Doyle, in *John Bull's Other Island*, act 1, comparing Ireland with England.

32   A people so individual in its genius, so tenacious in love or hate, so captivating in its nobler moods.

> F. E. SMITH, LORD BIRKENHEAD (1872–1930), British Conservative politician, lawyer. Speech, 23 Nov. 1920, House of Lords, London.

33   We Irish are too poetical to be poets; we are a nation of brilliant failures, but we are the greatest talkers since the Greeks.

> OSCAR WILDE (1854–1900), Anglo-Irish playwright, author. Said to poet W. B. Yeats, Christmas 1888. Quoted in: Richard Ellman, *Oscar Wilde*, ch. 11 (1987).

34   An entirely new factor has appeared in the social development of the country, and this factor is the Irish-American, and his influence. To mature its powers, to concentrate its action, to learn the secret of its own strength and of England's weakness, the Celtic intellect has had to cross the Atlantic. At home it had but learned the pathetic weakness of nationality; in a strange land it realised what indomitable forces nationality possesses. What captivity was to the Jews, exile has been to the Irish: America and American influence have educated them.

> OSCAR WILDE (1854–1900), Anglo-Irish playwright, author. Review of J. A. Froude, *The Two Chiefs of Dunboy: or an Irish Romance of the Last Century*, in *Pall Mall Gazette* (London, 13 April 1889).

35   Out of Ireland have we come,
Great hatred, little room
Maimed us at the start.
I carry from my mother's womb
A fanatic's heart.

> W. B. YEATS (1865–1939), Irish poet, playwright. *Remorse for Intemperate Speech.*

36   I am of a healthy long lived race, and our minds improve with age.

> W. B. YEATS (1865–1939), Irish poet. Letter, 24 June 1935 (published in *The Letters of W. B. Yeats*, ed. by Allan Wade, 1954).

See also Joyce on EXPATRIATES; Pearse on MARTYRDOM; Murdoch on WOMEN.

NORTHERN IRELAND

1   Belfast . . . as uncivilised as ever—savage black mothers in houses of dark red brick, friendly manufacturers too drunk to entertain you when you arrive. It amuses me till I get tired.

> E. M. FORSTER (1879–1970), British novelist, essayist. Letter from private collection, 3 May 1928, to T. E. Lawrence.

2   The Troubles are a pigmentation in our lives here, a constant irritation that detracts from real life. But life has to do with something else as well, and it's the other things which are the more permanent and real.

> BRIAN FRIEL (b. 1929), Irish playwright, author. *Vanity Fair* (New York, Oct. 1991).

3   The tragedy of Northern Ireland is that it is now a society in which the dead console the living.

> JACK HOLLAND (b. 1947), Irish poet, journalist. *New York Times Magazine* (15 July 1979).

4   For generations, a wide range of shooting in Northern Ireland has provided all sections of the population with a pastime which . . . has occupied a great deal of leisure time. Unlike many other countries, the outstanding characteristic of the sport has been that it was not confined to any one class.

> NORTHERN IRISH TOURIST BOARD, 1969. Quoted in: *New Statesman* (London, 29 Aug. 1969).

5 How could Southern Ireland keep a bridal North in the manner to which she is accustomed?

TERENCE O'NEILL (1914–90), Northern Irish politician, prime minister. Quoted in: *Irish Times* (Dublin, 16 Jan. 1971).

6 At all events, as she, Ulster, cannot have the *status quo*, nothing remains for her but complete union or the most extreme form of Home Rule; that is, separation from both England and Ireland.

GEORGE BERNARD SHAW (1856–1950), Anglo-Irish playwright, critic. *New Statesman* (London, 7 June 1913).

IRONY

1 Jesus wept; Voltaire smiled. From that divine tear and from that human smile is derived the grace of present civilization.

VICTOR HUGO (1802–85), French poet, dramatist, novelist. "Centenaire de Voltaire," address, 30 May 1878, on the centenary of Voltaire's death.

2 Irony is a disciplinarian feared only by those who do not know it, but cherished by those who do. He who does not understand irony and has no ear for its whispering lacks *eo ipso* what might called the absolute beginning of the personal life. He lacks what at moments is indispensable for the personal life, lacks both the regeneration and rejuvenation, the cleaning baptism of irony that redeems the soul from having its life in finitude though living boldly and energetically in finitude.

SØREN KIERKEGAARD (1813–1855), Danish philosopher. *The Concept of Irony*, pt. 2, "Irony as a Mastered Moment. The Truth of Irony" (1841; tr. 1966).

3 Sentimental irony is a dog that bays at the moon while pissing on graves.

KARL KRAUS (1874–1936), Austrian satirist. *Sprüche und Widersprüche*, ch. 6 (1909; repr. in *Half-Truths and One-And-A Half-Truths: Selected Aphorisms*, "Riddles Out of Solutions," ed. by Harry Zohn, 1976).

4 Humor brings insight and tolerance. Irony brings a deeper and less friendly understanding.

AGNES REPPLIER (1858–1950), U.S. author, social critic. *In Pursuit of Laughter*, ch. 9 (1936).

5 Irony is the form of paradox. Paradox is what is good and great at the same time.

FRIEDRICH SCHLEGEL (1772–1829), German philosopher, critic, writer. *Dialogue on Poetry and Literary Aphorisms*, "Selected Aphorisms from *The Lyceum*," aph. 48 (1968; first published 1797).

IRREVERENCE

1 Impiety. Your irreverence toward my deity.

AMBROSE BIERCE (1842–1914), U.S. author. *The Devil's Dictionary* (1881–1906).

2 Conventionality is not morality. Self-righteousness is not religion. To attack the first is not to assail the last. To pluck the mask from the face of the Pharisee is not to lift an impious hand to the Crown of Thorns.

CHARLOTTE BRONTË (1816–55), English novelist. *Jane Eyre*, Preface (1847).

3 In America few people will trust you unless you are irreverent.

NORMAN MAILER (b. 1923), U.S. author. *The Presidential Papers*, Preface (1963).

4 True irreverence is disrespect for another man's god.

MARK TWAIN (1835–1910), U.S. author. *Following the Equator*, ch. 53, "Pudd'nhead Wilson's New Calendar" (1897).

ISLAM AND THE MUSLIMS

1 Sooner or later we must absorb Islam if our own culture is not to die of anemia.

BASIL BUNTING (1900–1985), British poet. Omar Pound, *Arabic and Persian Poems*, Foreword (1970).

2 The exact objectives of Islam Inc. are obscure. Needless to say everyone involved has a different angle, and they all intend to cross each other up somewhere along the line.

WILLIAM BURROUGHS (b. 1914), U.S. author. *Naked Lunch*, "Islam Inc. and the Parties of Interzone" (1959).

3 There is not a Musselman alive who would not imagine that he was performing an action pleasing to God and his Holy Prophet by exterminating every Christian on earth, while the Christians are scarcely more tolerant on their side.

DENIS DIDEROT (1713–84), French philosopher. *Conversations with a Christian Lady* (written 1774; published 1777; repr. in *Selected Writings*, ed. by Lester G. Crocker, 1966).

4 There is nothing in our book, the Koran, that teaches us to suffer peacefully. Our religion teaches us to be intelligent. Be peaceful, be courteous, obey the law, respect everyone; but if someone puts his hand on you, send him to the cemetery. That's a good religion.

MALCOLM X (1925–65), U.S. black leader. "Message to the Grass Roots," speech, Nov. 1963, Detroit (published in *Malcolm X Speaks*, ch. 1, 1965).

5 Muhammad is the Messenger of God,
and those who are with him are hard
against the unbelievers, merciful
one to another. Thou seest them
bowing, prostrating, seeking bounty
from God and good pleasure. Their
mark is on their faces, the trace of
prostration. . . .
God has promised
those of them who believe and do deeds
of righteousness forgiveness and
a mighty wage.

QUR'AN. *Victory* 48:35 (ed. by Arthur J. Arberry, 1955).

6 Muhammad brought down from heaven and put into the Koran not religious doctrines only, but political maxims, criminal and civil laws, and scientific theories. The Gospels, on the other hand, deal only with the general relations between man and God and between man and man. Beyond that, they teach nothing and do not oblige people to believe anything. That alone, among a thousand reasons, is enough to show that Islam will not be able to hold its power long in ages of enlightenment and democracy, while Christianity is destined to reign in such ages, as in all others.

ALEXIS DE TOCQUEVILLE (1805–59), French social philosopher. *Democracy in America*, vol. 2, pt. 1, ch. 5 (1840).

7   As for those who think the Arab world promises freedom, the briefest study of its routine traditional treatment of blacks (slavery) and women (purdah) will provide relief from all illusion. If Malcom X had been a black woman his last message to the world would have been entirely different. The brotherhood of Moslem men—all colors—may exist there, but part of the glue that holds them together is the thorough suppression of women.

ALICE WALKER (b. 1944), U.S. author, critic. *In Search of Our Mothers' Gardens*, "To the Editors of *Ms.* Magazine" (1983).

ISOLATION

1   We allow our ignorance to prevail upon us and make us think we can survive alone, alone in patches, alone in groups, alone in races, even alone in genders.

MAYA ANGELOU (b. 1928), U.S. author. Address to Centenary College of Louisiana (reported in *New York Times,* 11 March 1990).

2   Life's an awfully lonesome affair. . . . You come into the world alone and you go out of the world alone yet it seems to me you are more alone while living than even going and coming.

EMILY CARR (1871–1945), Canadian artist. *Hundreds and Thousands: The Journals of Emily Carr,* "The Elephant" (1966), entry for 16 July 1933.

3   National isolation breeds national neurosis.

HUBERT H. HUMPHREY (1911–78), U.S. Democratic politician, vice president. Speech, 6 Jan. 1967, Buffalo, New York.

4   I am greatly pleased with the public, authentic isolation in which we two, you and I, now find ourselves. It is wholly in accord with our attitude and our principles.

KARL MARX (1818–83), German political theorist, social philosopher. Letter, 11 February 1851, to Engels (published in *Karl Marx and Friedrich Engels: Collected Works,* vol. 38, 1982). Marx referred to the strains of party politics after the collapse of the Communist League of which he was a leading member. He added, "The system of mutual concessions, half-measures tolerated for decency's sake, and the obligation to bear one's share of public ridicule in the party with all these jack-asses, is now over."

5   It isn't the oceans which cut us off from the world—it's the American way of looking at things.

HENRY MILLER (1891–1980), U.S. author. *The Air-Conditioned Nightmare,* "Letter to Lafayette" (1945).

6   Life is for each man a solitary cell whose walls are mirrors.

EUGENE O'NEILL (1888–1953), U.S. dramatist. Lazarus, in *Lazarus Laughed,* act 2, sc. 1.

7   Not only does democracy make every man forget his ancestors, but also clouds their view of their descendants and isolates them from their contemporaries. Each man is for ever thrown back on himself alone, and there is danger that he may be shut up in the solitude of his own heart.

ALEXIS DE TOCQUEVILLE (1805–59), French social philosopher. *Democracy in America*, vol. 2, pt. 2, ch. 2 (1840).

8   We're born alone, we live alone, we die alone. Only through our love and friendship can we create the illusion for the moment that we're not alone.

ORSON WELLES (1915–84), U.S. filmmaker, actor, producer. Definition of loneliness contributed by Welles to Henry Jaglom, *Someone to Love* (1985).

9   We're all of us sentenced to solitary confinement inside our own skins, for life!

TENNESSEE WILLIAMS (1914–83), U.S. dramatist. Val Xavier, in *Orpheus Descending,* act 2, sc. 1.

See also Proust on VICE.

ISRAEL

1   For in the division of the nations of the whole earth he set a ruler over every people; but Israel is the Lord's portion: whom, being his firstborn, he nourisheth with discipline, and giving him the light of his love doth not forsake him. Therefore all their works are as the sun before him, and his eyes are continually upon their ways.

APOCRYPHA. *Ecclesiasticus* 17:17–9.

2   My generation, dear Ron, swore on the Altar of God that whoever proclaims the intent of destroying the Jewish state or the Jewish people, or both, seals his fate.

MENACHEM BEGIN (1913–92), Israeli politician, prime minister. Letter to Reagan. Quoted in: *Observer* (London, 2 Jan. 1983).

3   In Israel, in order to be a realist you must believe in miracles.

DAVID BEN GURION (1886–1973), Israeli statesman. CBS-TV, 5 Oct. 1956.

4   The fathers have eaten sour grapes, and the children's teeth are set on edge.

BIBLE, HEBREW. Proverb reproach by God concerning the land of Israel, in *Ezekiel* 18:2.

5   Listen, my friend, I've just come back from Mississippi and over there when you talk about the West Bank they think you mean Arkansas.

PATRICK BUCHANAN (b. 1938), U.S. journalist, broadcaster, presidential candidate in 1992. *Spectator* (London, 13 March 1992).

6   Israel, and you who call yourself Israel, the Church that calls itself Israel, and the revolt that calls itself Israel, and every nation chosen to be a nation—none of these lands is yours, all of you are thieves of holiness, all of you at war with Mercy.

LEONARD COHEN (b. 1934), Canadian singer, poet, novelist. *Book of Mercy,* sct. 27 (1984).

7   The view of Jerusalem is the history of the world; it is more, it is the history of earth and of heaven.

> BENJAMIN DISRAELI (1804–81), English statesman, author. *Tancred*, bk. 3, ch. 4 (1847).

8   The security of Israel is a moral imperative for all free peoples.

> HENRY KISSINGER (b. 1923), U.S. Republican politician, Secretary of State. Speech, 13 Nov. 1977, at presentation of Stephen Wise Award to Golda Meir.

9   Still on Israel's head forlorn,
Every nation heaps its scorn.

> EMMA LAZARUS (1849–87), U.S. poet. *The World's Justice*.

10   We have always said that in our war with the Arabs we had a secret weapon—no alternative.

> GOLDA MEIR (1898–1978), Israeli politician, prime minister. *Life* (New York, 3 Oct. 1969).

11   The greatest security for Israel is to create new Egypts.

> RONALD REAGAN (b. 1911), U.S. Republican politician, president. Quoted in: *Observer* (London, 27 Feb. 1983).

12   Our image has undergone change from David fighting Goliath to being Goliath.

> YITZHAK SHAMIR (b. 1915), Israeli politician, prime minister. Quoted in: *Daily Telegraph* (London, 25 Jan. 1989).

13   There is Israel, for us at least. What no other generation had, we have. We have Israel in spite of all the dangers, the threats and the wars, we have Israel. We can go to Jerusalem. Generations and generations could not and we can.

> ELIE WIESEL (b. 1928), Rumanian-born U.S. writer. Interview in *Writers at Work* (Eighth Series, ed. by George Plimpton, 1988).

See also Meir on COMPROMISE; The MIDDLE EAST; Balfour on PALESTINE.

ITALY AND THE ITALIANS

1   Open my heart and you will see,
Graved inside of it, "Italy."

> ROBERT BROWNING (1812–89), English poet. *De Gustibus*, st. 2.

2   Don't forget that even our most obscene vices nearly always bear the seal of sullen greatness.

> GESUALDO BUFALINO (b. 1920), Sicilian author. *Guardian* (London, 21 May 1992), of the Sicilians.

3   It is unjust that Italy should claim musical pre-eminence, even forcing Italian on music as its international language, when Italy's genius is so visual. No nation can build towns as beautiful nor claim a better right to regard nature as a shapeless substance to be redeemed by urbifaction. The Italians are not Wordsworthian. Man fulfils himself in the town. There is too much wild nature in music, and it has to be tamed into simple four-square patterns, as in Verdi and Bellini. The tenor does not proclaim Byronically to the woods and hills: he is a kind of sexy politician for the town *piazza*. The Italians would listen to Aaron, but not to Moses.

> ANTHONY BURGESS (b. 1917), British author, critic. *You've Had Your Time*, pt. 4 (1990).

4   Travelling is the ruin of all happiness! There's no looking at a building here after seeing Italy.

> FANNY BURNEY (1752–1840), English author. Mr. Meadows, in *Cecilia*, bk. 4, ch. 2 (1782).

5   I love the language, that soft bastard Latin,
Which melts like kisses from a female mouth,
And sounds as if it should be writ on satin
With syllables which breathe of the sweet South.

> LORD BYRON (1788–1824), English poet. *Beppo*, st. 44.

6   Italia! oh Italia! thou who hast
The fatal gift of beauty.

> LORD BYRON (1788–1824), English poet. *Childe Harold's Pilgrimage*, cto. 4, st. 42, a loose translation of the sonnet *Italia*, by the 17th-century Italian poet Vincenza da Filicaja.

7   There is, in fact, no law or government at all; and it is wonderful how well things go on without them.

> LORD BYRON (1788–1824), English poet. Letter, 2 Jan. 1821, to the poet Thomas Moore, written from Ravenna during a period of great revolutionary ferment (published in *Byron's Letters and Journals*, vol. 8, ed. by Leslie A. Marchand, 1973–81).

8   Love and understand the Italians, for the people are more marvellous than the land.

> E. M. FORSTER (1879–1970), British novelist, essayist. Philip Herriton, in *Where Angels Fear to Tread*, ch. 1 (1905). This advice to Philip's sister-in-law Lilia was taken literally by her: his real views emerged when she decided to marry an Italian.

9   Italy is such a delightful place to live in if you happen to be a man. There one may enjoy that exquisite luxury of Socialism—that true Socialism which is based not on equality of income or character, but on the equality of manners. In the democracy of the *caffè* or the street the great question of our life has been solved, and the brotherhood of man is a reality. But it is accomplished at the expense of the sisterhood of women.

> E. M. FORSTER (1879–1970), British novelist, essayist. *Where Angels Fear to Tread*, ch. 3 (1905).

10   The traveller who has gone to Italy to study the tactile values of Giotto, or the corruption of the Papacy, may return remembering nothing but the blue sky and the men and women who live under it.

> E. M. FORSTER (1879–1970), British novelist, essayist. *A Room with a View*, ch. 2 (1908).

11   Italy is a poor country full of rich people.

> RICHARD GARDNER (b. 1927), U.S. diplomat, former ambassador in Rome. Quoted in: *Observer* (London, 16 Aug. 1981).

12   Everything in Italy that is particularly elegant and grand . . . borders upon insanity and absurdity—or at least is reminiscent of childhood.

> ALEXANDER HERZEN (1812–70), Russian journalist, political thinker. *My Past and Thoughts*, vol. 3, pt. 8, "Miscellaneous Pieces: Beyond the Alps" (1921; tr. by Constance Garnett 1924–27).

13   A man who has not been in Italy, is always conscious of an inferiority.

> SAMUEL JOHNSON (1709–84), English author, lexicographer. Said over supper with James Boswell and the Corsican patriot Pasquale Paoli. Quoted in: Boswell, *Life of Samuel Johnson*, 11 April 1776 (1791).

14 I am damnably sick of Italy, Italian and Italians, outrageously, illogically sick . . . I hate to think that Italians ever did anything in the way of art. . . . What did they do but illustrate a page or so of the New Testament! They themselves think they have a monopoly in the line. I am dead tired of their bello and bellezza.

JAMES JOYCE (1882–1941), Irish author. Letter, 7 Dec. 1906, to his brother from Rome (published in *Letters of James Joyce*, vol. 2, 1966).

15 And that is . . . how they are. So terribly physically all over one another. They pour themselves one over the other like so much melted butter over parsnips. They catch each other under the chin, with a tender caress of the hand, and they smile with sunny melting tenderness into each other's face.

D. H. LAWRENCE (1885–1930), British author. *Sea and Sardinia*, ch. 1 (1923), of the Sicilians.

16 For us to go to Italy and to penetrate into Italy is like a most fascinating act of self-discovery—back, back down the old ways of time. Strange and wonderful chords awake in us, and vibrate again after many hundreds of years of complete forgetfulness.

D. H. LAWRENCE (1885–1930), British author. *Sea and Sardinia*, ch. 6 (1923).

17 Christ never came this far, nor did time, nor the individual soul, nor hope, nor the relation of cause to effect, nor reason nor history.

CARLO LEVI (1902–75), Italian writer, painter. *Christ Stopped at Eboli*, ch. 1 (1945; tr. 1948), of Basilicata, in southern Italy. The book, describing Levi's internment in a small village as a consequence of his anti-fascist activities, was the first to publicize the true plight of the Italian South.

18 Italy is a geographical expression.

PRINCE METTERNICH (1773–1859), Austrian statesman. Letter, 6 Aug. 1847, to English statesman Lord Palmerston.

19 Report of fashions in proud Italy,
Whose manners still our tardy-apish nation
Limps after in base imitation.

WILLIAM SHAKESPEARE (1564–1616), English dramatist, poet. The Duke of York, in *Richard II*, act 2, sc. 1.

20 Thou Paradise of exiles, Italy!

PERCY BYSSHE SHELLEY (1792–1822), English poet. *Julian and Maddalo*.

21 Lump the whole thing! Say that the Creator made Italy from designs by Michael Angelo!

MARK TWAIN (1835–1910), U.S. author. Dan, in *The Innocents Abroad*, ch. 27 (1896). See Twain on ARTISTS.

22 I think sometimes that it is almost a pity to enjoy Italy as much as I do, because the acuteness of my sensations makes them rather exhausting; but when I see the stupid Italians I have met here, completely insensitive to their surroundings, and ignorant of the treasures of art and history among which they have grown up, I begin to think it is better to be an American, and bring to it all a mind and eye unblunted by custom.

EDITH WHARTON (1862–1937), U.S. author. Letter, 8 March 1903 (published in *The Letters of Edith Wharton*, 1988).

See also Byron on COURAGE; Lawrence on OPERA; ROME; VENICE.

HENRY JAMES

1 Few writers have had less journalistic talent than James, and this is his defect, for the supreme masters have one trait in common with the childish scribbling mass, the vulgar curiosity of a police-court reporter.

W. H. AUDEN (1907–73), Anglo-American poet. *The Dyer's Hand*, pt. 7, "The American Scene" (1962).

2 He was a young lady in so many ways. A Victorian lady. Somewhere inside him, there was an adolescent girl.

LEON EDEL (b. 1907), U.S. biographer, critic. Interview in *Writers at Work* (Eighth Series, ed. by George Plimpton, 1988).

3 The work of Henry James has always seemed divisible by a simple dynastic arrangement into three reigns: James I, James II, and the Old Pretender.

PHILIP GUEDALLA (1889–1944), British author. *Supers and Supermen*, "Some Critics" (1920).

4 Tell the boys to follow, to be faithful, to take me seriously.

HENRY JAMES (1843–1916), U.S. author. Quoted in: H. Montgomery Hyde, *Henry James at Home*, ch. 7, sct. 4 (1969). James spoke these words, according to Hyde, during one of his last conscious moments, when his mind was dwelling on his work.

5 A second-class mind dealing with third-class material is hardly a necessity of life.

HAROLD LASKI (1893–1950), British political scientist. Letter, 31 Aug. 1916, to Oliver Wendell Holmes, Jr. (published in *The Holmes-Laski Letters*, ed. by Mark DeWolfe Howe, 1953). Laski was referring to James's *The Ambassadors*.

6 Poor Henry, he's spending eternity wandering round and round a stately park and the fence is just too high for him to peep over and they're having tea just too far away for him to hear what the countess is saying.

W. SOMERSET MAUGHAM (1874–1965), British author. Edward Driffield, in *Cakes and Ale*, ch. 11 (1930).

7 He did not live, he observed life from a window, and too often was inclined to content himself with no more than what his friends told him they saw when *they* looked out of a window. . . . In the end the point of Henry James is neither his artistry nor his seriousness, but his personality, and this was curious and charming and a trifle absurd.

W. SOMERSET MAUGHAM (1874–1965), British author. *A Writer's Notebook* (1949), entry in 1937.

8 Well, well, Henry James is pretty good, though he is of the nineteenth century, and that glaringly.

ROBERT LOUIS STEVENSON (1850–94), Scottish novelist, essayist, poet. Letter, March 1889, to Henry James (published in *The Letters of Robert Louis Stevenson*, vol. 2, 1899).

9 James's great gift, of course, was his ability to tell a plot in shimmering detail with such delicacy of treatment and such fine aloofness—that is, reluctance to engage in any direct grappling with what, in the play or story, had actually "taken place"—that his listeners often did not, in the end, know what had, to put it in another way, "gone on."

JAMES THURBER (1894–1961), U.S. humorist, illustrator. *New Yorker* (17 June 1933).

10   We who knew him well know how great he would have been if he had never written a line.

> EDITH WHARTON (1862–1937), U.S. author. Letter of condolence, 1 March 1916, written the day after James's death (published in *The Letters of Edith Wharton*, 1988).

11   Mr. Henry James writes fiction as if it were a painful duty.

> OSCAR WILDE (1854–1900), Anglo-Irish playwright, author. Vivian, in "The Decay of Lying" (published in *Intentions*, 1891).

See also Woolf on LITERATURE.

JAPAN AND THE JAPANESE

1   The Japanese are, to the highest degree, both aggressive and unaggressive, both militaristic and aesthetic, both insolent and polite, rigid and adaptable, submissive and resentful of being pushed around, loyal and treacherous, brave and timid, conservative and hospitable to new ways.

> RUTH BENEDICT (1887–1948), U.S. anthropologist. *The Chrysanthemum and the Sword*, ch. 1 (1946).

2   There are times when they seem so small! And then again, although they never seem large, there is a vastness behind them, a past of indefinite complexity and marvel, an amazing power of absorbing and assimilating, which forces one to suspect some power in the race so different from our own that one cannot understand that power. And . . . whatever doubts or vexations one has in Japan, it is only necessary to ask oneself: "Well, who are the best people to live with?"

> LAFCADIO HEARN (1850–1904), U.S. journalist, author. Letter, Aug. 1891. Quoted in: Elizabeth Bisland, *The Life and Times of Lafcadio Hearn*, vol. 2 (1906). Hearn had moved to Japan the previous year, and he spent the rest of his life there.

3   For the building of a new Japan
Let's put our mind and strength together,
Doing our best to promote production,
Sending our goods to the peoples of the world,
Endlessly and continuously,
Like water gushing from a fountain.
Grow, industry, grow, grow, grow,
Harmony and sincerity. Matsushita Electrical.

> MATSUSHITA ELECTRICAL COMPANY. Company anthem, sung on official occasions. Quoted in: F. L. K. Hsu, *Iemoto, The Heart of Japan* (1975).

4   The Japanese have perfected good manners and made them indistinguishable from rudeness.

> PAUL THEROUX (b. 1941), U.S. novelist, travel writer. *The Great Railway Bazaar*, ch. 28 (1975).

5   In fact, the whole of Japan is a pure invention. There is no such country, there are no such people. . . . The Japanese people are . . . simply a mode of style, an exquisite fancy of art.

> OSCAR WILDE (1854–1900), Anglo-Irish playwright, author. Vivian, in "The Decay of Lying" (published in *Intentions*, 1891).

JARGON

1   Jargon is the verbal sleight of hand that makes the old hat seem newly fashionable; it gives an air of novelty and specious profundity to ideas that, if stated directly, would seem superficial, stale, frivolous, or false. The line between serious and spurious scholarship is an easy one to blur, with jargon on your side.

> DAVID LEHMAN (b. 1948), U.S. poet, editor, critic. *Signs of the Times*, ch. 3, "Archie Debunking" (1991).

2   Psychobabble is . . . a set of repetitive verbal formalities that kills off the very spontaneity, candor, and understanding it pretends to promote. It's an idiom that reduces psychological insight to a collection of standardized observations, that provides a frozen lexicon to deal with an infinite variety of problems.

> RICHARD DEAN ROSEN (b. 1949), U.S. journalist, critic. *Psychobabble: Fast Talk and Quick Cure in the Era of Feeling*, "Psychobabble" (1977), on "psychobabble," the term first coined by Rosen to describe the dialect or slang of the Bay Area of San Francisco.

JAZZ

1   The further jazz moves away from the stark blue continuum and the collective realities of Afro-American and American life, the more it moves into academic concert-hall lifelessness, which can be replicated by any middle class showing off its music lessons.

> IMAMU AMIRI BARAKA [LEROI JONES] (b. 1934), U.S. poet, playwright. *Daggers and Javelins*, "Jazz: Speech At Black Film Festival" (1984).

2   I've come close to matching the feeling of that night in 1944 in music, when I first heard Diz and Bird, but I've never got there. . . . I'm always looking for it, listening and feeling for it, though, trying to always feel it in and through the music I play everyday.

> MILES DAVIS (1926–91), U.S. jazz musician. *Miles: The Autobiography*, Prologue (1989).

3   It seems to me monstrous that anyone should believe that the jazz rhythm expresses America. Jazz rhythm expresses the primitive savage.

> ISADORA DUNCAN (1878–1927), U.S. dancer. *My Life*, ch. 30 (1927).

4   Playing "bop" is like playing Scrabble with all the vowels missing.

> DUKE ELLINGTON (1899–1974), U.S. jazz musician. *Look* (New York, 10 Aug. 1954).

5   Syncopations are no indication of light or trashy music, and to shy bricks at "hateful ragtime" no longer passes for musical culture.

> SCOTT JOPLIN (1868–1917), U.S. pianist, composer. *The School of Ragtime*, Preface (1908).

6   Jazz is the big brother of the blues. If a guy's playing blues like we play, he's in high school. When he starts playing jazz it's like going on to college, to a school of higher learning.

> B. B. KING (b. 1925), U.S. blues guitarist. *Sunday Times* (London, 4 Nov. 1984).

7 There's more bad music in jazz than any other form. Maybe that's because the audience doesn't really know what's happening.

> PAT METHENY (b. 1954), U.S. jazz guitarist. *International Herald Tribune* (Paris, 7 July 1992).

8 Jazz music is an intensified feeling of nonchalance.

> FRANÇOISE SAGAN (b. 1935), French novelist. Dominique, in *A Certain Smile*, pt. 1, ch. 7 (1956).

9 Today he plays jazz; tomorrow he betrays his country.

> STALINIST SLOGAN in the Soviet Union (1920s).

10 Something was still there, that something that distinguishes an artist from a performer: the revealing of self. Here I be. Not for long, but here I be. In sensing her mortality, we sensed our own.

> STUDS TERKEL (b. 1912), U.S. author, broadcaster. *Talking to Myself*, bk. 4, ch. 4 (1977), on seeing Billie Holiday perform in Chicago, 1956.

See also McRae on The BLUES; Holiday on SONG.

JEALOUSY

1 The "Green-Eyed Monster" causes much woe, but the absence of this ugly serpent argues the presence of a corpse whose name is Eros.

> MINNA ANTRIM (1861–?), U.S. epigrammist. *Naked Truth and Veiled Allusions,* (1901, p. 91).

2 The heart of the jealous knows the best and most satisfying love, that of the other's bed, where the rival perfects the lover's imperfections.

> DJUNA BARNES (1892–1982), U.S. author, poet, columnist. Doctor, in *Nightwood*, ch. 5 (1936).

3 Set me as a seal upon thine heart, as a seal upon thine arm: for love is strong as death; jealousy is cruel as the grave: the coals thereof are coals of fire, which hath a most vehement flame.

> BIBLE, HEBREW. *Song of Solomon* 8:6.

4 Jealousy is never satisfied with anything short of an omniscience that would detect the subtlest fold of the heart.

> GEORGE ELIOT (1819–80), English novelist. *The Mill on the Floss*, bk. 6, ch. 10 (1860).

5 There is a sort of jealousy which needs very little fire; it is hardly a passion, but a blight bred in the cloudy, damp despondency of uneasy egoism.

> GEORGE ELIOT (1819–80), English novelist. *Middlemarch*, bk. 2, ch. 21 (1871–72).

6 Jealousy, that dragon which slays love under the pretence of keeping it alive.

> HAVELOCK ELLIS (1859–1939), British psychologist. *On Life and Sex: Essays of Love and Virtue*, ch. 1 (1937).

7 Jealousy is indeed a poor medium to secure love, but it is a secure medium to destroy one's self-respect. For jealous people, like dope-fiends, stoop to the lowest level and in the end inspire only disgust and loathing.

> EMMA GOLDMAN (1869–1940), U.S. anarchist. "Jealousy: Causes and a Possible Cure," lecture (c. 1912; published in *Red Emma Speaks*, pt. 2, ed. by Alix Kates Shulman, 1972).

8 Jealousy is all the fun you *think* they had. . . .

> ERICA JONG (b. 1942), U.S. author. *How To Save Your Own Life*, "Bennett tells all in Woodstock . . .," epigraph (1977).

9 Jealousy contains more of self-love than of love.

> FRANÇOIS, DUC DE LA ROCHEFOUCAULD (1613–80), French writer, moralist. *Sentences et Maximes Morales*, no. 324 (1678).

10 Always remember, Peggy, it's matrimonial suicide to be jealous when you have a really good reason.

> CLARE BOOTHE LUCE (1903–87), U.S. diplomat, writer. Edith, in *The Women*, act 3 (1936).

11 To jealousy, nothing is more frightful than laughter.

> FRANÇOISE SAGAN (b. 1935), French novelist. Lucile, in *La Chamade*, ch. 9 (1965).

12 I had rather be a toad,
And live upon the vapour of a dungeon
Than keep a corner in the thing I love
For others' uses.

> WILLIAM SHAKESPEARE (1564–1616), English dramatist, poet. Othello, in *Othello*, act 3, sc. 3.

13 Never waste jealousy on a real man: it is the imaginary man that supplants us all in the long run.

> GEORGE BERNARD SHAW (1856–1950), Anglo-Irish playwright, critic. Hector Hushabye, in *Heartbreak House*, act 2.

See also Strindberg on INFIDELITY.

JESUS CHRIST

1 I am the bread of life: he that cometh to me shall never hunger; and he that believeth on me shall never thirst.

> BIBLE: NEW TESTAMENT. Jesus, in *John* 6:35.

2 Thinking as I do that the Creator of this world is a very cruel being, & being a worshipper of Christ, I cannot help saying: "the Son, O how unlike the Father!" First God Almighty comes with a thump on the head. Then Jesus Christ comes with a balm to heal it.

> WILLIAM BLAKE (1757–1827), English poet, painter, engraver. *A Vision of the Last Judgement* (1810; repr. in *Complete Writings*, ed. by Geoffrey Keynes, 1957).

3 A lot of people say to me, "Why did you kill Christ?" "I dunno . . . it was one of those parties, got out of hand, you know." "We killed him because he didn't want to become a doctor, that's why we killed him."

> LENNY BRUCE (1925–66), U.S. satirical comedian. *The Essential Lenny Bruce*, "The Jews" (ed. by John Cohen, 1967).

4 None speak of the bravery, the might, or the intellect of Jesus; but the devil is always imagined as a being of acute intellect, political cunning, and the fiercest courage. These universal and instinctive tendencies of the human mind reveal much.

> LYDIA M. CHILD (1802–80), U.S. abolitionist, writer. Let-

ter, Jan. 1843. Published in *Letters from New York*, vol. 1, letter 34 (1843).

5 The blood of Jesus Christ can cover a multitude of sins, it seems to me.

DENIS DIDEROT (1713–84), French philosopher. Mme de Maréchale, in *Conversation with a Christian Lady* (1777; repr. in *Selected Writings*, ed. by Lester G. Crocker, 1966).

6 A man who was completely innocent, offered himself as a sacrifice for the good of others, including his enemies, and became the ransom of the world. It was a perfect act.

MOHANDAS K. GANDHI (1869–1948), Indian political and spiritual leader. *Non-Violence in Peace and War*, vol. 2, ch. 166 (1949), referring to Jesus.

7 Jesus was the first socialist, the first to seek a better life for mankind.

MIKHAIL GORBACHEV (b. 1931), Soviet political leader. *Daily Telegraph* (London, 16 June 1992).

8 I wouldn't put it past God to arrange a virgin birth if He wanted, but I very much doubt if He would.

DAVID JENKINS (b. 1925), British ecclesiastic, bishop of Durham. *Church Times* (London, 4 May 1984).

9 He comes into the world God knows how, walks on the water, gets out of his grave and goes up off the Hill of Howth. What drivel is this?

JAMES JOYCE (1882–1941), Irish author. Stephen Daedalus, in *Stephen Hero*, ch. 21 (1944; rev. 1975).

10 Jesus was all right, but his disciples were thick and ordinary. It's them twisting it that ruins it for me.

JOHN LENNON (1940–80), British rock musician. *Evening Standard* (London, 4 March 1966).

11 The word "Christianity" is already a misunderstanding—in reality there has been only one Christian, and he died on the Cross.

FRIEDRICH NIETZSCHE (1844–1900), German philosopher. *The Anti-Christ*, aph. 39 (1895).

12 Jesus was a brilliant Jewish stand-up comedian, a phenomenal improvisor. His parables are great one-liners.

CAMILLE PAGLIA (b. 1947), U.S. author, critic, educator. *Harper's* (New York, March 1991).

13 A heroic figure . . . not wholly to blame for the religion that's been foisted on him.

EZRA POUND (1885–1972), U.S. poet, critic. Letter, 1914, to the father of Pound's bride-to-be, Dorothy Shakespear, explaining his reasons for not wanting a church wedding. Quoted in: Humphrey Carpenter, *A Serious Character*, pt. 2, ch. 13 (1988).

14 Never has any one been less a priest than Jesus, never a greater enemy of forms, which stifle religion under the pretext of protecting it. By this we are all his disciples and his successors; by this he has laid the eternal foundation-stone of true religion; and if religion is essential to humanity, he has by this deserved the Divine rank the world has accorded him.

ERNEST RENAN (1823–92), French writer, critic, scholar. *The Life of Jesus*, ch. 5 (1863).

15 Let us pardon him his hope of a vain apocalypse,

and of a second coming in great triumph upon the clouds of heaven. Perhaps these were the errors of others rather than his own; and if it be true that he himself shared the general illusion, what matters it, since his dream rendered him strong against death, and sustained him in a struggle to which he might otherwise have been unequal?

ERNEST RENAN (1823–1892), French writer, critic, scholar. *The Life of Jesus*, ch. 17 (1863).

16 The Galilean is not a favourite of mine. So far from owing him any thanks for his favour, I cannot avoid confessing that I owe a secret grudge to his carpentership.

PERCY BYSSHE SHELLEY (1792–1822), English poet. Letter, 24 April 1811 (published in *The Letters of Percy Bysshe Shelley*, vol. 1, ed. by Frederick L. Jones, 1964).

17 Thou has conquered, O pale Galilean.

A. C. SWINBURNE (1837–1909), English poet, critic. *Hymn to Proserpine*.

18 There is but one love of Jesus, as there is but one person in the poor — Jesus. We take vows of chastity to love Christ with undivided love; to be able to love him with undivided love we take a vow of poverty which frees us from all material possessions, and with that freedom we can love him with undivided love, and from this vow of undivided love we surrender ourselves totally to him in the person who takes his place.

MOTHER TERESA (b. 1910), Albanian-born Roman Catholic missionary. *A Gift for God*, "Carriers of Christ's Love" (1975).

19 Somewhere in the bible it say Jesus' hair was like lamb's wool, I say. Well, say Shug, if he came to any of these churches we talking bout he'd have to have it conked before anybody paid him any attention. The last thing niggers want to think about they God is that his hair kinky.

ALICE WALKER (b. 1944), U.S. author, critic. *The Color Purple* (1983).

20 Every time that I think of the crucifixion of Christ, I commit the sin of envy.

SIMONE WEIL (1909–43), French philosopher, mystic. *Waiting on God*, letter 4 (1950).

See also Nichols on FICTION; Brown on The MESSIAH; O'Connor on The SOUTH.

JEWELRY

1 Don't ever wear artistic jewelry; it wrecks a woman's reputation.

COLETTE (1873–1954), French author. Aunt Alicia, in *Gigi* (1944; tr. 1953). When asked (by Gilberte), "What is an artistic jewel?" Aunt Alicia replied, "It all depends. A mermaid in gold, with eyes of chrysoprase. An Egyptian scarab. A large engraved amethyst. A not very heavy bracelet said to have been chased by a master-hand. A lyre or star, mounted as a brooch. A studded tortoise. In a word, all of them frightful. Never wear baroque pearls, not even as hat-pins. Beware above all things, of family jewels!"

2 Let us not be too particular. It is better to have old second-hand diamonds than none at all.

MARK TWAIN (1835–1910), U.S. author. *Following the Equator*, ch. 34, "Pudd'nhead Wilson's New Calendar" (1897).

JEWS

See JUDAISM AND THE JEWS.

SAMUEL JOHNSON

1 My mind was, as it were, strongly impregnated with the Johnsonian aether.

> JAMES BOSWELL (1740–95), Scottish biographer, companion of Samuel Johnson. *Life of Samuel Johnson,* July 1763 (1791).

2 Figure him there, with his scrofulous diseases, with his great greedy heart, and unspeakable chaos of thoughts; stalking mournful as a stranger in this Earth; eagerly devouring what spiritual thing he could come at: school-languages and other merely grammatical stuff, if there were nothing better! The largest soul that was in all England.

> THOMAS CARLYLE (1795–1881), Scottish essayist, historian. *On Heroes and Hero-Worship,* lecture 5, "The Hero as a Man of Letters" (1841).

3 Perhaps Samuel Johnson was a great man; he was certainly a drumbling one.

> EDWARD DAHLBERG (1900–1977), U.S. author, critic. *Alms for Oblivion,* "Allen Tate, the Forlorn Demon" (1964).

4 If you were to make little fishes talk, they would talk like whales.

> OLIVER GOLDSMITH (1728–74), Anglo-Irish author, poet, playwright. Quoted in: James Boswell, *Life of Samuel Johnson,* entry for 27 April 1773 (1791), to Johnson.

5 Beyond all question, I might have had a wiser friend than he. The atmosphere in which alone he breathed was dense; his awful dread of death showed how much muddy imperfection was to be cleansed out of him, before he could be capable of spiritual existence; he meddled only with the surface of life, and never cared to penetrate further than to ploughshare depth; his very sense and sagacity were but a one-eyed clear-sightedness. . . . Dr. Johnson's morality was as English an article as a beefsteak.

> NATHANIEL HAWTHORNE (1804–1864), U.S. author. *Our Old Home,* "Lichfield and Uttoxeter" (1863). Henry James said that this formed part of a graceful tribute to Johnson who "certainly has nowhere else been more tenderly spoken of."

6 Dr. Johnson was a lazy learned man who liked to think and talk better than to read or write; who, however, wrote much and well, but too often by rote.

> WILLIAM HAZLITT (1778–1830), English essayist. *Lectures on the English Poets,* "On Swift, Young, Gray, Collins &c." (1818).

7 Now that the old lion is dead every ass thinks he may kick at him.

> SAMUEL PARR (1747–1825), English schoolteacher. Remark, 1784, while dining with painter Sir Joshua Reynolds. Quoted in: James Boswell, *Life of Samuel Johnson* (1791). Dr. Parr composed the Latin epitaph to Johnson in St. Paul's Cathedral, London.

8 Johnson's conversation was by much too strong for a person accustomed to obsequiousness and flattery; it was mustard in a young child's mouth.

> HESTER LYNCH THRALE [LATER PIOZZI] (1739–1821), English

writer. Quoted in: James Boswell, *Life of Samuel Johnson,* May 1781 (1791).

JOKES AND JOKERS

1 My life has been one great big joke,
A dance that's walked
A song that's spoke,
I laugh so hard I almost choke
When I think about myself.

> MAYA ANGELOU (b. 1928), U.S. author. *Just Give Me a Cool Drink of Water 'fore I Diiie,* "When I Think about Myself" (1971).

2 Witticism. A sharp and clever remark, usually quoted and seldom noted; what the Philistine is pleased to call a "joke."

> AMBROSE BIERCE (1842–1914), U.S. author. *The Devil's Dictionary* (1881–1906).

3 Being a funny person does an awful lot of things to you. You feel that you mustn't get serious with people. They don't expect it from you, and they don't want to see it. You're not entitled to be serious, you're a clown, and they only want you to make them laugh.

> FANNY BRICE (1891–1951), U.S. entertainer. Quoted in: Norman Katkov, *The Fabulous Fanny,* ch. 9 (1952).

4 I remain just one thing, and one thing only — and that is a clown. It places me on a far higher plane than any politician.

> CHARLIE CHAPLIN (1889–1977), British comic actor, filmmaker. Quoted in: *Observer* (London, 17 June 1960).

5 The old idea that the joke was not good enough for the company has been superseded by the new aristocratic idea that the company was not worthy of the joke. They have introduced an almost insane individualism into that one form of intercourse which is specially and uproariously communal. They have made even levities into secrets. They have made laughter lonelier than tears.

> G. K. CHESTERTON (1874–1936), British author. *All Things Considered,* "Demagogues and Mystagogues" (1908).

6 Prithee don't screw your wit beyond the compass of good manners.

> COLLEY CIBBER (1671–1757), English actor-manager, playwright. Narcissa, in *Love's Last Shift,* act 2, sc. 1.

7 His hilarity was like a scream from a crevasse.

> GRAHAM GREENE (1904–91), British novelist. *The Heart of the Matter,* bk. 3, pt. 1, ch. 1, sct. 1 (1948), of Major Scobie.

8 A pun does not commonly justify a blow in return. But if a blow were given for such cause, and death ensued, the jury would be judges both of the facts and of the pun, and might, if the latter were of an aggravated character, return a verdict of justifiable homicide.

> OLIVER WENDELL HOLMES, SR. (1809–94), U.S. writer, physician. *The Autocrat of the Breakfast-Table,* ch. 1 (1858).

9 I gleaned jests at home from obsolete farces.

> SAMUEL JOHNSON (1709–84), English author, lexicographer. *Rambler,* no. 141 (London, 23 July 1751).

10 The funniest line in English is "Get it?" When you say that, *everyone* chortles.

GARRISON KEILLOR (b. 1942), U.S. writer. *We Are Still Married,* Introduction (1989).

11 The teller of a mirthful tale has latitude allowed him. We are content with less than absolute truth.

CHARLES LAMB (1775–1834), English essayist, critic. *The Last Essays of Elia,* "Stage Illusion" (1833).

12 If all else fails, the character of a man can be recognized by nothing so surely as by a jest which he takes badly.

G. C. LICHTENBERG (1742–99), German physicist, philosopher. *Aphorisms,* "Notebook K," aph. 46 (written 1765–99; tr. by R. J. Hollingdale, 1990).

13 Jokes are grievances.

MARSHALL MCLUHAN (1911–80), Canadian communications theorist. Remark, June 1969, at American Booksellers Association luncheon, Washington, D.C. Quoted in: *Sun* (Vancouver, 7 June 1969).

14 A dirty joke is a sort of mental rebellion.

GEORGE ORWELL (1903–50), British author. "The Art of Donald McGill," in *Horizon* (London, Sept. 1941; repr. in *Collected Essays,* 1961).

15 I don't know jokes; I just watch the government and report the facts.

WILL ROGERS (1879–1935), U.S. humorist. "A Rogers Thesaurus," in *Saturday Review* (25 Aug. 1962).

16 Alas, poor Yorick! I knew him, Horatio: a fellow of infinite jest, of most excellent fancy. . . . Where be your jibes now, your gambols, your songs, your flashes of merriment that were wont to set the table on a roar?

WILLIAM SHAKESPEARE (1564–1616), English dramatist, poet. Hamlet, in *Hamlet,* act 5, sc. 1.

17 He jests at scars that never felt a wound.

WILLIAM SHAKESPEARE (1564–1616), English dramatist, poet. Romeo, in *Romeo and Juliet,* act 2, sc. 1, of Mercutio, who mocked Romeo's lovelorn state.

18 My way of joking is to tell the truth. It's the funniest joke in the world.

GEORGE BERNARD SHAW (1856–1950), Anglo-Irish playwright, critic. Keegan, in *John Bull's Other Island,* act 2.

19 Suppose the world were only one of God's jokes, would you work any the less to make it a good joke instead of a bad one?

GEORGE BERNARD SHAW (1856–1950), Anglo-Irish playwright, critic. Letter, 14 Feb. 1910, to Count Leo Tolstoy (published in *Collected Letters,* vol. 2, 1972). Tolstoy had criticized Shaw for his facetious tone in *Arms and the Man,* saying that one "should not speak jestingly of such a subject as the purpose of human life, the causes of its perversion, and the evil that fills the life of humanity today."

20 'Tis no extravagant arithmetic to say, that for every ten jokes, — thou hast got an hundred enemies; and till thou hast gone on, and raised a swarm of wasps about thine ears, and art half stung to death by them, thou wilt never be convinced it is so.

LAURENCE STERNE (1713–1768), English author. *Tristram Shandy,* bk. 1, ch. 12 (1760).

21 All womankind, from the highest to the lowest . . . love jokes; the difficulty is to know how they choose to have them cut; and there is no knowing that, but by trying, as we do with our artillery in the field, by raising or letting down their breeches, till we hit the mark.

LAURENCE STERNE (1713–68), English author. Trim, in *Tristram Shandy,* bk. 9, ch. 8 (1760–67).

22 All human race would fain be wits.
And millions miss, for one that hits.

JONATHAN SWIFT (1667–1745), Anglo-Irish satirist. *On Poetry: A Rhapsody.*

See also COMEDY AND COMEDIANS; HUMOR; PUNS; Goldsmith on The RICH; Twainon TRIALS.

JOURNALISM AND JOURNALISTS

1 Doctors bury their mistakes. Lawyers hang them. But journalists put theirs on the front page.

ANONYMOUS.

2 We may be scum, but at least we're *la crème de la scum.*

ANONYMOUS MEMBER OF THE ROYAL RATPACK—JOURNALISTS ASSIGNED TO REPORT ON THE BRITISH ROYAL FAMILY. Quoted in: *Sunday Times* (London, 13 Nov. 1988).

3 Journalism over here is not only an obsession but a drawback that cannot be overrated. Politicians are frightened of the press, and in the same way as bull-fighting has a brutalising effect upon Spain (of which she is unconscious), headlines of murder, rape, and rubbish, excite and demoralise the American public.

MARGOT ASQUITH (1864–1945), British socialite. *My Impressions of America,* ch. 10 (1922).

4 The lowest form of popular culture — lack of information, misinformation, disinformation, and a contempt for the truth or the reality of most people's lives — has overrun real journalism. Today, ordinary Americans are being stuffed with garbage.

CARL BERNSTEIN (b. 1944), U.S. journalist. *Guardian* (London, 3 June 1992).

5 Write the things which thou hast seen, and the things which are, and the things which shall be hereafter.

BIBLE: NEW TESTAMENT. *Revelation* 1:19.

6 We need not be theologians to see that we have shifted responsibility for making the world interesting from God to the newspaperman.

DANIEL J. BOORSTIN (b. 1914), U.S. historian. *The Image,* ch. 1 (1961).

7 I find I *journalize* too tediously. Let me try to abbreviate.

JAMES BOSWELL (1740–95), Scottish biographer. *Boswell: The Great Biographer* (1989), entry for 20 Aug. 1792.

8 Journalism could be described as turning one's enemies into money.

CRAIG BROWN (b. 1957), British journalist. *Daily Telegraph* (London, 28 Sept. 1990).

9 Journalism is popular, but it is popular mainly as fiction. Life is one world, and life seen in the newspapers another.

> G. K. CHESTERTON (1874–1936), British author. *All Things Considered*, "On the Cryptic and the Elliptic" (1908).

10 People accuse journalism of being too personal; but to me it has always seemed far too impersonal. It is charged with tearing away the veils from private life; but it seems to me to be always dropping diaphanous but blinding veils between men and men. The Yellow Press is abused for exposing facts which are private; I wish the Yellow Press did anything so valuable. It is exactly the decisive individual touches that it never gives; and a proof of this is that after one has met a man a million times in the newspapers it is always a complete shock and reversal to meet him in real life.

> G. K. CHESTERTON (1874–1936), British author. *Tremendous Trifles*, "A Great Man" (1909).

11 Evidently there are plenty of people in journalism who have neither got what they liked nor quite grown to like what they get. They write pieces they do not much enjoy writing, for papers they totally despise, and the sad process ends by ruining their style and disintegrating their personality, two developments which in a writer cannot be separate, since his personality and style must progress or deteriorate together, like a married couple in a country where death is the only permissible divorce.

> CLAUD COCKBURN (1904–81), British author, journalist. *Cockburn Sums Up*, "Mr. Capone, Philosopher" (1981).

12 He types his laboured column—weary drudge!
Senile fudge and solemn:
Spare, editor, to condemn
These dry leaves of his autumn.

> ROBERTSON DAVIES (b. 1913), Canadian novelist, journalist. *Haiku and Englyn*, in *Toronto Daily Star* (4 April 1959; repr. in *The Enthusiasms of Robertson Davies*, 1990).

13 Journalism without a moral position is impossible. Every journalist is a moralist. It's absolutely unavoidable. A journalist is someone who looks at the world and the way it works, someone who takes a close look at things every day and reports what she sees, someone who represents the world, the event, for others. She cannot do her work without judging what she sees.

> MARGUERITE DURAS (b. 1914), French author, filmmaker. *Outside: Selected Writings*, Foreword (1984).

14 I see journalists as the manual workers, the laborers of the word. Journalism can only be literature when it is passionate.

> MARGUERITE DURAS (b. 1914), French author, filmmaker. *Practicalities*, "Walesa's Wife" (1987; tr. 1990).

15 In journalism it is simpler to sound off than it is to find out. It is more elegant to pontificate than it is to sweat.

> HAROLD EVANS (b. 1928), British journalist, publisher. Said at memorial service for journalist David Blundy, 24 Jan. 1990. Quoted in: *Guardian* (London, 25 Jan 1990).

16 It was when "reporters" became "journalists" and when "objectivity" gave way to "searching for truth," that an aura of distrust and fear arose around the New Journalist.

> GEORGIE ANNE GEYER (b. 1935), U.S. author, columnist. "Whatever Happened to Lois Lane?" *Los Angeles Times* (4 Feb. 1979).

17 A petty reason perhaps why novelists more and more try to keep a distance from journalists is that novelists are trying to write the truth and journalists are trying to write fiction.

> GRAHAM GREENE (1904–91), British novelist. Letter, 18 Jan. 1981, to critic Stephen Pile at the London *Sunday Times* (published in *Yours, Etc: Letters to the Press, 1945–1989*, 1989).

18 If you can't get a job as a pianist in a brothel you become a royal reporter.

> MAX HASTINGS (b. 1945), British editor. *Daily Express* (London, 9 June 1992).

19 Personal columnists . . . are jackals and no jackal has been known to live on grass once he had learned about meat — no matter who killed the meat for him.

> ERNEST HEMINGWAY (1899–1961), U.S. author. "Old Newsman Writes: A Letter from Cuba," in *Esquire* (New York, Dec. 1934; repr. in *By-Line Ernest Hemingway*, ed. by William White, 1967).

20 Our job is like a baker's work — his rolls are tasty as long as they're fresh; after two days they're stale; after a week, they're covered with mould and fit only to be thrown out.

> RYSZARD KAPUSCINSKI (b. 1932), Polish journalist. *The Soccer War*, "The Plan of the Never-Written Book," sct. 33 (1990).

21 Journalist: a person without any ideas but with an ability to express them; a writer whose skill is improved by a deadline: the more time he has, the worse he writes.

> KARL KRAUS (1874–1936), Austrian satirist. *Pro Domo et Mundo*, ch. 3–4 (1912). Quoted in: Thomas Szasz, *Anti-Freud: Karl Kraus's Criticism of Psychoanalysis and Psychiatry*, ch. 8 (1976).

22 If the reporter has killed our imagination with his truth, he threatens our life with his lies.

> KARL KRAUS (1874–1936), Austrian satirist. "In These Great Times," speech, 19 Nov. 1914, Vienna (published in *Die Fackel*, Vienna, Dec. 1914; repr. in *In These Great Times: A Karl Kraus Reader*, ed. by Harry Zohn, 1976).

23 The man must have a rare recipe for melancholy, who can be dull in Fleet Street.

> CHARLES LAMB (1775–1834), English essayist, critic. Letter, 15 Feb. 1802.

24 More than illness or death, the American journalist fears standing alone against the whim of his owners or the prejudices of his audience. Deprive William Safire of the insignia of the *New York Times*, and he would have a hard time selling his truths to a weekly broadsheet in suburban Duluth.

> LEWIS H. LAPHAM (b. 1935), U.S. essayist, editor. *Money and Class in America*, ch. 9 (1988).

25 The journalists have constructed for themselves a little wooden chapel, which they also call the Temple of Fame, in which they put up and take down portraits all day long and make such a hammering you can't hear yourself speak.

G. C. LICHTENBERG (1742–99), German physicist, philosopher. *Aphorisms*, "Notebook D," aph. 20 (written 1765–99; tr. by R. J. Hollingdale, 1990).

26 What a squalid and irresponsible little profession it is. . . . Nothing prepares you for how bad Fleet Street really is until it craps on you from a great height.

KEN LIVINGSTONE (b. 1945), British Labour politician. Quoted in: *City Limits* (London, 1 May 1986).

27 Opinionated writing is always the most difficult . . . simply because it involves retaining in the cold morning-after crystal of the printed word the burning flow of molten feeling.

GAVIN LYALL (b. 1932), British journalist, novelist. Katharine Whitehorn, *Roundabout*, Introduction (1962).

28 Every journalist who is not too stupid or too full of himself to notice what is going on knows that what he does is morally indefensible. He is a kind of confidence man, preying on people's vanity, ignorance, or loneliness, gaining their trust and betraying them without remorse.

JANET MALCOLM (b. 1934), U.S. author. *The Journalist and the Murderer* (1990). The book discusses the case of journalist Joe McGinniss, who won the trust of an alleged murderer then wrote a best-seller, *Fatal Vision* (1984), proclaiming his guilt.

29 The dominant and most deep-dyed trait of the journalist is his timourousness. Where the novelist fearlessly plunges into the water of self-exposure, the journalist stands trembling on the shore in his beach robe. . . . The journalist confines himself to the clean, gentlemanly work of exposing the griefs and shames of others.

JANET MALCOLM (b. 1934), U.S. author. *The Journalist and the Murderer*, "Afterword" (1990).

30 I get up in the morning with an idea for a three-volume novel and by nightfall it's a paragraph in my column.

DON MARQUIS (1878–1937), U.S. humorist, journalist. Quoted in: E. Anthony, *O Rare Don Marquis*, ch. 6 (1962).

31 I think there ought to be a club in which preachers and journalists could come together and have the sentimentalism of the one matched with the cynicism of the other. That ought to bring them pretty close to the truth.

REINHOLD NIEBUHR (1892–1971), U.S. theologian, historian. *Leaves from the Notebook of a Tamed Cynic* (1930), 1928 entry.

32 Now he is a statesman, when what he really wants is to be what most reporters are, adult delinquents.

PEGGY NOONAN (b. 1950), U.S. author, presidential speech-writer. *What I Saw at the Revolution*, ch. 2 (1990), referring to Dan Rather.

33 I am a journalist and, under the modern journalist's code of Olympian objectivity (and total purity of motive), I am absolved of responsibility. We journalists don't have to step on roaches. All we have to do is turn on the kitchen light and watch the critters scurry.

P. J. O'ROURKE (b. 1947), U.S. journalist. *Parliament of Whores*, "Why God Is a Republican and Santa Claus Is a Democrat" (1991).

34 We now demand the light artillery of the intellect; we need the curt, the condensed, the pointed, the readily diffused — in place of the verbose, the detailed, the voluminous, the inaccessible. On the other hand, the lightness of the artillery should not degenerate into pop-gunnery — by which term we may designate the character of the greater portion of the newspaper press — their sole legitimate object being the discussion of ephemeral matters in an ephemeral manner.

EDGAR ALLAN POE (1809–45), U.S. poet, critic, short-story writer. *Marginalia*, "Magazine Literature" (1844–49; repr. in *The Centenary Poe*, ed. by Montagu Slater, 1949).

35 Journalists belong in the gutter because that is where the ruling classes throw their guilty secrets.

GERALD PRIESTLAND (b. 1927), British broadcaster. BBC Radio (London, 19 May 1988).

36 Europe has a press that stresses opinions; America a press, radio, and television that emphasize news.

JAMES RESTON (b. 1909), U.S. journalist. *The Artillery of the Press*, "The President and the Press" (1966).

37 In America journalism is apt to be regarded as an extension of history: in Britain, as an extension of conversation.

ANTHONY SAMPSON (b. 1926), British journalist, author. *Anatomy of Britain Today*, ch. 9 (1965).

38 I still believe that if your aim is to change the world, journalism is a more immediate short-term weapon.

TOM STOPPARD (b. 1937), British playwright. *Guardian* (London, 18 March 1988).

39 If I'd written all the truth I knew for the past ten years, about 600 people — including me — would be rotting in prison cells from Rio to Seattle today. Absolute truth is a very rare and dangerous commodity in the context of professional journalism.

HUNTER S. THOMPSON (b. 1939), U.S. journalist. "Fear and Loathing at the Superbowl," in *Rolling Stone* (New York, 15 Feb. 1973; repr. in *The Great Shark Hunt*, pt. 1, 1979).

40 *Gonzo* journalism is a style of "reporting" based on William Faulkner's idea that the best fiction is far more *true* than any kind of journalism—and the best journalists have always known this. . . . True *gonzo* reporting needs the talents of a master journalist, the eye of an artist/photographer and the heavy balls of an actor. Because the writer *must* be a participant in the scene, while he's writing it—or at least taping it, or even sketching it. Or all three. Probably the closest analogy to the ideal would be a film director/producer who writes his own scripts, does his own camera work and somehow manages to film himself in action, as the protagonist or at least a main character.

HUNTER S. THOMPSON (b. 1939), U.S. journalist. *The Great Shark Hunt*, "Jacket Copy for Fear and Loathing in Las Vegas" (1979).

41 If, for instance, they have heard something from the postman, they attribute it to "a semi-official statement"; if they have fallen into conversation with a stranger at a bar, they can conscientiously describe him as "a source that has hitherto proved unimpeachable." It is only when the journalist is reporting a whim of his own, and one to which he attaches minor importance, that he defines it as the opinion of "well-informed circles."

EVELYN WAUGH (1903–66), British novelist. "Well-Informed Circles and How to Move in Them" (1939; published in *The Essays, Articles and Reviews of Evelyn Waugh*, ed. by Donat Gallagher, 1983).

42 There is much to be said in favour of modern journalism. By giving us the opinions of the uneducated, it keeps us in touch with the ignorance of the community. By carefully chronicling the current events of contemporary life, it shows us of what very little importance such events really are. By invariably discussing the unnecessary, it makes us understand what things are requisite for culture, and what are not.

OSCAR WILDE (1854–1900), Anglo-Irish playwright, author. Gilbert, in *The Critic as Artist*, pt. 2 (published in *Intentions*, 1891).

43 It was a fatal day when the public discovered that the pen is mightier than the paving-stone, and can be made as offensive as the brickbat. They at once sought for the journalist, found him, developed him, and made him their industrious and well-paid servant. It is greatly to be regretted, for both their sakes.

OSCAR WILDE (1854–1900), Anglo-Irish playwright, author. *The Soul of Man under Socialism*, in *Fortnightly Review* (London, Feb. 1891; repr. 1895).

44 You cannot hope
to bribe or twist
(thank God!) the
British journalist.
But, seeing what
the man will do
unbribed, there's
no occasion to.

HUMBERT WOLFE (1885–1940), British poet, author. *The Uncelestial City*, bk. 1, "Over the Fire" (1930).

45 I hate journalists. There is nothing in them but tittering jeering emptiness. They have all made what Dante calls the Great Refusal. . . . The shallowest people on the ridge of the earth.

W. B. YEATS (1865–1939), Irish poet, playwright. Letter, 30 Aug. 1888, to writer Katharine Tynan (published in *The Collected Letters of W. B. Yeats*, vol. 1, ed. by John Kelly, 1986).

46 Most rock journalism is people who can't write, interviewing people who can't talk, for people who can't read.

FRANK ZAPPA (b. 1940), U.S. rock musician. *Chicago Tribune* (18 Jan. 1978).

See also NEWSPAPERS AND MAGAZINES; Stevenson on PLATITUDES; Wilde on The PRESIDENT; The PRESS: WAR CORRESPONDENTS.

JOY

1 He who binds to himself a joy
Does the winged life destroy;
But he who kisses the joy as it flies
Lives in Eternity's sunrise.

WILLIAM BLAKE (1757–1827), English poet, artist. *Eternity* (c. 1793; published in *Complete Writings*, ed. by Geoffrey Keynes, 1957).

2 Breathless, we flung us on the windy hill,
Laughed in the sun, and kissed the lovely grass.

RUPERT BROOKE (1887–1915), British poet. *The Hill*.

3 Our brightest blazes of gladness are commonly kindled by unexpected sparks.

SAMUEL JOHNSON (1709–84), English author, lexicographer. *The Idler*, no. 58, in *Universal Chronicle*, (London, 26 May 1759; repr. in *Works of Samuel Johnson*, vol. 2, ed. by W. J. Bate, John M. Bullitt, and L. F. Powell, 1963).

4 There are, as is known, insects that die in the moment of fertilization. So it is with all joy: life's highest, most splendid moment of enjoyment is accompanied by death.

SØREN KIERKEGAARD (1813–55), Danish philosopher. *Either/Or*, vol. 1, "Diapsalmata" (1843; tr. 1987).

5 Joy is prayer — Joy is strength — Joy is love — Joy is a net of love by which you can catch souls. God loves a cheerful giver. She gives most who gives with joy. The best way to show our gratitude to God and the people is to accept everything with joy. A joyful heart is the inevitable result of a heart burning with love. Never let anything so fill you with sorrow as to make you forget the joy of the Christ risen.

MOTHER TERESA (b. 1910), Albanian-born Roman Catholic missionary. *A Gift for God*, "Joy" (1975).

6 Grief can take care of itself, but to get the full value of a joy you must have somebody to divide it with.

MARK TWAIN (1835–1910), U.S. author. *Following the Equator*, ch. 12, "Pudd'nhead Wilson's New Calendar" (1897).

JAMES JOYCE

1 His writing is not about something. It is the thing itself.

SAMUEL BECKETT (1906–89), Irish dramatist, novelist. *Our Exagmination Round His Factification for Incamination of Work in Progress*, "Dante . . . Bruno. Vico . . . Joyce" (1929).

2 You should approach Joyce's *Ulysses* as the illiterate Baptist preacher approaches the Old Testament: with faith.

WILLIAM FAULKNER (1897–1962), U.S. novelist. Interview in *Writers at Work* (First Series, ed. by Malcolm Cowley, 1958).

3 *Ulysses* . . . is a dogged attempt to cover the universe with mud, an inverted Victorianism, an attempt to make crossness and dirt succeed where sweetness and light failed, a simplification of the human character in the interests of Hell.

E. M. FORSTER (1879–1970), British novelist, essayist. *Aspects of the Novel*, ch. 6, "Fantasy" (1927). Forster also called *Ulysses* "perhaps the most interesting literary experiment of our day."

4 Welcome, O life! I go to encounter for the millionth time the reality of experience and to forge in the smithy of my soul the uncreated conscience of my race.

JAMES JOYCE (1882–1941), Irish author. Stephen Dedalus, in the last lines of *A Portrait of the Artist as a Young Man* (1916), on his departure from Ireland.

5 At bottom there is in Joyce a profound hatred for

humanity — the scholar's hatred. One realizes that he has the neurotic's fear of entering the living world, the world of men and women in which he is powerless to function. He is in revolt not against institutions, but against mankind. . . . *Ulysses* is like a vomit spilled by a delicate child whose stomach has been overloaded with sweetmeats.

HENRY MILLER (1891–1980), U.S. author. *The Cosmological Eye,* "The Universe of Death" (1939).

6   Joyce for all his devotion to his art, terrible in its austerity, was a lad born with a song on one side of him, a dance on the other — two gay guardian angels every human ought to have.

SEAN O'CASEY (1884–1964), Irish dramatist. *Sunset and Evening Star,* "Shaw's Corner" (1954).

7   Joyce is a poet and also an elephantine pedant.

GEORGE ORWELL (1903–50), British author. *Inside the Whale and Other Essays,* "Inside the Whale" (1940).

8   In Ireland they try to make a cat cleanly by rubbing its nose in its own filth. Mr. Joyce has tried the same treatment on the human subject. I hope it may prove successful.

GEORGE BERNARD SHAW (1856–1950), Anglo-Irish playwright, critic. Letter, 10 Oct. 1921, to Joyce's publisher (published in *Letters of James Joyce,* vol. 3, 1966). Shaw, commenting on *Ulysses,* called it a "revolting record of a disgusting phase of civilisation; but it is a truthful one," though he refused the invitation to purchase a copy. In *The Table Talk of G.B.S.,* Shaw wrote, "I could not write the words Mr. Joyce uses: my prudish hands would refuse to form the letters."

9   It's a turgid welter of pornography (the rudest schoolboy kind) & unformed & unimportant drivel; & until the raw ingredients of a pudding *make* a pudding, I shall never believe that the raw material of sensation & thought can make a work of art without the cook's intervening.

EDITH WHARTON (1862–1937), U.S. author. Letter, 6 Jan. 1923, to art connoisseur and historian Bernard Berenson (published in *The Letters of Edith Wharton,* 1988). Wharton was commenting on *Ulysses,* which had been published in Paris the previous year. Shen went on, "The same applies to [T. S.] Eliot," whose *The Wasteland* had also been recently published.

10   Never did I read such tosh. As for the first two chapters we will let them pass, but the 3rd 4th 5th 6th — merely the scratching of pimples on the body of the bootboy at Claridges.

VIRGINIA WOOLF (1882–1941), British novelist. Letter, 24 April 1922, to Lytton Strachey. (published in *The Question of Things Happening: Letters, Vol. 2,* ed. by Nigel Nicolson, 1976), commenting on *Ulysses.*

See also Miller on READING.

JUDAISM AND THE JEWS

1   In early times every sort of advantage tends to become a military advantage; such is the best way, then, to keep it alive. But the Jewish advantage never did so; beginning in religion, contrary to a thousand analogies, it remained religious. *For* that we care for them; *from* that have issued endless consequences.

WALTER BAGEHOT (1826–77), English economist, critic. *Physics and Politics,* ch. 2, sct. 2 (1872).

2   We are all such accidents. We do not make up history and culture. We simply appear, not by our own choice. We make what we can of our condition with the means available. We must accept the mixture as we find it — the impurity of it, the tragedy of it, the hope of it.

SAUL BELLOW (b. 1915), Canadian-born U.S. novelist. *Great Jewish Short Stories,* introduction to the Dell paperback edition (1963), in which Bellow discusses the plight of the Jewish writer in American society.

3   That the Jews assumed a right exclusively to the benefits of God will be a lasting witness against them & the same will it be against Christians.

WILLIAM BLAKE (1757–1827), English poet, painter, engraver. Annotations to Bishop Watson, *An Apology for the Bible in a Series of Letters Addressed to Thomas Paine* (1798; published in *Complete Writings,* ed. by Geoffrey Keynes, 1957).

4   You can never betray the people who are dead, so you go on being a public Jew; the dead can't answer slurs, but I'm here. I would love to think that Jesus wants me for a sunbeam, but he doesn't.

ANITA BROOKNER (b. 1938), British novelist, art historian. *Novelists in Interview* (ed. by John Haffenden, 1985).

5   Now a Jew, in the dictionary, is one who is descended from the ancient tribes of Judea, or one who is regarded as descended from that tribe. That's what it says in the dictionary; but you and I know what a Jew is — *One Who Killed Our Lord.* . . . And although there should be a statute of limitations for that crime, it seems that those who neither have the actions nor the gait of Christians, pagan or not, will bust us out, unrelenting dues, for another deuce.

LENNY BRUCE (1925–66), U.S. satirical comedian. *The Essential Lenny Bruce,* "The Jews" (ed. by John Cohen, 1967).

6   Being a Jew, one learns to believe in the reality of cruelty and one learns to recognize indifference to human suffering as a fact.

ANDREA DWORKIN (b. 1946), U.S. feminist critic. *Letters from a War-Zone,* "A Feminist Looks At Saudi-Arabia" (1987; first published 1978).

7   The sons of Judah have to choose that God may again choose them. . . . The divine principle of our race is action, choice, resolved memory.

GEORGE ELIOT (1819–80), English novelist. Mordecai, in *Daniel Deronda,* bk. 6, ch. 42 (1876).

8   Chanuka and St. Nicholas Day came almost together this year—just one day's difference. We didn't make much fuss about Chanuka: we just gave each other a few little presents and then we had the candles. Because of the shortage of candles we only had them alight for ten minutes, but it is all right as long as you have the song.

ANNE FRANK (1929–45), German Jewish refugee, diarist. *The Diary of a Young Girl,* entry for 7 Dec. 1942 (1947; tr. 1952).

9   Is discord going to show itself while we are still fighting, is the Jew once again worth less than another? Oh, it is sad, very sad, that once more, for the umpteenth time, the old truth is confirmed: "What *one* Christian does is his own responsibility, what *one* Jew does is thrown back at all Jews.

ANNE FRANK (1929–45), German Jewish refugee, diarist. *The Diary of a Young Girl* (1947; tr. 1952), entry for 22 May 1944.

10 The Jews always complained, kvetching about false gods, and erected the biggest false God, Jehovah, in middle of western civilization.

ALLEN GINSBERG (b. 1926), U.S. poet. *World Karma* in *White Shroud* (1986).

11 *I determine who is a Jew.*

KARL LUEGER (1844–1910), Austrian lawyer, politician. Quoted in: Alan Bullock, *Hitler, a Study in Tyranny*, ch. 1, sct. 4 (1962). The statement has also been attributed to Nazi leader Hermann Goering.

12 From the outset, the Christian was the theorizing Jew, the Jew is therefore the practical Christian, and the practical Christian has become a Jew again.

KARL MARX (1818–83), German political theorist and social philosopher. *On the Jewish Question*, sct. 2 (1843; repr. in *Karl Marx and Friedrich Engels: Collected Works*, vol. 3, 1975).

13 Pessimism is a luxury that a Jew can never allow himself.

GOLDA MEIR (1898–1978), Israeli prime minister. Quoted in: *Observer* (London, 29 Dec. 1974).

14 Who hates the Jews more than the Jew?

HENRY MILLER (1891–1980), U.S. author. *Tropic of Cancer* (1979, p. 11).

15 A Jewish man with parents alive is a fifteen-year-old boy, and will remain a fifteen-year-old boy until *they die!*

PHILIP ROTH (b. 1933), U.S. novelist. *Portnoy's Complaint*, "Cunt Crazy" (1967).

16 A Jew without Jews, without Judaism, without Zionism, without Jewishness, without a temple or an army or even a pistol, a Jew clearly without a home, just the object itself, like a glass or an apple.

PHILIP ROTH (b. 1933), U.S. novelist. Nathan Zuckerman, in *The Counterlife*, ch. 5 (1986). Describing his newfound sense of difference after living in England, he explained, "England's made a Jew of me in only eight weeks, which, on reflection, might be the least painful method."

17 The Jews generally give value. They make you pay; but they deliver the goods. In my experience the men who want something for nothing are invariably Christians.

GEORGE BERNARD SHAW (1856–1950), Anglo-Irish playwright, critic. The Nobleman, in *Saint Joan*, sc. 4.

18 We found nothing grand in the history of the Jews nor in the morals inculcated in the Pentateuch. . . . I know of no other books that so fully teach the subjection and degradation of woman.

ELIZABETH CADY STANTON (1815–1902), U.S. campaigner for women's rights. *Eight Years and More*, ch. 24 (1898).

19 The Jew is neither a newcomer nor an alien in this country or on this continent; his Americanism is as original and ancient as that of any race or people with the exception of the American Indian and other aborigines. He came in the caravels of Columbus, and he knocked at the gates of New Amsterdam only thirty-five years after the Pilgrim Fathers stepped ashore on Plymouth Rock.

OSCAR SOLOMON STRAUS (1850–1926), U.S. diplomat, politi-

cian. "America and the Spirit of American Judaism," speech, 18 Jan. 1911, New York City.

20 Being a Jew is like walking in the wind or swimming: you are touched at all points and conscious everywhere.

LIONEL TRILLING (1905–1975), U.S. critic. 1928 Notebook entry, published in *Partisan Review 50th Anniversary Edition* (ed. by William Philips, 1985).

21 I marvel at the resilience of the Jewish people. Their best charactersitic is their desire to remember. No other people has such an obsession with memory.

ELIE WIESEL (b. 1928), Rumanian-born U.S. writer. *Daily Mail* (London, 15 July 1988).

See also Roth on CIRCUMCISION; Nemerov on FICTION; The HOLOCAUST; ISRAEL; Sontag on MINORITIES; Balfour on PALESTINE.

JUDGES

1 Judges don't age. Time decorates them.

ENID BAGNOLD (1889–1981), British novelist, playwright. Judge, in *The Chalk Garden*, act 2.

2 A day in thy courts is better than a thousand.

BIBLE, HEBREW. *Psalms* 84:10.

3 A Judge may be a farmer; but he is not to geld his own pigs. A Judge may play a little at cards for his own amusement; but he is not to play at marbles, or chuck farthing in the Piazza.

SAMUEL JOHNSON (1709–84), English author, lexicographer. Quoted in: James Boswell, *Life of Samuel Johnson*, 6 April 1775 (1791).

4 A judge is not supposed to know anything about the facts of life until they have been presented in evidence and explained to him at least three times.

LORD CHIEF JUSTICE PARKER (1900–1972), British judge. Quoted in: *Observer* (London, 12 March 1961).

5 I followed his argument with the blank uneasiness which one might feel in the presence of a logical lunatic.

VICTOR SERGE (1890–1947), Russian revolutionary author. "The Revolution at Dead-End (1926–1928)," in *Politics* (June 1944), written by Serge on meeting Konstantinov, examining magistrate for the Cheka, 1920. This quotation was noted by Wallace Stevens and used in *Esthéthique du Mal* (1945).

See also Marshall on RETIREMENT; Pope on TRIALS.

JUDGMENT

1 Human nature is so well disposed towards those who are in interesting situations, that a young person, who either marries or dies, is sure of being kindly spoken of.

JANE AUSTEN (1775–1817), English novelist. *Emma*, ch. 22 (1816).

2 A judgment about life has no meaning except the truth of the one who speaks last, and the mind is at ease only at the moment when everyone is shouting at once and no one can hear a thing.

GEORGES BATAILLE (1897–1962), French novelist, critic. *L'Abbé C*, pt. 2, ch. 17 (1950).

3 We are ashamed to seem evasive in the presence of

a straightforward man, cowardly in the presence of a brave one, gross in the eyes of a refined one, and so on. We always imagine, and in imagining share, the judgments of the other mind.

> CHARLES HORTON COOLEY (1864–1929), U.S. sociologist. *Human Nature and the Social Order*, ch. 5 (1902).

4   The judges of normality are present everywhere. We are in the society of the teacher-judge, the doctor-judge, the educator-judge, the "social worker"-judge.

> MICHEL FOUCAULT (1926–84), French philosopher. *Discipline and Punish: The Birth of the Prison*, pt. 4, ch. 3 (1975).

5   How easy it is to judge rightly after one sees what evil comes from judging wrongly!

> ELIZABETH GASKELL (1810–65), English novelist. Cynthia, in *Wives and Daughters*, ch. 43 (1866), of her misplaced attachment to Mr. Preston.

6   My guiding principle is this: Guilt is never to be doubted.

> FRANZ KAFKA (1883–1924), German novelist, short-story writer. In *The Penal Settlement*, "The Officer" (1919; tr. 1933; published in *Metamorphosis and Other Stories*, 1961).

7   Everyone complains of his memory, none of his judgment.

> FRANÇOIS, DUC DE LA ROCHEFOUCAULD (1613–80), French writer, moralist. *Sentences et Maximes Morales*, no. 89 (1678).

8   We judge ourselves by what we feel capable of doing, while others judge us by what we have already done.

> HENRY WADSWORTH LONGFELLOW (1807–82), U.S. poet. *Kavanagh*, bk. 1, ch. 1 (1849).

9   When one cannot appraise out of one's own experience, the temptation to blunder is minimized, but even when one can, appraisal seems chiefly useful as appraisal of the appraiser.

> MARIANNE MOORE (1887–1972), U.S. poet. "Comment," in *Dial*, no. 85 (New York, Oct. 1928; repr. in *Complete Prose*, 1987).

10   Judgments, value judgments concerning life, for or against, can in the last resort never be true: they possess value only as symptoms, they come into consideration only as symptoms—in themselves such judgments are stupidities.

> FRIEDRICH NIETZSCHE (1844–1900), German philosopher. *Twilight of the Idols*, "The Problem of Socrates," aph. 2 (1889).

11   It is a purely relative matter where one draws the plimsoll-line of condemnation, and . . . if you find the whole of humanity falls below it you have simply made a mistake and drawn it too high. And are probably below it yourself.

> FRANCES PARTRIDGE (b. 1900), British translator, author. *Julia*, ch. 17 (1983), entry for 3 Sept. 1959.

12   To say of men that they are bad is to say they are worse than we think we are, or worse than the ideal man whose image we have built up on the basis of a certain few.

> JEAN ROSTAND (1894–1977), French biologist, writer. *Carnets d'un Biologiste* (repr. in *The Substance of Man,*, 1962, p. 195).

13   Speak of me as I am. Nothing extenuate, Nor set down aught in malice.

> WILLIAM SHAKESPEARE (1564–1616), English dramatist, poet. Othello, in *Othello*, act 5, sc. 2, making an appeal to his arresting officers.

JUDGMENT DAY

1   Thou art weighed in the balances, and art found wanting.

> BIBLE, HEBREW. *Daniel* 5:27. Daniel interprets for Belshazzar the "writing on the wall."

2   And I saw the dead, small and great, stand before God; and the books were opened: and another book was opened, which is the book of life: and the dead were judged out of those things which were written in the books, according to their works.

> BIBLE: NEW TESTAMENT. *Revelation* 20:12.

3   A *material* resurrection seems strange and even absurd except for purposes of punishment, and all punishment which is to *revenge* rather than *correct* must be *morally* wrong, and when the World is at an end, what moral or warning purpose *can* eternal tortures answer?

> LORD BYRON (1788–1824), English poet. *Detached Thoughts*, no. 96 (1821–22; published in *Byron's Letters and Journals*, vol. 9, ed. by Leslie A. Marchand, 1979).

4   The world is full of judgment-days, and into every assembly that a man enters, in every action he attempts, he is gauged and stamped.

> RALPH WALDO EMERSON (1803–82), U.S. essayist, poet, philosopher. *Essays*, "Spiritual Laws" (First Series, 1841).

5   When the sun shall be darkened, when the stars shall be thrown down, when the mountains shall be set moving, when the pregnant camels shall be neglected, when the savage beasts shall be mustered, when the seas shall be set boiling, when the souls shall be coupled, when the buried infant shall be asked for what sin she was slain, when the scrolls shall be unrolled, when the heaven shall be stripped off, when Hell shall be set blazing, when Paradise shall be brought nigh, then shall a soul know what it has produced.

> QUR'AN. *The Darkening* 81:1–14 (ed. by Arthur J. Arberry, 1955)

See also Updike on CHRISTIANITY AND THE CHRISTIANS.

JURIES

1   "Write that down," the King said to the jury, and the jury eagerly wrote down all three dates on their slates, and then added them up, and reduced the answer to shillings and pence.

> LEWIS CARROLL (1832–98), English author, mathematician. *Alice's Adventures in Wonderland*, ch. 11 (1865).

2 Our civilization has decided . . . that determining the guilt or innocence of men is a thing too important to be trusted to trained men. . . . When it wants a library catalogued, or the solar system discovered, or any trifle of that kind, it uses up its specialists. But when it wishes anything done which is really serious, it collects twelve of the ordinary men standing round. The same thing was done, if I remember right, by the Founder of Christianity.

G. K. CHESTERTON (1874–1936), British author. *Tremendous Trifles,* "The Twelve Men" (1909).

3 I'm no idealist to believe firmly in the integrity of our courts and in the jury system — that is no ideal to me, it is a living, working reality. Gentlemen, a court is no better than each man of you sitting before me on this jury. A court is only as sound as its jury, and a jury is only as sound as the men who make it up.

HARPER LEE (b. 1926), U.S. author. Atticus Finch, in *To Kill a Mockingbird,* pt. 2, ch. 20 (1960), in his speech to the jury.

4 The jury, passing on the prisoner's life,
May have in the sworn twelve a thief or two
Guiltier than him they try.

WILLIAM SHAKESPEARE (1564–1616), English dramatist, poet. Angelo, in *Measure for Measure,* act 2, sc. 1.

See also Junius on PERSUASION; Pope on TRIALS.

JUSTICE

1 If we do not maintain Justice, Justice will not maintain us.

FRANCIS BACON (1561–1626), English philosopher, essayist, statesman. Speech for prosecution, as Attorney General, in Overbury murder case, Nov. 1615.

2 If one really wishes to know how justice is administered in a country, one does not question the policemen, the lawyers, the judges, or the protected members of the middle class. One goes to the unprotected—those, precisely, who need the laws's protection most!—and listens to their testimony.

JAMES BALDWIN (1924–1987), U.S. author. *The Price of the Ticket,* "No Name in the Street" (1972).

3 Justice in the hands of the powerful is merely a governing system like any other. Why call it justice? Let us rather call it injustice, but of a sly effective order, based entirely on cruel knowledge of the resistance of the weak, their capacity for pain, humiliation and misery. Injustice sustained at the exact degree of necessary tension to turn the cogs of the huge machine-for-the-making-of-rich-men, without bursting the boiler.

GEORGES BERNANOS (1888–1948), French novelist, political writer. M. Olivier, in *The Diary of a Country Priest,* ch. 7 (1936).

4 Blessed are they which do hunger and thirst after righteousness: for they shall be filled.

BIBLE: NEW TESTAMENT. *Matthew* 5:6.

5 It is better that ten guilty persons escape than that one innocent suffer.

SIR WILLIAM BLACKSTONE (1723–1780), English jurist. *Commentaries on the Laws of England,* vol. 4, ch. 27 (1765–69).

6 A good parson once said that where mystery begins religion ends. Cannot I say, as truly at least, of human laws, that where mystery begins justice ends?

EDMUND BURKE (1729–97), Irish philosopher, statesman. *A Vindication of Natural Society* (1756).

7 Absolute justice is achieved by the suppression of all contradiction: therefore it destroys freedom.

ALBERT CAMUS (1913–60), French-Algerian philosopher, author. *The Rebel,* pt. 5, "Historic Murder" (1951; tr. 1953).

8 Justice begins with the recognition of the necessity of sharing. The oldest law is that which regulates it, and this is still the most important law today and, as such, has remained the basic concern of all movements which have at heart the community of human activities and of human existence in general.

ELIAS CANETTI (b. 1905), Austrian novelist, philosopher. *Crowds and Power,* "Distiribution and Increase" (1960; tr. 1962).

9 If some beggar steals a bridle
he'll be hung by a man who's stolen a horse.
There's no surer justice in the world than that
which makes the rich thief hang the poor one.

PEIRE CARDENAL c. 1180–1272), French troubadour poet. "Las amairitz, qui encolpar las vol," published in *Songs of the Troubadours* (ed. and tr. by Anthony Bonner, 1972).

10 Justice consists in doing no injury to men; decency in giving them no offence.

CICERO (106–43 B.C.), Roman orator, philosopher. *De Officiis,* bk. 1, ch. 28, sct. 99.

11 It is not Justice the servant of men, but accident, hazard, Fortune — the ally of patient Time — that holds an even and scrupulous balance.

JOSEPH CONRAD (1857–1924), Polish-born English novelist. Marlow, in *Lord Jim,* ch. 34 (1900).

12 Let justice be done, though the world perish.

FERDINAND I (1503–64), King of Bohemia and Hungary, Holy Roman Emperor 1558–64. Motto adopted in the early 1530s.

13 Justice must always question itself, just as society can exist only by means of the work it does on itself and on its institutions.

MICHEL FOUCAULT (1926–84), French philosopher. "Vous Êtes Dangereux," in *Libération* (Paris, 30 June 1983; repr. in Didier Eribon, *Michel Foucault,* 1989; tr. 1991).

14 The first requisite of civilization . . . is that of justice.

SIGMUND FREUD (1856–1939), Austrian psychiatrist. *Civilization and Its Discontents,* ch. 3 (1930; repr. in *Complete Works,* ed. by James Strachey and Anna Freud, vol. 21, 1961).

15 A weak man is just by accident. A strong but non-violent man is unjust by accident.

MOHANDAS K. GANDHI (1869–1948), Indian political and spiritual leader. *Non-Violence in Peace and War,* vol. 1, ch. 354 (1942).

16 Justice . . . limps along, but it gets there all the same.

GABRIEL GARCÍA MÁRQUEZ (b. 1928), Colombian author. Guardiola, in *In Evil Hour* (1968; tr. 1979), to Judge Arcadio.

17 Justice should not only be done, but should manifestly and undoubtedly be seen to be done.

> LORD HEWART (1870–1943), British judge. Ruling on the quashing of a conviction on technical grounds, 9 Nov. 1923, in Rex v. Sussex Justices. Quoted in: *King's Bench Reports, 1924,* vol. 1.

18 Justice is a whore that won't let herself be stiffed, and collects the wages of shame even from the poor.

> KARL KRAUS (1874–1936) Austrian satirist. "The Good Conduct Medal" (1909; repr. in *In These Great Times: A Karl Kraus Reader,* ed. by Harry Zohn, 1976).

19 The love of justice is, in most men, nothing more than the fear of suffering injustice.

> FRANÇOIS, DUC DE LA ROCHEFOUCAULD (1613–80), French writer, moralist. *Sentences et Maximes Morales,* no. 78 (1678). Two hundred years later this aphorism was repeated with a slight variation by the French writer, Lautréamont, in *Poésies,* ch. 2 (1870): "Love of justice is for most men only the courage to suffer injustice."

20 The only justice is to follow the sincere intuition of the soul, angry or gentle. Anger is just, and pity is just, but judgement is never just.

> D. H. LAWRENCE (1885–1930), British author. *Studies in Classic American Literature,* ch. 2 (1924).

21 Injustice is relatively easy to bear; what stings is justice.

> H. L. MENCKEN (1880–1956), U.S. journalist. *Prejudices,* ch. 3 (Third Series, 1922).

22 Justice *is* conscience, not a personal conscience but the conscience of the whole of humanity. Those who clearly recognize the voice of their own conscience usually recognize also the voice of justice.

> ALEXANDER SOLZHENITSYN (b. 1918), Russian novelist. Letter, Oct. 1967, from Solzhenitsyn to three students (published in *Solzhenitsyn: A Documentary Record,* "The Struggle Intensifies," ed. by Leopold Labedz, 1970).

23 When justice has spoken, humanity must have its turn.

> PIERRE VERGNIAUD (1753–93), French revolutionary leader. Speech, 17 Jan. 1793, to the National Assembly, arguing in favor of executing Louis XVI. Four days later the king was guillotined, and in October of the same year, Vergniaud, as leader of the Girondist faction, met the same fate.

24 A rape! a rape! . . .
Yes, you have ravish'd justice;
Forc'd her to do your pleasure.

> JOHN WEBSTER (1580–1625), English dramatist. Vittoria, in *The White Devil,* act 3, sc. 2.

25 There is one, and only one, thing in modern society more hideous than crime — namely, repressive justice.

> SIMONE WEIL (1909–43), French philosopher, mystic. "Human Personality" (published in *La Table Ronde,* Dec. 1950; repr. in *Selected Essays,* ed. by Richard Rees, 1962).

See also McIlvanney on LAWS AND THE LAW; Bennett on The PRESS.

JOHN KEATS

1 Such writing is a sort of mental masturbation. . . . I don't mean that he is indecent but viciously soliciting his own ideas into a state which is neither poetry nor any-thing else but a Bedlam vision produced by raw pork and opium.

> LORD BYRON (1788–1824), English poet. Letter, 9 Nov. 1820, to the publisher John Murray (published in *Byron's Letters and Journals,* vol. 7, ed. by Leslie A. Marchand, 1973–81). Byron had previously called Keats's work "the Onanism of Poetry," but later retracted his attack, limiting his criticism to the younger Poet's style.

2 For awhile after you quit Keats all other poetry seems to be only whistling or humming.

> F. SCOTT FITZGERALD (1896–1940), U.S. author. Letter, 3 Aug. 1940, to his daughter Frances Scott Fitzgerald (published in *The Letters of F. Scott Fitzgerald,* ed. by Andrew Turnbull, 1963). Fitzgerald described *Ode on a Grecian Urn* as "unbearably beautiful with every syllable as inevitable as the notes in Beethoven's Ninth Symphony" (same source).

3 The opinion I have of the generality of women—who appear to me as children to whom I would rather give a sugar plum than my time, forms a barrier against matrimony which I rejoice in.

> JOHN KEATS (1795–1821), English poet. Letter, 14–31 Oct. 1818, to his brother and sister-in-law, George and Georgiana Keats (published in *Letters of John Keats,* no. 94, ed. by Frederick Page, 1954). Two years later (Aug. 1820) Keats wrote, "I am certain that I have said nothing in a spirit to displease any woman I would care to please; but still there is a tendency to class women in my books with roses and sweetmeats."

4 "If I should die," said I to myself, "I have left no immortal work behind me—nothing to make my friends proud of my memory—that I have loved the principle of beauty in all things, and if I had had time I would have made myself remembered."

> JOHN KEATS (1795–1821), English poet. Letter, Feb. 1820, to Fanny Brawne (published in *Letters of John Keats,* no. 186, ed. by Frederick Page, 1954), describing his thoughts during his illness.

THE KENNEDY FAMILY

1 One would never have guessed that the world had such a capacity for genuine grief. The most we can do is exploit our memories of his excellence.

> JOHN CHEEVER (1912–82), U.S. author. *John Cheever: The Journals,* "The Sixties" (ed. by Robert Gottlieb, 1991), 1963 entry on the assassination of John F. Kennedy.

2 There's never a dearth of reasons to shoot at the President.

> DON DELILLO (b. 1926), U.S. author. Larry Parmenter, in *Libra,* pt. 1, "26 April" (1988).

3 It all began so beautifully. After a drizzle in the morning, the sun came out bright and clear. We were driving into Dallas. In the lead car were President and Mrs. Kennedy.

> LADY BIRD JOHNSON (b. 1912), U.S. First Lady. *A White House Diary* (1970), first entry, 22 Nov. 1963.

4 Ask every person if he's heard the story,
And tell it strong and clear if he has not,
That once there was a fleeting wisp of glory
Called Camelot . . .
Don't let it be forgot
That once there was a spot
For one brief shining moment that was known
As Camelot.

> ALAN JAY LERNER (1918–86), U.S. composer, lyricist. Lyric from

title song of musical *Camelot* (1960). The song was named by Jackie Kennedy in an interview shortly after John F. Kennedy's assassination as one of which her husband was particularly fond. Official biographer William Manchester called his book *One Brief Shining Moment.*

5 What a terrible thing has happened to us all! To you there, to us here, to all everywhere. Peace who was becoming bright-eyed, now sits in the shadow of death; her handsome champion has been killed as he walked by her very side. Her gallant boy is dead. What a cruel, foul, and most unnatural murder! We mourn here with you, poor, sad American people.

> SEAN O'CASEY (1884–1964), Irish dramatist. Letter to Mrs. Rose Russell, leader of New York City Teachers Union (published in *New York Times,* 27 Nov. 1963), on President Kennedy's assassination.

6 We have no one to blame for the Kennedys but ourselves. We took the Kennedys to heart of our own accord. And it is my opinion that we did it not because we respected them or thought what they proposed was good, but because they were pretty. We, the electorate, were smitten by this handsome, vivacious family.... We wanted to hug their golden tousled heads to our dumpy breasts.

> P. J. O'ROURKE (b. 1947), U.S. journalist. *Give War a Chance,* "Mordred Had a Point—Camelot Revisited" (1992). "Two were shot," O'Rourke wrote of the Kennedy's, "but under the most romantic circumstances and not, as might have been hoped, after due process of law."

7 When we think of him, he is without a hat, standing in the wind and weather. He was impatient of topcoats and hats, preferring to be exposed, and he was young enough and tough enough to enjoy the cold and the wind of those times.... It can be said of him, as of few men in a like position, that he did not fear the weather, and did not trim his sails, but instead challenged the wind itself, to improve its direction and to cause it to blow more softly and more kindly over the world and its people.

> E. B. WHITE (1899–1985), U.S. author, editor. "John F. Kennedy," in *New Yorker* (30 Nov. 1963; repr. in *Writings from the New Yorker 1927–1976,* ed. by Rebecca M. Dale, 1991).

KILLING

1 There is no way of conveying to the corpse the reasons you have made him one—you have the corpse, and you are, thereafter, at the mercy of a fact which missed the truth, which means that the corpse has you.

> JAMES BALDWIN (1924–87), U.S. author. *The Price of The Ticket,* "The Devil Finds Work," sct. 2 (1985; first published 1976).

2 Modern conquerors can kill, but do not seem to be able to create. Artists know how to create but cannot really kill. Murderers are only very exceptionally found among artists.

> ALBERT CAMUS (1913–60), French-Algerian philosopher, author. *The Rebel,* pt. 4, "Creation and Revolution" (1951; tr. 1953).

3 It is not funny that a man should be killed, but it is sometimes funny that he should be killed for so little, and that his death should be the coin of what we call civilization.

> RAYMOND CHANDLER (1888–1959), U.S. author. *The Simple Art of Murder* (1950; first published in *Atlantic Monthly,* Boston, Dec. 1944).

4 A bestial and violent man will go so far as to kill because he is under the influence of drink, exasperated, or driven by rage and alcohol. He is paltry. He does not know the pleasure of killing, the charity of bestowing death like a caress, of linking it with the play of the noble wild beasts: every cat, every tiger, embraces its prey and licks it even while it destroys it.

> COLETTE (1873–1954), French author. "Assassins" (first published in *Quatre Saisons,* c. 1928; repr. in *Journey for Myself,* 1971).

5 The force of a death should be enormous but how can you know what kind of man you've killed or who was the braver and stronger if you have to peer through layers of glass that deliver the image but obscure the meaning of the act? War has a conscience or it's ordinary murder.

> DON DELILLO (b. 1926), U.S. author. Frank Vásquez, in *Libra,* pt. 2, "6 September" (1988).

6 I know for sure that there is only one step from insecticide to genocide.

> WERNER HERZOG (b. 1942), German film director. *New York Times* (11 Sept. 1977).

7 To kill a human being is, after all, the least injury you can do him.

> HENRY JAMES (1843–1916), U.S. author. George Bingham, having mistakenly shot a child,.in "My Friend Bingham," in *Atlantic Monthly* (Boston, March 1867; repr. in *The Complete Tales of Henry James,* vol. 1, ed. by Leon Edel, 1962).

8 There is no instant of time when one creature is not being devoured by another. Over all these numerous races of animals man is placed, and his destructive hand spares nothing that lives. He kills to obtain food and he kills to clothe himself; he kills to adorn himself; he kills in order to attack and he kills to defend himself; he kills to instruct himself and he kills to amuse himself; he kills to kill. Proud and terrible king, he wants everything and nothing resists him.

> JOSEPH DE MAISTRE (1753–1821), French diplomat, philosopher. The Senator, in *Les Soirées de Saint-Pétersbourg,* "Seventh Dialogue" (1821; repr. in *The Works of Joseph de Maistre,* ed. by Jack Lively, 1965).

9 For some men the power to destroy life becomes the equivalent to the female power to create life.

> MYRIAM MIEDZIAN, U.S. author. *Boys Will Be Boys,* ch. 4 (1991).

10 To live without killing is a thought which could electrify the world, if men were only capable of staying awake long enough to let the idea soak in.

> HENRY MILLER (1891–1980), U.S. author. *Sunday after the War,* "Reunion in Brooklyn" (1944).

11 Kill a man one is a murderer; kill a million, a conqueror; kill them all, a God.

> JEAN ROSTAND (1894–1977), French biologist, writer. *Pensées d'un Biologiste* (1939; repr. in *The Substance of Man,* 1962, p. 68).

12 As soon as men know that they can kill without fear of punishment or blame, they kill; or at least they encourage killers with approving smiles.

> SIMONE WEIL (1909–43), French philosopher, mystic. Letter, c.

1938, to author Georges Bernanos (published in *Selected Essays*, ed. by Richard Rees, 1962).

See also ASSASSINATION; MURDER.

KINDNESS

1 When kindness has left people, even for a few moments, we become afraid of them as if their reason had left them. When it has left a place where we have always found it, it is like shipwreck; we drop from security into something malevolent and bottomless.

> WILLA CATHER (1876–1947), U.S. author. *My Mortal Enemy* (1926; repr. 1963, p. 62).

2 A man without nobility cannot have kindliness; he can only have good nature.

> SÉBASTIEN-ROCH NICOLAS DE CHAMFORT (1741–94), French writer, wit. *Maxims and Considerations*, vol. 1, no. 116 (1796; tr. 1926).

3 Kindliness seems to exist primarily as an animal instinct, so deeply rooted that mental degeneracy, which works from the top down, does not destroy it until the mind sinks to the lower grades of idiocy.

> CHARLES HORTON COOLEY (1864–1929), U.S. sociologist. *Human Nature and the Social Order*, ch. 4 (1902).

4 Ignorant kindness may have the effect of cruelty; but to be angry with it as if it were direct cruelty would be an ignorant unkindness.

> GEORGE ELIOT (1819–80), English novelist, editor. *Daniel Deronda*, bk. 8, ch. 59 (1876).

5 True kindness presupposes the faculty of imagining as one's own the suffering and joys of others.

> ANDRÉ GIDE (1869–1951), French author. *Pretexts*, "Portraits and Aphorisms" (1903).

6 It is futile to judge a kind deed by its motives. Kindness can become its own motive. We are made kind by being kind.

> ERIC HOFFER (1902–83), U.S. philosopher. *The Passionate State of Mind*, aph. 123 (1955).

7 Human kindness is like a defective tap, the first gush may be impressive but the stream soon dries up.

> P. D. JAMES (b. 1920), British mystery writer. Jonah the tramp, in *Devices and Desires*, ch. 40 (1989).

8 One could laugh at the world better if it didn't mix tender kindliness with its brutality.

> D. H. LAWRENCE (1885–1930), British author. Letter, 3 Oct. 1910 (published in *The Letters of D. H. Lawrence*, vol. 1, ed. by James T. Boulton, 1979).

9 It is a terrible thing, this kindness that human beings do not lose. Terrible because when we are finally naked in the dark and cold, it is all we have. We who are so rich, so full of strength, wind up with that small change. We have nothing else to give.

> URSULA K. LE GUIN (b. 1929), U.S. author. *The Left Hand of Darkness*, ch. 13 (1969).

10 When you are young you take the kindness people show you as your right.

> W. SOMERSET MAUGHAM (1874–1965), British author. *Cakes and Ale*, ch. 12 (1930).

11 Kindness is a virtue neither modern nor urban. One almost unlearns it in a city. Towns have their own beatitude; they are not unfriendly; they offer a vast and solacing anonymity or an equally vast and solacing gregariousness. But one needs a neighbor on whom to practice compassion.

> PHYLLIS MCGINLEY (1905–78), U.S. poet, author. *The Province of the Heart*, "A Garland of Kindness" (1959).

12 If you stop to be kind, you must swerve often from your path.

> MARY WEBB (1881–1927), British author. *Precious Bane*, bk. 2, ch. 3 (1924).

13 One can always be kind to people about whom one cares nothing.

> OSCAR WILDE (1854–1900), Anglo-Irish playwright, author. Lord Henry, in the *The Picture of Dorian Gray*, ch. 1 (1891).

See also Gibran, Wordsworth on GOOD DEEDS.

MARTIN LUTHER KING, JR.

1 The secret lies, I think, in his intimate knowledge of the people he is addressing be they black or white, and in the forthrightness with which he speaks of those things which hurt and baffle them. . . . He allows them their self-respect—indeed, he insists on it.

> JAMES BALDWIN (1924–87), U.S. author. "The Dangerous Road Before Martin Luther King," in *Harper's* (New York, Feb. 1961; repr. in *The Price of The Ticket*, 1985).

2 When that devil's bullet lodged itself inside the body of Martin Luther King, he had already begun an astonishing mobilization of poor, Black, white, latino Americans who had nothing to lose. They would challenge our government to eliminate exploitative, merciless, and war-mongering policies, nationwide, or else "tie up the country" through "means of civil disobedience." Dr. King intended to organize those legions into "coercive direct actions" that would make of Babylon a dysfunctional behemoth begging for relief. Is it any wonder he was killed?

> JUNE JORDAN (b. 1939), U.S. poet, civil rights activist. "The Mountain and the Man Who Was Not God," lecture, 20 Jan. 1987, Stanford University, California (published in *Moving Towards Home: Political Essays*, 1989).

3 I don't think Dr. King helped racial harmony, I think he helped racial justice. What I profess to do is help the oppressed and if I cause a load of discomfort in the white community and the black community, that in my opinion means I'm being effective, because I'm not trying to make them comfortable. The job of an activist is to make people tense and cause social change.

> REV. AL SHARPTON (b. 1954), U.S. civil rights campaigner. *Independent on Sunday* (London, 21 April 1991).

KISSING

1 Kisses honeyed by oblivion.

GEORGE ELIOT (1819–80), English novelist. *The Spanish Gypsy*, bk. 3 (1868).

2 There used to be two kinds of kisses. First when girls were kissed and deserted; second, when they were engaged. Now there's a third kind, where the man is kissed and deserted. If Mr. Jones of the nineties bragged he'd kissed a girl, everyone knew he was through with her. If Mr. Jones of 1919 brags the same everyone knows it's because he can't kiss her any more. Given a decent start any girl can beat a man nowadays.

F. SCOTT FITZGERALD (1896–1940), U.S. author. Rosalind Connage, in *This Side of Paradise*, bk. 2, ch. 1 (1920).

3 The kiss originated when the first male reptile licked the first female reptile, implying in a subtle, complimentary way that she was as succulent as the small reptile he had for dinner the night before.

F. SCOTT FITZGERALD (1896–1940), U.S. author. *The Crack-Up*, "Notebook E" (ed. by Edmund Wilson, 1945).

4 But his kiss was so sweet, and so closely he pressed,
That I languished and pined till I granted the rest.

JOHN GAY (1685–1732), English dramatist. Lucy, in *The Beggar's Opera*, act 3, sc. 1, Air 41.

5 The kiss. There are all sorts of kisses, lad, from the sticky confection to the kiss of death. Of them all, the kiss of an actress is the most unnerving. How can we tell if she means it or if she's just practicing?

RUTH GORDON (b. 1896), U.S. playwright, actor. Benjy, in *The Leading Lady*, act 2 (1948).

6 Oh what lies lurk in kisses!

HEINRICH HEINE (1797–1856), German poet, journalist. *In den Küssen welche Lüge*, st. 1.

7 The sound of a kiss is not so loud as that of a cannon, but its echo lasts a great deal longer.

OLIVER WENDELL HOLMES, SR. (1809–94), U.S. writer, physician. *The Professor at the Breakfast-Table*, ch. 11 (1859).

8 What did that mean, to kiss? You put your face up like that to say goodnight and then his mother put her face down. That was to kiss. His mother put her lips on his cheek; her lips were soft and they wetted his cheek; and they made a tiny little noise: kiss. Why did people do that with their two faces?

JAMES JOYCE (1882–1941), Irish author. Stephen Dedalus, in *A Portrait of the Artist as a Young Man*, ch. 1 (1916).

9 When women kiss it always reminds one of prize-fighters shaking hands.

H. L. MENCKEN (1880–1956), U.S. journalist. *A Mencken Chrestomathy*, ch, 30 (1949).

10 A kiss is but a kiss now! and no wave
Of a great flood that whirls me to the sea.
But, as you will! we'll sit contentedly,
And eat our pot of honey on the grave.

GEORGE MEREDITH (1828–1909), English author. *Modern Love*, sonnet 29 (1862).

11 A kiss can be a comma, a question mark or an exclamation point. That's basic spelling that every woman ought to know.

MISTINGUETT (1874–1956), French dancer, singer. *Theatre Arts* (Dec. 1955).

12 He took the bride about the neck
And kissed her lips with such a clamorous smack
That at the parting all the church did echo.

WILLIAM SHAKESPEARE (1564–1616), English dramatist, poet. Gremio, in *The Taming of the Shrew*, act 3, sc. 3, of Petruccio and Katherine (Kate).

13 The social kiss is an exchange of insincerity between two combatants on the field of social advancement. It places hygiene before affection and condescension before all else.

SUNDAY CORRESPONDENT (London, 12 Aug. 1990).

14 Stephen's kiss was lost in jest,
Robin's lost in play,
But the kiss in Colin's eyes
Haunts me night and day.

SARA TEASDALE (1884–1933), U.S. poet. *The Look*, st. 2.

15 A kiss may ruin a human life.

OSCAR WILDE (1854–1900), Anglo-Irish playwright, author. Mrs. Arbuthnot, in *A Woman of No Importance*, act 4.

KITSCH

1 Kitsch . . . is one of the major categories of the modern object. Knick-knacks, rustic odds-and-ends, souvenirs, lampshades, and African masks: the kitsch-object is collectively this whole plethora of "trashy," sham or faked objects, this whole museum of junk which proliferates everywhere. . . . Kitsch is the equivalent to the "cliché" in discourse.

JEAN BAUDRILLARD (b. 1929), French semiologist. "Mass Media Culture" (published in *The Society of Consumption*, 1970; repr. in *Revenge of the Crystal: Selected Writings 1968–83*, ed. by Paul Foss and Julian Pefanis, 1990).

2 No matter how much we scorn it, kitsch is an integral part of the human condition.

MILAN KUNDERA (b. 1929), Czech author, critic. *The Unbearable Lightness of Being*, pt. 6, ch. 12 (1984).

3 So I say, if you cannot learn to love real art; at least learn to hate sham art and reject it. It is not because the wretched thing is so ugly and silly and useless that I ask you to cast it from you; it is much more because these are but the outward symbols of the poison that lies within them; look through them and see all that has gone to their fashioning, and you will see how vain labour, and sorrow, and disgrace have been their companions from the first—and all this for trifles that no man really needs!

WILLIAM MORRIS (1834–96), English artist, writer, printer. "The Decorative Arts: Their Relation to Modern Life and Progress," Morris's first public lecture (published in *Hopes and Fears for Art*, "The Lesser Arts," 1882).

4 Kitsch is the daily art of our time, as the vase or the hymn was for earlier generations. For the sensibility it has that arbitrariness and importance which works take on when they are no longer noticeable elements of the environment. In America kitsch is Nature. The Rocky Mountains have resembled fake art for a century.

HAROLD ROSENBERG (1906–78), U.S. art critic, author. *The Tradition of the New*, ch. 18 (1960).

KNOWLEDGE

1 The utmost extent of man's knowledge, is to know that he knows nothing.

JOSEPH ADDISON (1672–1719), English essayist. *Interesting Anecdotes, Memoirs, Allegories, Essays, and Poetical Fragments*, "Essay on Pride" (1794).

2 Can the knowledge deriving from reason even begin to compare with knowledge perceptible by sense? No doubt the number of people crass enough to reply exclusively on the former and scorn the latter are sufficient in themselves to explain the disfavor into which everything deriving from the senses has gradually fallen. But when the most scholarly of men have taught me that light is a vibration, or offered me any other fruits of their labors of reasoning, they will not have rendered me an account of what is important to me about light, of what my eyes have begun to teach me about it, of what makes me different from a blind man—things which are the stuff of miracles, not subject matter for reasoning.

LOUIS ARAGON (1897–1982), French poet. *Paris Peasant*, "Preface to a Modern Mythology" (first published 1926; repr. 1971).

3 All men by nature desire knowledge.

ARISTOTLE (384–322 B.C.), Greek philosopher. *Metaphysics*, bk. 1, ch. 1.

4 All human knowledge takes the form of interpretation.

WALTER BENJAMIN (1892–1940), German critic, philosopher. Letter, 9 Dec. 1923 (published in *Briefe*, no. 126, Frankfurt, 1966). Quoted in: Susan Sontag, "Under the Sign of Saturn," introductory essay to *One-Way Street and Other Writings* (1978).

5 There can be no knowledge without emotion. We may be aware of a truth, yet until we have felt its force, it is not ours. To the cognition of the brain must be added the experience of the soul.

ARNOLD BENNETT (1867–1931), British novelist. *The Journals of Arnold Bennett* (1932), entry for 18 March 1897.

6 For in much wisdom is much grief: and he that increaseth knowledge increaseth sorrow.

BIBLE, HEBREW. *Ecclesiastes* 1:18.

7 There be three things which are too wonderful for me, yea, four which I know not: the way of an eagle in the air; the way of a serpent upon a rock; the way of a ship in the midst of the sea; and the way of a man with a maid.

BIBLE, HEBREW. Agur, son of Jakeh, in *Proverbs* 30:18–19.

8 Knowledge puffeth up, but charity edifieth. And if any man think that he knoweth any thing, he knoweth nothing yet as he ought to know.

BIBLE: NEW TESTAMENT. *1 Corinthians* 8:1–2.

9 The real community of man . . . is the community of those who seek the truth, of the potential knowers.

ALLAN BLOOM (1930–92), U.S. educator, author. *The Closing of the American Mind*, pt. 3, "The Student and the University" (1987).

10 Sorrow is knowledge: they who know the most
Must mourn the deepest o'er the fatal truth,
The Tree of Knowledge is not that of life.

LORD BYRON (1788–1824), English poet. Manfred's opening speech in *Manfred*, act 1, sc. 1. As Michael Foot recorded in his biography, *The Politics of Paradise: A Vindication of Byron*, ch. 5 (1988), this speech was considered by Nietzsche to be "immortal" for stating the terrible fact that a man might bleed to death through the truth that he recognizes.

11 There's a theory, one I find persuasive, that the quest for knowledge is, at bottom, the search for the answer to the question: "Where was I before I was born." In the beginning was . . . what? Perhaps, in the beginning, there was a curious room, a room like this one, crammed with wonders; and now the room and all it contains are forbidden you, although it was made just for you, had been prepared for you since time began, and you will spend all your life trying to remember it.

ANGELA CARTER (1940–92), British author. *The Curious Room*, uncollected short story read at Basel University conference. Quoted in: *New Writing* (ed. by Malcolm Bradbury and Judy Cooke, 1992).

12 Knowledge, a rude unprofitable mass,
The mere materials with which wisdom builds,
Till smoothed and squared and fitted to its place,
Does but encumber whom it seems to enrich.
Knowledge is proud that he has learned so much;
Wisdom is humble that he knows no more.

WILLIAM COWPER (1731–1800), English poet. *The Task*, bk. 6 (1785).

13 To know all is not to forgive all. It is to despise everybody.

QUENTIN CRISP (b. 1908), British author. *The Naked Civil Servant*, ch. 11 (1968).

14 You have to believe in God before you can say there are things that man was not meant to know. I don't think there's anything man wasn't meant to know. There are just some stupid things that people shouldn't do.

DAVID CRONENBERG (b. 1943), Canadian filmmaker. *Cronenberg on Cronenberg*, ch. 1 (ed. by Chris Rodley, 1992).

15 Knowledge is not a passion from without the mind, but an active exertion of the inward strength, vigour and power of the mind, displaying itself from within.

RALPH J. CUDWORTH (1617–88), English theologian, philosopher. *Treatise Concerning Eternal and Immutable Morality*, bk. 4, ch. 1, sct. 1 (1731).

16 Knowledge is a polite word for dead but not buried imagination.

E. E. CUMMINGS (1894–1962), U.S. poet. *Jottings*, in *Wake*, no. 10 (1951; repr. in *A Miscellany*, ed. by George J. Firmage, 1958).

17 There are three principal means of acquiring knowledge available to us: observation of nature, reflection, and experimentation. Observation collects facts; reflection combines them; experimentation verifies the result of that combination. Our observation of nature must be diligent, our reflection profound, and our experiments exact. We rarely see these three means combined; and for this reason, creative geniuses are not common.

DENIS DIDEROT (1713–84), French philosopher. *On the Interpretation of Nature*, no. 15 (1753; repr. in *Selected Writings*, ed. by Lester G. Crocker, 1966).

18 Depend upon it there comes a time when for every addition of knowledge you forget something that you knew before. It is of the highest importance, therefore, not to have useless facts elbowing out the useful ones.

SIR ARTHUR CONAN DOYLE (1859–1930), English author. Sherlock Holmes, in *A Study in Scarlet*, ch. 2 (1887).

19 Of a truth, Knowledge is power, but it is a power reined by scruple, having a conscience of what must be and what may be; whereas Ignorance is a blind giant who, let him but wax unbound, would make it a sport to seize the pillars that hold up the long-wrought fabric of human good, and turn all the places of joy as dark as a buried Babylon.

GEORGE ELIOT (1819–80), English novelist, editor. *Daniel Deronda*, bk. 3, ch. 21 (1876).

20 For lust of knowing what should not be known,
We take the Golden Road to Samarkand.

JAMES ELROY FLECKER (1884–1915), British poet. Ishak, in *Hassan*, act 5, sc. 2 (1922).

21 It seems to me that man is made to act rather than to know: the principles of things escape our most persevering researches.

FREDERICK THE GREAT (1712–86), King of Prussia. Letter, 30 Sept. 1783, to mathematician and philosopher Jean le Rond d'Alembert.

22 A little knowledge that *acts* is worth infinitely more than much knowledge that is idle.

KAHLIL GIBRAN (1883–1931), Lebanese poet, novelist. *The Voice of the Master*, pt. 2, ch. 8 (1960; repr. in *A Second Treasury of Kahlil Gibran*, tr. by Anthony Ferris, 1962).

23 A man can only attain knowledge with the help of those who possess it. This must be understood from the very beginning. *One must learn from him who knows.*

GEORGE GURDJIEFF (c. 1877–1949), Greek-Armenian religious teacher, mystic. Quoted in: P. D. Ouspensky, *In Search of the Miraculous*, ch. 2 (1949).

24 All knowledge is ambiguous.

J. S. HABGOOD (b. 1927), British ecclesiastic, Archbishop of York. *Observer* (London, 14 April 1991).

25 Man is distinguished, not only by his reason; but also by this singular passion from other animals . . . which is a lust of the mind, that by a perseverance of delight in the continual and indefatigable generation of knowledge, exceeds the short vehemence of any carnal pleasure.

THOMAS HOBBES (1588–1679), English philosopher. *Leviathan*, pt. 1, ch. 6 (1651).

26 Knowledge about life is one thing; effective occupation of a place in life, with its dynamic currents passing through your being, is another.

WILLIAM JAMES (1842–1910), U.S. psychologist, philosopher. *The Varieties of Religious Experience*, lecture 20 (1902).

27 Man is not weak; knowledge is more than equivalent to force.

SAMUEL JOHNSON (1709–84), English author, lexicographer. Imlac, in *The History of Rasselas*, ch. 13 (1759).

28 Knowledge is happiness, because to have knowledge—broad, deep knowledge—is to know true ends from false, and lofty things from low. To know the thoughts and deeds that have marked man's progress is to feel the great heart-throbs of humanity through the centuries; and if one does not feel in these pulsations a heavenward striving, one must indeed be deaf to the harmonies of life.

HELEN KELLER (1880–1968), U.S. blind/deaf author, lecturer. *The Story of My Life*, pt. 1, ch. 20 (1903).

29 To know yet to think that one does not know is best;
Not to know yet to think that one knows will lead to difficulty.

LAO-TZU (6th century B.C.), Legendary Chinese philosopher. *Tao-te-ching*, bk. 2, ch. 71 (tr. by T. C. Lau, 1963).

30 Knowledge is what we get when an observer, preferably a scientifically trained observer, provides us with a copy of reality that we can all recognize.

CHRISTOPHER LASCH (b. 1932), U.S. historian. "The Lost Art of Political Argument" (first published as "Journalism, Publicity, and the Lost Art of Political Argument," in *Gannett Center Journal*, New York, Spring 1990; repr. in *Harper's*, New York, Sept. 1990).

31 Knowledge is and will be produced in order to be sold, it is and will be consumed in order to be valorized in a new production: in both cases, the goal is exchange. Knowledge ceases to be an end in itself, it loses its use-value.

JEAN FRANÇOIS LYOTARD (b. 1924), French philosopher. *The Postmodern Condition: A Report on Knowledge*, Introduction (1979).

32 If you want to know the taste of a pear, you must change the pear by eating it yourself. . . . If you want to know the theory and methods of revolution, you must take part in revolution. All genuine knowledge originates in direct experience.

MAO ZEDONG (1893–1976), Founder of the People's Republic of China. Speech, July 1937, Yenan, China.

33 Sin, guilt, neurosis—they are one and the same, the fruit of the tree of knowledge.

HENRY MILLER (1891–1980), U.S. author. *The Wisdom of the Heart*, "Creative Death" (1947).

34 The use of knowledge in our sex (beside the amusement of solitude) is to moderate the passions and learn to be contented with a small expense, which are the certain effects of a studious life and, it may be, preferable even to that fame which men have engrossed to themselves and will not suffer us to share.

LADY MARY WORTLEY MONTAGU (1689–1762), English society figure, letter writer. Letter, 28 Jan. 1753, to her daughter Lady Bute (published in *Selected Letters*, ed. by Robert Halsband, 1970).

35 "The tree of knowledge is not the tree of life!" And yet can we cast out of our spirits all the good or evil poured into them by so many learned generations? Ignorance cannot be learned.

GÉRARD DE NERVAL (1808–55), French novelist and poet. *Aurélia*, pt. 2, ch. 1 (1855; repr. in *Selected Writings*, ed. and tr. by Geoffrey Wagner, 1958).

36 We have no organ at all for *knowledge*, for "truth": we "know" (or believe or imagine) precisely as much as may be *useful* in the interest of the human herd, the species: and even what is here called "usefulness" is in the end only a belief, something imagined and perhaps precisely that most fatal piece of stupidity by which we shall one day perish.

FRIEDRICH NIETZSCHE (1844–1900), German philosopher. *The Gay Science*, aph. 354 (rev. ed., 1887).

37 Our treasure lies in the beehive of our knowledge. We are perpetually on the way thither, being by nature winged insects and honey gatherers of the mind.

FRIEDRICH NIETZSCHE (1844–1900), German philosopher. *The Genealogy of Morals*, "Preface," sct. 1 (1887; tr. 1956).

38 And all your future lies beneath your hat.

JOHN OLDHAM (1653–83), English poet. *Lines to a Friend About to Leave the University*.

39 Knowledge is ancient error reflecting on its youth.

FRANCIS PICABIA (1878–1953), French painter, poet. *491* (Paris, 4 March 1949; repr. in *Yes No: Poems and Sayings*, "Sayings," tr. by Rémy Hall, 1990).

40 Only divine love bestows the keys of knowledge.

ARTHUR RIMBAUD (1854–91), French poet. *Une Saison en Enfer*, "Mauvais Sang" (1874).

41 Children with Hyacinth's temperament don't know better as they grow older; they merely know more.

SAKI [H. H. MUNRO] (1870–1916), Scottish author. *The Toys of Peace*, "Hyacinth" (1919).

42 As the biggest library if it is in disorder is not as useful as a small but well-arranged one, so you may accumulate a vast amount of knowledge but it will be of far less value to you than a much smaller amount if you have not thought it over for yourself.

ARTHUR SCHOPENHAUER (1788–1860), German philosopher. *Parerga and Paralipomena*, vol. 2, ch. 22, sct. 257 (1851).

43 We are in fact convinced that if we are ever to have pure knowledge of anything, we must get rid of the body and contemplate things by themselves with the soul by itself. It seems, to judge from the argument, that the wisdom which we desire and upon which we profess to have set our hearts will be attainable only when we are dead and not in our lifetime.

SOCRATES (469–399 B.C.), Greek philosopher. Quoted in: Plato, *Phaedo*, sct. 65.

44 The knowledge of an unlearned man is living and luxuriant like a forest, but covered with mosses and lichens and for the most part inaccessible and going to waste; the knowledge of the man of science is like timber collected in yards for public works, which still supports a green sprout here and there, but even this is liable to dry rot.

HENRY DAVID THOREAU (1817–62), U.S. philosopher, author, naturalist. *Journals* (1906), entry for 7 Jan. 1851.

45 Knowledge is the most democratic source of power.

ALVIN TOFFLER (b. 1928), U.S. author. *Powershift: Knowledge, Wealth, and Violence at the Edge of the 21st Century*, pt. 1, ch. 2, "The Democratic Difference" (1990).

46 We have not the reverent feeling for the rainbow that a savage has, because we know how it is made. We have lost as much as we gained by prying into that matter.

MARK TWAIN (1835–1910), U.S. author. *A Tramp Abroad*, vol. 2, ch. 11 (1879).

47 Between us, we cover all knowledge; he knows all that can be known and I know the rest.

MARK TWAIN (1835–1910), U.S. author. *Autobiography*, ch. 59 (ed. by Charles Neider, 1959). "He knew more than any person I had met before," Twain wrote of Rudyard Kipling, "and I knew that he knew I knew less than any person he had met before."

48 Everything has been said yet few have taken advantage of it. Since all our knowledge is essentially banal, it can only be of value to minds that are not.

RAOUL VANEIGEM (b. 1934), Belgian Situationist philosopher. *The Revolution of Everyday Life*, Introduction (1967; tr. 1983).

49 The things we know best are the things we haven't been taught.

LUC, MARQUIS DE VAUVENARGUES (1715–47), French moralist. *Refléxions et Maximes*, no. 479 (1746).

50 When you see the abyss, and we have looked into it, then what? There isn't much room at the edge—one person, another, not many. If you are there, others cannot be there. If you are there, you become a protective wall. What happens? You become part of the abyss.

ELIE WIESEL (b. 1928), Rumanian-born U.S. writer. Interview in *Writers at Work* (Eighth Series, ed. by George Plimpton, 1988), discussing the experience of the Holocaust.

51 There are only two kinds of people who are really fascinating—people who know absolutely everything, and people who know absolutely nothing.

OSCAR WILDE (1854–1900), Anglo-Irish playwright, author. Lord Henry, in *The Picture of Dorian Gray*, ch. 7 (1891).

52 Knowledge is in the end based on acknowledgement.

LUDWIG WITTGENSTEIN (1889–1951), Austrian philosopher. *On Certainty*, sct. 378 (ed. by Anscombe and von Wright, 1969).

See also Watson on CURIOSITY; Johnson on INTEGRITY; Chesterfield, Emerson, Wilde on LEARNING; Spencer on SCIENCE; Lao-tzu on TRAVEL; Cudworth on WISDOM.

KORAN

See Qur'an.

LABOR

1 We've no use for intellectuals in this outfit. What we need is chimpanzees. Let me give you a word of advice: never say a word to us about being intelligent. We will think for you, my friend. Don't forget it.

LOUIS-FERDINAND CÉLINE (1894–1961), French author. Examining doctor at Ford auto factory in Detroit, where the narrator Ferdinand Bardamu (and Céline) worked, in *Journey to the End of the Night* (1932; tr. 1934; 1966 repre., p. 196).

2 I tell you, sir, the only safeguard of order and discipline in the modern world is a standardized worker with interchangeable parts. That would solve the entire problem of management.

JEAN GIRAUDOUX (1882–1944), French diplomat, author. The President, in *The Madwoman of Chaillot*, act 1.

3 Labor is prior to, and independent of, capital. Capital is only the fruit of labor, and could never have existed if labor had not first existed. Labor is the superior of capital, and deserves much the higher consideration.

ABRAHAM LINCOLN (1809–65), U.S. president. Message to Congress, 3 Dec. 1861 (published in *Collected Works*, vol. 5, ed. by Roy B. Basler, 1953).

4 It is not, truly speaking, the labour that is divided; but the men: divided into mere segments of men—broken into small fragments and crumbs of life, so that all the little piece of intelligence that is left in a man is not enough to make a pin, or a nail, but exhausts itself in making the point of a pin or the head of a nail.

JOHN RUSKIN (1819–1900), English art critic, author. *The Stones of Venice*, vol. 2, ch. 6 (1851–53), of division of labor.

LADIES

1 You may be a princess or the richest woman in the world, but you cannot be more than a lady.

JENNIE JEROME CHURCHILL (1854–1921), Anglo-American mother of Winston Churchill. *New York World* (13 Oct. 1908).

2 What soft—cherubic creatures—
These gentlewomen are—
One would as soon assault a plush—
Or violate a star—

EMILY DICKINSON (1830–86), U.S. poet. *The Complete Poems*, no. 401 (1955).

3 Ermined and minked and Persian-lambed,
Be-puffed (be-painted, too, alas!)
Be-decked, be-diamonded—be-damned!
The Women of the Better Class.

OLIVER HERFORD (1863–1935), U.S. poet, illustrator. *The Women of the Better Class*, st. 4.

4 Girls who put out are tramps. Girls who don't are ladies. This is, however, a rather archaic usage of the word. Should one of you boys happen upon a girl who doesn't put out, do not jump to the conclusion that you have found a lady. What you have probably found is a lesbian.

FRAN LEBOWITZ (b. 1951), U.S. journalist. *Metropolitan Life*, "The Word *Lady*: Most Often Used to Describe Someone You Wouldn't Want to Talk to for Even Five Minutes" (1978).

5 A lady is nothing very specific. One man's lady is another man's woman; sometimes, one man's lady is another man's wife. Definitions overlap but they almost never coincide.

RUSSELL LYNES (b. 1910), U.S. editor, critic. "Is There a Lady in the House," in *Look* (New York, 22 July 1958).

6 To behold her is an immediate check to loose behaviour; to love her is a liberal education.

SIR RICHARD STEELE (1672–1729), English dramatist, essayist, editor. *The Tatler*, no. 49, of Lady Elizabeth Hastings.

7 Give us that grand word "woman" once again,
And let's have done with "lady"; one's a term
Full of fine force, strong, beautiful, and firm,
Fit for the noblest use of tongue or pen;
And one's a word for lackeys.

ELLA WHEELER WILCOX (1855–1919), U.S. poet, journalist. *Woman*.

8 You've got many refinements. I don't think you need to worry about your failure at long division. I mean, after all, you got through short division, and short division is all that a lady ought to be called on to cope with.

TENNESSEE WILLIAMS (1914–83), U.S. dramatist. Silva to Baby Doll, in *Baby Doll*, set 43 (film script, 1957).

9 Women of quality are so civil, you can hardly distinguish love from good breeding.

WILLIAM WYCHERLEY (1640–1716), English dramatist. Horner, in *The Country Wife*, act 1.

LAISSEZ-FAIRE

1 Perhaps one of the most important accomplishments of my administration has been minding my own business.

CALVIN COOLIDGE (1872–1933), U.S. Republican politician, president. Remark to newspaper reporters, 1 March 1929, Washington, D.C.

2 What is laisser-faire but an orthodoxy? The most tyrannous and disastrous of all the orthodoxies, since it forbids you even to learn.

GEORGE BERNARD SHAW (1856–1950), Anglo-Irish playwright, critic. *The Doctor's Dilemma*, Preface, "The Technical Problem" (1911).

3 A man is rich in proportion to the number of things which he can afford to let alone.

HENRY DAVID THOREAU (1817–62), U.S. philosopher, author, naturalist. *Walden*, "Where I Lived, and What I Lived For" (1854).

4 The attitude is we live and let live. This is actually an amazing change in values in a rather short time and it's an example of freedom from religion.

TOM WOLFE (b. 1931), U.S. author, journalist. *International Herald Tribune* (Paris, 8 Sept. 1988).

LAKES

1 A lake is the landscape's most beautiful and expressive feature. It is earth's eye; looking into which the beholder measures the depth of his own nature.

HENRY DAVID THOREAU (1817–62), U.S. philosopher, author, naturalist. *Walden*, "The Ponds" (1854).

2 And I shall have some peace there, for peace comes dropping slow,
Dropping from the veils of the morning to where the cricket sings;

There midnight's all a glimmer, and noon a purple glow,
And evening full of the linnet's wings.

W. B. YEATS (1865–1939), Irish poet, playwright. *The Lake Isle of Innisfree*, st. 2.

THE LAND

1   To every people the land is given on condition. Perceived or not, there is a Covenant, beyond the constitution, beyond sovereign guarantee, beyond the nation's sweetest dreams of itself.

LEONARD COHEN (b. 1934), Canadian singer, poet, novelist. *Book of Mercy*, sct. 27 (1984).

2   Each blade of grass has its spot on earth whence it draws its life, its strength; and so is man rooted to the land from which he draws his faith together with his life.

JOSEPH CONRAD (1857–1924), Polish-born English novelist. Marlow, in *Lord Jim*, ch. 21 (1900).

3   This land is your land & this land is my land—sure—but the world is run by those that never listen to music anyway.

BOB DYLAN (b. 1941), U.S. singer, songwriter. *Tarantula*, "Sacred Cracked Voice & the Jingle Jangle Morning" (1970). See Guthrie, below.

4   If a man owns land, the land owns him.

RALPH WALDO EMERSON (1830–82), U.S. essayist, poet, philosopher. *The Conduct of Life*, "Wealth" (1860).

5   The land was ours before we were the land's.
She was our land more than a hundred years
Before we were her people.

ROBERT FROST (1874–1963), U.S. poet. *The Gift Outright*. Frost recited this poem at the inauguration of President John F. Kennedy (20 Jan. 1961).

6   This land is your land, this land is my land,
From California to the New York Island.
From the redwood forest to the Gulf Stream
   waters
This land was made for you and me.

WOODY GUTHRIE (1912–67), U.S. singer, songwriter. "This Land Is Your Land" (1956 song).

7   Topographically the country is magnificent—*and* terrifying. Why terrifying? Because nowhere else in the world is the divorce between man and nature so complete. Nowhere have I encountered such a dull, monotonous fabric of life as here in America. Here boredom reaches its peak.

HENRY MILLER (1891–1980), U.S. author. *The Air-Conditioned Nightmare*, Preface (1945).

8   Land is the only thing in the world that amounts to anything, for 'tis the only thing in this world that lasts, ... 'Tis the only thing worth working for, worth fighting for—worth dying for.

MARGARET MITCHELL (1900–1949), U.S. novelist. Gerald O'Hara, in *Gone with the Wind*, vol. 1, pt. 1, ch. 2 (1936).

9   O lands! O all so dear to me—what you are (what

ever it is), I become
part of that, whatever it is.

WALT WHITMAN (1819–92), U.S. poet. *American Feuillage*.

LANDLORDS

1   The best job that was ever offered to me was to become a landlord in a brothel. In my opinion it's the perfect milieu for an artist to work in.

WILLIAM FAULKNER (1897–1962), U.S. novelist. Interview in *Writers at Work* (First Series, ed. by Malcolm Cowley, 1958).

2   The Landlord is a gentleman . . . who does not earn his wealth. He has a host of agents and clerks that receive for him. He does not even take the trouble to *spend* his wealth. He has a host of people around him to do the actual spending. He never sees it until he comes to enjoy it. His sole function, his chief pride, is the stately consumption of wealth produced by others.

DAVID LLOYD GEORGE (1863–1945), Welsh Liberal politician, prime minister. Speech, 30 July 1909, Limehouse, London.

3   Landlords, like all other men, love to reap where they never sowed.

KARL MARX (1818–83), German political theorist, social philosopher. *Early Writings*, "First Manuscript" (ed. by T. B. Bottomore, 1884).

4   With one hand he put
A penny in the urn of poverty,
And with the other took a shilling out.

ROBERT POLLOK (1798–1827), Scottish poet. *The Course of Time*, bk. 8.

LANGUAGE

1   All true language
   is incomprehensible,
Like the chatter
   of a beggar's teeth.

ANTONIN ARTAUD (1896–1948), French theater producer, actor, theorist. *Ci-Gît* (1947; repr. in *Selected Writings*, pt. 36, *Indian Culture* and *Here Lies*, ed. by Susan Sontag, 1976).

2   A special kind of beauty exists which is born in language, of language, and for language.

GASTON BACHELARD (1884–1962), French scientist, philosopher, literary theorist. *Fragments of a Poetics of Fire*, "A Retrospective Glance at the Lifework of a Master of Books" (1988; tr. 1990).

3   All official institutions of language are repeating machines: school, sports, advertising, popular songs, news, all continually repeat the same structure, the same meaning, often the same words: the stereotype is a political fact, the major figure of ideology.

ROLAND BARTHES (1915–80), French semiologist. *The Pleasure of the Text*, "Modern" (1975).

4   Language is a skin: I rub my language against the other. It is as if I had words instead of fingers, or fingers at the tip of my words. My language trembles with desire.

ROLAND BARTHES (1915–80), French semiologist. *A Lovers Discourse: Fragments*, "Talking" (1977).

5 Never resist a sentence you like, in which language takes its own pleasure and in which, after having abused it for so long, you are stupefied by its innocence.

> JEAN BAUDRILLARD (b. 1929), French semiologist. *Cool Memories*, ch. 3 (1987; tr. 1990).

6 If everything is perfect, language is useless. This is true for animals. If animals don't speak, it's because everything's perfect for them. If one day they start to speak, it will be because the world has lost a certain sort of perfection.

> JEAN BAUDRILLARD (b. 1929), French semiologist. *Cool Memories*, ch. 3 (1987; tr. 1990).

7 No language is rude that can boast polite writers.

> AUBREY BEARDSLEY (1872–98), English illustrator, writer. *The Story of Venus and Tannhäuser or Under the Hill*, Dedicatory Epistle (1907).

8 One can say of language that it is potentially the only human home, the only dwelling place that cannot be hostile to man.

> JOHN BERGER (b. 1926), British author, critic. *And Our Faces, My Heart, Brief as Photos*, pt. 2 (1984).

9 Because language is the carrier of ideas, it is easy to believe that it should be very little else than such a carrier.

> LOUISE BOGAN (1897–1970), U.S. poet, critic. "A Revolution in European Poetry" (written 1941; published in *A Poet's Alphabet*, 1970).

10 Everything can change, but not the language that we carry inside us, like a world more exclusive and final than one's mother's womb.

> ITALO CALVINO (1923–85), Italian novelist, critic. *Grand Bazaar* (Milan, Sept.-Oct. 1980; repr. in *The Literature Machine*, 1987).

11 There is no such thing as an ugly language. Today I hear every language as if it were the only one, and when I hear of one that is dying, it overwhelms me as though it were the death of the earth.

> ELIAS CANETTI (b. 1905), Austrian novelist, philosopher. *The Secret Heart of the Clock: Notes, Aphorisms, Fragments 1973–1985*, "1976" (1991).

12 I speak Spanish to God, Italian to women, French to men and German to my horse.

> Attributed TO CHARLES V (1500–58), King of Spain, Holy Roman Emperor.

13 Language is a process of free creation; its laws and principles are fixed, but the manner in which the principles of generation are used is free and infinitely varied. Even the interpretation and use of words involves a process of free creation.

> NOAM CHOMSKY (b. 1928), U.S. linguist, political analyst. "Language and Freedom," lecture, Jan. 1970, delivered at Loyola University, Chicago (published in *For Reasons of State*, 1973).

14 One does not inhabit a country; one inhabits a language. That is our country, our fatherland—and no other.

> E. M. CIORAN (b. 1911), Rumanian-born French philosopher. *Anathemas and Admirations*, "On the Verge of Existence" (1986).

15 To a teacher of languages there comes a time when the world is but a place of many words and man appears a mere talking animal not much more wonderful than a parrot.

> JOSEPH CONRAD (1857–1924), Polish-born English novelist. The narrator, in *Under Western Eyes*, pt. 1, Prologue (1911).

16 The common faults of American language are an ambition of effect, a want of simplicity, and a turgid abuse of terms.

> JAMES FENIMORE COOPER (1789–1851), U.S. novelist. *The American Democrat*, "On Language" (1838).

17 It is still not enough for language to have clarity and content . . . it must also have a goal and an imperative. Otherwise from language we descend to chatter, from chatter to babble and from babble to confusion.

> RENÉ DAUMAL (1908–44), French poet, critic. *A Night of Serious Drinking*, Foreword (1938).

18 Curiously enough, it seems to be only in describing a mode of language which does not mean what it says that one can actually say what one means.

> PAUL DE MAN (1919–83), Belgian-born U.S. literary critic, "The Rhetoric of Temporality," sct. 2 (first published in *Interpretation*, ed. by Charles Singelton, 1969; repr. in *Blindness and Insight*, 1971, rev. 1983).

19 Male supremacy is fused into the language, so that every sentence both heralds and affirms it.

> ANDREA DWORKIN (b. 1946), U.S. feminist critic. *Pornography*, ch. 1 (1981).

20 There is the fear, common to all English-only speakers, that the chief purpose of foreign languages is to make fun of us. Otherwise, you know, why not just come out and *say* it?

> BARBARA EHRENREICH (b. 1941), U.S. author, columnist. *The Worst Years of Our Lives*, "Language Barrier" (1991; first published 1989).

21 Might, could, would—they are contemptible auxiliaries.

> GEORGE ELIOT (1819–80), English novelist. Mary Garth, in *Middlemarch*, bk. 2, ch. 14 (1872).

22 Language is the archives of history.

> RALPH WALDO EMERSON (1803–82), U.S. essayist, poet, philosopher. *Essays*, "The Poet" (Second Series, 1844).

23 I ascribe a basic importance to the phenomenon of language. . . . To speak means to be in a position to use a certain syntax, to grasp the morphology of this or that language, but it means above all to assume a culture, to support the weight of a civilization.

> FRANTZ FANON (1925–61), Martiniquan psychiatrist, philosopher, political activist. *Black Skins, White Masks*, "The Negro and Language" (1952; tr. 1967).

24 The style of an author should be the image of his mind, but the choice and command of language is the fruit of exercise.

> EDWARD GIBBON (1737–94), English historian. *Memoirs of My Life* (1796; repr. 1971, p. 98).

25 It is difficult for a woman to define her feelings in language which is chiefly made by men to express theirs.

> THOMAS HARDY (1840–1928), English novelist, poet. Bathsheba, in *Far from the Madding Crowd*, ch. 51 (1874).

26 Man acts as though *he* were the shaper and master of language, while in fact *language* remains the master of man.

> MARTIN HEIDEGGER (1889–1976), German philosopher. "Building Dwelling Thinking," lecture, 5 Aug. 1951 (published in *Poetry, Language, Thought,* 1971).

27 After all, when you come right down to it, how many people speak the same language even when they speak the same language?

> RUSSELL HOBAN (b. 1925), U.S. author. Boaz-Jachin, in *The Lion of Boaz-Jachin and Jachin-Boaz,* ch. 27 (1973).

28 Language is an archeological vehicle . . . the language we speak is a whole palimpsest of human effort and history.

> RUSSELL HOBAN (b. 1925), U.S. author. *Novelists in Interview* (ed. by John Haffenden, 1985).

29 Life and language are alike sacred. Homicide and *verbicide*—that is, violent treatment of a word with fatal results to its legitimate meaning, which is its life—are alike forbidden.

> OLIVER WENDELL HOLMES, SR. (1809–94), U.S. writer, physician. *The Autocrat of the Breakfast-Table,* ch. 1 (1858).

30 To rescue from oblivion even a fragment of a language which men have used and which is in danger of being lost—that is to say, one of the elements, whether good or bad, which have shaped and complicated civilization—is to extend the scope of social observation and to serve civilization.

> VICTOR HUGO (1802–85), French poet, dramatist, novelist. *Les Misérables,* pt. 4, bk. 7, ch. 1 (1862).

31 I am always sorry when any language is lost, because languages are the pedigree of nations.

> SAMUEL JOHNSON (1709–84), English author, lexicographer. Quoted in: James Boswell, *Tour to the Hebrides,* 18 Sept. 1773 (1785).

32 Language is political. That's why you and me, my Brother and Sister, that's why we sposed to choke our natural self into the weird, lying, barbarous, unreal, white speech and writing habits that the schools lay down like holy law. Because, in other words, the powerful don't play; they mean to keep that power, and those who are the powerless (you and me) better shape up—mimic/ape/suck—in the very image of the powerful, or the powerful will destroy you—you and our children.

> JUNE JORDAN (b. 1939), U.S. poet, civil rights activist. *Moving towards Home: Political Essays,* "White English/Black English: The Politics of Translation" (1989; first published 1972).

33 Language is the mother of thought, not its handmaiden.

> KARL KRAUS (1874–1936), Austrian satirist. *Die Fackel,* no. 288 (Vienna, 11 Oct. 1909). Quoted in: Thomas Szasz, *Anti-Freud: Karl Kraus's Criticism of Psychoanalysis and Psychiatry,* ch. 8 (1976).

34 My language is the common prostitute that I turn into a virgin.

> KARL KRAUS (1874–1936), Austrian satirist. *Pro Domo et Mundo,* ch. 7 (1912).

35 Public speaking is done in the public tongue, the national or tribal language; and the language of our tribe is the men's language. Of course women learn it. We're not dumb. If you can tell Margaret Thatcher from Ronald Reagan, or Indira Gandhi from General Somoza, by anything they say, tell me how. This is a man's world, so it talks a man's language.

> URSULA K. LE GUIN (b. 1929), U.S. author. "A Left-Handed Commencement Address," to Mills College Class of 1983, Oakland, Calif. (published in *Dancing at the Edge of the World,* 1989).

36 Language is a form of human reason, which has its internal logic of which man knows nothing.

> CLAUDE LÉVI-STRAUSS (b. 1908), French anthropologist. *The Savage Mind,* ch. 9 (1962).

37 Any language is necessarily a finite system applied with different degrees of creativity to an infinite variety of situations, and most of the words and phrases we use are "prefabricated" in the sense that we don't coin new ones every time we speak.

> DAVID LODGE (b. 1935), British author. *The State of the Language,* "Where It's At" (1980), defending Californian slang, or "psychobabble." See Rosen on SLANG.

38 Language, the machine of the poet, is best fitted for his purpose in its rudest state. Nations, like individuals, first perceive, and then abstract. They advance from particular images to general terms. Hence the vocabulary of an enlightened society is philosophical, that of a half-civilised people is poetical.

> THOMAS, LORD MACAULAY (1800–1859), English historian. "Milton," in *Edinburgh Review* (Aug. 1825; repr. in *Critical and Historical Essays,* 1843).

39 An art whose medium is language will always show a high degree of critical creativeness, for speech is itself a critique of life: it names, it characterizes, it passes judgment, in that it creates.

> THOMAS MANN (1875–1955), German author, critic. "Lessing," speech, 22 Jan. 1929, Prussian Academy of Art, Berlin (first published 1930; tr. 1933; repr. in *Essays of Three Decades,* 1942).

40 Syntax and vocabulary are overwhelming constraints—the rules that run us. Language is using *us* to talk—we think we're using the language, but language is doing the thinking, we're its slavish agents.

> HARRY MATHEWS (b. 1930), U.S. novelist. *City Limits* (London, 26 May 1988).

41 There is . . . in every child a painstaking teacher, so skilful that he obtains identical results in all children in all parts of the world. The only language men ever speak perfectly is the one they learn in babyhood, when no one can teach them anything!

> MARIA MONTESSORI (1870–1952), Italian educator. *The Absorbent Mind,* ch. 1 (1949).

42 The significance of language for the evolution of culture lies in this, that mankind set up in language a separate world beside the other world, a place it took to be so firmly set that, standing upon it, it could lift the rest of the world off its hinges and make itself master of it. To the extent that man has for long ages believed in the concepts and names of things as in *aeternae veritates* he has appropriated to himself that pride by which he raised himself above the animal: he really thought that in language he possessed knowledge of the world.

FRIEDRICH NIETZSCHE (1844–1900), German philosopher. *Human, All Too Human,* ch. 1, aph. 11 (1878).

43 Language ought to be the joint creation of poets and manual workers.

GEORGE ORWELL (1903–50), British author. "The English People" (1944; repr. in *The Collected Essays, Journalism and Letters of George Orwell,* vol. 3, ed. by Sonia Orwell and Ian Angus, 1968).

44 The great enemy of clear language is insincerity. When there is a gap between one's real and one's declared aims, one turns as it were instinctively to long words and exhausted idioms, like a cuttlefish squirting out ink.

GEORGE ORWELL (1903–50), British author. *Shooting an Elephant,* "Politics and the English Language" (1950).

45 Man, even man debased by the neocapitalism and pseudosocialism of our time, is a marvelous being because he sometimes *speaks.* Language is the mark, the sign, not of his fall but of his original innocence. Through the Word we may regain the lost kingdom and recover powers we possessed in the far-distant past.

OCTAVIO PAZ (b. 1914), Mexican poet. *Alternating Current,* "André Breton or the Quest of the Beginning" (1967).

46 You can't write about people out of textbooks, and you can't use jargon. You have to speak clearly and simply and purely in a language that a six-year-old child can understand; and yet have the meanings and the overtones of language, and the implications, that appeal to the highest intelligence.

KATHERINE ANNE PORTER (1890–1980), U.S. short-story writer, novelist. Interview in *Writers at Work* (Second Series, ed. by George Plimpton, 1963).

47 We might hypothetically possess ourselves of every technological resource on the North American continent, but as long as our language is inadequate, our vision remains formless, our thinking and feeling are still running in the old cycles, our process may be "revolutionary" but not transformative.

ADRIENNE RICH (b. 1929), U.S. poet. "Power and Danger: Works of a Common Woman," Introduction to *The Work of a Common Woman: The Collected Poetry of Judy Grahn, 1964–1977* (1977; repr. in *On Lies, Secrets, and Silence,* 1980).

48 When a language creates—as it does—a community within the present, it does so only by courtesy of a community between the present and the past.

CHRISTOPHER RICKS (b. 1933), British critic. *The State of the Language,* Preface (ed. by Ricks, 1980).

49 If you want to tell the untold stories, if you want to give voice to the voiceless, you've got to find a language. Which goes for film as well as prose, for documentary as well as autobiography. Use the wrong language, and you're dumb and blind.

SALMAN RUSHDIE (b. 1948), Indian-born British author. "*Songs Don't Know the Score,*" book review, in *Guardian* (London, 12 Jan. 1987).

50 Language furnishes the best proof that a law accepted by a community is a thing that is tolerated and not a rule to which all freely consent.

FERDINAND DE SAUSSURE (1857–1913), Swiss linguist. *Course in General Linguistics,* pt. 1, ch. 2, sct. 1 (1916). "Of all social institutions," de Saussure continued, "language is least amenable to initiative. It blends with the life of society, and the latter, inert by nature, is a prime conservative force."

51 A linguistic system is a series of differences of sound combined with a series of differences of ideas.

FERDINAND DE SAUSSURE (1857–1913), Swiss linguist. *Course in General Linguistics,* pt. 2, ch. 4, sct. 4 (1916).

52 The word of man is the most durable of all material.

ARTHUR SCHOPENHAUER (1788–1860), German philosopher. *Parerga and Paralipomena,* vol. 2, ch. 25, sct. 298 (1851).

53 Language can only deal meaningfully with a special, restricted segment of reality. The rest, and it is presumably the much larger part, is silence.

GEORGE STEINER (b. 1929), French-born U.S. critic, novelist. *Language and Silence,* "The Retreat from the Word" (1967).

54 The genius of democracies is seen not only in the great number of new words introduced but even more in the new ideas they express.

ALEXIS DE TOCQUEVILLE (1805–59), French social philosopher. *Democracy in America,* vol. 2, pt. 1, ch. 16 (1840).

55 Language is the amber in which a thousand precious and subtle thoughts have been safely embedded and preserved. It has arrested ten thousand lightning flashes of genius, which, unless thus fixed and arrested, might have been as bright, but would have also been as quickly passing and perishing, as the lightning.

RICHARD CHEVENIX TRENCH (1807–86), Irish ecclesiastic, archbishop of Dublin. *On the Study of Words,* Lecture 1 (1858).

56 The universal principle of etymology in all languages: words are carried over from bodies and from the properties of bodies to express the things of the mind and spirit. The order of ideas must follow the order of things.

GIAMBATTISTA VICO (1688–1744), Italian philosopher, historian. *The New Science,* bk. 1, para. 237–38 (ed. 1744; tr. 1968).

57 As societies grow decadent, the language grows decadent, too. Words are used to disguise, not to illuminate, action: you liberate a city by destroying it. Words are to confuse, so that at election time people will solemnly vote against their own interests.

GORE VIDAL (b. 1925), U.S. novelist, critic. *Armageddon? Essays 1983–1987,* "The Day the American Empire Ran Out of Gas" (1987).

58 A mind enclosed in language is in prison.

SIMONE WEIL (1909–43), French philosopher, mystic. "Human Personality" (written 1943; published in *La Table Ronde,* Dec. 1950; repr. in *Selected Essays,* ed. by Richard Rees, 1962).

59 The living language is like a cowpath: it is the creation of the cows themselves, who, having created it, follow it or depart from it according to their whims or their needs. From daily use, the path undergoes change. A cow is under no obligation to stay in the narrow path she helped make, following the contour of the land, but she often profits by staying with it and she would be handicapped if she didn't know where it was or where it led to.

> E. B. WHITE (1899–1985), U.S. author, editor. "The Living Language," in *New Yorker* (23 Feb. 1957; repr. in *Writings from the New Yorker 1927–1976*, ed. by Rebecca M. Dale, 1991).

60　Language is a part of our organism and no less complicated than it.

> LUDWIG WITTGENSTEIN (1889–1951), Austrian philosopher. *Notebooks 1914–1916*, entry for 14 May 1915 (ed. by Anscombe, 1961; later reformulated in Tractatus Logico-Philosophicus, sĕct. 4:002, 1921, tr. 1922). Also published in *Tractatus Logico-Philosophicus*, sct. 4:002 (1921; tr. 1922), "Everyday language is a part of the human organism and is no less complicated than it."

61　Methinks the human method of expression by sound of tongue is very elementary, & ought to be substituted for some ingenious invention which should be able to give vent to at least six coherent sentences at once.

> VIRGINIA WOOLF (1882–1941), British novelist. *A Terrible Tragedy in a Duckpond*, written when Woolf was seventeen, but not published until 1990.

See also Emerson on ANGELS; Koestler on CREATIVITY; Jargon; Calvino on LITERATURE; Auden on LITERATURE AND SOCIETY; Wittgenstein on MEANING; SLANG; Jonson on SPEECH.

LANGUAGE: ENGLISH

1　It is a mass language only in the same sense that its baseball slang is born of baseball players. That is, it is a language which is being molded by writers to do delicate things and yet be within the grasp of superficially educated people. It is not a natural growth, much as its proletarian writers would like to think so. But compared with it at its best, English has reached the Alexandrian stage of formalism and decay.

> RAYMOND CHANDLER (1888–1959), U.S. author. *The Notebooks of Raymond Chandler*, "Notes on English and American Style" (1976), on American English.

2　If English is spoken in heaven . . . God undoubtedly employs Cranmer as his speechwriter. The angels of the lesser ministries probably use the language of the New English Bible and the Alternative Service Book for internal memos.

> CHARLES, PRINCE OF WALES (b. 1948). Judging a reading competition. Quoted in: *Times* (London, 20 Dec. 1989).

3　And who in time knowes whither we may vent
The treasure of our tongue, to what strange shores
This gaine of our best glorie shal be sent,
T'inrich unknowing Nations with our stores?
What worlds in th'yet unformed Occident
May come refin'd with th'accents that are ours?

> SAMUEL DANIEL (c. 1562–1619), English poet, dramatist. *Musophilus*, in *Poetical Essays* (1599).

4　I like to be beholden to the great metropolitan English speech, the sea which receives tributaries from every region under heaven.

> RALPH WALDO EMERSON (1803–82), U.S. essayist, poet, philosopher. *Society and Solitude*, "Books" (1870).

5　Writing in English is the most ingenious torture ever devised for sins committed in previous lives. The English reading public explains the reason why.

> JAMES JOYCE (1882–1941), Irish author. Letter, 5 Sept. 1918 (published in *Selected Letters of James Joyce*, ed. by Richard Ellmann, 1975).

6　The problems of society will also be the problems of the predominant language of that society. It is the carrier of its perceptions, its attitudes, and its goals, for through it, the speakers absorb entrenched attitudes. The guilt of English then must be recognized and appreciated before its continued use can be advocated.

> NJABULO NDEBELE (b. 1948), Lesotho educator, writer. "The English Language and Social Change," keynote paper, 1986, delivered to the Jubilee Conference of the English Academy of Southern Africa, Johannesburg. Quoted in: Richard W. Bailey, "English at its Twilight," in *The State of the Language* (ed. by Christopher Ricks and Leonard Michaels, 1990).

7　To write or even speak English is not a science but an art. There are no reliable words. . . . Whoever writes English is involved in a struggle that never lets up even for a sentence. He is struggling against vagueness, against obscurity, against the lure of the decorative adjective, against the encroachment of Latin and Greek, and, above all, against the worn-out phrases and dead metaphors with which the language is cluttered up.

> GEORGE ORWELL (1903–50), British author. "The English People" (1944; repr. in *The Collected Essays, Journalism and Letters of George Orwell*, vol. 3, ed. by Sonia Orwell and Ian Angus, 1968). Consequently, Orwell explained, "The peculiarities of the English language make it almost impossible for anyone who has left school at fourteen to learn a foreign language after he has grown up."

8　My God! The English language is a *form of communication!* Conversation isn't just crossfire where you shoot and get shot at! Where you've got to duck for your life and aim to kill! Words aren't only bombs and bullets—no, they're little gifts, containing *meanings!*

> PHILIP ROTH (b. 1933), U.S. author. *Portnoy's Complaint*, "The Most Prevalent Form of Degradation in Erotic Life" (1967).

9　There is no such thing as "the Queen's English." The property has gone into the hands of a joint stock company and we own the bulk of the shares!

> MARK TWAIN (1835–1910), U.S. author. *Following the Equator*, ch. 24, "Pudd'nhead Wilson's New Calendar" (1897).

10　The English language is nobody's special property. It is the property of the imagination: it is the property of the language itself.

> DEREK WALCOTT (b. 1930), West Indian poet, playwright. Interview in *Writers at Work* (Eighth Series, ed. by George Plimpton, 1988).

11　Viewed freely, the English language is the accretion and growth of every dialect, race, and range of time, and is both the free and compacted composition of all.

> WALT WHITMAN (1819–92), U.S. poet. "Slang in America," in *North American Review* (Cedar Falls, Iowa, Nov. 1885).

12　We have really everything in common with America nowadays, except, of course, language.

> OSCAR WILDE (1854–1900), Anglo-Irish playwright, author. *The Canterville Ghost*, ch. 1 (first published in *Court and Society Review*, London, 23 Feb. and 2 March 1887).

See also Rushdie on DECOLINIZATION; Roosevelt on IMMIGRATION.

LATIN AMERICA

1 Brazil is bigger than Europe, wilder than Africa, and weirder than Baffin Land.

> LAWRENCE DURRELL (1912–90), British author. Letter, Dec. 1948, to Henry Miller (published in *The Durrell-Miller Letters 1935–80*, 1988).

2 Not only does the world scarcely know who the Latin American man is, the world has barely *cared*.

> GEORGIE ANNE GEYER (b. 1935), U.S. author, columnist. *The New Latins*, Introduction (1970).

3 Latin America can no longer tolerate being a haven for United States liberals who cannot make their point at home, an outlet for apostles too "apostolic" to find their vocation as competent professionals within their own community. The hardware salesman threatens to dump second-rate imitations of parishes, schools and catechisms—out-moded even in the United States—all around the continent. The traveling escapist threatens further to confuse a foreign world with his superficial protests, which are not viable even at home.

> IVAN ILLICH (b. 1926), Austrian-born U.S. theologian, author. *Celebration of Awareness*, ch. 5 (1969).

4 Latin America is very fond of the word "hope." We like to be called the "continent of hope." Candidates for deputy, senator, president, call themselves "candidates of hope." This hope is really something like a promise of heaven, an IOU whose payment is always being put off. It is put off until the next legislative campaign, until next year, until the next century.

> PABLO NERUDA (1904–73), Chilean poet. *Memoirs*, ch. 11 (1974; tr. 1977).

5 Violence has been Nicaragua's most important export to the world.

> RONALD REAGAN (b. 1911), U.S. Republican politician, president. Speech, 27 April 1983, to Congress (published in *Speaking My Mind*, 1989).

6 They are our brothers, these freedom fighters. . . . They are the moral equal of our Founding Fathers and the brave men and women of the French Resistance. We cannot turn away from them, for the struggle here is not right versus left; it is right versus wrong.

> RONALD REAGAN (b. 1911), U.S. Republican politician, president. Speech, 1 March 1985, to Conservative Political Action Conference, Washington, D.C. (published in *Speaking My Mind*, 1989), on the Nicaraguan contra fighters.

7 Mexico is a nineteenth-century country arranged for gaslight. Once brought into the harsh light of the twentieth-century media, Mexico can only seem false. In its male, in its public, its city aspect, Mexico is an arch-tranvestite, a tragic buffoon. Dogs bark and babies cry when Mother Mexico walks abroad in the light of day. The policeman, the Marxist mayor—Mother Mexico doesn't even bother to shave her mustachios. Swords and rifles and spurs and bags of money chink and clatter beneath her skirts. A chain of martyred priests dangles from her waist, for she is an austere, pious lady. Ay, how much—clutching her jangling bosoms; spilling cigars—how much she has suffered.

> RICHARD RODRIGUEZ (b. 1944), U.S. author, journalist. *Frontiers*, "Night and Day" (1990).

8 A happy people I call them still, whose peace and genuine morals have not been contaminated with European vices; and whose errors are only the errors of ignorance, and not the rooted depravity of a pretended civilization, and a spurious and mock Christianity.

> CAPTAIN J. G. STEDMAN (1744–97), British soldier, author, artist. *Narrative of a Five Years' Expedition against the Revolted Negroes of Surinam*, ch. 15 (1796; repr. 1971).

9 You must not judge people by their country. In South America, it is always wise to judge people by their altitude.

> PAUL THEROUX (b. 1941), U.S. novelist, travel writer. Quoting an old lady's advice, in *The Old Patagonian Express* (1979).

10 Americans living in Latin American countries are often more snobbish than the Latins themselves. The typical American has quite a bit of money by Latin American standards, and he rarely sees a countryman who doesn't. An American businessman who would think nothing of being seen in a sport shirt on the streets of his home town will be shocked and offended at a suggestion that he appear in Rio de Janeiro, for instance, in anything but a coat and tie.

> HUNTER S. THOMPSON (b. 1939), U.S. journalist. "Why Anti-Gringo Winds Often Blow South of the Border," in *National Observer* (Silver Spring, Md., 19 Aug. 1963; repr. in *The Great Shark Hunt*, 1979).

11 Since it is impossible to know what's really happening, we Peruvians lie, invent, dream and take refuge in illusion. Because of these strange circumstances, Peruvian life, a life in which so few actually do read, has become literary.

> MARIO VARGAS LLOSA (b. 1936), Peruvian novelist. The narrator, in *The Real Life of Alejandro Mayta*, ch. 9 (1984; tr. 1986).

See also Somoza on ELECTIONS; Reagan on FOREIGN COUNTRIES; Stedman on The NEW WORLD.

LAUGHTER

1 If we may believe our logicians, man is distinguished from all other creatures by the faculty of laughter. He has a heart capable of mirth, and naturally disposed to it.

> JOSEPH ADDISON (1672–1719), English essayist. *Spectator*, no. 494 (London, 26 Sept. 1712).

2 Laughter on American television has taken the place of the chorus in Greek tragedy. . . . In other countries, the business of laughing is left to the viewers. Here, their laughter is put on the screen, integrated into the show. It is the screen that is laughing and having a good time. You are simply left alone with your consternation.

> JEAN BAUDRILLARD (b. 1929), French semiologist. *America*, "Astral America" (1986; tr. 1988).

3 I hasten to laugh at everything for fear of being obliged to weep at it.

> PIERRE DE BEAUMARCHAIS (1732–99), French dramatist. Figaro, in *Le Barbier de Séville*, act 1, sc. 2. Byron expressed a similar idea in *Don Juan*, cto. 4, st. 4: "And if I laugh at any mortal thing, 'Tis that I may not weep."

4 We should laugh before being happy, for fear of dying without having laughed.

> JEAN DE LA BRUYÈRE (1645–96), French writer, moralist. *Characters,* "Of the Heart," aph. 63 (1688).

5 Nothing can confound
A wise man more than laughter from a dunce.

> LORD BYRON (1788–1824), English poet. *Don Juan,* cto. 16, st. 88.

6 No man who has once heartily and wholly laughed can be altogether irreclaimably bad.

> THOMAS CARLYLE (1795–1881), Scottish essayist, historian. *Sartor Resartus,* bk. 1, ch. 4 (1833–34).

7 Of all days, the day on which one has not laughed is the one most surely wasted.

> SÉBASTIEN-ROCH NICOLAS DE CHAMFORT (1741–94), French writer, wit. *Maxims and Considerations,* vol. 1, no. 80 (1796; tr. 1926).

8 In my mind, there is nothing so illiberal, and so ill-bred, as audible laughter.

> LORD CHESTERFIELD (1694–1773), English statesman, man of letters. Letter, 9 March 1748 (first published in 1774; repr. in *The Letters of the Earl of Chesterfield to His Son,* ed. by Charles Strachey, vol. 1, no. 144, 1901).

9 Observe it, the vulgar often laugh, but never smile, whereas well-bred people often smile, and seldom or never laugh. A witty thing never excited laughter, it pleases only the mind and never distorts the countenance.

> LORD CHESTERFIELD (1694–1773), English statesman, man of letters. Letter, 12 Dec. 1765 (published in *Lord Chesterfield's Letters to His Godson,* no. 135, ed. by Earl of Carnarvon, 1889).

10 There comes a time when suddenly you realize that laughter is something you remember and that *you* were the one laughing.

> MARLENE DIETRICH (1904–92), German-born U.S. film actor. *Marlene Dietrich's ABC,* "Laughter" (1962).

11 There exists a kind of laughter which is worthy to be ranked with the higher lyric emotions and is infinitely different from the twitchings of a mean merrymaker.

> NIKOLAI VASILYEVICH GOGOL (1809–52), Russian author, dramatist. *Dead Souls,* pt. 1, ch. 7 (1842).

12 The loud laugh that spoke the vacant mind.

> OLIVER GOLDSMITH (1728–74), Anglo-Irish playwright, author. *The Deserted Village.*

13 What provokes your risibility, Sir? Have I said anything that you understand? Then I ask pardon of the rest of the company.

> SAMUEL JOHNSON (1709–84), English author, lexicographer. Quoted in: Richard Cumberland, *Anecdotes* (first published in *Memoirs,* 1807; repr. in *Johnsonian Miscellanies,* vol. 2, ed. by George Birkbeck Hill, 1897, p. 77).

14 The sound of laughter is like the vaulted dome of a temple of happiness.

> MILAN KUNDERA (b. 1929), Czech author, critic. *The Book of Laughter and Forgetting,* pt. 3, ch. 2 (1978; tr. 1980).

15 Him, who incessantly laughs in the street, you may commonly hear grumbling in his closet.

> JOHANN KASPAR LAVATER (1741–1801), Swiss divine, poet. *Aphorisms on Man,* no. 305 (1788).

16 The sense of humour has other things to do than to make itself conspicuous in the act of laughter.

> ALICE MEYNELL (1847–1922), English poet, essayist. *Laughter.*

17 There is a kind of laughter that sickens the soul. Laughter when it is out of control: when it screams and stamps its feet, and sets the bells jangling in the next town. Laughter in all its ignorance and cruelty. Laughter with the seed of Satan in it. It tramples upon shrines; the belly-roarer. It roars, it yells, it is delirious: and yet it is as cold as ice. It has no humour. It is naked noise and naked malice.

> MERVYN PEAKE (1911–68), British author, artist. *Sometime, Never,* "Boy in Darkness" (1956).

18 Present mirth hath present laughter
What's to come is still unsure.

> WILLIAM SHAKESPEARE (1564–1616), English dramatist, poet. Feste's song to Sir Toby Belch and Sir Andrew Aguecheek, in *Twelfth Night,* act 2, sc. 3. The lines gave Noël Coward a title for his play, *Present Laughter.*

19 The laughter of man is more terrible than his tears, and takes more forms—hollow, heartless, mirthless, maniacal.

> JAMES THURBER (1894–1961), U.S. humorist, illustrator. *New York Times Magazine* (7 Dec. 1958).

20 We are a nation that has always gone in for the loud laugh, the wow, the yak, the belly laugh, and the dozen other labels for the roll-'em-in-the-aisles gagerissimo. This is the kind of laugh that delights actors, directors, and producers, but dismays writers of comedy because it is the laugh that often dies in the lobby. The appreciative smile, the chuckle, the soundless mirth, so important to the success of comedy, cannot be understood unless one sits among the audience and feels the warmth created by the quality of laughter that the audience takes home with it.

> JAMES THURBER (1894–1961), U.S. humorist, illustrator. *New York Times* (21 Feb. 1960).

See also Eliot on FOOLS AND FOLLIES; Sagan on JEALOUSY; SMILING.

D. H. LAWRENCE

1 If the Christ were content with humble toilers for disciples, that wasn't good enough for our Bert. He wanted dukes' half sisters and belted earls wiping his feet with their hair; grand apotheosis of the snob, to humiliate the objects of his own awe by making them venerate him.

> ANGELA CARTER (1940–92), British author. *New Society* (London, 3 June 1982).

2 No one can go on being a rebel too long without turning into an autocrat.

> LAWRENCE DURRELL (1912–90), British author. Pursewarden writing to Lawrence, in *Balthazar,* pt. 2, ch. 6 (1958).

3 For Lawrence, existence was one continuous convalescence; it was as though he were newly reborn from a mortal illness every day of his life. What these convalescent eyes saw, his most casual speech would reveal.

ALDOUS HUXLEY (1894–1963), British author. *The Olive Tree*, "D. H. Lawrence" (1936).

4 Isn't it remarkable how everyone who knew Lawrence has felt compelled to write about him? Why, he's had more books written about him than any writer since Byron!

ALDOUS HUXLEY (1894–1963), British author. Interview in *Writers at Work* (Second Series, ed. by George Plimpton, 1963).

5 I think . . . I have inside me a sort of answer to the *want* of today: to the real, deep want of the English people, not to just what they fancy they want. And gradually, I shall get my hold on them.

D. H. LAWRENCE (1885–1930), British author. Letter, 1 Feb. 1913, to writer and critic Edward Garnett, on the publication of Lawrence's novel *Sons and Lovers* (published in *The Letters of D. H. Lawrence*, vol. 1, ed. by James T. Boulton, 1979).

6 Primarily I am a passionately religious man, and my novels must be written from the depth of my religious experience.

D. H. LAWRENCE (1885–1930), British author. Letter, 22 April 1914, to writer and critic Edward Garnett (published in *The Letters of D. H. Lawrence*, vol. 2, ed. by George J. Zytaruk and James T. Boulton, 1981).

7 He is a man of one idea: *that life has a symbolic significance.* Which is to say that life and art are one.

HENRY MILLER (1891–1980), U.S. author. *The Wisdom of the Heart*, "Creative Death" (1947).

8 He's like an express train running through a tunnel—one shriek, sparks, smoke and gone.

VIRGINIA WOOLF (1882–1941), British novelist. Letter, 25 June 1935, to poet Stephen Spender (published in *The Sickle Side of the Moon: Letters vol. 5*, ed. by Nigel Nicolson, 1979).

See also Greer on ORGASM.

LAWS AND THE LAW

1 No civilization . . . would ever have been possible without a framework of stability, to provide the wherein for the flux of change. Foremost among the stabilizing factors, more enduring than customs, manners and traditions, are the legal systems that regulate our life in the world and our daily affairs with each other.

HANNAH ARENDT (1906–75), German-born U.S. political philosopher. *Crises of the Republic*, "Civil Disobedience" (1972).

2 Our law very often reminds one of those outskirts of cities where you cannot for a long time tell how the streets come to wind about in so capricious and serpentlike a manner. At last it strikes you that they grew up, house by house, on the devious tracks of the old green lanes; and if you follow on to the existing fields, you may often find the change half complete.

WALTER BAGEHOT (1826–77), English economist, critic. *The English Constitution*, ch. 9 (1867).

3 The law was made for one thing alone, for the exploitation of those who don't understand it, or are prevented by naked misery from obeying it.

BERTOLT BRECHT (1898–1956), German dramatist, poet. Peachum, in *The Threepenny Opera*, act 3, sc. 7.

4 Laws, like houses, lean on one another.

EDMUND BURKE (1729–97), Irish philosopher, statesman. *Tracts Relating to Popery Laws*, ch. 3, pt. 1 (1765; repr. in *The Writings and Speeches of Edmund Burke*, vol. 9, ed. by Paul Langford, 1991).

5 In effect, to follow, not to force the public inclination; to give a direction, a form, a technical dress, and a specific sanction, to the general sense of the community, is the true end of legislature.

EDMUND BURKE (1729–97), Irish philosopher, statesman. *Letter to the Sheriffs of Bristol*, 3 April 1777 (published in *Works*, vol. 2).

6 There is but one law for all, namely that law which governs all law, the law of our Creator, the law of humanity, justice, equity—the law of nature and of nations.

EDMUND BURKE (1729–97), Irish philosopher, statesman. Speech, 28 May 1794, Westminster Hall, at the impeachment of Warren Hastings.

7 As soon as you begin to say "We have always done things this way—perhaps *that* might be a better way," conscious law-making is beginning. As soon as you begin to say *We* do things this way—*they* do things that way—what is to be done about it?" men are beginning to feel towards justice, that resides between the endless jar of right and wrong.

HELEN M. CAM (1885–1968), British historian. "Law as It Looks to a Historian," lecture, 18 Feb. 1956, at Girton College, Cambridge University.

8 When the severity of the law is to be softened, let pity, not bribes, be the motive.

MIGUEL DE CERVANTES (1547–1616), Spanish writer. Don Quixote's advice to Sancho Panza, in *Don Quixote*, pt. 2, bk. 6, ch. 9 (1615; tr. by P. Motteux).

9 Some things are easier to legalize than to legitimate.

SÉBASTIEN-ROCH NICOLAS DE CHAMFORT (1741–94), French writer, wit. *Maxims and Considerations*, vol. 1, no. 134 (1796; tr. 1926).

10 Keep out of Chancery. . . . It's being ground to bits in a slow mill; it's being roasted at a slow fire; it's being stung to death by single bees; it's being drowned by drops; it's going mad by grains.

CHARLES DICKENS (1812–70), English novelist. Mr. Krook reporting Tom Jarndyce, in *Bleak House*, ch. 5 (1852).

11 The law isn't justice. It's a very imperfect mechanism. If you press exactly the right buttons and are also lucky, justice may show up in the answer. A mechanism is all the law was ever intended to be.

RAYMOND CHANDLER (1888–1959), U.S. author. Sewell Endicott, in *The Long Goodbye*, ch. 8 (1953).

12 The good of the people is the greatest law.

CICERO (106–43 B.C.), Roman orator, philosopher. *De Legibus*, bk. 3, ch. 3, sct. 8.

13 The law is simply expediency wearing a long white dress.

QUENTIN CRISP (b. 1908), British author. *Manners from Heaven,* ch. 8 (1984).

14 The decisions of law courts should never be printed: in the long run, they form a counterauthority to the law.

DENIS DIDEROT (1713–84), French philosopher. *Observations on the Drawing Up of Laws,* written in 1774 for Catherine the Great (first published 1921; repr. in *Selected Writings,* ed. by Lester G. Crocker, 1966).

15 We may not all break the Ten Commandments, but we are certainly all capable of it. Within us lurks the breaker of all laws, ready to spring out at the first real opportunity.

ISADORA DUNCAN (1878–1927), U.S. dancer. *My Life,* Introduction (1927).

16 The wise know that foolish legislation is a rope of sand, which perishes in the twisting.

RALPH WALDO EMERSON (1803–82), U.S. essayist, poet, philosopher. *Essays,* "Politics" (Second Series, 1844).

17 The law, in its majestic equality, forbids rich and poor alike to sleep under bridges, beg in the streets or steal bread.

ANATOLE FRANCE (1844–1924), French author. *The Red Lily,* ch. 7 (1894).

18 An unjust law is itself a species of violence. Arrest for its breach is more so.

MOHANDAS K. GANDHI (1869–1948), Indian political and spiritual leader. *Non-Violence in Peace and War,* vol. 2, ch. 150 (1949).

19 No great idea in its beginning can ever be within the law. How can it be within the law? The law is stationary. The law is fixed. The law is a chariot wheel which binds us all regardless of conditions or place or time.

EMMA GOLDMAN (1869–1940), U.S. anarchist. "Address to the Jury," in *Mother Earth* (New York, July 1917).

20 Law grinds the poor, and rich men rule the law.

OLIVER GOLDSMITH (1728–74), Anglo-Irish poet, essayist, playwright. *The Traveller.*

21 In a democracy—even if it is a so-called democracy like our white-élitist one—the greatest veneration one can show the rule of law is to keep a watch on it, and to reserve the right to judge unjust laws and the subversion of the function of the law by the power of the state. That vigilance is the most important proof of respect for the law.

NADINE GORDIMER (b. 1923), South African author. "Speak Out: The Necessity for Protest," lecture, 11 Aug. 1971, University of Natal, South Africa (published in *The Essential Gesture,* ed. by Stephen Clingman, 1988).

22 I know no method to secure the repeal of bad or obnoxious laws so effective as their stringent execution.

ULYSSES S. GRANT (1822–85), U.S. general, president. Inaugural address, 4 March 1869.

23 The law is only one of several imperfect and more or less external ways of defending what is better in life against what is worse. By itself, the law can never create anything better. . . . Establishing respect for the law does not automatically ensure a better life for that, after all, is a job for people and not for laws and institutions.

VÁCLAV HAVEL (b. 1936), Czech playwright, president. *Living in Truth,* pt. 1, "The Power of the Powerless," sct. 17 (1986).

24 We should have learnt by now that laws and court decisions can only point the way. They can establish criteria of right and wrong. And they can provide a basis for rooting out the evils of bigotry and racism. But they cannot wipe away centuries of oppression and injustice—however much we might desire it.

HUBERT H. HUMPHREY (1911–78), U.S. Democratic politician, vice president. Speech, 1 June 1966, White House Conference.

25 The only road to the highest stations in this country is that of the law.

SIR WILLIAM JONES (1746–94), English orientalist, jurist. Letter, 17 March 1771.

26 It may be true that the law cannot make a man love me, but it can keep him from lynching me, and I think that's pretty important.

MARTIN LUTHER KING, JR. (1929–68), U.S. clergyman, civil rights leader. *Wall Street Journal* (New York, 13 Nov. 1962).

27 Law and order exist for the purpose of establishing justice and . . . when they fail in this purpose they become the dangerously structured dams that block the flow of social progress.

MARTIN LUTHER KING, JR. (1929–68), U.S. clergyman, civil rights leader. "Letter from Birmingham Jail," in *Why We Can't Wait* (1963).

28 Laws are felt only when the individual comes into conflict with them.

SUZANNE LAFOLLETTE (1893–1983), U.S. editor, author. *Concerning Women,* "The Beginnings of Emancipation" (1926).

29 Let reverence for the laws be breathed by every American mother to the lisping babe that prattles on her lap. Let it be taught in schools, in seminaries, and in colleges. Let it be written in primers, spelling books, and in almanacs. Let it be preached from the pulpit, proclaimed in legislative halls, and enforced in the courts of justice. And, in short, let it become the political religion of the nation.

ABRAHAM LINCOLN (1809–65), U.S. president. Speech, 27 Jan. 1837, to the Young Men's Lyceum of Springfield, Ill.

30 A country survives its legislation. That truth should not comfort the conservative nor depress the radical. For it means that public policy can enlarge its scope and increase its audacity, can try big experiments without trembling too much over the result. This nation could enter upon the most radical experiments and could afford to fail in them.

WALTER LIPPMANN (1889–1974), U.S. journalist. *A Preface to Politics,* ch. 9 (1914).

31 Who thinks the law has anything to do with justice? It's what we have because we can't have justice.

WILLIAM MCILVANNEY (b. 1936), British novelist. Laidlaw, in *Laidlaw,* ch. 35 (1977).

32 The law is a sort of hocus-pocus science, that

smiles in yer face while it picks yer pocket: and the glorious uncertainty of it is of more use to the professors than the justice of it.

CHARLES MACKLIN (1690–1797), Irish actor, dramatist. Sir Archy MacSarcasm, in *Love à la Mode,* act 2. The part of Sir Archy was played by Macklin himself at the play's performance in Drury Lane, London, 12 Dec. 1759.

33 The business of the law is to make sense of the confusion of what we call human life—to reduce it to order but at the same time to give it possibility, scope, even dignity.

ARCHIBALD MACLEISH (1892–1982), U.S. poet. "Apologia," in *Harvard Law Review* (Cambridge, June 1972; repr. in *Riders on Earth,* as "Art and Law," 1978).

34 Laws and customs may be creative of vice; and should be therefore perpetually under process of observation and correction: but laws and customs cannot be creative of virtue: they may encourage and help to preserve it; but they cannot originate it.

HARRIET MARTINEAU (1802–76), English writer, social critic. *Society in America,* vol. 3, "Marriage" (1837).

35 All that makes existence valuable to any one depends on the enforcement of restraints upon the actions of other people.

JOHN STUART MILL (1806–73), English philosopher, economist. *On Liberty,* ch. 1 (1859).

36 Petty laws breed great crimes.

OUIDA (1839–1908), English novelist. *Pipistrello* (1880; published in *Wisdom, Wit and Pathos,* 1884).

37 Courts of law, and all the paraphernalia and folly of law . . . cannot be found in a rational state of society.

ROBERT OWEN (1771–1858), Welsh social reformer. Speech, 1 May 1833.

38 It is difficult to make our material condition better by the best law, but it is easy enough to ruin it by bad laws.

THEODORE ROOSEVELT (1858–1919), U.S. Republican (later Progressive) politician, president. Speech, 23 Aug. 1902, Providence, R.I.

39 Those laws, being forged for universal application, are in perpetual conflict with personal interest, just as personal interest is always in contradiction with the general interest. Good for society, our laws are very bad for the individuals whereof it is composed; for, if they one time protect the individual, they hinder, trouble, fetter him for three quarters of his life.

MARQUIS DE SADE (1740–1814), French author. Dolmancé, in *Philosophy in the Bedroom,* "Dialogue the Fifth" (1795).

40 Are not laws dangerous which inhibit the passions? Compare the centuries of anarchy with those of the strongest legalism in any country you like and you will see that it is only when the laws are silent that the greatest actions appear.

MARQUIS DE SADE (1740–1814), French author. Chigi, in *L'Histoire de Juliette, ou les Prospérités du Vice,* pt. 4 (1797).

41 The law often allows what honor forbids.

BERNARD JOSEPH SAURIN (1706–81), French dramatist. Blanche, in *Blanche et Guiscard,* act 5, sc. 6.

42 I have spent all my life under a Communist regime, and I will tell you that a society without any objective legal scale is a terrible one indeed. But a society with no other scale but the legal one is not quite worthy of man either.

ALEXANDER SOLZHENITSYN (b. 1918), Russian novelist. Commencement address, 7 June 1978, Harvard University.

43 Scarcely any political question arises in the United States that is not resolved, sooner or later, into a judicial question.

ALEXIS DE TOCQUEVILLE (1805–59), French social philosopher. *Democracy in America,* vol. 1, ch. 16 (1835).

44 The best laws cannot make a constitution work in spite of morals; morals can turn the worst laws to advantage. That is a commonplace truth, but one to which my studies are always bringing me back. It is the central point in my conception. I see it at the end of all my reflections.

ALEXIS DE TOCQUEVILLE (1805–59), French social philosopher. *Democracy in America,* "Concerning the Superiority of Morals to Laws," vol. 2, appendix 5 (1840).

45 The due process of law as we use it, I believe, rests squarely on the liberal idea of conflict and resolution.

JUNE L. TRAPP (b. 1930), U.S. psychologist, educator. *Psychology Today* (New York, May 1975).

46 To succeed in the other trades, capacity must be shown; in the law, concealment of it will do.

MARK TWAIN (1835–1910), U.S. author. *Following the Equator,* ch. 37, "Pudd'nhead Wilson's New Calendar" (1897).

See also King on PROTEST; Szasz on PUNISHMENT.

LAWYERS

1 Woe unto you, lawyers! for ye have taken away the key of knowledge: ye entered not in yourselves, and them that were entering in ye hindered.

BIBLE: NEW TESTAMENT. Jesus, in *Luke* 11:52.

2 Even an attorney of moderate talent can postpone doomsday year after year, for the system of appeals that pervades American jurisprudence amounts to a legalistic wheel of fortune, a game of chance, somewhat fixed in the favor of the criminal, that the participants play interminably.

TRUMAN CAPOTE (B 1924–84), U.S. author. *In Cold Blood,* ch. 4 (1965).

3 The kind of lawyer you hope the other fellow has.

RAYMOND CHANDLER (1888–1959), U.S. author. *The Long Goodbye,* ch. 17 (1954).

4 If there were no bad people there would be no good lawyers.

CHARLES DICKENS (1812–70), English novelist. Mr. Brass, in *The Old Curiosity Shop,* ch. 56 (1841).

5 When one wanted one's interests looking after whatever the cost, it was not so well for a lawyer to be over honest, else he might not be up to other people's tricks.

GEORGE ELIOT (1819–80), English novelist, editor. *Felix Holt, The Radical,* Author's Introduction (1866).

6 The good lawyer is not the man who has an eye to every side and angle of contingency, and qualifies all his qualifications, but who throws himself on your part so heartily, that he can get you out of a scrape.

RALPH WALDO EMERSON (1803–82), U.S. essayist, poet, philosopher. *The Conduct of Life*, "Power" (1860).

7 Amongst the learned the lawyers claim first place, the most self-satisfied class of people, as they roll their rock of Sisyphus and string together six hundred laws in the same breath, no matter whether relevant or not, piling up opinion on opinion and gloss on gloss to make their profession seem the most difficult of all. Anything which causes trouble has special merit in their eyes.

DESIDERIUS ERASMUS (c. 1466–1536), Dutch humanist. *Praise of Folly*, ch. 51 (1509).

8 A fox may steal your hens, Sir,
A whore your health and pence, Sir,
Your daughter rob your chest, Sir,
Your wife may steal your rest, Sir,
A thief your goods and plate.
But this is all but picking,
With rest, pence, chest and chicken;
It ever was decreed, Sir,
If lawyer's hand is fee'd, Sir,
He steals your whole estate.

JOHN GAY (1685–1732), English dramatist. Peachum, in *The Beggar's Opera*, act 1, sc. 9, Air 11.

9 I would be loath to speak ill of any person who I do not know deserves it, but I am afraid he is an *attorney*.

SAMUEL JOHNSON (1709–84), English author, lexicographer. Quoted in: Hester Piozzi, *Anecdotes of the Late Samuel Johnson* (1786; repr. in *Johnsonian Miscellanies*, vol. 1, p. 327, ed. by George Birkbeck Hill, 1891). Also quoted in: James Boswell, *Life of Samuel Johnson*, entry for 1770 (1791).

10 Lawyers know life practically. A bookish man should always have them to converse with.

SAMUEL JOHNSON (1709–84), English author, lexicographer. Said to the lawyer Oliver Edwards. Quoted in: James Boswell, *Life of Samuel Johnson*, 17 April 1778 (1791).

11 Lawyers are like rhinoceroses: thick skinned, short-sighted, and always ready to charge.

DAVID MELLOR (b. 1949), British Conservative politician. "Question Time," 3 Dec. 1992, BBC1.

12 A lawyer with his briefcase can steal more than a hundred men with guns.

MARIO PUZO (b. 1920), U.S. novelist. Oft-repeated dictum of Don Corleone, in *The Godfather*, bk. 1, ch. 1 (1969).

13 Lawyers enjoy a little mystery, you know. Why, if everybody came forward and told the truth, the whole truth, and nothing but the truth straight out, we should all retire to the workhouse.

DOROTHY L. SAYERS (1893–1957), British author. Sir Impey Biggs, in *Clouds of Witness*, ch. 3 (1926).

14 A lawyer without history or literature is a mechanic, a mere working mason; if he possesses some knowledge of these, he may venture to call himself an architect.

SIR WALTER SCOTT (1771–1832), Scottish novelist, poet. *Guy Mannering*, ch. 37 (1815).

15 Whenever you wish to do anything against the law, Cicely, always consult a good solicitor first.

GEORGE BERNARD SHAW (1856–1950), Anglo-Irish playwright, critic. Sir Howard, in *Captain Brassbound's Conversion*, act 1.

16 I said there was a society of men among us, bred up from their youth in the art of proving by words multiplied for the purpose, that white is black, and black is white, according as they are paid. To this society all the rest of the people are as slaves.

JONATHAN SWIFT (1667–1745), Anglo-Irish satirist. Gulliver, in *Gulliver's Travels*, pt. 4, "A Voyage to the Country of the Houyhnhnms," ch. 5 (1726), describing his native land.

17 Going to trial with a lawyer who considers your whole life-style a Crime in Progress is not a happy prospect.

HUNTER S. THOMPSON (b. 1939), U.S. journalist. "A Letter to *The Champion*: a publication of the National Assoc. of Criminal Defense Lawyers" (July 1990; repr. in *Songs of the Doomed*, 1991).

18 The lawyer's truth is not Truth, but consistency or a consistent expediency.

HENRY DAVID THOREAU (1817–62), U.S. philosopher, author, naturalist. *On the Duty of Civil Disobedience* (1849).

LAZINESS

1 Laziness. Unwarranted repose of manner in a person of low degree.

AMBROSE BIERCE (1842–1914), U.S. author. *The Devil's Dictionary* (1881–1906).

2 A lazy person, whatever the talents with which he set out, will have condemned himself to second-hand thoughts and to second-rate friends.

CYRIL CONNOLLY (1903–74), British critic. *The Unquiet Grave*, pt. 2 (1944; rev. 1951).

3 Turn on the prudent ant thy heedful eyes,
Observe her labours, sluggard, and be wise.

SAMUEL JOHNSON (1709–84), English author, lexicographer. Opening lines of *The Ant*, based on a passage in the Hebrew Bible, *Proverbs* 6:6: "Go to the ant, thou sluggard; consider her ways, and be wise."

4 My passions are all asleep from my having slumbered till nearly eleven and weakened the animal fibre all over me to a delightful sensation about three degrees on this sight of faintness—if I had teeth of pearl and the breath of lilies I should call it langour—but as I am I must call it laziness. In this state of effeminacy the fibres of the brain are relaxed in common with the rest of the body, and to such a happy degree that pleasure has no show of enticement and pain no unbearable frown. Neither poetry, nor ambition, nor love have any alertness of countenance as they pass by me.

JOHN KEATS (1795–1821), English poet. Letter, 14 Feb.-3 May 1819, to his brother and sister-in-law, George and Georgiana Keats (published in *Letters of John Keats*, no. 123, ed. by Frederick Page, 1954).

5 We seldom call anybody lazy, but such as we

reckon inferior to us, and of whom we expect some service.

> BERNARD MANDEVILLE (1670–1733), Dutch-born English author, physician. *The Fable of the Bees,* "Remark (V)" (1714; rev. 1723).

6 It is better to sit down than to stand, it is better to lie down than to sit, but death is the best of all.

> INDIAN PROVERB. Quoted in: Sébastien Roch de Chamfort, *Maxims and Considerations,* vol. 1, no. 155 (1796; tr. 1926).

7 Lazy people are always anxious to be doing something.

> LUC, MARQUIS DE VAUVENARGUES (1715–47), French moralist. *Refléxions et Maximes,* no. 458 (1746).

See also IDLENESS.

LEADERSHIP

1 Power tends to corrupt, and absolute power corrupts absolutely. Great men are almost always bad man.

> LORD ACTON (1834–1902), English historian. Letter, 3 April 1887, to Bishop Mandell Creighton (published in *The Life and Letters of Mandell Creighton,* 1904). William Pitt the Elder had previously said something to the same effect, in a speech to the House of Lords, 9 Jan. 1770: "Unlimited power is apt to corrupt the minds of those who possess it."

2 'Tis a dainty thing to command, though 'twere but a flock of sheep.

> MIGUEL DE CERVANTES (1547–1616), Spanish writer. Sancho Panza, in *Don Quixote,* pt. 2, bk. 6, ch. 9 (1615; tr. by P. Motteux).

3 To be a leader of men one must turn one's back on men.

> HAVELOCK ELLIS (1859–1939), British psychologist. Joris Karl Huysman, *Against the Grain,* Introduction (1884).

4 People try so hard to believe in leaders now, pitifully hard. But we no sooner get a popular reformer or politician or soldier or writer or philosopher—a Roosevelt, a Tolstoy, a Wood, a Shaw, a Nietzsche, than the cross-currents of criticism wash him away. My Lord, no man can stand prominence these days. It's the surest path to obscurity. People get sick of hearing the same name over and over.

> F. SCOTT FITZGERALD (1896–1940), U.S. author. Amory Blaine, in *This Side of Paradise,* bk. 2, ch. 2, "Restlessness" (1920).

5 All of the great leaders have had one characteristic in common: it was the willingness to confront unequivocally the major anxiety of their people in their time. This, and not much else, is the essence of leadership.

> JOHN KENNETH GALBRAITH (b. 1908), U.S. economist. *The Age of Uncertainty,* ch. 12 (1977), on his experience of the Nuremburg trials of Nazi war criminals.

6 The art of leadership . . . consists in consolidating the attention of the people against a single adversary and taking care that nothing will split up that attention. . . . The leader of genius must have the ability to make dif-ferent opponents appear as if they belonged to one category.

> ADOLF HITLER (1889–1945), German dictator. *Mein Kampf,* vol. 1, ch. 3 (1925).

7 Leadership in today's world requires far more than a large stock of gunboats and a hard fist at the conference table.

> HUBERT H. HUMPHREY (1911–78), U.S. Democratic politician, vice president. Speech, 20 Oct. 1966, Gainesville, Fla.

8 The wise man who is not heeded is counted a fool, and the fool who proclaims the general folly first and loudest passes for a prophet and Führer, and sometimes it is luckily the other way round as well, or else mankind would long since have perished of stupidity.

> CARL JUNG (1875–1961), Swiss psychiatrist. *Mysterium Coniunctionis* (1955–56; repr. in *Collected Works,* vol. 14, para. 783, ed. by William McGuire, 1963).

9 Blessed are the people whose leaders can look destiny in the eye without flinching but also without attempting to play God.

> HENRY KISSINGER (b. 1923), U.S. Republican politician, secretary of state. *Years of Upheaval,* ch. 25, "The End of the Road" (1982).

10 Most of the ladies and gentlemen who mourn the passing of the nation's leaders wouldn't know a leader if they saw one. If they had the bad luck to come across a leader, they would find out that he might demand something from them, and this impertinence would put an abrupt and indignant end to their wish for his return.

> LEWIS H. LAPHAM (b. 1935), U.S. essayist, editor. *Money and Class in America,* ch. 10 (1988). "Leadership," Lapham wrote, "consists not in degrees of technique but in traits of character; it requires moral rather than athletic or intellectual effort, and it imposes on both leader and follower alike the burdens of self-restraint."

11 The final test of a leader is that he leaves behind him in other men the conviction and the will to carry on. . . . The genius of a good leader is to leave behind him a situation which common sense, without the grace of genius, can deal with successfully.

> WALTER LIPPMANN (1889–1974), U.S. journalist. "Roosevelt Is Gone," in *New York Herald Tribune* (14 April 1945; repr. in *The Essential Lippman,* pt. 10, sct. 5, 1982).

12 There is no such thing as a perfect leader either in the past or present, in China or elsewhere. If there is one, he is only pretending, like a pig inserting scallions into its nose in an effort to look like an elephant.

> LIU SHAO-CH'I (b. 1898), Chinese leader. Said 13 July 1947. Quoted in: Stanley Karnow, *Mao and China: From Revolution to Revolution,* ch. 4 (1972).

13 That perfect bliss and sole felicity,
The sweet fruition of an earthly crown.

> CHRISTOPHER MARLOWE (1564–93), English dramatist, poet. Tamburlaine, in *Tamburlaine the Great,* pt. 1, act 2, sc. 7.

14 The most important quality in a leader is that of being acknowledged as such.

> ANDRÉ MAUROIS (1885–1967), French author, critic. *The Art of Living,* "The Art of Leadership" (1940).

15 That is no use at all. What I want is men who will support me when I am in the wrong.

> LORD MELBOURNE (1779–1848), English statesman, prime minister. Reply to a politician's pledge: "I will support you as long as you are in the right." Quoted in: David Cecil, *Lord M.,* ch. 4 (1954).

16 When I think of this life I have led; the desolation of solitude it has been; the masoned, walled-town of a Captain's exclusiveness, which admits but small entrance to any sympathy from the green country with-out—oh, weariness! heaviness! Guinea-coast slavery of solitary command!

> HERMAN MELVILLE (1819–91), U.S. author. Captain Ahab, in *Moby-Dick,* ch. 132 (1851).

17 The real leader has no need to lead—he is content to point the way.

> HENRY MILLER (1891–1980), U.S. author. *The Wisdom of the Heart,* title essay (1947).

18 Follow me if I advance! Kill me if I retreat! Revenge me if I die!

> NGO DINH DIEM (d. 1963), Vietnamese politician. Reported in *Time* (New York, 8 Nov. 1963), on becoming President of Vietnam, 1954. The same exhortation had been used by Mussolini to his officers after an attempt on his life 6 April 1926, by the Hon. Violet Gibson, an Irishwoman. Quoted in: Christopher Hibbert, *Benito Mussolini,* pt. 1, ch. 5 (1962).

19 I don't think that a leader can control to any great extent his destiny. Very seldom can he step in and change the situation if the forces of history are running in another direction.

> RICHARD M. NIXON (b. 1913), U.S. Republican politician, president. Quoted in: Earl Mazo, *Richard Nixon: A Political and Personal Portrait,* ch. 18 (1959).

20 The right man comes at the right time.

> ITALIAN PROVERB.

21 Perhaps in His wisdom the Almighty is trying to show us that a leader may chart the way, may point out the road to lasting peace, but that many leaders and many peoples must do the building.

> ELEANOR ROOSEVELT (1884–1962), U.S. columnist, lecturer. "My Day," syndicated newspaper column (16 April 1945).

22 People ask the difference between a leader and a boss. . . . The leader works in the open, and the boss in covert. The leader leads, and the boss drives.

> THEODORE ROOSEVELT (1858–1919), U.S. Republican (later Progressive) politician, president. Speech, 24 Oct. 1910, Binghamton, N.Y.

23 The secret of a leader lies in the tests he has faced over the whole course of his life and the *habit of action* he develops in meeting those tests.

> GAIL SHEEHY (b. 1937), U.S. journalist, author. *Gorbachev,* "Looking for Mikhail Gorbachev" (1991).

24 To be
Omnipotent but friendless is to reign.

> PERCY BYSSHE SHELLEY (1792–1822), English poet. Asia, in *Prometheus Unbound,* act 2, sc. 4.

25 No one would have doubted his ability to reign had he never been emperor.

> TACITUS (c. 55–c. 120), Roman historian. *The Histories,* bk. 1, sct. 49. This summary of Emperor Galba's character is regarded as a masterpiece of epigrammatic writing.

26 I am a leader by default, only because nature does not allow a vacuum.

> BISHOP DESMOND TUTU (b. 1931), South African prelate. *Christian Science Monitor* (Boston, 20 Dec. 1984).

27 It is very comforting to believe that leaders who do terrible things are, in fact, mad. That way, all we have to do is make sure we don't put psychotics in high places and we've got the problem solved.

> TOM WOLFE (b. 1931), U.S. journalist, author. *In Our Time,* ch. 2, "Jonestown" (1980).

See also Reagan on MANAGEMENT; Ledru-Rollin on MOBS; Sun Tzu on WINNING.

LEARNING

1 Learning. The kind of ignorance distinguishing the studious.

> AMBROSE BIERCE (1842–1914), U.S. author. *The Devil's Dictionary* (1881–1906).

2 With just enough of learning to misquote.

> LORD BYRON (1788–1824), English poet. *English Bards and Scotch Reviewers,* of critics.

3 For a man to attain to an eminent degree in learning costs him time, watching, hunger, nakedness, dizziness in the head, weakness in the stomach, and other inconveniences.

> MIGUEL DE CERVANTES (1547–1616), Spanish writer. Don Quixote, in *Don Quixote,* pt. 1, bk. 4, ch. 11 (1605; tr. by P. Motteux).

4 Never seem wiser, nor more learned, than the people you are with. Wear your learning, like your watch, in a private pocket: and do not merely pull it out and strike it; merely to show that you have one.

> LORD CHESTERFIELD (1694–1773), English statesman, man of letters. Letter, 22 Feb. 1748 (first published 1774; repr. in *The Letters of the Earl of Chesterfield to His Son,* vol. 1, no. 142, ed. by Charles Strachey, 1901).

5 All other men are specialists, but his specialism is omniscience.

> SIR ARTHUR CONAN DOYLE (1859–1930), English author. Sherlock Holmes, in *His Last Bow,* "The Bruce-Partington Plans" (1917), of his brother Mycroft.

6 The studious class are their own victims: they are thin and pale, their feet are cold, their heads are hot, the night is without sleep, the day a fear of interruption—pallor, squalor, hunger, and egotism.

> RALPH WALDO EMERSON (1803–82), U.S. essayist, poet, philosopher. *Representative Men,* ch. 4, "Montaigne" (1850).

7 This type of man who is devoted to the study of wisdom is always most unlucky in everything, and particularly when it comes to procreating children; I imagine this is because Nature wants to ensure that the evils of wisdom shall not spread further throughout mankind.

DESIDERIUS ERASMUS (c. 1466–1536), Dutch humanist. *Praise of Folly*, ch. 24 (1509).

8 I've studied now Philosophy
And Jurisprudence, Medicine—
And even, alas! Theology—
From end to end with labor keen;
And here, poor fool! with all my lore
I stand, no wiser than before.

JOHANN WOLFGANG VON GOETHE (1749–1832), German poet, dramatist. Faust, in *Faust*, pt. 1, "Night" (tr. by Bayard Taylor).

9 This is an age of intellectual sauces, of essence, of distillation. We have "conclusions" without deductions, "abridgments of history" and "abridgments of science" without leading facts. We have "animals" for literature, "Cabinet" Encyclopaedias, "Family" Libraries, "Diffusion" Societies, and heaven knows what else! What is all this for? Not to add knowledge to the learned, but to tell points to the ignorant, without giving them the trouble to acquire the links. Oh! it is sad work. And the result will be injurious to all classes.

BENJAMIN HAYDON (1786–1846), British artist. "Table Talk," in *Correspondence and Table-Talk*, vol. 2 (ed. by Frederic Wordsworth Haydon, 1876).

10 Learning is, in too many cases, but a foil to common sense; a substitute for true knowledge. Books are less often made use of as "spectacles" to look at nature with, than as blinds to keep out its strong light and shifting scenery from weak eyes and indolent dispositions . . . . The learned are mere literary drudges.

WILLIAM HAZLITT (1778–1830), English essayist. "On the Ignorance of the Learned," in *Edinburgh Magazine* (July 1818; repr. in *Table Talk*, 1821).

11 There are some things which cannot be learned quickly, and time, which is all we have, must be paid heavily for their acquiring. They are the very simplest things and because it takes a man's life to know them the little new that each man gets from life is very costly and the only heritage he has to leave.

ERNEST HEMINGWAY (1899–1961), U.S. author. *Death in the Afternoon*, ch. 16 (1932). This passage was used as the epigraph in A. E. Hotchner, *Papa Hemingway* (1955).

12 In a time of drastic change it is the learners who inherit the future. The learned usually find themselves equipped to live in a world that no longer exists.

ERIC HOFFER (1902–83), U.S. philosopher. *Reflections on the Human Condition*, aph. 32 (1973).

13 Their learning is like bread in a besieged town: every man gets a little, but no man gets a full meal.

SAMUEL JOHNSON (1709–84), English author, lexicographer. Quoted in: James Boswell, *Life of Samuel Johnson*, 18 April 1775 (1791), of the Scots.

14 Have you ever seen a pedant with a warm heart?

JOHANN KASPAR LAVATER (1741–1801), Swiss divine, poet. *Aphorisms on Man*, no. 260 (1788).

15 Erudition can produce foliage without bearing fruit.

G. C. LICHTENBERG (1742–99), German physicist, philosopher. *Aphorisms*, "Notebook C," aph. 26 (written 1765–99; tr. by R. J. Hollingdale, 1990).

16 I was brought up to believe that the only thing worth doing was to add to the sum of accurate information in the world.

MARGARET MEAD (1901–78), U.S. anthropologist. *New York Times* (9 Aug. 1964).

17 A little learning is a dangerous thing;
Drink deep, or taste not the Pierian spring:
There shallow draughts intoxicate the brain,
And drinking largely sobers us again.

ALEXANDER POPE (1688–1744), English satirical poet. *An Essay on Criticism*. Pieria was the fabled birthplace of the muses.

18 I would by no means wish a daughter of mine to be a progeny of learning; I don't think so much learning becomes a young woman: for instance, I would never let her meddle with Greek, or Hebrew, or algebra, or simony, or fluxions, or paradoxes, or such inflammatory branches of learning; nor will it be necessary for her to handle any of your mathematical, astronomical, diabolical instruments; but . . . I would send her, at nine years old, to a boarding-school, in order to learn a little ingenuity and artifice: then, sir, she would have a supercilious knowledge in accounts, and, as she grew up, I would have her instructed in geometry, that she might know something of the contagious countries: this . . . is what I would have a woman know; and I don't think there is a superstitious article in it.

RICHARD BRINSLEY SHERIDAN (1751–1816), Anglo-Irish dramatist. Mrs. Malaprop, in *The Rivals*, act 1, sc. 2.

19 Learning carries within itself certain dangers because out of necessity one has to learn from one's enemies.

LEON TROTSKY (1879–1940), Russian revolutionary. *Literature and Revolution*, ch. 6 (1924).

20 The mind of the thoroughly well-informed man is a dreadful thing. It is like a bric-à-brac shop, all monsters and dust, with everything priced above its proper value.

OSCAR WILDE (1854–1900), Anglo-Irish playwright, author. Lord Henry, in *The Picture of Dorian Gray*, ch. 1 (1891).

See also Montagu on KNOWLEDGE; Penn on READING; SCHOLARS AND SCHOLARSHIP; Hazlitt on SHAKESPEARE; Bible: New Testament on STUDENTS.

LEBANON

1 We are going to pull out the plug. We have reached the point where shells do not hurt us any more.

MICHEL AOUN (b. 1935), Lebanese army officer. *Independent* (London, 19 April 1989).

2 A process of genocide is being carried out before the eyes of the world.

JOHN PAUL II [KAROL WOJTYLA] (b. 1920), Polish ecclesiastic, pope. Quoted in: *Independent* (London, 16 Aug. 1989), of the situation in Beirut.

3 Here, even the law of the jungle has broken down.

> WALID JUMBLATT (b. 1949), Leader of the Druze. Quoted in: *Sunday Times* (London, 29 Dec. 1985).

See also The MIDDLE EAST.

LEISURE

1 It is already possible to imagine a society in which the majority of the population, that is to say, its laborers, will have almost as much leisure as in earlier times was enjoyed by the aristocracy. When one recalls how aristocracies in the past actually behaved, the prospect is not cheerful.

> W. H. AUDEN (1907–73), Anglo-American poet. *A Certain World*, "Work, Labor, and Play" (1970).

2 How many inner resources one needs to tolerate a life of leisure without fatigue

> NATALIE CLIFFORD BARNEY (1876–1972), U.S.-born French author. Quoted in: George Wickes, *The Amazon of Letters*, ch. 10 (1976).

3 Leisure is the mother of Philosophy.

> THOMAS HOBBES (1588–1679), English philosopher. *Leviathan*, pt. 4, ch. 46 (1651).

4 Money and time are the heaviest burdens of life, and . . . the unhappiest of all mortals are those who have more of either than they know how to use.

> SAMUEL JOHNSON (1709–84), English author, lexicographer. *The Idler*, no. 30, in *Universal Chronicle* (London, 11 Nov. 1758; repr. in *Works of Samuel Johnson*, vol. 2, ed. by W. J. Bate, John M. Bullitt, and L. F. Powell, 1963).

5 The most remarkable aspect of the transition we are living through is not so much the passage from want to affluence as the passage from labor to leisure. . . . Leisure contains the future, it is the new horizon. . . . The prospect then is one of unremitting labor to bequeath to future generations a chance of founding a society of leisure that will overcome the demands and compulsions of productive labor so that time may be devoted to creative activities or simply to pleasure and happiness.

> HENRI LEFEBVRE (b. 1901), French philosopher. *Everyday Life in the Modern World*, ch. 1, "What Should the New Society Be Called?" (1962).

6 The idea that leisure is of value in itself is only conditionally true. . . . The average man simply spends his leisure as a dog spends it. His recreations are all puerile, and the time supposed to benefit him really only stupefies him.

> H. L. MENCKEN (1880–1956), U.S. journalist. *Minority Report: H. L. Mencken's Notebooks*, no. 87 (1956).

7 To be able to fill leisure intelligently is the last product of civilization.

> BERTRAND RUSSELL (1872–1970), British philosopher, mathematician. *The Conquest of Happiness*, ch. 14 (1930). Russell added, "At present very few people have reached this level."

8 He enjoys true leisure who has time to improve his soul's estate.

> HENRY DAVID THOREAU (1817–62), U.S. philosopher, author, naturalist. *Journals* (1906), entry for 11 Feb. 1840.

9 A broad margin of leisure is as beautiful in a man's life as in a book. Haste makes waste, no less in life than in housekeeping. Keep the time, observe the hours of the universe, not of the cars. What are threescore years and ten hurriedly and coarsely lived to moments of divine leisure in which your life is coincident with the life of the universe?

> HENRY DAVID THOREAU (1817–62), U.S. philosopher, author, naturalist. *Journals* (1906), entry for 28 Dec. 1852.

10 People without imagination are beginning to tire of the importance attached to comfort, to culture, to leisure, to all that destroys imagination. This means that people are not really tired of comfort, culture and leisure, but of the use to which they are put, which is precisely what stops us enjoying them.

> RAOUL VANEIGEM (b. 1934), Belgian Situationist philosopher. *The Revolution of Everyday Life*, ch. 1, sct. 3 (1967; tr. 1983).

11 The basis on which good repute in any highly organized industrial community ultimately rests is pecuniary strength; and the means of showing pecuniary strength, and so of gaining or retaining a good name, are leisure and a conspicuous consumption of goods.

> THORSTEIN VEBLEN (1857–1929), U.S. social scientist. *The Theory of the Leisure Class*, ch. 4 (1899).

12 Cultivated leisure is the aim of man.

> OSCAR WILDE (1854–1900), Anglo-Irish playwright, author. *The Soul of Man under Socialism*, in *Fortnightly Review* (London, Feb. 1890).

13 It is most important that we should keep in this country a certain leisured class. . . . I am of the opinion of the ancient Jewish book which says "there is no wisdom without leisure."

> W. B. YEATS (1865–1939), Irish poet, playwright. Speech, 28 March 1923, to the Seanad Eireann, the Irish Senate

See also Johnson on PLAY; Bible, Hebrew, Bible: New Testament on WISDOM.

LENDING

See BAROWING AND LENDING

JOHN LENNON

1 John was a very political animal. The thing that politics did and that fame as an entertainer *didn't* do was provide you with an engine for propagating your theories and beliefs. The one thing John would have liked more than anything else was his own political machine. Even though he would profess that politics is bullshit, he just wouldn't call it "politics." He'd call it "peace."

> JOHN BROWER (b. 1946), Canadian rock impresario. Quoted in: Albert Goldman, *The Lives of John Lennon*, "A Vote for Peace is a Vote for Lennon" (1988).

2   I'm not gonna change the way I look or the way I feel to conform to anything. I've always been a freak. So I've been a freak all my life and I have to live with that, you know. I'm one of those people.

> JOHN LENNON (1940–80), British rock musician. Interview in *Playboy* (Chicago, Sept. 1980).

3   My role in society, or any artist or poet's role, is to try and express what we all feel. Not to tell people how to feel. Not as a preacher, not as a leader, but as a reflection of us all.

> JOHN LENNON (1940–80), British rock musician. Interview, 8 Dec. 1980, KFRC RKO Radio, given the day of his death.

4   The most important thing in my father's life? World peace. Me and my brother. My mom.

> SEAN TARO ONO LENNON (b. 1975). Interview, 21 Jan. 1988, in Andrew Solt and Sam Egan, *Imagine: John Lennon* (1988).

5   Maybe we were naïve, but still we were very honest about everything we did.

> YOKO ONO (b. 1933), Japanese-born U.S. artist. Interview, 8 Dec. 1980, KFRC RKO Radio, given a few hours before Lennon's death.

LESBIANISM

1   Then the question began to live under my blankets: How did lesbianism begin? What were the symptoms? The public library gave information on the finished lesbian—and that woefully sketchy—but on the growth of a lesbian, there was nothing. I did discover that the difference between hermaphrodites and lesbians was that hermaphrodites were "born that way." It was impossible to determine whether lesbians budded gradually, or burst into being with a suddenness that dismayed them as much as it repelled society.

> MAYA ANGELOU (b. 1928), U.S. author. *I Know Why the Caged Bird Sings*, vol. 1, ch. 35 (1969).

2   Between women love is contemplative; caresses are intended less to gain possession of the other than gradually to re-create the self through her; separateness is abolished, there is no struggle, no victory, no defeat; in exact reciprocity each is at once subject and object, sovereign and slave; duality become mutuality.

> SIMONE DE BEAUVOIR (1908–86), French novelist, essayist. *The Second Sex*, bk. 2, pt. 4, ch. 4 (1953).

3   I love, cherish, and respect women in my mind, in my heart, and in my soul. This love of women is the soil in which my life is rooted. It is the soil of our common life together. My life grows out of this soil. In any other soil, I would die. In whatever ways I am strong, I am strong because of the power and passion of this nurturant love.

> ANDREA DWORKIN (b. 1946), U.S. feminist critic. "Lesbian Pride," speech, 28 June 1975, Central Park, New York City (published in *Our Blood*, ch. 7, 1976).

4   "Lesbianism" would appear to be so little a threat at the moment that it is hardly ever mentioned. . . . Whatever its potentiality in sexual politics, female homosexuality is currently so dead an issue that while male homosexuality gains a grudging tolerance, in women the event is observed in scorn or in silence.

> KATE MILLET (b. 1934), U.S. feminist author. Note in *Sexual Politics*, pt. 3, ch. 8 (1970).

5   Gay men may seek sex without emotion; lesbians often end up in emotion without sex.

> CAMILLE PAGLIA (b. 1947), U.S. author, critic, educator. "Homosexuality at the Fin de Siècle," in *Esquire* (New York, Oct. 1991; repr. in *Sex, Art, and American Culture*, 1992).

6   It is . . . crucial that we understand lesbian/feminism in the deepest, most radical sense: as that love for ourselves and other women, that commitment to the freedom of all of us, which transcends the category of "sexual preference" and the issue of civil rights, to become a politics of *asking women's questions*, demanding a world in which the integrity of all women—not a chosen few—shall be honored and validated in every respect of culture.

> ADRIENNE RICH (b. 1929), U.S. poet. *On Lies, Secrets, and Silence*, Foreword (1980).

7   Lesbian existence comprises both the breaking of a taboo and the rejection of a compulsory way of life. It is also a direct or indirect attack on the male right of access to women.

> ADRIENNE RICH (b. 1929), U.S. poet. *Blood, Bread and Poetry*, "Compulsory Heterosexuality and Lesbian Existence" (1986).

8   I have decided to give up heterosexuality. I have decided that, while the project of altering the balance of power within heterosexual relationships is still a valid one, it is no longer one I can espouse—so to speak. There is no revolutionary hope for the heterosexual, and I have therefore decided to love myself and become a lesbian.

> MICHELENE WANDOR (b. 1940), British poet, playwright, critic. In conversation with her mother, in "Meet My Mother" (published in *Close Company: Stories of Mothers and Daughters*, ed. by Christine Park and Caroline Heaton, 1987).

See also HOMOSEXUALITY.

LIBERALS

1   Ultraliberalism today translates into a whimpering isolationism in foreign policy, a mulish obstructionism in domestic policy, and a pusillanimous pussyfooting on the critical issue of law and order.

> SPIRO AGNEW (b. 1918), U.S. Republican politician, vice president. Speech, 10 Sept. 1970, Springfield, Ill. (published in *Collected Speeches of Spiro Agnew*, 1971).

2   A liberal is a socialist with a wife and two children.

> ANONYMOUS (1930s). Quoted in: Alistair Cooke, "Letter from America," 8 April 1990, BBC Radio 4.

3   There are two kinds of liberalism. A liberalism which is always, subterraneously authoritative and paternalistic, on the side of one's good conscience. And then there is a liberalism which is more ethical than political; one would have to find another name for this. Something like a profound suspension of judgment.

> ROLAND BARTHES (1915–80), French semiologist. Interview with Bernard-Henri Lévy, in *Art and Text*, no. 8 (1977; repr. in

Discourses: Conversations in Postmodern Art and Culture, ed. by Russell Ferguson, et. al., 1990).

4   The liberals can understand everything but people who don't understand them.

> LENNY BRUCE (1925–66), U.S. satirical comedian. *The Essential Lenny Bruce,* "Politics" (ed. by John Cohen, 1967).

5   As with most liberal sexual ideas, what makes the world a better place for men invariably makes it a duller and more dangerous place for women.

> JULIE BURCHILL (b. 1960), British journalist, author. "Where's the Beef?" in *Arena* (London, 1988; repr. in *Sex and Sensibility,* 1992).

6   My objection to Liberalism is this—that it is the introduction into the practical business of life of the highest kind—namely, politics—of philosophical ideas instead of political principles.

> BENJAMIN DISRAELI (1804–81), English statesman, author. Speech, 5 June 1848, to House of Commons, London, on the expulsion of the British ambassador from Madrid.

7   Cosmopolitan critics, men who are the friends of every country save their own.

> BENJAMIN DISRAELI (1804–81), English statesman, author. Speech, 9 Nov. 1877, Guildhall, London.

8   The label of liberalism is hardly a sentence to public ignominy: otherwise Bruce Springsteen would still be rehabilitating used Cadillacs in Asbury Park and Jane Fonda, for all we know, would be just another overweight housewife.

> BARBARA EHRENREICH (b. 1941), U.S. author, columnist. *The Worst Years of Our Lives,* "The Liberals' Disappearing Act" (1991; first published in *Mother Jones,* 1986).

9   Liberalism, austere in political trifles, has learned ever more artfully to unite a constant protest against the government with a constant submission to it.

> ALEXANDER HERZEN (1812–70), Russian journalist, political thinker. Letter, 1862, to Ivan Turgenev (published in *My Past and Thoughts,* vol. 4, "Ends & Beginnings," 1921; tr. by Constance Garnett 1924–27).

10   Liberalism, above all, means emancipation—emancipation from one's fears, his inadequacies, from prejudice, from discrimination . . . from poverty.

> HUBERT H. HUMPHREY (1911–78), U.S. Democratic politician, vice president. Speech, 29 March 1967, New York City.

11   I have almost reached the regrettable conclusion that the Negro's great stumbling block in his stride toward freedom is not the White Citizen's Councilor or the Ku Klux Klanner, but the white moderate.

> MARTIN LUTHER KING, JR. (1929–68), U.S. clergyman, civil rights leader. "Letter from Birmingham Jail," in *Why We Can't Wait* (1963).

12   Before we blame we should first see whether we cannot excuse.

> G. C. LICHTENBERG (1742–99), German physicist, philosopher. *Aphorisms,* "Notebook K," aph. 39 (written 1765–99; tr. by R. J. Hollingdale, 1990).

13   The liberals have not softened their view of actuality to make themselves live closer to the dream, but instead sharpen their perceptions and fight to make the dream actuality or give up the battle in despair.

> MARGARET MEAD (1901–78), U.S. anthropologist. *Male and Female,* ch. 12 (1949).

14   The Liberal State is a mask behind which there is no face; it is a scaffolding behind which there is no building.

> BENITO MUSSOLINI (1883–1945), Italian dictator. Speech, 6 Oct. 1922, Milan, Italy.

15   The principle feature of American liberalism is sanctimoniousness. By loudly denouncing all bad things—war and hunger and date rape—liberals testify to their own terrific goodness. More important, they promote themselves to membership in a self-selecting elite of those who care deeply about such things. . . . It's a kind of natural aristocracy, and the wonderful thing about this aristocracy is that you don't have to be brave, smart, strong or even lucky to join it, you just have to be liberal.

> P. J. O'ROURKE (b. 1947), U.S. journalist. *Give War a Chance,* Introduction (1992).

16   Liberalism—it is well to recall this today—is the supreme form of generosity; it is the right which the majority concedes to minorities and hence it is *the noblest cry* that has ever resounded in this planet. It announces the determination to share existence with the enemy; more than that, with an enemy which is weak.

> JOSÉ ORTEGA Y GASSET (1883–1955), Spanish essayist, philosopher. *The Revolt of the Masses,* ch. 8 (1930).

17   Liberal—a power worshipper without power.

> GEORGE ORWELL (1903–50), British author. *Shooting an Elephant,* "Politics and the English Language" (1950).

18   When anything goes, it's women who lose.

> CAMILLE PAGLIA (b. 1947), U.S. author, critic, educator. *Observer* (London, 15 Dec. 1991).

19   The essence of the Liberal outlook lies not in *what* opinions are held, but in *how* they are held: instead of being held dogmatically, they are held tentatively, and with a consciousness that new evidence may at any moment lead to their abandonment.

> BERTRAND RUSSELL (1872–1970), British philosopher, mathematician. *Unpopular Essays,* "Philosophy and Politics" (1950).

20   I sit on a man's back, choking him and making him carry me, and yet assure myself and others that I am very sorry for him and wish to ease his lot by all possible means—except by getting off his back.

> LEO TOLSTOY (1828–1910), Russian novelist, philosopher. *What Then Must We Do?* ch. 16 (1886).

21   We who are liberal and progressive know that the poor are our equals in every sense except that of being equal to us.

> LIONEL TRILLING (1905–75), U.S. critic. *The Liberal Imagination,* "The Princess Casamassima" (1950).

22   The liberal holds that he is true to the republic when he is true to himself. (It may not be as cozy an attitude as it sounds.) He greets with enthusiasm the fact of the journey, as a dog greets a man's invitation to take a walk.

And he acts in the dog's way too, swinging wide, racing ahead, doubling back, covering many miles of territory that the man never traverses, all in the spirit of inquiry and the zest for truth. He leaves a crazy trail, but he ranges far beyond the genteel old party he walks with and he is usually in a better position to discover a skunk.

E. B. WHITE (1899–1985), U.S. author, editor. "Liberalism," in *New Yorker* (17 Jan. 1948; repr. in *Writings from the New Yorker 1927–1976*, ed. by Rebecca M. Dale, 1991).

23 A liberal is a conservative who has been arrested.

TOM WOLFE (b. 1931), U.S. author, journalist. *Bonfire of the Vanities*, ch. 24 (1987).

24 Why is it that right-wing bastards always stand shoulder to shoulder in solidarity, while liberals fall out among themselves?

YEVGENY YEVTUSHENKO (b. 1933), Russian poet. Quoted in: *Observer* (London, 15 Dec. 1991).

See also White on GENERATIONS.

LIBERTY

1 The ingrained idea that, because there is no king and they despise titles, the Americans are a free people is pathetically untrue. . . . There is a perpetual interference with personal liberty over there that would not be tolerated in England for a week.

MARGOT ASQUITH (1864–1945), British socialite. *My Impressions of America*, ch. 17 (1922).

2 I am truly free only when all human beings, men and women, are equally free. The freedom of other men, far from negating or limiting my freedom, is, on the contrary, its necessary premise and confirmation.

MIKHAIL BAKUNIN (1814–76), Russian political theorist. *God and the State* (1871; repr. in *Bakunin on Anarchism*, ed. by Sam Dolgoff, 1980).

3 You cannot have Liberty in this world without what you call Moral Virtue, & you cannot have Moral Virtue without the slavery of that half of the human race who hate what you call Moral Virtue.

WILLIAM BLAKE (1757–1827), English poet, painter, engraver. *A Vision of the Last Judgment* (c. 1810; repr. in *Complete Writings*, ed. by Geoffrey Keynes, 1957).

4 There is nothing with which it is so dangerous to take liberties as liberty itself.

ANDRÉ BRETON (1896–1966), French surrealist. *Surrealism and Painting* (1928).

5 The true danger is when liberty is nibbled away, for expedience, and by parts.

EDMUND BURKE (1729–97), Irish philosopher, statesman. Letter, 3 April 1777, to the Sheriffs of Bristol.

6 The effect of liberty to individuals is that they may do what they please: we ought to see what it will please them to do, before we risk congratulations.

EDMUND BURKE (1729–97), Irish philosopher, statesman. *Reflections on the Revolution in France* (1790).

7 It is not one man nor a million, but the *spirit* of liberty that must be preserved. The waves which dash upon the shore are, one by one, broken, but the *ocean* conquers nevertheless. It overwhelms the Armada, it wears out the rock. In like manner, whatever the struggle of individuals, the great cause will gather strength.

LORD BYRON (1788–1824), English poet. *Ravenna Journal* (11 Jan. 1821; published in *Letters and Journals*, vol. 5, ed. by Prothero, 1898–1901).

8 The condition upon which God hath given liberty to man is eternal vigilance; which condition if he break, servitude is at once the consequence of his crime, and the punishment of his guilt.

JOHN PHILPOT CURRAN (1750–1817), Irish lawyer, politician. "The Right of Election of the Lord Mayor of Dublin," speech, 10 July 1790, Dublin. See Orwell on LIBERTY.

9 The liberty of the individual is no gift of civilization. It was greatest before there was any civilization.

SIGMUND FREUD (1856–1939), Austrian psychiatrist. *Civilization and Its Discontents*, ch. 3 (1930; repr. in *Complete Works*, vol. 21, 1961).

10 The slaves of power mind the cause they have to serve, because their own interest is concerned; but the friends of liberty always sacrifice their cause, which is *only* the cause of humanity, to their own spleen, vanity, and self-opinion.

WILLIAM HAZLITT (1778–1830), English essayist. From a review of Byron, *Childe Harold*, cto. 4 (published in *Yellow Dwarf*, 2 May 1818).

11 When liberty is mentioned, we must always be careful to observe whether it is not really the assertion of private interests which is thereby designated.

GEORG HEGEL (1770–1831), German philosopher. *The Philosophy of History*, pt. 4, sct. 3, ch. 2 (1837).

12 I know not what course others may take; but as for me, give me liberty, or give me death.

PATRICK HENRY (1736–99), U.S. statesman. Speech, 23 March 1775, Virginia House of Delegates, Richmond. Quoted in: William Wirt, *Patrick Henry* (1818).

13 The boisterous sea of liberty is never without a wave.

THOMAS JEFFERSON (1743–1826), U.S. president. Letter, 20 Oct. 1820.

14 The deadliest foe of democracy is not autocracy but liberty frenzied.

OTTO KAHN (1867–1934), U.S. banker. Speech, 14 Jan. 1918, University of Wisconsin.

15 Then we are assured by Sartre that owing to the final disappearance of God our liberty is *absolute!* At this the entire audience waves its hat or claps its hands. But this natural enthusiasm is turned abruptly into something much less buoyant when it is learnt that this liberty weighs us down immediately with tremendous *responsibilities*. We now have to take all God's worries on our shoulders—now that we are become "men like gods." It is at this point that the Anxiety and Despondency begin, ending in utter despair.

WYNDHAM LEWIS (1882–1957), British author, painter. *The Writer and the Absolute*, "Twentieth Century Nihilism" (1952).

16 Liberty, as it is conceived by current opinion, has nothing inherent about it; it is a sort of gift or trust bestowed on the individual by the state pending *good behavior.*

> MARY MCCARTHY (1912–89), U.S. author, critic. Speech, 1952 (published in *On the Contrary*, "The Contagion of Ideas," 1961).

17 We are as great as our belief in human liberty—no greater. And our belief in human liberty is only ours when it is larger than ourselves.

> ARCHIBALD MACLEISH (1892–1982), U.S. poet. "Now Let Us Address the Main Question: Bicentennial of What?," in *New York Times* (3 July 1976; repr. in *Riders on Earth*, as "The Ghost of Thomas Jefferson," 1978).

18 An educational method that shall have *liberty* as its basis must intervene to help the child to a conquest of liberty. That is to say, his training must be such as shall help him to diminish as much as possible the *social bonds* which limit his activity.

> MARIA MONTESSORI (1870–1952), Italian educator. *The Montessori Method*, ch. 5 (1912).

19 I sometimes think that the price of liberty is not so much eternal vigilance as eternal dirt.

> GEORGE ORWELL (1903–50), British author. *The Road to Wigan Pier*, ch. 4 (1937). See Curran on LIBERTY.

20 A free spirit takes liberties even with liberty itself.

> FRANCIS PICABIA (1878–1953), French painter, poet. *591* (Paris, 21 Jan. 1952; repr. in *Écrits*, vol. 2, "1950–1953," ed. by Olivier Revault d'Allones and Dominique Bouissou, 1978).

21 How false is the conception, how frantic the pursuit, of that treacherous phantom which men call Liberty: most treacherous, indeed, of all phantoms; for the feeblest ray of reason might surely show us, that not only its attainment, but its being, was impossible. There is no such thing in the universe. There can never be. The stars have it not; the earth has it not; the sea has it not; and we men have the mockery and semblance of it only for our heaviest punishment.

> JOHN RUSKIN (1819–1900), English art critic, author. *The Seven Lamps of Architecture*, "The Lamp of Obedience," sct. 1 (1849).

22 What do we mean by setting a man free? You cannot free a man who dwells in a desert and is an unfeeling brute. There is no liberty except the liberty of some one making his way towards something. Such a man can be set free if you will teach him the meaning of thirst, and how to trace a path to a well. Only then will he embark upon a course of action that will not be without significance. You could not liberate a stone if there were no law of gravity—for where will the stone go, once it is quarried?

> ANTOINE DE SAINT-EXUPÉRY (1900–1944), French aviator, author. *Flight to Arras*, ch. 23 (1942).

23 It is not true that democracy will always safeguard freedom of conscience better than autocracy. Witness the most famous of all trials. Pilate was, from the standpoint of the Jews, certainly the representative of autocracy. Yet he tried to protect freedom. And he yielded to a democracy.

> JOSEPH A. SCHUMPETER (1883–1950), Austrian-American economist. *Capitalism, Socialism and Democracy*, note to ch. 20, sct. 3 (1942).

24 Liberty means responsibility. That is why most men dread it.

> GEORGE BERNARD SHAW (1856–1950), Anglo-Irish playwright, critic. *Man and Superman*, "Maxims for Revolutionists: Liberty and Equality" (1903).

25 Old England liberty—to be robbed by the Ministry, and insulted by the populace without redress.

> CAPTAIN J. G. STEDMAN (1744–97), British soldier, author, artist. *Journal*, ch. 10 (ed. by Stanbury Thompson, 1962), entry for 14 Feb. 1787.

26 It would seem that man was born a slave, and that slavery is his natural condition. At the same time nothing on earth can stop man from feeling himself born for liberty. Never, whatever may happen, can he accept servitude; for he is a thinking creature.

> SIMONE WEIL (1909–43), French philosopher, mystic. *Oppression and Liberty*, ch. 4 (1958).

27 The shallow consider liberty a release from all law, from every constraint. The wise man sees in it, on the contrary, the potent Law of Laws.

> WALT WHITMAN (1819–92), U.S. poet. *Notes Left Over*, "Freedom" (1881).

28 Liberty has never come from the government. Liberty has always come from the subjects of it. The history of liberty is a history of resistance.

> WOODROW WILSON (1856–1924), U.S. Democratic politician, president. Speech, 9 Sept. 1912, New York Press Club.

See also Burke, Gibbon on CORRUPTION; FREEDOM; Latin phrase on PATRIOTISM; Mamet on PRINCIPLES; Guizot on REVOLUTION; Wilde on TERRORISM.

LIBRARIES

1 We should burn all libraries and allow to remain only that which everyone knows by heart. A beautiful age of the legend would then begin.

> HUGO BALL (1886–1927), German Dadaist poet. *Flight out of Time: A Dada Diary* (1927), entry for 9 Jan. 1917.

2 The true university of these days is a collection of books.

> THOMAS CARLYLE (1795–1881), Scottish essayist, historian. *On Heroes and Hero-Worship*, Lecture 5, "The Hero as Man of Letters" (1841).

3 A man should keep his little brain attic stocked with all the furniture that he is likely to use, and the rest he can put away in the lumber room of his library, where he can get it if he wants it.

> SIR ARTHUR CONAN DOYLE (1859–1930), English author. Sherlock Holmes, in *The Adventures of Sherlock Holmes*, "The Five Orange Pips" (1892). Holmes expressed a similar idea in "A Study in Scarlet." See Doyle on THE MIND.

4 Meek young men grow up in libraries, believing it their duty to accept the views which Cicero, which Locke, which Bacon, have given, forgetful that Cicero, Locke, and Bacon were only young men in libraries, when they wrote these books. Hence, instead of Man Thinking, we have the book-worm.

> RALPH WALDO EMERSON (1803–82), U.S. essayist, poet, philosopher. Lecture, 31 Aug. 1837, delivered before the Phi Beta Kappa Society, Harvard University (published in *Nature, Addresses and Lectures,* "The American Scholar," 1849).

5 A man's library is a sort of harem.

> RALPH WALDO EMERSON (1803–82), U.S. essayist, poet, philosopher. *Society and Solitude,* "Books" (1870).

6 Be a little careful about your library. Do you foresee what you will do with it? Very little to be sure. But the real question is, What it will do with you? You will come here and get books that will open your eyes, and your ears, and your curiosity, and turn you inside out or outside in.

> RALPH WALDO EMERSON (1803–82), U.S. essayist, poet, philosopher. *Journals* (ed. by Joel Porte, 1982).

7 I've been drunk for about a week now, and I thought it might sober me up to sit in a library.

> F. SCOTT FITZGERALD (1896–1940), U.S. author. An unnamed guest at one of Gatsby's parties, in *The Great Gatsby,* ch. 3 (1925).

8 Libraries are reservoirs of strength, grace and wit, reminders of order, calm and continuity, lakes of mental energy, neither warm nor cold, light nor dark. The pleasure they give is steady, unorgastic, reliable, deep and long-lasting. In any library in the world, I am at home, unselfconscious, still and absorbed.

> GERMAINE GREER (b. 1939), Australian feminist writer. *Daddy, We Hardly Knew You,* "Still in Melbourne, January 1987" (1989).

9 Every library should try to be complete on something, if it were only the history of pinheads.

> OLIVER WENDELL HOLMES, SR. (1809–94), U.S. writer, physician. *The Poet at the Breakfast-Table,* ch. 8 (1872).

10 The great British Library—an immense collection of volumes of all ages and languages, many of which are now forgotten, and most of which are seldom read: one of these sequestered pools of obsolete literature to which modern authors repair, and draw buckets full of classic lore, or "pure English, undefiled" wherewith to swell their own scanty rills of thought.

> WASHINGTON IRVING (1783–1859), U.S. author. *The Sketch-Book,* "The Art of Book-Making" (1819–20).

11 No place affords a more striking conviction of the vanity of human hopes than a public library.

> SAMUEL JOHNSON (1709–84), English author, lexicographer. *Rambler,* no. 106 (London, 23 March 1751; repr. in *Works of Samuel Johnson,* vol. 4, ed. by W. J. Bate and Albrecht B. Strauss, 1969).

12 It is almost everywhere the case that soon after it is begotten the greater part of human wisdom is laid to rest in *repositories.*

> G. C. LICHTENBERG (1742–99), German physicist, philosopher. *Aphorisms,* "Notebook K," aph. 37 (written 1765–99; tr. by R. J. Hollingdale, 1990).

13 What is more important in a library than anything else—than everything else—is the fact that it exists.

> ARCHIBALD MACLEISH (1892–1982), U.S. poet. "The Premise of Meaning," in *American Scholar* (Washington, D.C., 5 June 1972; repr. in *Riders on Earth,* as "The Premise at the Center," 1978).

14 Some on commission, some for the love of learning,
Some because they have nothing better to do
Or because they hope these walls of books will deaden
The drumming of the demon in their ears.

> LOUIS MACNEICE (1907–63), British poet. *The British Museum Reading Room.*

15 What do we, as a nation, care about books? How much do you think we spend altogether on our libraries, public or private, as compared with what we spend on our horses?

> JOHN RUSKIN (1819–1900), English art critic, author. *Sesame and Lilies,* Lecture 1, sct. 32 (1865; repr. in *The Works of John Ruskin,* vol. 18, ed. by E. T. Cook and Alexander Weddesburn, 1905).

16 My library
Was dukedom large enough.

> WILLIAM SHAKESPEARE (1564–1616), English dramatist, poet. Prospero, in *The Tempest,* act 1, sc. 2.

17 Madam, a circulating library in a town is as an evergreen tree of diabolical knowledge; it blossoms through the year. And depend on it . . . that they who are so fond of handling the leaves, will long for the fruit at last.

> RICHARD BRINSLEY SHERIDAN (1751–1816), Anglo-Irish dramatist. Sir Anthony Absolute, in *The Rivals,* act 1, sc. 2.

18 I go into my library, and all history unrolls before me. I breathe the morning air of the world while the scent of Eden's roses yet lingered in it, while it vibrated only to the world's first brood of nightingales, and to the laugh of Eve. I see the pyramids building; I hear the shoutings of the armies of Alexander.

> ALEXANDER SMITH (1830–67), Scottish poet. *Dreamthorp,* "Books and Gardens" (1863).

19 To a historian libraries are food, shelter, and even muse. They are of two kinds: the library of published material, books, pamphlets, periodicals, and the archive of unpublished papers and documents.

> BARBARA TUCHMAN (1912–89), U.S. historian. *Practising History,* "The Houses of Research" (1981).

20 Here Greek and Roman find themselves
Alive along these crowded shelves;
And Shakespeare treads again his stage,
And Chaucer paints anew his age.

> JOHN GREENLEAF WHITTIER (1807–92), U.S. poet. *The Library,* st. 7.

See also RESEARCH.

LIES AND LYING

1 Husband a lie, and trump it up in some extraordinary emergency.

JOSEPH ADDISON (1672–1719), English essayist. *Spectator*, no. 507 (London, 11 Oct. 1712).

2 The difference between a saint and a hypocrite is that one lies for his religion, the other by it.

MINNA ANTRIM (b. 1861), U.S. epigrammist. *Naked Truth and Veiled Allusions* (1901, p. 30).

3 What does the truth matter? Haven't we mothers all given our sons a taste for lies, lies which from the cradle upwards lull them, reassure them, send them to sleep: lies as soft and warm as a breast!

GEORGES BERNANOS (1888–1948), French novelist, political writer. Madame la Comtesse, in *The Diary of a Country Priest*, ch. 5 (1936).

4 The best liar is he who makes the smallest amount of lying go the longest way.

SAMUEL BUTLER (1835–1902), English author. *The Way of All Flesh*, ch. 39 (1903).

5 I do not mind lying, but I hate inaccuracy.

SAMUEL BUTLER (1835–1902), English author. *Samuel Butler's Notebooks*, "Untraced Notes" (1951).

6 And, after all, what is a lie? 'Tis but
The truth in masquerade.

LORD BYRON (1788–1824), English poet. *Don Juan*, cto. 11, st. 37.

7 Someone who always has to lie discovers that every one of his lies is true.

ELIAS CANETTI (b. 1905), Austrian novelist, philosopher. *The Secret Heart of the Clock: Notes, Aphorisms, Fragments 1973–1985*, "1983" (1991).

8 I am a lie who always speaks the truth.

JEAN COCTEAU (1889–1963), French author, filmmaker. *Opéra*, "Le Paquet Rouge" (1925; repr. in *Collected Works*, vol. 4, 1947).

9 Of course I lie to people. But I lie altruistically—for our mutual good. The lie is the basic building block of good manners. That may seem mildly shocking to a moralist—but then what isn't?

QUENTIN CRISP (b. 1908), British author. *Manners from Heaven*, ch. 4 (1984).

10 Falsehood is invariably the child of fear in one form or another.

ALEISTER CROWLEY (1875–1947), British occultist. *The Confessions of Aleister Crowley*, ch. 49 (1929; rev. 1970).

11 Every violation of truth is not only a sort of suicide in the liar, but is a stab at the health of human society.

RALPH WALDO EMERSON (1803–82), U.S. essayist, poet, philosopher. *Essays*, "Prudence" (First Series, 1841).

12 He entered the territory of lies without a passport for return.

GRAHAM GREENE (1904–91), British novelist. *The Heart of the Matter*, bk. 2, pt. 3, ch. 2, sct. 1 (1948), of Major Scobie.

13 The great mass of people . . . will more easily fall victim to a big lie than to a small one.

ADOLF HITLER (1889–1945), German dictator. *Mein Kampf*, vol. 1, ch. 10 (1925).

14 Lying increases the creative faculties, expands the ego, lessens the friction of social contacts. . . . It is only in lies, wholeheartedly and bravely told, that human nature attains through words and speech the forebearance, the nobility, the romance, the idealism, that—being what it is—it falls so short of in fact and in deed.

CLARE BOOTHE LUCE (1903–87), U.S. diplomat, writer. *Vanity Fair* (New York, Oct. 1930).

15 Each day a few more lies eat into the seed with which we are born, little institutional lies from the print of newspapers, the shock waves of television, and the sentimental cheats of the movie screen.

NORMAN MAILER (b. 1923), U.S. author. *Advertisements for Myself*, "First Advertisement for Myself" (1959).

16 Good lies need a leavening of truth to make them palatable.

WILLIAM MCILVANNEY (b. 1936), British novelist. *The Papers of Tony Veitch*, ch. 17 (1983).

17 One can be absolutely truthful and sincere even though admittedly the most outrageous liar. Fiction and invention are of the very fabric of life.

HENRY MILLER (1891–1980), U.S. author. *The Wisdom of the Heart*, "Reflections on Writing" (1947).

18 Grow your tree of falsehood from a small grain of truth.
Do not follow those who lie in contempt of reality.
Let your lie be even more logical than the truth itself,
So the weary travelers may find repose.

CESLAW MILOSZ (b. 1911), Lithuanian-born Polish poet. *Child of Europe*, sct. 4, in *Selected Poems* (1973).

19 A lie will easily get you out of a scrape, and yet, strangely and beautifully, rapture possesses you when you have taken the scrape and left out the lie.

C. E. MONTAGUE (1867–1928), English author, journalist. *Disenchantment*, ch. 15, sct. 4 (1922).

20 No man lies so boldly as the man who is indignant.

FRIEDRICH NIETZSCHE (1844–1900), German philosopher. *Beyond Good and Evil*, ch. 2, aph. 26 (1886).

21 To the rulers of the state then, if to any, it belongs of right to use falsehood, to deceive either enemies or their own citizens, for the good of the state: and no one else may meddle with this privilege.

PLATO (c. 427–347 B.C.), Greek philosopher. *The Republic*, bk. 3, sct. 389.

22 Time passes, and little by little everything that we have spoken in falsehood becomes true.

MARCEL PROUST (1871–1922), French novelist. *Remembrance of Things Past*, vol. 3, "The Fugitive" (1925; tr. by Terence Kilmartin, 1981).

23 Telling lies is a fault in a boy, an art in a lover, an accomplishment in a bachelor, and second-nature in a married man.

HELEN ROWLAND (1875–1950), U.S. journalist. *A Guide to Men*, "Syncopations" (1922).

24 A little inaccuracy sometimes saves tons of explanation.

SAKI [H. H. MUNRO] (1870–1916), Scottish author. *The Square Egg*, "Clovis on the Alleged Romance of Business" (1924).

25 O, what a tangled web we weave,
When first we practise to deceive!

SIR WALTER SCOTT (1771–1832), Scottish novelist, poet. *Marmion*, cto. 6, st. 17 (1808). J. R. Pope, in *A Word of Encouragement*, added to this the lines, "But when we've practised quite a while/How vastly we improve our style."

26 Lying is like alcoholism. You are always recovering.

STEVEN SODERBERGH (b. 1963), U.S. filmmaker. Graham (James Spader) to Anne (Andie MacDowell), in the film *Sex, Lies and Videotape* (written and directed by Soderbergh, 1989). Quoted in: Norman K. Denzin, *Images of Postmodern Society*, ch. 8 (1991).

27 I would dodge, not lie, in the national interest.

LARRY SPEAKES (b. 1939), U.S. executive, former White House official. *New York Times* (10 Oct. 1986).

28 The cruellest lies are often told in silence. A man may have sat in a room for hours and not opened his mouth, and yet come out of that room a disloyal friend or a vile calumniator.

ROBERT LOUIS STEVENSON (1850–94), Scottish novelist, essayist, poet. *Virginibus Puerisque*, title essay, sct. 4 (1881).

29 You can fool too many of the people too much of the time.

JAMES THURBER (1894–1961), U.S. humorist, illustrator. *Fables for Our Time*, Moral of "The Owl Who Was God" (1940).

30 The liar at any rate recognizes that recreation, not instruction, is the aim of conversation, and is a far more civilised being than the blockhead who loudly expresses his disbelief in a story which is told simply for the amusement of the company.

OSCAR WILDE (1854–1900), Anglo-Irish playwright, author. "Aristotle at Afternoon Tea," in *Pall Mall Gazette* (London, 28 Feb. 1885; repr. in *Aristotle at Afternoon Tea: The Rare Oscar Wilde*, 1991).

31 As one knows the poet by his fine music, so one can recognise the liar by his rich rhythmic utterance, and in neither case will the casual inspiration of the moment suffice. Here, as elsewhere, practice must precede perfection.

OSCAR WILDE (1854–1900), Anglo-Irish playwright, author. Vivian, in "The Decay of Lying" (published in *Intentions*, 1891).

32 Mendacity is a system that we live in. Liquor is one way out an' death's the other.

TENNESSEE WILLIAMS (1914–83), U.S. dramatist. Brick, in *Cat on a Hot Tin Roof*, act 2.

33 Someone who knows too much finds it hard not to lie.

LUDWIG WITTGENSTEIN (1889–1951), Austrian philosopher.

Culture and Value (ed. by G. H. von Wright and Heikki Nyman, 1980), 1947 journal entry.

See also Bierce on CHILDHOOD; Brodsky on CONSCIOUSNESS AND THE SUB-CONSCIOUS; Williams on HYPOCRISY; Gay on MEN AND WOMEN; Shakespeare on OLD AGE; Lichtenberg on PROPAGANDA; Hoffer on SELF-DECEPTION; Disraeli on STATISTICS; Blake on TRUTH; Solzhenitsyn on VIOLENCE.

LIFE, LUST FOR

1 There is a very fine line between loving life and being greedy for it.

MAYA ANGELOU (b. 1928), U.S. author. Interview in *Black Scholar* (New York, Jan.-Feb. 1977).

2 Man wants to live, but it is useless to hope that this desire will dictate all his actions.

ALBERT CAMUS (1913–60), French-Algerian philosopher, author. *Resistance, Rebellion and Death*, "Reflections on the Guillotine" (1961), discussing the failure of capital punishment to act as a deterrent.

3 One should not confuse the craving for life with endorsement of it.

ELIAS CANETTI (b. 1905), Austrian novelist, philosopher. *The Secret Heart of the Clock: Notes, Aphorisms, Fragments 1973–1985*, "1981" (1991).

4 Life has no meaning unless one lives it with a will, at least to the limit of one's will. Virtue, good, evil are nothing but words, unless one takes them apart in order to build something with them; they do not win their true meaning until one knows how to apply them.

PAUL GAUGUIN (1848–1903), French artist. *Intimate Journals* (tr. by Van Wyck Brooks, 1923; 1930 ed., p. 194).

5 We quaff the cup of life with eager haste without draining it, instead of which it only overflows the brim—objects press around us, filling the mind with their magnitude and with the throng of desires that wait upon them, so that we have no room for the thoughts of death.

WILLIAM HAZLITT (1778–1830), English essayist. "On the Feeling of Immortality in Youth," published unsigned in *Monthly Magazine* (March 1827; repr. in *Complete Works*, vol. 17, ed. by P. P. Howe, 1932).

6 A life-worshipper's philosophy is comprehensive. . . . He is at one moment a positivist and at another a mystic: now haunted by the thought of death . . . and now a Dionysian child of nature; now a pessimist and now, with a change of lover or liver or even the weather, an exuberant believer that God's in his heaven and all's right with the world.

ALDOUS HUXLEY (1894–1963), British author. *Do What You Will*, "Pascal," sct. 23, "Summary of the Life-Worshipper's Creed" (1929).

7 Nothing can be meaner than the anxiety to live on, to live on anyhow and in any shape; a spirit with any honor is not willing to live except in its own way, and a spirit with any wisdom is not over-eager to live at all.

GEORGE SANTAYANA (1863–1952), U.S. philosopher, poet. *Winds of Doctrine* (1913; repr. in *Little Essays*, "The Intellect Out of Fashion," ed. by Logan Pearsall Smith, 1920)

See also VITALITY.

LIFE AND DEATH

1   Life, in my estimation, is a biological misadventure that we terminate on the shoulders of six strange men whose only objective is to make a hole in one with you.

> FRED ALLEN (1894–1957), U.S. radio comic. Quoted in: *Forbes* (New York, 1 Aug 1967).

2   Man that is born of woman hath but a short time to live, and is full of misery. He cometh up, and is cut down, like a flower; he fleeth as it were a shadow, and never continueth in one stay.

> BOOK OF COMMON PRAYER (1662). "Burial of the Dead," first anthem, derived from Hebrew Bible, *Job* 14:1–2.

3   Living is a sickness to which sleep provides relief every sixteen hours. It's a palliative. The remedy is death.

> SÉBASTIEN-ROCH NICOLAS DE CHAMFORT (1741–94), French writer, wit. *Maxims and Considerations* vol. 1, no. 113 (1796).

4   But there is good news yet to hear and fine things to be seen
Before we go to Paradise by way of Kensal Green.

> G. K. CHESTERTON (1874–1936), British author. "The Rolling English Road," in *The Flying Inn*, ch. 21 (1914).

5   The woods are lovely, dark and deep.
But I have promises to keep,
And miles to go before I sleep.

> ROBERT FROST (1874–1963), U.S. poet. *Stopping by Woods on a Snowy Evening.* These words were found on a scrap of paper on the desk of Indian prime minister Jawaharlal Nehru when he died.

6   Creation destroys as it goes, throws down one tree for the rise of another. But ideal mankind would abolish death, multiply itself million upon million, rear up city upon city, save every parasite alive, until the accumulation of mere existence is swollen to a horror.

> D. H. LAWRENCE (1885–1930), British author. *St. Mawr* (1925; repr. in *The Short Novels*, vol. 2, 1979).

7   Let us beware of saying that death is the opposite of life. The living being is only a species of the dead, and a very rare species.

> FRIEDRICH NIETZSCHE (1844–1900), German philosopher. *The Gay Science*, aph. 109 (rev. ed., 1887).

8   'Tis all a Chequer-board of Nights and Days
Where Destiny with Men for Pieces plays:
Hither and thither moves, and mates and slays,
And one by one back in the Closet lays.

> OMAR KHAYYAM (11–12th century), Persian astronomer, poet. *The Rubáiyát of Omar Khayyám*, st. 49 (tr. by Edward FitzGerald, 1859).

9   Death does determine life. . . . Once life is finished it acquires a sense; up to that point it has not got a sense; its sense is suspended and therefore ambiguous. However, to be sincere I must add that for me death is important only if it is not justified and rationalized by reason. For me death is the maximum of epicness and death.

> PIER PAOLO PASOLINI (1922–75), Italian filmmaker, author. *Pasolini on Pasolini: Interviews with Oswald Stack*, ch. 3 (1969).

10   A physician can sometimes parry the scythe of death, but has no power over the sand in the hourglass.

> HESTER PIOZZI [MRS. THRALE] (1741–1821), English writer. Letter, 12 Nov. 1781, to author Fanny Burney.

11   As flies to wanton boys, are we to th' gods;
They kill us for their sport.

> WILLIAM SHAKESPEARE (1564–1616), English dramatist, poet. Gloucester, in *King Lear*, act 4, sc. 1.

12   Life is the desert, life the solitude,
Death joins us to the great majority.

> EDWARD YOUNG (1683–1765), English poet, dramatist. Don Alonzo, in *The Revenge*, act 4, sc. 1 (1721).

LIFE AND LIVING

1   Life is divided up into the horrible and the miserable.

> WOODY ALLEN (b. 1935), U.S. filmmaker. Alvy Singer (Allen) to Annie Hall (Diane Keaton), in the film *Annie Hall* (directed by Woody Allen, scripted by Allen with Marshall Brickman, 1977; repr. in *Four Films of Woody Allen*, 1982).

2   Life loves the liver of it.

> MAYA ANGELOU (b. 1928), U.S. author. "The Black Scholar Interviews Maya Angelou" (Jan.-Feb. 1977; repr. in *Conversations with Maya Angelou*, 1989).

3   The drama of life begins with a wail and ends with a sigh.

> MINNA ANTRIM (b. 1861), U.S. epigrammist. *Naked Truth and Veiled Allusions* (1901).

4   When we speak the word "life," it must be understood we are not referring to life as we know it from its surface of fact, but to that fragile, fluctuating center which forms never reach.

> ANTONIN ARTAUD (1896–1948), French theater producer, actor, theorist. *The Theater and Its Double*, "Preface: The Theater and Culture" (1938; tr. 1958).

5   To live life well is to express life poorly; if one expresses life too well, one is living it no longer.

> GASTON BACHELARD (1884–1962), French scientist, philosopher, literary theorist. *Fragments of a Poetics of Fire*, "A Retrospective Glance at the Lifework of a Master of Books" (1988; tr. 1990).

6   Deep down, no one really believes they have a right to live. But this death sentence generally stays cosily tucked away, hidden beneath the difficulty of living. If that difficulty is removed from time to time, death is suddenly there, unintelligibly.

> JEAN BAUDRILLARD (b. 1929), French semiologist. *Cool Memories*, ch. 2 (1987; tr. 1990).

7   We have long forgotten the ritual by which the house of our life was erected. But when it is under assault and enemy bombs are already taking their toll, what enervated, perverse antiquities do they not lay bare in the foundations.

> WALTER BENJAMIN (1892–1940), German critic, philosopher. *One-Way Street*, "No. 113" (1928; repr. in *One-Way Street and Other Writings*, 1978).

8   The days of our years are threescore years and ten;

and if by reason of strength they be fourscore years, yet is their strength labour and sorrow; for it is soon cut off, and we fly away.

BIBLE, HEBREW. *Psalms* 90:10. *The Book of Common Prayer* has a variant version, *Psalms* 87:10 (1662).

9 For what is your life? It is even a vapour, that appeareth for a little time, and then vanisheth away.

BIBLE: NEW TESTAMENT. *James* 4:14.

10 Life. A spiritual pickle preserving the body from decay.

AMBROSE BIERCE (1842–1914), U.S. author. *The Devil's Dictionary* (1881–1906).

11 There's night and day, brother, both sweet things; sun, moon, and stars, brother, all sweet things; there's likewise a wind on the heath. Life is very sweet, brother; who would wish to die?

GEORGE BORROW (1803–81), English author. Jasper, in *Lavengro*, ch. 25 (1851).

12 Don't be afraid of death so much as an inadequate life.

BERTOLT BRECHT (1898–1956), German dramatist, poet. Pelagea Vlasova, in *The Mother*, sc. 10.

13 What should I say about life? That it's long and abhors transparence.

JOSEPH BRODSKY (b. 1940), Russian-born U.S. poet, critic. *May 24, 1980*, written on his 40th birthday.

14 Life is like playing a violin solo in public and learning the instrument as one goes on.

SAMUEL BUTLER (1835–1902), English author. Speech, 27 Feb. 1895, Somerville Club, London (published in *Samuel Butler's Notebooks*, 1951, p. 310).

15 Life is the art of drawing sufficient conclusions from insufficient premises.

SAMUEL BUTLER (1835–1902), English author. *Notebooks*, ch. 1 (1912).

16 Is life worth living? This is a question for an embryo not for a man.

SAMUEL BUTLER (1835–1902), English author. *Samuel Butler's Notebooks* (1951).

17 Between two worlds life hovers like a star,
'Twixt night and morn, upon the horizon's verge.

LORD BYRON (1788–1824), English poet. *Don Juan*, cto. 15, st. 99.

18 When one subtracts from life infancy (which is vegetation), sleep, eating and swilling, buttoning and unbuttoning—how much remains of downright existence? The summer of a dormouse.

LORD BYRON (1788–1824), English poet. *Byron's Letters and Journals*, vol. 3 (ed. by Leslie A. Marchand, 1974), entry for 7 Dec. 1813.

19 What is life? A frenzy. What is life? An illusion, a shadow, a fiction. And the greatest good is trivial; for all life is a dream and all dreams are dreams.

DON PEDRO CALDERÓN DE LA BARCA (1600–81), Spanish playwright. Sigismundo, in *La Vida es Sueño*, "2nd Day" (1636).

20 Accept life, take it as it is? Stupid. The means of doing otherwise? Far from our having to take it, it is life that possesses us and on occasion shuts our mouths.

ALBERT CAMUS (1913–60), French-Algerian philosopher, author. "Contradictions" (written c. 1933; published in *Youthful Writings*, 1976).

21 We get into the habit of living before acquiring the habit of thinking. In that race which daily hastens us towards death, the body maintains its irreparable lead.

ALBERT CAMUS (1913–60), French-Algerian philosopher, author. *The Myth of Sisyphus*, ch. 1 (1942; tr. 1955).

22 Living, just by itself—what a dirge that is! Life is a classroom and Boredom's the usher, there all the time to spy on you; whatever happens, you've got to look as if you were awfully busy all the time doing something that's terribly exciting—or he'll come along and nibble your brain.

LOUIS-FERDINAND CÉLINE (1894–1961), French author. The narrator (Ferdinand Bardamu), in *Journey to the End of the Night* (1932; tr. 1934; 1966 ed., p. 307).

23 Life is filigree work. . . . What is written clearly is not worth much, it's the transparency that counts.

LOUIS-FERDINAND CÉLINE (1894–1961), French author. *Féerie pour une Autre Fois* (1952). Quoted in: Patrick McCarthy, *Céline*, ch. 8 (1975).

24 Life is a horizontal fall.

JEAN COCTEAU (1889–1963), French author, filmmaker. *Opium* (1929; tr. 1932; ed. 1957, p. 21).

25 It's extraordinary how we go through life with eyes half shut, with dull ears, with dormant thoughts. Perhaps it's just as well; and it may be that it is this very dullness that makes life to the incalculable majority so supportable and so welcome.

JOSEPH CONRAD (1857–1924), Polish-born English novelist. Marlow, in *Lord Jim*, ch. 13 (1900).

26 Perhaps life is just that . . . a dream and a fear.

JOSEPH CONRAD (1857–1924), Polish-born English novelist. Razumov, in *Under Western Eyes*, pt. 4, ch. 2 (1911).

27 Life is too short to stuff a mushroom.

SHIRLEY CONRAN (b. 1932), British designer, journalist. *Superwoman*, Epigraph (1975).

28 Life was a funny thing that happened to me on the way to the grave.

QUENTIN CRISP (b. 1908), British author. *The Naked Civil Servant*, ch. 18 (1968).

29 The joy of life consists in the exercise of one's energies, continual growth, constant change, the enjoyment of every new experience. To stop means simply to die. The eternal mistake of mankind is to set up an attainable ideal.

ALEISTER CROWLEY (1875–1947), British occultist. *The Confessions of Aleister Crowley*, ch. 65 (1929; rev. 1970).

30 If one considered life as a simple loan, one would perhaps be less exacting. We possess actually nothing; everything goes through us.

EUGÈNE DELACROIX (1798–1863), French artist. Note, 22 Sept. 1844 (published in Supplement to *The Journal of Eugène Delacroix*, tr. by Walter Pach, 1937).

31 Life is infinitely stranger than anything which the mind of man could invent. We would not dare to conceive the things which are really merely commonplaces of existence. If we could fly out of that window hand in hand, hover over this great city, gently remove the roofs and peep in at the queer things which are going on, the strange coincidences, the planning, the cross-purposes, the wonderful chain of events, working through generations and leading to the most outre results, it would make all fiction with its conventionalities and foreseen conclusions most stale and unprofitable.

> SIR ARTHUR CONAN DOYLE (1859–1930), English author. Sherlock Holmes to Watson, in *The Adventures of Sherlock Holmes*, "A Case of Identity" (1892).

32 The dreamcrossed twilight between birth and dying.

> T. S. ELIOT (1888–1965), Anglo-American poet, critic. *Ash Wednesday*, pt. 6.

33 It has always been difficult for Man to realise that his life is all an art. It has been more difficult to conceive it so than to act it so. For that is always how he has more or less acted it.

> HAVELOCK ELLIS (1859–1939), British psychologist. *The Dance of Life*, ch. 1 (1923).

34 You are a little soul carrying around a corpse.

> EPICTETUS (c. 55–c. 135), Greek Stoic philosopher. *Epictetus—The Discourses, The Manual and Fragments*, "Fragments," no. 26, vol. 2 (ed. and tr. by W. Oldfather, 1928). Also quoted in: Marcus Aurelius, *Meditations*, bk. 4, no. 41.

35 Life is essentially a cheat and its conditions are those of defeat . . . the redeeming things are not "happiness and pleasure" but the deeper satisfactions that come out of struggle.

> F. SCOTT FITZGERALD (1896–1940), U.S. author. Letter, 5 Oct. 1940, to his daughter Frances Scott Fitzgerald (published in *The Letters of F. Scott Fitzgerald*, ed. by Andrew Turnbull, 1963).

36 Life.—No, I've nothing to teach you about it for the moment. May be writing about it another week.

> E. M. FORSTER (1879–1970), British novelist, essayist. Closing lines of letter, 3 May 1928, to soldier and scholar T. E. Lawrence.

37 I should have no objection to go over the same life from its beginning to the end: requesting only the advantage authors have, of correcting in a second edition the faults of the first.

> BENJAMIN FRANKLIN (1706–90), U.S. statesman, writer. *Autobiography*, ch. 1 (1868).

38 Life is hardly more than a fraction of a second. Such a little time to prepare oneself for eternity!!!

> PAUL GAUGUIN (1848–1903), French artist. *Intimate Journals* (tr. by Van Wyck Brooks, 1923; 1930, p. 2).

39 Life at the greatest and best is but a froward child, that must be humoured and coaxed a little till it falls asleep, and then all the care is over.

> OLIVER GOLDSMITH (1728–74), Anglo-Irish playwright, author. Croaker, in *The Good Natur'd Man*, act 1.

40 Life is an end in itself, and the only question as to whether it is worth living is whether you have had enough of it.

> OLIVER WENDELL HOLMES, JR. (1841–1935), U.S. jurist. Speech, 7 March 1900, at Bar Association Dinner, Boston.

41 Live all you can; it's a mistake not to. It doesn't so much matter what you do in particular, so long as you have your life. If you haven't had that what *have* you had?

> HENRY JAMES (1843–1916), U.S. author. Strether, in *The Ambassadors*, bk. 5, ch. 2 (1903).

42 We are doomed to cling to a life even while we find it unendurable.

> WILLIAM JAMES (1842–1910), U.S. psychologist, philosopher. *Vacations* (1873; repr. in "The Works of William James," vol. 17, pt. 1, 1987).

43 Life's splendor forever lies in wait about each one of us in all its fullness, but veiled from view, deep down, invisible, far off. It *is* there, though, not hostile, not reluctant, not deaf. If you summon it by the right word, by its right name, it will come.

> FRANZ KAFKA (1883–1924), German novelist, short-story writer. *The Diaries of Franz Kafka: 1910–1923* (ed. by Max Brod, 1948), entry for 18 Oct. 1921.

44 All of life is a foreign country.

> JACK KEROUAC (1922–69), U.S. author. Letter, 24 June 1949 (published in *The Beat Vision: A Primary Sourcebook*, ed. by Arthur and Kit Knight, 1987).

45 It is quite true what Philosophy says: that Life must be understood backwards. But that makes one forget the other saying: that it must be lived—forwards. The more one ponders this, the more it comes to mean that life in the temporal existence never becomes quite intelligible, precisely because at no moment can I find complete quiet to take the backward-looking position.

> SOREN KIERKEGAARD (1813–55), Danish philosopher. *The Diary of Søren Kierkegaard*, pt. 5, sct. 4, no. 136 (ed. by Peter Rohde, 1960), 1843 entry.

46 This is what is sad when one contemplates human life, that so many live out their lives in quiet lostness . . . they live, as it were, away from themselves and vanish like shadows. Their immortal souls are blown away, and they are not disquieted by the question of its immortality, because they are already disintegrated before they die.

> SØREN KIERKEGAARD (1813–55), Danish philosopher. *Either/Or*, vol. 2, "Balance between Esthetic and Ethical" (1843; tr. 1987).

47 The art of mastering life is the prerequisite for all further forms of expression, whether they are paintings, sculptures, tragedies, or musical compositions.

> PAUL KLEE (1879–1940), Swiss artist. *The Diaries of Paul Klee 1898–1918* (1957; tr. 1965), entry for 3 June 1902.

48 We only seem to learn from Life that Life doesn't matter so much as it seemed to do—it's not so burningly important, after all, what happens. We crawl, like blinking sea-creatures, out of the Ocean onto a spur of rock, we creep over the promontory bewildered and dazzled and hurting ourselves, then we drop in the ocean on the other side: and the little transit doesn't matter so much.

> D. H. LAWRENCE (1885–1930), British author. Letter, 13 Jan. 1911 (published in *The Letters of D. H. Lawrence*, vol. 1, ed. by James T. Boulton, 1979).

49 Life is what happens while you are making other plans.

> JOHN LENNON (1940–80), British rock musician. "Beautiful Boy," from the album *Starting Over* (1980).

50 Like a French poem is life; being only perfect in
> structure
When with the masculine rhymes mingled the
> feminine are.

> HENRY WADSWORTH LONGFELLOW (1807–82), U.S. poet. *Elegiac Verse*, st. 7.

51 Life is not a matter of place, things or comfort; rather, it concerns the basic human rights of family, country, justice and human dignity.

> IMELDA MARCOS (b. 1929), Filipino First Lady. Quoted in: *Newsweek* (New York, 12 June 1989).

52 Life is constantly providing us with new funds, new resources, even when we are reduced to immobility. In life's ledger there is no such thing as frozen assets.

> HENRY MILLER (1891–1980), U.S. author. *Quiet Days in Clichy* (1956; 1991 repr., p. 33).

53 My art and profession is to live.

> MICHEL DE MONTAIGNE (1533–92), French essayist. *Essays*, bk. 2, ch. 6, "Of Exercise or Practice" (1580–88; tr. by John Florio).

54 Life is a foreign language: all men mispronounce it.

> CHRISTOPHER MORLEY (1890–1957), U.S. novelist, journalist, poet. *Thunder on the Left*, ch. 14 (1925).

55 Life is a petty thing unless it is moved by the indominatable urge to extend its boundaries. Only in proportion as we are desirous of living more do we really live.

> JOSÉ ORTEGA Y GASSET (1883–1955), Spanish essayist, philosopher. *The Dehumanization of Art*, "Invitation to Understanding" (1925).

56 Life is an operation which is done in a forward direction. One lives *toward* the future, because to live consists inexorably in *doing*, in each individual life *making* itself.

> JOSÉ ORTEGA Y GASSET (1883–1955), Spanish essayist, philosopher. "In Search of Goethe from Within," in *Partisan Review* (New Brunswick, N.J., Dec. 1949; repr. in *The Dehumanization of Art and Other Essays*, 1968).

57 Living is like working out a long addition sum, and if you make a mistake in the first two totals you will never find the right answer. It means involving oneself in a complicated chain of circumstances.

> CESARE PAVESE (1908–50), Italian author, poet. *The Burning Brand: Diaries 1935–1950* (1952; tr. 1961), entry for 5 May 1936.

58 Every true man, sir, who is a little above the level of the beasts and plants does not live for the sake of living, without knowing how to live; but he lives so as to give a meaning and a value of his own to life.

> LUIGI PIRANDELLO (1867–1936), Italian author, playwright.

The Father, addressing the Manager, in *Six Characters in Search of an Author*, act 3.

59 Life—how curious is that habit that makes us think it is not here, but elsewhere.

> V. S. PRITCHETT (b. 1900), British author, critic. *Midnight Oil*, ch. 6 (1971). "Life is elsewhere" is a loose translation of Rimbaud's line *La vraie vie est absente. Nous ne sommes pas de monde*. from his poem "Délires." The words were used by Milan Kundera as the title of his novel written in 1969 (published 1973). In it he mentions its citation by André Breton at the conclusion of his Surrealist Manifesto, and by students in Paris, May 1968.

60 Life is a bridge. Cross over it, but build no house on it.

> INDIAN PROVERB. Quoted in: Bruce Chatwin, *The Songlines*, ch. 30, "From the Notebooks" (1987).

61 Life is like Sanskrit read to a pony.

> LOU REED (b. 1944), U.S. rock musician. "What's Good," from the album *Magic and Loss* (1992).

62 Life is the farce which everyone has to perform.

> ARTHUR RIMBAUD (1854–91), French poet. *Une Saison en Enfer*, "Mauvais Sang" (1874).

63 The life of man is a long march through the night, surrounded by invisible foes, tortured by weariness and pain, towards a goal that few can hope to reach, and where none may tarry long.

> BERTRAND RUSSELL (1872–1970), British philosopher, mathematician. *A Free Man's Worship and Other Essays*, ch. 1 (1976).

64 Each man must look to himself to teach him the meaning of life. It is not something discovered: it is something moulded.

> ANTOINE DE SAINT-EXUPÉRY (1900–1944), French aviator, author. *Wind, Sand, and Stars*, ch. 2, sct. 1 (1939).

65 There is no cure for birth and death save to enjoy the interval.

> GEORGE SANTAYANA (1863–1952), U.S. philosopher, poet. *Soliloquies in England*, "War Shrines" (1922).

66 It is a tale
Told by an idiot, full of sound and fury;
Signifying nothing.

> WILLIAM SHAKESPEARE (1564–1616), English dramatist, poet. Macbeth, in *Macbeth*, act 5, sc. 5.

67 Life is a disease; and the only difference between one man and another is the stage of the disease at which he lives. You are always at the crisis: I am always in the convalescent stage.

> GEORGE BERNARD SHAW (1856–1950), Anglo-Irish playwright, critic. Lubin, in *Back to Methuselah*, "The Gospel of the Brothers Barnabas," addressing his political rival Burge.

68 Life is obstinate and clings closest where it is most hated.

> MARY WOLLSTONECRAFT SHELLEY (1797–1851), English novelist. *Frankenstein*, ch. 23 (1818).

69 To find the point where hypothesis and fact meet; the delicate equilibrium between dream and reality; the place where fantasy and earthly things are metamorphosed into a work of art; the hour when faith in the future becomes knowledge of the past; to lay down one's power for others in need; to shake off the old ordeal and get ready for the new; to question, knowing that never can the full answer be found; to accept uncertainties quietly, even our incomplete knowledge of God; this is what man's journey is about, I think.

LILLIAN SMITH (1897–1966), U.S. author. *The Journey*, ch. 15 (1954).

70   There is one thing that matters—to set a chime of words tinkling in the minds of a few fastidious people.

LOGAN PEARSALL SMITH (1865–1946), Anglo-American essayist, aphorist. In answer to the question—asked two weeks before his death—whether he had discovered any meaning in life. Quoted by Cyril Connolly in: *New Statesman*, obituary (London, 9 March 1946).

71   The slightest living thing answers a deeper need than all the works of man because it is *transitory*. It has an evanescence of life, or growth, or change: it passes, as we do, from one stage to the another, from darkness to darkness, into a distance where we, too, vanish out of sight. A work of art is static; and its value and its weakness lie in being so: but the tuft of grass and the clouds above it belong to our own travelling brotherhood.

FREYA STARK (1893–1993), British travel writer. *Perseus in the Wind*, ch. 14 (1948).

72   I have done my fiddling so long under Vesuvius that I have almost forgotten to play, and can only wait for the eruption and think it long of coming. Literally no man has more wholly outlived life than I. And still it's good fun.

ROBERT LOUIS STEVENSON (1850–1894), Scottish novelist, essayist, poet. Closing lines of letter written a few months before Stevenson's death in Samoa (published in *Stevenson's Letters to Charles Baxter*, 1956).

73   Life is a means of extracting fiction.

ROBERT STONE (b. 1937), U.S. novelist. Interview in *Writers at Work* (Eighth Series, ed. by George Plimpton, 1988).

74   The force that through the green fuse drives the flower
Drives my green age; that blasts the roots of trees
Is my destroyer.

DYLAN THOMAS (1914–53), Welsh poet. *The Force that through the Green Fuse Drives the Flower*.

75   Life is like a B-movie. You don't want to leave in the middle of it but you don't want to see it again.

TED TURNER (b. 1938), U.S. broadcasting and sports executive. *International Herald Tribune* (Paris, 2 March 1990).

76   People need to be made more aware of the need to work at learning how to live because life is so quick and sometimes it goes away too quickly

ANDY WARHOL (1928–87), U.S. pop artist. Exhibition catalogue, Oct.-Nov. 1966, ICA, Boston.

77   Life is an offensive, directed against the repetitious mechanism of the Universe.

ALFRED NORTH WHITEHEAD (1861–1947), British philosopher. *Adventures of Ideas*, pt. 1, ch. 5. (1933).

78   Life, Lady Stutfield, is simply a *mauvais quart d'heure* made up of exquisite moments.

OSCAR WILDE (1854–1900), Anglo-Irish playwright, author. Mrs. Allonby, in *A Woman of No Importance*, act 2.

79   To live is the rarest thing in the world. Most people exist, that is all.

OSCAR WILDE (1854–1900), Anglo-Irish playwright, author. *The Soul of Man under Socialism*, in *Fortnightly Review* (London, Feb. 1890).

80   Life! Life! Don't let us go to life for our fulfilment or our experience. It is a thing narrowed by circumstances, incoherent in its utterance, and without that fine correspondence of form and spirit which is the only thing that can satisfy the artistic and critical temperament. It makes us pay too high a price for its wares, and we purchase the meanest of its secrets at a cost that is monstrous and infinite.

OSCAR WILDE (1854–1900), Anglo-Irish playwright, author. Gilbert, in *The Critic as Artist*, pt. 2 (published in *Intentions*, 1891).

81   I sit astride life like a bad rider on a horse. I only owe it to the horse's good nature that I am not thrown off at this very moment.

LUDWIG WITTGENSTEIN (1889–1951), Austrian philosopher. *Culture and Value* (ed. by G. H. von Wright with Heikki Nyman, 1980), 1939–40 entry.

82   Life is not a series of gig lamps symmetrically arranged; life is a luminous halo, a semi-transparent envelope surrounding us from the beginning of consciousness to the end.

VIRGINIA WOOLF (1882–1941), British novelist. *The Common Reader*, "Modern Fiction" (First Series, 1925).

83   The interest in life does not lie in what people do, nor even in their relations to each other, but largely in the power to communicate with a third party, antagonistic, enigmatic, yet perhaps persuadable, which one may call life in general.

VIRGINIA WOOLF (1882–1941), British novelist. *The Common Reader*, "On Not Knowing Greek" (First Series, 1925)

See also Eliot on CHANGE; Chaplin on COMEDY AND COMEDIANS; Latorgue on ENNUI; Johnson on RECREATION; Gourmont on SENSATION.

ABRAHAM LINCOLN

1   He saw Mr. Lincoln but once; at the melancholy function called an Inaugural Ball. Of course he looked anxiously for a sign of character. He saw a long, awkward figure; a plain, ploughed face; a mind, absent in part, and in part evidently worried by white kid gloves; features that expressed neither self-satisfaction nor any other familiar Americanism, but rather the same painful sense of becoming educated and of needing education that tormented a private secretary, above all a lack of apparent force. Any private secretary in the least fit for his business would have thought, as Adams did, that no man living needed so much education as the new President but that all the education he could get would not be enough.

HENRY B. ADAMS (1838–1918), U.S. historian. *The Education of Henry Adams*, ch. 7, "Treason" (1907), referring to Henry Adams's only encounter with Lincoln in March 1861, while serving as a private secretary in Washington, D.C.

2   Lincoln, six feet one in his stocking feet,

The lank man, knotty and tough as a hickory rail,
Whose hands were always too big for white-kid
  gloves,
Whose wit was a coonskin sack of dry, tall tales,
Whose weathered face was homely as a plowed
  field.

> STEPHEN VINCENT BENÉT (1898–1943), U.S. novelist, poet.
> *John Brown's Body.*

3 Our children shall behold his fame,
The kindly-earnest, brave, forseeing man,
Sagacious, patient, dreading praise, not blame,
New birth of our new soil, the first American.

> JAMES RUSSELL LOWELL (1819–91), U.S. poet, editor. *Ode
> Recited at Harvard Commemoration,* usually known as *Com-
> memoration Ode.*

4 I never see that man without feeling that he is one
to become personally attach'd to, for his combination of
purest, heartiest tenderness, and native western form of
manliness.

> WALT WHITMAN (1819–92), U.S. poet. "The Inauguration," 4
> March 1865, in *Specimen Days and Collect* (1882).

LITERACY

1 To learn to read is to light a fire; every syllable that
is spelled out is a spark.

> VICTOR HUGO (1802–85), French poet, dramatist, novelist. *Les
> Misérables,* pt. 4, bk. 7, ch. 1 (1862).

2 Showing up at school already able to read is like
showing up at the undertaker's already embalmed: people start worrying about being put out of their jobs.

> FLORENCE KING (b. 1936), U.S. author. *Reflections in a Jaun-
> diced Eye,* "Confessions of a Bloom & Hirsch Girl"(1989).

3 No amount of charters, direct primaries, or short
ballots will make a democracy out of an illiterate people.

> WALTER LIPPMANN (1889–1974), U.S. journalist. *A Preface to
> Politics,* ch. 9 (1914).

4 For this invention of yours will produce forgetfulness in the minds of those who learn it, by causing them
to neglect their memory, inasmuch as, from their confidence in writing, they will recollect by the external aid of
foreign symbols, and not by the internal use of their own
faculties. Your discovery, therefore, is a medicine not for
memory, but for recollection,—for recalling to, not for
keeping in mind.

> PLATO c. 427–347 B.C.), Greek philosopher. Socrates, in *Phae-
> drus,* sct. 275, recounting the response of the Egyptian god
> Thamus to Theuth's invention of letters. Socrates continued,
> "You are providing for your disciples a show of wisdom without
> the reality. For, acquiring by your means much information
> unaided by instruction, they will appear to possess much knowl-
> edge, while, in fact, they will, for the most part, know nothing at
> all; and, moreover, be disagreeable people to deal with, as hav-
> ing become wise in their own conceit, instead of truly wise."

5 An illiterate king is a crowned ass.

> MEDIEVAL ENGLISH PROVERB. Said by the chronicler William
> of Malmesbury to have been much used by King Henry I of Eng-
> land (1068–1135).

6 There is hardly a pioneer's hut which does not contain a few odd volumes of Shakespeare. I remember read-

ing the feudal drama of *Henry V* for the first time in a log
cabin.

> ALEXIS DE TOCQUEVILLE (1805–59), French social philosopher.
> *Democracy in America,* vol. 2, pt. 1, ch. 13 (1840), of the read-
> ing habits of Americans.

7 There is that indescribable freshness and unconsciousness about an illiterate person that humbles and
mocks the power of the noblest expressive genius.

> WALT WHITMAN (1819–92), U.S. poet. *Leaves of Grass,* Preface
> (1855).

LITERARY CRITICISM

1 I demand that my books be judged with utmost
severity, by knowledgeable people who know the rules
of grammar and of logic, and who will seek beneath the
footsteps of my commas the lice of my thought in the
head of my style.

> LOUIS ARAGON (1897–1982), French poet. *Treatise on Style,*
> pt. 1, "The Pen" (1928).

2 Genuine polemics approach a book as lovingly as a
cannibal spices a baby.

> WALTER BENJAMIN (1892–1940), German critic, philosopher.
> *One-Way Street,* "Post No Bills: The Critic's Technique in Thir-
> teen Theses" (1928; repr. in *One-Way Street and Other Writings,*
> 1978).

3 We have our little *theory* on all human and divine
things. Poetry, the workings of genius itself, which, in all
times, with one or another meaning, has been called
Inspiration, and held to be mysterious and inscrutable, is
no longer without its scientific exposition. The building
of the lofty rhyme is like any other masonry or bricklay-
ing: we have theories of its rise, height, decline and fall—
which latter, it would seem, is now near, among all people.

> THOMAS CARLYLE (1795–1881), Scottish essayist, historian.
> *Signs of the Times,* in *Edinburgh Review,* no. 98 (1829, repr. in
> *Critical and Miscellaneous Essays,* 1838).

4 Criticism is a misconception: we must read not to
understand others but to understand ourselves.

> E. M. CIORAN (b. 1911), Rumanian-born French philosopher.
> *Anathemas and Admirations,* "On the Verge of Existence" (1986).

5 The critical method which denies literary modernity would appear—and even, in certain respects, would
be—the most modern of critical movements.

> PAUL DE MAN (1919–83), Belgian-born U.S. literary critic. "Lit-
> erary History and Literary Modernity," lecture, Sept. 1969 (repr.
> in *Blindness and Insight,* 1971; rev. 1983).

6 There is then creative reading as well as creative
writing. When the mind is braced by labor and invention,
the page of whatever book we read becomes luminous
with manifold allusion. Every sentence is doubly significant, and the sense of our author is as broad as the world.

> RALPH WALDO EMERSON (1803–82), U.S. essayist, poet,
> philosopher. "The American Scholar," oration, 31 Aug. 1837,
> delivered to the Phi Beta Kappa Society at Harvard University
> (published in *The Works of Ralph Waldo Emerson,* 1889).

7 The "text" is merely one of the contexts of a piece
of literature, its lexical or verbal one, no more or less

important than the sociological, psychological, historical, anthropological or generic.

> LESLIE FIEDLER (b. 1917), U.S. critic. *Love and Death in the American Novel,* Preface (First Edition, 1960).

8 Unless criticism refuses to take itself quite so seriously or at least to permit its readers not to, it will inevitably continue to reflect the finicky canons of the genteel tradition and the depressing pieties of the Culture Religion of Modernism.

> LESLIE FIEDLER (b. 1917), U.S. critic. "Cross the Border—Close the Gap," in *Playboy* (Chicago, Dec. 1969; repr. in *Collected Essays,* vol. 2, 1971).

9 A reader who quarrels with postulates, who dislikes *Hamlet* because he does not believe that there are ghosts or that people speak in pentameters, clearly has no business in literature. He cannot distinguish fiction from fact, and belongs in the same category as the people who send cheques to radio stations for the relief of suffering heroines in soap operas.

> NORTHROP FRYE (1912-91), Canadian literary critic. *Anatomy of Criticism,* Essay 2, "Literal and Descriptive Phases" (1957).

10 Much literary criticism comes from people for whom extreme specialization is a cover for either grave cerebral inadequacy or terminal laziness, the latter being a much cherished aspect of academic freedom.

> JOHN KENNETH GALBRAITH (b. 1908), U.S. economist. "H. L. Mencken," in *Washington Post* (14 Sept. 1980; repr. in *A View from the Stands,* 1986).

11 You know lots of criticism is written by characters who are very academic and think it is a sign you are worthless if you make jokes or kid or even clown. I wouldn't kid Our Lord if he was on the cross. But I would attempt a joke with him if I ran into him chasing the money changers out of the temple.

> ERNEST HEMINGWAY (1899–1961), U.S. author. Letter, 21 June 1952 (published in *Selected Letters,* ed. by Carlos Baker, 1981).

12 The literary critic, or the critic of any other specific form of artistic expression, may detach himself from the world for as long as the work of art he is contemplating appears to do the same.

> CLIVE JAMES (b. 1939), Australian writer, critic. *Glued to the Box,* Introduction (1983).

13 Literary criticism can be no more than a reasoned account of the feeling produced upon the critic by the book he is criticizing. Criticism can never be a science: it is, in the first place, much too personal, and in the second, it is concerned with values that science ignores. The touchstone is emotion, not reason. We judge a work of art by its effect on our sincere and vital emotion, and nothing else. All the critical twiddle-twaddle about style and form, all this pseudoscientific classifying and analysing of books in an imitation-botanical fashion, is mere impertinence and mostly dull jargon.

> D. H. LAWRENCE (1885–1930), British author. *Phoenix: The Posthumous Papers of D. H. Lawrence,* pt. 4, "John Galsworthy" (ed. by E. McDonald, 1936).

14 There is an air of last things, a brooding sense of impending annihilation, about so much deconstructive activity, in so many of its guises; it is not merely postmodernist but preapocalyptic.

> DAVID LEHMAN (b. 1948), U.S. poet, editor, critic. *Signs of the Times,* ch. 1, "The End of the Word" (1991).

15 The great critic . . . must be a philosopher, for from philosophy he will learn serenity, impartiality, and the transitoriness of human things.

> W. SOMERSET MAUGHAM (1874–1965), British author. *The Summing Up,* ch. 60 (1938).

16 I have a dream: in my dream . . . Aretha Franklin, in her fabulous black-lipstick "Jumpin' Jack Flash" outfit, leaps from her seat at Maxim's and, shouting "Think!," blasts Lacan, Derrida and Foucault like dishrags against the wall, then leads thousands of freed academic white slaves in a victory parade down the Champs-Elysées.

> CAMILLE PAGLIA (b. 1947), U.S. author, critic, educator. *New York Times Book Review* (5 May 1991).

17 Interpretation is the revenge of the intellect upon art. Even more. It is the revenge of the intellect upon the world. To interpret is to impoverish, to deplete the world—in order to set up a shadow world of "meanings."

> SUSAN SONTAG (b. 1933), U.S. essayist. "Against Interpretation," sct. 4, in *Evergreen Review* (Dec. 1964; repr. in *Against Interpretation,* 1966)

See also CRITICISM AND THE ARTS; CRITICS.

LITERATURE

1 Literature is made upon any occasion that a challenge is put to the legal apparatus by conscience in touch with humanity.

> NELSON ALGREN (1909–81), U.S. author. Quoted in: *The Neon Wilderness,* Frontispiece (1947).

2 The writer in western civilization has become not a voice of his tribe, but of his individuality. This is a very narrow-minded situation.

> AHARON APPELFELD (b. 1932), Israeli novelist. *International Herald Tribune,* (Paris, 10 Aug. 1989).

3 Literary imagination is an aesthetic object offered by a writer to a lover of books.

> GASTON BACHELARD (1884–1962), French scientist, philosopher, literary theorist. *Fragments of a Poetics of Fire,* "A Retrospective Glance at the Lifework of a Master of Books" (1988; tr. 1990).

4 Literature is *without proofs.* By which it must be understood that it cannot prove, not only *what* it says, but even that it is worth the trouble of saying it.

> ROLAND BARTHES (1915–80), French semiologist. "Deliberation," in *Tel Quel* (Paris, Winter 1979; repr. in *Barthes: Selected Writings,* 1982).

5 In the present age, alas! our pens are ravished by unlettered authors and unmannered critics, that make a havoc rather than a building, a wilderness rather than a garden. But, alack! what boots it to drop tears upon the preterit?

> AUBREY BEARDSLEY (1872–98), English illustrator, writer. *The*

Story of Venus and Tannhäuser, or Under the Hill, Dedicatory Epistle (1907).

6 Literature is not exhaustible, for the sufficient and simple reason that a single book is not. A book is not an isolated entity: it is a narration, an axis of innumerable narrations. One literature differs from another, either before or after it, not so much because of the text as for the manner in which it is read.

JORGE LUIS BORGES (1899–1986), Argentinian author. *For Bernard Shaw* (1952; repr. in *Other Inquisitions*, 1960; tr. 1964).

7 English literature is a kind of training in social ethics. . . . English trains you to handle a body of information in a way that is conducive to action.

MARILYN BUTLER (b. 1937), British educator, author. *Guardian* (London, 3 March 1989).

8 The struggle of literature is in fact a struggle to escape from the confines of language; it stretches out from the utmost limits of what can be said; what stirs literature is the call and attraction of what is not in the dictionary.

ITALO CALVINO (1923–85), Italian author, critic. "Cybernetics and Ghosts," lecture, Nov. 1969, delivered in Turin (published in *The Literature Machine*, 1987).

9 There is a great discovery still to be made in literature, that of paying literary men by the quantity they *do not* write.

THOMAS CARLYLE (1795–1881), Scottish essayist, historian, in *London and Westminster Review*, 12 Nov. 1838 repr. in *Critical and Miscellaneous Essays* (1839).

10 When a book, any sort of book, reaches a certain intensity of artistic performance it becomes literature. That intensity may be a matter of style, situation, character, emotional tone, or idea, or half a dozen other things. It may also be a perfection of control over the movement of a story similar to the control a great pitcher has over the ball.

RAYMOND CHANDLER (1888–1959), U.S. author. Letter, 29 Jan. 1946, to crime writer Erle Stanley Gardner, refuting Gardner's denigration of his own books (published in *Raymond Chandler Speaking*, 1962).

11 Speak of the moderns without contempt, and of the ancients without idolatry.

LORD CHESTERFIELD (1694–1773), English statesman, man of letters. Letter, 22 Feb. 1748 (published 1774; repr. in *The Letters of the Earl of Chesterfield to His Son*, vol. 1, no. 142, ed. by Charles Strachey, 1901).

12 One learns little more about a man from his feats of literary memory than from the feats of his alimentary canal.

FRANK MOORE COLBY (1865–1925), U.S. editor, essayist. *The Colby Essays*, "Quotation and Allusion" (1926).

13 Literature exists at the same time in the modes of error and truth; it both betrays and obeys its own mode of being.

PAUL DE MAN (1919–83), Belgian-born U.S. literary critic. "Literary History and Literary Modernity," lecture, Sept. 1969 (repr. in *Blindness and Insight*, 1971; rev. 1983).

14 Literature . . . is condemned (or privileged) to be forever the most rigorous and, consequently, the most reliable of terms in which man names and transforms himself.

PAUL DE MAN (1919–83), Belgian-born U.S. literary critic. *Allegories Of Reading*, pt. 1, ch. 1, "Semiology and Rhetoric."

15 The test of literature is, I suppose, whether we ourselves live more intensely for the reading of it.

ELIZABETH DREW (1887–1965), Anglo-American author, critic. *The Modern Novel*, "Is There a 'Feminine' Fiction?" (1926).

16 Literature transforms and intensifies ordinary language, deviates systematically from everyday speech. If you approach me at a bus stop and murmur "Thou still unravished bride of quietness," then I am instantly aware that I am in the presence of the literary.

TERRY EAGLETON (b. 1943), British critic. *Literary Theory: An Introduction*, "What Is Literature?" (1983), of the Russian Formalists' view of "the literary."

17 The artist is of no importance. Only what he creates is important, since there is nothing new to be said. Shakespeare, Balzac, Homer have all written about the same things, and if they had lived one thousand or two thousand years longer, the publishers wouldn't have needed anyone since.

WILLIAM FAULKNER (1897–1962), U.S. novelist. Interview in *Writers at Work* (First Series, ed. by Malcolm Cowley, 1958).

18 To provoke dreams of terror in the slumber of prosperity has become the moral duty of literature.

ERNST FISCHER (1899–1972), Austrian editor, poet, critic. *Art against Ideology*, ch. 1 (1966; tr. 1969).

19 In our day the conventional element in literature is elaborately disguised by a law of copyright pretending that every work of art is an invention distinctive enough to be patented.

NORTHROP FRYE (1912-91), Canadian literary critic. *Anatomy of Criticism*, Second Essay, "Mythical Phase: Symbol as Archetype" (1957).

20 The world must be all fucked up when men travel first class and literature goes as freight.

GABRIEL GARCíA MÁRQUEZ (b. 1928), Colombian author. The Catalan bookstore owner in Macondo, in *100 Years of Solitude* (1967; tr. 1970; 1978 ed., p. 323).

21 One of the proud joys of the man of letters—if that man of letters is an artist—is to feel within himself the power to immortalize at will anything he chooses to immortalize. Insignificant though he may be, he is conscious of possessing a creative divinity. God creates lives; the man of imagination creates fictional lives which may make a profound and as it were more living impression on the world's memory.

EDMOND (1822–96) AND JULES DE GONCOURT (1830–70), French writers. *The Goncourt Journals* (1888–96; repr. in *Pages from the Goncourt Journal*, ed. by Robert Baldick, 1962), entry for 8 Feb. 1868.

22 A people's literature is the great textbook for real knowledge of them. The writings of the day show the quality of the people as no historical reconstruction can.

EDITH HAMILTON (1867–1963), U.S. classical scholar, translator. *The Roman Way*, Preface (1932).

23 [The] attempt to devote oneself to literature alone is a most deceptive thing, and . . . often, paradoxically, it is literature that suffers for it.

> VÁCLAV HAVEL (b. 1936), Czech playwright, president. *Disturbing the Peace*, ch. 3 (1986; tr. 1990).

24 It is a good lesson—though it may often be a hard one—for a man who has dreamed of literary fame, and of making for himself a rank among the world's dignitaries by such means, to step aside out of the narrow circle in which his claims are recognized, and to find how utterly devoid of all significance, beyond that circle, is all that he achieves, and all he aims at.

> NATHANIEL HAWTHORNE (1804–64), U.S. author. *The Scarlet Letter*, Introduction, "The Custom-House" (1850).

25 All modern American literature comes from one book by Mark Twain called *Huckleberry Finn*. American writing comes from that. There was nothing before. There has been nothing as good since.

> ERNEST HEMINGWAY (1899–1961), U.S. author. *The Green Hills of Africa*, ch. 1 (1935).

26 How simple the writing of literature would be if it were only necessary to write in another way what has been well written. It is because we have had such great writers in the past that a writer is driven far out past where he can go, out to where no one can help him.

> ERNEST HEMINGWAY (1899–1961), U.S. author. Address, 10 Dec. 1954, recorded for the Nobel Prize Committee, accepting the Nobel Prize for literature (published in Carlos Baker, *Hemingway: The Writer as Artist*, ch. 13, 1963 ed.).

27 Literature flourishes best when it is half a trade and half an art.

> W. R. INGE (1860–1954), Dean of St. Paul's, London. *Outspoken Essays*, "The Victorian Age" (Second Series, 1922).

28 It takes a great deal of history to produce a little literature.

> HENRY JAMES (1843–1916), U.S. author. *Hawthorne*, ch. 1 (1879).

29 Great literature cannot grow from a neglected or impoverished soil. Only if we actually tend or care will it transpire that every hundred years or so we might get a *Middlemarch*.

> P. D. JAMES (b. 1920), British mystery writer. *Daily Telegraph* (London, 14 April 1988).

30 The thing that teases the mind over and over for years, and at last gets itself put down rightly on paper—whether little or great, it belongs to Literature.

> SARAH ORNE JEWETT (1849–1909), U.S. author. Letter to author Willa Cather (published in *The Country of the Pointed Firs and Other Stories*, Preface, 1896).

31 Literature is my Utopia. Here I am not disfranchised. No barrier of the senses shuts me out from the sweet, gracious discourse of my book-friends. They talk to me without embarrassment or awkwardness.

> HELEN KELLER (1880–1968), U.S. author, lecturer. *The Story of My Life*, pt. 1, ch. 21 (1903).

32 In the electronic age, books, words and reading are not likely to remain sufficiently authoritative and central to knowledge to justify literature.

> ALVIN KERNAN (b. 1923), U.S. educator. *International Herald Tribune* (Paris, 12 Dec. 1990).

33 For a novelist, a given historic situation is an *anthropologic laboratory* in which he explores his basic question: *What is human existence?*

> MILAN KUNDERA (b. 1929), Czech author, critic. Postscript to *Life Is Elsewhere* (1986; first published 1973).

34 The present era grabs everything that was ever written in order to transform it into films, TV programmes; or cartoons. What is essential in a novel is precisely what can only be expressed in a novel, and so every adaptation contains nothing but the non-essential. If a person is still crazy enough to write novels nowadays and wants to protect them, he has to write them in such a way that they cannot be adapted, in other words, in such a way that they cannot be retold.

> MILAN KUNDERA (b. 1929), Czech author, critic. The narrator, in *Immortality*, pt. 5, ch. 9 (1991).

35 Literature is a toil and a snare, a curse that bites deep.

> D. H. LAWRENCE (1885–1930), British author. Letter, 25 Sept. 1911 (published in *The Letters of D. H. Lawrence*, vol. 1, ed. by James T. Boulton, 1979).

36 Oh literature, oh the glorious Art, how it preys upon the marrow in our bones. It scoops the stuffing out of us, and chucks us aside. Alas!

> D. H. LAWRENCE (1885–1930), British author. Letter, 10 June 1912, to poet and author Walter De La Mare (published in *The Letters of D. H. Lawrence*, vol. 1, ed. by James T. Boulton, 1979).

37 Literature is analysis after the event.

> DORIS LESSING (b. 1919), British novelist. Quoted in: *Children of Albion: Poetry of the Underground in Britain*, "Afterwords," sct. 2 (ed. by Michael Horovitz, 1969).

38 Our American professors like their literature clear and cold and pure and very dead.

> SINCLAIR LEWIS (1885–1951), U.S. novelist. Speech, 12 Dec. 1930, to Swedish Academy, accepting the Nobel Prize for Literature.

39 The pure work implies the disappearance of the poet as speaker, who hands over to the words.

> STÉPHANE MALLARMÉ (1842–98), French symbolist poet. *Variations sur un Sujet*, "Crise de Vers," in *La Revue Blanche* (Paris, Sept. 1895; repr. in *Mallarmé: The Poems*, ed. and tr. by Keith Bosley, 1977).

40 For whatever is truly wondrous and fearful in man, never yet was put into words or books.

> HERMAN MELVILLE (1819–91), U.S. author. *Moby-Dick*, ch. 110 (1851).

41 That is a very good question. I don't know the answer. But can you tell me the name of a classical Greek shoemaker?

> ARTHUR MILLER (b. 1915), U.S. dramatist. In reply to a shoe manufacturer who asked why Miller's job should be subsidized when his was not—recalled by Miller at London press conference. Quoted in: *Guardian* (London, 25 Jan. 1990).

42 What is not in the open street is false, derived, that is to say, *literature*.

> HENRY MILLER (1891–1980), U.S. author. *Black Spring*, "The Fourteenth Ward" (1936).

43 What makes literature interesting is that it does not survive its translation. The characters in a novel are made out of the sentences. That's what their substance is.

> JONATHAN MILLER (b. 1936), British doctor, humorist, director. *Sunday Times* (London, 12 Feb. 1989).

44 Literature, the most seductive, the most deceiving, the most dangerous of professions.

> JOHN, LORD MORLEY (1838–1923), English writer, Liberal politician. *Life of Burke*, ch. 1 (1879).

45 The existence of good bad literature—the fact that one can be amused or excited or even moved by a book that one's intellect simply refuses to take seriously—is a reminder that art is not the same thing as cerebration.

> GEORGE ORWELL (1903–50), British author. *Shooting an Elephant*, "Good Bad Books" (1950).

46 The truth is that literature, particularly fiction, is not the pure medium we sometimes assume it to be. Response to it is affected by things other than its own intrinsic quality; by a curiosity or lack of it about the people it deals with, their outlook, their way of life.

> VANCE PALMER (1885–1959), Australian author, poet. "Fragment of Autobiography" (1958; repr. in *Intimate Portraits*, ed. by H. P. Heseltine, 1969).

47 Literature is a defense against the attacks of life. It says to life: "You can't deceive me. I know your habits, foresee and enjoy watching all your reactions, and steal your secret by involving you in cunning obstructions that halt your normal flow."

> CESARE PAVESE (1908–50), Italian poet, novelist, translator. *The Burning Brand: Diaries 1935–1950* (1952; tr. 1961), entry for 5 May 1936.

48 Literature is the expression of a feeling of deprivation, a recourse against a sense of something missing. But the contrary is also true: language is what makes us human. It is a recourse against the meaningless noise and silence of nature and history.

> OCTAVIO PAZ (b. 1914), Mexican poet. *Alternating Current*, "The Exception to the Rule" (1967).

49 Whoever has the luck to be born a character can laugh even at death. Because a character will never die! A man will die, a writer, the instrument of creation: but what he has created will never die!

> LUIGI PIRANDELLO (1867–1936), Italian author, playwright. The Father, in *Six Characters in Search of an Author*, act 1 (1921).

50 The cultivation of literary pursuits forms the basis of all sciences, and in their perfection consist the reputation and prosperity of kingdoms.

> MARQUÉS DE POMBAL (1699–1782), Portuguese statesman. Quoted in: Conde da Carnota, *The Marquis of Pombal*, ch. 11 (1843).

51 The art of letters will come to an end before A.D. 2000. . . . I shall survive as a curiosity.

> EZRA POUND (1885–1972), U.S. poet, critic. Letter, 1 Jan. 1910, to Pound's mother. Quoted in: Humphrey Carpenter, *A Serious Character*, pt. 5, ch. 6 (1988).

52 Great literature is simply language charged with meaning to the utmost possible degree.

> EZRA POUND (1885–1972), U.S. poet, critic. *How to Read*, pt. 2 (1931).

53 Literature is news that STAYS news.

> EZRA POUND (1885–1972), U.S. poet, critic. *ABC of Reading*, ch. 2 (1934).

54 The party of God and the party of Literature have more in common than either will admit; their texts may conflict, but their bigotries coincide. Both insist on being the sole custodians of the true word and its only interpreters.

> FREDERIC RAPHAEL (b. 1931), British author, critic. *Sunday Times* (London, 12 Feb. 1989).

55 There can be no literary equivalent to truth.

> LAURA RIDING (1901–91), U.S. poet. *Extracts from Communications*.

56 Literature is where I go to explore the highest and lowest places in human society and in the human spirit, where I hope to find not absolute truth but the truth of the tale, of the imagination and of the heart.

> SALMAN RUSHDIE (b. 1947), Indian-born British author. Quoted in: *Observer* (London, 19 Feb. 1989).

57 The liveliness of literature lies in its exceptionality, in being the individual, idiosyncratic vision of one human being, in which, to our delight and great surprise, we may find our own vision reflected.

> SALMAN RUSHDIE (b. 1947), Indian-born British author. "In Good Faith," in *Independent on Sunday* (London, 4 Feb. 1990).

58 Of course the illusion of art is to make one believe that great literature is very close to life, but exactly the opposite is true. Life is amorphous, literature is formal.

> FRANÇOISE SAGAN (b. 1935), French novelist, playwright. Interview in *Writers at Work* (First Series, ed. by Malcolm Cowley, 1958).

59 If literature isn't *everything*, it's not worth a single hour of someone's trouble.

> JEAN-PAUL SARTRE (1905–80), French philosopher, author. Interview, 1960. Quoted in: Susan Sontag, Introduction to *Barthes: Selected Writings*, "Writing Itself: On Roland Barthes" (1982).

60 In literature the ambition of the novice is to acquire the literary language: the struggle of the adept is to get rid of it.

> GEORGE BERNARD SHAW (1856–1950), Anglo-Irish playwright, critic. Quoted in: Hesketh Pearson, *Bernard Shaw: His Life and Personality*, ch. 16 (1942).

61 How has the human spirit ever survived the terrific literature with which it has had to contend?

> WALLACE STEVENS (1879–1955), U.S. poet. *Opus Posthumous*, "Adagia" (1959).

62 Nothing could be more inappropriate to American

literature than its English source since the Americans are not British in sensibility.

> WALLACE STEVENS (1879–1955), U.S. poet. *Opus Posthumous,* "Adagia" (1959).

63   The function of literature, through all its mutations, has been to make us aware of the particularity of selves, and the high authority of the self in its quarrel with its society and its culture. Literature is in that sense subversive.

> LIONEL TRILLING (1905–75), U.S. critic. *Beyond Culture,* "Freud: Within and beyond Culture," sct. 2 (1965).

64   The rest, called *literature,* is a dossier of human imbecility for the guidance of future professors.

> TRISTAN TZARA (1896–1963), Rumanian-born French Dada theorist. "Note on Poetry," in *Dada 4/5* (Zurich, May 1919; repr. in *Lampisteries,* 1963).

65   Literature always anticipates life. It does not copy it, but moulds it to its purpose. The nineteenth century, as we know it, is largely an invention of Balzac.

> OSCAR WILDE (1854–1900), Anglo-Irish playwright, author. Vivian, in *The Decay of Lying* (published in *Intentions,* 1891).

66   Literature is the orchestration of platitudes.

> THORNTON WILDER (1897–1975), U.S. author. *Time* (New York, 12 Jan. 1953).

67   Professors of literature, who for the most part are genteel but mediocre men, can make but a poor defense of their profession, and the professors of science, who are frequently men of great intelligence but of limited interests and education, feel a politely disguised contempt for it; and thus the study of one of the most pervasive and powerful influences on human life is traduced and neglected.

> YVOR WINTERS (1900–68), U.S. literary critic. *In Defense of Reason,* Foreword (1960).

68   A good essay must have this permanent quality about it; it must draw its curtain round us, but it must be a curtain that shuts us in not out.

> VIRGINIA WOOLF (1882–1941), British novelist. *The Common Reader,* "The Modern Essay" (First Series, 1925).

69   Henry James seems most entirely in his element, doing that is to say what everything favours his doing, when it is a question of recollection. The mellow light which swims over the past, the beauty which suffuses even the commonest little figures of that time, the shadow in which the detail of so many things can be discerned which the glare of day flattens out, the depth, the richness, the calm, the humour of the whole pageant—all this seems to have been his natural atmosphere and his most abiding mood.

> VIRGINIA WOOLF (1882–1941), British novelist. *The Death of the Moth,* "The Old Order" (1942; first published 1917). Woolf added, "To Americans, indeed, to Henry James and to Hawthorne, we owe the best relish of the past in our literature, not the past of romance and chivalry, but the immediate past of vanished dignity and faded fashions."

See also Rushdie on ART; POETRY; POETS; Chandler on The PUBLIC; Pound on TRANSLATION; Le Guin on WOMEN AND THE ARTS; WRITERS; WRITING.

LITERATURE AND SOCIETY

1   If the most significant characteristic of man is the complex of biological needs he shares with all members of his species, then the best lives for the writer to observe are those in which the role of natural necessity is clearest, namely, the lives of the very poor.

> W. H. AUDEN (1907–73), Anglo-American poet. *The Dyer's Hand,* pt. 8, "Cav And Pag" (1962).

2   As a poet there is only one political duty, and that is to defend one's language against corruption. When it is corrupted, people lose faith in what they hear and this leads to violence.

> W. H. AUDEN (1907–73), Anglo-American poet. Quoted in: *Observer* (London, 31 Oct. 1971).

3   Do not worry about the incarnation of ideas. If you are a poet, your works will contain them without your knowledge—they will be both moral and national if you follow your inspiration freely.

> VISSARION BELINSKY (1810–48), Russian revolutionary writer. Quoted in: Nadine Gordimer, "The Essential Gesture," in *The Essential Gesture* (ed. by Stephen Clingman, 1988).

4   If a poet has any obligation toward society, it is to write well. Being in the minority, he has no other choice. Failing this duty, he sinks into oblivion. Society, on the other hand, has no obligation toward the poet. A majority by definition, society thinks of itself as having other options than reading verses, no matter how well written. Its failure to do so results in its sinking to that level of locution at which society falls easy prey to a demagogue or a tyrant. This is society's own equivalent of oblivion.

> JOSEPH BRODSKY (b. 1940), Russian-born U.S. poet, critic. *Less Than One: Selected Essays,* "To Please a Shadow," sct. 2 (1986; first published 1983).

5   When politicians and politically minded people pay too much attention to literature, it is a bad sign—a bad sign mostly for literature. . . . But it is also a bad sign when they don't want to hear the word mentioned.

> ITALO CALVINO (1923–85), Italian author, critic. "Right and Wrong Political Uses of Literature," lecture, Feb. 1976, delivered at Amherst College, Mass. (published in *The Literature Machine,* 1987).

6   Just as it is true that a stream cannot rise above its source, so it is true that a national literature cannot rise above the moral level of the social conditions of the people from whom it derives its inspiration.

> JAMES CONNOLLY (1870–1916), Irish syndicalist, Republican leader. *Labour in Irish History,* Foreword (1910).

7   The writer isn't made in a vacuum. Writers are witnesses. The reason we need writers is because we need witnesses to this terrifying century.

> E. L. DOCTOROW (b. 1931), U.S. novelist. Interview in *Writers at Work* (Eighth Series, ed. by George Plimpton, 1988).

8   Despair, feeding, as it always does, on phantasmagoria, is imperturbably leading literature to the rejection, *en masse,* of all divine and social laws, towards practical and theoretical evil.

> ISIDORE DUCASSE, COMTE DE LAUTRÉAMONT (1846–70), French author, poet. *Poems,* pt. 1 (1870).

9 When we read of human beings behaving in certain ways, with the approval of the author, who gives his benediction to this behaviour by his attitude towards the result of the behaviour arranged by himself, we can be influenced towards behaving in the same way.

T. S. ELIOT (1888–1965), Anglo-American poet, critic. "Religion and Literature" (1935; repr. in *Selected Essays*, 1951).

10 If you look at history you'll find that no state has been so plagued by its rulers as when power has fallen into the hands of some dabbler in philosophy or literary addict.

DESIDERIUS ERASMUS (c. 1466–1536), Dutch humanist. *Praise of Folly*, ch. 24 (1509).

11 Creative writers are always greater than the causes that they represent.

E. M. FORSTER (1879–1970), British novelist, essayist. *Two Cheers for Democracy*, "Gide and George" (1951).

12 It is the story-teller's task to elicit sympathy and a measure of understanding for those who lie outside the boundaries of State approval.

GRAHAM GREENE (1904–91), British novelist. Speech, 1969, on receiving the Shakespeare Prize awarded by the University of Hamburg, Germany.

13 A great number of the disappointments and mishaps of the troubled world are the direct result of literature and the allied arts. It is our belief that no human being who devotes his life and energy to the manufacture of fantasies can be anything but fundamentally inadequate

CHRISTOPHER HAMPTON (b. 1946), British playwright. Celia, in *The Philanthropist*, sc. 5.

14 I really do inhabit a system in which words are capable of shaking the entire structure of government, where words can prove mightier than ten military divisions.

VÁCLAV HAVEL (b. 1936), Czech playwright, president. Speech, Oct. 1989, Germany, accepting a peace prize. Quoted in: *Independent* (London, 9 Dec. 1989).

15 The hardest thing to do is to write straight honest prose on human beings. First you have to know the subject; then you have to know how to write. Both take a lifetime to learn, and anybody is cheating who takes politics as a way out. All the outs are too easy, and the thing itself is too hard to do.

ERNEST HEMINGWAY (1899–1961), U.S. author. "Old Newsman Writes: A Letter from Cuba," in *Esquire* (New York, Dec. 1934; repr. in *By-Line Ernest Hemingway*, ed. by William White, 1967).

16 Now a writer can make himself a nice career while he is alive by espousing a political cause, working for it, making a profession of believing in it, and if it wins he will be very well placed. All politics is a matter of working hard without reward, or with a living wage for a time, in the hope of booty later. A man can be a Fascist or a Communist and if his outfit gets in he can get to be an ambassador or have a million copies of his books printed by the Government or any of the other rewards the boys dream about.

ERNEST HEMINGWAY (1899–1961), U.S. author. "Old News-

man Writes: A Letter from Cuba," in *Esquire* (New York, Dec. 1934; repr. in *By-Line Ernest Hemingway*, ed. by William White, 1967).

17 There are events which are so great that if a writer has participated in them his obligation is to write truly rather than assume the presumption of altering them with invention.

ERNEST HEMINGWAY (1899–1961), U.S. author. Gustav Regler, *The Great Crusade*, Preface (1940).

18 All you can be sure about in a political-minded writer is that if his work should last you will have to skip the politics when you read it. Many of the so-called politically enlisted writers change their politics frequently .... Perhaps it can be respected as a form of the pursuit of happiness.

ERNEST HEMINGWAY (1899–1961), U.S. author. Interview in *Paris Review* (Flushing, N.Y., Spring 1958; repr. in *Writers at Work*, Second Series, ed. by George Plimpton, 1963).

19 The self-styled intellectual who is impotent with pen and ink hungers to write history with sword and blood.

ERIC HOFFER (1902–83), U.S. philosopher. *The Passionate State of Mind*, aph. 65 (1955).

20 The agitator seizes the word. The artist is seized by it.

KARL KRAUS (1874–1936), Austrian satirist. *Die Fackel*, no. 272/73 (Vienna, 15 Feb. 1909; quoted in Thomas Szasz, *Anti-Freud: Karl Kraus's Criticism of Psychoanalysis and Psychiatry*, ch. 8, 1976).

21 Literature must become Party literature. . . . Down with unpartisan litterateurs! Down with the superman of literature! Literature must become a part of the general cause of the proletariat.

VLADIMIR ILYICH LENIN (1870–1924), Russian revolutionary leader. *Party Organization and Party Literature* (1905). Quoted in: George Steiner, *Language and Silence*, "Marxism and the Literary Critic" (1967).

22 With a pen in my hand I have successfully stormed bulwarks from which others armed with sword and excommunication have been repulsed.

G. C. LICHTENBERG (1742–99), German physicist, philosopher. *Aphorisms*, "Notebook E," aph. 76 (written 1765–99; tr. by R. J. Hollingdale, 1990).

23 A good metaphor is something even the police should keep an eye on.

G. C. LICHTENBERG (1742–99), German physicist, philosopher. *Aphorisms*, "Notebook E," aph. 91 (written 1765–99; tr. by R. J. Hollingdale, 1990).

24 It is not the first duty of the novelist to provide blueprints for insurrection, or uplifting tales of successful resistance for the benefit of the opposition. The naming of what is there is what is important.

IAN MCEWAN (b. 1938), British author. *A Move Abroad*, Preface (1989).

25 The writer may very well serve a movement of history as its mouthpiece, but he cannot of course create it.

KARL MARX (1818–83), German political theorist, social philosopher. *Moralizing Criticism and Critical Morality* (1847;

repr. in *Karl Marx and Friedrich Engels: Collected Works*, vol. 6, 1976).

26 There was a time when the average reader read a novel simply for the moral he could get out of it, and however naïve that may have been, it was a good deal less naïve than some of the limited objectives he has now. Today novels are considered to be entirely concerned with the social or economic or psychological forces that they will by necessity exhibit, or with those details of daily life that are for the good novelist only means to some deeper end.

FLANNERY O'CONNOR (1925–64), U.S. author. "Some Aspects of the Grotesque in Southern Fiction," paper, Fall 1960, read at Wesleyan College for Women, Macon, Ga. (published in *Cluster Review*, 1965, Macon University; repr. in *Mystery and Manners*, ed. by Sally and Robert Fitzgerald, 1972).

27 The atmosphere of orthodoxy is always damaging to prose, and above all it is completely ruinous to the novel, the most anarchical of all forms of literature.

GEORGE ORWELL (1903–50), British author. *Inside the Whale and Other Essays*, "Inside the Whale" (1940).

28 If a nation's literature declines, the nation atrophies and decays.

EZRA POUND (1885–1972), U.S. poet, critic. *ABC of Reading*, ch. 3 (1934).

29 Literature does not exist in a vacuum. Writers as such have a definite social function exactly proportional to their ability *as writers*. This is their main use.

EZRA POUND (1885–1972), U.S. poet, critic. *ABC of Reading*, ch. 3 (1934).

30 Writers and politicians are natural rivals. Both groups try to make the world in their own images; they fight for the same territory.

SALMAN RUSHDIE (b. 1947), Indian-born British author. Quoted in: *Observer* (London, 19 Feb. 1989).

31 The only privilege literature deserves—and this privilege it requires in order to exist—is the privilege of being in the arena of discourse, the place where the struggle of our languages can be acted out.

SALMAN RUSHDIE (b. 1947), Indian-born British author. "Is Nothing Sacred?" Herbert Reade Memorial Lecture, 6 Feb. 1990.

32 Just as the office worker dreams of murdering his hated boss and so is saved from really murdering him, so it is with the author; with his great dreams he helps his readers to survive, to avoid their worst intentions. And society, without realizing it . . . respects and even exalts him, albeit with a kind of jealousy, fear and even repulsion, since few people want to discover the horrors that lurk in the depths of their souls. This is the highest mission of great literature, and there is no other.

ERNESTO SÁBATO (b. 1911), Argentinian novelist, essayist. *Independent* (London, 20 June 1992).

33 Writing is the continuation of politics by other means.

PHILIPPE SOLLERS (b. 1936), French author, critic. *Tel Quel: Théorie d'Ensemble*, "Ecriture et Révolution" (1968).

34 Literature that is not the breath of contemporary society, that dares not transmit the pains and fears of that society, that does not warn in time against threatening moral and social dangers—such literature does not deserve the name of literature; it is only a façade. Such literature loses the confidence of its own people, and its published works are used as wastepaper instead of being read.

ALEXANDER SOLZHENITSYN (b. 1918), Russian novelist. Open letter, 16 May 1967, to the Fourth Soviet Writers' Congress (repr. in *Solzhenitsyn: A Documentary Record*, "The Struggle Intensifies," ed. by Leopold Labedz, 1970).

35 For a country to have a great writer . . . is like having another government. That's why no régime has ever loved great writers, only minor ones.

ALEXANDER SOLZHENITSYN (b. 1918), Russian novelist. Innokenty, in *The First Circle*, ch. 57 (1968).

36 As life grows more terrible, its literature grows more terrible.

WALLACE STEVENS (1879–1955), U.S. poet. *Opus Posthumous*, "Adagia" (1959).

37 By and large the literature of a democracy will never exhibit the order, regularity, skill, and art characteristic of aristocratic literature; formal qualities will be neglected or actually despised. The style will often be strange, incorrect, overburdened, and loose, and almost always strong and bold. Writers will be more anxious to work quickly than to perfect details. Short works will be commoner than long books, wit than erudition, imagination than depth. There will be a rude and untutored vigor of thought with great variety and singular fecundity. Authors will strive to astonish more than to please, and to stir passions rather than to charm taste.

ALEXIS DE TOCQUEVILLE (1805–59), French social philosopher. *Democracy in America*, vol. 2, pt. 1, ch. 13 (1840).

38 Already the writers are complaining that there is too much freedom. They need some pressure. The worse your daily life, the better your art. If you have to be careful because of oppression and censorship, this pressure produces diamonds.

TATYANA TOLSTAYA (b. 1951), Russian author. *Independent* (London, 31 May 1990).

39 Any historian of the literature of the modern age will take virtually for granted the adversary intention, the actually subversive intention, that characterizes modern writing—he will perceive its clear purpose of detaching the reader from the habits of thought and feeling that the larger culture imposes, of giving him a ground and a vantage point from which to judge and condemn, and perhaps revise, the culture that produces him.

LIONEL TRILLING (1905–75), U.S. critic. *Beyond Culture*, Preface (1965).

40 There is an incompatibility between literary creation and political activity.

MARIO VARGAS LLOSA (b. 1936), Peruvian novelist. *International Herald Tribune* (Paris, 1 April 1988).

41 I have never known a novel that was good enough to be good in spite of its being adapted to the author's political views.

EDITH WHARTON (1862–1937), U.S. author. Letter, 19 Aug.

1927, to novelist and socialist Upton Sinclair (published in *The Letters of Edith Wharton*, 1988).

See also ART; Solzhenitsyn on CENSORSHIP; Hugo on DESPOTISM; Kundera on RIDICULE.

LITIGATION

1   Litigant. A person about to give up his skin for the hope of retaining his bones.

AMBROSE BIERCE (1842–1914), U.S. author. *The Devil's Dictionary* (1881–1906).

2   People are getting smarter nowadays; they are letting lawyers, instead of their conscience, be their guide.

WILL ROGERS (1879–1935), U.S. humorist. *The Illiterate Digest*, "Helping the Girls with Their Income Taxes" (1924).

3   The most important thing in their lives . . . was to have a lawsuit going. It was not a question of winning or losing it, and indeed it was vital to do neither, for otherwise the suit would be over and done with. A lawsuit was part of the personality, if not the only visible sign of it, to such an extent that there was often no real animosity between the litigants, because they both needed each other.

SALVATORE SATTA (1902–75), Italian jurist, novelist. *The Day of Judgment*, ch. 20 (1979), of the Nuorese in Sardinia. The novel recounts the lives of an inland mountain town in Sardinia around the turn of the century.

4   Come, agree, the law's costly.

JONATHAN SWIFT (1667–1745), Anglo-Irish satirist. *Polite Conversation*, Dialogue 1 (1738).

See also TRIALS.

LIVING TOGETHER

1   It is better to dwell in a corner of the housetop, than with a brawling woman in a wide house.

BIBLE, HEBREW. *Proverbs* 21:9.

2   Living en famille provides the strongest motives for rudeness combined with the maximum opportunity for displaying it.

QUENTIN CRISP (b. 1908), British author. *Manners from Heaven*, ch. 2 (1984).

3   One of the weaknesses in the cooperative is that it has never been sufficiently leavened by the imagination. This is a quick-silver faculty, and likely to be a cause of worry to any collective settlement.

EDWARD DAHLBERG (1900–77), U.S. author, critic. *Alms for Oblivion*, "Our Vanishing Cooperative Colonies" (1964).

4   I cannot live with You—
It would be Life—
And Life is over there—
Behind the Shelf.

EMILY DICKINSON (1830–86), U.S. poet. *The Complete Poems*, no. 640 (1955).

5   Do you think your mother and I should have lived comfortably so long together, if ever we had been married? Baggage!

JOHN GAY (1685–1732), English dramatist. Peachum, in *The Beggar's Opera*, act 1, sc. 8.

6   There would be no society if living together depended upon understanding each other.

ERIC HOFFER (1902–83), U.S. philosopher. *Reflections on the Human Condition*, aph. 143 (1973).

7   Come live with me, and be my love,
And we will all the pleasures prove.

CHRISTOPHER MARLOWE (1564–93), English dramatist, poet. *The Passionate Shepherd to His Love*.

8   In the old days, one married a wife; now one forms a company with a female partner, or moves in to live with a friend. And then one seduces the partner, or defiles the friend.

J. AUGUST STRINDBERG (1849–1912), Swedish dramatist, novelist, poet. Captain Adolf, in *The Father*, act 3, sc. 7.

See also Chesterfield on INTIMACY ilde on SELFISHNESS.

LOGIC

1   Logic is like the sword—those who appeal to it, shall perish by it.

SAMUEL BUTLER (1835–1902), English author. *Samuel Butler's Notebooks* (1951).

2   From a drop of water a logician could infer the possibility of an Atlantic or a Niagara without having seen or heard of one or the other.

SIR ARTHUR CONAN DOYLE (1859–1930), English author. Sherlock Holmes, in *A Study in Scarlet*, pt. 1, ch. 2 (1887).

3   The much vaunted male logic isn't logical, because they display prejudices—against half the human race—that are considered prejudices according to any dictionary definition.

EVA FIGES (b. 1932), British author. Interview in *Women Writers Talk* (ed. by Olga Kenyon, 1989).

4   Logic! Good gracious! What rubbish! How can I tell what I think till I see what I say?

E. M. FORSTER (1879–1970), British novelist, essayist. Riposte of "that old lady in the anecdote who was accused by her nieces of being illogical," in *Aspects of the Novel*, ch. 5, "The Plot" (1927).

5   The fact that logic cannot satisfy us awakens an almost insatiable hunger for the irrational.

A. N. WILSON (b. 1950), British author. Book review in *Guardian* (London, 30 Sept. 1989).

6   Logic takes care of itself; all we have to do is to look and see how it does it.

LUDWIG WITTGENSTEIN (1889–1951), Austrian philosopher. *Notebooks 1914–1916*, entry for 13 Oct. 1914.(ed. by Anscombe, 1961; also in *Tractatus Logico-Philosophicus*, sct. 5:473, 1921, tr. 1922).

7   The logic of the world is prior to all truth and falsehood.

LUDWIG WITTGENSTEIN (1889–1951), Austrian philosopher.

Notebooks 1914–1916, entry for 18 Oct. 1914. (ed. by Anscombe, 1961; later reformulated in *Tractatus Logico-Philosophicus*, sct. 5:552, 1921, tr. 1922) "Logic is *prior* to every experience—that something *is so*."

LONDON

1   The truth is, that in London it is always a sickly season. Nobody is healthy in London, nobody can be.

JANE AUSTEN (1775–1817), English novelist. Mr. Woodhouse, in *Emma*, ch. 12 (1816).

2   Finally, within a huge and sombre mass of things,
A blackened people, living and dying in silence.

HENRI AUGUSTE BARBIER (1805–82), French poet. *Londres.*

3   It is a damned place—to be sure—but the only one in the world (at least in the English world) for fun—though I have seen parts of the globe that I like better—still upon the whole it is the completest either to help one in feeling oneself alive, or forgetting that one is so.

LORD BYRON (1788–1824), English poet. Letter, 1 March 1816 (published in *Byron's Letters and Journals,* vol. 5, ed. by Leslie Marchand, 1973–81).

4   That monstrous tuberosity of civilised life, the capital of England.

THOMAS CARLYLE (1795–1881), Scottish essayist, historian. Teufelsdröckh, in *Sartor Resartus,* bk. 3, ch. 6 (1833–34).

5   London is a modern Babylon.

BENJAMIN DISRAELI (1804–81), English statesman, author. *Tancred,* bk. 5, ch. 5 (1847).

6   Unreal City
Under the brown fog of a winter dawn.

T. S. ELIOT (1888–1965), Anglo-American poet, critic. *The Wasteland,* "The Burial of the Dead" (1922).

7   The best bribe which London offers to-day to the imagination, is, that, in such a vast variety of people and conditions, one can believe there is room for persons of romantic character to exist, and that the poet, the mystic, and the hero may hope to confront their counterparts.

RALPH WALDO EMERSON (1803–82), U.S. essayist, poet, philosopher. *The Conduct of Life,* "Culture" (1860).

8   It is not the walls that make the city, but the people who live within them. The walls of London may be battered, but the spirit of the Londoner stands resolute and undismayed.

GEORGE VI (1895–1952), King of Great Britain and Northern Ireland. Broadcast, 23 Sept. 1940, to the Empire during German bomber offensive.

9   You find no man, at all intellectual, who is willing to leave London. No, Sir, when a man is tired of London, he is tired of life; for there is in London all that life can afford.

SAMUEL JOHNSON (1709–84), English author, lexicographer. Quoted in: James Boswell, *Life of Samuel Johnson,* 20 Sept. 1777 (1791).

10   Here falling houses thunder on your head,
And here a female atheist talks you dead.

SAMUEL JOHNSON (1709–84), English author, lexicographer. *London.*

11   I have passed all my days in London, until I have formed as many and intense local attachments as any of you mountaineers can have done with dead nature. The lighted shops of the Strand and Fleet Street, the innumerable trades, tradesmen, and customers, coaches, waggons, playhouses, all the bustle and wickedness round about Covent Garden, the very women of the town, the watchmen, drunken scenes, rattles,—life awake, if you awake, at all hours of the night, the impossibility of being dull in Fleet Street, the crowds, the very dirt and mud, the sun shining upon houses and pavements, the print shops, the old book stalls, parsons cheap'ning books, coffee houses, steam of soups from kitchens, pantomimes, London itself a pantomime and a masquerade,—all these things work themselves into my mind and feed me, without a power of satiating me. The wonder of these sights impels me into night-walks about her crowded streets, I often shed tears in the Strand from fullness of joy at so much life.

CHARLES LAMB (1775–1834), English essayist, critic. Letter, 30 Jan. 1801, to William Wordsworth (published in *Complete Works,* vol. 3, 1882).

12   Behold now this vast city; a city of refuge, the mansion house of liberty, encompassed and surrounded with his protection; the shop of war hath not there more anvils and hammers waking, to fashion out the plates and instruments of armed justice in defence of beleaguered truth, than there be pens and hands there, sitting by their studious lamps, musing, searching, revolving new notions.

JOHN MILTON (1608–74), English poet. *Areopagitica: A Speech for the Liberty of Unlicensed Printing to the Parliament of England* (1644), describing London during the English Civil War.

13   Dear damned distracting town.

ALEXANDER POPE (1688–1744), English satirical poet. *A Farewell to London.*

14   You are now
In London, that great sea, whose ebb and flow
At once is deaf and loud, and on the shore
Vomits its wrecks, and still howls on for more.
Yet in its depth what treasures!

PERCY BYSSHE SHELLEY (1792–1822), English poet. *Letter to Maria Gisborne.*

15   Hell is a city much like London—
A populous and a smoky city;
There are all sorts of people undone,
And there is little or no fun done;
Small justice shown, and still less pity.

PERCY BYSSHE SHELLEY (1792–1822), English poet. *Peter Bell the Third,* pt. 3, "Hell," st. 1.

16   I love London society! I think it has immensely improved. It is entirely composed now of beautiful idiots and brilliant lunatics. Just what Society should be.

OSCAR WILDE (1854–1900), Anglo-Irish playwright, author. Mabel Chiltern, in *An Ideal Husband,* act 1.

17   This melancholy London—I sometimes imagine that the souls of the lost are compelled to walk through its streets perpetually. One feels them passing like a whiff of air.

W. B. YEATS (1865–1939), Irish poet. Letter, 25 Aug. 1888, to writer Katharine Tynan—later Hinkson (published in *Collected Letters of W. B. Yeats*, vol. 1, ed. by John Kelly, 1986).

See also Forster on ACQUAINTANCE; CITIES AND CITY LIFE; De Quincey on SUNDAY.

LONELINESS

1 No one ever discovers the depths of his own loneliness.

GEORGES BERNANOS (1888–1948), French novelist, political writer. *The Diary of a Country Priest*, ch. 7 (1936).

2 Only in a house where one has learnt to be lonely does one have this solicitude for *things*. One's relation to them, the daily seeing or touching, begins to become love, and to lay one open to pain.

ELIZABETH BOWEN (1899–1973), Anglo-Irish novelist. *The Death of the Heart*, pt. 2, ch. 2 (1938).

3 A lonely man is a lonesome thing, a stone, a bone, a stick, a receptacle for Gilbey's gin, a stooped figure sitting at the edge of a hotel bed, heaving copious sighs like the autumn wind.

JOHN CHEEVER (1912–82), U.S. author. *John Cheever: The Journals*, "The Sixties" (ed. by Robert Gottlieb, 1991), 1966 entry.

4 Who knows what true loneliness is—not the conventional word, but the naked terror? To the lonely themselves it wears a mask. The most miserable outcast hugs some memory or some illusion. Now and then a fatal conjunction of events may lift the veil for an instant. For an instant only. No human being could bear a steady view of moral solitude without going mad.

JOSEPH CONRAD (1857–1924), Polish-born English novelist. *Under Western Eyes*, pt. 1, ch. 2 (1911).

5 What torments my soul is its loneliness. The more it expands among friends and the daily habits or pleasures, the more, it seems to me, it flees me and retires into its fortress. The poet who lives in solitude, but who produces much, is the one who enjoys those treasures we bear in our bosom, but which forsake us when we give ourselves to others. When one yields oneself completely to one's soul, it opens itself to one, and then it is that the capricious thing allows one the greatest of good fortunes . . . that of sympathizing with others, of studying itself, of painting itself constantly in its works.

EUGÈNE DELACROIX (1798–1863), French artist. *The Journal of Eugène Delacroix* (tr. by Walter Pach, 1937), entry for 14 May 1824.

6 One aged man—one man—can't fill a house.

ROBERT FROST (1874–1963), U.S. poet. *An Old Man's Winter Night*.

7 Loneliness is never more cruel than when it is felt in close propinquity with someone who has ceased to communicate.

GERMAINE GREER (b. 1939), Australian feminist writer. *The Female Eunuch*, "Security" (1970).

8 What makes loneliness an anguish
Is not that I have no one to share my burden,

But this:
I have only my own burden to bear.

DAG HAMMARSKJÖLD (1905–61), Swedish statesman, Secretary-General of U.N. *Markings*, "Night Is Drawing Nigh" (1964; written 1952).

9 It's a terrible thing to be alone—yes it is—it is—but don't lower your mask until you have another mask prepared beneath—as terrible as you like—but a *mask*.

KATHERINE MANSFIELD (1888–1923), New Zealand-born British author. Letter, July 1917, to her future husband, John Middleton Murry (published in *Collected Letters*, vol. 1, ed. by Vincent O'Sullivan and Margaret Scott, 1984).

10 All men are lonely. But sometimes it seems to me that we Americans are the loneliest of all. Our hunger for foreign places and new ways has been with us almost like a national disease. Our literature is stamped with a quality of longing and unrest, and our writers have been great wanderers.

CARSON MCCULLERS (1917–67), U.S. author. "Look Homeward, Americans," in *Vogue* (New York, 1 Dec. 1940; repr. in *The Mortgaged Heart*, ed. by Margarita G. Smith, 1972).

11 Man's loneliness is but his fear of life.

EUGENE O'NEILL (1888–1953), U.S. dramatist. Lazarus, in *Lazarus Laughed*, act. 3, sc. 2.

12 A man is never completely alone in this world. At the worst, he has the company of a boy, a youth, and by and by a grown man—the one he used to be.

CESARE PAVESE (1908–50), Italian poet, novelist, translator. *The Burning Brand: Diaries 1935–1950* (1952; tr. 1961), Winter 1941–42 entry.

13 When Christ said: "I was hungry and you fed me," he didn't mean only the hunger for bread and for food; he also meant the hunger to be loved. Jesus himself experienced this loneliness. He came amongst his own and his own received him not, and it hurt him then and it has kept on hurting him. The same hunger, the same loneliness, the same having no one to be accepted by and to be loved and wanted by. Every human being in that case resembles Christ in his loneliness; and that is the hardest part, that's real hunger.

MOTHER TERESA (b. 1910), Albanian-born Roman Catholic missionary. *A Gift for God*, "Imitation of Christ" (1975).

14 Be good and you will be lonesome.

MARK TWAIN (1835–1910), U.S. author. *Following the Equator*, caption for author's photograph in frontispiece (1897).

15 There is no God, no universe, no human race, no earthly life, no heaven, no hell. It is all a dream, a grotesque and foolish dream. Nothing exists but you. And you are but a *thought*—a vagrant thought, a useless thought, a homeless thought, wandering forlorn among the empty eternities!

MARK TWAIN (1835–1910), U.S. author. Satan's last words to Theodor Fischer, in "The Mysterious Stranger," ch. 11 (1916; repr. in *The Complete Short Stories*, ed. by Charles Neider, 1957).

16 The gift of loneliness is sometimes a radical vision of society or one's people that has not previously been taken into account.

ALICE WALKER (b. 1944), U.S. author, critic. Interview in *Interviews with Black Writers (ed. by John O'Brien, 1973; repr. in *In Search of Our Mothers' Gardens*, "From an Interview," 1983).

17 When so many are lonely as seem to be lonely, it would be inexcusably selfish to be lonely alone.

TENNESSEE WILLIAMS (1914–83), U.S. dramatist. Don Quixote, in *Camino Real*, "Prologue."

See also Eliot on SUSPICION.

LONG-WINDEDNESS

1 I dare say I am compelled, unconsciously compelled, now to write volume after volume, as in past years I was compelled to go to sea, voyage after voyage. Leaves must follow upon each other as leagues used to follow in the days gone by, on and on to the appointed end, which, being Truth itself, is One—one for all men and for all occupations.

JOSEPH CONRAD (1857–1924), Polish-born English novelist. *A Personal Record*, ch. 1 (1912).

2 One always tends to overpraise a long book, because one has got through it.

E. M. FORSTER (1879–1970), British novelist, essayist. "T. E. Lawrence," in *Abinger Harvest* (1936; first published 1935).

3 It wasn't by accident that the Gettysburg address was so short. The laws of prose writing are as immutable as those of flight, of mathematics, of physics.

ERNEST HEMINGWAY (1899–1961), U.S. author. Letter, 23 July 1945 (published in *Selected Letters*, ed. by Carlos Baker, 1981), said of the difficulties of sustaining an epic at a high pitch.

4 It is no great art to say something briefly when, like Tacitus, one has something to say; when one has nothing to say, however, and none the less writes a whole book and makes truth . . . into a liar—that I call an achievement.

G. C. LICHTENBERG (1742–99), German physicist, philosopher. *Aphorisms*, "Notebook E," aph. 59 (written 1765–99; tr. by R. J. Hollingdale, 1990).

5 Anybody can write a three-volume novel. It merely requires a complete ignorance of both life and literature.

OSCAR WILDE (1854–1900), Anglo-Irish playwright, author. Gilbert, in *The Critic as Artist*, pt. 1 (published in *Intentions*, 1891).

See also Jonson on OLD AGE; TALKATIVENESS.

LOS ANGELES

1 Just because you live in LA it doesn't mean you have to dress that way.

Advertising billboard campaign in Los Angeles, mounted by New York fashion house Charivari.

2 I don't wanna live in a city where the only cultural advantage is that you can make a right turn on a red light.

WOODY ALLEN (b. 1935), U.S. filmmaker. Alvy Singer (Allen) to Rob, comparing Los Angeles with Manhattan, in the film *Annie Hall* (directed by Allen, scripted by Allen with Marshall Brickman, 1977; repr. in *Four Films of Woody Allen*, 1982).

3 It is in love with its limitless horizontality, as New York may be with its verticality.

JEAN BAUDRILLARD (b. 1929), French semiologist. *America*, "Astral America" (1986; tr. 1988).

4 It's like a jumble of huts in a jungle somewhere. I don't understand how you can live there. It's really, completely dead. Walk along the street, there's nothing moving. I've lived in small Spanish fishing villages which were literally sunny all day long every day of the week, but they weren't as boring as Los Angeles.

TRUMAN CAPOTE (1924–84), U.S. author. *Conversations with Truman Capote*, ch. 7, "Hollywood" (ed. by Lawrence Grobel, 1985).

5 Billboards, billboards, drink this, eat that, use all manner of things, *everyone,* the best, the cheapest, the purest and most satisfying of all their available counterparts. Red lights flicker on every horizon, airplanes beware; cars flash by, more lights. Workers repair the gas main. Signs, signs, lights, lights, streets, streets.

NEAL CASSADY (1926–68), U.S. beat hero. "Leaving LA by Train at Night, High . . ." in *The First Third and Other Writings* (1971).

6 I used to like this town. . . . Los Angeles was just a big dry sunny place with ugly homes and no style, but good-hearted and peaceful. . . . Now . . . we've got the big money, the sharpshooters, the percentage workers, the fast dollar boys, the hoodlums out of New York and Chicago and Detroit—and Cleveland. We've got the flash restaurants and night clubs they run, and the hotels and apartment houses they own, and the grifters and con men and female bandits that live in them. The luxury trades, the pansy decorators, the Lesbian dress designers, the riff-raff of a big hardboiled city with no more personality than a paper cup.

RAYMOND CHANDLER (1888–1959), U.S. author. Philip Marlowe, in *The Little Sister*, ch. 26 (1949).

7 Twenty-four hours a day somebody is running, somebody else is trying to catch him. Out there in the night of a thousand crimes people were dying, being maimed, cut by flying glass, crushed against steering wheels or under heavy car tyres. People were being beaten, robbed, strangled, raped, and murdered. People were hungry, sick, bored, desperate with loneliness or remorse or fear, angry, cruel, feverish, shaken by sobs. A city no worse than others, a city rich and vigorous and full of pride, a city lost and beaten and full of emptiness.

RAYMOND CHANDLER (1888–1959), U.S. author. Philip Marlowe, in *The Long Goodbye*, ch. 38 (1953), describing Los Angeles.

8 The freeway experience . . . is the only secular communion Los Angeles has. . . . Actual participation requires a total surrender, a concentration so intense as to seem a kind of narcosis, a rapture-of-the-freeway. The mind goes clean. The rhythm takes over.

JOAN DIDION (b. 1935), U.S. essayist. *The White Album*, "The Bureaucrats" (1979; first published 1976).

9 Thought is barred in this City of Dreadful Joy and conversation is unknown.

ALDOUS HUXLEY (1894–1963), British novelist. *Jesting Pilate*, pt. 4 (1926).

10 Prejudices are useless. Call Los Angeles any dirty name you like—Six Suburbs in Search of a City, Paradise with a Lobotomy, anything—but the fact remains that you are already living in it before you get there.

CLIVE JAMES (b. 1939), Australian writer, critic. *Flying Visits,* "Postcard from Los Angeles 1" (1984; first published in *Observer,* London, 16 June 1979).

11 There are two modes of transport in Los Angeles: car and ambulance. Visitors who wish to remain inconspicuous are advised to choose the latter

FRAN LEBOWITZ (b. 1951), U.S. journalist. *Social Studies,* "Lesson 1" (1981).

12 If Los Angeles is not the one authentic rectum of civilization, then I am no anatomist. Any time you want to go out again and burn it down, count me in.

H. L. MENCKEN (1880–1956), U.S. journalist. Letter, 15 March 1927, to F. Scott and Zelda Fitzgerald on their return from working in Hollywood. Quoted in: James R. Mellon, *Invented Lives* (1984).

13 Los Angeles gives one the feeling of the future more strongly than any city I know of. A bad future, too, like something out of Fritz Lang's feeble imagination.

HENRY MILLER (1891–1980), U.S. author. *The Air-Conditioned Nightmare,* "Soirée in Hollywood" (1945).

14 It is hereby earnestly proposed that the USA. would be much better off if that big, sprawling, incoherent, shapeless, slobbering civic idiot in the family of American communities, the City of Los Angeles, could be declared incompetent and placed in charge of a guardian like any individual mental defective.

WESTBROOK PEGLER (1894–1969), U.S. journalist. *New York World Telegram* (22 Nov. 1938).

15 Of all the world's storied thoroughfares, it must be confessed that none produces quite the effect of Hollywood Boulevard. I have been downcast in Piccadilly, chopfallen on the Champs Elysée, and *doloroso* on the Via Veneto, but the avenues themselves were blameless. Hollywood Boulevard, on the contrary, creates an instant and malign impression in the breast of the beholder. Viewed in full sunlight, its tawdriness is unspeakable; in the torrential downpour of the rainy season, as we first saw it, it inspired an anguish similar to that produced by the engravings of Piranesi.

S. J. PERELMAN (1904–79), U.S. writer, humorist. *The Last Laugh,* "The Marx Brothers" (1981).

See also CALIFORNIA AND THE WEST; Baudrillard on CITIES AND CITY LIFE.

LOSING

1 One of the first businesses of a sensible man is to know when he is beaten, and to leave off fighting at once.

SAMUEL BUTLER (1835–1902), English author. *Samuel Butler's Notebooks* (1951).

2 Victory has a hundred fathers but defeat is an orphan.

GALEAZZO CIANO (1903–44), Italian Fascist leader. *Diario 1939–1943* (1946), entry for 9 Sept. 1942. President Kennedy is quoted as having made the same remark in the wake of the Bay of Pigs invasion in April 1961.

3 A real gentleman, even if he loses everything he owns, must show no emotion. Money must be so far beneath a gentleman that it is hardly worth troubling about.

FEODOR DOSTOYEVSKY (1821–81), Russian novelist. *The Gambler,* ch. 2 (1866).

4 We have resolved to endure the unendurable and suffer what is unsufferable.

HIROHITO (1901–89), Emperor of Japan. Quoted in: A. J. P. Taylor, *Listener* (London, 9 Sept. 1976), following the dropping of the atomic bomb on Hiroshima.

5 All th' world loves a good loser.

KIN [F. MCKINNEY] HUBBARD (1868–1930), U.S. humorist, journalist. *Abe Martin's Wisecracks* (ed. by E. V. Lucas, 1930).

6 What makes us so bitter against people who outwit us is that they think themselves cleverer than we are.

FRANÇOIS, DUC DE LA ROCHEFOUCAULD (1613–80), French writer, moralist. *Sentences et Maximes Morales,* no. 350 (1678).

7 Show me a good loser and I will show you a loser.

PAUL NEWMAN (b. 1925), U.S. screen actor. Quoted in: *Observer* (London, 2 Jan. 1982). The original source of these words is thought to be football coach Knute Rockne (1888–1931), who said to Wisconsin basketball coach Walter Meanwell in the 1920s, "Show me a good and gracious loser and I'll show you a failure."

8 There may be as much nobility in being last as in being first, because the two positions are equally necessary in the world, the one to complement the other.

JOSÉ ORTEGA Y GASSET (1883–1955), Spanish essayist, philosopher. *Meditations on Quixote,* "Preliminary Meditation" (1914).

9 We are not interested in the possibilities of defeat; they do not exist.

VICTORIA (1819–1901), Queen of Great Britain and Ireland. Letter, Dec. 1899, to statesman A. J. Balfour, during the "Black Week" of the Boer War.

10 Have you heard that it was good to gain the day?
I also say it is good to fall, battles are lost in the same spirit in which they are won.

WALT WHITMAN (1819–92), U.S. poet. *Song of Myself,* sct. 18, in *Leaves of Grass* (1855).

See also Eliot on BATTLES; Bragg on The BRITISH.

LOSS

1 The art of losing isn't hard to master;
so many things seem filled with the intent
to be lost that their loss is no disaster.

ELIZABETH BISHOP (1911–79), U.S. poet. *One Art.*

2 Never in any case say *I have lost* such a thing, but *I have returned it.* Is your child dead? It is a return. Is your wife dead? It is a return. Are you deprived of your estate? is not this also a return?

EPICTETUS (c. 55–c. 135), Greek Stoic philosopher. *Encheiridion,* no. 11 (tr. by T. W. H. Rolleston, 1881).

3 Take care to sell your horse before he dies. The art of life is passing losses on.

ROBERT FROST (1874–1963), U.S. poet. *The Poetry of Robert Frost*, "The Ingenuities of Debt" (1979).

4 Nothing that grieves us can be called little: by the eternal laws of proportion a child's loss of a doll and a king's loss of a crown are events of the same size.

MARK TWAIN (1835–1910), U.S. author. "Which Was the Dream?" unfinished story (written 1897; published in *Which Was the Dream and Other Symbolic Writings,* ed. by John S. Tuckey, 1967).

LOVE

1 Love is a great beautifier.

LOUISA MAY ALCOTT (1832–88), U.S. author. *Little Women,* pt. 2, ch. 1 (1869).

2 The Impossible Generalized Man today is the critic who believes in loving those unworthy of love as well as those worthy—yet believes this only insofar as no personal risk is entailed. Meaning he loves no one, worthy or no. This is what makes him impossible.

NELSON ALGREN (1909–81), U.S. author. *Notes from a Sea Diary: Hemingway All the Way,* "Prefatory" (1966).

3 There is love of course. And then there's life, its enemy.

JEAN ANOUILH (1910–87), French playwright. *Le Général,* in *Ardèle,* act 1.

4 Love is made by two people, in different kinds of solitude. It can be in a crowd, but in an oblivious crowd.

LOUIS ARAGON (1897–1982), French poet. Taped discussion in *La Révolution Surréaliste,* no. 11, Paris, 15 March 1928; repr. in *Recherches sur la Sexualité,* Jan. 1928– Aug. 1932, "Second Session, ed. by José Pierre (1990).

5 Love, by its very nature, is unworldly, and it is for this reason rather than its rarity that it is not only apolitical but antipolitical, perhaps the most powerful of all antipolitical human forces.

HANNAH ARENDT (1906–75), German-born U.S. political philosopher. *The Human Condition,* pt. 5, ch. 33 (1958).

6 Love is the victim's response to the rapist.

TI-GRACE ATKINSON (b. 1938?), U.S. feminist writer. Quoted in: *Sunday Times Magazine* (London, 14 Sept. 1969).

7 We are not commanded (or forbidden) to love our mates, our children, our friends, our country because such affections come naturally to us and are good in themselves, although we may corrupt them. We are commanded to love our neighbor because our "natural" attitude toward the "other" is one of either indifference or hostility.

W. H. AUDEN (1907–73), Anglo-American poet. *A Certain World,* "Neighbor, Love of One's" (1970).

8 For a crowd is not company; and faces are but a gallery of pictures; and talk but a tinkling cymbal, where there is no love.

FRANCIS BACON (1561–1626), English philosopher, essayist, statesman. *Essays,* "Of Friendship" (1597–1625).

9 The fate of love is that it always seems too little or too much.

AMELIA BARR (1831–1919), Anglo-American novelist. *The Belle of Bolling Green,* ch. 5 (1904).

10 To try to write love is to confront the *muck* of language: that region of hysteria where language is both *too much* and *too little,* excessive . . . and impoverished.

ROLAND BARTHES (1915–80), French semiologist. *A Lover's Discourse,* "Inexpressible Love" (1977; tr. 1979).

11 Naturally, love's the most distant possibility.

GEORGES BATAILLE (1897–1962), French novelist, critic. *La Somme Athéologique,* vol. 2, *Guilty,* "Alleluia," sct. 4 (1944).

12 It is unfortunately very true that, without leisure and money, love can be no more than an orgy of the common man. . . . Instead of being a sudden impulse full of ardour and reverie, it becomes a distastefully utilitarian affair.

CHARLES BAUDELAIRE (1821–67), French poet. "The Painter of Modern Life," sct. 9 (published in *L'Art Romantique,* 1869; repr. in *Selected Writings on Art and Artists,* ed. by P. E. Charvet, 1972).

13 To love someone is to isolate him from the world, wipe out every trace of him, dispossess him of his shadow, drag him into a murderous future. It is to circle around the other like a dead star and absorb him into a black light.

JEAN BAUDRILLARD (b. 1929), French semiologist. *Fatal Strategies,* "Ironic Strategies" (1983; tr. 1990).

14 If you say, I love you, then you have already fallen in love with language, which is already a form of break up and infidelity.

JEAN BAUDRILLARD (b. 1929), French semiologist. *Cool Memories,* ch. 4 (1987; tr. 1990).

15 When we understand that man is the only animal who must *create* meaning, who must open a wedge into neutral nature, we already understand the essence of love. Love is the problem of an animal who must *find* life, *create* a dialogue with nature in order to experience his own being.

ERNEST BECKER (1924–74), U.S. psychologist, cultural anthropologist. *The Structure of Evil,* pt. 2, ch. 9, "A Brief Ontology of Love" (1968).

16 Stay me with flagons, comfort me with apples: for I am sick of love.

BIBLE, HEBREW. *The Song of Solomon* 2:5.

17 There is no fear in love; but perfect love casteth out fear: because fear hath torment. He that feareth is not made perfect in love.

BIBLE: NEW TESTAMENT. *1 John* 4:18.

18 This is my commandment, that ye love one another.

BIBLE: NEW TESTAMENT. Jesus, in *John* 15:12.

19 Love seeketh only self to please,
To bind another to its delight,
Joys in another's loss of ease,
And builds a Hell in Heaven's despite.

WILLIAM BLAKE (1757–1827), English poet, painter, engraver. *Songs of Experience,* "The Clod & the Pebble" (1794), reply of the Pebble to the Clod of Clay's declaration that "Love seeketh not itself to please,/Nor for itself hath any care,/But for another gives its ease,/And builds a Heaven in Hell's despair."

20 To fall in love is to create a religion that has a fallible god.

JORGE LUIS BORGES (1899–1986), Argentinian author. *Other Inquisitions*, "The Meeting in a Dream" (1952).

21 If I place love above everything, it is because for me it is the most desperate, the most despairing state of affairs imaginable.

ANDRÉ BRETON (1896–1966), French Surrealist. Taped discussions, 3 March 1928 (published in *Recherches sur la Sexualité*, Jan. 1928–Aug. 1932, "Sixth Session," ed. by José Pierre, 1990).

22 When first we met we did not guess
That Love would prove so hard a master.

ROBERT BRIDGES (1844–1930), British poet. *Triolet*.

23 All the little emptiness of love!

RUPERT BROOKE (1887–1915), British poet. *Peace*.

24 Real love is a pilgrimage. It happens when there is no strategy, but it is very rare because most people are strategists.

ANITA BROOKNER (b. 1938), British novelist, art historian. Interview in *Women Writers Talk* (ed. by Olga Kenyon, 1989).

25 Whoso loves
Believes the impossible.

ELIZABETH BARRETT BROWNING (1806–61), English poet. *Aurora Leigh*, bk. 5 (1857).

26 If thou must love me, let it be for nought
Except for love's sake only. Do not say,
I love her for her smile . . . her look . . . her way
Of speaking gently . . . for a trick of thought
That falls in well with mine, and, certes, brought
A sense of pleasant ease on such a day—
For these things in themselves, Beloved, may
Be changed, or change for thee—and love so
    wrought,
May be unwrought so.

ELIZABETH BARRETT BROWNING (1806–61), English poet. *Sonnets from the Portuguese*, Sonnet 14.

27 We loved, sir—used to meet:
How sad and bad and mad it was—
But then, how it was sweet!

ROBERT BROWNING (1812–89), English poet. *Confessions*, st. 9.

28 O lyric Love, half angel and half bird
And all a wonder and a wild desire.

ROBERT BROWNING (1812–89), English poet. *The Ring and the Book*, bk. 1.

29 In love, as in gluttony, pleasure is a matter of the utmost precision.

ITALO CALVINO (1923–85), Italian author, critic. Charles Fourier, *Theory of the Four Movements*, Introduction (1971; repr. in *The Literature Machine*, 1987).

30 The desire for possession is insatiable, to such a point that it can survive even love itself. To love, therefore, is to sterilize the person one loves.

ALBERT CAMUS (1913–60), French-Algerian philosopher, author. *The Rebel*, pt. 4 (1951; tr. 1953).

31 Love, Arthur, is a poodle's chance of attaining the infinite, and personally I have my pride.

LOUIS-FERDINAND CÉLINE (1894–1961), French author. Ferdinand Bardamu, in *Journey to the End of the Night* (1932; tr. 1934; 1966, p. 8).

32 'Tis said of love that it sometimes goes, sometimes flies; runs with one, walks gravely with another; turns a third into ice, and sets a fourth in a flame: it wounds one, another it kills: like lightning it begins and ends in the same moment: it makes that fort yield at night which it besieged but in the morning; for there is no force able to resist it.

MIGUEL DE CERVANTES (1547–1616), Spanish writer. Leonela, in *Don Quixote*, pt. 1, bk. 4, ch. 7 (1605; tr. by P. Motteux).

33 Love and war are the same thing, and stratagems and policy are as allowable in the one as in the other.

MIGUEL DE CERVANTES (1547–1616), Spanish writer. Don Quixote, in *Don Quixote*, pt. 2, bk. 5, ch. 21 (1615; tr. by P. Motteux).

34 The lyf so short, the craft so longe to lerne,
Th'assay so hard, so sharp the conquerynge,
The dredful joye, alwey that slit so yerne;
Al this mene I be love.

GEOFFREY CHAUCER (1340–1400), English poet. First lines of *The Parlement of Foules*, in *The Works of Geoffrey Chaucer* (ed. by Alfred W. Pollard, et al., 1898).

35 If there's delight in love, 'tis when I see
That heart, which others bleed for, bleed for me.

WILLIAM CONGREVE (1670–1729), English dramatist. Song sung by Mrs. Hodgson, in *The Way of the World*, act 3, sc. 12.

36 Love is the extra effort we make in our dealings with those whom we do not like and once you understand that, you understand all. This idea that love overtakes you is nonsense. This is but a polite manifestation of sex. To love another you have to undertake some fragment of their destiny.

QUENTIN CRISP (b. 1908), British author. "Love Lies Bleeding," in *New Statesman & Society* (London, 9 Aug. 1991; first broadcast 6 Aug. 1991).

37 Men and women are not free to love decently until they have analysed themselves completely and swept away every mystery from sex; and this means the acquisition of a profound philosophical theory based on wide reading of anthropology and enlightened practice.

ALEISTER CROWLEY (1875–1947), British occultist. *The Confessions of Aleister Crowley*, ch. 44 (1929; rev. 1970).

38 If we seek the pleasures of love, passion should be occasional, and common sense continual.

ROBERTSON DAVIES (b. 1913), Canadian novelist, journalist. "The Pleasures of Love," in *Saturday Night* (Canada, 23 Dec. 1961; repr. in *The Enthusiasms of Robertson Davies*, 1990).

39 Love is not enough. It must be the foundation, the cornerstone—but not the complete structure. It is much too pliable, too yielding.

BETTE DAVIS (1908–89), U.S. screen actor. *The Lonely Life*, ch. 19 (1962).

40 Love was as subtly catched, as a disease;
But being got it is a treasure sweet,

Which to defend is harder than to get:
And ought not be prophaned on either part,
For though 'tis got by *chance*, 'tis kept by *art*.

> JOHN DONNE (c. 1572–1631), English divine, metaphysical poet. Last lines of *The Expostulation*.

41 Art is not necessary at all. All that is necessary to make this world a better place to live in is to love—to love as Christ loved, as Buddha loved.

> ISADORA DUNCAN (1878–1927), U.S. dancer. From the first chapter of her memoirs, dictated in Berlin in 1924 but never completed (published in *This Quarter*, Paris, Autumn 1929).

42 To love one child and to love all children, whether living or dead—somewhere these two loves come together. To love a no-good but humble punk and to love an honest man who believes himself to be an honest man—somewhere these, too, come together.

> MARGUERITE DURAS (b. 1914), French author, filmmaker. "The Path of Joyful Despair," interview, in *Le Monde* (Paris, 1977; repr. in *Outside: Selected Writings*, 1984).

43 It was the men I deceived the most that I loved the most.

> MARGUERITE DURAS (b. 1914), French author, filmmaker. *Practicalities*, "The Chimneys of *India Song*" (1987; tr. 1990).

44 It's unthinkable not to love—you'd have a severe nervous breakdown. Or you'd have to be Philip Larkin.

> LAWRENCE DURRELL (1912–90), British author. Interview in *Observer* (London, 11 Nov. 1990).

45 Romantic love, in pornography as in life, is the mythic celebration of female negation. For a woman, love is defined as her willingness to submit to her own annihilation. . . . The proof of love is that she is willing to be destroyed by the one whom she loves, for his sake. For the woman, love is always self-sacrifice, the sacrifice of identity, will, and bodily integrity, in order to fulfill and redeem the masculinity of her lover.

> ANDREA DWORKIN (b. 1946), U.S. feminist critic. "The Root Cause," speech, 26 Sept. 1975, Massachusetts Institute of Technology, Cambridge (published in *Our Blood*, ch. 9, 1976).

46 A supreme love, a motive that gives a sublime rhythm to a woman's life, and exalts habit into partnership with the soul's highest needs, is not to be had where and how she wills.

> GEORGE ELIOT (1819–80), English novelist, editor. *Felix Holt, The Radical*, ch. 48 (1866).

47 For what is love itself, for the one we love best?—an enfolding of immeasurable cares which yet are better than any joys outside our love.

> GEORGE ELIOT (1819–80), English novelist, editor. *Daniel Deronda*, bk. 8, ch. 69 (1876).

48 Love is most nearly itself
When here and now cease to matter.

> T. S. ELIOT (1888–1965), Anglo-American poet, critic. *East Coker*, pt. 5, in *Four Quartets*.

49 If only the strength of the love that people feel when it is reciprocated could be as intense and obsessive as the love we feel when it is not; then marriages would be truly made in heaven.

> BEN ELTON (b. 1959), British author, performer. *Stark*, "Private Investigations" (1989).

50 He who is in love is wise and is becoming wiser, sees newly every time he looks at the object beloved, drawing from it with his eyes and his mind those virtues which it possesses.

> RALPH WALDO EMERSON (1803–82), U.S. essayist, poet, philosopher. "The Method of Nature," oration, 11 Aug. 1841, delivered to the Society of the Adelphi, Waterville College, Me. (published in *The Works of Ralph Waldo Emerson*, 1889).

51 At any rate, let us love for a while, for a year or so, you and me. That's a form of divine drunkenness that we can all try.

> F. SCOTT FITZGERALD (1896–1940), U.S. author. John to Kismine, in *The Diamond as Big as the Ritz*, ch. 11 (1922).

52 I don't want to live—I want to love first, and live incidentally.

> ZELDA FITZGERALD (1900–48), U.S. writer. Letter, March 1919, to F. Scott Fitzgerald. Quoted in: Nancy Milford, *Zelda*, pt. 1, ch. 4 (1970).

53 The idea that nations should love one another, or that business concerns or marketing boards should love one another, or that a man in Portugal should love a man in Peru of whom he has never heard—it is absurd, unreal, dangerous. . . . The fact is we can only love what we know personally. And we cannot know much.

> E. M. FORSTER (1879–1970), British novelist, essayist. *Two Cheers for Democracy*, "Tolerance" (1951; first published 1941).

54 Well, love is insanity. The ancient Greeks knew that. It is the taking over of a rational and lucid mind by delusion and self-destruction. You lose yourself, you have no power over yourself, you can't even think straight.

> MARILYN FRENCH (b. 1929), U.S. author, critic. Valerie, in *The Women's Room*, ch. 4, sct. 10 (1977).

55 Love is often nothing but a favorable exchange between two people who get the most of what they can expect, considering their value on the personality market.

> ERICH FROMM (1900–80), U.S. psychologist. *The Sane Society*, ch. 5, "Alienation" (1955).

56 Immature love says: "I love you because I need you." Mature love says: "I need you because I love you."

> ERICH FROMM (1900–80), U.S. psychologist. *The Art of Loving*, ch. 2 (1956).

57 What then in love can woman do?
If we grow fond they shun us.
And when we fly them, they pursue:
But leave us when they've won us.

> JOHN GAY (1685–1732), English playwright. Polly and Lucy, in *The Beggar's Opera*, act 3, sc. 8, Air 49.

58 Love gives naught but itself and takes naught but
from itself.
Love possesses not nor would it be possessed;
For love is sufficient unto love.

> KAHLIL GIBRAN (1883–1931), Lebanese poet, novelist. *The Prophet* (1923).

59 Today I begin to understand what love must be, if it exists. . . . When we are parted, we each feel the lack of the other half of ourselves. We are incomplete like a book in two volumes of which the first has been lost.

That is what I imagine love to be: incompleteness in absence.

EDMOND (1822–96) AND JULES DE GONCOURT (1830–70), French writers. *The Goncourt Journals* (1888–96; repr. in *Pages from the Goncourt Journal*, ed. by Robert Baldick, 1962), entry for 15 Nov. 1859.

60 Love, love, love—all the wretched cant of it, masking egotism, lust, masochism, fantasy under a mythology of sentimental postures, a welter of self-induced miseries and joys, blinding and masking the essential personalities in the frozen gestures of courtship, in the kissing and the dating and the desire, the compliments and the quarrels which vivify its barrenness.

GERMAINE GREER (b. 1939), Australian feminist writer. *The Female Eunuch*, "Obsession" (1970).

61 One would always want to think of oneself as being on the side of love, ready to recognize it and wish it well—but, when confronted with it in others, one so often resented it, questioned its true nature, secretly dismissed the particular instance as folly or promiscuity. Was it merely jealousy, or a reluctance to admit so noble and enviable a sentiment in anyone but oneself?

SHIRLEY HAZZARD (b. 1931), Australian-American author. *The Evening of the Holiday*, ch. 9 (1965).

62 Madame, it is an old word and each one takes it new and wears it out himself. It is a word that fills with meaning as a bladder with air and the meaning goes out of it as quickly. It may be punctured as a bladder is punctured and patched and blown up again and if you have not had it it does not exist for you. All people talk of it, but those who have had it are marked by it, and I would not wish to speak of it further since of all things it is the most ridiculous to talk of and only fools go through it many times.

ERNEST HEMINGWAY (1899–1961), U.S. author. *Death in the Afternoon*, ch. 11 (1932).

63 Only the really plain people know about love—the very fascinating ones try so hard to create an impression that they very soon exhaust their talents.

KATHARINE HEPBURN (b. 1909), U.S. actor. *Look* (New York, 18 Feb. 1958).

64 Love's like the measles—all the worse when it comes late in life.

DOUGLAS JERROLD (1803–57), English playwright, humorist. *The Wit and Opinions of Douglas Jerrold*, "A Philanthropist" (1859). The author Jerome K. Jerome developed the idea in his *Idle Thoughts of an Idle Fellow*, "On Being in Love" (1889): "Love is like the measles; we all have to go through it. Also like the measles, we take it only once."

65 Love is the wisdom of the fool and the folly of the wise.

SAMUEL JOHNSON (1709–84), English author, lexicographer. Quoted in: William Cooke, *Life of Samuel Foote*, vol. 2 (repr. in *Johnsonian Miscellanies*, vol. 2, ed. by George Birkbeck Hill, 1897).

66 Do you want me to tell you something really subversive? Love *is* everything it's cracked up to be. That's why people are so cynical about it. . . . It really *is* worth fighting for, being brave for, risking everything for. And the trouble is, if you don't risk anything, you risk even *more*.

ERICA JONG (b. 1942), U.S. author. Hans, in *How to Save Your Own Life*, "Intuition, extuition . . ." (1977).

67 Love (understood as the desire of good for another) is in fact so unnatural a phenomenon that it can scarcely repeat itself, the soul being unable to become virgin again and not having energy enough to cast itself out again into the ocean of another's soul.

JAMES JOYCE (1882–1941), Irish author. Notes to the play *Exiles* (written 1914–15; published 1952).

68 'Tis very much like light, a thing that everybody knows, and yet none can tell what to make of it: 'Tis not money, fortune, joynture, raving, stabbing, hanging, romancing, flouncing, swearing, ramping, desiring, fighting, dying, though all those have been, are, and still will be mistaken and miscalled for it.

THE LADIES' DICTIONARY, "Love" (1694).

69 True love is like ghosts, which everyone talks about but few have seen.

FRANÇOIS, DUC DE LA ROCHEFOUCAULD (1613–80), French writer, moralist. *Sentences et Maximes Morales*, no. 76 (1678).

70 We are nearer loving those who hate us than those who love us more than we wish.

FRANÇOIS, DUC DE LA ROCHEFOUCAULD (1613–80), French writer, moralist. *Sentences et Maximes Morales*, no. 321 (1678).

71 The world is wonderful and beautiful and good beyond one's wildest imagination. Never, never, never could one conceive what love is, beforehand, never. Life *can* be great—quite god-like. It *can* be so. God be thanked I have proved it.

D. H. LAWRENCE (1885–1930), British author. Letter, 2 June 1912 (published in *The Letters of D. H. Lawrence*, vol. 1, ed. by James T. Boulton, 1979). Lawrence wrote the letter after eloping to Germany with Frieda von Richthofen, wife of his old university professor, whom he later married.

72 I shall always be a priest of love.

D. H. LAWRENCE (1885–1930), British author. Letter, 25 Dec. 1912 (published in *The Letters of D. H. Lawrence*, vol. 1, ed. by James T. Boulton, 1979).

73 We love in another's soul
whatever of ourselves
we can deposit in it;
the greater the deposit,
the greater the love.

IRVING LAYTON (b. 1912), Canadian poet. *The Whole Bloody Bird*, "Aphs" (1969).

74 We've got this gift of love, but love is like a precious plant. You can't just accept it and leave it in the cupboard or just think it's going to get on by itself. You've got to keep watering it. You've got to really look after it and nurture it.

JOHN LENNON (1940–80), British rock musician. *Man of the Decade*, broadcast, 30 Dec. 1969, ATV.

75 A man has only one escape from his old self: to see a different self—in the mirror of some woman's eyes.

CLARE BOOTHE LUCE (1903–87), U.S. diplomat, writer. Mrs. Morehead, in *The Women*, act 1 (1936).

76 Great passions, my dear, don't exist: they're liars' fantasies. What do exist are little loves that may last for a short or a longer while.

> ANNA MAGNANI (1918–73), Egyptian-born Italian actor. Quoted in: Oriana Fallaci, *The Egotists*, "Anna Magnani" (1963).

77 Nowadays men cannot love seven night but they must have all their desires: that love may not endure by reason; for where they be soon accorded and hasty, heat soon it cooleth. Right so fareth love nowadays, soon hot soon cold: this is no stability. But the old love was not so.

> SIR THOMAS MALORY (c. 1430–71), English author. *Le Morte d'Arthur*, bk. 18, ch. 25 (1485).

78 If there is any country on earth where the course of true love may be expected to run smooth, it is America.

> HARRIET MARTINEAU (1802–76), English writer, social critic. *Society in America*, "Marriage," vol. 3 (1837).

79 The love boat has crashed against the everyday.

> VLADIMIR MAYAKOVSKY (1893–1930), Russian poet, playwright. Untitled last poem found after his suicide (repr. in Viktor Shklovsky, *Mayakovsky and his Circle*, ch. 25, 1940; ed. and tr. by Lily Fieler, 1972).

80 Parrots, tortoises and redwoods
Live a longer life than men do,
Men a longer life than dogs do,
Dogs a longer life than love does.

> EDNA ST. VINCENT MILLAY (1892–1950), U.S. poet. *Pretty Love I Must Outlive You*.

81 No love is entirely without worth, even when the frivolous calls to the frivolous and the base to the base.

> IRIS MURDOCH (b. 1919), British novelist, philosopher. *The Nice and the Good*, ch. 39 (1968).

82 The spiritualization of sensuality is called *love*: it is a great triumph over Christianity.

> FRIEDRICH NIETZSCHE (1844–1900), German philosopher. *Twilight of the Idols*, "Morality as Anti-Nature," aph. 3 (1889).

83 Love is the final end of the world's history, the Amen of the universe.

> NOVALIS [FRIEDRICH VON HARDENBERG] (1772–1801), German poet, novelist. *Thoughts on Religion*, pt. 1 in *Hymns and Thoughts on Religion* (tr. and ed. by W. Hastie, 1888), from *Fragments* (1799–1800).

84 If love . . . means that one person absorbs the other, then no real relationship exists any more. Love evaporates; there is nothing left to love. The integrity of self is gone.

> ANN OAKLEY (b. 1944), British sociologist, author. *Taking It Like a Woman*, "Love: Irresolution" (1984).

85 To love, for us men, is to clasp one woman with our arms, feeling that she lives and breathes just as we do, suffers as we do, thinks with us, loves with us, and, above all, sins with us.

> BARONESS ORCZY (1865–1947), Hungarian-born British novelist, playwright. Sir Percy Blakeney, in *I Will Repay*, ch. 7 (1906).

86 To an ordinary human being, love means nothing if it does not mean loving some people more than others.

> GEORGE ORWELL (1903–50), British author. *Shooting an Elephant*, "Reflections on Gandhi" (1950).

87 Love is the cheapest of religions.

> CESARE PAVESE (1908–50), Italian poet, novelist, translator. *The Burning Brand: Diaries 1935–1950* (1952; tr. 1961), entry for 21 Dec. 1939.

88 People who are not in love fail to understand how an intelligent man can suffer because of a very ordinary woman. This is like being surprised that anyone should be stricken with cholera because of a creature so insignificant as the comma bacillus.

> MARCEL PROUST (1871–1922), French novelist. *Remembrance of Things Past*, vol. 2, "Swann's Way: Swann in Love" (1913; tr. by Scott Monkrieff, 1922).

89 In love, there is always one who kisses and one who offers the cheek.

> FRENCH PROVERB. George Bernard Shaw adapted this proverb in *Heartbreak House*, act 2: "One turns the cheek: the other kisses it. One provides the cash: the other spends it."

90 Love is the direct opposite of hate. By *definition* it's something you can't feel for more than a few minutes at a time, so what's all this bullshit about loving somebody for the rest of your life?

> JUDITH ROSSNER (b. 1935), U.S. author. *Nine Months in the Life of an Old Maid*, pt. 2 (1969).

91 Love, the quest; marriage, the conquest; divorce, the inquest.

> HELEN ROWLAND (1875–1950), U.S. journalist. *A Guide to Men*, "Syncopations" (1922).

92 Falling in love consists merely in uncorking the imagination and bottling the common-sense.

> HELEN ROWLAND (1875–1950), U.S. journalist. *A Guide to Men*, "Variations" (1922).

93 Many people when they fall in love look for a little haven of refuge from the world, where they can be sure of being admired when they are not admirable, and praised when they are not praiseworthy.

> BERTRAND RUSSELL (1872–1970), British philosopher, mathematician. *The Conquest of Happiness*, ch. 9 (1930).

94 Love does not consist in gazing at each other but in looking together in the same direction.

> ANTOINE DE SAINT-EXUPÉRY (1900–1944), French aviator, author. *Wind, Sand, and Stars*, ch. 8 (1939).

95 I regard as a mortal sin not only the lying of the senses in matters of love, but also the illusion which the senses seek to create where love is only partial. I say, I believe, that one must love with all of one's being, or else live, come what may, a life of complete chastity.

> GEORGE SAND (1804–76), French novelist. *The Story of My Life*, vol. 4, pt. 5, ch. 7 (1856). Men could never adhere to this principle, Sand added, but women, "helped by shame and public opinion," can easily accept the doctrine once convinced of its worth.

96 It is the privilege of those who fear love to murder those who do not fear it!

> MAY SARTON (b. 1912), U.S. poet, novelist. Hilary Stevens, in *Mrs. Stevens Hears the Mermaids Singing*, pt. 2 (1965).

97 Perhaps the old monks were right when they tried to root love out; perhaps the poets are right when they try to water it. It is a blood-red flower, with the colour of sin; but there is always the scent of a god about it.

> OLIVE SCHREINER (1855–1920), South African writer, feminist. *The Story of an African Farm*, pt. 2, ch. 8 (1883).

98 Men have died from time to time, and worms have eaten them, but not for love.

> WILLIAM SHAKESPEARE (1564–1616), English dramatist, poet. Rosalind, in *As You Like It*, act 4, sc. 1.

99 To say the truth, reason and love keep little company together now-a-days.

> WILLIAM SHAKESPEARE (1564–1616), English dramatist, poet. Bottom, in *A Midsummer Night's Dream*, act 3, sc. 1, on hearing Titania's declaration of love.

100 Love is a smoke made with the fume of sighs,
Being purged, a fire sparkling in lovers' eyes,
Being vexed, a sea nourished with lovers' tears.
What is it else? A madness most discreet,
A choking gall and a preserving sweet.

> WILLIAM SHAKESPEARE (1564–1616), English dramatist, poet. Romeo, in *Romeo and Juliet*, act 1, sc. 1.

101 Love is too young to know what conscience is.

> WILLIAM SHAKESPEARE (1564–1616), English dramatist, poet. *Sonnet* 151.

102 The fickleness of the women I love is only equalled by the infernal constancy of the women who love me.

> GEORGE BERNARD SHAW (1856–1950), Anglo-Irish playwright, critic. Charteris, in *The Philanderer*, act 2.

103 Love is free; to promise for ever to love the same woman is not less absurd than to promise to believe the same creed; such a vow in both cases excludes us from all inquiry.

> PERCY BYSSHE SHELLEY (1792–1822), English poet. *Even Love Is Sold*, a note from *Queen Mab* (1813).

104 Familiar acts are beautiful through love.

> PERCY BYSSHE SHELLEY (1792–1822), English poet. The Earth, in *Prometheus Unbound*, act 4.

105 When desire, having rejected reason and overpowered judgment which leads to right, is set in the direction of the pleasure which beauty can inspire, and when again under the influence of its kindred desires it is moved with violent motion towards the beauty of corporeal forms, it acquires a surname from this very violent motion, and is called love.

> SOCRATES (469–399 B.C.), Greek philosopher. Quoted in: Plato, *Phaedrus*.

106 True love makes the thought of death frequent, easy, without terrors; it merely becomes the standard of comparison, the price one would pay for many things.

> STENDHAL (1783–1842), French author. *De l'Amour*, "Various Fragments," sct. 46 (1822).

107 We often speak of love when we really should be speaking of the drive to dominate or to master, so as to confirm ourselves as active agents, in control of our own destinies and worthy of respect from others.

> THOMAS SZASZ (b. 1920), U.S. psychiatrist. *The Second Sin*, "Love" (1973).

108 I try to give to the poor people for love what the rich could get for money. No, I wouldn't touch a leper for a thousand pounds; yet I willingly cure him for the love of God.

> MOTHER TERESA (b. 1910), Albanian-born Roman Catholic missionary. *A Gift for God*, "Riches" (1975).

109 Love feels no burden, regards not labors, strives toward more than it attains, argues not of impossibility, since it believes that it may and can do all things. Therefore it avails for all things, and fulfils and accomplishes much where one not a lover falls and lies helpless.

> THOMAS à KEMPIS (1380–1471), German monk, mystic. *The Imitation of Christ*, pt. 3, ch. 6 (1471).

110 Love is life. All, everything that I understand, I understand only because I love. Everything is, everything exists, only because I love. Everything is united by it alone. Love is God, and to die means that I, a particle of love, shall return to the general and eternal source.

> LEO TOLSTOY (1828–1910), Russian novelist, philosopher. Prince Andrew, in *War and Peace*, bk. 12, ch. 4 (1868–69).

111 To love one person with a private love is poor and miserable: to love all is glorious.

> THOMAS TRAHERNE (1636–74), English clergyman, poet, mystic. *Centuries*, "Fourth Century," no. 69 (written c. 1672; first published 1908).

112 What is the main thing in love? to know and to hide. To know about the one you love and to hide that you love. At times the hiding (shame) overpowers the knowing (passion). The passion for the hidden—the passion for the revealed.

> MARINA TSVETAEVA (1892–1941), Russian poet. *The House at Old Pimen*, ch. 2 (1934; repr. in *A Captive Spirit: Selected Prose*, ed. and tr. by J. Marin King, 1980), on her youthful love for a girl.

113 For it is the suffering flesh, it is suffering, it is death, that lovers perpetuate upon the earth. Love is at once the brother, son, and father of death, which is its sister, mother, and daughter. And thus it is that in the depth of love there is a depth of eternal despair, out of which springs hope and consolation.

> MIGUEL DE UNAMUNO (1864–1936), Spanish philosophical writer. *The Tragic Sense of Life*, ch. 7 (1913).

114 An affair wants to spill, to share its glory with the world. No act is so private it does not seek applause.

> JOHN UPDIKE (b. 1932), U.S. author, critic. *Couples*, ch. 2 (1968).

115 Love is an act of endless forgiveness, a tender look which becomes a habit.

> PETER USTINOV (b. 1921), British actor, writer, director. *Christian Science Monitor* (Boston, 9 Dec. 1958).

116 I've only been in love with a beer bottle and a mirror.

> SID VICIOUS (1957–79), British punk rocker. *Sounds* (London, 9 Oct. 1976).

117 If somebody says, "I love you," to me, I feel as though I had a pistol pointed at my head. What can anybody reply under such conditions but that which the pistol-holder requires? "I love you, *too*."

> KURT VONNEGUT, JR. (b. 1922), U.S. novelist. *Wampeters,*

Foma and Granfalloons, "Address at Dedication of Wheaton College Library, 1973" (1974).

118 Fantasy love is much better than reality love. Never doing it is very exciting. The most exciting attractions are between two opposites that never meet.

> ANDY WARHOL (1928–87), U.S. pop artist . *From A to B and Back Again*, ch. 3 (1975).

119 A man in love is like a clipped coupon—it's time to cash in.

> MAE WEST (1892–1980), U.S. screen actor. *On Sex, Health and ESP*, "That Four-Letter Word!" (1975).

120 It has ever been since time began,
And ever will be, till time lose breath,
That love is a mood—no more—to man,
And love to a woman is life or death.

> ELLA WHEELER WILCOX (1855–1919), U.S. poet, journalist. *Blind*, st. 1.

121 When one is in love, one always begins by deceiving one's self, and one always ends by deceiving others. That is what the world calls a romance.

> OSCAR WILDE (1854–1900), Anglo-Irish playwright, author. Lord Henry, in *The Picture of Dorian Gray*, ch. 4 (1891). The same words reappeared spoken by Lord Illingworth in *A Woman of No Importance*, act 3.

122 Oh, Jacques, we're used to each other, we're a pair of captive hawks caught in the same cage, and so we've grown used to each other. That's what passes for love at this dim, shadowy end of the Camino Real.

> TENNESSEE WILLIAMS (1914–83), U.S. dramatist. Marguerite Gautier to Jacques Casanova, in *Camino Real*, Block 15.

123 However it is debased or misinterpreted, love is a redemptive feature. To focus on one individual so that their desires become superior to yours is a very cleansing experience.

> JEANETTE WINTERSON (b. 1959), British author. *Times* (London, 26 Aug. 1992).

124 For love . . . has two faces; one white, the other black; two bodies; one smooth, the other hairy. It has two hands, two feet, two tails, two, indeed, of every member and each one is the exact opposite of the other. Yet, so strictly are they joined together that you cannot separate them.

> VIRGINIA WOOLF (1882–1941), British novelist. *Orlando*, ch. 2 (1928).

125 A man falls in love through his eyes, a woman through her ears.

> WOODROW WYATT (b. 1918), British journalist. *To the Point*, "The Ears Have It" (1981). Wyatt's reasoning, apropos of women, was that "what is said to them and what they believe about a man's status is usually more important than the superficiality of good looks."

126 A pity beyond all telling
Is hid in the heart of love.

> W. B. YEATS (1865–1939), Irish poet. *The Pity of Love*

See also La Rochefoucauld on ABSENCE; Strindberg on ANTIPATHY; Shelley, Viorst on COMPATIBILITY; Marvell on DEATH AND DYING; Wilde on FIDELITY; De Vries on FELLOWSHIP, HUMAN; INFATUATION; Saint-Expéry on FLIRTING; Shaw on FOOD AND EATING; HEARTBREAK; Freud on ILLNESS;INFATUATION; Bible Hebrew on JEALOUSY; LOVERS; Russell on MARRIAGE. MARRIAGE AND LOVE; Keats on MARTYRDOM; Goldsmith on PASSION; Pascal on REASON; La Rochefoucauld on RELATIONSHIPS.

LOVE, ENDED

1 A bizarre sensation pervades a relationship of pretense. No truth seems true. A simple morning's greeting and response appear loaded with innuendo and fraught with implications. . . . Each nicety becomes more sterile and each withdrawal more permanent.

> MAYA ANGELOU (b. 1928), U.S. author. *Singin' and Swingin' and Gettin' Merry Like Christmas*, ch. 5 (1976).

2 I leave before being left. I decide.

> BRIGITTE BARDOT (b. 1933), French screen actor. Quoted in: *Newsweek* (New York, 5 March 1973).

3 When once estrangement has arisen between those who truly love each other, everything seems to widen the breach.

> MARY ELIZABETH BRADDON (1837–1915), English writer. *Run to Earth*, ch. 8 (1868).

4 And I shall find some girl perhaps,
And a better one than you,
With eyes as wise, but kindlier,
And lips as soft, but true,
And I daresay she will do.

> RUPERT BROOKE (1887–1915), British poet. *The Chilterns*.

5 Infinite hungers leap no more
In the chance swaying of your dress;
And love has changed to kindliness.

> RUPERT BROOKE (1887–1915), British poet. *Kindliness*.

6 The best way will be to avoid each other without appearing to do so—or if we jostle, at any rate not to bite.

> LORD BYRON (1788–1824), English poet. Letter, 25 April 1814, referring to his affair with Lady Caroline Lamb (published in *Byron's Letters and Journals*, vol. 4, ed. by Leslie Marchand, 1975).

7 It's afterwards you realize that the feeling of happiness you had with a man didn't necessarily prove that you loved him.

> MARGUERITE DURAS (b. 1914), French author, filmmaker. *Practicalities*, "The Chimneys of *India Song*" (1987; tr. 1990).

8 But that intimacy of mutual embarrassment, in which each feels that the other is feeling something, having once existed, its effect is not to be done away with.

> GEORGE ELIOT (1819–80), English novelist, editor. *Middlemarch*, bk. 3, ch. 27 (1871), of Rosamund and Lydgate.

9 Two separate, distinct personalities, not separate at all, but inextricably bound, soul and body and mind, to each other, how did we get so far apart so fast?

> JUDITH GUEST (b. 1936), U.S. author. *Ordinary People*, ch. 19 (1976).

10 There are few people who are not ashamed of their love affairs when the infatuation is over.

> FRANÇOIS, DUC DE LA ROCHEFOUCAULD (1613–80), French writer, moralist. *Sentences et Maximes Morales*, no. 71 (1678).

11 Were we positive, eager, real—alive? No, we were not. We were a nothingness shot with gleams of what might be.

> KATHERINE MANSFIELD (1888–1923), New Zealand-born British author. Letter, 11 Oct. 1922, to her husband, John Middleton Murry.

12   After all, my erstwhile dear,
My no longer cherished,
Need we say it was not love,
Now that love is perished?

> EDNA ST. VINCENT MILLAY (1892–1950), U.S. poet. *Passer Mortuus Est.*

13   I was never one to patiently pick up broken fragments and glue them together again and tell myself that the mended whole was as good as new. What is broken is broken—and I'd rather remember it as it was at its best than mend it and see the broken places as long as I lived.

> MARGARET MITCHELL (1900–1949), U.S. novelist. Rhett Butler's farewell to Scarlett O'Hara, in *Gone with the Wind*, vol. 2, pt. 5, ch. 63 (1936). The last words of his speech are: "I wish I could care what you do or where you go, but I can't. My dear, I don't give a damn."

14   I know a love may be revived which absence, inconstancy, or even infidelity has extinguished, but there is no returning from a *dégoût* given by satiety.

> LADY MARY WORTLEY MONTAGU (1689–1762), English society figure, letter writer. Letter, 25 April 1710, to her future husband (published in *Selected Letters*, ed. by Robert Halsband, 1970).

15   Falling out of love is chiefly a matter of *forgetting* how charming someone is.

> IRIS MURDOCH (b. 1919), British novelist, philosopher. Anderson Palmer, in *A Severed Head*, ch. 24 (1961).

16   In every question and every remark tossed back and forth between lovers who have not played out the last fugue, there is one question and it is this: "Is there someone new?"

> EDNA O'BRIEN (b. 1936), Irish author. *Lantern Slides*, "Long Distance" (1990).

17   In a separation it is the one who is not really in loved who says the more tender things.

> MARCEL PROUST (1871–1922), French novelist. *Remembrance of Things Past*, vol. 10, "The Captive," pt. 2, ch. 3 (1923; tr. by Ronald and Colette Cortie, 1988).

18   We who were loved will never
unlive that crippling fever.

> ADRIENNE RICH (b. 1929), U.S. poet. "After a Sentence in 'Malte Laurids Brigge,'" in *Snapshots of a Daughter-in-Law* (1963).

19   When love begins to sicken and decay
It useth an enforcèd ceremony

> WILLIAM SHAKESPEARE (1564–1616), English dramatist, poet. Brutus, in *Julius Caesar*, act 4, sc. 2.

20   She's gone. I am abused, and my relief
Must be to loathe her.

> WILLIAM SHAKESPEARE (1564–1616), English dramatist, poet. Othello, in *Othello*, act 3, sc. 3.

21   In love, unlike most other passions, the recollection of what you have had and lost is always better than what you can hope for in the future.

> STENDHAL (1783–1842), French author. *De l'Amour*, ch. 1 (1822).

22   I hated her now with a hatred more fatal than indifference because it was the other side of love.

> J. AUGUST STRINDBERG (1849–1912), Swedish dramatist, novelist, poet. *A Madman's Defense*, pt. 4, ch. 10 (1968).

23   When a man has once loved a woman, he will do anything for her, except continue to love her.

> OSCAR WILDE (1854–1900), Anglo-Irish playwright, author. Mrs. Cheveley, in *An Ideal Husband*, act 3

24   There is always something ridiculous about the emotions of people whom one has ceased to love.

> OSCAR WILDE (1854–1900), Anglo-Irish playwright, author. *The Picture of Dorian Gray*, ch. 7 (1891).

See also Lessing on HATE.

LOVE, FIRST

1   In her first passion woman loves her lover,
In all the others all she loves is love.

> LORD BYRON (1788–1824), English poet. *Don Juan*, cto. 3, st. 3. The words are from La Rochefoucauld, *Maximes*, no. 471 (1678).

2   We love but once, for once only are we perfectly equipped for loving.

> CYRIL CONNOLLY (1903–74), British critic. *The Unquiet Grave*, pt. 1 (1944; rev. 1951).

3   The magic of first love is our ignorance that it can ever end.

> BENJAMIN DISRAELI (1804–81), English statesman, author. *Henrietta Temple*, pt. 4, ch. 1 (1837).

4   First love is only a little foolishness and a lot of curiosity.

> GEORGE BERNARD SHAW (1856–1950), Anglo-Irish playwright, critic. Broadbent, in *John Bull's Other Island*, act 4.

LOVE AT FIRST SIGHT

1   The advantage of love at first sight is that it delays a second sight.

> NATALIE CLIFFORD BARNEY (1876–1972), U.S.-born French author. Quoted in: *Adam*, no. 299, "Samples from Almost Illegible Notebooks" (London, 1962).

2   I do not think that what is called *Love at first sight* is so great an absurdity as it is sometimes imagined to be. We generally make up our minds beforehand to the sort of person we should like, grave or gay, black, brown, or fair; with golden tresses or raven locks;—and when we meet with a complete example of the qualities we admire, the bargain is soon struck.

> WILLIAM HAZLITT (1778–1830), English essayist. *Table Talk*, vol. 2, "On the Knowledge of Character" (1822).

3   Where both deliberate, the love is slight:
Who ever lov'd, that lov'd not at first sight?

> CHRISTOPHER MARLOWE (1564–1593), English dramatist, poet. *Hero and Leander*, "First Sestiad."

4   Mine ear is much enamoured of thy note;
So is mine eye enthrallèd to thy shape;

And thy fair virtue's force perforce doth move me
On the first view to say, to swear, I love thee.

WILLIAM SHAKESPEARE (1564–1616), English dramatist, poet.
Titania to Bottom, while he is cursed with an ass's head, in *A
Midsummer Night's Dream,* act 3, sc. 1.

See also Shakespeare on ENGAGEMENT.

LOVERS

1   In every loving woman there is a priestess of the
past—a pious guardian of some affection, of which the
object has disappeared.

HENRI-FRÉDÉRIC AMIEL (1821–81), Swiss philosopher, poet.
Journal Intime (1882; tr. by Mrs. Humphrey Ward, 1892), entry
for 11 Dec. 1872.

2   One can be a soldier without dying, and a lover
without sighing.

SIR EDWIN ARNOLD (1832–1904), British dramatist, poet. Saka-
mune, in *Adzuma,* act 2, sc. 5.

3   Lovers should also have their days off.

NATALIE CLIFFORD BARNEY (1876–1972), U.S.-born French
author. Quoted in: George Wickes, *The Amazon of Letters,* ch.
10 (1976).

4   The lover of life makes the whole world into his
family, just as the lover of the fair sex creates his from all
the lovely women he has found, from those that could be
found, and those who are impossible to find.

CHARLES BAUDELAIRE (1821–67), French poet. "The Painter of
Modern life," sct. 3, in *L'Art Romantique* (1869; repr. in *Selected
Writings on Art and Artists,* ed. by P. E. Charvet, 1972).

5   There exists, between people in love, a kind of capital held by each. This is not just a stock of affects or
pleasure, but also the possibility of playing double or
quits with the share you hold in the other's heart.

JEAN BAUDRILLARD (b. 1929), French semiologist. *Cool Memories,* ch. 3 (1987; tr. 1990).

6   Love ceases to be a pleasure, when it ceases to be a
secret.

APHRA BEHN (1640–89), English playwright, poet. *The Lover's
Watch,* "Four O'Clock" (1686).

7   Pity the selfishness of lovers: it is brief, a forlorn
hope; it is impossible.

ELIZABETH BOWEN (1899–1973), Anglo-Irish novelist. *The
Death of the Heart,* pt. 2, ch. 4 (1938).

8   When Death to either shall come—
I pray it be first to me.

ROBERT BRIDGES (1844–1930), British poet. *When Death to
Either Shall Come.*

9   A man can go from being a lover to being a stranger
in three moves flat . . . but a woman under the guise of
friendship will engage in acts of duplicity which come to
light very much later. There are different species of self-
justification.

ANITA BROOKNER (b. 1938), British novelist, art historian. *Novelists in Interview* (ed. by John Haffenden, 1985).

10   Never the time and the place
And the loved one all together!

ROBERT BROWNING (1812–89), English poet. *Never the Time
and the Place.*

11   Nay but you, who do not love her,
Is she not pure gold, my mistress?

ROBERT BROWNING (1812–89), English poet. *Song.*

12   Lovers may be—and indeed generally are—enemies, but they never can be friends, because there must
always be a spice of jealousy and a something of Self in
all their speculations.

LORD BYRON (1788–1824), English poet. Letter, 1 Dec. 1822
(published in *Byron's Letters and Journals,* vol. 10, ed. by Leslie
A. Marchand, 1973–81).

13   One who has not only the four S's, which are
required in every good lover, but even the whole alphabet;
as for example . . . Agreeable, Bountiful, Constant, Dutiful, Easy, Faithful, Gallant, Honorable, Ingenious, Kind,
Loyal, Mild, Noble, Officious, Prudent, Quiet, Rich,
Secret, True, Valiant, Wise; the X indeed, is too harsh a
letter to agree with him, but he is Young and Zealous.

MIGUEL DE CERVANTES (1547–1616), Spanish writer. Camilla's
maid, Leonela, in *Don Quixote,* pt. 1, bk. 4, ch. 7 (1605; tr. by P.
Motteux). The "four S's" were "sightly, sprightly, sincere and
secret."

14   When a man and a woman have an overwhelming
passion for each other, it seems to me, in spite of such
obstacles dividing them as parents or husband, that they
belong to each other in the *name of Nature,* and are lovers
by *Divine right,* in spite of human convention or the laws.

SÉBASTIEN-ROCH NICOLAS DE CHAMFORT (1741–94), French
writer, wit. *Maxims and Considerations,* vol. 2, no. 357 (1796; tr.
1926).

15   There is no pain equal to that which two lovers can
inflict on one another. This should be made clear to all
who contemplate such a union. The avoidance of this
pain is the beginning of wisdom, for it is strong enough
to contaminate the rest of our lives.

CYRIL CONNOLLY (1903–74), British critic. *The Unquiet Grave,*
pt. 1 (1944; rev. 1951).

16   Busy old fool, unruly Sun,
Why dost thou thus,
Through windows and through curtains call on us?
Must to thy motions lovers' seasons run?

JOHN DONNE (c. 1572–1631), English divine, metaphysical
poet. *The Sun Rising.*

17   All mankind love a lover.

RALPH WALDO EMERSON (1803–82), U.S. essayist, poet,
philosopher. *Essays,* "Love" (First Series, 1841).

18   A lover, when he is admitted to cards, ought to be
solemnly silent, and observe the motions of his mistress.
He must laugh when she laughs, sigh when she sighs. In
short, he should be the shadow of her mind. A lady, in the
presence of her lover, should never want a looking-glass;
as a beau, in the presence of his looking-glass, never
wants a mistress.

HENRY FIELDING (1707–54), English novelist, dramatist. Lady
Matchless, in *Love in Several Masques,* act 2, sc. 11.

19 Lovers who love truly do not write down their happiness.

ANATOLE FRANCE (1844–1924), French author. *The Crime of Sylvestre Bonnard*, "The Log," 30 Nov. 1859 (1881).

20 O'er her warm cheek and rising bosom move
The bloom of young Desire and purple light of
Love.

THOMAS GRAY (1716–71), English poet. *The Progress of Poesy*, pt. 1, sct. 3.

21 Shall the dog lie where the deer once crouched?

NELL GWYNN (?1650–87), English actor, mistress of Charles II. Her alleged rejection of a lover after Charles II's death, 1685.

22 A lover without indiscretion is no lover at all. Circumspection and devotion are a contradiction in terms.

THOMAS HARDY (1840–1928), English novelist, poet. Ladywell, in *The Hand of Ethelberta*, ch. 20 (1875).

23 We can recognize the dawn and the decline of love by the uneasiness we feel when alone together.

JEAN DE LA BRUYÉRE (1645–96), French writer, moralist. *Characters*, "Of the Heart," aph. 33 (1688).

24 One seeks to make the loved one entirely happy, or, if that cannot be, entirely wretched.

JEAN DE LA BRUYÉRE (1645–96), French writer, moralist. *Characters*, "Of the Heart," aph. 39 (1688).

25 The more one loves a mistress, the more one is ready to hate her.

FRANÇOIS, DUC DE LA ROCHEFOUCAULD (1613–80), French writer, moralist. *Sentences et Maximes Morales*, no. 111 (1678).

26 My God, these folks don't know how to love—that's why they love so easily.

D. H. LAWRENCE (1885–1930), British author. Letter, 8 May 1909 (published in *The Letters of D. H. Lawrence*, vol. 1, ed. by James T. Boulton, 1979).

27 They are a curious mixture of Spanish tradition, American imitation, and insular limitation. This explains why they never catch on to themselves.

HELEN LAWRENSON (1904–82), U.S. author. "Latins Are Lousy Lovers," in *Esquire* (New York, Oct. 1939).

28 Queen Guenever, for whom I make here a little mention, that while she lived she was a true lover, and therefore she had a good end.

SIR THOMAS MALORY (c. 1430–71), English author. *Le Morte d'Arthur*, bk. 18, ch. 25 (1485).

29 I would not miss your face, your neck, your hands, your limbs, your bosom and certain other of your charms. Indeed, not to become boring by naming them all, I could do without you, Chloe, altogether.

MARTIAL (43–104), Roman poet. *Epigrams*, bk. 3, no. 53.

30 These two
Imparadised in one another's arms,
The happier Eden, shall enjoy their fill
Of bliss on bliss.

JOHN MILTON (1608–74), English poet. The devil, in *Paradise Lost*, bk. 4, of Adam and Eve.

31 Every man needs two women, a quiet home-maker, and a thrilling nymph.

IRIS MURDOCH (b. 1919), British novelist, philosopher. Gildas Hearne, in *The Message to the Planet*, pt. 1 (1989).

32 Scratch a lover, and find a foe.

DOROTHY PARKER (1893–1967), U.S. humorous writer. *Ballade of a Great Weariness*.

33 An orange on the table,
Your dress on the rug,
And you in my bed,
Sweet present of the present,
Cool of night,
Warmth of my life.

JACQUES PRÉVERT (1900–77), French poet. *Paroles*, "Alicante" (1946; tr. by Lawrence Ferlinghetti, 1958).

34 The difference is wide that the sheets will not decide.

ENGLISH PROVERB. Collected in: John Ray, *English Proverbs* (1670).

35 Between lovers a little confession is a dangerous thing.

HELEN ROWLAND (1875–1950), U.S. journalist. *Reflections of a Bachelor Girl*, (1903).

36 It is easier to keep half a dozen lovers guessing than to keep one lover after he has stopped guessing.

HELEN ROWLAND (1875–1950), U.S. journalist. *A Guide to Men*, "Third Interlude" (1922).

37 'Tis the most commonplace thing in the world, to love one man to distraction and to fuck frenziedly with another; you don't give your heart to him, just your body .... There are two manners of loving a man: morally and physically.

MARQUIS DE SADE (1740–1814), French author. Duvergier, in *L'Histoire de Juliette, ou les Prospérités du Vice*, pt. 1 (1797).

38 Age cannot wither her, nor custom stale
Her infinite variety. Other women cloy
The appetites they feed, but she makes hungry
Where most she satisfies.

WILLIAM SHAKESPEARE (1564–1616), English dramatist, poet. Enobarbus, in *Antony and Cleopatra*, act 2, sc. 2, of Cleopatra.

39 We that are true lovers run into strange capers.

WILLIAM SHAKESPEARE (1564–1616), English dramatist, poet. Touchstone, in *As You Like It*, act 2, sc. 4.

40 Modesty is a quality in a lover more praised by the women than liked.

RICHARD BRINSLEY SHERIDAN (1751–1816), Anglo-Irish dramatist. Sir Lucius O'Trigger, in *The Rivals*, act 2, sc. 2.

41 No one worth possessing
Can be quite possessed.

SARA TEASDALE (1884–1933), U.S. poet. *Advice to a Girl*.

42 You are my lover and I am your mistress and kingdoms and empires and governments have tottered and succumbed before now to that mighty combination.

VIOLET TREFUSIS (1894–1972), British novelist. Last words of letter March 1919 to author and critic Vita Sackville-West (published in *Letters to Vita Sackville-West*, 1989).

43 I'm a bit of a P. T. Barnum. I make stars out of everyone.

> DONALD TRUMP (b. 1946), U.S. businessman. On the women in his life. Quoted in: *Observer* (London, 7 July 1991).

44 There's nothing in the world like the devotion of a married woman. It's a thing no married man knows anything about.

> OSCAR WILDE (1854–1900), Anglo-Irish playwright, author. Cecil Graham, in *Lady Windermere's Fan*, act 3.

45 Mistresses are like books; if you pore upon them too much, they doze you and make you unfit for company; but if used discreetly, you are the fitter for conversation by 'em.

> WILLIAM WYCHERLEY (1640–1716), English dramatist. Harcourt, in *The Country Wife*, act 1.

See also Hugo on ABSENCE; France on DIARIES; Stendhal on MEN; Byron on MEN AND WOMEN; Catullus on PROMISES; Terence on QUARRELS; Walsh on SUICIDE.

LOYALTY

1 Total loyalty is possible only when fidelity is emptied of all concrete content, from which changes of mind might naturally arise.

> HANNAH ARENDT (1906–75), German-born U.S. political philosopher. *The Origins of Totalitarianism*, ch. 10, sct. 1 (1951).

2 Intreat me not to leave thee, or to return from following after thee: for whither thou goest, I will go; and where thou lodgest, I will lodge: thy people shall be my people, and thy God my God.

> BIBLE, HEBREW. Ruth to Naomi, in *Ruth* 1:16.

3 No man can serve two masters.

> BIBLE: NEW TESTAMENT. Jesus, in *Matthew* 6:24.

4 I'll take fifty percent efficiency to get one hundred percent loyalty.

> SAMUEL GOLDWYN (1882–1974), U.S. film producer. Remark to personnel who questioned his authority. Quoted in: Arthur Marx, *Goldwyn: The Man behind the Myth*, ch. 27 (1976).

5 We are all the President's men.

> HENRY KISSINGER (b. 1923), U.S. Republican politician, secretary of state. Said in 1970, after the invasion of Cambodia. Quoted in: *Sunday Times* (London, 4 May 1975).

6 Histories are more full of examples of the fidelity of dogs than of friends.

> ALEXANDER POPE (1688–1744), English satirical poet. Letter, 9 Oct. 1709.

7 Had I but served my God with half the zeal
I served my King, He would not in mine age
Have left me naked to mine enemies.

> WILLIAM SHAKESPEARE (1564–1616), English dramatist, poet. Cardinal Wolsey, in *Henry VIII*, act 3, sc. 2. These words, spoken in the play to Thomas Cromwell, were in fact recorded as Wolsey's dying words in Raphael Holinshed, *Chronicles* (1577), one of Shakespeare's main sources, where they appear in the form: "If I had served God as diligently as I have done the King, He would not have given me over in my grey hairs."

8 If you are not too long, I will wait here for you all my life.

> OSCAR WILDE (1854–1900), Anglo-Irish playwright, author. Gwendolen, in *The Importance of Being Earnest*, act 4.

See also FIDELITY; Himmler on HONOR; Shelley on LOVE; Elizabeth I on ROYALTY.

LUCK

1 The race is not to the swift, nor the battle to the strong, neither yet bread to the wise, nor yet riches to men of understanding, nor yet favour to men of skill; but time and chance happeneth to them all.

> BIBLE, HEBREW. *Ecclesiastes* 9:11.

2 There is death in the pot.

> BIBLE, HEBREW. *2 Kings* 4:40.

3 The Goddess Fortune is the devil's servant, ready to kiss any one's arse.

> WILLIAM BLAKE (1757–1827), English poet, painter, engraver. Notes on illustrations to Dante, "The Goddess Fortune" (1825–27; repr. in *Complete Writings*, ed. by Geoffrey Keynes, 1957).

4 What we call luck is the inner man externalized. We make things happen to us.

> ROBERTSON DAVIES (b. 1913), Canadian novelist, journalist. Simon Darcourt, in *What's Bred in the Bone*, pt. 1, "Who Asked the Question?" (1985).

5 Chance is the one thing you can't buy.... You have to pay for it and you have to pay for it with your life, spending a lot of time, you pay for it with time, not the wasting of time but the spending of time.

> ROBERT DOISNEAU (b. 1912), French photographer. *Weekend Guardian* (London, 4 April 1992).

6 There is no chance, and no anarchy, in the universe. All is system and gradation. Every god is there sitting in his sphere.

> RALPH WALDO EMERSON (1803–82), U.S. essayist, poet, philosopher. *The Conduct of Life*, "Illusions" (1860).

7 Chance does not speak essentially through words nor can it be seen in their convolution. It is the eruption of language, its sudden appearance. . . . It's not a night atwinkle with stars, an illuminated sleep, nor a drowsy vigil. It is the very edge of consciousness.

> MICHEL FOUCAULT (1926–84), French essayist, philosopher. *Death and the Labyrinth: The World of Raymond Roussel*, ch. 3 (1963; tr. 1986).

8 Some folk want their luck buttered.

> THOMAS HARDY (1840–1928), English novelist, poet. Mrs. Cuxcom, in *The Mayor of Casterbridge*, ch. 13 (1886).

9 Watch out w'en you'er gittin all you want. Fattenin' hogs ain't in luck.

> JOEL CHANDLER HARRIS (1848–1908), U.S. journalist. *Uncle Remus: His Songs and His Sayings*, "Plantation Proverbs" (1880).

10 In short, Luck's always to blame.

> JEAN DE LA FONTAINE (1621–95), French poet, fabulist. Moral of fable, "La Fortune et le Jeune Enfant," in *Fables*, bk. 5, no. 11 (1678–79).

11 The worst cynicism: a belief in luck.

JOYCE CAROL OATES (b. 1938), U.S. author. *Do What You Will*, pt. 2, ch. 15 (1970).

12 When God throws the dice are loaded.
GREEK PROVERB.

13 Fortune's a right whore.
If she give ought, she deals it in small parcels,
That she may take away all at one swoop.
JOHN WEBSTER (1580–1625), English dramatist. Lodovico, in *The White Devil*, act 1, sc. 1.

See also MISFORTUNE.

LUST

1 Lust is a mysterious wound in the side of humanity; or rather, at the very source of its life! To confound this lust in man with that desire which unites the sexes is like confusing a tumor with the very organ which it devours, a tumor whose very deformity horribly reproduces the shape.
GEORGES BERNANOS (1888–1948), French novelist, political writer. *The Diary of a Country Priest*, ch. 4 (1936).

2 Abstinence sows sand all over
The ruddy limbs and flaming hair,
But desire gratified
Plants fruits of life and beauty there.
WILLIAM BLAKE (1757–1827), English poet, painter, engraver. *Manuscript Notebooks*, "Poems and Fragments," no. 40 (1793; in *Complete Writings*, ed. by Geoffrey Keynes, 1957).

3 When Love's delirium haunts the glowing mind,
Limping Decorum lingers far behind.
LORD BYRON (1788–1824), English poet. *Answer to Some Elegant Verses Sent by a Friend.*

4 I have looked on a lot of women with lust. I've committed adultery in my heart many times. God recognizes I will do this and forgives me.
JIMMY CARTER (b. 1924), U.S. Democratic politician, president. Interview in *Playboy* (Chicago, Nov. 1976), during the presidential campaign against Gerald Ford.

5 He is every woman's man and every man's woman.
GAIUS SCRIBONIUS CURIO (d. 53 B.C.), Roman consul. Of Julius Caesar. Quoted in: Suetonius, *Lives of the Caesars*, "Julius," sct. 52.

6 What most men desire is a virgin who is a whore.
EDWARD DAHLBERG (1900–77), U.S. author, critic. *Reasons of the Heart*, "On Lust" (1965).

7 Down, wanton, down! Have you no shame
That at the whisper of Love's name,
Or Beauty's, presto! up you raise
Your angry head and stand at gaze?
ROBERT GRAVES (1895–1985), British poet, novelist. *Down, Wanton, Down!*

8 People will insist on treating the *mons Veneris* as though it were Mount Everest. Too silly!
ALDOUS HUXLEY (1894–1963), British author. Mary Amberly, in *Eyeless in Gaza*, ch. 30 (1936).

9 But the touch or company of any man whatsoever stirreth up their heat, which in their solitude was hushed and quiet, and lay as cinders raked up in ashes.
MICHEL DE MONTAIGNE (1533–92), French essayist. *Essays*, bk. 3, ch. 5, "Upon Some Verses of Virgil" (1588; tr. by John Florio).

10 If you live in rock and roll, as I do, you see the reality of sex, of male lust and women being aroused by male lust. It attracts women. It doesn't repel them.
CAMILLE PAGLIA (b. 1947), U.S. author, critic, educator. Interview in *Playboy* (Chicago, Oct. 1991; repr. in *Sex, Art, and American Culture*, "The Rape Debate," 1992).

11 Lust is to the other passions what the nervous fluid is to life; it supports them all, lends strength to them all . . . ambition, cruelty, avarice, revenge, are all founded on lust.
MARQUIS DE SADE (1740–1814), French author. Juliette, in *L'Histoire de Juliette, ou les Prospérités du Vice*, pt. 2 (1797).

12 Lust's passion will be served; it demands, it militates, it tyrannizes.
MARQUIS DE SADE (1740–1814), French author. Noirceuil, in *L'Histoire de Juliette, ou les Prospérités du Vice*, pt. 2 (1797).

13 This is the monstruosity in love, lady, that the will is infinite and the execution confined; that the desire is boundless, and the act a slave to limit.
WILLIAM SHAKESPEARE (1564–1616), English dramatist, poet. Troilus, in *Troilus and Cressida*, act 3, sc. 2.

14 It is no longer enough to be lusty. One must be a sexual gourmet.
GEORGE F. WILL (b. 1941), U.S. political columnist. *The Pursuit of Happiness, and Other Sobering Thoughts*, "The Ploy of Sex" (1978; first published 1974).

LUXURY

1 A slight daily unconscious luxury is hardly ever wanting to the dwellers in civilisation; like the gentle air of a genial climate, it is a perpetual minute enjoyment.
WALTER BAGEHOT (1826–77), English economist, critic. "The Waverley Novels" (1858; repr. in *Literary Studies*, vol. 2, 1878).

2 When you're not used to comfort and good things to eat, you're intoxicated by them in no time. Truth's only too pleased to leave you. Very little's ever needed for Truth to let go of you. And after all, you're not really very keen to keep hold of it.
LOUIS-FERDINAND CÉLINE (1894–1961), French author. The narrator (Ferdinand Bardamu), in *Journey to the End of the Night* (1932; tr. 1934; 1966 ed., p. 350).

3 The saddest thing I can imagine is to get used to luxury.
CHARLIE CHAPLIN (1889–1977), British comic actor, filmmaker. *My Autobiography*, ch. 22 (1964).

4 It is too great comfort which turns a man against himself. Life is most readily renounced at the time and among the classes where it is least harsh.
ÉMILE DURKHEIM (1858–1917), French sociologist. *Suicide*, bk. 3, ch. 1, sct. 1 (1897; tr. 1951).

5 The lust for comfort, that stealthy thing that enters the house a guest, and then becomes a host, and then a master.

> KAHLIL GIBRAN (1883–1931), Lebanese poet, novelist. *The Prophet*, "On Houses" (1923).

6 Give us the luxuries of life, and we will dispense with its necessaries.

> J. L. MOTLEY (1814–77), U.S. historian. Quoted in: Oliver Wendell Holmes, Sr., *The Autocrat of the Breakfast-Table*, ch. 6 (1858).

7 Most of the luxuries and many of the so-called comforts of life are not only not indispensable, but positive hindrances to the elevaton of mankind.

> HENRY DAVID THOREAU (1817–62), U.S. philosopher, author, naturalist. *Walden*, "Economy" (1854).

See also Shelley on WEALTH.

MACHINERY

1 Freedom from labor itself is not new; it once belonged among the most firmly established privileges of the few. In this instance, it seems as though scientific progress and technical developments had been only taken advantage of to achieve something about which all former ages dreamed but which none had been able to realize.

> HANNAH ARENDT (1906–75), German-born U.S. political philosopher. *The Human Condition*, Prologue (1958).

2 Man will never be enslaved by machinery if the man tending the machine be paid enough.

> KAREL CAPEK (1890–1938), Czech writer. Quoted in obituary, *News Chronicle* (27 Dec. 1938).

3 For man is not the creature and product of Mechanism; but, in a far truer sense, its creator and producer.

> THOMAS CARLYLE (1795–1881), Scottish essayist, historian. *Signs of the Times* , in *Edinburgh Review*, no. 98.(1829, repr. in Critical and Miscellaneous Essays, 1838).

4 The machine has had a pernicious effect upon virtue, pity, and love, and young men used to machines which induce inertia, and fear, are near impotents.

> EDWARD DAHLBERG (1900–1977), U.S. author, critic. *Alms for Oblivion*, "No Love and No Thanks" (1964).

5 By his machines man can dive and remain under water like a shark; can fly like a hawk in the air; can see atoms like a gnat; can see the system of the universe of Uriel, the angel of the sun; can carry whatever loads a ton of coal can lift; can knock down cities with his fist of gunpowder; can recover the history of his race by the medals which the deluge, and every creature, civil or savage or brute, has involuntarily dropped of its existence; and divine the future possibility of the planet and its inhabitants by his perception of laws of nature.

> RALPH WALDO EMERSON (1803–82), U.S. essayist, poet, philosopher. *Letters and Social Aims*, "Resources" (1876).

6 As machines become more and more efficient and perfect, so it will become clear that *imperfection is the greatness of man*.

> ERNST FISCHER (1899–1972), Austrian editor, poet, critic. *The Necessity of Art*, ch. 5 (1959; tr. 1963).

7 Nature is a self-made machine, more perfectly automated than any automated machine. To create something in the image of nature is to create a machine, and it was by learning the inner working of nature that man became a builder of machines.

> ERIC HOFFER (1902–1983), U.S. philosopher. *Reflections on the Human Condition*, aph. 6 (1973). See Hoffer on ANIMALS.

8 I'm afraid for all those who'll have the bread snatched from their mouths by these machines. . . . What business has science and capitalism got, bringing all these new inventions into the works, before society has produced a generation educated up to using them!

> HENRIK IBSEN (1828–1906), Norwegian dramatist. Aune, in *Pillars of Society*, act 2.

9 But remember please, the Law by which we live,
We are not built to comprehend a lie,
We can neither love nor pity nor forgive.
If you make a slip in handling us you die.

> RUDYARD KIPLING (1865–1936), British author, poet. *The Secret of the Machines*.

10 If the world *would only build temples to Machinery* in the abstract then everything would be perfect. The painter and sculptor would have plenty to do, and could, in complete peace and suitably honoured, pursue their trade without further trouble.

> WYNDHAM LEWIS (1882–1957), British author, painter. *The Caliph's Design*, "Machinery and Lions" (1920).

11 Machines were, it may be said, the weapon employed by the capitalists to quell the revolt of specialized labor.

> KARL MARX (1818–83), German political theorist, social philosopher. *The Poverty of Philosophy*, ch. 5, pt. 5 (1847; repr. in *Karl Marx and Friedrich Engels: Collected Works*, vol. 6, 1976).

12 The vast material displacements the machine has made in our physical environment are perhaps in the long run less important than its spiritual contributions to our culture.

> LEWIS MUMFORD (1895–1990), U.S. social philosopher. "The Drama of the Machines," in *Scribner's* (Aug. 1930; repr. in *Technics and Civilization*, Introduction, 1934; rev. ed., 1962).

13 The cycle of the machine is now coming to an end. Man has learned much in the hard discipline and the shrewd, unflinching grasp of practical possibilities that the machine has provided in the last three centuries: but we can no more continue to live in the world of the machine than we could live successfully on the barren surface of the moon.

> LEWIS MUMFORD (1895–1990), U.S. social philosopher. *The Culture of Cities*, ch. 7, sct. 16 (1938).

14 Machines are worshipped because they are beautiful and valued because they confer power; they are hated because they are hideous and loathed because they impose slavery.

> BERTRAND RUSSELL (1872–1970), British philosopher, mathematician. *Sceptical Essays*, "Machines and Emotions" (1928).

15 The machine does not isolate man from the great problems of nature but plunges him more deeply into them.

> ANTOINE DE SAINT-EXUPÉRY (1900–1944), French aviator, author. *Wind, Sand, and Stars*, ch. 3 (1939).

16 The machines that are first invented to perform any particular movement are always the most complex, and succeeding artists generally discover that, with fewer wheels, with fewer principles of motion, than had originally been employed, the same effects may be more easily produced. The first systems, in the same manner, are always the most complex.

> ADAM SMITH (1723–90), Scottish economist. *Essays on Philosophical Subjects*, sct. 4, "The Principles Which Lead and Direct Philosophical Inquiries" (1795); of philosophical systems.

17 Nothing is *less* instructive than a machine.

> SIMONE WEIL (1909–1943), French philosopher, mystic. *Factory Journal*, "The Mystery of the Factory" (1934–35; repr. in *La Condition Ouvrière*, 1951).

18 There is no country in the world where machinery is so lovely as in America.

> OSCAR WILDE (1854–1900), Anglo-Irish playwright, author. "Personal Impressions of America," lecture 10, July 1883. Wilde continued: "It was not until I had seen the water-works at Chicago that I realised the wonders of machinery; the rise and fall of the steel rods, the symmetrical motion of the great wheels is the most beautiful rhythmic thing I have ever seen."

19 I find it hard to believe that the machine would go into the creative artist's hand even were that magic hand in true place. It has been too far exploited by industrialism and science at expense to art and true religion.

> FRANK LLOYD WRIGHT (1869–1959), U.S. architect. *The Living City*, pt. 5, "Night Is but a Shadow Cast by the Sun" (1958).

See also TECHNOLOGY.

MADNESS

1 No great genius has ever existed without some touch of madness.

> ARISTOTLE (384–322 B.C.), Greek philosopher. Attributed by Seneca in *Moral Essays*, "De Tranquillitate Animi" (On Tranquility of Mind), sct. 17, subsct. 10.

2 And what is an authentic madman? It is a man who preferred to become mad, in the socially accepted sense of the word, rather than forfeit a certain superior idea of human honor. So society has strangled in its asylums all those it wanted to get rid of or protect itself from, because they refused to become its accomplices in certain great nastinesses. For a madman is also a man whom society did not want to hear and whom it wanted to prevent from uttering certain intolerable truths.

> ANTONIN ARTAUD (1896–1948), French theater producer, actor, theorist. *Van Gogh, the Man Suicided by Society*, (1947; repr. in *Selected Writings*, pt. 33, ed. by Susan Sontag, 1976).

3 In a completely sane world, *madness* is the only freedom!

> J. G. BALLARD (b. 1930), British author. Interview, 30 Oct. 1982, in *Re/Search*, no. 8/9 (San Francisco, 1984).

4 I have cultivated my hysteria with delight and terror. Now I suffer continually from vertigo, and today, 23rd of January, 1862, I have received a singular warning, I have felt the wind of the wing of madness pass over me.

> CHARLES BAUDELAIRE (1821–67), French poet. "My Heart Laid Bare" (written c. 1865; published in *Intimate Journals*, sct. 109, 1887; tr. by Christopher Isherwood, 1930; rev. by Don Bachardy, 1989).

5 The world has always gone through periods of madness so as to advance a bit on the road to reason.

> HERMANN BROCH (1886–1951), Austrian novelist. The doctor, in *The Spell*, ch. 11 (1976; tr. 1987).

6 One who shows signs of mental aberration is, inevitably, perhaps, but cruelly, shut off from familiar, thoughtless intercourse, partly excommunicated; his isolation is unwittingly proclaimed to him on every countenance by curiosity, indifference, aversion, or pity, and in so far as he is human enough to need free and equal communication and feel the lack of it, he suffers pain and loss of a kind and degree which others can only faintly imagine, and for the most part ignore.

> CHARLES HORTON COOLEY (1864–1929), U.S. sociologist. *Human Nature and the Social Order*, ch. 6 (1902).

7 Men are mad most of their lives; few live sane, fewer die so. . . . The acts of people are baffling unless we realize that their wits are disordered. Man is driven to justice by his lunacy.

> EDWARD DAHLBERG (1900–1977), U.S. author, critic. *The Carnal Myth*, ch. 2 (1968).

8 In this century the writer has carried on a conversation with madness. We might almost say of the twentieth-century writer that he aspires to madness. Some have made it, of course, and they hold special places in our regard. To a writer, madness is a final distillation of self, a final editing down. It's the drowning out of false voices.

> DON DELILLO (b. 1926), U.S. author. Owen Brademas, in *The Names*, ch. 5 (1982).

9 Much Madness is divinest Sense —
To a discerning Eye —
Much Sense—the starkest Madness —

> EMILY DICKINSON (1830–86), U.S. poet. *The Complete Poems*, no. 435 (1955).

10 Perhaps he was a bit different from other people, but what really sympathetic person is not a little mad?

> ISADORA DUNCAN (1878–1927), U.S. dancer. *My Life*, ch. 11 (1927), of Grand Duke Ferdinand of Hungary.

11 Madness is the absolute break with the work of art; it forms the constitutive moment of abolition, which dissolves in time the truth of the work of art.

> MICHEL FOUCAULT (1926–84), French essayist, philosopher. *Madness and Civilization*, Conclusion (1961; tr. 1965).

12 The experience and behaviour that gets labelled schizophrenic is a special strategy that a person invents in order to live in an unlivable situation.

> R. D. LAING (1927–89), British psychiatrist. *The Politics of Experience*, ch. 5 (1967).

13 Madness need not be all breakdown. It may also be break-through. It is potential liberation and renewal as well as enslavement and existential death.

> R. D. LAING (1927–89), British psychiatrist. *The Politics of Experience*, ch. 6 (1967).

14 Our society is run by insane people for insane objectives. . . . I think we're being run by maniacs for maniacal ends . . . and I think I'm liable to be put away as insane for expressing that. That's what's insane about it.

> JOHN LENNON (1940–80), British rock musician. Interview, 22 June 1968, BBC-TV.

15 The lightning flashes through my skull; mine eyeballs ache and ache; my whole beaten brain seems as beheaded, and rolling on some stunning ground.

> HERMAN MELVILLE (1819–91), U.S. author. Captain Ahab, in *Moby-Dick*, ch. 119 (1851).

16 Madness is tonic and invigorating. It makes the sane more sane. The only ones who are unable to profit by it are the insane.

> HENRY MILLER (1891–1980), U.S. author. *The Cosmological Eye*, "An Open Letter to Surrealists Everywhere" (1939).

17 The mind is its own place, and in itself
Can make a Heaven of Hell, a Hell of Heaven.

> JOHN MILTON (1608–74), English poet. Satan, in *Paradise Lost*, bk. 1.

18 Madness is something rare in individuals—but in groups, parties, peoples, ages it is the rule.

> FRIEDRICH NIETZSCHE (1844–1900), German philosopher. *Beyond Good and Evil*, "Maxims and Interludes," no. 156 (1886).

19 What can you do against the lunatic who is more intelligent than yourself, who gives your arguments a fair hearing and then simply persists in his lunacy?

> GEORGE ORWELL (1903–50), British author. Winston Smith, in *Nineteen Eighty-Four*, pt. 3, ch. 3 (1949), speaking of O'Brien.

20 The usefulness of madmen is famous: they demonstrate society's logic flagrantly carried out down to its last scrimshaw scrap.

> CYNTHIA OZICK (b. 1928), U.S. novelist, short-story writer. "The Hole/Birth Catalog," in *The First Ms. Reader* (ed. by Francine Klagsbrun, 1972).

21 I guess the definition of a lunatic is a man surrounded by them.

> EZRA POUND (1885–1972), U.S. poet, critic. Said to poet and critic Charles Olson in 1945, when Olson visited Pound in Howard Hall, the institution for the criminally insane in which Pound was detained pending a judgment on his wartime broadcasts from Rome. Quoted in: Catherine Seelye, *Charles Olson and Ezra Pound* (1975).

22 It's a question to ask ourselves if we're not mad. But who are the madmen, in God's name? Those who wonder about it, or the others? If we ever began to speak out loud, what would they do with us, tell me?

> VICTOR SERGE (1890–1947), Russian revolutionary author. *Birth of Our Power*, ch. 20 (1931; tr. 1968).

23 O what a noble mind is here o'erthrown!

> WILLIAM SHAKESPEARE (1564–1616), English dramatist, poet. Ophelia, in *Hamlet*, act 3, sc. 1.

24 O, let me not be mad, not mad, sweet heaven!
Keep me in temper. I would not be mad.

> WILLIAM SHAKESPEARE (1564–1616), English dramatist, poet. Lear, in *King Lear*, act 1, sc. 5.

25 We want a few mad people now. See where the sane ones have landed us!

> GEORGE BERNARD SHAW (1856–1950), Anglo-Irish playwright, critic. Poulengey, in *Saint Joan*, sc. 1.

26 In the past, men created witches; now they create mental patients.

> THOMAS SZASZ (b. 1920), U.S. psychiatrist. *The Manufacture of Madness*, Introduction (1971).

27 If the dead talk to you, you are a spiritualist; if God talks to you, you are a schizophrenic.

> THOMAS SZASZ (b. 1920), U.S. psychiatrist. *The Second Sin*, "Schizophrenia" (1973).

28 To think the world therefore a general Bedlam, or place of madmen, and oneself a physician, is the most necessary point of present wisdom: an important imagination, and the way to happiness.

> THOMAS TRAHERNE (1636–74), English clergyman, poet, mystic. *Centuries*, "Fourth Century," no. 20 (written c. 1672; published 1908).

See also Joyce on GENIUS; Shakespeare on POWER; Cocteau on WISDOM.

MADONNA (MADONNA LOUISE CICCIONE)

1 Effeminate men intrigue me more than anything in the world. I see them as my alter egos. I feel very drawn to them. I think like a guy, but I'm feminine. So I relate to feminine men.

> MADONNA (b. 1959), U.S. singer, actor. *Vanity Fair* (New York, April 1991).

2 I love meetings with suits. I *live* for meetings with suits. I love them because I know they had a really boring week and I walk in there with my orange velvet leggings and drop popcorn in my cleavage and then fish it out and eat it. I like that. I know I'm entertaining them and I know that they know. Obviously, the best meetings are with suits that are intelligent, because then things are operating on a whole other level.

> MADONNA (b. 1959), U.S. singer, actor. *Vanity Fair* (New York, April 1991).

3 Madonna is the true feminist. She exposes the puritanism and suffocating ideology of American feminism, which is stuck in an adolescent whining mode. Madonna has taught young women to be fully female and sexual while still excerising control over their lives.

CAMILLE PAGLIA (b. 1947), U.S. author, critic, educator. "Madonna 1: Animality and Artifice," in *New York Times* (14 Dec. 1991; repr. in *Sex, Art, and American Culture,* 1992).

MAGAZINES

See NEWSPAPERS AND MAGAZINES

MAGIC

1   The profession of magician, is one of the most perilous and arduous specialisations of the imagination. On the one hand there is the hostility of God and the police to be guarded against; on the other it is as difficult as music, as deep as poetry, as ingenious as stage-craft, as nervous as the manufacture of high explosives, and as delicate as the trade in narcotics.

WILLIAM BOLITHO (1890–1930), British author. *Twelve Against the Gods,* "Cagliostro (and Seraphina)" (1930).

2   Black magic operates most effectively in preconscious, marginal areas. Casual curses are the most effective.

WILLIAM BURROUGHS (b. 1914), U.S. author. *The Western Lands,* ch. 3 (1987).

3   Indubitably, Magick is one of the subtlest and most difficult of the sciences and arts. There is more opportunity for errors of comprehension, judgement and practice than in any other branch of physics.

ALEISTER CROWLEY (1875–1947), British occultist. *The Confessions of Aleister Crowley,* ch. 20 (1929; rev. 1970).

THE MAJORITY

1   The Government of the absolute majority instead of the Government of the people is but the Government of the strongest interests; and when not efficiently checked, it is the most tyrannical and oppressive that can be devised.

JOHN CALDWELL CALHOUN (1782–1850), U.S. statesman. Speech, 15 Feb. 1833, U.S. Senate.

2   Shall we then judge a country by the majority, or by the minority?

RALPH WALDO EMERSON (1803–82), U.S. essayist, poet, philosopher. *The Conduct of Life,* "Considerations by the Way" (1860).

3   Human life in common is only made possible when a majority comes together which is stronger than any separate individual and which remains united against all separate individuals. The power of this community is then set up as "right" in opposition to the power of the individual, which is condemned as "brute force."

SIGMUND FREUD (1856–1939), Austrian psychiatrist. *Civilization and its Discontents,* ch. 3 (1930; repr. in *Complete Works,* vol. 21, ed. by James Strachey and Anna Freud, 1961). Freud interpreted this replacement of the power of the individual by the power of the community as "the decisive step of civilization."

4   There is something wonderful in seeing a wrong-headed majority assailed by truth.

JOHN KENNETH GALBRAITH (b. 1908), U.S. economist. *Guardian* (London, 28 July 1989).

5   The worst enemy of truth and freedom in our society is the compact majority. Yes, the damned, compact, liberal majority.

HENRIK IBSEN (1828–1906), Norwegian dramatist. Dr. Stockmann, in *An Enemy of the People,* act 4.

6   The principle of majority rule is the mildest form in which the force of numbers can be exercised. It is a pacific substitute for civil war in which the opposing armies are counted and the victory is awarded to the larger before any blood is shed. Except in the sacred tests of democracy and in the incantations of the orators, we hardly take the trouble to pretend that the rule of the majority is not at bottom a rule of force.

WALTER LIPPMANN (1889–1974), U.S. journalist. "Why Should the Majority Rule?," in *Harper's Magazine* (New York, 1926; repr. in *The Essential Lippman,* pt. 1, sct. 1, 1982).

7   Majority rule is a precious, sacred thing worth dying for. But—like other precious, sacred things, such as the home and the family—it's not only worth dying for; it can make you wish you were dead. Imagine if all of life were determined by majority rule. Every meal would be a pizza. Every pair of pants, even those in a Brooks Brothers suit, would be stonewashed denim. Celebrity diet and exercise books would be the only thing on the shelves at the library. And—since women are a majority of the population—we'd all be married to Mel Gibson.

P J O'ROURKE (b. 1947), U.S. journalist. *Parliament of Whores,* "The Mystery of Government" (1991).

8   The moment a mere numerical superiority by either states or voters in this country proceeds to ignore the needs and desires of the minority, and for their own selfish purpose or advancement, hamper or oppress that minority, or debar them in any way from equal privileges and equal rights—that moment will mark the failure of our constitutional system.

FRANKLIN D. ROOSEVELT (1882–1945), U.S. Democratic politician, president. Radio broadcast, 2 March 1930.

See also Robbins on MINORITIES.

MALICE

1   In doing good, we are generally cold, and languid, and sluggish; and of all things afraid of being too much in the right. But the works of malice and injustice are quite in another style. They are finished with a bold, masterly hand; touched as they are with the spirit of those vehement passions that call forth all our energies, whenever we oppress and persecute.

EDMUND BURKE (1729–97), Irish philosopher, statesman. Speech at Bristol, prior to the 1780 election (published in *Works,* vol. 2, 1899).

2   It is remarkable by how much a pinch of malice

enhances the penetrating power of an idea or an opinion. Our ears, it seems, are wonderfully attuned to sneers and evil reports about our fellow men.

> ERIC HOFFER (1902–1983), U.S. philosopher. *The Passionate State of Mind*, aph. 167 (1955).

3 Malice is only another name for mediocrity.

> PATRICK KAVANAGH (1905–67), Irish poet, author. *Collected Prose*, "Signposts" (1967).

4 There's no possibility of being witty without a little ill-nature —
The malice of a good thing is the barb that makes it stick.

> RICHARD BRINSLEY SHERIDAN (1751–1816), Anglo-Irish dramatist. Lady Sneerwell, in *The School for Scandal*, act 1, sc. 1.

MANAGEMENT

1 A man is known by the company he organizes.

> AMBROSE BIERCE (1842–1914), U.S. author. *The Devil's Dictionary*, "Saw" (1881–1906).

2 Some great men owe most of their greatness to the ability of detecting in those they destine for their tools the exact quality of strength that matters for their work.

> JOSEPH CONRAD (1857–1924), Polish-born English novelist. Marlow, in *Lord Jim*, ch. 42 (1900).

3 You don't need a Harvard MBA to know that the bedroom and the boardroom are just two sides of the same ballgame.

> STEPHEN FRY (b. 1957), British comic actor, author. Stephen, in *A Bit of Fry & Laurie*, "Troubleshooters" (1990).

4 Damn the great executives, the men of measured merriment, damn the men with careful smiles, damn the men that run the shops, oh, damn their measured merriment.

> SINCLAIR LEWIS (1885–1951), U.S. novelist. Martin Arrowsmith, in *Arrowsmith* ch. 25 (1925).

5 A man may be a tough, concentrated, successful money-maker and never contribute to his country anything more than a horrible example. A manager may be tough and practical, squeezing out, while the going is good, the last ounce of profit and dividend, and may leave behind him an exhausted industry and a legacy of industrial hatred. A tough manager may never look outside his own factory walls or be conscious of his partnership in a wider world. I often wonder what strange cud such men sit chewing when their working days are over, and the accumulating riches of the mind have eluded them.

> ROBERT MENZIES (1894–1978), Australian Liberal politician, prime minister. First William Queale Memorial Lecture, 1954. Quoted in: *Wit and Wisdom of Robert Menzies* (ed. Colin Bingham, 1982).

6 Surround yourself with the best people you can find, delegate authority, and don't interfere.

> RONALD REAGAN (b. 1911), U.S. Republican politician, president. *Fortune* (New York, Sept. 1986). Quoted in: *Reagan's Reign of Error*, "Mission Impossible" (ed. by Mark Green and Gail MacColl, 1987).

See also BUSINESS AND COMMERCE.

MANNERS

1 Manners are the hypocrisy of a nation.

> HONORÉ DE BALZAC (1799–1850), French novelist. Quoted in: André Gide, *Journals 1889–1949* (ed. by Justin O'Brien, 1951), entry for 1911.

2 The English are polite by telling lies. The Americans are polite by telling the truth.

> MALCOLM BRADBURY (b. 1932), British author. Dr. Bernard Froelich, in *Stepping Westward*, bk. 2, ch. 5 (1965).

3 Manners are of more importance than laws. . . . Manners are what vex or soothe, corrupt or purify, exalt or debase, barbarize or refine us, by a constant, steady, uniform, insensible operation, like that of the air we breathe in.

> EDMUND BURKE (1729–97), Irish philosopher, statesman. *Letters on a Regicide Peace*, letter 1 (1796).

4 Manners must adorn knowledge, and smooth its way through the world.

> LORD CHESTERFIELD (1694–1773), English statesman, man of letters. Letter, 1 July 1748 (published 1774; repr. in *The Letters of the Earl of Chesterfield to His Son*, vol. 1, no. 155, ed. by Charles Strachey, 1901).

5 We are justified in enforcing good morals, for they belong to all mankind; but we are not justified in enforcing good manners, for good manners always mean our own manners.

> G. K. CHESTERTON (1874–1936), British author. *All Things Considered*, "Limericks and Counsels of Perfection" (1908).

6 Manners are love in a cool climate.

> QUENTIN CRISP (b. 1908), British author. *Manners from Heaven*, ch. 2 (1984).

7 There are men whose manners have the same essential splendor as the simple and awful sculpture on the friezes of the Parthenon, and the remains of the earliest Greek art.

> RALPH WALDO EMERSON (1803–82), U.S. essayist, poet, philosopher. *Essays*, "History" (First Series, 1841).

8 Manners are the happy way of doing things; each once a stroke of genius or of love—now repeated and hardened into usage. They form at last a rich varnish, with which the routine of life is washed, and its details adorned. If they are superficial, so are the dewdrops which give such depth to the morning meadows.

> RALPH WALDO EMERSON (1803–82), U.S. essayist, poet, philosopher. *The Conduct of Life*, "Behavior" (1860).

9 Good manners are made up of petty sacrifices.

> RALPH WALDO EMERSON (1803–82), U.S. essayist, poet, philosopher. *Letters and Social Aims*, "Social Aims" (1876).

10 In truth, politeness is artificial good humor, it covers the natural want of it, and ends by rendering habitual a substitute nearly equivalent to the real virtue.

> THOMAS JEFFERSON (1743–1826), U.S. president. Letter, 24 Nov. 1808, to his grandson Thomas Jefferson Randolph.

11 The purpose of polite behavior is never virtuous.

Deceit, surrender, and concealment: these are not virtues. The goal of the mannerly is comfort, per se.

> JUNE JORDAN (b. 1939), U.S. poet, civil rights activist. *Moving Towards Home: Political Essays*, "Civil Wars" (1989; first published 1981).

12 It is more *comfortable* for me, in the long run, to be rude than polite.

> WYNDHAM LEWIS (1882–1957), British author, painter. One of the "Imaginary Letters" exchanged between Lewis and Ezra Pound in *Little Review* (Chicago, May 1917).

13 I have always been of the mind that in a democracy manners are the only effective weapons against the bowie-knife.

> JAMES RUSSELL LOWELL (1819–91), U.S. poet, editor. Letter, 4 March 1873.

14 Manners are of such great consequence to the novelist that any kind will do. Bad manners are better than no manners at all, and because we are losing our customary manners, we are probably overly conscious of them; this seems to be a condition that produces writers.

> FLANNERY O'CONNOR (1925–64), U.S. author. "The Fiction Writer and His Country," in *The Living Novel: A Symposium* (ed. by Granville Hicks, 1957; repr. in *Mystery and Manners*, ed. by Sally and Robert Fitzgerald, 1972).

15 Manhood is melted into courtesies, valour into compliment, and men are only turned into tongue, and trim ones, too.

> WILLIAM SHAKESPEARE (1564–1616), English dramatist, poet. Beatrice, in *Much Ado About Nothing*, act 4, sc. 1.

16 The great secret, Eliza, is not having bad manners or good manners or any other particular sort of manners, but having the same manner for all human souls: in short, behaving as if you were in Heaven, where there are no third-class carriages, and one soul is as good as another.

> GEORGE BERNARD SHAW (1856–1950), Anglo-Irish playwright and critic. Henry Higgins to Eliza Doolittle, in *Pygmalion*, act 5.

17 He is the very pineapple of politeness!

> RICHARD BRINSLEY SHERIDAN (1751–1816), Anglo-Irish dramatist. Mrs. Malaprop, in *The Rivals*, act 3, sc. 3, speaking of Captain Absolute.

18 The highest perfection of politeness is only a beautiful edifice, built, from the base to the dome, of ungraceful and gilded forms of charitable and unselfish lying.

> MARK TWAIN (1835–1910), U.S. author. "On the Decay of the Art of Lying" (repr. in *The Complete Humorous Sketches and Tales of Mark Twain*, ed. by Charles Neider, 1961).

19 Good manners have much to do with the emotions. To make them ring true, one must feel them, not merely exhibit them.

> AMY VANDERBILT (1908–74), U.S. hostess, author. *New Complete Book of Etiquette*, pt. 2, Introduction (1963).

20 Manners are especially the need of the plain. The pretty can get away with anything.

> EVELYN WAUGH (1903–66), British novelist. Quoted in: *Observer* (London, 15 April 1962).

21 To the real artist in humanity, what are called bad manners are often the most picturesque and significant of all.

> WALT WHITMAN (1819–92), U.S. poet. *Notes Left Over*, "Emerson's Books" (1881).

See also COURTESY; Chesterfield on INTIMACY; TACT.

MARKETING

See SALES AND MARKETING.

MARRIAGE

1 When two people marry they become in the eyes of the law one person, and that one person is the husband!

> SHANA ALEXANDER (b. 1925), U.S. writer, editor. *State-by-State Guide to Women's Legal Rights*, Introduction (1975).

2 To marry a man out of pity is folly; and, if you think you are going to influence the kind of fellow who has "never had a chance, poor devil," you are profoundly mistaken. One can only influence the strong characters in life, not the weak; and it is the height of vanity to suppose that you can make an honest man of anyone.

> MARGOT ASQUITH (1864–1945), British socialite. *The Autobiography of Margot Asquith*, vol. 1, ch. 7 (1920).

3 In marriage there are no manners to keep up, and beneath the wildest accusations no real criticism. Each is familiar with that ancient child in the other who may erupt again. . . . We are not ridiculous to ourselves. We are ageless. That is the luxury of the wedding ring.

> ENID BAGNOLD (1889–1981), British novelist, playwright. *Autobiography*, ch. 6 (1969).

4 Marriage always demands the greatest understanding of the art of insincerity possible between two human beings.

> VICKI BAUM (1888–1960), U.S. writer. *And Life Goes On*, (1932, p. 141).

5 The curse which lies upon marriage is that too often the individuals are joined in their weakness rather than in their strength—each asking from the other instead of finding pleasure in giving. It is even more deceptive to dream of gaining through the child a plenitude, a warmth, a value, which one is unable to create for oneself; the child brings joy only to the woman who is capable of disinterestedly desiring the happiness of another, to one who without being wrapped up in self seeks to transcend her own existence.

> SIMONE DE BEAUVOIR (1908–86), French novelist, essayist. *The Second Sex*, bk. 2, pt. 5, ch. 2 (1949).

6 How many young hearts have revealed the fact that what they had been trained to imagine the highest earthly felicity was but the beginning of care, disappointment, and sorrow, and often led to the extremity of mental and physical suffering.

> CATHARINE ESTHER BEECHER (1800–1878), U.S. educator, writer. *Woman Suffrage and Women's Professions*, "Statistics of Female Health" (1871).

7 Therefore shall a man leave his father and mother, and shall cleave unto his wife: and they shall be one flesh.

BIBLE, HEBREW. *Genesis* 2:24.

8 For in the resurrection they neither marry, nor are given in marriage, but are as the angels of God in heaven.

BIBLE: NEW TESTAMENT. *Matthew* 22:30.

9 Incompatibility. In matrimony a similarity of tastes, particularly the taste for domination.

AMBROSE BIERCE (1842–1914), U.S. author. *The Devil's Dictionary* (1881–1906).

10 Marriage. The state or condition of a community consisting of a master, a mistress and two slaves, making in all, two.

AMBROSE BIERCE (1842–1914), U.S. author. *The Devil's Dictionary* (1881–1906).

11 The mere idea of marriage, as a strong possibility, if not always nowadays a reasonable likelihood, existing to weaken the will by distracting its straight aim in the life of practically every young girl, is the simple secret of their confessed inferiority in men's pursuits and professions to-day.

WILLIAM BOLITHO (1890–1930), British author. *Twelve Against the Gods*, "Isadora Duncan" (1930).

12 The aura of the theocratic death penalty for adultery still clings to America, even outside New England, and multiple divorce, which looks to the European like serial polygamy, is the moral solution to the problem of the itch. Love comes into it too, of course, but in Europe we tend to see marital love as an eternity which encompasses hate and also indifference: when we promise to love we really mean that we promise to honour a contract. Americans, seeming to take marriage with not enough seriousness, are really taking love and sex with too much.

ANTHONY BURGESS (b. 1917), British author, critic. *You've Had Your Time*, ch. 2 (1990).

13 One was never married, and that's his hell; another is, and that's his plague.

ROBERT BURTON (1577–1640), English clergyman, author. *Anatomy of Melancholy*, pt. 1, sct. 2 mem. 4, subsct. 7 (1621).

14 Though women are angels, yet wedlock's the devil.

LORD BYRON (1788–1824), English poet. *To Eliza*.

15 The deep, deep peace of the double-bed after the hurly-burly of the chaise-longue.

MRS. PATRICK CAMPBELL (1865–1940), British actress. Quoted in: Alexander Woollcott, *While Rome Burns*, "The First Mrs. Tanqueray" (1934). Woollcott commented of Mrs. Campbell, who is above describing her recent marriage, "Her failure to be polite took on the proportions of a magnificent gesture."

16 A man will teach his wife what is needed to arouse his desires. And there is no reason for a woman to know any more than what her husband is prepared to teach her. If she gets married knowing far too much about what she wants and doesn't want then she will be ready to find fault with her husband.

BARBARA CARTLAND (b. 1901), British novelist. Interview in Wendy Leigh, *Speaking Frankly* (1978).

17 There is a time for all things—Except Marriage my dear.

THOMAS CHATTERTON (1752–1770), English poet. Reply, 9 April 1770, to a note from an admirer who bade him be patient, "for there is a time for all things" (published in *The Complete Works of Thomas Chatterton*, vol. 1, 1971).

18 Except for poverty, incompatibility, opposition of parents, absence of love on one side and of desire to marry on both, nothing stands in the way of our happy union.

CYRIL CONNOLLY (1903–74), British critic. "The Journal of Cyril Connolly 1928–1937" (published in David Pryce-Jones, *Journal and Memoir*, 1983, p. 159).

19 Ven you're a married man, Samivel, you'll understand a good many things as you don't understand now; but vether it's worth while, goin' through so much, to learn so little, as the charity-boy said ven he got to the end of the alphabet, is a matter o' taste.

CHARLES DICKENS (1812–70), English novelist. Mr. Weller, in *The Pickwick Papers*, ch. 27 (1836–37).

20 Any intelligent woman who reads the marriage contract and then goes into it, deserves all the consequences.

ISADORA DUNCAN (1878–1927), U.S. dancer. *My Life*, ch. 19 (1927).

21 Marriage as an institution developed from rape as a practice. Rape, originally defined as abduction, became marriage by capture. Marriage meant the taking was to extend in time, to be not only use of but possession of, or ownership.

ANDREA DWORKIN (b. 1946), U.S. feminist critic. *Pornography*, ch. 1 (1981).

22 Marriage is socialism among two people.

BARBARA EHRENREICH (b. 1941), U.S. author, columnist. *The Worst Years of Our Lives*, "Socialism in One Household" (1991; first published in *Mother Jones*, 1987).

23 Marriage must be a relation either of sympathy or of conquest.

GEORGE ELIOT (1819–80), English novelist. *Romola*, ch. 48 (1863).

24 When the blind lead the blind, no wonder they both fall into—matrimony.

GEORGE FARQUHAR (1678–1707), Irish dramatist. Roebuck, in *Love and a Bottle*, act 5, sc. 1.

25 Wasn't marriage, like life, unstimulating and unprofitable and somewhat empty when too well ordered and protected and guarded? Wasn't it finer, more splendid, more nourishing, when it was, like life itself, a mixture of the sordid and the magnificent; of mud and stars; of earth and flowers; of love and hate and laughter and tears and ugliness and beauty and hurt?

EDNA FERBER (1887–1968), U.S. author. *Show Boat*, ch. 19 (1926).

26   One fool at least in every married couple.

HENRY FIELDING (1707–54), English novelist, dramatist. Dr. Harrison, in *Amelia*, vol. 3, bk. 9, ch. 4 (1751), speaking of Booth and Amelia.

27   Married life requires shared mystery even when all the facts are known.

RICHARD FORD (b. 1944), U.S. author. *The Sportswriter* (1987, p. 137).

28   Marriage accustomed one to the good things, so one came to take them for granted, but magnified the bad things, so they came to feel as painful as a grain in one's eye. An open window, a forgotten quart of milk, a TV set left blaring, socks on the bathroom floor could become occasions for incredible rage. And something happened sexually in marriage—the swearing to forsake all others, despite its slight observance, had a profound effect. Some people felt trapped by it, impelled to assert what they called freedom. Some accepted it like a rein, and in the effort to avoid pain in the form of hopeless desire, cut off occasions of desire, avoided having long talks at parties with attractive members of the opposite sex. In time, all feeling for the opposite sex was cut off, and intercourse limited to the barest politenesses. . . . But something happened to you when you did that, a kind of death seeped up from the genitals to the rest of the body, till it showed in the eyes, the gestures, in a certain lifelessness.

MARILYN FRENCH (b. 1929), U.S. author, critic. Mira, in *The Women's Room*, ch. 5, sct. 12 (1977).

29   Two such as you with such a master speed
Cannot be parted nor be swept away
From one another once you are agreed
That life is only life forevermore
Together wing to wing and oar to oar.

ROBERT FROST (1874–1963), U.S. poet. *The Master Speed*, inscribed on the gravestone of Frost and his wife, Elinor.

30   Deceive not thyself by over-expecting happiness in the married estate. . . . Remember the nightingales which sing only some months in the spring, but commonly are silent when they have hatched their eggs, as if their mirth were turned into care for their young ones.

THOMAS FULLER (1608–61), English cleric. *The Holy State and the Profane State*, bk. 3, "Of Marriage" (1642).

31   The problem with marriage is that it ends every night after making love, and it must be rebuilt every morning before breakfast.

GABRIEL GARCIA MÁRQUEZ (b. 1928)), Colombian writer. Dr. Urbino, in *Love in the Time of Cholera* (1985; Penguin ed., 1988, p. 209).

32   In taking out an insurance policy one pays for it in dollars and cents, always at liberty to discontinue payments. If, however, woman's premium is a husband, she pays for it with her name, her privacy, her self-respect, her very life, "until death doth part."

EMMA GOLDMAN (1869–1940), U.S. anarchist. *Anarchism and Other Essays*, "Marriage and Love" (1910).

33   Every time a woman makes herself laugh at her husband's often-told jokes she betrays him. The man who looks at his woman and says "What would I do without you?" is already destroyed.

GERMAINE GREER (b. 1939), Australian feminist writer. *The Female Eunuch*, "Egotism" (1970).

34   Marriage, for a woman at least, hampers the two things that made life to me glorious—friendship and learning.

JANE HARRISON (1850–1928), English classical scholar, writer. *Reminiscences of a Student's Life*, "Conclusion" (1925).

35   The married are those who have taken the terrible risk of intimacy and, having taken it, know life without intimacy to be impossible.

CAROLYN HEILBRUN (b. 1926), U.S. author, educator. "Marriage Is the Message," in *Ms.* (New York, Aug. 1974).

36   Only one marriage I regret. I remember after I got that marriage license I went across from the license bureau to a bar for a drink. The bartender said, "What will you have, sir?" And I said, "A glass of hemlock."

ERNEST HEMINGWAY (1899–1961), U.S. author. Quoted in: A. E. Hotchner, *Papa Hemingway*, pt. 2, ch. 5 (1966 ed.).

37   A marriage based on full confidence, based on complete and unqualified frankness on both sides; they are not keeping anything back; there's no deception underneath it all. If I might so put it, it's an agreement for the mutual forgiveness of sin.

HENRIK IBSEN (1828–1906), Norwegian dramatist. Hjalmar Ekdal, in *The Wild Duck*, act 4, referring to Mrs. Sörby's marriage.

38   Marriage is an act of will that signifies and involves a mutual gift, which unites the spouses and binds them to their eventual souls, with whom they make up a sole family—a domestic church.

JOHN PAUL II [KAROL WOJTYLA] (b. 1920), Polish ecclesiastic, pope. Quoted in: *Observer* (London, 31 Jan. 1982).

39   Marriage has many pains, but celibacy has no pleasures.

SAMUEL JOHNSON (1709–84), English author, lexicographer. Nekayah, in *The History of Rasselas*, ch. 26 (1759).

40   There is, indeed, nothing that so much seduces reason from vigilance, as the thought of passing life with an amiable woman.

SAMUEL JOHNSON (1709–84), English author, lexicographer. Letter, 21 Dec. 1762. Quoted in: James Boswell, *Life of Samuel Johnson* (1791).

41   There is a rhythm to the ending of a marriage just like the rhythm of a courtship—only backward. You try to start again but get into blaming over and over. Finally you are both worn out, exhausted, hopeless. Then lawyers are called in to pick clean the corpses. The death has occurred much earlier.

ERICA JONG (b. 1942), U.S. author. *How To Save Your Own Life*, "There Is a Rhythm to the Ending . . . " (1977).

42   Marrying a man is like buying something you've been admiring for a long time in a shop window. You may love it when you get it home, but it doesn't always go with everything else in the house.

JEAN KERR (b. 1923), U.S. author, playwright. *The Snake Has All the Lines*, "The Ten Worst Things About a Man" (1958).

43 Marriage brings one into fatal connection with custom and tradition, and traditions and customs are like the wind and weather, altogether incalculable.

SØREN KIERKEGAARD (1813–55), Danish philosopher. *Either/Or*, vol. 1, "The Rotation Method" (1843).

44 The American woman's concept of marriage is a clearly etched picture of something uninflated on the floor. A sleeping-bag without air, a beanbag without beans, a padded bra without pads. To work on it, you start pumping—what the magazines call "breathing life into your marriage." Do enough of this and the marriage becomes a kind of Banquo's ghost, a quasi-living entity.

FLORENCE KING (b. 1936), U.S. author. *Reflections in a Jaundiced Eye*, "From Captain Marvel to Captain Valium" (1989).

45 Matrimony is the union of meanness and martyrdom.

KARL KRAUS (1874–1936), Austrian satirist. *Die Fackel* (Vienna, 15 Dec. 1913). Quoted in: Thomas Szasz, *Anti-Freud: Karl Kraus's Criticism of Psychoanalysis and Psychiatry*, ch. 8 (1976).

46 Marriage, it seems, confines every man to his proper rank.

JEAN DE LA BRUYÈRE (1645–96), French writer, moralist. *Characters*, "Of Personal Merit," aph. 25 (1688).

47 All married couples should learn the art of battle as they should learn the art of making love. Good battle is objective and honest—never vicious or cruel. Good battle is healthy and constructive, and brings to a marriage the principle of equal partnership.

ANN LANDERS (b. 1918), U.S. columnist. *Ann Landers Says Truth Is Stranger . . .*, ch. 11 (1968).

48 My whole working philosophy is that the only stable happiness for mankind is that it shall live married in blessed union to woman-kind—intimacy, physical and psychical between a man and his wife. I wish to add that my state of bliss is by no means perfect.

D. H. LAWRENCE (1885–1930), British author. Letter, 4 Sept. 1913 (published in *The Letters of D. H. Lawrence*, vol. 2, ed. by George J. Zytaruk and James T. Boulton, 1981).

49 Progress of a marriage:
"There was a time when you couldn't
make me happy.
Now the time has come when you can't
make me unhappy."

IRVING LAYTON (b. 1912), Canadian poet. *The Whole Bloody Bird*, "Aphs" (1969).

50 Rituals are important. Nowadays it's hip not to be married. I'm not interested in being hip.

JOHN LENNON (1940–80), British rock musician. *Playboy* (Chicago, Sept. 1980).

51 There is, hidden or flaunted, a sword between the sexes till an entire marriage reconciles them.

C. S. LEWIS (1898–1963), British author. *A Grief Observed*, pt. 3 (1961).

52 The sum and substance of female education in America, as in England, is training women to consider marriage as the sole object in life, and to pretend that they do not think so.

HARRIET MARTINEAU (1802–76), English writer, social critic. *Society in America*, vol. 3, "Women" (1837).

53 A successful marriage is an edifice that must be rebuilt every day.

ANDRÉ MAUROIS (1885–1967), French author, critic. *The Art of Living*, "The Art of Marriage" (1940).

54 Say what you will, making marriage work is a woman's business. The institution was invented to do her homage; it was contrived for her protection. Unless she accepts it as such—as a beautiful, bountiful, but quite unequal association—the going will be hard indeed.

PHYLLIS MCGINLEY (1905–78), U.S. poet, author. *The Province of the Heart*, "The Honor of Being a Woman" (1959).

55 The institution of marriage in all societies is a pattern within which the strains put by civilization on males and females alike must be resolved, a pattern within which men must learn, in return for a variety of elaborate rewards, new forms in which sexual spontaneity is still possible, and women must learn to discipline their receptivity to a thousand other considerations.

MARGARET MEAD (1901–1978), U.S. anthropologist. *Male and Female*, ch. 10 (1949).

56 Whenever a husband and wife begin to discuss their marriage they are giving evidence at a coroner's inquest.

H. L. MENCKEN (1880–1956), U.S. journalist. *A Mencken Chrestomathy*, "Sententiæ: Masculum et Feminam Creavit Eos" (1949).

57 We cannot do without it, and yet we disgrace and vilify the same. It may be compared to a cage, the birds without despair to get in, and those within despair to get out.

MICHEL DE MONTAIGNE (1533–92), French essayist. *Essays*, bk. 3, ch. 5, "Upon Some Verses of Virgil" (tr. by John Florio, 1588).

58 In almost every marriage there is a selfish and an unselfish partner. A pattern is set up and soon becomes inflexible, of one person always making the demands and one person always giving way.

IRIS MURDOCH (b. 1919), British novelist, philosopher. Martin Lynch-Gibbons, in *A Severed Head*, ch. 2 (1961).

59 The best friend is likely to acquire the best wife, because a good marriage is based on the talent for friendship.

FRIEDRICH NIETZSCHE (1844–1900), German philosopher. *Human, All Too Human*, ch. 7, aph. 378 (1878).

60 It is obvious that all sense has gone out of modern marriage: which is, however, no objection to marriage but to modernity.

FRIEDRICH NIETZSCHE (1844–1900), German philosopher. *Twilight of the Idols*, "Expeditions of an Untimely Man," aph. 39 (1889).

61 God invented concubinage, Satan marriage.

FRANCIS PICABIA (1878–1953), French painter, poet. *Écrits*, vol. 2, "Sayings" (ed. by Olivier Revault d'Allones and Dominique Bouissou, 1978; repr. in *Yes No: Poems and Sayings*, ed. by Rémy Hall, 1990).

62 They dream in courtship, but in wedlock wake.

ALEXANDER POPE (1688–1744), English satirical poet. *The Wife of Bath.*

63 It ought to be illegal for an artist to marry. . . . If the artist must marry let him find someone more interested in art, or his art, or the artist part of him, than in him. After which let them take tea together three times a week.

EZRA POUND (1885–1972), U.S. poet, critic. Letter, 1909, to his mother. Quoted in: Humphrey Carpenter, *A Serious Character*, pt. 2, ch. 3 (1988).

64 When a girl marries, she exchanges the attentions of all the other men of her acquaintance for the inattention of just one.

HELEN ROWLAND (1875–1950), U.S. journalist. *Reflections of a Bachelor Girl* (1903).

65 After marriage, a woman's sight becomes so keen that she can see right through her husband without looking at him, and a man's so dull that he can look right through his wife without seeing her.

HELEN ROWLAND (1875–1950), U.S. journalist. *A Guide to Men*, "First Interlude" (1922).

66 Marriage is the operation by which a woman's vanity and a man's egotism are extracted without an anaesthetic.

HELEN ROWLAND (1875–1950), U.S. journalist. *A Guide to Men*, "Third Interlude" (1922).

67 Marriage is for women the commonest mode of livelihood, and the total amount of undesired sex endured by women is probably greater in marriage than in prostitution.

BERTRAND RUSSELL (1872–1970), British philosopher, mathematician. *Marriage and Morals*, "Prostitution" (1929).

68 The horror of wedlock, the most appalling, the most loathsome of all the bonds humankind has devised for its own discomfort and degradation.

MARQUIS DE SADE (1740–1814), French author. Noirceuil, in *L'Histoire de Juliette, ou les Prospérités du Vice*, pt. 2 (1797).

69 In our monogamous part of the world, to marry means to halve one's rights and double one's duties.

ARTHUR SCHOPENHAUER (1788–1860), German philosopher. *Parerga and Paralipomena*, vol. 2, ch. 27, sct. 370 (1851).

70 A little weeping, a little wheedling, a little self-degradation, a little careful use of our advantages, and then some man will say—".Come, be my wife!" With good looks and youth marriage is easy to attain. There are men enough; but a woman who has sold herself, even for a ring and a new name, need hold her skirt aside for no creature in the street. They both earn their bread in one way. Marriage for love is the beautifullest external symbol of the union of souls; marriage without it is the uncleanliest traffic that defiles the world.

OLIVE SCHREINER (1855–1920), South African writer, feminist. Lyndall, in *The Story of an African Farm*, pt. 2, ch. 4 (1883).

71 The world must be peopled. When I said I would die a bachelor, I did not think I should live till I were married.

WILLIAM SHAKESPEARE (1564–1616), English dramatist, poet.

Benedick, in *Much Ado About Nothing*, act 2, sc. 3, justifying his change of heart about marriage.

72 Marriage is popular because it combines the maximum of temptation with the maximum of opportunity.

GEORGE BERNARD SHAW (1856–1950), Anglo-Irish playwright, critic. *Man and Superman*, "Maxims for Revolutionists: Marriage" (1903).

73 There is no subject on which more dangerous nonsense is talked and thought than marriage.

GEORGE BERNARD SHAW (1856–1950), Anglo-Irish playwright, critic. *Getting Married*, Preface (1908).

74 When a man marries, dies, or turns Hindoo,
His best friends hear no more of him.

PERCY BYSSHE SHELLEY (1792–1822), English poet. *Letter to Maria Gisborne.*

75 Yes, *marriage* is hateful, detestable. A kind of ineffable, sickening disgust seizes my mind when I think of this most despotic, most unrequited fetter which prejudice has forged to confine its energies.

PERCY BYSSHE SHELLEY (1792–1822), English poet. Letter, 2 May 1811 (published in *The Letters of Percy Bysshe Shelley*, vol. 1, ed. by Frederick L. Jones, 1964). To the same correspondent (Thomas Jefferson Hogg), 21 June 1811, Shelley called matrimony ". . . the most horrible of all the means which the world has had recourse, to bind the noble to itself," but justified his own marriage in a letter to Hogg on Oct. 8 of that year on the grounds that, until considerable improvement of morals had been brought about, it would be advisable to maintain the institution of matrimony.

76 'Tis safest in matrimony to begin with a little aversion.

RICHARD BRINSLEY SHERIDAN (1751–1816), Anglo-Irish dramatist. Mrs. Malaprop, in *The Rivals*, act 1, sc. 2.

77 Chains do not hold a marriage together. It is threads, hundreds of tiny threads which sew people together through the years. That is what makes a marriage last—more than passion or even sex!

SIMONE SIGNORET (b. 1921), French film actor. *Daily Mail* (London, 4 July 1978).

78 It resembles a pair of shears, so joined that they cannot be separated, often moving in opposite directions, yet always punishing anyone who comes between them.

SYDNEY SMITH (1771–1845), English clergyman, writer. Quoted in: Hesketh Pearson, *The Smith of Smiths*, ch. 11 (1934).

79 The concerts you enjoy together
Neighbors you annoy together
Children you destroy together
That make marriage a joy

STEPHEN SONDHEIM (b. 1930), U.S. composer, lyricist. "The Little Things You Do Together," in *Company* (1970).

80 The marriage state, with and without the affection suitable to it, is the completest image of Heaven and Hell we are capable of receiving in this life.

SIR RICHARD STEELE (1672–1729), English dramatist, essayist, editor. *Spectator*, no. 480 (London, Sept. 1712).

81 Once you are married, there is nothing for you, not even suicide, but to be good.

ROBERT LOUIS STEVENSON (1850–94), Scottish novelist, essayist, poet. *Virginibus Puerisque*, title essay sec. 2, (1881). Stevenson referred to "matrimony at its lowest" as "no more than a sort of friendship recognised by the police."

82 Marriage is one long conversation, chequered by disputes.

ROBERT LOUIS STEVENSON (1850–1894), Scottish novelist, essayist, poet. *Talk and Talkers*, paper 2 (1882; repr. in *Memories and Portraits*, 1887).

83 Each coming together of man and wife, even if they have been mated for many years, should be a fresh adventure; each winning should necessitate a fresh wooing.

MARIE CARMICHAEL STOPES (1880–1958), British scientist, pioneer of birth control. *Married Love*, ch. 10 (1918).

84 A happy marriage perhaps represents the ideal of human relationship—a setting in which each partner, while acknowledging the need of the other, feels free to be what he or she by nature is: a relationship in which instinct as well as intellect can find expression; in which giving and taking are equal; in which each accepts the other, and I confronts Thou.

ANTHONY STORR (b. 1920), British psychiatrist. *The Integrity of the Personality*, ch. 9 (1960).

85 Every marriage tends to consist of an aristocrat and a peasant. Of a teacher and a learner.

JOHN UPDIKE (b. 1932), U.S. author, critic. *Couples*, ch. 1 (1968).

86 That a marriage ends is less than ideal; but all things end under heaven, and if temporality is held to be invalidating, then nothing real succeeds.

JOHN UPDIKE (b. 1932), U.S. novelist, critic. *Too Far To Go*, Foreword (1979).

87 I think people really marry far too much; it is such a lottery after all, and for a poor woman a very doubtful happiness.

VICTORIA (1819–1901), Queen of Great Britain and Ireland. Letter, 3 May 1858, to her daughter, Crown Princess Frederick William of Prussia (published in *Queen Victoria in Her Letters and Journals*, ed. by Christopher Hibbert, 1984).

88 A marriage is no amusement but a solemn act, and generally a sad one.

VICTORIA (1819–1901), Queen of Great Britain and Ireland. Letter, 9 Jan. 1879, to her daughter, Crown Princess Frederick William of Prussia. Quoted in: Elizabeth Longford, *Victoria R. I.*, ch. 28 (1964).

89 Marriage isn't a word—it's a sentence.

Caption from King Vidor's silent film, *The Crowd* (1926).

90 To many women marriage is only this. It is merely a physical change impinging on their ordinary nature, leaving their mentality untouched, their self-possession intact. They are not burnt by even the red fire of physical passion—far less by the white fire of love.

MARY WEBB (1881–1927), British novelist. *The Golden Arrow*, ch. 18 (1916).

91 I wonder, among all the tangles of this mortal coil, which one contains tighter knots to undo, & consequently suggests more tugging, & pain, & diversified elements of misery, than the marriage tie.

EDITH WHARTON (1862–1937), U.S. author. Letter, 12 Feb. 1909 (published in *The Letters of Edith Wharton*, 1988).

92 Twenty years of romance make a woman look like a ruin, but twenty years of marriage make her something like a public building.

OSCAR WILDE (1854–1900), Anglo-Irish playwright, author. Lord Illingworth, in *A Woman of No Importance*, act 1.

93 They flaunt their conjugal felicity in one's face, as if it were the most fascinating of sins.

OSCAR WILDE (1854–1900), Anglo-Irish playwright, author. Lord Henry, in *The Picture of Dorian Gray*, ch. 8 (1891).

94 Men marry because they are tired; women, because they are curious; both are disappointed.

OSCAR WILDE (1854–1900), Anglo-Irish playwright, author. Lord Henry, in *The Picture of Dorian Gray*, ch. 4 (1891).

95 On the whole, the great success of marriage in the States is due partly to the fact that no American man is ever idle, and partly to the fact that no American wife is considered responsible for the quality of her husband's dinners.

OSCAR WILDE (1854–1900), Anglo-Irish playwright, author. "The American Man," in *Court and Society Review* (London, 13 April 1887). In the same article, Wilde called marriage one of America's most popular institutions: "The American man marries early, and the American woman marries often; and they get on extremely well together."

96 Marriage is a bribe to make a housekeeper think she's a householder.

THORNTON WILDER (1897–1975), U.S. novelist, dramatist. Vandergelder, in *The Matchmaker*, act 1.

97 Arnold Bennett says that the horror of marriage lies in its "dailiness." All acuteness of relationship is rubbed away by this. The truth is more like this: life—say 4 days out of 7—becomes automatic; but on the 5th day a bead of sensation (between husband and wife) forms which is all the fuller and more sensitive because of the automatic customary unconscious days on either side. That is to say the year is marked by moments of great intensity. Hardy's "moments of vision." How can a relationship endure for any length of time except under these conditions?

VIRGINIA WOOLF (1882–1941), British novelist. *The Diary of Virginia Woolf*, vol. 3 (ed. by Anne O. Bell, 1980), entry for 2 Aug. 1926.

See also Clewlow, Shakespeare on ADULTERY; Moliere on BOOKS; Herbert on BREAKFAST; Butler on THOMAS CARLYLE; Stevenson on COMPATIBILITY; DIVORCE; ELOPEMENT; Jong on FRIENDS; Butler on FRIENDSHIP; HUSBANDS; keats on KEATS; Rowland on MEN, SINGLE; Shaw on the NINETEENTH CENTURY; Longfellow on SECTS; Shaw on VIRTUE; WIVES.

MARRIAGE, SECOND

1 To be sure a stepmother to a girl is a different thing to a second wife to a man!

ELIZABETH GASKELL (1810–65), English novelist. Squire Hamley, in *Wives and Daughters*, ch. 6 (1866).

2 By taking a second wife he pays the highest compliment to the first, by shewing that she made him so happy as a married man, that he wishes to be so a second time.

SAMUEL JOHNSON (1709–84), English author, lexicographer.

Quoted in: James Boswell, *Life of Samuel Johnson*, 30 Sept. 1769 (1791). On another occasion (1770), Johnson described the remarriage of "a gentleman who had been very unhappy in marriage" as "the triumph of hope over experience."

3   A bride at her second marriage does not wear a veil. She wants to *see* what she is getting.

HELEN ROWLAND (1875–1950), U.S. journalist. *A Guide to Men*, "Second Marriages" (1922).

4   When a woman marries again it is because she detested her first husband. When a man marries again it is because he adored his first wife. Women try their luck; men risk theirs.

OSCAR WILDE (1854–1900), Anglo-Irish playwright, author. Lord Henry, in *The Picture of Dorian Gray*, ch. 15 (1891).

MARRIAGE AND LOVE

1   Like everything which is not the involuntary result of fleeting emotion but the creation of time and will, any marriage, happy or unhappy, is infinitely more interesting than any romance, however passionate.

W. H. AUDEN (1907–73), Anglo-American poet. *A Certain World*, "Marriage" (1970).

2   I have great hopes that we shall love each other all our lives as much as if we had never married at all.

LORD BYRON (1788–1824), English poet. Letter, 5 Dec. 1814, to Annabella Milbanke, whom he married a month later (published in *Byron's Letters and Journals*, vol. 4, ed. by Leslie A. Marchand, 1975). Annabella left Byron after a year.

3   Love and marriage, love and marriage
Go together like a horse and carriage
Dad was told by mother
You can't have one without the other.

SAMMY CAHN (1913–93), U.S. songwriter. "Love and Marriage" (music by Jimmy Van Heusen).

4   A man in love is incomplete until he has married— then he's finished.

ZSA ZSA GABOR (b. 1919), Hungarian-born U.S. actor. *Newsweek* (New York, 28 March 1960).

5   Love, the stongest and deepest element in all life, the harbinger of hope, of joy, of ecstasy; love, the defier of all laws, of all conventions; love, the freest, the most powerful moulder of human destiny; how can such an all-compelling force be synonymous with that poor little State and Church-begotten weed, marriage?

EMMA GOLDMAN (1869–1940), U.S. anarchist. *Anarchism and Other Essays*, "Marriage and Love" (1910).

6   Love is moral even without legal marriage, but marriage is immoral without love.

ELLEN KEY (1849–1926), Swedish author, feminist. *The Morality of Woman and Other Essays*, "The Morality of Woman" (1911).

7   Nature admits of no permanence in the relation between man and woman. . . . It is only man's egoism that wants to keep woman like some buried treasure. All endeavors to introduce permanence in love, the most changeable thing in this changeable human existence, have gone shipwreck in spite of religious ceremonies, vows, and legalities.

LEOPOLD VON SACHER-MASOCH (1836–95), Austrian novel-

ist. Wanda, in *Venus in Furs*, "Confessions of a Supersensual Man" (1870; tr. 1928).

8   Marrying to increase love is like gaming to become rich; alas, you only lose what little stock you had before.

WILLIAM WYCHERLEY (1640–1716), English dramatist. Lucy, in *The Country Wife*, act 4

See Goldsmith on PASSION.

MARTYRDOM

1   But whether on the scaffold high,
Or in the battle's van,
The fittest place where man can die
Is where he dies for man.

MICHAEL J. BARRY (1817–89), Irish barrister. *The Place to Die*.

2   I am as content to die for God's eternal truth on the scaffold as in any other way.

JOHN BROWN (1800–1859), U.S. abolitionist. Letter, 2 Dec. 1859, to his children on the eve of his execution.

3   Martyrs, *cher ami*, must choose between being forgotten, mocked or made use of. As for being understood—never!

ALBERT CAMUS (1913–60), French-Algerian philosopher, author. The narrator (Jean-Baptiste Clamence), in *The Fall* (1956; ed. 1957, p. 57).

4   No human beings more dangerous than those who have suffered for a belief: the great persecutors are recruited from the martyrs not quite beheaded. Far from diminishing the appetite for power, suffering exasperates it.

E. M. CIORAN (b. 1911), Romanian-born French philosopher. *A Short History of Decay*, ch. 1, "Genealogy of Fanaticism" (1949).

5   The people who have really made history are the martyrs.

ALEISTER CROWLEY (1875–1947), British occultist. *The Confessions of Aleister Crowley*, ch. 4 (1929; rev. 1970).

6   We are not here to triumph by fighting, by stratagem, or by resistance,
Not to fight with beasts as men. We have fought the beast
And have conquered. We have only to conquer
Now, by suffering. This is the easier victory.

T. S. ELIOT (1888–1965), Anglo-American poet, critic. Thomas, in *Murder in the Cathedral*, pt. 2 (1935).

7   The martyr cannot be dishonored. Every lash inflicted is a tongue of fame; every prison a more illustrious abode.

RALPH WALDO EMERSON (1803–82), U.S. essayist, poet, philosopher. *Essays*,"Compensation" (First Series, 1841).

8   The torments of martyrdom are probably most keenly felt by the bystanders.

RALPH WALDO EMERSON (1803–82), U.S. essayist, poet, philosopher. *Society and Solitude*, "Courage" (1870).

9   Even if I died in the service of the nation, I would be proud of it. Every drop of my blood . . . will contribute to the growth of this nation and to make it strong and dynamic.

> INDIRA GANDHI (1917–84), Indian prime minster. Speech, 30 Oct. 1984, in Delhi on the eve of her assassination by Sikh militants.

10 While I do not suggest that humanity will ever be able to dispense with its martyrs, I cannot avoid the suspicion that with a little more thought and a little less belief their number may be substantially reduced.

> J. B. S. HALDANE (1892–1964), British scientist. *Possible Worlds,* "The Duty of Doubt" (1927).

11 What signify a few lives lost in a century or two? The tree of liberty must be refreshed from time to time with the blood of patriots and tyrants. It is its natural manure.

> THOMAS JEFFERSON (1743–1826), U.S. president. Letter, 13 Nov. 1787, referring to Daniel Shays's rebellion of poor farmers in Massachusetts. Jefferson, writing from Paris, was the only one of the American leaders not alarmed by news of the revolt.

12 I have been astonished that men could die martyrs for religion—I have shuddered at it. I shudder no more—I could be martyred for my religion—Love is my religion—I could die for that.

> JOHN KEATS (1795–1821), English poet. Letter, 13 Oct. 1819, to his fiancée Fanny Brawne (published in *Letters of John Keats,* no. 160, ed. by Frederick Page, 1954).

13 The difference between a man who faces death for the sake of an idea and an imitator who goes in search of martyrdom is that whilst the former expresses his idea most fully in death it is the strange feeling of bitterness which comes from failure that the latter really enjoys; the former rejoices in his victory, the latter in his suffering.

> SØREN KIERKEGAARD (1813–55), Danish philosopher. *The Journals of Søren Kierkegaard: A Selection,* no. 46 (ed. and tr. by Alexander Dru, 1938), March 1836 entry.

14 If a man hasn't discovered something that he will die for, he isn't fit to live.

> MARTIN LUTHER KING, JR. (1929–68), U.S. clergyman, civil rights leader. Speech, 23 June 1963, Detroit, Mich.

15 Play the man, Master Ridley; we shall this day light such a candle, by God's grace, in England, as I trust shall never be put out.

> BISHOP HUGH LATIMER (1485–1555), English churchman, Protestant martyr. Said 16 Oct. 1555 to Bishop Nicolas Ridley at their execution pyre in Oxford.

16 The martyr sacrifices *her*self (*him*self in a few instances) entirely in vain. Or rather not in vain; for she (or he) makes the selfish more selfish, the lazy more lazy, the narrow narrower.

> FLORENCE NIGHTINGALE (1820–1910), English nurse. Letter, c. 1867, to the scholar Benjamin Jowett (published in *Forever Yours, Florence Nightingale: Selected Letters,* ch. 4, 1989).

17 There are in every generation those who shrink from the ultimate sacrifice, but there are in every generation those who make it with joy and laughter and these are the salt of the generations.

> PATRICK HENRY PEARSE (1879–1916), Irish nationalist leader. Commemoration address, 2 March 1914, Brooklyn, N.Y., for Irish patriot Robert Emmet, executed in 1803 for his part in an abortive invasion of Ireland. Pearse was himself executed by the British in 1916 for his part in the Easter Rising, when he was proclaimed president of the provisional republican government.

18 I will soon be going out to shape all the singing tomorrows.

> GABRIEL PÉRI, French Communist leader. Letter, July 1942, written shortly before his execution by the Germans. Quoted in: *New York Times* (11 April 1943).

19 Martyrdom covers a multitude of sins.

> MARK TWAIN (1835–1910), U.S. author. *Notebook,* ch. 33 (ed. by Albert Bigelow Paine, 1935), entry for 23 May 1903.

20 A thing is not necessarily true because a man dies for it.

> OSCAR WILDE (1854–1900), Anglo-Irish playwright, author. Erskine, in *The Portrait of Mr. W. H.,* ch. 1 (first published in *Blackwood's Edinburgh Magazine,* July 1889).

21 No man dies for what he knows to be true. Men die for what they want to be true, for what some terror in their hearts tells them is not true.

> OSCAR WILDE (1854–1900), Anglo-Irish playwright, author. *The Portrait of Mr. W. H.,* ch. 1 (first published in *Blackwood's Edinburgh Magazine,* July 1889).

See also Dryden on CONFORMITY; Ewer on FREEDOM.

MARXISM

1 Our tradition of political thought had its definite beginning in the teachings of Plato and Aristotle. I believe it came to a no less definite end in the theories of Karl Marx.

> HANNAH ARENDT (1906–75), German-born U.S. political philosopher. *Between Past and Future,* ch. 1 (1961).

2 The point, as Marx saw it, is that dreams never come true.

> HANNAH ARENDT (1906–75), German-born U.S. political philosopher. *Crises of the Republic,* "On Violence," sct. 1, (1970), referring to the student rebellions in the 1960s.

3 The Marxist analysis has got nothing to do with what happened in Stalin's Russia: it's like blaming Jesus Christ for the Inquisition in Spain.

> TONY BENN (b. 1925), British Labour politician. Quoted in: *Observer* (London, 27 April 1980).

4 Marxism is not scientific: at the best, it has scientific prejudices.

> ALBERT CAMUS (1913–60), French-Algerian philosopher, author. *The Rebel,* pt. 3, "State Terrorism and Rational Terror" (1951; tr. 1953).

5 One good reason for the popularity of "reductionism" among the philosophical outposts of the Western Establishment is that it can be, and is, used as a device for trying to take the wind, so to speak, out of the sails of Marxism. . . . In essence reductionism is a kind of anti-Marxist caricature of Marxist determinism. It is what anti-Marxists pretend that Marxist determinism is.

> CLAUD COCKBURN (1904–81), British author, journalist. *Cockburn Sums Up,* "Days of Hope" (1981).

6 Ask anyone committed to Marxist analysis how

many angels on the head of a pin, and you will be asked in return to never mind the angels, tell me who controls the production of pins.

> JOAN DIDION (b. 1934), U.S. essayist. *The White Album*, "The Women's Movement" (1979).

7 It has been the acknowledged right of every Marxist scholar to read into Marx the particular meaning that he himself prefers and to treat all others with indignation.

> JOHN KENNETH GALBRAITH (b. 1908), U.S. economist. *The Age of Uncertainty*, ch. 3 (1977).

8 Workers of the world forgive me.

> GRAFFITO ON THE BUST OF KARL MARX IN BUCHAREST. Quoted in: *Times* (London, 4 May 1990).

9 When asked whether or not we are Marxists, our position is the same as that of a physicist or a biologist who is asked if he is a "Newtonian," or if he is a "Pasteurian."

> CHE [ERNESTO] GUEVARA (1928–67), Cuban revolutionary leader. Quoted in: *Radical Currents in Contemporary Philosophy* (ed. by David DeGrood, 1971).

10 Marxism is like a classical building that followed the Renaissance; beautiful in its way, but incapable of growth.

> HAROLD MACMILLAN (1894–1986), British Conservative politician, prime minister. Speech, 29 April 1981.

11 What I did that was new was to prove: (1) that the existence of classes is only bound up with particular, historic phases in the development of production; (2) that the class struggle necessarily leads to the dictatorship of the proletariat; (3) that this dictatorship itself only constitutes the transition to the abolition of all classes and to a classless society.

> KARL MARX (1818–83), German political theorist, social philosopher. Letter, 5 March 1852 (published in *Selected Works*, vol. 1, 1942).

12 All I know is I'm not a Marxist.

> KARL MARX (1818–83), German political theorist, social philosopher. Quoted by Engels in a letter, 5 Aug. 1890, to Conrad Schmidt. Engels had earlier quoted the same remark in French in a letter, 2–3 Nov. 1882, to Eduard Bernstein—"Ce qu'il y a de certain, c'est que moi je ne suis pas Marxiste" — recalling Marx's words to his son-in-law, French socialist Paul Lafargue, when he rejected the French "Marxists" of the late 1870s.

13 There's something about Marxism that brings out warts—the only kind of growth this economic system encourages.

> P. J. O'ROURKE (b. 1947), U.S. journalist. "The Death of Communism," in *Rolling Stone* (New York, Nov. 1989; repr. in *Give War A Chance*, 1992).

14 The moralist and the revolutionary are constantly undermining one another. Marx exploded a hundred tons of dynamite beneath the moralist position, and we are still living in the echo of that tremendous crash. But already, somewhere or other, the sappers are at work and fresh dynamite is being tamped in place to blow Marx at the moon. Then Marx, or somebody like him, will come back with yet more dynamite, and so the process continues, to an end we cannot foresee.

> GEORGE ORWELL (1903–50), British author. *Inside the Whale and Other Essays*, "Charles Dickens" (1940).

15 The Marxist vision of man without God must eventually be seen as an empty and a false faith—the second oldest in the world—first proclaimed in the Garden of Eden with whispered words of temptation: "Ye shall be as gods."

> RONALD REAGAN (b. 1911), U.S. Republican politician, president. Speech, 20 March 1981, to Conservative Political Action Conference, Washington, D.C. (published in *Speaking My Mind*, 1990).

16 Marxism is essentially a product of the bourgeois mind.

> JOSEPH A. SCHUMPETER (1883–1950), Austrian-American economist. *Capitalism, Socialism and Democracy*, ch. 1 (1942).

17 Marxism *is* a religion. To the believer it presents, first, a system of ultimate ends that embody the meaning of life and are absolute standards by which to judge events and actions; and, secondly, a guide to those ends which implies a plan of salvation and the indication of the evil from which mankind, or a chosen section of mankind, is to be saved.

> JOSEPH A. SCHUMPETER (1883–1950), Austrian-American economist. *Capitalism, Socialism and Democracy*, ch. 1 (1942).

See also COMMUNISM; SOCIALISM.

THE MASSES

1 What will happen once the authentic mass man takes over, we do not know yet, although it may be a fair guess that he will have more in common with the meticulous, calculated correctness of Himmler than with the hysterical fanaticism of Hitler, will more resemble the stubborn dulless of Molotov than the sensual vindictive cruelty of Stalin.

> HANNAH ARENDT (1906–75), German-born U.S. political philosopher. *The Origins of Totalitarianism*, ch. 10, sct. 2 (1951), referring to the masses in a totalitarian society.

2 The adjustment of reality to the masses and of the masses to reality is a process of unlimited scope, as much for thinking as for perception.

> WALTER BENJAMIN (1892–1940), German critic, philosopher. *The Work of Art in the Age of Mechanical Reproduction*, sct. 3 (1936; repr. in *Illuminations*, ed. by Hannah Arendt, 1968).

3 Civilization exists precisely so that there may be no masses but rather men alert enough never to constitute masses.

> GEORGES BERNANOS (1888–1948), French novelist, political writer. *The Last Essays of Georges Bernanos*, "Why Freedom?" (1955).

4 The only freedom supposed to be left to the masses is that of grazing on the ration of simulacra the system distributes to each individual.

> MICHEL DE CERTEAU (1925–86), French author, critic. *The Practice of Everyday Life*, ch. 12 (1974).

5 The English masses are lovable: they are kind, decent, tolerant, practical and not stupid. The tragedy is that they are too many of them, and that they are aimless, having outgrown the servile functions for which they were encouraged to multiply. One day these huge crowds will have to seize power because there will be nothing else for them to do, and yet they neither demand power nor are ready to make use of it; they will learn only to be bored in a new way.

CYRIL CONNOLLY (1903–74), British critic. *The Unquiet Grave*, pt. 1 (1944; rev. 1951).

6 The general interest of the masses might take the place of the insight of genius if it were allowed freedom of action.

DENIS DIDEROT (1713–84), French philosopher. *Observations on the Drawing up of Laws* (1921; repr. in *Selected Writings*, ed. by Lester G. Crocker, 1966), written 1774 for Catherine the Great.

7 Leave this hypocritical prating about the masses. Masses are rude, lame, unmade, pernicious in their demands and influence, and need not to be flattered, but to be schooled. I wish not to concede anything to them, but to tame, drill, divide, and break them up, and draw individuals out of them.

RALPH WALDO EMERSON (1803–82), U.S. essayist, poet, philosopher. *The Conduct of Life*, "Considerations by the Way" (1860).

8 None of us know all the potentialities that slumber in the spirit of the population, or all the ways in which that population can surprise us when there is the right interplay of events.

VÁCLAV HAVEL (b. 1936), Czech playwright, president. *Disturbing the Peace*, ch. 3 (1986; tr. 1990).

9 The broad masses of a population are more amenable to the appeal of rhetoric than to any other force.

ADOLF HITLER (1889–1945), German dictator. *Mein Kampf*, vol. 1, ch. 3 (1925).

10 There is a grandeur in the uniformity of the mass. When a fashion, a dance, a song, a slogan or a joke sweeps like wildfire from one end of the continent to the other, and a hundred million people roar with laughter, sway their bodies in unison, hum one song or break forth in anger and denunciation, there is the overpowering feeling that in this country we have come nearer the brotherhood of man than ever before.

ERIC HOFFER (1902–83), U.S. philosopher. *The Passionate State of Mind*, aph. 169 (1955).

11 Masses are always breeding grounds of psychic epidemics.

CARL JUNG (1875–1961), Swiss psychiatrist. *Concerning Rebirth* (1940; repr. in *Collected Works*, vol. 9, pt. 1, para. 227, ed. by William McGuire, 1959).

12 It's no go the Government grants, it's no go the
elections,
Sit on your arse for fifty years and hang your hat
on a pension.

LOUIS MACNEICE (1907–63), British poet. *Bagpipe Music*.

13 Take the ideas of the masses (scattered and unsystematic ideas) and concentrate them (through study turn them into concentrated and systematic ideas), then go to the masses and propagate and explain these ideas until the masses embrace them as their own, hold fast to them and translate them into action, and test the correctness of these ideas in such action. Then once again concentrate ideas from the masses and once again go to the masses so that the ideas are persevered in and carried through. And so on, over and over again in an endless spiral, with the ideas becoming more correct, more vital and richer each time. Such is the Marxist theory of knowledge.

MAO ZEDONG (1893–1976), Founder of the People's Republic of China. "Some Questions Concerning Methods of Leadership," June 1943 (published in *Selected Works*, vol. 3).

14 I have witnessed the tremendous energy of the masses. On this foundation it is possible to accomplish any task whatsoever.

MAO ZEDONG (1893–1976), Founder of the People's Republic of China. Said in Sept. 1958. Quoted in: Stanley Karnow, *Mao and China: From Revolution to Revolution*, ch. 5 (1972).

15 The only power deserving the name is that of masses, and of governments while they make themselves the organ of the tendencies and instincts of masses.

JOHN STUART MILL (1806–73), English philosopher, economist. *On Liberty*, ch. 3 (1859).

16 The exuberant fertility of the universal will.

FRIEDRICH NIETZSCHE (1844–1900), German philosopher. *The Birth of Tragedy*, ch. 17 (1872).

17 The mass believes that it has the right to impose and to give force of law to notions born in the café.

JOSÉ ORTEGA Y GASSET (1883–1955), Spanish essayist, philosopher. *The Revolt of the Masses*, ch. 1 (1930).

18 This leads us to note down in our psychological chart of the mass-man of today two fundamental traits: the free expansion of his vital desires, and, therefore, of his personality; and his radical ingratitude towards all that has made possible the ease of his existence. These traits together make up the well-known psychology of the spoilt child.

JOSÉ ORTEGA Y GASSET (1883–1955), Spanish essayist, philosopher. *The Revolt of the Masses*, ch. 6 (1930).

19 For men tied fast to the absolute, bled of their differences, drained of their dreams by authoritarian leeches until nothing but pulp is left, become a massive, sick Thing whose sheer weight is used ruthlessly by ambitious men. Here is the real enemy of the people: our own selves dehumanized into "the masses." And where is the David who can slay this giant?

LILLIAN SMITH (1897–1966), U.S. author. *The Journey*, Prologue (1954).

20 The mass never comes up to the standard of its best member, but on the contrary degrades itself to a level with the lowest.

HENRY DAVID THOREAU (1817–62), U.S. philosopher, author, naturalist. *Journals* (1906), entry for 14 March 1838.

21 The human animal cannot be trusted for anything *good* except en masse. The combined thought and action of the whole people of any race, creed or nationality, will always point in the right direction.

HARRY S TRUMAN (1884–1972), U.S. Democratic politician, president. Memorandum, 22 May 1945 (published in William Hillman, *Mr. President*, pt. 3, 1952).

22 The mind of the people is like mud,
From which arise strange and beautiful things.

W. J. TURNER (1889–1946), British poet. *Talking with Soldiers.*

23 The master minds of all nations, in all ages, have sprung in affluent multitude from the mass of the nation, and from the mass of the nation only—not from its privileged classes.

MARK TWAIN (1835–1910), U.S. author. *A Connecticut Yankee in King Arthur's Court,* ch. 25 (1889).

24 Our leading men are not of much account and never have been, but the average of the people is immense, beyond all history. Sometimes I think in all departments, literature and art included, that will be the way our superiority will exhibit itself. We will not have great individuals or great leaders, but a great average bulk, unprecedentedly great.

WALT WHITMAN (1819–92), U.S. poet. *Specimen Days and Collect,* "An Interviewer's Item" (1882).

See also Gladstone on CLASS; The PEOPLE; Warshow on POPULAR CULTURE.

MASTURBATION

1 Hey, don't knock masturbation! It's sex with someone I love.

WOODY ALLEN (b. 1935), U.S. filmmaker. Alvy Singer (Allen), in the film *Annie Hall* (directed by Woody Allen, scripted by Allen with Marshall Brickman, 1977; repr. in *Four Films of Woody Allen,* 1982).

2 The moment of desire! the moment of desire! The virgin
That pines for man shall awaken her womb to enormous joys
In the secret shadows of her chamber: the youth shut up from
The lustful joy shall forget to generate & create an amorous image
In the shadows of his curtains and in the folds of his silent pillow.
Are not these the places of religion, the rewards of continence,
The self-enjoyings of self-denial? why dost thou seek religion?
Is it because acts are not lovely that thou seekest solitude
Where the horrible darkness is impressed with reflections of desire?

WILLIAM BLAKE (1757–1827), English poet, painter, engraver. Oothoon, in *Visions of the Daughters of Albion,* plate 7 (1793; repr. in *Complete Writings,* ed. by Geoffrey Keynes, 1957).

3 Masturbation is not only an expression of self-regard: it is also the natural emotional outlet of those who . . . have already accepted as inevitable the wide gulf between their real futures and the expectations of their fantasies.

QUENTIN CRISP (b. 1908), British author. *The Naked Civil Servant,* ch. 2 (1968).

4 Removed from its more restrictive sense, mastur-bation has become an expression for everything that has proved, for lack of human contact, to be void of meaning. We have communication problems, suffer from egocentrism and narcissism, are frustrated by information glut and loss of environment; we stagnate despite the rising GNP.

GÜNTHER GRASS (b. 1927), German author. *From the Diary of a Snail,* "On Stasis in Progress" (1972).

5 The one thing that it seems impossible to escape from, once the habit is formed, is masturbation. It goes on and on, on into old age, in spite of marriage or love affairs or anything else. And it always carries this secret feeling of futility and humiliation, futility and humiliation. And this is, perhaps, the deepest and most dangerous cancer of our civilization. Instead of being a comparatively pure and harmless vice, masturbation is certainly the most dangerous sexual vice that a society can be afflicted with, in the long run. Comparatively pure it may be—purity being what it is. But harmless!!!

D. H. LAWRENCE (1885–1930), British author. *Pornography and Obscenity* (1930; repr. in *Phoenix: The Posthumous Papers of D. H. Lawrence,* pt. 3, ed. by E. McDonald, 1936).

6 In masturbation there is nothing but loss. There is no reciprocity. There is merely the spending away of a certain force, and no return. The body remains, in a sense, a corpse, after the act of self-abuse. There is no change, only deadening. There is what we call dead loss. And this is not the case in any act of sexual intercourse between two people. Two people may destroy one another in sex. But they cannot just produce the null effect of masturbation.

D. H. LAWRENCE (1885–1930), British author. *Pornography and Obscenity* (1930; repr. in *Phoenix: The Posthumous Papers of D H Lawrence,* pt. 3, ed. by E. McDonald, 1936).

7 Women are denied masturbation even more severely than men and that's another method of control—they're not taught to please themselves. . . . Most women—it takes them a while to warm up to the "situation," but once they get into it, I'm sure they're going to get just as hooked as—well, everyone I know is!

LYDIA LUNCH (b. 1959), U.S. rock vocalist. Interview in *Re/Search,* no. 13, *Angry Women* (San Francisco, 1991).

8 Masturbation: the primary sexual activity of mankind. In the nineteenth century, it was a disease; in the twentieth, it's a cure.

THOMAS SZASZ (b. 1920), U.S. psychiatrist. *The Second Sin,* "Sex" (1973).

MATERIALISM

1 The son will run away from the family not at eighteen but at twelve, emancipated by his gluttonous precocity; he will fly not to seek heroic adventures, not to deliver a beautiful prisoner from a tower, not to immortalize a garret with sublime thoughts, but to found a business, to enrich himself and to compete with his infamous papa.

CHARLES BAUDELAIRE (1821–67), French poet. "Squibs," in *Intimate Journals,* sct. 22 (1887; tr. by Christopher Isherwood, 1930; rev. by Don Bachardy, 1989).

2 Young people everywhere have been allowed to choose between love and a garbage disposal unit. Everywhere they have chosen the garbage disposal unit.

> GUY DEBORD (b. 1931), French Situationist philosopher. *The Incomplete Works of the Situationist International,* "Formula for a New City" (ed. by Christopher Gray, 1974).

3 Once one is caught up into the material world not one person in ten thousand finds the time to form literary taste, to examine the validity of philosophic concepts for himself, or to form what, for lack of a better phrase, I might call the wise and tragic sense of life.

> F. SCOTT FITZGERALD (1896–1940), U.S. author. Letter, 5 Oct. 1940, to his daughter, Frances Scott Fitzgerald (published in *The Letters of F. Scott Fitzgerald,* ed. by Andrew Turnbull, 1963).

4 Our life on earth is, and ought to be, material and carnal. But we have not yet learned to manage our materialism and carnality properly; they are still entangled with the desire for ownership.

> E. M. FORSTER (1879–1970), British novelist and essayist. (1926; repr. in *Abinger Harvest,* "My Wood" (1927).

5 When we of the so-called better classes are scared as men were never scared in history at material ugliness and hardship; when we put off marriage until our house can be artistic, and quake at the thought of having a child without a bank-account and doomed to manual labor, it is time for thinking men to protest against so unmanly and irreligious a state of opinion.

> WILLIAM JAMES (1842–1910), U.S. psychologist, philosopher. *The Varieties of Religious Experience,* Lectures 14 and 15 (1902).

6 Most men love money and security more, and creation and construction less, as they get older.

> JOHN MAYNARD KEYNES (1883–1946), British economist. *Essays in Persuasion,* "The Future" (1931).

7 The people recognize themselves in their commodities; they find their soul in their automobile, hi-fi set, split-level home, kitchen equipment.

> HERBERT MARCUSE (1898–1979), U.S. political philosopher. *One-Dimensional Man,* ch. 1 (1964).

8 The strongest argument for the un-materialistic character of American life is the fact that we tolerate conditions that are, from a negative point of view, intolerable. What the foreigner finds most objectionable in American life is its lack of basic comfort. No nation with any sense of material well-being would endure the food we eat, the cramped apartments we live in, the noise, the traffic, the crowded subways and buses. American life, in large cities, is a perpetual assault on the senses and the nerves; it is out of asceticism, out of unworldliness, precisely, that we bear it.

> MARY MCCARTHY (1912–89), U.S. author, critic. "America the Beautiful," in *Commentary* (New York, Sept. 1947; repr. in *On the Contrary,* 1961).

9 Freedom comes only to those who no longer ask of life that it shall yield them any of those personal goods that are subject to the mutations of time.

> BERTRAND RUSSELL (1872–1970), British philosopher, mathematician. *A Free Man's Worship and Other Essays,* ch. 1 (1976).

10 Any so-called material thing that you want is mere-ly a symbol: you want it not for *itself,* but because it will content your spirit for the moment.

> MARK TWAIN (1835–1910), U.S. author. Old Man, in *What Is Man?,* sct. 6 (1906; repr. in *Complete Essays,* ed. by Charles Neider, 1963).

11 When we try in good faith to believe in materialism, in the exclusive reality of the physical, we are asking our selves to step aside; we are disavowing the very realm where we exist and where all things precious are kept—the realm of emotion and conscience, of memory and intention and sensation.

> JOHN UPDIKE (b. 1932), U.S. author, critic. *Self-Consciousness: Memoirs,* ch. 6 (1989).

12 The organization controlling the material equipment of our everyday life is such that what in itself would enable us to construct it richly plunges us instead into a poverty of abundance, making alienation all the more intolerable as each convenience promises liberation and turns out to be only one more burden. We are condemned to slavery to the means of liberation.

> RAOUL VANEIGEM (b. 1934), Belgian Situationist philosopher. "Basic Banalities II," in *Internationale Situationiste,* no. 8 (Paris, Jan. 1963; repr. in *Situationist International Anthology,* ed. by Ken Knabb, 1981).

13 Production and consumption are the nipples of modern society. Thus suckled, humanity grows in strength and beauty; rising standard of living, all modern conveniences, distractions of all kinds, culture for all, the comfort of your dreams.

> RAOUL VANEIGEM (b. 1934), Belgian Situationist philosopher. *The Revolution of Everyday Life,* ch. 7, sct. 1 (1967; tr. 1983).

See also The CONSUMER SOCIETY; Tuchman on The NEW WORLD; Muggeridge on SEX.

MATHEMATICS

1 How happy the lot of the mathematician! He is judged solely by his peers, and the standard is so high that no colleague or rival can ever win a reputation he does not deserve. No cashier writes a letter to the press complaining about the incomprehensibility of Modern Mathematics and comparing it unfavorably with the good old days when mathematicians were content to paper irregularly shaped rooms and fill bathtubs without closing the waste pipe.

> W. H. AUDEN (1907–73), Anglo-American poet. *The Dyer's Hand,* pt. 1, "Writing" (1962).

2 All science requires mathematics. The knowledge of mathematical things is almost innate in us. . . . This is the easiest of sciences, a fact which is obvious in that no one's brain rejects it; for laymen and people who are utterly illiterate know how to count and reckon.

> ROGER BACON (c. 1214-C. 1294), English philosopher, scientist. *Opus Maius,* pt. 4, ch. 1 (1267).

3 I know that two and two make four—& should be glad to prove it too if I could—though I must say if by any sort of process I could convert 2 & 2 into *five* it would give me much greater pleasure.

> LORD BYRON (1788–1824), English poet. Letter, 1813, to

Annabella Milbanke, later Lady Byron (published in *Byron's Letters and Journals,* vol. 3, no. 10, ed. by Leslie A. Marchand, 1973–81).

4   Yet what are all such gaieties to me
Whose thoughts are full of indices and surds?

LEWIS CARROLL (1832–98), English author, mathematician. *Four Riddles,* no. 1 (1869; repr. in *Phantasmagoria and Other Poems,* 1919).

5   As far as the laws of mathematics refer to reality, they are not certain, and as far as they are certain, they do not refer to reality.

ALBERT EINSTEIN (1879–1955), German-born U.S. scientist. Quoted in: Fritjof Capra, *The Tao of Physics,* ch. 2 (1975).

6   Mathematics may be compared to a mill of exquisite workmanship, which grinds your stuff to any degree of fineness; but, nevertheless, what you get out depends on what you put in; and as the grandest mill in the world will not extract wheat flour from peascods, so pages of formulae will not get a definite result out of loose data.

THOMAS HENRY HUXLEY (1825–95), English biologist. "Geological Reform" (1869; published in *Collected Essays,* vol. 8, 1894).

7   I would advise you Sir, to study algebra, if you are not already an adept in it: your head would be less *muddy,* and you will leave off tormenting your neighbours about paper and packthread, while we all live together in a world that is bursting with sin and sorrow.

SAMUEL JOHNSON (1709–84), English author, lexicographer. Remark to a warehouse packer. Quoted in: Hester Piozzi, *Anecdotes of Samuel Johnson* (1786; repr. in *Johnsonian Miscellanies,* vol. 1, 1897, p. 301). Mrs. Piozzi also recorded that "when Mr. Johnson felt his fancy, or fancied he felt it, disordered, his constant recurrence was to the study of arithmetic."

8   Nobody before the Pythagoreans had thought that mathematical relations held the secret of the universe. Twenty-five centuries later, Europe is still blessed and cursed with their heritage. To non-European civilizations, the idea that numbers are the key to both wisdom and power, seems never to have occurred.

ARTHUR KOESTLER (1905–83), Hungarian-born British author. *The Sleepwalkers,* pt. 1, ch. 2, sct. 4 (1959).

9   Stand firm in your refusal to remain conscious during algebra. In real life, I assure you, there is no such thing as algebra.

FRAN LEBOWITZ (b. 1951), U.S. journalist. *Social Studies,* "Tips for Teens" (1981).

10   So-called professional mathematicians have, in their reliance on the relative incapacity of the rest of mankind, acquired for themselves a reputation for profundity very similar to the reputation for sanctity possessed by theologians.

G. C. LICHTENBERG (1742–99), German physicist, philosopher. *Aphorisms,* "Notebook K," aph. 52 (written 1765–99; tr. by R. J. Hollingdale, 1990).

11   Mathematics . . . would certainly have not come into existence if one had known from the beginning that there was in nature no exactly straight line, no actual circle, no absolute magnitude.

FRIEDRICH NIETZSCHE (1844–1900), German philosopher. *Human, All Too Human,* sct. 11 (1878).

12   I have hardly ever known a mathematician who was capable of reasoning.

PLATO c. 427–347 B.C.), Greek philosopher. *The Republic,* bk. 7, sct. 531e (tr. by Benjamin Jowett).

13   Mathematics may be defined as the subject in which we never know what we are talking about, nor whether what we are saying is true.

BERTRAND RUSSELL (1872–1970), British philosopher, mathematician. *Mysticism and Logic,* ch. 4 (1917; article first published in *International Monthly,* vol. 4, 1901). In a letter of March 1912 to Lady Ottoline Morrell, Russell wrote: "I like mathematics because it is not human and has nothing particular to do with this planet or with the whole accidental universe—because, like Spinoza's God, it won't love us in return."

14   Mathematics is not a book confined within a cover and bound between brazen clasps, whose contents it needs only patience to ransack; it is not a mine, whose treasures may take long to reduce into possession, but which fill only a limited number of veins and lodes; it is not a soil, whose fertility can be exhausted by the yield of successive harvests; it is not a continent or an ocean, whose area can be mapped out and its contour defined: it is limitless as that space which it finds too narrow for its aspirations; its possibilities are as infinite as the worlds which are forever crowding in and multiplying upon the astronomer's gaze.

JAMES JOSEPH SYLVESTER (1814–97), English mathematician, poet. Commemoration Day Address, 1877, at Johns Hopkins University.

15   In the midst of this chopping sea of civilized life, such are the clouds and storms and quicksands and thousand-and-one items to be allowed for, that a man has to live, if he would not founder and go to the bottom and not make his port at all, by dead reckoning, and he must be a great calculator indeed who succeeds.

HENRY DAVID THOREAU (1817–62), U.S. philosopher, author, naturalist. *Walden,* "Where I Lived, and What I Lived For" (1854).

16   Mathematics alone make us feel the limits of our intelligence. For we can always suppose in the case of an experiment that it is inexplicable because we don't happen to have all the data. In mathematics we have all the data . . . and yet we don't understand. We always come back to the contemplation of our human wretchedness. What force is in relation to our will, the impenetrable opacity of mathematics is in relation to our intelligence.

SIMONE WEIL (1909–43), French philosopher, mystic. *Notebooks,* vol. 2 (1952–55; repr. 1956, p. 511).

MATURITY

1   Ah, but I was so much older then,
I'm younger than that now.

BOB DYLAN (b. 1941), U.S. singer, songwriter. "My Back Pages," from the album *Another Side of Bob Dylan* (1964).

2   By the time a person has achieved years adequate for choosing a direction, the die is cast and the moment has long since passed which determined the future.

ZELDA FITZGERALD (1900–1948), U.S. writer. Alabama Beggs, in *Save Me the Waltz,* ch. 4, sct. 3 (1932).

3   Maturity: among other things, the unclouded happiness of the child at play, who takes it for granted that he is at one with his play-mates.

> DAG HAMMARSKJÖLD (1905–61), Swedish statesman, Secretary-General of U.N. *Markings*, "Night Is Drawing Nigh" (1963).

4   True maturity is only reached when a man realizes he has become a father figure to his girlfriends' boyfriends—and he accepts it.

> LARRY MCMURTRY (b. 1936), U.S. screenwriter, novelist, essayist. Danny Deck, in *Some Can Whistle*, pt. 1, ch. 12 (1989).

5   When the apple is ripe it will fall.

> IRISH PROVERB. An English equivalent to this might be, "To everything there is a season." See Hebrew Bible on TIME.

6   Your lordship, though not clean past your youth, have yet some smack of age in you, some relish of the saltness of time.

> WILLIAM SHAKESPEARE (1564–1616), English dramatist, poet. Falstaff, to the Lord Chief Justice, in *King Henry IV, Pt. 2*, act 1, sc. 2.

7   One does not get better but different and older and that is always a pleasure.

> GERTRUDE STEIN (1874–1946), U.S. author. Letter, 22 May 1925, to author F. Scott Fitzgerald (first published in *The Crack-Up*, ed. by Edmund Wilson, 1945).

8   If . . . boyhood and youth are but vanity, must it not be our ambition to become men?

> VINCENT VAN GOGH (1853–90), Dutch painter. Letter, 12 Sept. 1875, to his brother Theo (published in *The Complete Letters of Vincent Van Gogh*, vol. 1, 1958).

9   My experience is that as soon as people are old enough to know better, they don't know anything at all.

> OSCAR WILDE (1854–1900), Anglo-Irish playwright, author. Cecil Graham, in *Lady Windermere's Fan*, act 2.

See also ADULTHOOD.

MAXIMS

See PROVERBS AND MAXIMS.

MCCARTHYISM

1   They'll nail anyone who ever scratched his ass during the National Anthem.

> HUMPHREY BOGART (1899–1957), U.S. screen actor. Quoted on his death, 14 Jan. 1957, Bogart was referring to the House Un-American Activities Committee.

2   The junior senator from Wisconsin, by his reckless charges, has so preyed upon the fears and hatreds and prejudices of the American people that he has started a prairie fire which neither he nor anyone else may be able to control.

> J. WILLIAM FULBRIGHT (b. 1905), U.S. Democratic politician. Speech, 30 Nov. 1954, to U.S. Senate.

3   Every age develops its own peculiar forms of pathology, which express in exaggerated form its underlying character structure.

> CHRISTOPHER LASCH (b. 1932), U.S. historian. *The Culture of Narcissism*, ch. 2, "Social Influences on Narcissism" (1979).

4   There is a hate layer of opinion and emotion in America. There will be other McCarthys to come who will be hailed as its heroes.

> MAX LERNER (b. 1902), U.S. author, columnist. "McCarthyism: The Smell of Decay," in *New York Post* (5 April 1950; repr. in *The Unfinished Country*, pt. 4, 1959). The word "McCarthyism" was first coined in this article, as Lerner affirmed in a later column, 3 Feb. 1954: "For my own part I doubt seriously whether the word will outlast the political power of the man from whom it derives."

5   McCarthyism is Americanism with its sleeves rolled.

> JOSEPH MCCARTHY (1908–57), U.S. Republican politician. Speech, 1952, Wisconsin. Quoted in: Richard Rovere, *Senator Joe McCarthy*, ch. 1 (1973).

6   No one can terrorize a whole nation, unless we are all his accomplices.

> EDWARD R. MURROW (1908–65), U.S. newscaster. "See It Now," broadcast, 7 March 1954, CBS-TV.

7   The nation that complacently and fearfully allows its artists and writers to become suspected rather than respected is no longer regarded as a nation possessed with humor in depth.

> JAMES THURBER (1894–1961), U.S. humorist, illustrator. *New York Times Magazine* (7 Dec. 1958), in response to the question of whether humor was in decline in the United States.

MEANING

1   Everywhere one seeks to produce meaning, to make the world signify, to render it visible. We are not, however, in danger of lacking meaning; quite the contrary, we are gorged with meaning and it is killing us.

> JEAN BAUDRILLARD (b. 1929), French semiologist. *The Ecstasy of Communication*, "Seduction, or the Superficial Abyss" (1987).

2   Just as all thought, and primarily that of non-signification, signifies something, so there is no art that has no signification.

> ALBERT CAMUS (1913–60), French-Algerian philosopher, author. *The Rebel*, pt. 4 (1951; tr. 1953).

3   The fact that life has no meaning is a reason to live—moreover, the only one.

> E. M. CIORAN (b. 1911), Rumanian-born French philosopher. *Anathemas and Admirations*, "Fractures" (1986).

4   All meanings, we know, depend on the key of interpretation.

> GEORGE ELIOT (1819–80), English novelist, editor. *Daniel Deronda*, bk. 1, ch. 6 (1876).

5   The deeper the experience of an absence of meaning—in other words, of absurdity—the more energetically meaning is sought.

> VÁCLAV HAVEL (b. 1936), Czech playwright, president. *Disturbing the Peace*, ch. 5 (1986; tr. 1990).

6   Life has to be given a meaning because of the obvious fact that it has no meaning.

> HENRY MILLER (1891–1980), U.S. author. *The Wisdom of the Heart,* "Creative Death" (1947).

7   Social criticism begins with grammar and the re-establishing of meanings.

> OCTAVIO PAZ (b. 1914), Mexican poet. *The Other Mexico: Critique of the Pyramid,* "Development and Other Mirages" (1972).

8   After reading all that has been written, and after thinking all that can be thought, on the topics of God and the soul, the man who has a right to say that he thinks at all, will find himself face to face with the conclusion that, on these topics, the most profound thought is that which can be the least easily distinguished from the most superficial sentiment.

> EDGAR ALLAN POE (1809–45), U.S. poet, critic, short-story writer. *Marginalia,* in *Graham's Magazine* (Philadelphia, Feb. 1848; repr. in *Essays and Reviews,* 1984).

9   Those who talk on the razor-edge of double-meanings pluck the rarest blooms from the precipice on either side.

> LOGAN PEARSALL SMITH (1865–1946), U.S. essayist, aphorist. *Afterthoughts,* "In the World" (1931).

10   For a *large* class of cases—though not for all—in which we employ the word "meaning" it can be defined thus: the meaning of a word is its use in the language.

> LUDWIG WITTGENSTEIN (1889–1951), Austrian philosopher. *Philosophical Investigations,* pt. 1, sct. 43 (1953).

MEAT

1   To eat steak rare . . . represents both a nature and a morality.

> ROLAND BARTHES (1915–80), French semiologist. *Mythologies,* "Steak and Chips" (1957; tr. 1972).

2   Every moving thing that liveth shall be meat for you.

> BIBLE, HEBREW. God speaking to Noah, in *Genesis* 9:3.

3   But meat commendeth us not to God: for neither, if we eat, are we the better; neither, if we eat not, are we the worse.

> BIBLE: NEW TESTAMENT. St. Paul in *1 Corinthians* 8:8.

4   Any of us would kill a cow, rather than not have beef.

> SAMUEL JOHNSON (1709–84), English author, lexicographer. Quoted in: James Boswell, *Journal of a Tour to the Hebrides* (1785), entry for 23 Sept. 1773.

5   Methinks sometimes I have no more wit than a Christian or an ordinary man has; but I am a great eater of beef, and I believe that does harm to my wit.

> WILLIAM SHAKESPEARE (1564–1616), English dramatist, poet. Sir Andrew Aguecheek, in *Twelfth Night,* act 1, sc. 3, echoing a popular medical belief.

See also Vonnegut on UNITED STATES, PEOPLE OF THE.

THE MEDIA

1   The futility of everything that comes to us from the media is the inescapable consequence of the absolute inability of that particular stage to remain silent. Music, commercial breaks, news flashes, adverts, news broadcasts, movies, presenters—there is no alternative but to fill the screen; otherwise there would be an irremediable void. . . . That's why the slightest technical hitch, the slightest slip on the part of the presenter becomes so exciting, for it reveals the depth of the emptiness squinting out at us through this little window.

> JEAN BAUDRILLARD (b. 1929), French semiologist. *Cool Memories,* ch. 4 (1987; tr. 1990).

2   The media network has its idols, but its principal idol is its own style which generates an aura of winning and leaves the rest in darkness. It recognises neither pity nor pitilessness.

> JOHN BERGER (b. 1926), British author, critic. "The Third Week of August, 1991," in London *Guardian* (London, 4 Sept. 1991; repr. in *Keeping a Rendezvous,* 1992).

3   Society cannot share a common communication system so long as it is split into warring factions.

> BERTOLT BRECHT (1898–1956), German dramatist, poet. "A Short Organum for the Theatre," para. 55 (1949; repr. in *Brecht on Theatre,* ed. and tr. by John Willett, 1964).

4   Cinema, radio, television, magazines are a school of inattention: people look without seeing, listen in without hearing.

> ROBERT BRESSON (b. 1907), French film director. *Notes on the Cinematographer,* "1950–1958: Exercises" (1975).

5   The media transforms the great silence of things into its opposite. Formerly constituting a secret, the real now talks constantly. News reports, information, statistics, and surveys are everywhere.

> MICHEL DE CERTEAU (1925–86), French author, critic. *The Practice of Everyday Life,* ch. 13, "The Establishment of the Real" (1974).

6   The United States is unusual among the industrial democracies in the rigidity of the system of ideological control—"indoctrination," we might say—exercised through the mass media.

> NOAM CHOMSKY (b. 1928), U.S. linguist, political analyst. *Language and Responsibility,* "Politics" (1979).

7   The world is for thousands a freak show; the images flicker past and vanish; the impressions remain flat and unconnected in the soul. Thus they are easily led by the opinions of others, are content to let their impressions be shuffled and rearranged and evaluated differently.

> JOHANN WOLFGANG VON GOETHE (1749–1832), German poet, dramatist. *Aus Goethes Brieftasche,* "Third Pilgrimage to Erwin's Grave" (1776).

8   When distant and unfamiliar and complex things are communicated to great masses of people, the truth suffers a considerable and often a radical distortion. The complex is made over into the simple, the hypothetical into the dogmatic, and the relative into an absolute.

> WALTER LIPPMANN (1889–1974), U.S. journalist. *The Public Philosophy,* ch. 2, sct. 3 (1955).

9   The medium is the message. This is merely to say that the personal and social consequences of any medium—that is, of any extension of ourselves—result from the new scale that is introduced into our affairs by each extension of ourselves, or by any new technology.

> MARSHALL MCLUHAN (1911–80), Canadian communications theorist. *Understanding Media*, ch. 1 (1964).

10   Commercial jazz, soap opera, pulp fiction, comic strips, the movies set the images, mannerisms, standards, and aims of the urban masses. In one way or another, everyone is equal before these cultural machines; like technology itself, the mass media are nearly universal in their incidence and appeal. They are a kind of common denominator, a kind of scheme for pre-scheduled, mass emotions.

> C. WRIGHT MILLS (1916–62), U.S. sociologist. *White Collar*, ch. 15, sct. 3 (1951).

11   If I use the media, even with tricks, to publicize a black youth being shot in the back in Teaneck, New Jersey . . . then I should be praised for it, and it's more of a comment on them than me that it would take tricks to make them cover the loss of life.

> REV. AL SHARPTON (b. 1954), U.S. civil rights campaigner. *Independent on Sunday* (London, 21 April 1991).

12   We are eager to tunnel under the Atlantic and bring the Old World some weeks nearer to the New; but perchance the first news that will leak through into the broad, flapping American ear will be that the Princess Adelaide has the whooping cough.

> HENRY DAVID THOREAU (1817–62), U.S. philosopher, author, naturalist. *Walden*, "Economy" (1854).

13   The corporate grip on opinion in the United States is one of the wonders of the Western World. No First World country has ever managed to eliminate so entirely from its media all objectivity—much less dissent.

> GORE VIDAL (b. 1925), U.S. novelist, critic. *A View from the Diner's Club*, "Cue the Green God, Ted" (1991).

See also John Paul II on The CHURCH AND SOCIETY; CINEMA; Fischer on DISASTERS; Reagan on INFORMATION; NEWSPAPERS AND MAGAZINES; RADIO; The PRESS; TELEVISION.

MEDICINE

1   Vaccination is the medical sacrament corresponding to baptism.

> SAMUEL BUTLER (1835–1902), English author. *Samuel Butler's Notebooks* (1951).

2   The whole imposing edifice of modern medicine is like the celebrated tower of Pisa—slightly off balance.

> CHARLES, PRINCE OF WALES (b. 1948). Quoted in: *Observer* (London, 2 Jan. 1983).

3   Injections . . . are the best thing ever invented for feeding doctors.

> GABRIEL GARCÍA MÁRQUEZ (b. 1928), Colombian author. Doctor Giraldo, in *In Evil Hour* (1968; tr. 1979).

4   Some fell by laudanum, and some by steel,
And death in ambush lay in every pill.

> SIR SAMUEL GARTH (1661–1719), English physician, poet. *The Dispensary*, cto. 4.

5   The orthodox school has witnessed for centuries that nature itself has never once cured any existing disease with another *dissimilar* one, however intense. What must we think of this school, which nevertheless has continued to treat chronic diseases allopathically, with medicines and formulas that can only cause a disease condition—God knows which—*dissimilar* to the one being treated? Even if these physicians have not hitherto observed nature attentively enough, the miserable results of their treatment should have taught them that they were on the wrong road.

> SAMUEL HAHNEMANN (1755–1843), German physician, founder of homeopathy. *Organon of Medicine*, sct. 39 (written 1842; 6th ed., 1921).

6   We have to ask ourselves whether medicine is to remain a humanitarian and respected profession or a new but depersonalized science in the service of prolonging life rather than diminishing human suffering.

> ELISABETH KÜBLER-ROSS (b. 1926), Swiss-born U.S. psychiatrist. *On Death and Dying*, ch. 2 (1969).

7   I was not long since in a company where I wot not who of my fraternity brought news of a kind of pills, by true account, composed of a hundred and odd several ingredients; whereat we laughed very heartily, and made ourselves good sport; for what rock so hard were able to resist the shock or withstand the force of so thick and numerous a battery?

> MICHEL DE MONTAIGNE (1533–92), French essayist. *Essays*, bk. 2, ch. 37, "Of the Resemblance Between Children and Fathers" (1588, tr. by John Florio,).

8   The desire to take medicine is perhaps the greatest feature which distinguishes man from animals.

> SIR WILLIAM OSLER (1849–1919), Canadian physician. Quoted in: Harvey Cushing, *Life of Sir William Osler*, vol. 1, ch. 14 (1925).

See also DOCTORS; Rice, Shakespeare on HOPE.

MEDICINE, ALTERNATIVE

1   The Lord hath created medicines out of the earth: and he that is wise will not abhor them. Was not the water made sweet with wood, that the virtue thereof might be known?

> APOCRYPHA. *Ecclesiasticus* 38:4–5.

2   While Homeopathy itself is a perfect science, its truth is only partially known. The truth itself relates to the Divine, the knowledge relates to man.

> JAMES TYLER KENT (1849–1916), U.S. homeopathic teacher, physician. *Lectures on Homeopathic Philosophy*, lecture 37 (1900).

3   She saw she had fallen into the hands of one of those doctors who have strayed too far from aperients in the direction of the soul.

> REBECCA WEST (1892–1983), British author. *The Thinking Reed*, ch. 10 (1936).

MEDIOCRITY

1   The world is a republic of mediocrities, and always was.

THOMAS CARLYLE (1795–1881), Scottish essayist, historian. Letter, 13 May 1853, to Ralph Waldo Emerson.

2   Averageness is a quality we must put up with. Men march toward civilization in column formation, and by the time the van has learned to admire the masters the rear is drawing reluctantly away from the totem pole.

FRANK MOORE COLBY (1865–1925), U.S. editor, essayist. *The Colby Essays,* vol. 1, "The Reading Public" (1926).

3   The real antichrist is he who turns the wine of an original idea into the water of mediocrity.

ERIC HOFFER (1902–83), U.S. philosopher. *Reflections on the Human Condition,* aph. 109 (1973).

4   There are certain things in which mediocrity is intolerable: poetry, music, painting, public eloquence. What torture it is to hear a frigid speech being pompously declaimed, or second-rate verse spoken with all a bad poet's bombast!

JEAN DE LA BRUYÉRE (1645–96), French writer, moralist. *Characters,* "Of Books," aph. 7 (1688).

5   It is mediocrity which makes laws and sets mantraps and spring-guns in the realm of free song, saying thus far shalt thou go and no further.

JAMES RUSSELL LOWELL (1819–91), U.S. poet, editor. *Lowell's Early Prose Writings,* "Elizabethan Dramatists, Omitting Shakespear: John Webster" (1902; written 1843).

6   The general tendency of things throughout the world is to render mediocrity the ascendant power among mankind.

JOHN STUART MILL (1806–73), English philosopher, economist. *On Liberty,* ch. 3 (1859).

7   Take back the beauty and wit you bestow upon me; leave me my own mediocrity of agreeableness and genius, but leave me also my sincerity, my constancy, and my plain dealing; 'tis all I have to recommend me to the esteem either of others or myself.

LADY MARY WORTLEY MONTAGU (1689–1762), English society figure, letter writer. Letter, 21 Aug. 1709 (published in *Selected Letters,* ed. by Robert Halsband, 1970).

8   The world's made up of individuals who don't want to be heroes.

BRIAN MOORE (b. 1921), Irish novelist. *Sunday Times* (London, 15 April 1990).

9   They are good furniture pictures, unworthy of praise, and undeserving of blame.

JOHN RUSKIN (1819–1900), English art critic, author. *Modern Painters,* vol. 3, pt. 1, sct. 5, ch. 5 (1856).

10   One would like to be grand and heroic, if one could; but if not, why try at all? One wants to be *very* something, *very* great, *very* heroic; or if not that, then at least very stylish and very fashionable. It is this everlasting mediocrity that bores me.

HARRIET BEECHER STOWE (1811–96), U.S. novelist, anti-slavery campaigner. "Dress, or Who Makes the Fashions," in *Atlantic Monthly* (Boston, 1864).

11   The middlebrow is the man, or woman, of middle-bred intelligence who ambles and saunters now on this side of the hedge, now on that, in pursuit of no single object, neither art itself nor life itself, but both mixed indistinguishably, and rather nastily, with money, fame, power, or prestige.

VIRGINIA WOOLF (1882–1941), British novelist. *The Death of the Moth,* "Middlebrow" (1942). In contrast, see Woolf on INTELLECT AND INTELLECTUALS.

See also Melville on PATRIOTISM.

MEETINGS

1   No grand idea was ever born in a conference, but a lot of foolish ideas have died there.

F. SCOTT FITZGERALD (1896–1940), U.S. author. *The Crack-Up,* "Notebook E" (ed. by Edmund Wilson, 1945).

2   Meetings are a great trap. Soon you find yourself trying to get agreement and then the people who disagree come to think they have a right to be persuaded. . . . However, they are indispensable when you don't want to do anything.

JOHN KENNETH GALBRAITH (b. 1908), U.S. economist. *Ambassador's Journal,* ch. 5, (1969), written when serving as US ambassador to India 1961–63.

3   Whoever invented the meeting must have had Hollywood in mind. I think they should consider giving Oscars for meetings: Best Meeting of the Year, Best Supporting Meeting, Best Meeting Based on Material from Another Meeting.

WILLIAM GOLDMAN (b. 1931), U.S. screenwriter, novelist. *Adventures in the Screen Trade,* ch. 2 (1983).

4   I know, of course, how important it is not to keep a business engagement, if one wants to retain any sense of the beauty of life.

OSCAR WILDE (1854–1900), Anglo-Irish playwright, author. Cecily, in *The Importance of Being Earnest,* act 2.

See also COMMITTEES.

MELANCHOLY

1   Melancholy is at the bottom of everything, just as at the end of all rivers is the sea. Can it be otherwise in a world where nothing lasts, where all that we have loved or shall love must die? Is death, then, the secret of life? The gloom of an eternal mourning enwraps, more or less closely, every serious and thoughtful soul, as night enwraps the universe.

HENRI-FRÉDÉRIC AMIEL (1821–81), Swiss philosopher, poet. *Journal Intime* (1882; tr. by Mrs. Humphry Ward, 1892), entry for 16 Nov. 1864.

2   Man could not live if he were entirely impervious to sadness. Many sorrows can be endured only by being embraced, and the pleasure taken in them naturally has a somewhat melancholy character. So, melancholy is morbid only when it occupies too much place in life; but it is equally morbid for it to be wholly excluded from life.

ÉMILE DURKHEIM (1858–1917), French sociologist. *Suicide,* bk. 3, ch. 3, sct. 1 (1897; tr. 1951).

3   Melancholy, indeed, should be diverted by every means but drinking.

SAMUEL JOHNSON (1709–84), English author, lexicographer. Quoted in: James Boswell, *Life of Samuel Johnson,* 28 March 1776 (1791).

4   Sweet bird, that shunn'st the noise of folly,
Most musical, most melancholy!

JOHN MILTON (1608–74), English poet. *Il Penseroso* (1632).

MEMORY

1   But each day brings its petty dust
Our soon-chok'd souls to fill,
And we forget because we must,
And not because we will.

MATTHEW ARNOLD (1822–88), English poet, critic. *Absence.*

2   God gave us memory so that we might have roses in December.

J. M. BARRIE (1860–1937), British playwright. Rectorial address, 3 May 1922, St. Andrew's University, Scotland.

3   Like ultraviolet rays memory shows to each man in the book of life a script that invisibly and prophetically glosses the text.

WALTER BENJAMIN (1892–1940), German critic, philosopher. *One-Way Street,* "Madame Ariane—Second Courtyard on the Left" (1928; repr. in *One-Way Street and Other Writings,* 1978).

4   Memory is not an instrument for exploring the past but its theatre. It is the medium of past experience, as the ground is the medium in which dead cities lie interred.

WALTER BENJAMIN (1892–1940), German critic, philosopher. *A Berlin Chronicle* (written 1932; published 1970; repr. in *One-Way Street and Other Writings,* 1978).

5   The charm, one might say the genius of memory, is that it is choosy, chancy, and temperamental: it rejects the edifying cathedral and indelibly photographs the small boy outside, chewing a hunk of melon in the dust.

ELIZABETH BOWEN (1899–1973), Anglo-Irish novelist. *Vogue* (New York, 15 Sept. 1955).

6   I can only wait for the final amnesia, the one that can erase an entire life.

LUIS BUÑUEL (1900–1983), Spanish filmmaker. *My Last Sigh,* ch. 1 (1983).

7   You have to begin to lose your memory, if only in bits and pieces, to realize that memory is what makes our lives. Life without memory is no life at all, just as an intelligence without the possibility of expression is not really an intelligence. Our memory is our coherence, our reason, our feeling, even our action. Without it, we are nothing.

LUIS BUÑUEL (1900–1983), Spanish filmmaker. *My Last Sigh,* ch. 1 (1983).

8   It is singular how soon we lose the impression of what ceases to be *constantly* before us. A year impairs, a

lustre obliterates. There is little distinct left without an *effort* of memory, *then* indeed the lights are rekindled for a moment—but who can be sure that the Imagination is not the torch-bearer?

LORD BYRON (1788–1824), English poet. *Detached Thoughts,* no. 51 (1821–22; published in *Byron's Letters and Journals,* vol. 9, ed. by Leslie A. Marchand, 1979).

9   Our memories are card indexes consulted and then returned in disorder by authorities whom we do not control.

CYRIL CONNOLLY (1903–74), British critic. *The Unquiet Grave,* pt. 3 (1944; rev. 1951).

10   The difference between false memories and true ones is the same as for jewels: it is always the false ones that look the most real, the most brilliant.

SALVADOR DALI (1904–89), Spanish painter. *The Secret Life of Salvador Dali,* ch. 4 (1948).

11   You are told a lot about your education, but some beautiful, sacred memory, preserved since childhood, is perhaps the best education of all. If a man carries many such memories into life with him, he is saved for the rest of his days. And even if only one good memory is left in our hearts, it may also be the instrument of our salvation one day.

FEODOR DOSTOYEVSKY (1821–81), Russian novelist. Alyosha Karamazov, in *The Brothers Karamazov,* vol. 2, "Epilogue," sct. 3 (1880).

12   Memory is like a purse,—if it be over-full that it cannot shut, all will drop out of it. Take heed of a gluttonous curiosity to feed on many things, lest the greediness of the appetite of thy memory spoil the digestion thereof.

THOMAS FULLER (1608–61), English cleric. *The Holy State and the Profane State,* bk. 3, ch. 10 (1642).

13   People may correctly remember the events of twenty years ago (a remarkable feat), but who remembers his fears, his disgusts, his tone of voice? It is like trying to bring back the weather of that time.

MARTHA GELLHORN (b. 1908), U.S. journalist, author. *The Face of War,* "The War in Finland," Introduction (1959, rev. 1986).

14   The light of memory, or rather the light that memory lends to things, is the palest light of all. . . . I am not quite sure whether I am dreaming or remembering, whether I have lived my life or dreamed it. Just as dreams do, memory makes me profoundly aware of the unreality, the evanescence of the world, a fleeting image in the moving water.

EUGÉNE IONESCO (b. 1912), Rumanian-born French playwright. *Present Past—Past Present,* ch. 5 (1968).

15   The true art of memory is the art of attention.

SAMUEL JOHNSON (1709–84), English author, lexicographer. *The Idler,* no. 74, in *Universal Chronicle* (London, 15 Sept. 1759; repr. in *Works of Samuel Johnson,* vol. 2, ed. by W. J. Bate, John M. Bullitt and L. F. Powell, 1963).

16   The more a man can forget, the greater the number of metamorphoses which his life can undergo, the more he can remember the more divine his life becomes.

SØREN KIERKEGAARD (1813–55), Danish philosopher. *The

Journals of Søren Kierkegaard: A Selection, no. 429 (ed. and tr. by Alexander Dru, 1938), entry for 1842.

17 The struggle of man against power is the struggle of memory against forgetting.

MILAN KUNDERA (b. 1929), Czech author, critic. Mirek, in *The Book of Laughter and Forgetting*, pt. 1, ch. 2 (1978; tr. 1980).

18 Human memory is a marvelous but fallacious instrument. . . . The memories which lie within us are not carved in stone; not only do they tend to become erased as the years go by, but often they change, or even increase by incorporating extraneous features.

PRIMO LEVI (1919–87), Italian author. *The Drowned and the Saved*, ch. 1 (1988).

19 What a wonderful faculty is memory!—the most mysterious and inexplicable in the great riddle of life; that plastic tablet on which the Almighty registers with unerring fidelity the records of being, making it the depository of all our words, thoughts and deeds—this faithful witness against us for good or evil.

SUSANNA MOODIE (1803–85), Canadian author. *Life in the Clearing*, ch. 15 (1853).

20 The selective memory isn't selective enough.

BLAKE MORRISON (b. 1950), British poet and critic. *Independent on Sunday* (London, 16 June 1991).

21 Mournful and Never-ending Remembrance.

EDGAR ALLAN POE (1809–45), U.S. poet, critic, short-story writer. "The Philosophy of Composition," in *Graham's Magazine* (Philadelphia, April 1846; repr. in *Selected Writings*, ed. by David Galloway, 1967), explaining the meaning of the symbolic bird in his poem *The Raven*. The phrase was taken as the title of Kenneth Silverman's study of Poe (1992).

22 Our memory is like a shop in the window of which is exposed now one, now another photograph of the same person. And as a rule the most recent exhibit remains for some time the only one to be seen.

MARCEL PROUST (1871–1922), French novelist. *Remembrance of Things Past*, vol. 4, "Within a Budding Grove," pt. 2, "Seascape, with Frieze of Girls" (1918; tr. by Scott Monkrieff, 1924).

23 We are able to find everything in our memory, which is like a dispensary or chemical laboratory in which chance steers our hand sometimes to a soothing drug and sometimes to a dangerous poison.

MARCEL PROUST (1871–1922), French novelist. *Remembrance of Things Past*, vol. 10, "The Captive," pt. 2, ch. 3 (1923; tr. by Ronald and Colette Cortie, 1988).

24 A man's real possession is his memory. In nothing else is he rich, in nothing else is he poor.

ALEXANDER SMITH (1830–67), Scottish poet. *Dreamthorp*, "On Death and the Fear of Dying" (1863).

25 It's a pleasure to share one's memories. Everything remembered is dear, endearing, touching, precious. At least the past is safe—though we didn't know it at the time. We know it now. Because it's in the past; because we have survived.

SUSAN SONTAG (b. 1933), U.S. essayist. "Debriefing," in *American Review* (New York, Sept. 1973; repr. in *I, Etcetera*, 1978).

26 That is my major preoccupation—memory, the kingdom of memory. I want to protect and enrich that kingdom, glorify that kingdom and serve it.

ELIE WIESEL (b. 1928), Rumanian-born U.S. writer. Interview in *Writers at Work* (Eighth Series, ed. by George Plimpton, 1988). "God," Wiesel added, "from the religious point of view is part of that kingdom."

27 Memory . . . is the diary that we all carry about with us.

OSCAR WILDE (1854–1900), Anglo-Irish playwright, author. Miss Prism, in *The Importance of Being Earnest*, act 2.

28 In memory everything seems to happen to music.

TENNESSEE WILLIAMS (1914–83), U.S. dramatist. Tom, in *The Glass Menagerie*, sc. 1 (1944).

29 Life is all memory except for the one present moment that goes by you so quick you hardly catch it going.

TENNESSEE WILLIAMS (1914–83), U.S. dramatist. Mrs. Goforth, in *The Milk Train Doesn't Stop Here Anymore*, sc. 3 (1963).

30 The effectiveness of our memory banks is determined not by the total number of facts we take in, but the number we wish to reject.

JON WYNNE-TYSON (b. 1924), British author. *Food for a Future*, ch. 2 (1975).

31 The memory of most men is an abandoned cemetery where lie, unsung and unhonored, the dead whom they have ceased to cherish. Any lasting grief is reproof to their forgetfulness.

MARGUERITE YOURCENAR (1903–87), French novelist. *Memoirs of Hadrian*, "Saeculum Aureum" (1954).

See also Havel, La Rochefoucauld on ANECDOTES; NOSTALGIA; REMINISCENCE.

MEN

1 Poor little men, poor little cocks! As soon as they're old enough, they swell their plumage to be conquerors. . . . If they only knew that it's enough to be just a little bit wounded and sad in order to obtain everything without fighting for it.

JEAN ANOUILH (1910–87), French playwright. Araminthe, in *Cécile*.

2 Men are not to be told anything they might find too painful; the secret depths of human nature, the sordid physicalities, might overwhelm or damage them. For instance, men often faint at the sight of their own blood, to which they are not accustomed. For this reason you should never stand behind one in the line at the Red Cross donor clinic.

MARGARET ATWOOD (b. 1939), Canadian novelist, poet, critic. *Close Company: Stories of Mothers and Daughters*, "Significant Moments in the Life of my Mother" (ed. by Christine Park and Caroline Heaton, 1987), said of her mother's beliefs.

3 Left to itself the masculine imagination has very little appreciation for the here and now; it prefers to dwell on what is absent, on what has been or may be. If men are more punctual than women, it is because they know that, without the external discipline of clock time, they would never get anything done.

W. H. AUDEN (1907–73), Anglo-American poet. Phyllis McGinley, *Times Three: Selected Verse from Three Decades*, Foreword (1960).

4 Men's private self-worlds are rather like our geographical world's seasons, storm, and sun, deserts, oases, mountains and abysses, the endless-seeming plateaus, darkness and light, and always the sowing and the reaping.

FAITH BALDWIN (1893–1978), U.S. author. *Harvest of Hope*, "April" (1962).

5 The question arises as to whether it is possible *not* to live in the world of men and still to live in the world.

LOUISE BERNIKOW (b. 1940), U.S. journalist. *The World Split Open*, Introduction (1974).

6 Bloody men are like bloody buses—
You wait for about a year
And as soon as one approaches your stop
Two or three others appear.

WENDY COPE (b. 1945), British poet. *Serious Concerns*, "Bloody Men" (1992).

7 Before they're plumbers or writers or taxi drivers or unemployed or journalists, before everything else, men are men. Whether heterosexual or homosexual. The only difference is that some of them remind you of it as soon as you meet them, and others wait for a little while.

MARGUERITE DURAS (b. 1914), French author, filmmaker. *Practicalities*, "Men" (1987; tr. 1990).

8 You have to be very fond of men. Very, very fond. You have to be very fond of them to love them. Otherwise they're simply unbearable.

MARGUERITE DURAS (b. 1914), French author, filmmaker. *Practicalities*, "Men" (1987; tr. 1990).

9 Only when manhood is dead—and it will perish when ravaged femininity no longer sustains it—only then will we know what it is to be free.

ANDREA DWORKIN (b. 1946), U.S. feminist critic. "The Root Cause," speech, 26 Sept. 1975, at the Massachusetts Institute of Technology, Cambridge (published in *Our Blood*, ch. 9, 1976).

10 Considering the absence of legal coercion, the surprising thing is that men have for so long, and, on the whole, so reliably, adhered to what we might call the "breadwinner ethic."

BARBARA EHRENREICH (b. 1941), U.S. author, columnist. *The Hearts of Men*, ch. 1 (1983).

11 Men's men: gentle or simple, they're much of a muchness.

GEORGE ELIOT (1819–80), English novelist. Mrs. Girdle, in *Daniel Deronda*, bk. 4, ch. 31 (1874–76).

12 Providing for one's family as a good husband and father is a water-tight excuse for making money hand over fist. Greed may be a sin, exploitation of other people might, on the face of it, look rather nasty, but who can blame a man for "doing the best" for his children?

EVA FIGES (b. 1932), Anglo-German author. "A View of My Own," in *Nova* (Jan. 1973).

13 The intimate revelations of young men, or at least the terms in which they express them, are usually plagiaristic and marred by obvious suppressions.

F. SCOTT FITZGERALD (1896–1940), U.S. author. The narrator (Nick Carraway), in *The Great Gatsby*, ch. 1 (1925).

14 The world men inhabit . . . is rather bleak. It is a world full of doubt and confusion, where vulnerability must be hidden, not shared; where competition, not co-operation, is the order of the day; where men sacrifice the possibility of knowing their own children and sharing in their upbringing, for the sake of a job they may have chosen by chance, which may not suit them and which in many cases dominates their lives to the exclusion of much else.

ANNA FORD (b. 1943), British television journalist, presenter. *Men*, concluding chapter (1985).

15 All societies on the verge of death are masculine. A society can survive with only one man; no society will survive a shortage of women.

GERMAINE GREER (b. 1939), Australian feminist writer. *Sex and Destiny*, ch. 3 (1984).

16 All men are homosexual, some turn straight. It must be very odd to be a straight man because your sexuality is hopelessly defensive. It's like an ideal of racial purity.

DEREK JARMAN (b. 1942), British filmmaker, artist, author. *At Your Own Risk: A Saint's Testament*, "1940's" (1992).

17 During the feminist seventies men were caught between a rock and a hard-on; in the fathering eighties they are caught between good hugs and bad hugs.

FLORENCE KING (b. 1936), U.S. author. *Reflections in a Jaundiced Eye*, "From Captain Marvel to Captain Valium" (1989).

18 How beautiful maleness is, if it finds its right expression.

D. H. LAWRENCE (1885–1930), British author. *Sea and Sardinia*, ch. 3 (1923).

19 Next to the striking of fire and the discovery of the wheel, the greatest triumph of what we call civilization was the domestication of the human male.

MAX LERNER (b. 1902), U.S. author, columnist. *The Unfinished Country*, pt. 2, "The Revolt of the American Father" (1959; first published in *New York Post*, 16 June 1958).

20 The male has been persuaded to assume a certain onerous and disagreeable rôle with the promise of rewards—material and psychological. Women may in the first place even have put it into his head. BE A *MAN!* may have been, metaphorically, what Eve uttered at the critical moment in the garden of Eden.

WYNDHAM LEWIS (1882–1957), British author, painter. *The Art of Being Ruled*, "Call Yourself a Man!" (1926).

21 The male sex still constitute in many ways the most obstinate vested interest one can find.

LORD LONGFORD (b. 1905), British author, social reformer. Speech, 23 June 1963, House of Lords.

22 Sometimes I have a notion that what might improve the situation is to have women take over the occupations of government and trade and to give men their freedom. Let them do what they are best at. While we scrawl interoffice memos and direct national or extranational affairs, men could spend *all* their time inventing wheels, peering at stars, composing poems, carving statues, exploring continents—discovering, reforming, or crying out in a sacramental wilderness. Efficiency would probably increase, and no one would have to worry so much about the Gaza Strip or an election.

PHYLLIS MCGINLEY (1905–78), U.S. poet, author. *The Province of the Heart*, "Some of My Best Friends . . ." (1959).

23 As long as male behavior is taken to be the norm, there can be no serious questioning of male traits and behavior. A norm is by definition a standard for judging; it is not itself subject to judgment.

MYRIAM MIEDZIAN, U.S. author. *Boys Will Be Boys*, ch. 1 (1991).

24 A man that is ashamed of passions that are natural and reasonable is generally proud of those that are shameful and silly.

LADY MARY WORTLEY MONTAGU (1689–1762), English society figure, letter writer. Letter, c. 24 Nov. 1714, to her husband (published in *Selected Letters*, ed. by Robert Halsband, 1970).

25 It is much more easy to accuse the one sex than to excuse the other.

MICHEL DE MONTAIGNE (1533–92), French essayist. *Essays*, bk. 3, ch. 5, "Upon Some Verses of Virgil" (1588, tr. by John Florio).

26 Don't accept rides from strange men,
and remember that all men are as strange as hell.

ROBIN MORGAN (b. 1941), U.S. feminist author, poet. *Sisterhood is Powerful*, Introduction, "Letter to a Sister Underground" (1970).

27 I love the male body, it's better designed than the male mind.

ANDREA NEWMAN (b. 1938), British author. *Today* (London, 30 Sept. 1988).

28 Men are the enemies of women. Promising sublime intimacy, unequalled passion, amazing security and grace, they nevertheless exploit and injure in a myriad subtle ways. Without men the world would be a better place: softer, kinder, more loving; calmer, quieter, more humane.

ANN OAKLEY (b. 1944), British sociologist, author. *Taking It Like a Woman*, "A French Letter" (1984).

29 Men know they are sexual exiles. They wander the earth seeking satisfaction, craving and despising, never content. There is nothing in that anguished motion for women to envy.

CAMILLE PAGLIA (b. 1947), U.S. author, critic, educator. *Sexual Personae*, ch. 1 (1990).

30 Reading, solitude, idleness, a soft and sedentary life, intercourse with women and young people, these are perilous paths for a young man, and these lead him constantly into danger.

JEAN-JACQUES ROUSSEAU (1712–78), Swiss-born French philosopher, political theorist. *Emile*, bk. 4 (1762).

31 There's so much saint in the worst of them,
And so much devil in the best of them,
That a woman who's married to one of them,
Has nothing to learn of the rest of them.

HELEN ROWLAND (1875–1950), U.S. journalist. *A Guide to Men*, "The Refrain" (1922).

32 Most men act so tough and strong on the outside because on the inside, we are scared, weak, and fragile. Men, not women, are the weaker sex.

JERRY RUBIN (b. 1938), U.S. essayist, radical leader. *Chicago Tribune* (16 March 1978).

33 To call a man an animal is to flatter him; he's a machine, a walking dildo.

VALERIE SOLANAS (b. 1940), U.S. artist, writer. *The SCUM Manifesto* (1968). The acronym *SCUM* stood for "Society for Cutting Up Men."

34 It is funny the two things most men are proudest of is the thing that any man can do and doing does in the same way, that is being drunk and being the father of their son.

GERTRUDE STEIN (1874–1946), U.S. author. *Everybody's Autobiography*, ch. 2 (1937).

35 Since I am a man, my heart is three or four times less sensitive, because I have three or four times as much power of reason and experience of the world—a thing which you women call hard-heartedness. As a man, I can take refuge in having mistresses. The more of them I have, and the greater the scandal, the more I acquire reputation and brilliance in society.

STENDHAL (1783–1842), French author. Letter to his sister Pauline, 29 Aug. 1804, exhorting her not to throw away her virtue.

36 One of the things being in politics has taught me is that men are not a reasoned or reasonable sex.

MARGARET THATCHER (b. 1925), British Conservative politician, prime minister. BBC interview, 14 Jan. 1972.

37 I think we're a kind of desperation. We're sort of a maddening luxury. The basic and essential human is the woman, and all that we're doing is trying to brighten up the place. That's why all the birds who belong to our sex have prettier feathers—because males have got to try and justify their existence.

ORSON WELLES (1915–84), U.S. filmmaker, actor, producer. Interview in David Frost, *The Americans*, "Can a Martian Survive by Pretending to Be a Leading American Actor?" (1970).

38 The Ideal Man should talk to us as if we were goddesses, and treat us as if we were children. He should refuse all our serious requests, and gratify every one of our whims. He should encourage us to have caprices, and forbid us to have missions. He should always say much more than he means, and always mean much more than he says.

OSCAR WILDE (1854–1900), Anglo-Irish playwright, author. Mrs. Allonby, in *A Woman of No Importance*, act 2.

See also Dworkin on The BODY; Dworkin on DEFINITION; Meynell on DRESS; Westwood on ELEGANCE; GENDER; HOMOSEXUALITY; MEN AND WOMEN; Billings; Dworkin on PORNOGRAPHY; Solanas on SELF-ABSORPTION; Dworkin on VIOLENCE; Douglas on WIVES; WOMEN AND MEN.

MEN, SINGLE

1 It is a truth universally acknowledged, that a single man in possession of a good fortune must be in want of a wife.

> JANE AUSTEN (1775–1817), English novelist. *Pride and Prejudice* (1813), opening words.

2 Certainly the best works, and of greatest merit for the public, have proceeded from the unmarried, or childless men.

> FRANCIS BACON (1561–1626), English philosopher, essayist, statesman. *Essays*, "Of Marriage and Single Life" (1597).

3 Show me a man who lives alone and has a perpetually clean kitchen, and 8 times out of 9 I'll show you a man with detestable spiritual qualities.

> CHARLES BUKOWSKI (b. 1920), U.S. author, poet. *Tales of Ordinary Madness*, "Too Sensitive" (1967).

4 James Bond in his Sean Connery days . . . was the first well-known bachelor on the American scene who was not a drifter or a degenerate and did not eat out of cans.

> BARBARA EHRENREICH (b. 1941), U.S. author, columnist. "Socialism in One Household," in *Mother Jones* (1987; repr. in *The Worst Years of Our Lives*, 1991).

5 The most threatened group in human societies as in animal societies is the unmated male: the unmated male is more likely to wind up in prison or in an asylum or dead than his mated counterpart. He is less likely to be promoted at work and he is considered a poor credit risk.

> GERMAINE GREER (b. 1939), Australian feminist writer. *Sex and Destiny*, ch. 2 (1984).

6 They that have grown old in a single state are generally found to be morose, fretful and captious; tenacious of their own practices and maxims; soon offended by contradiction or negligence; and impatient of any association but with those that will watch their nod, and submit themselves to unlimited authority.

> SAMUEL JOHNSON (1709–84), English author, lexicographer. *Rambler*, no. 112 (London, 13 April 1751; repr. in *Works of Samuel Johnson*, vol. 4, ed. by W. J. Bate and Albrecht B. Strauss, 1969).

7 Bachelors know more about women than married men. If they didn't they'd be married, too.

> H. L. MENCKEN (1880–1956), U.S. journalist. *A Mencken Chrestomathy*, "Sententiæ: Masculam et Feminam Creavit Eos" (1949).

8 "Come, come," said Tom's father, "at your time
> of life,
There's no longer excuse for thus playing the
> rake—
"It is time you should think, boy, of taking a
> wife."
"Why, so it is, father—whose wife shall I take?"

> THOMAS MOORE (1779–1852), Irish poet. *A Joke Versified.*

9 Let sinful bachelors their woes deplore;
Full well they merit all they feel, and more:

Unaw'd by precepts, human or divine,
Like birds and beasts, promiscuously they join.

> ALEXANDER POPE (1688–1744), English satirical poet. *January and May.*

10 Marrying an old bachelor is like buying second-hand furniture.

> HELEN ROWLAND (1875–1950), U.S. journalist. *Reflections of a Bachelor Girl* (1903; repr.1909, p. 13).

11 A Bachelor of Arts is one who makes love to a lot of women, and yet has the art to remain a bachelor.

> HELEN ROWLAND (1875–1950), U.S. journalist. *A Guide to Men*, "Bachelors" (1922).

12 Somehow, a bachelor never quite gets over the idea that he is a thing of beauty and a boy for ever!

> HELEN ROWLAND (1875–1950), U.S. journalist. *A Guide to Men*, "Bachelors" (1922).

13 By persistently remaining single, a man converts himself into a permanent public temptation. Men should be more careful.

> OSCAR WILDE (1854–1900), Anglo-Irish playwright, author. Miss Prism, in *The Importance of Being Earnest*, act 2.

14 Nowadays, all the married men live like bachelors, and all the bachelors like married men.

> OSCAR WILDE (1854–1900), Anglo-Irish playwright, author. Lady Hunstanton, in *A Woman of No Importance*, act 2. The aphorism also appeared in *The Picture of Dorian Gray*, ch. 15 (1891).

See also CELIBACY.

MEN: THE NEW MAN

1 Like many other women, I could not understand why every man who changed a diaper has felt impelled, in recent years, to write a book about it.

> BARBARA EHRENREICH (b. 1941), U.S. author, columnist. "Wimps," in *New York Times* (1985; repr. in *The Worst Years of Our Lives*, 1991).

2 It is the marketplace that calls most clearly for men to be softer, more narcissistic and receptive, and the new man is the result.

> BARBARA EHRENREICH (b. 1941), U.S. author, columnist. "At Last, a New Man," in *New York Times* (1984; repr. in *The Worst Years of Our Lives*, 1991).

See also FEMINISM.

MEN AND MASCULINITY

1 The masculine imagination lives in a state of perpetual revolt against the limitations of human life. In theological terms, one might say that all men, left to themselves, become gnostics. They may swagger like peacocks, but in their heart of hearts they all think sex an indignity and wish they could beget themselves on themselves. Hence the aggressive hostility toward women so manifest in most club-car stories.

> W. H. AUDEN (1907–73), Anglo-American poet. Phyllis McGin-

ley, *Times Three: Selected Verse from Three Decades,* Foreword (1960).

2 The American ideal of masculinity . . . has created cowboys and Indians, good guys and bad guys, punks and studs, tough guys and softies, butch and faggot, black and white. It is an ideal so paralytically infantile that it is virtually forbidden—as an unpatriotic act—that the American boy evolves into the complexity of manhood.

> JAMES BALDWIN (1924–87), U.S. author. *The Price of the Ticket,* "Here Be Dragons" (1985).

3 The man, most man,
Works best for men: and, if most man indeed,
He gets his manhood plainest from his soul.

> ELIZABETH BARRETT BROWNING (1806–61), English poet. *Aurora Leigh,* bk. 9 (1857).

4 Because it is in the nature of things that they become extreme, we have passed down from manliness to cruelty. If I had been told when I was 20 that there was a tavern in the town where the brave and the cruel were gathered together, I would have run all the way and I would have gone up to the largest and leatheriest of the denizens and said: "If you truly love me, kill the bartender."

> QUENTIN CRISP (b. 1908), British author. "Love Lies Bleeding," broadcast, 6 Aug. 1991 (published in *New Statesman & Society,* London, 9 Aug. 1991).

5 In this society, the norm of masculinity is phallic aggression. Male sexuality is, by definition, intensely and rigidly phallic. A man's identity is located in his conception of himself as the possessor of a phallus; a man's worth is located in his *pride* in phallic identity. The main characteristic of phallic identity is that *worth* is entirely contingent on the possession of a phallus. Since men have no other criteria for worth, no other notion of identity, those who do not have phalluses are not recognized as fully human.

> ANDREA DWORKIN (b. 1946), U.S. feminist critic. "The Rape Atrocity and the Boy Next Door," speech, 1 March 1975, State University of New York, Stony Brook (published in *Our Blood,* ch. 4, 1976).

6 Masculinity can only be experienced, achieved, recognized, and embodied in opposition to femininity. When men posit sex, violence, and death as elemental erotic truths, they mean this—that sex, or fucking, is the act which enables them to experience their own reality, or identity, or masculinity most concretely; that violence, or sadism, is the means by which they actualize that reality, or identity, or masculinity; and that death, or negation, or nothingness, or contamination by the female is what they risk each time they penetrate into what they imagine to be the emptiness of the female hole.

> ANDREA DWORKIN (b. 1946), U.S. feminist critic. "The Root Cause," speech, 26 Sept. 1975, Massachusetts Institute of Technology, Cambridge (published in *Our Blood,* ch. 9, 1976).

7 Someone has to stand up for wimps.

> BARBARA EHRENREICH (b. 1941), U.S. author, columnist. "Wimps," in *New York Times* (1985; repr. in *The Worst Years of Our Lives,* 1991).

8 The things a man has to have are hope and confidence in himself against odds, and sometimes he needs somebody, his pal or his mother or his wife or God, to give him that confidence. He's got to have some inner standards worth fighting for or there won't be any way to bring him into conflict. And he must be ready to choose death before dishonor without making too much song and dance about it. That's all there is to it.

> CLARK GABLE (1901–60), U.S. film actor. Quoted in: Adela Rogers St. Johns, *The Honeycomb (1969).*

9 Unlike femininity, relaxed masculinity is at bottom empty, a limp nullity. While the female body is full of internal potentiality, the male is internally barren. . . . Manhood at the most basic level can be validated and expressed only in action.

> GEORGE GILDER (b. 1939), U.S. editor, speechwriter, author. *Sexual Suicide,* pt. 1, ch. 1 (1973).

10 The tragedy of machismo is that a man is never quite man enough.

> GERMAINE GREER (b. 1939), Australian feminist writer. "My Mailer Problem," in *Esquire* (New York, Sept. 1971; repr. in *The Madwoman's Underclothes,* 1986).

11 A hairy body, and arms stiff with bristles, give promise of a manly soul.

> JUVENAL (40–125), Roman satiric poet. *Satires,* Satire 2.

12 Men were only made into "men" with great difficulty even in primitive society: the male is not naturally "a man" any more than the woman. He has to be propped up into that position with some ingenuity, and is always likely to collapse.

> WYNDHAM LEWIS (1882–1957), British author, painter. *The Art of Being Ruled,* "Call Yourself a Man!" (1926).

13 Masculinity is not something given to you, but something you gain. And you gain it by winning small battles with honor.

> NORMAN MAILER (b. 1923), U.S. author. *Cannibals and Christians,* "Petty Notes on Some Sex in America" (1966; first published in Playboy 1961-62).

14 In the United States adherence to the values of the masculine mystique makes intimate, self-revealing, deep friendships between men unusual.

> MYRIAM MIEDZIAN, U.S. author. *Boys Will Be Boys,* Introduction (1991).

15 The true man wants two things: danger and play. For that reason he wants woman, as the most dangerous plaything.

> FRIEDRICH NIETZSCHE (1844–1900), German philosopher. *Thus Spoke Zarathustra,* pt. 1, "Of Old and Young Women" (1883–92; tr. 1961).

16 A woman simply is, but a man must become. Masculinity is risky and elusive. It is achieved by a revolt from woman, and it is confirmed only by other men. . . . Manhood coerced into sensitivity is no manhood at all.

> CAMILLE PAGLIA (b. 1947), U.S. author, critic, educator. "Alice in Muscle Land," book review, in *Boston Globe* (27 Jan. 1991; repr. in *Sex, Art, and American Culture,* 1992).

17 He may have hair upon his chest
But, sister, so has Lassie.

COLE PORTER (1891–1964), U.S. composer, lyricist. *Kiss Me Kate*, "I Hate Men" (1948).

18 I'm not the man to baulk at a low smell,
I'm not the man to insist on asphodel.
This sounds like a He-fellow, don't you think?
It sounds like that. I belch, I bawl, I drink.

EDITH SITWELL (1887–1964), British poet, critic. *One-Way Song*.

19 Not only is it harder to be a man, it is also harder to become one.

ARIANNA STASSINOPOULOS (b. 1950), Greek author. *The Female Woman*, "The Male Man" (1973).

20 There is hardly an American male of my generation who has not at one time or another tried to master the victory cry of the great ape as it issued from the androgynous chest of Johnny Weissmuller, to the accompaniment of thousands of arms and legs snapping during attempts to swing from tree to tree in the backyards of the Republic.

GORE VIDAL (b. 1925), U.S. novelist, critic. "The Waking Dream: Tarzan Revisited," in *Esquire* (New York, Dec. 1963).

21 How dwarfed against his manliness
She sees the poor pretension,
The wants, the aims, the follies, born
Of fashion and convention!

JOHN GREENLEAF WHITTIER (1807–92), U.S. poet. *Among the Hills.*

MEN AND WOMEN

1 When a woman is very, very bad, she is awful, but when a man is correspondingly good, he is weird.

MINNA ANTRIM (1861–?), U.S. epigrammist. *Naked Truth and Veiled Allusions* (1901, p. 16).

2 By this also ye must know that women have dominion over you: do ye not labour and toil, and give and bring all to the woman? Yea, a man taketh his sword, and goeth his way to rob and to steal, to sail upon the sea and upon rivers; and looketh upon a lion, and goeth in the darkness; and when he hath stolen, spoiled, and robbed, he bringeth it to his love.

APOCRYPHA. Zorobabel, in *Esdras I* 4:22–24.

3 So it is naturally with the male and the female; the one is superior, the other inferior; the one governs, the other is governed; and the same rule must necessarily hold good with respect to all mankind.

ARISTOTLE (384–322 B.C.), Greek philosopher. *Politics*, bk. 1, ch. 5, sct. 1254b.

4 With men he can be rational and unaffected, but when he has ladies to please, every feature works.

JANE AUSTEN (1775–1817), English novelist. Mr. John Knightley, in *Emma*, ch. 13 (1816), describing Mr. Elton.

5 I think that if most guys in America could somehow get their fave-rave poster girl in bed and have total license to do whatever they wanted with this legendary body for one afternoon, at least 75 percent of the guys in the country would elect to beat her up.

LESTER BANGS (1948–82), U.S. rock journalist. Quoted in: Simon Frith, *Sound Effects: Youth, Leisure and the Politics of Rock*, ch. 10 (1979).

6 Men act and women appear. Men look at women. Women watch themselves being looked at.

JOHN BERGER (b. 1926), British author, critic. *Ways of Seeing*, ch. 3 (1972).

7 I think the worst woman that ever existed would have made a *man* of very passable reputation—they are all better than us & their faults such as they are must originate with ourselves.

LORD BYRON (1788–1824), English poet. Letter, 6 Sept. 1813, to Annabella Millbanke—later Lady Byron (published in *Byron's Letters and Journals*, vol. 3, ed. by Leslie Marchand, 1974).

8 A woman who . . . gives any advantage to a man may expect a lover—but will sooner or later find a tyrant.

LORD BYRON (1788–1824), English poet. Letter, 1 Dec. 1822 (published in *Byron's Letters and Journals*, vol. 10, ed. by Leslie Marchand, 1973–81). Byron added, "This may not perhaps be the man's fault neither—but is the necessary and natural result of the circumstances of society."

9 The nearer society approaches to divine order, the less separation will there be in the characters, duties, and pursuits of men and women. Women will not become less gentle and graceful, but men will become more so. Women will not neglect the care and education of their children, but men will find themselves ennobled and refined by sharing those duties with them; and will receive, in return, co-operation and sympathy in the discharge of various other duties, now deemed inappropriate to women. The more women become rational companions, partners in business and in thought, as well as in affection and amusement, the more highly will men appreciate home.

LYDIA M. CHILD (1802–80), U.S. abolitionist, writer, editor. Letter, Jan. 1843 (published in *Letters from New York*, vol. 1, letter 34, 1843).

10 The woman is the home. That's where she used to be, and that's where she still is. You might ask me, What if a man tries to be part of the home—will the woman let him? I answer yes. Because then he becomes one of the children.

MARGUERITE DURAS (b. 1914), French author, filmmaker. *Practicalities*, "House and Home" (1987; tr. 1990).

11 Upscale young men seem to go for the kind of woman who plays with a full deck of credit cards, who won't cry while she's knocked to the ground while trying to board the six o'clock Eastern shuttle, and whose schedule doesn't allow for a sexual encounter lasting more than twelve minutes.

BARBARA EHRENREICH (b. 1941), U.S. author, columnist. "The Cult of Busyness," in *New York Times* (1985; repr. in *The Worst Years of Our Lives*, 1991).

12 Given the cultural barriers to intersex conversation, the amazing thing is that we would even expect women and men to have anything to say to each other for more than ten minutes at a stretch. The barriers are ancient—

perhaps rooted, as some paleontologist may soon discover, in the contrast between the occasional guttural utterances exchanged in male hunting bands and the extended discussions characteristic of female food-gathering groups.

> BARBARA EHRENREICH (b. 1941), U.S. author, columnist. "Tales of the Man Shortage," in *Mother Jones* (1986; repr. in *The Worst Years of Our Lives*, 1991).

13 I tell you there isn't a thing under the sun that needs to be done at all, but what a man can do better than a woman, unless it's bearing children, and they do that in a poor make-shift way; it had better ha' been left to the men.

> GEORGE ELIOT (1819–80), English novelist. Bartle Massey, in *Adam Bede*, bk. 2, ch. 21 (1859).

14 Where women love each other, men learn to smother their mutual dislike.

> GEORGE ELIOT (1819–80), English novelist, editor. *Middlemarch*, "Finale" (1871).

15 Men get to be a mixture of the charming mannerisms of the women they have known.

> F. SCOTT FITZGERALD (1896–1940), U.S. author. *The Crack-Up*, "Notebook G" (ed. by Edmund Wilson, 1945).

16 Whatever they may be in public life, whatever their relations with men, in their relations with women, all men are rapists and that's all they are. They rape us with their eyes, their laws, their codes.

> MARILYN FRENCH (b. 1929), U.S. author. Valerie, in *The Woman's Room*, ch. 5, sct. 19 (1977).

17 Woman submits to her fate; man makes his.

> ÉMILE GABORIAU (1835–73), French author. Mlle. Lucienne, in *Other People's Money*, pt. 1, ch. 27.

18 Sure men were born to lie, and women to believe them!

> JOHN GAY (1685–1732), English dramatist. Lucy, in *The Beggar's Opera*, act 2, sc. 13.

19 I have always been principally interested in men for sex. I've always thought any sane woman would be a lover of women because loving men is such a mess. I have always wished I'd fall in love with a woman. Damn.

> GERMAINE GREER (b. 1939), Australian feminist writer. *New York Times Book Review* (11 Oct. 1992).

20 Men should be saying "I want to become a woman." The world would be a far better place if more men wanted to become women, than women wanted to become men.

> ALBERT HALSEY (b. 1923), British author, educator. *Independent* (London, 14 Oct. 1992).

21 Men greet each other with a sock on the arm, women with a hug, and the hug wears better in the long run.

> EDWARD HOAGLAND (b. 1932), U.S. novelist, essayist. "Heaven and Nature," in *Harper's* (March 1988; repr. in *Heart's Desire*, 1988).

22 Sometimes I think that the biggest difference between men and women is that more men need to seek out some terrible lurking thing in existence and hurl themselves upon it. . . . Women know where it lives but they can let it alone.

> RUSSELL HOBAN (b. 1925), U.S. author. Neaera, in *Turtle Diary*, ch. 18 (1975).

23 The superiority of one man's opinion over another's is never so great as when the opinion is about a woman.

> HENRY JAMES (1843–1916), U.S. author. *The Tragic Muse*, ch. 9 (1890).

24 Men know that women are an over-match for them, and therefore they choose the weakest or most ignorant. If they did not think so, they never could be afraid of women knowing as much as themselves.

> SAMUEL JOHNSON (1709–84), English author, lexicographer. Quoted in: James Boswell, *Tour to the Hebrides* (1785), 19 Sept. 1773.

25 Men and women, women and men. It will never work.

> ERICA JONG (b. 1942), U.S. author. The narrator (Isadora Wing), in *Fear of Flying*, ch. 16 (1973).

26 The source of all life and knowledge is in man and woman, and the source of all living is in the interchange and the meeting and mingling of these two: man-life and woman-life, man-knowledge and woman-knowledge, man-being and woman-being.

> D. H. LAWRENCE (1885–1930), British author. Letter, 2 June 1914 (published in *The Letters of D. H. Lawrence*, vol. 2, ed. by George J. Zytaruk and James T. Boulton, 1981).

27 The great living experience for every man is his adventure into the woman. . . . The man embraces in the woman all that is not himself, and from that one resultant, from that embrace, comes every new action.

> D. H. LAWRENCE (1885–1930), British author. Letter, 24 Feb. 1915, to Bertrand Russell (published in *The Letters of D. H. Lawrence*, vol. 2. ed. by George J. Zytaruk and James T. Boulton, 1981).

28 Women have . . . by imitating the life condition of men, surrendered a very strong position of their own. Men are afraid of virgins, but they have a cure for their own fear and the virgin's virginity: fucking. Men are afraid of crones, so afraid that their cure for virginity fails them; they know it won't work. Faced with the fulfilled crone, all but the bravest men wilt and retreat, crestfallen and cockadroop.

> URSULA K. LE GUIN (b. 1929), U.S. author. "The Space Crone," in *The Co-Evolution Quarterly* (Summer 1976; repr. in *Dancing at the Edge of the World*, 1989).

29 Much can be inferred about a man from his mistress: in her one beholds his weaknesses and his dreams.

> G.C. LICHTENBERG (1742–99), German physicist, philosopher. *Aphorisms*, "Notebook F," aph. 88 (written 1765–99; tr. by R. J. Hollingdale, 1990).

30 I really think that American gentlemen are the best after all, because kissing your hand may make you feel very very good but a diamond and a sapphire bracelet lasts forever.

> ANITA LOOS (1893–1981), U.S. novelist, screenwriter. Lorelei Lee's journal entry for 27 April, in *Gentlemen Prefer Blondes*, "Paris is Divine" (1925).

31 I do not know who first invented the myth of sexual equality. But it is a myth willfully fostered and nourished by certain semi-scientists and other fiction writers. And it has done more, I suspect, to unsettle marital happiness than any other false doctrine of this myth-ridden age.

> PHYLLIS MCGINLEY (1905–78), U.S. poet, author. *The Province of the Heart,* "The Honor of Being a Woman" (1959).

32 Coming to terms with the rhythms of women's lives means coming to terms with life itself, accepting the imperatives of the body rather than the imperatives of an artificial, man-made, perhaps transcendentally beautiful civilization. Emphasis on the male work-rhythm is an emphasis on infinite possibilities; emphasis on the female rhythms is an emphasis on a defined pattern, on limitation.

> MARGARET MEAD (1901–78), U.S. anthropologist. *Male and Female,* ch. 8 (1949).

33 Men have a much better time of it than women. For one thing, they marry later, for another thing, they die earlier.

> H. L. MENCKEN (1880–1956), U.S. journalist. *A Mencken Chrestomathy,* "Sententiæ: Masculum et Feminam Creavit Eos" (1949).

34 Because of our social circumstances, male and female are really two cultures and their life experiences are utterly different.

> KATE MILLET (b. 1934), U.S. feminist author. *Sexual Politics,* ch. 2, sct. 2 (1970).

35 For the woman, the man is a means: the end is always the child.

> FRIEDRICH NIETZSCHE (1844–1900), German philosopher. *Thus Spoke Zarathustra,* pt. 1, "Of Old and Young Women" (1883–92; tr. 1961).

36 It is not her body that he wants but it is only through her body that he can take possession of another human being, so he must labor upon her body, he must enter her body, to make his claim.

> JOYCE CAROL OATES (b. 1938), U.S. author. *Unholy Loves,* "In the Founders' Room" (1979).

37 The incomprehensibleness of women is an old theory, but what is that to the curious wondering observation with which wives, mothers, and sisters watch the other unreasoning animal in those moments when he has snatched the reins out of their hands, and is not to be spoken to! . . . It is best to let him come to, and feel his own helplessness.

> MARGARET OLIPHANT (1828–97), English novelist, historian. Mrs. Proctor, in *The Rector,* ch. 4 (1863), first of *Chronicles of Carlingford.*

38 Men are gentle, honest and straightforward. Women are convoluted, deceptive and dangerous.

> ERIN PIZZEY (b. 1939), British civil rights activist. *Daily Mail* (London, 24 Aug. 1988).

39 In our civilization, men are afraid that they will not be men enough and women are afaid that they may be considered only women.

> THEODOR REIK (1888–1969), U.S. psychologist. *Esquire* (New York, Nov. 1958).

40 The great renewal of the world will perhaps consist in this, that man and maid, freed of all false feelings and reluctances, will seek each other not as opposites, but as brother and sister, as neighbors, and will come together as *human* beings.

> RAINER MARIA RILKE (1875–1926), German poet. Letter, 16 July 1903 (published in *Letters to a Young Poet,* 1934; rev. 1954).

41 Man is the one who desires, woman the one who is desired. This is woman's entire but decisive advantage. Through man's passions, nature has given man into woman's hands, and the woman who does not know how to make him her subject, her slave, her toy, and how to betray him with a smile in the end is not wise.

> LEOPOLD VON SACHER-MASOCH (1835–95), Austrian novelist. Madame Venus, in *Venus in Furs* (1870; tr. 1928).

42 When men and women agree, it is only in their conclusions; their reasons are always different.

> GEORGE SANTAYANA (1863–1952), U.S. philosopher, poet. *The Life of Reason,* "Reason in Society," ch. 6, (1905–6).

43 We all enter the world little plastic beings, with so much natural force, perhaps, but for the rest—blank; and the world tells us what we are to be, and shapes us by the ends it sets before us. To you it says—*Work;* and to us it says—*Seem!* To you it says—As you approximate to man's highest ideal of God, as your arm is strong and your knowledge great, and the power to labour is with you, so you shall gain all that human heart desires. To us it says—Strength shall not help you, nor knowledge, nor labour. You shall gain what men gain, but by other means. And so the world makes men and women.

> OLIVE SCHREINER (1855–1920), South African writer, feminist. Lyndall, in *The Story of an African Farm,* pt. 2, ch. 4 (1883).

44 There is very little difference between men and women in space.

> HELEN SHARMAN (b. 1963), British scientist, astronaut. *Independent on Sunday* (London, 9 June 1991). Sharman was Britain's first astronaut in space.

45 Man, born of woman, has found it a hard thing to forgive her for giving him birth. The patriarchal protest against the ancient matriarch has borne strange fruit through the years.

> LILLIAN SMITH (1897–1966), U.S. author. *Killers of the Dream,* pt. 2, ch. 4 (1949; rev. 1961).

46 Just as humans have a prior right to existence over dogs by virtue of being more highly evolved and having a superior consciousness, so women have a prior right to existence over men. The elimination of any male is, therefore, a righteous and good act, an act highly beneficial to women as well as an act of mercy.

> VALERIE SOLANAS (b. 1940), U.S. artist, writer. *The SCUM Manifesto* (1968).

47 What is most beautiful in virile men is something feminine; what is most beautiful in feminine women is something masculine.

> SUSAN SONTAG (b. 1933), U.S. essayist. *Against Interpretation,* "Notes on 'Camp'," Note 9 (1966; first published 1964).

48 The great majority of men, especially in France, both desire and possess a fashionable woman, much in the way one might own a fine horse—as a luxury befitting a young man.

> STENDHAL (1783–1842), French author. *De l'Amour*, ch. 1 (1822).

49   A woman is a branchy tree
And man a singing wind;
And from her branches carelessly
He takes what he can find.

> JAMES STEPHENS (1882–1950), Irish poet, author. *A Woman is a Branchy Tree.*

50   The little rift between the sexes is astonishingly widened by simply teaching one set of catchwords to the girls and another to the boys.

> ROBERT LOUIS STEVENSON (1850–94), Scottish novelist, essayist, poet. *Virginibus Puerisque*, sct. 2 (1881).

51   'Tis strange what a man may do, and a woman yet think him an angel.

> WILLIAM MAKEPEACE THACKERAY (1811–63), English author. *The History of Henry Esmond*, bk. 1, ch. 7 (1852).

52   The anger that appears to be building up between the sexes becomes more virulent with every day that passes. And far from women taking the blame . . . the fact is that men are invariably portrayed as the bad guys. Being a good man is like being a good Nazi.

> DAVID THOMAS (b. 1959), British editor. "Fifth Column," Oct. 1991, BBC2. Quoted in: *Independent on Sunday* (London, 22 March 1992).

53   For a man to strike any women is most brutal, and I, as well as everyone else, think this far worse than any attempt to shoot, which, wicked as it is, is at least more comprehensible and more courageous.

> VICTORIA (1819-1901), Queen of Great Britain and Ireland. In *Victoria, Her Letters and Journals* (ed. by Christopher Hibbert, 1984), entry for 2 July 1850. Victoria had survived two assassination attemps.

54   It is well within the order of things
That man should listen when his mate sings;
But the true male never yet walked
Who liked to listen when his mate talked.

> ANNA WICKHAM (1884–1947), British poet. *The Affinity*, in *The Contemplative Quarry* (1915).

55   A man can be happy with any woman, as long as he does not love her.

> OSCAR WILDE (1854–1900), Anglo-Irish playwright, author. Lord Henry, in *The Picture of Dorian Gray*, ch. 15 (1891).

56   Women love us for our defects. If we have enough of them, they will forgive us everything, even our gigantic intellects.

> OSCAR WILDE (1854–1900), Anglo-Irish playwright, author. Lord Illingworth, in *A Woman of No Importance*, act 3. The remark had also appeared, two years earlier, in *The Picture of Dorian Gray*, ch. 15 (1891).

See also Collins on AGE AND AGING; Wilde on COMPLIMENTS; Bron on FALLIBILITY; Byron, Wilde on FRIENDSHIP; GENDER; Oliphant on GENTLEMEN; Dworkin, McGinley on GOSSIP; De Wolfe on HOME AND HOUSES; Longfellow on LIFE AND LIVING; Wyatt on LOVE; Brookner on LOVERS; Staël on PUBLIC OPINION; Clewlow on SEX; Zetterling on SENSUALITY; Spacks on VANITY; WOMEN AND MEN.

MENOPAUSE

1   Though her years were waning,
Her climacteric teased her like her teens.

> LORD BYRON (1788–1824), English poet. *Don Juan*, cto. 10, st. 47.

2   The climacteric marks the end of apologizing. The chrysalis of conditioning has once for all to break and the female woman finally to emerge.

> GERMAINE GREER (b. 1939), Australian feminist writer. *The Change: Women, Aging and the Menopause*, ch. 17 (1991).

3   The menopause is probably the least glamorous topic imaginable; and this is interesting, because it is one of the very few topics to which cling some shreds and remnants of taboo. A serious mention of menopause is usually met with uneasy silence; a sneering reference to it is usually met with relieved sniggers. Both the silence and the sniggering are pretty sure indications of taboo.

> URSULA K. LE GUIN (b. 1929), U.S. author. "The Space Crone," in *The Co-Evolution Quarterly* (Summer 1976; repr. in *Dancing at the Edge of the World*, 1989).

MENSTRUATION

1   If you think you are emancipated, you might consider the idea of tasting your menstrual blood—if it makes you sick, you've a long way to go, baby.

> GERMAINE GREER (b. 1939), Australian feminist writer. *The Female Eunuch*, "The Wicked Womb" (1970).

2   Each month
the blood sheets down
like good red rain.

> ERICA JONG (b. 1942), U.S. author. *Gardener*, in *Half Lives* (1973).

3   It is not menstrual blood per se which disturbs the imagination—unstanchable as that red flood may be—but rather the albumen in the blood, the uterine shreds, placental jellyfish of the female sea. This is the chthonian matrix from which we rose. We have an evolutionary revulsion from slime, our site of biologic origins. Every month, it is woman's fate to face the abyss of time and being, the abyss which is herself.

> CAMILLE PAGLIA (b. 1947), U.S. author, critic, educator. *Sexual Personae*, ch. 1 (1990).

4   In man, the shedding of blood is always associated with injury, disease, or death. Only the female half of humanity was seen to have the magical ability to bleed profusely and still rise phoenix-like each month from the gore.

> ESTELLE R. RAMEY (b. 1917), U.S. scientist, educator. "Men's Monthly Cycles (They Have Them Too, You Know)," in *The First Ms. Reader* (ed. by Francine Klagsbrun, 1972).

5   When people say women can't be trusted because they cycle every month, my response is that men cycle every day, so they should only be allowed to negotiate peace treaties in the evening.

> JUNE REINISCH (b. 1943), U.S. psychologist. *Times* (London, 20 Jan. 1992).

6 If men could menstruate . . . clearly, menstruation would become an enviable, boast-worthy, masculine event: Men would brag about how long and how much. . . . Sanitary supplies would be federally funded and free. Of course, some men would still pay for the prestige of such commercial brands as Paul Newman Tampons, Muhammed Ali's Rope-a-Dope Pads, John Wayne Maxi Pads, and Joe Namath Jock Shields—"For Those Light Bachelor Days."

GLORIA STEINEM (b. 1934), U.S. feminist writer, editor. "If Men Could Menstruate," in *Ms.* (Oct. 1978; repr. in *Outrageous Acts and Everyday Rebellions,* 1983).

7 Stupid word, that. Period. In America it means "full stop," like in punctuation. That's stupid as well. A period isn't a full stop. It's a new beginning. I don't mean all that creativity, life-giving force, earth-mother stuff, I mean it's a new beginning to the month, relief that you're not pregnant, when you don't have to have a child.

MICHELENE WANDOR (b. 1940), British poet, playwright, critic. *Guests in the Body,* "Mother's Pride" (1986).

MENTAL ILLNESS

1 Nothing defines the quality of life in a community more clearly than people who regard themselves, or whom the consensus chooses to regard, as mentally unwell.

RENATA ADLER (b. 1938), U.S. author, film critic. *Toward a Radical Middle,* "The Thursday Group" (1971; first published 1967).

2 It is thus that the few rare lucid well-disposed people who have had to struggle on the earth find themselves at certain hours of the day or night in the depth of certain authentic and waking nightmare states, surrounded by the formidable suction, the formidable tentacular oppression of a kind of civic magic which will soon be seen appearing openly in social behavior.

ANTONIN ARTAUD (1896–1948), French theater producer, actor, theorist. *Van Gogh, the Man Suicided by Society* (1947; repr. in *Selected Writings,* pt. 33, ed. by Susan Sontag, 1976).

3 Schizophrenia cannot be understood without understanding despair.

R. D. LAING (1927–89), British psychiatrist. *The Divided Self,* ch. 2 (1959).

4 There is no such "condition" as "schizophrenia," but the label is a social fact and the social fact a *political event.*

R. D. LAING (1927–89), British psychiatrist. *The Politics of Experience,* ch. 5 (1967).

5 Schizophrenia may be a necessary consequence of literacy.

MARSHALL MCLUHAN (1911–80), Canadian communications theorist. *The Gutenberg Galaxy,* "Typographic Man Can Express But Is Helpless to Read the Configuration of Print Technology" (1962).

6 Doubt is to certainty as neurosis is to psychosis. The neurotic is in doubt and has fears about persons and things; the psychotic has convictions and makes claims about them. In short, the neurotic has problems, the psychotic has solutions.

THOMAS SZASZ (b. 1920), U.S. psychiatrist. *The Second Sin,* "Mental Illness" (1973).

7 No further evidence is needed to show that "mental illness" is not the name of a biological condition whose nature awaits to be elucidated, but is the name of a concept whose purpose is to obscure the obvious.

THOMAS SZASZ (b. 1920), U.S. psychiatrist. *The Second Sin,* "Mental Illness" (1973).

See also INSANITY; MADNESS.

MERIT

1 'Tis not in mortals to command success,
But we'll do more, Sempronius, we'll deserve it.

JOSEPH ADDISON (1672–1719), English essayist. Portius, in *Cato,* act 1, sc. 2. "Curse on the stripling!" responds Sempronius, father of Portius, ". . . ambitiously sententious."

2 Arrogance on the part of the meritorious is even more offensive to us than the arrogance of those without merit: for merit itself is offensive.

FRIEDRICH NIETZSCHE (1844–1900), German philosopher. *Human, All Too Human,* aph. 332 (1878).

3 What is merit? The opinion one man entertains of another.

LORD PALMERSTON (1784–1865), English politician, prime minister. Quoted in: Thomas Carlyle, *Critical and Miscellaneous Essays,* vol. 8, "Shooting Niagara" (1838).

THE MESSIAH

1 The Old Testament teems with prophecies of the Messiah, but nowhere is it intimated that that Messiah is to stand as a God to be worshipped. He is to bring peace on earth, to build up the waste places—to comfort the broken-hearted, but nowhere is he spoken of as a deity.

OLYMPIA BROWN (1835–1900), U.S. minister (first woman ordained in US). Sermon, c. 13 Jan. 1895, Mukwonago, Wisc. (" in Olympia Brown, An Autobiography," ed. by Gwendolen B. Willis, 1960; published in *Annual Journal of the Universalist Historical Society,* vol. 4, 1963).

2 You will never get the crowd to cry Hosanna until you ride into town on an ass.

FRIEDRICH NIETZSCHE (1844–1900), German philosopher. *Assorted Opinions and Maxims,* aph. 313 (1879).

3 I think the Messianic concept, which is the Jewish offering to mankind, is a great victory. What does it mean? It means that history has a sense, a meaning, a direction; it goes somewhere, and necessarily in a good direction—the Messiah.

ELIE WIESEL (b. 1928), Rumanian-born US writer. Interview in *Writers at Work* (Eighth Series, ed. by George Plimpton, 1988).

METAPHYSICS

1 I was thrown out of N.Y.U. my freshman year . . .

for cheating on my metaphysics final. You know, I looked within the soul of the boy sitting next to me.

> WOODY ALLEN (b. 1935), U.S. filmmaker. Alvy Singer (Allen), in the film *Annie Hall* (directed by Woody Allen, scripted by Allen with Marshall Brickman, 1977; published in *Four Films of Woody Allen*, 1982), doing standup comedy in front of a college audience.

2 Two half philosophers will probably never a whole metaphysician make.

> GASTON BACHELARD (1884–1962), French scientist, philosopher, literary theorist. *Fragments of a Poetics of Fire*, "A Retrospective Glance at the Lifework of a Master of Books" (1988; tr. 1990).

3 Metaphysics is the finding of bad reasons for what we believe upon instinct; but to find these reasons is no less an instinct.

> F. H. BRADLEY (1846–1924), English philosopher. *Appearance and Reality*, Preface (1893).

4 Metaphysics means nothing but an unusually obstinate effort to think clearly.

> WILLIAM JAMES (1842–1910), U.S. psychologist, philosopher. *Principles of Psychology*, vol. 1, ch. 6 (1890).

5 A little cooling down of animal excitability and instinct, a little loss of animal toughness, a little irritable weakness and descent of the pain-threshold, will bring the worm at the core of all our usual springs of delight into full view, and turn us into melancholy metaphysicians.

> WILLIAM JAMES (1842–1910), U.S. psychologist, philosopher. *The Varieties of Religious Experience*, lectures 6 and 7 (1902).

6 The most heterogeneous ideas are yoked by violence together; nature and art are ransacked for illustrations, comparisons, and allusions; their learning instructs, and their subtlety surprises; but the reader commonly thinks his improvement dearly bought and, though he sometimes admires, is seldom pleased.

> SAMUEL JOHNSON (1709–84), English author, lexicographer. *Lives of the English Poets*, "Cowley" (1779–81), on metaphysical poets.

7 A metaphysician is one who, when you remark that twice two makes four, demands to know what you mean by twice, what by two, what by makes, and what by four. For asking such questions metaphysicians are supported in oriental luxury in the universities, and respected as educated and intelligent men.

> H. L. MENCKEN (1880–1956), U.S. journalist. *A Mencken Chrestomathy*, pt. 2, "The Metaphysician" (1949).

8 That's metaphysics, my dear fellow. It's forbidden me by my doctor, my stomach won't take it.

> BORIS PASTERNAK (1890–1960), Russian poet, novelist, translator. Ivan Ivanovich, in *Doctor Zhivago*, ch. 1, sct. 5 (1957).

9 Metaphysics abstracts the mind from the senses, and the poetic faculty must submerge the whole mind in the senses. Metaphysics soars up to universals, and the poetic faculty must plunge deep into particulars.

> GIAMBATTISTA VICO (1688–1744), Italian philosopher, historian. *The New Science*, bk. 3, ch. 4, para. 821 (ed. 1744; tr. 1984).

METHOD

1 There is no method but to be very intelligent.

> T. S. ELIOT (1888–1965), Anglo-American poet, critic. *The Perfect Critic* (1920; repr. in *Selected Prose of T. S. Eliot*, ed. by Frank Kermode, 1975), said of Aristotle, who exemplified not method so much as intelligence itself.

2 There is a point at which methods devour themselves.

> FRANTZ FANON (1925–61), Martiniquan psychiatrist, philosopher, political activist. *Black Skins, White Masks*, Introduction (1952; tr. 1967).

3 Art is the beautiful way of doing things. Science is the effective way of doing things. Business is the economic way of doing things.

> ELBERT HUBBARD (1856–1915), U.S. author. *Selected Writings*, vol. 1, "Index" (1921).

4 No delusion is greater than the notion that method and industry can make up for lack of mother-wit, either in science or in practical life.

> THOMAS HENRY HUXLEY (1825–95), English biologist. "On the Advisableness of Improving Natural Knowledge" (1866; repr. in *Collected Essays*, vol. 1, 1893).

MIDDLE AGE

1 The only time you really live fully is from thirty to sixty. . . . The young are slaves to dreams; the old servants of regrets. Only the middle-aged have all their five senses in the keeping of their wits.

> HERVEY ALLEN (1889–1949), U.S. novelist, poet, biographer. *Anthony Adverse*, ch. 31 (1933).

2 To think, when one is no longer young, when one is not yet old, that one is no longer young, that one is not yet old, that is perhaps something.

> SAMUEL BECKETT (1906–89), Irish dramatist, novelist. *Watt* (written 1944, 1953).

3 She was a handsome woman of forty-five and would remain so for many years.

> ANITA BROOKNER (b. 1938), British novelist, art historian. *Hotel du Lac*, ch. 4 (1984).

4 Of all the barbarous middle ages, that
Which is most barbarous is the middle age
Of man! it is—I really scarce know what;
But when we hover between fool and sage,
And don't know justly what we would be at—
A period something like a printed page,
Black letter upon foolscap, while our hair
Grows grizzled, and we are not what we were.

> LORD BYRON (1788–1824), English poet. *Don Juan*, cto. 12, st. 1 (1823).

5 Youth is the period in which a man can be hopeless. The end of every episode is the end of the world. But the power of hoping through everything, the knowledge that the soul survives its adventures, that great inspiration comes to the middle-aged.

> G. K. CHESTERTON (1874–1936), British author. *Charles Dickens*, "The Boyhood of Dickens" (1906).

6   By the time we hit fifty, we have learned our hardest lessons. We have found out that only a few things are really important. We have learned to take life seriously, but never ourselves.

> MARIE DRESSLER (1873–1934), U.S. actor. *My Own Story*, ch. 17 (1934).

7   Few women, I fear, have had such reason as I have to think the long sad years of youth were worth living for the sake of middle age.

> GEORGE ELIOT (1819–80), English novelist. Letter, 31 Dec. 1857 (published in *George Eliot's Life as Related in Her Letters and Journals*, 1900).

8   In the multitude of middle-aged men who go about their vocations in a daily course determined for them much in the same way as the tie of their cravats, there is always a good number who once meant to shape their own deeds and alter the world a little.

> GEORGE ELIOT (1819–80), English novelist. *Middlemarch*, bk. 2, ch. 15 (1871–72).

9   The years between fifty and seventy are the hardest. You are always being asked to do things, and yet you are not decrepit enough to turn them down.

> T. S. ELIOT (1888–1965), Anglo-American poet, critic. *Time* (New York, 23 Oct. 1950).

10   The misery of the middle-aged woman is a grey and hopeless thing, born of having nothing to live for, of disappointment and resentment at having been gypped by consumer society, and surviving merely to be the butt of its unthinking scorn.

> GERMAINE GREER (b. 1939), Australian feminist writer. *The Change: Women, Ageing and the Menopause*, Introduction (1991).

11   Every man who has lived for fifty years has buried a whole world or even two; he has grown used to its disappearance and accustomed to the new scenery of another act: but suddenly the names and faces of a time long dead appear more and more often on his way, calling up series of shades and pictures kept somewhere, "just in case," in the endless catacombs of the memory, making him smile or sigh, and sometimes almost weep.

> ALEXANDER HERZEN (1812–70), Russian journalist, political thinker. *My Past and Thoughts*, vol. 3, pt. 8, "Miscellaneous Pieces: From the Other World and from This" (1921; tr. by Constance Garnett, 1924–27).

12   I think middle-age is the best time, if we can escape the fatty degeneration of the conscience which often sets in at about fifty.

> W. R. INGE (1860–1954), Dean of St Paul's, London. Quoted in: *Observer* (London, 8 June 1930).

13   At last now you can be
What the old cannot recall
And the young long for in dreams,
Yet still include them all.

> ELIZABETH JENNINGS (b. 1926), British poet. *Accepted*, in *Growing Pains* (1975).

14   From the middle of life onward, only he remains vitally alive who is ready to *die with life*.

> CARL JUNG (1875–1961), Swiss psychiatrist. *The Soul and*

Death (1934; repr. in *Collected Works*, vol. 8, para. 800, ed. by William McGuire, 1960).

15   Middle age is the time when a man is always thinking that in a week or two he will feel as good as ever.

> DON MARQUIS (1878–1937), U.S. humorist, journalist. Quoted in: E. Anthony, *O Rare Don Marquis*, ch. 11 (1962).

16   Men of my age live in a state of continual desperation.

> TREVOR MCDONALD (b. 1939), British journalist, broadcaster. *Today* (London, 8 Dec. 1989).

17   In mid-life the man wants to see how irresistible he still is to younger women. How they turn their hearts to stone and more or less commit a murder of their marriage I just don't know, but they do.

> PATRICIA NEAL (b. 1926), U.S. screen actor. *Daily Telegraph* (London, 22 June 1988).

18   The youth gets together his materials to build a bridge to the moon, or, perchance, a palace or temple on the earth, and, at length, the middle-aged man concludes to build a woodshed with them.

> HENRY DAVID THOREAU (1817–62), U.S. philosopher, author, naturalist. *Journal* (1906), entry for 14 July 1852.

19   In middle life, the human back is spoiling for a technical knockout and will use the flimsiest excuse, even a sneeze, to fall apart.

> E. B. WHITE (1899–1985), U.S. author, editor. "Radiography," in *New Yorker* (24 Feb. 1951; repr. in *Writings from the New Yorker 1927–1976*, ed. by Rebecca M. Dale, 1991).

20   At 46 one must be a miser; only have time for essentials.

> VIRGINIA WOOLF (1882–1941), British novelist. *The Diary of Virginia Woolf*, vol. 3 (ed. by Anne O. Bell, 1980), entry for 22 March 1928.

21   Be wise with speed;
A fool at forty is a fool indeed.

> EDWARD YOUNG (1683–1765), English poet, dramatist. *Love of Fame: The Universal Passion*, Satire 2 (1725–28).

See also Fitzgerald on FRIENDS.

THE MIDDLE CLASS

1   The most perfect political community must be amongst those who are in the middle rank, and those states are best instituted wherein these are a larger and more respectable part, if possible, than both the other; or, if that cannot be, at least than either of them separate.

> ARISTOTLE (384–322 B.C.), Greek philosopher. *Politics*, bk. 4, ch. 11, sct. 1295b (c. 343 B.C.).

2   This miserable state is borne by the wretched souls of those who lived without disgrace and without praise.

> DANTE ALIGHIERI (1265–1321), Italian poet. *The Divine Comedy*, "The Inferno," cto. 3 (completed 1321).

3   What I call middle-class society is any society that becomes rigidified in predetermined forms, forbidding all evolution, all gains, all progress, all discovery. I call middle-class a closed society in which life has no taste, in which the air is tainted, in which ideas and men are corrupt. And I think that a man who takes a stand against this death is in a sense a revolutionary.

> FRANTZ FANON (1925–61), Martiniquan psychiatrist, philosopher, political activist. *Black Skins, White Masks,* ch. 8 (1952; tr. 1967).

4   What I always hated and detested and cursed above all things was this contentment, this healthiness and comfort, this carefully preserved optimism of the middle classes, this fat and prosperous brood of mediocrity.

> HERMANN HESSE (1877–1962), German novelist, poet. *Steppenwolf,* "For Madmen Only" (1927).

5   The prevalent fear of poverty among the educated classes is the worst moral disease from which our civilization suffers.

> WILLIAM JAMES (1842–1910), U.S. psychologist, philosopher. *The Varieties of Religious Experience,* lectures 14–15, "The Value of Saintliness" (1902).

6   We of the sinking middle class . . . may sink without further struggles into the working class where we belong, and probably when we get there it will not be so dreadful as we feared, for, after all, we have nothing to lose but our aitches.

> GEORGE ORWELL (1903–50), British author. *The Road to Wigan Pier,* ch. 13 (1937).

7   I have to live for others and not for myself: that's middle-class morality.

> GEORGE BERNARD SHAW (1856–1950), Anglo-Irish playwright, critic. Alfred Doolittle, in *Pygmalion,* act 5.

8   I simply contend that the middle-class ideal which demands that people be affectionate, respectable, honest and content, that they avoid excitements and cultivate serenity is the ideal that appeals to me, it is in short the ideal of affectionate family life, of honorable business methods.

> GERTRUDE STEIN (1874–1946), U.S. author. *Q.E.D.,* bk. 1, "Adele" (1903).

9   It is to the middle-class we must look for the safety of England.

> WILLIAM MAKEPEACE THACKERAY (1811–63), English author. *The Four Georges,* "George the Third" (1855).

10   A theory of the middle class: that it is not to be determined by its financial situation but rather by its relation to government. That is, one could shade down from an actual ruling or governing class to a class hopelessly out of relation to government, thinking of gov't as beyond its control, of itself as wholly controlled by gov't. Somewhere in between and in gradations is the group that has the sense that gov't exists for it, and shapes its consciousness accordingly.

> LIONEL TRILLING (1905–75), U.S. critic. Notebook entry, 1945, in *Partisan Review 50th Anniversary Edition* (ed. by William Philips, 1985).

See also Sutton on CLASS; Friel on REPRESSION.

THE MIDDLE EAST

1   I saw the Arab map.

It resembled a mare shuffling on, dragging its history like saddlebags, nearing its tomb and the pitch of hell.

> ADONIS [ALI AHMED SAID] (b. 1930), Syrian poet. *The Desert (Diary of Beirut under Siege, 1982).*

2   It is not possible to create peace in the Middle East by jeopardizing the peace of the world.

> ANEURIN BEVAN (1897–1960), British Labour politician. Speech, 4 Nov. 1956, at rally protesting Britain's armed intervention in the Suez dispute.

3   The Persians are called the French of the East; we will call the Arabs Oriental Italians. A gifted noble people; a people of wild strong feelings, and of iron restraint over these: the characteristic of noblemindedness, of genius.

> THOMAS CARLYLE (1795–1881), Scottish essayist, historian. *On Heroes and Hero-Worship,* "The Hero as Prophet" (1841).

4   The picture. A great plain, comprising the entire Jerusalem district, where is the supreme Commander-in-Chief of the forces of good, Christ our Lord: another plain near Babylon, where Lucifer is, at the head of the enemy.

> ST. IGNATIUS OF LOYOLA (1491–1556), Spanish churchman, founder of the Society of Jesus. *Spiritual Exercises,* "Second Week," no. 138 (1548).

5   America is the world's policeman, all right—a big, dumb, mick flatfoot in the middle of the one thing cops dread most, a "domestic disturbance."

> P. J. O'ROURKE (b. 1947), U.S. journalist. "Jordan," in *Rolling Stone* (New York, Aug. 1990; repr. in *Give War a Chance,* 1992).

6   It is crystal clear to me that if Arabs put down a draft resolution blaming Israel for the recent earthquake in Iran it would probably have a majority, the US would veto it and Britain and France would abstain.

> AMOS OZ (b. 1939), Israeli novelist. *Times* (London, 24 Oct. 1990).

7   The tormenting dilemma of the Middle East is this: either we have one people too many, or one state too few.

> AFIF SAFIEH, London representative of PLO. Quoted by Neal Ascherson in: *Independent on Sunday* (London, 3 March 1991)

See also IRAQ AND THE GULF WAR; ISRAEL; LEBANON; PALESTINE.

HENRY MILLER

1   Miller is not really a writer but a non-stop talker to whom someone has given a typewriter.

> GERALD BRENAN (1894–1987), British author. *Thoughts in a Dry Season,* "Literature" (1978).

2   It is true I swim in a perpetual sea of sex but the actual excursions are fairly limited.

> HENRY MILLER (1891–1980), U.S. author. Letter, 1 Feb. 1932 (published in *Letters to Anaïs Nin,* pt. 1, 1965).

3   Miller does have something highly important to tell us; his virulent sexism is beyond question an honest contribution to social and psychological understanding which we can hardly afford to ignore. But to confuse this neurotic hostility, this frank abuse, with sanity, is pitiable. To confuse it with freedom were vicious, were it not so very sad.

> KATE MILLETT (b. 1934), U.S. feminist author. *Sexual Politics*, ch. 6 (1970).

4 I never liked the language of Henry Miller. I don't think pornography has added to our sensual life.

> ANAÏS NÍN (1903–77), Franco-American novelist, diarist. Quoted in: *Times* (London, 1 June 1970). Nin had a ten-year relationship with Miller in France and the United States.

5 He is fiddling while Rome is burning, and, unlike the enormous majority of people who do this, fiddling with his face towards the flames.

> GEORGE ORWELL (1903–50), British author. *Inside the Whale and Other Essays*, "Inside the Whale," sct.1 (1940). "It is as though you could hear a voice speaking to you," Orwell wrote of Miller, "a friendly American voice, with no humbug in it, no moral purpose, merely an implicit assumption that we are all alike."

6 Here is a dirty book worth reading . . . a bawdy which will be very useful to put Wyndham and J. J. into their proper cubby holes; cause Miller is sore and without kinks.

> EZRA POUND (1885–1972), U.S. poet, critic. Letter, 1 Dec. 1934, referring to *Tropic of Cancer*. Quoted in: Karl Shapiro, "The Greatest Living Author," Preface to *Tropic of Cancer*. The book was first published in Paris in 1934, but suppressed in the U.S. until 1961, when it became a bestseller. "Wyndham" was Wyndham Lewis, J. J., James Joyce.

See also Miller on WRITING.

JOHN MILTON

1 The reason Milton wrote in fetters when he wrote of Angels & God, and at liberty when of Devils & Hell, is because he was a true Poet, and of the Devil's party without knowing it.

> WILLIAM BLAKE (1757–1827), English poet, painter, engraver. *The Marriage of Heaven and Hell*, plates 5–6 (1790–3).

2 Milton, Madam, was a genius that could cut a Colossus from a rock; but he could not carve heads upon cherry-stones.

> SAMUEL JOHNSON (1709–84), English author, lexicographer. Quoted in: Boswell, *Life of Samuel Johnson*, 13 June 1784 (1791), said to author Hannah More when she wondered how a poet capable of writing *Paradise Lost* had written such poor sonnets.

3 Milton! thou should'st be living at this hour: England hath need of thee.

> WILLIAM WORDSWORTH (1770–1850), English poet. *London* (1807).

THE MIND

1 What impresses men is not mind, but the result of mind.

> WALTER BAGEHOT (1826–77), English economist, critic. *The English Constitution*, ch. 8 (1867).

2 He has the lucidity which is the by-product of a fundamentally sterile mind. . . . He does not have to struggle . . . with the crowded pulsations of a fecund imagination. On the contrary he is almost devoid of imagination.

> ANEURIN BEVAN (1897–1960), British Labour politician. Quoted in: Michael Foot, *Aneurin Bevan*, vol. 1, ch. 8 (1962), referring to Prime Minister Neville Chamberlain.

3 Everything tends to make us believe that there exists a certain point of the mind at which life and death, the real and the imagined, past and future, the communicable and the incommunicable, high and low, cease to be perceived as contradictions.

> ANDRÉ BRETON (1896–1966), French surrealist. "Second Manifesto of Surrealism" (1930; repr. in *Manifestos of Surrealism*, 1969).

4 The mind is the result of the torments the flesh undergoes or inflicts upon itself.

> E. M. CIORAN (b. 1911), Rumanian-born French philosopher. *The Temptation to Exist*, title essay (1956).

5 The mind is not a hermit's cell, but a place of hospitality and intercourse.

> CHARLES HORTON COOLEY (1864–1929), U.S. sociologist. *Human Nature and the Social Order*, ch. 3 (1902).

6 Sense is a line, the mind *is a circle*. Sense is like a line which is the flux of a point running out from itself, but intellect like a circle that keeps within itself.

> RALPH J. CUDWORTH (1617–88), English theologian, philosopher. *Treatise Concerning Eternal and Immutable Morality*, bk. 3, ch. 3, sct. 4 (1731).

7 The Brain—is wider than the Sky—.

> EMILY DICKINSON (1830–86), U.S. poet. *The Complete Poems*, no. 632 (1955).

8 I consider that a man's brain originally is like a little empty attic, and you have to stock it with such furniture as you choose.

> SIR ARTHUR CONAN DOYLE (1859–1930), English author. Sherlock Holmes, in A Study in Scarlet, ch. 2 (1887). Holmes made a similar comparison in The Five Orange Pips. See Doyle on LIBRARIES.

9 Give up the belief that mind is, even temporarily, compressed within the skull, and you will quickly become more manly or womanly. You will understand yourself and your Maker better than before.

> MARY BAKER EDDY (1821–1910), U.S. founder of the Christian Science movement. *Science and Health*, ch. 12 (1875).

10 The human head is bigger than the globe. It conceives itself as containing more. It can think and rethink itself and ourselves from any desired point outside the gravitational pull of the earth. It starts by writing one thing and later reads itself as something else. The human head is monstrous.

> GÜNTHER GRASS (b. 1927), German author. "Racing with the Utopias," in *Die Zeit* (16 June 1978; repr. in *On Writing and Politics 1967–1983*, 1984; tr. 1985).

11 We live in the mind, in ideas, in fragments. We no longer drink in the wild outer music of the streets—we *remember* only.

> HENRY MILLER (1891–1980), U.S. author. *Black Spring*, "The Fourteenth Ward" (1936).

12 Is there no way out of the mind?

SYLVIA PLATH (1932–63), U.S. poet. *Apprehensions.*

13 What is mind but motion in the intellectual sphere?

OSCAR WILDE (1854–1900), Anglo-Irish playwright, author. Gilbert, in *The Critic as Artist*, pt. 2 (published in *Intentions*, 1891).

14 Where the Mind is biggest, the Heart, the Senses, Magnanimity, Charity, Tolerance, Kindliness, and the rest of them scarcely have room to breathe.

VIRGINIA WOOLF (1882–1941), British novelist. *Orlando*, ch. 4 (1928).

15 My own brain is to me the most unaccountable of machinery—always buzzing, humming, soaring roaring diving, and then buried in mud. And why? What's this passion for?

VIRGINIA WOOLF (1882–1941), British novelist. Letter, 28 Dec. 1932 (published in *The Sickle Side of the Moon: Letters*, vol. 5, ed. by Nigel Nicolson, 1979).

16 Not Chaos, not
The darkest pit of lowest Erebus,
Nor aught of blinder vacancy, scooped out
By help of dreams—can breed such fear and awe
As fall upon us often when we look
Into our Minds, into the Mind of Man.

WILLIAM WORDSWORTH (1770–1850), English poet. *The Excursion*, Preface.

See also Santayana on The BODY; Lowell on INTROSPECTION.

MINORITIES

1 We cannot discuss the state of our minorities until we first have some sense of what we are, who we are, what our goals are, and what we take life to be. The question is not what we can do now for the hypothetical Mexican, the hypothetical Negro. The question is what we really want out of life, for ourselves, what we think is real.

JAMES BALDWIN (1924–87), U.S. author. Address, 1960, Kalamazoo College (published in *Nobody Knows My Name*, 1961).

2 All history is a record of the power of minorities, and of minorities of one.

RALPH WALDO EMERSON (1803–82), U.S. essayist, poet, philosopher. "Progress of Culture," address, 18 July 1867, read before the Harvard University Phi Beta Kappa Society, Cambridge, Massachusetts (published in *Letters and Social Aims*, 1876).

3 A dissenting minority feels free only when it can impose its will on the majority: what it abominates most is the dissent of the majority.

ERIC HOFFER (1902–83), U.S. philosopher. *Reflections on the Human Condition*, aph. 40 (1973).

4 Niggerization is the result of oppression—and it doesn't just apply to the black people. Old people, poor people, and students can also get niggerized.

FLORYNCE R. KENNEDY (b. 1916), U.S. lawyer, civil rights activist. Quoted in: Gloria Steinem, "The Verbal Karate of Florynce R. Kennedy, Esq.," in *Ms.* (New York, March 1973).

5 Truth always rests with the minority, and the minority is always stronger than the majority, because the minority is generally formed by those who really have an opinion, while the strength of a majority is illusory, formed by the gangs who have no opinion—and who, therefore, in the next instant (when it is evident that the minority is the stronger) assume *its* opinion . . . while Truth again reverts to a new minority.

SØREN KIERKEGAARD (1813–55), Danish philosopher. *The Diary of Søren Kierkegaard*, pt. 5, sct. 3, no. 128 entry from 1850, ed. by Peter Rohde, 1960.

6 In making the great experiment of governing people by consent rather than by coercion, it is not sufficient that the party in power should have a majority. It is just as necessary that the party in power should never outrage the minority.

WALTER LIPPMANN (1889–1974), U.S. journalist. "The Indispensable Opposition," in *Atlantic Monthly* (Boston, 1939; repr. in *The Essential Lippman*, pt. 6, sct. 2, 1982).

7 What characterizes a member of a minority group is that he is forced to see himself as both exceptional and insignificant, marvelous and awful, good and evil.

NORMAN MAILER (b. 1923), U.S. author. *Cannibals and Christians*, "A Speech at Berkeley on Vietnam Day" (1966).

8 How a minority,
Reaching majority,
Seizing authority,
Hates a minority!

LEONARD H. ROBBINS (1877–1947), U.S. author. *Minorities.*

9 No democracy can long survive which does not accept as fundamental to its very existence the recognition of the rights of minorities.

FRANKLIN D. ROOSEVELT (1882–1945), U.S. Democratic politician, president. Letter, 25 June 1938, to the National Association for the Advancement of Colored People.

10 Jews and homosexuals are the outstanding creative minorities in contemporary urban culture. Creative, that is, in the truest sense: they are creators of sensibilities. The two pioneering forces of modern sensibility are Jewish moral seriousness and homosexual aestheticism and irony.

SUSAN SONTAG (b. 1933), U.S. essayist. *Against Interpretation*, "Notes on 'Camp'," note 51 (1966; first published 1964).

11 A minority is powerless while it conforms to the majority; it is not even a minority then; but it is irresistible when it clogs by its whole weight.

HENRY DAVID THOREAU (1817–62), U.S. philosopher, author, naturalist. *On the Duty of Civil Disobedience* (1849).

12 You cannot become thorough Americans if you think of yourselves in groups. America does not consist of groups. A man who thinks of himself as belonging to a particular national group in America has not yet become an American.

WOODROW WILSON (1856–1924), U.S. Democratic politician, president. Speech, 10 May 1915, Philadelphia, Pa.

MIRACLES

1 God is a character, a real and consistent being, or

He is nothing. If God did a miracle He would deny His own nature and the universe would simply blow up, vanish, become nothing.

> JOYCE CARY (1888–1957), British author. Interview in *Writers at Work* (First Series, ed. by Malcolm Cowley, 1958).

2 The miracles of the church seem to me to rest not so much upon faces or voices or healing power coming suddenly near to us from afar off, but upon our perceptions being made finer, so that for a moment our eyes can see and our ears can hear what is there about us always.

> WILLA CATHER (1873–1947), U.S. author. *Death Comes for the Archbishop*, bk. 1, ch. 4 (1927).

3 Miracle me no miracles.

> MIGUEL DE CERVANTES (1547–1616), Spanish writer. Sancho Panza, in *Don Quixote*, pt. 2, bk. 5, ch. 3 (1615; tr. by P. Motteux).

4 I do not think our successes can compete with those of Lourdes. There are so many more people who believe in the miracles of the Blessed Virgin than in the existence of the unconscious.

> SIGMUND FREUD (1856–1939), Austrian psychiatrist. *New Introductory Lectures on Psychoanalysis*, lecture 34, "Explanations, Applications and Orientations" (1933; repr. in *Complete Works*, vol. 22, ed. by James Strachey and Anna Freud, 1964).

5 An act of God was defined as "*something which no reasonable man could have expected.*"

> A. P. HERBERT (1890–1971), British author, politician. Mr. David, in *Uncommon Law*, "Act of God" (1935).

6 If the grace of God miraculously operates, it probably operates through the subliminal door.

> WILLIAM JAMES (1842–1910), U.S. psychologist, philosopher. *The Varieties of Religious Experience*, lectures 11, 12 and 13, "Saintliness" (1902).

7 Moralities, ethics, laws, customs, beliefs, doctrines—these are of trifling import. All that matters is that the miraculous become the norm.

> HENRY MILLER (1891–1980), U.S. author. *The World of Sex* (1940; ed. 1970, p. 118).

8 Everything is a miracle. It is a miracle that one does not dissolve in one's bath like a lump of sugar.

> PABLO PICASSO (1881–1973), Spanish artist. Quoted in: Jean Cocteau, *Opium* (1929; tr. 1932; ed. 1957, p. 29).

9 A miracle is an event which creates faith. That is the purpose and nature of miracles. . . . Frauds deceive. An event which creates faith does not deceive: therefore it is not a fraud, but a miracle.

> GEORGE BERNARD SHAW (1856–1950), Anglo-Irish playwright, critic. The Archbishop, in *Saint Joan*, sc. 2.

See also Jenkins on JESUS CHRIST.

MISANTHROPY

1 I hate mankind, for I think myself one of the best of them, and I know how bad I am.

> ANONYMOUS. A "foreign friend" of Samuel Johnson. Quoted in: James Boswell, *Life of Samuel Johnson*, Feb. 1776 (1791).

2 All men are intrinsical rascals, and I am only sorry that not being a dog I can't bite them.

> LORD BYRON (1788–1824), English poet. Letter, 20 Oct. 1821, to the publisher John Murray (published in *Byron's Letters and Journals*, vol. 8, ed. by Leslie Marchand, 1973–81).

3 When we have ceased to love the stench of the human animal, either in others or in ourselves, then are we condemned to misery, and clear thinking can begin.

> CYRIL CONNOLLY (1903–74), British critic. *The Unquiet Grave*, pt. 3 (1944; rev. 1951).

4 To think ill of mankind and not wish ill to them, is perhaps the highest wisdom and virtue.

> WILLIAM HAZLITT (1778–1830), English essayist. *Characteristics: In the Manner of Rochefoucault's Maxims*, no. 241 (1823; repr. in *The Complete Works of William Hazlitt*, vol. 9, ed. by P. P. Howe, 1932).

5 It is a sign of creeping inner death when we can no longer praise the living.

> ERIC HOFFER (1902–83), U.S. philosopher. *Reflections on the Human Condition*, aph. 147 (1973).

6 Since I no longer expect
anything from mankind except
madness,
meanness, and mendacity;
egotism,
cowardice,
and
self-delusion,
I have stopped
being a
misanthrope.

> IRVING LAYTON (b. 1912), Canadian poet. *The Whole Bloody Bird*, "Aphs" (1969).

7 It disturbs me no more to find men base, unjust, or selfish than to see apes mischievous, wolves savage, or the vulture ravenous for its prey.

> MOLIÉRE (1622–73), French dramatist. Philinte, in *Le Misanthrope*, act 1, sc. 1.

8 It is true that we are weak and sick and ugly and quarrelsome but if that is all we ever were, we would millenniums ago have disappeared from the face of the earth.

> JOHN STEINBECK (1902–68), U.S. author. *Writers at Work*, "On Intent" (Fourth Series, ed. by George Plimpton, 1977).

9 Principally I hate and detest that animal called man; although I heartily love John, Peter, Thomas, and so forth.

> JONATHAN SWIFT (1667–1745), Anglo-Irish satirist. Letter, 29 Sept. 1725, to Alexander Pope.

MISERLINESS

1 To the eyes of a miser a guinea is more beautiful than the sun, and a bag worn with the use of money has more beautiful proportions than a vine filled with grapes.

> WILLIAM BLAKE (1757–1827), English poet, painter, engraver. Letter, 23 Aug. 1799 (published in *Complete Writings*, ed. by Geoffrey Keynes, 1957).

2 Man hoards himself when he has nothing to give away.

> EDWARD DAHLBERG (1900–1977), U.S. author, critic. *Reasons of the Heart*, "On Love and Friendship" (1965).

3 Some men have a necessity to be mean, as if they were exercising a faculty which they had to partially neglect since early childhood.

> F. SCOTT FITZGERALD (1896–1940), U.S. author. *The Crack-Up*, "Notebook O" (ed. by Edmund Wilson, 1945).

4 A soul that is reluctant to share does not as a rule have much of its own. Miserliness is here a symptom of meagerness.

> ERIC HOFFER (1902–83), U.S. philosopher. *The Passionate State of Mind*, aph. 132 (1955).

5 Do not discourage your children from hoarding, if they have a taste to it; whoever lays up his penny rather than part with it for a cake, at least is not the slave of gross appetite; and shows besides a preference always to be esteemed, of the future to the present moment.

> SAMUEL JOHNSON (1709–84), English author, lexicographer. Quoted in: Hester Piozzi, *Anecdotes of the Late Samuel Johnson* (1786; repr.in *Johnsonian Miscellanies*, vol. 1, ed. by George Birkbeck Hill, 1891, pp. 251–52).

6 The sage does not hoard.
Having bestowed all he has on others, he has yet
   more;
Having given all he has to others, he is richer still.

> LAO-TZU (6th century B.C.), Legendary Chinese philosopher. *Tao-te-ching*, bk. 2, ch. 81 (tr. by T. C. Lau, 1963).

7 While the miser is merely a capitalist gone mad, the capitalist is a rational miser.

> KARL MARX (1818–83), German political theorist, social philosopher. *Capital*, vol. 1, ch. 4 (1867).

8 Oh, I wish I were a miser; being a miser must be so occupying.

> GERTRUDE STEIN (1874–1946), U.S. author. Quoted by Thornton Wilder in: *Writers at Work* (First Series, ed. by Malcom Cowley, 1958).

9 It was said of old Sarah, Duchess of Marlborough, that she never puts dots over her i's, to save ink.

> HORACE WALPOLE (1717–97), English author. Letter, 4 Oct. 1785.

10 There are many things that we would throw away if we were not afraid that others might pick them up.

> OSCAR WILDE (1854–1900), Anglo-Irish playwright, author. Lord Henry, in *The Picture of Dorian Gray*, ch. 4 (1891).

See also ECONOMIZING.

MISERY

1 I am as comfortless as a pilgrim with peas in his shoes—and as cold as Charity, Chastity or any other Virtue.

> LORD BYRON (1788–1824), English poet. Letter, 16 Nov. 1814, to Annabella Milbanke—later Lady Byron (published in *Byron's Letters and Journals*, vol. 4, ed. by Leslie A. Marchand, 1975).

2 'Tis the only comfort of the miserable to have partners in their woes.

> MIGUEL DE CERVANTES (1547–1616), Spanish writer. *Don Quixote*, pt. 1, bk. 3, ch. 10 (1605; tr. by P. Motteux).

3 To long for that which comes not. To lie a-bed and sleep not. To serve well and please not. To have a horse that goes not. To have a man obeys not. To lie in jail and hope not. To be sick and recover not. To lose one's way and know not. To wait at door and enter not, and to have a friend we trust not: are ten such spites as hell hath not.

> JOHN FLORIO (c. 1553–1625), English author, translator. Nolano, in *Second Frutes*, ch.1 (1591).

4 People talk about the courage of condemned men walking to the place of execution: sometimes it needs as much courage to walk with any kind of bearing towards another person's habitual misery.

> GRAHAM GREENE (1904–91), British novelist. *Heart of the Matter*, bk. 1, pt. 1, ch. 2, sct. 3 (1948).

5 Friends *love* misery, in fact. Sometimes, especially if we are too lucky or too successful or too pretty, our misery is the only thing that endears us to our friends.

> ERICA JONG (b. 1942), U.S. author. *How to Save Your Own Life*, "A day in the life . . . " (1977).

6 Man hands on misery to man.
It deepens like a coastal shelf.
Get out as early as you can,
And don't have any kids yourself.

> PHILIP LARKIN (1922–85), British poet. *This Be the Verse*.

7 Part of every misery is, so to speak, the misery's shadow or reflection: the fact that you don't merely suffer but have to keep on thinking about the fact that you suffer. I not only live each endless day in grief, but live each day thinking about living each day in grief.

> C. S. LEWIS (1898–1963), British author. *A Grief Observed*, pt. 1 (1961).

8 Maybe men are separated from each other only by the degree of their misery.

> FRANCIS PICABIA (1878–1953), French painter, poet. *591* (Paris, 21 Jan 1952; repr. in *Écrits*, vol. 2, "1950–1953," ed. by Olivier Revault d'Allones and Dominique Bouissou, 1978).

9 Misery acquaints a man with strange bedfellows.

> WILLIAM SHAKESPEARE (1564–1616), English dramatist, poet. Trinculo, in *The Tempest*, act 2, sc. 2.

MISFORTUNE

1 Misfortune is never mournful to the soul that accepts it; for such do always see that every cloud is an angel's face. Every man deems that he has precisely the trials and temptations which are the hardest of all others for him to bear; but they are so, simply because they are the very ones he most needs.

> LYDIA M. CHILD (1802–80), U.S. abolitionist, writer, editor. Letter, 27 April 1843 (published in *Letters from New York*, vol. 1, Letter 39, 1843).

2 My fortune somewhat resembled that of a person who should entertain an idea of committing suicide, and, altogether beyond his hopes, meet with the good hap to be murdered.

> NATHANIEL HAWTHORNE (1804–64), U.S. author. *The Scarlet Letter*, Introduction, "The Custom-House" (1850). Hawthorne was here relating the loss of his job as a customs surveyor in Salem, Massachusetts, as a result of political maneuvering; the blow was mitigated by his "previous weariness of office, and vague thoughts of resignation."

3 now and then
there is a person born
who is so unlucky
that he runs into accidents
which started out to happen
to somebody else.

> DON MARQUIS (1878–1937), U.S. humorist, journalist. *archy says*, in *archys life of mehitabel* (1933).

4 Affliction is enamoured of thy parts,
And thou art wedded to calamity.

> WILLIAM SHAKESPEARE (1564–1616), English dramatist, poet. Friar Laurence, speaking to Romeo, in *Romeo and Juliet*, act 3, sc. 3.

5 There is always something infinitely mean about other people's tragedies.

> OSCAR WILDE (1854–1900), Anglo-Irish playwright, author. Lord Henry, in *The Picture of Dorian Gray*, ch. 4 (1891).

See also HARD TIMES; LUCK.

MISSIONARIES

1 Let the saints be joyful in glory: let them sing aloud upon their beds. Let the high praises of God be in their mouth, and a two-edged sword in their hand; to execute vengeance upon the heathen, and punishments upon the people; to bind their kings with chains and their nobles with fetters of iron; to execute upon them the judgment written.

> BIBLE, HEBREW. *Psalms* 149:5–9.

2 Firm, faithful, and devoted, full of energy and zeal, and truth, he labours for his race; he clears their painful way to improvement; he hews down like a giant the prejudices of creed and caste that encumber it. He may be stern; he may be exacting; he may be ambitious yet; but his is the sternness of the warrior Greatheart, who guards his pilgrim convoy from the onslaught of Apollyon. His is the exaction of the apostle, who speaks but for Christ, when he says, "Whosoever will come after Me, let him deny himself, and take up his cross and follow Me." His is the ambition of the high master-spirit, which aims to fill a place in the first rank of those who are redeemed from the earth—who stand without fault before the throne of God, who share the last mighty victories of the Lamb, who are called, and chosen, and faithful.

> CHARLOTTE BRONTË (1816–55), English novelist. *Jane Eyre*, ch. 38 (1847), of the missionary St. John Rogers.

3 Go practise if you please
With men and women: leave a child alone
For Christ's particular love's sake!

> ROBERT BROWNING (1812–89), English poet. *The Ring and the Book*, bk. 3.

4 The missionary is no longer a man, a conscience. He is a corpse, in the hands of a confraternity, without family, without love, without any of the sentiments that are dear to us. . . . Emasculated, in a sense, by his vow of chastity, he offers us the distressing spectacle of a man deformed and impotent or engaged in a stupid and useless struggle with the sacred needs of the flesh, a struggle which, seven times out of ten, leads him to sodomy, the gallows, or prison.

> PAUL GAUGUIN (1848–1903), French artist. *Intimate Journals* (tr. by Van Wyck Brooks, 1923; ed. 1930, p. 143).

5 Exporting Church employees to Latin America masks a universal and unconscious fear of a new Church. North and South American authorities, differently motivated but equally fearful, become accomplices in maintaining a clerical and irrelevant Church. Sacralizing employees and property, this Church becomes progressively more blind to the possibilities of sacralizing person and community.

> IVAN ILLICH (b. 1926), Austrian-born U.S. theologian, author. *Celebration of Awareness*, ch. 5 (1969).

6 The Christian missionary may preach the gospel to the poor naked heathen, but the spiritual heathen who populate Europe have as yet heard nothing of Christianity.

> CARL JUNG (1875–1961), Swiss psychiatrist. *Psychology and Alchemy* (1944; repr. in *Collected Works*, vol. 12, para. 13, ed. by William McGuire, 1953).

7 If he have faith, the believer cannot be restrained. He betrays himself. He breaks out. He confesses and teaches this gospel to the people at the risk of life itself.

> MARTIN LUTHER (1483–1546), German leader of the Protestant Reformation. Preface to his translation of the New Testament (1522).

8 As each Sister is to become a Co-Worker of Christ in the slums, each ought to understand what God and the Missionaries of Charity expect from her. Let Christ radiate and live his life in her and through her in the slums. Let the poor, seeing her, be drawn to Christ and invite him to enter their homes and their lives. Let the sick and suffering find in her a real angel of comfort and consolation. Let the little ones of the streets cling to her because she reminds them of him, the friend of the little ones.

> MOTHER TERESA (b. 1910), Albanian-born Roman Catholic missionary. *A Gift for God*, "Carriers of Christ's Love" (1975).

See also Illich on SILENCE.

MITIGATION

1 Friar Barnadine: Thou hast committed—
Barabas: Fornication? But that was in another country; and besides, the wench is dead.

> CHRISTOPHER MARLOWE (1564–93), English dramatist, poet. *The Jew of Malta*, act 4, sc. 1.

2 If weakness may excuse,
What murtherer, what traitor, parricide,
Incestuous, sacrilegious, but may plead it?

All wickedness is weakness: that plea therefore
With God or man will gain thee no remission.
JOHN MILTON (1608–1674), English poet. Samson, in *Samson Agonistes* (1671), to Dalila.

3 I will be deaf to pleading and excuses.
Nor tears nor prayers shall purchase out abuses.
WILLIAM SHAKESPEARE (1564–1616), English dramatist, poet. Prince Escalus, in *Romeo and Juliet*, act 3, sc. 1, after Romeo's killing of Tybalt.

MOBS

1 Certain lewd fellows of the baser sort.
BIBLE: NEW TESTAMENT. *Acts* 17:5.

2 The tyranny of a multitude is a multiplied tyranny.
EDMUND BURKE (1729–97), Irish philosopher, statesman. Letter, 26 Feb. 1790.

3 Are we aware of our obligations to a mob? It is the mob that labour in your fields and serve in your houses— that man your navy, and recruit your army—that have enabled you to defy the world, and can also defy you when neglect and calamity have driven them to despair. You may call the people a mob; but do not forget that a mob too often speaks the sentiments of the people.
LORD BYRON (1788–1824), English poet. Maiden speech to the House of Lords, 27 Feb. 1812, on the subject of the Luddite machine-wreckers.

4 The mob is man voluntarily descending to the nature of the beast. Its fit hour of activity is night. Its actions are insane like its whole constitution. It persecutes a principle; it would whip a right; it would tar and feather justice, by inflicting fire and outrage upon the houses and persons of those who have these. It resembles the prank of boys, who run with fire-engines to put out the ruddy aurora streaming to the stars.
RALPH WALDO EMERSON (1803–82), U.S. essayist, poet, philosopher. *Essays*, "Compensation" (First Series, 1841).

5 I'm their leader, I've got to follow them.
ALEXANDRE LEDRU-ROLLIN (1807–64), French politician, revolutionary. Quoted in: *Histoire Contemporaine*, no. 79 (1857), while among the Paris mob at the barricades, 1848.

6 The nose of a mob is its imagination. By this, at any time, it can be quietly led.
EDGAR ALLAN POE (1809–45), U.S. poet, critic, short-story writer. *Marginalia*, in *Southern Literary Messenger* (Richmond, Va., July 1849; repr. in *Essays and Reviews*, 1984).

7 The mob has many heads but no brains.
ENGLISH PROVERB (17th-century). Collected in Thomas Fuller, *Gnomologia* (1732).

See also RIOTS.

MODELS AND MODELING

1 Model. Two mobile eyes in a mobile head, itself on a mobile body.
ROBERT BRESSON (b. 1907), French film director. *Notes on the Cinematographer*, "1950–1958: On Automatism" (1975).

2 Among all the modernized aspects of the most luxurious of industries, the model, a vestige of voluptuous barbarianism, is like some plunder-laden prey. She is the object of unbridled regard, a living bait, the passive realization of an ideal. . . . No other female occupation contains such potent impulses to moral disintegration as this one, applying as it does the outward signs of riches to a poor and beautiful girl.
COLETTE (1873–1954), French author. "Models," in *Vogue* (1925–27; repr. in *Journey for Myself*, 1971).

3 A good model can advance fashion by ten years.
YVES SAINT LAURENT (b. 1936), French couturier. *Ritz*, no. 85 (London, 1984).

4 It's not that I don't want to be a beauty, that I don't yearn to be dripping with glamor. It's just that I can't see how any woman can find time to do to herself all the things that must apparently be done to make herself beautiful and, having once done them, how anyone without the strength of mind of a foreign missionary can keep up such a regime.
CORNELIA OTIS SKINNER (1901–79), U.S. author, actor. *Dithers and Jitters*, "The Skin-Game" (1937).

5 For an artist to marry his model is as fatal as for a *gourmet* to marry his cook: the one gets no sittings, and the other gets no dinners.
OSCAR WILDE (1854–1900), Anglo-Irish playwright, author. "London Models," in *English Illustrated Magazine* (London, Jan. 1889; repr. in *Aristotle at Afternoon Tea: The Rare Oscar Wilde*, 1991).

MODERATION

1 My God, Mr. Chairman, at this moment I stand astonished at my own moderation!
ROBERT CLIVE (1725–74), British soldier, colonial administrator. Speech, March 1773, to a select committee of the House of Commons, defending himself against charges of embezzlement. Clive was cleared of the charge but committed suicide by stabbing himself in November 1774.

2 Tell a man whose house is on fire to give a moderate alarm; tell him to moderately rescue his wife from the hands of the ravisher; tell the mother to gradually extricate her babe from the fire into which it has fallen; but urge me not to use moderation in a case like the present.
WILLIAM LLOYD GARRISON (1805–79), U.S. abolitionist. Editorial, 1 Jan. 1831, launching the newspaper, *The Liberator*, in his antislavery campaign.

3 Moderation is a virtue only in those who are thought to have an alternative.
HENRY KISSINGER (b. 1923), U.S. Republican politician, secretary of state. Quoted in: *Observer* (London, 24 Jan. 1982).

4 Moderation in people who are contented comes from that calm that good fortune lends to their spirit.
FRANÇOIS, DUC DE LA ROCHEFOUCAULD (1613–80), French writer, moralist. Sentences et Maximes Morales, no. 17 (1678).

5 Any plan conceived in moderation must fail when the circumstances are set in extremes.
PRINCE METTERNICH (1773–1859), Austrian statesman. Letter, 2 Dec. 1822.

6   That moderation which nature prescribes, which limits our desires by resources restricted to our needs, has abandoned the field; it has now come to this–that to want only what is enough is a sign both of boorishness and of utter destitution.

> SENECA (c. 5 B.C.–A.D. c. 65), Roman writer, philosopher, statesman. *Epistulae ad Lucilium*, Epistle 90.

See also Dickenson on ABSTINENCE; Wilde on EXCESS.

MODERN TIMES

1   This strange disease of modern life,
With its sick hurry, its divided aims.

> MATTHEW ARNOLD (1822–88), English poet, critic. *The Scholar-Gipsy*, st. 21.

2   We are becoming like cats, slyly parasitic, enjoying an indifferent domesticity. Nice and snug in "the social," our historic passions have withdrawn into the glow of an artificial cosiness, and our half-closed eyes now seek little other than the peaceful parade of television pictures.

> JEAN BAUDRILLARD (b. 1929), French semiologist. *Cool Memories*, ch. 1 (1987; tr. 1990).

3   I am prisoner of a gaudy and unlivable present, where all forms of human society have reached an extreme of their cycle and there is no imagining what new forms they may assume.

> ITALO CALVINO (1923–85), Italian author, critic. The Great Khan in *Invisible Cities*, (1972; tr. 1974, pp. 135–36).

4   The modern mind is in complete disarray. Knowledge has streched itself to the point where neither the world nor our intelligence can find any foot-hold. It is a fact that we are suffering from nihilism.

> ALBERT CAMUS (1913–60), French-Algerian philosopher, author. *Notebooks 1942–1951* (1964), entry for March/Aug. 1942.

5   No man lives without jostling and being jostled; in all ways he has to elbow himself through the world, giving and receiving offence.

> THOMAS CARLYLE (1795–1881), Scottish essayist, historian. "Sir Walter Scott," in *London and Westminster Review* (12 Nov. 1838; reprinted in *Critical and Miscellaneous Essays*).

6   Now here, you see, it takes all the running you can do, to keep in the same place. If you want to get somewhere else, you must run at least twice as fast as that!

> LEWIS CARROLL (1832–98), English author, mathematician. The Red Queen in *Through the Looking-Glass*, ch. 2, (1872).

7   Don't bother about being modern. Unfortunately it is the one thing that, whatever you do, you cannot avoid.

> SALVADOR DALI (1904–89), Spanish painter. *Diary of a Genius*, (1966), entry for 15 July 1952.

8   In societies where modern conditions of production prevail, all of life presents itself as an immense accumulation of *spectacles*. Everything that was directly lived has moved away into a representation.

> GUY DEBORD (b. 1931), French Situationist philosopher. *The Society of the Spectacle*, ch. 1, sct. 1 (1967; tr. 1970).

9   It cannot be denied that for a society which has to create scarcity to save its members from starvation, to whom abundance spells disaster, and to whom unlimited energy means unlimited power for war and destruction, there is an ominous cloud in the distance though at present it be no bigger than a man's hand.

> ARTHUR STANLEY EDDINGTON (1882–1944), British astronomer, physicist. *New Pathways in Science*, ch. 8 (1935).

10   It takes a kind of shabby arrogance to survive in our time, and a fairly romantic nature to want to.

> EDGAR Z. FRIEDENBERG (b. 1921), U.S. sociologist. *The Vanishing Adolescent*, Title chapter (1959).

11   The reason for the sadness of this modern age and the men who live in it is that it looks for the truth in everything and finds it.

> EDMOND (1822–96) AND JULES DE GONCOURT (1830–70), French writers, journalists. *The Goncourt Journals* (1956; repr. in *Pages from the Goncourt Journal*, ed. by Robert Baldick, 1962), entry for 23 Oct. 1864.

12   If work and leisure are soon to be subordinated to this one utopian principle—absolute busyness—then utopia and melancholy will come to coincide: an age without conflict will dawn, perpetually busy—and without consciousness.

> GÜNTHER GRASS (b. 1927), German author. *From the Diary of a Snail*, "On Stasis in Progress" (1972).

13   I am truly horrified by modern man. Such absence of feeling, such narrowness of outlook, such lack of passion and information, such feebleness of thought.

> ALEXANDER HERZEN (1812–70), Russian journalist, political thinker. *From the Other Shore*, "Epilogue 1849" (1855).

14   When you automate an industry you modernize it; when you automate a life you primitivize it.

> ERIC HOFFER (1902–83), U.S. philosopher. *Reflections on the Human Condition*, aph. 8 (1973).

15   Even in a time of elephantine vanity and greed, one never has to look far to see the campfires of gentle people.

> GARRISON KEILLOR (b. 1942), U.S. author. *We Are Still Married*, "The Meaning of Life" (1989).

16   In these great times which I knew when they were this small; which will become small again, provided they have time left for it . . . in these times in which things are happening that could not be imagined and in which what can no longer be *imagined* must *happen*, for if one could imagine it, it would not happen; in these serious times which have died laughing at the thought that they might become serious; which, surprised by their own tragedy, are reaching for diversion and, catching themselves red-handed, are groping for words . . . in these times you should not expect any words of my own from me—none but these words which barely manage to prevent silence from being misinterpreted.

> KARL KRAUS (1874–1936), Austrian satirist. "In These Great Times," speech, 19 Nov. 1914, in Vienna (first published in *Die Fackel*, Vienna, Dec. 1914; repr. in *In These Great Times: A Karl Kraus Reader*, ed. by Harry Zohn, 1976).

17 The trouble with our age is that it is all signpost and no destination.

> LOUIS KRONENBERGER (1904–80), U.S. critic, editor, author. *Company Manners,* "The Spirit of the Age" (1954).

18 In the society of men the truth resides now less in what things are than in what they are not. Our social realities are so ugly if seen in the light of exiled truth, and beauty is no longer possible if it is not a lie.

> R. D. LAING (1927–89), British psychiatrist. *The Politics of Experience,* Introduction (1967).

19 It is a tribute to the peculiar horror of contemporary life that it makes the worst features of earlier times—the stupefaction of the masses, the obsessed and driven lives of the bourgeoisie—seem attractive by comparison.

> CHRISTOPHER LASCH (b. 1932), U.S. historian. *The Culture of Narcissism,* ch. 4, "No Exit" (1979).

20 Our own epoch is determining, day by day, its own style. Our eyes, unhappily, are unable yet to discern it.

> LE CORBUSIER (1887–1965), Swiss-born French architect. *Toward a New Architecture,* ch. 1, "Eyes Which Do Not See" (1923; tr. 1946).

21 The sickness of our times for me has been just this damn thing that everything has been getting smaller and smaller and less and less important, that the romantic spirit has dried up, that there is no shame today. . . . We're all getting so mean and small and petty and ridiculous, and we all live under the threat of extermination.

> NORMAN MAILER (b. 1923), U.S. author. "Hip, Hell, and the Navigator," in *Western Review,* no. 23 (Winter 1959; repr. in *Conversations with Norman Mailer,* ed. by J. Michael Lennon, 1988).

22 Unable to create a meaningful life for itself, the personality takes its own revenge: from the lower depths comes a regressive form of spontaneity: raw animality forms a counterpoise to the meaningless stimuli and the vicarious life to which the ordinary man is conditioned. Getting spiritual nourishment from this chaos of events, sensations, and devious interpretations is the equivalent of trying to pick through a garbage pile for food.

> LEWIS MUMFORD (1895–1990), U.S. social philosopher. *The Conduct Of Life,* ch. 1 (1951), remarking on the condition of life in the modern city.

23 You don't have to be old in America to say of a world you lived in: That world is gone.

> PEGGY NOONAN (b. 1950), U.S. author, presidential speechwriter. *What I Saw at the Revolution,* ch. 1 (1990).

24 The atom bombs are piling up in the factories, the police are prowling through the cities, the lies are streaming from the loudspeakers, but the earth is still going round the sun.

> GEORGE ORWELL (1903–50), British author. *Shooting an Elephant,* "Thoughts on the Common Toad" (1950).

25 Today we all speak, if not the same tongue, the same universal language. There is no one center, and time has lost its former coherence: East and West, yesterday and tomorrow exist as a confused jumble in each

one of us. Different times and different spaces are combined in a here and now that is everywhere at once.

> OCTAVIO PAZ (b. 1914), Mexican poet. *Alternating Current,* "Invention, Underdevelopment, Modernity" (1967).

26 Anyone who lives in this time is concerned with grottiness.

> PETER READING (b. 1946), British poet. *International Herald Tribune* (Paris, 10 March 1988).

27 For we which now behold these present days
Have eyes to wonder, but lack tongues to praise.

> WILLIAM SHAKESPEARE (1564–1616), English dramatist, poet. Sonnet 106.

28 There is something terribly wrong with a culture inebriated by noise and gregariousness.

> GEORGE STEINER (b. 1929), French-born U.S. critic, novelist. *Daily Telegraph* (London, 23 May 1989).

29 The fate of our times is characterized by rationalization and intellectualization and, above all, by the "disenchantment of the world." Precisely the ultimate and most sublime values have retreated from public life either into the transcendental realm of mystic life or into the brotherliness of direct and personal human relations. It is not accidental that our greatest art is intimate and not monumental.

> MAX WEBER (1864–1920), German sociologist. "Science as a Vocation" (1919; repr. in *Essays in Society,* ed. by H. H. Gerth and C. Wright Mills, 1946).

30 A multitude of causes unknown to former times are now acting with a combined force to blunt the discriminating powers of the mind, and unfitting it for all voluntary exertion to reduce it to a state of almost savage torpor.

> WILLIAM WORDSWORTH (1770–1850), English poet. *Lyrical Ballads,* Preface (2nd ed., 1801). Among the causes Wordsworth perceived were, "the great national events which are daily taking place, and the increasing accumulation of men in cities, where the uniformity of their occupations produces a craving for extraordinary incident which the rapid communication of intelligence hourly gratifies."

See also Einstein on ENDS AND MEANS; Phaedrus on HASTE; Reagan on INFORMATION; Sontag on MINORITIES; Sandburg on OPTIMISM; The TWENTIETH CENTURY.

MODERNISM AND POST-MODERNISM

1 Postmodernism is, almost by definition, a transitional cusp of social, cultural, economic and ideological history when modernism's high-minded principles and preoccupations have ceased to function, but before they have been replaced with a totally new system of values. It represents a moment of suspension before the batteries are recharged for the new millennium, an acknowledgment that preceding the future is a strange and hybrid interregnum that might be called the last gasp of the past.

> GILBERT ADAIR, British author, critic. *Sunday Times: Books* (London, 21 April 1991).

2 Modernism may be seen as an attempt to reconstruct the world in the absence of God.

> BRYAN APPLEYARD (b.1951), British author. *The Culture Club: Crisis in the Arts*, ch. 6 (1984).

3 Modernity is the transient, the fleeting, the contingent; it is one half of art, the other being the eternal and the immovable.

> CHARLES BAUDELAIRE (1821–67), French poet. *L'Art Romantique*, sct. 4, "The Painter of Modern Life" (1869; repr. in *Selected Writings on Art and Artists*, ed. by P. E. Charvet, 1972).

4 You are born modern, you do not become so.

> JEAN BAUDRILLARD (b. 1929), French semiologist. *America*, "Astral America" (1986; tr. 1988).

5 Postmodernity is the simultaneity of the destruction of earlier values and their reconstruction. It is renovation within ruination.

> JEAN BAUDRILLARD (b. 1929), French semiologist. *Cool Memories*, ch. 4 (1987; tr. 1990).

6 A "modern" man has nothing to add to modernism, if only because he has nothing to oppose it with. The well-adapted drop off the dead limb of time like lice.

> ELIAS CANETTI (b. 1905), Austrian novelist, philosopher. *The Secret Heart of the Clock: Notes, Aphorisms, Fragments 1973–1985*, "1980" (1991).

7 I think the adjective "post-modernist" really means "mannerist." Books about books is fun but frivolous.

> ANGELA CARTER (1940–92), British author. *Novelists in Interview* (ed. by John Haffenden, 1985).

8 By Modernism I mean the positive rejection of the past and the blind belief in the process of change, in novelty for its own sake, in the idea that progress through time equates with cultural progress; in the cult of individuality, originality and self-expression.

> DAN CRUICKSHANK (b. 1949), British architectural critic. *Commerce and Culture*, ch. 4 (1989).

9 Modernity exists in the form of a desire to wipe out whatever came earlier, in the hope of reaching at least a point that could be called a true present, a point of origin that marks a new departure.

> PAUL DE MAN (1919–83), Belgian-born U.S. literary critic. "Literary History and Literary Modernity," lecture, Sept. 1969 (published in *Blindness and Insight*, 1971; rev. 1983).

10 Postmodernism is among other things a sick joke at the expense of . . . revolutionary avant-gardism.

> TERRY EAGLETON (b. 1943), British critic. *Against the Grain*, ch. 9, "Capitalism, Modernism and Postmodernism" (1986; first published 1985).

11 The postmodern reply to the modern consists of recognizing that the past, since it cannot really be destroyed, because its destruction leads to silence, must be revisited: but with irony, not innocently. I think of the postmodern attitude as that of a man who loves a very cultivated woman and knows he cannot say to her, "I love you madly," because he knows that she knows (and that she knows that he knows) that these words have already been written by Barbara Cartland. Still, there is a solution. He can say, "As Barbara Cartland would put it, I love you madly."

> UMBERTO ECO (b. 1932), Italian semiologist, novelist. *Reflections on the Name of the Rose*, "Postmodernism, Irony, the Enjoyable" (1983; tr. 1984).

12 Post-modernism is modernism with the optimism taken out.

> ROBERT HEWISON (b. 1943), British cultural historian. *The Heritage Industry*, ch. 6 (1987).

13 A work can become modern only if it is first postmodern. Postmodernism thus understood is not modernism at its end but in the nascent state, and this state is constant.

> JEAN FRANÇOIS LYOTARD (b. 1924), French philosopher. "Answering the Question: What is Postmodernism?," in *Critique*, no. 419 (Paris, April 1982; repr. in *The Postmodern Condition: A Report on Knowledge*, 1979; rev. 1986).

14 One cannot spend one's time in being modern when there are so many more important things to be.

> WALLACE STEVENS (1879–1955), U.S. poet. *Opus Posthumous*, "Adagia" (1959).

15 I don't think we can ignore the Modern Movement. But I wouldn't have minded at all if it hadn't happened. I think the world would be a much nicer place.

> QUINLAN TERRY (b. 1937), British architect. *International Herald Tribune* (Paris, 25 April 1988).

16 It is only the modern that ever becomes old-fashioned.

> OSCAR WILDE (1854–1900), Anglo-Irish playwright, author. Vivian, in *The Decay of Lying* (published in *Intentions*, 1891).

17 Postmodernism refuses to privilege any one perspective, and recognizes only difference, never inequality, only fragments, never conflict.

> ELIZABETH WILSON (b. 1936), British journalist, author. *Hallucinations*, ch. 23 (1988).

18 Not "Seeing is Believing," you ninny, but "Believing is Seeing." For modern art has become completely literary: the paintings and other works exist only to illustrate the text.

> TOM WOLFE (b. 1931), U.S. journalist, author. *The Painted Word*, ch. 1 (1975).

MODESTY

1 Conceit spoils the finest genius. There is not much danger that real talent or goodness will be overlooked long; even if it is, the consciousness of possessing and using it well should satisfy one, and the great charm of all power is modesty.

> LOUISA MAY ALCOTT (1832–88), U.S. author. Mrs. March to her daughter Amy, in *Little Women*, pt. 1, ch. 7 (1868).

2 He seems determined to make a trumpet sound like a tin whistle.

> ANEURIN BEVAN (1897–1960), British Labour politician. Quoted in: Michael Foot, *Aneurin Bevan*, vol. 1, ch. 14 (1962), referring to Labour politician (later prime minister) Clement Attlee. Attlee, said Bevan, had "consistently underplayed his position and opportunities" (by, in this case, playing second fiddle to Conservative Anthony Eden when the two were delegated British

representatives at the forthcoming U.N. conference in San Francisco). "He brings to the fierce struggle of politics the tepid enthusiasm of a lazy summer afternoon at a cricket match," Bevan added. See Churchill's Verdict on Attley, below.

3 Modesty is the only sure bait when you angle for praise.

LORD CHESTERFIELD (1694–1773), English statesman, man of letters. Letter, 17 May 1750 (first published 1774; repr. in *The Letters of the Earl of Chesterfield to His Son*, vol. 2, no. 225, ed. by Charles Strachey, 1901).

4 He is a modest little man who has a good deal to be modest about.

SIR WINSTON CHURCHILL (1874–1965), British statesman, writer. Quoted in: *Chicago Sunday Tribune Magazine of Books* (27 June 1954), referring to Labour politician and prime minister Clement Attlee.

5 That is the consolation of a little mind; you have the fun of changing it without impeding the progress of mankind.

FRANK MOORE COLBY (1865–1925), U.S. editor, essayist. *The Colby Essays*, vol. 1, "Simple Simon" (1926).

6 If there is anybody in this land who thoroughly believes that the meek shall inherit the earth they have not often let their presence be known.

W. E. B. DU BOIS (1868–1963), U.S. civil rights leader, author. *The Gift of Black Folk*, ch. 9 (1924).

7 Modesty is the lowest of the virtues, and is a real confession of the deficiency it indicates. He who undervalues himself is justly undervalued by others.

WILLIAM HAZLITT (1778–1830), English essayist. *Table Talk*, vol. 2, "On the Knowledge of Character" (1822).

8 No truly great man ever thought himself so.

WILLIAM HAZLITT (1778–1830), English essayist. "Common Places," no. 20, in *Literary Examiner* (London, 13 Sept. 1823; repr. in *Collected Works*, vol. 11, ed. by A. R. Waller and Arnold Glover, 1904).

9 I don't like to write like God. It is only because you never do it, though, that the critics think you can't do it.

ERNEST HEMINGWAY (1899–1961), U.S. author. Letter, 26 Aug. 1940 (published in *Selected Letters*, ed. by Carlos Baker, 1981).

10 Great things happen in small places. Jesus was born in Bethlehem. Jesse Jackson was born in Greenville.

JESSE JACKSON (b. 1941), U.S. clergyman, civil rights leader. *Daily Mail* (London, 9 March 1988).

11 Because impudence is a vice, it does not follow that modesty is a virtue; it is built upon shame, a passion in our nature, and may be either good or bad according to the actions performed from that motive.

BERNARD MANDEVILLE (1670–1733), Dutch-born English author, physician. *The Fable of the Bees* Remark ("c") (1714; rev. 1723).

12 Fidelity to conscience is inconsistent with retiring modesty. If it be so, let the modesty succumb. It can be only a false modesty which can be thus endangered.

HARRIET MARTINEAU (1802–76), English writer, social critic. *Society in America*, vol. 3, "Women" (1837).

13 Be plain in dress, and sober in your diet;
In short, my deary, kiss me and be quiet.

LADY MARY WORTLEY MONTAGU (1689–1762), English society figure, letter writer. *A Summary of Lord Lyttelton's Advice*.

14 We must watch over our modesty in the presence of those who cannot understand its grounds.

JEAN ROSTAND (1894–1977), French biologist, writer. *Pensées d'un Biologiste* (1939; repr. in *The Substance of Man*, "A Biologist's Thoughts," ch. 8, 1962).

15 Although modesty is natural to man, it is not natural to children. Modesty only begins with the knowledge of evil.

JEAN-JACQUES ROUSSEAU (1712–78), Swiss-born French philosopher, political theorist. *Emile*, bk. 4 (1762).

16 I have often wished I had time to cultivate modesty . . . . But I am too busy thinking about myself.

DAME EDITH SITWELL (1887–1964), British poet. Quoted in: *Observer* (London, 30 April 1950).

17 The man who is ostentatious of his modesty is twin to the statue that wears a fig-leaf.

MARK TWAIN (1835–1910), U.S. author. *Following the Equator*, ch. 50, "Pudd'nhead Wilson's New Calendar" (1897).

See also Sheridan on LOVERS; Gilbert on SELF-IMAGE.

MONEY

1 Money is better than poverty, if only for financial reasons.

WOODY ALLEN (b. 1935), U.S. filmmaker. *Without Feathers*, "The Early Essays" (1976).

2 Money doesn't mind if we say it's evil, it goes from strength to strength. It's a fiction, an addiction, and a tacit conspiracy.

MARTIN AMIS (b. 1949), British author. *Novelists in Interview* (ed. by John Haffenden, 1985).

3 Money is like muck, not good except it be spread.

FRANCIS BACON (1561–1626), English philosopher, statesman, essayist. *Essays*, "Of Seditions and Troubles" (1597–1625).

4 A feast is made for laughter, and wine maketh merry: but money answereth all things.

BIBLE, HEBREW. *Ecclesiastes* 10:19.

5 Whether he admits it or not, a man has been brought up to look at money as a sign of his virility, a symbol of his power, a bigger phallic symbol than a Porsche.

VICTORIA BILLINGS (b. 1945), U.S. journalist, author. *The Womansbook*, "Getting It Together" (1974).

6 The money complex is the demonic, and the demonic is God's ape; the money complex is therefore the heir to and substitute for the religious complex, an attempt to find God in things.

NORMAN O. BROWN (b. 1913), U.S. philosopher. *Life against Death*, ch. 15, "Sacred and Secular" (1959), referring to the Protestant view toward money.

7 We all need money, but there are degrees of desperation.

ANTHONY BURGESS (b. 1917), British author, critic. *Face* (London, Dec. 1984).

8 The want of money is the root of all evil.

> SAMUEL BUTLER (1835–1902), English author. *Samuel Butler's Notebooks* (1951). The aphorism, which has also been credited to Mark Twain, reappeared in Butler's novel, *Erewhon*, ch. 20 (1872).

9 Yes! ready money *is* Aladdin's lamp.

> LORD BYRON (1788–1824), English poet. *Don Juan*, cto. 12, st. 12.

10 I have imbibed such a love for money that I keep some sequins in a drawer to count, & cry over them once a week.

> LORD BYRON (1788–1824), English poet. Letter, 27 Jan. 1819 (published in *Byron's Letters and Journals*, vol. 6, ed. by Leslie A. Marchand, 1976).

11 Cash-payment never was, or could except for a few years be, the union-bond of man to man. Cash never yet paid one man fully his deserts to another; nor could it, nor can it, now or henceforth to the end of the world.

> THOMAS CARLYLE (1795–1881), Scottish essayist, historian. *Past and Present*, bk. 3, ch. 10 (1843).

12 Preoccupation with money is the great test of small natures, but only a small test of great ones.

> SÉBASTIEN-ROCH NICOLAS DE CHAMFORT (1741–94), French writer, wit. *Maxims and Considerations*, vol. 1, no. 164 (1796; tr. 1926).

13 However toplofty and idealistic a man may be, he can always rationalize his right to earn money.

> RAYMOND CHANDLER (1888–1959), U.S. author. Letter, 15 Nov. 1951, to his New York literary agent Carl Brandt (published in *Raymond Chandler Speaking*, 1962).

14 There is a strange and mighty race of people called the Americans who are rapidly becoming the coldest in the world because of this cruel, maneating idol, lucre.

> EDWARD DAHLBERG (1900–1977), U.S. author, critic. *Alms for Oblivion*, "Florentine Codex" (1964).

15 Comparatively few people know what a million dollars actually is. To the majority it is a gaseous concept, swelling or decreasing as the occasion suggests. In the minds of politicians, perhaps more than anywhere, the notion of a million dollars has this accordion-like ability to expand or contract; if they are disposing of it, the million is a pleasing sum, reflecting warmly upon themselves; if somebody else wants it, it becomes a figure of inordinate size, not to be compassed by the rational mind.

> ROBERTSON DAVIES (b. 1913), Canadian novelist, journalist. *What's Bred in the Bone*, pt. 6 (1985).

16 Dollars! All their cares, hopes, joys, affections, virtues, and associations seemed to be melted down into dollars. Whatever the chance contributions that fell into the slow cauldron of their talk, they made the gruel thick and slab with dollars. Men were weighed by their dollars, measures were gauged by their dollars; life was auctioneered, appraised, put up, and knocked down for its dollars. The next respectable thing to dollars was any venture having their attainment for its end. The more of that worthless ballast, honour and fair-dealing, which any man cast overboard from the ship of his Good Nature and Good Intent, the more ample stowage-room he had for dollars. Make commerce one huge lie and mighty theft. Deface the banner of the nation for an idle rag; pollute it star by star; and cut out stripe by stripe as from the arm of a degraded soldier. Do anything for dollars! What is a flag to *them*!

> CHARLES DICKENS (1812–70), English novelist. *Martin Chuzzlewit*, ch. 16 (1844), remarking on a company of New Yorkers.

17 In any country where talent and virtue produce no advancement, money will be the national god. Its inhabitants will either have to possess money or make others believe that they do. Wealth will be the highest virtue, poverty the greatest vice. Those who have money will display it in every imaginable way. If their ostentation does not exceed their fortune, all will be well. But if their ostentation does exceed their fortune they will ruin themselves. In such a country, the greatest fortunes will vanish in the twinkling of an eye. Those who don't have money will ruin themselves with vain efforts to conceal their poverty. That is one kind of affluence: the outward sign of wealth for a small number, the mask of poverty for the majority, and a source of corruption for all.

> DENIS DIDEROT (1713–84), French philosopher. *Observations on the Drawing Up of Laws* (1921; repr. in *Selected Writings*, ed. by Lester G. Crocker, 1966), written 1774 for Catherine the Great.

18 Money speaks, but it speaks with a male voice.

> ANDREA DWORKIN (b. 1946), U.S. feminist critic. *Pornography*, ch. 1 (1981).

19 Money doesn't talk, it swears.

> BOB DYLAN (b. 1941), U.S. singer, songwriter. "It's Alright Ma (I'm Only Bleeding)," on the album *Bringing It All Back Home* (1965).

20 Money, which represents the prose of life, and which is hardly spoken of in parlors without an apology, is, in its effects and laws, as beautiful as roses.

> RALPH WALDO EMERSON (1803–82), U.S. essayist, poet, philosopher. *Essays*, "Nominalist and Realist" (Second Series, 1844).

21 Money is the sinews of love, as of war.

> GEORGE FARQUHAR (1678–1707), Irish dramatist. Roebuck, in *Love and a Bottle*, act 2, sc. 1.

22 Sir, money, money, the most charming of all things; money, which will say more in one moment than the most elegant lover can in years. Perhaps you will say a man is not young; I answer he is rich. He is not genteel, handsome, witty, brave, good-humoured, but he is rich, rich, rich, rich, rich—that one word contradicts everything you can say against him.

> HENRY FIELDING (1707–54), English novelist, dramatist. Mariana, in *The Miser*, act 3, sc. 7.

23 Money is a singular thing. It ranks with love as man's greatest source of joy. And with death as his greatest source of anxiety. Over all history it has oppressed nearly all people in one of two ways: either it has been abundant and very unreliable, or reliable and very scarce.

> JOHN KENNETH GALBRAITH (b. 1908), U.S. economist. *The Age of Uncertainty*, ch. 6 (1977).

24 But money, wife, is the true Fuller's Earth for reputations, there is not a spot or a stain but what it can take out.

> JOHN GAY (1685–1732), English dramatist. Peachum, in *The Beggar's Opera*, act 1, sc. 9.

25 Money's a horrid thing to follow, but a charming thing to meet.

> HENRY JAMES (1843–1916), U.S. author. Gilbert Osmond, in *The Portrait of a Lady*, ch. 35 (1881), speaking of Isabel Archer's fortune.

26 There are few ways in which a man can be more innocently employed than in getting money.

> SAMUEL JOHNSON (1709–84), English author, lexicographer. Quoted in: James Boswell, *Life of Samuel Johnson*, 27 March 1775 (1791).

27 It is better that a man should tyrannise over his bank balance than over his fellow-citizens and whilst the former is sometimes denounced as being but a means to the latter, sometimes at least it is an alternative.

> JOHN MAYNARD KEYNES (1883–1946), British economist. *The General Theory of Employment, Interest and Money*, ch. 24, "Concluding Notes" (1936).

28 We might make a public moan in the newspapers about the decay of conscience, but in private conversation, no matter what crimes a man may have committed or how cynically he may have debased his talent or his friends, variations on the answer "Yes, but I did it for the money," satisfy all but the most tiresome objections.

> LEWIS H. LAPHAM (b. 1935), U.S. essayist, editor. *Money and Class in America*, ch. 4 (1988).

29 Money is like fire, an element as little troubled by moralizing as earth, air and water. Men can employ it as a tool or they can dance around it as if it were the incarnation of a god. Money votes socialist or monarchist, finds a profit in pornography or translations from the Bible, commissions Rembrandt and underwrites the technology of Auschwitz. It acquires its meaning from the uses to which it is put.

> LEWIS H. LAPHAM (b. 1935), U.S. essayist, editor. *Money and Class in America*, ch. 8 (1988).

30 There is no intrinsic worth in money but what is alterable with the times, and whether a guinea goes for twenty pounds or for a shilling, it is . . . the labour of the poor and not the high and low value that is set on gold or silver, which all the comforts of life must arise from.

> BERNARD MANDEVILLE (1670–1733), Dutch-born English author, physician. *The Fable of the Bees*, "An Essay on Charity, and Charity-Schools" (1714; rev. 1723).

31 All social rules and all relations between individuals are eroded by a cash economy, avarice drags Pluto himself out of the bowels of the earth.

> KARL MARX (1818–83), German political theorist, social philosopher. *Capital*, vol. 1, ch. 3 (1867).

32 Money is like a sixth sense without which you cannot make a complete use of the other five.

> W. SOMERSET MAUGHAM (1874–1966), British author. Monsieur Foinet, in *Of Human Bondage*, ch. 51 (1915).

33 Money is a poor man's credit card.

> MARSHALL MCLUHAN (1911–80), Canadian communications theorist. Quoted in: *Maclean's* (Toronto, June 1971).

34 Money couldn't buy friends, but you got a better class of enemy.

> SPIKE MILLIGAN (b. 1918), British comedian, humorous writer. *Puckoon*, ch. 6 (1963).

35 Americans want action for their money. They are fascinated by its self-reproducing qualities if it's put to work. . . . Gold-hoarding goes against the American grain; it fits in better with European pessimism than with America's traditional optimism.

> PAULA NELSON (b. 1945), U.S. business executive. *The Joy of Money*, ch. 15 (1975).

36 Having money is rather like being a blond. It is more fun but not vital.

> MARY QUANT (b. 1936), British fashion designer. Quoted in: *Observer* (London, 2 Nov. 1986).

37 I know of nothing more despicable and pathetic than a man who devotes all the hours of the waking day to the making of money for money's sake.

> JOHN D. ROCKEFELLER (1839–1937), U.S. industrialist, philanthropist. Quoted in: Lewis H. Lapham, *Money and Class in America*, note to ch. 8 (1988).

38 Money is human happiness in the abstract: he, then, who is no longer capable of enjoying human happiness in the concrete devotes his heart entirely to money.

> ARTHUR SCHOPENHAUER (1788–1860), German philosopher. *Parerga and Paralipomena*, vol. 2, ch. 26, sct. 320 (1851).

39 The universal regard for money is the one hopeful fact in our civilisation. Money is the most important thing in the world. It represents health, strength, honour, generosity and beauty. . . . Not the least of its virtues is that it destroys base people as certainly as it fortifies and dignifies noble people.

> GEORGE BERNARD SHAW (1856–1950), Anglo-Irish playwright, critic. *Major Barbara*, Preface (1905).

40 All things are sold: the very light of Heaven
Is venal; earth's unsparing gifts of love,
The smallest and most despicable things
That lurk in the abysses of the deep,
All objects of our life, even life itself,
And the poor pittance which the laws allow
Of liberty, the fellowship of man,
Those duties which his heart of human love
Should urge him to perform instinctively,
Are bought and sold as in a public mart
Of undisguising selfishness, that sets
On each its price, the stamp-mark of her reign.

> PERCY BYSSHE SHELLEY (1792–1822), English poet. *Queen Mab*, pt. 5 (1813).

41 There are few sorrows, however poignant, in which a good income is of no avail.

> LOGAN PEARSALL SMITH (1865–1946), U.S. essayist, aphorist. *Afterthoughts*, "Life and Human Nature" (1931).

42 There is only one class in the community that

thinks more about money than the rich, and that is the poor. The poor can think of nothing else.

> OSCAR WILDE (1854–1900), Anglo-Irish playwright, author. *The Soul of Man under Socialism*, in *Fortnightly Review* (London, Feb. 1891; repr. 1895).

43   You can be young without money but you can't be old without it.

> TENNESSEE WILLIAMS (1914–83), U.S. dramatist. Margaret, in *Cat on a Hot Tin Roof*, act 1.

See also Holmes on BANKING; Bible: New Testament on GREED; Emerson on INHERITANCE; Thatcher on INTENTIONS; Shaw on POVERTY.

MONKS

1   They give themselves to God when the Devil will no longer have them.

> SOPHIE ARNOULD (1740–1802), French actor, operatic soprano. Quoted in: Robert B. Douglas, *Sophie Arnould: Actress and Wit*, ch. 4 (1898).

2   They can never have known old monks, wise, shrewd, unerring in judgment, and yet aglow with passionate insight, so very tender in their humanity. What miracle enables these semi-lunatics, these prisoners of their own dreams, these sleepwalkers, apparently to enter more deeply each day into the pain of others? An odd sort of dream, an unusual opiate which, far from turning him back into himself and isolating him from his fellows, unites the individual with mankind in the spirit of universal charity!

> GEORGES BERNANOS (1888–1948), French novelist, political writer. *The Diary of a Country Priest*, ch. 4 (1936), remarking on the attitude of skeptical scientists.

3   Monasticism, as it existed in Spain and still exists in Tibet, is a wasting disease of civilization. It puts a stop to life. Quite simply, it depopulates. Claustration is castration. It has been the scourge of Europe. Add to this the violence so often inflicted on the conscience, the enforced vocations . . . the closed mouths and minds, so much intelligence condemned to the imprisonment of vows for life, the burial of living souls. No matter who you are, the thought of so much suffering and degradation must cause you to shudder at the sight of a veil or cassock, those two shrouds of human invention.

> VICTOR HUGO (1802–85), French poet, dramatist, novelist. *Les Misérables*, pt. 2, bk. 7, ch. 3 (1862).

4   The monk in hiding himself from the world becomes not less than himself, not less of a person, but more of a person, more truly and perfectly himself: for his personality and individuality are perfected in their true order, the spiritual, interior order, of union with God, the principle of all perfection.

> THOMAS MERTON (1915–68), U.S. religious writer, poet. *The Seven Storey Mountain*, pt. 3, ch. 2 (1948), describing Merton's impressions following his first visit to the Trappist monastery which he later joined.

See also NUNS.

MONOPOLIES

1   (1) Never give anything away for nothing. (2) Never give more than you have to give (always catch the buyer hungry and always make him wait). (3) Always take everything back if you possibly can.

> WILLIAM BURROUGHS (b. 1914), U.S. author. *The Naked Lunch*, Introduction (1959), describing the basic principles of monopoly, as followed by dealers of heroin.

2   Like many businessmen of genius he learned that free competition was wasteful, monopoly efficient. And so he simply set about achieving that efficient monopoly.

> MARIO PUZO (b. 1920), U.S. novelist. *The Godfather*, bk. 3, ch. 14 (1969), referring to Don Vito Corleone.

MARILYN MONROE

1   The essence of the physicality of the most famous blonde in the world is a wholesome eroticism blurred a little round the edges by the fact she is not quite sure what eroticism is. This gives her her tentative luminosity and what makes her, somehow, always more like her own image in the mirror than she is like herself.

> ANGELA CARTER (1940–92), British author. *The Sadeian Woman*, "Desecration of the Temple" (1979).

2   Monroe, the consummate sexual doll, is empowered to act but afraid to act, perhaps because no amount of acting, however inspired, can convince the actor herself that her ideal female life is not a dreadful form of dying.

> ANDREA DWORKIN (b. 1946), U.S. feminist critic. *Right-Wing Women*, ch. 1 (1978).

3   All my energy and attention were devoted to trying to help her solve her problems. Unfortunately I didn't have much success.

> ARTHUR MILLER (b. 1915), U.S. dramatist. *International Herald Tribune* (Paris, 5 Aug. 1992).

4   My work is the only ground I've ever had to stand on. I seem to have a whole superstructure with no foundation—but I'm working on the foundation.

> MARILYN MONROE (1926–62), U.S. screen actor. Quoted in: *Marilyn Monroe in Her Own Words*, "Acting" (1990).

5   I remember her on the screen, huge as a colossus doll, mincing and whispering and simply hoping her way into total vulnerability.

> GLORIA STEINEM (b. 1934), U.S. feminist writer, editor. "Marilyn Monroe: The Woman Who Died Too Soon," *Ms.* (New York, Aug. 1972; repr. in *Outrageous Acts and Everyday Rebellions*, 1983).

6   Ah, Marilyn, Hollywood's Joan of Arc, our Ultimate Sacrificial Lamb. Well, let me tell you, she was mean, terribly mean. The meanest woman I have ever known in this town. I am appalled by this Marilyn Monroe cult. Perhaps it's getting to be an act of courage to say the truth about her. Well, let me be courageous. I have never met anyone as utterly mean as Marilyn Monroe. Nor as utterly fabulous on the screen, and that includes Garbo.

> BILLY WILDER (b. 1906), U.S. film director. Interview in *Los*

Angeles Times (1968). Quoted in: Maurice Zolotow, Billy Wilder in Hollywood, ch. 19 (1977).

MONUMENTS

1 America loves the representation of its heroes to be not just larger than life, but stupendously, awesomely bigger than anything else. If blue whales built statues to each other they'd be smaller then these.

SIMON HOGGART (b. 1946), British journalist. *America: A User's Guide*, ch. 11 (1990), remarking on Mount Rushmore.

2 If a man needs an elaborate tombstone in order to remain in the memory of his country, it is clear that his living at all was an act of absolute superfluity.

OSCAR WILDE (1854–1900), Anglo-Irish playwright, author. Public letter, read 15 Jan. 1885, at Funeral and Mourning Reform meeting, Leicester, England.

THE MOON

1 That's one small step for a man, one giant leap for mankind.

NEIL ARMSTRONG (b. 1930), U.S. astronaut. Remark, 10:56 P.M. (E.D.T.), 20 July 1969, on making his first steps on the moon's surface. Quoted in: *New York Times* (21 July 1969). Armstrong's message—possibly garbled or obscured by static—was originally understood to be, "one small step for man, one giant leap for mankind."

2 So there he is at last. Man on the moon. The poor magnificent bungler! He can't even get to the office without undergoing the agonies of the damned, but give him a little metal, a few chemicals, some wire and twenty or thirty billion dollars and, vroom! there he is, up on a rock a quarter of a million miles up in the sky.

RUSSELL BAKER (b. 1925), U.S. journalist. *New York Times* (21 July 1969).

3 There is something haunting in the light of the moon; it has all the dispassionateness of a disembodied soul, and something of its inconceivable mystery.

JOSEPH CONRAD (1857–1924), Polish-born English novelist. Marlow, in *Lord Jim*, ch. 24 (1900).

4 The moon is nothing
But a circumambulating aphrodisiac
Divinely subsidized to provoke the world
Into a rising birth-rate.

CHRISTOPHER FRY (b. 1907), British playwright. Thomas Mendip, in *The Lady's Not for Burning*, act 3.

5 The moon is a white strange world, great, white, soft-seeming globe in the night sky, and what she actually communicates to me across space I shall never fully know. But the moon that pulls the tides, and the moon that controls the menstrual periods of women, and the moon that touches the lunatics, she is not the mere dead lump of the astronomist.... When we describe the moon as dead, we are describing the deadness in ourselves. When we find space so hideously void, we are describing our own unbearable emptiness.

D. H. LAWRENCE (1885–1930), British author. "Introduction to *The Dragon of the Apocalypse* by Frederick Carter," in *London Mercury* (July 1930; repr. in *Phoenix: The Posthumous Papers of D. H. Lawrence*, pt. 4, ed. by E. McDonald, 1936). Carter's book eventually appeared under a different title and without Lawrence's introduction.

6 Moon!
Moon!
I am prone before you.
Pity me,
And drench me in loneliness.

AMY LOWELL (1874–1925), U.S. poet. *On a Certain Critic*.

7 Treading the soil of the moon, palpating its pebbles, tasting the panic and splendor of the event, feeling in the pit of one's stomach the separation from terra . . . these form the most romantic sensation an explorer has ever known . . . this is the only thing I can say about the matter. The utilitarian results do not interest me.

VLADIMIR NABOKOV (1899–1977), Russian-born U.S. novelist, poet. Quoted in: *New York Times* (21 July 1969), referring to the first moon-landing.

8 This is the greatest week in the history of the world since the Creation, because as a result of what happened in this week, the world is bigger, infinitely.

RICHARD M. NIXON (b. 1913), U.S. Republican politician, president. Remark, 24 July 1969, on *U.S.S. Hornet*, welcoming back the crew of Apollo 11 four days after the first moon-landing. Quoted in: Stephen Ambrose, *Nixon: The Triumph of a Politician*, ch. 13 (1989). A few days later, Ambrose narrates, the evangelist Billy Graham mentioned three greater days: Christ's birth, Christ's death, and Christ's resurrection. Nixon's scribbled response was: "Tell Billy R.N. referred to a *week* not a *day*."

9 Here Men from The Planet Earth
First Set Foot upon The Moon
July, 1969 AD
We Came in Peace for All Mankind

Plaque left behind on the moon's surface by the crew of Apollo 11.

See also Picasso on INDIFFERENCE.

MORALISTS

1 Ah! How neatly tied, in these people, is the umbilical cord of morality! Since they left their mothers they have never sinned, have they? They are apostles, they are the descendants of priests; one can only wonder from what source they draw their indignation, and above all how much they have pocketed to do this, and in any case what it has done for them.

ANTONIN ARTAUD (1896–1948), French theatre producer, actor, theorist. *General Security: The Liquidation of Opium* (1925; repr. in *Selected Writings*, pt. 10, ed. by Susan Sontag, 1976).

2 Compound for sins they are inclined to
By damning those they have no mind to.

SAMUEL BUTLER (1612–80), English poet. *Hudibras*.

3 The disesteem into which moralists have fallen is due at bottom to their failure to see that in an age like this one the function of the moralist is not to exhort men to be good but to elucidate what the good is. The problem of sanctions is secondary.

> WALTER LIPPMANN (1889–1974), U.S. journalist. *A Preface to Morals,* ch. 15 (1929).

4 What I have absolutely no sympathy with is the legislator, the man who seeks, for his own profit, to exploit the weaknesses of those who are unable to help themselves and then to fasten some moral superscription upon it. This I loathe so much that I cannot conceivably explain how much it is.

> MALCOLM LOWRY (1909–57), British novelist. Letter, 1937 (published in *Selected Letters of Malcolm Lowry,* 1967). Lowry was fulminating against his persecution by "spies and dogs" in Oaxaca, Mexico, where he was drinking heavily while writing *Under the Volcano.*

5 Moralistic is not moral. And as for truth—well, it's like brown—it's not in the spectrum. . . . Truth is *sui generis.*

> IRIS MURDOCH (b. 1919), British novelist, philosopher. Rozanov, in *The Philosopher's Pupil,* "The Events in Our Town" (1983).

6 Dost thou think because thou art virtuous there shall be no more cakes and ale?

> WILLIAM SHAKESPEARE (1564–1616), English dramatist, poet. Sir Toby Belch to Malvolio, in *Twelfth Night,* act 2, sc. 3. "Cakes and Ale" was used by W. Somerset Maugham as the title of a novel in 1930.

7 A man who moralises is usually a hypocrite, and a woman who moralises is invariably plain.

> OSCAR WILDE (1854–1900), Anglo-Irish playwright, author. Cecil Graham, in *Lady Windermere's Fan,* act 3.

8 I never approve, or disapprove, of anything now. It is an absurd attitude to take towards life. We are not sent into the world to air our moral prejudices. I never take any notice of what common people say, and I never interfere with what charming people do.

> OSCAR WILDE (1854–1900), Anglo-Irish playwright, author. Lord Henry, in the *The Picture of Dorian Gray,* ch. 6 (1891).

See also PURITANS.

MORALITY

1 The only immorality . . . is not to do what one has to do when one has to do it.

> JEAN ANOUILH (1910–87), French playwright. Thomas à Becket, in *Becket,* act 2.

2 The moral virtues, then, are produced in us neither by nature nor against nature. Nature, indeed, prepares in us the ground for their reception, but their complete formation is the product of habit.

> ARISTOTLE (384–322 B.C.), Greek philosopher. *The Ethics of Aristotle,* bk. 3, ch. 1 (1953).

3 While moral rules may be propounded by authority the fact that these were so propounded would not validate them.

> A. J. AYER (1910–89), British philosopher. *The Meaning of Life and Other Essays,* title essay (1990).

4 The essence of morality is a questioning about morality; and the decisive move of human life is to use ceaselessly all light to look for the origin of the opposition between good and evil.

> GEORGES BATAILLE (1897–1962), French novelist, critic. "Du Rapport entre le Divin et le Mal," in *Critique* (Paris, March 1947; quoted. in Denis Hollier, "The Duallist Materialism of Georges Bataille," in *On Bataille,* ed. by Allan Stoekl, 1990).

5 Though sages may pour out their wisdom's treasure,
There is no sterner moralist than pleasure.

> LORD BYRON (1788–1824), English poet. *Don Juan,* cto. 3, st. 65.

6 For the "superior morality," of which we hear so much, we too would desire to be thankful: at the same time, it were but blindness to deny that this "superior morality" is properly rather an "inferior criminality," produced not by greater love of Virtue, but by greater perfection of Police; and of that far subtler and stronger Police, called Public Opinion.

> THOMAS CARLYLE (1795–1881), Scottish essayist, historian. *Signs of the Times* (first published in *Edinburgh Review,* no. 98, repr. in Critical and Miscellaneous Essays, 1838).

7 It is far easier for a woman to lead a blameless life than it is for a man; all she has to do is to avoid sexual intercourse like the plague.

> ANGELA CARTER (1940–92), British author. *Wayward Girls and Wicked Women,* Introduction (ed. by Angela Carter, 1986).

8 Ordinary morality is only for ordinary people.

> ALEISTER CROWLEY (1875–1947), British occultist. *The Confessions of Aleister Crowley,* ch. 22 (1929; rev. 1970).

9 Modern morality and manners suppress all natural instincts, keep people ignorant of the facts of nature and make them fighting drunk on bogey tales.

> ALEISTER CROWLEY (1875–1947), British occultist. *The Confessions of Aleister Crowley,* ch. 57 (1929; rev. 1970).

10 Morals are in all countries the result of legislation and government; they are not African or Asian or European: they are good or bad.

> DENIS DIDEROT (1713–84), French philosopher. *Observations on the Drawing Up of Laws* (1921; repr. in *Selected Writings,* ed. by Lester G. Crocker, 1966), written 1774 for Catherine the Great.

11 When we start deceiving ourselves into thinking not that we want something or need something, not that it is a pragmatic necessity for us to have it, but that it is a *moral imperative* that we have it, then is when we join the fashionable madmen, and then is when the thin whine of hysteria is heard in the land, and then is when we are in bad trouble.

> JOAN DIDION (b. 1934), U.S. essayist. *Slouching Towards Bethlehem,* "On Morality" (1968).

12 We moralise among ruins.

> BENJAMIN DISRAELI (1804–81), English statesman, author. *Tancred,* bk. 5, ch. 5 (1847).

13 A woman can look both moral and exciting—if she also looks as if it was quite a struggle.

> EDNA FERBER (1887–1968), U.S. writer. Quoted in: *The Reader's Digest* (Dec. 1954).

14 It is safe to say that no other superstition is so detrimental to growth, so enervating and paralyzing to the minds and hearts of the people, as the superstition of Morality.

EMMA GOLDMAN (1869–1940), U.S. anarchist. "Victims of Morality," in *Mother Earth* (New York, March 1913; repr. in *Red Emma Speaks*, pt. 2, ed. by Alix Kates Shulman, 1972).

15 Don't let us make imaginary evils, when you know we have so many real ones to encounter.

OLIVER GOLDSMITH (1728–74), Anglo-Irish playwright, author. Leontine, in *The Good Natur'd Man,* act 1.

16 Morality comes with the sad wisdom of age, when the sense of curiosity has withered.

GRAHAM GREENE (1904–91), British novelist. *A Sort of Life,* ch. 7, sct. 1 (1971).

17 We may pretend that we're basically moral people who make mistakes, but the whole of history proves otherwise.

TERRY HANDS (b. 1941), British theater and opera director. *Times* (London, 11 Aug. 1992).

18 Morality and expediency coincide more than the cynics allow.

ROY HATTERSLEY (b. 1932), British Labour politician. *Guardian* (London, 30 Sept. 1988).

19 Every man, in his own opinion, forms an exception to the ordinary rules of morality.

WILLIAM HAZLITT (1778–1830), English essayist. *Characteristics: In the Manner of Rochefoucault's Maxims,* no. 305 (1823; repr. in *The Complete Works Of William Hazlitt,* vol. 9, ed. by P. P. Howe, 1932).

20 About morals, I know only that what is moral is what you feel good after and what is immoral is what you feel bad after.

ERNEST HEMINGWAY (1899–1961), U.S. author. *Death in the Afternoon,* ch. 1 (1932).

21 However great an evil immorality may be, we must not forget that it is not without its beneficial consequences. It is only through extremes that men can arrive at the middle path of wisdom and virtue.

KARL WILHELM VON HUMBOLDT (1767–1835), German statesman, philologist. *The Limits of State Action,* ch. 8 (1792; repr. 1854; tr. and ed. by J. W. Burrow, 1969).

22 Moral choices do not depend on personal preference and private decision but on right reason and, I would add, divine order.

BASIL HUME (b. 1923), British cardinal, Archbishop of Westminster. *Times* (London, 16 March 1990).

23 Morality is always the product of terror; its chains and strait-waistcoats are fashioned by those who dare not trust others, because they dare not trust themselves, to walk in liberty.

ALDOUS HUXLEY (1894–1963), British author. *Do What You Will,* "Pascal" sct. 23, "Summary of the Life-Worshipper's Creed" (1929).

24 The quality of moral behaviour varies in inverse ratio to the number of human beings involved.

ALDOUS HUXLEY (1894–1963), British author. *Grey Eminence,* ch. 10 (1941).

25 For morality life is a war, and the service of the highest is a sort of cosmic patriotism which also calls for volunteers.

WILLIAM JAMES (1842–1910), U.S. psychologist, philosopher. *The Varieties of Religious Experience,* lecture 2, "Circumscription of the Topic" (1902).

26 There are few things more disturbing than to find, in somebody we detest, a moral quality which seems to us demonstrably superior to anything we ourselves possess. It augurs not merely an unfairness on the part of creation, but a lack of artistic judgement. . . . Sainthood is acceptable only in saints.

PAMELA HANSFORD JOHNSON (1912–81) , British author, critic. *Night and Silence, Who is Here?—An American Comedy,* ch. 23 (1963).

27 Morality is a venereal disease. Its primary stage is called virtue; its secondary stage, boredom; its tertiary stage, syphilis.

KARL KRAUS (1874–1936), Austrian satirist. *Die Fackel* (Vienna, Nov. 1906; repr. in *Morality and Criminal Justice,* "The Riehl Case," 1908).

28 The immorality of men triumphs over the amorality of women.

KARL KRAUS (1874–1936), Austrian satirist. *Sprüche und Widersprüche,* ch. 2 (1909; repr. in *Half-Truths and One-And-A Half-Truths: Selected Aphorisms,* ed. by Harry Zohn, "Not for Women but Against Men," 1976).

29 There's always the hyena of morality at the garden gate, and the real wolf at the end of the street.

D. H. LAWRENCE (1885–1930), British author. Letter, 17 Jan. 1913 (published in *The Letters of D. H. Lawrence,* vol. 1, ed. by James T. Boulton, 1979).

30 Every man has his moral backside which he refrains from showing unless he has to and keeps covered as long as possible with the trousers of decorum.

G. C. LICHTENBERG (1742–99), German physicist, philosopher. *Aphorisms,* "Notebook B," aph. 12 (written 1765–99; tr. by R. J. Hollingdale, 1990).

31 There is nothing so bad but it can masquerade as moral.

WALTER LIPPMANN (1889–1974), U.S. journalist. *A Preface to Politics,* ch. 6 (1914).

32 Morality without religion is only a kind of dead reckoning—an endeavor to find our place on a cloudy sea by measuring the distance we have run, but without any observation of the heavenly bodies.

HENRY WADSWORTH LONGFELLOW (1807–82), U.S. poet. *Kavanagh,* bk. 1, ch. 13 (1849), meditation of Mr. Churchill, inscribed on his pulpit.

33 We know no spectacle so ridiculous as the British public in one of its periodical fits of morality.

THOMAS BABINGTON MACAULAY (1800–1859), English historian, Whig politician. "Moore's *Life of Lord Byron,*" in *Edinburgh Review* (June 1831; repr. in *Critical and Historical Essays,* 1843).

34 Morality is the theory that every human act must be either right or wrong, and that 99% of them are wrong.

H. L. MENCKEN (1880–1956), U.S. journalist. *A Mencken Chrestomathy,* "Sententiæ: The Mind of Men" (1949).

35   We become moral when we are unhappy.

> MARCEL PROUST (1871–1922), French novelist. *Remembrance of Things Past*, vol. 3, "Within a Budding Grove," pt. 1, "Madame Swann at Home" (1918; tr. by Ronald and Colette Cortie, 1988).

36   The greater part of humanity is too much harassed and fatigued by the struggle with want, to rally itself for a new and sterner struggle with error.

> FRIEDRICH VON SCHILLER (1759–1805), German dramatist, poet, essayist. *On the Aesthetic Education of Man*, "Eighth Letter" (1795).

37   He that has not religion to govern his morality, is not a dram better than my mastiff-dog; so long as you stroke him, and please him, and do not pinch him, he will play with you as finely as may be, he is a very good moral mastiff; but if you hurt him, he will fly in your face, and tear out your throat.

> JOHN SELDEN (1584–1654), English jurist, statesman. *Table Talk*, "Moral Honesty" (1686).

38   An Englishman thinks he is moral when he is only uncomfortable.

> GEORGE BERNARD SHAW (1856–1950), Anglo-Irish playwright, critic. The Devil, in *Man and Superman*, act 3.

39   A system of morality which is based on relative emotional values is a mere illusion, a thoroughly vulgar conception which has nothing sound in it and nothing true.

> SOCRATES (469–399 B.C.), Greek philosopher. Quoted in: Plato, *Phaedo* sct. 68c–69d.

40   Unfortunately, moral beauty in art—like physical beauty in a person—is extremely perishable. It is nowhere so durable as artistic or intellectual beauty. Moral beauty has a tendency to decay very rapidly into sententiousness or untimeliness.

> SUSAN SONTAG (b. 1933), U.S. essayist. *Against Interpretation*, "Camus' Notebooks" (1966; first published 1963).

41   If your morals make you dreary, depend upon it they are wrong. I do not say "give them up," for they may be all you have; but conceal them like a vice, lest they should spoil the lives of better and simpler people.

> ROBERT LOUIS STEVENSON (1850–94), Scottish novelist, essayist, poet. *Across the Plains*, "A Christmas Sermon," sct. 2 (1892).

42   Our whole life is startlingly moral. There is never an instant's truce between virtue and vice.

> HENRY DAVID THOREAU (1817–62), U.S. philosopher, author, naturalist. *Walden*, "Higher Laws" (1854).

43   To set up as a standard of public morality a notion which can neither be defined nor conceived is to open the door to every kind of tyranny.

> SIMONE WEIL (1909–43), French philosopher, mystic. "Human Personality," in *La Table Ronde* (Dec. 1950; repr. in *Selected Essays*, ed. by Richard Rees, 1962).

44   Morality is simply the attitude we adopt towards people we personally dislike.

> OSCAR WILDE (1854–1900), Anglo-Irish playwright, author. Mrs. Cheveley, in *An Ideal Husband*, act 2.

45   There is no such thing as morality or immorality in thought. There is immoral emotion.

> OSCAR WILDE (1854–1900), Anglo-Irish playwright, author. In answer to Edward Carson, Q.C., during Wilde's prosecution of the Marquess of Queensberry for criminal libel, in *Regina (Wilde) v. Queensberry* (3 April 1895).

46   Moral power is probably best when it is not used. The less you use it the more you have.

> ANDREW YOUNG (b. 1932), U.S. Democratic politician, diplomat. *Observer* (London, 8 Sept. 1979).

See also Butler on ALCOHOL: DRUNKENNESS; Twain on ANIMALS; Smith on CONSCIENCE; Spencer on HEALTH; Blake on LIBERTY; Taylor on PUNISHMENT; Arnold, Shaw on RELIGION; Whitlam on SELF-INTEREST; Stevenson on TABOO.

MOTHERS

1   What *do* girls do who haven't any mothers to help them through their troubles?

> LOUISA MAY ALCOTT (1832–88), U.S. author. Jo March, in *Little Women*, pt. 2, ch. 23 (1869).

2   The best thing that could happen to motherhood already has. Fewer women are going into it.

> VICTORIA BILLINGS (b. 1945), U.S. journalist, author. *The Womansbook*, "Meeting Your Personal Needs" (1974).

3   When a woman is twenty, a child deforms her; when she is thirty, he preserves her; and when forty, he makes her young again.

> LÉON BLUM (1872–1950), French Socialist statesman. *Du Mariage*, ch. 6 (1907).

4   Women know
The way to rear up children (to be just),
They know a simple, merry, tender knack
Of tying sashes, fitting baby-shoes,
And stringing pretty words that make no sense,
And kissing full sense into empty words.

> ELIZABETH BARRETT BROWNING (1806–61), English poet. *Aurora Leigh*, bk. 1 (1857).

5   There are lots of things that you can brush under the carpet about yourself until you're faced with somebody whose needs won't be put off.

> ANGELA CARTER (1940–92), British author. Interview in *Marxism Today* (London; Jan. 1985), on being a mother for the first time, at age 43.

6   The kind of power mothers have is enormous. Take the skyline of Istambul—enormous breasts, pathetic little willies, a final revenge on Islam. I was so scared I had to crouch in the bottom of the boat when I saw it.

> ANGELA CARTER (1940–92), British author. Interview by Lorna Sage, published in *New Writing* (ed. by Malcolm Bradbury and Judy Cooke, 1992).

7   Nobody can misunderstand a boy like his own mother. . . . Mothers at present can bring children into the world, but this performance is apt to mark the end of their capacities. They can't even attend to the elementary animal requirements of their offspring. It is quite surprising how many children survive in spite of their mothers.

> NORMAN DOUGLAS (1868–1952), British author. Mr. Keith, in *South Wind*, ch. 22 (1917).

8 For that's what a woman, a mother wants—to teach her children to take an interest in life. She knows it's safer for them to be interested in other people's happiness than to believe in their own.

MARGUERITE DURAS (b. 1914), French author, filmmaker. *Practicalities,* "House and Home" (1987; tr. 1990).

9 I believe that always, or almost always, in all childhoods and in all the lives that follow them, the mother represents madness. Our mothers always remain the strangest, craziest people we've ever met.

MARGUERITE DURAS (b. 1914), French author, filmmaker. *Practicalities,* "House and Home" (1987; tr. 1990).

10 The fact that we are all trained to be mothers from infancy on means that we are all trained to devote our lives to men, whether they are our sons or not; that we are all trained to force other women to exemplify the lack of qualities which characterizes the cultural construct of femininity.

ANDREA DWORKIN (b. 1946), U.S. feminist critic. "The Sexual Politics of Fear and Courage," speech, delivered 12 March 1975, Queens College, City University of New York (published in *Our Blood,* ch. 5, 1976).

11 Take motherhood: nobody ever thought of putting it on a moral pedestal until some brash feminists pointed out, about a century ago, that the pay is lousy and the career ladder nonexistent.

BARBARA EHRENREICH (b. 1941), U.S. author, columnist. *The Worst Years of Our Lives,* "Premature Pragmatism" (1991; first published in *Ms.,* New York, 1986).

12 No culture on earth outside of mid-century suburban America has ever deployed one woman per child without simultaneously assigning her such major productive activities as weaving, farming, gathering, temple maintenance, and tent-building. The reason is that full-time, one-on-one child-raising is not good for women *or* children.

BARBARA EHRENREICH (b. 1941), U.S. author, columnist. *The Worst Years of Our Lives,* "Stop Ironing the Diapers" (1991; first published 1989).

13 But the mother's yearning, that completest type of the life in another life which is the essence of real human love, feels the presence of the cherished child even in the debased, degraded man.

GEORGE ELIOT (1819–80), English novelist. *Adam Bede,* bk. 5, ch. 43 (1859).

14 The lullaby is the spell whereby the mother attempts to transform herself back from an ogre to a saint.

JAMES FENTON (b. 1949), British poet, critic. "Ars Poetica," no. 7, in *Independent on Sunday* (London, 11 March 1990).

15 The mother as a social servant instead of a home servant will not lack in true mother duty. . . . From her work, loved and honored though it is, she will return to her home life, the child life, with an eager, ceaseless pleasure, cleansed of all the fret and fraction and weariness that so mar it now.

CHARLOTTE PERKINS GILMAN (1860–1935), U.S. feminist, writer. *Women and Economics,* ch. 13 (1898).

16 Morality and its victim, the mother—what a terrible picture! Is there indeed anything more terrible, more criminal, than our glorified sacred function of motherhood?

EMMA GOLDMAN (1869–1940), U.S. anarchist. "Victims of Morality," in *Mother Earth* (New York, March 1913; repr. in *Red Emma Speaks,* pt. 2, ed. by Alix Kates Shulman, 1972).

17 All that remains to the mother in modern consumer society is the role of scapegoat; psychoanalysis uses huge amounts of money and time to persuade analysands to foist their problems on to the absent mother, who has no opportunity to utter a word in her own defence. Hostility to the mother in our societies is an index of mental health.

GERMAINE GREER (b. 1939), Australian feminist writer. *The Change: Women, Ageing and the Menopause,* ch. 3 (1991).

18 One must leave one's parents early, especially one's mother. Mothers are never any good for their daughters. They forget they were just as ugly and silly and scraggy when they were little girls.

MRS. ROBERT HENREY (b. 1906), French author. Paloma, in *Paloma,* ch. 3 (1951).

19 Whatever else is unsure in this stinking dunghill of a world a mother's love is not.

JAMES JOYCE (1882–1941), Irish author. Cranly, in *A Portrait of the Artist as a Young Man,* ch. 5 (1916).

20 Few misfortunes can befall a boy which bring worse consequences than to have a really affectionate mother.

W. SOMERSET MAUGHAM (1874–1966), British author. *A Writer's Notebook* (1949), entry for 1896.

21 The Enemy, who wears
Her mother's usual face
And confidential tone,
Has access; doubtless stares
Into her writing case
And listens on the phone.

PHYLLIS MCGINLEY (1905–78), U.S. poet, author. *Fourteenth Birthday,* in *Times Three* (1960).

22 Clearly, society has a tremendous stake in insisting on a woman's natural fitness for the career of mother: the alternatives are all too expensive.

ANN OAKLEY (b. 1944), British sociologist, author. *Woman's Work: The Housewife, Past and Present,* ch. 8 (1974).

23 Every man must define his identity against his mother. If he does not, he just falls back into her and is swallowed up.

CAMILLE PAGLIA (b. 1947), U.S. author, critic, educator. "Homosexuality at the Fin de Siècle," in *Esquire* (New York, Oct. 1991; repr. in *Sex, Art, and American Culture,* 1992).

24 He that would the daughter win
Must with the mother first begin.

ENGLISH PROVERB (17th-century).
Collected in J. Ray, *English Proverbs* (1670).

25 God could not be everywhere and therefore he made mothers.

JEWISH PROVERB.

26 Maternity is on the face of it an unsocial experi-

ence. The selfishness that a woman has learned to stifle or to dissemble where she alone is concerned, blooms freely and unashamed on behalf of her offspring.

EMILY JAMES PUTNAM (1865–1944), U.S. educator, author. *The Lady*, Introduction (1910).

27 The worker can unionize, go out on strike; mothers are divided from each other in homes, tied to their children by compassionate bonds; our wildcat strikes have most often taken the form of physical or mental breakdown.

ADRIENNE RICH (b. 1929), U.S. poet. *Of Woman Born*, ch. 2 (1976).

28 As her sons have seen her: the mother in patriarchy: controlling, erotic, castrating, heart-suffering, guilt-ridden, and guilt-provoking; a marble brow, a huge breast, an avid cave; between her legs snakes, swampgrass, or teeth; on her lap a helpless infant or a martyred son. She exists for one purpose: to bear and nourish the son.

ADRIENNE RICH (b. 1929), U.S. poet. *Of Woman Born*, ch. 8 (1976).

29 Biological *possibility* and desire are not the same as biological *need*. Women have childbearing equipment. For them to choose not to use the equipment is no more blocking what is instinctive than it is for a man who, muscles or no, chooses not to be a weightlifter.

BETTY ROLLIN (b. 1936), U.S. journalist, author. "Motherhood: Who Needs It?," in *Look* (New York, 16 May 1971).

30 Only in America . . . do these peasants, our mothers, get their hair dyed platinum at the age of sixty, and walk up and down Collins Avenue in Florida in pedal-pushers and mink stoles—and with opinions on every subject under the sun. It isn't their fault they were given a gift like speech—look, if cows could talk, they would say things just as idiotic.

PHILIP ROTH (b. 1933), U.S. novelist. *Portnoy's Complaint*, "Cunt Crazy" (1967).

31 There was never a great man who had not a great mother.

OLIVE SCHREINER (1855–1920), South African writer, feminist. Lyndall, in *The Story of an African Farm*, pt. 2, ch. 4 (1883).

32 Men never think, at least seldom think, what a hard task it is for us women to go through this very often. God's will be done, and if He decrees that we are to have a great number of children why we must try to bring them up as useful and exemplary members of society.

VICTORIA (1819–1901), Queen of Great Britain and Ireland. Letter, 5 Jan. 1841, to her uncle King Leopold of the Belgians, written after the birth of her first child (published in *Queen Victoria in Her Letters and Journals*, ed. by Christopher Hibbert, 1984). Leopold had expressed the hope that Princess Victoria would be the first of many children; Victoria eventually mothered nine. See Victoria on CHILDBIRTH.

33 How simple a thing it seems to me that to know ourselves as we are, we must know our mothers' names.

ALICE WALKER (b. 1944), U.S. author, critic. "A Letter to the Editor of *Ms.*," in *Ms.* (New York, Aug. 1974; repr. in *In Search of Our Mothers' Gardens*, 1983).

34 Young women especially have something invested in being *nice people*, and it's only when you have chil-

dren that you realise you're not a nice person at all, but generally a selfish bully.

FAY WELDON (b. 1933), British novelist. *Independent on Sunday* (London, 5 May 1991).

35 Motherhood is the strangest thing, it can be like being one's own Trojan horse.

REBECCA WEST (1892–1983), British author. Letter, 20 Aug. 1959. Quoted in: Victoria Glendinning, *Rebecca West: A Life*, pt. 5, ch. 8 (1987).

36 Lord Illingworth: All women become like their mothers. That is their tragedy.
Mrs. Allonby: No man does. That is his.

OSCAR WILDE (1854–1900), Anglo-Irish playwright, author. *A Woman of No Importance*, act 2. This aphorism was also spoken by Algernon in *The Importance of Being Earnest*, act 1.

See also Jones on HOUSEWORK; PARENTS; Dworkin, Freud on SONS.

MOTIVATION

1 But what we strive to gratify, though we may call it a distant hope, is an immediate desire; the future estate for which men drudge up city alleys exists already in their imagination and love.

GEORGE ELIOT (1819–80), English novelist, editor. *Middlemarch*, bk. 4, ch. 42 (1871).

2 In these years we are witnessing the gigantic spectacle of innumerable human lives wandering about lost in their own labyrinths, through not having anything to which to give themselves.

JOSÉ ORTEGA Y GASSET (1883–1955) , Spanish essayist, philosopher. *The Revolt of the Masses*, ch. 14, sct. 4 (1930).

3 It's that—the thought of the few, simple things we want and the knowledge that we're going to get them in spite of you know Who and His spites and tempers—that keeps us living I think.

DYLAN THOMAS (1914–53), Welsh poet. Letter, late 1936, to Caitlin, later Thomas's wife (published in *The Collected Letters of Dylan Thomas*, 1985).

MOTIVES

1 Never ascribe to an opponent motives meaner than your own.

J. M. BARRIE (1860–1937), British playwright. Rectorial address, 3 May 1922, St. Andrew's University, Scotland.

2 We are all selfish & I no more trust myself than others with a good motive.

LORD BYRON (1788–1824), English poet. Letter, 28 Sept. 1813 (published in *Byron's Letters and Journals*, vol. 3, ed. by Leslie Marchand, 1974).

3 A man's most open actions have a secret side to them.

JOSEPH CONRAD (1857–1924), Polish-born English novelist. Razumov, in *Under Western Eyes*, pt. 1, ch. 2 (1911).

4 Every woman is supposed to have the same set of motives, or else to be a monster.

GEORGE ELIOT (1819–80), English novelist, editor. Deronda's

mother, in *Daniel Deronda*, bk. 7, ch. 51 (1876), speaking of society's expectations of women.

5 To read between the lines was easier than to follow the text.

HENRY JAMES (1843–1916), U.S. author. Ralph Touchett, in *The Portrait of a Lady*, ch. 13 (1881), giving his appraisal of Henrietta Stackpole.

6 We should often be ashamed of our finest actions if the world understood all the motives behind them.

FRANÇOIS, DUC DE LA ROCHEFOUCAULD (1613–80), French writer, moralist. *Sentences et Maximes Morales*, no. 409 (1678).

7 Let it be your constant method to look into the design of people's actions, and see what they would be at, as often as it is practicable; and to make this custom the more significant, practice it first upon yourself.

MARCUS AURELIUS (121–180), Roman emperor, philosopher. *Meditations*, bk. 10, sct. 37.

8 There's an enduring American compulsion to be on the side of the angels. Expediency alone has never been an adequate American reason for doing anything. When actions are judged, they go before the bar of God, where Mom and the Flag closely flank His presence.

JONATHAN RABAN (b. 1942), British author, critic. *For Love and Money*, pt. 2 (1987).

9 He never does a proper thing without giving an improper reason for it.

GEORGE BERNARD SHAW (1856–1950), Anglo-Irish playwright, critic. Lady Britomart, in *Major Barbara*, act 3, speaking of Andrew Undershaft.

10 From his cradle to his grave a man never does a single thing which has any FIRST AND FOREMOST object but one—to secure peace of mind, spiritual comfort, for HIMSELF.

MARK TWAIN (1835–1910), U.S. author. Old Man, in *What Is Man?* sct. 2 (1906; repr. in *Complete Essays*, ed. by Charles Neider, 1963).

11 Whenever a man does a thoroughly stupid thing, it is always from the noblest motives.

OSCAR WILDE (1854–1900), Anglo-Irish playwright, author. Lord Henry, in *The Picture of Dorian Gray*, ch. 6 (1891)

See also Eliot on GOOD DEEDS; Blake on TRUTH.

MOTTOS

1 Never let the other fellow set the agenda.

JAMES BAKER (b. 1930), U.S. Republican politician, Secretary of State. *Daily Telegraph* (London, 15 Nov. 1988).

2 If you have to be in a soap opera try not to get the worst role.

BOY GEORGE (b. 1961), British rock singer. *Face* (London, Dec. 1984).

3 Early to bed, early to rise, work like hell and organize.

ALBERT GORE, JR. (b. 1948), U.S. Democratic politician, vice president. Quoted in: *Daily Telegraph* (London, 2 Feb. 1988), as his presidential campaign slogan.

4 If you want to get along, go along.

SAM RAYBURN (1882–1961), U.S. legislator, Democratic politician. Often-repeated maxim.

5 Early to rise and early to bed makes a male healthy and wealthy and dead.

JAMES THURBER (1894–1961), U.S. humorist, illustrator. "The Shrike and the Chipmunks," in *New Yorker* (18 Feb. 1939; repr. in *Fables for our Time*, 1940).

6 Life is not a dress rehearsal.

ROSE TREMAIN (b. 1943), British author. *Sunday Correspondent* (London, 24 Dec. 1989).

7 Never be the only one, except, possibly, in your own home.

ALICE WALKER (b. 1944), U.S. author, critic. "Breaking Chains and Encouraging Life," in *Ms.* (New York, April 1980; repr. in *In Search of our Mothers' Gardens*, 1983).

8 It is vain to do with more what can be done with less.

Attributed to WILLIAM OF OCCAM (c. 1285–1349), English monk, philosopher. *Occam's Razor*.

MOUNTAINS

1 The ordinary man looking at a mountain is like an illiterate person confronted with a Greek manuscript.

ALEISTER CROWLEY (1875–1947), British occultist. *The Confessions of Aleister Crowley*, ch. 10 (1929; rev. 1970), referring to mountaineering.

2 Separate from the pleasure of your company, I don't much care if I never see another mountain in my life.

CHARLES LAMB (1775–1834), English essayist, critic. Letter, 30 Jan. 1801, to William Wordsworth (published in *Complete Works*, vol. 3, 1882).

3 I can't do with mountains at close quarters—they are always in the way, and they are so stupid, never moving and never doing anything but obtrude themselves.

D. H. LAWRENCE (1885–1930), British author. Letter, 23 Oct. 1913 (published in *The Letters of D. H. Lawrence*, vol. 2, ed. by George J. Zytaruk and James T. Boulton, 1981).

4 Mountains are to the rest of the body of the earth, what violent muscular action is to the body of man. The muscles and tendons of its anatomy are, in the mountain, brought out with force and convulsive energy, full of expression, passion, and strength.

JOHN RUSKIN (1819–1900), English art critic, author. *Modern Painters*, vol. 1, pt. 2, sct. 4, ch. 1, para. 3 (1843).

5 Thou hast a voice, great Mountain, to repeal
Large codes of fraud and woe; not understood
By all, but which the wise, and great, and good
Interpret, or make felt, or deeply feel.

PERCY BYSSHE SHELLEY (1792–1822), English poet. *Mont Blanc*.

MOURNING

1 Weep bitterly, and make great moan, and use lamentation, as he is worthy, and that a day or two, lest thou be evil spoken of: and then comfort thyself for thy heaviness. For of heaviness cometh death, and the heaviness of the heart breaketh strength.

APOCRYPHA. *Ecclesiasticus* 38:17–18.

2   Friends make pretence of following to the grave
But before one is in it, their minds are turned
And making the best of their way back to life
And living people and things they understand.

ROBERT FROST (1874–1963), U.S. poet. *Home Burial.*

3   To be remembered after we are dead, is but poor recompense for being treated with contempt while we are living.

WILLIAM HAZLITT (1778–1830), English essayist. *Characteristics: In the Manner of Rochefoucault's Maxims*, no. 429 (1823; repr. in *The Complete Works Of William Hazlitt*, vol. 9, ed. by P. P. Howe, 1932).

4   The grief of the keen is no personal complaint for the death of one woman over eighty years, but seems to contain the whole passionate rage that lurks somewhere in every native of the island. In this cry of pain the inner consciousness of the people seems to lay itself bare for an instant, and to reveal the mood of beings who feel their isolation in the face of a universe that wars on them with winds and seas.

J. M. SYNGE (1871–1909), Irish poet, dramatist. *The Aran Islands*, pt. 1 *(1907)*, referring to the burial of an inhabitant of Inishmaan, one of the Aran Islands off the western coast of Ireland. Synge made several visits to the Aran Islands after his return from Paris, where W. B. Yeats encouraged him to go back to Ireland to study and assimilate the country's folk culture and dialects.

See also BEREAVEMENT.

MOVIES

See CINEMA.

MULTICULTURALISM

1   The establishment of democracy on the American continent was scarcely as radical a break with the past as was the necessity, which Americans faced, of broadening this concept to include black men.

JAMES BALDWIN (1924–87), U.S. author. "Stranger In The Village," in *Harper's* (New York, Oct. 1953; repr. in *Notes of a Native Son*, 1955).

2   We become not a melting pot but a beautiful mosaic. Different people, different beliefs, different yearnings, different hopes, different dreams.

JIMMY CARTER (b. 1924), U.S. Democratic politician, president. Speech, 27 Oct. 1976, Pittsburgh, Pa.

3   We Americans have the chance to become someday a nation in which all radical stocks and classes can exist in their own selfhoods, but meet on a basis of respect and equality and live together, socially, economically, and politically. We can become a dynamic equilibrium, a harmony of many different elements, in which

the whole will be greater than all its parts and greater than any society the world has seen before. It can still happen.

SHIRLEY CHISHOLM (b. 1924), U.S. educator, congresswoman. *The Good Fight*, ch. 14 (1973).

4   Once the visitor was told rather repetitively that this city was the melting pot; never before in history had so many people of such varied languages, customs, colors and culinary habits lived so amicably together. Although New York remains peaceful by most standards, this self-congratulation is now less often heard, since it was discovered some years ago that racial harmony depended unduly on the willingness of the blacks (and latterly the Puerto Ricans) to do for the other races the meanest jobs at the lowest wages and then to return to live by themselves in the worst slums.

JOHN KENNETH GALBRAITH (b. 1908), U.S. economist. "The United States," in *New York* (15 Nov. 1971; repr. in *A View from the Stands*, 1986), referring to New York City.

5   Fortunately, the time has long passed when people liked to regard the United States as some kind of melting pot, taking men and women from every part of the world and converting them into standardized, homogenized Americans. We are, I think, much more mature and wise today. Just as we welcome a world of diversity, so we glory in an America of diversity—an America all the richer for the many different and distinctive strands of which it is woven.

HUBERT H. HUMPHREY (1911–78), U.S. Democratic politician, vice president. "All-America Tribute to Archbishop Iakovos," speech, 15 Jan. 1967, Chicago, Ill.

6   I hear that melting-pot stuff a lot, and all I can say is that we haven't melted.

JESSE JACKSON (b. 1941), U.S. clergyman, civil rights leader. *Playboy* (Chicago, Nov. 1969).

7   It's just like when you've got some coffee that's too black, which means it's too strong. What do you do? You integrate it with cream, you make it weak. But if you pour too much cream in it, you won't even know you ever had coffee. It used to be hot, it becomes cool. It used to be strong, it becomes weak. It used to wake you up, now it puts you to sleep.

MALCOLM X (1925–65), U.S. black leader. "Message to the Grass Roots," speech, Nov. 1963, Detroit (published in *Malcolm X Speaks*, ch. 1, 1965).

8   Of course I'm a black writer. . . . I'm not *just* a black writer, but categories like black writer, woman writer and Latin American writer aren't marginal anymore. We have to acknowledge that the thing we call "literature" is more pluralistic now, just as society ought to be. The melting pot never worked. We ought to be able to accept on equal terms everybody from the Hasidim to Walter Lippmann, from the Rastafarians to Ralph Bunche.

TONI MORRISON (b. 1931), U.S. novelist, editor. Quoted in: *Newsweek* (New York, 30 March 1981).

9   O unbelievers,
I serve not what you serve
and you are not serving what I serve,
nor am I serving what you have served,

neither are you serving what I serve.
To you your religion, and to me my religion!

QUR'AN. *The Unbelievers,* 109:1–5 (ed. by Arthur J. Arberry, 1955).

10 There can be no fifty-fifty Americanism in this country. There is room here for only 100% Americanism, only for those who are Americans and nothing else.

THEODORE ROOSEVELT (1858–1919), U.S. Republican (later Progressive) politician, president. Speech, 19 July 1918, to the State Republican Party Convention, Saratoga, New York.

11 Though it is very important for man as an individual that his religion should be true, that is not the case for society. Society has nothing to fear or hope from another life; what is most important for it is not that all citizens profess the true religion but that they should profess religion.

ALEXIS DE TOCQUEVILLE (1805–59), French social philosopher. *Democracy in America,* vol. 1, pt. 2, ch. 9 (1835).

12 If there were only one religion in England there would be danger of despotism, if there were two, they would cut each other's throats, but there are thirty, and they live in peace and happiness.

VOLTAIRE (1694–1778), French philosopher, author. *Letters on England,* Letter 6, "On the Presbyterians" (1732).

13 America is God's Crucible, the great Melting-Pot where all the races of Europe are melting and re-forming!

ISRAEL ZANGWILL (1864–1926), British playwright, novelist. David Quixano, in *The Melting Pot,* act 1. With this play, Zangwill introduced the term "melting-pot" into the language.

See also DIVERSITY.

MURDER

1 Lizzie Borden took an axe
And gave her mother forty whacks;
When she saw what she had done,
She gave her father forty-one.

ANONYMOUS BALLAD (Late 19th century). The quatrain refers to the famous case of Lizzie Borden, tried for the murder of her father and step-mother on 4 Aug. 1892, in Fall River, Massachusetts. Though she was found innocent, there were many who contested the verdict, occasioning a prodigious output of articles and books, including, most recently, Frank Spiering's *Lizzie* (1985), which points the finger at Lizzie's elder sister, Emma.

2 It's frightening how easy it is to commit murder in America. Just a drink too much. I can see myself doing it. In England, one feels all the social restraints holding one back. But here, anything can happen.

W. H. AUDEN (1907–73), Anglo-American poet. *The Table Talk of W. H. Auden,* "November 16, 1946" (comp. by Alan Ansen, ed. by Nicholas Jenkins, 1990).

3 Murder is unique in that it abolishes the party it injures, so that society has to take the place of the victim and on his behalf demand atonement or grant forgiveness; it is the one crime in which society has a direct interest.

W. H. AUDEN (1907–73), Anglo-American poet. "The Guilty Vicarage," in *Harper's* (New York, May 1948; repr. in *The Dyer's Hand,* pt. 3, 1962).

4 After all, every murderer when he kills runs the risk of the most dreadful of deaths, whereas those who kill him risk nothing except promotion.

ALBERT CAMUS (1913–60), French-Algerian philosopher, author. *Resistance, Rebellion and Death,* "Reflections on the Guillotine" (1961).

5 The boys with their feet on the desks know that the easiest murder case in the world to break is the one somebody tried to get very cute with; the one that really bothers them is the murder somebody only thought of two minutes before he pulled it off.

RAYMOND CHANDLER (1888–1959), U.S. author. *The Simple Art of Murder,* in *Atlantic Monthly* (Boston, Dec. 1944; repr. 1950).

6 If once a man indulges himself in murder, very soon he comes to think little of robbing; and from robbing he comes next to drinking and Sabbath-breaking, and from that to incivility and procrastination.

THOMAS DE QUINCEY (1785–1859), English author. *Murder Considered as One of the Fine Arts* (1827).

7 Murders are exciting and lift people into a heartbeating awe as religion is supposed to do, after seeing one in the street young couples will go back to bed and make love, people will cross themselves and thank God for the gift of their stuporous lives, old folks will talk to each other over cups of hot water with lemon because murders are enlivened sermons to be analyzed and considered and relished, they speak to the timid of the dangers of rebellion, murders are perceived as momentary descents of God and so provide joy and hope and righteous satisfaction to parishioners, who will talk about them for years afterward to anyone who will listen.

E. L. DOCTOROW (b. 1931), U.S. novelist. *Billy Bathgate,* ch. 19 (1989).

8 Murder in the murderer is no such ruinous thought as poets and romancers will have it; it does not unsettle him, or fright him from his ordinary notice of trifles; it is an act quite easy to be contemplated.

RALPH WALDO EMERSON (1803–82), U.S. essayist, poet, philosopher. *Essays,* "Experience" (Second Series, 1844).

9 I love the old way best, the simple way
Of poison, where we too are strong as men.

EURIPIDES (c. 480–406 BC), Greek tragedian. Medea, in *Medea* (tr. by Gilbert Murray).

10 A murderer is regarded by the conventional world as something almost monstrous, but a murderer to himself is only an ordinary man. . . . It is only if the murderer is a good man that he can be regarded as monstrous.

GRAHAM GREENE (1904–91), British novelist. *The Ministry of Fear,* bk. 1, ch. 7, sct. 1 (1943).

11 Every murder turns on a bright hot light, and a lot of people . . . have to walk out of the shadows.

MARK HELLINGER (1903–47), U.S. journalist, scriptwriter, producer. Narrating his last production, *The Naked City* (scripted by Albert Maltz and Marvin Wald, 1948).

12 It takes two to make a murder. There are born victims, born to have their throats cut, as the cut-throats are born to be hanged.

> ALDOUS HUXLEY (1894–1963), British author. Maurice Spandrell, in *Point Counter Point*, ch. 12 (1928).

13 Cruel with guilt, and daring with despair,
The midnight murderer bursts the faithless bar;
Invades the sacred hour of silent rest
And leaves, unseen, a dagger in your breast.

> SAMUEL JOHNSON (1709–84), English author, lexicographer. *London*.

14 Under the rules of a society that cannot distinguish between profit and profiteering, between money defined as necessity and money defined as luxury, murder is occasionally obligatory and always permissible.

> LEWIS H. LAPHAM (b. 1935), U.S. essayist, editor. *Money and Class in America*, ch. 4 (1988).

15 It is a question whether, when we break a murderer on the wheel, we do not fall into the error a child makes when it hits the chair it has bumped into.

> G. C. LICHTENBERG (1742–99), German physicist, philosopher. *Aphorisms*, "Notebook J," aph. 146 (written 1765–99; tr. by R. J. Hollingdale, 1990).

16 Murder is born of love, and love attains the greatest intensity in murder.

> OCTAVE MIRBEAU (1850–1917), French journalist, author. *The Torture Garden*, "The Manuscript" (1899).

17 You can always count on a murderer for a fancy prose style.

> VLADIMIR NABOKOV (1899–1977), Russian-born U.S. novelist, poet. *Lolita*, pt. 1, ch. 1 (1955).

18 Murder is a horror, but an often necessary horror, never criminal, which it is essential to tolerate in a republican State. . . . Is it or is it not a crime? If it is not, why make laws for its punishment? And if it is, by what barbarous logic do you, to punish it, duplicate it by another crime?

> MARQUIS DE SADE (1740–1814), French author. Dolmancé, in *Philosophy in the Bedroom*, "Dialogue the Fifth: Yet Another Effort, Frenchmen, If You Would Become Republicans" (1795).

19 Yet who would have thought the old man to have had so much blood in him?

> WILLIAM SHAKESPEARE (1564–1616), English dramatist, poet. Lady Macbeth, in *Macbeth*, act 5, sc. 1, of the murdered Duncan.

20 When once a certain class of people has been placed by the temporal and spiritual authorities outside the ranks of those whose life has value, then nothing comes more naturally to men than murder.

> SIMONE WEIL (1909–43), French philosopher, mystic. Letter, c. 1938, to author Georges Bernanos (published in *Selected Essays*, ed. by Richard Rees, 1962).

21 Murder is always a mistake. One should never do anything that one cannot talk about after dinner.

> OSCAR WILDE (1854–1900), Anglo-Irish playwright, author. Lord Henry, in *The Picture of Dorian Gray*, ch. 19 (1891).

See also ASSASSINATION; Porteus on GENERALS; KILLING; Hitchcock on TELEVISION.

MUSEUMS AND GALLERIES

1 The Museum is not meant either for the wanderer to see by accident or for the pilgrim to see with awe. It is meant for the mere slave of a routine of self-education to stuff himself with every sort of incongruous intellectual food in one indigestible meal.

> G. K. CHESTERTON (1874–1936), British author. *All Is Grist*, "On Sightseeing" (1931).

2 The Louvre is a morgue; you go there to identify your friends.

> JEAN COCTEAU (1889–1963), French author, filmmaker. Quoted in: Roger Shattuck, "A Native Son of Paris" in *Jean Cocteau and the French Scene* (1984).

3 That which, perhaps, hears more nonsense than anything in the world, is a picture in a museum.

> EDMOND (1822–96) AND JULES DE GONCOURT (1830–70), French writers. *The Goncourt Journals 1851–1870* (ed. by Lewis Galantière, 1937), entry for 1866.

4 In public buildings set aside for the care and maintenance of the goods of the middle ages, a staff of civil service art attendants praise all the dead, irrelevant scribblings and scrawlings that, at best, have only historical interest for idiots and layabouts.

> GEORGE GROSZ (1893–1959), German artist. *Der Gegner*, vol. 1, nos. 10–12, "The Art Scab" (1920; repr. in *Art Is in Danger*, tr. by Paul Gorrell, 1987).

5 Yesterday I went out at about twelve, and visited the British Museum; an exceedingly tiresome affair. It quite crushes a person to see so much at once; and I wandered from hall to hall with a weary and heavy heart, wishing (Heaven forgive me!) that the Elgin marbles and the frieze of the Parthenon were all burnt into lime, and that the granite Egyptian statues were hewn and squared into building stones, and that the mummies had all turned to dust, two thousand years ago; and, in fine, that all the material relics of so many successive ages had disappeared with the generations that produced them. The present is burthened too much with the past.

> NATHANIEL HAWTHORNE (1804–64), U.S. author. *English Notebooks* (1870; rev. 1941), entry for 27 March 1856.

6 Individually, museums are fine institutions, dedicated to the high values of preservation, education and truth; collectively, their growth in numbers points to the imaginative death of this country.

> ROBERT HEWISON (b. 1943), British cultural historian. *The Heritage Industry*, Introduction (1987).

7 In museums and palaces we are alternate radicals and conservatives.

> HENRY JAMES (1843–16), U.S. author. *Italian Hours*, "Florentine Notes," sct. 3 (1909).

8 Museums and art stores are also sources of pleasure and inspiration. Doubtless it will seem strange to many that the hand unaided by sight can feel action, sentiment, beauty in the cold marble; and yet it is true that I derive genuine pleasure from touching great works of art. As my finger tips trace line and curve, they discover the thought and emotion which the artist has portrayed.

> HELEN KELLER (1880–1968), U.S. blind/deaf author, lecturer. *The Story of My Life*, pt. 1, ch. 22 (1903).

9 I never can pass by the Metropolitan Museum of Art in New York without thinking of it not as a gallery of living portraits but as a cemetery of tax-deductible wealth.

> LEWIS H. LAPHAM (b. 1935), U.S. essayist, editor. *Money and Class in America*, ch. 9 (1988).

10 Museums, museums, museums, object-lessons rigged out to illustrate the unsound theories of archaeologists, crazy attempts to co-ordinate and get into a fixed order that which has no fixed order and will not be co-ordinated! It is sickening! Why must all experience be systematized? . . . A museum is not a first-hand contact: it is an illustrated lecture. And what one wants is the actual vital touch.

> D. H. LAWRENCE (1885–1930), British author. *Etruscan Places*, ch. 6 (1932), bemoaning the removal of excavated Etruscan tombs to the archaeological museum in Florence.

11 Nothing seems more like a whorehouse to me than a museum. In it you find the same equivocal aspect, the same frozen quality.

> MICHEL LEIRIS (1901–90), French anthropologist, author. *Manhood*, ch. 2, "Brothels and Museums" (1946; tr. 1963).

12 Attitudes to museums have changed. If it had Marilyn Monroe's knickers or Laurence Olivier's jockstrap they would flock to it.

> JONATHAN MILLER (b. 1936), British doctor, humorist, director. *Daily Telegraph* (London, 7 June 1989), commenting on the low attendances at his recently opened Theatre Museum.

13 Museums are just a lot of lies, and the people who make art their business are mostly imposters. . . . We have infected the pictures in museums with all our stupidities, all our mistakes, all our poverty of spirit. We have turned them into petty and ridiculous things.

> PABLO PICASSO (1881–1973), Spanish artist. "Conversation avec Picasso," in *Cahiers d'Art*, vol. 10, no. 10 (Paris, 1935; tr. in Alfred H. Barr, Jr., *Picasso: Fifty Years of His Art*, 1946).

14 One ought not to hoard culture. It should be adapted and infused into society as a leaven. Liberality of culture does not mean illiberality of its benefits.

> WALLACE STEVENS (1879–1955), U.S. poet. *Souvenirs and Prophecies: the Young Wallace Stevens*, ch. 3 (ed. by Holly Stevens, 1977), journal entry for 20 June 1899.

MUSIC

1 Mozart has the classic purity of light and the blue ocean; Beethoven the romantic grandeur which belongs to the storms of air and sea, and while the soul of Mozart seems to dwell on the ethereal peaks of Olympus, that of Beethoven climbs shuddering the storm-beaten sides of a Sinai. Blessed be they both! Each represents a moment of the ideal life, each does us good. Our love is due to both.

> HENRI-FRÉDÉRIC AMIEL (1821–81), Swiss philosopher, poet.

Journal Intime (1882; tr. by Mrs. Humphrey Ward, 1892), entry for 17 Dec. 1856.

2 Today, music heralds . . . the establishment of a society of repetition in which nothing will happen anymore.

> JACQUES ATTALI (b. 1943), Algerian-born French economist, writer. *Noise: The Political Economy of Music*, ch. 1 (1977).

3 A verbal art like poetry is reflective; it stops to think. Music is immediate, it goes on to become.

> W. H. AUDEN (1907–73), Anglo-American poet. *The Dyer's Hand*, pt. 8, "Notes on Music and Opera" (1962).

4 The English may not like music, but they absolutely love the noise it makes.

> SIR THOMAS BEECHAM (1879–1961), British conductor. *New York Herald Tribune* (9 March 1961).

5 Great music is that which penetrates the ear with facility and leaves the memory with difficulty. Magical music never leaves the memory.

> SIR THOMAS BEECHAM (1879–1961), British conductor. Quoted in: *Sunday Times* (London, 16 Sept. 1962).

6 It is cruel, you know, that music should be so beautiful. It has the beauty of loneliness & of pain: of strength & freedom. The beauty of disappointment & never-satisfied love. The cruel beauty of nature, & everlasting beauty of monotony.

> BENJAMIN BRITTEN (1913–76), British composer. Letter, 29 June 1937 (published in *Letters from a Life: Letters and Diaries of Benjamin Britten*, vol. 1, "A Working Life," 1991). Britten wrote this while listening to the "Abschied"—the finale of Mahler's song cycle *Das Lied von der Erde*.

7 It is a wise tune that knows its own father, and I like my music to be the legitimate offspring of respectable parents.

> SAMUEL BUTLER (1835–1902), English author. *Samuel Butler's Notebooks* (1951, p. 237).

8 It is better to make a piece of music than to perform one, better to perform one than to listen to one, better to listen to one than to misuse it as a means of distraction, entertainment, or acquisitiuon of "culture."

> JOHN CAGE (1912–92), U.S. composer. "Forerunners of Modern Music; At Random," in *Tiger's Eye* (New York, March 1949; repr. in *Silence*, 1961).

9 Truly fertile Music, the only kind that will move us, that we shall truly appreciate, will be a Music conducive to Dream, which banishes all reason and analysis. One must not wish first to understand and then to feel. Art does not tolerate Reason.

> ALBERT CAMUS (1913–60), French-Algerian philosopher, author. "Essay on Music," in *Sud* (Algiers, June 1932; repr. in *Youthful Writings*, 1976).

10 Alas! all music jars when the soul's out of tune.

> MIGUEL DE CERVANTES (1547–1616), Spanish writer. Altisidora, in *Don Quixote*, pt. 2, bk. 6, ch. 11 (1615; tr. by P. Motteux).

11 All good music resembles something. Good music stirs by its mysterious resemblance to the objects and feelings which motivated it.

> JEAN COCTEAU (1889–1963), French author, filmmaker. *Le*

Rappel àl'Ordre, "Le Coq et l'Arlequin" (1926; repr. in *Collected Works*, vol. 9, 1950).

12 Music has charms to soothe a savage breast,
To soften rocks, or bend a knotted oak.

WILLIAM CONGREVE (1670–1729), English dramatist. Almeria, in *The Mourning Bride*, act 1, sc. 1.

13 The Americans . . . are almost ignorant of the art of music, one of the most elevating, innocent and refining of human tastes, whose influence on the habits and morals of a people is of the most beneficial tendency.

JAMES FENIMORE COOPER (1789–1851), U.S. novelist. *The American Democrat*, "On Civilization" (1838).

14 Nothing separates the generations more than music. By the time a child is eight or nine, he has developed a passion for his own music that is even stronger than his passions for procrastination and weird clothes.

BILL COSBY (b. 1937), U.S. comedian, actor. *Fatherhood*, ch. 10 (1986).

15 Good music is very close to primitive language.

DENIS DIDEROT (1713–84), French philosopher. *Elements of Physiology*, "Correspondence of Ideas with the Motion of Organs" (written 1774–80; published 1875; repr. in *Selected Writings*, ed. by Lester G. Crocker, 1966).

16 Music was invented to confirm human loneliness.

LAWRENCE DURRELL (1912–90), British author. Clea, in *Clea*, ch. 1, sct. 4 (1960).

17 I always seem to have a vague feeling that he is a Satan among musicians, a fallen angel in the darkness who is perpetually seeking to fight his way back to happiness.

HAVELOCK ELLIS (1859–1939), British psychologist. *Impressions and Comments* (1914), entry for 3 Sept. 1913, referring to Beethoven.

18 Perhaps all music, even the newest, is not so much something discovered as something that re-emerges from where it lay buried in the memory, inaudible as a melody cut in a disc of flesh. A composer lets me hear a song that has always been shut up silent within me.

JEAN GENET (1910–86), French playwright, novelist. *Prisoner of Love*, pt. 1 (1986; tr. 1989).

19 Music and dancing (the more's the pity) have become so closely associated with ideas of riot and debauchery among the less cultivated classes, that a taste for them, for their own sakes, can hardly be said to exist, and before they can be recommended as innocent or safe amusements, a very great change of ideas must take place.

SIR JOHN HERSCHEL (1792–1871), English scientist. Quoted in: Ronald Pearsall, *Victorian Popular Music* (1973, p. 199).

20 I am fond of music I think because it is so amoral. Everything else is moral and I am after something that isn't. I have always found moralizing intolerable.

HERMANN HESSE (1877–1962), German novelist, poet. Sinclair, in *Demian*, ch. 5 (1960).

21 It is the stretched soul that makes music, and souls are stretched by the pull of opposites—opposite bents, tastes, yearnings, loyalties. Where there is no polarity—

where energies flow smoothly in one direction—there will be much doing but no music.

ERIC HOFFER (1902–83), U.S. philosopher. *Reflections on the Human Condition*, aph. 108 (1973).

22 It is the only sensual pleasure without vice.

SAMUEL JOHNSON (1709–84), English author, lexicographer. Quoted in: "Anecdotes by William Seward," in *European Magazine* (1795; repr. in *Johnsonian Miscellanies*, vol. 2, ed. by George Birkbeck Hill, 1897, p. 301).

23 Difficult do you call it, Sir? I wish it were impossible.

SAMUEL JOHNSON (1709–84), English author, lexicographer. Quoted in: *Anecdotes of Distinguished Persons*, "Anecdotes by William Seward" (repr. in *Johnsonian Miscellanies*, vol. 2, ed. by George Birkbeck Hill, 1897, p. 308), remarking on a violinist's playing.

24 'Tis the common disease of all your musicians that they know no mean, to be entreated, either to begin or end.

BEN JONSON (1573–1637), English dramatist, poet. Julia, in *The Poetaster*, act 2, sc. 2.

25 Heard melodies are sweet, but those unheard
Are sweeter.

JOHN KEATS (1795–1821), English poet. *Ode on a Grecian Urn*, st. 2.

26 Since music is a language with some meaning at least for the immense majority of mankind, although only a tiny minority of people are capable of formulating a meaning in it, and since it is the only language with the contradictory attributes of being at once intelligible and untranslatable, the musical creator is a being comparable to the gods, and music itself the supreme mystery of the science of man, a mystery that all the various disciplines come up against and which holds the key to their progress.

CLAUDE LÉVI-STRAUSS (b. 1908), French anthropologist. *The Raw and the Cooked*, "Overture" (1964).

27 The musical emotion springs precisely from the fact that at each moment the composer withholds or adds more or less than the listener anticipates on the basis of a pattern that he thinks he can guess, but that he is incapable of wholly divining. . . . If the composer withholds more than we anticipate, we experience a delicious falling sensation; we feel we have been torn from a stable point on the musical ladder and thrust into the void. . . . When the composer withholds less, the opposite occurs: he forces us to perform gymnastic exercises more skillful than our own.

CLAUDE LÉVI-STRAUSS (b. 1908), French anthropologist. *The Raw and the Cooked*, "Overture" (1964).

28 People whose sensibility is destroyed by music in trains, airports, lifts, cannot concentrate on a Beethoven Quartet.

WITOLD LUTOSLAWSKI (b. 1913), Polish composer. *Independent on Sunday* (London, 13 Jan. 1991).

29 A woman's two cents worth is worth two cents in the music business.

LORETTA LYNN (b. 1930), U.S. singer. Quoted in: *Los Angeles Times* (26 May 1974).

30 There is something suspicious about music, gentlemen. I insist that she is, by her nature, equivocal. I shall not be going too far in saying at once that she is politically suspect.

> THOMAS MANN (1875–1955), German author, critic. Herr Settembrini, in *The Magic Mountain*, ch. 4, "Politically Suspect" (1924).

31 Music is a beautiful opiate, if you don't take it too seriously.

> HENRY MILLER (1891–1980), U.S. author. *The Air-Conditioned Nightmare*, "With Edgar Varèse in the Gobi Desert" (1945).

32 Music is spiritual. The music business is not.

> VAN MORRISON (b. 1945), Irish rock musician. *Times* (London, 6 July 1990).

33 Music is your own experience, your own thoughts, your own wisdom. If you don't live it, it won't come out of your horn. They teach you there's a boundary line to music. But, man, there's no boundary line to art.

> CHARLIE PARKER (1920–55), U.S. jazz musician. Quoted in: *Children of Albion: Poetry of the Underground in Britain*, "Afterwords," sct. 3 (ed. by Michael Horovitz, 1969).

34 All art constantly aspires towards the condition of music.

> WALTER PATER (1839–94), English essayist, critic. *Studies in the History of the Renaissance*, "The School of Giorgione" (1873).

35 For the introduction of a new kind of music must be shunned as imperiling the whole state; since styles of music are never disturbed without affecting the most important political institutions.

> PLATO (c. 427–347 B.C.), Greek philosopher. Socrates, in *The Republic*, bk. 4, sct. 424. He continued: "It is here in music that our guardians should erect their guard-house." Adeimantus replied: "At any rate it is here that lawlessness easily creeps in unawares."

36 The author's conviction on this day of New Year is that music begins to atrophy when it departs too far from the dance; that poetry begins to atrophy when it gets too far from music; but this must not be taken as implying that all good music is dance music or all poetry lyric. Bach and Mozart are never too far from physical movement.

> EZRA POUND (1885–1972), U.S. poet, critic. *ABC of Reading*, prefatory "Warning" (1934).

37 There once was a brainy baboon
Who always breathed down a bassoon,
For he said, "It appears
That in billions of years
I shall certainly hit on a tune."

> EZRA POUND (1885–1972), U.S. poet, critic. Letter to Huntingdon Cairns of the National Gallery of Art in Washington, 21 July 1949. Quoted in: Humphrey Carpenter, *A Serious Character*, pt. 2, ch. 16 (1988). Pound took up the bassoon for a few months in 1921.

38 If anyone has conducted a Beethoven performance, and then doesn't have to go to an osteopath, then there's something wrong.

> SIMON RATTLE (b. 1955), British conductor. *Guardian* (London, 31 May 1990).

39 The notes I handle no better than many pianists. But the pauses between the notes—ah, that is where the art resides.

> ARTUR SCHNABEL (1882–1951), German-born U.S. pianist. Quoted in: *Chicago Daily News* (11 June 1958).

41 Is it not strange that sheep's guts should hale souls out of men's bodies?

> WILLIAM SHAKESPEARE (1564–1616), English dramatist, poet. Benedick, in *Much Ado about Nothing*, act 2, sc. 3.

40 The man that hath no music in himself,
Nor is not moved with concord of sweet sounds,
Is fit for treasons, stratagems, and spoils.
The motions of his spirit are dull as night,
And his affections dark as Erebus.
Let no such man be trusted.

> WILLIAM SHAKESPEARE (1564–1616), English dramatist, poet. Lorenzo, in *The Merchant of Venice*, act 5, sc. 1, responding to Jessica's remark, "I am never merry when I hear sweet music."

42 Hell is full of musical amateurs: music is the brandy of the damned.

> GEORGE BERNARD SHAW (1856–1950), Anglo-Irish playwright, critic. Don Juan, in *Man and Superman*, act 3.

43 I think no woman I have had ever gave me so sweet a moment, or at so light a price, as the moment I owe to a newly heard musical phrase.

> STENDHAL (1783–1842), French author. Letter, 29 Oct. 1808, to his sister Pauline.

44 They said, "You have a blue guitar,
You do not play things as they are."
The man replied, "Things as they are
Are changed upon a blue guitar."

> WALLACE STEVENS (1879–1955), U.S. poet. *The Man with the Blue Guitar*.

45 The most perfect expression of human behavior is a string quartet.

> JEFFREY TATE (b. 1943), British conductor. *New Yorker* (30 April 1990).

46 Music is the effort we make to explain to ourselves how our brains work. We listen to Bach transfixed because this is listening to a human mind.

> LEWIS THOMAS (b. 1913), U.S. physician, educator. *The Medusa and the Snail*, "On Thinking about Thinking" (1979).

47 We all drew on the comfort which is given out by the major works of Mozart, which is as real and material as the warmth given up by a glass of brandy.

> REBECCA WEST (1892–1983), British author. *Black Lamb and Grey Falcon*, "Serbia" (1942).

48 Musical people are so absurdly unreasonable. They always want one to be perfectly dumb at the very moment when one is longing to be absolutely deaf.

> OSCAR WILDE (1854–1900), Anglo-Irish playwright, author. Mabel Chiltern, in *An Ideal Husband*, act 2.

49 There's a basic rule which runs through all kinds of music, kind of an unwritten rule. I don't know what it is. But I've got it.

> RON WOOD (b. 1947), British rock musician. *Independent* (London, 10 Sept. 1992).

50 Hearing often-times
The still, sad music of humanity,
Nor harsh nor grating, though of ample power
To chasten and subdue.

WILLIAM WORDSWORTH (1770–1850), English poet. *Lines Composed a Few Miles above Tintern Abbey.*

51 Music, in performance, is a type of sculpture. The air in the performance is sculpted into something.

FRANK ZAPPA (b. 1940), U.S. rock musician. *The Real Frank Zappa Book*, ch. 8 (1989; written with Peter Occhiogrosso).

52 The manner in which Americans "consume" music has a lot to do with leaving it on their coffee tables, or using it as wallpaper for their lifestyles, like the score of a movie—it's consumed that way without any regard for how and why it's made.

FRANK ZAPPA (b. 1940), U.S. rock musician. Interview in: *The Real Frank Zappa Book*, ch. 11 (1989; written with Peter Occhiogrosso).

See also Pater on ART; Stravinsky on CINEMA; OPERA; POPULAR MUSIC; RAP MUSIC; ROCK 'N' ROLL; SONG; Simon on SPONTANEITY; Bernstein on TECHNIQUE; Zappa on TIME.

MUSIC COMPOSITION

1 In writing songs I've learned as much from Cézanne as I have from Woody Guthrie.

BOB DYLAN (b. 1941), U.S. singer, songwriter. Quoted in: Clinton Heylin, *Dylan: Behind the Shades*, ch. 25 (1991).

2 A nation creates music—the composer only arranges it.

MIKHAIL GLINKA (1804–57), Russian composer. Quoted in: *Theatre Arts Magazine* (New York, June 1958).

3 Composing a piece of music is very feminine. It is sensitive, emotional, contemplative. By comparison, doing housework is positively masculine.

BARBARA KOLB (b. 1939), U.S. composer. Quoted in: *Time* (10 Nov. 1975).

4 Songwriting is about getting the demon out of me. It's like being possessed. You try to go to sleep, but the song won't let you. So you have to get up and make it into something, and then you're allowed to sleep. It's always in the middle of the bloody night, or when you're half-awake or tired, when your critical faculties are switched off. So letting go is what the whole game is. Every time you try to put your finger on it, it slips away. You turn on the lights and the cockroaches run away. You can never grasp them.

JOHN LENNON (1940–80), British rock musician. *Playboy* (Chicago, Sept. 1980).

5 Before I compose a piece, I walk around it several times, accompanied by myself.

ERIK SATIE (1866–1925), French composer, pianist. *Bulletin des Éditions Musicales* (Paris, Dec. 1913). Quoted in: Alan M. Gillmor, *Erik Satie*, ch. 5 (1988).

6 A composer is a guy who goes around forcing his will on unsuspecting air molecules, often with the assistance of unsuspecting musicians.

FRANK ZAPPA (b. 1940), U.S. rock musician. *The Real Frank Zappa Book*, ch. 8 (1989; written with Peter Occhiogrosso).

MUSLIMS

See ISLAM AND THE MUSLIMS.

MYSTICS AND MYSTICISM

1 The mystic purchases a moment of exhilaration with a lifetime of confusion; and the confusion is infectious and destructive. It is confusing and destructive to try and explain anything in terms of anything else, poetry in terms of psychology.

BASIL BUNTING (1900–1985), British poet. Letter, Sept. 1932, to poet Louis Zukofsky. Quoted in: Victoria Forde, *The Poetry of Basil Bunting*, ch. 2 (1991).

2 The most beautiful emotion we can experience is the mystical. It is the power of all true art and science. He to whom this emotion is a stranger, who can no longer wonder and stand rapt in awe, is as good as dead. To know that what is impenetrable to us really exists, manifesting itself as the highest wisdom and the most radiant beauty, which our dull faculties can comprehend only in their most primitive forms—this knowledge, this feeling, is at the center of true religiousness. In this sense, and in this sense only, I belong to the rank of devoutly religious men.

ALBERT EINSTEIN (1879–1955), German-born U.S. theoretical physicist. Quoted in: Philipp Frank, *Einstein: His Life and Times*, ch. 12, sct. 5 (1947).

3 One does not become a guru by accident.

JAMES FENTON (b. 1949), British poet, critic. *Times* (London, 9 Aug. 1984), referring to playwright Samuel Beckett.

4 Uncontrolled, the hunger and thirst after God may become an obstacle, cutting off the soul from what it desires. If a man would travel far along the mystic road, he must learn to desire God intensely but in stillness, passively and yet with all his heart and mind and strength.

ALDOUS HUXLEY (1894–1963), British author. *Grey Eminence*, ch. 9 (1941).

5 We follow the mystics. They know where they are going. They, too, go astray, but when they go astray they do so in a way that is mystical, dark, and mysterious.

RYSZARD KAPUSCINSKI (b. 1932), Polish journalist. "A Warsaw Diary" in *Granta*, no. 15 (Cambridge, England, 1985).

6 Just as in earthly life lovers long for the moment when they are able to breathe forth their love for each other, to let their souls blend in a soft whisper, so the mystic longs for the moment when in prayer he can, as it were, creep into God.

SØREN KIERKEGAARD (1813–1855), Danish philosopher. *Either/Or*, vol. 2, "Balance between Esthetic and Ethical" (1843; tr. 1987).

7 Mysticism and exaggeration go together. A mystic must not fear ridicule if he is to push all the way to the limits of humility or the limits of delight.

MILAN KUNDERA (b. 1929), Czech author, critic. *The Book of Laughter and Forgetting*, pt. 3, ch. 2 (1978; tr. 1980).

8 What does mysticism really mean? It means the

way to attain knowledge. It's close to philosophy, except in philosophy you go horizontally while in mysticism you go vertically.

ELIE WIESEL (b. 1928), Rumanian-born U.S. writer. Interview in *Writers at Work* (Eighth Series, ed. by George Plimpton, 1988).

9   Mysticism has been in the past & probably ever will be one of the great powers of the world & it is bad scholarship to pretend the contrary. You may argue against it but you should no more treat it with disrespect than a perfectly cultivated writer would treat (say) the Catholic Church or the Church of Luther no matter how much he disliked them.

W. B. YEATS (1865–1939), Irish poet, playwright. Letter, 10 Oct. 1893, to author Laurence Housman (published in *Collected Letters*, vol. 1, ed. by John Kelly, 1986). In an earlier letter (23 July 1892), Yeats had written: "The mystical life is the centre of all that I do & all that I think & all that I write. . . . I have always considered myself a voice of what I believe to be a greater renaissance—the revolt of the soul against the intellect."

MYTH

1   Myth is neither a lie nor a confession: it is an inflexion.

ROLAND BARTHES (1915–80), French semiologist. *Mythologies*, "Myth Today: Reading and Deciphering Myth" (1957; tr. 1972).

2   Myth is the hidden part of every story, the buried part, the region that is still unexplored because there are as yet no words to enable us to get there. . . . Myth is nourished by silence as well as by words.

ITALO CALVINO (1923–85), Italian author, critic. "Cybernetics and Ghosts," lecture, Nov. 1969, Turin (published in *The Literature Machine*, 1987).

3   There is nothing truer than myth: history, in its attempt to "realize" myth, distorts it, stops halfway; when history claims to have "succeeded," this is nothing but humbug and mystification. Everything we dream is "realizable." Reality does not have to be: it is simply what it is.

EUGÈNE IONESCO (b. 1912), Rumanian-born French playwright. "Experience of the Theatre," in *Nouvelle N.R.F*, no. 62 (Paris, 1958; repr. in *Notes and Counter Notes*, 1962).

4   The great enemy of the truth is very often not the lie—deliberate, contrived and dishonest—but the myth—persistent, persuasive and unrealistic.

JOHN F. KENNEDY (1917–63), U.S. Democratic politician, president. Commencement address, 11 June 1962, Yale University, New Haven, Conn.

5   Myth is an attempt to narrate a whole human experience, of which the purpose is too deep, going too deep in the blood and soul, for mental explanation or description.

D. H. LAWRENCE (1885–1930), British author. "Introduction to *The Dragon of the Apocalypse* by Frederick Carter," in *London Mercury* (July 1930; repr. in *Phoenix: The Posthumous Papers of D. H. Lawrence*, pt. 4, ed. by E. McDonald, 1936). Carter's book eventually appeared under a different title and without Lawrence's introduction.

6   I therefore claim to show, not how men think in myths, but how myths operate in men's minds without their being aware of the fact.

CLAUDE LÉVI-STRAUSS (b. 1908), French anthropologist. *The Raw and the Cooked*, "Overture," sct. 1 (1964).

7   It is a sure sign that a culture has reached a dead end when it is no longer intrigued by its myths.

GREIL MARCUS (b. 1945), U.S. rock journalist. *Mystery Train*, "Elvis: Presliad" (1976).

8   The primary function of myth is to validate an existing social order. Myth enshrines conservative social values, raising tradition on a pedestal. It expresses and confirms, rather than explains or questions, the sources of cultural attitudes and values. . . . Because myth anchors the present in the past it is a sociological charter for a future society which is an exact replica of the present one.

ANN OAKLEY (b. 1944), British sociologist, author. *Woman's Work: The Housewife, Past and Present*, ch. 7 (1974).

9   Myths which are believed in tend to become true.

GEORGE ORWELL (1903–50), British author. "The English People" (1944; repr. in *The Collected Essays, Journalism and Letters of George Orwell*, vol. 3, ed. by Sonia Orwell and Ian Angus, 1968).

10   Sometimes legends make reality, and become more useful than the facts.

SALMAN RUSHDIE (b. 1947), Indian-born British author. *Midnight's Children*, bk. 1, "Hit-the-spittoon" (1981).

11   All the great things have been denied and we live in an intricacy of new and local mythologies, political, economic, poetic, which are asserted with an ever-enlarging incoherence.

WALLACE STEVENS (1879–1955), U.S. poet. *The Necessary Angel*, "The Noble Rider and the Sound of Words" (1951; first published 1942).

12   The poets were not alone in sanctioning myths, for long before the poets the states and the lawmakers had sanctioned them as a useful expedient. . . . They needed to control the people by superstitious fears, and these cannot be aroused without myths and marvels.

STRABO (c. 58 B.C.-c. 24 A.D.), Greek geographer. *Geographia*, bk. 1, sct. 2, subsct. 8.

13   Myths and legends die hard in America. We love them for the extra dimension they provide, the illusion of near-infinite possibility to erase the narrow confines of most men's reality. Weird heroes and mould-breaking champions exist as living proof to those who need it that the tyranny of "the rat race" is not yet final.

HUNTER S. THOMPSON (b. 1939), U.S. journalist. "Those Daring Young Men in their Flying Machines . . . Ain't What They Used to Be!" in *Pageant* (Sept. 1969; repr. in *The Great Shark Hunt*, pt. 3, 1979).

14   One may as well preach a respectable mythology as anything else.

MRS. HUMPHREY WARD (1851–1920), British novelist. Edward Langham, in *Robert Elsmere*, bk. 1, ch. 5 (1888)

See also Don DeLillo on The UNITED STATES

NAGGING

1   Mrs. Van Daan's grizzling is absolutely unbearable; now she can't any longer drive us crazy over the invasion, she nags us the whole day long about the bad weather. It really would be nice to dump her in a bucket of cold water and put her up in the loft.

> ANNE FRANK (1929–45), German Jewish refugee, diarist. *The Diary of a Young Girl* (1947; tr. 1952), entry for 9 June 1944, referring to a fellow refugee in the "secret Annex" in Amsterdam.

2   Naggers always know what they are doing. They weigh up the risks, then they go on and on and on until they get what they want or until they get punched.

> JOOLS HOLLAND (b. 1958), British rock musician, television broadcaster. Quoted in: *Independent on Sunday* (London, 4 Oct. 1992).

3   Nagging is the repetition of unpalatable truths.

> EDITH, LADY SUMMERSKILL (1901–80), British Labour politician. Speech, 14 July 1960, to Married Women's Association, House of Commons, London.

NAÏVETÉ

1   Naïveté in grownups is often charming; but when coupled with vanity it is indistinguishable from stupidity.

> ERIC HOFFER (1902–83), U.S. philosopher. *The Passionate State of Mind*, aph. 269 (1955).

2   A child-like man is not a man whose development has been arrested; on the contrary, he is a man who has given himself a chance of continuing to develop long after most adults have muffled themselves in the cocoon of middle-aged habit and convention.

> ALDOUS HUXLEY (1894–1963), British author. "Vulgarity in Literature" (1930; repr. in *Music at Night and Other Essays*, 1949).

3   The fact is that we all seem capable of living, because at some time or other we have taken refuge in a lie, in blindness, in enthusiasm, in optimism, in some conviction, in pessimism or something of the sort. He has never taken refuge in anything. He is absolutely incapable of lying. . . . He has nothing to take refuge in, no shelter. It's as if he were naked and everyone else had clothes on.

> MILENA JESENSKÁ (1896–1944), Czech translator, political journalist. Letter to Max Brod, referring to Franz Kafka. Quoted in: Margarete Buber-Neumann, *Milena*, ch. 7 (1989).

NAMES

1   Proper names are poetry in the raw. Like all poetry they are untranslatable.

> W. H. AUDEN (1907–73), Anglo-American poet. *A Certain World*, "Names, Proper" (1970).

2   Miss. A title with which we brand unmarried women to indicate that they are in the market. Miss, Missis (Mrs.) and Mister (Mr.) are the three most distinctly disagreeable words in the language, in sound and sense. Two are corruptions of Mistress, the other of Master. . . . If we must have them, let us be consistent and give one to the unmarried man. I venture to suggest Mush, abbreviated to Mh.

> AMBROSE BIERCE (1842–1914), U.S. author. *The Devil's Dictionary* (1881–1906).

3   In real life, unlike in Shakespeare, the sweetness of the rose depends upon the name it bears. Things are not only what they are. They are, in very important respects, what they seem to be.

> HUBERT H. HUMPHREY (1911–78), U.S. Democratic politician, vice president. Speech, 26 March 1966, Washington, D.C.

4   These names: gay, queer, homosexual are limiting. I would love to finish with them. We're going to have to decide which terms to use and where we use them. . . . For me to use the word "queer" is a liberation; it was a word that frightened me, but no longer.

> DEREK JARMAN (b. 1942), British filmmaker, artist, author. *At Your Own Risk: A Saint's Testament*, "1950's" (1992).

5   To name oneself is the first act of both the poet and the revolutionary. When we take away the right to an individual name, we symbolically take away the right to be an individual. Immigration officials did this to refugees; husbands routinely do it to wives.

> ERICA JONG (b. 1942), U.S. author. *How to Save Your Own Life*, "My Posthumous Life. . ." Epigraph (1977).

6   I think a child should be allowed to take his father's or mother's name at will on coming of age. Paternity is a legal fiction.

> JAMES JOYCE (1882–1941), Irish author. Letter, 18 Sept. 1905, to his brother Stanislaus (published in *Selected Letters*, ed. by Richard Ellmann, 1975).

7   I shall write a book some day about the appropriateness of names. Geoffrey Chaucer has a ribald ring, as is proper and correct, and Alexander Pope was inevitably Alexander Pope. Colley Cibber was a silly little man without much elegance and Shelley was very Percy and very Bysshe.

> JAMES JOYCE (1882–1941), Irish author. Quoted in: Frederic Prokosch, *Voices: A Memoir*, "At Sylvia's" (1983). Joyce was replying to a question from the young author and poet Prokosch, "What do you think of Virginia Woolf?" Joyce answered that it was "an impressive name . . . she married her wolfish husband purely in order to change her name. Virginia Stephens is not a name for an exploratory authoress."

8   We don't know when our name came into being or how some distant ancestor acquired it. We don't understand our name at all, we don't know its history and yet we bear it with exalted fidelity, we merge with it, we like it, we are ridiculously proud of it as if we had thought it up ourselves in a moment of brilliant inspiration.

> MILAN KUNDERA (b. 1929), Czech author, critic. Agnes, in *Immortality*, pt. 1, ch. 7 (1991).

9   I don't like your miserable lonely single "front name." It is so limited, so meagre; it has no versatility; it is weighted down with the sense of responsibility; it is worn threadbare with much use; it is as bad as having only one jacket and one hat; it is like having only one relation, one blood relation, in the world. Never set a child afloat on the flat sea of life with only one sail to catch the wind.

> D. H. LAWRENCE (1885–1930), British author. Letter, 13 May

1908 (published in *The Letters of D. H. Lawrence,* vol. 1, ed. by James T. Boulton, 1979). Lawrence added, "I am called Bertie, Bert, David, Herbert, Billy, William and Dick; I am a full-rigged schooner; I have a wardrobe as complete as the man's-about-town."

10 I sometimes think I was born to live up to my name. How could I be anything else but what I am having been named Madonna? I would either have ended up a nun or this.

MADONNA (b. 1959), U.S. singer, actor. *Vanity Fair* (April 1991). Madonna Ciccone was named after her mother.

11 The name of a man is a numbing blow from which he never recovers.

MARSHALL MCLUHAN (1911–80), Canadian communications theorist. *Understanding Media,* ch. 2 (1964).

12 I came to live in a country I love; some people label me a defector. I have loved men and women in my life; I've been labelled "the bisexual defector" in print. Want to know another secret? I'm even ambidextrous. I don't like labels. Just call me Martina.

MARTINA NAVRATILOVA (b. 1956), Czech-born U.S. tennis player. *Martina Navratilova—Being Myself,* ch. 1 (1985).

13 Names, once they are in common use, quickly become mere sounds, their etymology being buried, like so many of the earth's marvels, beneath the dust of habit.

SALMAN RUSHDIE (b. 1947), Indian-born British author. *The Satanic Verses,* "Ayesha" (1988).

14 A name pronounced is the recognition of the individual to whom it belongs. He who can pronounce my name aright, he can call me, and is entitled to my love and service.

HENRY DAVID THOREAU (1817–62), U.S. philosopher, author, naturalist. *A Week on the Concord and Merrimack Rivers,* "Wednesday" (1849).

15 If the fairest features of the landscape are to be named after men, let them be the noblest and worthiest men alone.

HENRY DAVID THOREAU (1817–62), U.S. philosopher, author, naturalist. *Walden,* "The Ponds" (1854).

16 It is a sad truth, but we have lost the faculty of giving lovely names to things. Names are everything. I never quarrel with actions. My one quarrel is with words. . . . The man who could call a spade a spade should be compelled to use one. It is the only thing he is fit for.

OSCAR WILDE (1854–1900), Anglo-Irish playwright, author. Lord Henry, in *The Picture of Dorian Gray,* ch. 17 (1891).

See also Cheever on DIVORCE; Berger on NATIONALISM.

NAMES: NICKNAMES

1 A nickname is the heaviest stone that the devil can throw at a man. It is a bugbear to the imagination, and, though we do not believe in it, it still haunts our apprehensions.

WILLIAM HAZLITT (1778–1830), English essayist. *Sketches and Essays,* "On Nicknames" (1839).

2 In its purest sense, nicknaming is an elitist ritual practiced by those who cherish hierarchy. For preppies it's a smoke signal that allows Bunny to tell Pooky that they belong to the same tribe, while among the good ole boys it serves the cause of masculine dominance by identifying Bear and Wrecker as Alpha males.

FLORENCE KING (b. 1936), U.S. author. *Reflections in a Jaundiced Eye,* "Democracy" (1989).

NAPOLEON BONAPARTE

1 He looked as if he wished to rive new war material out of the wombs of the mothers.

ANONYMOUS. Quoted in: Ellen Key, *War, Peace and the Future,* ch. 9 (1916).

2 Napoleon never wished to be justified. He killed his enemy according to Corsican traditions [*le droit corse*] and if he sometimes regretted his mistake, he never understood that it had been a crime.

GUILLAUME-PROSPER, BARON DE BARANTE (1782–1866), French diplomat. *Souvenirs,* vol. 7 (1865), of the execution of the Duc d'Enghien, 1804.

3 Napoleon has not been conquered by men. He was greater than any of us. God punished him because he relied solely on his own intelligence until that incredible instrument was so strained that it broke.

JEAN BAPTISTE BERNADOTTE (1763–1844), French general, king of Sweden (1818–44). Speech, 1821, on hearing of the death of Napoleon, his former commander.

4 Napoleon is a torrent which as yet we are unable to stem. Moscow will be the sponge that will suck him dry.

MIKHAIL KUTUZOV (1745–1813), Russian general. Speech, 13 Sept. 1812, to the Russian army commanders at Fili, the day before Napoleon entered Moscow, which he was obliged to abandon a month later.

5 I am the successor, not of Louis XVI, but of Charlemagne.

NAPOLEON BONAPARTE (1769–1821), French general, emperor. Remark, 2 Dec. 1804, to Pope Pius VII in Paris, on Napoleon's coronation as emperor of France.

6 France has more need of me than I have need of France.

NAPOLEON BONAPARTE (1769–1821), French general, emperor. Speech, 31 Dec. 1813, to Corps Législatif, Paris.

See also Shelley on VEGETARIANISM.

NARCISSISM

1 Narcissus does not fall in love with his reflection because it is beautiful, but because it is *his.* If it were his beauty that enthralled him, he would be set free in a few years by its fading.

W. H. AUDEN (1907–73), Anglo-American poet. *The Dyer's Hand,* pt. 3, "Hic et Ille," sct. A (1962).

2 As individuals and as a nation, we now suffer from social narcissism. The beloved Echo of our ancestors, the virgin America, has been abandoned. We have fallen in love with our own image, with images of our making, which turn out to be images of ourselves.

> DANIEL J. BOORSTIN (b. 1914), U.S. historian. *The Image*, ch. 6 (1961).

3   Nobody can be kinder than the narcissist while you react to life in his own terms.

> ELIZABETH BOWEN (1899–1973), Anglo-Irish novelist. *The Death of the Heart*, pt. 3, ch. 3 (1938).

4   Self-love for ever creeps out, like a snake, to sting anything which happens . . . to stumble upon it.

> LORD BYRON (1788–1824), English poet. *Ravenna Journal* (published in *Byron's Letters and Journals*, vol. 8, ed. by Leslie A. Marchand, 1973–81), entry for 11 Jan. 1821.

5   It is possible to have a strong self-love without any self-satisfaction, rather with a self-discontent which is the more intense because one's own little core of egoistic sensibility is a supreme care.

> GEORGE ELIOT (1819–80), English novelist, editor. *Daniel Deronda*, bk. 1, ch. 2 (1876).

6   Self-love is often rather arrogant than blind; it does not hide our faults from ourselves, but persuades us that they escape the notice of others.

> SAMUEL JOHNSON (1709–84), English author, lexicographer. *Rambler*, no. 155 (London, 10 Sept. 1751; repr. in *Works of Samuel Johnson*, vol. 5, ed. by W. J. Bate and Albrecht B. Strauss, 1969).

7   Self-love depressed becomes self-loathing.

> SALLY KEMPTON (b. 1943), U.S. author. "Cutting Loose," in *Esquire* (New York, July 1970).

8   He who is enamored of himself will at least have the advantage of being inconvenienced by few rivals.

> G. C. LICHTENBERG (1742–99), German physicist, philosopher. *Aphorisms*, "Notebook H," aph. 10 (written 1765–99; tr. by R. J. Hollingdale, 1990).

9   Self-love seems so often unrequited.

> ANTHONY POWELL (b. 1905), British novelist. The narrator (Nicholas Jenkins), in *The Acceptance World*, ch. 1 (1955).

10   Narcissist: psychoanalytic term for the person who loves himself more than his analyst; considered to be the manifestation of a dire mental disease whose successful treatment depends on the patient learning to love the analyst more and himself less.

> THOMAS SZASZ (b. 1920), U.S. psychiatrist. *The Second Sin*, "Psychoanalysis" (1973).

11   Had we not loved ourselves at all, we could never have been obliged to love anything. So that self-love is the basis of all love.

> THOMAS TRAHERNE (1636–74), English clergyman, poet, mystic. *Centuries*, "Fourth Century," no. 55 (written c. 1672; published 1908).

12   A narcissist is someone better looking than you are.

> GORE VIDAL (b. 1925), U.S. novelist, critic. Quoted in: *San Francisco Chronicle* (12 April 1981).

13   It is not love that should be depicted as blind, but self-love.

> VOLTAIRE (1694–1778), French philosopher, author. Letter, 11 May 1764.

14   I dote on myself, there is that lot of me and all so luscious.

> WALT WHITMAN (1819–92), U.S. poet. *Song of Myself*, sct. 24, in *Leaves of Grass* (1855).

15   To love oneself is the beginning of a life-long romance.

> OSCAR WILDE N1854–1900), Anglo-Irish playwright, author. Lord Goring, in *An Ideal Husband*, act 3. The quip had already appeared in *Phrases and Philosophies for the Use of the Young*, in *Chameleon* (London, Dec. 1894).

THE NATIONAL DEBT

1   Solvency is maintained by means of a national debt, on the principle, "If you will not lend me the money, how can I pay you?

> RALPH WALDO EMERSON (1803–82), U.S. essayist, poet, philosopher. *English Traits*, "Ability" (1856).

2   A national debt, if it is not excessive, will be to us a national blessing.

> ALEXANDER HAMILTON (1757–1804), U.S. statesman. Letter, 30 April 1781. Later, as secretary of the treasury (1789–95), Hamilton sponsored legislation to pay off the debt of the Continental Congress, and to charter the short-lived Bank of the United States.

3   On 16 September 1985, when the Commerce Department announced that the United States had become a debtor nation, the American Empire died.

> GORE VIDAL (b. 1925), U.S. novelist, critic. *Armageddon? Essays 1983–1987*, "The Day the American Empire Ran out of Gas" (1987).

See also Cobbett on TAXATION.

NATIONALISM

1   Patriotism is a lively sense of collective responsibility. Nationalism is a silly cock crowing on its own dunghill and calling for larger spurs and brighter beaks. I fear that nationalism is one of England's many spurious gifts to the world.

> RICHARD ALDINGTON (1892–1962), British author. Purfleet, in *The Colonel's Daughter*, pt. 1, ch. 6 (1931).

2   All nationalisms are at heart deeply concerned with names: with the most immaterial and original human invention. Those who dismiss names as a detail have never been displaced; but the peoples on the peripheries are always being displaced. That is why they insist upon their continuity—their links with their dead and the unborn.

> JOHN BERGER (b. 1926), British author, critic. "The Soul and the Operator," in *Expressen* (Stockholm, 19 March 1990; repr. in *Keeping a Rendezvous*, 1992).

3   It is a well-known fact that we always recognize our homeland when we are about to lose it.

> ALBERT CAMUS (1913–60), French-Algerian philosopher, author. "Summer in Algiers," in *Nuptials* (1939; repr. in *Selected Essays and Notebooks*, ed. and tr. by Philip Thody, 1970).

4   Historians are to nationalism what poppy-growers

in Pakistan are to heroin-addicts: we supply the essential raw material for the market.

E. J. HOBSBAWM (b. 1917), British historian. Lecture to the American Anthropological Association (published in *Anthropology Today*, Feb. 1992).

5 Nationalist pride, like other variants of pride, can be a substitute for self-respect.

ERIC HOFFER (1902–83), U.S. philosopher. *The Passionate State of Mind,* aph. 38 (1955).

6 Pervading nationalism imposes its dominion on man today in many different forms and with an aggressiveness that spares no one. . . . The challenge that is already with us is the temptation to accept as true freedom what in reality is only a new form of slavery.

JOHN PAUL II [KAROL WOJTYLA] (b. 1920), Polish ecclesiastic, Pope. Address, 29 Sept. 1979, Dublin, Ireland.

7 All the isms are wasms—except one, the most powerful ism of this century, indeed, of the entire democratic age, which is nationalism.

JOHN LUKACS (b. 1924), Hungarian-born U.S. historian. "The Stirrings of History," in *Harper's* (New York, Aug. 1990).

8 Without Country you have neither name, token, voice, nor rights, no admission as brothers into the fellowship of the Peoples. You are the bastards of Humanity. Soldiers without a banner, Israelites among the nations, you will find neither faith nor protection; none will be sureties for you. Do not beguile yourselves with the hope of emancipation from unjust social conditions if you do not first conquer a Country for yourselves.

GIUSEPPE MAZZINI (1805–72), Italian nationalist leader. *The Duties of Man,* ch. 5 (1844–58; tr. 1907).

9 It is humiliating to remain with our hands folded while others write history. It matters little who wins. To make a people great it is necessary to send them to battle even if you have to kick them in the pants. That is what I shall do.

BENITO MUSSOLINI (1883–1945), Italian dictator. Said to his son-in-law and minister for foreign affairs, Count Galeazzo Ciano. Quoted in: Ciano, *Diario 1939–1943* (1946), entry for 11 April 1940. Mussolini declared war on 10 June 1940.

10 Nationalism is power hunger tempered by self-deception.

GEORGE ORWELL (1903–50), British author. *Notes on Nationalism* (1945; repr. in *Collected Essays,* 1961).

11 No man has a right to fix the boundary of the march of a nation; no man has a right to say to his country, "Thus far shalt thou go and no further."

CHARLES STEWART PARNELL (1846–91), Irish nationalist politician. Speech, 21 Jan. 1885, Cork, Ireland.

12 Nations whose nationalism is destroyed are subject to ruin.

COLONEL MUAMMAR QADDAFI (b. 1938), Libyan leader. *The Green Book,* pt. 3, "The Social Basis of the Third Universal Theory" (1976–79).

NATIONS

1 In every particular state of the world, those nations which are strongest tend to prevail over the others; and in certain marked peculiarities the strongest tend to be the best.

WALTER BAGEHOT (1826–77), English economist, critic. *Physics and Politics,* ch. 2, sct. 1 (1872).

2 Righteousness exalteth a nation: but sin is a reproach to any people.

BIBLE, HEBREW. *Proverbs* 14:34.

3 Nations, like men, have their infancy.

HENRY ST. JOHN, VISCOUNT BOLINGBROKE (1678–1751), English politician, author. *On the Study and Uses of History,* Letter 4 (1752).

4 A country grows in history not only because of the heroism of its troops on the field of battle, it grows also when it turns to justice and to right for the conservation of its interests.

ARISTIDE BRIAND (1862–1932), French prime minister. Speech, 10 Sept. 1926, in Geneva, welcoming Germany into the League of Nations.

5 A nation is not conquered which is perpetually to be conquered.

EDMUND BURKE (1729–97), Irish philosopher, statesman. Speech, 22 March 1775, on conciliation with America.

6 A strong nation, like a strong person, can afford to be gentle, firm, thoughtful, and restrained. It can afford to extend a helping hand to others. It's a weak nation, like a weak person, that must behave with bluster and boasting and rashness and other signs of insecurity.

JIMMY CARTER (b. 1924), U.S. Democratic politician, president. Speech, 14 Oct. 1976, New York City.

7 I do not call the sod under my feet my country; but language—religion—government—blood—identity in these makes men of one country.

SAMUEL TAYLOR COLERIDGE (1772–1834), English poet, critic. *Table Talk,* 27 May 1830, in *Specimens of the Table Talk of Samuel Taylor Coleridge* (ed. by Henry Nelson Coleridge, 1835; repr. in *Collected Works,* vol. 14, ed. by Kathleen Coburn, 1990).

8 Nations have always good reasons for being what they are, and the best of all is that they cannot be otherwise.

MARQUIS DE CUSTINE (1790–1857), French traveler, author. *Empire of the Czar: A Journey Through Eternal Russia,* ch. 37 (1843; rev. 1989).

9 The wealth and prosperity of the country are only the comeliness of the body, the fullness of the flesh and fat; but the spirit is independent of them; it requires only muscle, bone and nerve for the true exercise of its functions. We cannot lose our liberty, because we cannot cease to think.

SIR HUMPHRY DAVY (1778–1829), English chemist, physicist. Letter, 28 Aug. 1807.

10 Nationality is the miracle of political independence; race is the principle of physical analogy.

BENJAMIN DISRAELI (1804–81), English statesman, author. Speech, 9 Aug. 1848, to House of Commons.

11 Shall we then judge a country by the majority, or by the minority? By the minority, surely. 'Tis pedantry to estimate nations by the census, or by square miles of land, or other than by their importance to the mind of the time.

RALPH WALDO EMERSON (1803–82), U.S. essayist, poet, philosopher. *The Conduct of Life,* "Considerations by the Way" (1860).

12 The principle of all sovereignty resides essentially in the nation.

FRENCH NATIONAL ASSEMBLY. *Declaration of the Rights of Man* (Sept. 1791).

13 In the true sense one's native land, with its background of tradition, early impressions, reminiscences and other things dear to one, is not enough to make sensitive human beings feel at home.

EMMA GOLDMAN (1869–1940), U.S. anarchist. "The Individual, Society and the State" (published c. 1940; repr. in *Red Emma Speaks,* pt. 1, ed. by Alix Kates Shulman, 1972).

14 If nations always moved from one set of furnished rooms to another—and always into a better set—things might be easier, but the trouble is that there is no one to prepare the new rooms. The future is worse than the ocean—there is nothing there. It will be what men and circumstances make it.

ALEXANDER HERZEN (1812–70), Russian journalist, political thinker. *From the Other Shore,* ch. 3 (1849).

15 Nations without a past are contradictions in terms. What makes a nation *is* the past, what justifies one nation against others is the past, and historians are the people who produce it.

E. J. HOBSBAWM (b. 1917), British historian. Lecture to the American Anthropological Association (published in *Anthropology Today,* Feb. 1992).

16 Nations, like stars, are entitled to eclipse. All is well, provided the light returns and the eclipse does not become endless night. Dawn and resurrection are synonymous. The reappearance of the light is the same as the survival of the soul.

VICTOR HUGO (1802–85), French poet, dramatist, novelist. *Les Misérables,* pt. 5, bk. 1, ch. 20 (1862).

17 The history of any nation follows an undulatory course. In the trough of the wave we find more or less complete anarchy; but the crest is not more or less complete Utopia, but only, at best, a tolerably humane, partially free and fairly just society that invariably carries within itself the seeds of its own decadence.

ALDOUS HUXLEY (1894–1963), British author. *Grey Eminence,* ch. 10 (1941).

18 A nation is the same people living in the same place.

JAMES JOYCE (1882–1941), Irish author. Leopold Bloom, in *Ulysses,* ch. 12 (1922).

19 A people always ends by resembling its shadow.

RUDYARD KIPLING (1865–1936), British author, poet. Said to author and critic André Maurois c. 1930, on the subject of the transformation of Germany. Quoted in: Maurois, *The Art of Writing,* "The Writer's Craft," sct. 2 (1960).

20 The great nations have always acted like gangsters, and the small nations like prostitutes.

STANLEY KUBRICK (b. 1928), U.S. filmmaker. Quoted in: *Guardian* (London, 5 June 1963).

21 God how I hate new countries: They are older than the old, more sophisticated, much more conceited, only young in a certain puerile vanity more like senility than anything.

D. H. LAWRENCE (1885–1930), British author. Letter, 30 May 1922, written from Australia (published in *The Letters of D. H. Lawrence,* vol. 4, ed. by James T. Boulton, E. Mansfield, and W. Roberts, 1987).

22 States that rise quickly, just as all the other things of nature that are born and grow rapidly, cannot have roots and ramifications; the first bad weather kills them.

NICCOLÒ MACHIAVELLI (1469–1527), Italian political philosopher, statesman. *The Prince,* ch. 4 (1514).

23 A Country is not a mere territory; the particular territory is only its foundation. The Country is the idea which rises upon that foundation; it is the sentiment of love, the sense of fellowship which binds together all the sons of that territory.

GIUSEPPE MAZZINI (1805–72), Italian nationalist leader. *The Duties of Man,* ch. 5 (1844–58; tr. 1907).

24 Methinks I see in my mind a noble and puissant nation rousing herself like a strong man after sleep, and shaking her invincible locks. Methinks I see her as an eagle mewing her mighty youth, and kindling her undazzled eyes at the full midday beam.

JOHN MILTON (1608–74), English poet. *Areopagitica: A Speech for the Liberty of Unlicensed Printing to the Parliament of England* (1644).

25 Without a country, I am not a man.

NAWAF AL-NASIR AL-SABAH, Grandnephew of the Emir of Kuwait. Quoted in: *Guardian* (London, 9 Aug. 1990).

26 If there be no nobility of descent in a nation, all the more indispensable is it that there should be nobility of ascent—a character in them that bear rule, so fine and high and pure, that as men come within the circle of its influence, they involuntarily pay homage to that which is the one pre-eminent distinction, the Royalty of Virtue.

HENRY CODMAN POTTER (1835–1908), U.S. bishop. Speech, 30 April 1889, on the centennial of Washington, D.C.

27 National character is only another name for the particular form which the littleness, perversity and baseness of mankind take in every country. Every nation mocks at other nations, and all are right.

ARTHUR SCHOPENHAUER (1788–1860), German philosopher. *Parerga and Paralipomena,* "Aphorisms on the Wisdom of Life" (1851).

28 Poor nations are hungry, and rich nations are proud; and pride and hunger will ever be at variance.

JONATHAN SWIFT (1667–1745), Anglo-Irish satirist. *Gulliver's Travels,* pt. 4, "A Voyage to the Country of the Houyhnhnms," ch. 5 (1726).

29 Nations! What are nations? Tartars! and Huns! and Chinamen! Like insects they swarm. The historian strives in vain to make them memorable. It is for want of a man that there are so many men. It is individuals that populate the world.

HENRY DAVID THOREAU (1817–62), U.S. philosopher, author, naturalist. *Journals* (1906), entry for 1 May 1851.

30 Nations do not *think*, they only *feel*. They get their feelings at second hand through their temperaments, not their brains. A nation can be brought—by force of circumstances, not argument—to reconcile itself to *any kind of government or religion that can be devised*; in time it will fit itself to the required conditions; later it will prefer them and will fiercely fight for them.

MARK TWAIN (1835–1910), U.S. author. Old Man, in *What Is Man?*, sct. 6 (1906; repr. in *Complete Essays*, ed. by Charles Neider, 1963).

31 It is true that men themselves made this world of nations . . . but this world without doubt has issued from a mind often diverse, at times quite contrary, and always superior to the particular ends that men had proposed to themselves.

GIAMBATTISTA VICO (1688–1744), Italian philosopher, historian. *The New Science*, Conclusion, para. 1108 (ed. 1744; tr. 1984).

32 I suffer more from the humiliations inflicted by my country than from those inflicted on her.

SIMONE WEIL (1909–43), French philosopher, mystic. Letter (1938?) to author Georges Bernanos (published in *Selected Essays*, ed. by Richard Rees, 1962).

See also Douglas on ADVERTISING; Wilson on INTERNATIONAL RELATIONS; Lao-tzu on PATRIOTISM; Belloc on PROPAGANDA; Weil on WAR.

NATIVE AMERICANS

1 Bury my heart at Wounded Knee.

STEPHEN VINCENT BENÉT (1898–1943), U.S. poet, author. *American Names*. Wounded Knee, a creek in South Dakota, was site of the last major battle of the Indian Wars, 1890.

2 The Indians knew that life was equated with the earth and its resources, that America was a paradise, and they could not comprehend why the intruders from the East were determined to destroy all that was Indian as well as America itself.

DEE BROWN (b. 1908), U.S. author. *Bury My Heart at Wounded Knee* (1970).

3 Land of opportunity, land for the huddled masses—where would the opportunity have been without the genocide of those Old Guard, bristling Indian tribes?

EDWARD HOAGLAND (b. 1932), U.S. novelist, essayist. "Lament the Red Wolf," in *Sports Illustrated* (New York, 14 Jan. 1974; repr. in *Heart's Desire*, 1988).

4 Luxury spreads its ample board before their eyes; but they are excluded from the banquet. Plenty revels over the fields; but they are starving in the midst of its abundance: the whole wilderness has blossomed into a garden; but they feel as reptiles that infest it.

WASHINGTON IRVING (1783–1859), U.S. author. *The Sketch-Book*, "Traits of Indian Character" (1819–20).

5 If you tie a horse to a stake, do you expect he will grow fat? If you pen an Indian up on a small spot of earth, and compel him to stay there, he will not be contented, nor will he grow and prosper. I have asked some of the great white chiefs where they get their authority to say to the Indian that he shall stay in one place, while he sees white men going where they please. They can not tell me.

CHIEF JOSEPH (c. 1840–1904), Nez Percé leader. *North American Review* (Cedar Falls, Iowa, April 1879).

6 Not that the Red Indian will ever possess the broad lands of America. At least I presume not. But his ghost will.

D. H. LAWRENCE (1885–1930), British author. *Studies in Classic American Literature*, ch. 4 (1924).

7 Whoever the last true cowboy in America turns out to be, he's likely to be an Indian.

WILLIAM LEAST HEAT MOON [WILLIAM TROGDON] (b. 1939), U.S. author. *Blue Highways: A Journey into America*, pt. 5, ch. 2 (1983).

8 The Indian is one of Nature's gentlemen—he never says or does a rude or vulgar thing. The vicious, uneducated barbarians, who form the surplus of overpopulous European countries, are far behind the wild man in delicacy of feeling or natural courtesy.

SUSANNA MOODIE (1803–85), Canadian author. *Roughing It in the Bush*, ch. 1 (1852).

9 We do not understand when the buffalo are all slaughtered, the wild horses are tamed, the secret corners of the forest heavy with scent of many men, and the view of the ripe hills blotted by talking wires. Where is the thicket? Gone. Where is the eagle? Gone. The end of living and the beginning of survival.

Attributed to SEATTLE (c. 1784–1866), Chief of the Dwamish, Suquamish and allied Indian tribes. Letter, 1854, to President Franklin Pierce (published in *Brother Eagle, Sister Sky: A Message from Chief Seattle*, 1990). The letter, in which Seattle pleaded that his name should die with the ceding of the Washington State territories, was shown in 1992 to have been largely a forgery, devised by television scriptwriter Ted Perry for a historical epic in 1971.

10 We drove the Indians out of the land,
But a dire revenge those Redmen planned,
For they fastened a name to every nook,
And every boy with a spelling book
Will have to toil till his hair turns gray
Before he can spell them the proper way.

EVA MARCH TAPPAN (1854–1930), U.S. writer, poet, historian. *On the Cape*, st. 1.

NATURE

1 Nature has no mercy at all. Nature says, "I'm going to snow. If you have on a bikini and no snowshoes, that's tough. I am going to snow anyway."

MAYA ANGELOU (b. 1928), U.S. author. "Maya Angelou: An Interview" (first published Oct. 1974; repr. in *Conversations with Maya Angelou*, 1989).

2 The plastic virtues: purity, unity, and truth, keep nature in subjection.

GUILLAUME APOLLINAIRE (1880–1918), Italian-born French poet, critic. *The Cubist Painters*, "On Painting" (1913).

3　To sit in the shade on a fine day, and look upon verdure is the most perfect refreshment.

> JANE AUSTEN (1775–1817), English novelist. Fanny Price, in *Mansfield Park*, ch. 9 (1814).

4　Nature . . . is nothing but the inner voice of self-interest.

> CHARLES BAUDELAIRE (1821–67), French poet. "The Painter of Modern Life," sct. 11, in *L'Art Romantique* (1869; repr. in *Selected Writings on Art and Artists*, ed. by P. E. Charvet, 1972).

5　The tree which moves some to tears of joy is in the eyes of others only a green thing that stands in the way. Some see nature all ridicule and deformity . . . and some scarce see nature at all. But to the eyes of the man of imagination, nature is imagination itself.

> WILLIAM BLAKE (1757–1827), English poet, painter, engraver. Letter, 23 Aug. 1799 (published in *The Letters of William Blake*, 1956).

6　Man masters nature not by force but by understanding. This is why science has succeeded where magic failed: because it has looked for no spell to cast over nature.

> JACOB BRONOWSKI (1908–74), British scientist, author. "The Creative Mind," lecture, delivered 26 Feb. 1953, at the Massachusetts Institute of Technology (published in *Science and Human Values*, sct. 4, 1961).

7　All things are artificial, for nature is the art of God.

> SIR THOMAS BROWNE (1605–82), English physician, author. *Religio Medici*, pt. 1, sct. 16 (1643).

8　As long as I retain my feeling and my passion for Nature, I can partly soften or subdue my other passions and resist or endure those of others.

> LORD BYRON (1788–1824), English poet. Letter, 10 June 1822, to author Isaac D'Israeli (published in *Byron's Letters and Journals*, vol. 9, ed. by Leslie A. Marchand, 1979).

9　If only nature is real and if, in nature, only desire and destruction are legitimate, then, in that all humanity does not suffice to assuage the thirst for blood, the path of destruction must lead to universal annihilation.

> ALBERT CAMUS (1913–60), French-Algerian philosopher, author. *The Rebel*, pt. 2, "The Sons of Cain" (1951; tr. 1953), discussing the philosophy of the Marquis de Sade.

10　The "control of nature" is a phrase conceived in arrogance, born of the Neanderthal age of biology and the convenience of man.

> RACHEL CARSON (1907–64), U.S. marine biologist, author. *The Silent Spring*, ch. 17 (1962).

11　That man's best works should be such bungling imitations of Nature's infinite perfection, matters not much; but that he should make himself an imitation, this is the fact which Nature moans over, and deprecates beseechingly. Be spontaneous, be truthful, be free, and thus be individuals! is the song she sings through warbling birds, and whispering pines, and roaring waves, and screeching winds.

> LYDIA M. CHILD (1802–80), U.S. abolitionist, writer, editor. Letter, 17 March 1843 (published in *Letters from New York*, vol. 1, Letter 38, 1843).

12　Nature, like us is sometimes caught
Without her diadem.

> EMILY DICKINSON (1830–86), U.S. poet. *The Complete Poems*, no. 1075 (1955).

13　I am against nature. I don't dig nature at all. I think nature is very unnatural. I think the truly natural things are dreams, which nature can't touch with decay.

> BOB DYLAN (b. 1941), U.S. singer, songwriter. Quoted in: Robert Shelton, *No Direction Home*, ch. 1, "Kaddish" (1986).

14　Nature is an endless combination and repetition of a very few laws. She hums the old well-known air through innumerable variations.

> RALPH WALDO EMERSON (1803–82), U.S. essayist, poet, philosopher. *Essays*, "History" (First Series, 1841).

15　The best remedy for those who are afraid, lonely or unhappy is to go outside, somewhere where they can be quiet, alone with the heavens, nature and God. Because only then does one feel that all is as it should be and that God wishes to see people happy, amidst the simple beauty of nature. As long as this exists, and it certainly always will, I know that then there will always be comfort for every sorrow, whatever the circumstances may be. And I firmly believe that nature brings solace in all troubles.

> ANNE FRANK (1929–45), German Jewish refugee, diarist. *The Diary of a Young Girl* (1947; tr. 1952), entry for 23 Feb. 1944.

16　Nature is a collective idea, and, though its essence exist in each individual of the species, can never in its perfection inhabit a single object.

> HENRY FUSELI (1741–1825), Swiss-born English artist, critic. *Lectures on Painting*, "First Lecture" (1801). Quoted in: *The Mind of Henry Fuseli*, pt. 4, ch. 1, "Nature, a Collective Idea" (ed. by Eudo C. Mason, 1951).

17　You may drive out nature with a pitchfork, yet she'll be constantly running back.

> HORACE (65–8 B.C.), Roman poet. *Epistles*, bk. 1, Epistle 10.

18　The mountains, the forest, and the sea, render men savage; they develop the fierce, but yet do not destroy the human.

> VICTOR HUGO (1802–85), French poet, dramatist, novelist. *Les Misérables*, bk. 2, ch. 6, "Fantine" (1862).

19　A man who lives with nature is used to violence and is companionable with death. There is more violence in an English hedgerow than in the meanest streets of a great city.

> P. D. JAMES (b. 1920), British mystery writer. Jonah the tramp, in *Devices and Desires*, ch. 40 (1989).

20　Nature is garrulous to the point of confusion, let the artist be truly taciturn.

> PAUL KLEE (1879–1940), Swiss artist. *The Diaries of Paul Klee 1898–1918*, no. 857 (1957: tr. 1965), 1909 entry.

21　We cannot remember too often that when we observe nature, and especially the ordering of nature, it is always ourselves alone we are observing.

> G. C. LICHTENBERG (1742–99), German physicist, philosopher. *Aphorisms*, "Notebook J," aph. 65 (written 1765–99; tr. by R. J. Hollingdale, 1990).

22　The Laws of Nature are just, but terrible. There is

no weak mercy in them. Cause and consequence are inseparable and inevitable. The elements have no forbearance. The fire burns, the water drowns, the air consumes, the earth buries. And perhaps it would be well for our race if the punishment of crimes against the Laws of Man were as inevitable as the punishment of crimes against the Laws of Nature—were Man as unerring in his judgments as Nature.

HENRY WADSWORTH LONGFELLOW (1807–82), U.S. poet. *Drift-Wood*, "Table-Talk" (ed. 1857; repr. in *Complete Works*, vol. 1, 1886).

23 It is absolutely impossible to transcend the laws of nature. What can change in historically different circumstances is only the form in which these laws expose themselves.

KARL MARX (1818–83), German political theorist, social philosopher. Letter, 11 July 1868, to Dr. Kugelmann (published in *Karl Marx and Friedrich Engels: Collected Works*, vol. 38, 1982).

24 Men have an extraordinarily erroneous opinion of their position in nature; and the error is ineradicable.

W. SOMERSET MAUGHAM (1874–1966), British author. *A Writer's Notebook* (1949), 1896 entry.

25 It is easy to replace man, and it will take no great time, when Nature has lapsed, to replace Nature.

ALICE MEYNELL (1847–1922), English poet, essayist. *Essays*, "The True Colour of Life" (1914).

26 Let us beware of saying there are laws in nature. There are only necessities: there is no one to command, no one to obey, no one to transgress. When you realize there are no goals or objectives, then you realize, too, that there is no chance: for only in a world of objectives does the word "chance" have any meaning.

FRIEDRICH NIETZSCHE (1844–1900), German philosopher. *The Gay Science*, aph. 109 (rev. ed., 1887).

27 Nature is unfair? So much the better, inequality is the only bearable thing, the monotony of equality can only lead us to boredom.

FRANCIS PICABIA (1878–1953), French painter, poet. "L'Humour Poetique," in *La Nef*, no. 71–72 (Paris, Dec. 1950/Jan. 1951; repr. in *Yes No: Poems and Sayings*, "Sayings," ed. by Rémy Hall, 1990).

28 Nature uses human imagination to lift her work of creation to even higher levels.

LUIGI PIRANDELLO (1867–1936), Italian author, playwright. The Father, in *Six Characters in Search of an Author*, act 1 (1921).

29 Nature breaks through the eyes of the cat.

IRISH PROVERB.

30 Of all the things that oppress me, this sense of the evil working of nature herself—my disgust at her barbarity—clumsiness—darkness—bitter mockery of herself—is the most desolating.

JOHN RUSKIN (1819–1900), English art critic, author. Letter, 3 April 1871. Quoted in: *Ruskin Today*, sct. 115 (ed. by Kenneth Clark, 1964).

31 Nature allows all, by its murderous laws;
Incest and rape, all theft and parricide,

All sodom's pleasures, Sappho's lesbian games,
All that destroys and sends men to their graves.

MARQUIS DE SADE (1740–1814), French author. *The Truth* (1787; repr. in Donald Thomas, *The Marquis de Sade*, "The Prisoner," 1976).

32 Nature, who for the perfect maintenance of the laws of her general equilibrium, has sometimes need of vices and sometimes of virtues, inspires now this impulse, now that one, in accordance with what she requires.

MARQUIS DE SADE (1740–1814), French author. Dolmancé, in *Philosophy in the Bedroom*, "Dialogue the Seventh" (1795).

33 From our earliest hour we have been taught that the thought of the heart, the shaping of the rain-cloud, the amount of wool that grows on a sheep's back, the length of a drought, and the growing of the corn, depend on nothing that moves immutable, at the heart of all things; but on the changeable will of a changeable being, whom our prayers can alter. To us, from the beginning, Nature has been but a poor plastic thing, to be toyed with this way or that, as man happens to please his deity or not; to go to church or not; to say his prayers right or not; to travel on a Sunday or not. Was it possible for us in an instant to see Nature as she is—the flowing vestment of an unchanging reality?

OLIVE SCHREINER (1855–1920), South African writer, feminist. *The Story of an African Farm*, pt. 2, ch. 1 (1883).

34 Nature in America has always been suspect, on the defensive, cannibalized by progress. In America, every specimen becomes a relic.

SUSAN SONTAG (b. 1933), U.S. essayist. *On Photography*, "Melancholy Objects" (1977).

35 I know no subject more elevating, more amazing, more ready to the poetical enthusiasm, the philosophical reflection, and the moral sentiment than the works of nature. Where can we meet such variety, such beauty, such magnificence?

JAMES THOMSON (1700–1748), Scottish poet. *The Seasons*, Preface. The poem's novel attitude toward nature anticipated the Romantic movement.

36 We can never have enough of nature. We must be refreshed by the sight of inexhaustible vigor, vast and titanic features, the sea-coast with its wrecks, the wilderness with its living and its decaying trees, the thundercloud, and the rain which lasts three weeks and produces freshets. We need to witness our own limits transgressed, and some life pasturing freely where we never wander.

HENRY DAVID THOREAU (1817–62), U.S. philosopher, author, naturalist. *Walden*, "Spring" (1854).

37 However much you knock at nature's door, she will never answer you in comprehensible words.

IVAN TURGENEV (1818–83), Russian author. Shubin, in *On the Eve*, ch. 1 (1860), comparing nature to "life" (in fact women).

38 Our task is not to rediscover nature but to remake it.

RAOUL VANEIGEM (b. 1934), Belgian Situationist philosopher. *The Revolution of Everyday Life*, ch. 9, sct. 2 (1967; tr. 1983).

39 I believe a leaf of grass is no less than the journey-work of the stars.

WALT WHITMAN (1819–92), U.S. poet. *Song of Myself*, sct. 31, in *Leaves of Grass* (1855).

40 After you have exhausted what there is in business, politics, conviviality, and so on—have found that none of these finally satisfy, or permanently wear—what remains? Nature remains.

WALT WHITMAN (1819–92), U.S. poet. *Specimen Days and Collect*, "New Themes Entered Upon" (1882).

41 For I have learned
To look on nature, not as in the hour
Of thoughtless youth, but hearing oftentimes
The still, sad music of humanity.

WILLIAM WORDSWORTH (1770–1850), English poet. *Lines Written a Few Miles Above Tintern Abbey*, in *Lyrical Ballads* (1798).

See also Apollinaire, Chagall, Frye, Longfellow, Nietzsche, Poe, Schiller, Van Gogh, Whistler, Wilde on ART; Berger on EVIL; Hegel on GOODNESS; Stein on IMITATION; Hoffer on MACHINERY; SCIENCE AND NATURE.

THE NAVY

1 There is something about going to sea. A little bit of discipline, self-discipline and humility are required.

PRINCE ANDREW, DUKE OF YORK (b. 1960). *Daily Telegraph* (London, 7 Oct. 1988).

2 How happy is the sailor's life,
From coast to coast to roam;
In every port he finds a wife,
In every land a home.

ISAAC BICKERSTAFFE (c.1735–1812), Irish playwright. *Thomas and Sally*.

3 Admiral. That part of a warship which does the talking while the figurehead does the thinking.

AMBROSE BIERCE (1842–1914), U.S. author. *The Devil's Dictionary* (1881–1906).

4 The Royal Navy of England hath ever been its greatest defence and ornament; it is its ancient and natural strength; the floating bulwark of the island.

SIR WILLIAM BLACKSTONE (1723–80), English jurist. *Commentaries on the Laws of England*, bk. 1, ch. 13 (1765).

5 Don't talk to me about naval tradition. It's nothing but rum, sodomy and the lash.

SIR WINSTON CHURCHILL (1874–1965), British statesman, writer. Remark made in 1911. Quoted in: Sir Peter Gretton, *Former Naval Person*, ch. 1 (1968).

6 There is nothing more enticing, disenchanting, and enslaving than the life at sea.

JOSEPH CONRAD (1857–1924), Polish-born English novelist. *Lord Jim*, ch. 2 (1900).

7 I must have the gentleman to haul and draw with the mariner, and the mariner with the gentleman . . . I would know him, that would refuse to set his hand to a rope, but I know there is not any such here.

SIR FRANCIS DRAKE (1540–96), English navigator. Speech, May 1578, to his crew off Puerto San Julian, Argentina, shortly before entering the Magellan Straits. Drake sailed the Pacific to become the first Englishman to circumnavigate the globe.

8 The wonder is always new that any sane man can be a sailor.

RALPH WALDO EMERSON (1803–82), U.S. essayist, poet, philosopher. *English Traits*, "Voyage to England" (1856).

9 The most advanced nations are always those who navigate the most.

RALPH WALDO EMERSON (1803–82), U.S. essayist, poet, philosopher. *Society and Solitude*, "Civilization" (1870).

10 He was begotten in the galley and born under a gun. Every hair was a rope yarn, every finger a fish-hook, every tooth a marline-spike, and his blood right good Stockholm tar.

NAVAL EPITAPH.

11 We are as near to heaven by sea as by land.

SIR HUMPHREY GILBERT (1537?–83), English soldier, navigator, explorer. Said during a storm on his last, fatal voyage back from Newfoundland, Sept. 1583. Quoted in: Richard Hakluyt, *The Principal Navigations, Voyages, Traffics and Discoveries of the English Nation*, vol. 3 (1600).

12 No man will be a sailor who has contrivance enough to get himself into a jail; for being in a ship is being in a jail, with the chance of being drowned. . . . A man in a jail has more room, better food and commonly better company.

SAMUEL JOHNSON (1709–84), English author, lexicographer. Quoted in: James Boswell, *Life of Samuel Johnson*, 16 March 1759 (1791). On another occasion (10 April 1778), when told, "We find people fond of being sailors," Johnson replied, "I cannot account for that, any more than I can account for other strange perversions of imagination."

13 There were gentlemen and there were seamen in the navy of Charles the Second. But the seamen were not gentlemen; and the gentlemen were not seamen.

THOMAS BABINGTON MACAULAY (1800–1859), English historian, Whig politician. *History of England*, vol. 1, ch. 3 (1849).

14 Visit the Navy-Yard, and behold a marine, such a man as an American government can make, or such as it can make a man with its black arts—a mere shadow and reminiscence of humanity, a man laid out alive and standing, and already, as one may say, buried under arms with funeral accompaniments.

HENRY DAVID THOREAU (1817–62), U.S. philosopher, author, naturalist. *On the Duty of Civil Disobedience* (1849).

15 In this country it's a good thing to kill an admiral now and then to encourage the others.

VOLTAIRE (1694–1778), French philosopher, author. English bystanders at the execution of an admiral, in *Candide*, ch. 23 (1759). On 14 March 1757, Admiral John Byng was executed for failing to relieve the island of Minorca, besieged by the French.

See also Johnson on The SEA.

NAZISM

1 Everything I do is done within sight of the Führer, so that my faults or mistakes are never hidden from him. I do my very utmost to live and act in such a manner that the Führer should remain satisfied with me; I am hardworking; but whether I shall always be able to cope with the tasks entrusted to me in the future as well, is an open question.

> MARTIN BORMANN (1900–1945), German Nazi leader. Letter, 6 July 1943, to his wife, Gerda (published in *The Bormann Letters,* ed. by Hugh Trevor-Roper, 1954).

2　A régime which invented a biological foreign policy was obviously acting against its own best interests. But at least it obeyed its own particular logic.

> ALBERT CAMUS (1913–60), French-Algerian philosopher, author. *The Rebel,* pt. 3, "State Terrorism and Irrational Terror" (1951; tr. 1953).

3　There is no independence of law against National Socialism. Say to yourselves at every decision which you make: "How would the Führer decide in my place?" In every decision ask yourselves: "Is this decision compatible with the National Socialist conscience of the German people?" Then you will have a firm iron foundation which, allied with the unity of the National Socialist People's State and with your recognition of the eternal nature of the will of Adolf Hitler, will endow your own sphere of decision with the authority of the Third Reich, and this for all time.

> HANS FRANK (1900–1946), German Nazi politician. Speech to jurists in 1936. Quoted in: William L. Shirer, *The Rise and Fall of the Third Reich,* ch. 8, "Justice in the Third Reich" (1959). Frank was at the time commissioner of justice and president of the German Law Academy; later he became governor-general of Poland, where he established concentration camps and conducted a policy of persecution and extermination.

4　Hermann Goering, Joachim von Ribbentrop, Albert Speer, Walther Frank, Julius Streicher and Robert Ley did pass under my inspection and interrogation in 1945 but they only proved that National Socialism was a gangster interlude at a rather low order of mental capacity and with a surprisingly high incidence of alcoholism.

> JOHN KENNETH GALBRAITH (b. 1908), U.S. economist. *The Age of Uncertainty,* ch. 12 (1977).

5　When an opponent declares, "I will not come over to your side," I calmly say, "Your child belongs to us already. . . . What are you? You will pass on. Your descendants, however, now stand in the new camp. In a short time they will know nothing else but this new community."

> ADOLF HITLER (1889–1945), German dictator. Speech, 6 Nov. 1933. Quoted in: William L. Shirer, *The Rise and Fall of the Third Reich,* ch. 8, "Education in the Third Reich" (1959).

6　What we call National-Socialism is the poisonous perversion of ideas which have a long history in German intellectual life.

> THOMAS MANN (1875–1955), German author, critic. Speech, delivered in 1940 (published in *Order of the Day,* "The War and the Future," 1942).

7　Left-wing movements have tended to be unisex, and asexual in their imagery. Right-wing movements, however puritanical and repressive the realities they usher in, have an erotic surface. Certainly Nazism is "sexier" than communism.

> SUSAN SONTAG (b. 1933), U.S. essayist. *Under the Sign of Saturn,* "Fascinating Fascism" (1980; first published 1974). This fact, Sontag parenthetically added, "is not to the Nazis' credit, but rather shows something of the nature and limits of the sexual imagination." See Sontag on SADOMASOCHISM.

See also FASCISM; ADOLF HITLER.

NECESSITY

1　Man cannot be free if he does not know that he is subject to necessity, because his freedom is always won in his never wholly successful attempts to liberate himself from necessity.

> HANNAH ARENDT (1906–75), German-born U.S. political philosopher. *The Human Condition,* pt. 3, ch. 16 (1958).

2　We come into the world laden with the weight of an infinite necessity.

> ALBERT CAMUS (1913–60), French-Algerian philosopher, author. *Resistance, Rebellion and Death,* "Reflections on the Guillotine" (1961).

3　Arguably the only goods people need these days are food and nappies.

> SIR TERENCE CONRAN (b. 1931), British businessman, designer. *Observer* (London, 21 Feb. 1988).

4　Necessity hath no law.

> OLIVER CROMWELL (1599–1658), Parliamentarian general, Lord Protector of England. Speech, 12 Sept. 1654, to Parliament.

5　Must! Is *must* a word to be addressed to princes? Little man, little man! thy father, if he had been alive, durst not have used that word.

> ELIZABETH I (1533–1603), Queen of England. Attributed remonstrance to Sir Robert Cecil, who had urged her to go to bed in her last illness, March 1603. Both Robert and his father, William Cecil (Lord Burghley), were secretaries of state to Elizabeth.

6　We do what we must, and call it by the best names.

> RALPH WALDO EMERSON (1803–82), U.S. essayist, poet, philosopher. *The Conduct of Life,* "Considerations by the Way" (1860).

7　Necessity has the face of a dog.

> GABRIEL GARCÍA MÁRQUEZ (b. 1928), Colombian author. Mina, in *In Evil Hour* (1968; tr. 1979).

8　The necessary has never been man's top priority. The passionate pursuit of the nonessential and the extravagant is one of the chief traits of human uniqueness. Unlike other forms of life, man's greatest exertions are made in the pursuit not of necessities but of superfluities.

> ERIC HOFFER (1902–83), U.S. philosopher. *New York Times* (21 July 1969).

9　Fact I know; and Law I know; but what is this Necessity, save an empty shadow of my own mind's throwing?

> THOMAS HENRY HUXLEY (1825–95), English biologist. "On the Physical Basis Of Life" (1868; published in *Collected Essays,* vol. 1, 1893).

10　If people should ever start to do only what is necessary millions would die of hunger.

> G. C. LICHTENBERG (1742–99), German physicist, philosopher. *Aphorisms,* "Notebook C," aph. 54 (written 1765–99; tr. by R. J. Hollingdale, 1990).

11 Nothing is necessary except God, and nothing is less necessary than pain.

> JOSEPH DE MAISTRE (1753–1821), French diplomat, philosopher. The Senator, in *Les Soirées de Saint-Pétersbourg*, "Fifth Dialogue" (1821; repr. in *The Works of Joseph de Maistre*, ed. by Jack Lively, 1965).

12 Nobody should trust their virtue with necessity, the force of which is never known till it is felt, and it is therefore one of the first duties to avoid the temptation of it.

> LADY MARY WORTLEY MONTAGU (1689–1762), English society figure, letter writer. Letter, 22 June 1752, to her daughter, Lady Bute (published in *Selected Letters*, ed. by Robert Halsband, 1970).

13 Only useless things are indispensable.

> FRANCIS PICABIA (1878–1953), French painter, poet. "Dactylocoque," in *Littérature* (Second Series, Paris, 1 Dec. 1922; repr. in *Yes / No: Poems and Sayings*, "Sayings," ed. by Rémy Hall, 1990).

14 Necessity is the plea for every infringement of human freedom. It is the argument of tyrants; it is the creed of slaves.

> WILLIAM PITT THE YOUNGER (1759–1806), English statesman. Speech, 18 Nov. 1783, to the House of Commons, on the India Bill. A month later, aged 24, Pitt was appointed prime minister, a position he retained until his resignation 17 years later.

15 Foul water will quench fire.

> ENGLISH PROVERB (16th century).

16 We live in an age when unnecessary things are our only necessities.

> OSCAR WILDE (1854–1900), Anglo-Irish playwright, author. *The Picture of Dorian Gray*, ch. 8 (1891).

See also Cassady on ART; Seneca on FUTILITY; Schlegel on HISTORY.

NEGOTIATION

1 Let us never negotiate out of fear, but let us never fear to negotiate.

> JOHN F. KENNEDY (1917–63), U.S. Democratic politician, president. Inaugural address, 20 Jan. 1961. Quoted in: Theodore C. Sorenson, *Kennedy*, pt. 3, ch. 9 (1965).

2 Jaw-jaw is better than war-war.

> HAROLD MACMILLAN (1894–1986), British Conservative politician, prime minister. Speech, 30 Jan. 1958, Canberra, Australia.

3 Only free men can negotiate. Prisoners cannot enter into contracts.

> NELSON MANDELA (b. 1918), South African political leader. Statement, 10 Feb. 1985, refusing the terms offered for his release by South African president P. W. Botha (published in Fatima Meer, *Higher Than Hope*, pt. 4, ch. 30, 1988). The statement was read by Zindzi Mandela, Nelson's daughter, at a U.D.F. rally at the Jabulani Stadium, Soweto.

4 We were not born to sue, but to command.

> WILLIAM SHAKESPEARE (1564–1616), English dramatist, poet. King Richard, in *Richard II*, act 1, sc. 1.

See also Shakespeare on AGENTS.

NEIGHBORS

1 For what do we live, but to make sport for our neighbours, and laugh at them in our turn?

> JANE AUSTEN (1775–1817), English novelist. Mr. Bennet, in *Pride and Prejudice*, ch. 57 (1813).

2 A good neighbour, even in this,
Is fatal sometimes, cuts your morning up
To mince-meat of the very smallest talk,
Then helps to sugar her bohea at night
With your reputation.

> ELIZABETH BARRETT BROWNING (1806–61), English poet. *Aurora Leigh*, bk. 4 (1857).

3 Sometimes a neighbor whom we have disliked a lifetime for his arrogance and conceit lets fall a single commonplace remark that shows us another side, another man, really; a man uncertain, and puzzled, and in the dark like ourselves.

> WILLA CATHER (1873–1947), U.S. author. *Shadows on the Rock*, Epilogue (1931).

4 Your next-door neighbour . . . is not a man; he is an environment. He is the barking of a dog; he is the noise of a pianola; he is a dispute about a party wall; he is drains that are worse than yours, or roses that are better than yours.

> G. K. CHESTERTON (1874–1936), British author. *The Uses of Diversity*, "The Irishman" (1920).

5 Keeping up with the Joneses was a full-time job with my mother and father. It was not until many years later when I lived alone that I realized how much cheaper it was to drag the Joneses down to my level.

> QUENTIN CRISP (b. 1908), British author. *The Naked Civil Servant*, ch. 1 (1968).

6 The supreme satisfaction is to be able to despise one's neighbour and this fact goes far to account for religious intolerance. It is evidently consoling to reflect that the people next door are headed for hell.

> ALEISTER CROWLEY (1875–1947), British occultist. *The Confessions of Aleister Crowley*, ch. 3 (1929; rev. 1970).

7 In great cities men are brought together by the desire of gain. They are not in a state of co-operation, but of isolation, as to the making of fortunes; and for all the rest they are careless of neighbours. Christianity teaches us to love our neighbour as ourself; modern society acknowledges no neighbour.

> BENJAMIN DISRAELI (1804–81), English statesman, author. Stephen Morley, in *Sybil*, bk. 2, ch. 5 (1845).

8 Good fences make good neighbors.

> ROBERT FROST (1874–1963), U.S. poet. *Mending Wall*.

9 My neighbour
doesn't want to be loved
as much as
he wants to be envied.

> IRVING LAYTON (b. 1912), Canadian poet. *The Whole Bloody Bird*, "Aphs" (1969).

10 Love your neighbour, yet pull not down your hedge.

> ENGLISH PROVERB. Collected in: George Herbert, *Jacula Prudentum* (1651).

11   It is grossly selfish to require of one's neighbour that he should think in the same way, and hold the same opinions. Why should he? If he can think, he will probably think differently. If he cannot think, it is monstrous to require thought of any kind from him.

> OSCAR WILDE (1854–1900), Anglo-Irish playwright, author. *The Soul of Man Under Socialism,* in *Fortnightly Review* (London, Feb. 1891; repr. 1895).

See also McGinley on KINDNESS.

NEUROSIS

1   You mistake me, my dear. I have a high repect for your nerves. They are my old friends. I have heard you mention them with consideration these twenty years at least.

> JANE AUSTEN (1775–1817), English novelist. Mr. Bennet, in *Pride and Prejudice,* ch. 1 (1813), in answer to Mrs. Bennet's accusation that he had "no compassion on my poor nerves."

2   I have three phobias which, could I mute them, would make my life as slick as a sonnet, but as dull as ditch water: I hate to go to bed, I hate to get up, and I hate to be alone.

> TALLULAH BANKHEAD (1903–68), U.S. screen actor. *Tallulah,* ch. 1 (1952).

3   The anguish of the neurotic individual is the same as that of the *saint.* The neurotic, the saint are engaged in the same battle. Their blood flows from similar wounds. But the first one gasps and the other one gives.

> GEORGES BATAILLE (1897–1962), French novelist, critic. *Inner Experience,* "Notes: To Whomever Wishes Truly to Hear Me," sct. 1 (1942), comprising the first volume of a trilogy published in France under the title *La Somme Athéologique.*

4   If you get hung up on everybody else's hang-ups, then the whole world's going to be nothing more than one huge gallows.

> RICHARD BRAUTIGAN (1935–84), U.S. novelist, poet. *The Abortion: An Historical Romance 1966* (1970, p. 63).

5   Oh the nerves, the nerves; the mysteries of this machine called man! Oh the little that unhinges it, poor creatures that we are!

> CHARLES DICKENS (1812–70), English novelist. Alderman Cute, in *The Chimes,* "Third Quarter" (1844).

6   As every man is hunted by his own daemon, vexed by his own disease, this checks all his activity.

> RALPH WALDO EMERSON (1803–82), U.S. essayist, poet, philosopher. *The Conduct of Life,* "Fate" (1860).

7   The expectation that every neurotic phenomenon can be cured may, I suspect, be derived from the layman's belief that the neuroses are something quite unnecessary which have no right whatever to exist. Whereas in fact they are severe, constitutionally fixed illnesses, which rarely restrict themselves to only a few attacks but persist as a rule over long periods throughout life.

> SIGMUND FREUD (1856–1939), Austrian psychiatrist. *New Introductory Lectures on Psychoanalysis,* Lecture 34, "Explanations, Applications and Orientations" (1933; repr. in *Complete Works,* vol. 22, ed. by James Strachey and Anna Freud, 1964).

8   A certain degree of neurosis is of inestimable value as a drive, especially to a psychologist.

> SIGMUND FREUD (1856–1939), Austrian psychiatrist. Quoted in: Joseph Wortis, *Fragments of an Analysis with Freud,* ch. 3, 22 "Jan. 1935" (1954).

9   Neurosis is always a substitute for legitimate suffering.

> CARL JUNG (1875–1961), Swiss psychiatrist. *Psychology and Religion* (1938; repr. in *Collected Works,* vol. 9, para. 129, ed. by William McGuire, 1958).

10   If neurotic is wanting two mutually exclusive things at one and the same time, then I'm neurotic as hell. I'll be flying back and forth between one mutually exclusive thing and another for the rest of my days.

> SYLVIA PLATH (1932–63), U.S. poet. The narrator, in *The Bell Jar,* ch. 8 (1963).

11   Everything great in the world comes from neurotics. They alone have founded our religions and composed our masterpieces.

> MARCEL PROUST (1871–1922), French novelist. *Remembrance of Things Past,* vol. 5, "The Guermantes Way," pt. 1 (1921; tr. by Scott Monkrieff, 1925).

12   Neurosis has an absolute genius for malingering. There is no illness which it cannot counterfeit perfectly. If it is capable of deceiving the doctor, how should it fail to deceive the patient?

> MARCEL PROUST (1871–1922), French novelist. *Remembrance of Things Past,* vol. 5, "The Guermantes Way," pt. 1 (1921; tr. by Scott Monkrieff, 1925).

13   Every neurosis is a primitive form of legal proceeding in which the accused carries on the prosecution, imposes judgment and executes the sentence: *all to the end that someone else should not perform the same process.*

> LIONEL TRILLING (1905–75), U.S. critic. Notebook entry, 1946 (published in *Partisan Review 50th Anniversary Edition,* ed. by William Philips, 1985).

See also Freud on BELIEF; PARANOIA.

THE NEW AGE

1   A sociosphere of contact, control, persuasion and dissuasion, of exhibitions of inhibitions in massive or homeopathic doses . . . : this is obscenity. All structures turned inside out and exhibited, all operations rendered visible. In America this goes all the way from the bewildering network of aerial telephone and electric wires. . . to the concrete multiplication of all the bodily functions in the home, the litany of ingredients on the tiniest can of food, the exhibition of income or IQ.

> JEAN BAUDRILLARD (b. 1929), French semiologist. *Fatal Strategies,* "Figures of the Transpolitical" (1983; tr. 1990).

2   The appropriation of radical thinking by lazy, self-obsessed hippies is a public relations disaster that could cost the earth.

> BEN ELTON (b. 1959), British author, performer. *Stark,* "Court, Hippies and Love at First Sight" (1989).

3 The New Age? It's just the old age stuck in a microwave oven for fifteen seconds.

> JAMES RANDI (b. 1928), Canadian-born U.S. magician, psychic investigator, author. *Observer* (London, 14 April 1991).

NEW ENGLAND

1 The New England conscience . . . does not stop you from doing what you shouldn't—it just stops you from enjoying it.

> CLEVELAND AMORY (b. 1917), U.S. author. *New York* (5 May 1980).

2 Just specimens is all New Hampshire has,
One each of everything as in a show-case
Which naturally she doesn't care to sell.

> ROBERT FROST (1874–1963), U.S. poet. *New Hampshire.*

3 The most serious charge which can be brought against New England is not Puritanism but February.

> JOSEPH WOOD KRUTCH (1893–1970), U.S. author, editor. *Twelve Seasons,* "February" (1949).

4 The East is the hearthside of America. Like any home, therefore, it has the defects of its virtues. Because it is a long-lived-in house, it bursts its seams, is inconvenient, needs constant refurbishing. And some of the family resources have been spent. To attain the privacy that grown-up people find so desirable, Easterners live a harder life than people elsewhere. Today it is we and not the frontiersman who must be rugged to survive.

> PHYLLIS MCGINLEY (1905–78), U.S. poet, author. *The Province of the Heart,* "The Happy Exile" (1959).

5 Philadelphians are every whit as mediocre as their neighbors, but they seldom encourage each other in mediocrity by giving it a more agreeable name.

> AGNES REPPLIER (1858–1950), U.S. author, social critic. *Philadelphia: The Place and the People,* Introduction (1898).

6 I reverently believe that the Maker who made us all makes everything in New England but the weather. I don't know who makes that, but I think it must be raw apprentices in the weather-clerk's factory who experiment and learn how. . . . In the spring I have counted one hundred and thirty-six different kinds of weather inside of four-and-twenty hours.

> MARK TWAIN (1835–1910), U.S. author. "The Weather," speech, at the New England Society's 71st Annual Dinner, New York City (published in *Mark Twain's Speeches,* ed. by Albert Bigelow Paine, 1923).

7 There is no pleasing New Englanders, my dear, their soil is all rocks and their hearts are bloodless absolutes.

> JOHN UPDIKE (b. 1932), U.S. author, critic. The Statesman Buchanan, in *Buchanan Dying,* act 2 (1974).

See also BOSTON.

THE NEW WORLD

1 What passes for identity in America is a series of myths about one's heroic ancestors. It's astounding to me, for example, that so many people really seem to believe that the country was founded by a band of heroes who wanted to be free. That happens not to be true. What happened was that some people left Europe because they couldn't stay there any longer and had to go someplace else to make it. They were hungry, they were poor, they were convicts.

> JAMES BALDWIN (1924–87), U.S. author. "A Talk to Teachers," 16 Oct. 1963 (published in *The Price of the Ticket,* 1985).

2 If you are prepared to accept the consequences of your dreams . . . then you must still regard America today with the same naive enthusiasm as the generations that discovered the New World.

> JEAN BAUDRILLARD (b. 1929), French semiologist. *America,* "Utopia Achieved" (1986; tr. 1988).

3 At least the Pilgrim Fathers used to shoot Indians: the Pilgrim Children merely punch time clocks.

> E. E. CUMMINGS (1894–1962), U.S. poet. "The Tabloid Newspaper," in *Vanity Fair* (New York, Dec. 1926; repr. in *A Miscellany,* ed. by George J. Firmage, 1958).

4 I asked the captain what his name was
And how come he didn't drive a truck
He said his name was Columbus
I just said, "Good luck."

> BOB DYLAN (b. 1941), U.S. singer, songwriter. "Bob Dylan's 115th Dream," on the album *Bringing It All Back Home* (1965).

5 The pious ones of Plymouth who, reaching the Rock, first fell upon their own knees and then upon the aborigines.

> WILLIAM M. EVARTS (1818–1901), U.S. statesman. Quoted by Henry Watterson in: *Louisville Courier-Journal* (4 July 1913; also attributed to various others, including Oliver Wendell Holmes, Sr., and Bill Nye).

6 I am not belittling the brave pioneer men but the sunbonnet as well as the sombrero has helped to settle this glorious land of ours.

> EDNA FERBER (1887–1968), U.S. author. Sabra Cravat, in *Cimarron,* ch. 23 (1929).

7 For a transitory enchanted moment man must have held his breath in the presence of this continent, compelled into an aesthetic contemplation he neither understood nor desired, face to face for the last time in history with something commensurate to his capacity for wonder.

> F. SCOTT FITZGERALD (1896–1940), U.S. author. The narrator (Nick Carraway), in *The Great Gatsby,* ch. 9 (1926).

8 The founders of a new colony, whatever Utopia of human virtue and happiness they might originally project, have invariably recognized it among their earliest practical necessities to allot a portion of the virgin soil as a cemetery, and another portion as the site of a prison.

> NATHANIEL HAWTHORNE (1804–64), U.S. author. *The Scarlet Letter,* ch. 1 (1850).

9 America is, therefore the land of the future, where, in the ages that lie before us, the burden of the World's history shall reveal itself. It is a land of desire for all those who are weary of the historical lumber-room of Old Europe.

GEORG HEGEL (1770–1831), German philosopher. *The Philosophy of History,* Introduction (1832).

10 Then hail! thou noble conquerer!
That, when tyranny oppressed,
Hewed for our fathers from the wild
A land wherein to rest.

MARY ELIZABETH HEWITT (1818–?), U.S. poet. *The Axe of the Settler,* st. 5.

11 Christopher Columbus, as everyone knows, is honoured by posterity because he was the last to discover America.

JAMES JOYCE (1882–1941), Irish author. "The Mirage of the Fisherman of Aran," in *Piccolo della Sera* (Trieste, 5 Sept. 1912; repr. in *Critical Writings,* sct. 46, ed. by Ellsworth Mason and Richard Ellmann, 1959).

12 Being human signifies, for each one of us, belonging to a class, a society, a country, a continent and a civilization; and for us European earth-dwellers, the adventure played out in the heart of the New World signifies in the first place that it was not our world and that we bear responsibility for the crime of its destruction.

CLAUDE LÉVI-STRAUSS (b. 1908), French anthropologist. *Tristes Tropiques,* ch. 38 (1955).

13 The American who first discovered Columbus made a bad discovery.

G. C. LICHTENBERG (1742–99), German physicist, philosopher. *Aphorisms,* "Notebook G," aph. 42 (written 1765–99; tr. by R. J. Hollingdale, 1990).

14 A new world is not made simply by trying to forget the old. A new world is made with a new spirit, with new values. Our world may have begun that way, but today it is caricatural. Our world is a world of *things.* . . . What we dread most, in the face of the impending débâcle, is that we shall be obliged to give up our gewgaws, our gadgets, all the little comforts that have made us so uncomfortable. . . . We are not peaceful souls; we are smug, timid, queasy and quakey.

HENRY MILLER (1891–1980), U.S. author. *The Air-Conditioned Nightmare,* Preface (1945).

15 The settlement of America had its origins in the unsettlement of Europe. America came into existence when the European was already so distant from the ancient ideas and ways of his birthplace that the whole span of the Atlantic did not widen the gulf.

LEWIS MUMFORD (1895–1990), U.S. social philosopher. *The Golden Day,* "The Origins of the American Mind" (1926; repr. in *The Lewis Mumford Reader,* 1986).

16 Other nations have tried to check . . . the fulfilment of our manifest destiny to overspread the continent allotted by Providence for the free development of our yearly multiplying millions.

JOHN L. O'SULLIVAN (1813–95), U.S. editor. Editorial in *U.S. Magazine & Democratic Review,* vol. 17 (July-Aug 1845), supporting the annexation of Texas.

17 Europe and the U.K. are yesterday's world. Tomorrow is in the United States.

R. W. "TINY" ROWLAND (b. 1917), British businessman. Quoted in: *Observer* (London, 16 Jan. 1983).

18 I have, indeed, even omitted facts, which, on account of their singularity, must in the eyes of some have appeared to border on the marvellous. But in the forests of South America such extraordinary realities are to be found, that there is assuredly no need to have recourse to fiction or the least exaggeration.

CAPTAIN J. G. STEDMAN (1744–97), British soldier, author, artist. *Narrative of a Five Years' Expedition Against the Revolted Negroes of Surinam,* ch. 29 (1796; repr. 1971).

19 The open frontier, the hardships of homesteading from scratch, the wealth of natural resources, the whole vast challenge of a continent waiting to be exploited, combined to produce a prevailing materialism and an American drive bent as much, if not more, on money, property, and power than was true of the Old World from which we had fled.

BARBARA TUCHMAN (1912–89), U.S. historian. "On Our Birthday—America as Idea," in *Newsweek* (New York, 12 July 1976).

20 The next Augustan age will dawn on the other side of the Atlantic. There will, perhaps, be a Thucydides at Boston, a Xenophon at New York, and, in time, a Virgil at Mexico, and a Newton at Peru. At last, some curious traveller from Lima will visit England and give a description of the ruins of St Paul's, like the editions of Balbec and Palmyra.

HORACE WALPOLE (1717–97), English author. Letter, 24 Nov. 1774.

THE NEW WORLD ORDER

1 If America does not wish to end her days in the same nursing home as Britannia she had best end this geo-babble about new world orders. Our war, the Cold War, is over. It is time for America to come home.

PATRICK BUCHANAN (b. 1938), U.S. journalist, broadcaster, presidential candidate in 1992. *Observer* (London, 15 Dec. 1991).

2 If the Soviet Union can give up the Brezhnev Doctrine for the Sinatra Doctrine, the United States can give up the James Monroe Doctrine for the Marilyn Monroe Doctrine: Let's all go to bed wearing the perfume we like best.

CARLOS FUENTES (b. 1928), Mexican novelist, short-story writer. Quoted in: *Times* (London, 23 Feb. 1990).

3 People have passed through a very dark tunnel at the end of which there was a light of freedom. Unexpectedly they passed through the prison gates and found themselves in a square. They are now free and they don't know where to go.

VÁCLAV HAVEL (b. 1936), Czech playwright, president. Address to Institute of Contemporary Arts, London. Quoted in: *Independent* (London, 22 March 1990).

4 Ideology, politics and journalism, which luxuriate in failure, are impotent in the face of hope and joy.

P. J. O'ROURKE (b. 1947), U.S. journalist. "The Death of Communism," in *Rolling Stone* (New York, Nov. 1989; repr. in *Give War a Chance,* 1992).

See also Havel, Maiziere, Plesu on EUROPE, EASTERN.

NEW YEAR

1 The only way to spend New Year's Eve is either quietly with friends or in a brothel. Otherwise when the evening ends and people pair off, someone is bound to be left in tears.

> W. H. AUDEN (1907–73), Anglo-American poet. *The Table Talk of W. H. Auden,* "31 December, 1947" (comp. by Alan Ansen, ed. by Nicholas Jenkins, 1990).

2 Then sing, young hearts that are full of cheer,
With never a thought of sorrow;
The old goes out, but the glad young year
Comes merrily in tomorrow.

> EMILY MILLER (1833–1913), U.S. journalist, writer, poet. *New Year Song.*

3 Every New Year is the direct descendant, isn't it, of a long line of proven criminals?

> OGDEN NASH (1902–71), U.S. poet. *Good-by, Old Year, You Oaf or Why Don't They Pay the Bonus?,* in *The Primrose Path,* (1935).

4 Each age has deemed the new-born year
The fittest time for festal cheer.

> SIR WALTER SCOTT (1771–1832), Scottish novelist, poet. *Marmion,* cto. 6, Introduction.

NEW YORK

1 New York is a woman
holding, according to history,
a rag called liberty with one hand
and strangling the earth with the other.

> ADONIS [ALI AHMED SAID] (b. 1930), Syrian poet. *The Funeral of New York.*

2 New York is the meeting place of the peoples, the only city where you can hardly find a typical American.

> DJUNA BARNES (1892–1982), U.S. author, poet, columnist. "Greenwich Village As It Is," in *Pearson's Magazine* (Oct. 1916; repr. in *Djuna Barnes's New York,* 1989).

3 New York . . . is a city of geometric heights, a petrified desert of grids and lattices, an inferno of greenish abstraction under a flat sky, a real Metropolis from which man is absent by his very accumulation.

> ROLAND BARTHES (1915–80), French semiologist. "Buffet Finishes off New York," in *Arts* (Paris, 1959; repr. in *The Eiffel Tower and Other Mythologies,* tr. by Richard Howard, 1979).

4 It is a world completely rotten with wealth, power, senility, indifference, puritanism and mental hygiene, poverty and waste, technological futility and aimless violence, and yet I cannot help but feel it has about it something of the dawning of the universe.

> JEAN BAUDRILLARD (b. 1929), French semiologist. *America,* "New York" (1986; tr. 1988).

5 There is no human reason to be here, except for the sheer ecstasy of being crowded together.

> JEAN BAUDRILLARD (b. 1929), French semiologist. *America,* "New York" (1986; tr. 1988).

6 I think that New York is not the cultural center of America, but the business and administrative center of American culture.

> SAUL BELLOW (b. 1915), U.S. author. BBC radio interview (published in *Listener,* London, 22 May 1969).

7 Everybody ought to have a lower East Side in their life.

> IRVING BERLIN (1888–1989), U.S. songwriter. *Vogue* (New York, 1 Nov. 1962).

8 I like it here in New York. I like the idea of having to keep eyes in the back of your head all the time.

> JOHN CALE (b. 1940), British rock musician. *Times* (London, 27 Sept. 1989).

9 Manhattan. Sometimes from beyond the skyscrapers, across the hundreds of thousands of high walls, the cry of a tugboat finds you in your insomnia in the middle of the night, and you remember that this desert of iron and cement is an island.

> ALBERT CAMUS (1913–60), French-Algerian philosopher, author. *American Journals* (1978; tr. 1988), April/May 1946 entry.

10 In Africa I had indeed found a sufficiently frightful kind of loneliness but the isolation of this American ant heap was even more shattering.

> LOUIS-FERDINAND CÉLINE (1894–1961), French author. The narrator (Ferdinand Bardamu), in *Journey to the End of the Night* (1932; tr. 1934; ed. 1966, p. 179).

11 New York has never learnt the art of growing old by playing on all its pasts. Its present invents itself, from hour to hour, in the act of throwing away its previous accomplishments and challenging the future. A city composed of paroxysmal places in monumental reliefs.

> MICHEL DE CERTEAU (1925–86), French author, critic. *The Practice of Everyday Life,* ch. 7 (1974).

12 There was a time when all these things would have passed me by, like the flitting figures of a theatre, sufficient for the amusement of an hour. But now, I have lost the power of looking merely on the surface. Everything seems to me to come from the Infinite, to be filled with the Infinite, to be tending toward the Infinite. Do I see crowds of men hastening to extinguish a fire? I see not merely uncouth garbs, and fantastic, flickering lights, of lurid hue, like a trampling troop of gnomes—but straightway my mind is filled with thoughts about mutual helpfulness, human sympathy, the common bond of brotherhood, and the mysteriously deep foundations on which society rests; or rather, on which it now reels and totters.

> LYDIA M. CHILD (1802–80), U.S. abolitionist, writer, editor. Letter, 19 Aug. 1841 (published in: *Letters from New York,* vol. 1, Letter 1, 1843), referring to street life in New York.

13 New York is more now than the sum of its people and buildings. It makes sense only as a mechanical intelligence, a transporter system for the daily absorbing and nightly redeploying of the human multitudes whose services it requires.

> PETER CONRAD (b. 1948), Australian critic, author. *The Art of the City,* ch. 13 (1984).

14 In Manhattan, every flat surface is a potential stage and every inattentive waiter an unemployed, possibly unemployable, actor.

QUENTIN CRISP (b. 1908), British author. "Love Lies Bleeding," broadcast, 6 Aug. 1991 (published in *New Statesman & Society*, London, 9 Aug. 1991).

15 New York, you are an Egypt! But an Egypt turned inside out. For she erected pyramids of slavery to death, and you erect pyramids of democracy with the vertical organ-pipes of your skyscrapers all meeting at the point of infinity of liberty!

SALVADOR DALI (1904–89), Spanish painter. *The Secret Life of Salvador Dali*, ch. 11 (1948).

16 New York is full of people . . . with a feeling for the tangential adventure, the risky adventure, the interlude that's not likely to end in any double-ring ceremony.

JOAN DIDION (b. 1934), U.S. essayist. *Mademoiselle* (New York, Feb. 1961).

17 It is often said that New York is a city for only the very rich and the very poor. It is less often said that New York is also, at least for those of us who came there from somewhere else, a city for only the very young.

JOAN DIDION (b. 1934), U.S. essayist. *Slouching Towards Bethlehem*, "Goodbye to All That" (1968; first published 1967).

18 New York is a sucked orange.

RALPH WALDO EMERSON (1803–82), U.S. essayist, poet, philosopher. *The Conduct of Life*, "Culture" (1860).

19 The City of New York is currently undergoing a grave experiment that affects the comfort and, on occasion, the safety of even the most casual visitor. The experiment consists in seeing whether a city of that size can be operated on a far smaller amount of money than would make its life tolerable and a still smaller amount than would make it agreeable. The richer New Yorkers . . . are cooperating with an enthusiasm that the affluent rarely show for social experiment, and at great personal expense. They are paying for private security guards in unprecedented numbers and costly private schooling for their children . . . and they are accepting numerous other costs and inconveniences in order to show that private affluence is consistent with public squalor.

JOHN KENNETH GALBRAITH (b. 1908), U.S. economist. "The United States," in *New York* (15 Nov. 1971; repr. in *A View from the Stands*, 1986).

20 New York is something awful, something monstrous. I like to walk the streets, lost, but I recognize that New York is the world's greatest lie. New York is Senegal with machines.

FEDERICO GARCÍA LORCA (1898–1936), Spanish poet, playwright. Interview, 1931. Quoted in: *Poet in New York*, Introduction (1940; tr. 1988). Also published in: *Obras Completas*, vol. 3 (1986).

21 New York is a meeting place for every race in the world, but the Chinese, Armenians, Russians, and Germans remain foreigners. So does everyone except the blacks. There is no doubt but that the blacks exercise great influence in North America, and, no matter what anyone says, they are the most delicate, spiritual element in that world.

FEDERICO GARCÍA LORCA (1898–1936), Spanish poet, playwright. "A Poet in New York," lecture, March 1932, Madrid (published in *Poet in New York*, 1940; tr. 1988).

22 We New Yorkers see more death and violence than most soldiers do, grow a thick chitin on our backs, grimace like a rat and learn to do a disappearing act. Long ago we outgrew the need to be blowhards about our masculinity; we leave that to the Alaskans and Texans, who have more time for it.

EDWARD HOAGLAND (b. 1932), U.S. novelist, essayist. "City Rat," in *Audience* (Hollywood, March 1972; repr. in *Heart's Desire*, 1988).

23 Living in New York is like being at some terrible late-night party. You're tired, you've had a headache since you arrived, but you can't leave because then you'd miss the party.

SIMON HOGGART (b. 1946), British journalist. *America: A User's Guide*, ch. 1 (1990).

24 Here at our sea-washed, sunset gates shall stand
A mighty woman with a torch, whose flame
Is the imprisoned lightning, and her name
Mother of exiles.

EMMA LAZARUS (1849–87), U.S. poet. *The New Colossus*.

25 A hundred times have I thought New York is a catastrophe . . . it is a beautiful catastrophe.

LE CORBUSIER (1887–1965), Swiss-born French architect. Quoted in: *New York Herald Tribune* (6 Aug. 1961).

26 New York is what Paris was in the twenties . . . the center of the art world. And we want to be in the center. It's the greatest place on earth . . . I've got a lot of friends here and I even brought my own cash.

JOHN LENNON (1940–80), British rock musician. *The Tomorrow Show*, April 1975, NBC-TV. Lennon was finally given residency status in the U.S. the following year.

27 It is the place where all the aspirations of the Western World meet to form one vast master aspiration, as powerful as the suction of a steam dredge. It is the icing on the pie called Christian civilization.

H. L. MENCKEN (1880–1956), U.S. journalist. *Prejudices*, ch. 9 (Sixth Series, 1927).

28 The City of New York is like an enormous citadel, a modern Carcassonne. Walking between the magnificent skyscrapers one feels the presence on the fringe of a howling, raging mob, a mob with empty bellies, a mob unshaven and in rags.

HENRY MILLER (1891–1980), U.S. author. *The Cosmological Eye*, "Glittering Pie" (1939).

29 New York has a trip-hammer vitality which drives you insane with restlessness, if you have no inner stabilizer. . . . In New York I have always felt lonely, the loneliness of the caged animal, which brings on crime, sex, alcohol and other madnesses.

HENRY MILLER (1891–1980), U.S. author. *The Colossus of Maroussi*, pt. 3 (1941).

30 If ever there was an aviary overstocked with jays it is that Yaptown-on-the-Hudson, called New York.

> O. HENRY [WILLIAM SYDNEY PORTER] (1862–1910), U.S. short-story writer. *The Gentle Grafter*, "A Tempered Wind" (1908).

31 And New York is the most beautiful city in the world? It is not far from it. No urban night is like the night there. . . . Squares after squares of flame, set up and cut into the aether. Here is our poetry, for we have pulled down the stars to our will.

> EZRA POUND (1885–1972), U.S. poet, critic. "Patria Mia," in *New Age* (London, 18 Sept. 1912).

32 New York will be a great place when they finish it.

> NEW YORK SAYING.

33 This city is neither a jungle nor the moon. . . . In long shot: a cosmic smudge, a conglomerate of bleeding energies. Close up, it is a fairly legible printed circuit, a transistorized labyrinth of beastly tracks, a data bank for asthmatic voice-prints.

> SUSAN SONTAG (b. 1933), U.S. essayist. "Debriefing," in *American Review* (New York, Sept. 1973; repr. in *I, Etcetera*, 1978).

34 New York, home of the vivisectors of the mind, and of the mentally vivisected still to be reassembled, of those who live intact, habitually wondering about their states of sanity, and home of those whose minds have been dead, bearing the scars of resurrection.

> MURIEL SPARK (b. 1918), British novelist. *The Hothouse by the East River*, ch. 1 (1973).

35 New York is a field of tireless and antagonistic interests—undoubtedly fascinating but horribly unreal. Everybody is looking at everybody else—a foolish crowd walking on mirrors.

> WALLACE STEVENS (1879–1955), U.S. poet. *Souvenirs and Prophecies: The Young Wallace Stevens*, ch. 4 (ed. by Holly Stevens, 1977), journal entry for 15 June 1900.

36 The siren south is well enough, but New York, at the beginning of March, is a hoyden we would not care to miss—a drafty wench, her temperature up and down, full of bold promises and dust in the eye.

> E. B. WHITE (1899–1985), U.S. author, editor. "New York in March," in *New Yorker* (2 March 1935; repr. in *Writings from the New Yorker 1927–1976*, ed. by Rebecca M. Dale, 1991).

37 Though one can dine in New York, one could not dwell there.

> OSCAR WILDE (1854–1900), Anglo-Irish playwright, author. "The American Invasion," in *Court and Society Review* (London, March 1887).

38 It was a cruel city, but it was a lovely one, a savage city, yet it had such tenderness, a bitter, harsh, and violent catacomb of stone and steel and tunneled rock, slashed savagely with light, and roaring, fighting a constant ceaseless warfare of men and of machinery; and yet it was so sweetly and so delicately pulsed, as full of warmth, of passion, and of love, as it was full of hate.

> THOMAS WOLFE (1900–1938), U.S. author. Monk, in *The Web and the Rock*, ch. 30 (1939).

39 New York is the biggest mouth in the world. It appears to be prime example of the herd instinct, leading

the universal urban conspiracy to beguile man from his birthright (the good ground), to hang him by his eyebrows from skyhooks above hard pavement, to crucify him, sell him, or be sold by him.

> FRANK LLOYD WRIGHT (1869–1959), U.S. architect. *The Living City*, pt. 1, "The-Shadow-of-the-Wall—Primitive Instincts Still Alive" (1958).

See also Baudrillard on CITIES AND CITY LIFE; Wharton on DIVORCE; Galbraith on MULTICULTURALISM; Cummings on SKYSCRAPERS.

NEWS

1 Flash'd from his bed the electric tidings came,
He is no better, he is much the same.

> ANONYMOUS. Parody of the style of poet laureate Alfred Austin (1835–1913) by a Dublin undergraduate c. 1871, describing the illness of the Prince of Wales (later Edward VII).

2 Between what matters and what seems to matter, how should the world we know judge wisely?

> E. C. BENTLEY (1875–1956), British novelist, journalist. Opening words of *Trent's Last Case* (1912).

3 The greatest felony in the news business today is to be behind, or to miss a big story. So speed and quantity substitute for thoroughness and quality, for accuracy and context. The pressure to compete, the fear somebody else will make the splash first, creates a frenzied environment in which a blizzard of information is presented and serious questions may not be raised.

> CARL BERNSTEIN (b. 1944), U.S. journalist. *Guardian* (London, 3 June 1992).

4 News is the first rough draft of history.

> PHILIP L. GRAHAM (1915–63), U.S. newspaper publisher. This aphorism has also been attributed to *Washington Post* editor Ben C. Bradlee, but Bradlee, in an interview in *Vanity Fair* (New York, Sept. 1991) credited it to Graham, formerly his boss at the *Post*.

5 News reports stand up as people, and people wither into editorials. Clichés walk around on two legs while men are having theirs shot off.

> KARL KRAUS (1874–1936), Austrian satirist. See also Austrian satirist, Grumbler, in *The Last Days of Mankind*, Prologue (1915–22; repr. in *In These Great Times: A Karl Kraus Reader*, ed. by Harry Zohn, 1976).

6 Listening to a news broadcast is like smoking a cigarette and crushing the butt in the ashtray.

> MILAN KUNDERA (b. 1929), Czech author, critic. Paul, in *Immortality*, pt. 3, "The Brilliant Ally of His Own Gravediggers" (1991).

7 I do not like to get the news, because there has never been an era when so many things were going so right for so many of the wrong persons.

> OGDEN NASH (1902–71), U.S. poet. *Everybody Tells Me Everything*, in *The Face Is Familiar* (1940).

8 Newsmen believe that news is a tacitly acknowledged fourth branch of the federal system. This is why most news about government sounds as if it were federally mandated—serious, bulky and blandly worthwhile, like a high-fiber diet set in type.

> P. J. O'ROURKE (b. 1947), U.S. journalist. *Parliament of Whores*,

"The Dictatorship of Boredom: The Winners Go to Washington, D.C." (1991).

9 The conflict between the men who make and the men who report the news is as old as time. News may be true, but it is not truth, and reporters and officials seldom see it the same way. . . . In the old days, the reporters or couriers of bad news were often put to the gallows; now they are given the Pulitzer Prize, but the conflict goes on.

JAMES RESTON (b. 1909), U.S. journalist. *The Artillery of the Press,* "The Tug of History" (1966).

10 To a philosopher all *news,* as it is called, is gossip, and they who edit it and read it are old women over their tea.

HENRY DAVID THOREAU (1817–62), U.S. philosopher, author, naturalist. *Walden,* "Where I Lived, and What I Lived For" (1854).

11 In the case of news, we should always wait for the sacrament of confirmation.

VOLTAIRE (1694–1778), French philosopher, author. Letter, 28 Aug. 1760.

12 News is what a chap who doesn't care much about anything wants to read. And it's only news until he's read it. After that it's dead.

EVELYN WAUGH (1903–66), British novelist. Corker, in *Scoop,* bk. 1, ch. 5, sct. 1 (1938).

13 It is always the unreadable that occurs.

OSCAR WILDE (1854–1900), Anglo-Irish playwright, author. Vivian, in "The Decay of Lying" (published in *Intentions,* 1891).

See also Lebowitz on DISC JOCKEYS.

NEWSPAPERS AND MAGAZINES

1 Reading someone else's newspaper is like sleeping with someone else's wife. Nothing seems to be precisely in the right place, and when you find what you are looking for, it is not clear then how to respond to it.

MALCOLM BRADBURY (b. 1932), British author. Dr. Jochum, in *Stepping Westward,* bk. 1, ch. 1 (1965).

2 Rage is the only quality which has kept me, or anybody I have ever studied, writing columns for newspapers.

JIMMY BRESLIN (b. 1929), U.S. journalist, author. *Times* (London, 9 May 1990).

3 Frankly, despite my horror of the press, I'd love to rise from the grave every ten years or so and go buy a few newspapers.

LUIS BUÑUEL (1900–1983), Spanish filmmaker. *My Last Sigh,* ch. 21 (1983).

4 I sometimes think of what future historians will say of us. A single sentence will suffice for modern man: he fornicated and read the papers.

ALBERT CAMUS (1913–60), French-Algerian philosopher, author. The narrator (Jean-Baptiste Clamence), in *The Fall* (1956; ed. 1957, p. 7).

5 A journal produced by office-boys for office-boys.

ROBERT CECIL, MARQUIS OF SALISBURY (1830–1903), English

Conservative politician, prime minister. Of the London *Daily Mail.* Quoted in: H. Hamilton Fyfe, *Northcliffe: An Intimate Biography,* ch. 4 (1930).

6 Their constant yelping about a free press means, with a few honorable exceptions, freedom to peddle scandal, crime, sex, sensationalism, hate, innuendo and the political and financial uses of propaganda. A newspaper is a business out to make money through advertising revenue. That is predicated on the circulation and you know what circulation depends on.

RAYMOND CHANDLER (1888–1959), U.S. author. Harlan Potter, in *The Long Goodbye,* ch. 32 (1954).

7 A magazine or a newspaper is a shop. Each is an experiment and represents a new focus, a new ratio between commerce and intellect.

JOHN JAY CHAPMAN (1862–1933), U.S. author. *Practical Agitation,* ch. 4 (1898).

8 I believe it has been said that one copy of *The Times* contains more useful information than the whole of the historical works of Thucydides.

RICHARD COBDEN (1804–65), English radical politician. Speech, 27 Dec. 1850.

9 To read a newspaper is to refrain from reading something worth while. The first discipline of education must therefore be to refuse resolutely to feed the mind with canned chatter.

ALEISTER CROWLEY (1875–1947), British occultist. *The Confessions of Aleister Crowley,* ch. 23 (1929; rev. 1970).

10 Certainly the most obvious . . . example of the strictly infantile essence of America's all-conquering mentality greets our eyes daily, anywhere and everywhere, in the guise of the tabloid newspaper. The tabloid newspaper actually means to the typical American of the era what the Bible is popularly supposed to have meant to the typical Pilgrim Father: *viz.* a very present help in times of trouble, plus a means of keeping out of trouble via harmless, since vicarious, indulgence in the pomps and vanities of this wicked world.

E. E. CUMMINGS (1894–1962), U.S. poet. "The Tabloid Newspaper," in *Vanity Fair* (New York, Dec. 1926; repr. in *A Miscellany,* ed. by George J. Firmage, 1958).

11 The newspaper has debauched the American until he is a slavish, simpering, and angerless citizen; it has taught him to be a lump mass-man toward fraud, simony, murder, and lunacies more vile than those of Commodus or Caracalla.

EDWARD DAHLBERG (1900–1977), U.S. author, critic. *Alms for Oblivion,* "Peopleless Fiction" (1964).

12 They are so filthy and bestial that no honest man would admit one into his house for a water-closet doormat.

CHARLES DICKENS (1812–70), English novelist. Comment on the U.S. press, March 1842, while on an American tour. Quoted in: Hesketh Pearson, *Dickens,* ch. 8 (1949).

13 Any rich, unprogressive old party with that particularly grasping, acquisitive form of mentality known as financial genius can own a paper that is the intellectual meat and drink of thousands of tired, hurried men, men too involved in the business of modern living to swallow anything but predigested food. For two cents the voter buys his politics, prejudices, and philosophy. A year later there is a new political ring or a change in the paper's ownership, consequence: more confusion, more contradiction, a sudden inrush of new ideas, their tempering, their distillation, the reaction against them.

> F. SCOTT FITZGERALD (1896–1940), U.S. author. Amory Blaine, in *This Side of Paradise*, bk. 2, ch. 2, "Restlessness" (1920).

14   Everything known before it happens; and headlines twice the size of the events.

> JOHN GALSWORTHY (1867–1933), English novelist, playwright. General Cherrell, in *Over the River*, ch. 27 (1933), the last of *The Forsythe Chronicles*.

15   The newspaper is the natural enemy of the book, as the whore is of the decent woman.

> EDMOND (1822–96) AND JULES DE GONCOURT (1830–70), French writers, journalists. *The Goncourt Journals* (1888–96; repr. in *Pages from the Goncourt Journal*, ed. by Robert Baldick, 1962), July 1858 entry.

16   Whate'er men do, or say, or think, or dream,
Our motley paper seizes for its theme.

> JUVENAL (40–125), Roman satiric poet. *Satires*, Satire 1 (tr. and embellished by Alexander Pope), used as the epigraph of the "Prospectus" in the first issue of Richard Steele's *Tatler* (12 April 1709), outlining the general principles on which the paper was to be published.

17   What appears in newspapers is often new but seldom true.

> PATRICK KAVANAGH (1905–67), Irish poet, author. *Collected Pruse*, "Signposts" (1967).

18   A good newspaper is never nearly good enough but a lousy newspaper is a joy forever.

> GARRISON KEILLOR (b. 1942), U.S. author. "That Old 'Picayune-Moon,'" in *Harper's* (New York, Sept. 1990).

19   It is uplifting to lose one's faith in a reality which looks the way it is described in a newspaper.

> KARL KRAUS (1874–1936), Austrian satirist. "In Praise of a Topsy-Turvy Lifestyle," in *Simplicissimus*, (Munich, 1908; repr. in *In These Great Times: A Karl Kraus Reader*, ed. by Harry Zohn, 1976).

20   If one reads a newspaper only for information, one does not learn the truth, not even the truth about the paper. The truth is that the newspaper is not a statement of contents but the contents themselves; and more than that, it is an instigator.

> KARL KRAUS (1874–1936), Austrian satirist. "In These Great Times," speech, 19 Nov. 1914, Vienna (published in: *Die Fackel*, Vienna, Dec. 1914; repr. in *In These Great Times: A Karl Kraus Reader*, ed. by Harry Zohn, 1976).

21   Newspapers always excite curiosity. No one ever lays one down without a feeling of disappointment.

> CHARLES LAMB (1775–1834), English essayist, critic. *The Last Essays of Elia*, "Detached Thoughts on Books and Reading" (1833).

22   The art of newspaper paragraphing is to stroke a platitude until it purrs like an epigram.

> DON MARQUIS (1878–1937), U.S. humorist, journalist. Quoted in: E. Anthony, *O Rare Don Marquis*, ch. 11 (1962).

23   The tabloids are like animals, with their own behavioural patterns. There's no point in complaining about them, any more than complaining that lions might eat you.

> DAVID MELLOR (b. 1949), British Conservative politician. *Independent* (London, 3 Nov. 1992). Mellor was forced to resign his government position in 1992, largely as a result of pressure from the British press.

24   All successful newpapers are ceaselessly querulous and bellicose. They never defend anyone or anything if they can help it; if the job is forced upon them, they tackle it by denouncing someone or something else.

> H. L. MENCKEN (1880–1956), U.S. journalist. *Prejudices*, ch. 13, First Series (1919).

25   A good newspaper, I suppose, is a nation talking to itself.

> ARTHUR MILLER (b. 1915), U.S. dramatist. Quoted in: *Observer* (London, 26 Nov. 1961).

26   To read a newspaper for the first time is like coming into a film that has been on for an hour. Newspapers are like serials. To understand them you have to take knowledge to them; the knowledge that serves best is the knowledge provided by the newspaper itself.

> V. S. NAIPAUL (b. 1932), Trinidad-born British writer. *The Enigma of Arrival*, "The Journey" (1987), referring to *The New York Times*.

27   We live under a government of men and morning newspapers.

> WENDELL PHILLIPS (1811–84), U.S. abolitionist, orator. "The Press," speech (28 Jan. 1852).

28   People are always dying in the *Times* who don't seem to die in other papers, and they die at greater length and maybe even with a little more grace.

> JAMES RESTON (b. 1909), U.S. journalist. *New Leader* (New York, 7 Jan. 1963).

29   Newspapers are the second hand of history. This hand, however, is usually not only of inferior metal to the other hands, it also seldom works properly.

> ARTHUR SCHOPENHAUER (1788–1860), German philosopher. *Parerga and Paralipomena*, vol. 2, ch. 19, sct. 233 (1851).

30   Neither in what it gives, nor in what it does not give, nor in the mode of presentation, must the unclouded face of truth suffer wrong. Comment is free, but facts are sacred.

> C. P. SCOTT (1846–1932), British author, journalist. Editorial in *Manchester Guardian* (5 May 1921), marking the paper's first hundred years. Scott served as editor of the *Manchester Guardian* for fifty-nine years—the longest editorship of a national newspaper anywhere in the world..

31   Newspapers are unable, seemingly, to discriminate between a bicycle accident and the collapse of civilisation.

> GEORGE BERNARD SHAW (1856–1950), Anglo-Irish playwright, critic. *Too True to Be Good*, Preface (1931).

32   That's where *Time* magazine lives . . . way out there on the puzzled, masturbating edge, peering through the keyhole and selling what they see to the big wide world of chamber of commerce voyeurs who support the public prints.

HUNTER S. THOMPSON (b. 1939), U.S. journalist. "The Ultimate Free Lancer," in *Distant Drummer* (Nov. 1967; repr. in *The Great Shark Hunt*, 1979).

33 I have no time to read newspapers. If you chance to live and move and have your being in that thin stratum in which the events which make the news transpire—thinner than the paper on which it is printed—then these things will fill the world for you; but if you soar above or dive below that plane, you cannot remember nor be reminded of them.

HENRY DAVID THOREAU (1817–62), U.S. philosopher, author, naturalist. *Journals* (1906), entry for 3 April 1853.

34 I consider that that "that" that worries us so much should be forgotten. Rats desert a sinking ship. Thats infest a sinking magazine.

JAMES THURBER (1894–1961), U.S. humorist, illustrator. Memo to *New Yorker* (1959; published in *New York Times Book Review*, 4 Dec. 1988).

35 *You* try to tell *me* anything about the newspaper business! Sir, I have been through it from Alpha to Omaha, and I tell you that the less a man knows the bigger the noise he makes and the higher the salary he commands.

MARK TWAIN (1835–1910), U.S. author. "How I Edited an Agricultural Paper" (1870; repr. in *The Complete Short Stories*, ed. by Charles Neider, 1957).

36 When other helpers fail and comforts flee, when the senses decay and the mind moves in a narrower and narrower circle, when the grasshopper is a burden and the postman brings no letters, and even the Royal Family is no longer quite what it was, an obituary column stands fast.

SYLVIA TOWNSEND WARNER (1893–1978), British author. *Autumn River*, "Their Quiet Lives" (1966).

38 Newspapers . . . give us the bald, sordid, disgusting facts of life. They chronicle, with degrading avidity, the sins of the second-rate, and with the conscientiousness of the illiterate give us accurate and prosaic details of the doings of people of absolutely no interest whatsoever.

OSCAR WILDE (1854–1900), Anglo-Irish playwright, author. Gilbert, in *The Critic as Artist*, pt. 2 (published in *Intentions*, 1891).

39 There should be a law that no ordinary newspaper should be allowed to write about art. The harm they do by their foolish and random writing it would be impossible to overestimate—not to the artist but to the public. . . . Without them we would judge a man simply by his work; but at present the newspapers are trying hard to induce the public to judge a sculptor, for instance, never by his statues but by the way he treats his wife; a painter by the amount of his income and a poet by the colour of his necktie.

OSCAR WILDE (1854–1900), Anglo-Irish playwright, author. "Art and the Handicraftsman," manuscript written 1882 in Philadelphia for a lecture (published in *Aristotle at Afternoon Tea: The Rare Oscar Wilde*, 1991)

See also EDITORS; JOURNALISM AND JOURNALISTS; The PRESS.

SIR ISAAC NEWTON

1 Nature and nature's laws lay hid in night;
God said *Let Newton be!* and all was light.

ALEXANDER POPE (1688–1744), English satirical poet. *Epitaph Intended for Sir Isaac Newton in Westminster Abbey*. British author J. C. (Sir John) Squire (1884–1958) coined the following in answer to Pope's: It did not last: the Devil, howling *Ho! / Let Einstein be!* restored the status quo.

2 Where the statue stood
Of Newton with his prism and silent face,
The marble index of a mind for ever
Voyaging through strange seas of thought, alone.

WILLIAM WORDSWORTH (1770–1850), English poet. *The Prelude*, bk. 3, of the statue of Newton at Trinity College, Cambridge University.

NIGHT

1 The night is a skin pulled over the head of day that the day may be in torment.

DJUNA BARNES (1892–1982), U.S. author, poet, columnist. Doctor, in *Nightwood*, ch. 5 (1936).

2 I cannot walk through the suburbs in the solitude of the night without thinking that the night pleases us because it suppresses idle details, just as our memory does.

JORGE LUIS BORGES (1899–1986), Argentinian author. *Labyrinths*, "A New Refutation of Time" (1964).

3 For the night
Shows stars and women in a better light.

LORD BYRON (1788–1824), English poet. *Don Juan*, cto. 2, st. 152.

4 Night makes no difference 'twixt the Priest and Clerk;
Joan as my Lady is as good i'th'dark.

ROBERT HERRICK (1591–1674), English poet, critic. *No Difference i' th' Dark*.

5 Whoever thinks of going to bed before twelve o'clock is a scoundrel.

SAMUEL JOHNSON (1709–84), English author, lexicographer. Quoted in: *Works*, vol. 9, "Apophthegms" (ed. by John Hawkins, 1787–89) and *Johnsonian Miscellanies*, vol. 2 (ed. by George Birkbeck Hill, 1897, p. 19).

6 Beware thoughts that come in the night. They aren't turned properly; they come in askew, free of sense and restriction, deriving from the most remote of sources.

WILLIAM LEAST HEAT MOON [WILLIAM TROGDON] (b. 1939), U.S. author. Opening words of *Blue Highways: A Journey into America* (1983).

7 And the night shall be filled with music,
And the cares, that infest the day,
Shall fold their tents, like the Arabs,
And as silently steal away.

HENRY WADSWORTH LONGFELLOW (1807–82), U.S. poet. *The Day Is Done*.

8 Blemishes are hid by night and every fault forgiven; darkness makes any woman fair.

OVID (43 B.C.–A.D. 17), Roman poet. *Ars Amatoria,* bk. 1.

9 Night, the beloved. Night, when words fade and things come alive. When the destructive analysis of day is done, and all that is truly important becomes whole and sound again. When man reassembles his fragmentary self and grows with the calm of a tree.

ANTOINE DE SAINT-EXUPÉRY (1900–1944), French aviator, author. *Flight to Arras,* ch. 1 (1942).

10 O comfort-killing night, image of hell,
Dim register and notary of shame,
Black stage for tragedies and murders fell,
Vast sin-concealing chaos, nurse of blame!

WILLIAM SHAKESPEARE (1564–1616), English dramatist, poet. *The Rape of Lucrece.*

11 Night is a dead monotonous period under a roof; but in the open world it passes lightly, with its stars and dews and perfumes, and the hours are marked by changes in the face of Nature. What seems a kind of temporal death to people choked between walls and curtains, is only a light and living slumber to the man who sleeps afield.

ROBERT LOUIS STEVENSON (1850–94), Scottish novelist, essayist, poet. *Travels with a Donkey,* "A Night Among the Pines" (1879).

12 Press close bare-bosom'd night—press close magnetic nourishing night!
Night of south winds! night of the large few stars!
Still nodding night! mad naked summer night.

WALT WHITMAN (1819–92), U.S. poet. *Song of Myself,* sct. 21, in *Leaves of Grass* (1855).

13 By night an atheist half believes a God.

EDWARD YOUNG (1683–1765), English poet, dramatist. *Night Thoughts,* "The Complaint: Night V" (1742–46).

See also McLaughlin on PLANNING.

NIHILISM

1 Nihilism is not only despair and negation, but above all the desire to despair and to negate.

ALBERT CAMUS (1913–60), French-Algerian philosopher, author. *The Rebel,* pt. 2, "The Rejection of Salvation" (1951; tr. 1953).

2 All roads are blocked to a philosophy which reduces everything to the word "no." To "no" there is only one answer and that is "yes." Nihilism has no substance. There is no such thing as nothingness, and zero does not exist. Everything is something. Nothing is nothing. Man lives more by affirmation than by bread.

VICTOR HUGO (1802–85), French poet, dramatist, novelist. *Les Misérables,* pt. 2, bk. 7, ch. 6 (1862).

3 Nothing requires a greater effort of thought than arguments to justify the rule of non-thought.

MILAN KUNDERA (b. 1929), Czech author, critic. The Bear, in *Immortality,* pt. 3, "The Brilliant Ally of His Own Gravediggers" (1991).

4 What every artist should try to prevent is the car, in which is our civilized life, plunging over the side of the precipice—the exhibitionist extremist promoter driving the whole bag of tricks into a nihilistic nothingness or zero.

WYNDHAM LEWIS (1882–1957), British author, painter. *The Demon of Progress in the Arts,* "There Is a Limit, Beyond Which There Is Nothing" (1954).

5 Nihilism is best done by professionals.

IGGY POP (b. 1947), U.S. rock singer. *Independent* (London, 12 July 1990).

6 When there's no future
How can there be sin
We're the flowers in the dustbin
We're the poison in your human machine
We're the future
Your future
God Save the Queen.

THE SEX PISTOLS (1976–79), British punk band. "God Save the Queen," from the album *Never Mind the Bollocks . . . Here's the Sex Pistols* (1977).

THE NINETEENTH CENTURY

1 A population sodden with drink, steeped in vice, eaten up by every social and physical malady, these are the denizens of Darkest England amidst whom my life has been spent.

WILLIAM BOOTH (1829–1912), English evangelist, founder of the Salvation Army. *In Darkest England, and the Way Out,* pt. 1, ch. 1 (1890).

2 This we take it is the grand characteristic of our age. By our skill in Mechanism, it has come to pass, that in the management of external things we excel all other ages; while in whatever respects the pure moral nature, in true dignity of soul and character, we are perhaps inferior to most civilised ages.

THOMAS CARLYLE (1795–1881), Scottish essayist, historian. *Signs of the Times* in *Edinburgh Review,* no. 98 (1829; repr. in *Critical and Miscellaneous Essays,* 1839) .

3 The nineteenth century planted the words which the twentieth ripened into the atrocities of Stalin and Hitler. There is hardly an atrocity committed in the twentieth century that was not foreshadowed or even advocated by some noble man of words in the nineteenth.

ERIC HOFFER (1902–83), U.S. philosopher. *Reflections on the Human Condition,* aph. 64 (1973).

4 The three great problems of this century, the degradation of man in the proletariat, the subjection of women through hunger, the atrophy of the child by darkness.

VICTOR HUGO (1802–85), French poet, dramatist, novelist. *Les Misérables,* Preface (1862).

5 There is one great fact, characteristic of this our nineteenth century, a fact which no party dares deny. On the one hand, there have started into life industrial and scientific forces which no epoch of former human history had ever suspected. On the other hand, there exist symptoms of decay, far surpassing the horrors recorded of the latter times of the Roman empire. In our days everything seems pregnant with its contrary.

> KARL MARX (1818–83), German social philosopher, revolutionary. Speech, 14 April 1856, London (published in *People's Paper*, London, 19 April 1856; repr. in *Surveys from Exile*, 1973).

6 The most revolutionary invention of the Nineteenth Century was the artificial sterilization of marriage.

> GEORGE BERNARD SHAW (1856–1950), Anglo-Irish playwright, critic. *Man and Superman*, "Maxims for Revolutionists: Marriage" (1903).

7 The history of the Victorian Age will never be written: we know too much about it.

> LYTTON STRACHEY (1880–1932), British biographer, historian. *Eminent Victorians*, Preface (1918).

9 The nineteenth century is a turning point in history, simply on account of the work of two men, Darwin and Renan, the one the critic of the Book of Nature, the other the critic of the books of God. Not to recognise this is to miss the meaning of one of the most important eras in the progress of the world.

> OSCAR WILDE (1854–1900), Anglo-Irish playwright, author. Gilbert, in *The Critic as Artist*, pt. 2 (published in *Intentions*, 1891).

8 Death and vulgarity are the only two facts in the nineteenth century that one cannot explain away.

> OSCAR WILDE (1854–1900), Anglo-Irish playwright, author. Lord Henry, in *The Picture of Dorian Gray*, ch. 19 (1891).

10 Men felt a chill in their hearts; a damp in their minds. In a desperate effort to snuggle their feelings into some sort of warmth, one subterfuge was tried after another. . . sentences swelled, adjectives multiplied, lyrics became epics.

> VIRGINIA WOOLF (1882–1941), British novelist. *Orlando*, ch. 5 (1928), referring to the onset of the Victorian age.

See also Wilde on LITERATURE.

RICHARD MILHOUS NIXON

1 I think that Richard Nixon will go down in history as a true folk hero, who struck a vital blow to the whole diseased concept of the revered image and gave the American virtue of irreverence and skepticism back to the people.

> WILLIAM BURROUGHS (b. 1914), U.S. author. *The Adding Machine*, "A Word to the Wise Guy" (1985).

2 Do you realize the responsibility I carry? I'm the only person between Nixon and the White House.

> JOHN F. KENNEDY (1917–63), U.S. Democratic politician, president. Teasing remark to a liberal supporter during the 1960 election campaign. Quoted in: Theodore C. Sorensen, *Kennedy*, pt. 2, ch. 7 (1965). Nixon won 49.6 percent of the total vote.

3 To have striven so hard, to have molded a public personality out of so amorphous an identity, to have sustained that superhuman effort only to end with every weakness disclosed and every error compounding the downfall—that was a fate of biblical proportions. Evidently the Deity would not tolerate the presumption that

all can be manipulated; an object lesson of the limits of human presumption was necessary.

> HENRY KISSINGER (b. 1923), U.S. Republican politician, secretary of state. *Years of Upheaval*, ch. 25, "The End of the Road" (1982), on the downfall of Richard Nixon.

4 Nixon is the kind of politician who would cut down a redwood tree, then mount the stump for a speech on conservation.

> ADLAI STEVENSON (1900–1965), U.S. Democratic politician. Quoted in: Leon Harris, *The Fine Art of Political Wit*, ch. 10 (1965).

5 The trouble with Nixon is that he's a serious *politics junkie*. He's totally hooked . . . and like any other junkie, he's a bummer to have around: especially as President.

> HUNTER S. THOMPSON (b. 1939), U.S. journalist. *The Great Shark Hunt*, "Jacket Copy for Fear and Loathing in Las Vegas" (1979).

NOISE

1 For twenty-five centuries, Western knowledge has tried to look upon the world. It has failed to understand that the world is not for the beholding. It is for hearing. It is not legible, but audible. Our science has always desired to monitor, measure, abstract, and castrate meaning, forgetting that life is full of noise and that death alone is silent: work noise, noise of man, and noise of beast. Noise bought, sold, or prohibited. Nothing essential happens in the absence of noise.

> JACQUES ATTALI (b. 1943), Algerian-born French economist, writer. *Noise: The Political Economy of Music*, ch. 1 (1977).

2 The world is never quiet, even its silence eternally resounds with the same notes, in vibrations which escape our ears. As for those that we perceive, they carry sounds to us, occasionally a chord, never a melody.

> ALBERT CAMUS (1913–60), French-Algerian philosopher, author. *The Rebel*, "Rebellion and Art" (1951; tr. 1953).

3 In antiquity there was only silence. In the nineteenth century, with the invention of the machine, Noise was born. Today, Noise triumphs and reigns supreme over the sensibility of men.

> LUIGI RUSSOLO (1885–1947), Italian painter, Futurist. "The Art of Noise," in *Futurist Manifesto* (Milan, 1913; repr. in Michael Kirby, *Futurist Performance*, 1971).

See also Attali on MUSIC.

NONCONFORMITY

1 If you are cast in a different mould to the majority, it is no merit of yours: Nature did it.

> CHARLOTTE BRONTË (1816–55), English novelist. Mr. Rochester in *Jane Eyre*, ch. 14 (1847).

2 Caprice, independence and rebellion, which are opposed to the social order, are essential to the good health of an ethnic group. We shall measure the good health of this group by the number of its delinquents.

Nothing is more immobilizing than the spirit of *deference*.

> JEAN DUBUFFET (1901–85), French sculptor, painter. *Asphyxiating Culture* (1968; repr. in *Asphyxiating Culture and Other Writings*, 1986; tr. 1988).

3 What forests of laurel we bring, and the tears of mankind, to those who stood firm against the opinion of their contemporaries!

> RALPH WALDO EMERSON (1803–82), U.S. essayist, poet, philosopher. *The Conduct of Life,* "Culture" (1860).

4 So much they scorn the crowd, that if the throng
By chance go right, they purposely go wrong.

> ALEXANDER POPE (1688–1744), English satirical poet. *Essay on Criticism* (1711).

5 If someone does something we disapprove of, we regard him as bad if we believe we can deter him from persisting in his conduct, but we regard him as mad if we believe we cannot. In either case, the crucial issue is our control of the other: the more we lose control over him, and the more he assumes control over himself, the more, in case of conflict, we are likely to consider him mad rather than just bad.

> THOMAS SZASZ (b. 1920), U.S. psychiatrist. *The Second Sin,* "Control and Self-control" (1973).

See also DISSENT.

NONVIOLENCE

1 It is my contention that civil disobedients are nothing but the latest form of voluntary association, and that they are thus quite in tune with the oldest traditions of the country.

> HANNAH ARENDT (1906–75), German-born U.S. political philosopher. *Crises of the Republic,* "Civil Disobedience" (1972).

2 The only thing that's been a worse flop than the organization of non-violence has been the organization of violence.

> JOAN BAEZ (b. 1941), U.S. singer. *Daybreak,* "What Would You Do?" (1968).

3 Hurt a fly!
He would not for the world: he's pitiful
To flies even. "Sing," says he, "and tease me still,
If that's your way, poor insect."

> ELIZABETH BARRETT BROWNING (1806–61), English poet. *Aurora Leigh,* bk. 4 (1857), of Aurora's cousin Romney Leigh.

4 The people in power will not disappear voluntarily, giving flowers to the cops just isn't going to work. This thinking is fostered by the establishment; they like nothing better than love and nonviolence. The only way I like to see cops given flowers is in a flower pot from a high window.

> WILLIAM BURROUGHS (b. 1914), U.S. author. *The Job: Interviews with Daniel Odier,* "Prisoners of the Earth Come Out" (1969).

5 Only a philosophy of eternity, in the world today, could justify non-violence.

> ALBERT CAMUS (1913–60), French-Algerian philosopher, author. *The Rebel,* pt. 5, "Historic Murder" (1951; tr. 1953).

6 It is my hope that as the Negro plunges deeper into the quest for freedom and justice he will plunge even deeper into the philosophy of non-violence. The Negro all over the South must come to the point that he can say to his white brother: "We will match your capacity to inflict suffering with our capacity to endure suffering. We will meet your physical force with soul force. We will not hate you, but we will not obey your evil laws. We will soon wear you down by pure capacity to suffer."

> MARTIN LUTHER KING, JR. (1929–68), U.S. clergyman, civil rights leader. Letter, 28 Oct. 1957.

7 To be deeply committed to negotiations, to be opposed to a particular war or military action, is not only considered unpatriotic, it also casts serious doubt on one's manhood.

> MYRIAM MIEDZIAN, U.S. author. *Boys Will Be Boys,* ch. 2 (1991).

See also King on PROTEST; Thoreau on TAXATION.

NORMALITY

1 Nothing is poetical if plain daylight is not poetical; and no monster should amaze us if the normal man does not amaze.

> G. K. CHESTERTON (1874–1936), British author. *All Is Grist,* "On Experience" (1931).

2 Every normal person, in fact, is only normal on the average. His ego approximates to that of the psychotic in some part or other and to a greater or lesser extent.

> SIGMUND FREUD (1856–1939), Austrian psychiatrist. *Analysis Terminable and Interminable,* sct. 5 (1937; repr. in *Complete Works,* vol. 23, ed. by James Strachey and Anna Freud, 1964).

3 Normality highly values its normal man. It educates children to lose themselves and to become absurd, and thus to be normal. Normal men have killed perhaps 100,000,000 of their fellow normal men in the last fifty years.

> R. D. LAING (1927–89), British psychiatrist. *The Politics of Experience,* ch. 1 (1967).

NOSES

1 A large nose is the mark of a witty, courteous, affable, generous, and liberal man.

> CYRANO DE BERGERAC (1619–55), French author, playwright. A "lunarian," in *The Other World: States and Empires of the Moon,* ch. 8 (1656). Here, the inhabitants of the moon tell the time by using a natural sundial formed by their long noses, which project their shadows onto the "dial" of their teeth. The speech was taken almost verbatim by Edmond Rostand in his 1897 dramatization of Cyrano's life, *Cyrano de Bergerac,* act 1, sc. 4.

2 Thy nose is as the tower of Lebanon which looketh toward Damascus.

> BIBLE, HEBREW. *Song of Solomon* 7:4.

3 The modern nose, like the modern eye, has developed a sort of microscopic, intercellular intensity which makes our human contacts painful and revolting.

MARSHALL MCLUHAN (1911–80), Canadian communications theorist. *The Mechanical Bride,* "How Not to Offend" (1951).

4 A nose, kind sir! Sure, Mother Nature,
With all her freaks, ne'er formed this feature.
If such were mine, I'd try and trade it,
And swear the gods had never made it.

SUSANNA MOODIE (1803–85), Canadian author. *Roughing It in the Bush,* ch. 6, "Old Satan and Tom Wilson's Nose" (1852).

5 There is nothing so difficult to marry as a large nose.

OSCAR WILDE (1854–1900), Anglo-Irish playwright, author. Lady Markby, in *An Ideal Husband,* act 1.

NOSTALGIA

1 To look backward for a while is to refresh the eye, to restore it, and to render it the more fit for its prime function of looking forward.

MARGARET FAIRLESS BARBER (1869–1901), English author. *The Roadmender,* vol. 3, ch. 3 (1900).

2 The "good old times"—all times when old are good.

LORD BYRON (1788–1824), English poet. *The Age of Bronze.*

3 I wept as I remembered how often you and I
Had tired the sun with talking and sent him down the sky.

CALLIMACHUS (c. 305–240 B.C.), Greek poet, grammarian. *Heraclitus* (tr. by William Johnson Cory).

4 Those who weep for the happy periods which they encounter in history acknowledge what they want; not the alleviation but the silencing of misery.

ALBERT CAMUS (1913–60), French-Algerian philosopher, author. *The Rebel,* pt. 3, "Rebellion and Revolution" (1951; tr. 1953).

5 Oh, how cruelly sweet are the echoes that start
When Memory plays an old tune on the heart!

ELIZA COOK (1818–89), English poet. *Old Dobbin,* st. 16.

6 That is the land of lost content,
I see it shining plain,
The happy highways where I went
And cannot come again.

A. E. HOUSMAN (1859–1936), British poet, classical scholar. *A Shropshire Lad,* no. 40.

7 People have this obsession. They want you to be like you were in 1969. They want you to, because otherwise their youth goes with you. . . . It's very selfish, but it's understandable.

MICK JAGGER (b. 1942), British rock musician. Quoted in: *Observer* (London, 10 Jan. 1993).

8 Time has lost all meaning in that nightmare alley of the Western world known as the American mind. We wallow in nostalgia but manage to get it all wrong. True nostalgia is an ephemeral composition of disjointed

memories . . . but American-style nostalgia is about as ephemeral as copyrighted déjà vu.

FLORENCE KING (b. 1936), U.S. author. *Reflections in a Jaundiced Eye,* "Déjà Views" (1989).

9 Ah tell me not that memory
Sheds gladness o'er the past;
What is recalled by faded flowers
Save that they did not last?

LETITIA ELIZABETH LANDON (1802–38), English poet, novelist. *Despondency.*

10 A society that has made "nostalgia" a marketable commodity on the cultural exchange quickly repudiates the suggestion that life in the past was in any important way better than life today.

CHRISTOPHER LASCH (b. 1932), U.S. historian. *The Culture of Narcissism,* Preface (1979).

11 A feeling of sadness and longing
That is not akin to pain,
And resembles sorrow only
As the mist resembles the rain.

HENRY WADSWORTH LONGFELLOW (1807–82), U.S. poet. *The Day Is Done,* st. 3.

12 It is a curious emotion, this certain homesickness I have in mind. With Americans, it is a national trait, as native to us as the rollercoaster or the jukebox. It is no simple longing for the home town or country of our birth. The emotion is Janus-faced: we are torn between a nostalgia for the familiar and an urge for the foreign and strange. As often as not, we are homesick most for the places we have never known.

CARSON MCCULLERS (1917–67), U.S. author. "Look Homeward, Americans," in *Vogue* (New York, 1 Dec. 1940; repr. in *The Mortgaged Heart,* ed. by Margarita G. Smith, 1972).

13 I don't like nostalgia unless it's mine.

LOU REED (b. 1944), U.S. rock musician. *Evening Standard* (London, 8 June 1989).

14 Remembrance of things past.

WILLIAM SHAKESPEARE (1564–1616), English dramatist, poet. *Sonnet 30.* This title was chosen by Scott Moncrieff for his translation of Proust's *À La Recherche du Temps Perdu.*

15 What joy can the years bring half so sweet as the unhappiness they've taken away?

LOGAN PEARSALL SMITH (1865–1946), U.S. essayist, aphorist. *All Trivia,* "Last Words" (1933).

16 Even while I protest the assembly-line production of our food, our songs, our language, and eventually our souls, I know that it was a rare home that baked good bread in the old days. Mother's cooking was with rare exceptions poor, that good unpasteurized milk touched only by flies and bits of manure crawled with bacteria, the healthy old-time life was riddled with aches, sudden death from unknown causes, and that sweet local speech I mourn was the child of illiteracy and ignorance. It is the nature of a man as he grows older, a small bridge in time, to protest against change, particularly change for the better.

JOHN STEINBECK (1902–68), U.S. author. *Travels with Charley: In Search of America,* pt. 2 (1962).

17 For us, the best time is always yesterday.

TATYANA TOLSTAYA (b. 1951), Russian author. *Independent* (London, 31 May 1990), said of the Russians.

18 Oh, for boyhood's painless play,
Sleep that wakes in laughing day,
Health that mocks the doctor's rules,
Knowledge never learned of schools.

JOHN GREENLEAF WHITTIER (1807–92), U.S. poet. *The Barefoot Boy.*

19 What though the radiance which was once so
bright
Be now for ever taken from my sight,
Though nothing can bring back the hour
Of splendour in the grass, of glory in the flower;
We will grieve not, rather find
Strength in what remains behind.

WILLIAM WORDSWORTH (1770–1850), English poet. *Intimations of Immortality.*

20 When you are old and gray and full of sleep,
And nodding by the fire, take down this book
And slowly read, and dream of the soft look
Your eyes had once, and of their shadows deep.

W. B. YEATS (1865–1939), Irish poet, playwright. *When You Are Old.*

See also Smith on HAPPINESS.

NOVELTY

1 The new always happens against the overwhelming odds of statistical laws and their probability, which for all practical, everyday purposes amounts to certainty; the new therefore always appears in the guise of a miracle.

HANNAH ARENDT (1906–75), German-born U.S. political philosopher. *The Human Condition*, pt. 5, ch. 24 (1958).

2 The New is not a fashion, it is a value.

ROLAND BARTHES (1915–80), French semiologist. *The Pleasure of the Text*, "Modern" (1975).

3 An old thing becomes new if you detach it from what usually surrounds it.

ROBERT BRESSON (b. 1907), French film director. *Notes on the Cinematographer*, "1950–1958: On Poverty" (1975).

4 We do not quite say that the new is more valuable because it fits in; but its fitting in is a test of its value—a test, it is true, which can only be slowly and cautiously applied, for we are none of us infallible judges of conformity.

T. S. ELIOT (1888–1965), Anglo-American poet, critic. "Tradition and the Individual Talent," sct. 1, in *Egoist* (London, Sept. and Dec. 1919; repr. in *Selected Prose of T. S. Eliot*, ed. by Frank Kermode, 1975).

5 To the old, the new is usually bad news.

ERIC HOFFER (1902–83), U.S. philosopher. *The Passionate State of Mind*, aph. 268 (1955).

6 The birth of the new constitutes a crisis, and its mastery calls for a crude and simple cast of mind—the mind of a fighter—in which the virtues of tribal cohesion and fierceness and infantile credulity and malleability are paramount. Thus every new beginning recapitulates in some degree man's first beginning.

ERIC HOFFER (1902–83), U.S. philosopher. *Reflections on the Human Condition*, aph. 120 (1973).

7 The new always carries with it the sense of violation, of sacrilege. What is dead is sacred; what is new, that is *different*, is evil, dangerous, or subversive.

HENRY MILLER (1891–1980), U.S. author. *The Air-Conditioned Nightmare*, "With Edgar Varèse in the Gobi Desert" (1945).

See also Canetti on IDEAS; Twain on ORIGINALITY.

THE NUCLEAR AGE

1 If you ask a member of this generation two simple questions: "How do you want the world to be in fifty years?" and "What do you want your life to be like five years from now?" the answers are quite often preceded by "Provided there is still a world" and "Provided I am still alive." . . . To the often-heard question, Who are they, this new generation? one is tempted to answer, Those who hear the ticking. And to the other question, Who are they who utterly deny them? the answer may well be, Those who do not know, or refuse to face, things as they really are.

HANNAH ARENDT (1906–75), German-born U.S. political philosopher. *Crises of the Republic*, "On Violence, sct. 1 (1972).

2 REST IN PEACE. THE MISTAKE SHALL NOT BE REPEATED.

CENOTOPH Hiroshima, Japan Inscription.

3 Although personally I am quite content with existing explosives, I feel we must not stand in the path of improvement.

SIR WINSTON CHURCHILL (1874–1965), British statesman, writer. Minutes, taken 30 Aug. 1941, of report of the MAUD Committee that it would be possible to make a uranium bomb. Quoted in: Churchill, *The Second World War*, vol. 3 (1950).

4 It sometimes strikes me that the whole of science is a piece of impudence; that nature can afford to ignore our impertinent interference. If our monkey mischief should ever reach the point of blowing up the earth by decomposing an atom, and even annihilated the sun himself, I cannot really suppose that the universe would turn a hair.

ALEISTER CROWLEY (1875–1947), British occultist. *The Confessions of Aleister Crowley*, ch. 14 (1929; rev. 1970).

5 No country without an atom bomb could properly consider itself independent.

CHARLES DE GAULLE (1890–1970), French statesman, soldier. Quoted in: *New York Times Magazine* (12 May 1968).

6 The unleashed power of the atom has changed everything save our modes of thinking and we thus drift toward unparalleled catastrophe.

ALBERT EINSTEIN (1879–1955), German-born U.S. scientist. Telegram, 24 May 1946, sent to prominent Americans (published in *New York Times*, 25 May 1946).

7 What has kept the world safe from the bomb since

1945 has not been deterrence, in the sense of fear of specific weapons, so much as it's been memory. The memory of what happened at Hiroshima.

> JOHN HERSEY (b. 1914), U.S. novelist, journalist. Interview in *Writers at Work* (Eighth Series, ed. by George Plimpton, 1988).

8 The base emotions Plato banned
have left a radio-active and not radiant land.

> LIBBY HOUSTON (b. 1941), British poet. *At the Mercy*, "Judging Lear" (1981).

9 For the first time in the history of mankind, one generation literally has the power to destroy the past, the present and the future, the power to bring time to an end.

> HUBERT H. HUMPHREY (1911–78), U.S. Democratic politician, vice president. Speech, 29 Oct. 1964, New York City.

10 What happened at Hiroshima was not only that a scientific breakthrough . . . had occurred and that a great part of the population of a city had been burned to death, but that the problem of the relation of the triumphs of modern science to the human purposes of man had been explicitly defined.

> ARCHIBALD MACLEISH (1892–1982), U.S. poet. "The Great American Frustration," in *Saturday Review* (9 July 1968; repr. in *Riders on Earth* as "Return from the Excursion," 1978).

11 The flame from the angel's sword in the garden of Eden has been catalysed into the atom bomb; God's thunderbolt became blunted, so man's dunderbolt has become the steel star of destruction.

> SEAN O'CASEY (1884–1964), Irish dramatist. *Sunset and Evening Star* "And Evening Star" (1954).

12 There are no accidents, only nature throwing her weight around. Even the bomb merely releases energy that nature has put there. Nuclear war would be just a spark in the grandeur of space. Nor can radiation "alter" nature: she will absorb it all. After the bomb, nature will pick up the cards we have spilled, shuffle them, and begin her game again.

> CAMILLE PAGLIA (b. 1947), U.S. author, critic, educator. *Sexual Personae*, ch. 1 (1990).

13 There is no evil in the atom; only in men's souls.

> ADLAI STEVENSON (1900–1965), U.S. Democratic politician. Speech, 18 Sept, 1952, Hartford, Conn.

14 The atom bomb was no "great decision." . . . It was merely another powerful weapon in the arsenal of righteousness.

> HARRY S TRUMAN (1884–1972), U.S. Democratic politician, president. Seminar, 28 April 1959, Columbia University, New York City.

15 The terror of the atom age is not the violence of the new power but the speed of man's adjustment to it—the speed of his acceptance.

> E. B. WHITE (1899–1985), U.S. author, editor. *The Second Tree from the Corner*, "Notes on Our Time" (1954).

See also Mason on THE ARMS RACE; Oppenheimer on TECHNOLOGY.

NUCLEAR ARMAGEDDON

1 For myself and my loved ones, I want the heat, which comes at the speed of light. I don't want to have to hang about for the blast, which idles along at the speed of sound.

> MARTIN AMIS (b. 1949), British author. *Einstein's Monsters*, Introduction (1987).

2 It is a secret from nobody that the famous random event is most likely to arise from those parts of the world where the old adage "There is no alternative to victory" retains a high degree of plausibility.

> HANNAH ARENDT (1906–75), German-born U.S. political philosopher. *Crises of the Republic*, sct. 1, "On Violence" (1972).

3 For they have sown the wind, and they shall reap the whirlwind.

> BIBLE, HEBREW. *Hosea* 8:7 Referring to idolaters.

4 Today every inhabitant of this planet must contemplate the day when this planet may no longer be habitable. Every man, woman and child lives under a nuclear sword of Damocles, hanging by the slenderest of threads, capable of being cut at any moment by accident or miscalculation or madness.

> JOHN F. KENNEDY (1917–63), U.S. Democratic politician, president. Address, Sept. 1961, to the United Nations Assembly, New York City.

5 We have had our last chance. If we do not devise some greater and more equitable system, Armageddon will be at our door.

> DOUGLAS MACARTHUR (1880–1964), U.S. general. Speech, 2 Sept. 1945, broadcast shortly after atomic bombs fell on Hiroshima and Nagasaki and the subsequent surrender of Japan, ending the Second World War.

6 If the Third World War is fought with nuclear weapons, the fourth will be fought with bows and arrows.

> LORD LOUIS MOUNTBATTEN (1900–1979), British admiral, member of Royal Family. *Maclean's* (Toronto, 17 Nov. 1975).

7 At last, after innumerable glamorous and frightful years, mankind approaches a war which is *totally predictable from beginning to end.*

> FREDERIC RAPHAEL (b. 1931), British author, critic. *New Society* (London, 10 May 1984).

8 That even an apocalypse can be made to seem part of the ordinary horizon of expectation constitutes an unparalleled violence that is being done to our sense of reality, to our humanity.

> SUSAN SONTAG (b. 1933), U.S. essayist. *AIDS and Its Metaphors*, ch. 8 (1989).

9 Cogito ergo boom.

> SUSAN SONTAG (b. 1933), U.S. essayist. Parenthetical comment in *Styles of Radical Will*, "'Thinking Against Oneself': Reflections on Cioran" (1969), on our sense that we stand "in the ruins of thought, and on the verge of the ruins of history and of man himself."

10 We are heading towards catastrophe. I think the world is going to pieces. I am very pessimistic. Why? Because the world hasn't been punished yet, and the only punishment that could be adequate is the nuclear destruction of the world.

> ELIE WIESEL (b. 1928), Rumanian-born U.S. writer. Interview in *Writers at Work* (Eighth Series, ed. by George Plimpton, 1988).

See also THE END OF THE WORLD.

NUDITY

1 Nakedness reveals itself. Nudity is placed on display. . . . The nude is condemned to never being naked. Nudity is a form of dress.

> JOHN BERGER (b. 1926), British critic. *Ways of Seeing*, ch. 3 (1972).

2 And they were both naked, the man and his wife, and were not ashamed.

> BIBLE, HEBREW. *Genesis* 2:25.

3 Naked came I out of my mother's womb, and naked shall I return thither.

> BIBLE, HEBREW. Job, in *Job* 1:21. Almost identical words are used in *Aesop's Fables*, no. 120, written in the 6th century B.C.

4 Art can never exist without naked beauty displayed.

> WILLIAM BLAKE (1757–1827), English poet, painter, engraver. Notes on *The Laocoön* (engraved c. 1820; repr. in *Complete Writings*, ed. by Geoffrey Keynes, 1957).

5 There are those who so dislike the nude that they find something indecent in the naked truth.

> F. H. BRADLEY (1846–1924), English philosopher. *Aphorisms*, no. 88 (1930).

6 In the NUDE, all that is not beautiful is obscene.

> ROBERT BRESSON (b. 1907), French film director. *Notes on the Cinematographer*, "Further Notes 1960–1974" (1975).

7 Full nakedness! All my joys are due to thee,
As souls unbodied, bodies unclothed must be,
To taste whole joys.

> JOHN DONNE (c. 1572–1631), English divine, metaphysical poet. *Elegies*, "To His Mistress Going to Bed" (1669), composed 1590–1600.

8 To see you naked is to recall the Earth.

> FEDERICO GARCÍA LORCA (1899–1936), Spanish poet, playwright. *Casida de la Mujer Tendida*.

9 Nudity is the uniform of the other side. . . nudity is a shroud.

> MILAN KUNDERA (b. 1929), Czech author, critic. *The Book of Laughter and Forgetting*, pt. 7, ch. 8 (1978; tr. 1980).

10 You know, it's just like being a peddler. You want two breasts? Well, here you are—two breasts. . . . We must see to it that the man looking at the picture has at hand everything he needs to paint a nude. If you really give him everything he needs—and the best—he'll put everything where it belongs, with his own eyes. Each person will make for himself the kind of nude he wants, with the nude that I will have made for him.

> PABLO PICASSO (1881–1973), Spanish artist. Quoted in: Hélène Parmelin, *Picasso: The Artist and His Model, and Other Recent Works* (1965, p. 16).

11 To be sure an European woman would blush to her fingers' ends at the very idea of appearing publicly stark naked; but education and prejudice are everything, since it is an axiom, that where there is no feeling of self-reproach, there can assuredly be no shame.

> CAPTAIN J. G. STEDMAN (1744–97), British soldier, author, artist. *Narrative of a Five Years' Expedition Against the Revolted Negroes of Surinam*, ch. 15 (1796; repr. 1971), referring to the Indians of Surinam.

12 We shift and bedeck and bedrape us,
Thou art noble and nude and antique.

> A. C. SWINBURNE (1837–1909), English poet, critic. *Dolores*, st. 7.

13 Being naked approaches being revolutionary; going barefoot is mere populism.

> JOHN UPDIKE (b. 1932), U.S. novelist, critic. *On the Vineyard*, "Going Barefoot" (1980; repr. in *Hugging the Shore*, 1983).

14 My advice to those who think they have to take off their clothes to be a star is, once you're boned, what's left to create the illusion? Let 'em wonder. I never believed in givin' them too much of me.

> MAE WEST (1892–1980), U.S. screen actor. *On Sex, Health and ESP*, "Biographical Study," ch. 4 (1975).

See also Thoreau on DRESS; Carlyle on PARLIAMENT: THE HOUSE OF LORDS; Dylan on The PRESIDENT; Hawthorne on SCULPTURE.

NUNS

1 Convent. A place of retirement for women who wish for leisure to meditate upon the sin of idleness.

> AMBROSE BIERCE (1842–1914), U.S. author. *The Devil's Dictionary* (1881–1906).

2 The convent, which belongs to the West as it does to the East, to antiquity as it does to the present time, to Buddhism and Muhammadanism as it does to Christianity, is one of the optical devices whereby man gains a glimpse of infinity.

> VICTOR HUGO (1802–85), French poet, dramatist, novelist. *Les Misérables*, pt. 2, bk. 7, ch. 1 (1862).

3 A nun, at best, is only half a woman, just as a priest is only half a man.

> H. L. MENCKEN (1880–1956), U.S. journalist. *Minority Report: H. L. Mencken's Notebooks*, no. 221 (1956).

4 Come, pensive nun, devout and pure,
Sober, steadfast, and demure,
All in a robe of darkest grain,
Flowing with majestic train.

> JOHN MILTON (1608–74), English poet. *Il Penseroso*.

5 She gave up beauty in her tender youth,
Gave all her hope and joy and pleasant ways;
She covered up her eyes lest they should gaze
On vanity, and chose the bitter truth.

> CHRISTINA ROSSETTI (1830–94), English poet, lyricist. *A Portrait*.

6 The sight of a Black nun strikes their sentimentality; and, as I am unalterably rooted in native ground, they consider me a work of primitive art, housed in a magical color; the incarnation of civilized, anti-heathenism, and the fruit of a triumphing idea.

ALICE WALKER (b. 1944), U.S. author. "The Diary of an African Nun," in *Freedomways* (New York, Summer 1968).

See also MONKS; Barbarito on SPORT.

OBEDIENCE

1   For rulers are not a terror to good works, but to the evil. Wilt thou then not be afraid of the power?

BIBLE: NEW TESTAMENT. *Romans* 13:3.

2   The reason why men do not obey us is because they see the mud at the bottom of our eye.

RALPH WALDO EMERSON (1803–82), U.S. essayist, poet, philosopher. *The Conduct of Life,* "Behavior" (1860).

3   The doctrine of blind obedience and unqualified submission to any human power, whether civil or ecclesiastical, is the doctrine of despotism, and ought to have no place 'mong Republicans and Christians.

ANGELINA GRIMKÉ (1805–79), U.S. abolitionist, feminist. "Appeal to the Christian Women of the South," in *Anti-Slavery Examiner* (Sept 1836; repr. in *The Oven Birds: American Women on Womanhood 1820–1920,* ed. by Gail Parker, 1972).

4   I have thought about it a great deal, and the more I think, the more certain I am that obedience is the gateway through which knowledge, yes, and love, too, enter the mind of the child.

ANNE SULLIVAN (1866–1936), U.S. educator of deaf and blind. Letter, 11 March 1887 (published in: Helen Keller, *The Story of My Life,* pt. 3, ch. 1, 1903). Her student Helen Keller, Sullivan wrote, had "tyrannized over everybody . . . like all tyrants she holds tenaciously to her divine right to do as she pleases."

5   It is much safer to obey, than to govern.

THOMAS À KEMPIS (1380–1471), German monk, mystic. *The Imitation of Christ,* pt. 1, ch. 9 (1471).

6   There can be a true grandeur in any degree of submissiveness, because it springs from loyalty to the laws and to an oath, and not from baseness of soul.

SIMONE WEIL (1909–43), French philosopher, mystic. "The Great Beast," pt. 3, in *Selected Essays* (ed. by Richard Rees, 1962).

7   Disobedience, in the eyes of any one who has read history, is man's original virtue. It is through disobedience that progress has been made, through disobedience and through rebellion.

OSCAR WILDE (1854–1900), Anglo-Irish playwright, author. *The Soul of Man Under Socialism,* in *Fortnightly Review* (London, Feb. 1891; repr. 1895).

OBESITY

1   Outside every fat man there was an even fatter man trying to close in.

KINGSLEY AMIS (b. 1922), British novelist. Roger Micheldene, "a shortish fat Englishman of forty," in *One Fat Englishman,* ch. 3 (1963), musing over a particularly heavy lunch. For the probable inspiration of this, see Connolly on OBESITY.

2   The obese is . . . in a total delirium. For he is not only large, of a size opposed to normal morphology: he is larger than large. He no longer makes sense in some distinctive opposition, but in his excess, his redundancy.

JEAN BAUDRILLARD (b. 1929), French semiologist. *Fatal Strategies,* "Figures of the Transpolitical" (1983; tr. 1990).

3   Every day the fat woman dies a series of small deaths.

SHELLEY BOVEY, U.S. author. *Being Fat Is Not a Sin,* ch. 1 (1989).

4   I don't mind that I'm fat. You still get the same money.

MARLON BRANDO (b. 1924), U.S. screen actor. *International Herald Tribune* (Paris, 9 Oct. 1989).

5   Imprisoned in every fat man a thin one is wildly signalling to be let out.

CYRIL CONNOLLY (1903–1974), British critic. *The Unquiet Grave,* pt. 2 (1944; rev. 1951). Orwell had made a similar observation in *Coming up for Air,* pt. 1, ch. 3 (1939): "I'm fat, but I'm thin inside. Has it ever struck you that there's a thin man inside every fat man, just as they say there's a statue inside every block of stone?" See Amis on OBESITY for a later variant.

6   I have always wanted a mistress who was fat, and I have never found one. To make a fool of me, they are always pregnant.

PAUL GAUGUIN (1848–1903), French artist. *Intimate Journals* (tr. by Van Wyck Brooks, 1923; repr. 1930, p. 3).

7   it's a sex object if you're pretty
and no love
or love and no sex if you're fat

NIKKI GIOVANNI (b. 1943), U.S. poet. *Woman Poem,* in *Black Feeling/Black Talk/Black Judgement* (1970).

8   Who ever hears of fat men heading a riot, or herding together in turbulent mobs?—No—no, ''tis your lean, hungry men who are continually worrying society, and setting the whole community by the ears.

WASHINGTON IRVING (1783–1859), U.S. author. *A History of New York,* bk. 3, ch. 2 (1809), written under the pseudonym Diedrich Knickerbocker.

9   Some people are born to fatness. Others have to get there.

LES MURRAY (b. 1938), Australian poet. *Independent on Sunday* (London, 15 April 1990).

10   How easy for those who do not bulge
To not overindulge!

OGDEN NASH (1902–1971), U.S. poet. *A Necessary Dirge,* in *I'm a Stranger Here Myself* (1938).

11   Fat is a social disease, and fat is a feminist issue.

SUSIE ORBACH (b. 1946), U.S. psychotherapist, feminist author. *Fat Is a Feminist Issue,* Introduction (1978).

12   Fat is a way of saying "no" to powerlessness and self-denial.

SUSIE ORBACH (b. 1946), U.S. psychotherapist, feminist author. *Fat is a Feminist Issue,* Introduction (1978).

13   There is no need to worry about mere size. We do not necessarily respect a fat man more than a thin man.

Sir Isaac Newton was very much smaller than a hippopotamus, but we do not on that account value him less.

> BERTRAND RUSSELL (1872–1970), British philosopher, mathematician. "The Expanding Mental Universe," in *Saturday Evening Post* (New York, July 1959).

14 Thou seest I have more flesh than another man, and therefore more frailty.

> WILLIAM SHAKESPEARE (1564–1616), English dramatist, poet. Sir John Oldcastle [Falstaff], in *King Henry IV, Pt. 1*, act 3, sc. 3.

15 Let me have men about me that are fat,
Sleek-headed men and such as sleep a-nights.
Yon Cassius has a lean and hungry look.
He thinks too much. Such men are dangerous.

> WILLIAM SHAKESPEARE (1564–1616), English dramatist, poet. Caesar, in *Julius Caesar*, act 1, sc. 2.

16 I find no sweeter fat than sticks to my own bones.

> WALT WHITMAN (1819–92), U.S. poet. *Song of Myself*, sct. 50, in *Leaves of Grass* (1855).

See also Eagleton on POLITICAL CORRECTNESS.

OBSCENITY

1 The reading or non-reading a book will never keep down a single petticoat.

> LORD BYRON (1788–1824), English poet. Letter, 29 Oct. 1819, discussing Byron's poem *Don Juan*, which women had been warned not to read (published in *Byron's Letters and Journals*, vol. 6, ed. by Leslie A. Marchand, 1976).

2 My English text is chaste, and all licentious passages are left in the obscurity of a learned language.

> EDWARD GIBBON (1737–94), English historian. *Memoirs of my Life* (1796; published in World's Classics as *Autobiography*). This has also been misquoted with the phrase "decent obscurity," following a parody in *The Anti-Jacobin Review and Magazine* of the time.

3 Here is the piece. If you can't say fornicate can you say copulate or if not that can you say co-habit? If not that would have to say consummate I suppose. Use your own good taste and judgment.

> ERNEST HEMINGWAY (1899–1961), U.S. author. Letter, 11 April 1935, to *Esquire* editor Arnold Gingrich (published in *Selected Letters*, ed. by Carlos Baker, 1981).

4 Since obscenity is the truth of our passion today, it is the only stuff of art—or almost the only stuff.

> D. H. LAWRENCE (1885–1930), British author. Letter, 9 Oct. 1916 (published in *The Letters of D. H. Lawrence*, vol. 2, ed. by George J. Zytaruk and James T. Boulton, 1981). See Lawrence on CENSORSHIP.

5 Obscenity is a moral concept in the verbal arsenal of the Establishment, which abuses the term by applying it, not to expressions of its own morality but to those of another.

> HERBERT MARCUSE (1898–1979), U.S. political philosopher. *An Essay on Liberation*, ch. 1 (1969).

6 Not when truth is dirty, but when it is shallow, does the enlightened man dislike to wade into its waters.

> FRIEDRICH NIETZSCHE (1844–1900), German philosopher. *Thus Spoke Zarathustra*, pt. 1, "Of Chastity" (1883–92; tr. 1961).

7 Obscenity is whatever happens to shock some elderly and ignorant magistrate.

> BERTRAND RUSSELL (1872–1970), British philosopher, mathematician. *Look* (New York, 23 Feb. 1954).

8 Obscenity, which is ever blasphemy against the divine beauty in life, . . . is a monster for which the corruption of society forever brings forth new food, which it devours in secret.

> PERCY BYSSHE SHELLEY (1792–1822), English poet. *A Defence of Poetry* (written 1821; published 1840).

9 Shocking writing is like murder: the questions the jury must decide are the questions of motive and intent.

> E. B. WHITE (1899–1985), U.S. author, editor. Interview in *Writers at Work* (Eighth Series, 1988).

10 The sign of a Philistine age is the cry of immorality against art.

> OSCAR WILDE (1854–1900), Anglo-Irish playwright, author. "Lecture Delivered to the Art Students of the Royal Academy, June 30 1883," in *Essays and Lectures* (1908).

See also Miller on PORNOGRAPHY.

OBSCURITY

1 The obscure only exists that it may cease to exist. In it lies the opportunity of all victory and all progress. Whether it call itself fatality, death, night, or matter, it is the pedestal of life, of light, of liberty and the spirit. For it represents *resistance*—that is to say, the fulcrum of all activity, the occasion for its development and its triumph.

> HENRI-FRÉDÉRIC AMIEL (1821–81), Swiss philosopher, poet. *Journal Intime* (1882; tr. by Mrs. Humphrey Ward, 1892), entry for 27 Oct. 1856.

2 What is grand is necessarily obscure to weak men. That which can be made explicit to the idiot is not worth my care.

> WILLIAM BLAKE (1757–1827), English poet, painter, engraver. Letter, 23 Aug. 1799 (published in *Complete Writings*, ed. by Geoffrey Keynes, 1957).

3 The growing good of the world is partly dependent on unhistoric acts; and that things are not so ill with you and me as they might have been, is half owing to the number who lived faithfully a hidden life, and rest in unvisited tombs.

> GEORGE ELIOT (1819–1880), English novelist. *Middlemarch*, bk. 8, "Finale" (1871–72).

4 Everybody is so talented nowadays that the only people I care to honour as deserving real distinction are those who remain in obscurity.

> THOMAS HARDY (1840–1928), English novelist, poet. Neigh, in *The Hand of Ethelberta*, ch. 9 (1876).

5 More significant than the fact that poets write abstrusely, painters paint abstractly, and composers compose unintelligible music is that people should admire what they cannot understand; indeed, admire that which has no meaning or principle.

> ERIC HOFFER (1902–1983), U.S. philosopher. *Reflections on the Human Condition*, aph. 104 (1973).

6 Obscurantism is the academic theorist's revenge on society for having consigned him or her to relative obscurity—a way of proclaiming one's superiority in the face of one's diminished influence.

> DAVID LEHMAN (b. 1948), U.S. poet, editor, critic. *Signs of the Times*, ch. 3, "Archie Debunking" (1991).

7 Be wary of passing the judgment: *obscure*. To find something obscure poses no difficulty: elephants and poodles find many things obscure.

> G. C. LICHTENBERG (1742–99), German physicist, philosopher. *Aphorisms*, "Notebook E," aph. 36 (written 1765–99; tr. by R. J. Hollingdale, 1990).

8 Darkness is to space what silence is to sound, i.e., the interval.

> MARSHALL MCLUHAN (1911–80), Canadian communications theorist. *Through the Vanishing Point*, "Toward a Spatial Dialogue," ch. 16 (1968; written with Harley Parker, 1968).

9 The great work must inevitably be obscure, except to the very few, to those who like the author himself are initiated into the mysteries. Communication then is secondary: it is perpetuation which is important. For this only one good reader is necessary.

> HENRY MILLER (1891–1980), U.S. author. *The Wisdom of the Heart*, "Reflections on Writing" (1947).

10 The mind's passion is all for singling out. Obscurity has another tale to tell.

> ADRIENNE RICH (b. 1929), U.S. poet. *Focus*, st. 7, in *Necessities of Life* (1966).

11 Obscurity is the realm of error.

> LUC, MARQUIS DE VAUVENARGUES (1715–47), French moralist. *Réflexions et Maximes*, no. 5 (1746).

See also Gellner on PARIS; Chesterton on WORSHIP.

OBSESSION

1 Anger and jealousy can no more bear to lose sight of their objects than love.

> GEORGE ELIOT (1819–80), English novelist. *The Mill on the Floss*, bk. 1, ch. 10 (1860).

2 I envy people who can just look at a sunset. I wonder how you can shoot it. There is nothing more grotesque to me than a vacation.

> DUSTIN HOFFMAN (b. 1937), U.S. screen actor. *Observer* (London, 19 Feb. 1989).

3 Single-mindedness is all very well in cows or baboons; in an animal claiming to belong to the same species as Shakespeare it is simply disgraceful.

> ALDOUS HUXLEY (1894–1963), British author. *Do What You Will*, "Pascal," sct. 24 (1929).

4 It's no longer a warmth hidden in my veins: it's Venus entire and whole fastening on her prey.

> JEAN RACINE (1639–99), French dramatist. Phèdre, in *Phèdre*, act 1, sc. 3 (1677).

See also Johnson on ERROR.

OBSTINACY

1 [He] has a brilliant mind until it is made up.

> VIOLET BONHAM-CARTER (LADY ASQUITH) (1887–1969), British Liberal politician. Quoted in: Leon Harris, *The Fine Art of Political Wit*, ch. 12 (1964), referring to British Labour politician Sir Stafford Cripps.

2 Obstinacy in a bad cause is but constancy in a good.

> SIR THOMAS BROWNE (1605–82), English physician, author. *Religio Medici*, pt. 1, sct. 25 (1643).

3 They defend their errors as if they were defending their inheritance.

> EDMUND BURKE (1729–97), Irish philosopher, statesman. Speech, 11 Feb. 1780, to the House of Commons.

4 For every why he had a wherefore.

> SAMUEL BUTLER (1612–80), English poet. *Hudibras*.

5 Firmness yclept in heroes, kings and seamen,
That is, when they succeed; but greatly blamed
As *obstinacy*, both in men and women,
Whene'er their triumph pales, or star is tamed —
And 'twill perplex the casuist in morality
To fix the due bounds of this dangerous quality.

> LORD BYRON (1788–1824), English poet. *Don Juan*, cto. 14, st. 89. In stanza 90, Byron added:
> Had Buonaparte won at Waterloo,
> It had been firmness; now 'tis pertinacity.

6 Certainly, the mistakes that we male and female mortals make when we have our own way might fairly raise some wonder that we're so fond of it.

> GEORGE ELIOT (1819–80), English novelist, editor. *Middlemarch*, bk. 1, ch. 9 (1871).

7 Like all weak men he laid an exaggerated stress on not changing one's mind.

> W. SOMERSET MAUGHAM (1874–1966), British author. *Of Human Bondage*, ch. 39 (1915), of the vicar of Blackstable.

8 He says NO! in thunder; but the Devil himself cannot make him say *yes*.

> HERMAN MELVILLE (1819–91), U.S. author. Letter to Hawthorne about Melville, 16 April 1851 (published in *The Letters of Herman Melville*, ed. by Merrell R. Davis and William H. Gilman, 1960). Melville added, "For all men who say *yes*, lie; and all men who say *no*,—why, they are in the happy condition of judicious, unencumbered travelers in Europe; they cross the frontiers into Eternity with nothing but a carpet bag."

9 Who is so deaf or so blind as he
That wilfully will neither hear nor see?

> SIXTEENTH-CENTURY ENGLISH PROVERB. Collected in J. Heywood, *Dialogue of Proverbs* (1546).

10 Obstinacy is the result of the will forcing itself into the place of the intellect.

> ARTHUR SCHOPENHAUER (1788–1860), German philosopher. *Parerga and Paralipomena*, vol. 2, ch. 26, sct. 321 (1851).

11 The obstinacy of cleverness and reason is nothing to the obstinacy of folly and inanity.

> HARRIET BEECHER STOWE (1811–96), U.S. novelist, anti-slavery campaigner. *Little Foxes*, ch. 4 (1865).

See also Hogarth on HUSBANDS; Blake on OPINION.

THE OBVIOUS

1   To spell out the obvious is often to call it in question.

> ERIC HOFFER (1902–83), U.S. philosopher. *The Passionate State of Mind*, aph. 220 (1955).

2   In saying what is obvious, never choose cunning. Yelling works better.

> CYNTHIA OZICK (b. 1928), U.S. novelist, short-story writer. "We Are the Crazy Lady and Other Feisty Feminist Fables," in *The First Ms. Reader* (ed. by Francine Klagsbrun, 1972).

THE OFFICE

1   A molehill man is a pseudo-busy executive who comes to work at 9 am and finds a molehill on his desk. He has until 5 pm to make this molehill into a mountain. An accomplished molehill man will often have his mountain finished before lunch.

> FRED ALLEN (1894–1957), U.S. radio comic. *Treadmill to Oblivion*, pt. 2 (1954).

2   Here is a pen and here is a pencil,
Here's a typewriter, here's a stencil,
Here is a list of today's appointments,
And all the flies in all the ointments,
The daily woes that a man endures —
Take them, George, they're yours!

> OGDEN NASH (1902–1971), U.S. poet. *Let George Do It, If You Can Find Him*, in *The Primrose Path* (1935).

3   He [Robert Benchley] and I had an office so tiny that an inch smaller and it would have been adultery.

> DOROTHY PARKER (1893–1967), U.S. humorous writer. Interview in *Writers at Work* (First Series, ed. by Malcolm Cowley, 1958). Benchley probably originated this remark, ascribed to him in the *New Yorker* (5 Jan. 1946): "One square foot less and it would be adulterous."

4   My desk, most loyal friend
thank you. You've been with me on
every road I've taken.
My scar and my protection.

> MARINA TSVETAEVA (1892–1941), Russian poet. *Desk* (tr. by Elaine Fernstein).

5   An office party is not, as is sometimes supposed, the Managing Director's chance to kiss the tea-girl. It is the tea-girl's chance to kiss the Managing Director (however bizarre an ambition this may seem to anyone who has seen the Managing Director face on). Bringing down the mighty from their seats is an agreeable and necessary pastime, but no one supposes that the mighty, having struggled so hard to get seated, will enjoy the dethronement.

> KATHARINE WHITEHORN (b. 1926), British journalist. *Roundabout*, "The Office Party" (1962).

OLD AGE

1   Men of age object too much, consult too long, adventure too little, repent too soon, and seldom drive business home to the full period, but content themselves with a mediocrity of success.

> FRANCIS BACON (1561–1626), English philosopher, essayist, statesman. *Essays*, "Of Youth and Age" (1597–1625).

2   Old age is the verdict of life.

> AMELIA BARR (1831–1919), Anglo-American novelist. *All the Days of My Life*, ch. 26 (1913).

3   A man is not old until regrets take the place of dreams.

> JOHN BARRYMORE (1882–1942), U.S. actor. Quoted in: Gene Fowler, *Good Night, Sweet Prince* (1943).

4   To me, old age is always fifteen years older than I am.

> BERNARD BARUCH (1870–1965), U.S. financier. *Observer* (London, 21 Aug. 1955).

5   Since it is the Other within us who is old, it is natural that the revelation of our age should come to us from outside—from others. We do not accept it willingly.

> SIMONE DE BEAUVOIR (1908–86), French novelist, essayist. *The Coming of Age*, pt. 2, ch. 5 (1970; tr. 1972).

6   It is old age, rather than death, that is to be contrasted with life. Old age is life's parody, whereas death transforms life into a destiny: in a way it preserves it by giving it the absolute dimension. . . . Death does away with time.

> SIMONE DE BEAUVOIR (1908–86), French novelist, essayist. *The Coming of Age*, Conclusion (1970; tr. 1972).

7   We lose our hair, our teeth! Our bloom, our ideals.

> SAMUEL BECKETT (1906–89), Irish dramatist and novelist. Hamm, in *Endgame* (1958, p. 16).

8   I hope I never get so old I get religious.

> INGMAR BERGMAN (b. 1918), Swedish stage and film writer-director. *International Herald Tribune* (Paris, 8 Sept. 1989).

9   With the ancient is wisdom; and in length of days understanding.

> BIBLE, HEBREW. *Job* 12:12.

10   Age. That period of life in which we compound for the vices that remain by reviling those we have no longer the vigor to commit.

> AMBROSE BIERCE (1842–1914), U.S. author. *The Devil's Dictionary* (1881–1906).

11   In the name of Hippocrates, doctors have invented the most exquisite form of torture ever known to man: survival.

> LUIS BUÑUEL (1900–1983), Spanish filmmaker. *My Last Sigh*, ch. 21 (1983).

12   What is the worst of woes that wait on age?
What stamps the wrinkle deeper on the brow?
To view each loved one blotted from life's page,
And be alone on earth, as I am now.

> LORD BYRON (1788–1824), English poet. *Childe Harold's Pilgrimage*, cto. 2, st. 98 (1812–18).

13   It is not all bad, this getting old, ripening. After the fruit has got its growth it should juice up and mellow.

God forbid I should live long enough to ferment and rot and fall to the ground in a squash.

> EMILY CARR (1871–1945), Canadian artist. *Hundreds and Thousands: The Journals of Emily Carr* (1966), entry for 12 Dec. 1933; written on the eve of her 62nd birthday.

14 The heart never grows better by age; I fear rather worse, always harder. A young liar will be an old one, and a young knave will only be a greater knave as he grows older.

> LORD CHESTERFIELD (1694–1773), English statesman, man of letters. Letter, 17 May 1750 (1774; repr. in *The Letters of the Earl of Chesterfield to His Son*, vol. 2, no. 225, ed. by Charles Strachey, 1901).

15 Old age isn't so bad when you consider the alternative.

> MAURICE CHEVALIER (1888–1972), French singer, actor. *New York Times* (9 Oct. 1960).

16 Childhood itself is scarcely more lovely than a cheerful, kind, sunshiny old age.

> LYDIA M. CHILD (1802–80), U.S. abolitionist, writer, editor. Letter, March 1843 (published in *Letters from New York*, vol. 1, Letter 37, 1843).

17 No one is so old as to think he cannot live one more year.

> CICERO (106–43 BC), Roman orator, philosopher. *De Senectute*, ch. 7, sct. 24 (44 B.C.).

18 Father Time is not always a hard parent, and, though he tarries for none of his children, often lays his hand lightly upon those who have used him well; making them old men and women inexorably enough, but leaving their hearts and spirits young and in full vigour. With such people the grey head is but the impression of the old fellow's hand in giving them his blessing, and every wrinkle but a notch in the quiet calendar of a well-spent life.

> CHARLES DICKENS (1812–70), English novelist. *Barnaby Rudge*, ch. 2 (1841).

19 For in all the world there are no people so piteous and forlorn as those who are forced to eat the bitter bread of dependency in their old age, and find how steep are the stairs of another man's house. Wherever they go they know themselves unwelcome. Wherever they are, they feel themselves a burden. There is no humiliation of the spirit they are not forced to endure. Their hearts are scarred all over with the stabs from cruel and callous speeches.

> DOROTHY DIX (1861–1951), U.S. columnist. *Dorothy Dix, Her Book*, ch. 69 (1926).

20 Old age is an insult. It's like being smacked.

> LAWRENCE DURRELL (1912–90), British author. *Sunday Times* (London, 20 Nov. 1988).

21 We do not count a man's years until he has nothing else to count.

> RALPH WALDO EMERSON (1803–82), U.S. essayist, poet, philosopher. *Society and Solitude*, "Old Age" (1870).

22 The nearer people approach old age the closer they return to a semblance of childhood, until the time comes for them to depart this life, again like children, neither tired of living nor aware of death.

> DESIDERIUS ERASMUS (c. 1466–1536), Dutch humanist. *Praise of Folly*, ch. 14 (1509).

23 An ... important antidote to American democracy is American gerontocracy. The positions of eminence and authority in Congress are allotted in accordance with length of service, regardless of quality. Superficial observers have long criticized the United States for making a fetish of youth. This is unfair. Uniquely among modern organs of public and private administration, its national legislature rewards senility.

> JOHN KENNETH GALBRAITH (b. 1908), U.S. economist. "The United States," in *New York* (15 Nov. 1971; repr. in *A View from the Stands*, 1986).

24 The older woman's love is not love of herself, nor of herself mirrored in a lover's eyes, nor is it corrupted by need. It is a feeling of tenderness so still and deep and warm that it gilds every grassblade and blesses every fly. It includes the ones who have a claim on it, and a great deal else besides. I wouldn't have missed it for the world.

> GERMAINE GREER (b. 1939), Australian feminist writer. *The Change: Women, Ageing and the Menopause*, Introduction (1991).

25 The value of old age depends upon the person who reaches it. To some men of early performance it is useless. To others, who are late to develop, it just enables them to finish the job.

> THOMAS HARDY (1840–1928), English novelist, poet. "Birthday Notes." Quoted in: Florence Emily Hardy, *The Later Years of Thomas Hardy*, ch. 17 (1930).

26 A woman would rather visit her own grave than the place where she has been young and beautiful after she is aged and ugly.

> CORRA MAY HARRIS (1869–1935), U.S. author. *Eve's Second Husband*, ch. 14 (1910).

27 Old age, believe me, is a good and pleasant thing. It is true you are gently shouldered off the stage, but then you are given such a comfortable front stall as spectator.

> JANE HARRISON (1850–1928), English classical scholar, writer. *Reminiscences of a Student's Life*, "Conclusion" (1925).

28 The end comes when we no longer talk with ourselves. It is the end of genuine thinking and the beginning of the final loneliness.

> ERIC HOFFER (1902–83), U.S. philosopher. *Reflections on the Human Condition*, aph. 150 (1973).

29 Old age equalizes—we are aware that what is happening to us has happened to untold numbers from the beginning of time. When we are young we act as if we were the first young people in the world.

> ERIC HOFFER (1902–83), U.S. philosopher. *Reflections on the Human Condition*, aph. 165 (1973).

30 I don't generally feel anything until noon, then it's time for my nap.

> BOB HOPE (b. 1903), U.S. comedian. *International Herald Tribune* (Paris, 3 Aug. 1990).

31 Wrecked on the lee shore of age.

> SARAH ORNE JEWETT (1849–1909), U.S. author. *The Country of the Pointed Firs and Other Stories*, ch. 7 (1896).

32 Talking is the disease of age.

BEN JONSON (1573–1637), English dramatist, poet. *Timber, or Discoveries Made upon Men and Matter,* para. 46, "Lingua Sapientis" (1641).

33 Old age realizes the dreams of youth: look at Dean Swift; in his youth he built an asylum for the insane, in his old age he was himself an inmate.

SØREN KIERKEGAARD (1813–55), Danish philosopher. *Either/Or,* vol. 1, sct. 1 (1843; tr. 1987).

34 For the last third of life there remains only work. It alone is always stimulating, rejuvenating, exciting and satisfying.

KÄTHE KOLLWITZ (1867–1945), German artist. *Diaries and Letters* (ed. by Hans Kollwitz, 1955), entry for 1 Jan. 1912.

35 Old age is not a disease—it is strength and survivorship, triumph over all kinds of vicissitudes and disappointments, trials and illnesses.

MAGGIE KUHN (b. 1905), U.S. civil rights activist, author. Quoted in: *New Age* (Feb. 1979).

36 Old people love to give good advice to console themselves for no longer being able to set a bad example.

FRANÇOIS, DUC DE LA ROCHEFOUCAULD (1613–1680), French writer, moralist. *Sentences et Maximes Morales,* no. 93 (1678).

37 Few people know how to be old.

FRANÇOIS, DUC DE LA ROCHEFOUCAULD (1613–80), French writer, moralist. *Sentences et Maximes Morales,* no. 423 (1678).

38 O what a thing is age! Death without death's quiet.

WALTER SAVAGE LANDOR (1775–1864), English author. *Imaginary Conversations,* "Epicurus, Leontion, and Ternissa" (1824–29).

39 Perhaps being old is having lighted rooms
Inside your head, and people in them, acting.
People you know, yet can't quite name.

PHILIP LARKIN (1922–85), British poet. *The Old Fools.*

40 The great secret that all old people share is that you really haven't changed in seventy or eighty years. Your body changes, but you don't change at all. And that, of course, causes great confusion.

DORIS LESSING (b. 1919), British novelist. *Sunday Times: Books* (London, 10 May 1992).

41 Age is opportunity no less
Than youth itself, though in another dress,
And as the evening twilight fades away
The sky is filled with stars, invisible by day.

HENRY WADSWORTH LONGFELLOW (1807–82), U.S. poet. *Morituri Salutamus.*

42 Whatever poet, orator, or sage
May say of it, old age is still old age.

HENRY WADSWORTH LONGFELLOW (1807–82), U.S. poet. *Morituri Salutamus.*

43 Age is not a particularly interesting subject. Anyone can get old. All you have to do is live long enough.

GROUCHO MARX (1895–1977), U.S. comic actor. *Groucho and Me,* ch. 1 (1959).

44 The complete life, the perfect pattern, includes old age as well as youth and maturity. The beauty of the morning and the radiance of noon are good, but it would be a very silly person who drew the curtains and turned on the light in order to shut out the tranquillity of the evening. Old age has its pleasures, which, though different, are not less than the pleasures of youth.

W. SOMERSET MAUGHAM (1874–1965), British author. *The Summing Up,* ch. 73 (1938).

45 Old age is far more than white hair, wrinkles, the feeling that it is too late and the game finished, that the stage belongs to the rising generations. The true evil is not the weakening of the body, but the indifference of the soul.

ANDRÉ MAUROIS (1885–1967), French author, critic. *The Art of Living,* "The Art of Living" (1940).

46 If you associate enough with older people who do enjoy their lives, who are not stored away in any golden ghettos, you will gain a sense of continuity and of the possibility for a full life.

MARGARET MEAD (1901–78), U.S. anthropologist. Quoted in: *Family Circle* (26 July 1977).

47 Old age is always wakeful; as if, the longer linked with life, the less man has to do with aught that looks like death.

HERMAN MELVILLE (1819–91), U.S. author. *Moby-Dick,* ch. 29 (1851).

48 Not till the fire is dying in the grate,
Look we for any kinship with the stars.
Oh, wisdom never comes when it is gold,
And the great price we paid for it full worth:
We have it only when we are half earth.
Little avails that coinage to the old!

GEORGE MEREDITH (1828–1909), English author. *Modern Love,* sonnet 4 (1862). Cecil Day Lewis, professor of poetry at Oxford, wrote of this extract, in his Introduction to 1948 ed. of the volume, that it was not originality that made it memorable, "it is a commonplace, whose force we are at last made to feel, through and through, by the inner conviction and the expressive grandeur of its utterance."

49 Nature should have been pleased to have made this age miserable, without making it also ridiculous.

MICHEL DE MONTAIGNE (1533–92), French essayist. *Essays,* bk. 3, ch. 5, "Upon Some Verses of Virgil" (tr. by John Florio, 1588). Montaigne was referring to the age of the "eleventh *lustre,*" or fifty-five—his own age.

50 When you get to my age life seems little more than one long march to and from the lavatory.

JOHN MORTIMER (b. 1923), British barrister, novelist. Haverford Downs, in *Summer's Lease,* pt. 2, ch. 3 (1988).

51 Old women snore violently. They are like bodies into which bizarre animals have crept at night; the animals are vicious, bawdy, noisy. How they snore! There is no shame to their snoring. Old women turn into old men.

JOYCE CAROL OATES (b. 1938), U.S. author. "What is the Connection Between Men and Women?," in *Mademoiselle* (New York, Feb. 1970).

52 Here, with whitened hair, desires failing, strength ebbing out of him, with the sun gone down and with only the serenity and the calm warning of the evening star left to him, he drank to Life, to all it had been, to what it was, to what it would be. Hurrah!

> SEAN O'CASEY (1884–1964), Irish dramatist. *Sunset and Evening Star*, final paragraph (1954).

53 The old—like children—talk to themselves, for they have reached that hopeless wisdom of experience which knows that though one were to cry it in the streets to multitudes, or whisper it in the kiss to one's beloved, the only ears that can ever hear one's secrets are one's own!

> EUGENE O'NEILL (1888–1953), U.S. dramatist. Tiberius, in *Lazarus Laughed*, act 4, sc. 1. See Hoffer, above, on talking to oneself.

54 He who is of a calm and happy nature will hardly feel the pressure of age, but to him who is of an opposite disposition youth and age are equally a burden.

> PLATO c. 427–347 B.C.), Greek philosopher. Cephalus, in *The Republic*, bk. 1, sct. 329.

55 Time and trouble will tame an advanced young woman, but an advanced old woman is uncontrollable by any earthly force.

> DOROTHY L. SAYERS (1893–1957), British author. Sir Impey Biggs, in *Clouds of Witness*, ch. 16 (1926).

56 My age is as a lusty winter,
Frosty but kindly.

> WILLIAM SHAKESPEARE (1564–1616), English dramatist, poet. Adam, in *As You Like It*, act 2, sc. 3.

57 Have you not a moist eye, a dry hand, a yellow cheek, a white beard, a decreasing leg, an increasing belly? Is not your voice broken, your wind short, your chin double, your wit single, and every part about you blasted with antiquity?

> WILLIAM SHAKESPEARE (1564–1616), English dramatist, poet. Lord Chief Justice, in *King Henry IV, Pt. 2*, act 1, sc. 2.

58 Lord, Lord, how subject we old men are to this vice of lying!

> WILLIAM SHAKESPEARE (1564–1616), English dramatist, poet. Falstaff, in *King Henry IV, Pt. 2*, act 3, sc. 2.

59 I have lived long enough. My way of life
Is fall'n into the sere, the yellow leaf,
And that which should accompany old age,
As honour, love, obedience, troops of friends,
I must not look to have.

> WILLIAM SHAKESPEARE (1564–1616), English dramatist, poet. Macbeth, in *Macbeth*, act 5, sc. 3.

60 Old men are dangerous: it doesn't matter to them what is going to happen to the world.

> GEORGE BERNARD SHAW (1856–1950), Anglo-Irish playwright, critic. Captain Shotover, in *Heartbreak House*, act 2. Ellie responds: "I should have thought nothing else mattered to old men. They can't be very interested in what is going to happen to themselves."

61 How earthy old people become—mouldy as the grave! Their wisdom smacks of the earth. There is no foretaste of immortality in it. They remind me of earthworms and mole crickets.

> HENRY DAVID THOREAU (1817–62), U.S. philosopher, author, naturalist. *Journal* (1906), entry for 16 Aug. 1853.

62 Old age is the most unexpected of all things that happen to a man.

> LEON TROTSKY (1879–1940), Russian revolutionary. *Diary in Exile* (1959), entry for 8 May 1935.

63 I am admonished in many ways that time is pushing me inexorably along. I am approaching the threshold of age; in 1977 I shall be 142. This is no time to be flitting about the earth. I must cease from the activities proper to youth and begin to take on the dignities and gravities and inertia proper to that season of honorable senility which is on its way.

> MARK TWAIN (1835–1910), U.S. author. Letter, 19 July 1901 (published in *Letters of Mark Twain*, ed. by Albert Bigelow Paine, 1917), refusing an invitation to attend 80th anniversary celebrations of the state of Missouri.

64 They are all gone into the world of light,
And I alone sit lingering here.

> HENRY VAUGHAN (1622–95), Welsh poet. *They Are All Gone.*

65 You end up as you deserve. In old age you must put up with the face, the friends, the health, and the children you have earned.

> FAY WELDON (b. 1933), British novelist. The narrator (Praxis Duveen), in *Praxis*, ch. 21 (1978).

66 There's no such thing as old age, there is only sorrow.

> EDITH WHARTON (1862–1937), U.S. author. *A Backward Glance*, "A First Word" (1934).

67 Old age, calm, expanded, broad with the haughty breadth of the universe,
Old age flowing free with the delicious near-by freedom of death.

> WALT WHITMAN (1819–92), U.S. poet. *Song of the Open Road*, verse 12 (1856).

68 O Time and Change!—with hair as gray
As was my sire's that winter day,
How strange it seems, with so much gone
Of life and love, to still live on!

> JOHN GREENLEAF WHITTIER (1807–92), U.S. poet. *Snow-Bound.*

69 The tragedy of old age is not that one is old, but that one is young.

> OSCAR WILDE (1854–1900), Anglo-Irish playwright, author. Lord Henry, in *The Picture of Dorian Gray*, ch. 19 (1891).

70 But an old age serene and bright,
And lovely as a Lapland night,
Shall lead thee to thy grave.

> WILLIAM WORDSWORTH (1770–1850), English poet. *To a Young Lady* (1805).

71 An aged man is but a paltry thing,
A tattered coat upon a stick

> W. B. YEATS (1865–1939), Irish poet, playwright. *Sailing to Byzantium*, st. 2.

See also Smith on ACQUAINTANCE; Holmes on ADVICE; Nicklaus on AGE AND AGING; Colette, Lichtenberg on AGE AND AGING: THE SIXTIES; AGE AND AGING: THE SEVENTIES; Disraeli on ANECDOTES; Vauvenargues on AWARENESS; Shakespeare on BEAUTY; Jenkins on BELIEF; Thomas on DEATH AND DYING; Winegarten on DECAY; Johnson on MEN, SINGLE; Yeats on NOSTALGIA; Hoffer on NOVELTY; Plato on SEX; Read on SIN; YOUTH AND AGE.

OLD AGE AND AGING

1   Forty years on, growing older and older,
Shorter in wind, as in memory long,
Feeble of foot, and rheumatic of shoulder
What will it help you that once you were strong?

> E. E. BOWEN (1836–1901), English schoolmaster. "Forty Years On" (Harrow School song).

2   My days are in the yellow leaf;
The flowers and fruits of Love are gone;
The worm—the canker, and the grief
Are mine alone!

> LORD BYRON (1788–1824), English poet. *On This Day I Complete My Thirty-Sixth Year* (published in *Byron's Letters and Journals*, vol. 11, ed. by Leslie A. Marchand, 1981). The poem was the final entry in Byron's last journal, written in Greece. He died three months later.

3   Age wins and one must learn to grow old. . . . I must learn to walk this long unlovely wintry way, looking for spectacles, shunning the cruel looking-glass, laughing at my clumsiness before others mistakenly condole, not expecting gallantry yet disappointed to receive none, apprehending every ache of shaft of pain, alive to blinding flashes of mortality, unarmed, totally vulnerable.

> [LADY] DIANA COOPER (1892–1986), British actor, author, society figure. *Trumpets from the Steep*, ch. 8 (1960).

4   What a wretched lot of old shrivelled creatures we shall be by-and-by. Never mind—the uglier we get in the eyes of others, the lovelier we shall be to each other; that has always been my firm faith about friendship.

> GEORGE ELIOT (1819–80), English novelist. Letter, 27 May 1852.

5   The best part of the art of living is to know how to grow old gracefully.

> ERIC HOFFER (1902–83), U.S. philosopher. *The Passionate State of Mind*, aph. 235 (1955).

6   Certainly the effort to remain unchanged, young, when the body gives so impressive a signal of change as the menopause, is gallant; but it is a stupid, self-sacrificial gallantry, better befitting a boy of twenty than a woman of forty-five or fifty. Let the athletes die young and laurel-crowned. Let the soldiers earn the Purple Hearts. Let women die old, white-crowned, with human hearts.

> URSULA K. LE GUIN (b. 1929), U.S. author. "The Space Crone," in *The Co-Evolution Quarterly* (Summer 1976; repr. in *Dancing at the Edge of the World*, 1989).

7   Nothing makes one old so quickly as the ever-present thought that one is growing older . . .

> G. C. LICHTENBERG (1742–99), German physicist, philosopher. *Aphorisms*, "Notebook K," aph. 13 (written 1765–99; tr. by R. J. Hollingdale, 1990).

8   Growing old is no more than a bad habit which a busy man has no time to form.

> ANDRÉ MAUROIS (1885–1967), French author, critic. *The Art of Living*, "The Art of Growing Old" (1940).

9   Self-parody is the first portent of age.

> LARRY MCMURTRY (b. 1936), U.S. screenwriter, novelist, essayist. Danny Deck, in *Some Can Whistle*, pt. 1, ch. 14 (1989).

10   I dread no more the first white in my hair,
Or even age itself, the easy shoe,
The cane, the wrinkled hands, the special chair:
Time, doing this to me, may alter too
My anguish, into something I can bear.

> EDNA ST. VINCENT MILLAY (1892–1950), U.S. poet. *Time, That Renews the Tissues of This Frame*.

11   Time has the same effect on the mind as on the face; the predominant passion and the strongest feature become more conspicuous from the others' retiring.

> LADY MARY WORTLEY MONTAGU (1689–1762), English society figure, letter writer. Letter, 5 Sept. 1758, to her daughter Lady Bute (published in *Selected Letters*, ed. by Robert Halsband, 1970).

12   Growing old's like being increasingly penalized for a crime you haven't committed.

> ANTHONY POWELL (b. 1905), British novelist. Dick Umfraville, in *Temporary Kings*, ch. 1 (1973); eleventh in the novel sequence, *A Dance to the Music of Time*.

13   The secret of a long life is knowing when it's time to go.

> MICHELE SHOCKED (b. 1962), U.S. singer, songwriter. "The Secret of a Long Life" on album *Campfire Tapes* (rerecorded on *Arkansas Traveler*, 1992).

14   Growing old is no gradual decline, but a series of tumbles, full of sorrow, from one ledge to another. Yet when we pick ourselves up we find no bones are broken; while not unpleasing is the new terrace which stretches out unexplored before us.

> LOGAN PEARSALL SMITH (1865–1946), U.S. essayist, aphorist. *All Trivia*, "Last Words" (1933).

15   I see in you the estuary that enlarges and spreads itself grandly as it
pours in the great sea.

> WALT WHITMAN (1819–1892), U.S. poet. *To Old Age*.

16   It haunts me, the passage of time. I think time is a merciless thing. I think life is a process of burning oneself out and time is the fire that burns you. But I think the spirit of man is a good adversary.

> TENNESSEE WILLIAMS (1914–83), U.S. dramatist. *New York Post* (30 April 1958).

See also Thomas on DEATH AND DYING.

OPERA

1   Nothing is capable of being well set to music that is not nonsense.

> JOSEPH ADDISON (1672–1719), English essayist. *Spectator*, no. 18 (London, 21 March 1711), on the effect of Italian opera on the English stage.

2   If music in general is an imitation of history, opera in particular is an imitation of human willfulness; it is rooted in the fact that we not only have feelings but insist upon having them at whatever cost to ourselves. . . . The quality common to all the great operatic roles, e.g., Don Giovanni, Norma, Lucia, Tristan, Isolde, Brünnhilde, is that each of them is a passionate and willful state of being. In real life they would all be bores, even Don Giovanni.

W. H. AUDEN (1907–73), Anglo-American poet. *The Dyer's Hand*, pt. 8, "Notes on Music And Opera" (1962).

3   Opera once was an important social instrument—especially in Italy. With Rossini and Verdi people were listening to opera together and having the same catharsis with the same story, the same moral dilemmas. They were holding hands in the darkness. That has gone. Now perhaps they are holding hands watching television.

LUCIANO BERIO (b. 1925), Italian composer. Interview in *Observer Review* (London, 5 Feb. 1989).

4   Opera, next to Gothic architecture, is one of the strangest inventions of Western man. It could not have been foreseen by any logical process.

KENNETH, LORD CLARK (1903–83), British art historian. *Civilisation*, ch. 9 (1970).

5   A Librettist is a mere drudge in the world of opera.

ROBERTSON DAVIES (b. 1913), Canadian novelist, journalist. "The Happy Intervention of Robertson Davies," in *Opera Canada* (Spring, 1982; repr. in *The Enthusiasms of Robertson Davies*, 1990).

6   I never was an opera fan—about twenty-five musically supreme masterpieces in this curious medium apart.

HANS KELLER (1919–85), Austrian-born British musicologist. *Criticism*, Preface (ed. by Julian Hogg, 1987).

7   The Opera is obviously the first draft of a fine spectacle; it suggests the idea of one.

JEAN DE LA BRUYÈRE (1645–96), French writer, moralist. *Characters*, "Of Books," aph. 47 (1688).

8   I love Italian opera—it's so reckless. Damn Wagner, and his bellowings at Fate and death. Damn Debussy, and his averted face. I like the Italians who run all on impulse, and don't care about their immortal souls, and don't worry about the ultimate.

D. H. LAWRENCE (1885–1930), British author. Letter, 1 April 1911 (published in *The Letters of D. H. Lawrence*, vol. 1, ed. by James T. Boulton, 1979).

9   Going to the opera, like getting drunk, is a sin that carries its own punishment with it.

HANNAH MORE (1745–1833), English writer, reformer, philanthropist. Letter, 1775, to her sister (published in *The Letters of Hannah More*, 1925).

10   I never can hear a crowd of people singing and gesticulating, all together, at an Italian opera, without fancying myself at Athens, listening to that particular tragedy, by Sophocles, in which he introduces a full chorus of turkeys, who set about bewailing the death of Meleager.

EDGAR ALLAN POE (1809–45), U.S. poet, critic, short-story writer. "Marginalia," in *Southern Literary Messenger* (Richmond, Va., July 1849; repr. in *Essays and Reviews*, 1984).

11   If I weren't reasonably placid, I don't think I could cope with this sort of life. To be a diva, you've got to be absolutely like a horse.

JOAN SUTHERLAND (b. 1926), Australian opera singer. Quoted in: Winthrop Sargeant, *Divas: Impressions of Six Opera Superstars*, "Joan Sutherland" (1959).

12   I have always believed that opera is a planet where the muses work together, join hands and celebrate all the arts.

FRANCO ZEFFIRELLI (b. 1922), Italian stage and film director. *International Herald Tribune* (Paris, 21 March 1990).

OPINION

1   Opinions are formed in a process of open discussion and public debate, and where no opportunity for the forming of opinions exists, there may be moods—moods of the masses and moods of individuals, the latter no less fickle and unreliable than the former—but no opinion.

HANNAH ARENDT (1906–75), German-born U.S. political philosopher. *On Revolution*, ch. 6 (1963).

2   Where an opinion is general, it is usually correct.

JANE AUSTEN (1775–1817), English novelist. Mary Crawford, in *Mansfield Park*, ch. 11 (1814).

3   Opinions are to the vast apparatus of social existence what oil is to machines: one does not go up to a turbine and pour machine oil over it; one applies a little to hidden spindles and joints that one has to know.

WALTER BENJAMIN (1892–1940), German critic and philosopher. *One-Way Street*, "Filling Station" (1928; repr. in *One-Way Street and Other Writings*, 1978).

4   The man who never alters his opinion is like standing water, and breeds reptiles of the mind.

WILLIAM BLAKE (1757–1827), English poet, painter, engraver. *The Marriage of Heaven and Hell*, plates 17–20, "A Memorable Fancy" (1790; repr. in *Complete Writings*, ed. by Geoffrey Keynes, 1957).

5   Men get opinions as boys learn to spell,
By reiteration chiefly.

ELIZABETH BARRETT BROWNING (1806–61), English Poet. *Aurora Leigh*, bk. 6 (1857).

6   The public buys its opinions as it buys its meat, or takes in its milk, on the principle that it is cheaper to do this than to keep a cow. So it is, but the milk is more likely to be watered.

SAMUEL BUTLER (1835–1902), English author. *Notebooks*, ch. 17 (1912).

7   Opinions have vested interests just as men have.

SAMUEL BUTLER (1835–1902), English author. *Samuel Butler's Notebooks*, (1951, p. 221).

8   Opinions are made to be changed—or how is truth to be got at?

LORD BYRON (1788–1824), English poet. Letter, 9 May 1817, to publisher John Murray (published in *Byron's Letters and Journals*, vol. 5, ed. by Leslie A. Marchand, 1973–81).

9   No two men see the world exactly alike, and different temperaments will apply in different ways a principle that they both acknowledge. The same man will, indeed, often see and judge the same things differently on different occasions: early convictions must give way to more mature ones. Nevertheless, may not the opinions that a man holds and expresses withstand all trials, if he only remains true to himself and others?

JOHANN WOLFGANG VON GOETHE (1749–1832), German poet, dramatist. *Propyläen* Introduction (1798), a periodical founded by Goethe that took its title from the gateway to the Acropolis of Athens.

10 It rarely adds anything to say, "In my opinion"— not even modesty. Naturally a sentence is only your opinion; and you are not the Pope.

PAUL GOODMAN (1911–1972), U.S. author, poet, critic. *Five Years*, "1959," sct. 2 (1966).

11 The only means of strengthening one's intellect is to make up one's mind about nothing—to let the mind be a thoroughfare for all thoughts. Not a select party.

JOHN KEATS (1795–1821), English poet. Letter, 17–27 Sept. 1819, to his brother and sister-in-law, George and Georgiana Keats (published in *Letters of John Keats*, no. 156, ed. by Frederick Page, 1954).

12 A study of the history of opinion is a necessary preliminary to the emancipation of the mind.

JOHN MAYNARD KEYNES (1883–1946), British economist. *The End of Laissez-Faire*, ch. 1 (1926).

13 I have remarked very clearly that I am often of one opinion when I am lying down and of another when I am standing up. . .

G. C. LICHTENBERG (1742–99), German physicist, philosopher. *Aphorisms*, "Notebook F," aph. 73 (written 1765–99; tr. by R. J. Hollingdale, 1990).

14 We accumulate our opinions at an age when our understanding is at its weakest.

G. C. LICHTENBERG (1742–99), German physicist, philosopher. *Aphorisms*, "Notebook H," aph. 4 (written 1765–99; tr. by R. J. Hollingdale, 1990).

15 New opinions are always suspected, and usually opposed, without any other reason but because they are not already common.

JOHN LOCKE (1632–1704), English philosopher. Dedicatory Epistle to *An Enquiry Concerning Human Understanding* (1690).

16 False opinions are like false money, struck first of all by guilty men and thereafter circulated by honest people who perpetuate the crime without knowing what they are doing.

JOSEPH DE MAISTRE (1753–1821), French diplomat, philosopher. The Count, in *Les Soirées de Saint-Pétersbourg*, "First Dialogue" (1821; repr. in *The Works of Joseph de Maistre*, ed. by Jack Lively, 1965).

17 A point of view can be a dangerous luxury when substituted for insight and understanding.

MARSHALL MCLUHAN (1911–80), Canadian communications theorist. *The Gutenberg Galaxy*, "Typographic Man Can Express but Is Helpless to Read the Configuration of Print Technology" (1962).

18 The peculiar evil of silencing the expression of an opinion is, that it is robbing the human race; posterity as well as the existing generation; those who dissent from the opinion, still more than those who hold it. If the opinion is right, they are deprived of the opportunity of exchanging error for truth: if wrong, they lose, what is

almost as great a benefit, the clearer perception and livelier impression of truth, produced by its collision with error.

JOHN STUART MILL (1806–73), English philosopher, economist. *On Liberty*, ch. 2 (1859).

19 It's not that I don't have opinions, rather that I'm paid not to think aloud.

YITZHAK NAVON (b. 1921), Israeli politician, president. Quoted in: *Observer* (London, 16 Jan. 1983).

20 Altered opinions do not alter a man's character (or do so very little); but they do illuminate individual aspects of the constellation of his personality which with a different constellation of opinions had hitherto remained dark and unrecognizable.

FRIEDRICH NIETZSCHE (1844–1900), German philosopher. *Assorted Opinions and Maxims*, aph. 58 (1879).

21 We would not let ourselves be burned to death for our opinions: we are not sure enough of them for that. But perhaps for the right to have our opinions and to change them.

FRIEDRICH NIETZSCHE (1844–1900), German philosopher. *The Wanderer and His Shadow*, aph. 333 (1880).

22 It takes a very deep-rooted opinion to survive unexpressed.

JEAN ROSTAND (1894–1977), French biologist, writer. *Carnets d'un Biologiste* (repr. in *The Substance of Man*, 1962, p. 192).

23 The sound of tireless voices is the price we pay for the right to hear the music of our own opinions.

ADLAI STEVENSON (1900–1965), U.S. Democratic politician. Speech, 28 Aug. 1952, New York City.

24 Hardly a man in the world has an opinion upon morals, politics or religion which he got otherwise than through his associations and sympathies. Broadly speaking, there are none but corn-pone opinions. And broadly speaking, Corn-Pone stands for Self-Approval. Self-approval is acquired mainly from the approval of other people. The result is Conformity.

MARK TWAIN (1835–1910), U.S. author. "Corn-Pone Opinions" (1923; repr. in *What Is Man?*, ed. by Paul Baender, 1973).

25 The more opinions you have, the less you see.

WIM WENDERS (b. 1945), German filmmaker. *Evening Standard* (London, 25 April 1990).

26 No work of art ever puts forward views. Views belong to people who are not artists.

OSCAR WILDE (1854–1900), Anglo-Irish playwright, author. In answer to Edward Carson, Q.C., during Wilde's prosecution of the Marquess of Queensberry for criminal libel, in *Regina (Wilde) v. Queensberry*, 3 April 1895.

See also Nietzsche on ARGUMENT; Butler on CHRISTIANITY AND THE CHRISTIANS; Emerson on CONFORMITY; Twain on DISSENT; Emerson on INCONSISTENCY; Lichtenberg on INDIFFERENCE; Mill on REPRESSION.

OPPORTUNITY

1 This American system of ours . . . call it Americanism, call it capitalism, call it what you like, gives to each and every one of us a great opportunity if we only seize it with both hands and make the most of it.

AL CAPONE (1899–1947), U.S. gangster. Interview with Claud Cockburn, in *Cockburn Sums Up*, "Mr. Capone, Philosopher" (1981).

2 Thou strong seducer, Opportunity!

JOHN DRYDEN (1631–1700), English poet, dramatist, critic. Almahide, in *The Conquest of Granada*, pt. 2, act 4, sc. 3.

3 I go the way that Providence dictates with the assurance of a sleepwalker.

ADOLF HITLER (1889–1945), German dictator. Speech, 15 March 1936, Munich, Germany.

4 It still holds true that man is most uniquely human when he turns obstacles into opportunities.

ERIC HOFFER (1902–83), U.S. philosopher. *Reflections on the Human Condition*, aph. 27 (1973).

5 How oft the sight of means to do ill deeds
Makes deeds ill done!

WILLIAM SHAKESPEARE (1564–1616), English dramatist, poet. King John, in *King John*, act 4, sc. 2.

6 There is a tide in the affairs of men
Which, taken at the flood, leads on to fortune;
Omitted, all the voyage of their life
Is bound in shallows and in miseries.

WILLIAM SHAKESPEARE (1564–1616), English dramatist, poet. Brutus, in *Julius Caesar*, act 4, sc. 2.

7 People think that at the top there isn't much room. They tend to think of it as an Everest. My message is that there is tons of room at the top.

MARGARET THATCHER (b. 1925), British Conservative politician, prime minister. *Daily Telegraph* (London, 30 Sept. 1988). Thatcher's words echo those attributed to Daniel Webster c. 1801, rejecting advice that he stay out of the crowded legal profession: "There is always room at the top."

OPPOSITES

1 Light is meaningful only in relation to darkness, and truth presupposes error. It is these mingled opposites which people our life, which make it pungent, intoxicating. We only exist in terms of this conflict, in the zone where black and white clash.

LOUIS ARAGON (1897–1982), French poet. *Paris Peasant*, "Preface to a Modern Mythology" (1926).

2 The world is not dialectical—it is sworn to extremes, not to equilibrium, sworn to radical antagonism, not to reconciliation or synthesis. This is also the principle of evil.

JEAN BAUDRILLARD (b. 1929), French semiologist. *Fatal Strategies*, "Ecstasy and Inertia" (1983; tr. 1990).

3 Without contraries is no progression. Attraction and repulsion, reason and energy, love and hate, are necessary to human existence.

WILLIAM BLAKE (1757–1827), English poet, painter, engraver. *The Marriage of Heaven and Hell*, plate 3 (1790–93; repr. in *Complete Writings*, ed. by Geoffrey Keynes, 1957).

4 The beginning, middle, and end of the birth, growth, and perfection of whatever we behold is from contraries, by contraries, and to contraries; and whatever contrarity is, there is action and reaction, there is motion, diversity, multitude, and order, there are degrees, succession and vicissitude.

GIORDANO BRUNO (1548–1600), Italian philosopher. *The Expulsion of the Triumphant Beast*, "First Dialogue," Introduction (1588). Quoted in: Giordano Bruno, *Cause, Principle, and Unity*, sct. 7 (ed. and tr. by Jack Lindsay, 1962).

5 In me the tiger sniffs the rose.

SIEGFRIED SASSOON (1886–1967), British poet. *The Heart's Journey*, no. 7 (1928).

See also CONTRADICTION.

OPPOSITION

1 Opposition is true friendship.

WILLIAM BLAKE (1757–1827), English poet, painter, engraver. *The Marriage of Heaven and Hell*, plates 17–20, "A Memorable Fancy" (1790–93).

2 He that wrestles with us strengthens our nerves, and sharpens our skill. Our antagonist is our helper. This amicable conflict with difficulty helps us to an intimate acquaintance with our object, and compels us to consider it in all its relations. It will not suffer us to be superficial.

EDMUND BURKE (1729–97), Irish philosopher, statesman. *Reflections on the Revolution in France* (1790).

3 I respect only those who resist me; but I cannot tolerate them.

CHARLES DE GAULLE (1890–1970), French general, president. Quoted in: *New York Times Magazine* (12 May 1966).

4 No Government can be long secure without a formidable Opposition. It reduces their supporters to that tractable number which can be managed by the joint influences of fruition and hope. It offers vengeance to the discontented, and distinction to the ambitious; and employs the energies of aspiring spirits, who otherwise may prove traitors in a division or assassins in a debate.

BENJAMIN DISRAELI (1804–81), English statesman, author. *Coningsby*, bk. 2, ch. 1 (1844).

5 Opposition may become sweet to a man when he has christened it persecution.

GEORGE ELIOT (1819–80), English novelist. *Janet's Repentance*, ch. 8 (first published in *Blackwood's Magazine*, 1857; repr. in *Scenes of Clerical Life*, 1858).

6 But most of us are apt to settle within ourselves that the man who blocks our way is odious, and not to mind causing him a little of the disgust which his personality excites in ourselves.

GEORGE ELIOT (1819–1880), English novelist, editor. *Middlemarch*, bk. 5, ch. 47 (1871).

7 Opposition is not necessarily enmity; it is merely misused and made an *occasion* for enmity.

SIGMUND FREUD (1856–1939), Austrian psychiatrist. *Civilization and Its Discontents*, ch. 5 (1930; repr. in *Complete Works*, vol. 21, ed. by James Strachey and Anna Freud, 1961).

8 The opposition is indispensable. A good statesman, like any other sensible human being, always learns more from his opponents than from his fervent supporters. For his supporters will push him to disaster unless his opponents show him where the dangers are. So if he is wise he will often pray to be delivered from his friends, because they will ruin him. But though it hurts, he ought also to pray never to be left without opponents; for they keep him on the path of reason and good sense.

WALTER LIPPMANN (1889–1974), U.S. journalist. "The Indispensable Opposition," in *Atlantic Monthly* (Boston, 1939; repr. in *The Essential Lippman*, pt. 6, sct. 2, 1982).

9 If it is once again one against forty-eight, then I am very sorry for the forty-eight.

MARGARET THATCHER (b. 1925), British Conservative politician, prime minister. Quoted in: *Daily Telegraph* (London, 25 Oct. 1989), referring to the 1989 Commonwealth Conference.

10 It is easy and dismally enervating to think of opposition as merely perverse or actually evil—far more invigorating to see it as essential for honing the mind, and as a positive good in itself. For the day that moral issues cease to be fought over is the day the word "human" disappears from the race.

JILL TWEEDIE (b. 1936), British author, journalist. *Independent* (London, May 1989).

See also Kennedy on PROTEST.

OPPRESSION

1 You know, it's not the world that was my oppressor, because what the world does to you, if the world does it to you long enough and effectively enough, you begin to do to yourself.

JAMES BALDWIN (1924–87), U.S. author. *A Dialogue* (1973; with Nikki Giovanni), from a conversation in London, 4 Nov. 1971.

2 Everybody knows there is no fineness or accuracy of suppression; if you hold down one thing, you hold down the adjoining.

SAUL BELLOW (b. 1915), U.S. novelist. *The Adventures of Augie Marsh*, ch. 1 (1949).

3 Ours is the century of enforced travel . . . of disappearances. The century of people helplessly seeing others, who were close to them, disappear over the horizon.

JOHN BERGER (b. 1926), British author, critic. "Ev'ry Time We Say Goodbye," in *Expressen* (Stockholm, 3 Nov. 1990); repr. in *Keeping a Rendezvous*, 1992).

4 Nature in darkness groans
And men are bound to sullen contemplation in the night:
Restless they turn on beds of sorrow; in their inmost brain
Feeling the crushing wheels, they rise, they write the bitter words
Of stern philosophy & knead the bread of knowledge with tears & groans.

WILLIAM BLAKE (1757–1827), English poet, painter, engraver.

The Four Zoas, "Night the Ninth" (1795–1804; repr. in *Complete Writings*, ed. by Geoffrey Keynes, 1957).

5 They have given us into the hand of new unhappy lords,
Lords without anger and honour, who dare not carry their swords.
They fight by shuffling papers; they have bright dead alien eyes;
They look at our labour and laughter as a tired man looks at flies.

G. K. CHESTERTON (1874–1936), British author. *The Secret People.*

6 Tyranny destroys or strengthens the individual; freedom enervates him, until he becomes no more than a puppet. Man has more chances of saving himself by hell than by paradise.

E. M. CIORAN (b. 1911), Rumanian-born French philosopher. *Anathemas and Admirations*, "On the Verge of Existence" (1986).

7 Where justice is denied, where poverty is enforced, where ignorance prevails, and where any one class is made to feel that society is in an organized conspiracy to oppress, rob, and degrade them, neither persons nor property will be safe.

FREDERICK DOUGLASS (c. 1817–95), U.S. abolitionist. Speech, April 1886, Washington, D.C., on the 24th anniversary of emancipation in the District of Columbia.

8 The will to domination is a ravenous beast. There are never enough warm bodies to satiate its monstrous hunger. Once alive, this beast grows and grows, feeding on all the life around it, scouring the earth to find new sources of nourishment. This beast lives in each man who battens on female servitude.

ANDREA DWORKIN (b. 1946), U.S. feminist critic. "Our Blood: The Slavery of Women in Amerika," speech, 23 Aug. 1975, to the National Organization for Women, Washington, D.C. (published in *Our Blood*, ch. 8, 1976).

9 You may try but you can never imagine what it is to have a man's form of genius in you, and to suffer the slavery of being a girl.

GEORGE ELIOT (1819–80), English novelist, editor. Deronda's mother, in *Daniel Deronda*, bk. 7, ch. 51 (1874–76).

10 We fight, get beat, rise, and fight again.

NATHANAEL GREENE (1742–86), U.S. Revolutionary general. Letter, April 1781, to French ambassador to the United States Chevalier del la Luzerne, following the Battle of Hobkirk's Hill, S.C.

11 True enough, the country is calm. Calm as a morgue or a grave, would you not say?

VÁCLAV HAVEL (b. 1936), Czech playwright, president. *Living in Truth*, pt. 1, "Letter to Dr. Gustáv Husák" (1986), referring to the situation in Czechoslovakia under the communist régime.

12 Do not be misled by the fact that you are at liberty and relatively free; that for the moment you are not under lock and key: you have simply been granted a reprieve.

RYSZARD KAPUSCINSKI (b. 1932), Polish journalist. "A Warsaw Diary," in *Granta*, no. 15 (Cambridge, England, 1985).

13 Loss of freedom seldom happens overnight. Oppression doesn't stand on the doorstep with tooth-brush moustache and swastika armband—it creeps up insidiously . . . step by step, and all of a sudden the unfortunate citizen realises that it is gone.

> BARON LANE (b. 1918), British judge, Lord Chief Justice of England. Quoted in: *Independent* (London, 3 Feb. 1990), referring to proposed legal reforms.

14 A handful of soldiers is always better than a mouthful of arguments.

> G. C. LICHTENBERG (1742–99), German physicist, philosopher. *Aphorisms*, "Notebook E," aph. 19 (written 1765–99; tr. by R. J. Hollingdale, 1990).

15 The web of domination has become the web of Reason itself, and this society is fatally entangled in it.

> HERBERT MARCUSE (1898–1979), U.S. political philosopher. *One-Dimensional Man*, ch. 5 (1964).

16 Even today a crude sort of persecution is all that is required to create an *honorable* name for any sect, no matter how indifferent in itself.

> FRIEDRICH NIETZSCHE (1844–1900), German philosopher. *The Anti-Christ*, aph. 53 (1895).

17 If you want a vision of the future, imagine a boot stamping on a human face—forever.

> GEORGE ORWELL (1903–50), British author. O'Brien to Winston Smith, in *Nineteen Eighty-Four*, pt. 3, ch. 3 (1949).

18 First we kill all the subversives; then, their collaborators; later, those who sympathize with them; afterward, those who remain indifferent; and finally, the undecided.

> GENERAL IBERICO SAINT JEAN, Argentinian soldier, politician. Quoted in: *Boletin de las Madres de Plaza de Mayo*, vol. 1, no. 6 (May 1985; repr. in Robin Morgan, *The Demon Lover*, ch. 4, 1989). General Iberico Saint Jean was governor of the province of Buenos Aires during the military rule in Argentina.

20 Human beings are so made that the ones who do the crushing feel nothing; it is the person crushed who feels what is happening. Unless one has placed oneself on the side of the oppressed, to feel with them, one cannot understand.

> SIMONE WEIL (1909–43), French philosopher, mystic. *Lectures on Philosophy*, pt. 3, ch. 2 (1978).

19 Oppression that is clearly inexorable and invincible does not give rise to revolt but to submission.

> SIMONE WEIL (1909–43), French philosopher, mystic. *Factory Journal*, "The Mystery of the Factory" (1934–35; repr. in *La Condition Ouvrière*, 1951).

See also Konrad on COURAGE; DESPOTISM; Tolstoy on LIBERALS; Szasz on MADNESS; REPRESSION; TYRANNY.

OPTIMISM

1 Optimism. The doctrine or belief that everything is beautiful, including what is ugly.

> AMBROSE BIERCE (1842–1914), U.S. author. *The Devil's Dictionary* (1881–1906).

2 The world is the best of all possible worlds, and everything in it is a necessary evil.

> F. H. BRADLEY (1846–1924), English philosopher. *Appearance and Reality*, Preface (1893).

3 If Christianity is pessimistic as to man, it is optimistic as to human destiny. Well, I can say that, pessimistic as to human destiny, I am optimistic as to man.

> ALBERT CAMUS (1913–60), French-Algerian philosopher, author. Address, 1948, to monks of Latour-Maubourg (published in *Resistance, Rebellion and Death*, "The Unbeliever and Christians," 1961).

4 These are not dark days: these are great days—the greatest days our country has ever lived.

> SIR WINSTON CHURCHILL (1874–1965), English statesman, writer. Speech, 29 Oct. 1941, Harrow School, England.

5 Too cheerful a morality is a loose morality; it is appropriate only to decadent peoples and is found only among them.

> EMILE DURKHEIM (1858–1917), French sociologist. *Suicide*, bk. 3, ch. 3, sct. 1 (1897; tr. 1951).

6 Optimism is the content of small men in high places.

> F. SCOTT FITZGERALD (1896–1940), U.S. author. *The Crack-Up*, "Notebook E" (ed. by Edmund Wilson, 1945).

7 I'm a pessimist because of intelligence, but an optimist because of will.

> ANTONIO GRAMSCI (1891–1937), Italian political theorist. Letter, 19 Dec. 1929 (published in *Gramsci: Letters from Prison*, tr. by Raymond Rosenthal, 1993).

8 Optimism is the opium of the people.

> MILAN KUNDERA (b. 1929), Czech author, critic. *The Joke*, pt. 3, ch. 3 (1967; tr. 1982). The line, written by Ludvik on a postcard, was used by the Party as incriminating evidence against him, though it was only meant as "a joke."

9 Let us be of good cheer, however, remembering that the misfortunes hardest to bear are those which never come.

> JAMES RUSSELL LOWELL (1819–91), U.S. poet, editor. "On Democracy," speech, 6 Oct. 1884, Birmingham, England (published in *Democracy and Other Addresses*, 1886).

10 an optimist is a guy
who has never had
much experience.

> DON MARQUIS (1878–1937), U.S. humorist, journalist. *archy and mehitabel*, "certain maxims of archy" (1927).

11 The happy ending is our national belief.

> MARY MCCARTHY (1912–89), U.S. author, critic. *On the Contrary*, pt. 1, "America the Beautiful: The Humanist in the Bathtub" (1962; first published Sept. 1947).

12 Nothing bad's going to happen to us. If we get fired, it's not failure; its a midlife vocational reassessment.

> P. J. O'ROURKE (b. 1947), U.S. journalist. *Rolling Stone* (New York, 30 Nov. 1989).

13 Man's real life is happy, chiefly because he is ever expecting that it soon will be so.

> EDGAR ALLAN POE (1809–45), U.S. poet, critic, short-story writer. *Marginalia*, "Re-Living the Old Life," (1844–49; repr. in *The Centenary Poe*, ed. by Montagu Slater, 1949).

14 In these times you have to be an optimist to open your eyes when you wake in the morning.

> CARL SANDBURG (1878–1967), U.S. poet. *New York Post* (9 Sept. 1960).

15   Oh yet we trust that somehow good
Will be the final goal of ill!

     ALFRED LORD TENNYSON (1809–92), English poet. *In Memoriam A.H.H.*, cto. 54.

16   As both capitalist and communist states—not to mention the technological world—have evolved under the illusion that men purposefully built them, ideological optimism seeps into every niche of our lives. It is made worse by mass culture which feeds our most destructive illusions, fostering the belief that if we're only justified (and who isn't?)—if we only calculate things correctly, if we only *do the right thing* (and who doesn't?)—then the future must yield the desired results. There must always be a way. And so hubris turns to false certainties, everyone expects to be a winner, and each morning is a mind-blowing surprise.

     STEPHEN VIZINCZEY (b. 1933), Hungarian novelist, critic. "One of the Very Few," an appreciation of Stendhal, in *Times* (London, 11 May 1968; repr. in *Truth and Lies in Literature*, 1986).

17   The basis of optimism is sheer terror.

     OSCAR WILDE (1854–1900), Anglo-Irish playwright, author. Lord Henry, in *The Picture of Dorian Gray*, ch. 6 (1891).

See also Marquis on MIDDLE AGE.

ORDER

1   That man is a creature who needs order yet yearns for change is the creative contradiction at the heart of the laws which structure his conformity and define his deviancy.

     FREDA ADLER (b. 1934), U.S. educator, author. *Sisters in Crime*, ch. 8 (1975).

2   However fiercely opposed one may be to the present order, an old respect for the idea of order itself often prevents people from distinguishing between order and those who stand for order, and leads them in practise to respect individuals under the pretext of respecting order itself.

     ANTONIN ARTAUD (1896–1948), French theater producer, actor, theorist. Letter, 10 Feb. 1935, to André Gide (repr. in *Selected Writings*, pt. 24, ed. by Susan Sontag, 1976).

3   When we walk the streets at night in safety, it does not strike us that this might be otherwise. This habit of feeling safe has become second nature, and we do not reflect on just how this is due solely to the working of special institutions. Commonplace thinking often has the impression that force holds the state together, but in fact its only bond is the fundamental sense of order which everybody possesses.

     GEORG HEGEL (1770–1831), German philosopher. *The Philosophy of Right*, "The State," addition 160 (1821; tr. 1942).

4   There is a quality even meaner than outright ugliness or disorder, and this meaner quality is the dishonest mask of pretended order, achieved by ignoring or suppressing the real order that is struggling to exist and to be served.

     JANE JACOBS (b. 1916), U.S. author. *The Death and Life of Great American Cities*, Introduction (1961).

5   The attitude that nature is chaotic and that the artist puts order into it is a very absurd point of view, I think. All that we can hope for is to put some order into ourselves.

     WILLEM DE KOONING (b. 1904), Dutch-born US artist. "The Renaissance and Order," lecture, 1950, New York City (published in *Collected Writings*, ed. by George Scrivani, 1988).

6   Neatness begets order; but from order to taste there is the same difference as from taste to genius, or from love to friendship.

     JOHANN KASPAR LAVATER (1741–1801), Swiss divine, poet. *Aphorisms on Man*, no. 583 (1788).

7   An Englishman, even if he is alone, forms an orderly queue of one.

     GEORGE MIKES (b. 1912), Hungarian-born British humorist. *How to Be an Alien*, ch. 1, sct. 14 (1946).

8   If we can, when we have established individual discipline, arrange the children, sending each one to *his own place, in order*, trying to make them understand the idea that thus placed they look well, and that it is a *good thing* to be thus placed in order, that it is a *good and pleasing arrangement in the room*, this ordered and tranquil adjustment of theirs—then their remaining in their places, *quiet* and *silent*, is the result of a species of lesson, not an *imposition*. To make them understand the idea, without calling their attention too forcibly to the practise, to have them *assimilate a principle of collective order*—that is the important thing.

     MARIA MONTESSORI (1870–1952), Italian educator. *The Montessori Method*, ch. 5 (1912).

9   Despite crime's omnipresence, things *work* in society, because biology compels it. Order eventually restores itself, by psychic equilibrium.

     CAMILLE PAGLIA (b. 1947), U.S. author, critic, educator. *Sex, Art, and American Culture*, "Sexual Personae: The Cancelled Preface" (1992).

10   There seems to be a kind of order in the universe, in the movement of the stars and the turning of the earth and the changing of the seasons, and even in the cycle of human life. But human life itself is almost pure chaos. Everyone takes his stance, asserts his own rights and feelings, mistaking the motives of others, and his own.

     KATHERINE ANNE PORTER (1890–1980), U.S. short-story writer, novelist. Interview in *Writers at Work* (Second Series, ed. by George Plimpton, 1963).

11   His vocation was orderliness, which is the basis of creation. Accordingly, when a letter came, he would turn it over in his hands for a long time, gazing at it meditatively; then he would put it away in a file without opening it, because everything had its own time.

     SALVATORE SATTA (1902–1975), Italian jurist, novelist. *The Day of Judgment*, ch. 20 (1979), of Ludovico.

ORGANIZATION

1 The more highly public life is organized the lower does its morality sink.

E. M. FORSTER (1879–1970), British novelist, essayist. *Two Cheers for Democracy*, "What I Believe" (1951).

2 Any consideration of the life and larger social existence of the modern corporate man . . . begins and also largely ends with the effect of one all-embracing force. That is organization—the highly structured assemblage of men, and now some women, of which he is a part. It is to this, at the expense of family, friends, sex, recreation and sometimes health and effective control of alcoholic intake, that he is expected to devote his energies.

JOHN KENNETH GALBRAITH (b. 1908), U.S. economist. "Corporate Man," in *New York Times* (22 Jan. 1984; repr. in *A View from the Stands*, 1986).

3 One of the many reasons for the bewildering and tragic character of human existence is the fact that social organization is at once necessary and fatal. Men are forever creating such organizations for their own convenience and forever finding themselves the victims of their home-made monsters.

ALDOUS HUXLEY (1894–1963), British author. *Themes and Variations*, "Variations on a Philosopher," sct. 2 (1950).

ORGASM

1 I may not be a great actress but I've become the greatest at screen orgasms. Ten seconds of heavy breathing, roll your head from side to side, simulate a slight asthma attack and die a little.

CANDICE BERGEN (b. 1946), U.S. screen actor. Quoted in: Leslie Halliwell, *Halliwell's Filmgoer's Companion* (1984).

2 There is the pleasurable orgasm, like a rising sales graph, and there is the unpleasurable orgasm, slumping ominously like the Dow Jones in 1929.

WILLIAM BURROUGHS (b. 1914), U.S. author. *The Adding Machine*, "My Exeriences with Wilhelm Reich's Orgone Box" (1985).

3 An enema under the influence of Ecstasy would probably feel much like this.

GERMAINE GREER (b. 1939), Australian feminist writer. Quoted in: *Independent on Sunday* (London, 3 June 1990), referring to D. H. Lawrence's description of the female orgasm in *Lady Chatterley's Lover*.

4 An orgasm joins you to the past. Its timelessness becomes the brotherhood; the brethren are lovers; they extend the "family." I share that sexuality. It was then, is now and will be in the future.

DEREK JARMAN (b. 1942), British filmmaker, artist, author. *At Your Own Risk: A Saint's Testament*, "1950's" (1992).

5 Oh Doris Lessing, my dear—your Anna is *wrong* about orgasms. They are no proof of love—any more than that other Anna's fall under the wheels of that Russian train was a proof of love. It's all female shenanigans, cultural *mishegoss*, conditioning, brainwashing, male mythologizing. What does a woman want? She wants what she has been told she ought to want. Anna Wulf wants orgasm, Anna Karenina, death. Orgasm is no proof of anything. Orgasm is proof of orgasm. Someday every woman will have orgasms—like every family has color TV—and we can all get on with the real business of life.

ERICA JONG (b. 1942), U.S. author. *How to Save Your Own Life*, "The Street Where I Lived . . ." (1977).

6 The orgasm has replaced the Cross as the focus of longing and the image of fulfillment.

MALCOLM MUGGERIDGE (1903–1990), British broadcaster. *Tread Softly for You Tread on My Jokes*, "Down with Sex" (1966).

7 Electric flesh-arrows . . . traversing the body. A rainbow of color strikes the eyelids. A foam of music falls over the ears. It is the gong of the orgasm.

ANAÏS NIN (1903–1977), Franco-American novelist, diarist. *The Diary of Anaïs Nin*, vol. 2 (1967), entry for Oct. 1937.

8 The pleasure of living and the pleasure of the orgasm are identical. Extreme orgasm anxiety forms the basis of the general fear of life.

WILHELM REICH (1897–1957), Austrian-born U.S. psychoanalyst, biophysicist. *The Function of the Orgasm*, ch. 5, sct. 4 (1927; tr. 1942).

ORIGINALITY

1 Nearly all our originality comes from the stamp that time impresses upon our sensibility.

CHARLES BAUDELAIRE (1821–67), French poet. "The Painter of Modern Life," sct. 4, in *L'Art Romantique* (1869; repr. in *Selected Writings on Art and Artists*, ed. by P. E. Charvet, 1972).

2 The true is inimitable, the false untransformable.

ROBERT BRESSON (b. 1907), French film director. *Notes on the Cinematographer*, "1950–1958: The Real" (1975).

3 When a work appears to be ahead of its time, it is only the time that is behind the work.

JEAN COCTEAU (1889–1963), French author, filmmaker. *Le Rappel à l'Ordre*, "Le Coq et l'Arlequin" (1926; first published 1918; repr. in *Collected Works*, vol. 9, 1950).

4 The first man to compare the cheeks of a young woman to a rose was obviously a poet; the first to repeat it was possibly an idiot.

SALVADOR DALI (1904–89), Spanish painter. *Dialogues with Marcel Duchamp*, Preface (ed. by Pierre Cabanne, 1968; tr. 1971).

5 It is a matter of perfect indifference where a thing originated; the only question is: "Is it true in and for itself?"

GEORG HEGEL (1770–1831), German philosopher. *The Philosophy of History*, pt. 3, sct. 3, ch. 2 (1837).

6 Perhaps our originality manifests itself most strikingly in what we do with that which we did not originate. To discover something wholly new can be a matter of chance, of idle tinkering, or even of the chronic dissatisfaction of the untalented.

ERIC HOFFER (1902–83), U.S. philosopher. *Reflections on the Human Condition*, aph. 93 (1973).

7   A thought is often original, though you have uttered it a hundred times.

OLIVER WENDELL HOLMES, SR. (1809–1894), U.S. writer, physician. *The Autocrat of the Breakfast-Table*, ch. 1 (1858).

8   A man is original when he speaks the truth that has always been known to all good men.

PATRICK KAVANAGH (1905–67), Irish poet, author. *Collected Pruse*, "Signposts" (1967).

9   Everything has been said, and we have come too late, now that men have been living and thinking for seven thousand years and more.

JEAN DE LA BRUYÈRE (1645–96), French writer, moralist. *Characters*, "Of Books," aph. 1 (1688).

10   Original thought is like original sin: both happened before you were born to people you could not have possibly met.

FRAN LEBOWITZ (b. 1951), U.S. journalist. *Social Studies*, "People" (1981).

11   We are obliged to regard many of our original minds as crazy at least until we have become as clever as they are.

G. C. LICHTENBERG (1742–99), German physicist, philosopher. *Aphorisms*, "Notebook D," aph. 97 (written 1765–99; tr. by R. J. Hollingdale, 1990).

12   No one can be profoundly original who does not avoid eccentricity.

ANDRÉ MAUROIS (1885–1967), French author, critic. *The Art of Writing*, "Turgenev" (1960).

13   A society made up of individuals who were all capable of original thought would probably be unendurable.

H. L. MENCKEN (1880–1956), U.S. journalist. *Minority Report: H. L. Mencken's Notebooks*, no. 13 (1956).

14   The more intelligent one is, the more men of originality one finds. Ordinary people find no difference between men.

BLAISE PASCAL (1623–62), French scientist, philosopher. *Pensées* (1670; no. 510 ed. by Krailsheimer, no. 7 ed. by Brunschvicg).

15   Originality consists in trying to be like everybody else—and failing.

RAYMOND RADIGUET (1903–1923), French novelist. Quoted by Jean Cocteau in his acceptance speech to the French Academy, Oct. 1955. Quoted in: Joseph Brennan, *Three Philosophical Novelists*, "Thomas Mann" (1964).

16   The man with a new idea is a crank until the idea succeeds.

MARK TWAIN (1835–1910), U.S. author. *Following the Equator*, ch. 32, "Pudd'nhead Wilson's New Calendar" (1897).

See also Cocteau on IMITATION.

ORTHODOXY

1   All orthodox opinion—that is, today, "revolutionary" opinion either of the pure or the impure variety—is anti-man.

WYNDHAM LEWIS (1882–1957), British author, painter. *The Art of Being Ruled*, "The Family and Feminism," ch. 10 (1926).

2   Universal orthodoxy is enriched by every new discovery of truth: what at first appeared universal, by wishing to stand still, sooner or later becomes a sect.

EDGAR QUINET (1803–75), French poet, historian, politician. *Ultramontanism, or The Roman Church and Modern Society*, "The Roman Church and History—Vico" (1845).

3   Nothing, it is true, is more common than for both Science and Art to pay homage to the spirit of the age, and for creative taste to accept the law of critical taste.

FRIEDRICH VON SCHILLER (1759–1805), German dramatist, poet, essayist. *On the Aesthetic Education of Man*, "Eighth Letter" (1795).

4   When an opinion has taken root in a democracy and established itself in the minds of the majority, if afterward persists by itself, needing no effort to maintain it since no one attacks it. Those who at first rejected it as false come in the end to adopt it as accepted, and even those who still at the bottom of their hearts oppose it keep their views to themselves, taking great care to avoid a dangerous and futile contest.

ALEXIS DE TOCQUEVILLE (1805–59), French social philosopher. *Democracy in America*, vol. 2, pt. 3, ch. 21 (1840).

OTHER PEOPLE

1   It is when we try to grapple with another man's intimate need that we perceive how incomprehensible, wavering, and misty are the beings that share with us the sight of the stars and the warmth of the sun.

JOSEPH CONRAD (1857–1924), Polish-born English novelist. Marlow, in *Lord Jim*, ch. 16 (1900).

2   A man's real life is that accorded to him in the thoughts of other men by reason of respect or natural love.

JOSEPH CONRAD (1857–1924), Polish-born English novelist. The narrator, in *Under Western Eyes*, pt. 1, ch. 1 (1911).

3   We have no higher life that is really apart from other people. It is by imagining them that our personality is built up; to be without the power of imagining them is to be a low-grade idiot.

CHARLES HORTON COOLEY (1864–1929), U.S. sociologist. *Human Nature and the Social Order*, ch. 3 (1902).

4   If one had to worry about one's actions in respect of other people's ideas, one might as well be buried alive in an antheap or married to an ambitious violinist. Whether that man is the prime minister, modifying his opinions to catch votes, or a bourgeois in terror lest some harmless act should be misunderstood and outrage some petty convention, that man is an inferior man and I do not want to have anything to do with him any more than I want to eat canned salmon.

ALEISTER CROWLEY (1875–1947), British occultist. *The Confessions of Aleister Crowley*, ch. 4 (1929; rev. 1970).

5   What we know of other people

Is only our memory of the moments
During which we knew them.

> T. S. ELIOT (1888–1965), Anglo-American poet, critic. Unidentified Guest, later identified as Sir Henry Harcourt-Reilly, in *The Cocktail Party*, act 1, sc. 3.

6 Other men are lenses through which we read our own minds. Each man seeks those of different quality from his own, and such as are good of their kind; that is, he seeks other men, and the *otherest*.

> RALPH WALDO EMERSON (1803–82), U.S. essayist, poet, philosopher. *Representative Men*, "Uses of Great Men" (1850).

7 And finally I twist my heart round again, so that the bad is on the outside and the good is on the inside, and keep on trying to find a way of becoming what I would so like to be, and could be, if . . . there weren't any other people living in the world.

> ANNE FRANK (1929–1945), German Jewish refugee, diarist. *The Diary of a Young Girl* (1947; tr. 1952), last words of last entry, 1 Aug. 1944. Three days after writing this entry, Anne Frank was arrested and sent to a concentration camp in Germany.

8 The time comes when each one of us has to give up as illusions the expectations which, in his youth, he pinned upon his fellow-men, and when he may learn how much difficulty and pain has been added to his life by their ill-will.

> SIGMUND FREUD (1856–1939), Austrian psychiatrist. *Civilization and Its Discontents*, ch. 5 (1930; repr. in *Complete Works*, vol. 21, ed. by James Strachey and Anna Freud, 1961).

9 Any man who does not see everything in terms of self, that is to say who wants to be something in respect of other men, to do good to them or simply give them something to do, is unhappy, disconsolate, and accursed.

> EDMOND (1822–96) AND JULES DE GONCOURT (1830–70), French writers. *The Goncourt Journals* (1888–96; repr. in *Pages from the Goncourt Journal*, ed. by Robert Baldick, 1962), entry for 30 July 1861.

10 The only thing that could spoil a day was people. . . . People were always the limiters of happiness except for the very few that were as good as spring itself.

> ERNEST HEMINGWAY (1899–1961), U.S. author. *A Moveable Feast*, ch. 6 (1964).

11 The remarkable thing is that we really love our neighbor as ourselves: we do unto others as we do unto ourselves. We hate others when we hate ourselves. We are tolerant toward others when we tolerate ourselves. We forgive others when we forgive ourselves. We are prone to sacrifice others when we are ready to sacrifice ourselves.

> ERIC HOFFER (1902–83), U.S. philosopher. *The Passionate State of Mind*, aph. 100 (1955).

12 We demand that people should be true to the pictures we have of them, no matter how repulsive those pictures may be: we prefer the true portrait (as we have conceived it), in all its homogeneity, to one with a detail added which refuses to fit in.

> PAMELA HANSFORD JOHNSON (1912–81), British author, critic. *Night and Silence, Who Is Here?—An American Comedy*, ch. 23 (1963).

13 One can no longer live with people: it is too hideous and nauseating. Owners and owned, they are like the two sides of a ghastly disease.

> D. H. LAWRENCE (1885–1930), British author. Letter, 3 Aug. 1915 (published in *The Letters of D. H. Lawrence*, vol. 2, ed. by George J. Zytaruk and James T. Boulton, 1981).

14 I am convinced we do not only love ourselves in others but hate ourselves in others too.

> G. C. LICHTENBERG (1742–99), German physicist, philosopher. *Aphorisms*, "Notebook F," aph. 54 (written 1765–99; tr. by R. J. Hollingdale, 1990).

15 Hell is other people.

> JEAN-PAUL SARTRE (1905–1980), French philosopher, author. Garcin, in *No Exit*, sc. 5.

16 Men often treat others worse than they treat themselves, but they rarely treat anyone better. It is the height of folly to expect consideration and decency from a person who mistreats himself.

> THOMAS SZASZ (b. 1920), U.S. psychiatrist. *The Second Sin*, "Personal Conduct" (1973).

17 You know about a person who deeply interests you more than you can be told. A look, a gesture, an act, which to everybody else is insignificant tells you more about that one than words can.

> HENRY DAVID THOREAU (1817–62), U.S. philosopher, author, naturalist. *Journals* (1906), entry for 20 Feb. 1859.

18 I wonder if we are all wrong about each other, if we are just composing unwritten novels about the people we meet?

> REBECCA WEST (1892–1983), British author. Letter, 1917. Quoted as epigraph to Victoria Glendinning, *Rebecca West: A Life* (1987).

19 It is absurd to divide people into good and bad. People are either charming or tedious.

> OSCAR WILDE (1854–1900), Anglo-Irish playwright, author. Lord Darlington, in *Lady Windermere's Fan*, act 1.

20 The eyes of others our prisons; their thoughts our cages.

> VIRGINIA WOOLF (1882–1941), British novelist. *Monday or Tuesday*, "An Unwritten Novel" (1921).

21 Each had his past shut in him like the leaves of a book known to him by heart; and his friends could only read the title, James Spalding, or Charles Budgeon, and the passengers going the opposite way could read nothing at all—save "a man with a red moustache," "a young man in grey smoking a pipe."

> VIRGINIA WOOLF (1882–1941), British novelist. *Jacob's Room*, ch. 5 (1922), of passengers on an omnibus.

See also Renard on The BOURGEOISIE; Wilde on VULGARITY.

OUTCASTS

1 His hand will be against every man, and every man's hand against him.

> BIBLE, HEBREW. The prophecy given to Hagar of her unborn son, Ishmael, in *Genesis* 16:12. Ishmael was sent into the desert, giving the name the connotation of "outcast."

2   For they had golden earrings, because they were Ishmaelites.

> BIBLE, HEBREW. *Judges* 8:24.

3   In an expanding universe, time is on the side of the outcast. Those who once inhabited the suburbs of human contempt find that without changing their address they eventually live in the metropolis.

> QUENTIN CRISP (b. 1908), British author. *The Naked Civil Servant*, ch. 1 (1968).

4   I am an invisible man. . . . I am a man of substance, of flesh and bone, fiber and liquids—and I might even be said to possess a mind. I am invisible, understand, simply because people refuse to see me.

> RALPH ELLISON (b. 1914), U.S. author. The narrator, in *The Invisible Man*, Prologue (1952).

5   What a life! True life is elsewhere. We are not in the world.

> ARTHUR RIMBAUD (1854–1891), French poet. *Une Saison en Enfer*, "Délires I" (1874).

6   In this world, only those people who have fallen to the lowest degree of humiliation, far below beggary, who are not just without any social consideration but are regarded by all as being deprived of that foremost human dignity, reason itself—only those people, in fact, are capable of telling the truth. All the others lie.

> SIMONE WEIL (1909–43), French philosopher, mystic. Letter, 4 Aug. 1943, to her parents (published in *Seventy Letters*, 1965).

7   For his mourners will be outcast men,
And outcasts always mourn.

> OSCAR WILDE (1854–1900), Anglo-Irish playwright, author. *The Ballad of Reading Gaol*, sct. 4, inscribed on Wilde's tomb.

PACIFISM

1   Bullets cannot be recalled. They cannot be uninvented. But they can be taken out of the gun.

> MARTIN AMIS (b. 1949), British author. *Einstein's Monsters*, Introduction (1987).

2   The wolf also shall dwell with the lamb, and the leopard shall lie down with the kid; and the calf and the young lion and the fatling together; and a little child shall lead them.

> BIBLE, HEBREW. *Isaiah* 11:6.

3   All that a pacifist can undertake—but it is a very great deal—is to refuse to kill, injure or otherwise cause suffering to another human creature, and untiringly to order his life by the rule of love though others may be captured by hate.

> VERA BRITTAIN (1896–1970), British author, pacifist. "What Can We Do In Wartime?," in *Forward* (Scotland, 9 Sept. 1939; repr. in *Wartime Chronicle: Vera Brittain's Diary 1939–1945*, 1989).

4   There is no shadow of protection to be had by sheltering behind the slender stockades of visionary speculation, or by hiding behind the wagon-wheels of pacific theories.

> MADAME CHIANG KAI-SHEK (b. 1898), Chinese educator, reformer. Quoted in: *New York Herald Tribune* (21 March 1938).

5   Mental violence has no potency and injures only the person whose thoughts are violent. It is otherwise with mental non-violence. It has potency which the world does not yet know.

> MOHANDAS K. GANDHI (1869–1948), Indian political and spiritual leader. *Non-Violence in Peace and War*, vol. 1, ch. 256 (1942).

6   I now understand what Christ suffered in Gethsemane as well as any man living.

> JAMES KEIR HARDIE (1856–1915), First British Labour Party member of parliament. Remark to friends, 6 Aug. 1914, after being howled down in Aberdare, Wales, for speaking against the First World War.

7   It is useless for the sheep to pass resolutions in favour of vegetarianism, while the wolf remains of a different opinion.

> W. R. INGE (1860–1954), Dean of St. Paul's, London. *Outspoken Essays*, "Patriotism" (First Series, 1919; first published 1915).

8   You either get tired fighting for peace, or you die.

> JOHN LENNON (1940–80), British rock musician. Press conference, June 1970, Toronto, Canada (published in *The Ballad of John and Yoko*, pt. 2, "John, Yoko and Year One," ed. by Jonathan Cott and Christine Doudna, 1982).

9   War can only be abolished through war, and in order to get rid of the gun it is necessary to take up the gun.

> MAO ZEDONG (1893–1976), Founder of the People's Republic of China. "Problems of War and Strategy" (6 Nov. 1938; published in *Selected Works*, vol. 2, 1961).

10   If the Nazis have really been guilty of the unspeakable crimes circumstantially imputed to them, then—let us make no mistake—pacifism is faced with a situation with which it cannot cope. The conventional pacifist conception of a reasonable or generous peace is irrelevant to this reality.

> JOHN MIDDLETON MURRY (1889–1957), British critic, editor. *Peace News* (London, 22 Sept. 1944). Editor of *Peace News* (1940–46), Murry was a prominent pacifist and radical Christian.

11   The pacifist is as surely a traitor to his country and to humanity as is the most brutal wrongdoer.

> THEODORE ROOSEVELT (1858–1919), U.S. Republican (later Progressive) politician, president. Speech, 27 July 1917, Pittsburgh, Pa.

12   This idea of weapons of mass extermination s utterly horrible and is something which no one with one spark of humanity can tolerate. I will not pretend to obey a government which is organising a mass massacre of mankind.

> BERTRAND RUSSELL (1872–1970), British philosopher, mathematician. Speech, 15 April 1961, Birmingham, England, encouraging civil disobedience in support of nuclear disarmament.

13   Sometime they'll give a war and nobody will come.

> CARL SANDBURG (1878–1967), U.S. poet. *The People, Yes*.

14   We can best help you to prevent war not by repeating your words and following your methods but by finding new words and creating new methods.

> VIRGINIA WOOLF (1882–1941), British novelist. *Three Guineas* (1938, p. 164).

PAGANISM

1   So much of truth, only under an ancient obsolete vesture, but the spirit of it still true, do I find in the Paganism of old nations. Nature is still divine, the revelation of the workings of God; the Hero is still worshipable: this, under poor cramped incipient forms, is what all Pagan religions have struggled, as they could, to set forth.

> THOMAS CARLYLE (1795–1881), Scottish essayist, historian. *On Heroes and Hero-Worship*, Lecture 1, "The Hero as Divinity" (1841).

2   Paganism is wholesome because it faces the facts of life.

> ALEISTER CROWLEY (1875–1947), British occultist. *The Confessions of Aleister Crowley*, ch. 8 (1929; rev. 1970).

3   And so we ask for peace for the gods of our fathers, for the gods of our native land. It is reasonable that whatever each of us worships is really to be considered one and the same. We gaze up at the same stars, the sky covers us all, the same universe compasses us. What does it matter what practical systems we adopt in our search for the truth. Not by one avenue only can we arrive at so tremendous a secret.

> QUINTUS AURELIUS SYMMACHUS (A.D. c. 340–c. 402), Roman senator. Letter, written 384, to the Christian Emperor Valentinian II, pleading for the continuation of pagan ceremonies (published in Finley Hooper and Matthew Schwartz, *Roman Letters: History from a Personal Point of View*, ch. 10, 1991).

See also MAGIC; WITCHCRAFT.

PAIN

1   After great pain, a formal feeling comes—
The Nerves sit ceremonious, like Tombs—

> EMILY DICKINSON (1830–86), U.S. poet. *The Complete Poems*, no. 341 (1955).

2   There is much pain that is quite noiseless; and vibrations that make human agonies are often a mere whisper in the roar of hurrying existence. There are glances of hatred that stab and raise no cry of murder; robberies that leave man or woman for ever beggared of peace and joy, yet kept secret by the sufferer—committed to no sound except that of low moans in the night, seen in no writing except that made on the face by the slow months of suppressed anguish and early morning tears. Many an inherited sorrow that has marred a life has been breathed into no human ear.

> GEORGE ELIOT (1819–80), English novelist, editor. *Felix Holt, the Radical*, Introduction (1866).

3   The art of life is the art of avoiding pain; and he is the best pilot, who steers clearest of the rocks and shoals with which it is beset.

> THOMAS JEFFERSON (1743–1826), U.S. president. Letter, 12 Oct. 1786, to Maria Cosway.

4   All pain is a punishment, and every punishment is inflicted for love as much as for justice.

> JOSEPH DE MAISTRE (1753–1821), French diplomat, philosopher. The Senator, in *Les Soirées de Saint-Pétersbourg*, "Fifth Dialogue" (1821; repr. in *The Works of Joseph de Maistre*, ed. by Jack Lively, 1965).

5   Strictly speaking, there is but one real evil: I mean acute pain. All other complaints are so considerably diminished by time that it is plain the grief is owing to our passion, since the sensation of it vanishes when that is over.

> LADY MARY WORTLEY MONTAGU (1689–1762), English society figure, letter writer. Letter, 19 Feb. 1750, to her daughter Lady Bute (published in *Selected Letters*, ed. by Robert Halsband, 1970).

6   This horror of pain is a rather low instinct and . . . if I think of human beings I've known and of my own life, such as it is, I can't recall any case of pain which didn't, on the whole, enrich life.

> MALCOLM MUGGERIDGE (1903–90), British broadcaster. "Meeting Point," 11 Aug. 1963, BBC television broadcast. Quoted in: *Muggeridge through the Microphone*, "The Problem of Pain" (1967).

7   Life is pain and the enjoyment of love is an anesthetic.

> CESARE PAVESE (1908–50), Italian poet, novelist, translator. *The Burning Brand: Diaries 1935–1950* (1952; tr. 1961), entry for 19 Jan. 1938.

8   They can rule the world while they can persuade us
our pain belongs in some order.
Is death by famine worse than death by suicide,
than a life of famine and suicide . . . ?

> ADRIENNE RICH (b. 1929), U.S. poet. *The Dream of a Common Language*, pt. 1, "Power. Hunger." (1978).

9   There is no more lively sensation than that of pain; its impressions are certain and dependable, they never deceive as may those of the pleasure women perpetually feign and almost never experience.

> MARQUIS DE SADE (1740–1814), French author. Clément, in *Justine, ou les Malheurs de la Vertu* (1791).

10   Pain, scorned by yonder gout-ridden wretch, endured by yonder dyspeptic in the midst of his dainties, borne bravely by the girl in travail. Slight thou art, if I can bear thee, short thou art if I cannot bear thee!

> SENECA (c. 5 B.C.–A.D. c. 65), Roman writer, philosopher, statesman. *Epistulae ad Lucilium*, Epistle 24.

11   For we are born in other's pain,
And perish in our own.

> FRANCIS THOMPSON (1859–1907), English poet. *Daisy*.

12   Do not undervalue the headache. While it is at its sharpest it seems a bad investment; but when relief begins, the unexpired remainder is worth $4 a minute.

> MARK TWAIN (1835–1910), U.S. author. *Following the Equator*, ch. 54, "Pudd'nhead Wilson's New Calendar" (1897).

13   Pain with the thousand teeth.

> SIR WILLIAM WATSON (1858–1935), British poet. *The Dream of Man*.

14   Evil being the root of mystery, pain is the root of knowledge.

> SIMONE WEIL (1909–43), French philosopher, mystic. *New York*

Notebook (written 1942; published 1950; repr. in *First and Last Notebooks*, pt. 3, ed. by Richard Rees, 1970).

15 There is no detachment where there is no pain. And there is no pain endured without hatred or lying unless detachment is present too.

SIMONE WEIL (1909–43), French philosopher, mystic. *Gravity and Grace*, "Illusions" (1947; tr. 1952).

16 Pain is real when you get other people to believe in it. If no one believes in it but you, your pain is madness or hysteria.

NAOMI WOLF (b. 1962), U.S. author. *The Beauty Myth*, "Violence" (1990).

17 On the outskirts of every agony sits some observant fellow who points.

VIRGINIA WOOLF (1882–1941), British novelist. Bernard, in *The Waves* (1931; repr. 1943, p. 205).

See also Arendt on EXERCISE; Nietzsche on ILLNESS.

PAINTING

1 Painting throughout its history has served many purposes, has been flat and has used perspective, has been framed and has been left borderless, has been explicit and has been mysterious. But one act of faith has remained a constant. . . . The act of faith consisted in believing that the visible contained hidden secrets, that to study the visible was to learn something more than could be seen in a glance. . . . Jackson Pollock was driven by a despair which was partly his and partly that of the times which nourished him, to refuse this act of faith: to insist, with all his brilliance as a painter, that there was nothing behind, that there was only *that which was done to the canvas on the side facing us.*

JOHN BERGER (b. 1926), British author, critic. "A Kind of Sharing," in ital/*Guardian* (London, 23 Nov. 1989; repr. in *Keeping a Rendezvous*, 1992).

2 It is impossible for me to envisage a picture as being other than a window, and why my first concern is then to know what it *looks out* on.

ANDRÉ BRETON (1896–1966), French surrealist. *Surrealism and Painting* (1928).

3 You must recollect however that I know nothing of painting & that I detest it, unless it reminds me of something I have seen or think it possible to see. . . . Depend upon it of all the arts it is the most artificial & unnatural—& that by which the nonsense of mankind is the most imposed upon.

LORD BYRON (1788–1824), English poet. Letter, 14 April 1817, to the publisher John Murray (published in *Byron's Letters and Journals*, vol. 5, 1973–81).

4 The foreground in a picture is always unattractive . . . Art demands that the interest of the canvas should be placed in the far distance, where lies take refuge, those dreams which blossom out of fact and are man's only love.

LOUIS-FERDINAND CÉLINE (1894–1961), French author. The narrator (Ferdinand Bardamu), in *Journey to the End of the Night*

(1932; tr. 1934; repr. 1966, p. 70), voicing the opinions of landscape painter Claude Lorraine.

5 If you pick up some paint with your brush and make somebody's nose with it, this is rather ridiculous when you think of it, theoretically or philosophically. It's really absurd to make an image, like a human image, with paint, today.

WILLEM DE KOONING (b. 1904), Dutch-born U.S. artist. "Painting As Self Discovery," interview, 30 Dec. 1960, BBC (first published as "Content Is a Glimpse . . .," in *Location*, New York, Spring 1963). Quoted in: Diane Waldman, *William de Kooning* (1988).

6 The studio has become the crucible where human genius at the apogee of its development brings back to question not only that which is, but creates anew a fantastic and conventional nature which our weak minds, impotent to harmonize it with existing things, adopt by preference, because the miserable work is our own.

EUGÈNE DELACROIX (1798–1863), French artist. Note, c. 1829 (published in Supplement to *The Journal of Eugène Delacroix*, tr. by Walter Pach, 1937).

7 My weakness has always been to prefer the large intention of an unskilful artist to the trivial intention of an accomplished one: in other words, I am more interested in the high ideas of a feeble executant than in the high execution of a feeble thinker.

THOMAS HARDY (1840–1928), English novelist, poet. Letter, 8 July 1901 (published in Florence Emily Hardy, *The Later Years of Thomas Hardy*, ch. 7, 1930).

8 The humblest painter is a true scholar; and the best of scholars—the scholar of nature.

WILLIAM HAZLITT (1778–1830), English essayist. *Table Talk*, vol. 1, "On the Pleasure of Painting" (1821).

9 Painting consumes labour not disproportionate to its effect; but a fellow will hack half a year at a block of marble to make something in stone that hardly resembles a man. The value of statuary is owing to its difficulty. You would not value the finest head cut upon a carrot.

SAMUEL JOHNSON (1709–84), English author, lexicographer. Quoted in: James Boswell, *Life of Samuel Johnson*, 19 March 1776 (1791).

10 If people only knew as much about painting as I do, they would never buy my pictures.

EDWIN LANDSEER (1802–73), English painter of animals. Quoted in: Campbell Lennie, *Landseer the Victorian Paragon*, ch. 12 (1976).

11 I don't very much enjoy looking at paintings in general. I know too much about them. I take them apart.

GEORGIA O'KEEFFE (1887–1986), U.S. artist. Quoted in: *San Francisco Examiner and Chronicle* (16 March 1971).

13 Painting is a *jeu d'esprit.*

PABLO PICASSO (1881–1973), Spanish artist. *Arts* (Paris, 29 June 1935). Quoted in: Alfred H. Barr, Jr., *Picasso: Fifty Years of His Art* (1946, p. 241).

14 Painting is a blind man's profession. He paints not what he sees, but what he feels, what he tells himself about what he has seen.

PABLO PICASSO (1881–1973), Spanish artist. Quoted in: Jean Cocteau, *Journals*, pt. 1, "War and Peace" (1956).

15 The method of painting is the natural growth out of a need. I want to express my feelings rather than illustrate them. Technique is just a means of arriving at a statement. . . . I *can* control the flow of paint: there is no accident, just as there is no beginning and no end.

> JACKSON POLLOCK (1912–56), U.S. artist. Narrative, for film by Hans Nemuth and Paul Falkenberg (1951; repr. in Bryan Robertson, *Jackson Pollock*, 1960).

16 To me, a painter, if not the most useful, is the least harmful member of our society.

> MAN RAY (1890–1976), U.S. photographer. *Self Portrait*, ch. 6 (1963).

17 A thousand moral paintings I can show
That shall demonstrate these quick blows of Fortune's
More pregnantly than words.

> WILLIAM SHAKESPEARE (1564–1616), English dramatist, poet. Painter, in *Timon of Athens*, act 1, sc. 1.

18 It's easier to replace a dead man than a good picture.

> GEORGE BERNARD SHAW (1856–1950), Anglo-Irish playwright, critic. Ridgeon, in *The Doctor's Dilemma*, act 2.

19 When love of painting (late a passion) came,
With kindling zeal he caught the novel flame;
To joys unfelt before with rapture sprung,
Forgot his age and found he still was young.

> SIR MARTIN ARCHER SHEE (1769–1850), Irish portrait painter, president of Royal Academy. *Rhymes on Art, or the Remonstrance of a Painter*, pt. 2 (1805).

20 Let us shun self-analyzation, self-consciousness, morbidness, affectation, attitudinizing. Let us look ahead as little as possible, keeping our eyes on our brushes and on the world of beauty around us.

> MARIANA GRISWOLD VAN RENSSELAER (1851–1934), U.S. art critic. "Some Aspects of Contemporary Art," in *Lippincott's* (Philadelphia, Dec. 1878).

21 To say of a picture, as is often said in its praise, that it shows great and earnest labour, is to say that it is incomplete and unfit for view.

> JAMES MCNEILL WHISTLER (1834–1903), U.S. artist. *The Gentle Art of Making Enemies*, "Propositions no. 2" (1890).

22 Frankly, these days, without a theory to go with it, I can't *see* a painting.

> TOM WOLFE (b. 1931), U.S. journalist, author. *The Painted Word*, ch. 1 (1975).

See also ART; Rilke on COLOR; PHOTOGRAPHY AND PAINTING; PORTRAITS.

PALESTINE

1 Palestine is the cement that holds the Arab world together, or it is the explosive that blows it apart.

> YASIR ARAFAT (b. 1929), Palestinian leader. Quoted in: *Time* (New York, 11 Nov. 1974).

2 We are not asking for the moon.

> YASIR ARAFAT (b. 1929), Palestinian leader. Quoted in: *Observer* (London, 7 Feb. 1982).

3 His Majesty's Government views with favour the establishment in Palestine of a national home for the Jewish people.

> A. J. BALFOUR (1848–1930), British statesman. Letter, 2 Nov. 1917. This document, which became known as the "Balfour Declaration," committed British support for a Jewish national home in Palestine.

4 Should there be maniacs ho raise the idea, they will encounter an iron fist which will leave no trace of such attempts.

> YITZHAK SHAMIR (b. 1915), Israeli politician, prime minister. Quoted in: *Times* (London, 11 Aug. 1988), on advocates of Palestinian self-government.

5 Even the pyramids might one day disappear, but not the Palestinians longing for their homeland.

> EDUARD SHEVARDNADZE (b. 1927), Soviet politician, diplomat. *Daily Telegraph* (London, 24 Feb. 1989).

See also The MIDDLE EAST.

PARADISE

1 It gets to seem as if way back in the Garden of Eden after the Fall, Adam and Eve had begged the Lord to forgive them and He, in his boundless exasperation, had said, "All right, then. Stay. Stay in the Garden. Get civilized. Procreate. Muck it up." And they did.

> DIANE ARBUS (1923–71), U.S. photographer. Remarks on a nudist camp, from classes given in 1971 (published in *Diane Arbus: An Aperture Monograph*, 1972).

2 Santa Barbara is a paradise; Disneyland is a paradise; the U.S. is a paradise. Paradise is just paradise. Mournful, monotonous, and superficial though it may be, it is paradise. There is no other.

> JEAN BAUDRILLARD (b. 1929), French semiologist. *America*, "Utopia Achieved" (1986; tr. 1988).

3 A fool's paradise is a wise man's hell!

> THOMAS FULLER (1608–61), English cleric. *The Holy State and the Profane State*, bk. 4, ch. 20 (1642).

4 The abominable effort to take one's sins with one to paradise.

> ANDRÉ GIDE (1869–1951), French author. *Journals 1889–1949*, "Detached Pages" (ed. by Justin O'Brien, 1951), entry for 1913.

5 A beautiful vacuum filled with wealthy monogamists, all powerful and members of the best families all drinking themselves to death.

> ERNEST HEMINGWAY (1899–1961), U.S. author. Letter, 1 July 1925, to F. Scott Fitzgerald, describing Fitzgerald's version of heaven (published in *Ernest Hemingway: Selected Letters*, 1981). Hemingway depicts Fitzgerald's *hell* as "an ugly vacuum full of poor polygamists unable to obtain booze or with chronic stomach disorders that they called secret sorrows." For Hemingway's own idea of paradise, see HEAVEN.

6 From the very fountain of enchantment there arises a taste of bitterness to spread anguish amongst the flowers.

> LUCRETIUS (c. 99–c. 55 B.C.), Roman poet, philosopher. *De Rerum Natura*, bk. 4.

7   Everyone who has ever built anywhere a "new heaven" first found the power thereto in his own hell.

> FRIEDRICH NIETZSCHE (1844–1900), German philosopher. *The Genealogy of Morals*, Essay 3, aph. 10 (1887).

8   Here with a Loaf of Bread beneath the Bough,
A Flask of Wine, a Book of Verse—and Thou
Beside me singing in the Wilderness—
And Wilderness is Paradise enow.

> OMAR KHAYYÁM (11th–12th century), Persian astronomer, poet. *The Rubáiyát of Omar Khayyám*, st. 11 (tr. by Edward FitzGerald; first ed., 1859).

9   It is difficult to write a paradiso when all the superficial indications are that you ought to write an apocalypse. It is obviously much easier to find inhabitants for an inferno or even a purgatorio.

> EZRA POUND (1885–1972), U.S. poet, critic. Interview in *Writers at Work* (Second Series, ed. by George Plimpton, 1963).

10   We, who have already borne on the road to Paradise the lives of the best among us, want a difficult, erect, implacable Paradise; a Paradise where one can never rest and which has, beside the threshold of the gates, angels with swords.

> J. A. PRIMO DE RIVERA (1903–36), Spanish Falangist politician. Quoted in: Stanley Payne, *Falange*, ch. 7 (1962).

11   I should have no use for a paradise in which I should be deprived of the right to prefer hell.

> JEAN ROSTAND (1894–1977), French biologist, writer. *Pensées d'un Biologiste* (1939; repr. in *The Substance of Man*, "A Biologist's Thoughts," ch. 10, 1962).

12   It is a curious thing that every creed promises a paradise which will be absolutely uninhabitable for anyone of civilised taste.

> EVELYN WAUGH (1903–66), British novelist. Ambrose, in *Put Out More Flags*, ch. 1, sct. 7 (1942).

13   We must prefer real hell to an imaginary paradise.

> SIMONE WEIL (1909–43), French philosopher, mystic. *Gravity and Grace*, "Illusions" (1947; tr. 1952).

See also Macaulay on ENGLAND AND THE ENGLISH.

PARADOX

1   Play not with paradoxes. That caustic which you handle in order to scorch others may happen to sear your own fingers and make them dead to the quality of things.

> GEORGE ELIOT (1819–80), English novelist, editor. Mr. Lyon, in *Felix Holt, The Radical*, ch. 13 (1866).

2   The paradox is really the *pathos* of intellectual life and just as only great souls are exposed to passions it is only the great thinker who is exposed to what I call paradoxes, which are nothing else than grandiose thoughts in embryo.

> SØREN KIERKEGAARD (1813–55), Danish philosopher. *The Journals of Søren Kierkegaard: A Selection*, no. 206 (ed. and tr. by Alexander Dru, 1938), entry for 1838.

3   The paradoxes of today are the prejudices of tomorrow, since the most benighted and the most deplorable prejudices have had their moment of novelty when fashion lent them its fragile grace.

> MARCEL PROUST (1871–1922), French novelist. *Pleasures and Regrets*, "Regrets, Reveries, Changing Skies," no. 5 (1896; tr. 1948).

4   The way of paradoxes is the way of truth. To test Reality we must see it on the tight-rope. When the Verities become acrobats we can judge them.

> OSCAR WILDE (1854–1900), Anglo-Irish playwright, author. Mr. Erskine, in *The Picture of Dorian Gray*, ch. 3 (1891).

See also Eliot on EXPERIENCE; Schlegel on IRONY.

PARANOIA

1   Separate thyself from thine enemies, and take heed of thy friends.

> APOCRYPHA. *Ecclesiasticus* 6:13.

2   A paranoiac . . . like a poet, is born, not made.

> LUIS BUÑUEL (1900–1983), Spanish filmmaker. *My Last Sigh*, ch. 18 (1983).

3   The paranoiac is the exact image of the ruler. The only difference is their position in the world. . . . One might even think the paranoiac the more impressive of the two because he is sufficient unto himself and cannot be shaken by failure.

> ELIAS CANETTI (b. 1905), Austrian novelist, philosopher. *Crowds And Power*, "The Case of Schreber: II" (1960; tr. 1962).

4   Even a paranoid can have enemies.

> HENRY KISSINGER (b. 1923), U.S. Republican politician, secretary of state. Quoted in: *Time* (New York, 24 Jan. 1977).

5   I envy paranoids; they actually feel people are paying attention to them.

> SUSAN SONTAG (b. 1933), U.S. essayist. Quoted in: *Time Out* (London, 19 Aug. 1992).

PARASITES

1   You had no right to be born; for you make no use of life. Instead of living for, in, and with yourself, as a reasonable being ought, you seek only to fasten your feebleness on some other person's strength.

> CHARLOTTE BRONTË (1816–55), English novelist. Eliza Reed to her sister Georgiana, in *Jane Eyre*, ch. 21 (1847).

2   People who get through life dependent on other people's possessions are always the first to lecture you on how little possessions count.

> BEN ELTON (b. 1959), British author, performer. *Stark*, "Strategic Decisions" (1989).

3   I have often told you that I am that little fish who swims about under a shark and, I believe, lives indelicately on its offal. Anyway, that is the way I am. Life moves over me in a vast black shadow and I swallow whatever it drops with relish, having learned in a very hard school that one cannot be both a parasite and enjoy self-nourishment without moving in worlds too fantastic for even my disordered imagination to people with meaning.

ZELDA FITZGERALD (1900–48), U.S. writer. Letter, c. March 1932, to F. Scott Fitzgerald. Quoted in: Nancy Milford, *Zelda*, pt. 3, ch. 15 (1970).

4 Man is the only animal which esteems itself rich in proportion to the number and voracity of its parasites.

GEORGE BERNARD SHAW (1856–1950), Anglo-Irish playwright, critic. *Man and Superman*, "Maxims for Revolutionists: Servants" (1903).

PARENTS

1 The unjustifiable severity of a parent is loaded with this aggravation, that those whom he injures are always in his sight.

JOSEPH ADDISON (1672–1719), English essayist. *Interesting Anecdotes, Memoirs, Allegories, Essays, and Poetical Fragments*, "The Cruelty of Parental Tyranny" (1794).

2 It's a sad moment, really, when parents first become a bit frightened of their children.

AMA ATA AIDOO (b. 1942), Ghanaian author. "The Message," in *Fragment from a Lost Diary and Other Stories* (ed. by Naomi Katz and Nancy Milton, 1973).

3 It's frightening to think that you mark your children merely by being yourself. . . . It seems unfair. You can't assume the responsibility for everything you do—or don't do.

SIMONE DE BEAUVOIR (1908–86), French novelist, essayist. *Les Belles Images*, ch. 3 (1966; tr. 1968).

4 Let me go to hell, that's all I ask, and go on cursing them there, and them look down and hear me, that might take some of the shine off their bliss.

SAMUEL BECKETT (1906–89), Irish dramatist, novelist. *From an Abandoned Work* (1958).

5 He that curseth his father, or his mother, shall surely be put to death.

BIBLE, HEBREW. *Exodus* 21:17.

6 Fathers and mothers have lost the idea that the highest aspiration they might have for their children is for them to be wise . . . specialized competence and success are all that they can imagine.

ALLAN BLOOM (1930–92), U.S. educator, author. *The Closing of the American Mind*, pt. 1, "The Clean Slate" (1987).

7 Parenthood is not an object of appetite or even desire. It is an object of will. There is no appetite for parenthood; there is only a purpose or intention of parenthood.

R. G. COLLINGWOOD (1889–1943), British philosopher. *The New Leviathan*, pt. 2, ch. 23, aph. 85 (1942).

8 No matter how calmly you try to referee, parenting will eventually produce bizarre behavior, and I'm not talking about the kids. *Their* behavior is always normal.

BILL COSBY (b. 1937), U.S. comedian, actor. *Fatherhood*, ch. 4 (1986).

9 My mother protected me from the world and my father threatened me with it.

QUENTIN CRISP (b. 1908), British author. *The Naked Civil Servant*, ch. 5 (1968).

10 How selfhood begins with a walking away,
And love is proved in the letting go.

C. DAY LEWIS (1904–72), British poet, author. *Walking Away*.

11 There are times when parenthood seems nothing but feeding the mouth that bites you.

PETER DE VRIES (b. 1910), U.S. author. *The Tunnel of Love*, ch. 5 (1954).

12 The thing that impresses me most about America is the way parents obey their children.

EDWARD, DUKE OF WINDSOR (1894–1972), King Edward VIII of Great Britain and Northern Ireland. *Look* (New York, 5 March 1957).

13 You don't have to deserve your mother's love. You have to deserve your father's. He's more particular. . . . The father is always a Republican towards his son, and his mother's always a Democrat.

ROBERT FROST (1874–1963), U.S. poet. Interview in *Writers at Work* (Second Series, ed. by George Plimpton, 1963).

14 A wise parent humours the desire for independent action, so as to become the friend and advisor when his absolute rule shall cease.

ELIZABETH GASKELL (1810–65), English novelist. Mr. Hale, in *North and South*, ch. 15 (1855).

15 Do they know they're old,
These two who are my father and my mother
Whose fire from which I came, has now grown cold?

ELIZABETH JENNINGS (b. 1926), British poet. *One Flesh*.

16 Selective ignorance, a cornerstone of child rearing. You don't put kids under surveillance: it might frighten you. Parents should sit tall in the saddle and look upon their troops with a noble and benevolent and extremely nearsighted gaze.

GARRISON KEILLOR (b. 1942), U.S. author. *Leaving Home*, "Easter" (1987).

17 They fuck you up, your mum and dad.
They may not mean to, but they do.
They fill you with the faults they had
And add some extra, just for you.

PHILIP LARKIN (1922–1985), British poet. *This Be the Verse*, st. 1. In a letter, 6 June 1982 (published in *Selected Letters*, 1992), Larkin complained of the notoriety of this poem, which "will clearly be my 'Lake Isle of Innisfree.' I fully expect to hear it recited by a thousand Girl Guides before I die."

18 Your responsibility as a parent is not as great as you might imagine. You need not supply the world with the next conqueror of disease or major motion-picture star. If your child simply grows up to be someone who does not use the word "collectible" as a noun, you can consider yourself an unqualified success.

FRAN LEBOWITZ (b. 1951), U.S. journalist. *Social Studies*, "Parental Guidance" (1981).

19 The pressures of being a parent are equal to any pressure on earth. To be a conscious parent, and really look to that little being's mental and physical health, is a responsibility which most of us, including me, avoid most of the time because it's too hard.

> JOHN LENNON (1940–80), British rock musician. *Playboy* (Chicago, Sept. 1980). Lennon added, "To put it loosely, the reason why kids are crazy is because nobody can face the responsibility of bringing them up."

20 Oh, high is the price of parenthood,
And daughters may cost you double.
You dare not forget, as you thought you could,
That youth is a plague and a trouble.

> PHYLLIS MCGINLEY (1905–78), U.S. poet, author. *Homework for Anabelle*, in *Times Three* (1960).

21 I wish you would moderate that fondness you have for your children. I do not mean you should abate any part of your care, or not do your duty to them in its utmost extent, but I would have you early prepare yourself for disappointments, which are heavy in proportion to their being surprising.

> LADY MARY WORTLEY MONTAGU (1689–1762), English society figure, letter writer. Letter, 19 Feb. 1750, to her daughter Lady Bute (published in *Selected Letters*, ed. by Robert Halsband, 1970).

22 The most loving parents and relatives commit murder with smiles on their faces. They force us to destroy the person we really are: a subtle kind of murder.

> JIM MORRISON (1943–71), U.S. rock musician. Quoted in: Andrew Doe and John Tobler, *In Their Own Words: The Doors*, ch. 1 (1988).

23 If you bungle raising your children, I don't think whatever else you do well matters very much.

> JACQUELINE KENNEDY ONASSIS (b. 1929), U.S. First Lady. Quoted in: Theodore C. Sorenson, *Kennedy* pt. 4, ch. 15 (1965).

24 Parents . . . are sometimes a bit of a disappointment to their children. They don't fulfil the promise of their early years.

> ANTHONY POWELL (b. 1905), British novelist. Stringham, in *A Buyer's Market*, ch. 2 (1952; second in the novel sequence, *A Dance to the Music of Time*). Stringham found stepparents "especially" disappointing.

25 I am the slave of my baptism. Parents, you have caused my misfortune, and you have caused your own.

> ARTHUR RIMBAUD (1854–91), French poet. *Une Saison en Enfer*, "Nuit de l'Enfer" (1874; repr. in *Collected Poems*, ed. by Oliver Bernard, 1962).

26 Parents lend children their experience and a vicarious memory; children endow their parents with a vicarious immortality.

> GEORGE SANTAYANA (1863–1952), U.S. philosopher, poet. *The Life of Reason*, "Reason in Society," ch. 2 (1905–6; rev. ed., 1953).

27 The question that is so clearly in many potential parents' minds: "Why should we stunt our ambitions and impoverish our lives in order to be insulted and looked down upon in our old age?"

> JOSEPH A. SCHUMPETER (1883–1950), Austrian-American economist. *Capitalism, Socialism and Democracy*, ch. 14 (1942).

28 Perhaps the best function of parenthood is to teach the young creature to love with *safety*, so that it may be able to venture unafraid when later emotion comes; the thwarting of the instinct to love is the root of all sorrow and not sex only but divinity itself is insulted when it is repressed. To disapprove, to condemn—the human soul shrivels under barren righteousness.

> FREYA STARK (b. 1893–1993), British travel writer. *Traveller's Prelude*, ch. 10 (1950).

29 I wish either my father or my mother, or indeed both of them, as they were in duty both equally bound to it, had minded what they were about when they begot me.

> LAURENCE STERNE (1713–68), English author. *Tristram Shandy*, bk. 1, ch. 1 (1760–67), opening words.

30 To lose one parent may be regarded as a misfortune . . . to lose both seems like carelessness.

> OSCAR WILDE (1854–1900), Anglo-Irish playwright, author. Lady Bracknell, in *The Importance of Being Earnest*, act 1.

31 Children begin by loving their parents. After a time they judge them. Rarely, if ever, do they forgive them.

> OSCAR WILDE (1854–1900), Anglo-Irish playwright, author. Lord Illingworth, in *A Woman of No Importance*, act 2. Wilde had used almost the same words in *The Picture of Dorian Gray*, ch. 5 (1891).

32 No test tube can breed love and affection. No frozen packet of semen ever read a story to a sleepy child.

> SHIRLEY WILLIAMS (b. 1930), British Liberal-Democrat politician. *Daily Mirror* (London, 2 March 1978).

See also FATHERS; MOTHERS; Schreiner on PROCREATION.

PARIS

1 Good Americans, when they die, go to Paris.

> THOMAS APPLETON (1812–84), U.S. author. Quoted in: Oliver Wendell Holmes, Sr., *The Autocrat of the Breakfast-Table*, ch. 6 (1858). The saying also found its way into Oscar Wilde, *The Picture of Dorian Gray*, ch. 3 (1891) and *A Woman of No Importance*, act 1.

2 The heart of Paris is like nothing so much as the unending interior of a house. Buildings become furniture, courtyards become carpets and arrases, the streets are like galleries, the boulevards conservatories. It is a house, one or two centuries old, rich, bourgeois, distinguished. The only way of going out, or shutting the door behind you, is to leave the centre.

> JOHN BERGER (b. 1926), British author, critic. "Imagine Paris," in *Harper's* (New York, Jan. 1987; repr. in *Keeping a Rendezvous*, 1992).

3 Paris is a mighty schoolmaster, a grand enlightener of the provincial intellect.

> MARY ELIZABETH BRADDON (1837–1915), English writer. *The Cloven Foot*, ch. 4 (1879).

4 And trade is art, and art's philosophy,
In Paris.

> ELIZABETH BARRETT BROWNING (1806–61), English poet. *Aurora Leigh*, bk. 6 (1857).

5 Paris: a city of pleasures and amusements where four-fifths of the people die of grief.

> SÉBASTIEN-ROCH NICOLAS DE CHAMFORT (1741–94), French

writer, wit. *Maxims and Considerations*, vol. 2, no. 496 (1796; tr. 1926).

6 No one can understand Paris and its history who does not understand that its fierceness is the balance and justification of its frivolity. It is called a city of pleasure; but it may also very specially be called a city of pain. The crown of roses is also a crown of thorns. Its people are too prone to hurt others, but quite ready also to hurt themselves. They are martyrs for religion, they are martyrs for irreligion; they are even martyrs for immorality.

> G. K. CHESTERTON (1874–1936), British author. *Tremendous Trifles*, "Humanity: an Interlude" (1909).

7 In Paris, everybody wants to be an actor; nobody is content to be a spectator.

> JEAN COCTEAU (1889–1963), French author, filmmaker. *Le Rappel àL'Ordre*, "Le Coq et l'Arlequin" (1926; repr. in *Collected Works*, vol. 9, 1950).

8 Nowhere is one more alone than in Paris . . . and yet surrounded by crowds. Nowhere is one more likely to incur greater ridicule. And no visit is more essential.

> MARGUERITE DURAS (b. 1914), French author, filmmaker. "Tourists in Paris," in *France-Observateur* (Paris, 1957; repr. in *Outside: Selected Writings*, 1984).

9 Paradoxically, the freedom of Paris is associated with a persistent belief that nothing ever changes. Paris, they say, is the city that changes least. After an absence of twenty or thirty years, one still recognizes it.

> MARGUERITE DURAS (b. 1914), French journalist, author. "Tourists in Paris," in *France-Observateur* (Paris, 1957; repr. in *Outside: Selected Writings*, 1984).

10 The best of America drifts to Paris. The American in Paris is the best American. It is more fun for an intelligent person to live in an intelligent country. France has the only two things toward which we drift as we grow older—intelligence and good manners.

> F. SCOTT FITZGERALD (1896–1940), U.S. author. *New York World* (3 April 1927). Quoted in: Matthew J. Bruccoli, *Some Sort of Epic Grandeur*, ch. 33 (1981).

11 The production of obscurity in Paris compares to the production of motor cars in Detroit in the great period of American industry.

> ERNEST GELLNER (b. 1925), British anthropologist and philosopher. "The Late Show," 15 Oct. 1992, BBC2 television broadcast. Quoted in: *Observer Review* (London, 18 Oct. 1992).

12 If you are lucky enough to have lived in Paris as a young man, then wherever you go for the rest of your life it stays with you, for Paris is a moveable feast.

> ERNEST HEMINGWAY (1899–1961), U.S. author. Quoted in: A. E. Hotchner, *Papa Hemingway*, pt. 1, ch. 3 (1966 ed.). The words "a moveable feast" were used—on Hotchner's recommendation—as the title for Hemingway's posthumously published Paris memoirs. This quotation appeared as the book's epigraph.

13 The Parisian is to the French what the Athenian was to the Greeks: no one sleeps better than he, no one is more openly frivolous and idle, no one appears more heedless. But this is misleading. He is given to every kind of listlessness, but when there is glory to be won he may be inspired with every kind of fury. Give him a pike and he will enact the tenth of August, a musket and you have

Austerlitz. He was the springboard of Napoleon and the mainstay of Danton. At the cry of "*la patrie*" he enrols, and at the call of liberty he tears up the pavements. Beware of him!

> VICTOR HUGO (1802–85), French poet, dramatist, novelist. *Les Misérables*, pt. 1, bk. 3, ch. 5 (1862).

14 As an artist, a man has no home in Europe save in Paris.

> FRIEDRICH NIETZSCHE (1844–1900), German philosopher. *Ecce Homo*, "Why I Am So Clever," sct. 5 (1888).

15 There is but one Paris and however hard living may be here, and if it became worse and harder even—the French air clears up the brain and does good—a world of good.

> VINCENT VAN GOGH (1853–90), Dutch painter. Letter, Summer 1886, to an English artist considering a move to Paris (published in *The Complete Letters of Vincent Van Gogh*, vol. 2, 1958). Van Gogh adds, "What is to be gained is *progress* and what[ever] the deuce that is, it is to be found here."

16 Napoleon wanted to turn Paris into Rome under the Caesars, only with louder music and more marble. And it was done. His architects gave him the Arc de Triomphe and the Madeleine. His nephew Napoleon III wanted to turn Paris into Rome with Versailles piled on top, and it was done. His architects gave him the Paris Opera, an addition to the Louvre, and miles of new boulevards.

> TOM WOLFE (b. 1931), U.S. journalist, author. *From Bauhaus to Our House*, Introduction (1981).

See also Paglia on STRUCTURALISM AND DECONSTRUCTION.

PARLIAMENT

1 Parliament is not a *congress* of ambassadors from different and hostile interests; which interests each must maintain, as an agent and advocate, against other agents and advocates; but parliament is a *deliberative* assembly of *one* nation, with *one* interest, that of the whole; where, not local purposes, not local prejudices ought to guide, but the general good, resulting from the general reason of the whole. You choose a member indeed; but when you have chosen him, he is not a member of Bristol, but he is a member of *parliament*.

> EDMUND BURKE (1729–97), Irish philosopher, statesman. Speech, 3 Nov. 1774, to the Electors of Bristol, England.

2 You have sat too long for any good you have been doing. Depart, I say, and let us have done with you. In the name of God, go!

> OLIVER CROMWELL (1599–1658), Parliamentarian general, Lord Protector of England. Address, 20 April 1653, dismissing the rump of the Long Parliament. Cromwell later justified his action: "When I was there, I did not think to have done this. But perceiving the Spirit of God so strong upon me, I would not consult flesh and blood." On 7 May 1940, Conservative politician Leo Amery used Cromwell's words in a speech in Parliament to the government of Neville Chamberlain, which stepped down in favor of Winston Churchill's wartime coalition government three days later.

3 You behold a range of exhausted volcanoes. Not a flame flickers on a single pallid crest.

> BENJAMIN DISRAELI (1804–81), English statesman, author.

Speech, 3 April 1872, Manchester, England, criticizing the government Treasury Bench.

4 Kings govern by popular assemblies only when they cannot do without them.

CHARLES JAMES FOX (1749–1806), English Whig politician. Speech, 31 Oct. 1776, to House of Commons.

5 Would it be possible to stand still on one spot more majestically—while simulating a triumphant march forward—than it is done by the two English Houses of Parliament?

ALEXANDER HERZEN (1812–70), Russian journalist, political thinker. *My Past and Thoughts*, vol. 2, pt. 5, ch. 38, "Post Scriptum" (1921; tr. by Constance Garnett 1924–27).

6 I would walk from here to Drogheda and back to see the man who is blockhead enough to expect anything except injustice from an English Parliament.

DANIEL O'CONNELL (1775–1847), Irish political leader. Speech, 16 March 1843, Trim, Ireland.

7 A Parliament is that to the Commonwealth which the soul is to the body. . . . It behoves us therefore to keep the facility of that soul from distemper.

JOHN PYM (1584–1643), English Parliamentarian leader. Speech, 17 April 1640, to House of Commons.

8 This place is the longest running farce in the West End.

CYRIL SMITH (b. 1928), British Liberal politician. Comment, July 1973. Quoted in: *Big Cyril*, ch. 8 (1977).

9 Parliament must not be told a direct untruth, but it's quite possible to allow them to mislead themselves.

NORMAN TEBBIT (b. 1931), British Conservative politician. Quoted in: *Observer* (London, 17 March 1991).

PARLIAMENT: THE HOUSE OF COMMONS

1 You see how this House of Commons has begun to verify all the ill prophecies that were made of it— low, vulgar, meddling with everything, assuming universal competency, and flattering every base passion— and sneering at everything noble refined and truly national. The direct tyranny will come on by and by, after it shall have gratified the multitude with the spoil and ruin of the old institutions of the land.

SAMUEL TAYLOR COLERIDGE (1772–1834), English poet, critic. *Table Talk*, 8 April 1833 (published in *Specimens of the Table Talk of Samuel Taylor Coleridge*, ed. by Henry Nelson Coleridge, 1835; repr. in *Collected Works*, vol. 14, ed. by Kathleen Coburn, 1990).

2 The House of Commons starts its proceedings with a prayer. The chaplain looks at the assembled members with their varied intelligence and then prays for the country.

LORD DENNING (b. 1899), British judge. *Daily Telegraph* (London, 12 Oct. 1989).

3 Anybody who enjoys being in the House of Commons probably needs psychiatric care.

KEN LIVINGSTONE (b. 1945), British Labour politician. *Evening Standard* (London, 26 Feb. 1988).

4 The Commons, faithful to their system, remained in a wise and masterly inactivity.

SIR JAMES MACKINTOSH (1765–1832), Scottish philosopher. *Vindiciae Gallicae*, ch. 1 (1791).

PARLIAMENT: THE HOUSE OF LORDS

1 A severe though not unfriendly critic of our institutions said that "the cure for admiring the House of Lords was to go and look at it."

WALTER BAGEHOT (1826–77), English economist, critic. *The English Constitution*, ch. 4 (1867).

2 The House of Lords is the British Outer Mongolia for retired politicians.

TONY BENN (b. 1925), British Labour politician. Comment during his campaign to disclaim his hereditary peerage. Quoted in: *New York Times* (11 February 1962).

3 Lives the man that can figure a naked Duke of Windlestraw addressing a naked House of Lords?

THOMAS CARLYLE (1795–1881), Scottish essayist and historian. *Sartor Resartus*, bk. 1, ch. 9 (1833–34).

4 Twenty thousand thieves landed at Hastings. These founders of the House of Lords were greedy and ferocious dragoons, sons of greedy and ferocious pirates. They were all alike, they took everything they could carry, they burned, harried, violated, tortured, and killed until everything English was brought to the verge of ruin. Such, however, is the illusion of antiquity and wealth, that decent and dignified men now existing boast their descent from these filthy thieves, who showed a far juster conviction of their own merits, by assuming for their types the swine, goat, jackal, leopard, wolf, and snake, which they severally resembled.

RALPH WALDO EMERSON (1803–82), U.S. essayist, poet, philosopher. *English Traits*, "Race" (1856).

5 We are fortunate to have inherited an institution (the House of Lords) which we certainly should never have had the intelligence to create. We might have been landed with something like the American Senate.

LORD ESHER (b. 1913), British architect. *Wall Street Journal* (2 May 1963).

6 Five hundred men, ordinary men, chosen accidentally from among the unemployed.

DAVID LLOYD GEORGE (1863–1945), British Liberal politician, prime minister. Speech, 9 Oct. 1909, Newcastle, England.

7 Where might is, the right is:
Long purses make strong swords.
Let weakness learn meekness:
God save the House of Lords!

A. C. SWINBURNE (1837–1909), English poet, critic. *A Word for the Country*, st. 1.

8 My Lord Bath, you and I are now two as insignificant men as any in England.

SIR ROBERT WALPOLE (1676–1745), English statesman.

Remark, Feb. 1742, to Pulteney, earl of Bath, on their elevation to the House of Lords. Quoted in: William King, *Political and Literary Anecdotes* (1819, p. 43).

PARTIES

1 Like other parties of the kind, it was first silent, then talky, then argumentative, then disputatious, then unintelligible, then altogethery, then inarticulate, and then drunk. When we had reached the last step of this glorious ladder, it was difficult to get down again without stumbling.

LORD BYRON (1788–1824), English poet. Letter, 31 Oct. 1815, to poet Thomas Moore (published in *Byron's Letters and Journals*, vol. 4, ed. by Leslie A. Marchand, 1975).

2 On with the dance! let joy be unconfined;
No sleep till morn, when Youth and Pleasure meet
To chase the glowing hours with flying feet.

LORD BYRON (1788–1824), English poet. *Childe Harold's Pilgrimage*, cto. 3, st. 22.

3 And thus they give the time, that Nature meant
For peaceful sleep and meditative snores,
To ceaseless din and mindless merriment
And waste of shoes and floors.

LEWIS CARROLL (1832–98), English author, mathematician. *Four Riddles*, no. 1 (first published 1869; repr. in *Phantasmagoria and Other Poems*, 1919).

4 We give lovely parties that last through the night,
I dress as a woman and scream with delight,
We wake up at lunch time and find we're still tight.
What could be duller than that?

NOËL COWARD (1899–1973), British playwright, actor, composer. *Bright Young People*, in *Collected Sketches and Lyrics* (1931).

5 Whether a party can have much success without a woman present I must ask others to decide, but one thing is certain, no party is any fun unless seasoned with folly.

DESIDERIUS ERASMUS (c. 1466–1536), Dutch humanist. *Praise of Folly*, ch. 18 (1509).

6 At every party there are two kinds of people—those who want to go home and those who don't. The trouble is, they are usually married to each other.

ANN LANDERS (b. 1918), U.S. advice columnist. *International Herald Tribune* (Paris, 19 June 1991).

7 Drink, and dance and laugh and lie,
Love the reeling midnight through,
For tomorrow we shall die!
(But, alas, we never do.)

DOROTHY PARKER (1893–1967), U.S. writer, wit. *The Flaw in Paganism*.

8 Enjoyed it! One more drink and I'd have been under the host.

DOROTHY PARKER (1893–1967), U.S. writer, wit. Remark, on being asked whether she enjoyed a party. Quoted in: *Wit's End* (ed. by Robert E. Drennan, 1968).

9 Whenever, at a party, I have been in the mood to study fools, I have always looked for a great beauty: they always gather round her like flies around a fruit stall.

JEAN PAUL RICHTER (1763–1825), German novelist. *Hesperus*, ch. 21 (1795).

10 I am for those who believe in loose delights, I share the midnight orgies of young men,
I dance with the dancers and drink with the drinkers.

WALT WHITMAN (1819–92), U.S. poet. *Native Moments*.

See also Byron on SOCIALIZING.

PARTING

See DEPARTURE AND PARTING.

PARTNERSHIP

1 Mr. Morgan buys his partners; I grow my own.

ANDREW CARNEGIE (1835–1919), U.S. industrialist, philanthropist. Quoted in: Burton J. Hendrick, *Life of Andrew Carnegie*, vol. 1, ch. 15, sct. 2 (1932).

2 And so we plough along, as the fly said to the ox.

HENRY WADSWORTH LONGFELLOW (1807–82), U.S. poet. Chispa, in *The Spanish Student*, act 3, sc. 6 (1840).

3 By the time a partnership dissolves, it has dissolved.

JOHN UPDIKE (b. 1932), U.S. author, critic. *Couples*, ch. 5 (1968).

PASSION

1 Without passion man is a mere latent force and possibility, like the flint which awaits the shock of the iron before it can give forth its spark.

HENRI-FRÉDÉRIC AMIEL (1821–81), Swiss philosopher, poet. *Journal Intime* (1882; tr. by Mrs. Humphrey Ward, 1892), entry for 17 Dec. 1856.

2 To hide a passion totally (or even to hide, more simply, its excess) is inconceivable: not because the human subject is too weak, but because passion is in essence made to be seen: the hiding must be seen: *I want you to know that I am hiding something from you*, that is the active paradox I must resolve: *at one and the same time* it must be known and not known: I want you to know that I don't want to show my feelings: that is the message I address to the other.

ROLAND BARTHES (1915–80), French semiologist. *A Lover's Discourse*, "Dark Glasses," sct. 2 (1977; tr. 1979).

3 What is passion? It is surely the becoming of a person. Are we not, for most of our lives, marking time? Most of our being is at rest, unlived. In passion, the body and the spirit seek expression outside of self. Passion is all that is other from self. Sex is only interesting when it releases passion. The more extreme and the more expressed that passion is, the more unbearable does life seem without it. It reminds us that if passion dies or is denied, we are partly dead and that soon, come what may, we will be wholly so.

> JOHN BOORMAN (b. 1933), British filmmaker. *Projections* (ed. by John Boorman and Walter Donohue, 1992), entry for 16 May 1991.

4 There is no such thing as a life of passion any more than a continuous earthquake, or an eternal fever. Besides, who would ever *shave* themselves in such a state?

> LORD BYRON (1788–1824), English poet. Letter, 5 July 1821, to the poet Thomas Moore (published in *Byron's Letters and Journals*, vol. 8, 1973–81).

5 There is only one passion, the passion for happiness.

> DENIS DIDEROT (1713–84), French philosopher. *Elements of Physiology*, "Will, Freedom" (notes written 1774–80, first published 1875; repr. in *Selected Writings*, ed. by Lester G. Crocker, 1966).

6 Our passions do not live apart in locked chambers but dress in their small wardrobe of notions, bring their provisions to a common table and mess together, feeding out of the common store according to their appetite.

> GEORGE ELIOT (1819–80), English novelist, editor. *Middlemarch*, bk. 2, ch. 16 (1871–72).

7 Passion, though a bad regulator, is a powerful spring.

> RALPH WALDO EMERSON (1803–82), U.S. essayist, poet, philosopher. *The Conduct of Life*, "Considerations by the Way" (1860).

8 Jupiter, not wanting man's life to be wholly gloomy and grim, has bestowed far more passion than reason— you could reckon the ration as twenty-four to one. Moreover, he confined reason to a cramped corner of the head and left all the rest of the body to the passions.

> DESIDERIUS ERASMUS c. 1466–1536), Dutch humanist. *Praise of Folly*, ch. 16 (1509).

9 It seemed to me pretty plain, that they had more of love than matrimony in them.

> OLIVER GOLDSMITH (1728–74), Anglo-Irish author, poet, playwright. Dr. Charles Primrose, in *The Vicar of Wakefield*, ch. 16 (1766).

10 You can no more bridle passions with logic than you can justify them in the law courts. Passions are facts and not dogmas.

> ALEXANDER HERZEN (1812–70), Russian journalist, political thinker. *My Past and Thoughts*, vol. 2, pt. 5, ch. 41 (1921; tr. by Constance Garnett, 1924–27).

11 There is in most passions a shrinking away from ourselves. The passionate pursuer has all the earmarks of a fugitive.

> ERIC HOFFER (1902–83), U.S. philosopher. *The Passionate State of Mind*, aph. 1 (1955).

12 The passions are the only orators which always persuade.

> FRANÇOIS, DUC DE LA ROCHEFOUCAULD (1613–80), French writer, moralist. *Sentences et Maximes Morales*, no. 8 (1678).

13 If we resist our passions, it is more because of their weakness than because of our strength.

> FRANÇOIS, DUC DE LA ROCHEFOUCAULD (1613–80), French writer, moralist. *Sentences et Maximes Morales*, no. 122 (1678).

14 Man is to be found in reason, God in the passions.

> G. C. LICHTENBERG (1742–99), German physicist, philosopher. *Aphorisms*, "Notebook K," aph. 21 (written 1765–99; tr. by Hollingdale, 1990).

15 Passions spin the plot:
We are betrayed by what is false within.

> GEORGE MEREDITH (1828–1909), English author. *Modern Love*, Sonnet 43 (1862).

16 As a bathtub lined with white porcelain,
When the hot water gives out or goes tepid,
So is the slow cooling of our chivalrous passion,
O my much praised but-not-altogether-satisfactory lady.

> EZRA POUND (1885–1972), U.S. poet, critic. "The Bath Tub," in *Lustra* (1916). The poem is thought to have been about Pound's fiancée Dorothy Shakespear, whom he married in April 1914.

17 They declaim against the passions without bothering to think that it is from their flame philosophy lights its torch.

> MARQUIS DE SADE (1740–1814), French author. Delbène, in *L'Histoire de Juliette, ou les Prospérités du Vice*, pt. 1 (1797).

18 Anyone who seeks to destroy the passions instead of controlling them is trying to play the angel.

> VOLTAIRE (1694–1778), French philosopher, author. *Letters on England*, letter 18, "On the *Pensées* of Pascal" (1732), note to Pascal's aphorism no. 358 (numbered 52 by Voltaire): "Man is neither angel nor brute, and the pity of it is that he who wants to play the angel acts the brute."

See also Disraeli on REASON.

THE PAST

1 One must always maintain one's connection to the past and yet ceaselessly pull away from it. To remain in touch with the past requires a love of memory. To remain in touch with the past requires a constant imaginative effort.

> GASTON BACHELARD (1884–1962), French scientist, philosopher, literary theorist. *Fragments of a Poetics of Fire*, "A Retrospective Glance at the Lifework of a Master of Books" (1988; tr. 1990).

2 A safe but sometimes chilly way of recalling the past is to force open a crammed drawer. If you are searching for anything in particular you don't find it, but something falls out at the back that is often more interesting.

> J. M. BARRIE (1860–1937), British playwright. *Peter Pan*, "To the Five—A Dedication" (1902).

3 The true picture of the past flits by. The past can be seized only as an image which flashes up at the instant when it can be recognized and is never seen again.

> WALTER BENJAMIN (1892–1940), German critic, philosopher. *Illuminations*, "Theses on the Philosophy of History," no. 5 (1955; ed. by Hannah Arendt, 1968).

4 The past grows gradually around one, like a placenta for dying.

> JOHN BERGER (b. 1926), British author, critic. *And Our Faces, My Heart, Brief As Photos*, pt. 2 (1984).

5   The past is the only dead thing that smells sweet.

CYRIL CONNOLLY (1903–74), British critic. Quoted in: David Pryce-Jones, *Journal and Memoir*, Epilogue (1983).

6   We are well advised to keep on nodding terms with the people we used to be, whether we find them attractive company or not. Otherwise they turn up unannounced and surprise us, come hammering on the mind's door at 4am of a bad night and demand to know who deserted them, who betrayed them, who is going to make amends. We forget all too soon the things we thought we could never forget.

JOAN DIDION (b. 1934), U.S. essayist. *Slouching Towards Bethlehem*, "On Keeping a Notebook" (1968).

7   With memory set smarting like a reopened wound, a man's past is not simply a dead history, an outworn preparation of the present: it is not a repented error shaken loose from the life: it is a still quivering part of himself, bringing shudders and bitter flavours and the tinglings of a merited shame.

GEORGE ELIOT (1819–80), English novelist, editor. *Middlemarch*, bk. 6, ch. 61 (1871).

8   It is sadder to find the past again and find it inadequate to the present than it is to have it elude you and remain forever a harmonious conception of memory.

F. SCOTT FITZGERALD (1896–1940), U.S. author. *The Crack-Up*, "Show Mr. and Mrs. F to Number—" (written with Zelda Fitzgerald, ed. by Edmund Wilson, 1945; first published in *Esquire*, New York, June 1934).

9   It's very expressive of myself. I just lump everything in a great heap which I have labeled "the past," and, having thus emptied this deep reservoir that was once myself, I am ready to continue.

ZELDA FITZGERALD (1900–1948), U.S. writer. Alabama Beggs, in *Save Me the Waltz*, ch. 4, sct. 3 (1932).

10   It is not the literal past, the "facts" of history, that shape us, but images of the past embodied in language.

BRIAN FRIEL (b. 1929), Irish playwright, author. Hugh, in *Translations*, act 3.

11   We live in a world where amnesia is the most wished-for state. When did history become a bad word?

JOHN GUARE (b. 1938), U.S. playwright. *International Herald Tribune* (Paris, 13 June 1990).

12   The past is a foreign country; they do things differently there.

L. P. HARTLEY (1895–1972), British author. *The Go-Between*, Prologue (1953).

13   If the only new thing we have to offer is an improved version of the past, then today can only be inferior to yesterday. Hypnotised by images of the past, we risk losing all capacity for creative change.

ROBERT HEWISON (b. 1943), British cultural historian. *The Heritage Industry*, Introduction (1987).

14   If the past cannot teach the present and the father cannot teach the son, then history need not have bothered to go on, and the world has wasted a great deal of time.

RUSSELL HOBAN (b. 1925), U.S. author. Jachin-Boaz, in *The Lion of Boaz-Jachin and Jachin-Boaz*, ch. 1 (1973).

15   Nothing changes more constantly than the past; for the past that influences our lives does not consist of what actually happened, but of what men believe happened.

GERALD W. JOHNSON (1890–1980), U.S. author. *American Heroes and Hero-Worship*, ch. 1 (1943).

16   The past is necessarily inferior to the future. That is how we wish it to be. How could we acknowledge any merit in our most dangerous enemy: the past, gloomy prevaricator, execrable tutor?

TOMMASO MARINETTI (1876–1944), Italian playwright, founder of Futurism. *War, the World's Only Hygiene*, "We Abjure Our Symbolist Masters . . .," (1911–15; repr. in *Marinetti: Selected Writings*, ed. by R. W. Flint, 1972).

17   Man . . . cannot learn to forget, but hangs on the past: however far or fast he runs, that chain runs with him.

FRIEDRICH NIETZSCHE (1844–1900), German philosopher. *The Use and Abuse of History*, sct. 1 (1874).

18   Because men really respect only that which was founded of old and has developed slowly, he who wants to live on after his death must take care not only of his posterity but even more of his past.

FRIEDRICH NIETZSCHE (1844–1900), German philosopher. *Assorted Opinions and Maxims*, aph. 307 (published as first supplement to *Human, All Too Human*, 1879).

19   Who controls the past controls the future: who controls the present controls the past.

GEORGE ORWELL (1903–50), British author. *Nineteen Eighty-Four*, pt. 1, ch. 3 (1949), Ingsoc party slogan.

20   We do NOT know the past in chronological sequence. It may be convenient to lay it out anesthetized on the table with dates pasted on here and there, but what we know we know by ripples and spirals eddying out from us and from our own time.

EZRA POUND (1885–1972), U.S. poet, critic. *Guide to Kulchur*, pt. 1, ch. 5, "ZWECK or the AIM" (1938).

21   The moments of the past do not remain still; they retain in our memory the motion which drew them towards the future, towards a future which has itself become the past, and draw us on in their train.

MARCEL PROUST (1871–1922), French novelist. *Remembrance of Things Past*, vol. 11, "The Sweet Cheat Gone," ch. 1 (1925; tr. by Scott Moncrieff, 1930).

22   Whoso desireth to know what will be hereafter, let him think of what is past, for the world hath ever been in a circular revolution; whatsoever is now, was heretofore; and things past or present, are no other than such as shall be again: *Redit orbis in orbem.*

SIR WALTER RALEGH (1552–1618), English author, soldier, explorer. *The Cabinet Council*, ch. 25, "A Collection of Political Observations" (repr. in *The Works of Sir Walter Raleigh*, vol. 1, 1751).

23   Every journey into the past is complicated by delusions, false memories, false namings of real events.

ADRIENNE RICH (b. 1929), U.S. poet. *Of Woman Born*, Foreword (1976).

24 The past itself, as historical change continues to accelerate, has become the most surreal of subjects—making it possible . . . to see a new beauty in what is vanishing.

> SUSAN SONTAG (b. 1933), U.S. essayist. *On Photography*, "Melancholy Objects" (1977).

25 It is not the literal past that rules us, save, possibly, in a biological sense. It is images of the past. . . . Each new historical era mirrors itself in the picture and active mythology of its past or of a past borrowed from other cultures. It tests its sense of identity, of regress or new achievement against that past.

> GEORGE STEINER (b. 1929), French-born U.S. critic, novelist. *In Bluebeard's Castle*, ch. 1 (1971).

26 The past is only the present become invisible and mute; and because it is invisible and mute, its memoried glances and its murmurs are infinitely precious. We are tomorrow's past.

> MARY WEBB (1881–1927), British author. *Precious Bane*, Foreword (1924).

27 The Past—the dark unfathom'd retrospect!
The teeming gulf—the sleepers and the shadows!
The past! the infinite greatness of the past!
For what is the present after all but a growth out of the past?

> WALT WHITMAN (1819–92), U.S. poet. *Passage to India*, verse 1.

28 One's past is what one is. It is the only way by which people should be judged.

> OSCAR WILDE (1854–1900), Anglo-Irish playwright, author. Lady Chiltern, in *An Ideal Husband*, act 1.

See also Chesterton; Walden on HISTORY; Hobsbawm on NATIONS; Sontag on PHOTOGRAPHY.

PATERNITY

1 There was a young man in Rome that was very like Augustus Caesar; Augustus took knowledge of it and sent for the man, and asked him "Was your mother never at Rome?" He answered "No Sir; but my father was."

> FRANCIS BACON (1561–1626), English philosopher, essayist, statesman. *Apothegms*, no. 87 (1624).

2 He that bulls the cow must keep the calf.

> ENGLISH PROVERB (16th century).

See also FATHERS; ILLEGITIMACY; PARENTS.

PATIENCE

1 With close-lipp'd Patience for our only friend,
Sad Patience, too near neighbour to Despair.

> MATTHEW ARNOLD (1822–88), English poet, critic. *The Scholar-Gipsy*, st. 20.

2 Perhaps there is only one cardinal sin: impatience. Because of impatience we were driven out of Paradise, because of impatience we cannot return.

> W. H. AUDEN (1907–73), Anglo-American poet. *The Dyer's Hand*, pt. 3, "The I Without a Self" (1962).

3 Patience. A minor form of despair disguised as a virtue.

> AMBROSE BIERCE (1842–1914), U.S. author. *The Devil's Dictionary* (1881–1906).

4 Beware the fury of a patient man.

> JOHN DRYDEN (1631–1700), English poet, dramatist, critic. *Absalom and Achitophel*, pt. 1.

5 Patience, that blending of moral courage with physical timidity.

> THOMAS HARDY (1840–1928), English novelist, poet. *Tess of the D'Urbervilles*, ch. 43 (1891).

6 All human errors are impatience, a premature breaking off of methodical procedure, an apparent fencing-in of what is apparently at issue.

> FRANZ KAFKA (1883–1924), German novelist, short-story writer. *The Collected Aphorisms* (Oct. 1917–Feb. 1918), no. 2 (published in *Shorter Works*, vol. 1, ed. and tr. by Malcolm Pasley, 1973).

7 Patience, the beggar's virtue,
Shall find no harbour here.

> PHILIP MASSINGER (1583–1640), English dramatist. Sir Giles Overreach, "a cruel extortioner," in *A New Way To Pay Old Debts*, act 5, sc. 1.

8 They also serve who only stand and wait.

> JOHN MILTON (1608–74), English poet. Sonnet 16, *On His Blindness*.

9 That which in mean men we entitle patience
Is pale cold cowardice in noble breasts.

> WILLIAM SHAKESPEARE (1564–1616), English dramatist, poet. Duchess of Gloucester, in *Richard II*, act 1, sc. 2.

10 I am extraordinarily patient provided I get my own way in the end.

> MARGARET THATCHER (b. 1925), British Conservative politician, prime minister. Quoted in: *Observer* (London, 2 Jan. 1983).

PATRIOTISM

1 True patriots we; for be it understood
We left our country for our country's good.

> Attributed to GEORGE BARRINGTON (1755–1810), Irish-born convict, Australian historian. Prologue, 16 Jan. 1796, to celebrate the opening of the first playhouse in Sydney, New South Wales. Most of the actors were former convicts. (Barrington himself had been a celebrated pickpocket before his transportion to Botany Bay). Quoted in: *Australian Encyclopedia* (1958, pp. 438–39). The verse is ascribed to Henry Carter (d. 1806), "a gentleman of Leicester" (England).

2 Patriotism. Combustible rubbish ready to the torch of any one ambitious to illuminate his name.

> AMBROSE BIERCE (1842–1914), U.S. author. *The Devil's Dictionary* (1881–1906). Bierce defined *Patriot* as: "One to whom the interests of a part seem superior to those of the whole. The dupe of statesmen and the tool of conquerors."

3 Next to the love of God, the love of country is the best preventive of crime.

GEORGE BORROW (1803–81), English author. *The Bible in Spain*, ch. 4 (1843). "He who is proud of his country," Borrow explained, "will be particularly cautious not to do anything which is calculated to disgrace it."

4   God and Country are an unbeatable team; they break all records for oppression and bloodshed.

LUIS BUÑUEL (1900–1983), Spanish filmmaker. *My Last Sigh*, ch. 14 (1983).

5   To make us love our country, our country ought to be lovely.

EDMUND BURKE (1729–97), Irish philosopher, statesman. *Reflections on the Revolution in France* (1790).

6   I realise that patriotism is not enough. I must have no hatred or bitterness towards anyone.

EDITH CAVELL (1865–1915), British nurse. Inscription, Cavell monument, London. Guilty of breaking the rules of war by using her status as a Red Cross nurse to help Allied prisoners escape from German-occupied territory, Cavell spoke these words to her chaplain, Rev. Stirling Gahan, shortly before her execution in Brussels as a spy (11 Oct. 1915).

7   "My country, right or wrong" is a thing that no patriot would think of saying except in a desperate case. It is like saying "My mother, drunk or sober."

G. K. CHESTERTON (1874–1936), British author. *The Defendant*, "Defence of Patriotism" (1901).

8   The love of their country is with them only a mode of flattering its master; as soon as they think that master can no longer hear, they speak of everything with a frankness which is the more startling because those who listen to it become responsible.

MARQUIS DE CUSTINE (1790–1857), French traveler, author. *Empire of the Czar: A Journey Through Eternal Russia*, ch. 7 (1843; rev. 1989), of the Russians.

9   Our country! In her intercourse with foreign nations, may she always be in the right; but our country, right or wrong.

STEPHEN DECATUR (1779–1820), U.S. naval commander. Toast, April 1816, proposed at a banquet in Norfolk, Virginia to celebrate Decatur's victory over Algerian "Barbary pirates." Quoted in: A. S. Mackenzie, *Life of Decatur*, ch. 14. The words were revived in a speech by Carl Schurz (1829–1906), German orator and later U.S. general and senator, to the U.S. Senate (17 Jan. 1872): "Our country right or wrong. When right, to be kept right; when wrong, to be put right." See Chesterton above.

10   Patriotism is an ephemeral motive that scarcely ever outlasts the particular threat to society that aroused it.

DENIS DIDEROT (1713–84), French philosopher. *Observations on the Drawing Up of Laws* (written 1774 for Catherine the Great; first published 1921; repr. in *Selected Writings*, ed. by Lester G. Crocker, 1966).

11   Never was patriot yet, but was a fool.

JOHN DRYDEN (1631–1700), English poet, dramatist, critic. *Absalom and Achitophel*, pt. 1.

12   Everyone loathes his own country and countrymen if he is any sort of artist.

LAWRENCE DURRELL (1912–1990), British author. Letter, March 1948, to Henry Miller (published in *The Durrell-Miller Letters 1935–80*, 1988).

13   No matter that patriotism is too often the refuge of scoundrels. Dissent, rebellion, and all-around hell-raising remain the true duty of patriots.

BARBARA EHRENREICH (b. 1941), U.S. author, columnist. *The Worst Years of Our Lives*, "Family Values" (1991).

14   Nationalism is our form of incest, is our idolatry, is our insanity. "Patriotism" is its cult. It should hardly be necessary to say, that by "patriotism" I mean that attitude which puts the own nation above humanity, above the principles of truth and justice; not the loving interest in one's own nation, which is the concern with the nation's spiritual as much as with its material welfare—never with its power over other nations. Just as love for one individual which excludes the love for others is not love, love for one's country which is not part of one's love for humanity is not love, but idolatrous worship.

ERICH FROMM (1900–1980), U.S. psychologist. *The Sane Society*, ch. 3, "Rootedness—Brotherliness vs. Incest" (1955).

15   The citizen who criticizes his country is paying it an implied tribute.

J. WILLIAM FULBRIGHT (b. 1905), U.S. Democratic politician. Speech, 28 April 1966, to the American Newspaper Publishers Association.

16   I only regret that I have but one life to lose for my country.

NATHAN HALE (1755–76), U.S. revolutionary soldier. Speech, 22 Sept. 1776, before being executed as a spy by the British. In his play *Cato*, act 4, sc. 4, Joseph Addison had written similar words: "What pity is it/ That we can die but once to serve our country!"

17   I wonder that we Americans love our country at all, it having no limits and no oneness; and when you try to make it a matter of the heart, everything falls away except one's native State;—neither can you seize hold of that, unless you tear it out of the Union, bleeding and quivering.

NATHANIEL HAWTHORNE (1804–64), U.S. author. *Italian Notebook*, 11 Oct. 1858 (published in *Works*, vol. 14, ed. by Thomas Woodson, 1980). "Yet," Hawthorne added, "unquestionably we do stand by our national flag as stoutly as any people in the world; and I myself have felt the heart-throb at sight of it, as sensibly as other men."

18   I've seen a lot of patriots and they all died just like anybody else if it hurt bad enough and once they were dead their patriotism was only good for legends; it was bad for their prose and made them write bad poetry. If you are going to be a great patriot i.e. loyal to any existing order of government (not one who wishes to destroy the existing for something better) you want to be killed early if your life and works won't stink.

ERNEST HEMINGWAY (1899–1961), U.S. author. Letter, 12 Jan. 1936 (published in *Selected Letters*, ed. by Carlos Baker, 1981).

19   It seems that American patriotism measures itself against an outcast group. The right Americans are the right Americans because they're not like the wrong Americans, who are not really Americans.

ERIC HOBSBAWM (b. 1917), British historian. *Marxism Today* (London, Jan. 1988).

20   Patriotism is the last refuge of a scoundrel.

SAMUEL JOHNSON (1709–84), English author, lexicographer. Quoted in: James Boswell, *Life of Samuel Johnson*, 7 April 1775

(1791). Under Ambrose Bierce's entry for *Patriotism* in his *Devil's Dictionary* (see above), Bierce added: "In Dr. Johnson's famous dictionary patriotism is defined as the last resort of a scoundrel. With all due respect to an enlightened but inferior lexicographer I beg to submit that it is the first." See Ehrenreich on PATRIOTISM.

21   My fellow Americans, ask not what your country can do for you—ask what you can do for your country.

JOHN F. KENNEDY (1917–63), U.S. president. Inaugural address, 20 Jan. 1961, Washington, D.C. Kennedy continued, "My fellow citizens of the world, ask not what America will do for you, but what together we can do for the freedom of man." Many antecedents to these words have been cited, including Oliver Wendell Holmes, Sr. in his Memorial Day Address, 1884: "It is now the moment . . . to recall what our country has done for each of us, and to ask ourselves what we can do for our country in return." Kennedy himself expressed the same idea in a televised campaign address, 20 Sept 1960, quoted in: Theodore C. Sorenson, *Kennedy*, pt. 3, ch. 9 (1965).

22   When a nation is filled with strife, then do patriots flourish.

LAO-TZU (6TH CENTURY B.C.), Legendary Chinese philosopher. *Tao-te-ching*, bk. 1, ch. 18 (tr. by T. C. Lau, 1963).

23   Intellectually I know that America is no better than any other country; emotionally I know she is better than every other country.

SINCLAIR LEWIS (1885–1951), U.S. novelist. Interview, 29 Dec. 1930, Berlin, Germany.

24   God has given you your country as cradle, and humanity as mother; you cannot rightly love your brethren of the cradle if you love not the common mother.

GIUSEPPE MAZZINI (1805–72), Italian nationalist leader. Speech, 25 July 1848, Milan, Italy.

25   O my Brothers! love your Country. Our Country is our home, the home which God has given us, placing therein a numerous family which we love and are loved by, and with which we have a more intimate and quicker communion of feeling and thought than with others; a family which by its concentration upon a given spot, and by the homogeneous nature of its elements, is destined for a special kind of activity.

GIUSEPPE MAZZINI (1805–72), Italian nationalist leader. *The Duties of Man*, ch. 5 (1844–58; tr. 1907).

26   Let America first praise mediocrity even, in her children, before she praises . . . the best excellence in the children of any other land.

HERMAN MELVILLE (1819–91), U.S. author. "Hawthorne And His Mosses," in *Literary World* (17–24 Aug. 1850).

27   Whenever you hear a man speak of his love for his country, it is a sign that he expects to be paid for it.

H. L. MENCKEN (1880–1956), U.S. journalist. *A Mencken Chrestomathy*, "Sententiæ: The Mind of Men" (1949).

28   The summer soldier and the sunshine patriot will, in this crisis, shrink from the service of his country; but he that stands it NOW deserves the love and thanks of man and woman.

THOMAS PAINE (1737–1809), Anglo-American political theorist, writer. Introduction to the first of a series of pamplets entitled "The American Crisis" (23 Dec. 1776; first published in *Pennsylvania Journal*, 19 Dec. 1776). George Washington ordered this paper to be read to his troops, 26 Dec. 1776, on the eve of the Battle of Trenton, New Jersey.

29   Where liberty dwells there is my country.

LATIN PHRASE OF UNKNOWN AUTHORSHIP. Adopted as a motto by U.S. patriot and orator James Otis (1725–83), and before him by Algernon Sydney (c. 1640).

30   A man who is good enough to shed his blood for his country is good enough to be given a square deal afterwards. More than that no man is entitled to, and less than that no man shall have.

THEODORE ROOSEVELT (1858–1919), U.S. Republican (later Progressive) politician, president. Speech, 4 June 1903, Springfield, Ill.

31   Patriotism, when it wants to make itself felt in the domain of learning, is a dirty fellow who should be thrown out of doors.

ARTHUR SCHOPENHAUER (1788–1860), German philosopher. *Parerga and Paralipomena*, vol. 2, ch. 21, sct. 255 (1851).

32   What do we mean by patriotism in the context of our times? I venture to suggest that what we mean is a sense of national responsibility . . . a patriotism which is not short, frenzied outbursts of emotion, but the tranquil and steady dedication of a lifetime.

ADLAI STEVENSON (1900–1965), U.S. Democratic politician. "The Nature of Patriotism," speech, 27 Aug. 1952, to American Legion Convention, New York City.

33   Yet some can be patriotic who have no *self-respect*, and sacrifice the greater to the less. They love the soil which makes their graves, but have no sympathy with the spirit which may still animate their clay. Patriotism is a maggot in their heads.

HENRY DAVID THOREAU (1817–62), U.S. philosopher, author, naturalist. *Walden*, "Conclusion" (1854).

34   I do not mean to exclude altogether the idea of patriotism. I know it exists, and I know it has done much in the present contest. But I will venture to assert, that a great and lasting war can never be supported on this principle alone. It must be aided by a prospect of interest, or some reward.

GEORGE WASHINGTON (1732–99), U.S. general, president. Letter, 21 April 1778.

35   He was inordinately proud of England and he abused her incessantly.

H. G. WELLS (1866–1946), British author. *Mr. Britling Sees it Through*, bk. 1, ch. 2, sct. 2.

36   How much longer are we going to think it necessary to be "American" before (or in contradistinction to) being cultivated, being enlightened, being humane, & having the same intellectual discipline as other civilized countries? It is really too easy a disguise for our shortcomings to dress them up as a form of patriotism!

EDITH WHARTON (1862–1937), U.S. author. Letter, 19 July 1919 (published in *The Letters of Edith Wharton*, 1988).

See also Kinnock on The ARMS RACE; Walpole on ENGLAND AND THE ENGLISH; Canning on INTERNATIONALISM; Aldington on NATIONALISM; Hayes on POLITICAL PARTIES.

PATRONAGE

1 If thou be invited of a mighty man, withdraw thyself, and so much the more will he invite thee. Press thou not upon him, lest thou be put back; stand not far off, lest thou be forgotten.

APOCRYPHA. *Ecclesiasticus* 13:9–10.

2 If it were not for the intellectual snobs who pay—in solid cash—the tribute which philistinism owes to culture, the arts would perish with their starving practitioners. Let us thank heaven for hypocrisy.

ALDOUS HUXLEY (1894–1963), British novelist. *Jesting Pilate,* pt. 1 (1926).

3 Is not a patron, my lord, one who looks with unconcern on a man struggling for life in the water, and, when he has reached ground, encumbers him with help? The notice which you have been pleased to take of my labours, had it been early, had been kind; but it has been delayed till I am indifferent, and cannot enjoy it; till I am solitary, and cannot impart it; till I am known, and do not want it.

SAMUEL JOHNSON (1709–84), English author, lexicographer. Letter, 7 Feb. 1755, to his patron Lord Chesterfield (published in James Boswell, *Life of Samuel Johnson,* 1791).

4 Patron: One who countenances, supports or protects. Commonly a wretch who supports with insolence, and is paid with flattery.

SAMUEL JOHNSON (1709–84), English author, lexicographer. *Dictionary of the English Language* (1755).

5 Every time I bestow a vacant office I make a hundred discontented persons and one ingrate.

LOUIS XIV (1638–1715), King of France. Remark made following the disgrace of the Duke of Lauzun, c. 1669. Quoted in: Voltaire, *Le Siècle de Louis XIV,* ch. 26 (1751).

6 If a patron buys from an artist who needs money (needs money to buy tools, time, food), the patron then makes himself equal to the artist; he is building art into the world; he creates.

EZRA POUND (1885–1972), U.S. poet, critic. Letter, 8 March 1915 (published in *The Letters of Ezra Pound 1907–1941,* ed. by D. D. Paige, 1951). Pound urged U.S. collector John Quinn to assist the new renaissance of the arts that Pound believed would happen.

7 I would rather have as my patron a host of anonymous citizens digging into their own pockets for the price of a book or a magazine than a small body of enlightened and responsible men administering public funds. I would rather chance my personal vision of truth striking home here and there in the chaos of publication that exists than attempt to filter it through a few sets of official, honorably public-spirited scruples.

JOHN UPDIKE (b. 1932), U.S. author, critic. Testimony, 30 Jan. 1978, given before the Subcommittee on Select Education of the House of Representatives Committee on Education and Labor, Boston (published in *Hugging the Shore,* 1983).

PAYMENT

1 Alas! how deeply painful is all payment!

LORD BYRON (1788–1824), English poet. *Don Juan,* cto. 10, st. 79.

2 Cash-payment is not the sole nexus of man with man.

THOMAS CARLYLE (1795–1881), Scottish essayist, historian. *Past and Present,* bk. 3, ch. 9 (1843).

3 I can't afford to pay them any other way.

ANDREW CARNEGIE (1835–1919), U.S. industrialist, philanthropist. In reply to a banker's question, "How can you afford to pay your men so well?" Quoted in: Burton J. Hendrick, *Life of Andrew Carnegie,* vol. 1, ch. 15, sct. 2 (1932).

4 When you overpay small people you frighten them. They know that their merits or activites entitle them to no such sums as they are receiving. As a result their boss soars out of economic into magic significance. He becomes a source of blessings rather than wages. Criticism is sacrilege, doubt is heresy.

BEN HECHT (1893–1964), U.S. journalist, author, screenwriter. *A Child of the Century,* bk. 5, "The Captive Muse" (1954).

5 Better see rightly on a pound a week than squint on a million.

GEORGE BERNARD SHAW (1856–1950), Anglo-Irish playwright, critic. to *Plays Pleasant and Unpleasant,* Preface (1898).

See also Byron on BILLS.

PEACE

1 They shall beat their swords into plowshares, and their spears into pruninghooks: nation shall not lift up sword against nation, neither shall they learn war any more.

BIBLE, HEBREW. *Isaiah* 2:4.

2 The United States is not a nation to which peace is a necessity.

GROVER CLEVELAND (1837–1908), U.S. Democratic politician, president. Annual Message to Congress, 7 Dec. 1896.

3 I take it that what all men are really after is some form or perhaps only some formula of peace.

JOSEPH CONRAD (1857–1924), Polish-born English novelist. The narrator, in *Under Western Eyes,* Prologue to pt. 1 (1911).

4 That doctrine [of peace at any price] has done more mischief than any I can well recall that have been afloat in this country. It has occasioned more wars than any of the most ruthless conquerors. It has disturbed and nearly destroyed that political equilibrium so necessary to the liberties and the welfare of the world.

BENJAMIN DISRAELI (1804–81), English statesman, author. Speech, 24 April 1844, to the House of Lords.

5 There never was a good war or a bad peace.

BENJAMIN FRANKLIN (1706–90), U.S. statesman, writer. Letters to Sir Joseph Banks, 27 July 1783, and Josiah Quincy, 11 Sept. 1783 (published in *Complete Works,* vol. 8, ed. by John Bigelow, 1887–88).

6 Mankind has grown strong in eternal struggles and it will only perish through eternal peace.

ADOLF HITLER (1889–1945), German dictator. *Mein Kampf,* vol. 1, ch. 4 (1925).

7 The pursuit of peace resembles the building of a great cathedral. It is the work of a generation. In concept it requires a master-architect; in execution, the labors of many.

> HUBERT H. HUMPHREY (1911–78), U.S. Democratic politician, vice president. Remarks, 17 Feb. 1965, New York City.

8 It is an unfortunate fact that we can secure peace only by preparing for war.

> JOHN F. KENNEDY (1917–63), U.S. Democratic politician, president. Speech, 6 Sept. 1960, while campaigning for presidency, Seattle, Wash.

9 Peace hath her victories
No less renowned than War.

> JOHN MILTON (1608–74), English poet. *To the Lord General Cromwell, May 1652.*

10 War is pillage versus resistance and if illusions of magnitude could be transmuted into ideals of magnanimity, peace might be realized.

> MARIANNE MOORE (1887–1972), U.S. poet. "Comment," in *Dial,* no. 86 (New York, April 1929; repr. in *Complete Prose,* 1987).

11 Peace is no more than a dream as long as we need the comfort of the clan.

> PETER NICOLS (b. 1927), British playwright. *Independent* (London, 1 Sept. 1990).

12 The greatest honor history can bestow is that of peacemaker.

> RICHARD M. NIXON (b. 1913), U.S. Republican politician, president. First inaugural address, 20 Jan. 1969.

13 Peace is normally a great good, and normally it coincides with righteousness, but it is righteousness and not peace which should bind the conscience of a nation as it should bind the conscience of an individual; and neither a nation nor an individual can surrender conscience to another's keeping.

> THEODORE ROOSEVELT (1858–1919), U.S. Republican (later Progressive) politician, president. Sixth annual message to Congress, 4 Dec. 1906.

14 You may either win your peace or buy it: win it, by resistance to evil; buy it, by compromise with evil.

> JOHN RUSKIN (1819–1900), English art critic, author. *The Two Paths,* Lecture 5 (1859).

15 To many men . . . the miasma of peace seems more suffocating than the bracing air of war.

> GEORGE STEINER (b. 1929), French-born U.S. critic, novelist. "Has Truth a Future?," Bronowski Memorial Lecture, 1978.

16 They make a wilderness and call it peace.

> TACITUS (c. 55–c. 120), Roman historian. Tacitus quoting the British chief Calgalus, speaking of the Romans, in *Agricola,* sct. 30.

17 I would rather have peace in the world than be President.

> HARRY S TRUMAN (1884–1972), U.S. Democratic politician, president. Christmas Message, 24 Dec. 1948, Independence, Mo.

18 Since wars begin in the minds of men, it is in the minds of men that the defences of peace must be constructed.

> UNITED NATIONS EDUCATIONAL, SCIENTIFIC, AND CULTURAL ORGANIZATION (UNESCO), Constitution, 1945.

See also APPEASEMENT; Vegetius on The ARMS RACE; Mussolini on FASCISM; Jiang Qing on IDEOLOGY; PACIFISM; Franklin on WAR; WAR AND PEACE.

PEOPLE, THE

1 What's important is promising something to the people, not actually keeping those promises. . . . The people have always lived on hope alone.

> HERMANN BROCH (1886–1951), Austrian novelist. Mother Gisson, in *The Spell,* ch. 13 (1976; tr. 1987).

2 If the people are happy, united, wealthy, and powerful, we presume the rest. We conclude that to be good from whence good is derived.

> EDMUND BURKE (1729–97), Irish philosopher, statesman. *Reflections on the Revolution in France* (1790).

3 But we are the people of England; and we have not spoken yet.
Smile at us, pay us, pass us. But do not quite forget.

> G. K. CHESTERTON (1874–1936), British author. *The Secret People,* closing lines.

4 Only when human sorrows are turned into a toy with glaring colors will baby people become interested— for a while at least. The people are a very fickle baby that must have new toys every day.

> EMMA GOLDMAN (1869–1940), U.S. anarchist. *Anarchism and Other Essays,* "The Traffic in Women" (1910).

5 If all power is in the people, if there is no higher law than their will, and if by counting their votes, their will may be ascertained—then the people may entrust all their power to anyone, and the power of the pretender and the usurper is then legitimate. It is not to be challenged since it came originally from the sovereign people.

> WALTER LIPPMANN (1889–1974), U.S. journalist. "The American Idea," address, 3 Feb. 1947, delivered at the unveiling of the statue of George Washington in the Washington Cathedral (published in a shortened version in *New York Herald Tribune,* 22 Feb. 1954; repr. in *The Essential Lippman,* pt. 1, sct. 1, 1982).

6 The people, and the people alone, are the motive force in the making of world history.

> MAO ZEDONG (1893–1976) Founder of the People's Republic of China. "On Coalition Government," 24 April 1945 (published in *Selected Works,* vol. 3).

7 There used to be a thing or a commodity we put great store by. It was called the People. Find out where the People have gone. I don't mean the square-eyed toothpaste-and-hair-dye people or the new-car-or-bust people, or the success-and-coronary people. Maybe they never existed, but if there ever were the People, that's the commodity the Declaration was talking about, and Mr. Lincoln.

> JOHN STEINBECK (1902–1968), U.S. author. A political correspondent conversing with Steinbeck, in *Travels With Charley: in Search of America,* pt. 3 (1962).

8 The genius of the United States is not best or most in its executives or legislatures, nor in its ambassadors or authors or colleges, or churches, or parlors, nor even in its newspapers or inventors, but always most in the common people.

WALT WHITMAN (1819–92), U.S. poet. *Leaves of Grass*, Preface (1855).

See also The MASSES.

PERCEPTION

1 To perceive means to immobilize . . . we seize, in the act of perception, something which outruns perception itself.

HENRI BERGSON (1859–1941), French philosopher. *Matter and Memory*, ch. 4, sct. 4 (1896; tr. 1911).

2 Nothing exists until or unless it is observed. An artist is making something exist by observing it. And his hope for other people is that they will also make it exist by observing it. I call it "creative observation." Creative viewing.

WILLIAM BURROUGHS (b. 1914), U.S. author. *Painting and Guns*, "The Creative Observer" (1992).

3 However, no two people see the external world in exactly the same way. To every separate person a thing is what he thinks it is—in other words, not a thing, but a think.

PENELOPE FITZGERALD (b. 1916), British author. Shippey, in *The Gate of Angels*, ch. 6 (1990).

PERFECTION

1 No one ever approaches perfection except by stealth, and unknown to themselves.

WILLIAM HAZLITT (1778–1830), English essayist. *Sketches and Essays*, "On Taste" (1839).

2 Perfection is a trifle dull. It is not the least of life's ironies that this, which we all aim at, is better not quite achieved.

W. SOMERSET MAUGHAM (1874–1965), British author. *The Summing Up*, ch. 76 (1938).

3 The essence of being human is that one does not seek perfection, that one *is* sometimes willing to commit sins for the sake of loyalty, that one does not push asceticism to the point where it makes friendly intercourse impossible, and that one is prepared in the end to be defeated and broken up by life, which is the inevitable price of fastening one's love upon other human individuals.

GEORGE ORWELL (1903–50), British author. *Shooting an Elephant*, "Reflections on Gandhi" (1950).

4 I have no faith in human perfectability. I think that human exertion will have no appreciable effect upon humanity. Man is now only more active—not more happy—nor more wise, than he was 6000 years ago.

EDGAR ALLAN POE (1809–45), U.S. poet, critic, short-story writer. Letter, 2 July 1844, to poet and critic James Russell Low-

ell. Quoted in: Julian Symons, *The Tell-Tale Heart: The Life and Works of Edgar Allan Poe*, pt. 1, ch. 11 (1978).

5 No barber shaves so close but another finds his work.

ENGLISH PROVERB. Collected in George Herbert, *Outlandish Proverbs* (1640).

6 Perfection is finally attained not when there is no longer anything to add but when there is no longer anything to take away, when a body has been stripped down to its nakedness.

ANTOINE DE SAINT-EXUPÉRY (1900–1944), French aviator, writer. *Wind, Sand, and Stars*, ch. 3.

7 Striving to better, oft we mar what's well.

WILLIAM SHAKESPEARE (1564–1616), English dramatist, poet. Albany, in *King Lear*, act 1, sc. 4.

8 The indefatigable pursuit of an unattainable perfection—even though nothing more than the pounding of an old piano—is what alone gives a meaning to our life on this unavailing star.

LOGAN PEARSALL SMITH (1865–1946), U.S. essayist, aphorist. *Afterthoughts*, "Art and Letters" (1931).

9 "Finality is death. Perfection is finality. Nothing is perfect. There are lumps in it," said the Philosopher.

JAMES STEPHENS (1882–1950), Irish poet, author. *The Crock of Gold*, ch. 4 (1912).

10 Faultily faultless, icily regular, splendidly null,
Dead perfection, no more.

LORD TENNYSON (1809–72), English poet. *Maud*, pt. 1, sct. 2.

11 The condition of perfection is idleness: the aim of perfection is youth.

OSCAR WILDE (1854–1900), Anglo-Irish playwright, author. *Phrases and Philosophies for the Use of the Young*, in *Chameleon* (London, Dec. 1894).

12 The intellect of man is forced to choose
Perfection of the life, or of the work,
And if it take the second must refuse
A heavenly mansion, raging in the dark.

W. B. YEATS (1865–1939), Irish poet. *The Choice*.

See also Fischer on MACHINERY; Chandler on WRITING: SCRIPTS AND SCREENPLAYS.

PERSECUTION

1 It is a very rare man who does not victimize the helpless.

JAMES BALDWIN (1924–87), U.S. author. *The Price of the Ticket*, "No Name in the Street" (1985; first published 1972).

2 The history of persecution is a history of endeavors to cheat nature, to make water run up hill, to twist a rope of sand.

RALPH WALDO EMERSON (1803–82), U.S. essayist, poet, philosopher. *Essays*, "Compensation" (First Series, 1841).

3 That which corrodes the souls of the persecuted is the monstrous inner agreement with the prevailing prejudice against them.

ERIC HOFFER (1902–83), U.S. philosopher. *The Passionate State of Mind*, aph. 127 (1955).

4   To punish a man because he has committed a crime, or because he is believed, though unjustly, to have committed a crime, is not persecution. To punish a man, because we infer from the nature of some doctrine which he holds, or from the conduct of other persons who hold the same doctrines with him, that he will commit a crime, is persecution, and is, in every case, foolish and wicked.

> THOMAS BABINGTON MACAULAY (1800–1859), English historian. "Hallam's Constitutional History," in *Edinburgh Review* (Sept. 1828; repr. in *Critical and Historical Essays*, 1843).

5   Miserable creatures, thrown for a moment on the surface of this little pile of mud, is it decreed that one half of the flock should be the persecutor of the other? Is it for you, mankind, to pronounce on what is good and what is evil?

> MARQUIS DE SADE (1740–1814), French author. Letter, 26 Jan. 1782, from Vincennes prison (published in *Selected Letters*, no. 10, ed. by Margaret Crosland, 1965).

See also Eliot on OPPOSITION.

PERSEVERANCE

1   Sure I am of this, that you have only to endure to conquer. You have only to persevere to save yourselves.

> SIR WINSTON CHURCHILL (1874–1965), British statesman, writer. First wartime address, 4 Sept. 1914, Guildhall, London.

2   God Almighty hates a quitter.

> SAMUEL FESSENDEN (1847–1908), U.S. lawyer, politician. Speech, June 1896, Republican National Convention, St. Louis, Mo.

3   Vitality shows in not only the ability to persist but the ability to start over.

> F. SCOTT FITZGERALD (1896–1940), U.S. author. *The Crack-Up*, "Notebook E" (ed. by Edmund Wilson, 1945).

4   In the fell clutch of circumstance,
I have not winced nor cried aloud:
Under the bludgeonings of chance
My head is bloody, but unbowed.

> W. E. HENLEY (1849–1903), English poet, critic, editor. *Invictus: In Memoriam R. T. Hamilton Bruce*.

5   The troubles of our proud and angry dust
Are from eternity, and shall not fail.
Bear them we can, and if we can we must.
Shoulder the sky, my lad, and drink your ale.

> A. E. HOUSMAN (1859–1936), British poet, classical scholar. *Last Poems*, no. 9 (1922).

6   Patience and tenacity of purpose are worth more than twice their weight of cleverness.

> THOMAS HENRY HUXLEY (1825–95), English biologist. "On Medical Education," address, 1870, at University College, London (published in *Collected Essays*, vol. 3, 1893).

7   Neither evil tongues,
Rash judgements, nor the sneers of selfish men,
Nor greetings where no kindness is, nor all
The dreary intercourse of daily life,
Shall e'er prevail against us.

> WILLIAM WORDSWORTH (1770–1850), English poet. *Lines Written a Few Miles Above Tintern Abbey*.

See also OBSTINACY.

PERSONALITY

1   I am what is mine. Personality is the original personal property.

> NORMAN O. BROWN (b. 1913), U.S. philosopher. *Love's Body*, ch. 8 (1967).

2   Personality is an unbroken series of successful gestures.

> F. SCOTT FITZGERALD (1896–1940), U.S. author. The narrator (Nick Carraway), in *The Great Gatsby*, ch. 1 (1925).

3   Man's main task in life is to give *birth* to himself, to become what he potentially is. The most important product of his effort is his own personality.

> ERICH FROMM (1900–1980), U.S. psychologist. *Man For Himself*, ch. 4 (1947).

4   Personality is only ripe when a man has made the truth his own.

> SøREN KIERKEGAARD (1813–55), Danish philosopher. *The Journals of Søren Kierkegaard: A Selection*, no. 432 (ed. and tr. by Alexander Dru, 1938), 1843 entry.

5   Personality is the glitter that sends your little gleam across the footlights and the orchestra pit into that big black space where the audience is.

> MAE WEST (1892–1980), U.S. screen actor. Quoted in: David Ray Johnson, *On Sex, Health and ESP*, ch. 2, appendix to "Biographical Study" (1975).

See also Wilde on TECHNIQUE.

PERSUASION

1   We are not won by arguments that we can analyse but by tone and temper, by the manner which is the man himself.

> SAMUEL BUTLER (1835–1902), English author. *Samuel Butler's Notebooks* (1951).

2   He who wants to persuade should put his trust not in the right argument, but in the right word. The power of sound has always been greater than the power of sense.

> JOSEPH CONRAD (1857–1924), Polish-born English novelist. *A Personal Record*, "A Familiar Preface" (1912).

3   Roughly speaking, any man with energy and enthusiasm ought to be able to bring at least a dozen others round to his opinion in the course of a year no matter how absurd that opinion might be. We see every day in politics, in business, in social life, large masses of people brought to embrace the most revolutionary ideas, sometimes within a few days. It is all a question of getting hold of them in the right way and working on their weak points.

> ALEISTER CROWLEY (1875–1947), British occultist. *The Confessions of Aleister Crowley*, ch. 56 (1929; rev. 1970).

4   The measure of a master is his success in bringing all men round to his opinion twenty years later.

> RALPH WALDO EMERSON (1803–82), U.S. essayist, poet, philosopher. *The Conduct of Life*, "Culture" (1860).

5   "For your own good" is a persuasive argument that will eventually make a man agree to his own destruction.

> JANET FRAME (b. 1924), New Zealand novelist, poet. *Faces in the Water*, ch. 4 (1961).

6   The real persuaders are our appetites, our fears and above all our vanity. The skillful propagandist stirs and coaches these internal persuaders.

> ERIC HOFFER (1902–83), U.S. philosopher. *The Passionate State of Mind*, aph. 218 (1955).

7   As there is no worse lie than a truth misunderstood by those who hear it, so reasonable arguments, challenges to magnanimity, and appeals to sympathy or justice, are folly when we are dealing with human crocodiles and boa-constrictors.

> WILLIAM JAMES (1842–1910), U.S. psychologist, philosopher. *The Varieties of Religious Experience*, Lectures 14–15, "The Value of Saintliness" (1902).

8   There is a holy, mistaken zeal in politics, as well as in religion. By persuading others, we convince ourselves.

> JUNIUS (18th century). Letter, 19 Dec. 1769.

9   There are two levers for moving men—interest and fear.

> NAPOLEON BONAPARTE (1769–1821), French general, emperor. Quoted in: Ralph Waldo Emerson, *Representative Men*, "Napoleon; or The Man of the World" (1850).

10   He that winna be ruled by the rudder maun be ruled by the rock.

> SCOTTISH PROVERB.

11   One of the best ways to persuade others is with your ears—by listening to them.

> DEAN RUSK (b. 1909), U.S. Democratic politician. *The Reader's Digest* (Pleasantville, N.Y., July 1961).

12   Hence to fight and conquer in all your battles is not supreme excellence; supreme excellence consists in breaking the enemy's resistance without fighting.

> SUN TZU (6th–5th century B.C.), Chinese general. *The Art of War*, ch. 3, axiom 2 (c. 490 B.C.; ed. by James Clavell, 1981).

See also Morley on ARGUMENT; Newman on FAITH; La Rochefoucauld on PASSION; Macaulay on SPEECHES AND SPEECHMAKING.

PESSIMISM

1   Pessimists are the people who have no hope for themselves or for others. Pessimists are also people who think the human race is beneath their notice, that they're better than other human beings.

> JAMES BALDWIN (1924–87), U.S. author. *A Dialogue* (1973; with Nikki Giovanni), from a conversation, 4 Nov 1971, in London.

2   Pessimists are not boring. Pessimists are right. Pessimists are superfluous.

> ELIAS CANETTI (b. 1905), Austrian novelist, philosopher. *The*

Secret Heart of the Clock: Notes, Aphorisms, Fragments 1973–1985, "1982" (1991).

3   Only one endowed with restless vitality is susceptible to pessimism. You become a pessimist—a demonic, elemental, bestial pessimist—only when life has been defeated many times in its fight against depression.

> E. M. CIORAN (b. 1911), Rumanian-born French philosopher. *On the Heights of Despair*, "Capitulation" (1934).

4   It is a quite remarkable fact that the great religions of the most civilized peoples are more deeply fraught with sadness than the simpler beliefs of earlier societies. This certainly does not mean that the current of pessimism is eventually to submerge the other, but it proves that it does not lose ground and that it does not seem destined to disappear.

> EMILE DURKHEIM (1858–1917), French sociologist. *Suicide*, bk. 3, ch. 3, sct. 1 (1897; tr. 1951).

5   It is wisdom in prosperity, when all is as thou wouldst have it, to fear and suspect the worst.

> DESIDERIUS ERASMUS c. 1466–1536), Dutch humanist. *Proverbs or Adages of Erasmus*, fol. 32 (ed. by Richard Taverner, 1545).

6   Man, at least when educated, is a pessimist. He believes it safer not to reflect on his achievements; Jove is known to strike such people down.

> JOHN KENNETH GALBRAITH (b. 1908), U.S. economist. *The Age of Uncertainty*, ch. 12 (1977).

7   Pessimism . . . is, in brief, playing the sure game. You cannot lose at it; you may gain. It is the only view of life in which you can never be disappointed. Having reckoned what to do in the worst possible circumstances, when better arise, as they may, life becomes child's play.

> THOMAS HARDY (1840–1928), English novelist, poet. Note written 1 Jan. 1902 (published in Florence Emily Hardy, *The Later Years of Thomas Hardy*, ch. 7, 1930).

8   If we see light at the end of the tunnel,
It's the light of the oncoming train.

> ROBERT LOWELL (1917–77), U.S. poet. *Since 1939*.

9   One has to have the courage of one's pessimism.

> IAN MCEWAN (b. 1948), British author. *Guardian* (London, 26 May 1983).

10   The pessimist . . . is seldom an agitating individual. His creed breeds indifference to others, and he does not trouble himself to thrust his views upon the unconvinced.

> AGNES REPPLIER (1858–1950), U.S. author, social critic. *Books and Men*, "Some Aspects of Pessimism" (1888).

11   The taste for worst-case scenarios reflects the need to master fear of what is felt to be uncontrollable. It also expresses an imaginative complicity with disaster.

> SUSAN SONTAG (b. 1933), U.S. essayist. *AIDS and Its Metaphors*, ch. 8 (1989).

12   There is no sadder sight than a young pessimist, except an old optimist.

> MARK TWAIN (1835–1910), U.S. author. *Notebook*, ch. 34 (ed. by Albert Bigelow Paine, 1935), entry for 27 Dec. 1903.

See also Gramsci on OPTIMISM.

PHILANTHROPY

1 Philanthropist. A rich (and usually bald) old gentleman who has trained himself to grin while his conscience is picking his pocket.

> AMBROSE BIERCE (1842–1914), U.S. author. *The Devil's Dictionary* (1881–1906).

2 If the barricades went up in our streets and the poor became masters, I think the priests would escape, I fear the gentlemen would; but I believe the gutters would simply be running with the blood of philanthropists.

> G. K. CHESTERTON (1874–1936), British author. *Charles Dickens*, "Dickens and Christmas" (1906).

3 I love my fellow creatures—I do all the good
  I can—
  Yet everybody says I'm such a disagreeable man!

> W. S. GILBERT (1836–1911), English librettist. King Gama, in *Princess Ida*, act 1 (1884).

4 Are there not thousands in the world . . .
  Who love their fellows even to the death,
  Who feel the giant agony of the world,
  And more, like slaves to poor humanity,
  Labour for mortal good?

> JOHN KEATS (1795–1821), English poet. *The Fall of Hyperion*, cto. 1.

5 All philanthropy . . . is only a savory fumigation burning at the mouth of a sewer. This incense offering makes the air more endurable to passers-by, but it does not hinder the infection in the sewer from spreading.

> ELLEN KEY (1849–1926), Swedish author, feminist. *The Century of the Child*, ch. 2 (1909).

6 Philanthropic people lose all sense of humanity. It is their distinguishing characteristic.

> OSCAR WILDE (1854–1900), Anglo-Irish playwright, author. Lord Henry, in *The Picture of Dorian Gray*, ch. 3 (1891).

7 Boredom is the legitimate kingdom of the philanthropic.

> VIRGINIA WOOLF (1882–1941), British novelist. Letter, 10 Sept. 1918 (published in *The Diary of Virginia Woolf*, vol. 1, ed. by Anne O. Bell, 1977).

See also ALTRUISM; BENEFACTORS.

PHILOSOPHERS

1 The philosopher is like a man fasting in the midst of universal intoxication. He alone perceives the illusion of which all creatures are the willing playthings; he is less duped than his neighbor by his own nature. He judges more sanely, he sees things as they are. It is in this that his liberty consists—in the ability to see clearly and soberly, in the power of mental record.

> HENRI-FRÉDÉRIC AMIEL (1821–81), Swiss philosopher, poet. *Journal Intime* (1882; tr. by Mrs. Humphrey Ward, 1892), entry for 30 Aug. 1872.

2 The traditional disputes of philosophers are, for the most part, as unwarranted as they are unfruitful.

> A. J. AYER (1910–89), British philosopher. *Language, Truth and Logic*, ch. 1 (1936), opening sentence.

3 We are much beholden to Machiavel and others, that write what men do, and not what they ought to do.

> FRANCIS BACON (1561–1626), English philosopher, essayist, statesman. *The Advancement of Learning*, bk. 2, ch. 21, sct. 9 (1605).

4 Pythagoras, Locke, Socrates—but pages
  Might be filled up, as vainly as before,
  With the sad usage of all sorts of sages,
  Who in his life-time, each was deemed a bore!
  The loftiest minds outrun their tardy ages.

> LORD BYRON (1788–1824), English poet. *Don Juan*, cto. 17, st. 9.

5 The profoundest thoughts of the philosophers have something tricklike about them. A lot disappears in order for something to suddenly appear in the palm of the hand.

> ELIAS CANETTI (b. 1905), Austrian novelist, philosopher. *The Secret Heart of the Clock: Notes, Aphorisms, Fragments 1973–1985*, "1973" (1991).

6 The most dangerous criminal now is the entirely lawless modern philosopher. Compared to him, burglars and bigamists are essentially moral men.

> G. K. CHESTERTON (1874–1936), British author. A policeman, in *The Man Who Was Thursday*, ch. 4 (1908).

7 There is nothing so absurd but some philosopher has said it.

> CICERO (106–43 B.C.), Roman orator, philosopher. *De Divinatione*, bk. 2, sct. 58.

8 In it he proves that all things are true and states how the truths of all contradictions may be reconciled physically, such as for example that white is black and black is white; that one can be and not be at the same time; that there can be hills without valleys; that nothingness is something and that everything, which is, is not. But take note that he proves all these unheard-of paradoxes wihout any fallacious or sophistical reasoning.

> CYRANO DE BERGERAC (1619–55), French author, playwright. A "lunarian," describing a work of philosophy "composed by one of the best brains under the sun," in *The Other World: States and Empires of the Moon*, ch. 8 (1656).

9 The philosopher has never killed any priests, whereas the priest has killed a great many philosophers.

> DENIS DIDEROT (1713–84), French philosopher. *Observations on Drawing Up of Laws* (1774; repr. in *Selected Writings*, ed. by Lester G. Crocker, 1966).

10 Of what use is a philosopher who doesn't hurt anybody's feelings?

> DIOGENES OF SINOPE ["THE CYNIC"] (c. 410–c. 320 B.C.), Greek philosopher, moralist. *Herakleitos and Diogenes*, pt. 2, Fragment 10 (tr. by Guy Davenport, 1976).

11 I have tried too in my time to be a philosopher; but, I don't know how, cheerfulness was always breaking in.

> OLIVER EDWARDS (1711–91), English lawyer. Quoted in: James Boswell, *Life of Samuel Johnson*, 17 April 1778 (1791).

12 If you set your heart upon philosophy, you must straightway prepare yourself to be laughed at and mocked by many who will say *Behold a philosopher arisen among us!* or *How came you by that brow of scorn?* But do you cherish no scorn, but hold to those things which seem to you the best, as one set by God in that place. Remember too, that if you abide in those ways, those who first mocked you, the same shall afterwards reverence you; but if you yield to them, you will be laughed at twice as much as before.

EPICTETUS (c. 55–c. 135), Greek Stoic philosopher. *Encheiridion*, no. 22 (tr. by T. W. H. Rolleston, 1881).

13 As an example of just how useless these philosophers are for any practice in life there is Socrates himself, the one and only wise man, according to the Delphic Oracle. Whenever he tried to do anything in public he had to break off amid general laughter. While he was philosophizing about clouds and ideas, measuring a flea's foot and marveling at a midge's humming, he learned nothing about the affairs of ordinary life.

DESIDERIUS ERASMUS c. 1466–1536), Dutch humanist. *Praise of Folly*, ch. 24 (1509).

14 I have always taken as the standard of the mode of teaching and writing, not the abstract, particular, professional philosopher, but universal man, that I have regarded *man* as the criterion of truth, and not this or that founder of a system, and have from the first placed the highest excellence of the philosopher in this, that he abstains, both as a man and as an author, from the ostentation of philosophy, *i.e.*, that he is a philosopher only in reality, not formally, that he is a quiet philosopher, not a loud and still less a brawling one.

LUDWIG FEUERBACH (1804–72), German philosopher. *The Essence of Christianity*, Preface (1843 ed.).

15 To be a real philosopher all that is necessary is to *hate* some one else's type of thinking.

WILLIAM JAMES (1842–1910), U.S. psychologist, philosopher. Letter, 29 Jan. 1909 (published in *The Letters of William James*, vol. 2, 1920).

16 When philosophers try to be politicians they generally cease to be philosophers.

WALTER LIPPMANN (1889–1974), U.S. journalist. *A Preface to Politics*, ch. 3 (1914).

17 The philosophers have only *interpreted* the world in various ways; the point, however, is to *change* it.

KARL MARX (1818–83), German political theorist, social philosopher. *Theses on Feuerbach*, no. 11 (written 1845; published 1888; repr. in *Selected Works*, vol. 1, 1942). The observation also appeared in Marx, *The German Ideology* (1846), and was inscribed as the epitaph on his tomb in Highgate Cemetery, London.

18 The philosopher believes that the value of his philosophy lies in the whole, in the building: posterity discovers it in the bricks with which he built and which are then often used again for better building: in the fact, that is to say, that that building can be destroyed and *nonetheless* possess value as material.

FRIEDRICH NIETZSCHE (1844–1900), German philosopher. *Assorted Opinions and Maxims*, aph. 201 (1879).

19 *Actual philosophers . . . are commanders and lawgivers:* they say "thus it *shall* be!", it is they who determine the Wherefore and Whither of mankind, and they possess for this task the preliminary work of all the philosophical labourers, of all those who have subdued the past—they reach for the future with creative hand, and everything that is or has been becomes for them a means, an instrument, a hammer. Their "knowing" is *creating*, their creating is a lawgiving, their will to truth is—*will to power*. Are their such philosophers today? Have there been such philosophers? *Must* there not be such philosophers?

FRIEDRICH NIETZSCHE (1844–1900), German philosopher. *Beyond Good and Evil*, aph. 211 (1886).

20 The usual picture of Socrates is of an ugly little plebeian who inspired a handsome young nobleman to write long dialogues on large topics.

RICHARD RORTY (b. 1931), U.S. philosopher. *Contingency, Irony, and Solidarity*, ch. 6, "From Ironist Theory to Private Allusions" (1989).

21 For there was never yet philosopher
That could endure the toothache patiently.

WILLIAM SHAKESPEARE (1564–1616), English dramatist, poet. Leonato, in *Much Ado About Nothing*, act 5, sc. 1.

22 Bishop Berkeley destroyed this world in one volume octavo; and nothing remained, after his time, but mind; which experienced a similar fate from the hand of Mr. Hume in 1737.

SYDNEY SMITH (1771–1845), English writer, clergyman. *Sketches of Moral Philosophy*, Introduction (1850).

23 The philosopher proves that the philosopher exists. The poet merely enjoys existence.

WALLACE STEVENS (1879–1955), U.S. poet. "The Figure of the Youth as Virile Poet," speech, delivered Aug. 1943 (published in *The Necessary Angel*, 1951).

24 Perhaps it is of more value to infuriate philosophers than to go along with them.

WALLACE STEVENS (1879–1955), U.S. poet. *Opus Posthumous*, "Adagia" (1959).

25 Reason, progress, unselfishness, a wide historical perspective, expansiveness, generosity, enlightened self-interest. I had heard it all my life, and it filled me with despair.

KATHERINE TAIT (b. 1923), Daughter of Bertrand Russell. Quoted in: Caroline Moorehead, *Bertrand Russell*, Afterword (1992), said of her life with Bertrand Russell.

26 Then, like an old-time orator
Impressively he rose;
I make the most of all that comes
And the least of all that goes.

SARA TEASDALE (1884–1933), U.S. poet. *The Philosopher*, st. 4.

27 To be a philosopher is not merely to have subtle thoughts, nor even to found a school, but so to love wisdom as to live according to its dictates a life of simplicity, independence, magnanimity, and trust. It is to solve some of the problems of life, not only theoretically, but practically.

HENRY DAVID THOREAU (1817–62), U.S. philosopher, author, naturalist. *Walden*, "Economy" (1854).

28 It is one of the chief skills of the philosopher not to occupy himself with questions which do not concern him.

LUDWIG WITTGENSTEIN (1889–1951), Austrian philosopher. *Notebooks 1914–1916* 1 May 1915 (ed. by Anscombe, 1961).

29 Englishmen are babes in philosophy and so prefer faction-fighting to the labour of its unfamiliar thought.

> W. B. YEATS (1865–1939), Irish poet, playwright. Letter, 24 March 1927 (published in *The Letters of W. B. Yeats*, ed. by Allan Wade, 1954).

See also Vizinczey on CONSISTENCY; Russell on EVOLUTION; Nietzsche on GREECE AND THE GREEKS; Thucydides on HISTORY; Hobbes on LEISURE; PHILOSOPHY; Coleridge on POETS; James on PRAISE.

PHILOSOPHY

1 Unintelligible answers to insoluble problems.

> HENRY B. ADAMS (1838–1918), U.S. historian. Adams's definition of philosophy. Quoted in: Bert Leston Taylor, *The So-Called Human Race* (1922).

2 Existentialism is about being a saint without God; being your own hero, without all the sanction and support of religion or society.

> ANITA BROOKNER (b. 1938), British novelist, art historian. Interview in *Writers at Work* (Eighth Series, ed. by George Plimpton, 1988).

3 To philosophize is only another way of being afraid and leads hardly anywhere but to cowardly make-believe.

> LOUIS-FERDINAND CÉLINE (1894–1961), French author. The narrator (Ferdinand Bardamu), in *Journey to the End of the Night* (1932; tr. 1934; repr. 1966, p. 180).

4 Philosophy, like medicine, has plenty of drugs, few good remedies, and hardly any specific cures.

> SÉBASTIEN-ROCH NICOLAS DE CHAMFORT (1741–94), French writer, wit. *Maxims and Considerations*, vol. 1, no. 17 (1796).

5 A new philosophy generally means in practice the praise of some old vice.

> G. K. CHESTERTON (1874–1936), British author. *All Things Considered*, "The Methuselahite" (1908).

6 And new Philosophy calls all in doubt,
The element of fire is quite put out;
The Sun is lost, and th'earth, and no mans wit
Can well direct him where to look for it.

> JOHN DONNE (c. 1572–1631), English divine, metaphysical poet. *An Anatomie of the World: First Anniversary*.

7 Art requires philosophy, just as philosophy requires art. Otherwise, what would become of beauty?

> PAUL GAUGUIN (1848–1903), French artist. *Intimate Journals* (tr. by Van Wyck Brooks, 1923; repr. 1930, p. 193).

8 Truth in philosophy means that concept and external reality correspond.

> GEORG HEGEL (1770–1831), German philosopher. *The Philosophy of Right*, "Introduction," Addition 16 (1821; tr. 1942).

9 I know that you, ladies and gentlemen, have a philosophy, each and all of you, and that the most interesting and important thing about you is the way in which it determines the perspective in your several worlds.

> WILLIAM JAMES (1842–1910), U.S. psychologist, philosopher. *Pragmatism*, Lecture 1, "The Present Dilemma in Philosophy" (1907).

10 Philosophy is at once the most sublime and the most trivial of human pursuits.

> WILLIAM JAMES (1842–1910), U.S. psychologist, philosopher. *Pragmatism*, Lecture 1, "The Present Dilemma in Philosophy" (1907).

11 All the interests of my reason, speculative as well as practical, combine in the three following questions:
1. What can I know?
2. What ought I to do?
3. What may I hope?

> IMMANUEL KANT (1724–1804), German philosopher. *Critique of Pure Reason*, "Transcendental Doctrine of Method," ch. 2, sct. 2 (1781).

12 Do not all charms fly
At the mere touch of cold philosophy?
There was an awful rainbow once in heaven:
We know her woof, her texture; she is given
In the dull catalogue of common things.
Philosophy will clip an angel's wings,
Conquer all mysteries by rule and line,
Empty the haunted air, and gnomed mine
Unweave a rainbow.

> JOHN KEATS (1795–1821), English poet. *Lamia*, pt. 2.

13 Philosophy always requires something more, requires the eternal, the true, in contrast to which even the fullest existence as such is but a happy moment.

> SøREN KIERKEGAARD (1813–55), Danish philosopher. *The Concept of Irony*, Introduction to pt. 1 (1841; tr. 1966).

14 In the information age, you don't teach philosophy as they did after feudalism. You perform it. If Aristotle were alive today he'd have a talk show.

> TIMOTHY LEARY (b. 1920), U.S. psychologist. *Evening Standard* (London, 8 Feb. 1989).

15 If this is philosophy it is at any rate a philosophy that is not in its right mind.

> G. C. LICHTENBERG (1742–99), German physicist, philosopher. *Aphorisms*, "Notebook L," aph. 23 (written 1765–99; tr. by R. J. Hollingdale, 1990).

16 We often have need of a profound philosophy to restore to our feelings their original state of innocence, to find *our* way out of the rubble of things alien to us, to begin to feel for *ourselves* and to speak *ourselves*, and I might almost say to exist ourselves.

> G. C. LICHTENBERG (1742–99), German physicist, philosopher. *Aphorisms*, "Notebook B," aph. 49 (written 1765–99; tr. by R. J. Hollingdale, 1990). "Even if my philosophy does not extend to discovering anything new," Lichtenberg wrote, "it does nevertheless possess the courage to regard as questionable what has long been thought true."

17 There is no philosophy without the art of ignoring objections.

> JOSEPH DE MAISTRE (1753–1821), French diplomat, philosopher. The Count, in *Les Soirées de Saint-Pétersbourg*, "Fifth Dialogue" (1821; repr. in *The Works of Joseph de Maistre*, ed. by Jack Lively, 1965).

18 Philosophy stands in the same relation to the study of the actual world as masturbation to sexual love.

> KARL MARX (1818–83) AND FRIEDRICH ENGELS (1820–95), German social philosophers, revolutionaries. *The German Ideology*, sct. 2 (1845–46).

19 Why, ever since Adam, who has got to the meaning of this great allegory—the world? Then we pygmies must be content to have out paper allegories but ill comprehended.

HERMAN MELVILLE (1819–91), U.S. author. Letter, 17 Nov. 1851, to Nathaniel Hawthorne (published in *The Letters of Herman Melville*, ed. by Merrell R. Davis and William H. Gilman, 1960).

20 Philosophy consists very largely of one philosopher arguing that all others are jackasses. He usually proves it, and I should add that he also usually proves that he is one himself.

H. L. MENCKEN (1880–1956), U.S. journalist. *Minority Report: H. L. Mencken's Notebooks*, no. 57 (1956).

21 Any genuine philosophy leads to action and from action back again to wonder, to the enduring fact of mystery.

HENRY MILLER (1891–1980), U.S. author. *The Wisdom of the Heart*, "The Absolute Collective" (1947).

22 How charming is divine philosophy!
Not harsh and crabbèd, as dull fools suppose,
But musical as is Apollo's lute,
And a perpetual feast of nectared sweets,
Where no crude surfeit reigns.

JOHN MILTON (1608–74), English poet. Second brother, in *Comus* (1634).

23 In philosophy if you aren't moving at a snail's pace you aren't moving at all.

IRIS MURDOCH (b. 1919), British novelist, philosopher. Socrates, in *Acastos: Two Platonic Dialogues*, "Above the Gods: A Dialogue about Religion" (1986).

24 Philosophy! Empty thinking by ignorant conceited men who think they can digest without eating!

IRIS MURDOCH (b. 1919), British novelist, philosopher. Levquist, in *The Book and the Brotherhood*, pt. 1, "Midsummer" (1987).

25 To have no time for philosophy is to be a true philosopher.

BLAISE PASCAL (1623–62), French scientist, philosopher. *Pensées* (1670; no. 513 ed. by Krailsheimer, no. 4 ed. by Brunschvicg).

26 The philosophic spirit of inquiry may be traced to brute curiosity, and that to the habit of examining all things in search of food.

W. WINWOOD READE (1838–75), English traveler, author. *The Martyrdom of Man*, ch. 3, "Materials of Human History" (1872).

27 The ultimate triumph of philosophy would be to cast light upon the mysterious ways in which Providence moves to achieve the designs it has for man.

MARQUIS DE SADE (1740–1814), French author. *The Misfortunes of Virtue* (1787), opening lines.

28 How very paltry and limited the normal human intellect is, and how little lucidity there is in the human consciousness, may be judged from the fact that, despite the ephemeral brevity of human life, the uncertainty of our existence and the countless enigmas which press upon us from all sides, everyone does not continually and ceaselessly philosophize, but that only the rarest of exceptions do.

ARTHUR SCHOPENHAUER (1788–1860), German philosopher. *Parerga and Paralipomena*, vol. 2, ch. 3, sct. 39 (1851).

29 Ordinary people seem not to realize that those who really apply themselves in the right way to philosophy are directly and of their own accord preparing themselves for dying and death.

SOCRATES (469–399 B.C.), Greek philosopher. Quoted in: Plato, *Phaedo*, sct. 62.

30 A writer must always try to have a philosophy and he should also have a psychology and a philology and many other things. Without a philosophy and a psychology and all these various other things he is not really worthy of being called a writer. I agree with Kant and Schopenhauer and Plato and Spinoza and that is quite enough to be called a philosophy. But then of course a philosophy is not the same thing as a style.

GERTRUDE STEIN (1874–1946), U.S. author. Quoted in: Frederic Prokosch, *Voices: A Memoir*, "Style" (1983).

31 The proper method of philosophy consists in clearly conceiving the insoluble problems in all their insolubility and then in simply contemplating them, fixedly and tirelessly, year after year, without any hope, patiently waiting.

SIMONE WEIL (1909–43), French philosopher, mystic. "London Notebook" (1943; published in *First and Last Notebooks*, ed. by Richard Rees, 1970).

32 Every philosophy is tinged with the colouring of some secret imaginative background, which never emerges explicitly into its train of reasoning.

ALFRED NORTH WHITEHEAD (1861–1947), British philosopher. *Science and the Modern World*, ch. 1 (1926).

33 Philosophy is like trying to open a safe with a combination lock: each little adjustment of the dials seems to achieve nothing, only when everything is in place does the door open.

LUDWIG WITTGENSTEIN (1889–1951), Austrian philosopher. *Personal Recollections*, ch. 6 (ed. by Rush Rhees, 1981), said in conversation in 1930.

34 The real discovery is the one which enables me to stop doing philosophy when I want to.—The one that gives philosophy peace, so that it is no longer tormented by questions which bring *itself* into question.

LUDWIG WITTGENSTEIN (1889–1951), Austrian philosopher. *Philosophical Investigations*, pt. 1, sct. 133 (1953).

See also Karl Marx on GREECE AND THE GREEKS; Seneca on INVENTION; LOGIC; METAPHYSICS.

PHOTOGRAPHY

1 I have often thought that if photography were *difficult* in the true sense of the term—meaning that the creation of a simple photograph would entail as much time and effort as the production of a good watercolor or etching—there would be a vast improvement in total output.

The sheer ease with which we can produce a superficial image often leads to creative disaster.

> ANSEL ADAMS (1902–84), U.S. photographer. "A Personal Credo," in *American Annual of Photography*, vol. 58 (1944; repr. in *Photographers on Photography*, ed. by Nathan Lyons, 1966).

2 If I were just curious, it would be very hard to say to someone, "I want to come to your house and have you talk to me and tell me the story of your life." I mean people are going to say, "You're crazy." Plus they're going to keep mighty guarded. But the camera is a kind of license. A lot of people, they want to be paid that much attention and that's a reasonable kind of attention to be paid.

> DIANE ARBUS (1923–71), U.S. photographer. Remarks made in class, 1971 (published in *Diane Arbus: An Aperture Monograph*, 1972).

3 A photograph is a secret about a secret. The more it tells you the less you know.

> DIANE ARBUS (1923–71), U.S. photographer. Quoted in: Patricia Bosworth, *Diane Arbus: A Biography*, Preface (1985).

4 The virtue of the camera is not the power it has to transform the photographer into an artist, but the impulse it gives him to keep on looking.

> BROOKS ATKINSON (1894–1984), U.S. critic, essayist. *Once Around the Sun* (1951), entry for 28 Aug.

5 It takes a lot of imagination to be a good photographer. You need less imagination to be a painter, because you can invent things. But in photography everything is so ordinary; it takes a lot of looking before you learn to see the ordinary.

> DAVID BAILEY (b. 1938), British photographer. *Face* (London, Dec. 1984).

6 The photographic image . . . *is a message without a code.*

> ROLAND BARTHES (1915–80), French semiologist. "The Photographic Message," in *Communications*, no. 1 (Paris, 1961; repr. in *Image Music Text*, 1977).

7 If photography is allowed to stand in for art in some of its functions it will soon supplant or corrupt it completely thanks to the natural support it will find in the stupidity of the multitude. It must return to its real task, which is to be the servant of the sciences and the arts, but the very humble servant, like printing and shorthand which have neither created nor supplanted literature.

> CHARLES BAUDELAIRE (1821–67), French poet. "Salon of 1859," sct. 2, in *Curiosités Esthétiques* (1868; repr. in *The Mirror of Art*, ed. by Jonathan Mayne, 1955).

8 Too many photographers try too hard. They try to lift photography into the realm of Art, because they have an inferiority complex about their Craft. You and I would see more interesting photography if they would stop worrying, and instead, apply horse-sense to the problem of recording the look and feel of their own era.

> JESSIE TARBOX BEALS (1870–1942), U.S. photographer. Quoted in: *PM* (New York, April 1941).

9 The camera introduces us to unconscious optics as does psychoanalysis to unconscious impulses.

> WALTER BENJAMIN (1892–1940), German critic, philosopher. *The Work of Art in the Age of Mechanical Reproduction*, sct. 13 (1936; repr. in *Illuminations*, ed. by Hannah Arendt, 1968).

10 Most things in life are moments of pleasure and a lifetime of embarrassment; photography is a moment of embarrassment and a lifetime of pleasure.

> TONY BENN (b. 1925), British Labour politician. Quoted in: *Independent* (London, 21 Oct. 1989).

11 The camera relieves us of the burden of memory. It surveys us like God, and it surveys for us. Yet no other god has been so cynical, for the camera records in order to forget.

> JOHN BERGER (b. 1926), British novelist, critic. *About Looking*, "Uses of Photography" (1980).

12 Unlike any other visual image, a photograph is not a rendering, an imitation or an interpretation of its subject, but actually a trace of it. No painting or drawing, however naturalist, *belongs* to its subject in the way that a photograph does.

> JOHN BERGER (b. 1926), British novelist, critic. *About Looking*, "Uses of Photography (1980).

13 The camera can photograph thought. It's better than a paragraph of sweet polemic.

> DIRK BOGARDE (b. 1921), British actor. Quoted in: *Independent* (London, 28 Jan. 1990).

14 The most refined skills of color printing, the intricate techniques of wide-angle photography, provide us pictures of trivia bigger and more real than life. We forget that we see trivia and notice only that the reproduction is so good. Man fulfils his dream and by photographic magic produces a precise image of the Grand Canyon. The result is not that he adores nature or beauty the more. Instead he adores his camera—and himself.

> DANIEL J. BOORSTIN (b. 1914), U.S. historian. *The Image*, ch. 4 (1961).

15 It is not merely the likeness which is precious . . . but the association and the sense of nearness involved in the thing . . . the fact of the *very shadow of the person* lying there fixed forever! It is the very sanctification of portraits I think—and it is not at all monstrous in me to say . . . that I would rather have such a memorial of one I dearly loved, than the noblest Artist's work ever produced.

> ELIZABETH BARRETT BROWNING (1806–61), English poet. Letter, 7 Dec. 1843, to Mary Russell Mitford (published in *Elizabeth Barrett to Miss Mitford*, 1954).

16 Blessed be the inventor of photography! I set him above even the inventor of chloroform! It has given more positive pleasure to poor suffering humanity than anything else that has "cast up" in my time or is like to—this art by which even the "poor" can possess themselves of tolerable likenesses of their absent dear ones. And mustn't it be acting favourably on the morality of the country?

> JANE WELSH CARLYLE (1801–66), Scottish poet. Letter, 21 Oct. 1859 (published in *The Collected Letters of Thomas and Jane Welsh Carlyle*, 1970).

17 The camera is a killing chamber, which speeds up the time it claims to be conserving. Like coffins exhumed and prised open, the photographs put on show what we were and what we will be again.

> PETER CONRAD (b. 1948), Australian critic, author. *Down Home: Revisiting Tasmania*, pt. 5, "Seeing Tasmania" (1988).

18 A hundredth of a second here, a hundredth of a second there—even if you put them end to end, they still only add up to one, two, perhaps three seconds, snatched from eternity.

> ROBERT DOISNEAU (b. 1912), French photographer. *Weekend Guardian* (London, 4 April 1992).

19 The camera has an interest in turning history into spectacle, but none in reversing the process. At best, the picture leaves a vague blur in the observer's mind; strong enough to send him into battle perhaps, but not to have him understand why he is going.

> DENIS DONOGHUE (b. 1928), Irish educator, author. *The State of the Language*, "Radio Talk" (1980).

20 The magic of photography is metaphysical. What you see in the photograph isn't what you saw at the time. The real skill of photography is organised visual lying.

> TERENCE DONOVAN (b. 1936), British photographer. *Guardian* (London, 19 Nov. 1983).

21 We have crossed the Andes, ascended Tenerife, entered Japan, "done" Niagara and the Thousand Isles, drunk delight of battle with our peers (at shop windows), sat at the councils of the mighty, grown familiar with kings, emperors and queens, prima donnas, pets of the ballet, and "well graced actors." Ghosts have we seen and have not trembled; stood before royalty and have not uncovered; and looked, in short, through a three-inch lens at every single pomp and vanity of this wicked but beautiful world.

> "D.P.", English columnist. *Once a Week* (London, 1 June 1861).

22 The camera is an instrument that teaches people how to see without a camera.

> DOROTHEA LANGE (1895–1979), U.S. photographer. Quoted in: *Los Angeles Times* (13 Aug. 1978).

23 Photographers never have much incentive to show the world as it is.

> WILLIAM LEITH (b. 1960), British journalist. *Independent on Sunday* (London, 13 Sept. 1992).

24 Any one who knows what the worth of family affection is among the lower classes, and who has seen the array of little portraits stuck over a labourer's fireplace ... will perhaps feel with me that in counteracting the tendencies, social and industrial, which every day are sapping the healthier family affections, the sixpenny photograph is doing more for the poor than all the philanthropists in the world.

> *MACMILLAN'S MAGAZINE* (London, Sept. 1871).

25 Giving a camera to Diane Arbus is like putting a live grenade in the hands of a child.

> NORMAN MAILER (b. 1923), U.S. author. *Newsweek* (New York, 22 Oct. 1984).

26 I have no fear of photography as long as it cannot be used in heaven and in hell.

> EDVARD MUNCH (1863–1944), Norwegian artist. "Saint Cloud Declaration" (1889–90). Quoted in: Aaron Scharf, *Art and Photography*, ch. 11 (1968). All the same, in 1902, Munch bought a Kodak, and experimented with photography.

27 Sometimes you can tell a large story with a tiny subject.

> ELIOT PORTER (1901–90), U.S. photographer. Quoted in: *Guardian* (London, 6 Nov. 1990).

28 That the outer man is a picture of the inner, and the face an expression and revelation of the whole character, is a presumption likely enough in itself, and therefore a safe one to go on; borne out as it is by the fact that people are always anxious to see anyone who has made himself famous. . . . Photography . . . offers the most complete satisfaction of our curiosity.

> ARTHUR SCHOPENHAUER (1788–1860), German philosopher. *Parerga and Paralipomena*, vol. 2, ch. 29, sct. 377 (1851).

29 The camera can represent flesh so superbly that, if I dared, I would never photograph a figure without asking that figure to take its clothes off.

> GEORGE BERNARD SHAW (1856–1950), Anglo-Irish playwright, critic. "Some Criticisms of the Exhibitions," in *Amateur Photographer* (London, 16 Oct. 1902; repr. in *Bernard Shaw on Photography*, 1989).

30 In America, the photographer is not simply the person who records the past, but the one who invents it.

> SUSAN SONTAG (b. 1933), U.S. essayist. *On Photography*, "Melancholy Objects" (1977).

31 It is not altogether wrong to say that there is no such thing as a bad photograph—only less interesting, less relevant, less mysterious ones.

> SUSAN SONTAG (b. 1933), U.S. essayist. *On Photography*, "The Heroism of Vision" (1977).

32 Most modern reproducers of life, even including the camera, really repudiate it. We gulp down evil, choke at good.

> WALLACE STEVENS (1879–1955), U.S. poet. *Opus Posthumous*, "Adagia" (1959).

33 Photography suits the temper of this age—of active bodies and minds. It is a perfect medium for one whose mind is teeming with ideas, imagery, for a prolific worker who would be slowed down by painting or sculpting, for one who sees quickly and acts decisively, accurately.

> EDWARD WESTON (1886–1958), U.S. photographer. *The Daybooks of Edward Weston*, vol. 3, pt. 3, ch. 10 (ed. by Nancy Newhall, 1925), June 1934 entry.

34 We *regard* the photograph, the picture on our wall, as the object itself (the man, landscape, and so on) depicted there. This need not have been so. We could easily imagine people who did not have this relation to such pictures. Who, for example, would be repelled by photographs, because a face without color and even perhaps a face in reduced proportions struck them as inhuman.

> LUDWIG WITTGENSTEIN (1889–1951), Austrian philosopher. *Philosophical Investigations*, pt. 2, sct. 11 (1953).

See also Sontag on TOURISM.

PHOTOGRAPHY AND PAINTING

1 All photographs are there to remind us of what we forget. In this—as in other ways—they are the opposite of paintings. Paintings record what the painter remembers. Because each one of us forgets different things, a photo more than a painting may change its meaning according to who is looking at it.

> JOHN BERGER (b. 1926), British novelist, critic. *Keeping a Rendezvous*, "How Fast Does It Go?" (1992).

2 Now at least we know everything that painting isn't.

> PABLO PICASSO (1881–1973), Spanish artist. Remark, 1949, in answer to whether painting figures was still possible after photography, cinema, etc.; reported by artist Renato Guttuso in his journals. Quoted in: Mario De Micheli, *Scritti di Picasso* (1964).

3 I paint what cannot be photographed, that which comes from the imagination or from dreams, or from an unconscious drive. I photograph the things that I do not wish to paint, the things which already have an existence.

> MAN RAY (1890–1976), U.S. photographer. Interview in *Caméra* (Paris; repr. in *Man Ray: Photographer*, ed. by Philippe Sers, 1981).

4 The painter constructs, the photographer discloses.

> SUSAN SONTAG (b. 1933), U.S. essayist. *On Photography*, "The Heroism of Vision" (1977).

PHYSICS

1 To see a world in a grain of sand
And a heaven in a wild flower,
Hold infinity in the palm of your hand
And eternity in an hour.

> WILLIAM BLAKE (1757–1827), English poet, painter, engraver. *Auguries of Innocence*, in *Poems from the Pickering Manuscript* (c. 1808; repr. in *Complete Writings*, ed. by Geoffrey Keynes, 1957).

2 No atomic physicist has to worry, people will always want to kill other people on a mass scale. Sure, he's got the fridge full of sausages and spring water.

> WILLIAM BURROUGHS (b. 1914), U.S. author. *The Adding Machine*, "A Word to the Wise Guy" (1985).

3 We must be physicists in order . . . to be creative since so far codes of values and ideals have been constructed in ignorance of physics or even in contradiction to physics.

> FRIEDRICH NIETZSCHE (1844–1900), German philosopher. *The Gay Science*, aph. 335 (1887 ed.).

4 In some sort of crude sense, which no vulgarity, no humor, no overstatement can quite extinguish, the physicists have known sin; and this is a knowledge which they cannot lose.

> J. ROBERT OPPENHEIMER (1904–67), U.S. physicist. "Physics in the Contemporary World," lecture, 25 Nov. 1947, delivered at Massachusetts Institute of Technology (published in *Technology Review*, no. 50, 1948). The remark became notorious when it was quoted in *Time* (23 Feb. 1948 and 8 Nov. 1948).

5 It would be a poor thing to be an atom in a universe without physicists, and physicists are made of atoms. A physicist is an atom's way of knowing about atoms.

> GEORGE WALD (b. 1906), U.S. biochemist. Foreword to L. J. Henderson, *The Fitness of the Environment* (1959).

PABLO PICASSO

1 If surrealism ever comes to adopt a particular line of moral conduct, it has only to accept the discipline that Picasso has accepted and will continue to accept.

> ANDRÉ BRETON (1896–1966), French surrealist. *Surrealism and Painting* (1928).

2 No theoretician, no writer on art, however interesting he or she might be, could be as interesting as Picasso. A good writer on art may give you an insight to Picasso, but, after all, Picasso was there first.

> DAVID HOCKNEY (b. 1937), British artist. *Hockney On Photography*, "Mexico City: May 1984" (ed. by Wendy O. Brown, 1988), from conversations with Paul Joyce.

3 If all the ways I have been along were marked on a map and joined up with a line, it might represent a minotaur.

> PABLO PICASSO (1881–1973), Spanish artist. Official catalog of the Musée d'Antibes, known as the Musée Picasso, France. Quoted in: Dor de la Souchère, *Picasso in Antibes* (1960).

4 Today, as you know, I am famous and very rich. But when I am alone with myself, I haven't the courage to consider myself an artist, in the great and ancient sense of that word . . . I am only a public entertainer, who understands his age.

> PABLO PICASSO (1881–1973), Spanish artist. *Le Spectacle du Monde* (Paris, Nov. 1962; repr. in Duncan Williams, *The Trousered Ape*, ch. 2, 1971).

5 A painter like Picasso, who runs through many periods and phases, ends up by saying all those things which are on the tip of the tongue of the age to say, and finally sterilizes the originality of his contemporaries and juniors.

> NORBERT WIENER (1894–1964), U.S. mathematician, educator, founder of cybernetics. *The Human Use of Human Beings*, ch. 7 (1950).

PIETY

1 Bernard always had a few prayers in the hall and some whiskey afterwards as he was rather pious.

> DAISY ASHFORD (1881–1972), British writer. *The Young Visiters*, "The First Evening" (written when the author was aged nine; published 1919).

2 You smile with pomp & rigor, you talk of
benevolence & virtue;
I act with benevolence & virtue & get murdered
time after time.

> WILLIAM BLAKE (1757–1827), English poet, painter, engraver. *Jerusalem*, ch. 4, Plate 91 (1804–20; repr. in *Complete Writings*, ed. by Geoffrey Keynes, 1957).

3 Their sighin', cantin', grace-proud faces,
Their three-mile prayers, and half-mile graces.

> ROBERT BURNS (1759–96), Scottish poet. *To the Rev. John M'Math*.

4 How holy people look when they are sea-sick!

> SAMUEL BUTLER (1835–1902), English author. *Notebooks*, "Written Sketches" (1912).

5 Piety practised in solitude, like the flower that blooms in the desert, may give its fragrance to the winds of heaven, and delight those unbodied spirits that survey the works of God and the actions of men; but it bestows no assistance upon earthly beings, and however free from taints of impurity, yet wants the sacred splendour of beneficence.

SAMUEL JOHNSON (1709–84), English author, lexicographer. *Adventurer*, no. 126, (London, 19 Jan. 1754; repr. in *The Works of Samuel Johnson*, vol. 2, ed. by W. J. Bate, John M. Bullitt, and L. F. Powell, 1963).

6 A wicked fellow is the most pious when he takes to it. He'll beat you all at piety.

SAMUEL JOHNSON (1709–84), English author, lexicographer. Quoted in: James Boswell, *Life of Samuel Johnson*, 10 June 1784 (1791).

7 I judge a man by his actions with men, much more than by his declarations Godwards—When I find him to be envious, carping, spiteful, hating the successes of others, and complaining that the world has never done enough for him, I am apt to doubt whether his humility before God will atone for his want of manliness.

ANTHONY TROLLOPE (1815–82), English novelist. Letter, 8 June 1876 (published in *The Letters of Anthony Trollope*, vol. 2, 1983).

See also Jung on SPIRITUALITY.

PITY

1 Nobody can tell what I suffer! But it is always so. Those who do not complain are never pitied.

JANE AUSTEN (1775–1817), English novelist. Mrs. Bennett, in *Pride and Prejudice*, ch. 20 (1813).

2 More helpful than all wisdom is one draught of simple human pity that will not forsake us.

GEORGE ELIOT (1819–80), English novelist. *The Mill on the Floss*, bk. 7, ch. 1 (1860).

3 When Man evolved Pity, he did a queer thing— deprived himself of the power of living life as it is without wishing it to become something different.

JOHN GALSWORTHY (1867–1933), English novelist and playwright. Letter, 27 March 1910, to Thomas Hardy.

4 If a madman were to come into this room with a stick in his hand, no doubt we should pity the state of his mind; but our primary consideration would be to take care of ourselves. We should knock him down first, and pity him afterwards.

SAMUEL JOHNSON (1709–84), English author, lexicographer. Quoted in: James Boswell, *Life of Samuel Johnson*, 3 April 1776 (1791).

5 Pity is treason.

MAXIMILIEN ROBESPIERRE (1758–94), French revolutionary leader. Speech, 26 Feb. 1794, to the National Convention, Paris.

6 Humane sentiments are baseless, mad, and improper; they are incredibly feeble; never do they withstand the gainsaying passions, never do they resist bare necessity.

MARQUIS DE SADE (1740–1814), French author. Noirceuil, in *L'Histoire de Juliette, ou les Prospérités du Vice*, pt. 1 (1797).

7 Pity is for living, envy is for dead.

MARK TWAIN (1835–1910), U.S. author. *Following the Equator*, ch. 19, "Pudd'nhead Wilson's New Calendar" (1897).

8 To love with the spirit is to pity, and he who pities most loves most.

MIGUEL DE UNAMUNO (1864–1936), Spanish philosophical writer. *The Tragic Sense of Life*, ch. 7 (1913).

PLACES

1 One does not love a place the less for having suffered in it, unless it has been all suffering, nothing but suffering.

JANE AUSTEN (1775–1817), English novelist. Anne Elliot, in *Persuasion*, ch. 20 (1818).

2 The local is a shabby thing. There's nothing worse than bringing us back down to our own little corner, our own territory, the radiant promiscuity of the face to face. A culture which has taken the risk of the universal, must perish by the universal.

JEAN BAUDRILLARD (b. 1929), French semiologist. *Cool Memories*, ch. 3 (1987; tr. 1990).

3 A place belongs forever to whoever claims it hardest, remembers it most obsessively, wrenches it from itself, shapes it, renders it, loves it so radically that he remakes it in his own image.

JOAN DIDION (b. 1934), U.S. essayist. *The White Album*, "In the Islands" (1979).

4 God gives all men all earth to love,
But, since man's heart is small,
Ordains for each one spot shall prove
Belovèd over all.

RUDYARD KIPLING (1865–1936), British author, poet. *Sussex*.

5 The accent of one's birthplace remains in the mind and in the heart as in one's speech.

FRANÇOIS, DUC DE LA ROCHEFOUCAULD (1613–80), French writer, moralist. *Sentences et Maximes Morales*, no.342 (1678).

See also Meynell on TRAVEL.

PLAGIARISM

1 And for the citation of so many authors, 'tis the easiest thing in nature. Find out one of these books with an alphabetical index, and without any farther ceremony, remove it verbatim into your own . . . there are fools enough to be thus drawn into an opinion of the work; at least, such a flourishing train of attendants will give your book a fashionable air, and recommend it for sale.

MIGUEL DE CERVANTES (1547–1616), Spanish writer. Prologue to *Don Quixote*, pt. 1 (1605; tr. by P. Motteux). It is thought that Cervantes was alluding to Lope de Vega's book, *El Peregrino y el Isidro*, which included a list of cited authors in alphabetical order.

2 Ideas improve. The meaning of words participates in the improvement. Plagiarism is necessary. Progress implies it. It embraces an author's phrase, makes use of his expressions, erases a false idea, and replaces it with the right idea.

> GUY DEBORD (b. 1931), French situationist philosopher. *The Society of the Spectacle*, ch. 8, sct. 207 (1967; tr. 1977).

3 He invades authors like a monarch; and what would be theft in other poets is only victory in him.

> JOHN DRYDEN (1631–1700), English poet, dramatist, critic. Neander, in *Essay of Dramatic Poesy* (1668), speaking of dramatist Ben Jonson.

4 Stealing things is a glorious occupation, particularly in the artworld.

> MALCOLM MCLAREN (b. 1946), British rock impresario. "Punk and History," transcript of discussion, 24 Sept. 1988, New York City (published in *Discourses: Conversations in Postmodern Art and Culture*, ed. by Russell Ferguson et. al., 1990).

5 If you steal from one author, it's plagiarism; if you steal from many, it's research.

> WILSON MIZNER (1876–1933), U.S. dramatist, wit. Quoted in: Alva Johnston, *The Legendary Mizners*, ch. 4 (1953).

6 Most writers steal a good thing when they can,
And when 'tis safely got 'tis worth the winning.
The worst of 't is we now and then detect 'em,
Before they ever dream that we suspect 'em.

> BRYAN WALLER PROCTOR (1787–1874), English poet. *Diego de Montillo*.

7 The human plagiarism which is most difficult to avoid, for individuals . . . is the plagiarism of ourself.

> MARCEL PROUST (1871–1922), French novelist. *Remembrance of Things Past*, vol. 11, "The Sweet Cheat Gone," ch. 1 (1925; tr. 1930).

8 Whatever is well said by another, is mine.

> SENECA (c. 5 A.D.–B.C. c. 65), Roman writer, philosopher, statesman. *Epistulae ad Lucilium*, Epistle 16, sct. 7.

9 So much of what I am I got from you. I had no idea how much of it was secondhand.

> PETE TOWNSHEND (b. 1945), British rock musician. Remarks, Jan. 1989, at the 1989 Rock & Roll Hall of Fame induction dinner. Quoted in: *Rolling Stone* (New York, 8 Feb. 1990), on the Rolling Stones.

10 Immature artists imitate. Mature artists steal.

> LIONEL TRILLING (1905–75), U.S. critic. *Esquire* (New York, Sept. 1962).

See also Fitzgerald on F. SCOTT FITZGERALD.

PLANNING

1 I have never yet seen any plan which has not been mended by the observations of those who were much inferior in understanding to the person who took the lead in the business.

> EDMUND BURKE (1729–97), Irish philosopher, statesman. *Reflections on the Revolution in France* (1790).

2 To have his path made clear for him is the aspiration of every human being in our beclouded and tempestuous existence.

> JOSEPH CONRAD (1857–1924), Polish-born English novelist. *The Mirror of the Sea*, ch. 27 (1906).

3 In preparing for battle I have always found that plans are useless, but planning is indispensable.

> DWIGHT D. EISENHOWER (1890–1969), U.S. general, Republican politician, president. One of Eisenhower's favorite maxims. Quoted by Richard Nixon in: *Six Crises*, "Krushchev" (1962).

4 I have always thought that one man of tolerable abilities may work great changes, and accomplish great affairs among mankind, if he first forms a good plan, and, cutting off all amusements or other employments that would divert his attention, make the execution of that same plan his sole study and business.

> BENJAMIN FRANKLIN (1706–90), U.S. statesman, writer. *Autobiography*, ch. 7 (written 1771–90; published 1868).

5 For the happiest life, days should be rigorously planned, nights left open to chance.

> MIGNON MCLAUGHLIN (b. 1915?), U.S. author, editor. *Atlantic* (Boston, July 1965).

6 Planning ahead is a measure of class. The rich and even the middle class plan for future generations, but the poor can plan ahead only a few weeks or days.

> GLORIA STEINEM (b. 1934), U.S. feminist writer, editor. "The Time Factor," in *Ms.* (New York, March 1980; repr. in *Outrageous Acts and Everyday Rebellions*, 1983).

7 If we had had more time for discussion we should probably have made a great many more mistakes.

> LEON TROTSKY (1879–1940), Russian revolutionary. *My Life*, ch. 36 (1930), of the discussions in the Central Committee of the Soviet Communist Party about the proposed development of the Red Army.

PLATITUDES

1 In spite of his practical ability, some of his experience had petrified into maxims and quotations.

> GEORGE ELIOT (1819–80), English novelist. *Daniel Deronda*, bk. 2, ch. 15 (1874–76), of the Rector (Gwendolen Harleth's uncle).

2 The Republicans stroke platitudes until they purr like epigrams.

> ADLAI STEVENSON (1900–1966), U.S. Democratic politician. Quoted in: Leon Harris, *The Fine Art of Political Wit*, ch. 1 (1964). Stevenson borrowed the phrase from humorist Don Marquis. See Marquis on NEWSPAPERS AND MAGAZINES.

3 . . . exchanging platitudes, as Frenchmen do, for the pleasure of feeling their mouths full of the good meat of common sense.

> REBECCA WEST (1892–1983), British author. *The Thinking Reed*, ch. 3 (1936), of the inn-keeper and Marc.

4 In modern life nothing produces such an effect as a good platitude. It makes the whole world kin.

> OSCAR WILDE (1854–1900), Anglo-Irish playwright, author. Mrs. Cheveley, in *An Ideal Husband*, act 1.

See also Wilder on LITERATURE.

PLAY

1 If there is a species which is more maltreated than children, then it must be their toys, which they handle in an incredibly off-hand manner. . . . Toys are thus the end point in that long chain in which all the conditions of despotic high-handedness are in play which enchain beings one to another, from one species to another—cruel divinities to their sacrificial victims, from masters to slaves, from adults to children, and from children to their objects.

> JEAN BAUDRILLARD (b. 1929), French semiologist. *Cool Memories*, ch. 3 (1987; tr. 1990).

2 The true object of all human life is play. Earth is a task garden; heaven is a playground.

> G. K. CHESTERTON (1874–1936), British author. *All Things Considered*, "Oxford from Without" (1908).

3 It is the child in man that is the source of his uniqueness and creativeness, and the playground is the optimal milieu for the unfolding of his capacities and talents.

> ERIC HOFFER (1902–83), U.S. philosopher. *Reflections on the Human Condition*, aph. 27 (1973).

4 Life isn't all beer and skittles, but beer and skittles, or something better of the same sort, must form a good part of every Englishman's education.

> THOMAS HUGHES (1822–96), English author. *Tom Browne's Schooldays*, pt. 1, ch. 2 (1857).

5 Life must be filled up, and the man who is not capable of intellectual pleasures must content himself with such as his senses can afford.

> SAMUEL JOHNSON (1709–84), English author, lexicographer. Quoted in: Hester Piozzi, *Anecdotes of Samuel Johnson*, vol. 1 (1786; repr. in *Johnsonian Miscellanies*, ed. by George Birkbeck Hill, 1897, p. 251).

6 Man only plays when in the full meaning of the word he is a man, and *he is only completely a man when he plays.*

> FRIEDRICH VON SCHILLER (1759–1805), German dramatist, poet, essayist. *On the Aesthetic Education of Man*, "Fifteenth Letter" (1795).

7 If all the year were playing holidays,
To sport would be as tedious as to work.

> WILLIAM SHAKESPEARE (1564–1616), English dramatist, poet. Prince Harry [Hal], in *Henry IV, Pt. 1*, act 1, sc. 2.

8 A stereotyped but unconscious despair is concealed even under what are called the games and amusements of mankind.

> HENRY DAVID THOREAU (1817–62), U.S. philosopher, author, naturalist. *Walden*, "Economy" (1854).

See also BASEBALL; CARDS; Thackeray on CHILDHOOD; Montaigne on CHILDREN; FOOTBALL; GAMBLING; GAMES; GOLF; LEISURE; PLEASURE; RECREATION; SPORT.

PLEASURE

1 The important question is not, what will yield to man a few scattered pleasures, but what will render his life happy on the whole amount.

> JOSEPH ADDISON (1672–1719), English essayist. *Interesting Anecdotes, Memoirs, Allegories, Essays, and Poetical Fragments*, "Happiness Not Independent" (1794).

2 A fool bolts pleasure, then complains of moral indigestion.

> MINNA ANTRIM (1861–?), U.S. epigrammist. *Naked Truth and Veiled Allusions* (1901, p. 9).

3 One half of the world cannot understand the pleasures of the other.

> JANE AUSTEN (1775–1817), English novelist. Emma, in *Emma*, ch. 9 (1816).

4 Pleasure is continually disappointed, reduced, deflated, in favor of strong, noble values: Truth, Death, Progress, Struggle, Joy, etc. Its victorious rival is Desire: we are always being told about Desire, never about Pleasure.

> ROLAND BARTHES (1915–80), French semiologist. *The Pleasure of the Text*, "Oppositions" (1975).

5 Pleasure only starts once the worm has got into the fruit, to become delightful happiness must be tainted with poison.

> GEORGES BATAILLE (1897–1962), French novelist, critic. The Mother, in *My Mother* (1966; tr. 1979, p. 65).

6 Stolen waters are sweet, and bread eaten in secret is pleasant.

> BIBLE, HEBREW. "A foolish woman," in *Proverbs* 9:17.

7 For most men, and most circumstances, pleasure—tangible material prosperity in this world—is the safest test of virtue. Progress has ever been through the pleasures rather than through the extreme sharp virtues, and the most virtuous have leaned to excess rather than to asceticism.

> SAMUEL BUTLER (1835–1902), English author. *The Way of All Flesh*, ch. 19 (1903).

8 Whenever I meet with anything agreeable in this world it surprises me so much—and pleases me so much (when my passions are not interested in one way or the other) that I go on wondering for a week to come.

> LORD BYRON (1788–1824), English poet. Letter, 6 June 1819 (published in *Byron's Letters and Journals*, vol. 6, ed. by Leslie A. Marchand, 1976).

9 Do not bite at the bait of pleasure, till you know there is no hook beneath it.

> THOMAS JEFFERSON (1743–1826), U.S. president. Letter, 12 Oct. 1786.

10 If pleasure was not followed by pain, who would forbear it?

> SAMUEL JOHNSON (1709–84), English author, lexicographer. *The Idler*, no. 89, in *Universal Chronicle* (London, 29 Dec 1759; repr. in *Works of Samuel Johnson*, vol. 2, ed. by W. J. Bate, John M. Bullitt and L. F. Powell, 1963).

11 Give me books, fruit, French wine and fine weather and a little music out of doors, played by someone I do not know. . . . I admire lolling on a lawn by a water-lilied pond to eat white currants and see goldfish: and go to the fair in the evening if I'm good. There is not hope for that—one is sure to get into some mess before evening.

> JOHN KEATS (1795–1821), English poet. Letter, 28 Aug. 1819, to

his sister Fanny Keats (published in *Letters of John Keats*, no. 146, ed. by Frederick Page, 1954).

12 Most men pursue pleasure with such breathless haste that they hurry past it.

SØREN KIERKEGAARD (1813–55), Danish philosopher. *Either/Or*, vol. 1, "Diapsalmata" (1843; tr. 1987).

13 Pleasure that isn't paid for is as insipid as everything else that's free.

ANITA LOOS (1893–1981), U.S. novelist, screenwriter. *Kiss Hollywood Good-by*, ch. 2 (1974).

14 Scratching is one of nature's sweetest gratifications, and the one nearest at hand.

MICHEL DE MONTAIGNE (1533–92), French essayist. *Essays*, bk. 3, ch. 13, "Of Experience" (1588).

15 The truth is, I do indulge myself a little the more in pleasure, knowing that this is the proper age of my life to do it; and, out of my observation that most men that do thrive in the world do forget to take pleasure during the time that they are getting their estate, but reserve that till they have got one, and then it is too late for them to enjoy it.

SAMUEL PEPYS (1633–1703), English diarist. Diary entry, 10 March 1666, written at age 33.

16 Physical pleasure is a sensual experience no different from pure seeing or the pure sensation with which a fine fruit fills the tongue; it is a great unending experience, which is given us, a knowing of the world, the fullness and the glory of all knowing. And not our acceptance of it is bad; the bad thing is that most people misuse and squander this experience and apply it as a stimulant at the tired spots of their lives and as distraction instead of a rallying toward exalted moments.

RAINER MARIA RILKE (1875–1926), German poet. Letter, 16 July 1903 (published in *Letters to a Young Poet*, 1934; rev. 1954).

17 Pleasures are all alike simply considered in themselves: he that hunts, or he that governs the commonwealth, they both please themselves alike, only we commend that, whereby we ourselves receive some benefit.

JOHN SELDEN (1584–1654), English jurist, statesman. *Table Talk*, "Pleasure" (1686).

18 Your enjoyment of the world is never right, till every morning you awake in Heaven: see yourself in your Father's palace; and look upon the skies, the earth, and the air as celestial joys: having such a reverend esteem of all, as if you were among the angels.

THOMAS TRAHERNE (1636–74), English clergyman, poet, mystic. *Centuries*, "First Century," no. 28 (written c. 1672; published 1908).

19 The eruption of lived pleasure is such that in losing myself I find myself; forgetting that I exist, I realize myself.

RAOUL VANEIGEM (b. 1934), Belgian situationist philosopher. *The Revolution of Everyday Life*, ch. 20, sct. 2 (1967; tr. 1983).

20 The vocabulary of pleasure depends on the imagery of pain.

MARINA WARNER (b. 1946), British author, critic. "Fighting Talk," in *The State of the Language* (ed. by Christopher Ricks and Leonard Michaels, 1990).

21 Pleasure is Nature's test, her sign of approval. When man is happy, he is in harmony with himself and his environment.

OSCAR WILDE (1854–1900), Anglo-Irish playwright, author. *The Soul of Man Under Socialism*, in *Fortnightly Review* (London, Feb. 1891; repr. 1895).

22 All the things I really like to do are either immoral, illegal, or fattening.

ALEXANDER WOOLLCOTT (1887–1943), U.S. columnist, critic. Quoted in: *Wit's End* (ed. by Robert E. Drennan, 1968).

See also HEDONISM; Johnson on HUNTING; Johnson on HYPOCRISY; Calvino on LOVE; Shakespeare on PLAY; Shelley on SORROW; Huxley on SPEED.

EDGAR ALLAN POE

1 Poor Poe! At first so forgotten that his grave went without a tomb-stone twenty-six years . . . today in danger of becoming the life study of a few professors.

W. H. AUDEN (1907–73), Anglo-American poet. Introduction to *Edgar Allan Poe* (1950; repr. in *The Recognition of Edgar Allen Poe*, ed. by E. W. Carlson, 1970).

2 There comes Poe, with his raven, like Barnaby
        Rudge,
  Three-fifths of him genius, and two-fifths sheer
        fudge.
  Who talks like a book of iambs and pentameters,
  In a way to make people of common sense damn
        metres,
  Who has written some things quite the best of
        their kind,
  But the heart somehow seems all squeezed out by
        the mind.

JAMES RUSSELL LOWELL (1819–91), U.S. poet, editor. *A Fable for Critics*, in *Poe and Longfellow*.

3 Like a wild stranger out of wizard-land
  He dwelt a little with us, and withdrew;
  Black and unblossomed were the ways he knew,
  Dark was the glass through which his fire eye
        shined.

EDWIN ARLINGTON ROBINSON (1869–1935), U.S. author. *For a Copy of Poe's Poems* (1894; repr. in *The Recognition of Edgar Allan Poe*, ed. by E. W. Carlson, 1970).

4 Poe is the only impeccable writer. He was never mistaken.

PAUL VALÉRY (1871–1945), French poet, essayist. Letter to writer André Gide. Quoted in: Julian Symons, *The Tell-Tale Heart: The Life and Works of Edgar Allan Poe*, pt. 1, Epilogue (1978).

5 Poe gives the sense for the first time in America, that literature is serious, not a matter of courtesy but of truth.

WILLIAM CARLOS WILLIAMS (1883–1963), U.S. poet. *The Recognition of Edgar Allan Poe*, "In the American Grain" (ed. by E. W. Carlson, 1970; first published 1925).

POETRY

1 Written poetry is worth reading once, and then

should be destroyed. Let the dead poets make way for others. Then we might even come to see that it is our veneration for what has already been created, however beautiful and valid it may be, that petrifies us.

ANTONIN ARTAUD (1896–1948), French theater producer, actor, theorist. *The Theater and Its Double,* ch. 6 (1938; tr. 1958).

2   There is the view that poetry should improve your life. I think people confuse it with the Salvation Army.

JOHN ASHBERY (b. 1927), U.S. poet, critic. *International Herald Tribune* (Paris, 2 Oct. 1989).

3   Rhymes, meters, stanza forms, etc., are like servants. If the master is fair enough to win their affection and firm enough to command their respect, the result is an orderly happy household. If he is too tyrannical, they give notice; if he lacks authority, they become slovenly, impertinent, drunk and dishonest.

W. H. AUDEN (1907–73), Anglo-American poet. *The Dyer's Hand,* pt. 1, "Writing" (1962).

4   I cannot accept the doctrine that in poetry there is a "suspension of belief." A poet must never make a statement simply because it is sounds poetically exciting; he must also believe it to be true.

W. H. AUDEN (1907–73), Anglo-American poet. *A Certain World,* "Writing" (1970).

5   Poetry is one of the destinies of speech. . . . One would say that the poetic image, in its newness, opens a future to language.

GASTON BACHELARD (1884–1962), French scientist, philosopher, literary theorist. *The Poetics of Reverie,* "Introduction," sct. 2 (1960; tr. 1969).

6   Who among us has not, in moments of ambition, dreamt of the miracle of a form of poetic prose, musical but without rhythm and rhyme, both supple and staccato enough to adapt itself to the lyrical movements of our souls, the undulating movements of our reveries, and the convulsive movements of our consciences? This obsessive ideal springs above all from frequent contact with enormous cities, from the junction of their innumerable connections.

CHARLES BAUDELAIRE (1821–67), French poet. Dedication of *Le Spleen de Paris,* in *La Presse* (Paris, 26 Aug. 1862; repr. in *Complete Works,* vol. 1, "Shorter Prose Poems," ed. by Yves-Gérard le Dantec; rev. by Claude Pichois, 1953).

7   Poetry and progress are like two ambitious men who hate one another with an instinctive hatred, and when they meet upon the same road, one of them has to give place.

CHARLES BAUDELAIRE (1821–67), French poet. "Salon of 1859," sct. 2, in *Curiosités Esthétiques* (1868; repr. in *The Mirror of Art,* ed. by Jonathan Mayne, 1955).

8   In the works of the better poets you get the sensation that they're not talking to people any more, or to some seraphical creature. What they're doing is simply talking back to the language itself—as beauty, sensuality, wisdom, irony—those aspects of language of which the poet is a clear mirror. Poetry is not an art or a branch of art, it's something more. If what distinguishes us from other species is speech, then poetry, which is the supreme

linguistic operation, is our anthropological, indeed genetic, goal. Anyone who regards poetry as an entertainment, as a "read," commits an anthropological crime, in the first place, against himself.

JOSEPH BRODSKY (b. 1940), Russian-born U.S. poet, critic. Interview in *Writers at Work* (Eighth Series, ed. by George Plimpton, 1988).

9   I by no means rank poetry high in the scale of intelligence—this may look like affectation but it is my real opinion. It is the lava of the imagination whose eruption prevents an earthquake.

LORD BYRON (1788–1824), English poet. Letter, 29 Nov. 1813, to Annabella Milbanke, later Lady Byron (published in *Byron's Letters and Journals,* vol. 3, ed. by Leslie Marchand, 1974).

10   As to "Don Juan," confess . . . that it is the sublime of that there sort of writing; it may be bawdy, but is it not good English? It may be profligate, but is it not life, is it not the thing? Could any man have written it who has not lived in the world? and tooled in a post-chaise? in a hackney coach? in a Gondola? against a wall? in a court carriage? in a vis a vis? on a table? and under it?

LORD BYRON (1788–1824), English poet. Letter, 26 Oct. 1819, written from Venice (published in *Byron's Letters and Journals,* vol. 6, ed. by Leslie A. Marchand, 1976).

11   An age which is incapable of poetry is incapable of any kind of literature except the cleverness of a decadence.

RAYMOND CHANDLER (1888–1959), U.S. author. Letter, 5 Jan. 1947, to *Atlantic Monthly* editor Charles W. Morton (published in *Raymond Chandler Speaking,* 1962).

12   Little do such men know the toil, the pains,
The daily, nightly racking of the brains,
To range the thoughts, the matter to digest,
To cull fit phrases, and reject the rest.

CHARLES CHURCHILL (1731–64), English clergyman, poet. *Gotham,* bk. 2.

13   Such is the role of poetry. It unveils, in the strict sense of the word. It lays bare, under a light which shakes off torpor, the surprising things which surround us and which our senses record mechanically.

JEAN COCTEAU (1889–1963), French author, filmmaker. *Le Rappel à l'Ordre,* "Le Secret Professionnel" (1926; repr. in *Collected Works,* vol. 9, 1950).

14   Poetry is indispensable—if I only knew what for.

JEAN COCTEAU (1889–1963), French author, filmmaker. Quoted in: Ernst Fischer, *The Necessity of Art,* ch. 1 (1959).

15   That willing suspension of disbelief for the moment, which constitutes poetic faith.

SAMUEL TAYLOR COLERIDGE (1772–1834), English poet, critic. *Biographia Literaria,* ch. 14 (1817).

16   I wish our clever young poets would remember my homely definitions of prose and poetry; that is, prose = words in their best order;—poetry = the *best* words in the best order.

SAMUEL TAYLOR COLERIDGE (1772–1834), English poet, critic. *Table Talk,* 12 July 1827 (published in *Specimens of the Table Talk of Samuel Taylor Coleridge,* ed. by Henry Nelson Coleridge, 1835; repr. in *Collected Works,* vol. 14, ed. by Kathleen Coburn, 1990).

17 It is with roses and locomotives (not to mention acrobats Spring electricity Coney Island the 4th of July the eyes of mice and Niagara Falls) that my "poems" are competing.

> E. E. CUMMINGS (1894–1962), U.S. poet. Foreword to *is 5* (1926).

18 Poetry must have something in it that is barbaric, vast and wild.

> DENIS DIDEROT (1713–84), French philosopher. *On Dramatic Poetry* (1758; repr. in *Selected Writings*, ed. by Lester G. Crocker, 1966).

19 We read poetry because the poets, like ourselves, have been haunted by the inescapable tyranny of time and death; have suffered the pain of loss, and the more wearing, continuous pain of frustration and failure; and have had moods of unlooked-for release and peace. They have known and watched in themselves and others.

> ELIZABETH DREW (1887–1965), Anglo-American author, critic. *Poetry: A Modern Guide to Its Understanding and Enjoyment*, pt. 2, ch. 7 (1959).

20 Poetry, the genre of purest beauty, was born of a truncated woman: her head severed from her body with a sword, a symbolic penis.

> ANDREA DWORKIN (b. 1946), U.S. feminist critic. *Pornography*, ch. 4 (1981).

21 I would define the poetic effect as the capacity that a text displays for continuing to generate different readings, without ever being completely consumed.

> UMBERTO ECO (b. 1932), Italian semiologist, novelist. *Reflections on the Name of the Rose*, "Telling the Process" (1983; tr. 1984).

22 Here undoubtedly lies the chief poetic energy:—in the force of imagination that pierces or exalts the solid fact, instead of floating among cloud-pictures.

> GEORGE ELIOT (1819–80), English novelist, editor. *Daniel Deronda*, bk. 4, ch. 33 (1876).

23 Each venture
Is a new beginning, a raid on the inarticulate
With shabby equipment always deteriorating
In the general mess of imprecision of feeling.

> T. S. ELIOT (1888–1965), Anglo-American poet, critic. *East Coker*, pt. 5, in *Four Quartets*.

24 It seems just possible that a poem might happen
To a very young man: but a poem is not poetry—
That is a life.

> T. S. ELIOT (1888–1965), Anglo-American poet, critic. *A Note on War Poetry*, st. 4.

25 Poetry is not a turning loose of emotion, but an escape from emotion; it is not the expression of personality, but an escape from personality. But, of course, only those who have personality and emotions know what it means to want to escape from these things.

> T. S. ELIOT (1888–1965), Anglo-American poet, critic. *Tradition and the Individual Talent*, sct. 1, in *Egoist* (London, Sept. and Dec. 1919; repr. in *Selected Prose of T. S. Eliot*, ed. by Frank Kermode, 1975).

26 We must believe that "emotion recollected in tranquillity" is an inexact formula. For it is neither emotion, nor recollection, nor without distortion of meaning, tranquillity. It is a concentration, and a new thing resulting from the concentration of a very great number of experiences which to the practical and active person would not seem to be experiences at all; it is a concentration which does not happen consciously or of deliberation. These experiences are not "recollected" and they finally unite in an atmosphere which is "tranquil" only in that it is a passive attending upon the event.

> T. S. ELIOT (1888–1965), Anglo-American poet, critic. "Tradition and the Individual Talent," sct. 2, in *Egoist* (London, Sept. and Dec. 1919; repr. in *Selected Prose of T. S. Eliot*, ed. by Frank Kermode, 1975). See below, for Wordsworth's original formulation of his theory of poetry.

27 Only poetry inspires poetry.

> RALPH WALDO EMERSON (1803–82), U.S. essayist, poet, philosopher. *Society and Solitude*, "Books" (1870).

28 Poetry is a mere drug, Sir.

> GEORGE FARQUHAR (1678–1707), Irish dramatist. Pamphlet, in *Love and a Bottle*, act 3, sc. 2.

29 The writing of a poem is like a child throwing stones into a mineshaft. You compose first, then you listen for the reverberation.

> JAMES FENTON (b. 1949), British poet, critic. *Ars Poetica*, no. 22, in *Independent on Sunday* (London, 24 June 1990).

30 Poetry is either something that lives like fire inside you—like music to the musician or Marxism to the Communist—or else it is nothing, an empty formalized bore around which pedants can endlessly drone their notes and explanations.

> F. SCOTT FITZGERALD (1896–1940), U.S. author. Letter, 3 Aug. 1940, to his daughter Frances Scott Fitzgerald (published in *The Letters of F. Scott Fitzgerald*, ed. by Andrew Turnbull, 1963).

31 Poetry is at least an elegance and at most a revelation.

> ROBERT FITZGERALD (1910–85), U.S. scholar, translator. *Writers at Work* (Eighth Series, ed. by George Plimpton, 1988).

32 A poem . . . begins as a lump in the throat, a sense of wrong, a homesickness, a lovesickness. . . . It finds the thought and the thought finds the words.

> ROBERT FROST (1874–1963), U.S. poet. Letter, 1 Jan. 1916, to poet and anthologist Louis Untermeyer (published in *The Letters of Robert Frost to Louis Untermeyer*, 1963).

33 Writing free verse is like playing tennis with the net down.

> ROBERT FROST (1874–1963), U.S. poet. Address, 17 May 1935, Milton Academy, Mass.

34 Poetry is a way of taking life by the throat.

> ROBERT FROST (1874–1963), U.S. poet. Quoted in: Elizabeth S. Sergeant, *Robert Frost: the Trial by Existence*, ch. 18 (1960).

35 Poetry is the language in which man explores his own amazement . . . says heaven and earth in one word . . . speaks of himself and his predicament as though for the first time. It has the virtue of being able to say twice as much as prose in half the time, and the drawback, if you do not give it your full attention, of seeming to say half as much in twice the time.

> CHRISTOPHER FRY (b. 1907), British playwright. *Time* (New York, 3 April 1950).

36 Between religion's "this is" and poetry's "but suppose *this* is," there must always be some kind of tension, until the possible and the actual meet at infinity.

> NORTHROP FRYE (1912–91), Canadian literary critic. *Anatomy of Criticism,* second essay, "Anagogic Phase: Symbol as Monad" (1957).

37 Just as a new scientific discovery manifests something that was already latent in the order of nature, and at the same time is logically related to the total structure of the existing science, so the new poem manifests something that was already latent in the order of words.

> NORTHROP FRYE (1912–91), Canadian literary critic. *Anatomy of Criticism,* second essay, "Mythical Phase: Symbol as Archetype" (1957).

38 I have a new method of poetry. All you got to do is look over your notebooks . . . or lay down on a couch, and think of anything that comes into your head, especially the miseries. . . . Then arrange in lines of two, three or four words each, don't bother about sentences, in sections of two, three or four lines each.

> ALLEN GINSBERG (b. 1926), U.S. poet. Letter, 1952, to Jack Kerouac and Neal Cassady (published in Barry Miles, *Ginsberg: A Biography,* ch. 5, 1989).

39 Poetry is not an expression of the party line. It's that time of night, lying in bed, thinking what you really think, making the private world public, that's what the poet does.

> ALLEN GINSBERG (b. 1926), U.S. poet. Quoted in: Barry Miles, *Ginsberg: A Biography,* ch. 17 (1989).

40 If there's no money in poetry, neither is there poetry in money.

> ROBERT GRAVES (1895–1985), British poet, novelist. Speech, 6 Dec. 1963, London School of Economics.

41 Poetry is emotion put into measure. The emotion must come by nature, but the measure can be acquired by art.

> THOMAS HARDY (1840–1928), English novelist, poet. Note written 1899. Quoted in: Florence Emily Hardy, *The Later Years of Thomas Hardy,* ch. 6 (1930).

42 Poetry is the universal language which the heart holds with nature and itself. He who has a contempt for poetry, cannot have much respect for himself, or for anything else.

> WILLIAM HAZLITT (1778–1830), English essayist. *Lectures on the English Poets,* "On Poetry in General" (1818).

43 The poetical impression of any object is that uneasy, exquisite sense of beauty or power that cannot be contained within itself; that is impatient of all limit; that (as flame bends to flame) strives to link itself to some other image of kindred beauty or grandeur; to enshrine itself, as it were, in the highest forms of fancy, and to relieve the aching sense of pleasure by expressing it in the boldest manner.

> WILLIAM HAZLITT (1778–1830), English essayist. *Lectures on the English Poets,* "On Poetry in General" (1818).

44 Poetry, even when apparently most fantastic, is always a revolt against artifice, a revolt, in a sense, against actuality.

> JAMES JOYCE (1882–1941), Irish author. "James Clarence Mangan," lecture, 15 Feb. 1902, University College, Dublin (first published 1902; repr. in *Critical Writings,* sct. 8, ed. by Ellsworth Mason and Richard Ellmann, 1959).

45 Poetry should be great and unobtrusive, a thing which enters into one's soul, and does not startle it or amaze it with itself, but with its subject.

> JOHN KEATS (1795–1821), English poet. Letter, 3 Feb. 1818 (published in *Letters of John Keats,* no. 44, ed. by Frederick Page, 1954).

46 Poetry should surprise by a fine excess and not by singularity—it should strike the reader as a wording of his own highest thoughts, and appear almost a remembrance.

> JOHN KEATS (1795–1821), English poet. Letter, 27 Feb. 1818 (published in *Letters of John Keats,* no. 51, ed. by Frederick Page, 1954).

47 When power leads man towards arrogance, poetry reminds him of his limitations. When power narrows the area of man's concern, poetry reminds him of the richness and diversity of existence. When power corrupts, poetry cleanses.

> JOHN F. KENNEDY (1917–63), U.S. Democratic politician, president. Last major public address, 26 Oct. 1963, at dedication of Robert Frost Library, Amherst College.

48 Prose on certain occasions can bear a great deal of poetry; on the other hand, poetry sinks and swoons under a moderate weight of prose.

> WALTER SAVAGE LANDOR (1775–1864), English author. *Imaginary Conversations,* "Archdeacon Hare and Walter Landor" (1824–29).

49 Perhaps no person can be a poet, or can even enjoy poetry, without a certain unsoundness of mind.

> THOMAS BABINGTON MACAULAY (1800–1859), English historian, Whig politician. "Milton," in *Edinburgh Review* (Aug. 1825; repr. in *Critical and Historical Essays,* 1843).

50 There is only beauty—and it has only one perfect expression—Poetry. All the rest is a lie—except for those who live by the body, love, and, that love of the mind, friendship. . . . For me, Poetry takes the place of love, because it is enamored of itself, and because its sensual delight falls back deliciously in my soul.

> STÉPHANE MALLARMÉ (1842–98), French Symbolist poet. Letter, 14 May 1867. Quoted in: Frederic Chase St. Aubyn, *Mallarmé,* ch. 1 (1969).

51 The poetic act consists of suddenly seeing that an idea splits up into a number of equal motifs and of grouping them; they rhyme.

> STÉPHANE MALLARMÉ (1842–98), French Symbolist poet. *Variations sur un sujet,* "Crise de Vers," in *La Revue Blanche* (Paris, Sept. 1895; repr. in *Mallarmé: The Poems,* ed. and tr. by Keith Bosley, 1977).

52 Writing a book of poetry is like dropping a rose petal down the Grand Canyon and waiting for the echo.

> DON MARQUIS (1878–1937), U.S. humorist, journalist. Quoted in: E. Anthony, *O Rare Don Marquis,* ch. 6 (1962). This aphorism emerged as the distillation of what had been a long piece on the futility of writing poetry for Don Marquis's "Sun Dial" column, which he rejected on the grounds of it being too much a plaint, publishing instead this one sentence.

53 Poetry is what Milton saw when he went blind.

> DON MARQUIS (1878–1937), U.S. humorist, journalist. Quoted in: E. Anthony, *O Rare Don Marquis*, ch. 11 (1962).

54 The crown of literature is poetry. It is its end and aim. It is the sublimest activity of the human mind. It is the achievement of beauty and delicacy. The writer of prose can only step aside when the poet passes.

> W. SOMERSET MAUGHAM (1874–1966), British author. *Saturday Review* (New York, 20 July 1957).

55 My verse
has brought me
no roubles to spare:
no craftsmen have made
mahogany chairs for my house.

> VLADIMIR MAYAKOVSKY (1893–1930), Russian poet, dramatist. *At the Top of My Voice* (tr. by George Reavey).

56 Most people ignore most poetry
because
most poetry ignores most people.

> ADRIAN MITCHELL (b. 1932), British poet, author. Epigraph to *Poems* (1964).

57 Poetry, that is to say the poetic, is a primal necessity.

> MARIANNE MOORE (1887–1972), U.S. poet. "Comment," in *Dial*, no. 81 (New York, Aug. 1926; repr. in *Complete Prose*, 1987).

58 I see no reason for calling my work poetry except that there is no other category in which to put it.

> MARIANNE MOORE (1887–1972), U.S. poet. On accepting the National Book Award for poetry. Quoted in: *New York Mirror* (31 May 1959).

59 I've never read a political poem that's accomplished anything. Poetry makes things happen, but rarely what the poet wants.

> HOWARD NEMEROV (1920–91), U.S. poet, novelist, critic. *International Herald Tribune* (Paris, 14 Oct. 1988).

60 Poetry has become the higher algebra of metaphors.

> JOSÉ ORTEGA Y GASSET (1883–1955), Spanish essayist, philosopher. *The Dehumanization of Art*, "More about the Dehumanization of Art" (1925).

61 Poetry is adolescence fermented, and thus preserved.

> JOSÉ ORTEGA Y GASSET (1883–1955), Spanish essayist, philosopher. "In Search of Goethe from Within," in *Partisan Review* (New Brunswick, N.J., Dec. 1949; repr. in *The Dehumanization of Art and Other Essays*, 1968).

62 It is no longer possible for lyric poetry to express the immensity of our experience. Life has grown too cumbersome, too complicated. We have acquired values which are best expressed in prose.

> BORIS PASTERNAK (1890–1960), Russian poet, novelist, translator. Interview in *Writers at Work* (Second Series, ed. by George Plimpton, 1963).

63 When in public poetry should take off its clothes and wave to the nearest person in sight; it should be seen in the company of thieves and lovers rather than that of journalists and publishers.

> BRIAN PATTEN (b. 1946), British poet. "Prosepoem Towards a Definition of Itself."

64 To read a poem is to hear it with our eyes; to hear it is to see it with our ears.

> OCTAVIO PAZ (b. 1914), Mexican poet. *Alternating Current*, "Recapitulations" (1967).

65 Colloquial poetry is to the real art as the barber's wax dummy is to sculpture.

> EZRA POUND (1885–1972), U.S. poet, critic. *Selected Prose 1909–1965*, pt. 1, "I Gather the Limbs of Osiris" (ed. by William Cookson, 1973).

66 In verse one can take any damn constant one likes, one can alliterate, or assone, or rhyme, or quant, or smack, only one MUST leave the other elements irregular.

> EZRA POUND (1885–1972), U.S. poet, critic. Letter, 30 July 1920, to Ford Madox Ford (published in *Pound/Ford: The Story of a Literary Friendship*, ed. by Brita Lindberg-Seyersted, 1982).

67 No verse is *libre* for the man who wants to do a good job.

> EZRA POUND (1885–1972), U.S. poet, critic. Interview in *Writers at Work* (Second Series, ed. by George Plimpton, 1963).

68 Poetry is a very complex art. . . . It is an art of pure sound bound in through an art of arbitrary and conventional symbols.

> EZRA POUND (1885–1972), U.S. poet, critic. *Selected Prose 1909–1965*, pt. 1, "I Gather the Limbs of Osiris" (ed. by William Cookson, 1973).

69 No one lives in this room
without confronting the whiteness of the wall
behind the poems, planks of books,
photographs of dead heroines.
Without contemplating last and late
the true nature of poetry. The drive
to connect. The dream of a common language.

> ADRIENNE RICH (b. 1929), U.S. poet. *Origins and History of Consciousness*, in *The Dream of a Common Language* (1978).

70 To a poet the mere making of a poem can seem to solve the problem of truth . . . but only a problem of art is solved in poetry.

> LAURA RIDING (1901–91), U.S. poet. Preface to *Selected Poems: In Five Sets* (1975).

71 I invented the colors of the vowels!—*A* black, *E* white, *I* red, *O* blue, *U* green—I made rules for the form and movement of each consonant, and, and with instinctive rhythms, I flattered myself that I had created a poetic language accessible, some day, to all the senses.

> ARTHUR RIMBAUD (1854–91), French poet. *Une Saison en Enfer*, "Délires II: Alchimie du Verbe" (1874; repr. in *Collected Poems*, ed. by Oliver Bernard, 1962).

72 Poetry is truth in its Sunday clothes.

> JOSEPH ROUX (1834–86), French priest, writer. *Meditations of a Parish Priest*, pt. 1, no. 76 (1886).

73 He who draws noble delights from the sentiments of poetry is a true poet, though he has never written a line in all his life.

> GEORGE SAND (1804–76), French novelist. *The Haunted Pool*, ch. 2 (1851).

74 Ordering a man to write a poem is like commanding a pregnant woman to give birth to a red-headed child.

CARL SANDBURG (1878–1967), U.S. poet. Quoted in: *The Reader's Digest* (Pleasantville, N.Y., Feb. 1978).

75 Every age has its own poetry; in every age the circumstances of history choose a nation, a race, a class to take up the torch by creating situations that can be expressed or transcended only through poetry.

JEAN-PAUL SARTRE (1905–80), French philosopher, author. *Anthologie de la Nouvelle Poésie Nègre et Malgache*, "Orphée Noir," Preface (1948).

76 Much is the force of heaven-bred poesy.

WILLIAM SHAKESPEARE (1564–1616), English dramatist, poet. The Duke of Milan, in *The Two Gentlemen of Verona*, act 3, sc. 2. In the Renaissance period, poetry, like love, was thought to be a divine *furor*.

77 Not marble nor the gilded monuments
Of princes shall outlive this powerful rhyme.

WILLIAM SHAKESPEARE (1564–1616), English dramatist, poet. *Sonnet 55*.

78 A story of particular facts is a mirror which obscures and distorts that which should be beautiful; poetry is a mirror which makes beautiful that which it distorts.

PERCY BYSSHE SHELLEY (1792–1822), English poet. *A Defence of Poetry* (written 1821; published 1840).

79 Poetry is a sword of lightning, ever unsheathed, which consumes the scabbard that would contain it.

PERCY BYSSHE SHELLEY (1792–1822), English poet. *A Defence of Poetry* (written 1821; published 1840).

80 Poetry lifts the veil from the hidden beauty of the world, and makes familiar objects be as if they were not familiar.

PERCY BYSSHE SHELLEY (1792–1822), English poet. *A Defence of Poetry* (written 1821; published 1840).

81 If poetry should address itself to the same needs and aspirations, the same hopes and fears, to which the Bible addresses itself, it might rival it in distribution.

WALLACE STEVENS (1879–1955), U.S. poet. *The Necessary Angel*, "Imagination as Value" (1951; first published 1949).

82 A poem need not have a meaning and like most things in nature often does not have.

WALLACE STEVENS (1879–1955), U.S. poet. *Opus Posthumous*, "Adagia" (1959).

83 Poetry is the supreme fiction, madame.

WALLACE STEVENS (1879–1955), U.S. poet. *A High-Toned Old Christian Woman*.

84 One merit of poetry few persons will deny: it says more and in fewer words than prose.

VOLTAIRE (1694–1778), French philosopher, author. *Dictionnaire Philosophique*, "Poets" (1764).

85 The United States themselves are essentially the greatest poem.

WALT WHITMAN (1819–92), U.S. poet. Preface to *Leaves of Grass* (1855).

86 All bad poetry springs from genuine feeling. To be natural is to be obvious, and to be obvious is to be inartistic.

OSCAR WILDE (1854–1900), Anglo-Irish playwright, author. Gilbert, in *The Critic as Artist*, pt. 2 (published in *Intentions*, 1891).

87 We have been able to have fine poetry in England because the public do not read it, and consequently do not influence it. The public like to insult poets because they are individual, but once they have insulted them, they leave them alone.

OSCAR WILDE (1854–1900), Anglo-Irish playwright, author. *The Soul of Man under Socialism*, in *Fortnightly Review* (London, Feb. 1891; repr. 1895).

88 I want the concentration & the romance, & the words all glued together, fused, glowing: have no time to waste any more on prose.

VIRGINIA WOOLF (1882–1941), British novelist. *The Diary of Virginia Woolf*, vol. 2 (ed. by Anne O. Bell, 1978), entry for 15 Aug. 1924.

89 Yet, it is true, poetry is delicious; the best prose is that which is most full of poetry.

VIRGINIA WOOLF (1882–1941), British novelist. *The Common Reader*, "Montaigne" (First Series, 1925).

90 All good poetry is the spontaneous overflow of powerful feelings: it takes its origin from emotion recollected in tranquillity.

WILLIAM WORDSWORTH (1770–1850), English poet. Preface to *Lyrical Ballads* (2nd ed., 1801). This sentiment, which is a central tenet in Wordsworth's criticism, has parallels in Schiller, *Über Bürgers Gedichte*, as well as Coleridge, *Notebooks*, in which he speaks of "recalling passion in tranquillity."

91 All things can tempt me from this craft of verse:
One time it was a woman's face, or worse—
The seeming needs of my fool-driven land.

W. B. YEATS (1865–1939), Irish poet, playwright. *All Things Can Tempt Me*.

92 We make out of the quarrel with others, rhetoric, but of the quarrel with ourselves, poetry.

W. B. YEATS (1865–1939), Irish poet, playwright. *Essays*, "Anima Hominis," sct. 5 (1924).

See also Graves on AWARDS; MacLeish on FOOTBALL; Brodsky on INFINITY; Vico on METAPHYSICS; Auden on MUSIC; Pound on PARADISE; Byron on POETS; Hamilton on TRAGEDY; Frost, Shelley on TRANSLATIONS; Yeats on WORDS.

POETS

1 Poets . . . are the only people to whom love is not only a crucial, but an indispensable experience, which entitles them to mistake it for a universal one.

HANNAH ARENDT (1906–75), German-born U.S. political philosopher. *The Human Condition*, "Action," footnote to ch. 33 (1958).

2 Earth receive an honoured guest:
William Yeats is laid to rest.
Let the Irish vessel lie
Emptied of its poetry.

W. H. AUDEN (1907–73), Anglo-American poet. *In Memory of W. B. Yeats*.

3 Every American poet feels that the whole responsibility for contemporary poetry has fallen upon his shoulders, that he is a literary aristocracy of one.

> W. H. AUDEN (1907–73), Anglo-American poet. *Faber Book of Modern American Verse*, Introduction (1956).

4 It is a sad fact about our culture that a poet can earn much more money writing or talking about his art than he can by practicing it.

> W. H. AUDEN (1907–73), Anglo-American poet. Opening words of Foreword to *The Dyer's Hand* (1962).

5 You will be a poet because you will always be humiliated.

> W. H. AUDEN (1907–73), Anglo-American poet. Remark remembered by poet Stephen Spender in *Journals 1939–1983* (1985), entry for 11 April 1979, reminiscing on his first meeting with Auden at Oxford.

6 A poet is a combination of an instrument and a human being in one person, with the former gradually taking over the latter. The sensation of this takeover is responsible for timbre; the realization of it, for destiny.

> JOSEPH BRODSKY (b. 1940), Russian-born U.S. poet, critic. *Less Than One: Selected Essays*, "A Poet and Prose," sct. 2 (1986; first published 1979).

7 Every individual ought to know at least one poet from cover to cover: if not as a guide through the world, then as a yardstick for the language.

> JOSEPH BRODSKY (b. 1940), Russian-born U.S. poet, critic. *Less Than One: Selected Essays*, "To Please a Shadow," sct. 5 (1986; first published 1983). Brodsky recommended W. H. Auden as qualified on both counts.

8 For the poet the credo or doctrine is not the point of arrival but is, on the contrary, the point of departure for the metaphysical journey.

> JOSEPH BRODSKY (b. 1940), Russian-born U.S. poet, critic. Interview in *Writers at Work* (Eighth Series, ed. by George Plimpton, 1988).

9 What's this, Aurora Leigh,
You write so of the poets and not laugh?
Those virtuous liars, dreamers after dark,
Exaggerators of the sun and moon,
And soothsayers in a tea-cup? I write so
Of the only speakers of essential truth,
Opposed to relative, comparative,
And temporal truths; . . .
The only teachers who instruct mankind,
From just a shadow on a charnel-wall.

> ELIZABETH BARRETT BROWNING (1806–61), English poet. *Aurora Leigh*, bk. 1 (1857).

10 Nay, if there's room for poets in this world
A little overgrown (I think there is),
Their sole work is to represent the age,
Their age, not Charlemagne's,—this live,
    throbbing age.
That brawls, cheats, maddens, calculates, aspires,
And spends more passion, more heroic heat,
Betwixt the mirrors of its drawing-rooms,
Than Roland with his knights.

> ELIZABETH BARRETT BROWNING (1806–61), English poet. *Aurora Leigh*, bk. 5 (1857).

11 Some rhyme a neebor's name to lash;
Some rhyme (vain thought!) for needfu' cash;
Some rhyme to court the country clash,
An' raise a din;
For me, an aim I never fash;
I rhyme for fun.

> ROBERT BURNS (1759–96), Scottish poet. *Epistle to James Smith*.

12 I can never get people to understand that poetry is the expression of *excited passion*, and that there is no such thing as a life of passion any more than a continuous earthquake, or an eternal fever. Besides, who would ever *shave* themselves in such a state?

> LORD BYRON (1788–1824), English poet. Letter, 5 July 1821, to the poet Thomas Moore, of the reactions of an American visitor. Quoted in: Moore's biography of Byron (1830; repr. in Doris Langley Moore, *The Late Lord Byron*, ch. 8, 1961, rev. 1976).

13 Many are poets but without the name,
For what is poesy but to create
From overfeeling good or ill; and aim
At an external life beyond our fate,
And be the new Prometheus of new men.

> LORD BYRON (1788–1824), English poet. *The Prophecy of Dante*, cto. 4.

14 They raise their minds by brooding over and embellishing their sufferings, from one degree of fervid exaltation and dreary greatness to another, till at length they run amuck entirely, and whoever meets them would do well to run them thro' the body.

> THOMAS CARLYLE (1795–1881), Scottish essayist, historian. Letter, 28 Jan. 1821 (published in *Collected Letters of Thomas and Jane Welsh Carlyle*, vol. 1, 1970–81), referring specifically to the Romantics.

15 Modesty, 'tis a virtue not often found among poets, for almost every one of them thinks himself the greatest in the world.

> MIGUEL DE CERVANTES (1547–1616), Spanish writer. Don Quixote, in *Don Quixote*, pt. 2, bk. 5, ch. 18 (1615; tr. by P. Motteux).

16 Poets don't draw. They unravel their handwriting and then tie it up again, but differently.

> JEAN COCTEAU (1889–1963), French author, filmmaker. *Dessins* (1924). Quoted in: Pierre Chanel, "A Thousand Flashes of Genius," in *Jean Cocteau and the French Scene* (1984).

17 The worst tragedy for a poet is to be admired through being misunderstood.

> JEAN COCTEAU (1889–1963), French author, filmmaker. *Le Rappel à l'Ordre*, "Le Coq et l'Arlequin" (repr. in *Collected Works*, vol. 9, 1950).

18 No man was ever yet a great poet, without being at the same time a profound philosopher.

> SAMUEL TAYLOR COLERIDGE (1772–1834), English poet, critic. *Biographia Literaria*, ch. 15 (1817).

19 A young Apollo, golden-haired,
Stands dreaming on the verge of strife,
Magnificently unprepared
For the long littleness of life.

> FRANCES CORNFORD (1886–1960), British poet. *Rupert Brooke*, on poet Rupert Brooke.

20 If a poet is anybody, he is somebody to whom things made matter very little—somebody who is obsessed by Making.

> E. E. CUMMINGS (1894–1962), U.S. poet. Foreword to *is 5* (1926).

21 Look at this poet William Carlos Williams: he is primitive and native, and his roots are in raw forest and violent places; he is word-sick and place-crazy. He admires strength, but for what? Violence! This is the cult of the frontier mind.

> EDWARD DAHLBERG (1900–1977), U.S. author, critic. *Alms for Oblivion,* "Word-Sick And Place-Crazy" (1964).

22 The earnings of a poet could be reckoned by a metaphysician rather than a bookkeeper.

> EDWARD DAHLBERG (1900–1977), U.S. author, critic. *Alms for Oblivion,* "For Sale" (1964).

23 The bad poet is a toady mimicking nature.

> EDWARD DAHLBERG (1900–1977), U.S. author, critic. *The Carnal Myth,* ch. 5 (1968).

24 They who in folly or mere greed
Enslaved religion, markets, laws,
Borrow our language now and bid
Us to speak up in freedom's cause.

> C. DAY LEWIS (1904–72), British poet, author. *Where Are the War Poets?,* st. 1.

25 The poet . . . like the lover . . . is a person unable to reconcile what he knows with what he feels. His peculiarity is that he is under a certain compulsion to do so.

> BABETTE DEUTSCH (1895–1982), U.S. poet, critic. "Poetry at the Mid-Century," in *The Writers Book* (ed. by Helen Hull, 1950).

26 No man ever walked down to posterity with so small a book under his arm.

> CHARLES DICKENS (1812–70), English novelist. Quoted in: Hesketh Pearson, *Dickens,* ch. 20 (1949), of poet Thomas Gray.

27 When shall we see poets born? After a time of disasters and great misfortunes, when harrowed nations begin to breathe again. And then, shaken by the terror of such spectacles, imaginations will paint things entirely strange to those who have not witnessed them.

> DENIS DIDEROT (1713–84), French philosopher. *On Dramatic Poetry* (1758; repr. in *Selected Writings,* ed. by Lester G. Crocker, 1966).

28 I am two fools, I know,
For loving, and for saying so
In whining Poetry.

> JOHN DONNE (c. 1572–1631), English divine, metaphysical poet. *The Triple Fool.*

29 Chaucer was a class traitor
Shakespeare hated the mob
Donne sold out a bit later
Sidney was a nob.

> TERRY EAGLETON (b. 1943), British critic. *Against The Grain,* ch. 14, "The Ballad of English Literature" (1986; to the tune of *Land of Hope and Glory*).

30 To be a poet is to have a soul so quick to discern, that no shade of quality escapes it, and so quick to feel, that discernment is but a hand playing with finely-ordered variety on the chords of emotion—a soul in which knowledge passes instantaneously into feeling, and feeling flashes back as a new organ of knowledge. One may have that condition by fits only.

> GEORGE ELIOT (1819–80), English novelist. Will Ladislaw, in *Middlemarch,* bk. 2, ch. 22 (1871–72).

31 The bad poet is usually unconscious where he ought to be conscious, and conscious where he ought to be unconscious.

> T. S. ELIOT (1888–1965), Anglo-American poet, critic. "Tradition and the Individual Talent," sct. 2, in *Egoist* (London, Sept. and Dec. 1919; repr. in *Selected Prose of T. S. Eliot,* ed. by Frank Kermode, 1975).

32 The business of the poet is not to find new emotions, but to use the ordinary ones and, in working them up into poetry, to express feelings which are not in actual emotions at all.

> T. S. ELIOT (1888–1965), Anglo-American poet, critic. "Tradition and the Individual Talent," sct. 2, in *Egoist* (London, Sept. and Dec. 1919; repr. in *Selected Prose of T. S. Eliot,* ed. by Frank Kermode, 1975).

33 Constantly risking absurdity
and death
whenever he performs
above the heads
of his audience
the poet like an acrobat
climbs on rime
to a high wire of his own making.

> LAWRENCE FERLINGHETTI (b. 1919), U.S. poet, publisher. *A Coney Island of the Mind,* sct. 15 (1958).

34 Is encouragement what the poet needs? Open question. Maybe he needs discouragement. In fact, quite a few of them need more discouragement, the most discouragement possible.

> ROBERT FITZGERALD (1910–85), U.S. scholar, translator. Interview in *Writers at Work* (Eighth Series, ed. by George Plimpton, 1988).

35 No wonder poets sometimes have to *seem*
So much more business-like than business men.
Their wares are so much harder to get rid of.

> ROBERT FROST (1874–1963), U.S. poet. *New Hampshire.*

36 He repeated until his dying day that there was no one with more common sense, no stonecutter more obstinate, no manager more lucid or dangerous, than a poet.

> GABRIEL GARCÍA MÁRQUEZ (b. 1928), Colombian writer. *Love in the Time of Cholera* (1985; tr. 1988, p. 168).

37 Could a man live by it, it were not unpleasant employment to be a poet.

> OLIVER GOLDSMITH (1728–74), Anglo-Irish playwright, author. Letter, Feb. 1759, to his brother Henry Goldsmith.

38 To be a poet is a condition rather than a profession.

> ROBERT GRAVES (1895–1985), British poet, novelist. Reply to questionnaire, "The Cost of Letters," in *Horizon* (London, Sept. 1946).

39 Nine-tenths of English poetic literature is the result either of vulgar careerism or of a poet trying to keep his hand in. Most poets are dead by their late twenties.

ROBERT GRAVES (1895–1985), British poet, novelist. Quoted in: *Observer* (London, 11 Nov. 1962).

40 My opinion is that a poet should express the emotion of all the ages and the thought of his own.

THOMAS HARDY (1840–1928), English novelist, poet. Remark, 1918. Quoted in: Florence Emily Hardy, *The Later Years of Thomas Hardy,* ch. 15 (1930).

41 He is to the great poet, what an excellent mimic is to a great actor. There is no determinate impression left on the mind by reading his poetry. . . . A great mind is one that moulds the minds of others.

WILLIAM HAZLITT (1778–1830), English essayist. *Lectures on the English Poets,* "On the Living Poets" (1818), of Sir Walter Scott.

42 He indeed cloys with sweetness; he obscures with splendour; he fatigues with gaiety. We are stifled on beds of roses.

WILLIAM HAZLITT (1778–1830), English essayist. *The Spirit of the Age,* "Mr. T. Moore—Mr. Leigh Hunt" (1825), of the poet Thomas Moore.

43 The poet's place, it seems to me, is with the Mr. Hydes of human nature.

ALDOUS HUXLEY (1894–1963), British author. Do What You Will, "Wordsworth in the Tropics" (1929). See Huxley on ARTISTS.

44 Happy you poets who can be present and *so* present by a simple flicker of your genius, and not, like the clumsier race, have to lay a train and pile up faggots that may not after prove in the least combustible!

HENRY JAMES (1843–1916), U.S. author. Letter, 25 Aug. 1915, to poet W. B. Yeats, from private collection. This passage was later incorporated into Yeats's poem, "In Memory of Major Robert Gregory."

45 In this nadir of poetic repute, when the only verse that most people read from one year's end to the next is what appears on greetings cards, it is well for us to stop and consider our poets. . . . Poets are the leaven in the lump of civilization.

ELIZABETH JANEWAY (b. 1913), U.S. author and critic. *The Writer's Book,* ch. 30 (ed. by Helen Hull, 1950).

46 I should tell you that honestly, on my honour of a Nearwicked, I always think in a wordsworth's of that primed favourite continental poet, Daunty, Gouty and Shopkeeper, A. G., whom the generality admoyers in this that is and that this is to come.

JAMES JOYCE (1882–1941), Irish author. *Finnegans Wake,* pt. 3 (1939).

47 With a great poet the sense of Beauty overcomes every other consideration, or rather obliterates all consideration.

JOHN KEATS (1795–1821), English poet. Letter, 21 Dec. 1817, to his brothers George and Thomas Keats (published in *Letters of John Keats,* no. 32, ed. by Frederick Page, 1954).

48 What is a poet? An unhappy person who conceals profound anguish in his heart but whose lips are so

formed that as sighs and cries pass over them they sound like beautiful music.

SØREN KIERKEGAARD (1813–55), Danish philosopher. Opening lines of *Either/Or,* vol. 1, "Diapsalmata" (1843; tr. 1987).

49 It is a curious thing how poets tend to become ascetics. . . . Even a debauch for them is a self-flagellation. They go on the loose in cruelty against themselves, admitting that they are pandering to, and despising, the lower self.

D. H. LAWRENCE (1885–1930), British author. Letter, 31 Oct. 1913 (published in *The Letters of D. H. Lawrence,* vol. 2, ed. by George J. Zytaruk and James T. Boulton, 1981).

50 It seems to me a purely lyric poet gives himself, right down to his sex, to his mood, utterly and abandonedly, whirls himself round . . . till he spontaneously combusts into verse. He has nothing that goes on, no passion, only a few intense moods, separate like odd stars, and when each has burned away, he must die.

D. H. LAWRENCE (1885–1930), British author. Letter, 2 Dec. 1913 (published in *The Letters of D. H. Lawrence,* vol. 2, ed. by George J. Zytaruk and James T. Boulton, 1981).

51 The Helicon of too many poets is not a hill crowned with sunshine and visited by the Muses and the Graces, but an old, mouldering house, full of gloom and haunted by ghosts.

HENRY WADSWORTH LONGFELLOW (1807–82), U.S. poet. "Table-Talk," in *Drift-Wood* (ed. 1857; repr. in *Complete Works,* vol. 1, 1886).

52 He who, in an enlightened and literary society, aspires to be a great poet, must first become a little child. He must take to pieces the whole web of his mind. He must unlearn much of that knowledge which has perhaps constituted hitherto his chief title to superiority. His very talents will be a hindrance to him.

THOMAS BABINGTON MACAULAY (1800–1859), English historian. "Milton," in *Edinburgh Review* (Aug. 1825; repr. in *Critical and Historical Essays,* 1843).

53 His imagination resembled the wings of an ostrich. It enabled him to run, though not to soar.

THOMAS BABINGTON MACAULAY (1800–1859), English historian. "John Dryden," in *Edinburgh Review* (Jan. 1828; repr. in *Critical and Historical Essays,* 1843), of Dryden.

54 Auden, MacNeice, Day Lewis, I have read them all,
Hoping against hope to hear the authentic call . . .
And know the explanation I must pass is this
—You cannot light a match on a crumbling wall.

HUGH MACDIARMID (1892–1978), Scottish poet, critic. *British Leftist Poetry, 1930–1940.*

55 Poets . . . are literal-minded men who will squeeze a word till it hurts.

ARCHIBALD MACLEISH (1892–1982), U.S. poet. "Apologia," in *Harvard Law Review* (Cambridge, June 1972; repr. in *Riders on Earth* as "Art and Law," 1978).

56 The poet begins where the man ends. The man's lot is to live his human life, the poet's to invent what is nonexistent.

JOSÉ ORTEGA Y GASSET (1883–1955), Spanish essayist,

philosopher. *The Dehumanization of Art,* "More about the Dehumanization of Art" (1925).

57 Poets utter great and wise things which they do not themselves understand.

> PLATO (c. 427–347 B.C.), Greek philosopher. *The Republic,* bk. 2, sct. 5.

58 Cibber! write all thy Verses upon Glasses,
The only way to save 'em from our Arses.

> ALEXANDER POPE (1688–1744), English satirical poet. *Epigrams Occasioned by Cibber's Verses in Praise of Nash,* no. 2. Colley Cibber, dramatist and poet (1671–1757), was Poet Laureate for 27 years from 1730, and is generally considered one of the worst poets to hold the office, admitting himself that he was given the post principally for being a good Whig.

59 Sir, I admit your general rule,
That every poet is a fool,
But you yourself may serve to show it,
That every fool is not a poet.

> ALEXANDER POPE (1688–1744), English satirical poet. *Epigram from the French.*

60 I
Am here a Poet, that doth drink of life
As lesser men drink wine.

> EZRA POUND (1885–1972), U.S. poet, critic. *And Thus in Nineveh.*

61 In case I conk out, this is provisionally what I have to do: I must clarify obscurities; I must make clearer definite ideas or dissociations. I must find a verbal formula to combat the rise of brutality—the principle of order versus the split atom.

> EZRA POUND (1885–1972), U.S. poet, critic. Interview in *Writers at Work* (Second Series, ed. by George Plimpton, 1963).

62 Narrowed-down by her early editors and anthologists, reduced to quaintness or spinsterish oddity by many of her commentators, sentimentalized, fallen-in-love with like some gnomic Garbo, still unread in the breadth and depth of her full range of work, she was, and is, a wonder to me when I try to imagine myself into that mind.

> ADRIENNE RICH (b. 1929), U.S. poet. "Vesuvius at Home: The Power of Emily Dickinson," in *Parnassus: Poetry in Review* (New York, Fall-Winter 1976; repr. in *On Lies, Secrets, and Silence,* 1980), of Emily Dickinson.

63 The poet makes himself a *seer* by a long, prodigious, and rational *disordering* of *all the senses.* Every form of love, of suffering, of madness; he searches himself, he consumes all the poisons in him, and keeps only their quintessences.

> ARTHUR RIMBAUD (1854–91), French poet. Letter, 15 May 1871 (published in *Collected Poems,* ed. by Oliver Bernard, 1962).

64 A poet's work is to name the unnameable, to point at frauds, to take sides, start arguments, shape the world, and stop it going to sleep.

> SALMAN RUSHDIE (b. 1947), Indian-born British author. Quoted in: *Independent* (London, 18 Feb. 1989).

65 The poet must be free to love or hate as the spirit moves him, free to change, free to be a chameleon, free to be an *enfant terrible.* He must above all never worry about his effect on other people. Power requires that one do just that all the time. Power requires that the inner person never be unmasked. No, we poets have to go naked. And since this is so, it is better that we stay private people; a naked public person would be rather ridiculous, what?

> MAY SARTON (b. 1912), U.S. poet, novelist. Hilary Stevens, in *Mrs. Stevens Hears the Mermaids Singing,* pt. 2 (1965).

66 Write till your ink be dry, and with your tears
Moist it again, and frame some feeling line
That may discover such integrity.

> WILLIAM SHAKESPEARE (1564–1616), English dramatist, poet. Proteus, in *The Two Gentlemen of Verona,* act 3, sc. 2, giving advice to Thurio.

67 That is what all poets do: they talk to themselves out loud; and the world overhears them. But it's horribly lonely not to hear someone else talk sometimes.

> GEORGE BERNARD SHAW (1856–1950), Anglo-Irish playwright, critic. Marchbanks, in *Candida,* act 2.

68 After Shelley, Byron and Scott, you know, one cannot care about other poets.

> HELLEN SHELLEY (1799–c. 1870), sister of Percy Bysshe Shelley. Remark at dinner with William Allingham. Quoted in: *Diaries of William Allingham,* ch. 6 (1907), entry for 29 Oct. 1864.

69 A poet, as he is the author to others of the highest wisdom, pleasure, virtue, and glory, so he ought personally to be the happiest, the best, the wisest, and the most illustrious of men.

> PERCY BYSSHE SHELLEY (1792–1822), English poet. *A Defence of Poetry* (written 1821; published 1840).

70 A poet is a nightingale, who sits in darkness and sings to cheer its own solitude with sweet sounds; his auditors are as men entranced by the melody of an unseen musician, who feel that they are moved and softened, yet know not whence or why.

> PERCY BYSSHE SHELLEY (1792–1822), English poet. *A Defence of Poetry* (written 1821; published 1840).

71 Poets are the hierophants of an unapprehended inspiration; the mirrors of the gigantic shadows which futurity casts upon the present; the words which express what they understand not; the trumpets which sing to battle and feel not what they inspire; the influence which is moved not, but moves. Poets are the unacknowledged legislators of the world.

> PERCY BYSSHE SHELLEY (1792–1822), English poet. Last words of *A Defence of Poetry* (written 1821; published 1840). In his *History of Rasselas,* ch. 10 (1759), Samuel Johnson similarly wrote that the poet "must write as the interpreter of nature, and the legislator of mankind, and consider himself as presiding over the thoughts and manners of future generations." In our own century, W. H. Auden wrote—in *The Dyer's Hand*—"'The unacknowledged legislators of the world' describes the secret police, not the poets."

72 So I soon made up my mind about the poets too: I decided that it was not wisdom that enabled them to write their poetry, but a kind of instinct or inspiration, such as you find in seers and prophets who deliver all their sublime messages without knowing in the least what they mean.

> SOCRATES (469–399 B.C.), Greek philosopher. Quoted in: Plato, *Apology,* sct. 21.

73   What poet would not grieve to see
His brother write as well as he?
But rather than they should excel,
He'd wish his rivals all in Hell.

> JONATHAN SWIFT (1667–1745), Anglo-Irish satirist. *Verses on the Death of Dr. Swift.*

74   At a time when pimpery, lick-spittlery, and picking the public's pocket are the order of the day—indeed, officially proclaimed as virtue—the poet must play the madcap to keep his balance. And ours.

> STUDS TERKEL (b. 1912), U.S. author, broadcaster. *Talking to Myself,* bk. 4, ch. 4 (1977), said of author Nelson Algren.

75   The poet is a man who lives at last by watching his moods. An old poet comes at last to watch his moods as narrowly as a cat does a mouse.

> HENRY DAVID THOREAU (1817–62), U.S. philosopher, author, naturalist. *Journals* (1906), entry for 28 Aug. 1851.

76   A farmer, a hunter, a soldier, a reporter, even a philosopher, may be daunted; but nothing can deter a poet, for he is actuated by pure love. Who can predict his comings and goings? His business calls him out at all hours, even when doctors sleep.

> HENRY DAVID THOREAU (1817–62), U.S. philosopher, author, naturalist. *Walden,* "Winter Visitors" (1854).

77   I hate the whole race . . . . There is no believing a word they say—your professional poets, I mean—there never existed a more worthless set than Byron and his friends for example.

> DUKE OF WELLINGTON (1769–1852), English soldier, prime minister. Quoted in: Lady Salisbury's diary, 26 Oct. 1833.

78   I sound my barbaric yawp over the roofs of the world.

> WALT WHITMAN (1819–92), U.S. poet. *Song of Myself,* sct. 52, in *Leaves of Grass* (1855).

79   The proof of a poet is that his country absorbs him as affectionately as he has absorbed it.

> WALT WHITMAN (1819–92), U.S. poet. *Leaves of Grass,* Preface (1855).

80   The poet is the supreme artist, for he is the master of colour and of form, and the real musician besides, and is lord over all life and all arts.

> OSCAR WILDE (1854–1900), Anglo-Irish playwright, author. "Mr. Whistler's Ten O'Clock," in *Pall Mall Gazette* (London, 21 Feb. 1885).

81   Good artists exist simply in what they make, and consequently are perfectly uninteresting in what they are. A really great poet is the most unpoetical of all creatures. But inferior poets are absolutely fascinating. The worse their rhymes are, the more picturesque they look. The mere fact of having published a book of second-rate sonnets makes a man quite irresistible. He lives the poetry that he cannot write. The others write the poetry that they dare not realise.

> OSCAR WILDE (1854–1900), Anglo-Irish playwright, author. Lord Henry, in *The Picture of Dorian Gray,* ch. 4 (1891).

82   Personality must be accepted for what it is. You mustn't mind that a poet is a drunk, rather that drunks are not always poets.

> OSCAR WILDE (1854–1900), Anglo-Irish playwright, author.

Quoted in: Richard Ellman, *Oscar Wilde,* ch. 21 (1987), of poet Ernest Dowson.

83   You know what? Poets are being pursued by the philosophers today out of the poverty of philosophy. God damn it, you might think a man had no business to be writing, to be a poet unless some philosophic stinker gave him permission.

> WILLIAM CARLOS WILLIAMS (1883–1963), U.S. poet. Letter, 14 Jan. 1944, to James Laughlin (published in *William Carlos Williams and James Laughlin—Selected Letters,* ed. by H. Witemeyer, 1989).

84   We poets in our youth begin in gladness;
But thereof comes in the end despondency and madness.

> WILLIAM WORDSWORTH (1770–1850), English poet. *Resolution and Independence,* st. 7.

85   Irish poets, learn your trade,
Sing whatever is well made,
Scorn the sort now growing up
All out of shape from toe to top.

> W. B. YEATS (1865–1939), Irish poet. *Under Ben Bulben,* sct. 5 (written five months before Yeats's death)

See also Whitman on AUDIENCES; BYRON; SAMUEL TAYLOR COLERIDGE; Hardy on CUSTOM; DANTE; Johnson on DULLNESS; Wilde on IRELAND AND THE IRISH; JOHN KEATS; Auden, Brodsky on LITERATURE AND SOCIETY; JOHN MILTON; Stevens on PHILOSOPHERS; Dryden on PLAGIARISM; EZRA POUND; Wilde on PUBLISHING AND PUBLISHERS; WILLIAM SHAKESPEARE; PERCY BYSSHE SHELLEY; Shelley on SIN; Pound on VENICE; Yeats on WAR; WALT WHITMAN; Rimbaud, Wolfe on WOMEN AND THE ARTS; WILLIAM WORDSWORTH; Auden on WRITERS.

POLAND AND THE POLISH

1   It is often said that Poland is a country where there is anti-semitism and no Jews, which is pathology in its purest state.

> BRONISLAW GEREMEK (b. 1932), Polish politician, historian. *International Herald Tribune* (Paris, 17 Feb. 1992).

2   In Poland a man must be one thing: white or black, here or there, with us or against us—clearly, openly, without hesitations. . . . We lack the liberal, democratic tradition rich in all its gradations. We have instead the tradition of struggle: the extreme situation, the final gesture.

> RYSZARD KAPUSCINSKI (b. 1932), Polish journalist. "A Warsaw Diary," in *Granta,* no. 15 (Cambridge, England, 1985).

3   The Poles do not know how to hate, thank God.

> CARDINAL STEFAN WYSZYNSKI (1901–81), Primate of Poland, archbishop. Quoted in: *Observer* (London, 8 June 1986).

4   Poverty was an ornament on a learned man like a red ribbon on a white horse.

> ANZIA YEZIERSKA (c. 1881–1970), Polish author. *Red Ribbon on a White Horse,* ch. 9 (1950), of Poland, in letter from Boruch Shlomoe Mayer to Anzia Yezierska.

THE POLICE

1   He may be a very nice man. But I haven't got the time to figure that out. All I know is, he's got a uniform and a gun and I have to relate to him that way. That's the only way to relate to him because one of us may have to die.

JAMES BALDWIN (1924–87), U.S. author. *A Dialogue* (1973; with Nikki Giovanni), said of the police in a conversation in London, 4 Nov. 1971.

2   A *functioning* police state needs no police.

WILLIAM BURROUGHS (b. 1914), U.S. author. Dr. Benway, in *The Naked Lunch*, "Benway" (1959).

3   A really good detective never gets married.

RAYMOND CHANDLER (1888–1959), U.S. author. "Casual Notes on the Mystery Novel" (1949; first published in *Raymond Chandler Speaking*, 1962).

4   However low a man sinks he never reaches the level of the police.

QUENTIN CRISP (b. 1908), British author. *The Naked Civil Servant*, ch. 12 (1968).

5   There is nothing more unaesthetic than a policeman.

SIR ARTHUR CONAN DOYLE (1859–1930), English author. Thaddeus Sholto, in *The Sign of Four*, ch. 4 (1889).

6   We now in the United States have more security guards for the rich than we have police services for the poor districts. If you're looking for personal security, far better to move to the suburbs than to pay taxes in New York.

JOHN KENNETH GALBRAITH (b. 1908), U.S. economist. *Guardian* (London, 23 May 1992).

7   With their souls of patent leather,
they come down the road.
Hunched and nocturnal,
Where they breathe they impose,
silence of dark rubber,
and fear of fine sand.

FEDERICO GARCÍA LORCA (1898–1936), Spanish poet, playwright. *Romance de la Guardia Civil Española*.

8   I'm not against the police; I'm just afraid of them.

ALFRED HITCHCOCK (1899–1980), Anglo-American filmmaker. Quoted in: *New Society* (London, 10 May 1984).

9   If it were possible to make an accurate calculation of the evils which police regulations occasion, and of those which they prevent, the number of the former would, in all cases, exceed that of the latter.

KARL WILHELM VON HUMBOLDT (1767–1835), German statesman, philologist. *The Limits of State Action*, ch. 8 (1792; repr. 1854; tr. and ed. by J. W. Burrow, 1969).

10   Every society gets the kind of criminal it deserves. What is equally true is that every community gets the kind of law enforcement it insists on.

ROBERT KENNEDY (1925–68), U.S. Attorney General, Democratic politician. *The Pursuit of Justice*, pt. 3, "Eradicating Free Enterprise in Organized Crime" (1964).

11   At one time my only wish was to be a police official. It seemed to me to be an occupation for my sleepless intriguing mind. I had the idea that there, among criminals, were people to fight: clever, vigorous, crafty fellows. Later I realized that it was good that I did not

become one, for most police cases involve misery and wretchedness—not crimes and scandals.

SØREN KIERKEGAARD (1813–55), Danish philosopher. *Journals and Papers*, vol. 5, entry no. 6016 (ed. by Howard V. Hong and Edna H. Hong, 1978). Kierkegaard found his vocation instead as—in his words—"a spy in the service of the highest."

12   Policemen so cherish their status as keepers of the peace and protectors of the public that they have occasionally been known to beat to death those citizens or groups who question that status.

DAVID MAMET (b. 1947), U.S. playwright. *Writing in Restaurants*, "Some Thoughts on Writing in Restaurants" (1986).

13   Rain is the best policeman.

POLICE MOTTO.

14   The art of the police is not to see what it is useless that it should see.

NAPOLEON BONAPARTE (1769–1821), French general, emperor. Letter, 24 May 1800.

15   As far as I can see, the Polis as Polis, in this city, is Null an' Void!

SEAN O'CASEY (1884–1964), Irish dramatist. Mrs. Madigan, of Dublin during the Irish Civil War in 1922, in *Juno and the Paycock*, act 3.

16   You are thought here to be the most senseless and fit man for the constable of the watch, therefore bear you the lantern.

WILLIAM SHAKESPEARE (1564–1616), English dramatist, poet. Dogberry to the First Watchman, in *Much Ado About Nothing*, act 3, sc. 3, venting one of his many malapropisms ("senseless" for sensible).

See also DETECTIVES; Dickens on UNIFORMS.

POLICY

1   A policy is a temporary creed liable to be changed, but while it holds good it has got to be pursued with apostolic zeal.

MOHANDAS K. GANDHI (1869–1948), Indian political and spiritual leader. Letter, 8 March 1922, to the general secretary of the Congress Party, India.

2   Policy is the people you work with.

WILLIAM GASKILL (b. 1930), British stage director. *Times* (London, 6 Sept. 1989), said of his job as theater director.

3   My esoteric doctrine, is that if you entertain any doubt, it is safest to take the unpopular side in the first instance. Transit from the unpopular, is easy . . . but from the popular to the unpopular is so steep and rugged that it is impossible to maintain it.

LORD MELBOURNE (1779–1848), English statesman, prime minister. Quoted in: David Cecil, *Lord M*, ch. 4 (1954).

4   You do the policy, I'll do the politics.

DAN QUAYLE (b. 1947), U.S. Republican politician, vice president. Remark to aide. Quoted in: *International Herald Tribune* (Paris, 13 Jan. 1992)

See also Richard Nixon on PUBLIC OFFICE.

POLITICAL CORRECTNESS

1 It is silly to call fat people "gravitationally challenged"—a self-righteous fetishism of language which is no more than a symptom of political frustration.

TERRY EAGLETON (b. 1943), British critic. *Guardian* (London, 27 Oct. 1992).

2 During the years 1945–1965 (I am referring to Europe), there was a certain way of thinking correctly, a certain style of political discourse, a certain ethics of the intellectual. One had to be on familiar terms with Marx, not let one's dreams stray too far from Freud. . . . These were the . . . requirements that made the strange occupation of writing and speaking a measure of truth about oneself and one's time acceptable.

MICHEL FOUCAULT (1926–84), French philosopher. Gilles Deleuze and Félix Guattari, *Anti-Oedipus*, Preface (1972).

3 We have needed to define ourselves by reclaiming the words that define us. They have used language as weapons. When we open ourselves to what they say and how they say it, our narrow prejudices evaporate and we are nourished and armed.

SELMA JAMES (b. 1930), U.S. author, political activist. *The Ladies and the Mammies: Jane Austen and Jean Rhys*, ch. 1 (1983).

4 Political correctness is the natural continuum from the party line. What we are seeing once again is a self-appointed group of vigilantes imposing their views on others. It is a heritage of communism, but they don't seem to see this.

DORIS LESSING (b. 1919), British novelist. *Sunday Times: Books* (London, 10 May 1992).

5 If you do not regard feminism with an uplifting sense of the gloriousness of woman's industrial destiny, or in the way, in short, that it is prescribed, by the rules of the political publicist, that you should, that will be interpreted by your opponents as an attack on *woman*.

WYNDHAM LEWIS (1882–1957), British author, painter. *The Art of Being Ruled*, "The Family and Feminism," ch. 6 (1926).

6 All . . . forms of consensus about "great" books and "perennial" problems, once stabilized, tend to deteriorate eventually into something philistine. The real life of the mind is always at the frontiers of "what is already known." Those great books don't only need custodians and transmitters. To stay alive, they also need adversaries. The most interesting ideas are heresies.

SUSAN SONTAG (b. 1933), U.S. essayist. Interview, April 1975, *Salmagundi* (Fall 1975-Winter 1976; repr. in *A Susan Sontag Reader*, 1982).

7 It seems our fate to be incorrect (look where we live, for example), and in our incorrectness stand.

ALICE WALKER (b. 1944), U.S. author, critic. Interview in *Interviews with Black Writers* (ed. by John O'Brien, 1973; repr. in *In Search of Our Mothers' Gardens*, "From an Interview," 1983).

8 The thing has been blown up out of all proportion. PC language is *not* enjoined on one and all—there are a lot more places where you can say "spic" and "bitch" with impunity than places where you can smoke a cigarette.

KATHARINE WHITEHORN (b. 1926), British journalist. *Observer* (London, 25 Aug. 1991)

See also ORTHODOXY.

POLITICAL PARTIES

1 Growing older, I have lost the need to be political, which means, in this country, the need to be left. I am driven into grudging toleration of the Conservative Party because it is the party of non-politics, of resistance to politics.

KINGSLEY AMIS (b. 1922), British novelist. *Sunday Telegraph* (London, 2 July 1967).

2 All political parties die at last of swallowing their own lies.

JOHN ARBUTHNOT (1667–1735), Scottish writer, physician. Quoted in: Richard Garnett, *Life of Emerson*, ch. 7 (1888).

3 When great questions end, little parties begin.

WALTER BAGEHOT (1826–77), English economist, critic. *The English Constitution*, ch. 8 (1867).

4 We are not just here to manage capitalism but to change society and to define its finer values.

TONY BENN (b. 1925), British Labour politician. Speech, 1 Oct. 1975, to Labour Party Conference.

5 Political organizations have slowly substituted themselves for the Churches as the places for believing practices. . . . Politics has once again become religious.

MICHEL DE CERTEAU (1925–86), French cultural theorist, critic. *The Practice of Everyday Life*, ch. 13, "An Archaeology: The Transits of Believing" (1974).

6 A political organization is a transferable commodity. You could not find a better way of killing virtue than by packing it into one of these contraptions which some gang of thieves is sure to find useful.

JOHN JAY CHAPMAN (1862–1933), U.S. author. *Practical Agitation*, ch. 1 (1898).

7 Every clique is a refuge for incompetence. It fosters corruption and disloyalty, it begets cowardice, and consequently is a burden upon and a drawback to the progress of the country. Its instincts and actions are those of the pack.

MADAME CHIANG KAI-SHEK (b. 1898), Chinese educator, reformer. *China Shall Rise Again*, pt. 1, ch. 8 (1941).

8 Party leads to vicious, corrupt and unprofitable legislation, for the sole purpose of defeating party.

JAMES FENIMORE COOPER (1789–1851), U.S. novelist. *The American Democrat*, "On Party" (1838).

9 The bright old day now dawns again; the cry runs
through the the land,
In England there shall be dear bread—in Ireland,
sword and brand;
And poverty, and ignorance, shall swell the rich
and grand,
So, rally round the rulers with the gentle iron
hand,
Of the fine old English Tory days;
Hail to the coming time!

CHARLES DICKENS (1812–70), English novelist. *The Fine Old English Gentleman* (1841; published in *The Poems and Verse of Charles Dickens*, ed. by F. G. Kitton, 1903; repr. in *The Faber Book of Ballads*, 1965).

10 A Conservative government is an organised hypocrisy.

BENJAMIN DISRAELI (1804–81), English statesman, author. Speech, 17 March 1845, addressing prime minister Sir Robert Peel in the House of Commons, London.

11 Things must be done by parties, not by persons using parties as tools.

BENJAMIN DISRAELI (1804–81), English statesman, author. Letter, 17 Dec. 1846, referring to the tactics of prime minister Sir Robert Peel.

12 A sect or a party is an elegant incognito, devised to save a man from the vexation of thinking.

RALPH WALDO EMERSON (1803–82), U.S. essayist, poet, philosopher. *Journals* (1909–14), entry for 20 June 1831.

13 The aim of every political association is the preservation of the natural and imprescriptible rights of man. These rights are liberty, property, security and resistance to oppression.

FRENCH NATIONAL ASSEMBLY. *Declaration of the Rights of Man* (drafted and discussed Aug. 1789; published Sept. 1791).

14 Let us not forget that we can never go farther than we can persuade at least half of the people to go.

HUGH GAITSKELL (1906–63), British Labour Politician. Speech, 3 Oct. 1961, to Labour Party Conference, Brighton.

15 He serves his party best who serves his country best.

RUTHERFORD B. HAYES (1822–93), U.S. president. Inaugural address, 5 March 1877.

16 We are the trade union for pensioners and children, the trade union for the disabled and the sick . . . the trade union for the nation as a whole.

EDWARD HEATH (b. 1916), British Conservative politician, prime minister. Election campaign speech, 20 Feb. 1974, Manchester, England, said of the Conservative Party.

17 The two-party system has given this country the war of Lyndon Johnson, the Watergate of Nixon, and the incompetence of Carter. Saying we should keep the two-party system simply because it is working is like saying the Titanic voyage was a success because a few people survived on life-rafts.

EUGENE J. McCARTHY (b. 1916), U.S. senator. *Chicago Tribune* (10 Sept. 1978).

18 As usual the Liberals offer a mixture of sound and original ideas. Unfortunately none of the sound ideas is original and none of the original ideas is sound.

HAROLD MACMILLAN (1894–1986), British Conservative politician, prime minister. Speech, 7 March 1961, London.

19 As in private life one differentiates between what a man thinks and says of himself and what he really is and does, so in historical struggles one must still more distinguish the language and the imaginary aspirations of parties from their real organism and their real interests, their conception of themselves from their reality.

KARL MARX (1818–83), German political theorist, social philosopher. *The Eighteenth Brumaire of Louis Bonaparte*, sct. 3 (1852; repr. in *Karl Marx and Friedrich Engels: Collected Works*, vol. 11, 1979).

20 The Tories in England had long imagined that they were enthusiastic about the monarchy, the church and beauties of the old English Constitution, until the day of danger wrung from them the confession that they are enthusiastic only about rent.

KARL MARX (1818–83), German political theorist, social philosopher. *The Eighteenth Brumaire of Louis Bonaparte*, sct. 3 (1852; repr. in *Karl Marx and Friedrich Engels: Collected Works*, vol. 11, 1979).

21 A party of order or stability, and a party of progress or reform, are both necessary elements of a healthy state of political life.

JOHN STUART MILL (1806–73), English philosopher, economist. *On Liberty*, ch. 2 (1859).

22 The Empress is Legitimist, my cousin is Republican, Morny is Orleanist, I am a socialist; the only Bonapartist is Persigny, and he is mad.

NAPOLEON III (1808–73), French emperor. Attributed conversational remark, late 1850s, of the leading figures in the Second Empire.

23 The newspaper reader says: this party will ruin itself if it makes errors like this. My *higher* politics says: a party which makes errors like this is already finished—it is no longer secure in its instincts.

FRIEDRICH NIETZSCHE (1844–1900), German philosopher. *Twilight of the Idols*, "The Four Great Errors," aph. 2 (1889).

24 I find myself . . . hoping a total end of all the unhappy divisions of mankind by party-spirit, which at best is but the madness of many for the gain of a few.

ALEXANDER POPE (1688–1744), English satirical poet. Letter, 27 Aug. 1714.

25 The old parties are husks, with no real soul within either, divided on artificial lines, boss-ridden and privilege-controlled, each a jumble of incongruous elements, and neither daring to speak out wisely and fearlessly on what should be said on the vital issues of the day.

THEODORE ROOSEVELT (1858–1919), U.S. Republican (later Progressive) politician, president. Speech, 6 Aug. 1912, at the Progressive party convention, Chicago.

26 In order to remain true to oneself one ought to renounce one's party three times a day.

JEAN ROSTAND (1894–1977), French biologist, writer. *Pensées d'un Biologiste* (1939; repr. in *The Substance of Man*, "A Biologist's Thoughts," ch. 10, 1962).

27 We have never yet had a Labour Government that knew what taking power really means; they always act like second-class citizens.

DORA RUSSELL (1894–1986), British author, campaigner. Quoted in: *Observer* (London, 30 Jan. 1983).

28 The lounge of the main hotel is full of jollity, with large comfortable men sitting in braces; the bar is packed with talkative intellectuals, full of witty disloyalties. . . . The next week the main hotel is suddenly full of dinner-jackets and large hats. The girls are dressed as if for a weekend in the country. . . . When one of the great men of the party comes through, the crowd edges respectfully away, murmuring loyal noises.

> ANTHONY SAMPSON (b. 1926), British journalist, author. *The Anatomy of Britain Today*, ch. 5 (1965), describing repectively the Labour and Conservative Party Conferences.

29 You are pitiful isolated individuals; you are bankrupts; your role is played out. Go where you belong from now on—into the dustbin of history!

> LEON TROTSKY (1879–1940), Russian revolutionary. *History of the Russian Revolution*, vol. 3, ch. 10 (1933), of the Mensheviks.

30 When the doctrine of allegiance to party can utterly up-end a man's moral constitution and make a temporary fool of him besides, what excuse are you going to offer for preaching it, teaching it, extending it, perpetuating it? Shall you say, the best good of the country demands allegiance to party? Shall you also say it demands that a man kick his truth and his conscience into the gutter, and become a mouthing lunatic, besides?

> MARK TWAIN (1835–1910), U.S. author. "Consistency," paper, read at Hartford, Connecticut in 1884 (published 1923; repr. in *Complete Essays*, ed. by Charles Neider, 1963).

31 The two real political parties in America are the *Winners* and the *Losers*. The people don't acknowledge this. They claim membership in two imaginary parties, the *Republicans* and the *Democrats*, instead.

> KURT VONNEGUT, JR. (b. 1922), U.S. novelist. *Wampeters, Foma and Granfalloons*, "In a Manner that Must Shame God Himself" (1974).

32 I adore political parties. They are the only place left to us where people don't talk politics.

> OSCAR WILDE (1854–1900), Anglo-Irish playwright, author. Lord Goring, in *An Ideal Husband*, act 1.

33 This Party is a moral crusade or it is nothing.

> HAROLD WILSON, LORD RIVEAULX (b. 1916), British Labour politician, prime minister. Speech, 1 Oct. 1962, to Labour Party Conference. Said of the Labour Party.

34 The success of a party means little more than that the Nation is using the party for a large and definite purpose. . . . It seeks to use and interpret a change in its own plans and point of view.

> WOODROW WILSON (1856–1924), U.S. Democratic politician, president. Inaugural address, 1913

See also Burke on ALLIANCES; The DEMOCRATIC PARTY; Gingrich on ELECTIONS; The REPUBLICAN PARTY.

POLITICIANS

1 He could not see a belt without hitting below it.

> MARGOT ASQUITH (1864–1945), British socialite. Quoted in: Mark Bonham Carter's Introduction to Margot Asquith, *Autobiography* (first published 1936; repr. 1962), of former prime minister David Lloyd George.

2 It is as hard and severe a thing to be a true politician as to be truly moral.

> FRANCIS BACON (1561–1626), English philosopher, essayist, statesman. *Advancement of Learning*, bk. 2 (1605).

3 The apparent rulers of the English nation are like the imposing personages of a splendid procession: it is by them the mob are influenced; it is they whom the spectators cheer. The real rulers are secreted in second-rate carriages; no one cares for them or asks after them, but they are obeyed implicitly and unconsciously by reason of the splendour of those who eclipsed and preceded them.

> WALTER BAGEHOT (1826–77), English economist, critic. *The English Constitution*, ch. 8 (1867).

4 A political leader must keep looking over his shoulder all the time to see if the boys are still there. If they aren't still there, he's no longer a political leader.

> BERNARD BARUCH (1870–1965), U.S. financier. Quoted in: his obituary, *New York Times* (21 June 1965).

5 Politicians—power itself—are abject because they merely embody the profound contempt people have for their own lives. . . . One should be grateful to the politicians for accepting the abjectness of power, and ridding others of its burden. This inevitably kills them but they get their revenge by passing onto others the corpse of power.

> JEAN BAUDRILLARD (b. 1929), French semiologist. *Cool Memories*, ch. 1 (1987; tr. 1990).

6 It only takes a politician believing in what he says for the others to stop believing him.

> JEAN BAUDRILLARD (b. 1929), French semiologist. *Cool Memories*, ch. 5 (1987; tr. 1990).

7 The Prime Minister has an absolute genius for putting flamboyant labels on empty luggage.

> ANEURIN BEVAN (1897–1960), British Labour politician. Quoted in: Michael Foot, *Aneurin Bevan*, vol. 2, ch. 16 (1973), said of Harold Macmillan, in Queen's Speech debate, House of Commons, 3 Nov. 1959.

8 The history of American politics is littered with bodies of people who took so pure a position that they had no clout at all.

> BEN C. BRADLEE (b. 1921), U.S. editor. Quoted in: Studs Terkel, *Talking to Myself*, bk. 1, ch. 7 (1977).

9 No wonder that, when a political career is so precarious, men of worth and capacity hesitate to embrace it. They cannot afford to be thrown out of their life's course by a mere accident.

> JAMES BRYCE (1838–1922), British historian, politician, diplomat. *The American Commonwealth*, vol. 2, ch. 58 (1888).

10 Your representative owes you, not his industry only, but his judgement; and he betrays instead of serving you if he sacrifices it to your opinion.

> EDMUND BURKE (1729–97), Irish philosopher, statesman. Speech, 3 Nov. 1774, to the electors of Bristol, England.

11 Away with the cant of "Measures, not men!"—the idle supposition that it is the harness and not the horses that draw the chariot along. No, Sir, if the comparison must be made, if the distinction must be taken, men are everything, measures comparatively nothing.

> GEORGE CANNING (1770–1827), English statesman, prime minister. Speech, 9 Dec. 1802, House of Commons.

12 Little other than a redtape Talking-machine, and unhappy Bag of Parliamentary Eloquence.

THOMAS CARLYLE (1795–1881), Scottish essayist, historian. *Latter-Day Pamphlets*, no. 1, "The Present Time" (1850).

13 Now, we deny not, but that politicians may sometimes abuse religion, and make it serve for the promoting of their own private interests and designs; which yet they could not do so well neither, were the thing itself a mere cheat and figment of their own, and had no reality at all in nature, nor anything solid at the bottom of it.

RALPH J. CUDWORTH (1617–88), English theologian, philosopher. *The True Intellectual System of the Universe*, bk. 1, ch. 5 (1678; repr. 1820).

14 a politician is an arse upon
which everyone has sat except a man.

E. E. CUMMINGS (1894–1962), U.S. poet. *1 x 1*, no. 10 (1944).

15 A sophistical rhetorician, inebriated with the exuberance of his own verbosity, and gifted with an egotistical imagination that can at all times command an interminable and inconsistent series of arguments to malign an opponent and to glorify himself.

BENJAMIN DISRAELI (1804–81), English statesman, author. Speech, 27 July 1878, Knightsbridge, London, said of Prime Minister Gladstone.

16 Resolv'd to ruin or to rule the state.

JOHN DRYDEN (1631–1700), English poet, dramatist, critic. *Absolom and Achitophel*, pt. 1.

17 It is our experience that political leaders do not always mean the opposite of what they say.

ABBA EBAN (b. 1915), Israeli politician. Quoted in: *Observer* (London, 5 Dec. 1971).

18 Heads of state are notoriously ill prepared for their mature careers; think of Adolf Hitler (landscape painter), Ho Chi Minh (seaman), and our own Ronald Reagan.

BARBARA EHRENREICH (b. 1941), U.S. author, columnist. *The Worst Years of Our Lives*, "Premature Pragmatism" (1991; first published *Ms.*, 1986).

19 Nothing is so foolish, they say, as for a man to stand for office and woo the crowd to win its vote, buy its support with presents, court the applause of all those fools and feel self-satisfied when they cry their approval, and then in his hour of triumph to be carried round like an effigy for the public to stare at, and end up cast in bronze to stand in the market place.

DESIDERIUS ERASMUS (c. 1466–1536), Dutch humanist. *Praise of Folly*, ch. 27 (1509).

20 My life's work has been accomplished. I did all that I could.

MIKHAIL GORBACHEV (b. 1931), Soviet political leader. Quoted in: *Observer* (London, 15 Dec. 1991), on being ousted as Soviet president.

21 A Whig is properly what is called a Trimmer—that is, a coward to both sides of the question, who dare not be a knave nor an honest man, but is a sort of whiffling, shuffling, cunning, silly, contemptible, unmeaning negation of the two.

WILLIAM HAZLITT (1778–1830), English essayist. *Political Essays*, Preface (1819; repr. in *Complete Works*, vol. 7, ed. by P. P. Howe, 1932).

22 You know, what I very well know, that I bought you. And I know, what perhaps you think I don't know, you are now selling yourselves to somebody else; and I know, what you do not know, that I am buying another borough. May God's curse light upon you all: may your houses be as open and common to all Excise Officers as your wifes and daughters were to me, when I stood for your scoundrel corporation.

ANTHONY HENLEY (d. 1745), English M.P. for Southampton. Letter to his constituents, 1734 (published in *Notes and Queries*, Second Series, 1861).

23 A politician never forgets the precarious nature of elective life. We have never established a practice of tenure in public office.

HUBERT H. HUMPHREY (1911–78), U.S. Democratic politician, vice president. Speech, 23 Aug. 1965, University of Wisconsin.

24 Idealism is the noble toga that political gentlemen drape over their will to power.

ALDOUS HUXLEY (1894–1963), British novelist. Quoted in: *New York Herald Tribune* (25 Nov. 1963).

25 You slam a politician, you make out he's the devil, with horns and hoofs. But his wife loves him, and so did all his mistresses.

PAMELA HANSFORD JOHNSON (1912–81), British author, critic. Dr. Wohlgemutt, in *Night and Silence, Who is Here?—An American Comedy*, ch. 23 (1963).

26 Politicians are the same all over: they promise to build a bridge even where there is no river.

NIKITA KHRUSHCHEV (1894–1971), Soviet premier. Press conference, Oct. 1960, Glen Cove, N.Y.

27 The ordinary politician has a very low estimate of human nature. In his daily life he comes into contact chiefly with persons who want to get something or to avoid something. Beyond this circle of seekers after privileges, individuals and organized minorities, he is aware of a large unorganized, indifferent mass of citizens who ask nothing in particular and rarely complain. The politician comes after a while to think that the art of politics is to satisfy the seekers after favors and to mollify the inchoate mass with noble sentiments and patriotic phrases.

WALTER LIPPMANN (1889–1974), U.S. journalist. "The New Congress," in *New York Herald Tribune* (8 Dec 1931; repr. in *The Essential Lippman*, pt. 3, sct. 6, 1982).

28 Successful democratic politicians are insecure and intimidated men. They advance politically only as they placate, appease, bribe, seduce, bamboozle, or otherwise manage to manipulate the demanding and threatening elements in their constituencies. The decisive consideration is not whether the proposition is good but whether it is popular—not whether it will work well and prove itself but whether the active talking constituents like it immediately. Politicians rationalize this servitude by saying that in a democracy public men are the servants of the people.

WALTER LIPPMANN (1889–1974), U.S. journalist. *The Public Philosophy*, ch. 2, sct. 4 (1955).

29 At home you always have to be a politician. When you're abroad you almost feel yourself a statesman.

> HAROLD MACMILLAN (1894–1986), British Conservative politician, prime minister. Speech, 17 Feb. 1958, Melbourne, Australia, during the first visit to Australia by a British prime minister. Quoted in: *Look* (15 April 1958).

30 The politician who never made a mistake never made a decision.

> JOHN MAJOR (b. 1943), British Conservative politician, prime minister. "World This Weekend" Interview, 25 Nov. 1990, on BBC Radio 4 (UK).

31 Did you ever
notice that when
a politician
does get an idea
he usually
gets it all wrong.

> DON MARQUIS (1878–1937), U.S. humorist, journalist. *archy's life of mehitabel*, ch. 11 (1934).

32 Nothing is so abject and pathetic as a politician who has lost his job, save only a retired stud-horse.

> H. L. MENCKEN (1880–1956), U.S. journalist. *A Mencken Chrestomathy*, "Sententiæ: The Citizen and the State" (1949).

33 One has to be a lowbrow, a bit of a murderer, to be a politician, ready and willing to see people sacrificed, slaughtered, for the sake of an idea, whether a good one or a bad one.

> HENRY MILLER (1891–1980), U.S. author. Interview in *Writers at Work* (Second Series, ed. by George Plimpton, 1963).

34 Political image is like mixing cement. When it's wet, you can move it around and shape it, but at some point it hardens and there's almost nothing you can do to reshape it.

> WALTER F. MONDALE (b. 1928), U.S. Democratic politician. Quoted in: *Independent on Sunday* (London, 12 May 1991).

35 Whether elected or appointed
He considers himself the Lord's annointed,
And indeed the ointment lingers on him
So thick you can't get your fingers on him.

> OGDEN NASH (1902–71), U.S. poet. *I'm a Stranger Here Myself*, "The Politician" (1938).

36 Don't fall in love with politicians, they're all a disappointment. They can't help it, they just are.

> PEGGY NOONAN (b. 1950), U.S. author, presidential speechwriter. *What I Saw at the Revolution*, "Another Epilogue" (1990).

37 I do not deny that there may be other well-founded causes for the hatred which various classes feel toward politicians, but the *main one seems to me that politicians are symbols of the fact that every class must take every other class into account.*

> JOSÉ ORTEGA Y GASSET (1883–1955), Spanish essayist, philosopher. *Invertebrate Spain*, ch. 2, "Direct Action" (1921).

38 We assume that politicians are without honor. We read their statements trying to crack the code. The scandals of their politics: not so much that men in high places lie, only that they do so with such indifference, so endlessly, still expecting to be believed. We are accustomed to the contempt inherent in the political lie.

> ADRIENNE RICH (b. 1929), U.S. poet. "Women and Honor: Some Notes on Lying," paper read at Hartwick College, New York, June 1975 (first published 1977; repr. in *On Lies, Secrets, and Silence*, 1980).

39 People start parades—politicians just get out in front and act like they're leading.

> DANA GILLMAN RINEHART (b. 1946), U.S. politician, mayor of Columbus, Ohio. Quoted in: *Observer* (London, 22 May 1988).

40 We all know that Prime Ministers are wedded to the truth, but like other wedded couples they sometimes live apart.

> SAKI [H. H. MUNRO] (1870–1916), Scottish author. Lady Caroline, in *The Unbearable Bassington*, ch. 13 (1912).

41 Get thee glass eyes,
And, like a scurvy politician, seem
To see the things thou dost not.

> WILLIAM SHAKESPEARE (1564–1616), English dramatist, poet. Lear, in *King Lear*, act 4, sc. 5.

42 There have been many great men that have flattered the people who ne'er loved them.

> WILLIAM SHAKESPEARE (1564–1616), English dramatist, poet. Second Officer, in *Coriolanus*, act 2, sc. 2.

43 He knows nothing and he thinks he knows everything. That points clearly to a political career.

> GEORGE BERNARD SHAW (1856–1950), Anglo-Irish playwright, critic. Undershaft, in *Major Barbara*, act 3.

44 We mustn't be stiff and stand-off, you know. We must be thoroughly democratic, and patronize everybody without distinction of class.

> GEORGE BERNARD SHAW (1856–1950), Anglo-Irish playwright, critic. Broadbent, in *John Bull's Other Island*, act 4.

45 A politician is a statesman who approaches every question with an open mouth.

> ADLAI STEVENSON (1900–1965), U.S. Democratic politician. Quoted in: Leon Harris, *The Fine Art of Political Wit*, ch. 10 (1964).

46 He speaks to Me as if I was a public meeting.

> VICTORIA (1819–1901), Queen of Great Britain and Ireland. Attributed remark of Prime Minister W. E. Gladstone. Quoted in: G. W. E. Russell, *Collections and Recollections*, ch. 14 (1898). "No image except that of a flood can convey the notion of Mr. Gladstone's table-talk," Russell observed.

47 Politics makes strange bed-fellows.

> CHARLES DUDLEY WARNER (1829–1900), U.S. editor, author. *My Summer in a Garden*, "Fifteenth Week" (1871).

48 People with high ideals don't necessarily make good politicians. If clean politics is so important, we should leave the job to scientists and the clergy.

> MICHIO WATANABE (b. 1923), Japanese Liberal Democratic politician. Quoted in: *Newsweek* (New York, 12 June 1989).

49 It is my settled opinion, after some years as a political correspondent, that no one is attracted to a political career in the first place unless he is socially or emotionally crippled.

> AUBERON WAUGH (b. 1939), British journalist, author. Quoted in: Richard Reeves, *A Ford, Not a Lincoln*, ch. 1 (1975).

50 One can say that three pre-eminent qualities are decisive for the politician: passion, a feeling of responsibility, and a sense of proportion.

MAX WEBER (1864–1920), German sociologist. *Essays in Sociology*, "Politics as a Vocation" (ed. by H. H. Gerth and C. Wright Mills, 1946; first published 1919).

51 He thinks like a Tory, and talks like a Radical, and that's so important nowadays.

OSCAR WILDE (1854–1900), Anglo-Irish playwright, author. Mrs. Erlynne, in *Lady Windermere's Fan*, act 2.

52 A politician's words reveal less about what he thinks about his subject than what he thinks about his audience.

GEORGE F. WILL (b. 1941), U.S. political columnist. Quoted in: Richard Reeves, *A Ford, Not a Lincoln*, ch. 1 (1975).

See also Layton on ASSASSINATION; Ortega y Gasset on CHAOS; Pope on COFFEE; Major on CONSENSUS; Vanderbilt on CORRUPTION; Kissinger on CRISIS; Hazlitt on DISSENT; Huxley on IDEALISM; Calvino on LITERATURE AND SOCIETY; RICHARD NIXON; Lippmann on PHILOSOPHERS; The PRESIDENT; Brenton, Hare on The PRESS; RONALD REAGAN; Russell on RELIGION; Nixon on SPEECHES AND SPEECH-MAKING; STATESMANSHIP; MARGARET THATCHER.

POLITICS

1 Practical politics consists in ignoring facts.

HENRY B. ADAMS (1838–1918), U.S. historian. *The Education of Henry Adams*, ch. 22 (1907).

2 Nothing is irreparable in politics.

JEAN ANOUILH (1910–87), French playwright. Warwick, in *The Lark*, pt. 1.

3 Man is by nature a political animal.

ARISTOTLE (384–322 B.C.), Greek philosopher. *Politics*, bk. 1, ch. 2, sct. 1253a (c. 343 B.C.).

4 Politics is about putting yourself in a state of grace.

PADDY ASHDOWN (b. 1941), British Liberal Democrat politician. *Daily Telegraph* (London, 16 Sept. 1992).

5 The belief that politics can be scientific must inevitably produce tyrannies. Politics cannot be a science, because in politics theory and practice cannot be separated, and the sciences depend upon their separation. . . . Empirical politics must be kept in bounds by democratic institutions, which leave it up to the subjects of the experiment to say whether it shall be tried, and to stop it if they dislike it, because, in politics, there is a distinction, unknown to science, between Truth and Justice.

W. H. AUDEN (1907–73), Anglo-American poet. *A Certain World*, "Tyranny" (1970).

6 Every political system is an accumulation of habits, customs, prejudices, and principles that have survived a long process of trial and error and of ceaseless response to changing circumstances. If the system works well on the whole, it is a lucky accident—the luckiest, indeed, that can befall a society.

EDWARD C. BANFIELD (b. 1916), U.S. political scientist. Quoted in: *Newsweek* (New York, 12 June 1989).

7 The era of the political was one of *anomie*: crisis, violence, madness and revolution. The era of the transpolitical is that of anomaly: an aberration of no conse-

quence, contemporaneous with the event of no consequence.

JEAN BAUDRILLARD (b. 1929), French semiologist. *Fatal Strategies*, "Figures of the Transpolitical" (1983; tr. 1990).

8 The abjection of our political situation is the only true challenge today. Only facing up to this situation in all its desperation can help us get out of it.

JEAN BAUDRILLARD (b. 1929), French semiologist. *Cool Memories*, ch. 5 (1987; tr. 1990).

9 Politics is not an exact science.

PRINCE OTTO VON BISMARCK (1815–98), Prussian statesman. Speech, 18 Dec. 1863, to Prussian legislature.

10 I am really sorry to see my countrymen trouble themselves about politics. If men were wise, the most arbitrary princes could not hurt them. If they are not wise, the freest government is compelled to be a tyranny. Princes appear to me to be fools. Houses of Commons & Houses of Lords appear to me to be fools; they seem to me to be something else besides human life.

WILLIAM BLAKE (1757–1827), English poet, painter, engraver. *Public Address* (c. 1810; repr. in *Complete Writings*, ed. by Geoffrey Keynes, 1957).

11 I am invariably of the politics of the people at whose table I sit, or beneath whose roof I sleep.

GEORGE BORROW (1803–81), English author. *The Bible in Spain*, ch. 16 (1843).

12 Politics are usually the executive expression of human immaturity.

VERA BRITTAIN (1893–1970), British author. *The Rebel Passion*, ch. 1 (1964).

13 A passion for politics stems usually from an insatiable need, either for power, or for friendship and adulation, or a combination of both.

FAWN M. BRODIE (1915–81), U.S. biographer. *Thomas Jefferson*, ch. 1 (1974).

14 Magnanimity in politics is not seldom the truest wisdom; and a great empire and little minds go ill together.

EDMUND BURKE (1729–97), Irish philosopher, statesman. "Speech on Conciliation with America," 22 March 1775.

15 Circumstances . . . give in reality to every political principle its distinguishing colour and discriminating effect. The circumstances are what render every civil and political scheme beneficial or noxious to mankind.

EDMUND BURKE (1729–97), Irish philosopher, statesman. *Reflections on the Revolution in France* (1790).

16 I have simplified my politics into an utter detestation of all existing governments; and, as it is the shortest and most agreeable and summary feeling imaginable, the first moment of an universal republic would convert me into an advocate for single and uncontradicted despotism. The fact is, riches are power, and poverty is slavery all over the earth, and one sort of establishment is no better, nor worse, for a *people* than another.

LORD BYRON (1788–1824), English poet. *Byron's Letters and Journals*, vol. 3 (ed. by Leslie A. Marchand, 1974), entry for 16 Jan. 1814.

17 Religion is organized to satisfy and guide the soul—politics does the same thing for the body.

> JOYCE CARY (1888–1957), British author. Interview in *Writers at Work* (First Series, ed. by Malcolm Cowley, 1958).

18 If American politics does not look to you like a joke, a tragic dance; if you have enough blindness left in you, on any plea, on any excuse, to vote for the Democratic Party or the Republican Party (for at present machine and party are one), or for any candidate who does not stand for a new era,—then you yourself pass into the slide of the magic-lantern; you are an exhibit, a quaint product, a curiosity of the American soil. You are part of the problem.

> JOHN JAY CHAPMAN (1862–1933), U.S. author. *Practical Agitation*, ch. 7 (1898).

19 The average educated man in America has about as much knowledge of what a political idea is as he has of the principles of counterpoint. Each is a thing used in politics or music which those fellows who practise politics or music manipulate somehow. Show him one and he will deny that it is politics at all. It must be corrupt or he will not recognize it. He has only seen dried figs. He has only thought dried thoughts. A live thought or a real idea is against the rules of his mind.

> JOHN JAY CHAPMAN (1862–1933), U.S. author. *Practical Agitation*, ch. 7 (1898).

20 Half a truth is better than no politics.

> G. K. CHESTERTON (1874–1936), British author. *All Things Considered*, "The Boy" (1908).

21 Politics is a place of humble hopes and strangely modest requirements, where all are good who are not criminal and all are wise who are not ridiculously otherwise.

> FRANK MOORE COLBY (1865–1925), U.S. editor, essayist. *The Colby Essays*, vol. 1, "On Seeing Ten Bad Plays" (1926).

22 In politics, what begins in fear usually ends in folly.

> SAMUEL TAYLOR COLERIDGE (1772–1834), English poet, critic. *Table Talk* (published in *Specimens of the Table Talk of Samuel Taylor Coleridge*, ed. by Henry Nelson Coleridge, 1835; repr. in *Collected Works*, ed. by Kathleen Coburn, vol. 14, 1990), entry for 5 Oct. 1830.

23 The work of the political activist inevitably involves a certain tension between the requirement that position be taken on current issues as they arise and the desire that one's contributions will somehow survive the ravages of time.

> ANGELA DAVIS (b. 1944), U.S. political activist. *Women, Culture and Politics*, Introduction (1989).

24 Finality is not the language of politics.

> BENJAMIN DISRAELI (1804–81), English statesman, author. Speech to House of Commons, 28 Feb. 1859.

25 Politics ought to be the part-time profession of every citizen who would protect the rights and privileges of free people and who would preserve what is good and fruitful in our national heritage.

> DWIGHT D. EISENHOWER (1890–1969), U.S. general, Republican politician, president. Broadcast speech, 28 Jan. 1954.

26 Mediocrity in politics is not to be despised. Greatness is not needed.

> HANS MAGNUS ENZENSBERGER (b. 1929), German poet, critic. "The Late Show," 5 Nov. 1990, BBC2.

27 Politics is not the art of the possible. It consists in choosing between the disastrous and the unpalatable.

> JOHN KENNETH GALBRAITH (b. 1908), U.S. economist. Letter, 2 March 1962, to President Kennedy, while Galbraith was serving as U.S. ambassador in India (published in his *Ambassador's Journal*, 1969). Galbraith was referring to Bismarck's celebrated saying, "Politics is the art of the possible."

28 Politics is the reflex of the business and industrial world.

> EMMA GOLDMAN (1869–1940), U.S. anarchist. *Anarchism and Other Essays*, "The Tragedy of Women's Emancipation" (1910).

29 The political arena leaves one no alternative, one must either be a dunce or a rogue.

> EMMA GOLDMAN (1869–1940), U.S. anarchist. *Anarchism and Other Essays*, "Anarchism: What It Really Stands For" (1910).

30 In politics, being ridiculous is more damaging than being extreme.

> ROY HATTERSLEY (b. 1932), British Labour politician. *Evening Standard* (London, 9 May 1989).

31 Politics is a choice of enemas. You're gonna get it up the ass, no matter what you do.

> GEORGE V. HIGGINS (b. 1939), U.S. novelist. Ed Cobb, in *Victories*, ch. 7 (1991).

32 Cant is always rather nauseating; but before we condemn political hypocrisy, let us remember that it is the tribute paid by men of leather to men of God, and that the acting of the part of someone better than oneself may actually commit one to a course of behaviour perceptibly less evil than what would be normal and natural in an avowed cynic.

> ALDOUS HUXLEY (1894–1963), British author. "On The Natural Inequality Of Men" (1890; published in *Collected Essays*, vol. 1, 1893).

33 There is no sea more dangerous than the ocean of practical politics—none in which there is more need of good pilotage and of a single, unfaltering purpose when the waves rise high.

> THOMAS HENRY HUXLEY (1825–95), English biologist. "On the Natural Inequality of Men" (1890; published in *Collected Essays*, vol. 1, 1893).

34 My constituency is the desperate, the damned, the disinherited, the disrespected and the despised.

> JESSE JACKSON (b. 1941), U.S. clergyman, civil rights leader. Speech, 17 July 1984, Democratic National Convention, San Francisco.

35 Son, in politics you've got to learn that overnight chicken shit can turn to chicken salad.

> LYNDON B. JOHNSON (1908–73), U.S. Democratic politician, president. Quoted in: Fawn Brodie, *Richard Nixon: The Shaping of his Character*, ch. 25 (1983), in reply to reporter who had questioned him on his embracing Richard Nixon on Nixon's return from his vice presidential tour of South America, where he had stood up to being mobbed by an angry crowd in Caracas, Venezuela, May 1958. Johnson had previously referred to Nixon as "chicken shit." Reactions to the incident were not all favorable: Walter Lippmann called the tour "a diplomatic Pearl Har-

bor" and the Boston *Globe* said it was "one of the most ineptly handled episodes in this country's foreign relations."

36 Politics are now nothing more than means of rising in the world. With this sole view do men engage in politics, and their whole conduct proceeds upon it.

SAMUEL JOHNSON (1709–84), English author, lexicographer. · Quoted in: James Boswell, *Life of Samuel Johnson*, 17 April 1775 (1791).

37 Most of us are conditioned for many years to have a political veiwpoint—Republican or Democratic, liberal, conservative, or moderate. The fact of the matter is that most of the problems . . . that we now face are technical problems, are administrative problems. They are very sophisticated judgments, which do not lend themselves to the great sort of passionate movements which have stirred this country so often in the past. [They] deal with questions which are now beyond the comprehension of most men.

JOHN F. KENNEDY (1917–63), U.S. Democratic politician, president. Press conference, May 1962. Quoted in: David Eakins, *A New History of Leviathan*, "Policy-Planning for the Establishment" (ed. by Ronald Radosh and Murray Rothbard, 1972).

38 Politics can be relatively fair in the breathing spaces of history; at its critical turning points there is no other rule possible than the old one, that the end justifies the means.

ARTHUR KOESTLER (1905–83), Hungarian-born British author. Extract from Rubashov's diary, in *Darkness at Noon*, "The Second Hearing," ch. 1 (1940).

39 To rely upon conviction, devotion, and other excellent spiritual qualities—that is not to be taken seriously in politics.

VLADIMIR ILYICH LENIN (1870–1924), Russian revolutionary leader. Address to the 11th Party Congress, March 1922.

40 The first requirement of politics is not intellect or stamina but patience. Politics is a very long run game and the tortoise will usually beat the hare.

JOHN MAJOR (b. 1943), British Conservative politician, prime minister. *Daily Express* (London, 25 July 1989).

41 Politics is war without bloodshed while war is politics with bloodshed.

MAO ZEDONG (1893–1976), Founder of the People's Republic of China. "On Protracted War," lecture, May 1938 (published in *Selected Works*, vol. 2, 1965).

42 The human being is in the most literal sense a political animal, not merely a gregarious animal, but an animal which can individuate itself only in the midst of society.

KARL MARX (1818–83), German political theorist, social philosopher. *Grundrisse*, notebook 1, sct. 1 (1857–58).

43 In the domain of Political Economy, free scientific inquiry meets not merely the same enemies as in all other domains. The peculiar nature of the material it deals with, summons as foes into the field of battle the most violent, mean and malignant passions of the human breast, the Furies of private interest.

KARL MARX (1818–83), German political theorist, social philosopher. Preface to the first German edition of *Capital* (1867).

44 In politics, it seems, retreat is honorable if dictated by military considerations and shameful if even *suggested* for ethical reasons.

MARY MCCARTHY (1912–89), U.S. author, critic. *Vietnam*, "Solutions" (1967).

45 Politics is the enemy of the imagination.

IAN MCEWAN (b. 1948), British author. Quoted in: *Independent on Sunday* (London, 5 July 1992).

46 Politics will eventually be replaced by imagery. The politician will be only too happy to abdicate in favor of his image, because the image will be much more powerful than he could ever be.

MARSHALL MCLUHAN (1911–80), Canadian communications theorist. Quoted in: *Maclean's* (Toronto, June 1971).

47 I played by the rules of politics as I found them.

RICHARD M. NIXON (b. 1913), U.S. Republican politician, president. *Times* (London, 26 March 1990).

48 The one thing sure about politics is that what goes up comes down and what goes down often comes up.

RICHARD M. NIXON (b. 1913), U.S. Republican politician, president. Quoted in: Earl Mazo, *Richard Nixon: A Political and Personal Portrait*, ch. 17 (1959).

49 Beware the politically obsessed. They are often bright and interesting, but they have something missing in their natures; there is a hole, an empty place, and they use politics to fill it up. It leaves them somehow misshapen.

PEGGY NOONAN (b. 1950), U.S. author, presidential speechwriter. *What I Saw at the Revolution*, "Another Epilogue" (1990).

50 Politics are for foreigners with their endless wrongs and paltry rights. Politics are a lousy way to get things done. Politics are, like God's infinite mercy, a last resort.

P. J. O'ROURKE (b. 1947), U.S. journalist. *Parliament of Whores*, Author's Preface to the British Edition (1991).

51 In our time, political speech and writing are largely the defence of the indefensible.

GEORGE ORWELL (1903–50), British author. "Politics and the English Language" (1946; repr. in *Shooting an Elephant*, 1950).

52 In politics people give you what they think you deserve and deny you what they think you want.

CECIL PARKINSON (b. 1932), British Conservative politician. Television interview, 19 Nov. 1990, ITV.

53 Politics is just like show business, you have a hell of an opening, coast for a while and then have a hell of a close.

RONALD REAGAN (b. 1911), U.S. Republican politician, president. Quoted in: *There He Goes Again* (ed. by Mark Green and Gail MacColl, 1983), said in 1966 to aide Stuart Spencer.

54 Politics in the United States consists of the struggle between those whose change has been arrested by success or failure, on one side, and those who are still engaged in changing themselves, on the other. Agitators of arrested metamorphosis versus agitators of continued metamorphosis. The former have the advantage of numbers (since most people accept themselves as successes or failures quite early), the latter of vitality and visibility (since self-transformation, though it begins from within, with ideology, religion, drugs, tends to express itself publicly through costume and jargon).

> HAROLD ROSENBERG (1906–78), U.S. art critic, author. *Discovering the Present*, pt. 4, ch. 24 (1973).

55 In politics, yesterday's lie is attacked only to flatter today's.

> JEAN ROSTAND (1894–1977), French biologist, writer. *Pensées d'un Biologiste* (1939; repr. in *The Substance of Man*, "A Biologist's Thoughts," ch. 10, 1962).

56 To "know your place" is a good idea in politics. That is not to say "stay in your place" or "hang on to your place," because ambition or boredom may dictate upward or downward mobility, but a sense of place—a feel for one's own position in the control room—is useful in gauging what you should try to do.

> WILLIAM SAFIRE (b. 1929), U.S. journalist. *Before The Fall*, Prologue (1975).

57 We mean by "politics" the people's business—the most important business there is.

> ADLAI STEVENSON (1900–1965), U.S. Democratic politician. Speech, 19 Nov. 1955, Chicago.

58 In the school of political projectors, I was but ill entertained, the professors appearing, in my judgment, wholly out of their senses; which is a scene that never fails to make me melancholy. These unhappy people were proposing schemes for persuading monarchs to choose favourites upon the score of their wisdom, capacity, and virtue; of teaching ministers to consult the public good; of rewarding merit, great abilities, and eminent services, of instructing princes to know their true interest, by placing it on the same foundation with that of their people; of choosing for employment persons qualified to exercise them; with many other wild impossible chimeras, that never entered before into the heart of man to conceive; and confirmed in me the old observation, that there is nothing so extravagant and irrational which some philosophers have not maintained for truth.

> JONATHAN SWIFT (1667–1745), Anglo-Irish satirist. *Gulliver's Travels*, pt. 3, "A Voyage to Laputa," ch. 6 (1726).

59 I am in politics because of the conflict between good and evil, and I believe that in the end good will triumph.

> MARGARET THATCHER (b. 1925), British Conservative politician. prime minister. Quoted in: *Guardian* (London, 23 Oct. 1990).

60 Only he has the calling for politics who is sure that he will not crumble when the world from his point of view is too stupid or base for what he wants to offer. Only he who in the face of all this can say "In spite of all!" has the calling for politics.

> MAX WEBER (1864–1920), German sociologist. *Essays in Sociology*, "Politics as a Vocation" (ed. by H. H. Gerth and C. Wright Mills, 1946; first published 1919).

61 Only very intelligent people don't wish they were in politics, and I'm dumb enough to want to be in there.

> ORSON WELLES (1915–84), U.S. filmmaker, actor, producer. Interview in David Frost, *The Americans*, "Can a Martian Survive by Pretending to be a Leading American Actor?" (1970).

62 Politics should share one purpose with religion: the steady emancipation of the individual through the education of his passions.

> GEORGE F. WILL (b. 1941), U.S. political columnist. *Statecraft as Soulcraft: What Government Does*, ch. 2 (1984).

63 All politics takes place on a slippery slope. The most important four words in politics are "up to a point."

> GEORGE F. WILL (b. 1941), U.S. political columnist. *Statecraft as Soulcraft: What Government Does*, ch. 4 (1984).

See also Miller on ALIENATION; CONGRESS; Nixon on ELECTIONS; GOVERNMENT; PARLIAMENT; Junius on PERUSASION; McLuhan on PROPAGANDA; STATESMAN-SHIP.

POLLS

1 I did not enter the Labour Party forty-seven years ago to have our manifesto written by Dr. Mori, Dr. Gallup and Mr. Harris.

> TONY BENN (b. 1925), British Labour politician. *Guardian* (London, 13 June 1988).

2 The so-called science of poll-taking is not a science at all but mere necromancy. People are unpredictable by nature, and although you can take a nation's pulse, you can't be sure that the nation hasn't just run up a flight of stairs.

> E. B. WHITE (1899–1985), U.S. author, editor. "Polling," in *New Yorker* (13 Nov. 1948; repr. in *Writings from the New Yorker 1927–1976*, ed. by Rebecca M. Dale, 1991).

3 The total collapse of the public opinion polls shows that this country is in good health. A country that developed an airtight system of finding out in advance what was in people's minds would be uninhabitable.

> E. B. WHITE (1899–1985), U.S. author, editor. "Polling," in *New Yorker* (13 Nov. 1948; repr. in *Writings from the New Yorker 1927–1976*, ed. by Rebecca M. Dale, 1991), commenting on Truman's surprise victory in the 1948 presidential election.

POLLUTION

1 Raise a million filters and the rain will not be clean, until the longing for it be refined in deep confession. And still we hear, If only this nation had a soul, or, Let us change the way we trade, or, Let us be proud of our region.

> LEONARD COHEN (b. 1934), Canadian singer, poet, novelist. *Book of Mercy*, sct. 30 (1984).

2 Unfortunately, our affluent society has also been an effluent society.

> HUBERT H. HUMPHREY (1911–78), U.S. Democratic politician, vice president. Speech, 11 Oct. 1966, Gannon College, Erie, Penn.

3 Approximately 80% of our air pollution stems from hydrocarbons released by vegetation, so let's not go overboard in setting and enforcing tough emission standards from man-made sources.

> RONALD REAGAN (b. 1911), U.S. Republican politician, president. *Sierra* (10 Sept. 1980). Reagan later amended this figure to 93%—both statements quoted in *Reagan's Reign of Error*, "Killer Trees" (ed. by Mark Green and Gail MacColl, 1987).

4 I durst not laugh for fear of opening my lips and receiving the bad air.

> WILLIAM SHAKESPEARE (1564–1616), English dramatist, poet. Casca, in *Julius Caesar*, act 1, sc. 2.

5 The new American finds his challenge and his love in the traffic-choked streets, skies nested in smog, choking with the acids of industry, the screech of rubber and houses leashed in against one another while the townlets wither a time and die.

> JOHN STEINBECK (1902–68), U.S. author. *Travels With Charley: in Search of America*, pt. 2 (1961). Steinbeck added, "This is not offered in criticism but only as observation. And I am sure that, as all pendulums reverse their swing, so eventually will the swollen cities rupture like dehiscent wombs and disperse their children back to the countryside."

See also ECOLOGY; THE ENVIRONMENT.

THE POPE

1 I like his holiness very much, particularly since an order, which I understand he has lately given, that no more miracles shall be performed.

> LORD BYRON (1788–1824), English poet. Quoted in: James Kennedy, *Conversations on Religion with Lord Byron* (1830; repr. in Doris Langley Moore, *The Late Lord Byron*, ch. 10, 1961, rev. 1976).

2 For them it's out-of-date and outmoded to perform miracles; teaching the people is too like hard work, interpreting the holy scriptures is for schoolmen and praying is a waste of time; to shed tears is weak and womanish, to be needy is degrading; to suffer defeat is a disgrace and hardly fitting for one who scarcely permits the greatest of kings to kiss the toes of his sacred feet; and finally, death is an unattractive prospect, and dying on a cross would be an ignominious end.

> DESIDERIUS ERASMUS c. 1466–1536), Dutch humanist. *Praise of Folly*, ch. 59 (1509).

3 The Papacy is no other than the ghost of the deceased Roman empire, sitting crowned upon the grave thereof.

> THOMAS HOBBES (1588–1679), English philosopher. *Leviathan*, pt. 4, ch. 47 (1651).

4 Christians are to be taught that the pope would and should wish to give of his own money, even though he had to sell the basilica of St. Peter, to many of those from whom certain hawkers of indulgences cajole money.

> MARTIN LUTHER (1483–1546), German leader of the Protestant Reformation. No. 51 of the Ninety-Five Theses pinned onto the door of the castle church at Wittenberg, Germany, 31 Oct. 1517.

5 It is an error to believe that the Roman Pontiff can and ought to reconcile himself to, and agree with, progress, liberalism, and contemporay civilization.

> PIUS IX (1792–1878), Italian ecclesiastic, pope. *Syllabus of Errors* (1876).

6 I wouldn't take the Pope too seriously. He's a Pole first, a pope second, and maybe a Christian third.

> MURIEL SPARK (b. 1918), British novelist. *International Herald Tribune* (Paris, 29 May 1989).

7 The Pope? How many divisions has he got?

> JOSEF STALIN (1879–1953), Soviet leader. Winston Churchill, *The Second World War*, vol. 1, "The Gathering Storm," ch. 8, (1948), said, 13 May 1935, to French Foreign Minister Pierre Laval, in reply to a suggestion that the Soviet Union should encourage Catholicism in order to propitiate the Pope.

POPULAR CULTURE

1 Popular art is the dream of society; it does not examine itself.

> MARGARET ATWOOD (b. 1939), Canadian novelist, poet, critic. "A Question Of Metamorphosis," interview in *Malahat Review*, no. 41 (1977; repr. in *Conversations*, ed. by Earl G. Ingersoll, 1990).

2 The bastard form of mass culture is humiliated repetition . . . always new books, new programs, new films, news items, but always the same meaning.

> ROLAND BARTHES (1915–80), French semiologist. *The Pleasure of the Text*, "Modern" (1975).

3 Popular art is normally decried as vulgar by the cultivated people of its time; then it loses favor with its original audience as a new generation grows up; then it begins to merge into the softer lighting of "quaint," and cultivated people become interested in it, and finally it begins to take on the archaic dignity of the primitive.

> NORTHROP FRYE (1912–91), Canadian literary critic. *Anatomy of Criticism*, second essay, "Mythical Phase: Symbol as Archetype" (1957).

4 There is no comparing the brutality and cynicism of today's pop culture with that of forty years ago: from *High Noon* to *Robocop* is a long descent.

> CHARLES KRAUTHAMMER (b. 1950), U.S. editor, columnist. *International Herald Tribune* (Paris, 31 Oct. 1990).

5 Popular culture is the new Babylon, into which so much art and intellect now flow. It is our imperial sex theater, supreme temple of the western eye. We live in the age of idols. The pagan past, never dead, flames again in our mystic hierarchies of stardom.

> CAMILLE PAGLIA (b. 1947), U.S. author, critic, educator. *Sexual Personae*, ch. 4 (1990).

6 The fact is popular art dates. It grows quaint. How many people feel strongly about Gilbert and Sullivan today compared to those who felt strongly in 1890?

> STEPHEN SONDHEIM (b. 1930), U.S. composer, lyricist. *International Herald Tribune* (Paris, 20 June 1989).

7 The violent illiteracies of the graffiti, the clenched silence of the adolescent, the nonsense cries from the stage-happening, are resolutely strategic. The insurgent and the freak-out have broken off discourse with a cultural system which they despise as a cruel, antiquated fraud. They will not bandy words with it. Accept, even momentarily, the conventions of literate linguistic exchange, and you are caught in the net of the old values, of the grammars that can condescend or enslave.

> GEORGE STEINER (b. 1929), French-born U.S. critic, novelist. *In Bluebeard's Castle*, ch. 4 (1971).

8 We now have a whole culture based on the assumption that people know nothing and so anything can be said to them.

> STEPHEN VIZINCZEY (b. 1933), Hungarian novelist, critic. *Observer Review* (London, 24 June 1990).

9 Nobody seriously questions the principle that it is the function of mass culture to maintain public morale, and certainly nobody in the mass audience objects to having his morale maintained.

> ROBERT WARSHOW (1917–55), U.S. author. "The Gangster as Tragic Hero," in *Partisan Review* (New Brunswick, N.J., 1948; repr. in *The Immediate Experience*, 1970).

See also POPULAR MUSIC.

POPULAR MUSIC

1 James Brown and Frank Sinatra are two different quantities in the universe. They represent two different experiences of the world.

> IMAMU AMIRI BARAKA [LEROI JONES] (b. 1934), U.S. poet, playwright. Interview in David Frost, *The Americans*, "Is Democracy a White Man's Word?" (1970).

2 Extraordinary how potent cheap music is.

> NOËL COWARD (1899–1973), British actor, playwright, composer. Amanda, in *Private Lives*, act 1.

3 We fight our way through the massed and leveled collective safe taste of the Top 40, just looking for a little something we can call our own. But when we find it and jam the radio to hear it again it isn't just ours—it is a link to thousands of others who are sharing it with us. As a matter of a single song this might mean very little; as culture, as a way of life, you can't beat it.

> GREIL MARCUS (b. 1945), U.S. rock journalist. *Mystery Train*, "Randy Newman" (1976).

4 The new sound-sphere is global. It ripples at great speed across languages, ideologies, frontiers and races. . . . The economics of this musical esperanto is staggering. Rock and pop breed concentric worlds of fashion, setting and life-style. Popular music has brought with it sociologies of private and public manner, of group solidarity. The politics of Eden come loud.

> GEORGE STEINER (b. 1929), French-born U.S. critic, novelist. *In Bluebeard's Castle*, ch. 4 (1971).

See also The BLUES; JAZZ; RAP MUSIC; ROCK 'N' ROLL.

POPULARITY

1 Everybody hates me because I'm so universally liked.

> PETER DE VRIES (b. 1910), U.S. author. The narrator, Joe Sandwich, in *The Vale of Laughter*, pt. 1, ch. 1 (1967).

2 I have never wished to cater to the crowd; for what I know they do not approve, and what they approve I do not know.

> EPICURUS (341–270 B.C.), Greek philosopher. *Fragments*, no. 187.

3 I've given parties that have made Indian rajahs green with envy. I've had prima donnas break $10,000 engagements to come to my smallest dinners. When you were still playing button back in Ohio, I entertained on a cruising trip that was so much fun that I had to sink my yacht to make my guests go home.

> F. SCOTT FITZGERALD (1896–1940), U.S. author. *The Crack-Up*, "Notebook K" (ed. by Edmund Wilson, 1945).

4 What most people in our culture mean by being lovable is essentially a mixture between being popular and having sex appeal.

> ERICH FROMM (1900–1980), U.S. psychologist. *The Art of Loving*, ch. 1 (1956).

5 Beware of over-great pleasure in being popular or even beloved.

> MARGARET FULLER (1810–50), U.S. writer, lecturer. Letter, 20 Dec. 1840, to her brother. Quoted in: Alice Rossi, *The Feminist Papers* (1973).

6 He cast off his friends as a huntsman his pack,
For he knew when he pleas'd he could whistle them back.

> OLIVER GOLDSMITH (1728–74), Anglo-Irish author, poet, playwright. *Retaliation*.

7 Popularity? It's glory's small change.

> VICTOR HUGO (1802–85), French poet, dramatist, novelist. Don Salluste, in *Ruy Blas*, act 3, sc. 5.

8 I would jump down Etna for any public good—but I hate a mawkish popularity.

> JOHN KEATS (1795–1821), English poet. Letter, 9 April 1818 (published in *Letters of John Keats*, no. 60, ed. by Frederick Page, 1954).

9 A few more days, and this essay will follow the *Defensio Populi* to the dust and silence of the upper shelf. . . . For a month or two it will occupy a few minutes of chat in every drawing-room, and a few columns in every magazine; and it will then . . . be withdrawn, to make room for the forthcoming novelties.

> THOMAS BABINGTON MACAULAY (1800–1859), English historian, Whig politician. "Milton," in *Edinburgh Review* (Aug. 1825; repr. in *Critical and Historical Essays*, 1843), of Milton's long lost "Treatise on the Doctrines of Christianity".

10 My books are water; those of the great geniuses is wine. Everybody drinks water.

> MARK TWAIN (1835–1910), U.S. author. *Mark Twain's Notebooks and Journals*, vol. 3 (ed. by Frederick Anderson, 1979), entry in Notebook 26, March 1886–June 1887.

11 By common consent of all the nations and all the ages the most valuable thing in this world is the homage of men, whether deserved or undeserved.

> MARK TWAIN (1835–1910), U.S. author. "At the Shrine of St. Wagner" (1891; repr. in *Complete Essays*, ed. by Charles Neider, 1963).

12 Popularity is the crown of laurel which the world puts on bad art. Whatever is popular is wrong.

> OSCAR WILDE (1854–1900), Anglo-Irish playwright, author. Lecture, 30 June 1883, to students of the Royal Academy, London (published in *Aristotle at Afternoon Tea: The Rare Oscar Wilde*, 1991).

13 Popularity is the only insult that has not yet been offered to Mr. Whistler.

OSCAR WILDE (1854–1900), Anglo-Irish playwright, author. Quoted by Whistler in: *The Gentle Art of Making Enemies*, "Mr. Whistler and His Critics, a Catalogue" (1890).

POPULATION

1 If government knew how, I should like to see it check, not multiply, the population. When it reaches its true law of action, every man that is born will be hailed as essential.

RALPH WALDO EMERSON (1803–82), U.S. essayist, poet, philosopher. *The Conduct of Life*, "Considerations by the Way" (1860).

2 The purpose of population is not ultimately peopling earth. It is to fill heaven.

GRAHAM D. LEONARD (b. 1921), Bishop of London (1983). Speech, 10 Feb. 1983, Church of England Synod.

3 Think of the earth as a living organism that is being attacked by billions of bacteria whose numbers double every forty years. Either the host dies, or the virus dies, or both die.

GORE VIDAL (b. 1925), U.S. novelist, critic. "Gods and Greens," in *Observer* (London, 27 Aug. 1989; repr. in *A View from the Diner's Club*, 1991).

PORNOGRAPHY

1 What I wanted to get at is the value difference between pornographic playing-cards when you're a kid, and pornographic playing-cards when you're older. It's that when you're a kid you use the cards as a substitute for a real experience, and when you're older you use real experience as a substitute for the fantasy.

EDWARD ALBEE (b. 1928), U.S. playwright. Jerry, in *The Zoo Story*.

2 There's only one good test of pornography. Get twelve normal men to read the book, and then ask them, "Did you get an erection?" If the answer is "Yes" from a majority of the twelve, then the book is pornographic.

W. H. AUDEN (1907–73), Anglo-American poet. *The Table Talk of W. H. Auden*, "March 17, 1947" (comp. by Alan Ansen, ed. by Nicholas Jenkins, 1990).

3 A widespread taste for pornography means that nature is alerting us to some threat of extinction.

J. G. BALLARD (b. 1930), British author. *Myths of the Near Future*, "News from the Sun" (1982).

4 Pornography is the quadrophonics of sex. It adds a third and fourth track to the sexual act. It is the hallucination of detail that rules. Science has already habituated us to this microscopics, this excess of the real in its microscopic detail, this voyeurism of exactitude.

JEAN BAUDRILLARD (b. 1929), French semiologist. *Seduction*, ch. 1 (1979; tr. 1990).

5 At male strip shows, it is still the women that we watch, the audience of women and their eager faces. They are more obscene than if they were dancing naked themselves.

JEAN BAUDRILLARD (b. 1929), French semiologist. *Cool Memories*, ch. 2 (1987; tr. 1990).

6 Pornographers are the enemies of women only because our contemporary ideology of pornography does not encompass the possibility of change, as if we were the slaves of history and not its makers. . . . Pornography is a satire on human pretensions.

ANGELA CARTER (1940–92), British author. *The Sadeian Woman*, "Polemical Preface" (1979).

7 Pornography is rather like trying to find out about a Beethoven symphony by having somebody tell you about it and perhaps hum a few bars.

ROBERTSON DAVIES (b. 1913), Canadian novelist, journalist. *The Enthusiasms of Robertson Davies*, "The Table Talk of Robertson Davies" (1990).

8 The utopian male concept which is the premise of male pornography is this—since manhood is established and confirmed over and against the brutalized bodies of women, men need not aggress against each other; in other words, women absorb male aggression so that men are safe from it.

ANDREA DWORKIN (b. 1946), U.S. feminist critic. "The Root Cause," speech, 26 Sept. 1975, Massachusetts Institute of Technology, Cambridge (published in *Our Blood*, ch. 9, 1976).

9 Women, for centuries not having access to pornography and now unable to bear looking at the muck on the supermarket shelves, are astonished. Women do not believe that men believe what pornography says about women. But they do. From the worst to the best of them, they do.

ANDREA DWORKIN (b. 1946), U.S. feminist critic. *Pornography*, ch. 5 (1981).

10 Those Romans who perpetrated the rape of the Sabines, for example, did not work themselves up for the deed by screening *Debbie Does Dallas*, and the monkish types who burned a million or so witches in the Middle Ages had almost certainly not come across *Boobs and Buns* or related periodicals.

BARBARA EHRENREICH (b. 1941), U.S. author, columnist. *The Worst Years of Our Lives*, "Our Neighborhood Porn Committee" (1991; first published 1986).

11 It's red hot, mate. I hate to think of this sort of book getting in the wrong hands. As soon as I've finished this, I shall recommend they ban it.

TONY HANCOCK (1924–68), British comedian. "The Missing Page," on "Hancock's Half-Hour," BBC broadcast, 26 Feb. 1960.

12 Pornography is literature designed to be read with one hand.

ANGELA LAMBERT (b. 1940), British journalist. *Independent on Sunday* (London, 18 Feb. 1990).

13 Pornography is the attempt to insult sex, to do dirt on it.

D. H. LAWRENCE (1885–1930), British author. *Pornography and Obscenity* (1930; repr. in *Phoenix: The Posthumous Papers of D. H. Lawrence*, pt. 3, ed. by E. McDonald, 1936). Lawrence admitted, however, that the definition of pornography varied according to the individual: "What is pornography to one man is the laughter of genius to another."

14 The pornography of violence of course far exceeds,

in volume and general acceptance, sexual pornography, in this Puritan land of ours. Exploiting the apocalypse, selling the holocaust, is a pornography. . . . For the ultimate selling job on ultimate violence one must read those works of fiction issued by our government as manuals of civil defense, in which . . . you learn that there's nothing to be afraid of if you've stockpiled lots of dried fruit.

> URSULA K. LE GUIN (b. 1929), U.S. author. "Facing It," address, Dec. 1982, Portland Fellowship Of Reconciliation, Maine (repr. in *Dancing at the Edge of the World*, 1989).

15 There's a subterranean impetus towards pornography so powerful that half the business world is juiced by the sort of half sex that one finds in advertisements.

> NORMAN MAILER (b. 1923), U.S. author. "Petty Notes on Some Sex in America," interview in *Playboy* (Chicago, 1962–63; repr. in *Cannibals and Christians*, 1966).

16 Obscenity is a cleansing process, whereas pornography only adds to the murk.

> HENRY MILLER (1891–1980), U.S. author. *Writers at Work* (Second Series, ed. by George Plimpton, 1963). Miller is quoted as saying, "I am for obscenity and against pornography."

17 The violence and obscenity are left unadulterated, as manifestation of the mystery and pain which ever accompanies the act of creation.

> ANAÏS NIN (1903–77) Franco-American novelist, diarist. Preface to Henry Miller, *Tropic of Cancer* (1934).

18 Pornography is human imagination in tense theatrical action; its violations are a protest against the violations of our freedom by nature.

> CAMILLE PAGLIA (b. 1947), U.S. author, critic, educator. *Sexual Personae*, ch. 1 (1990).

19 Nine-tenths of the appeal of pornography is due to the indecent feelings concerning sex which moralists inculcate in the young; the other tenth is physiological, and will occur in one way or another whatever the state of the law may be.

> BERTRAND RUSSELL (1872–1970), British philosopher, mathematician. *Marriage and Morals*, "The Taboo on Sex Knowledge" (1929).

20 What pornographic literature does is precisely to drive a wedge between one's existence as a full human being and one's existence as a sexual being—while in ordinary life a healthy person is one who prevents such a gap from opening up. Normally we don't experience, at least don't want to experience, our sexual fulfillment as distinct from or opposed to our personal fulfillment. But perhaps in part they are distinct, whether we like it or not.

> SUSAN SONTAG (b. 1933), U.S. essayist. "The Pornographic Imagination," sct. 3, in *Partisan Review* (New Brunswick, N.J., repr. in *Styles of Radical Will*, 1969).

21 What pornography is really about, ultimately, isn't sex but death.

> SUSAN SONTAG (b. 1933), U.S. essayist. "The Pornographic Imagination," sct. 4, in *Partisan Review* (New Brunswick, N.J.; repr. in *Styles of Radical Will*, 1969).

22 Pornographers subvert this last, vital privacy; they do our imagining for us. They take away the words that were of the night and shout them over the roof-tops, making them hollow.

> GEORGE STEINER (b. 1929), French-born U.S. critic, novelist. *Language and Silence,* "Nightworks" (1967).

See also Murdoch on FANTASY.

PORTRAITS

1 It seems to be a law of nature that no man, unless he has some obvious physical deformity, ever is loth to sit for his portrait.

> SIR MAX BEERBOHM (1872–1956), British author. *And Even Now,* "Quia Imperfectum" (1920).

2 Mr. Lely, I desire you would use all your skill to paint my picture truly like me, and not flatter me at all; but remark all these roughnesses, pimples, warts, and everything as you see me, otherwise I will never pay a farthing for it.

> OLIVER CROMWELL (1599–1658), Parliamentarian general, Lord Protector of England. Quoted in: Horace Walpole, *Anecdotes of Painting in England*, ch. 12 (1762–71), to painter Sir Peter Lely, c. 1657.

3 There are only two styles of portrait painting; the serious and the smirk.

> CHARLES DICKENS (1812–70), English novelist. Miss La Creevy, in *Nicholas Nickleby*, ch. 10 (1838–9).

4 Sir Joshua would have been glad to take her portrait; and he would have had an easier task than the historian at least in this, that he would not have had to represent the truth of change—only to give stability to one beautiful moment.

> GEORGE ELIOT (1819–80), English novelist, editor. *Daniel Deronda*, bk. 2, ch. 11 (1876).

5 The explanation of the propensity of the English people to portrait painting is to be found in their relish for a Fact. Let a man do the grandest things, fight the greatest battles, or be distinguished by the most brilliant personal heroism, yet the English people would prefer his portrait to a painting of the great deed. The likeness they can judge of; his existence is a Fact. But the truth of the picture of his deeds they cannot judge of, for they have no imagination.

> BENJAMIN HAYDON (1786–1846), British artist. "Table Talk," in *Correspondence and Table-Talk*, vol. 2 (ed. by Frederic Wordsworth Haydon, 1876).

6 I had rather see the portrait of a dog that I know, than all the allegorical paintings they can show me in the world.

> SAMUEL JOHNSON (1709–84), English author, lexicographer. Quoted in: "Apophthegms, Sentiments, Opinions," in *Works*, vol. 11 (ed. by Sir John Hawkins, 1787–9; repr. in *Johnsonian Miscellanies*, vol. 2, p.15, ed. by George Birkbeck Hill, 1891).

7 Some will not recognize the truthfulness of my mirror. Let them remember that I am not here to reflect the surface . . . but must penetrate inside. My mirror probes down to the heart. I write words on the forehead and around the corners of the mouth. My human faces are truer than the real ones.

> PAUL KLEE (1879–1940), Swiss artist. *The Diaries of Paul Klee 1898–1918*, no. 136 (1957; tr. 1965), entry, Munich 1901.

8 When you start with a portrait and search for a pure form, a clear volume, through successive eliminations, you arrive inevitably at the egg. Likewise, starting with the egg and following the same process in reverse, one finishes with the portrait.

> PABLO PICASSO (1881–1973), Spanish artist. *Intransigeant* (Paris, 15 June 1932).

9 Few persons who have ever sat for a portrait can have felt anything but inferior while the process is going on.

> ANTHONY POWELL (b. 1905), British novelist. Quoted in: *Observer* (London, 9 Jan. 1983).

10 He reproduced himself with so much humble objectivity, with the unquestioning, matter of fact interest of a dog who sees himself in a mirror and thinks: there's another dog.

> RAINER MARIA RILKE (1875–1926), German poet. Letter, 23 Oct. 1907 (published in *Letters on Cézanne*, 1952, tr. 1985), on Cézanne.

11 I *hate* to paint portraits! I hope never to paint another portrait in my life. . . . Portraiture may be all right for a man in his youth, but after forty I believe that manual dexterity deserts one, and, besides, the colour-sense is less acute. Youth can better stand the exactions of a personal kind that are inseparable from portraiture. I have had enough of it.

> JOHN SINGER SARGENT (1856–1925), U.S. artist. Quoted in: Walter Tittle, "My Recollections of John Sargent," in *Illustrated London News*, vol. 166, no. 724 (1925; repr. in Richard Ormond, *John Singer Sargent*, ch. 6, 1970). Sargent frequently inveighed against what he called "paughtraights" and "mugs" though these were the basis of his reputation. Many, however, were poorly received, and the remark "Every time I paint a portrait I lose a friend" has been attributed to him.

12 Every portrait that is painted with feeling is a portrait of the artist, not of the sitter.

> OSCAR WILDE (1854–1900), Anglo-Irish playwright, author. Basil Hallward, in *The Picture of Dorian Gray*, ch. 1 (1891).

13 Most of our modern portrait painters are doomed to absolute oblivion. They never paint what they see. They paint what the public sees, and the public never sees anything.

> OSCAR WILDE (1854–1900), Anglo-Irish playwright, author. Vivian, in *The Decay of Lying* (published in *Intentions*, 1891).

POSSESSIONS

1 Why grab possessions like thieves, or divide them like socialists when you can ignore them like wise men?

> NATALIE CLIFFORD BARNEY (1876–1972), U.S.-born French author. Quoted in: "My Country 'tis of Thee," in *Adam*, no. 299 (London, 1962).

2 Americans are uneasy with their possessions, guilty about power, all of which is difficult for Europeans to perceive because they are themselves so truly materialistic, so versed in the uses of power.

> JOAN DIDION (b. 1934), U.S. essayist. *Slouching Towards Bethlehem*, "7000 Romaine, Los Angeles" (1967; repr. 1968).

3 All my possessions for a moment of time.

> ELIZABETH I (1533–1603), Queen of England. Alleged last words.

4 Some men are born to own, and can animate all their possessions. Others cannot: their owning is not graceful; seems to be a compromise of their character: they seem to steal their own dividends.

> RALPH WALDO EMERSON (1803–82), U.S. essayist, poet, philosopher. *The Conduct of Life*, "Wealth" (1860).

5 Possession, it is true, crowns exertion with rest; but it is only in the illusions of fancy that it has power to charm us.

> KARL WILHELM VON HUMBOLDT (1767–1835), German statesman, philologist. *The Limits of State Action*, ch. 1 (1792, repr. 1854; tr. and ed. by J. W. Burrow, 1969).

6 Many possessions, if they do not make a man better, are at least expected to make his children happier; and this pathetic hope is behind many exertions.

> GEORGE SANTAYANA (1863–1952), U.S. philosopher, poet. *The Life of Reason*, "Reason in Society," ch. 3 (1905–6).

POSSIBILITY

1 I dwell in Possibility—
A fairer House than Prose—
More numerous of Windows—
Superior—for Doors—.

> EMILY DICKINSON (1830–86), U.S. poet. *The Complete Poems*, no. 657 (1955).

2 If I were to wish for anything, I should not wish for wealth and power, but for the passionate sense of the potential, for the eye which, ever young and ardent, sees the possible. Pleasure disappoints, possibility never. And what wine is so sparkling, what so fragrant, what so intoxicating, as possibility!

> SØREN KIERKEGAARD (1813–55), Danish philosopher. *Either/Or*, vol. 1, "Diapsalmata" (1843; tr. 1987).

3 Today Americans are overcome not by the sense of endless possibility but by the banality of the social order they have erected against it.

> CHRISTOPHER LASCH (b. 1932), U.S. historian. *The Culture of Narcissism*, ch. 1, "The Therapeutic Sensibility" (1979).

4 I am neither an optimist nor pessimist, but a possibilist.

> MAX LERNER (b. 1902), U.S. author, columnist. Entry in *Who's Who in America* (1992).

5 The becoming of man is the history of the exhaustion of his possibilities.

> SUSAN SONTAG (b. 1933), U.S. essayist. *Styles of Radical Will*, "'Thinking Against Oneself': Reflections on Cioran" (1969).

POSTERITY

1 "We are always doing," says he, "something for posterity, but I would fain see posterity do something for us."

> JOSEPH ADDISON (1672–1719), English essayist. *Spectator*, no. 583 (London, 20 Aug. 1714), said in the style of an old fellow of a college.

2 After being Turned Down by numerous Publishers, he had decided to write for Posterity.

> GEORGE ADE (1866–1944), U.S. humorist, playwright. *Fables in*

Slang, "The Fable of the Bohemian who had Hard Luck" (1899), said of the "main Bohemian."

3　The flattery of posterity is not worth much more than contemporary flattery, which is worth nothing.

> JORGE LUIS BORGES (1899–1986), Argentinian author. *Dreamtigers,* "Dead Men's Dialogue" (1964).

4　A blot in thy scutcheon to all futurity.

> MIGUEL DE CERVANTES (1547–1616), Spanish writer. Merlin's Nymph curse to Sancho Panza, in *Don Quixote,* pt. 2, bk. 6, ch. 2 (1615; tr. by P. Motteux).

5　History is fond of her grandchildren, for it offers them the marrow of the bones, which the previous generation had hurt its hands in breaking.

> NIKOLAI GAVRILOVICH CHERNYSHEVSKY (1828–89), Russian writer, philosopher. Quoted by Isaiah Berlin in his Introduction to Franco Venturi, *Roots of Revolution* (1952; tr. 1960).

6　Few can be induced to labor exclusively for posterity; and none will do it enthusiastically. Posterity has done nothing for us; and theorize on it as we may, practically we shall do very little for it, unless we are made to think we are at the same time doing something for ourselves.

> ABRAHAM LINCOLN (1809–65), U.S. president. Speech, 22 Feb. 1842, Washingtonian Temperance Society, Springfield, Ill. (published in *The Collected Works of Abraham Lincoln,* vol. 1, ed. by Roy P. Basler, 1953).

7　Men of genius are not to be analyzed by commonplace rules. The rest of us who have been or are leaders, more commonplace in our quality, will do well to remember two things. One is *never to forget posterity when devising a policy.* The other is *never to think of posterity when making a speech.*

> ROBERT MENZIES (1894–1978), Australian Liberal politician, prime minister. *The Measure of The Years,* ch. 1 (1970).

8　When we are planning for posterity, we ought to remember that virtue is not hereditary.

> THOMAS PAINE (1737–1809), Anglo-American political theorist, writer. *Common Sense,* ch. 4 (1776).

POSTMODERNISM

See MODERNISM AND POSTMODERNISM.

POTENTIAL

1　When you know what men are capable of you marvel neither at their sublimity nor their baseness. There are no limits in either direction apparently.

> HENRY MILLER (1891–1980), U.S. author. *The Air-Conditioned Nightmare,* "The Soul of Anaesthesia" (1945).

2　And what is the potential man, after all? Is he not the sum of all that is human? *Divine,* in other words?

> HENRY MILLER (1891–1980), U.S. author. *A Devil in Paradise* (1956; repr. in *Big Sur and the Oranges of Hieronymus Bosch,* pt. 3, "Paradise Lost," 1957) .

3　Our being is subject to all the chances of life. There are so many things we are capable of, that we could be or do. The potentialities are so great that we never, any of us, are more than one-fourth fulfilled.

> KATHERINE ANNE PORTER (1890–1980), U.S. short-story writer, novelist. Interview in *Writers at Work* (Second Series, ed. by George Plimpton, 1963).

4　For he was likely, had he been put on,
To have proved most royally.

> WILLIAM SHAKESPEARE (1564–1616), English dramatist, poet. Fortinbras's closing speech, on the death of Hamlet, in *Hamlet,* act 5, sc. 2.

5　I only wish that ordinary people had an unlimited capacity for doing harm; then they might have an unlimited power for doing good.

> SOCRATES (469–399 B.C.), Greek philosopher. Quoted in: Plato, *Crito,* sct. 43.

6　One's prime is elusive. You little girls, when you grow up, must be on the alert to recognize your prime at whatever time of your life it may occur. You must then live it to the full.

> MURIEL SPARK (b. 1918), British novelist. Miss Brodie, in *The Prime of Miss Jean Brodie,* ch. 1 (1961).

7　We are not what we are, nor do we treat or esteem each other for such, but for what we are capable of being.

> HENRY DAVID THOREAU (1817–62), U.S. philosopher, author, naturalist. Letter, 2 March 1842, to Mrs. Lucy Brown (published in *The Correspondence of Henry David Thoreau,* 1958).

EZRA POUND

1　Ezra was right half the time, and when he was wrong, he was so wrong you were never in any doubt about it.

> ERNEST HEMINGWAY (1899–1961), U.S. author. Quoted in: *New Republic* (Washington, D.C., 11 Nov. 1936).

2　Pound's crazy. All poets are. . . . They have to be. You don't put a poet like Pound in the loony bin. For history's sake we shouldn't keep him there.

> ERNEST HEMINGWAY (1899–1961), U.S. author. Quoted in: *New York Post* (24 Jan. 1957), said of Pound's detention in St. Elizabeth's Hospital in Washington, D.C.

3　Somebody said that I am the last American living the tragedy of Europe.

> EZRA POUND (1885–1972), U.S. poet, critic. Interview in *Writers at Work* (Second Series, ed. by George Plimpton, 1963).

4　Ezra Pound still lives in a village and his world is a kind of village and people keep explaining things when they live in a village. . . . I have come not to mind if certain people live in villages and some of my friends still appear to live in villages and a village can be cozy as well as intuitive but must one really keep perpetually explaining and elucidating?

> GERTRUDE STEIN (1874–1946), U.S. author. Reply to Thornton Wilder, who has asked her what she meant by calling Pound "a village explainer." Quoted in: Frederic Prokosch, *Voices: A Memoir,* "The Evil Corner" (1983).

5　He doesn't know a damn thing about China . . . That's what makes him an expert. He knows nothing about music, being tone deaf. That's what makes him a musician . . . And he's batty in the head. That's what makes him a philosopher.

> WILLIAM CARLOS WILLIAMS (1883–1963), U.S. poet. *Ezra Pound in Melbourne: Helix 13/14* (1983). Quoted in: Humphrey Carpenter, *A Serious Character*, pt. 5, ch. 6 (1988).

See also Pound on LITERATURE.

POVERTY AND THE POOR

1 Poverty is an anomaly to rich people. It is very difficult to make out why people who want dinner do not ring the bell.

> WALTER BAGEHOT (1826–77), English economist, critic. "The Waverley Novels" (1858; repr. in *Literary Studies*, vol. 2, 1878).

2 The poverty of our century is unlike that of any other. It is not, as poverty was before, the result of natural scarcity, but of a set of priorities imposed upon the rest of the world by the rich. Consequently, the modern poor are not pitied . . . but written off as trash. The twentieth-century consumer economy has produced the first culture for which a beggar is a reminder of nothing.

> JOHN BERGER (b. 1926), British author, critic. "The Soul and the Operator," in *Expressen* (Stockholm; 19 March 1990; repr. in *Keeping a Rendezvous*, 1992).

3 A poor man with nothing in his belly needs hope, illusion, more than bread.

> GEORGES BERNANOS (1888–1948), French novelist, political writer. The Curé de Torcy, in *The Diary of a Country Priest*, ch. 2 (1936).

4 For unto every one that hath shall be given, and he shall have abundance; but from him that hath not shall be taken away even that which he hath.

> BIBLE: NEW TESTAMENT. *Matthew* 25:29.

5 The Poor Man whom everyone speaks of, the Poor Man whom everyone pities, one of the repulsive Poor from whom "charitable" souls keep their distance, he has still said nothing. Or, rather, he has spoken through the voice of Victor Hugo, Zola, Richepin. At least, they said so. And these shameful impostures fed their authors. Cruel irony, the Poor Man tormented with hunger feeds those who plead his case.

> ALBERT CAMUS (1913–60), French-Algerian philosopher, author. "Jehan Rictus, Poet of Poverty," in *Sud* (Algiers, May 1932; repr. in *Youthful Writings*, 1976).

6 There's a point of poverty at which the spirit isn't with the body all the time. It finds the body really too unbearable. So it's almost as if you were talking to the soul itself. And a soul's not properly responsible.

> LOUIS-FERDINAND CÉLINE (1894–1961), French author. The narrator, Ferdinand Bardamu, in *Journey to the End of the Night* (1932; tr. 1934; 1966, p. 196).

7 The honest poor can sometimes forget poverty. The honest rich can never forget it.

> G. K. CHESTERTON (1874–1936), British author. *All Things Considered*, "Cockneys and their Jokes" (1908).

8 To suppose such a thing possible as a society, in which men, who are able and willing to work, cannot support their families, and ought, with a great part of the women, to be *compelled* to lead a life of celibacy, for fear of having children to be starved; to suppose such a thing possible is monstrous.

> WILLIAM COBBETT (1762–1835), English journalist, reformer. "To Parson Malthus," in *Political Register* (London, 8 May 1819; repr. in *The Opinions of William Cobbett*, ch. 9, ed. by G. D. H. and Margaret Cole, 1944).

9 The poverty from which I have suffered could be diagnosed as "Soho" poverty. It comes from having the airs and graces of a genius and no talent.

> QUENTIN CRISP (b. 1908), British author. *The Naked Civil Servant*, ch. 7 (1968).

10 To be a poor man is hard, but to be a poor race in a land of dollars is the very bottom of hardships.

> W. E. B. DU BOIS (1868–1963), U.S. civil rights leader, author. *The Souls of Black Folk*, ch. 1 (1903).

11 There's no scandal like rags, nor any crime so shameful as poverty.

> GEORGE FARQUHAR (1678–1707), Irish dramatist. Archer, a "gentleman of broken fortunes," in *The Beaux' Stratagem*, act 1, sc. 1.

12 I used to think I was poor. Then they told me I wasn't poor, I was needy. Then they told me it was self-defeating to think of myself as needy, I was deprived. Then they told me deprived was a bad image, I was underprivileged. Then they told me underprivileged was overused, I was disadvantaged. I still don't have a dime. But I sure have a great vocabulary.

> JULES FEIFFER (b. 1929), U.S. cartoonist. Cartoon caption, 1965. Quoted in: William Safire, *Political Dictionary*, "Disadvantaged" (1968; rev. 1978).

13 We are not concerned with the very poor. They are unthinkable, and only to be approached by the statistician or the poet.

> E. M. FORSTER (1879–1970), British novelist, essayist. *Howards End*, ch. 6 (1910).

14 Grant me the treasure of sublime poverty: permit the distinctive sign of our order to be that it does not possess anything of its own beneath the sun, for the glory of your name, and that it have no other patrimony than begging.

> ST. FRANCIS OF ASSISI (1182?–1226), Italian friar, founder of the Franciscan Order. Prayer. Quoted in: Maurice Keen, *A History of Medieval Europe*, ch. 11 (1967).

15 Too poor for a bribe, and too proud to importune,
> He had not the method of making a fortune.

> THOMAS GRAY (1716–71), English poet. *Sketch of his Own Character*.

16 That the poor are invisible is one of the most important things about them. They are not simply neglected and forgotten as in the old rhetoric of reform; what is much worse, they are not seen.

> MICHAEL HARRINGTON (1928–89), U.S. social scientist, author. *The Other America*, ch. 1, sct. 1 (1962).

17 Poverty in itself does not make men into a rabble; a rabble is created only when there is joined to poverty a disposition of mind, an inner indignation against the rich, against society, against the government.

> GEORG HEGEL (1770–1831), German philosopher. *The Philosophy of Right*, "The State," Addition 149 (1821; tr. 1942).

18 Oh, God! that bread should be so dear!
And flesh and blood so cheap!

> THOMAS HOOD (1799–1845), English poet. *The Song of the Shirt.*

19 We have grown literally afraid to be poor. We despise anyone who elects to be poor in order to simplify and save his inner life. If he does not join the general scramble and pant with the money-making street, we deem him spiritless and lacking in ambition.

> WILLIAM JAMES (1842–1910), U.S. psychologist, philosopher. *The Varieties of Religious Experience,* Lectures 14–15, "The Value of Saintliness" (1902).

20 It is easy enough to say that poverty is no crime. No; if it were men wouldn't be ashamed of it. It is a blunder, though, and is punished as such. A poor man is despised the whole world over.

> JEROME K. JEROME (1859–1927), British author. *Idle Thoughts of an Idle Fellow,* "On Being Hard Up" (1889).

21 Resolve not to be poor: whatever you have, spend less. Poverty is a great enemy to human happiness; it certainly destroys liberty, and it makes some virtues impracticable, and others extremely difficult.

> SAMUEL JOHNSON (1709–84), English author, lexicographer. Letter, 7 Dec. 1782, to James Boswell. Quoted in: James Boswell, *Life of Samuel Johnson* (1791).

22 This mournful truth is ev'rywhere confessed,
Slow rises worth by poverty depressed.

> SAMUEL JOHNSON (1709–84), English author, lexicographer. *London.*

23 Here we all live in a state of ambitious poverty.

> JUVENAL (47–138 A.D.), Roman satiric poet. *Satires,* Satire 3.

24 If a free society cannot help the many who are poor, it cannot save the few who are rich.

> JOHN F. KENNEDY (1917–63), U.S. Democratic politician, president. Inaugural address, 20 Jan. 1961, Washington, D.C.

25 You don't seem to realize that a poor person who is unhappy is in a better position than a rich person who is unhappy. Because the poor person has hope. He thinks money would help.

> JEAN KERR (b. 1923), U.S. author, playwright. Sydney, in *Poor Richard,* act 1.

26 Four spectres haunt the Poor—Old Age, Accident, Sickness and Unemployment. We are going to exorcise them. We are going to drive hunger from the hearth. We mean to banish the workhouse from the horizon of every workman in the land.

> DAVID LLOYD GEORGE (1863–1945), Welsh Liberal politician, prime minister. Speech, 1 Jan. 1910, Reading, England.

27 In verity . . . we are the poor. This humanity we would claim for ourselves is the legacy, not only of the Enlightenment, but of the thousands and thousands of European peasants and poor townspeople who came here bringing their humanity and their sufferings with them. It is the absence of a stable upper class that is responsible for much of the vulgarity of the American scene. Should we blush before the visitor for this deficiency?

> MARY MCCARTHY (1912–89), U.S. author, critic. "America the Beautiful," in *Commentary* (New York, Sept. 1947; repr. in *On the Contrary,* 1961).

28 Poverty is not a shame, but the being ashamed of it is.

> ENGLISH PROVERB. Collected in Thomas Fuller, *Gnomologia,* no. 3908 (1732).

29 The poorest He that is in England hath a life to live as the greatest He.

> THOMAS RAINEBOROUGH (d. 1648), English Puritan soldier, politician. Speech, 29 Oct. 1647, Putney, England, during the "Army debates."

30 The forgotten man at the bottom of the economic pyramid.

> FRANKLIN D. ROOSEVELT (1882–1945), U.S. Democratic politician, president. Radio broadcast, 7 April 1932.

31 Poverty keeps together more homes than it breaks up.

> SAKI [H. H. MUNRO] (1870–1916), Scottish author. The Baroness, in "Esmé," in *The Chronicles of Clovis* (1911).

32 O world, how apt the poor are to be proud!

> WILLIAM SHAKESPEARE (1564–1616), English dramatist, poet. Olivia, in *Twelfth Night,* act 3, sc. 1.

33 The seven deadly sins. . . . Food, clothing, firing, rent, taxes, respectability and children. Nothing can lift those seven millstones from Man's neck but money; and the spirit cannot soar until the millstones are lifted.

> GEORGE BERNARD SHAW (1856–1950), Anglo-Irish playwright, critic. Undershaft, in *Major Barbara,* act 3.

34 Our life of poverty is as necessary as the work itself. Only in heaven will we see how much we owe to the poor for helping us to love God better because of them.

> MOTHER TERESA (b. 1910), Albanian-born Roman Catholic missionary. *A Gift for God,* "Carriers of Christ's Love" (1975).

35 Give me the poverty that enjoys true wealth.

> HENRY DAVID THOREAU (1817–62), U.S. philosopher, author, naturalist. *Walden,* "The Ponds" (1854).

36 As poverty has been reduced in terms of mere survival, it has become more profound in terms of our way of life.

> RAOUL VANEIGEM (b. 1934), Belgian Situationist philosopher. "Basic Banalities I," in *Internationale Situationiste 7* (April 1962; repr. in *Situationist International Anthology,* ed. by K. Knabb, 1981).

37 At present cats have more purchasing power and influence than the poor of this planet. Accidents of geography and colonial history should no longer determine who gets the fish.

> DEREK WALL (b. 1965), British ecologist. *Getting There,* ch. 1 (1990).

38 What a devil art thou, Poverty! How many desires—how many aspirations after goodness and truth—how many noble thoughts, loving wishes toward our fellows, beautiful imaginings thou hast crushed under thy heel, without remorse or pause!

> WALT WHITMAN (1819–92), U.S. poet. "Death Of McDonald Clarke," in *New York Aurora* (8 March 1842; repr. in *Walt Whitman of the New York Aurora,* pt. 4, 1950).

39 In going to America one learns that poverty is not a necessary accompaniment to civilisation.

> OSCAR WILDE (1854–1900), Anglo-Irish playwright, author. "Personal Impressions of America," lecture, 10 July 1883.

40 As for the virtuous poor, one can pity them, of course, but one cannot possibly admire them. They have made private terms with the enemy, and sold their birthright for very bad pottage. They must also be extraordinarily stupid.

> OSCAR WILDE (1854–1900), Anglo-Irish playwright, author. *The Soul of Man Under Socialism*, in *Fortnightly Review* (London, Feb. 1891; repr. 1895).

See also Pound on BOHEMIA; Harrington on DRESS; O'Connor on FICTION; Pitt on HOME AND HOUSES; Disraeli on INEQUALITY; Butler, Wilde on MONEY; Friel on REPRESSION; Johnson on UNEMPLOYMENT; Johnson on WELFARE.

POWER

1 A friend in power is a friend lost.

> HENRY B. ADAMS (1838–1918), U.S. historian. *The Education of Henry Adams*, ch. 7 "Treason" (1907), said of the rupture with Senator Charles Sumner.

2 Power is not only what you have but what the enemy thinks you have.

> SAUL ALINSKY (1909–72), U.S. radical activist. *Rules for Radicals*, "Tactics" (1971).

3 Power tires only those who do not have it.

> GIULIO ANDREOTTI (b. 1919), Italian Christian Democrat politician, prime minister. Reply when asked how he had survived in power so long. Quoted in: *Independent on Sunday* (London, 5 April 1992).

4 It is a strange desire, to seek power, and to lose liberty; or to seek power over others, and to lose power over a man's self.

> FRANCIS BACON (1561–1626), English philosopher, essayist, statesman. *Essays*, "Of Great Place" (1597–1625).

5 But the relationship of morality and power is a very subtle one. Because ultimately power without morality is no longer power.

> JAMES BALDWIN (1924–87), U.S. author. *A Dialogue* (1973; with Nikki Giovanni), from a conversation in London, 4 Nov. 1971.

6 I call the discourse of power any discourse that engenders blame, hence guilt, in its recipient.

> ROLAND BARTHES (1915–80), French semiologist. Inaugural lecture, 7 Jan. 1977, Collège de France (published as *Leçon*, 1978; repr. in *Barthes: Selected Writings*, 1982).

7 Contact with men who wield power and authority still leaves an intangible sense of repulsion. It's very like being in close proximity to faecal matter, the faecal embodiment of something unmentionable, and you wonder what it is made of and when it acquired its historically sacred character.

> JEAN BAUDRILLARD (b. 1929), French semiologist. *Cool Memories*, ch. 3 (1987; tr. 1990).

8 The purpose of getting power is to be able to give it away.

> ANEURIN BEVAN (1897–1960), British Labour politician. Quoted in: Michael Foot, *Aneurin Bevan*, vol. 1, ch. 1 (1962).

9 Those who have been once intoxicated with power, and have derived any kind of emolument from it, even though but for one year, never can willingly abandon it. They may be distressed in the midst of all their power; but they will never look to anything but power for their relief.

> EDMUND BURKE (1729–97), Irish philosopher, statesman. *A Letter to a Member of the National Assembly*, 19 Jan. 1791.

10 From Paul to Stalin, the popes who have chosen Caesar have prepared the way for Caesars who quickly learn to despise popes.

> ALBERT CAMUS (1913–60), French-Algerian philosopher, author. *The Rebel*, pt. 2, "The Rejection of Salvation" (1951; tr. 1953).

11 The need to exert power, when thwarted in the open fields of life, is the more likely to assert itself in trifles.

> CHARLES HORTON COOLEY (1864–1929), U.S. sociologist. *Human Nature and the Social Order*, ch. 5 (1902).

12 Power has only one duty—to secure the social welfare of the People.

> BENJAMIN DISRAELI (1804–81), English statesman, author. *Sybil*, bk. 4, ch. 14 (1845).

13 All personal, psychological, social, and institutionalized domination on this earth can be traced back to its source: the phallic identities of men.

> ANDREA DWORKIN (b. 1946), U.S. feminist critic. "The Rape Atrocity and the Boy Next Door," speech, 1 March 1975, at State University of New York, Stony Brook (published in *Our Blood*, ch. 4, 1976).

14 Power is not an institution, and not a structure; neither is it a certain strength we are endowed with; it is the name that one attributes to a complex strategical situation in a particular society.

> MICHEL FOUCAULT (1926–84), French philosopher. *The History of Sexuality*, vol. 1, pt. 4, ch. 2 (1976).

15 In the United States, though power corrupts, the expectation of power paralyzes.

> JOHN KENNETH GALBRAITH (b. 1908), U.S. economist. "The United States," *New York* (15 Nov. 1971; repr. in *A View from the Stands*, 1986).

16 "Power may be at the end of a gun," but sometimes it's also at the end of the shadow or the image of a gun.

> JEAN GENET (1910–86), French playwright, novelist. *Prisoner of Love*, pt. 1 (1986; tr. 1989). Genet was here taking issue with the notion that armed struggle is the only way to achieve revolutionary change. See Mao on POWER.

17 The exercise of power is determined by thousands of interactions between the world of the powerful and that of the powerless, all the more so because these worlds are never divided by a sharp line: everyone has a small part of himself in both.

> VÁCLAV HAVEL (b. 1936), Czech playwright, president. *Disturbing the Peace*, ch. 5 (1986; tr. 1990).

18 Those in possession of absolute power can not only prophesy and make their prophecies come true, but they can also lie and make their lies come true.

ERIC HOFFER (1902–83), U.S. philosopher. *The Passionate State of Mind*, aph. 78 (1955).

19 I hope our wisdom will grow with our power, and teach us, that the less we use our power the greater it will be.

THOMAS JEFFERSON (1743–1826), U.S. president. Letter, 12 June 1815.

20 Power is the great aphrodisiac.

HENRY KISSINGER (b. 1923), U.S. Republican politician, Secretary of State. Quoted in: *New York Times* (19 Jan. 1971).

21 We should keep silent about those in power; to speak well of them almost implies flattery; to speak ill of them while they are alive is dangerous, and when they are dead is cowardly.

JEAN DE LA BRUYÈRE (1645–96), French writer, moralist. *Characters*, "Of Great Nobles," aph. 56 (1688).

22 The quality of the will to power is, precisely, growth. Achievement is its cancellation. To be, the will to power must increase with each fulfillment, making the fulfillment only a step to a further one. The vaster the power gained the vaster the appetite for more.

URSULA K. LE GUIN (b. 1929), U.S. author. *The Lathe of Heaven*, ch. 9 (1971).

23 Power? It's like a Dead Sea fruit. When you achieve it, there is nothing there.

HAROLD MACMILLAN (1894–1986), British Conservative politician, prime minister. Quoted in: Anthony Sampson, *The New Anatomy of Britain*, ch. 37 (1971).

24 Political power grows out of the barrel of a gun.

MAO ZEDONG (1893–1976), Founder of the People's Republic of China. "Problems of War and Strategy," speech, 6 Nov. 1938 (published in *Selected Works*, vol. 2, 1961).

25 I love power. But it is as an artist that I love it. I love it as a musician loves his violin, to draw out its sounds and chords and harmonies.

NAPOLEON BONAPARTE (1769–1821), French general, emperor. Quoted in: Havelock Ellis, *The Dance of Life* (1923).

26 Not necessity, not desire—no, the love of power is the demon of men. Let them have everything—health, food, a place to live, entertainment—they are and remain unhappy and low-spirited: for the demon waits and waits and will be satisfied.

FRIEDRICH NIETZSCHE (1844–1900), German philosopher. *Daybreak*, aph. 262 (1881).

27 Power is not a means, it is an end. One does not establish a dictatorship in order to safeguard a revolution; one makes the revolution in order to establish the dictatorship.

GEORGE ORWELL (1903–50), British author. O'Brien to Winston Smith, in *Nineteen Eighty-Four*, pt. 3, ch. 3 (1949).

28 Power-worship blurs political judgement because it leads, almost unavoidably, to the belief that present trends will continue. Whoever is winning at the moment will always seem to be invincible.

GEORGE ORWELL (1903–50), British author. *Shooting an Elephant*, "Second Thoughts on James Burnham" (1950).

29 A cock has great influence on his own dunghill.

PUBLILIUS SYRUS (1st century B.C.), Latin writer of mimes. *Sententiae*, no. 397.

30 All, or the greatest part of men that have aspired to riches or power, have attained thereunto either by force or fraud, and what they have by craft or cruelty gained, to cover the foulness of their fact, they call purchase, as a name more honest. Howsoever, he that for want of will or wit useth not those means, must rest in servitude and poverty.

SIR WALTER RALEGH (1552–1618), English author, soldier, explorer. *The Cabinet Council*, ch. 25, "A Collection of Political Observations" (repr. in *The Works of Sir Walter Raleigh*, vol. 1, 1751).

31 The least one can say of power is that a vocation for it is suspicious.

JEAN ROSTAND (1894–1977), French biologist, writer. *Pensées d'un Biologiste* (1939; repr. in *The Substance of Man*, "A Biologist's Thoughts," ch. 10, 1962).

32 The fundamental concept in social science is Power, in the same sense in which Energy is the fundamental concept in physics.

BERTRAND [EARL] RUSSELL (1872–1970), British philosopher, mathematician. *Power*, ch. 1, "The Impulse to Power" (1938).

33 Power! Did you ever hear of men being asked whether other souls should have power or not? It is born in them. You may dam up the fountain of water, and make it a stagnant marsh, or you may let it run free and do its work; but *you* cannot say whether it shall be there; *it is there.* And it will act, if not openly for good, then covertly for evil; but it will act.

OLIVE SCHREINER (1855–1920), South African writer, feminist. Lyndall, in *The Story of an African Farm*, pt. 2, ch. 4 (1883).

34 Madness in great ones must not unwatched go.

WILLIAM SHAKESPEARE (1564–1616), English dramatist, poet. Claudius, in *Hamlet*, act 3, sc. 1.

35 You cannot have power for good without having power for evil too. Even mother's milk nourishes murderers as well as heroes.

GEORGE BERNARD SHAW (1856–1950), Anglo-Irish playwright, critic. Cusins, in *Major Barbara*, act 3.

36 Power, like a desolating pestilence,
Pollutes whate'er it touches.

PERCY BYSSHE SHELLEY (1792–1822), English poet. *Queen Mab*, pt. 3.

37 You only have power over people so long as you don't take *everything* away from them. But when you've robbed a man of *everything* he's no longer in your power—he's free again.

ALEXANDER SOLZHENITSYN (b. 1918), Russian novelist. Bobynin, in *The First Circle*, ch. 17 (1968).

38 Power can be taken, but not given. The process of the taking is empowerment in itself.

GLORIA STEINEM (b. 1934), U.S. feminist writer, editor. "Far From the Opposite Shore," in *Ms.* (New York, July 1978 and July/Aug. 1982; repr. in *Outrageous Acts and Everyday Rebellions*, 1983).

39 I shan't be pulling the levers there but I shall be a very good back-seat driver.

MARGARET THATCHER (b. 1925), British Conservative politician, prime minister. *Independent* (London, 27 Nov. 1990), on the appointment of her Cabinet colleague, John Major, as the next Prime Minister.

40 Purchasing power is a license to purchase power.

> RAOUL VANEIGEM (b. 1934), Belgian Situationist philosopher. *The Revolution of Everyday Life*, ch. 7, sct. 3 (1967; tr. 1983).

41 It is difficult to find a reputable American historian who will acknowledge the crude fact that a Franklin Roosevelt, say, wanted to be President merely to wield power, to be famed and to be feared. To learn this simple fact one must wade through a sea of evasions: history as sociology, leaders as teachers, bland benevolence as a motive force, when, finally, power *is* an end to itself, and the instinctive urge to prevail the most important single human trait, the necessary force without which no city was built, no city destroyed.

> GORE VIDAL (b. 1925), U.S. novelist, critic. *Rocking the Boat*, "Robert Graves and the Twelve Caesars" (1963).

42 Powerful men in particular suffer from the delusion that human beings have no memories. I would go so far as to say that the distinguishing trait of powerful men is the psychotic certainty that people forget acts of infamy as easily as their parents' birthdays.

> STEPHEN VIZINCZEY (b. 1933), Hungarian novelist, critic. "Commentary on a Poem," in *Horizon* (London, Oct. 1976; repr. in *Truth and Lies in Literature*, 1986).

43 Alexander at the head of the world never tasted the true pleasure that boys of his own age have enjoyed at the head of a school.

> HORACE WALPOLE (1717–97), English author. Letter, 6 May 1736.

44 The appetite for power, even for universal power, is only insane when there is no possibility of indulging it; a man who sees the possibility opening before him and does not try to grasp it, even at the risk of destroying himself and his country, is either a saint or a mediocrity.

> SIMONE WEIL (1909–43), French philosopher, mystic. "Cold War Policy in 1939" (written 1939; published in *Selected Essays*, ed. by Richard Rees, 1962).

45 To get power over is to defile. To possess is to defile.

> SIMONE WEIL (1909–43), French philosopher, mystic. *New York Notebook* (written 1942; published 1950; repr. in *First and Last Notebooks*, pt. 3, ed. by Richard Rees, 1970).

46 The good old rule
Sufficeth them, the simple plan,
That they should take, who have the power,
And they should keep who can.

> WILLIAM WORDSWORTH (1770–1850), English poet. *Rob Roy's Grave*, st. 9.

See also Hoffer on GOD; Nietzsche on GOODNESS; Korean proverb on INFLUENCE; Acton on LEADERSHIP; Adams on The PRESIDENT; Baldwin on The PRESS.

PRAISE

1 Praise is not seemly in the mouth of a sinner, for it was not sent him of the Lord.

> APOCRYPHA. *Ecclesiasticus* 15:9.

2 Eulogy. Praise of a person who has either the advantages of wealth and power, or the consideration to be dead.

> AMBROSE BIERCE (1842–1914), U.S. author. *The Devil's Dictionary* (1881–1906).

3 Praise out of season, or tactlessly bestowed, can freeze the heart as much as blame.

> PEARL S. BUCK (1892–1973), U.S. author. *To My Daughters, With Love*, "First Meeting" (1967).

4 The advantage of doing one's praising for oneself is that one can lay it on so thick and exactly in the right places.

> SAMUEL BUTLER (1835–1902), English author. *The Way of All Flesh*, ch. 34 (1903).

5 One should use praise to recognize what one is not.

> ELIAS CANETTI (b. 1905), Austrian novelist, philosopher. *The Secret Heart Of The Clock: Notes, Aphorisms, Fragments 1973–1985*, "1976" (1991).

6 By recognizing a favorable opinion of yourself, and taking pleasure in it, you in a measure give yourself and your peace of mind into the keeping of another, of whose attitude you can never be certain. You have a new source of doubt and apprehension.

> CHARLES HORTON COOLEY (1864–1929), U.S. sociologist. *Human Nature and the Social Order*, ch. 6 (1902).

7 What every genuine philosopher (every genuine man, in fact) craves most is *praise*—although the philosophers generally call it "recognition"!

> WILLIAM JAMES (1842–1910), U.S. psychologist, philosopher. Letter, 13 June 1907, to philosopher Henri Bergson (published in *The Letters of William James*, vol. 2, 1920).

8 A continual feast of commendation is only to be obtained by merit or by wealth: many are therefore obliged to content themselves with single morsels, and recompense the infrequency of their enjoyment by excess and riot, whenever fortune sets the banquet before them.

> SAMUEL JOHNSON (1709–84), English author, lexicographer. *Rambler*, no. 193 (London, 21 Jan. 1752; repr. in *Works of Samuel Johnson*, vol. 5, ed. by W. J. Bate and Albrecht B. Strauss, 1969).

9 He who praises everybody, praises nobody.

> SAMUEL JOHNSON (1709–84), English author, lexicographer. *Works* vol. 11 (1787, p. 216). Quoted in: James Boswell, *Life of Samuel Johnson*, note to vol. 3 (ed. by George Birkbeck Hill, rev. L. F. Powell, 1934).

10 A heap of epithets is poor praise: the praise lies in the facts, and in the way of telling them.

> JEAN DE LA BRUYÈRE (1645–96), French writer, moralist. *Characters*, "Of Books," aph. 13 (1688).

11 So long as you are praised think only that you are not yet on your own path but on that of another.

> FRIEDRICH NIETZSCHE (1844–1900), German philosopher. *Assorted Opinions and Maxims*, aph. 340 (1879).

12 I love eulogies. They are the most moving kind of speech because they attempt to pluck meaning from the fog, and on short order, when the emotions are still ragged and raw and susceptible to leaps.

PEGGY NOONAN (b. 1950), U.S. author, presidential speech-writer. *What I Saw at the Revolution,* ch. 13 (1990).

13 Fondly we think we honour merit then,
When we but praise ourselves in other men.

ALEXANDER POPE (1688–1744), English satirical poet. *An Essay on Criticism.*

14 I will praise any man that will praise me.

WILLIAM SHAKESPEARE (1564–1616), English dramatist, poet. Enobarbus, in *Antony and Cleopatra,* act 2, sc. 6.

15 Among the smaller duties of life I hardly know any one more important than that of not praising where praise is not due.

SYDNEY SMITH (1771–1845), English writer, clergyman. *Sketches of Moral Philosophy,* Lecture 9 (1850).

16 Men sometimes feel injured by praise because it assigns a limit to their merit; few people are modest enough not to take offense that one appreciates them.

LUC, MARQUIS DE VAUVENARGUES (1715–47), French moralist. *Refléxions et Maximes,* no. 66 (1746).

See also La Rochefoucauld on COMPLIMENTS; Johnson on FLATTERY; Chesterfield on MODESTY.

PRAYER

1 O Lord! thou knowest how busy I must be this day: if I forget thee, do not thou forget me.

SIR JACOB ASTLEY (1579–1652), English Royalist soldier. Uttered before the Battle of Edgehill, 23 Oct. 1642, in the English Civil War.

2 To pray is to pay attention to something or someone other than oneself. Whenever a man so concentrates his attention—on a landscape, a poem, a geometrical problem, an idol, or the True God—that he completely forgets his own ego and desires, he is praying. . . . The primary task of the schoolteacher is to teach children, in a secular context, the technique of prayer.

W. H. AUDEN (1907–73), Anglo-American poet. *A Certain World,* "Prayer, Nature of" (1970).

3 Spiritual favors are not always to be looked for, and not always to be relied on.

AMELIA BARR (1831–1919), Anglo-American novelist. *All the Days of My Life,* ch. 19 (1913).

4 The man who says his evening prayer is a captain posting his sentinels. He can sleep.

CHARLES BAUDELAIRE (1821–67), French poet. *My Heart Laid Bare* (written c. 1865; published in *Intimate Journals,* sct. 116, 1887; tr. by Christopher Isherwood, 1930; rev. by Don Bachardy, 1989).

5 The wish to pray is a prayer in itself . . . God can ask no more than that of us.

GEORGES BERNANOS (1888–1948), French novelist, political writer. *The Diary of a Country Priest,* ch. 4 (1936).

6 Therefore I say unto you, What things soever ye desire, when ye pray, believe that ye receive them, and ye shall have them.

BIBLE: NEW TESTAMENT. Jesus, in *Mark* 11:24.

7 Pray. To ask the laws of the universe to be annulled on behalf of a single petitioner confessedly unworthy.

AMBROSE BIERCE (1842–1914), U.S. author. *The Devil's Dictionary* (1881–1906).

8 A childish soul not inoculated with compulsory prayer is a soul open to any religious infection.

ALEXANDER COCKBURN (b. 1941), Anglo-Irish journalist. *Corruptions of Empire,* pt. 1, "Heatherdown" (1988; first published 1985).

9 Prayer is translation. A man translates himself into a child asking for all there is in a language he has barely mastered.

LEONARD COHEN (b. 1934), Canadian singer, poet, novelist. "F.," in *Beautiful Losers,* sct. 18 (1970).

10 I throw myself down in my chamber, and I call in, and invite God, and his Angels thither, and when they are there, I neglect God and his Angels, for the noise of a fly, for the rattling of a coach, for the whining of a door.

JOHN DONNE (c. 1572–1631), English divine, metaphysical poet. *Eighty Sermons,* no. 80, sct. 3 (1640; preached 12 Dec. 1626).

11 Audible prayer can never do the works of spiritual understanding, which regenerates; but silent prayer, watchfulness, and devout obedience enable us to follow Jesus' example. Long prayers, superstition, and creeds clip the strong pinions of love, and clothe religion in human forms. Whatever materializes worship hinders man's spiritual growth and keeps him from demonstrating his power over error.

MARY BAKER EDDY (1821–1910), U.S. founder of the Christian Science movement. *Science and Health,* ch. 1 (1875).

12 Prayer is not an old woman's idle amusement. Properly understood and applied, it is the most potent instrument of action.

MOHANDAS K. GANDHI (1869–1948), Indian political, spiritual leader. *Non-Violence in Peace and War,* vol. 2, ch. 77 (1948).

13 Prayer is not asking. It is a longing of the soul. It is daily admission of one's weakness. . . . It is better in prayer to have a heart without words than words without a heart.

MOHANDAS K. GANDHI (1869–1948), Indian political, spiritual leader. *Young India* (23 Jan. 1930).

14 Old hands soil, it seems, whatever they caress, but they too have their beauty when they are joined in prayer. Young hands were made for caresses and the sheathing of love. It is a pity to make them join too soon.

ANDRÉ GIDE (1869–1951), French author. *Journals 1889–1949* (ed. by Justin O'Brien, 1951), entry for 21 Jan. 1929.

15 I have not placed reading before praying because I regard it more important, but because, in order to pray aright, we must understand what we are praying for.

ANGELINA GRIMKÉ (1805–79), U.S. abolitionist, feminist. "Appeal to the Christian Women of the South," in *Anti-Slavery Examiner* (Sept. 1836; repr. in *The Oven Birds: American Women on Womanhood 1820–1920,* ed. by Gail Parker, 1972).

16 Your cravings as a human animal do not become a prayer just because it is God whom you ask to attend to them.

> DAG HAMMARSKJÖLD (1905–61), Swedish statesman, Secretary-General of U.N. *Markings*, "The Middle Years" (1963; written 1941–42).

17 Our nada who art in nada, nada be thy name thy kingdom nada thy will be nada in nada as it is in nada. Give us this nada our daily nada and nada us our nada as we nada our nadas and nada us not into nada but deliver us from nada; pues nada. Hail nothing full of nothing, nothing is with thee.

> ERNEST HEMINGWAY (1899–1961), U.S. author. The older waiter, in "A Clean, Well-Lighted Place" (published in *Winner Take Nothing*, 1932).

18 There are thoughts which are prayers. There are moments when, whatever the posture of the body, the soul is on its knees.

> VICTOR HUGO (1802–85), French poet, dramatist, novelist. Marius, in *Les Misérables*, pt. 4, bk. 5, ch. 4 (1862).

19 There is no greater distance than that between a man in prayer and God.

> IVAN ILLICH (b. 1926), Austrian-born U.S. theologian, author. *Celebration of Awareness*, ch. 4 (1969).

20 Father in Heaven! When the thought of thee wakes in our hearts let it not awaken like a frightened bird that flies about in dismay, but like a child waking from its sleep with a heavenly smile.

> SØREN KIERKEGAARD (1813–55), Danish philosopher. *The Journals of Søren Kierkegaard: A Selection*, no. 248 (ed. and tr. by Alexander Dru, 1938), entry for 6 Jan. 1839.

21 The fates are not quite obdurate;
They have a grim, sardonic way
Of granting them who supplicate
The thing they wanted yesterday.

> ROSELLE MERCIER MONTGOMERY (1874–1933), U.S. writer. *The Fates*.

22 Prayer should be short, without giving God Almighty reasons why he should grant this, or that; he knows best what is good for us.

> JOHN SELDEN (1584–1654), English jurist, statesman. *Table Talk*, "Prayer" (1686).

23 We often want one thing and pray for another, not telling the truth even to the gods.

> SENECA (c. 5 B.C.–A.D. c. 65), Roman writer, philosopher, statesman. *Epistulae ad Lucilium*, Epistle 95, sct. 2.

24 Bow, stubborn knees!

> WILLIAM SHAKESPEARE (1564–1616), English dramatist, poet. Claudius, in *Hamlet*, act 3, sc. 3.

25 Whatsoever we beg of God, let us also work for it.

> JEREMY TAYLOR (1613–67), English churchman, devotional writer. *The Rule and Exercises of Holy Living*, ch. 4, sct. 7 (4th ed., 1654).

26 I hate it when people pray on the screen. It's not because I hate praying, but whenever I see an actor forld his hands and look up in the spotlight, I'm lost. There's only one other thing in the movies I hate as much, and that's sex. You just can't get in bed or pray to God and convince me on the screen.

> ORSON WELLES (1915–84), U.S. filmmaker, actor, producer. Interview in David Frost, *The Americans*, "Can a Martian Survive by Pretending to be a Leading American Actor?" (1970).

27 When the gods wish to punish us they answer our prayers.

> OSCAR WILDE (1854–1900), Anglo-Irish playwright, author. Sir Robert Chiltern, in *An Ideal Husband*, act 2.

See also Irish proverb on AGE AND AGING; CONTEMPLATION; Cowper on The DEVIL; Voltaire on ENEMIES; Beckett on GOD; Browne on SLEEP.

PREACHING

1 I preached as never sure to preach again,
And as a dying man to dying men.

> RICHARD BAXTER (1615–91), English Nonconformist cleric. *Love Breathing Thanks and Praise*.

2 Every accent, every emphasis, every modulation of voice, was so perfectly well turned and well placed, that, without being interested in the subject, one could not help being pleased with the discourse; a pleasure of much the same kind with that received from an excellent piece of music. This is an advantage itinerant preachers have over those who are stationary, as the latter can not well improve their delivery of a sermon by so many rehearsals.

> BENJAMIN FRANKLIN (1706–90), U.S. statesman, writer. *Autobiography*, ch. 8 (written 1771–90; published 1868), said of the Irish itinerant preacher the Reverend Mr. Whitefield, who arrived in Philadelphia in 1739.

3 It is hardly to be believed how spiritual reflections when mixed with a little physics can hold people's attention and give them a livelier idea of God than do the often ill-applied examples of his wrath.

> G. C. LICHTENBERG (1742–99), German physicist, philosopher. *Aphorisms*, "Notebook A," aph. 11 (written 1765–99; tr. by R. J. Hollingdale, 1990).

4 Preach in the name of God. The learned will smile; ask the learned what they have done for their country. The priests will excommunicate you; say to the priests that you know God better than all of them together do, and that between God and His law you have no need of any intermediary. The people will understand you, and repeat with you: *We believe in God the Father, who is Intelligence and Love, Creator and Teacher of Humanity.* And in this saying you and the People will conquer.

> GIUSEPPE MAZZINI (1805–72), Italian nationalist leader. *The Duties of Man*, ch. 2 (1844–58; tr. 1907).

5 To preach long, loud, and Damnation, is the way to be cried up. We love a man that damns us, and we run after him again to save us.

> JOHN SELDEN (1584–1654), English jurist, statesman. *Table Talk*, "Damnation" (1686).

6 But, good my brother,
Do not, as some ungracious pastors do,
Show me the steep and thorny way to heaven
Whilst like a puffed and reckless libertine

Himself the primrose path of dalliance treads
And recks not his own rede.

WILLIAM SHAKESPEARE (1564–1616), English dramatist, poet. Ophelia's response to the lengthy advice given her by her brother Polonius before his departure for France, in *Hamlet*, act 1, sc. 3; the last line means "heeds not his own advice."

7 That we should practise what we preach is generally admitted; but anyone who preaches what he and his hearers practise must incur the gravest moral disapprobation.

LOGAN PEARSALL SMITH (1865–1946), U.S. essayist, aphorist. *Afterthoughts*, "Life and Human Nature" (1931).

See also Cervantes on EXAMPLE; Niebuhr on JOURNALISM AND JOURNALISTS.

PRECEDENT

1 It is in the very nature of things human that every act that has once made its appearance and has been recorded in the history of mankind stays with mankind as a potentiality long after its actuality has become a thing of the past.

HANNAH ARENDT (1906–75), German-born U.S. political philosopher. *Eichmann in Jerusalem*, Epilogue (1963).

2 Judicial judgment must take deep account . . . of the day before yesterday in order that yesterday may not paralyze today.

FELIX FRANKFURTER (1882–1965), U.S. associate justice of the Supreme Court. Quoted in: *National Observer* (Silver Spring, Md., 1 March 1965).

3 The man who will follow precedent, but never create one, is merely an obvious example of the routineer. You find him desperately numerous in the civil service, in the official bureaus. To him government is something given as unconditionally, as absolutely as ocean or hill. He goes on winding the tape that he finds. His imagination has rarely extricated itself from under the administrative machine to gain any sense of what a human, temporary contraption the whole affair is. What he thinks is the heavens above him is nothing but the roof.

WALTER LIPPMANN (1889–1974), U.S. journalist. *A Preface to Politics*, ch. 1 (1913).

4 The glory of each generation is to make its own precedents.

BELVA LOCKWOOD (1830–1917), U.S. lawyer, feminist. Quoted in: Mary Virginia Fox, *Lady for the Defense*, pt. 3, ch. 13 (1975). Lockwood was arguing in favor of admitting women to practice in the U.S. Supreme Court, for which there was no precedent. In 1879 she became the first woman to practice there.

5 To say that a thing has never yet been done among men is to erect a barrier stronger than reason, stronger than discussion.

THOMAS BRACKETT REED (1839–1902), U.S. Republican politician. Speech, 12 April 1878, to the House of Representatives.

6 It is a maxim among these lawyers, that whatever hath been done before, may legally be done again: and therefore they take special care to record all the decisions formerly made against common justice and the general reason of mankind.

JONATHAN SWIFT (1667–1745), Anglo-Irish satirist. Gulliver, in *Gulliver's Travels*, "A Voyage to the Country of the Houyhnhnms," pt. 4, ch. 5 (1726), describing his native land.

7 To do something, say something, see something, before *anybody* else—these are things that confer a pleasure compared with which other pleasures are tame and commonplace, other ecstacies cheap and trivial.

MARK TWAIN (1835–1910), U.S. author. *The Innocents Abroad*, ch. 26 (1869).

PREDICTION

1 Predictions of the future are never anything but projections of present automatic processes and procedures, that is, of occurrences that are likely to come to pass if men do not act and if nothing unexpected happens; every action, for better or worse, and every accident necessarily destroys the whole pattern in whose frame the prediction moves and where it finds its evidence.

HANNAH ARENDT (1906–75), German-born U.S. political philosopher. *Crises of the Republic*, "On Violence," sct. 1 (1972).

2 No one can possibly know what is about to happen: it is happening, each time, for the first time, for the only time.

JAMES BALDWIN (1924–87), U.S. author. *The Price Of The Ticket*, "The Devil Finds Work," sct. 1 (1985; first published 1976).

3 He who asks fortune-tellers the future unwittingly forfeits an inner intimation of coming events that is a thousand times more exact than anything they may say. He is impelled by inertia, rather than curiosity, and nothing is more unlike the submissive apathy with which he hears his fate revealed than the alert dexterity with which the man of courage lays hands on the future.

WALTER BENJAMIN (1892–1940), German critic, philosopher. *One-Way Street*, "Madame Ariane—Second Courtyard on the Left" (1928; repr. in *One-Way Street and Other Writings*, 1978).

4 The unpredictability inherent in human affairs is due largely to the fact that the by-products of a human process are more fateful than the product.

ERIC HOFFER (1902–83), U.S. philosopher. *Reflections on the Human Condition*, aph. 122 (1973).

5 Legends of prediction are common throughout the whole Household of Man. Gods speak, spirits speak, computers speak. Oracular ambiguity or statistical probability provides loopholes, and discrepancies are expunged by Faith.

URSULA K. LE GUIN (b. 1929), U.S. author. *The Left Hand of Darkness*, ch. 4 (1969).

PREGNANCY

1 Childbearing is glorified in part because women die from it.

ANDREA DWORKIN (b. 1946), U.S. feminist critic. *Pornography*, ch. 2 (1981).

2 If men were equally at risk from this condition—if they knew their bellies might swell as if they were suffering from end-stage cirrhosis, that they would have to go nearly a year without a stiff drink, a cigarette, or even an aspirin, that they would be subject to fainting spells and unable to fight their way onto commuter trains—then I am sure that pregnancy would be classified as a sexually transmitted disease and abortions would be no more controversial than emergency appendectomies.

> BARBARA EHRENREICH (b. 1941), U.S. author, columnist. *The Worst Years of Our Lives*, "Their Dilemma and Mine" (1991).

3   These wretched babies don't come until they are ready.

> ELIZABETH II (b. 1926), Queen of Great Britain and Northern Ireland. Quoted in: *Today* (London, 4 Aug. 1988), said of the expected birth of her fifth grandchild and the first child of the Duke and Duchess of York. A girl, Beatrice, was born five days later.

4   If men could get pregnant, abortion would be a sacrament.

> FLORYNCE R. KENNEDY (b. 1916), U.S. lawyer, civil rights activist. Quoted in: Gloria Steinem, "The Verbal Karate of Florynce R. Kennedy, Esq.," in *Ms.* (New York, March 1973).

5   Pregnant women! They had that weird frisson, an aura of magic that combined awkwardly with an earthy sense of duty. Mundane, because they were nothing unique on the suburban streets; ethereal because their attention was ever somewhere else. Whatever you said was trivial. And they had that preciousness which they imposed wherever they went, compelling attention, constantly reminding you that they carried the future inside, its contours already drawn, but veiled, private, an inner secret.

> RUTH MORGAN (1920–78), U.S. novelist. Evelina, in *Andrew's Revenge*, ch. 13 (1975).

6   Pregnancy demonstrates the deterministic character of woman's sexuality. Every pregnant woman has body and self taken over by a chthonian force beyond her control. In the welcome pregnancy, this is a happy sacrifice. But in the unwanted one, initated by rape or misadventure, it is a horror. Such unfortunate women look directly into nature's heart of darkness. For a fetus is a benign tumor, a vampire who steals in order to live. The so-called miracle of birth is nature getting her own way.

> CAMILLE PAGLIA (b. 1947), U.S. author, critic, educator. *Sexual Personae*, ch. 1 (1990). Paglia explains "chthonian" as "my symbol for unregenerate nature."

7   Good work, Mary. We all knew you had it in you.

> DOROTHY PARKER (1893–1967), U.S. humorous writer. Telegram to a friend who had belatedly given birth. Quoted in: Alexander Woollcott, *While Rome Burns*, "Our Mrs. Parker" (1934).

8   I am nothing but a miserable, crushed worm, whom no one wants, whom no one loves, a useless creature with morning sickness, and a big belly, two rotten teeth, and a bad temper, a battered sense of dignity, and a love which nobody wants and which nearly drives me insane.

> SOPHIE TOLSTOY (1844–1919), Russian diarist. *A Diary of Tolstoy's Wife, 1860–1891* (1928), entry for 12 September 1867.

9   I positively think that ladies who are always *enceinte* quite disgusting; it is more like a rabbit or guinea-pig than anything else and really it is not very nice.

> VICTORIA (1819–1901), Queen of Great Britain and Ireland. Let-

ter, 15 June 1859, to her daughter Princess Frederick William (published in *Queen Victoria in Her Letters and Journals*, ed. by Christopher Hibbert, 1984).

10   Most of a modest woman's life was spent, after all, in denying what, in one day at least of every year, was made obvious.

> VIRGINIA WOOLF (1882–1941), British novelist. *Orlando*, ch. 6 (1928), on pregnancy in Victorian times.

PREJUDICE

1   Prejudice. A vagrant opinion without visible means of support.

> AMBROSE BIERCE (1842–1914), U.S. author. *The Devil's Dictionary* (1881–1906).

2   Prejudices, it is well known, are most difficult to eradicate from the heart whose soil has never been loosened or fertilized by education; they grow there, firm as weeds among stones.

> CHARLOTTE BRONTë (1816–55), English novelist. *Jane Eyre*, ch. 29 (1847).

3   It is just as impossible to help reform by conciliating prejudice as it is by buying votes. Prejudice is the enemy. Whoever is not for you is against you.

> JOHN JAY CHAPMAN (1862–1933), U.S. author. *Practical Agitation*, ch. 1 (1898).

4   Our prejudices are our mistresses; reason is at best our wife, very often heard indeed, but seldom minded.

> LORD CHESTERFIELD (1694–1773), English statesman, man of letters. Letter, 13 April 1752 (first published 1774; repr. in *The Letters of the Earl of Chesterfield to His Son*, vol. 2, no. 276, ed. by Charles Strachey, 1901).

5   America owes most of its social prejudices to the exaggerated religious opinions of the different sects which were so instrumental in establishing the colonies.

> JAMES FENIMORE COOPER (1789–1851), U.S. novelist. *The American Democrat*, "On Prejudice" (1838).

6   It is not the simple statement of facts that ushers in freedom; it is the constant repetition of them that has this liberating effect. Tolerance is the result not of enlightenment, but of boredom.

> QUENTIN CRISP (b. 1908), British author. *The Naked Civil Servant*, ch. 28 (1968).

7   He who has a task to perform must know how to take sides, or he is quite unworthy of it.

> JOHANN WOLFGANG VON GOETHE (1749–1832), German poet, dramatist. *Propyläen*, Introduction (1798). This periodical, founded by Goethe, took its title from the gateway to the Acropolis of Athens.

8   Man associates ideas not according to logic or verifiable exactitude, but according to his pleasure and interests. It is for this reason that most truths are nothing but prejudices.

> RÉMY DE GOURMONT (1858–1915), French critic, novelist. "The Dissociation of Ideas" (1899; repr. in *Selected Writings*, ed. and tr. by Glen S. Burne, 1966).

9   There is no prejudice so strong as that which arises from a fancied exemption from all prejudice.

> WILLIAM HAZLITT (1778–1830), English essayist. *The Round Table*, "On the Tendency of Sects" (1817).

10   No wise man can have a contempt for the prejudices of others; and he should even stand in a certain awe of his own, as if they were aged parents and monitors. They may in the end prove wiser than he.

> WILLIAM HAZLITT (1778–1830), English essayist. *Characteristics: in the Manner of Rochefoucault's Maxims*, no. 132 (1823; repr. in *Collected Works*, vol. 2, ed. by A. R. Waller and Arnold Glover, 1902).

11   Sometimes we feel the loss of a prejudice as a loss of vigor.

> ERIC HOFFER (1902–83), U.S. philosopher. *Reflections on the Human Condition*, aph. 166 (1973).

12   Prejudices are so to speak the mechanical instincts of men: through their prejudices they do without any effort many things they would find too difficult to think through to the point of resolving to do them.

> G. C. LICHTENBERG (1742–99), German physicist, philosopher. *Aphorisms*, "Notebook A," aph. 17 (written 1765–99; tr. by R. J. Hollingdale, 1990).

13   The tendency of the casual mind is to pick out or stumble upon a sample which supports or defies its prejudices, and then to make it the representative of a whole class.

> WALTER LIPPMANN (1889–1974), U.S. journalist. *Public Opinion*, ch. 3, sct. 10 (1929).

14   One may no more live in the world without picking up the moral prejudices of the world than one will be able to go to hell without perspiring.

> H. L. MENCKEN (1880–1956), U.S. journalist. *Prejudices*, "Scientific Examination of a Popular Virtue" (Second Series, 1920).

15   Stupidity, outrage, vanity, cruelty, iniquity, bad faith, falsehood—we fail to see the whole array when it is facing in the same direction as we.

> JEAN ROSTAND (1894–1977), French biologist, writer. *Pensées d'un Biologiste* (1939; repr. in *The Substance of Man*, "A Biologist's Thoughts," ch. 10, 1962).

16   Prejudice is the sole author of infamies: how many acts are so qualified by an opinion forged out of nought but prejudice!

> MARQUIS DE SADE (1740–1814), French author. Mme Delbène, in *L'Histoire de Juliette, ou les Prospérités du Vice*, pt. 1 (1797).

17   The discovery of truth is prevented more effectively, not by the false appearance things present and which mislead into error, not directly by weakness of the reasoning powers, but by preconceived opinion, by prejudice.

> ARTHUR SCHOPENHAUER (1788–1860), German philosopher. *Parerga and Paralipomena*, vol. 2, ch. 1, sct. 17 (1851).

See also Hazlitt on CUSTOM; Twain on HISTORY; Figes on LOGIC; Proust on PARADOX.

THE PRESENT

1   The pleasure we derive from the representation of the present is due, not only to the beauty it can be clothed in, but also to its essential quality of being the present.

> CHARLES BAUDELAIRE (1821–67), French poet. "The Painter of Modern Life," sct. 1 (published in *L'Art Romantique*, 1869; repr. in *Selected Writings on Art and Artists*, ed. by P. E. Charvet, 1972).

2   We were wise indeed, could we discern truly the signs of our own time; and by knowledge of its wants and advantages, wisely adjust our own position in it. Let us, instead of gazing idly into the obscure distance, look calmly around us, for a little, on the perplexed scene where we stand. Perhaps, on a more serious inspection, something of its perplexity will disappear, some of ts distinctive characters and deeper tendencies more clearly reveal themselves; whereby our own relations to it, our own true aims and endeavours in it, may also become clearer.

> THOMAS CARLYLE (1795–1881), Scottish essayist, historian. *Signs of the Times* (1829; first published in *Edinburgh Review*, no. 98).

3   Time past and time future
What might have been and what has been
Point to one end, which is always present.

> T. S. ELIOT (1888–1965), Anglo-American poet, critic. *Four Quartets*, "Burnt Norton," pt. 1.

4   Give me insight into today and you may have the antique and future worlds.

> RALPH WALDO EMERSON (1803–82), U.S. essayist, poet, philosopher. Lecture, 31 Aug. 1837, delivered before the Phi Beta Kappa Society, Harvard University (repr. in *Nature, Addresses and Lectures*, "The American Scholar," 1849).

5   The present reeks of mediocrity and the atom bomb.

> RENÉ MAGRITTE (1898–1967), Belgian surrealist painter. Quoted in: Suzi Gablik, *Magritte*, ch. 5 (1970). "I don't want to belong to my own time, or for that matter, to any other," Magritte added.

6   We shall be better prepared for the future if we see how terrible, how *doomed* the present is.

> IRIS MURDOCH (b. 1919), British novelist, philosopher. David Crimond, in *The Book and the Brotherhood*, pt. 2, "Midwinter" (1987).

7   The obscurest epoch is to-day.

> ROBERT LOUIS STEVENSON (1850–94), Scottish novelist, essayist, poet. *The Day After Tomorrow* (first published 1887; repr. in *Complete Works*, vol. 26, 1924).

8   He to whom the present is the only thing that is present, knows nothing of the age in which he lives.

> OSCAR WILDE (1854–1900), Anglo-Irish playwright, author. Review of Walter Pater, *Appreciations, with an Essay on Style*, in *Speaker* (London, 22 Mar. 1890).

9   The present is the ever moving shadow that divides yesterday from tomorrow. In that lies hope.

> FRANK LLOYD WRIGHT (1869–1959), U.S. architect. Closing words of *The Living City*, pt. 5, "Night is but a Shadow Cast by the Sun" (1958).

See also Wittgenstein on ETERNITY; Orwell on The PAST.

THE PRESIDENT

1 Power is poison. It's effect on Presidents had always been tragic.

> HENRY B. ADAMS (1838–1918), U.S. historian. *The Education of Henry Adams*, ch. 28 (1907).

2 Under a Presidential government, a nation has, except at the electing moment, no influence; it has not the ballot-box before it; its virtue is gone, and it must wait till its instant of despotism again returns.

> WALTER BAGEHOT (1826–77), English economist, critic. *The English Constitution*, ch. 1 (1867).

3 You don't need to know who's playing on the White House tennis court to be a good president. A president has many roles.

> JAMES BAKER (b. 1930), U.S. Republican politician, Secretary of State. Remark made while serving as White House Chief of Staff, on the president's overall knowledge and accountability. Quoted in: Joan Didion, *Miami*, ch. 15 (1987).

4 Wilson adventured for the whole of the human race. Not as a servant, but as a champion. So pure was this motive, so unflecked with anything that his worst enemies could find, except the mildest and most excusable, a personal vanity, practically the minimum to be human, that in a sense his adventure is that of humanity itself. In Wilson, the whole of mankind breaks camp, sets out from home and wrestles with the universe and its gods.

> WILLIAM BOLITHO (1890–1930), British author. *Twelve Against the Gods*, "Woodrow Wilson" (1930).

5 We have had triumphs, we have made mistakes, we have had sex.

> GEORGE BUSH (b. 1924), U.S. Republican politician, president. Gaffe reported in *International Herald Tribune* (Paris, 13 May 1988), said of the Reagan-Bush administration.

6 All Presidents start out to run a crusade but after a couple of years they find they are running something less heroic and much more intractable: namely the presidency. The people are well cured by then of election fever, during which they think they are choosing Moses. In the third year, they look on the man as a sinner and a bumbler and begin to poke around for rumours of another Messiah.

> ALISTAIR COOKE (b. 1908), British broadcaster, journalist. *Talk About America*, ch. 31 (1968).

7 When I was a boy I was told that anybody could become President. I'm beginning to believe it.

> CLARENCE DARROW (1857–1938), U.S. lawyer, writer. Quoted in: Irving Stone, *Clarence Darrow for the Defence*, ch. 6 (1941).

8 But even the President of the United States
Sometimes must have
To stand naked.

> BOB DYLAN (b. 1941), U.S. singer, songwriter. "It's Alright Ma (I'm Only Bleeding)," on the album *Bringing it all Back Home* (1965).

9 The President has paid dear for his White House. It has commonly cost him all his peace, and the best of his manly attributes. To preserve for a short time so conspicuous an appearance before the world, he is content to eat dust before the real masters who stand erect behind the throne.

> RALPH WALDO EMERSON (1803–82), U.S. essayist, poet, philosopher. *Essays*, "Compensation" (First Series, 1841).

10 I feel very proud, even though they didn't elect me, to be President of the Argentines.

> GENERAL LEOPOLDO GALTIERI (b. 1927), Argentine soldier, president. Quoted in: *Observer* (London, 2 Jan. 1983).

11 I don't have any problem with a reporter or a news person who says the President is uninformed on this issue or that issue. I don't think any of us would challenge that. I do have a problem with the singular focus on this, as if that's the only standard by which we ought to judge a president. What we learned in the last administration was how little having an encyclopedic grasp of all the facts has to do with governing.

> DAVID R. GERGEN (b. 1942), U.S. editor, former White House communications director. *New York Times* (10 Jan. 1984).

12 If you want to see your plays performed the way you wrote them, become President.

> VáCLAV HAVEL (b. 1936), Czech playwright, president. Address to Institute of Contemporary Arts, London. Quoted in: *Independent* (London, 24 March 1990).

13 The President is the people's lobbyist.

> HUBERT H. HUMPHREY (1911–78), U.S. Democratic politician, vice president. Address, 8 Dec. 1965, at Rockefeller Public Service Awards, Washington, D.C.

14 No man will ever bring out of that office the reputation which carries him into it. The honeymoon would be as short in that case as in any other, and its moments of ecstasy would be ransomed by years of torment and hatred.

> THOMAS JEFFERSON (1743–1826), U.S. president. Letter, 27 Dec. 1796. Jefferson was shortly to begin a four-year term as vice-president followed by eight years as president.

15 Jerry Ford is so dumb he can't fart and chew gum at the same time.

> LYNDON B. JOHNSON (1908–73), U.S. Democratic politician, president. Quoted in: Richard Reeves, *A Ford, Not a Lincoln*, ch. 1 (1975). Reeves alleges that Johnson's remark was "cleaned up" by "the late President's aides and history."

16 Frankly, I don't mind not being president. I just mind that someone else is.

> EDWARD KENNEDY (b. 1932), U.S. Democratic politician. Speech, 22 Mar. 1986, Gridiron Club, Washington, D.C. Kennedy unsuccessfully challenged Jimmy Carter for the 1980 Democratic presidential nomination.

17 When we got into office, the thing that surprised me most was to find that things were just as bad as we'd been saying they were.

> JOHN F. KENNEDY (1917–63), U.S. Democratic politician, president. Speech, 27 May 1961, at dinner honoring Kennedy's 44th birthday, Washington, D.C.

18 We want a president who is as much like an American tourist as possible. Someone with the same goofy grin, the same innocent intentions, the same naive trust; a president with no conception of foreign policy and no discernible connection to the U.S. government, whose

Nice Guyism will narrow the gap between the U.S. and us until nobody can tell the difference.

FLORENCE KING (b. 1936), U.S. author. *Reflections in a Jaundiced Eye*, "Nice Guyism" (1989).

19 A President is best judged by the enemies he makes when he has really hit his stride.

MAX LERNER (b. 1902), U.S. author, columnist. *The Unfinished Country*, pt. 4, "The Education of Harry Truman" (1959; first published in *New York Star*, 9 Jan. 1949).

20 The power confided in me will be used to hold, occupy and possess the property and places belonging to the government, and to collect the duties and imposts.

ABRAHAM LINCOLN (1809–65), U.S. president. First Inaugural Address, 4 March 1861.

21 When the President does it, that means that it is not illegal.

RICHARD M. NIXON (b. 1913), U.S. Republican politician, president. TV interview with David Frost, 20 May 1977. Quoted in: Frost's account of the Nixon interviews, *I Gave Them a Sword*, ch. 8 (1978).

22 In our brief national history we have shot four of our presidents, worried five of them to death, impeached one and hounded another out of office. And when all else fails, we hold an election and assassinate their character.

P. J. O'ROURKE (b. 1947), U.S. journalist. *Parliament of Whores*, "The President" (1991).

23 A president, however, must stand somewhat apart, as all great presidents have known instinctively. Then the language which has the power to survive its own utterance is the most likely to move those to whom it is immediately spoken.

J. R. POLE (b. 1922), British historian. *The State of the Language*, "The Language of American Presidents" (1980).

24 We're an ideal political family, as accessible as Disneyland.

MAUREEN REAGAN (b. 1941), Daughter of Ronald Reagan. Quoted in: *Guardian* (London, 24 Dec. 1984).

25 But there are advantages to being elected President. The day after I was elected, I had my high school grades classified Top Secret.

RONALD REAGAN (b. 1911), U.S. Republican politician, president. Address, 19 June 1986, to the graduating class of Glassboro High School, New Jersey.

26 All Coolidge had to do in 1924 was to keep his mean trap shut, to be elected. All Harding had to do in 1920 was repeat "Avoid foreign entanglements." All Hoover had to do in 1928 was to endorse Coolidge. All Roosevelt had to do in 1932 was to point to Hoover.

ROBERT E. SHERWOOD (1896–1955), U.S. playwright. Quoted in: *Wit's End* (ed. by Robert E. Drennan, 1968).

27 From now on, I think it is safe to predict, neither the Democratic nor the Republican Party will ever nominate for President a candidate without good looks, stage presence, theatrical delivery, and a sense of timing.

JAMES THURBER (1894–1961), U.S. humorist, illustrator. From an unpublished manuscript, dated 20 March 1961, later published in *James Thurber Collecting Himself* (1989), said of the Kennedy-Nixon TV debates.

28 The buck stops here.

HARRY S TRUMAN (1884–1972), U.S. Democratic politician, president. Motto on Truman's desk at the White House. Quoted in: Alfred Steinberg, *The Man from Missouri* (1962).

29 When you get to be President, there are all those things, the honors, the twenty-one gun salutes, all those things. You have to remember it isn't for you. It's for the Presidency.

HARRY S TRUMAN (1884–1972), U.S. Democratic politician, president. Quoted in: Merle Miller, *Plain Speaking: Conversations with Harry S Truman*, ch. 15 (1973).

30 To be President of the United States, sir, is to act as advocate for a blind, venomous, and ungrateful client; still, one must make the best of the case, for the purposes of Providence.

JOHN UPDIKE (b. 1932), U.S. author, critic. President James Polk, in *Buchanan Dying*, act 2 (1974).

31 In America the President reigns for four years, and Journalism governs for ever and ever.

OSCAR WILDE (1854–1900), Anglo-Irish playwright, author. *The Soul of Man Under Socialism*, in *Fortnightly Review* (London, Feb. 1891; repr. 1895).

See also The FIRST LADY; DeLillo on The KENNEDY FAMILY; Kissinger on LOYALTY; RICHARD NIXON; Reagan on QUOTATION; RONALD REAGAN.

ELVIS PRESLEY

1 When I first heard Elvis's voice I just knew that I wasn't going to work for anybody and nobody was gonna be my boss. Hearing him for the first time was like busting out of jail.

BOB DYLAN (b. 1941), U.S. singer, songwriter. Comment on the anniversary of Presley's death, in *US* (New York, Aug. 1987).

2 Commercial to the core, Elvis was the kind of singer dear to the heart of the music business. For him to sing a song was to sell a song. His G clef was a dollar sign.

ALBERT GOLDMAN (b. 1927), U.S. author, critic. *Elvis*, ch. 14 (1981).

3 Distorting hackneyed words in hackneyed songs
He turns revolt into a style, prolongs
The impulse to a habit of the time.

THOM GUNN (b. 1929), British poet. *Elvis Presley*, in *The Sense of Movement* (1957). The poem gave George Melly the title for his study of the pop arts in Britain, *Revolt into Style* (1970).

4 Elvis' disappearing body is like a flashing event horizon at the edge of the black hole that is America today.

ARTHUR KROKER (b. 1945), MARILOUISE KROKER (birth date unknown), DAVID COOK (b. 1946), Canadian sociologists. *Panic Encyclopedia*, "Why Panic?" (1989).

5 Elvis transcends his talent to the point of dispensing with it altogether.

GREIL MARCUS (b. 1945), U.S. rock journalist. *Mystery Train*, "Elvis: Presliad" (1976).

6 I wish not to be given a title or an appointed position. I can and will do more good if I were made a Federal Agent at Large, and I will help best by doing it my way through my communications with people of all ages. First and Foremost I am an entertainer but all I need is the Federal Credentials.

ELVIS PRESLEY (1935–77), U.S. singer. Letter, 19 Dec. 1970, to President Nixon, offering Presley's services as a Federal Agent to work to curb drug abuse by young people. Elvis was made an agent of the Bureau of Narcotics and Dangerous Drugs by Nixon, receiving an enamel shield which, according to biographer Albert Goldman, became one of his most treasured possessions.

THE PRESS

1   Power without responsibility—the prerogative of the harlot throughout the ages.

STANLEY BALDWIN (1867–1947), British Conservative politician, prime minister. Speech, 17 March 1931, attacking press barons Lords Beaverbrook and Rothermere.

2   It is precisely the purpose of the public opinion generated by the press to make the public incapable of judging, to insinuate into it the attitude of someone irresponsible, uninformed.

WALTER BENJAMIN (1892–1940), German critic, philosopher. "Karl Kraus," in *Frankfurter Zeitung*, no. 76 (Frankfurt, 1931; repr. in *Reflections*, ed. by Peter Demetz, 1978).

3   The price of justice is eternal publicity.

ARNOLD BENNETT (1867–1931), British novelist. *Things That Have Interested Me*, "Secret Trials" (Second Series, 1923).

4   The press and politicians. A delicate relationship. Too close, and danger ensues. Too far apart and democracy itself cannot function without the essential exchange of information. Creative leaks, a discreet lunch, interchange in the Lobby, the art of the unattributable telephone call, late at night.

HOWARD BRENTON (b. 1942) AND DAVID HARE (b. 1947), British playwrights. Quince, in *Pravda*, act 1, sc. 4.

5   The most important service rendered by the press and the magazines is that of educating people to approach printed matter with distrust.

SAMUEL BUTLER (1835–1902), English author. *Samuel Butler's Notebooks* (1951).

6   The very hirelings of the press, whose trade it is to buoy up the spirits of the people . . . have uttered falsehoods so long, they have played off so many tricks, that their budget seems, at last, to be quite empty.

WILLIAM COBBETT (1762–1835), English journalist, reformer. "The Last Ten Years," in *Political Register* (London, 4 Jan. 1812; repr. in *The Opinions of William Cobbett*, ch. 6, ed. by G. D. H. and Margaret Cole, 1944).

7   It is a misfortune that necessity has induced men to accord greater license to this formidable engine, in order to obtain liberty, than can be borne with less important objects in view; for the press, like fire, is an excellent servant, but a terrible master.

JAMES FENIMORE COOPER (1789–1851), U.S. novelist. *The American Democrat*, "On the Press."

8   Belief is with them mechanical, voluntary: they believe what they are paid for—they swear to that which turns to account. Do you suppose, that after years spent in this manner, they have any feeling left answering to the difference between truth and falsehood?

WILLIAM HAZLITT (1778–1830), English essayist. Writing of the Tory press, in *London Weekly Review* (17 May 1828).

9   I sometimes compare press officers to riflemen on the Somme—mowing down wave upon wave of distortion, taking out rank upon rank of supposition, deduction and gossip.

BERNARD INGHAM (b. 1932), British government press officer. *Independent* (London, 8 Feb. 1990).

10   No government ought to be without censors; and where the press is free no one ever will.

THOMAS JEFFERSON (1743–1826), U.S. president. Letter, 9 Sept. 1792, to George Washington.

11   The liberty of the Press is the *Palladium* of all the civil, political and religious rights of an Englishman.

JUNIUS (*fl.* 1769–72). Anonymous pseudonym of English political writer. Dedicatory notice in The Letters of Junius (1772).

12   It is impossible to read the daily press without being diverted from reality. You are full of enthusiasm for the eternal verities—life is worth living, and then out of sinful curiosity you open a newspaper. You are disillusioned and wrecked.

PATRICK KAVANAGH (1905–67), Irish poet, author. *Collected Pruse*, "Signposts" (1967).

13   There is a a terrific disadvantage in not having the abrasive quality of the press applied to you daily. . . . Even though we never like it, and even though we wish they didn't write it, and even though we disapprove, there isn't any doubt that we could not do the job at all in a free society without a very, very active press.

JOHN F. KENNEDY (1917–63), U.S. Democratic politician, president. Quoted in: Theodore C. Sorensen, *Kennedy*, pt. 3, ch. 12 (1965), said of Khruschev's control of the Soviet press.

14   The press, that goiter of the world, swells up with the desire for conquest and bursts with the achievements which every day brings. A week has room for the boldest climax of the human drive for expansion.

KARL KRAUS (1874–1936), Austrian satirist. "The Discovery of the North Pole," in *Die Fackel*, no. 287 (Vienna, Sept. 1909; repr. in *In These Great Times: A Karl Kraus Reader*, ed. by Harry Zohn, 1976).

15   The job of the press is to encourage debate, not to supply the public with information.

CHRISTOPHER LASCH (b. 1932), U.S. historian. "Journalism, Publicity, and the Lost Art of Political Argument," in *Gannett Center Journal* (New York, Spring 1990; repr. as "The Lost Art of Political Argument," in *Harper's*, New York, Sept. 1990).

16   The press is no substitute for institutions. It is like the beam of a searchlight that moves restlessly about, bringing one episode and then another out of darkness into vision. Men cannot do the work of the world by this light alone. They cannot govern society by episodes, incidents, and eruptions. It is only when they work by a steady light of their own, that the press, when it is turned upon them, reveals a situation intelligible enough for a popular decision.

WALTER LIPPMANN (1889–1974), U.S. journalist. *Public Opinion*, ch. 24 (1922).

17   The rising power of the United States in world affairs . . . requires, not a more compliant press, but a relentless barrage of facts and criticism. . . . Our job in this age, as I see it, is not to serve as cheerleaders for our side in the present world struggle but to help the largest possible number of people to see the realities of the changing and convulsive world in which American policy must operate.

> JAMES RESTON (b. 1909), U.S. journalist. *The Artillery of the Press*, Introduction (1966).

18   The men with the muck-rake are often indispensable to the well-being of society, but only if they know when to stop raking the muck.

> THEODORE ROOSEVELT (1858–1919), U.S. Republican (later Progressive) politician, president. Speech, 14 April 1906, Washington, D.C.

19   Report me and my cause aright.

> WILLIAM SHAKESPEARE (1564–1616), English dramatist, poet. Hamlet, in *Hamlet*, act 5, sc. 2.

20   Hastiness and superficiality are the psychic diseases of the twentieth century, and more than anywhere else this disease is reflected in the press.

> ALEXANDER SOLZHENITSYN (b. 1918), Russian novelist. Commencement Address, 7 June 1978, Harvard University.

21   The press today is an army with carefully organized weapons, the journalists its officers, the readers its soldiers. But, as in every army, the soldier obeys blindly, and the war aims and operating plans change without his knowledge. The reader neither knows nor is supposed to know the purposes for which he is used and the role he is to play. There is no more appalling caricature of freedom of thought. Formerly no one was allowed to think freely; now it is permitted, but no one is capable of it any more. Now people want to think only what they are supposed to want to think, and this they consider freedom.

> OSWALD SPENGLER (1880–1936), German historian. *The Decline of the West*, vol. 2, ch. 12, sct. 4 (1926).

22   There are only two forces that can carry light to all the corners of the globe . . . the sun in the heavens and the Associated Press down here.

> MARK TWAIN (1835–1910), U.S. author. "Spelling and Pictures," speech, 18 Sept. 1906, to Associated Press, New York City (published in *Mark Twain's Speeches*, ed. by Albert Bigelow Paine, 1923).

23   On leaf of palm, on sedge-wrought roll;
On plastic clay and leathern scroll,
Man wrote his thoughts; the ages passed,
And lo! the Press was found at last!

> JOHN GREENLEAF WHITTIER (1807–92), U.S. poet. *The Library*, st. 4.

24   In old days men had the rack. Now they have the Press.

> OSCAR WILDE (1854–1900), Anglo-Irish playwright, author. *The Soul of Man Under Socialism*, in *Fortnightly Review* (London, Feb. 1891; repr. 1895).

See also MacKenzie on EDITORS; JOURNALISM AND JOURNALISTS; NEWSPAPERS AND MAGAZINES.

PRIDE

1   He that toucheth pitch shall be defiled therewith; and he that hath fellowship with a proud man shall be like unto him.

> APOCRYPHA. *Ecclesiasticus* 13:1.

2   It's a fine thing to rise above pride, but you must have pride in order to do so.

> GEORGES BERNANOS (1888–1948), French novelist, political writer. *The Diary of a Country Priest*, ch. 7 (1936).

3   Pride goeth before destruction, and an haughty spirit before a fall.

> BIBLE, HEBREW. *Proverbs* 16:18.

4   I cannot dig; to beg I am ashamed.

> BIBLE: NEW TESTAMENT. The unjust steward, in the Parable of the Unjust Steward, in *Luke* 16:3.

5   Proud people breed sad sorrows for themselves.

> EMILY BRONTË (1818–48), English novelist, poet. Nelly, in *Wuthering Heights*, ch. 7 (1847).

6   It is my PRIDE, my damn'd, native, unconquerable Pride, that plunges me into Distraction. You must know that 19–20th of my Composition is Pride. I must either live a Slave, a Servant; to have no Will of my own, no Sentiments of my own which I may freely declare as such;—or DIE—perplexing alternative!

> THOMAS CHATTERTON (1752–70), English poet. Letter, April 1770. Quoted in: John Cranstoun Nevill, *Thomas Chatterton* (1948).

7   And the Devil did grin, for his darling sin
Is pride that apes humility.

> SAMUEL TAYLOR COLERIDGE (1772–1834), English poet, critic. *The Devil's Thoughts* (written with Robert Southey).

8   My family pride is something inconceivable. I can't help it. I was born sneering.

> W. S. GILBERT (1836–1911), English librettist. Pooh-Bah, in *The Mikado*, act 1.

9   I will give you a definition of a proud man: he is a man who has neither vanity nor wisdom—one filled with hatreds cannot be vain, neither can he be wise.

> JOHN KEATS (1795–1821), English poet. Letter, 23 Aug. 1819 (published in *Letters of John Keats*, no. 144, ed. by Frederick Page, 1954). Keats condoned his own pride in the same letter: "This pride and egotism will enable me to write finer things than anything else could—so I will indulge it."

10   The sin of pride may be a small or a great thing in someone's life, and hurt vanity a passing pinprick, or a self-destroying or ever murderous obsession.

> IRIS MURDOCH (b. 1919), British novelist, philosopher. *The Philosopher's Pupil*, "The Events in Our Town" (1983).

11   Nothing has been purchased more dearly than the little bit of reason and sense of freedom which now constitutes our pride.

> FRIEDRICH NIETZSCHE (1844–1900), German philosopher. *The Dawn*, aph. 18 (1881).

12   Man, proud man,
Drest in a little brief authority,
Most ignorant of what he's most assur'd,
His glassy essence, like an angry ape,

Plays such fantastic tricks before high heaven,
As make the angels weep.

WILLIAM SHAKESPEARE (1564–1616), English dramatist, poet. Isabella, in *Measure for Measure*, act 2, sc. 2.

See also Shelley on LORD BYRON; Shakespeare on POVERTY AND THE POOR.

PRIMITIVE LIFE

1 No arts; no letters; no society; and which is worst of all, continual fear, and danger of violent death; and the life of man, solitary, poor, nasty, brutish, and short.

THOMAS HOBBES (1588–1679), English philosopher. *Leviathan,* pt. 1, ch. 13 (1651), said of the state "wherein men live without other security, than what their own strength and their own invention shall furnish them."

2 By all odds, earliest man, so naked to the elements and to deadly enemies, should have existed in a state of constant shock. We find him instead the only lighthearted being in a deadly serious universe. . . . He alone, with childish carelessness, tinkered and played, and exerted himself more in the pursuit of superfluities than of necessities. Yet the tinkering and playing, and the fascination with the nonessential, were a chief source of the inventiveness which enabled man to prevail over better-equipped and more-purposeful animals.

ERIC HOFFER (1902–83), U.S. philosopher. *Reflections on the Human Condition,* aph. 27 (1973).

3 So often among so-called "primitives" one comes across spiritual personalities who immediately inspire respect, as though they were the fully matured products of an undisturbed fate.

CARL JUNG (1875–1961), Swiss psychiatrist. *Marriage as a Psychological Relationship* (1925; repr. in *Collected Works,* vol. 17, para. 336, ed. by William McGuire, 1954).

4 Destroy your primitivity, and you will most probably get along well in the world, maybe achieve great success—but Eternity will reject you. Follow up your primitivity, and you will be shipwrecked in temporality, but accepted by Eternity.

SøREN KIERKEGAARD (1813–55), Danish philosopher. *The Diary of Søren Kierkegaard,* pt. 6, sct. 3, no. 196 (ed. by Peter Rohde, 1960), 1854 entry.

5 Oh yes, there is a vast difference between the savage and the civilized man, but it is never apparent to their wives until after breakfast.

HELEN ROWLAND (1875–1950), U.S. journalist. *A Guide to Men,* "Cymbals and Kettle-drums" (1922).

6 By this you may see who are the rude and barbarous Indians: for verily there is no savage nation under the cope of Heaven, that is more absurdly barbarous than the Christian World. They that go naked and drink water and live upon roots are like Adam, or Angels in comparison of us.

THOMAS TRAHERNE (1636–74), English clergyman, poet, mystic. *Centuries,* "Third Century," no. 12 (written c. 1672; first published 1908).

7 But the nature of our civilized minds is so detached from the senses, even in the vulgar, by abstractions corresponding to all the abstract terms our languages abound in, and so refined by the art of writing, and as it were spiritualized by the use of numbers, because even the vulgar know how to count and reckon, that it is naturally beyond our power to form the vast image of this mistress called "Sympathetic Nature."

GIAMBATTISTA VICO (1688–1744), Italian philosopher, historian. *The New Science,* bk. 2, para. 378 (ed. 1744; tr. 1984).

8 Human beings *will* be happier—not when they cure cancer or get to Mars or eliminate racial prejudice or flush Lake Erie but when they find ways to inhabit primitive communities again. That's my utopia.

KURT VONNEGUT, JR. (b. 1922), U.S. novelist. *Wampeters, Foma and Granfalloons,* "Playboy Interview, 1973" (1974).

9 There is the old brute, too, the savage, the hairy man who dabbles his fingers in ropes of entrails; and gobbles and belches; whose speech is guttural, visceral—well, he is here. He squats in me.

VIRGINIA WOOLF (1882–1941), British novelist. Bernard, in *The Waves* (1931; p. 205 of Hogarth ed., 1943).

PRINCIPLES

1 It is always easier to fight for one's principles than to live up to them.

ALFRED ADLER (1870–1937), Austrian psychiatrist. Quoted in: Phyllis Bottome, *Alfred Adler: Apostle of Freedom,* ch. 5 (1939). The quote was used by Adlai Stevenson in a speech, 27 Aug. 1952, in New York.

2 The principles which men give to themselves end by overwhelming their noblest intentions.

ALBERT CAMUS (1913–60), French-Algerian philosopher, author. *The Rebel,* pt. 3, "State Terrorism and Rational Terror" (1951; tr. 1953).

3 To abandon oneself to principles is really to die—and to die for an impossible love which is the contrary of love.

ALBERT CAMUS (1913–60), French-Algerian philosopher, author. *The Rebel,* pt. 3, "The Regicides" (1951; tr. 1953).

4 Amid the pressure of great events, a general principle gives no help.

GEORG HEGEL (1770–1831), German philosopher. *The Philosophy of History,* "Introduction," sct. 2 (1837).

5 Almost anything that can be praised or advocated has been put to some disgusting use. There is no principle, however immaculate, that has not had its compromising manipulator.

WYNDHAM LEWIS (1882–1957), British author, painter. *The Art of Being Ruled,* ch. 8, "The Family and Feminism" (1926).

6 The proclamation and repetition of first principles is a constant feature of life in our democracy. Active adherence to these principles, however, has always been considered un-American. We recipients of the boon of liberty have always been ready, when faced with discomfort, to discard any and all first principles of liberty, and, further, to indict those who do not freely join with us in happily arrogating those principles.

DAVID MAMET (b. 1947), U.S. playwright. *Writing in Restaurants,* "First Principles" (1986).

7 Nobody ever did anything very foolish except from some strong principle.

> LORD MELBOURNE (1779–1848), English statesman, prime minister. Quoted in: David Cecil, *The Young Melbourne*, ch. 9 (1939).

8 Every principle is a judgment, every judgment the outcome of experience, and experience is only acquired by the exercise of the senses; whence it follows that religious principles bear upon nothing whatever and are not in the slightest innate. . . . Ignorance and fear, you will repeat to them, ignorance and fear—those are the twin bases of every religion.

> MARQUIS DE SADE (1740–1814), French author. Dolmancé, in *Philosophy in the Bedroom*, "Dialogue the Fifth: Yet Another Effort, Frenchmen, If You Would Become Republicans" (1795).

9 I find that principles have no real force except when one is well fed.

> MARK TWAIN (1835–1910), U.S. author. Adam, in *Extracts from Adam's Diary*, "Wednesday" (1893).

10 Principles aren't of much account anyway, except at election time. After that you hang them up to let them season.

> MARK TWAIN (1835–1910), U.S. author. "Municipal Corruption," speech, 4 Jan. 1901 (published in *Mark Twain's Speeches*, ed. by Albert Bigelow Paine, 1923).

11 Americans are willing to go to enormous trouble and expense defending their principles with arms, very little trouble and expense advocating them with words. Temperamentally we are ready to die for certain principles (or, in the case of overripe adults, send youngsters to die), but we show little inclination to advertise the reasons for dying.

> E. B. WHITE (1899–1985), U.S. author, editor. "The Thud of Ideas," in *New Yorker* (23 Sept. 1950; repr. in *Writings from the New Yorker 1927–1976*, ed. by Rebecca M. Dale, 1991).

12 I like persons better than principles, and I like persons with no principles better than anything else in the world.

> OSCAR WILDE (1854–1900), Anglo-Irish playwright, author. Lord Henry, in *The Picture of Dorian Gray*, ch. 1 (1891).

See also Shaw on ENGLAND AND THE ENGLISH; Disraeli on TRADITION.

PRISON

1 To assert in any case that a man must be absolutely cut off from society because he is absolutely evil amounts to saying that society is absolutely good, and no-one in his right mind will believe this today.

> ALBERT CAMUS (1913–60), French-Algerian philosopher, author. *Resistance, Rebellion and Death*, "Reflections on the Guillotine" (1961).

2 In jail a man has no personality. He is a minor disposal problem and a few entries on reports. Nobody cares who loves or hates him, what he looks like, what he did with his life. Nobody reacts to him unless he gives trouble. Nobody abuses him. All that is asked of him is that he go quietly to the right cell and remain quiet when he gets there. There is nothing to fight against, nothing to be mad at. The jailers are quiet men without animosity or sadism. All this stuff you read about men yelling and screaming, beating against the bars, running spoons along them, guards rushing in with clubs—all that is for the big house. A good jail is one of the quietest places in the world. . . . Life in jail is in suspension.

> RAYMOND CHANDLER (1888–1959), U.S. author. *The Long Goodbye*, ch. 8 (1953).

3 In prison, those things withheld from and denied to the prisoner become precisely what he wants most of all.

> ELDRIDGE CLEAVER (b. 1935), U.S. black leader, writer. *Soul on Ice*, "On Becoming" (1968), written from Folsom Prison, 25 June 1965.

4 We are all conceived in close prison; in our mothers' wombs, we are close prisoners all; when we are born, we are born but to the liberty of the house; prisoners still, though within larger walls; and then all our life is but a going out to the place of execution, to death.

> JOHN DONNE (c. 1572–1631), English divine, metaphysical poet. *Eighty Sermons*, ser. 27 (1640).

5 Prison continues, on those who are entrusted to it, a work begun elsewhere, which the whole of society pursues on each individual through innumerable mechanisms of discipline.

> MICHEL FOUCAULT (1926–84), French philosopher. *Discipline and Punish: The Birth of the Prison*, pt. 4, ch. 3 (1975).

6 *There is a close relationship between flowers and convicts.* The fragility and delicacy of the former are of the same nature as the brutal insensitivity of the latter.

> JEAN GENET (1910–86), French playwright, novelist. *The Thief's Journal* (1949; tr. 1965).

7 I turn and turn in my cell like a fly that doesn't know where to die.

> ANTONIO GRAMSCI (1891–1937), Italian political theorist. Letter, 20 July 1931 (published in *Gramsci: Letters from Prison*, no. 199, tr. by Raymond Rosenthal, 1993). Gramsci had been in prison since 1926, when Mussolini had outlawed the Communist Party, and spent the rest of his life there.

8 He that is taken and put into prison or chains is not conquered, though overcome; for he is still an enemy.

> THOMAS HOBBES (1588–1679), English philosopher. *Leviathan*, "A Review and Conclusion" (1651).

9 Such is the remorseless progression of human society, shedding lives and souls as it goes on its way. It is an ocean into which men sink who have been cast out by the law and consigned, with help most cruelly withheld, to moral death. The sea is the pitiless social darkness into which the penal system casts those it has condemned, an unfathomable waste of misery. The human soul, lost in those depths, may become a corpse. Who shall revive it?

> VICTOR HUGO (1802–85), French poet, dramatist, novelist. *Les Misérables*, pt. 1, bk. 2, ch. 8 (1862).

10 A forest bird never wants a cage.

> HENRIK IBSEN (1828–1906), Norwegian dramatist. Hilde, in *The Master Builder*, act 3.

11 Stone walls do not a prison make
Nor iron bars a cage;
Minds innocent and quiet take
That for an hermitage.

> RICHARD LOVELACE (1618–58), English poet. *To Althea, from Prison*.

12 A prisoner has no sex. He is God's own private eunuch.

HENRY MILLER (1891–1980), U.S. author. *The Air-Conditioned Nightmare*, "The Soul of Anaesthesia" (1945).

13 The prisoner is not the one who has commited a crime, but the one who clings to his crime and lives it over and over.

HENRY MILLER (1891–1980), U.S. author. *Sexus*, ch. 14 (1949).

14 The most anxious man in a prison is the governor.

GEORGE BERNARD SHAW (1856–1950), Anglo-Irish playwright, critic. *Man and Superman*, "Maxims for Revolutionists: Crime and Punishment" (1903).

15 Under a government which imprisons any unjustly, the true place for a just man is also a prison.

HENRY DAVID THOREAU (1817–62), U.S. philosopher, author, naturalist. *On the Duty of Civil Disobedience* (1849). Thoreau spent one night in jail in the summer of 1846 for non-payment of the poll tax, a gesture against the Mexican War declared that year.

16 It isn't true that convicts live like animals: animals have more room to move around.

MARIO VARGAS LLOSA (b. 1936), Peruvian novelist. *The Real Life of Alejandro Mayta*, ch. 10 (1984; tr. 1986).

17 Anyone who has been to an English public school will always feel comparatively at home in prison. It is the people brought up in the gay intimacy of the slums . . . who find prison so soul-destroying.

EVELYN WAUGH (1903–66), British novelist. *Decline and Fall*, pt. 3, ch. 4 (1928).

18 I know not whether Laws be right
Or whether Laws be wrong;
All that we know who live in gaol
Is that the wall is strong;
And that each day is like a year,
A year whose days are long.

OSCAR WILDE (1854–1900), Anglo-Irish playwright, author. *The Ballad of Reading Gaol*, pt. 5, st. 1.

19 We who live in prison, and in whose lives there is no event but sorrow, have to measure time by throbs of pain, and the record of bitter moments.

OSCAR WILDE (1854–1900), Anglo-Irish playwright, author. *De Profundis* (1905). Wilde himself spent two years in prison.

20 A man will be imprisoned in a room with a door that's unlocked and opens inwards; as long as it does not occur to him to pull rather than push.

LUDWIG WITTGENSTEIN (1889–1951), Austrian philosopher. *Culture and Value* (ed. by G. H. von Wright and Heikki Nyman, 1980), 1942 entry.

See also Greer on INSECURITY; Gramsci on HYPOCHONDRIA.

PRIVACY

1 Bourgeois existence is the regime of private affairs . . . and the family is the rotten, dismal edifice in whose closets and crannies the most ignominious instincts are deposited. Mundane life proclaims the total subjugation of eroticism to privacy.

WALTER BENJAMIN (1892–1940), German critic, philosopher. One-Way Street, "Betting Office" (1928; repr. in *One-Way Street and Other Writings*, 1978).

2 Privacy is not something that I'm merely entitled to, it's an absolute prerequisite.

MARLON BRANDO (b. 1924), U.S. film actor. Quoted in: David Shipman, *Marlon Brando*, ch. 11 (1974; rev. 1989).

3 There is no private life which has not been determined by a wider public life.

GEORGE ELIOT (1819–80), English novelist, editor. *Felix Holt, The Radical*, ch. 3 (1866).

4 Who could deny that privacy is a jewel? It has always been the mark of privilege, the distinguishing feature of a truly urbane culture. Out of the cave, the tribal tepee, the pueblo, the community fortress, man emerged to build himself a house of his own with a shelter in it for himself and his diversions. Every age has seen it so. The poor might have to huddle together in cities for need's sake, and the frontiersman cling to his neighbors for the sake of protection. But in each civilization, as it advanced, those who could afford it chose the luxury of a withdrawing-place.

PHYLLIS MCGINLEY (1905–78), U.S. poet, author. *The Province of the Heart*, "A Lost Privilege" (1959).

5 Isn't privacy about keeping taboos in their place?

KATE MILLET (b. 1934), U.S. feminist author. Speech, 22 March 1975, Women Writer's Conference, Los Angeles.

6 Today, the degradation of the inner life is symbolized by the fact that the only place sacred from interruption is the private toilet.

LEWIS MUMFORD (1895–1990), U.S. social philosopher. *The Culture of Cities*, ch. 1, sct. 5 (1938).

7 May we agree that private life is irrelevant? Multiple, mixed, ambiguous at best—out of it we try to fashion the crystal clear, the singular, the absolute, and that is what *is* relevant; that is what matters.

MAY SARTON (b. 1912), U.S. poet, novelist. Hilary Stevens, in *Mrs. Stevens Hears the Mermaids Singing*, pt. 2 (1965).

PRIVILEGE

1 I perceive that God is no respecter of persons.

BIBLE: NEW TESTAMENT. Peter, in *Acts* 10:34.

2 What men prize most is a privilege, even if it be that of chief mourner at a funeral.

JAMES RUSSELL LOWELL (1819–91), U.S. poet, editor. "Democracy," address, 6 Oct. 1884, Birmingham, England (published in *Democracy and Other Addresses*, 1886).

3 What men value in this world is not rights but privileges.

H. L. MENCKEN (1880–1956), U.S. journalist. *Minority Report: H. L. Mencken's Notebooks*, no. 36 (1956).

4 If you don't have a policeman to stop traffic and let you walk across the street like you are somebody, how are you going to know you are somebody?

JOHN C. WHITE (b. 1924), U.S. Democratic politician. *International Herald Tribune* (Paris, 23 March 1992), said of the perks of Washington, D.C.

See also Hill on FREEDOM; Galbraith on YUPPIES.

PROBLEMS

1 I have yet to see any problem, however complicated, which, when you looked at it in the right way, did not become still more complicated.

> POUL ANDERSON (b. 1926), U.S. science fiction writer. *New Scientist* (London, 25 Sept. 1969).

2 He that will not apply new remedies, must expect new evils: for Time is the greatest innovator: and if Time, of course, alter things to the worse, and wisdom and counsel shall not alter them to the better, what shall be the end?.

> FRANCIS BACON (1561–1626), English philosopher, essayist, statesman. *Essays*, "Of Innovations" (1597–1625).

3 But Jesus, when you don't have any money, the problem is food. When you have money, it's sex. When you have both, it's health, you worry about getting ruptured or something. If everything is simply jake then you're frightened of death.

> J. P. DONLEAVY (b. 1926), U.S. author. O'Keefe, in *The Ginger Man*, ch. 5 (1955).

4 It is characteristic of all deep human problems that they are not to be approached without some humor and some bewilderment.

> FREEMAN DYSON (b. 1923), British-born U.S. physicist, author. *Disturbing the Universe*, pt. 1, ch. 1 (1979).

5 Any solution to a problem changes the problem.

> R. W. JOHNSON (b. 1916), U.S. journalist, newspaper executive. *Washingtonian* (Nov. 1979).

6 It is one of man's curious idiosyncrasies to create difficulties for the pleasure of resolving them.

> JOSEPH DE MAISTRE (1753–1821), French diplomat, philosopher. *Study on Sovereignty*, bk. 1, ch. 2 (1884; repr. in *The Works of Joseph de Maistre*, ed. by Jack Lively, 1965).

7 The problems of the world, AIDS, cancer, nuclear war, pollution, are, finally, no more solvable than the problem of a tree which has borne fruit: the apples are overripe and they are falling—what can be done? . . . *Nothing* can be done, and nothing needs to be done. Something *is* being done—the organism is preparing to rest.

> DAVID MAMET (b. 1947), U.S. playwright. *Writing in Restaurants*, "Decay: Some Thoughts for Actors" (1986).

8 All problems are finally scientific problems.

> GEORGE BERNARD SHAW (1856–1950), Anglo-Irish playwright, critic. *The Doctor's Dilemma*, Preface, "The Technical Problem" (1911).

9 The problems of this world are only truly solved in two ways: by extinction or duplication.

> SUSAN SONTAG (b. 1933), U.S. essayist. *I, Etcetera*, "The Dummy" (1978).

10 When a contradiction is impossible to resolve except by a lie, then we know that it is really a door.

> SIMONE WEIL (1909–43), French philosopher, mystic. *New York Notebook* (written 1942; published 1950; repr. in *First and Last Notebooks*, pt. 3, ed. by Richard Rees, 1970).

11 Almost everybody in the neighborhood had "troubles," frankly localized and specified; but only the chosen had "complications." To have them was in itself a distinction, though it was also, in most cases, a death warrant. People struggled on for years with "troubles," but they almost always succumbed to "complications."

> EDITH WHARTON (1862–1937), U.S. author. *Ethan Frome*, ch. 7 (1911).

12 Don't get involved in partial problems, but always take flight to where there is a free view over the whole *single* great problem, even if this view is still not a clear one.

> LUDWIG WITTGENSTEIN (1889–1951), Austrian philosopher. *Notebooks 1914–1916*, entry for 1 Nov. 1914 (ed. by Anscombe, 1961).

PROCRASTINATION

1 The truth is that we live out our lives putting off all that can be put off; perhaps we all know deep down that we are immortal and that sooner or later all men will do and know all things.

> JORGE LUIS BORGES (1899–1986), Argentinian author. *Labyrinths*, "Funes the Memorious" (1964).

2 Delay always breeds danger; and to protract a great design is often to ruin it.

> MIGUEL DE CERVANTES (1547–1616), Spanish writer. Don Quixote, in *Don Quixote*, pt. 1, bk. 4, ch. 2 (1605; tr. by P. Motteux).

3 My evil genius Procrastination has whispered me to tarry 'til a more convenient season.

> MARY TODD LINCOLN (1818–82), U.S. First Lady. Letter, June 1841 (published in *Mary Todd Lincoln: Her Life and Letters*, 1972).

4 procrastination is the
art of keeping
up with yesterday

> DON MARQUIS (1878–1937), U.S. humorist, journalist. *archy and mehitabel*, "certain maxims of archy" (1927).

5 Life, as it is called, is for most of us one long postponement.

> HENRY MILLER (1891–1980), U.S. author. *The Wisdom of the Heart*, "The Enormous Womb" (1947).

6 Procrastination is the thief of time.

> EDWARD YOUNG (1683–1765), English poet, dramatist. *Night Thoughts*, "The Complaint: Night 1" (1742–46).

See also Wells on REFORM.

PROCREATION

1 Living substance conquers the frenzy of destruction only in the ecstasy of procreation.

> WALTER BENJAMIN (1892–1940), German critic, philosopher. *One-Way Street*, "To the Planetarium" (1928; repr. in *One-Way Street and Other Writings*, 1978).

2 Luckless is the country in which the symbols of procreation are the objects of shame, while the agents of destruction are honored! And yet you call that member your pudendum, or shameful part, as if there were anything more glorious than creating life, or anything more atrocious than taking it away.

CYRANO DE BERGERAC (1619–55), French author, playwright. A "lunarian," in *The Other World: States and Empires of the Moon*, ch. 8 (1656). ·

3 I could be content that we might procreate like trees, without conjunction, or that there were any way to perpetuate the world without this trivial and vulgar way of coition.

SIR THOMAS BROWNE (1605–82), English physician, author. *Religio Medici*, pt. 2, sct. 9 (1643).

4 A hen is only an egg's way of making another egg.

SAMUEL BUTLER (1835–1902), English author. *Life and Habit*, ch. 8 (1877).

5 What a strange thing is the propagation of life! A bubble of seed which may be spilt in a whore's lap, or in the orgasm of a voluptuous dream, might (for aught we know) have formed a Caesar or a Buonaparte—there is nothing remarkable recorded of their sires, that I know of.

LORD BYRON (1788–1824), English poet. *Detached Thoughts*, no. 102 (1821–22; published in *Byron's Letters and Journals*, vol. 9, ed. by Leslie A. Marchand, 1979).

6 Sperm is a bandit in its pure state.

E. M. CIORAN (b. 1911), Rumanian-born French philosopher. *Syllogismes de L'Amertune*, "Aux Sources du Vide" (1952).

7 Media mystifications should not obfuscate a simple, perceivable fact; Black teenage girls do not create poverty by having babies. Quite the contrary, they have babies at such a young age precisely because they are poor—because they do not have the opportunity to acquire an education, because meaningful, well-paying jobs and creative forms of recreation are not accessible to them . . . because safe, effective forms of contraception are not available to them.

ANGELA DAVIS (b. 1944), U.S. political activist. "Facing Our Common Foe," address, 15 Nov. 1987 (published in *Women, Culture and Politics*, 1989).

8 It would be one of the greatest triumphs of humanity, one of the most tangible liberations from the constraints of nature to which mankind is subject, if we could succeed in raising the responsible act of procreating children to the level of a deliberate and intentional activity and in freeing it from its entanglement with the necessary satisfaction of a natural need.

SIGMUND FREUD (1856–1939), Austrian psychiatrist. *Sexuality in the Aetiology of the Neuroses* (1898; repr. in *Complete Works, Standard Edition*, vol. 3, ed. by James Strachey and Anna Freud, 1962).

9 I should consent to breed under pressure, if I were convinced in any way of the reasonableness of reproducing the species. But my nerves and the nerves of any woman I could live with three months, would produce only a victim . . . lacking in impulse, a mere bundle of

discriminations. If I were wealthy I might subsidize a stud of young peasants, or a tribal group in Tahiti.

EZRA POUND (1885–1972), U.S. poet, critic. Quoted in: *Little Review* (Sept. 1917).

10 Wilful sterility is, from the standpoint of the nation, from the standpoint of the human race, the one sin for which the penalty is national death, race death; a sin for which there is no atonement. . . . No man, no woman, can shirk the primary duties of life, whether for love of ease and pleasure, or for any other cause, and retain his or her self-respect.

THEODORE ROOSEVELT (1858–1919), U.S. Republican (later Progressive) politician, president. Sixth Annual Message to Congress, 3 Dec. 1906.

11 Let us make no mistake about it, this propagation was never one of her laws, nothing she ever demanded of us, but at the very most something she tolerated; I have told you so. Why! what difference would it make to her were the race of men entirely to be extinguished upon earth, annihilated! she laughs at our pride when we persuade ourselves all would be over and done with were this misfortune to occur!

MARQUIS DE SADE (1740–1814), French author. Dolmancé, describing Nature's laws, in *Philosophy in the Bedroom*, "Dialogue the Fifth" (1795).

12 Do not breed. Nothing gives less pleasure than childbearing. Pregnancies are damaging to health, spoil the figure, wither the charms, and it's the cloud of uncertainty forever hanging over these events that darkens a husband's mood.

MARQUIS DE SADE (1740–1814), French author. Mme Delbène, in *L'Histoire de Juliette, ou les Prospérités du Vice*, pt. 1 (1797).

13 I have no conscience, none, but I would not like to bring a soul into this world. When it sinned and when it suffered something like a dead hand would fall on me,— "You did it, you, for your own pleasure you created this thing! See your work!" If it lived to be eighty it would always hang like a millstone round my neck, have the right to demand good from me, and curse me for its sorrow. A parent is only like to God: if his work turns out bad so much the worse for him; he *dare* not wash his hands of it. Time and years can never bring the day when you can say to your child, "Soul, what have I to do with you?"

OLIVE SCHREINER (1855–1920), South African writer, feminist. Lyndall, in *The Story of an African Farm*, pt. 2, ch. 6 (1883).

14 He plough'd her, and she cropp'd.

WILLIAM SHAKESPEARE (1564–1616), English dramatist, poet. Agrippa, in *Antony and Cleopatra*, act 2, sc. 2, said of Caesar and Cleopatra.

15 We have been God-like in our planned breeding of our domesticated plants and animals, but we have been rabbit-like in our unplanned breeding of ourselves.

A. J. TOYNBEE (1889–1975), British historian. On growths in population, to World Food Congress in Washington. Quoted in: *National Observer* (10 June 1963).

16 It is so characteristic, that just when the mechanics of reproduction are so vastly improved, there are fewer and fewer people who know how the music should be played.

LUDWIG WITTGENSTEIN (1889–1951), Austrian philosopher. Conversation in 1949 (published in *Personal Recollections*, ch. 6, ed. by Rush Rhees, 1981).

See also Mumford on BABIES; Keynes on FERTILITY; Leonard on POPULATION.

PRODUCTION

1 The myth of unlimited production brings war in its train as inevitably as clouds announce a storm.

ALBERT CAMUS (1913–60), French-Algerian philosopher, author. *The Rebel*, pt. 4, "Creation and Revolution" (1951; tr. 1953).

2 The society based on production is only productive, not creative.

ALBERT CAMUS (1913–60), French-Algerian philosopher, author. *The Rebel*, pt. 4, "Creation and Revolution" (1951; tr. 1953).

3 Constant revolutionizing of production . . . distinguish the bourgeois epoch from all earlier ones. All fixed, fast-frozen relations, with their train of ancient and venerable prejudices are swept away, all new-formed ones become antiquated before they can ossify. All that is solid melts into air, all that is holy is profaned, and man is at last compelled to face with sober senses, his real conditions of life, and his relations with his kind.

KARL MARX (1818–83) AND FRIEDRICH ENGELS (1820–95), German social philosophers, revolutionaries. *The Communist Manifesto*, sct. 1 (1848).

PROFESSIONS

1 The best augury of a man's success in his profession is that he thinks it the finest in the world.

GEORGE ELIOT (1819–80), English novelist. The Rector, in *Daniel Deronda*, bk. 8, ch. 58 (1876).

2 Through all the employments of life
Each neighbour abuses his brother;
Whore and rogue they call husband and wife:
All professions be-rogue one another.

JOHN GAY (1685–1732), English dramatist. Peachum, in *The Beggar's Opera*, act 1, sc. 1.

3 The bond between a man and his profession is similar to that which ties him to his country; it is just as complex, often ambivalent, and in general it is understood completely only when it is broken: by exile or emigration in the case of one's country, by retirement in the case of a trade or profession.

PRIMO LEVI (1919–87), Italian chemist, author. *Other People's Trades*, "Ex-Chemist" (1985; tr. 1989).

4 All things will be produced in superior quantity and quality, and with greater ease, when each man works at a single occupation, in accordance with his natural gifts, and at the right moment, without meddling with anything else.

PLATO c. 427–347 B.C.), Greek philosopher. Socrates, in *The Republic*, bk. 2, sct. 370.

5 All professions are conspiracies against the laity.

GEORGE BERNARD SHAW (1856–1950), Anglo-Irish playwright, critic. Sir Patrick Cullen, in *The Doctor's Dilemma*, act 1 (1911).

6 And there is no trade or employment but the young man following it may become a hero.

WALT WHITMAN (1819–92), U.S. poet. *Song of Myself*, sct. 48, in *Leaves of Grass* (1855).

7 There is something tragic about the enormous number of young men there are in England at the present moment who start life with perfect profiles, and end by adopting some useful profession.

OSCAR WILDE (1854–1900), Anglo-Irish playwright, author. *Phrases and Philosophies for the Use of the Young*, in *Chameleon* (London, Dec. 1894).

8 To depend upon a profession is a less odious form of slavery than to depend upon a father.

VIRGINIA WOOLF (1882–1941), British novelist. *Three Guineas* (1938; p. 20 of Penguin ed.).

See also CAREERS.

PROFIT

1 Civilization and profits go hand in hand.

CALVIN COOLIDGE (1872–1933), U.S. Republican politician, president. Speech, 27 Nov. 1920, New York City.

2 What is a man if he is not a thief who openly charges as much as he can for the goods he sells?

MOHANDAS K. GANDHI (1869–1948), Indian political and spiritual leader. *Non-Violence in Peace and War*, vol. 2, ch. 124 (1949).

3 Profit *and* morality are a hard combination to beat.

HUBERT H. HUMPHREY (1911–78), U.S. Democratic politician, vice president. Speech, 26 Jan. 1967, Washington, D.C., to international newspaper advertising executives.

4 I respect not his labors, his farm where everything has its price, who would carry the landscape, who would carry his God, to market, if he could get anything for him; who goes to market *for* his god as it is; on whose farm nothing grows free, whose fields bear no crops, whose meadows no flowers, whose trees no fruits, but dollars.

HENRY DAVID THOREAU (1817–62), U.S. philosopher, author, naturalist. *Walden*, "The Ponds" (1854).

5 As one digs deeper into the national character of the Americans, one sees that they have sought the value of everything in this world only in the answer to this single question: how much money will it bring in?

ALEXIS DE TOCQUEVILLE (1805–59), French social philosopher. Letter, 9 June 1831 (published in *Selected Letters on Politics and Society*, 1985).

PROGRESS

1 Progress would not have been the rarity it is if the early food had not been the late poison.

WALTER BAGEHOT (1826–77), English economist, critic. *Physics and Politics*, ch. 2, sct. 3 (1872).

2 It's the same each time with progress. First they ignore you, then they say you're mad, then dangerous, then there's a pause and then you can't find anyone who disagrees with you.

> TONY BENN (b. 1925), British Labour politician. Quoted in: *Observer* (London, 6 Oct. 1991).

3 All progress is based upon a universal innate desire on the part of every organism to live beyond its income.

> SAMUEL BUTLER (1835–1902), English author. *Notebooks*, ch. 1 (1912).

4 All progress is experimental.

> JOHN JAY CHAPMAN (1862–1933), U.S. author. *Practical Agitation*, ch. 1 (1898).

5 The reason for the slow progress of the world seems to lie in a single fact. Every man is born under the yoke, and grows up beneath the oppressions of his age. He can only get a vision of the unselfish forces in the world by appealing to them, and every appeal is a call to arms. If he fights he must fight, not one man, but a conspiracy. He is always at war with a civilization. On his side is proverbial philosophy, a galaxy of invisible saints and sages, and the half-developed consciousness and professions of everybody. Against him is the world, and every selfish passion in his own heart.

> JOHN JAY CHAPMAN (1862–1933), U.S. author. *Practical Agitation*, ch. 7 (1898).

6 Nothing recedes like progress.

> E E CUMMINGS (1894–1962), U.S. poet. *Jottings*, in *Wake*, no. 10 (1951; repr. in *A Miscellany*, ed. by George J. Firmage, 1958).

7 Perhaps the best definition of progress would be the continuing efforts of men and women to narrow the gap between the convenience of the powers that be and the unwritten charter.

> NADINE GORDIMER (b. 1923), South African author. "Speak Out: The Necessity for Protest," lecture, 11 Aug. 1971, University of Natal, South Africa (published in *The Essential Gesture*, ed. by Stephen Clingman, 1988). Gordimer is referring to a passage by Mohandas K. Gandhi in *Satyagraha in South Africa* (rev. 1928): "The convenience of the powers that be is the law in the final analysis."

8 Progress everywhere today does seem to come so *very* heavily disguised as Chaos.

> JOYCE GRENFELL (1910–79), British actor, writer. *Stately as a Galleon*, "English Lit." (1978).

9 Human development is a form of chronological unfairness, since late-comers are able to profit by the labors of their predecessors without paying the same price.

> ALEXANDER HERZEN (1812–70), Russian journalist, political thinker. Quoted by Isaiah Berlin in: Franco Venturi, *Roots of Revolution*, Introduction (1952; tr. 1960).

10 The slogan of progress is changing from the full dinner pail to the full garage.

> HERBERT HOOVER (1874–1964), U.S. Republican politician, president. Speech, 22 Oct. 1928, New York City.

11 Progress is the life-style of man. The general life of the human race is called Progress, and so is its collective march. Progress advances, it makes the great human and earthly journey towards what is heavenly and divine; it has its pauses, when it rallies the stragglers, its stopping places when it meditates, contemplating some new and splendid promised land that has suddenly appeared on its horizon. It has its nights of slumber; and it is one of the poignant anxieties of the thinker to see the human spirit lost in shadow, and to grope in the darkness without being able to awake sleeping progress.

> VICTOR HUGO (1802–85), French poet, dramatist, novelist. *Les Misérables*, pt. 5, bk. 1, ch. 20 (1862).

12 The United States has to move very fast to even stand still.

> JOHN F. KENNEDY (1917–63), U.S. president. Quoted in: *Observer* (London, 21 July 1963).

13 Progress celebrates Pyrrhic victories over nature. Progress makes purses out of human skin. When people were traveling in mail coaches, the world got ahead better than it does now that salesmen fly through the air. What good is speed if the brain has oozed out on the way? How will the heirs of this age be taught the most basic motions that are necessary to activate the most complicated machines? Nature can rely on progress; it will avenge it for the outrage it has perpetrated on it.

> KARL KRAUS (1874–1936), Austrian satirist. "The Discovery of the North Pole," in *Die Fackel*, no. 287 (Vienna, Sept. 1909; repr. in *In These Great Times: A Karl Kraus Reader*, ed. by Harry Zohn, 1976).

14 Progress, under whose feet the grass mourns and the forest turns into paper from which newspaper plants grow, has subordinated the purpose of life to the means of subsistence and turned us into the nuts and bolts for our tools.

> KARL KRAUS (1874–1936), Austrian satirist. "In These Great Times," speech, 19 Nov. 1914, Vienna (first published in *Die Fackel*, Dec. 1914; repr. in *In These Great Times: A Karl Kraus Reader*, ed. by Harry Zohn, 1976).

15 Enthusiastic partisans of the idea of progress are in danger of failing to recognize . . . the immense riches accumulated by the human race. . . . By underrating the achievements of the past, they devalue all those which still remain to be accomplished.

> CLAUDE LÉVI-STRAUSS (1908–90), French anthropologist. *Tristes Tropiques*, ch. 38 (1955).

16 It is curious to note the old sea-margins of human thought! Each subsiding century reveals some new mystery; we build where monsters used to hide themselves.

> HENRY WADSWORTH LONGFELLOW (1807–82), U.S. poet. One of the meditations of Mr. Churchill, inscribed on his pulpit, in *Kavanagh*, bk. 1, ch. 13 (1849).

17 Time advances: facts accumulate; doubts arise. Faint glimpses of truth begin to appear, and shine more and more unto the perfect day. The highest intellects, like the tops of mountains, are the first to catch and to reflect the dawn. They are bright, while the level below is still in darkness. But soon the light, which at first illuminated only the loftiest eminences, descends on the plain, and penetrates to the deepest valley. First come hints, then fragments of systems, then defective systems, then complete and harmonious systems. The sound opinion, held for a time by one bold speculator, becomes the opinion of a small minority, of a strong minority, of a majority of mankind. Thus, the great progress goes on.

THOMAS BABINGTON MACAULAY (1800–1859), English historian. "History of the Revolution in England," in *Edinburgh Review* (July 1835; repr. in *Lord Macaulay's Essays*, 1889).

18 Whatever there be of progress in life comes not through adaptation but through daring, through obeying the blind urge.

HENRY MILLER (1891–1980), U.S. author. *The Wisdom of the Heart*, "Reflections on Writing" (1947).

19 Today, the notion of progress in a single line without goal or limit seems perhaps the most parochial notion of a very parochial century.

LEWIS MUMFORD (1895–1990), U.S. social philosopher. *Technics and Civilization*, ch. 8, sct. 12 (1934).

20 Progress is not an illusion, it happens, but it is slow and invariably disappointing.

GEORGE ORWELL (1903–50), British author. *Inside the Whale and Other Essays*, "Charles Dickens" (1940).

21 You can't say that civilization don't advance . . . for in every war they kill you a new way.

WILL ROGERS (1879–1935), U.S. humorist. *The Autobiography of Will Rogers*, ch. 14 (1949).

22 A process which led from the amoeba to man appeared to the philosophers to be obviously a progress—though whether the amoeba would agree with this opinion is not known.

BERTRAND RUSSELL (1872–1970), British philosopher, mathematician. *A Free Man's Worship and Other Essays*, ch. 2 (1976).

23 Progress, far from consisting in change, depends on retentiveness. When change is absolute there remains no being to improve and no direction is set for possible improvement: and when experience is not retained, as among savages, infancy is perpetual.

GEORGE SANTAYANA (1863–1952), U.S. philosopher, poet. *The Life of Reason*, ch. 12, "Reason in Common Sense" (1905–6).

24 The reasonable man adapts himself to the world; the unreasonable one persists in trying to adapt the world to himself. Therefore, all progress depends on the unreasonable man.

GEORGE BERNARD SHAW (1856–1950), Anglo-Irish playwright, critic. *Man and Superman*, "Maxims for Revolutionists: Reason" (1903).

25 All progress has resulted from people who took unpopular positions.

ADLAI STEVENSON (1900–1965), U.S. Democratic politician. Speech, 22 March 1954, Princeton University.

26 Only mediocrities progress. An artist revolves in a cycle of masterpieces, the first of which is no less perfect than the last.

OSCAR WILDE (1854–1900), Anglo-Irish playwright, author. Letter to the Editor, in *Pall Mall Gazette* (London, 25 Sept. 1894).

27 A radical is one of whom people say "He goes too far." A conservative, on the other hand, is one who "doesn't go far enough." Then there is the reactionary, "one who doesn't go at all." All these terms are more or less objectionable, wherefore we have coined the term "progressive." I should say that a progressive is one who insists upon recognizing new facts as they present themselves—one who adjusts legislation to these new facts.

WOODROW WILSON (1856–1924), U.S. Democratic politician, president. Speech, 29 Jan. 1911, Kansas Society of New York, New York City.

28 Our civilization is characterized by the word "progress." Progress is its form rather than making progress being one of its features. Typically it constructs. It is occupied with building an ever more complicated structure. And even clarity is sought only as a means to this end, not as an end in itself. For me on the contrary clarity, perspicuity are valuable in themselves.

LUDWIG WITTGENSTEIN (1889–1951), Austrian philosopher. *Culture and Value* (ed. by G. H. von Wright and Heikki Nyman, 1980), 1930 entry.

See also Hooker on CHANGE; Weil on DESTINY; Cioran on INJUSTICE; Gladstone on REFORM; Hugo on REVOLUTION.

PROHIBITION

1 But the cheerful Spring came kindly on
And show'rs began to fall:
John Barleycorn got up again
And sore surpris'd them all.

ROBERT BURNS (1759–96), Scottish poet. *John Barleycorn*, st. 3.

2 Prohibition will work great injury to the cause of temperance. It is a species of intemperance within itself, for it goes beyond the bounds of reason in that it attempts to control a man's appetite by legislation, and makes a crime out of things that are not crimes. A Prohibition law strikes a blow at the very principles upon which our government was founded.

ABRAHAM LINCOLN (1809–65), U.S. president. Speech, 18 Dec. 1840, to Illinois House of Representatives.

3 Whether or not the world would be vastly benefited by a total banishment from it of all intoxicating drinks seems not now an open question. Three-fourths of mankind confess the affirmative with their tongues, and I believe all the rest acknowledge it in their hearts.

ABRAHAM LINCOLN (1809–65), U.S. president. Speech, 22 Feb. 1842, Washingtonian Temperance Society, Springfield, Ill. (published in *The Collected Works of Abraham Lincoln*, vol. 1, ed. by Roy P. Basler, 1953).

4 prohibition makes you
want to cry
into your beer and
denies you the beer
to cry into

DON MARQUIS (1878–1937), U.S. humorist, journalist. *archy and mehitabel*, "certain maxims of archy" (1927).

5 Of old all invitations ended
With the well-known *R.S.V.P.*,
But now our laws have been amended
The hostess writes *B.Y.O.B.*

CHRISTOPHER MORLEY (1890–1957), U.S. novelist, journalist, poet. *Thoughts on Being Invited to Dinner*.

6 The prohibition law, written for weaklings and derelicts, has divided the nation, like Gaul, into three parts—wets, drys, and hypocrites.

FLORENCE SABIN (1871–1953), U.S. anatomist, teacher. Speech, 9 Feb. 1931.

PROJECTS

1 Every man is the son of his own works.

MIGUEL DE CERVANTES (1547–1616), Spanish writer. Don Quixote, in *Don Quixote*, pt. 1, bk. 1, ch. 4 (1605; tr. by P. Motteux).

2 Mankind always sets itself only such tasks as it can solve; since, looking at the matter more closely, we will always find that the task itself arises only when the material conditions necessary for its solution already exist or are at least in the process of formation.

KARL MARX (1818–83), German political theorist, social philosopher. *A Contribution to the Critique of Political Economy*, Preface (1859; repr. in *Selected Works*, vol. 1, 1942).

3 To finish a work? To finish a picture? What nonsense! To finish it means to be through with it, to kill it, to rid it of its soul, to give it its final blow . . . the *coup de grâce* for the painter as well as for the picture.

PABLO PICASSO (1881–1973), Spanish artist. Quoted in: Jaime Sabartés, *Picasso: portraits et souvenirs*, ch. 7 (1946).

4 The road to hell is paved with works-in-progress.

PHILIP ROTH (b. 1933), U.S. author. *New York Times Book Review* (15 July 1979).

5 There are two things to be considered with regard to any scheme. In the first place, "Is it good in itself?" In the second, "Can it be easily put into practise?"

JEAN-JACQUES ROUSSEAU (1712–78), Swiss-born French philosopher, political theorist. *Emile*, Preface (1762).

PROMISCUITY

1 To sleep around is absolutely wrong for a woman; it's degrading and it completely ruins her personality. Sooner or later it will destroy all that is feminine and beautiful and idealistic in her.

BARBARA CARTLAND (b. 1901), British novelist. Interview in Wendy Leigh, *Speaking Frankly* (1978).

2 As bees their sting, so the promiscuous leave behind them in each encounter something of themselves by which they are made to suffer.

CYRIL CONNOLLY (1903–74), British critic. *The Unquiet Grave*, pt. 2 (1944; rev. 1951).

3 Elyot: It doesn't suit women to be promiscuous. Amanda: It doesn't suit men for women to be promiscuous.

NOËL COWARD (1899–1973), British playwright, actor, composer. *Private Lives*, act 2.

4 What happens is that, as with drugs, he needs a stronger shot each time, and women are just women. The consumption of one woman is the consumption of all. You can't double the dose.

IAN FLEMING (1908–64), British author. Notebook entry, describing a man's progress from woman to woman. Quoted in: John Pearson, *The Life of Ian Fleming*, ch. 8, sct. 1 (1966).

5 I have known a number of Don Juans who were good studs and who cavorted between the sheets without a psychiatrist to guide them. But most of the busy lovemakers I knew were looking for masculinity rather than practicing it. They were fellows of dubious lust.

BEN HECHT (1893–1964), U.S. journalist, author, screenwriter. *A Child of the Century*, bk. 5, "Don Juan in Hollywood" (1954), said of sex in Hollywood. In regard to Don Juan's "conquests," Hecht noted "a similar lack": "Their female sexuality was nearly all in their clothes, their mannerisms and their reputations. . . . The ladies hopping from lover to lover brought more ambition to bed than passion."

6 If you still behave in dancing rooms and other societies as I have seen you—I do not want to live—if you have done so I wish this coming night may be my last. I cannot live without you, and not only you but *chaste you; virtuous you.*

JOHN KEATS (1795–1821), English poet. Letter, May/June 1820, to Fanny Brawne (published in *Letters of John Keats*, no. 220, ed. by Frederick Page, 1954).

7 Be not too liberal; it doth belong
To dogs alone to fuck the whole day long.

FRIEDRICH NIETZSCHE (1844–1900), German philosopher. "Timon Says," in *Maxims 1882–1885* (published in *The Genealogy of Morals*, 1899).

8 You were born with your legs apart. They'll send you to the grave in a Y-shaped coffin.

JOE ORTON (1933–67), British playwright. Dr. Prentice to Mrs. Prentice, in *What the Butler Saw*, act 1.

9 When sexual indulgence has reduced a man to the shape of Lord Hailsham, sexual continence involves no more than a sense of the ridiculous.

REGINALD PAGET (1908–90), British Labour politician. Speech, 17 June 1963, House of Commons, during the debate on the Profumo scandal.

10 Promiscuity in men may cheapen love but sharpen thought. Promiscuity in women is illness, a leakage of identity. The promiscuous woman is self-contaminated and incapable of clear ideas. She has ruptured the ritual integrity of her body.

CAMILLE PAGLIA (b. 1947), U.S. author, critic, educator. *Sexual Personae*, ch. 1 (1990).

11 That woman speaks eighteen languages and can't say No in any of them.

DOROTHY PARKER (1893–1967), U.S. humorous writer. Quoted in: Alexander Woollcot, *While Rome Burns*, "Our Mrs. Parker" (1934), said of a departing guest.

12 The sexual freedom of today for most people is really only a convention, an obligation, a social duty, a social anxiety, a necessary feature of the consumer's way of life.

PIER PAOLO PASOLINI (1922–75), Italian film director, essayist. "Sono Contro l'Aborto," in *Corriere della Sera* (Milan, 19 Jan. 1975; repr. in *Scritti Corsari*, 1975).

13 Chaste to her Husband, frank to all beside,
A teeming Mistress, but a barren Bride.

ALEXANDER POPE (1688–1744), English satirical poet. *Epistle to a Lady*.

14 Variety is the spice of love.

HELEN ROWLAND (1875–1950), U.S. journalist. *Reflections of a Bachelor Girl* (1903; p. 3).

PROMISES

1 It is not the oath that makes us believe the man, but the man the oath.

AESCHYLUS (525–456 B.C.), Greek dramatist. *Fragments*, no. 385.

2 Promises are the uniquely human way of ordering the future, making it predictable and reliable to the extent that this is humanly possible.

HANNAH ARENDT (1906–75), German-born U.S. political philosopher. *Crises of the Republic*, "Civil Disobedience" (1972).

3 The rule is, jam tomorrow and jam yesterday—but never jam today.

LEWIS CARROLL [CHARLES LUTWIDGE DODGSON] (1832–98), English writer, mathematician. The White Queen, in *Through the Looking-Glass*, ch. 5 (1872).

4 What a woman says to her avid lover
Should be written in wind and running water.

CATULLUS (87–54 B.C.), Roman lyric poet. *Odes*, Ode 70.

5 The man who promises everything is sure to fulfil nothing, and everyone who promises too much is in danger of using evil means in order to carry out his promises, and is already on the road to perdition.

CARL JUNG (1875–1961), Swiss psychiatrist. *After the Catastrophe* (1945; repr. in *Collected Works*, vol. 10, para. 413, ed. by William McGuire, 1964).

6 A prince never lacks legitimate reasons to break his promise.

NICCOLÓ MACHIAVELLI (1469–1527), Italian political philosopher, statesman. *The Prince*, ch. 18 (1514).

7 One promises much, to avoid giving little.

LUC, MARQUIS DE VAUVENARGUES (1715–47), French moralist. *Refléxions et Maximes*, no. 436 (1746).

8 Good resolutions are useless attempts to interfere with scientific laws. Their origin is pure vanity. Their result is absolutely nil. . . . They are simply cheques that men draw on a bank where they have no account.

OSCAR WILDE (1854–1900), Anglo-Irish playwright, author. Lord Henry, in *The Picture of Dorian Gray*, ch. 8 (1891).

PROMOTION

1 Upon the creatures we have made,
We are, ourselves, at last, dependent.

JOHANN WOLFGANG VON GOETHE (1749–1832), German poet, dramatist. Mephistopheles, in *Faust*, pt. 2, act 2, sc. 2, "Laboratorium."

2 It is easier to appear worthy of a position one does not hold, than of the office which one fills.

FRANÇOIS, DUC DE LA ROCHEFOUCAULD (1613–80), French writer, moralist. *Sentences et Maximes Morales*, no. 164 (1678).

3 I don't say 'tis impossible for an impudent man not to rise in the world, but a moderate merit with a large share of impudence is more probable to be advanced than the greatest qualifications without it.

LADY MARY WORTLEY MONTAGU (1689–1762), English society figure, letter writer. Letter, c. 24 Sept. 1714, to her husband (published in *Selected Letters*, ed. by Robert Halsband, 1970).

4 The hope, and not the fact, of advancement, is the spur to industry.

SIR HENRY TAYLOR (1800–1886), English author. *The Statesman*, ch. 23 (1836).

5 When I give a man an office, I watch him carefully to see whether he is swelling or growing.

WOODROW WILSON (1856–1924), U.S. Democratic politician, president. Speech, 15 May 1916, to National Press Club, Washington, D.C.

See also Carnegie on PARTNERSHIP.

PROPAGANDA

1 Propaganda is a soft weapon; hold it in your hands too long, and it will move about like a snake, and strike the other way.

JEAN ANOUILH (1910–87), French playwright. Warwick, in *The Lark* (adapted by Lillian Hellman, 1955).

2 It is sometimes necessary to lie damnably in the interests of the nation.

HILAIRE BELLOC (1870–1953), British author. Letter, 12 Dec. 1917, to G. K. Chesterton. Quoted in: Robert Speaight, *Life of Hilaire Belloc* (1957). Belloc was a zealous propagandist during World War I.

3 Propaganda is that branch of the art of lying which consists in nearly deceiving your friends without quite deceiving your enemies.

F. M. CORNFORD (1874–1943), British author, poet. Quoted in: *New Statesman* (London, 15 Sept. 1978).

4 Propaganda has a bad name, but its root meaning is simply to disseminate through a medium, and all writing therefore is propaganda for *something*. It's a seeding of the self in the consciousness of others.

ELIZABETH DREW (1887–1965), Anglo-American author, critic. *Poetry: A Modern Guide to Its Understanding and Enjoyment*, pt. 2, ch. 10 (1959).

5 All propaganda or popularization involves a putting of the complex into the simple, but such a move is instantly deconstructive. For if the complex *can* be put into the simple, then it cannot be as complex as it seemed in the first place; and if the simple can be an adequate medium of such complexity, then it cannot after all be as simple as all that.

TERRY EAGLETON (b. 1943), British critic. *Against The Grain*, ch. 10, "The Critic as Clown" (1986).

6 As soon as by one's own propaganda even a glimpse of right on the other side is admitted, the cause for doubting one's own right is laid.

ADOLF HITLER (1889–1945), German dictator. *Mein Kampf*, vol. 1, ch. 6 (1925).

7 Propaganda does not deceive people; it merely helps them to deceive themselves.

> ERIC HOFFER (1902–83), U.S. philosopher. *The Passionate State of Mind*, aph. 260 (1955).

8 Propaganda, to be effective, must be believed. To be believed, it must be credible. To be credible, it must be true.

> HUBERT H. HUMPHREY (1911–78), U.S. Democratic politician, vice president. Speech, 6 Dec. 1965, Medford, Mass.

9 The most dangerous untruths are truths slightly distorted.

> G. C. LICHTENBERG (1742–99), German physicist, philosopher. *Aphorisms*, "Notebook H," aph. 7 (written 1765–99; tr. by R. J. Hollingdale, 1990).

10 The successor to politics will be propaganda. Propaganda, not in the sense of a message or ideology, but as the impact of the whole technology of the times.

> MARSHALL MCLUHAN (1911–80), Canadian communications theorist. Quoted in: *Maclean's* (Toronto, June 1971).

11 Why is propaganda so much more successful when it stirs up hatred than when it tries to stir up friendly feeling?

> BERTRAND RUSSELL (1872–1970), British philosopher, mathematician. *The Conquest of Happiness*, ch. 6 (1930).

12 In our country the lie has become not just a moral category but a pillar of the State.

> ALEXANDER SOLZHENITSYN (b. 1918), Russian novelist. Quoted in: *Observer* (London, 29 Dec. 1974).

13 Words that are saturated with lies or atrocity, do not easily resume life.

> GEORGE STEINER (b. 1929), French-born U.S. critic, novelist. *Language and Silence*, "K" (1967; first published 1963).

14 Get your facts first, and then you can distort them as much as you please.

> MARK TWAIN (1835–1910), U.S. author. Quoted in: Rudyard Kipling, *From Sea to Sea*, Letter 37 (1899).

15 The current flows fast and furious. It issues in a spate of words from the loudspeakers and the politicians. Every day they tell us that we are a free people fighting to defend freedom. That is the current that has whirled the young airman up into the sky and keeps him circulating there among the clouds. Down here, with a roof to cover us and a gasmask handy, it is our business to puncture gasbags and discover the seeds of truth.

> VIRGINIA WOOLF (1882–1941), British novelist. *New Republic* (21 Oct. 1940).

PROPERTY

1 Thieves respect property. They merely wish the property to become their property that they may more perfectly respect it.

> G. K. CHESTERTON (1874–1936), British author. Policeman, in *The Man Who Was Thursday*, ch. 4 (1908).

2 No man acquires property without acquiring with it a little arithmetic also.

> RALPH WALDO EMERSON (1803–82), U.S. essayist, poet, philosopher. *Representative Men*, "Montaigne" (1850).

3 Property is an intellectual production. The game requires coolness, right reasoning, promptness, and patience in the players.

> RALPH WALDO EMERSON (1803–82), U.S. essayist, poet, philosopher. *The Conduct of Life*, "Wealth" (1860).

4 Seeing is believing, and if an American success is to count for anything in the world it must be clothed in the raiment of property. As often as not it isn't the money itself that means anything; it is the use of money as the currency of the soul.

> LEWIS H. LAPHAM (b. 1935), U.S. essayist, editor. *Money and Class in America*, ch. 8 (1988).

5 Government has no other end but the preservation of Property.

> JOHN LOCKE (1632–1704), English philosopher. *Second Treatise on Civil Government*, ch. 6 (written 1681; published 1690).

6 Property is theft.

> PIERRE-JOSEPH PROUDHON (1809–65), French political theorist. *What is Property?*, ch. 1 (1840).

7 How can you buy or sell the sky, the warmth of the land? The idea is strange to us. If we do not own the freshness of the air and the sparkle of the water, how can you buy them? Every part of the earth is sacred to my people.

> Attributed to SEATTLE (c. 1784–1866), Chief of the Dwamish, Suquamish and allied Indian tribes. Letter, 1854, to President Franklin Pierce (published in *Brother Eagle, Sister Sky: A Message from Chief Seattle*, 1990). The letter, in which Seattle pleaded that his name should die with the ceding of the Washington State territories, was shown in 1992 to have been largely a forgery, devised by television scriptwriter Ted Perry for a historical epic in 1971.

8 Next to the right of liberty, the right of property is the most important individual right guaranteed by the Constitution and the one which, united with that of personal liberty, has contributed more to the growth of civilization than any other institution established by the human race.

> WILLIAM HOWARD TAFT (1857–1930), U.S. Republican politician, president. *Popular Government*, ch. 3 (1913).

9 In no other country in the world is the love of property keener or more alert than in the United States, and nowhere else does the majority display less inclination toward doctrines which in any way threaten the way property is owned.

> ALEXIS DE TOCQUEVILLE (1805–59), French social philosopher. *Democracy in America*, vol. 2, pt. 3, ch. 21 (1840).

10 What between the duties expected of one during one's lifetime, and the duties exacted from one after one's death, land has ceased to be either a profit or a pleasure. It gives one position, and prevents one from keeping it up. That's all that can be said about land.

> OSCAR WILDE (1854–1900), Anglo-Irish playwright, author. Lady Bracknell, in *The Importance of Being Earnest*, act 1.

11 If property had simply pleasures, we could stand it;

but its duties make it unbearable. In the interest of the rich we must get rid of it.

> OSCAR WILDE (1854–1900), Anglo-Irish playwright, author. *The Soul of Man Under Socialism,* in *The Fortnightly Review* (London, Feb. 1891; repr. 1895).

See also Emerson on CIVILIZATION; Frost on COMMUNICATION; Freud on COMMUNISM; LANDLORDS.

PROPHECY

1 Man has an incurable habit of not fulfilling the prophecies of his fellow men.

> ALISTAIR COOKE (b. 1908), British broadcaster, journalist. *Talk About America,* ch. 8 (1968).

2 Among all forms of mistake, prophecy is the most gratuitous.

> GEORGE ELIOT (1819–80), English novelist. *Middlemarch,* bk. 1, ch. 10 (1872).

3 Prophecy today is hardly the romantic business that it used to be. The old tools of the trade, like the sword, the hair shirt, and the long fast in the wilderness, have given way to more contemporary, mundane instruments of doom—the book, the picket and the petition, the sit-in . . . at City Hall.

> JANE KRAMER (b. 1938), U.S. author. *Off Washington Square,* "The Ranks and Rungs of Mrs. Jacobs' Ladder" (1963).

4 With prophecies the commentator is often a more important man than the prophet.

> G. C. LICHTENBERG (1742–99), German physicist, philosopher. *Aphorisms,* "Notebook H," aph. 23 (written 1765–99; tr. by R. J. Hollingdale, 1990).

5 Ages when custom is unsettled are necessarily ages of prophecy. The moralist cannot teach what is revealed; he must reveal what can be taught. He has to seek insight rather than to preach.

> WALTER LIPPMANN (1889–1974), U.S. journalist. *A Preface to Morals,* ch. 15 (1929).

PROPHETS

1 He is despised and rejected of men; a man of sorrows, and acquainted with grief: and we hid as it were our faces from him. . . . Surely he hath borne our griefs, and carried our sorrows.

> BIBLE, HEBREW. *Isaiah* 53:3–4.

2 The people who were honored in the Bible were the false prophets. It was the ones we call the prophets who were jailed and driven into the desert, and so on.

> NOAM CHOMSKY (b. 1928), U.S. linguist, political analyst. Interview in *Guardian* (London, 23 Nov. 1992).

3 Fear prophets . . . and those prepared to die for the truth, for as a rule they make many others die with them, often before them, at times instead of them.

> UMBERTO ECO (b. 1932), Italian semiologist, novelist. Brother William, in *The Name of the Rose,* "Seventh Day: Night (2)" (1980; tr. 1983).

4 There exists a species of transcendental ventrilo-

quism by means of which men can be made to believe that something said on earth comes from Heaven.

> G. C. LICHTENBERG (1742–99), German physicist, philosopher. *Aphorisms,* "Notebook F," aph. 84 (written 1765–99; tr. by R. J. Hollingdale, 1990).

5 The prophet who fails to present a bearable alternative and yet preaches doom is part of the trap that he postulates. Not only does he picture us caught in a tremendous man-made or God-made trap from which there is no escape, but we must also listen to him day in, day out, describe how the trap is inexorably closing. To such prophecies the human race, as presently bred and educated and situated, is incapable of listening. So some dance and some immolate themselves as human torches; some take drugs and some artists spill their creativity in sets of randomly placed dots on a white ground.

> MARGARET MEAD (1901–78), U.S. anthropologist. *Culture and Commitment,* Introduction (1970).

6 There is no question but that if Jesus Christ, or a great prophet from another religion, were to come back today, he would find it virtually impossible to convince anyone of his credentials . . . despite the fact that the vast evangelical machine on American television is predicated on His imminent return among us sinners.

> PETER USTINOV (b. 1921), British actor, writer, director. Quoted in: *Independent* (London, 25 Feb. 1989).

See also Humphrey on HERESY; Lichtenberg on SCOTLAND AND THE SCOTS; VISIONARIES.

PROSTITUTION

1 What it comes down to is this: the grocer, the butcher, the baker, the merchant, the landlord, the druggist, the liquor dealer, the policeman, the doctor, the city father and the politician—these are the people who make money out of prostitution, these are the real reapers of the wages of sin.

> POLLY ADLER (1900–1962), U.S. brothel-keeper. *A House Is Not a Home,* ch. 9 (1953).

2 The women who take husbands not out of love but out of greed, to get their bills paid, to get a fine house and clothes and jewels; the women who marry to get out of a tiresome job, or to get away from disagreeable relatives, or to avoid being called an old maid—these are whores in everything but name. The only difference between them and my girls is that my girls gave a man his money's worth.

> POLLY ADLER (1900–1962), U.S. brothel-keeper. *A House Is Not a Home,* ch. 10 (1953).

3 Prisons are built with stones of law, brothels with bricks of religion.

> WILLIAM BLAKE (1757–1827), English poet, painter, engraver. *The Marriage of Heaven and Hell,* plate 8 (1790–93).

4 The profession of a prostitute is the only career in which the maximum income is paid to the newest apprentice. It is the one calling in which at the beginning the only exertion is that of self-indulgence; all the prizes are at the commencement. It is the ever-new embodiment of the old fable of the sale of the soul to the Devil. The tempter offers wealth, comfort, excitement, but in return the victim must sell her soul, nor does the other party forget to exact his due to the uttermost farthing.

WILLIAM BOOTH (1829–1912), English evangelist, founder of the Salvation Army. *In Darkest England, and the Way Out,* pt. 1, ch. 6 (1890).

5 Prostitution is the supreme triumph of capitalism. . . . Worst of all, prostitution reinforces all the old dumb clichés about women's sexuality; that they are not built to enjoy sex and are little more than walking masturbation aids, things to be DONE TO, things so sensually null and void that they have to be *paid* to indulge in fornication, that women can be had, bought, as often as not sold from one man to another. When the sex war is won prostitutes should be shot as collaborators for their terrible betrayal of all women, for the moral tarring and feathering they give indigenous women who have had the bad luck to live in what they make their humping ground.

JULIE BURCHILL (b. 1960), British journalist, author. *Damaged Gods,* "Born Again Cows" (1986).

6 The whore is despised by the hypocritical world because she has made a realistic assessment of her assets and does not have to rely on fraud to make a living. In an area of human relations where fraud is regular practice between the sexes, her honesty is regarded with a mocking wonder.

ANGELA CARTER (1940–92), British author. *The Sadeian Woman,* "Desecration of the Temple" (1979).

7 A country without bordels is like a house without bathrooms.

MARLENE DIETRICH (1904–92), German-born U.S. film actor. *Marlene Dietrich's ABC,* "Bordel" (1962).

8 Actually, if my business was legitimate, I would deduct a substantial percentage for depreciation of my body.

XAVIERA HOLLANDER (b. 1936), U.S. prostitute. *The Happy Hooker,* ch. 14 (1972; written with Robin Moore and Yvonne Dunleavy).

9 We say that slavery has vanished from European civilization, but this is not true. Slavery still exists, but now it applies only to women and its name is prostitution.

VICTOR HUGO (1802–85), French poet, dramatist, novelist. *Les Misérables,* pt. 1, bk. 5, ch. 11 (1862).

10 I was like a social worker for lepers. My clients had a chunk of their body they wanted to give away; for a price I was there to receive it. Crimes, sins, nightmares, hunks of hair: it was surprising how many of them has something to dispose of. The more I charged, the easier it was for them to breathe freely once more.

TAMA JANOWITZ (b. 1957), U.S. author. *Slaves of New York,* "Modern Saint 271" (1986).

11 If a woman hasn't got a tiny streak of a harlot in her, she's a dry stick as a rule.

D. H. LAWRENCE (1885–1930), British author. *Pornography and Obscenity* (1930; repr. in *Phoenix: The Posthumous Papers of D. H. Lawrence,* pt. 3, ed. by E. McDonald, 1936).

12 If courtesans and strumpets were to be prosecuted with as much rigour as some silly people would have it, what locks or bars would be sufficient to preserve the honour of our wives and daughters?

BERNARD MANDEVILLE (1670–1733), Dutch-born English author, physician. *The Fable of the Bees,* "Remark (H)" (1714; rev. 1723).

13 Prostitution, when unmotivated by economic need, might well be defined as a species of psychological addiction, built on self-hatred through repetitions of the act of sale by which a whore is defined.

KATE MILLETT (b. 1934), U.S. feminist author. *Sexual Politics,* ch. 3 (1970).

14 Prostitution is not just a service industry, mopping up the overflow of male demand, which always exceeds female supply. Prostitution testifies to the amoral power struggle of sex, which religion has never been able to stop. Prostitutes, pornographers, and their patrons are marauders in the forest of archaic night.

CAMILLE PAGLIA (b. 1947), U.S. author, critic, educator. *Sexual Personae,* ch. 1 (1990).

15 The prostitute is not, as feminists claim, the victim of men but rather their conqueror, an outlaw who controls the sexual channel between nature and culture.

CAMILLE PAGLIA (b. 1947), U.S. author, critic, educator. "Elizabeth Taylor: Hollywood's Pagan Queen," in *Penthouse* (New York, March 1992; repr. in *Sex, Art, and American Culture,* 1992).

16 If you want to buy my wares
Follow me and climb the stairs . . .
Love for sale.

COLE PORTER (1893–1964), U.S. composer, lyricist. *Love For Sale,* in the show *The New Yorkers* (1930).

17 Punishing the prostitute promotes the rape of all women. When prostitution is a crime, the message conveyed is that women who are sexual are "bad", and therefore legitimate victims of sexual assault. Sex becomes a weapon to be used by men.

MARGO ST. JAMES (b. 1937), U.S. prostitute, activist. Quoted in: *San Francisco Examiner* (29 April 1979).

18 There is no more defiant denial of one man's ability to possess one woman exclusively than the prostitute who refuses to redeemed.

GAIL SHEEHY (b. 1937), U.S. author and critic. *Hustling,* ch. 1 (1971).

19 So do not think of helpful whores
as aberrational blots;
I could not love you half so well
without my practice shots.

JAMES STEWART ALEXANDER SIMMONS (b. 1933), Northern Irish poet. *Cavalier Lyric.*

20 Be composed—be at ease with me—I am Walt Whitman, liberal and lusty
as Nature,
Not till the sun excludes you do I exclude you,
Not till the waters refuse to glisten for you and the
  leaves to rustle for you,
do my words refuse to glisten and rustle for you.

WALT WHITMAN (1819–92), U.S. poet. *To a Common Prostitute.*

See also Dahlberg on LUST; Dworkin, Prince Philip on WIVES.

PROTEST

1 There is all the difference in the world between the criminal's avoiding the public eye and the civil disobedient's taking the law into his own hands in open defiance. This distinction between an open violation of the law, performed in public, and a clandestine one is so glaringly obvious that it can be neglected only by prejudice or ill will.

HANNAH ARENDT (1906–75), German-born U.S. political philosopher. *Crises of the Republic,* "Civil Disobedience" (1972).

2 If you attack the establishment long enough and hard enough, they will make you a member of it.

ART BUCHWALD (b. 1925), U.S. humorist. *International Herald Tribune* (Paris, 24 May 1989).

3 Resistance is feasible even for those who are not heroes by nature, and it is an obligation, I believe, for those who fear the consequences and detest the reality of the attempt to impose American hegemony.

NOAM CHOMSKY (b. 1928), U.S. linguist, political analyst. "Supplement to *On Resistance,*" in *New York Review of Books* (1 Feb. 1968; repr. in *American Power and the New Mandarins,* 1969).

4 While there is a lower class, I am in it; while there is a criminal element, I am of it; and while there is a soul in prison, I am not free.

EUGENE V. DEBS (1855–1926), U.S. trade unionist. Speech, 16 June 1913, from the dock at Canton, Ohio. Debs was defending himself against charges of violating the 1917 Espionage Act.

5 An ass may bray a good while before he shakes the stars down.

GEORGE ELIOT (1819–80), English novelist. *Romola,* ch. 50 (1863).

6 A great wind swept over the ghetto, carrying away shame, invisibility and four centuries of humiliation. But when the wind dropped people saw it had been only a little breeze, friendly, almost gentle.

JEAN GENET (1910–86), French playwright, novelist. *Prisoner of Love,* pt. 1 (1986; tr. 1989), said of the rise and fall of the Black Panthers.

7 Even a purely moral act that has no hope of any immediate and visible political effect can gradually and indirectly, over time, gain in political significance.

VÁCLAV HAVEL (b. 1936), Czech playwright, president. Letter, Aug. 1969, to Czech leader Alexander Dubcek. Quoted by Havel in: *Disturbing the Peace,* ch. 3 (1986; tr. 1990).

8 The dissident does not operate in the realm of genuine power at all. He is not seeking power. He has no desire for office and does not gather votes. He does not attempt to charm the public, he offers nothing and promises nothing. He can offer, if anything, only his own skin—and he offers it solely because he has no other way of affirming the truth he stands for. His actions simply articulate his dignity as a citizen, regardless of the cost.

VÁCLAV HAVEL (b. 1936), Czech playwright, president. *Living in Truth,* pt. 1, "An Anatomy of Reticence," sct. 10 (1986). See Havel on DISSENT.

9 We all have private ails. The troublemakers are they who need public cures for their private ails.

ERIC HOFFER (1902–83), U.S. philosopher. *Reflections on the Human Condition,* aph. 43 (1973).

10 One-fifth of the people are against everything all the time.

ROBERT KENNEDY (1925–68), U.S. Attorney General, Democratic politician. Speech, 6 May 1964, University of Pennsylvania.

11 One who breaks an unjust law that conscience tells him is unjust, and who willingly accepts the penalty of imprisonment in order to arouse the conscience of the community over its injustice, is in reality expressing the highest respect for law.

MARTIN LUTHER KING, JR. (1929–68), U.S. clergyman, civil rights leader. "Letter from Birmingham Jail," in *Why We Can't Wait* (1963).

12 We who in engage in nonviolent direct action are not the creators of tension. We merely bring to the surface the hidden tension that is already alive.

MARTIN LUTHER KING, JR. (1929–68), U.S. clergyman, civil rights leader. "Letter from Birmingham Jail," in *Why We Can't Wait* (1963).

13 Unfortunately, I am involved in a freedom ride protesting the loss of the minority rights belonging to the few remaining earthbound stars. All we demanded was our right to twinkle.

MARILYN MONROE (1926–62), U.S. screen actor. Telegram, 13 June 1962, to Mr. and Mrs. Robert Kennedy, turning down a party invitation.

14 I pondered all these things, and how men fight and lose the battle, and the thing that they fought for comes about in spite of their defeat, and when it comes turns out not to be what they meant, and other men have to fight for what they meant under another name.

WILLIAM MORRIS (1834–96), English artist, writer, printer. *A Dream of John Ball,* ch. 4 (1888).

15 We are here, not because we are law-breakers; we are here in our efforts to become law-makers.

EMMELINE PANKHURST (1858–1928), English suffragette. Speech, 21 Oct. 1908, at her trial in London.

16 I quietly declare war with the State, after my fashion, though I will still make use and get advantage of her as I can, as is usual in such cases.

HENRY DAVID THOREAU (1817–62), U.S. philosopher, author, naturalist. *On the Duty of Civil Disobedience* (1849).

See also Czech slogan on REVOLUTION; Spock on VIETNAM.

PROTESTANTISM

1 A single friar who goes counter to all Christianity for a thousand years must be wrong.

CHARLES V (1500–1558), Spanish king, Holy Roman Emperor. Answer to Protestant reformer Martin Luther at the Diet of Worms, 19 April 1521.

2 Alas the Church of England! What with Popery on one hand, and schismatics on the other, how has she been crucified between two thieves!

DANIEL DEFOE (1659–1731), English writer. *The Shortest Way with the Dissenters* (1702). Publication of this satire resulted in Defoe's imprisonment.

3 The Anglican Church is marked by the grace and good sense of its forms, by the manly grace of its clergy. The gospel it preaches is, "By taste are ye saved." . . . It is not in ordinary a persecuting church; it is not inquisitorial, not even inquisitive, is perfectly well bred and can shut its eyes on all proper occasions. If you let it alone, it will let you alone. But its instinct is hostile to all change in politics, literature, or social arts.

RALPH WALDO EMERSON (1803–82), U.S. essayist, poet, philosopher. *English Traits*, "Religion" (1856).

4 The White Protestant's ultimate sympathy must be with science, factology, and committee rather than with sex, birth, heat, flesh, creation, the sweet and the funky; they must vote, manipulate, control, and direct, these Protestants who are the center of power in our land, they must go for what they believe is reason when it is only the Square logic of the past.

NORMAN MAILER (b. 1923), U.S. author. *Advertisements for Myself*, pt. 5, "Advertisement for 'Games and Ends'" (1959).

5 The chief contribution of Protestantism to human thought is its massive proof that God is a bore.

H. L. MENCKEN (1880–1956), U.S. journalist. *Minority Report: H. L. Mencken's Notebooks*, no. 309 (1956).

6 This is what the Church is said to want, not party men, but sensible, temperate, sober, well-judging persons, to guide it through the channel of no-meaning, between the Scylla and Charybdis of Aye and no.

CARDINAL JOHN NEWMAN (1801–90), English churchman, theologian. *Apologia Pro Vita Sua*, "History of My Religious Opinions from 1839–1841" (1864).

7 Place before your eyes two Precepts, and two only. One is, Preach the Gospel; and the other is—Put down enthusiasm! . . . The Church of England in a nutshell.

MRS. HUMPHREY WARD (1851–1920), British novelist. Mr. Wendover, quoting Archbishop Manners Sutton, in *Robert Elsmere*, bk. 2, ch. 17 (1888). The last sentence is Wendover's own comment.

MARCEL PROUST

1 After Proust, there are certain things that simply cannot be done again. He marks off for you the boundaries of your talent.

FRANÇOISE SAGAN (b. 1935), French novelist, playwright. Interview in *Writers at Work* (First Series, ed. by Malcolm Cowley, 1958).

2 Oh, I love Proust. We all learned from him how to go back in time. The difference is that Proust stayed in his room, and he observed himself. He was Proust lying in his bed looking at Proust at the window who was looking at Proust in bed. In our generation's case, we are always in the middle. We are never on the outside. Whatever happens, happens to us.

ELIE WIESEL (b. 1928), Rumanian-born U.S. writer. Interview in *Writers at Work* (Eighth Series, ed. by George Plimpton, 1988).

3 The thing about Proust is his combination of the utmost sensibility with the utmost tenacity. He searches out these butterfly shades to the last grain. He is as tough as catgut and as evanescent as a butterfly's bloom.

VIRGINIA WOOLF (1882–1941), British novelist. *The Diary of Virginia Woolf*, vol. 3 (ed. by Anne O. Bell, 1980), entry for 8 April 1925.

PROVERBS AND MAXIMS

1 Until a friend or relative has applied a particular proverb to your own life, or until you've watched him apply the proverb to his own life, it has no power to sway you.

NICHOLSON BAKER (b. 1957), U.S. author. *U. And I: A True Story*, ch. 4 (1991).

2 I believe there's no proverb but what is true; they are all so many sentences and maxims drawn from experience, the universal mother of sciences.

MIGUEL DE CERVANTES (1547–1616), Spanish author. Don Quixote, in *Don Quixote*, pt. 1, bk. 3, ch. 7 (1605; tr. by P. Motteux).

3 I do not say a proverb is amiss when aptly and reasonably applied, but to be forever discharging them, right or wrong, hit or miss, renders conversation insipid and vulgar.

MIGUEL DE CERVANTES (1547–1616), Spanish author. Don Quixote, in *Don Quixote*, pt. 2, ch. 43 (1615).

4 No people require maxims so much as the American. The reason is obvious: the country is so vast, the people always going somewhere, from Oregon apple valley to boreal New England, that we do not know whether to be temperate orchards or sterile climate.

EDWARD DAHLBERG (1900–1977), U.S. author, critic. *Alms For Oblivion*, "Word-Sick And Place-Crazy" (1964).

5 What is all wisdom save a collection of platitudes? Take fifty of our current proverbial sayings—they are so trite, so threadbare, that we can hardly bring our lips to utter them. None the less they embody the concentrated experience of the race and the man who orders his life according to their teaching cannot go far wrong.

NORMAN DOUGLAS (1868–1952), British author. Count Caloveglia's "old teacher," in *South Wind*, ch. 16 (1917).

6 For proverbs are the pith, the proprieties, the proofs, the purities, the elegancies, as the commonest so the commendablest phrases of a language. To use them is a grace, to understand them a good.

JOHN FLORIO (c. 1553–1625), English author, translator. *Second Frutes*, Preface (1591).

7 Don't you go believing in sayings, Picotee: they are all made by men, for their own advantages. Women who use public proverbs as a guide through events are those who have not ingenuity enough to make private ones as each event occurs.

THOMAS HARDY (1840–1928), English novelist, poet. Ethelberta, in *The Hand of Ethelberta*, ch. 20 (1875).

8 Proverbs are always platitudes until you have personally experienced the truth of them.

ALDOUS HUXLEY (1894–1963), British novelist. *Jesting Pilate*, pt. 4 (1926).

9 A country can be judged by the quality of its proverbs.

GERMAN PROVERB.

10 Although none of the rules for becoming more alive is valid, it is healthy to keep on formulating them.

SUSAN SONTAG (b. 1933), U.S. essayist. "Debriefing," in *American Review* (Sept. 1973; repr. in *I, Etcetera*, 1978).

11 I can't make head or tail of Life. Love is a fine thing, Art is a fine thing, Nature is a fine thing; but the average human mind and spirit are confusing beyond measure. Sometimes I think that all our learning is the little learning of the maxim. To laugh at a Roman awestricken in a sacred grove is to laugh at something today.

WALLACE STEVENS (1879–1955), U.S. poet. Journal entry for 5 Feb. 1906 (published in *Letters of Wallace Stevens*, no. 107, ed. by Holly Stevens, 1967).

12 Most of our pocket wisdom is conceived for the use of mediocre people, to discourage them from ambitious attempts, and generally console them in their mediocrity.

ROBERT LOUIS STEVENSON (1850–94), Scottish novelist, essayist, poet. *Virginibus Puerisque*, "Crabbed Age and Youth" (1881).

PROVINCIALISM

1 When I was growing up I used to think that the best thing about coming from Des Moines was that it meant you didn't come from anywhere else in Iowa. By Iowa standards, Des Moines is a mecca of cosmopolitanism, a dynamic hub of wealth and education, where people wear three-piece suits and dark socks, often simultaneously.

BILL BRYSON (b. 1951), U.S. author, journalist. *The Lost Continent: Travels in Small Town America*, ch. 1 (1989).

2 Being a Georgia author is a rather specious dignity, on the same order as, for the pig, being a Talmadge ham.

FLANNERY O'CONNOR (1925–64), U.S. author. "The Regional Writer," in *Esprit* (University of Scranton, Penn., Winter 1963; repr. in *Mystery and Manners*, ed. by Sally and Robert Fitzgerald, 1972).

THE PSYCHE

1 Instead of being at the mercy of wild beasts, earthquakes, landslides, and inundations, modern man is battered by the elemental forces of his own psyche. This is the World Power that vastly exceeds all other powers on earth. The Age of Enlightenment, which stripped nature and human institutions of gods, overlooked the God of Terror who dwells in the human soul.

CARL JUNG (1875–1961), Swiss psychiatrist. *The Development of Personality* (1934; repr. in *Collected Works*, vol. 17, para. 302, ed. by William McGuire, 1954).

2 No great inner event befalls those who summon it not.

MAURICE MAETERLINCK (1862–1949), Belgian author. *Wisdom and Destiny*, p. 32 (1898; tr. by Alfred Sutro, 1912).

3 In every one of us there are two ruling and directing principles, whose guidance we follow wherever they may lead; the one being an innate desire of pleasure; the other, an acquired judgment which aspires after excellence.

SOCRATES (469–399 B.C.), Greek philosopher. Quoted in: Plato, *Phaedrus*.

4 The darkest pit
Of the profoundest hell, chaos, night,
Nor aught of blinder vacancy scooped out
By help of dreams can breed such fear and awe
As fall upon us often when we look
Into our minds, into the mind of man.

WILLIAM WORDSWORTH (1770–1850), English poet. *Home at Grasmere* (written 1800; published as *The Recluse*, 1888).

PSYCHIATRIC INSTITUTIONS

1 I myself spent nine years in an insane asylum and I never had the obsession of suicide, but I know that each conversation with a psychiatrist, every morning at the time of his visit, made me want to hang myself, realizing that I would not be able to cut his throat.

ANTONIN ARTAUD (1896–1948), French theater producer, actor, theorist. *Van Gogh, the Man Suicided by Society* (1947; repr. in *Selected Writings*, pt. 33, ed. by Susan Sontag, 1976).

2 Every morning I woke in dread, waiting for the day nurse to go on her rounds and announce from the list of names in her hand whether or not I was for shock treatment, the new and fashionable means of quieting people and of making them realize that orders are to be obeyed and floors are to be polished without anyone protesting and faces are to be made to be fixed into smiles and weeping is a crime.

JANET FRAME (b. 1924), New Zealand novelist, poet. *Faces in the Water*, ch. 1 (1961).

3 Involuntary mental hospitalization is like slavery. Refining the standards for commitment is like prettifying the slave plantations. The problem is not how to improve commitment, but how to abolish it.

THOMAS SZASZ (b. 1920), U.S. psychiatrist. *The Second Sin*, "Mental Hospitalization" (1973).

PSYCHIATRY

1 It is almost impossible to be a doctor and an honest man, but it is obscenely impossible to be a psychiatrist without at the same time bearing the stamp of the most incontestable madness: that of being unable to resist that old atavistic reflex of the mass of humanity, which makes any man of science who is absorbed by this mass a kind of natural and inborn enemy of all genius.

ANTONIN ARTAUD (1896–1948), French theater producer, actor, theorist. *Van Gogh, the Man Suicided by Society* (1947; repr. in *Selected Writings*, pt. 33, ed. by Susan Sontag, 1976).

2 If the nineteenth century was the age of the editorial chair, ours is the century of the psychiatrist's couch.

> MARSHALL MCLUHAN (1911–80), Canadian communications theorist. *Understanding Media*, Introduction (1964).

3 If you are well off and can afford to spend ten or twenty-five dollars a day to hire some patient soul to listen to your troubles you can be réadjusted to the crazy scheme of things and spare yourself the humiliation of becoming a Christian Scientist. You can have your ego trimmed or removed, as you wish, just like a wart or bunion.

> HENRY MILLER (1891–1980), U.S. author. *The Air-Conditioned Nightmare*, "With Edgar Varèse in the Gobi Desert" (1945).

4 Canst thou not minister to a mind diseased,
Pluck from the memory a rooted sorrow,
Raze out the written troubles of the brain,
And with some sweet oblivious antidote
Cleanse the fraught bosom of that perilous stuff
Which weighs upon the heart?

> WILLIAM SHAKESPEARE (1564–1616), English dramatist, poet. Macbeth to the Doctor of Physic, in *Macbeth*, act 5, sc. 3.

5 A psychiatrist is a man who goes to the Folies-Bergère and looks at the audience.

> BISHOP MERVYN STOCKWOOD (b. 1913), British ecclesiastic, author. Quoted in: *Observer* (London, 15 Oct. 1961).

6 The professional must learn to be moved and touched emotionally, yet at the same time stand back objectively: I've seen a lot of damage done by tea and sympathy.

> ANTHONY STORR (b. 1920), British psychiatrist. Quoted in: *Times* (London, 22 Oct. 1992).

7 Institutional psychiatry is a continuation of the Inquisition. All that has really changed is the vocabulary and the social style. The vocabulary conforms to the intellectual expectations of our age: it is a pseudo-medical jargon that parodies the concepts of science. The social style conforms to the political expectations of our age: it is a pseudo-liberal social movement that parodies the ideals of freedom and rationality.

> THOMAS SZASZ (b. 1920), U.S. psychiatrist. *The Manufacture of Madness*, ch. 1 (1971).

8 Psychiatric expert testimony: mendacity masquerading as medicine.

> THOMAS SZASZ (b. 1920), U.S. psychiatrist. *The Second Sin*, "Law" (1973).

PSYCHOANALYSIS

1 Freud thought he was bringing the plague to the U.S.A., but the U.S.A. has victoriously resisted the psychoanalytical frost by real deep freezing, by mental and sexual refrigeration. They have countered the black magic of the Unconscious with the white magic of "doing your own thing," air conditioning, sterilization, mental frigidity and the cold media of information.

> JEAN BAUDRILLARD (b. 1929), French semiologist. *Cool Memories*, ch. 2 (1987; tr. 1990).

2 Psycho-analysis pretends to investigate the Unconscious. The Unconscious by definition is what you are not conscious of. But the Analysts already know what's in it—they should, because they put it all in beforehand.

> SAUL BELLOW (b. 1915), U.S. novelist. Albert Corde, in *The Dean's December*, ch. 18 (1982).

3 The human mind is indeed a cave swarming with strange forms of life, most of them unconscious and unilluminated. Unless we can understand something as to how the motives that issue from this obscurity are generated, we can hardly hope to foresee or control them.

> CHARLES HORTON COOLEY (1864–1929), U.S. sociologist. *Human Nature and the Social Order*, ch. 6 (1902).

4 Psychoanalysis can unravel some of the forms of madness; it remains a stranger to the sovereign enterprise of unreason. It can neither limit nor transcribe, nor most certainly explain, what is essential in this enterprise.

> MICHEL FOUCAULT (1926–84), French essayist, philosopher. *Madness and Civilization*, "The Birth of the Asylum" (1961; tr. 1965).

5 The analytic psychotherapist thus has a threefold battle to wage—in his own mind against the forces which seek to drag him down from the analytic level; outside the analysis, against opponents who dispute the importance he attaches to the sexual instinctual forces and hinder him from making use of them in his scientific technique; and inside the analysis, against his patients, who at first behave like opponents but later on reveal the overvaluation of sexual life which dominates them, and who try to make him captive to their socially untamed passion.

> SIGMUND FREUD (1856–1939), Austrian psychiatrist. *Observations on Transference-Love* (1915; repr. in *Complete Works*, vol. 12, ed. by James Strachey and Anna Freud, 1958).

6 Analysis does not set out to make pathological reactions impossible, but to give the patient's ego *freedom* to decide one way or another.

> SIGMUND FREUD (1856–1939), Austrian psychiatrist. *The Ego and the Id*, ch. 5, note (1923; repr. in *Complete Works*, vol. 19, ed. by James Strachey and Anna Freud, 1961).

7 Where *id* was, there *ego* shall be.

> SIGMUND FREUD (1856–1939), Austrian psychiatrist. *New Introductory Lectures on Psychoanalysis*, Lecture 31, "The Dissection of the Psychical Personality" (1933; repr. in *Collected Works*, vol. 22, ed. by James Strachey and Anna Freud, 1964). The intention of psychoanalysis, Freud explained, is "to strengthen the ego, to make it more independent of the super-ego, to widen its field of perception and enlarge its organization, so that it can appropriate fresh portions of the id. . . . It is a work of culture," he added in the closing words of the lecture, "not unlike the draining of the Zuider Zee."

8 Freud is the father of psychoanalysis. It had no mother.

> GERMAINE GREER (b. 1939), Australian feminist author. *The Female Eunuch*, "The Psychological Sell" (1970).

9 Psychoanalysis cannot be considered a method of education if by education we mean the topiary art of clipping a tree into a beautiful artificial shape. But those who have a higher conception of education will prize most the method of cultivating a tree so that it fulfils to perfection its own natural conditions of growth.

> CARL JUNG (1875–1961), Swiss psychiatrist. *The Theory of Psychoanalysis* (1913; repr. in *Collected Works*, vol. 4, para. 442, ed. by William McGuire, 1961).

10 The psychoanalysts pick our dreams as if they were our pockets.

> KARL KRAUS (1874–1936), Austrian satirist. *Die Fackel*, no. 376/77 (Vienna, 30 May 1913; repr. in Thomas Szasz, *Anti-Freud: Karl Kraus's Criticism of Psychoanalysis and Psychiatry*, ch. 6, 1976).

11 The ultimate aim of psychoanalysis is to attribute art to mental weakness, and then to trace the weakness back to the point where, according to analytic dogma, it originated—namely, the lavatory.

> KARL KRAUS (1874–1936), Austrian satirist. *Die Fackel*, no. 381/83 (Vienna, 19 Sept. 1913; repr. in Thomas Szasz, *Anti-Freud: Karl Kraus's Criticism of Psychoanalysis and Psychiatry*, ch. 6, 1976).

12 Considered in its entirety, psychoanalysis won't do. It's an end product, moreover, like a dinosaur or a zeppelin; no better theory can ever be erected on its ruins, which will remain for ever one of the saddest and strangest of all landmarks in the history of twentieth-century thought.

> SIR PETER MEDAWAR (1915–87), British immunologist. *The Hope of Progress*, "Further Comments on Psychoanalysis" (1972).

13 Analysis brings no curative powers in its train; it merely makes us conscious of the existence of an evil, which, oddly enough, is consciousness.

> HENRY MILLER (1891–1980), U.S. author. *The Cosmological Eye*, "An Open Letter to Surrealists Everywhere" (1939).

14 Aided and abetted by corrupt analysts, patients who have nothing better to do with their lives often use the psychoanalytic situation to transform insignificant childhood hurts into private shrines at which they worship unceasingly the enormity of the offenses committed against them. This solution is immensely flattering to the patients—as are all forms of unmerited self-aggrandizement; it is immensely profitable for the analysts—as are all forms pandering to people's vanity; and it is often immensely unpleasant for nearly everyone else in the patient's life.

> THOMAS SZASZ (b. 1920), U.S. psychiatrist. *The Second Sin*, "Psychoanalysis" (1973).

15 Psychoanalysis is an attempt to examine a person's self-justifications. Hence it can be undertaken only with the patient's cooperation and can succeed only when the patient has something to gain by abandoning or modifying his system of self-justification.

> THOMAS SZASZ (b. 1920), U.S. psychiatrist. *The Second Sin*, "Psychoanalysis" (1973).

16 The more one analyses people, the more all reasons for analysis disappear. Sooner or later one comes to that dreadful universal thing called human nature.

> OSCAR WILDE (1854–1900), Anglo-Irish playwright, author. Vivian, in "The Decay of Lying" (published in *Intentions*, 1891).

See also Freud on DOCTORS; SIGMUND FREUD; Freud on MIRACLES.

PSYCHOLOGY

1 Always this same morbid interest in other people and their doings, their privacies, their dirty linen, always this air of alertness for personal happenings, personalities, personalities, personalities. Always this subtle criticism and appraisal of other people, this analysis of other people's motives. If anatomy presupposes a corpse, then psychology presupposes a world of corpses. Personalities, which means personal criticism and analysis, presuppose a whole world laboratory of human psyches waiting to be vivisected. If you cut a thing up, of course it will smell. Hence, nothing raises such an infernal stink, at last, as human psychology.

> D. H. LAWRENCE (1885–1930), British author. *St. Mawr* (1925; repr. in *The Short Novels*, vol. 2, 1979), said of Mrs. Witt, the "fiendish psychologist."

2 We have lost the art of living; and in the most important science of all, the science of daily life, the science of behaviour, we are complete ignoramuses. We have psychology instead.

> D. H. LAWRENCE (1885–1930), British author. *Etruscan Places*, ch. 4 (1932).

3 A large part of the popularity and persuasiveness of psychology comes from its being a sublimated spiritualism: a secular, ostensibly scientific way of affirming the primacy of "spirit" over matter.

> SUSAN SONTAG (b. 1933), U.S. essayist. *Illness As Metaphor*, ch. 7 (1978).

4 There is no psychology; there is only biography and autobiography.

> THOMAS SZASZ (b. 1920), U.S. psychiatrist. *The Second Sin*, "Psychology" (1973).

5 In an extensive reading of recent books by psychologists, psychoanalysts, psychiatrists, and inspirationalists, I have discovered that they all suffer from one or more of these expression-complexes: italicizing, capitalizing, exclamation-pointing, multiple-interrogating, and itemizing. These are all forms of what the psychos themselves would call, if they faced their condition frankly, Rhetorical-Over-Compensation.

> JAMES THURBER (1894–1961), U.S. humorist, illustrator. *Collecting Himself*, "Peace, It's Wonderful" (1989).

See also BEHAVIORISM.

THE PUBLIC

1 The approval of the public is to be avoided like the plague. It is absolutely essential to keep the public from *entering* if one wishes to avoid confusion. I must add that the public must be kept panting in expectation at the gate by a system of challenges and provocations.

> ANDRÉ BRETON (1896–1966), French surrealist. "Second Manifesto of Surrealism" (1930; repr. in *Manifestos of Surrealism*, 1969).

2 The reading public is intellectually adolescent at best, and it is obvious that what is called "significant literature" will only be sold to this public by exactly the same methods as are used to sell it toothpaste, cathartics and automobiles.

RAYMOND CHANDLER (1888–1959), U.S. author. Letter, 29 Jan. 1946, to crime novelist Erle Stanley Gardner (published in *Raymond Chandler Speaking*, 1962).

3   I don't believe that the public knows what it wants; this is the conclusion that I have drawn from my career.

CHARLIE CHAPLIN (1889–1977), British comic actor, filmmaker. Quoted in: *Cinema: Art and Industry*, ch. 10 (1976).

4   The basic idea which runs right through modern history and modern liberalism is that the public has got to be marginalized. The general public are viewed as no more than ignorant and meddlesome outsiders, a bewildered herd.

NOAM CHOMSKY (b. 1928), U.S. linguist, political analyst. Interview in *Guardian* (London, 23 Nov. 1992).

5   No decent career was ever founded on a public.

F. SCOTT FITZGERALD (1896–1940), U.S. author. "Early Success," in *American Cavalcade* (Oct. 1937; repr. in *The Crack-Up*, ed. by Edmund Wilson, 1945).

6   The urgent consideration of the public safety may undoubtedly authorise the violation of every positive law. How far that or any other consideration may operate to dissolve the natural obligations of humanity and justice, is a doctrine of which I still desire to remain ignorant.

EDWARD GIBBON (1737–94), English historian. *The Decline and Fall of the Roman Empire*, vol. 3 (1776–88; repr. 1910, ch. 26).

7   There is not a more mean, stupid, dastardly, pitiless, selfish, spiteful, envious, ungrateful animal than the Public. It is the greatest of cowards, for it is afraid of itself.

WILLIAM HAZLITT (1778–1830), English essayist. *Table Talk*, "On Living to One's Self" (1821–22).

8   The Public . . . a thing I cannot help looking upon as an enemy, and which I cannot address without feelings of hostility.

JOHN KEATS (1795–1821), English poet. Letter, 9 April 1818 (published in *Letters of John Keats*, no. 60, ed. by Frederick Page, 1954). Keats continued, "I never wrote one single line of poetry with the least shadow of public thought." See Keats on CRITICISM: PROFESSIONAL.

9   The public seldom forgive twice.

JOHANN KASPAR LAVATER (1741–1801), Swiss divine, poet. *Aphorisms on Man*, no. 595 (1788).

10   The public, with its mob yearning to be instructed, edified and pulled by the nose, demands certainties; it must be told definitely and a bit raucously that this is true and that is false. But there *are* no certainties.

H. L. MENCKEN (1880–1956), U.S. journalist. *Prejudices*, ch. 3 (First Series, 1919).

11   If you have got the public in the palm of your hand, you can be sure that is where they want to be.

CLIFF RICHARD (b. 1940), British singer. Quoted in: *Observer* (London, 4 Dec. 1988).

12   It has taken me nearly twenty years of studied self-restraint, aided by the natural decay of my faculties, to make myself dull enough to be accepted as a serious person by the British public; and I am not sure that I am not still regarded as a suspicious character in some quarters.

GEORGE BERNARD SHAW (1856–1950), Anglo-Irish playwright, critic. Quoted in: Hesketh Pearson, *Bernard Shaw: His Life and Personality*, ch. 16 (1942).

13   The English public, as a mass, takes no interest in a work of art until it is told that the work in question is immoral.

OSCAR WILDE (1854–1900), Anglo-Irish playwright, author. Letter to the editor of *St. James's Gazette* (London, 27 June 1890), answering criticisms leveled at Wilde's *The Picture of Dorian Gray*.

14   Yes; the public is wonderfully tolerant. It forgives everything except genius.

OSCAR WILDE (1854–1900), Anglo-Irish playwright, author. Gilbert, in *The Critic as Artist*, pt. 1 (published in *Intentions*, 1891).

See also Cocteau on CRITICISM; The MASSES; Butler on OPINION; The PEOPLE; Wilde on PORTRAITS.

PUBLIC LIFE

1   You're not an M.P., you're a gastronomic pimp.

ANEURIN BEVAN (1897–1960), British Labour politician. Quoted in: Michael Foot, *Aneurin Bevan*, vol. 2, ch. 6 (1973), said to a colleague who complained of attending too many public dinners.

2   The measure of your quality as a public person, as a citizen, is the gap between what you do and what you say.

RAMSEY CLARK (b. 1927), U.S. attorney general. *International Herald Tribune* (Paris, 18 June 1991).

3   We are not here to laugh.

CHARLES DE GAULLE (1890–1970), French general, president. Quoted in: *Independent* (London, 21 April 1990), on the centenary of his birth.

4   Everywhere I go I smell fresh paint.

DIANA, PRINCESS OF WALES (b. 1961). Quoted in: *Daily Telegraph* (London, 28 Jan. 1988), commenting on her royal duties.

5   A man in public life expects to be sneered at—it is the fault of his elewated sitiwation, and not of himself.

CHARLES DICKENS (1812–70), English novelist. Mr. Kenwigs, in *Nicholas Nickleby*, ch. 14 (1838–39).

6   How dreary—to be—Somebody!
How public—like a frog—
To tell one's name—the livelong June—
To an admiring Bog!

EMILY DICKINSON (1830–86), U.S. poet. *The Complete Poems*, no. 288 (1955).

7   I never know when I press these whether I am going to blow up Massachusetts or start the project.

JOHN F. KENNEDY (1917–63), U.S. Democratic politician, president. Speech, Sept. 1963, at airport in Salt Lake City, Utah, where Kennedy pulled the switch to activate generators at the Green River in the Colorado River basin, 150 miles distant.

8   The worthiest man to be known, and for a pattern to be presented to the world, he is the man of whom we have most certain knowledge. He hath been declared and enlightened by the most clear-seeing men that ever were; the testimonies we have of him are in faithfulness and sufficiency most admirable.

> MICHEL DE MONTAIGNE (1533–92), French essayist. *Essays*, ch. 12, bk. 3, "Of Physiognomy" (tr. by John Florio, 1588).

9 The more you stay in this kind of job, the more you realize that a public figure, a major public figure, is a lonely man.

> RICHARD M. NIXON (b. 1913), U.S. Republican politician, president. Interview with Stewart Alsop. Quoted in: Alsop, *Nixon and Rockefeller: A Double Portrait*, "A Talk with Nixon," appendix (1960), said during his term as vice-president.

10 The General has dedicated himself so many times, he must feel like the cornerstone of a public building.

> ADLAI STEVENSON (1900–1965), U.S. Democratic politician. Quoted in: Leon Harris, *The Fine Art of Political Wit*, ch. 10 (1964), said of President Eisenhower.

11 For such will be our ruin if you, in the immensity of your public abstractions, forget the private figure, or if we in the intensity of our private emotions forget the public world. Both houses will be ruined, the public and the private, the material and the spiritual, for they are inseparably connected.

> VIRGINIA WOOLF (1882–1941), British novelist. *Three Guineas* (1938, p. 163).

See also Levater on The PUBLIC.

PUBLIC OFFICE

1 Nominee. A modest gentleman shrinking from the distinction of private life and diligently seeking the honorable obscurity of public office.

> AMBROSE BIERCE (1842–1914), U.S. author. *The Devil's Dictionary* (1881–1906).

2 If a large city can, after intense intellectual efforts, choose for its mayor a man who merely will not steal from it, we consider it a triumph of the suffrage.

> FRANK MOORE COLBY (1865–1925), U.S. editor, essayist. *The Colby Essays*, vol. 1, "On Seeing Ten Bad Plays" (1926).

3 The State, in choosing men to serve it, takes no notice of their opinions. If they be willing faithfully to serve it, that satisfies.

> OLIVER CROMWELL (1599–1658), Parliamentarian general, Lord Protector of England. Speech, 2 July 1644, to the Parliamentarian army before the Battle of Marston Moor.

4 When you give power to an executive you do not know who will be filling that position when the time of crisis comes.

> ERNEST HEMINGWAY (1899–1961), U.S. author. "Notes on the Next War: A Serious Topical Letter," in *Esquire* (New York, Sept. 1935; repr. in *By-Line Ernest Hemingway*, ed. by William White, 1967).

5 I am not a perfect servant. I am a public servant doing my best against the odds. As I develop and serve, be patient. God is not finished with me yet.

> JESSE JACKSON (b. 1941), U.S. clergyman, civil rights leader.

Speech, 16 July 1984, at the Democratic National Convention, San Francisco.

6 Public employment contributes neither to advantage nor happiness. It is but honorable exile from one's family and affairs.

> THOMAS JEFFERSON (1743–1826), U.S. president. Letter, 18 April 1790 (published in *The Papers of Thomas Jefferson*, vol. 16, ed. by Julian P. Boyd, 1961).

7 Lofty posts make great men greater still, and small men much smaller.

> JEAN DE LA BRUYÈRE (1645–96), French writer, moralist. *Characters*, "Of Man," aph. 95 (1688).

8 We say that someone occupies an official position, whereas it is the official position that occupies him.

> G. C. LICHTENBERG (1742–99), German physicist, philosopher. *Aphorisms*, "Notebook F," aph. 47 (written 1765–99; tr. by R. J. Hollingdale, 1990).

9 In government offices which are sensitive to the vehemence and passion of mass sentiment public men have no sure tenure. They are in effect perpetual office seekers, always on trial for their political lives, always required to court their restless constituents.

> WALTER LIPPMANN (1889–1974), U.S. journalist. *The Public Philosophy*, ch. 2, sct. 4 (1955).

10 A public man must never forget that he loses his usefulness when he as an individual, rather than his policy, becomes the issue.

> RICHARD M. NIXON (b. 1913), U.S. Republican politician, president. *Life* (New York, 8 June 1959). This observation appeared in a tribute to Secretary of State John Foster Dulles following his death. Dulles, Nixon asserted, recognized this "fundamental truth."

11 No people is wholly civilized where a distinction is drawn between stealing an office and stealing a purse.

> THEODORE ROOSEVELT (1858–1919), U.S. Republican (later Progressive) politician, president. Acceptance Speech, 22 June 1912, Chicago, Illinois, upon his nomination for president on an independent ticket.

12 You don't have power if you surrender all your principles—you have office.

> RON TODD (b. 1927), British trade unionist. Quoted in: *Daily Telegraph* (London, 17 June 1988).

PUBLIC OPINION

1 Opinions are a private matter. The public has an interest only in judgments.

> WALTER BENJAMIN (1892–1940), German critic, philosopher. "Karl Kraus," in *Frankfurter Zeitung*, no. 76 (Frankfurt, 1931; repr. in *Reflections*, ed. by Peter Demetz, 1978).

2 We must live for the few who know and appreciate us, who judge and absolve us, and for whom we have the same affection and indulgence. The rest I look upon as a mere crowd, lively or sad, loyal or corrupt, from whom there is nothing to be expected but fleeting emotions, either pleasant or unpleasant, which leave no trace behind them.

> SARAH BERNHARDT (1844–1923), French actor. *The Memoirs of Sarah Bernhardt*, ch. 9 (1977).

3 The world will only, in the end, follow those who have despised as well as served it.

SAMUEL BUTLER (1835–1902), English author. *Samuel Butler's Notebooks* (1951).

4 Wonderful "Force of Public Opinion!" We must act and walk in all points as it prescribes; follow the traffic it bids us, realise the sum of money, the degree of "influence" it expects of us, *or* we shall be lightly esteemed; certain mouthfuls of articulate wind will be blown at us, and this what mortal courage can front?

THOMAS CARLYLE (1795–1881), Scottish essayist, historian. *Signs of the Times* (1829; first published in *Edinburgh Review*, no. 98).

5 There are certain times when public opinion is the worst of all opinions.

SÉBASTIEN-ROCH NICOLAS DE CHAMFORT (1741–94), French writer, wit. *Maxims and Considerations*, vol. 1, no. 92 (1796).

6 It is a besetting vice of democracies to substitute public opinion for law. This is the usual form in which masses of men exhibit their tyranny.

JAMES FENIMORE COOPER (1789–1851), U.S. novelist. *The American Democrat*, "On the Disadvantages of Democracy" (1838).

7 They look for a victim to chivy, and howl him down, and finally lynch him in a sheer storm of sexual frenzy which they honestly imagine to be moral indignation, patriotic passion or some equally avowable emotion, it may be an innocent Negro, a Jew like Leo Frank, a harmless half-witted German; a Christ-like idealist of the type of Debs, an enthusiastic reformer like Emma Goldman.

ALEISTER CROWLEY (1875–1947), British occultist. *The Confessions of Aleister Crowley*, ch. 58 (1929; rev. 1970), on the popular mood when inflamed by newspapers.

8 Public opinion contains all kinds of falsity and truth, but it takes a great man to find the truth in it. The great man of the age is the one who can put into words the will of his age, tell his age what its will is, and accomplish it. What he does is the heart and the essence of his age, he actualizes his age. The man who lacks sense enough to despise public opinion expressed in gossip will never do anything great.

GEORG HEGEL (1770–1831), German philosopher. *The Philosophy of Right*, "The State," addition 186 (1821; tr. 1942).

9 American public opinion is like an ocean—it cannot be stirred by a teaspoon.

HUBERT H. HUMPHREY (1911–78), U.S. Democratic politician, vice president. Speech, 11 Oct. 1966, Gannon College, Erie, Pa.

10 Public opinion, a vulgar, impertinent, anonymous tyrant who deliberately makes life unpleasant for anyone who is not content to be the average man.

W. R. INGE (1860–1954), Dean of St. Paul's, London. *Outspoken Essays*, "Our Present Discontents" (First Series), 1919).

11 Ah! Sir, a boy's being flogged is not so severe as a man's having the hiss of the world against him.

SAMUEL JOHNSON (1709–84), English author, lexicographer. Quoted in: James Boswell, *Life of Samuel Johnson*, 21 July 1763 (1791).

12 The private citizen, beset by partisan appeals for the loan of his Public Opinion, will soon see, perhaps, that these appeals are not a compliment to his intelligence, but an imposition on his good nature and an insult to his sense of evidence.

WALTER LIPPMANN (1889–1974), U.S. journalist. *Public Opinion*, ch. 17 (1922).

13 Where mass opinion dominates the government, there is a morbid derangement of the true functions of power. The derangement brings about the enfeeblement, verging on paralysis, of the capacity to govern. This breakdown in the constitutional order is the cause of the precipitate and catastrophic decline of Western society. It may, if it cannot be arrested and reversed, bring about the fall of the West.

WALTER LIPPMANN (1889–1974), U.S. journalist. *The Public Philosophy*, ch. 1, sct. 4 (1955).

14 If forty million people say a foolish thing it does not become a wise one, but the wise man is foolish to give them the lie.

W. SOMERSET MAUGHAM (1874–1966), British author. *A Writer's Notebook* (1949), entry for 1901.

15 A man must know how to fly in the face of opinion; a woman to submit to it.

MADAME DE STAËL (1766–1817), Swiss-French writer, wit. *Delphine*, Epigraph (1802).

16 It is the folly of too many to mistake the echo of a London coffee-house for the voice of the kingdom.

JONATHAN SWIFT (1667–1745), Anglo-Irish satirist. *The Conduct of the Allies* (1711).

17 Public Opinion . . . an attempt to organise the ignorance of the community, and to elevate it to the dignity of physical force.

OSCAR WILDE (1854–1900), Anglo-Irish playwright, author. Gilbert, in *The Critic as Artist*, pt. 2 (published in *Intentions*, 1891).

See also Carlyle on MORALITY.

PUBLICITY

1 All publicity is good, except an obituary notice.

BRENDAN BEHAN (1923–64), Irish playwright. Quoted in: *Sunday Express* (London, 5 Jan. 1964).

2 Publicity is the life of this culture—in so far as without publicity capitalism could not survive—and at the same time publicity is its dream.

JOHN BERGER (b. 1926), British critic. *Ways of Seeing*, ch. 7 (1972).

3 The monster of advertisement . . . is a sort of octopus with innumerable tentacles. It throws out to right and left, in front and behind, its clammy arms, and gathers in, through its thousand little suckers, all the gossip and slander and praise afloat, to spit out again at the public.

SARAH BERNHARDT (1844–1923), French actor. *The Memoirs of Sarah Bernhardt*, ch. 7 (1977).

4 The cult of individuality and personality, which promotes painters and poets only to promote itself, is really a business. The greater the "genius" of the personage, the greater the profit.

> GEORGE GROSZ (1893–1959), German artist. "Instead of a Biography," in *Der Gegner*, vol. 2, no. 3 (Berlin, 1920; repr. in *Art Is In Danger*, tr. 1987).

5 With publicity comes humiliation.

> TAMA JANOWITZ (b. 1957), U.S. author. Quoted in: *International Herald Tribune* (Paris, 8 Sept. 1992).

6 Of course I'm a publicity hound. Aren't all crusaders? How can you accomplish anything unless people know what you are trying to do?

> VIVIEN KELLEMS (1896–1975), U.S. industrialist, lecturer. Quoted in: *The Reader's Digest* (Pleasantville, N.Y., Oct. 1975).

7 To have news value is to have a tin can tied to one's tail.

> T. E. LAWRENCE (1888–1935), British soldier, scholar. Letter, 1 April 1935 (published in *The Letters of T. E. Lawrence*, ed. by Malcolm Brown, 1988).

8 We endeavour more that men should speak of us, than how and what they speak, and it sufficeth us that our name run in men's mouths, in what manner soever. It seemeth that to be known is in some sort to have life and continuance in other men's keeping.

> MICHEL DE MONTAIGNE (1533–92), French essayist. *Essays*, bk. 2, ch. 16, "Of Glory" (tr. by John Florio, 1580).

9 I have bought
Golden opinions from all sorts of people.

> WILLIAM SHAKESPEARE (1564–1616), English dramatist, poet. Macbeth, in *Macbeth*, act 1, sc. 7.

10 In America, the race goes to the loud, the solemn, the hustler. If you think you're a great writer, you must say that you are.

> GORE VIDAL (b. 1925), U.S. novelist, critic. Interview in *Writers at Work* (Fifth Series, ed. by George Plimpton, 1981).

11 Publicity in women is detestable. Anonymity runs in their blood. The desire to be veiled still possesses them. They are not even now as concerned about the health of their fame as men are, and, speaking generally, will pass a tombstone or a signpost without feeling an irresistible desire to cut their names on it.

> VIRGINIA WOOLF (1882–1941), British novelist. *A Room Of One's Own*, ch. 3 (1929)

See also Mills on FAME; Bennett on The PRESS.

PUBLISHING AND PUBLISHERS

1 Some said, John, print it; other said, Not so:
Some said, It might do good; others said, no.

> JOHN BUNYAN (1628–88), English Baptist preacher, author. *The Pilgrim's Progress*, pt. 1, "Author's Apology" (1678).

2 The minute you try to talk business with him he takes the attitude that he is a gentleman and a scholar, and the moment you try to approach him on the level of his moral integrity he starts to talk business.

> RAYMOND CHANDLER (1888–1959), U.S. author. Letter, 2

June 1947, to editor Dale Warren (published in *Raymond Chandler Speaking*, 1962), commenting on publishers.

3 In matters of truth the fact that you don't want to publish something is, nine times out of ten, a proof that you ought to publish it.

> G. K. CHESTERTON (1874–1936), British author. *A Miscellany of Men*, "The Nameless Man" (1912).

4 As repressed sadists are supposed to become policemen or butchers so those with an irrational fear of life become publishers.

> CYRIL CONNOLLY (1903–74), British critic. *Enemies of Promise*, pt. 2, ch. 10 (1938).

5 To me a book is a message from the gods to mankind; or, if not, should never be published at all. . . . A message from the gods should be delivered at once. It is damnably blasphemous to talk about the autumn season and so on. How dare the author or publisher demand a price for doing his duty, the highest and most honourable to which a man can be called?

> ALEISTER CROWLEY (1875–1947), British occultist. *The Confessions of Aleister Crowley*, ch. 68 (1929; rev. 1970).

6 A publisher is a specialised form of bank or building society, catering for customers who cannot cope with life and are therefore forced to write about it.

> COLIN HAYCRAFT (b. 1929), British publisher. Letter, to *Sunday Times* (London, 11 Feb. 1990). "Hype," added Haycraft, "springs eternal in every publisher's breast."

7 Having books published is very destructive to writing. It is even worse than making love too much. Because when you make love too much at least you get a damned clarte that is like no other light. A very clear and hollow light.

> ERNEST HEMINGWAY (1899–1961), U.S. author. Letter, 2 Oct. 1952, to poet and critic Bernard Berenson (published in *Selected Letters*, ed. by Carlos Baker, 1981).

8 If another Messiah was born he could hardly do so much good as the printing-press.

> G. C. LICHTENBERG (1742–99), German physicist, philosopher. *Aphorisms*, "Golden Notebook," aph. 8 (written 1765–99; tr. by R. J. Hollingdale, 1990).

9 When you publish a book, it's the world's book. The world edits it.

> PHILP ROTH (b. 1933), U.S. author. *New York Times Book Review* (2 Sept. 1979).

10 Publishers are notoriously slothful about numbers, unless they're attached to dollar signs—unlike journalists, quarterbacks, and felony criminal defendents who tend to be keenly aware of numbers at all times.

> HUNTER S. THOMPSON (b. 1939), U.S. journalist. "A Letter to *The Champion*: a publication of the National Assoc. of Criminal Defense Lawyers" (July 1990; repr. in *Songs Of The Doomed*, 1991).

11 No publisher should ever express an opinion on the value of what he publishes. That is a matter entirely for the literary critic to decide. . . . I can quite understand how any ordinary critic would be strongly prejudiced against a work that was accompanied by a premature and unnecessary panegyric from the publisher. A publisher is simply a useful middle-man. It is not for him to anticipate the verdict of criticism.

> OSCAR WILDE (1854–1900), Anglo-Irish playwright, author. Letter to the editor of *St. James's Gazette* (London, 30 June 1890).

12 Accursed who brings to light of day
The writings I have cast away.

> W. B. YEATS (1865–1939), Irish poet, playwright. *Untitled*, in *Variorum edition*, "Poems Not Included in the Definitive Edition" (ed. by Peter Allt and Russell Alspach, 1957).

See also McGovern on GREATNESS; Auden on MEN AND MASCULINITY.

PUNCTUALITY

1 Punctuality is the soul of business.

> THOMAS C. HALIBURTON (1796–1865), Canadian jurist, humorist. *Sam Slick's Wise Saws*, ch. 3 (1853).

2 Few things tend more to alienate friendship than a want of punctuality in our engagements. I have known the breach of a promise to dine or sup to break up more than one intimacy.

> WILLIAM HAZLITT (1778–1830), English essayist. "On the Spirit of Obligations" (1824; repr. in *The Plain Speaker*, 1826).

3 Punctuality is the politeness of kings.

> LOUIS XVIII (1755–1824), King of France. Attributed, c. 1814, in *Souvenirs de Jean Lafitte*, bk. 1, ch. 3 (1844).

4 I've been on a calendar, but never on time.

> MARILYN MONROE (1926–62), U.S. screen actor. Quoted in: *Look* (16 Jan. 1962).

5 Punctuality is the virtue of the bored.

> EVELYN WAUGH (1903–66), British novelist. *The Diaries of Evelyn Waugh* (ed. by Michael Davie, 1976), entry for 26 March 1962.

6 He was always late on principle, his principle being that punctuality is the thief of time.

> OSCAR WILDE (1854–1900), Anglo-Irish playwright, author. *The Picture of Dorian Gray*, ch. 4 (1891), commenting on Lord Henry.

PUNISHMENT

1 The generality of men are naturally apt to be swayed by fear rather than reverence, and to refrain from evil rather because of the punishment that it brings than because of its own foulness.

> ARISTOTLE (384–322 B.C.), Greek philosopher. *Nicomachean Ethics*, bk. 10, ch. 9.

2 As a man chasteneth his son, so the Lord thy God chasteneth thee.

> BIBLE, HEBREW. *Deuteronomy* 8:5.

3 I should be very willing to redress
Men's wrongs, and rather check than punish crimes,
Had not Cervantes, in that all too true tale
Of Quixote, shown how all such efforts fail.

> LORD BYRON (1788–1824), English poet. *Don Juan*, cto. 13, st. 8.

4 Retaliation is related to nature and instinct, not to law. Law, by definition, cannot obey the same rules as nature.

> ALBERT CAMUS (1913–60), French-Algerian philosopher, author. *Resistance, Rebellion and Death*, "Reflections on the Guillotine" (1961).

5 Better build schoolrooms for "the boy,"
Than cells and gibbets for "the man."

> ELIZA COOK (1818–89), English poet. *A Song for the Ragged Schools*, st. 12.

6 Thwackum was for doing justice, and leaving mercy to Heaven.

> HENRY FIELDING (1707–54), English novelist, dramatist. *Tom Jones*, bk. 3, ch. 10 (1749).

7 In its function, the power to punish is not essentially different from that of curing or educating.

> MICHEL FOUCAULT (1926–84), French philosopher. *Discipline and Punish: The Birth of the Prison*, pt. 4, ch. 3 (1975).

8 Well, there's no one at all, they do be saying, but is deserving of some punishment from the very minute of his birth.

> LADY GREGORY (1859–1932), Irish playwright, director. O'Malley, in *Shanwalla*, act 2.

9 Let us have compassion for those under chastisement. Alas, who are we ourselves? Who am I and who are you? Whence do we come and is it quite certain that we did nothing before we were born? This earth is not without some resemblance to a gaol. Who knows but that man is a victim of divine justice? Look closely at life. It is so constituted that one senses punishment everywhere.

> VICTOR HUGO (1802–85), French poet, dramatist, novelist. *Les Misérables*, pt. 4, bk. 7, ch. 1 (1862).

10 Our system is the height of absurdity, since we treat the culprit both as a child, so as to have the right to punish him, and as an adult, in order to deny him consolation.

> CLAUDE LÉVI-STRAUSS (b. 1908), French anthropologist. *Tristes Tropiques*, ch. 38 (1955), commenting on the system of justice.

11 All in all, punishment hardens and renders people more insensible; it concentrates; it increases the feeling of estrangement; it strengthens the power of resistance.

> FRIEDRICH NIETZSCHE (1844–1900), German philosopher. *The Genealogy of Morals*, essay 2, aph. 14 (1887).

12 Distrust everyone in whom the impulse to punish is powerful!

> FRIEDRICH NIETZSCHE (1844–1900), German philosopher. *Thus Spoke Zarathustra*, pt. 2, ch. 29 (1883–91).

13 If your buttocks burn, you know you have done wrong.

> WHITE SOUTH AFRICAN PROVERB.

14 Any punishment that does not correct, that can merely rouse rebellion in whoever has to endure it, is a piece of gratuitous infamy which makes those who impose it more guilty in the eyes of humanity, good sense and reason, nay a hundred times more guilty than the victim on whom the punishment is inflicted.

> MARQUIS DE SADE (1740–1814), French author. Letter, 21 May

1781, to his wife from Vincennes prison (published in *Selected Letters*, no. 8, ed. by Margaret Crosland, 1965).

15 Men are not hanged for stealing horses, but that horses may not be stolen.

GEORGE SAVILE, LORD HALIFAX (1633–95), English statesman, author. *Political, Moral, and Miscellaneous Thoughts and Reflections*, "Of Punishment" (1750).

16 And where th'offence is, let the great axe fall.

WILLIAM SHAKESPEARE (1564–1616), English dramatist, poet. Claudius, in *Hamlet*, act 4, sc. 5.

17 Whipping and abuse are like laudanum: you have to double the dose as the sensibilities decline.

HARRIET BEECHER STOWE (1811–96), U.S. novelist, anti-slavery campaigner. *Uncle Tom's Cabin*, ch. 20 (1852).

18 If he who breaks the law is not punished, he who obeys it is cheated. This, and this alone, is why lawbreakers ought to be punished: to authenticate as good, and to encourage as useful, law-abiding behavior. The aim of criminal law cannot be correction or deterrence; it can only be the maintenance of the legal order.

THOMAS SZASZ (b. 1920), U.S. psychiatrist. *The Second Sin*, "Punishment" (1973).

19 We have found that morals are not, like bacon, to be cured by hanging; nor, like wine, to be improved by sea voyages; nor, like honey, to be preserved in cells.

WILLIAM COOKE TAYLOR (1800–1849), Irish author. Remark, 1849. Quoted in: James Walvin, *Victorian Values*, ch. 6 (1987).

20 Whenever a human being, through the commission of a crime, has become exiled from good, he needs to be reintegrated with it through suffering. The suffering should be inflicted with the aim of bringing the soul to recognize freely some day that its infliction was just.

SIMONE WEIL (1909–43), French philosopher, mystic. "Draft for a Statement of Human Obligations" (written 1943; repr. in *Selected Essays*, ed. by Richard Rees, 1962).

21 One is absolutely sickened, not by the crimes that the wicked have committed, but by the punishments that the good have inflicted; and a community is infinitely more brutalised by the habitual employment of punishment than it is by the occasional occurence of crime.

OSCAR WILDE (1854–1900), Anglo-Irish playwright, author. *The Soul of Man Under Socialism*, in *Fortnightly Review* (London, Feb. 1891; repr. 1895).

See also CAPITAL PUNISHMENT; Mao on ERROR.

PUNISHMENT, CORPORAL

1 Withold not correction from the child: for if thou beatest him with the rod, he shall not die. Thou shalt beat him with the rod, and shalt deliver his soul from hell.

BIBLE, HEBREW. *Proverbs* 23:13–14.

2 And he smote his enemies in the hinder parts: he put them to a perpetual reproach.

BIBLE, HEBREW. *Psalms* 78:66.

3 Then spare the rod and spoil the child.

SAMUEL BUTLER (1612–80), English poet. *Hudibras*, pt. 2, cto. 1 (1663–78).

4 Hold you there, neither a strange hand nor my own, neither heavy nor light shall touch my bum.

MIGUEL DE CERVANTES (1547–1616), Spanish author. Sancho Panza, in *Don Quixote*, pt. 2, bk. 6, ch. 2 (1615; tr. by P. Motteux).

5 Why not whip the teacher when the pupil misbehaves?

DIOGENES OF SINOPE ["THE CYNIC"] (c. 410–c. 320 B.C.), Greek philosopher, moralist. *Herakleitos and Diogenes*, pt. 2, Fragment 99 (tr. by Guy Davenport, 1976).

6 Corporal punishment is as humiliating for him who gives it as for him who receives it; it is ineffective besides. Neither shame nor physical pain have any other effect than a hardening one.

ELLEN KEY (1849–1926), Swedish author, feminist. *The Century of the Child*, ch. 7 (1909).

7 He must have known me if he had seen me as he was wont to see me, for he was in the habit of flogging me constantly. Perhaps he did not recognise me by my face.

ANTHONY TROLLOPE (1815–82), English novelist. *Autobiography*, ch. 1 (1883).

8 I'm all for bringing back the birch, but only between consenting adults.

GORE VIDAL (b. 1925), U.S. novelist, critic. TV interview with David Frost. Quoted in: *Sunday Times Magazine* (London, 16 Sept. 1973).

PUNK

1 At its best New Wave/punk represents a fundamental and age-old Utopian dream: that if you give people the license to be as outrageous as they want in absolutely any fashion they can dream up, *they'll be creative about it*, and do something good besides.

LESTER BANGS (1948–82), U.S. rock journalist. *New Musical Express* (London, 24 Dec. 1977).

2 Punks in their silly leather jackets are a cliché. I have never liked the term and have never discussed it. I just got on with it and got out of it when it became a competition.

JOHN LYDON [formerly JOHNNY ROTTEN] (b. 1957), British rock musician. *Observer* (London, 4 May 1986).

3 Punk to me was a form of free speech. It was a moment when suddenly all kinds of strange voices that no reasonable person could ever have expected to hear in public were being heard all over the place.

GREIL MARCUS (b. 1945), U.S. rock journalist. *Discourses: Conversations in Postmodern Art and Culture*, "Punk and History" (ed. by Russell, Ferguson et. al., 1990). The essay is the transcript of a discussion, 24 Sept. 1988, New York.

PUNS

1 For my own part I think no innocent species of wit or pleasantry should be suppressed: and that a good pun may be admitted among the smaller excellencies of lively conversation.

> JAMES BOSWELL (1709–84), Scottish author. *Life of Samuel Johnson,* entry for 19 June 1784 (1791).

2 A man who could make so vile a pun would not scruple to pick a pocket.

> JOHN DENNIS (1657–1734), English playwright, critic. *Gentleman's Magazine,* vol. 51 (1781).

3 People who make puns are like wanton boys that put coppers on the railroad tracks. They amuse themselves and other children, but their little trick may upset a freight train of conversation for the sake of a battered witticism.

> OLIVER WENDELL HOLMES, SR. (1809–94), U.S. writer, physician. *The Autocrat of the Breakfast-Table,* ch. 1 (1858).

4 A pun is not bound by the laws which limit nicer wit. It is a pistol let off at the ear; not a feather to tickle the intellect.

> CHARLES LAMB (1775–1834), English essayist, critic. *Last Essays of Elia,* "Popular Fallacies: That the Worst Puns are the Best" (1833).

See also Holmes on JOKES AND JOKERS.

PURITANS

1 A puritan is a person who pours righteous indignation into the wrong things.

> G. K. CHESTERTON (1874–1936), British author. *New York Times* (21 Nov. 1930).

2 The Puritan through Life's sweet garden goes
To pluck the thorn and cast away the rose.

> KENNETH HARE (1888–1962), British poet, author. *The Puritan.*

3 The Puritan hated bearbaiting, not because it gave pain to the bear, but because it gave pleasure to the spectators.

> THOMAS BABINGTON MACAULAY (1800–1859), English historian. *History of England,* vol. 1, ch. 2 (1849).

4 The truth is, as every one knows, that the great artists of the world are never Puritans, and seldom even ordinarily respectable. No virtuous man—that is, virtuous in the Y.M.C.A. sense—has ever painted a picture worth looking at, or written a symphony worth hearing, or a book worth reading, and it is highly improbable that the thing has ever been done by a virtuous woman.

> H. L. MENCKEN (1880–1956), U.S. journalist. *Prejudices,* "The Blushful Mystery: Art and Sex" (First Series, 1919).

5 Puritanism: The haunting fear that someone, somewhere, may be happy.

> H. L. MENCKEN (1880–1956), U.S. journalist. *A Book of Burlesques,* "Sententiae" (1920).

6 What the Puritans gave the world was not thought, but action.

> WENDELL PHILLIPS (1811–84), U.S. abolitionist, orator. "The Pilgrims," speech, 21 Dec. 1855.

PURITY

1 To insist on purity is to baptize instinct, to humanize art, and to deify personality.

> GUILLAUME APOLLINAIRE (1880–1918), Italian-born French poet, critic. *The Cubist Painters,* "On Painting" (1913).

2 No one is more dangerous than he who imagines himself pure in heart: for his purity, by definition, is unassailable.

> JAMES BALDWIN (1924–87), U.S. author. "The Black Boy Looks at the White Boy," in *Esquire* (New York, May 1961; repr. in *Nobody Knows My Name,* 1961).

3 Purity is not imposed upon us as though it were a kind of punishment, it is one of those mysterious but obvious conditions of that supernatural knowledge of ourselves in the Divine, which we speak of as faith. Impurity does not destroy this knowledge, it slays our need for it.

> GEORGES BERNANOS (1888–1948), French novelist, political writer. *The Diary of a Country Priest,* ch. 4 (1936).

4 In order for the wheel to turn, for life to be lived, impurities are needed, and the impurities of impurities in the soil, too, as is known, if it is to be fertile. Dissension, diversity, the grain of salt and mustard are needed: Fascism does not want them, forbids them, and that's why you're not a Fascist; it wants everybody to be the same, and you are not. But immaculate virtue does not exist either, or if it exists it is detestable.

> PRIMO LEVI (1919–87), Italian chemist, author. *The Periodic Table,* "Zinc" (1975; tr. 1984).

5 We are not naïve enough to ask for pure men; we ask merely for men whose impurity does not conflict with the obligations of their job.

> JEAN ROSTAND (1894–1977), French biologist, writer. *Pensées d'un Biologiste* (1939; repr. in *The Substance of Man,* ch. 10, "A Biologist's Thoughts," 1962).

6 What stronger breastplate than a heart untainted?
Thrice is he armed that hath his quarrel just;
And he but naked, though locked up in steel,
Whose conscience with injustice is corrupted.

> WILLIAM SHAKESPEARE (1564–1616), English dramatist, poet. King Henry, in *King Henry VI, pt. 2,* act 3, sc. 2.

7 My strength is as the strength of ten,
Because my heart is pure.

> LORD TENNYSON (1809–92), English poet. *Sir Galahad.*

8 The purity men love is like the mists which envelope the earth, and not like the azure ether beyond.

> HENRY DAVID THOREAU (1817–62), U.S. philosopher, author, naturalist. *Walden,* "Conclusion" (1854).

9 Mud-pies gratify one of our first and best instincts. So long as we are dirty, we are pure.

> CHARLES D. WARNER (1829–1900), U.S. author. *My Summer in a Garden,* "Preliminary" (1817).

10 Life does not need to mutilate itself in order to be pure.

> SIMONE WEIL (1909–43), French philosopher, mystic. *The Pre-War Notebook* (1933–39; published in *First and Last Notebooks,* ed. by Richard Rees, 1970).

11 Purity is the power to contemplate defilement.

SIMONE WEIL (1909–43), French philosopher, mystic. *Gravity and Grace*, "Attention and Will" (1947; tr. 1952).

12 The sick do not ask if the hand that smoothes their pillow is pure, nor the dying care if the lips that touch their brow have known the kiss of sin.

OSCAR WILDE (1854–1900), Anglo-Irish playwright, author. Mrs. Arbuthnot, in *A Woman of No Importance*, act 4.

PURPOSE

1 The only failure a man ought to fear is failure in cleaving to the purpose he sees to be best.

GEORGE ELIOT (1819–80), English novelist, editor. Felix Holt, in *Felix Holt, The Radical*, ch. 45 (1866).

2 We need not only a purpose in life to give meaning to our existence but also something to give meaning to our suffering. We need as much something to suffer for as something to live for.

ERIC HOFFER (1902–83), U.S. philosopher. *Reflections on the Human Condition*, aph. 153 (1973).

3 The aims of life are the best defense against death.

PRIMO LEVI (1919–87), Italian author. *The Drowned and the Saved*, ch. 6 (1988).

4 Every man is occasionally visited by the suspicion that the planet on which he is riding is not really going anywhere; that the Force which controls its measured eccentricities hasn't got anything special in mind. If he broods on this somber theme long enough he gets the doleful idea that the laughing children on a merry-go-round or the thin, fine hands of a lady's watch are revolving more purposely than he is.

JAMES THURBER (1894–1961), U.S. humorist, illustrator. *Collecting Himself*, "Thinking Ourselves Into Trouble," pt. 1 (1989).

QUARRELS

1 Contemplative and bookish men must of necessitie be more quarrelsome than others, because they contend not about matter of fact, nor can determine their controversies by any certain witnesses, nor judges. But as long as they goe towards peace, that is Truth, it is no matter which way.

JOHN DONNE (c. 1572–1631), English divine, metaphysical poet. *Biathanatos*, Preface (written c. 1608; published 1646; repr. in *Complete Poetry and Selected Prose*, ed. by John Hayward, 1929).

2 The falling out of faithful friends, renewing is of love.

RICHARD EDWARDES (c. 1523–66), English poet. *Amantium Irae*. This last line of each of the poem's stanzas is an echo of an older line, from which the poem's Latin title is taken. See Terence below.

3 In all private quarrels the duller nature is triumphant by reason of dullness.

GEORGE ELIOT (1819–80), English novelist. *Felix Holt, the Radical*, ch. 9 (1866).

4 Quarrel? Nonsense; we have not quarrelled. If one is not to get into a rage sometimes, what is the good of being friends?

GEORGE ELIOT (1819–80), English novelist, editor. Mary, to Rosamond, in *Middlemarch*, bk. 1, ch. 12 (1871). Rosamond has questioned Mary about her feelings for Mr. Lydgate.

5 The last sound on the worthless earth will be two human beings trying to launch a homemade spaceship and already quarreling about where they are going next.

WILLIAM FAULKNER (1897–1962), U.S. novelist. Speech to UNESCO Commission. Quoted in: *New York Times* (3 Oct. 1959).

6 The longer a man lives in this world the more he must be convinced that all domestic quarrels had better never be obtruded on the public; for, let the husband be right, or let him be wrong, there is always a sympathy existing for women which is certain to give the man the worst of it.

BENJAMIN HAYDON (1786–1846), British artist. "Table Talk," in *Correspondence and Table-Talk*, vol. 2 (ed. by Frederic Wordsworth Haydon, 1876).

7 The foolish race of mankind
Are swarming below in the night;
They shriek and rage and quarrel—
And all of them are right.

HEINRICH HEINE (1797–1856), German poet, journalist. *Katharina*, sct. 4, in *New Poems* (1844).

8 The enemy is like a woman, weak in face of opposition, but correspondingly strong when not opposed. In a quarrel with a man, it is natural for a woman to lose heart and run away when he faces up to her; on the other hand, if the man begins to be afraid and to give ground, her rage, vindictiveness and fury overflow and know no limit.

ST. IGNATIUS OF LOYOLA (1491–1556), Spanish churchman, founder of the Society of Jesus. *Spiritual Exercises*, no. 325 (1548).

9 Though a quarrel in the streets is a thing to be hated, the energies displayed in it are fine; the commonest man shows a grace in his quarrel.

JOHN KEATS (1795–1821), English poet. Letter, written 14 Feb.–3 May 1819, to his brother and sister-in-law, George and Georgiana Keats (published in *Letters of John Keats*, no. 123, ed. by Frederick Page, 1954).

10 The most terrible fight is not when there is one opinion against another, the most terrible is when two men say the same thing—and fight about the interpretation, and this interpretation involves a difference of quality.

SØREN KIERKEGAARD (1813–55), Danish philosopher. *The Journals of Søren Kierkegaard: A Selection*, no. 1057 (ed. and tr. by Alexander Dru, 1938), 1850 entry.

11 I strove with none; for none was worth my strife.

WALTER SAVAGE LANDOR (1775–1864), English author. *Finis*.

12 Quarrel not at all. No man resolved to make the most of himself can spare time for personal contention. Still less can he afford to take all the consequences, including the vitiating of his temper and loss of self control. Yield larger things to which you can show no more than equal right; and yield lesser ones, though clearly your own. Better give your path to a dog than be bitten by him in contesting for the right. Even killing the dog would not cure the bite.

ABRAHAM LINCOLN (1809–1865), U.S. president. Letter, 26 Oct. 1863.

13 The same reason that makes us chide and brawl and fall out with any of our neighbours, causeth a war to follow between Princes.

MICHEL DE MONTAIGNE (1533–92), French essayist. *Essays,* bk. 2, ch. 12, "An Apology of Raimond Sebond" (tr. by John Florio, 1580).

14 I find my wife hath something in her gizzard, that only waits an opportunity of being provoked to bring up; but I will not, for my content-sake, give it.

SAMUEL PEPYS (1633–1703), English diarist. Diary entry, 17 June 1668.

15 I against my brother
I and my brother against our cousin
I, my brother and our cousin against the neighbors
All of us against the foreigner.

BEDOUIN PROVERB. Quoted by Bruce Chatwin in: *The Songlines,* ch. 30, "From the Notebooks" (1987).

16 The course of true love never did run smooth.

WILLIAM SHAKESPEARE (1564–1616), English dramatist, poet. Lysander, in *A Midsummer Night's Dream,* act 1, sc. 1.

17 The test of a man or woman's breeding is how they behave in a quarrel.

GEORGE BERNARD SHAW (1856–1950), Anglo-Irish playwright, critic. Colonel Craven, in *The Philanderer,* act 4.

18 Lovers' quarrels are the renewal of love.

TERENCE (c. 190–159 B.C.). Roman dramatist. Chremes, in *Andria,* act 3, sc. 3.

19 Break a vase, and the love that reassembles the fragments is stronger than that love which took its symmetry for granted when it was whole.

DEREK WALCOTT (b. 1930), West Indian poet, playwright. "Dissolving the Sigh of History," in *Guardian* (London, 16 Dec. 1992).

See also Fitzgerald on FAMILY; Gay on INTERVENTION; Proverb on LOVERS; Yeats on POETRY.

QUOTATION

1 One must be a wise reader to quote wisely and well.

A. BRONSON ALCOTT (1799–1888), U.S. educator, social reformer. *Table Talk,* bk. 1, "Quotation" (1877).

2 Quotes from Mao, Castro, and Che Guevara . . . are as germane to our highly technological, computerized society as a stagecoach on a jet runway at Kennedy airport.

SAUL ALINSKY (1909–72), U.S. radical activist. *Rules for Radicals,* Prologue (1971).

3 When one begins to live by habit and by quotation, one has begun to stop living.

JAMES BALDWIN (1924–87), U.S. author. "White Racism or World Community?," in *Ecumenical Review* (Oct. 1968; repr. in *The Price of The Ticket,* 1985).

4 Quotations in my work are like wayside robbers who leap out armed and relieve the stroller of his conviction.

WALTER BENJAMIN (1892–1940), German critic and philosopher. *One-Way Street,* "Hardware" (1928; repr. in *One-Way Street and Other Writings,* 1978).

5 Life itself is a quotation.

JORGE LUIS BORGES (1899–1986), Argentinian author. Heard by Jean Baudrillard at a lecture given in Paris. Quoted in: Baudrillard, *Cool Memories,* ch. 5 (1987; tr. 1990).

6 Ah, yes, I wrote the "Purple Cow"—
I'm sorry, now, I wrote it!
But I can tell you, anyhow,
I'll kill you if you quote it.

GELETT BURGESS (1866–1951), U.S. humorist, illustrator. *Cinq Ans Après.*

7 It is a good thing for an uneducated man to read books of quotations. . . . The quotations, when engraved upon the memory, give you good thoughts. They also make you anxious to read the authors and look for more.

SIR WINSTON CHURCHILL (1874–1965), British statesman, writer. *My Eary Life,* ch. 9 (1930).

8 One learns little more about a man from the feats of his literary memory than from the feats of his alimentary canal.

FRANK MOORE COLBY (1865–1925), U.S. editor, essayist. *The Colby Essays,* vol. 1, "Quotation and Allusion" (1926).

9 Too much traffic with a quotation book begets a conviction of ignorance in a sensitive reader. Not only is there a mass of quotable stuff he never quotes, but an even vaster realm of which he has never heard.

ROBERTSON DAVIES (b. 1913), Canadian novelist, journalist. "Dangerous Jewels," in *Toronto Daily Star* (1 Oct. 1960; repr. in *The Enthusiasms of Robertson Davies,* 1990). "To be apt in quotation," Davies wrote, "is a splendid and dangerous gift. Splendid, because it ornaments a man's speech with other men's jewels; dangerous, for the same reason."

10 Quotations are useful in periods of ignorance or obscurantist beliefs.

GUY DEBORD (b. 1931), French Situationist philosopher. *Panegyric,* vol. 1, pt. 1 (1989).

11 The wisdom of the wise, and the experience of ages, may be preserved by quotation.

ISAAC D'ISRAELI (1766–1848), English author. *Curiosities of Literature,* "Quotation" (1791–1834).

12 I hate quotations. Tell me what you know.

RALPH WALDO EMERSON (1803–82), U.S. essayist, poet, philosopher. *Journals and Miscellaneous Notebooks,* vol. 2 (ed. by William H. Gillman, Alfred R. Ferguson, and Merrell R. Davis, 1961), May 1849 entry.

13 Next to the originator of a good sentence is the first quoter of it. Many will read the book before one thinks of quoting a passage. As soon as he has done this, that line will be quoted east and west.

RALPH WALDO EMERSON (1803–82), U.S. essayist, poet, philosopher. *Journals,* vol. 16 (ed. by Ronald Bosco and Glen Johnson, 1982), 1867 entry. The passage later appeared in *Letters and Social Aims*, "Quotation and Originality" (1876), in which Emerson wrote, "By necessity, by proclivity, and by delight, we all quote."

14   Quotation . . . A writer expresses himself in words that have been used before because they give his meaning better than he can give it himself, or because they are beautiful or witty, or because he expects them to touch a cord of association in his reader, or because he wishes to show that he is learned and well read. Quotations due to the last motive are invariably ill-advised; the discerning reader detects it and is contemptuous; the undiscerning is perhaps impressed, but even then is at the same time repelled, pretentious quotations being the surest road to tedium.

HENRY W. FOWLER (1859–1933), English lexicographer. *A Dictionary of Modern English Usage* (1926).

15   Quotations offer one kind of break in what the eye can see, the ear can hear.

IHAB HASSAN (b. 1925), U.S. critic. *The Right Promethean Fire*, Preface (1980).

16   We rarely quote nowadays to appeal to authority . . . though we quote sometimes to display our sapience and erudition. Some authors we quote against. Some we quote not at all, offering them our scrupulous avoidance, and so make them part of our "white mythology." Other authors we constantly invoke, chanting their names in cerebral rituals of propitiation or ancestor worship.

IHAB HASSAN (b. 1925), U.S. critic. "The Critic as Innovator," in *Chicago Review* (Winter 1977; repr. in *The Right Promethean Fire*, 1980).

17   Every quotation contributes something to the stability or enlargement of the language.

SAMUEL JOHNSON (1709–84), English author, lexicographer. *Dictionary of the English Language*, Preface (1755).

18   Classical quotation is the *parole* of literary men all over the world.

SAMUEL JOHNSON (1709–84), English author, lexicographer. Quoted in: James Boswell, *Life of Samuel Johnson*, 8 May 1781 (1791).

19   He wrapped himself in quotations—as a beggar would enfold himself in the purple of Emperors.

RUDYARD KIPLING (1865–1936), British author, poet. *Many Inventions*, "The Finest Story in the World" (1893).

20   Fidelity to the subject's thought and to his characteristic way of expressing himself is the sine qua non of journalistic quotation.

JANET MALCOLM (b. 1934), U.S. author. *The Journalist and the Murderer*, "Afterword" (1990). Malcolm was at the center of a legal dispute in which she was accused of fabricating quotations. In her book, she argued that accurate quotation is impossible: "When we talk with somebody, we are not aware of the language we are speaking. Our ear takes it in as English, and only if we see it transcribed verbatim do we realize that it is a kind of foreign tongue."

See also Eliot on CARICATURE; Byron on LEARNING.

21   Great speeches have always had great soundbites. The problem now is that the young technicians who put together speeches are paying attention only to the soundbite, not to the text as a whole, not realizing that all great soundbites happen by accident, which is to say, all great soundbites are yielded up inevitably, as part of the natural expression of the text. They are part of the tapestry, they aren't a little flower somebody sewed on.

PEGGY NOONAN (b. 1950), U.S. author, presidential speechwriter. *What I Saw at the Revolution*, ch. 5 (1990).

22   A book that furnishes no quotations is, *me judice*, no book — it is a plaything.

THOMAS LOVE PEACOCK (1785–1866), English author. Dr. Folliot, in *Crotchet Castle*, ch. 9 (1831).

23   Misquotation is, in fact, the pride and privilege of the learned. A widely-read man never quotes accurately, for the rather obvious reason that he has read too widely.

HESKETH PEARSON (1887–1964), British biographer. *Common Misquotations*, Introduction (1934). "Misquotations," Pearson wrote, "are the only quotations that are never misquoted.".

24   That's the nice thing about this job. You get to quote yourself shamelessly. If you don't, Larry Speakes will.

RONALD REAGAN (b. 1911), U.S. Republican politician, president. *Daily Telegraph* (London, 14 April 1988).

25   Quotations—always inexact. I don't trust people who cannot even copy out.

JEAN ROSTAND (1894–1977), French biologist, writer. *Carnets d'un Biologiste* (repr. in *The Substance of Man*, 1962, p. 191).

26   In quoting of books, quote such authors as are usually read; others you may read for your own satisfaction, but not name them.

JOHN SELDEN (1584–1654), English jurist, statesman. *Table Talk*, "Books; Authors" (1686).

27   To be occasionally quoted is the only fame I care for.

ALEXANDER SMITH (1830–67), Scottish poet. *Dreamthorp*, "Men of Letters" (1863).

28   The habit some writers indulge in of perpetual quotation is one it behoves lovers of good literature to protest against, for it is an insidious habit which in the end must cloud the stream of thought, or at least check spontaneity. If it be true that *le style c'est l'homme*, what is likely to happen if *l'homme* is for ever eking out his own personality with that of some other individual?

DAME ETHEL SMYTH (1858–1944), British composer and feminist. *Streaks of Life*, "The Quotation-Fiend" (1924).

29   The taste for quotations (and for the juxtaposition of incongruous quotations) is a Surrealist taste.

SUSAN SONTAG (b. 1933), U.S. essayist. *On Photography*, "Melancholy Objects" (1977).

30   Though collecting quotations could be considered as merely an ironic mimetism—victimless collecting, as it were . . . in a world that is well on its way to becoming one vast quarry, the collector becomes someone engaged in a pious work of salvage. The course of modern history having already sapped the traditions and shattered the living wholes in which precious objects once found their place, the collector may now in good conscience go about excavating the choicer, more emblematic fragments.

SUSAN SONTAG (b. 1933), U.S. essayist. *On Photography*,

"Melancholy Objects" (1977). Sontag adds, "But the old world cannot be renewed—certainly not by quotations."

31 In the dying world I come from quotation is a national vice. It used to be the classics, now it's lyric verse.

> EVELYN WAUGH (1903–66), British novelist. Dennis Barlow, in *The Loved One* (1948; ed. 1951, p. 108).

32 One has to secrete a jelly in which to slip quotations down people's throats—and one always secretes too much jelly.

> VIRGINIA WOOLF (1882–1941), British novelist. Letter, 4 July 1938 (published in *Leave the Letters Till We're Dead: Letters, Vol. 6*, ed. by Nigel Nicolson, 1980).

33 Some, for renown, on scraps of learning dote,
And think they grow immortal as they quote.

> EDWARD YOUNG (1683–1765), English poet. *Love of Fame*, Satire. 1.

RACE

1 At bottom, to be colored means that one has been caught in some utterly unbelievable cosmic joke, a joke so hideous and in such bad taste that it defeats all categories and definitions.

> JAMES BALDWIN (1924–87), U.S. author. "Color," in *Esquire* (New York, Dec. 1962; repr. in *The Price of the Ticket*, 1985).

2 It is a great shock at the age of five or six to find that in a world of Gary Coopers you are the Indian.

> JAMES BALDWIN (1924–87), U.S. author. Speech, 17 Feb. 1965, Cambridge Union, Cambridge University.

3 The true worth of a race must be measured by the character of its womanhood.

> MARY MCLEOD BETHUNE (1875–1955), U.S. educator. "A Century of Progress of Negro Women," address, 3 June 1933, to Chicago Women's Federation (published in *Black Women in White America*, ed. by Gerda Lerner, 1972).

4 Whites must be made to realize that they are only human, not superior. Same with blacks. They must be made to realize that they are also human, not inferior.

> STEVE BIKO (1946–77), South African political leader. Quoted in: *Boston Globe* (26 Oct. 1977).

5 Race prejudice is not only a shadow over the colored—it is a shadow over all of us, and the shadow is darkest over those who feel it least and allow its evil effects to go on.

> PEARL BUCK (1892–1973), U.S. novelist. *What America Means to Me*, ch. 1 (1943).

6 The new grammar of race is constructed in a way that George Orwell would have appreciated, because its rules make some ideas impossible to express—unless, of course, one wants to be called a racist.

> STEPHEN CARTER (b. 1954), U.S. lawyer, author. *Reflections of an Affirmative Action Baby*, ch. 8 (1992).

7 The North will at least preserve your flesh for you; Northerners are pale for good and all. There's very little difference between a dead Swede and a young man who's had a bad night. But the Colonial is full of maggots the day after he gets off the boat.

> LOUIS-FERDINAND CÉLINE (1894–1961), French author. The narrator (Ferdinand Bardamu), in *Journey to the End of the Night* (1932; tr. 1934; repr. 1966, p. 101).

8 Today I see more clearly than yesterday that back of the problem of race and color, lies a greater problem which both obscures and implements it: and that is the fact that so many civilized persons are willing to live in comfort even if the price of this is poverty, ignorance and disease of the majority of their fellowmen; that to maintain this privilege men have waged war until today war tends to become universal and continuous, and the excuse for this war continues largely to be color and race.

> W. E. B. DU BOIS (1868–1963), U.S. civil rights leader, author. Preface to 1969 ed. of *The Souls of Black Folk* (1903).

9 In fact, there is clear evidence of black intellectual superiority: in 1984, 92 percent of blacks voted to retire Ronald Reagan, compared to only 36 percent of whites.

> BARBARA EHRENREICH (b. 1941), U.S. author, columnist. *The Worst Years of Our Lives*, "The Unbearable Being Of Whiteness" (1991; first published 1988).

10 Purity of race does not exist. Europe is a continent of energetic mongrels.

> H. A. L. FISHER (1865–1940), British historian, politician. *A History of Europe*, ch. 1 (1935).

11 There are only two races on this planet—the intelligent and the stupid.

> JOHN FOWLES (b. 1926), British novelist. *Daily Telegraph* (London, 15 Aug. 1991).

12 No race has the last word on culture and on civilization. You do not know what the black man is capable of; you do not know what he is thinking and therefore you do not know what the oppressed and suppressed Negro, by virtue of his condition and circumstance, may give to the world as a surprise.

> MARCUS GARVEY (1887–1940), Jamaican black nationalist leader. Speech, 6 June 1928, Royal Albert Hall, London. Quoted in: Adolph Edwards, *Marcus Garvey* (1967).

13 A white face goes with a white mind. Occasionally a black face goes with a white mind. Very seldom a white face will have a black mind.

> NIKKI GIOVANNI (b. 1943), U.S. poet. *A Dialogue* (1973; with James Baldwin), from a conversation in London, 4 Nov. 1971.

14 We can rejoice that the time has arrived when millions of Negro Americans can step out of the shadows, and walk forthrightly into the bright sunshine of human rights.

> HUBERT H. HUMPHREY (1911–78), U.S. Democratic politician, vice president. Address, 14 July 1948, to Democratic National Convention, Philadelphia, supporting his Civil Rights Amendment to the Party Platform. Humphrey was currently mayor of Minneapolis.

15 No one has been barred on account of his race from fighting or dying for America—there are no "white" or "colored" signs on the foxholes or graveyards of battle.

> JOHN F. KENNEDY (1917–63), U.S. Democratic politician, president. Message to Congress, 19 June 1963, on proposed civil rights bill.

16 I have a dream that my four little children will one

day live in a nation where they will not be judged by the color of their skin but by the content of their character.

> MARTIN LUTHER KING, JR. (1929–68), U.S. clergyman, civil rights leader. Speech, 15 June 1963, at civil rights demonstration, Washington, D.C.

17 I have no purpose to introduce political and social equality between the white and black races. There is a physical difference between the two, which, in my judgement, will probably for ever forbid their living together upon the footing of perfect equality; and inasmuch as it becomes a necessity that there must be a difference, I . . . am in favour of the race to which I belong having the superior position.

> ABRAHAM LINCOLN (1809–65), U.S. president. Speech, 21 Aug. 1858, Ottawa, Ill., during his debates with Stephen A. Douglas for election to the Senate.

18 In this country American means white. Everybody else has to hyphenate.

> TONI MORRISON (b. 1931), U.S. novelist, editor. *Guardian* (London, 29 Jan. 1992).

19 There's no such thing as a race and barely such a thing as an ethnic group. If we were dogs, we'd be the same breed. . . . Trouble doesn't come from Slopes, Kikes, Niggers, Spics or White Capitalist Pigs; it comes from the heart.

> P. J. O'ROURKE (b. 1947), U.S. journalist. *Holidays in Hell*, Introduction (1988).

20 Seems fairly clear that you fix a breed by LIMITING the amount of alien infiltration. You make a race by homogeneity and by avoiding INbreeding . . . No argument has ever been sprouted against it. You like it in dogs and horses.

> EZRA POUND (1885–1972), U.S. poet, critic. War broadcast from Rome, 28 June 1942 (published in *"Ezra Pound Speaking": Radio Speeches of World War II*, 1978).

21 No person who examines and reflects, can avoid seeing that there is but one race of people on the earth, who differ from each other only according to the soil and the climate in which they live.

> CAPTAIN J. G. STEDMAN (1744–97), British soldier, author, artist. *Narrative of a Five Years' Expedition Against the Revolted Negroes of Surinam*, ch. 15 (1796; repr. 1971).

22 Native always means people who belong somewhere else, because they had once belonged somewhere. That shows that the white race does not really think they belong anywhere because they think of everybody else as native.

> GERTRUDE STEIN (1874–1946), U.S. author. *Everybody's Autobiography*, ch. 1 (1937).

23 Please stop using the word "Negro." . . . We are the only human beings in the world with fifty-seven variety of complexions who are classed together as a single racial unit. Therefore, we are really truly colored people, and that is the only name in the English language which accurately describes us.

> MARY CHURCH TERRELL (1863–1954), U.S. educator, suffragist. Letter to the Editor, *The Washington Post* (14 May 1949).

24 To me, the black black woman is our essential mother—the blacker she is the more us she is—and to see

the hatred that is turned on her is enough to make me despair, almost entirely, of our future as a people.

> ALICE WALKER (b. 1944), U.S. author, critic. *In Search of our Mothers' Gardens*, "If the Present Looks Like the Past, What Does the Future Look Like?" (1983; first published July 1982).

See also Gregory on CIVIL RIGHTS; King on FELLOWSHIP, HUMAN; King on LIBERALS; Hitler on The UNITED STATES; Greene on The WORLD.

RACISM

1 Racism is an *ism* to which everyone in the world today is exposed; for or against, we must take sides. And the history of the future will differ according to the decision which we make.

> RUTH BENEDICT (1887–1948), U.S. anthropologist. *Race: Science and Politics*, ch. 1 (1940).

2 Racism? But isn't it only a form of misanthropy?

> JOSEPH BRODSKY (b. 1940), Russian-born U.S. poet, critic. *Less Than One: Selected Essays*, "Flight from Byzantium," sct. 9 (1986).

3 The problem of the twentieth century is the problem of the color-line—the relation of the darker to the lighter races of men in Asia and Africa, in America and the islands of the sea. It was a phase of this problem that caused the Civil War.

> W. E. B. DU BOIS (1868–1963), U.S. civil rights leader, author. *The Souls of Black Folk*, ch. 2 (1903). Du Bois discussed the problem of "the color-line" on a number of occasions, incorporating the concept in a speech, January 1900, at the first Pan-African Conference, London.

4 What I did not yet know so intensely was te hatred of the white American for the black, a hatred so deep that I wonder if every white man in this country, when he plants a tree, doesn't see *Negroes* hanging from its branches.

> JEAN GENET (1910–86), French playwright, novelist. *Soledad Brother: The Prison Letters of George Jackson*, Introduction (1970).

5 As the global expansion of Indian and Chinese restaurants suggests, xenophobia is directed against foreign people, not foreign cultural imports.

> E. J. HOBSBAWM (b. 1917), British historian. Lecture to the American Anthropological Association (published in *Anthropology Today*, Feb. 1992).

6 Racism as a form of skin worship, and as a sickness and a pathological anxiety for America, is so great, until the poor whites—rather than fighting for jobs or educaiton—fight to remain pink and fight to remain white. And therefore they cannot see an alliance with people that they feel to be inherently inferior.

> JESSE JACKSON (b. 1941), U.S. clergyman, civil rights leader. Interview with David Frost in Frost, *The Americans*, "When Whites Are Unemployed, It's Called a Depression" (1970).

7 As you grow older, you'll see white men cheat black men every day of your life, but let me tell you something and don't you forget it—whenever a white man does that to a black man, no matter who he is, how rich he is, or how fine a family he comes from, that white man is trash.

> HARPER LEE (b. 1926), U.S. author. Atticus Finch to his son Jem, in *To Kill a Mockingbird*, pt. 2, ch. 23 (1960).

8 Racism is when you have laws set up, systematically put in a a way to keep people from advancing, to stop the advancement of a people. Black people have never had the power to enforce racism, and so this is something that white America is going to have to work out themselves. If they decide they want to stop it, curtail it, or to do the right thing . . . then it will be done, but not until then.

SPIKE LEE (b. 1956), U.S. filmmaker. Interview in *Roger Ebert's Home Movie Companion* (1990).

9 Anti-Semitism is a horrible disease from which nobody is immune, and it has a kind of evil fascination that makes an enlightened person draw near the source of infection, supposedly in a scientific spirit, but really to sniff the vapors and dally with the possibility.

MARY McCARTHY (1912–89), U.S. author, critic. *On the Contrary*, pt. 3, "Settling the Colonel's Hash" (1961; first published 1954).

10 Until the philosophy which holds one race superior and another inferior is finally and permanently discredited and abandoned, everywhere is war . . . and until there are no longer first-class and second-class citizens of any nation, until the color of a man's skin is of no more significance than the color of his eyes, me seh war. And until the basic human rights are equally guaranteed to all without regard to race, there is war. And until that day, the dream of lasting peace, world citizenship, rule of international morality, will remain but a fleeting illusion to be pursued, but never attained . . . now everywhere is war.

BOB MARLEY (1945–81), Jamaican reggae musician. "War," on the album *Rastaman Vibration* (1976). The words of the song are based on a speech given to the United Nations by the Ethiopian emperor Haile Selassie in 1968.

11 The worst mistake I made was that stupid, suburban prejudice of anti-Semitism.

EZRA POUND (1885–1972), U.S. poet, critic. Quoted in: Humphrey Carpenter, *A Serious Character*, pt. 5 (1988), said in conversation with Allen Ginsberg in June 1968.

12 I do not think white America is committed to granting equality to the American Negro . . . this is a passionately racist country; it will continue to be so in the foreseeable future.

SUSAN SONTAG (b. 1933), U.S. essayist. "What's Happening in America (1966)," in *Partisan Review* (New Brunswick, N.J., Winter 1967; repr. in *Styles of Radical Will*, 1969).

13 I am obliged to confess that I do not regard the abolition of slavery as a means of warding off the struggle of the two races in the Southern states. The Negroes may long remain slaves without complaining; but if they are once raised to the level of freemen, they will soon revolt at being deprived of almost all their civil rights; and as they cannot become the equals of the whites, they will speedily show themselves as enemies.

ALEXIS DE TOCQUEVILLE (1805–59), French social philosopher. *Democracy in America*, vol. 1, ch. 18 (1835).

14 I am fifty-two years of age. I am a bishop in the Anglican Church, and a few people might be constrained to say that I was reasonably responsible. In the land of my birth I cannot vote, whereas a young person of eighteen can vote. And why? Because he or she possesses that wonderful biological attribute—a white skin.

BISHOP DESMOND TUTU (b. 1931), South African prelate. Quoted in: *Guardian Weekly* (London, 8 April 1984).

See also AFFIRMATIVE ACTION; Jordan on SOUTH AFRICA.

RADICALS

1 *Radical* simply means "grasping things at the root."

ANGELA DAVIS (b. 1944), U.S. political activist. *Let Us All Rise Together*, address, Spellman College, 25 June 1987 (repr. in *Women, Culture and Politics*, 1989).

2 The spirit of our American radicalism is destructive and aimless; it is not loving; it has no ulterior and divine ends; but is destructive only out of hatred and selfishness.

RALPH WALDO EMERSON (1803–82), U.S. essayist, poet, philosopher. *Essays*, "Politics" (Second Series, 1844).

3 My generation of radicals and breakers-down never found anything to take the place of the old virtues of work and courage and the old graces of courtesy and politeness.

F. SCOTT FITZGERALD (1896–1940), U.S. author. Letter, July 1938, to his daughter Frances Scott Fitzgerald (published in *The Letters of F. Scott Fitzgerald*, ed. by Andrew Turnbull, 1963).

4 I never dared to be radical when young
For fear it would make me conservative when old.

ROBERT FROST (1874–1963), U.S. poet. *Precaution*.

5 The force of what was called Panther rhetoric or wordmongering resided not in elegant discourse but in strength of affirmation (or denial), in anger of tone and timbre. When the anger led to action there was no turgidity or over-emphasis. Anyone who has witnessed political rows among the Whites . . . will have to admit that the Whites aren't overburdened with poetic imagination.

JEAN GENET (1910–86), French playwright, novelist. *Prisoner of Love*, pt. 1 (1986; tr. 1989).

6 To the indefinite, uncertain mind of the American radical the most contradictory ideas and methods are possible. The result is a sad chaos in the radical movement, a sort of intellectual hash, which has neither taste nor character.

EMMA GOLDMAN (1869–1940), U.S. anarchist. "Syndicalism: Its Theory and Practice," in *Mother Earth* (New York, Jan. 1913; repr. in *Red Emma Speaks*, pt. 1, ed. by Alix Kates Shulman, 1972).

7 So much of left-wing thought is a kind of playing with fire by people who don't even know that fire is hot.

GEORGE ORWELL (1903–50), British author. *Inside the Whale and Other Essays*, "Inside the Whale" (1940).

8 The radical invents the views. When he has worn them out the conservative adopts them.

MARK TWAIN (1835–1910), U.S. author. *Notebook*, ch. 31 (ed. by Albert Bigelow Paine, 1935), 1898 entry.

See also Emerson on CONSERVATIVES.

RADIO

1   The radio . . . goes on early in the morning and is listened to at all hours of the day, until nine, ten and often eleven o'clock in the evening. This is certainly a sign that the grown-ups have infinite patience, but it also means that the power of absorption of their brains is pretty limited, with exceptions, of course—I don't want to hurt anyone's feelings. One or two news bulletins would be ample per day! But the old geese, well—I've said my piece!

> ANNE FRANK (1929–45), German Jewish refugee, diarist. *The Diary of a Young Girl* (1947; tr. 1952), entry for 27 March 1944.

2   TV gives everyone an image, but radio gives birth to a million images in a million brains.

> PEGGY NOONAN (b. 1950), U.S. author, presidential speechwriter. *What I Saw at the Revolution*, ch. 2 (1990).

3   I don't so much write as I roar; a Newtechnique/vurry funny after WRITING.

> EZRA POUND (1885–1972), U.S. poet, critic. Letter, 18 June 1941, to his U.S. publisher, James Laughlin, remarking on his wartime broadcasts from Rome. Quoted in: Humphrey Carpenter, *A Serious Character*, pt. 2, ch. 13 (1988).

RAIN

1   There's always a period of curious fear between the first sweet-smelling breeze and the time when the rain comes cracking down.

> DON DELILLO (b. 1926), U.S. author. James Axton, in *The Names*, ch. 12 (1982).

2   Nature, like man, sometimes weeps from gladness.

> BENJAMIN DISRAELI (1804–81), English statesman, author. *Coningsby*, bk. 7, ch. 5 (1844).

3   Still falls the Rain—
Dark as the world of man, black as our loss—
Blind as the nineteen hundred and forty nails
Upon the Cross.

> EDITH SITWELL (1887–1964), British writer, poet. *Still Falls the Rain: The Raids, 1940. Night and Dawn.*

4   To watch this crystal globe just sent from heaven to associate with me. While these clouds and this sombre drizzling weather shut all in, we two draw nearer and know one another. The gathering in of the clouds with the last rush and dying breath of the wind, and then the regular dripping of twigs and leaves the country o'er, the impression of inward comfort and sociableness, the drenched stubble and trees that drop beads on you as you pass, their dim outline seen through the rain on all sides drooping in sympathy with yourself. These are my undisputed territory. This is Nature's English comfort.

> HENRY DAVID THOREAU (1817–62), U.S. philosopher, author, naturalist. *Journals* (1906), entry for 30 March 1840.

5   Rain is grace; rain is the sky condescending to the earth; without rain, there would be no life.

> JOHN UPDIKE (b. 1932), U.S. author, critic. *Self-Consciousness: Memoirs*, ch. 1 (1989).

See also Police motto on The POLICE; WEATHER.

RAP MUSIC

1   I started off rapping for people just like myself, people who were in awe of wealth and flash. It was a conversation between me and them. But now most of those who buy my records are listening in on others' conversation. They are the aural equivalent of voyeurs, thrilled at this crazy world that has nothing to do with their experience.

> ICE-T [TRACY MARROW], U.S. rapper. *Observer* (London, 27 Oct. 1991).

2   Rap is poetry to music—like beatniks without beards and bongos.

> DAVE LEE ROTH (b. 1955), U.S. rock musician. Quoted in: *Rolling Stone* (New York, Dec. 1990).

RAPE

1   It is little wonder that rape is one of the least-reported crimes. Perhaps it is the only crime in which the victim becomes the accused and, in reality, it is she who must prove her good reputation, her mental soundness, and her impeccable propriety.

> FREDA ADLER (b. 1934), U.S. educator, author. *Sisters in Crime*, ch. 9 (1975).

2   Rape is a culturally fostered means of suppressing women. Legally we say we deplore it, but mythically we romanticize and perpetuate it, and privately we excuse and overlook it.

> VICTORIA BILLINGS (b. 1945), U.S. journalist, author. *The Womansbook*, "Sex: We Need Another Revolution" (1974).

3   Rape is no excess, no aberration, no accident, no mistake—it embodies sexuality as the culture defines it. As long as these definitions remain intact—that is, as long as men are defined as sexual aggressors and women are defined as passive receptors lacking integrity—men who are exemplars of the norm will rape women.

> ANDREA DWORKIN (b. 1946), U.S. feminist critic. "The Rape Atrocity and the Boy Next Door," speech, 1 March 1975, at State University of New York, Stony Brook (published in *Our Blood*, ch. 4, 1976).

4   As long as there is rape . . . there is not going to be any peace or justice or equality or freedom. You are not going to become what you want to become or who you want to become. You are not going to live in the world you want to live in.

> ANDREA DWORKIN (b. 1946), U.S. feminist critic. "Feminism: An Agenda," speech, 8 April 1983 (published in *Letters from a War-Zone*, 1987).

5   I don't want to know about the constitution of the rapist—I want to kill him! I don't care if he is white or black, if he is middle-class or poor, if his mother hung him from the clothesline by his balls: I only want to *kill* him! Any woman who has been raped will agree.

> DIAMANDA GALÁS (b. 1955), U.S. singer. Interview in *Re/Search*, no. 13, "Angry Women" (San Francisco, 1991).

6   Rape is a part of war; but it may be more accurate to say that the capacity for dehumanizing another which so corrodes male sexuality is carried over from sex into war.

ADRIENNE RICH (b. 1929), U.S. poet. "Caryatid," in *American Poetry Review* (Philadelphia, May-June 1973; repr. in *On Lies, Secrets, and Silence*, 1980).

See also French on MEN AND WOMEN; Dworkin on SEDUCTION.

REACTIONARIES

1   He is a man walking backwards with his face to the future.

ANEURIN BEVAN (1897–1960), British Labour politician. Quoted in: Leon Harris, *The Fine Art of Political Wit*, ch. 9 (1964), of Conservative politician Sir Walter Elliot.

2   The march of the human mind is slow.

EDWARD BURKE (1729–97), Irish philosopher, statesman. *Speech on Conciliation with America: The Thirteen Resolutions*, 22 March 1775, House of Commons, London.

3   Like other revolutionaries I can thank God for the reactionaries. They clarify the issue.

R. G. COLLINGWOOD (1889–1943), British philosopher. *An Autobiography*, ch. 6 (1939).

4   All the reputedly powerful reactionaries are merely paper tigers. The reason is that they are divorced from the people. Look! Was not Hitler a paper tiger? Was Hitler not overthrown? . . . U.S. imperialism has not yet been overthrown and it has the atomic bomb. I believe it also will be overthrown. It, too, is a paper tiger.

MAO ZEDONG (1893–1976), Founder of the People's Republic of China. Speech, 18 Nov. 1957, to International Congress of Communist and Workers' Parties, Moscow (published in *Selected Works*, vol. 4, 1961). Mao's first recorded reference to "paper tigers" was in 1946, in "Talk with the American Correspondent Anna Louise Strong," Aug. 1946.

5   A reactionary is a somnambulist walking backwards.

FRANKLIN D. ROOSEVELT (1882–1945), U.S. Democratic politician, president. Radio broadcast, 26 Oct. 1939.

6   Those old faces, in Pasadena, California, and Tucson, Arizona, and Dallas, crumpling in hatred and fear at the mention of the United Nations or those liberals in government who constitute for them the fifth column of communism, yearn for an America that is as far from the society of the present as is the extended family system in village India.

RONALD SEGAL (b. 1932), South African author. *America's Receding Future*, ch. 1 (1968).

See also Mill on CUSTOM; Rostand on The FUTURE; Hitler on REVOLUTIONARIES.

READING

1   Of all the diversions of life, there is none so proper to fill up its empty spaces as the reading of useful and entertaining authors.

JOSEPH ADDISON (1672–1719), English essayist. *Spectator*, no. 93 (London, 16 June 1711).

2   He had read much, if one considers his long life; but his contemplation was much more than his reading. He was wont to say that if he had read as much as other men he should have known no more than other men.

JOHN AUBREY (1626–97), English antiquarian, writer. *Brief Lives*, "Thomas Hobbes" (1813; repr. in *Brief Lives and Other Selected Writings by John Aubrey*, ed. by Anthony Powell, 1949), of Thomas Hobbes.

3   To feel most beautifully alive means to be reading something beautiful, ready always to apprehend in the flow of language the sudden flash of poetry.

GASTON BACHELARD (1884–1962), French scientist, philosopher, literary theorist. *Fragments of a Poetics of Fire*, "A Retrospective Glance at the Lifework of a Master of Books" (1988; tr. 1990).

4   Read not to contradict and confute; nor to believe and take for granted; nor to find talk and discourse; but to weigh and consider.

FRANCIS BACON (1561–1626), English philosopher, essayist, statesman. *Essays*, "Of Studies" (1597–1625).

5   The world may be full of fourth-rate writers but it's also full of fourth-rate readers.

STAN BARSTOW (b. 1928), British novelist, playwright. *Daily Mail* (London, 15 Aug. 1989).

6   Hypocrite reader—my fellow—my brother!

CHARLES BAUDELAIRE (1821–67), French poet. *Les Fleurs du Mal*, Preface (1857).

7   The power of a text is different when it is read from when it is copied out. . . . Only the copied text thus commands the soul of him who is occupied with it, whereas the mere reader never discovers the new aspects of his inner self that are opened by the text, that road cut throught the interior jungle forever closing behind it: because the reader follows the movement of his mind in the free flight of day-dreaming, whereas the copier submits it to command.

WALTER BENJAMIN (1892–1940), German critic, philosopher. *One-Way Street*, "Chinese Curios" (1928; repr. in *One-Way Street and Other Writings*, 1978).

8   Does there, I wonder, exist a being who has read all, or approximately all, that the person of average culture is supposed to have read, and that not to have read is a social sin? If such a being does exist, surely he is an old, a very old man.

ARNOLD BENNETT (1867–1931), British novelist. *The Journals of Arnold Bennett* (ed. by Frank Swinnerton, 1932), entry for 15 Oct. 1896.

9   When we read a story, we inhabit it. The covers of the book are like a roof and four walls. What is to happen next will take place within the four walls of the story. And this is possible because the story's voice makes everything its own.

JOHN BERGER (b. 1926), British author, critic. "Ev'ry Time We Say Goodbye," in *Expressen* (Stockholm, 3 Nov. 1990; repr. in *Keeping a Rendezvous*, 1992).

10   Reading is not a duty, and has consequently no business to be made disagreeable.

AUGUSTINE BIRRELL (1850–1933), English essayist, Liberal

politician. *Obiter Dicta*, "The Office of Literature" (Second Series), 1887).

11 The failure to read good books both enfeebles the vision and strengthens our most fatal tendency—the belief that the here and now is all there is.

ALLAN BLOOM (1930–92), U.S. educator, author. *The Closing of the American Mind*, pt. 1, "Books" (1987).

12 A conventional good read is usually a bad read, a relaxing bath in what we know already. A true good read is surely an act of innovative creation in which we, the readers, become conspirators.

MALCOLM BRADBURY (b. 1932), British author, critic. *Sunday Times* (London, 29 Nov. 1987).

13 Americans will listen, but they do not care to read. *War and Peace* must wait for the leisure of retirement, which never really comes: meanwhile it helps to furnish the living room. Blockbusting fiction is bought as furniture. Unread, it maintains its value. Read, it looks like money wasted. Cunningly, Americans know that books contain a person, and they want the person, not the book.

ANTHONY BURGESS (b. 1917), British author, critic. *You've Had Your Time*, ch. 2 (1990).

14 Reading a book is like re-writing it for yourself. . . . You bring to a novel, anything you read, all your experience of the world. You bring your history and you read it in your own terms.

ANGELA CARTER (1940–92), British author. *Marxism Today* (London, Jan. 1985).

15 The novel can't compete with cars, the movies, television, and liquor. A guy who's had a good feed and tanked up on good wine gives his old lady a kiss after supper and his day is over. Finished.

LOUIS-FERDINAND CÉLINE (1894–1961), French author. Interview, 1 June 1960 (repr. in *Critical Essays on Louis-Ferdinand Céline*, ed. by William F. Buckley, 1989).

16 Let blockheads read what blockheads wrote.

LORD CHESTERFIELD (1694–1773), English statesman, man of letters. Letter, 1 Nov. 1750 (first published 1774; repr. in *The Letters of the Earl of Chesterfield to His Son*, vol. 2, no. 232, ed. by Charles Strachey, 1901).

17 The mere brute pleasure of reading—the sort of pleasure a cow must have in grazing.

G. K. CHESTERTON (1874–1936), British author. Quoted in: Dudley Barker, *G. K. Chesterton* (1973).

18 Perhaps there are none more lazy, or more truly ignorant, than your everlasting readers.

WILLIAM COBBETT (1762–1835), English journalist, reformer. *Advice to Young Men and to Young Women*, Letter 5, "To a Father" (1829; repr. 1930). Cobbett added, "with regard to young women, everlasting book-reading is absolutely a *vice.*"

19 A person of mature years and ripe development, who is expecting nothing from literature but the corroboration and renewal of past ideas, may find satisfaction in a lucidity so complete as to occasion no imaginative excitement, but young and ambitious students are not content with it. They seek the excitement because they are capable of the growth that it accompanies.

CHARLES HORTON COOLEY (1864–1929), U.S. sociologist. *Human Nature and the Social Order*, ch. 9 (1902).

20 He ate and drank the precious Words,
His Spirit grew robust;
He knew no more that he was poor,
Nor that his frame was Dust.

EMILY DICKINSON (1830–86), U.S. poet. *A Book (1)*, in *The Complete Poems*, no. 1587 (1955).

21 You will, I am sure, agree with me that . . . if page 534 only finds us in the second chapter, the length of the first one must have been really intolerable.

SIR ARTHUR CONAN DOYLE (1859–1930), English author. Sherlock Holmes, in *The Valley of Fear*, ch. 1 (1915).

22 Readers are less and less seen as mere non-writers, the subhuman "other" or flawed derivative of the author; the lack of a pen is no longer a shameful mark of secondary status but a positively enabling space, just as within every writer can be seen to lurk, as a repressed but contaminating antithesis, a reader.

TERRY EAGLETON (b. 1943), British critic. *Against The Grain*, ch. 13, "The Revolt of the Reader" (1986; first published 1982).

23 Never read any book that is not a year old.

RALPH WALDO EMERSON (1803–82), U.S. essayist, poet, philosopher. *Society and Solitude*, "Books" (1870), one of Emerson's three "practical rules" for reading.

24 'Tis the good reader that makes the good book; a good head cannot read amiss: in every book he finds passages which seem confidences or asides hidden from all else and unmistakeably meant for his ear.

RALPH WALDO EMERSON (1803–82), U.S. essayist, poet, philosopher. *Society and Solitude*, "Success" (1870).

25 No tears in the writer, no tears in the reader.

ROBERT FROST (1874–1963), U.S. poet. *Collected Poems*, "The Figure a Poem Makes," Preface (1939).

26 As writers become more numerous, it is natural for readers to become more indolent; whence must necessarily arise a desire of attaining knowledge with the greatest possible ease.

OLIVER GOLDSMITH (1728–74), Anglo-Irish playwright, author. "Upon Unfortunate Merit," in *The Bee*, no. 5 (London, 3 Nov. 1759).

27 I read part of it all the way through.

SAMUEL GOLDWYN (1882–1974), U.S. film producer. Quoted in: Arthur Marx, *Goldwyn: the Man Behind the Myth*, ch. 27 (1976).

28 The only obligation to which in advance we may hold a novel, without incurring the accusation of being arbitrary, is that it be interesting.

HENRY JAMES (1843–1916), U.S. author. *The Art of Fiction* (1884; repr. in *Partial Portraits*, 1888).

29 A man ought to read just as his inclination leads him; for what he reads as a task will do him little good.

SAMUEL JOHNSON (1709–84), English author, lexicographer. Quoted in: James Boswell, *Life of Samuel Johnson*, 14 July 1763 (1791). Johnson continued, however, by prescribing that, "A young man should read five hours in a day, and so may acquire a great deal of knowledge."

30 What is written without effort is in general read without pleasure.

SAMUEL JOHNSON (1709–84), English author, lexicographer.

Quoted in: *Johnsonian Miscellanies,* vol. 2, "Anecdotes by William Seward" (ed. by George Birkbeck Hill, 1897).

31 He has left off reading altogether, to the great improvement of his originality.

CHARLES LAMB (1775–1834), English essayist, critic. *The Last Essays of Elia,* "Detached Thoughts on Books and Reading" (1833).

32 After all, the world is *not* a stage—not to me: nor a theatre: nor a show-house of any sort. And art, especially novels, are not little theatres where the reader sits aloft and watches . . . and sighs, commiserates, condones and smiles.—That's what you want a book to be: because it leaves you so safe and superior, with your two-dollar ticket to the show. And that's what my books are not and never will be. . . . Whoever reads me will be in the thick of the scrimmage, and if he doesn't like it—if he wants a safe seat in the audience—let him read someone else.

D. H. LAWRENCE (1885–1930), British author. Letter, 22 Jan. 1925 (published in *The Letters of D. H. Lawrence,* vol. 5, ed. by James T. Boulton, 1987).

33 Until I feared I would lose it, I never loved to read. One does not love breathing.

HARPER LEE (b. 1926), U.S. author. Scout, in *To Kill a Mockingbird,* pt. 1, ch. 2 (1960).

34 The unread story is not a story; it is little black marks on wood pulp. The reader, reading it, makes it live: a live thing, a story.

URSULA K. LE GUIN (b. 1929), U.S. author. *Dancing at the Edge of the World,* "Where Do You Get Your Ideas From?" (1989).

35 There are very many people who read simply to prevent themselves from thinking.

G. C. LICHTENBERG (1742–99), German physicist, philosopher. *Aphorisms,* "Notebook G," aph. 29 (written 1765–99; tr. by R. J. Hollingdale, 1990).

36 Many readers judge of the power of a book by the shock it gives their feelings—as some savage tribes determine the power of muskets by their recoil; that being considered best which fairly prostrates the purchaser.

HENRY WADSWORTH LONGFELLOW (1807–82), U.S. poet. One of the meditations of Mr. Churchill, inscribed on his pulpit, in *Kavanagh,* bk. 1, ch. 13 (1849).

37 Readers are plentiful: thinkers are rare.

HARRIET MARTINEAU (1802–76), English writer, social critic. *Society in America,* vol. 3, "Occupation" (1837).

38 All my good reading, you might say, was done in the toilet. . . . There are passages in *Ulysses* which can be read only in the toilet—if one wants to extract the full flavor of their content.

HENRY MILLER (1891–1980), U.S. author. *Black Spring,* "A Saturday Afternoon" (1936).

39 No entertainment is so cheap as reading, nor any pleasure so lasting. She will not want new fashions nor regret the loss of expensive diversions or variety of company if she can be amused with an author in her closet.

LADY MARY WORTLEY MONTAGU (1689–1762), English society figure, letter writer. Letter, 22 June 1752, to her daughter Lady Bute, advising her on bringing up Lady Bute's own daughter (published in *Selected Letters,* ed. by Robert Halsband, 1970).

40 The worst readers are those who behave like plundering troops: they take away a few things they can use, dirty and confound the remainder, and revile the whole.

FRIEDRICH NIETZSCHE (1844–1900), German philosopher. *Assorted Opinions and Maxims,* aph. 137 (1879).

41 Early in the morning, at break of day, in all the freshness and dawn of one's strength, to read a *book*—I call that vicious!

FRIEDRICH NIETZSCHE (1844–1900), German philosopher. *Ecce Homo,* "Why I Am So Clever," aph. 8 (1908).

42 Much reading is an oppression of the mind, and extinguishes the natural candle, which is the reason of so many senseless scholars in the world.

WILLIAM PENN (1644–1718), English religious leader, founder of Pennsylvania. *Advice to His Children* (1699).

43 With one day's reading a man may have the key in his hands.

EZRA POUND (1885–1972), U.S. poet, critic. *Pisan Cantos,* cto. 74 (1948). In contrast, Pound had once confided to William Carlos Williams that, "It is not necessary to read everything in a book in order to speak intelligently of it," adding, "Don't tell everybody I said so." Quoted in: Williams, *Kora in Hell,* p. 13 (1920).

44 She could give herself up to the written word as naturally as a good dancer to music or a fine swimmer to water. The only difficulty was that after finishing the last sentence she was left with a feeling at once hollow and uncomfortably full. Exactly like indigestion.

JEAN RHYS (1894–1979), British author. "The Insect World," in *Sleep It Off, Lady* (1976).

45 Prerequisite for rereadability in books: that they be forgettable.

JEAN ROSTAND (1894–1977), French biologist, writer. *Carnets d'un Biologiste* (repr. in *The Substance of Man,* 1962, p. 195).

46 Be sure that you go to the author to get at *his* meaning, not to find yours.

JOHN RUSKIN (1819–1900), English art critic, author. *Sesame and Lilies,* lecture 1, sct. 13, no. 2 (1865; repr. in *The Works of John Ruskin,* vol. 18, ed. by E. T. Cook and Alexander Wedderburn, 1905).

47 *Reading* is equivalent to thinking with someone else's head instead of with one's own.

ARTHUR SCHOPENHAUER (1788–1860), German philosopher. *Parerga and Paralipomena,* vol. 2, ch. 22, sct. 261 (1851).

48 How can you dare teach a man to read until you've taught him everything else first?

GEORGE BERNARD SHAW (1856–1950), Anglo-Irish playwright, critic. Lord Summerhays, in *Misalliance.*

49 People say that life is the thing, but I prefer reading.

LOGAN PEARSALL SMITH (1865–1946), U.S. essayist, aphorist. *Afterthoughts,* "Myself" (1931).

50 Digressions, incontestably, are the sunshine;—they are the life, the soul of reading!—take them out of this book, for instance,—you might as well take the book along with them;—one cold external winter would reign in every page of it; restore them to the writer;—he steps forth like a bridegroom,—bids All-hail; brings in variety, and forbids the appetite to fail.

LAURENCE STERNE (1713–68), English author. *Tristram Shandy*, bk. 1, ch. 22 (1760–67).

51 A great book should leave you with many experiences, and slightly exhausted at the end. You live several lives while reading it.

WILLIAM STYRON (b. 1925), U.S. novelist. Interview in *Writers at Work* (First Series, ed. by George Plimpton, 1958).

52 Read the best books first, or you may not have a chance to read them at all.

HENRY DAVID THOREAU (1817–62), U.S. philosopher, author, naturalist. *A Week on the Concord and Merrimack Rivers*, "Sunday" (1849).

53 To read well, that is, to read true books in a true spirit, is a noble exercise, and one that will task the reader more than any other exercise which the customs of the day esteem. It requires a training such as the athletes underwent, the steady intention almost of the whole life to this object.

HENRY DAVID THOREAU (1817–62), U.S. philosopher, author, naturalist. *Walden*, "Reading" (1854).

54 I always begin at the left with the opening word of the sentence and read toward the right and I recommend this method.

JAMES THURBER (1894–1961), U.S. humorist, illustrator. Memo to *New Yorker* (1959; repr. in *New York Times Book Review*, 4 Dec. 1988), on editors' reading habits.

55 Education . . . has produced a vast population able to read but unable to distinguish what is worth reading, an easy prey to sensations and cheap appeals.

G. M. TREVELYAN (1876–1962), British historian. *English Social History*, ch. 18 (1942).

56 There are books so alive that you're always afraid that while you weren't reading, the book has gone and changed, has shifted like a river; while you went on living, it went on living too, and like a river moved on and moved away. No one has stepped twice into the same river. But did anyone ever step twice into the same book?

MARINA TSVETAEVA (1892–1941), Russian poet. *Pushkin and Pugachev* (1937; repr. in *A Captive Spirit: Selected Prose*, ed. and tr. by J. Marin King, 1980).

57 When the Day of Judgement dawns and the great conquerors and lawyers and statesmen come to receive their rewards—their crowns, their laurels, their names carved indelibly upon imperishable marble—the Almighty will turn to Peter and will say, not without a certain envy when he sees us coming with our books under our arms, "Look, these need no reward. We have nothing to give them here. They have loved reading."

VIRGINIA WOOLF (1882–1941), British novelist. *The Common Reader*, "How Should One Read a Book?" (Second Series, 1932).

58 Somewhere, everywhere, now hidden, now apparent in what ever is written down, is the form of a human being. If we seek to know him, are we idly occupied?

VIRGINIA WOOLF (1882–1941), British novelist. *The Captain's Death Bed*, "Reading" (1950)

See also Lichtenberg on BARBARISM; Bacon, Kempis on BOOKS; Smith on CRITICISM AND THE ARTS; Grimke on PRAYER; Chandler on The PUBLIC.

RONALD REAGAN

1 Are you more likely to tolerate drivel than you were four years ago? I think the answer is yes. Four years of Reagan has deadened the senses against a barrage of uninterrupted nonsense.

ALEXANDER COCKBURN (b. 1941), Anglo-Irish journalist. "Balancing Acts," in *Nation* (New York, 27 Oct. 1984; repr. in *Corruptions of Empire*, pt. 2, 1988).

2 Someday our grandchidren will look up at us and say, "Where were you, Grandma, and what were you doing when you first realized that President Reagan was, er, not playing with a full deck?"

BARBARA EHRENREICH (b. 1941), U.S. author and columnist. *The Worst Years of Our Lives*, "The Unfastened Head of State" (1991; first published 1987).

3 Reagan was a flesh and blood version of any other mute national emblem, say the Statue of Liberty. Everyone knows what she represents, but no one would dream of asking her opinion.

SIMON HOGGART (b. 1946), British journalist. *America: A User's Guide*, ch. 11 (1990).

4 The battle for the mind of Ronald Reagan was like the trench warfare of World War I: never have so many fought so hard for such barren terrain.

PEGGY NOONAN (b. 1950), U.S. author, presidential speechwriter. *What I Saw at the Revolution*, ch. 14 (1990). Noonan worked as a special assistant and speechwriter to Reagan, 1984–88.

5 As the age of television progresses the Reagans will be the rule, not the exception. To be perfect for television is all a President has to be these days.

GORE VIDAL (b. 1925), U.S. novelist, critic. Quoted in: *Observer* (London, 7 Feb. 1982). In the same newspaper, 26 April 1981, Vidal was quoted as describing Reagan as "a triumph of the embalmer's art."

REALISM

1 Literary works cannot be taken over like factories, or literary forms of expression like industrial methods. Realist writing, of which history offers many widely varying examples, is likewise conditioned by the question of how, when and for what class it is made use of.

BERTOLT BRECHT (1898–1956), German dramatist, poet. "The Popular and the Realistic" (written 1938; published 1958; repr. in *Brecht on Theatre*, ed. and tr. by John Willett, 1964).

2 This sort of adoration of the real
Is but a heightening of the *beau ideal*.

LORD BYRON (1788–1824), English poet. *Don Juan*, cto. 2, st. 211.

3 Realism should only be the means of expression of religious genius . . . or, at the other extreme, the artistic expressions of monkeys which are quite satisfied with mere imitation. In fact, art is never realistic though sometimes it is tempted to be. To be really realistic a description would have to be endless.

ALBERT CAMUS (1913–60), French-Algerian philosopher, author. *The Rebel*, pt. 4, "Rebellion and Style."

4 True realism consists in revealing the surprising things which habit keeps covered and prevents us from seeing.

> JEAN COCTEAU (1889–1963), French author, filmmaker. *Le Mystère Laïc (1928; repr. in Collected Works,* vol. 10, 1950).

5 To be realistic today is to be visionary. To be realistic is to be starry-eyed.

> HUBERT H. HUMPHREY (1911–78), U.S. Democratic politician, vice president. Speech, 29 Nov. 1965, White House Conference on International Cooperation.

6 Realism, whether it be socialist or not, falls short of reality. It shrinks it, attenuates it, falsifies it; it does not take into account our basic truths and our fundamental obsessions: love, death, astonishment. It presents man in a reduced and estranged perspective. Truth is in our dreams, in the imagination.

> EUGÉNE IONESCO (b. 1912), Romanian-born French playwright. "Experience of the Theatre," in *Nouvelle N.R.F.,* no. 62 (Paris, 1958; repr. in *Notes and Counter Notes,* 1962).

7 The genuine artist is never "true to life." He sees what is real, but not as we are normally aware of it. We do not go storming through life like actors in a play. Art is never real life.

> WALLACE STEVENS (1879–1955), U.S. poet. *Opus Posthumous,* "On Poetic Truth" (1959).

8 I hate vulgar realism in literature. The man who could call a spade a spade should be compelled to use one. It is the only thing he is fit for.

> OSCAR WILDE (1854–1900), Anglo-Irish playwright, author. Lord Henry, in the *The Picture of Dorian Gray,* ch. 17 (1891).

REALITY

1 As opposed to the incoherent spectacle of the world, the real is what is expected, what is obtained and what is discovered by our own movement. It is what is sensed as being within our own power and always responsive to our action.

> ALAIN [ÉMILE-AUGUSTE CHARTIER] (1868–1951), French philosopher. *The Gods,* bk. 1, ch. 3 (1934; tr. 1988).

2 Given that external reality is a fiction, the writer's role is almost superfluous. He does not need to invent the fiction because it is already there.

> J. G. BALLARD (b. 1930), British author. Interview in *Friends* (London, 30 Oct. 1970; repr. in *Re/Search,* no. 8/9, San Francisco, 1984).

3 There are . . . intangible realities which float near us, formless and without words; realities which no one has thought out, and which are excluded for lack of interpreters.

> NATALIE CLIFFORD BARNEY (1876–1972), U.S.-born French author. Quoted in: "On Writing and Writers," in *Adam,* no. 299 (London, 1962; tr. by Ezra Pound).

4 The very definition of the real becomes: *that of which it is possible to give an equivalent reproduction. . . . The real is not only what can be reproduced, but that which is always already reproduced.* The hyperreal.

> JEAN BAUDRILLARD (b. 1929), French semiologist. *Simulations,* pt. 2, "The Hyperrealism of Simulation" (1983). Baudrillard goes

on to say, "Reality no longer has the time to take on the appearance of reality. It no longer even surpasses fiction: it captures every dream even before it takes on the appearance of a dream."

5 To hell with reality! I want to die in music, not in reason or in prose. People don't deserve the restraint we show by not going into delirium in front of them. To hell with *them!*

> LOUIS-FERDINAND CÉLINE (1894–1961), French author. Letter, 30 June 1947 (published in *Critical Essays on Louis-Ferdinand Céline,* ed. by William K. Buckley, 1989).

6 Facts as facts do not always create a spirit of reality, because reality is a spirit.

> G. K. CHESTERTON (1874–1936), British author. *Come to Think of It,* "On the Classics" (1930).

7 In an age of synthetic images and synthetic emotions, the chances of an accidental encounter with reality are remote indeed.

> SERGE DANEY (1944–92), French film critic. "Falling out of Love" (repr. in *Sight and Sound,* London, July 1992).

8 Reality is that which, when you stop believing in it, doesn't go away.

> PHILIP K. DICK (1928–82), U.S. science fiction writer. Definition given in 1972. Quoted by Dick in: *I Hope I Shall Arrive Soon,* "How to Build a Universe That Doesn't Fall Apart Two Days Later," Introduction (1986).

9 Human kind
Cannot bear very much reality.

> T. S. ELIOT (1888–1965), Anglo-American poet, critic. *Burnt Norton,* pt. 1, in *Four Quartets.* The words also appeared in Eliot, *Murder in the Cathedral,* pt. 2, spoken by Thomas.

10 Reality in our century is not something to be faced.

> GRAHAM GREENE (1904–91), British novelist. Hasselbacher, in *Our Man in Havana,* pt. 1, ch. 1, sct. 1 (1958).

11 Reality leaves a lot to the imagination.

> JOHN LENNON (1940–80), British rock musician. "The Way It Is," CBC-TV, June 1969.

12 Reality is not protected or defended by laws, proclamations, ukases, cannons and armadas. Reality is that which is sprouting all the time out of death and disintegration.

> HENRY MILLER (1891–1980), U.S. author. *The Air-Conditioned Nightmare,* "With Edgar Varèse in the Gobi Desert" (1945).

13 Reality is a prison, where . . . one vegetates and always will. All the rest—thought, action—is just a pastime, mental or physical. What counts then, is to come to grips with reality. The rest can go.

> CESARE PAVESE (1908–50), Italian poet, novelist, translator. *The Burning Brand: Diaries 1935–1950* (1952; tr. 1961), entry for 28 Dec. 1936.

14 Whatever is a reality today, whatever you touch and believe in and that seems real for you today, is going to be—like the reality of yesterday—an illusion tomorrow.

> LUIGI PIRANDELLO (1867–1936), Italian author, playwright. The Father, in *Six Characters in Search of an Author,* act 3 (1921).

15 I prefer the honest jargon of reality to the outright lies of books.

> JEAN ROSTAND (1894–1977), French biologist, writer. *Pensées*

d'un Biologiste (1939; repr. in *The Substance of Man*, "A Biologist's Thoughts," ch. 8, 1962).

16 Reality is a question of perspective; the further you get from the past, the more concrete and plausible it seems—but as you approach the present, it inevitably seems incredible.

> SALMAN RUSHDIE (b. 1948), Indian-born British author. *Midnight's Children*, bk. 2, "All-India Radio" (1981).

17 The unreal is natural, so natural that it makes of unreality the most natural of anything natural. That is what America does, and that is what America is.

> GERTRUDE STEIN (1874–1946), U.S. author. "I Came and Here I Am," in *Cosmopolitan* (New York, Feb. 1936; repr. in *How Writing Is Written*, ed. by Robert Bartlett Haas, 1974).

18 What our eyes behold may well be the text of life but one's meditations on the text and the disclosures of these meditations are no less a part of the structure of reality.

> WALLACE STEVENS (1879–1955), U.S. poet. *The Necessary Angel*, "Three Academic Pieces," no. 1 (1951; first published 1947).

19 In the American metaphysic, reality is always material reality, hard, resistant, unformed, impenetrable, and unpleasant.

> LIONEL TRILLING (1905–75), U.S. critic. *The Liberal Imagination*, "Reality in America" (1950).

20 Why is it that reality, when set down untransposed in a book, sounds false?

> SIMONE WEIL (1909–43), French philosopher, mystic. "London Notebook" (1943; published in *First and Last Notebooks*, ed. by Richard Rees, 1970).

21 A test of what is real is that it is hard and rough. Joys are found in it, not pleasure. What is pleasant belongs to dreams.

> SIMONE WEIL (1909–43), French philosopher, mystic. *Gravity and Grace*, "Illusions" (1947; tr. 1952).

22 What is meant by "reality"? It would seem to be something very erratic, very undependable—now to be found in a dusty road, now in a scrap of newspaper in the street, now a daffodil in the sun. It lights up a group in a room and stamps some casual saying. It overwhelms one walking home beneath the stars and makes the silent world more real than the world of speech—and then there it is again in an omnibus in the uproar of Piccadilly. Sometimes, too, it seems to dwell in shapes too far away for us to discern what their nature is. But whatever it touches, it fixes and makes permanent. That is what remains over when the skin of the day has been cast into the hedge; that is what is left of past time and of our loves and hates.

> VIRGINIA WOOLF (1882–1941), British novelist. *A Room Of One's Own*, ch. 6 (1929).

REASON

1 Reason itself is fallible, and this fallibility must find a place in our logic.

> NICOLA ABBAGNANO (1901–90), Italian philosopher. Quoted in: *Daily Telegraph* (London, 14 Sept. 1990).

2 O reason, reason, abstract phantom of the waking state, I had already expelled you from my dreams, now I have reached a point where those dreams are about to become fused with apparent realities: now there is only room here for myself.

> LOUIS ARAGON (1897–1982), French poet. *Paris Peasant*, "Preface to a Modern Mythology" (1926).

3 There are strange flowers of reason to match each error of the senses.

> LOUIS ARAGON (1897–1982), French poet. *Paris Peasant*, "Preface to a Modern Mythology" (1926).

4 Everything that is beautiful and noble is the product of reason and calculation.

> CHARLES BAUDELAIRE (1821–67), French poet. "The Painter of Modern life," sct. 11, in *L'Art Romantique* (1869; repr. in *Selected Writings on Art and Artists*, ed. by P. E. Charvet, 1972).

5 As if *reasoning* were *any kind* of writing or talking which tends to convince people that some doctrine or measure is true and right.

> CATHARINE ESTHER BEECHER (1800–1878), U.S. educator, writer. *Woman Suffrage and Women's Professions*, "An Address to the Christian Women of America" (1871).

6 Reason transformed into prejudice is the worst form of prejudice, because reason is the only instrument for liberation from prejudice.

> ALLAN BLOOM (1930–92), U.S. educator, author. *The Closing of the American Mind*, pt. 3, "From Socrates' *Apology* to Heidegger's *Rektoratsrede*" (1987).

7 Reason sits firm and holds the reins, and she will not let the feelings burst away and hurry her to wild chasms. The passions may rage furiously, like true heathens, as they are; and the desires may imagine all sorts of vain things: but judgement shall still have the last word in every argument, and the casting vote in every decision.

> CHARLOTTE BRONTË (1816–55), English novelist. Mr. Rochester, disguised as a fortune teller, in *Jane Eyre*, ch. 19 (1847), reading the character of Jane Eyre.

8 People are governed with the head; kindness of heart is little use in chess.

> SÉBASTIEN-ROCH NICOLAS DE CHAMFORT (1741–94), French writer, wit. *Maxims and Considerations*, vol. 2, no. 522 (1796; tr. 1926).

9 The more you reason the less you create.

> RAYMOND CHANDLER (1888–1959), U.S. author. Letter, 28 Oct. 1947, to *Atlantic Monthly* editor Charles W. Morton (published in *Raymond Chandler Speaking*, 1962).

10 If you can once engage people's pride, love, pity, ambition (or whatever is their prevailing passion) on your side, you need not fear what their reason can do against you.

> LORD CHESTERFIELD (1694–1773), English statesman, man of letters. Letter, 8 Feb. 1746 (first published 1774; repr. in *The Letters of the Earl of Chesterfield to His Son*, vol. 1, no. 105, ed. by Charles Strachey, 1901).

11 Reason is a whore, surviving by simulation, versatility, and shamelessness.

> E. M. CIORAN (b. 1911), Rumanian-born French philosopher.

The Temptation to Exist, "Rages and Resignations: Luther" (1956).

12 The trouble with Reason is that it becomes meaningless at the exact point where it refuses to act.

> BERNARD DEVOTO (1897–1955), U.S. historian, critic. "The Easy Chair," in *Harper's* (New York, May 1941).

13 It was not reason that besieged Troy; it was not reason that sent forth the Saracen from the desert to conquer the world; that inspired the crusades; that instituted the monastic orders; it was not reason that produced the Jesuits; above all, it was not reason that created the French Revolution. Man is only great when he acts from the passions; never irresistible but when he appeals to the imagination.

> BENJAMIN DISRAELI (1804–81), English statesman, author. Sidonia, in *Coningsby*, bk. 4, ch. 13 (1844).

14 Just as love is an orientation which refers to all objects and is incompatible with the restriction to one object, so is reason a human faculty which must embrace the whole of the world with which man is confronted.

> ERICH FROMM (1900–1980), U.S. psychologist. *The Sane Society*, ch. 3, "The Need for a Frame of Orientation and Devotion—Reason vs. Irrationality" (1955).

15 Rationalists are admirable beings, rationalism is a hideous monster when it claims for itself omnipotence. Attribution of omnipotence to reason is as bad a piece of idolatry as is worship of stock and stone believing it to be God. I plead not for the suppression of reason, but for a due recognition of that in us which sanctifies reason.

> MOHANDAS K. GANDHI (1869–1948), Indian political, spiritual leader. *Young India* (14 Oct. 1926).

16 I'll not listen to reason. . . . Reason always means what someone else has got to say.

> ELIZABETH GASKELL (1810–65), English novelist. Miss Matty's maid, Martha, in *Cranford*, ch. 14 (1853).

17 As soon as man began considering himself the source of the highest meaning in the world and the measure of everything, the world began to lose its human dimension, and man began to lose control of it.

> VÁCLAV HAVEL (b. 1936), Czech playwright, president. *Disturbing the Peace*, ch. 1 (1986; tr. 1990).

18 To him who looks upon the world rationally, the world in its turn presents a rational aspect. The relation is mutual.

> GEORG HEGEL (1770–1831), German philosopher. *The Philosophy of History*, "Introduction," sct. 3 (1837).

19 Reason is a supple nymph, and slippery as a fish by nature. She had as leave give her kiss to an absurdity any day, as to syllogistic truth. The absurdity may turn out truer.

> D. H. LAWRENCE (1885–1930), British author. "Introduction to *The Dragon of the Apocalypse* by Frederick Carter," in *London Mercury* (July 1930; repr. in *Phoenix: The Posthumous Papers of D. H. Lawrence*, pt. 4, ed. by E. McDonald, 1936). Carter's book eventually appeared under a different title and without Lawrence's introduction.

20 Reason is a faculty far larger than mere objective force. When either the political or the scientific discourse announces itself as the voice of reason, it is playing God, and should be spanked and stood in the corner.

> URSULA K. LE GUIN (b. 1929), U.S. author. Commencement Address, Bryn Mawr (1986; published in *Dancing at the Edge of the World*, 1989).

21 Reason now gazes above the realm of the dark but warm feelings as the Alpine peaks do above the clouds. They behold the sun more clearly and distinctly, but they are cold and unfruitful.

> G. C. LICHTENBERG (1742–99), German physicist, philosopher. *Aphorisms*, "Notebook L," aph. 50 (written 1765–99; tr. by R. J. Hollingdale, 1990).

22 Our reason may prove what it will: our reason is only a feeble ray that has issued from Nature.

> MAURICE MAETERLINCK (1862–1949), Belgian author. *Wisdom and Destiny* (1898; tr. by Alfred Sutro, 1912, p. 15).

23 The heart has its reasons of which reason knows nothing: we know this in countless ways.

> BLAISE PASCAL (1623–62), French scientist, philosopher. *Pensées* (1670; no. 423 ed. by Karailshemer, no. 277 ed. by Brunschvicg).

24 Whenever a person strives, by the help of dialectic, to start in pursuit of every reality by a simple process of reason, independent of all sensuous information—never flinching, until by an act of the pure intelligence he has grasped the real nature of good—he arrives at the very end of the intellectual world.

> PLATO (c. 427–347 B.C.), Greek philosopher. Socrates, in *The Republic*, bk. 7, sct. 532.

25 Reason is a harmonising, controlling force rather than a creative one.

> BERTRAND RUSSELL (1872–1970), British philosopher, mathematician. *A Free Man's Worship and Other Essays*, ch. 2 (1976).

26 The irrational in the human has something about it altogether repulsive and terrible, as we see in the maniac, the miser, the drunkard or the ape.

> GEORGE SANTAYANA (1863–1952), U.S. philosopher, poet. *The Life of Reason*, "Reason in Society," ch. 3 (1905–6).

27 Sure, he, that made us with such large discourse,
Looking before and after, gave us not
That capability and god-like reason,
To fust in us unused.

> WILLIAM SHAKESPEARE (1564–1616), English dramatist, poet. Hamlet, in *Hamlet*, act 4, sc. 4. This passage is absent from the 1623 Folio edition.

28 I can stand brute force, but brute reason is quite unbearable. There is something unfair about its use. It is hitting below the intellect.

> OSCAR WILDE (1854–1900), Anglo-Irish playwright, author. Lord Henry, in *The Picture of Dorian Gray*, ch. 3 (1891).

29 The only business of the head in the world is to bow a ceaseless obeisance to the heart.

> W. B. YEATS (1865–1939), Irish poet, playwright. Letter, late summer 1886 (published in *Collected Letters*, vol. 1, ed. by John Kelly, 1986). "I hate reasonable people," Yeats wrote, explaining

his dislike for the novelist George Eliot; "the activity of their brains sucks up all the blood out of their hearts."

See also Jefferson on AGNOSTICS; Niebuhr on FAITH; Greek proverb on HUNGER; Fromm on INTELLIGENCE; Shakespeare on LOVE; Chesterfield on PREJUDICE; Shaw on PROGRESS; Bloom on UNIVERSITIES AND COLLEGES.

REBELLION

1   Whoever thinks of stopping the uprising before it achieves its goals, I will give him ten bullets in the chest.

> YASIR ARAFAT (b. 1929), Palestinian leader. Quoted in: *Daily Telegraph* (London, 19 Jan. 1989), on the Intifada.

2   For as the interposition of a rivulet, however small, will occasion the line of the phalanx to fluctuate, so any trifling disagreement will be the cause of seditions; but they will not so soon flow from anything else as from the disagreement between virtue and vice, and next to that between poverty and riches.

> ARISTOTLE (384–322 B.C.), Greek philosopher. *Politics*, bk. 5, ch. 3, sct. 1303b (c. 343 B.C.).

3   To revolt is a natural tendency of life. Even a worm turns against the foot that crushes it. In general, the vitality and relative dignity of an animal can be measured by the intensity of its instinct to revolt.

> MIKHAIL BAKUNIN (1814–76), Russian political theorist. *The International and Karl Marx* (1872; repr. in *Bakunin on Anarchism*, ed. by Sam Dolgoff, 1980).

4   Insurrection. An unsuccessful revolution; disaffection's failure to substitute misrule for bad government.

> AMBROSE BIERCE (1842–1914), U.S. author. *The Devil's Dictionary* (1881–1906).

5   Rebellion to tyrants is obedience to God.

> JOHN BRADSHAW (1602–59), English lawyer, regicide. Inscription at Bradshaw's final burial place near Martha Bay, Jamaica. Bradshaw, the President of the Parliamentary Commission which tried and sentenced King Charles I, was originally buried in Westminster Abbey, but his remains, along with those of Cromwell and Ireton, were dug up in 1660, and hanged at Tyburn, London, where rebels and common criminals were executed. Both Benjamin Franklin and Thomas Jefferson were attributed with sayings similar to Bradshaw's epitaph.

6   Every act of rebellion expresses a nostalgia for innocence and an appeal to the essence of being.

> ALBERT CAMUS (1913–60), French-Algerian philosopher, author. *The Rebel*, pt. 3 (1951; tr. 1953).

7   The rebel can never find peace. He knows what is good and, despite himself, does evil. The value which supports him is never given to him once and for all—he must fight to uphold it, unceasingly.

> ALBERT CAMUS (1913–60), French-Algerian philosopher, author. *The Rebel*, pt. 5, "Nihilistic Murder" (1951; tr. 1953).

8   It's not wise to violate rules until you know how to observe them.

> T. S. ELIOT (1888–1965), Anglo-American poet, critic. Interview in *Writers at Work* (Second Series, ed. by George Plimpton, 1963).

9   Most commonly revolt is born of material circumstances; but insurrection is always a moral phenomenon.

Revolt is Masaniello, who led the Neapolitan insurgents in 1647; but insurrection is Spartacus. Insurrection is a thing of the spirit, revolt is a thing of the stomach.

> VICTOR HUGO (1802–85), French poet, dramatist, novelist. *Les Misérables*, pt. 4, bk. 10, ch. 2 (1862).

10   I hold it that a little rebellion, now and then, is a good thing, and as necessary in the political world as storms in the physical. . . . It is a medicine necessary for the sound health of government.

> THOMAS JEFFERSON (1743–1826), U.S. president. Letter, 30 Jan. 1787, to statesman James Madison, speaking of Shays's Rebellion.

11   Anyone who can be proved to be a seditious person is an outlaw befoe God and the emperor; and whoever is the first to put him to death does right and well . . . . Therefore let everyone who can, smite, slay and stab, secretly or openly, remembering that nothing can be more poisonous, hurtful, or devilish than a rebel.

> MARTIN LUTHER (1483–1546), German leader of the Protestant Reformation. *Against the Robbing and Murdering Hordes of Peasants*, pamphlet of May 1525 against the Peasants' Revolt in Germany (1524–25), a stand that lost much popular support for the Reformation.

12   I wouldn't have turned out the way I was if I didn't have all those old-fashioned values to rebel against.

> MADONNA (b. 1959), U.S. singer, actor. *Time* (New York, 17 Dec. 1990). Quoted in: Mark Bego, *Madonna: Blonde Ambition*, ch. 11 (1992).

13   Insurrection: . . . insurrection as soon as circumstances allow: insurrection, strenuous, ubiquitous: the insurrection of the masses: the holy war of the oppressed: the republic to make republicans: the people in action to initiate progress. Let the insurrection announce with its awful voice the decrees of God: let it clear and level the ground on which its own immortal structure shall be raised. Let it, like the Nile, flood all the country that it is destined to make fertile.

> GIUSEPPE MAZZINI (1805–72), Italian nationalist leader. *Faith and the Future*, sct. 2 (1835; tr. in *Essays by Joseph Mazzini*, ed. by Bolton King, 1894).

14   There is something that Governments care for far more than human life, and that is the security of property, and so it is through property that we shall strike the enemy. . . . Be militant each in your own way. . . . I incite this meeting to rebellion.

> EMMELINE PANKHURST (1858–1928), British suffragette. Speech, 17 Oct. 1912, Albert Hall, London.

15   When the sword of rebellion is drawn, the sheath should be thrown away.

> ENGLISH PROVERB. Quoted by painter John Singleton Copley in letter, 6 Aug. 1775, on the subject of the American Revolution.

16   In the relations of a weak Government and a rebellious people there comes a time when every act of the authorities exasperates the masses, and every refusal to act excites their contempt.

> JOHN REED (1887–1920), U.S. journalist, author. *Ten Days That Shook the World*, ch. 3 (1919).

17   The burning of rebellious thoughts in the little

breast, of internal hatred and opposition, could not long go on without slight whiffs of external smoke, such as mark the course of subterranean fire.

> HARRIET BEECHER STOWE (1811–96), U.S. novelist, anti-slavery campaigner. *Old Town Folks*, ch. 2 (1869).

18 The greater part of what my neighbors call good I believe in my soul to be bad, and if I repent of anything, it is very likely to be my good behavior. What demon possessed me that I behaved so well? You may say the wisest thing you can, old man,—you who have lived seventy years, not without honor of a kind,—I hear an irresistible voice which invites me away from all that.

> HENRY DAVID THOREAU (1817–62), U.S. philosopher, author, naturalist. *Walden*, "Economy" (1854).

19 Insurrection is an art, and like all arts has its own laws.

> LEON TROTSKY (1879–1940), Russian revolutionary. *The History of the Russian Revolution*, vol. 3, ch. 6 (1933).

20 All men should have a drop of treason in their veins, if nations are not to go soft like so many sleepy pears.

> REBECCA WEST (1892–1983), British author. *The Meaning of Treason*, pt. 4, "Conclusion" (1949)

See also Durrell on D. H. LAWRENCE; REVOLUTION.

RECESSION

1 Can anybody remember when the times were not hard, and money not scarce?

> RALPH WALDO EMERSON (1803–82), U.S. essayist, poet, philosopher. *Society and Solitude*, "Works and Days" (1870).

2 Few can believe that suffering, especially by others, is in vain. Anything that is disagreeable must surely have beneficial economic effects.

> JOHN KENNETH GALBRAITH (b. 1908), U.S. economist. *The Age of Uncertainty*, ch. 7 (1977), on the solutions proposed by politicians to ride out a recession.

3 In a society of little economic development, universal inactivity accompanies universal poverty. You survive not by struggling against nature, or by increasing production, or by relentless labour; instead you survive by expending as little energy as possible, by striving constantly to achieve a state of immobility.

> RYSZARD KAPUSCINSKI (b. 1932), Polish journalist. "A Warsaw Diary," in *Granta*, no. 15 (Cambridge, England, 1985).

4 So-called "austerity," the stoic injunction, is the path towards universal destruction. It is the old, the fatal, competitive path. "Pull in your belt" is a slogan closely related to "gird up your loins," or the guns-butter metaphor.

> WYNDHAM LEWIS (1882–1957), British author, painter. *America and Cosmic Man*, "The Case Against Roots" (1948).

5 If we can "boondoggle" ourselves out of this depression, that word is going to be enshrined in the hearts of the American people for years to come.

> FRANKLIN D. ROOSEVELT (1882–1945), U.S. Democratic politician, president. Speech, 18 Jan. 1936, to the New Jersey State Emergency Council, Newark.

6 I see one-third of a nation ill-housed, ill-clad, ill-nourished.

> FRANKLIN D. ROOSEVELT (1882–1945), U.S. Democratic politician, president. Second Inaugural Address, 20 Jan. 1937.

RECREATION

1 The bow cannot always stand bent, nor can human frailty subsist without some lawful recreation.

> MIGUEL DE CERVANTES (1547–1616), Spanish writer. The Canon, in *Don Quixote*, pt. 1, bk. 4, ch. 21 (1605; tr. by P. Motteux).

2 The effect of having other interests beyond those domestic works well. The more one does and sees and feels, the more one is able to do, and the more genuine may be one's appreciation of fundamental things like home, and love, and understanding companionship.

> AMELIA EARHART (1897–1937), U.S. aviator, author. Quoted in: Mary S. Lovell, *The Sound of Wings*, ch. 11 (1989).

3 One way of getting an idea of our fellow-countrymen's miseries is to go and look at their pleasures.

> GEORGE ELIOT (1819–80), English novelist. *Felix Holt, the Radical*, ch. 28 (1866).

4 I still need more healthy rest in order to work at my best. My health is the main capital I have and I want to administer it intelligently.

> ERNEST HEMINGWAY (1899–1961), U.S. author. Letter, 21 Feb. 1952 (published in *Selected Letters*, ed. by Carlos Baker, 1981).

5 If I had no duties, and no reference to futurity, I would spend my life in driving briskly in a post-chaise with a pretty woman.

> SAMUEL JOHNSON (1709–84), English author, lexicographer. Quoted in: James Boswell, *Life of Samuel Johnson*, 19 Sept. 1777 (1791).

6 Surely life, if it be not long, is tedious, since we are forced to call in the assistance of so many trifles to rid us of our time, of that time which never can return.

> SAMUEL JOHNSON (1709–84), English author, lexicographer. Letter, 10 June 1761. Quoted in: James Boswell, *Life of Samuel Johnson* (1791).

7 Have you known how to take rest? You have done more than he who hath taken empires and cities.

> MICHEL DE MONTAIGNE (1533–92), French essayist. *Essays*, bk. 3, ch. 13, "Of Experience" (tr. by John Florio, 1588).

See also Prince Charles on The ENVIRONMENT.

REFORM

1 You begin saving the world by saving one man at a time; all else is grandiose romanticism or politics.

> CHARLES BUKOWSKI (b. 1920), U.S. author, poet. *Tales of Ordinary Madness*, "Too Sensitive" (1967).

2 To reform a world, to reform a nation, no wise man will undertake; and all but foolish men know, that the only solid, though a far slower reformation, is what each begins and perfects on *himself*.

> THOMAS CARLYLE (1795–1881), Scottish essayist, historian.

Closing words of *Signs of the Times* (1829; first published in *Edinburgh Review*, no. 98).

3 People who love soft methods and hate iniquity forget this,—that reform consists in taking a bone from a dog. Philosophy will not do it.

JOHN JAY CHAPMAN (1862–1933), U.S. author. *Practical Agitation*, ch. 7 (1898).

4 Every reform, however necessary, will by weak minds be carried to an excess, which will itself need reforming.

SAMUEL TAYLOR COLERIDGE (1772–1834), English poet, critic. *Biographia Literaria*, ch. 1 (1817).

5 Every reform was once a private opinion, and when it shall be a private opinion again, it will solve the problem of the age.

RALPH WALDO EMERSON (1803–82), U.S. essayist, poet, philosopher. *Essays*, "History" (First Series, 1841).

6 You cannot fight against the future. Time is on our side.

W. E. GLADSTONE (1809–98), English statesman. Speech, 27 April 1866, to the House of Commons, on the Reform Bill.

7 Until politics are a branch of science we shall do well to regard political and social reforms as experiments rather than short-cuts to the millennium.

J. B. S. HALDANE (1892–1964), British scientist. *Possible Worlds*, "Science and Politics" (1927).

8 No one is to blame. It is neither their fault nor ours. It is the misfortune of being born when a whole world is dying.

ALEXANDER HERZEN (1812–70), Russian journalist, political thinker. *From the Other Shore*, "Epilogue 1849," of the failure of the revolutionary movements in Europe after 1848.

9 The amelioration of the world cannot be achieved by sacrifices in moments of crisis; it depends on the efforts made and constantly repeated during the humdrum, uninspiring periods, which separate one crisis from another, and of which normal lives mainly consist.

ALDOUS HUXLEY (1894–1963), British author. *Grey Eminence*, ch. 10 (1941).

10 Why, Sir, most schemes of political improvement are very laughable things.

SAMUEL JOHNSON (1709–84), English author, lexicographer. Quoted in: James Boswell, *Life of Samuel Johnson*, 26 Oct. 1769 (1791).

11 Unless the reformer can invent something which substitutes attractive virtues for attractive vices, he will fail.

WALTER LIPPMANN (1889–1974), U.S. journalist. *A Preface to Politics*, ch. 2 (1913).

12 Turn where we may, within, around, the voice of great events is proclaiming to us, Reform, that you may preserve!

THOMAS BABINGTON MACAULAY (1800–1859), English historian, Whig politician. Speech, 2 March 1831, to the House of Commons, on the Reform Bill.

13 If it was not absolutely necessary, it was the foolishest thing ever done.

LORD MELBOURNE (1779–1848), English statesman, prime minister. Comment on the Reform Bill of 1832. Quoted in: David Cecil, *Lord M*, ch. 4 (1954).

14 Of all follies there is none greater than wanting to make the world a better place.

MOLIÈRE (1622–73), French dramatist. Philinte, in *Le Misanthrope*, act 1, sc. 1.

15 You have to make more noise than anybody else, you have to make yourself more obtrusive than anybody else, you have to fill all the papers more than anybody else, in fact you have to be there all the time and see that they do not snow you under, if you are really going to get your reform realized.

EMMELINE PANKHURST (1858–1928), English suffragette. "When Civil War Is Waged by Women," speech, 13 Nov. 1913 (published in *My Own Story*, 1914).

16 If there are people who feel that God wants them to change the structures of society, that is something between them and their God. We must serve him in whatever way we are called. I am called to help the individual; to love each poor person. Not to deal with institutions. I am in no position to judge.

MOTHER TERESA (b. 1910), Albanian-born Roman Catholic missionary. *A Gift for God*, "Carriers of Christ's Love" (1975).

17 I believe that what so saddens the reformer is not his sympathy with his fellows in distress, but, though he be the holiest son of God, is his private ail. Let this be righted, let the spring come to him, the morning rise over his couch, and he will forsake his generous companions without apology.

HENRY DAVID THOREAU (1817–62), U.S. philosopher, author, naturalist. *Walden*, "Economy" (1854).

18 Nothing so needs reforming as other people's habits.

MARK TWAIN (1835–1910), U.S. author. *Pudd'nhead Wilson*, ch. 15, "Pudd'nhead Wilson's Calendar" (1894).

19 In England we have come to rely upon a comfortable time-lag of fifty years or a century intervening between the perception that something ought to be done and a serious attempt to do it.

H. G. WELLS (1866–1946), British author. *The Work, Wealth and Happiness of Mankind*, ch. 2 (1931).

20 Men must be capable of imagining and executing and insisting on social change if they are to reform or even maintain civilization, and capable too of furnishing the rebellion which is sometimes necessary if society is not to perish of immobility.

REBECCA WEST (1892–1983), British author. *The Meaning of Treason*, pt. 4, "Conclusion" (1949).

See also Hooker on CHANGE; Burke on INNOVATION; Crisp on PREJUDICE; Shaw on REVOLUTION; Burke on The STATE.

REFUGEES

See EMIGRANTS AND REFUGEES.

REGRET

1   I believe that he was really sorry that people would not believe he was sorry that he was not more sorry.

> SAMUEL BUTLER (1835–1902), English author. *Samuel Butler's Notebooks* (1951, p. 193).

2   It's the things I might have said that fester.

> CLEMENCE DANE (1888–1965), British playwright, novelist. Margaret, in *A Bill of Divorcement*, act 2.

3   There is no greater sorrow than to recall a happy time in the midst of wretchedness.

> DANTE ALIGHIERI (1265–1321), Italian poet. *The Divine Comedy*, "The Inferno," cto. 5 (completed 1321).

4   Remorse—is Memory—awake—
Her Parties all astir—
A Presence of Departed Acts—
At window—and at Door—

> EMILY DICKINSON (1830–86), U.S. poet. *The Complete Poems*, no. 744 (1955).

5   Footfalls echo in the memory
Down the passage which we did not take
Towards the door we never opened
Into the rose-garden.

> T. S. ELIOT (1888–1965), Anglo-American poet, critic. *Burnt Norton*, pt. 1, in *Four Quartets*.

6   Maybe all one can do is hope to end up with the right regrets.

> ARTHUR MILLER (b. 1915), U.S. dramatist. Tom, in *The Ride Down Mount Morgan*, act 1 (1991).

7   There is no man, however wise, who has not at some period of his youth said things, or lived in a way the consciousness of which is so unpleasant to him in later life that he would gladly, if he could, expunge it from his memory.

> MARCEL PROUST (1871–1922), French novelist. Elstir, in *Remembrance of Things Past*, vol. 4, "Within a Budding Grove," pt. 2, "Seascape, with Frieze of Girls" (1918; tr. by Scott Monkrieff, 1924).

8   Make the most of your regrets; never smother your sorrow, but tend and cherish it till it come to have a separate and integral interest. To regret deeply is to live afresh.

> HENRY DAVID THOREAU (1817–62), U.S. philosopher, author, naturalist. *Journals* (1906), entry for 13 Nov. 1839.

9   For of all sad words of tongue or pen,
The saddest are these: "It might have been!"

> JOHN GREENLEAF WHITTIER (1807–92), U.S. poet. *Maud Muller*.

10   Hindsight is always twenty-twenty.

> BILLY WILDER (b. 1906), U.S. film director. Quoted in: *Wit and Wisdom of the Moviemakers*, ch. 7 (ed. by John Robert Columbo, 1979).

11   Only in your imagination can you revise.

> FAY WRAY (b. 1907), U.S. screen actor. *International Herald Tribune* (Paris, 22 Feb. 1989).

See also Barrymore on OLD AGE; Huxley on REPENTANCE.

REJECTION

1   Any man who does not accept the conditions of human life sells his soul.

> CHARLES BAUDELAIRE (1821–67), French poet. *Les Paradis Artificiels*, "The Poem of Hashish," ch. 5 (1860).

2   Negation is the mind's first freedom, yet a negative habit is fruitful only so long as we exert ourselves to overcome it, adapt it to our needs; once *acquired* it can imprison us.

> E. M. CIORAN (b. 1911), Rumanian-born French philosopher. *The Temptation to Exist*, title essay (1956).

3   To be no part of any body, is to be nothing.

> JOHN DONNE (c. 1572–1631), English divine and metaphysical poet. Letter, Sept. 1608, to Sir Henry Goodyer (published in *Complete Poetry and Selected Prose*, ed. by John Hayward, 1929).

4   Dear to us are those who love us . . . but dearer are those who reject us as unworthy, for they add another life; they build a heaven before us whereof we had not dreamed, and thereby supply to us new powers out of the recesses of the spirit, and urge us to new and unattempted performances.

> RALPH WALDO EMERSON (1803–82), U.S. essayist, poet, philosopher. *Essays*, "New England Reformers" (Second Series, 1844).

5   Anyone who cannot come to terms with his life while he is alive needs one hand to ward off a little his despair over his fate . . . but with his other hand he can note down what he sees among the ruins.

> FRANZ KAFKA (1883–1924), German novelist, short-story writer. *The Diaries of Franz Kafka: 1910–1923* (ed. by Max Brod, 1948), entry for 19 Oct. 1921.

6   In so far as one denies what is, one is possessed by what is not, the compulsions, the fantasies, the terrors that flock to fill the void.

> URSULA K. LE GUIN (b. 1929), U.S. author. *The Lathe of Heaven*, ch. 10 (1971).

7   Over emphatic negatives always suggest that what is being denied may be what is really being asserted.

> JONATHAN RABAN (b. 1942), British author, critic. *Counterblasts* (1989).

RELATIONSHIPS

1   A relationship, I think, is like a shark, you know? It has to constantly move forward or it dies. And I think what we got on our hands is a dead shark.

> WOODY ALLEN (b. 1935), U.S. filmmaker. Alvy Singer (Allen), in the film *Annie Hall* (directed by Woody Allen, scripted by Allen with Marshall Brickman, 1977; repr. in *Four Films of Woody Allen*, 1982), reaching the end of his affair with Annie Hall (Diane Keaton).

2   You must go to bed with friends or whores, where money makes up the difference in beauty or desire.

> W. H. AUDEN (1907–73), Anglo-American poet. *The Table Talk of W. H. Auden*, "10 December, 1947" (comp. by Alan Ansen, ed. by Nicholas Jenkins, 1990).

3   The highest level of sexual excitement is in a monogamous relationship.

> WARREN BEATTY (b. 1937), U.S. screen actor. Quoted in: *Observer* (London, 27 Oct. 1991).

4   The only way of knowing a person is to love them without hope.

> WALTER BENJAMIN (1892–1940), German critic and philosopher. *One-Way Street,* "Arc Lamp" (1928; repr. in *One-Way Street and Other Writings,* 1978).

5   Constant togetherness is fine—but only for Siamese twins.

> VICTORIA BILLINGS (b. 1945), U.S. journalist, author. *The Womansbook,* "A Love to Believe In" (1974).

6   Now the whole dizzying and delirious range of sexual possibilities has been boiled down to that one big, boring, bulimic word. RELATIONSHIP.

> JULIE BURCHILL (b. 1960), British journalist, author. "The Dead Zone," in *Arena* (London, 1988; repr. in *Sex and Sensibility,* 1992).

7   My attachment has neither the blindness of the beginning, nor the microscopic accuracy of the close of such liaisons.

> LORD BYRON (1788–1824), English poet. Letter, 10 Jan. 1820 (published in *Byron's Letters and Journals,* vol. 7, ed. by Leslie A. Marchand, 1973–81).

8   Human relationships always help us to carry on because they always presuppose further developments, a future—and also because we live as if our only task was precisely to have relationships with other people.

> ALBERT CAMUS (1913–60), French-Algerian philosopher, author. *Notebooks 1942–1951* (1964), Jan. 1943 entry.

9   People who are having a love-sex relationship are continuously lying to each other because the very nature of the relationship demands that they do, because you have to make a love object of this person, which means that you editorialize about them. . . . You cut out what you don't want to see, you add this if it isn't there. And so therefore you're building a lie.

> TRUMAN CAPOTE (1924–84), U.S. author. Interview with David Frost in Frost, *The Americans,* "When Does a Writer Become a Star?" (1970).

10   In the mythic schema of all relations between men and women, man proposes, and woman is disposed of.

> ANGELA CARTER (1940–92), British author. *The Sadeian Woman,* "Polemical Preface" (1979).

11   It is explained that all relationships require a little give and take. This is untrue. Any partnership demands that we give and give and give and at the last, as we flop into our graves exhausted, we are told that we didn't give enough.

> QUENTIN CRISP (b. 1908), British author. *How to Become a Virgin,* ch. 4 (1981).

12   The formula for achieving a successful relationship is simple: you should treat all disasters as if they were trivialities but never treat a triviality as if it were a disaster.

> QUENTIN CRISP (b. 1908), British author. *Manners from Heaven,* ch. 7 (1984).

13   The thing that's between us is fascination, and the fascination resides in our being alike. Whether you're a man or a woman, the fascination resides in finding out that we're alike.

> MARGUERITE DURAS (b. 1914), French author, filmmaker. *Practicalities,* "Men" (1987; tr. 1990).

14   Surely there must be some way to find a husband or, for that matter, merely an escort, without sacrificing one's privacy, self-respect, and interior decorating scheme. For example, men could be imported from the developing countries, many parts of which are suffering from a man excess, at least in relation to local food supply.

> BARBARA EHRENREICH (b. 1941), U.S. author, columnist. *The Worst Years of Our Lives,* "Tales of the Man Shortage" (1991; first published in *Mother Jones,* 1986).

15   It is easier to live through someone else than to become complete yourself.

> BETTY FRIEDAN (b. 1921), U.S. feminist writer. *The Feminine Mystique,* ch. 14 (1963).

16   Kindness and intelligence don't always deliver us from the pitfalls and traps: there are always failures of love, of will, of imagination. There is no way to take the danger out of human relationships.

> BARBARA GRIZZUTI HARRISON (1941), U.S. author, publicist. "Secrets Women Tell Each Other," in *McCall's* (New York, Aug. 1975).

17   We can never establish with certainty what part of our relations with others is the result of our emotions—love, antipathy, charity, or malice—and what part is predetermined by the constant power play among individuals.

> MILAN KUNDERA (b. 1929), Czech author, critic. *The Unbearable Lightness of Being,* pt. 7, ch. 2 (1984).

18   One can find women who have never had one love affair, but it is rare indeed to find any who have had only one.

> FRANÇOIS, DUC DE LA ROCHEFOUCAULD (1613–80), French writer, moralist. *Sentences et Maximes Morales,* no. 73 (1678).

19   I want relations which are not purely personal, based on purely personal qualities; but relations based upon some unanimous accord in truth or belief, and a harmony of *purpose,* rather than of personality. I am weary of personality. . . . Let us be easy and impersonal, not forever fingering over our own souls, and the souls of our acquaintances, but trying to create a new life, a new common life, a new complete tree of life from the roots that are within us.

> D. H. LAWRENCE (1885–1930), British author. Letter, 12 Dec. 1915, to author Katherine Mansfield (published in *The Letters of D. H. Lawrence,* vol. 2, ed. by George J. Zytaruk and James T. Boulton, 1981).

20   Long-term commitment to an intimate relationship with one person of whatever sex is an essential need that people have in order to breed the qualities out of which nurturant thought can rise.

> GERDA LERNER (b. 1920), U.S. educator, author. Quoted in: *Ms.* (New York, Sept. 1981).

21 There is no substitute for the comfort supplied by the utterly taken-for-granted relationship.

> IRIS MURDOCH (b. 1919), British novelist, philosopher. Martin Lynch-Gibbons, in *A Severed Head,* ch. 28 (1961).

22 If we are a metaphor of the universe, the human couple is the metaphor par excellence, the point of intersection of all forces and the seed of all forms. The couple is time recaptured, the return to the time before time.

> OCTAVIO PAZ (b. 1914), Mexican poet. *Alternating Current,* "André Breton or the Quest of the Beginning" (1967).

23 Nowadays love is a matter of chance, matrimony a matter of money and divorce a matter of course.

> HELEN ROWLAND (1875–1950), U.S. journalist. *Reflections of a Bachelor Girl* (1903). The epigram reappeared in Rowland, *A Guide to Men,* "Cymbals and Kettle-Drums" (1922).

24 It is only when we no longer compulsively need someone that we can have a real relationship with them.

> ANTHONY STORR (b. 1920), British psychiatrist. *The Integrity of the Personality,* ch. 9 (1960).

RELATIVITY

1 Each of us is incomplete compared to someone else—an animal's incomplete compared to a person . . . and a person compared to God, who is complete only to be imaginary.

> GEORGES BATAILLE (1897–1962), French novelist, critic. *La Somme Athéologique,* vol. 2, *Guilty,* "Friends," ch. 3 (1944).

2 God keep me from the divinity of Yes and No . . . the Yea Nay Creeping Jesus, from supposing Up and Down to be the same thing as all experimentalists must suppose.

> WILLIAM BLAKE (1757–1827), English poet, painter, engraver. Letter, 12 April 1827 (published in *The Letters of William Blake,* 1956).

3 When you are courting a nice girl an hour seems like a second. When you sit on a red-hot cinder a second seems like an hour. That's relativity.

> ALBERT EINSTEIN (1879–1955), German-American theoretical physicist. Quoted in: *News Chronicle* (14 March 1949).

4 Perspective, as its inventor remarked, is a beautiful thing. What horrors of damp huts, where human beings languish, may not become picturesque through aerial distance! What hymning of cancerous vices may we not languish over as sublimest art in the safe remoteness of a strange language and artificial phrase! Yet we keep a repugnance to rheumatism and other painful effects when presented in our personal experience.

> GEORGE ELIOT (1819–80), English novelist, editor. *Daniel Deronda,* bk. 2, ch. 14 (1876).

RELIGION

1 If religion is only human, and its form is man's form, it follows that everything in religion is true.

> ALAIN [EMILE-AUGUSTE CHARTIER] (1868–1951), French philosopher. Note written 1911. Quoted in: Richard Pever, *The Gods,* Introduction (1934; tr. 1974).

2 Of all possible sexual perversions, religion is the only one to have ever been scientifically systematized.

> LOUIS ARAGON (1897–1982), French poet. *Treatise on Style,* pt. 1, "The Pen" (1928).

3 The true meaning of religion is thus, not simply *morality,* but *morality touched by emotion.*

> MATTHEW ARNOLD (1822–88), English poet, critic. *Literature and Dogma,* ch. 1, sct. 2 (1873).

4 The first revolt is against the supreme tyranny of theology, of the phantom of God. As long as we have a master in heaven, we will be slaves on earth.

> MIKHAIL BAKUNIN (1814–76), Russian political theorist. *God and the State* (1871; repr. in *Bakunin on Anarchism,* ed. by Sam Dolgoff, 1980).

5 Pure religion and undefiled before God and the Father is this, To visit the fatherless and widows in their affliction, and to keep himself unspotted from the world.

> BIBLE: NEW TESTAMENT. James 1:27.

6 Religion. A daughter of Hope and Fear, explaining to Ignorance the nature of the Unknowable.

> AMBROSE BIERCE (1842–1914), U.S. author. *The Devil's Dictionary* (1881–1906).

7 And lips say "God be pitiful,"
Who ne'er said, "God be praised."

> ELIZABETH BARRETT BROWNING (1806–61), English poet. *The Cry of the Human,* st. 1.

8 Nothing is so fatal to religion as indifference which is, at least, half infidelity.

> EDMUND BURKE (1729–97), Irish philosopher, statesman. Letter, 29 Jan. 1795 (published in *The Writings and Speeches of Edmund Burke,* vol. 9, ed. by Paul Langford, 1991).

9 I am always most religious upon a sunshiny day. . .

> LORD BYRON (1788–1824), English poet. *Detached Thoughts,* no. 99 (written 1821–22; published in *Byron's Letters and Journals,* vol. 9, ed. by Leslie A. Marchand, 1979).

10 A cosmic philosophy is not constructed to fit a man; a cosmic philosophy is constructed to fit a cosmos. A man can no more possess a private religion than he can possess a private sun and moon.

> G. K. CHESTERTON (1874–1936), British author. *G. K. C. as M. C.,* "The Book of Job" (1929).

11 A religion, that is, a true religion, must consist of ideas and facts both; not of ideas alone without facts, for then it would be mere Philosophy;—nor of facts alone without ideas, of which those facts are symbols, or out of which they arise, or upon which they are grounded: for then it would be mere History.

> SAMUEL TAYLOR COLERIDGE (1772–1834), English poet, critic. *Table Talk,* 3 Dec. 1831 (1835; published in *Specimens of the Table Talk of Samuel Taylor Coleridge,* ed. by Henry Nelson Coleridge, 1835; repr. in *Collected Works,* vol. 14, ed. by Kathleen Coburn, 1990).

12 Religion! what treasure untold
Resides in that heavenly word!

> WILLIAM COWPER (1731–1800), English poet. *Verses Supposed to Be Written by Alexander Selkirk.*

13 Man is made to adore and to obey: but if you will

not command him, if you give him nothing to worship, he will fashion his own divinities, and find a chieftain in his own passions.

BENJAMIN DISRAELI (1804–81), English statesman, author. Sidonia, in *Coningsby*, bk. 4, ch. 13 (1844).

14 Religion is the dream of the human mind. But even in dreams we do not find ourselves in emptiness or in heaven, but on earth, in the realm of reality; we only see real things in the entrancing splendor of imagination and caprice, instead of in the simple daylight of reality and necessity.

LUDWIG FEUERBACH (1804–72), German philosopher. Preface to 1843 ed. of *The Essence of Christianity* (1841).

15 Our knowledge of the historical worth of certain religious doctrines increases our respect for them, but does not invalidate our proposal that they should cease to be put forward as the reasons for the precepts of civilization. On the contrary! Those historical residues have helped us to view religious teachings, as it were, as neurotic relics, and we may now argue that the time has probably come, as it does in an analytic treatment, for replacing the effects of repression by the results of the rational operation of the intellect.

SIGMUND FREUD (1856–1939), Austrian psychiatrist. *The Future of an Illusion*, ch. 8 (1927; repr. in *Complete Works*, vol. 21, ed. by James Strachey and Anna Freud, 1961). Two paragraphs earlier, Freud called religion "the universal obsessional neurosis of humanity," arising, "like the obsessional neuroses of children . . . out of the Oedipus complex," though he never actually used the words—often quoted in anthologies—"Religion is comparable to a childhood neurosis.".

16 Culture's essential service to a religion is to destroy intellectual idolatry, the recurrent tendency in religion to replace the object of its worship with its present understanding and forms of approach to that object.

NORTHROP FRYE (1912–91), Canadian literary critic. *Anatomy of Criticism*, Second Essay, "Anagogic Phase: Symbol as Monad" (1957).

17 Religion is doing; a man does not merely *think* his religion or feel it, he "lives" his religion as much as he is able, otherwise it is not religion but fantasy or philosophy.

GEORGE GURDJIEFF (c. 1877–1949), Greek-Armenian religious teacher, mystic. Quoted in: P. D. Ouspensky, *In Search of the Miraculous*, ch. 15 (1949).

18 All religions have based morality on obedience, that is to say, on voluntary slavery. That is why they have always been more pernicious than any political organisation. For the latter makes use of violence, the former—of the corruption of the will.

ALEXANDER HERZEN (1812–70), Russian journalist, political thinker. *From the Other Shorem*, "Omnia Mea Mecum Porto" (1855).

19 It's incongruous that the older we get, the more likely we are to turn in the direction of religion. Less vivid and intense ourselves, closer to the grave, we begin to conceive of ourselves as immortal.

EDWARD HOAGLAND (b. 1932), U.S. novelist, essayist. "The Ridge-Slope Fox and The Knife-Thrower," in *Harper's* (New York, Jan. 1977; repr. in *Heart's Desire*, 1988).

20 For it is with the mysteries of our religion, as with wholesome pills for the sick, which swallowed whole, have the virtue to cure; but chewed, are for the most part cast up again without effect.

THOMAS HOBBES (1588–1679), English philosopher. *Leviathan*, pt. 3, ch. 32 (1651).

21 To know a person's religion we need not listen to his profession of faith but must find his brand of intolerance.

ERIC HOFFER (1902–83), U.S. philosopher. *The Passionate State of Mind*, aph. 215 (1955).

22 Give us a religion that will help us to live—we can die without assistance.

ELBERT HUBBARD (1856–1915), U.S. author. *Selected Writings*, vol. 1, "Index" (1921).

23 We are on the side of religion as opposed to religions, and we are among those who believe in the wretched inadequacy of sermons and the sublimity of prayer.

VICTOR HUGO (1802–85), French poet, dramatist, novelist. *Les Misérables*, pt. 2, bk. 7, ch. 8 (1862).

24 You never see animals going through the absurd and often horrible fooleries of magic and religion. . . . Dogs do not ritually urinate in the hope of persuading heaven to do the same and send down rain. Asses do not bray a liturgy to cloudless skies. Nor do cats attempt, by abstinence from cat's meat, to wheedle the feline spirits into benevolence. Only man behaves with such gratuitous folly. It is the price he has to pay for being intelligent but not, as yet, quite intelligent enough.

ALDOUS HUXLEY (1894–1963), British author. *Texts and Pretexts*, "Amor Fati" (1932).

25 There must be something solemn, serious, and tender about any attitude which we denominate religious. If glad, it must not grin or snicker; if sad, it must not scream or curse.

WILLIAM JAMES (1842–1910), U.S. psychologist, philosopher. *The Varieties of Religious Experience*, Lecture 2 (1902).

26 When a culture feels that its end has come, it sends for a priest.

KARL KRAUS (1874–1936), Austrian satirist. *Pro Domo et Mundo*, ch. 7 (1912).

27 There is nothing more innately human than the tendency to transmute what has become customary into what has been divinely ordained.

SUZANNE LAFOLLETTE (1893–1983), U.S. editor, author. *Concerning Women*, "The Beginnings of Emancipation" (1926).

28 A man has no religion who has not slowly and painfully gathered one together, adding to it, shaping it; and one's religion is never complete and final, it seems, but must always be undergoing modification.

D. H. LAWRENCE (1885–1930), British author. Letter, 3 Dec. 1907 (published in *The Letters of D. H. Lawrence*, vol. 1, ed. by James T. Boulton, 1979). Lawrence added, "So I contend that true Socialism is religion; that honest, fervent politics are religion; that whatever a man will labour for earnestly and in some measure unselfishly is religion."

29 Talk to me about the truth of religion and I'll listen gladly. Talk to me about the duty of religion and I'll listen submissively. But don't come talking to me about the consolations of religion or I shall suspect that you don't understand.

C. S. LEWIS (1898–1963), British author. *A Grief Observed*, pt. 2 (1961).

30 A church is disaffected when it is persecuted, quiet when it is tolerated, and actively loyal when it is favoured and cherished.

THOMAS BABINGTON MACAULAY (1800–1859), English historian, Whig politician. "Hallam," in *Edinburgh Review* (Sept. 1828; repr. in *Critical and Historical Essays*, 1843).

31 Wherever an altar is found, there civilization exists.

JOSEPH DE MAISTRE (1753–1821), French diplomat, philosopher. The Count, in *Les Soirées de Saint-Pétersbourg*, "Second Dialogue" (1821; repr. in *The Works of Joseph de Maistre*, ed. by Jack Lively, 1965).

32 I count religion but a childish toy,
And hold there is no sin but innocence.

CHRISTOPHER MARLOWE (1564–93), English dramatist, poet. Machiavel, in *The Jew of Malta*, "Prologue." The lines are often modernized:
I count religion but a childish toy,
And hold there is no sin but ignorance.

33 But is it not the fact that religion emanates from the nature, from the moral state of the individual? Is it not therefore true that unless the nature be completely exercised, the moral state harmonised, the religion cannot be healthy?

HARRIET MARTINEAU (1802–76), English writer, social critic. *Society in America*, vol. 3, "Occupation" (1837).

34 Religion is a temper, not a pursuit.

HARRIET MARTINEAU (1802–76), English writer, social critic. *Society in America*, vol. 3, "Women" (1837).

35 Religion is the sigh of the oppressed creature, the heart of a heartless world, and the soul of soulless conditions. It is the *opium* of the people.

KARL MARX (1818–83), German political theorist, social philosopher. *A Contribution to the Critique of Hegel's Philosophy of Right*, Preface (1844). The formulation has invited many variations, including the observation by Edmund Wilson in *Letters on Literature and Politics* (1977): "Marxism is the opium of the intellectuals," and, according to psychiatrist Thomas Szasz writing about drugs in *The Second Sin* (1973): "In the United States today, opiates are the religion of the people."

36 Nobody can deny but religion is a comfort to the distressed, a cordial to the sick, and sometimes a restraint on the wicked; therefore whoever would argue or laugh it out of the world without giving some equivalent for it ought to be treated as a common enemy.

LADY MARY WORTLEY MONTAGU (1689–1762), English society figure, letter writer. Letter, 23 June 1754, to her daughter Lady Bute (published in *Selected Letters*, ed. by Robert Halsband, 1970).

37 Oh senseless man, who cannot possibly make a worm, and yet will make Gods by dozens.

MICHEL DE MONTAIGNE (1533–92), French essayist. *Essays*, bk. 2, ch. 12, "An Apology of Raimond Sebond" (tr. by John Florio, 1580).

38 When the soul drifts uncertainly between life and

the dream, between the mind's disorder and the return to cool reflection, it is in religious thought that we should seek consolation.

GÉRARD DE NERVAL (1808–55), French novelist, poet. *Aurélia*, pt. 2, ch. 1, (1855; repr. in *Selected Writings*, ed. and tr. by Geoffrey Wagner, 1958).

39 From the age of fifteen, dogma has been the fundamental principle of my religion: I know no other religion; I cannot enter into the idea of any other sort of religion; religion, as a mere sentiment, is to me a dream and a mockery.

CARDINAL JOHN NEWMAN (1801–90), English churchman, theologian. *Apologia Pro Vita Sua*, "History of My Religious Opinions from 1833–1839" (1864).

40 A wise architect observed that you could break the laws of architectural art provided you had mastered them first. That would apply to religion as well as to art. Ignorance of the past does not guarantee freedom from its imperfections.

REINHOLD NIEBUHR (1892–1971), U.S. theologian, historian. *Leaves from the Notebook of a Tamed Cynic* (1930), 1928 entry.

41 After coming into contact with a religious man I always feel I must wash my hands.

FRIEDRICH NIETZSCHE (1844–1900), German philosopher. *Ecce Homo*, "Why I Am a Destiny" (1888).

42 There's no reason to bring religion into it. I think we ought to have as great a regard for religion as we can, so as to keep it out of as many things as possible.

SEAN O'CASEY (1884–1964), Irish dramatist. Fluther Good, in *The Plough and the Stars*, act 1.

43 Every religion is good that teaches man to be good; and I know of none that instructs him to be bad.

THOMAS PAINE (1737–1809), Anglo-American political theorist, writer. *The Rights of Man*, pt. 2, ch. 5 (1792). Shelley echoed this sentiment in his *Address to the Irish People* (1812): "All religions are good which make men good.".

44 All national institutions of churches, whether Jewish, Christian or Turkish, appear to me no other than human inventions, set up to terrify and enslave mankind, and monopolize power and profit.

THOMAS PAINE (1737–1809), Anglo-American political theorist, writer. *The Age of Reason*, pt. 1, "The Author's Profession of Faith" (1794).

45 Men despise religion. They hate it and are afraid it may be true.

BLAISE PASCAL (1623–62), French scientist, philosopher. *Pensées* (1670; no. 12 ed. by Krailsheimer, no. 187 ed. by Brunschvicg).

46 Religion, oh, just another of those numerous failures resulting from an attempt to popularize art.

EZRA POUND (1885–1972), U.S. poet, critic. Letter (undated), to Pound's fiancée, Mary Moore (from the Van Pelt Library, University of Pennsylvania). Quoted in: Humphrey Carpenter, *A Serious Character*, pt. 1, ch. 8 (1988).

47 A maker of idols is never an idolater.

CHINESE PROVERB.

48 It is certain that if you would have the whole secret of a people, you must enter into the intimacy of their religion.

> EDGAR QUINET (1803–75), French poet, historian, politician. "The Roman Church and History—Vico," lecture, 15 May 1844 (published in *Ultramontanism, or The Roman Church and Modern Society*, 1845).

49 It is not God that is worshipped but the group or authority that claims to speak in His name. Sin becomes disobedience to authority not violation of integrity.

> SIR SARVEPALLI RADHAKRISHNAN (1888–1975), Indian philosopher, statesman. Quoted in: J. A. C. Brown, *Techniques of Persuasion*, ch. 11 (1965), speaking of organized religion.

50 The idea of the sacred is quite simply one of the most conservative notions in any culture, because it seeks to turn other ideas—uncertainty, progress, change—into crimes.

> SALMAN RUSHDIE (b. 1947), Indian-born British author. *Is Nothing Sacred?*, Herbert Reade Memorial Lecture, 6 Feb. 1990.

51 Religions, which condemn the pleasures of sense, drive men to seek the pleasures of power. Throughout history power has been the vice of the ascetic.

> BERTRAND RUSSELL (1872–1970), British philosopher, mathematician. *New York Herald-Tribune Magazine* (6 May 1938).

52 Religions are the cradles of despotism.

> MARQUIS DE SADE (1740–1814), French author. Dolmancé, in *Philosophy in the Bedroom*, "Dialogue the Fifth: Yet Another Effort, Frenchmen, If You Would Become Republicans" (1795).

53 All the sweetness of religion is conveyed to the world by the hands of story-tellers and image-makers. Without their fictions the truths of religion would for the multitude be neither intelligible nor even apprehensible; and the prophets would prophesy and the teachers teach in vain.

> GEORGE BERNARD SHAW (1856–1950), Anglo-Irish playwright, critic. *Back to Methusaleh*, Preface (1921).

54 I think that the leaf of a tree, the meanest insect on which we trample, are in themselves arguments more conclusive than any which can be adduced that some vast intellect animates Infinity.

> PERCY BYSSHE SHELLEY (1792–1822), English poet. Letter, 3 Jan. 1811.

55 Religion is probably, after sex, the second oldest resource which human beings have available to them for blowing their minds.

> SUSAN SONTAG (b. 1933), U.S. essayist. "The Pornographic Imagination," sct. 3, in *Partisan Review* (New Brunswick, N.J.; repr. in *Styles of Radical Will*, 1969).

56 Religion is the state of being grasped by an ultimate concern, a concern which qualifies all other concerns as preliminary and which itself contains the answer to the question of a meaning of our life.

> PAUL TILLICH (1886–1965), German-born U.S. theologian. *Christianity and the Encounter of the World Religions*, ch. 1 (1963).

57 The main business of religions is to purify, control, and restrain that excessive and exclusive taste for well-being which men acquire in times of equality.

> ALEXIS DE TOCQUEVILLE (1805–59), French social philosopher. *Democracy in America*, vol. 2, pt. 1, ch. 5 (1840).

58 I cannot see how a man of any large degree of humorous perception can ever be religious—except he purposely shut the eyes of his mind & keep them shut by force.

> MARK TWAIN (1835–1910), U.S. author. *Mark Twain's Notebooks and Journals*, vol. 3, (ed. by Frederick Anderson, 1979), Notebook 27 (Aug. 1887–July 1888).

59 It is a good and gentle religion, but inconvenient.

> MARK TWAIN (1835–1910), U.S. author. *Following the Equator*, ch. 49 (1897), of Hinduism.

60 Religion enables us to ignore nothingness and get on with the jobs of life.

> JOHN UPDIKE (b. 1932), U.S. author, critic. *Self-Consciousness: Memoirs*, ch. 6 (1989).

61 Religion is love; in no case is it logic.

> BEATRICE POTTER WEBB (1858–1943), British socialist, author. *My Apprenticeship*, Introduction (1926).

62 Religions die when they are proved to be true. Science is the record of dead religions.

> OSCAR WILDE (1854–1900), Anglo-Irish playwright, author. "Phrases and Philosophies for the Use of the Young," in *Chameleon* (London, Dec. 1894).

63 For a truly religious man nothing is tragic.

> LUDWIG WITTGENSTEIN (1889–1951), Austrian philosopher. Conversation in 1930 (published in *Personal Recollections*, ch. 6, ed. by Rush Rhees, 1981).

64 Not every religion has to have St. Augustine's attitude to sex. Why even in our culture marriages are celebrated in a church, everyone present knows what is going to happen that night, but that doesn't prevent it being a religious ceremony.

> LUDWIG WITTGENSTEIN (1889–1951), Austrian philosopher. Conversation in 1943 (published in *Personal Recollections*, ch. 6, ed. by Rush Rhees, 1981).

See also Colton on BIGOTRY; BUDDHISM; CHRISTIANITY AND THE CHRISTIANS; Byron on CONTENTMENT; Twain on FAITH; Selden on MORALITY; Tocqueville, Voltaire on MULTICULTURALISM; Bergman on OLD AGE ; Diderot on REVOLUTIONARIES; Barrie on SUCCESS; Burke on SUPERSTITION; More on TOLERANÉ.

REMINISCENCE

1 To look back is to relax one's vigil.

> BETTE DAVIS (1908–89), U.S. screen actor. *The Lonely Life*, ch. 1 (1962).

2 One man's remorse is another man's reminiscence.

> OGDEN NASH (1902–71), U.S. poet. *A Clean Conscience Never Relaxes*, in *I'm a Stranger Here Myself* (1938).

3 That translucent alabaster of our memories.

> MARCEL PROUST (1871–1922), French novelist. *Remembrance of Things Past*, vol. 10, "The Captive," pt. 2, ch. 2 (1923; tr. by Scott Monkrieff, 1929).

4 Reminiscences make one feel so deliciously aged and sad.

> GEORGE BERNARD SHAW (1856–1950), Anglo-Irish playwright, critic. *The Irrational Knot*, ch. 14 (1905).

5   Perhaps one day this too will be pleasant to remember.

> VIRGIL (70–19 B.C.), Roman poet. *Aeneid*, bk. 1.

See also NOSTALGIA.

THE RENAISSANCE

1   The mind of the Renaissance was not a pilgrim mind, but a sedentary city mind, like that of the ancients.

> GEORGE SANTAYANA (1863–1952), U.S. philosopher, poet. *The Genteel Tradition at Bay*, ch. 1 (1931).

2   *Who* is this Renaissance? Where did he come from? Who gave him permission to cram the Republic with his execrable daubs?

> MARK TWAIN (1835–1910), U.S. author. *The Innocents Abroad*, ch. 23 (1869), of sightseeing in Venice.

REPENTANCE

1   True penitence condemns to silence. What a man is ready to recall he would be willing to repeat.

> F. H. BRADLEY (1846–1924), English philosopher. *Aphorisms*, no. 10 (1930).

2   Repentance is but want of power to sin.

> JOHN DRYDEN (1631–1700), English poet, dramatist, critic. *Palamon and Arcite*, bk. 3.

3   Classic remorse, as all the moralists are agreed, is a most undesirable sentiment. If you have behaved badly, repent, make what amends you can and address yourself to the task of behaving better next time. On no account brood over your wrongdoing. ROLLING IN THE MUCK IS NOT THE BEST WAY OF GETTING CLEAN.

> ALDOUS HUXLEY (1894–1963), British author. Introduction to 1946 ed. of *Brave New World* (1932).

4   One may disavow and disclaim vices that surprise us, and whereto our passions transport us; but those which by long habits are rooted in a strong and . . . powerful will are not subject to contradiction. Repentance is but a denying of our will, and an opposition of our fantasies.

> MICHEL DE MONTAIGNE (1533–92), French essayist. *Essays*, bk. 3, ch. 2, "Of Repenting" (1588; tr. by John Florio).

5   Remorse is a violent dyspepsia of the mind.

> OGDEN NASH (1902–71), U.S. poet. *A Clean Conscience Never Relaxes*, in *I'm a Stranger Here Myself* (1938).

REPRESSION

1   In the groves of their academy, at the end of every vista, you see nothing but the gallows.

> EDMUND BURKE (1729–97), Irish philosopher, statesman. *Reflections on the Revolution in France* (1790), of the aftermath of the French Revolution.

2   The only justification for repressive institutions is material and cultural deficit. But such institutions, at certain stages of history, perpetuate and produce such a deficit, and even threaten human survival.

> NOAM CHOMSKY (b. 1928), U.S. linguist, political analyst. "Language and Freedom," lecture, delivered Jan. 1970, at Loyola University, Chicago (first published 1970; repr. in *For Reasons of State*, 1973).

3   If repression has indeed been the fundamental link between power, knowledge, and sexuality since the classical age, it stands to reason that we will not be able to free ourselves from it except at a considerable cost.

> MICHEL FOUCAULT (1926–84), French philosopher. *The History of Sexuality*, vol. 1, pt. 1 (1976).

4   What progress we are making. In the Middle Ages they would have burned me. Now they are content with burning my books.

> SIGMUND FREUD (1856–1939), Austrian psychiatrist. Comment on the public burning of his books in Berlin in 1933. Quoted in: Ernest Jones, *Sigmund Freud: Life and Work*, vol. 3, pt. 1, ch. 4 (1957).

5   People with a culture of poverty suffer much less from repression than we of the middle class suffer and indeed, if I may make the suggestion with due qualification, they often have a hell of a lot more fun than we have.

> BRIAN FRIEL (b. 1929), Irish playwright, author. Dodds, in *The Freedom of the City*, act 1.

6   Life cannot be destroyed for good, neither . . . can history be brought entirely to a halt. A secret streamlet trickles on beneath the heavy lid of inertia and pseudo-events, slowly and inconspicuously undercutting it. It may be a long process, but one day it must happen: the lid will no longer hold and will start to crack. This is the moment when something once more begins visibly to *happen*, something truly new and unique . . . something truly historical, in the sense that *history* again demands to be heard.

> VÁCLAV HAVEL (b. 1936), Czech playwright, president. *Living in Truth*, pt. 1, "Letter to Dr. Gustáv Husák," 8 April 1975 (1986).

7   We can never be sure that the opinion we are endeavouring to stifle is a false opinion; and even if we were sure, stifling it would be an evil still.

> JOHN STUART MILL (1806–73), English philosopher, economist. *On Liberty*, ch. 2 (1859).

8   Blow the dust off the clock. Your watches are behind the times. Throw open the heavy curtains which are so dear to you—you do not even suspect that the day has already dawned outside.

> ALEXANDER SOLZHENITSYN (b. 1918), Russian novelist. Letter, 12 Nov. 1969, to the Secretariat of the Soviet Writers' Union (published in *Solzhenitsyn: A Documentary Record*, "Expulsion," ed. by Leopold Labedz, 1970)

See also Konrád on COURAGE; Hugo on DESPOTISM; OPPRESSION.

U.S. REPUBLICAN PARTY

1   The Republicans hardly need a party and the cumbersome cadre of low-level officials that form one; they have a bankroll as large as the Pentagon's budget, dozens of fatted PACs, and the well-advertised support of the Christian deity.

BARBARA EHRENREICH (b. 1941), U.S. author, columnist. *The Worst Years of Our Lives*, "The Liberals' Disappearing Act" (1991; first published in *Mother Jones*, 1986).

2 The Republican convention, an event with the intellectual content of a Guns'n'Roses lyric attended by every ofay insurance broker in America who owns a pair of white shoes.

P. J. O'ROURKE (b. 1947), U.S. journalist. *Parliament of Whores*, "On the Blandwagon" (1991).

3 The Republicans have a "me too" candidate running on a "yes but" platform, advised by a "has been" staff.

ADLAI STEVENSON (1900–1965), U.S. Democratic politician. Quoted in: Leon Harris, *The Fine Art of Political Wit*, ch. 10 (1964).

4 No one has ever seen a Republican mass meeting that was devoid of the perception of the ludicrous.

MARK TWAIN (1835–1910), U.S. author. Closing words of "Turncoats," speech, 1884 (published in *Mark Twain's Speeches*, ed. by Albert Bigelow Paine, 1923).

REPUBLICANISM

1 We all have the republican spirit in our veins, like syphilis in our bones. We are democratized and venerealized.

CHARLES BAUDELAIRE (1821–67), French poet. Epilogue to *Sur la Belgique*, a never completed book on Belgium (published in *Complete Works*, vol. 2, ed. by Yves-Gérard le Dantec; rev. by Claude Pichois, 1976).

2 A Republican by principle and devotion, I will, until my death, oppose all Royalists . . . and all enemies of my Government and the Republic.

JEAN BAPTISTE BERNADOTTE (1763–1844), French general and later King of Sweden. Letter, Sept. 1797, to the French Directory. Thirteen years later he was invited to lead the Swedish government, later becoming Charles XIV (1818–1844) of Sweden and Norway, enemy of Napoleon (in whose defeat at Leipzig he took part in 1813), and founder of the present Swedish royal house.

3 A Republic! Look in the history of the Earth . . . To be the first man—not the Dictator, not the Sylla, but the Washington or the Aristides, the leader in talent and truth—is next to the Divinity!

LORD BYRON (1788–1824), English poet. *Byron's Letters and Journals*, vol. 3, (ed. by Leslie A. Marchand, 1974), entry for 23 Nov. 1813.

4 The king-times are fast finishing. There will be blood shed like water, and tears like mist; but the peoples will conquer in the end. I shall not live to see it, but I foresee it.

LORD BYRON (1788–1824), English poet. *Byron's Letters and Journals*, vol. 8, Ravenna Journal (ed. by Leslie A. Marchand, 1973–81), entry for 13 Jan. 1821.

5 People think they have taken quite an extraordinarily bold step forward when they have rid themselves of belief in hereditary monarchy and swear by the democratic republic. In reality, however, the state is nothing but a machine for the oppression of one class by another, and

indeed in the democratic republic no less than in the monarchy.

FRIEDRICH ENGELS (1820–95), German social philosopher. Introduction to 1891 ed. of Karl Marx, *The Civil War in France* (1871; repr. in *Karl Marx: Selected Works*, vol. 2, 1942).

6 The republican is the only form of government which is not eternally at open or secret war with the rights of mankind.

THOMAS JEFFERSON (1743–1826), U.S. president. Letter, 11 March 1790.

7 The republic, as I at least understand it, means association, of which liberty is only an element, a necessary antecedent. It means association, a new philosophy of life, a divine Ideal that shall move the world, the only means of regeneration vouchsafed to the human race.

GIUSEPPE MAZZINI (1805–72), Italian nationalist leader. *Faith and the Future*, sct. 1 (1835; tr. in *Essays by Joseph Mazzini*, ed. by Bolton King, 1894).

8 The Republican form of government is the highest form of government; but because of this it requires the highest type of human nature—a type nowhere at present existing.

HERBERT SPENCER (1820–1903), English philosopher. *Essays*, "The Americans" (1891).

9 Grant me thirty years of equal division of inheritances and a free press, and I will provide you with a republic.

ALEXIS DE TOCQUEVILLE (1805–59), French social philosopher. *Democracy in America*, vol. 2, Appendix 5, "About Virtue in Republics" (1840).

10 Yes, I am a thorough republican. No other form of government is so favorable to the growth of art.

OSCAR WILDE (1854–1900), Anglo-Irish playwright, author. Remark, 21 Feb. 1882, Louisville, Ky. Quoted in: Richard Ellman, *Oscar Wilde*, ch. 7 (1987).

REPUTATION

1 A good name is better than precious ointment.

BIBLE, HEBREW. *Ecclesiastes* 7:1.

2 It ain't often that a man's reputashun outlasts his munny.

JOSH BILLINGS [HENRY WHEELER SHAW] (1818–85), U.S. humorist. *Josh Billings, His Sayings*, ch. 39 (1865).

3 The easiest way to get a reputation is to go outside the fold, shout around for a few years as a violent atheist or a dangerous radical, and then crawl back to the shelter.

F. SCOTT FITZGERALD (1896–1940), U.S. author. *The Crack-Up*, "Notebook O" (ed. by Edmund Wilson, 1945).

4 The great difficulty is first to win a reputation; the next to keep it while you live; and the next to preserve it after you die, when affection and interest are over, and nothing but sterling excellence can preserve your name. Never suffer youth to be an excuse for inadequacy, nor age and fame to be an excuse for indolence.

BENJAMIN HAYDON (1786–1846), British artist. "Table Talk,"

in *Correspondence and Table-Talk,* vol. 2 (ed. by Frederic Wordsworth Haydon, 1876).

5   How many people live on the reputation of the reputation they might have made!

OLIVER WENDELL HOLMES, SR. (1809–94), U.S. writer, physician. *The Autocrat of the Breakfast-Table,* ch. 3 (1858).

6   The blaze of reputation cannot be blown out, but it often dies in the socket; a very few names may be considered as perpetual lamps that shine unconsumed.

SAMUEL JOHNSON (1709–84), English author, lexicographer. Letter, 1 May 1780, to Hester Thrale. Quoted in: James Boswell, *Life of Samuel Johnson* (1791).

7   For God's sake (I never was more serious) don't make me ridiculous any more by terming me gentle-hearted in print . . . substitute drunken dog, ragged head, seld-shaven, odd-eyed, stuttering, or any other epithet which truly and properly belongs to the gentleman in question.

CHARLES LAMB (1775–1834), English essayist, critic. Letter, Aug. 1800, to Samuel Taylor Coleridge, referring to lines Coleridge had inserted in his poem *This Lime Tree Bower My Prison:*

For thee, my gentle-hearted Charles, to whom
No sound is dissonant which tells of life.

8   My reputation is a media creation.

JOHN LYDON [formerly JOHNNY ROTTEN] (b. 1957), British rock musician. *Observer* (London, 4 May 1986).

9   Until you've lost your reputation, you never realize what a burden it was or what freedom really is.

MARGARET MITCHELL (1900–1949), U.S. novelist. Rhett Butler, in *Gone with the Wind,* vol. 1, pt. 2, ch. 9 (1936).

10   Character is much easier kept than recovered.

THOMAS PAINE (1737–1809), Anglo-American political theorist, writer. *The American Crisis,* no. 13 (19 April 1783).

11   No man can understand why a woman shouldn't prefer a good reputation to a good time.

HELEN ROWLAND (1875–1950), U.S. journalist. *Reflections of a Bachelor Girl* (1903, p. 10).

12   Reputation, reputation, reputation! O, I ha' lost my reputation, I ha' lost the immortal part of myself, and what remains is bestial!

WILLIAM SHAKESPEARE (1564–1616), English dramatist, poet. Cassio, in *Othello,* act 2, sc. 3.

13   Your women of honour, as you call'em, are only chary of their reputations, not their persons; and 'tis scandal that they would avoid, not men.

WILLIAM WYCHERLEY (1640–1716), English dramatist. Horner, in *The Country Wife,* act 1.

See also Pope, on GOSSIP.

RESEARCH

1   Not many appreciate the ultimate power and potential usefulness of basic knowledge accumulated by obscure, unseen investigators who, in a lifetime of intensive study, may never see any practical use for their findings but who go on seeking answers to the unknown without thought of financial or practical gain.

EUGENIE CLARK (b. 1922), U.S. marine biologist, author. *The Lady and the Sharks,* ch. 1 (1969).

2   After all, the ultimate goal of all research is not objectivity, but truth.

HELENE DEUTSCH (1884–1982), U.S. psychiatrist. *The Psychology of Women,* vol. 1, Preface (1944–45).

3   To write it, it took three months; to conceive it—three minutes; to collect the data in it—all my life.

F. SCOTT FITZGERALD (1896–1940), U.S. author. *The Author's Apology,* a letter to the Booksellers' Convention, April 1920 (published in *The Letters of F. Scott Fitzgerald,* ed. by Andrew Turnbull, 1963), referring to his novel *This Side of Paradise.*

4   Data is what distinguishes the dilettante from the artist.

GEORGE V. HIGGINS (b. 1939), U.S. novelist. *Guardian* (London, 17 June 1988).

5   Knowledge is of two kinds. We know a subject ourselves, or we know where we can find information upon it.

SAMUEL JOHNSON (1709–84), English author, lexicographer. Quoted in: James Boswell, *Life of Samuel Johnson,* 18 April 1775 (1791).

6   If politics is the art of the possible, research is surely the art of the soluble. Both are immensely practical-minded affairs.

SIR PETER MEDAWAR (1915–87), British immunologist. "The Act of Creation," in *New Statesman* (London, 19 June 1964; repr. in *The Art of the Soluble,* 1967).

7   Research is usually a policeman stopping a novel from progressing.

BRIAN MOORE (b. 1921), Irish novelist. *Sunday Times* (London, 15 April 1990).

8   Just as the largest library, badly arranged, is not so useful as a very moderate one that is well arranged, so the greatest amount of knowledge, if not elaborated by our own thoughts, is worth much less than a far smaller volume that has been abundantly and repeatedly thought over.

ARTHUR SCHOPENHAUER (1788–1860), German philosopher. *Parerga and Paralipomena,* vol. 2, ch. 22, sct. 257 (1851).

9   Fools make researches and wise men exploit them.

H. G. WELLS (1866–1946), British author. *A Modern Utopia,* ch. 2, sct. 5 (1905; repr. in *The Works of H. G. Wells,* vol. 9, 1925).

10   Lost in a gloom of uninspired research.

WILLIAM WORDSWORTH (1770–1850), English poet. *The Excursion,* bk. 4.

See also Mizner on PLAGIARISM; Johnson on WRITING.

RESENTMENT

1   I was angry with my friend:
I told my wrath, my wrath did end.
I was angry with my foe:
I told it not, my wrath did grow.

WILLIAM BLAKE (1757–1827), English poet, painter, engraver. *Songs of Experience,* "A Poison Tree" st. 1 (1794).

2   In ceremonies of the horsemen,
Even the pawn must hold a grudge.

> BOB DYLAN (b. 1941), U.S. singer, songwriter. "Love Minus Zero/No Limit," on the album *Bringing It All Back Home* (1965).

3   To have a grievance is to have a purpose in life.

> ERIC HOFFER (1902–83), U.S. philosopher. *The Passionate State of Mind*, aph. 166 (1955). Hoffer adds: "It not infrequently happens that those who hunger for hope give their allegiance to him who offers them a grievance."

4   You gave him an opportunity of showing greatness of character and he did not seize it. He will never forgive you for that.

> FRIEDRICH NIETZSCHE (1844–1900), German philosopher. *Assorted Opinions and Maxims*, aph. 384 (1879).

RESERVE

1   There is safety in reserve, but no attraction. One cannot love a reserved person.

> JANE AUSTEN (1775–1817), English novelist. Frank Churchill, in *Emma*, ch. 24 (1816). Emma replies, "Not till the reserve ceases towards one's self; and then the attraction may be the greater."

2   I would not unduly praise the virtue of restraint. It is often merely temperamental. But it is not always a sign of coldness. It may be pride. There can be nothing more humiliating than to see the shaft of one's emotion miss the mark of either laughter or tears. Nothing more humiliating! And this for the reason that should the mark be missed, should the open display of emotion fail to move, then it must perish unavoidably in disgust or contempt.

> JOSEPH CONRAD (1857–1924), Polish-born English novelist. *A Personal Record*, "A Familiar Preface" (1912).

3   I like people and I like them to like me, but I wear my heart where God put it—on the inside.

> F. SCOTT FITZGERALD (1896–1940), U.S. author. Monroe Stahr, in *The Last Tycoon*, ch. 1 (1941).

RESIGNATION

1   At fifteen life had taught me undeniably that surrender, in its place, was as honorable as resistance, especially if one had no choice.

> MAYA ANGELOU (b. 1928), U.S. author. *I Know Why the Caged Bird Sings*, ch. 31 (1969).

2   Fatalism is the lazy man's way of accepting the evitable.

> NATALIE CLIFFORD BARNEY (1876–1972), U.S.-born French author. Quoted in: George Wickes, *The Amazon of Letters*, ch. 10 (1976).

3   Make sense who may. I switch off.

> SAMUEL BECKETT (1906–89), Irish dramatist, novelist. Bam, in *What Where* (1984).

4   Resignation, not mystic, not detached, but resignation open-eyed, conscious, and informed by love, is the only one of our feelings for which it is impossible to become a sham.

> JOSEPH CONRAD (1857–1924), Polish-born English novelist. to *A Personal Record*, "A Familiar Preface" (1912).

5   We'd like to fight but we fear defeat,
We'd like to work but we're feeling too weak,
We'd like to be sick but we'd get the sack,
We'd like to behave, we'd like to believe,
We'd like to love, but we've lost the knack.

> CECIL DAY LEWIS (1904–72), British poet. *The Magnetic Mountain: 33*.

6   Give up the feeling of responsibility, let go your hold, resign the care of your destiny to higher powers, be genuinely indifferent as to what becomes of it all and you will find not only that you gain a perfect inward relief, but often also, in addition, the particular goods you sincerely thought you were renouncing.

> WILLIAM JAMES (1842–1910), U.S. psychologist, philosopher. *The Varieties of Religious Experience*, Lectures 4–5, "The Religion of Healthy-Mindedness" (1902).

7   Mankind are more disposed to suffer, while evils are sufferable, than to right themselves by abolishing the forms to which they are accustomed.

> THOMAS JEFFERSON (1743–1826), U.S. president. *The Declaration of Independence*, 4 July 1776.

8   I can imagine no more comfortable frame of mind for the conduct of life than a humorous resignation.

> W. SOMERSET MAUGHAM (1874–1966), British author. *A Writer's Notebook* (1949), 1902 entry.

9   We learn resignation not by our own suffering, but by the suffering of others.

> W. SOMERSET MAUGHAM (1874–1965), British author. *The Summing Up*, ch. 19 (1938). Maugham was writing of his experiences as a medical student and the suffering he witnessed then: "Suffering did not ennoble; it degraded. It made men selfish, mean, petty and suspicious. It absorbed them in small things . . . it made them less than men."

10   What is called resignation is confirmed desperation.

> HENRY DAVID THOREAU (1817–62), U.S. philosopher, author, naturalist. *Walden*, "Economy" (1854).

RESOLVE

1   I am in earnest—I will not equivocate—I will not excuse—I will not retreat a single inch—and I will be heard!

> WILLIAM LLOYD GARRISON (1805–79), U.S. abolitionist. Salutatory address of Garrison's anti-slavery newspaper, *The Liberator* (1 Jan. 1831).

2   The myths have always condemned those who "looked back." Condemned them, whatever the paradise may have been which they were leaving. Hence this shadow over each departure from your decision.

> DAG HAMMARSKJÖLD (1905–61), Swedish statesman, Secretary-General of the U.N. *Markings*, "Night is Drawing Nigh" (1963; written 1957).

3   A resolution to avoid an evil is seldom framed till the evil is so far advanced as to make avoidance impossible.

> THOMAS HARDY (1840–1928), English novelist, poet. *Far from the Madding Crowd*, ch. 18 (1874).

4   I think the worst thing this nation could do for

humanity would be to leave any uncertainty as to our will, our purpose and our capacity to carry out our purpose.

> HUBERT H. HUMPHREY (1911–78), U.S. Democratic politician, vice president. "Meet the Press," 13 March 1965, NBC-TV.

5 Having thus chosen our course, without guile and with pure purpose, let us renew our trust in God, and go forward without fear and with manly hearts.

> ABRAHAM LINCOLN (1809–65), U.S. president. Message to Congress, 4 July 1861.

6 What reinforcement we may gain from hope;
If not, what resolution from despair.

> JOHN MILTON (1608–74), English poet. Satan, in *Paradise Lost*, bk. 1.

7 Good resolutions are useless attempts to interfere with scientific laws. Their origin is pure vanity. Their result is absolutely *nil*. They give us, now and then, some of those luxurious sterile emotions that have a certain charm for the weak. . . . They are simply cheques that men draw on a bank where they have no account.

> OSCAR WILDE (1854–1900), Anglo-Irish playwright, author. Lord Henry, in *The Picture of Dorian Gray*, ch. 8 (1891).

See also Herford on CAPRICE.

RESPECT

1 Eminence without merit earns deference without esteem.

> SÉBASTIEN-ROCH NICOLAS DE CHAMFORT (1741–94), French writer, wit. *Maxims and Considerations*, vol. 1, no. 60 (1796; tr. 1926).

2 Trust men, and they will be true to you; treat them greatly, and they will show themselves great.

> RALPH WALDO EMERSON (1803–82), U.S. essayist, poet, philosopher. *Essays*, "Prudence" (First Series, 1841).

3 Attention and respect give pleasure, however late, or however useless. But they are not useless, when they are late, it is reasonable to rejoice, as the day declines, to find that it has been spent with the approbation of mankind.

> SAMUEL JOHNSON (1709–84), English author, lexicographer. Letter, 31 Dec. 1783, to Hester Thrale (published in *The Letters of Samuel Johnson*, vol. 3, no. 922, ed. by R. W. Chapman, 1952).

4 Honest people will respect us for our merit: the public, for our luck.

> FRANÇOIS, DUC DE LA ROCHEFOUCAULD (1613–80), French writer, moralist. *Sentences et Maximes Morales*, no. 165 (1678).

5 Where there is reverence there is fear, but there is not reverence everywhere that there is fear, because fear presumably has a wider extension than reverence.

> SOCRATES (469–399 B.C.), Greek philosopher. Quoted in: Plato, *Euthyphro*, sct. 11.

6 When people do not respect us we are sharply offended; yet deep down in his private heart no man much respects himself.

> MARK TWAIN (1835–1910), U.S. author. *Following the Equator*, ch. 29, "Pudd'nhead Wilson's New Calendar" (1897).

RESPECTABILITY

1 The enquiry in England is not whether a man has talents & genius, but whether he is passive & polite & a virtuous ass & obedient to noblemen's opinions in art & science. If he is, he is a good man. If not, he must be starved.

> WILLIAM BLAKE (1757–1827), English poet, painter, engraver. Annotations to Sir Joshua Reynolds, *Discourses* (c. 1808; repr. in *Complete Writings*, ed. by Geoffrey Keynes, 1957).

2 Since when was genius found respectable?

> ELIZABETH BARRETT BROWNING (1806–61), English Poet. *Aurora Leigh*, bk. 6 (1857).

3 Decency . . . must be an even more exhausting state to maintain than its opposite. Those who succeed seem to need a stupefying amount of sleep.

> QUENTIN CRISP (b. 1908), British author. *The Naked Civil Servant*, ch. 9 (1968).

4 In order to acquire a growing and lasting respect in society, it is a good thing, if you possess great talent, to give, early in your youth, a very hard kick to the right shin of the society that you love. After that, be a snob.

> SALVADOR DALI (1904–89), Spanish painter. *Diary of a Genius* (1966), entry for 11 May 1956.

5 Your home is regarded as a model home, your life as a model life. But all this splendor, and you along with it . . . it's just as though it were built upon a shifting quagmire. A moment may come, a word can be spoken, and both you and all this splendor will collapse.

> HENRIK IBSEN (1828–1906), Norwegian dramatist. Lona Hessel, in *Pillars of Society*, act 3.

6 A mere literary man is a *dull* man; a man who is solely a man of business is a *selfish* man; but when literature and commerce are united, they make a *respectable* man.

> SAMUEL JOHNSON (1709–84), English author, lexicographer. Quoted by Robert Barclay in: James Boswell, *Life of Samuel Johnson*, Appendix (ed. by John Wilson Croker, 1847).

7 I shall be glad when you have strangled the invincible respectability that dogs your steps.

> D. H. LAWRENCE (1885–1930), British author. Letter, 2 June 1915, to Bertrand Russell (published in *The Letters of D. H. Lawrence*, vol. 2, ed. by George J. Zytaruk and James T. Boulton, 1981).

8 Prestige is the shadow of money and power. Where these are, there it is. Like the national market for soap or automobiles and the enlarged arena of federal power, the national cash-in area for prestige has grown, slowly being consolidated into a truly national system.

> C. WRIGHT MILLS (1916–62), U.S. sociologist. *The Power Elite*, ch. 4 (1956).

9 My life has been one long descent into respectability.

> MANDY RICE-DAVIES (b. 1944), Call girl in British political scandal, 1963. Quoted by journalist Lynn Barber in: *Independent on Sunday* (London, 31 March 1991), in connection with reports that Rice-Davies was on social terms with Sir Denis Thatcher, husband of ex-prime minister Margaret Thatcher.

10 Well, dearie, men have to do some awfully mean things to keep up their respectability. But you can't blame them for that, can you?

> GEORGE BERNARD SHAW (1856–1950), Anglo-Irish playwright, critic. Dora Delaney, in *Fanny's First Play*, act 3.

11 The more things a man is ashamed of, the more respectable he is.

> GEORGE BERNARD SHAW (1856–1950), Anglo-Irish playwright, critic. Tanner, in *Man and Superman*, act 1.

12 The older one grows the more one likes indecency.

> VIRGINIA WOOLF (1882–1941), British novelist. *Monday or Tuesday*, "The String Quartet" (1921).

See also Updike on CUSTOM; Wilde on GOODNESS; Peacock on SNOBBERY.

RESPONSIBILITY

1 Responsibility is what awaits outside the Eden of Creativity.

> NADINE GORDIMER (b. 1923), South African author. "The Essential Gesture," lecture, 12 Oct. 1984, University of Michigan (published in *The Tanner Lectures on Human Values*, ed. by Sterling M. McMurrin, 1985; repr. in *The Essential Gesture*, ed. by Stephen Clingman, 1988).

2 We are responsible for actions performed in response to circumstances for which we are not responsible.

> ALLAN MASSIE (b. 1938), British author. Etienne, in *A Question of Loyalties*, pt. 3, ch. 22 (1989).

3 To be a man is . . . to be responsible. It is to feel shame at the sight of what seems to be unmerited misery. It is to take pride in a victory won by one's comrades. It is to feel, when setting one's stone, that one is contributing to the building of the world.

> ANTOINE DE SAINT-EXUPÉRY (1900–1944), French aviator, writer. *Wind, Sand, and Stars*, ch. 2, sct. 2 (1939; tr. by Galantière).

4 I am responsible for everything . . . except for my very responsibility, for I am not the foundation of my being. Therefore everything takes place as if I were compelled to be responsible. I am *abandoned* in the world . . . in the sense that I find myself suddenly alone and witout help, engaged in a world for which I bear the whole responsibility without being able, whatever I do, to tear myself away from this responsibility for an instant.

> JEAN-PAUL SARTRE (1905–80), French philosopher, author. *Being and Nothingness*, "Being and Doing: Freedom," sct. 3 (1943; tr. 1965).

See also Dylan on HEROES; Shaw on LIBERTY; Baldwin on The PRESS.

RESTAURANTS

1 In the United States all business not transacted over the telephone is accomplished in conjunction with alcohol or food, often under conditions of advanced intoxication. This is a fact of the utmost importance for the visitor of limited funds . . . for it means that the most expensive restaurants are, with rare exceptions, the worst.

> JOHN KENNETH GALBRAITH (b. 1908), U.S. economist. "The United States," in *New York* (15 Nov. 1971; repr. in *A View from the Stands*, 1986).

2 A restaurant is a fantasy—a kind of living fantasy in which diners are the most important members of the cast.

> WARNER LEROY, Founder of Maxwell's Plum restaurant, New York City. *New York Times* (9 July 1976).

3 In a restaurant one is both observed and unobserved. Joy and sorrow can be displayed and observed "unwittingly," the writer scowling naively and the diners wondering, What the *hell* is he doing?

> DAVID MAMET (b. 1947), U.S. playwright. *Writing in Restaurants*, "Some Thoughts on Writing in Restaurants" (1986).

4 She tried to found a *salon*, and only succeeded in opening a restaurant.

> OSCAR WILDE (1854–1900), Anglo-Irish playwright, author. Lord Henry, in *The Picture of Dorian Gray*, ch. 1 (1891), of Lady Brandon.

RETIREMENT

1 Lord Tyrawley and I have been dead these two years, but we don't choose to have it known.

> LORD CHESTERFIELD (1694–1773), English statesman, man of letters. Quoted in: James Boswell, *Life of Samuel Johnson*, 3 April 1773 (1791).

2 I am a free man. I feel as light as a feather.

> JAVIER PÉREZ DE CUÉLLAR (b. 1920), Peruvian diplomat, Secretary-General of U.N. Quoted in: *Times* (London, 2 Jan. 1992), on stepping down as Secretary-General of U.N.

3 We had no revolutions to fear, nor fatigues to undergo; all our adventures were by the fireside, and all our migrations from the blue bed to the brown.

> OLIVER GOLDSMITH (1728–74), Anglo-Irish author, poet, playwright. The narrator (Dr. Charles Primrose), in *The Vicar of Wakefield*, ch. 1 (1766).

4 Don't you stay at home of evenings?
Don't you love a cushioned seat
In a corner, by the fireside, with your slippers on your feet?

> OLIVER WENDELL HOLMES, SR. (1809–94), U.S. writer, physician. *The Archbishop and Gil Blas*.

5 Men and women approaching retirement age should be recycled for public service work, and their companies should foot the bill. We can no longer afford to scrap-pile people.

> MAGGIE KUHN (b. 1905), U.S. civil rights activist, author. "Gray Panthers Versus Ageism," in *Ms.* (New York, July 1973).

6 I have a lifetime appointment and I intend to serve it. I expect to die at 110, shot by a jealous husband.

> JUSTICE THURGOOD MARSHALL (1908–1993), U.S. judge. *International Herald Tribune* (Paris, 15 Jan. 1990).

7 Eating's going to be a whole new ball game. I may even have to buy a new pair of trousers.

> LESTER PIGGOTT (b. 1935), British champion jockey. On his retirement. Quoted in: *Sunday Times* (London, 29 Dec. 1985). Piggott later came out of retirement.

8 Learn to live well, or fairly make your will;
You've played, and loved, and ate, and drunk your fill:
Walk sober off; before a sprightlier age

Comes tittering on, and shoves you from the
   stage:
Leave such to trifle with more grace and ease,
Whom Folly pleases, and whose Follies please.

> ALEXANDER POPE (1688–1744), English satirical poet. Last lines of *Imitations of Horace*, bk. 2, Epistle 2.

9   Fear no more the heat o' th' sun,
Nor the furious winter's rages.
Thou thy worldly task hast done,
Home art gone and ta'en thy wages.

> WILLIAM SHAKESPEARE (1564–1616), English dramatist, poet. Song from *Cymbeline*, act 4, sc. 2, sung by Guiderius and Arviragus.

10   I feel nothing but the accursed happiness I have dreaded all my life long: the happiness that comes as life goes, the happiness of yielding and dreaming instead of resisting and doing, the sweetness of the fruit that is going rotten.

> GEORGE BERNARD SHAW (1856–1950), Anglo-Irish playwright, critic. Captain Shotover, in *Heartbreak House*, act 2.

11   As to that leisure evening of life, I must say that I do not want it. I can conceive of no contentment of which toil is not to be the immediate parent.

> ANTHONY TROLLOPE (1815–82), English novelist. Letter, 8 June 1876 (published in *The Letters of Anthony Trollope*, vol. 2, 1983).

12   I advise you to go on living solely to enrage those who are paying your annuities. It is the only pleasure I have left.

> VOLTAIRE (1694–1778), French philosopher, author. Letter, 23 April 1754, to Madame du Deffand.

13   I anticipate with pleasing expectations that retreat in which I promise myself to realize, without alloy, the sweet enjoyment of partaking, in the midst of my fellow citizens, the benign influence of good laws under a free government, the ever favorite object of my heart, and the happy reward, as I trust, of our mutual cares, labors, and dangers.

> GEORGE WASHINGTON (1732–99), U.S. general, president. Farewell Address, 17 Sept. 1796.

REVENGE

1   Revenge is a kind of wild justice, which the more a man's nature runs to, the more ought law to weed it out.

> FRANCIS BACON (1561–1626), English philosopher, essayist, statesman. *Essays*, "Of Revenge" (1597–1625). "A man that studieth revenge," Bacon added later in the essay, "keeps his own wounds green."

2   And if any mischief follow, then thou shalt give life for life, eye for eye, tooth for tooth, hand for hand, foot for foot, burning for burning, wound for wound, stripe for stripe.

> BIBLE, HEBREW. *Exodus* 21:23.

3   The land cannot be cleansed of the blood that is shed therein, but by the blood of him that shed it.

> BIBLE, HEBREW. *Numbers* 35:33.

4   Something of vengeance I had tasted for the first time; as aromatic wine it seemed, on swallowing, warm and racy: its after-flavour, metallic and corroding, gave me a sensation as if I had been poisoned.

> CHARLOTTE BRONTË (1816–55), English novelist. *Jane Eyre*, ch. 4 (1847).

5   And, re-assembling our afflicted powers,
Consult how we may henceforth most offend.

> JOHN MILTON (1608–74), English poet. Satan, in *Paradise Lost*, bk. 1.

6   If you prick us do we not bleed? If you tickle us do we not laugh? If you poison us do we not die? And if you wrong us shall we not revenge?

> WILLIAM SHAKESPEARE (1564–1616), English dramatist, poet. Shylock, in *The Merchant of Venice*, act 3, sc. 1.

7   Revenge is the naked idol of the worship of a semi-barbarous age.

> PERCY BYSSHE SHELLEY (1792–1822), English poet. *A Defence of Poetry* (written 1821; published 1840).

8   No more tears now; I will think upon revenge.

> MARY STUART (1542–87), Queen of Scotland (Mary Queen of Scots) (1542–67). Attributed remark, 9 March 1566, after the murder of her favorite, David Rizzio, by an opposing faction led by Mary's husband, Lord Darnley, who was himself murdered the following year.

See also Camus on PUNISHMENT.

REVIVALISM

1   The Americans have always been food, sex, and spirit revivalists.

> EDWARD DAHLBERG (1900–1977), U.S. author, critic. *Alms for Oblivion*, "Our Vanishing Cooperative Colonies" (1964).

2   The deadly monotony of Christian country life where there are no beggars to feed, no drunkards to credit, which are among the moral duties of Christians in cities, leads as naturally to the outvent of what Methodists call "revivals" as did the backslidings of the people in those days.

> CORRA MAY HARRIS (1869–1935), U.S. author. *A Circuit Rider's Wife*, ch. 3 (1910).

See also EVANGELISM.

REVOLUTION

1   The Revolution was effected before the War commenced. The Revolution was in the minds and hearts of the people; a change in their religious sentiments of their duties and obligations. . . . This radical change in the principles, opinions, sentiments, and affections of the people, was the real American Revolution.

> JOHN ADAMS (1735–1826), U.S. statesman, president. Letter, 13 Feb. 1818.

2   Inferiors revolt in order that they may be equal, and equals that they may be superior. Such is the state of mind which creates revolutions.

> ARISTOTLE (384–322 B.C.), Greek philosopher. *Politics,* bk. 5, ch. 2 (written c. 343 B.C.; tr. by Benjamin Jowett).

3   I, John Brown, am now quite certain that the crimes of this guilty land will never be purged away but with Blood.

> JOHN BROWN (1800–1859), U.S. abolitionist. Last statement, written on the day of his execution, 2 Dec. 1859.

4   I had such a wonderful feeling last night, walking beneath the dark sky while cannon boomed on my right and guns on my left . . . the feeling that I could change the world only by being there.

> VIORICA BUTNARIU, Student at Bucharest University, Rumania. Letter, 23 Dec. 1989, to American friend (published in *Observer,* London, 31 Dec. 1989), on the Romanian revolution.

5   The dead have been awakened—shall I sleep?
The world's at war with tyrants—shall I crouch?
The harvest's ripe—and shall I pause to reap?
I slumber not; the thorn is in my couch;
Each day a trumpet soundeth in mine ear,
Its echo in my heart.

> LORD BYRON (1788–1824), English poet. First item of *Journal in Cephalonia,* 19 June 1823 (published in *Byron's Letters and Journals,* vol. 9, ed. by Leslie A. Marchand, 1979). The journal was written during Byron's last journey to aid the Greek revolt.

6   More and more, revolution has found itself delivered into the hands of its bureaucrats and doctrinaires on the one hand, and to the enfeebled and bewildered masses on the other.

> ALBERT CAMUS (1913–60), French-Algerian philosopher, author. *The Rebel,* pt. 3, "State Terrorism and Rational Terror" (1951; tr. 1953).

7   Revolution, in order to be creative, cannot do without either a moral or metaphysical rule to balance the insanity of history.

> ALBERT CAMUS (1913–60), French-Algerian philosopher, author. *The Rebel,* pt. 3, "Rebellion and Revolution" (1951; tr. 1953).

8   You can never have a revolution in order to establish a democracy. You must have a democracy in order to have a revolution.

> G. K. CHESTERTON, British author. *Tremendous Trifles,* "The Wind and the Trees" (1909).

9   Our cause is just. Our union is perfect.

> JOHN DICKINSON (1732–1808), U.S. statesman, essayist. *Declaration on the Causes and Necessity of Taking up Arms* (1775).

10   I have been ever of opinion that revolutions are not to be evaded.

> BENJAMIN DISRAELI (1804–81), English Statesman, author. Sidonia, in *Coningsby,* bk. 4, ch. 11 (1844).

11   Normal life cannot sustain revolutionary attitudes for long.

> MILOVAN DJILAS (b. 1911), Yugoslav political leader, writer. *Guardian* (London, 9 April 1990).

12   If there is any period one would desire to be born in, is it not the age of Revolution; when the old and the new stand side by side, and admit of being compared; when

the energies of all men are searched by fear and by hope; when the historic glories of the old can be compensated by the rich possibilities of the new era?

> RALPH WALDO EMERSON (1803–82), U.S. essayist, poet, philosopher. "The American Scholar," lecture, 31 Aug. 1837, delivered before the Phi Beta Kappa Society, Harvard University (published in *Nature, Addresses and Lectures,* 1849).

13   The worst of revolutions is a restoration.

> CHARLES JAMES FOX (1749–1806), English Whig politician. Speech, 10 Dec. 1785, to the House of Commons.

14   All successful revolutions are the kicking in of a rotten door. The violence of revolutions is the violence of men who charge into a vacuum.

> JOHN KENNETH GALBRAITH (b. 1908), U.S. economist. *The Age of Uncertainty,* ch. 3 (1977).

15   The main object of a revolution is the liberation of man . . . not the interpretation and application of some transcendental ideology.

> JEAN GENET (1910–86), French playwright, novelist. *Prisoner of Love,* pt. 1 (1986; tr. 1989).

16   The surest guide to the correctness of the path that women take is *joy in the struggle.* Revolution is the festival of the oppressed.

> GERMAINE GREER (b. 1939), Australian feminist writer. *The Female Eunuch,* "Revolution" (1970).

17   The spirit of revolution, the spirit of insurrection, is a spirit radically opposed to liberty.

> FRANÇOIS GUIZOT (1787–1874), French statesman, historian. Speech, 29 Dec. 1830, Paris.

18   All great movements are popular movements. They are the volcanic eruptions of human passions and emotions, stirred into activity by the ruthless Goddess of Distress or by the torch of the spoken word cast into the midst of the people.

> ADOLF HITLER (1889–1945), German dictator. *Mein Kampf,* vol. 1, ch. 3 (1925).

19   The main effect of a real revolution is perhaps that it sweeps away those who do not know how to wish, and brings to the front men with insatiable appetites for action, power and all that the world has to offer.

> ERIC HOFFER (1902–83), U.S. philosopher. *The Passionate State of Mind,* aph. 23 (1955).

20   We used to think that revolutions are the cause of change. Actually it is the other way around: change prepares the ground for revolution.

> ERIC HOFFER (1902–83), U.S. philosopher. *The Temper of Our Time,* "A Time of Juveniles" (1967).

21   The brutalities of progress are called revolutions. When they are over we realize this: that the human race has been roughly handled, but that it has advanced.

> VICTOR HUGO (1802–85), French poet, dramatist, novelist. The old revolutionary, in *Les Misérables,* pt. 1, bk. 1, ch. 10 (1862).

22   If we glance at the most important revolutions in history, we see at once that the greatest number of these originated in the periodical revolutions of the human mind.

> KARL WILHELM VON HUMBOLDT (1767–1835), German

statesman and philologist. *The Limits of State Action*, ch. 16 (written 1792; first published 1854; tr. and ed. by J. W. Burrow, 1969).

23   History teaches us that the great revolutions aren't started by people who are utterly down and out, without hope and vision. They take place when people begin to live a little better—and when they see how much yet remains to be achieved.

HUBERT H. HUMPHREY (1911–78), U.S. Democratic politician, vice president. Speech, 2 April 1966, Durham, N.C.

24   Revolutions are notorious for allowing even non-participants—even women!—new scope for telling the truth since they are themselves such massive moments of truth, moments of such massive participation.

SELMA JAMES (b. 1930), U.S. author and political activist. *The Ladies and the Mammies: Jane Austen & Jean Rhys*, ch. 1 (1983).

25   And then, Sir, there is this consideration, that if the abuse be enormous, Nature will rise up, and claiming her original rights, overturn a corrupt political system.

SAMUEL JOHNSON (1709–84), English author, lexicographer. Quoted in: James Boswell, *Life of Samuel Johnson*, 6 July 1763 (1791).

26   Although a system may cease to exist in the legal sense or as a structure of power, its values (or anti-values), its philosophy, its teachings remain in us. They rule our thinking, our conduct, our attitude to others. The situation is a demonic paradox: we have toppled the system but we still carry its genes.

RYSZARD KAPUSCINSKI (b. 1932), Polish journalist. *Independent on Sunday* (London, 1 Sept. 1991).

27   Those who make peaceful revolution impossible will make violent revolution inevitable.

JOHN F. KENNEDY (1917–63), U.S. Democratic politician, president. Speech, 13 March 1962, the White House.

28   Revolutions are not made for export.

NIKITA KHRUSHCHEV (1894–1971), Soviet premier. Speech, 27 Jan. 1959, 21st Communist Party Congress, Moscow.

29   The children of the revolution are always ungrateful, and the revolution must be grateful that it is so.

URSULA K. LE GUIN (b. 1929), U.S. author. "Reciprocity of Prose and Poetry," address, 1983 in Poetry Series, Folger Shakespeare Library, Washington, D.C. (published in *Dancing at the Edge of the World*, 1989).

30   You cannot make a revolution in white gloves.

VLADIMIR ILYICH LENIN (1870–1924), Russian revolutionary leader. Lenin to Kropotkin, May 1919. Quoted in: Tamara Deutsche, *Not By Politics Alone*, ch. 2 (1973).

31   "Revolution" today is taken for granted, and in consequence becomes rather dull.

WYNDHAM LEWIS (1882–1957), British author, painter. *The Art of Being Ruled*, "Revolution and Progress," ch. 5 (1926).

32   At the crash of economic collapse of which the rumblings can already be heard, the sleeping soldiers of the proletariat will awake as at the fanfare of the Last Judgment and the corpses of the victims of the struggle will arise and demand an accounting from those who are loaded down with curses.

KARL LIEBKNECHT (1871–1919), German jurist, politician.

Quoted in: Albert Camus, *The Rebel*, pt. 3, "State Terrorism and Rational Terror" (1951; tr. 1953).

33   A revolution is not a dinner party, or writing an essay, or painting a picture, or doing embroidery; it cannot be so refined, so leisurely and gentle, so temperate, kind, courteous, restrained and magnanimous. A revolution is an insurrection, an act of violence by which one class overthrows another.

MAO ZEDONG (1893–1976), Founder of the People's Republic of China. Report, March 1927 (published in *Selected Works*, vol. 1, 1954).

34   It is easier to run a revolution than a government.

FERDINAND E. MARCOS (1917–81), Filipino politician, president. *Time* (New York, 6 June 1977).

35   A revolution does not last more than fifteen years, the period which coincides with the flourishing of a generation.

JOSÉ ORTEGA Y GASSET (1883–1955), Spanish essayist, philosopher. *The Revolt of the Masses*, ch. 10 (1930).

36   The word "revolution" itself has become not only a dead relic of Leftism, but a key to the deadendedness of male politics: the "revolution" of a wheel which returns in the end to the same place; the "revolving door" of a politics which has "liberated" women only to use them, and only within the limits of male tolerance.

ADRIENNE RICH (b. 1929), U.S. poet. "Power and Danger: Works of a Common Woman," Introduction to *The Work of a Common Woman: The Collected Poetry of Judy Grahn, 1964–1977* (1977; repr. in *On Lies, Secrets, and Silence*, 1980).

37   The differences between revolution in art and revolution in politics are enormous. . . . Revolution in art lies not in the will to destroy but in the revelation of what has already been destroyed. Art kills only the dead.

HAROLD ROSENBERG (1906–78), U.S. art critic, author. *The Tradition of the New*, ch. 6 (1960).

38   No one makes a revolution by himself; and there are some revolutions . . . which humanity accomplishes without quite knowing how, because it is everybody who takes them in hand.

GEORGE SAND (1804–76), French novelist. *The Haunted Pool*, Preface (1851).

39   When the people contend for their liberty they seldom get anything by their victory but new masters.

GEORGE SAVILE, LORD HALIFAX (1633–95), English statesman, author. *Political, Moral and Miscellaneous Thoughts and Reflections*, "Of Prerogative, Power and Liberty" (1750).

40   Revolutions have never lightened the burden of tyranny: they have only shifted it to another shoulder.

GEORGE BERNARD SHAW (1856–1950), Anglo-Irish playwright, critic. *Man and Superman*, Preface, "The Revolutionist's Handbook" (1903).

41   A nation grown free in a single day is a child born with the limbs and the vigour of a man, who would take a drawn sword for his rattle, and set the house in a blaze that he might chuckle over the splendour.

SYDNEY SMITH (1771–1845), English clergyman, writer. Quoted in: Hesketh Pearson, *The Smith of Smiths*, ch. 11 (1934), of the French.

42 The old order changeth, yielding place to new,
And God fulfils himself in many ways.

> LORD TENNYSON (1809–92), English poet. King Arthur, in *The Idylls of the King*, "The Passing of Arthur."

43 It is almost never when a state of things is the most detestable that it is smashed, but when, beginning to improve, it permits men to breathe, to reflect, to communicate their thoughts with each other, and to gauge by what they already have the extent of their rights and their grievances. The weight, although less heavy, seems then all the more unbearable.

> ALEXIS DE TOCQUEVILLE (1805–59), French social philosopher. Letter, 23 Sept. 1853 (published in *Selected Letters on Politics and Society*, 1985).

44 Revolutions are always verbose.

> LEON TROTSKY (1879–1940), Russian revolutionary. *The History of the Russian Revolution*, vol. 2, ch. 12 (1933).

See also Ellis on CIVILIZATION; Alinsky on HISTORY; Orwell on POWER; REBELLION; REVOLUTIONARIES; Khrushchev on The USSR.

REVOLUTIONARIES

1 I must study politics and war that my sons may have liberty to study mathematics and philosophy.

> JOHN ADAMS (1735–1826), U.S. statesman, president. Letter, 12 May 1780, to his wife Abigail Adams.

2 On the first day of a revolution he is a treasure; on the second he ought to be shot.

> ANONYMOUS. Said of anarchist Mikhail Bakunin during the Paris Revolt of 1848. Quoted in: *Benét's Reader's Encyclopedia* (3rd ed., 1987).

3 The most radical revolutionary will become a conservative the day after the revolution.

> HANNAH ARENDT (1906–75), German-born U.S. political philosopher. *New Yorker* (12 Sept. 1970).

4 Every revolutionary ends by becoming either an oppressor or a heretic.

> ALBERT CAMUS (1913–60), French-Algerian philosopher and author. *The Rebel*, ch. 3, "Rebellion and Revolution" (1951; tr. 1953).

5 I feel my belief in sacrifice and struggle getting stronger. I despise the kind of existence that clings to the miserly trifles of comfort and self-interest. I think that a man should not live beyond the age when he begins to deteriorate, when the flame that lighted the brightest moment of his life has weakened.

> FIDEL CASTRO (b. 1926), Cuban revolutionary, premier. Letter, 19 Dec. 1953 (published in Carlos Franqui, *Diary of the Cuban Revolution*, 1980, p. 67).

6 I began revolution with 82 men. If I had [to] do it again, I do it with 10 or 15 and absolute faith. It does not matter how small you are if you have faith and plan of action.

> FIDEL CASTRO (b. 1926), Cuban revolutionary, premier. *New York Times* (22 April 1959).

7 The scrupulous and the just, the noble, humane, and devoted natures; the unselfish and the intelligent may begin a movement—but it passes away from them. They are not the leaders of a revolution. They are its victims.

> JOSEPH CONRAD (1857–1924), Polish-born English novelist. The narrator, in *Under Western Eyes*, pt. 2, ch. 3 (1911).

8 The revolutionary spirit is mighty convenient in this, that it frees one from all scruples as regards ideas. Its hard absolute optimism is repulsive to my mind by the menace of fanaticism and intolerance it contains. No doubt one should smile at these things; but, imperfect Esthete, I am no better Philosopher. All claim to special righteousness awakens in me that scorn and anger from which a philosophical mind should be free.

> JOSEPH CONRAD (1857–1924), Polish-born English novelist. *A Personal Record*, "A Familiar Preface" (1912).

9 Clemency is also a revolutionary measure.

> CAMILLE DESMOULINS (1760–94), French journalist, revolutionary leader. Speech, 14 July 1789, to a crowd outside Palais Royal, Paris, recalled by Desmoulins in his newspaper *Le Vieux Cordelier* (5 Jan. 1794). Desmoulins was guillotined together with his friend Danton.

10 Disturbances in society are never more fearful than when those who are stirring up the trouble can use the pretext of religion to mask their true designs.

> DENIS DIDEROT (1713–84), French philosopher. *Observations on the Drawing up of Laws* (written 1774 for Catherine the Great; first published 1921; repr. in *Selected Writings*, ed. by Lester G. Crocker, 1966).

11 The successful revolutionary is a statesman, the unsuccessful one a criminal.

> ERICH FROMM (1900–1980), U.S. psychologist. *Escape From Freedom*, ch. 7 (1941).

12 True revolutionaries are like God—they create the world in their own image. Our awesome responsibility to ourselves, to our children, and to the future is to create ourselves in the image of goodness, because the future depends on the nobility of our imaginings.

> BARBARA GRIZZUTI HARRISON (b. 1941), U.S. author, publicist. *Unlearning the Lie: Sexism in School*, ch. 9 (1973).

13 We have wasted our spirit in the regions of the abstract and general just as the monks let it wither in the world of prayer and contemplation.

> ALEXANDER HERZEN (1812–70), Russian journalist, political thinker. *From the Other Shore*, "Epilogue 1849" (1855), of the failure of the revolutionary movements in Europe after 1848.

14 If today I stand here as a revolutionary, it is as a revolutionary against the Revolution.

> ADOLF HITLER (1889–1945), German dictator. Speech, 26 Feb. 1924, while on trial for involvement in the unsuccessful *putsch* against the Republican government in Munich, Germany, which had itself overthrown the Bavarian monarchy in 1918.

15 He that goeth about to persuade a multitude that they are not so well governed as they ought to be shall never want attentive and favourable hearers.

> RICHARD HOOKER (1554–1600), English theologian. *Of the Laws of Ecclesiastical Polity*, bk. 1, ch. 1 (1594).

16 It is better to die on your feet than to live on your knees.

> DOLORES IBÁRRURI, *LA PASIONARIA* (1895–1989), Spanish Communist leader. Radio broadcast, 3 Sept. 1936, from Paris,

calling on the women of Spain to defend the Republic. In her autobiography (1966), she stated that she had first used the words in an earlier broadcast in Spain 18 July, the same broadcast in which she said *No pasarán*. Both expressions, which became slogans in the ensuing civil war, have earlier attributions, the first to Mexican revolutionary Emiliano Zapata (c. 1877–1919), the second to Marshal Pétain (1856–1951) during World War I.

17 Revolutionary politics, revolutionary art, and oh, the revolutionary mind, is the dullest thing on earth. When we open a "revolutionary" review, or read a "revolutionary" speech, we yawn our heads off. It is true, there is nothing else. Everything is correctly, monotonously, dishearteningly "revolutionary." What a stupid word! What a stale fuss!

WYNDHAM LEWIS (1882–1957), British author, painter. *The Art of Being Ruled* "Revolution and Progress," ch. 5 (1926).

18 In every revolution there intrude, at the side of its true agents, men of a different stamp; some of them survivors of and devotees to past revolutions, without insight into the present movement, but preserving popular influence by their known honesty and courage, or by the sheer force of tradition; others mere brawlers, who, by dint of repeating year after year the same set of stereotyped declamations against the government of the day, have sneaked into the reputation of revolutionists of the first water. . . . They are an unavoidable evil: with time they are shaken off.

KARL MARX (1818–83), German political theorist, social philosopher. *Address of the General Council of the International Working Men's Association on "The Civil War in France"* (1871; published in *Selected Works*, vol. 2, 1942).

19 Revolutions are brought about by men, by men who think as men of action and act as men of thought.

KWAME NKRUMAH (1900–1972), Ghanaian president. *Consciencism*, ch. 2 (1964).

20 Most revolutionaries are potential Tories, because they imagine that everything can be put right by altering the *shape* of society; once that change is effected, as it sometimes is, they see no need for any other.

GEORGE ORWELL (1903–50), British author. *Inside the Whale and Other Essays*, "Charles Dickens" (1940).

21 All revolutions devour their own children.

ERNST RÖHM (1887–1934), German Nazi leader. Remark, 30 June 1933, to lawyer (later Nazi leader) Hans Frank, recorded by Frank in his memoirs (1955). Quoted in: Joachim C. Fest, *The Face of the Third Reich*, pt. 2, "Ernst Röhm and the Lost Generation" (1963; tr. 1970). Röhm was executed without trial a year later, in the Night of the Long Knives, for his alleged part in the plot to assassinate Hitler.

22 If not us, who? If not now, when?

SLOGAN BY CZECH UNIVERSITY STUDENTS IN PRAGUE, Nov. 1989. Quoted in: *Observer* (London, 26 Nov. 1989).

23 People who talk about revolution and class struggle without referring explicitly to everyday life, without understanding what is subversive about love and what is positive in the refusal of constraints, such people have a corpse in their mouth.

RAOUL VANEIGEM (b. 1934), Belgian Situationist philosopher. *The Revolution of Everyday Life*, ch. 1, sct. 4 (1967; tr. 1983).

24 All partisan movements add to the fullness of our understanding of society as a whole. They never detract; or, in any case, one must not allow them to do so. Experience adds to experience.

ALICE WALKER (b. 1944), U.S. author, critic. "Can I Be My Brother's Sister?," in *Ms.* (New York, Oct. 1975; repr. in *In Search of our Mothers' Gardens*, "Brothers and Sisters," 1983).

25 You said, "They're harmless dreamers and they're loved by the people."—"What," I asked you, "is harmless about a dreamer, and what," I asked you, "is harmless about the love of the people?—Revolution only needs good dreamers who remember their dreams."

TENNESSEE WILLIAMS (1914–1983), U.S. dramatist. Gutman, in *Camino Real*, block 2, speaking to the Generalissimo.

See also Collingwood on REACTIONARIES.

REWARD

1 Vice is its own reward. It is virtue which, if it is to be marketed with consumer appeal, must carry Green Shield stamps.

QUENTIN CRISP (b. 1908), British author. *The Naked Civil Servant*, ch. 2 (1968).

2 People think that if a man has undergone any hardship, he should have a reward; but for my part, if I have done the hardest possible day's work, and then come to sit down in a corner and eat my supper comfortably— why, then I don't think I deserve any reward for my hard day's work—for am I not now at peace? Is not my supper good?

HERMAN MELVILLE (1819–1891), U.S. author. Letter, 17 Nov. 1851, to Nathaniel Hawthorne (published in *The Letters of Herman Melville*, ed. by Merrell R. Davis and William H. Gilman, 1960).

3 What are we hoping to get out of it, what's it all in aid of—is it really just for the sake of a gloved hand waving at you from a golden coach?

JOHN OSBORNE (b. 1929), British playwright. Jean, in *The Entertainer*, no. 10.

THE RICH

1 Every man thinks God is on his side. The rich and powerful know he is.

JEAN ANOUILH (1910–87), French playwright. Charles, in *The Lark* (adapted by Lillian Hellman, 1955).

2 Have you never been moved by poor men's fidelity, the image of you they form in their simple minds? Why should you always talk of their *envy*, without understanding that what they ask of you is not so much your worldly goods, as something very hard to define, which they themselves can put no name to; yet at times it consoles their loneliness; a dream of splendor, of magnificence, a tawdry dream, a poor man's dream—and yet God blesses it!

GEORGES BERNANOS (1888–1948), French novelist, political writer. The priest to Madame la Comtesse, in *The Diary of a Country Priest*, ch. 5 (1936).

3   He that maketh haste to be rich shall not be innocent.

> BIBLE, HEBREW. *Proverbs* 28:20.

4   About the only difference between the poor and the
ritch, is this, the poor *suffer* mizery, while the ritch hav tu
enjoy it.

> JOSH BILLINGS [HENRY WHEELER SHAW] (1818–85), U.S.
> humorist. *Josh Billings, His Sayings*, ch. 71 (1865).

5   This, then, is held to be the duty of the man of
wealth: First, to set an example of modest, unostentatious
living, shunning display or extravagance; to provide
moderately for the legitimate wants of those dependent
upon him; and, after doing so, to consider all surplus revenues which come to him simply as trust funds, which he
is called upon to administer, and strictly bound as a matter of duty to administer in the manner which, in his judgment, is best calculated to produce the most beneficial
results for the community—the man of wealth thus
becoming the mere trustee and agent for his poorer
brethren, bringing to their service his superior wisdom,
experience and ability to administer, doing for them better than they would or could do for themselves.

> ANDREW CARNEGIE (1835–1919), U.S. industrialist, philan-
> thropist. "The Gospel of Wealth," in *North American Review*
> (June 1889). Quoted in: Burton J. Hendrick, *Life of Andrew
> Carnegie*, vol. 1, ch. 17 (1932).

6   The poor have sometimes objected to being governed badly; the rich have always objected to being governed at all.

> G. K. CHESTERTON (1874–1936), British author. Ratcliffe, in
> *The Man Who Was Thursday*, ch. 11 (1908).

7   Among the Very Rich you will never find a really
generous man, even by accident. They may give their
money away, but they will never give themselves away;
they are egoistic, secretive, dry as old bones. To be smart
enough to get all that money you must be dull enough to
want it.

> G. K. CHESTERTON (1874–1936), British author. *A Miscellany
> of Men*, "A Miscellany of Men" (1912).

8   In a rich man's house there is no place to spit but his
face.

> DIOGENES OF SINOPE ["THE CYNIC"] c. 410–C. 320 B.C.),
> Greek philosopher and moralist. *Herakleitos and Diogenes*, pt. 2,
> Fragment 56 (tr. by Guy Davenport, 1976).

9   Her voice is full of money.

> F. SCOTT FITZGERALD (1896–1940), U.S. author. Gatsby, in
> *The Great Gatsby*, ch. 7 (1925), describing Daisy Buchanan. The
> narrator (Nick Carraway) adds, "that was the inexhaustible charm
> that rose and fell in it, the jingle of it, the cymbals' song of it."

10   Let me tell you about the very rich. They are different from you and me. They possess and enjoy early,
and it does something to them, makes them soft where
we are hard, and cynical where we are trustful, in a way
that, unless you were born rich, it is very difficult to
understand. They think, deep in their hearts, that they are
better than we are because we had to discover the compensations and refuges of life for ourselves. Even when
they enter deep into our world or sink below us, they still
think that they are better than we are. They are different.

> F. SCOTT FITZGERALD (1896–1940), U.S. author. *All the Sad*

Young Men, "The Rich Boy" (1926). The first line also occurs in
Fitzgerald's notebooks, published in *The Crack-Up*, "Notebook
E" (1945), and was taken up by Hemingway in his story "The
Snows of Kilimanjaro" (1936). See Hemingway on THE RICH,
and Fitzgerald on WEALTH, for his riposte to Hemingway's jibe.

11   Of all classes the rich are the most noticed and the
least studied.

> JOHN KENNETH GALBRAITH (b. 1908), U.S. economist. *The
> Age of Uncertainty*, ch. 2 (1977).

12   No, not rich. I am a poor man with money, which is
not the same thing.

> GABRIEL GARCÍA MÁRQUEZ (b. 1928), Colombian writer.
> Uncle Leo XII, in *Love in the Time of Cholera* (1985; tr. 1988,
> p. 167).

13   The jests of the rich are ever successful.

> OLIVER GOLDSMITH (1728–74), Anglo-Irish author, poet, play-
> wright. The narrator (Dr. Charles Primrose), in *The Vicar of
> Wakefield*, ch. 7 (written 1761–62; published 1766).

14   The rich were dull and they drank too much or they
played too much backgammon. They were dull and they
were repetitious. He remembered poor Julian and his
romantic awe of them and how he had started a story
once that began, "The very rich are different from you
and me." And how someone had said to Julian, "Yes,
they have more money."

> ERNEST HEMINGWAY (1899–1961), U.S. author. "The Snows of
> Kilimanjaro," in *Esquire* (New York, Aug. 1936; collected in *The
> Fifth Column and the First Forty-Nine Stories*, 1938). In its origi-
> nal publication, "Julian" was named as F. Scott Fitzgerald, who
> had written in his 1926 story "The Rich Boy": "Let me tell you
> about the very rich. They are different from you and me" (see
> Fitzgerald, above).

15   A sumptuous dwelling the rich man hath.
And dainty is his repast;
But remember that luxury's prodigal hand
Keeps the furnace of toil in blast.

> MARY ELIZABETH HEWITT (1818–?), U.S. poet. *A Plea for the
> Rich Man*, st. 3.

16   It is wonderful to think how men of very large
estates not only spend their yearly income, but are often
actually in want of money. It is clear, they have not value
for what they spend.

> SAMUEL JOHNSON (1709–84), English author, lexicographer.
> Quoted in: James Boswell, *Life of Samuel Johnson*, 10 April 1778
> (1791).

17   Nothing more clearly shows how little God esteems
his gift to men of wealth, money, position and other
worldly goods, than the way he distributes these, and the
sort of men who are most amply provided with them.

> JEAN DE LA BRUYÈRE (1645–96), French writer, moralist. *Char-
> acters*, "Of Worldly Goods," aph. 24 (1688).

18   A certain kind of rich man afflicted with the symptoms of moral dandyism sooner or later comes to the conclusion that it isn't enough merely to make money. He
feels obliged to hold views, to espouse causes and elect
Presidents, to explain to a trembling world how and why
the world went wrong. The spectacle is nearly always
comic.

> LEWIS H. LAPHAM (b. 1935), U.S. essayist, editor. *Money and
> Class in America*, ch. 7 (1988).

19 Among all the emotions, the rich have the least talent for love. It is possible to love one's dog, dress or duck-shooting hat, but a human being presents a more difficult problem. The rich might wish to experience feelings of affection, but it is almost impossible to chip away the enamel of their narcissism. They take up all the space in all the mirrors in the house. Their children, who represent the most present and therefore the most annoying claim on their attention, usually receive the brunt of their irritation.

LEWIS H. LAPHAM (b. 1935), U.S. essayist, editor. *Money and Class in America*, ch. 9 (1988).

20 He must have killed a lot of men to have made so much money.

MOLIÉRE (1622–73), French dramatist. Toinette, in *Le Malade Imaginaire* ("The Imaginary Invalid"), act 1, sc. 5, of the doctor M. Purgon.

21 Of rich men it telleth, and strange is the story
How they have, and they hanker, and grip far and wide;
And they live and they die, and the earth and its glory
Has been but a burden they scarce might abide.

WILLIAM MORRIS (1834–96), English artist, writer, printer. *The Pilgrims of Hope*, "The Message of the March Wind" (1885).

22 I don't mind their having a lot of money, and I don't care how they employ it,
But I do think that they damn well ought to admit they enjoy it.

OGDEN NASH (1902–71), U.S. poet. *The Terrible People*, in *Happy Days* (1933).

23 For just as poets love their own works, and fathers their own children, in the same way those who have created a fortune value their money, not merely for its uses, like other persons, but because it is their own production. This makes them moreover disagreeable companions, because they will praise nothing but riches.

PLATO (c. 427–347 B.C.), Greek philosopher. Socrates, in *The Republic*, bk. 1, sct. 330.

24 A fool and her money are soon courted.

HELEN ROWLAND (1875–1950), U.S. journalist. *A Guide to Men*, "First Interlude" (1922).

25 No one has ever said it, but how painfully true it is that the poor have us always with them.

SAKI [H. H. MUNRO] (1870–1916), Scottish author. Lady Caroline, in *The Unbearable Bassington*, ch. 7 (1912).

26 O, what a world of vile ill-favoured faults,
Looks handsome in three hundred pounds a year!

WILLIAM SHAKESPEARE (1564–1616), English dramatist, poet. Anne, in *The Merry Wives of Windsor*, act 3, sc. 4.

27 The more I see of the moneyed classes, the more I understand the guillotine.

GEORGE BERNARD SHAW (1856–1950), Anglo-Irish playwright, critic. Letter, 25 Sept. 1899 (published in *Collected Letters*, vol. 2, 1972).

28 The wretchedness of being rich is that you live with rich people. . . . To suppose, as we all suppose, that we could be rich and not behave as the rich behave, is like supposing that we could drink all day and stay sober.

LOGAN PEARSALL SMITH (1865–1946), U.S. essayist, aphorist. *Afterthoughts*, "In the World" (1931).

29 If Heaven had looked upon riches to be a valuable thing, it would not have given them to such a scoundrel.

JONATHAN SWIFT (1667–1745), Anglo-Irish satirist. Letter, 12 Aug. 1720.

30 Even the rich are hungry for love, for being cared for, for being wanted, for having someone to call their own.

MOTHER TERESA (b. 1910), Albanian-born Roman Catholic missionary. *A Gift for God*, "Carriers of Christ's Love" (1975).

31 The trouble is that rich people, well-to-do people, very often don't really know who the poor are; and that is why we can forgive them, for knowledge can only lead to love, and love to service. And so, if they are not touched by them, it's because they do not know them.

MOTHER TERESA (b. 1910), Albanian-born Roman Catholic missionary. *A Gift for God*, "Riches" (1975).

32 The rich man . . . is always sold to the institution which makes him rich. Absolutely speaking, the more money, the less virtue.

HENRY DAVID THOREAU (1817–62), U.S. philosopher, author, naturalist. *On the Duty of Civil Disobedience* (1849).

33 What is most important for democracy is not that great fortunes should not exist, but that great fortunes should not remain in the same hands. In that way there are rich men, but they do not form a class.

ALEXIS DE TOCQUEVILLE (1805–59), French social philosopher. *Democracy in America*, vol. 2, Appendix 5, "Democracy" (1840).

34 To be rich nowadays merely means to possess a large number of poor objects.

RAOUL VANEIGEM (b. 1934), Belgian Situationist philosopher. *The Revolution of Everyday Life*, ch. 7, sct. 2 (1967; tr. 1983).

35 He rides in the Row at ten o'clock in the morning, goes to the Opera three times a week, changes his clothes at least five times a day, and dines out every night of the season. You don't call that leading an idle life, do you?

OSCAR WILDE (1854–1900), Anglo-Irish playwright, author. Mabel Chiltern, in *An Ideal Husband*, act 1.

See also Dobell on FUNERALS; Saki on GIFTS AND GIVING; Disraeli on INEQUALITY; France, Goldsmith on LAWS AND THE LAW; LUXURY; Bagehot on POVERTY AND THE POOR; TYCOONS; WEALTH.

RIDICULE

1 One cannot be always laughing at a man without now and then stumbling on something witty.

JANE AUSTEN (1775–1817), English novelist. Elizabeth Bennet, in *Pride and Prejudice*, ch. 40.

2 It is commonly said . . . that ridicule is the best test of truth; for that it will not stick where it is not just. I deny it. A truth learned in a certain light, and attacked in certain words, by men of wit and humour, may, and often doth, become ridiculous, at least so far, that the truth is only remembered and repeated for the sake of the ridicule.

LORD CHESTERFIELD (1694–1773), English statesman, man of letters. Letter, 6 Feb. 1752 (first published 1774; repr. in *The Letters of the Earl of Chesterfield to His Son*, vol. 2, no. 270, ed. by Charles Strachey, 1901).

3   I believe they talked of me, for they laughed consumedly.

GEORGE FARQUHAR (1678–1707), Irish dramatist. Scrub, in *The Beaux' Stratagem*, act 3, sc. 1.

4   We grow tired of everything but turning others into ridicule, and congratulating ourselves on their defects.

WILLIAM HAZLITT (1778–1830), English essayist. *The Plain Speaker*, "On the Pleasure of Hating" (1826).

5   Resort is had to ridicule only when reason is against us.

THOMAS JEFFERSON (1743–1826), U.S. president. Letter, 1813, to Jefferson's successor as president, James Madison.

6   No great movement designed to change the world can bear to be laughed at or belittled. Mockery is a rust that corrodes all it touches.

MILAN KUNDERA (b. 1929), Czech author, critic. Kostka, in *The Joke*, pt. 6, ch. 18 (1967; tr. 1982).

7   When a person can no longer laugh at himself, it is time for others to laugh at him.

THOMAS SZASZ (b. 1920), U.S. psychiatrist. *The Second Sin*, "Social Relations" (1973).

8   No God and no religion can survive ridicule. No political church, no nobility, no royalty or other fraud, can face ridicule in a fair field, and live.

MARK TWAIN (1835–1910), U.S. author. *Mark Twain's Notebooks and Journals*, vol. 3 (ed. by Frederick Anderson, 1979), Notebook 28 (July 1888–May 1889).

RIOTS

1   With society and its public, there is no longer any other language than that of bombs, barricades, and all that follows.

ANTONIN ARTAUD (1896–1948), French theater producer, actor, theorist. Remark to André Breton. Quoted in: *Le Monde* (Paris, 11 Sept. 1970; repr. in Renee Weingarten, *Writers and Revolution*, ch. 15, 1974).

2   Some punishment seems preparing for a people who are ungratefully abusing the best constitution and the best King any nation was ever blessed with, intent on nothing but luxury, licentiousness, power, places, pensions, and plunder; while the ministry, divided in their counsels, with little regard for each other, worried by perpetual oppositions, in continual apprehension of changes, intent on securing popularity in case they should lose favor, have for some years past had little time or inclination to attend to our small affairs, whose remoteness makes them appear even smaller.

BENJAMIN FRANKLIN (1706–90), U.S. statesman, writer. Letter, 14 May 1768, written while in London during the riots following the arrest of John Wilkes, when "all respect to law and government seems to be lost among the common people, who are moreover continually inflamed by seditious scibblers, to trample on authority and every thing that used to keep them in order"

(published in *Complete Works*, vol. 4, ed. by John Bigelow, 1887–88).

3   Perhaps having built a barricade when you're sixteen provides you with a sort of safety rail. If you've once taken part in building one, even inadvertently, doesn't its usually latent image reappear like a warning signal whenever you're tempted to join the police, or support any manifestation of Law and Order?

JEAN GENET (1910–86), French playwright, novelist. *Prisoner of Love*, pt. 1 (1986: tr. 1989).

4   A rioter with a Molotov cocktail in his hands is not fighting for civil rights any more than a Klansman with a sheet on his back and a mask on his face.

LYNDON B. JOHNSON (1908–73), U.S. Democratic politician, president. Speech, 20 Aug. 1965, Washington, D.C.

5   The tumultous populace of large cities are ever to be dreaded. Their indiscriminate violence prostrates for the time all public authority, and its consequences are sometimes extensive and terrible.

GEORGE WASHINGTON (1732–99), U.S. general, president. Letter, 28 July 1791, to the Marquis de Lafayette.

See also MOBS.

RISK

1   The man who knows it can't be done counts the risk, not the reward.

ELBERT HUBBARD (1856–1915), U.S. author. *Selected Writings*, vol. 1, "Index" (1921).

2   Risk! Risk anything! Care no more for the opinion of others, for those voices. Do the hardest thing on earth for you. Act for yourself. Face the truth.

KATHERINE MANSFIELD (1888–1923), New Zealand-born British author. Journal entry, 14 Oct. 1922, in THE JOURNAL OF KATHERINE MANSFIELD (1927).

3   To save all we must risk all.

FRIEDRICH VON SCHILLER (1759–1805), German dramatist, poet, essayist. Fiesco, in *Fiesco*, act 4, sc. 6.

RITUAL

1   Ritual will always mean throwing away something: *destroying* our corn or wine upon the altar of our gods.

G. K. CHESTERTON (1874–1936), British author. *Tremendous Trifles*, "The Secret of a Train" (1909).

2   Any serious attempt to try to do something worthwhile is ritualistic.

DEREK WALCOTT (b. 1930), West Indian poet, playwright. Interview in *Writers at Work* (Eighth Series, ed. by George Plimpton, 1988).

See also Gonzalez-Crussi on CEREMONY.

RIVERS

1   A river seems a magic thing. A magic, moving, living part of the very earth itself—for it is from the soil, both from its depth and from its surface, that a river has its beginning.

> LAURA GILPIN (1891–1979), U.S. photographer. *The Rio Grande*, Introduction (1949).

2 By shallow rivers, to whose falls,
Melodious birds sing madrigals.

> CHRISTOPHER MARLOWE (1564–93), English dramatist, poet. *The Passionate Shepherd to His Love.* These lines also appeared in Shakespeare, *The Merry Wives of Windsor,* sung by Evans in act 3, sc. 1.

3 Sweete Themmes! runne softly, till I end my Song.

> EDMUND SPENSER, English poet (c. 1522–99). *Prothalamion.* The line recurred in T. S. Eliot's *The Waste Land.*

4 I was born upon thy bank, river,
My blood flows in thy stream,
And thou meanderest forever
At the bottom of my dream.

> HENRY DAVID THOREAU (1817–62), U.S. philosopher, author, naturalist. *Journals* (1906), 1842 entry.

5 The face of the water, in time, became a wonderful book—a book that was a dead language to the uneducated passenger, but which told its mind to me without reserve, delivering its most cherished secrets as clearly as if it uttered them with a voice. And it was not a book to be read once and thrown aside, for it had a new story to tell every day.

> MARK TWAIN (1835–1910), U.S. author. *Life on the Mississippi,* ch. 9 (1883), of learning to pilot a steamboat on the Mississippi. Nonetheless, Twain went on to explain, "All the grace, the beauty, the poetry had gone out of the majestic river! . . . All the value any feature had for me now was the amount of usefulness it could furnish toward compassing the safe piloting of a steamboat."

ROCK 'N' ROLL

1 A lot of pop music is about stealing pocket money from children.

> IAN ANDERSON (b. 1947), British rock musician. *Rolling Stone* (New York, 30 Nov. 1989).

2 As I define it, rock & roll is dead. The attitude isn't dead, but the music is no longer vital. It doesn't have the same meaning. The attitude, though, is still very much alive—and it still informs other kinds of music.

> DAVID BYRNE (b. 1952), U.S. rock musician, composer. Quoted in: *Rolling Stone* (New York, Dec. 1990).

3 Rock music should be gross: that's the fun of it. It gets up and drops its trousers.

> BRUCE DICKINSON (b. 1958), British rock guitarist. *Guardian* (London, 10 Jan. 1991).

4 What we do is as American as lynch mobs. America has always been a complex place.

> JERRY GARCIA (b. 1942), U.S. rock musician. *Rolling Stone* (New York, 30 Nov. 1989).

5 There are two kinds of artists left: those who endorse Pepsi and those who simply won't.

> ANNIE LENNOX (b. 1954), British singer. *Guardian* (London, 30 Nov. 1990).

6 Awop-bop-a-loo-mop alop-bam-boom!

> LITTLE RICHARD (b. 1932), U.S. rock'n'roll musician. *Tutti-Frutti* (1955). The song is credited to Little Richard (named Richard Penniman), J. Lubin, and Dorothy La Bostrie.

7 Rock 'n' roll is a combination of good ideas dried up by fads, terrible junk, hideous failings in taste and judgment, gullibility and manipulation, moments of unbelievable clarity and invention, pleasure, fun, vulgarity, excess, novelty and utter enervation.

> GREIL MARCUS (b. 1945), U.S. rock journalist. *Mystery Train,* "Randy Newman" (1976).

8 Rock & roll doesn't necessarily mean a band. It doesn't mean a singer, and it doesn't mean a lyric, really. . . . It's that question of trying to be immortal.

> MALCOLM MCLAREN (b. 1946), British rock impresario. "Punk and History," transcript of discussion, 24 Sept. 1988, New York City (published in *Discourses: Conversations in Postmodern Art and Culture,* ed. by Russell Ferguson, et al., 1990).

9 Music for the neck downwards.

> KEITH RICHARDS (b. 1943), British rock guitarist. Quoted in: Simon Frith, *Sound Effects: Youth, Leisure and the Politics of Rock,* ch. 7 (1979).

10 The most brutal, ugly, desperate, vicious form of expression it has been my misfortune to hear.

> FRANK SINATRA (b. 1915), U.S. singer, actor. Quoted in: Simon Frith, *Sound Effects: Youth, Leisure and the Politics of Rock,* ch. 5 (1979).

11 No change in musical style will survive unless it is accompanied by a change in clothing style. Rock is to dress up to.

> FRANK ZAPPA (b. 1940), U.S. rock musician. *The Real Frank Zappa Book,* ch. 9 (1989; written with Peter Occhiogrosso).

See also Zappa on JOURNALISM AND JOURNALISTS.

ROMANCE

1 The essence of romantic love is that wonderful beginning, after which sadness and impossibility may become the rule.

> ANITA BROOKNER (b. 1938), British novelist, art historian. Rachel, in *A Friend From England,* ch. 10 (1987), referring to Michael Sandberg.

2 Love stories are only fit for the solace of people in the insanity of puberty. No healthy adult human being can really care whether so-and-so does or does not succeed in satisfying his physiological uneasiness by the aid of some particular person or not.

> ALEISTER CROWLEY (1875–1947), British occultist. *The Confessions of Aleister Crowley,* ch. 50 (1929; rev. 1970).

3 Any walk through a park that runs between a double line of mangy trees and passes brazenly by the ladies' toilet is invariably known as "Lover's Lane."

> F. SCOTT FITZGERALD (1896–1940), U.S. author. *The Crack-Up,* "Notebook E" (ed. by Edmund Wilson, 1945).

4 Rather would I have the love songs of romantic ages, rather Don Juan and Madame Venus, rather an elopement by ladder and rope on a moonlight night, followed by the father's curse, mother's moans, and the moral comments of neighbors, than correctness and propriety measured by yardsticks.

EMMA GOLDMAN (1869–1940), U.S. anarchist. *Anarchism and Other Essays,* "The Tragedy of Woman's Emancipation" (1910).

5   Romance, like the rabbit at the dog track, is the elusive, fake, and never attained reward which, for the benefit and amusement of our masters, keeps us running and thinking in safe circles.

BEVERLY JONES (b. 1927), U.S. feminist writer. *The Florida Paper on Women's Liberation,* "The Dynamics of Marriage and Motherhood" (1970).

6   And what's romance? Usually, a nice little tale where you have everything As You Like It, where rain never wets your jacket and gnats never bite your nose and it's always daisy-time.

D. H. LAWRENCE (1885–1930), British author. *Studies in Classic American Literature,* ch. 7 (1924).

7   The concept of romantic love affords a means of emotional manipulation which the male is free to exploit, since love is the only circumstance in which the female is (ideologically) pardoned for sexual activity.

KATE MILLET (b. 1934), U.S. feminist author. *Sexual Politics,* ch. 2, sct. 4 (1970).

8   He must have a truly romantic nature, for he weeps when there is nothing at all to weep about.

OSCAR WILDE (1854–1900), Anglo-Irish playwright, author. The Catherine Wheel, in "The Remarkable Rocket," in *The Happy Prince and Other Tales* (1888).

9   Nothing spoils a romance so much as a sense of humour in the woman.

OSCAR WILDE (1854–1900), Anglo-Irish playwright, author. Lord Illingworth, in *A Woman of No Importance,* act 1.

10   Romance should never begin with sentiment. It should begin with science and end with a settlement.

OSCAR WILDE (1854–1900), Anglo-Irish playwright, author. Mrs. Cheveley, in *An Ideal Husband,* act 3.

See also Wilde on MARRIAGE.

ROMANTICISM

1   To say the word Romanticism is to say modern art—that is, intimacy, spirituality, color, aspiration towards the infinite, expressed by every means available to the arts.

CHARLES BAUDELAIRE (1821–67), French poet. "Salon of 1846," sct. 2 (published in *Curiosités Esthétiques,* 1868; repr. in *The Mirror of Art,* ed. by Jonathan Mayne, 1955). "Romanticism," Baudelaire judged, "is the most recent, the most contemporary expression of beauty."

2   Romanticism is not just a mode; it literally eats into every life. Women will never get rid of just waiting for the right man.

ANITA BROOKNER (b. 1938), British novelist, art historian. Interview in *Women Writers Talk* (ed. by Olga Kenyon, 1989).

3   I'm a romantic—a sentimental person thinks things

will last—a romantic person hopes against hope that they won't.

F. SCOTT FITZGERALD (1896–1940), U.S. author. Amory Blaine, in *This Side of Paradise,* bk. 2, ch. 1 (1920).

See also Connolly on STYLE.

ROME

1   Rome took all the vanity out of me; for after seeing the wonders there, I felt too insignificant to live, and gave up all my foolish hopes in despair.

LOUISA MAY ALCOTT (1832–88), U.S. author. Amy March, in *Little Women,* pt. 2, ch. 16 (1869).

2   Everyone soon or late comes round by Rome.

ROBERT BROWNING (1812–89), English poet. *The Ring and the Book,* bk. 5.

3   Rome, the city of visible history, where the past of a whole hemisphere seems moving in funeral procession with strange ancestral images and trophies gathered from afar.

GEORGE ELIOT (1819–80), English novelist. *Middlemarch,* bk. 2, ch. 20 (1871–72).

4   What is there in Rome for me to see that others have not seen before me? What is there for me to touch that others have not touched? What is there for me to feel, to learn, to hear, to know, that shall thrill me before it pass to others? What can I discover?—Nothing. Nothing whatsoever. One charm of travel dies here.

MARK TWAIN (1835–1910), U.S. author. *The Innocents Abroad,* ch. 26 (1869).

ROYALTY

1   The supreme, the merciless, the destroyer of opposition, the exalted King, the shepherd, the protector of the quarters of the world, the King the word of whose mouth destroys mountains and seas, who by his lordly attack has forced mighty and merciless Kings from the rising of the sun to the setting of the same to acknowledge one supremacy.

ASHURNASIRPAL II (r. 883–59 B.C.), King of Assyria. Cuneiform inscription on alabaster relief from palace at Nimrud (Iraq), now in Bristol City Museum, England.

2   A *family* on the throne is an interesting idea. . . . It brings down the pride of sovereignty to the level of petty life.

WALTER BAGEHOT (1826–77), English economist, critic. *The English Constitution,* ch. 2 (1867).

3   Royalty is a government in which the attention of the nation is concentrated on one person doing interesting actions.

WALTER BAGEHOT (1826–1877), English economist, critic. *The English Constitution,* "The Monarchy" (1867).

4   The best reason why Monarchy is a strong government, is that it is an intelligible government. The mass of mankind understand it, and they hardly anywhere in the world understand any other.

> WALTER BAGEHOT (1826–77), English economist, critic. *The English Constitution*, ch. 2 (1867).

5 The Sovereign has, under a constitutional monarchy such as ours, three rights—the right to be consulted, the right to encourage, the right to warn. And a king of great sense and sagacity would want no others.

> WALTER BAGEHOT (1826–77), English economist, critic. *The English Constitution*, ch. 2 (1867). Bagehot construed the formula, "I do not oppose, it is my duty not to oppose; but observe that I warn," as a notional statement by a British constitutional sovereign.

6 Put not your trust in princes.

> BIBLE, HEBREW. *Psalms* 146:3.

7 All the time I feel I must justify my existence.

> CHARLES, PRINCE OF WALES (b. 1948). Quoted in: *Observer* (London, 2 Jan. 1983).

8 I have nothing against the Queen of England. Even in my heart I never resented her for not being Jackie Kennedy. She is, to my mind, a very gallant lady, victimized by whoever it is who designs the tops of her uniforms.

> LEONARD COHEN (b. 1934), Canadian singer, poet, novelist. *Beautiful Losers*, bk. 2, "A Long Letter from F" (1970).

9 A monarchy is the most expensive of all forms of government, the regal state requiring a costly parade, and he who depends on his own power to rule, must strengthen that power by bribing the active and enterprising whom he cannot intimidate.

> JAMES FENIMORE COOPER (1789–1851), U.S. novelist. *The American Democrat*, "On the Disadvantages of a Monarchy" (1838).

10 Everyone likes flattery; and when you come to Royalty you should lay it on with a trowel.

> BENJAMIN DISRAELI (1804–81), English statesman, author. Remark to critic and poet Matthew Arnold, c. 1880. Quoted in: G. W. E. Russell, *Collections and Recollections*, ch. 23.

11 I cannot be indifferent to the assassination of a member of my profession, We should be obliged to shut up business if we, the Kings, were to consider the assassination of Kings as of no consequence at all.

> EDWARD VII (1841–1910), King of Great Britain and Northern Ireland. Remark, 1903, refusing to recognize the Karageorgevic régime in Serbia after the murder of King Alexander and the extermination of the Obrenovic dynasty. Quoted in: *Anatomy of Britain Today*, pt. 1, ch. 2 (1965).

12 I have found it impossible to carry the heavy burden of responsibility and to discharge my duties as King as I would wish to do without the help and support of the woman I love. . . . I now quit altogether public affairs, and I lay down my burden.

> EDWARD VIII (1894–1972), King of Great Britain and Northern Ireland. Abdication speech, broadcast 11 Dec. 1936.

13 I am your anointed Queen. I will never be by violence constrained to do anything. I thank God I am endued with such qualities that if I were turned out of the

Realm in my petticoat I were able to live in any place in Christendom.

> ELIZABETH I (1533–1603), Queen of England. Speech, Oct. 1566, to Deputation of Lords and Commons.

14 Though God hath raised me high, yet this I count the glory of my crown: that I have reigned with your loves. . . . And though you have had, and may have, many mightier and wiser princes sitting in this seat; yet you never had, nor shall have any that will love you better.

> ELIZABETH I (1533–1603), Queen of England. "The Golden Speech," 30 Nov. 1601, House of Commons.

15 Like all the best families, we have our share of eccentricities, of impetuous and wayward youngsters and of family disagreements.

> ELIZABETH II (b. 1926), Queen of Great Britain and Northern Ireland. Quoted in: *Daily Mail* (London, 19 Oct. 1989).

16 I'm glad we've been bombed. It makes me feel I can look the East End in the face.

> ELIZABETH, THE QUEEN MOTHER (b. 1900), Wife of King George VI of Great Britain and Northern Ireland. Said after the bombing of Buckingham Palace in September 1940. Quoted in: John Wheeler-Bennett, *King George VI*, pt. 3, ch. 6 (1958). The East End—predominantly working-class—bore the brunt of the bombing during the blitz on London in World War II.

17 Picture the prince, such as most of them are today: a man ignorant of the law, well-nigh an enemy to his people's advantage, while intent on his personal convenience, a dedicated voluptary, a hater of learning, freedom and truth, without a thought for the interests of his country, and measuring everything in terms of his own profit and desires.

> DESIDERIUS ERASMUS c. 1466–1536), Dutch humanist. *Praise of Folly*, ch. 55 (1509).

18 In a few years there will be only five kings in the world—the King of England and the four kings in a pack of cards.

> FAROUK I (1920–65), King of Egypt. Remark to Lord Boyd-Orr. Quoted in: *Life* (New York, 10 April 1950).

19 Don't forget your great guns, which are the most respectable arguments of the rights of kings.

> FREDERICK THE GREAT (1712–86), King of Prussia. Letter, 21 April 1759, to his brother Prince Henry.

20 The metaphor of the king as the shepherd of his people goes back to ancient Egypt. Perhaps the use of this particular convention is due to the fact that, being stupid, affectionate, gregarious, and easily stampeded, the societies formed by sheep are most like human ones.

> NORTHROP FRYE (1912–91), Canadian literary critic. *Anatomy of Criticism*, Third Essay, "Theory of Archetypal Meaning" (1957).

21 Who does not know that kings and rulers sprang from men who were ignorant of God, who assumed because of blind greed and intolerable presumption to make themselves masters of other men, their equals, by means of pride, violence, bad faith, murder, and almost every other kind of crime? Surely the devil drove them on.

> POPE GREGORY VII c. 1020–1085). Letter, 15 March 1081, on the right of the pope to excommunicate the German king and

Holy Roman Emperor Henry IV. Gregory excommunicated Henry twice, in 1076 and 1080, and was in turn excommunicated by him.

22   From his childhood onwards this boy will be surrounded by sycophants and flatterers. . . . In due course, following the precedent which has already been set, he will be sent on a tour of the world and probably rumours of a morganatic marriage alliance will follow, and the end of it will be the country will be called upon to pay the bill.

JAMES KEIR HARDIE (1856–1915), First British Labour Party Member of Parliament. Speech, 28 June 1894, to the House of Commons, opposing a motion congratulating Queen Victoria on the birth of the future Edward VIII.

23   The state of monarchy is the supremest thing upon earth: for kings are not only God's Lieutenants upon earth, and sit upon God's throne, but even by God himself they are called Gods.

KING JAMES I OF ENGLAND, JAMES VI OF SCOTLAND (1566–1625). Address to Parliament, 21 March 1609.

24   There is not a single crowned head in Europe whose talents or merit would entitle him to be elected a vestryman by the people of any parish in America.

THOMAS JEFFERSON (1743–1826), U.S. president. Letter, 2 May 1788, to George Washington, from Paris.

25   A king should die on his feet.

LOUIS XVIII (1755–1824), King of France. Alleged remark on his deathbed.

26   What are kings, when regiment is gone,
But perfect shadows in a sunshine day?

CHRISTOPHER MARLOWE (1564–93), English dramatist, poet. Edward, in *Edward II*, act 5, sc. 1.

27   And what, in a mean man, I should call folly,
Is in your majesty remarkable wisdom.

PHILIP MASSINGER (1583–1640), English dramatist. Eubulus, advisor to King Ladislaus of Hungary, in *The Picture*, act 1, sc. 2 (1630).

28   Princes give me sufficiently if they take nothing from me, and do me much good if they do me no hurt; it is all I require of them.

MICHEL DE MONTAIGNE (1533–92), French essayist. *Essays*, bk. 3, ch. 9, "Of Vanity" (1588; tr. by John Florio).

29   We live in what virtually amounts to a museum—which does not happen to a lot of people.

PHILIP, DUKE OF EDINBURGH (b. 1921). Remark, 25 Feb. 1964. Quoted in: Anthony Sampson, *Anatomy of Britain Today*, pt. 1, ch. 2 (1965).

30   There is something behind the throne greater than the King himself.

WILLIAM PITT THE ELDER, LORD CHATHAM (1708–78), English statesman. Speech, 2 March 1770, to House of Lords.

31   Once you touch the trappings of monarchy, like opening an Egyptian tomb, the inside is liable to crumble.

ANTHONY SAMPSON (b. 1926), British journalist, author. *Anatomy of Britain Today*, pt. 1, ch. 2 (1965).

32   A king is a thing men have made for their own sakes, for quietness' sake. Just as in a family one man is appointed to buy the meat.

JOHN SELDEN (1584–1654), English jurist, statesman. *Table Talk*, "King" (1686).

33   Uneasy lies the head that wears a crown.

WILLIAM SHAKESPEARE (1564–1616), English dramatist, poet. King Henry, in *Henry IV, Part 2*, act 3, sc. 1.

34   Kings are not born: they are made by artificial hallucination.

GEORGE BERNARD SHAW (1856–1950), Anglo-Irish playwright, critic. *Man and Superman*, "Maxims for Revolutionists: Royalty" (1903).

35   Vulgarity in a king flatters the majority of the nation.

GEORGE BERNARD SHAW (1856–1950), Anglo-Irish playwright, critic. *Man and Superman*, "Maxims for Revolutionists: Royalty" (1903).

36   Divine right of kings means the divine right of anyone who can get uppermost.

HERBERT SPENCER (1820–1903), English philosopher. *Social Statistics*, pt. 2, ch. 6, sct. 3 (1850).

37   All I say is, kings is kings, and you got to make allowances. Take them all around, they're a mighty ornery lot. It's the way they're raised.

MARK TWAIN (1835–1910), U.S. author. Huck, in *Huckleberry Finn*, ch. 23 (1884).

38   A monarch, when good, is entitled to the consideration which we accord to a pirate who keeps Sunday School between crimes; when bad, he is entitled to none at all.

MARK TWAIN (1835–1910), U.S. author. *Mark Twain's Notebooks and Journals*, vol. 3 (ed. by Frederick Anderson, 1979), Notebook 28 (July 1888–May 1889).

39   I am every day more convinced that *we* women, *if we are* to be *good* women, *feminine* and *amiable* and *domestic*, are *not fitted to reign;* at least it is *contre gré* that they drive themselves to the *work* which it entails.

VICTORIA (1819–1901), Queen of Great Britain and Ireland. Letter, 17 Feb. 1852, to Leopold I, King of the Belgians (published in *Letters of Queen Victoria*, vol. 2, ch. 21, ed. by A. C. Benson and Viscount Esher, 1907).

40   There is no necessity to separate the monarch from the mob; all authority is equally bad.

OSCAR WILDE (1854–1900), Anglo-Irish playwright, author. *The Soul of Man Under Socialism*, in *Fortnightly Review* (London, Feb. 1891; repr. 1895).

41   If your job is to leaven ordinary lives with elevating spectacle, be elevating or be gone.

GEORGE F. WILL (b. 1941), U.S. political columnist. *International Herald Tribune* (Paris, 25 June 1992), of the British royal family.

42   Here lies our Sovereign Lord, the King
Whose word no man relies on:
He never said a foolish thing
Nor ever did a wise one.

JOHN WILMOT, SECOND EARL OF ROCHESTER (1647–80), English poet, courtier. *The King's Epitaph*, written on the door of Charles II's bedchamber. On seeing it, the king is said to have replied, "This is very true: for my words are my own, and my actions are my ministers'.".

See also Tennyson on DEATH AND DYING; Marlowe on GLORY; Jonson on HORSES; Anonymous journalist, Hastings on JOURNALISM AND JOURNALISTS; Marlowe on LEADERSHIP; Elizabeth I on NECESSITY; Bernadotte on REPUBLICANISM; Elizabeth II on TRAINING; Burke, Fox on TYRANNY; QUEEN VICTORIA; Bagehot on WEDDINGS; Elizabeth I on WOMEN AND POLITICS.

RUSSIA AND THE RUSSIANS

1   Moscow, breathing fire like a human volcano with its smouldering lava of passion, ambition and politics, its hurly-burly of meetings and entertainment. . . . Moscow seethes and bubbles and gasps for air. It's always thirsting for something new, the newest events, the latest sensation. Everyone wants to be the first to know. It's the rhythm of life today.

SVETLANA ALLILUYEVA (b. 1925), Russian writer. *Twenty Letters to a Friend,* "Introduction" (1967; first published 1963).

2   Don't you forget what's divine in the Russian soul—and that's resignation.

JOSEPH CONRAD (1857–1924), Polish-born English novelist. Victor Haldin, in *Under Western Eyes,* pt. 1, ch. 1 (1911).

3   I do not believe I am exaggerating in affirming that the empire of Russia is a country whose inhabitants are the most miserable on earth, because they suffer at one and the same time the evils of barbarism and of civilization.

MARQUIS DE CUSTINE (1790–1857), French traveler, author. *Empire of the Czar: A Journey Through Eternal Russia,* ch. 37 (1843; rev. 1989).

4   In Russia, whatever be the appearance of things, violence and arbitrary rule is at the bottom of them all. Tyranny rendered calm by the influence of terror is the only kind of happiness which this government is able to afford its people.

MARQUIS DE CUSTINE (1790–1857), French traveler, author. *Empire of the Czar: A Journey Through Eternal Russia,* ch. 37 (1843; rev. 1989). De Custine went on to say of the Russians, "If they wish to be recognized by the European nations, and treated as equals, they must begin by submitting to hear themselves judged."

5   The so-called new Russian man is characterized mainly by his complete exhaustion. You may find yourself wondering if he has the strength to enjoy his new-found freedom. He is like a long-distance runner who, on reaching the finishing line, is incapable even of raising his hands in a gesture of victory.

RYSZARD KAPUSCINSKI (b. 1932), Polish journalist. *Independent on Sunday* (London, 27 Oct. 1991).

6   Let it be clearly understood that the Russian is a delightful person till he tucks in his shirt. As an Oriental he is charming. It is only when he insists on being treated as the most easterly of western peoples instead of the most westerly of easterns that he becomes a racial anomaly extremely difficult to handle.

RUDYARD KIPLING (1865–1936), British author, poet. *Life's Handicap,* "The Man Who Was" (1891).

7   One question that people always ask at home is never asked here: "What happened to Communism in Russia?" Everybody yawns when a visitor brings it up, because the answer is so obvious to every Russian. The answer is that there never was Communism in Russia; there were only communists.

ARTHUR KOESTLER (1905–83), Hungarian-born British author. *The Trail of the Dinosaur,* pt. 2, "The Shadow of a Tree" (1955; first published 1953).

8   There is no man who desires as passionately as a Russian. If we could imprison a Russian desire beneath a fortress, that fortress would explode.

JOSEPH DE MAISTRE (1753–1821), French diplomat, philosopher. *Four Chapters on Russia,* ch. 1. Quoted in: Isaiah Berlin, *The Crooked Timber of Humanity* (1990).

9   But these Russians are too romantic—too *exaltés*; they give way to a morbid love of martyrdom; they think they can do no good to mankind unless they are uncomfortable.

H. SETON MERRIMAN (1862–1903), English novelist. Steinmetz, in *The Sowers,* ch. 1 (1896).

10   My fellow Americans, I am pleased to tell you today that I've signed legislation which outlaws Russia forever. The bombing begins in five minutes.

RONALD REAGAN (b. 1911), U.S. Republican politician, president. Radio test broadcast, 11 Aug. 1984. Quoted in: *Reagan's Reign of Error,* "Defense and Russia" (ed. by Mark Green and Gail MacColl, 1987).

11   I suddenly realized that the devout Russian people no longer needed priests to pray them into heaven. On earth they were building a kingdom more bright than any heaven had to offer, and for which it was a glory to die.

JOHN REED (1887–1920), U.S. journalist, author. *Ten Days That Shook the World,* ch. 10 (1926), on the mass burial of five hundred soldiers and workers in Red Square, Nov 1917.

12   In Russia, people suffer from the stillness of time.

TATYANA TOLSTAYA (b. 1951), Russian author. *Independent* (London, 31 May 1990).

13   From being a patriotic myth, the Russian people have become an awful reality.

LEON TROTSKY (1879–1940), Russian revolutionary. *The History of the Russian Revolution,* vol. 3, ch. 7, on the chaotic aftermath of the October Revolution, 1917.

14   Nothing is impossible in Russia but reform.

OSCAR WILDE (1854–1900), Anglo-Irish playwright, author. Michael, in *Vera, or The Nihilists* (1880).

See also Thurber on APATHY; Custine on BUREAUCRACY; Attlee on COMMUNISM; Anon on CONSTITUTIONS; Tolstaya on NOSTALGIA; Custine on PATRIOTISM; The RUSSIAN REVOLUTION; The USSR.

THE RUSSIAN REVOLUTION

1   Others loved themselves, money, theories, power: Lenin loved his fellow men. . . . Lenin was God, as Christ was God, because God is Love and Christ and Lenin were all Love!

ISADORA DUNCAN (1878–1927), U.S. dancer. From the first chapter of her memoirs, dictated in Berlin in 1924 but never completed (published in *This Quarter,* Paris, Autumn 1929).

2 That is Lenin. Look at the self-willed, stubborn head. A real Russian peasant's head with a few faintly Asiatic lines. That man will try to overturn mountains. Perhaps he will be crushed by them. But he will never yield.

> ROSA LUXEMBURG (1871–1919), German revolutionary. Remark to Klara Zetkin. Quoted in: Zetkin, *Reminiscences of Lenin* (1929; repr. in *Not By Politics Alone*, ch. 4, ed. by Tamara Deutsch, 1973).

3 Everything established, settled, everything to do with home and order and the common round, has crumbled into dust and been swept away in the general upheaval and reorganization of the whole of society. The whole human way of life has been destroyed and ruined. All that's left is the bare, shivering human soul, stripped to the last shred, the naked force of the human psyche for which nothing has changed because it was always cold and shivering and reaching out to its nearest neighbor, as cold and lonely as itself.

> BORIS PASTERNAK (1890–1960), Russian poet, novelist, translator. Lara, in *Doctor Zhivago*, ch. 13, sct. 13 (1957).

4 In the language, in the slogans posted everywhere, in the only two newspapers published, among the men, we discovered one enormous uniformity of a single way of thinking, imperious, almost despotic, but supreme, terribly true, made flesh and blood at each moment through action. We found not the passionate mobs going forward under new flags to struggles begun anew each day in tragic and fruitful confusions, but a sort of vast administration, an army, a machine in which the most burning energies and the clearest intelligences were coldly integrated and which performed its task inexorably.

> VICTOR SERGE (1890–1947), Russian revolutionary author. *Birth of Our Power*, ch. 35 (1931; tr. 1968).

5 There is no example in history of a revolutionary movement involving such gigantic masses being so bloodless.

> LEON TROTSKY (1879–1940), Russian revolutionary. *The History of the Russian Revolution*, vol. 2, ch. 7 (1933), on the initial stages of the Russian Revolution (which included the storming of Moscow's Winter Palace).

See also Leon Trotsky on RUSSIA AND THE RUSSIANS.

SACRIFICE

1 Sacrifice is nothing other than the production of *sacred* things.

> GEORGES BATAILLE (1897–1962), French novelist, critic. "The Notion of Expenditure," in *La Critique Sociale* (Paris, Jan. 1933; repr. in *Visions of Excess: Selected Writings 1927–1939*, ed. by Allan Stoekl, 1985).

2 He who never sacrificed a present to a future good or a personal to a general one can speak of happiness only as the blind do of colors.

> OLYMPIA BROWN (1835–1900), U.S. minister (first woman ordained in U.S.). Sermon, c. 13 Jan. 1895, Mukwonago, Wis. (published in *Olympia Brown, An Autobiography*, ed. by Gwendolen B. Willis, 1960; repr. in *Annual Journal of the Universalist Historical Society*, vol. 4, 1963).

3 The stern hand of fate has scourged us to an elevation where we can see the great everlasting things which matter for a nation—the great peaks we had forgotten, of Honour, Duty, Patriotism, and clad in glittering white, the great pinnacle of Sacrifice pointing like a rugged finger to Heaven.

> DAVID LLOYD GEORGE (1863–1945), Welsh Liberal politician, prime minister. Speech, 19 Sept. 1914, Queen's Hall, London, shortly after the start of the First World War.

4 There is no moral authority like that of sacrifice.

> NADINE GORDIMER (b. 1923), South African author. "The Essential Gesture," lecture, 12 Oct. 1984, University of Michigan (first published in *The Tanner Lectures on Human Values*, ed. by Sterling M. McMurrin, 1985; repr. in *The Essential Gesture*, ed. by Stephen Clingman, 1988).

5 There's only one effectively redemptive sacrifice, the sacrifice of self-will to make room for the knowledge of God.

> ALDOUS HUXLEY (1894–1963), British author. Bruno Rontini, in *Time Must Have a Stop*, ch. 30 (1944).

6 When looking at any significant work of art, remember that a more significant one probably has had to be sacrificed.

> PAUL KLEE (1879–1940), Swiss artist. *The Diaries of Paul Klee 1898–1918*, no. 583 (1957; tr. 1965), Dec. 1904 entry.

7 A man must be sacrificed now and again
To provide for the next generation of men.

> AMY LOWELL (1874–1925), U.S. poet. *A Critical Fable*, st. 2.

8 The whole earth, perpetually steeped in blood, is nothing but an immense altar on which every living thing must be sacrificed without end, without restraint, without respite until the consummation of the world, the extinction of evil, the death of death.

> JOSEPH DE MAISTRE (1753–1821), French diplomat, philosopher. The Senator, in *Les Soirées de Saint-Pétersbourg*, "Seventh Dialogue" (1821; repr. in *The Works of Joseph de Maistre*, ed. by Jack Lively, 1965).

9 The whole point of a sacrifice is that you give up something you never really wanted in the first place. . . . People are doing it around you all the time. They give up their careers, say—or their beliefs—or sex.

> JOHN OSBORNE (b. 1929), British playwright. Jimmy Porter, in *Look Back in Anger*, act 3, sc. 1.

10 Only he can understand what a farm is, what a country is, who shall have sacrificed part of himself to his farm or country, fought to save it, struggled to make it beautiful. Only then will the love of farm or country fill his heart.

> ANTOINE DE SAINT-EXUPÉRY (1900–1944), French aviator, author. *Flight to Arras*, ch. 23 (1942).

11 Self-sacrifice enables us to sacrifice other people without blushing.

> GEORGE BERNARD SHAW (1856–1950), Anglo-Irish playwright, critic. *Man and Superman*, "Maxims for Revolutionists: Self-Sacrifice" (1903).

12 Greater love hath no man than this, that he lay down his friends for his life.

> JEREMY THORPE (b. 1929), British Liberal politician. Remark,

1962. Quoted in: D. E. Butler and Anthony King, *The General Election of 1964*, ch. 1 (1965), said in response to a Cabinet "reorganization" in which many members of the Cabinet were sacked by Prime Minister Harold Macmillan. The remark is a play on the words of Jesus in *St. Mark* 15:13, "Greater love hath no man than this, that a man lay down his life for his friends."

13 Too long a sacrifice
Can make a stone of the heart.

W. B. YEATS (1865–1939), Irish poet, playwright. *Easter 1916*.

See also Lenin on CAPITALISM; Emerson on MANNERS; Chesterton, Shaw on SELF-DENIAL.

SADOMASOCHISM

1 Sade has a curious ability to render every aspect of sexuality suspect, so that we see how the chaste kiss of the sentimental lover differs only in degree from the vampirish love-bite that draws blood, we understand that a disinterested caress is only quantitatively different from a disinterested flogging.

ANGELA CARTER (1940–92), British author. *The Sadeian Woman*, "Polemical Preface" (1979).

2 Sexual sadism actualizes male identity. Women are tortured, whipped, and chained; women are bound and gagged, branded and burned, cut with knives and wires; women are pissed on and shit on; red-hot needles are driven into breasts, bones are broken, rectums are torn, mouths are ravaged, cunts are savagely bludgeoned by penis after penis, dildo after dildo—and all of this to establish in the male a viable sense of his own worth.

ANDREA DWORKIN (b. 1946), U.S. feminist critic. "The Root Cause," speech, 26 Sept. 1975, Massachusetts Institute of Technology, Cambridge (published in *Our Blood*, ch. 9, 1976).

3 "Must we burn Sade?" asks Mme de Beauvoir. Now that you mention it, why not? The world is littered with literature. And Sade teaches us little about human nature which we couldn't gather from a few minutes of honest introspection.

D. J. ENRIGHT (b. 1920), British poet, critic. *Conspirators and Poets*, "The Marquis and the Madame" (1966; first published 1953).

4 The practice of S/M is the creation of pleasure.... And that's why S/M is really a subculture. It's a process of invention. S/M is the *use* of a strategic relationship as a source of pleasure.

MICHEL FOUCAULT (1926–84), French philosopher. "Sex, Power and the Politics of Identity," interview, Oct. 1982 (first published in *Advocate*, 7 Aug. 1984; repr. in Didier Eribon, *Michel Foucault*, 1989; tr. 1991).

5 Sadism is the necessary outcome of the belief that one sex is passive and suffers sex at the hands of another. If we are to escape any of the hideous effects of this mythology, effects which include war and capital punishment, we must regain the power of the cunt.

GERMAINE GREER (b. 1939), Australian feminist writer. "Lady Love Your Cunt," in *Suck* (London, 1971; repr. in *The Madwoman's Underclothes*, 1986).

6 De Sade is the one completely consistent and thoroughgoing revolutionary of history.

ALDOUS HUXLEY (1894–1963), British author. *Ends and Means*, ch. 14 (1937).

7 The safest and most suitable form of penance seems to be that which causes pain in the flesh but does not penetrate to the bones, that is, which causes suffering but not sickness. So the best way seems to be to scourge oneself with thin cords which hurt superficially, rather than to use some other means which might produce serious internal injury.

ST. IGNATIUS OF LOYOLA (1491–1556), Spanish churchman, founder of the Society of Jesus. *Spiritual Exercises*, "First Week," no. 86 (1548).

8 The debility to which Nature condemned women incontestably proves that her design is for man, who then more than ever enjoys his strength, to exercise it in all the violent forms that suit him best, by means of tortures, if he be so inclined, or worse.

MARQUIS DE SADE (1740–1814), French author. Dolmancé, in *Philosophy in the Bedroom*, "Dialogue the Fifth" (1795).

9 Sadomasochism has always been the furthest reach of the sexual experience: when sex becomes most purely sexual, that is, severed from personhood, from relationships, from love. It should not be surprising that it has become attached to Nazi symbolism in recent years. Never before was the relation of masters and slaves so consciously aestheticized. Sade had to make up his theater of punishment and delight from scratch, improvising the decor and costumes and blasphemous rites. Now there is a master scenario available to everyone. The color is black, the material is leather, the seduction is beauty, the justification is honesty, the aim is ecstasy, the fantasy is death.

SUSAN SONTAG (b. 1933), U.S. essayist. *Under the Sign of Saturn*, "Fascinating Fascism" (1980; first published 1974).

SAINTS

1 Saintliness is also a temptation.

JEAN ANOUILH (1910–87), French playwright. Thomas à Becket, in *Becket*, act 3.

2 It's impossible to represent a saint [in Art]. It becomes boring. Perhaps because he is, like the *Saturday Evening Post* people, in the position of having almost infinitely free will.

W. H. AUDEN (1907–73), Anglo-American poet. *The Table Talk of W. H. Auden*, "November 16, 1946" (comp. by Alan Ansen, ed. by Nicholas Jenkins, 1990).

3 I have fought a good fight, I have finished my course, I have kept the faith.

BIBLE: NEW TESTAMENT. Paul, in *2 Timothy* 4:7.

4 Saint. A dead sinner revised and edited.

AMBROSE BIERCE (1842–1914), U.S. author. *The Devil's Dictionary* (1881–1906).

5 A saint addicted to excessive self-abnegation is a dangerous associate; he may infect you with poverty, and a stiffening of those joints which are needed for advancement—in a word, with more renunciation than you care for—and so you flee the contagion.

> VICTOR HUGO (1802–85), French poet, dramatist, novelist. *Les Misérables,* pt. 1, bk. 1, ch. 12 (1862).

6 God creates out of *nothing,* wonderful, you say: yes, to be sure, but he does what is still more wonderful: he makes saints out of sinners.

> SØREN KIERKEGAARD (1813–55), Danish philosopher. *The Journals of Soren Kierkegaard: A Selection,* no. 209 (ed. and tr. by Alexander Dru, 1938), 1838 entry.

7 People who are born even-tempered, placid and untroubled—secure from violent passions or temptations to evil—those who have never needed to struggle all night with the Angel to emerge lame but victorious at dawn, never become great saints.

> EVA LE GALLIENNE (b. 1899), U.S. actor, producer. *The Mystic in the Theatre: Eleanora Duse,* ch. 1 (1965).

8 Your mock saint who stands in a niche is not a woman if she have not suffered, still less a woman if she have not sinned. Fall at the feet of your idol as you wish, but drag her down to your level after that—the only level she should ever reach, that of your heart.

> BARONESS ORCZY (1865–1947), Hungarian-born British novelist, playwright. Sir Percy Blakeney, in *I Will Repay,* ch. 7 (1906).

9 Saints should always be judged guilty until they are proved innocent.

> GEORGE ORWELL (1903–50), British author. *Shooting an Elephant,* "Reflections on Gandhi" (1950), opening words of the essay. Orwell was deeply skeptical of the desire for sainthood: "It is probable," he wrote, "that some who achieve or aspire to sainthood have never felt much temptation to be human beings."

10 It is easier to make a saint out of a libertine than out of a prig.

> GEORGE SANTAYANA (1863–1952), U.S. philosopher, poet. *The Life of Reason,* "Reason in Religion," ch. 11 (1905–6).

11 What makes saintliness in my view, as distinguished from ordinary goodness, is a certain quality of magnanimity and greatness of soul that brings life within the circle of the heroic.

> HARRIET BEECHER STOWE (1811–96), U.S. novelist, anti-slavery campaigner. "The Cathedral," in *Atlantic Monthly* (Boston, 1846).

12 We must have a real living determination to reach holiness. "I will be a saint" means I will despoil myself of all that is not God; I will strip my heart of all created things; I will live in poverty and detachment; I will renounce my will, my inclinations, my whims and fancies, and make myself a willing slave to the will of God.

> MOTHER TERESA (b. 1910), Albanian-born Roman Catholic missionary. *A Gift for God,* "Willing Slaves to the Will of God" (1975).

13 Our manners have been corrupted by communication with the saints.

> HENRY DAVID THOREAU (1817–62), U.S. philosopher, author, naturalist. *Walden,* "Economy" (1854).

14 Saints are simply men & women who have fulfilled their natural obligation which is to approach God.

> EVELYN WAUGH (1903–66), British novelist. Letter, 26 Aug.

1946, to author Nancy Mitford (published in *The Letters of Evelyn Waugh,* 1980).

15 Every perfect life is a parable invented by God.

> SIMONE WEIL (1909–43), French philosopher, mystic. *New York Notebook* (1942; published in *First and Last Notebooks,* ed. by Richard Rees, 1970).

16 It is well for his peace that the saint goes to his martyrdom. He is spared the sight of the horror of his harvest.

> OSCAR WILDE (1854–1900), Anglo-Irish playwright, author. Gilbert, in *The Critic as Artist,* pt. 1 (1890).

17 The only difference between the saint and the sinner is that every saint has a past, and every sinner has a future.

> OSCAR WILDE (1854–1900), Anglo-Irish playwright, author. Lord Illingworth, in *A Woman of No Importance,* act 3.

See also See also Cowper on The DEVIL.

SALES AND MARKETING

1 In fast-moving, progress-conscious America, the consumer expects to be dizzied by progress. If he could completely understand advertising jargon he would be badly disappointed. The half-intelligibility which we expect, or even hope, to find in the latest product language personally reassures each of us that progress *is* being made: that the pace exceeds our ability to follow.

> DANIEL J. BOORSTIN (b. 1914), U.S. historian. *The Image,* ch. 5 (1961).

2 Bold knaves thrive without one grain of sense,
But good men starve for want of impudence.

> JOHN DRYDEN (1631–1700), English poet, dramatist, critic. *Constantine the Great: Epilogue.*

3 A commodity appears at first sight an extremely obvious, trivial thing. But its analysis brings out that it is a very strange thing, abounding in metaphysical subtleties and theological niceties.

> KARL MARX (1818–83), German political theorist, social philosopher. *Capital,* vol. 1, ch. 1 (1867).

4 Today the tyrant rules not by club or fist, but, disguised as a market researcher, he shepherds his flocks in the ways of utility and comfort.

> MARSHALL MCLUHAN (1911–80), Canadian communications theorist. *The Mechanical Bride,* Preface (1951).

5 When producers want to know what the public wants, they graph it as curves. When they want to tell the public what to get, they say it in curves.

> MARSHALL MCLUHAN (1911–80), Canadian communications theorist. *The Mechanical Bride,* "Eye Appeal" (1951).

6 Nobody dast blame this man. . . . For a salesman, there is no rock bottom to the life. He don't put a bolt to a nut, he don't tell you the law or give you medicine. He's a man way out there in the blue, riding on a smile and a shoeshine. And when they start not smiling back—that's an earthquake. And then you get yourself a couple of spots on your hat, and you're finished. Nobody dast blame this man. A salesman is got to dream, boy. It comes with the territory.

> ARTHUR MILLER (b. 1915), U.S. dramatist. Charley, in *Death of a Salesman,* "Requiem."

SALVATION

1 Judge none blessed before his death.

> APOCRYPHA. *Ecclesiasticus* 11:28.

2 To get a man soundly saved it is not enough to put on him a pair of new breeches, to give him regular work, or even to give him a University education. These things are all outside a man, and if the inside remains unchanged you have wasted your labour. You must in some way or other graft upon the man's nature a new nature, which has in it the element of the Divine.

> WILLIAM BOOTH (1829–1912), English evangelist, founder of the Salvation Army. *In Darkest England, and the Way Out,* pt. 1, ch. 5 (1890).

3 When you have understood that nothing *is,* that things do not even deserve the status of appearances, you no longer need to be saved, you are saved, and miserable forever.

> E. M. CIORAN (b. 1911), Rumanian-born French philosopher. *The New Gods,* "Encounters with Suicide" (1969; tr. 1974).

4 It is the final proof of God's omnipotence that he need not exist in order to save us.

> PETER DE VRIES (b. 1910), U.S. author. The Reverend Andrew Mackerel, in *The Mackerel Plaza,* ch. 1 (1958). "This aphorism," De Vries added, "seemed to his hearers so much better than anything Voltaire had said on the subject that he was given an immediate hike in pay and invited out to more dinners than he could possibly eat."

5 Don't matter how much money you got, there's only two kinds of people: there's saved people and there's lost people.

> BOB DYLAN (b. 1941), U.S. singer, songwriter. On stage, 26 Nov. 1979, in Tempe, Arizona. Quoted in: *Wanted Man,* "Saved: Bob Dylan's Conversion to Christianity" (ed. by John Bauldie, 1990).

6 The salvation of this human world lies nowhere else than in the human heart, in the human power to reflect, in human meekness and human responsibility.

> VáCLAV HAVEL (b. 1936), Czech playwright, president. *International Herald Tribune* (Paris, 21 Feb. 1990).

7 The savior who wants to turn men into angels is as much a hater of human nature as the totalitarian despot who wants to turn them into puppets.

> ERIC HOFFER (1902–83), U.S. philosopher. *Reflections on the Human Condition,* aph. 13 (1973).

8 We do not want our world to perish. But in our quest for knowledge, century by century, we have placed all our trust in a cold, impartial intellect which only brings us nearer to destruction. We have heeded no wisdom offering guidance. Only by learning to love one another can our world be saved. Only love can conquer all.

> DORA RUSSELL (1894–1986), British author, campaigner. *Chal-lenge to the Cold War,* vol. 3, ch. 14 (1985), final words of final volume of her autobiography.

SAN FRANCISCO

1 I'd never set foot in San Francisco. Of all the Sodoms and Gomorrahs in our modern world, it is the worst. There are not 10 righteous (and courageous) men there. It needs another quake, another whiff of fire—and—more than all else—a steady trade wind of grapeshot. . . . That moral penal colony of the world.

> AMBROSE BIERCE (1842–1914), U.S. author. Letter, 25 June 1907.

2 A madhouse of frenzied moneymaking and frenzied pleasure-seeking, with none of the corners chipped off. It is beautifully situated and the air reminds one curiously of Edinburgh.

> ALEISTER CROWLEY (1875–1947), British occultist. *The Confessions of Aleister Crowley,* ch. 25 (1929; rev. 1970), said of San Francisco in 1898. Later, in 1917, Crowley's impressions had changed: "The old charm had vanished completely. It had become a regular fellow. The earthquake had swallowed up romance, and the fire burnt up the soul of the city to ashes. The phoenix had perished and from the cinders had arisen a turkey buzzard." (*Confessions,* ch. 77).

3 Drop down, O fleecy Fog and hide
Her skeptic sneer, and all her pride!

> FRANCIS BRET HARTE (1836–1902), U.S. author, journalist, poet. *San Francisco from the Sea.*

4 San Francisco is a mad city—inhabited for the most part by perfectly insane people whose women are of a remarkable beauty.

> RUDYARD KIPLING (1865–1936), British author, poet. *American Notes* (1891).

5 San Francisco is where gay fantasies come true, and the problem the city presents is whether, after all, we wanted these particular dreams to be fulfilled—or would we have preferred others? Did we know what price these dreams would exact? Did we anticipate the ways in which, vivid and continuous, they would unsuit us for the business of daily life? Or should our notion of daily life itself be transformed?

> EDMUND WHITE (b. 1940), U.S. author. *States of Desire: Travels in Gay America,* ch. 2 (1980).

6 It is an odd thing, but every one who disappears is said to be seen at San Francisco. It must be a delightful city, and possess all the attractions of the next world.

> OSCAR WILDE (1854–1900), Anglo-Irish playwright, author. Lord Henry, in *The Picture of Dorian Gray,* ch. 18 (1891).

SANITY

1 Sanity is the lot of those who are most obtuse, for lucidity destroys one's equilibrium: it is unhealthy to honestly endure the labors of the mind which incessantly contradict what they have just established.

> GEORGES BATAILLE (1897–1962), French novelist, critic. *L'Abbé C,* pt. 2, ch. 17 (1950).

2   Sanity is a madness put to good uses; waking life is a dream controlled.

> GEORGE SANTAYANA (1863–1952), U.S. philosopher, poet. *Interpretations of Poetry and Religion,* "The Elements of Poetry" (1900; repr. in *Little Essays,* ed. by Logan Pearsall Smith, 1920).

SARCASM

1   What I claim is to live to the full the contradiction of my time, which may well make sarcasm the condition of truth.

> ROLAND BARTHES (1915–80), French semiologist. *Mythologies,* Preface.

2   Sarcasm I now see to be, in general, the language of the Devil; for which reason I have long since as good as renounced it.

> THOMAS CARLYLE (1795–1881), Scottish essayist, historian. *Sartor Resartus,* bk. 2, ch. 4 (1833–34).

3   Sarcasm: the last refuge of modest and chaste-souled people when the privacy of their soul is coarsely and intrusively invaded.

> FEODOR DOSTOYEVSKY (1821–81), Russian novelist. *Notes from Underground,* ch. 2, sct. 4 (1864).

SATIRE

1   Satire is tragedy plus time. You give it enough time, the public, the reviewers will allow you to satirize it. Which is rather ridiculous, when you think about it.

> LENNY BRUCE (1925–66), U.S. satirical comedian. *The Essential Lenny Bruce,* "Performing and the Art of Comedy" (ed. by John Cohen, 1967).

2   Fools are my theme, let satire be my song.

> LORD BYRON (1788–1824), English poet. *English Bards and Scotch Reviewers.*

3   The satirist is prevented by repulsion from gaining a better knowledge of the world he is attracted to, yet he is forced by attraction to concern himself with the world that repels him.

> ITALO CALVINO (1923–85), Italian author, critic. "Definitions of Territories: Comedy," in *Il Caffè* (Rome, Feb. 1967; repr. in *The Literature Machine,* 1987).

4   What arouses the indignation of the honest satirist is not, unless the man is a prig, the fact that people in positions of power or influence behave idiotically, or even that they behave wickedly. It is that they conspire successfully to impose upon the public a picture of themselves as so very sagacious, honest and well-intentioned.

> CLAUD COCKBURN (1904–81), British author, journalist. *Cockburn Sums Up,* "The Worst Possible Taste" (1981).

5   By rights, satire is a lonely and introspective occupation, for nobody can describe a fool to the life without much patient self-inspection.

> FRANK MOORE COLBY (1865–1925), U.S. editor, essayist. *The Colby Essays,* vol. 1, "Simple Simon" (1926).

6   I believe no satirist could breathe this air. If another Juvenal or Swift could rise up among us tomorrow, he would be hunted down. If you have any knowledge of our literature, and can give me the name of any man, American born and bred, who has anatomised our follies as a people, and not as this or that party; and who has escaped the foulest and most brutal slander, the most inveterate hatred and intolerant pursuit; it will be a strange name in my ears, believe me.

> CHARLES DICKENS (1812–70), English novelist. Mr. Bevan, in *Martin Chuzzlewit,* ch. 16 (1844).

7   Satirists gain the applause of others through fear, not through love.

> WILLIAM HAZLITT (1778–1830), English essayist. *Characteristics: In the Manner of Rochefoucault's Maxims,* no. 77 (1823; repr. in *The Complete Works Of William Hazlitt,* vol. 9, ed. by P. P. Howe, 1932).

8   It is difficult not to write satire.

> JUVENAL (c. 60–130), Roman satiric poet. *Satires,* Satire 1.

9   Satire must not be a kind of superfluous ill will, but ill will from a higher point of view. Ridiculous man, divine God. Or else, hatred against the bogged-down vileness of average man as against the possible heights that humanity might attain.

> PAUL KLEE (1879–1940), Swiss artist. *The Diaries of Paul Klee 1898–1918,* no. 420 (1957; tr. 1965), 1902 entry.

10   It is said that truth comes from the mouths of fools and children: I wish every good mind which feels an inclination for satire would reflect that the finest satirist always has something of both in him.

> G. C. LICHTENBERG (1742–99), German physicist, philosopher. *Aphorisms,* "Notebook J," aph. 157 (written 1765–99; tr. by R. J. Hollingdale, 1990).

11   Satire is a sort of glass, wherein beholders do generally discover everybody's face but their own; which is the chief reason for that kind of reception it meets in the world, and that so very few are offended with it.

> JONATHAN SWIFT (1667–1745), Anglo-Irish satirist. *The Battle of the Books,* Preface (written 1697; published 1704).

12   The satirist who writes nothing but satire should write but little—or it will seem that his satire springs rather from his own caustic nature than from the sins of the world in which he lives.

> ANTHONY TROLLOPE (1815–82), English novelist. *Autobiography,* ch. 10 (1883). Trollope was writing of William Makepeace Thackeray, on his death (Christmas Day, 1863): "It was perhaps his chief fault as a writer that he could never abstain from that dash of satire which he felt to be demanded by the weaknesses which he saw around him."

13   Out of the unconscious lips of babes and sucklings are we satirized.

> MARK TWAIN (1835–1910), U.S. author. "Which Was the Dream?" an unfinished story (written 1897, published in *Which Was the Dream?* ed. by John S Tuckey, 1967).

14   Laughing at someone else is an excellent way of learning how to laugh at oneself; and questioning what seem to be the absurd beliefs of another group is a good way of recognizing the potential absurdity of many of one's own cherished beliefs.

> GORE VIDAL (b. 1925), U.S. novelist, critic. "Satire in the 1950's," in *Nation* (New York, 26 April 1958; repr. in *Homage to Daniel Shays: Collected Essays 1952–1972,* 1974).

SCANDAL

1 Mistakes, scandals, and failures no longer signal catastrophe. The crucial thing is that they be made credible, and that the public be made aware of the efforts being expended in that direction. The "marketing" immunity of governments is similar to that of the major brands of washing powder.

JEAN BAUDRILLARD (b. 1929), French semiologist. *America*, "The End of U.S. Power?" (1986; tr. 1988).

2 There are persons who, when they cease to shock us, cease to interest us.

F. H. BRADLEY (1846–1924), English philosopher. *Aphorisms*, no. 20 (1930).

3 An event has happened, upon which it is difficult to speak, and impossible to be silent.

EDMUND BURKE (1729–97), Irish philosopher, statesman. Speech, 5 May 1789, Westminster Hall, London, at the impeachment of Warren Hastings.

4 Scandal is an importunate wasp, against which we must make no movement unless we are quite sure that we can kill it; otherwise it will return to the attack more furious than ever.

SÉBASTIEN-ROCH NICOLAS DE CHAMFORT (1741–94), French writer, wit. *Maxims and Considerations*, vol. 2, no. 302 (1796; tr. 1926).

5 In the case of scandal, as in that of robbery, the receiver is always thought as bad as the thief.

LORD CHESTERFIELD (1694–1773), English statesman, man of letters. Letter, 19 Oct. 1748 (first published 1774; repr. in *The Letters of the Earl of Chesterfield to His Son*, vol. 1, no. 166, ed. by Charles Strachey, 1901).

6 I have Dalinian thought: the one thing the world will never have enough of is the outrageous.

SALVADOR DALI (1904–89), Spanish painter. *Diary of a Genius* (1966), entry for 30 Aug. 1953.

7 Scandal begins when the police put a stop to it.

KARL KRAUS (1874–1936), Austrian satirist. *Sprüche und Widersprüche*, ch. 2 (1901; tr. in *Half-Truths and One-And-A Half-Truths: Selected Aphorisms*, "Lord, Forgive Them," ed. by Harry Zohn, 1976).

8 History is made in the class struggle and not in bed.

ALEX MITCHELL, British left-wing journalist. Quoted in: *Sunday Times* (London, 29 Dec. 1985), following deposition of Gerry Healey, leader of the Workers' Revolutionary Party, in the wake of a sex scandal.

9 It is the public scandal that offends; to sin in secret is no sin at all.

MOLIÉRE (1622–73), French dramatist. Tartuffe, in *Le Tartuffe*, act 4, sc. 5.

10 Scandal is merely the compassionate allowance which the gay make to the humdrum. Think how many blameless lives are brightened by the blazing indiscretions of other people.

SAKI [H. H. MUNRO] (1870–1916), Scottish author. Reginald, in *Reginald*, "Reginald at the Carlton" (1904).

11 Nor do they trust their tongue alone,
But speak a language of their own;
Can read a nod, a shrug, a look,
Far better than a printed book;
Convey a libel in a frown,
And wink a reputation down.

JONATHAN SWIFT (1667–1745), Anglo-Irish satirist. *The Journal of a Modern Lady*.

12 Certain it is that scandal is good brisk talk, whereas praise of one's neighbour is by no means lively hearing. An acquaintance grilled, scored, devilled, and served with mustard and cayenne pepper excites the appetite; whereas a slice of cold friend with currant jelly is but a sickly, unrelishing meat.

WILLIAM MAKEPEACE THACKERAY (1811–63), English author. *The Roundabout Papers*, "On a Hundred Years Hence" (1863).

13 There are no good girls gone wrong, just bad girls found out.

MAE WEST (1892–1980), U.S. screen actor. *On Sex, Health and E.S.P.*, "Last Word" (1975).

14 Gossip is charming! History is merely gossip. But scandal is gossip made tedious by morality.

OSCAR WILDE (1854–1900), Anglo-Irish playwright, author. Cecil Graham, in *Lady Windermere's Fan*, act 3.

15 One should never make one's *debut* with a scandal. One should reserve that to give an interest to one's old age.

OSCAR WILDE (1854–1900), Anglo-Irish playwright, author. Lord Henry, in the *The Picture of Dorian Gray*, ch. 8 (1891).

See also GOSSIP; SLANDER; Fielding on TEA.

SCAPEGOATS

1 The savages set up gods to which they pray, and which they punish if one of their prayers is not answered . . . . That is what is happening at this moment. . . . Yesterday Kerensky; today Lenin and Trotsky; another tomorrow.

VICTOR MIKHAILOVICH CHERNOV (1873–1972), Russian socialist revolutionary. Speech, 28 Nov. 1917, Peasants' Congress, Petrograd. Quoted in: John Reed, *Ten Days that Shook the World*, ch. 12 (1926).

2 As some day it may happen that a victim must be
    found,
I've got a little list—I've got a little list
Of society offenders who might well be under
    ground,
And who never would be missed—who never
    would be missed!
There's the pestilential nuisances who write for
    autographs—
All people who have flabby hands and irritating
    laughs—
All children who are up in dates, and floor you
    with 'em flat—
All persons who in shaking hands, shake hands
    with you like *that*—
And all third persons who on spoiling *tête-à-têtes*
    insist—

They'd none of 'em be missed—they'd none of
'em be missed

W. S. GILBERT (1836–1911), English librettist. Ko-Ko, in *The
Mikado*, act 1.

3 Authoritarian political ideologies have a vested
interest in promoting fear, a sense of the imminence of
takeover by aliens—and real diseases are useful material.

SUSAN SONTAG (b. 1933), U.S. essayist. *AIDS and Its
Metaphors*, ch. 6 (1989).

SCHOLARS AND SCHOLARSHIP

1 The ceaseless, senseless demand for original scholarship in a number of fields, where only erudition is now
possible, has led either to sheer irrelevancy, the famous
knowing of more and more about less and less, or to the
development of a pseudo-scholarship which actually
destroys its object.

HANNAH ARENDT (1906–75), German-born U.S. political
philosopher. *Crises of the Republic*, "On Violence" (1972).

2 In the same way that we need statesmen to spare us
the abjection of exercising power, we need scholars to
spare us the abjection of learning.

JEAN BAUDRILLARD (b. 1929), French semiologist. *Cool Memories*, ch. 5 (1987; tr. 1990).

3 Of making many books there is no end; and much
study is a weariness of the flesh.

BIBLE, HEBREW. *Ecclesiastes* 12:12.

4 Erudition. Dust shaken out of a book into an empty
skull.

AMBROSE BIERCE (1842–1914), U.S. author. *The Devil's Dictionary* (1881–1906).

5 The professors laugh at themselves, they laugh at
life; they long ago abjured the bitch-goddess Success,
and the best of them will fight for his scholastic ideals
with a courage and persistence that would shame a soldier. The professor is not afraid of words like *truth*; in
fact he is not afraid of words at all.

CATHERINE DRINKER BOWEN (1897–1973), U.S. author.
Adventures of a Biographer, ch. 5 (1946).

6 By the worldly standards of public life, all scholars
in their work are of course oddly virtuous. They do not
make wild claims, they do not cheat, they do not try to
persuade at any cost, they appeal neither to prejudice nor
to authority, they are often frank about their ignorance,
their disputes are fairly decorous, they do not confuse
what is being argued with race, politics, sex or age, they
listen patiently to the young and to the old who both
know everything. These are the general virtues of scholarship, and they are peculiarly the virtues of science.

JACOB BRONOWSKI (1908–74), British scientist, author. "The
Sense of Human Dignity," lecture, 19 March 1953, the Massa-
chusetts Institute of Technology (published in *Science and
Human Values*, pt. 3, sct. 4, 1961).

7 And let a scholar all earth's volumes carry,

He will be but a walking dictionary:
A mere articulate clock.

GEORGE CHAPMAN (1559–1634), English dramatist, translator.
The Tears of Peace.

8 I am an old scholar, better-looking now than when
I was young. That's what sitting on your ass does to your
face.

LEONARD COHEN (b. 1934), Canadian singer, poet, novelist.
Beautiful Losers, bk. 1, "The History of Them All" (1970).

9 The office of the scholar is to cheer, to raise, and to
guide men by showing them facts amidst appearances.
He plies the slow, unhonored, and unpaid task of observation. . . . He is the world's eye.

RALPH WALDO EMERSON (1803–82), U.S. essayist, poet,
philosopher. "The American Scholar," lecture, 31 Aug. 1837, to
Phi Beta Kappa Society, Harvard University (published in *Nature,
Addresses and Lectures*, 1849).

10 I cannot forgive a scholar his homeless despondency.

RALPH WALDO EMERSON (1803–82), U.S. essayist, poet,
philosopher. *Lectures and Biographical Sketches*, "The Man of
Letters" (1883).

11 People who use their erudition to write for a learned
minority . . . don't seem to me favored by fortune but
rather to be pitied for their continuous self-torture. They
add, change, remove, lay aside, take up, rephrase, show
to their friends, keep for nine years and are never satisfied. And their futile reward, a word of praise from a
handful of people, they win at such a cost—so many late
nights, such loss of sleep, sweetest of all things, and so
much sweat and anguish . . . their health deteriorates,
their looks are destroyed, they suffer partial or total
blindness, poverty, ill-will, denial of pleasure, premature
old age and early death.

DESIDERIUS ERASMUS (c. 1466–1536), Dutch humanist. *Praise
of Folly*, ch. 50 (1509).

12 He has the common feeling of his profession. He
enjoys a statement twice as much if it appears in fine
print, and anything that turns up in a footnote . . . takes on
the character of divine revelation.

MARGARET HALSEY (b. 1910), U.S. author. *With Malice
Toward Some*, pt. 2, "June 26" (1938), said of her husband.

13 The learner always begins by finding fault, but the
scholar sees the positive merit in everything.

GEORG HEGEL (1770–1831), German philosopher. *The Philosophy of Right*, "The State," Addition 160 (1821; tr. 1942).

14 The world's great men have not commonly been
great scholars, nor its great scholars great men.

OLIVER WENDELL HOLMES, SR. (1809–94), U.S. writer, physician. *The Autocrat of the Breakfast-Table*, ch. 6 (1858).

15 I am not able to instruct you. I can only tell that I
have chosen wrong. I have passed my time in study without experience; in the attainment of sciences which can,
for the most part, be but remotely useful to mankind. I
have purchased knowledge at the expense of all the common comforts of life: I have missed the endearing elegance of female friendship, and the happy commerce of
domestic tenderness.

SAMUEL JOHNSON (1709–84), English author, lexicographer.
The astronomer, in *The History of Rasselas*, ch. 46 (1759).

16 There mark what ills the scholar's life assail,
Toil, envy, want, the patron, and the gaol.

> SAMUEL JOHNSON (1709–84), English author, lexicographer. *The Vanity of Human Wishes*. In his *Life of Samuel Johnson* (1791), James Boswell noted that the second line of Johnson's couplet had read, "Toil, envy, want, the *garret*, and the gaol," but that Johnson had changed it "after experiencing the uneasiness which Lord Chesterfield's fallacious patronage made him feel."

For further views of Chesterfield and patrons in general, see Johnson on PATRONAGE.

17 One cannot demand of a scholar that he show himself a scholar everywhere in society, but the whole tenor of his behavior must none the less betray the thinker, he must always be instructive, his way of judging a thing must even in the smallest matters be such that people can see what it will amount to when, quietly and self-collected, he puts this power to scholarly use.

> G. C. LICHTENBERG (1742–99), German physicist, philosopher. *Aphorisms*, "Notebook J," aph. 85 (written 1765–99; tr. by R. J. Hollingdale, 1990).

18 People often become scholars for the same reason they become soldiers: simply because they are unfit for any other station. Their right hand has to earn them a livelihood; one might say they lie down like bears in winter and seek sustenance from their paws.

> G. C. LICHTENBERG (1742–99), German physicist, philosopher. *Aphorisms*, "Notebook B," aph. 41 (written 1765–99; tr. by R. J. Hollingdale, 1990).

19 A reading machine, always wound up and going,
He mastered whatever was not worth the knowing.

> JAMES RUSSELL LOWELL (1819–91), U.S. poet, editor. *A Fable for Critics*.

20 He was a rake among scholars, and a scholar among rakes.

> THOMAS BABINGTON MACAULAY (1800–1859), English historian. Aiken, *Life and Writings of Addison*, in *Edinburgh Review* (July 1843; repr. in *Critical and Historical Essays*, 1843), referring to essayist and dramatist Sir Richard Steele.

21 Gloom and solemnity are entirely out of place in even the most rigorous study of an art originally intended to make glad the heart of man.

> EZRA POUND (1885–1972), U.S. poet, critic. *ABC of Reading*, Prefatory "Warning" (1934).

22 I'm a good scholar when it comes to reading but a blotting kind of writer when you give me a pen.

> J. M. SYNGE (1871–1909), Irish poet, dramatist. From "Notebook 16." Quoted in: *The Collected Works of J. M. Synge*, vol. 1, Introduction (1962).

23 The success of great scholars and thinkers is commonly a courtier-like success, not kingly, not manly.

> HENRY DAVID THOREAU (1817–62), U.S. philosopher, author, naturalist. *Walden*, "Economy" (1854).

SCHOOL

1 I was allowed to ring the bell for five minutes until everyone was in assembly. It was the beginning of power.

> JEFFREY ARCHER (b. 1940), British Conservative politician, nov-

elist. *Daily Telegraph* (London, 16 March 1988), said of his school days.

2 A school is not a factory. Its raison d'être is to provide opportunity for experience.

> J. L. CARR (b. 1912), British novelist. *The Harpole Report*, ch. 6 (1972).

3 It is always safe to learn, even from our enemies; seldom safe to venture to instruct, even our friends.

> C. C. COLTON (1780–1832), English author, clergyman. *Lacon*, vol. 1, no. 286 (1820).

4 I was asked to memorise what I did not understand; and, my memory being so good, it refused to be insulted in that manner.

> ALEISTER CROWLEY (1875–1947), British occultist. *The Confessions of Aleister Crowley*, ch. 5 (1929; rev.1970), of geometry lessons.

5 In the schoolroom her quick mind had taken readily that strong starch of unexplained rules and disconnected facts which saves ignorance from any painful sense of limpness.

> GEORGE ELIOT (1819–80), English novelist, editor. *Daniel Deronda*, bk. 1, ch. 4 (1876), referring to Gwendolen Harleth.

6 School divides life into two segments, which are increasingly of comparable length. As much as anything else, schooling implies custodial care for persons who are declared undesirable elsewhere by the simple fact that a school has been built to serve them.

> IVAN ILLICH (b. 1926), Austrian-born U.S. theologian, author. *Celebration of Awareness*, ch. 8 (1969).

7 School-days, I believe, are the unhappiest in the whole span of human existence. They are full of dull, unintelligible tasks, new and unpleasant ordinances, brutal violations of common sense amd common decency. It doesn't take a reasonably bright boy long to discover that most of what is rammed into him is nonsense, and that no one really cares very much whether he learns it or not.

> H. L. MENCKEN (1880–1956), U.S. journalist. "Travail," in *Baltimore Evening Sun* (8 Oct. 1928; repr. in *A Mencken Chrestomathy*, pt. 17, 1949).

8 The first idea that the child must acquire, in order to be actively disciplined, is that of the difference between *good* and *evil*; and the task of the educator lies in seeing that the child does not confound *good* with *immobility*, and *evil* with *activity*.

> MARIA MONTESSORI (1870–1952), Italian educationist. *The Montessori Method*, ch. 5 (1912).

9 My plan of instruction is extremely simple and limited. They learn, on week-days, such coarse works as may fit them for servants. I allow of no writing for the poor. My object is not to make fanatics, but to train up the lower classes in habits of industry and piety.

> HANNAH MORE (1745–1833), English writer, reformer, philanthropist. Letter, 1801, to the Bishop of Bath and Wells (published in *The Letters of Hannah More*, 1925).

10 No one can look back on his schooldays and say with truth that they were altogether unhappy.

> GEORGE ORWELL (1903–50), British author. "Such, Such were the Joys" (1947; repr. in *The Collected Essays, Journalism and*

Letters of George Orwell, ed. by Sonia Orwell and Ian Angus, 1968).

11 No trace of slavery ought to mix with the studies of the freeborn man. . . . No study, pursued under compulsion, remains rooted in the memory.

> PLATO (c. 427–347 B.C.), Greek philosopher. Socrates, in *The Republic*, bk. 7, sct. 536

12 My dear dear Mother,
If you don't let me come home I die—I am all over ink,
and my fine clothes have been spoilt—I have been
  tost in a blanket,
and seen a ghost.
I remain, my dear dear Mother,
Your dutiful and most unhappy son,
Freddy.
P.S. Remember me to my Father.

> Frederick Reynolds, schoolboy letter, on his second day of school. (written 1775; published in Westminster School's magazine, The Elizabethan, (London, Feb. 1983).

13 Thou hast most traitorously corrupted the youth of the realm in erecting a grammar school.

> WILLIAM SHAKESPEARE (1564–1616), English dramatist, poet. Jack Cade, in *King Henry VI, pt. 2*, act 4, sc. 7.

14 The whining schoolboy, with his satchel
And shining morning face, creeping like snail
Unwillingly to school.

> WILLIAM SHAKESPEARE (1564–1616), English dramatist, poet. Jaques, in *As You Like It*, act 2, sc. 7, describing the second age of man.

15 Art and religion first; then philosophy; lastly science. That is the order of the great subjects of life, that's their order of importance.

> MURIEL SPARK (b. 1918), British novelist. Miss Brodie, in *The Prime of Miss Jean Brodie*, ch. 2 (1961).

16 I owe everything to a system that made me learn by heart till I wept. As a result I have thousands of lines of poetry by heart. I owe everything to this.

> GEORGE STEINER (b. 1929), French-born U.S. critic, novelist. *Guardian* (London, 26 March 1992).

17 In the first place God made idiots. This was for practice. Then He made School Boards.

> MARK TWAIN (1835–1910), U.S. author. *Following the Equator*, ch. 61, "Pudd'nhead Wilson's New Calendar" (1897).

18 The Founding Fathers in their wisdom decided that children were an unnatural strain on parents. So they provided jails called schools, equipped with tortures called an education. School is where you go between when your parents can't take you and industry can't take you.

> JOHN UPDIKE (b. 1932), U.S. author, critic. George Caldwell, in *The Centaur*, ch. 4 (1963).

19 You send a boy to school in order to make friends—the right sort.

> VIRGINIA WOOLF (1882–1941), British novelist. *The Diary of Virginia Woolf*, vol. 2 (ed. by Anne O. Bell, 1978), entry for 16 Nov. 1921. Woolf was here quoting the reaction of Maurice Baring and his wife to Lady Cromer sending her son to Winchester, which was not considered elite enough.

See also EDUCATION; Walpole on POWER; TEACHERS; UNIVERSITIES AND COLLEGES.

SCHOOL, PRIVATE

1 What we must look for here is, 1st, religious and moral principles; 2ndly, gentlemanly conduct; 3rdly, intellectual ability.

> THOMAS ARNOLD (1795–1842), English educator, scholar. Address to Rugby School. Quoted in: *The Life and Correspondence of Thomas Arnold, D.D.*, vol. 1, ch. 3 (1845).

2 Were I to deduce any system from my feelings on leaving Eton, it might be called *The Theory of Permanent Adolescence*. It is the theory that the experiences undergone by boys at the great public schools, their glories and disappointments, are so intense as to dominate their lives and to arrest their development. From these it results that the greater part of the ruling class remains adolescent, school-minded, self-conscious, cowardly, sentimental, and in the last analysis homosexual.

> CYRIL CONNOLLY (1903–74), British critic. *Enemies of Promise*, pt. 3, ch. 24 (1938).

3 Minerva House . . . was "a finishing establishment for young ladies," where some twenty girls of the ages from thirteen to nineteen inclusive, acquired a smattering of everything and a knowledge of nothing.

> CHARLES DICKENS (1812–70), English novelist. *Sketches by Boz*, "Tales," ch. 3, "Sentiment" (1833–35).

4 I have found it; I have discovered the cause of all the misfortunes which befell him. A public school, Joseph, was the cause of all the calamaties which he afterwards suffered. Public schools are the nurseries of all vice and immorality.

> HENRY FIELDING (1707–54), English novelist, dramatist. Abraham Adams, in *Joseph Andrews*, bk. 3, ch. 5 (1742), speaking of his host, Wilson.

5 Probably the battle of Waterloo *was* won on the playing-fields of Eton, but the opening battles of all subsequent wars have been lost there.

> GEORGE ORWELL (1903–50), British author. *The Lion and the Unicorn*, pt. 1, "England Your England" (1941).

6 Of all cursed places under the sun, where the hungriest soul can hardly pick up a few grains of knowledge, a girls' boarding-school is the worst. They are called finishing schools, and the name tells accurately what they are. They finish everything but imbecility and weakness, and that they cultivate. They are nicely adapted machines for experimenting on the question, "Into how little space a human being can be crushed?" I have seen some souls so compressed that they would have fitted into a small thimble, and found room to move there—wide room. A woman who has been for many years at one of those places carries the mark of the beast on her till she dies.

> OLIVE SCHREINER (1855–1920), South African writer, feminist. Lyndall, in *The Story of an African Farm*, pt. 2, ch. 4 (1883).

7 That's the public-school system all over. They may kick you out, but they never let you down.

> EVELYN WAUGH (1903–66), British novelist. Captain Grimes, in *Decline and Fall*, pt. 1, ch. 3 (1928). Paul Pennyfeather, to whom these words are addressed, had been given a letter of recommendation by his housemaster after being expelled from school.

See also Waugh on PRISON.

SCIENCE

1 Rather than have it the principal thing in my son's mind, I would gladly have him think that the sun went round the earth, and that the stars were so many spangles set in the bright blue firmament.

THOMAS ARNOLD (1795–1842), English educator, scholar. Letter, 9 May 1836 (published in *The Life and Correspondence of Thomas Arnold, D.D.*, vol. 2, 1845), on the teaching of Physical Science. Arnold welcomed that his children be well versed in science only if "in due subordination to the fulness and freshness of their knowledge on moral subjects"—an ideal he could not believe in.

2 Science knows only one commandment—contribute to science.

BERTOLT BRECHT (1898–1956), German dramatist, poet. Andrea, in *The Life of Galileo*, sc. 14 (1938–39; tr. by Howard Brenton 1980).

3 Science has nothing to be ashamed of even in the ruins of Nagasaki. The shame is theirs who appeal to other values than the human imaginative values which science has evolved.

JACOB BRONOWSKI (1908–74), British scientist, author. "The Sense of Human Dignity," lecture, 19 March 1953, Massachusetts Institute of Technology (published in *Science and Human Values*, pt. 3, sct. 11, 1961).

4 That is the essence of science: ask an impertinent question, and you are on the way to a pertinent answer.

JACOB BRONOWSKI (1908–74), British scientist, author. *The Ascent of Man*, ch. 4 (1973).

5 The more we learn of science, the more we see that its wonderful mysteries are all explained by a few simple laws so connected together and so dependent upon each other, that we see the same mind animating them all.

OLYMPIA BROWN (1835–1900), U.S. minister (first woman ordained in U.S.). Sermon, c. 13 Jan. 1895, Mukwonago, Wis. (published in *Olympia Brown, An Autobiography*, ed. by Gwendolen B. Willis, 1960; repr. in *Annual Journal of the Universalist Historical Society*, vol. 4, 1963).

6 Science has a simple faith, which transcends utility. Nearly all men of science, all men of learning for that matter, and men of simple ways too, have it in some form and in some degree. It is the faith that it is the privilege of man to learn to understand, and that this is his mission. If we abandon that mission under stress we shall abandon it forever, for stress will not cease. Knowledge for the sake of understanding, not merely to prevail, that is the essence of our being. None can define its limits, or set its ultimate boundaries.

VANNEVAR BUSH (1890–1974), U.S. electrical engineer, physicist. *Science Is Not Enough*, "The Search for Understanding" (1967). Vannevar Bush was a zealous believer in the "missionary" function of science: during World War II, he led the U.S. Office of Scientific Research and Development, directing such programs as the development of the first atomic bomb.

7 Science, after all, is only an expression for our ignorance of our own ignorance.

SAMUEL BUTLER (1835–1902), English author. *Samuel Butler's Notebooks* (1951, p. 233).

8 O Star-eyed Science! hast thou wandered there,
To waft us home the message of despair?

THOMAS CAMPBELL (1777–1844), Scottish poet. *Pleasures of Hope*, pt. 2.

9 Science in the modern world has many uses; its chief use, however, is to provide long words to cover the errors of the rich.

G. K. CHESTERTON (1874–1936), British author. *Heretics*, "Celts and Celtophiles" (1905).

10 The latest refinements of science are linked with the cruelties of the Stone Age.

SIR WINSTON CHURCHILL (1874–1965), British statesman, writer. Speech, 26 March 1942, London, on the effects of war.

11 "Faith" is a fine invention
When Gentleman can *see*—
But *Microscopes* are prudent
In an Emergency

EMILY DICKINSON (1830–86), U.S. poet. *The Complete Poems*, no. 185 (1955).

12 Do you see this egg? With this you can topple every theological theory, every church or temple in the world.

DENIS DIDEROT (1713–84), French philosopher. *D'Alembert's Dream*, "Conversation between d'Alembert and Diderot" (written 1769; published 1830; repr. in *Selected Writings*, ed. by Lester G. Crocker, 1966).

13 The pursuit of science leads only to the insoluble.

BENJAMIN DISRAELI (1804–81), English statesman, author. Cardinal Grandison, in *Lothair*, ch. 17 (1870).

14 Let me arrest thy thoughts; wonder with me,
Why plowing, building, ruling and the rest,
Or most of those arts, whence our lives are blest,
By cursed *Cain's* race invented be,
And blest *Seth* vexed us with Astronomie.

JOHN DONNE (c. 1572–1631), English divine, metaphysical poet. *The Progress of the Soul*, st. 52.

15 Thus will the fondest dream of Phallic science be realized: a pristine new planet populated entirely by little boy clones of great scientific entrepeneurs . . . free to smash atoms, accelerate particles, or, if they are so moved, build pyramids—without any social relevance or human responsibility at all.

BARBARA EHRENREICH (b. 1941), U.S. author, columnist. *The Worst Years of Our Lives*, "Phallic Science" (1991; first published 1988).

16 The whole of science is nothing more than a refinement of everyday thinking.

ALBERT EINSTEIN (1879–1955), German-born U.S. theoretical physicist. *Out of My Later Years*, ch. 12 (1950).

17 What terrible questions we are learning to ask! The former men believed in magic, by which temples, cities, and men were swallowed up, and all trace of them gone. We are coming on the secret of a magic which sweeps out of men's minds all vestige of theism and beliefs which they and their fathers held and were framed upon.

RALPH WALDO EMERSON (1803–82), U.S. essayist, poet, philosopher. *The Conduct of Life*, "Illusions" (1860).

18 Furnished as all Europe now is with Academies of Science, with nice instruments and the spirit of experiment, the progress of human knowledge will be rapid and discoveries made of which we have at present no conception. I begin to be almost sorry I was born so soon, since I cannot have the happiness of knowing what will be known a hundred years hence.

> BENJAMIN FRANKLIN (1706–90), U.S. statesman, writer. Letter, 27 July 1783, to naturalist Sir Joseph Banks, President of the Royal Society (published in *Complete Works*, vol. 8, ed. by John Bigelow, 1887–88).

19 The pace of science forces the pace of technique. Theoretical physics forces atomic energy on us; the successful production of the fission bomb forces upon us the manufacture of the hydrogen bomb. *We* do not choose our problems, we do not choose our products; we are pushed, we are forced—by what? By a system which has no purpose and goal transcending it, and which makes man its appendix.

> ERICH FROMM (1900–1980), U.S. psychologist. *The Sane Society*, ch. 5, "Nineteenth-Century Capitalism" (1955).

20 The real accomplishment of modern science and technology consists in taking ordinary men, informing them narrowly and deeply and then, through appropriate organization, arranging to have their knowledge combined with that of other specialized but equally ordinary men. This dispenses with the need for genius. The resulting performance, though less inspiring, is far more predictable.

> JOHN KENNETH GALBRAITH (b. 1908), U.S. economist. *The New Industrial State*, ch. 6 (1967).

21 Science is analytical, descriptive, informative. Man does not live by bread alone, but by science he attempts to do so. Hence the deadliness of all that is purely scientific.

> ERIC GILL (1882–1940), British sculptor, engraver, writer and typographer. *Essays*, "Art" (1948).

22 Science is the only truth and it is the great lie. It knows nothing, and people think it knows everything. It is misrepresented. People think that science is electricity, automobilism, and dirigible balloons. It is something very different. It is life devouring itself. It is the sensibility transformed into intelligence. It is the need to know stifling the need to live. It is the genius of knowledge vivisecting the vital genius.

> RÉMY DE GOURMONT (1858–1915), French critic, novelist. "Art and Science," in *Promenades Philosophiques* (1905–9; repr. in *Selected Writings*, ed./tr. by Glen S. Burne, 1966).

23 Since we are assured that the all-wise Creator has observed the most exact proportions of number, weight and measure in the make of all things, the most likely way therefore to get any insight into the nature of those parts of the Creation which come within our observation must in all reason be to number, weigh and measure.

> STEPHEN HALES (1677–1761), English scientist. *Vegetable Staticks*, Introduction (1727). The work followed his own precepts of scrupulous scholarship, containing exact details of the weighing, measuring and recording he carried out in his experiments on plants.

24 Science, which cuts its way through the muddy pond of daily life without mingling with it, casts its wealth to right and left, but the puny boatmen do not know how to fish for it.

> ALEXANDER HERZEN (1812–70), Russian journalist, political

thinker. *My Past and Thoughts*, vol. 3, pt. 8, "Miscellaneous Pieces: Swiss Views" (1921; tr. by Constance Garnett, 1924–27).

25 Science is the knowledge of consequences, and dependence of one fact upon another.

> THOMAS HOBBES (1588–1679), English philosopher. *Leviathan*, pt. 1, ch. 5 (1651).

26 To overturn orthodoxy is no easier in science than in philosophy, religion, economics, or any of the other disciplines through which we try to comprehend the world and the society in which we live.

> RUTH HUBBARD (b. 1924), U.S. biologist. "Have Only Men Evolved?" in *Women Look at Biology Looking At Women* (ed. by Ruth Hubbard, Mary Sue Henifin and Barbara Fried, 1979).

27 Science has "explained" nothing; the more we know the more fantastic the world becomes and the profounder the surrounding darkness.

> ALDOUS HUXLEY (1894–1963), British author. *Along the Road*, pt. 2, "Views of Holland" (1925).

28 Man lives for science as well as bread.

> WILLIAM JAMES (1842–1910), U.S. psychologist, philosopher. *Vivisection*, (1875; repr. in "The Works of William James," vol. 17, pt. 1, 1987).

29 Nevertheless, in order to imbue civilization with sound principles and enliven it with the spirit of the gospel, it is not enough to be illumined with the gift of faith and enkindled with the desire of forwarding a good cause. For this end it is necessary to take an active part in the various organizations and influence them from within. And since our present age is one of outstanding scientific and technical progress and excellence, one will not be able to enter these organizations and work effectively from within unless he is scientifically competent, technically capable and skilled in the practice of his own profession.

> POPE JOHN XXIII (1881–1963). Encyclical, 10 April 1963 (published in *Pacem in Terris*, pt. 5).

30 In everything that relates to *science*, I am a whole Encyclopaedia behind the rest of the world.

> CHARLES LAMB (1775–1834), English essayist, critic. *The Essays of Elia*, "The Old and the New Schoolmaster" (1820–23).

31 Science is all metaphor.

> TIMOTHY LEARY (b. 1920), U.S. psychologist. Interview, 24 Sept. 1980, published in *Contemporary Authors*, vol. 107, Metaphor.

32 The scientific mind does not so much provide the right answers as ask the right questions.

> CLAUDE LÉVI-STRAUSS (b. 1908), French anthropologist. *The Raw and the Cooked*, "Overture," sct. 1 (1964).

33 When we say "science" we can either mean any manipulation of the inventive and organizing power of the human intellect: or we can mean such an extremely different thing as the *religion of science*, the vulgarized derivative from this pure activity manipulated by a sort of priestcraft into a great religious and political weapon.

> WYNDHAM LEWIS (1882–1957), British author, painter. *The Art of Being Ruled*, "Revolution and Progress," ch. 1 (1926).

34 The most heated defenders of a science, who cannot endure the slightest sneer at it, are commonly those who have not made very much progress in it and are secretly aware of this defect.

> G. C. LICHTENBERG (1742–99), German physicist, philosopher. *Aphorisms,* "Notebook F," aph. 8 (written 1765–99; tr. by R. J. Hollingdale, 1990).

35   There is no greater impediment to progress in the sciences than the desire to see it take place too quickly.

> G. C. LICHTENBERG (1742–99), German physicist, philosopher. *Aphorisms,* "Notebook K," aph. 72 (written 1765–99; tr. by R. J. Hollingdale, 1990).

36   Natural science will in time incorporate into itself the science of man, just as the science of man will incorporate into itself natural science: there will be *one* science.

> KARL MARX (1818–83), German political theorist, social philosopher. *Economic and Philosophic Manuscripts of 1844* (1844; repr. in *Karl Marx and Friedrich Engels: Collected Works,* vol. 3, 1975).

37   The product of mental labor—science—always stands far below its value, because the labor-time necessary to reproduce it has no relation at all to the labor-time required for its original production.

> KARL MARX (1818–83), German political theorist, social philosopher. *Theories of Surplus Value,* vol. 1, Addendum, "Hobbes on Labor, on Value and on the Economic Role of Science" (1862–63).

38   From man or angel the great Architect
Did wisely to conceal, and not divulge
His secrets to be scanned by them who ought
Rather admire; or if they list to try
Conjecture, he his fabric of the heav'ns
Hath left to their disputes, perhaps to move
His laughter at their quaint opinions wide
Hereafter, when they come to model heav'n
And calculate the stars, how they will wield
The mighty frame, how build, unbuild, contrive
To save appearances, how gird the sphere
With centric and eccentric scribbled o'er,
Cycle and epicycle, orb in orb.

> JOHN MILTON (1608–74), English poet. The angel Raphael, in *Paradise Lost,* bk. 8.

39   Oh, how much is today hidden by science! Oh, how much it is expected to hide!

> FRIEDRICH NIETZSCHE (1844–1900), German philosopher. *The Genealogy of Morals,* essay 3, "What Do Ascetic Ideals Mean?" aph. 23 (1887).

40   There does not exist a category of science to which one can give the name applied science. There are science and the applications of science, bound together as the fruit of the tree which bears it.

> LOUIS PASTEUR (1822–95), French chemist. "Pourquoi la France n'a pas trouvé d'hommes supérieurs au moment du péril," in *Revue Scientifique* (Paris, 1871).

41   Traditional scientific method has always been at the very *best,* 20–20 hindsight. It's good for seeing where you've been. It's good for testing the truth of what you think you know, but it can't tell you where you *ought* to go.

> ROBERT M. PIRSIG (b. 1928), U.S. author. *Zen and the Art of Motorcycle Maintenance,* pt. 3, ch. 24 (1974).

42   If the study of all these sciences which we have enumerated, should ever bring us to their mutual association and relationship, and teach us the nature of the ties which bind them together, I believe that the diligent treatment of them will forward the objects which we have in view, and that the labor, which otherwise would be fruitless, will be well bestowed.

> PLATO (c. 427–347 B.C.), Greek philosopher. Socrates, in *The Republic,* bk. 7, sct. 531.

43   One science only will one genius fit;
So vast is art, so narrow human wit.

> ALEXANDER POPE (1688–1744), English satirical poet. *An Essay on Criticism.*

44   Science may be described as the art of systematic over-simplification.

> KARL POPPER (b. 1902), Anglo-Austrian philosopher. Quoted in: *Observer* (London, 1 Aug. 1982).

45   It is sometimes important for science to know how to forget the things she is surest of.

> JEAN ROSTAND (1894–1977), French biologist, writer. *Pensées d'un Biologiste* (1939; repr. in *The Substance of Man,* "A Biologist's Thoughts," ch. 7, 1962).

46   In science men have discovered an activity of the very highest value in which they are no longer, as in art, dependent for progress upon the appearance of continually greater genius, for in science the successors stand upon the shoulders of their predecessors; where one man of supreme genius has invented a method, a thousand lesser men can apply it.

> BERTRAND RUSSELL (1872–1970), British philosopher, mathematician. *A Free Man's Worship and Other Essays,* ch. 3 (1976).

47   Science becomes dangerous only when it imagines that it has reached its goal.

> GEORGE BERNARD SHAW (1856–1950), Anglo-Irish playwright, critic. *The Doctor's Dilemma,* Preface, "The Latest Theories" (1911).

48   Science is organized knowledge.

> HERBERT SPENCER (1820–1903), English philosopher. *Education,* ch. 2 (1861).

49   True science investigates and brings to human perception such truths and such knowledge as the people of a given time and society consider most important. Art transmits these truths from the region of perception to the region of emotion.

> LEO TOLSTOY (1828–1910), Russian novelist, philosopher. *What Is Art?* ch. 10 (1898; repr. in *Tolstoy on Art,* ed. by Aylmer Maude, 1924).

50   Science is a cemetery of dead ideas.

> MIGUEL DE UNAMUNO (1864–1936), Spanish philosophical writer. *The Tragic Sense of Life,* ch. 5 (1913).

51   Science means simply the aggregate of all the recipes that are always successful. All the rest is literature.

> PAUL VALÉRY (1871–1945), French poet, essayist. *Moralités* (1932; repr. in *Collected Works,* vol. 14, "Analects," ed. by J. Matthews, 1970).

52   To us, men of the West, a very strange thing happened at the turn of the century; without noticing it, we lost science, or at least the thing that had been called by that name for the last four centuries. What we now have in place of it is something different, radically different, and we don't know what it is. Nobody knows what it is.

> SIMONE WEIL (1909–43), French philosopher, mystic. "Classical Science and After" (written 1941; published in *On Science, Necessity, and the Love of God*, ed. by Richard Rees, 1968).

53 The effort to understand the universe is one of the very few things that lifts human life a little above the level of farce, and gives it some of the grace of tragedy.

> STEVEN WEINBERG (b. 1933), U.S. theoretical physicist. *The First Three Minutes*, ch. 8 (1977), closing sentence.

54 Man has to awaken to wonder—and so perhaps do peoples. Science is a way of sending him to sleep again.

> LUDWIG WITTGENSTEIN (1889–1951), Austrian philosopher. *Culture and Value* (ed. by G. H. von Wright with Heikki Nyman, 1980), 1930 entry.

See also Huxley on BOOKS; CHEMISTRY; Lamb on The COSMOS; ENGINEERING; Huxley on EXPERTS; Bronowski on NATURE; PHYSICS; Lichtenberg on PREACHING; Shaw on PROBLEMS; Wilde on RELIGION; SCIENTISTS; The SOCIAL SCIENCES; TECHNOLOGY.

SCIENCE AND ART

1 There are two kinds of truth; the truth that lights the way and the truth that warms the heart. The first of these is science, and the second is art. . . . Without art science would be as useless as a pair of high forceps in the hands of a plumber. Without science art would become a crude mess of folklore and emotional quackery.

> RAYMOND CHANDLER (1888–1959), U.S. author. *The Notebooks of Raymond Chandler*, "Great Thought" (1976).

2 Today the function of the artist is to bring imagination to science and science to imagination, where they meet, in the myth.

> CYRIL CONNOLLY (1903–74), British critic. *The Unquiet Grave*, pt. 3 (1944; rev. 1951).

3 Art has a double face, of expression and illusion, just like science has a double face: the reality of error and the phantom of truth.

> RENÉ DAUMAL (1908–44), French poet, critic. "The Lie of the Truth" (written 1938; published in *Essais et Notes*, vol. 2, ed. by Claudio Rugafiori, 1972; repr. in *The Lie of the Truth*, tr. by Phil Powrie, 1989).

4 The worst state of affairs is when science begins to concern itself with art.

> PAUL KLEE (1879–1940), Swiss artist. *The Diaries of Paul Klee 1898–1918*, no. 747 (1957; tr. 1965), Jan. 1906 entry.

5 Science is spectral analysis. Art is light synthesis.

> KARL KRAUS (1874–1936), Austrian satirist. *Pro Domo et Mundo*, ch. 4 (1912; repr. in *Half-Truths and One-And-A Half-Truths: Selected Aphorisms*, "Riddles out of Solutions," ed. by Harry Zohn, 1976).

6 Science is for those who learn; poetry, for those who know.

> JOSEPH ROUX (1834–86), French priest, writer. *Meditations of a Parish Priest*, pt. 1, no. 71 (1886).

7 Science is feasible when the variables are few and

can be enumerated; when their combinations are distinct and clear. We are tending toward the condition of science and aspiring to do it. The artist works out his own formulas; the interest of science lies in the *art* of making science.

> PAUL VALÉRY (1871–1945), French poet, essayist. *Moralités* (1932; repr. in *Collected Works*, vol. 14, "Analects," ed. by J. Matthews, 1970).

SCIENCE AND NATURE

1 Whatever the scientists may say, if we take the supernatural out of life, we leave only the unnatural.

> AMELIA BARR (1831–1919), Anglo-American novelist. *All the Days of My Life*, ch. 26 (1913).

2 Our ideas must be as broad as Nature if they are to interpret Nature.

> SIR ARTHUR CONAN DOYLE (1859–1930), English author. Sherlock Holmes, in *A Study in Scarlet*, ch. 5 (1888).

3 Well: what we gain by science is, after all, sadness, as the Preacher saith. The more we know of the laws & nature of the Universe the more ghastly a business we perceive it all to be—& the non-necessity of it.

> THOMAS HARDY (1840–1928), English novelist, poet. Letter, 27 Feb. 1902 (published in *Collected Letters*, vol. 3, ed. by Richard Little Purdy and Michael Millgate, 1982). Hardy's reference to "the Preacher" is to *Ecclesiastes* 1:18. See Hebrew Bible on KNOWLEDGE.

4 Every formula which expresses a law of nature is a hymn of praise to God.

> MARIA MITCHELL (1818–89), U.S. astronomer. Quoted as inscription on her bust in the Hall of Fame (1905).

5 If we knew all the laws of Nature, we should need only one fact, or the description of one actual phenomenon, to infer all the particular results at that point. Now we know only a few laws, and our result is vitiated, not, of course, by any confusion or irregularity in Nature, but by our ignorance of essential elements in the calculation. Our notions of law and harmony are commonly confined to those instances which we detect; but the harmony which results from a far greater number of seemingly conflicting, but really concurring, laws, which we have not detected, is still more wonderful. The particular laws are as our points of view, as, to the traveler, a mountain outline varies with every step, and it has an infinite number of profiles, though absolutely but one form. Even when cleft or bored through it is not comprehended in its entirety.

> HENRY DAVID THOREAU (1817–62), U.S. philosopher, author, naturalist. *Walden*, "The Pond in Winter" (1854).

SCIENCE AND SOCIETY

1 Dissent is the native activity of the scientist, and it has got him into a good deal of trouble in the last years. But if that is cut off, what is left will not be a scientist. And I doubt whether it will be a man.

> JACOB BRONOWSKI (1908–74), British scientist, author. "The Sense of Human Dignity," lecture, 19 March 1953, the Massachusetts Institute of Technology (published in Jacob Bronowski, *Science and Human Values*, pt. 3, sct. 5, 1961).

2 No science is immune to the infection of politics and the corruption of power.

> JACOB BRONOWSKI (1908–74), British scientist, author. *Encounter* (London, July 1971).

3 I hate Science. It denies a man's responsibility for his own deeds, abolishes the brotherhood that springs from God's fatherhood. It is a hectoring, dictating expertise, which makes the least lovable of the Church Fathers seem liberal by contrast. It is far easier for a Hitler or a Stalin to find a mock-scientific excuse for persecution than it was for Dominic to find a mock-Christian one.

> BASIL BUNTING (1900–1985), British poet. Letter, 1 Jan. 1947, to poet Louis Zukofsky. Quoted in: Victoria Forde, *The Poetry of Basil Bunting*, ch. 6 (1991).

4 Science is an integral part of culture. It's not this foreign thing, done by an arcane priesthood. It's one of the glories of the human intellectual tradition.

> STEPHEN JAY GOULD (b. 1941), U.S. scientist. *Independent* (London, 24 Jan. 1990).

5 We are living now, not in the delicious intoxication induced by the early successes of science, but in a rather grisly morning-after, when it has become apparent that what triumphant science has done hitherto is to improve the means for achieving unimproved or actually deteriorated ends.

> ALDOUS HUXLEY (1894–1963), British author. *Ends and Means*, ch. 14 (1937).

6 We have genuflected before the god of science only to find that it has given us the atomic bomb, producing fears and anxieties that science can never mitigate.

> MARTIN LUTHER KING, JR. (1929–68), U.S. clergyman, civil rights leader. *Strength Through Love*, ch. 13 (1963).

7 The future of humanity is uncertain, even in the most prosperous countries, and the quality of life deteriorates; and yet I believe that what is being discovered about the infinitely large and infinitely small is sufficient to absolve this end of the century and millennium. What a very few are acquiring in knowledge of the physical world will perhaps cause this period not to be judged as a pure return of barbarism.

> PRIMO LEVI (1919–87), Italian chemist, author. *Other People's Trades*, "News from The Sky" (1985; tr. 1989).

8 The puritanical potentialities of science have never been forecast. If it evolves a body of organized rites, and is established as a religion, hierarchically organized, things more than anything else will be done in the name of "decency." The coarse fumes of tobacco and liquors, the consequent tainting of the breath and staining of white fingers and teeth, which is so offensive to many women, will be the first things attended to.

> WYNDHAM LEWIS (1882–1957), British author, painter. *The Art of Being Ruled*, "The Family and Feminism," ch. 7 (1926).

9 The negative cautions of science are never popular. If the experimentalist would not commit himself, the social philosopher, the preacher, and the pedagogue tried the harder to give a short-cut answer.

> MARGARET MEAD (1901–78), U.S. anthropologist. *Coming of Age in Samoa*, ch. 1 (1928).

10 Science is intimately integrated with the whole social structure and cultural tradition. They mutually support one other—only in certain types of society can science flourish, and conversely without a continuous and healthy development and application of science such a society cannot function properly.

> TALCOTT PARSONS (1902–79), U.S. sociologist. *The Social System*, ch. 8 (1951). Parsons, a functionalist, argued that social practises had to be studied in terms of their function in maintaining society.

11 *Vanity of science.* Knowledge of physical science will not console me for ignorance of morality in time of affliction, but knowledge of morality will always console me for ignorance of physical science.

> BLAISE PASCAL (1623–62), French scientist, philosopher. *Pensées* (1670; no. 23 ed. by Krailsheimer, no. 67 ed. by Brunschvicg).

12 Science is Christian, not when it condemns itself to the letter of things, but when, in the infinitely little, it discovers as many mysteries and as much depth and power as in the infinitely great.

> EDGAR QUINET (1803–75), French poet, historian, politician. "The Roman Church and Science—Galileo," lecture, 7 May 1844 (published in *Ultramontanism, or The Roman Church and Modern Society*, 1845).

13 Can a society in which thought and technique are scientific persist for a long period, as, for example, ancient Egypt persisted, or does it necessarily contain within itself forces which must bring either decay or explosion?

> BERTRAND RUSSELL (1872–1970), British philosopher, mathematician. "Can a Scientific Community be Stable?" Lloyd Roberts Lecture to the Royal Society of Medicine, 29 Nov. 1949, London.

SCIENCE FICTION

1 Science fiction writers foresee the inevitable, and although problems and catastrophes may be inevitable, solutions are not.

> ISAAC ASIMOV (1920–92), Russian-born U.S. author. "How Easy to See the Future," in *Natural History* (New York, April 1975; repr. in *Asimov on Science Fiction*, 1981).

2 Individual science fiction stories may seem as trivial as ever to the blinder critics and philosophers of today—but the core of science fiction, its essence . . . has become crucial to our salvation if we are to be saved at all.

> ISAAC ASIMOV (1920–92), Russian-born U.S. author. "My Own View," in *The Encyclopedia of Science Fiction* (ed. by Robert Holdstock, 1978; repr. in *Asimov on Science Fiction*, 1981).

3 Everything is becoming science fiction. From the margins of an almost invisible literature has sprung the intact reality of the 20th century.

> J. G. BALLARD (b. 1930), British author. "Fictions of Every Kind," in *Books and Bookmen* (London, Feb. 1971; repr. in *Re/Search*, no. 8/9, San Francisco, 1984). Ballard continued: "Even the worst science fiction is better . . . than the best conventional fiction. The future is a better key to the present than the past."

4 Science fiction writers, I am sorry to say, really do not know anything. We can't talk about science, because our knowledge of it is limited and unofficial, and usually our fiction is dreadful.

> PHILIP K. DICK (1928–82), U.S. science fiction writer. *I Hope I Shall Arrive Soon*, Introduction, "How to Build a Universe That Doesn't Fall Apart Two Days Later" (1986).

5 The fancy that extraterrestrial life is by definition of a higher order than our own is one that soothes all children, and many writers.

> JOAN DIDION (b. 1934), U.S. essayist. *The White Album*, "Doris Lessing" (1979).

6 A predilection for genre fiction is symptomatic of a kind of arrested development.

> THOMAS M. DISCH (b. 1940), U.S. author, ex-science fiction writer. Quoted in: *Face* (London, March 1986).

7 In sci-fi convention, life-forms that hadn't developed space travel were mere prehistory—horse-shoe crabs of the cosmic scene—and something of the humiliation of being stuck on a provincial planet in a galactic backwater has stayed with me ever since.

> BARBARA EHRENREICH (b. 1941), U.S. author, columnist. *The Worst Years of Our Lives*, "Blocking the Gates to Heaven" (1991; first published 1986).

8 Where everything is possible miracles become commonplaces, but the familiar ceases to be self-evident.

> ERIC HOFFER (1902–83), U.S. philosopher. *The Passionate State of Mind*, aph. 228 (1955).

9 What the hell is nostalgia doing in a science-fiction film? With the whole universe and all the future to play in, Lucas took his marvelous toys and crawled under the fringed cloth on the parlor table, back into a nice safe hideyhole, along with Flash Gordon and the Cowardly Lion and Huck Skywalker and the Flying Aces and the Hitler Jugend. If there's a message there, I don't think I want to hear it.

> URSULA K. LE GUIN (b. 1929), U.S. author. "Close Encounters, Star Wars, and the Tertium Quid," in *Future* (Aug. 1978; repr. in *Dancing at the Edge of the World*, 1989), of the film *Star Wars*.

10 If science fiction is the mythology of modern technology, then its myth is tragic.

> URSULA K. LE GUIN (b. 1929), U.S. author. "The Carrier Bag Theory of Fiction" (written 1986; first published in *Women of Vision*, ed. by Denise M. Du Pont, 1988; repr. in *Dancing at the Edge of the World*, 1989).

11 Space or science fiction has become a dialect for our time.

> DORIS LESSING (b. 1919), British novelist. *Guardian* (London, 7 Nov. 1988).

12 Science fiction films are not about science. They are about disaster, which is one of the oldest subjects of art.

> SUSAN SONTAG (b. 1933), U.S. essayist. *Against Interpretation*, "The Imagination of Disaster" (1966).

13 I have been a soreheaded occupant of a file drawer labeled "Science Fiction" . . . and I would like out, particularly since so many serious critics regularly mistake the drawer for a urinal.

> KURT VONNEGUT, JR. (b. 1922), U.S. novelist. *Wampeters, Foma and Granfalloons*, "Science Fiction" (1974).

SCIENTISTS

1 We vivisect the nightingale
To probe the secret of his note.

> THOMAS BAILEY ALDRICH (1836–1907), U.S. writer, editor. *Realism*.

2 But how is one to make a scientist understand that there is something unalterably deranged about differential calculus, quantum theory, or the obscene and so inanely liturgical ordeals of the precession of the equinoxes.

> ANTONIN ARTAUD (1896–1948), French theater producer, actor, theorist. *Van Gogh, the Man Suicided by Society* (1947; repr. in *Selected Writings*, pt. 33, ed. by Susan Sontag, 1976).

3 When I am in the company of scientists, I feel like a shabby curate who has strayed by mistake into a drawing room full of dukes.

> W. H. AUDEN (1907–73), Anglo-American poet. *The Dyer's Hand*, pt. 2, "The Poet and the City" (1963).

4 It doesn't matter whether you're talking about bombs or the intelligence quotients of one race as against another . . . if a man is a scientist, like me, he'll always say "Publish and be damned."

> JACOB BRONOWSKI (1908–74), British scientist, author. Quoted by George Steiner in the Bronowski Memorial Lecture, 1978.

5 They tend to be suspicious, bristly, paranoid-type people with huge egos they push around like some elephantiasis victim with his distended testicles in a wheelbarrow terrified no doubt that some skulking ingrate of a clone student will sneak into his very brain and steal his genius work.

> WILLIAM BURROUGHS (b. 1914), U.S. author. *The Adding Machine*, "Immortality" (1985).

6 The ordinary scientific man is strictly a sentimentalist. He is a sentimentalist in this essential sense, that he is soaked and swept away by mere associations.

> G. K. CHESTERTON (1874–1936), British author. *Orthodoxy*, "The Logic of Elfland" (1908).

7 Researchers, with science as their authority, will be able to cut [animals] up, alive, into small pieces, drop them from a great height to see if they are shattered by the fall, or deprive them of sleep for sixteen days and nights continuously for the purposes of an iniquitous monograph. . . . "Animal trust, undeserved faith, when at last will you turn away from us? Shall we never tire of deceiving, betraying, tormenting animals before they cease to trust us?"

> COLETTE (1873–1954), French author. "Animals," in *Quatre Saisons* (c. 1928; repr. in *Journey for Myself*, 1971).

8 A man ceases to be a beginner in any given science and becomes a master in that science when he has learned that . . . he is going to be a beginner all his life.

> R. G. COLLINGWOOD (1889–1943), British philosopher. *The New Leviathan*, pt. 1, ch. 1, aph. 46 (1942).

9 Everybody's a mad scientist, and life is their lab. We're all trying to experiment to find a way to live, to solve problems, to fend off madness and chaos.

> DAVID CRONENBERG (b. 1943), Canadian filmmaker. *Cronenberg On Cronenberg*, ch. 1 (ed. by Chris Rodley, 1992).

10 The man of science is a poor philosopher.

> ALBERT EINSTEIN (1879–1955), German-born U.S. theoretical physicist. *Out of My Later Years*, ch. 12 (1950).

11 If they don't depend on true evidence, scientists are no better than gossips.

> PENELOPE FITZGERALD (b. 1916), British author. Herbert Flowerdew to Fred Fairly, in *The Gate of Angels*, ch. 3 (1990).

12 There is not much that even the most socially responsible scientists can do as individuals, or even as a group, about the social consequences of their activities.

> E. J. HOBSBAWM (b. 1917), British historian. *New York Review of Books* (19 Nov. 1970).

13 The mythology of science asserts that with many different scientists all asking their own questions and evaluating the answers independently, whatever personal bias creeps into their individual answers is cancelled out when the large picture is put together. This might conceivably be so if scientists were women and men from all sorts of different cultural and social backgrounds who came to science with very different ideologies and interests. But since, in fact, they have been predominantly university-trained white males from privileged social backgrounds, the bias has been narrow and the product often reveals more about the investigator than about the subject being researched.

> RUTH HUBBARD (b. 1924), U.S. biologist. "Have Only Men Evolved?," in *Women Look at Biology Looking At Women* (ed. by Ruth Hubbard, Mary Sue Henifin and Barbara Fried, 1979).

14 There comes a time when every scientist, even God, has to write off an experiment.

> P. D. JAMES (b. 1920), British mystery writer. Jonah the tramp, in *Devices and Desires*, ch. 40 (1989).

15 For undemocratic reasons and for motives not of State,
They arrive at their conclusions—largely inarticulate.
Being void of self-expression they confide their views to none;
But sometimes in a smoking room, one learns why things were done.

> RUDYARD KIPLING (1865–1936), British author, poet. *The Puzzler*.

16 It is a good morning exercise for a research scientist to discard a pet hypothesis every day before breakfast. It keeps him young.

> KONRAD LORENZ (1903–89), Austrian ethologist. *On Aggression*, ch. 2 (1963; tr. 1966).

17 I seem to have been only like a boy playing on the seashore, and diverting myself in now and then finding a smoother pebble or a prettier shell than ordinary, whilst the great ocean of truth lay all undiscovered before me.

> SIR ISAAC NEWTON (1642–1727), English mathematician, physicist. *Memoirs of Newton*, vol. 2, ch. 27 (ed. by David Brewster, 1855).

18 A body of work such as Pasteur's is inconceivable in our time: no man would be given a chance to create a whole science. Nowadays a path is scarcely opened up when the crowd begins to pour in.

> JEAN ROSTAND (1894–1977), French biologist, writer. *Pensées d'un Biologiste* (1939; repr. in *The Substance of Man*, ch. 6, 1962).

19 It is not easy to imagine how little interested a scientist usually is in the work of any other, with the possible exception of the teacher who backs him or the student who honors him.

> JEAN ROSTAND (1894–1977), French biologist, writer. *Carnets d'un Biologiste*, in *The Substance of Man* (1962, p. 195).

20 When a scientist is ahead of his times, it is often through misunderstanding of current, rather than intuition of future truth. In science there is never any error so gross that it won't one day, from some perspective, appear prophetic.

> JEAN ROSTAND (1894–1977), French biologist, writer. *Pensées d'un Biologiste* (1939; repr. in *The Substance of Man*, "A Biologist's Thoughts," ch. 7, 1962).

21 Nothing leads the scientist so astray as a premature truth.

> JEAN ROSTAND (1894–1977), French biologist, writer. *Pensées d'un Biologiste* (1939; repr. in *The Substance of Man*, "A Biologist's Thoughts," ch. 7, 1962).

22 Aristotle could have avoided the mistake of thinking that women have fewer teeth than men, by the simple device of asking Mrs. Aristotle to keep her mouth open while he counted.

> BERTRAND RUSSELL (1872–1970), British philosopher, mathematician. *Unpopular Essays*, "An Outline of Intellectual Rubbish" (1950).

23 He had been eight years upon a project for extracting sunbeams out of cucumbers, which were to be put into vials hermetically sealed, and let out to warm the air in raw, inclement summers.

> JONATHAN SWIFT (1667–1745), Anglo-Irish satirist. A scientist at the grand academy of Lagado, in *Gullivers Travels*, "A Voyage to Laputa," ch. 5 (1726).

24 Scientists have odious manners, except when you prop up their theory; then you can borrow money of them.

> MARK TWAIN (1835–1910), U.S. author. *The Bee* (first published 1917; repr. in *Complete Essays*, ed. by Charles Neider, 1963).

See also SIR ISAAC NEWTON.

SCOTLAND AND THE SCOTS

1 I've sometimes thought . . . that the difference between us and the English is that the Scotch are hard in all other respects but soft with women, and the English are hard with women but soft in all other respects.

> J. M. BARRIE (1860–1937), Scottish playwright. Maggie Wylie, in *What Every Woman Knows*, act 2.

2 There are few more impressive sights in the world than a Scotsman on the make.

> J. M. BARRIE (1860–1937), Scottish playwright. David Wylie, in *What Every Woman Knows*, act 2.

3 A land of meanness, sophistry and mist.

Each breeze from foggy mount and marshy plain
Diluteds with drivel every drizzly brain.

LORD BYRON (1788–1824), English poet. *The Curse of Minerva.*

4   Sir, let me tell you, the noblest prospect which a
Scotchman ever sees is the high road that leads him to
England.

SAMUEL JOHNSON (1709–84), English author, lexicographer.
Quoted in: James Boswell, *Life of Samuel Johnson*, 6 July 1763
(1791).

5   Much . . . may be made of a Scotchman, if he be
caught young.

SAMUEL JOHNSON (1709–84), English author, lexicographer.
Quoted in: James Boswell, *Life of Samuel Johnson*, Spring 1772
(1791).

6   I have been trying all my life to like Scotchmen,
and am obliged to desist from the experiment in despair.

CHARLES LAMB (1775–1834), English essayist, critic. *The Essays
of Elia*, "Imperfect Sympathies" (1820–23).

7   The "second sight" possessed by the Highlanders in
Scotland is actually a foreknowledge of future events. I
believe they possess this gift because they don't wear
trousers.

G. C. LICHTENBERG (1742–99), German physicist, philosopher.
Aphorisms, "Notebook L," aph. 26 (written 1765–99; tr. by R. J.
Hollingdale, 1990). Lichtenberg added, "That is also why in all
countries women are more prone to utter prophecies."

8   Beautiful, glorious Scotland, has spoilt me for
every other country!

MARY TODD LINCOLN (1818–82), U.S. First Lady. Letter, 21
Aug. 1869 (published in *The Mary Lincoln Letters*, 1956).

9   In all my travels I never met with any one Scotchman but what was a man of sense: I believe everybody of
that country that has any, leaves it as fast as they can.

FRANCIS LOCKIER (1668–1740), English prelate, man of letters.
Quoted in: Joseph Spence, *Anecdotes*, pt. 2, "1730–32" (1820).

10   That garret of the earth—that knuckle-end of England—that land of Calvin, oat-cakes, and sulphur.

SYDNEY SMITH (1771–1845), English clergyman, writer. Quoted
in: Lady Holland, *Memoir*, vol. 1, ch. 2 (1855).

11   It requires a surgical operation to get a joke well
into a Scotch understanding. The only idea of wit, or
rather that inferior variety of the electric talent which
prevails occasionally in the North, and which, under the
name of "Wut," is so infinitely distressing to people of
good taste, is laughing immoderately at stated intervals.

SYDNEY SMITH (1771–1845), English clergyman, writer. Quoted
in: Lady Holland, *Memoir*, vol. 1, ch. 2 (1855)

See also Franklin on ARGUMENT.

SCULPTURE

1   Every young sculptor seems to think that he must
give the world some specimen of indecorous womanhood, and call it Eve, Venus, a Nymph, or any name that
may apologize for a lack of decent clothing.

NATHANIEL HAWTHORNE (1804–64), U.S. author. Miriam, in
The Marble Faun, ch. 14 (1860).

2   I sometimes wonder if the hand is not more sensitive to the beauties of sculpture than the eye. I should
think the wonderful rhythmical flow of lines and curves
could be more subtly felt than seen. Be this as it may, I
know that I can feel the heart-throbs of the ancient
Greeks in their marble gods and goddesses.

HELEN KELLER (1880–1968), U.S. blind/deaf author, lecturer.
The Story of My Life, pt. 1, ch. 22 (1903).

3   The marble not yet carved can hold the form
Of every thought the greatest artist has.

MICHELANGELO BUONARROTI (1475–1564), Italian sculptor,
painter, poet. Sonnet 15 (tr. by Elizabeth Jennings).

4   Sculpture is the art of the intelligence.

PABLO PICASSO (1881–1973), Spanish artist. *Masses and Mainstream* (New York, March 1948).

5   Sculpture is the best comment that a painter can
make on painting.

PABLO PICASSO (1881–1973), Spanish artist. Remark, 2 Feb.
1964 Quoted by artist Renato Guttuso in his journals (repr. in
Mario De Micheli, *Scritti di Picasso*, 1964).

6   The jargon of these sculptors is beyond me. I do
not know precisely why I admire a green granite female,
apparently pregant monster with one eye going around a
square corner.

EZRA POUND (1885–1972), U.S. poet, critic. *Egoist* (London, 15
Feb. 1914).

THE SEA

1   Hitherto shalt thou come, but no further: and here
shall thy proud waves be stayed.

BIBLE, HEBREW. God speaking to Job of his laying of his "foundations of the earth," in *Job* 38:11.

2   They that go down to the sea in ships, that do business in great waters, these see the works of the Lord and
his wonders in the deep.

BIBLE, HEBREW. *Psalms* 107:23–24.

3   Those who live by the sea can hardly form a single
thought of which the sea would not be part.

HERMANN BROCH (1886–1951), Austrian novelist. *The Spell*,
Foreword (1976; tr. 1987).

4   As usual I finish the day before the sea, sumptuous
this evening beneath the moon, which writes Arab symbols with phosphorescent streaks on the slow swells.
There is no end to the sky and the waters. How well they
accompany sadness!

ALBERT CAMUS (1913–60), French-Algerian philosopher,
author. *American Journals* (1978; tr. 1988), written 3 July 1949,
while crossing the Atlantic en route to South America.

5   The sea has never been friendly to man. At most it
has been the accomplice of human restlessness.

JOSEPH CONRAD (1857–1924), Polish-born English novelist.
The Mirror of the Sea, ch. 35 (1906).

6   The sea—this truth must be confessed—has no
generosity. No display of manly qualities—courage,
hardihood, endurance, faithfulness—has ever been
known to touch its irresponsible consciousness of power.

JOSEPH CONRAD (1857–1924), Polish-born English novelist.
The Mirror of the Sea, ch. 36 (1906).

7   for whatever we lose (like a you or a me)
it's always ourselves we find in the sea

E. E. CUMMINGS (1894–1962), U.S. poet. *maggie and milly and molly and may.*

8   To me, the sea is like a person—like a child that I've known a long time. It sounds crazy, I know, but when I swim in the sea I talk to it. I never feel alone when I'm out there.

GERTRUDE EDERLE (b. 1906), U.S. swimmer. *New York Post* (5 Sept. 1956), remark made 30 years after becoming the first woman to swim the English Channel.

9   The sea, washing the equator and the poles, offers its perilous aid, and the power and empire that follow it. ... "Beware of me," it says, "but if you can hold me, I am the key to all the lands."

RALPH WALDO EMERSON (1803–82), U.S. essayist, poet, philosopher. *The Conduct of Life,* "Wealth" (1860).

10   I hate to be near the sea, and to hear it roaring and raging like a wild beast in its den. It puts me in mind of the everlasting efforts of the human mind, struggling to be free, and ending just where it began.

WILLIAM HAZLITT (1778–1830), English essayist. "Common Places," no. 60, in *Literary Examiner* (London, 8 Nov. 1823; repr. in *Collected Works,* vol. 11, ed. by A. R. Waller and Arnold Glover, 1904).

11   When men come to like a sea-life, they are not fit to live on land.

SAMUEL JOHNSON (1709–84), English author, lexicographer. Quoted in: James Boswell, *Life of Samuel Johnson,* 18 March 1776 (1791).

12   The snotgreen sea. The scrotumtightening sea.

JAMES JOYCE (1882–1941), Irish author. Buck Mulligan, in *Ulysses,* ch. 1 (1986 ed.).

13   Wide sea, that one continuous murmur breeds
Along the pebbled shore of memory!

JOHN KEATS (1795–1821), English poet. *Endymion,* bk. 2.

14   There is nothing so desperately monotonous as the sea, and I no longer wonder at the cruelty of pirates.

JAMES RUSSELL LOWELL (1819–91), U.S. poet, editor. *Fireside Travels,* "At Sea" (1864).

15   It is only when we are very happy that we can bear to gaze merrily upon the vast and limitless expanse of water, rolling on and on with such persistent, irritating monotony, to the accompaniment of our thoughts, whether grave or gay. When they are gay, the waves echo their gaiety; but when they are sad, then every breaker, as it rolls, seems to bring additional sadness, and to speak to us of hopelessness and of the pettiness of all our joys.

BARONESS ORCZY (1865–1947), British author, playwright. *The Scarlet Pimpernel,* ch. 21 (1905).

16   There is hope from the sea, but none from the grave.

IRISH PROVERB.

17   The ocean, whose tides respond, like women's menses, to the pull of the moon, the ocean which corresponds to the amniotic fluid in which human life begins, the ocean on whose surface vessels (personified as female) can ride but in whose depth sailors meet their death and monsters conceal themselves ... it is unstable and threatening as the earth is not; it spawns new life daily, yet swallows up lives; it is changeable like the moon, unregulated, yet indestructible and eternal.

ADRIENNE RICH (b. 1929), U.S. poet. *Of Woman Born,* ch. 4 (1976).

18   The sea speaks a language polite people never repeat. It is a colossal scavenger slang and has no respect.

CARL SANDBURG (1878–1967), U.S. poet. *Two Nocturnes.*

19   The sea is mother-death and she is a mighty female, the one who wins, the one who sucks us all up.

ANNE SEXTON (1928–74), U.S. poet. *The Poet's Story,* "A Small Journal" (ed. by Howard Moss, 1974), entry for 19 Nov. 1971.

20   The Mediterranean has the color of mackerel, changeable I mean. You don't always know if it is green or violet, you can't even say it's blue, because the next moment the changing reflection has taken on a tint of rose or gray.

VINCENT VAN GOGH (1853–90), Dutch painter. Letter, June 1888, to his brother Theo Van Gogh (published in *The Letters of Vincent Van Gogh,* ed. by M. Roskill, 1927).

See also Conrad on The NAVY; Butler on PIETY.

THE SEASONS

1   One of the joys our technological civilisation has lost is the excitement with which seasonal flowers and fruits were welcomed; the first daffodil, strawberry or cherry are now things of the past, along with their precious moment of arrival. Even the tangerine—now a satsuma or clementine—appears de-pipped months before Christmas.

DEREK JARMAN (b. 1942), British filmmaker, artist, author. *Modern Nature: The Journals of Derek Jarman* (1991), entry for 7 Feb. 1989.

2   Indoors or out, no one relaxes
In March, that month of wind and taxes,
The wind will presently disappear,
The taxes last us all the year.

OGDEN NASH (1902–71), U.S. poet. *Thar She Blows,* in *Versus* (1949).

3   To be interested in the changing seasons is, in this middling zone, a happier state of mind than to be hopelessly in love with spring.

GEORGE SANTAYANA (1863–1952), U.S. philosopher, poet. *The Life of Reason,* "Reason in Art" (1905; repr. in *Little Essays,* "The Need of Discipline," ed. by Logan Pearsall Smith, 1920).

4   January gray is here,
Like a sexton by her grave;
February bears the bier,
March with grief doth howl and rave,
And April weeps—but, O ye hours!
Follow with May's fairest flowers.

PERCY BYSSHE SHELLEY (1792–1822), English poet. *Dirge for the Year.*

5 Live in each season as it passes; breathe the air, drink the drink, taste the fruit, and resign yourself to the influences of each. Let them be your only diet drink and botanical medicines.

> HENRY DAVID THOREAU (1817–62), U.S. philosopher, author, naturalist. *Journals* (1906), entry for 23 Aug. 1853.

See also AUTUMN; SPRING; SUMMER; WINTER.

SECRETS

1 Every thing secret degenerates, even the administration of justice; nothing is safe that does not show how it can bear discussion and publicity.

> LORD ACTON (1834–1902), English historian. Letter, 23 Jan. 1861 (published in *Lord Acton and his Circle*, Letter 74, ed. by Abbot Gasquet, 1906).

2 Our true history is scarcely ever deciphered by others. The chief part of the drama is a monologue, or rather an intimate debate between God, our conscience, and ourselves. Tears, griefs, depressions, disappointments, irritations, good and evil thoughts, decisions, uncertainties, deliberations—all these belong to our secret, and are almost all incommunicable and intransmissible, even when we try to speak of them, and even when we write them down.

> HENRI-FRÉDÉRIC AMIEL (1821–81), Swiss philosopher, poet. *Journal Intime* (1882; tr. by Mrs. Humphrey Ward, 1892), entry for 27 Oct. 1856.

3 You know there are no secrets in America. It's quite different in England, where people think of a secret as a shared relation between two people.

> W. H. AUDEN (1907–73), Anglo-American poet. *The Table Talk of W. H. Auden*, "16 March, 1948" (comp. by Alan Ansen, ed. by Nicholas Jenkins, 1990).

4 What one hides is worth neither more nor less than what one finds. And what one hides from oneself is worth neither more nor less than what one allows others to find.

> ANDRÉ BRETON (1896–1966), French surrealist. *Surrealism and Painting* (1928).

5 Secrecy is the badge of fraud.

> SIR JOHN CHADWICK (b. 1941), British judge. *Independent* (London, 26 July 1990).

6 Men with secrets tend to be drawn to each other, not because they want to share what they know but because they need the company of the like-minded, the fellow afflicted.

> DON DELILLO (b. 1926), U.S. author. Walter Everett, Jr., in *Libra*, pt. 1, "17 April" (1988).

7 A wonderful fact to reflect upon, that every human creature is constituted to be that profound secret and mystery to every other.

> CHARLES DICKENS (1812–70), English novelist. *A Tale of Two Cities*, bk. 1, ch. 3 (1859).

8 His mind of man, a secret makes
I meet him with a start

He carries a circumference
In which I have no part.

> EMILY DICKINSON (1830–86), U.S. poet. *The Complete Poems*, no. 1663 (1955).

9 He that has eyes to see and ears to hear may convince himself that no mortal can keep a secret. If his lips are silent, he chatters with his fingertips; betrayal oozes out of him at every pore.

> SIGMUND FREUD (1856–1939), Austrian psychiatrist. *Fragment of an Analysis of a Case of Hysteria*, "The First Dream" (1905; repr. in *Complete Works*, vol. 7, ed. by James Strachey and Anna Freud, 1953). Freud thus justified his interest in symbolism; "and thus the task of making conscious the most hidden recesses of the mind is one which it is quite possible to accomplish."

10 We dance round in a ring and suppose,
But the Secret sits in the middle and knows.

> ROBERT FROST (1874–1963), U.S. poet. *The Secret Sits*.

11 Women's propensity to share confidences is universal. We confirm our reality by sharing.

> BARBARA GRIZZUTI HARRISON (1941), U.S. author, publicist. "Secrets Women Tell Each Other," in *McCall's* (New York, Aug. 1975).

12 The secret thoughts of a man run over all things, holy, profane, clean, obscene, grave, and light, without shame or blame.

> THOMAS HOBBES (1588–1679), English philosopher. *Leviathan*, pt. 1, ch. 8 (1651).

13 The vanity of being known to be trusted with a secret is generally one of the chief motives to disclose it.

> SAMUEL JOHNSON (1709–84), English author, lexicographer. *Rambler*, no. 13 (London, 1 May 1750; repr. in *Works of Samuel Johnson*, vol. 3, ed. by W. J. Bate and Albrecht B. Strauss, 1969).

14 When a friend, then, indulges in the joy of unburdening a secret on to another friend's bosom, he makes the latter, in his turn, feel the urge to taste the same joy himself. He implores him, it is true, not to tell a soul; but if such a condition were taken absolutely literally, it would at once cut off the flow of these joys at their very source. The general practice is for the secret to be confided only to an equally trustworthy friend, the same conditions being imposed on him. And so from trustworthy friend to trustworthy friend the secret goes moving on round that immense chain, until finally it reaches the ears of just the very person or persons whom the first talker had expressly intended it never should reach.

> ALESSANDRO MANZONI (1785–1873), Italian novelist, poet, dramatist. *The Betrothed*, ch. 11 (1827; tr. 1951).

15 But he that hides a dark soul and foul thoughts
Benighted walks under the mid-day sun;
Himself is his own dungeon.

> JOHN MILTON (1608–74), English poet. Second brother, in *Comus* (1634).

16 Secrecy is the first essential in affairs of the State.

> CARDINAL DE RICHELIEU (1585–1642), French statesman. *Testament Politique*, "Maxims" (1641).

17 The first step towards vice is to shroud innocent actions in mystery, and whoever likes to conceal something sooner or later has reason to conceal it.

> JEAN-JACQUES ROUSSEAU (1712–78), Swiss-born French

philosopher, political theorist. *La Nouvelle Héloïse,* pt. 4, Letter 6 (1791).

18 There are no secrets better kept than the secrets everybody guesses.

> GEORGE BERNARD SHAW (1856–1950), Anglo-Irish playwright, critic. Sir George Crofts, in *Mrs. Warren's Profession,* act 3.

19 If you wish to preserve your secret, wrap it up in frankness.

> ALEXANDER SMITH (1830–67), Scottish poet. *Dreamthorp,* "On the Writing of Essays" (1863).

20 O divine art of subtlety and secrecy! Through you we learn to be invisible, through you inaudible and hence we can hold the enemy's fate in our hands.

> SUN TZU (6th-5th century B.C.), Chinese general. *The Art of War,* ch. 6, axiom 9 (c. 490 B.C.; ed. by James Clavell, 1981).

21 Shy and unready men are great betrayers of secrets; for there are few wants more urgent for the moment than the want of something to say.

> SIR HENRY TAYLOR (1800–1886), English author. *The Statesman,* ch. 18 (1836).

See also Colton on GOSSIP; Behn on LOVERS; Conrad on MOTIVES; Hebrew Bible on PLEASURE; Proust on THINGS, TRIVIAL.

SECTS

1 The multiplication of individual sects should not fool us: the important point is that the whole of America is preoccupied with the sect as a moral institution, with its immediate demand for beatification, its material efficacity, its compulsion for justification, and doubtless also with its madness and frenzy.

> JEAN BAUDRILLARD (b. 1929), French semiologist. *America,* "Utopia Achieved" (1986; tr. 1988).

2 Sekts and creeds ov religion, are like pocket compesses, good enuff tu pinte out the direction, but the nearer the pole yu git the wuss tha wurk.

> JOSH BILLINGS [HENRY WHEELER SHAW] (1818–85), U.S. humorist. *Josh Billings, His Sayings,* ch. 39 (1865).

3 One seems to believe almost all that they believe; and when they stop short and call it a Religion, and you pass on, and call it only a reminiscence of one, should you not part with the kiss of peace?

> THOMAS CARLYLE (1795–1881), Scottish essayist, historian. Letter, 10 Sept. 1833, to John Stuart Mill (published in *Letters of Thomas Carlyle,* 1923), on the Unitarians, following a meeting with Ralph Waldo Emerson.

4 In America the taint of sectarianism lies broad upon the land. Not content with acknowledging the supremacy as the Diety, and with erecting temples in his honor, where all can bow down with reverence, the pride and vanity of human reason enter into and pollute our worship, and the houses that should be of God and for God, alone, where he is to be honored with submissive faith, are too often merely schools of metaphysical and useless distinctions. The nation is sectarian, rather than Christian.

> JAMES FENIMORE COOPER (1789–1851), U.S. novelist. *The American Democrat,* "On Religion" (1838).

5 'Tis a strange thing, Sam, that among us people can't agree the whole week, because they go different ways upon *Sundays.*

> GEORGE FARQUHAR (1678–1707), Irish dramatist. Letter, 15 Oct. 1700 (published in *Love and Business,* 1701).

6 Like a man traveling in foggy weather, those at some distance before him on the road he sees wrapped up in the fog, as well as those behind him, and also the people in the fields on each side, but near him all appears clear, though in truth he is as much in the fog as any of them.

> BENJAMIN FRANKLIN (1706–90), U.S. statesman, writer. *Autobiography,* ch. 8 (written 1771–90; published 1868), of the delusions of those in sects. Franklin was, however, struck by the "modesty" of the Quakers, in contrast to other sects.

7 Almost every sect of Christianity is a perversion of its essence, to accomodate it to the prejudices of the world.

> WILLIAM HAZLITT, English essayist. *The Round Table,* "On the Causes of Methodism" (1817).

8 I see and hear daily that you of the Clergy preach one against another, teach one contrary to another, inveigh one against another without charity or discretion. Some be too stiff in their old mumpsimus, others be too busy and curious in their new sumpsimus. Thus all men almost be in variety and discord . . .

> HENRY VIII (1491–1547), King of England (1509–47). Speech, 24 Dec. 1545, to Parliament.

9 Fanatics have their dreams, wherewith they weave
A paradise for a sect.

> JOHN KEATS (1795–1821), English poet. First lines of *The Fall of Hyperion.*

10 Every sect is a moral check on its neighbour. Competition is as wholesome in religion as in commerce.

> WALTER SAVAGE LANDOR (1775–1864), English author. *Imaginary Conversations,* "Martin and Jack" (1824–9).

11 The Mormons make the marriage ring, like the ring of Saturn, fluid, not solid, and keep it in its place by numerous satellites.

> HENRY WADSWORTH LONGFELLOW (1807–82), U.S. poet. *Drift-Wood,* "Table-Talk" (1857 ed.; repr. in *Complete Works,* vol. 1, 1886).

12 Nothing does more to activate Christian divisions than talk about Christian unity.

> CONOR CRUISE O'BRIEN (b. 1917), Irish diplomat, writer. *Times* (London, 3 Oct. 1989).

13 If I could believe the Quakers banned music because church music is so damn bad, I should view them with approval.

> EZRA POUND (1885–1972), U.S. poet, critic. Letter, 23 Aug. 1917, to Pound's father. Quoted in: Humphrey Carpenter, *A Serious Character,* pt. 1, ch. 2 (1988). Pound's grandfather was a Quaker.

14 A general loathing of a gang or sect usually has some sound basis in instinct.

> EZRA POUND (1885–1972), U.S. poet, critic. *New English Weekly* (London, 14 May 1936).

15 And when religious sects ran mad,

He held, in spite of all their learning,
That if a man's belief is bad,
It will not be improved by burning.

> WINTHROP MACKWORTH PRAED (1802–39), English poet.
> *The Vicar.*

16 The Methodists love your big sinners, as proper subjects to work upon.

> HORACE WALPOLE (1717–97), English author. Letter, 3 May 1749.

SEDUCTION

1 Man proposes, woman forecloses.

> MINNA ANTRIM (1861-?), U.S. epigrammist. *Naked Truth and Veiled Allusions*, (1901, p. 45).

2 When a woman wants a man and lusts after him, the lover need not bother to conjure up opportunities, for she will find more in an hour than we men could think of in a century.

> PIERRE DE BOURDEILLE, ABBÉ DE BRANTÔME c. 1530–1614), French courtier, soldier, author. *The Lives of Gallant Ladies*, "First Essay" (1659).

3 I should like to know *who* has been carried off, except poor dear me—I have been more ravished myself than anybody since the Trojan war.

> LORD BYRON (1788–1824), English poet. Letter, 29 Oct. 1819, answering accusations of debauchery (published in *Byron's Letters and Journals*, vol. 6, ed. by Leslie A. Marchand, 1976).

4 A gentleman doesn't pounce . . . he glides. If a woman sits on a piece of furniture which permits your sitting beside her, you are free to regard this as an invitation, though not an unequivocal one.

> QUENTIN CRISP (b. 1908), British author. *Manners from Heaven*, ch. 6 (1984).

5 License my roving hands, and let them go
Before, behind, between, above, below.

> JOHN DONNE (c. 1572–1631), English divine, metaphysical poet. *Elegies*, "To His Mistress Going to Bed."

6 Seduction is often difficult to distinguish from rape. In seduction, the rapist often bothers to buy a bottle of wine.

> ANDREA DWORKIN (b. 1946), U.S. feminist critic. *Letters from a War-Zone*, "Sexual Economics: The Terrible Truth" (1987; speech 1976).

7 He in a few minutes ravished this fair creature, or at least would have ravished her, if she had not, by a timely compliance, prevented him.

> HENRY FIELDING (1707–54), English novelist, dramatist. *Jonathan Wild*, bk. 3, ch. 7 (1743; rev. 1754), of Fireblood's conquest of Laetitia.

8 Can love be controlled by advice?
Will Cupid our mothers obey?
Though my heart were as frozen as ice,
At his flame 'twould have melted away.
When he kissed me so closely he pressed,
'Twas so sweet that I must have complied:
So I thought it both safest and best
To marry, for fear you should chide.

> JOHN GAY (1685–1732), English dramatist. Polly, in *The Beggar's Opera*, act 1, sc. 8 (Air 8).

9 When lovely woman stoops to folly,
And finds too late that men betray,
What charm can soothe her melancholy,
What art can wash her guilt away?

> OLIVER GOLDSMITH (1728–74), Anglo-Irish author, poet, playwright. Song sung by Olivia, in *The Vicar of Wakefield*, ch. 24 (written 1761–62; published 1766).

10 Weep not for little Leonie,
Abducted by a French Marquis!
Though loss of honour was a wrench,
Just think how it's improved her French.

> HARRY GRAHAM (1874–1936), British author, rhymster. *Compensation.*

11 You have to penetrate a woman's defenses. Getting into her head is a prerequisite to getting into her body.

> BOB GUCCIONE (b. 1930), U.S. publisher. Interview in Wendy Leigh, *Speaking Frankly* (1978).

12 To seduce a woman famous for strict morals, religious fervour and the happiness of her marriage: what could possibly be more prestigious?

> CHRISTOPHER HAMPTON (b. 1946), British playwright. Valmont, in *Dangerous Liaisons* (screenplay, 1989).

13 The trouble with Ian is that he gets off with women because he can't get on with them.

> ROSAMOND LEHMANN (1903–90), British author. Quoted in: John Pearson, The Life of Ian Fleming, ch. 8, sct. 1 (1966), said of novelist Ian Fleming. The remark echoes one first made, in a different context, by Irish author Elizabeth Bowen. Fleming is described as having a voracious—and cynical—sexual appetite. See Fleming on PROMISCUITY and SEX.

14 Had we but world enough, and time,
This coyness, lady, were no crime.

> ANDREW MARVELL (1621–78), English metaphysical poet. *To His Coy Mistress.*

15 Let this great maxim be my virtue's guide—
In part she is to blame that has been tried:
He comes too near that comes to be denied.

> LADY MARY WORTLEY MONTAGU (1689–1762), English society figure, letter writer. *The Lady's Resolve.*

16 Pursuit and seduction are the essence of sexuality. It's part of the sizzle.

> CAMILLE PAGLIA (b. 1947), U.S. author, critic, educator. Interview in *Playboy* (Chicago, Oct. 1991; repr. in *Sex, Art, and American Culture*, "The Rape Debate," 1992).

17 He saw, he wish'd, and to the prize aspir'd.
Resolv'd to win, he meditates the way,
By force to ravish, or by fraud betray;
For when success a lover's toil attends,
Few ask, if fraud or force attain'd his ends.

> ALEXANDER POPE (1688–1744), English satirical poet. *The Rape of the Lock*, cto. 2.

18 Slowly, but very deliberately, the brooding edifice of seduction, creaking and incongruous, came into being, a vast Heath Robinson mechanism, dually controlled by them and lumbering gloomily down vistas of triteness. With a sort of heavy-fisted dexteritry the mutually adapted emotions of each of them became synchronised, until the unavoidable anti-climax was at hand.

> ANTHONY POWELL (b. 1905), British novelist. *Afternoon Men*, ch. 9 (1931), of Lola and Atwater.

19 She's beautiful, and therefore to be wooed;
She is a woman, therefore to be won.

> WILLIAM SHAKESPEARE (1564–1616), English dramatist, poet. Suffolk, in *Henry VI Part 1*, act 5, sc. 5.Demetrius voices a similar thought in *Titus Andronicus*, act 2, sc. 1:
> She is a woman, therefore may be wooed;
> She is a woman, therefore may be won;
> She is Lavinia, therefore must be loved.

20 A wise woman never yields by appointment. It should always be an unforeseen happiness.

> STENDHAL (1783–1842), French author. *On Love*, ch. 60 (1822).

SEGREGATION

1 The difference between *de jure* and *de facto* segregation is the difference open, forthright bigotry and the shamefaced kind that works through unwritten agreements between real estate dealers, school officals, and local politicians.

> SHIRLEY CHISHOLM (b. 1924), U.S. educator, congresswoman. *Unbought and Unbossed*, pt. 4, ch. 14 (1970).

2 In America, you can segregate the people, but the problems will travel. From slavery to equal rights, from state suppression of dissent to crime, drugs and unemployment, I can't think of a supposedly Black issue that hasn't wasted the original Black target group and then spread like measles to outlying white experience.

> JUNE JORDAN (b. 1939), U.S. poet, civil rights activist. *Moving Towards Home: Political Essays*, "Problems of Language in a Democratic State" (1989; first published 1982).

3 Segregation now, segregation tomorrow and segregation forever!

> GEORGE C. WALLACE (b. 1919), U.S. Democratic politician. Inaugural address, Jan. 1963, as Governor of Alabama. Wallace persisted in refusing to implement President Kennedy's desegregation laws. Wallace's speechwriter, Asa Carter (1926–79), was a Klu Klux Klansman who went on to have literary success under the name of Forrest Carter, with two books: one, *Gone to Texas*, was made into a film by Clint Eastwood, *The Outlaw Josey Wales* (1976); the other, *The Education of Little Tree* (1976), purported to be Carter's memoir describing his upbringing by Cherokee grandparents, and became a bestseller as a work of Native American literature. In 1991 the book became the first in the history of the *New York Times* to be switched from the non-fiction grid on the bestseller charts.

SELF

1 The boundary line between self and external world bears no relation to reality; the distinction between ego and world is made by spitting out part of the inside, and swallowing in part of the outside.

> NORMAN O. BROWN (b. 1913), U.S. philosopher. *Love's Body*, ch. 8 (1967).

2 We are all serving a life-sentence in the dungeon of self.

> CYRIL CONNOLLY (1903–74), British critic. *The Unquiet Grave*, pt. 2 (1944; rev. 1951).

3 The self . . . might be regarded as a sort of citadel of the mind, fortified without and containing selected treasures within, while love is an undivided share in the rest of the universe. In a healthy mind each contributes to the growth of the other: what we love intensely or for a long time we are likely to bring within the citadel, and to assert as part of ourself. On the other hand, it is only on the basis of a substantial self that a person is capable of progressive sympathy or love.

> CHARLES HORTON COOLEY (1864–1929), U.S. sociologist. *Human Nature and the Social Order*, ch. 5 (1902).

4 It is ironic that the one thing that all religions recognize as separating us from our creator—our very self-consciousness—is also the one thing that divides us from our fellow creatures. It was a bitter birthday present from evolution.

> ANNIE DILLARD (b. 1945), U.S. author, poet. *Pilgrim at Tinker Creek*, ch. 6 (1974).

5 Human beings have an inalienable right to invent themselves; when that right is pre-empted it is called brain-washing.

> GERMAINE GREER (b. 1939), Australian feminist writer. *Times* (London, 1 Feb. 1986).

6 Me, what's that after all? An arbitrary limitation of being bounded by the people before and after and on either side. Where they leave off, I begin, and vice versa.

> RUSSELL HOBAN (b. 1925), U.S. author. William G, in *Turtle Diary*, ch. 11 (1975).

7 My self . . . is a dramatic ensemble. Here a prophetic ancestor makes his appearance. Here a brutal hero shouts. Here an alcoholic bon vivant argues with a learned professor. Here a lyric muse, chronically love-struck, raises her eyes to heaven. Her papa steps forward, uttering pedantic protests. Here the indulgent uncle intercedes. Here the aunt babbles gossip. Here the maid giggles lasciviously. And I look upon it all with amazement, the sharpened pen in my left hand.

> PAUL KLEE (1879–1940), Swiss artist. *The Diaries of Paul Klee 1898–1918*, no. 638 (1957: tr. 1965), Jan. 1963 entry.

8 I suppose everyone continues to be interested in the quest for the self, but what you feel when you're older, I think, is that . . . you really must *make* the self. It is absolutely useless to look for it, you won't find it, but it's possible in some sense to make it. I don't mean in the sense of making a mask, a Yeatsian mask. But you finally begin in some sense to make and choose the self you want.

> MARY MCCARTHY (1912–89), U.S. author, critic. Interview in *Writers at Work* (Second Series, ed. by George Plimpton, 1963).

9 You have for company the best companion you will ever have—the modest, defeated, plodding workaday self which has a name and can be identified in public registers in case of accident or death. But the real self, the one who has taken over the reins, is almost a stranger. He is the one who is filled with ideas; he is the one who is writing in the air; he is the one who, if you become too fascinated with his exploits, will finally expropriate the old, worn-out self, taking over your name, your address, your wife, your past, your future.

> HENRY MILLER (1891–1980), U.S. author. *Sexus*, ch. 2 (1949).

10   Active, successful natures act, not according to the dictum "know thyself," but as if there hovered before them the commandment: *will* a self and thou shalt *become* a self.

> FRIEDRICH NIETZSCHE (1844–1900), German philosopher. *Assorted Opinions and Maxims*, aph. 366 (1879).

11   Man is not merely the sum of his masks. Behind the shifting face of personality is a hard nugget of self, a genetic gift. . . . The self is malleable but elastic, snapping back to its original shape like a rubber band. Mental illness is no myth, as some have claimed. It is a disturbance in our sense of possession of a stable inner self that survives its personae.

> CAMILLE PAGLIA (b. 1947), U.S. author, critic, educator. *Sex, Art, and American Culture*, "Sexual Personae: The Cancelled Preface" (1992).

12   The more the development of late capitalism renders obsolete or at least suspect the real possibilities of self, self-fulfillment and actualization, the more they are emphasized as if they could spring to life through an act of will alone.

> RICHARD DEAN ROSEN (b. 1949), U.S. journalist, critic. *Psychobabble: Fast Talk and Quick Cure in the Era of Feeling*, "Psychobabble" (1977).

13   All I can tell you with certainty is that I, for one, have no self, and that I am unwilling or unable to perpetrate upon myself the joke of a self. . . . What I have instead is a variety of impersonations I can do, and not only of myself—a troupe of players that I have internalised, a permanent company of actors that I can call upon when a self is required. . . . I am a theater and nothing more than a theater.

> PHILIP ROTH (b. 1933), U.S. novelist. Nathan Zuckerman, in *The Counterlife*, ch. 5 (1986), writing to Maria.

14   Can one thus resume one's self? Can one know one's self? Is one ever *somebody*? I don't know anything about it any more. It now seems to me that one changes from day to day and that every few years one becomes a new being.

> GEORGE SAND (1804–76), French novelist. *The Intimate Journal of George Sand*, "Final Comment by George Sand" (1929), Sept. 1868 entry.

15   Man who man would be,
Must rule the empire of himself; in it
Must be supreme, establishing his throne
On vanquished will, quelling the anarchy
Of hopes and fears, being himself alone.

> PERCY BYSSHE SHELLEY (1792–1822), English poet. *Political Greatness*.

16   People often say that this or that person has not yet found himself. But the self is not something one finds; it is something one creates.

> THOMAS SZASZ (b. 1920), U.S. psychiatrist. *The Second Sin*, "Personal Conduct" (1973).

17   The philosophical I is not the human being, not the human body or the human soul with the psychological properties, but the metaphysical subject, the boundary (not a part) of the world.

> LUDWIG WITTGENSTEIN (1889–1951), Austrian philosopher. *Notebooks 1914–1916*, entry for 2 Sept. 1915. (ed. by Anscombe, 1961). Wittgenstein reformulated this idea in *Tractatus Logico-Philosophicus* sct. 5: 641 (1921; tr. 1922): "The philosophical self is not the human being, not the human body, or the human soul with which psychology deals, but rather the metaphysical subject, the limit of the world—not a part of it."

See also Cioran, Debord, Repplier, Thoreau on EGOTISM; Murdoch on HAPPINESS.

SELF-ABSORPTION

1   For an introvert his environment is himself and can never be subject to startling or unforeseen change.

> QUENTIN CRISP (b. 1908), British author. *The Naked Civil Servant*, ch. 24 (1968).

2   My own thoughts
Are my companions; my designs and labors
And aspirations are my only friends.

> HENRY WADSWORTH LONGFELLOW (1807–82), U.S. poet. *The Masque of Pandora*.

3   Happiness lies outside yourself, is achieved through interacting with others. Self-forgetfulness should be one's goal, not self-absorption. The male, capable of only the latter, makes a virtue of an irremediable fault and sets up self-absorption, not only as a good but as a Philosophical Good.

> VALERIE SOLANAS (b. 1940), U.S. artist, writer. *The SCUM Manifesto* (1968).

See also INTROSPECTION.

SELF-CONFIDENCE

1   Name me an Emperor who was ever struck by a cannonball.

> CHARLES V (1500–1558), Spanish king, Holy Roman Emperor. Alleged remark, 23 April 1547, to his military commanders before the Battle of Mühlberg.

2   Self-confidence is apt to address itself to an imaginary dullness in others; as people who are well off speak in a cajoling tone to the poor.

> GEORGE ELIOT (1819–80), English novelist, editor. *Daniel Deronda*, bk. 1, ch. 5 (1876).

3   Trust thyself: every heart vibrates to that iron string.

> RALPH WALDO EMERSON (1803–82), U.S. essayist, poet, philosopher. *Essays*, "Self-Reliance" (First Series, 1841).

4   The people I respect most behave as if they were immortal and as if society was eternal.

> E. M. FORSTER (1879–1970), British novelist, essayist. *Two Cheers for Democracy*, "What I Believe" (1951).

5   Those who believe that they are exclusively in the right are generally those who achieve something.

> ALDOUS HUXLEY (1894–1963), British author. *Proper Studies*, "A Note on Dogma: Varieties of Human Type" (1927).

6 I wish I was as cocksure of anything as Tom Macaulay is of everything.

> LORD MELBOURNE (1779–1848), English statesman, prime minister. Quoted in: Earl Cowper, *Lord Melbourne's Papers*, Preface (1889), reported by Melbourne's nephew.

7 True it is that she who escapeth safe and unpolluted from out the school of freedom, giveth more confidence of herself than she who cometh sound out of the school of severity and restraint.

> MICHEL DE MONTAIGNE (1533–92), French essayist. *Essays*, bk. 3, ch. 5, "Upon Some Verses of Virgil" (tr. by John Florio, 1588).

8 It is easy—terribly easy—to shake a man's faith in himself. To take advantage of that to break a man's spirit is devil's work.

> GEORGE BERNARD SHAW (1856–1950), Anglo-Irish playwright, critic. Morell, in *Candida*, act 1.

9 Without self-confidence we are as babes in the cradles. And how can we generate this imponderable quality, which is yet so invaluable most quickly? By thinking that other people are inferior to oneself.

> VIRGINIA WOOLF (1882–1941), British novelist. *A Room Of One's Own*, ch. 2 (1929).

See also Tolstoy on COMPLACENCY.

SELF-CONTROL

1 A little kingdom I possess,
Where thoughts and feelings dwell;
And very hard the task I find
Of governing it well.

> LOUISA MAY ALCOTT (1832–88), U.S. author. *My Kingdom*, st. 1

2 The highest possible stage in moral culture is when we recognize that we ought to control our thoughts.

> CHARLES DARWIN (1809–82), English naturalist. *The Descent of Man*, ch. 4 (1871).

3 He that would govern others, first should be
The master of himself.

> PHILIP MASSINGER (1583–1640), English dramatist. Timoleon, in *The Bondman*, act 1, sc. 3 (1624).

4 Why are we so full of restraint? Why do we not give in all directions? Is it fear of losing ourselves? Until we do lose ourselves there is no hope of finding ourselves.

> HENRY MILLER (1891–1980), U.S. author. *The World of Sex*, (1940; repr. 1970, p. 105).

5 He who cannot obey himself will be commanded. That is the nature of living creatures.

> FRIEDRICH NIETZSCHE (1844–1900), German philosopher. *Thus Spoke Zarathustra*, pt. 2, "Of Self-Overcoming" (1883–92; tr. 1961).

6 O, it is excellent
To have a giant's strength, but it is tyrannous
To use it like a giant.

> WILLIAM SHAKESPEARE (1564–1616), English dramatist, poet. Isabella, in *Measure for Measure*, act 2, sc. 2.

7 When angry, count four; when very angry, swear.

> MARK TWAIN (1835–1910), U.S. author. *Pudd'nhead Wilson*, ch. 10, "Pudd'nhead Wilson's Calendar" (1894).

See also Dickens on ABSTINENCE; Boileau on WRITERS.

SELF-CRITICISM

1 Yet how proud we are,
In daring to look down upon ourselves!

> ELIZABETH BARRETT BROWNING (1806–61), English poet. *Aurora Leigh*, bk. 5 (1857).

2 Think of, and look at, your work as though it were done by your enemy. If you look at it to admire it you are lost.

> SAMUEL BUTLER (1835–1902), English author. *Samuel Butler's Notebooks* (1951, p. 119).

3 The cleverest of all, in my opinion, is the man who calls himself a fool at least once a month.

> FEODOR DOSTOYEVSKY (1821–81), Russian novelist. Ivan Ivanovich, in "Bobok," in *A Writer's Diary* (1873).

4 He who undervalues himself is justly undervalued by others.

> WILLIAM HAZLITT (1778–1830), English essayist. *Table Talk*, "On the Knowledge of Character" (1821).

5 You see it's awfully hard to talk or write about your own stuff because if it is any good you yourself know about how good it is—but if you say so yourself you feel like a shit.

> ERNEST HEMINGWAY (1899–1961), U.S. author. Letter, 17 Oct. 1945, to poet and critic Malcolm Cowley (published in *Selected Letters*, ed. by Carlos Baker, 1981).

SELF-DECEPTION

1 Most of our platitudes notwithstanding, self-deception remains the most difficult deception. The tricks that work on others count for nothing in that very well-lit back alley where one keeps assignations with oneself: no winning smiles will do here, no prettily drawn lists of good intentions.

> JOAN DIDION (b. 1934), U.S. essayist. *Slouching Towards Bethlehem*, "On Self-Respect" (1968).

2 We lie loudest when we lie to ourselves.

> ERIC HOFFER (1902–83), U.S. philosopher. *The Passionate State of Mind*, aph. 70 (1955).

3 Take the life-lie away from the average man and straight away you take away his happiness.

> HENRIK IBSEN (1828–1906), Norwegian dramatist. Reilling, in *The Wild Duck*, act 5.

4 The surest way to be deceived is to consider oneself cleverer than others.

> FRANÇOIS, DUC DE LA ROCHEFOUCAULD (1613–80), French writer, moralist. *Sentences et Maximes Morales*, no. 127 (1678).

5 We run heedlessly into the abyss after putting something in front of us to stop us seeing it.

> BLAISE PASCAL (1623–62), French scientist, philosopher. *Pensées*, (1670; no 166 ed. by Krailsheimer, no. 166 ed. by Brunschvicg).

6 The heart deceives, because it is never anything but the expression of the mind's miscalculations . . . I don't know what the heart is, not I: I only use the word to denote the mind's frailties.

> MARQUIS DE SADE (1740–1814), French author. Dolmancé, in *Philosophy in the Bedroom*, "Dialogue the Fifth" (1795).

7 Nothing is so difficult as not deceiving oneself.

> LUDWIG WITTGENSTEIN (1889–1951), Austrian philosopher. *Culture and Value* (ed. by G. H. von Wright with Heikki Nyman, 1980), 1938 entry.

See also Demosthenes on CREDULITY; Wilde on LOVE.

SELF-DESTRUCTIVENESS

1 Destroy yourselves, you who are desperate, and you who are tortured in body and soul, abandon all hope. There is no more solace for you in this world. The world lives off your rotting flesh.

> ANTONIN ARTAUD (1896–1948), French theater producer, actor, theorist. "General Security: The Liquidation of Opium" (1925; repr. in *Selected Writings*, pt. 10, ed. by Susan Sontag, 1976).

2 Yet is every man his own greatest enemy, and as it were his own executioner.

> SIR THOMAS BROWNE (1605–82), English physician, author. *Religio Medici*, pt. 2, sct. 4 (1643).

3 When the beginnings of self-destruction enter the heart it seems no bigger than a grain of sand.

> JOHN CHEEVER (1912–82), U.S. author. *John Cheever: The Journals*, "The Late Forties and the Fifties" (ed. by Robert Gottlieb, 1991), 1952 entry.

4 when man determined to destroy
himself he picked the was
of shall and finding only why
smashed it into because

> E. E. CUMMINGS (1894–1962), U.S. poet. *when god decided to invent.*

5 But I do nothing upon myself, and yet am mine own Executioner.

> JOHN DONNE (c. 1572–1631), English divine, metaphysical poet. *Devotions upon Emergent Occasions*, "Meditation 12" (1624).

6 If destruction be our lot, we must ourselves be its author and finisher. As a nation of freemen, we must live through all time, or die by suicide.

> ABRAHAM LINCOLN (1809–65), U.S. president. "The Perpetuation of Our Political Institutions," speech, 27 Jan. 1837, Springfield, Ill.

See also Kapuscinski on STRUGGLE; SUICIDE.

SELF-EXPRESSION

1 I will tell you what I will do and what I will not do. I will not serve that in which I no longer believe, whether it call itself my home, my fatherland, or my church: and I will try to express myself in some mode of life or art as freely as I can and as wholly as I can, using for my defence the only arms I allow myself to use—silence, exile and cunning.

> JAMES JOYCE (1882–1941), Irish author. Stephen Dedalus, in *A Portrait of the Artist as a Young Man*, ch. 5 (1916).

2 To me, the whole process of being a brushstroke in someone else's painting is a little difficult.

> MADONNA (b. 1959), U.S. singer, actor. *Vanity Fair* (New York, April 1991).

3 I fear chiefly lest my expression may not be *extra-vagant* enough, may not wander far enough beyond the narrow limit of my daily experience, so as to be adequate to the truth of which I have been convinced. *Extra vagance!* it depends on how you are yarded.

> HENRY DAVID THOREAU (1817–62), U.S. philosopher, author, naturalist. *Walden*, "Conclusion" (1854).

4 Life has been your art. You have set yourself to music. Your days are your sonnets.

> OSCAR WILDE (1854–1900), Anglo-Irish playwright, author. Lord Henry to Dorian Gray, in *The Picture of Dorian Gray*, ch. 19 (1891).

SELF-HELP

1 Welcome evermore to gods and men is the self-helping man. For him all doors are flung wide: him all tongues greet, all honors crown, all eyes follow with desire. Our love goes out to him and embraces him, because he did not need it. We solicitously and apologetically caress and celebrate him, because he held on his way and scorned our disapprobation. The gods loved him because men hated him.

> RALPH WALDO EMERSON (1803–82), U.S. essayist, poet, philosopher. *Essays*, "Self-Reliance" (First Series, 1841).

2 Self-help books are making life downright unsafe. Women desperate to catch a man practice all the ploys recommended by these authors. Bump into him, trip over him, knock him down, spill something on him, scald him, but *meet him*.

> FLORENCE KING (b. 1936), U.S. author. *Reflections in a Jaundiced Eye*, "Does Your Child Taste Salty?" (1989).

3 But you think . . . that it is time for me to have done with the world, and so I would if I could get into a better before I was called into the best, and not die here in a rage, like a poisoned rat in a hole.

> JONATHAN SWIFT (1667–1745), Anglo-Irish satirist. Letter, 21 March 1729, to statesman and author Viscount Bolingbroke.

SELF-IMAGE

1 I think it's one of the scars in our culture that we have too high an opinion of ourselves. We align ourselves with the angels instead of the higher primates.

> ANGELA CARTER (1940–92), British author. *Marxism Today* (London, Jan. 1985).

2 If we could see ourselves as others see us, we would vanish on the spot.

> E. M. CIORAN (b. 1911), Rumanian-born French philosopher. *The Trouble with Being Born*, ch. 3 (1973).

beings reflection, but have no assurance of the tranquillity of the waters in which we see it.

> CHARLES HORTON COOLEY (1864–1929), U.S. sociologist. *Human Nature and the Social Order,* ch. 6 (1902).

4 The very purpose of existence is to reconcile the glowing opinion we have of ourselves with the appalling things that other people think about us.

> QUENTIN CRISP (b. 1908), British author. *How to Become a Virgin,* ch. 2 (1981).

5 To see ourselves as others see us can be eye-opening. To see others as sharing a nature with ourselves is the merest decency. But it is from the far more difficult achievement of seeing ourselves amongst others, as a local example of the forms human life has locally taken, a case among cases, a world among worlds, that the largeness of mind, without which objectivity is self-congratulation and tolerance a sham, comes.

> CLIFFORD GEERTZ (b. 1926), U.S. anthropologist. *Local Knowledge,* Introduction (1983).

6 You've no idea what a poor opinion I have of myself—and how little I deserve it.

> W. S. GILBERT (1836–1911), English librettist. Sir Ruthven Murgatroyd (disguised as Robin Oakapple), in *Ruddigore,* act 1.

7 We can bear to be deprived of everything but our self-conceit.

> WILLIAM HAZLITT (1778–1830), English essayist. *Characteristics: In the Manner of Rochefoucault's Maxims,* no. 421 (1823; repr. in *The Complete Works Of William Hazlitt,* vol. 9, ed. by P. P. Howe, 1932).

8 Self-esteem and self-contempt have specific odors; they can be smelled.

> ERIC HOFFER (1902–83), U.S. philosopher. *The Passionate State of Mind,* aph. 246 (1955).

9 No matter what our achievements might be, we think well of ourselves only in rare moments. We need people to bear witness against our inner judge, who keeps book on our shortcomings and transgressions. We need people to convince us that we are not as bad as we think we are.

> ERIC HOFFER (1902–83), U.S. philosopher. *Reflections on the Human Condition,* aph. 144 (1973).

10
$$\text{Self-esteem} = \frac{\text{Success}}{\text{Pretensions}}.$$

> WILLIAM JAMES (1842–1910), U.S. psychologist, philosopher. *The Principles of Psychology,* vol. 1, ch. 10 (1890).

11 The world has become uglier since it began to look into a mirror every day; so let us settle for the mirror image and do without an inspection of the original.

> KARL KRAUS (1874–1936), Austrian satirist. "In Praise of a Topsy-Turvy Lifestyle," in *Simplicissimus* (Munich, 1908; repr. in *In These Great Times: A Karl Kraus Reader,* ed. by Harry Zohn, 1976).

12 It is terrible to destroy a person's picture of himself in the interests of truth or some other abstraction.

> DORIS LESSING (b. 1919), British novelist. *The Grass is Singing,* ch. 2 (1950).

13 Neither man nor woman can be worth anything until they have discovered that they are fools. This is the first step towards becoming either estimable or agreeable; and until it be taken there is no hope. The sooner the discovery is made the better, as there is more time and power for taking advantage of it. Sometimes the great truth is found out too late to apply to it any effectual remedy. Sometimes it is never found at all; and these form the desperate and inveterate causes of folly, self-conceit, and impertinence.

> LORD MELBOURNE (1779–1848), English statesman, prime minister. Quoted in: David Cecil, *The Young Melbourne,* ch. 9 (1939).

14 As you see yourself, I once saw myself; as you see me now, you will be seen.

> MEXICAN PROVERB. Quoted in: Richard Rodriguez, *Frontiers,* "Night and Day" (1990).

15 I think I am one of those who can manage not to take on a completely different appearance under their own glance.

> JEAN ROSTAND (1894–1977), French biologist, writer. *Carnets d'un Biologiste,* in *The Substance of Man* (1962, p. 192).

16 Public opinion is a weak tyrant compared with our own private opinion. What a man thinks of himself, that it is which determines, or rather indicates, his fate.

> HENRY DAVID THOREAU (1817–62), U.S. philosopher, author, naturalist. *Walden,* "Economy" (1854).

17 I have nothing to declare except my genius.

> OSCAR WILDE (1854–1900), Anglo-Irish playwright, author. Comment, 3 Jan. 1882, at the New York Customs. Quoted in: Richard Ellman, *Oscar Wilde,* ch. 6 1987). There is no contemporary evidence for the remark.

18 It is curious how instinctively one protects the image of oneself from idolatry or any other handling that could make it ridiculous, or too unlike the original to be believed any longer.

> VIRGINIA WOOLF (1882–1941), British novelist. *A Haunted House,* "The Mark on the Wall" (1944).

See also NARCISSISM; Hazlitt on MODESTY.

SELF-IMPROVEMENT

1 There's only one corner of the universe you can be certain of improving, and that's your own self.

> ALDOUS HUXLEY (1894–1963), British author. Carlo Malpighi (quoting Bruno Rontini), in *Time Must Have a Stop,* ch. 7 (1944).

2 I am a bad, wicked man, but I am practising moral self-purification; I don't eat meat any more, I now eat rice cutlets.

> VLADIMIR ILYICH LENIN (1870–1924), Russian revolutionary leader. Quoted in: Tamara Deutsche, *Not By Politics Alone,* ch. 4 (1973).

3 He was always smoothing and polishing himself, and in the end he became blunt before he was sharp.

> G. C. LICHTENBERG (1742–99), German physicist, philosopher. *Aphorisms,* "Notebook L," aph. 70 (written 1765–99; tr. by R. J. Hollingdale, 1990).

4   Whoever will cultivate their own mind will find full employment. Every virtue does not only require great care in the planting, but as much daily solicitude in cherishing as exotic fruits and flowers; the vices and passions (which I am afraid are the natural product of the soil) demand perpetual weeding. Add to this the search after knowledge . . . and the longest life is too short.

> LADY MARY WORTLEY MONTAGU (1689–1762), English society figure, letter writer. Letter, 6 March 1753, to her daughter Lady Bute (published in *Selected Letters*, ed. by Robert Halsband, 1970).

5   To affect the quality of the day, that is the highest of arts. Every man is tasked to make his life, even in its details, worthy of the contemplation of his most elevated and critical hour.

> HENRY DAVID THOREAU (1817–62), U.S. philosopher, author, naturalist. *Walden*, "Where I Lived, and What I Lived For" (1854).

SELF-INTEREST

1   Self-interest is but the survival of the animal in us. Humanity only begins for man with self-surrender.

> HENRI-FRÉDÉRIC AMIEL (1821–81), Swiss philosopher, poet. *Journal Intime* (1882; tr. by Mrs. Humphrey Ward, 1892), entry for 17 Dec. 1856.

2   The ruin of the human heart is self-interest, which the American merchant calls self-service. We have become a self-service populace, and all our specious comforts—the automatic elevator, the escalator, the cafeteria—are depriving us of volition and moral and physical energy.

> EDWARD DAHLBERG (1900–1977), U.S. author, critic. *Alms for Oblivion*, "No Love and No Thanks" (1964).

3   Remember how often you have postponed minding your interest, and let slip those opportunities the gods have given you. It is now high time to consider what sort of world you are part of, and from what kind of governor of it you are descended; that you have a set period assigned you to act in, and unless you improve it to brighten and compose your thoughts, it will quickly run off with you, and be lost beyond recovery.

> MARCUS AURELIUS (121–80), Roman emperor, philosopher. *Meditations*, bk. 2, sct. 4.

4   It is not from the benevolence of the butcher, the brewer, or the baker, that we expect our dinner, but from their regard to their own interest. We address ourselves, not to their humanity but to their self-love, and never talk to them of our necessities but of their advantages.

> ADAM SMITH (1723–90), Scottish economist. *The Wealth of Nations*, vol. 1, bk. 1, ch. 2 (1776).

5   The punters know that the horse named Morality rarely gets past the post, whereas the nag named Self-Interest always runs a good race.

> GOUGH WHITLAM (b. 1916), Australian Labor politician, prime minister. *Daily Telegraph* (London, 19 Oct. 1989).

6   Long before Einstein told us that matter is energy, Machiavelli and Hobbes and other modern political philosophers defined man as a lump of matter whose most politically relevant attribute is a form of energy called "self-interestedness." This was not a portrait of man "warts and all." It was all wart.

> GEORGE F. WILL (b. 1941), U.S. political columnist. *Statecraft as Soulcraft: What Government Does*, ch. 2 (1984).

7   A little group of wilful men reflecting no opinion but their own have rendered the great Government of the United States helpless and contemptible.

> WOODROW WILSON (1856–1924), U.S. Democratic politician, president. Statement, 4 March 1917, referring to a successful filibuster against Wilson's bill to arm U.S. merchant ships against German submarine attacks.

SELF-KNOWLEDGE

1   He who seeks to approach his own buried past must conduct himself like a man digging. . . . He must not be afraid to return again and again to the same matter; to scatter it as one scatters earth, to turn it over as one turns over soil. For the matter itself is only a deposit, a stratum, which yields only to the most meticulous examination what constitutes the real treasure hidden within the earth: the images, severed from all earlier associations, that stand—like precious fragments or torsos in a collector's gallery—in the prosaic rooms of our later understanding.

> WALTER BENJAMIN (1892–1940), German critic, philosopher. *A Berlin Chronicle* (written 1932; first published 1970; repr. in *One-Way Street and Other Writings*, 1978).

2   Many a man who has known himself at ten forgets himself utterly between ten and thirty.

> CATHERINE DRINKER BOWEN (1897–1973), U.S. author. *Friends and Fiddlers*, ch. 9 (1934).

3   The one self-knowledge worth having is to know one's own mind.

> F. H. BRADLEY (1846–1924), English philosopher. *Aphorisms*, no. 8 (1930).

4   To know oneself, one should assert oneself. Psychology is action, not thinking about oneself. We continue to shape our personality all our life. If we knew ourselves perfectly, we should die.

> ALBERT CAMUS (1913–60), French-Algerian philosopher, author. *Notebooks 1935–1942* (1962), entry for May 1937.

5   The self-explorer, whether he wants to or not, becomes the explorer of everything else. He learns to see himself, but suddenly, provided he was honest, all the rest appears, and it is as rich as he was, and, as a final crowning, richer.

> ELIAS CANETTI (b. 1905), Austrian novelist, philosopher. *The Secret Heart Of The Clock: Notes, Aphorisms, Fragments 1973–1985*, "1975" (1991).

6   The most excellent and divine counsel, the best and most profitable advertisement of all others, but the least practised, is to study and learn how to know ourselves. This is the foundation of wisdom and the highway to whatever is good. . . . God, Nature, the wise, the world, preach man, exhort him both by word and deed to the study of himself.

> PIERRE CHARRON (1541–1603), French philosopher. *Of Wisdom*, bk. 1, Preface (1601), first words.

7 One may understand the cosmos, but never the ego; the self is more distant than any star.

> G. K. CHESTERTON (1874–1936), British author. *Orthodoxy*, "The Logic of Elfland" (1908).

8 Know thyself.

> INSCRIPTION on the Oracle of Apollo at Delphi, Greece (6th century B.C.).

9 It is, I fear, but a vain show of fulfilling the heathen precept, "Know thyself," and too often leads to a self-estimate which will subsist in the absence of that fruit by which alone the quality of the tree is made evident.

> GEORGE ELIOT (1819–80), English novelist, editor. Mr. Lyon, the independent minister, in *Felix Holt, The Radical*, ch. 5 (1866), said of the pitfalls of scrutinizing oneself too closely.

10 If people can be educated to see the lowly side of their own natures, it may be hoped that they will also learn to understand and to love their fellow men better. A little less hypocrisy and a little more tolerance towards oneself can only have good results in respect for our neighbor; for we are all too prone to transfer to our fellows the injustice and violence we inflict upon our own natures.

> CARL JUNG (1875–1961), Swiss psychiatrist. *Two Essays on Analytical Psychology: New Paths in Psychology* (1912; repr. in *Collected Works*, vol. 7, para. 439, ed. by William McGuire, 1953).

11 He knows the universe and does not know himself.

> JEAN DE LA FONTAINE (1621–95), French poet, fabulist. *Fables*, bk. 8, fable 26 (1678–79).

12 He who knows others is clever;
He who knows himself has discernment.

> LAO-TZU (6th century B.C.), Legendary Chinese philosopher. *Tao-te-ching*, bk. 1, ch. 33 (tr. by T. C. Lau, 1963).

13 To grow wiser means to learn to know better and better the faults to which this instrument with which we feel and judge can be subject.

> G. C. LICHTENBERG (1742–99), German physicist, philosopher. *Aphorisms*, "Notebook A," aph. 38 (written 1765–99; tr. by R. J. Hollingdale, 1990).

14 We forge gradually our greatest instrument for understanding the world—introspection. We discover that humanity may resemble us very considerably—that the best way of knowing the inwardness of our neighbors is to know ourselves.

> WALTER LIPPMANN (1889–1974), U.S. journalist. *A Preface to Politics*, ch. 4 (1914).

15 'Tis not need we *know* our every thought
Or see the work shop where each mask is wrought
Wherefrom we view the world of box and pit,
Careless of wear, just so the mask shall fit
And serve our jape's turn for a night or two.

> EZRA POUND (1885–1972), U.S. poet, critic. *Fifine Answers*.

16 Our lives teach us who we are.

> SALMAN RUSHDIE (b. 1947), Indian-born British author. *Independent on Sunday* (London, 4 Feb. 1990).

17 An humble knowledge of thyself is a surer way to God than a deep search after learning.

> THOMAS À KEMPIS (1380–1471), German monk, mystic. *The Imitation of Christ*, pt. 1, ch. 3 (1471).

18 Nay, be a Columbus to whole new continents and worlds within you, opening new channels, not of trade, but of thought. Every man is the lord of a realm beside which the earthly empire of the Czar is but a petty state, a hummock left by the ice.

> HENRY DAVID THOREAU (1817–62), U.S. philosopher, author, naturalist. *Walden*, "Conclusion" (1854).

19 You never know yourself till you know more than your body.

> THOMAS TRAHERNE (1636–74), English clergyman, poet, mystic. *Centuries*, "First Century," no. 19 (written c. 1672; first published 1908).

See also James on INTROSPECTION; SELF-IMAGE; Bradley on VIRTUE.

SELF-PITY

1 Self-pity in its early stage is as snug as a feather mattress. Only when it hardens does it become uncomfortable.

> MAYA ANGELOU (b. 1928), U.S. author. *Gather Together in My Name*, vol. 2, ch. 6 (1974).

2 The fool saith, I have no friends, I have no thank for all my good deeds, and they that eat my bread speak evil of me.

> APOCRYPHA. *Ecclesiasticus* 20:16.

3 The dupe of friendship, and the fool of love; have I not reason to hate and to despise myself? Indeed I do; and chiefly for not having hated and despised the world enough.

> WILLIAM HAZLITT (1778–1830), English essayist. *The Plain Speaker*, "On the Pleasure of Hating" (1826).

4 Forget your personal tragedy. We are all bitched from the start and you especially have to be hurt like hell before you can write seriously. But when you get the damned hurt use it—don't cheat with it.

> ERNEST HEMINGWAY (1899–1961), U.S. author. Quoted in: Andrew Turnbull, *Scott Fitzgerald*, ch. 14 (1962).

5 I never saw a wild thing
Sorry for itself.
A small bird will drop frozen dead
From a bough
Without ever having felt sorry for itself.

> D. H. LAWRENCE (1885–1930), British author. *Self-Pity*.

6 Self-pity comes so naturally to all of us, that the most solid happiness can be shaken by the compassion of a fool.

> ANDRÉ MAUROIS (1885–1967), French author, critic. *Ariel*, ch. 16 (1924).

SELF-PROMOTION

1 To establish oneself in the world, one does all one can to seem established there already.

> FRANÇOIS, DUC DE LA ROCHEFOUCAULD (1613–80), French writer, moralist. *Sentences et Maximes Morales*, no. 56 (1678).

2 The final key to the way I promote is bravado. I play to people's fantasies. People may not always think big themselves, but they can still get very excited by those who do. That's why a little hyperbole never hurts.

> DONALD TRUMP (b. 1946), U.S. businessman. *Trump: The Art of the Deal*, ch. 2 (1987; written with Tony Schwartz).

SELF-RESPECT

1 To have that sense of one's intrinsic worth which constitutes self-respect is potentially to have everything: the ability to discriminate, to love and to remain indifferent. To lack it is to be locked within oneself, paradoxically incapable of either love or indifference.

> JOAN DIDION (b. 1934), U.S. essayist. *Slouching Towards Bethlehem*, "On Self-Respect" (1968).

2 Let a man then know his worth, and keep things under his feet. Let him not peep or steal, or skulk up and down with the air of a charity-boy, a bastard, or an interloper.

> RALPH WALDO EMERSON (1803–82), U.S. essayist, poet, philosopher. *Essays*, "Self-Reliance" (First Series, 1841).

3 Self-repect—The secure feeling that no one, as yet, is suspicious.

> H. L. MENCKEN (1880–1956), U.S. journalist. *A Mencken Chrestomathy*, "Sententiæ: The Mind of Men" (1949).

4 Self-respect is nothing to hide behind. When you need it most it isn't there.

> MAY SARTON (b. 1912), U.S. poet, novelist. Hilary Stevens, in *Mrs. Stevens Hears the Mermaids Singing*, "Epilogue: Mar" (1965).

See also Shaw on CRAFTS; Twain on RESPECT.

SELF-SUFFICIENCY

1 I needed a drink, I needed a lot of life insurance, I needed a vacation, I needed a home in the country. What I had was a coat, a hat and a gun.

> RAYMOND CHANDLER (1888–1959), U.S. author. Philip Marlowe, in *Farewell, My Lovely*, ch. 34 (1940).

2 Be thine own palace, or the world's thy jail.

> JOHN DONNE (c. 1572–1631), English divine, metaphysical poet. *Verse Letter to Sir Henry Wotton*.

3 The history of this country was made largely by people who wanted to be left alone. Those who could not thrive when left to themselves never felt at ease in America.

> ERIC HOFFER (1902–83), U.S. philosopher. *Reflections on the Human Condition*, aph. 53 (1973).

4 My pet, the world can forgive practically anything except people who mind their own business.

> MARGARET MITCHELL (1900–1949), U.S. novelist. Rhett Butler, in *Gone with the Wind*, vol. 2, pt. 4, ch. 47 (1936).

5 The greatest thing of the world is for a man to know how to be his own.

> MICHEL DE MONTAIGNE (1533–92), French essayist. *Essays*, bk. 1, ch. 38, "Of Solitariness" (tr. by John Florio, 1580).

6 The proverb warns that "You should not bite the hand that feeds you." But maybe you should, if it prevents you from feeding yourself.

> THOMAS SZASZ (b. 1920), U.S. psychiatrist. *The Second Sin*, "Control and Self-control" (1973).

7 We must cultivate our own garden. . . . When man was put in the garden of Eden he was put there so that he should work, which proves that man was not born to rest.

> VOLTAIRE (1694–1778), French philosopher, author. Candide and Pangloss, in the Conclusion to *Candide*, ch. 30 (1759), exchanging the fruits of their experience. This passage is held to encapsulate Voltaire's philosophy of common sense as against the complacency of "optimism."

SELFISHNESS

1 You have no idea how promising the world begins to look once you have decided to have it all for yourself. And how much healthier your decisions are once they become entirely selfish.

> ANITA BROOKNER (b. 1938), British novelist, art historian. Mr. Neville, in *Hotel du Lac*, ch. 7 (1984).

2 If love closes, the self contracts and hardens: the mind having nothing else to occupy its attention and give it that change and renewal it requires, busies itself more and more with self-feeling, which takes on narrow and disgusting forms, like avarice, arrogance and fatuity.

> CHARLES HORTON COOLEY (1864–1929), U.S. sociologist. *Human Nature and the Social Order*, ch. 5 (1902).

3 Her unselfishness came in pretty small packages well wrapped.

> F. SCOTT FITZGERALD (1896–1940), U.S. author. *The Crack-Up*, "Notebook E" (ed. by Edmund Wilson, 1945).

4 Selfish persons are incapable of loving others, but they are not capable of loving themselves either.

> ERICH FROMM (1900–1980), U.S. psychologist. *Man for Himself*, ch. 4 (1947).

5 An' if tha does owt for nowt, do it for thysen. (And if you do anything for nothing, do it for yourself.)

> YORKSHIRE PROVERB.

6 Consider any individual at any period of his life, and you will always find him preoccupied with fresh plans to increase his comfort. Do not talk to him about the interests and rights of the human race; that little private business of his for the moment absorbs all his thoughts, and he hopes that public disturbances can be put off to some other time.

> ALEXIS DE TOCQUEVILLE (1805–59), French social philosopher. *Democracy in America*, vol. 2, pt. 3, ch. 21 (1840).

7 Selfishness is not living as one wishes to live, it is asking others to live as one wishes to live.

> OSCAR WILDE (1854–1900), Anglo-Irish playwright, author. *The Soul of Man Under Socialism*, in *Fortnightly Review* (London, Feb. 1891; repr. 1895).

See also Byron on MOTIVES.

SENSATION

1　The great object in life is Sensation—to feel that we exist, even though in pain; it is this "craving void" which drives us to gaming, to battle, to travel, to intemperate but keenly felt pursuits of every description whose principal attraction is the agitation inseparable from their accomplishment.

> LORD BYRON (1788–1824), English poet. Letter, 6 Sept. 1813, written to Annabella Millbanke—later Lady Byron (published in *Byron's Letters and Journals*, vol. 3, ed. by Leslie A. Marchand, 1974). The "craving void" was described by Alexander Pope in *Epistle from Eloisa to Abelard.*

2　Reciprocity of sensation is not possible because to share is to be robbed.

> ANGELA CARTER (1940–92), British author. *The Sadeian Woman,* "Speculative Finale" (1979).

3　A sensation must have fallen very low to deign to turn into an idea.

> E. M. CIORAN (b. 1911), Rumanian-born French philosopher. *Anathemas and Admirations,* "On the Verge of Existence" (1986).

4　Life is a series of sensations connected to different states of consciousness.

> RÉMY DE GOURMONT (1858–1915), French critic, novelist. "The Value of Education," in *Le Chemin de Velours* (1902; repr. in *Selected Writings,* ed. and tr. by Glen S. Burne, 1966).

5　Every pleasure or pain has a sort of rivet with which it fastens the soul to the body and pins it down and makes it corporeal, accepting as true whatever the body certifies.

> SOCRATES (469–399 B.C.), Greek philosopher. Quoted in: Plato, *Phaedo,* sct. 81.

THE SENSES

1　We are all instruments endowed with feeling and memory. Our senses are so many strings that are struck by surrounding objects and that also frequently strike themselves.

> DENIS DIDEROT (1713–84), French philosopher. *D'Alembert's Dream,* "Conversation Between D'Alembert and Diderot" (written 1769; published 1830; repr. in *Selected Writings,* ed. by Lester G. Crocker, 1966).

2　Our ideas are the offspring of our senses; we are not more able to create the form of a being we have not seen, without retrospect to one we know, than we are able to create a new sense. He whose fancy has conceived an idea of the most beautiful form must have composed it from actual existence.

> HENRY FUSELI (1741–1825), Swiss-born English artist, critic. *Lectures on Painting,* "First Lecture" (1801). Quoted in: *The Mind of Henry Fuseli,* pt. 3, ch. 1, "Is Art Creation?" (ed. by Eudo C. Mason, 1951).

3　"Reason" is the cause of our falsification of the evidence of the senses. In so far as the senses show becoming, passing away, change, they do not lie.

> FRIEDRICH NIETZSCHE (1844–1900), German philosopher. *Twilight of the Idols,* "'Reason' in Philosophy," aph. 2 (1889).

4　Each day I live in a glass room
Unless I break it with the thrusting
Of my senses and pass through
The splintered walls to the great landscape.

> MERVYN PEAKE (1911–68), British author, artist. *A Reverie of Bone,* "Each Day I Live in a Glass Room" (1967).

5　I was afraid that by observing objects with my eyes and trying to comprehend them with each of my other senses I might blind my soul altogether.

> SOCRATES (469–399 B.C.), Greek philosopher. Quoted in: Plato, *Phaedo,* sct. 98.

6　Nothing can cure the soul but the senses, just as nothing can cure the senses but the soul.

> OSCAR WILDE (1854–1900), Anglo-Irish playwright, author. Lord Henry, in the *The Picture of Dorian Gray,* ch. 2 (1891).

SENSITIVITY

1　It is . . . axiomatic that we should all think of ourselves as being more sensitive than other people because, when we are insensitive in our dealings with others, we cannot be aware of it at the time: conscious insensitivity is a self-contradiction.

> W. H. AUDEN (1907–73), Anglo-American poet. Dag Hammarskjöld, *Markings,* Foreword (1964).

2　If we had a keen vision and feeling of all ordinary human life, it would be like hearing the grass grow and the squirrel's heart beat, and we should die of that roar which lies on the other side of silence. As it is, the best of us walk about well wadded with stupidity.

> GEORGE ELIOT (1819–80), English novelist. *Middlemarch,* bk. 2, ch. 20 (1872).

3　It is all a question of sensitiveness. Brute force and overbearing may make a terrific effect. But in the end, that which lives lives by delicate sensitiveness. If it were a question of brute force, not a single human baby would survive for a fortnight. It is the grass of the field, most frail of all things, that supports all life all the time. But for the green grass, no empire would rise, no man would eat bread: for grain is grass; and Hercules or Napoleon or Henry Ford would alike be denied existence.

> D. H. LAWRENCE (1885–1930), British author. *Etruscan Places,* ch. 2 (1932).

4　One of the effects of a safe and civilised life is an immense oversensitiveness which makes all the primary emotions somewhat disgusting. Generosity is as painful as meanness, gratitude as hateful as ingratitude.

> GEORGE ORWELL (1903–50), British author. "Looking Back on the Spanish War" (1943; repr. in *Collected Essays,* 1961).

5　How frail the human heart must be—
a mirrored pool of thought . . .

> SYLVIA PLATH (1932–63), U.S. poet. *I Thought I Could Not Be Hurt.* Quoted in: Aurelia Schober Plath, *Letters Home: Correspondence 1950–1963,* Introduction (1975). This was Plath's first poem, written at age 14.

6　What we think of as our sensitivity is only the higher evolution of terror in a poor dumb beast. We suffer for nothing. Our own death wish is our only real tragedy.

> MARIO PUZO (b. 1920), U.S. novelist. Merlyn, in *Fools Die,* ch. 55 (1978).

7 The finest qualities of our nature, like the bloom on fruits, can be preserved only by the most delicate handling. Yet we do not treat ourselves nor one another thus tenderly.

> HENRY DAVID THOREAU (1817–62), U.S. philosopher, author, naturalist. *Walden*, "Economy" (1854).

8 A person who, because he has corns himself, always treads on other people's toes.

> OSCAR WILDE (1854–1900), Anglo-Irish playwright, author. The Roman Candle, answering the question, "What is a sensitive person?" in "The Remarkable Rocket," in *The Happy Prince and Other Tales* (1888).

9 I can't stand a naked light bulb, any more than I can a rude remark or a vulgar action.

> TENNESSEE WILLIAMS (1914–83), U.S. dramatist. Blanche DuBois, in *A Streetcar Named Desire*, sc. 3 (1947).

10 It's not catastrophes, murders, deaths, diseases, that age and kill us; it's the way people look and laugh, and run up the steps of omnibuses.

> VIRGINIA WOOLF (1882–1941), British novelist. *Jacob's Room*, ch. 9 (1922).

See also Guppy on ARTISTS; Eliot on TEMPER.

SENSUALITY

1 So must pure lovers' souls descend
T'affections, and to faculties,
Which sense may reach and apprehend,
Else a great Prince in prison lies.

> JOHN DONNE (c. 1572–1631), English divine, metaphysical poet. *The Extasie*.

2 A woman can look both moral and exciting—if she also looks as if it was quite a struggle.

> EDNA FERBER (1887–1968), U.S. author. Quoted in: *The Reader's Digest* (Dec. 1954).

3 Sensuality reconciles us with the human race. The misanthropy of the old is due in large part to the fading of the magic glow of desire.

> ERIC HOFFER (1902–83), U.S. philosopher. *Reflections on the Human Condition*, aph. 138 (1973).

4 Sex appeal is fifty percent what you've got and fifty percent what people think you've got.

> SOPHIA LOREN (b. 1934), Italian actor. Quoted in: Leslie Halliwell, *Halliwell's Filmgoer's Companion* (1984).

5 How nicely the bitch Sensuality knows how to beg for a piece of the spirit, when a piece of flesh is denied her.

> FRIEDRICH NIETZSCHE (1844–1900), German philosopher. *Thus Spoke Zarathustra*, pt. 1, "Of Chastity" (1883–92; tr. 1961).

6 Sensual excess drives out pity in man.

> MARQUIS DE SADE (1740–1814), French author. *The Misfortunes of Virtue* (1787).

7 I am over-run, jungled in my bed, I am infested with a menagerie of desires: my heart is eaten by a dove, a cat scrambles in the cave of my sex, hounds in my bed obey a whipmaster who cries nothing but havoc as the hours test my endurance with an accumulation of tortures. Who, if I cried, would hear me among the angelic orders?

> ELIZABETH SMART (1913–86), Canadian author, poet. *By Grand Central Station I Sat Down and Wept*, pt. 1 (1945).

8 Being a sex symbol has to do with an attitude, not looks. Most men think it's looks, most women know otherwise.

> KATHLEEN TURNER (b. 1956), U.S. actor. Quoted in: *Observer* (London, 27 April 1986).

9 Women are on the whole more sensual than sexual, men are more sexual than sensual.

> MAI ZETTERLING (b. 1925), Swedish actor, director. *Times* (London, 17 May 1989).

See also SEXUALITY; Humboldt on SPIRITUALITY.

SENTIMENTALITY

1 Sentimentality is a form of fatigue.

> LEONORA CARRINGTON (b. 1917), British surrealist artist, writer. The Happy Corpse, in "The Happy Corpse Story" (written 1971; first published in a French translation in *Le Nouveau Commerce*, no. 31, 1975; repr. in *The Seventh Horse and Other Tales*, 1988).

2 It is as healthy to enjoy sentiment as to enjoy jam.

> G. K. CHESTERTON (1874–1936), British author. *Generally Speaking*, "On Sentiment" (1928).

3 Sentimentalists . . . adopt whatever merit is in good repute, and almost make it hateful with their praise. The warmer their expressions, the colder we feel. . . . Cure the drunkard, heal the insane, mollify the homicide, civilize the Pawnee, but what lessons can be devised for the debauchee of sentiment?

> RALPH WALDO EMERSON (1803–82), U.S. essayist, poet, philosopher. *Letters and Social Aims*, "Social Aims" (1876).

4 The psychiatrist knows only too well how each of us becomes the helpless but not pitiable victim of his own sentiments. Sentimentality is the superstructure erected upon brutality.

> CARL JUNG (1875–1961), Swiss psychiatrist. *Ulysses: A Monologue* (1932; repr. in *Collected Works*, vol. 15, ed. by William McGuire, 1966).

5 Sentimentality is the emotional promiscuity of those who have no sentiment.

> NORMAN MAILER (b. 1923), U.S. author. *Cannibals and Christians*, pt. 1, "My Hope for America" (1966), review of book by Lyndon B. Johnson.

6 Sentimentality is only sentiment that rubs you up the wrong way.

> W. SOMERSET MAUGHAM (1874–1965), British author. *A Writer's Notebook* (1949), 1941 entry.

7 Sentimentalists are they who seek to enjoy without incurring the Immense Debtorship for a thing done.

> GEORGE MEREDITH (1828–1909), English author. Sir Austin Feverel, quoting the "Pilgrim's Scrip," in: *The Ordeal of Richard Feverel*, ch. 24, "Of the Spring Primrose and the Autumnal" (1859). Speaking of sentimentalism, Sir Austin continued, "It is a happy pastime and an important science to the timid, the idle,

and the heartless; but a damning one to them who have anything to forfeit." James Joyce, for whom Meredith was an early influence, quoted this aphorism in *Ulysses*, ch. 9 (1922).

8 This, mayhap, was not logic, but it was something more potent, more real than logic—the soft insinuating voice of Sentiment . . .

BARONESS ORCZY (1865–1947), British author, playwright. *Leatherface*, bk. 2, ch. 5 (1918).

9 A sentimentalist, my dear Darlington, is a man who sees an absurd value in everything, and doesn't know the market price of any single thing.

OSCAR WILDE (1854–1900), Anglo-Irish playwright, author. Cecil Graham, in *Lady Windermere's Fan*, act 3.

See also Lowell on ACTION; Burroughs on GRIEF; Byron on WOMEN.

SERVANTS

1 We are beginning to wonder whether a servant girl hasn't the best of it after all. She knows how the salad tastes without the dressing, and she knows how life's lived before it gets to the parlor door.

DJUNA BARNES (1892–1982), U.S. author, poet, columnist. "The Home Club: For Servants Only," in *Brooklyn Daily Eagle* (12 Oct. 1913; repr. in *Djuna Barnes's New York*, 1989).

2 His lordship may compel us to be equal upstairs, but there will never be equality in the servants' hall.

J. M. BARRIE (1860–1937), British playwright. Crichton, in *The Admirable Crichton*, act 1 (1914).

3 One of the most considerable advantages the great have over their inferiors is to have servants as good as themselves.

MIGUEL DE CERVANTES (1547–1616), Spanish writer. Don Quixote, in *Don Quixote*, pt. 2, bk. 5, ch. 31 (1615; tr. by P. Motteux).

4 Me? What am I? Nothing. The legs on which dinner comes to the table, the arms by which cocktails enter the living room, the hands that drive cars. I am the eyes that see nothing, the ears that don't hear. I'm invisible too. They look and don't see me. When they move, I have to guess their direction and get myself out of the way.

SHIRLEY ANN GRAU (b. 1929), U.S. author. *The Condor Passes*, "Stanley" (1971).

5 The highest panegyric, therefore, that private virtue can receive, is the praise of servants.

SAMUEL JOHNSON (1709–84), English author, lexicographer. *Rambler*, no. 68 (London, 10 Nov. 1750; repr. in *Works of Samuel Johnson*, vol. 3, ed. by W. J. Bate and Albrecht B. Strauss, 1969).

6 For my own part, I had rather suffer any inconvenience from having to work occasionally in chambers and kitchen . . . than witness the subservience in which the menial class is held in Europe.

HARRIET MARTINEAU (1802–76), English writer, social critic. *Society in America*, vol. 3, "Occupation" (1837).

7 Few men have been admired of their familiars.

MICHEL DE MONTAIGNE (1533–92), French essayist. *Essays*, bk. 3, ch. 2, "Of Repenting" (tr. by John Florio, 1588).

8 Ladies and gentleman are permitted to have friends in the kennel, but not in the kitchen.

GEORGE BERNARD SHAW (1856–1950), Anglo-Irish playwright, critic. *Man and Superman*, "Maxims for Revolutionists: Servants" (1903).

SEX

1 The Englishman can get along with sex quite perfectly so long as he can pretend that it isn't sex but something else.

JAMES AGATE (1877–1947), British drama critic. *The Selective Ego*, "Ego 1" (ed. by Tim Beaumont, 1976), entry for 14 Oct. 1932.

2 That was the most fun I've ever had without laughing.

WOODY ALLEN (b. 1935), U.S. filmmaker. Alvy Singer (Allen), in the film *Annie Hall* (directed by Woody Allen, scripted by Allen with Marshall Brickman, 1977; repr. in *Four Films of Woody Allen*, 1982), complimenting Annie Hall (Diane Keaton).

3 You have to see the sex act comically, as a child.

W. H. AUDEN (1907–73), Anglo-American poet. *The Table Talk of W. H. Auden*, "March 17, 1947" (comp. by Alan Ansen, ed. by Nicholas Jenkins, 1990).

4 Sex—the great inequality, the great miscalculator, the great Irritator.

ENID BAGNOLD (1889–1981), British novelist, playwright. *Autobiography*, ch. 6 (1969).

5 The question of sexual dominance can exist only in the nightmare of that soul which has armed itself, totally, against the possibility of the changing motion of conquest and surrender, which is love.

JAMES BALDWIN (1924–87), U.S. author. *The Price Of The Ticket*, "The Devil Finds Work," sct. 2 (1985; first published 1976).

6 I believe that organic sex, body against body, skin area against skin area, is becoming no longer possible, simply because if anything is to have any meaning for us it must take place in terms of the values and experiences of the media landscape. . . . What we're getting is a whole new order of sexual fantasies, involving a different order of experiences, like car crashes, like travelling in jet aircraft, the whole overlay of new technologies, architecture, interior design, communications, transport, merchandising. These things are beginning to reach into our lives and change the interior design of our sexual fantasies. We've got to recognize that what one sees through the window of the TV screen is as important as what one sees through a window on the street.

J. G. BALLARD (b. 1930), British author. Interview in *Penthouse* (London, Sept. 1970; repr. in *Re/Search*, no. 8/9, San Francisco, 1984).

7 I've tried several varieties of sex. The conventional position makes me claustrophobic and the others give me a stiff neck or lockjaw.

TALLULAH BANKHEAD (1903–68), U.S. screen actor. Quoted in: Lee Israel, *Miss Tallulah Bankhead* (1972).

8 Sex pleasure in woman . . . is a kind of magic spell;

it demands complete abandon; if words or movements oppose the magic of caresses, the spell is broken.

> SIMONE DE BEAUVOIR (1908–86), French novelist, essayist. *The Second Sex*, bk. 2, pt. 4, ch. 3 (1953).

9 Embraces are cominglings from the head even to
the feet,
And not a pompous high priest entering by a
secret place.

> WILLIAM BLAKE (1757–1827), English poet, painter, engraver. *Jerusalem*, ch. 3, plate 69 (1804–20; repr. in *Complete Writings*, ed. by Geoffrey Keynes, 1957).

10 For once you must try not to shirk the facts:
Mankind is kept alive by bestial acts.

> BERTOLT BRECHT (1898–1956), German dramatist, poet. *The Threepenny Opera*, act 2, sc. 6, "What Keeps Mankind Alive?"

11 If the devil were to offer me a resurgence of what is commonly called virility, I'd decline. "Just keep my liver and lungs in good working order," I'd reply, "so I can go on drinking and smoking!"

> LUIS BUÑUEL (1900–1983), Spanish filmmaker. *My Last Sigh*, ch. 6 (1983).

12 It is true from early habit, one must make love mechanically as one swims; I was once very fond of both, but now as I never swim unless I tumble into the water, I don't make love till almost obliged.

> LORD BYRON (1788–1824), English poet. Letter, 10 Sept. 1812 (published in *Byron's Letters and Journals*, vol. 2, ed. by Leslie A. Marchand, 1973–81).

13 We do not go to bed in single pairs; even if we choose not to refer to them, we still drag there with us the cultural impedimenta of our social class, our parents' lives, our bank balances, our sexual and emotional expectations, our whole biographies—all the bits and pieces of our unique existences.

> ANGELA CARTER (1940–92), British author. *The Sadeian Woman*, "Polemical Preface" (1979).

14 Every man has been brought up with the idea that decent women don't pop in and out of bed; he has always been told by his mother that "nice girls don't." He finds, of course, when he gets older that this may be untrue— but only in a certain section of society.

> BARBARA CARTLAND (b. 1901), British novelist. Interview in Wendy Leigh, *Speaking Frankly* (1978).

15 Much more than our other needs and endeavors, it is sexuality that puts us on an even footing with our kind: the more we practice it, the more we become like everyone else: it is in the performance of a reputedly bestial function that we prove our status as citizens: nothing is more *public* than the sexual act.

> E. M. CIORAN (b. 1911), Rumanian-born French philosopher. *The Temptation to Exist*, "Rages and Resignations: Gogol" (1956).

16 The real problem between the sexes is that for men, sex is a gender-underliner, they need it for their egos. We don't need sex to make us feel we are the person we need to be.

> CAROL CLEWLOW (b. 1947), British novelist. Interview in *Observer* (London, 19 Feb. 1989).

17 The more developed sexual passion, in both sexes, is very largely an emotion of power, domination, or appropriation. There is no state of feeling that says "mine, mine," more fiercely.

> CHARLES HORTON COOLEY (1864–1929), U.S. sociologist. *Human Nature and the Social Order*, ch. 5 (1902).

18 Sex is the last refuge of the miserable.

> QUENTIN CRISP (b. 1908), British author. *The Naked Civil Servant*, ch. 8 (1968).

19 Sex is a short cut to everything.

> ANNE CUMMING (b. 1917), British author. *The Love Quest*, ch. 1 (1991), opening line of her autobiography.

20 The act of sex, gratifying as it may be, is God's joke on humanity. It is man's last desperate stand at superintendency.

> BETTE DAVIS (1908–89), U.S. screen actor. *The Lonely Life*, ch. 20 (1962).

21 Women's Liberation calls it enslavement but the real truth about the sexual revolution is that it has made of sex an almost chaotically limitless and therefore unmanageable realm in the life of women.

> MIDGE DECTER (b. 1927), U.S. author, editor, social critic. *The New Chastity and Other Arguments Against Women's Liberation*, ch. 2 (1972).

23 Sex. In America an obsession. In other parts of the world a fact.

> MARLENE DIETRICH (1904–92), German-born U.S. film actor. *Marlene Dietrich's ABC*, "Sex" (1962).

24 You can't remember sex. You can remember the fact of it, and recall the setting, and even the details, but the sex of the sex cannot be remembered, the substantive truth of it, it is by nature self-erasing, you can remember its anatomy and be left with a judgment as to the degree of your liking of it, but whatever it is as a splurge of being, as a loss, as a charge of the conviction of love stopping your heart like your execution, there is no memory of it in the brain, only the deduction that it happened and that time passed, leaving you with a silhouette that you want to fill in again.

> E. L. DOCTOROW (b. 1931), U.S. novelist. The narrator (Billy Bathgate), in *Billy Bathgate*, ch. 16 (1989).

25 No woman needs intercourse; few women escape it.

> ANDREA DWORKIN (b. 1946), U.S. feminist critic. *Right-Wing Women*, ch. 3 (1978).

26 What will happen to sex after liberation? Frankly, I don't know. It is a great mystery to all of us.

> NORA EPHRON (b. 1941), U.S. author, journalist. "Women," in *Esquire* (New York, July 1972).

27 We do not understand these Americans who, like adolescents, always speak of sex, and who, like adolescents, all of a sudden have discovered that sex is good not only for procreating children.

> ORIANA FALLACI (b. 1930), Italian author. *The Egotists*, "Hugh Hefner" (1963).

28 Sex is two plus two making five, rather than four. Sex is the X ingredient that you can't define, and it's that

X ingredient between two people that make both a man and a woman good in bed. It's all relative. There are no rules.

MARTY FELDMAN (1933–82), British comedian. Interview in Wendy Leigh, *Speaking Frankly* (1978).

29 Older women are best, because they always think they may be doing it for the last time.

IAN FLEMING (1908–64), British author. Notebook entry. Quoted in: John Pearson, *The Life of Ian Fleming*, ch. 8, sct. 1 (1966).

30 Marital intercourse is certainly holy, lawful and praiseworthy in itself and profitable to society, yet in certain circumstances it can prove dangerous, as when through excess the soul is made sick with venial sin, or through the violation and perversion of its primary end, killed by mortal sin; such perversion, detestable in proportion to its departure from the true order, being always mortal sin, for it is never lawful to exclude the primary end of marriage which is the procreation of children.

ST. FRANCIS DE SALES (1567–1622), French churchman, devotional writer. *Introduction to the Devout Life*, pt. 3, ch. 39 (1609).

31 We must reckon with the possibility that something in the nature of the sexual instinct itself is unfavorable to the realization of complete satisfaction.

SIGMUND FREUD (1856–1939), Austrian psychiatrist. *On the Universal Tendency to Debasement in the Sphere of Love*, sct. 3 (1912; repr. in *Complete Works*, vol. 11, ed. by James Strachey and Anna Freud, 1957).

32 Sexual love is undoubtedly one of the chief things in life, and the union of mental and bodily satisfaction in the enjoyment of love is one of its culminating peaks. Apart from a few queer fanatics, all the world knows this and conducts its life accordingly; science alone is too delicate to admit it.

SIGMUND FREUD (1856–1939), Austrian psychiatrist. *Observations on Transference-Love* (1915; repr. in *Complete Works*, vol. 12, ed. by James Strachey and Anna Freud, 1958).

33 Instead of fulfilling the promise of infinite orgastic bliss, sex in the America of the feminine mystique is becoming a strangely joyless national compulsion, if not a contemptuous mockery.

BETTY FRIEDAN (b. 1921), U.S. feminist writer. *The Feminine Mystique*, ch. 11 (1963).

34 If I were asked for a one line answer to the question "What makes a woman good in bed?" I would say, "A man who is good in bed."

BOB GUCCIONE (b. 1930), U.S. publisher. Interview in Wendy Leigh, *Speaking Frankly* (1978).

35 Sex can no longer be the germ, the seed of fiction. Sex is an episode, most properly conveyed in an episodic manner, quickly, often ironically. It is a bursting forth of only one of the cells in the body of the omnipotent "I," the one who hopes by concentration of tone and voice to utter the sound of reality.

ELIZABETH HARDWICK (b. 1916), U.S. critic, author. "Seduction and Betrayal," address, 1972, Vassar College (published in *Seduction And Betrayal: Women and Literature*, 1974).

36 The human spirit sublimates
the impulses it thwarts:

a healthy sex life mitigates
the lust for other sports.

PIET HEIN (b. 1905), Dutch inventor, poet. *Grooks*, "Hint and Suggestion" (1966), admonitory grook addressed to youth.

37 I find it extraordinary that a straightforward if inelegant device for ensuring the survival of the species should involve human beings in such emotional turmoil. Does sex have to be taken so seriously?

P. D. JAMES (b. 1920), British mystery writer. Alice, in *Devices and Desires*, ch. 16 (1989).

38 I can live without it all—
love with its blood pump,
sex with its messy hungers,
men with their peacock strutting,
their silly sexual baggage,
their wet tongues in my ear.

ERICA JONG (b. 1942), U.S. author. "Becoming a Nun," in *About Women* (ed. by Stephen Berg and S. J. Marks, 1973).

39 Intercourse with a woman is sometimes a satisfactory substitute for masturbation. But it takes a lot of imagination to make it work.

KARL KRAUS (1874–1936), Austrian satirist. *Die Fackel*, no. 229 (Vienna, 2 July 1907; repr. in Thomas Szasz, *Anti-Freud: Karl Kraus's Criticism of Psychoanalysis and Psychiatry*, ch. 8, 1976).

40 Sexual intercourse began
In nineteen sixty-three
(Which was rather late for me)—
Between the end of the *Chatterley* ban
And the Beatles' first LP.

PHILIP LARKIN (1922–85), British poet. *Annus Mirabilis*.

41 I am sure no other civilization, not even the Romans, has showed such a vast proportion of ignominious and degraded nudity, and ugly, squalid dirty sex. Because no other civilization has driven sex into the underworld, and nudity to the W.C.

D. H. LAWRENCE (1885–1930), British author. *Pornography and Obscenity* (1930; repr. in *Phoenix: The Posthumous Papers of D. H. Lawrence*, pt. 3, ed. by E. McDonald, 1936).

42 That our popular art forms have become so obsessed with sex has turned the U.S.A into a nation of hobbledehoys; as if grown people don't have more vital concerns, such as taxes, inflation, dirty politics, earning a living, getting an education, or keeping out of jail.

ANITA LOOS (1893–1981), U.S. novelist, screenwriter. *Kiss Hollywood Good-by*, ch. 21 (1974).

43 There is nothing safe about sex. There never will be.

NORMAN MAILER (b. 1923), U.S. author. *International Herald Tribune* (Paris, 24 Jan. 1992).

44 The passion between the sexes has appeared in every age to be so nearly the same, that it may always be considered, in algebraic language as a given quantity.

THOMAS ROBERT MALTHUS (1766–1834), English economist, sociologist. *An Essay on the Principle of Population*, ch. 8 (1798).

45 For those for whom the sex act has come to seem mechanical and merely the meeting and manipulation of body parts, there often remains a hunger which can be called metaphysical but which is not recognized as such, and which seeks satisfaction in physical danger, or sometimes in torture, suicide, or murder.

> MARSHALL MCLUHAN (1911–80), Canadian communications theorist. *The Mechanical Bride,* title essay (1951).

46 Continental people have sex lives; the English have hot-water bottles.

> GEORGE MIKES (b. 1912), Hungarian-born British humorist. *How to be an Alien,* ch. 1, sct. 6 (1946).

47 What holds the world together, as I have learned from bitter experience, is sexual intercourse.

> HENRY MILLER (1891–1980), U.S. author. *Tropic of Capricorn* (1938; repr. 1966, p. 174).

48 Sex is one of the nine reasons for reincarnation. The other eight are unimportant.

> HENRY MILLER (1891–1980), U.S. author. *Sexus,* ch. 21 (1949).

49 Coitus can scarcely be said to take place in a vacuum; although of itself it appears a biological and physical activity, it is set so deeply within the larger context of human affairs that it serves as a charged microcosm of the variety of attitudes and values to which culture subscribes. Among other things, it may serve as a model of sexual politics on an individual or personal plane.

> KATE MILLETT (b. 1934), U.S. feminist author. *Sexual Politics,* ch. 2 (1970).

50 After mature deliberation of counsel, the good Queen to establish a rule and imitable example unto all posterity, for the moderation and required modesty in a lawful marriage, ordained the number of six times a day as a lawful, necessary and competent limit.

> MICHEL DE MONTAIGNE (1533–92), French essayist. *Essays,* bk. 3, ch. 5, "Upon Some Verses of Virgil" (tr. by John Florio, 1588), of the Queen of Aragon.

51 Sex is the mysticism of materialism and the only possible religion in a materialistic society.

> MALCOLM MUGGERIDGE (1903–90), British broadcaster. Television broadcast, BBC1, 21 Oct. 1965. Quoted in: *Muggeridge Through the Microphone,* "The American Way of Sex" (1967).

52 Skill makes love unending.

> OVID (43 B.C.-17 A.D.), Roman poet. *Ars Amatoria,* bk. 3.

53 You have to accept the fact that part of the sizzle of sex comes from the danger of sex. You can be overpowered.

> CAMILLE PAGLIA (b. 1947), U.S. author, critic, educator. Interview in *San Francisco Examiner* (7 July 1991; repr. in *Sex, Art, and American Culture,* "The Rape Debate," 1992).

54 We should teach general ethics to both men and women, but sexual relationships themselves must not be policed. Sex, like the city streets, would be risk-free only in totalitarian regimes.

> CAMILLE PAGLIA (b. 1947), U.S. author, critic, educator. *Sex, Art, and American Culture,* Introduction (1992).

55 I know it does make people happy, but to me it is just like having a cup of tea.

> CYNTHIA PAYNE (b. 1934), British housewife, brothel-keeper. Remark, 8 Nov. 1987. Quoted in: *Sunday Correspondent* (London, 24 Dec. 1989), after Paine was acquitted of running a brothel in Streatham, South London, in the "sex-for-luncheon-vouchers" case.

56 In particular I may mention Sophocles the poet, who was once asked in my presence, "How do you feel about love, Sophocles? are you still capable of it?" to which he replied, "Hush! if you please: to my great delight I have escaped from it, and feel as if I had escaped from a frantic and savage master." I thought then, as I do now, that he spoke wisely. For unquestionably old age brings us profound repose and freedom from this and other passions.

> PLATO. (c. 427–347 B.C.), Greek philosopher. Cephalus, in *The Republic,* bk. 1, sct. 329.

57 There goes a saying, and 'twas shrewdly said,
Old fish at table, but young flesh in bed.

> ALEXANDER POPE (1688–1744), English satirical poet. *January and May,* a translation of Geoffrey Chaucer, *The Merchant's Tale,* written aged sixteen or seventeen.

58 Your daughter is old enough to do what she pleases . . . she likes to fuck, loves to fuck . . . she was born to fuck, and . . . if you do not wish to be fucked yourself, the best thing for you to do is to let her do what she wants.

> MARQUIS DE SADE (1740–1814), French author. Dolmancé, in *Philosophy in the Bedroom,* "Dialogue the Seventh" (1795), to Madame de Saint-Ange.

59 "Sex" is as important as eating or drinking and we ought to allow the one appetite to be satisfied with as little restraint or false modesty as the other.

> MARQUIS DE SADE (1740–1814), French author. Mme Delbène, in *L'Histoire de Juliette, ou les Prospérités du Vice,* pt. 1 (1797).

60 A mutual and satisfied sexual act is of great benefit to the average woman, the magnetism of it is health giving. When it is not desired on the part of the woman and she gives no response, it should not take place. The submission of her body without love or desire is degrading to the woman's finer sensibility, all the marriage certificates on earth to the contrary notwithstanding.

> MARGARET SANGER (1883–1966), U.S. pioneer of birth control movement. *Family Limitation,* "Coitus Interruptus" (1914).

61 Making love? It's a communion with a woman. The bed is the holy table. There I find passion—and purification.

> OMAR SHARIF (b. 1932), Egyptian screen actor. Quoted in: *City Limits* (London, 18 Dec. 1986).

62 All nature's creatures join to express nature's purpose. Somewhere in their mounting and mating, rutting and butting is the very secret of nature itself.

> GRAHAM SWIFT (b. 1949), British novelist, short-story writer. *Shuttlecock,* ch. 11 (1981).

63 The law of God, as quite plainly expressed in woman's construction, is this: There shall be no limit put upon your intercourse with the other sex sexually, at any time of life. . . . During twenty-three days in every month (in the absence of pregnancy) from the time a woman is seven years old till she dies of old age, she is ready for action, and *competent.* As competent as the candlestick is to receive the candle. Competent every day, competent every night. Also, she *wants* that candle—yearns for it, longs for it, hankers after it, as commanded by the law of God in her heart.

> MARK TWAIN (1835–1910), U.S. author. Satan, in *Letters from the Hearth,* Letter 8 (ed. by Bernard De Voto, 1962). As for men, "The law of god, as quite plainly expressed in man's construction, is this: During your entire life you shall be under inflexible limits and restrictions, sexually."

64 Sex is like money; only too much is enough.

> JOHN UPDIKE (b. 1932), U.S. author, critic. Piet Hanema, in *Couples,* ch. 5 (1968).

65 What more fiendish proof of cosmic irresponsibility than a Nature which, having invented sex as a way to mix genes, then permits to arise, amid all its perfumed and hypnotic inducements to mate, a tireless tribe of spirochetes and viruses that torture and kill us for following orders?

> JOHN UPDIKE (b. 1932), U.S. author, critic. *Self-Consciousness: Memoirs,* ch. 6 (1989).

66 Sex is a conversation carried out by other means. If you get on well out of bed, half the problems of bed are solved.

> PETER USTINOV (b. 1921), British actor, writer, director. Interview in Wendy Leigh, *Speaking Frankly* (1978).

67 Painting and fucking a lot are not compatible; it weakens the brain.

> VINCENT VAN GOGH (1853–90), Dutch painter. Letter, June 1888 (published in *The Complete Letters of Vincent Van Gogh,* vol. 3, no. B7, 1958).

68 Sex is. There is nothing more to be done about it. Sex builds no roads, writes no novels and sex certainly gives no meaning to anything in life but itself.

> GORE VIDAL (b. 1925), U.S. novelist, critic. "Norman Mailer's Self-Advertisements," in *Nation* (New York, 2 Jan. 1960; repr. in *Homage to Daniel Shays: Collected Essays 1952–1972,* 1974).

69 Sex is more exciting on the screen and between the pages than between the sheets.

> ANDY WARHOL (1928–87), U.S. Pop artist. *From A to B and Back Again,* ch. 3 (1975).

70 All this fuss about sleeping together. For physical pleasure I'd sooner go to my dentist any day.

> EVELYN WAUGH (1903–66), British novelist. Nina Blount, in *Vile Bodies,* ch. 6 (1930), to her fiancé Adam Fenwick-Symes.

71 There comes a moment in the day when you have written your pages in the morning, attended to your correspondence in the afternoon, and have nothing further to do. Then comes that hour when you are bored; that's the time for sex.

> H. G. WELLS (1866–1946), British author. Quoted in: Charlie Chaplin, *My Autobiography,* ch. 16 (1964).

72 I am, I must confess, suspicious of those who denounce others for having "too much" sex. At what point does a "healthy" amount become "too much"? There are, of course, those who suffer because their desire for sex has become compulsive; in their case the drive (loneliness, guilt) is at fault, not the activity as such. . . . When "morality" is discussed I invariably discover, halfway into the conversation, that what is meant are not the great ethical questions . . . but the rather dreary business of sexual habit, which to my mind is an aesthetic rather than an ethical issue.

> EDMUND WHITE (b. 1940), U.S. author. *States of Desire: Travels in Gay America,* ch. 2 (1980).

73 Sex contains all, bodies, souls,
Meanings, proofs, purities, delicacies, results, promulgations,
Songs, commands, health, pride, the maternal mystery, the seminal milk,
All hopes, benefactions, bestowals, all the passions, loves, beauties,
delights of the earth.

> WALT WHITMAN (1819–92), U.S. poet. *A Woman Waits for Me.*

See also Bagnold on AFFECTION; Pope on ENNUI; Freud on EXCREMENT AND EXCRETION; Cartland on FOOD AND EATING; Loos on FRANCE AND THE FRENCH; FRIGIDITY; IMPOTENCE; MASTURBATION; ORGASM; PROMISCUITY; Burchill on RELATIONSHIPS; Wittgenstein on RELIGION; Donne on SEDUCTION; SEXUAL DEVIATION.

SEXISM

1 In the beginning, I wanted to enter what was essentially a man's field. I wanted to prove I could do it. Then I found that when I did as well as the men in the field I got more credit for my work because I am a woman, which seems unfair.

> EUGENIE CLARK (b. 1922), U.S. marine biologist, author. Quoted in: *Ms.* (New York, Aug. 1979).

2 Sexism is the foundation on which all tyranny is built. Every social form of hierarchy and abuse is modeled on male-over-female domination.

> ANDREA DWORKIN (b. 1946), U.S. feminist critic. "Redefining Nonviolence," speech, 5 April 1975, Boston College (published in *Our Blood,* ch. 6, 1976).

3 A woman is handicapped by her sex, and handicaps society, either by slavishly copying the pattern of man's advance in the professions, or by refusing to compete with man at all.

> BETTY FRIEDAN (b. 1921), U.S. feminist writer. *The Feminine Mystique,* ch. 14 (1963).

4 If any of us hopes to survive, s/he must meet the extremity of the American female condition with immediate and political response. The thoroughly destructive and indefensible subjugation of the majority of Americans cannot continue except at the peril of the entire body politic.

> JUNE JORDAN (b. 1939), U.S. poet, civil rights activist. *Moving Towards Home: Political Essays,* "The Case for the Real Majority" (1989; first published 1982).

5 There are very few jobs that actually require a penis or vagina. All other jobs should be open to everybody.

> FLORYNCE R. KENNEDY (b. 1916), U.S. lawyer, civil rights activist. Quoted in: John Brady, "Freelancer with No Time to Write," in *Writer's Digest* (Cincinnati, Feb. 1974).

6 The misogyny that shapes every aspect of our civilization is the institutionalized form of male fear and hatred of what they have denied and therefore cannot know, cannot share: that wild country, the being of women.

> URSULA K. LE GUIN (b. 1929), U.S. author. "Woman/Wilderness," speech, June 1986, University of California at Davis (published in *Dancing at the Edge of the World*, 1989).

7 Much of the ill-tempered railing against women that has characterized the popular writing of the last two years is a half-hearted attempt to find a way back to a more balanced relationship between our biological selves and the world we have built. So women are scolded both for being mothers and for not being mothers, for wanting to eat their cake and have it too, and for not wanting to eat their cake and have it too.

> MARGARET MEAD (1901–78), U.S. anthropologist. *Male and Female*, ch. 8 (1949).

8 However muted its present appearance may be, sexual dominion obtains nevertheless as perhaps the most pervasive ideology of our culture and provides its most fundamental concept of power.

> KATE MILLET (b. 1934), U.S. feminist author. *Sexual Politics*, ch. 2 (1970).

9 No man can call himself liberal, or radical, or even a conservative advocate of fair play, if his work depends in any way on the unpaid or underpaid labor of women at home, or in the office.

> GLORIA STEINEM (b. 1934), U.S. feminist writer, editor. *New York Times* (26 Aug. 1971).

10 Any woman who chooses to behave like a full human being should be warned that the armies of the status quo will treat her as something of a dirty joke. That's their natural and first weapon. She will *need* her sisterhood.

> GLORIA STEINEM (b. 1934), U.S. feminist writer, editor. "Sisterhood," in *Ms.* (New York, 1972; repr. in *Outrageous acts and Everyday Rebellions*, 1983).

11 Society's double behavioral standard for women and for men is, in fact, a more effective deterrent than economic discrimination because it is more insidious, less tangible. Economic disadvantages involve ascertainable amounts, but the very nature of societal value judgments makes them harder to define, their effects harder to relate.

> ANNE TUCKER (b. 1945), U.S. editor, critic. *The Woman's Eye*, Introduction (1973).

12 Inevitably we look upon society, so kind to you, so harsh to us, as an ill-fitting form that distorts the truth; deforms the mind; fetters the will.

> VIRGINIA WOOLF (1882–1941), British novelist. *Three Guineas* (1938, p. 121).

See also MEN AND WOMEN; Eliot on OPPRESSION; Lerner on THEORY; WOMEN AND MEN.

SEXUAL ABUSE

1 Children's bodies aren't like automobiles with the assailant's fingerprints lingering on the wheel. The world of sexual abuse is quintessentially secret. It is the perfect crime.

> BEATRIX CAMPBELL (b. 1947), British journalist. *Unofficial Secrets*, ch. 2 (1988). In the book's introduction, Campbell quotes a police source on the subject: "Sexual abuse is like a corpse on a slab, saying nothing. You've got nothing to go on. It's a police officer's nightmare. You just want it to go away."

2 In most cases an act of unwelcome sex is no more bother than being vaccinated, so there's no point going on about it as if it were a fate worse than death. With skill and good manners you can avoid having to make the sacrifice, but should you find yourself in a compromising situation largely of your own making, you should stop defending your virtue and start worrying about your maturity. It will give you something to think about while the savage pumper bangs away.

> QUENTIN CRISP (b. 1908), British author. *Manners from Heaven*, ch. 6 (1984).

3 A man assumes that a woman's refusal is just part of a game. Or, at any rate, a lot of men assume that. When a man says no, it's no. When a woman says no, it's yes, or at least maybe. There is even a joke to that effect. And little by little, women begin to believe in this view of themselves.

> ERICA JONG (b. 1942), U.S. author. The narrator (Isadora Wing), in *Fear of Flying*, ch. 16 (1973).

4 Profanation and violation are part of the perversity of sex, which never will conform to liberal theories of benevolence. Every model of morally or politically correct sexual behavior *will be subverted*, by nature's daemonic law.

> CAMILLE PAGLIA (b. 1947), U.S. author, critic, educator. *Sexual Personae*, ch. 1 (1990).

See also CHILD ABUSE; INCEST; RAPE.

SEXUAL DEVIATION

1 There is no such thing as a value-free concept of deviance; to say homosexuals are deviant because they are a statistical minority is, in practice, to stigmatize them. Nuns are rarely classed as deviants for the same reason, although if they obey their vows they clearly differ very significantly from the great majority of people.

> DENNIS ALTMAN (b. 1943), Australian sociologist. *The Homosexualization of America*, ch. 1 (1982).

2 People will begin to explore all the sidestreets of sexual experience, but they will do it intellectually. . . . Sex won't take place in the bed, necessarily—it'll take place in the head!

> J. G. BALLARD (b. 1930), British author. Interview in *Penthouse* (London, Sept. 1970; repr. in *Re/Search*, no. 8/9, San Francisco, 1984).

3 Part of the public horror of sexual irregularity so-called is due to the fact that everyone knows himself essentially guilty.

> ALEISTER CROWLEY (1875–1947), British occultist. *The Confessions of Aleister Crowley*, ch. 50 (1929; rev. 1970).

4 How many modern transsexuals are unacknowledged shamans? Perhaps it is to poets they should go for counsel, rather than surgeons.

CAMILLE PAGLIA (b. 1947), U.S. author, critic, educator. *Sexual Personae*, ch. 2 (1990).

5 One must feel sorry for those who have strange tastes, but never insult them. Their wrong is Nature's too; they are no more responsible for having come into the world with tendencies unlike ours than are we for being born bandy-legged or well-proportioned.

MARQUIS DE SADE (1740–1814), French author. Le Chevalier, in *Philosophy in the Bedroom*, "Dialogue the Fifth" (1795).

6 Variety, multiplicity are the two most powerful vehicles of lust.

MARQUIS DE SADE (1740–1814), French author. Mme Delbène, in *L'Histoire de Juliette, ou les Prospérités du Vice*, pt. 1 (1797).

7 The variables are surprisingly few. . . . One can whip or be whipped; one can eat excrement or quaff urine; mouth and private part can be meet in this or that commerce. After which there is the gray of morning and the sour knowledge that things have remained fairly generally the same since man first met goat and woman.

GEORGE STEINER (b. 1929), French-born U.S. critic, novelist. *Language and Silence*, "Nightworks" (1967).

See also CHILD ABUSE; INCEST; SADOMASOCHISM.

SEXUALITY

1 The American *ideal* . . . of sexuality appears to be rooted in the American ideal of masculinity. This idea has created cowboys and Indians, good guys and bad guys, punks and studs, tough guys and softies, butch and faggot, black and white. It is an ideal so paralytically infantile that it is virtually forbidden—as an unpatriotic act—that the American boy evolve into the complexity of manhood.

JAMES BALDWIN (1924–87), U.S. author. "Freaks and the American Ideal of Manhood," in *Playboy* (Chicago, Jan. 1985; repr. in *The Price of the Ticket*, "Here Be Dragons," 1985).

2 Sexual liberation, as a slogan, turns out to be another kind of bondage. For a woman it offers orgasm as her ultimate and major fulfillment; it's better than motherhood.

VICTORIA BILLINGS (b. 1945), U.S. journalist, author. *The Womansbook*, "What Is Individuality?" (1974).

3 Admittedly, a homosexual can be conditioned to react sexually to a woman, or to an old boot for that matter. In fact, both homo- and heterosexual experimental subjects *have* been conditioned to react sexually to an old boot, and you can save a lot of money that way.

WILLIAM BURROUGHS (b. 1914), U.S. author. *The Adding Machine*, "Civilian Defense" (1985).

4 It is essential that we realize once and for all that man is much more of a sex creature than a moral creature. The former is inherent, the other is grafted on.

EMMA GOLDMAN (1869–1940), U.S. anarchist. "The Social Importance of the Modern School," lecture c. 1912 (first published in *Red Emma Speaks*, pt. 2, ed. by Alix Kates Shulman, 1972).

5 Understand that sexuality is as wide as the sea. Understand that your morality is not law. Understand that we are you. Understand that if we decide to have sex whether safe, safer, or unsafe, it is our decision and you have no rights in our lovemaking.

DEREK JARMAN (b. 1942), British filmmaker, artist, author. *At Your Own Risk: A Saint's Testament*, "1940's" (1992).

6 Back in the days when men were hunters and chest-beaters and women spent their whole lives worrying about pregnancy or dying in childbirth, they often had to be taken against their will. Men complained that women were cold, unresponsive, frigid. . . . They wanted their women wanton. They wanted their women wild. Now women were finally learning to be wanton and wild—and what happened? The men wilted.

ERICA JONG (b. 1942), U.S. author. The narrator (Isadora Wing), in *Fear of Flying*, ch. 16 (1973).

7 Sexuality poorly repressed unsettles some families; well repressed, it unsettles the whole world.

KARL KRAUS (1874–1936), Austrian satirist. *Die Fackel*, no. 315/16 (Vienna, 26 Jan. 1911; repr. in Thomas Szasz, *Anti-Freud: Karl Kraus's Criticism of Psychoanalysis and Psychiatry*, ch. 8, 1976).

8 Everyone probably thinks that I'm a raving nymphomaniac, that I have an *insatiable* sexual appetite, when the truth is I'd rather read a book.

MADONNA (b. 1959), U.S. singer, actor. *Q Magazine* (London, June 1991).

9 WHAT am I suffering from? Sexuality. . . . Will it destroy me? . . . How can I rid myself of Sexuality?

THOMAS MANN (1875–1955), German author, critic. Quoted in: Marcel Reich-Ranicki, *Thomas Mann and His Family*, "Thomas Mann—The Genius and His Helpers" (1987; tr. 1989), written at age 21.

10 In libertinage, nothing is frightful, because everything libertinage suggests is also a natural inspiration; the most extraordinary, the most bizarre acts, those which most arrantly seem to conflict with every law, every human institution . . . even those that are not frightful, and there is not one amongst them all that cannot be demonstrated within the boundaries of nature.

MARQUIS DE SADE (1740–1814), French author. Dolmancé, in *Philosophy in the Bedroom*, "Dialogue the Fifth" (1795).

11 The sexual parts are not only vivid examples of the body's dominion; they are also apertures whose damp emissions and ammoniac smells testify to the mysterious putrefaction of the body.

ROGER SCRUTON (b. 1944), British philosopher, author. *Sexual Desire*, ch. 6 (1986).

12 Tamed as it may be, sexuality remains one of the demonic forces in human consciousness—pushing us at intervals close to taboo and dangerous desires, which range from the impulse to commit sudden arbitrary violence upon another person to the voluptuous yearning for the extinction of one's consciousness, for death itself.

Even on the level of simple physical sensation and mood, making love surely resembles having an epileptic fit at least as much as, if not more than, it does eating a meal or conversing with someone.

> SUSAN SONTAG (b. 1933), U.S. essayist. *Styles of Radical Will,* "The Pornographic Imagination," sct. 3 (1969).

13 Fear of sexuality is the new, disease-sponsored register of the universe of fear in which everyone now lives.

> SUSAN SONTAG (b. 1933), U.S. essayist. *AIDS and Its Metaphors,* ch. 7 (1989).

14 In asking forgiveness of women for our mythologizing of their bodies, for being *unreal* about them, we can only appeal to their own sexuality, which is different but not basically different, perhaps, from our own. For women, too, there seems to be that tangle of supplication and possessiveness, that descent toward infantile undifferentiation, that omnipotent helplessness, that merger with the cosmic mother-warmth, that flushed pulse-quickened leap into overestimation, projection, general mix-up.

> JOHN UPDIKE (b. 1932), U.S. author, critic. "The Female Body," in *Michigan Quarterly Review* (1990; repr. in "The Best American Essays, 1991," ed. by Joyce Carol Oates, 1991).

15 There is no such thing as a homosexual or a heterosexual person. There are only homo- or heterosexual acts. Most people are a mixture of impulses if not practices.

> GORE VIDAL (b. 1925), U.S. novelist, critic. *Armageddon? Essays 1983–1987,* sct. 1, "Tennessee Williams: Someone to Laugh at the Squares With" (1987).

16 I believe that it's better to be looked over than it is to be overlooked.

> MAE WEST (1892–1980), U.S. screen actor. *On Sex, Health and ESP,* "Last Word" (1975). Mae West first said said these words in the 1934 film, *Belle of the Nineties,* which she scripted.

See also SENSUALITY.

WILLIAM SHAKESPEARE

1 But Shakespeare one gets acquainted with without knowing how. It is a part of an Englishman's constitution. His thoughts and beauties are so spread abroad that one touches them everywhere; one is intimate with him by instinct.

> JANE AUSTEN (1775–1817), English novelist. Henry Crawford, in *Mansfield Park,* ch. 34 (1814).

2 Shakespeare's name, you may depend on it, stands absurdly too high and will go down.

> LORD BYRON (1788–1824), English poet. Letter, 24 March 1814, to poet James Hogg (published in *Selected Letters and Journals,* ed. by Leslie A. Marchand, 1982).

3 I look upon him to be the *worst* of models—though the most extraordinary of writers.

> LORD BYRON (1788–1824), English poet. Letter, 14 July 1821, to the publisher John Murray (published in *Byron's Letters and Journals,* vol. 8, ed. by Leslie A. Marchand, 1973–81).

4 It would be unjust, and moreover Utopian, for Shakespeare to direct the shoemakers' union. But it would be equally disastrous for the shoemakers' union to ignore Shakespeare.

> ALBERT CAMUS (1913–60), French-Algerian philosopher, author. *The Rebel,* pt. 4, "Creation and Revolution" (1951; tr. 1953).

5 Alive today he would undoubtedly have written and directed motion pictures, plays and God knows what. Instead of saying "This medium is not good," he would have used it and made it good. If some people called some of his work cheap (which some of it is), he wouldn't have cared a rap, because he would know that without some vulgarity there is no complete man.

> RAYMOND CHANDLER (1888–1959), U.S. author. Letter, 22 April 1949, to publisher Hamish Hamilton (published in *Raymond Chandler Speaking,* 1962).

6 Shakespeare's fault is not the greatest into which a poet may fall. It merely indicates a deficiency of taste.

> DENIS DIDEROT (1713–84), French philosopher. *On Dramatic Poetry* (1758; repr. in *Selected Writings,* ed. by Lester G. Crocker, 1966).

7 He was the man who of all modern, and perhaps ancient poets, had the largest and most comprehensive soul. . . . He needed not the spectacles of books to read Nature; he looked inwards, and found her there.

> JOHN DRYDEN (1631–1700), English poet, dramatist, critic. Neander, in *An Essay of Dramatic Poesy* (1668).

8 Shakespeare—whetting, frustrating, surprising and gratifying.

> F. SCOTT FITZGERALD (1896–1940), U.S. author. *The Crack-Up,* "Notebook L" (ed. by Edmund Wilson, 1945).

9 The remarkable thing about Shakespeare is that he is really very good—in spite of all the people who say he is very good.

> ROBERT GRAVES (1895–1985), British poet, novelist. Quoted in: *Observer* (London, 6 Dec. 1964).

10 If we wish to know the force of human genius, we should read Shakespeare. If we wish to see the insignificance of human learning, we may study his commentators.

> WILLIAM HAZLITT (1778–1830), English essayist. "On the Ignorance of the Learned," in *Edinburgh Magazine* (July 1818; repr. in *Table Talk,* 1821).

11 Shakespeare was the great one before us. His place was between God and despair.

> EUGÈNE IONESCO (b. 1912), Rumanian-born French playwright. *International Herald Tribune* (Paris, 17 June 1988).

12 A quibble is to Shakespeare what luminous vapours are to the traveller: he follows it at all adventures; it is sure to lead him out of his way and sure to engulf him in the mire.

> SAMUEL JOHNSON (1709–84), English author, lexicographer. *Plays of William Shakespeare,* Preface (1765).

13 He was not of an age, but for all time!

> BEN JONSON (1573–1637), English dramatist, poet. *To the Memory of My Beloved, the Author, Master William Shakespeare.*

14 For I loved the man and do honour his memory, on this side of idolatry, as much as any.

> BEN JONSON (1573–1637), English dramatist, poet. *Timber, or Discoveries Made upon Men and Matter,* "De Shakespeare Nostrati" (1641).

15 Shakespeare is one of the last books one should like to give up, perhaps the one just before the Dying Service in a large Prayer book.

> CHARLES LAMB (1775–1834), English essayist, critic. Letter, 1 Feb. 1806, to William Wordsworth (published in *Bibliophile,* 1840).

16 If I had any doubts at all about the justice of my dislike for Shakespeare, that doubt vanished completely. What a crude, immoral, vulgar, and senseless work Hamlet is. The whole thing is based on pagan vengeance; the only aim is to gather together as many effects as possible; there is no rhyme or reason about it.

> LEO TOLSTOY (1828–1910), Russian novelist, philosopher. Letter, Jan. 1896 (published in *Tolstoy's Letters,* vol. 2, ed. and tr. by R. F. Christian, 1978). Tolstoy continued, "The author was so concerned with the effects that he didn't even bother to give the main person any character, and everybody decided that it was a brilliant portrayal of a characterless man. I never understood so clearly the utter helplessness of the crowd in making judgements, and how they can deceive themselves."

17 Shakespeare, who was considered the English Corneille, flourished at about the time of Lope de Vega. He had a strong and fertile genius, full of naturalness and sublimity, without the slightest spark of good taste or the least knowledge of the rules. . . . After two hundred years most of the outlandish and monstrous ideas of this author have acquired the right to be considered sublime, and almost all modern authors have copied him. . . . It does not occur to people that they should not copy him, and the lack of success of their copies simply makes people think that he is inimitable.

> VOLTAIRE (1694–1778), French philosopher, author. *Letters on England,* letter 18, "On Tragedy" (1732).

18 We become lovers when we see Romeo and Juliet, and Hamlet makes us students. The blood of Duncan is upon our hands, with Timon we rage against the world, and when Lear wanders out upon the heath the terror of madness touches us. Ours is the white sinlessness of Desdemona, and ours, also, the sin of Iago.

> OSCAR WILDE (1854–1900), Anglo-Irish playwright, author. *The Portrait of Mr. W. H.,* ch. 1, in *Blackwood's Edinburgh Magazine* (July 1889).

19 This is not "writing" at all. Indeed, I could say that Shakespeare surpasses literature altogether, if I knew what I meant.

> VIRGINIA WOOLF (1882–1941), British novelist. *The Diary of Virginia Woolf,* vol. 3, (ed. by Anne O. Bell, 1980), entry for 13 April 1930.

See also Tocqueville on LITERACY.

SHAME

1 Whilst shame keeps its watch, virtue is not wholly extinguished in the heart; nor will moderation be utterly exiled from the minds of tyrants.

> EDMUND BURKE (1729–97), Irish philosopher, statesman. *Reflections on the Revolution in France* (1790).

2 What a man is ashamed of is always at bottom himself; and he is ashamed of himself at bottom always for being afraid.

> R. G. COLLINGWOOD (1889–1943), British philosopher. *The New Leviathan,* pt. 1, ch. 10, aph. 49 (1942).

3 See! those fiendish lineaments graven on the darkness, the writhed lip of scorn, the mockery of that living eye, the pointed finger, touching the sore place in your heart! Do you remember any act of enormous folly, at which you would blush, even in the remotest cavern of the earth? Then recognize youur Shame.

> NATHANIEL HAWTHORNE (1804–64), U.S. author. *Twice-Told Tales,* "The Haunted Mind" (1851; repr. in *Works,* vol. 9, 1974).

4 The basis of shame is not some personal mistake of ours, but the ignominy, the humiliation we feel that we must be what we are without any choice in the matter, and that this humiliation is seen by everyone.

> MILAN KUNDERA (b. 1929), Czech author, critic. *Immortality,* pt. 5, ch. 12 (1991).

5 Ashamed of the many frailties they feel within, all men endeavour to hide themselves, their ugly nakedness, from each other, and wrapping up the true motives of their hearts in the specious cloak of sociableness, and their concern for the public good, they are in hopes of concealing their filthy appetites and the deformity of their desires.

> BERNARD MANDEVILLE (1670–1733), Dutch-born English author, physician. *The Fable of the Bees,* "Remark (T)" (1714; rev. 1723).

6 We live in an atmosphere of shame. We are ashamed of everything that is real about us; ashamed of ourselves, of our relatives, of our incomes, of our accents, of our opinions, of our experience, just as we are ashamed of our naked skins.

> GEORGE BERNARD SHAW (1856–1950), Anglo-Irish playwright, critic. Tanner, in *Man and Superman,* act 1.

See also La Rochefoucauld on LOVERS; Hebrew Bible on NUDITY; Proverb on POVERTY AND THE POOR; Shaw on RESPECTABILITY.

GEORGE BERNARD SHAW

1 Shaw's plays are the price we pay for Shaw's prefaces.

> JAMES AGATE (1877–1947), British drama critic. *Ego* (1935), journal entry for 10 March 1933.

2 As a teacher, as a propagandist, Mr. Shaw is no good at all, even in his own generation. But as a personality, he is immortal.

> SIR MAX BEERBOHM (1872–1956), British author. *Around Theatres,* "A Cursory Conspectus of G.B.S." (1924), closing words of essay written 1901. Shaw was Beerbohm's predecessor as dramatic critic on the London weekly, *Saturday Review.*

3 To be made to hold his tongue is the greatest insult

you can offer him—though he might be ready with a poker to make you hold yours.

> MRS. PATRICK CAMPBELL (1865–1940), British actress. *My Life and Some Letters*, ch. 16 (1922).

4 A good man fallen among Fabians.

> VLADIMIR ILYICH LENIN (1870–1924), Russian revolutionary leader. Remark to Arthur Ransome. Quoted in: Arthur Ransome, *Russia in 1919*, "Notes of a Conversation with Lenin" (1919).

5 Kind man, brave man, wise soul, indomitable spirit of the indomitable Irishry.

> SEAN O'CASEY (1884–1964), Irish dramatist. *Sunset and Evening Star*, vol. 6, "Shaw's Corner" (1954), written on the death of George Bernard Shaw.

6 A buzz of recognition came from the front rows of the pit, together with a craning of necks on the part of those in less favoured seats. It heralded the arrival of Sherard Blaw, the dramatist who had discovered himself, and who had given so ungrudgingly of his discovery to the world.

> SAKI [H. H. MUNRO] (1870–1916), Scottish author. *The Unbearable Bassington*, ch. 13 (1912). Lady Caroline, in the audience, commented: "They say the poor man is haunted by the fear that he will die during a general election, and that his obituary notices will be seriously curtailed by the space taken up by the election results. The curse of our party system, from his point of view, is that it takes up so much room in the press."

7 All we can get out of a Shaw play is two hours and a half of mental exhilaration. We are, inscrutably, denied the pleasure of wondering what Shaw means, or whether he is sincere.

> BERT LESTON TAYLOR (1866–1921), U.S. humorist, newspaper columnist. *The So-Called Human Race* (1922, p. 164).

8 An excellent man; he has no enemies; and none of his friends like him.

> OSCAR WILDE (1854–1900), Anglo-Irish playwright, author. Quoted by Shaw in a letter, 25 Sept. 1896, to actor Ellen Terry (published in *Bernard Shaw: Collected Letters*, vol. 1, 1965).

9 I agree about Shaw—he is haunted by the mystery he flouts. He is an atheist who trembles in the haunted corridor.

> W. B. YEATS (1865–1939), Irish poet, playwright. Letter, 1 July 1921, to author George Russell (published in *The Letters of W. B. Yeats*, ed. by Allan Wade, 1954). Yeats expressed ambiguous views toward Shaw in his *Autobiography* (1938): "We all hated him with the left side of our heads, while admiring him immensely with the right side."

PERCY BYSSHE SHELLEY

1 The man Shelley, in very truth, is not entirely sane, and Shelley's poetry is not entirely sane either. The Shelley of actual life is a vision of beauty and radiance, indeed, but availing nothing, effecting nothing. And in poetry, no less than in life, he is "a beautiful *and ineffectual* angel, beating in the void his luminous wings in vain."

> MATTHEW ARNOLD (1822–88), English poet, critic. Closing words of "Shelley," a review (first published 1886; repr. in *Essays in Criticism*, Second Series, 1888). The quotation is to be found in another essay by Arnold, "Byron"—also collected in this volume. Arnold was appalled at what he considered the depravity of Shelley's personal life: "What a set! what a world! . . . One feels sickened for ever of the subject of irregular relations."

2 Shelley is *truth* itself—and *honour* itself—notwithstanding his out-of-the-way notions about religion.

> LORD BYRON (1788–1824), English poet. Letter, 2 June 1821 (published in *Byron's Letters and Journals*, vol. 8, ed. by Leslie A. Marchand, 1973–81).

SHIPS AND BOATS

1 My experience of ships is that on them one makes an interesting discovery about the world. One finds one can do without it completely.

> MALCOLM BRADBURY (b. 1932), British author. Dr. Jochum, in *Stepping Westward*, bk. 1, ch. 2 (1965).

2 A modern fleet of ships does not so much make use of the sea as exploit a highway.

> JOSEPH CONRAD (1857–1924), Polish-born English novelist. *The Mirror of the Sea*, ch. 22 (1906).

3 There is *nothing*—absolutely nothing—half so much worth doing as simply messing about in boats.

> KENNETH GRAHAME (1859–1932), British essayist, writer of children's books. Rat, in *The Wind in the Willows*, ch. 1 (1908). Rat continued, "In or out of 'em, it doesn't matter. Nothing seems really to matter, that's the charm of it. Whether you get away, or whether you don't; whether you arrive at your destination or whether you reach somewhere else, or whether you never get anywhere at all, you're always busy, and you never do anything in particular; and when you've done it there's always something else to do, and you can do it if you like, but you'd much better not."

4 Ships at a distance have every man's wish on board.

> ZORA NEALE HURSTON (1907–60), U.S. author, anthropologist. *Their Eyes Were Watching God*, ch. 1 (1937).

5 Ha, ha, my ship! thou mightest well be taken now for the sea-chariot of the sun. Ho, ho! all ye nations before my prow, I bring the sun to ye! Yoke on the further billows . . . I drive the sea!

> HERMAN MELVILLE (1819–91), U.S. author. Captain Ahab, in *Moby-Dick*, ch. 124 (1851).

SHOES

1 Shoes are the first adult machines we are given to master.

> NICHOLSON BAKER (b. 1957), U.S. author. *The Mezzanine*, ch. 2 (1988).

2 It is the fragrant lack of practicality that makes high-heeled shoes so fascinating: in terms of static mechanics they induce a sort of insecurity which some find titillating. If a woman wears a high-heeled shoe it changes the apparent musculature of the leg so that you get an effect of twanging sinew, of tension needing to be released. Her bottom sticks out like an offering. At the same time, the lofty perch is an expression of vulnerability, she is effectively hobbled and unable to escape. There is something arousing about this declaration that she is prepared to sacrifice function for form.

> STEPHEN BAYLEY (b. 1951), British design critic. *Taste*, pt. 2, "Fashion: Being and Dressing" (1991).

3 Boots and shoes are the greatest trouble of my life. Everything else one can turn and turn about, and make old look like new; but there's no coaxing boots and shoes to look better than they are.

> GEORGE ELIOT (1819–80), English novelist. Mrs. Barton, in *Amos Barton*, ch. 2 (first published in *Blackwood's Magazine*, 1857; repr. in *Scenes of Clerical Life*, 1858).

SHOPPING

1 In an age robbed of religious symbols, going to the shops replaces going to the church. . . . We have a free choice, but at a price. We can win experience, but never achieve innocence. Marx knew that the epic activities of the modern world involve not lance and sword but dry goods.

> STEPHEN BAYLEY (b. 1951), British design critic. *Taste*, pt. 2, "The Sport of Things" (1991).

2 Americans are fascinated by their own love of shopping. This does not make them unique. It's just that they have more to buy than most other people on the planet. And it's also an affirmation of faith in their country, its prosperity and limitless bounty. They have shops the way that lesser countries have statues.

> SIMON HOGGART (b. 1946), British journalist. *America: A User's Guide*, ch. 6 (1990).

SHOPPING MALLS

1 The new shopping malls make possible the synthesis of all consumer activities, not least of which are shopping, flirting with objects, idle wandering, and all the permutations of these.

> JEAN BAUDRILLARD (b. 1929), French semiologist. "Consumer Society," in *La Société de Consommation* (1970; repr. in *Selected Writings*, ed. by Mark Poster, 1988).

2 Shopping malls are liquid TVs for the end of the twentieth century. A whole micro-circuitry of desire, ideology and expenditure for processed bodies drifting through the cyber-space of ultracapitalism.

> ARTHUR KROKER (b. 1945), MARILOUISE KROKER (birth date unknown), AND DAVID COOK (b. 1946), Canadian sociologists. *Panic Encyclopedia*, "Panic (Shopping) Malls" (1989).

SHOW BUSINESS

1 All my shows are great. Some of them are bad. But they are all great.

> LORD GRADE (b. 1906), British film and television entrepreneur. Quoted in: *Observer* (London, 6 Sept. 1981).

2 Show business offers more solid promises than Catholicism.

> JOHN GUARE (b. 1938), U.S. playwright. *Independent* (London, 25 April 1992).

3 That's what show business is—sincere insincerity

> BENNY HILL (1925–92), British comedian. Quoted in: *Observer* (London, 12 June 1977).

4 Show business is the best possible therapy for remorse.

> ANITA LOOS (1888–1981), U.S. novelist, screenwriter. *Kiss Hollywood Good-by*, ch. 13 (1974).

5 Show business is really 90 per cent luck and 10 per cent being able to handle it when it gets offered to you.

> TOMMY STEELE (b. 1936), British actor, singer. *Listener* (London, 10 Oct. 1974).

See also Levant on HOLLYWOOD.

SHYNESS

1 The bashful are always aggressive at heart.

> CHARLES HORTON COOLEY (1864–1929), U.S. sociologist. *Human Nature and the Social Order*, ch. 5 (1902).

2 And indeed there will be time
To wonder, "Do I dare?" and, "Do I dare?"
Time to turn back and descend the stair,
With a bald spot in the middle of my hair . . .
Do I dare
Disturb the universe?

> T. S. ELIOT (1888–1965), Anglo-American poet, critic. *The Love Song of J. Alfred Prufrock*.

3 The shy man does have some slight revenge upon society for the torture it inflicts upon him. He is able, to a certain extent, to communicate his misery. He frightens other people as much as they frighten him. He acts like a damper upon the whole room, and the most jovial spirits become, in his presence, depressed and nervous.

> JEROME K. JEROME (1859–1927), British author. *Idle Thoughts of an Idle Fellow*, "On Being Shy" (1889).

4 Shyness is just egotism out of its depth.

> PENELOPE KEITH (b. 1939), British actor. *Daily Mail* (London, 27 June 1988).

5 Shy and proud men . . . are more liable than any others to fall into the hands of parasites and creatures of low character. For in the intimacies which are formed by shy men, they do not choose, but are chosen.

> SIR HENRY TAYLOR (1800–1886), English author. *The Statesman*, ch. 4 (1836).

See also Taylor on SECRETS.

SIGNS

See SYMBOLS AND SIGNS.

SILENCE

1 Soon silence will have passed into legend. Man has turned his back on silence. Day after day he invents machines and devices that increase noise and distract humanity from the essence of life, contemplation, meditation. . . . Tooting, howling, screeching, booming, crashing, whistling, grinding, and trilling bolster his ego. His anxiety subsides. His inhuman void spreads monstrously like a gray vegetation.

> JEAN ARP (1887–1948), French-German artist, poet. *On My Way*, "Sacred Silence" (ed. by Robert Motherwell, 1948).

2   I shall state silences more competently than ever a better man spangled the butterflies of vertigo.

> SAMUEL BECKETT (1906–89), Irish dramatist, novelist. Belacqua, in *Dream of Fair to Middling Women* (written 1932; published 1992).

3   Even a fool, when he holdeth his peace, is counted wise: and he that shutteth his lips is esteemed a man of understanding.

> BIBLE, HEBREW. *Proverbs* 17:28

4   And when he had opened the seventh seal, there was silence in heaven about the space of half an hour.

> BIBLE: NEW TESTAMENT. *Revelation* 8:1

5   Under all speech that is good for anything there lies a silence that is better. Silence is deep as Eternity; speech is shallow as Time.

> THOMAS CARLYLE (1795–1881), Scottish essayist, historian. *Critical and Miscellaneous Essays*, vol. 4, "Sir Walter Scott" (1839; first published 1838).

6   Speech and silence. We feel safer with a madman who talks than with one who cannot open his mouth.

> E. M. CIORAN (b. 1911), Rumanian-born French philosopher. *The New Gods*, "Strangled Thoughts," sct. 3 (*Le Mauvais Démiurge*, 1969; tr. 1974).

7   These be
Three silent things:
The Falling snow . . . the hour
Before the dawn . . . the mouth of one
Just dead.

> ADELAIDE CRAPSEY (1878–1914), U.S. poet. *Cinquain: Triad.* The "cinquain" was a poetic form, originated by Crapsey, comprising five unrhyming lines of, respectively, 2, 4, 6, 8 and 2 syllables.

8   Speech is often barren; but silence also does not necessarily brood over a full nest. Your still fowl, blinking at you without remark, may all the while be sitting on one addled egg; and when it takes to cackling will have nothing to announce but that addled delusion.

> GEORGE ELIOT (1819–80), English novelist. *Felix Holt*, ch. 15 (1866).

9   That man's silence is wonderful to listen to.

> THOMAS HARDY (1840–1928), English novelist, poet. Spinks, in *Under the Greenwood Tree*, pt. 2, ch. 5 (1872). Some editions have the variation: "That man's dumbness is wonderful to listen to."

10   And Silence, like a poultice, comes
To heal the blows of sound.

> OLIVER WENDELL HOLMES, SR. (1809–94), U.S. writer, physician. *The Music-Grinders*, st. 10.

11   Silence is as full of potential wisdom and wit as the unhewn marble of great sculpture. The silent bear no witness against themselves.

> ALDOUS HUXLEY (1894–1963), British author. Walter Bidlake, in *Point Counter Point*, ch. 1 (1928).

12   It takes more time and effort and delicacy to learn the silence of a people than to learn its sounds. Some people have a special gift for this. Perhaps this explains why some missionaries, notwithstanding their efforts, never come to speak properly, to communicate delicately through silences. Although they "speak with the accent of natives" they remain forever thousands of miles away. The learning of the grammar of silence is an art much more difficult to learn than the grammar of sounds.

> IVAN ILLICH (b. 1926), Austrian-born U.S. theologian, author. *Celebration of Awareness*, ch. 4 (1969).

13   Silence is the element in which great things fashion themselves.

> MAURICE MAETERLINCK (1862–1949), Belgian author. *The Treasure of the Humble*, "Silence" (1896; tr. by Alfred Sutro, 1908).

14   Do not the most moving moments of our lives find us all without words?

> MARCEL MARCEAU (b. 1923), French mime artist. *The Reader's Digest* (June 1958).

15   A silent mouth is melodious.

> IRISH PROVERB.

16   His enemies might have said before that he talked rather too much; but now he has occasional flashes of silence, that make his conversation perfectly delightful.

> SYDNEY SMITH (1771–1845), English clergyman, writer. Quoted in: Lady Holland, *Memoir*, vol. 1, ch. 11 (1855), of historian Thomas Macaulay.

17   We need to find God, and he cannot be found in noise and restlessness. God is the friend of silence. See how nature—trees, flowers, grass—grows in silence; see the stars, the moon and the sun, how they move in silence. . . . We need silence to be able to touch souls.

> MOTHER TERESA (b. 1910), Albanian-born Roman Catholic missionary. *A Gift for God*, "Willing Slaves to the Will of God" (1975).

18   I have been breaking silence these twenty-three years and have hardly made a rent in it.

> HENRY DAVID THOREAU (1817–62), U.S. philosopher, author, naturalist. *Journals* (1904), entry for 9 Feb. 1841.

19   Silence is the universal refuge, the sequel to all dull discourses and all foolish acts, a balm to our every chagrin, as welcome after satiety as after disappointment; that background which the painter may not daub, be he master or bungler, and which, however awkward a figure we may have made in the foreground, remains ever our inviolable asylum, where no indignity can assail, no personality can disturb us.

> HENRY DAVID THOREAU (1817–62), U.S. philosopher, author, naturalist. *A Week on the Concord and Merrimac Rivers*, "Friday" (1849).

20   Whereof one cannot speak, thereof one must be silent.

> LUDWIG WITTGENSTEIN (1889–1951), Austrian philosopher. *Tractatus Logico-Philosophicus*, sct. 7 (1921). Wittgenstein had elaborated in the book's Preface: "What can be said at all can be said clearly, and what we cannot talk about we must pass over in silence." Karl Popper, in his *Conjectures and Refutations* (1963), reported Franz Urbach's rejoinder to this: "But it is only here that speaking becomes worthwhile."

21 I have often repented speaking, but never of holding my tongue.

> XENOCRATES (396–315 B.C.), Greek philosopher. Quoted by Valerius Maximus in: *Annals*, bk. 7, ch. 2, sct. 7. Plutarch has attributed the remark to Simonides.

See also King on ACCEPTANCE; Emerson on APPLAUSE; De Gaulle on AUTHORITY; COMPLICITY; Steiner on LANGUAGE; Stevenson on LIES AND LYING.

SIMPLICITY

1 The price we pay for the complexity of life is too high. When you think of all the effort you have to put in—telephonic, technological and relational—to alter even the slightest bit of behaviour in this strange world we call social life, you are left pining for the straightforwardness of primitive peoples and their physical work.

> JEAN BAUDRILLARD (b. 1929), French semiologist. *Cool Memories*, ch. 4 (1987; tr. 1990).

2 Simplicity is a pleasant thing in children, or at any age, but it is not necessariy admirable, nor is affectation altogether a thing of evil. To be normal, to be at home in the world, with a prospect of power, usefulness, or success, the person must have that imaginative insight into other minds that underlies tact and *savoir-faire*, morality and beneficence. This insight involves sophistication, some understanding and sharing of the clandestine impulses of human nature. A simplicity that is merely the lack of this insight indicates a sort of defect.

> CHARLES HORTON COOLEY (1864–1929), U.S. sociologist. *Human Nature and the Social Order*, ch. 5 (1902).

3 A refined simplicity is the characteristic of all high bred deportment, in every country, and a considerate humanity should be the aim of all beneath it.

> JAMES FENIMORE COOPER (1789–1851), U.S. novelist. *The American Democrat*, "On Deportment" (1838).

4 A taste for simplicity cannot endure for long.

> EUGÈNE DELACROIX (1798–1863), French artist. *The Journal of Eugène Delacroix* (tr. by Walter Pach, 1937), 1847 entry.

5 Behind the complicated details of the world stand the simplicities: God is good, the grown-up man or woman knows the answer to every question, there is such a thing as truth, and justice is as measured and faultless as a clock. Our heroes are simple: they are brave, they tell the truth, they are good swordsmen and they are never in the long run really defeated. That is why no later books satisfy us like those which were read to us in childhood—for those promised a world of great simplicity of which we knew the rules, but the later books are complicated and contradictory with experience; they are formed out of our own disappointing memories.

> GRAHAM GREENE (1904–91), British novelist. *The Ministry of Fear*, bk. 1, ch. 7, sct. 1 (1943).

6 I hate American simplicity. I glory in the piling up of complications of every sort. If I could pronounce the name James in any different or more elaborate way I should be in favour of doing it.

> HENRY JAMES (1843–1916), U.S. author. Quoted by Leon Edel in: *Letters of Henry James*, vol. 4, Introduction (1984), said to James's niece Peggy (Margaret Mary James).

7 Life will not bear refinement. You must do as other people do.

> SAMUEL JOHNSON (1709–84), English author, lexicographer. Quoted in: James Boswell, *Life of Samuel Johnson*, 19 Sept. 1777 (1791). Johnson was advising Boswell not to "refine" in the education of his children.

8 Outward simplicity befits ordinary men, like a garment made to measure for them; but it serves as an adornment to those who have filled their lives with great deeds: they might be compared to some beauty carelessly dressed and thereby all the more attractive.

> JEAN DE LA BRUYÈRE (1645–96), French writer, moralist. *Characters*, "Of Personal Merit," aph. 17 (1688).

9 The noble simplicity in the works of nature only too often originates in the noble shortsightedness of him who observes it.

> G. C. LICHTENBERG (1742–99), German physicist, philosopher. *Aphorisms*, "Notebook H," aph. 1 (written 1765–99; tr. by R. J. Hollingdale, 1990).

10 Simplicity of life, even the barest, is not a misery, but the very foundation of refinement; a sanded floor and whitewashed walls and the green trees, and flowery meads, and living waters outside; or a grimy palace amid the same with a regiment of housemaids always working to smear the dirt together so that it may be unnoticed; which, think you, is the most refined, the most fit for a gentleman of those two dwellings?

> WILLIAM MORRIS (1834–96), English artist, writer, printer. "The Decorative Arts: Their Relation to Modern Life and Progress," Morris's first public lecture (published in *Hopes and Fears for Art*, "The Lesser Arts," 1882).

11 Simplicity, simplicity, simplicity! I say, let your affairs be as two or three, and not a hundred or a thousand; instead of a million count half a dozen, and keep your accounts on your thumb-nail.

> HENRY DAVID THOREAU (1817–62), U.S. philosopher, author, naturalist. *Walden*, "Where I Lived, and What I Lived For" (1854).

12 When a thought is too weak to be expressed simply, it should be rejected.

> LUC, MARQUIS DE VAUVENARGUES (1715–47), French moralist. *Réfléxions et Maximes*, no. 3 (1746).

13 The art of art, the glory of expression and the sunshine of the light of letters, is simplicity.

> WALT WHITMAN (1819–92), U.S. poet. *Leaves of Grass*, Preface (1855).

14 I adore simple pleasures. They are the last refuge of the complex.

> OSCAR WILDE (1854–1900), Anglo-Irish playwright, author. Lord Illingworth, in *A Woman of No Importance*, act 1.

SIN

1 True Civilization does not lie in gas, nor in steam, nor in turn-tables. It lies in the reduction of the traces of original sin.

> CHARLES BAUDELAIRE (1821–67), French poet. *My Heart Laid Bare* (written c. 1865; published in *Intimate Journals*, 1887; tr. by Christopher Isherwood, 1930; rev. by Don Bachardy, 1989).

2 Who are you to condemn another's sin? He who condemns sin becomes part of it, espouses it.

> GEORGES BERNANOS (1888–1948), French novelist, political writer. *The Diary of a Country Priest*, ch. 4 (1936).

3 These six things doth the Lord hate: yea, seven are an abomination unto him: A proud look, a lying tongue, and hands that shed innocent blood, an heart that deviseth wicked imaginations, feet that be swift in running to mischief, a false witness that speaketh lies, and he that soweth discord among brethren.

> BIBLE, HEBREW. *Proverbs* 6:16–19.

4 One leak will sink a ship: and one sin will destroy a sinner.

> JOHN BUNYAN (1628–88), English Baptist preacher, author. The Interpreter, in *The Pilgrim's Progress*, pt. 2 (1684).

5 When the righteous man turneth away from his righteousness that he hath committed and doeth that which is neither lawful nor quite right, he will generally be found to have gained in amiability what he has lost in holiness.

> SAMUEL BUTLER (1835–1902), English author. *Notebooks*, ch. 2 (1912).

6 A private sin is not so prejudicial in this world, as a public indecency.

> MIGUEL DE CERVANTES (1547–1616), Spanish writer. Don Quixote, in *Don Quixote*, pt. 2, bk. 5, ch. 22 (1615; tr. by P. Motteux).

7 Sin in this country has been always said to be rather calculating than impulsive.

> FRANK MOORE COLBY (1865–1925), U.S. editor, essayist. *The Colby Essays*, vol. 1, "The Two Alleged Generations" (1926).

8 Those of us who were brought up as Christians and have lost our faith have retained the sense of sin without the saving belief in redemption. This poisons our thought and so paralyses us in action.

> CYRIL CONNOLLY (1903–74), British critic. *The Unquiet Grave*, pt. 1 (1944; rev. 1951).

9 That which we call sin in others, is experiment for us.

> RALPH WALDO EMERSON (1803–82), U.S. essayist, poet, philosopher. *Essays*, "Experience" (Second Series, 1844).

10 He that falls into sin is a man; that grieves at it, is a saint; that boasteth of it, is a devil.

> THOMAS FULLER (1608–61), English cleric. *The Holy State and the Profane State*, "Of Self-Praising" (1642).

11 For God's sake, if you sin, take pleasure in it,
And do it for the pleasure . . .

> GERALD GOULD (1885–1936), British poet. Sonnet 21, in *Collected Poems* (1929).

12 A "sin" is something which is not necessary.

> GEORGE GURDJIEFF c. 1877–1949), Greek-Armenian religious teacher, mystic. Quoted in: P. D. Ouspensky, *In Search of the Miraculous*, ch. 17 (1949).

13 People of substance may sin without being exposed for their stolen pleasure; but servants and the poorer sort of women have seldom an opportunity of concealing a big belly, or at least the consequences of it.

> BERNARD MANDEVILLE (1670–1733), Dutch-born English author, physician. *The Fable of the Bees*, "Remark (C)" (1714; rev. 1723).

14 Sin has always been an ugly word, but it has been made so in a new sense over the last half-century. It has been made not only ugly but passé. People are no longer sinful, they are only immature or underprivileged or frightened or, more particularly, sick.

> PHYLLIS MCGINLEY (1905–78), U.S. poet, author. *The Province of the Heart*, "In Defense of Sin" (1959).

15 There are only two kinds of men: the righteous who think they are sinners and the sinners who think they are righteous.

> BLAISE PASCAL (1623–62), French scientist, philosopher. *Pensées*, (1670; no. 562 ed. by Krailsheimer, no. 534 ed. by Brunschvicg).

16 If it were possible to have a life absolutely free from every feeling of sin, what a terrifying vacuum it would be!

> CESARE PAVESE (1908–50), Italian poet, novelist, translator. *The Burning Brand: Diaries 1935–1950* (1952; tr. 1961), entry for 17 March 1940.

17 Sins become more subtle as you grow older: you commit sins of despair rather than lust.

> PIERS PAUL READ (b. 1941), British author. *Daily Telegraph* (London, 3 Oct. 1990).

18 Commit a sin twice and it will not seem a crime.

> JEWISH SAYING.

19 A large part of mankind is angry not with the sins, but with the sinners.

> SENECA (c. 5 B.C.–A.D. c. 65), Roman writer, philosopher, statesman. *De Ira*, bk. 2, sct. 28.

20 It makes a great deal of difference whether one wills not to sin or has not the knowledge to sin.

> SENECA (c. 5 B.C.–A.D. c. 65), Roman writer, philosopher, statesman. *Epistulae ad Lucilium*, Epistle 90, sct. 46.

21 Few love to hear the sins they love to act.

> WILLIAM SHAKESPEARE (1564–1616), English dramatist, poet. Pericles, in *Pericles*, sc. 1.

22 We cannot well do without our sins; they are the highway of our virtue.

> HENRY DAVID THOREAU (1817–62), U.S. philosopher, author, naturalist. *Journals* (1906), entry for 22 March 1842.

23 After the first blush of sin comes its indifference.

> HENRY DAVID THOREAU (1817–62), U.S. philosopher, author, naturalist. *On the Duty of Civil Disobedience* (1849).

24 The body sins once, and has done with its sin, for action is a mode of purification. Nothing remains then but the recollection of a pleasure, or the luxury of a regret.

> OSCAR WILDE (1854–1900), Anglo-Irish playwright, author. Lord Henry, in *The Picture of Dorian Gray*, ch. 2 (1891).

25 What is termed Sin is an essential element of progress. Without it the world would stagnate, or grow old, or become colourless. By its curiosity Sin increases the experience of the race. Through its intensified assertion of individualism it saves us from monotony of type. In its rejection of the current notions about morality, it is one with the higher ethics.

> OSCAR WILDE (1854–1900), Anglo-Irish playwright, author. Gilbert, in *The Critic as Artist*, pt. 1 (published in *Intentions*, 1891).

See also Wilde on EVANGELISM; Shelley on FORGIVENESS; Marlowe on MITIGATION; Twain on PREACHING; Marlowe on RELIGION; Dryden on REPENTANCE.

SINCERITY

1 Sincerity may be *humble*, but she cannot be servile.

> LORD BYRON (1788–1824), English poet. Letter, 29 May 1823, to Stendhal (published in Doris Langley Moore, *The Late Lord Byron*, ch. 11, 1961).

2 A wit should no more be sincere, than a woman constant; one argues a decay of parts, as t'other of beauty.

> WILLIAM CONGREVE (1670–1729), English dramatist. Witwoud, in *The Way of the World*, act 1, sc. 1 (1700).

3 Truth of a modest sort I can promise you, and also sincerity. That complete, praiseworthy sincerity which, while it delivers one into the hands of one's enemies, is as likely as not to embroil one with one's friends.

> JOSEPH CONRAD (1857–1924), Polish-born English novelist. *A Personal Record*, "A Familiar Preface" (1912).

4 What is earnest is not always true; on the contrary, error is often more earnest than truth.

> BENJAMIN DISRAELI (1804–81), English statesman, author. Letter, 4 Nov. 1868, to Queen Victoria.

5 Sincerity is the luxury allowed, like diadems and authority, only to the highest rank. . . . Every man alone is sincere. At the entrance of a second person, hypocrisy begins.

> RALPH WALDO EMERSON (1803–82), U.S. essayist, poet, philosopher. *Essays*, "Friendship" (First Series, 1841).

6 Nay, Madam, when you are declaiming, declaim; and when you are calculating, calculate.

> SAMUEL JOHNSON (1709–84), English author, lexicographer. Retort to Hester Thrale, quoted in: James Boswell, *Life of Samuel Johnson*, 26 April 1776 (1791).

7 Sincerity is impossible, unless it pervade the whole being, and the pretence of it saps the very foundation of character.

> JAMES RUSSELL LOWELL (1819–91), U.S. poet, editor. "Essay on Pope," lecture (1855; published in *Lectures on English Poets*, 1897).

8 Sincerity: if you can fake it, you've got it made.

> DANIEL SCHORR (1916–93), U.S. journalist, broadcaster. *International Herald Tribune* (Paris, 18 May 1992).

9 It is dangerous to be sincere unless you are also stupid.

> GEORGE BERNARD SHAW (1856–1950), Anglo-Irish playwright, critic. *Man and Superman*, "Maxims for Revolutionists: Stray Sayings" (1903).

10 I only desire sincere relations with the worthiest of my acquaintance, that they may give me an opportunity once in a year to speak the truth.

> HENRY DAVID THOREAU (1817–62), U.S. philosopher, author, naturalist. *Journals* (1906), entry for 24 Aug. 1851.

11 A little sincerity is a dangerous thing, and a great deal of it is absolutely fatal.

> OSCAR WILDE (1854–1900), Anglo-Irish playwright, author. Gilbert, in *The Critic as Artist*, pt. 2 (published in *Intentions*, 1891).

12 Everyone says he's sincere, but everyone isn't sincere. If everyone was sincere who says he's sincere there wouldn't be half so many insincere ones in the world and there would be lots, lots, lots more really sincere ones!

> TENNESSEE WILLIAMS (1914–83), U.S. dramatist. Esmeralda, in *Camino Real*, block 12.

See also Wilde on ACTING.

SKEPTICISM

1 If I am fool, it is, at least, a doubting one; and I envy no one the certainty of his self-approved wisdom.

> LORD BYRON (1788–1824), English poet. *Byron's Letters and Journals*, vol. 3 (ed. by Leslie A. Marchand, 1974), entry for 27 Nov. 1813.

2 Scepticism, as I said, is not intellectual only; it is moral also; a chronic atrophy and disease of the whole soul. A man lives by believing something; not by debating and arguing about many things. A sad case for him when all that he can manage to believe is something he can button in his pocket, and with one or the other organ eat and digest! Lower than that he will not get.

> THOMAS CARLYLE (1795–1881), Scottish essayist, historian. *On Heroes and Hero-Worship*, Lecture 5, "The Hero as a Man of Letters" (1841).

3 A mind that questions everything, unless strong enough to bear the weight of its ignorance, risks questioning itself and being engulfed in doubt. If it cannot discover the claims to existence of the objects of its questioning—and it would be miraculous if it so soon succeeded in solving so many mysteries—it will deny them all reality, the mere formulation of the problem already implying an inclination to negative solutions. But in so doing it will become void of all positive content and, finding nothing which offers it resistance, will launch itself perforce into the emptiness of inner revery.

> EMILE DURKHEIM (1858–1917), French sociologist. *Suicide*, bk. 2, ch. 6, sct. 1 (1897; tr. 1951).

4 "Skepticism," is that anything more than we used to mean when we said, "Well, what have we here?"

> ROBERT FROST (1874–1963), U.S. poet. Quoted by critic Lionel Trilling in: *Partisan Review 50th Anniversary Edition* (ed. by William Philips, 1985), 1946 entry.

5 Truth, Sir, is a cow which will yield such people no more milk, and so they are gone to milk the bull.

> SAMUEL JOHNSON (1709–84), English author, lexicographer. Quoted in: James Boswell, *Life of Samuel Johnson*, 21 July 1763

(1791), said of the philosopher David Hume "and other sceptical innovators."

6 Cautiousness in judgment is nowadays to be recommended to each and every one: if we gained only one incontestable truth every ten years from each of our philosophical writers the harvest we reaped would be sufficient.

G. C. LICHTENBERG (1742–99), German physicist, philosopher. *Aphorisms,* "Notebook A," aph. 38 (written 1765–99; tr. by R. J. Hollingdale, 1990).

7 We, when we sow the seeds of doubt deeper than the most up-to-date and modish free-thought has ever dreamed of doing, we well know what we are about. Only out of radical skepsis, out of moral chaos, can the Absolute spring, the anointed Terror of which the time has need.

THOMAS MANN (1875–1955), German author, critic. Leo Naphta, in *The Magic Mountain,* ch. 7, "Hysterica Passio" (1924).

8 There is a kind of courtesy in skepticism. It would be an offense against polite conventions to press our doubts too far.

GEORGE SANTAYANA (1863–1952), U.S. philosopher, poet. *The Life of Reason,* "Reason in Common Sense," ch. 4 (1905–6).

9 The skeptic does not mean him who doubts, but him who investigates or researches, as opposed to him who asserts and thinks that he has found.

MIGUEL DE UNAMUNO (1864–1936), Spanish philosophical writer. *Essays and Soliloquies,* "My Religion" (1924).

10 The poison of skepticism becomes, like alcholism, tuberculosis, and some other diseases, much more virulent in a hitherto virgin soil.

SIMONE WEIL (1909–43), French philosopher, mystic. "East and West" (written 1943; first published in *Selected Essays,* ed. by Richard Rees, 1962).

11 Scepticism is the beginning of Faith.

OSCAR WILDE (1854–1900), Anglo-Irish playwright, author. Dorian Gray, in *The Picture of Dorian Gray,* ch. 17 (1891).

See also Carlyle on GREATNESS.

THE SKY

1 To see the Summer Sky
Is Poetry, though never in a Book it lie—
True Poems flee—

EMILY DICKINSON (1830–86), U.S. poet. *The Complete Poems,* no. 1472 (1955).

2 The sky is the daily bread of the eyes.

RALPH WALDO EMERSON (1803–82), U.S. essayist, poet, philosopher. *Journal,* vol. 6 (1911), entry for 25 May 1843.

3 And that inverted Bowl we call The Sky,
Whereunder crawling coop't we live and die,
Lift not thy hands to *It* for help—for It
Rolls impotently on as Thou or I.

OMAR KHAYYáM (11–12TH CENTURY), Persian astronomer, poet. *The Rubáiyát of Omar Khayyám,* st. 52 (tr. by Edward Fitzgerald, 1859).

4 I never saw a man who looked
With such a wistful eye
Upon that little tent of blue
Which prisoners call the sky.

OSCAR WILDE (1854–1900), Anglo-Irish playwright, author. *The Ballad of Reading Gaol,* pt. 1.

SKYSCRAPERS

1 The skyscraper establishes the block, the block creates the street, the street offers itself to man.

ROLAND BARTHES (1915–80), French semiologist. "Buffet Finishes off New York," in *Arts* (Paris, 1959); repr. in *The Eiffel Tower and Other Mythologies,* tr. by Richard Howard, 1979).

2 The sensual mysticism of entire vertical being.

E. E. CUMMINGS (1894–1962), U.S. poet. Quoted in: *Architectural Digest* (Sept. 1986), said of New York City.

3 Are we not madder than those first inhabitants of the plain of Sennar? We know that the distance separating the earth from the sky is infinite, and yet we do not stop building our tower.

DENIS DIDEROT (1713–84), French philosopher. *On the Interpretation of Nature,* ch. 4 (1753; repr. in *Selected Writings,* ed. by Lester G. Crocker, 1966).

4 There is nothing more poetic and terrible than the skyscrapers' battle with the heavens that cover them. Snow, rain, and mist highlight, drench, or conceal the vast towers, but those towers, hostile to mystery and blind to any sort of play, shear off the rain's tresses and shine their three thousand swords through the soft swan of the fog.

FEDERICO GARCIA LORCA (1898–1936), Spanish poet, playwright. "A Poet in New York," lecture, March 1932, Madrid (published in *Poet in New York,* 1940; tr. 1988).

5 The sardonic funeral towers of metropolitan finance.

LEWIS MUMFORD (1895–1990), U.S. social philosopher. *The Culture of Cities,* Introduction (1938).

SLANDER

1 Our disputants put me in mind of the scuttlefish that, when he is unable to extricate himself, blackens the water about him till he becomes invisible.

JOSEPH ADDISON (1672–1719), English essayist. *Spectator,* no. 476 (London, 5 Sept. 1712).

2 Backbite. To "speak of a man as you find him" when he can't find you.

AMBROSE BIERCE (1842–1914), U.S. author. *The Devil's Dictionary* (1881–1906).

3 I don't care what anybody says about me as long as it isn't true.

TRUMAN CAPOTE (1924–84), U.S. author. Interview with David Frost published in *The Americans,* "When Does a Writer Become a Star?" (1970).

4 I am about courting a girl I have had but little acquaintance with. How shall I come to a knowledge of her faults, and whether she has the virtues I imagine she has?

Answer. Commend her among her female acquaintances.

> BENJAMIN FRANKLIN (1706–90), U.S. statesman, writer. *Complete Works*, vol. 1, "Miscellaneous Observations" (ed. by John Bigelow, 1887–88).

5 A man calumniated is doubly injured—first by him who utters the calumny, and then by him who believes it.

> HERODOTUS (c. 484–c. 425 B.C.), Greek historian. Artabanus, in *Histories*, bk. 7 (c. 430 B.C.), said of the disparagement of the Greeks by Mardonius.

6 If a man could say nothing against a character but what he can prove, history could not be written.

> SAMUEL JOHNSON (1709–84), English author, lexicographer. Quoted in: James Boswell, *Life of Samuel Johnson*, 3 April 1776 (1791).

7 Slander-mongers and those who listen to slander, if I had my way, would all be strung up, the talkers by the tongue, the listeners by the ears.

> PLAUTUS (254–184 B.C.), Roman playwright. Callipho, in *Pseudolus*, act 1, sc. 5.

8 To vilify a great man is the readiest way in which a little man can himself attain greatness.

> EDGAR ALLAN POE (1809–45), U.S. poet, critic, short-story writer. *Marginalia*, in *Southern Literary Messenger* (Richmond, Va., July 1849; repr. in *Essays and Reviews*, 1984).

9 Be thou as chaste as ice, as pure as snow, thou shalt not escape calumny.

> WILLIAM SHAKESPEARE (1564–1616), English dramatist, poet. Hamlet, in *Hamlet*, act 3, sc. 1, berating Ophelia.

10 I will make a bargain with the Republicans. If they will stop telling lies about Democrats, we will stop telling the truth about them.

> ADLAI STEVENSON (1900–1965), U.S. Democratic politician. Campaign speech, 1952 Quoted in: Leon Harris, *The Fine Art of Political Wit*, ch. 10 (1964). In the speech, Stevenson attributes the remark first to Republican Chauncey Depew, though with the party-names reversed.

11 It is harder to kill a whisper than even a shouted calumny.

> MARY STEWART (b. 1916), British novelist. *The Last Enchantment*, bk. 1, ch. 1 (1979).

12 The slanders poured down like Niagara. If you take into consideration the setting—the war and the revolution—and the character of the accused—revolutionary leaders of millions who were conducting their party to the sovereign power—you can say without exaggeration that July 1917 was the month of the most gigantic slander in world history.

> LEON TROTSKY (1879–1940), Russian revolutionary. *The History of the Russian Revolution*, vol. 2, ch. 4 (1933).

13 It is perfectly monstrous the way people go about nowadays saying things against one behind one's back that are absolutely and entirely true.

> OSCAR WILDE (1854–1900), Anglo-Irish playwright, author. Lord Henry, in *The Picture of Dorian Gray*, ch. 15 (1891). The words reappeared in *A Woman of No Importance*, act 1.

14 What is said of a man is nothing. The point is, who says it.

> OSCAR WILDE (1854–1900), Anglo-Irish playwright, author. *De Profundis* (1905), a letter to Lord Alfred Douglas following the scandal that ruined Wilde.

15 If you know somebody is going to be awfully annoyed by something you write, that's obviously very satisfying, and if they howl with rage or cry, that's honey.

> A. N. WILSON (b. 1950), British author. Quoted in: *Independent on Sunday* (London, 13 Sept. 1992).

SLANG

1 By such innovations are languages enriched, when the words are adopted by the multitude, and naturalized by custom.

> MIGUEL DE CERVANTES (1547–1616), Spanish writer. Don Quixote, in *Don Quixote*, pt. 2, bk. 6, ch. 10 (1615; tr. by P. Motteux).

2 I've found that there are only two kinds that are any good: slang that has established itself in the language, and slang that you make up yourself. Everything else is apt to be passé before it gets into print.

> RAYMOND CHANDLER (1888–1959), U.S. author. Letter, 18 March 1949 (published in *Raymond Chandler Speaking*, 1962).

3 All slang is metaphor, and all metaphor is poetry.

> G. K. CHESTERTON (1874–1936), British author. *The Defendant*, "A Defence of Slang" (1901).

4 The language of the younger generation . . . has the brutality of the city and an assertion of threatening power at hand, not to come. It is military, theatrical, and at its most coherent probably a lasting repudiation of empty courtesy and bureaucratic euphemism.

> ELIZABETH HARDWICK (b. 1916), U.S. critic, author. *Bartleby in Manhattan and Other Essays*, "The Apotheosis of Martin Luther King" (1983; first published 1968).

5 Dialect words—those terrible marks of the beast to the truly genteel.

> THOMAS HARDY (1840–1928), English novelist, poet. *The Mayor of Casterbridge*, ch. 20 (1886).

6 Nothing can be more depressing than to expose, naked to the light of thought, the hideous growth of argot. Indeed it is like a sort of repellent animal intended to dwell in darkness which has been dragged out of its cloaca. One seems to see a horned and living creature viciously struggling to be restored to the place where it belongs. One word is like a claw, another like a sightless and bleeding eye; and there are phrases which clutch like the pincers of a crab. And all of it is alive with the hideous vitality of things that have organized themselves amid disorganization.

> VICTOR HUGO (1802–85), French poet, dramatist, novelist. *Les Misérables*, pt. 4, bk. 7, ch. 1 (1862).

7 Slang is a language that rolls up its sleeves, spits on its hands and goes to work.

> CARL SANDBURG (1878–1967), U.S. poet. *New York Times* (13 Feb. 1959).

See also Lodge on LANGUAGE.

SLAVERY

1   Slavery is so intolerable a condition that the slave can hardly escape deluding himself into thinking that he is choosing to obey his master's commands when, in fact, he is obliged to. Most slaves of habit suffer from this delusion and so do some writers, enslaved by an all too "personal" style.

> W. H. AUDEN (1907–73), Anglo-American poet. *The Dyer's Hand*, pt. 1, "Writing" (1962).

2   Slavery can only be abolished by raising the character of the people who compose the nation; and *that* can be done only by showing them a higher one.

> MARIA WESTON CHAPMAN (1806–85), U.S. abolitionist. "How Can I Help to Abolish Slavery," speech, 1855, New York.

3   It cannot in the opinion of His Majesty's Government be classified as slavery in the extreme acceptance of the word without some risk of terminological inexactitude.

> SIR WINSTON CHURCHILL (1874–1965), British statesman, writer. Speech, 22 Feb. 1906, to the House of Commons, on the position of indented Chinese laborers working in the Rand mines in the Transvaal, South Africa, made soon after assuming office of Under-Secretary for the Colonies. Of Churchill's last phrase, former colonial secretary Joseph Chamberlain commented: "Eleven syllables, many of them of Latin or Greek derivation, when one good English word, a Saxon word of a single syllable, would do!."

4   Slavery is no more sinful, by the Christian code, than it is sinful to wear a whole coat, while another is in tatters, to eat a better meal than a neighbor, or otherwise to enjoy ease and plenty, while our fellow creatures are suffering and in want.

> JAMES FENIMORE COOPER (1789–1851), U.S. novelist. *The American Democrat*, "On Slavery" (1838).

5   Forced from home, and all its pleasures,
Afric's coast I left forlorn;
To increase a stranger's treasures,
O'er the raging billows borne.
Men from England bought and sold me,
Paid my price in paltry gold;
But, though theirs they have enroll'd me,
Minds are never to be sold.

> WILLIAM COWPER (1731–1800), English poet. *The Negro's Complaint* (written 1788; published 1793).

6   I pity them greatly, but I must be mum,
For how could we do without sugar and rum?

> WILLIAM COWPER (1731–1800), English poet. *Pity for Poor Africans* (written 1788; published 1800).

7   The art of being a slave is to rule one's master.

> DIOGENES OF SINOPE ["THE CYNIC"] (c. 410–c. 320 B.C.), Greek philosopher, moralist. *Herakleitos and Diogenes*, fragment 20, pt. 2 (tr. by Guy Davenport, 1976). Diogenes followed his own advice when in later life he was captured by pirates while on a voyage and sold as a slave to Xeniades of Corinth. The philosopher was appointed tutor to the children of Xeniades, remaining in Corinth for the rest of his life.

8   The genius of any slave system is found in the dynamics which isolate slaves from each other, obscure the reality of a common condition, and make united rebellion against the oppressor inconceivable.

> ANDREA DWORKIN (b. 1946), U.S. feminist critic. "Our Blood: The Slavery of Women in Amerika," speech, 23 Aug. 1975, for the National Organization for Women, Washington, D.C. (published in *Our Blood*, ch. 8, 1976).

9   Slavery is the first step towards civilization. In order to develop it is necessary that things should be much better for some and much worse for others, then those who are better off can develop at the expense of others.

> ALEXANDER HERZEN (1812–1870), Russian journalist, political thinker. *From the Other Shore*, "Consolatio" (1855).

10   To relive the relationship between owner and slave we can consider how we treat our cars and dogs—a dog exercising a somewhat similar leverage on our mercies and an automobile being comparable in value to a slave in those days.

> EDWARD HOAGLAND (b. 1932), U.S. novelist, essayist. "Virginie and the Slaves," in *Travel and Leisure* (New York, Feb. 1976; repr. in *Heart's Desire*, 1988).

11   You can be up to your boobies in white satin, with gardenias in your hair and no sugar cane for miles, but you can still be working on a plantation.

> BILLIE HOLIDAY (1915–1959), U.S. blues singer. *Lady Sings the Blues*, ch. 11 (written with William Dufty, 1956; rev. 1975).

12   The whole commerce between master and slave is a perpetual exercise of the most boisterous passions, the most unremitting despotism on the one part, and degrading submissions on the other. Our children see this, and learn to imitate it.

> THOMAS JEFFERSON (1743–1826), U.S. president. *Notes on the State of Virginia*, Query 18 (1784; written 1781).

13   Slavery is founded on the selfishness of man's nature—opposition to it on his love of justice. These principles are in eternal antagonism; and when brought into collision so fiercely as slavery extension brings them, shocks and throes and convulsions must ceaselessly follow.

> ABRAHAM LINCOLN (1809–65), U.S. president. Comment, 16 Oct. 1854, Peoria, Ill., during a debate with Stephen Douglas.

14   In giving freedom to the slave, we assure freedom to the free—honorable alike in what we give and what we preserve.

> ABRAHAM LINCOLN (1809–65), U.S. president. Annual Message to Congress, 1 Dec. 1862.

15   The distinguishing sign of slavery is to have a price, and to be bought for it.

> JOHN RUSKIN (1819–1900), English art critic, author. *The Crown of Wild Olive*, "War" (1866).

16   The slave is doomed to worship time and fate and death, because they are greater than anything he finds in himself, and because all his thoughts are of things which they devour.

> BERTRAND RUSSELL (1872–1970), British philosopher, mathematician. *A Free Man's Worship and Other Essays*, ch. 1 (1976).

17   Slavery may, perhaps, be best compared to the infantile disease of measles; a complaint which so commonly attacks the young of humanity in their infancy, and when gone through at that period leaves behind it so few fatal marks; but which when it normally attacks the fully developed adult becomes one of the most virulent and toxic of diseases, often permanently poisoning the constitution where it does not end in death.

OLIVE SCHREINER (1855–1920), South African writer, feminist. *Thoughts on South Africa*, ch. 1 (1892).

18 So long as the law considers all these human beings, with beating hearts and living affections, only as so many *things* belonging to the master—so long as the failure, or misfortune, or imprudence, or death of the kindest owner, may cause them any day to exchange a life of kind protection and indulgence for one of hopeless misery and toil—so long it is impossible to make anything beautiful or desirable in the best-regulated administration of slavery.

HARRIET BEECHER STOWE (1811–96), U.S. novelist, anti-slavery campaigner. *Uncle Tom's Cabin*, ch. 1 (1852).

19 Nobody had ever instructed him that a slave-ship, with a procession of expectant sharks in its wake, is a missionary institution, by which closely-packed heathen are brought over to enjoy the light of the Gospel.

HARRIET BEECHER STOWE (1811–96), U.S. novelist, anti-slavery campaigner. *The Minister's Wooing*, ch. 1 (1859).

20 Talk about slavery! It is not the peculiar institution of the South. It exists wherever men are bought and sold, wherever a man allows himself to be made a mere thing or a tool, and surrenders his inalienable rights of reason and conscience. Indeed, this slavery is more complete than that which enslaves the body alone. . . . I never yet met with, or heard of, a judge who was not a slave of this kind, and so the finest and most unfailing weapon of injustice. He fetches a slightly higher price than the black men only because he is a more valuable slave.

HENRY DAVID THOREAU (1817–62), U.S. philosopher, author, naturalist. *Journals* (1906), entry for 4 Dec. 1860 .

21 Mister Ward, don't yur blud bile at the thawt that three million and a half of your culled brethren air a clanking their chains in the South?—Sez I, not a bile! Let 'em clank!

ARTEMUS WARD (1834–67), U.S. journalist. *His Book*, "Oberlin" (1862).

22 The fact is, that civilisation requires slaves. . . . Human slavery is wrong, insecure, and demoralising. On mechanical slavery, on the slavery of the machine, the future of the world depends.

OSCAR WILDE (1854–1900), Anglo-Irish playwright, author. *The Soul of Man Under Socialism*, in *Fortnightly Review* (London, Feb. 1891; repr. 1895).

See also Emerson on WOMEN.

SLEEP

1 The repose of sleep refreshes only the body. It rarely sets the soul at rest. The repose of the night does not belong to us. It is not the possession of our being. Sleep opens within us an inn for phantoms. In the morning we must sweep out the shadows.

GASTON BACHELARD (1884–1962), French scientist, philosopher and literary theorist. *The Poetics of Reverie*, ch. 2, sct. 3 (1960; tr. 1969).

2 Sleep demands of us a guilty immunity. There is not one of us who, given an eternal incognito, a thumbprint nowhere set against our souls, would not commit rape, murder and all abominations.

DJUNA BARNES (1892–1982), U.S. author, poet, columnist. Doctor, in *Nightwood*, ch. 5 (1936).

3 There is between sleep and us something like a pact, a treaty with no secret clauses, and according to this convention it is agreed that, far from being a dangerous, bewitching force, sleep will become domesticated and serve as an instrument of our power to act. We surrender to sleep, but in the way that the master entrusts himself to the slave who serves him.

MAURICE BLANCHOT (b. 1907), French literary theorist, author. *The Space of Literature*, Appendices, "Sleep, Night" (1955; tr. 1982).

4 We term sleep a death . . . by which we may be literally said to die daily; *in fine*, so like death, I dare not trust it without my prayers.

SIR THOMAS BROWNE (1605–82), English physician, author. *Religio Medici*, pt. 2, sct. 12 (1643).

5 Sleep hath its own world,
And a wide realm of wild reality.
And dreams in their development have breath,
And tears, and tortures, and the touch of joy.

LORD BYRON (1788–1824), English poet. *The Dream*, sct. 1

6 Now blessings light on him that first invented this same sleep: it covers a man all over, thoughts and all, like a cloak; 'tis meat for the hungry, drink for the thirsty, heat for the cold, and cold for the hot. 'Tis the current coin that purchases all the pleasures of the world cheap; and the balance that sets the king and the shepherd, the fool and the wise-man even. There is only one thing . . . that I dislike in sleep; 'tis that it resembles death; there's very little difference between a man in his first sleep, and a man in his last sleep.

MIGUEL DE CERVANTES (1547–1616), Spanish writer. Sancho Panza, in *Don Quixote*, pt. 2, bk. 6, ch. 35 (1615; tr. by P. Motteux).

7 Oh Sleep! it is a gentle thing,
Beloved from pole to pole,
To Mary Queen the praise be given!
She sent the gentle sleep from Heaven,
That slid into my soul.

SAMUEL TAYLOR COLERIDGE (1772–1834), English poet and critic. *The Ancient Mariner*, pt. 5.

8 Sleep is when all the unsorted stuff comes flying out as from a dustbin upset in a high wind.

WILLIAM GOLDING (1911–93), British author. *Pincher Martin*, ch. 6 (1956).

9 We are not hypocrites in our sleep.

WILLIAM HAZLITT (1778–1830), English essayist. *The Plain Speaker*, "On Dreams" (1826).

10 Even sleepers are workers and collaborators on what goes on in the universe.

HERACLITUS (c. 535–c. 475 B.C.), Greek philosopher. *The Cosmic Fragments*, no. 90 (c. 480 B.C.).

11   I divide my time as follows: half the time I sleep, the other half I dream. I never dream when I sleep, for that would be a pity, for sleeping is the highest accomplishment of genius.

SØREN KIERKEGAARD (1813–55), Danish philosopher. *Either/Or*, vol. 1, "Diapsalmata" (1843; tr. 1987).

12   He who sleeps half a day has won half a life.

KARL KRAUS (1874–1936), Austrian satirist. "In Praise of a Topsy-Turvy Lifestyle," in *Simplicissimus* (Munich, 1908; repr. in *In These Great Times: A Karl Kraus Reader*, ed. by Harry Zohn, 1976).

13   Sleep is a reward for some, a punishment for others. For all, it is a sanction.

ISIDORE DUCASSE, COMTE DE LAUTRÉAMONT (1846–70), French author, poet. *Poésies*, ch. 2 (1870).

14   And if tonight my soul may find her peace
in sleep, and sink in good oblivion,
and in the morning wake like a new-opened flower
then I have been dipped again in God, and new-created.

D. H. LAWRENCE (1885–1930), British author. *Shadows*.

15   Sleep, dear Sleep, sweet harlot of the senses,
Delilah of the spirit.

CHRISTOPHER MORLEY (1890–1957), U.S. novelist, journalist, poet. *Sleep*.

16   The first moments of sleep are an image of death; a hazy torpor grips our thoughts and it becomes impossible for us to determine the exact instant when the "I," under another form, continues the task of existence.

GÉRARD DE NERVAL (1808–55), French novelist, poet. *Aurélia*, pt. 1, ch. 1 (1855).

17   All men whilst they are awake are in one common world: but each of them, when he is asleep, is in a world of his own.

PLUTARCH (46–120), Greek essayist, biographer. *Morals*, "Of Superstition."

18   Six hours for a man, seven for a woman, and eight for a fool.

ENGLISH PROVERB (18th century).

19   No matter what time it is, wake me, even if it's in the middle of a Cabinet meeting.

RONALD REAGAN (b. 1911), U.S. Republican politician, president. Remark, 13 April 1984, at the annual dinner of the White House Correspondents' Association.

20   A nap, my friend, is a brief period of sleep which overtakes superannuated persons when they endeavour to entertain unwelcome visitors or to listen to scientific lectures.

GEORGE BERNARD SHAW (1856–1950), Anglo-Irish playwright, critic. The Elderly Gentleman, in *Back to Methuselah*, "Tragedy of an Elderly Gentleman."

21   Come Sleep! Oh Sleep, the certain knot of peace,
The baiting-place of wit, the balm of woe,
The poor man's wealth, the prisoner's release,
Th' indifferent judge between the high and low.

SIR PHILIP SIDNEY (1554–86), English poet, critic, soldier. *Astrophel and Stella*, Sonnet 39 (1591).

22   The city sleeps and the country sleeps,
The living sleep for their time, the dead sleep for their time,
The old husband sleeps by his wife and the young husband sleeps by his wife;
And these tend inward to me, and I tend outward to them,
And such as it is to be of these more or less I am,
And of these one and all I weave the song of myself.

WALT WHITMAN (1819–92), U.S. poet. *Song of Myself*, sct. 15 in *Leaves of Grass* (1855).

23   Come, cuddle your head on my shoulder, dear,
Your head like the golden-rod,
And we will go sailing away from here
To the beautiful land of Nod.

ELLA WHEELER WILCOX (1855–1919), U.S. poet, journalist. *The Beautiful Land of Nod*.

24   Sleep, that deplorable curtailment of the joy of life.

VIRGINIA WOOLF (1882–1941), British novelist. *The Common Reader*, "Montaigne" (First Series, 1925).

See also DREAMS; Chamfort on LIFE AND DEATH; Oates on OLD AGE; Baudelaire on PRAYER.

SLUMS

1   Life is lived in common, but not in community.

MICHAEL HARRINGTON (1928–89), U.S. social scientist, author. *The Other America*, ch. 7, sct. 4 (1962), of life in the slums.

2   Slumism is the pent-up anger of people living on the outside of affluence. Slumism is decay of structure and deterioration of the human spirit. Slumism is a virus which spreads through the body politic. As other "isms," it breeds disorder and demagoguery and hate.

HUBERT H. HUMPHREY (1911–78), U.S. Democratic politician, vice president. Speech, 13 June 1966, U.S. Conference of Mayors, Dallas, Texas.

3   Mankind which began in a cave and behind a windbreak will end in the disease-soaked ruins of a slum.

H. G. WELLS (1866–1946), British author. *The Fate of Man*, ch. 26 (1939).

SMELLS

1   A man has his distinctive personal scent which his wife, his children and his dog can recognize. A crowd has a generalized stink. The public is odorless.

W. H. AUDEN (1907–73), Anglo-American poet. *The Dyer's Hand*, pt. 2, "The Poet and the City" (1962).

2   They haven't got no noses
The fallen sons of Eve;
Even the smell of roses
Is not what they supposes;
But more than mind discloses
And more than men believe.

G. K. CHESTERTON (1874–1936), British author. *The Flying Inn*, ch. 15, "The Song of Quoodle" (1914).

3   I counted two and seventy stenches,
All well defined, and several stinks!

> SAMUEL TAYLOR COLERIDGE (1772–1834), English poet, critic. *Cologne*, referring to the city of Cologne.

4   The lovesick, the betrayed, and the jealous all smell alike.

> COLETTE (1873–1954), French author. *Break of Day* (1961; repr. in *Earthly Paradise*, pt. 4, "The South of France," ed. by Robert Phelps, 1966).

5   The rankest compound of villainous smell that ever offended nostril.

> WILLIAM SHAKESPEARE (1564–1616), English dramatist, poet. Sir John Falstaff, in *The Merry Wives of Windsor*, act 3, sc. 5.

See also Artaud on EXCREMENT AND EXCRETION.

SMILING

1   If you have only one smile in you, give it to the people you love. Don't be surly at home, then go out in the street and start grinning "Good morning" at total strangers.

> MAYA ANGELOU (b. 1928), U.S. author. *Singin' and Swingin' and Gettin' Merry Like Christmas*, vol. 3, ch. 5 (1976), quoting her mother's advice.

2   Smile and others will smile back. Smile to show how transparent, how candid you are. Smile if you have nothing to say. Most of all, do not hide the fact you have nothing to say nor your total indifference to others. Let this emptiness, this profound indifference shine out spontaneously in your smile.

> JEAN BAUDRILLARD (b. 1929), French semiologist. *America*, "Astral America" (1986; tr. 1988).

3   She gave me a smile I could feel in my hip pocket.

> RAYMOND CHANDLER (1888–1959), U.S. author. Philip Marlowe, in *Farewell, My Lovely*, ch. 18 (1940), said of Helen Grayle.

See also Twain on FACES.

SMOKING

1   The Germans are the most philosophic people in the world, and the greatest smokers: now I trace their philosophy to their smoking. . . . Smoking has a sedative effect upon the nerves, and enables a man to bear the sorrows of this life (of which every one has his share) not only decently, but dignifiedly.

> GEORGE BORROW (1803–81), English author. An "elderly individual," in *Lavengro*, ch. 23 (1851).

2   If alcohol is queen, then tobacco is her consort. It's a fond companion for all occasions, a loyal friend through fair weather and foul. People smoke to celebrate a happy moment, or to hide a bitter regret. Whether you're alone or with friends, it's a joy for all the senses. What lovelier sight is there than that double row of white cigarettes, lined up like soldiers on parade and wrapped in silver paper? . . . I love to touch the pack in my pocket, open it,

savor the feel of the cigarette between my fingers, the paper on my lips, the taste of tobacco on my tongue. I love to watch the flame spurt up, love to watch it come closer and closer, filling me with its warmth.

> LUIS BUÑUEL (1900–1983), Spanish filmmaker. *My Last Sigh*, ch. 6 (1983). Buñuel concludes this eulogy: "Finally, dear readers, allow me to end these ramblings on tobacco and alcohol, delicious fathers of abiding friendships and fertile reveries, with some advice: Don't drink and don't smoke. It's bad for your health."

3   Tobacco, divine, rare, superexcellent tobacco, which goes far beyond all the panaceas, potable gold, and philosophers' stones, a sovereign remedy to all diseases . . . but as it is commonly abused by most men, which take it as tinkers do ale, 'tis a plague, a mischief, a violent purger of goods, lands, health; hellish, devilish and damned tobacco, the ruin and overthrow of body and soul.

> ROBERT BURTON (1577–1640), English clergyman, author. *Anatomy of Melancholy*, pt. 2, sct. 4, memb. 2, subsct. 1 (1621).

4   Sublime tobacco! which from east to west
Cheers the tar's labour or the Turkman's rest.

> LORD BYRON (1788–1824), English poet. *The Island*, cto. 2, st. 19.

5   Go mad, and beat their wives;
Plunge (after shocking lives)
Razors and carving knives
Into their gizzards.

> C. S. CALVERLEY (1831–84), English poet. *Ode to Tobacco*. This is possibly a reference to a letter in the medical journal *Lancet*, 14 Feb. 1857: "[Dr. Webster] distinctly enumerates tobacco as one of the causes of insanity. . . . Two brothers in one family had become deranged from smoking tobacco, and in that state had committed suicide."

6   Smokers, male and female, inject and excuse idleness in their lives every time they light a cigarette.

> COLETTE (1873–1954), French author. *The Pure and the Impure* (1933; repr. in *Earthly Paradise*, pt. 2, "Freedom," 1966).

7   The pipe, with solemn interposing puff,
Makes half a sentence at a time enough;
The dozing sages drop the drowsy strain,
Then pause, and puff—and speak, and pause again.

> WILLIAM COWPER (1731–1800), English poet. *Conversation* (written 1781; published 1782).

8   I doused the fatal instrument with lightning promptitude, but it was a good seven minutes before the last indignant handkerchief had folded its wings and gone back to its reticule and the last manufactured cough died protestingly away.

> MARGARET HALSEY (b. 1910), U.S. author. *With Malice Toward Some*, pt. 2, "20 June" (1938), on smoking in a London hotel.

9   Pull out a Monte Cristo at a dinner party and the political liberal turns into the nicotine fascist.

> MARTYN HARRIS (b. 1952), British journalist, author. *Daily Telegraph* (London, 20 Jan. 1989).

10   But when I don't smoke I scarcely feel as if I'm living. I don't feel as if I'm living unless I'm killing myself.

> RUSSELL HOBAN (b. 1925), U.S. author. William G, in *Turtle Diary*, ch. 7 (1975).

11   A custom loathsome to the eye, hateful to the nose, harmful to the brain, dangerous to the lungs, and in the black, stinking fume thereof nearest resembling the horrible Stygian smoke of the pit that is bottomless.

> JAMES I OF ENGLAND, JAMES VI OF SCOTLAND (1566–1625). *A Counter-blaste to Tobacco* (1604). The passage was written shortly after Sir Walter Raleigh introduced tobacco to England from the Americas.

12   I attribute the quarrelsome nature of the Middle Ages young men entirely to the want of the soothing weed.

> JEROME K. JEROME (1859–1927), British author. *Idle Thoughts of an Idle Fellow*, "On Being Idle" (1889).

13   There's nothing quite like tobacco: it's the passion of decent folk, and whoever lives without tobacco doesn't deserve to live.

> MOLIÈRE (1622–73), French dramatist. Sganarelle, in *Don Juan*, act 1, sc. 1 (1665).

14   There are some circles in America where it seems to be more socially acceptable to carry a hand-gun than a packet of cigarettes.

> KATHARINE WHITEHORN (b. 1926), British journalist. *Observer* (London, 30 Oct. 1988).

15   A cigarette is the perfect type of a perfect pleasure. It is exquisite, and it leaves one unsatisfied. What more can one want?

> OSCAR WILDE (1854–1900), Anglo-Irish playwright, author. Lord Henry, in *The Picture of Dorian Gray*, ch. 6 (1891).

SMUGNESS

1   Of all the horrid, hideous notes of woe,
Sadder than owl-songs or the midnight blast,
Is that portentous phrase, "I told you so,"
Uttered by friends, those prophets of the past.

> LORD BYRON (1788–1824), English poet. *Don Juan*, cto. 14, st. 50.

2   And then in the fulness of joy and hope,
Seemed washing his hands with invisible soap,
In imperceptible water.

> THOMAS HOOD (1799–1845), English poet. *Miss Kilmansegg*, "Her Christening" (1841–43).

3   I do not object to Gladstone's always having the ace of trumps up his sleeve, but only to his pretence that God had put it there.

> HENRY LABOUCHERE (1831–1912), English journalist, politician. Quoted in: *Dictionary of National Biography* (1912–21).

4   He knew that he was precisely what he himself would have chosen to be had God consulted him on the subject of his birth; he fully appreciated and approved what had been bestowed, and realized that he couldn't have done the job better himself, in fact he would not have changed a single item.

> MICHEÁL MACLIAMMÓIR (1899–1978), Irish actor. *All for Hecuba*, ch. 4, "Changes" (1947), on first meeting Orson Welles.

SNOBBERY

1   Snobbery? But it's only a form of despair.

> JOSEPH BRODSKY (b. 1940), Russian-born U.S. poet, critic. *Less Than One: Selected Essays*, "Flight from Byzantium," sct. 9 (1986).

2   There are few who would not rather be taken in adultery than in provincialism.

> ALDOUS HUXLEY (1894–1963), British author. Mr. Boldero, in *Antic Hay*, ch. 10 (1923).

3   Nothing succeeds like address.

> FRAN LEBOWITZ (b. 1951), U.S. journalist. *Metropolitan Life*, "The Nail Bank: Not Just Another Clip Joint" (1978).

4   Heaven grant him now some noble nook,
For, rest his soul! he'd rather be
Genteelly damn'd beside a Duke,
Than sav'd in vulgar company.

> THOMAS MOORE (1779–1852), Irish poet. *Epitaph on a Tuft-Hunter*.

5   Respectable means rich, and decent means poor. I should die if I heard my family called decent.

> THOMAS LOVE PEACOCK (1785–1866), English author. Lady Clarinda, in *Crotchet Castle*, ch. 3 (1831).

6   The word snob belongs to the sour-grape vocabulary.

> LOGAN PEARSALL SMITH (1865–1946), U.S. essayist, aphorist. *Afterthoughts*, "Other People" (1931).

7   It is impossible, in our condition of Society, not to be sometimes a Snob.

> WILLIAM MAKEPEACE THACKERAY (1811–63), English author. *The Book of Snobs*, ch. 3 (1848).

8   Laughter would be bereaved if snobbery died.

> PETER USTINOV (b. 1921), British actor, writer, director. Quoted in: *Observer* (London, 13 March 1955).

See also Saint Laurent on ELEGANCE.

SNUBS

1   No more fiendish punishment could be devised, were such a thing physically possible, than that one should be turned loose in society and remain absolutely unnoticed.

> WILLIAM JAMES (1842–1910), U.S. psychologist, philosopher. *The Principles of Psychology*, vol. 1, ch. 10 (1890).

2   Mrs. Montagu has dropt me. Now, Sir, there are people whom one should like very well to drop, but would not wish to be dropt by.

> SAMUEL JOHNSON (1709–84), English author, lexicographer. Quoted in: James Boswell, *Life of Samuel Johnson*, March 1781 (1791), of Mary Wortley Montagu.

3   When an acquaintance goes by I often step back from my window, not so much to spare him the effort of acknowledging me as to spare myself the embarrassment of seeing that he has not done so.

> G. C. LICHTENBERG (1742–99), German physicist, philosopher.

Aphorisms, "Notebook F," aph. 155 (written 1765–99; tr. by R. J. Hollingdale, 1990).

4　There are some persons we could not cut down to size without diminishing ourselves as well.

JEAN ROSTAND (1894–1977), French biologist, writer. *Carnets d'un Biologiste*, in *The Substance of Man* (1962, p. 193).

SOAP OPERAS

1　In its artless cruelty, *Dallas* is superior to any "intelligent" critique that can be made of it. That is why intellectual snobbery meets its match here.

JEAN BAUDRILLARD (b. 1929), French semiologist. *Cool Memories*, ch. 3 (1987; tr. 1990).

2　A sceptic finds Dallas absurd. A cynic thinks the public doesn't.

CLIVE JAMES (b. 1939), Australian writer, critic. *Glued To The Box*, Introduction (1983).

3　I've finally figured out why soap operas are, and logically should be, so popular with generations of housebound women. *They are the only place in our culture where grown-up men take seriously all the things that grown-up women have to deal with all day long.*

GLORIA STEINEM (b. 1934), U.S. feminist writer, editor. "Night Thoughts of a Media Watcher," in *Ms.* (New York, Nov. 1981; repr. in *Outrageous Acts and Everyday Rebellions*, 1983).

SOCIABILITY

1　I only go out to get me a fresh appetite for being alone.

LORD BYRON (1788–1824), English poet. *Byron's Letters and Journals*, vol. 3 (ed. by Leslie A. Marchand, 1974), entry for 12 Dec. 1813.

2　We would not be interested in human beings if we did not have the hope of someday meeting someone worse off than ourselves.

E. M. CIORAN (b. 1911), Rumanian-born French philosopher. *The New Gods*, "Strangled Thoughts," sct. 3 (1969; tr. 1974).

3　Lions, wolves, and vultures don't live together in herds, droves or flocks. Of all animals of prey, man is the only sociable one. Every one of us preys upon his neighbour, and yet we herd together.

JOHN GAY (1685–1732), English dramatist. Lockit, in *The Beggar's Opera*, act 3, sc. 2.

4　A man has as many social selves as there are individuals who recognize him.

WILLIAM JAMES (1842–1910), U.S. psychologist, philosopher. *The Principles of Psychology*, vol. 1, ch. 10 (1890).

5　Men of genius are often dull and inert in society; as the blazing meteor, when it descends to earth, is only a stone.

HENRY WADSWORTH LONGFELLOW (1807–82), U.S. poet. One of the meditations of Mr. Churchill, inscribed on his pulpit, in *Kavanagh*, bk. 1, ch. 13 (1849).

6　Rascals are always sociable—more's the pity! and

the chief sign that a man has any nobility in his character is the little pleasure he takes in others' company.

ARTHUR SCHOPENHAUER (1788–1860), German philosopher. *Parerga and Paralipomena*, vol. 1, "Aphorisms on the Wisdom of Life," ch. 5, sct. 9 (1851).

7　What men call social virtues, good fellowship, is commonly but the virtue of pigs in a litter, which lie close together to keep each other warm.

HENRY DAVID THOREAU (1817–62), U.S. philosopher, author, naturalist. Journal entry, 23 Oct. 1852.

See also Dickens on COMPANY; Burns on FRIENDLINESS; SOCIALIZING.

THE SOCIAL SCIENCES

1　The true science and study of man, is man himself.

PIERRE CHARRON (1541–1603), French philosopher. *Of Wisdom*, bk. 1, Preface (1601).

2　The circumstances of human society are too complicated to be submitted to the rigour of mathematical calculation.

MARQUIS DE CUSTINE (1790–1857), French traveler, author. *Empire of the Czar: A Journey Through Eternal Russia*, ch. 29 (1843; rev. 1989).

3　Like the Pentagon, our social science often reduces all phenomena to dollars and body counts. Sexuality, family unity, kinship, masculine solidarity, maternity, motivation, nurturing, all the rituals of personal identity and development, all the bonds of community, seem "sexist," "superstitious," "mystical," "inefficient," "discriminatory." And, of course, they are—and they are also indispensable to a civilized society.

GEORGE GILDER (b. 1939), U.S. editor, speechwriter, author. *Sexual Suicide*, Introduction (1973).

4　There are no better terms available to describe [the] difference between the approach of the natural and the social sciences than to call the former "objective" and the latter "subjective." . . . While for the natural scientist the contrast between objective facts and subjective opinions is a simple one, the distinction cannot as readily be applied to the object of the social sciences. The reason for this is that the object, the "facts" of the social sciences are also opinions—not opinions of the student of the social phenomena, of course, but opinions of those whose actions produce the object of the social scientist.

FRIEDRICH AUGUST VON HAYEK (1899–1992), Austrian-born British economist. *The Counter-Revolution of Science*, pt. 1, ch. 3 (1952).

See also SOCIOLOGY.

SOCIALISM

1　Socialists make the mistake of confusing individual worth with success. They believe you cannot allow people to succeed in case those who fail feel worthless.

KENNETH BAKER (b. 1934), British Conservative politician. Quoted in: *Observer* (London, 13 July 1986).

2 I pass the test that says a man who isn't a socialist at 20 has no heart, and a man who is a socialist at 40 has no head.

> WILLIAM CASEY (1913–87), U.S. intelligence chief, director of the C.I.A. Quoted in his obituary, in: *Washington Post* (7 May 1987). The saying referred to by Casey was attributed to French socialist politician and premier Aristide Briand.

3 One is a socialist because one *used to be* one, no longer going to demonstations, attending meetings, sending in one's dues, in short, without paying.

> MICHEL DE CERTEAU (1925–86), French author, critic. *The Practice of Everyday Life*, ch. 13 (1974).

4 Real socialism is inside man. It wasn't born with Marx. It was in the communes of Italy in the Middle Ages. You can't say it is finished.

> DARIO FO (b. 1926), Italian playwright, actor. *Times* (London, 6 April 1992).

5 Socialism can only arrive by bicycle.

> JOSÉ ANTONIO VIERA GALLO (b. 1943), Chilean politician in Allende's government. Quoted in: Ivan Illich, *Energy and Equity*, Foreword (1974).

6 This socialism will develop in all its phases until it reaches its own extremes and absurdities. Then once again a cry of denial will break from the titanic chest of the revolutionary minority and again a mortal struggle will begin, in which socialism will play the role of contemporary conservatism and will be overwhelmed in the subsequent revolution, as yet unknown to us.

> ALEXANDER HERZEN (1812–70), Russian journalist, political thinker. *From the Other Shore*, "Epilogue 1849" (1855).

7 If Socialism can only be realized when the intellectual development of all the people permits it, then we shall not see Socialism for at least five hundred years.

> VLADIMIR ILYICH LENIN (1870–1924), Russian revolutionary leader. Speech, 27 Nov. 1917, at Peasants' Congress, Petrograd. Quoted in: John Reed, *Ten Days That Shook the World*, ch. 12 (1919).

8 Every reasonable human being should be a moderate Socialist.

> THOMAS MANN (1875–1955), German author, critic. *New York Times* (18 June 1950). Quoted in: R. J. Hollingdale, *Thomas Mann: A Critical Study*, ch. 2 (1971).

9 By concentrating on what is good in people, by appealing to their idealism and their sense of justice, and by asking them to put their faith in the future, socialists put themselves at a severe disadvantage.

> IAN MCEWAN (b. 1948), British author. *City Limits* (London, 27 May 1983).

10 As with the Christian religion, the worst advertisement for Socialism is its adherents.

> GEORGE ORWELL (1903–50), British author. *The Road to Wigan Pier*, ch. 11 (1937).

11 Whether considered as a doctrine, or as an historical fact, or as a movemement, socialism, if it really remains socialism, cannot be brought into harmony with the dogmas of the Catholic church. . . . Religious socialism, Christian socialism, are expressions implying a contradiction in terms.

> PIUS XI [ACHILLE RATTI] (1857–1939), Italian ecclesiastic, pope. From the encyclical, *Quadragesimo Anno* (1931).

12 WOT IZZA COMIN'?
I'll tell you wot izza comin'
Sochy-lism is a-comin'.

> EZRA POUND (1885–1972), U.S. poet. *Canto 77*.

13 Great Socialist statesmen aren't made, they're stillborn.

> SAKI [H. H. MUNRO] (1870–1916), Scottish author. Courtenay Youghal, in *The Unbearable Bassington*, ch. 13 (1912).

14 Socialism proposes no adequate substitute for the motive of enlightened selfishness that to-day is at the basis of all human labor and effort, enterprise and new activity.

> WILLIAM HOWARD TAFT (1857–1930), U.S. Republican politician, president. *Popular Government*, ch. 3 (1913).

15 It is certainly safe, in view of the movement to the right of intellectuals and political thinkers, to pronounce the brain death of socialism.

> NORMAN TEBBIT (b. 1931), British Conservative politician. *Times* (London, 26 April 1988).

16 The only hope of socialism resides in those who have already brought about in themselves, as far as is possible in the society of today, that union between manual and intellectual labor which characterizes the society we are aiming at.

> SIMONE WEIL (1909–43), French philosopher, mystic. *Oppression and Liberty*, ch. 1 (1958).

17 To make men Socialists is nothing, but to make Socialism human is a great thing.

> OSCAR WILDE (1854–1900), Anglo-Irish playwright, author. Review of *Chants of Labour: A Song-Book of the People*, in *Pall Mall Gazette* (London, 15 Feb. 1889; ed. by Edward Carpenter).

18 It wasn't idealism that made me, from the beginning, want a more secure and rational society. It was an intellectual judgement, to which I still hold. When I was young its name was socialism. We can be deflected by names. But the need was absolute, and is still absolute.

> RAYMOND WILLIAMS (1921–88), British novelist, critic. Norman Braose, in *Loyalties*, pt. 5, ch. 5 (1985). This was Williams's last novel.

See also COMMUNISM; Galbraith on ECONOMICS; Gorbachev on JESUS CHRIST; MARXISM.

SOCIALIZING

1 People nowadays like to be together not in the old-fashioned way of, say, mingling on the piazza of an Italian Renaissance city, but, instead, huddled together in traffic jams, bus queues, on escalators and so on. It's a new kind of togetherness which may seem totally alien, but it's the togetherness of modern technology.

> J. G. BALLARD (b. 1930), British author. Interview in *Penthouse* (London, April 1979; repr. in *Re/Search*, no. 8/9, San Francisco, 1984).

2 Last night, *party* at Lansdowne-House. Tonight, *party* at Lady Charlotte Greville's—deplorable waste of time, and something of temper. Nothing imparted—nothing acquired—talking without ideas—if any thing like thought in my mind, it was not on the subjects on which we were gabbling. Heigho!—and in this way half London pass what is called life.

LORD BYRON (1788–1824), English poet. *Byron's Letters and Journals,* vol. 3 (ed. by Leslie A. Marchand, 1974), entry for 22 March 1814.

3 A great social success is a pretty girl who plays her cards as carefully as if she were plain.

F. SCOTT FITZGERALD (1896–1940), U.S. author. Letter (undated) to his daughter Frances Scott Fitzgerald (first published in *The Crack-Up,* ed. by Edmund Wilson, 1945).

4 A successful social technique consists perhaps in finding unobjectionable means for individual self-assertion.

ERIC HOFFER (1902–83), U.S. philosopher. *The Passionate State of Mind,* aph. 26 (1955).

5 You're looking exceptionally ugly tonight, Madam, is it because we have company?

ALFRED JARRY (1873–1907), French playwright, author. Father Ubu, in *Ubu Rex,* act 1, sc. 2 (1896).

6 We are persons of quality, I assure you, and women of fashion, and come to see and to be seen.

BEN JONSON (1573–1637), English dramatist, poet. Mirth, in *The Staple of News,* "Induction" (1625).

7 When one pays a visit it is for the purpose of wasting other people's time, not one's own.

OSCAR WILDE (1854–1900), Anglo-Irish playwright, author. Lord Goring, in *An Ideal Husband,* act 4.

See also SOCIABILITY; COMPANY; FRIENDLINESS.

SOCIETY

1 American society is a sort of flat, fresh-water pond which absorbs silently, without reaction, anything which is thrown into it.

HENRY B. ADAMS (1838–1918), U.S. historian. Letter, 20 Sept. 1911.

2 Nor was civil society founded merely to preserve the lives of its members; but that they might live well: for otherwise a state might be composed of slaves, or the animal creation . . . nor is it an alliance mutually to defend each other from injuries, or for a commercial intercourse. . . . But whosoever endeavors to establish wholesome laws in a state, attends to the virtues and vices of each individual who composes it; from whence it is evident, that the first care of him who would found a city, truly deserving that name, and not nominally so, must be to have his citizens virtuous.

ARISTOTLE (384–322 B.C.), Greek philosopher. *Politics,* bk. 3, ch. 9, sct. 1280 (c. 343 B.C.).

3 Society is held together by our need; we bind it together with legend, myth, coercion, fearing that without it we will be hurled into that void, within which, like the earth before the Word was spoken, the foundations of society are hidden.

JAMES BALDWIN (1924–87), U.S. author. "Everybody's Protest Novel," in *Partisan Review* (New Brunswick, N.J., June 1949; repr. in *Notes of a Native Son,* pt. 1, 1955).

4 I am now quite cured of seeking pleasure in society, be it country or town. A sensible man ought to find sufficient company in himself.

EMILY BRONTË (1818–48), English novelist, poet. Mr. Lockwood, in *Wuthering Heights,* ch. 3 (1847).

5 Society is indeed a contract. . . . It is a partnership in all science; a partnership in all art; a partnership in every virtue, and in all perfection. As the ends of such a partnership cannot be obtained in many generations, it becomes a partnership not only between those who are living, but between those who are living, those who are dead, and those who are to be born.

EDMUND BURKE (1729–97), Irish philosopher, statesman. *Reflections on the Revolution in France* (1790).

6 We call it a Society; and go about professing openly the totalest separation, isolation. Our life is not a mutual helpfulness; but rather, cloaked under due laws-of-war, named "fair competition" and so forth, it is a mutual hostility.

THOMAS CARLYLE (1795–1881), Scottish essayist, historian. *Past and Present,* bk. 3, ch. 2 (1843).

7 We can imagine a society in which no one could survive as a social being because it does not correspond to biologically determined perceptions and human social needs. For historical reasons, existing societies might have such properties, leading to various forms of pathology.

NOAM CHOMSKY (b. 1928), U.S. linguist, political analyst. *Language and Responsibility,* "A Philosophy of Language" (1979).

8 Man's characteristic privilege is that the bond he accepts is not physical but moral; that is, social. He is governed not by a material environment brutally imposed on him, but by a conscience superior to his own, the superiority of which he feels. Because the greater, better part of his existence transcends the body, he escapes the body's yoke, but is subject to that of society.

EMILE DURKHEIM (1858–1917), French sociologist. *Suicide,* bk. 2, ch. 5, sct. 2 (1897; tr. 1951).

9 Society never advances. It recedes as fast on one side as it gains on the other. . . . Society acquires new arts, and loses old instincts.

RALPH WALDO EMERSON (1803–82), U.S. essayist, poet, philosopher. *Essays,* "Self-Reliance" (First Series, 1841).

10 Society is a masked ball, where every one hides his real character, and reveals it by hiding.

RALPH WALDO EMERSON (1803–82), U.S. essayist, poet, philosopher. *The Conduct of Life,* "Worship" (1860).

11 It is always possible to bind together a considerable number of people in love, so long as there are other people left over to receive the manifestations of their aggression.

SIGMUND FREUD (1856–1939), Austrian psychiatrist. *Civilization and its Discontents,* ch. 5 (1930; repr. in *Complete Works,* vol. 21, ed. by James Strachey and Anna Freud, 1961).

12 Compare society to a boat. Her progress through

the water will not depend upon the exertion of her crew, but upon the exertion devoted to propelling her. This will be lessened by any expenditure of force in fighting among themselves, or in pulling in different directions.

> HENRY GEORGE (1839–97), U.S. economist. *Progress and Poverty,* bk. 10, ch. 3 (1879).

13 Social improvement is attained more readily by a concern with the quality of results than with the purity of motives.

> ERIC HOFFER (1902–83), U.S. philosopher. *Reflections on the Human Condition,* aph. 25 (1973).

14 The spirit of truth and the spirit of freedom—these are the pillars of society.

> HENRIK IBSEN (1828–1906), Norwegian dramatist. Lona Hessel, in *Pillars of Society,* act 4.

15 No society has been able to abolish human sadness, no political system can deliver us from the pain of living, from our fear of death, our thirst for the absolute. It is the human condition that directs the social condition, not vice versa.

> EUGèNE IONESCO (b. 1912), Rumanian-born French playwright. "The Playwright's Role," in *Observer* (London, 29 June 1958; repr. in *Notes and Counter-Notes,* pt. 2, 1962).

16 The principles of the good society call for a concern with an order of being—which cannot be proved existentially to the sense organs—where it matters supremely that the human person is inviolable, that reason shall regulate the will, that truth shall prevail over error.

> WALTER LIPPMANN (1889–1974), U.S. journalist. *The Public Philosophy,* ch. 11, sct. 4 (1955).

17 Society does not consist of individuals but expresses the sum of interrelations, the relations within which these individuals stand.

> KARL MARX (1818–1883), German political theorist, social philosopher. *Grundrisse,* "Notebook 2" (written 1857–58; first published 1939). The *Grundrisse,* or outline, is a rough draft of Marx's master work, *Capital.* It was unknown until its publication in 1939, when it caused great controversy amongst academics, revealing as it does (along with other previously lost works) an apparently more philosophical and humanist Marx.

18 We have two American flags always: one for the rich and one for the poor. When the rich fly it it means that things are under control; when the poor fly it it means danger, revolution, anarchy.

> HENRY MILLER (1891–1980), U.S. author. *The Air-Conditioned Nightmare,* "Good News! God is Love!" (1945).

19 Any relations in a social order will endure, if there is infused into them some of that spirit of human sympathy which qualifies life for immortality.

> GEORGE W. RUSSELL (A. E.) (1867–1965), Irish writer. Open letter to the Masters of Dublin, in *Irish Times* (7 Oct. 1913).

20 Society is like the air, necessary to breathe but insufficient to live on.

> GEORGE SANTAYANA (1863–1952), U.S. philosopher, poet. *The Life of Reason,* "Reason in Society," ch. 8 (1905–6).

21 What is called good society is usually nothing but a mosaic of polished caricatures.

> FRIEDRICH SCHLEGEL (1772–1829), German philosopher, critic, writer. *Dialogue on Poetry and Literary Aphorisms,* from "Selected Aphorisms," in *The Athenaeum,* aph. 5 (1968; first published 1798).

22 Our society is not a community, but merely a collection of isolated family units.

> VALERIE SOLANAS (b. 1940), U.S. artist, writer. *The SCUM Manifesto* (1968).

23 One set of messages of the society we live in is: Consume. Grow. Do what you want. Amuse yourselves. The very working of this economic system, which has bestowed these unprecedented liberties, most cherished in the form of physical mobility and material prosperity, depends on encouraging people to defy limits.

> SUSAN SONTAG (b. 1933), U.S. essayist. *AIDS and Its Metaphors,* ch. 7 (1989).

24 There is no such thing as society: there are individual men and women, and there are families.

> MARGARET THATCHER (b. 1925), British Conservative politician, prime minister. *Woman's Own* (London, 31 Oct. 1987).

25 Never speak disrespectfully of Society, Algernon. Only people who can't get into it do that.

> OSCAR WILDE (1854–1900), Anglo-Irish playwright, author. Lady Bracknell, in *The Importance of Being Earnest,* act 4.

See also Lennon on MADNESS.

SOCIOLOGY

1 Social movements are at once the symptoms and the instruments of progress. Ignore them and statesmanship is irrelevant; fail to use them and it is weak.

> WALTER LIPPMANN (1889–1974), U.S. journalist. *A Preface to Politics,* ch. 9 (1914).

2 To understand the true quality of people, you must look into their minds, and examine their pursuits and aversions.

> MARCUS AURELIUS (121–80), Roman emperor, philosopher. *Meditations,* bk. 4, sct. 38.

3 He . . . was a sociologist; he had got into an intellectual muddle early on in life and never managed to get out.

> IRIS MURDOCH (b. 1919), British novelist, philosopher. *The Philosopher's Pupil,* "The Events in Our Town" (1983).

4 No sociologist . . . should think himself too good, even in his old age, to make tens of thousands of quite trivial computations in his head and perhaps for months at a time. One cannot with impunity try to transfer this task entirely to mechanical assistants if one wishes to figure something, even though the final result is often small indeed.

> MAX WEBER (1864–1920), German sociologist. *Essays in Sociology,* "Science as a Vocation" (ed. by H. H. Gerth and C. Wright Mills, 1946; first published 1919).

See also The SOCIAL SCIENCES.

SOLEMNITY

1 There are people who believe everything is sane and sensible that is done with a solemn face.

> G. C. LICHTENBERG (1742–99), German physicist, philosopher. *Aphorisms,* "Notebook E," aph. 59 (written 1765–99; tr. by R. J. Hollingdale, 1990).

2 Seriousness is stupidity sent to college.

P. J. O'ROURKE (b. 1947), U.S. journalist. *Give War A Chance,* "A Serious Problem" (1992).

3 Everything has two sides—the outside that is ridiculous, and the inside that is solemn.

OLIVE SCHREINER (1855–1920), South African writer, feminist. Lyndall, in *The Story of an African Farm,* pt. 2, ch. 4 (1883).

See also Byron on HISTORIANS.

SOLITUDE

1 Whosoever is delighted in solitude is either a wild beast or a god.

FRANCIS BACON (1561–1626), English philosopher, essayist, statesman. Quoting an anonymous source, in: *Essays,* "Of Friendship" (1597–1625).

2 A writer who writes, "I am alone" . . . can be considered rather comical. It is comical for a man to recognize his solitude by addressing a reader and by using methods that prevent the individual from being alone. The word *alone* is just as general as the word *bread.* To pronounce it is to summon to oneself the presence of everything the word excludes.

MAURICE BLANCHOT (b. 1907), French literary theorist, author. "From Dread to Language," in *Faux Pas* (1943; repr. in *The Gaze of Orpheus,* ed. by P. Adams Sitney, 1981).

3 In solitude, where we are *least* alone.

LORD BYRON (1788–1824), English poet. *Childe Harold,* cto. 3, st. 90.

4 Ah, *mon cher,* for anyone who is alone, without God and without a master, the weight of days is dreadful.

ALBERT CAMUS (1913–60), French-Algerian philosopher, author. The narrator (Jean-Baptiste Clamence), in *The Fall* (1956; repr. 1957, p. 99).

5 The whole business of your life overwhelms you when you live alone. One's stupefied by it. To get rid of it you try to daub some of it off on to people who come to see you, and they hate that. To be alone trains one for death.

LOUIS-FERDINAND CÉLINE (1894–1961), French author. The narrator (Ferdinand Bardamu), in *Journey to the End of the Night* (1932; tr. 1934; ed. 1966, p. 328).

6 Alone, even doing nothing, you do not waste your time. You do, almost always, in company. No encounter with yourself can be altogether sterile: Something necessarily emerges, even if only the hope of some day meeting yourself again.

E. M. CIORAN (b. 1911), Rumanian-born French philosopher. *The New Gods,* "Strangled Thoughts," sct. 2 (1969; tr. 1974).

7 The worst vice of the solitary is the worship of his food.

CYRIL CONNOLLY (1903–74), British critic. Quoted in: David Pryce-Jones, *Journal and Memoir,* ch. 12 (1983).

8 We are a most solitary people, and we live, repelled by one another, in the gray, outcast cities of Cain.

EDWARD DAHLBERG (1900–1977), U.S. author, critic. *Alms for Oblivion,* "No Love and No Thanks" (1964).

9 In the tumult of men and events, solitude was my temptation; now it is my friend. What other satisfaction can be sought once you have confronted History?

CHARLES DE GAULLE (1890–1970), French general, president. *War Memoirs,* vol. 3, ch. 7 (1959; tr. 1960).

10 By all means use sometimes to be alone.
Salute thyself: see what thy soul doth wear.
Dare to look in thy chest; for 'tis thine own:
And tumble up and down what thou find'st there.
Who cannot rest till he good fellows find,
He breaks up house, turns out of doors his mind.

GEORGE HERBERT (1593–1633), English clergyman, poet. *The Church Porch,* st. 25.

11 True solitude is a din of birdsong, seething leaves, whirling colors, or a clamor of tracks in the snow.

EDWARD HOAGLAND (b. 1932), U.S. novelist, essayist. *Weekend Guardian* (London, 20–21 Jan. 1990).

12 With some people solitariness is an escape not from others but from themselves. For they see in the eyes of others only a reflection of themselves.

ERIC HOFFER (1902–83), U.S. philosopher. *The Passionate State of Mind,* aph. 211 (1955).

13 A man by himself is in bad company.

ERIC HOFFER (1902–83), U.S. philosopher. *The Passionate State of Mind,* aph. 262 (1955).

14 The more powerful and original a mind, the more it will incline towards the religion of solitude.

ALDOUS HUXLEY (1894–1963), British author. *Proper Studies,* "The Essence of Religion: Solitaries and Sociables" (1927).

15 If you are idle, be not solitary; if you are solitary, be not idle.

SAMUEL JOHNSON (1709–84), English author, lexicographer. Letter, 27 Oct. 1779, to James Boswell. Quoted in: James Boswell, *Life of Samuel Johnson* (1791).

16 Solitude is dangerous to reason, without being favourable to virtue. . . . Remember that the solitary mortal is certainly luxurious, probably superstitious, and possibly mad.

SAMUEL JOHNSON (1709–84), English author, lexicographer. Quoted in: Hester Piozzi, *Anecdotes of the Late Samuel Johnson* (1786; repr. in *Johnsonian Miscellanies,* vol. 1, ed. by George Birkbeck Hill, 1891, p. 219).

17 Solitude is un-American.

ERICA JONG (b. 1942), U.S. author. *Fear of Flying,* ch. 1 (1973).

18 Though the most beautiful creature were waiting for me at the end of a journey or a walk; though the carpet were of silk, the curtains of the morning clouds; the chairs and sofa stuffed with cygnet's down; the food manna, the wine beyond claret, the window opening on Winander Mere, I should not feel—or rather my happiness would not be so fine, as my solitude is sublime.

JOHN KEATS (1795–1821), English poet. Letter, 14–31 Oct. 1818, to his brother and sister-in-law, George and Georgiana Keats (published in *Letters of John Keats,* ed. by Frederick Page, no. 94, 1954).

19 Solitude: a sweet absence of looks.

MILAN KUNDERA (b. 1929), Czech author, critic. *Immortality,* pt. 1, ch. 6 (1991).

20 A solitude is the audience-chamber of God.

WALTER SAVAGE LANDOR (1775–1864), English author. *Imaginary Conversations*, "Lord Brooke and Sir Philip Sidney" (1824–29).

21 Ships that pass in the night, and speak each other in passing,
Only a signal shown, and a distant voice in the darkness;
So on the ocean of life, we pass and speak one another,
Only a look and a voice, then darkness again and a silence.

HENRY WADSWORTH LONGFELLOW (1807–82), U.S. poet. *Tales of a Wayside Inn*, pt. 3, "The Theologian's Tale: Elizabeth" (1874).

22 Two Paradises 'twere in one,
To live in Paradise alone.

ANDREW MARVELL (1621–78), English poet. *The Garden*, st. 8.

23 An artist is always alone—if he *is* an artist. No, what the artist needs is *loneliness*.

HENRY MILLER (1891–1980), U.S. author. *Tropic of Cancer* (1934; 1979, p. 72).

24 What call'st thou solitude? Is not the earth
With various living creatures, and the air
Replenished, and all these at thy command
To come and play before thee?

JOHN MILTON (1608–74), English poet. God, in *Paradise Lost*, bk. 8, responding to Adam's plea for a companion in Eden—"In solitude/What happiness? Who can enjoy alone/Or all enjoying, what contentment find?" The plea is finally granted by the creation of Eve.

25 Solitude begets whimsies.

LADY MARY WORTLEY MONTAGU (1689–1762), English society figure, letter writer. Letter, 19 July 1759 (published in *Selected Letters*, ed. by Robert Halsband, 1970).

26 Life without a friend is death without a witness.

SPANISH PROVERB.

27 The strong man is strongest when alone.

FRIEDRICH VON SCHILLER (1759–1805), German dramatist, poet, historian. Tell, in *Wilhelm Tell*, act 1, sc. 3 (tr. by Sir Thomas Martin).

28 One can acquire everything in solitude except character.

STENDHAL (1783–1842), French author. *On Love*, "Miscellaneous Fragments" (1822).

29 I never found the companion that was so companionable as solitude.

HENRY DAVID THOREAU (1817–62), U.S. philosopher, author, naturalist. *Walden*, "Solitude" (1854). Yet, in his journal (23 Dec. 1851), Thoreau noted, "It would give me such joy to know that a friend had come to see me, and yet that pleasure I seldom if ever experience."

30 In solitude we are in the presence of mere matter (even the sky, the stars, the moon, trees in blossom), things of less value (perhaps) than a human spirit. Its value lies in the greater possibility of attention. If we could be attentive to the same degree in the presence of a human being . . .

SIMONE WEIL (1909–43), French philosopher, mystic. *Gravity and Grace*, "Attention and Will" (1947; tr. 1952).

See also Osborne on ATHEISM; Cather on FRIENDSHIP; Garbo on GARBO; Eliot on HELL; HERMITS; HOBOS; Vaughan on OLD AGE; Byron on SOCIABILITY.

SOLUTIONS

1 The best way out is always through.

ROBERT FROST (1874–1963), U.S. poet. *A Servant to Servants*.

2 Increasingly in recent times we have come first to identify the remedy that is most agreeable, most convenient, most in accord with major pecuniary or political interest, the one that reflects our available faculty for action; then we move from the remedy so available or desired back to a cause to which that remedy is relevant.

JOHN KENNETH GALBRAITH (b. 1908), U.S. economist. "The Convenient Reverse Logic of Our Time," commencement address, 1984, American University (published in *A View from the Stands*, 1986).

3 America's present need is not heroics but healing; not nostrums but normalcy; not revolution but restoration.

WARREN GAMALIEL HARDING (1865–1923), U.S. Republican politician, president. Speech, June 1920, Boston. "Back to normalcy" was Harding's campaign slogan in that year.

4 The fact that I have no remedy for all the sorrows of the world is no reason for my accepting yours. It simply supports the strong probability that yours is a fake.

H. L. MENCKEN (1880–1956), U.S. journalist. *Minority Report: H. L. Mencken's Notebooks*, no. 78 (1956).

5 In this age, which believes that there is a short cut to everything, the greatest lesson to be learned is that the most difficult way is, in the long run, the easiest.

HENRY MILLER (1891–1980), U.S. author. *The Books in My Life*, Preface (1951).

SONG

1 Precisely because we do not communicate by singing, a song can be out of place but not out of character; it is just as credible that a stupid person should sing beautifully as that a clever person should do so.

W. H. AUDEN (1907–73), Anglo-American poet. *The Dyer's Hand*, pt. 8, "Notes on Music and Opera" (1962).

2 It is the best of all trades, to make songs, and the second best to sing them.

HILAIRE BELLOC (1870–1953), British author. *On Everything*, "On Song" (1909).

3 That's the wise thrush; he sings each song twice over,
Lest you should think he never could recapture
The first fine careless rapture!

ROBERT BROWNING (1812–89), English poet. *Home Thoughts, From Abroad*.

4 Swans sing before they die—'twere no bad thing
Did certain persons die before they sing.

> SAMUEL TAYLOR COLERIDGE (1772–1834), English poet, critic. *Epigram on a Volonteer Singer.*

5 I can't stand to sing the same song the same way two nights in succession, let alone two years or ten years. If you can, then it ain't music, it's close-order drill or exercise or yodeling or something, not music.

> BILLIE HOLIDAY (1915–59), U.S. blues singer. *Lady Sings the Blues*, ch. 4 (1956; written with William Dufty; rev. 1975).

6 This is a fault common to all singers, that among their friends they will never sing when they are asked; unasked, they will never desist.

> HORACE (65–8 B.C.), Roman poet. *Satires*, bk. 1, Satire 3 (c. 35 B.C.).

7 Singing has always seemed to me the most perfect means of expression. It is so spontaneous. And after singing, I think the violin. Since I cannot sing, I paint.

> GEORGIA O'KEEFFE (1887–1986), U.S. artist. Quoted in: *New York Sun* (5 Dec. 1922; repr. in Laurie Lisle, *Portrait of an Artist*, 1986).

8 There are few cases in which mere popularity should be considered a proper test of merit; but the case of song-writing is, I think, one of the few.

> EDGAR ALLAN POE (1809–45), U.S. poet, critic, short-story writer. *Marginalia*, in *Southern Literary Messenger* (Richmond, Va., April 1849; repr. in *Essays and Reviews*, 1984).

9 Odds life! must one swear to the truth of a song?

> MATTHEW PRIOR (1664–1721), English poet, diplomat. *A Better Answer.*

10 When Satan makes impure verses, Allah sends a divine tune to cleanse them.

> GEORGE BERNARD SHAW (1856–1950), Anglo-Irish playwright, critic. The Arab, in *The Adventures of the Black Girl in Her Search for God* (1932).

11 I would rather be remembered by a song than by a victory.

> ALEXANDER SMITH (1830–67), Scottish poet. *Dreamthorp*, "Men of Letters" (1863).

See also Dylan, Lennon on MUSIC COMPOSITION.

SONS

1 He followed in his father's footsteps, but his gait was somewhat erratic.

> NICOLAS BENTLEY (1907–78), British artist, author, publisher. Quoted in: Evan Esar, *Treasury of Humorous Quotations* (ed. by Nicolas Bentley, 1951).

2 Correct thy son, and he shall give thee rest; yea, he shall give delight unto thy soul.

> BIBLE, HEBREW. *Proverbs* 29:17.

3 For a mother the *project* of raising a boy is the most fulfilling project she can hope for. She can watch him, as a child, play the games she was not allowed to play; she can invest in him her ideas, aspirations, ambitions, and values—or whatever she has left of them; she can watch her son, who came from her flesh and whose life was sustained by her work and devotion, embody her in the world. So while the project of raising a boy is fraught with ambivalence and leads inevitably to bitterness, it is the only project that allows a woman *to be*—to be *through* her son, to live through her son.

> ANDREA DWORKIN (b. 1946), U.S. feminist critic. "The Sexual Politics of Fear and Courage," speech, first delivered 12 March 1975, Queens College, City University of New York (published in *Our Blood*, ch. 5, 1976).

4 If a man has been his mother's undisputed darling he retains throughout life the triumphant feeling, the confidence in success, which not seldom brings actual success along with it.

> SIGMUND FREUD (1856–1939), Austrian psychiatrist. *A Childhood Recollection*, in *Dichtung und Wahrheit* (1917; repr. in *Complete Works*, vol. 17, ed. by James Strachey and Anna Freud, 1955). Freud expressed the same idea on other occasions.

5 He didn't come out of my belly, but my God, I've made his bones, because I've attended to every meal, and how he sleeps, and the fact that he swims like a fish because I took him to the ocean. I'm so proud of all those things. But he is my biggest pride.

> JOHN LENNON (1940–80), British rock musician. Interview in *Playboy* (Chicago, Sept. 1980), said of his son, Sean Taro Ono Lennon.

6 How we dwelt in two worlds
the daughters and the mothers
in the kingdom of the sons.

> ADRIENNE RICH (b. 1929), U.S. poet. *The Dream of a Common Language*, "Sibling Mysteries" (1978).

7 It takes one woman twenty years to make a man of her son—and another woman twenty minutes to make a fool of him.

> HELEN ROWLAND (1875–1950), U.S. journalist. *A Guide to Men*, "Prelude" (1922).

8 In the middle classes the gifted son of a family is always the poorest—usually a writer or artist with no sense for speculation—and in a family of peasants, where the average comfort is just over penury, the gifted son sinks also, and is soon a tramp on the roadside.

> J. M. SYNGE (1871–1909), Irish poet, dramatist. *The Vagrants of Wicklow* (written 1901–2; first published in *The Shanachie*, Dublin, Autumn 1906).

See also FATHERS AND SONS.

SOPHISTICATION

1 I have always thought of sophistication as rather a feeble substitute for decadence.

> CHRISTOPHER HAMPTON (b. 1946), British playwright. Braham, in *The Philanthropist*, sc. 3.

2 Hip is the sophistication of the wise primitive in a giant jungle.

> NORMAN MAILER (b. 1923), U.S. author. "The White Negro," sct. 3, in *Dissent* (Summer 1957; repr. in *Advertisements for Myself*, 1959).

3 Sophistication might be described as the ability to

cope gracefully with a situation involving the presence of a formidable menace to one's poise and prestige (such as the butler, or the man under the bed—but never the husband).

> JAMES THURBER (1894–1961), U.S. humorist, illustrator. *New Yorker* (2 Aug. 1930). Thurber was referring specifically to sophistication in cartoon-drawing.

See also Santayana on SPIRIT.

SORROW

1   Some say that happiness is not good for mortals, & they ought to be answered that sorrow is not fit for immortals & is utterly useless to any one; a blight never does good to a tree, & if a blight kill not a tree but it still bear fruit, let none say that the fruit was in consequence of the blight.

> WILLIAM BLAKE (1757–1827), English poet, painter, engraver. Letter, 7 Oct. 1803 (published in *Complete Writings*, ed. by Geoffrey Keynes, 1957).

2   To fight aloud is very brave,
But *gallanter*, I know,
Who charge within the bosom
The Cavalry of Woe.

> EMILY DICKINSON (1830–86), U.S. poet. *The Complete Poems*, no. 126 (1955).

3   Sadness does not inhere in things; it does not reach us from the world and through mere contemplation of the world. It is a product of our own thought. We create it out of whole cloth.

> EMILE DURKHEIM (1858–1917), French sociologist. *Suicide*, bk. 2, ch. 6, sct. 1 (1897; tr. 1951).

4   Sorrow makes us all children again, destroys all differences of intellect. The wisest knows nothing.

> RALPH WALDO EMERSON (1803–82), U.S. essayist, poet, philosopher. *Journals*, vol. 8 (1909–1914), entry for 30 Jan. 1842.

5   Sorrow is a kind of rust of the soul, which every new idea contributes in its passage to scour away. It is the putrefaction of stagnant life, and is remedied by exercise and motion.

> SAMUEL JOHNSON (1709–84), English author, lexicographer. *Rambler*, no. 47 (London, 28 Aug. 1750; repr. in *Works of Samuel Johnson*, vol. 3, ed. by W. J. Bate and Albrecht B. Strauss, 1969).

6   There is no wisdom in useless and hopeless sorrow, but there is something in it so like virtue, that he who is wholly without it cannot be loved.

> SAMUEL JOHNSON (1709–84), English author, lexicographer. Letter, 12 April 1781, to Hester Thrale (published in *The Letters of Samuel Johnson*, vol. 2, no. 722, ed. by R. W. Chapman, 1952).

7   Since my earliest childhood a barb of sorrow has lodged in my heart. As long as it stays I am ironic—if it is pulled out I shall die.

> SØREN KIERKEGAARD (1813–55), Danish philosopher. *The Diary of Soren Kierkegaard*, pt. 1, no. 26 (ed. by Peter Rohde, 1960), 1847 entry.

8   Melancholy and sadness are the start of doubt . . .

doubt is the beginning of despair; despair is the cruel beginning of the differing degrees of wickedness.

> ISIDORE DUCASSE, COMTE DE LAUTRÉAMONT (1846–70), French author, poet. *Poésies*, ch. 1 (1870).

9   The lives of happy people are dense with their own doings—crowded, active, thick. . . . But the sorrowing are nomads, on a plain with few landmarks and no boundaries; sorrow's horizons are vague and its demands are few.

> LARRY MCMURTRY (b. 1936), U.S. screenwriter, novelist, essayist. *Some Can Whistle*, pt. 4, ch. 9 (1989).

10   Jesus, Buddha, Mahommed, great as each may be, their highest comfort given to the sorrowful is a cordial introduction into another's woe. Sorrow's the great community in which all men born of woman are members at one time or another.

> SEAN O'CASEY (1884–1964), Irish dramatist. *Rose and Crown*, vol. 5, "Wild Life in New Amsterdam" (1952).

11   Sorrow is tranquility remembered in emotion.

> DOROTHY PARKER (1893–1967), U.S. humorous writer. *The Portable Dorothy Parker*, "Sentiment" (1944).

12   But, truly, I have wept too much! The Dawns are heartbreaking. Every moon is atrocious and every sun bitter.

> ARTHUR RIMBAUD (1854–91), French poet. *Le Bateau Ivre*, in *Collected Poems* (ed. by Oliver Bernard, 1962).

13   When sorrows come they come not single spies,
But in battalions.

> WILLIAM SHAKESPEARE (1564–1616), English dramatist, poet. Claudius, in *Hamlet*, act 4, sc. 5.

14   The pleasure that is in sorrow is sweeter than the pleasure of pleasure itself.

> PERCY BYSSHE SHELLEY (1792–1822), English poet. *A Defence of Poetry* (written 1821; published 1840).

15   Pain and fear and hunger are effects of causes which can be foreseen and known: but sorrow is a debt which someone else makes for us.

> FREYA STARK (1893–1993), British travel writer. *Perseus in the Wind*, ch. 16 (1948).

16   Sorrow has the fortunate peculiarity that it preys upon itself. It dies of starvation. Since it is essentially an interruption of habits, it can be replaced by new habits. Constituting, as it does, a void, it is soon filled up by a real "horror vacui."

> J. AUGUST STRINDBERG (1849–1912), Swedish dramatist, novelist, poet. *The Son of a Servant*, vol. 1 (1886; tr. 1913, p. 99).

17   With no matter what human being, taken individually, I always find reasons for concluding that sorrow and misfortune do not suit him; either because he seems too mediocre for anything so great, or, on the contrary, too precious to be destroyed.

> SIMONE WEIL (1909–43), French philosopher, mystic. *Waiting on God*, Letter 4 (1950).

See also DESPAIR; GRIEF; Smith on MONEY; UNHAPPINESS.

THE SOUL

1   One certainly has a soul; but how it came to allow itself to be enclosed in a body is more than I can imagine. I only know if once mine gets out, I'll have a bit of a tussle before I let it get in again to that of any other.

> LORD BYRON (1788–1824), English poet. Letter, 11 April 1817, to the poet Thomas Moore (published in *Byron's Letters and Journals*, vol. 5, ed. by Leslie A. Marchand, 1973–81).

2   It must be admitted that there are some parts of the soul which we must entirely *paralyse* before we can live happily in this world.

> SÉBASTIEN-ROCH NICOLAS DE CHAMFORT (1741–94), French writer, wit. *Maxims and Considerations*, vol. 1, no. 124 (1796; tr. 1926).

3   The Soul unto itself
Is an imperial friend—
Or the most agonizing Spy—
An Enemy—could send—.

> EMILY DICKINSON (1830–86), U.S. poet. *The Complete Poems*, no. 683 (1955).

4   Developing the muscles of the soul demands no competitive spirit, no killer instinct, although it may erect pain barriers that the spiritual athlete must crash through.

> GERMAINE GREER (b. 1939), Australian feminist writer. *The Change: Women, Ageing and the Menopause*, ch. 2 (1991).

5   The weakness of a soul is proportionate to the number of truths that must be kept from it.

> ERIC HOFFER (1902–83), U.S. philosopher. *The Passionate State of Mind*, aph. 61 (1955).

6   Why do you hasten to remove anything which hurts your eye, while if something affects your soul you postpone the cure until next year?

> HORACE (65–8 B.C.), Roman poet. *Epistles*, bk. 1, Epistle 2.

7   A good soul like a good body should be as unobtrusive as possible; in so far as it functions properly, it should not be noticed for good or for ill.

> C. E. M. JOAD (1891–1953), British author, academic. *The Book of Joad*, ch. 2, "Food and Women" (1932).

8   My soul is my great asset and my great misfortune.

> D. H. LAWRENCE (1885–1930), British author. Letter, 13 May 1908 (published in *The Letters of D. H. Lawrence*, vol. 1, ed. by James T. Boulton, 1979).

9   The human being is a most curious creature. He thinks he has got one soul, and he has got dozens.

> D. H. LAWRENCE (1885–1930), British author. *Sea and Sardinia*, ch. 8 (1923).

10   The soul's a sort of sentimental wife,
That prays and whimpers of the higher life.

> RICHARD LE GALLIENNE (1866–1947), British poet. *The Decadent to his Soul*.

11   Every soul is a melody which needs renewing.

> STÉPHANE MALLARMÉ (1842–98), French Symbolist poet. *Variations sur un sujet*, "Crise de Vers" (first published in *La Revue Blanche*, Paris, Sept. 1895).

12   On the pavement
of my trampled soul
the soles of madmen
stamp the prints of rude, crude words.

> VLADIMIR MAYAKOVSKY (1893–1930), Russian poet, dramatist. *1*, in *Listen!: Early poems 1913–1918* (tr. by Maria Enzenberger, 1987).

13   Our souls belong to our bodies, not our bodies to our souls.

> HERMAN MELVILLE (1819–91), U.S. author. Babbalanja, in *Mardi: and a Voyage Thither*, ch. 155 (1849).

14   Our souls are like those orphans whose unwedded mothers die in bearing them: the secret of our paternity lies in their grave, and we must there to learn it.

> HERMAN MELVILLE (1819–91), U.S. author. *Moby-Dick*, ch. 114 (1851).

15   The soul can split the sky in two,
And let the face of God shine through.

> EDNA ST. VINCENT MILLAY (1892–1950), U.S. poet. *Renascence*, st. 8.

16   When one tears away the veils and shows them naked, people's souls give off such a pungent smell of decay.

> OCTAVE MIRBEAU (1850–1917), French journalist, author. *The Diary of a Chambermaid*, "14 September" (1900).

17   Your soul . . . is a dark forest. But the trees are of a particular species, they are genealogical trees.

> MARCEL PROUST (1871–1922), French novelist. *Pleasures and Regrets*, "Fragments From Italian Comedy," no. 7, sct. 4 (1896; tr. 1948).

18   There is nothing deep down inside us except what we have put there ourselves.

> RICHARD RORTY (b. 1931), U.S. philosopher. *Consequences of Pragmatism*, "Pragmatism and Philosophy" (1982). Rorty was arguing here against the notion that there is some metaphysical "truth" about human beings—i.e. some kind of answer within us to the problems presented to us by the world.

19   A soul is but the last bubble of a long fermentation in the world.

> GEORGE SANTAYANA (1863–1952), U.S. philosopher, poet. *The Life of Reason*, "Reason in Religion," ch. 10 (1905–6).

20   We know now that the soul is the body, and the body the soul. They tell us they are different because they want to persuade us that we can keep our souls if we let them make slaves of our bodies.

> GEORGE BERNARD SHAW (1856–1950), Anglo-Irish playwright, critic. Ellie, in *Heartbreak House*, act 2.

21   Most people sell their souls, and live with a good conscience on the proceeds.

> LOGAN PEARSALL SMITH (1865–1946), U.S. essayist, aphorist. *Afterthoughts*, "Other People" (1931).

22   However intense my experience, I am conscious of the presence and criticism of a part of me, which, as it were, is not a part of me, but a spectator, sharing no experience, but taking note of it, and that is no more I than it is you. When the play, it may be the tragedy, of life is over, the spectator goes his way. It was a kind of fiction, a work of the imagination only, so far as he was concerned.

> HENRY DAVID THOREAU (1817–62), U.S. philosopher, author, naturalist. *Walden*, "Solitude" (1854).

23 How strange a thing this is! The Priest telleth me that the Soul is worth all the gold in the world, and the merchants say that it is not worth a clipped piece of silver.

> OSCAR WILDE (1854–1900), Anglo-Irish playwright, author. The young fisherman, in "The Fisherman and his Soul" (published in *A House of Pomegranates*, 1891).

24 We are truly indefatigable in providing for the needs of the body, but we starve the soul.

> ELLEN WOOD (1813–87), English playwright, writer, journalist. *About Ourselves*, ch. 1 (1883).

25 This soul, or life within us, by no means agrees with the life outside us. If one has the courage to ask her what she thinks, she is always saying the very opposite to what other people say.

> VIRGINIA WOOLF (1882–1941), British novelist. *The Common Reader*, "Montaigne" (First Series, 1925).

See also Keats on ADVERSITY; Meredith on CERTAINTY; Woolf on CONFORMITY; Bellow on CONFUSION; Byron on IMMORTALITY; Jung on The PSYCHE; Wilde on The SENSES; Bloom on TEACHERS; Carlyle on UNHAPPINESS.

THE SOUTH

1 The South *is* very beautiful but its beauty makes one sad because the lives that people live here, and have lived here, are so ugly.

> JAMES BALDWIN (1924–87), U.S. author. "They Can't Turn Back," in *Mademoiselle* (New York, Aug. 1960; repr. in *The Price of the Ticket*, 1985).

2 The average Southerner has the speech patterns of someone slipping in and out of consciousness. I can change my shoes and socks faster than most people in Mississippi can speak a sentence.

> BILL BRYSON (b. 1951), U.S. author, journalist. *The Lost Continent: Travels in Small Town America*, ch. 7 (1989).

3 Southerners can never resist a losing cause.

> MARGARET MITCHELL (1900–1949), U.S. novelist. Rhett Butler, in *Gone with the Wind*, vol. 2, pt. 4, ch. 34 (1936).

4 While the South is hardly Christ-centered, it is most certainly Christ-haunted.

> FLANNERY O'CONNOR (1925–64), U.S. author. "Some Aspects of the Grotesque in Southern Fiction," paper, read at Wesleyan College for Women, Fall 1960, Macon, Georgia (published in *Cluster Review*, 1965; repr. in *Mystery and Manners*, ed. by Sally and Robert Fitzgerald, 1972).

5 Storytelling and copulation are the two chief forms of amusement in the South. They're inexpensive and easy to procure.

> ROBERT PENN WARREN (b. 1905), U.S. poet, novelist. Quoted in: *Newsweek* (New York, 25 Aug. 1980).

6 O magnet-south! O glistening, perfumed South!
>   my South!
> O quick mettle, rich blood, impulse and love!
> Good and evil! O all dear
>   to me!

> WALT WHITMAN (1819–92), U.S. poet. *O Magnet-south*.

See also Twain on The CIVIL WAR; O'Connor on The GROTESQUE; O'Connor on PROVINCIALISM.

SOUTH AFRICA

1 Christ in this country would quite likely have been arrested under the Suppression of Communism act.

> JOOST DE BLANK (1908–68), South African cleric. Quoted in: *Observer* (London, 27 Oct. 1963). Joost de Blank was Archbishop of Cape Town, 1957–63.

2 There is only one element that can break the Afrikaner, and that is the Afrikaner himself. It is when the Afrikaner, like a baboon shot in the stomach, pulls out his own intestines. We must guard against that.

> P. W. BOTHA (b. 1916), South African politician, prime minister. Speech, 26 April 1984.

3 South Africa used to seem so far away. Then it came home to me. It began to signify the meaning of white hatred here. That was what the sheets and the suits and the ties covered up, not very well. That was what the cowardly guys calling me names from their speeding truck wanted to happen to me, to all of me: to my people. That was what would happen to me if I walked around the corner into the wrong neighborhood. That was Birmingham. That was Brooklyn. That was Reagan. That was the end of reason. South Africa was how I came to understand that I am not against war; I am against losing the war.

> JUNE JORDAN (b. 1939), U.S. poet, civil rights activist. *Moving Towards Home: Political Essays*, "South Africa: Bringing It All Back Home" (written 1981; first published 1985; repr. 1989).

4 The drama can only be brought to its climax in one of two ways—through the selective brutality of terrorism or the impartial horrors of war.

> KENNETH KAUNDA (b. 1924), Zambian politician, president. *Kaunda on Violence*, pt. 2 (1980), of the situation in South Africa.

5 Together, hand in hand, with that stick of matches, with our necklace, we shall liberate this country.

> WINNIE MANDELA (b. 1934), South African political leader. Speech in black townships. Quoted in: *Guardian* (London, 15 April 1986).

6 If Nature here wishes to make a mountain, she runs a range for five hundred miles; if a plain, she levels eighty; if a rock, she tilts five thousand feet of strata on end; our skies are higher and more intensely blue; our waves larger than others; our rivers fiercer. There is nothing measured, small nor petty in South Africa.

> OLIVE SCHREINER (1855–1920), South African writer, feminist. *Thoughts on South Africa*, ch. 1 (1892).

7 Is not our role to stand for the one thing which means our own salvation here but with which it will also be possible to save the world, and with which Europe will be able to save itself, namely the preservation of the white man and his state?

> HENDRIK VERWOERD (1901–66), South African Nationalist politician, prime minister. Speech, 1964 Quoted in: *Oxford History of South Africa*, vol. 2, ch. 10 (ed. by M. Wilson and L. Thompson, 1971).

8 As far as criticism is concerned, we don't resent that unless it is absolutely biased, as it is in most cases.

> JOHN VORSTER (1915–83), South African politician, prime minister. Quoted in: *Observer* (London, 9 Nov. 1969).

See also Macmillan on DECOLONIZATION.

SPACE

1   Man is an artifact designed for space travel. He is not designed to remain in his present biologic state any more than a tadpole is designed to remain a tadpole.

> WILLIAM BURROUGHS (b. 1914), U.S. author. *The Adding Machine*, "Civilian Defense" (1985).

2   Until they come to see us from their planet, I wait patiently. I hear them saying: Don't call us, we'll call you.

> MARLENE DIETRICH (1904–92), German-born U.S. film actor. *Marlene Dietrich's ABC*, "Venus" (1962).

3   The question that will decide our destiny is not whether we shall expand into space. It is: shall we be one species or a million? A million species will not exhaust the ecological niches that are awaiting the arrival of intelligence.

> FREEMAN DYSON (b. 1923), British-born U.S. physicist, author. *Disturbing the Universe*, pt. 1, ch. 21 (1979).

4   Our passionate preoccupation with the sky, the stars, and a God somewhere in outer space is a homing impulse. We are drawn back to where we came from.

> ERIC HOFFER (1902–83), U.S. philosopher. *New York Times* (21 July 1969), on the first moon-landing.

5   Space isn't remote at all. It's only an hour's drive away if your car could go straight upwards.

> SIR FRED HOYLE (b. 1915), British astronomer. *Observer* (London, 9 Sept. 1979).

6   Space is the stature of God.

> JOSEPH JOUBERT (1754–1824), French essayist, moralist. *Pensées*, no. 183 (1842).

7   Prometheus is reaching out for the stars with an empty grin on his face.

> ARTHUR KOESTLER (1905–83), Hungarian-born British author. *New York Times* (21 July 1969), on the first moon-landing.

8   Oh! I have slipped the surly bonds of earth,
And danced the skies on laughter-silvered wings
. . .
And while with silent lifting mind I've trod
The high, untrespassed sanctity of space,
Put out my hand and touched the face of God.

> JOHN GILLESPIE MAGEE (c.1922–41), U.S.-born pilot with Royal Canadian Air Force. First and last lines of the sonnet *High Flight* (written 1941). Magee died while on a bombing mission over Germany. The verse was later quoted by President Ronald Reagan following the Challenger space shuttle disaster in 1986.

9   No matter how vast, how total, the failure of man here on earth, the work of man will be resumed elsewhere. War leaders talk of resuming operations on this front and that, but man's front embraces the whole universe.

> HENRY MILLER (1891–1980), U.S. author. *Sunday after the War*, "Reunion in Brooklyn" (1944).

10   The eternal silence of these infinite spaces fills me with dread.

> BLAISE PASCAL (1623–62), French scientist, philosopher. *Pensées*, (1670; no. 201 ed. by Krailsheimer, no. 206 ed. by Brunschvicg).

11   Space is almost infinite. As a matter of fact, we think it is infinite.

> DAN QUAYLE (b. 1947), U.S. Republican politician, vice president. *Daily Telegraph* (London, 8 March 1989).

12   It is marvelous indeed to watch on television the rings of Saturn close; and to speculate on what we may yet find at galaxy's edge. But in the process, we have lost the human element; not to mention the high hope of those quaint days when flight would create "one world." Instead of one world, we have "star wars," and a future in which dumb dented human toys will drift mindlessly about the cosmos long after our small planet's dead.

> GORE VIDAL (b. 1925), U.S. novelist, critic. *Armageddon*, "On Flying," sct. 3 (1987).

13   Don't tell me that man doesn't belong out there. Man belongs wherever he wants to go—and he'll do plenty well when he gets there.

> WERNHER VON BRAUN (1912–77), German-born U.S. rocket engineer. *Time* (New York, 17 Feb. 1958), of space flights.

14   It was a thunderingly beautiful experience—voluptuous, sexual, dangerous, and expensive as hell.

> KURT VONNEGUT, JR. (b. 1922), U.S. novelist. *Wampeters, Foma and Granfalloons*, "Playboy Interview, 1973" (1974), of the Apollo launches.

See also Lamb on The COSMOS; The MOON; Lessing on SCIENCE FICTION.

SPAIN AND THE SPANISH

1   The genius of the Spanish people is exquisitely subtle, without being at all acute; hence there is so much humour and so little wit in their literature.

> SAMUEL TAYLOR COLERIDGE (1772–1834), English poet, critic. *Table Talk*, 23 April 1832 (published in *Specimens of the Table Talk of Samuel Taylor Coleridge*, ed. by Henry Nelson Coleridge, 1835; repr. in *Collected Works*, vol. 14, ed. by Kathleen Coburn, 1990).

2   In Spain, the dead are more alive than the dead of any other country in the world.

> FEDERICO GARCÍA LORCA (1898–1936), Spanish poet, playwright. *Poet in New York*, "The Duende: Theory and Divertissement, Appendix 6" (1940).

3   Honor to a Spaniard, no matter how dishonest, is as real a thing as water, wine, or olive oil. There is honor among pickpockets and honor among whores. It is simply that the standards differ.

> ERNEST HEMINGWAY (1899–1961), U.S. author. *Death in the Afternoon*, ch. 9 (1932).

4   Spain is an overflow of sombreness . . . a strong and threatening tide of history meets you at the frontier.

> WYNDHAM LEWIS (1882–1957), British author, painter. *The Wild Body*, "A Soldier of Humour" (1927).

5   Three Spaniards, four opinions.

> SPANISH PROVERB.

SPECULATION

1   Another great evil arising from this desire to be

thought rich; or rather, from the desire not to be thought poor, is the destructive thing which has been honoured by the name of "speculation"; but which ought to be called Gambling.

> WILLIAM COBBETT (1762–1835), English journalist, reformer. *Advice to Young Men and to Young Women*, Letter 2, "To a Young Man" (1829; repr. 1930).

2 I never guess. It is a shocking habit—destructive to the logical faculty.

> SIR ARTHUR CONAN DOYLE (1859–1930), English author. Sherlock Holmes, in *The Sign of Four*, ch. 1 (1890).

3 If the world were good for nothing else, it is a fine subject for speculation.

> WILLIAM HAZLITT (1778–1830), English essayist. *Characteristics: in the Manner of Rochefoucault's Maxims*, no. 302 (1823; repr. in *Collected Works*, vol. 2, ed. by A. R. Waller and Arnold Glover, 1902).

4 When speculation has done its worst, two and two still make four.

> SAMUEL JOHNSON (1709–84), English author, lexicographer. *The Idler*, no. 36, in *Universal Chronicle* (London, 23 Dec. 1758; repr. in *Works of Samuel Johnson*, vol. 2, ed. by W. J. Bate, John M. Bullitt, and L. F. Powell, 1963).

5 What most people don't seem to realize is that there is just as much money to be made out of the wreckage of a civilization as from the upbuilding of one.

> MARGARET MITCHELL (1900–1949), U.S. novelist. Rhett Butler, in *Gone with the Wind*, vol. 1, pt. 2, ch. 9 (1936).

6 There are two times in a man's life when he should not speculate: when he can't afford it, and when he can.

> MARK TWAIN (1835–1910), U.S. author. *Following the Equator*, ch. 56, "Pudd'nhead Wilson's New Calendar" (1897).

SPEECH

1 It's a damn shame we have this immediate ticking off in the mind about how people sound. On the other hand, how many people really want to be operated upon by a surgeon who talks broad cockney?

> EILEEN AITKINS (b. 1934), British stage and screen actor. *Daily Telegraph* (London, 5 Feb. 1992).

2 The stroke of the whip maketh marks in the flesh: but the stroke of the tongue breaketh the bones. Many have fallen by the edge of the sword: but not so many as have fallen by the tongue.

> APOCRYPHA. *Ecclesiasticus* 28:17–18.

3 Wherever the relevance of speech is at stake, matters become political by definition, for speech is what makes man a political being.

> HANNAH ARENDT (1906–75), German-born U.S. political philosopher. *The Human Condition*, Prologue (1958).

4 Language is legislation, speech is its code. We do not see the power which is in speech because we forget that all speech is a classification, and that all classifications are oppressive.

> ROLAND BARTHES (1915–80), French semiologist. *Leçon*, Inaugural Lecture, 7 Jan. 1977, Collège de France (published 1978; repr. in *Barthes: Selected Writings*, 1982).

5 Let your speech be always with grace, seasoned with salt, that ye may know how ye ought to answer every man.

> BIBLE: NEW TESTAMENT. *Colossians* 4:6.

6 The basic rule of human nature is that powerful people speak slowly and subservient people quickly—because if they don't speak fast nobody will listen to them.

> MICHAEL CAINE (b. 1933), British stage and screen actor. *Times* (London, 26 Aug. 1992).

7 From my earliest days I have enjoyed an attractive impediment in my speech. I have never permitted the use of the word "stammer." I can't say it myself.

> PATRICK CAMPBELL (1913–80), Irish humorist. *The P-p-Penguin Patrick Campbell*, "Unaccustomed As I Am" (1965).

8 The only happy talkers are dandies who extract pleasure from the very perishability of their material and who would not be able to tolerate the isolation of all other forms of composition; for most good talkers, when they have run down, are miserable; they know that they have betrayed themselves, that they have taken material which should have a life of its own, to dispense it in noises upon the air.

> CYRIL CONNOLLY (1903–74), British critic. *Enemies of Promise*, pt. 2, ch. 13 (1938).

9 Speech is power: speech is to persuade, to convert, to compel. It is to bring another out of his bad sense into your good sense.

> RALPH WALDO EMERSON (1803–82), U.S. essayist, poet, philosopher. *Letters and Social Aims*, "Social Aims" (1876).

10 Speech is an arrangement of notes that will never be played again.

> F. SCOTT FITZGERALD (1896–1940), U.S. author. The narrator (Nick Carraway), in *The Great Gatsby*, ch. 1 (1925), describing Daisy Buchanan's "low, thrilling voice . . . the kind of voice that the ear follows up and down."

11 For mankind, speech with a capital S is especially meaningful and committing, more than the content communicated. The outcry of the newborn and the sound of the bells are fraught with mystery more than the baby's woeful face or the venerable tower.

> PAUL GOODMAN (1911–72), U.S. author, poet, critic. *Five Years*, "Summer 1957, in Europe," sct. 3 (1966).

12 Speak clearly, if you speak at all;
Carve every word before you let it fall.

> OLIVER WENDELL HOLMES, SR. (1809–94), U.S. writer, physician. *A Rhymed Lesson*.

13 Sweet Benjamin, since thou art young,
And hast not yet the use of tongue,
Make it thy slave, while thou art free;
Imprison it, lest it do thee.

> JOHN HOSKINS (1566–1638), English lawyer, wit. *To His Son*, written from prison in the Tower of London.

14 Language most shews a man: Speak, that I may see thee.

> BEN JONSON (1573–1637), English dramatist, poet. *Timber, or*

Discoveries Made upon Men and Matter, para. 121, "Explorata: Oratio Imago Animi" (1641).

15 Be still when you have nothing to say; when genuine passion moves you, say what you've got to say, and say it hot.

D. H. LAWRENCE (1885–1930), British author. *Studies in Classic American Literature,* ch. 2 (1924).

16 What has influenced my life more than any other single thing has been my stammer. Had I not stammered I would probably . . . have gone to Cambridge as my brothers did, perhaps have become a don and every now and then published a dreary book about French literature.

W. SOMERSET MAUGHAM (1874–1965), English author. *Newsweek* (New York, 23 May 1960).

17 Let us speak, though we show all our faults and weaknesses,—for it is a sign of strength to be weak, to know it, and out with it,—not in a set way and ostentatiously, though, but incidentally and without premeditation.

HERMAN MELVILLE (1819–91), U.S. author. Letter, 29 June 1851, to Nathaniel Hawthorne (published in *The Letters of Herman Melville,* ed. by Merrell R. Davis and William H. Gilman, 1960).

18 Man does not speak because he thinks; he thinks because he speaks. Or rather, speaking is no different than thinking: to speak is to think.

OCTAVIO PAZ (b. 1914), Mexican poet. *Alternating Current,* "André Breton or the Quest of the Beginning" (1967).

19 People resent articulacy, as if articulacy were a form of vice.

FREDERIC RAPHAEL (b. 1931), British author, critic. *Guardian* (London, 8 June 1989).

20 The world does not speak. Only we do. The world can, once we have programmed ourselves with a language, cause us to hold beliefs. But it cannot propose a language for us to speak. Only other human beings can do that.

RICHARD RORTY (b. 1931), U.S. philosopher. *Contingency, Irony, and Solidarity,* ch. 1, "The Contingency of Language" (1989).

21 I don't want to talk grammar. I want to talk like a lady.

GEORGE BERNARD SHAW (1856–1950), Anglo-Irish playwright, critic. Liza Doolittle, in *Pygmalion,* act 2.

22 All speech, written or spoken, is a dead language, until it finds a willing and prepared hearer.

ROBERT LOUIS STEVENSON (1850–94), Scottish novelist, essayist, poet. *Reflections and Remarks on Human Life,* sct. 3 (first published 1878; repr. in *Complete Works,* vol. 26, 1924).

23 Speech is for the convenience of those who are hard of hearing; but there are many fine things which we cannot say if we have to shout.

HENRY DAVID THOREAU (1817–62), U.S. philosopher, author, naturalist. *Walden,* "Visitors" (1854).

24 Speech is the twin of my vision, it is unequal to measure itself,
It provokes me forever, it says sarcastically,

Walt you contain enough, why don't you let it out then?

WALT WHITMAN (1819–92), U.S. poet. *Song of Myself,* sct. 25, in *Leaves of Grass* (1855).

25 Many great writers have been extraordinarily awkward in daily exchange, but the greatest give the impression that their style was nursed by the closest attention to colloquial speech.

THORNTON WILDER (1897–1975), U.S. novelist, dramatist. Interview in *Writers at Work* (First Series, ed. by Malcolm Cowley, 1958).

26 There are remarks that sow and remarks that reap.

LUDWIG WITTGENSTEIN (1889–1951), Austrian philosopher. *Culture and Value* (ed. by G. H. von Wright and Heikki Nyman, 1980), 1948 entry.

See also Holmes on CONVERSATION; Mann on LANGUAGE; Carlyle on SILENCE; Kierkegaard on TALKITIVENESS; WORDS.

SPEECHES AND SPEECHMAKING

1 Let thy speech be short, comprehending much in few words.

APROCRYPHA. *Ecclesiasticus* 32:8.

2 I do not object to people looking at their watches when I am speaking. But I strongly object when they start shaking them to make certain they are still going.

LORD BIRKETT (1883–1962), British lawyer, Liberal politician. Quoted in: *Observer* (London, 30 Oct. 1960).

3 For, if a "good speaker," never so eloquent, does not see into the fact, and is not speaking the truth of that . . . is there a more horrid kind of object in creation?

THOMAS CARLYLE (1795–1881), Scottish essayist, historian. "Inaugural Address at Edinburgh," 2 April 1866 (published in *Scottish and Other Miscellanies,* 1915), on being installed as Rector of the University at Edinburgh.

4 Most people have ears, but few have judgment; tickle those ears, and depend upon it you will catch their judgments, such as they are.

LORD CHESTERFIELD (1694–1773), English statesman, man of letters. Letter, 9 Dec. 1749 (first published 1774; repr. in *The Letters of the Earl of Chesterfield to His Son,* vol. 1, no. 206, ed. by Charles Strachey, 1901).

5 Adepts in the speaking trade
Keep a cough by them ready made.

CHARLES CHURCHILL (1731–64), English clergyman, poet. *The Ghost,* bk. 2.

6 He is one of those orators of whom it was well said, "Before they get up, they do not know what they are going to say; when they are speaking, they do not know what they are saying; and when they have sat down, they do not know what they have said."

SIR WINSTON CHURCHILL (1874–1965), English statesman, writer. Speech, 20 Dec. 1912, to the House of Commons, said of naval commander Lord Charles Beresford.

7 A man may lack everything but tact and conviction and still be a forcible speaker; but without these nothing will avail. . . . Fluency, grace, logical order, and the like, are merely the decorative surface of oratory.

CHARLES HORTON COOLEY (1864–1929), U.S. sociologist. *Human Nature and the Social Order*, ch. 9 (1902).

8 If we use common words on a great occasion, they are the more striking, because they are felt at once to have a particular meaning, like old banners, or everyday clothes, hung up in a sacred place.

GEORGE ELIOT (1819–80), English novelist. Maggie Tulliver, in *The Mill on the Floss*, bk. 6, ch. 2 (1860).

9 When a man gets up to speak, people listen, then look. When a woman gets up, people *look*; then, if they like what they see, they listen.

PAULINE FREDERICK (1883–1938), U.S. stage and screen actor. Quoted in: Jilly Cooper and Tom Hartman, *Violets and Vinegar*, "Mrs. Crankhurst" (1980).

10 Commencement oratory . . . must eschew anything that smacks of partisan politics, political preference, sex, religion or unduly firm opinion. Nonetheless, there must be a speech: speeches in our culture are the vacuum that fills a vacuum.

JOHN KENNETH GALBRAITH (b. 1908), U.S. economist. Commencement address, American University, Washington, D.C. (published in *Time*, 18 June 1984).

11 I feel like Zsa Zsa Gabor's fifth husband. I know what I'm supposed to do but I don't know if I can make it interesting.

ALBERT GORE, JR. (b. 1948), U.S. Democratic politician, vice president. Quoted in: *Today* (London, 1 March 1989), on being the 23rd speaker at a political dinner.

12 Amplification is the vice of modern oratory. It is an insult to an assembly of reasonable men, disgusting and revolting instead of persuading. Speeches measured by the hour, die by the hour.

THOMAS JEFFERSON (1743–1826), U.S. president. Letter, 20 April 1824.

13 There may be other reasons for a man's not speaking in publick than want of resolution: he may have nothing to say.

SAMUEL JOHNSON (1709–84), English author, lexicographer. Quoted in: James Boswell, *Life of Samuel Johnson*, 5 April 1775 (1791).

14 The object of oratory alone is not truth, but persuasion.

THOMAS BABINGTON MACAULAY (1800–1859), English historian. *The Works of Lord Macaulay*, vol. 11, "Essay on Athenian Orators" (1898).

15 So having said, a while he stood, expecting
Their universal shout and high applause
To fill his ear; when contrary, he hears,
On all sides, from innumerable tongues
A dismal universal hiss, the sound
Of public scorn.

JOHN MILTON (1608–74), English poet. *Paradise Lost*, bk. 10, of Satan.

16 He's a wonderful talker, who has the art of telling you nothing in a great harangue.

MOLIÈRE (1622–73), French dramatist. Célimène, in *Le Misanthrope*, act 2 sc. 5.

17 The mark of a true politician is that he is never at a loss for words because he is always half-expecting to be asked to make a speech.

RICHARD M. NIXON (b. 1913), U.S. Republican politician, president. *Six Crises*, "The Campaign of 1960" (1962).

18 A speech is poetry: cadence, rhythm, imagery, sweep! A speech reminds us that words, like children, have the power to make dance the dullest beanbag of a heart.

PEGGY NOONAN (b. 1950), U.S. author, presidential speechwriter. *What I Saw at the Revolution*, ch. 5 (1990).

19 Few speeches which have produced an electrical effect on an audience can bear the colourless photography of a printed record.

LORD ROSEBERY (1847–1929), English Liberal politician, prime minister. *The Life of William Pitt*, ch. 13 (1891). Rosebery himself was an effective and distinguished orator.

20 Speak the speech . . . trippingly on the tongue; but if you mouth it . . . I had as lief the town crier had spoke my lines. Nor do not saw the air too much with your hand, thus, but use all gently; for in the very torrent, tempest, and as I may say the whirlwind of your passion, you must acquire and beget a temperance that may give it smoothness.

WILLIAM SHAKESPEARE (1564–1616), English dramatist, poet. Hamlet, in the opening lines of *Hamlet*, act 3, sc. 2, instructing the player how to give the speech he has written.

21 Sure, if I reprehend anything in this world, it is the use of my oracular tongue, and a nice derangement of epitaphs.

RICHARD BRINSLEY SHERIDAN (1751–1816), Anglo-Irish dramatist. Mrs. Malaprop, in *The Rivals*, act 3, sc. 3.

22 The sanity of the average banquet speaker lasts about two and a half months; at the end of that time he begins to mutter to himself, and calls out in his sleep.

JAMES THURBER (1894–1961), U.S. humorist, illustrator. *New Yorker* (29 March 1930).

23 The right word may be effective, but no word was ever as effective as a rightly timed pause.

MARK TWAIN (1835–1910), U.S. author. Quoted in: *Mark Twain's Speeches*, Introduction (ed. by Albert Bigelow Paine, 1923).

24 O the orator's joys!
To inflate the chest, to roll the thunder of the
    voice out from the ribs and throat,
To make the people rage, weep, hate, desire, with
    yourself,
To lead America—to quell America with a great
    tongue.

WALT WHITMAN (1819–92), U.S. poet. *Calamus: A Song of Joys* (1855), in *Leaves of Grass*.

See also La Rochefoucauld on PASSION; Franklin on PREACHING; Noonan on QUOTATION.

SPEED

1 Speed, it seems to me, provides the one genuinely modern pleasure.

ALDOUS HUXLEY (1894–1963), British author. *Music at Night and Other Essays*, "Wanted, a New Pleasure" (1949).

2 A new beauty has been added to the splendor of the world—the beauty of speed.

> TOMMASO MARINETTI (1876–1944), Italian playwright. "Foundation and Manifesto of Futurism," in *Figaro* (Paris, 20 Feb. 1909; repr. in *Marinetti: Selected Writings*, ed. by R. W. Flint, 1971).

3 Speed is scarcely the noblest virtue of graphic composition, but it has its curious rewards. There is a sense of getting somewhere fast, which satisfies a native American urge.

> JAMES THURBER (1894–1961), U.S. humorist, illustrator. *A Thurber Garland*, Preface (1955).

SPIES

1 And ye shall know the truth, and the truth shall make you free.

> BIBLE: NEW TESTAMENT. *John* 8:32. These words of Jesus are inscribed on the wall of the main lobby at the C.I.A. headquarters, Langley, Va.

2 Kings have many ears and many eyes. . . . They have ears that listen a hundred miles from them; they have eyes that espy out more things than men would think. Wherefore, it is wisdom for subjects not only to keep their princes' laws and ordinances in the face of the world but also privily . . . for conscience sake.

> DESIDERIUS ERASMUS (c. 1466–1536), Dutch humanist. *Proverbs or Adages of Erasmus*, folio 4–5 (ed. by Richard Taverner, 1545).

3 What do you think spies are: priests, saints and martyrs? They're a squalid procession of vain fools, traitors too, yes; pansies, sadists and drunkards, people who play cowboys and Indians to brighten their rotten lives.

> JOHN LE CARRÉ (b. 1931), British novelist. Leamas, in *The Spy Who Came in From the Cold*, ch. 25 (1963).

4 It's easy to forget what intelligence consists of: luck and speculation. Here and there a windfall, here and there a scoop.

> JOHN LE CARRÉ (b. 1931), British novelist. Leclerc, in *The Looking-Glass War*, pt. 2, ch. 9 (1965).

5 There are some who become spies for money, or out of vanity and megalomania, or out of ambition, or out of a desire for thrills. But the malady of our time is of those who become spies out of idealism.

> MAX LERNER (b. 1902), U.S. author, columnist. *The Unfinished Country*, pt. 4, "The Tragedy of the Rosenbergs" (1959; first published in *New York Post*, 9 April 1952), of the atomic secrets spy, Julius Rosenberg.

6 It is only the enlightened ruler and the wise general who will use the highest intelligence of the army for the purposes of spying, and thereby they achieve great results.

> SUN TZU (6–5th century B.C.), Chinese general. *The Art of War*, ch. 13, axiom 27 (c. 490 B.C.; ed. by James Clavell, 1981).

7 I cannot think that espionage can be recommended as a technique for building an impressive civilisation. It's a lout's game.

> REBECCA WEST (1892–1983), British author. Introduction to 1982 ed. of *The Meaning of Treason* (first published 1949).

8 He smiled rather too much. He smiled at breakfast, you know.

> CHARLES WHEELER (b. 1923), British journalist, broadcaster. "Inside Story," BBC-1 TV. Quoted in: *Independent* (London, 20 Sept. 1990), remembering the spy George Blake.

SPIRIT

1 Spirit borrows from matter the perceptions on which it feeds and restores them to matter in the form of movements which it has stamped with its own freedom.

> HENRI BERGSON (1859–1941), French philosopher. Last sentence in *Matter and Memory*, "Summary and Conclusion," sct. 9 (1896; tr. 1988).

2 There are incalculable resources in the human spirit, once it has been set free.

> HUBERT H. HUMPHREY (1911–78), U.S. Democratic politician, vice president. Speech, 10 Dec. 1966, Adas Israel Synagogue, Washington, D.C.

3 Once spirit was God, then it became man, and now it is even becoming mob.

> FRIEDRICH NIETZSCHE (1844–1900), German philosopher. *Thus Spoke Zarathustra*, pt. 1, "Of Reading and Writing" (1883).

4 But the thing that I saw in your face
No power can disinherit:
No bomb that ever burst
Shatters the crystal spirit.

> GEORGE ORWELL (1903–50), British author. Poem, 1943, included in Orwell's essay, "Looking Back on the Spanish War," sct. 7 (first published in *England Your England*, 1953).

5 The spirit's foe in man has not been simplicity, but sophistication.

> GEORGE SANTAYANA (1863–1952), U.S. philosopher, poet. *The Life of Reason*, "Reason in Religion," ch. 11 (1905–6).

6 But those rare souls whose spirit gets magically into the hearts of men, leave behind them something more real and warmly personal than bodily presence, an ineffable and eternal thing. It is everlasting life touching us as something more than a vague, recondite concept. The sound of a great name dies like an echo; the splendor of fame fades into nothing; but the grace of a fine spirit pervades the places through which it has passed, like the haunting loveliness of mignonette.

> JAMES THURBER (1894–1961), U.S. humorist, illustrator. *Collecting Himself*, "The Book-End" (1989; first published 1923).

See also Hugo on HUMAN RIGHTS; Bloom on The UNITED STATES.

SPIRITUALITY

1 His spiritual life has been exaggerated by a chronic attack of mental gallstones.

> OLIVER ST. JOHN GOGARTY (1878–1957), Irish physician, senator, author. Speech, 12 Dec. 1922, to Seanad Eireann, the Irish Senate, said of lawyer and politician Lord Carson.

2 The sensual and spiritual are linked together by a mysterious bond, sensed by our emotions, though hidden from our eyes. To this double nature of the visible and invisible world—to the profound longing for the latter, coupled with the feeling of the sweet necessity for the former, we owe all sound and logical systems of philosophy, truly based on the immutable principles of our nature, just as from the same source arise the most senseless enthusiasms.

> KARL WILHELM VON HUMBOLDT (1767–1835), German statesman, philologist. *The Limits of State Action*, ch. 8 (1792; repr. 1854; tr. and ed. by J. W. Burrow, 1969).

3 Pure Spirit, one hundred degrees proof—that's a drink that only the most hardened contemplation-guzzlers indulge in. Bodhisattvas dilute their Nirvana with equal parts of love and work.

> ALDOUS HUXLEY (1894–1963), British author. Susila, in *Island*, ch. 15 (1962).

4 Nothing is more repulsive than a furtively prurient spirituality; it is just as unsavory as gross sensuality.

> CARL JUNG (1875–1961), Swiss psychiatrist. *Marriage as a Psychological Relationship* (1925; repr. in *Collected Works*, vol. 17, para. 336, ed. by William McGuire, 1954).

5 The most spiritual human beings, assuming they are the most courageous, also experience by far the most painful tragedies: but it is precisely for this reason that they honor life, because it brings against them its most formidable weapons.

> FRIEDRICH NIETZSCHE (1844–1900), German philosopher. *Twilight of the Idols*, "Expeditions of an Untimely Man," aph. 17 (1889).

6 He whom God has touched will always be a being apart: he is, whatever he may do, a stranger among men; he is marked by a sign.

> ERNEST RENAN (1823–92), French writer, critic, scholar. Last lines of *L'Avenir de la Science* (1890; repr. in *Oeuvres Complètes*, vol. 3).

See also Jung, Watts on BUDDHISM.

SPONTANEITY

1 Our spontaneous action is always the best. You cannot, with your best deliberation and heed, come so close to any question as your spontaneous glance shall bring you.

> RALPH WALDO EMERSON (1803–82), U.S. essayist, poet, philosopher. *Essays*, "Intellect" (First Series, 1841).

2 Fools rush in where Angels fear to tread.

> ALEXANDER POPE (1688–1744), English poet. *An Essay on Criticism* (1711).

3 Improvisation is too good to leave to chance.

> PAUL SIMON (b. 1941), U.S. rock musician. *International Herald Tribune* (Paris, 12 Oct. 1990).

4 Through spontaneity we are re-formed into ourselves. It creates an explosion that for the moment frees us from handed-down frames of reference, memory choked with old facts and information and undigested theories and techniques of other people's findings. Spontaneity is the moment of personal freedom when we are faced with reality, and see it, explore it and act

accordingly. In this reality the bits and pieces of ourselves function as an organic whole. It is the time of discovery, of experiencing, of creative expression.

> VIOLA SPOLIN (b. 1911), U.S. theatrical director, producer. *Improvisation for the Theater*, ch. 1 (1963).

SPORT

1 We want beans, not goals.

> MEXICAN STEELWORKERS' BANNER AT OPENING CEREMONY OF 1986 WORLD CUP SOCCER CHAMPIONSHIP.

2 Playing snooker gives you firm hands and helps to build up character. It is the ideal recreation for dedicated nuns.

> ARCHBISHOP LUIGI BARBARITO (b. 1922), Italian cleric. *Daily Telegraph* (London, 15 Nov. 1989).

3 There are people who think that wrestling is an ignoble sport. Wrestling is not sport, it is a spectacle, and it is no more ignoble to attend a wrestled performance of suffering than a performance of the sorrows of Arnolphe or Andromaque.

> ROLAND BARTHES (1915–80), French semiologist. *Mythologies*, "The World of Wrestling" (1957; tr. 1972). "What wrestling is above all meant to portray," Barthes added, "is a purely moral concept: that of justice. The idea of 'paying' is essential to wrestling, and the crowd's 'Give it to him' means above all else 'Make him pay.'"

4 For man, maximum excitement is the confrontation of death and the skillful defiance of it by watching others fed to it as he survives transfixed with rapture.

> ERNEST BECKER (1924–74), U.S. psychologist, cultural anthropologist. *Escape from Evil*, ch. 8, "The Logic of Scapegoating" (1975).

5 By Heaven! it is a splendid sight to see
(For one who hath no friend, no brother there)
Their rival scarfs of mix'd embroidery,
Their various arms that glitter in the air!

> LORD BYRON (1788–1824), English poet. *Childe Harold's Pilgrimage*, cto. 1, st. 40.

6 So you wish to conquer in the Olympic games, my friend? And I too, by the Gods, and a fine thing it would be! But first mark the conditions and the consequences, and then set to work. You will have to put yourself under discipline; to eat by rule, to avoid cakes and sweetmeats; to take exercise at the appointed hour whether you like it or no, in cold and heat; to abstain from cold drinks and from wine at your will; in a word, to give yourself over to the trainer as to a physician. Then in the conflict itself you are likely enough to dislocate your wrist or twist your ankle, to swallow a great deal of dust, or to be severely thrashed, and, after all these things, to be defeated.

> EPICTETUS (c. 55–c. 135), Greek Stoic philosopher. *Encheiridion*, no. 29b (tr. by T. W. H. Rolleston, 1881).

7 Bullfighting is the only art in which the artist is in danger of death and in which the degree of brilliance in the performance is left to the fighter's honor.

> ERNEST HEMINGWAY (1899–1961), U.S. author. *Death in the Afternoon*, ch. 9 (1932).

8   Two things only the people anxiously desire,
       Bread and the Circus games.
       JUVENAL (40–125), Roman satirical poet. *Satires,* Satire 10.

9   Unlike any other business in the United States,
sports must preserve an illusion of perfect innocence.
The mounting of this illusion defines the purpose and
accounts for the immense wealth of American sports. It
is the ceremony of innocence that the fans pay to see—
not the game or the match or the bout, but the ritual portrayal of a world in which time stops and all hope remains
plausible, in which everybody present can recover the
blameless expectations of a child, where the forces of
light always triumph over the powers of darkness.
       LEWIS H. LAPHAM (b. 1935), U.S. essayist, editor. *Money and
       Class in America,* ch. 5, sct. 2 (1988).

10   Sport in the sense of a mass-spectacle, with death to
add to the underlying excitement, comes into existence
when a population has been drilled and regimented and
depressed to such an extent that it needs at least a vicarious participation in difficult feats of strength or skill or
heroism in order to sustain its waning life-sense.
       LEWIS MUMFORD (1895–1990), U.S. social philosopher. *Tech-
       nics and Civilization,* ch. 6, sct. 11 (1934).

11   People in the States used to think that if girls were
good at sports their sexuality would be affected. Being
feminine meant being a cheerleader, not being an athlete.
The image of women is changing now. You don't have
to be pretty for people to come and see you play. At the
same time, if you're a good athlete, it doesn't mean
you're not a woman.
       MARTINA NAVRATILOVA (b. 1956), Czech-born U.S. tennis
       player. *Martina Navratilova—Being Myself,* ch. 8 (1985).

12   Serious sport has nothing to do with fair play. It is
bound up with hatred, jealousy, boastfulness, disregard
of all rules and sadistic pleasure in witnessing violence:
in other words it is war minus the shooting.
       GEORGE ORWELL (1903–50), British author. "The Sporting Spir-
       it" (1945; repr. in *The Collected Essays, Journalism and Letters of
       George Orwell,* vol. 4, ed. by Sonia Orwell and Ian Angus,
       1968).

13   Sport inevitably creates deadness of feeling. No one
could take pleasure in it who was sensitive to suffering; and
therefore its pursuit by women is much more to be regretted than its pursuit by men, because women pursue much
more violently and recklessly what they pursue at all.
       OUIDA [MARIE LOUISE DE LA RAMÉE] (1839–1908), English
       novelist. *Critical Studies,* "The Quality of Mercy" (1900).

14   I don't think I can be expected to take seriously any
game which takes less than three days to reach its conclusion.
       TOM STOPPARD (b. 1937), British playwright, cricket enthusi-
       ast. Quoted in: *Guardian* (London, 24 Dec. 1984), of baseball.

See also BASEBALL; BOXING; FOOTBALL; GOLF; HUNTING; TENNIS.

SPRING

1   April is the cruellest month, breeding
       Lilacs out of the dead land, mixing

       Memory and desire, stirring
       Dull roots with spring rain.
       T. S. ELIOT (1888–1965), Anglo-American poet, critic. Opening
       lines of *The Waste Land,* pt. 1, "The Burial of the Dead" (1922).

2   Ask of her, the mighty mother:
       Her reply puts this other
       Question: What is Spring?—
       Growth in everything.
       GERARD MANLEY HOPKINS (1844–89), English poet, Jesuit
       priest. *The May Magnificat,* st. 4

3   Nothing is so beautiful as spring—
       When weeds, in wheels, shoot long and lovely and
          lush;
       Thrush's eggs look little low heavens, and thrush
       Through the echoing timber does so rinse and
          wring
       The ear, it strikes like lightning to hear him sing.
       GERARD MANLEY HOPKINS (1844–89), English poet, Jesuit
       priest. *Spring,* st. 1.

4   For like as herbs and trees bringen forth fruit and
flourish in May, in likewise every lusty heart that is in
any manner a lover, springeth and flourisheth in lusty
deeds.
       SIR THOMAS MALORY (c. 1430–71), English author. *Le Morte
       d'Arthur,* bk. 18, ch. 25 (1485).

5   Rough winds do shake the darling buds of May.
       WILLIAM SHAKESPEARE (1564–1616), English dramatist, poet.
       Sonnet 18, "Shall I Compare Thee to a Summer's Day?"

6   Poor, dear, silly Spring, preparing her annual surprise!
       WALLACE STEVENS (1879–1955), U.S. poet. *Souvenirs and
       Prophecies: the Young Wallace Stevens,* ch. 8 (ed. by Holly
       Stevens, 1977), entry for 4 March 1906.

7   April, April,
       Laugh thy girlish laughter;
       Then, the moment after,
       Weep thy girlish tears!
       SIR WILLIAM WATSON (1858–1935), British poet. *April.*

See also Shelley on WINTER.

JOSEF STALIN

1   He is gone, but his shadow still stands over all of
us. It still dictates to us and we, very often, obey.
       SVETLANA ALLILUEVYA (b. 1925), Russian writer. *Twenty Let-
       ters to a Friend,* ch. 2 (1967). Alliluevya is the daughter of Josef
       Stalin.

2   He gives the impression of a strong mind which is
composed and wise. His brown eye is exceedingly kindly and gentle. A child would like to sit in his lap and a
dog would sidle up to him. It is difficult to associate his
personality and this impression of kindness and gentle
simplicity with what has occurred here in connection
with these purges and shootings of the Red Army generals, and so forth.
       JOSEPH DAVIES (1876–1958), U.S. ambassador to Moscow. Let-

ter to daughter, 1936 Quoted in: *Stalin*, pt. 2, ch. 4 (ed. by T. H. Rigby, 1966).

3 Everyone can err, but Stalin considered that he never erred, that he was always right. He never acknowledged to anyone that he made any mistake, large or small, despite the fact that he made not a few mistakes in the matter of theory and in his practical activity.

NIKITA KHRUSHCHEV (1894–1971), Soviet premier. Speech, Feb. 1956, to 20th Congress of Soviet Communist Party. Quoted in: *Stalin*, pt. 2, ch. 6 (ed. by T. H. Rigby, 1966).

4 Each thick finger, a fattened worm, gesticulates,
And his words strike you like they were many-
     pound weights.
His full cockroach moustache hints a laughter
     benigning,
And the shafts of his boots: always spotlessly
     shining.

OSIP MANDELSTAM (1891–1938), Russian poet. *We exist in a country grown unreal and strange* (tr. by Vladimir Markov and Merrill Sparks). This satire of Stalin led to Mandelstam's arrest and exile to a concentration camp.

5 To choose one's victims, to prepare one's plan minutely, to slake an implacable vengeance, and then to go to bed . . . there is nothing sweeter in the world.

JOSEF STALIN (1879–1953), Soviet leader. Remark to colleague before signing almost 40,000 death warrants. Quoted in: Robert Conquest, "Lenin's Guffaw," in *New Republic* (Washington, D.C., 15 Sept. 1986).

6 It was the supreme expression of the mediocrity of the apparatus that Stalin himself rose to his position.

LEON TROTSKY (1879–1940), Russian revolutionary. *My Life*, ch. 40 (1930).

7 In Stalin each [Soviet bureaucrat] easily finds himself. But Stalin also finds in each one a small part of his own spirit. Stalin is the personification of the bureaucracy. That is the substance of his political personality.

LEON TROTSKY (1879–1940), Russian revolutionary. *The Revolution Betrayed*, ch. 11 (1937).

8 Our party's most outstanding mediocrity.

LEON TROTSKY (1879–1940), Russian revolutionary. Quoted in: Dmitri Volkogonov, *Stalin: Triumph and Tragedy*, Foreword (1989; tr. 1991). In his last book, *Stalin*, Trotsky wrote: "Our paths diverged so long ago and so far, and in my eyes he is so much the instrument of historical forces that are alien and hostile to me, that my feelings towards him differ little from those I have towards Hitler or the Mikado. The personal element burned out long ago." Trotsky was assassinated on Stalin's orders before the book could be finished.

See also Khrushchev on INDIVIDUALITY.

STARDOM

1 There is not a more unhappy being than a superannuated idol.

JOSEPH ADDISON (1672–1719), English essayist. *Spectator*, no. 73 (London, 24 May 1711).

2 Thy name is an ointment poured forth, therefore do the virgins love thee.

BIBLE, HEBREW. *The Song of Solomon* 1:3.

3 I stopped believing in Santa Claus when I was six. Mother took me to see him in a department store and he asked for my autograph.

SHIRLEY TEMPLE BLACK (b. 1928), U.S. screen actor. Quoted in: Leslie Halliwell, *Halliwell's Filmgoer's Companion* (1984).

4 He whose face gives no light, shall never become a star.

WILLIAM BLAKE (1757–1827), English poet, painter, engraver. *The Marriage of Heaven and Hell*, plate 7, "Proverbs of Hell" (1790–93).

5 You're not a star until they can spell your name in Karachi.

HUMPHREY BOGART (1899–1957), U.S. screen actor. Quoted in: David Brown, *Star Billing* (1985, p. 5).

6 The star is the ultimate American verification of Jean Jacques Rousseau's *Emile*. His mere existence proves the perfectability of any man or woman. Oh wonderful pliability of human nature, in a society where anyone can become a celebrity! And where any celebrity . . . may become a star!

DANIEL J. BOORSTIN (b. 1914), U.S. historian. *The Image*, ch. 4 (1961).

7 Richard Burton is now my epitaph, my cross, my title, my image. I have achieved a kind of diabolical fame. It has nothing to do with my talents as an actor. That counts for little now. I am the diabolically famous Richard Burton.

RICHARD BURTON (1925–84), British stage and screen actor. Interview, 1963. Quoted in: Ruth Waterbury, *Elizabeth Taylor*, ch. 21 (1964).

8 Being at the centre of a film is a burden one takes on with innocence—the first time. Thereafter, you take it on with trepidation.

DANIEL DAY LEWIS (b. 1957), British stage and screen actor. *City Limits* (London, 7 April 1988).

9 No memory of having starred
Atones for later disregard,
Or keeps the end from being hard.

ROBERT FROST (1874–1963), U.S. poet. *Two Tramps in Mud Time*, st. 9.

10 God makes stars. I just produce them.

SAMUEL GOLDWYN (1882–1974), U.S. film producer. Quoted in: *Daily Express* (London, 16 May 1939).

11 Much more frequent in Hollywood than the emergence of Cinderella is her sudden vanishing. At our party, even in those glowing days, the clock was always striking twelve for someone at the height of greatness; and there was never a prince to fetch her back to the happy scene.

BEN HECHT (1893–1964), U.S. journalist, author, screenwriter. *A Child of the Century*, bk. 5, "My Poverty Row" (1954), writing of Hollywood 1925–45.

12 One thing about being successful is that I stopped being afraid of dying. Once you're a star you're dead already. You're embalmed.

DUSTIN HOFFMAN (b. 1937), U.S. screen actor. Quoted in: Leslie Halliwell, *Halliwell's Filmgoer's Companion* (1984).

13 You have to know exactly what you want out of your career. If you want to be a star, you don't bother with other things.

MARILYN HORNE (b. 1934), U.S. opera singer. Quoted in: Winthrop Sargeant, *Divas: Impressions of Six Opera Superstars* (1959).

14 It's nice to be a part of history but people should get it right. I may not be perfect, but I'm bloody close.

JOHN LYDON [FORMERLY JOHNNY ROTTEN] (b. 1957), British rock musician. *Observer* (London, 4 May 1986).

15 I *am* big. It's the pictures that got small.

GLORIA SWANSON (1897–1983), U.S. screen actor. As Norma Desmond, in Billy Wilder, *Sunset Boulevard* (scripted by Wilder, Charles Brackett and D. M. Marsham, Jr., 1950).

16 The stars are the apexes of what triangles!

HENRY DAVID THOREAU (1817–62), U.S. philosopher, author, naturalist. *Journals* (1906), entry for 5 Oct. 1847. Thinking of Ralph Waldo Emerson, who had just set out on his second voyage to England, Thoreau wrote: "I just looked up at a fine twinkling star and thought that a voyager whom I know, now many days' sail from this coast, might possibly be looking up at that same star with me."

17 Do we really want to know HOW Michael Jackson makes his music? NO. We want to understand why he needs the bones of the Elephant Man—and, until he tells us, it doesn't make too much difference whether or not he really is "bad."

FRANK ZAPPA (b. 1940), U.S. rock musician. *The Real Frank Zappa Book*, ch. 11 (1989; written with Peter Occhiogrosso).

See also Goldman on CINEMA; FAME.

THE STATE

1 If nationality is consent, the state is compulsion.

HENRI-FRÉDÉRIC AMIEL (1821–81), Swiss philosopher, poet. *Journal Intime* (1882; tr. by Mrs. Humphrey Ward, 1892), entry for 17 Dec. 1856.

2 A state without the means of some change is without the means of its conservation.

EDMUND BURKE (1729–97), Irish philosopher, statesman. *Reflections on the Revolution in France* (1790).

3 In the twentieth century one of the most personal relationships to have developed is that of the person and the state. . . . It's become a fact of life that governments have become very intimate with people, most always to their detriment.

E. L. DOCTOROW (b. 1931), U.S. novelist. Interview in *Writers at Work* (Eighth Series, ed. by George Plimpton, 1988).

4 The State has but one face for me: that of the police. To my eyes, all of the State's ministries have this single face, and I cannot imagine the ministry of culture other than as the police of culture, with its prefect and commissioners.

JEAN DUBUFFET (1901–85), French sculptor, painter. *Asphyxiating Culture* (1968; repr. in *Asphyxiating Culture and Other Writings*, 1986; tr. 1988).

5 While the State becomes inflated and hypertrophied in order to obtain a firm enough grip upon individuals, but without succeeding, the latter, without mutual relationships, tumble over one another like so many liquid molecules, encountering no central energy to retain, fix and organize them.

EMILE DURKHEIM (1858–1917), French sociologist. *Suicide*, bk. 3, ch. 3, sct. 4 (1897; tr. 1951).

6 The State must follow, and not lead, the character and progress of the citizen.

RALPH WALDO EMERSON (1803–82), U.S. essayist, poet, philosopher. *Essays,* "Politics" (Second Series, 1844).

7 The State is the altar of political freedom and, like the religious altar, it is maintained for the purpose of human sacrifice.

EMMA GOLDMAN (1869–1940), U.S. anarchist. *Anarchism and Other Essays,* "Anarchism: What It Really Stands For" (1910).

8 The essence of the modern state is that the universal be bound up with the complete freedom of its particular members and with private well-being, that thus the interests of family and civil society must concentrate themselves on the state. . . . It is only when both these moments subsist in their strength that the state can be regarded as articulated and genuinely organized.

GEORG HEGEL (1770–1831), German philosopher. *The Philosophy of Right,* "The State," addition 154 (1821; tr. 1942).

9 As high as mind stands above nature, so high does the state stand above physical life. Man must therefore venerate the state as a secular deity. . . . The march of God in the world, that is what the State is.

GEORG HEGEL (1770–1831), German philosopher. *The Philosophy of Right,* "The State," addition 164 (1821; tr. 1942).

10 The obligation of subjects to the sovereign is understood to last as long, and no longer, than the power lasteth by which he is able to protect them.

THOMAS HOBBES (1588–1679), English philosopher. *Leviathan,* pt. 2, ch. 21 (1651).

11 While the State exists there can be no freedom; when there is freedom there will be no State.

VLADIMIR ILYICH LENIN (1870–1924), Russian Revolutionary Leader. *The State and Revolution,* ch. 5, sct. 4 (1919).

12 In a free society the state does not administer the affairs of men. It administers justice among men who conduct their own affairs.

WALTER LIPPMANN (1889–1974), U.S. journalist. *The Good Society,* ch. 12 (1937).

13 The worth of a State, in the long run, is the worth of the individuals composing it . . . a State which dwarfs its men, in order that they may be more docile instruments in its hands even for beneficial purposes—will find that with small men no great thing can really be accomplished.

JOHN STUART MILL (1806–73), English philosopher, economist. *On Liberty,* ch. 5 (1859).

14 There will never be a really free and enlightened State until the State comes to recognize the individual as a higher and independent power, from which all its own power and authority are derived, and treats him accordingly. I please myself with imagining a State at last which can afford to be just to all men, and to treat the individual with respect as a neighbor; which even would not think it inconsistent with its own repose if a few went to live aloof from it, not meddling with it, nor embraced by it, who fulfilled all the duties of neighbors and fellow-men. A State which bore this kind of fruit, and suffered it to drop off as fast as it ripened, would prepare the way for a still more perfect and glorious State, which also I have imagined, but not yet anywhere seen.

> HENRY DAVID THOREAU (1817–62), U.S. philosopher, author, naturalist. Closing lines of *On the Duty of Civil Disobedience* (1849). The passage relates to Thoreau's refusal to pay a poll tax, for which he went to jail for one night in July 1846. This essay was often quoted by Gandhi in his campaign of passive resistance. Later, Thoreau wrote, "I was never molested by any person but those who represented the State" (*Walden*, "The Village," 1854). See Thoreau on PROTEST.

15 Every new development for the last three centuries has brought men closer to a state of affairs in which absolutely nothing would be recognized in the whole world as possessing a claim to obedience except the authority of the State. The majority of people in Europe obey nothing else.

> SIMONE WEIL (1909–43), French philosopher, mystic. "The Great Beast: Conclusion" (written 1939–40; published in *Selected Essays*, ed. by Richard Rees, 1962).

16 The State is to make what is useful. The individual is to make what is beautiful.

> OSCAR WILDE (1854–1900), Anglo-Irish playwright, author. *The Soul of Man under Socialism*, in *Fortnightly Review* (London, Feb. 1891; repr. 1895).

17 Statecraft is soulcraft. Just as all education is moral education because learning conditions conduct, much legislation is moral legislation because it conditions the action and the thought of the nation in broad and important spheres of life.

> GEORGE F. WILL (b. 1941), U.S. political columnist. *Statecraft as Soulcraft: What Government Does*, ch. 1 (1984).

See also Cromwell on PUBLIC OFFICE; Lewis on FAMILY; Kaunda on FORCE; Thoreau on PROTEST.

STATESMANSHIP

1 What the statesman is most anxious to produce is a certain moral character in his fellow citizens, namely a disposition to virtue and the performance of virtuous actions.

> ARISTOTLE (384–322 B.C.), Greek philosopher. *The Ethics of Aristotle*, bk. 1, ch. 9 (1953).

2 A constitutional statesman is in general a man of common opinions and uncommon abilities.

> WALTER BAGEHOT (1826–77), English economist, critic. *Biographical Studies*, "The Character of Sir Robert Peel" (1856).

3 A disposition to preserve, and an ability to improve, taken together, would be my standard of a statesman.

> EDMUND BURKE (1729–97), Irish philosopher, statesman. *Reflections on the Revolution in France* (1790).

4 The essence of statesmanship is not a rigid adherence to the past, but a prudent and probing concern for the future.

> HUBERT H. HUMPHREY (1911–78), U.S. Democratic politician, vice president. Speech, 30 March 1967, Bonn, Germany.

5 The chief element in the art of statesmanship under modern conditions is the ability to elucidate the confused and clamorous interests which converge upon the seat of government. It is an ability to penetrate from the naïve self-interest of each group to its permanent and real interest.... Statesmanship ... consists in giving the people not what they want but what they will learn to want.

> WALTER LIPPMANN (1889–1974), U.S. journalist. *A Preface to Morals*, ch. 13 (1929).

6 A man who is a politician at forty is a statesman at three score and ten. It is at this age, when he would be too old to be a clerk or a gardener or a police-court magistrate, that he is ripe to govern a country.

> W. SOMERSET MAUGHAM (1874–1965), British author. Ashenden, in *Cakes and Ale*, ch. 11 (1930).

7 A politician is a man who understands government and it takes a politician to run a government. A statesman is a politician who's been dead ten or fifteen years.

> HARRY S TRUMAN (1884–1972), U.S. Democratic politician, president. Address, 11 April 1958, to the Reciprocity Club, Washington, D.C. Quoted in: *New York World-Telegram and Sun* (12 April 1958).

8 In statesmanship get the formalities right, never mind about the moralities.

> MARK TWAIN (1835–1910), U.S. author. *Following the Equator*, ch. 65, "Pudd'nhead Wilson's New Calendar" (1897).

STATISTICS

1 Like dreams, statistics are a form of wish fulfillment.

> JEAN BAUDRILLARD (b. 1929), French semiologist. *Cool Memories*, ch. 4 (1987; tr. 1990).

2 There are three kinds of lies: lies, damned lies and statistics.

> BENJAMIN DISRAELI (1804–81), English statesman, author. Quoted in: Mark Twain, *Autobiography*, ch. 29 (ed. by Charles Neider, 1959).

3 He uses statistics as a drunken man uses lampposts—for support rather than illumination.

> ANDREW LANG (1844–1912), Scottish author. Quoted in: Alan L. Mackay, *The Harvest of a Quiet Eye* (1977).

4 I will stand on, and continue to use, the figures I have used, because I believe they are correct. Now, I'm not going to deny that you don't now and then slip up on something; no one bats a thousand.

> RONALD REAGAN (b. 1911), U.S. Republican politician, president. News conference, Philadelphia. Quoted in: *Washington Post* (20 April 1980).

See also Smith on FACTS.

THE STATUS QUO

1   The order of the world is always right—such is the judgment of God. For God has departed, but he has left his judgment behind, the way the Cheshire Cat left his grin.

JEAN BAUDRILLARD (b. 1929), French semiologist. *Cool Memories*, ch. 1 (1987; tr. 1990).

2   The powers that be are ordained of God.

BIBLE: NEW TESTAMENT. *Romans* 13:1.

3   Status quo, you know, that is Latin for "the mess we're in."

RONALD REAGAN (b. 1911), U.S. Republican politician, president. Address, 16 March 1981 to Associated General Contractors of America.

STEREOTYPES

1   All stereotypes turn out to be true. This is a horrifying thing about life. All those things you fought against as a youth: you begin to realize they're stereotypes because they're true.

DAVID CRONENBERG (b. 1943), Canadian filmmaker. *Cronenberg On Cronenberg*, ch. 1 (ed. by Chris Rodley, 1992).

2   Nothing is ever simple. What do you do when you discover you *like* parts of the role you're trying to escape?

MARILYN FRENCH (b. 1929), U.S. author, critic. Mira, in *The Women's Room*, ch. 5, sct. 6 (1977).

3   Out with stereotypes, feminism proclaims. But stereotypes are the west's stunning sexual personae, the vehicles of art's assault against nature. The moment there is imagination, there is myth.

CAMILLE PAGLIA (b. 1947), U.S. author, critic, educator. *Sexual Personae*, ch. 1 (1990).

4   Do you really have to be the ice queen intellectual or the slut whore? Isn't there some way to be both?

SUSAN SARANDON (b. 1946), U.S. screen actor. *Observer* (London, 14 Sept. 1991).

THE STOCK MARKET

1   The terrible, cold, cruel part is Wall Street. Rivers of gold flow there from all over the earth, and death comes with it. There, as nowhere else, you feel a total absence of the spirit: herds of men who cannot count past three, herds more who cannot get past six, scorn for pure science and demoniacal respect for the present. And the terrible thing is that the crowd that fills the street believes that the world will always be the same and that it is their duty to keep that huge machine running, day and night, forever. This is what comes of a Protestant morality, that I, as a (thank God) typical Spaniard, found unnerving.

FEDERICO GARCIA LORCA (1898–1936), Spanish poet, playwright. "A Poet in New York," lecture, March 1932, Madrid (published in *Poet in New York*, 1940; tr. 1988).

2   The freedom to make a fortune on the Stock Exchange has been made to sound more alluring than freedom of speech.

JOHN MORTIMER (b. 1923), British barrister, novelist. Quoted in: *Independent* (London, 29 Oct. 1988).

3   October. This is one of the peculiarly dangerous months to speculate in stocks in. The others are July, January, September, April, November, May, March, June, December, August, and February.

MARK TWAIN (1835–1910), U.S. author. *Pudd'nhead Wilson*, ch. 13, "Pudd'nhead Wilson's Calendar" (1894).

4   The only reason to invest in the market is because you think you know something others don't.

R. FOSTER WINANS (b. 1948), U.S. journalist. *Newsweek* (New York, 1 Dec. 1986). Winans, a *Wall Street Journal* reporter, was tried and convicted for "insider trading."

STORY-TELLING

1   We construct a narrative for ourselves, and that's the thread that we follow from one day to the next. People who disintegrate as personalities are the ones who lose that thread.

PAUL AUSTER (b. 1947), U.S. author, translator. *Sunday Times* (London, 16 April 1989).

2   The art of storytelling is reaching its end because the epic side of truth, wisdom, is dying out.

WALTER BENJAMIN (1892–1940), German critic, philosopher. *The Storyteller*, sct. 4 (1936; repr. in *Illuminations*, ed. by Hannah Arendt, 1968).

3   Death is the sanction of everything the story-teller can tell. He has borrowed his authority from death.

WALTER BENJAMIN (1892–1940), German critic, philosopher. *The Storyteller*, sct. 11 (1936; repr. in *Illuminations*, ed. by Hannah Arendt, 1968).

4   There are only two or three human stories, and they go on repeating themselves as fiercely as if they had never happened before.

WILLA CATHER (1876–1947), U.S. author. *O Pioneers!* pt. 2, ch. 4 (1913).

5   A good story cannot be devised; it has to be distilled.

RAYMOND CHANDLER (1888–1959), U.S. author. Letter, 7 March 1947 (published in *Raymond Chandler Speaking*, 1962).

6   Listen, little Elia: draw your chair up close to the edge of the precipice and I'll tell you a story.

F. SCOTT FITZGERALD (1896–1940), U.S. author. *The Crack-Up*, "Notebook N" (ed. by Edmund Wilson, 1945).

7   Nobody has any conscience about adding to the improbabilities of a marvelous tale.

NATHANIEL HAWTHORNE (1804–64), U.S. author. *The Marble Faun*, ch. 4 (1860).

8   Madame, all stories, if continued far enough, end in death, and he is no true-story teller who would keep that from you.

ERNEST HEMINGWAY (1899–1961), U.S. author. *Death in the Afternoon*, ch. 11 (1932).

9 Man is eminently a storyteller. His search for a purpose, a cause, an ideal, a mission and the like is largely a search for a plot and a pattern in the development of his life story—a story that is basically without meaning or pattern.

ERIC HOFFER (1902–83), U.S. philosopher. *The Passionate State of Mind*, aph. 97 (1955).

10 We inherit plots. . . . There are only two or three in the world, five or six at most. We ride them like treadmills.

JANETTE TURNER HOSPITAL (b. 1942), Australian author. *Independent* (London, 7 April 1990).

11 The book which the reader now holds in his hands, from one end to the other, as a whole and in its details, whatever gaps, exceptions, or weaknesses it may contain, treats of the advance from evil to good, from injustice to justice, from falsity to truth, from darkness to daylight, from blind appetite to conscience, from decay to life, from bestiality to duty, from Hell to Heaven, from limbo to God. Matter itself is the starting-point, and the point of arrival is the soul. Hydra at the beginning, an angel at the end.

VICTOR HUGO (1802–85), French poet, dramatist, novelist. *Les Misérables*, pt. 5, bk. 1, ch. 20 (1862).

12 One mark of a second-rate mind is to be always telling stories.

JEAN DE LA BRUYÈRE (1645–96), French writer, moralist. *Characters*, "Of Opinions," aph. 52 (1688).

13 In the tale, in the telling, we are all one blood. Take the tale in your teeth, then, and bite till the blood runs, hoping it's not poison; and we will all come to the end together, and even to the beginning: living, as we do, in the middle.

URSULA K. LE GUIN (b. 1929), U.S. author. "It Was A Dark and Stormy Night; Or, Why Are We Huddling About the Campfire?," speech, 1979, University of Chicago (repr. in *Dancing at the Edge of the World*, 1989).

14 We ought to esteem it of the greatest importance that the fictions which children first hear should be adapted in the most perfect manner to the promotion of virtue.

PLATO (c. 427–347 B.C.), Greek philosopher. Socrates, in *The Republic*, bk. 2, sct. 378.

15 We are lonesome animals. We spend all our life trying to be less lonesome. One of our ancient methods is to tell a story begging the listener to say—and to feel—"Yes, that's the way it is, or at least that's the way I feel it. You're not as alone as you thought."

JOHN STEINBECK (1902–68), U.S. author. "In Awe of Words," in *The Exonian*, 75th anniversary edition (Exeter University; repr. in *Writers at Work*, Fourth Series, ed. by George Plimpton, 1977).

16 The first law of story-telling. . . . Every man is bound to leave a story better than he found it.

MRS. HUMPHREY WARD (1851–1920), British novelist. Dr. Baker, in *Robert Elsmere*, bk. 1, ch. 3 (1888).

STRANGERS

1 Every time a man unburdens his heart to a stranger he reaffirms the love that unites humanity.

GERMAINE GREER (b. 1939), Australian feminist writer. *The Female Eunuch*, "The Ideal" (1970).

2 It was his peculiar happiness that he scarcely ever found a stranger whom he did not leave a friend; but it must likewise be added, that he had not often a friend long without obliging him to become a stranger.

SAMUEL JOHNSON (1709–84), ENGLISH AUTHOR, LEXICOGRAPHER. *Lives of the English Poets*, "Savage" (1779–81), of the poet Richard Savage.

3 The moment one accosts a stranger or is accosted by him is above all in this life the moment of drama. . . . Whoever we meet watches us intently at the quick, strange moment of meeting, to see whether we are disposed to be friendly.

HANIEL LONG (1888–1956), U.S. author, poet, journalist. *Interlinear to Cabeza de Vaca* (1936; repr. 1987, p. 41).

4 I do desire we may be better strangers.

WILLIAM SHAKESPEARE (1564–1616), English dramatist, poet. Orlando, in *As You Like It*, act 3, sc. 2.

5 I have always depended on the kindness of strangers.

TENNESSEE WILLIAMS (1914–83), U.S. dramatist. Blanche DuBois' final words, in *A Streetcar Named Desire*, sc. 11 (1947).

STRESS

1 When you suffer an attack of nerves you're being attacked by the nervous system. What chance has a man got against a system?

RUSSELL HOBAN (b. 1925), U.S. author. The bookshop owner, in *The Lion of Boaz-Jachin and Jachin-Boaz*, ch. 13 (1973).

2 In this world without quiet corners, there can be no easy escapes from history, from hullabaloo, from terrible, unquiet fuss.

SALMAN RUSHDIE (b. 1947), Indian-born British author. *Outside the Whale* (1984).

3 If you can't stand the heat, get out of the kitchen.

HARRY S TRUMAN (1884–1972), U.S. Democratic politician, president. Quoted in: *Mr. Citizen*, ch. 15 (1960). A favorite saying of Truman's, he had previously ascribed this motto to an adviser.

STRIKES

1 The General Strike has taught the working class more in four days than years of talking could have done.

A. J. BALFOUR (1848–1930), British Conservative politician, prime minister. Speech, 7 May 1926 Five days later, the Trades Unions Congress was forced to call off the General Strike, which, though bringing the country to a virtual standstill, was unable to prevent volunteers from manning essential services.

2 Ensnared in his starvation, Chaplin-man is always just below political awareness. A strike is a catastrophe for him because it threatens a man truly blinded by his hunger; this man achieves an awareness of the working-class condition only when the poor man and the proletarian coincide under the gaze (and the blows) of the the police.

ROLAND BARTHES (1915–1980), French semiologist. *Mythologies*, "The Poor and the Proletariat" (1957; tr. 1972), of Charlie Chaplin's character on film.

3 One of the great reasons for the popularity of strikes is that they give the suppressed self a sense of power. For once the human tool knows itself a man, able to stand up and speak a word or strike a blow.

CHARLES HORTON COOLEY (1864–1929), U.S. sociologist. *Human Nature and the Social Order*, ch. 6 (1902).

See also ACTIVISM.

STRUCTURALISM AND DECONSTRUCTION

1 I would say that deconstruction is affirmation rather than questioning, in a sense which is not positive: I would distinguish between the positive, or positions, and affirmations. I think that deconstruction is affirmative rather than questioning: this affirmation goes *through* some radical questioning, but it is not questioning in the field of analysis.

JACQUES DERRIDA (b. 1930), Algerian-born French literary theorist. Interview, 1985, in *Criticism in Society* (ed. by Imre Salusinski, 1987).

2 Deconstruction . . . insists not that truth is illusory but that it is institutional.

TERRY EAGLETON (b. 1943), British critic. *Against The Grain*, ch. 6, "Frère Jacques: The Politics of Deconstruction" (1986; first published 1984).

3 Post-structuralism is among other things a kind of theoretical hangover from the failed uprising of '68—a way of keeping the revolution warm at the level of language, blending the euphoric libertarianism of that moment with the stoical melancholia of its aftermath.

TERRY EAGLETON (b. 1943), British critic. *Guardian* (London, 27 Oct. 1992).

4 The (post) structuralist temper requires too great a depersonalization of the writing/speaking subject. Writing becomes plagiarism; speaking becomes quoting. Meanwhile, we do write, we do speak.

IHAB HASSAN (b. 1925), U.S. critic. "The Re-Vision of Literature," in *New Literary History* (Autumn 1976; repr. in *The Right Promethean Fire*, 1980).

5 French rhetorical models are too narrow for the English tradition. Most pernicious of French imports is the notion that there is no person behind a text. Is there anything *more* affected, aggressive, and relentlessly concrete than a Parisan intellectual behind his/her turgid text? The Parisian is a provincial when he pretends to speak for the universe.

CAMILLE PAGLIA (b. 1947), U.S. author, critic, educator. *Sexual Personae*, ch. 1 (1990). In her Introduction to *Sex, Art, and American Culture* (1992), Paglia writes scathingly of "French post-structuralism, whose pedantic jargon, clumsy convolutions, prissy abstractions have spread throughout academe and the arts and

are now blighting the most promising minds of the next generation."

6 The fall into the abyss of deconstruction inspires us with as much pleasure as fear. We are intoxicated with the prospect of never hitting bottom.

GAYATRI CHAKRAVORTY SPIVAK (b. 1942), Indian-born U.S. educator, author, translator. Jacques Derrida, *Of Grammatology*, Translator's Preface (1967).

7 By day, Structuralists constructed the structure of meaning and pondered the meaning of structure. By night, Deconstructivists pulled the cortical edifice down. And the next day the Structuralists started in again.

TOM WOLFE (b. 1931), U.S. journalist, author. *From Bauhaus to Our House*, ch. 5 (1981).

STRUGGLE

1 My darling girl, Unfortunately this earth is not . . . a fairy-land, but a struggle for life, perfectly natural and therefore extremely harsh. All the same, or precisely for this reason, it is happiness and comfort for us men to have a precious sweetheart—and I have the most precious, the dearest and best of all!

MARTIN BORMANN (1900–1945), German Nazi leader. Letter, 19 July 1944, to his wife Gerda (published in *The Bormann Letters*, ed. by Hugh Trevor-Roper, 1954).

2 The struggle itself towards the heights is enough to fill a man's heart. One must imagine Sisyphus happy.

ALBERT CAMUS (1913–60), French-Algerian philosopher, author. Last words of *The Myth of Sisyphus*, "The Myth of Sisyphus" (1942; tr. 1955).

3 Struggle is the father of all things. . . . It is not by the principles of humanity that man lives or is able to preserve himself above the animal world, but solely by means of the most brutal struggle.

ADOLF HITLER (1889–1945), German dictator. Speech, 5 Feb. 1928, Kulmbach, Germany. Quoted in: Alan Bullock, *Hitler, a Study in Tyranny*, ch. 1, sct. 3 (1962).

4 When man meets an obstacle he can't destroy, he destroys himself.

RYSZARD KAPUSCINSKI (b. 1932), Polish journalist. "A Warsaw Diary," in *Granta*, no. 15 (Cambridge, England; 1985).

5 It may be that the most interesting American struggle is the struggle to set oneself free from the limits one is born to, and then to learn something of the value of those limits.

GREIL MARCUS (b. 1945), U.S. rock journalist. *Mystery Train*, "Robert Johnson, 1938" (1976).

6 There is no longer beauty except in the struggle. No more masterpieces without an aggressive character. Poetry must be a violent assault against the unknown forces in order to overcome them and prostrate them before men.

TOMMASO MARINETTI (1876–1944), Italian playwright. "The Founding and Manifesto of Futurism," in *Figaro* (Paris, 20 Feb. 1909; repr. in *Marinetti: Selected Writings*, ed. by R. W. Flint, 1972).

7 As regards the celebrated "struggle for *life*," it

seems to me for the present to have been rather asserted than proved. It does occur, but as the exception; the general aspect of life is *not* hunger and distress, but rather wealth, luxury, even absurd prodigality—where there is a struggle it is a struggle for *power*.

> FRIEDRICH NIETZSCHE (1844–1900), German philosopher. *Twilight of the Idols*, "Expeditions of an Untimely Man," aph. 14 (1889).

8 In a serious struggle there is no worse cruelty than to be magnanimous at an inopportune time.

> LEON TROTSKY (1879–1940), Russian revolutionary. *The History of the Russian Revolution*, vol. 2, ch. 7 (1933).

9 I've never forgotten for long at a time that living is struggle. I know that every good and excellent thing in the world stands moment by moment on the razor-edge of danger and must be fought for—whether it's a field, or a home, or a country.

> THORNTON WILDER (1897–1975), U.S. novelist, dramatist. Antrobus, in *The Skin of Our Teeth*, act 3.

STUDENTS

1 The greatest significance of the present student generation is that it is through them that the point of view of the subjugated is finally and inexorably being expressed.

> JAMES BALDWIN (1924–87), U.S. author. "They Can't Turn Back," in *Mademoiselle* (New York, Aug. 1960; repr. in *The Price of the Ticket*, 1985).

2 Paul, thou art beside thyself; much learning doth make thee mad.

> BIBLE: NEW TESTAMENT. Festus, the Roman Procurator, in *Acts* 26:24.

3 Study to be quiet, and to do your own business.

> BIBLE: NEW TESTAMENT. *1 Thessalonians* 4:11.

4 It were a real increase of human happiness, could all young men from the age of nineteen be covered under barrels, or rendered otherwise invisible; and there left to follow their lawful studies and callings, till they emerged, sadder and wiser, at the age of twenty-five.

> THOMAS CARLYLE (1795–1881), Scottish essayist, historian. *Sartor Resartus*, bk. 2, ch. 4 (1833–34). Carlyle's ostensible narrator, Teufelsdröckh, disclaims this opinion, but agrees that "as young ladies are, to mankind, precisely the most delightful in those years; so young gentlemen do then attain their maximum of detestability."

5 The average Ph.D. thesis is nothing but a transference of bones from one graveyard to another.

> J. FRANK DOBIE (1888–1964), U.S. author. *A Texan in England*, ch. 1 (1945).

6 My own experience is that a certain kind of genius among students is best brought out in bed.

> ALLEN GINSBERG (b. 1926), U.S. poet. Interview, Feb. 1981, with Nancy Bunge at Michigan State University, in *Washington Post* (29 July 1984).

7 The mind is refrigerated by interruption; the thoughts are diverted from the principle subject; the read-er is weary, he suspects not why; and at last throws away the book, which he has too diligently studied.

> SAMUEL JOHNSON (1709–84), English author, lexicographer. *Preface to Shakespeare* (1765; repr. in *Works of Samuel Johnson*, vol. 7, ed. by Arthur Sherbo, 1968), of textual notes.

8 What is the student but a lover courting a fickle mistress who ever eludes his grasp?

> SIR WILLIAM OSLER (1849–1919), Canadian physician. *Aequanimitas*, "The Student Life," sct. 1 (1906).

9 The democratic youth . . . lives along day by day, gratifying the desire that occurs to him, at one time drinking and listening to the flute, at another downing water and reducing, now practising gymnastic, and again idling and neglecting everything; and sometimes spending his time as though he were occupied in philosophy.

> PLATO (c. 427–347 B.C.), Greek philosopher. *The Republic*, bk. 8, sct. 561 c-d (tr. by Benjamin Jowett).

10 Generally young men are regarded as radicals. This is a popular misconception. The most conservative persons I ever met are college undergraduates. The radicals are the men past middle life.

> WOODROW WILSON (1856–1924), U.S. Democratic politician, president. Speech, 19 Nov. 1905, New York City.

See also EXAMINATIONS; SCHOOL; UNIVERSITIES AND COLLEGES.

STUPIDITY

1 It is against Stupidity in every shape and form that we have to wage our eternal battle. But how can we wonder at the want of sense on the part of those who have had no advantages, when we see such plentiful absence of that commodity on the part of those who have had all the advantages?

> WILLIAM BOOTH (1829–1912), English evangelist, founder of the Salvation Army. *In Darkest England, and the Way Out*, pt. 1, ch. 5 (1890).

2 The Cardinal is at his wit's end—it is true that he had not far to go.

> LORD BYRON (1788–1824), English poet. Letter, 22 July 1820, to the publisher John Murray (published in *Byron's Letters and Journals*, vol. 7, ed. by Leslie A. Marchand, 1973–81).

3 The key to the age may be this, or that, or the other, as the young orators describe; the key to all ages is—Imbecility; imbecility in the vast majority of men, at all times, and, even in heroes, in all but certain eminent moments; victims of gravity, custom, and fear.

> RALPH WALDO EMERSON (1803–82), U.S. essayist, poet, philosopher. *The Conduct of Life*, "Power" (1860).

4 The question now is: Can we understand our stupidity? This is a test of intellect, not of character.

> JOHN KING FAIRBANK (1907–91), U.S. historian, educator. Quoted in: *Observer* (London, 4 May 1975).

5 We never really know what stupidity is until we have experimented on ourselves.

> PAUL GAUGUIN (1848–1903), French artist. *Intimate Journals* (tr. by Van Wyck Brooks, 1923; repr. 1930, p. 132).

6 There is no one thoroughly despicable. We cannot descend much lower than an idiot; and an idiot has some advantages over a wise man.

WILLIAM HAZLITT (1778–1830), English essayist. *Characteristics: In the Manner of Rochefoucauld's Maxims*, no. 222 (1823; repr. in *The Complete Works Of William Hazlitt*, vol. 9, ed. by P. P. Howe, 1932).

7 An empty head is not really empty; it is stuffed with rubbish. Hence the difficulty of forcing anything into an empty head.

ERIC HOFFER (1902–83), U.S. philosopher. *Reflections on the Human Condition*, aph. 88 (1973).

8 Stupidity gets up early; that is why events are accustomed to happening in the morning.

KARL KRAUS (1874–1936), Austrian satirist. "In Praise of a Topsy-Turvy Lifestyle," in *Simplicissimus* (Munich, 1908; repr. in *In These Great Times: A Karl Kraus Reader*, ed. by Harry Zohn, 1976).

9 To accuse another of having weak kidneys, lungs, or heart, is not a crime; on the contrary, saying he has a weak brain is a crime. To be considered stupid and to be told so is more painful than being called gluttonous, mendacious, violent, lascivious, lazy, cowardly: every weakness, every vice, has found its defenders, its rhetoric, its ennoblement and exaltation, but stupidity hasn't.

PRIMO LEVI (1919–87), Italian chemist, author. *Other People's Trades*, "The Irritable Chess-players" (1985; tr. 1989).

10 Just as the performance of the vilest and most wicked deeds requires spirit and talent, so even the greatest demand a certain insensitivity which under other circumstances we would call stupidity.

G. C. LICHTENBERG (1742–99), German physicist, philosopher. *Aphorisms*, "Notebook F," aph. 87 (written 1765–99; tr. by R. J. Hollingdale, 1990).

11 Strange as it may seem, no amount of learning can cure stupidity, and formal education positively fortifies it.

STEPHEN VIZINCZEY (b. 1933), Hungarian novelist, critic. "Europe's Inner Demons," review of Norman Cohn, *An Inquiry Inspired by the Great Witch-Hunt*, in *Sunday Telegraph* (London, 2 March 1975; repr. in *Truth and Lies in Literature*, 1986).

12 The only thing that ever consoles man for the stupid things he does is the praise he always gives himself for doing them.

OSCAR WILDE (1854–1900), Anglo-Irish playwright, author. Review of *Chuang Tsu: Mystic, Moralist and Social Reformer* (tr. by Herbert A. Giles; published in *Speaker*, London, 8 Feb. 1890).

13 There is no sin except stupidity.

OSCAR WILDE (1854–1900), Anglo-Irish playwright, author. Gilbert, in *The Critic as Artist*, pt. 2 (published in *Intentions*, 1891).

14 Our greatest stupidities may be very wise.

LUDWIG WITTGENSTEIN (1889–1951), Austrian philosopher. *Culture and Value* (ed. by G. H. von Wright and Heikki Nyman, 1980), 1940 entry.

STYLE

1 Style is not neutral; it gives moral directions.

MARTIN AMIS (b. 1949), British author. *Novelists in Interview* (ed. by John Haffenden, 1985).

2 Behold, Esau my brother is a hairy man, and I am a smooth man.

BIBLE, HEBREW. Jacob, in *Genesis* 27:11.

3 The most durable thing in writing is style, and style is the most valuable investment a writer can make with his time. It pays off slowly, your agent will sneer at it, your publisher will misunderstand it, and it will take people you have never heard of to convince them by slow degrees that the writer who puts his individual mark on the way he writes will always pay off.

RAYMOND CHANDLER (1888–1959), U.S. author. Letter, 7 March 1947 (published in *Raymond Chandler Speaking*, 1962).

4 A style does not go out of style as long as it adapts itself to its period. When there is an incompatibility between the style and a certain state of mind, it is never the style that triumphs.

COCO CHANEL (1883–1971), French couturière. Quoted in: Marcel Haedrich, *Coco Chanel: Her Life, Her Secrets*, ch. 21 (1971).

5 Style is the dress of thoughts; and let them be ever so just, if your style is homely, coarse, and vulgar, they will appear to as much disadvantage, and be as ill received, as your person, though ever so well-proportioned, would if dressed in rags, dirt, and tatters.

LORD CHESTERFIELD (1694–1773), English statesman, man of letters. Letter, 24 Nov. 1749 (first published 1774; repr. in *The Letters of the Earl of Chesterfield to His Son*, vol. 1, no. 203, ed. by Charles Strachey, 1901).

6 What is line? It is life. A line must live at each point along its course in such a way that the artist's presence makes itself felt above that of the model. . . . With the writer, line takes precedence over form and content. It runs through the words he assembles. It strikes a continuous note unperceived by ear or eye. It is, in a way, the soul's style, and if the line ceases to have a life of its own, if it only describes an arabesque, the soul is missing and the writing dies.

JEAN COCTEAU (1889–1963), French author, filmmaker. *The Difficulty of Being*, "De la Ligne" (1947).

7 Classical and romantic: private language of a family quarrel, a dead dispute over the distribution of emphasis between man and nature.

CYRIL CONNOLLY (1903–74), British critic. *The Unquiet Grave*, pt. 3 (1944; rev. 1951).

8 Style is a fraud. I always felt the Greeks were hiding behind their columns.

WILLEM DE KOONING (b. 1904), Dutch-born U.S. artist. "A Desperate View," lecture, 1949, New York (published in *Collected Writings*, ed. by George Scrivani, 1988).

9 Style is the image of character.

EDWARD GIBBON (1737–94), English historian. *Memoirs of my Life*, Introduction (1796; repr. as *Autobiography*, 1971).

10 To me style is just the outside of content, and content the inside of style, like the outside and the inside of the human body—both go together, they can't be separated.

JEAN-LUC GODARD (b. 1930), French filmmaker, author. Quoted in: Richard Roud, *Godard,* Introduction (1970; first published 1967).

11 I might say that what amateurs call a style is usually only the unavoidable awkwardnesses in first trying to make something that has not heretofore been made.

ERNEST HEMINGWAY (1899–1961), U.S. author. Interview in *Paris Review* (Flushing, N.Y., Spring 1958; repr. in *Writers at Work,* Second Series, ed. by George Plimpton, 1963).

12 'Tisn't beauty, so to speak, nor good talk necessarily. It's just IT. Some women'll stay in a man's memory if they once walked down a street.

RUDYARD KIPLING (1865–1936), British author, poet. Mr. Pyecroft, in "Mrs. Bathurst," in *Traffics and Discoveries* (1904), said of Mrs. Bathurst.

13 He has found his style, when he cannot do otherwise.

PAUL KLEE (1879–1940), Swiss artist. *The Diaries of Paul Klee 1898–1918,* no. 825 (1957; tr. 1965), 1908 entry.

14 Always, however brutal an age may actually have been, its style transmits its music only.

ANDRÉ MALRAUX (1901–76), French man of letters, statesman. Quoted in: Lillian Smith, *The Journey,* ch. 15 (1955).

15 Style [is] the hallmark of a temperament stamped on the material in hand.

ANDRÉ MAUROIS (1885–1967), French author, critic. *The Art of Writing,* "The Writer's Craft," sct. 2 (1960).

16 Happy the society whose deepest divisions are ones of style.

PETER MCKAY (b. 1940), British Conservative politician. *Evening Standard* (London, 31 Jan. 1990).

17 "To give style" to one's character—a great and rare art! He exercises it who surveys all that his nature presents in strength and weakness and then moulds it to an artistic plan until everything appears as art and reason, and even the weaknesses delight the eye.

FRIEDRICH NIETZSCHE (1844–1900), German philosopher. *The Gay Science,* aph. 290 (rev. ed., 1887).

18 Oh, never mind the fashion. When one has a style of one's own, it is always twenty times better.

MARGARET OLIPHANT (1828–97), English novelist, historian. Miss Marjoribanks, in *Miss Marjoribanks,* ch. 31 (1866), fourth of *Chronicles of Carlingford.*

19 A cultivated style would be like a mask. Everybody knows it's a mask, and sooner or later you must show yourself—or at least, you show yourself as someone who could not afford to show himself, and so created something to hide behind. . . . You do not create a style. You work, and develop yourself; your style is an emanation from your own being.

KATHERINE ANNE PORTER (1890–1980), U.S. short-story writer, novelist. Interview in *Writers at Work* (Second Series, ed. by George Plimpton, 1963).

20 No good poetry is ever written in a manner twenty years old, for to write in such a manner shows conclusively that the writer thinks from books, convention and cliché, not from real life.

EZRA POUND (1885–1972), U.S. poet, critic. "Prolegomena," in *Poetry Review* (London, Feb. 1912).

21 Fashions fade, style is eternal.

YVES SAINT LAURENT (b. 1936), French couturier. *Andy Warhol's Interview* (New York, 13 April 1975).

22 I do not much dislike the matter, but
The manner of his speech.

WILLIAM SHAKESPEARE (1564–1616), English dramatist, poet. Octavius Caesar, in *Antony and Cleopatra,* act 2, sc. 2

23 In the final analysis, "style" is art. And art is nothing more or less than various modes of stylized, dehumanized representation.

SUSAN SONTAG (b. 1933), U.S. essayist. *Against Interpretation,* "On Style" (1966).

24 Style is not something applied. It is something that permeates. It is of the nature of that in which it is found, whether the poem, the manner of a god, the bearing of a man. It is not a dress.

WALLACE STEVENS (1879–1955), U.S. poet. *Opus Posthumous,* "Two or Three Ideas" (1959; first published 1951).

25 He most honors my style who learns under it to destroy the teacher.

WALT WHITMAN (1819–92), U.S. poet. *Song of Myself,* sct. 47, in *Leaves of Grass* (1855).

26 While one should always study the method of a great artist, one should never imitate his manner. The manner of an artist is essentially individual, the method of an artist is absolutely universal. The first is personality, which no one should copy; the second is perfection, which all should aim at.

OSCAR WILDE (1854–1900), Anglo-Irish playwright, author. *Dramatic Review* (London, 20 Feb. 1886).

See also FASHION; TECHNIQUE; Pascal on WRITING.

SUBCONSCIOUS

See CONSCIOUSNESS AND THE SUBCONSCIOUS.

SUBJECTIVITY

1 Bias and impartiality is in the eye of the beholder.

LORD BARNETT (b. 1923), British Conservative politician. *Independent* (London, 12 July 1990).

2 I see every thing I paint in this world, but everybody does not see alike. To the eyes of a miser a guinea is more beautiful than the sun, and a bag worn with the use of money has more beautiful proportions than a vine filled with grapes.

WILLIAM BLAKE (1757–1827), English poet, painter, engraver. Letter, 23 Aug. 1799 (published in *The Letters of William Blake,* 1956).

3 When you're in the muck you can only see muck. If you somehow manage to float above it, you still see the muck but you see it from a different perspective. And you see other things too. That's the consolation of philosophy.

DAVID CRONENBERG (b. 1943), Canadian filmmaker. *Cronenberg On Cronenberg,* ch. 3 (ed. by Chris Rodley, 1992).

4 Nobody, I think, ought to read poetry, or look at pictures or statues, who cannot find a great deal more in them than the poet or artist has actually expressed. Their highest merit is suggestiveness.

NATHANIEL HAWTHORNE (1804–64), U.S. author. Hilda, in *The Marble Faun*, ch. 41 (1860).

5 I shut my eyes and all the world drops dead;
I lift my eyes and all is born again.

SYLVIA PLATH (1932–63), U.S. poet. *Mad Girl's Love Song.*

6 He that is giddy thinks the world turns round.

WILLIAM SHAKESPEARE (1564–1616), English dramatist, poet. The Widow, in *The Taming of the Shrew*, act 5, sc. 2.

7 A little grit in the eye destroyeth the sight of the very heavens, and a little malice or envy a world of joys. One wry principle in the mind is of infinite consequence.

THOMAS TRAHERNE (1636–74), English clergyman, poet, mystic. *Centuries*, "Fourth Century," no. 17 (written c. 1672; first published 1908).

SUBMISSION

1 The sovereign being is burdened with a servitude *that crushes him,* and the condition of free men is deliberate servility.

GEORGES BATAILLE (1897–1962), French novelist, critic. *L'Abbé C*, pt. 4, "The Diary of Chianine" (1950).

2 There is a sort of subjection which is the peculiar heritage of largeness and of love; and strength is often only another name for willing bondage to irremediable weakness.

GEORGE ELIOT (1819–80), English novelist, editor. *Felix Holt, The Radical*, ch. 5 (1866).

3 There're two people in the world that are not likeable: a master and a slave.

NIKKI GIOVANNI (b. 1943), U.S. poet. *A Dialogue* (1973; with James Baldwin), from a conversation in London, 4 Nov. 1971.

4 If every day a man takes orders in silence from an incompetent superior, if every day he solemnly performs ritual acts which he privately finds ridiculous, if he unhesitatingly gives answers to questionnaires which are contrary to his real opinions and is prepared to deny his own self in public, if he sees no difficulty in feigning sympathy or even affection where, in fact, he feels only indifference or aversion, it still does not mean that he has entirely lost the use of one of the basic human senses, namely, the sense of *humiliation.*

VÁCLAV HAVEL (b. 1936), Czech playwright, president. *Living in Truth*, pt. 1, "Letter to Dr. Gustáv Husák," 8 April 1975 (1986).

5 My reason is not framed to bend or stoop: my knees are.

MICHEL DE MONTAIGNE (1533–92), French essayist. *Essays*, bk. 3, ch. 8, "Of the Art of Conferring" (tr. by John Florio, 1588).

6 Progress and reaction have both turned out to be swindles. Seemingly, there is nothing left but quietism—robbing reality of its terrors by simply submitting to it.

GEORGE ORWELL (1903–50), British author. *Inside the Whale and Other Essays*, "Inside the Whale" (1940).

7 It does not matter what the whip is; it is none the less a whip, because you have cut thongs for it out of your own souls.

JOHN RUSKIN (1819–1900), English art critic, author. Address, 1865, Royal Military Academy (published in *Crown of Wild Olives*, Lecture 3, sct. 119, 1865; repr. in *The Works of John Ruskin*, vol. 18, ed. by E. T. Cook and Alexander Weddesburn, 1905).

8 Never may an act of possession be exercised upon a free being; the exclusive possession of a woman is no less unjust than the possession of slaves; all men are born free, all have equal rights: never should we lose sight of those principles; according to which never may there be granted to one sex the legitimate right to lay monopolizing hands upon the other, and never may one of the sexes, or classes, arbitrarily possess the other.

MARQUIS DE SADE (1740–1814), French author. Dolmancé, in *Philosophy in the Bedroom*, "Dialogue the Fifth: Yet Another Effort, Frenchmen, If You Would Become Republicans" (1795).

9 We are like horses who hurt themselves as soon as they pull on their bits—and we bow our heads. We even lose consciousness of the situation, we just submit. Any re-awakening of thought is then painful.

SIMONE WEIL (1909–43), French philosopher, mystic. *Factory Journal* (1934–35; repr. in *La Condition Ouvrière*, 1951).

SUBURBIA

1 Everywhere—all over Africa and South America . . . you see these suburbs springing up. They represent the optimum of what people want. There's a certain sort of logic leading towards these immaculate suburbs. And they're terrifying, because they are the *death of the soul.* . . . *This* is the prison this planet is being turned into.

J. G. BALLARD (b. 1930), British author. Interview, 30 Oct. 1982, in *Re/Search*, no. 8/9 (San Francisco, 1984).

2 They were as fed horses in the morning: every one neighed after his neighbour's wife.

BIBLE, HEBREW. *Jeremiah* 5:8.

3 The women there do all they ought;
The men observe the Rules of Thought.
They love the Good; they worship Truth;
They laugh uproariously in youth;
(And when they get to feeling old,
They up and shoot themselves, I'm told).

RUPERT BROOKE (1887–1915), British poet. *The Old Vicarage, Grantchester*, of the people of Grantchester, outside Cambridge, England.

4 Slums may well be breeding-grounds of crime, but middle-class suburbs are incubators of apathy and delirium.

CYRIL CONNOLLY (1903–74), British critic. *The Unquiet Grave*, pt. 1 (1944; rev. 1951).

5 Let's face it, we became ingrown, clannish, and retarded. Cut off from the mainstream of humanity, we came to believe that pink is "flesh-color", that mayonnaise is a nutrient, and that Barry Manilow is a musician.

BARBARA EHRENREICH (b. 1941), U.S. author, columnist. *The Worst Years of Our Lives*, "The Unbearable Being Of Whiteness"

(1991; first published 1981), of the effects on the white middle class of moving out to the suburbs.

6 All urbanization, pushed beyond a certain point, automatically becomes suburbanization. . . . Every great city is just a collection of suburbs. Its inhabitants . . . do not *live* in their city; they merely inhabit it.

ALDOUS HUXLEY (1894–1963), British author. *Beyond the Mexique Bay,* "Oaxaca" (1934).

7 The future of America may or may not bring forth a black President, a woman President, a Jewish President, but it most certainly always will have a suburban President. A President whose senses have been defined by the suburbs, where lakes and public baths mutate into back yards and freeways, where walking means driving, where talking means telephoning, where watching means TV, and where living means real, imitation life.

ARTHUR KROKER (b. 1945), MARILOUISE KROKER (birth date unknown) AND DAVID COOK (b. 1946), Canadian sociologists. *Panic Encyclopedia,* "Panic Suburbs" (1989).

8 Heaven is not built of country seats
But little queer suburban streets.

CHRISTOPHER MORLEY (1890–1957), U.S. novelist, journalist, poet. *To the Little House,* st. 4.

9 With four walk-in closets to walk in,
Three bushes, two shrubs, and one tree,
The suburbs are good for the children,
But no place for grown-ups to be.

JUDITH VIORST (b. 1935), U.S. poet, journalist. *The Suburbs Are Good For The Children,* in *It's Hard to Be Hip Over Thirty and Other Tragedies of Married Life* (1968).

SUCCESS

1 One's religion is whatever he is most interested in, and yours is Success.

J. M. BARRIE (1860–1937), British playwright. Kate, in *The Twelve-Pound Look* (1910).

2 The toughest thing about success is that you've got to keep on being a success. Talent is only a starting point in this business. You've got to keep on working that talent. Someday I'll reach for it and it won't be there.

IRVING BERLIN (1888–1989), U.S. songwriter. *Theatre Arts* (Feb. 1958).

3 Success is the space one occupies in the newspaper. Success is one day's insolence.

ELIAS CANETTI (b. 1905), Austrian novelist, philosopher. *The Secret Heart Of The Clock: Notes, Aphorisms, Fragments 1973–1985,* "1974" (1991).

4 There's terrific merit in having no sense of humour, no sense of irony, practically no sense of anything at all. If you're born with these so-called defects you have a very good chance of getting to the top.

PETER COOK (b. 1937), British comedian. Quoted in: Ronald Bergan, *Beyond the Fringe . . . and Beyond,* pt. 4 (1989).

5 Success is counted sweetest
By those who ne'er succeed.
To comprehend a nectar
Requires sorest need.

EMILY DICKINSON (1830–86), U.S. poet. *The Complete Poems,* no. 67, st. 1 (1955).

6 There is a vast difference between success at twenty-five and success at sixty. At sixty, nobody envies you. Instead, everybody rejoices generously, sincerely, in your good fortune.

MARIE DRESSLER (1873–1934), U.S. actor. *My Own Story,* ch. 17 (1934).

7 In the United States there's a Puritan ethic and a mythology of success. He who is successful is good. In Latin countries, in Catholic countries, a successful person is a sinner.

UMBERTO ECO (b. 1932), Italian semiologist, novelist. *International Herald Tribune* (Paris, 14 Dec. 1988).

8 If A is a success in life, then A equals x plus y plus z. Work is x; y is play; and z is keeping your mouth shut.

ALBERT EINSTEIN (1879–1955), German-born U.S. scientist. Quoted in: *Observer* (London, 15 Jan. 1950).

9 The compensation of a very early success is a conviction that life is a romantic matter. In the best sense one stays young.

F. SCOTT FITZGERALD (1896–1940), U.S. author. *The Crack-Up,* "Early Success" (ed. by Edmund Wilson, 1945; essay first published in *American Cavalcade,* Oct. 1937).

10 Nothing recedes like success.

BRYAN FORBES (b. 1926), British author, actor, filmmaker. Quoted in: *Observer* (London, 19 Dec. 1971).

11 Success is more dangerous than failure, the ripples break over a wider coastline.

GRAHAM GREENE (1904–91), British novelist. *Independent* (London, 4 April 1991). The quote was recalled at Greene's death by critic Miriam Allot.

12 As long as she is young and personable, every woman may cherish the dream that she may leap up the social ladder and dim the sheen of luxury by sheer natural loveliness; the few examples of such a feat are kept before the eye of the public.

GERMAINE GREER (b. 1939), Australian feminist writer. *The Female Eunuch,* "The Stereotype" (1970).

13 Success isn't everything but it makes a man stand straight.

LILLIAN HELLMAN (1905–84), U.S. playwright. Julian, in *Toys in the Attic,* act 1 (1959).

14 If you have a success, you have it for the wrong reasons. If you become popular it is always because of the worst aspects of your work.

ERNEST HEMINGWAY (1899–1961), U.S. author. Quoted in: Morley Callaghan, *That Summer in Paris,* ch. 13 (1963).

15 The moral flabbiness born of the exclusive worship of the bitch-goddess SUCCESS. That—with the squalid cash interpretation put on the word success—is our national disease.

WILLIAM JAMES (1842–1910), U.S. psychologist, philosopher. Letter, 11 Sept. 1906, to H. G. Wells (published in: *The Letters of William James,* vol. 2, 1920).

16 Think of all the really successful men and women you know. Do you know a single one who didn't learn very young the trick of calling attention to himself in the right quarters?

STORM JAMESON (1891–1986), British author. The College Master, in *A Cup of Tea for Mr. Thorgill,* ch. 7 (1957).

17 Success is somebody else's failure. Success is the American Dream we can keep dreaming because most people in most places, including thirty million of ourselves, live wide awake in the terrible reality of poverty.

URSULA K. LE GUIN (b. 1929), U.S. author. "A Left-Handed Commencement Address," to Mills College Class of 1983 (published in: *Dancing at the Edge of the World,* 1989).

18 Success makes men rigid and they tend to exalt stability over all the other virtues; tired of the effort of willing they become fanatics about conservatism.

WALTER LIPPMANN (1889–1974), U.S. journalist. *A Preface to Politics,* ch. 1 (1913).

19 The common idea that success spoils people by making them vain, egotistic, and self-complacent is erroneous; on the contrary, it makes them, for the most part, humble, tolerant, and kind. Failure makes people cruel and bitter.

W. SOMERSET MAUGHAM (1874–1965), British author. *The Summing Up,* ch. 48 (1938).

20 No illusion is more crucial than the illusion that great success and huge money buy you immunity from the common ills of mankind, such as cars that won't start.

LARRY McMURTRY (b. 1936), U.S. screenwriter, novelist, essayist. Danny Deck, in *Some Can Whistle,* pt. 1, ch. 11 (1989).

21 The logic of worldly success rests on a fallacy: the strange error that our perfection depends on the thoughts and opinions and applause of other men! A weird life it is, indeed, to be living always in somebody else's imagination, as if that were the only place in which one could at last become real!

THOMAS MERTON (1915–68), U.S. religious writer, poet. *The Seven Storey Mountain,* pt. 3, ch. 2 (1948).

22 Success, instead of giving freedom of choice, becomes a way of life. There's no country I've been to where people, when you come into a room and sit down with them, so often ask you, "What do you do?" And, being American, many's the time I've almost asked that question, then realized it's good for my soul not to know. For a while! Just to let the evening wear on and see what I think of this person without knowing what he does and how successful he is, or what a failure. We're *ranking* everybody every minute of the day.

ARTHUR MILLER (b. 1915), U.S. dramatist. *Paris Review* (Flushing, N.Y., Summer 1966).

23 There's no point in success if you don't let it go to your head. That's what it's for.

JOHN OTWAY (b. 1953), British rock musician. Quoted in: *Sunday Correspondent* (London, 6 May 1990). Otway spent recklessly after receiving a large sum, at the age of 24, when he signed a contract with the record company Polydor. His purchases included a Bentley, which he was never able to drive.

24 If you are a genius and unsuccessful, everybody treats you as if you were a genius, but when you come to be successful, when you commence to earn money, when you are really successful, then your family and everybody no longer treats you like a genius, they treat you like a man who has become successful.

PABLO PICASSO (1881–1973), Spanish artist. Quoted in: Gertrude Stein, *Picasso* (1938; repr. 1959, p. 27).

25 Success is dangerous. One begins to copy oneself, and to copy oneself is more dangerous than to copy others. It leads to sterility.

PABLO PICASSO (1881–1973), Spanish artist. *Vogue* (New York, 1 Nov. 1956).

26 There are many paths to the top of the mountain, but the view is always the same.

CHINESE PROVERB.

27 People are beginning to see that the first requisite to success in life is to be a good animal.

HERBERT SPENCER (1820–1903), English philosopher. *Education,* ch. 2 (1861).

28 Your success story is a bigger story than whatever you're trying to say on stage. . . . Success makes life easier. It doesn't make *living* easier.

BRUCE SPRINGSTEEN (b. 1949), U.S. rock musician. *Q* (London, Aug. 1992).

29 Success to me is having ten honeydew melons, and eating only the top half of each one.

BARBRA STREISAND (b. 1942), U.S. singer, actor. *Life* (New York, 20 Sept. 1963).

30 People seldom see the halting and painful steps by which the most insignificant success is achieved.

ANNE SULLIVAN (1866–1936), U.S. educator of the deaf and blind. Letter, 30 Oct. 1887 (published in Helen Keller, *The Story of My Life,* 1903), of teaching Helen Keller.

31 God doesn't require us to succeed; he only requires that you try.

MOTHER TERESA (b. 1910), Roman Catholic missionary in India. Quoted by Robert F. Kennedy, Jr. in: *Rolling Stone* (New York, Dec. 1992).

32 If the day and the night are such that you greet them with joy, and life emits a fragrance like flowers and sweet-scented herbs, is more elastic, more starry, more immortal—that is your success. All nature is your congratulation, and you have cause momentarily to bless yourself.

HENRY DAVID THOREAU (1817–62), U.S. philosopher, author, naturalist. *Walden,* "Higher Laws" (1854).

33 Human nature is the same everywhere; it deifies success, it has nothing but scorn for defeat.

MARK TWAIN (1835–1910), U.S. author. *Joan of Arc,* bk. 1, ch. 8 (1896).

34 Whenever a friend succeeds a little something in me dies.

GORE VIDAL (b. 1925), U.S. novelist, critic. Quoted in: *Sunday Times Magazine* (London, 16 Sept. 1973).

35 Success can make you go one of two ways. It can make you a prima donna, or it can smooth the edges, take away the insecurities, let the nice things come out.

BARBARA WALTERS (b. 1931), U.S. journalist, broadcaster. Quoted in: *Newsweek* (New York, 6 May 1974).

36 In the deeper layers of the modern consciousness . . . every attempt to succeed is an act of aggression, leaving one alone and guilty and defenseless among enemies: one is *punished* for success. This is our intolerable dilemma: that failure is a kind of death and success is evil and dangerous, is—ultimately—impossible.

ROBERT WARSHOW (1917–55), U.S. author. "The Gangster as Tragic Hero," in *Partisan Review* (New Brunswick, N.J., 1948; repr. in *The Immediate Experience*, 1970).

37   There has been something crude and heartless and unfeeling in our haste to succeed and be great. Our thought has been "Let every man look out for himself, let every generation look out for itself," while we reared giant machinery which made it impossible that any but those who stood at the levers of control should have any chance to look out for themselves.

WOODROW WILSON (1856–1924), U.S. Democratic politician, president. First inaugural address, 4 March 1913.

See also Marcus on CLICHÉS; Twain on FOOLS AND FOLLIES; Baker on SOCIALISM.

SUFFERING

1   You are outside life, you are above life, you have miseries which the ordinary man does not know, you exceed the normal level, and it is for this that men refuse to forgive you, you poison their peace of mind, you undermine their stability. You have irrepressible pains whose essence is to be inadaptable to any known state, indescribable in words. You have repeated and shifting pains, incurable pains, pains beyond imagining, pains which are neither of the body nor of the soul, *but which partake of both*. And I share your suffering, and I ask you: who dares to ration our relief? . . . We are not going to kill ourselves just yet. In the meantime, leave us the hell alone.

ANTONIN ARTAUD (1896–1948), French theater producer, actor, theorist. *General Security: The Liquidation of Opium* (1925; repr. in *Selected Writings*, pt. 10, ed. by Susan Sontag, 1976), plea for free use of opium for sufferers including "lucid madmen, spastics, cancer patients, chronic meningitis cases."

2   It is by a wise economy of nature that those who suffer without change, and whom no one can help, become uninteresting. Yet so it may happen that those who need sympathy the most often attract it the least.

F. H. BRADLEY (1846–1924), English philosopher. *Aphorisms*, no. 22 (1930).

3   In default of inexhaustible happiness, eternal suffering would at least give us a destiny. But we do not even have that consolation, and our worst agonies come to an end one day.

ALBERT CAMUS (1913–60), French-Algerian philosopher, author. *The Rebel*, pt. 4 (1951; tr. 1953).

4   Is suffering so very serious? I have come to doubt it. It may be quite childish, a sort of undignified pastime—I'm referring to the kind of suffering a man inflicts on a woman or a woman on a man. It's extremely painful. I agree that it's hardly bearable. But I very much fear that this sort of pain deserves no consideration at all. It's no more worthy of respect than old age or illness.

COLETTE (1873–1954), French author. *Break of Day* (1961; repr. in *Earthly Paradise*, pt. 4, "The South of France," ed. by Robert Phelps, 1966).

5   I like a look of Agony,
Because I know it's true—
Men do not sham Convulsion,
Nor simulate, a Throe—

EMILY DICKINSON (1830–86), U.S. poet. *The Complete Poems*, no. 241 (1955).

6   Affliction is a treasure, and scarce any man hath enough of it.

JOHN DONNE (c. 1572–1631), English divine, metaphysical poet. *Devotions Upon Emergent Occasions*, Meditation 17 (1624).

7   One writes of scars healed, a loose parallel to the pathology of the skin, but there is no such thing in the life of an individual. There are open wounds, shrunk sometimes to the size of a pin-prick but wounds still. The marks of suffering are more comparable to the loss of a finger, or the sight of an eye. We may not miss them, either, for one minute in a year, but if we should there is nothing to be done about it.

F. SCOTT FITZGERALD (1896–1940), U.S. author. *Tender is the Night*, bk. 2, ch. 11 (1934).

8   We are threatened with suffering from three directions: from our own body, which is doomed to decay and dissolution and which cannot even do without pain and anxiety as warning signals; from the external world, which may rage against us with overwhelming and merciless forces of destruction; and finally from our relations to other men. The suffering which comes from this last source is perhaps more painful than any other.

SIGMUND FREUD (1856–1939), Austrian psychiatrist. *Civilization and its Discontents*, ch. 2 (1930; repr. in *Complete Works*, vol. 21, ed. by James Strachey and Anna Freud, 1961).

9   A man will renounce any pleasures you like but he will not give up his suffering.

GEORGE GURDJIEFF (c. 1877–1949), Greek-Armenian religious teacher, mystic. Quoted in: P. D. Ouspensky, *In Search of the Miraculous*, ch. 13 (1949).

10   Every age, every culture, every custom and tradition has its own character, its own weakness and its own strength, its beauties and cruelties; it accepts certain sufferings as matters of course, puts up patiently with certain evils. Human life is reduced to real suffering, to hell, only when two ages, two cultures and religions overlap.

HERMANN HESSE (1877–1962), German novelist, poet. *Steppenwolf*, Preface (1927).

11   You can hold yourself back from the sufferings of the world, that is something you are free to do and it accords with your nature, but perhaps this very holding back is the one suffering you could avoid.

FRANZ KAFKA (1883–1924), German novelist, short-story writer. *The Collected Aphorisms*, no. 103 (Oct. 1917–Feb. 1918; repr. in *Shorter Works*, vol. 1, ed. and tr. by Malcolm Pasley, 1973).

12   There is not much sense in suffering, since drugs can be given for pain, itching, and other discomforts. The belief has long died that suffering here on earth will be rewarded in heaven. Suffering has lost its meaning.

ELISABETH KÜBLER-ROSS (b. 1926), Swiss-born U.S. psychiatrist. *On Death and Dying*, ch. 2 (1969).

13 Oh, fear not in a world like this,
And thou shalt know erelong,
Know how sublime a thing it is
To suffer and be strong.

> HENRY WADSWORTH LONGFELLOW (1807–82), U.S. poet.
> *The Light of Stars,* in *Knickerbocker* (Jan. 1839).

14 Everything in life that we really accept undergoes a change. So suffering must become Love. That is the mystery.

> KATHERINE MANSFIELD (1888–1923), New Zealand-born British author. *The Journal of Katherine Mansfield* (1927), entry for 19 Dec. 1920.

15 It is not true that suffering ennobles the character; happiness does that sometimes, but suffering, for the most part, makes men petty and vindictive.

> W. SOMERSET MAUGHAM (1874–1965), British author. *The Moon and Sixpence,* ch. 17 (1919).

16 Who feareth to suffer suffereth already, because he feareth.

> MICHEL DE MONTAIGNE (1533–92), French essayist. *Essays,* bk. 3, ch. 13, "Of Experience" (tr. by John Florio, 1588).

17 Most people get a fair amount of fun out of their lives, but on balance life is suffering, and only the very young or the very foolish imagine otherwise.

> GEORGE ORWELL (1903–50), British author. *Shooting an Elephant,* "Lear, Tolstoy and the Fool" (1950).

18 To choose a hardship for ourselves is our only defence against that hardship. *This* is what is meant by accepting suffering. . . . Those who, by their very nature, can suffer completely, utterly, have an advantage. That is how we can disarm the power of suffering, make it our own creation, our own choice; submit to it. A justification for suicide.

> CESARE PAVESE (1908–50), Italian poet, novelist, translator. *The Burning Brand: Diaries 1935–1950* 1952; tr. 1961), entry for 10 Nov. 1938. Suicide was a continuing theme in Pavese's diaries; he took his own life on 27 Aug. 1950, shortly after being awarded the Strega Prize for literature.

19 Suffering is by no means a privilege, a sign of nobility, a reminder of God. Suffering is a fierce, bestial thing, commonplace, uncalled for, natural as air. It is intangible; no one can grasp it or fight against it; it dwells in time—is the same thing as time; if it comes in fits and starts, that is only so as to leave the sufferer more defenseless during the moments that follow, those long moments when one relives the last bout of torture and waits for the next.

> CESARE PAVESE (1908–50), Italian poet, novelist, translator. *The Burning Brand: Diaries 1935–1950,* 1952; tr. 1961), entry for 30 Oct. 1940.

20 It is not suffering as such that is most deeply feared but suffering that degrades.

> SUSAN SONTAG (b. 1933), U.S. essayist. *AIDS and Its Metaphors,* ch. 4 (1989).

21 Without out suffering, our work would just be social work, very good and helpful, but it would not be the work of Jesus Christ, not part of the Redemption. . . . All the desolation of the poor people, not only their material poverty, but their spiritual destitution, must be redeemed. And we must share it, for only by being one with them can we redeem them by bringing God into their lives and bringing them to God.

> MOTHER TERESA (b. 1910), Albanian-born Roman Catholic missionary. *A Gift for God,* "Suffering" (1975).

22 There is no true love save in suffering, and in this world we have to choose either love, which is suffering, or happiness. . . . Man is the more man—that is, the more divine—the greater his capacity for suffering, or rather, for anguish.

> MIGUEL DE UNAMUNO (1864–1936), Spanish philosophical writer. *The Tragic Sense of Life,* ch. 9 (1913).

23 The afflicted are not listened to. They are like someone whose tongue has been cut out and who occasionally forgets the fact. When they move their lips no ear perceives any sound. And they themselves soon sink into impotence in the use of language, because of the certainty of not being heard.

> SIMONE WEIL (1909–43), French philosopher, mystic. "Human Personality" (written 1943; published in *La Table Ronde,* Dec. 1950; repr. in *Selected Essays,* ed. by Richard Rees, 1962).

24 Don't look forward to the day you stop suffering, because when it comes you'll *know* you're dead.

> TENNESSEE WILLIAMS (1914–83), U.S. dramatist. Quoted in: *Observer* (London, 26 Jan. 1958).

See also Weil on DISSATISFACTION; Byatt on GRIEF; Austen on PLACES; Weil on PUNISHMENT; Hoffer on PURPOSE.

SUICIDE

1 No one is promiscuous in his way of dying. A man who has decided to hang himself will never jump in front of a train.

> A. ALVAREZ (b. 1929), British critic, poet, novelist. *The Savage God,* pt. 5 (1971).

2 If I commit suicide, it will not be to destroy myself but to put myself back together again. Suicide will be for me only one means of violently reconquering myself, of brutally invading my being, of anticipating the unpredictable approaches of God. By suicide, I reintroduce my design in nature, I shall for the first time give things the shape of my will.

> ANTONIN ARTAUD (1896–1948), French theater producer, actor, theorist. "On Suicide," in *Le Disque Vert,* no. 1 (Paris, 1925; repr. in *Artaud Anthology,* ed. by Jack Hirschman, 1965).

3 Let the day perish wherein I was born, and the night in which it was said, There is a man child conceived.

> BIBLE, HEBREW. Job, in *Job* 3:3.

4 If you must commit suicide . . . always contrive to do it as decorously as possible; the decencies, whether of life or of death, should never be lost sight of.

> GEORGE BORROW (1803–81), English author. An "elderly individual," in *Lavengro,* ch. 23 (1851).

5 One said of suicide, "As long as one has brains one should not blow them out." And another answered, "But when one has ceased to have them, too often one cannot."

> F. H. BRADLEY (1846–1924), English philosopher. *Aphorisms,* no. 48 (1930).

6 There is but one truly serious philosophical problem and that is suicide. Judging whether life is or is not worth living amounts to answering the fundamental question of philosophy. All the rest—whether or not the world has three dimensions, whether the mind has nine or twelve categories—comes afterwards. These are games; one must first answer.

ALBERT CAMUS (1913–60), French-Algerian philosopher, author. *The Myth of Sisyphus*, "Absurdity and Suicide" (1942; tr. 1955).

7 Men are never convinced of your reasons, of your sincerity, of the seriousness of your sufferings, except by your death. So long as you are alive, your case is doubtful; you have a right only to your skepticism.

ALBERT CAMUS (1913–60), French-Algerian philosopher, author. The narrator (Jean-Baptiste Clamence), in *The Fall* (1956; repr. 1957, p. 56).

9 It is not worth the bother of killing yourself, since you always kill yourself *too late*.

E. M. CIORAN (b. 1911), Rumanian-born French philosopher. *The Trouble with Being Born*, ch. 2 (1973).

8 The obsession with suicide is characteristic of the man who can neither live nor die, and whose attention never swerves from this double impossibility.

E. M. CIORAN (b. 1911), Rumanian-born French philosopher. *The New Gods*, "Encounters with Suicide" (1969; tr. 1974).

10 It appears I am destined for something; I will live.

ROBERT CLIVE (1725–74), English soldier, colonial administrator. Alleged comment, 1744, in Madras, after the pistol with which he intended to shoot himself would not fire on two attempts. Subsequently, after a glorious career, he succeeded in killing himself after accusations of embezzlement and corruption were made against him, though all charges had been dropped.

11 There are many who dare not kill themselves for fear of what the neighbours will say.

CYRIL CONNOLLY (1903–74), British critic. *The Unquiet Grave*, pt. 2 (1944; rev. 1951).

12 Whensoever any affliction assails me, mee thinks I have the keyes of my prison in mine owne hand, and no remedy presents it selfe so soone to my heart, as mine own sword. Often meditation of this hath wonne me to a charitable interpretation of their action, who dy so: and provoked me a little to watch and exagitate their reasons, which pronounce so peremptory judgements upon them.

JOHN DONNE (c. 1572–1631), English divine, metaphysical poet. *Biathanatos*, Preface (written c. 1608; published 1646; repr. in *Complete Poetry and Selected Prose*, ed. by John Hayward, 1929).

13 Each victim of suicide gives his act a personal stamp which expresses his temperament, the special conditions in which he is involved, and which, consequently, cannot be explained by the social and general causes of the phenomenon.

EMILE DURKHEIM (1858–1917), French sociologist. *Suicide*, bk. 2, ch. 6 (1897; tr. 1951).

14 The prevalence of suicide, without doubt, is a test of height in civilization; it means that the population is winding up its nervous and intellectual system to the utmost point of tension and that sometimes it snaps.

HAVELOCK ELLIS (1859–1939), British psychologist. *The Dance of Life*, ch. 7 (1923).

15 Would Hamlet have felt the delicious fascination of suicide if he hadn't had an audience, and lines to speak?

JEAN GENET (1910–86), French playwright, novelist. *Prisoner of Love*, pt. 1 (1986; tr. 1989).

16 Human life consists in mutual service. No grief, pain, misfortune, or "broken heart," is excuse for cutting off one's life while any power of service remains. But when all usefulness is over, when one is assured of an unavoidable and imminent death, it is the simplest of human rights to choose a quick and easy death in place of a slow and horrible one.

CHARLOTTE PERKINS GILMAN (1860–1935), U.S. feminist, writer. Suicide note, 17 Aug. 1935. Quoted in: Jilly Cooper and Tom Hartman, *Violets and Vinegar*, "The Happy Dead" (1980).

17 However great a man's fear of life, suicide remains the courageous act, the clear-headed act of a mathematician. The suicide has judged by the laws of chance—so many odds against one that to live will be more miserable than to die. His sense of mathematics is greater than his sense of survival. But think how a sense of survival must clamour to be heard at the last moment, what excuses it must present of a totally unscientific nature.

GRAHAM GREENE (1904–91), British novelist. Dr. Magiot, in *The Comedians*, pt. 1, ch. 4, sct. 1 (1966).

18 Fatigue dulls the pain, but awakes enticing thoughts of death. So! *that* is the way in which you are tempted to overcome your loneliness—by making the ultimate escape from life.—No! It may be that death is to be your ultimate gift to life: it must not be an act of treachery against it.

DAG HAMMARSKJÖLD (1905–61), Swedish statesman, Secretary-General of U.N. *Markings*, "Night is Drawing Nigh" (1963; written 1952).

19 Sometimes I wonder if suicides aren't in fact sad guardians of the meaning of life.

VÁCLAV HAVEL (b. 1936), Czech playwright, president. *Disturbing the Peace*, ch. 5 (1986; tr. 1990).

20 It requires courage not to surrender oneself to the ingenious or compassionate counsels of despair that would induce a man to eliminate himself from the ranks of the living; but it does not follow from this that every huckster who is fattened and nourished in self-confidence has more courage than the man who yielded to despair.

SØREN KIERKEGAARD (1813–55), Danish philosopher. *The Concept Of Irony*, pt. 2, "Irony as a Mastered Moment. The Truth of Irony" (1841; tr. 1966).

21 If you are of the opinion that the contemplation of suicide is sufficient evidence of a poetic nature, do not forget that actions speak louder than words.

FRAN LEBOWITZ (b. 1951), U.S. journalist. *Metropolitan Life*, "Letters" (1978).

22 Here take back the stuff that I am, nature, knead it back into the dough of being, make of me a bush, a cloud, whatever you will, even a man, only no longer make me me.

G. C. LICHTENBERG (1742–99), German physicist, philosopher. "Speech of a suicide composed shortly before the act," in *Aphorisms*, "Notebook B," aph. 37 (written 1765–99; tr. by R. J. Hollingdale, 1990).

23   Death hath
had a thousand doors to let out life,
I shall find one . . . From a loath'd life,
I'll not an hour outlive.

PHILIP MASSINGER (1583–1640), English dramatist. Almera (daughter of the Viceroy of Sicily), in *A Very Women*, act 5, sc. 4 (1655). This image of death was a common one, used by Massinger and John Fletcher in *The Custom of the Country*, John Webster in *The Duchess of Malfi*, and much earlier by Seneca in *Phoenissae* (1st century A.D.).

24   It is the part of cowardliness, and not of virtue, to seek to squat itself in some hollow lurking hole, or to hide herself under some massive tomb, thereby to shun the strokes of fortune.

MICHEL DE MONTAIGNE (1533–92), French essayist. *Essays*, bk. 2, ch. 3, "A Custom of the Isle of Cea" (1580–88; tr. by John Florio).

25   And one of his partners asked "Has he vertigo?" and the other glanced out and down and said "Oh no, only about ten feet more."

OGDEN NASH (1902–71), U.S. poet. *Mr. Artesian's Conscientiousness*, in *The Face is Familiar* (1940).

26   It is always consoling to think of suicide: in that way one gets through many a bad night.

FRIEDRICH NIETZSCHE (1844–1900), German philosopher. *Beyond Good and Evil*, ch. 4, aph. 157 (1886).

27   When one *does away with* oneself one does the most estimable thing possible: one thereby almost deserves to live.

FRIEDRICH NIETZSCHE (1844–1900), German philosopher. *Twilight of the Idols*, "Expeditions of an Untimely Man," aph. 36 (1889).

28   I am just going outside and may be some time.

LAWRENCE OATES (1880–1912), English soldier, explorer. Quoted in: *Scott's Last Expedition*, vol. 1, ch. 20 (ed. by L. Huxley, 1913), diary entry for 16–17 March 1912 These were Oates' last words, before walking out into an Antarctic blizzard on Captain Scott's ill-fated expedition to the South Pole. Scott recorded, "We knew it was the act of a brave man and an English gentleman."

29   Razors pain you;
Rivers are damp;
Acids stain you;
And drugs cause cramp.
Guns aren't lawful;
Nooses give;
Gas smells awful;
You might as well live.

DOROTHY PARKER (1893–1967), U.S. humorous writer. *Résumé.*

30   No one ever lacks a good reason for suicide.

CESARE PAVESE (1908–50), Italian poet, novelist, translator. *The Burning Brand: Diaries 1935–1950* (1952; tr. 1961), entry for 23 March 1938. Suicide was a continuing theme in Pavese's diaries;

he took his own life on 27 Aug. 1950, shortly after being awarded the Strega Prize for literature.

31   At great periods you have always felt, deep within you, the temptation to commit suicide. *You gave yourself to it,* breached your own defenses. You were a child. The idea of suicide was a protest against life; by dying, you would escape this longing for death.

CESARE PAVESE (1908–50), Italian poet, novelist, translator. *The Burning Brand: Diaries 1935–1950* (1952; tr. 1961), entry for 1 Jan. 1950.

32   The woman is perfected
Her dead
Body wears the smile of accomplishment.

SYLVIA PLATH (1932–63), U.S. poet. First lines of *Edge*. This was Plath's last poem, written a week before her suicide.

33   I have always thought the suicide shd/ bump off at least one swine before taking off for parts unknown.

EZRA POUND (1885–1972), U.S. poet, critic. Letter, 10 Sept. 1956, to poet Archibald MacLeish. Quoted in: Humphrey Carpenter, *A Serious Character*, pt. 5, ch. 3 (1988).

34   Suicide may also be regarded as an experiment—a question which man puts to Nature, trying to force her to answer. The question is this: What change will death produce in a man's existence and in his insight into the nature of things? It is a clumsy experiment to make; for it involves the destruction of the very consciousness which puts the question and awaits the answer.

ARTHUR SCHOPENHAUER (1788–1860), German philosopher. *Parerga and Paralipomena*, vol. 2, ch. 13, sct. 160 (1851).

35   Then is it sin
To rush into the secret house of death
Ere death dare come to us?

WILLIAM SHAKESPEARE (1564–1616), English dramatist, poet. Cleopatra, in *Antony and Cleopatra*, act 4, sc. 16, on the death of Antony.

36   He who does not accept and respect those who want to reject life does not truly accept and respect life itself.

THOMAS SZASZ (b. 1920), U.S. psychiatrist. *The Second Sin*, "Suicide" (1973).

37   A lover forsaken
A new love may get,
But a neck when once broken
Can never be set.

WILLIAM WALSH (1663–1708), English poet. *The Despairing Lover.*

See also Webster on CONFESSION; Artaud on PSYCHIATRIC INSTITUTIONS; SELF-DESTRUCTIVENESS.

SUMMER

1   Ah, summer, what power you have to make us suffer and like it.

RUSSELL BAKER (b. 1925), U.S. journalist. *New York Times* (27 June 1965).

2   Summer has set in with its usual severity.

SAMUEL TAYLOR COLERIDGE (1772–1834), English poet, critic. Quoted by essayist Charles Lamb, in letter, 9 May 1826.

3 Summer's lease hath all too short a date.

> WILLIAM SHAKESPEARE (1564–1616), English dramatist, poet. *Sonnet* 18.

4 Summer set lip to earth's bosom bare
And left the flushed print in a poppy there.

> FRANCIS THOMPSON (1859–1907), English poet. *The Poppy.*

THE SUN

1 The sun was like a great visiting presence that stimulated and took its due from all animal energy. When it flung wide its cloak and stepped down over the edge of the fields at evening, it left behind it a spent and exhausted world.

> WILLA CATHER (1873–1947), U.S. author. *One of Ours*, bk. 2, ch. 6 (1922).

2 The Sun, the hearth of affection and life, pours burning love on the delighted earth.

> ARTHUR RIMBAUD (1854–1891), French poet. *Soleil et Chair*, sct. 1, in *Collected Poems* (ed. by Oliver Bernard, 1962).

3 The day of the sun is like the day of a king. It is a promenade in the morning, a sitting on the throne at noon, a pageant in the evening.

> WALLACE STEVENS (1879–1955), U.S. poet. *Souvenirs and Prophecies: the Young Wallace Stevens*, ch. 6 (ed. by Holly Stevens, 1966), entry for 20 April 1920.

4 The sun is but a morning star.

> HENRY DAVID THOREAU (1817–62), U.S. philosopher, author, naturalist. *Walden*, "Conclusion" (1854), last sentence.

5 Nobody of any real culture, for instance, ever talks nowadays about the beauty of sunset. Sunsets are quite old fashioned. . . . To admire them is a distinct sign of provincialism of temperament. Upon the other hand they go on.

> OSCAR WILDE (1854–1900), Anglo-Irish playwright, author. Vivian, in *The Decay of Lying* (published in *Intentions*, 1891).

SUNDAY

1 Sunday clears away the rust of the whole week.

> JOSEPH ADDISON (1672–1719), English essayist. *Spectator*, no. 112 (London, 9 July 1711).

2 Sabbath. A weekly festival having its origin in the fact that God made the world in six days and was arrested on the seventh.

> AMBROSE BIERCE (1842–1914), U.S. author. *The Devil's Dictionary* (1881–1906).

3 The boredom of Sunday afternoon, which drove de Quincey to drink laudanum, also gave birth to surrealism: hours propitious for making bombs.

> CYRIL CONNOLLY (1903–74), British critic. *The Unquiet Grave*, pt. 3 (1944; rev. 1951).

4 It was a Sunday afternoon, wet and cheerless; and a duller spectacle this earth of ours has not to show than a rainy Sunday in London.

> THOMAS DE QUINCEY (1785–1859), English author. *Confes-*

sions of an English Opium-Eater, "The Pleasures of Opium" (1822), recalling the day in 1804 when he first took opium.

5 Some keep the Sabbath going to Church—
I keep it, staying at Home—
With a Bobolink for a Chorister—
And an Orchard, for a Dome.

> EMILY DICKINSON (1830–86), U.S. poet. *The Complete Poems*, no. 324 (1955).

6 Sometimes there's nothing but Sundays for weeks on end. Why can't they move Sunday to the middle of the week so you could put it in the OUT tray on your desk?

> RUSSELL HOBAN (b. 1925), U.S. author. "The tightly furled man," in *The Lion of Boaz-Jachin and Jachin-Boaz*, ch. 13 (1973). "Forgive us our Sundays," he adds, "as we forgive those who Sunday against us."

7 Why do I do this every Sunday? Even the book reviews seem to be the same as last week's. Different books—same reviews.

> JOHN OSBORNE (b. 1929), British playwright. Jimmy, in opening words of *Look Back in Anger*, act 1.

8 Sunday—the doctor's paradise! Doctors at country clubs, doctors at the seaside, doctors with mistresses, doctors with wives, doctors in church, doctors in yachts, doctors everywhere resolutely being people, not doctors.

> SYLVIA PLATH (1932–1963), U.S. poet. The narrator, in *The Bell Jar*, ch. 19 (1963).

9 The feeling of Sunday is the same everywhere, heavy, melancholy, standing still. Like when they say, "As it was in the beginning, is now, and ever shall be, world without end."

> JEAN RHYS (1894–1979), British author. The narrator (Anna Morgan), in *Voyage in the Dark*, act 4 (1934).

10 Anybody can observe the Sabbath, but making it holy surely takes the rest of the week.

> ALICE WALKER (b. 1944), U.S. author, critic. *In Search of Our Mothers' Gardens*, "To the Editors of *Ms.* Magazine" (1983).

See also WEEKENDS.

SUPERIORITY

1 I still lack to a considerable degree that naturally superior kind of manner that I would dearly like to possess.

> HEINRICH HIMMLER (1900–1945), German Nazi leader. Diary entry, Nov. 1921. Quoted in: Derek Raymond, *The Hidden Files* (1992).

2 The most perfect ape cannot draw an ape; only man can do that; but, likewise, only man regards the ability to do this as a sign of superiority.

> G. C. LICHTENBERG (1742–99), German physicist, philosopher. *Aphorisms*, "Notebook J," aph. 115 (written 1765–99; tr. by R. J. Hollingdale, 1990).

3 There it is: it doesn't make any difference who we are or what we are, there's always *somebody* to look down on! somebody to hold in light esteem, somebody to be indifferent about.

> MARK TWAIN (1835–1910), U.S. author. "Three Thousand Years Among the Microbes," ch. 15 (written 1905; published in *Which Was the Dream?* ed. by John S. Tuckey, 1967).

4 If a person tells me he has been to the worst places I have no reason to judge him; but if he tells me it was his superior wisdom that enabled him to go there, then I know he is a fraud.

> LUDWIG WITTGENSTEIN (1889–1951), Austrian philosopher. Conversation, 1930 (published in *Personal Recollections*, ch. 6, ed. by Rush Rhees, 1981).

SUPERSTITION

1 I have, thanks to my travels, added to my stock all the superstitions of other countries. I know them all now, and in any critical moment of my life, they all rise up in armed legions for or against me.

> SARAH BERNHARDT (1844–1923), French actor. *The Memoirs of Sarah Bernhardt*, ch. 8 (1977 ed.).

2 Superstition is the religion of feeble minds.

> EDMUND BURKE (1729–97), Irish philosopher, statesman. *Reflections on the Revolution in France* (1790).

3 When superstition is allowed to perform the task of old age in dulling the human temperament, we can say goodbye to all excellence in poetry, in painting, and in music.

> DENIS DIDEROT (1713–84), French philosopher. *Philosophic Thoughts*, ch. 3 (1746; repr. in *Selected Writings*, ed. by Lester G. Crocker, 1966).

4 Superstitions are habits rather than beliefs.

> MARLENE DIETRICH (1904–92), German-born U.S. film actor. *Marlene Dietrich's ABC*, "Superstition" (1962).

5 Mankind are an incorrigible race. Give them but bugbears and idols—it is all that they ask; the distinctions of right and wrong, of truth and falsehood, of good and evil, are worse than indifferent to them.

> WILLIAM HAZLITT (1778–1830), English essayist. "Common Places," no. 76, in *Literary Examiner* (London, 29 Nov. 1823; repr. in *Collected Works*, vol. 11, ed. by A. R. Waller and Arnold Glover, 1904).

6 Superstition, bigotry and prejudice, ghosts though they are, cling tenaciously to life; they are shades armed with tooth and claw. They must be grappled with unceasingly, for it is a fateful part of human destiny that it is condemned to wage perpetual war against ghosts. A shade is not easily taken by the throat and destroyed.

> VICTOR HUGO (1802–85), French poet, dramatist, novelist. *Les Misérables*, pt. 2, bk. 7, ch. 3 (1862).

7 No one is so thoroughly superstitious as the godless man.

> HARRIET BEECHER STOWE (1811–96), U.S. novelist, anti-slavery campaigner. *Uncle Tom's Cabin*, ch. 39 (1852).

8 Let me make the superstitions of a nation and I care not who makes its laws or its songs either.

> MARK TWAIN (1835–1910), U.S. author. *Following the Equator*, ch. 51, "Pudd'nhead Wilson's New Calendar" (1897).

9 We would be a lot safer if the Government would take its money out of science and put it into astrology and the reading of palms. . . . Only in superstition is there hope. If you want to become a friend of civilization, then become an enemy of the truth and a fanatic for harmless balderdash.

> KURT VONNEGUT, JR. (b. 1922), U.S. novelist. *Wampeters, Foma and Granfalloons*, "When I Was Twenty-One" (1974).

10 There is no such thing as an omen. Destiny does not send us heralds. She is too wise or too cruel for that.

> OSCAR WILDE (1854–1900), Anglo-Irish playwright, author. Lord Henry, in *The Picture of Dorian Gray*, ch. 17 (1891).

See also Stewart on The ARMY.

SURPRISE

1 Be astonished, O ye heavens, at this, and be horribly afraid.

> BIBLE, HEBREW. *Jeremiah* 2:12.

2 Stupefaction, when it persists, becomes stupidity.

> JOSÉ ORTEGA Y GASSET (1883–1955), Spanish essayist, philosopher. "In Search of Goethe from Within," in *Partisan Review* (New Brunswick, N.J., Dec. 1949; repr. in *The Dehumanization of Art and Other Essays*, 1968).

3 The husband who decides to surprise his wife is often very much surprised himself.

> VOLTAIRE (1694–1778), French philosopher, author. Mrs. Gripon, in *La Femme Qui a Raison*, act 2, sc. 2.

SURREALISM

1 The vice named *surrealism* is the immoderate and impassioned use of the stupefacient *image*, or rather of the uncontrolled provocation of the image for its own sake and for the element of unpredictable perturbation and of metamorphosis which it introduces into the domain of representation; for each image on each occasion forces you to revise the entire Universe.

> LOUIS ARAGON (1897–1982), French poet. *Paris Peasant*, "The Passage de l'Opéra" (1926; repr. 1971).

2 Surrealism, n. Pure psychic automatism, by which it is intended to express, whether verbally or in writing, or in any other way, the real process of thought. Thought's dictation, free from any control by the reason, independent of any aesthetic or moral proccupation.

> ANDRÉ BRETON (1896–1966), French surrealist. "Manifesto of Surrealism" (1924; repr. in *Manifestos of Surrealism*, 1969).

3 An aesthetic movement with a revolutionary dynamism and no popular appeal should proceed quite otherwise than by public scandal, publicity stunt, noisy expulsion and excommunication.

> CYRIL CONNOLLY (1903–74), British critic. *The Unquiet Grave*, pt. 3 (1944; rev. 1951).

4 Instead of stubbornly attempting to use surrealism for purposes of subversion, it is necessary to try to make of surrealism something as solid, complete and classic as the works of museums.

> SALVADOR DALI (1904–89), Spanish painter. *The Secret Life of Salvador Dali*, ch. 14 (1948).

5 *Le surréalisme, c'est moi.*

> SALVADOR DALI (1904–1989), Spanish painter. Quoted in: Saranne Alexandrian, *Surrealist Art*, ch. 5 (1969).

6 Like all revolutions, the surrealist revolution was a reversion, a restitution, an expression of vital and indispensable spiritual needs.

> EUGÈNE IONESCO (b. 1912), Rumanian-born French playwright. "Experience of the Theatre," in *N.R.F.*, no. 62 (Paris, Feb. 1958; repr. in *Notes and Counter Notes*, pt. 1, 1962).

7 To be a surrealist . . . means barring from your mind all remembrance of what you have seen, and being always on the lookout for what has never been.

> RENÉ MAGRITTE (1898–1967), Belgian surrealist painter. *Time* (New York, 21 April 1947). Quoted in: Uwe M. Scheede, "Sightless Vision," in *Max Ernst* (ed. by Werner Spies, 1991).

8 Surrealism . . . is the forbidden flame of the proletariat embracing the insurrectional dawn—enabling us to rediscover at last the revolutionary moment: the radiance of the workers' councils as a life profoundly adored by those we love.

> MANIFESTO OF THE ARAB SURREALIST MOVEMENT (1975). Quoted in: *What is Surrealism?* "Surrealist Glossary" (ed. by Franklin Rosemont, 1971).

9 Surrealism is merely the reflection of the death process. It is one of the manifestations of a life becoming extinct, a virus which quickens the inevitable end.

> HENRY MILLER (1891–1980), U.S. author. *The Cosmological Eye*, "An Open Letter to Surrealists Everywhere" (1939). On the subject of surrealism, Miller wrote earlier in the same essay, "I was writing Surrealistically in America before I had ever heard the word."

10 Surrealism is not a school of poetry but a movement of liberation. . . . A way of rediscovering the language of innocence, a renewal of the primordial pact, poetry is the basic text, the foundation of the human order. Surrealism is revolutionary because it is a return to the beginning of all beginnings.

> OCTAVIO PAZ (b. 1914), Mexican poet. *Alternating Current*, "André Breton or the Quest of the Beginning" (1967).

11 The simplest surrealist gesture consists in going out into the street, gun in hand, and taking pot shots at the crowd!

> SURREALIST SLOGAN FROM THE 1920S. Quoted by Luis Buñuel in: *My Last Sigh*, ch. 10 (1983). The slogan was revived in Paris in 1968, during the May uprising.

12 Surrealism is a bourgeois disaffection; that its militants thought it universal is only one of the signs that it is typically bourgeois.

> SUSAN SONTAG (b. 1933), U.S. essayist. *On Photography*, "Melancholy Objects" (1977). For Sontag, "surrealism in painting amounted to little more than the contents of a meagerly stocked dream world: a few witty fantasies, mostly wet dreams and agoraphobic nightmares."

SURVIVAL

1 Mi advise tu them who are about tu begin, in arnest, the jurney ov life, is tu take their harte in one hand and a club in the other.

> JOSH BILLINGS [HENRY WHEELER SHAW] (1818–85), U.S. humorist. *Josh Billings, His Sayings*, ch. 71 (1865).

2 The values by which we are to survive are not rules for just and unjust conduct, but are those deeper illuminations in whose light justice and injustice, good and evil, means and ends are seen in fearful sharpness of outline.

> JACOB BRONOWSKI (1908–74), British scientist, author. Concluding sentence of "The Sense of Human Dignity," lecture, 19 March 1953, the Massachusetts Institute of Technology (published in *Science and Human Values*, pt. 3, sct. 11, 1961).

3 Survival, with honor, that outmoded and all-important word, is as difficult as ever and as all-important to a writer. Those who do not last are always more beloved since no one has to see them in their long, dull, unrelenting, no-quarter-given-and-no-quarter-received, fights that they make to do something as they believe it should be done before they die. Those who die or quit early and easy and with every good reason are preferred because they are understandable and human. Failure and well-disguised cowardice are more human and more beloved.

> ERNEST HEMINGWAY (1899–1961), U.S. author. Interview in *Paris Review* (Flushing, N.Y., Spring 1958; repr. in *Writers at Work*, Second Series, ed. by George Plimpton, 1963).

4 A population weakened and exhausted by battling against so many obstacles—whose needs are never satisfied and desires never fulfilled—is vulnerable to manipulation and regimentation. The struggle for survival is, above all, an exercise that is hugely time-consuming, absorbing and debilitating. If you create these "anti-conditions," your rule is guaranteed for a hundred years.

> RYSZARD KAPUSCINSKI (b. 1932), Polish journalist. "A Warsaw Diary," in *Granta*, no. 15 (Cambridge, England, 1985).

5 Self-preservation, nature's first great law,
All the creatures, except man, doth awe.

> ANDREW MARVELL (1621–1678), English metaphysical poet. *Hodge's Vision*.

6 The conciousness of being deemed dead, is next to the presumable unpleasantness of being so in reality. One feels like his own ghost unlawfully tenanting a defunct carcass.

> HERMAN MELVILLE (1819–91), U.S. author. *Mardi: and a Voyage Thither*, ch. 9 (1849), on being lost at sea.

7 The notion that one will not survive a particular catastrophe is, in general terms, a comfort since it is equivalent to abolishing the catastrophe.

> IRIS MURDOCH (b. 1919), British novelist, philosopher. Franca Sheerwater, in *The Message to the Planet*, pt. 6 (1989).

8 Once one determines that he or she has a mission in life, that's it's not going to be accomplished without a great deal of pain, and that the rewards in the end may not outweigh the pain—if you recognize historically that that always happens, then when it comes, you survive it.

> RICHARD M. NIXON (b. 1913), U.S. Republican politician, pres-

ident. Remark to interviewer, Sept. 1980. Quoted in: Robert Sam Anson, *Exile: The Unquiet Oblivion of Richard M. Nixon,* ch. 17 (1984).

9 All I'm trying to do is not join my ancestral spirits just yet.

JOSHUA NKOMO (b. 1917), Zimbabwean politician. *Observer* (London, 20 March 1983).

10 To survive it is often necessary to fight and to fight you have to dirty yourself.

GEORGE ORWELL (1903–50), British author. "Looking Back on the Spanish War" (1943; repr. in *Collected Essays,* 1961).

11 I believe that all the survivors are mad. One time or another their madness will explode. You cannot absorb that much madness and not be influenced by it. That is why the children of survivors are so tragic. I see them in school. They don't know how to handle their parents. They see that their parents are traumatized: they scream and don't react normally.

ELIE WIESEL (b. 1928), Rumanian-born U.S. writer. Interview in *Writers at Work* (Eighth Series, ed. by George Plimpton, 1988), referring to the survivors of the Holocaust.

12 Nobody is stonger, nobody is weaker than someone who came back. There is nothing you can do to such a person because whatever you could do is less than what has already been done to him. We have already paid the price.

ELIE WIESEL (b. 1928), Rumanian-born U.S. writer. Interview in *Writers at Work* (Eighth Series, ed. by George Plimpton, 1988).

13 One can survive anything these days, except death, and live down anything except a good reputation.

OSCAR WILDE (1854–1900), Anglo-Irish playwright, author. Lord Illingworth, in *A Woman of No Importance,* act 1. Lord Henry uttered similar sentiments in Wilde's *The Picture of Dorian Gray,* ch. 19 (1891).

See also Mumford on BABIES; Santayana on LUST FOR LIFE; Buñuel on OLD AGE.

SUSPICION

1 Suspicion is not less an enemy to virtue than to happiness; he that is already corrupt is naturally suspicious, and he that becomes suspicious will quickly be corrupt.

JOSEPH ADDISON (1672–1719), English essayist. *Interesting Anecdotes, Memoirs, Allegories, Essays, and Poetical Fragments,* "On Suspicion" (1794).

2 There is nothing makes a man suspect much, more than to know little.

FRANCIS BACON (1561–1626), English philosopher, essayist, statesman. *Essays,* "Of Suspicion" (1597–1625).

3 What loneliness is more lonely than distrust?

GEORGE ELIOT (1819–80), English novelist. *Middlemarch,* bk. 5, ch. 44 (1872).

4 The suspicious mind believes more than it doubts. It believes in a formidable and ineradicable evil lurking in every person.

ERIC HOFFER (1902–83), U.S. philosopher. *The Passionate State of Mind,* aph. 184 (1955).

5 A new disease? I know not, new or old,
But it may well be called poor mortals' plague:
For, like a pestilence, it doth infect
The houses of the brain . . .
Till not a thought, or motion, in the mind,
Be free from the black poison of suspect.

BEN JONSON (1573–1637), English dramatist, poet. Kitely, in *Every Man in His Humour,* act 2, sc. 3.

6 Suspicion is the companion of mean souls, and the bane of all good society.

THOMAS PAINE (1737–1809), Anglo-American political theorist, writer. *Common Sense* (1776).

7 Suspicion . . . is one of the morbid reactions by which an organism defends itself and seeks another equilibrium.

NATHALIE SARRAUTE (b. 1900), French novelist. *The Age of Suspicion,* title essay (1956; first published 1950).

8 If you ask a Negro where he's been, he'll tell you where he's going.

BLACK AMERICAN SAYING. Quoted by Maya Angelou in: *I Know Why the Caged Bird Sings,* vol. 1, ch. 25 (1969), mentioned to describe her mother's sense of caution.

9 We are paid for our suspicions by finding what we suspected.

HENRY DAVID THOREAU (1817–62), U.S. philosopher, author, naturalist. *A Week on the Concord and Merrimack Rivers,* "Wednesday" (1849).

10 We have to distrust each other. It is our only defence against betrayal.

TENNESSEE WILLIAMS (1914–83), U.S. dramatist. Marguerite Gautier, in *Camino Real,* Block 10.

See also Cowper on TRUST.

SWEARING

1 Take not God's name in vain; select
A time when it will have effect.

AMBROSE BIERCE (1842–1914), U.S. author. *The Devil's Dictionary,* "The Decalogue Revised" (1881–1906).

2 'Twas but my tongue, 'twas not my soul that swore.

EURIPIDES (480–406 B.C.), Greek dramatist. Hippolytus, in *Hippolytus* (tr. by Gilbert Murray).

3 Grant me some wild expressions, Heavens, or I shall burst.

GEORGE FARQUHAR (1678–1707), Irish dramatist. Lady Lurewell, in *The Constant Couple,* act 5, sc. 3.

4 Ethelberta breathed a sort of exclamation, not right out, but stealthily, like a parson's damn.

THOMAS HARDY (1840–1928), English novelist, poet. *The Hand of Ethelberta,* ch. 26 (1876).

5 I've tried to reduce profanity but I reduced so much profanity when writing the book that I'm afraid not much could come out. Perhaps we will have to consider it simply as a profane book and hope that the next book will be less profane or perhaps more sacred.

ERNEST HEMINGWAY (1899–1961), U.S. author. Letter, 21 Aug.

1926 (published in: *Selected Letters*, ed. by Carlos Baker, 1981), of his book, *The Sun Also Rises*.

6   Oaths are the fossils of piety.

GEORGE SANTAYANA (1863–1952), U.S. philosopher, poet. "The Absence of Religion in Shakespeare," in *New World* Journal, issue 5.

7   A whoreson jackanapes must take me up for swearing; as if I borrowed mine oaths of him and might not spend them at my pleasure. . . . When a gentleman is disposed to swear, it is not for any standers-by to curtail his oaths, ha?

WILLIAM SHAKESPEARE (1564–1616), English dramatist, poet. Cloten, in *Cymbeline*, act 2, sc. 1.

8   Swear me, Kate, like a lady as thou art,
A good mouth-filling oath.

WILLIAM SHAKESPEARE (1564–1616), English dramatist, poet. Hotspur to his wife (Lady Percy), in *King Henry IV, pt. 1*, act 3, sc. 1.

9   It comes to pass oft that a terrible oath, with a swaggering accent sharply twanged off, gives manhood more approbation than ever proof itself would have earned him.

WILLIAM SHAKESPEARE (1564–1616), English dramatist, poet. Sir Toby Belch, in *Twelfth Night*, act 3, sc. 4.

10   Ay, ay, the best terms will grow obsolete: damns have had their day.

RICHARD BRINSLEY SHERIDAN (1751–1816), Anglo-Irish dramatist. Acres, in *The Rivals*, act 2, sc. 1.

11   A footman may swear; but he cannot swear like a lord. He can swear as often: but can he swear with equal delicacy, propriety, and judgment?

JONATHAN SWIFT (1667–1745), Anglo-Irish satirist. *Polite Conversation*, Introduction (1738).

See also Twain on SELF-CONTROL.

SWITZERLAND AND THE SWISS

1   Switzerland is a country where very few things begin, but many things end.

F. SCOTT FITZGERALD (1896–1940), U.S. author. *The Crack-Up*, "Notebook E" (ed. by Edmund Wilson, 1945).

2   Switzerland is a small, steep country, much more up and down than sideways, and is all stuck over with large brown hotels built on the cuckoo clock style of architecture.

ERNEST HEMINGWAY (1899–1961), U.S. writer. Quoted in: *Toronto Star Weekly* (4 March 1922).

3   This is a strange little complacent country, in many ways a U.S.A in miniature but of course nearer the center of disturbance!

ELEANOR ROOSEVELT (1884–1962), U.S. columnist, lecturer. Letter, 2 May 1951, to her daughter Anna from Geneva (published in *Mother and Daughter: The Letters of Eleanor and Anna Roosevelt*, 1982).

4   In Italy for thirty years under the Borgias they had warfare, terror, murder, bloodshed—they produced Michelangelo, Leonardo da Vinci and the Renaissance. In Switzerland they had brotherly love, five hundred years of democracy and peace, and what did they produce? The cuckoo clock!

ORSON WELLES (1915–84), U.S. filmmaker, actor. Contributed by Welles to Graham Greene's screenplay of the film *The Third Man* (1949), in which Welles starred. Welles later claimed that the speech was based on a fragment of an old Hungarian play.

5   I don't like Switzerland; it has produced nothing but theologians and waiters.

OSCAR WILDE (1854–1900), Anglo-Irish playwright, author. Quoted in: H. Montgomery Hyde, *Oscar Wilde*, ch. 9 (1976), said during his exile in Europe.

SYMBOLS AND SIGNS

1   The symbolic view of things is a consequence of long absorption in images. Is sign language the real language of Paradise?

HUGO BALL (1886–1927), German Dadaist poet. *Flight out of Time: A Dada Diary*, (1927), entry for 8 April 1917.

2   The whole visible universe is but a storehouse of images and signs to which the imaginaton will give a relative place and value; it is a sort of pasture which the imagination must digest and transform.

CHARLES BAUDELAIRE (1821–67), French poet. "Salon of 1859," sct. 3, in *Curiosités Esthétiques* (1868; repr. in *The Mirror of Art*, ed. by Jonathan Mayne, 1955).

3   The society of merchants can be defined as a society in which things disappear in favor of signs. When a ruling class measures its fortunes, not by the acre of land or the ingot of gold, but by the number of figures corresponding ideally to a certain number of exchange operations, it thereby condemns itself to setting a certain kind of humbug at the center of its experience and its universe. A society founded on signs is, in its essence, an artificial society in which man's carnal truth is handled as something artificial.

ALBERT CAMUS (1913–60), French-Algerian philosopher, author. Lecture, Dec. 1957, University of Uppsala, Sweden (published as "Create Dangerously," in *Resistance, Rebellion and Death*, 1961).

4   In a symbol there is concealment and yet revelation: here therefore, by silence and by speech acting together, comes a double significance. . . . In the symbol proper, what we can call a symbol, there is ever, more or less distinctly and directly, some embodiment and revelation of the Infinite; the Infinite is made to blend itself with the Finite, to stand visible, and as it were, attainable there. By symbols, accordingly, is man guided and commanded, made happy, made wretched.

THOMAS CARLYLE (1795–1881), Scottish essayist, historian. Teufelsdröckh, in *Sartor Resartus*, bk. 3, ch. 3 (1833–34).

5   If you are to reach masses of people in this world, you must do it by a sign language. Whether your vehicle be commerce, literature, or politics, you can do nothing but raise signals, and make motions to the people.

JOHN JAY CHAPMAN (1862–1933), U.S. author. *Practical Agitation*, ch. 5 (1898).

6 All abstract sciences are nothing but the study of relations between signs.

DENIS DIDEROT (1713–84), French philosopher. Dr. Théophile de Bordeu, in *D'Alembert's Dream*, "Conversation Between D'Alembert and Diderot" (written 1769; published 1830; repr. in *Selected Writings*, ed. by Lester G. Crocker, 1966).

7 The present age . . . prefers the sign to the thing signified, the copy to the original, fancy to reality, the appearance to the essence . . . for in these days *illusion* only is *sacred, truth profane.*

LUDWIG FEUERBACH (1804–72), German philosopher. Preface to 1843 ed. of *The Essence of Christianity* (1841).

8 There isn't any symbolism. The sea is the sea. The old man is an old man. The boy is a boy and the fish is a fish. The shark are all sharks no better and no worse. All the symbolism that people say is shit. What goes beyond is what you see beyond when you know.

ERNEST HEMINGWAY (1899–1961), U.S. author. Letter, 13 Sept. 1952, to the critic Bernard Berenson (published in *Selected Letters*, ed. by Carlos Baker, 1981), of *The Old Man and the Sea*, published that year.

9 Every sign is subject to the criteria of ideological evaluation. . . . The domain of ideology coincides with the domain of signs. They equate with one another. Wherever a sign is present, ideology is present, too. *Everything ideological possesses semiotic value.*

V. N. VOLOSINOV (1905–60), Russian linguist. *Marxism and the Philosophy of Language*, ch. 1 (1929).

SYMPATHY

1 Strengthen me by sympathizing with my strength, not my weakness.

A. BRONSON ALCOTT (1799–1888), U.S. educator, social reformer. *Table Talk*, "Sympathy" (1877).

2 One cannot weep for the entire world, it is beyond human strength. One must choose.

JEAN ANOUILH (1910–87), French playwright. Le Chevalier, in *Cécile.*

3 The force of truth that a statement imparts, then, its prominence among the hordes of recorded observations that I may optionally apply to my own life, depends, in addition to the sense that it is argumentatively defensible, on the sense that someone like me, and someone I like, whose voice is audible and who is at least notionally in the same room with me, does or can possibly hold it to be compellingly true.

NICHOLSON BAKER (b. 1957), U.S. author. *U And I: A True Story*, ch. 4 (1991).

4 The delicate and infirm go for sympathy, not to the well and buoyant, but to those who have suffered like themselves.

CATHARINE ESTHER BEECHER (1800–1878), U.S. educator, writer. *Woman Suffrage and Women's Professions*, "Statistics of Female Health" (1871).

5 Women have no sympathy . . . and my experience of women is almost as large as Europe.

FLORENCE NIGHTINGALE (1820–1910), English nurse. Letter, 13 Dec. 1861 (published in *Forever Yours, Florence Nightingale:*

Selected Letters, ch. 3, 1989). Florence Nightingale was refuting the argument that women had been more sympathetic to her work than men.

6 Is there anything more dangerous than sympathetic understanding?

PABLO PICASSO (1881–1973), Spanish artist. Quoted in: Hélène Parmelin, *Picasso Says . . .*, "Solitude" (1966; tr. 1969).

7 The capacity to give one's attention to a sufferer is a very rare and difficult thing; it is almost a miracle; it *is* a miracle. Nearly all those who think they have this capacity do not possess it. Warmth of heart, impulsiveness, pity are not enough.

SIMONE WEIL (1909–43), French philosopher, mystic. *Waiting on God*, "Reflections on the Right Use of School Studies" (1950).

8 And whoever walks a furlong without sympathy walks to his own funeral drest in his shroud.

WALT WHITMAN (1819–92), U.S. poet. *Song of Myself*, sct. 48, in *Leaves of Grass* (1855).

9 There is something terribly morbid in the modern sympathy with pain. One should sympathise with the colour, the beauty, the joy of life. The less said about life's sores the better.

OSCAR WILDE (1854–1900), Anglo-Irish playwright, author. Lord Henry, in *The Picture of Dorian Gray*, ch. 3 (1891).

10 Sympathy with joy intensifies the sum of sympathy in the world, sympathy with pain does not really diminish the amount of pain.

OSCAR WILDE (1854–1900), Anglo-Irish playwright, author. *The Soul of Man Under Socialism*, in *Fortnightly Review* (London, Feb. 1891; repr. 1895).

See also Phelps on GRIEF; Russell on SOCIETY.

1 The type of fig leaf which each culture employs to cover its social taboos offers a twofold description of its morality. It reveals that certain unacknowledged behavior exists and it suggests the form that such behavior takes.

FREDA ADLER (b. 1934), U.S. educator, author. *Sisters in Crime*, ch. 3 (1975).

2 The old guard may grumble and occasionally sue, but in a society where *Portnoy's Complaint* is a record-breaking best-seller sexual permissiveness is no longer an issue. The real resistance now is to an art which forces its audience to recognize and accept imaginatively, in their nerve-ends, not the facts of life but the facts of death and violence: absurd, random, gratuitous, unjustified, and inescapably part of the society we have created.

A. ALVAREZ (b. 1929), British critic, poet, novelist. *The Savage God*, pt. 4, "The Savage God" (1971).

3 We find many things to which the prohibition of them constitutes the only temptation.

WILLIAM HAZLITT (1778–1830), English essayist. *Characteristics: In the Manner of Rochefoucault's Maxims*, no. 140 (1823; repr. in *The Complete Works Of William Hazlitt*, vol. 9, ed. by P. P. Howe, 1932).

4 I think the greatest taboos in America are faith and failure.

MICHAEL MALONE (b. 1942), U.S. author. *Guardian* (London, 7 July 1989).

5   Whenever a taboo is broken, something good happens, something vitalizing. . . . Taboos after all are only hangovers, the product of diseased minds, you might say, of fearsome people who hadn't the courage to live and who under the guise of morality and religion have imposed these things upon us.

> HENRY MILLER (1891–1980), U.S. author. Interview in *Writers at Work* (Second Series, ed. by George Plimpton, 1963).

6   To make our idea of morality centre on forbidden acts is to defile the imagination and to introduce into our judgements of our fellow-men a secret element of gusto.

> ROBERT LOUIS STEVENSON (1850–94), Scottish novelist, essayist, poet. *Across the Plains*, ch. 12 (1892).

See also DISGRACE; Le Guin on MENOPAUSE.

TACT

1   A soft answer turneth away wrath: but grievous words stir up anger.

> BIBLE, HEBREW. *Proverbs* 15:1.

2   It is tact that is golden, not silence.

> SAMUEL BUTLER (1835–1902), English author. *Samuel Butler's Notebooks* (1951, p. 229).

3   'Tis ill talking of halters in the house of a man that was hanged.

> MIGUEL DE CERVANTES (1547–1616), Spanish writer. Sancho Panza, in *Don Quixote*, pt. 1, bk. 3, ch. 11 (1605; tr. by P. Motteux).

4   The art of the parenthesis is one of the greatest secrets of eloquence in Society.

> SÉBASTIEN-ROCH NICOLAS DE CHAMFORT (1741–94), French writer, wit. *Maxims and Considerations*, vol. 1, no. 243 (1796; tr. 1902).

5   Tact in audacity consists in knowing how far we may go too far.

> JEAN COCTEAU (1889–1963), French author, filmmaker. *Le Rappel àL'Ordre*, "Le Coq et l'Arlequin" (1926; repr. in *Collected Works*, vol. 9, 1950).

6   Euphemisms are not, as many young people think, useless verbiage for that which can and should be said bluntly; they are like secret agents on a delicate mission, they must airily pass by a stinking mess with barely so much as a nod of the head, make their point of constructive criticism and continue on in calm forbearance. Euphemisms are unpleasant truths wearing diplomatic cologne.

> QUENTIN CRISP (b. 1908), British author. *Manners from Heaven*, ch. 5 (1984).

7   Experience was to be taken as showing that one might get a five-pound note as one got a light for a cigarette; but one had to check the friendly impulse to ask for it in the same way.

> HENRY JAMES (1843–1916), U.S. author. *The Awkward Age*, bk. 4, ch. 1 (1899).

8   Tact is after all a kind of mind reading.

> SARAH ORNE JEWETT (1849–1909), U.S. author. *The Country of the Pointed Firs and Other Stories*, ch. 10 (1896).

9   Forbear to mention what thou canst not praise.

> MATTHEW PRIOR (1664–1721), English poet, diplomat. *Carmen Seculare*.

10   So long as the laws remain such as they are today, employ some discretion: loud opinion forces us to do so; but in privacy and silence let us compensate ourselves for that cruel chastity we are obliged to display in public.

> MARQUIS DE SADE (1740–1814), French author. Mme de Saint-Ange, in *Philosophy in the Bedroom*, "Dialogue the Third" (1795).

11   'Tis not seasonable to call a man traitor, that has an army at his heels.

> JOHN SELDEN (1584–1654), English jurist, statesman. *Table Talk*, "Traitor" (1686).

12   Give thy thoughts no tongue,
Nor any unproportioned thought his act.
Be thou familiar but by no means vulgar.

> WILLIAM SHAKESPEARE (1564–1616), English dramatist, poet. Polonius, in *Hamlet*, act 1, sc. 3, giving advice to his son Laertes, departing for France. ["unproportioned." means "inappropriate."]

See also Wilde on CONVERSATION.

TALENT

1   Talent isn't genius, and no amount of energy can make it so. I want to be great, or nothing. I won't be a commonplace dauber, so I don't intend to try any more.

> LOUISA MAY ALCOTT (1832–88), U.S. author. Amy March, in *Little Women*, pt. 2, ch. 16 (1869).

2   It takes little talent to see clearly what lies under one's nose, a good deal of it to know in which direction to point that organ.

> W. H. AUDEN (1907–73), Anglo-American poet. *The Dyer's Hand*, pt. 1, "Writing" (1962).

3   There are two kinds of talent, man-made talent and God-given talent. With man-made talent you have to work very hard. With God-given talent, you just touch it up once in a while.

> PEARL BAILEY (1918–90), U.S. singer, writer, diplomat. *Newsweek* (New York, 4 Dec. 1967).

4   Whom the gods wish to destroy they first call promising.

> CYRIL CONNOLLY (1903–74), British critic. *Enemies of Promise*, pt. 2, ch. 13 (1938).

5   Ordinary people think that talent must be always on its own level and that it arises every morning like the sun, rested and refreshed, ready to draw from the same storehouse—always open, always full, always abundant—new treasures that it will heap up on those of the day before; such people are unaware that, as in the case of all mortal things, talent has its increase and decrease, and that independently of the career it takes, like everything that breathes . . . it undergoes all the accidents of health, of sickness, and of the dispositions of the soul—its gaiety or its sadness. . . . As with our perishable flesh . . . talent is obliged constantly to keep guard over itself, to combat, and to keep perpetually on the alert amid the obstacles that witness the exercise of its singular power.

EUGÈNE DELACROIX (1798–1863), French artist. Note, c. 1857 (published in Supplement to *The Journal of Eugène Delacroix*, tr. by Walter Pach, 1937).

6 If a man can write a better book, preach a better sermon, or make a better mouse-trap, than his neighbor, though he build his house in the woods, the world will make a beaten path to his door.

RALPH WALDO EMERSON (1803–82), U.S. essayist, poet, philosopher. Ascribed to Emerson by Sarah Yule in the anthology *Borrowings* (1889), later said by her to have been culled from a lecture given by Emerson in 1871. The remark's authorship was also claimed by Elbert Hubbard in *A Thousand and One Epigrams* (1911).

7 Talent is an amalgam of high sensitivity; easy vulnerability; high sensory equipment (seeing, hearing, touching, smelling, tasting—*intensely*); a vivid imagination as well as a grip on reality; the desire to communicate one's own experience and sensations, to make one's self heard and seen.

UTA HAGEN (b. 1919), U.S. actor. *Respect for Acting*, pt. 1, ch. 1 (1973).

8 We are told that talent creates its own opportunities. But it sometimes seems that intense desire creates not only its own opportunities, but its own talents.

ERIC HOFFER (1902–83), U.S. philosopher. *The Passionate State of Mind*, aph. 18 (1955).

9 If you have this enormous talent, it's got you by the balls, it's a *demon*. You can't be a family man and a husband and a caring person and *be* that animal. Dickens wan't that nice a guy.

DUSTIN HOFFMAN (b. 1937), U.S. screen actor. *Empire* (London, Aug. 1992).

10 Everyone has talent. What is rare is the courage to follow the talent to the dark place where it leads.

ERICA JONG (b. 1942), U.S. author. "The Artist as Housewife," in *The First Ms. Reader* (ed. by Francine Kragbrun, 1972).

11 The great rule: If the little bit you have is nothing special in itself, at least find a way of saying it that is a little bit special.

G. C. LICHTENBERG (1742–99), German physicist, philosopher. *Aphorisms*, "Notebook E," aph. 55 (written 1765–99; tr. by R. J. Hollingdale, 1990).

12 The American white man (not to speak of the Indian, the negro, the Mexican) hasn't a ghost of a chance. If he has any talent he's doomed to have it crushed one way or another. The American way is to seduce a man by bribery and make a prostitute of him. Or else to ignore him, starve him into submission and make a hack of him.

HENRY MILLER (1891–1980), U.S. author. *The Air-Conditioned Nightmare*, "Letter to Lafayette" (1945).

13 A man with a talent does what is expected of him, makes his way, constructs, is an engineer, a composer, a builder of bridges. It's the natural order of things that he construct objects outside himself and his family. The woman who does so is aberrant. . . . We have to *expiate* for this cursed talent someone handed out to us, by mistake, in the black mystery of genetics.

MAY SARTON (b. 1912), U.S. poet, novelist. Hilary Stevens, in *Mrs. Stevens Hears the Mermaids Singing*, pt. 2 (1965).

14 Talent is nothing but a prolonged period of attention and a shortened period of mental assimilation.

KONSTANTIN STANISLAVSKY (1863–1938), Russian theatrical director, actor, theorist. *The Art of the Stage*, "System and Methods of Creative Art," ch. 22 (1950).

15 If a man has a talent and cannot use it, he has failed. If he has a talent and uses only half of it, he has partly failed. If he has a talent and learns somehow to use the whole of it, he has gloriously succeeded, and won a satisfaction and a triumph few men ever know.

THOMAS WOLFE (1900–1938), U.S. author. *The Web and the Rock*, ch. 29 (1939).

See also Amiel, Calvino, Conan Doyle on GENIUS; Emerson on WRITERS.

TALK SHOWS

1 The failures of the press have contributed immensely to the emergence of a talk-show nation, in which public discourse is reduced to ranting and raving and posturing. We now have a mainstream press whose news agenda is increasingly influenced by this netherworld.

CARL BERNSTEIN (b. 1944), U.S. journalist. *Guardian* (London, 3 June 1992).

2 He has a nasty instinct for the exposed groin, and always puts his knee in just to stir things up.

AUSTIN MITCHELL (b. 1934), British Labour politician. *Evening Standard* (London, 2 Feb. 1989), said of fellow M.P. and talkshow host Norman Tebbit.

3 The talk shows are stuffed full of sufferers who have regained their health — congressmen who suffered through a serious spell of boozing and skirt-chasing, White House aides who were stricken cruelly with overweening ambition, movie stars and baseball players who came down with acute cases of wanting to trash hotel rooms while under the influence of recreational drugs. Most of them have found God, or at least a publisher.

CALVIN TRILLIN (b. 1935), U.S. journalist, author. "Diseases of the Mighty," *Nation* (New York, 19 Oct. 1985).

TALKATIVENESS

1 The habit of common and continuous speech is a symptom of mental deficiency. It proceeds from not knowing what is going on in other people's minds.

WALTER BAGEHOT (1826–77), English economist, critic. "Hartley Coleridge" (1852; repr. in *Literary Studies*, vol. 1, 1878).

2 I prefer tongue-tied knowledge to ignorant loquacity.

CICERO (106–43 B.C.), Roman orator, philosopher. *De Oratore*, bk. 3, sct. 142 (55 B.C.).

3 Blessed is the man who, having nothing to say, abstains from giving us wordy evidence of the fact.

GEORGE ELIOT (1819–80), English novelist. *Impressions of Theophrastus Such*, ch. 4 (1879).

4 Well, well, perhaps I am a bit of a talker. A popular fellow such as I am—my friends get round me—we chaff, we sparkle, we tell witty stories—and somehow my tongue gets wagging. I have the gift of conversation. I've been told I ought to have a *salon*, whatever that may be.

KENNETH GRAHAME (1859–1932), British essayist, writer of children's books. Toad, in *The Wind in the Willows*, ch. 11 (1908).

5 We never say so much as when we do not quite know what we want to say. We need few words when we have something to say, but all the words in all the dictionaries will not suffice when we have nothing to say and want desperately to say it.

ERIC HOFFER (1902–83), U.S. philosopher. *Reflections on the Human Condition*, aph. 173 (1973).

6 How ironical that it is by means of speech that man can degrade himself below the level of dumb creation—for a chatterbox is truly of a lower category than a dumb creature.

SØREN KIERKEGAARD (1813–55), Danish philosopher. *The Last Years: Journals 1853–55* (ed. and tr. by Ronald G. Smith, 1965).

7 My great-grandfather used to say to his wife, my great-grandmother, who in turn told her daughter, my grandmother, who repeated it to her daughter, my mother, who used to remind her daughter, my own sister, that to talk well and eloquently was a very great art, but that an equally great one was to know the right moment to stop.

WOLFGANG AMADEUS MOZART (1756–91), Austrian composer. Letter, 4 Nov. 1787 (published in *The Letters of Mozart and His Family*, 2nd ed., ed. by Emily Anderson, 1966).

8 They never taste who always drink;
They always talk who never think.

MATTHEW PRIOR (1664–1721), English poet, diplomat. *Upon This Passage in Scaligerana*.

9 To talk without thinking is to shoot without aiming.

ENGLISH PROVERB (18th-century).

10 A good old man, sir. He will be talking. As they say, when the age is in, the wit is out.

WILLIAM SHAKESPEARE (1564–1616), English dramatist, poet. Dogberry, in *Much Ado about Nothing*, act 3, sc. 5.

11 I like to do all the talking myself. It saves time, and prevents arguments.

OSCAR WILDE (1854–1900), Anglo-Irish playwright, author. The Frog, in "The Remarkable Rocket," in *The Happy Prince and Other Tales* (1888).

see also LONG-WINDEDNESS.

TASTE

1 What is exhilarating in bad taste is the aristocratic pleasure of giving offense.

CHARLES BAUDELAIRE (1821–67), French poet. *Squibs*, in *Intimate Journals*, sct. 18 (1887; tr. by Christopher Isherwood, 1930; rev. by Don Bachardy, 1989).

2 Everyone has taste, yet it is more of a taboo subject than sex or money. The reason for this is simple: claims about your attitudes to or achievements in the carnal and financial arenas can be disputed only by your lover and your financial advisers, whereas by making statements about your taste you expose body and soul to terrible scrutiny. Taste is a merciless betrayer of social and cultural attitudes. Thus, while anybody will tell you as much (and perhaps more than) you want to know about their triumphs in bed and at the bank, it is taste that gets people's nerves tingling.

STEPHEN BAYLEY (b. 1951), British design critic. *Taste*, pt. 1, "Taste: The Story of an Idea" (1991).

3 Taste is more to do with manners than *appearances*. Taste is both myth and reality; it is not a style.

STEPHEN BAYLEY (b. 1951), British design critic. *Taste*, pt. 1, "Taste: The Story of an Idea" (1991).

4 Lovers of painting and lovers of music are people who openly display their preference like a delectable ailment that isolates them and makes them proud.

MAURICE BLANCHOT (b. 1907), French literary theorist, author. "Reading," in *The Space of Literature* (1955; repr. in *The Gaze of Orpheus, and Other Literary Essays*, ed. by P. Adams Sitney, 1981).

5 People care more about being thought to have taste than about being thought either good, clever or amiable.

SAMUEL BUTLER (1835–1902), English author. *Samuel Butler's Notebooks* (1951).

6 The aim of life is appreciation; there is no sense in not appreciating things; and there is no sense in having more of them if you have less appreciation of them.

G. K. CHESTERTON (1874–1936), British author. *Autobiography*, ch. 11 (1936).

7 No taste is so acquired as that for someone else's quality of mind.

CYRIL CONNOLLY (1903–74), British critic. David Pryce-Jones, *Journal and Memoir*, "The Journal of Cyril Connolly 1928–1937" (1983, p.230).

8 A man is known by the books he reads, by the company he keeps, by the praise he gives, by his dress, by his tastes, by his distastes, by the stories he tells, by his gait, by the notion of his eye, by the look of his house, of his chamber; for nothing on earth is solitary but every thing hath affinities infinite.

RALPH WALDO EMERSON (1803–82), U.S. essayist, poet, philosopher. *Journals* (1909–14), entry for 24 June 1830

9 Every orientation presupposes a disorientation.

HANS MAGNUS ENZENSBERGER (b. 1929), German poet, critic. "Topological Studies in Modern Literature," in *Sur* (Buenos Aires, May–June 1966).

10 I love everything that's old: old friends, old times, old manners, old books, old wines; and, I believe, Dorothy, you'll own I have been pretty fond of an old wife.

OLIVER GOLDSMITH (1728–74), Anglo-Irish author, poet, playwright. Hardcastle, in *She Stoops to Conquer*, act 1, sc. 1.

11 One of the surest evidences of an elevated taste is the power of enjoying works of impassioned terrorism, in poetry, and painting. The man who can look at impassioned subjects of terror with a feeling of exultation may be certain he has an elevated taste.

BENJAMIN HAYDON (1786–1846), British artist. Table Talk", in

Correspondence and Table-Talk, vol. 2 (ed. by Frederic Wordsworth Haydon, 1876).

12 Taste is nothing but an enlarged capacity for receiving pleasure from works of imagination.

WILLIAM HAZLITT (1778–1830), English essayist. *Sketches and Essays*, "On Taste" (1839).

13 It is conventional to call "monster" any blending of dissonant elements. . . . I call "monster" every original inexhaustible beauty.

ALFRED JARRY (1873–1907), French playwright, author. *L'Ymagier* (Paris, 1894; repr. in Roger Shattuck, *The Banquet Years*, ch. 8, 1958).

14 Between good sense and good taste there lies the difference between a cause and its effect.

JEAN DE LA BRUYèRE (1645–96), French writer, moralist. *Characters*, "Of Opinions," aph. 56 (1688).

15 Taste is the fundamental quality which sums up all the other qualities. It is the *nec plus ultra* of the intelligence. Through this alone is genius the supreme health and balance of all the faculties.

ISIDORE DUCASSE, COMTE DE LAUTRÉAMONT (1846–70), French author, poet. *Poésies*, ch. 1 (1870).

16 I cannot cure myself of that most woeful of youth's follies—thinking that those who care about us will care for the things that mean much to us.

D. H. LAWRENCE (1885–1930), British author. Letter, 4 May 1908 (published in *The Letters of D. H. Lawrence*, vol. 1, ed. by James T. Boulton, 1979).

17 I wish you all manner of prosperity, with a little more taste.

ALAIN-RENÉ LE SAGE (1668–1747), French playwright, novelist. *The Archbishop of Grenada*, in *The Adventures of Gil Blas*, bk. 7, ch. 4 (1715–35), on dismissing Gil Blas, who had incurred the Archbishop's disfavor by criticizing one of his sermons.

18 Good taste is either that which agrees with my taste or that which subjects itself to the rule of reason. From this we can see how useful it is to employ reason in seeking out the laws of taste.

G. C. LICHTENBERG (1742–99), German physicist, philosopher. *Aphorisms*, "Notebook E," aph. 69 (written 1765–99; tr. by R. J. Hollingdale, 1990).

19 Errors of taste are very often the outward sign of a deep fault of sensibility.

JONATHAN MILLER (b. 1936), British doctor, humorist, director. *Guardian* (London, 21 May 1992).

20 Taste is tiring like good company.

FRANCIS PICABIA (1878–1953), French painter, poet. *Écrits*, vol. 2 (ed. by Olivier Revault d'Allones and Dominique Bouissou, 1978; repr. in *Yes No: Poems and Sayings*, "Sayings," ed. by Rémy Hall, 1990).

21 Ah, good taste! What a dreadful thing! Taste is the enemy of creativeness.

PABLO PICASSO (1881–1973), Spanish artist. *Quote* (Anderson, S.C., 24 March 1957).

22 For a long time I . . . found the celebrities of modern painting and poetry ridiculous. I loved absurd pictures, fanlights, stage scenery, mountebanks' backcloths, inn-signs, cheap colored prints; unfashionable literature, church Latin, pornographic books badly spelt, grandmothers' novels, fairy stories, little books for children, old operas, empty refrains, simple rhythms.

ARTHUR RIMBAUD (1854–91), French poet. *Une Saison en Enfer*, "Délires II: Alchimie du Verbe" (1874).

23 A man of great common sense and good taste—meaning thereby a man without originality or moral courage.

GEORGE BERNARD SHAW (1856–1950), Anglo-Irish playwright, critic. *Caesar and Cleopatra*, "Notes: Julius Caesar" (1906).

24 The discovery of the good taste of bad taste can be very liberating. The man who insists on high and serious pleasures is depriving himself of pleasure; he continually restricts what he can enjoy; in the constant exercise of his good taste he will eventually price himself out of the market, so to speak. Here Camp taste supervenes upon good taste as a daring and witty hedonism. It makes the man of good taste cheerful, where before he ran the risk of being chronically frustrated. It is good for the digestion.

SUSAN SONTAG (b. 1933), U.S. essayist. *Against Interpretation* "Notes on 'Camp'," Note 54 (1964; repr. 1966).

25 The hard truth is that what may be acceptable in elite culture may not be acceptable in mass culture, that tastes which pose only innocent ethical issues as the property of a minority become corrupting when they become more established. Taste is context, and the context has changed.

SUSAN SONTAG (b. 1933), U.S. essayist. *Under the Sign of Saturn*, "Fascinating Fascism" (1980; first published 1974), on the fashion for "fascist art."

26 I think "taste" is a social concept and not an artistic one. I'm willing to show good taste, if I can, in somebody else's living room, but our reading life is too short for a writer to be in any way polite. Since his words enter into another's brain in silence and intimacy, he should be as honest and explicit as we are with ourselves.

JOHN UPDIKE (b. 1932), U.S. author, critic. Interview in *New York Times Book Review* (10 April 1977; repr. in *Hugging the Shore*, Appendix, 1984).

27 Absolute catholicity of taste is not without its dangers. It is only an auctioneer who should admire all schools of art.

OSCAR WILDE (1854–1900), Anglo-Irish playwright, author. *Pall Mall Gazette* (London, 8 Feb. 1886).

See also Yeats on DESIGN; KITSCH.

TAXATION

1 To tax and to please, no more than to love and to be wise, is not given to men.

EDMUND BURKE (1729–97), Irish philosopher, statesman. "First Speech on Conciliation with America: American Taxation," 19 April 1774.

2 Nothing is so well calculated to produce a death-like torpor in the country as an extended system of taxation and a great national debt.

> WILLIAM COBBETT (1762–1835), English journalist, reformer. Letter, 10 Feb. 1804.

3 We don't pay taxes. Only the little people pay taxes.

> LEONA HELMSLEY (b. 1920), U.S. businesswoman. Quoted by Helmsley's former housekeeper during her trial for tax evasion, in *New York Times* (12 July 1989). In March 1992, Leona Helmsley was sentenced to four years' imprisonment.

4 Our tax law is a 1,598-page hydra-headed monster and I'm going to attack and attack and attack until I have ironed out every fault in it.

> VIVIEN KELLEMS (1896–1975), U.S. industrialist, lecturer. Quoted in: *Los Angeles Times* (26 Jan. 1975).

5 Civil servants and priests, soldiers and ballet-dancers, schoolmasters and police constables, Greek museums and Gothic steeples, civil list and services list—the common seed within which all these fabulous beings slumber in embryo is taxation.

> KARL MARX (1818–83), German political theorist, social philosopher. *Moralizing Criticism and Critical Morality* (1847; repr. in *Karl Marx and Friedrich Engels: Collected Works*, vol. 6, 1976).

6 All money nowadays seems to be produced with a natural homing instinct for the Treasury.

> PRINCE PHILIP, DUKE OF EDINBURGH (b. 1921). Quoted in: Observer (London, 26 May 1963).

7 A government which robs Peter to pay Paul can always depend on the support of Paul.

> GEORGE BERNARD SHAW (1856–1950), Anglo-Irish playwright, critic. *Everybody's Political What's What*, ch. 30 (1944).

8 I have with me two gods, Persuasion and Compulsion.

> THEMISTOCLES (c. 528–462 B. C.), Athenian statesman. On demanding tribute from the people of Andros; the historian Herodotus described it thus in his *Histories*, bk. 8: "He had put it to them that they would be unable to avoid paying, because the Athenians had the support of two powerful deities, one called Persuasion and the other Compulsion, and the Andrians replied that Athens was lucky to have two such useful gods, who were obviously responsible for her wealth and greatness; unfortunately, however, they themselves, in their small and inadequate land, had two utterly useless deities, who refused to leave the island . . . and their names were Poverty and Inability. With the support of these, no money would be forthcoming." (tr. by Aubrey de Sélincourt).

9 If a thousand men were not to pay their tax-bills this year, that would not be a violent and bloody measure, as it would be to pay them, and enable the State to commit violence and shed innocent blood. This is, in fact, the definition of a peaceable revolution, if any such is possible.

> HENRY DAVID THOREAU (1817–62), U.S. philosopher, author, naturalist. *On the Duty of Civil Disobedience* (1849). Thoreau by his account paid no poll tax for six years, for which he spent a night in jail in the summer of 1846, a gesture against the Mexican War declared that year.

10 In other words, a democratic government is the only one in which those who vote for a tax can escape the obligation to pay it.

> ALEXIS DE TOCQUEVILLE (1805–59), French social philosopher. *Democracy in America*, vol. 1, pt. 2, ch. 5 (1840).

11 I know all those people. I have friendly, social, and criminal relations with the whole lot of them.

> MARK TWAIN (1835–1910), U.S. author. "Taxes and Morals," speech, 22 Jan. 1906, Carnegie Hall, New York City (published in *Complete Essays of Mark Twain*, ed. by Charles Neider, 1963), on tax evaders.

12 In general, the art of government consists in taking as much money as possible from one party of the citizens to give to the other.

> VOLTAIRE (1694–1778), French philosopher, author. *Dictionnaire Philosophique*, "Money" (1764).

See also Franklin on CERTAINTY; Nash on The SEASONS; Dickens on TRUTH.

TEA

1 Is there no Latin word for Tea? Upon my soul, if I had known that I would have let the vulgar stuff alone.

> HILAIRE BELLOC (1870–1953), British author. *On Nothing*, "On Tea" (1908).

2 Tea! Thou soft, thou sober, sage, and venerable liquid, thou innocent pretence for bringing the wicked of both sexes together in a morning; thou female tongue-running, smile-smoothing, heart-opening, wink-tipping cordial, to whose glorious insipidity I owe the happiest moment of my life, let me fall prostrate thus, and . . . adore thee.

> COLLEY CIBBER (1671–1757), English actor-manager, playwright. Lord George, in *The Lady's Last Stake*, act 1, sc. 1 Lord George's "happiest moment" was sipping tea in the company of Lady Gentle.

3 Tea, though ridiculed by those who are naturally coarse in their nervous sensibilities . . . will always be the favourite beverage of the intellectual.

> THOMAS DE QUINCEY (1785–1859), English author. *Confessions of an English Opium-Eater*, "The Pleasures of Opium" (1822).

4 Love and scandal are the best sweeteners of tea.

> HENRY FIELDING (1707–54), English novelist, dramatist. Lady Matchless, in *Love in Several Masques*, act 4, sc. 11.

5 Under certain circumstances there are few hours in life more agreeable than the hour dedicated to the ceremony known as afternoon tea.

> HENRY JAMES (1843–1916), U.S. author. Opening words of *The Portrait of a Lady* (1881).

6 Its proper use is to amuse the idle, and relax the studious, and dilute the full meals of those who cannot use exercise, and will not use abstinence.

> SAMUEL JOHNSON (1709–84), English author, lexicographer. "Review of A Journal of Eight Days' Journey," in *Literary Magazine*, vol. 2, no. 13 (London, 1757; repr. in *Works*, vol. 6, 1825). Nonetheless, Johnson confessed in the article to being "a hardened and shameless tea-drinker, who has, for twenty years, diluted his meals with only the infusion of this fascinating plant; whose kettle has scarcely time to cool; who with tea amuses the evening, with tea solaces the midnight, and, with tea, welcomes the morning." James Boswell vouched for this passion in his *Life of Samuel Johnson*: "I suppose no person ever enjoyed with more relish the infusion of that fragrant leaf than Johnson" (entry for 1756).

7 The best quality tea must have creases like the

leathern boot of Tartar horsemen, curl like the dewlap of a mighty bullock, unfold like a mist rising out of a ravine, gleam like a lake touched by a zephyr, and be wet and soft like a fine earth newly swept by rain.

LU YU (d. 804), Chinese sage, hermit. Quoted in: Jason Goodwin, *The Gunpowder Gardens,* Introduction (1990), from the *Cha Ching.*

8 The trouble with tea is that originally it was quite a good drink. So a group of the most eminent British scientists put their heads together, and made complicated biological experiments to find a way of spoiling it. To the eternal glory of British science their labour bore fruit.

GEORGE MIKES (b. 1912), Hungarian-born British humorist. *How To Be An Alien,* ch. 1, sct. 5 (1946).

9 Our trouble is that we drink too much tea. I see in this the slow revenge of the Orient, which has diverted the Yellow River down our throats.

J. B. PRIESTLEY (1894–1984), British author. Quoted in: *Observer* (London, 15 May 1949).

10 It has been well said that tea is suggestive of a thousand wants, from which spring the decencies and luxuries of civilization.

AGNES REPPLIER (1858–1950), U.S. author, social critic. *To Think of Tea!* ch. 2 (1932).

See also Holmes on COFFEE.

TEACHERS

1 A teacher affects eternity; he can never tell where his influence stops.

HENRY B. ADAMS (1838–1918), U.S. historian. *The Education of Henry Adams,* ch. 20 (1907).

2 The true teacher defends his pupils against his own personal influence. He inspires self-distrust. He guides their eyes from himself to the spirit that quickens him. He will have no disciple.

A. BRONSON ALCOTT (1799–1888), U.S. educator, social reformer. *Orphic Sayings,* "The Teacher" (1840).

3 To know how to suggest is the great art of teaching. To attain it we must be able to guess what will interest; we must learn to read the childish soul as we might a piece of music. Then, by simply changing the key, we keep up the attraction and vary the song.

HENRI-FRÉDÉRIC AMIEL (1821–81), Swiss philosopher, poet. *Journal Intime* (1882; tr. by Mrs. Humphry Ward, 1892), entry for 16 Nov. 1864.

4 My object will be, if possible, to form Christian men, for Christian boys I can scarcely hope to make.

THOMAS ARNOLD (1795–1842), English educator, scholar. Letter, 2 March 1828 (published in *The Life and Correspondence of Thomas Arnold, D.D.,* vol. 1, 1845), on appointment as headmaster of Rugby School.

5 A schoolmaster should have an atmosphere of awe, and walk wonderingly, as if he was amazed at being himself.

WALTER BAGEHOT (1826–77), English economist, critic. "Hartley Coleridge" (1852; repr. in *Literary Studies,* vol. 1, 1878).

6 Teaching is not a lost art, but the regard for it is a lost tradition.

JACQUES BARZUN (b. 1907), U.S. scholar. *Newsweek* (New York, 5 Dec. 1955).

7 The schoolmaster is abroad! And I trust to him armed with his primer against the soldier in full military array.

JEREMY BENTHAM (1748–1832), English philosopher, political theorist, jurist. Speech, 29 Jan. 1828, to House of Commons, on educational reform.

8 Life is amazing: and the teacher had better prepare himself to be a medium for that amazement.

EDWARD BLISHEN (b. 1920), British author. *Donkey Work,* pt. 2, ch. 5 (1983).

9 There is no real teacher who in practise does not believe in the existence of the soul, or in a magic that acts on it through speech.

ALLAN BLOOM (1930–92), U.S. educator, author. *The Closing of the American Mind,* Preface (1987).

10 The world of knowledge takes a crazy turn
When teachers themselves are taught to learn.

BERTOLT BRECHT (1898–1956), German dramatist, poet. *The Life of Galileo,* sc. 6 (tr. by Howard Brenton, 1980).

11 Housework is a breeze. Cooking is a pleasant diversion. Putting up a retaining wall is a lark. But teaching is like climbing a mountain.

FAWN M. BRODIE (1915–81), U.S. biographer. Quoted in: *Los Angeles Times Home Magazine* (20 Feb. 1977).

12 Arrogance, pedantry, and dogmatism . . . the occupational diseases of those who spend their lives directing the intellects of the young.

HENRY S. CANBY (1878–1961), U.S. author, editor. *Alma Mater,* ch. 5 (1936).

13 Once more I would adopt the graver style—
A teacher should be sparing of his smile.

WILLIAM COWPER (1731–1800), English poet. *Charity* (written 1781, published 1782).

14 It is the supreme art of the teacher to awaken joy in creative expression and knowledge.

ALBERT EINSTEIN (1879–1955), German-born U.S. physicist. Motto for the astronomy building of Junior College, Pasadena, California.

15 We love the precepts for the teacher's sake.

GEORGE FARQUHAR (1678–1707), Irish dramatist. Sir Harry Wildair, in *The Constant Couple,* act 5, sc. 3

16 Well had the boding tremblers learned to trace
The day's disasters in his morning face.

OLIVER GOLDSMITH (1728–74), Anglo-Irish author, poet, playwright. *The Deserted Village,* of the village schoolmaster.

17 I swear . . . to hold my teacher in this art equal to my own parents; to make him partner in my livelihood; when he is in need of money to share mine with him; to consider his family as my own brothers and to teach them this art, if they want to learn it, without fee or indenture.

HIPPOCRATES (c. 460–c. 370 B.C.), Greek physician. *The Hippocratic Oath.*

18 One looks back with appreciation to the brilliant teachers, but with gratitude to those who touched our human feelings. The curriculum is so much necessary raw material, but warmth is the vital element for the growing plant and for the soul of the child.

> CARL JUNG (1875–1961), Swiss psychiatrist. *The Gifted Child* (1943; repr. in *Collected Works*, vol. 17, para. 249, ed. by William McGuire, 1954).

19 Why are we never quite at ease in the presence of a schoolmaster? Because we are conscious that he is not quite at his ease in ours. He is awkward, and out of place in the society of his equals. He comes like Gulliver from among his little people, and he cannot fit the stature of his understanding to yours.

> CHARLES LAMB (1775–1834), English essayist, critic. *Essays of Elia*, "The Old and the New Schoolmaster" (1820–23). Of the schoolmaster, Lamb wrote: "He can receive no pleasure from a casual glimpse of Nature, but must catch at it as an object of instruction. . . . The Universe—that Great Book, as it has been called—is to him, indeed, to all intents and purposes, a book out of which he is doomed to read tedious homilies to distasting schoolboys."

20 A schoolteacher or professor cannot educate individuals, he educates only species.

> G. C. LICHTENBERG (1742–99), German physicist, philosopher. *Aphorisms*, "Notebook J," aph. 10 (written 1765–99; tr. by R. J. Hollingdale, 1990).

21 What office is there which involves more responsibility, which requires more qualifications, and which ought, therefore, to be more honourable, than that of teaching?

> HARRIET MARTINEAU (1802–76), English writer, social critic. *Society in America*, vol. 3, "Occupation" (1837).

22 The truth is that the average schoolmaster, on all the lower levels, is and always must be essentially and next door to an idiot, for how can one imagine an intelligent man engaging in so puerile an avocation?

> H. L. MENCKEN (1880–1956), U.S. journalist. The Educational Process," in *New York Evening Mail* (23 Jan. 1918; repr. in *Prejudices*, Third Series, 1922).

23 The teacher must derive not only the capacity, but the desire, to observe natural phenomena. In our system, she must become a passive, much more than an active, influence, and her passivity shall be composed of anxious scientific curiosity and of absolute *respect* for the phenomenon which she wishes to observe. The teacher must understand and *feel* her position of observer: the *activity* must lie in the *phenomenon*.

> MARIA MONTESSORI (1870–1952), Italian educationist. *The Montessori Method*, ch. 5 (1912). On the importance of observation for the teacher, Montessori continued: "The observation of the way in which the children pass from the first disordered movements to those which are *spontaneous and ordered*—this is the book of the teacher; this is the book which must inspire her actions; it is the only one in which she must read and study if she is to become a real educator."

24 We teachers can only help the work going on, as servants wait upon a master.

> MARIA MONTESSORI (1870–1952), Italian educationist. *The Absorbent Mind*, ch. 1 (1949).

25 He who wishes to teach us a truth should not tell it to us, but simply suggest it with a brief gesture, a gesture which starts an ideal trajectory in the air along which we glide until we find ourselves at the feet of the new truth.

> JOSÉ ORTEGA Y GASSET (1883–1955), Spanish essayist, philosopher. *Meditations on Quixote*, "Preliminary Meditation" (1914).

26 No bubble is so iridescent or floats longer than that blown by the successful teacher.

> SIR WILLIAM OSLER (1849–1919), Canadian physician. Address, 4 Oct. 1911, Glasgow (quoted in: Harvey Cushing, *Life of Sir William Osler*, vol. 2, ch. 31, 1925).

27 You must train the children to their studies in a playful manner, and without any air of constraint, with the further object of discerning more readily the natural bent of their respective characters.

> PLATO (c. 427–347 B.C.), Greek philosopher. Socrates, in *The Republic*, bk. 7, sct. 537.

28 I have trailed the pike of composition work and directed the small-sword play of debate. I have carried the musket on the long historical trail from Beowulf to Browning, and now, after many years of happy duty in the pleasant Elizabethan country, I am still serving, with such effect as may be, the big guns of Shakespeare.

> FELIX E. SCHELLING (1858–1945), U.S. educator. *Pedagogically Speaking*, ch. 8 (1929).

29 He who can, does. He who cannot, teaches.

> GEORGE BERNARD SHAW (1856–1950), Anglo-Irish playwright, critic. *Man and Superman*, "Maxims for Revolutionists: Education" (1903).

30 Give me a girl at an impressionable age, and she is mine for life!

> MURIEL SPARK (b. 1918), British novelist. Miss Brodie, in *The Prime of Miss Jean Brodie*, ch. 1 (1961).

31 A teacher should have maximal authority, and minimal power.

> THOMAS SZASZ (b. 1920), U.S. psychiatrist. *The Second Sin*, "Education" (1973).

32 We schoolmasters must temper discretion with deceit.

> EVELYN WAUGH (1903–66), British novelist. Dr. Fagan, in *Decline and Fall*, pt. 1, ch. 2 (1928).

33 Everybody who is incapable of learning has taken to teaching.

> OSCAR WILDE (1854–1900), Anglo-Irish playwright, author. Vivian, in "The Decay of Lying" (published in *Intentions*, 1891).

See also EDUCATION; Trollope on PUNISHMENT, CORPORAL; SCHOOL; STUDENTS.

TECHNIQUE

1 Technique is communication: the two words are synonymous in conductors.

> LEONARD BERNSTEIN (1918–90), U.S. composer, conductor. *Times* (London, 27 June 1989).

2 The moment a man begins to talk about technique that's proof that he is fresh out of ideas.

> RAYMOND CHANDLER (1888–1959), U.S. author. Letter, 5

May 1939, to crime novelist Erle Stanley Gardner (published in *Raymond Chandler Speaking*, 1962).

3   The more technique you have, the less you have to worry about it. The more technique there is, the less there is.

PABLO PICASSO (1881–1973), Spanish artist. Quoted in: Hélène Parmelin, *Picasso Plain*, ch. 4 (published in France, 1959; repr. 1963). Picasso described himself as "a painter without style," explaining: "Style is often something which locks the painter into the same vision, the same technique, the same formula during years and years, sometimes during one's whole lifetime." (quoted in: prefatory text to exhibition catalog, Geneva, 1963).

4   Technique is the test of sincerity. If a thing isn't worth getting the technique to say, it is of inferior value.

EZRA POUND (1885–1972), U.S. poet, critic. Interview in *Writers at Work* (Second Series, ed. by George Plimpton, 1963).

5   Technique is noticed most markedly in the case of those who have not mastered it.

LEON TROTSKY (1879–1940), Russian revolutionary. *Literature and Revolution*, ch. 6 (1924), referring to the "breathless literary schools that followed the revolution."

6   Technique is really personality. That is the reason why the artist cannot teach it, why the pupil cannot learn it, and why the aesthetic critic can understand it. To the great poet, there is only one method of music—his own. To the great painter, there is only one manner of painting—that which he himself employs. The aesthetic critic, and the aesthetic critic alone, can appreciate all forms and all modes. It is to him that Art makes her appeal.

OSCAR WILDE (1854–1900), Anglo-Irish playwright, author. Gilbert, in *The Critic as Artist*, pt. 2 (published in *Intentions*, 1891).

TECHNOLOGY

1   Science and technology multiply around us. To an increasing extent they dictate the languages in which we speak and think. Either we use those languages, or we remain mute.

J. G. BALLARD (b. 1930), English novelist. Introduction, 1974, to the French edition of *Crash* (1973).

2   When we can drain the Ocean into mill-ponds, and bottle up the Force of Gravity, to be sold by retail, in gas jars; then may we hope to comprehend the infinitudes of man's soul under formulas of Profit and Loss; and rule over this too, as over a patent engine, by checks, and valves, and balances.

THOMAS CARLYLE (1795–1881), Scottish essayist, historian. *Signs of the Times* (1829; first published in *Edinburgh Review* no. 98).

3   We are always talking about being together, and yet whatever we invent destroys the family, and makes us wild, touchless beasts feeding on technicolor prairies and rivers.

EDWARD DAHLBERG (1900–1977), U.S. author, critic. *Alms for Oblivion*, "No Love and No Thanks" (1964).

4   If we had a reliable way to label our toys good and bad, it would be easy to regulate technology wisely. But we can rarely see far enough ahead to know which road leads to damnation. Whoever concerns himself with big technology, either to push it forward or to stop it, is gambling in human lives.

FREEMAN DYSON (b. 1923), British-born U.S. physicist, author. *Disturbing the Universe*, pt. 1, ch. 1 (1979).

5   Technology . . . the knack of so arranging the world that we don't have to experience it.

MAX FRISCH (b. 1911), Swiss author, architect. Hanna, in *Homo Faber*, "Second Stop" (1957; tr. 1959).

6   I claim that in losing the spinning wheel we lost our left lung. We are, therefore, suffering from galloping consumption. The restoration of the wheel arrests the progress of the fell disease.

MOHANDAS K. GANDHI (1869–1948), Indian political and spiritual leader. "Young India," speech, 13 Oct. 1921.

7   If there is technological advance without social advance, there is, almost automatically, an increase in human misery, in impoverishment.

MICHAEL HARRINGTON (1928–89), U.S. social scientist, author. *The Other America*, Appendix, sct. 1 (1962).

8   Where there is the necessary technical skill to move mountains, there is no need for the faith that moves mountains.

ERIC HOFFER (1902–83), U.S. philosopher. *The Passionate State of Mind*, aph. 12 (1955).

9   From coupler-flange to spindle-guide I see Thy
      Hand, O God—
    Predestination in the stride o' yon connectin'-rod.

RUDYARD KIPLING (1865–1936), British author, poet. *McAndrew's Hymn*.

10   Space-ships and time machines are no escape from the human condition. Let Othello subject Desdemona to a lie-detector test; his jealousy will still blind him to the evidence. Let Oedipus triumph over gravity; he won't triumph over his fate.

ARTHUR KOESTLER (1905–83), Hungarian-born British author. *The Trail of the Dinosaur*, pt. 2, "The Boredom of Fantasy" (1955; first published 1953).

11   Persons grouped around a fire or candle for warmth or light are less able to pursue independent thoughts, or even tasks, than people supplied with electric light. In the same way, the social and educational patterns latent in automation are those of self-employment and artistic autonomy.

MARSHALL MCLUHAN (1911–80), Canadian communications theorist. *Understanding Media*, ch. 33 (1964).

12   However far modern science and technics have fallen short of their inherent possibilities, they have taught mankind at least one lesson: Nothing is impossible.

LEWIS MUMFORD (1895–1990), U.S. social philosopher. *Technics and Civilization*, ch. 8, sct. 13 (1934).

13   By his very success in inventing labor-saving devices, modern man has manufactured an abyss of boredom that only the privileged classes in earlier civilizations have ever fathomed.

LEWIS MUMFORD (1895–1990), U.S. social philosopher. *The Conduct of Life*, "The Challenge of Renewal" (1951).

14   The press, the machine, the railway, the telegraph are premises whose thousand-year conclusion no one has yet dared to draw.

> FRIEDRICH NIETZSCHE (1844–1900), German philosopher. *The Wanderer and His Shadow*, aph. 278 (1880).

15   When you see something that is technically sweet, you go ahead and do it and you argue about what to do about it only after you have had your technical success. That is the way it was with the atomic bomb.

> J. ROBERT OPPENHEIMER (1904–67), U.S. physicist. *In the Matter of J. Robert Oppenheimer, USAEC Transcript of Hearing Before Personnel Security Board* (1954, p. 81), said during hearings investigating allegations of past communist associations in connection with his involvement in the Los Alamos project to develop the atomic bomb.

16   Men are only as good as their technical development allows them to be.

> GEORGE ORWELL (1903–50), British author. *Inside the Whale and Other Essays*, "Charles Dickens" (1940).

17   Technology is not an image of the world but a way of operating on reality. The nihilism of technology lies not only in the fact that it is the most perfect expression of the will to power . . . but also in the fact that it lacks meaning.

> OCTAVIO PAZ (b. 1914), Mexican poet. *Alternating Current*, "The Channel and the Signs" (1967).

18   The Church welcomes technological progress and receives it with love, for it is an indubitable fact that technological progress comes from God and, therefore, can and must lead to Him.

> PIUS XII [EUGENIO PACELLI] (1876–1958), Italian ecclesiastic, pope. Christmas message, 1953.

19   There are three roads to ruin; women, gambling and technicians. The most pleasant is with women, the quickest is with gambling, but the surest is with technicians.

> GEORGES POMPIDOU (1911–74), French president. Quoted in: *Sunday Telegraph* (London, 26 May 1968).

20   In health of mind and body, men should see with their own eyes, hear and speak without trumpets, walk on their feet, not on wheels, and work and war with their arms, not with engine-beams, nor rifles warranted to kill twenty men at a shot before you can see them.

> JOHN RUSKIN (1819–1900), English art critic, author. *Praeterita*, vol. 2, sct. 200 (1855–59). Quoted in: *Ruskin Today*, sct. 65, ed. by Kenneth Clark, 1964).

21   I have no doubt that it is possible to give a new direction to technological development, a direction that shall lead it back to the real needs of man, and that also means: *to the actual size of man.* Man is small, and, therefore, small is beautiful. To go for giantism is to go for self-destruction.

> E. F. SCHUMACHER (1911–77), German-born British economist. *Small is Beautiful*, pt. 2, ch. 10 (1973).

22   Our inventions are wont to be pretty toys, which distract our attention from serious things. They are but improved means to an unimproved end.

> HENRY DAVID THOREAU (1817–62), U.S. philosopher, author, naturalist. *Walden*, "Economy" (1854).

See also Fischer on MACHINERY; SCIENCE; TOOLS; Gallo on SOCIALISM.

TEETH

1   Americans may have no identity, but they do have wonderful teeth.

> JEAN BAUDRILLARD (b. 1929), French semiologist. *America*, "Astral America" (1986; tr. 1988).

2   I had very good dentures once. Some magnificent gold work. It's the only form of jewelry a man can wear that women fully appreciate.

> GRAHAM GREENE (1904–91), British novelist. Mr. Visconti, in *Travels With My Aunt*, pt. 2, ch. 7 (1969).

3   The best of friends fall out, and so
> His teeth had done some years ago.

> THOMAS HOOD (1799–1845), English poet. *A True Story*.

See also Roux on CRYING; Byron on The DEAD; Russell on SCIENCE.

TELEVISION

1   There is nothing more mysterious than a TV set left on in an empty room. It is even stranger than a man talking to himself or a woman standing dreaming at her stove. It is as if another planet is communicating with you.

> JEAN BAUDRILLARD (b. 1929), French semiologist. *America*, "Astral America" (1986; tr. 1988).

2   Television knows no night. It is perpetual day. TV embodies our fear of the dark, of night, of the other side of things.

> JEAN BAUDRILLARD (b. 1929), French semiologist. *Cool Memories*, ch. 4 (1987; tr. 1990).

3   Sometimes, because of its immediacy, television produces a kind of electronic parable. Berlin, for instance, on the day the Wall was opened. Rostropovich was playing his cello by the Wall that no longer cast a shadow, and a million East Berliners were thronging to the West to shop with an allowance given them by West German banks! At that moment the whole world saw how materialism had lost its awesome historic power and become a shopping list.

> JOHN BERGER (b. 1926), British author, critic. "The Soul and the Operator," in *Expressen* (Stockholm, 19 March 1990; repr. in *Keeping a Rendezvous*, 1992).

4   Television's perfect. You turn a few knobs, a few of those mechanical adjustments at which the higher apes are so proficient, and lean back and drain your mind of all thought. And there you are watching the bubbles in the primeval ooze. You don't have to concentrate. You don't have to react. You don't have to remember. You don't miss your brain because you don't need it. Your heart and liver and lungs continue to function normally. Apart from that, all is peace and quiet. You are in the man's nirvana. And if some poor nasty minded person comes along and says you look like a fly on a can of garbage, pay him no mind. He probably hasn't got the price of a televion set.

> RAYMOND CHANDLER (1888–1959), U.S. author. Letter, 22 Nov. 1950, to *Atlantic Monthly* editor Charles W. Morton (published in *Raymond Chandler Speaking*, 1962).

5 So by all means let's have a television show quick and long, even if the commercial has to be delivered by a man in a white coat with a stethoscope hanging around his neck, selling ergot pills. After all the public is entitled to what it wants, isn't it? The Romans knew that and even they lasted four hundred years after they started to putrefy.

RAYMOND CHANDLER (1888–1959), U.S. author. Letter, 15 Nov. 1951 (published in *Raymond Chandler Speaking*, 1962).

6 What is a television apparatus to man, who has only to shut his eyes to see the most inaccessible regions of the seen and the never seen, who has only to imagine in order to pierce through walls and cause all the planetary Baghdads of his dreams to rise from the dust.

SALVADOR DALI (1904–89), Spanish painter. *The Secret Life of Salvador Dali* ch. 11 (1948).

7 Television thrives on unreason, and unreason thrives on television. It strikes at the emotions rather than the intellect.

SIR ROBIN DAY (b. 1915), British broadcaster. *Financial Times* (London, 8 Nov. 1989).

8 You have debased [my] child. . . . You have made him a laughingstock of intelligence . . . a stench in the nostrils of the gods of the ionosphere.

DR. LEE DE FOREST (1873–1961), U.S. inventor of the audion tube. To National Association of Broadcasters. Quoted in: his obituary in *Time* (New York, 7 July 1963).

9 So why do people keep on watching? The answer, by now, should be perfectly obvious: we love television because television brings us a world in which television does not exist. In fact, deep in their hearts, this is what the spuds crave most: a rich, new, participatory life.

BARBARA EHRENREICH (b. 1941), U.S. author, columnist. *The Worst Years of Our Lives*, "Spudding Out" (1991; first published 1988), of "couch potatoes."

10 It is a medium of entertainment which permits millions of people to listen to the same joke at the same time, and yet remain lonesome.

T. S. ELIOT (1888–1965), Anglo-American poet, critic. *New York Post* (22 Sept. 1963).

11 Let's face it, there are no plain women on television.

ANNA FORD (b. 1943), British television personality. Quoted in: *Observer* (London, 23 Sept. 1979).

12 Television is an excellent system when one has nothing to lose, as is the case with a nomadic and rootless country like the United States, but in Europe the affect of television is that of a bulldozer which reduces culture to the lowest possible denominator.

MARC FUMAROLI (b. 1932), French commentator. *Observer* (London, 27 Oct. 1991).

13 A three- to four- to five-hour experience with nothingness.

FREDERIC GLEZER (b. 1937), U.S. literacy lobbyist, librarian. Quoted in: *Newsweek* (New York, 1 Dec. 1986), on watching TV.

14 Television has brought back murder into the home—where it belongs.

ALFRED HITCHCOCK (1899–1980), Anglo-American filmmaker. *Observer* (London, 19 Dec. 1965).

15 Television is becoming a collage—there are so many channels that you move through them making a collage yourself. In that sense, everyone sees something a bit different.

DAVID HOCKNEY (b. 1937), British artist. *Hockney On Photography*, "New York: November 1985" (ed. by Wendy Brown, 1988), conversations with Paul Joyce.

16 Anyone afraid of what he thinks television does to the world is probably just afraid of the world.

CLIVE JAMES (b. 1939), Australian writer, critic. *Glued To The Box*, Introduction (1983).

17 Watching old movies is like spending an evening with those people next door. They bore us, and we wouldn't go out of our way to see them; we drop in on them because they're so close. If it took some effort to see old movies, we might try to find out which were the good ones, and if people saw only the good ones maybe they would still respect old movies. As it is, people sit and watch movies that audiences walked out on thirty years ago. Like Lot's wife, we are tempted to take another look, attracted not by evil but by something that seems much more shameful—our own innocence.

PAULINE KAEL (b. 1919), U.S. film critic. *Kiss Kiss Bang Bang*, "Movies on Television" (1968).

18 Television, despite its enormous presence, turns out to have added pitifully few lines to the communal memory.

JUSTIN KAPLAN (b. 1925), U.S. literary historian, biographer, editor. Quoted in: *Observer* (London, 9 June 1991), on editing the 1992 edition of *Bartlett's Familiar Quotations*.

19 There's a good deal in common between the mind's eye and the TV screen, and though the TV set has all too often been the boobtube, it could be, it can be, the box of dreams.

URSULA K. LE GUIN (b. 1929), U.S. author. "Working on 'The Lathe'," in *Horizon* (New York, 1980; repr. in *Dancing at the Edge of the World*, 1989).

20 Do not, on a rainy day, ask your child what he feels like doing, because I assure you that what he feels like doing, you won't feel like watching.

FRAN LEBOWITZ (b. 1951), U.S. journalist. *Social Studies*, "Parental Guidance" (1981).

21 The difference between writing a book and being on television is the difference between conceiving a child and having a baby made in a test tube.

NORMAN MAILER (b. 1923), U.S. author. "The Siege of Mailer: Hero to Historian," in *Village Voice* (New York, 21 Jan. 1971; repr. in *Conversations with Norman Mailer*, ed. by J. Michael Lennon, 1988).

22 I find television very educational. Every time someone switches it on I go into another room and read a good book.

GROUCHO MARX (1895–1977), U.S. comic actor. Quoted in: Leslie Halliwell, *Halliwell's Filmgoer's Companion* (1984).

23 In the theater, while you recognized that you were

looking at a house, it was a house in quotation marks. On screen, the quotation marks tend to be blotted out by the camera.

> ARTHUR MILLER (b. 1915), U.S. dramatist. *New York Times* (15 Sept. 1985), on a television production of *Death of a Salesman*.

24   Television was not invented to make human beings vacuous, but is an emanation of their vacuity.

> MALCOLM MUGGERIDGE (1903–90), British broadcaster. *Tread Softly For You Tread on My Jokes,* "I Like Dwight" (1966).

25   Much of what passes for quality on British television is no more than a reflection of the narrow elite which controls it and has always thought that its tastes were synonymous with quality.

> RUPERT MURDOCH (b. 1931), Australian-born U.S. media magnate. Address, 1989, to the Edinburgh Television Festival. Quoted in: *Guardian* (London, 1 Jan. 1990).

26   The television screen, so unlike the movie screen, sharply reduced human beings, revealed them as small, trivial, flat, in two banal dimensions, drained of color. Wasn't there something reassuring about it!—that human beings were in fact merely images of a kind registered in one another's eyes and brains, phenomena composed of microscopic flickering dots like atoms. They *were* atoms—nothing more. A quick switch of the dial and they disappeared and who could lament the loss?

> JOYCE CAROL OATES (b. 1938), U.S. author. *You Must Remember This,* pt. 1, ch. 13 (1987).

27   Man watches his history on the screen with apathy and an occasional passing flicker of horror or indignation.

> CONOR CRUISE O'BRIEN (b. 1917), Irish historian, critic, diplomat. Quoted in: *Irish Times* (Dublin, 16 July 1969).

28   Television is actually closer to reality than anything in books. The madness of TV is the madness of human life.

> CAMILLE PAGLIA (b. 1947), U.S. author, critic, educator. *Harper's* (New York, March 1991).

29   Already we Viewers, when not viewing, have begun to whisper to one another that the more we elaborate our means of communication, the less we communicate.

> J. B. PRIESTLEY (1894–1984), British author. *Thoughts in the Wilderness,* "Televiewing" (1957).

30   The great networks are there to prove that ideas can be canned like spaghetti. If everything ends up by tasting like everything else, is that not the evidence that it has been properly cooked?

> FREDERIC RAPHAEL (b. 1931), British author, critic. "The Language of Television," in *The State of the Language* (ed. by Christopher Ricks, 1980).

31   If we had had the right technology back then, you would have seen Eva Braun on the Donahue show and Adolf Hitler on Meet the Press.

> ED TURNER (b. 1935), U.S. broadcast executive, author. Quoted in: *Daily Telegraph* (London, 5 Sept. 1990).

32   I hate television. I hate it as much as peanuts. But I can't stop eating peanuts.

> ORSON WELLES (1915–85), U.S. filmmaker. *New York Herald Tribune* (12 Oct. 1956).

33   Television hangs on the questionable theory that whatever happens anywhere should be sensed everywhere. If everyone is going to be able to see everything, in the long run all sights may lose whatever rarity value they once possessed, and it may well turn out that people, being able to see and hear practically everything, will be specially interested in almost nothing.

> E. B. WHITE (1899–1985), U.S. author, editor. "Television," in *New Yorker* (4 Dec. 1948; repr. in *Writings from the New Yorker 1927–1976,* ed. by Rebecca M. Dale, 1991).

34   The most puzzling thing about TV is the steady advance of the sponsor across the line that has always separated news from promotion, entertainment from merchandising. The advertiser has assumed the role of originator, and the performer has gradually been eased into the role of peddler.

> E. B. WHITE (1899–1985), U.S. author, editor. "Split Personalities," in *New Yorker* (19 Feb. 1955; repr. in *Writings from the New Yorker 1927–1976,* ed. by Rebecca M. Dale, 1991).

35   What do a few lies on TV matter? They can be swallowed, digested and excreted, or follow people when they doze off to sink into oblivion.

> ZHANG JIE (b. 1937), Chinese author. Teacher Li, in *As Long as Nothing Happens, Nothing Will,* "What's Wrong with Him?" (1981).

See also James on CINEMA; Raphael on CRITICS; The MEDIA; SOAP OPERA.

TEMPER

1   Many people lose their tempers merely from seeing you keep yours.

> FRANK MOORE COLBY (1865–1925), U.S. editor, essayist. *The Colby Essays,* vol. 1, "Trials of an Encyclopedist" (1926).

2   A fretful temper will divide
The closest knot that may be tied,
By ceaseless sharp corrosion;
A temper passionate and fierce
May suddenly your joys disperse
At one immense explosion.

> WILLIAM COWPER (1731–1800), English poet. *Friendship* (written 1781; published 1800).

3   A lady of what is commonly called an uncertain temper—a phrase which being interpreted signifies a temper tolerably certain to make everybody more or less uncomfortable.

> CHARLES DICKENS (1812–70), English novelist. Of Martha Varden, in *Barnaby Rudge,* ch. 7 (1841).

4   It was not that she was out of temper, but that the world was not equal to the demands of her fine organism.

> GEORGE ELIOT (1819–80), English novelist, editor. *Daniel Deronda,* bk. 1, ch. 7 (1876), of Gwendolen Harleth.

5   There is a great deal of unmapped country within us which would have to be taken into account in an explanation of our gusts and storms.

> GEORGE ELIOT (1819–80), English novelist. *Daniel Deronda,* bk. 3, ch. 24 (1876).

6   We boil at different degrees.

> RALPH WALDO EMERSON (1803–82), U.S. essayist, poet, philosopher. *Society and Solitude,* "Eloquence" (1870).

7 A tart temper never mellows with age, and a sharp tongue is the only edged tool that grows keener with constant use.

> WASHINGTON IRVING (1783–1859), U.S. author. *The Sketch Book of Geoffrey Crayon, Gent.*, "Rip Van Winkle" (1820).

8 I have never known anyone worth a damn who wasn't irascible.

> EZRA POUND (1885–1972), U.S. poet, critic. Remark, 1917 Quoted in: Humphrey Carpenter, *A Serious Character*, pt. 2, ch. 17 (1988).

9 Take care; you know I am compliance itself, when I am not thwarted! No one more easily led, when I have my own way; but don't put me in a phrenzy.

> RICHARD BRINSLEY SHERIDAN (1751–1816), Anglo-Irish dramatist. Sir Anthony Absolute, in *The Rivals*, act 2, sc. 1.

See also Butler on ARGUMENT.

TEMPTATION

1 The force of the blow depends on the resistance. It is sometimes better not to struggle against temptation. Either fly or yield at once.

> F. H. BRADLEY (1846–1924), English philosopher. *Aphorisms*, no. 75 (1930).

2 Can a moment of madness make up for
an age of consent?

> BASIL BUNTING (1900–1985), British poet. *The Well of Lycopolis*.

3 No temptation can ever be measured by the value of its object.

> COLETTE (1873–1954), French author. "Temptations," in *Earthly Paradise*, pt. 4, "Human Nature" (ed. by Robert Phelps, 1966).

4 You oughtn't to yield to temptation.
Well, somebody must, or the thing becomes
absurd.

> ANTHONY HOPE [ANTHONY HOPE HAWKINS] (1863–1933), British author. Dolly Foster and Mr. Carter, in *The Dolly Dialogues*, no. 14 (1894).

5 We love to overlook the boundaries which we do not wish to pass.

> SAMUEL JOHNSON (1709–84), English author, lexicographer. *Rambler*, no. 114 (London, 20 April 1751; repr. in *Works of Samuel Johnson*, vol. 4, ed. by W. J. Bate and Albrecht B. Strauss, 1969).

6 The most successful tempters and thus the most dangerous are the deluded deluders.

> G. C. LICHTENBERG (1742–99), German physicist, philosopher. *Aphorisms*, "Notebook F," aph. 120 (written 1765–99; tr. by R. J. Hollingdale, 1990).

7 Man is so muddled, so dependent on the things immediately before his eyes, that every day even the most submissive believer can be seen to risk the torments of the afterlife for the smallest pleasure.

> JOSEPH DE MAISTRE (1753–1821), French diplomat, philosopher. The Senator, in *Les Soirées de Saint-Pétersbourg*, "First Dialogue" (1821; repr. in *The Works of Joseph de Maistre*, ed. by Jack Lively, 1965).

8 Taste this, and be henceforth among the Gods Thyself a Goddess.

> JOHN MILTON (1608–74), English poet. Satan to Eve, in *Paradise Lost*, bk. 5.

9 Temptations come, as a general rule, when they are sought.

> MARGARET OLIPHANT (1828–97), English novelist, historian. *Miss Marjoribanks*, ch. 47 (1866), fourth of *Chronicles of Carlingford*.

10 O mischief, thou art swift
To enter in the thoughts of desperate men!

> WILLIAM SHAKESPEARE (1564–1616), English dramatist, poet. Romeo, in *Romeo and Juliet*, act 5, sc. 1.

11 There are several good protections against temptations but the surest is cowardice.

> MARK TWAIN (1835–1910), U.S. author. *Following the Equator*, ch. 36, "Pudd'nhead Wilson's New Calendar" (1897). The epigram also appeared as an entry in 1898 in Twain, *Notebook*, ch. 31 (ed. by Albert Bigelow Paine, 1935).

12 Do you really think, Arthur, that it is weakness that yields to temptation? I tell you that there are terrible temptations that it requires strength, strength and courage, to yield to.

> OSCAR WILDE (1854–1900), Anglo-Irish playwright, author. Sir Robert Chiltern to Lord Goring, in *An Ideal Husband*, act 2
> On the same theme, Wilde wrote, in *The Picture of Dorian Gray*, ch. 2: "The only way to get rid of a temptation is to yield to it."

13 I can resist everything except temptation.

> OSCAR WILDE (1854–1900), Anglo-Irish playwright, author. Lord Darlington, in *Lady Windermere's Fan*, act 1.

See also Wilde on RESOLVE.

TENNIS

1 New Yorkers love it when you spill your guts out there. Spill your guts at Wimbledon and they make you stop and clean it up.

> JIMMY CONNORS (b. 1952), U.S. tennis player. Quoted in: *Guardian* (London, 24 Dec. 1984).

2 Good shot, bad luck and hell are the five basic words to be used in a game of tennis, though these, of course, can be slightly amplified.

> VIRGINIA GRAHAM (b. 1912), U.S. author, commentator. *Say Please*, ch. 8 (1949).

3 Tennis is more than just a sport. It's an art, like the ballet. Or like a performance in the theater. When I step on the court I feel like Anna Pavlova. Or like Adelina Patti. Or even like Sarah Bernhardt. I see the footlights in front of me. I hear the whisperings of the audience. I feel an icy shudder. Win or die! Now or never! It's the crisis of my life.

> BILL TILDEN (1893–1953), U.S. tennis player. Said to Frederic Prokosch. Quoted in: Prokosch, *Voices: A Memoir*, "A Bernhardt" (1983).

TERRORISM

1 It's not the bullet with my name on it that worries me. It's the one that says "To whom it may concern."

> ANONYMOUS BELFAST RESIDENT. Quoted in: *Guardian* (London, 16 Oct. 1991).

2 The man who throws a bomb is an artist, because he prefers a great moment to everything.

> G. K. CHESTERTON (1874–1936), British author. Gregory, in *The Man Who Was Thursday*, ch. 1 (1908).

3 Civilization is maintained by a very few people in a small number of places and we need only some bombs and a few prisons to blot it out altogether.

> CYRIL CONNOLLY (1903–74), British critic. *The Unquiet Grave*, pt. 2 (1944, rev. ed. 1951).

4 Imagine that leader of all the enemy, in that great plain of Babylon, sitting on a sort of throne of smoking flame, a horrible and terrifying sight. Watch him calling together countless devils, to despatch them into different cities till the whole world is covered, forgetting no province or locality, no class or single individual.

> ST. IGNATIUS OF LOYOLA (1491–1556), Spanish churchman, founder of the Society of Jesus. *Spiritual Exercises*, "Second Week," no. 140–41 (1548).

5 The greatest danger of bombs is in the explosion of stupidity that they provoke.

> OCTAVE MIRBEAU (1850–1917), French journalist, author. "Pour Jean Grave," in *Le Journal* (19 Feb. 1894), referring to a bombing campaign, which Jean Grave had allegedly incited by his inflammatory anarchist pamphlets, and for which he was to be tried the following week.

6 The terrible thing about terrorism is that ultimately it destroys those who practise it. Slowly but surely, as they try to extinguish life in others, the light within them dies.

> TERRY WAITE (b. 1939), British religious adviser, hostage in Lebanon. *Guardian* (London, 20 Feb. 1992).

7 When liberty comes with hands dabbled in blood it is hard to shake hands with her.

> OSCAR WILDE (1854–1900), Anglo-Irish playwright, author. Comment to reporters on the murder in Dublin of the new Irish chief secretary, Lord Frederick Cavendish, by Fenian nationalists, May 1882. Quoted in: Richard Ellman, *Oscar Wilde*, ch. 7 (1987).

8 Fighting terrorism is like being a goalkeeper. You can make a hundred brilliant saves but the only shot that people remember is the one that gets past you.

> PAUL WILKINSON (b. 1937), British scholar, author on terrorism. *Daily Telegraph* (London, 1 Sept. 1992).

See also Marighella on GUERRILLA WARFARE.

TEXAS

1 It is very considerably smaller than Australia and British Somaliland put together. As things stand at present there is nothing much the Texans can do about this, and . . . they are inclined to shy away from the subject in ordinary conversation, muttering defensively about the size of oranges.

> ALEX ATKINSON, British humorous writer. *The Eyes of Texas Are Upon You*, in *Punch* (London, 1959; repr. in *Present Laughter*, ed. by Alan Coren, 1982).

2 It was part of the Texas ritual. We're rich as son-of-a-bitch stew but look how homely we are, just as plain-folksy as Grandpappy back in 1836. We know about champagne and caviar but we talk hog and hominy.

> EDNA FERBER (1887–1968), U.S. author. *Giant*, ch. 2 (1952).

3 If a man's from Texas, he'll tell you. If he's not, why embarrass him by asking?

> JOHN GUNTHER (1901–70), U.S. journalist. Quoted in: *Inside U.S.A.*, ch. 47, "Some Texas Jokes" (1947).

4 Many people have believed that they were Chosen, but none more baldly than the Texans.

> EDWARD HOAGLAND (b. 1932), U.S. novelist, essayist. "Lament the Red Wolf," in *Sports Illustrated* (New York, 14 Jan. 1974; repr. in *Heart's Desire*, 1988).

5 Fish have water, the bushmen of the Kalahari have sand, and Houstonians have interior décor.

> SIMON HOGGART (b. 1946), British journalist. *America: A User's Guide*, ch. 1 (1990).

6 Texas is a state of mind. Texas is an obsession. Above all, Texas is a nation in every sense of the word. And there's an opening convey of generalities. A Texan outside of Texas is a foreigner.

> JOHN STEINBECK (1902–68), U.S. author. *Travels With Charley: in Search of America*, pt. 4 (1962).

7 For most Northerners, Texas is the home of real men. The cowboys, the rednecks, the outspoken self-made right-wing millionaires strike us as either the best or worst examples of American manliness. . . . The ideal is not an illusion nor is it contemptible, no matter what damage it may have done. Many people who scorn it in conversation want to submit to it in bed. Those who believe machismo reeks of violence alone choose to forget it once stood for honor as' well.

> EDMUND WHITE (b. 1940), U.S. author. *States of Desire: Travels in Gay America*, ch. 5 (1980).

MARGARET THATCHER

1 What Mrs. Thatcher did for women was to demonstrate that if a woman had enough desire she could do what she wanted, do anything a man could do. . . . Mrs. Thatcher did not have one traditional feminine cell in her body.

> JULIE BURCHILL (b. 1960), British journalist, author. *Damaged Gods*, "Born Again Cows" (1986).

2 I am not prepared to accept the economics of a housewife.

> JACQUES CHIRAC (b. 1932), French politician, prime minister. Quoted in: *Sunday Times* (London, 27 Dec. 1987), of Margaret Thatcher.

3 For us she is not the iron lady. She is the kind, dear Mrs. Thatcher.

> ALEXANDER DUBCEK (b. 1921), Czechoslovakian politician. Quoted in: *Independent on Sunday* (London, 30 Dec. 1990).

4 This woman is headstrong, obstinate and dangerously self-opinionated.

> REPORT BY PERSONNEL OFFICER AT I.C.I., REJECTING MRS. THATCHER FOR A JOB IN 1948.

5 She's the best man in England.

> RONALD REAGAN (b. 1911), U.S. Republican politician, president. Quoted in: *Observer* (London, 16 Jan. 1983).

6 She really is a woman just like my mum.

> CLIFF RICHARD (b. 1940), British singer. *Guardian* (London, 17 Aug. 1988).

7 I'll stay until I'm tired of it. So long as Britain needs me, I shall never be tired of it.

> MARGARET THATCHER (b. 1925), British Conservative politician, prime minister. Said in 1982. Quoted in: *Observer* (London, 2 Jan. 1983).

8 It was then that the iron entered my soul.

> MARGARET THATCHER (b. 1925), British Conservative politician, prime minister. Quoted in: *Observer* (London, 27 March 1983), on her time in Edward Heath's cabinet. Thatcher and Heath were later to become irreconcilable political opponents.

See also Thatcher on OPPOSITION.

THEATER

1 The theater, which is in *no thing,* but makes use of everything—gestures, sounds, words, screams, light, darkness—rediscovers itself at precisely the point where the mind requires a language to express its manifestations. . . . To break through language in order to touch life is to create or recreate the theatre.

> ANTONIN ARTAUD (1896–1948), French theater producer, actor, theorist. *The Theater and its Double,* "Preface: The Theater and Culture" (1938; tr. 1958).

2 *Theater of cruelty* means a theater difficult and cruel for myself first of all. And, on the level of performance, it is not the cruelty we can exercise upon each other by hacking at each other's bodies, carving up our personal anatomies, or, like Assyrian emperors, sending parcels of human ears, noses, or neatly detached nostrils through the mail, but the much more terrible and necessary cruelty which things can exercise against us. We are not free. And the sky can still fall on our heads. And the theater has been created to teach us that first of all.

> ANTONIN ARTAUD (1896–1948), French theater producer, actor, theorist. *The Theater and Its Double,* ch. 1 (1938; tr. 1958).

3 Drama is based on the Mistake. I think someone is my friend when he really is my enemy, that I am free to marry a woman when in fact she is my mother, that this person is a chambermaid when it is a young nobleman in disguise, that this well-dressed young man is rich when he is really a penniless adventurer, or that if I do this such and such a result will follow when in fact it results in something very different. All good drama has two movements, first the making of the mistake, then the discovery that it was a mistake.

> W. H. AUDEN (1907–73), Anglo-American poet. *The Dyer's Hand,* pt. 8, "Notes on Music And Opera" (1962).

4 The theatre is a gross art, built in sweeps and over-emphasis. Compromise is its second name.

> ENID BAGNOLD (1889–1981), British novelist, playwright. *Autobiography,* ch. 3 (1969).

5 It's one of the tragic ironies of the theatre that only one man in it can count on steady work—the night watchman.

> TALLULAH BANKHEAD (1903–68), U.S. screen actor. *Tallulah,* ch. 1 (1952).

6 I submit all my plays to the National Theatre for rejection. To assure myself I am seeing clearly.

> HOWARD BARKER (b. 1946), British poet, playwright. *Guardian* (London, 13 Feb. 1992).

7 We need a type of theatre which not only releases the feelings, insights and impulses possible within the particular historical field of human relations in which the action takes place, but employs and encourages those thoughts and feelings which help transform the field itself.

> BERTOLT BRECHT (1898–1956), German dramatist, poet. "A Short Organum for the Theatre," para.35 (1949; repr. in *Brecht on Theatre,* ed. and tr. by John Willett, 1964).

8 Theatergoing is a communal act, moviegoing a solitary one.

> ROBERT BRUSTEIN (b. 1927), U.S. stage director, author, critic. *Who Needs Theatre,* Introduction (1987).

9 The primary function of a theater is not to please itself, or even to please its audience. It is to serve talent.

> ROBERT BRUSTEIN (b. 1927), U.S. stage director, author, critic. *Who Needs Theatre,* pt. 3, "The Humanist and the Artist" (1987).

10 For my part, I confess I seldom listen to the players: one has so much to do, in looking about and finding out one's acquaintance, that, really, one has no time to mind the stage. . . . One merely comes to meet one's friends, and shew that one's alive.

> FANNY BURNEY (1752–1840), English author. Mr. Lovel, in *Evelina,* Letter 20 (1778).

11 All tragedies are finish'd by a death,
All comedies are ended by a marriage.

> LORD BYRON (1788–1824), English poet. *Don Juan,* cto. 3, st. 9.

12 The stage is life, music, beautiful girls, legs, breasts, not talk or intellectualism or dried-up academics.

> HAROLD CLURMAN (1901–80), U.S. stage director, critic. Quoted in: Robert Brustein, *Who Needs Theatre,* pt. 1, "The Vitality of Harold Clurman" (1987).

13 Theater people are always pining and agonizing because they're afraid that they'll be forgotten. And in America they're quite right. They will be.

> AGNES DE MILLE (b. 1908), U.S. choreographer, dancer. Quoted in: *Life* (New York, 15 Nov. 1963).

14 The pit of a theatre is the one place where the tears of virtuous and wicked men alike are mingled.

> DENIS DIDEROT (1713–84), French philosopher. *On Dramatic Poetry* (1758; repr. in *Selected Writings,* ed. by Lester G. Crocker, 1966).

15 I had learned to have a perfect nausea for the theatre: the continual repetition of the same words and the same gestures, night after night, and the caprices, the way of looking at life, and the entire rigmarole disgusted me.

> ISADORA DUNCAN (1878–1927), U.S. dancer. *My Life,* ch. 5 (1927).

16 To save the theatre, the theatre must be destroyed, the actors and actresses must all die of the plague. They poison the air, they make art impossible. It is not drama that they play, but pieces for the theatre. We should return to the Greeks, play in the open air; the drama dies of stalls and boxes and evening dress, and people who come to digest their dinner.

ELEANOR DUSE (1859–1924), Italian actor. Quoted in: Arthur Symons, *Studies in Seven Arts*, "Eleanora Duse" (1906).

17 The theatre is the best way of showing the gap between what is said and what is seen to be done, and that is why, ragged and gap-toothed as it is, it has still a far healthier potential than some poorer, abandoned arts.

DAVID HARE (b. 1947), British playwright. *The Playwright as Historian*, in *Sunday Times Magazine* (26 Nov. 1978).

18 I think theatre should always be somewhat suspect.

VÁCLAV HAVEL (b. 1936), Czech playwright, president. *Disturbing the Peace*, ch. 2 (1986; tr. 1990).

19 Drama assumes an order. If only so that it might have—by disrupting that order—a way of surprising.

VáCLAV HAVEL (b. 1936), Czech playwright, president. *Disturbing the Peace*, ch. 5 (1986; tr. 1990).

20 Drama is life with the dull bits cut out.

ALFRED HITCHCOCK (1899–1980), Anglo-American filmmaker. Quoted in: Leslie Halliwell, *Halliwell's Filmgoer's Companion* (1984).

21 The novel is more of a whisper, whereas the stage is a shout.

ROBERT HOLMAN (b. 1936), British dramatist. *Independent* (London, 8 Oct. 1990).

22 To treat a "big" subject in the intensely summarized fashion demanded by an evening's traffic of the stage when the evening, freely clipped at each end, is reduced to two hours and a half, is a feat of which the difficulty looms large.

HENRY JAMES (1843–1916), U.S. author. *Theatricals: Second Series*, Prefatory Note (1894).

23 The theater, bringing impersonal masks to life, is only for those who are virile enough to create new life: either as a conflict of passions subtler than those we already know, or as a complete new character.

ALFRED JARRY (1873–1907), French playwright, author. "Twelve Theatrical Topics," Topic 4, in *Dossiers Acénonètes due Collège de Pataphysique*, no. 5 (Paris, 1960; repr. in *Selected Works of Alfred Jarry*, ed. by Roger Shattuck and Simon Watson Taylor, 1965).

24 The virtue of dress rehearsals is that they are a free show for a select group of artists and friends of the author, and where for one unique evening the audience is almost expurgated of idiots.

ALFRED JARRY (1873–1907), French playwright, author. "Twelve Theatrical Topics," Topic 8 (1960; repr. in *Selected Works of Alfred Jarry*, ed. by Roger Shattuck and Simon Watson Taylor, 1965).

25 The drama's laws, the drama's patrons give,
For we that live to please, must please to live.

SAMUEL JOHNSON (1709–84), English author, lexicographer. *Prologue at the Opening of the Theatre in Drury Lane.*

26 I write plays for people who wouldn't be seen dead in the theatre.

BARRIE KEEFFE (b. 1945), British playwright. *Evening Standard* (London, 8 June 1989).

27 A dramatic experience concerned with the mundane may inform but it cannot release; and one concerned essentially with the *aesthetic politics* of its creators may divert or anger, but it cannot enlighten.

DAVID MAMET (b. 1947), U.S. playwright. *Writing in Restaurants*, "A National Dream-Life" (1986).

28 By whatever means it is accomplished, the prime business of a play is to arouse the passions of its audience so that by the route of passion may be opened up new relationships between a man and men, and between men and Man. Drama is akin to the other inventions of man in that it ought to help us to know more, and not merely to spend our feelings.

ARTHUR MILLER (b. 1915), U.S. dramatist. *Collected Plays*, Introduction, sct. 7 (1958).

29 A playwright . . . is . . . the litmus paper of the arts. He's got to be, because if he isn't working on the same wave length as the audience, no one would know what in hell he was talking about. He is a kind of psychic journalist, even when he's great.

ARTHUR MILLER (b. 1915), U.S. dramatist. *Paris Review* (Flushing, N.Y., Summer 1966).

30 Farce is tragedy played at a thousand revolutions per minute.

JOHN MORTIMER (b. 1923), British barrister, novelist. *Times* (London, 9 Sept. 1992).

31 The drama's altar isn't on the stage: it is candlesticked and flowered in the box office. There is the gold, though there be no frankincense or myrrh; and the gospel for the day always The Play will Run for a Year. The Dove of Inspiration, of the desire for inspiration, has flown away from it; and on it's roof, now, the commonplace crow caws candidly.

SEAN O'CASEY (1884–1964), Irish dramatist. From his autobiography, *Sunset and Evening Star*, "And Evening Star" (1954).

32 It hath evermore been the notorious badge of prostituted Strumpets and the lewdest Harlots, to ramble abroad to Plays, to Playhouses; whither no honest, chaste or sober Girls or Women, but only branded Whores and infamous Adulteresses, did usually resort in ancient times.

WILLIAM PRYNNE (1600–1669), English Puritan pamphleteer. *Histriomastix* (1632).

33 The theatre, for all its artifices, depicts life in a sense more truly than history, because the medium has a kindred movement to that of real life, though an artificial setting and form.

GEORGE SANTAYANA (1863–1952), U.S. philosopher, poet. *Skepticism and the Animal Mind*, p.102.

34 Good drama must be drastic.

FRIEDRICH SCHLEGEL (1772–1829), German philosopher, critic, writer. *Dialogue on Poetry and Literary Aphorisms*, "Selected Aphorisms from *The Athenaeum*," aph. 42 (1968; first published 1798).

35 Can this cock-pit hold
The vasty fields of France?

WILLIAM SHAKESPEARE (1564–1616), English dramatist, poet.
Chorus, in *King Henry V*, Prologue.

36 In a drama of the highest order there is little food for censure or hatred; it teaches rather self-knowledge and self-respect.

PERCY BYSSHE SHELLEY (1792–1822), English poet. *A Defence of Poetry* (written 1821; published 1840).

37 I open with a clock striking, to beget an awful attention in the audience—it also marks the time, which is four o'clock in the morning, and saves a description of the rising sun, and a great deal about gilding the eastern hemisphere.

RICHARD BRINSLEY SHERIDAN (1751–1816), Anglo-Irish dramatist. Puff, in *The Critic*, act 2, sc. 2.

38 All this class of pleasures inspires me with the same nausea as I feel at the sight of rich plum-cake or sweetmeats; I prefer the driest bread of common life.

SYDNEY SMITH (1771–1845), English journalist, clergyman.
Quoted in: Hesketh Pearson, *The Smith of Smiths*, ch. 13 (1934), of the theatrical arts.

39 In a good play every speech should be as fully flavoured as a nut or apple.

JOHN MILLINGTON SYNGE (1871–1909), Irish poet and dramatist. *The Playboy of the Western World*, Introduction (1907).

40 If a playwright tried to see eye to eye with everybody, he would get the worst case of strabismus since Hannibal lost an eye trying to count his nineteen elephants during a snowstorm while crossing the Alps.

JAMES THURBER (1894–1961), U.S. humorist, illustrator. *New York Times* (21 Feb. 1960).

41 A talent for drama is not a talent for writing, but is an ability to articulate human relationships.

GORE VIDAL (b. 1925), U.S. novelist, critic. *New York Times* (17 June 1956).

42 The theater needs continual reminders that there is nothing more debasing than the work of those who do well what is not worth doing at all.

GORE VIDAL (b. 1925), U.S. novelist, critic. *Newsweek* (New York, 25 March 1968).

43 I want to give the audience a *hint* of a scene. No more than that. Give them too much and they won't contribute anything themselves. Give them just a suggestion and you get them working with you. That's what gives the theater meaning: when it becomes a social act.

ORSON WELLES (1915–84), U.S. filmmaker, actor, producer.
Quoted in: Frank Brady, *Citizen Welles*, ch. 8 (1989).

44 The stage is not merely the meeting place of all the arts, but is also the return of art to life.

OSCAR WILDE (1854–1900), Anglo-Irish playwright, author.
Nineteenth Century (London, May 1885).

45 A dramatist is one who believes that the pure event, an action involving human beings, is more arresting than any comment that can be made upon it.

THORNTON WILDER (1897–1975), U.S. novelist, dramatist.

Interview in *Writers at Work* (First Series, ed. by Malcolm Cowley, 1958).

46 The theatre is supremely fitted to say: "Behold! These things are." Yet most dramatists employ it to say: "This moral truth can be learned from beholding this action."

THORNTON WILDER (1897–1975), U.S. novelist, dramatist.
Interview in *Writers at Work* (First Series, ed. by Malcolm Cowley, 1958).

47 Every now and then, when you're on stage, you hear the best sound a player can hear. It's a sound you can't get in movies or in television. It is the sound of a wonderful, deep silence that means you've hit them where they live.

SHELLEY WINTERS (b. 1922), U.S. stage and screen actor. *Theatre Arts* (June 1956).

See also Day Lewis, MacLiammoir on ACTING; Mamet, Miller on AUDIENCES; Miller on BROADWAY; Tynan on CRITICISM AND THE ARTS; Berger on ENTERTAINMENT; Hall on WRITERS.

THEOLOGY

1 Dogmatic theological statements are neither logical propositions nor poetic utterances. They are "shaggy dog" stories; they have a point, but he who tries too hard to get it will miss it.

W. H. AUDEN (1907–73), Anglo-American poet. *A Certain World*, "God" (1970).

2 Only a very bad theologian would confuse the certainty that follows revelation with the truths that are revealed. They are entirely different things.

DENIS DIDEROT (1713–84), French philosopher. *Apology for the Abbé de Prades* (1752) repr. in *Selected Writings* (ed. by Lester G. Crocker, 1966).

3 Christians would show sense if they dispatched these argumentative Scotists and pigheaded Ockhamists and undefeated Albertists along with the whole regiment of Sophists to fight the Turks and Saracens instead of sending those armies of dull-witted soldiers with whom they've long been carrying on war with no result.

DESIDERIUS ERASMUS c. 1466–1536), Dutch humanist. *Praise of Folly*, ch. 53 (1509).

4 It's the generally accepted privilege of theologians to stretch the heavens, that is the Scriptures, like tanners with a hide.

DESIDERIUS ERASMUS c. 1466–1536), Dutch humanist. *Praise of Folly*, ch. 64 (1509).

5 Theology—An effort to explain the unknowable by putting it into terms of the not worth knowing.

H. L. MENCKEN (1880–1956), U.S. journalist. *A Mencken Chrestomathy*, "Sententiæ: Arcana Coelestia" (1949).

6 To judge from the notions expounded by theologians, one must conclude that God created most men simply with a view to crowding hell.

MARQUIS DE SADE (1740–1814), French author. Juliette, in *L'Histoire de Juliette, ou les Prospérités du Vice*, pt. 2 (1797).

7 There was never a century nor a country that was

short of experts who knew the Deity's mind and were willing to reveal it.

> MARK TWAIN (1835–1910), U.S. author. "As Concerns Interpreting the Deity" (1905; repr. in *What Is Man?*, ed. by Paul Baender, 1973).

THEORY

1   There never comes a point where a theory can be said to be true. The most that one can claim for any theory is that it has shared the successes of all its rivals and that it has passed at least one test which they have failed.

> A. J. AYER (1910–89), British philosopher. *Philosophy in the Twentieth Century*, ch. 4 (1982).

2   It is not enough for theory to describe and analyse, it must itself be an event in the universe it describes. In order to do this theory must partake of and become the acceleration of this logic. It must tear itself from all referents and take pride only in the future. Theory must operate on time at the cost of a deliberate distortion of present reality.

> JEAN BAUDRILLARD (b. 1929), French semiologist. *The Ecstasy of Communication*, "Why Theory?" (1987).

3   To insure the adoration of a theorem for any length of time, faith is not enough, a police force is needed as well.

> ALBERT CAMUS (1913–60), French-Algerian philosopher, author. *The Rebel*, pt. 3, "The Regicides" (1951; tr. 1953).

4   The world can doubtless never be well known by theory: practice is absolutely necessary; but surely it is of great use to a young man, before he sets out for that country, full of mazes, windings, and turnings, to have at least a general map of it, made by some experienced traveller.

> LORD CHESTERFIELD (1694–1773), English statesman, man of letters. Letter, 30 Aug. 1749 (first published 1774; repr. in *The Letters of the Earl of Chesterfield to His Son*, vol. 1, no. 190, ed. by Charles Strachey, 1901).

5   In order to shake a hypothesis, it is sometimes not necessary to do anything more than push it as far as it will go.

> DENIS DIDEROT (1713–84), French philosopher. *On the Interpretation of Nature*, no. 50 (1753; repr. in *Selected Writings*, ed. by Lester G. Crocker, 1966).

6   It is a capital mistake to theorize before one has data.

> SIR ARTHUR CONAN DOYLE (1859–1930), English author. Sherlock Holmes, in *The Adventures of Sherlock Holmes*, "Scandal in Bohemia" (1892). In *A Study in Scarlet*, ch. 3, Holmes reiterated, "It is a capital mistake to theorize before you have all the evidence. It biases the judgement."

7   No theory is good unless it permits, not rest, but the greatest work. No theory is good except on condition that one use it to go on beyond.

> ANDRÉ GIDE (1869–1951), French author. *Journals 1889–1949*, "Detached Pages" (ed. by Justin O'Brien, 1951), journal entry 1913.

8   The wise man regulates his conduct by the theories both of religion and science. But he regards these theories not as statements of ultimate fact but as art-forms.

> J. B. S. HALDANE (1892–1964), British scientist. Closing words of "Science and Theology as Art-Forms" in *Possible Worlds and Other Essays* (1927).

9   Theories that go counter to the facts of human nature are foredoomed.

> EDITH HAMILTON (1867–1963), U.S. classical scholar, translator. *The Roman Way*, ch. 1 (1932).

10   Unaware of the absurdity of it, we introduce our own petty household rules into the economy of the universe for which the life of generations, peoples, of entire planets, has no importance in relation to the general development.

> ALEXANDER HERZEN (1812–70), Russian journalist, political thinker. *From the Other Shore*, "Year LVII of the Republic" (1855).

11   Every theory is a self-fulfilling prophecy that orders experience into the framework it provides.

> RUTH HUBBARD (b. 1924), U.S. biologist. "Have Only Men Evolved?" in *Women Look at Biology Looking At Women* (ed. by Ruth Hubbard, Mary Sue Henifin and Barbara Fried, 1979).

12   Everything that explains the world has in fact explained a world that does not exist, a world in which men are at the center of the human enterprise and women are at the margin "helping" them. Such a world does not exist—never has.

> GERDA LERNER (b. 1920), U.S. educator, author. Quoted in: *Ms.* (New York, Sept. 1981).

13   Delight at having understood a very abstract and obscure system leads most people to believe in the truth of what it demonstrates.

> G. C. LICHTENBERG (1742–99), German physicist, philosopher. *Aphorisms* "Notebook J," aph. 77 (written 1765–99; tr. by R. J. Hollingdale, 1990).

14   One must credit an hypothesis with all that has had to be discovered in order to demolish it.

> JEAN ROSTAND (1894–1977), French biologist, writer. *Pensées d'un Biologiste* (1939; repr. in *The Substance of Man*, "A Biologist's Thoughts," ch. 7, 1962).

15   A conception not reducible to the small change of daily experience is like a currency not exchangeable for articles of consumption; it is not a symbol, but fraud.

> GEORGE SANTAYANA (1863–1952), U.S. philosopher, poet. *The Life of Reason*, "Reason in Society," ch. 8 (1905–6).

16   Let us work without theorizing, 'tis the only way to make life endurable.

> VOLTAIRE (1694–1778), French philosopher, author. Martin, in *Candide*, ch. 30 (1759).

See also Engels on ACTION; Proust on ART.

THINGS

1   Inanimate objects are classified scientifically into three major categories—those that don't work, those that break down and those that get lost.

> RUSSELL BAKER (b. 1925), U.S. journalist. *New York Times* (18 June 1968).

2   Every passion borders on the chaotic, but the collector's passion borders on the chaos of memories.

> WALTER BENJAMIN (1892–1940), German critic, philosopher. *Unpacking my Library* (1931; repr. in *Illuminations*, ed. by Hannah Arendt, 1968).

3   Once I planned to write a book of poems entirely about the things in my pocket. But I found it would be too long; and the age of the great epics is past.

> G. K. CHESTERTON (1874–1936), British author. *Tremendous Trifles*, "A Piece of Chalk" (1909).

4   I can never bring you to realize the importance of sleeves, the suggestiveness of thumb-nails, or the great issues that may hang from a boot-lace.

> SIR ARTHUR CONAN DOYLE (1859–1930), English author. Sherlock Holmes, in *The Adventures of Sherlock Holmes*, "A Case of Identity" (1892).

5   We live in a world of things, and our only connection with them is that we know how to manipulate or to consume them.

> ERICH FROMM (1900–1980), U.S. psychologist. *The Sane Society*, ch. 5 (1955).

6   We must not discriminate between things. Where things are concerned there are no class distinctions. We must pick out what is good for us where we can find it.

> PABLO PICASSO (1881–1973), Spanish artist. *Conversation avec Picasso*, in *Cahiers d'Art*, vol. 10 (Paris, 1935; tr. in Alfred H. Barr, Jr., *Picasso: Fifty Years of His Art*, 1946).

7   Fewer and fewer Americans possess objects that have a patina, old furniture, grandparents' pots and pans—the used things, warm with generations of human touch, . . . essential to a human landscape. Instead, we have our paper phantoms, transistorized landscapes. A featherweight portable museum.

> SUSAN SONTAG (b. 1933), U.S. essayist. *On Photography*, "Melancholy Objects" (1977).

8   I believe in the total depravity of inanimate things . . . the elusiveness of soap, the knottiness of strings, the transitory nature of buttons, the inclination of suspenders to twist and of hooks to forsake their lawful eyes, and cleave only unto the hairs of their hapless owner's head.

> KATHARINE WALKER (1840–1916), U.S. author. *Atlantic Monthly* (Boston, Sept. 1864).

See also Bowen on LONELINESS.

THINGS, TRIVIAL

1   What we call little things are merely the causes of great things; they are the beginning, the embryo, and it is the point of departure which, generally speaking, decides the whole future of an existence. One single black speck may be the beginning of a gangrene, of a storm, of a revolution.

> HENRI-FRÉDÉRIC AMIEL (1821–81), Swiss philosopher, poet. *Journal Intime* (1882; tr. by Mrs. Humphry Ward, 1892), entry for 16 March 1868.

2   My own idear is that these things are as piffle before the wind.

> DAISY ASHFORD (1881–1972), British writer. The Earl of Clincham, in *The Young Visiters*, "The Crystal Palace" (1919), written when the author was aged nine.

3   It has long been an axiom of mine that the little things are infinitely the most important.

> SIR ARTHUR CONAN DOYLE (1859–1930), English author. Sherlock Holmes, in *The Adventures of Sherlock Holmes*, "A Case of Identity" (1892).

4   It is in these acts called trivialities that the seeds of joy are forever wasted, until men and women look round with haggard faces at the devastation their own waste has made, and say, the earth bears no harvest of sweetness—calling their denial knowledge.

> GEORGE ELIOT (1819–80), English novelist, editor. *Middlemarch*, bk. 4, ch. 42 (1871).

5   You'll come to learn a great deal if you study the Insignificant in depth.

> ODYSSEUS ELYTIS (b. 1911), Greek poet, essayist. *To Axion Asti—It Is Worthy* (1959), quoted as Epigraph to Roman Baczynski, *Discontent and Liberal Opinion* (1987).

6   There is nothing, Sir, too little for so little a creature as man. It is by studying little things that we attain the great art of having as little misery and as much happiness as possible.

> SAMUEL JOHNSON (1709–84), English author, lexicographer. Quoted in: James Boswell, *Life of Samuel Johnson*, 14 July 1763 (1791). Johnson was replying to Boswell's fear that, should he keep a journal (as Johnson proposed), he would put into it too many little incidents.

7   As the few adepts in such things well know, universal morality is to be found in little everyday penny-events just as much as in great ones. There is so much goodness and ingenuity in a raindrop that an apothecary wouldn't let it go for less than half-a-crown . . .

> G. C. LICHTENBERG (1742–99), German physicist, philosopher. *Aphorisms*, "Notebook B," aph. 33 (written 1765–99; tr. by R. J. Hollingdale, 1990).

8   The human tendency to regard little things as important has produced very many great things.

> G. C. LICHTENBERG (1742–99), German physicist, philosopher. *Aphorisms*, "Notebook G," aph. 46 (written 1765–99; tr. by R. J. Hollingdale, 1990).

9   It has been rightly said that nothing is unimportant, nothing powerless in the universe; a single atom can dissolve everything, and save everything! What terror! There lies the eternal distinction between good and evil.

> GÉRARD DE NERVAL (1808–55), French novelist, poet. *Aurélia*, pt. 2, ch. 6 (1855; repr. in *Selected Writings*, ed. and tr. by Geoffrey Wagner, 1958).

10   For the person for whom small things do not exist, the great is not great.

> JOSÉ ORTEGA Y GASSET (1883–1955), Spanish essayist, philosopher. *Meditations on Quixote*, "To the Reader" (1914).

11   What a profound significance small things assume when the woman we love conceals them from us.

> MARCEL PROUST (1871–1922), French novelist. *Remembrance*

of Things Past, vol. 9, "The Captive," pt. 1, ch. 1 (1923; tr. by Ronald and Colette Cortie, 1988).

12 How full of trifles everything is! It is only one's thoughts that fill a room with something more than furniture.

> WALLACE STEVENS (1879–1955), U.S. poet. Letter, 16 May 1907, to his future wife Elsie Moll Kachel (published in *Souvenirs and Prophecies: the Young Wallace Stevens*, ch. 9, ed. by Holly Stevens, 1977).

13 There is no object so soft but it makes a hub for the wheel'd universe.

> WALT WHITMAN (1819–92), U.S. poet. *Leaves of Grass*, "Song of Myself," sct. 48 (1855).

See also INSIGNFICANCE; Johnson on RECREATION.

THE THIRD WORLD

1 From all around the Third World,
You hear the same story;
Rulers
Asleep to all things at
All times—
Conscious only of
Riches, which they gather in a
Coma—
Intravenously

> AMA ATA AIDOO (b. 1942), Ghanaian scholar, poet. *The Plum*, in *Wayward Girls and Wicked Women* (ed. by Angela Carter, 1986).

2 The Third World is not a reality but an ideology.

> HANNAH ARENDT (1906–75), German-born U.S. political philosopher. *Crises of the Republic*, "On Violence," sct. 1 (1972).

3 History is strewn with the wrecks of nations which have gained a little progressiveness at the cost of a great deal of hard manliness, and have thus prepared themselves for destruction as soon as the movements of the world gave a chance for it.

> WALTER BAGEHOT (1826–77), English economist, critic. *Physics and Politics*, ch. 2, sct. 2 (1872).

4 Remember the rights of the savage, as we call him. Remember that the happiness of his humble home, remember that the sanctity of life in the hill villages of Afghanistan, among the winter snows, is as inviolable in the eye of Almighty God, as can be your own.

> W. E. GLADSTONE (1809–88), English Liberal prime minister, statesman. Speech, 26 Nov. 1879, Dalkeith, Scotland.

5 People in places many of us never heard of, whose names we can't pronounce or even spell, are speaking up for themselves. They speak in languages we once classified as "exotic" but whose mastery is now essential for our diplomats and businessmen. But what they say is very much the same the world over. They want a decent standard of living. They want human dignity and a voice in their own futures. They want their children to grow up strong and healthy and free.

> HUBERT H. HUMPHREY (1911–78), U.S. Democratic politician, vice president. Speech, 4 June 1966, Faribault, Minn.

6 The great battleground for the defence and expansion of freedom today is the whole southern half of the globe . . . the lands of the rising peoples. Their revolution is the greatest in human history. They seek an end to injustice, tyranny and exploitation. More than an end, they seek a beginning.

> JOHN F. KENNEDY (1917–63), U.S. Democratic politician, president. Supplementary State of the Union Message to Congress, 25 May 1961.

7 To the United States the Third World often takes the form of a black woman who has been made pregnant in a moment of passion and who shows up one day in the reception room on the forty-ninth floor threatening to make a scene. The lawyers pay the woman off; sometimes uniformed guards accompany her to the elevators.

> LEWIS H. LAPHAM (b. 1935), U.S. essayist, editor. *Money and Class in America*, ch. 5, sct. 1 (1988).

8 We face neither East nor West: we face forward.

> KWAME NKRUMAH (1900–1972), Ghanaian president. Conference speech, 7 April 1960, Accra.

HENRY DAVID THOREAU

1 Henry David Thoreau, who never earned much of a living or sustained a relationship with any woman that wasn't brotherly—who lived mostly under his parents' roof . . . who advocated one day's work and six days "off" as the weekly round and was considered a bit of a fool in his hometown . . . is probably the American writer who tells us best how to live comfortably with our most constant companion, ourselves.

> EDWARD HOAGLAND (b. 1932), U.S. novelist, essayist. "Bragging For Humanity," in *American Heritage* (New York, July 1988; repr. in *Heart's Desire*, 1988).

2 Whatever question there may be of his talent, there can be none, I think, of his genius. It was a slim and crooked one, but it was eminently personal. He was unperfect, unfinished, inartistic; he was worse than provincial—he was parochial.

> HENRY JAMES (1843–1916), U.S. author. *Hawthorne*, ch. 4 (1879).

3 If I were confined to a corner of a garret all my days, like a spider, the world would be just as large to me while I had my thoughts about me.

> HENRY DAVID THOREAU (1817–62), U.S. philosopher, author, naturalist. *Walden*, "Conclusion" (1854). This reflection was carried over from Thoreau's journals, in the entry for Oct. 1850.

See also Edel on WRITERS.

THOUGHT AND THINKING

1 Thought is a kind of opium; it can intoxicate us, while still broad awake; it can make transparent the mountains and everything that exists.

> HENRI-FRÉDÉRIC AMIEL (1821–81), Swiss philosopher, poet. *Journal Intime* (1882; tr. by Mrs. Humphry Ward, 1892), entry for 3 Feb. 1857.

2 The surprises of thought are like those of love: they

wear out. But here too you can carry on for a long time doing your conjugal duty.

> JEAN BAUDRILLARD (b. 1929), French semiologist. *Cool Memories*, ch. 5 (1987; tr. 1990).

3 A thought which does not result in an action is nothing much, and an action which does not proceed from a thought is nothing at all.

> GEORGES BERNANOS (1888–1948), French novelist, political writer. *The Last Essays of Georges Bernanos*, "France Before the World of Tomorrow" (1955).

4 One thought fills immensity.

> WILLIAM BLAKE (1757–1827), English poet, painter, engraver. *The Marriage of Heaven and Hell*, Plate 8 (1790–93).

5 Like many rich men, he thought in anecdotes; like many simple women, she thought in terms of biography.

> ANITA BROOKNER (b. 1938), British novelist, art historian. *The Misalliance*, ch. 1 (1986), of Bertie and Blanche Vernon.

6 There is nothing so unthinkable as thought, unless it be the entire absence of thought.

> SAMUEL BUTLER (1835–1902), English author. *Samuel Butler's Notebooks* (1951, p. 154). In a later entry, Butler wrote; "Thought pure and simple is as near to God as we can get, it is through this that we are linked with God."

7 For in itself a thought,
A slumbering thought, is capable of years,
And curdles a long life into one hour.

> LORD BYRON (1788–1824), English poet. *The Dream*, sct. 1 (1816).

8 Thought once awakened does not again slumber; unfolds itself into a System of Thought; grows, in man after man, generation after generation,—till its full stature is reached, and *such* System of Thought can grow no farther, but must give place to another.

> THOMAS CARLYLE (1795–1881), Scottish essayist, historian. *On Heroes and Hero-Worship*, Lecture 1, "The Hero as Divinity" (1841).

9 Our goodness comes solely from thinking on goodness; our wickedness from thinking on wickedness. We too are the victims of our own contemplation.

> JOHN JAY CHAPMAN (1862–1933), U.S. author. *Practical Agitation*, ch. 7 (1898).

10 To think is to act.

> RALPH WALDO EMERSON (1803–82), U.S. essayist, poet, philosopher. *Essays*, "Spiritual Laws" (First Series, 1841).

11 The revelation of Thought takes men out of servitude into freedom.

> RALPH WALDO EMERSON (1803–82), U.S. essayist, poet, philosopher. *The Conduct of Life*, "Fate" (1860).

12 Either you think—or else others have to think for you and take power from you, pervert and discipline your natural tastes, civilize and sterilize you.

> F. SCOTT FITZGERALD (1896–1940), U.S. author. Nicole's thoughts, in *Tender is the Night*, bk. 3, ch. 7 (1934).

13 It is clear that all verbal structures with meaning are verbal imitations of that elusive psychological and physiological process known as thought, a process stumbling through emotional entanglements, sudden irrational convictions, involuntary gleams of insight, rationalized prejudices, and blocks of panic and inertia, finally to reach a completely incommunicable intuition.

> NORTHROP FRYE (1912-91), Canadian literary critic. *Anatomy of Criticism*, Second Essay, "Formal Phase: Symbol as Image" (1957).

14 It was at a particular moment in the history of my own rages that I saw the Western world conditioned by the images of Marx, Darwin and Freud; and Marx, Darwin and Freud are the three most crashing bores of the Western world. The simplistic popularization of their ideas has thrust our world into a mental straitjacket from which we can only escape by the most anarchic violence.

> WILLIAM GOLDING (1911-93), British author. "Belief and Creativity," lecture, 11 April 1980, Hamburg, Germany (repr. in *A Moving Target*, 1982).

15 Thought would destroy their paradise.

> THOMAS GRAY (1716–71), English poet. *Ode on a Distant Prospect of Eton College*.

16 Little-minded people's thoughts move in such small circles that five minutes' conversation gives you an arc long enough to determine their whole curve.

> OLIVER WENDELL HOLMES, SR. (1809–94), U.S. writer, physician. *The Autocrat of the Breakfast-Table*, ch. 1 (1858).

17 Most of one's life is one prolonged effort to prevent oneself thinking.

> ALDOUS HUXLEY (1894–1963), British author. Mr. Topes, in *Mortal Coils*, "Green Tunnels" (1922).

18 Thought must be divided against itself before it can come to any knowledge of itself.

> ALDOUS HUXLEY (1894–1963), British author. *Do What You Will*, "Wordsworth in the Tropics" (1929).

19 All thought must, directly or indirectly, by way of certain characters, relate ultimately to intuitions, and therefore, with us, to sensibility, because in no other way can an object be given to us.

> IMMANUEL KANT (1724–1804), German philosopher. *Critique of Pure Reason*, "Transcendental Doctrine of Elements: Introduction to Transcendental Aesthetics," A.20/B.34 (1781).

20 When I write down my thoughts, they do not escape me. This action makes me remember my strength which I forget at all times. I educate myself proportionately to my captured thought. I aim only to distinguish the contradiction between my mind and nothingness.

> ISIDORE DUCASSE, COMTE DE LAUTRÉAMONT (1846–70), French author, poet. *Poésies*, ch. 2 (1870).

21 Rational free spirits are the light brigade who go on ahead and reconnoitre the ground which the heavy brigade of the orthodox will eventually occupy.

> G. C. LICHTENBERG (1742–99), German physicist, philosopher. *Aphorisms*, "Notebook H," aph. 36 (written 1765–99; tr. by R. J. Hollingdale, 1990).

22 Man cannot produce a single work without the assistance of the slow, assiduous, corrosive worm of thought.

> EUGENIO MONTALE (1896–1981), Italian poet. *Poet In Our Time* (1972).

23 Thoughts are the shadows of our sensations—always darker, emptier, simpler than these.

> FRIEDRICH NIETZSCHE (1844–1900), German philosopher. *The Gay Science*, aph. 179 (rev. ed. 1887).

24 We do not live to think, but, on the contrary, we think in order that we may succeed in surviving.

> JOSÉ ORTEGA Y GASSET (1883–1955), Spanish essayist, philosopher. "In Search of Goethe from Within," in *Partisan Review* (New Brunswick, N.J., Dec. 1949; repr. in *The Dehumanization of Art and Other Essays*, 1968).

25 Man is obviously made for thinking. Therein lies all his dignity and his merit; and his whole duty is to think as he ought.

> BLAISE PASCAL (1623–62), French scientist, philosopher. *Pensées* (1670; no. 620 ed. by Krailsheimer, no. 146 ed. by Brunschvicg). Pascal expanded on this idea in another aphorism: "All our dignity consists in thought. It is on thought that we must depend for our reovery, not on space and time which we could never fill. Let us then strive to think well; that is the basic principle of morality." (no. 200 ed. by Krailsheimer, no. 347 ed. by Brunschvicg).

26 Modern man likes to pretend that his thinking is wide-awake. But this wide-awake thinking has led us into the mazes of a nightmare in which the torture chambers are endlessly repeated in the mirrors of reason.

> OCTAVIO PAZ (b. 1914), Mexican poet, essayist. *The Labyrinth of Solitude*, ch. 9 (1950; tr. 1961).

27 Man
You beheld the saddest and dreariest of all the
flowers of the earth
And as with other flowers you gave it a name
You called it Thought.

> JACQUES PRÉVERT (1900–1977), French poet. *Paroles*, "Flowers and Wreaths" (1946; tr. by Lawrence Ferlinghetti, 1958).

28 To reflect is to disturb one's thoughts.

> JEAN ROSTAND (1894–1977), French biologist, writer. *Pensées d'un Biologiste* (1939; repr. in *The Substance of Man*, ch. 10, 1962).

29 The birth of thought in the depths of the spirit, the shaping and ordering of it into periods, the translation into signs, and above all the transference of it from one spirit to another, the communication that is, if only for an instant, the meeting of two beings, with the unforeseeable consequences that such a meeting always causes, is in fact a miracle; except that the moment one stops to think about it one can't even write a letter.

> SALVATORE SATTA (1902–75), Italian jurist, novelist. *The Day of Judgment*, ch. 20 (1979).

30 It is difficult, if not impossible, for most people to think otherwise than in the fashion of their own period.

> GEORGE BERNARD SHAW (1856–1950), Anglo-Irish playwright, critic. *Saint Joan*, Preface (1923).

31 Thought is an infection. In the case of certain thoughts, it becomes an epidemic.

> WALLACE STEVENS (1879–1955), U.S. poet. *Opus Posthumous*, "Adagia" (1959).

32 Having each some shingles of thought well dried, we sat and whittled them.

> HENRY DAVID THOREAU (1817–62), U.S. philosopher, author, naturalist. *Walden*, "Winter Visitors" (1854).

33 Thought is made in the mouth.

> TRISTAN TZARA (1896–1963), Rumanian-born French Dada theorist. "Dada Manifesto on Feeble Love and Bitter Love," sct. 4, in *La Vie des Lettres*, no. 4 (Paris, 1921; repr. in *The Dada Painters and Poets*, ed. by Robert Motherwell, 1951).

34 They use thought only to justify their injustices, and speech only to disguise their thoughts.

> VOLTAIRE (1694–1778), French philosopher, author. Le Chapon, in *Dialogues*, "Le Chapon et la Poularde" (1765), describing the ways of men.

35 Thinking is the most unhealthy thing in the world, and people die of it just as they die of any other disease. Fortunately, in England at any rate, thought is not catching. Our splendid physique as a people is entirely due to our national stupidity.

> OSCAR WILDE (1854–1900), Anglo-Irish playwright, author. Vivian, in *The Decay of Lying* (published in *Intentions*, 1891).

36 In order to be able to set a limit to thought, we should have to find both sides of the limit thinkable (i.e. we should have to be able to think what cannot be thought).

> LUDWIG WITTGENSTEIN (1889–1951), Austrian philosopher. *Tractatus Logico-Philosophicus*, Preface (1921).

37 A man's thinking goes on within his consciousness in a seclusion in comparison with which any physical seclusion is an exhibition to public view.

> LUDWIG WITTGENSTEIN (1889–1951), Austrian philosopher. *Philosophical Investigations*, pt. 2, sct. 2 (1953).

38 We all indulge in the strange, pleasant process called thinking, but when it comes to saying, even to someone opposite, what we think, then how little we are able to convey! The phantom is through the mind and out of the window before we can lay salt on its tail, or slowly sinking and returning to the profound darkness which it has lit up momentarily with a wandering light.

> VIRGINIA WOOLF (1882–1941), British novelist. *The Common Reader*, "Montaigne" (First Series, 1925).

See also Longfellow on PROGRESS: Vauvenargues on SIMPLICITY.

TIME

1 The geometry of landscape and situation seems to create its own systems of time, the sense of a dynamic element which is cinematising the events of the canvas, translating a posture or ceremony into dynamic terms. The greatest movie of the 20th century is the Mona Lisa, just as the greatest novel is *Gray's Anatomy*.

> J. G. BALLARD (b. 1930), British author. "The Thousand Wounds and Flowers," review of J. T. Frazer, *The Voices of Time*, in *New Worlds*, no. 191 (London, June 1969; repr. in *Re/Search*, no. 8/9, San Francisco, 1984).

2 We are weighed down, every moment, by the conception and the sensation of Time. And there are but two means of escaping and forgetting this nightmare: pleasure and work. Pleasure consumes us. Work strengthens us. Let us choose.

> CHARLES BAUDELAIRE (1821–67), French poet. *My Heart Laid Bare* (written c. 1865; published in *Intimate Journals*, sct. 111,

1887; tr. by Christopher Isherwood 1930; rev. by Don Bachardy 1989).

3 Modern thought has transferred the spectral character of Death to the notion of time itself. Time has become Death triumphant over all.

> JOHN BERGER (b. 1926), British author, critic. "That Which Is Held," in *Village Voice* (New York, 13 April 1982; repr. in *Keeping a Rendezvous*, 1992).

4 To everything there is a season, and a time to every purpose under the heaven: a time to be born and a time to die; a time to plant, and a time to pluck up that which is planted; a time to kill, and a time to heal; a time to break down, and a time to build up; a time to weep, and a time to laugh; a time to mourn and a time to dance; a time to cast away stones, and a time to gather stones together; a time to embrace, and a time to refrain from embracing; a time to get, and a time to lose; a time to keep, and a time to cast away; a time to rend, and a time to sew; a time to keep silence, and a time to speak; a time to love, and a time to hate; a time of war, and a time of peace.

> BIBLE, HEBREW. *Ecclesiastes* 3:1–8.

5 The hours of folly are measured by the clock, but of wisdom no clock can measure.

> WILLIAM BLAKE (1757–1827), English poet, painter, engraver. *The Marriage of Heaven and Hell*, Plate 7, "Proverbs of Hell" (1790).

6 Time is the substance from which I am made. Time is a river which carries me along, but I am the river; it is a tiger that devours me, but I am the tiger; it is a fire that consumes me, but I am the fire.

> JORGE LUIS BORGES (1899–1986), Argentinian author. *Labyrinths*, "A New Refutation of Time" (1964).

7 Oh Time! the beautifier of the dead,
Adorner of the ruin, comforter
And only healer when the heart hath bled;
. . . Time, the avenger!

> LORD BYRON (1788–1824), English poet. *Childe Harold's Pilgrimage*, cto. 4, st. 130.

8 The illimitable, silent, never-resting thing called Time, rolling, rushing on, swift, silent, like an all-embracing ocean-tide, on which we and all the universe swim like exhalations, like apparitions which *are,* and then *are not*: this is forever very literally a miracle; a thing to strike us dumb, for we have no word to speak about it.

> THOMAS CARLYLE (1795–1881), Scottish essayist, historian. *On Heroes and Hero-Worship*, Lecture 1, "The Hero as Divinity" (1841).

9 I recommend to you to take care of the minutes; for hours will take care of themselves.

> LORD CHESTERFIELD (1694–1773), English statesman, man of letters. Letter, 6 Nov. 1747 (first published 1774; repr. in *The Letters of the Earl of Chesterfield to His Son*, vol. 1, no. 131, ed. by Charles Strachey, 1901).

10 Nods from the Gilded pointers—
Nods from the Seconds slim—
Decades of Arrogance between

The Dial life—
And Him—

> EMILY DICKINSON (1830–86), U.S. poet. *The Complete Poems*, no. 287 (1955).

11 Time goes, you say? Ah, no!
Alas, Time stays, *we* go.

> AUSTIN DOBSON (1840–1921), British author. *The Paradox of Time.*

12 The best way to fill time is to waste it.

> MARGUERITE DURAS (b. 1914), French author, filmmaker. *Practicalities*, "Wasting Time" (1987; tr. 1990).

13 The surest poison is time.

> RALPH WALDO EMERSON (1803–82), U.S. essayist, poet, philosopher. *Society and Solitude*, "Old Age" (1870).

14 City people try to buy time as a rule, when they can, whereas country people are prepared to kill time, although both try to cherish in their mind's eye the notion of a better life ahead.

> EDWARD HOAGLAND (b. 1932), U.S. novelist, essayist. "The Ridge-Slope Fox and The Knife-Thrower," in *Harper's* (New York, Jan. 1977; repr. in *Heart's Desire*, 1988).

15 Time, you old gypsy man,
Will you not stay,
Put up your caravan
Just for one day?

> RALPH HODGESON (1871–1962), British poet. *Time, You Old Gypsy Man.*

16 O, for an engine, to keep back all clocks,
Or make the sun forget his motion!

> BEN JONSON (1573–1637), English dramatist, poet. Lady Frampul, in *The New Inn*, act 4, sc. 3.

17 We must use time as a tool, not as a couch.

> JOHN F. KENNEDY (1917–63), U.S. Democratic politician, president. Quoted in: *Observer* (London, 10 Dec. 1961).

18 We all run on two clocks. One is the outside clock, which ticks away our decades and brings us ceaselessly to the dry season. The other is the inside clock, where you are your own timekeeper and determine your own chronology, your own internal weather and your own rate of living. Sometimes the inner clock runs itself out long before the outer one, and you see a dead man going through the motions of living.

> MAX LERNER (b. 1902), U.S. author, columnist. "Fifty," in *New York Post* (18 Dec. 1952; repr. in *The Unfinished Country*, pt. 1, 1959).

19 Time! Joyless emblem of the greed
Of millions, robber of the best
Which earth can give . . .

> AMY LOWELL (1874–1925), U.S. poet. *New York at Night.*

20 But at my back I always hear
Time's wingèd chariot hurrying near.

> ANDREW MARVELL (1621–78), English metaphysical poet. *To His Coy Mistress.*

21 We should not say that one man's hour is worth another man's hour, but rather that one man during an hour is worth just as much as another man during an hour. Time is everything, man is nothing: he is at the most time's carcass.

> KARL MARX (1818–83), German political theorist, social philosopher. *The Poverty of Philosophy*, ch. 1, pt. 2 (1847; repr. in *Karl Marx and Friedrich Engels: Collected Works*, vol. 6, 1976).

22 While time,
The endless idiot, runs screaming 'round the world.

> CARSON MCCULLERS (1917–67), U.S. author. *When We Are Lost*, st. 2.

23 For tribal man space was the uncontrollable mystery. For technological man it is time that occupies the same role.

> MARSHALL MCLUHAN (1911–80), Canadian communications theorist. *The Mechanical Bride*, "Magic that Changes Mood" (1951).

24 Time is a great legalizer, even in the field of morals.

> H. L. MENCKEN (1880–1956), U.S. journalist. *A Book of Prefaces*, ch. 4, sct. 6 (1917).

25 Time and I against any two.

> SPANISH PROVERB. Quoted by Cardinal Mazarin during the minority of Louis XIV.

26 American time has stretched around the world. It has become the dominant tempo of modern history, especially of the history of Europe.

> HAROLD ROSENBERG (1906–78), U.S. art critic, author. *The Tradition of the New*, ch. 14 (1960).

27 A truer image of the world, I think, is obtained by picturing things as entering into the stream of time from an eternal world outside, than from a view which regards time as the devouring tyrant of all that is.

> BERTRAND RUSSELL (1872–1970), British philosopher, mathematician. *A Free Man's Worship and Other Essays*, ch. 2 (1976).

28 Everything passes, everything perishes, everything palls.

> FRENCH SAYING.

29 O, call back yesterday, bid time return.

> WILLIAM SHAKESPEARE (1564–1616), English dramatist, poet. Salisbury, in *Richard II*, act 3, sc. 2.

30 And thus the whirligig of time brings in his revenges.

> WILLIAM SHAKESPEARE (1564–1616), English dramatist, poet. Feste, in *Twelfth Night*, act 5, sc. 1.

31 Time is the only critic without ambition.

> JOHN STEINBECK (1902–68), U.S. author. *Writers at Work*, "On Critics" (Fourth Series, ed. by George Plimpton, 1977).

32 The longest day must have its close—the gloomiest night will wear on to a morning. An eternal, inexorable lapse of moments is ever hurrying the day of the evil to an eternal night, and the night of the just to an eternal day.

> HARRIET BEECHER STOWE (1811–96), U.S. novelist, anti-slavery campaigner. *Uncle Tom's Cabin*, ch. 40 (1852).

33 Time turns the old days to derision,
Our loves into corpses or wives;

And marriage and death and division
Make barren our lives.

> A. C. SWINBURNE (1837–1909), English poet. *Dolores*, st. 20.

34 As if you could kill time without injuring eternity.

> HENRY DAVID THOREAU (1817–62), U.S. philosopher, author, naturalist. *Walden*, "Economy" (1854).

35 When as a child I laughed and wept,
Time crept.
When as a youth I waxed more bold,
Time *strolled*.
When I became a full-grown man,
Time RAN.
When older still I daily grew,
Time FLEW.
Soon I shall find, in passing on,
Time *gone*.
O Christ! wilt Thou have saved me then?
Amen.

> HENRY TWELLS (1823–1900), English rhymster. *Time's Paces*, poem fixed to the front of the clock-case in the North Transept of Chester Cathedral. Quoted in: Alan L. Mackay, *The Harvest of a Quiet Eye* (1977).

36 Here or henceforward it is all the same to me, I accept Time absolutely.

> WALT WHITMAN (1819–92), U.S. poet. *Leaves of Grass*, "Song of Myself," sct. 23 (1855).

37 Time is waste of money.

> OSCAR WILDE (1854–1900), Anglo-Irish playwright, author. "Phrases and Philosophies for the Use of the Young," in *Chameleon* (London, Dec. 1894).

38 For time is the longest distance between two places.

> TENNESSEE WILLIAMS (1914–83), U.S. dramatist. Tom, in *The Glass Menagerie*, sc. 7.

39 Time rushes toward us with its hospital tray of infinitely varied narcotics, even while it is preparing us for its inevitably fatal operation.

> TENNESSEE WILLIAMS (1914–83), U.S. dramatist. *The Rose Tattoo*, "The Timeless World of a Play" (1951).

40 We are always acting on what has just finished happening. It happened at least 1/30th of a second ago. We think we're in the present, but we aren't. The present we know is only a movie of the past.

> TOM WOLFE (b. 1931), U.S. author, journalist. Ken Kesey's philosophy, as explained in *The Electric Kool-Aid Acid Test*, ch. 11 (1968).

41 The years like great black oxen tread the world,
And God the herdsman treads them on behind,
And I am broken by their passing feet.

> W. B. YEATS (1865–1939), Irish poet, playwright. *The Countess Cathleen*, act 4.

42 Without music to decorate it, time is just a bunch of boring production deadlines or dates by which bills must be paid.

> FRANK ZAPPA (b. 1940), U.S. rock musician. *The Real Frank Zappa Book*, ch. 8 (1989; written with Peter Occhiogrosso).

See also Munro on DAY; Shakespeare on FAME; PUNCTUALITY.

TOASTS

1 Here's to the maiden of bashful fifteen;
Here's to the widow of fifty;
Here's to the flaunting extravagant queen;
And here's to the housewife that's thrifty.
Let the toast pass,—
Drink to the lass,
I'll warrant she'll prove an excuse for the glass.

RICHARD BRINSLEY SHERIDAN (1751–1816), Anglo-Irish dramatist. Chorus, in *The School for Scandal,* act 3, sc. 3.

2 May you live all the days of your life.

JONATHAN SWIFT (1667–1745), Anglo-Irish satirist. The Colonel, in *Polite Conversation,* Dialogue 2 (1738).

See also Bossidy on BOSTON.

TOLERANCE

1 For ye suffer fools gladly, seeing ye yourselves are wise.

BIBLE: NEW TESTAMENT. Paul, in *2 Corinthians* 11:19.

2 Persecution was at least a sign of personal interest. Tolerance is composed of nine parts of apathy to one of brotherly love.

FRANK MOORE COLBY (1865–1925), U.S. editor, essayist. *The Colby Essays,* vol. 1, "Trials of an Encyclopedist" (1926).

3 Tolerance is a very dull virtue. It is boring. Unlike love, it has always had a bad press. It is negative. It merely means putting up with people, being able to stand things.

E. M. FORSTER (1879–1970), British novelist, essayist. *Two Cheers for Democracy,* "Tolerance" (1951). The essay, written in 1941, looked ahead to the post-war world, and the necessity to accept former enemies. "I don't . . . regard tolerance as a great eternally established divine principle . . ." Forster wrote. "It is just a makeshift, suitable for an overcrowded and overheated planet . . . . It's dull. And yet it entails imagination."

4 Toleration is the greatest gift of the mind; it requires the same effort of the brain that it takes to balance oneself on a bicycle.

HELEN KELLER (1880–1968), U.S. blind/deaf author, lecturer. *The Story of My Life,* pt. 3, "Personality" (1903).

5 Tolerance is only another name for indifference.

W. SOMERSET MAUGHAM (1874–1966), British author. *A Writer's Notebook* (1949), entry for 1896.

6 For this is one of the ancientest laws among them; that no man shall be blamed for reasoning in the maintenance of his own religion.

THOMAS MORE (1478–1535), English statesman, author. *Utopia,* bk. 2, "Of the Religions in Utopia" (1516).

See also Crisp on PREJUDICE.

TOOLS

1 And if thou wilt make me an altar of stone, thou shalt not build it of hewn stone: for if thou lift up thy tool upon it, thou hast polluted it.

BIBLE, HEBREW. *Exodus* 20:25.

2 Man is a tool-using animal. . . . Without tools he is nothing, with tools he is all.

THOMAS CARLYLE (1795–1881), Scottish essayist, historian. *Sartor Resartus,* bk. 1, ch. 5 (1833–34). Benjamin Franklin was also quoted as defining man as a *tool-making* animal in James Boswell, *Life of Samuel Johnson,* 7 April 1778 (1791).

3 There is a great satisfaction in building good tools for other people to use.

FREEMAN DYSON (b. 1923), British-born U.S. physicist, author. *Disturbing the Universe,* pt. 1, ch. 1 (1979).

4 A worker may be the hammer's master, but the hammer still prevails. A tool knows exactly how it is meant to be handled, while the user of the tool can only have an approximate idea.

MILAN KUNDERA (b. 1929), Czech author, critic. *The Book of Laughter and Forgetting,* pt. 7, ch. 8 (1978; tr. 1980).

5 But lo! men have become the tools of their tools.

HENRY DAVID THOREAU (1817–62), U.S. philosopher, author, naturalist. *Walden,* "Economy" (1854).

TORTURE

1 One of the most horrible, yet most important, discoveries of our age has been that, if you really wish to destroy a person and turn him into an automaton, the surest method is not physical torture, in the strict sense, but simply to keep him awake, i.e., in an existential relation to life without intermission.

W. H. AUDEN (1907–73), Anglo-American poet. *The Dyer's Hand,* pt. 3, "Hic et Ille," sct. C (1962).

2 Torment, for some men, is a need, an appetite, and an accomplishment.

E. M. CIORAN (b. 1911), Rumanian-born French philosopher. *The New Gods,* "Strangled Thoughts," sct. 3 (1969; tr. 1974).

3 There is only one thing that arouses animals more than pleasure, and that is pain. Under torture you are as if under the dominion of those grasses that produce visions. Everything you have heard told, everything you have read returns to your mind, as if you were being transported, not toward heaven, but toward hell. Under torture you say not only what the inquisitor wants, but also what you imagine might please him, because a bond (this, truly, diabolical) is established between you and him.

UMBERTO ECO (b. 1932), Italian semiologist, novelist. Brother William, in *The Name of the Rose,* "First Day: Sext" (1980; tr. 1983).

4 The healthy man does not torture others—generally it is the tortured who turn into torturers.

CARL JUNG (1875–1961), Swiss psychiatrist. "Return to the Simple Life," in *DU,* vol. 1 (Zurich, May 1941; repr. in *Collected Works,* vol. 18, ed. by William McGuire).

5 Man torturing man is a fiend beyond description. You turn a corner in the dark and there he is. You congeal into a bundle of inanimate fear. You become the

very soul of anaesthesia. But there is no escaping him. It is your turn now . . .

HENRY MILLER (1891–1980), U.S. author. *The Air-Conditioned Nightmare*, "The Soul of Anaesthesia" (1945).

6 The universe appears to me like an immense, inexorable torture-garden. . . . Passions, greed, hatred, and lies; law, social institutions, justice, love, glory, heroism, and religion: these are its monstrous flowers and its hideous instruments of eternal human suffering.

OCTAVE MIRBEAU (1850–1917), French journalist, author. *The Torture Garden*, "The Garden," ch. 9 (1899).

7 Pain forces even the innocent to lie.

PUBLILIUS SYRUS (1st century B.C.), Roman writer of mimes. *Sententiae*, no. 171.

8 I've already told you: the only way to a woman's heart is along the path of torment. I know none other as sure.

MARQUIS DE SADE (1740–1814), French author. Oxtiern, in *Oxtiern, ou les Malheurs du Libertinage*, act 2, sc. 1 (1791; repr. in *120 Days of Sodom, and Other Writings*, ed. and tr. by Austryn Wainhouse and Richard Seaver, 1966).

TOTALITARIANISM

1 Only the mob and the elite can be attracted by the momentum of totalitarianism itself. The masses have to be won by propaganda.

HANNAH ARENDT (1906–75), German-born U.S. political philosopher. *The Origins of Totalitarianism*, ch. 3, sct. 11 (1951).

2 Totalitarianism is never content to rule by external means, namely, through the state and a machinery of violence; thanks to its peculiar ideology and the role assigned to it in this apparatus of coercion, totalitarianism has discovered a means of dominating and terrorizing human beings from within.

HANNAH ARENDT (1906–75), German-born U.S. political philosopher. *The Origins of Totalitarianism*, ch. 10, sct. 1 (1951).

3 One leader, one people, signifies one master and millions of slaves.

ALBERT CAMUS (1913–60), French-Algerian philosopher, author. *The Rebel*, pt. 3, "State Terrorism and Irrational Terror" (1951; tr. 1953).

4 People who live in the post-totalitarian system know only too well that the question of whether one or several political parties are in power, and how these parties define and label themselves, is of far less importance than the question of whether or not it is possible to live like a human being.

VÁCLAV HAVEL (b. 1936), Czech playwright, president. *Living in Truth*, pt. 1, "The Power of the Powerless," sct. 11 (1986). "Post-totalitarianism" is the term used by Havel—writing before the dissolution of the Iron Curtain—to describe Czechoslovakia and other East European states: "totalitarian in a way fundamentally different from classical dictatorships."

5 There is a totalitarian regime inside every one of us. We are ruled by a ruthless politburo which sets our norms and drives us from one five-year plan to another. The

autonomous individual who has to justify his existence by his own efforts is in eternal bondage to himself.

ERIC HOFFER (1902–83), U.S. philosopher. *The Passionate State of Mind*, aph. 28 (1955).

6 Man is more disposed to domination than freedom; and a structure of dominion not only gladdens the eye of the master who rears and protects it, but even its servants are uplifted by the thought that they are members of a whole, which rises high above the life and strength of single generations.

KARL WILHELM VON HUMBOLDT (1767–1835), German statesman, philologist. *The Limits of State Action*, ch. 16 (written 1792; published 1854; tr. and ed. by J. W. Burrow, 1969).

7 The only successful revolution of this century is totalitarianism.

BERNARD-HENRI LEVY (b. 1948), French philosopher. *Time* (New York, 12 Sep. 1977).

8 Unless democracy is to commit suicide by consenting to its own destruction, it will have to find some formidable answer to those who come to it saying: "I demand from you in the name of your principles the rights which I shall deny to you later in the name of my principles."

WALTER LIPPMANN (1889–1974), U.S. journalist. "Mr. John Strachey's Case and the Law," in *New York Herald Tribune* (13 Oct. 1938; repr. in *The Essential Lippman*, pt. 2, sct. 4, 1982).

9 Without general elections, without unrestricted freedom of press and assembly, without a free struggle of opinion, life dies out in every public institution, becomes a mere semblance of life, in which only the bureaucracy remains as the active element. Public life gradually falls asleep, a few dozen party leaders of inexhaustible energy and boundless experience direct and rule. . . . Such conditions must inevitably cause a brutalization of public life: attempted assassinations, shootings of hostages, etc.

ROSA LUXEMBURG (1870–1919), German revolutionary. Prison notes, 1918 (published in *The Russian Revolution*, ch. 6, 1922; tr. 1961).

10 Since it is difficult to join them together, it is safer to be feared than to be loved when one of the two must be lacking.

NICCOLÒ MACHIAVELLI (1469–1527), Italian political philosopher, statesman. *The Prince*, ch. 17 (1514).

TOUCH

1 All disgust is originally disgust at touching.

WALTER BENJAMIN (1892–1940), German critic, philosopher. *One-Way Street*, "Gloves" (1928; repr. in *One-Way Street and Other Writings*, 1978).

2 O why do you walk through the fields in gloves,
Missing so much and so much?
O fat white woman whom nobody loves,
Why do you walk through the fields in gloves
When the grass is soft as the breast of doves
And shivering sweet to the touch?

FRANCES CORNFORD (1886–1960), British poet. *To a Fat Lady Seen from a Train*.

TOURISM

1 The time to enjoy a European tour is about three weeks after you unpack.

> GEORGE ADE (1866–1944), U.S. humorist, playwright. *Forty Modern Fables*, "The Hungry Man from the Bird Center" (1901).

2 The American arrives in Paris with a few French phrases he has culled from a conversational guide or picked up from a friend who owns a beret.

> FRED ALLEN (1894–1957), U.S. radio comic. Introduction to Art Buchwald, *Paris After Dark* (1954).

3 I am leaving the town to the invaders: increasingly numerous, mediocre, dirty, badly behaved, shameless tourists.

> BRIGITTE BARDOT (b. 1933), French screen actor. Quoted in: *International Herald Tribune* (Paris, 10 Aug. 1989), on leaving her home at Saint Tropez.

4 For the perfect idler, for the passionate observer it becomes an immense source of enjoyment to establish his dwelling in the throng, in the ebb and flow, the bustle, the fleeting and the infinite. To be away from home and yet to feel at home anywhere; to see the world, to be at the very center of the world, and yet to be unseen of the world, such are some of the minor pleasures of those independent, intense and impartial spirits, who do not lend themselves easily to linguistic definitions. The observer is a prince enjoying his incognito wherever he goes.

> CHARLES BAUDELAIRE (1821–67), French poet. "The Painter of Modern life," sct. 3, in *L'Art Romantique* (1869; repr. in *Selected Writings on Art and Artists*, ed. by P. E. Charvet, 1972).

5 The traveller, however virginal and enthusiastic, does not enjoy an unbroken ecstasy. He has periods of gloom, periods when he asks himself the object of all these exertions, and puts the question whether or not he is really experiencing pleasure. At such times he suspects that he is not seeing the right things, that the characteristic, the right aspects of these strange scenes are escaping him. He looks forward dully to the days of his holiday yet to pass, and wonders how he will dispose of them. He is disgusted because his money is not more, his command of the language so slight, and his capacity for enjoyment so limited.

> ARNOLD BENNETT (1867–1931), British novelist. *The Journals of Arnold Bennett* (1932), entry for 25 Oct. 1897.

6 Should we have stayed at home and thought of here?
Where should we be today?
Is it right to be watching strangers in a play
in this strangest of theatres?

> ELIZABETH BISHOP (1911–79), U.S. poet. *Questions of Travel*. Bishop, an avid traveler, spent the last 16 years of her life in Brazil.

7 Modern tourist guides have helped raised tourist expectations. And they have provided the natives—from Kaiser Wilhelm down to the villagers of Chichacestenango—with a detailed and itemized list of what is expected of them and when. These are the up-to-date scripts for actors on the tourists' stage.

> DANIEL J. BOORSTIN (b. 1914), U.S. historian. *The Image*, ch. 3 (1961).

8 The modern American tourist now fills his experience with pseudo-events. He has come to expect both more strangeness and more familiarity than the world naturally offers. He has come to believe that he can have a lifetime of adventure in two weeks and all the thrills of risking his life without any real risk at all.

> DANIEL J. BOORSTIN (b. 1914), U.S. historian. *The Image*, ch. 3 (1961).

9 I swims in the Tagus all across at once, and I rides on an ass or a mule, and swears Portuguese, and have got a diarrhoea and bites from the mosquitoes. But what of that? Comfort must not be expected by folks that go a pleasuring.

> LORD BYRON (1788–1824), English poet. Letter, 16 July 1809 (published in *Byron's Letters and Journals*, vol. 1, ed. by Leslie A. Marchand, 1973).

10 The idea that seeing life means going from place to place and doing a great variety of obvious things is an illusion natural to dull minds.

> CHARLES HORTON COOLEY (1864–1929), U.S. sociologist. *Human Nature and the Social Order*, ch. 4 (1902).

11 The *personal appropriation of clichés* is a condition for the spread of cultural tourism.

> SERGE DANEY (1944–92), French film critic. "Falling out of Love," in *Sight and Sound*, vol. 2, no. 3 (London, July 1992).

12 Tourism, human circulation considered as consumption . . . is fundamentally nothing more than the leisure of going to see what has become banal.

> GUY DEBORD (b. 1931), French Situationist philosopher. *The Society of the Spectacle*, ch. 7, sct. 168 (1967; tr. 1977).

13 To be a tourist is to escape accountability. Errors and failings don't cling to you the way they do back home. You're able to drift across continents and languages, suspending the operation of sound thought. Tourism is the march of stupidity. You're expected to be stupid. The entire mechanism of the host country is geared to travelers acting stupidly. You walk around dazed, squinting into fold-out maps. You don't know how to talk to people, how to get anywhere, what the money means, what time it is, what to eat or how to eat it. Being stupid is the pattern, the level and the norm. You can exist on this level for weeks and months without reprimand or dire consequence. Together with thousands, you are granted immunities and broad freedoms. You are an army of fools, wearing bright polyesters, riding camels, taking pictures of each other, haggard, dysenteric, thirsty. There is nothing to think about but the next shapeless event.

> DON DELILLO (b. 1926), U.S. author. James Axton, in *The Names*, ch. 3 (1982).

14 Sailin' 'round the world in a dirty gondola
Oh, to be back in the land of Coca-Cola!

> BOB DYLAN (b. 1941), U.S. singer, songwriter. "When I Paint My Masterpiece" (1971; on the album *More Greatest Hits*, 1972).

15 The country of the tourist pamphlet always is another country, an embarrassing abstraction of the desirable that, thank God, does not exist on this planet, where there are always ants and bad smells and empty Coca-Cola bottles to keep the grubby finger-print of reality upon the beautiful.

> NADINE GORDIMER (b. 1923), South African author. *A World of Strangers*, ch. 1 (1958).

16 Though there are some disagreeable things in Venice there is nothing so disagreeable as the visitors.

> HENRY JAMES (1843–1916), U.S. author. *Italian Hours*, "Venice," sct. 2 (1909; written 1882).

17 Worth seeing? Yes; but not worth going to see.

> SAMUEL JOHNSON (1709–84), English author, lexicographer. Quoted in: James Boswell, *Life of Samuel Johnson* 12 Oct. 1779 (1791), in response to James Boswell's question, "Is not the Giant's Causeway worth seeing?."

18 Behold then Septimus Dodge returning to Dodgetown victorious. Not crowned with laurel, it is true, but wreathed in lists of things he has seen and sucked dry. Seen and sucked dry, you know: Venus de Milo, the Rhine or the Coloseum: swallowed like so many clams, and left the shells.

> D. H. LAWRENCE (1885–1930), British author. *Studies in Classic American Literature*, ch. 4 (1924).

19 The tourist who moves about to see and hear and open himself to all the influences of the places which condense centuries of human greatness is only a man in search of excellence.

> MAX LERNER (b. 1902), U.S. author, columnist. "Lo, the Poor Sightseer," in *New York Post* (15 Sept. 1954; repr. in *The Unfinished Country*, pt. 1, 1959).

20 Does this boat go to Europe, France?

> ANITA LOOS (1888–1981), U.S. novelist, screenwriter. Marilyn Monroe, in the film *Gentlemen Prefer Blondes* (directed by Howard Hawkes, screenplay by Charles Lederer, based on an original novel by Anita Loos, 1953).

21 As for pictures and museums, that don't trouble me. The worst of going abroad is that you've always got to look at things of that sort. To have to do it at home would be beyond a joke.

> MARGARET OLIPHANT (1828–97), English novelist, historian. Clarence Copperhead, in *Phoebe, Junior*, ch. 26 (1876), the fifth of *Chronicles of Carlingford*.

22 In the middle ages people were tourists because of their religion, whereas now they are tourists because tourism is their religion.

> ROBERT RUNCIE (b. 1921), British ecclesiastic, Archbishop of Canterbury. Quoted in: *Independent* (London, 7 Dec. 1988).

23 Using a camera appeases the anxiety which the work-driven feel about not working when they are on vacation and supposed to be having fun. They have something to do that is like a friendly imitation of work: they can take pictures.

> SUSAN SONTAG (b. 1933), U.S. essayist. *On Photography*, "Plato's Cave" (1977).

24 Inter-railers are the ambulatory equivalent of McDonalds, walking testimony to the erosion of French culture.

> ALICE THOMPSON (b. 1963), British travel writer, journalist. *Ticket to Ride the Rails of France*, in *Times* (London, 16 July 1992).

25 You perceive I generalize with intrepidity from single instances. It is the tourist's custom.

> MARK TWAIN (1835–1910), U.S. author. *Mark Twain's Notebooks and Journals*, vol. 2 (ed. by Frederick Anderson, 1975), Notebook 18.

26 I was disappointed in Niagara—most people must be disappointed in Niagara. Every American bride is taken there, and the sight of the stupendous waterfall must be one of the earliest, if not the keenest, disappointments in American married life.

> OSCAR WILDE (1854–1900), Anglo-Irish playwright, author. "Personal Impressions of America," lecture, 10 July 1883.

See also Morley on The BRITISH; Burney on ITALY AND THE ITALIANS; TRAVEL.

TOWN AND COUNTRY

1 If you would be known, and not know, vegetate in a village; if you would know, and not be known, live in a city.

> C. C. COLTON (1780–1832), English author. *Lacon*, vol. 1, no. 334 (1820).

2 God the first garden made, and the first city Cain.

> ABRAHAM COWLEY (1618–67), English essayist, poet. *The Garden* (1666).

3 When a village ceases to be a community, it becomes oppressive in its narrow conformity. So one becomes an individual and migrates to the city. There, finding others likeminded, one re-establishes a village community. Nowadays only New Yorkers are yokels.

> PAUL GOODMAN (1911–72), U.S. author, poet, critic. *Five Years*, "Winter and Spring 1956–1957," sct. 8 (1966).

4 Country people tend to consider that they have a corner on righteousness and to distrust most manifestations of cleverness, while people in the city are leery of righteousness but ascribe to themselves all manner of cleverness.

> EDWARD HOAGLAND (b. 1932), U.S. novelist, essayist. "The Ridge-Slope Fox and The Knife-Thrower," in *Harper's* (New York, Jan. 1977; repr. in *Heart's Desire*, 1988).

5 How soon country people forget. When they fall in love with a city it is forever, and it is like forever. As though there never was a time when they didn't love it. The minute they arrive at the train station or get off the ferry and glimpse the wide streets and the wasteful lamps lighting them, they know they are born for it. There, in a city, they are not so much new as themselves: their stronger, riskier selves.

> TONI MORRISON (b. 1931), U.S. novelist, editor. *Jazz*, ch. 2 (1991).

6 Long ago the country bore the country-town and nourished it with her best blood. Now the giant city sucks the country dry, insatiably and incessantly demanding and devouring fresh streams of men, till it wearies and dies in the midst of an almost uninhabited waste of country.

> OSWALD SPENGLER (1880–1936), German historian. *The Decline of the West*, vol. 2, ch. 4, sct. 5 (1926).

See also CITIES AND CITY LIFE; COUNTRY LIFE.

TRADE

1 This instinctive repulsion which tradespeople inspire in men of sensitive feeling is one of the very rare consolations for being so impoverished which are given to those of us who don't sell anything to anybody.

> LOUIS-FERDINAND CÉLINE (1894–1961), French author. The narrator (Ferdinand Bardamu), in *Journey to the End of the Night*, (1932; tr. 1934; repr. 1966, p. 90).

2 Is there something in trade that dessicates and flattens out, that turns men into dried leaves at the age of forty? Certainly there is. It is not due to trade but to intensity of self-seeking, combined with narrowness of occupation.... Business has destroyed the very knowledge in us of all other natural forces except business.

> JOHN JAY CHAPMAN (1862–1933), U.S. author. *Practical Agitation*, ch. 2 (1898).

3 Protection is not a principle but an expedient.

> BENJAMIN DISRAELI (1804–81), English statesman, author. Speech, 17 March 1845, to House of Commons. Disreali said exactly the opposite in a speech two years earlier, 25 April 1843.

4 We rail at trade, but the historian of the world will see that it was the principle of liberty; that it settled America, and destroyed feudalism, and made peace and keeps peace; that it will abolish slavery.

> RALPH WALDO EMERSON (1803–82), U.S. essayist, poet, philosopher. *Journals* (1909–1914), entry for Jan. 1844.

5 The greatest meliorator of the world is selfish, huckstering Trade.

> RALPH WALDO EMERSON (1803–82), U.S. essayist, poet, philosopher. *Society and Solitude*, "Works and Days" (1870).

6 Merchants have no country. The mere spot they stand on does not constitute so strong an attachment as that from which they draw their gains.

> THOMAS JEFFERSON (1743–1826), U.S. president. Letter, 17 March 1814.

7 Trade is the natural enemy of all violent passions. Trade loves moderation, delights in compromise, and is most careful to avoid anger. It is patient, supple, and insinuating, only resorting to extreme measures in cases of absolute necessity. Trade makes men independent of one another and gives them a high idea of their personal importance: it leads them to want to manage their own affairs and teaches them to succeed therein. Hence it makes them inclined to liberty but disinclined to revolution.

> ALEXIS DE TOCQUEVILLE (1805–59), French social philosopher. *Democracy in America*, vol. 2, pt. 3, ch. 21 (1840).

TRADE UNIONS

1 The most conservative man in the world is the British Trade Unionist when you want to change him.

> ERNEST BEVIN (1881–1951), British Labour politician. Speech, 8 Sept. 1927, to Trades Union Congress, Edinburgh.

2 Without the power of the Industrial Union behind it, Democracy can only enter the State as the victim enters the gullet of the Serpent.

> JAMES CONNOLLY (1870–1916), Irish syndicalist, Republican leader. *The Re-Conquest of Ireland*, ch. 9 (1915).

3 With all their faults, trade-unions have done more for humanity than any other organization of men that ever existed. They have done more for decency, for honesty, for education, for the betterment of the race, for the developing of character in man, than any other association of men.

> CLARENCE DARROW (1857–1938), U.S. lawyer, writer. *The Railroad Trainman* (Nov. 1909).

4 The methods by which a trade union can alone act, are necessarily destructive; its organization is necessarily tyrannical.

> HENRY GEORGE (1839–97), U.S. economist. *Progress and Poverty*, bk. 6, ch. 1 (1879).

5 Unionism seldom, if ever, uses such power as it has to insure better work; almost always it devotes a large part of that power to safeguarding bad work.

> H. L. MENCKEN (1880–1956), U.S. journalist. *Prejudices*, ch. 4 (Third Series, 1922).

6 It is essential that there should be organization of labor. This is an era of organization. Capital organizes and therefore labor must organize.

> THEODORE ROOSEVELT (1858–1919), U.S. Republican (later Progressive) politician, president. Speech, 14 Oct. 1912, Milwaukee, Wis.

7 Men don't and can't live by exchanging articles, but by producing them. They don't live by trade, but by work. Give up that foolish and vain title of Trades Unions; and take that of Labourers' Unions.

> JOHN RUSKIN (1819–1900), English art critic, author. Open letter to the Trades Unions of England, 31 Aug. 1880 (published in *Fors Clavigera*, vol. 8, 29 Sep 1880).

8 No king on earth is as safe in his job as a Trade Union official. There is only one thing that can get him sacked; and that is drink. Not even that, as long as he doesn't actually fall down.

> GEORGE BERNARD SHAW (1856–1950), Anglo-Irish playwright, critic. Boanerges, in *The Apple Cart*, act 1.

9 People of the same trade seldom meet together, even for merriment and diversion, but the conversation ends in a conspiracy against the public, or in some contrivance to raise prices.

> ADAM SMITH (1723–90), Scottish economist. *The Wealth of Nations*, vol. 1, bk. 1, ch. 10 (1776).

TRADITION

1 In America nothing dies easier than tradition.

> RUSSELL BAKER (b. 1925), U.S. journalist. *New York Times* (14 May 1991).

2 The assumption must be that those who can see value only in tradition, or versions of it, deny man's ability to adapt to changing circumstances.

> STEPHEN BAYLEY (b. 1951), British design critic. *Commerce and Culture*, ch. 3 (1989).

3 As soon as tradition has come to be recognized as tradition, it is dead.

> ALLAN BLOOM (1930–92), U.S. educator, author. *The Closing of the American Mind*, pt. 1, "The Clean Slate" (1987).

4 People will not look forward to posterity, who never look backward to their ancestors.

> EDMUND BURKE (1729–97), Irish philosopher, statesman. *Reflections on the Revolution in France* (1790).

5 Tradition means giving votes to the most obscure of all classes—our ancestors. It is the democracy of the dead. Tradition refuses to submit to the small and arrogant oligarchy of those who merely happen to be walking around.

> G. K. CHESTERTON (1874–1936), British author. *Orthodoxy*, ch. 4, "The Ethics of England" (1909).

6 Tradition! We scarcely know the word anymore. We are afraid to be either proud of our ancestors or ashamed of them. We scorn nobility in name and in fact. We cling to a bourgeois mediocrity which would make it appear we are all Americans, made in the image and likeness of George Washington.

> DOROTHY DAY (1897–1980), U.S. religious leader. *The Long Loneliness*, pt. 1 (1952).

7 A precedent embalms a principle.

> BENJAMIN DISRAELI (1804–81), English statesman, author. Speech, 22 Feb. 1848, House of Commons. This axiom was also ascribed to the lawyer Lord Stowell (William Scott), from whom Disraeli may have borrowed it.

8 It cannot be inherited, and if you want it you must obtain it by great labour.

> T. S. ELIOT (1888–1965), Anglo-American poet, critic. *Tradition and the Individual Talent*, sct. 1, in *Egoist* (London, Sept. and Dec. 1919; repr. in *Selected Prose of T. S. Eliot*, ed. by Frank Kermode, 1975), of tradition.

9 There is nothing in the world more stubborn than a corpse: you can hit it, you can knock it to pieces, but you cannot convince it.

> ALEXANDER HERZEN (1812–70), Russian journalist, political thinker. *My Past and Thoughts*, vol. 3, pt. 6, ch. 10 (1921; tr. by Constance Garnett 1924–7).

10 To keep up even a worthwhile tradition means vitiating the idea behind it which must necessarily be in a constant state of evolution: it is mad to try to express new feelings in a "mummified" form.

> ALFRED JARRY (1873–1907), French playwright, author. "Twelve Theatrical Topics," Topic 10, in *Dossiers Acénonètes due Collège de Pataphysique*, no. 5 (Paris, 1960; repr. in *The Selected Works of Alfred Jarry*, ed. by Roger Shattuck and Simon Watson Taylor, 1965).

See also Gonzalez-Crussi on CEREMONY; Lippmann on CONSERVATIVES; Mills on CUSTOM.

TRAGEDY

1 It is restful, tragedy, because one knows that there is no more lousy hope left. You know you're caught, caught at last like a rat with all the world on its back. And the only thing left to do is shout—not moan, or complain, but yell out at the top of your voice whatever it was you had to say. What you've never said before. What perhaps you don't even know till now.

> JEAN ANOUILH (1910–87), French playwright. The Chorus, in *Antigone*.

2 Tragedy on the stage is no longer enough for me, I shall bring it into my own life.

> ANTONIN ARTAUD (1896–1948), French theater producer, actor, theorist. Quoted in: the memoirs of Jean-Louis Barrault, *Memories for Tomorrow*, pt. 2, "The Grenier des Grands-Augustins" (1972; tr. 1974).

3 None but a poet can write a tragedy. For tragedy is nothing less than pain transmuted into exaltation by the alchemy of poetry.

> EDITH HAMILTON (1867–1963), U.S. classical scholar, translator. *The Greek Way*, ch. 11 (1930).

4 Tragedy is like strong acid—it dissolves away all but the very gold of truth.

> D. H. LAWRENCE (1885–1930), British author. Letter, 1 April 1911 (published in *The Letters of D. H. Lawrence*, vol. 1, ed. by James T. Boulton, 1979).

5 Ours is essentially a tragic age, so we refuse to take it tragically.

> D. H. LAWRENCE (1885–1930), British author. Opening words of *Lady Chatterley's Lover* (written 1928; published 1959).

6 Commonplace people dislike tragedy because they dare not suffer and cannot exult.

> JOHN MASEFIELD (1874–1967), British poet, playwright. *The Tragedy of Nan*, Preface (1908).

7 The closer a man approaches tragedy the more intense is his concentration of emotion upon the fixed point of his commitment, which is to say the closer he approaches what in life we call fanaticism.

> ARTHUR MILLER (b. 1915), U.S. dramatist. *Collected Plays*, Introduction, sct. 1 (1958).

8 A tragic situation exists precisely when virtue does *not* triumph but when it is still felt that man is nobler than the forces which destroy him.

> GEORGE ORWELL (1903–50), British author. *Shooting an Elephant*, "Lear, Tolstoy and the Fool" (1950).

9 It's not the tragedies that kill us, it's the messes.

> DOROTHY PARKER (1893–1967), U.S. humorous writer. Interview in *Writers at Work* (First Series, ed. by Malcolm Cowley, 1958).

10 Laughter is ever young, whereas tragedy, except the very highest of all, quickly becomes haggard.

> MARGARET SACKVILLE (1881–1963), British poet. *The Works of Susan Ferrier*, vol. 1, Introduction (1929).

11 Tragedy delights by affording a shadow of the pleasure which exists in pain.

> PERCY BYSSHE SHELLEY (1792–1822), English poet. *A Defence of Poetry* (written 1821, published 1840).

12 When you close your eyes to tragedy, you close your eyes to greatness.

> STEPHEN VIZINCZEY (b. 1933), Hungarian novelist, critic. "Who Killed Kleist?," review of Joachim Maass, *Kleist: A Biogra-*

phy, in *Sunday Telegraph* (London, 5 Jan. 1984; repr. in *Truth and Lies in Literature*, 1986).

13 It often happens that the real tragedies of life occur in such an inartistic manner that they hurt us by their crude violence, their absolute incoherence, their absurd want of meaning, their entire lack of style.

OSCAR WILDE (1854–1900), Anglo-Irish playwright, author. Lord Henry, in *The Picture of Dorian Gray*, ch. 8 (1891).

14 You get tragedy where the tree, instead of bending, breaks.

LUDWIG WITTGENSTEIN (1889–1951), Austrian philosopher. *Culture and Value*, (ed. by G. H. von Wright with Heikki Nyman, 1980), journal entry for 1929.

See also Baldwin on EUROPE AND AMERICA; Voltaire on WOMEN AND THE ARTS.

TRAINING

1 Reading maketh a full man; conference a ready man; and writing an exact man.

FRANCIS BACON (1561–1626), English philosopher, essayist, statesman. *Essays*, "Of Studies" (1597–1625).

2 It's all to do with the training: you can do a lot if you're properly trained.

ELIZABETH II (b. 1926), Queen of Great Britain and Northern Ireland. Television documentary, BBC1, 6 Feb. 1992.

3 Training is everything. The peach was once a bitter almond; cauliflower is nothing but cabbage with a college education.

MARK TWAIN (1835–1910), U.S. author. *Pudd'nhead Wilson*, ch. 5, "Pudd'nhead Wilson's Calendar" (1894).

4 A man can seldom—very, very, seldom—fight a winning fight against his training; the odds are too heavy.

MARK TWAIN (1835–1910), U.S. author. *As Regards Patriotism* (written c. 1911; published 1923; repr. in *Complete Essays*, ed. by Charles Neider, 1963).

TRAINS

1 The only way of catching a train I have ever discovered is to miss the train before.

G. K. CHESTERTON (1874–1936), British author. *Tremendous Trifles*, "The Prehistoric Railway Station" (1909).

2 Railway termini . . . are our gates to the glorious and the unknown. Through them we pass out into adventure and sunshine, to them, alas! we return.

E. M. FORSTER (1879–1970), British novelist, essayist. *Howards End*, ch. 2 (1910).

3 frseeeeeeeefronnnng train somewhere whistling the strength those engines have in them like big giants and the water rolling all over and out of them all sides like the end of Loves old sweeeetsonnnng the poor men that have to be out all the night from their wives and families in those roasting engines.

JAMES JOYCE (1882–1941), Irish author. Molly Bloom's final soliloquy, in *Ulysses*, ch. 18 (1922).

4 Along the iron veins that traverse the frame of our country, beat and flow the fiery pulses of its exertion, hotter and faster every hour. All vitality is concentrated through those throbbing arteries into the central cities; the country is passed over like a green sea by narrow bridges, and we are thrown back in continually closer crowds on the city gates.

JOHN RUSKIN (1819–1900), English art critic, author. *The Seven Lamps of Architecture*, "The Lamp of Memory," sct. 20 (1849).

5 We who have lived before railways were made belong to another world. . . . It was only yesterday, but what a gulf between now and then! *Then* was the old world. Stage-coaches, more or less swift, riding-horses, pack-horses, highwaymen, knights in armour, Norman invaders, Roman legions, Druids, Ancient Britons painted blue, and so forth—all these belong to the old period. . . . But your railroad starts the new era, and we of a certain age belong to the new time and the old one. . . . We who lived before railways, and survive out of the ancient world, are like Father Noah and his family out of the Ark.

WILLIAM MAKEPEACE THACKERAY (1811–63), English author. *The Roundabout Papers*, "De Juventute" (1863).

6 That devilish Iron Horse, whose ear-rending neigh is heard throughout the town, has muddied the Boiling Spring with his foot, and he it is that has browsed off all the woods on Walden shore, that Trojan horse, with a thousand men in his belly, introduced by mercenary Greeks! Where is the country's champion, the Moore of Moore Hall, to meet him at the Deep Cut and thrust an avenging lance between the ribs of the bloated pest?

HENRY DAVID THOREAU (1817–62), U.S. philosopher, author, naturalist. *Walden*, "The Ponds" (1854).

TRANQUILITY

1 Like water, we are truest to our nature in repose.

CYRIL CONNOLLY (1903–74), British critic. *The Unquiet Grave*, pt. 3 (1944; rev. 1951).

2 You must learn to be still in the midst of activity and to be vibrantly alive in repose.

INDIRA GANDHI (1917–1984), Indian politician, prime minister. Quoted in: *People* (New York, 30 June 1975).

3 There is no such thing as perpetual tranquillity of mind while we live here; because life itself is but motion, and can never be without desire, nor without fear, no more than without sense.

THOMAS HOBBES (1588–1679), English philosopher. *Leviathan*, pt. 1, ch. 6 (1651).

4 Tranquility is the old man's milk.

THOMAS JEFFERSON (1743–1826), U.S. president. Letter, 24 June 1797.

5 There is no such thing as inner peace. There is only nervousness or death. Any attempt to prove otherwise constitutes unacceptable behavior.

FRAN LEBOWITZ (b. 1951), U.S. journalist. *Metropolitan Life*, "Manners" (1978).

See also Bronte on ACTION.

TRANSLATION

1 Any translation which intends to perform a transmitting function cannot transmit anything but information—hence, something inessential. This is the hallmark of bad translations.

> WALTER BENJAMIN (1892–1940), German critic, philosopher. *Illuminations,* "The Task of the Translator" (1955; ed. by Hannah Arendt, 1968).

2 Nor ought a genius less than his that writ
Attempt translation.

> SIR JOHN DENHAM (1615–69), English poet. *To Sir Richard Fanshaw upon his translation of Pastor Fido.* The poem begins: "Such is our pride, our folly, or our fate, That few but such as cannot write, translate."

3 God employs several translators; some pieces are translated by age, some by sickness, some by war, some by justice.

> JOHN DONNE (c. 1572–1631), English divine, metaphysical poet. *Devotions Upon Emergent Occasions,* Meditation 17 (1624).

4 I do not hesitate to read . . . all good books in translations. What is really best in any book is translatable—any real insight or broad human sentiment.

> RALPH WALDO EMERSON (1803–82), U.S. essayist, poet, philosopher. *Society and Solitude,* "Books" (1870).

5 The test of a given phrase would be: Is it worthy to be immortal? To "make a beeline" for something. That's worthy of being immortal and is immortal in English idiom. "I guess I'll split" is not going to be immortal and is excludable, therefore excluded.

> ROBERT FITZGERALD (1910–85), U.S. scholar, translator. *Writers at Work* (Eighth Series, ed. by George Plimpton, 1988), on his criteria for translating Homeric Greek. Fitzgerald's translations of Homer's *Odyssey* and *The Iliad* appeared in 1961 and 1974.

6 Poetry is what is lost in translation.

> ROBERT FROST (1874–1963), U.S. poet. Quoted in: Louis Untermeyer, *Robert Frost: a Backward Look,* ch. 1 (1964). Samuel Taylor Coleridge wrote, in *Biographia Literaria,* ch. 22 (1817): "In poetry, in which every line, every phrase, may pass the ordeal of deliberation and deliberate choice, it is possible, and barely possible, to attain that *ultimatum* which I have ventured to propose as the infallible test of a blameless style; namely: its *untranslatableness* in words of the same language without injury to the meaning."

7 To translate, one must have a style of his own, for otherwise the translation will have no rhythm or nuance, which come from the process of artistically thinking through and molding the sentences; they cannot be reconstituted by piecemeal imitation. The problem of translation is to retreat to a simpler tenor of one's own style and creatively adjust this to one's author.

> PAUL GOODMAN (1911–72), U.S. author, poet, critic. *Five Years,* "Summer 1957, in Europe," sct. 8 (1966).

8 There are few efforts more conducive to humility than that of the translator trying to communicate an incommunicable beauty. Yet, unless we do try, something unique and never surpassed will cease to exist except in the libraries of a few inquisitive book lovers.

> EDITH HAMILTON (1867–1963), U.S. classical scholar, translator. Introduction to *Three Greek Plays* (1937).

9 Translation is entirely mysterious. Increasingly I have felt that the art of writing is itself translating, or more like translating than it is like anything else. What is the other text, the original? I have no answer. I suppose it is the source, the deep sea where ideas swim, and one catches them in nets of words and swings them shining into the boat . . . where in this metaphor they die and get canned and eaten in sandwiches.

> URSULA K. LE GUIN (b. 1929), U.S. author. "Reciprocity of Prose and Poetry," address, 1983 in Poetry Series, Folger Shakespeare Library, Washington, D.C. (published in *Dancing at the Edge of the World,* 1989).

10 Translation is the paradigm, the exemplar of all writing. . . . It is translation that demonstrates most vividly the yearning for transformation that underlies every act involving speech, that supremely human gift.

> HARRY MATHEWS (b. 1930), U.S. novelist. *Country Cooking and Other Stories,* "The Dialect of the Tribe" (1980).

11 As far as modern writing is concerned, it is rarely rewarding to translate it, although it might be easy. . . . Translation is very much like copying paintings.

> BORIS PASTERNAK (1890–1960), Russian poet, novelist, translator. Interview in *Writers at Work* (Second Series, ed. by George Plimpton, 1963). "The only interesting sort of translating is that of classics," Pasternak believed.

12 A great age of literature is perhaps always a great age of translations.

> EZRA POUND (1885–1972), U.S. poet, critic. *Egoist* (London, Oct. 1917).

13 Translators, traitors.

> ITALIAN PROVERB.

14 The best thing on translation was said by Cervantes: translation is the other side of a tapestry.

> LEONARDO SCIASCIA (1921–89), Italian writer. *Guardian* (London, 5 Aug. 1988).

15 It were as wise to cast a violet into a crucible that you might discover the formal principle of its colour and odour, as seek to transfuse from one language into another the creations of a poet. The plant must spring again from its seed, or it will bear no flower—and this is the burthen of the curse of Babel.

> PERCY BYSSHE SHELLEY (1792–1822), English poet. *A Defence of Poetry* (written 1821; published 1840).

16 Woe to the makers of literal translations, who by rendering every word weaken the meaning! It is indeed by so doing that we can say the letter kills and the spirit gives life.

> VOLTAIRE (1694–1778), French philosopher, author. *Letters on England,* Letter 18, "On Tragedy" (1732). Earlier in the essay, Voltaire prefaced a translated extract from Shakespeare ("To be or not to be") with the words: "Have pity on the copy for the sake of the original, and always bear in mind when you see a translation that you are only looking at a feeble print of a great picture."

17 Humour is the first of the gifts to perish in a foreign tongue.

> VIRGINIA WOOLF (1882–1941), British novelist. *The Common Reader,* "On Not Knowing Greek" (First Series, 1925).

TRANSPORTATION

1 I have done almost every human activity inside a taxi which does not require main drainage.

ALAN BRIEN (b. 1925), British novelist, humorist. *Punch* (London, 5 July 1972).

2 What is this that roareth thus?
Can it be a Motor Bus?
Yes, the smell and hideous hum
Indicat Motorem Bum . . .
omine, defende nos
Contra hos Motores Bos!

ALFRED D. GODLEY (1856–1925), British scholar. *The Motor Bus.*

3 A solitary traveller can sleep from state to state, from day to night, from day to day, in the long womb of its controlled interior. It is the cradle that never stops rocking after the lullaby is over. It is the biggest sleeping tablet in the world, and no one need ever swallow the pill, for it swallows them.

LISA ST. AUBIN DE TERáN (b. 1953), British author. *Off the Rails,* ch. 15 (1989), on trains in the U.S.

4 I am struck by the way people behave on the Tube. They look at each other beadily and inquisitively, and something goes on in their thoughts which must be equivalent to the way dogs and other animals, when they meet, sniff each other's arses and nuzzle each other's fur.

GRAHAM SWIFT (b. 1949), British novelist, short-story writer. *Shuttlecock,* ch. 3 (1981)

See also BICYCLES; CARS; Greer on ENGLAND AND THE ENGLISH; SHIPS AND BOATS; TRAINS.

TRAVEL

1 Of all possible subjects, travel is the most difficult for an artist, as it is the easiest for a journalist.

W. H. AUDEN (1907–73), Anglo-American poet. *The Dyer's Hand,* pt. 6, "The American Scene" (1962).

2 A part, a large part, of travelling is an engagement of the ego v. the world. . . . The world is hydra headed, as old as the rocks and as changing as the sea, enmeshed inextricably in its ways. The ego wants to arrive at places safely and on time.

SYBILLE BEDFORD (b. 1911), British author. "The Quality of Travel," in *Esquire* (New York, Nov. 1961; repr. in *As It Was,* 1990).

3 In America there are two classes of travel—first class and with childen.

ROBERT BENCHLEY (1889–1945), U.S. humorous writer. Quoted in: *The Algonquin Wits* (ed. by Robert E. Drennan, 1968).

4 I have been a stranger in a strange land.

BIBLE, HEBREW. Moses, in *Exodus* 2:22.

5 What childishness is it that while there's breath of life
in our bodies, we are determined to rush
to see the sun the other way around?

ELIZABETH BISHOP (1911–79), U.S. poet. *Questions of Travel.*

Bishop, an avid traveler, spent the last 16 years of her life in Brazil.

6 Not so many years ago there there was no simpler or more intelligible notion than that of going on a journey. Travel—movement through space—provided the universal metaphor for change. . . . One of the subtle confusions—perhaps one of the secret terrors—of modern life is that we have lost this refuge. No longer do we move through space as we once did.

DANIEL J. BOORSTIN (b. 1914), U.S. historian. *The Image,* ch. 3 (1961).

7 I am so convinced of the advantages of looking at mankind instead of reading about them, and of the bitter effects of staying at home with all the narrow prejudices of an Islander, that I think there should be a law amongst us to set our young men abroad for a term among the few allies our wars have left us.

LORD BYRON (1788–1824), English poet. Letter, 14 Jan. 1811, to his mother (published in *Byron's Letters and Journals,* vol. 2, ed. by Leslie A. Marchand, 1973–81).

8 Traveling, you realize that differences are lost: each city takes to resembling all cities, places exchange their form, order, distances, a shapeless dust cloud invades the continents.

ITALO CALVINO (1923–85), Italian author, critic. Marco Polo, in *Invisible Cities* (1972; tr. 1974, p. 137).

9 The whole object of travel is not to set foot on foreign land; it is at last to set foot on one's own country as a foreign land.

G. K. CHESTERTON (1874–1936), British author. *Tremendous Trifles,* "The Riddle of the Ivy" (1909).

10 The travel writer seeks the world we have lost—the lost valleys of the imagination.

ALEXANDER COCKBURN (b. 1941), Anglo-Irish journalist. "Bwana Vistas," in *Harper's* (New York, Aug. 1985; repr. in *Corruptions of Empire,* pt. 1, 1988).

11 When one realizes that his life is worthless he either commits suicide or travels.

EDWARD DAHLBERG (1900–1977), U.S. author, critic. *Reasons of the Heart,* "On Futility" (1965).

12 Journeys, like artists, are born and not made. A thousand differing circumstances contribute to them, few of them willed or determined by the will—whatever we may think.

LAWRENCE DURRELL (1914–91), British author. *Bitter Lemons,* "Towards an Eastern Landfall" (1957), opening words.

13 Our instructed vagrancy, which has hardly time to linger by the hedgerows, but runs away early to the tropics, and is at home with palms and banyans—which is nourished on books of travel, and stretches the theatre of its imagination to the Zambesi.

GEORGE ELIOT (1819–80), English novelist. *The Mill on the Floss,* bk. 3, ch. 9 (1860).

14 Traveling is a fool's paradise. Our first journeys discover to us the indifference of places.

RALPH WALDO EMERSON (1803–82), U.S. essayist, poet, philosopher. *Essays,* "Self-Reliance" (First Series, 1841).

15 I am not much an advocate for traveling, and I observe that men run away to other countries because they are not good in their own, and run back to their own because they pass for nothing in the new places. For the most part, only the light characters travel. Who are you that have no task to keep you at home?

RALPH WALDO EMERSON (1803–82), U.S. essayist, poet, philosopher. *The Conduct of Life*, "Culture" (1860).

16 It would be nice to travel if you knew where you were going and where you would live at the end or do we ever know, do we ever live where we live, we're always in other places, lost, like sheep.

JANET FRAME (b. 1924), New Zealand novelist, poet. *You Are Now Entering the Human Heart*, "The Day of the Sheep" (1983).

17 A man who leaves home to mend himself and others is a philosopher; but he who goes from country to country, guided by the blind impulse of curiosity, is a vagabond.

OLIVER GOLDSMITH (1728–74), Anglo-Irish author, poet, playwright. *The Citizen of the World*, Letter 7 (1762).

18 The important thing about travel in foreign lands is that it breaks the speech habits and makes you blab less, and breaks the habitual space-feeling because of different village plans and different landscapes. It is less important that there are different mores, for you counteract these with your own reaction-formations.

PAUL GOODMAN (1911–72), U.S. author, poet, critic. *Five Years*, "Summer 1957, in Europe," sct. 3 (1966).

19 Writing and travel broaden your ass if not your mind and I like to write standing up.

ERNEST HEMINGWAY (1899–1961), U.S. author. Letter, 9 July 1950 (published in *Selected Letters*, ed. by Carlos Baker, 1981).

20 Your true traveller finds boredom rather agreeable than painful. It is the symbol of his liberty—his excessive freedom. He accepts his boredom, when it comes, not merely philosophically, but almost with pleasure.

ALDOUS HUXLEY (1894–1963), British author. *Along the Road*, pt. 1, "Why Not Stay at Home?" (1925).

21 He that travels in theory has no inconveniences; he has shade and sunshine at his disposal, and wherever he alights finds tables of plenty and looks of gaiety. These ideas are indulged till the day of departure arrives, the chaise is called, and the progress of happiness begins. A few miles teach him the fallacies of imagination. The road is dusty, the air is sultry, the horses are sluggish, and the postilion brutal. He longs for the time of dinner that he may eat and rest. The inn is crowded, his orders are neglected, and nothing remains but that he devour in haste what the cook has spoiled, and drive on in quest of better entertainment. He finds at night a more commodious house, but the best is always worse than he expected.

SAMUEL JOHNSON (1709–84), English author, lexicographer. *The Idler*, no. 58, in *Universal Chronicle* (London, 26 May 1759; repr. in *Works of Samuel Johnson*, vol. 2, ed. by W. J. Bate, John M. Bullitt and L. F. Powell, 1963).

22 As the Spanish proverb says, "He who would bring home the wealth of the Indies, must carry the wealth of the Indies with him." So it is in travelling; a man must carry knowledge with him, if he would bring home knowledge.

SAMUEL JOHNSON (1709–84), English author, lexicographer. Quoted in: James Boswell, *Life of Samuel Johnson*, 17 April 1778 (1791).

23 Much have I travelled in the realms of gold,
And many goodly states and kingdoms seen.

JOHN KEATS (1795–1821), English poet. *On First Looking into Chapman's Homer*, opening lines.

24 People commonly travel the world over to see rivers and mountains, new stars, garish birds, freak fish, grotesque breeds of human; they fall into an animal stupor that gapes at existence and they think they have seen something.

SØREN KIERKEGAARD (1813–55), Danish philosopher. *Fear and Trembling*, "Preamble from the Heart" (1843; tr. 1985).

25 A route differs from a road not only because it is solely intended for vehicles, but also because it is merely a line that connects one point with another. A route has no meaning in itself; its meaning derives entirely from the two points that it connects. A road is a tribute to space. Every stretch of road has meaning in itself and invites us to stop. A route is the triumphant devaluation of space, which thanks to it has been reduced to a mere obstacle to human movement and a waste of time.

MILAN KUNDERA (b. 1929), Czech author, critic. *Immortality*, pt. 5, ch. 3 (1991).

26 Without stirring abroad,
One can know the whole world;
Without looking out of the window
One can see the way of heaven.
The further one goes
The less one knows.

LAO-TZU (6th century B.C.), Legendary Chinese philosopher. *Tao-te-ching*, bk. 2, ch. 47 (tr. by T. C. Lau, 1963).

27 Comes over one an absolute necessity to move. And what is more, to move in some particular direction. A double necessity then: to get on the move, and to know whither.

D. H. LAWRENCE (1885–1930), British author. *Sea and Sardinia* (1923), opening words.

28 Spirit of place! It is for this we travel, to surprise its subtlety; and where it is a strong and dominant angel, that place, seen once, abides entire in the memory with all its own accidents, its habits, its breath, its name.

ALICE MEYNELL (1847–1922), English poet, essayist. *Essays*, "The Spirit of Place" (1914).

29 The fabric of my faithful love
No power shall dim or ravel
Whilst I stay here—but oh, my dear,
If I should ever travel!

EDNA ST. VINCENT MILLAY (1892–1950), U.S. poet. *To The Not Impossible Him*.

30 If we are always arriving and departing, it is also true that we are eternally anchored. One's destination is never a place but rather a new way of looking at things.

HENRY MILLER (1891–1980), U.S. author. *Big Sur and the*

Oranges of Hieronymous Bosch, "The Oranges of the Millennium" (1957).

31 We travellers are in very hard circumstances. If we say nothing but what has been said before us, we are dull and have observed nothing. If we tell anything new, we are laughed at as fabulous and romantic.

LADY MARY WORTLEY MONTAGU (1689–1762), English society figure, letter writer. Letter, 10 March 1718 (published in *Selected Letters,* ed. by Robert Halsband 1970).

32 A man should ever . . . be ready booted to take his journey.

MICHEL DE MONTAIGNE (1533–92), French essayist. *Essays,* bk. 1, ch. 19, "That to Philosophise is to Learn How to Die" (1580–88; tr. by John Florio).

33 Life, as the most ancient of all metaphors insists, is a journey; and the travel book, in its deceptive simulation of the journey's fits and starts, rehearses life's own fragmentation. More even than the novel, it embraces the contingency of things.

JONATHAN RABAN (b. 1942), British author, critic. *For Love and Money,* pt. 5 (1987).

34 Travel is the most private of pleasures. There is no greater bore than the travel bore. We do not in the least want to hear what he has seen in Hong-Kong.

VITA SACKVILLE-WEST (1892–1962), British novelist, poet. *Passenger to Teheran,* ch. 1 (1926).

35 Journeys end in lovers meeting.

WILLIAM SHAKESPEARE (1564–1616), English dramatist, poet. Feste's song to Sir Toby Belch and Sir Andrew Aguecheek, in *Twelfth Night,* act 2, sc. 3.

36 Life on board a pleasure steamer violates every moral and physical condition of healthy life except fresh air. . . . It is a guzzling, lounging, gambling, dog's life. The only alternative to excitement is irritability.

GEORGE BERNARD SHAW (1856–1950), Anglo-Irish playwright, critic. Letter, 17 Oct. 1899 (published in *Collected Letters,* vol. 2, 1972), written while on a six-week Mediterranean cruise aboard the *S.S. Lusitania.*

37 An involuntary return to the point of departure is, without doubt, the most disturbing of all journeys.

IAIN SINCLAIR (b. 1943), British author. *Downriver,* "Riverside Opportunities," sct. 9 (1991).

38 Travelling is like flirting with life. It's like saying, "I would stay and love you, but I have to go; this is my station."

LISA ST. AUBIN DE TERÁN (b. 1953), British author. *Off the Rails,* ch. 2 (1989).

39 A journey is like marriage. The certain way to be wrong is to think you control it.

JOHN STEINBECK (1902–68), U.S. author. *Travels With Charley: in Search of America,* pt. 1 (1961).

40 When I was very young and the urge to be someplace was on me, I was assured by mature people that maturity would cure this itch. When years described me as mature, the remedy prescribed was middle age. In middle age I was assured that greater age would calm my fever and now that I am fifty-eight perhaps senility will do the job. Nothing has worked. . . . In other words, I

don't improve, in further words, once a bum always a bum. I fear the disease is incurable.

JOHN STEINBECK (1902–68), U.S. author. *Travels With Charley: in Search of America,* pt. 1 (1961).

41 For my part, I travel not to go anywhere, but to go. I travel for travel's sake. The great affair is to move; to feel the needs and hitches of our life more nearly; to come down off this feather-bed of civilisation, and find the globe granite underfoot and strewn with cutting flints.

ROBERT LOUIS STEVENSON (1850–94), Scottish novelist, essayist, poet. *Travels with a Donkey,* "Cheylard and Luc" (1879).

42 To travel hopefully is a better thing than to arrive.

ROBERT LOUIS STEVENSON (1850–94), Scottish novelist, essayist, poet. *Virginibus Puerisque,* "El Dorado" (1881).

43 Extensive traveling induces a feeling of encapsulation, and travel, so broadening at first, contracts the mind.

PAUL THEROUX (b. 1941), U.S. novelist, travel writer. *The Great Railway Bazaar,* ch. 21 (1975).

44 Travel is glamorous only in retrospect.

PAUL THEROUX (b. 1941), U.S. novelist, travel writer. Quoted in: *Observer* (London, 7 Oct. 1979).

45 He who is only a traveler learns things at secondhand and by the halves, and is poor authority. We are most interested when science reports what those men already know practically or instinctively, for that alone is a true *humanity,* or account of human experience.

HENRY DAVID THOREAU (1817–62), U.S. philosopher, author, naturalist. *Walden,* "Higher Laws" (1854).

46 I have found out that there ain't no surer way to find out whether you like people or hate them than to travel with them.

MARK TWAIN (1835–1910), U.S. author. *Tom Sawyer Abroad,* ch. 11 (1894).

47 Commuter—one who spends his life
In riding to and from his wife;
A man who shaves and takes a train,
And then rides back to shave again.

E. B. WHITE (1899–1985), U.S. author, editor. *The Commuter.*

48 O public road, I say back I am not afraid to leave you, yet I love you,
You express me better than I can express myself.

WALT WHITMAN (1819–92), U.S. poet. *Song of the Open Road,* sct. 4 (1856).

49 I travelled among unknown men,
In lands beyond the sea;
Nor England! did I know till then
What love I bore to thee.

WILLIAM WORDSWORTH (1770–1850), English poet. *I Travelled Among Unknown Men* (written 1801, published 1807).

See also Emerson on DISSATISFACTION; Thoreau on EXPLORATION; Falk on FOREIGN COUNTRIES; Kipling on HERMITS; Thoreau on INDEPENDENCE; TOURISM; TRANSPORTATION; Byron on WORLDLINESS.

TREACHERY

1 All his usual formalites of perfidy were observed with scrupulous technique.

> SIR WINSTON CHURCHILL (1874–1965), British statesman, writer. Radio broadcast, 21 June 1941, of Hitler's invasion of Russia.

2 Treason doth never prosper: what's the reason?
For if it prosper, none dare call it treason.

> SIR JOHN HARINGTON (1561–1612), English writer, courtier. *Epigrams*, bk. 4, *Of Treason* (1618).

3 The treason pleases, but the traitors are odious.

> SPANISH PROVERB. Quoted in: Miguel de Cervantes, *Don Quixote*, pt. 1, bk. 4, ch. 7 (1605; tr. by P. Motteux).

4 Treason implies responsibility for something, control over something, influence upon something, knowledge of something. Treason in our time is a proof of genius. Why, I want to know, are not traitors decorated?

> ANTOINE DE SAINT-EXUPÉRY (1900–1944), French aviator, author. *Flight to Arras*, ch. 13 (1942).

See also BETRAYAL.

TREES

1 What do we plant when we plant the tree?
We plant the ship that will cross the sea,
We plant the mast to carry the sails,
We plant the planks to withstand the gales—
The keel, the keelson, and beam and knee—
We plant the ship when we plant the tree.

> HENRY ABBEY (1842–1911), U.S. poet. *What Do We Plant?*

2 I like trees because they seem more resigned to the way they have to live than other things do.

> WILLA CATHER (1876–1947), U.S. author. *O Pioneers!* pt. 2, ch. 8 (1913).

3 Tall poplars—human beings of this earth!

> PAUL CELAN (1920–70), German poet, translator. "Landscape," in *Von Schwelle zu Schwelle* (1955; repr. in *Paul Celan: Poems*, ed. and tr. by Michael Hamburger, 1980).

4 Tree at my window, window tree,
My sash is lowered when night comes on;
But let there never be curtain drawn
Between you and me.

> ROBERT FROST (1874–1963), U.S. poet. *Tree at My Window*, st. 1.

5 My aspens dear, whose airy cages quelled,
Quelled or quenched in leaves the leaping sun,
All felled, felled, are all felled;
Of a fresh and following folded rank
Not spared, not one
That dandled a sandalled
Shadow that swam or sank
On meadow and river and wind-wandering weed-
winding bank.

> GERARD MANLEY HOPKINS (1844–89), English poet, Jesuit priest. *Binsey Poplars*, st. 1.

6 He who plants a tree
Plants a hope.

> LUCY LARCOM (1826–93), U.S. poet. *Plant a Tree*, st. 1.

7 We have nothing to fear and a great deal to learn from trees, that vigorous and pacific tribe which without stint produces strengthening essences for us, soothing balms, and in whose gracious company we spend so many cool, silent and intimate hours.

> MARCEL PROUST (1871–1922), French novelist. *Pleasures and Regrets*, "Regrets, Reveries, Changing Skies," no. 26 (1896; tr. 1948).

8 A tree's a tree. How many more do you need to look at?

> RONALD REAGAN (b. 1911), U.S. Republican politician, president. Speech, 12 Sept. 1965. Quoted in: *Sacramento Bee* (California, 12 March 1966). Reagan later denied having made this statement.

9 Why are there trees I never walk under but large and melodious thoughts descend upon me?

> WALT WHITMAN (1819–92), U.S. poet. *Song of the Open Road*, sct. 7 (1856).

10 One impulse from a vernal wood
May teach you more of man,
Of moral evil and of good,
Than all the ages can.

> WILLIAM WORDSWORTH (1770–1850), English poet. *The Tables Turned*, st. 6.

TRIALS

1 Appeal. In law, to put the dice into the box for another throw.

> AMBROSE BIERCE (1842–1914), U.S. author. *The Devil's Dictionary* (1881–1906).

2 Trial. A formal inquiry designed to prove and put upon record the blameless characters of judges, advocates and jurors.

> AMBROSE BIERCE (1842–1914), U.S. author. *The Devil's Dictionary* (1881–1906).

3 When the judge calls the criminal's name out he stands up, and they are immediately linked by a strange biology that makes them both opposite and complementary. The one cannot exist without the other. Which is the sun and which is the shadow? It's well known some criminals have been great men.

> JEAN GENET (1910–86), French playwright, novelist. *Prisoner Of Love*, pt. 1 (1986; tr. 1989).

4 A criminal trial is like a Russian novel: it starts with exasperating slowness as the characters are introduced to a jury, then there are complications in the form of minor witnesses, the protagonist finally appears and contradictions arise to produce drama, and finally as both jury and spectators grow weary and confused the pace quickens, reaching its climax in passionate final argument.

> CLIFFORD IRVING (b. 1930), U.S. author, notorious hoaxer. *Sunday Times* (London, 14 Aug. 1988).

5 I gather from a lawyer that there was a rehearsal

yesterday. We haven't a hope. I know the presiding judge too: I've had the misfortune to sleep with his wife. He was specially picked.

ALPHONSE KARR (1808–90), French journalist, novelist. Quoted in: *The Goncourt Journal* (tr. 1962), entry for 20 Feb. 1853 Karr was on trial together with Edmond and Jules de Goncourt, accused of writing articles offensive to public morals.

6 I'm trusting in the Lord and a good lawyer.

OLIVER NORTH (b. 1943), U.S. marine officer. Quoted in: *Observer* (London, 7 Dec. 1986).

7 The hungry judges soon the sentence sign,
And wretches hang that jurymen may dine.

ALEXANDER POPE (1688–1744), English satirical poet. *The Rape of the Lock*, cto. 3.

8 Ladies and gentlemen, let me tell you again what you are to presume. [The defendant] is innocent. I am the judge. I am telling you that. Presume he is innocent. When you sit there, I want you to look and say to yourself, There sits an innocent man.

SCOTT L. TUROW (b. 1949), U.S. lawyer, author. Judge Larren Lyttle addressing the jury, in *Presumed Innocent*, ch. 26 (1987). Judge Lyttle began the selection of the jury by asking one member whether the defendant committed the crime, and, on receiving the answer, "I wouldn't know, Judge," dismissed the juror.

9 A joke, even if it be a lame one, is nowhere so keenly relished or quickly applauded as in a murder trial.

MARK TWAIN (1835–1910), U.S. author. *The Gilded Age*, ch. 54 (1873; written with Charles Dudley Warner).

10 He maintained that the case was lost or won by the time the final juror had been sworn in; his summation was set in his mind before the first witness was called. It was all in the orchestration, he claimed: in knowing how and where to pitch each and every particular argument; who to intimidate; who to trust, who to flatter and court; who to challenge; when to underplay and exactly when to let out all the stops.

DOROTHY UHNAK (b. 1933), U.S. novelist. *The Investigation*, pt. 1, ch. 14 (1977).

11 All trials are trials for one's life, just as all sentences are sentences of death.

OSCAR WILDE (1854–1900), Anglo-Irish playwright, author. *De Profundis* (1905). Wilde was tried for homosexual practices in 1895, and served a two-year sentence with hard labor, during which *De Profundis*—Wilde's letter of confession and reminiscence to his lover—was written.

See also JUDGES; JURIES; Thompson on LAWYERS; LITIGATION.

TROUBLE

1 Trouble has no necessary connection with discouragement—discouragement has a germ of its own, as different from trouble as arthritis is different from a stiff joint.

F. SCOTT FITZGERALD (1896–1940), U.S. author. "Handle With Care," in *Esquire* (New York, March 1936, as second part of Fitzgerald, *Crack-Up* series; repr. in *The Crack-Up*, ed. by Edmund Wilson, 1945).

2 Women like to sit down with trouble as if it were knitting.

ELLEN GLASGOW (1874–1945), U.S. novelist. Jenny Blair, in *The Sheltered Life*, pt. 3, sct. 3 (1932).

3 Worry is interest paid on trouble before it falls due.

W. R. INGE (1860–1954), Dean of St. Paul's, London. *Observer* (London, 14 Feb. 1932).

4 Lately . . . Americans have begun to understand that trouble does not start somewhere on the other side of town. It seems to originate inside the absolute middle of the homemade cherry pie. In our history, the state has failed to respond to the weak. . . . You could be white, male, Presbyterian and heterosexual besides, but if you get fired or if you get sick tomorrow, you might as well be Black, for all the state will want to hear from you.

JUNE JORDAN (b. 1939), U.S. poet, civil rights activist. *Moving Towards Home: Political Essays*, "Problems of Language in a Democratic State" (1989; first published 1982).

5 Death and taxes and childbirth! There's never any convenient time for any of them!

MARGARET MITCHELL (1900–1949), U.S. novelist. Scarlett O'Hara, in *Gone with the Wind*, vol. 2, pt. 4, ch. 38 (1936).

See also PROBLEMS.

TRUST

1 Who would not rather trust and be deceived?

ELIZA COOK (1818–89), English poet. *Love On.*

2 Candid and generous and just,
Boys care but little whom they trust,
An error soon corrected—
For who but learns in riper years,
That man, when smoothest he appears,
Is most to be suspected?

WILLIAM COWPER (1731–1800), English poet. *Friendship* (written 1781; published 1800).

3 Trust everybody, but cut the cards.

FINLEY PETER DUNNE (1867–1936), U.S. journalist, humorist. *Mr. Dooley's Philosophy*, "Casual Observations" (1900).

4 The highest compact we can make with our fellow is—"Let there be truth between us two forevermore."

RALPH WALDO EMERSON (1803–82), U.S. essayist, poet, philosopher. *The Conduct of Life*, "Behavior" (1870).

5 It is impossible to go through life without trust: that is to be imprisoned in the worst cell of all, oneself.

GRAHAM GREENE (1904–91), British novelist. *The Ministry of Fear*, bk. 1, ch. 3, sct. 2 (1943).

6 I cannot give them my confidence; pardon me, gentlemen, confidence is a plant of slow growth in an aged bosom: youth is the season of credulity.

WILLIAM PITT THE ELDER, LORD CHATHAM (1708–78), English statesman. Speech, 14 Jan 1766, to House of Commons, attacking the Rockingham ministry.

7 It is an equal failing to trust everybody, and to trust nobody.

ENGLISH PROVERB (18th century).

8 Never trust a husband too far, nor a bachelor too near.

> HELEN ROWLAND (1875–1950), U.S. journalist. *A Guide to Men*, "Finale" (1922).

9 The only way to make a man trustworthy is to trust him.

> HENRY LEWIS STIMSON (1867–1930), U.S. statesman. Quoted in: *International Herald Tribune* (Paris, 30 Sept. 1992).

10 You may have your suspicions, your fears, you may even believe there is something, somewhere, terribly, drastically wrong, but because someone else is in charge, because there is a part of the system above you which you don't know, you don't question it, you even distrust your own doubts.

> GRAHAM SWIFT (b. 1949), British novelist, short-story writer. *Shuttlecock*, ch. 4 (1981).

11 At the bottom of the heart of every human being from earliest infancy until the tomb, there is something that goes on indomitably expecting, in the teeth of all experience of crimes committed, suffered, and witnessed, that good and not evil will be done to him. It is this above all that is sacred in every human being.

> SIMONE WEIL (1909–43), French philosopher, mystic. "Human Personality" (written 1943; published in *Selected Essays*, ed. by Richard Rees, 1962).

See also Hebrew Bible on ROYALTY; Aeschylus on TYRANNY; Wilde on WIVES.

TRUTH

1 Too much *Truth*
Is uncouth.

> FRANKLIN P. ADAMS (1881–1960), U.S. journalist, humorist. *Nods and Becks*, "From the New England Primer" (1944).

2 The first wrote, wine is the strongest. The second wrote, the king is strongest. The third wrote, women are strongest: but above all things truth beareth away the victory.

> APOCRYPHA. *I Esdras* 3:10–2.

3 The trouble with lying and deceiving is that their efficiency depends entirely upon a clear notion of the truth that the liar and deceiver wishes to hide. In this sense, truth, even if it does not prevail in public, possesses an ineradicable primacy over all falsehoods.

> HANNAH ARENDT (1906–75), German-born U.S. political philosopher. *Crises of the Republic*, "Lying in Politics" (1972).

4 Plato is dear to me, but dearer still is truth.

> Attributed to ARISTOTLE (384–322 B.C.), Greek philosopher.

5 What is truth? said jesting Pilate; and would not stay for an answer.

> FRANCIS BACON (1561–1626), English philosopher, essayist, statesman. *Essays*, "Of Truth" (1597–1625), opening words.

6 It is a pleasure to stand upon the shore, and to see ships tost upon the sea: a pleasure to stand in the window of a castle, and to see a battle and the adventures thereof below: but no pleasure is comparable to standing upon

the vantage ground of truth . . . and to see the errors, and wanderings, and mists, and tempests, in the vale below.

> FRANCIS BACON (1561–1626), English philosopher, essayist, statesman. *Essays*, "Of Truth" (1597–1625).

7 With the truth, you need to get rid of it as soon as possible and pass it on to someone else. As with illness, this is the only way to be cured of it. The person who keeps truth in his hands has lost.

> JEAN BAUDRILLARD (b. 1929), French semiologist. *Cool Memories*, ch. 1 (1987; tr. 1990).

8 Nothing is poorer than a truth expressed as it was thought. Committed to writing in such cases, it is not even a bad photograph. . . . Truth wants to be startled abruptly, at one stroke, from her self-immersion, whether by uproar, music or cries for help.

> WALTER BENJAMIN (1892–1940), German critic, philosopher. *One-Way Street*, "Technical Aid" (1928; repr. in *One-Way Street and Other Writings*, 1978).

9 A truth that's told with bad intent
Beats all the lies you can invent.

> WILLIAM BLAKE (1757–1827), English poet, painter, engraver. *Auguries of Innocence*, in *Poems from the Pickering Manuscript* (c. 1803; repr. in *Complete Writings*, ed. by Geoffrey Keynes, 1957).

10 When I tell any truth it is not for the sake of convincing those who do not know it, but for the sake of defending those who do.

> WILLIAM BLAKE (1757–1827), English poet, painter, engraver. *Public Address* (written c. 1810; published in *Complete Writings*, ed. by Geoffrey Keynes, 1957).

11 *Eclecticism.* Every truth is so true that any truth must be false.

> F. H. BRADLEY (1846–1924), English philosopher. *Aphorisms*, no. 6 (1930).

12 A man may be in as just possession of truth as of a city, and yet be forced to surrender.

> SIR THOMAS BROWNE (1605–82), English physician, author. *Religio Medici*, pt. 1, sct. 6 (c. 1635).

13 Truth that peeps
Over the glasses' edge when dinner's done.

> ROBERT BROWNING (1812–89), English poet. *Bishop Blougram's Apology*.

14 Truth is used to vitalize a statement rather than devitalize it. Truth implies more than a simple statement of fact. "I don't have any whisky," may be a fact but it is not a truth.

> WILLIAM BURROUGHS (b. 1914), U.S. author. *The Adding Machine*, "On Coincidence" (1985).

15 There is no such source of error as the pursuit of absolute truth.

> SAMUEL BUTLER (1835–1902), English author. *Samuel Butler's Notebooks* (1951, p. 120).

16 We don't arrive at it by standing on one leg or on the first day of our setting out—but though we may jostle one another on the way that is no reason why we should strike or trample—*elbowing's* enough.

> LORD BYRON (1788–1824), English poet. Letter, 9 May 1817, to

publisher John Murray (published in *Byron's Letters and Journals*, vol. 5, ed. by Leslie A. Marchand, 1973–81).

17 Such is Truth! Men dare not look her in the face, except by degrees: they mistake her for a Gorgon, instead of knowing her to be a Minerva.

LORD BYRON (1788–1824), English poet. Letter, 10 June 1822, to author Isaac D'Israeli (published in *Byron's Letters and Journals*, vol. 9, ed. by Leslie A. Marchand, 1973–81).

18 Truth is a pain which will not stop. And the truth of this world is to die. You must choose: either dying or lying. Personally, I have never been able to kill myself.

LOUIS-FERDINAND CÉLINE (1894–1961), French author. The narrator (Ferdinand Bardamu), in *Journey to the End of the Night* (1932; tr. 1934; repr. 1966, p. 176).

19 Truth indeed rather alleviates than hurts, and will always bear up against falsehood, as oil does above water.

MIGUEL DE CERVANTES (1547–1616), Spanish author. *Don Quixote*, pt. 2, bk. 5, ch. 10 (1615; tr. by P. Motteux).

20 Man may aspire to virtue, but he cannot reasonably aspire to truth.

SÉBASTIEN-ROCH NICOLAS DE CHAMFORT (1741–94), French writer, wit. *Maxims and Considerations*, vol. 2, no. 342 (1796; tr. 1926).

21 There are truths which one can only say after having won the right to say them.

JEAN COCTEAU (1889–1963), French author, filmmaker. *Le Rappel àL'Ordre*, "Le Coq et l'Arlequin" (1926; repr. in *Collected Works*, vol. 9, 1950).

22 Truth is the most unbending and uncompliable, the most necessary, firm, immutable, and *adamantine* thing in the world.

RALPH J. CUDWORTH (1617–88), English theologian, philosopher. *Treatise Concerning Eternal and Immutable Morality*, bk. 4, ch. 5, sct. 3 (1731).

23 It was as true as taxes is. And nothing's truer than them.

CHARLES DICKENS (1812–70), English novelist. Mr. Barkis, in *David Copperfield*, ch. 21 (1849–50). This remark echoes Benjamin Franklin's famous gloomy observation on the inevitability of taxes. See Franklin on CERTAINTY.

24 When you have eliminated the impossible, whatever remains, *however improbable*, must be the truth.

SIR ARTHUR CONAN DOYLE (1859–1930), English author. Sherlock Holmes, in *The Sign of Four*, ch. 6 (1889).

25 Perhaps our only sickness is to desire a truth which we cannot bear rather than to rest content with the fictions we manufacture out of each other.

LAWRENCE DURRELL (1912–90), British author. *Justine*, in *Clea*, ch. 1, sct. 3 (1960).

26 Perhaps the mission of those who love mankind is to make people laugh at the truth, *to make truth laugh*, because the only truth lies in learning to free ourselves from insane passion for the truth.

UMBERTO ECO (b. 1932), Italian semiologist, novelist. Brother William, in *The Name of the Rose*, "Seventh Day: Night (2)" (1980; tr. 1983).

27 Truth has rough flavours if we bite it through.

GEORGE ELIOT (1819–80), English novelist, editor. Graf Dornberg, in *Armgart*, sc. 2 (1871).

28 God offers to every mind its choice between truth and repose. Take which you please; you can never have both.

RALPH WALDO EMERSON (1803–82), U.S. essayist, poet, philosopher. *Essays*, "Intellect" (First Series, 1841).

29 The business man who assumes that his life is everything, and the mystic who asserts that it is nothing, fail, on this side and on that, to hit the truth. . . . No; truth, being alive . . . was only to be found by continuous excursions into either realm, and though proportion is the final secret, to espouse it at the outset is to ensure sterility.

E. M. FORSTER (1879–1970), British novelist, essayist. *Howards End*, ch. 23 (1910).

30 The truth isn't always beauty, but the hunger for it is.

NADINE GORDIMER (b. 1923), South African author. "A Bolter and the Invincible Summer," in *London Magazine* (May 1963; repr. in *The Essential Gesture*, ed. by Stephen Clingman, 1988).

31 Man, in spite of his tendency towards mendacity, has a great respect for what he calls the truth. Truth is his staff in his voyage through life; commonplaces are the bread in his bag and the wine in his jug.

RÉMY DE GOURMONT (1858–1915), French critic, novelist. "The Dissociation of Ideas" (1899; repr. in *Selected Writings*, ed. and tr. by Glen S. Burne, 1966).

32 The truth has never been of any real value to any human being—it is a symbol for mathematicians and philosophers to pursue. In human relations kindness and lies are worth a thousand truths.

GRAHAM GREENE (1904–91), British novelist. Scobie, in *Heart of the Matter*, bk. 1, pt. 1, ch. 2, sct. 4 (1948).

33 There are times when we must sink to the bottom of our misery to understand truth, just as we must descend to the bottom of a well to see the stars in broad daylight.

VÁCLAV HAVEL (b. 1936), Czech playwright, president. *Living in Truth*, pt. 1, "The Power of the Powerless," sct. 16 (1986).

34 The truth is not simply what you think it is; it is also the circumstances in which it is said, and to whom, why, and how it is said.

VÁCLAV HAVEL (b. 1936), Czech playwright, president. *Disturbing the Peace*, ch. 2 (1986; tr. 1990).

35 Such truth, as opposeth no man's profit, nor pleasure, is to all men welcome.

THOMAS HOBBES (1588–1679), English philosopher. *Leviathan*, "A Review and Conclusion" (1651).

36 Truth is tough. It will not break, like a bubble, at a touch; nay, you may kick it about all day like a football, and it will be round and full at evening.

OLIVER WENDELL HOLMES, SR. (1809–94), U.S. writer, physician. *The Professor at the Breakfast Table*, ch. 5 (1860).

37 It doesn't do to be quixotic. Telling the truth to people who misunderstand you is really promoting falsehood.

ANTHONY HOPE [ANTHONY HOPE HAWKINS] (1863–1933),

British author. The narrator (Mr. Carter), in *The Dolly Dialogues*, no. 14 (1894).

38   I'm plotting revolution against this lie that the majority has a monopoly of the truth.   What are these truths that always bring the majority rallying round? Truths so elderly they are practically senile.   And when a truth is as old as that, gentlemen, you can hardly tell it from a lie.

HENRIK IBSEN (1828–1906), Norwegian dramatist. Dr. Stockmann, in *An Enemy of the People*, act 4.

39   It is always the best policy to speak the truth, unless of course you are an exceptionally good liar.

JEROME K. JEROME (1859–1927), British author. *Idler* (London, Feb. 1892).

40   Truth must be the foundation stone, the cement to solidify the entire social edifice.

JOHN PAUL II [KAROL WOJTYLA] (b. 1920), Polish ecclesiastic, pope. *Times* (London, 18 May 1988).

41   In order to swim one takes off all one's clothes—in order to aspire to the truth one must undress in a far more inward sense, divest oneself of all one's inward clothes, of thoughts, conceptions, selfishness etc. before one is sufficiently naked.

SØREN KIERKEGAARD (1813–55), Danish philosopher. *The Journals of Soren Kierkegaard: A Selection*, no. 1395, (ed. and tr. by Alexander Dru, 1938), entry for 1854.

42   The truth is a snare: you cannot have it, without being caught. You cannot have the truth in such a way that you catch it, but only in such a way that it catches you.

SØREN KIERKEGAARD (1813–55), Danish philosopher. *The Papers of Soren Kierkegaard*, vol. 11, pt. 1, sct. 352 (ed. by P. A. Heiberg and V. Kuhr, 1909; repr. in *The Last Years: Journals 1853–55*, ed. and tr. by Ronald G. Smith, 1965).

43   The ultimate truth is penultimately always a falsehood. He who will be proved right in the end appears to be wrong and harmful before it.

ARTHUR KOESTLER (1905–83), Hungarian-born British author. Extract from Rubashov's diary, in *Darkness at Noon*, "The Second Hearing," ch. 1 (1940).

44   Truth is a clumsy servant that breaks the dishes while washing them.

KARL KRAUS (1874–1936), Austrian satirist. *Sprüche und Widersprüche*, ch. 9 (1909; tr. in *Half-Truths and One-And-A Half-Truths*, "Lord, Forgive Them . . ." ed. by Harry Zohn, 1976).

45   I maintain that Truth is a pathless land, and you cannot approach it by any path whatsoever, by any religion, by any sect.

JIDDU KRISHNAMURTI (1895–1986), Indian mystic. Speech, 3 Aug. 1929, Holland. Quoted in: Lilly Heber, *Krishnamurti*, ch. 2 (1931).

46   All vital truth contains the memory of all that for which it is not true.

D. H. LAWRENCE (1885–1930), British author. Letter, 20 Dec. 1914 (published in *The Letters of D. H. Lawrence*, vol. 2, ed. by George J. Zytaruk and James T. Boulton, 1981).

47   If it were true what in the end would be gained? Nothing but another truth.   Is this such a mighty advantage?   We have enough old truths still to digest, and even these we would be quite unable to endure if we did not sometimes flavor them with lies.

G. C. LICHTENBERG (1742–99), German physicist, philosopher. *Aphorisms*, "Notebook E," aph. 10 (written 1765–99; tr. by R. J. Hollingdale, 1990).

48   Closest to the truth are those who deal lightly with it because they know it is inexhaustible.

GOLO MANN (b. 1909), German historian, son of Thomas Mann. Quoted in: Marcel Reich-Ranicki, *Thomas Mann and His Family*, "Golo Mann: The Liberation of an Unloved One" (1987; tr. 1989), of satirist Heinrich Heine.

49   There are no new truths, but only truths that have not been recognized by those who have perceived them without noticing.   A truth is something that everybody can be shown to know and to have known, as people say, all along.

MARY MCCARTHY (1912–89), U.S. author, critic. "The Vita Activa," in *New Yorker* (18 Oct. 1958; repr. in *On the Contrary*, 1961).

50   What does it matter how one comes by the truth so long as one pounces upon it and lives by it?

HENRY MILLER (1891–1980), U.S. author. *Tropic of Capricorn* (1939; repr. 1966, p. 159).

51   Truth . . . never comes into the world but like a Bastard, to the ignominy of him that brought her forth.

JOHN MILTON (1608–74), English poet. *The Doctrine and Discipline of Divorce*, Introduction (1643).

52   I speak truth, not my belly-full, but as much as I dare; and I dare the more the more I grow into years.

MICHEL DE MONTAIGNE (1533–92), French essayist, moralist. *Essays*, bk. 3, ch. 2, "Of Repenting" (1580–8; tr. by John Florio).

53   You cannot have both truth and what you call civilisation.

IRIS MURDOCH (b. 1919), British novelist, philosopher. Honor Klein, in *A Severed Head*, ch. 9 (1961).

54   Let us begin by committing ourselves to the truth— to see it like it is, and tell it like it is—to find the truth, to speak the truth, and to live the truth.

RICHARD M. NIXON (b. 1913), U.S. Republican politician, president. Speech, 9 Aug. 1968, Miami, accepting the presidential nomination.

55   I preach there are all kinds of truth, your truth and somebody else's.   But behind all of them there is only one truth and that is that there's no truth.

FLANNERY O'CONNOR (1925–64), U.S. author. The preacher Hazel Motes, in *Wise Blood*, ch. 10 (1952).

56   If there were only one truth, you couldn't paint a hundred canvases on the same theme.

PABLO PICASSO (1881–1973), Spanish artist. Quoted in: Hélène Parmelin, *Picasso Says . . .,* "Truth" (1966; tr. 1969).

57   Where there are no rights, there are no duties.   To tell the truth is thus a duty; but it is a duty only in respect to one who has a right to the truth.

HENRI BENJAMIN CONSTANT DE REBECQUE (1767–1830), French writer, orator, statesman. "On Political Reactions," in the journal *France*, pt. 6, no. 1 (1797).

58   In morals, truth is but little prized when it is a mere sentiment, and only attains its full value when realized in the world as fact.

> ERNEST RENAN (1823–92), French writer, critic, scholar. *The Life of Jesus*, ch. 5 (1863).

59   You may take great comfort from the fact that suffering inwardly for the sake of truth proves abundantly that one loves it and marks one out as being of the elect.

> ERNEST RENAN (1823–92), French writer, critic, scholar. Quoted in: H. W. Wardman, *Ernest Renan: a Critical Biography*, "Saint Sulpice and the Hidden God" (1964).

60   Truth is simply a compliment paid to sentences seen to be paying their way.

> RICHARD RORTY (b. 1931), U.S. philosopher. Quoted in: *New York Times Magazine* (12 Feb. 1990).

61   There are moments when very little truth would be enough to shape opinion. One might be hated at extremely low cost.

> JEAN ROSTAND (1894–1977), French biologist, writer. *Pensées d'un Biologiste* (1939; repr. in *The Substance of Man*, "A Biologist's Thoughts," ch. 10, 1962).

62   Truth titillates the imagination far less than fiction.

> MARQUIS DE SADE (1740–1814), French author. Friar Claude, in *L'Histoire de Juliette, ou les Prospérités du Vice*, pt. 3 (1797).

63   It is not because the truth is too difficult to see that we make mistakes. It may even lie on the surface; but we make mistakes because the easiest and most comfortable course for us is to seek insight where it accords with our emotions—especially selfish ones.

> ALEXANDER SOLZHENITSYN (b. 1918), Russian novelist. "Peace and Violence," sct. 2, in *Index*, no. 4 (London, 1973; repr. in *Solzhenitsyn: A Documentary Record*, "Trials in Détente," ed. by Leopold Labedz, 1974).

64   The truth is always something that is told, not something that is known. If there were no speaking or writing, there would be no truth about anything. There would only be what is.

> SUSAN SONTAG (b. 1933), U.S. essayist. *The Benefactor*, ch. 1 (1963).

65   The truth is balance, but the opposite of truth, which is unbalance, may not be a lie.

> SUSAN SONTAG (b. 1933), U.S. essayist. *Against Interpretation*, "Simone Weil" (1966).

66   We have been a little insane about the truth. We have had an obsession.

> WALLACE STEVENS (1879–1955), U.S. poet. *The Necessary Angel*, "The Noble Rider and the Sound of Words" (1951; lecture first published 1942).

67   It takes two to speak the truth—one to speak and another to hear.

> HENRY DAVID THOREAU (1817–62), U.S. philosopher, author, naturalist. *A Week on the Concord and Merrimack Rivers*, "Wednesday" (1849).

68   They who know of no purer sources of truth, who have traced up its stream no higher, stand, and wisely stand, by the Bible and the Constitution, and drink at it there with reverence and humility; but they who behold where it comes trickling into this lake or that pool, gird up their loins once more, and continue their pilgrimage toward its fountainhead.

> HENRY DAVID THOREAU (1817–62), U.S. philosopher, author, naturalist. *On the Duty of Civil Disobedience* (1849).

69   Truth is the most valuable thing we have. Let us economize it.

> MARK TWAIN (1835–1910), U.S. author. *Following the Equator*, ch. 7, "Pudd'nhead Wilson's New Calendar" (1897).

70   Familiarity breeds contempt. How accurate that is. The reason we hold truth in such respect is because we have so little opportunity to get familiar with it.

> MARK TWAIN (1835–1910), U.S. author. *Notebook* ch. 31 (ed. by Albert Bigelow Paine, 1935), entry for 1898.

71   Truth should not be forced; it should simply manifest itself, like a woman who has in her privacy reflected and coolly decided to bestow herself upon a certain man.

> JOHN UPDIKE (b. 1932), U.S. author, critic. *Self-Consciousness: Memoirs*, ch. 6 (1989).

72   The truth is really an ambition which is beyond us.

> PETER USTINOV (b. 1921), British actor, writer, director. *International Herald Tribune* (Paris, 12 March 1990).

73   The only way into truth is through one's own annihilation; through dwelling a long time in a state of extreme and total humiliation.

> SIMONE WEIL (1909–43), French philosopher, mystic. "Human Personality" (written 1943; published in *La Table Ronde*, Dec. 1950; repr. in *Selected Essays*, ed. by Richard Rees, 1962).

74   There are no whole truths; all truths are half-truths. It is trying to treat them as whole truths that plays the devil.

> ALFRED NORTH WHITEHEAD (1861–1947), British philosopher. *Dialogues of Alfred North Whitehead*, Prologue (ed. by Lucien Price, 1954).

75   A truth ceases to be true when more than one person believes in it.

> OSCAR WILDE (1854–1900), Anglo-Irish playwright, author. *Phrases and Philosophies for the Use of the Young*, in *Chameleon* (London, Dec. 1894). Shortly afterwards, under cross-examination by Edward Carson, Q.C., during Wilde's prosecution of the Marquess of Queensberry for criminal libel (*Regina v. Queensberry*, 3 April 1895), Wilde explained this aphorism: "That would be my metaphysical definition of truth; something so personal that the same truth could never be appreciated by two minds."

76   The truth is rarely pure and never simple. Modern life would be very tedious if it were either, and modern literature a complete impossibility!

> OSCAR WILDE (1854–1900), Anglo-Irish playwright, author. Algernon, in *The Importance of Being Earnest*, act 1.

77   When one is frightened of the truth . . . then it is never the *whole* truth that one has an inkling of.

> LUDWIG WITTGENSTEIN (1889–1951), Austrian philosopher. *Notebooks 1914–1916* (ed. by Anscombe, 1961), entry for 15 Oct. 1914.

78   Let a man get up and say, "Behold, this is the truth," and instantly I perceive a sandy cat filching a piece of fish in the background. Look, you have forgotten the cat, I say.

> VIRGINIA WOOLF (1882–1941), British novelist. Bernard, in *The Waves* (1931).

79 Man can embody truth but he cannot know it.

> W. B. YEATS (1865–1939), Irish poet, playwright. Letter, 4 Jan. 1939 (published in *The Letters of W. B. Yeats*, ed. by Allan Wade, 1954) Yeats died 28 Jan. 1939.

See also Keats on BEAUTY; Huxley on COMMON SENSE; Brookner on CONFESSION; Voltaire on The DEAD; Arnold on DEATH AND DYING; Daumal on ERROR; Hugo on EXAGGERATION; Lichtenberg on FASHION; Johnson on FREEDOM OF SPEECH; Hazlitt on INJURY; Byron on LIES AND LYING; Galbraith on The MAJORITY; Murdoch on MORALISTS; Scott on NEWSPAPERS AND MAGAZINES; Hegel on ORIGINALITY; Chesterfield on RIDICULE.

THE TWENTIETH CENTURY

1 The marriage of reason and nightmare which has dominated the 20th century has given birth to an ever more ambiguous world. Across the communications landscape move the specters of sinister technologies and the dreams that money can buy. Thermonuclear weapons systems and soft drink commercials coexist in an overlit realm ruled by advertising and pseudoevents, science and pornography. Over our lives preside the great twin leitmotifs of the 20th century—sex and paranoia.

> J. G. BALLARD (b. 1930), English novelist. Introduction, 1974, to the French edition of *Crash* (1973).

2 At no previous period has mankind been faced by a half-century which so paradoxically united violence and progress. Its greater and lesser wars and long series of major assassinations have been strangely combined with the liberation of more societies and individuals than ever before in history, and by the transformation of millions of second-class citizens—women, workers and the members of subject races—to a stage at which first-rate achievement is no longer inhibited even if opportunities are not yet complete.

> VERA BRITTAIN (1893–1970), British author. *The Rebel Passion*, ch. 12 (1964).

3 The real passion of the twentieth century is servitude.

> ALBERT CAMUS (1913–60), French-Algerian philosopher, author. *The Rebel*, pt. 3, "State Terrorism and Rational Terror" (1951; tr. 1953).

4 In the nineteenth century the problem was that *God is dead;* in the twentieth century the problem is that *man is dead*.

> ERICH FROMM (1900–1980), U.S. psychologist. *The Sane Society*, ch. 9 (1955).

5 By all but the pathologically romantic, it is now recognized that this is not the age of the small man.

> JOHN KENNETH GALBRAITH (b. 1908), U.S. economist. *The New Industrial State*, ch. 3 (1967).

6 I was lucky enough to see with my own eyes the recent stock-market crash, where they lost several million dollars, a rabble of dead money that went sliding off into the sea. Never as then, amid suicides, hysteria, and groups of fainting people, have I felt the sensation of real death, death without hope, death that is nothing but rottenness, for the spectacle was terrifying but devoid of greatness. . . . I felt something like a divine urge to bombard that whole canyon of shadow, where ambulances collected suicides whose hands were full of rings.

> FEDERICO GARCÍA LORCA (1898–1936), Spanish poet, playwright. "A Poet in New York," lecture, March 1932, Madrid (published in *Poet in New York*, 1940; tr. 1988).

7 The horror of the Twentieth Century was the size of each new event, and the paucity of its reverberation.

> NORMAN MAILER (b. 1923), U.S. author. *A Fire on the Moon*, pt. 1, ch. 1 (1970).

8 It is the mission of the twentieth century to elucidate the irrational.

> MAURICE MERLEAU-PONTY (1907–61), French philosopher. Quoted in: Lev Braun, *Witness of Decline*, ch. 8 (1974).

9 The new man is born too old to tolerate the new world. The present conditions of life have not yet erased the traces of the past. We run too fast, but we still do not move enough. . . . He looks but he does not contemplate, he sees but he does not think. He runs away from time, which is made of thought, and yet all he can feel is his own time, the present.

> EUGENIO MONTALE (1896–1981), Italian poet. *Poet In Our Time* (1972).

10 This filthy twentieth century. I hate its guts.

> A. L. ROWSE (b. 1903), British historian, critic. *Time* (New York, 13 Nov. 1978).

11 All in all, I would not have missed this century for the world.

> GORE VIDAL (b. 1925), U.S. novelist, critic. *Observer* (London, 31 Dec. 1989).

See also Rushdie on DOUBT; MODERN TIMES; Eric Hoffer on NINETEENTH CENTURY; Solzhenitsyn on The PRESS.

THE TWENTIETH CENTURY: THE 1920s

1 The early twenties when we drank wood alcohol and every day in every way grew better and better, and there was a first abortive shortening of the skirts, and girls all looked alike in sweater dresses, and people you didn't want to know said "Yes, we have no bananas," and it seemed only a question of a few years before the older people would step aside and let the world be run by those who saw things as they were—and it all seems rosy and romantic to us who were young then, because we will never feel quite so intensely about our surroundings any more.

> F. SCOTT FITZGERALD (1896–1940), U.S. author. "Echoes of the Jazz Age," in *Scribner's* (New York, Nov. 1931; repr. in *The Crack-Up*, ed. by Edmund Wilson, 1945).

2 Though the Jazz Age continued it became less and less an affair of youth. The sequel was like a children's party taken over by the elders.

> F. SCOTT FITZGERALD (1896–1940), U.S. author. "Echoes of the Jazz Age," in *Scribner's* (New York, Nov. 1931; repr. in *The Crack-Up*, ed. by Edmund Wilson, 1945).

3 The age demanded that we dance
And jammed us into iron pants.

And in the end the age was handed
The sort of shit that it demanded.

> ERNEST HEMINGWAY (1899–1961), U.S. author. "The Age Demanded," in *Der Querschnitt* (Feb. 1925). Quoted in: Noel Riley Fitch, *Sylvia Beach and the Lost Generation*, ch. 9 (1983).

THE TWENTIETH CENTURY: THE 1940s

1   To say "I accept" in an age like our own is to say that you accept concentration-camps, rubber truncheons, Hitler, Stalin, bombs, aeroplanes, tinned food, machine guns, putsches, purges, slogans, Bedaux belts, gasmasks, submarines, spies, provocateurs, press-censorship, secret prisons, aspirins, Hollywood films and political murder.

> GEORGE ORWELL (1903–50), British author. *Inside the Whale and Other Essays*, "Inside the Whale" (1940).

THE TWENTIETH CENTURY: THE 1950s

1   These are the fifties, you know. The disgusting, posturing fifties.

> HANNAH ARENDT (1906–75), German-born U.S. political philosopher. Quoted in: Frederic Prokosch, *Voices: A Memoir*, "The Monster" (1983), said to author and poet Prokosch.

2   Our civilization survives in the complacency of cowardly or malignant minds—a sacrifice to the vanity of ageing adolescents. . . . In 1953, excess is always a comfort, and sometimes a career.

> ALBERT CAMUS (1913–60), French-Algerian philosopher, author. *The Rebel*, pt. 5, "Moderation and Excess" (1951; tr. 1953).

3   We were that generation called "silent," but we were silent neither, as some thought, because we shared the period's official optimism nor, as others thought, because we feared its official repression. We were silent because the exhilaration of social action seemed to many of us just one more way of escaping the personal, of masking for a while that dread of the meaningless which was man's fate.

> JOAN DIDION (b. 1935), U.S. essayist. *The White Album*, "On the Morning After the Sixties" (1979; first published 1970).

4   The 1950s to me is darkness, hidden history, perversion behind most doors waiting to creep out. The 1950s to most people is kitsch and Mickey Mouse watches and all this intolerable stuff . . .

> JAMES ELLROY (b. 1948), U.S. crime author. Quoted in: John Williams, *Into The Badlands*, ch. 4 (1991).

5   The fifties—they seem to have taken place on a sunny afternoon that asked nothing of you except a drifting belief in the moment and its power to satisfy.

> ELIZABETH HARDWICK (b. 1916), U.S. critic, author. *Bartleby in Manhattan and Other Essays*, "Domestic Manners" (1983).

THE TWENTIETH CENTURY: THE 1960s

1   The defiance of established authority, religious and secular, social and political, as a world-wide phenomenon may well one day be accounted the outstanding event of the last decade.

> HANNAH ARENDT (1906–75), German-born U.S. political philosopher. *Crises of the Republic*, "Civil Disobedience" (1972).

2   All that Swinging Sixties nonsense, we all thought it was passé at the time.

> DAVID BAILEY (b. 1938), British photographer. *Face* (London, Dec. 1984).

3   The white youth of today have begun to react to the fact that the "American Way of Life" is a fossil of history. What do they care if their old baldheaded and crewcut elders don't dig their caveman mops? They couldn't care less about the old, stiffassed honkies who don't like their new dances: Frug, Monkey, Jerk, Swim, Watusi. All they know is that it feels good to swing to way-out body-rhythms instead of dragassing across the dance floor like zombies to the dead beat of mind-smothered Mickey Mouse music.

> ELDRIDGE CLEAVER (b. 1935), U.S. black leader, writer. *Soul on Ice*, "The White Race and Its Heroes" (1968).

4   Many people I know in Los Angeles believe that the Sixties ended abruptly on August 9, 1969, ended at the exact moment when word of the murders on Cielo Drive traveled like brushfire through the community, and in a sense this is true. The tension broke that day. The paranoia was fulfilled.

> JOAN DIDION (b. 1935), U.S. essayist. "The White Album: A Chronicle of Survival in the Sixties," in *New West* (4 June 1979), of the Charles Manson murders.

5   People today are still living off the table scraps of the sixties. They are still being passed around—the music and the ideas.

> BOB DYLAN (b. 1941), U.S. singer, songwriter. *Guardian* (London, 13 Feb. 1992).

6   For me, the lame part of the Sixties was the political part, the social part. The real part was the spiritual part.

> JERRY GARCIA (b. 1942), U.S. rock musician. *Rolling Stone* (New York, 30 Nov. 1989).

7   It is in our interests to let the police and their employers go on believing that the Underground is a conspiracy, because it increases their paranoia and their inability to deal with what is really happening. As long as they look for ringleaders and documents they will miss their mark, which is that proportion of every personality which belongs in the Underground.

> GERMAINE GREER (b. 1939), Australian feminist writer. "The Million-Dollar Underground," in *Oz* (London, July 1969; repr. in *The Madwoman's Underclothes*, 1986).

8   The Great Society is a place where every child can find knowledge to enrich his mind and to enlarge his talents. . . . It is a place where the city of man serves not only the needs of the body and the demands of commerce but the desire for beauty and the hunger for community. . . . It is a place where men are more concerned with the quality of their goals than the quantity of their goods.

> LYNDON B. JOHNSON (1908–73), U.S. Democratic politician, president. Speech, 22 May 1964, Ann Arbor, Mich. According to Hugh Sidey, in *A Very Personal Presidency* (1968), the slogan

"Great Society" had been current for several years, but was adopted for Johnson by Richard N. Goodwin, Secretary General of the International Peace Corps Secretariat and occasional speechwriter. It became a keynote of Johnson's presidency, stressed by him in his acceptance speech at the Democratic Party National Convention, August 1964.

9 We stand today on the edge of a new frontier—the frontier of the 1960s, a frontier of unknown opportunities and perils, a frontier of unfulfilled hopes and threats. . . . The new frontier of which I speak is not a set of promises—it is a set of challenges.

JOHN F. KENNEDY (1917–63), U.S. Democratic politician, president. Speech, 13 July 1960, at the Democratic Convention, Los Angeles, accepting the presidential nomination. Theodore C. Sorensen took credit for drafting this speech, in his biography *Kennedy*, ch. 6 (1965).

10 My advice to people today is as follows: If you take the game of life seriously, if you take your nervous system seriously, if you take your sense organs seriously, if you take the energy process seriously, you must turn on, tune in, and drop out.

TIMOTHY LEARY (b. 1920), U.S. psychologist. Lecture, 1966 (published in *The Politics of Ecstasy*, ch. 21, 1968).

11 We were all on this ship in the sixties, our generation, a ship going to discover the New World. And the Beatles were in the crow's nest of that ship.

JOHN LENNON (1940–80), British rock musician. Interview, March 1974, for French TV by François Vallee.

12 The thing the sixties did was to show us the possibilities and the responsibility that we all had. It wasn't the answer. It just gave us a glimpse of the possibility.

JOHN LENNON (1940–80), British rock musician. Interview, 8 Dec. 1980, for KFRC RKO Radio, given the day of Lennon's death.

13 It has to be acknowledged that in capitalist society, with its herds of hippies, originality has become a sort of fringe benefit, a *mere* convention, accepted obsolescence, the Beatnik model being turned in for the Hippie model, as though strangely obedient to capitalist laws of marketing.

MARY MCCARTHY (1912–1989), U.S. author, critic. *Hanoi*, "Language" (1968).

14 I like to think of my behavior in the sixties as a "learning experience." Then again, I like to think of anything stupid I've done as a "learning experience." It makes me feel less stupid.

P. J. O'ROURKE (b. 1947), U.S. journalist. "Second Thoughts About the Sixties," Speech, Oct. 1987, Second Thoughts Conference, Washington, D.C. (repr. in *Give War A Chance*, 1992).

15 My generation of the Sixties, with all our great ideals, destroyed liberalism, because of our excesses.

CAMILLE PAGLIA (b. 1947), U.S. author, critic, educator. "The M.I.T. Lecture: Crisis in the American Universities," 19 Sept. 1991 (published in *Sex, Art, and American Culture*, 1992).

16 The Sixties, of course, was the worst time in the world to try and bring up a child. They were exposed to all these crazy things going on.

NANCY REAGAN (b. 1923), U.S. First Lady. Quoted in: *Parade* (New York, 8 Nov. 1981).

17 I knew the youthfulness of the sixties: Talitha and Paul Getty lying on a starlit terrace in Marrakesh, beautiful and damned, and a whole generation assembled as if for eternity where the curtain of the past seemed to lift before an extraordinary future.

YVES SAINT LAURENT (b. 1936), French couturier. *Ritz*, no. 85 (London, 1984).

18 History is hard to know, because of all the hired bullshit, but even without being sure of "history" it seems entirely reasonable to think that every now and then the energy of a whole generation comes to a head in a long fine flash, for reasons that nobody really understands at the time—and which never explain, in retrospect, what actually happened.

HUNTER S. THOMPSON (b. 1939), U.S. journalist. *Fear and Loathing in Las Vegas*, ch. 8 (1971).

19 Never before has a civilization reached such a degree of a contempt for life; never before has a generation, drowned in mortification, felt such a rage to live.

RAOUL VANEIGEM (b. 1934), Belgian Situationist philosopher. *The Revolution of Everyday Life*, ch. 5 (1967; tr. 1983).

20 Infantilism is possibly the hallmark of our generation.

JOHN WELLS (b. 1936), British writer, actor, director. Quoted in: Ronald Bergan, *Beyond the Fringe . . . and Beyond*, pt. 4 (1989)

See also Arendt on The NUCLEAR AGE.

THE TWENTIETH CENTURY: THE 1970s

1 If anything characterizes the cultural life of the seventies in America, it is an insistence on preventing failures of communication.

RICHARD DEAN ROSEN (b. 1949), U.S. journalist, critic. *Psychobabble: Fast Talk and Quick Cure in the Era of Feeling*, "Psychobabble" (1977).

THE TWENTIETH CENTURY: THE 1980s

1 Maybe in the '90s or possibly in the next century people will look upon the '80s as the age of masturbation, when it was taken to the limit; that might be all that's going on right now in a big way.

BOB DYLAN (b. 1941), U.S. singer, songwriter. Interview, 1985, with Cameron Crowe, for *Biograph*, box set (1985), notes to "Every Grain of Sand."

2 In economics, we borrowed from the Bourbons; in foreign policy, we drew on themes fashioned by the nomad warriors of the Eurasian steppes. In spiritual matters, we emulated the braying intolerance of our archenemies, the Shi'ite fundamentalists.

BARBARA EHRENREICH (b. 1941), U.S. author, columnist. *The Worst Years of Our Lives*, "Family Values" (1991), of the "traditional values" adopted by Americans in the eighties. These values formed "part of what may someday be known as the 'Reagan renovation,' that finely balanced mix of cosmetic refinement and moral coarseness which brought $200,000 china to the White House dinner table and mayhem to the beleaguered peasantry of Central America."

3   We can safely abandon the doctrine of the eighties, namely that the rich were not working because they had too little money, the poor because they had much.

> JOHN KENNETH GALBRAITH (b. 1908), U.S. economist. *Guardian* (London, 20 Nov. 1991).

4   I wouldn't wish the eighties on anyone, it was the time when all that was rotten bubbled to the surface. If you were not at the receiving end of this mayhem you could be unaware of it. It was possible to live through the decade preoccupied by the mortgage and the pence you saved on your income tax. It was also possible for those of us who saw what was happening to turn our eyes in a different direction; but what, in another decade, had been a trip to the clap clinic was now a trip to the mortuary.

> DEREK JARMAN (b. 1942), British filmmaker, artist, author. *At Your Own Risk: A Saint's Testament*, "1980's" (1992).

5   The last best hope of earth, two trillion dollars in debt, is spinning out of control, and all we can do is stare at a flickering cathode-ray tube as Ollie "answers" questions on TV while the press, resolutely irrelevant as ever, asks politicians if they have committed adultery. From V-J Day 1945 to this has been, my fellow countrymen, a perfect nightmare.

> GORE VIDAL (b. 1925), U.S. novelist, critic. *A View from the Diner's Club*, "Ollie" (1991).

THE TWENTIETH CENTURY THE 1990s

1   As the end of the century approaches, all our culture is like the culture of flies at the beginning of winter. Having lost their agility, dreamy and demented, they turn slowly about the window in the first icy mists of morning. They give themselves a last wash and brush-up, their ocellated eyes roll, and they fall down the curtains.

> JEAN BAUDRILLARD (b. 1929), French semiologist. *Cool Memories*, ch. 5 (1987; tr. 1990).

2   I confidently predict the collapse of capitalism and the beginning of history. Something will go wrong in the machinery that converts money into money, the banking system will collapse totally, and we will be left having to barter to stay alive. Those who can dig in their garden will have a better chance than the rest. I'll be all right; I've got a few veg.

> MARGARET DRABBLE (b. 1939), British novelist. Predictions for the year, in *Guardian* (London, 2 Jan. 1993).

3   The 1990s, after the reign of terror of academic vandalism, will be a decade of restoration: restoration of meaning, value, beauty, pleasure, and emotion to art and restoration of art to its audience.

> CAMILLE PAGLIA (b. 1947), U.S. author, critic, educator. "The Critic at Graceful Ease," book review in *Washington Post Book World* (10 March 1991; repr. in *Sex, Art, and American Culture*, 1992).

TYCOONS

1   The rights and interests of the laboring man will be protected and cared for, not by the labor agitators, but by the Christian men to whom God in His infinite wisdom has given control of the property interests of the country.

> GEORGE BAER (1842–1914), U.S. railroad magnate. Open letter to the press, Oct. 1902, during the Pennsylvania miners' strike.

2   It is impossible to think of Howard Hughes without seeing the apparently bottomless gulf between what we say we want and what we do want, between what we officially admire and secretly desire, between, in the largest sense, the people we marry and the people we love. In a nation which increasingly appears to prize social virtues, Howard Hughes remains not merely antisocial but grandly, brilliantly, surpassingly, asocial. He is the last private man, the dream we no longer admit.

> JOAN DIDION (b. 1934), U.S. essayist. *Slouching towards Bethlehem*, "7000 Romaine, Los Angeles" (1968; first published 1967).

3   There's a certain part of the contented majority who love anybody who is worth a billion dollars.

> JOHN KENNETH GALBRAITH (b. 1908), U.S. economist. *Guardian* (London, 23 May 1992), of millionaire presidential candidate H. Ross Perot.

4   My religion? Well, my dear, I am a Millionaire. That is my religion.

> GEORGE BERNARD SHAW (1856–1950), Anglo-Irish playwright, critic. Undershaft, in *Major Barbara*, act 2.

5   I wasn't satisfied just to earn a good living. I was looking to make a statement.

> DONALD TRUMP (b. 1946), U.S. businessman. *Trump: The Art of the Deal*, ch. 2 (1987; written with Tony Schwartz).

See also The RICH.

TYRANNY

1   In every tyrant's heart there springs in the end
This poison, that he cannot trust a friend.

> AESCHYLUS (525–456 B.C.), Greek dramatist. Prometheus, in *Prometheus Bound* (tr. by Gilbert Murray).

2   The tyrant grinds down his slaves and they don't turn against him, they crush those beneath them.

> EMILY BRONTË (1818–48), English novelist, poet. Heathcliff, in *Wuthering Heights*, ch. 11 (1847).

3   Kings will be tyrants from policy, when subjects are rebels from principle.

> EDMUND BURKE (1729–97), Irish philosopher, statesman. *Reflections on the Revolution in France* (1790).

4   If we must have a tyrant, let him at least be a gentleman who has been bred to the business, and let us fall by the axe and not by the butcher's cleaver.

> LORD BYRON (1788–1824), English poet. Letter, 21 Feb. 1820, to publisher John Murray (published in *Byron's Letters and Journals*, vol. 7, ed. by Leslie A. Marchand, 1973–81).

5   I have sworn upon the altar of God eternal hostility against every form of tyranny over the mind of man.

> THOMAS JEFFERSON (1743–1826), U.S. president. Letter, 23 Sept. 1800.

6   No government power can be abused long.

Mankind will not bear it. . . . There is a remedy in human nature against tyranny, that will keep us safe under every form of government.

> SAMUEL JOHNSON (1709–84), English author, lexicographer. Quoted in: James Boswell, *Life of Samuel Johnson*, 31 March 1772 (1791).

7 The people always have some champion whom they set over them and nurse into greatness. . . . This and no other is the root from which a tyrant springs; when he first appears he is a protector.

> PLATO (c. 427–347 B.C.), Greek philosopher. Socrates, in *The Republic*, bk. 8, sct. 565

8 Like Cato, give his little senate laws,
And sit attentive to his own applause.

> ALEXANDER POPE (1688–1744), English satirical poet. A portrait of essayist Joseph Addison, in *Epistle to Dr. Arbuthnot* (1735).

9 Rulers, who neither see, nor feel, nor know,
But leech-like to their fainting country cling,
Till they drop, blind in blood, without a blow,—
A people starved and stabbed in the untilled field . . .

> PERCY BYSSHE SHELLEY (1792–1822), English poet. *Sonnet: England in 1819.*

10 The worst form of tyranny the world has ever known . . . the tyranny of the weak over the strong. It is the only tyranny that lasts.

> OSCAR WILDE (1854–1900), Anglo-Irish playwright, author. Lord Illingworth, in *A Woman of No Importance*, act 3, referring to the "tyranny" of women.

UGLINESS

1 It's nothing to be born ugly. Sensibly, the ugly woman comes to terms with her ugliness and exploits it as a grace of nature. To become ugly means the beginning of a calamity, self-willed most of the time.

> COLETTE (1873–1954), French author. "Beauties," in *Quatre Saisons* (c. 1928; repr. in *Journey for Myself*, 1971).

2 I seated ugliness on my knee, and almost immediately grew tired of it.

> SALVADOR DALI (1904–89), Spanish painter. The Diary of a Genius (1966), entry for 1 Aug 1953. Dali almost certainly drew his inspiration for this sentiment from Rimbaud. see Rimbaud on BEAUTY.

3 The secret of ugliness consists not in irregularity, but in being uninteresting.

> RALPH WALDO EMERSON (1803–82), U.S. essayist, poet, philosopher. *The Conduct of Life*, "Beauty" (1860).

4 Against the beautiful and the clever and the successful, one can wage a pitiless war, but not against the unattractive: then the millstone weighs on the breast.

> GRAHAM GREENE (1904–91), British novelist. *The Heart of the Matter*, bk. 1, pt. 1, ch. 2, sct. 2 (1948).

5 Reckoned physiologically, everything ugly weakens and afflicts man. It recalls decay, danger, impotence; he actually suffers a loss of energy in its presence. The effect of the ugly can be measured with a dynamometer. Whenever man feels in any way depressed, he senses the proximity of something "ugly." His feeling of power, his will to power, his courage, his pride—they decline with the ugly, they increase with the beautiful.

> FRIEDRICH NIETZSCHE (1844–1900), German philosopher. *Twilight of the Idols*, "Expeditions of an Untimely Man," aph. 20 (1889).

6 There is nothing in machinery, there is nothing in embankments and railways and iron bridges and engineering devices to oblige them to be ugly. Ugliness is the measure of imperfection.

> H. G. WELLS (1866–1946), British author. *A Modern Utopia*, ch. 3, sct. 8 (1905; repr. in *The Works of H. G. Wells*, vol. 9, 1925).

7 The ugly and the stupid have the best of it in this world. They can sit at their ease and gape at the play. If they know nothing of victory, they are at least spared the knowledge of defeat.

> OSCAR WILDE (1854–1900), Anglo-Irish playwright, author. Basil Hallward, in *The Picture of Dorian Gray*, ch. 1 (1891).

See also Colette on HOME AND HOUSES.

UNCERTAINTY

1 Uncertainty is the refuge of hope.

> HENRI-FRÉDÉRIC AMIEL (1821–81), Swiss philosopher, poet. *Journal Intime* (1882; tr. by Mrs. Humphry Ward, 1892), entry for 23 Jan. 1881.

2 The grand Perhaps! We look on helplessly,
There the old misgivings, crooked questions are.

> ROBERT BROWNING (1812–89), English poet. *Bishop Blougram's Apology.*

3 The quest for certainty blocks the search for meaning. Uncertainty is the very condition to impel man to unfold his powers.

> ERICH FROMM (1900–1980), U.S. psychologist. *Man for Himself*, ch. 3 (1947).

4 Hesitation increases in relation to risk in equal proportion to age.

> ERNEST HEMINGWAY (1899–1961), U.S. author. Quoted in: A. E. Hotchner, *Papa Hemingway*, pt. 1, ch. 3 (1966 ed.).

See also DOUBT.

UNDERSTANDING

1 The world only goes round by misunderstanding.

> CHARLES BAUDELAIRE (1821–67), French poet. "My Heart Laid Bare," in *Intimate Journals*, sct. 99 (1887; tr. by Christopher Isherwood, 1930; rev. by Don Bachardy, 1989).

2 Perhaps I am doomed to retrace my steps under the illusion that I am exploring, doomed to try and learn what I should simply recognize, learning a mere fraction of what I have forgotten.

> ANDRÉ BRETON (1896–1966), French surrealist. *Nadja* (1928).

3 If you do not understand a man you cannot crush

him. And if you do understand him, very probably you will not.

> G. K. CHESTERTON (1874–1936), British author. *All Things Considered,* "Humanitarianism and Strength" (1908).

4 In the long course of history, having people who understand your thought is much greater security than another submarine.

> J. WILLIAM FULBRIGHT (b. 1905), U.S. Democratic politician. *New York Times* (26 June 1986), of the Fulbright scholarship program.

5 If you don't understand yourself you don't understand anybody else.

> NIKKI GIOVANNI (b. 1943), U.S. poet. *A Dialogue* (1973; with James Baldwin), from a conversation, 4 Nov. 1971, in London.

6 If the secret of being a bore is to tell all, the secret of pleasing is to say just enough to be—not understood, but divined.

> RÉMY DE GOURMONT (1858–1915), French critic, novelist. "On Style and Writing," sct. 6, in *La Culture des Idées* (1900; repr. in *Selected Writings,* ed. and tr. by Glen S. Burne, 1966).

7 The thing is plain. All that men really understand, is confined to a very small compass; to their daily affairs and experience; to what they have an opportunity to know, and motives to study or practise. The rest is affectation and imposture.

> WILLIAM HAZLITT (1778–1830), English essayist. "On the Ignorance of the Learned," in *Edinburgh Magazine* (July 1818; repr. in *Table Talk,* 1821).

8 Sir, I have found you an argument; but I am not obliged to find you an understanding.

> SAMUEL JOHNSON (1709–84), English author, lexicographer. Quoted in: James Boswell, *Life of Samuel Johnson,* 19 June 1784 (1791).

9 If one does not understand a person, one tends to regard him as a fool.

> CARL JUNG (1875–1961), Swiss psychiatrist. *Mysterium Coniunctionis* (1955–56; repr. in *Collected Works,* vol. 14, para. 147, ed. by William McGuire, 1963).

10 A first sign of the beginning of understanding is the wish to die.

> FRANZ KAFKA (1883–1924), German novelist and short–story writer. *The Collected Aphorisms,* no. 13 (Oct 1917-Feb 1918; published in *Shorter Works,* vol. 1, ed. and tr. by Malcolm Pasley, 1973).

11 It is the duty of the human understanding to understand that there are things which it cannot understand, and what those things are. Human understanding has vulgarly occupied itself with nothing but understanding, but if it would only take the trouble to understand itself at the same time it would simply have to posit the paradox.

> SØREN KIERKEGAARD (1813–1855), Danish philosopher. *The Journals of Sören Kierkegaard: A Selection,* no. 1395 (ed. and tr. by Alexander Dru, 1938), 1854 entry.

12 Shallow understanding from people of good will is more frustrating than absolute misunderstanding from people of ill-will.

> MARTIN LUTHER KING, JR. (1929–68), U.S. clergyman and civil rights leader. "Letter from Birmingham Jail" (published in *Why We Can't Wait,* 1963).

13 I still understand a few words in life, but I no longer think they make a sentence.

> JEAN ROSTAND (1894–1977), French biologist, writer. *Pensées d'un Biologiste* (1939; repr. in *The Substance of Man,* 1962, p. 83).

14 Is an intelligent human being likely to be much more than a large-scale manufacturer of misunderstanding?

> PHILIP ROTH (b. 1933), U.S. novelist. Nathan Zuckerman, in *The Counterlife,* ch. 5 (1986).

15 The theoretical understanding of the world, which is the aim of philosophy, is not a matter of great practical importance to animals, or to savages, or even to most civilised men.

> BERTRAND RUSSELL (1872–1970), British philosopher, mathematician. *A Free Man's Worship and Other Essays,* ch. 1 (1976).

16 Where I am not understood, it shall be concluded that something very useful and profound is couched underneath.

> JONATHAN SWIFT (1667–1745), Anglo-Irish satirist. *The Tale of a Tub,* Preface (1704).

17 We shall see but little way if we require to understand what we see. How few things can a man measure with the tape of his understanding! How many greater things might he be seeing in the meanwhile!

> HENRY DAVID THOREAU (1817–62), U.S. philosopher, author, naturalist. *Journals* (1906), entry for 14 Feb. 1851.

See also INTELLIGIBILITY.

UNEMPLOYMENT

1 A man's labour is not only his capital but his life. When it passes it returns never more. To utilise it, to prevent its wasteful squandering, to enable the poor man to bank it up for use hereafter, this surely is one of the most urgent tasks before civilisation.

> WILLIAM BOOTH (1829–1912), English evangelist, founder of the Salvation Army. *In Darkest England, and the Way Out,* pt. 1, ch. 4 (1890).

2 A man willing to work, and unable to find work, is perhaps the saddest sight that fortune's inequality exhibits under this sun.

> THOMAS CARLYLE (1795–1881), Scottish essayist and historian. *Chartism,* ch. 4 (1839).

3 When we're unemployed, we're called lazy; when the whites are unemployed it's called a depression.

> JESSE JACKSON (b. 1941), U.S. clergyman and civil rights leader. Interview with David Frost, in Frost, *The Americans,* "When Whites Are Unemployed, It's Called a Depression" (1970).

4 To be idle and to be poor have always been reproaches, and therefore every man endeavours with his utmost care to hide his poverty from others, and his idleness from himself.

> SAMUEL JOHNSON (1709–84), English author, lexicographer.

Idler, no. 17 (London, 5 Aug 1758; repr. in *The Works of Samuel Johnson*, vol. 2, ed. by W. J. Bate, John M. Bullitt, and L. F. Powell, 1963).

5   We believe that if men have the talent to invent new machines that put men out of work, they have the talent to put those men back to work.

> JOHN F. KENNEDY (1917–63), U.S. Democratic politician, president. Speech, 27 Sept 1962, Wheeling, W.Va.

6   The production of too many useful things results in too many useless people.

> KARL MARX (1818–83), German political theorist and social philosopher. *Economic and Philosophic Manuscripts* (1844; repr. in *Karl Marx and Friedrich Engels: Collected Works*, vol. 3).

7   An "unemployed" existence is a worse negation of life than death itself.

> JOSÉ ORTEGA Y GASSET (1883–1955), Spanish essayist, philosopher. *The Revolt of the Masses*, ch. 14, sct. 2 (1930).

8   Better wear out shoes than sheets.

> SCOTTISH PROVERB (18th century). Collected in: J. Kelly, *Complete Collection of Scottish Proverbs* (1721).

9   Unemployment insurance is a pre-paid vacation for freeloaders.

> RONALD REAGAN (b. 1911), U.S. Republican politician, president. *Sacramento Bee* (28 April 1966). Nonetheless, on 31 March 1982, Reagan claimed that, "We have, in some of the hardest-hit states, extended the unemployment insurance. There's nothing that strikes to my heart more than the unemployed." Quoted in: *Reagan's Reign of Error*, "Want Ads" (ed. by Mark Green and Gail MacColl, 1987), where the Labor Department is quoted as estimating that changes in the eligibility formula in the 1981 budget in fact reduced extended benefits for 1.5 million jobless workers.

10   Not only our future economic soundness but the very soundness of our democratic institutions depends on the determination of our government to give employment to idle men.

> FRANKLIN D. ROOSEVELT (1882–1945), U.S. Democratic politician, president. "Fireside Chat," radio broadcast, 14 April 1938.

11   I don't pity any man who does hard work worth doing. I admire him. I pity the creature who does not work, at whichever end of the social scale he may regard himself as being.

> THEODORE ROOSEVELT (1858–1919), U.S. Republican (later Progressive) politician, president. Speech, 8 Sept 1902, Chattanooga, Tenn.

12   You take my life
When you do take the means whereby I live.

> WILLIAM SHAKESPEARE (1564–1616), English dramatist, poet. Shylock, in *The Merchant of Venice*, act 4, sc. 1.

13   A man who has no office to go to—I don't care who he is—is a trial of which you can have no conception.

> GEORGE BERNARD SHAW (1856–1950), Anglo-Irish playwright, critic. *The Irrational Knot*, ch. 18 (1905).

14   He didn't riot. He got on his bike and looked for work.

> NORMAN TEBBIT (b. 1931), British Conservative politician. Speech, 15 Oct. 1981, Conservative Party Conference, Blackpool, England, on his unemployed father during the Depression. Tebbit's speech, contrasting his father's self-help approach with

the attitude of rioters in Britain during the previous summer, was received with a rousing ovation at the conference, but provoked widespread controversy in the country at a time when unemployment stood at three million.

UNHAPPINESS

1   Nothing is funnier than unhappiness, I grant you that. . . . Yes, yes, it's the most comical thing in the world.

> SAMUEL BECKETT (1906–1989), Irish dramatist and novelist. Nell, in *Endgame* (1958, p. 20).

2   Let no one till his death
Be called unhappy. Measure not the work
Until the day's out and the labour done.

> ELIZABETH BARRETT BROWNING (1806–1861), English poet. *Aurora Leigh*, bk. 5 (1857).

3   Man's unhappiness, as I construe, comes of his greatness; it is because there is an Infinite in him, which with all his cunning he cannot quite bury under the Finite.

> THOMAS CARLYLE (1795–1881), Scottish essayist and historian. Teufelsdröckh, in *Sartor Resartus*, bk. 2, ch. 9 (1833–34).

4   Never believe straight off in a man's unhappiness. Ask him if he can still sleep. If the answer's "yes," all's well. That is enough.

> LOUIS-FERDINAND CÉLINE (1894–1961), French author. The narrator (Ferdinand Bardamu), in *Journey to the End of the Night* (1932; tr. 1934; 1966, p. 371).

5   Unhappiness is best defined as the difference between our talents and our expectations.

> EDWARD DE BONO (b. 1933), British writer on thinking processes. Quoted in: *Observer* (London, 12 June 1977).

6   He felt the loyalty we feel to unhappiness—the sense that that is where we really belong.

> GRAHAM GREENE (1904–91), British novelist. *The Heart of the Matter*, bk. 2, pt. 2, ch. 1, sct. 1 (1948), referring to Harris.

7   The world will never be long without some good reason to hate the unhappy; their real faults are immediately detected, and if those are not sufficient to sink them into infamy, an additional weight of calumny will be superadded.

> SAMUEL JOHNSON (1709–84), English author, lexicographer. *Adventurer*, no. 99 (London, 16 Oct. 1753; repr. in *The Works of Samuel Johnson*, vol. 2, ed. by W. J. Bate, John M. Bullitt, and L. F. Powell, 1963).

8   Men who are unhappy, like men who sleep badly, are always proud of the fact.

> BERTRAND RUSSELL (1872–1970), British philosopher, mathematician. *The Conquest of Happiness*, ch. 1 (1930).

9   The secret of being miserable is to have leisure to bother about whether you are happy or not. The cure for it is occupation.

> GEORGE BERNARD SHAW (1856–1950), Anglo-Irish playwright, critic. *Parents and Children*, "Children's Happiness" (1914).

10   Those who are unhappy have no need for anything

in this world but people capable of giving them their attention.

SIMONE WEIL (1909–1943), French philosopher and mystic. *Waiting on God*, "Reflections on the Right Use of School Studies" (1950). See Weil on SYMPATHY

See also James on DEPRESSION; DESPAIR; GRIEF; SORROW.

UNIFORMS

1 Iconic clothing has been secularized. . . . A guardsman in a dress uniform is ostensibly an icon of aggression; his coat is red as the blood he hopes to shed. Seen on a coat-hanger, with no man inside it, the uniform loses all its blustering significance and, to the innocent eye seduced by decorative colour and tactile braid, it is as abstract in symbolic information as a parasol to an Eskimo. It becomes simply magnificent.

ANGELA CARTER (1940–1992), British author. "Notes for a Theory of Sixties Style," in *New Society* (London, 1967; repr. in *Arts in Society*, ed. by Paul Barker, 1977).

2 *We* know, Mr. Weller—we, who are men of the world—that a good uniform must work its way with the women, sooner or later.

CHARLES DICKENS (1812–1870), English novelist. "The Gentleman in Blue," in *The Pickwick Papers*, ch. 37 (1836–37).

3 This death's livery which walled its bearers from ordinary life was sign that they have sold their wills and bodies to the State: and contracted themselves into a service not the less abject for that its beginning was voluntary.

T. E. LAWRENCE (1888–1935), British soldier, scholar. *The Revolt in the Desert*, ch. 35 (1927).

4 The connection between dress and war is not far to seek; your finest clothes are those you wear as soldiers.

VIRGINIA WOOLF (1882–1941), British novelist. *Three Guineas* (1938, p. 25).

UNITED NATIONS

1 The U.N. is not just a product of do-gooders. It is harshly real. The day will come when men will see the U.N. and what it means clearly. Everything will be all right—you know when? When people, just people, stop thinking of the United Nations as a weird Picasso abstraction, and see it as a drawing they made themselves.

DAG HAMMARSKJÖLD (1905–61), Swedish statesman, Secretary-General of the U.N. *Time* (London, 27 June 1955).

2 The heroes of the world community are not those who withdraw when difficulties ensue, not those who can envision neither the prospect of success nor the consequence of failure—but those who stand the heat of battle, the fight for world peace through the United Nations.

HUBERT H. HUMPHREY (1911–1978), U.S. Democratic politician, vice president. Speech, 17 Nov. 1965, New York City.

3 This organization is created to prevent you from going to hell. It isn't created to take you to heaven.

HENRY CABOT LODGE, JR. (1902–85), U.S. senator, representative to the U.N. *New York Times* (28 Jan. 1954).

4 The United Nations cannot do anything, and never could; it is not an animate entity or agent. It is a place, a stage, a forum and a shrine . . . a place to which powerful people can repair when they are fearful about the course on which their own rhetoric seems to be propelling them.

CONOR CRUISE O'BRIEN (b. 1917), Irish historian, critic and diplomat. *New Republic* (Washington, D.C., 4 Nov. 1985).

5 I am like a doctor. I have written a prescription to help the patient. If the patient doesn't want all the pills I've recommended that's up to him. But I must warn that next time I will have to come as a surgeon with a knife.

JAVIER PÉREZ DE CUÉLLAR (b. 1920), Peruvian diplomat, Secretary-General of the U.N. Quoted in: *Guardian* (London, 10 May 1986).

THE UNITED STATES

1 America fears the unshaven legs, the unshaven men's cheeks, the aroma of perspiration, and the limp prick. Above all it fears the limp prick.

WALTER ABISH (b. 1931), Austrian-born U.S. author. *In The Future Perfect*, "In So Many Words" (1975).

2 As for America, it is the ideal fruit of all your youthful hopes and reforms. Everybody is fairly decent, respectable, domestic, bourgeois, middle-class, and tiresome. There is absolutely nothing to revile except that it's a bore.

HENRY B. ADAMS (1838–1918), U.S. historian. Letter, 17 Dec. 1908.

3 I always consider the settlement of America with reverence and wonder, as the opening of a grand scene and design in providence, for the illumination of the ignorant and the emancipation of the slavish part of mankind all over the earth.

JOHN ADAMS (1735–1826), U.S. statesman, president. Notes for *A Dissertation on the Canon and Feudal Law* (1765).

4 God bless the USA, so large,
So friendly, and so rich.

W. H. AUDEN (1907–73), Anglo-American poet. *On the Circuit*.

5 America, thou half-brother of the world;
With something good and bad of every land.

PHILIP BAILEY (1816–1902), British poet. *Festus*, st. 10.

6 The American Dream has run out of gas. The car has stopped. It no longer supplies the world with its images, its dreams, its fantasies. No more. It's over. It supplies the world with its nightmares now: the Kennedy assassination, Watergate, Vietnam . . .

J. G. BALLARD (b. 1930), British author. Interview in *Métaphors*, no. 7 (1983; repr. in *Re/Search*, San Francisco, no. 8/9, 1984).

7 Deep down, the US, with its space, its technological refinement, its bluff good conscience, even in those spaces which it opens up for simulation, is the *only remaining primitive society*.

JEAN BAUDRILLARD (b. 1929), French semiologist. *America*, "Vanishing Point" (1986; tr. 1988).

8 What you have to do is enter the fiction of America,

enter America as fiction. It is, indeed, on this fictive basis that it dominates the world.

> JEAN BAUDRILLARD (b. 1929), French semiologist. *America,* "Astral America" (1986; tr. 1988).

9 It is a noble land that God has given us: a land that can feed and clothe the world; a land whose coastlines would enclose half the countries of Europe; a land set like a sentinel between the two imperial oceans of the globe.

> ALBERT J. BEVERIDGE (1862–1927), U.S. politician and historian. Speech, 16 Sept. 1898, Indianapolis, Ind.

10 The spirit is at home, if not entirely satisfied, in America.

> ALLAN BLOOM (1930–92), U.S. educator, author. *The Closing of the American Mind,* pt. 2, "Two Revolutions and Two States of Nature" (1987).

11 Of all the nations in the world, the United States was built in nobody's image. It was the land of the unexpected, of unbounded hope, of ideals, of quest for an unknown perfection. It is all the more unfitting that we should offer ourselves in images. And all the more fitting that the images which we make wittingly or unwittingly to sell America to the world should come back to haunt and curse us.

> DANIEL J. BOORSTIN (b. 1914), U.S. historian. *The Image,* ch. 6 (1961).

12 The most important American addition to the World Experience was the simple surprising fact of America. We have helped prepare mankind for all its later surprises.

> DANIEL J. BOORSTIN (b. 1914), U.S. historian. Reith Lectures, Oct. 1975, Lecture 6 (published in *The Exploring Spirit: America and the World Experience,* 1976).

13 Young man, there is America, which at this day serves for little more than to amuse you with stories of savage men and uncouth manners.

> EDMUND BURKE (1729–1797), Irish philosopher, statesman. *Second Speech on Conciliation with America,* 22 March 1775, to House of Commons.

14 America is not a young land: it is old and dirty and evil before the settlers, before the Indians. The evil is there waiting.

> WILLIAM BURROUGHS (b. 1914), U.S. author. *The Naked Lunch* (1959; repr. 1990, p. 24).

15 America is not so much a nightmare as a *non-dream.* The American non-dream is precisely a move to wipe the dream out of existence. The dream is a spontaneous happening and therefore dangerous to a control system set up by the non-dreamers.

> WILLIAM BURROUGHS (b. 1914), U.S. author. *The Job: Interviews with Daniel Odier,* "Prisoners of the Earth Come Out" (1969).

16 America is a model of force and freedom & moderation—with all the coarseness and rudeness of its people.

> LORD BYRON (1788–1824), English poet. Letter, 12 Oct. 1821 (published in *Byron's Letters and Journals,* vol. 8, ed. by Leslie A. Marchand, 1973–81).

17 I have no further use for America. I wouldn't go back there if Jesus Christ was President.

> CHARLIE CHAPLIN (1889–1977), British comic actor, filmmaker. Quoted in: Leslie Halliwell, *Halliwell's Filmgoer's Companion* (1984).

18 America is the only nation in history which, miraculously, has gone directly from barbarism to degeneration without the usual interval of civilization.

> ATTR. TO GEORGES CLEMENCEAU (1841–1929), French statesman. Quoted in: *Saturday Review of Literature* (New York, 1 Dec. 1945).

19 The business of America is business.

> CALVIN COOLIDGE (1872–1933), U.S. Republican politician, president. Speech, 17 Jan. 1925, to the Society of American Newspaper Editors.

20 in every language even deafanddumb
thy sons acclaim your glorious name by gorry
by jing by gee by gosh by gum

> E. E. CUMMINGS (1894–1962), U.S. poet. *next to of course god america i.*

21 America makes prodigious mistakes, America has colossal faults, but one thing cannot be denied: America is always on the move. She may be going to Hell, of course, but at least she isn't standing still.

> E. E. CUMMINGS (1894–1962), U.S. poet. "Why I Like America," in *Vanity Fair* (New York, May 1927; repr. in *A Miscellany,* ed. by George J. Firmage, 1958).

22 America is the world's living myth. There's no sense of wrong when you kill an American or blame America for some local disaster. This is our function, to be character types, to embody recurring themes that people can use to comfort themselves, justify themselves and so on. We're here to accommodate. Whatever people need, we provide. A myth is a useful thing.

> DON DELILLO (b. 1926), U.S. author. James Axton, in *The Names,* ch. 5 (1982).

23 If its individual citizens, to a man, are to be believed, it always *is* depressed, and always *is* stagnated, and always *is* at an alarming crisis, and never was otherwise; though as a body, they are ready to make oath upon the Evangelists, at any hour of the day or night, that it is the most thriving and prosperous of all countries on the habitable globe.

> CHARLES DICKENS (1812–70), English novelist. *Martin Chuzzlewit,* ch. 16 (1844).

24 I like America, just as everybody else does. I love America, I gotta say that. But America will be judged.

> BOB DYLAN (b. 1941), U.S. singer, songwriter. On stage, 26 Nov. 1979, in Tempe, Ariz. Quoted in: *Wanted Man,* "Saved: Bob Dylan's Conversion to Christianity" (ed. by John Bauldie, 1990).

25 The ideology of this America wants to establish reassurance through Imitation. But profit defeats ideology, because the consumers want to be thrilled not only by the guarantee of the Good but also by the shudder of the Bad.

> UMBERTO ECO (b. 1932), Italian semiologist and novelist. *Travels in Hyperreality,* "Ecology 1984 and Coca-Cola Made Flesh" (1986).

26 I hate this shallow Americanism which hopes to get rich by credit, to get knowledge by raps on midnight tables, to learn the economy of the mind by phrenology, or skill without study, or mastery without apprenticeship.

> RALPH WALDO EMERSON (1803–1882), U.S. essayist, poet, philosopher. *Society and Solitude,* "Success" (1870).

27 America—rather, the United States—seems to me to be the Jew among the nations. It is resourceful, adaptable, maligned, envied, feared, imposed upon. It is warm-hearted, overfriendly; quick-witted, lavish, colorful; given to extravagant speech and gestures; its people are travelers and wanderers by nature, moving, shifting, restless; swarming in Fords, in ocean liners; craving entertainment; volatile. The *schnuckle* among the nations of the world.

> EDNA FERBER (1887–1968), U.S. writer. *A Peculiar Treasure,* ch. 1 (1939). Compare this quote with Herman Melville's "We Americans are the peculiar, chosen people—the Israel of our time; we bear the ark of the liberties of the world" (from *White-Jacket,* 1850).

28 France was a land, England was a people, but America, having about it still that quality of the idea, was harder to utter—it was the graves at Shiloh and the tired, drawn, nervous faces of its great men, and the country boys dying in the Argonne for a phrase that was empty before their bodies withered. It was a willingness of the heart.

> F. SCOTT FITZGERALD (1896–1940), U.S. author. "The Swimmers," in *Saturday Evening Post* (New York, 19 Oct. 1929; repr. in *Bits of Paradise,* ed. by Matthew J. Bruccoli and Scottie Fitzgerald Smith, 1973). The passage also appeared in *The Crack-Up,* "Notebook O" (ed. by Edmund Wilson, 1945).

29 America is rather like life. You can usually find in it what you look for. . . . It will probably be interesting, and it is sure to be large.

> E. M. FORSTER (1879–1970), British novelist and essayist. "Impressions of the United States," in *Listener* (London, 4 Sept. 1947; repr. in *Two Cheers for Democracy,* "The United States," 1951).

30 America is the most grandiose experiment the world has seen, but, I am afraid, it is not going to be a success.

> SIGMUND FREUD (1856–1939), Austrian psychiatrist. Quoted in: Ronald W. Clark, *Freud: the Man and His Cause,* pt. 3, ch. 12 (1980). More famously, to his colleague and biographer Ernest Jones (*Memories of a Psycho-analyst,* ch. 9, 1959), Freud said: "Yes, America is gigantic, but a gigantic mistake."

31 What the United States does best is to understand itself. What it does worst is understand others.

> CARLOS FUENTES (b. 1928), Mexican novelist, short-story writer. *Time* (London, 16 June 1986).

32 America is still mostly xenophobic and racist. That's the nature of America, I think.

> JERRY GARCIA (b. 1942), U.S. rock musician. *Rolling Stone* (New York, 30 Nov. 1989).

33 I can never suppose this country so far lost to all ideas of self-importance as to be willing to grant America independence; if that could ever be adopted I shall despair of this country being ever preserved from a state of inferiority and consequently falling into a very low class among the European States.

> GEORGE III (1738–1820), King of Great Britain and Ireland. Letter, 7 March 1780, to his prime minister Lord North.

34 America does not concern itself now with Impressionism. We own no involved philosophy. The psyche of the land is to be found in its movement. It is to be felt as a dramatic force of energy and vitality. We move; we do not stand still. We have not yet arrived at the stock-taking stage.

> MARTHA GRAHAM (1894–1991), U.S. dancer, choreographer. "The American Dance," in *Modern Dance* (ed. by Virginia Stewart, 1935).

35 Ours is the only country deliberately founded on a good idea.

> JOHN GUNTHER (1901–1970), U.S. journalist. *Inside USA,* Foreword (1947).

36 No author, without a trial, can conceive of the difficulty of writing a romance about a country where there is no shadow, no antiquity, no mystery, no picturesque and gloomy wrong, nor anything but a commonplace prosperity, in broad and simple daylight, as is happily the case with my dear native land.

> NATHANIEL HAWTHORNE (1804–1864), U.S. author. *The Marble Faun,* Preface (1860).

37 I don't see much future for the Americans. . . . Everything about the behavior of American society reveals that it's half Judaized, and the other half negrified. How can one expect a State like that to hold together?

> ADOLF HITLER (1889–1945), German dictator. *Hitler's Table Talk,* pt. 2 (1953).

38 The face of nature and civilization in this our country is to a certain point a very sufficient literary field. But it will yield its secrets only to a really *grasping* imagination. . . . To write well and worthily of American things one need even more than elsewhere to be a *master.*

> HENRY JAMES (1843–1916), U.S. author. Letter, 16 Jan. 1871, to editor and critic Charles Eliot Norton.

39 No sovereign, no court, no personal loyalty, no aristocracy, no church, no clergy, no army, no diplomatic service, no country gentlemen, no palaces, no castles, nor manors, nor old country-houses, nor parsonages, nor thatched cottages nor ivied ruins; no cathedrals, nor abbeys, nor little Norman churches; no great Universities nor public schools—no Oxford, nor Eton, nor Harrow; no literature, no novels, no museums, no pictures, no political society, no sporting class—no Epsom nor Ascot! Some such list as that might be drawn up of the absent things in American life.

> HENRY JAMES (1843–1916), U.S. author. *Hawthorne,* ch. 2 (1879). "The American knows that a good deal remains," added James:. " What it is that remains—that is his secret, his joke, as one may say." Nearly thirty-five years later, in a letter (1 April 1913) to his sister-in-law, James wrote, "Dearest Alice, I could come back to America (could be carried on a stretcher) to die—but never, never to live."

40 I pray we are still a young and courageous nation, that we have not grown so old and so fat and so prosperous that all we can think about is to sit back with our arms around our moeny bags. If we choose to do that I have no doubt that the smoldering fires will burst into flame and consume us—dollars and all.

> LYNDON B. JOHNSON (1908–73), U.S. Democratic politician, president. Speech, 7 May 1947, to Congress.

41   For this is what America is all about. It is the uncrossed desert and the unclimbed ridge. It is the star that is not reached and the harvest that is sleeping in the unplowed ground.

> LYNDON B. JOHNSON (1908–1973), U.S. president. Inaugural address, 20 Jan. 1965.

42   America is not a democracy, it's an absolute monarchy ruled by King Kid. In a nation of immigrants, the child is automatically more of an American than his parents. . . . Americans regard children as what Mr. Hudson in "Upstairs, Downstairs" called "betters." Aping their betters, American adults do their best to turn themselves into children. Puerility exercises *droit de seigneur* everywhere.

> FLORENCE KING (b. 1936), U.S. author. *Reflections in a Jaundiced Eye*, "Good King Herod" (1989).

43   America does to me what I knew it would do: it just *bumps* me. . . . The people charge at you like trucks coming down on you—no awareness. But one tries to dodge aside in time. Bump! bump! go the trucks. And that is human contact.

> D. H. LAWRENCE (1885–1930), British author. Letter, 19 Oct. 1922, to poet Amy Lowell (published in *The Letters of D. H. Lawrence*, vol. 4, ed. by James T. Boulton, E. Mansfield, and W. Roberts, 1987).

44   I feel most at home in the United States, not because it is intrinsically a more interesting country, but because no one really belongs there any more than I do. We are all there together in its wholly excellent vacuum.

> WYNDHAM LEWIS (1882–1957), British author, painter. *America and Cosmic Man*, "The Case Against Roots" (1948).

45   To me Americanism means . . . an imperative duty to be nobler than the rest of the world.

> MEYER LONDON (1871–1926), U.S. labor leader. Speech, 18 Jan 1916, to Congress.

46   America is promises to
Take!
America is promises to
Us
To take them
Brutally
With love but
Take them.

> ARCHIBALD MACLEISH (1892–1982), U.S. poet. *America Was Promises* (1940).

47   There is one expanding horror in American life. It is that our long odyssey toward liberty, democracy and freedom-for-all may be achieved in such a way that utopia remains forever closed, and we live in freedom and hell, debased of style, not individual from one another, void of courage, our fear rationalized away.

> NORMAN MAILER (b. 1923), U.S. author. *Cannibals and Christians*, pt. 1, "My Hope for America" (1966).

48   I don't see America as a mainland, but as a sea, a big ocean. Sometimes a storm arises, a formidable current develops, and it seems it will engulf everything. Wait a moment, another current will appear and bring the first one to naught.

> JACQUES MARITAIN (1882–1973), French philosopher. *Reflections on America*, ch. 4 (1948).

49   America is like one of those old-fashioned six-cylinder truck engines that can be missing two spark-plugs and have a broken flywheel and have a crankshaft that's 5000 millimetres off fitting properly, and two bad ball-bearings, and still runs. We're in that kind of situation. We can have substantial parts of the population committing suicide, and still run and look fairly good.

> THOMAS McGUANE (b. 1939), U.S. novelist. *Sunday Correspondent* (London, 1 April 1990).

50   I see America spreading disaster. I see America as a black curse upon the world. I see a long night settling in and that mushroom which has poisoned the world withering at the roots.

> HENRY MILLER (1891–1980), U.S. author. *Black Spring*, "Third or Fourth Day of Spring" (1936).

51   I have never been able to look upon America as young and vital but rather as prematurely old, as a fruit which rotted before it had a chance to ripen.

> HENRY MILLER (1891–1980), U.S. author. *The Air-Conditioned Nightmare*, "Dr. Souchon: Surgeon-Painter" (1945).

52   Is America a land of God where saints abide for ever? Where golden fields spread fair and broad, where flows the crystal river? Certainly not flush with saints, and a good thing, too, for the saints sent buzzing into man's ken now are but poor-mouthed ecclesiastical film stars and cliché-shouting publicity agents.

> Their little knowledge bringing them nearer to their ignorance,
> Ignorance bringing them nearer to death,
> But nearness to death no nearer to God.

> SEAN O'CASEY (1884–1964), Irish dramatist. *Rose And Crown*, vol. 5, "Only Five Minutes More" (1952).

53   Our democracy, our culture, our whole way of life is a spectacular triumph of the blah. Why *not* have a political convention without politics to nominate a leader who's out in front of nobody? . . . Maybe our national mindlessness is the very thing that keeps us from turning into one of those smelly European countries full of pseudo-reds and crypto-fascists and greens who dress like forest elves.

> P. J. O'ROURKE (b. 1947), U.S. journalist. *Parliament of Whores*, "On the Blandwagon" (1991).

54   I take SPACE to be the central fact to man born in America. . . . I spell it large because it comes large here. Large and without mercy.

> CHARLES OLSON (1910–1970), U.S. poet, critic. *Call Me Ishmael*, sct. 1 (1947).

55   It is capitalist America that produced the modern independent woman. Never in history have women had more freedom of choice in regard to dress, behavior, career, and sexual orietation.

> CAMILLE PAGLIA (b. 1947), U.S. author, critic, educator. "The Big Udder," in *Philadelphia Enquirer* (12 May 1991; repr. in *Sex, Art, and American Culture*, 1992).

56 The voice of America has no undertones or overtones in it. It repeats its optimistic catchwords in a tireless monologue that has the slightly metallic sound of a gramophone.

> VANCE PALMER (1885–1959), Australian author and poet. "Literary America" (1923; repr. in *Intimate Portraits*, ed. by H. P. Heseltine, 1969).

57 The North American system only wants to consider the positive aspects of reality. Men and women are subjected from childhood to an inexorable process of adaptation; certain principles, contained in brief formulas are endlessly repeated by the Press, the radio, the churches, and the schools, and by those kindly, sinister beings, the North American mothers and wives. A person imprisoned by these schemes is like a plant in a flowerpot too small for it: he cannot grow or mature.

> OCTAVIO PAZ (b. 1914), Mexican poet and essayist. *The Labyrinth of Solitude*, ch. 1 (1950; tr. 1961).

58 The things that will destroy America are prosperity-at-any-price, peace-at-any-price, safety-first instead of duty-first, the love of soft living, and the get-rich-quick theory of life.

> THEODORE ROOSEVELT (1858–1919), U.S. Republican (later Progressive) politician, president. Letter, 10 Jan. 1917.

59 America is a young country with an old mentality.

> GEORGE SANTAYANA (1863–1952), U.S. philosopher, poet. *Winds of Doctrine*, ch. 6 (1913).

60 It is veneer, rouge, aetheticism, art museums, new theaters, etc. that make America impotent. The good things are football, kindness, and jazz bands.

> GEORGE SANTAYANA (1863–1952), U.S. philosopher, poet. Letter, 22 May 1927, to critic Van Wyck Brooks.

61 That land is like an Eagle, whose young gaze
Feeds on the noontide beam, whose golden plume
Floats moveless on the storm, and in the blaze
Of sunrise gleams when Earth is wrapped in
  gloom;
An epitaph of glory for the tomb
Of murdered Europe may thy fame be made,
Great People! as the sands shalt thou become;
Thy growth is swift as morn, when night must
  fade;
The multitudinous Earth shall sleep beneath thy
  shade.

> PERCY BYSSHE SHELLEY (1792–1822), English poet. *The Revolt of Islam*, cto. 11, "America."

62 The quality of American life is an insult to the possibilities of human growth . . . the pollution of American space, with gadgetry and cars and TV and box architecture, brutalizes the senses, making gray neurotics of most of us, and perverse spiritual athletes and strident self-transcenders of the best of us.

> SUSAN SONTAG (b. 1933), U.S. essayist. "What's Happening in America (1966)," in *Partisan Review* (New Brunswick, N.J., Winter 1967; repr. in *Styles of Radical Will*, 1969).

63 It's like Britain, only with buttons.

> RINGO STARR (b. 1940), British drummer. Interview, 1965, BBC-TV.

64 The United States is just now the oldest country in the world, there always is an oldest country and she is it, it is she who is the mother of the twentieth century civilization. She began to feel herself as it just after the Civil War. And so it is a country the right age to have been born in and the wrong age to live in.

> GERTRUDE STEIN (1874–1946), U.S. author. "Why I Do Not Live In America," in *Transition* (Fall 1928; repr. in *How Writing Is Written*, ed. by Robert Bartlett Haas, 1974).

65 This monster of a land, this mightiest of nations, this spawn of the future, turns out to be the macrocosm of microcosm me.

> JOHN STEINBECK (1902–68), U.S. author. *Travels With Charley: in Search of America*, pt. 3 (1962).

66 The biggest difference between ancient Rome and the USA is that in Rome the common man was treated like a dog. In America he sets the tone. This is the first country where the common man could stand erect.

> I. F. STONE (1907–89), U.S. author. Quoted in: Clive James, *Flying Visits*, "Postcard from Washington" (1984).

67 In a nation ruled by swine, all pigs are upward-mobile—and the rest of us are fucked until we can put our acts together: not necessarily to win, but mainly to keep from losing completely. We owe that to ourselves and our crippled self-image as something better than a nation of panicked sheep.

> HUNTER S. THOMPSON (b. 1939), U.S. journalist. *The Great Shark Hunt*, "Jacket Copy for Fear and Loathing in Las Vegas" (1979).

68 Two things in America are astonishing: the changeableness of most human behavior and the strange stability of certain principles. Men are constantly on the move, but the spirit of humanity seems almost unmoved.

> ALEXIS DE TOCQUEVILLE (1805–59), French social philosopher. *Democracy in America*, vol. 2, pt. 3, ch. 21 (1840).

69 America is a large, friendly dog in a very small room. Every time it wags its tail, it knocks over a chair.

> A. J. TOYNBEE (1889–1975), British historian. News summaries, 14 July 1954.

70 It was wonderful to find America, but it would have been more wonderful to miss it.

> MARK TWAIN (1835–1910), U.S. author. *Pudd'nhead Wilson*, Conclusion, "Pudd'nhead Wilson's Calendar" (1894).

71 In Boston they ask, "How much does he know?" In New York, "How much is he worth?" In Philadelphia, "Who were his parents?"

> MARK TWAIN (1835–1910), U.S. author. Reporting a joke quoted by French critic Paul Bourget in: "What Paul Bourget Thinks Of Us," in *North American Review* (Cedar Falls, Iowa, Jan. 1895; repr. in *Complete Essays*, ed. by Charles Neider, 1963).

72 America is a vast conspiracy to make you happy.

> JOHN UPDIKE (b. 1932), U.S. author, critic. *Problems*, "How to Love America and Leave it at the Same Time" (1980).

73 It's the movies that have really been running things in America ever since they were invented. They show you what to do, how to do it, when to do it, how to feel about it, and how to look how you feel about it. Everybody has their own America, and then they have the pieces of a fantasy America that they think is out there but they can't see.

ANDY WARHOL (1928–1987), U.S. Pop artist. Quoted in: Victor Bokris, *Warhol*, "The Education of Andy Warhol 1937–45" (1989).

74 I despair of the Republic! Such dreariness, such whining sallow women, such utter absence of the amenities, such crass food, crass manners, crass landscape!! . . . What a horror it is for a whole nation to be developing without the sense of beauty, & eating bananas for breakfast.

EDITH WHARTON (1862–1937), U.S. author. Letter, 19 Aug. 1904, to Sara Norton, daughter of distinguished scholar Charles Eliot Norton (published in *The Letters of Edith Wharton*, 1988).

75 A man is not expected to love his country, lest he make an ass of himself. Yet our country, seen through the mists of smog, is curiously lovable, in somewhat the way an individual who has got himself into an unconscionable scrape seems lovable—or at least deserving of support.

E. B. WHITE (1899–1985), U.S. author, editor. "A Busy Place," in *New Yorker* (5 July 1976; repr. in *Writings from the New Yorker 1927–1976*, ed. by Rebecca M. Dale, 1991).

76 The youth of America is their oldest tradition. It has been going on now for three hundred years.

OSCAR WILDE (1854–1900), Anglo-Irish playwright, author. Lord Illingworth, in *A Woman of No Importance*, act 1.

77 The gap between ideals and actualities, between dreams and achievements, the gap that can spur strong men to increased exertions, but can break the spirit of others—this gap is the most conspicuous, continuous land mark in American history. It is conspicuous and continuous not because Americans achieve little, but because they dream grandly. The gap is a standing reproach to Americans; but it marks them off as a special and singularly admirable community among the world's peoples.

GEORGE F. WILL (b. 1941), U.S. political columnist. *Statecraft as Soulcraft: What Government Does*, ch. 4 (1984).

78 America lives in the heart of every man everywhere who wishes to find a region where he will be free to work out his destiny as he chooses.

WOODROW WILSON (1856–1924), U.S. Democratic politician, president. Speech, 6 April 1912, Chicago.

79 Sometimes people call me an idealist. Well, that is the way I know I am an American. . . . America is the only idealistic nation in the world.

WOODROW WILSON (1856–1924), U.S. Democratic politician, president. Speech, 8 Sept. 1919, Sioux Falls, N. Dak.

See also Miller on ARTISTS; Rosenberg on CHANGE; James on CIVILIZATION; Stevenson on THE CONSUMER SOCIETY; Baudrillard on CULTURE; Thurber on DISSENT; Brodsky on EXILE; Pound on EXPATRIATES; Butler on GENIUS; HAWAII; Sullivan on HEROES; Lazarus, Lippman on IMMIGRATION; Wilson on INDIVIDUALITY; Mailer on IRREVERENCE; Asquith on JOURNALISM; Miller on THE LAND; Martineau on LOVE; MULTICULTURALISM; Sontag on NATURE; The NEW WOLRD; NEW YORK; Lewis on PATRIOTISM; Cleveland on PEACE; Wilde on POVERTY AND THE POOR; Kennedy on PROGRESS; Tocqueville on PROPERTY; Morrison on RACE; Baudrillard on SECTS; Jordon on SEGREGATION; James on SIMPLICITY; Eco, James, Wilson on SUCCESS; TEXAS; Dahlberg on WAR; Wilde on GEORGE WASHINGTON; Jordon on WHITES; Jong on WOMEN; Miller on YOUTH.

UNITED STATES, PEOPLE OF THE

1 Our society distributes itself into Barbarians, Philistines and Populace; and America is just ourselves with the Barbarians quite left out, and the Populace nearly.

MATTHEW ARNOLD (1822–1888), English poet, critic. *Culture and Anarchy*, Preface (1869). Arnold held that literature was of paramount importance for the education of the "Philistines."

2 It is always dangerous to generalise, but the American people, while infinitely generous, are a hard and strong race and, but for the few cemeteries I have seen, I am inclined to think they never die.

MARGOT ASQUITH (1864–1945), British socialite. *My Impressions of America*, ch. 14 (1922).

3 The Americans are violently oral. . . . That's why in America the mother is all-important and the father has no position at all—isn't respected in the least. Even the American passion for laxatives can be explained as an oral manifestation. They want to get rid of any unpleasantness taken in through the mouth.

W. H. AUDEN (1907–1973), Anglo-American poet. *The Table Talk of W. H. Auden*, "Halloween 1947" (comp. by Alan Ansen, ed. by Nicholas Jenkins, 1990).

4 Americans, unhappily, have the most remarkable ability to alchemize all bitter truths into an innocuous but piquant confection and to transform their moral contradictions, or public discussion of such contradictions, into a proud decoration, such as are given for heroism on the battle field.

JAMES BALDWIN (1924–1987), U.S. author. "Many Thousands Gone," in *Partisan Review* (New Brunswick, N.J., Nov.-Dec. 1951; repr. in *Notes of a Native Son*, pt. 1, 1955).

5 A people who are still, as it were, but in the gristle, and not yet hardened into the bone of manhood.

EDMUND BURKE (1729–1797), Irish philosopher, statesman. "On Conciliation with America," speech, 22 March 1775.

6 I would rather . . . have a nod from an American, than a snuff-box from an emperor.

LORD BYRON (1788–1824), English poet. Letter, 8 June 1822, to poet Thomas Moore (published in *Byron's Letters and Journals*, vol. 9, ed. by Leslie A. Marchand, 1979).

7 The keynote of American civilization is a sort of warm-hearted vulgarity. The Americans have none of the irony of the English, none of their cool poise, none of their manner. But they do have friendliness. Where an Englishman would give you his card, an American would very likely give you his shirt.

RAYMOND CHANDLER (1888–1959), U.S. author. *The Notebooks of Raymond Chandler*, "Beginning of an Essay" (1976).

8 There is nothing the matter with Americans except their ideals. The real American is all right; it is the ideal American who is all wrong.

G. K. CHESTERTON (1874–1936), British author. *New York Times* (1 Feb. 1931).

9 There is a constant in the average American imagination and taste, for which the past must be preserved and celebrated in full-scale authentic copy; a philosophy of immortality as duplication. It dominates the relation with the self, with the past, not infrequently with the present, always with History and, even, with the European tradition.

> UMBERTO ECO (b. 1932), Italian semiologist and novelist. *Travels in Hyperreality*, "The Fortresses Of Solitude" (1986).

10 We are a puny and fickle folk. Avarice, hesitation, and following are our diseases.

> RALPH WALDO EMERSON (1803–82), U.S. essayist, poet, philosopher. *Nature, Addresses and Lectures*, "The Method of Nature" (1849).

11 In America the geography is sublime, but the men are not; the inventions are excellent, but the inventors one is sometimes ashamed of.

> RALPH WALDO EMERSON (1803–82), U.S. essayist, poet, philosopher. *The Conduct of Life*, "Considerations by the Way" (1860).

12 If we Americans are to survive it will have to be because we choose and elect and defend to be first of all Americans; to present to the world one homogeneous and unbroken front, whether of white Americans or black ones or purple or blue or green. . . . If we in America have reached that point in our desperate culture when we must murder children, no matter for what reason or what color, we don't deserve to survive, and probably won't.

> WILLIAM FAULKNER (1897–1962), U.S. novelist. Interview in *Writers at Work* (First Series, ed. by Malcolm Cowley, 1958).

13 To be an American (unlike being English or French or whatever) is precisely to *imagine* a destiny rather than to inherit one; since we have always been, insofar as we are Americans at all, inhabitants of myth rather than history.

> LESLIE FIEDLER (b. 1917), U.S. critic. "Cross the Border—Close the Gap," in *Playboy* (Chicago, Dec. 1969; repr. in *Collected Essays*, vol. 2, 1971).

14 There are no second acts in American lives.

> F. SCOTT FITZGERALD (1896–1940), U.S. author. Notes for *The Last Tycoon*, "Hollywood, ETC." (1941).

15 Americans see history as a straight line and themselves standing at the cutting edge of it as representatives for all mankind. They believe in the future as if it were a religion; they believe that there is nothing they cannot accomplish, that solutions wait somewhere for all problems, like brides.

> FRANCES FITZGERALD (b. 1940), U.S. journalist and author. *Fire in the Lake*, pt. 1, ch. 1 (1972).

16 We are more thoroughly an enlightened people, with respect to our political interests, than perhaps any other under heaven. Every man among us reads, and is so easy in his circumstances as to have leisure for conversations of improvement and for acquiring information.

> BENJAMIN FRANKLIN (1706–1790), U.S. statesman, writer. Letter, 6 Sept. 1783 (published in *Complete Works*, vol. 8, ed. by John Bigelow, 1887–88).

17 Knavery seems to be so much a the striking feature of its inhabitants that it may not in the end be an evil that they will become aliens to this kingdom.

> GEORGE III (1738–1820), King of Great Britain and Ireland. Letter, 10 Nov. 1782.

18 The superficiality of the American is the result of his hustling. It needs leisure to think things out; it needs leisure to mature. People in a hurry cannot think, cannot grow, nor can they decay. They are preserved in a state of perpetual puerility.

> ERIC HOFFER (1902–1983), U.S. philosopher. *The Passionate State of Mind*, aph. 172 (1955).

19 In every American there is an air of incorrigible innocence, which seems to conceal a diabolical cunning.

> A. E. HOUSMAN (1859–1936), British poet, classical scholar. Quoted in: Prokosch, *Voices: A Memoir*, "The Sneeze" (1983). Housman asked Prokosch, whose volume *The Asiatics* had been published to critical acclaim, "Is your air of simplicity just a part of your cunning, or is your cunning just an aspect of your inner simplicity."

20 It is, I think, an indisputable fact that Americans are, as Americans, the most self-conscious people in the world, and the most addicted to the belief that the other nations of the earth are in a conspiracy to under value them.

> HENRY JAMES (1843–1916), U.S. author. *Hawthorne*, ch. 6 (1879).

21 Sir, they are a race of convicts, and ought to be thankful for anything we allow them short of hanging.

> SAMUEL JOHNSON (1709–1784), English author, lexicographer. Quoted in: Boswell, *Life of Samuel Johnson*, 21 March 1776 (1791).

22 I am willing to love all mankind, *except an American.*

> SAMUEL JOHNSON (1709–1784), English author, lexicographer. Quoted in: Boswell, *Life of Samuel Johnson*, 15 April 1778 (1791).

23 America is neither free nor brave, but a land of tight, iron-clanking little wills, everybody trying to put it over everybody else, and a land of men absolutely devoid of the real courage of trust, trust in life's sacred spontaneity. They can't *trust* life until they can *control* it.

> D. H. LAWRENCE (1885–1930), British author. Letter, 27 Sept. 1922 (published in *The Letters of D. H. Lawrence*, vol. 4, ed. by James T. Boulton, E. Mansfield and W. Roberts, 1987).

24 No American worth his salt should go around looking for a root. I advance this in all modesty, as a not unreasonable opinion.

> WYNDHAM LEWIS (1882–1957), British author, painter. *America and Cosmic Man*, "The Case Against Roots" (1948).

25 The American mood, perhaps even the American character, has changed. There are few manifestations any longer of the old American self-assurance which so irritated Dickens. . . . Instead, there is a sense of frustration so perceptible that even our politicians . . . have attempted to exploit it.

> ARCHIBALD MACLEISH (1892–1982), U.S. poet. "The Great American Frustration," in *Saturday Review* (New York, 9 July 1968; repr. in *Riders on Earth*, as "Return from the Excursion," 1978).

26 Sitting at the table doesn't make you a diner, unless you eat some of what's on that plate. Being here in America doesn't make you an American. Being born here in America doesn't make you an American.

> MALCOLM X (1925–1965), U.S. black leader. "The Ballot or the Bullet," speech, 3 April 1964, Cleveland, Ohio (published in *Malcolm X Speaks*, ch. 3, 1965).

27 The American character looks always as if it had just had a rather bad haircut, which gives it, in our eyes at any rate, a greater humanity than the European, which even among its beggars has an all too professional air.

> MARY MCCARTHY (1912–1989), U.S. author, critic. "America the Beautiful," in *Commentary* (New York, Sept. 1947; repr. in *On the Contrary*, 1961).

28 People in America, of course, live in all sorts of fashions, because they are foreigners, or unlucky, or depraved, or without ambition; people live like that, but *Americans* live in white detached houses with green shutters. Rigidly, blindly, the dream takes precedence.

> MARGARET MEAD (1901–1978), U.S. anthropologist. *Male and Female*, ch. 12 (1949).

29 Actually we are a vulgar, pushing mob whose passions are easily mobilized by demagogues, newspaper men, religious quacks, agitators and such like. To call this a society of free peoples is blasphemous. What have we to offer the world besides the superabundant loot which we recklessly plunder from the earth under the maniacal delusion that this insane activity represents progress and enlightenment?

> HENRY MILLER (1891–1980), U.S. author. *The Air-Conditioned Nightmare*, Preface (1945).

30 Perhaps I am still very much of an American. That is to say, naïve, optimistic, gullible. . . . In the eyes of a European, what am I but an American to the core, an American who exposes his Americanism like a sore. Like it or not, I am a product of this land of plenty, a believer in superabundance, a believer in miracles.

> HENRY MILLER (1891–1980), U.S. author. *Big Sur and the Oranges of Hieronymous Bosch*, pt. 3, "Paradise Lost" (1957; also published separately as *A Devil in Paradise*, 1956).

31 Being blunt with your feelings is very American. In this big country, I can be as brash as New York, as hedonistic as Los Angeles, as sensuous as San Francisco, as brainy as Boston, as proper as Philadelphia, as brawny as Chicago, as warm as Palm Springs, as friendly as my adopted home town of Dallas, Fort Worth, and as peaceful as the inland waterway that rubs up against my former home in Virginia Beach.

> MARTINA NAVRATILOVA (b. 1956), Czech-born U.S. tennis player. *Martina Navratilova—Being Myself*, ch. 1 (1985).

32 It is impossible for a stranger traveling through the United States to tell from the appearance of the people or the country whether he is in Toledo, Ohio, or Portland, Oregon. Ninety million Americans cut their hair in the same way, eat each morning exactly the same breakfast, tie up the small girls' curls with precisely the same kind of ribbon fashioned into bows exactly alike; and in every way all try to look and act as much like all the others as they can.

> ALFRED HARMSWORTH, LORD NORTHCLIFFE (1865–1922), Irish journalist and newspaper magnate. Quoted in: William E. Carson, *Northcliffe*, ch. 10 (1918).

33 One can not be an American by going about saying that one is an American. It is necessary to feel America, like America, love America and then work.

> GEORGIA O'KEEFFE (1887–1986), U.S. artist. Quoted in: *Chicago Evening Post* (2 March 1926; repr. in Laurie Lisle, *Portrait of an Artist*, 1986).

34 A trait no other nation seems to possess in quite the same degree that we do—namely, a feeling of almost childish injury and resentment unless the world as a whole recognizes how innocent we are of anything but the most generous and harmless intentions.

> ELEANOR ROOSEVELT (1884–1962), U.S. columnist, lecturer. "My Day," syndicated newspaper column (11 Nov. 1946).

35 The American people abhor a vacuum.

> THEODORE ROOSEVELT (1858–1919), U.S. Republican (later Progressive) politician, president. Speech, 3 Oct. 1907, Cairo, Ill.

36 The story of Americans is the story of arrested metamorphoses. Those who achieve success come to a halt and accept themselves as they are. Those who fail become resigned and accept themselves as they are.

> HAROLD ROSENBERG (1906–78), U.S. art critic and author. *Discovering the Present*, pt. 4, ch. 24 (1973).

37 We know that the white man does not understand our ways. One portion of land is the same to him as the next, for he is a stranger who comes in the night and takes from the land whatever he needs. The earth is not his brother, but his enemy, and when he has conquered it, he moves on.

> Attributed to SEATTLE c. 1784–1866), Chief of the Dwamish, Suquamish & allied Indian tribes. Letter, 1854, to President Franklin Pierce (published in *Brother Eagle, Sister Sky: A Message from Chief Seattle*, 1990). The letter, in which Seattle pleaded that his name should die with the ceding of the Washington State territories, was shown in 1992 to have been largely a forgery, devised by television scriptwriter Ted Perry for a historical epic in 1971.

38 American "energy." . . is the energy of violence, of free-floating resentment and anxiety unleashed by chronic cultural dislocations which must be, for the most part, ferociously sublimated. This energy has mainly been sublimated into crude materialism and acquisitiveness. Into hectic philanthropy. Into benighted moral crusades, the most spectacular of which was Prohibition. Into an awesome talent for uglifying countryside and cities. Into the loquacity and torment of a minority of gadflies: artists, prophets, muckrakers, cranks, and nuts. And into self-punishing neuroses. But the naked violence keeps breaking through, throwing everything into question.

> SUSAN SONTAG (b. 1933), U.S. essayist. "What's Happening in America (1966)," in *Partisan Review* (New Brunswick, N.J., Winter 1967; repr. in *Styles of Radical Will*, 1969).

39 I have met charming people, lots who would be charming if they hadn't got a complex about the British and everyone has pleasant and cheerful manners and I like most of the American voices. On the other hand I don't believe they have any God and their hats are frightful. On balance I prefer the Arabs.

> FREYA STARK (1893–1993), British travel writer. Letter, 19 Feb.

1944, to Field-Marshal Lord Wavell, written in Los Angeles (published in *Over the Rim of the World: Selected Letters*, ed. by Caroline Moorehead, 1988). "One ought not to make sweeping statements about countries one doesn't know," Stark added, "but a people that *prides* itself on monotony deserves it."

40 Americans are very friendly and very suspicious, that is what Americans are and that is what always upsets the foreigner, who deals with them, they are so friendly how can they be so suspicious they are so suspicious how can they be so friendly but they just are.

> GERTRUDE STEIN (1874–1946), U.S. author. "The Capital and Capitals of the United States of America," in *New York Herald Tribune* (9 March 1935; repr. in *How Writing Is Written*, ed. by Robert Bartlett Haas, 1974).

41 The whole life of an American is passed like a game of chance, a revolutionary crisis, or a battle.

> ALEXIS DE TOCQUEVILLE (1805–1859), French social philosopher. *Democracy in America*, vol. 1, ch. 18 (1835).

42 There isn't a single human characteristic that can be safely labeled as "American."

> MARK TWAIN (1835–1910), U.S. author. *What Paul Bourget Thinks of Us* (first published in *North American Review*, Cedar Falls, Ia., Jan. 1895; repr. in *Complete Essays*, ed by Charles Neider, 1963)).

43 Being American is to eat a lot of beef steak, and boy, we've got a lot more beef steak than any other country, and that's why you ought to be glad you're an American. And people have started looking at these big hunks of bloody meat on their plates, you know, and wondering what on earth they think they're doing.

> KURT VONNEGUT, JR. (b. 1922), U.S. novelist. *City Limits* (London, 11 March 1983).

44 The ideal American type is perfectly expressed by the Protestant, individualist, anti-conformist, and this is the type that is in the process of disappearing. In reality there are few left.

> ORSON WELLES (1915–84), U.S. filmmaker, actor, producer. Interview in *Hollywood Voices* (ed. by Andrews Sarris, 1971).

45 Their manners, speech, dress, friendships,—the freshness and candor of their physiognomy—the picturesque looseness of their carriage—their deathless attachment to freedom—their aversion to anything indecorous or soft or mean—the practical acknowledgment of the citizens of one state by the citizens of all other states—the fierceness of their roused resentment—their curiosity and welcome of novelty—their self-esteem and wonderful sympathy—their susceptibility to a slight—the air they have of persons who never knew how it felt to stand in the presence of superiors—the fluency of their speech—their delight in music, a sure symptom of manly tenderness and native elegance of soul—their good temper and open-handedness—the terrible significance of their elections, the President's taking off his hat to them, not they to him—these too are unrhymed poetry. It awaits the gigantic and generous treatment worthy of it.

> WALT WHITMAN (1819–92), U.S. poet. *Leaves of Grass*, Preface (1855).

46 No . . . the real American has not yet arrived. He is only in the Crucible, I tell you—he will be the fusion of all races, perhaps the coming superman.

> ISRAEL ZANGWILL (1864–1926), British playwright and novelist. David Quixano, in *The Melting Pot*, act 1.

See Falk on ABROAD; Illich on ALTRUISM; Whitehorn on CHILDREN; Dahlberg on CRITICISM; Duncan on DANCE; Auden on DISSATISFACTION; Russell on EQUALITY; Emerson, Pound on EUROPE AND AMERICA; Will on EXCESS; Dickens on GENTLEMEN; Wilde on HERO-WORSHIP; Will on HISTORY; Gallico on INSULTS; Cleaver on INTERVENTION; Geldof on IRELAND AND THE IRISH; Asquith on LIBERTY; McCullers on LONELINESS; Burgess, Wilde on MARRIAGE; Wilson on MINORITIES; Dahlberg on MONEY; Roth on MOTHERS ; Zangwill on MULTICULTURALISM; Dahlberg on NEWSPAPERS AND MAGAZINES; Appleton on PARIS; Hobsbawm on PATRIOTISM; Tocqueville on PROFIT; Burgess on READING; Dahlberg on REVIVALISM; Dickens on SATIRE; Fallaci on SEX; Hoggart on SHOPPING; James on SIMPLICITY; Baudrillard on TEETH; Sontag on THINGS; Tocqueville on WOMEN; Child on WORSHIP.

THE UNIVERSE

1 The universe is then one, infinite, immobile. . . . It is not capable of comprehension and therefore is endless and limitless, and to that extent infinite and indeterminable, and consequently immoblie.

> GIORDANO BRUNO (1548–1600), Italian philosopher. Teofilo, in *Cause, Principle, and Unity*, "Fifth Dialogue" (1588; ed and tr. by Jack Lindsay, 1962).

2 This is a war universe. War all the time. That is its nature. There may be other universes based on all sorts of other principles, but ours seems to be based on war and games.

> WILLIAM BURROUGHS (b. 1914), U.S. author. "The War Universe," taped conversation (first published in *Grand Street*, no. 37, New York; repr. in *Painting and Guns*, 1992, in a slightly different form).

3 I don't pretend to understand the Universe—it's a great deal bigger than I am.

> THOMAS CARLYLE (1795–1881), Scottish essayist and historian. Quoted by poet and diarist William Allingham in: *A Diary*, ch. 10 (ed. by H. Allingham and D. Radford, 1907), entry for 28 Dec. 1868.

4 I have never grown out of the infantile belief that the universe was made for me to suck.

> ALEISTER CROWLEY (1875–1947), British occultist. *The Confessions of Aleister Crowley*, ch. 54 (1929; rev. 1970).

5 Anyone informed that the universe is expanding and contracting in pulsations of eighty billion years has a right to ask, "What's in it for me?"

> PETER DE VRIES (b. 1910), U.S. author. The narrator (Jim Tickler), in *The Glory of the Hummingbird*, ch. 1 (1939).

6 If that's how it all started, then we might as well face the fact that what's left out there is a great deal of shrapnel and a whole bunch of cinders (one of which is, fortunately, still hot enough and close enough to be good for tanning).

> BARBARA EHRENREICH (b. 1941), U.S. author and columnist. *The Worst Years of Our Lives*, "Blocking the Gates to Heaven" (1991; first published 1986), referring to the Big Bang.

7 They cannot scare me with their empty spaces
Between stars—on stars where no human race is.
I have it in me so much nearer home
To scare myself with my own desert places.

> ROBERT FROST (1874–1963), U.S. poet. *Desert Places*.

8   Now my own suspicion is that the Universe is not only queerer than we suppose, but queerer than we can suppose.

> J. B. S. HALDANE (1892–1964), British scientist. *Possible Worlds*, title essay (1927).

9   The universe seems to me infinitely strange and foreign. At such a moment I gaze upon it with a mixture of anguish and euphoria; separate from the universe, as though placed at a certain distance outside it; I look and I see pictures, creatures that move in a kind of timeless time and spaceless space, emitting sounds that are a kind of language I no longer understand or ever register.

> EUGèNE IONESCO (b. 1912), Rumanian-born French playwright. *Notes and Counter-Notes*, pt. 2, "Interviews: Brief Notes for Radio" (1962).

10   Whatever universe a professor believes in must at any rate be a universe that lends itself to lengthy discourse. A universe definable in two sentences is something for which the professorial intellect has no use. No faith in anything of that cheap kind!

> WILLIAM JAMES (1842–1910), U.S. psychologist, philosopher. *Pragmatism*, Lecture 1, "The Present Dilemma in Philosophy" (1907).

11   Just as the individual is not alone in the group, nor any one in society alone among the others, so man is not alone in the universe.

> CLAUDE LÉVI-STRAUSS (b. 1908), French anthropologist. *Tristes Tropiques*, ch. 40 (1955).

12   It is only too clear that man is not at home in this universe, and yet he is not good enough to deserve a better.

> PERRY MILLER (1905–63), U.S. historian. *The New England Mind: The Seventeenth Century*, ch. 1 (1939).

13   Nothing is accidental in the universe—this is one of my Laws of Physics—except the entire universe itself, which is Pure Accident, pure divinity.

> JOYCE CAROL OATES (b. 1938), U.S. author. *Do What You Will*, "The Summing Up: Meredith Dawe" (1970).

14   The universe is asymmetric and I am persuaded that life, as it is known to us, is a direct result of the asymmetry of the universe or of its indirect consequences. The universe is asymmetric.

> LOUIS PASTEUR (1822–95), French chemist. *Comptes Rendus de l'Académie des Sciences* (1 June 1874; repr. in *Works*, vol. 1).

15   The universe is one of God's thoughts.

> FRIEDRICH VON SCHILLER (1759–1805), German dramatist, poet and essayist. *Philosophische Briefe*, "Letter 4: Theosophy of Julius" (published in *Essays: Aesthetical and Philosophical*, 1884).

16   The universe is wider than our views of it.

> HENRY DAVID THOREAU (1817–62), U.S. philosopher, author, naturalist. *Walden*, "Conclusion" (1854).

17   The more the universe seems comprehensible, the more it also seems pointless.

> STEVEN WEINBERG (b. 1933), U.S. theoretical physicist. *The First Three Minutes*, ch. 8 (1977).

18   I heard what was said of the universe,

Heard it and heard it of several thousand years;
It is middling well as far as it goes—but is that all?

> WALT WHITMAN (1819–92), U.S. poet. *Song of Myself*, sct. 41, in *Leaves of Grass* (1855).

UNIVERSITIES AND COLLEGES

1   To be sure, nothing is more important to the integrity of the universities . . . than a rigorously enforced divorce from war-oriented research and all connected enterprises.

> HANNAH ARENDT (1906–75), German-born U.S. political philosopher. *Crises of the Republic*, "On Violence," sct. 1 (1972). "But," Arendt added, "it would be naïve to expect this to change the nature of modern science or hinder the war effort, naïve also to deny that the resulting limitation might well lead to a lowering of university standards."

2   Home of lost causes, and forsaken beliefs, and unpopular names, and impossible loyalties!

> MATTHEW ARNOLD (1822–88), English poet, critic. *Essays in Criticism* (First Series, 1865).

3   The race of prophets is extinct. Europe is becoming set in its ways, slowly embalming itself beneath the wrappings of its borders, its factories, its law-courts and its universities. The frozen Mind cracks between the mineral staves which close upon it. The fault lies with your mouldy systems, your logic of $2 + 2 = 4$. The fault lies with you, Chancellors, caught in the net of syllogisms. You manufacture engineers, magistrates, doctors, who know nothing of the true mysteries of the body or the cosmic laws of existence. False scholars blind outside this world, philosophers who pretend to reconstruct the mind. The least act of spontaneous creation is a more complex and revealing world than any metaphysics.

> ANTONIN ARTAUD (1896–1948), French theater producer, actor, theorist. *Letter to the Chancellors of the European Universities* (published in *Collected Works*, vol. 1, pt. 2, 1956; tr. 1968).

4   I was a modest, good-humoured boy. It is Oxford that has made me insufferable.

> SIR MAX BEERBOHM (1872–1956), British author. *More*, "Going Back to School" (1899).

5   Remote and ineffectual don.

> HILAIRE BELLOC (1870–1953), British author. *Lines to a Don*.

6   The most important function of the university in an age of reason is to protect reason from itself.

> ALLAN BLOOM (1930–92), U.S. educator, author. *The Closing of the American Mind*, pt. 3, "From Socrates' Apology to Heidegger's Rektoratsrede" (1987).

7   This place is the *Devil*, or at least his principal residence, they call it the University, but any other appellation would have suited it much better, for study is the last pursuit of the society; the Master eats, drinks, and sleeps, the Fellows drink, dispute and pun, the employments of the undergraduates you will probably conjecture without my description.

> LORD BYRON (1788–1824), English poet. Letter, 23 Nov 1805 (published in *Byron's Letters and Journals*, vol. 1, ed. by Leslie Marchand, 1973).

8   'Tis well enough for a servant to be bred at an University. But the education is a little too pedantic for a gentleman.

> WILLIAM CONGREVE (1670–1729), English dramatist. Tattle, in *Love for Love*, act 5, sc. 1.

9   The greatest gift that Oxford gives her sons is, I truly believe, a genial irreverence toward learning, and from that irreverence love may spring.

> ROBERTSON DAVIES (b. 1913), Canadian novelist, journalist. "Shakespeare over the Port," in *Stratford Papers on Shakespeare* (1960; repr. in *The Enthusiasms of Robertson Davies*, 1979).

10   Within the university . . . you can study without waiting for any efficient or immediate result. You may search, just for the sake of searching, and try for the sake of trying. So there is a possibility of what I would call playing. It's perhaps the only place within society where play is possible to such an extent.

> JACQUES DERRIDA (b. 1930), Algerian-born French literary theorist. Interview in *Criticism in Society* (ed. by Imre Salusinski, 1987).

11   I am not impressed by the Ivy League establishments. Of course they graduate the best—it's all they'll take, leaving to others the problem of educating the country. They will give you an education the way the banks will give you money—provided you can prove to their satisfaction that you don't need it.

> PETER DE VRIES (b. 1910), U.S. author. The narrator (Joe Sandwich), in *The Vale of Laughter*, pt. 1, ch. 4 (1967).

12   A University should be a place of light, of liberty, and of learning.

> BENJAMIN DISRAELI (1804–81), English statesman and author. Speech, 11 March 1873, to House of Commons.

13   One of the benefits of a college education is to show the boy its little avail.

> RALPH WALDO EMERSON (1803–82), U.S. essayist, poet, philosopher. *The Conduct of Life*, "Culture" (1870).

14   The men—the undergraduates of Yale and Princeton are cleaner, healthier, better-looking, better dressed, wealthier and more attractive than any undergraduate body in the country.

> F. SCOTT FITZGERALD (1896–1940), U.S. author. Letter, 3 June 1920, to John Grier Hibben, president of Princeton University (published in *The Letters of F. Scott Fitzgerald*, ed. by Andrew Turnbull, 1963). Hibben had written Fitzgerald a letter lamenting the portrayal of the University in his recently-published first novel, *This Side of Paradise*.

15   Looking back over a decade one sees the ideal of a university become a myth, a vision, a meadow lark among the smoke stacks. Yet perhaps it is there at Princeton, only more elusive than under the skies of the Prussian Rhineland or Oxfordshire; or perhaps some men come upon it suddenly and possess it, while others wander forever outside. Even these seek in vain through middle age for any corner of the republic that preserves so much of what is fair, gracious, charming and honorable in American life.

> F. SCOTT FITZGERALD (1896–1940), U.S. author. "Princeton" (1927; repr. in *Afternoon of an Author*, ed. by Arthur Mizener, 1957). Quoted in: Matthew J. Bruccoli, *Some Sort of Epic Grandeur*, ch. 33 (1981).

16   Scratch a Yale man with both hands and you'll be lucky to find a coast-guard. Usually you find nothing at all.

> F. SCOTT FITZGERALD (1896–1940), U.S. author. *The Crack-Up*, "Notebook O" (ed. by Edmund Wilson, 1945). Fitzgerald himself studied at Princeton.

17   Oxford is—Oxford: not a mere receptacle for youth, like Cambridge. Perhaps it wants its inmates to love it rather than to love one another.

> E. M. FORSTER (1879–1970), British novelist, essayist. *Howards End*, ch. 12 (1910).

18   Master and Doctor are my titles;
For ten years now, without repose,
I've held my erudite recitals
And led my pupils by the nose.

> JOHANN WOLFGANG VON GOETHE (1749–1832), German poet and dramatist. Faust, in *Faust*, pt. 1, "Night" (tr. by Philip Wayne).

19   I had always imagined that Cliché was a suburb of Paris, until I discovered it to be a street in Oxford.

> PHILIP GUEDALLA (1889–1944), British author. *Supers and Supermen*, "Some Historians" (1920).

20   I often think how much easier the world would have been to manage if Herr Hitler and Signor Mussolini had been at Oxford.

> EDWARD F. WOOD, VISCOUNT HALIFAX (1881–1959), British politician, diplomat. Speech, 4 Nov. 1937, York, England. Wood was at the time chancellor of Oxford University.

21   If the factory people outside the colleges live under the discipline of narrow means, the people inside live under almost every other kind of discipline except that of narrow means—from the fruity austerities of learning, through the iron rations of English gentlemanhood, down to the modest disadvantages of occupying cold stone buildings without central heating and having to cross two or three quadrangles to take a bath.

> MARGARET HALSEY (b. 1910), U.S. author. *With Malice Toward Some*, pt. 2, "June 24" (1938).

22   Towery city and branchy between towers;
Cuckoo-echoing, bell-swarmèd, lark-charmèd,
rook-racked, river-rounded.

> GERARD MANLEY HOPKINS (1844–89), English poet, Jesuit priest. *Duns Scotus's Oxford*, st.1.

23   The medieval university looked backwards; it professed to be a storehouse of old knowledge. . . . The modern university looks forward, and is a factory of new knowledge.

> THOMAS HENRY HUXLEY (1825–1895), English biologist. Letter, 11 April 1892.

24   University degrees are a bit like adultery: you may not want to get involved with that sort of thing, but you don't want to be thought incapable.

> SIR PETER IMBERT (b. 1933), British police commissioner. *Times* (London, 11 Oct. 1992).

25   It might be said now that I have the best of both worlds: a Harvard education and a Yale degree.

> JOHN F. KENNEDY (1917–63), U.S. Democratic politician, pres-

ident. Yale Commencement Address, 11 June 1962, on being awarded an honorary degree.

26 They were evidently small men, all wind and quibbles, flinging out their chaffy grain to us with far less interest than a farm-wife feels as she scatters corn to her fowls.

> D. H. LAWRENCE (1885–1930), British author. Letter, 4 May 1908 (published in *The Letters of D. H. Lawrence,* vol. 1, ed. by James T. Boulton, 1979), on Lawrence's university professors. Lawrence added, "I deeply respect some of our Professors, but I revere none."

27 I am told that today rather more than 60 per cent of the men who go to university go on a Government grant. This is a new class that has entered upon the scene. It is the white-collar proletariat. . . . They do not go to university to acquire culture but to get a job, and when they have got one, scamp it. They have no manners and are woefully unable to deal with any social predicament. Their idea of a celebration is to go to a public house and drink six beers. They are mean, malicious and envious . . . . They are scum.

> W. SOMERSET MAUGHAM (1874–1965), British author. *Sunday Times* (London, 25 Dec. 1955), on the generation of "Angry Young Men" as portrayed in Kingsley Amis's 1954 novel *Lucky Jim.* These people, Amis continued, "will in due course leave the university. Some will doubtless sink back, perhaps with relief, into the modest social class from which they emerged; some will take to drink, some to crime and go to prison. . . . A few will go into Parliament, become Cabinet Ministers and rule the country. I look upon myself as fortunate that I shall not live to see it."

28 I am . . . willing to admit that some people might live there for years, or even a lifetime, so protected that they never sense the sweet stench of corruption that is all around them—the keen, thin scent of decay that pervades everything and accuses with a terrible accusation the superficial youthfulness, the abounding undergraduate noise, that fills those ancient buildings.

> THOMAS MERTON (1915–68), U.S. religious writer, poet. *The Seven Storey Mountain,* pt. 1, ch. 3 (1948), describing his undergraduate days.

29 American universities are organized on the principle of the nuclear rather than the extended family. Graduate students are grimly trained to be technicians rather than connoisseurs. The old German style of universal scholarship has gone.

> CAMILLE PAGLIA (b. 1947), U.S. author, critic, educator. *Sex, Art, and American Culture,* "Sexual Personae: The Cancelled Preface" (1992).

30 Our major universities are now stuck with an army of pedestrian, toadying careerists, Fifties types who wave around Sixties banners to conceal their record of ruthless, beaverlike tunneling to the top.

> CAMILLE PAGLIA (b. 1947), U.S. author, critic, educator. *Sex, Art, and American Culture,* Introduction (1992).

31 Apparently, the most difficult feat for a Cambridge male is to accept a woman not merely as feeling, not merely as thinking, but as managing a complex, vital interweaving of both.

> SYLVIA PLATH (1932–63), U.S. poet. *Isis* (Oxford, 6 May 1956), written while Plath was a student at Cambridge.

32 It is dangerous sending a young man who is beautiful to Oxford.

> DUDLEY RYDER (1691–1756), Lord Chief Justice of the King's Bench, diarist. Quoted in: Arthur Marwick, *Beauty in History,* "The Private Sphere," ch. 4 (1988).

33 Oxford, the paradise of dead philosophies.

> GEORGE SANTAYANA (1863–1952), U.S. philosopher, poet. *Egotism in German Philosophy* (1916, p. 144).

34 Socrates gave no diplomas or degrees, and would have subjected any disciple who demanded one to a disconcerting catechism on the nature of true knowledge.

> G. M. TREVELYAN (1876–1962), British historian. *History of England,* bk. 2, ch. 4 (1926).

35 In spite of the roaring of the young lions at the Union, and the screaming of the rabbits in the home of the vivisector, in spite of Keble College, and the tramways, and the sporting prints, Oxford still remains the most beautiful thing in England, and nowhere else are life and art so exquisitely blended, so perfectly made one.

> OSCAR WILDE (1854–1900), Anglo-Irish playwright, author. *Dramatic Review* (London, 23 May 1885).

36 The exquisite art of idleness, one of the most important things that any University can teach.

> OSCAR WILDE (1854–1900), Anglo-Irish playwright, author. Review of Laurence Binyon, Manmohan Ghose, Stephen Phillips and Arthur Cripps, *Primavera: Poems* (published in *Pall Mall Gazette,* London, 24 May 1890).

37 The first duty of a lecturer—to hand you after an hour's discourse a nugget of pure truth to wrap up between the pages of your notebooks and keep on the mantlepiece for ever.

> VIRGINIA WOOLF (1882–1941), British novelist. *A Room of One's Own,* ch. 1 (1929).

38 If we help an educated man's daughter to go to Cambridge are we not forcing her to think not about education but about war?—not how she can learn, but how she can fight in order that she might win the same advantages as her brothers?

> VIRGINIA WOOLF (1882–1941), British novelist. *Three Guineas* (1938, p. 36).

39 I wonder anybody does anything at Oxford but dream and remember, the place is so beautiful. One almost expects the people to sing instead of speaking. It is all . . . like an opera.

> W. B. YEATS (1865–1939), Irish poet, playwright. Letter, 25 Aug. 1888, to writer Katherine Tynan—later Hinkson (published in *The Collected Letters of W. B. Yeats,* vol. 1, ed. by John Kelly, 1986).

THE UNKNOWN

1 There is nothing that man fears more than the touch of the unknown. He wants to *see* what is reaching towards him, and to be able to recognize or at least classify it. Man always tends to avoid physical contact with anything strange.

> ELIAS CANETTI (b. 1905), Austrian novelist and philosopher. *Crowds And Power,* "The Fear of Being Touched" (1960; tr. 1962), opening lines.

2   Mystery has its own mysteries, and there are gods above gods. We have ours, they have theirs. That is what's known as infinity.

> JEAN COCTEAU (1889–1963), French author and filmmaker. *Anubis*, in *The Infernal Machine*, act 2 (1932; repr. in *Collected Works*, vol. 5, 1948).

3   The mind loves the unknown. It loves images whose meaning is unknown, since the meaning of the mind itself is unknown.

> RENÉ MAGRITTE (1898–1967), Belgian surrealist painter. Quoted in: Suzi Gablik, *Magritte*, ch. 1 (1970).

4   Only the unknown frightens men. But once a man has faced the unknown, that terror becomes the known.

> ANTOINE DE SAINT-EXUPÉRY (1900–1944), French aviator and author. *Wind, Sand, and Stars* (published in *Terre des Hommes*, ch. 2, sct. 2, 1939).

5   The fundament upon which all our knowledge and learning rests is the inexplicable.

> ARTHUR SCHOPENHAUER (1788–1860), German philosopher. *Parerga and Paralipomena*, vol. 2, ch. 1, sct. 1 (1851).

6   It is the unknown that excites the ardor of scholars, who, in the known alone, would shrivel up with boredom.

> WALLACE STEVENS (1879–1955), U.S. poet. "The Irrational Element in Poetry," lecture (c. 1937; published in *Opus Posthumous*, 1959).

7   At the same time that we are earnest to explore and learn all things, we require that all things be mysterious and unexplorable, that land and sea be infinitely wild, unsurveyed and unfathomed by us because unfathomable.

> HENRY DAVID THOREAU (1817–62), U.S. philosopher, author, naturalist. *Walden*, "Spring" (1854).

See also Lichtenberg on DISCOVERY.

UPBRINGING

1   Anyone who has a child today should train him to be either a physicist or a ballet dancer. Then he'll escape.

> W. H. AUDEN (1907–73), Anglo-American poet. *The Table Talk of W. H. Auden*, "January 15, 1947" (comp. by Alan Ansen, ed. by Nicholas Jenkins, 1990).

2   Tew bring up a child in the wa he should go—travel that wa yourself.

> JOSH BILLINGS [HENRY WHEELER SHAW] (1818–85), U.S. humorist. *Josh Billings, His Sayings*, ch. 78 (1865).

3   Good breeding ... differs, if at all, from high breeding only as it gracefully remembers the rights of others, rather than gracefully insists on its own rights.

> THOMAS CARLYLE (1795–1881), Scottish essayist and historian. *Sartor Resartus*, bk. 3, ch. 6 (1833–34).

4   I suffer whenever I see that common sight of a parent or senior imposing his opinion and way of thinking and being on a young soul to which they are totally unfit. Cannot we let people be themselves, and enjoy life in their own way? You are trying to make that man another *you*. One's enough.

> RALPH WALDO EMERSON (1803–1882), U.S. essayist, poet, philosopher. *Lectures and Biographical Sketches*, "Education" (1883).

5   It is the common error of builders and parents to follow some plan they think beautiful (and perhaps is so) without considering that nothing is beautiful that is misplaced.

> LADY MARY WORTLEY MONTAGU (1689–1762), English society figure, letter writer. Letter, 28 Jan. 1753, to her daughter Lady Bute (published in *Selected Letters*, ed. by Robert Halsband, 1970).

6   Permissiveness is the principle of treating children as if they were adults; and the tactic of making sure they never reach that stage.

> THOMAS SZASZ (b. 1920), U.S. psychiatrist. *The Second Sin*, "Social Relations" (1973).

THE UPPER CLASS

1   Real good breeding, as the people have it here, is one of the finest things now going in the world. The careful avoidance of all discussion, the swift hopping from topic to topic, does not agree with me; but the graceful style they do it with is beyond that of minuets!

> THOMAS CARLYLE (1795–1881), Scottish essayist and historian. Letter, 17 July 1844, to his wife Jane Welsh Carlyle. Quoted in: Fred Kaplan, *Thomas Carlyle: A Biography* (1983).

2   I am ... by tradition and long study a complete snob. P. Marlowe and I do not despise the upper classes because they take baths and have money; we despise them because they are phony.

> RAYMOND CHANDLER (1888–1959), U.S. author. Letter, 7 Jan. 1945, to editor Dale Warren (published in *Raymond Chandler Speaking*, 1962).

3   People of quality know everything without ever having learned anything.

> MOLIÈRE (1622–73), French dramatist. Mascarille, in *Les Précieuses Ridicules*, sc. 9

See also ARISTOCRACY; SNOBBERY.

THE USSR

1   As a result of half a century of Soviet rule people have been weaned from a belief in human kindness.

> SVETLANA ALLILUEVYA (b. 1925), Russian writer, daughter of Josef Stalin. *Only One Year*, "The Journey's End" (1969).

2   I cannot forecast to you the action of Russia. It is a riddle wrapped in a mystery inside an enigma.

> SIR WINSTON CHURCHILL (1874–1965), British statesman, writer. Radio broadcast, 1 Oct. 1939. Churchill added: "But perhaps there is a key ... Russian national interest."

3   I believe, as Lenin said, that this revolutionary chaos may yet crystallize into new forms of life.

> MIKHAIL GORBACHEV (b. 1931), Soviet political leader. Quoted in: *Times* (London, 18 May 1990), to journalists, of the Soviet Union's regional difficulties.

4 *Perestroika* basically is creating material incentives for the individual. Some of the comrades deny that, but I can't see it any other way. In that sense human nature kinda goes backwards. It's a step backwards. You have to realize the people weren't quite ready for a socialist production system.

> GUS HALL (b. 1910), General secretary of the Communist Party of U.S.A. *Independent* (London, 19 May 1990).

5 Nothing an interested foreigner may have to say about the Soviet Union today can compare with the scorn and fury of those who inhabit the ruin of a dream.

> CHRISTOPHER HOPE (b. 1944), South African author. *Sunday Times* (London, 15 April 1990).

6 Visitors who come from the Soviet Union and tell you how marvellous it is to be able to look at public buildings without advertisements stuck all over them are just telling you that they can't decipher the cyrillic alphabet.

> CLIVE JAMES (b. 1939), Australian writer, critic. *Glued To The Box*, Introduction (1983).

7 When your house is on fire, you can't be bothered with the neighbors. Or, as we say in chess, if your king is under attack you don't worry about losing a pawn on the queen's side.

> GARY KASPAROV (b. 1963), Russian chess player. Interview in *Observer* (London, 3 Dec. 1989), of Mikhail Gorbachev's attitude to changes in Eastern Europe.

8 Those who wait for that must wait until a shrimp learns to whistle.

> NIKITA KHRUSHCHEV (1894–1971), Soviet premier. Speech, 17 Sept. 1955, Moscow, on the possibility of the Soviet Union rejecting communism.

9 If we were to promise people nothing better than only revolution, they would scratch their heads and say: "Is it not better to have good goulash?"

> NIKITA KHRUSHCHEV (1894–1971), Soviet premier. Quoted in: *Observer* (London, 12 Sept. 1971).

10 The Régime did not want Communists; it wanted robots. It will take at least a generation to change them back into humans again.

> ARTHUR KOESTLER (1905–83), Hungarian-born British author. *The Trail of the Dinosaur*, pt. 2, "The Shadow of a Tree" (1955).

11 You ask can we ever trust the Bear? . . . I will give you several answers at once. The first is no, we can never trust the Bear. For one reason, the Bear doesn't trust himself. The Bear is threatened and the Bear is frightened and the Bear is falling apart. The Bear is disgusted with his past, sick of his present and scared stiff of his future. He often was. The Bear is broke, lazy, volatile, incompetent, slippery, dangerously proud, dangerously armed, sometimes brilliant, often ignorant. Without his claws, he'd be just another chaotic member of the Third World. . . . The second answer is yes, we can trust the Bear completely. The Bear has never been so trustworthy. The Bear is begging to be part of us, to submerge his problems in us, to have his own bank account with us, to shop in our High Street and be accepted as a dignified member of our forest as well as his. . . . The Bear needs us so desperately that we may safely trust him to need us.

> JOHN LE CARRÉ (b. 1931), British novelist. Smiley, in *The Secret Pilgrim*, ch. 12 (1990).

12 Comrade life,
let us
march faster,
March
faster through what's left
of the five-year plan.

> VLADIMIR MAYAKOVSKY (1893–1930), Russian poet and dramatist. *At the top of my voice* (tr. by George Reavey).

13 Let us be aware that while they preach the supremacy of the state, declare its omnipotence over individual man, and predict its eventual domination of all peoples of the earth—they are the focus of evil in the modern world.

> RONALD REAGAN (b. 1911), U.S. Republican politician, president. Statement, 8 March 1983 Quoted in: *Reagan's Reign of Error*, "Focus of Evil" (ed. by Mark Green and Gail MacColl, 1987).

14 If the Soviet Union let another political party come into existence, they would still be a one-party state, because everybody would join the other party.

> RONALD REAGAN (b. 1911), U.S. Republican politician, president. Remark, 23 June 1983, to Polish Americans in Chicago (published in *Speaking My Mind*, "The Wit and Wisdom of Ronald Reagan," 1989).

15 Democratization is not democracy; it is a slogan for the temporary liberalization handed down from an autocrat. Glasnost is not free speech; only free speech, consitutionally guaranteed, is free speech.

> GAIL SHEEHY (b. 1937), U.S. journalist and author. *Gorbachev*, "Looking for Mikhail Gorbachev" (1991).

16 In the Soviet Union everything happens slowly. Always remember that.

> A. N. SHEVCHENKO (b. 1930), defecting Soviet diplomat. Quoted in: *Observer* (London, 2 Jan. 1983).

17 I have not had major experience of talking with people once pronounced brain-dead, but I think we could be safe in saying he did not have great zip.

> SIR HOWARD SMITH (b. 1919), Ex-British ambassador to Moscow. *Times* (London, 8 Sept. 1988), of Soviet premier Leonid Brezhnev.

18 For us in Russia, communism is a dead dog, while, for many people in the West, it is still a living lion.

> ALEXANDER SOLZHENITSYN (b. 1918), Russian novelist. Radio broadcast, BBC Russian service (published in *Listener*, London, 15 Feb. 1979).

19 The clock of communism has stopped striking. But its concrete building has not yet come crashing down. For that reason, instead of freeing ourselves, we must try to save ourselves from being crushed by its rubble.

> ALEXANDER SOLZHENITSYN (b. 1918), Russian novelist. Opening sentence of essay, "How We Must Rebuild Russia" (published in Soviet Union's biggest-selling daily newspaper, *Komsomolskaya Pravda*, 18 Sept. 1990).

20 I have been over into the future, and it works.

> LINCOLN STEFFENS (1866–1936), U.S. writer, editor. Remark to financier Bernard Baruch, on his return from the Soviet Union in

1919. Quoted in: Steffens, *Autobiography*, ch. 18 (1931). He made the same remark in a letter, 3 April 1919.

21 They were right. The Soviet régime is not the embodiment of evil as you think in the West. They have laws and I broke them. I hate tea and they love tea. Who is wrong?

> ALEXANDER ZINOVIEV (b. 1922), Soviet philosopher. *Sunday Times* (London, 3 May 1981), on his forced exile from the Soviet Union.

See also Attlee, Lenin on COMMUNISM; Solzhenitsyn on PROPAGANDA; RUSSIA AND THE RUSSIANS.

UTOPIA

1 In our wildest aberrations we dream of an equilibrium we have left behind and which we naively expect to find at the end of our errors. Childish presumption which justifies the fact that child-nations, inheriting our follies, are now directing our history.

> ALBERT CAMUS (1913–60), French-Algerian philosopher and author. *The Myth of Sisyphus & Other Essays*, "Helen's Exile" (1955; first published 1948).

2 Utopias are presented for our inspection as a critique of the human state. If they are to be treated as anything but trivial exercises of the imagination, I suggest there is a simple test we can apply. . . . We must forget the whole paraphernalia of social description, demonstration, expostulation, approbation, condemnation. We have to say to ourselves, "How would I myself live in this proposed society? How long would it be before I went stark staring mad?"

> WILLIAM GOLDING (1911-93), British author. "Utopias And Antiutopias," address, 13 Feb. 1977, to Les Anglicistes, Lille, France (repr. in *A Moving Target*, 1982).

3 Every daring attempt to make a great change in existing conditions, every lofty vision of new possibilities for the human race, has been labeled Utopian.

> EMMA GOLDMAN (1869–1940), U.S. anarchist. "Socialism: Caught in the Political Trap," lecture (c. 1912; first published in *Red Emma Speaks*, pt. 1, ed. by Alix Kates Shulman, 1972).

4 I shall speak of . . . how melancholy and utopia preclude one another. How they fertilize one another. . . . Of the revulsion that follows one insight and precedes the next. . . . Of superabundance and surfeit. Of stasis in progress. And of myself, for whom melancholy and utopia are heads and tails of the same coin.

> GÜNTHER GRASS (b. 1927), German author. *From the Diary of a Snail*, "On Stasis in Progress" (1972).

5 We are at heart so profoundly anarchistic that the only form of state we can imagine living in is Utopian; and so cynical that the only Utopia we can believe in is authoritarian.

> LIONEL TRILLING (1905–75), U.S. critic. Notebook entry, 1948 (published in *Partisan Review 50th Anniversary Edition*, ed. by William Philips, 1985).

VACATION

1 Holidays are in no sense an alternative to the congestion and bustle of cities and work. Quite the contrary. People look to escape into an intensification of the conditions of ordinary life, into a deliberate aggravation of those conditions: further from nature, nearer to artifice, to abstraction, to total pollution, to well above average levels of stress, pressure, concentration and monotony—this is the ideal of popular entertainment. No one is interested in overcoming alienation; the point is to plunge into it to the point of ecstasy. That is what holidays are for.

> JEAN BAUDRILLARD (b. 1929), French semiologist. *Cool Memories*, ch. 2 (1987; tr. 1990).

2 To get away from one's working environment is, in a sense, to get away from one's self; and this is often the chief advantage of travel and change.

> CHARLES HORTON COOLEY (1864–1929), U.S. sociologist. *Human Nature and the Social Order*, ch. 6 (1902).

3 Total physical and mental inertia are highly agreeable, much more so than we allow ourselves to imagine. A beach not only permits such inertia but enforces it, thus neatly eliminating all problems of guilt. It is now the only place in our overly active world that does.

> JOHN KENNETH GALBRAITH (b. 1908), U.S. economist. Foreword to Gloria Steinem, *The Beach Book* (1963; repr. in *A View from the Stands*, 1986).

4 Every man who possibly can should force himself to a holiday of a full month in a year, whether he feels like taking it or not.

> WILLIAM JAMES (1842–1910), U.S. psychologist, philosopher. *Vacations* (1873; repr. in *The Works of William James*, vol. 17, pt. 1, 1987).

5 *Fact:* Girls who are having a good sex thing stay in New York. The rest want to spend their summer vacations in Europe.

> GAIL PARENT (b. 1941), U.S. author. *Sheila Levine is Dead and Living in New York*, "Europe" (1972).

6 A perpetual holiday is a good working definition of hell.

> GEORGE BERNARD SHAW (1856–1950), Anglo-Irish playwright, critic. *Parents and Children*, "Children's Happiness" (1914).

VALUE

1 That which costs little is less valued.

> MIGUEL DE CERVANTES (1547–1616), Spanish writer. *Don Quixote*, pt. 1, bk. 4, ch. 7 (1605; tr. by P. Motteux).

2 Value is the most invincible and impalpable of ghosts, and comes and goes unthought of while the visible and dense matter remains as it was.

> W. STANLEY JEVONS (1835–82), British economist, logician. *Investigations in Currency and Finance*, pt. 2, ch. 4 (1884).

3 All sciences are now under the obligation to prepare the ground for the future task of the philosopher, which is to solve the problem of value, to determine the true hierarchy of values.

> FRIEDRICH NIETZSCHE (1844–1900), German philosopher. *The Genealogy of Morals*, "First Essay," sct. 17 (1887).

4 What we obtain too cheap we esteem too lightly; it is dearness only that gives everything its value.

THOMAS PAINE (1737–1809), Anglo-American political theorist, writer. "The American Crisis," pamphlet (23 Dec. 1776; first published in *Pennsylvania Journal*, 19 Dec. 1776).

5 Ruskin's counsel: The labour of two days . . . is that for which you ask two hundred guineas?

Whistler: No. I ask it for the knowledge of a lifetime.

JAMES MCNEILL WHISTLER (1834–1903), U.S. artist. Altercation during critic John Ruskin's lawsuit against Whistler, 15 Nov. 1878 Quoted in: Whistler, *The Gentle Art of Making Enemies*, "The action" (1890). See Ruskin on ART for the inflammatory remark that led to the suit, which Whistler won, though it left him nearly penniless.

6 Nowadays people know the price of everything and the value of nothing.

OSCAR WILDE (1854–1900), Anglo-Irish playwright, author. Lord Henry Wotton, in *The Picture of Dorian Gray*, ch. 4 (1891). A similar wording was used in *Lady Windermere's Fan*.

See Wilde on CYNICS.

VALUES

1 The three most important things a man has are, briefly, his private parts, his money, and his religious opinions.

SAMUEL BUTLER (1835–1902), English author. *Samuel Butler's Notebooks*, "Untraced Notes" (1951).

2 The least pain in our little finger gives us more concern and uneasiness than the destruction of millions of our fellow-beings.

WILLIAM HAZLITT (1778–1830), English essayist. "American Literature—Dr. Channing," in *Edinburgh Review* (Oct. 1829; repr. in *Complete Works*, vol. 16, ed. by P. P. Howe, 1932).

3 First you destroy those who create values. Then you destroy those who know what the values are, and who also know that those destroyed before were in fact the creators of values. But real barbarism begins when no one can any longer judge or know that what he does is barbaric.

RYSZARD KAPUSCINSKI (b. 1932), Polish journalist. "A Warsaw Diary," in *Granta*, no. 15 (Cambridge, England, 1985).

4 You can't appreciate home till you've left it, money till it's spent, your wife till she's joined a woman's club, nor Old Glory till you see it hanging on a broomstick on the shanty of a consul in a foreign town.

O. HENRY [WILLIAM SYDNEY PORTER] (1862–1910), U.S. short-story writer. *Roads of Destiny*, "The Fourth in Salvador" (1909).

5 Values are tapes we play on the Walkman of the mind: any tune we choose so long as it does not disturb others.

JONATHAN SACKS (b. 1948), British Chief Rabbi. "The Persistence of Faith," 1990 Reith Lecture.

VINCENT VAN GOGH

1 It is not a certain conformity of manners that the painting of Van Gogh attacks, but rather the conformity of institutions themselves. And even external nature, with her climates, her tides, and her equinoctial storms, cannot, after van Gogh's stay upon earth, maintain the same gravitation.

ANTONIN ARTAUD (1896–1948), French theatre producer, actor, theorist. *Van Gogh, the Man Suicided by Society* (1947; repr. in *Selected Writings*, pt. 33, ed. by Susan Sontag, 1976).

2 When he painted a road, the roadmakers were there in his imagination. When he painted the turned earth of a ploughed field, the gesture of the blade turning the earth was included in his own act. Wherever he looked he saw the labour of existence; and this labour, recognized as such, was what constituted reality for him.

JOHN BERGER (b. 1926), British author, critic. *And Our Faces, My Heart, Brief As Photos*, pt. 2 (1984).

3 But I owe something to Vincent, and that is, in the consciousness of having been useful to him, the confirmation of my own original ideas about painting. And also, at difficult moments, the remembrance that one finds others unhappier than oneself.

PAUL GAUGUIN (1848–1903), French artist. *Intimate Journals* (tr. by Van Wyck Brooks, 1923; repr. 1930, p. 16).

4 Here a brain is consumed by the fire of a star. It frees itself in its work just before the catastrophe. Deepest tragedy takes place here, real tragedy, natural tragedy, exemplary tragedy.

PAUL KLEE (1879–1940), Swiss artist. *The Diaries of Paul Klee 1898–1918*, no. 816 (1957: tr.1965), entry for March 1908.

VANITY

1 Looking at yourself in a mirror isn't exactly a study of life.

LAUREN BACALL (b. 1924), U.S. actor. *Daily Mail* (London, 1 Nov. 1990).

2 To say that a man is vain means merely that he is pleased with the effect he produces on other people. A conceited man is satisfied with the effect he produces on himself.

SIR MAX BEERBOHM (1872–1956), British author. *And Even Now*, "Quia Imperfectum" (1920).

3 Vanity of vanities, saith the Preacher, vanity of vanities; all is vanity.

BIBLE, HEBREW. *Ecclesiastes* 1:2 *passim*.

4 Vanity is as ill at ease under indifference as tenderness is under a love which it cannot return.

GEORGE ELIOT (1819–80), English novelist, editor. *Daniel Deronda*, bk. 1, ch. 10 (1876).

5 Most people dislike vanity in others, whatever share they have of it themselves; but I give it fair quarter, wherever I meet with it, being persuaded that it is often productive of good to the possessor, and to others who are within his sphere of action: and therefore, in many cases, it would not be altogether absurd if a man were to thank God for his *vanity* among the other comforts of life.

BENJAMIN FRANKLIN (1706–90), U.S. statesman, writer. *Autobiography*, ch. 1 (1868).

6 If there is a single quality that is shared by all great men, it is vanity. But I mean by "vanity" only that they appreciate their own worth. Without this kind of vanity they would not be great. And with vanity alone, of course, a man is nothing.

YOUSEF KARSH (b. 1908), Turkish-born Canadian photographer. *Cosmopolitan* (New York, Dec. 1955).

7 Throughout the centuries, man has considered himself beautiful. . . . I rather suppose that man only believes in his own beauty out of pride; that he is not really beautiful and he suspects this himself; for why does he look on the face of his fellow-man with such scorn?

ISIDORE DUCASSE, COMTE DE LAUTRÉAMONT (1846–70), French author, poet. *Maldoror*, bk. 1, ch. 9 (1870; tr. 1978).

8 Possibly, more people kill themselves and others out of hurt vanity than out of envy, jealousy, malice or desire for revenge.

IRIS MURDOCH (b. 1919), British novelist, philosopher. *The Philosopher's Pupil*, "The Events in Our Town" (1983).

9 What is the vanity of the vainest man compared with the vanity which the most modest possesses when, in the midst of nature and the world, he feels himself to be "man"!

FRIEDRICH NIETZSCHE (1844–1900), German philosopher. *The Wanderer and His Shadow*, aph. 304 (1880).

10 There was never yet fair woman but she made mouths in a glass.

WILLIAM SHAKESPEARE (1564–1616), English dramatist, poet. Fool, in *King Lear*, act 3, sc. 2.

11 Vanity is a vital aid to nature: completely and absolutely necessary to life. It is one of nature's ways to bind you to the earth.

ELIZABETH SMART (1913–86), Canadian author, poet. *Necessary Secrets*, pt. 1, ch. 2 (ed. by Alice Van Wart, 1991), journal entry for 25 June 1933.

12 The vanity of men, a constant insult to women, is also the ground for the implicit feminine claim of superior sensitivity and morality.

PATRICIA MEYER SPACKS (b. 1929), U.S. literary critic. *The Female Imagination*, ch. 1 (1975).

13 There are no grades of vanity, there are only grades of ability in concealing it.

MARK TWAIN (1835–1910), U.S. author. *Notebook*, ch. 31 (ed. by Albert Bigelow Paine, 1935), 1898 entry.

14 Cure yourself of the affliction of caring how you appear to others. Concern yourself only with how you appear before God, concern yourself only with the idea that God may have of you.

MIGUEL DE UNAMUNO (1864–1936), Spanish philosophical writer. *The Life of Don Quixote and Sancho*, "The Sepulcher of Don Quixote" (1905).

See also Johnson on SECRETS.

VEGETARIANISM

1 Behold I have given you every herb bearing seed which is upon the face of all the earth, and every tree, in which is the fruit of a tree yielding seed; to you it shall be for meat.

BIBLE, HEBREW. *Genesis* 1:29 But in a later context, God told the disgraced Adam, "and thou shalt eat the herb of the field" (*Genesis* 3:18).

2 Never would it occur to a child that a sheep, a pig, a cow or a chicken was good to eat, while, like Milton's Adam, he would eagerly make a meal off fruits, nuts, thyme, mint, peas and broad beans which penetrate further and stimulate not only the appetite but other vague and deep nostalgias. We are closer to the Vegetable Kingdom than we know; is it not for man alone that mint, thyme, sage, and rosemary exhale "crush me and eat me!"—for us that opium poppy, coffee-berry, teaplant and vine perfect themselves? Their aim is to be absorbed by us, even if it can only be achieved by attaching themselves to roast mutton.

CYRIL CONNOLLY (1903–74), British critic. *The Unquiet Grave*, pt. 2 (1944; rev. 1951).

3 Most vegetarians I ever see looked enough like their food to be classed as cannibals.

FINLEY PETER DUNNE (1867–1936), U.S. journalist, humorist. *Mr. Dooley's Philosophy*, "Casual Observations" (1900).

4 A man of my spiritual intensity does not eat corpses.

GEORGE BERNARD SHAW (1856–1950), Anglo-Irish playwright, critic. Quoted in: Hesketh Pearson, *Bernard Shaw: His Life and Personality*, ch. 9 (1942). Shaw, Pearson reported, believed vegetarians had radically different experiences from meat-eaters: "The odd thing about being a vegetarian is, not that the things that happen to other people don't happen to me—they all do—but that they happen differently: pain is different, pleasure different, fever different, cold different, even love different."

5 It is impossible that had Buonaparte descended from a race of vegetable feeders that he could have had either the inclination or the power to ascend the throne of the Bourbons.

PERCY BYSSHE SHELLEY (1792–1822), English poet. *A Vindication of Natural Diet*, a note in *Queen Mab* (1813). Shelley became a vegetarian in 1812, remaining so until his death.

6 I have no doubt that it is a part of the destiny of the human race, in its gradual improvement, to leave off eating animals, as surely as the savage tribes have left off eating each other when they came in contact with the more civilized.

HENRY DAVID THOREAU (1817–62), U.S. philosopher, author, naturalist. *Walden*, "Higher Laws" (1854). Thoreau believed that "every man who has ever been earnest to preserve his higher or poetic faculties in the best condition has been particularly inclined to abstain from animal food, and from much food of any kind" (same source).

7 One farmer says to me, "You cannot live on vegetable food solely, for it furnishes nothing to make bones with;" and so he religiously devotes a part of his day to supplying his system with the raw material of bones; walking all the while he talks behind his oxen, which, with vegetable-made bones, jerk him and his lumbering plow along in spite of every obstacle.

HENRY DAVID THOREAU (1817–62), U.S. philosopher, author, naturalist. *Walden*, "Economy" (1854).

VENICE

1   My beautiful, my own
My only Venice—this is breath! Thy breeze
Thine Adrian sea-breeze, how it fans my face!
Thy very winds feel native to my veins,
And cool them into calmness!

> LORD BYRON (1788–1824), English poet. Jacopo Foscari, in *The Two Foscari*, act 1, sc. 1.

2   The greenest island of my imagination.

> LORD BYRON (1788–1824), English poet. Letter, 17 Nov. 1816, to poet Thomas Moore (published in *Byron's Letters and Journals*, vol. 5, ed. by Leslie A. Marchand, 1973–81).

3   Venice is like eating an entire box of chocolate liqueurs at one go.

> TRUMAN CAPOTE (1924–84), U.S. author. Quoted in: *Observer* (London, 26 Nov. 1961).

4   You desire to embrace it, to caress it, to possess it; and finally a soft sense of possession grows up and your visit becomes a perpetual love affair.

> HENRY JAMES (1843–1916), U.S. author. *Italian Hours,* "Venice," sct. 2 (1909; written 1882). James visited Venice seven times between 1869 and 1907. For the city's downside, see James on TOURISM.

5   The things of *this* world reveal their essential absurdity when they are put in the Venetian context. In the unreal realm of the canals, as in a Swiftian Lilliput, the real world, with its contrivances, appears as a vast folly.

> MARY MCCARTHY (1912–89), U.S. author, critic. *Venice Observed*, ch. 1 (1956).

6   A wholly materialistic city is nothing but a dream incarnate. Venice is the world's unconscious, a miser's glittering hoard, guarded by a Beast whose eyes are made of white agate, and by a saint who is really a prince who has just slain a dragon.

> MARY MCCARTHY (1912–89), U.S. author, critic. *Venice Observed*, ch. 2 (1956).

7   A fit abode for a poet. Stage setting at least correct.

> EZRA POUND (1885–1972), U.S. poet, critic. Letter, summer 1908 Quoted in: Humphrey Carpenter, *A Serious Character*, pt. 2, ch. 1 (1988). Pound spent four months in Venice before settling in London.

8   I'm glad to find that you dislike Venice because I thought it detestable when we were there, both times—once it might be due to insanity but not twice, so I thought it must be my fault. I suppose the obscurer reaches might be beautiful.

> VIRGINIA WOOLF (1882–1941), British novelist. Letter, 25 April 1913, to Vanessa Bell (published in *The Question of Things Happening: Letters, vol. 2*, ed. by Nigel Nicolson, 1976).

VICE

1   Alas, human vices, however horrible one might imagine them to be, contain the proof (were it only in their infinite expansion) of man's longing for the infinite; but it is a longing that often takes the wrong route. . . . It is my belief that the reason behind all culpable excesses lies in this depravation of the sense of the infinite.

> CHARLES BAUDELAIRE (1821–67), French poet. *Les Paradis Artificiels,* "The Poem of Hashish," ch. 1 (1860).

2   There are men so incorrigibly lazy that no inducement that you can offer will tempt them to work; so eaten up by vice that virtue is abhorrent to them, and so inveterably dishonest that theft is to them a master passion. When a human being has reached that stage, there is only one course that can be rationally pursued. Sorrowfully, but remorselessly, it must be recognised that he has become lunatic, morally demented, incapable of self-government, and that upon him, therefore, must be passed the sentence of permanent seclusion from a world in which he is not fit to be at large.

> WILLIAM BOOTH (1829–1912), English evangelist, founder of the Salvation Army. *In Darkest England, and the Way Out*, pt. 2, ch. 5, sct. 10 (1890).

3   Tobacco and alcohol, delicious fathers of abiding friendships and fertile reveries.

> LUIS BUÑUEL (1900–1983), Spanish filmmaker. *My Last Sigh*, ch. 6 (1983).

4   It is the function of vice to keep virtue within reasonable bounds.

> SAMUEL BUTLER (1835–1902), English author. *Samuel Butler's Notebooks* (1951, p. 219).

5   Every day confirms my opinion on the superiority of a vicious life—and if Virtue is not its own reward I don't know any other stipend annexed to it.

> LORD BYRON (1788–1824), English poet. Letter, 18 Dec. 1813 (published in *Byron's Letters and Journals*, vol. 3, ed. by Leslie A. Marchand, 1974).

6   Vice, in its true light, is so deformed, that it shocks us at first sight; and would hardly ever seduce us, if it did not at first wear the mask of some virtue.

> LORD CHESTERFIELD (1694–1773), English statesman, man of letters. Letter, 22 Feb. 1748 (first published 1774; repr. in *The Letters of the Earl of Chesterfield to His Son*, vol. 1, no. 142, ed. by Charles Strachey, 1901).

7   So much of our lives is given over to the consideration of our imperfections that there is no time to improve our imaginary virtues. The truth is we only perfect our vices, and man is a worse creature when he dies than he was when he was born.

> EDWARD DAHLBERG (1900–1977), U.S. author, critic. *Alms for Oblivion,* "Moby-Dick: A Hamitic Dream" (1964).

8   Vices are sometimes only virtues carried to excess!

> CHARLES DICKENS (1812–70), English novelist. Mr. Morfin, in *Dombey and Son*, ch. 58 (1848).

9   Vice is a creature of such hideous mien . . . that the more you see it the better you like it.

> FINLEY PETER DUNNE (1867–1936), U.S. journalist, humorist. *Mr. Dooley's Opinions,* "The Crusade Against Vice" (1901).

10   Most vices . . . demand considerable self-sacrifices. There is no greater mistake than to suppose that a vicious life is a life of uninterrupted pleasure. It is a life almost as wearisome and painful—if strenuously led—as Christian's in *The Pilgrim's Progress*.

> ALDOUS HUXLEY (1894–1963), British author. *Along the Road*, pt. 1, "Why Not Stay at Home?" (1925).

11 A prince must be prudent enough to know how to escape the bad reputation of those vices that would lose the state for him, and must protect himself from those that will not lose it for him, if this is possible; but if he cannot, he need not concern himself unduly if he ignores these less serious vices.

> NICCOLÒ MACHIAVELLI (1469–1527), Italian political philosopher, statesman. *The Prince*, ch. 15 (1514).

12 It's true Heaven forbids some pleasures, but a compromise can usually be found.

> MOLIÈRE (1622–73), French dramatist. Tartuffe, in *Le Tartuffe*, act 4, sc. 5.

13 Life is extraordinarily suave and sweet with certain natural, witty, affectionate people who have unusual distinction and are capable of every vice, but who make a display of none in public and about whom no one can affirm they have a single one. There is something supple and secret about them. Besides, their perversity gives spice to their most innocent occupations, such as taking a walk in the garden at night.

> MARCEL PROUST (1871–1922), French novelist. *Pleasures and Regrets*, "Fragments From Italian Comedy," no. 5 (1896; tr. 1948).

14 No exile at the South Pole or on the summit of Mont Blanc separates us more effectively from others than the practice of a hidden vice.

> MARCEL PROUST (1871–1922), French novelist. *Remembrance of Things Past*, vol. 10, pt. 2, ch. 2, "The Captive" (1922; tr. by Scott Monkrieff, 1929).

15 Here am I: at one stroke incestuous, adulteress, sodomite, and all that in a girl who only lost her maidenhead today! . . . What progress, my friends! . . . with what rapidity I advance along the thorny road of vice!

> MARQUIS DE SADE (1740–1814), French author. Eugénie, in *Philosophy in the Bedroom*, "Dialogue the Seventh" (1795).

16 Time, which alone makes the reputation of men, ends by making their defects respectable.

> VOLTAIRE (1694–1778), French philosopher, author. *Letters on England*, Letter 18, "On Tragedy" (1732).

17 Never support two weaknesses at the same time. It's your combination sinners—your lecherous liars and your miserly drunkards—who dishonor the vices and bring them into bad repute.

> THORNTON WILDER (1897–1975), U.S. novelist, dramatist. Malachi, in *The Matchmaker*, act 3.

See also Shaw on ABSTINENCE. La Rochefoucald on HYPOCRISY; Bierce on OLD AGE; Woolcott on PLEASURE; Montaigne on REPENTANCE; Crisp on REWARD.

THE VICE PRESIDENT

1 That's the really neat thing about Dan Quayle, as you must have realized from the first moment you looked into those lovely blue eyes: *impeachment insurance.*

> BARBARA EHRENREICH (b. 1941), U.S. author, columnist. *The Worst Years of Our Lives*, "My Reply to George" (1991; first published 1981), essay addressed to George Bush.

2 The President has only 190 million bosses. The Vice President has 190 million and one.

> HUBERT H. HUMPHREY (1911–78), U.S. Democratic politician, vice president. *American Salesman Magazine* (1966). Quoted in: *The Quotable Hubert Humphrey*.

3 Quayle was a twink. He got all the way through the sixties without dying from an overdose, being institutionalized by his parents or getting arrested for nude violation of the Mann act on a motorcycle. At least he was a draft-dodger—although Dan timidly joined the National Guard instead of bravely going to his physical in panty hose.

> P. J. O'ROURKE (b. 1947), U.S. journalist. *Parliament of Whores*, "Attack of the Midget Vote Suckers" (1991).

VICTIMS

1 Oh, the holiness of always being the injured party. The historically oppressed can find not only sanctity but safety in the state of victimization. When access to a better life has been denied often enough, and successfully enough, one can use the rejection as an excuse to cease all efforts. After all, one reckons, "they" don't want me, "they" accept their own mediocrity and refuse my best, "they" don't deserve me.

> MAYA ANGELOU (b. 1928), U.S. author. *Singin' and Swingin' and Gettin' Merry Like Christmas*, vol. 3, ch. 9 (1976).

2 Sympathy for victims is always counter-balanced by an equal and opposite feeling of resentment towards them.

> BEN ELTON (b. 1959), British author, performer. *Stark*, "On the Business of Stark" (1989).

3 Once victim, always victim—that's the law!

> THOMAS HARDY (1840–1928), English novelist, poet. Tess, in *Tess of the D'Urbervilles*, ch. 47 (1891).

4 Don't agonize. Organize.

> FLORYNCE R. KENNEDY (b. 1916), U.S. lawyer, civil rights activist. Quoted in: Gloria Steinem, "The Verbal Karate of Florynce R. Kennedy, Esq.," in *Ms.* (New York, March 1973).

5 I am a man more sinned against than sinning.

> WILLIAM SHAKESPEARE (1564–1616), English dramatist, poet. Lear, in *King Lear*, act 3, sc. 2..

6 Victims suggest innocence. And innocence, by the inexorable logic that governs all relational terms, suggests guilt.

> SUSAN SONTAG (b. 1933), U.S. essayist. *AIDS and Its Metaphors*, ch. 1 (1989).

7 When a man's life is destroyed or damaged by some wound or privation of soul or body, which is due to other men's actions or negligence, it is not only his sensibility that suffers but also his aspiration toward the good. Therefore there has been sacrilege towards that which is sacred in him.

> SIMONE WEIL (1909–43), French philosopher, mystic. "Draft for a Statement of Human Obligation" (written 1943; published in *Selected Essays*, ed. by Richard Rees, 1962).

QUEEN VICTORIA

1   What's the use? She would only want me to take a message to dear Albert.

> BENJAMIN DISRAELI (1804–81), English statesman, author. Quoted in: W. H. Auden, *A Certain World*, "Words, Last" (1970), attributed last words on hearing that Victoria would like to see him.

2   Today 23 years ago dear Grandmama died. I wonder what she would have thought of a Labour Government.

> GEORGE V (1865–1936), King of Great Britain and Ireland. Diary entry, 22 Jan. 1924, after having invited Ramsay Macdonald to form Britain's first Labour government.

3   I mourn the safe and motherly old middle-class queen, who held the nation warm under the fold of her big, hideous Scotch-plaid shawl and whose duration had been so extraordinarily convenient and beneficent. I felt her death much more than I should have expected; she was a sustaining symbol—and the wild waters are upon us now.

> HENRY JAMES (1843–1916), U.S. author. Letter, 20 Feb. 1901, to jurist Oliver Wendell Holmes, Jr. (published in *Letters of Henry James*, vol. 4, 1984).

4   Knew her own mind. But the mind radically commonplace, only its inherited force, & cumulative sense of power, making it remarkable.

> VIRGINIA WOOLF (1882–1941), British novelist. *The Diary of Virginia Woolf*, vol. 3 (ed. by Anne O. Bell, 1980), entry for 27 Dec. 1930 on Queen Victoria.

VICTORY

1   The problems of victory are more agreeable than the problems of defeat, but they are no less difficult.

> SIR WINSTON CHURCHILL (1874–1965), British statesman, writer. Speech, 11 Nov. 1942, House of Commons.

2   Victory is gay only back home. Up front it is joyless.

> MARLENE DIETRICH (1904–92), German-born U.S. film actor. *Marlene Dietrich's ABC*, "Victory" (1962).

3   Even victors are by victories undone.

> JOHN DRYDEN (1631–1700), English poet, dramatist, critic. *Epistle to John Driden of Chesterton*.

4   Democracies are notorious for a tendency to obey the feelings rather than the mind; thus the nature of democracies often makes it difficult to conclude a peace after a hard-won war. Generous victors are rare.

> AMOS ELON (b. 1926), Israeli author, journalist. *New Yorker* (23 April 1990).

5   You may be always victorious if you will never enter into any contest where the issue does not wholly depend upon yourself.

> EPICTETUS (c. 55-c. 135), Greek Stoic philosopher. *Encheiridion*, no. 19 (tr. by T. W. H. Rolleston, 1881).

6   The moment of victory is much too short to live for that and nothing else.

> MARTINA NAVRATILOVA (b. 1956), Czech-born U.S. tennis player. *Guardian* (London, 21 June 1989).

7   It is not the cause for which men took up arms that makes a victory more just or less, it is the order that is established when arms have been laid down.

> SIMONE WEIL (1909–43), French philosopher, mystic. "The Great Beast: Conclusion" (written 1939–40; published in *Selected Essays*, ed. by Richard Rees, 1962).

See also Saint-Exupery on DEFEAT; Smith on SONG; WINNING.

VIETNAM

1   The war was won on both sides: by the Vietnamese on the ground, by the Americans in the electronic mental space. And if the one side won an ideological and political victory, the other made *Apocalypse Now* and that has gone right around the world.

> JEAN BAUDRILLARD (b. 1929), French semiologist. *America*, "Astral America" (1986; tr. 1988).

2   There is the guilt all soldiers feel for having broken the taboo against killing, a guilt as old as war itself. Add to this the soldier's sense of shame for having fought in actions that resulted, indirectly or directly, in the deaths of civilians. Then pile on top of that an attitude of social opprobrium, an attitude that made the fighting man feel personally morally responsible for the war, and you get your proverbial walking time bomb.

> PHILIP CAPUTO (b. 1941), U.S. author, journalist, Vietnam veteran. *Playboy* (Chicago, Jan. 1982).

3   You have a row of dominoes set up; you knock over the first one, and what will happen to the last one is that it will go over very quickly.

> DWIGHT D. EISENHOWER (1890–1969), U.S. general, Republican politician, president. Address, 7 April 1954, to press conference, on the situation in south-east Asia after the defeat of the French by the Viet-Minh.

4   Saigon was an addicted city, and we were the drug: the corruption of children, the mutilation of young men, the prostitution of women, the humiliation of the old, the division of the family, the division of the country—it had all been done in our name. . . . The French city . . . had represented the opium stage of the addiction. With the Americans had begun the heroin phase.

> JAMES FENTON (b. 1949), British poet, critic. "The Fall of Saigon," in *Granta*, no. 15 (Cambridge, England, 1985; repr. in *All the Wrong Places*, 1988).

5   By intervening in the Vietnamese struggle the United States was attempting to fit its global strategies into a world of hillocks and hamlets, to reduce its majestic concerns for the containment of communism and the security of the Free World to a dimension where governments rose and fell as a result of arguments between two colonels' wives.

> FRANCES FITZGERALD (b. 1940), U.S. journalist, author. *Fire in the Lake*, pt. 1, ch. 1 (1972).

6   America has made no reparation to the Vietnamese, nothing. We are the richest people in the world and they are among the poorest. We savaged them, though they had never hurt us, and we cannot find it in our hearts, our honor, to give them help—because the government of Vietnam is Communist. And perhaps because they won.

> MARTHA GELLHORN (b. 1908), U.S. journalist, author. *The Face of War*, "The War in Vietnam—Vietnam Again, 1986" (1959; rev. 1986). Gellhorn went on to say, "After all this time I still cannot think calmly about that war. It was the only war I reported on the wrong side."

7 Vietnam was what we had instead of happy childhoods.

> MICHAEL HERR (b. 1940), U.S. journalist. *Dispatches*, "Colleagues," sct. 3 (1977).

8 All the wrong people remember Vietnam. I think all the people who remember it should forget it, and all the people who forgot it should remember it.

> MICHAEL HERR (b. 1940), U.S. journalist. *Observer* (London, 15 Jan. 1989).

9 This is not a jungle war, but a struggle for freedom on every front of human activity.

> LYNDON B. JOHNSON (1908–73), U.S. Democratic politician, president. Television broadcast, 4 Aug. 1964.

10 Now we have a problem in making our power credible, and Vietnam is the place.

> JOHN F. KENNEDY (1917–63), U.S. Democratic politician, president. Remark, June 1961, to journalist James Reston, following Kennedy's meeting with Soviet premier Khrushchev.

11 Vietnam presumably taught us that the United States could not serve as the world's policeman; it should also have taught us the dangers of trying to be the world's midwife to democracy when the birth is scheduled to take place under conditions of guerrilla war.

> JEANE KIRKPATRICK (b. 1926), U.S. public official. "Dictatorship and Double Standards," in *Commentary* (New York, Nov. 1979).

12 Some of the critics viewed Vietnam as a morality play in which the wicked must be punished before the final curtain and where any attempt to salvage self-respect from the outcome compounded the wrong. I viewed it as a genuine tragedy. No one had a monopoly on anguish.

> HENRY KISSINGER (b. 1923), U.S. Republican politician, Secretary of State. *The White House Years*, ch. 8 (1979).

13 Above all, Vietnam was a war that asked everything of a few and nothing of most in America.

> MYRA MACPHERSON, U.S. author. *Long Time Passing: Vietnam and the Haunted Generation*, Epilogue (1984).

14 Television brought the brutality of war into the comfort of the living room. Vietnam was lost in the living rooms of America—not on the battlefields of Vietnam.

> MARSHALL MCLUHAN (1911–80), Canadian communications theorist. Quoted in: *Montreal Gazette* (16 May 1975).

15 Let us understand: North Vietnam cannot defeat or humiliate the United States. Only Americans can do that.

> RICHARD M. NIXON (b. 1913), U.S. Republican politician, president. Television broadcast, 3 Nov. 1969. Quoted in: Stephen Ambrose, *Nixon: The Triumph of a Politician*, vol. 2, ch. 14 (1989). In his *Memoirs*, Nixon commented: "Very few speeches actually influence the course of history. The November 3 speech was one of them."

16 No event in American history is more misunderstood than the Vietnam War. It was misreported then, and it is misremembered now.

> RICHARD M. NIXON (b. 1913), U.S. Republican politician, president. "No More Vietnams," in *New York Times* (28 March 1985).

17 We are at war with the most dangerous enemy that has ever faced mankind in his long climb from the swamp to the stars, and it has been said if we lose that war, and in so doing lose this way of freedom of ours, history will record with the greatest astonishment that those who had the most to lose did the least to prevent its happening.

> RONALD REAGAN (b. 1911), U.S. Republican politician, president. "A Time for Choosing," television address, 27 Oct. 1964 (published in *Speaking My Mind*, 1989).

18 We should declare war on North Vietnam. . . . We could pave the whole country and put parking strips on it, and still be home by Christmas.

> RONALD REAGAN (b. 1911), U.S. Republican politician, president. *Fresno Bee* (10 Oct. 1965). Quoted in: *Reagan's Reign of Error*, "Vietnam, a Noble Cause" (ed. by Mark Green and Gail MacColl, 1987).

19 I was proud of the youths who opposed the war in Vietnam because they were my babies.

> BENJAMIN SPOCK (b. 1903), U.S. pediatrician, author. *Times* (London, 2 May 1988).

20 The war against Vietnam is only the ghastliest manifestation of what I'd call imperial provincialism, which afflicts America's whole culture—aware only of its own history, insensible to everything which isn't part of the local atmosphere.

> STEPHEN VIZINCZEY (b. 1933), Hungarian novelist, critic. "Condemned World, Literary Kingdom," review of Norman Mailer, *Armies of the Night*, in *Times Saturday Review* (London, 21 Sept. 1968; repr. in *Truth and Lies in Literature*, 1986).

VILLAINS

1 It takes a certain courage and a certain greatness to be truly base.

> JEAN ANOUILH (1910–87), French playwright. Le Générale, in *Ardèle*, act 1.

2 As for an authentic villain, the real thing, the absolute, the artist, one rarely meets him even once in a lifetime. The ordinary bad hat is always in part a decent fellow.

> COLETTE (1873–1954), French author. *Break of Day* (1961; repr. in *Earthly Paradise*, pt. 4, "The South of France," ed. by Robert Phelps, 1966).

3 I have known a vast quantity of nonsense talked about bad men not looking you in the face. Don't trust that conventional idea. Dishonesty will stare honesty out of countenance any day in the week, if there is anything to be got by it.

> CHARLES DICKENS (1812–70), English novelist. The narrator (Mr. Sampson), in *Hunted Down*, ch. 2, *New York Ledger* (1859; repr. in *All the Year Round*, 1860).

4 As there is a use in medicine for poisons, so the world cannot move without rogues.

RALPH WALDO EMERSON (1803–82), U.S. essayist, poet, philosopher. *The Conduct of Life*, "Power" (1860).

5 Gamesters and highwaymen are generally very good to their whores, but they are very devils to their wives.

JOHN GAY (1685–1732), English dramatist. Peachum, in *The Beggar's Opera*, act 1, sc. 4.

6 In the old days villains had moustaches and kicked the dog. Audiences are smarter today. They don't want their villain to be thrown at them with green limelight on his face. They want an ordinary human being with failings.

ALFRED HITCHCOCK (1899–1980), Anglo-American filmmaker. Quoted in: Leslie Halliwell, *Halliwell's Filmgoer's Companion* (1984).

7 The Cad is the entire epitome, the complete blossom and fruit in one, of what we are told is an age of culture. Behold him in the vélodrome as he yells insanely after his kind as they tear along on their tandem machines in a match, and then ask yourself candidly, O my reader, if any age before this in all the centuries of earth ever produced any creature so utterly low and loathsome, so physically, mentally, individually, and collectively hideous?

OUIDA [MARIE LOUISE DE LA RAMÉE] (1839–1908), English novelist. *Critical Studies*, "The Ugliness of Modern Life" (1900).

8 A villain must be a thing of power, handled with delicacy and grace. He must be wicked enough to excite our aversion, strong enough to arouse our fear, human enough to awaken some transient gleam of sympathy. We must triumph in his downfall, yet not barbarously nor with contempt, and the close of his career must be in harmony with all its previous development.

AGNES REPPLIER (1858–1950), U.S. author, social critic. *Essays in Miniature*, "A Short Defense of Villains" (1892).

9 When it comes to the point, really bad men are just as rare as really good ones.

GEORGE BERNARD SHAW (1856–1950), Anglo-Irish playwright, critic. Lady Cicely, in *Captain Brassbound's Conversion*, act 2.

10 The experience of the gangster *as an experience of art* is universal to Americans. There is almost nothing we understand better or react to more readily or with quicker intelligence. . . . In ways that we do not easily or willingly define, the gangster speaks for us, expressing that part of the American psyche which rejects the qualities and the demands of modern life, which rejects "Americanism" itself.

ROBERT WARSHOW (1917–55), U.S. author. "The Gangster as Tragic Hero," in *Partisan Review* (New Brunswick, N.J., 1948; repr. in *The Immediate Experience*, 1970).

See also Shakespeare on CORRUPTION; Johnson on PIETY.

VIOLENCE

1 Power and violence are opposites; where the one rules absolutely, the other is absent. Violence appears where power is in jeopardy, but left to its own course it ends in power's disappearance.

HANNAH ARENDT (1906–75), German-born U.S. political philosopher. *Crises of the Republic*, "On Violence" (1972).

2 The more dubious and uncertain an instrument violence has become in international relations, the more it has gained in reputation and appeal in domestic affairs, specifically in the matter of revolution.

HANNAH ARENDT (1906–75), German-born U.S. political philosopher. *Crises of the Republic*, "On Violence" (1972).

3 Perhaps violence, like pornography, is some kind of an evolutionary standby system, a last-resort device for throwing a wild joker into the game?

J. G. BALLARD (b. 1930), British author. *Myths of the Near Future*, "News from the Sun" (1982).

4 I write about violence as naturally as Jane Austen wrote about manners. Violence shapes and obsesses our society, and if we do not stop being violent we have no future.

EDWARD BOND (b. 1934), British playwright. *Lear*, Preface (1972). Two of Bond's plays were banned for their violent content in the 1960s, provoking a furor which contributed to ending censorship on the stage in Britain.

5 We are supposed to be the children of Seth; but Seth is too much of an effete nonentity to deserve ancestral regard. No, we are the sons of Cain, and with violence can be associated the attacks on sound, stone, wood and metal that produced civilisation.

ANTHONY BURGESS (b. 1917), British author, critic. Book review in *Observer* (London, 26 Nov. 1989).

6 Violence does, in truth, recoil upon the violent, and the schemer falls into the pit which he digs for another.

SIR ARTHUR CONAN DOYLE (1859–1930), English author. Sherlock Holmes, in *The Adventures of Sherlock Holmes*, "The Speckled Band" (1892), having driven a poisonous snake to return fatally upon its owner, Dr. Grimesby Roylott.

7 Men are rewarded for learning the practice of violence in virtually any sphere of activity by money, admiration, recognition, respect, and the genuflection of others honoring their sacred and proven masculinity. In male culture, police are heroic and so are outlaws; males who enforce standards are heroic and so are those who violate them.

ANDREA DWORKIN (b. 1946), U.S. feminist critic. *Pornography*, ch. 2 (1981).

8 There are situations in life to which the only satisfactory response is a physically violent one. If you don't make that response, you continually relive the unresolved situation over and over in your life.

RUSSELL HOBAN (b. 1925), U.S. author. *Novelists in Interview* (ed. by John Haffenden, 1985).

9 A society that presumes a norm of violence and celebrates aggression, whether in the subway, on the football field, or in the conduct of its business, cannot help making celebrities of the people who would destroy it.

LEWIS H. LAPHAM (b. 1935), U.S. essayist, editor. "Citizen Goetz," in *Harper's* (New York, March 1985).

10 In America all too few blows are struck into flesh.

We kill the spirit here, we are experts at that. We use psychic bullets and kill each other cell by cell.

> NORMAN MAILER (b. 1923), U.S. author. *The Presidential Papers*, "The Fourth Presidential Paper—Foreign Affairs: Letter To Castro" (1963), contrasting the U.S. with Cuba, where "hatred runs over into the love of blood."

11 In the whole vast dome of living nature there reigns an open violence, a kind of prescriptive fury which arms all the creatures to their common doom: as soon as you leave the inanimate kingdom you find the decree of violent death inscribed on the very frontiers of life.

> JOSEPH DE MAISTRE (1753–1821), French diplomat, philosopher. The Senator, in *Les Soirées de Saint-Pétersbourg*, "Seventh Dialogue" (1821; repr. in *The Works of Joseph de Maistre*, ed. by Jack Lively, 1965).

12 If violence is wrong in America, violence is wrong abroad. If it is wrong to be violent defending black women and black children and black babies and black men, then it is wrong for America to draft us, and make us violent abroad in defense of her. And if it is right for America to draft us, and teach us how to be violent in defense of her, then it is right for you and me to do whatever is necessary to defend our own people right here in this country.

> MALCOLM X (1925–65), U.S. black leader. Speech, Nov. 1963, New York City.

13 In violence we forget who we are.

> MARY MCCARTHY (1912–89), U.S. author, critic. *On the Contrary*, pt. 3, "Characters in Fiction" (1961).

14 If human beings are to survive in a nuclear age, committing acts of violence may eventually have to become as embarrassing as urinating or defecating in public are today.

> MYRIAM MIEDZIAN, U.S. author. *Boys Will Be Boys*, ch. 3 (1991).

15 If you strike a child, take care that you strike it in anger, even at the risk of maiming it for life. A blow in cold blood neither can nor should be forgiven.

> GEORGE BERNARD SHAW (1856–1950), Anglo-Irish playwright, critic. *Man and Superman*, "Maxims for Revolutionists: How to Beat Children" (1903).

16 Violence can only be concealed by a lie, and the lie can only be maintained by violence. Any man who has once proclaimed violence as his method is inevitably forced to take the lie as his principle.

> ALEXANDER SOLZHENITSYN (b. 1918), Russian novelist. Nobel Prize lecture, 1973 (published in *Solzhenitsyn: A Documentary Record*, ed. by Leopold Labedz, 1974).

17 Rambo isn't violent. I see Rambo as a philanthropist.

> SYLVESTER STALLONE (b. 1946), U.S. actor, filmmaker. *Today* (London, 27 May 1988).

18 Under all conditions well-organized violence seems to him the shortest distance between two points.

> LEON TROTSKY (1879–1940), Russian revolutionary. Unfinished biography, *Stalin*, ch. 3 (1947), of Stalin.

See also Burgess on DELINQUENCY; James on NATURE; NON-VIOLENCE.

VIRGINITY

1 Gaze not on a maid, that thou fall not be by those things that are precious to her.

> APOCRYPHA. *Ecclesiasticus* 9:5.

2 Because her instinct has told her, or because she has been reliably informed, the faded virgin knows that the supreme joys are not for her; she knows by a process of the intellect; but she can feel her deprivation no more than the young mother can feel the hardship of the virgin's lot.

> ARNOLD BENNETT (1867–1931), British novelist. *The Journals of Arnold Bennett* (1932), entry for 18 March 1897.

3 An isolated outbreak of virginity . . . is a rash on the face of society. It arouses only pity from the married, and embarrassment from the single.

> CHARLOTTE BINGHAM (b. 1942), British author. *Lucinda*, ch. 1 (1966).

4 The great majority of people in England and America are modest, decent and pure-minded and the amount of virgins in the world today is stupendous.

> BARBARA CARTLAND (b. 1901), British novelist. Interview in Wendy Leigh, *Speaking Frankly* (1978). But on another occasion, Cartland was reported as saying: "Only the English and the Americans are improper. East of Suez everyone wants a virgin."

5 If love the virgin's heart invade,
How, like a moth, the simple maid
Still plays about the flame!

> JOHN GAY (1685–1732), English dramatist. Mrs. Peachum, in *The Beggar's Opera*, act 1, sc. 4, air 4.

6 I always thought of losing my virginity as a career move.

> MADONNA (b. 1959), U.S. singer, actor. Quoted in: Christopher Andersen, *Madonna Unauthorized*, Epilogue (1991).

7 She had already allowed her delectable lover to pluck that flower which, so different from the rose to which it is nevertheless sometimes compared, has not the same faculty of being reborn each spring.

> MARQUIS DE SADE (1740–1814), French author. "The Mystified Magistrate" (written 1787; first published in *Historiettes, Contes et Fabliaux*, 1926).

See also Le Guin on MEN AND WOMEN.

VIRTUE

1 A homely face and no figure have aided many women heavenward.

> MINNA ANTRIM (b. 1861), U.S. epigrammist. *Naked Truth and Veiled Allusions* (1901, p. 16).

2 Most virtue is a demand for greater seduction.

> NATALIE CLIFFORD BARNEY (1876–1972), U.S.-born French author. Quoted in: "My Country 'tis of Thee" in *Adam*, no. 299 (London, 1962).

3 The deadliest foe to virtue would be complete self-knowledge.

> F. H. BRADLEY (1846–1924), English philosopher. *Aphorisms*, no. 68 (1930).

4 Virtue is simply happiness, and happiness is a by-product of function. You are happy when you are functioning.

> WILLIAM BURROUGHS (b. 1914), U.S. author. *Painting and Guns,* "The Creative Observer" (1992).

5 Rare virtues are like rare plants or animals, things that have not been able to hold their own in the world. A virtue to be serviceable must, like gold, be alloyed with some commoner but more durable metal.

> SAMUEL BUTLER (1835–1902), English author. *The Way of All Flesh,* ch. 19 (1903).

6 Virtue knows that it is impossible to get on without compromise, and tunes herself, as it were, a trifle sharp to allow for an inevitable fall in playing.

> SAMUEL BUTLER (1835–1902), English author. *Samuel Butler's Notebooks* (1951).

7 Virtue cannot separate itself from reality without becoming a principle of evil.

> ALBERT CAMUS (1913–60), French-Algerian philosopher, author. *The Rebel,* pt. 5, "Moderation and Excess" (1951; tr. 1953).

8 Virtue is the truest nobility.

> MIGUEL DE CERVANTES (1547–1616), Spanish writer. Dorothea, in *Don Quixote,* pt. 1, bk. 4, ch. 9 (1605; tr. by P. Motteux).

9 The chief assertion of religious morality is that white is a colour. Virtue is not the absence of vices or the avoidance of moral dangers; virtue is a vivid and separate thing, like pain or a particular smell.

> G. K. CHESTERTON (1874–1936), British author. *Tremendous Trifles,* "A Piece of Chalk" (1909).

10 Man seems to be capable of great virtues but not of small virtues; capable of defying his torturer but not of keeping his temper.

> G. K. CHESTERTON (1874–1936), British author. *Autobiography,* ch. 11 (1936).

11 Nothing in our times has become so unattractive as virtue.

> EDWARD DAHLBERG (1900–1977), U.S. author, critic. *Alms for Oblivion,* "The Expatriates: A Memoir" (1964).

12 People praise virtue, but they hate it, they run away from it. It freezes you to death, and in this world you've got to keep your feet warm.

> DENIS DIDEROT (1713–84), French philosopher. Rameau's nephew, in *Rameau's Nephew* (written 1762; published 1821; repr. in *Selected Writings,* ed. by Lester G. Crocker, 1966).

13 Virtuous people are simply those who have . . . not been tempted sufficiently, because they live in a vegetative state, or because their purposes are so concentrated in one direction that they have not had the leisure to glance around them.

> ISADORA DUNCAN (1878–1927), U.S. dancer. *My Life,* Introduction (1927).

14 The less a man thinks or knows about his virtues, the better we like him.

> RALPH WALDO EMERSON (1803–82), U.S. essayist, poet, philosopher. *Essays,* "Spiritual Laws" (First Series, 1841).

15 The virtues of society are vices of the saint. The terror of reform is the discovery that we must cast away our virtues, or what we have always esteemed such, into the same pit that has consumed our grosser vices.

> RALPH WALDO EMERSON (1803–82), U.S. essayist, poet, philosopher. *Essays,* "Circles" (First Series, 1841).

16 Every one suspects himself of at least one of the cardinal virtues.

> F. SCOTT FITZGERALD (1896–1940), U.S. author. The narrator (Nick Carraway), in *The Great Gatsby,* ch. 3 (1925).

17 People who are in a fortunate position always attribute virtue to what makes them so happy.

> JOHN KENNETH GALBRAITH (b. 1908), U.S. economist. *Guardian* (London, 23 May 1992).

18 To a superior race of being the pretensions of mankind to extraordinary sanctity and virtue must seem . . . ridiculous.

> WILLIAM HAZLITT (1778–1830), English essayist. *Characteristics: In the Manner of Rochefoucault's Maxims,* no. 191 (1823; repr. in *The Complete Works Of William Hazlitt,* vol. 9, ed. by P. P. Howe, 1932).

19 Often devotion to virtue arises from sated desire.

> LAURENCE HOPE [ADELA FLORENCE CORY NICOLSON] (1865–1904), British poet. *I Arise and Go Down to the River,* st. 6

20 Virtue is too often merely local.

> SAMUEL JOHNSON (1709–84), English author, lexicographer. *The Idler,* no. 53, in *Universal Chronicle* (London, 21 April 1759; repr. in *Works of Samuel Johnson,* vol. 2, ed. by W. J. Bate, John M. Bullitt and L. F. Powell, 1963).

21 I cannot love anyone if I hate myself. That is the reason why we feel so extremly uncomfortable in the presence of people who are noted for their special virtuousness, for they radiate an atmosphere of the torture they inflict on themselves. That is not a virtue but a vice.

> CARL JUNG (1875–1961), Swiss psychiatrist. Basel seminar, multigraphed for private circulation by the Psychology Club, Zurich (1934, p. 88; repr. in *Collected Works,* vol. 18, ed. by William McGuire).

22 Virtue by premeditation isn't worth much.

> G. C. LICHTENBERG (1742–99), German physicist, philosopher. *Aphorisms,* "Notebook H," aph. 13 (written 1765–99; tr. by R. J. Hollingdale, 1990).

23 The fact is that a man who wants to act virtuously in every way necessarily comes to grief among so many who are not virtuous.

> NICCOLÒ MACHIAVELLI (1469–1527), Italian political philosopher, statesman. *The Prince,* ch. 15 (1514).

24 I cannot praise a fugitive and cloistered virtue, unexercised and unbreathed, that never sallies out and sees her adversary, but slinks out of the race where that immortal garland is to be run for, not without dust and heat.

> JOHN MILTON (1608–74), English poet. *Areopagitica: a Speech for the Liberty of Unlicensed Printing to the Parliament of England* (1644).

25 Virtue rejects facility to be her companion. . . . She requires a craggy, rough and thorny way.

MICHEL DE MONTAIGNE (1533–92), French essayist. *Essays*, bk. 2, ch. 11, "Of Cruelty" (1580–88; tr. by John Florio).

26 All art is a struggle to be, in a particular sort of way, virtuous.

IRIS MURDOCH (b. 1919), British novelist, philosopher. Quoted in: *Novelists in Interview* (ed. by John Haffenden, 1985).

27 We do not place especial value on the possession of a virtue until we notice its total absence in our opponent.

FRIEDRICH NIETZSCHE (1844–1900), German philosopher. *Human, All Too Human*, aph. 302 (1878).

28 Ah, Eugénie, have done with virtues! Among the sacrifices that can be made to those counterfeit divinities, is there one worth an instant of the pleasures one tastes in outraging them?

MARQUIS DE SADE (1740–1814), French author. Dolmancé, in *Philosophy in the Bedroom*, "Dialogue the Third" (1795).

29 Virtue is reason which has become energy.

FRIEDRICH SCHLEGEL (1772–1829), German philosopher, critic, writer. *Dialogue on Poetry and Literary Aphorisms*, "Ideas," aph. 23 (1968; first published 1799–1800).

30 Assume a virtue if you have it not.

WILLIAM SHAKESPEARE (1564–1616), English dramatist, poet. Hamlet, in *Hamlet*, act 3, sc. 4, to Gertrude.

31 Men's evil manners live in brass, their virtues
We write in water.

WILLIAM SHAKESPEARE (1564–1616), English dramatist, poet. Griffith, in *King Henry VIII*, act 4, sc. 2.

32 What is virtue but the Trade Unionism of the married?

GEORGE BERNARD SHAW (1856–1950), Anglo-Irish playwright, critic. Don Juan, in *Man and Superman*, act 3.

33 There are nine hundred and ninety-nine patrons of virtue to one virtuous man.

HENRY DAVID THOREAU (1817–62), U.S. philosopher, author, naturalist. *On the Duty of Civil Disobedience* (1849).

34 Be virtuous and you will be eccentric.

MARK TWAIN (1835–1910), U.S. author. Motto, in *Mental Photographs* (first published 1869; repr. in *Complete Humourous Sketches and Tales*, ed. by Charles Neider, 1961).

See also La Rochefoucauld, Montaigne on CHASTITY; Twain on EXAMPLE; Wordsworth on GOOD DEEDS; La Rochefoucauld on GOODNESS; Martineau on LAWS & THE LAW; Montagu on NECESSITY; Butler on PLEASURE; Paine on POSTERITY; Crisp on REWARD; Butler, Dahlberg on VICE.

VIRTUE AND VICE

1 There are in every man, always, two simultaneous allegiances, one to God, the other to Satan. Invocation of God, or Spirituality, is a desire to climb higher; that of Satan, or animality, is delight in descent.

CHARLES BAUDELAIRE (1821–67), French poet. *My Heart Laid Bare* (written c. 1865; published in *Intimate Journals*, sct. 41, 1887; tr. by Christopher Isherwood, 1930; rev. by Don Bachardy, 1989).

2 I begin to find out that nothing but virtue will do in this damned world. I am tolerably sick of vice which I have tried in its agreeable varieties, and mean on my return to cut all my dissolute acquaintance and leave off wine and "carnal company," and betake myself to politics and Decorum.

LORD BYRON (1788–1824), English poet. Letter, 5 May 1810 (published in *Byron's Letters and Journals*, vol. 1, ed. by Leslie A. Marchand, 1973). For the opposite view, see Byron on VICE.

3 If he does really think that there is no distinction between virtue and vice, why, Sir, when he leaves our houses let us count our spoons.

SAMUEL JOHNSON (1709–84), English author, lexicographer. Quoted in: James Boswell, *Life of Samuel Johnson*, 14 July 1763 (1791).

4 All good things were at one time bad things; every original sin has developed into an original virtue.

FRIEDRICH NIETZSCHE (1844–1900), German philosopher. *The Genealogy of Morals*, Essay 3, "What Do Ascetic Ideals Mean?," aph. 9 (1887).

5 Nature has not got two voices, you know, one of them condemning all day what the other commands.

MARQUIS DE SADE (1740–1814), French author. Dolmancé, in *Philosophy in the Bedroom*, "Dialogue the Fifth" (1795).

6 It is queer how it is always one's virtues and not one's vices that precipitate one into disaster.

REBECCA WEST (1892–1983), British author. *There Is No Conversation*, ch. 1 (1935).

VISION

1 Perhaps our eyes are merely a blank film which is taken from us after our deaths to be developed elsewhere and screened as our life story in some infernal cinema or despatched as microfilm into the sidereal void.

JEAN BAUDRILLARD (b. 1929), French semiologist. *Cool Memories*, ch. 2 (1987; tr. 1990).

2 As a man is, so he sees. As the eye is formed, such are its powers.

WILLIAM BLAKE (1757–1827), English poet, painter, engraver. Letter, 23 Aug. 1799 (published in *The Letters of William Blake*, 1956).

3 One eye sees, the other feels.

PAUL KLEE (1879–1940), Swiss artist. *The Diaries of Paul Klee 1898–1918*, no. 937 (1957; tr. 1965), 1914 entry.

4 If only we could pull out our brain and use only our eyes.

PABLO PICASSO (1881–1973), Spanish artist. *Saturday Review* (1 Sept. 1956).

VISIONARIES

1 How beautiful upon the mountains are the feet of him that bringeth good tidings, that publisheth peace.

BIBLE, HEBREW. *Isaiah* 52:7.

2 Where there is no vision, the people perish.

BIBLE, HEBREW. *Proverbs* 29:18. President John F. Kennedy had quoted this passage on the eve of his assassination in Dallas, Texas. Quoted in: Theodore C. Sorenson, *Kennedy*, Epilogue (1965).

3 "When the sun rises, do you not see a round disc of fire somewhat like a guinea?" O no, no, I see an innumerable company of the heavenly host crying "Holy, Holy, Holy is the Lord God Almighty."

> WILLIAM BLAKE (1757–1827), English poet, painter, engraver. *A Vision of the Last Judgement* (1810; repr. in *Complete Writings*, ed. by Geoffrey Keynes, 1957).

4   The world values the seer above all men, and has always done so. Nay, it values all men in proportion as they partake of the character of seers. The Elgin Marbles and a decision of John Marshall are valued for the same reason. What we feel in them is a painstaking submission to facts beyond the author's control, and to ideas imposed upon him by his vision. So with Beethoven's Symphonies, with Adam Smith's "Wealth of Nations"—with any conceivable output of the human mind of which you approve. You love them because you say, "These things were not made, they were seen."

> JOHN JAY CHAPMAN (1862–1933), U.S. author. *Practical Agitation*, ch. 6 (1898).

5   Nothing is so easy to fake as the inner vision.

> ROBERTSON DAVIES (b. 1913), Canadian novelist, journalist. Saraceni, in *What's Bred in the Bone*, pt. 4, "What Would Not out of the Flesh?" (1985).

6   I have nothing new to teach the world. Truth and Non-violence are as old as the hills. All I have done is to try experiments in both on as vast a scale as I could.

> MOHANDAS K. GANDHI (1869–1948), Indian political and spiritual leader. *Harijan* (28 March 1936).

7   The business of a seer is to see; and if he involves himself in the kind of God-eclipsing activities which make seeing impossible, he betrays the trust which his fellows have tacitly placed in him.

> ALDOUS HUXLEY (1894–1963), British novelist. *Grey Eminence*, ch. 10 (1941).

8   I just want to do God's will. And He's allowed me to go up to the mountain. And I've looked over, and I've seen the Promised Land.

> MARTIN LUTHER KING, JR. (1929–68), U.S. clergyman, civil rights leader. Speech, 3 April 1968, Memphis, Tenn., the day before his assassination. The epitaph on King's tomb, in South View Cemetery, Atlanta, Georgia, reads: Free at last, Free at last/ Thank God Almighty/ I'm free at last (a reference to the spiritual with which King often closed his speeches).

9   There are lone figures armed only with ideas, sometimes with just one idea, who blast away whole epochs in which we are enwrapped like mummies. Some are powerful enough to resurrect the dead. Some steal on us unawares and put a spell over us which it takes centuries to throw off. Some put a curse on us, for our stupidity and inertia, and then it seems as if God himself were unable to lift it.

> HENRY MILLER (1891–1980), U.S. author. *The Air-Conditioned Nightmare*, "With Edgar Varèse in the Gobi Desert" (1945).

10   St. Teresa of Avila described our life in this world as like a night at a second-class hotel.

> MALCOLM MUGGERIDGE (1903–90), British broadcaster. Quoted in: *Observer* (London, 20 March 1983).

11   I know my fate. One day there will be associated with my name the recollection of something frightful—of a crisis like no other before on earth, of the profound-

est collision of conscience, of a decision evoked *against* everything that until then had been believed in, demanded, sanctified. I am not a man I am dynamite.

> FRIEDRICH NIETZSCHE (1844–1900), German philosopher. *Ecce Homo*, "Why I Am a Destiny" (1888).

12   Lycurgus, Numa, Moses, Jesus Christ, Mohammed, all these great rogues, all these great thought-tyrants, knew how to associate the divinities they fabricated with their own boundless ambition.

> MARQUIS DE SADE (1740–1814), French author. Dolmancé, in *Philosophy in the Bedroom*, "Dialogue the Fifth: Yet Another Effort, Frenchmen, If You Would Become Republicans" (1795).

13   You see things; and you say "Why?" But I dream things that never were; and I say "Why not?"

> GEORGE BERNARD SHAW (1856–1950), Anglo-Irish playwright, critic. The Serpent, in *Back to Methuselah*, "In the Beginning," act 1. These words are often associated with Robert Kennedy after they were quoted by him in an address to the Irish Parliament in Dublin, June 1963, and attributed to him by Edward Kennedy at Robert's funeral service in 1968.

See also Rushdie on ART; Hebrew Bible on PROPHETS.

VITALITY

1   We derive our vitality from our store of madness.

> E. M. CIORAN (b. 1911), Rumanian-born French philosopher. *The Temptation to Exist*, title essay (1956).

2   Of all natural forces, vitality is the incommunicable one. . . . Vitality never "takes." You have it or you haven't it, like health or brown eyes or a baritone voice.

> F. SCOTT FITZGERALD (1896–1940), U.S. author. "The Crack-Up," in *Esquire* (1936; repr. in *The Crack-Up*, ed. by Edmund Wilson, 1945). Fitzgerald illustrated this view of vitality with a biblical quote: see Bible: New Testament on DISCIPLES.

3   I'm tired of everlastingly being unnatural and never doing anything I want to do. I'm tired of acting like I don't eat more than a bird, and walking when I want to run and saying I feel faint after a waltz, when I could dance for two days and never get tired. I'm tired of saying, "How wonderful you are!" to fool men who haven't got one-half the sense I've got, and I'm tired of pretending I don't know anything, so men can tell me things and feel important while they're doing it.

> MARGARET MITCHELL (1900–1949), U.S. novelist. Scarlett O'Hara, in *Gone with the Wind*, vol. 1, pt. 1, ch. 5 (1936).

4   The only virtue a character needs to possess between hardcovers, even if he bears a real person's name, is vitality: if he comes to life in our imaginations, he passes the test.

> STEPHEN VIZINCZEY (b. 1933), Hungarian novelist, critic. "Condemned World, Literary Kingdom," review of Mailer, *Armies of the Night*, in *Times Saturday Review* (London, 21 Sept. 1968; repr. in *Truth and Lies in Literature*, 1986).

See also LIFE, LUST FOR; Fitzgerald on PERSEVERANCE.

VOCATION

1   There is no way to penetrate the surface of life but by attacking it earnestly at a particular point.

> CHARLES HORTON COOLEY (1864–1929), U.S. sociologist. *Human Nature and the Social Order*, ch. 4 (1902).

2   Once you get into this great stream of history you can't get out. You can drown. Or you can be pulled ashore by the tide. But it is awfully hard to get out when you are in the middle of the stream—if it is intended that you stay there.

> RICHARD M. NIXON (b. 1913), U.S. Republican politician, president. Quoted in: Earl Mazo, *Richard Nixon: A Political and Personal Portrait*, ch. 10 (1959), on revoking his decision to retire in 1954.

3   This is the true joy in life, the being used for a purpose recognized by yourself as a mighty one; the being thoroughly worn out before you are thrown on the scrap heap; the being a force of Nature instead of a feverish selfish little clod of ailments and grievances complaining that the world will not devote itself to making you happy.

> GEORGE BERNARD SHAW (1856–1950), Anglo-Irish playwright, critic. *Man and Superman*, "Epistle Dedicatory" (1903).

4   The test of a vocation is the love of the drudgery it involves.

> LOGAN PEARSALL SMITH (1865–1946), U.S. essayist, aphorist. *Afterthoughts*, "Art and Letters" (1931).

5   Many people mistake our work for our vocation. Our vocation is the love of Jesus.

> MOTHER TERESA (b. 1910), Roman Catholic missionary in India. From documentary film, *Mother Teresa*. Quoted in: *New York Times* (28 Nov. 1986).

6   Sweetest Lord, make me appreciative of the dignity of my high vocation, and its many responsibilities. Never permit me to disgrace it by giving way to coldness, unkindness, or impatience.

> MOTHER TERESA (b. 1910), Albanian-born Roman Catholic missionary. *A Gift for God*, "Love to Pray" (1975).

VOTING

1   Suffrage is the pivotal right.

> SUSAN B. ANTHONY (1820–1906), U.S. suffragette. "The Status of Women, Past, Present and Future," in *Arena* (May 1897).

2   The fact that a man is to vote forces him to think. You may preach to a congregation by the year and not affect its thought because it is not called upon for definite action. But throw your subject into a campaign and it becomes a challenge.

> JOHN JAY CHAPMAN (1862–1933), U.S. author. *Practical Agitation*, ch. 7 (1898).

3   The average man votes below himself; he votes with half a mind or a hundredth part of one. A man ought to vote with the whole of himself, as he worships or gets married. A man ought to vote with his head and heart, his soul and stomach, his eye for faces and his ear for music; also (when sufficiently provoked) with his hands and feet. If he has ever seen a fine sunset, the crimson colour of it should creep into his vote. . . . The question is not so much whether only a minority of the electorate votes. The point is that only a minority of the voter votes.

> G. K. CHESTERTON (1874–1936), British author. *Tremendous Trifles*, "A Glimpse of My Country" (1909).

4   Constantly choosing the lesser of two evils is still choosing evil.

> JERRY GARCIA (b. 1942), U.S. rock musician. *Rolling Stone* (New York, 30 Nov. 1989).

5   The ignorance of one voter in a democracy impairs the security of all.

> JOHN F. KENNEDY (1917–63), U.S. Democratic politician, president. Speech, 18 May 1963, Vanderbilt University, Nashville, Tenn.

6   The ballot is stronger than the bullet.

> ABRAHAM LINCOLN (1809–65), U.S. president. Speech, 19 May 1856, Bloomington, Ill.

7   The effort to calculate exactly what the voters want at each particular moment leaves out of account the fact that when they are troubled the thing the voters most want is to be told what to want.

> WALTER LIPPMANN (1889–1974), U.S. journalist. "The Bogey of Public Opinion," in *Vanity Fair* (New York, Dec. 1931).

8   It's not the voting that's democracy, it's the counting.

> TOM STOPPARD (b. 1937), British playwright. Dotty, in *Jumpers*, act 1.

9   All voting is a sort of gaming, like checkers or backgammon, with a slight moral tinge to it, a playing with right and wrong.

> HENRY DAVID THOREAU (1817–62), U.S. philosopher, author, naturalist. *On the Duty of Civil Disobedience* (1849).

10   Voters don't decide issues, they decide *who* will decide issues.

> GEORGE F. WILL (b. 1941), U.S. political columnist. *Newsweek* (New York, 8 March 1976).

See also ELECTIONS.

VULGARITY

1   The vulgar man is always the most distinguished, for the very desire to be distinguished is vulgar.

> G. K. CHESTERTON (1874–1936), British author. *All Things Considered*, "The Boy" (1908).

2   It's only with great vulgarity that you can achieve real refinement, only out of bawdry that you can get tenderness.

> LAWRENCE DURRELL (1912–1990), British author. Interview in *Writers at Work* (Second Series, ed. by George Plimpton, 1963).

3   Very notable was his distinction between coarseness and vulgarity (coarseness, revealing something; vulgarity, concealing something).

> E. M. FORSTER (1879–1970), British novelist, essayist. *The Longest Journey*, ch. 26 (1907), on Anthony Eustace Failing's *Essays*.

4   It is an immense loss to have all robust and sustaining expletives refined away from one! At . . . moments of trial refinement is a feeble reed to lean upon.

> ALICE JAMES (1848–92), U.S. diarist, sister of Henry and William James. Letter, 12 Dec. 1889 to her brother, psychologist William James (published in *The Diary of Alice James*, ed. by Leon Edel, 1964).

5   coarse
jocosity
catches the crowd
shakespeare
and i
are often
low browed

> DON MARQUIS (1878–1937), U.S. humorist, journalist. *archy and mehitabel*, "archy confesses" (1927).

6   The higher a man stands, the more the word "vulgar" becomes unintelligible to him.

> JOHN RUSKIN (1819–1900), English art critic, author. *Modern Painters*, vol. 3, pt. 4, ch. 7, sct. 9 (1856).

7   Vulgarity is, in reality, nothing but a modern, chic, pert descendant of the goddess Dullness.

> EDITH SITWELL (1887–1964), British poet, critic. *Taken Care Of*, ch. 19 (1965).

8   Vulgarity is simply the conduct of other people.

> OSCAR WILDE (1854–1900), Anglo-Irish playwright, author. Lord Goring, in *An Ideal Husband*, act 3. Wilde uttered similar words himself in responding to criticisms of his house as "vulgar," when he said, "Vulgarity is the conduct of others." Quoted in: H. Montgomery Hyde, *Oscar Wilde*, ch. 3 (1976).

9   Whatever harsh criticisms may be passed on the construction of her sentences, she at least possesses that one touch of vulgarity that makes the whole world kin.

> OSCAR WILDE (1854–1900), Anglo-Irish playwright, author. Book review, in *Pall Mall Gazette* (London, 28 Oct. 1886).

WALES AND THE WELSH

1   Lovely the woods, waters, meadows, combes, vales,
All the air things wear that build this world of Wales.

> GERARD MANLEY HOPKINS (1844–89), English poet, Jesuit priest. *In the Valley of the Elwy*, st. 2.

2   An impotent people,
Sick with inbreeding,
Worrying the carcase of an old song.

> R. S. THOMAS (b. 1913), Welsh poet, clergyman. *Welsh Landscape*.

3   We can trace almost all the disasters of English history to the influence of Wales.

> EVELYN WAUGH (1903–66), British novelist. Dr. Fagan, in *Decline and Fall*, pt. 1, ch. 8 (1928).

WALKING

1   When one walks, one is brought into touch first of all with the essential relations between one's physical powers and the character of the country; one is com-pelled to see it as its natives do. Then every man one meets is an individual. One is no longer regarded by the whole population as an unapproachable and uninterest-ing animal to be cheated and robbed.

> ALEISTER CROWLEY (1875–1947), British occultist. *The Confessions of Aleister Crowley*, ch. 67 (1929; rev. 1970).

2   If a walker is indeed an individualist there is nowhere he can't go at dawn and not many places he can't go at noon. But just as it demeans life to live alongside a great river you can no longer swim in or drink from, to be crowded into safer areas and hours takes much of the gloss off walking—one sport you shouldn't have to reserve a time and a court for.

> EDWARD HOAGLAND (b. 1932), U.S. novelist, essayist. "City Walking," in *New York Times Book Review* (1 June 1975; repr. in "Heart's Desire," 1988).

3   The true charm of pedestrianism does not lie in the walking, or in the scenery, but in the talking. The walking is good to time the movement of the tongue by, and to keep the blood and the brain stirred up and active; the scenery and the woodsy smells are good to bear in upon a man an unconscious and unobtrusive charm and solace to eye and soul and sense; but the supreme pleasure comes from the talk.

> MARK TWAIN (1835–1910), U.S. author. *A Tramp Abroad*, ch. 23 (1880).

WAR

1   O can't you see, brother—
Death's a congested road for fighters now,
and hero a cheap label.

> C. D. ANDREWS (1913–92), British poet, scholar. *To a Pilot Lost in Aragón*, in *London Town*, no. 459 (March 1938).

2   The chief reason warfare is still with us is neither a secret death-wish of the human species, nor an irrepress-ible instinct of aggression, nor, finally and more plausi-bly, the serious economic and social dangers inherent in disarmament, but the simple fact that no substitute for this final arbiter in international affairs has yet appeared on the political scene.

> HANNAH ARENDT (1906–75), German-born U.S. political philosopher. *Crises of the Republic*, sct. 1, "On Violence" (1972).

3   From the happy expression on their faces you might have supposed that they welcomed the war. I have met with men who loved stamps, and stones, and snakes, but I could not imagine any man loving war.

> MARGOT ASQUITH (1864–1945), British socialite. *The Autobiography of Margot Asquith*, vol. 2, ch. 7 (1922), said of the crowds outside Downing Street, 3 Aug. 1914, the eve of the declaration of World War I.

4   War both needs and generates certain virtues; not the highest, but what may be called the preliminary virtues, as valour, veracity, the spirit of obedience, the habit of discipline. Any of these, and of others like them, when possessed by a nation, and no matter how generated, will give them a military advantage, and make them more likely to *stay* in the race of nations.

WALTER BAGEHOT (1826–77), English economist, critic. *Physics and Politics,* ch. 2, sct. 3 (1872).

5 The cannon thunders . . . limbs fly in all directions . . . one can hear the groans of victims and the howling of those performing the sacrifice . . . it's Humanity in search of happiness.

CHARLES BAUDELAIRE (1821–67), French poet. Appendix to *Prose Poems,* "Plans and Notes: For Civil War" (published in *Complete Works,* vol. 1, "Shorter Prose Poems," ed. by Yves-Gérard le Dantec; rev. by Claude Pichois, 1953).

6 It takes twenty years or more of peace to make a man; it takes only twenty seconds of war to destroy him.

BAUDOUIN I (b. 1930), King of Belgium from 1951. Address, 12 May 1959, to joint session of U.S. Congress.

7 If we justify war, it is because all peoples always justify the traits of which they find themselves possessed, not because war will bear an objective examination of its merits.

RUTH BENEDICT (1887–1948), U.S. anthropologist. *Patterns of Culture,* ch. 1 (1934).

8 All war represents a failure of diplomacy.

TONY BENN (b. 1925), British Labour politician. Speech, 28 Feb. 1991, to House of Commons, the day the Gulf War ended.

9 The inevitableness, the idealism, and the blessing of war, as an indispensable and stimulating law of development, must be repeatedly emphasized.

FRIEDRICH VON BERNHARDI (1849–1930), German soldier, military writer. *Germany and the Next War,* ch. 1 (1912). This book, translated and widely diffused in cheap editions, did much to exacerbate anti-German sentiments before and during World War I.

10 Saul hath slain his thousands, and David his ten thousands.

BIBLE, HEBREW. *1 Samuel* 18:7.

11 Anyone who has ever looked into the glazed eyes of a soldier dying on the battlefield will think hard before starting a war.

OTTO VON BISMARCK (1815–98), Prussian statesman. Speech, Aug. 1867, Berlin.

12 Hell and damnation,
life is such fun
with a ragged greatcoat
and a Jerry gun!

ALEXANDER BLOK (1880–1921), Russian poet. *The Twelve,* sct. 3

13 The wrong war, at the wrong place, at the wrong time, and with the wrong enemy.

OMAR BRADLEY (1893–1981), U.S. general. Speech, May 1951, to Senate inquiry into General MacArthur's proposal to carry the Korean conflict into China.

14 The Angel of Death has been abroad throughout the land, you may almost hear the beating of his wings.

JOHN BRIGHT (1811–89), English radical politician. Speech, 23 Feb. 1855, to the House of Commons, appealing for an armistice in the Crimean War.

15 "Let there be light!" said God, and there was light! "Let there be blood!" says man, and there's a sea!

LORD BYRON (1788–1824), English poet. *Don Juan,* cto. 7, st. 41

16 War's a brain-spattering, windpipe-slitting art.

LORD BYRON (1788–1824), English poet. *Don Juan,* cto. 9, st. 4.

17 We used to wonder where war lived, what it was that made it so vile. And now we realize that we know where it lives, that it is inside ourselves.

ALBERT CAMUS (1913–60), French-Algerian philosopher, author. *Notebooks,* vol. 3 (1966), entry for 7 Sept. 1939

18 There is nothing so subject to the inconstancy of fortune as war.

MIGUEL DE CERVANTES (1547–1616), Spanish writer. Don Quixote, in *Don Quixote,* pt. 1, bk. 1, ch. 8 (1605; tr. by P. Motteux).

19 The sinews of war, a limitless supply of money.

CICERO (106–43 B.C.), Roman orator, philosopher. *Philippics,* Oration 5, sct. 5.

20 War is regarded as nothing but the continuation of politics by other means.

KARL VON CLAUSEWITZ (1780–1831), Prussian soldier, strategist. *On War,* Preface (1832).

21 A "just war" is hospitable to every self-deception on the part of those waging it, none more than the certainty of virtue, under whose shelter every abomination can be committed with a clear conscience.

ALEXANDER COCKBURN (b. 1941), Anglo-Irish journalist. *New Statesman and Society* (London, 8 Feb. 1991).

22 That strange feeling we had in the war. Have you found anything in your lives since to equal it in strength? A sort of splendid carelessness it was, holding us together.

NOËL COWARD (1899–1973), British playwright, actor, composer. John Cavan, in *Post-Mortem,* sc. 6.

23 Our young people have come to look upon war as a kind of beneficent deity, which not only adds to the national honor but uplifts a nation and develops patriotism and courage. That is all true. But it is only fair, too, to let them know that the garments of the deity are filthy and that some of her influences debase and befoul a people.

REBECCA HARDING DAVIS (1831–1910), U.S. writer, journalist. *Bits of Gossip,* ch. 5 (1904).

24 War is the trade of Kings.

JOHN DRYDEN (1631–1700), English poet, dramatist, critic. Arthur, in *King Arthur,* act 2, sc. 2.

25 America is addicted to wars of distraction.

BARBARA EHRENREICH (b. 1941), U.S. author, columnist. *Times* (London, 22 April 1991).

26 War is not a life: it is a situation,
One which may neither be ignored nor accepted.

T. S. ELIOT (1888–1965), Anglo-American poet, critic. *A Note on War Poetry,* st. 5.

27 Those who actually set out to see the fall of a city . . . or those who choose to go to a front line, are obviously asking themselves to what extent they are cowards. But the tests they set themselves—there is a dead body, can you bear to look at it?—are nothing in comparison with the tests that are sprung on them. It is not the obvious tests that matter (do you go to pieces in a mortar attack?) but the unexpected ones (here is a man on the run, seeking your help—can you face him honestly?).

JAMES FENTON (b. 1949), British poet, critic. "The Fall of Saigon," in *Granta*, no. 15 (Cambridge, England, 1985; repr. in *All the Wrong Places*, 1988).

28 I don't believe that the big men, the politicians and the capitalists alone are guilty of the war. Oh, no, the little man is just as keen, otherwise the people of the world would have risen in revolt long ago! There is an urge and rage in people to destroy, to kill, to murder, and until all mankind, without exception, undergoes a great change, wars will be waged, everything that has been built up, cultivated and grown, will be destroyed and disfigured, after which mankind will have to begin all over again.

ANNE FRANK (1929–45), German Jewish refugee, diarist. *The Diary of a Young Girl* (1947; tr. 1952), entry for 3 May 1944.

29 What vast additions to the conveniences and comforts of living might mankind have acquired, if the money spent in wars had been employed in works of public utility; what an extension of agriculture even to the tops of our mountains; what rivers rendered navigable, or joined by canals; what bridges, acqueducts, new roads, and other public works, edifices, and improvements . . . might not have been obtained by spending those millions in doing good, which in the last war have been spent in doing mischief.

BENJAMIN FRANKLIN (1706–90), U.S. statesman, writer. Letter, 27 July 1783, to Sir Joseph Banks, President of the Royal Society, after the American War of Independence (published in *Complete Works*, vol. 8, ed. by John Bigelow, 1887–88).

30 Morality is contraband in war.

MOHANDAS K. GANDHI (1869–1948), Indian political and spiritual leader. *Non-Violence in Peace and War*, vol. 1, ch. 268 (1942).

31 Unless they are immediate victims, the majority of mankind behaves as if war was an act of God which could not be prevented; or they behave as if war elsewhere was none of their business. It would be a bitter cosmic joke if we destroy ourselves due to atrophy of the imagination.

MARTHA GELLHORN (b. 1908), U.S. journalist, author. *The Face of War*, Introduction (1959; rev. 1967).

32 I feel sure that *coups d'état* would go much better if there were seats, boxes, and stalls so that one could see what was happening and not miss anything.

EDMOND (1822–96) AND JULES DE GONCOURT (1830–70), French writers, journalists. *The Goncourt Journals* (1888–96; repr. in *Pages from the Goncourt Journal*, ed. by Robert Baldick, 1962), Dec. 1851 entry.

33 War is the great scavenger of thought. It is the sovereign disinfectant, and its red stream of blood is the Condy's Fluid that cleans out the stagnant pools and clotted channels of the intellect. . . . We have awakened from an opium-dream of comfort, of ease, of that miserable poltroonery of "the sheltered life." Our wish for indulgence of every sort, our laxity of manners, our wretched sensitiveness to personal inconvenience, these are suddenly lifted before us in their true guise as the spectres of national decay; and we have risen from the lethargy of our dilettantism to lay them, before it is too late, by the flashing of the unsheathed sword.

SIR EDMUND GOSSE (1849–1928), English poet, critic. *Inter Arma*, "War and Literature" (1916).

34 Frankly, I'd like to see the government get out of war altogether and leave the whole field to private industry.

JOSEPH HELLER (b. 1923), U.S. novelist. Milo Minderbinder, in *Catch-22*, ch. 24 (1955).

35 I was always embarrassed by the words sacred, glorious and sacrifice and the expression in vain. We had heard them, sometimes standing in the rain almost out of earshot, so that only the shouted words came through, and had read them, on proclamations that were slapped up by billposters over other proclamations, now for a long time, and I had seen nothing sacred, and the things that were glorious had no glory and the sacrifices were like the stockyards at Chicago if nothing was done with the meat except to bury it.

ERNEST HEMINGWAY (1899–1961), U.S. author. Frederic Henry, in *A Farewell to Arms*, ch. 27 (1929).

36 Force, and fraud, are in war the two cardinal virtues.

THOMAS HOBBES (1588–1679), English philosopher. *Leviathan*, pt. 1, ch. 13 (1651).

37 War has been the most convenient pseudo-solution for the problems of twentieth-century capitalism. It provides the incentives to modernisation and technological revolution which the market and the pursuit of profit do only fitfully and by accident, it makes the unthinkable (such as votes for women and the abolition of unemployment) not merely thinkable but practicable. . . . What is equally important, it can re-create communities of men and give a temporary sense to their lives by uniting them against foreigners and outsiders. This is an achievement beyond the power of the private enterprise economy . . . when left to itself.

E. J. HOBSBAWM (b. 1917), British historian. *Observer* (London), 26 May 1968).

38 Here dead lie we because we did not choose
To live and shame the land from which we sprung.
Life, to be sure, is nothing much to lose;
But young men think it is, and we were young.

A. E. HOUSMAN (1859–1936), British poet, classical scholar. *More Poems*, no. 36 (1936).

39 War seems to be one of the most salutary phenomena for the culture of human nature; and it is not without regret that I see it disappearing more and more from the scene.

KARL WILHELM VON HUMBOLDT (1767–1835), German statesman, philologist. *Limits of State Action*, ch. 5 (1792; repr. 1854; tr. and ed. by J. W. Burrow, 1969).

40 A democracy which makes or even effectively prepares for modern, scientific war must necessarily cease to be democratic. No country can be really well prepared for modern war unless it is governed by a tyrant, at the head of a highly trained and perfectly obedient bureaucracy.

> ALDOUS HUXLEY (1894–1963), British author. *Ends and Means,* ch. 7 (1937).

41 What we believe is more important than our material existence, therefore warfare is a legitimate extension of values.

> EDWARD JOHNSON (b. 1915), U.S. author, educator. *Independent* (London, 26 April 1988).

42 Oh, the brave Music of a distant Drum!

> OMAR KHAYYÁM (11th–12th century A.D.), Persian astronomer, poet. *The Rubáiyát of Omar Khayyám,* st. 12 (tr. by Edward Fitzgerald; first ed. 1859).

43 If any question why we died,
Tell them, because our fathers lied.

> RUDYARD KIPLING (1865–1936), British author, poet. *Common Form.*

44 The most persistent sound which reverberates through man's history is the beating of war drums.

> ARTHUR KOESTLER (1905–83), Hungarian-born British novelist, essayist. *Janus: A Summing Up,* "Prologue: The New Calendar," sct. 1 (1978).

45 Where do all the women who have watched so carefully over the lives of their beloved ones get the heroism to send them to face the cannon?

> KÄTHE KOLLWITZ (1867–1945), German artist. *Diaries and Letters* (ed. by Hans Kollwitz, 1955), entry for 27 Aug. 1914, made at the start of World War I.

46 War: first, one hopes to win; then one expects the enemy to lose; then, one is satisfied that he too is suffering; in the end, one is surprised that everyone has lost.

> KARL KRAUS (1874–1936), Austrian satirist. *Die Fackel,* no. 462/71 (Vienna, 9 Oct. 1917; repr. in Thomas Szasz, *Anti-Freud: Karl Kraus's Criticism of Psychoanalysis and Psychiatry,* ch. 8, 1976).

47 How is the world ruled and led to war? Diplomats lie to journalists and believe these lies when they see them in print.

> KARL KRAUS (1874–1936), Austrian satirist. *Nachts,* ch. 5 (1918; repr. in *Half-Truths and One-And-A Half-Truths: Selected Aphorisms,* "In this War we are Dealing . . .," ed. by Harry Zohn, 1976).

48 Those who have been immersed in the tragedy of massive death during wartime, and who have faced it squarely, never allowing their senses and feelings to become numbed and indifferent, have emerged from their experiences with growth and humanness greater than that achieved through almost any other means.

> ELISABETH KÜBLER-ROSS (b. 1926), Swiss-born U.S. psychiatrist. *Death: The Final Stage of Growth,* ch. 5 (1975).

49 The more prosperous and settled a nation, the more readily it tends to think of war as a regrettable accident; to nations less fortunate the chance of war presents itself as a possible bountiful friend.

> LEWIS H. LAPHAM (b. 1935), U.S. essayist, editor. "Notebook: Brave New World," in *Harper's* (New York, March 1991).

50 The war is dreadful. It is the business of the artist to follow it home to the heart of the individual fighters—not to talk in armies and nations and numbers—but to track it home.

> D. H. LAWRENCE (1885–1930), British author. Letter, 18 Nov. 1914, to editor Harriet Monroe (published in *The Letters of D. H. Lawrence,* vol. 2, ed. by George J. Zytaruk and James T. Boulton, 1981). Harriet Monroe had just published an issue of her magazine *Poetry* that featured war poems.

51 Of course in war all madnesses come out in a man, that is the fault of *war* not of a *man* or a *nation.*

> FRIEDA LAWRENCE (1879–1956), German wife of D. H. Lawrence. Letter, c. 13 Sept. 1914 (published in *The Letters of D. H. Lawrence,* vol. 2, ed. by George J. Zytaruk and James T. Boulton, 1981). Frieda's brother was the celebrated pilot Manfred von Richthofen—the "Red Baron."

52 There is no avoiding war; it can only be postponed to the advantage of others.

> NICCOLO MACHIAVELLI (1469–1527), Italian political philosopher, statesman. *The Prince,* ch. 3 (1514).

53 War is thus divine in itself, since it is a law of the world. War is divine through its consequences of a supernatural nature which are as much general as particular. . . . War is divine in the mysterious glory that surrounds it and in the no less inexplicable attraction that draws us to it. . . . War is divine by the manner in which it breaks out.

> JOSEPH DE MAISTRE (1753–1821), French diplomat, philosopher. *The Senator,* in *Les Soirées de Saint-Pétersbourg,* "Seventh Dialogue" (1821; repr. in *The Works of Joseph de Maistre,* ed. by Jack Lively, 1965).

54 Blunders are an inescapable feature of war, because choice in military affairs lies generally between the bad and the worse.

> ALLAN MASSIE (b. 1938), British author. Marshal Pétain, in *A Question of Loyalties,* pt. 3, ch. 11 (1989).

55 War will never cease until babies begin to come into the world with larger cerebrums and smaller adrenal glands.

> H. L. MENCKEN (1880–1956), U.S. journalist. *Minority Report: H. L. Mencken's Notebooks,* no. 164 (1956).

56 War is an ugly thing, but not the ugliest of things: the decayed and degraded state of moral and patriotic feeling which thinks nothing *worth* a war, is worse. . . . A war to protect other human beings against tyrannical injustice; a war to give victory to their own ideas of right and good, and which is their own war, carried on for an honest purpose by their own free choice—is often the means of their regeneration.

> JOHN STUART MILL (1806–73), English philosopher, economist. *Dissertations and Discussions,* "The Contest in America" (1859), written to oppose England's siding with the Confederacy during the American Civil War.

57 I regard almost all quarrels of princes on the same footing, and I see nothing that marks man's unreason so positively as war. Indeed, what folly to kill one another for interests often imaginary, and always for the pleasure of persons who do not think themselves even obliged to those who sacrifice themselves for them!

> LADY MARY WORTLEY MONTAGU (1689–1762), English society figure, letter writer. Letter, 12 July 1744 (published in *Selected Letters,* ed. by Robert Halsband, 1970).

58 War is the supreme drama of a completely mechanized society.

> LEWIS MUMFORD (1895–1990), U.S. social philosopher. *Technics and Civilization*, ch. 6, sct. 11 (1934).

59 War alone brings up to their highest tension all human energies and imposes the stamp of nobility upon the peoples who have the courage to make it.

> BENITO MUSSOLINI (1883–1945), Italian dictator. "The Political and Social Doctrine of Fascism," in the *Enciclopedia Italiana* (1932).

60 War has always been the grand sagacity of every spirit which has grown too inward and too profound; its curative power lies even in the wounds one receives.

> FRIEDRICH NIETZSCHE (1844–1900), German philosopher. *Twilight of the Idols*, Foreword (1889).

61 What the horrors of war are, no one can imagine. They are not wounds and blood and fever, spotted and low, or dysentery, chronic and acute, cold and heat and famine. They are intoxication, drunken brutality, demoralisation and disorder on the part of the inferior . . . jealousies, meanness, indifference, selfish brutality on the part of the superior.

> FLORENCE NIGHTINGALE (1820–1910), English nurse. Letter, 5 May 1855, to her family (published in *Forever Yours, Florence Nightingale: Selected Letters*, ch. 2, 1989), written while nursing on the Black Sea.

62 There is hardly such a thing as a war in which it makes no difference who wins. Nearly always one side stands more or less for progress, the other side more or less for reaction.

> GEORGE ORWELL (1903–50), British author. "Looking Back on the Spanish War" (1943; repr. in *Collected Essays*, 1961).

63 The quickest way of ending a war is to lose it.

> GEORGE ORWELL (1903–50), British author. "Second Thoughts on James Burnham," in *Polemic* (May 1946; repr. in *Shooting an Elephant*, 1950).

64 What passing-bells for these who die as cattle? Only the monstrous anger of the guns.

> WILFRED OWEN (1893–1918), British poet. *Anthem for Doomed Youth*.

65 To establish any mode to abolish war, however advantageous it might be to Nations, would be to take from such Government the most lucrative of its branches.

> THOMAS PAINE (1737–1809), Anglo-American political theorist, writer. *The Rights of Man*, pt. 1, "Conclusion" (1791).

66 The real trouble with war (modern war) is that it gives no one a chance to kill the right people.

> EZRA POUND (1885–1972), U.S. poet, critic. "Gaudier: A Postscript," in *Esquire* (New York, Aug. 1934; repr. in *Gaudier-Brzeska: a Memoir*, 1916; rev. 1960).

67 Wars are made to make debt.

> EZRA POUND (1885–1972), U.S. poet, critic. Interview in *Writers at Work* (Second Series, ed. by George Plimpton, 1963).

68 War begets quiet, quiet idleness, idleness disorder, disorder ruin; likewise ruin order, order virtue, virtue glory, and good fortune.

> SIR WALTER RALEGH (1552–1618), English author, soldier, explorer. *The Cabinet Council*, ch. 25, "A Collection of Political Observations" (repr. in *The Works of Sir Walter Raleigh*, vol. 1, 1751).

69 You can no more win a war than you can win an earthquake.

> JEANNETTE RANKIN (1880–1973), U.S. suffragist, politician. Quoted in: Hannah Josephson, *Jeanette Rankin: First Lady in Congress*, ch. 8 (1974).

70 Of the four wars in my lifetime, none came about because the U.S. was too strong.

> RONALD REAGAN (b. 1911), U.S. Republican politician, president. Quoted in: *Observer* (London, 29 June 1980).

71 War is a contagion.

> FRANKLIN D. ROOSEVELT (1882–1945), U.S. Democratic politician, president. Speech, 5 Oct. 1937, Chicago.

72 More than an end to war, we want an end to the beginnings of all wars.

> FRANKLIN D. ROOSEVELT (1882–1945), U.S. Democratic politician, president. Speech, 13 April 1945, prepared for Jefferson Day broadcast, the day after Roosevelt's sudden death at Warm Springs, Ga.

73 Those who dare to interpret God's will must never claim Him as an asset for one nation or group rather than another. War springs from the love and loyalty which should be offered to God being applied to some God substitute, one of the most dangerous being nationalism.

> ROBERT RUNCIE (b. 1921), British ecclesiastic, Archbishop of Canterbury. Sermon, 26 July 1982, at the Falkland Islands Thanksgiving Service, St. Paul's Cathedral, London.

74 I had supposed until that time that it was quite common for parents to love their children, but the war persuaded me that it is a rare exception. I had supposed that most people liked money better than almost anything else, but I discovered that they liked destruction even better. I had supposed that intellectuals frequently loved truth, but I found here again that not ten per cent of them prefer truth to popularity.

> BERTAND RUSSELL (1872–1970), British philosopher, mathematician. *The Autobiography of Bertrand Russell*, vol. 2, ch. 1 (1968), of World War I.

75 Are wars . . . anything but the means whereby a nation is nourished, whereby it is strengthened, whereby it is buttressed?

> MARQUIS DE SADE (1740–1814), French author. Dolmancé, in *Philosophy in the Bedroom*, "Dialogue the Fifth: Yet Another Effort, Frenchmen, If You Would Become Republicans" (1795).

76 War is not a true adventure. It is a mere ersatz. Where ties are established, where problems are set, where creation is stimulated—there you have adventure. But there is no adventure in heads-or-tails, in betting that the toss will come out of life or death. War is not an adventure. It is a disease. It is like typhus.

> ANTOINE DE SAINT-EXUPÉRY (1900–1944), French aviator, author. *Flight to Arras*, ch. 8 (1942).

77 To delight in war is a merit in the soldier, a dangerous quality in the captain, and a positive crime in the statesman.

> GEORGE SANTAYANA (1863–1952), U.S. philosopher, poet. *The Life of Reason*, "Reason in Society," ch. 3 (1905–6).

78 If it were not for the war,
This war
Would suit me down to the ground.
DOROTHY L. SAYERS (1893–1957), British author. "London Calling: Lord I Thank Thee."

79 We go to gain a little patch of ground
That hath in it no profit but the name.
WILLIAM SHAKESPEARE (1564–1616), English dramatist, poet. Captain, in *Hamlet*, act 4, sc. 4 (the passage in which the Captain's speech occurs is absent from the 1623 Folio ed.).

80 Cry "havoc!" and let loose the dogs of war,
That this foul deed shall smell above the earth
With carrion men, groaning for burial.
WILLIAM SHAKESPEARE (1564–1616), English dramatist, poet. Antony, in *Julius Caesar*, act 3, sc. 1.

81 In the arts of life man invents nothing; but in the arts of death he outdoes Nature herself, and produces by chemistry and machinery all the slaughter of plague, pestilence, and famine.
GEORGE BERNARD SHAW (1856–1950), Anglo-Irish playwright, critic. The Devil, in *Man and Superman*, act 3.

82 War is the statesman's game, the priest's delight,
The lawyer's jest, the hired assassin's trade.
PERCY BYSSHE SHELLEY (1792–1822), English poet. *Queen Mab*, pt. 4.

83 War-making is one of the few activities that people are not supposed to view "realistically;" that is, with an eye to expense and practical outcome. In all-out war, expenditure is all-out, unprudent—war being defined as an emergency in which no sacrifice is excessive.
SUSAN SONTAG (b. 1933), U.S. essayist. *AIDS and Its Metaphors*, ch. 1 (1989).

84 Hence that general is skilful in attack whose opponent does not know what to defend; and he is skilful in defense whose opponent does not know what to attack.
SUN TZU (6–5TH CENTURY B.C.), Chinese general. *The Art of War*, ch. 6, Axiom 9 (c. 490 B.C.; ed. by James Clavell, 1981).

85 I have a deep sympathy with war, it so apes the gait and bearing of the soul.
HENRY DAVID THOREAU (1817–62), U.S. philosopher, author, naturalist. *Journals* (1906), entry for 30 June 1840.

86 There are two things which will always be very difficult for a democratic nation: to start a war and to end it.
ALEXIS DE TOCQUEVILLE (1805–59), French social philosopher. *Democracy in America*, vol. 2, pt. 3, ch. 22 (1840). Tocqueville added, "All those who seek to destroy the freedom of the democratic nations must know that war is the surest and shortest means to accomplish this. That is the very first axiom of their science."

87 O Lord our God, help us to tear their soldiers to bloody shreds with our shells; help us to cover their smiling fields with the pale forms of their patriot dead; help us to drown the thunder of the guns with the shrieks of their wounded, writhing in pain; help us to lay waste their humble homes with a hurricane of fire; help us to wring the hearts of their unoffending widows with unavailing grief . . . for our sakes who adore Thee, Lord, blast their hopes, blight their lives, protract their bitter pilgrimage, make heavy their steps, water their way with their tears, stain the white snow with the blood of their wounded feet! We ask it, in the spirit of love, of Him Who is the Source of Love, and Who is the ever-faithful refuge and friend of all that are sore beset and seek His aid with humble and contrite hearts. Amen.
MARK TWAIN (1835–1910), U.S. author. The aged stranger, claiming to be God's messenger verbalizing a congregation's unspoken prayer, in *The War Prayer* (dictated 1904–5; published in *Complete Essays of Mark Twain*, ed. by Charles Neider, 1963).

88 To say that war is madness is like saying that sex is madness: true enough, from the standpoint of a stateless eunuch, but merely a provocative epigram for those who must make their arrangements in the world as given.
JOHN UPDIKE (b. 1932), U.S. author, critic. *Self-Consciousness: Memoirs*, ch. 4 (1989).

89 What war has always been is a puberty ceremony. It's a very rough one, but you went away a boy and came back a man, maybe with an eye missing or whatever but godammit you were a man and people had to call you a man thereafter.
KURT VONNEGUT, JR (b. 1922), U.S. novelist. *City Limits* (London, 11 March 1983).

90 A self-respecting nation is ready for anything, including war, except for a renunciation of its option to make war.
SIMONE WEIL (1909–43), French philosopher, mystic. "The Power of Words," in *Nouveaux Cahiers* (1 and 15 April 1937; repr. in *Selected Essays*, ed. by Richard Rees, 1962).

91 What a country calls its vital economic interests are not the things which enable its citizens to live, but the things which enable it to make war. Petrol is more likely than wheat to be a cause of international conflict.
SIMONE WEIL (1909–43), French philosopher, mystic. "The Power of Words," in *Nouveaux Cahiers* (1 and 15 April 1937; repr. in *Selected Essays*, ed. by Richard Rees, 1962).

92 As long as war is regarded as wicked, it will always have its fascination. When it is looked upon as vulgar, it will cease to be popular.
OSCAR WILDE (1854–1900), Anglo-Irish playwright, author. Gilbert, in *The Critic as Artist*, pt. 2 (published in *Intentions*, 1891).

93 If you insist upon fighting to protect me, or "our" country, let it be understood soberly and rationally between us that you are fighting to gratify a sex instinct which I cannot share; to procure benefits which I have not shared and probably will not share.
VIRGINIA WOOLF (1882–1941), British novelist. *Three Guineas* (1938; repr. 1977, p. 197).

94 I think it better that in times like these
A poet's mouth be silent, for in truth
We have no gift to set a statesman right.
W. B. YEATS (1865–1939), Irish poet, playwright. *On Being Asked for a War Poem*.

See also THE AMERICAN CIVIL WAR; Vegetius on THE ARMS RACE; Clemenceau, O'Casey on THE ARMY; Nietzsche on CAUSES; Dryden on CONQUEST; Croesus on FATHERS AND SONS; Napoleon on GENERALS; Lincoln on GLORY; Cleaver on GODS AND GODDESSES; GUERRILLA WARFARE; IRAQ AND THE SECOND GULF WAR; DeLillo on KILLING; Mussolini on NATIONALISM; THE NUCLEAR AGE: ARMAGEDDON; PACIFISM; Mao Zedong on POLITICS; Rich on RAPE; Lloyd George on SACRIFICE; Burroughs on THE UNIVERSE; VIETNAM; WAR AND PEACE; WAR CORRESPONDENTS; WAR CRIMES; WORLD WAR I; WORLD WAR II.

WAR AND PEACE

1 It is far easier to make war than to make peace.

GEORGES CLEMENCEAU (1841–1929), French statesman. Speech, 14 July 1919, Verdun, France.

2 No country has suffered so much from the ruins of war while being at peace as the American.

EDWARD DAHLBERG (1900–1977), U.S. author, critic. *Alms for Oblivion*, "No Love and No Thanks" (1964).

3 The triumphs of peace have been in some proximity to war. Whilst the hand was still familiar with the sword-hilt, whilst the habits of the camp were still visible in the port and complexion of the gentleman, his intellectual power culminated; the compression and tension of these stern conditions is a training for the finest and softest arts, and can rarely be compensated in tranquil times, except by some analogous vigor drawn from occupations as hardy as war.

RALPH WALDO EMERSON (1803–82), U.S. essayist, poet, philosopher. *The Conduct of Life*, "Power" (1860).

4 It is open to a war resister to judge between the combatants and wish success to the one who has justice on his side. By so judging he is more likely to bring peace between the two than by remaining a mere spectator.

MOHANDAS K. GANDHI (1869–1948), Indian political and spiritual leader. *Non-Violence in Peace and War*, vol. 1, ch. 241 (1942).

5 War is hell and all that, but it has a good deal to recommend it. It wipes out all the small nuisances of peacetime.

IAN HAY (1876–1952), British playwright, novelist. Wagstaffe, in *The First Hundred Thousand*, ch. 10 (1916). Among the "small nuisances," Wagstaffe listed suffragettes, futurism, the tango, party politics and golf-maniacs.

WAR CORRESPONDENTS

1 News of battle! News of battle!
Hark. 'Tis ringing down the street
And the archways and the pavement
Bear the clang of hurrying feet.
News of battle. Who has brought it?

W. E. AYTOUN (1813–65), Scottish poet. *Lays of the Scottish Cavaliers*.

2 Who could not be moved by the sight of that poor, demoralized rabble, outwitted, outflanked, outmanoeuvered by the U.S. military? Yet, given time, I think the press will bounce back.

JAMES BAKER (b. 1930), U.S. Republican politician, Secretary of State. Quoted in: *Guardian* (London, 26 March 1991), said of war correspondents in the Second Gulf War.

3 It took nine years, and a great depression, and two wars ending in defeat, and one surrender without war, to break my faith in the benign power of the press. Gradually I came to realize that people will more readily swallow lies than truth, as if the taste of lies was homey, appetizing: a habit.

MARTHA GELLHORN (b. 1908), U.S. journalist, author. *The Face of War*, Introduction (1959).

4 We came to fear something more complicated than death, an annihilation less final but more complete, and we got out. Because . . . we all knew that if you stayed too long you became one of those poor bastards who had to have a war on all the time, and where was that?

MICHAEL HERR (b. 1940), U.S. journalist. *Dispatches*, "Colleagues," sct. 3 (1977).

5 In a time of war the nation is always of one mind, eager to hear something good of themselves and ill of the enemy. At this time the task of news-writers is easy, they have nothing to do but to tell that a battle is expected, and afterwards that a battle has been fought, in which we and our friends, whether conquering or conquered, did all, and our enemies did nothing.

SAMUEL JOHNSON (1709–84), English author, lexicographer. *The Idler*, no. 30, in *Universal Chronicle* (London, 11 Nov. 1758; repr. in *Works of Samuel Johnson*, vol. 2, ed. by W. J. Bate, John M. Bullitt and L. F. Powell, 1963).

6 The heroes of obtrusiveness, people with whom no soldier would lie down in the trenches, though he has to submit to being interviewed by them, break into recently abandoned royal castles so that they can report, "We got there first!" It would be far less shameful to be paid for committing atrocities than for fabricating them.

KARL KRAUS (1874–1936), Austrian satirist. "In These Great Times," speech, 19 Nov. 1914, in Vienna (first published in *Die Fackel*, Vienna, Dec. 1914; repr. in *In These Great Times: A Karl Kraus Reader*, ed. by Harry Zohn, 1976).

7 I am no longer an artist, interested and curious. I am a messenger who will bring back word from the men who are fighting to those who want the war to go on for ever. Feeble, inarticulate, will be my message, but it will have a bitter truth, and may it burn their lousy souls.

PAUL NASH (1889–1946), British artist. Letter, 13 Nov. 1917, to his wife (published in *Outline: An Autobiography and Other Writings*, 1949).

8 I will put in my poems, that with you is heroism, upon land and sea—And
I will report all heroism from an American point of view.

WALT WHITMAN (1819–92), U.S. poet. *Starting From Paumanok*, sct. 7.

WAR CRIMES

1 I do not know a method of drawing up an indictment against a whole people.

EDMUND BURKE (1729–97), Irish philosopher, statesman. Speech, 22 March 1775, on conciliation with America.

2 A trial cannot be conducted by announcing the general culpability of a civilization. Only the actual deeds which, at least, stank in the nostrils of the entire world were brought to judgment.

ALBERT CAMUS (1913–60), French-Algerian philosopher, author. *The Rebel*, pt. 3, "State Terrorism and Irrational Terror" (1951; tr. 1953).

3 You cannot do justice to the dead. When we talk about doing justice to the dead we are talking about retribution for the harm done to them. But retribution and justice are two different things.

WILLIAM, LORD SHAWCROSS (b. 1902), British lawyer. *Daily Telegraph* (London, 1 May 1991), discussing the War Crimes Bill, which proposed to prosecute ex-Nazis living in Britain. Lord Shawcross was a prosecutor in the Nuremberg Trials following World War II.

4   There is no such thing as collective guilt.

KURT WALDHEIM (b. 1918), Austrian diplomate president. *International Herald Tribune* (Paris, 11 March 1988), on the charges of collaboration with the Nazi regime in Austria during World War II.

ANDY WARHOL

1   Ultimately Warhol's private moral reference was to the supreme kitsch of the Catholic church.

ALLEN GINSBERG (b. 1926), U.S. poet. *Andy Warhol: A Retrospective*, "A Collective Portrait of Andy Warhol" (1986).

2   Andy passes through things, but so do we. He sat down and had a talk with me. "You gotta decide what you want to do. Do you want to keep just playing museums from now on and the art festivals? Or do you want to start moving into other areas? Lou, don't you think you should think about it?" So I thought about it, and I fired him.

LOU REED (b. 1944), U.S. rock musician. Interview in *Rolling Stone* (New York, 4 May 1989).

3   My image is a statement of the symbols of the harsh, impersonal products and brash materialistic objects on which America is built today. It is a projection of everything that can be bought and sold, the practical but impermanent symbols that sustain us.

ANDY WARHOL (1928–87), U.S. Pop artist. "New Talent USA," in *Art in America*, vol. 50, no. 1 (New York, 1962).

4   If you want to know all about Andy Warhol, just look at the surface: of my paintings and films and me, and there I am. There's nothing behind it.

ANDY WARHOL (1928–87), U.S. Pop artist. "Warhol in his own Words," in *Los Angeles Free Press* (17 March 1967; repr. in *Andy Warhol: A Retrospective*, 1986).

5   The man whose heart is as warm as a hanky soaked in ethyl chloride.

EDMUND WHITE (b. 1940), U.S. author. *States of Desire: Travels in Gay America*, ch. 1 (1980).

GEORGE WASHINGTON

1   His mind was great and powerful, without being of the very first order; his penetration strong, though not so acute as that of a Newton, Bacon, or Locke; and as far as he saw, no judgment was ever sounder. It was slow in operation, being little aided by invention or imagination, but sure in conclusion.

THOMAS JEFFERSON (1743–1826), U.S. president. Letter, Jan. 1814.

2   As to you, sir, treacherous to private friendship (for so you have been to me, and that in the day of danger) and a hypocrite in public life, the world will be puzzled

to decide whether you are an apostate or an imposter, whether you have abandoned good principles or whether you ever had any.

THOMAS PAINE (1737–1809), Anglo-American political theorist, writer. Letter, 30 July 1796, to George Washington. Paine believed that Washington had abandoned him to imprisonment in France during the Reign of Terror.

3   We have exchanged the Washingtonian dignity for the Jeffersonian simplicity, which in due time came to be only another name for the Jacksonian vulgarity.

HENRY CODMAN POTTER (1835–1908), U.S. ecclesiastic. Speech, 30 April 1889, on the centennial of Washington, D.C.

4   The crude commercialism of America, its materialising spirit, its indifference to the poetical side of things, and its lack of imagination and of high unattainable ideals, are entirely due to that country having adopted for its national hero a man who, according to his own confession, was incapable of telling a lie, and it is not too much to say that the story of George Washington and the cherry-tree has done more harm, and in a shorter space of time, than any other moral tale in the whole of literature.

OSCAR WILDE (1854–1900), Anglo-Irish playwright, author. Vivian, in "The Decay of Lying" (published in *Intentions*, 1891).

See also Cooke on FESTIVALS.

WASHINGTON, D.C.

1   It is sometimes called the City of Magnificent Distances, but it might with greater propriety be termed the City of Magnificent Intentions. . . . Spacious avenues, that begin in nothing, and lead nowhere; streets, mile-long, that only want houses, roads, and inhabitants; public buildings that need but a public to be complete; and ornaments of great thoroughfares, which only lack great thoroughfares to ornament—are its leading features.

CHARLES DICKENS (1812–70), English novelist. *American Notes*, ch. 8 (1842).

2   In Washington, success is just a training course for failure.

SIMON HOGGART (b. 1946), British journalist. *America: A User's Guide*, ch. 1 (1990).

3   Washington is a city of Southern efficiency and Northern charm.

JOHN F. KENNEDY (1917–63), U.S. Democratic politician, president. Remark, quoted in: William Manchester, *Portrait of a President*, 1962).

4   Look a here people, listen to me,
Don't try to find no home in Washington, D.C.
Lord, it's a bourgeois town, it's a bourgeois town.

HUDDIE "LEADBELLY" LEDBETTER (1889–1949), U.S. blues musician. *Bourgeois Blues*. The song was written in collaboration with musicologist Alan Lomax, who had recorded Leadbelly in Louisiana State Prison in 1933 and 1934, and helped to obtain his pardon from there.

5   For the people in government, rather than the people who pester it, Washington is an early-rising, hard-working city. It is a popular delusion that the government wastes vast amounts of money through inefficiency and sloth. Enormous effort and elaborate planning are required to waste this much money.

> P. J. O'ROURKE (b. 1947), U.S. journalist. *Parliament of Whores*, "The Winners Go to Washington, D.C." (1991).

6 As a colored woman I might enter Washington any night, a stranger in a strange land, and walk miles without finding a place to lay my head. . . . The colored man alone is thrust out of the hotels of the national capital like a leper. . . . Surely nowhere in the world do oppression and persecution based solely on the color of the skin appear more hateful and hideous than in the capital of the United States, because the chasm between the principles upon which this Government was founded, in which it still professes to believe, and those which are daily practiced under the protection of the flag, yawn so wide and deep.

> MARY CHURCH TERRELL (1863–1954), U.S. educator, suffragist. "What It Means to Be Colored in the Capital of the United States" (1907; repr. in *A Colored Woman in a White World*, 1940).

7 Washington isn't a city, it's an abstraction.

> DYLAN THOMAS (1914–53), Welsh poet. Quoted in: John Malcolm Brinnin, *Dylan Thomas in America*, ch. 1 (1956).

8 Washington is a very easy city for you to forget where you came from and why you got there in the first place.

> HARRY S TRUMAN (1884–1972), U.S. Democratic politician, president. Quoted in: Merle Miller, *Plain Speaking: Conversations with Harry S. Truman*, ch. 11 (1973).

9 I date the end of the old republic and the birth of the empire to the invention, in the late thirties, of air conditioning. Before air conditioning, Washington was deserted from mid-June to September. . . . But after air conditioning and the Second World War arrived, more or less at the same time, Congress sits and sits while the presidents—or at least their staffs—never stop making mischief.

> GORE VIDAL (b. 1925), U.S. novelist, critic. *Armageddon? Essays 1983–1987*, "At Home in Washington, D.C." (1987).

10 Political life at Washington is like political life in a suburban vestry.

> OSCAR WILDE (1854–1900), Anglo-Irish playwright, author. "The American Invasion," in *Court and Society Review* (March 1887).

See also Wilde on CITIES AND CITY LIFE; Hoggarton DINNER PARTIES.

WASTE

1 The word which gives the key to the national vice is waste. And people who are wasteful are not wise, neither can they remain young and vigorous. In order to transmute energy to higher and more subtle levels one must first conserve it.

> HENRY MILLER (1891–1980), U.S. author. *The Air-Conditioned Nightmare*, "Dr. Souchon: Surgeon-Painter" (1945).

2 The waste of plenty is the resource of scarcity.

> THOMAS LOVE PEACOCK (1785–1866), English author. *Melincourt*, ch. 24 (1817).

3 We waste our lights in vain, like lamps by day.

> WILLIAM SHAKESPEARE (1564–1616), English dramatist, poet. Mercutio, in *Romeo and Juliet*, act 1, sc. 4, l. 45.

WATER

1 When the water of a place is bad it is safest to drink none that has not been filtered through either the berry of a grape, or else a tub of malt. These are the most reliable filters yet invented.

> SAMUEL BUTLER (1835–1902), English author. *Samuel Butler's Notebooks* (1951, p. 255).

2 A pool is, for many of us in the West, a symbol not of affluence but of order, of control over the uncontrollable. A pool is water, made available and useful, and is, as such, infinitely soothing to the western eye.

> JOAN DIDION (b. 1934), U.S. essayist. *The White Album*, "Holy Water" (1979; first published 1977).

3 No poems can please for long or live that are written by water-drinkers.

> HORACE (65–8 B.C.), Roman poet. *Epistles*, bk. 1, Epistle 19.

4 In the world there is nothing more submissive and weak than water. Yet for attacking that which is hard and strong nothing can surpass it.

> LAO-TZU (6TH CENTURY B.C.), Legendary Chinese philosopher. *Tao-te-ching* bk. 2, ch. 78 (tr. by T. C. Lau, 1963).

5 So let man consider of what he was created;
> he was created of gushing water
> issuing between the loins and the breast-bones.

> QUR'AN. *The Night-Star*, 86:5–7 (ed. by Arthur J. Arberry, 1955).

See also Horace, Spanish proverb on WINE.

WATERGATE AFFAIR

1 If the national security is involved, *anything goes*. There are no rules. There are people so lacking in roots about what is proper and what is improper that they don't know there's anything wrong in breaking into the headquarters of the opposition party.

> HELEN GAHAGAN DOUGLAS (1900–1980), U.S. author, actor, congresswoman. Quoted in: *Ms.* (New York, Oct. 1973).

2 There had been no thievery or venality. We had all simply wandered into a situation unthinkingly, trying to protect ourselves from what we saw as a political problem. Now, suddenly, it was like a Rorschach ink blot: others, looking at our actions, pointed out a pattern that we ourselves had not seen.

> RICHARD M. NIXON (b. 1913), U.S. Republican politician, president. *The Memoirs of Richard Nixon*, "The Presidency 1973" (1978).

3 Maybe this is like the Old Testament. It was visited upon us and maybe we're going to benefit from it.

> NELSON A. ROCKEFELLER (1908–79), U.S. Republican politician, vice president. Speech, 17 July 1973, New York City.

WEAKNESS

1 The weak have one weapon: the errors of those who think they are strong.

GEORGES BIDAULT (1899–1983), French resistance leader, statesman. Quoted in: *Observer* (London, 15 July 1962).

2 The weak are the most treacherous of us all. They come to the strong and drain them. They are bottomless. They are insatiable. They are always parched and always bitter. They are everyone's concern and like vampires they suck our life's blood.

BETTE DAVIS (1908–89), U.S. screen actor. *The Lonely Life*, ch. 20 (1962).

3 The weak are more likely to make the strong weak than the strong are likely to make the weak strong.

MARLENE DIETRICH (1904–92), German-born U.S. film actor. *Marlene Dietrich's ABC*, "Weakness" (1962).

4 Man's biological weakness is the condition of human culture.

ERICH FROMM (1900–1980), U.S. psychologist. *Escape from Freedom*, ch. 2 (1941).

5 Power corrupts the few, while weakness corrupts the many. . . . The resentment of the weak does not spring from any injustice done to them but from the sense of their inadequacy and impotence. They hate not wickedness but weakness. When it is in their power to do so, the weak destroy weakness wherever they see it.

ERIC HOFFER (1902–83), U.S. philosopher. *The Passionate State of Mind*, aph. 41 (1955).

6 It is a talent of the weak to persuade themselves that they suffer for something when they suffer from something; that they are showing the way when they are running away; that they see the light when they feel the heat; that they are chosen when they are shunned.

ERIC HOFFER (1902–83), U.S. philosopher. *The Passionate State of Mind*, aph. 49 (1955).

7 Union of the weakest develops strength
Not wisdom. Can all men, together, avenge
One of the leaves that have fallen in autumn?
But the wise man avenges by building his city in
snow.

WALLACE STEVENS (1879–1955), U.S. poet. *Like Decorations in a Nigger Cemetery*, sct. 50, in *Ideas of Order* (1936).

8 She lacks the indefinable charm of weakness.

OSCAR WILDE (1854–1900), Anglo-Irish playwright, author. Lord Henry, in *The Picture of Dorian Gray*, ch. 15 (1891), said of the Duchess of Monmouth.

See also Hebrew Bible on FOOLS AND FOLLIES.

WEALTH

1 But lay up for yourselves treasures in heaven, where neither moth nor rust doth corrupt, and where thieves do not break through nor steal.

BIBLE: NEW TESTAMENT. *Matthew* 6:20.

2 It is, generally, in the season of prosperity that men discover their real temper, principles, and designs.

EDMUND BURKE (1729–97), Irish philosopher, statesman. *First Letter on a Regicide Peace* (1796); published in *The Writings and Speeches of Edmund Burke*, vol. 9, ed. by Paul Langford, 1991).

3 The day is not far distant when the man who dies leaving behind him millions of available wealth, which was free for him to administer during life, will pass away "unwept, unhonored, and unsung," no matter to what uses he leave the dross which he cannot take with him. Of such as these the public verdict will then be: "The man who dies thus rich dies disgraced." Such, in my opinion, is the true gospel concerning wealth, obedience to which is destined some day to solve the problem of the rich and the poor.

ANDREW CARNEGIE (1835–1919), U.S. industrialist, philanthropist. "The Gospel of Wealth," in *North American Review* (Cedar Falls, Iowa, June 1889). Quoted in: Burton J. Hendrick, *Life of Andrew Carnegie*, vol. 1, ch. 17 (1932).

4 There are many definite methods, honest and dishonest, which make people rich; the only "instinct" I know of which does it is that instinct which theological Christianity crudely describes as "the sin of avarice."

G. K. CHESTERTON (1874–1936), British author. *All Things Considered*, "The Fallacy of Success" (1908).

5 If prosperity is regarded as the reward of virtue it will be regarded as the symptom of virtue.

G. K. CHESTERTON (1874–1936), British author. *G.K.C. as M.C.*, "The Book of Job" (1929).

6 Wealth is an inborn attitude of mind, like poverty. The pauper who has made his pile may flaunt his spoils, but cannot wear them plausibly.

JEAN COCTEAU (1889–1963), French author, filmmaker. *Les Enfants Terribles* (tr. by Rosamond Lehmann, 1929).

7 Prosperity is only an instrument to be used, not a deity to be worshiped.

CALVIN COOLIDGE (1872–1933), U.S. Republican politician, president . Speech, 11 June 1928, Boston.

8 Wealth, howsoever got, in England makes
Lords of mechanics, gentlemen of rakes;
Antiquity and birth are needless here;
'Tis impudence and money makes a peer.

DANIEL DEFOE (c. 1661–1731), English author. *The True-Born Englishman*, pt. 1.

9 The secret point of money and power in America is neither the things that money can buy nor power for power's sake . . . but absolute personal freedom, mobility, privacy. It is the instinct which drove America to the Pacific, all through the nineteenth century, the desire to be able to find a restaurant open in case you want a sandwich, to be a free agent, live by one's own rules.

JOAN DIDION (b. 1934), U.S. essayist. *Slouching Towards Bethlehem*, "7000 Romaine, Los Angeles" (1968; first published 1967).

10 There is a gigantic difference between earning a great deal of money and being rich.

MARLENE DIETRICH (1904–92), German-born U.S. film actor. *Marlene Dietrich's ABC*, "Earning" (1962).

11 Wealth is in applications of mind to nature; and the art of getting rich consists not in industry, much less in saving, but in a better order, in timeliness, in being at the right spot.

> RALPH WALDO EMERSON (1803–82), U.S. essayist, poet, philosopher. *The Conduct of Life*, "Wealth" (1860).

12 Riches have *never* fascinated me, unless combined with the greatest charm or distinction.

> F. SCOTT FITZGERALD (1896–1940), U.S. author. Letter, Aug. 1936, to Ernest Hemingway (published in *The Letters of F. Scott Fitzgerald*, ed. by Andrew Turnbull, 1963). Fitzgerald was defending himself against an attack by Hemingway in "The Snows of Kilimanjaro" published in *Esquire* of that month, in which he named Fitzgerald as feeling a "romantic awe" for the rich. When the story was collected in *The Fifth Column and the First Forty-Nine Stories* in 1938, Fitzgerald became the character "Julian." See Hemingway on THE RICH.

13 Wealth is not without its advantages and the case to the contrary, although it has often been made, has never proved widely persuasive.

> JOHN KENNETH GALBRAITH (b. 1908), U.S. economist. *The Affluent Society*, ch. 1, sct. 1 (1958).

14 Wealth, in even the most improbable cases, manages to convey the aspect of intelligence.

> JOHN KENNETH GALBRAITH (b. 1908), U.S. economist. *Sydney Morning Herald* (22 May 1982).

15 If you can actually count your money, then you are not really a rich man.

> J. PAUL GETTY (1892–1976), U.S. oil millionaire, arts patron. Quoted in: *Observer* (London, 3 Nov. 1957).

16 Ill fares the land, to hast'ning ills a prey,
Where wealth accumulates, and men decay.

> OLIVER GOLDSMITH (1728–74), Anglo-Irish author, poet, playwright. *The Deserted Village*.

17 Wealth is so much the greatest good that Fortune has to bestow that in the Latin and English languages it has usurped her name.

> LORD MELBOURNE (1779–1848), English statesman, prime minister. Notebook entry. Quoted in: David Cecil, *The Young Melbourne*, ch. 9 (1939).

18 Let none admire
That riches grow in hell; that soil may best
Deserve the precious bane.

> JOHN MILTON (1608–74), English poet. *Paradise Lost*, bk. 1.

19 'Tis a sort of duty to be rich, that it may be in one's power to do good, riches being another word for power.

> LADY MARY WORTLEY MONTAGU (1689–1762), English society figure, letter writer. Letter, c. 24 Sept. 1714, to her husband (published in *Selected Letters*, ed. by Robert Halsband, 1970).

20 Wealth often takes away chances from men as well as poverty. There is none to tell the rich to go on striving, for a rich man makes the law that hallows and hollows his own life.

> SEAN O'CASEY (1884–1964), Irish dramatist. *Rose and Crown*, vol. 5, "Pennsylvanian Visit" (1952).

21 But Satan now is wiser than of yore,
And tempts by making rich, not making poor.

> ALEXANDER POPE (1688–1744), English satirical poet. *Epistle to Lord Bathurst*.

22 Probably the greatest harm done by vast wealth is the harm that we of moderate means do ourselves when we let the vices of envy and hatred enter deep into our own natures.

> THEODORE ROOSEVELT (1858–1919), U.S. Republican (later Progressive) politician, president. Speech, 23 Aug. 1902, Providence, R.I.

23 What difference does it make how much you have? What you do not have amounts to much more.

> SENECA (c. 5 B.C.–A.D. c. 65), Roman writer, philosopher, statesman. Attributed, in *Noctes Atticae*, bk. 12, ch. 2, sct. 13, by second-century Roman grammarian Aulus Gellius.

24 The odious and disgusting aristocracy of wealth is built upon the ruins of all that is good in chivalry or republicanism; and luxury is the forerunner of a barbarism scarcely capable of cure.

> PERCY BYSSHE SHELLEY (1792–1822), English poet. *A Vindication of Natural Diet*, a Note in *Queen Mab* (1813).

25 There must be a reason why some people can afford to live well. They must have worked for it. I only feel angry when I see waste. When I see people throwing away things that we could use.

> MOTHER TERESA (b. 1910), Albanian-born Roman Catholic missionary. *A Gift for God*, "Riches" (1975).

26 Superfluous wealth can buy superfluities only. Money is not required to buy one necessary of the soul.

> HENRY DAVID THOREAU (1817–62), U.S. philosopher, author, naturalist. *Walden*, "Conclusion" (1854).

27 What is the most important for democracy is not that great fortunes should not exist, but that great fortunes should not remain in the same hands. In that way there are rich men, but they do not form a class.

> ALEXIS DE TOCQUEVILLE (1805–59), French social philosopher. *Democracy in America*, vol. 2, Appendix 5, "Democracy" (1840).

28 Every man of ambition has to fight his century with its own weapons. What this century worships is wealth. The God of this century is wealth. To succeed one must have wealth. At all costs one must have wealth.

> OSCAR WILDE (1854–1900), Anglo-Irish playwright, author. Sir Robert Chiltern, in *An Ideal Husband*, act 2.

See also Burke on BUSINESS AND COMMERCE; LUXURY; Smith on MONEY; THE RICH; TYCOONS.

WEAPONS

1 After a shooting spree, they always want to take the guns away from the people who *didn't* do it. I sure as hell wouldn't want to live in a society where the only people allowed guns are the police and the military.

> WILLIAM BURROUGHS (b. 1914), U.S. author. "The War Universe," taped conversation (published in *Grand Street*, no. 37; repr. in *Painting and Guns*, 1992, in a slightly different form).

2 A well-regulated militia being necessary to the

security of a free State, the right of the people to keep and bear arms shall not be infringed.

> U.S. CONSTITUTION, Second Amendment.

3 The Prospero of poisons, the Faustus of the front, bringing mental magic to modern armament.

> TONY HARRISON (b. 1953), British poet. *Square Rounds*. The speaker is intended to be the German chemist Fritz Haber, Nobel Prize winner and father of chemical warfare.

4 When I hold you in my arms
And I feel my finger on your trigger
I know no one can do me no harm
Because happiness is a warm gun.

> JOHN LENNON (1940–1980) AND PAUL MCCARTNEY (b. 1942), British rock musicians. "Happiness is a Warm Gun," from *Beatles White Album*, (1968).

5 Cannons and fire-arms are cruel and damnable machines; I believe them to have been the direct suggestion of the Devil. If Adam had seen in a vision the horrible instruments his children were to invent, he would have died of grief.

> MARTIN LUTHER (1483–1546), German leader of the Protestant Reformation. *Table Talk*, sct. 820 (1569).

6 The main foundations of every state, new states as well as ancient or composite ones, are good laws and good arms . . . you cannot have good laws without good arms, and where there are good arms, good laws inevitably follow.

> NICCOLÒ MACHIAVELLI (1469–1527), Italian political philosopher, statesman. *The Prince*, ch. 12 (1514).

7 For among other evils caused by being disarmed, it renders you contemptible; which is one of those disgraceful things which a prince must guard against.

> NICCOLÒ MACHIAVELLI (1469–1527), Italian political philosopher, statesman. *The Prince*, ch. 14 (1514).

8 Weapons are an important factor in war, but not the decisive factor; it is people, not things, that are decisive. The contest of strength is not only a contest of military and economic power, but also a contest of human power and morale. Military and economic power is necessarily wielded by people.

> MAO ZEDONG (1893–1976), Founder of the People's Republic of China. "On Protracted War" (May 1938; published in *Selected Works*, vol. 2, 1961).

WEATHER

1 What dreadful hot weather we have! It keeps me in a continual state of inelegance.

> JANE AUSTEN (1775–1817), English novelist. Letter, 18 Sept. 1796.

2 He maketh his sun to rise on the evil and on the good, and sendeth rain on the just and on the unjust.

> BIBLE: NEW TESTAMENT. *Matthew* 5:45.

3 The weather is like the government, always in the wrong.

> JEROME K. JEROME (1859–1927), British author. *Idle Thoughts of an Idle Fellow*, "On the Weather" (1889).

4 A change in the weather is sufficient to recreate the world and ourselves.

> MARCEL PROUST (1871–1922), French novelist. *Remembrance of Things Past*, vol. 6, "The Guermantes Way," pt. 2, ch. 2 (1921; cit. by Ronald and Colette Cortie, 1988).

5 Heat, ma'am! It was so dreadful here that I found there was nothing left for it but to take off my flesh and sit in my bones.

> SYDNEY SMITH (1771–1845), English writer, clergyman. Quoted in: Lady Holland, *Memoir*, vol. 1, ch. 9 (1855).

6 Everybody talks about the weather, but nobody does anything about it.

> Attributed to MARK TWAIN (1835–1910), U.S. author. Quoted in: an editorial by Charles D. Warner in *Hartford Courant* (27 Aug. 1897). Warner's actual words were: "A well-known U.S. writer once said that while everyone talked about the weather, nobody seemed to do anything about it." The remark is generally ascribed to Twain, with whom Warner collaborated on the novel, *The Gilded Age* (1873).

7 All we need is a meteorologist who has once been soaked to the skin without ill effect. No one can write knowingly of the weather who walks bent over on wet days.

> E. B. WHITE (1899–1985), U.S. author, editor. "Dismal?," in *New Yorker* (25 Feb. 1950; repr. in *Writings from the New Yorker 1927–1976*, ed. by Rebecca M. Dale, 1991).

8 People get a bad impression of it by continually trying to treat it as if it was a bank clerk, who ought to be on time on Tuesday next, instead of philosophically seeing it as a painter, who may do anything so long as you don't try to predict what.

> KATHARINE WHITEHORN (b. 1926), British journalist. *Observer* (London, 7 Aug. 1966), of the English climate.

9 Pray don't talk to me about the weather, Mr. Worthing. Whenever people talk to me about the weather, I always feel quite certain that they mean something else.

> OSCAR WILDE (1854–1900), Anglo-Irish playwright, author. Gwendolen, in *The Importance of Being Earnest*, act 1.

10 It was so cold I almost got married.

> SHELLEY WINTERS (b. 1922), U.S. stage and screen actor. Quoted in: *New York Times* (29 April 1956).

See also Byron, Coleridge, Walpole on ENGLAND AND THE ENGLISH; Twain on NEW ENGLAND; RAIN.

DANIEL WEBSTER

1 A terrible, beetle-browed, mastiff-mouthed, yellow-skinned, broad-bottomed, grim-taciturn individual; with a pair of dull-cruel-looking black eyes, and as much Parliamentary intellect and silent-rage in him . . . as I have ever seen in any man.

> THOMAS CARLYLE (1795–1881), Scottish essayist, historian. Letter, 24 June 1824, to his brother (published in *New Letters of Thomas Carlyle*, 1904).

2 Daniel Webster struck me much like a steam-engine in trousers.

> SYDNEY SMITH (1771–1845), English writer, clergyman. Quoted in: Lady Holland, *Memoir*, vol. 1, ch. 9 (1855).

3 God is only the president of the day, and Webster is his orator.

> HENRY DAVID THOREAU (1817–62), U.S. philosopher, author, naturalist. *Walden*, "Conclusion" (1854).

WEDDINGS

1 A princely marriage is the brilliant edition of a universal fact, and, as such, it rivets mankind.

> WALTER BAGEHOT (1826–77), English economist, critic. *The English Constitution*, ch. 2 (1867).

2 That is ever the way. 'Tis all jealousy to the bride and good wishes to the corpse.

> J. M. BARRIE (1860–1937), British playwright. Miss Susan, in *Quality Street*, act 1.

3 Bride. A woman with a fine prospect of happiness behind her.

> AMBROSE BIERCE (1842–1914), U.S. author. *The Devil's Dictionary* (1881–1906).

4 Girls usually have a papier mâché face on their wedding day.

> COLETTE (1873–1954), French author. "Wedding Day," in *Earthly Paradise*, pt. 2 (ed. by Robert Phelps, 1966).

5 Strange, to see what delight we married people have to see these poor fools decoyed into our condition, every man and wife gazing and smiling at them.

> SAMUEL PEPYS (1633–1703), English diarist. Diary entry, 25 Dec. 1665.

6 Wedding: the point at which a man stops toasting a woman and begins roasting her.

> HELEN ROWLAND (1875–1950), U.S. journalist. *A Guide to Men*, "Syncopations" (1922).

7 A gloomy guest fits not a wedding feast.

> FRIEDRICH VON SCHILLER (1759–1805), German dramatist, poet, historian. Tell, in *Wilhelm Tell*, act 4, sc. 3, (tr. by Sir Thomas Martin).

8 Of all actions of a man's life, his marriage does least concern other people, yet of all actions of our life 'tis most meddled with by other people.

> JOHN SELDEN (1584–1654), English jurist, statesman. *Table Talk*, "Marriage" (1686).

See also Shakespeare on KISSING.

WEEKENDS

1 The rhythm of the weekend, with its birth, its planned gaieties, and its announced end, followed the rhythm of life and was a substitute for it.

> F. SCOTT FITZGERALD (1896–1940), U.S. author. *The Crack-Up*, "Notebook D" (ed. by Edmund Wilson, 1945).

2 One non-revolutionary weekend is infinitely more bloody than a month of permanent revolution.

> GRAFFITI, School of Oriental Languages, London 1968. Quoted in: *Leaving the 20th Century: The Incomplete Work of the Situationist International* (ed. and tr. by Christopher Gray, 1974).

3 Your hair may be brushed, but your mind's
    untidy,
You've had about seven hours' sleep since Friday,
No wonder you feel that lost sensation;
You're sunk from a riot of relaxation.

> OGDEN NASH (1902–71), U.S. poet. *We'll All Feel Better By Wednesday*, in *Versus* (1949).

4 How pleasant is Saturday night,
When I've tried all the week to be good,
And not spoke a word that was bad,
And obliged everyone that I could.

> NANCY SPROAT (1766–1827), U.S. writer of verse for children. *Saturday Night*.

See also Rorty on EXCELLENCE; SUNDAY.

WELFARE

1 To drive men from independence to live on alms, is itself great cruelty.

> EDMUND BURKE (1729–97), Irish philosopher, statesman. *Reflections on the Revolution in France* (1790).

2 And having looked to government for bread, on the very first scarcity they will turn and bite the hand that fed them. To avoid that evil, government will redouble the causes of it; and then it will become inveterate and incurable.

> EDMUND BURKE (1729–97), Irish philosopher, statesman. *Thoughts and Details on Scarcity* (Nov. 1795; published in *Works*, vol. 5), cautioning against the "attempt to feed the people out of the hands of the magistrates."

3 Religion was nearly dead because there was no longer real belief in future life; but something was struggling to take its place—service—social service—the ants' creed, the bees' creed.

> JOHN GALSWORTHY (1867–1933), English novelist, playwright. Sir Lawrence Mont, in *Over the River*, ch. 11 (bk. 3 of *End of the Chapter*, the last installment of *The Forsyte Chronicles*, 1933).

4 Mothers born on relief have their babies on relief. Nothingness, truly, seems to be the condition of these New York people. . . . They are nomads going from one rooming house to another, looking for a toilet that functions.

> ELIZABETH HARDWICK (b. 1916), U.S. author, critic. *A View of My Own*, "The Insulted and Injured: Books About Poverty" (1962; first published 1961).

5 A decent provision for the poor is the true test of civilization.

> SAMUEL JOHNSON (1709–84), English author, lexicographer. Quoted by the Rev. Dr. Maxwell in: James Boswell, *Life of Samuel Johnson* (1791), 1770 entry.

6 Social Security is a government program with a constituency made up of the old, the near old and those who hope or fear to grow old. After 215 years of trying, we have finally discovered a special interest that includes 100 percent of the population. Now we can vote ourselves rich.

P. J. O'ROURKE (b. 1947), U.S. journalist. *Parliament of Whores,* "Graft for the Millions: Social Security" (1991).

7 Public money is like holy water; everyone helps himself to it.

ITALIAN PROVERB. Graham Hancock, *Lords of Poverty,* pt. 5, epigraph (1989).

8 'Tis not enough to help the feeble up,
But to support him after.

WILLIAM SHAKESPEARE (1564–1616), English dramatist, poet. Timon, in *Timon of Athens,* act 1, sc. 1.

THE WEST

1 Modern Western thought will pass into history and be incorporated in it, will have its influence and its place, just as our body will pass into the composition of grass, of sheep, of cutlets, and of men. We do not like that kind of immortality, but what is to be done about it?

ALEXANDER HERZEN (1812–70), Russian journalist, political thinker. *My Past and Thoughts,* vol. 2, pt. 5, ch. 38 (1921; tr. by Constance Garnett 1924–27).

2 A society which is clamoring for choice, which is filled with many articulate groups, each urging its own brand of salvation, its own variety of economic philosophy, will give each new generation no peace until all have chosen or gone under, unable to bear the conditions of choice. The stress is in our civilization.

MARGARET MEAD (1901–78), U.S. anthropologist. *Coming of Age in Samoa,* ch. 14 (1928).

3 So-called Western Civilization, as practised in half of Europe, some of Asia and a few parts of North America, is better than anything else available. Western civilization not only provides a bit of life, a pinch of liberty and the occasional pursuance of happiness, it's also the only thing that's ever tried to. Our civilization is the first in history to show even the slightest concern for average, undistinguished, none-too-commendable people like us.

P. J. O'ROURKE (b. 1947), U.S. journalist. *Holidays in Hell,* Introduction (1988).

4 Western man represents himself, on the political or psychological stage, in a spectacular world-theater. Our personality is innately cinematic, light-charged projections flickering on the screen of Western consciousness.

CAMILLE PAGLIA (b. 1947), U.S. author, critic, educator. *Sex, Art, and American Culture,* "Sexual Personae: The Cancelled Preface" (1992).

5 Thank God we're living in a country where the sky's the limit, the stores are open late and you can shop in bed thanks to television.

JOAN RIVERS (b. 1935), U.S. comedian. *International Herald Tribune* (Paris, 31 May 1989).

6 You in the West have a problem. You are unsure when you are being lied to, when you are being tricked. We do not suffer from this; and unlike you, we have acquired the skill of reading between the lines.

ZDENEK URBÁNAK (b. 1917), Czech translator, essayist. Interview, Aug. 1977, with journalist John Pilger. Quoted in: *Guardian* (London, 12 Feb. 1990).

7 Who wants a world in which the guarantee that we shall not die of starvation entails the risk of dying of boredom?

RAOUL VANEIGEM (b. 1934), Belgian Situationist philosopher. *The Revolution of Everyday Life,* Introduction (1967; tr. 1983).

8 You have riches and freedom here but I feel no sense of faith or direction. You have so many computers, why don't you use them in the search for love?

LECH WALESA (b. 1943), Polish trade union leader, politician. Quoted in: *Daily Telegraph* (London, 14 Dec. 1988), said in Paris on his first visit out of the Soviet Bloc.

WESTERNS

1 In Westerns you were permitted to kiss your horse but never your girl.

GARY COOPER (1901–61), U.S. screen actor. "Well, It Was This Way," in *Saturday Evening Post* (New York, 17 March 1958).

2 I wouldn't say when you've seen one Western you've seen the lot; but when you've seen the lot you get the feeling you've seen one.

KATHARINE WHITEHORN (b. 1926), British journalist. *Sunday Best,* "Decoding the West" (1976).

WHITES

1 The white man regards the universe as a gigantic machine hurtling through time and space to its final destruction: individuals in it are but tiny organisms with private lives that lead to private deaths: personal power, success and fame are the absolute measures of values, the things to live for. This outlook on life divides the universe into a host of individual little entities which cannot help being in constant conflict thereby hastening the approach of the hour of their final destruction.

POLICY STATEMENT, 1944, of the Youth League of the African National Congress (published in Fatima Meer's biography of Nelson Mandela, *Higher than Hope,* pt. 2, ch. 4, 1988).

2 As far as I knew white women were never lonely, except in books. White men adored them, Black men desired them and Black women worked for them.

MAYA ANGELOU (b. 1928), U.S. author. *Singin' and Swingin' and Gettin' Merry Like Christmas,* vol. 3, ch. 1 (1976).

3 The reason people think it's important to be white is that they think it's important not to be black.

JAMES BALDWIN (1924–87), U.S. author. *A Dialogue* (1973; with Nikki Giovanni), from a conversation, 4 Nov. 1971, in London.

4 Every time I embrace a black woman I'm embracing slavery, and when I put my arms around a white woman, well, I'm hugging freedom. The white man forbade me to have the white woman on pain of death. . . . I will not be free until the day I can have a white woman in my bed.

ELDRIDGE CLEAVER (b. 1935), U.S. black leader, writer. Lazarus, in *Soul on Ice,* "Allegory of the Black Eunuchs" (1968).

5 It is exasperating to see little brown men and little yellow men from the mysterious Orient, and the opaque black men of Africa (to say nothing of those impudent American Negroes!) who come to the U.N. and talk smart to us, who are scurrying all over *our* globe in their strange modes of dress—much as if they were new, unpleasant arrivals from another planet. Many whites believe in their ulcers that it is only a matter of time before the Marines get the signal to round up these truants and put them back securely in their cages.

> ELDRIDGE CLEAVER (b. 1935), U.S. black leader, writer. *Soul on Ice*, "The White Race and Its Heroes" (1968).

6 Collective guilt is borne by what is conventionally called the scapegoat. Now the scapegoat for white society—which is based on myths of progress, civilization, liberalism, education, enlightenment, refinement—will be precisely the force that opposes the expansion and the triumph of these myths. This brutal opposing force is supplied by the Negro.

> FRANTZ FANON (1925–61), Martiniquan psychiatrist, philosopher, political activist. *Black Skins, White Masks*, ch. 6 (1952; tr. 1967).

7 The so called white races are really pinko-grey.

> E. M. FORSTER (1879–1970), British novelist, essayist. Mr. Fielding, in *A Passage to India*, pt. 1, ch. 7 (1924). This aside caused scandal at Fielding's Anglo-Indian club.

8 We do not deride the fears of prospering white America. A nation of violence and private property has every reason to dread the violated and the deprived.

> JUNE JORDAN (b. 1939), U.S. poet, civil rights activist. *Black Studies: Bringing Back the Person*, in *Evergreen Review* (Oct. 1969; repr. in *Moving Towards Home: Political Essays*, 1989).

9 In the tropics the white feels weakened, or downright weak, whence comes the heightened tendency to outbursts of aggression. People who are polite, modest or even humble in Europe fall easily into a rage here, get into fights, destroy other people, start feuds, fall prey to megalomania, grow touchy about their prestige and significance and go around completely devoid of self-criticism, bragging about the position and the influence they have at home.

> RYSZARD KAPUSCINSKI (b. 1932), Polish journalist. *The Soccer War*, "The Plan of the Never-Written Book," sct. 32 (1990).

10 The fact that white people readily and proudly call themselves "white," glorify all that is white, and whitewash all that is glorified, becomes unnatural and bigoted in its intent only when these same whites deny persons of African heritage who are Black the natural and inalienable right to readily—proudly—call themselves "black," glorify all that is black, and blackwash all that is glorified.

> ABBEY LINCOLN (b. 1930), U.S. singer. "Who Will Revere the Black Woman?," in *Negro Digest* (Sept. 1966).

11 What are the characters that I discern most clearly in the so-called Anglo-Saxon type of man? I may answer at once that two stick out above all others. One is his curious and apparently incurable incompetence—his congenital inability to do any difficult thing easily and well, whether it be isolating a bacillus or writing a sonata. The other is his astounding susceptibility to fears and alarms—in short, his hereditary cowardice. . . . There is no record in history of any Anglo-Saxon nation entering upon any great war without allies.

> H. L. MENCKEN (1880–1956), U.S. journalist. "The Anglo-Saxon," in *Baltimore Evening Sun* (16 July 1923; repr. in *Prejudices*, Fourth Series, 1924).

12 When I think of some of the Persians, the Hindus, the Arabs I knew, when I think of the character they revealed, their grace, their tenderness, their intelligence, *their holiness*, I spit on the white conquerors of the world, the degenerate British, the pigheaded Germans, the smug self-satisfied French.

> HENRY MILLER (1891–1980), U.S. author. *Tropic of Capricorn* (1939; repr. 1966, p. 31).

13 At the ground of all these noble races, the beast of prey, the splendid, *blond beast,* lustfully roving in search of spoils and victory, cannot be mistaken.

> FRIEDRICH NIETZSCHE (1844–1900), German philosopher. *The Genealogy of Morals*, Essay 1, aph. 11 (1887; tr. 1899).

14 The truth is that Mozart, Pascal, Boolean algebra, Shakespeare, parliamentary government, baroque churches, Newton, the emancipation of women, Kant, Marx, and Balanchine ballets don't redeem what this particular civilization has wrought upon the world. The white race *is* the cancer of human history.

> SUSAN SONTAG (b. 1933), U.S. essayist. "What's Happening in America (1966)," in *Partisan Review* (New Brunswick, N.J., Winter 1967; repr. in *Styles of Radical Will*, 1969).

15 Be nice to the whites, they need you to rediscover their humanity.

> BISHOP DESMOND TUTU (b. 1931), South African prelate. Quoted in: *New York Times* (19 Oct. 1984).

16 The good news may be that Nature is phasing out the white man, but the bad news is that's who She thinks we all are.

> ALICE WALKER (b. 1944), U.S. author, critic. "Nuclear Madness: What You Can Do," in *Black Scholar* (New York, Spring 1982; repr. in *In Search of our Mothers' Gardens*, 1983).

See also Gordimer on AFRICA AND THE AFRICANS; Jordan on ELECTIONS; Morrison on RACE; Jackson on RACISM.

WALT WHITMAN

1 While the light burning within may have been divine, the outer case of the lamp was assuredly cheap enough. Whitman was, from first to last, a boorish, awkward *poseur*.

> REBECCA HARDING DAVIS (1831–1910), U.S. writer, journalist. *Bits of Gossip*, ch. 8 (1904).

2 I greet you at the beginning of a great career, which must yet have had a long foreground somewhere, for such a start. I rubbed my eyes a little to see if this sunbeam were no illusion; but the solid sense of the book is a sober certainty. It has the best merits, namely, of fortifying and encouraging.

> RALPH WALDO EMERSON (1803–82), U.S. essayist, poet, philosopher. Letter, 21 July 1855, on the appearance of *Leaves of Grass*.

3 Mr. Whitman's muse is at once indecent and ugly, lascivious and gawky, lubricious and coarse.

LAFCADIO HEARN (1850–1904), U.S. journalist, author. *New Orleans Times-Democrat* (30 July 1882), of Whitman's *Leaves of Grass.*

4 It exhibits the effort of an essentially prosaic mind to lift itself, by a prolonged muscular strain, into poetry.

HENRY JAMES (1843–1916), U.S. author. Review of *Drum Taps,* Whitman's volume of impressions of the Civil War (1865; repr. in *Views and Reviews,* 1908). James later came to be more tolerant of Whitman's verse.

5 Whitman is like a human document, or a wonderful treatise in human self revelation. It is neither art nor religion nor truth: Just a self revelation of a man who could not live, and so had to write himself.

D. H. LAWRENCE (1885–1930), British author. Letter, 22 Dec. 1913 (published in *The Letters of D. H. Lawrence,* vol. 2, ed. by George J. Zytaruk and James T. Boulton, 1981). In his essay on Whitman in *Studies in Classic American Literature,* Lawrence wrote of, "This awful Whitman. This post-mortem poet. This poet with the private soul leaking out of him all the time. All his privacy leaking out in a sort of dribble, oozing into the universe."

6 Walt Whitman, a Kosmos, of Manhattan the son,
Turbulent, fleshy, sensual, eating, drinking and
breeding,
No sentimentalist, no stander above men and
women or apart from them,
No more modest than immodest.

WALT WHITMAN (1819–92), U.S. poet. *Song of Myself,* sct. 24, in *Leaves of Grass* (1855).

7 In his very rejection of art Walt Whitman is an artist. He tried to produce a certain effect by certain means and he succeeded. . . . He stands apart, and the chief value of his work is in its prophecy, not in its performance. He has begun a prelude to larger themes. He is the herald to a new era. As a man he is the precursor of a fresh type. He is a factor in the heroic and spiritual evolution of the human being. If Poetry has passed him by, Philosophy will take note of him.

OSCAR WILDE (1854–1900), Anglo-Irish playwright, author. Review of Whitman, *November Boughs,* in *Pall Mall Gazette* (London, 25 Jan. 1889).

WICKEDNESS

1 Wicked is not much worse than indiscreet.

JOHN DONNE(c. 1572–1631), English divine, metaphysical poet. *An Anatomy of the World,* "The First Anniversary" (1611).

2 A wicked mortal is not the idea of God. He is little else than the expression of error. To suppose that sin, lust, hatred, envy, hypocrisy, revenge, have life abiding in them, is a terrible mistake. Life and Life's idea, Truth and Truth's idea, never make men sick, sinful, or mortal.

MARY BAKER EDDY (1821–1910), U.S. founder of the Christian Science movement. *Science and Health,* ch. 10 (1875).

3 It is a fact that cannot be denied: the wickedness of others becomes our own wickedness because it kindles something evil in our own hearts.

CARL JUNG (1875–1961), Swiss psychiatrist. *After the Catastrophe* (1945; repr. in *Collected Works,* vol. 10, para. 408, ed. by William McGuire, 1964).

4 Behold, my love, behold all that I simultaneously do: scandal, seduction, bad example, incest, adultery, sodomy! Oh, Satan! one and unique God of my soul, inspire thou in me something yet more, present further perversions to my smoking heart, and then shalt thou see how I shall plunge myself into them all!

MARQUIS DE SADE (1740–1814), French author. Mme de Saint-Ange, in *Philosophy in the Bedroom,* "Dialogue the Fifth" (1795).

5 It is safest to be moderately base—to be flexible in shame, and to be always ready for what is generous, good and just, when anything is to be gained by virtue.

SYDNEY SMITH (1771–1845), English writer, clergyman. *Essays,* "The Catholic Question" (1877).

6 Wickedness is a myth invented by good people to account for the curious attractiveness of others.

OSCAR WILDE (1854–1900), Anglo-Irish playwright, author. "Phrases and Philosophies for the Use of the Young," in *Chameleon* (London, Dec. 1894).

7 As a wicked man I am a complete failure. Why, there are lots of people who say I have never really done anything wrong in the whole course of my life. Of course they only say it behind my back.

OSCAR WILDE (1854–1900), Anglo-Irish playwright, author. Lord Darlington, in *Lady Windermere's Fan,* act 1.

See also EVIL; Johnson on PIETY; Apocrypha on WOMEN.

WIDOWHOOD

1 Give unto them beauty for ashes, the oil of joy for mourning.

BIBLE, HEBREW. *Isaiah* 61:3.

2 Take example by your father, my boy, and be wery careful o' vidders all your life, specially if they've kept a public house, Sammy.

CHARLES DICKENS (1812–70), English novelist. Mr. Weller, in *The Pickwick Papers,* ch. 20 (1836–37).

3 The comfortable estate of widowhood is the only hope that keeps up a wife's spirits.

JOHN GAY (1685–1732), English dramatist. Peachum, in *The Beggar's Opera,* act 1, sc. 10.

4 There is no lonelier man in death, except the suicide, than that man who has lived many years with a good wife and then outlived her. If two people love each other there can be no happy end to it.

ERNEST HEMINGWAY (1899–1961), U.S. author. *Death in the Afternoon,* ch. 11 (1932).

5 He that outlives a wife whom he has long loved, sees himself disjoined from the only mind that has the same hopes, and fears, and interest; from the only companion with whom he has shared much good and evil; and with whom he could set his mind at liberty, to retrace the past or anticipate the future. The continuity of being is lacerated; the settled course of sentiment and action is stopped; and life stands suspended and motionless.

SAMUEL JOHNSON (1709–84), English author, lexicographer. Letter, 20 Jan. 1780. Quoted in: James Boswell, *Life of Samuel Johnson* (1791).

6 Widow. The word consumes itself . . .

> SYLVIA PLATH (1932–63), U.S. poet. *Widow*, in *Crossing the Water* (1971).

7 Sorrow for a husband is like a pain in the elbow, sharp and short.

> ENGLISH PROVERB. Collected in Thomas Fuller, *Gnomologia*, no. 4231 (1732).

8 Widows are divided into two classes—the bereaved and relieved.

> VICTOR ROBINSON (1886–1947), U.S. physician, medical historian. *Truth Seeker* (6 Jan. 1906).

9 A widow is a fascinating being with the flavor of maturity, the spice of experience, the piquancy of novelty, the tang of practised coquetry, and the halo of one man's approval.

> HELEN ROWLAND (1875–1950), U.S. journalist. *A Guide to Men*, "Widows" (1922).

10 There is nothing on earth so easy as to forget, if a person chooses to set about it. I'm sure I have as much forgot your poor, dear uncle, as if he had never existed; and I thought it my duty to do so.

> RICHARD BRINSLEY SHERIDAN (1751–1816), Anglo-Irish dramatist. Mrs. Malaprop, in *The Rivals*, act 1, sc. 2.

11 The poor fatherless baby of eight months is now the utterly broken-hearted and crushed widow of forty-two! My *life* as a *happy* one is *ended*! the world is gone for *me*! If I *must live* on (and I will do nothing to make me worse than I am), it is henceforth for our poor fatherless children—for my unhappy country, which has lost *all* in losing him—and in *only* doing what I know and *feel* he would wish.

> VICTORIA (1819–1901), Queen of Great Britain and Ireland. Letter, 20 Dec. 1861, to Leopold I, King of the Belgians (published in *Letters of Queen Victoria*, vol. 3, ch. 30, ed. by A. C. Benson and Viscount Esher, 1907), of the death of Albert, the Prince Consort. Victoria's three-year seclusion and long mourning earned her the sobriquet of "the Widow of Windsor."

12 He first deceased; she for a little tried
To live without him, liked it not, and died.

> SIR HENRY WOTTON (1568–1639), English diplomat, poet. *Death of Sir Albertus Moreton's Wife*.

See also BEREAVEMENT; GRIEF.

OSCAR WILDE

1 To be kind was why he flattered—but woe to any fool who *accepted* the flattery.

> GORDON CRAIG (1872–1966), British theatrical designer, producer, actor. Quoted in: Richard Ellman, *Oscar Wilde*, ch. 22 (1987), said of Oscar Wilde.

2 He left behind, as his essential contribution to literature, a large repertoire of jokes which survive because of their sheer neatness, and because of a certain intriguing uncertainty—which extends to Wilde himself—as to whether they really mean anything.

> GEORGE ORWELL (1903–50), British author. *Lady Windermere's Fan*—A Commentary," 21 Nov. 1943, BBC broadcast.

3 If, with the literate, I am
Impelled to try an epigram,
I never seek to take the credit;
We all assume that Oscar said it.

> DOROTHY PARKER (1893–1967), U.S. humorous writer. *A Pig's-Eye View of Literature: Oscar Wilde*.

THE WILDERNESS

1 What would the world be, once bereft
Of wet and wildness? Let them be left,
O let them be left, wildness and wet;
Long live the weeds and the wilderness yet.

> GERARD MANLEY HOPKINS (1844–89), English poet, Jesuit priest. *Inversnaid*, st. 4.

2 There is in every American, I think, something of the old Daniel Boone—who, when he could see the smoke from another chimney, felt himself too crowded and moved further out into the wilderness.

> HUBERT H. HUMPHREY (1911–78), U.S. Democratic politician, vice president. Speech, 14 Jan. 1966, University of Chicago.

3 Wildness and silence disappeared from the countryside, sweetness fell from the air, not because anyone wished them to vanish or fall but because throughways had to floor the meadows with cement to carry the automobiles which advancing technology produced. . . . Tropical beaches turned into high-priced slums where thousand-room hotels elbowed each other for glimpses of once-famous surf not because those who loved the beaches wanted them there but because enormous jets could bring a million tourists every year—and therefore did.

> ARCHIBALD MACLEISH (1892–1982), U.S. poet. "The Great American Frustration," in *Saturday Review* (New York, 9 July 1968; repr. in *Riders on Earth* as "Return from the Excursion," 1978), of the advance of technology in the U.S.

4 We need the tonic of wildness, to wade sometimes in marshes where the bittern and the meadow-hen lurk, and hear the booming of the snipe; to smell the whispering sedge where only some wilder and more solitary fowl builds her nest, and the mink crawls with its belly close to the ground.

> HENRY DAVID THOREAU (1817–62), U.S. philosopher, author, naturalist. *Walden*, "Spring" (1854).

5 In wildness is the preservation of the world.

> HENRY DAVID THOREAU (1817–62), U.S. philosopher, author, naturalist. "Walking," in *Atlantic Monthly* (Boston, June 1862).

See also THE DESERT.

THE WIND

1 The wind goeth toward the south, and turneth about unto the north; it whirleth about continually, and the wind returneth again according to his circuits.

> BIBLE, HEBREW. *Ecclesiastes* 1:6.

2 The Westerly Wind asserting his sway from the south-west quarter is often like a monarch gone mad, driving forth with wild imprecations the most faithful of his courtiers to shipwreck, disaster, and death.

> JOSEPH CONRAD (1857–1924), Polish-born English novelist. *The Mirror of the Sea*, ch. 26 (1906).

3 The East Wind, an interloper in the dominions of Westerly Weather, is an impassive-faced tyrant with a sharp poniard held behind his back for a treacherous stab.

> JOSEPH CONRAD (1857–1924), Polish-born English novelist. *The Mirror of the Sea*, ch. 28 (1906).

4 Who has seen the wind?
Neither you nor I:
But when the trees bow down their heads,
The wind is passing by.

> CHRISTINA ROSSETTI (1830–94), English poet, lyricist. *Who Has Seen the Wind?*, st. 2.

5 The wind that gave our grandfather his first breath also receives his last sigh.

> Attributed to SEATTLE (c. 1784–1866), Chief of the Dwamish, Suquamish and allied Indian tribes. Letter, to President Franklin Pierce, 1854 (published in *Brother Eagle, Sister Sky: A Message from Chief Seattle*, 1990). The letter, in which Seattle pleaded that his name should die with the ceding of the Washington State territories, was shown in 1992 to have been largely a forgery, devised by television scriptwriter Ted Perry for an historical epic in 1971.

See also Shakespeare on SPRING; Shelley on WINTER.

WINE

1 Wine is a part of society because it provides a basis not only for a morality but also for an environment; it is an ornament in the slightest ceremonials of French daily life, from the snack . . . to the feast, from the conversation at the local café to the speech at a formal dinner.

> ROLAND BARTHES (1915–80), French semiologist. *Mythologies*, "Wine and Milk" (1957; tr. 1972).

2 Drink no longer water, but use a little wine for thy stomach's sake and thine often infirmities.

> BIBLE: NEW TESTAMENT. *1 Timothy* 5:23.

3 I may not here omit those two main plagues, and common dotages of human kind, wine and women, which have infatuated and besotted myriads of people. They go commonly together.

> ROBERT BURTON (1577–1640), English clergyman, author. *The Anatomy of Melancholy*, pt. 1, sct. 2, Member 3, subsct. 13 (1621).

4 It is a maudlin and indecent verity that comes out through the strength of wine.

> JOSEPH CONRAD (1857–1924), Polish-born English novelist. *A Personal Record*, ch. 6 (1912).

5 This wine is too good for toast-drinking, my dear. You don't want to mix emotions up with a wine like that. You lose the taste.

> ERNEST HEMINGWAY (1899–1961), U.S. author. Count Mippipopolous, in *The Sun Also Rises*, bk. 1, ch. 7 (1926).

6 Wine gives a man nothing. It neither gives him knowledge nor wit; it only animates a man, and enables him to bring out what a dread of the company has repressed. It only puts in motion what had been locked up in frost.

> SAMUEL JOHNSON (1709–84), English author, lexicographer. Quoted in: James Boswell, *Life of Samuel Johnson*, 28 April 1778 (1791).

7 Wine makes a man better pleased with himself. I do not say that it makes him more pleasing to others. . . . This is one of the disadvantages of wine, it makes a man mistake words for thoughts.

> SAMUEL JOHNSON (1709–84), English author, lexicographer. Quoted in: James Boswell, *Life of Samuel Johnson*, 28 April 1778 (1791).

8 You know, my Friends, with what a brave Carouse
I made a Second Marriage in my house;
Divorced old barren Reason from my Bed,
And took the Daughter of the Vine to Spouse.

> OMAR KHAYYÁM (11th–12th century A.D.), Persian astronomer, poet. *The Rubáiyát of Omar Khayyám*, st. 55 (tr. by Edward Fitzgerald, 1879).

9 Water for oxen, wine for kings.

> SPANISH PROVERB.

10 Nothing equals the joy of the drinker, except the joy of the wine in being drunk.

> FRENCH SAYING.

11 O thou invisible spirit of wine, if thou hast no name to be known by, let us call thee devil.

> WILLIAM SHAKESPEARE (1564–1616), English dramatist, poet. Cassio, in *Othello*, act 2, sc. 3.

12 It's a naïve domestic Burgundy without any breeding, but I think you'll be amused by its presumption.

> JAMES THURBER (1894–1961), U.S. humorist, illustrator. Cartoon caption in *New Yorker* (27 March 1937).

13 If you have a grateful heart (which is a miracle amongst you statesmen), show it by directing the bearer to the best wine in town, and pray let not this highest point of sacred friendship be performed slightly, but go about it with all due deliberation and care, as holy priests to sacrifice, or as discreet thieves to the wary performance of burglary and shop-lifting. Let your well-discerning palate (the best judge about you) travel from cellar to cellar and then from piece to piece till it has lighted on wine fit for its noble choice and my approbation.

> JOHN WILMOT, SECOND EARL OF ROCHESTER (1647–80), English poet, courtier. Letter, to the diplomat Henry Savile, 1673–74 (published in *The Letters of John Wilmot, Earl of Rochester*, 1980).

See also Milton on THE ARISTOCRACY; DRINK.

WINNING

1 We will get everything out of her that you can squeeze out of a lemon and a bit more. . . . I will squeeze her until you can hear the pips squeak.

> SIR ERIC GEDDES (1875–1937), British Conservative politician. Speech, 9 Dec. 1918, the Guildhall, Cambridge, England, on German war reparations following World War I. Geddes repeat-

ed the speech the following night, adding, "My only doubt is not whether we can squeeze hard enough, but whether there is enough juice."

2 The only way to win is to fight on the side of your adversaries.

FRANCIS PICABIA (1878–1953), French painter, poet. *Who Knows: Poems and Aphorisms* (1950; repr. 1986, p. 46).

3 Therefore the skilful leader subdues the enemy's troops without any fighting; he captures their cities without laying siege to them; he overthrows their kingdom without lengthy operations in the field.

SUN TZU (6th–5th century B.C.), Chinese general. *The Art of War*, ch. 3, axiom 6 (c. 490 B.C.; ed. by James Clavell, 1981).

4 Resting on your laurels is as dangerous as resting when you are walking in the snow. You doze off and die in your sleep.

LUDWIG WITTGENSTEIN (1889–1951), Austrian philosopher. *Culture and Value* (ed. by G. H. von Wright and Heikki Nyman, 1980), 1939–40 journal entry.

See also Shakespeare on CHEATING; Khrushchev on THE COLD WAR; VICTORY.

WINTER

1 The English winter—ending in July,
To recommence in August.

LORD BYRON (1788–1824), English poet. *Don Juan,* cto. 13, st. 42

2 Winter lies too long in country towns; hangs on until it is stale and shabby, old and sullen.

WILLA CATHER (1873–1947), U.S. author. *My Antonia,* bk. 2, ch. 7 (1918).

3 January, month of empty pockets! . . . Let us endure this evil month, anxious as a theatrical producer's forehead.

COLETTE (1873–1954), French author. "Empty Pockets," in *Quatre Saisons* (1928; repr. in *Journey for Myself,* 1971).

4 Often in winter the end of the day is like the final metaphor in a poem celebrating death: there is no way out.

AGUSTIN GOMEZ-ARCOS (b. 1939), Spanish author. *A Bird Burned Alive,* ch. 1 (1988).

5 Winter is icummen in,
Lhude sing Goddamm,
Raineth drop and staineth slop,
And how the wind doth ramm!
Sing: Goddamm.

EZRA POUND (1885–1972), U.S. poet, critic. *Ancient Music.* The poem—originally dropped from Pound's 1916 edition of *Lustra* when it was considered offensive, later reinstated—is a pastiche of an anonymous 13th-century hymn sung annually at Reading Abbey, England:
Sumer is icumen in,
Lhude sing cuccu!
Groweth sed, and bloweth med,
And springeth the wude nu.

6 O, Wind,
If Winter comes, can Spring be far behind?

PERCY BYSSHE SHELLEY (1792–1822), English poet. *Ode to the West Wind.*

7 Many of the phenomena of Winter are suggestive

of an inexpressible tenderness and fragile delicacy. We are accustomed to hear this king described as a rude and boisterous tyrant; but with the gentleness of a lover he adorns the tresses of Summer.

HENRY DAVID THOREAU (1817–62), U.S. philosopher, author, naturalist. *Walden,* "Spring" (1854).

WISDOM

1 The wisdom of a learned man cometh by opportunity of leisure: and he that hath little business shall become wise.

APOCRYPHA. *Ecclesiasticus* 38:25.

2 For it is not possible to join serpentine wisdom with columbine innocency, except men know exactly all the conditions of the serpent: his baseness and going upon his belly, his volubility and lubricity, his envy and sting, and the rest; that is, all forms and natures of evil: for without this, virtue lieth open and unfenced.

FRANCIS BACON (1561–1626), English philosopher, essayist, statesman. *The Advancement of Learning,* bk. 2, ch. 21, sct. 9 (1605). Bacon was referring to Jesus's words to the Apostles in *Matthew* 10:16: "Behold, I send you forth as sheep in the midst of wolves: be ye therefore wise as serpents, and harmless as doves."

3 The fear of the Lord is the beginning of wisdom.

BIBLE, HEBREW. *Psalms* 111:10.

4 Let no man deceive himself. If any man among you seemeth to be wise in this world, let him become a fool, that he may be wise. For the wisdom of this world is foolishness with God.

BIBLE: NEW TESTAMENT. *1 Corinthians* 3:18–19.

5 Mixing one's wines may be a mistake, but old and new wisdom mix admirably.

BERTOLT BRECHT (1898–1956), German dramatist, poet. The Singer, in *The Caucasian Chalk Circle,* Prologue (1944).

6 Wisdom we know is the knowledge of good and evil—not the strength to choose between the two.

JOHN CHEEVER (1912–82), U.S. author. *John Cheever: The Journals,* "The Late Forties and the Fifties" (ed. by Robert Gottlieb, 1991), 1956 entry.

7 The extreme limit of wisdom—that's what the public calls madness.

JEAN COCTEAU (1889–1963), French author, filmmaker. *Le Rappel àL'Ordre,* "Le Coq et l'Arlequin" (1926; repr. in *Collected Works,* vol. 9, 1950).

8 No one over thirty-five is worth meeting who has not something to teach us,—something more than we could learn for ourselves, from a book.

CYRIL CONNOLLY (1903–74), British critic. *The Unquiet Grave,* pt. 1 (1944; rev. 1951).

9 Now all the knowledge and wisdom that is in creatures, whether angels or men, is nothing else but a participation of that one eternal, immutable and increated wisdom of God, or several signatures of that one archetypal seal, or like so many multiplied reflections of one and the same face, made in several glasses, whereof some are clearer, some obscurer, some standing nearer, some further off.

> RALPH J. CUDWORTH (1617–88), English theologian, philosopher. *Treatise Concerning Eternal and Immutable Morality,* bk. 1, ch. 3, sct. 7 (1731).

10 History teaches us that men and nations behave wisely once they have exhausted all other alternatives.

> ABBA EBAN (b. 1915), Israeli politician. Speech, 16 Dec. 1970, London.

11 Raphael paints wisdom; Handel sings it, Phidias carves it, Shakespeare writes it, Wren builds it, Columbus sails it, Luther preaches it, Washington arms it, Watt mechanizes it.

> RALPH WALDO EMERSON (1803–82), U.S. essayist, poet, philosopher. *Society and Solitude,* "Art" (1870).

12 Wisdom is like electricity. There is no permanently wise man, but men capable of wisdom, who, being put into certain company, or other favorable conditions, become wise for a short time, as glasses rubbed acquire electric power for a while.

> RALPH WALDO EMERSON (1803–82), U.S. essayist, poet, philosopher. *Society and Solitude,* "Clubs" (1870).

13 Truth from his lips prevailed with double sway,
And fools, who came to scoff, remained to pray.

> OLIVER GOLDSMITH (1728–74), Anglo-Irish author, poet, playwright. *The Deserted Village,* of the village preacher.

14 There often seems to be a playfulness to wise people, as if either their equanimity has as its source this playfulness or the playfulness flows from the equanimity; and they can persuade other people who are in a state of agitation to calm down and manage a smile.

> EDWARD HOAGLAND (b. 1932), U.S. novelist, essayist. "Other Lives," in *Harper's* (New York, July 1973; repr. in *Heart's Desire,* 1988).

15 Such is the nature of men, that howsoever they may acknowledge many others to be more witty, or more eloquent, or more learned; yet they will hardly believe there be many so wise as themselves.

> THOMAS HOBBES (1588–1679), English philosopher. *Leviathan,* pt. 1, ch. 13 (1651).

16 The wisdom of others remains dull till it is writ over with our own blood. We are essentially apart from the world; it bursts into our consciousness only when it sinks its teeth and nails into us.

> ERIC HOFFER (1902–83), U.S. philosopher. *The Passionate State of Mind,* aph. 188 (1955).

17 It is the province of knowledge to speak, and it is the privilege of wisdom to listen.

> OLIVER WENDELL HOLMES, SR. (1809–94), U.S. writer, physician. *The Poet at the Breakfast Table,* ch. 10 (1872).

18 Experiences are savings which a miser puts aside. Wisdom is an inheritance which a wastrel cannot exhaust.

> KARL KRAUS (1874–1936), Austrian satirist. *Sprüche und Widersprüche,* ch. 4 (1909; tr. in *Half-Truths and One-And-A Half-Truths,* "Lord, Forgive Them . . . ," ed. by Harry Zohn, 1976).

19 It's the height of folly to want to be the only wise one.

> FRANÇOIS, DUC DE LA ROCHEFOUCAULD (1613–80), French writer, moralist. *Sentences et Maximes Morales,* no. 231 (1678).

20 We have no words for speaking of wisdom to the stupid. He who understands the wise is wise already.

> G. C. LICHTENBERG (1742–99), German physicist, philosopher. *Aphorisms,* "Notebook E," aph. 49 (written 1765–99; tr. by R. J. Hollingdale, 1990).

21 Wisdom hath her excesses, and no less need of moderation than folly.

> MICHEL DE MONTAIGNE (1533–92), French essayist. *Essays,* bk. 3, ch. 5, "Upon some Verses of Virgil" (tr. by John Florio, 1588).

22 Does wisdom perhaps appear on the earth as a raven which is inspired by the smell of carrion?

> FRIEDRICH NIETZSCHE (1844–1900), German philosopher. *Twilight of the Idols,* "The Problem of Socrates," aph. 1 (1889).

23 The heart of the wise man lies quiet like limpid water.

> CAMEROUNIAN PROVERB.

24 Nine-tenths of wisdom consists in being wise in time.

> THEODORE ROOSEVELT (1858–1919), U.S. Republican (later Progressive) politician, president. Speech, 14 June 1917, Lincoln, Nebr.

25 They would need to be already wise, in order to love wisdom.

> FRIEDRICH VON SCHILLER (1759–1805), German dramatist, poet, essayist. *On the Aesthetic Education of Man,* "Eighth Letter" (1795).

26 So wise so young, they say, do never live long.

> WILLIAM SHAKESPEARE (1564–1616), English dramatist, poet. Gloucester (later Richard III), in *Richard III,* act 3, sc. 1, speaking of Prince Edward. Edward is dead by act 4, sc. 3.

27 Well I am certainly wiser than this man. It is only too likely that neither of us has any knowledge to boast of; but he thinks that he knows something which he does not know, whereas I am quite concious of my ignorance. At any rate it seems that I am wiser than he is to this small extent, that I do not think that I know what I do not know.

> SOCRATES (469–399 B.C.), Greek philosopher. Quoted in: Plato, *Apology,* sct. 19, of "a gentleman with a reputation for wisdom."

28 It seems to me that, in every culture, I come across a chapter headed "Wisdom." And then I know exactly what is going to follow: "Vanity of vanities, all is vanity."

> LUDWIG WITTGENSTEIN (1889–1951), Austrian philosopher. Conversation, 1934 (published in *Personal Recollections,* ch. 6, ed. by Rush Rhees, 1981), of philosophy books.

See also Paz on CHANGE; Hein on ERROR; Blake on EXCESS; Apochrypha on FARMING AND FARMERS; Maugham on GENERATIONS; Gray on IGNORANCE; Emerson on INCONSISTENCY; Cowper on KNOWLEDGE; Meredith on OLD AGE; Bloom on PARENTS; Massinger on ROYALTY; Lichtenberg on SELF-KNOWLEDGE; Chesterfield on YOUTH.

WISHING

1 When we get to wishing a great deal for ourselves,

whatever we get soon turns into mere limitation and exclusion.

> GEORGE ELIOT (1819–80), English novelist, editor. *Daniel Deronda*, bk. 2, ch. 14 (1876).

2 Oh, the secret life of man and woman—dreaming how much better we would be than we are if we were somebody else or even ourselves, and feeling that our estate has been unexploited to its fullest.

> ZELDA FITZGERALD (1900–1948), U.S. writer. *Save Me the Waltz*, ch. 4, sct. 3 (1932).

WIT

1 Wit is educated insolence.

> ARISTOTLE (384–322 B.C.), Greek philosopher. *The Art of Rhetoric*, bk. 2, sct. 12, subsct. 16.

2 Wit. The salt with which the American humorist spoils his intellectual cookery by leaving it out.

> AMBROSE BIERCE (1842–1914), U.S. author. *The Devil's Dictionary* (1881–1906).

3 Wit is so shining a quality that everybody admires it; most people aim at it, all people fear it, and few love it unless in themselves. A man must have a good share of wit himself to endure a great share of it in another.

> LORD CHESTERFIELD (1694–1773), English statesman, man of letters. Letter, 18 Dec. 1765 (published in *Lord Chesterfield's Letters to His Godson*, no. 136, ed. by Earl of Carnarvon, 1889).

4 Humour is consistent with pathos, whilst wit is not.

> SAMUEL TAYLOR COLERIDGE (1772–1834), English poet, critic. "Table Talk," 1821, reported by Thomas Allsop in *Letters and Conversations of S. T. Coleridge*, vol. 1 (1836; repr. in *Collected Works*, vol. 14, ed. by Kathleen Coburn, 1990).

5 A man renowned for repartee
Will seldom scruple to make free
With friendship's finest feeling,
Will thrust a dagger at your breast,
And say he wounded you in jest,
By way of balm for healing.

> WILLIAM COWPER (1731–1800), English poet. *Friendship*.

6 You can make a sordid thing sound like a brilliant drawing-room comedy. Probably a fear we have of facing up to the real issues. Could you say we were guilty of Noel Cowardice?

> PETER DE VRIES (b. 1910), U.S. author. *Comfort Me With Apples*, ch. 15 (1956).

7 Wit is the salt of conversation, not the food.

> WILLIAM HAZLITT (1778–1830), English essayist. *Lectures on the English Comic Writers*, "On Wit and Humour" (1819).

8 The witty woman is a tragic figure in American life. Wit destroys eroticism and eroticism destroys wit, so women must choose between taking lovers and taking no prisoners.

> FLORENCE KING (b. 1936), U.S. author. *Reflections in a Jaundiced Eye*, "The State of the Funny Bone" (1989).

9 There's a helluva distance between wisecracking and wit. Wit has truth in it; wisecracking is simply calisthenics with words.

> DOROTHY PARKER (1893–1967), U.S. humorous writer. Inter-

view in *Writers at Work* (First Series, ed. by Malcolm Cowley, 1958).

10 True wit is nature to advantage dressed,
What oft was thought, but ne'er so well expressed.

> ALEXANDER POPE (1688–1744), English satirical poet. *An Essay on Criticism*.

11 Brevity is the soul of wit,
And tediousness the limbs and outward flourishes.

> WILLIAM SHAKESPEARE (1564–1616), English dramatist, poet. Polonius, in *Hamlet*, act 2, sc. 2.

12 He's winding up the watch of his wit. By and by it will strike.

> WILLIAM SHAKESPEARE (1564–1616), English dramatist, poet. Sebastian, in *The Tempest* act 2, sc. 1, on Gonzalo's attempts to cheer up Alonso.

13 Wit lies in recognising the resemblance among things which differ and the difference between things which are alike.

> MADAME DE STAËL (1766–1817), Swiss-French writer, wit. *Germany*, pt. 3, ch. 8 (1813).

14 Sometimes we are inclined to class those who are once-and-a-half witted with the half-witted, because we appreciate only a third part of their wit.

> HENRY DAVID THOREAU (1817–62), U.S. philosopher, author, naturalist. *Walden*, "Conclusion" (1854).

15 Humor does not include sarcasm, invalid irony, sardonicism, innuendo, or any other form of cruelty. When these things are raised to a high point they can become wit, but unlike the French and the English, we have not been much good at wit since the days of Benjamin Franklin.

> JAMES THURBER (1894–1961), U.S. humorist, illustrator. Letter, 25 June 1954, to Walter Landau (published in *Horn Book Magazine*, April 1962).

16 Wit and Humor—if any difference, it is in *duration*—lightning and electric light. Same material, apparently; but one is vivid, and can do damage—the other fools along and enjoys elaboration.

> MARK TWAIN (1835–1910), U.S. author. *Mark Twain's Notebooks and Journals*, vol. 3 (ed. by Frederick Anderson, 1979), Notebook 24, April-Aug. 1885.

WITCHCRAFT

1 Every old woman with a wrinkled face, a furr'd brow, a hairy lip, a gobber tooth, a squint eye, a squeaking voice, or a scolding tongue . . . a dog or cat by her side, is not only suspected but pronounced for a witch.

> JOHN GAULE (fl. 1640–60), Vicar of Great Stoughton, Huntingdonshire, England. *Sermons on Witchcraft* (30 June 1646), on the activities of Witch-Finder General Matthew Hopkins.

2 A witch is one who worketh by the Devil or by some curious art either healing or revealing things secret, or foretelling things to come which the Devil hath devised to ensnare men's souls withal unto damnation. The conjurer, the enchanter, the sorcerer, the diviner, and whatever other sort there is encompassed within this circle.

> GEORGE GIFFORD (16th century), English clergyman. *A Dis-*

course Concerning the Subtle Practices of Devils by Witches and Sorcerers (1587).

3 Why not walk in the aura of magic that gives to the small things of life their uniqueness and importance? Why not befriend a toad today?

GERMAINE GREER (b. 1939), Australian feminist writer. *The Change: Women, Ageing and the Menopause,* ch. 16 (1991).

4 What are these,
So withered, and so wild in their attire,
That look not like th'inhabitants o'th' earth,
And yet are on't?

WILLIAM SHAKESPEARE (1564–1616), English dramatist, poet. Banquo, in *Macbeth,* act 1, sc. 3, referring to the three witches.

5 For when girls have been corrupted, and have been scorned by their lovers after they have immodestly copulated with them in the hope and promise of marriage with them, and have found themselves disappointed in all their hopes and everywhere despised, they turn to the help and protection of devils; either for the sake of vengeance by bewitching those lovers or the wives they have married, or for the sake of giving themselves up to every sort of lechery. Alas! experience tells us that there is no number to such girls, and consequently the witches that spring from this class are innumerable.

JACOB SPRENGER AND HEINRICH KRÄMER (15th century), German theologians, Dominican monks. *Malleus Maleficarum,* pt. 2, ch. 1 (c. 1486; ed. by Pennethorne Hughes, 1968).

WIVES

1 Wives are young men's mistresses, companions for middle age, and old men's nurses.

FRANCIS BACON (1561–1626), English philosopher, essayist, statesman. *Essays,* "Of Marriage and Single Life" (1597–1625).

2 Whoso findeth a wife findeth a good thing, and obtaineth favour of the Lord.

BIBLE, HEBREW. *Proverbs* 18:22.

3 "Adam knew Eve his wife and she conceived." It is a pity that this is still the only knowledge of their wives at which some men seem to arrive.

F. H. BRADLEY (1846–1924), English philosopher. *Aphorisms,* no. 94 (1930).

4 Meek wifehood is no part of my profession;
I am your friend, but never your possession.

VERA BRITTAIN (1896–1970), British author, pacifist. *Married Love.*

5 The fact is that my wife if she had common sense would have more power over me than any other whatsoever, for my heart always alights upon the nearest perch.

LORD BYRON (1788–1824), English poet. Letter, 30 April 1814 (published in *Byron's Letters and Journals,* vol. 4, ed. by Leslie A. Marchand, 1973–81).

6 She'd have you spew up what you've drunk when you were out.

CAECILIUS (2nd century B.C.), Roman poet. *Plocium.*

7 A woman asking "Am *I* good? Am I satisfied?" is extremely selfish. The less women fuss about themselves, the less they talk to other women, the more they try to please their husbands, the happier the marriage is going to be.

BARBARA CARTLAND (b. 1901), British novelist. Interview in Wendy Leigh, *Speaking Frankly* (1978).

8 Variability is one of the virtues of a woman. It avoids the crude requirement of polygamy. So long as you have one good wife you are sure to have a spiritual harem.

G. K. CHESTERTON (1874–1936), British author. *Alarms and Discursions,* "The Glory of Grey" (1910).

9 The true index of a man's character is the health of his wife.

CYRIL CONNOLLY (1903–74), British critic. *The Unquiet Grave,* pt. 2 (1944; rev. 1951).

10 The majority of persons choose their wives with as little prudence as they eat. They see a trull with nothing else to recommend her but a pair of thighs and choice hunkers, and so smart to void their seed that they marry her at once. They imagine they can live in marvelous contentment with handsome feet and ambrosial buttocks. Most men are accredited fools shortly after they leave the womb.

EDWARD DAHLBERG (1900–1977), U.S. author, critic. *The Carnal Myth,* ch. 1 (1968).

11 Many a promising career has been wrecked by marrying the wrong sort of woman. The right sort of woman can distinguish between Creative Lassitude and plain shiftlessness.

ROBERTSON DAVIES (b. 1913), Canadian novelist, journalist. "The Writer's Week," in *Toronto Daily Star* (28 March 1959; repr. in *The Enthusiasms of Robertson Davies,* 1990).

12 Accidents will occur in the best regulated families; and in families not regulated by that pervading influence which sanctifies while it enhances the—a—I would say, in short, by the influence of Woman, in the lofty character of Wife, they may be expected with confidence, and must be borne with philosophy.

CHARLES DICKENS (1812–70), English novelist. Mr. Micawber, in *David Copperfield,* ch. 28 (1849–50).

13 It's my old girl that advises. She has the head. But I never own to it before her. Discipline must be maintained.

CHARLES DICKENS (1812–70), English novelist. Mr. Bagnet, in *Bleak House,* ch. 27 (1852).

14 A man would prefer to come home to an unmade bed and a happy woman than to a neatly made bed and an angry woman.

MARLENE DIETRICH (1904–92), German-born U.S. film actor. *Marlene Dietrich's ABC,* "Unmade Bed" (1962).

15 If you want to know about a man you can find out an awful lot by looking at who he married.

KIRK DOUGLAS (b. 1916), U.S. screen actor. *Daily Mail* (London, 9 Sept. 1988).

16 Nature meant me
A wife, a silly harmless household Dove,
Fond without art; and kind without deceit.

JOHN DRYDEN (1631–1700), English poet, dramatist, critic. Cleopatra, in *All for Love*, act 4, sc. 1 (1678).

17 The argument between wives and whores is an old one; each one thinking that whatever she is, at least she is not the other.

ANDREA DWORKIN (b. 1946), U.S. feminist critic. *Right-Wing Women*, ch. 2 (1978).

18 That's what a man wants in a wife, mostly; he wants to make sure o' one fool as 'ull tell him he's wise.

GEORGE ELIOT (1819–80), English novelist. Mrs. Poyser, in *Adam Bede*, bk. 6, ch. 53 (1859).

19 He knows little, who will tell his wife all he knows.

THOMAS FULLER (1608–61), English cleric. *The Holy State and the Profane State*, bk. 1, "The Good Husband" (1642).

20 I . . . chose my wife as she did her wedding-gown, not for a fine glossy surface, but such qualities as would wear well.

OLIVER GOLDSMITH (1728–74), Anglo-Irish author, poet, playwright. The narrator (Dr. Charles Primrose), in *The Vicar of Wakefield*, ch. 1 (1766).

21 In that second it dawned on me that I had been living here for eight years with a strange man and had borne him three children.

HENRIK IBSEN (1828–1906), Norwegian dramatist. Nora Helmer, in *A Doll's House*, act 3, speaking to her husband Torvald Helmer shortly before shooting herself.

22 In your power, all the same. Subject to your will and your demands. No longer free! No! That's a thought I'll never endure! Never.

HENRIK IBSEN (1828–1906), Norwegian dramatist. Hedda Gabler's final speech before shooting herself, in *Hedda Gabler*, act 4.

23 A man is in general better pleased when he has a good dinner upon his table, than when his wife talks Greek.

SAMUEL JOHNSON (1709–84), English author, lexicographer. *Works*, vol. 11, "Apophthegms" (ed. by John Hawkins, 1787–89). Quoted in: *Johnsonian Miscellanies*, vol. 2 (ed. by George Birkbeck Hill, 1897, p. 11).

24 Those graceful acts,
Those thousand decencies, that daily flow
From all her words and actions, mixed with love
And sweet compliance, which declare unfeigned
Union of mind, or in us both one soul.

JOHN MILTON (1608–74), English poet. Adam, in *Paradise Lost*, bk. 8, describing Eve.

25 A pretty wife is something for the fastidious vanity of a *roué* to retire upon.

THOMAS MOORE (1779–1852), Irish poet. Quoted by Lord Byron in a letter, 16 Jan. 1814 (published in *Byron's Letters and Journals*, vol. 4, 1975).

26 If you are really Master of your Fate,
It shouldn't make any difference to you whether
Cleopatra or the Bearded Lady is your mate.

OGDEN NASH (1902–71), U.S. poet. *The Anatomy of Happiness*, in *I'm a Stranger Here Myself* (1938).

27 I don't think a prostitute is more moral than a wife, but they are doing the same thing.

PRINCE PHILIP, DUKE OF EDINBURGH (b. 1921). Speech, 6 Dec. 1988. Quoted in: *Daily Mail* (London, 7 Dec. 1988). Prince Philip was discussing the morality of hunting.

28 Marry a mountain girl and you marry the whole mountain.

IRISH PROVERB.

29 No girl who is going to marry need bother to win a college degree; she just naturally becomes a "Master of Arts" and a "Doctor of Philosophy" after catering to an ordinary man for a few years.

HELEN ROWLAND (1875–1950), U.S. journalist. *A Guide to Men*, "Cymbals and Kettle-drums" (1922).

30 To suckle fools, and chronicle small beer.

WILLIAM SHAKESPEARE (1564–1616), English dramatist, poet. Iago, in *Othello*, act 2, sc. 1, describing the role of "a deserving woman." Desdemona calls this a "most lame and impotent conclusion."

31 This comes of James teaching me to think for myself, and never to hold back out of fear of what other people may think of me. It works beautifully as long as I think the same things as he does.

GEORGE BERNARD SHAW (1856–1950), Anglo-Irish playwright, critic. Candida, in *Candida*, act 2, of her husband Morell.

32 I'm sorry to say my dear wife is a dreamer,
And as she dreams she gets paler and leaner.
Then be off to your Dream, with his fly-away hat,
I'll stay with the girls who are happy and fat.

STEVIE SMITH (1902–71), British poet. *BE OFF!*

33 Such indeed is the superior longevity of the fair females of Surinam, compared to that of the males (owing chiefly, as I said, to their excesses of all sorts) that I have frequently known wives who have buried four husbands, but never met a man in this country who had survived two wives.

CAPTAIN J. G. STEDMAN (1744–97), British soldier, author, artist. *Narrative of a Five Years' Expedition Against the Revolted Negroes of Surinam*, ch. 1 (1796; repr. 1971).

34 An ideal wife is any woman who has an ideal husband.

BOOTH TARKINGTON (1869–1946), U.S. novelist, playwright. Gallup, in "The Hopeful Pessimist," in *Looking Forward and Others* (1926).

35 He will hold thee, when his passion shall have spent its novel force,
Something better than his dog, a little dearer than his horse.

LORD TENNYSON (1809–92), English poet. *Locksley Hall*.

36 In America a woman loses her independence for ever in the bonds of matrimony. While there is less constraint on girls there than anywhere else, a wife submits to stricter obligations. For the former, her father's house is a home of freedom and pleasure; for the latter, her husband's is almost a cloister.

ALEXIS DE TOCQUEVILLE (1805–59), French social philosopher. *Democracy in America*, vol. 2, pt. 3, ch. 10 (1840).

37 When I think of a merry, happy, free young girl— and look at the ailing, aching state a young wife generally is doomed to—which you can't deny is the penalty of marriage.

VICTORIA (1819–1901), Queen of Great Britain and Ireland. Letter, 16 May 1860, to her daughter Princess Frederick William (published in *Queen Victoria in Her Letters and Journals*, ed. by Christopher Hibbert, 1984).

38   London is full of women who trust their husbands. One can always recognise them. They look so thoroughly unhappy.

OSCAR WILDE (1854–1900), Anglo-Irish playwright, author. Lady Windermere, in *Lady Windermere's Fan*, act 2.

39   The clog of all pleasure, the luggage of life,
Is the best can be said for a very good wife.

JOHN WILMOT, SECOND EARL OF ROCHESTER (1647–80), English poet, courtier. *On a Wife*.

40   He's a fool that marries, but he's a greater that does not marry a fool; what is wit in a wife good for, but to make a man a cuckold?

WILLIAM WYCHERLEY (1640–1716), English dramatist. Pinchwife, in *The Country Wife*, act 1.

See also Prince Philip on CHIVALRY; Gilbert on FIDELITY; Mencken on FLIRTING; HUSBANDS; MARRIAGE; WIDOWHOOD.

WOMEN

1   A new kind of woman with deep-rooted values is changing the way we live. Market researchers call it "neo-traditionalism." To us it's a woman who has found her identity in herself, her home, her family. . . . She is part of an extraordinary social movement that is profoundly changing the way Americans look at living— and the way products are marketed. The home is again the center of American life, oatmeal is back on the breakfast table, families are vacationing together, watching movies at home, playing Monopoly again. Even the perfume ads are suddenly glorifying commitment.

ADVERTISEMENT for *Good Housekeeping*, in *New York Times* (17 Nov. 1988). Quoted in: Norman K. Denzin, *Images of Postmodern Society*, ch. 1 (1991).

2   All wickedness is but little to the wickedness of a woman.

APOCRYPHA. *Ecclesiasticus* 7:26.

3   A woman, especially, if she have the misfortune of knowing anything, should conceal it as well as she can.

JANE AUSTEN (1775–1817), English novelist. *Northanger Abbey*, ch. 14 (1818).

4   The being who, for most men, is the source of the most lively, and even, be it said, to the shame of philosophical delights, the most lasting joys; the being towards or for whom all their efforts tend . . . for whom and by whom fortunes are made and lost; for whom, but especially by whom, artists and poets compose their most delicate jewels; from whom flow the most enervating pleasures and the most enriching sufferings—woman, in a word, is not, for the artist in general . . . only the female of the human species. She is rather a divinity, a star.

CHARLES BAUDELAIRE (1821–67), French poet. "The Painter of

Modern Life," sct. 10, in *L'Art Romantique* (1869; repr. in *Selected Writings on Art and Artists*, ed. by P. E. Charvet, 1972).

5   We have dreamt of every woman there is, and dreamt too of the miracle that would bring us the pleasure of being a woman, for women have all the qualities— courage, passion, the capacity to love, cunning—whereas all our imagination can do is naively pile up the illusion of courage.

JEAN BAUDRILLARD (b. 1929), French semiologist. *Cool Memories*, ch. 1 (1987; tr. 1990).

6   One is not born, but rather becomes, a woman.

SIMONE DE BEAUVOIR (1908–86), French novelist, essayist. *The Second Sex*, bk. 2, pt. 4, ch. 1 (1953).

7   Who can find a virtuous woman? for her price is far above rubies.

BIBLE, HEBREW. *Proverbs* 31:10.

8   I will therefore . . . that women adorn themselves in modest apparel, with shamefacedness and sobriety; not with broided hair, or gold, or pearls, or costly array; but (which becometh women professing godliness) with good works. Let the woman learn in silence with all subjection. But I suffer not a woman to teach, nor to usurp authority over the man, but to be in silence. For Adam was first formed, then Eve. And Adam was not deceived, but the woman being deceived was in the transgression. Notwithstanding she shall be saved in childbearing, if they continue in faith and charity and holiness with sobriety.

BIBLE: NEW TESTAMENT. *1 Timothy* 3:8–15.

9   Women have no wilderness in them
They are provident instead
Content in the tight hot cell of their hearts
To eat dusty bread.

LOUISE BOGAN (1897–1970), U.S. poet, critic. *Women*.

10   Good women always think it is their fault when someone else is being offensive. Bad women never take the blame for anything.

ANITA BROOKNER (b. 1938), British author. Mr. Neville, in *Hotel du Lac*, ch. 7 (1984).

11   A complete woman is probably not a very admirable creature. She is manipulative, uses other people to get her own way, and works within whatever system she is in.

ANITA BROOKNER (b. 1938), British novelist, art historian. Interview in *Writers at Work* (Eighth Series, ed. by George Plimpton, 1988).

12   It will be a pity if women in the more conventional mould are to be phased out, for there will never be anyone to go home to.

ANITA BROOKNER (b. 1938), British novelist, art historian. Rachel, in *A Friend From England*, ch. 10 (1987), of women's lifestyles.

13   A woman cannot do the thing she ought,
Which means whatever perfect thing she can,
In life, in art, in science, but she fears
To let the perfect action take her part
And rest there: she must prove what she can do

Before she does it,—prate of woman's rights,
Of woman's mission, woman's function, till
The men (who are prating, too, on their side) cry,
"A woman's function plainly is . . . to talk."
Poor souls, they are very reasonably vexed!

ELIZABETH BARRETT BROWNING (1806–61), English poet.
Aurora Leigh, bk. 8 (1857).

14 Eve is a twofold mystery.

ELIZABETH BARRETT BROWNING (1806–61), English Poet. *The Poet's Vow*, pt. 1, st. 1.

15 Women hate everything which strips off the tinsel of sentiment, and they are right, or it would rob them of their weapons.

LORD BYRON (1788–1824), English poet. Letter, 12 Oct. 1820, to publisher John Murray (published in *Byron's Letters and Journals*, vol. 7, ed. by Leslie A. Marchand, 1973–81).

16 If *Miss* means respectably unmarried, and *Mrs.* respectably married, then *Ms.* means nudge, nudge, wink, wink.

ANGELA CARTER (1940–92), British author. "The Language of Sisterhood," in *The State of the Language* (1980).

17 I have always found women difficult. I don't really understand them. To begin with, few women tell the truth.

BARBARA CARTLAND (b. 1901), British novelist. *The Isthmus Years*, ch. 1 (1942).

18 Women are a sisterhood. They make common cause in behalf of the sex; and, indeed, this is natural enough, when we consider the vast power that the law gives us over them.

WILLIAM COBBETT (1762–1835), English journalist, reformer. *Advice to Young Men and to Young Women*, Letter 4, "To a Husband" (1829; repr. 1930).

19 Don't you realize that as long as you have to sit down to pee, you'll never be a dominant force in the world? You'll never be a convincing technocrat or middle manager. Because people will know. She's in there *sitting down.*

DON DELILLO (b. 1926), U.S. author. James Axton to his wife Kathryn, in *The Names*, ch. 5 (1982).

20 All observations point to the fact that the intellectual woman is masculinized; in her, warm, intuitive knowledge has yielded to cold unproductive thinking.

HELENE DEUTSCH (1884–1982), U.S. psychiatrist. *The Psychology of Women*, vol. 1, ch. 8 (1944–45).

21 Impenetrable in their dissimulation, cruel in their vengeance, tenacious in their purposes, unscrupulous as to their methods, animated by profound and hidden hatred for the tyranny of man—it is as though there exists among them an ever-present conspiracy toward domination, a sort of alliance like that subsisting among the priests of every country.

DENIS DIDEROT (1713–84), French philosopher. *On Women* (1772; repr. in *Selected Writings*, ed. by Lester G. Crocker, 1966).

22 I do not know if you remember the tale of the girl who saves the ship under mutiny by sitting on the powder barrel with her lighted torch . . . and all the time

knowing that it is empty? This has seemed to me a charming image of the women of my time. There they were, keeping the world in order . . . by sitting on the mystery of life, and knowing themselves that there was no mystery.

ISAK DINESEN [KAREN BLIXEN] (1885–1962), Danish author. *Seven Gothic Tales*, "The Old Chevalier" (1934).

23 Women are most fascinating between the ages of thirty-five and forty, after they have won a few races and know how to pace themselves. Since few women ever pass forty, maximum fascination can continue indefinitely.

CHRISTIAN DIOR (1905–57), French couturier. *Collier's Magazine* (10 June 1955).

24 It's only women who are not really quite women at all, frivolous women who have no idea, who neglect repairs.

MARGUERITE DURAS (b. 1914), French author, filmmaker. *Practicalities*, "House and Home" (1987; tr. 1990).

25 There are only three things to be done with a woman. You can love her, suffer for her, or turn her into literature.

LAWRENCE DURRELL (1912–90), British author. Clea, in *Justine*, pt. 1 (1957).

26 Woman is not born: she is made. In the making, her humanity is destroyed. She becomes symbol of this, symbol of that: mother of the earth, slut of the universe; but she never becomes herself because it is forbidden for her to do so.

ANDREA DWORKIN (b. 1946), U.S. feminist critic. *Pornography*, ch. 4 (1981).

27 The woman who can create her own job is the woman who will win fame and fortune.

AMELIA EARHART (1897–1937), U.S. aviator, author. *New York Times* (29 July 1928). Quoted in: Mary S. Lovell, *The Sound of Wings*, ch. 12 (1989), of openings for women in aviation.

28 The happiest women, like the happiest nations, have no history.

GEORGE ELIOT (1819–80), English novelist. *The Mill on the Floss*, bk. 6, ch. 3 (1860).

29 We women are always in danger of living too exclusively in the affections; and though our affections are perhaps the best gifts we have, we ought also to have our share of the more independent life—some joy in things for their own sake. It is piteous to see the helplessness of some sweet women when their affections are disappointed—because all their teaching has been, that they can only delight in study of any kind for the sake of a personal love. They have never contemplated an independent delight in ideas as an experience which they could confess without being laughed at. Yet surely women need this defence against passionate affliction even more than men.

GEORGE ELIOT (1819–80), English novelist. Letter, 8 July 1870 (published in *The George Eliot Letters*, vol. 5, 1954).

30 A woman's heart must be of such a size and no larger, else it must be pressed small, like Chinese feet; her happiness is to be made as cakes are, by a fixed receipt.

GEORGE ELIOT (1819–80), English novelist, editor. Deronda's mother, in *Daniel Deronda*, bk. 7, ch. 51 (1876), on society's expectations of women.

31 Slavery it is that makes slavery; freedom, freedom. The slavery of women happened when the men were slaves of kings.

RALPH WALDO EMERSON (1803–82), U.S. essayist, poet, philosopher. "Women," lecture, 1855 (published in *Miscellanies*, 1884).

32 Of all things upon earth that bleed and grow,
A herb most bruised is woman.

EURIPIDES (c. 480–406 B.C.), Greek tragedian. Medea, in *Medea* (tr. by Gilbert Murray).

33 When a woman behaves like a man why doesn't she behave like a nice man?

DAME EDITH EVANS (1888–1976), British actor. Quoted in: *Observer* (London, 30 Sept. 1956).

34 Observe this, that tho' a woman swear, forswear, lie, dissemble, back-bite, be proud, vain, malicious, anything, if she secures the main chance, she's still virtuous; that's a maxim.

GEORGE FARQUHAR (1678–1707), Irish dramatist. Lady Lurewell, in *The Constant Couple*, act 1, sc. 2.

35 They talk about a woman's sphere,
As though it had a limit.
There's not a place in earth or heaven.
There's not a task to mankind given . . .
Without a woman in it.

KATE FIELD (1838–96), U.S. writer. *Woman's Spirit.*

36 Women, despite the fact that nine out of ten of them go through life with a death-bed air either of snatching-the-last-moment or with martyr-resignation, do not die tomorrow—or the next day. They have to live on to any one of many bitter ends.

ZELDA FITZGERALD (1900–1948), U.S. writer. "Eulogy on the Flapper," in *Metropolitan Magazine* (New York, June 1922).

37 Women sometimes seem to share a quiet, unalterable dogma of persecution that endows even the most sophisticated of them with the inarticulate poignancy of the peasant.

ZELDA FITZGERALD (1900–1948), U.S. writer. *Save Me the Waltz*, ch. 2 (1932).

38 The great question that has never been answered, and which I have not yet been able to answer, despite my thirty years of research into the feminine soul, is "What does a woman want?"

SIGMUND FREUD (1856–1939), Austrian psychiatrist. Said to friend and disciple Marie Bonaparte. Quoted in: Ernest Jones, *Sigmund Freud: Life and Work*, vol. 2, pt. 3, ch. 16 (1955). Freud's views on women are summed up in Peter Gay, *Freud: A Life of Our Time*, pt. 10 (1988). See Wilde on WOMEN, below.

39 The especial genius of women I believe to be electrical in movement, intuitive in function, spiritual in tendency.

MARGARET FULLER (1810–50), U.S. writer, lecturer. "The Great Lawsuit," in *The Dial* (July 1843).

40 The Woman-Soul leadeth us
Upward and on!

JOHANN WOLFGANG VON GOETHE (1749–1832), German poet, dramatist. Last lines of *Faust*, pt. 2, act 5, sc. 7 (1832; tr. by Bayard Taylor), spoken by Chorus Mysticus.

41 The higher mental development of woman, the less possible it is for her to meet a congenial male who will see in her, not only sex, but also the human being, the friend, the comrade and strong individuality, who cannot and ought not lose a single trait of her character.

EMMA GOLDMAN (1869–1940), U.S. anarchist. *Anarchism and Other Essays*, "The Tragedy of Women's Emancipation" (1910).

42 Maybe I couldn't make it. Maybe I don't have a pretty smile, good teeth, nice tits, long legs, a cheeky arse, a sexy voice. Maybe I don't know how to handle men and increase my market value, so that the rewards due to the feminine will accrue to me. Then again, maybe I'm sick of the masquerade. I'm sick of pretending eternal youth. I'm sick of belying my own intelligence, my own will, my own sex. I'm sick of peering at the world through false eyelashes, so everything I see is mixed with a shadow of bought hairs; I'm sick of weighting my head with a dead mane, unable to move my neck freely, terrified of rain, of wind, of dancing too vigorously in case I sweat into my lacquered curls. I'm sick of the Powder Room. I'm sick of pretending that some fatuous male's self-important pronouncements are the objects of my undivided attention, I'm sick of going to films and plays when someone else wants to, and sick of having no opinions of my own about either. I'm sick of being a transvestite. I refuse to be a female impersonator. I am a woman, not a castrate.

GERMAINE GREER (b. 1939), Australian feminist writer. *The Female Eunuch*, "Soul: The Stereotype" (1970).

43 A woman might claim to retain some of the child's faculties, although very limited and defused, simply because she has not been encouraged to learn methods of thought and develop a disciplined mind. As long as education remains largely induction ignorance will retain these advantages over learning and it is time that women impudently put them to work.

GERMAINE GREER (b. 1939), Australian feminist writer. *The Female Eunuch*, "Womanpower" (1970).

44 What breadth, what beauty and power of human nature and development there must be in a woman to get over all the palisades, all the fences, within which she is held captive!

ALEXANDER HERZEN (1812–70), Russian journalist, political thinker. *My Past and Thoughts*, vol. 2, pt. 5, ch. 41 (1921; tr. by Constance Garnett, 1924–27).

45 If it were not somewhat fanciful to suppose that every human excellence is presented, as it were, in one kind of being, we might believe that the whole treasure of morality and order is enshrined in the female character.

KARL WILHELM VON HUMBOLDT (1767–1835), German statesman, philologist. *Limits of State Action*, ch. 3 (1792; repr. 1854; tr. and ed. by J. W. Burrow, 1969).

46 A woman's whole life is a history of the affections. The heart is her world: it is there her ambition strives for empire; it is there her avarice seeks for hidden treasures. She sends forth her sympathies on adventure; she embarks her whole soul on the traffic of affection; and if shipwrecked, her case is hopeless—for it is a bankruptcy of the heart.

> WASHINGTON IRVING (1783–1859), U.S. author. *The Sketch-Book,* "The Broken Heart" (1819–20).

47 It is not women's fault if we are so tender. It is in the nature of the lives *we* live. And further, it would be a terrible catastrophe if men had to live men's lives and women's also. Which is precisely what has happened today—to women.

> SELMA JAMES (b. 1930), U.S. author, political activist. *The Ladies and the Mammies: Jane Austen and Jean Rhys,* ch. 1 (1983).

48 Like their personal lives, women's history is fragmented, interrupted; a shadow history of human beings whose existence has been shaped by the efforts and the demands of others.

> ELIZABETH JANEWAY (b. 1913), U.S. author, critic. *Women: Their Changing Roles,* "Reflections on the History of Women" (1973).

49 Nature has given women so much power that the law has very wisely given them little.

> SAMUEL JOHNSON (1709–84), English author, lexicographer. Letter, 18 Aug. 1763 (published in *The Letters of Samuel Johnson,* vol. 1, no. 157, ed. by R. W. Chapman, 1952).

50 Growing up female in America. What a liability! You grew up with your ears full of cosmetic ads, love songs, advice columns, whoreoscopes, Hollywood gossip, and moral dilemmas on the level of TV soap operas. What litanies the advertisers of the good life chanted at you! What curious catechisms!

> ERICA JONG (b. 1942), U.S. author. The narrator (Isadora Wing), in *Fear of Flying,* ch. 1 (1973).

51 The real thinking of woman . . . is pre-eminently practical and applied. It is something we describe as sound common sense, and is usually directed to what is close at hand and personal. . . . In general, it can be said that feminine mentality manifests an undeveloped, child-like, or primitive character; instead of the thirst for knowledge, curiosity; instead of judgment, prejudice; instead of thinking, imagination or dreaming; instead of will, wishing. Where a man takes up objective problems, a woman contents herself with solving riddles; where he battles for knowledge and understanding, she contents herself with faith or superstition, or else she makes assumptions.

> EMMA JUNG (1882–1955), Swiss scholar, lecturer. "On the Nature of Animus" (1931; repr. in *Animus and Anima,* 1957).

52 Women are natural guerrillas. Scheming, we nestle into the enemy's bed, avoiding open warfare, watching the options, playing the odds.

> SALLY KEMPTON (b. 1943), U.S. author. "Cutting Loose," in *Esquire* (New York, July 1970).

53 The Monstrous Regiment of Women.

> JOHN KNOX (1505–72), Scottish Presbyterian leader. From title of pamphlet *The First Blast of the Trumpet Against the Monstrous Regiment of Women* (1558). In it, Knox wrote, "Nature doth paint them further to be weak, frail, impatient, feeble and foolish; and experience hath declared them to be unconstant, variable, cruel, and lacking the spirit of counsel."

54 Woman is the future of man. That means that the world which was once formed in man's image will now be transformed to the image of woman. The more technical and mechanical, cold and metallic it becomes, the more it will need the kind of warmth that only the woman can give it. If we want to save the world, we must adapt to the woman, let ourselves be led by the woman, let ourselves be penetrated by the *Ewigweiblich,* the eternally feminine!

> MILAN KUNDERA (b. 1929), Czech author, critic. Paul, in *Immortality,* pt. 7, ch. 3 (1991).

55 The chief thing about a woman—who is much of a woman—is that in the long run she is not to be had. . . . She is not to be caught by any of the catch-words, love, beauty, honor, duty, worth, work, salvation—none of them—not in the long run. In the long run she only says "Am I satisified, or is there some beastly unsatisfaction gnawing and gnawing inside me." And if there is some unsatisfaction, it is physical, at least as much as psychic, sex as much as soul.

> D. H. LAWRENCE (1885–1930), British author. Letter, 31 Oct. 1913 (published in *The Letters of D. H. Lawrence,* vol. 2, ed. by George J. Zytaruk and James T. Boulton, 1981).

56 The one woman who *never* gives herself is your free woman, who is always giving herself.

> D. H. LAWRENCE (1885–1930), British author. Letter, 2 Sept. 1922 (published in *The Letters of D. H. Lawrence,* vol. 4, ed. by James T. Boulton, E. Mansfield and W. Roberts, 1987).

57 To me the "female principle" is, or at least historically has been, basically anarchic. It values order without constraint, rule by custom not by force. It has been the male who enforces order, who constructs power structures, who makes, enforces, and breaks laws.

> URSULA K. LE GUIN (b. 1929), U.S. author. "Is Gender Necessary?," in *Aurora* (ed. by Susan Anderson and Vonda McIntyre, 1976; repr. in *Dancing at the Edge of the World,* 1989).

58 We are volcanoes. When we women offer our experience as our truth, as human truth, all the maps change. There are new mountains.

> URSULA K. LE GUIN (b. 1929), U.S. author. Bryn Mawr Commencement Address, 1986 (published in *Dancing at the Edge of the World,* 1989).

59 A Woman is home caring for her children! even if she can't. Trapped in this well-built trap, A Woman blames her mother for luring her into it, while ensuring that her own daughter never gets out; she recoils from the idea of sisterhood and doesn't believe women have friends, because it probably means something unnatural, and anyhow, A Woman is afraid of women. She's a male construct, and she's afraid women will deconstruct her. She's afraid of everything, because she can't change. Thighs forever thin and shining hair and shining teeth and she's my Mom, too, all seven percent of her. And she never grows old.

> URSULA K. LE GUIN (b. 1929), U.S. author. Bryn Mawr Commencement Address, 1986 (published in *Dancing at the Edge of the World,* 1989).

60 Being a woman is of special interest only to aspiring male transsexuals. To actual women it is merely a good excuse not to play football.

FRAN LEBOWITZ (b. 1951), U.S. journalist. *Metropolitan Life,* "Letters" (1978).

61   Woman is the Nigger of the World.

JOHN LENNON (1940–80) AND YOKO ONO (b. 1933), British rock musician, U.S. artist. Song title, on the album *Some Time in New York City* (1972).

62   But if God had wanted us to think just with our wombs, why did He give us a brain?

CLARE BOOTHE LUCE (1903–87), U.S. playwright, diplomat. Nora, in *Slam the Door Softly* (1970).

63   There are many examples of women that have excelled in learning, and even in war, but this is no reason we should bring 'em all up to *Latin* and *Greek* or else military discipline, instead of needle-work and housewifry.

BERNARD MANDEVILLE (1670–1733), Dutch-born English author, physician. *The Fable of the Bees,* "Essay on Charity and Charity-Schools" (1714; rev. 1723).

64   If a test of civilization be sought, none can be so sure as the condition of that half of society over which the other half has power.

HARRIET MARTINEAU (1802–76), English writer, social critic. *Society in America,* vol. 3, "Women" (1837).

65   The angel of the Family is Woman. Mother, wife, or sister, Woman is the caress of life, the soothing sweetness of affection shed over its toils, a reflection for the individual of the loving providence which watches over Humanity. In her there is treasure enough of consoling tenderness to allay every pain. Moreover for every one of us she is the initiator of the future. The mother's first kiss teaches the child love; the first holy kiss of the woman he loves teaches man hope and faith in life; and love and faith create a desire for perfection and the power of reaching towards it step by step; create the future, in short, of which the living symbol is the child, link between us and the generations to come. Through her the Family, with its divine mystery of reproduction, points to Eternity.

GIUSEPPE MAZZINI (1805–72), Italian nationalist leader. *The Duties of Man,* ch. 6 (1844–58; tr. 1907).

66   Women are the fulfilled sex. Through our children we are able to produce our own immortality, so we lack that divine restlessness which sends men charging off in pursuit of fortune or fame or an imagined Utopia. That is why we number so few geniuses among us. The wholesome oyster wears no pearl, the healthy whale no ambergris, and as long as we can keep on adding to the race, we harbor a sort of health within ourselves.

PHYLLIS MCGINLEY (1905–78), U.S. poet, author. *The Province of the Heart,* "Some of My Best Friends . . ." (1959).

67   I expect that Woman will be the last thing civilised by Man.

GEORGE MEREDITH (1828–1909), English author. An aphorism from the "Pilgrim's Scrip," in *The Ordeal of Richard Feverel,* ch. 1 (1859).

68   The great mass of women throughout history have been confined to the cultural level of animal life in pro-

viding the male with sexual outlet and exercising the animal functions of reproduction and care of the young.

KATE MILLETT (b. 1934), U.S. feminist author. *Sexual Politics,* ch. 3 (1970).

69   Aren't women prudes if they don't and prostitutes if they do?

KATE MILLET (b. 1934), U.S. feminist author. Speech, 22 March 1975, Women Writers' Conference, Los Angeles.

70   We are educated in the grossest ignorance, and no art omitted to stifle our natural reason; if some few get above their nurses' instructions, our knowledge must rest concealed and be as useless to the world as gold in the mine.

LADY MARY WORTLEY MONTAGU (1689–1762), English society figure, letter writer. Letter, 10 Oct. 1753, to her daughter Lady Bute (published in *Selected Letters,* ed. by Robert Halsband, 1970).

71   I think being a woman is like being Irish. . . . Everyone says you're important and nice, but you take second place all the same.

IRIS MURDOCH (b. 1919), British novelist, philosopher. Frances Bellman, in *The Red and the Green,* ch. 2 (1965). Iris Murdoch was born in Dublin.

72   We admire a woman for the courage to show herself to the world as she is, and in the end it's the courage we find attractive.

NEW YORKER (30 April 1990).

73   Women are considered deep—why? Because one can never discover any bottom to them. Women are not even shallow.

FRIEDRICH NIETZSCHE (1844–1900), German philosopher. *Twilight of the Idols,* "Maxims and Arrows," no. 27 (1889).

74   If a woman possesses manly virtues one should run away from her; and if she does not possess them she runs away from herself.

FRIEDRICH NIETZSCHE (1844–1900), German philosopher. *Twilight of the Idols,* "Maxims and Arrows," no. 28 (1889).

75   Woman does not forget she needs the fecundator, she does not forget that everything that is born of her is planted in her.

ANAÏS NIN (1903–77), Franco-American novelist, diarist. *The Diary of Anaïs Nin,* vol. 2 (1967), Aug. 1937 entry.

76   Woman is the dominant sex. Men have to do all sorts of stuff to prove that they are worthy of woman's attention.

CAMILLE PAGLIA (b. 1947), U.S. author, critic, educator. Interview in *SPIN,* "The Rape Debate" (Sept. 1991; repr. in *Sex, Art, and American Culture,* 1992). Later in the essay, Paglia writes, "Women's sexual powers are enormous. All cultures have seen it. Men know it. Women know it. The only people who don't know it are feminists. Desensualized, desexualized, neurotic women."

77   If civilization had been left in female hands we would still be living in grass huts.

CAMILLE PAGLIA (b. 1947), U.S. author, critic, educator. *Sex, Art, and American Culture,* Introduction (1992).

78   Woman—for example, look at her case! She turns tantalizing inviting glances on you. You seize her. No sooner does she feel herself in your grasp than she closes her eyes. It is a sign of her mission, the sign by which she says to man: "Blind yourself, for I am blind."

> LUIGI PIRANDELLO (1867–1936), Italian author, playwright. The Father addressing the Step-daughter, in *Six Characters in Search of an Author,* act 1.

79   Most women have no characters at all.

> ALEXANDER POPE (1688–1744), English satirical poet. *Epistle to a Lady.*

80   The individual woman is required . . . a thousand times a day to choose either to accept her appointed role and thereby rescue her good disposition out of the wreckage of her self-respect, or else follow an independent line of behavior and rescue her self-respect out of the wreckage of her good disposition.

> JEANNETTE RANKIN (1880–1973), U.S. suffragist, politician. Quoted in: Hannah Josephson, *Jeanette Rankin: First Lady in Congress,* ch. 3 (1974).

81   A woman is like a teabag—only in hot water do you realize how strong she is.

> NANCY REAGAN (b. 1923), U.S. First Lady. Quoted in: *Observer* (London, 29 March 1981).

82   No woman is really an insider in the institutions fathered by masculine consciousness. When we allow ourselves to believe we are, we lose touch with parts of ourselves defined as unacceptable by that consciousness; with the vital toughness and visionary strength of the angry grandmothers, the shamanesses, the fierce market-women of the Ibo's Women's War, the marriage-resisting women silkworkers of prerevolutionary China, the millions of widows, midwives, and the women healers tortured and burned as witches for three centuries in Europe.

> ADRIENNE RICH (b. 1929), U.S. poet. *Blood, Bread and Poetry,* "What Does a Woman Need to Know?" (1986).

83   Woman! The peg on which the wit hangs his jest, the preacher his text, the cynic his grouch, and the sinner his justification!

> HELEN ROWLAND (1875–1950), U.S. journalist. *A Guide to Men,* "Second Interlude" (1922).

84   For my part I distrust *all* generalizations about women, favourable and unfavourable, masculine and feminine, ancient and modern; all alike, I should say, result from paucity of experience.

> BERTRAND RUSSELL (1872–1970), British philosopher, mathematician. *Unpopular Essays,* "An Outline of Intellectual Rubbish" (1950).

85   Woman's destiny is to be wanton, like the bitch, the she-wolf; she must belong to all who claim her.

> MARQUIS DE SADE (1740–1814), French author. Mme de Saint-Ange, in *Philosophy in the Bedroom,* "Dialogue the Third" (1795).

86   If they are ignorant, they are despised, if learned, mocked. In love they are reduced to the status of courtesans. As wives they are treated more as servants than as companions. Men do not love them: they make use of

them, they exploit them, and expect, in that way, to make them subject to the law of fidelity.

> GEORGE SAND (1804–76), French novelist. *Almanach du Mois,* "La Fauvette du Docteur," Nov. 1844 (1844).

87   Only a male intellect clouded by the sexual drive could call the stunted, narrow-shouldered, broad-hipped and short-legged sex the fair sex.

> ARTHUR SCHOPENHAUER (1788–1860), German philosopher. *Parerga and Paralipomena,* vol. 2, ch. 27, sct. 369 (1851).

88   The only way for a woman to provide for herself decently is for her to be good to some man that can afford to be good to her.

> GEORGE BERNARD SHAW (1856–1950), Anglo-Irish playwright, critic. Mrs. Warren, in *Mrs. Warren's Profession,* act 2.

89   The cliché that women, more consistently than men, turn inward for sustenance seems to mean, in practice, that women have richly defined the ways in which imagination creates possibility; possibility that society denies.

> PATRICIA MEYER SPACKS (b. 1929), U.S. literary critic. *The Female Imagination,* "Afterword" (1975).

90   The great and almost only comfort about being a woman is that one can always pretend to be more stupid than one is and no one is surprised.

> FREYA STARK (b. 1893–1993), British travel writer. *The Valleys of the Assassins,* ch. 2 (1934).

91   Most women defend themselves. It is the female of the species—it is the tigress and lioness in you—which tends to defend when attacked.

> MARGARET THATCHER (b. 1925), British Conservative politician, prime minister. *Daily Mail* (London, 4 May 1989).

92   It requires nothing less than a chivalric feeling to sustain a conversation with a lady.

> HENRY DAVID THOREAU (1817–62), U.S. philosopher, author, naturalist. *Journals* (1906), entry for 31 Dec. 1851.

93   I have no hesitation in saying that although the American woman never leaves her domestic sphere and is in some respects very dependent within it, nowhere does she enjoy a higher station. And . . . if anyone asks me what I think the chief cause of the extraordinary prosperity and growing power of this nation, I should answer that it is due to the superiority of their women.

> ALEXIS DE TOCQUEVILLE (1805–59), French social philosopher. *Democracy in America,* vol. 2, pt. 3, ch. 12 (1840).

94   I repeat, sir, that in whatever position you place a woman she is an ornament to society and a treasure to the world. As a sweetheart, she has few equals and no superiors; as a cousin, she is convenient; as a wealthy grandmother with an incurable distemper, she is precious; as a wet-nurse, she has no equal among men. What, sir, would the people of the earth be without woman? They would be scarce, sir, almighty scarce.

> MARK TWAIN (1835–1910), U.S. author. "Woman—an Opinion," speech, to Washington Correspondents' Club (published in *Mark Twain's Speeches,* ed. by Albert Bigelow Paine, 1923).

95   A typical minority group stereotype—woman as

nigger—if she knows her place (home), she is really a quite lovable, loving creature, happy and childlike.

NAOMI WEISSTEIN (b. 1939), U.S. psychologist, author. "Woman as Nigger," in *Psychology Today* (New York, Oct. 1969).

96 The New Women! I could barely recognise them as being of the same sex as myself, their buttocks arrogant in tight jeans, openly inviting, breasts falling free and shameless and feeling no apparent obligation to smile, look pleasant or keep their voices low. And how they live! Just look at them to know how! If a man doesn't bring them to orgasm, they look for another who does. If by mistake they fall pregnant, they abort by vacuum aspiration. If they don't like the food, they push the plate away. If the job doesn't suit them, they hand in their notice. They are satiated by everything, hungry for nothing. They are what I wanted to be; they are what I worked for them to be: and now I see them, I hate them.

FAY WELDON (b. 1933), British novelist. The narrator (Praxis Duveen), in *Praxis*, ch. 2 (1978).

97 If there hadn't been women we'd still be squatting in a cave eating raw meat, because we made civilization in order to impress our girl friends. And they tolerated it and let us go ahead and play with our toys.

ORSON WELLES (1915–84), U.S. filmmaker, actor, producer. Interview in David Frost, *The Americans*, "Can a Martian Survive by Pretending to be a Leading American Actor?" (1970).

98 We have now traced the history of women from Paradise to the nineteenth century and have heard nothing through the long roll of the ages but the clank of their fetters.

LADY JANE WILDE (1821–96), Irish author, poet, translator. *Social Studies*, "The Bondage of Women" (1893).

99 The strength of women comes from the fact that psychology cannot explain us. Men can be analysed, women . . . merely adored.

OSCAR WILDE (1854–1900), Anglo-Irish playwright, author. Mrs. Cheveley, in *The Ideal Husband*, act 1.

100 There is only one real tragedy in a woman's life. The fact that her past is always her lover, and her future invariably her husband.

OSCAR WILDE (1854–1900), Anglo-Irish playwright, author. Mrs. Cheveley, in *An Ideal Husband*, act 3.

101 Every woman is a rebel, and usually in wild revolt against herself.

OSCAR WILDE (1854–1900), Anglo-Irish playwright, author. Lord Illingworth, in *A Woman of No Importance*, act 3.

102 The truth is, I often like women. I like their unconventionality. I like their completeness. I like their anonymity.

VIRGINIA WOOLF (1882–1941), British novelist. *A Room Of One's Own*, ch. 6 (1929).

103 Young women . . . you are, in my opinion, disgracefully ignorant. You have never made a discovery of any sort of importance. You have never shaken an empire or led an army into battle. The plays by Shakespeare are not by you, and you have never introduced a barbarous race to the blessings of civilization. What is your excuse?

VIRGINIA WOOLF (1882–1941), British novelist. *A Room Of One's Own*, ch. 6 (1929). This was originally a paper read to the women students of Cambridge University.

104 To be born woman is to know—
Although they do not speak of it at school—
Women must labour to be beautiful.

W. B. YEATS (1865–1939), Irish poet, playwright. *Adam's Curse*, observation by a "beautiful mild woman," actually the sister of Irish freedom fighter Maud Gonne.

See also ABORTION; Bierce on ABSENCE; Angelou on AFRICAN AMERICANS; Browning, Collins, Engel on AGE AND AGING; Greer on AGE AND AGING: FIFTIES; Coleridge on AGE AND AGING: SEVENTIES; Duras on ALCOHOL: DRUNKENNESS; Pugh on ANTIPATHY; Greer on APPEARANCE; Florio, Wollstonecraft on BEAUTY; Angelou on BLACK CULTURE; Atwood, Cohen on The BODY; CHILDBIRTH; Hawthorne, La Rochefoucauld on CHASTITY; Kasparov on CHESS; Daly on The CHURCH; Fairbairns on CLASS; Wolfe on COOKING; Jong on COSMETICS; Colette on COUNTRY LIFE; Byron, Shakespeare, Wilde on CRYING; Rosenstein on DESTINY; Hebrew Bible on DISCRETION; Steinem on DRESS; Burgess on ENGLAND AND THE ENGLISH; Saint Laurent on FASHION; FEMINISM; FERTILITY; Byron on FOOD AND EATING; Connolly on FRIENDS; Steinem on GAMBLING; GENDER; GIRLS; Bible: New Testament, Carter, Schiller on GODS AND GODDESSES; Conrad on HONOR; Browning, Bowen on INTIMACY; Sterne on JOKES AND JOKERS; Keats on KEATS; Mistinguett on KISSING; Montagu on KNOWLEDGE; LADIES; LESBIANISM;Byron on LOVE, FIRST; Lunch on MASTURBATION; MEN AND WOMEN; MENOPAUSE; MENSTRUATION; Greer on MIDDLE AGE; Carter on MORALITY; MOTHERS; Eliot on MOTIVES; Lynn on MUSIC; Greer, Le Guin on OLD AGE AND AGING; Jong on ORGASM; Dworkin on POETRY; PROSTITUTION; Woolf on PUBLICITY; Bethune on RACE; La Rochefoucauld on RELATIONSHIPS; Dworkin, Twain on SEX; Updike on SEXUALITY; Steinem on SOAP OPERAS; Nightingale on SYMPATHY; Burton on WINE; King on WIT; WIVES; Jong on WOMEN, SINGLE.

WOMEN, SINGLE

1 There is simply no dignified way for a woman to live alone. Oh, she can get along financially perhaps (though not nearly as well as a man), but emotionally she is never left in peace. Her friends, her family, her fellow workers never let her forget that her husbandlessness, her childlessness—her *selfishness*, in short—is a reproach to the American way of life.

ERICA JONG (b. 1942), U.S. author. Isadora Wing, the narrator in *Fear of Flying*, ch. 1 (1973).

2 He travels fastest who travels alone, and that goes double for she. Real feminism is spinsterhood.

FLORENCE KING (b. 1936), U.S. author. *Reflections in a Jaundiced Eye*, "Spinsterhood Is Powerful" (1989).

3 I'm anal retentive. I'm a workaholic. I have insomnia. And I'm a control freak. That's why I'm not married. Who could stand me?

MADONNA (b. 1959), U.S. singer, actor. Quoted in: Christopher Andersen, *Madonna Unauthorized*, ch. 22 (1991).

See also Shaw on WOMEN AND POLITICS.

WOMEN AND FEMININITY

1 Femininity appears to be one of those pivotal qualities that is so important no one can define it.

CAROLINE BIRD (b. 1915), U.S. author, social commentator. *Born Female*, ch. 11 (1968).

2 The feminine mystique has succeeded in burying millions of American women alive.

BETTY FRIEDAN (b. 1921), U.S. feminist writer. *The Feminine Mystique*, ch. 13 (1963).

3 Older women can afford to agree that femininity is a charade, a matter of coloured hair, écru lace and whalebones, the kind of slap and tat that transvestites are in love with, and no more.

GERMAINE GREER (b. 1939), Australian feminist writer. *The Change: Women, Ageing and the Menopause*, ch. 2 (1991).

See also Westwood on ELEGANCE.

WOMEN AND MEN

1 The white American man makes the white American woman maybe not superfluous but just a little kind of decoration. Not really important to turning around the wheels of the state. Well the black American woman has never been able to feel that way. No black American man at any time in our history in the United States has been able to feel that he didn't need that black woman right against him, shoulder to shoulder—in that cotton field, on the auction block, in the ghetto, wherever.

MAYA ANGELOU (b. 1928), U.S. author. "A Conversation with Maya Angelou," interview, 21 Nov. 1973 (published in *Conversations with Maya Angelou*, 1989).

2 Man forgives women anything save the wit to outwit him.

MINNA ANTRIM (b. 1861), U.S. epigrammist. *Naked Truth and Veiled Allusions*, p. 41 (1901).

3 She even had a kind of special position among men: she was an exception, she fitted none of the categories they commonly used when talking about girls; she wasn't a cock-teaser, a cold fish, an easy lay or a snarky bitch; she was an honorary person. She had grown to share their contempt for most women.

MARGARET ATWOOD (b. 1939), Canadian novelist, poet, critic. "The Man From Mars," in *Ontario Review* (1977; repr. in *Dancing Girls*, 1984).

4 Every woman is like a timezone. She is a nocturnal fragment of your journey. She brings you unflaggingly closer to the next night.

JEAN BAUDRILLARD (b. 1929), French semiologist. *Cool Memories*, ch. 5 (1987; tr. 1990).

5 A woman who looks like a girl and thinks like a man is the best sort, the most enjoyable to be and the most pleasurable to have and to hold.

JULIE BURCHILL (b. 1960), British journalist, author. *Damaged Gods*, "Born again Cows" (1986).

6 But as to women, who can penetrate
The real sufferings of their she condition?
Man's very sympathy with their estate
Has much of selfishness and more suspicion.
Their love, their virtue, beauty, education,
But form good housekeepers, to breed a nation.

LORD BYRON (1788–1824), English poet. *Don Juan*, cto. 14, st. 24. See Byron on MEN AND WOMEN.

7 There is something to me very softening in the presence of a woman, some strange influence, even if one is not in love with them, which I cannot at all account for, having no very high opinion of the sex. But yet, I always feel in better humour with myself and every thing else, if there is a woman within ken.

LORD BYRON (1788–1824), English poet. *Byron's Letters and Journals*, vol 3 (ed. by Leslie A. Marchand, 1974), entry for 27 Feb. 1814.

8 A woman should say: "Have I made *him* happy? Is *he* satisfied? Does he love me more than he loved me before? Is he likely to go to bed with another woman?" If he does, then it's the wife's fault because she is not trying to make him happy.

BARBARA CARTLAND (b. 1901), British novelist. Interview in Wendy Leigh, *Speaking Frankly* (1978).

9 Whatever evil a man may think of women, there is no woman but thinks more.

SÉBASTIEN-ROCH NICOLAS DE CHAMFORT (1741–94), French writer, wit. *Maximes et Pensées*, vol. 2, no. 414 (1796).

10 A man of sense only trifles with them, plays with them, humours and flatters them, as he does with a sprightly and forward child; but he neither consults them about, nor trusts them with, serious matters.

LORD CHESTERFIELD (1694–1773), English statesman, man of letters. Letter, 5 Sept. 1748 (first published 1774; repr. in *The Letters of the Earl of Chesterfield to His Son*, vol 1, no. 161, ed. by Charles Strachey, 1901).

11 It seems as though women keep growing. Eventually they can have little or nothing in common with the men they chose long ago.

EUGENIE CLARK (b. 1922), U.S. marine biologist, author. Quoted in: *Ms.* (New York, Aug. 1979).

12 A pretty little collection of weaknesses and a terror of spiders are our indispensable stock-in-trade with the men.

COLETTE (1873–1954), French author. Aunt Alicia, in *Gigi* (1944; tr. 1953); when asked why, Aunt Alicia replied, "Because nine men out of ten are superstitious, nineteen out of twenty believe in the evil eye, and ninety-eight out of a hundred are afraid of spiders. They forgive us—oh! for many things, but not for the absence in us of their own feelings."

13 There is no kind of harassment that a man may not inflict on a woman with impunity in civilized societies.

DENIS DIDEROT (1713–84), French philosopher. *On Women* (1772; repr. in *Selected Writings*, ed. by Lester G. Crocker, 1966).

14 To be completely woman you need a master, and in him a compass for your life. You need a man you can look up to and respect. If you dethrone him it's no wonder that you are discontented, and discontented women are not loved for long.

MARLENE DIETRICH (1904–92), German-born U.S. film actor. *Marlene Dietrich's ABC*, "Married Love" (1962).

15 Once a man is on hand, a woman tends to stop believing in her own beliefs.

COLETTE DOWLING (b. 1939), U.S. author. *The Cinderella Complex*, ch. 6 (1981).

16 Women are an enslaved population—the crop we harvest is children, the fields we work are houses.

Women are forced into committing sexual acts with men that violate integrity because the universal religion—contempt for women—has as its first commandment that women exist purely as sexual fodder for men.

ANDREA DWORKIN (b. 1946), U.S. feminist critic. "Pornography: The New Terrorism," speech, 1977, University of Massachusetts (published in *Letters From A War-Zone*, 1988). This was Dworkin's first public speech exclusively on the subject of pornography.

17 Women must try to do things as men have tried. When they fail their failure must be but a challenge to others.

AMELIA EARHART (1897–1937), U.S. aviator, author. Quoted in: Mary S. Lovell, *The Sound of Wings*, ch. 21 (1989).

18 I should like to know what is the proper function of women, if it is not to make reasons for husbands to stay at home, and still stronger reasons for bachelors to go out.

GEORGE ELIOT (1819–80), English novelist. Stephen Guest, in *The Mill on the Floss*, bk. 6, ch. 6 (1860).

19 And when a woman's will is as strong as the man's who wants to govern her, half her strength must be concealment.

GEORGE ELIOT (1819–80), English novelist. Deronda's mother on society's expectations of women, in *Daniel Deronda*, bk. 7, ch. 51 (1876).

20 I must have women—there is nothing unbends the mind like them.

JOHN GAY (1685–1732), English dramatist. Macheath, in *The Beggar's Opera*, act 2, sc. 3.

21 The female of the genus homo is economically dependent on the male. He is her food supply.

CHARLOTTE PERKINS GILMAN (1860–1935), U.S. feminist, writer. *Women and Economics*, ch. 1 (1898).

22 Man made one grave mistake: in answer to vaguely reformist and humanitarian agitation he admitted women to politics and the professions. The conservatives who saw this as the undermining of our civilization and the end of the state and marriage were right after all; it is time for the demolition to begin.

GERMAINE GREER (b. 1939), Australian feminist writer. *The Female Eunuch*, "Revolution" (1970).

23 Perhaps . . . women have always been in closer contact with reality than men: it would seem to be the just recompense for being deprived of idealism.

GERMAINE GREER (b. 1939), Australian feminist writer. *The Female Eunuch*, "Womanpower" (1970).

24 To be womanly is one thing, and one only; it is to be sensitive to man, to be highly endowed with the sex instinct; to be manly is to be sensitive to woman.

JANE HARRISON (1850–1928), English classical scholar, writer. *Alpha and Omega*, "Homo Sum" (1915).

25 Women receive
the insults of men
with tolerance,
having been bitten
in the nipple
by their toothless gums.

DILYS LAING (1906–60), Canadian poet, editor. *Veterans.*

26 Once women begin to question the inevitability of their subordination and to reject the conventions formerly associated with it, they can no longer retreat to the safety of those conventions. The woman who rejects the stereotype of feminine weakness and dependence can no longer find much comfort in the cliché that all men are beasts. She has no choice except to believe, on the contrary, that men are human beings, and she finds it hard to forgive them when they act like animals.

CHRISTOPHER LASCH (b. 1932), U.S. historian. *The Culture of Narcissism*, ch. 8, "Feminism and the Intensification of Sexual Warfare" (1979).

27 The cruellest thing a man can do to a woman is to portray her as perfection.

D. H. LAWRENCE (1885–1930), British author. Letter, 17 May 1913, to writer and critic Edward Garnett (published in *The Letters of D. H. Lawrence*, vol. 1, ed. by James T. Boulton, 1979).

28 A lady is smarter than a gentleman, maybe,
She can sew a fine seam, she can have a baby,
She can use her intuition instead of her brain,
But she can't fold a paper in a crowded train.

PHYLLIS MCGINLEY (1905–78), U.S. poet, author. *Trial and Error.*

29 A man's women folk, whatever their outward show of respect for his merit and authority, always regard him secretly as an ass, and with something akin to pity. His most gaudy sayings and doings seldom deceive them; they see the actual man within, and know him for a shallow and pathetic fellow. In this fact, perhaps, lies one of the best proofs of feminine intelligence, or, as the common phrase makes it, feminine intuition.

H. L. MENCKEN (1880–1956), U.S. journalist. *In Defense of Women*, "The Feminine Mind" (1918; rev. 1922; repr. in *A Mencken Chrestomathy*, pt. 3, 1949).

30 Nature has not placed us in an inferior rank to men, no more than the females of other animals, where we see no distinction of capacity, though I am persuaded if there was a commonwealth of rational horses . . . it would be an established maxim amongst them that a mare could not be taught to pace.

LADY MARY WORTLEY MONTAGU (1689–1762), English society figure, letter writer. Letter, 6 March 1753, to her daughter Lady Bute (published in *Selected Letters*, ed. by Halsband, 1970).

31 "Stupid as a man" say the women: "cowardly as a woman" say the men. Stupidity is in woman the *unwomanly.*

FRIEDRICH NIETZSCHE (1844–1900), German philosopher. *The Wanderer and His Shadow*, aph. 273 (1880).

32 If man knew how women pass the time when they are alone, they'd never marry.

O. HENRY [WILLIAM SYDNEY PORTER] (1862–1910), U.S. short-story writer. "Memoirs of a Yellow Dog," in *The Four Million* (1906).

33 She plucked from my lapel the invisible strand of lint (the universal act of woman to proclaim ownership).

O. HENRY [WILLIAM SYDNEY PORTER] (1862–1910), U.S. short-story writer. *Strictly Business*, "A Ramble in Aphasia" (1910).

34 There are always women who will take men on

their own terms. If I were a man I wouldn't bother to change while there are women like that around.

> ANN OAKLEY (b. 1944), British sociologist, author. Quoted in: *Observer* (London, 27 Oct. 1991).

35 Let us leave pretty women to men devoid of imagination.

> MARCEL PROUST (1871–1922), French novelist. *Remembrance of Things Past,* vol 11, "The Sweet Cheat Gone," ch. 1 (1925; tr. by Scott Monkrieff, 1930).

36 Men are the managers of the affairs of women
for that God has preferred in bounty
one of them over another, and for that
they have expended of their property.
Righteous women are therefore obedient,
guarding the secret for God's guarding.
And those you fear may be rebellious
admonish; banish them to their couches,
and beat them.

> QUR'AN. *Women* 4:38 (ed. by Arthur J. Arberry, 1955).

37 Some women can be fooled all of the time, and all women can be fooled some of the time, but the same woman can't be fooled by the same man in the same way more than half of the time.

> HELEN ROWLAND (1875–1950), U.S. journalist. *A Guide to Men,* "Intermezzo" (1922).

38 Men are like the earth and we are the moon; we turn always one side to them, and they think there is no other, because they don't see it—but there is.

> OLIVE SCHREINER (1855–1920), South African writer, feminist. Lyndall, in *The Story of an African Farm,* pt. 2, ch. 4 (1883).

39 If women were as fastidious as men, morally or physically, there would be an end of the race.

> GEORGE BERNARD SHAW (1856–1950), Anglo-Irish playwright, critic. *Man and Superman,* "Epistle Dedicatory" (1903).

40 The desire of the man is for the woman, but the desire of the woman is for the desire of the man.

> Attributed to MADAME DE STAËL (1766–1817), Swiss-French writer, wit.

41 Some of us are becoming the men we wanted to marry.

> GLORIA STEINEM (b. 1934), U.S. feminist writer, editor. Speech, Sept. 1981, Yale University, New Haven, Conn.

42 The cocks may crow, but it's the hen that lays the egg.

> MARGARET THATCHER (b. 1925), British Conservative politician, prime minister. Quoted in: *Sunday Times* (London, 9 April 1989).

43 No men who really think deeply about women retain a high opinion of them; men either despise women or they have never thought seriously about them.

> OTTO WEININGER (1880–1903), Austrian philosopher. *Sex and Character,* ch. 11 (1906).

44 The fact is, you have fallen lately, Cecily, into a bad habit of thinking for yourself. You should give it up. It is not quite womanly.... Men don't like it.

> OSCAR WILDE (1854–1900), Anglo-Irish playwright, author. Miss Prism, in *The Importance of Being Earnest,* act 3.

45 Women are told from their infancy, and taught by the example of their mothers, that a little knowledge of human weakness, justly termed cunning, softness of temper, *outward* obedience and a scrupulous attention to a puerile kind of propriety, will obtain for them the protection of man.

> MARY WOLLSTONECRAFT (1759–97), English feminist writer. *A Vindication of the Rights of Women,* ch. 2 (1792).

46 Women have served all these centuries as lookingglasses possessing the magic and delicious power of reflecting the figure of man at twice its natural size.

> VIRGINIA WOOLF (1882–1941), British novelist. *A Room Of One's Own,* ch. 2 (1929).

47 Why are women . . . so much more interesting to men than men are to women?

> VIRGINIA WOOLF (1882–1941), British novelist. *A Room Of One's Own,* ch. 2 (1929).

48 Women serve but to keep a man from better company.

> WILLIAM WYCHERLEY (1640–1716), English dramatist. Horner, in *The Country Wife,* act 1.

See also MEN AND WOMEN; Dworkin on PORNOGRAPHY; Coward on PROMISCUITY; Rich on REVOLUTION; Zetterling on SEX.

WOMEN AND POLITICS

1 I can conceive of nothing worse than a man-governed world—except a woman-governed world.

> NANCY ASTOR (1879–1964), British politician. *My Two Countries,* ch. 1, "America" (1923).

2 I see little hope for a peaceful world until men are excluded from the realm of foreign policy altogether and all decisions concerning international relations are reserved for women, preferably married ones.

> W. H. AUDEN (1907–73), Anglo-American poet. *A Certain World,* "Penis Rivalry" (1970).

3 Women—one half the human race at least—care fifty times more for a marriage than a ministry.

> WALTER BAGEHOT (1826–77), English economist, critic. *The English Constitution,* ch. 2 (1867).

4 Like all successful politicians I married above myself.

> DWIGHT D. EISENHOWER (1890–1969), U.S. general, Republican politician, president. Quoted by Richard Nixon in: *Six Crises,* "The Campaign of 1960" (1962).

5 I know I have the body of a weak and feeble woman, but I have the heart and stomach of a king, and of a king of England too.

> ELIZABETH I (1533–1603), Queen of England. Speech, 8 Aug. 1588, to troops at Tilbury, England, on the approach of the Spanish Armada.

6 If American politics are too dirty for women to take part in, there's something wrong with American politics.

> EDNA FERBER (1887–1968), U.S. author. Sabra Cravat, in *Cimarron,* ch. 23 (1929).

7 The woman who can't influence her husband to vote the way she wants ought to be ashamed of herself.

E. M. FORSTER (1879–1970), British novelist, essayist. Mrs. Plynlimmon, in *Howards End,* ch. 26 (1910).

8 My father was a statesman, I'm a political woman. My father was a saint. I'm not.

INDIRA GANDHI (1917–84), Indian politician, prime minister. Of her father Pandit Jawaharlal Nehru. Quoted in: Oriana Fallaci, "Indira's Coup," in *New York Review of Books* (18 Sept. 1975).

9 There is no hope even that woman, with her right to vote, will ever purify politics.

EMMA GOLDMAN (1869–1940), U.S. anarchist. *Anarchism and Other Essays,* "The Tragedy of Women's Emancipation" (1910).

10 I'm always rather nervous about how you talk about women who are active in politics, whether they want to be talked about as women or as politicians.

JOHN F. KENNEDY (1917–63), U.S. Democratic politician, president. To a group of women delegates to the United Nations who had suggested that there might one day be a woman President. Quoted in: Bill Adler, *The Wit of President Kennedy,* "The Presidency" (1964).

11 To promote a woman to bear rule, superiority, dominion or empire, above any realm, nation, or city, is repugnant to nature; contumely to God, a thing most contrarious to his revealed will and approved ordinance, and finally it is the subversion of good order, of all equity and justice.

JOHN KNOX (1505–72), Scottish Presbyterian leader. *First Blast of the Trumpet Against the Monstrous Regiment of Women*— pamphlet published 1558, the first year of Elizabeth I's reign.

12 To put a woman on the ticket would challenge the loyalty of women everywhere to their sex, because it would be made to seem that the defeat of the ticket meant the defeat for a hundred years of women's chance to be truly equal with men in politics.

CLARE BOOTHE LUCE (1903–87), U.S. diplomat, writer. Quoted in: *New York World-Telegram* (28 June 1948).

13 It certainly must have been a relief for the women of the country to realize that one could be a woman and a lady and yet be thoroughly political.

AGNES MEYER (1887–1970), U.S. author, journalist. Letter, 25 July 1952 to Eleanor Roosevelt. Quoted in: Joseph P. Lash, *Eleanor: The Years Alone* (1972).

14 Now, in my opinion, a woman has no business with Power—Power admits no equal, and dismisses friendship for flattery. Besides, it keeps the men at a distance, and that is not always what we wish.

EDWARD MOORE (1712–57), English fabulist, dramatist. Fidelia, in *The Foundling,* act 1, sc. 2.

15 Give women the vote, and in five years there will be a crushing tax on bachelors.

GEORGE BERNARD SHAW (1856–1950), Anglo-Irish playwright, critic. *Man and Superman,* "Epistle Dedicatory" (1903).

16 But you must know the class of sweet women— who are always so happy to declare "they have all the rights they want"; "they are perfectly willing to let their husbands vote for them"—are and always have been numerous, though it is an occasion for thankfulness that they are becoming less so.

ELIZA "MOTHER" STEWART (1816–1908), U.S. temperance leader. *Memories of the Crusade,* ch. 7 (1888).

17 No woman in my time will be Prime Minister or Chancellor or Foreign Secretary—not the top jobs. Anyway I wouldn't want to be Prime Minister. You have to give yourself 100%.

MARGARET THATCHER (b. 1925), British Conservative politician, prime minister. Interview in *Sunday Telegraph* (London, 26 Oct. 1969), on her appointment as Shadow Education Spokesman.

18 In politics if you want anything said, ask a man. If you want anything done, ask a woman.

MARGARET THATCHER (b. 1925), British Conservative politician. prime minister. *People* (New York, 15 Sept. 1975).

19 We women are not *made* for governing–and if we are good women, we must *dislike* these masculine occupations; but there are times which force one to take *interest* in them *mal gré bon gré,* and *I* do, of course, *intensely.*

VICTORIA (1819–1901), Queen of Great Britain and Ireland. Letter, 3 Feb. 1852, to Leopold I, King of the Belgians (published in *Letters of Queen Victoria,* vol. 2, ch. 21, ed. by A. C. Benson and Viscount Esher, 1907).

See also THE FIRST LADY; Victoria on ROYALTY; MARGARET THATCHER.

WOMEN AND THE ARTS

1 All I ask, is the privilege for my masculine part the poet in me. . . . If I must not, because of my sex, have this freedom . . . I lay down my quill and you shall hear no more of me.

APHRA BEHN (1640–89), English author, adventuress. *The Lucky Chance,* Preface (1686).

2 I am obnoxious to each carping tongue
Who says my hand a needle better fits,
A poet's pen all scorn I should thus wrong
For such despite they cast on female wits;
If what I do prove well, it won't advance,
They'll say it's stolen, or else it was by chance.

ANNE BRADSTREET (c. 1612–72), U.S. poet. *Several Poems Compiled with Great Variety of Wit and Learning,* Prologue (1678).

3 Regularity and Decorum. 'Tis what we women-authors, in particular, have been thought greatly deficient in; and I should be concerned to find it an objection not to be removed.

ELIZABETH COOPER (fl. 1730s), British playwright, anthologist. *The Rival Widows; or, Fair Libertine,* Preface (1735).

4 I think it's a question which particularly arises over women writers: whether it's better to have a happy life or a good supply of tragic plots.

WENDY COPE (b. 1945), British poet. *Independent* (London, 9 March 1992).

5 Men like women who write. Even though they don't say so. A writer is a foreign country.

MARGUERITE DURAS (b. 1914), French author, filmmaker. *Practicalities,* "The M.D. Uniform" (1987; tr. 1990).

6 Since art is the expression of beauty and beauty can be understood only in the form of the material elements of the true idea it contains, art has become almost uniquely feminine. Beauty is woman, and also art is woman.

RÉMY DE GOURMONT (1858–1915), French critic, novelist. "The Dissociation of Ideas" (1899; repr. in *Selected Writings*, ed. and tr. by Glen S. Burne, 1966).

7   To be a woman and a writer
is double mischief, for
the world will slight her
who slights "the servile house," and who would
   rather
make odes than beds.

DILYS LAING (1906–60), Canadian poet, editor. *Sonnet to a Sister in Error*, st. 6.

8   Literature takes shape and life in the body, in the wombs of the mother tongue: always: and the Fathers of Culture get anxious about paternity. They start talking about legitimacy. They steal the baby. They ensure by every means that the artist, the writer, is male. This involves intellectual abortion by centuries of women artists, infanticide of works by women writers, and a whole medical corps of sterilizing critics working to purify the Canon, to reduce the subject matter and style of literature to something Ernest Hemingway could have understood.

URSULA K. LE GUIN (b. 1929), U.S. author. Bryn Mawr Commencement Address, 1986 (published in *Dancing at the Edge of the World*, 1989).

9   If you want your writing to be taken seriously, don't marry and have kids, and above all, don't die. But if you have to die, commit suicide. They approve of that.

URSULA K. LE GUIN (b. 1929), U.S. author. "Prospects for Women in Writing," address, Sept. 1986, Conference on Women in the Year 2000, Portland, Maine (published in *Dancing at the Edge of the World*, 1989).

10   I'm a writer first and a woman after.

KATHERINE MANSFIELD (1888–1923), New Zealand-born British author. Letter, 3 Dec. 1920, to her husband John Middleton Murry.

11   America is essentially a woman's country — why shouldn't the leading novelists be women?

HENRY MILLER (1891–1980), U.S. author. "Reunion in Brooklyn," in *Sunday After the War* (1944; repr. in *The Best of Henry Miller*, ed. by Lawrence Durrell, 1960).

12   The literary woman, unsatisfied, agitated, desolate in heart and entrails, listening every minute with painful curiosity to the imperative which whispers from the depths of her organism "*aut liberi aut libri.*"

FRIEDRICH NIETZSCHE (1844–1900), German philosopher. *Twilight of the Idols*, "Expeditions of an Untimely Man," aph. 27 (1889). *Aut liberi aut libri* = "either children or books."

13   Before I put a brush to canvas, I question, "Is this mine? . . . Is it influenced by some idea which I have acquired from some man?" . . . I am trying with all my skill to do a painting that is all of women, as well as all of me.

GEORGIA O'KEEFFE (1887–1986), U.S. artist. Debate reported in *New York World* (16 March 1930). Quoted in: Laurie Lisle, *Portrait Of An Artist* (1986).

14   There is no female Mozart because there is no female Jack the Ripper.

CAMILLE PAGLIA (b. 1947), U.S. author, critic, educator. *International Herald Tribune* (Paris, 26 April 1991).

15   As artists they're rot, but as providers they're oil wells; they gush. Norris said she never wrote a story unless it was fun to do. I understand Ferber whistles at her typewriter. And there was that poor sucker Flaubert rolling around on his floor for three days looking for the right word.

DOROTHY PARKER (1893–1967), U.S. humorous writer. Interview in *Writers at Work* (First Series, ed. by Malcolm Cowley, 1958).

16   There shall be poets! When woman's unmeasured bondage shall be broken, when she shall live for and through herself, man — hitherto detestable — having let her go, she, too, will be poet! Woman will find the unknown! Will her ideational worlds be different from ours? She will come upon strange, unfathomable, repellent, delightful things; we shall take them, we shall comprehend them.

ARTHUR RIMBAUD (1854–1891), French poet. Letter, 15 May 1871 (published in *Collected Poems*, ed. by Oliver Bernard, 1962).

17   The woman who needs to create works of art is born with a kind of psychic tension in her which drives her unmercifully to find a way to balance, to make herself whole. Every human being has this need: in the artist it is mandatory. Unable to fulfill it, he goes mad. But when the artist is a woman she fulfills it at the *expense* of herself as a woman.

MAY SARTON (b. 1912), U.S. poet, novelist. Hilary Stevens, in *Mrs. Stevens Hears the Mermaids Singing*, pt. 2 (1965).

18   What a revolting contrast exists in England between the slavery of women and the intellectual superiority of women writers.

FLORA TRISTAN (1803–44), French novelist. *Promenades Dans Londres*, ch. 17 (1840).

19   The composition of a tragedy requires *testicles.*

VOLTAIRE (1694–1778), French philosopher, author. Attributed by Byron in his letter, 2 April 1817, to publisher John Murray. The quote was Voltaire's reply when asked why no woman had ever written a tolerable tragedy.

20   There had been a time on earth when poets had been young and dead and famous — and were men. But now the poet as the tragic child of grandeur and destiny had changed. The child of genius was a woman, now, and the man was gone.

THOMAS WOLFE (1900–1938), U.S. author. *The Web and the Rock*, ch. 30 (1939), of the poetess Rosalind Bailey.

21   A woman must have money and a room of her own if she is to write fiction.

VIRGINIA WOOLF (1882–1941), British novelist. *A Room Of One's Own*, ch. 1 (1929).

22   Who shall measure the heat and violence of the poet's heart when caught and tangled in a woman's body?

VIRGINIA WOOLF (1882–1941), British novelist. *A Room Of*

One's Own, ch. 3 (1929). Woolf added: "The indifference of the world which Keats and Flaubert and other men of genius have found so hard to bear was in her case not indifference but hostility. The world did not say to her as it said to them, Write if you choose; it makes no difference to me. The world said with a guffaw, Write? What's the good of you writing?"

See also Woolf on WRITING.

WORDS

1 Words convey the mental treasures of one period to the generations that follow; and laden with this, their precious freight, they sail safely across gulfs of time in which empires have suffered shipwreck and the languages of common life have sunk into oblivion.

ANONYMOUS. Quoted in: Richard Chevenix Trench, *On the Study of Words*, Lecture 1 (1858).

2 I am a dreamer of words, of written words. I think I am reading; a word stops me. I leave the page. The syllables of the word begin to move around. Stressed accents begin to invert. The word abandons its meaning like an overload which is too heavy and prevents dreaming. Then words take on other meanings as if they had the right to be young. And the words wander away, looking in the nooks and crannies of vocabulary for new company, bad company.

GASTON BACHELARD (1884–1962), French scientist, philosopher, literary theorist. *The Poetics of Reverie*, "Introduction," sct. 6 (1960; tr. 1969).

3 The words of the world want to make sentences.

GASTON BACHELARD (1884–1962), French scientist, philosopher, literary theorist. *The Poetics of Reverie*, ch. 5, sct. 4 (1960; tr. 1969).

4 Today the discredit of words is very great. Most of the time the media transmit lies. In the face of an intolerable world, words appear to change very little. State power has become congenitally deaf, which is why—but the editorialists forget it—terrorists are reduced to bombs and hijacking.

JOHN BERGER (b. 1926), British author, critic. "Lost Off Cape Wrath," in *Threepenny Review* (Winter 1988; repr. in *Keeping a Rendezvous*, 1992).

5 My general theory since 1971 has been that the word is literally a virus, and that it has not been recognised as such because it has achieved a state of relatively stable symbiosis with its human host; that is to say, the word virus (the Other Half) has established itself so firmly as an accepted part of the human organism that it can now sneer at gangster viruses like smallpox and turn them in to the Pasteur Institute.

WILLIAM BURROUGHS (b. 1914), U.S. author. *The Adding Machine*, "Ten Years and a Billion Dollars" (1985).

6 Words are not as satisfactory as we should like them to be, but, like our neighbours, we have got to live with them and must make the best and not the worst of them.

SAMUEL BUTLER (1835–1902), English author. *Samuel Butler's Notebooks* (1951).

7 But words are things, and a small drop of ink,
Falling like dew, upon a thought, produces
That which makes thousands, perhaps millions, think.

LORD BYRON (1788–1824), English poet. *Don Juan*, cto. 3, st. 88

8 "When *I* use a word," Humpty Dumpty said in rather a scornful tone, "it means just what I choose it to mean—neither more nor less."

LEWIS CARROLL (1832–98), English author, mathematician. *Through the Looking-Glass*, ch. 6 (1872).

9 Give the people a new word and they think they have a new fact.

WILLA CATHER (1876–1947), U.S. author. *On Writing*, "Four Letters: Escapism" (written 1936; published 1949).

10 Words today are like the shells and rope of seaweed which a child brings home glistening from the beach and which in an hour have lost their lustre.

CYRIL CONNOLLY (1903–74), British critic. *The Unquiet Grave*, pt. 3 (1944; rev. 1951).

11 A word carries far—very far—deals destruction through time as the bullets go flying through space.

JOSEPH CONRAD (1857–1924), Polish-born English novelist. Marlow, in *Lord Jim*, ch. 15 (1900).

12 Words, as is well known, are the great foes of reality.

JOSEPH CONRAD (1857–1924), Polish-born English novelist. The narrator, in *Under Western Eyes*, Prologue, pt. 1 (1911).

13 Words are made for a certain exactness of thought, as tears are for a certain degree of pain. What is least distinct cannot be named; what is clearest is unutterable.

RENÉ DAUMAL (1908–44), French poet, critic. *A Night of Serious Drinking*, Foreword (1938).

14 The basic tool for the manipulation of reality is the manipulation of words. If you can control the meaning of words, you can control the people who must use the words.

PHILIP K. DICK (1928–82), U.S. science fiction writer. *I Hope I Shall Arrive Soon*, Introduction, "How to Build a Universe That Doesn't Fall Apart Two Days Later" (1986).

15 A word is dead
When it is said,
Some say.
I say it just
Begins to live
That day.

EMILY DICKINSON (1830–86), U.S. poet. *The Complete Poems*, no. 1212 (1955).

16 Our words have wings, but fly not where we would.

GEORGE ELIOT (1819–80), English novelist. *The Spanish Gypsy*, bk. 3 (1868).

17 For last year's words belong to last year's language
And next year's words await another voice.

T. S. ELIOT (1888–1965), Anglo-American poet, critic. *Little Gidding*, pt. 2, in *Four Quartets*.

18 You can stroke people with words.

F. SCOTT FITZGERALD (1896–1940), U.S. author. *The Crack-Up,* "Notebook O" (ed. by Edmund Wilson, 1945).

19   I haven't much opinion of words.... They're apt to set fire to a dry tongue, that's what I say.

ELLEN GLASGOW (1874–1945), U.S. novelist. Sam Murray, in *The Deliverance,* bk. 2, ch. 4 (1904).

20   In fact, words are well adapted for description and the arousing of emotion, but for many kinds of precise thought other symbols are much better.

J. B. S. HALDANE (1892–1964), British scientist. *The Inequality of Man,* "God-Makers" (1932).

21   There can be no doubt that distrust of words is less harmful than unwarranted trust in them. Besides, to distrust words, and indict them for the horrors that might slumber unobtrusively within them—isn't this, after all, the true vocation of the intellectual?

VÁCLAV HAVEL (b. 1936), Czech playwright, president. Speech, Oct. 1989, Germany, accepting a peace prize. Quoted in: *Independent* (London, 9 Dec. 1989).

22   All our words from loose using have lost their edge.

ERNEST HEMINGWAY (1899–1961), U.S. author. *Death in the Afternoon,* ch. 7 (1932).

23   All my life I've looked at words as though I were seeing them for the first time.

ERNEST HEMINGWAY (1899–1961), U.S. author. Letter, 9 April 1945 (published in *Selected Letters,* ed. by Carlos Baker, 1981).

24   Poor Faulkner. Does he really think big emotions come from big words? He thinks I don't know the ten-dollar words. I know them all right. But there are older and simpler and better words, and those are the ones I use.

ERNEST HEMINGWAY (1899–1961), U.S. author. Quoted in: A. E. Hotchner, *Papa Hemingway,* pt. 1, ch. 4 (1966 ed.), of William Faulkner. Hemingway's assessment was made after being informed (by Hotchner) that Faulkner considered that Hemingway "had no courage" and "had never been known to use a word that might send the reader to the dictionary."

25   Words are wise men's counters, they do but reckon by them: but they are the money of fools.

THOMAS HOBBES (1588–1679), English philosopher. *Leviathan,* pt. 1, ch. 4 (1651).

26   Without words to objectify and categorize our sensations and place them in relation to one another, we cannot evolve a tradition of what is real in the world.

RUTH HUBBARD (b. 1924), U.S. biologist. "Have Only Men Evolved?," in *Women Look at Biology Looking at Women* (ed. by Ruth Hubbard, Mary Sue Henifin, and Barbara Fried, 1979).

27   As a poet and writer, I deeply love and I deeply hate words. I love the infinite evidence and change and requirements and possibilities of language; every human use of words that is joyful, or honest or new, because experience is new.... But as a Black poet and writer, I hate words that cancel my name and my history and the freedom of my future: I hate the words that condemn and refuse the language of my people in America.

JUNE JORDAN (b. 1939), U.S. poet, civil rights activist. *Moving towards Home: Political Essays,* "White English/Black English: The Politics of Translation" (1989; first published 1972).

28   Words are, of course, the most powerful drug used by mankind.

RUDYARD KIPLING (1865–1936), British author, poet. Speech, 14 Feb. 1923 (published in *Times,* London, 15 Feb. 1923).

29   The closer the look one takes at a word, the greater distance from which it looks back.

KARL KRAUS (1874–1936), Austrian satirist. *Pro Domo et Mundo,* ch. 7 (1912).

30   Truthful words are not beautiful; beautiful words are not truthful. Good words are not persuasive; persuasive words are not good.

LAO-TZU (6th century B.C.), Legendary Chinese philosopher. *Tao-te-ching,* bk. 2, ch. 81 (tr. by T. C. Lau, 1963).

31   Words can have no single fixed meaning. Like wayward electrons, they can spin away from their initial orbit and enter a wider magnetic field. No one owns them or has a proprietary right to dictate how they will be used.

DAVID LEHMAN (b. 1948), U.S. poet, editor, critic. *Signs of the Times,* ch. 1, "The End of the Word" (1991).

32   A wise man hears one word and understands two.

YIDDISH PROVERB.

33   A good word is as a good tree—
   its roots are firm,
   and its branches are in heaven;
   it gives its produce every season
   by the leave of its Lord.

QUR'AN. *Abraham* 14:29–30 (ed. by Arthur J. Arberry, 1955).

34   There is no greater impediment to the advancement of knowledge than the ambiguity of words.

THOMAS REID (1710–69), Scottish philosopher. *Essays on the Intellectual Powers of Man,* Essay 1, "Explication of Words" (1785).

35   One of our defects as a nation is a tendency to use what have been called "weasel words." When a weasel sucks eggs the meat is sucked out of the egg. If you use a "weasel word" after another there is nothing left of the other.

THEODORE ROOSEVELT (1858–1919), U.S. Republican (later Progressive) politician, president. Speech, 31 May 1916, St. Louis, Miss., referring to Woodrow Wilson's proposal for "universal voluntary military training."

36   The volatile truth of our words should continually betray the inadequacy of the residual statement.

HENRY DAVID THOREAU (1817–62), U.S. philosopher, author, naturalist. *Walden,* "Conclusion" (1854).

37   An average English word is four letters and a half. By hard, honest labor I've dug all the large words out of my vocabulary and shaved it down till the average is three and a half.... I never write "metropolis" for seven cents, because I can get the same money for "city." I never write "policeman," because I can get the same price for "cop."... I never write "valetudinarian" at all, for not even hunger and wretchedness can humble me to the point where I will do a word like that for seven cents; I wouldn't do it for fifteen.

MARK TWAIN (1835–1910), U.S. author. "Spelling and Pictures," speech, 18 Sept. 1906, to Associated Press, New York

City (published in *Mark Twain's Speeches,* ed. by A. B. Paine, 1923).

38 The supply of words in the world market is plentiful but the demand is falling. Let deeds follow words now.

LECH WALESA (b. 1943), Polish trade union leader, politician. *Newsweek* (New York, 27 Nov. 1989).

39 One forgets words as one forgets names. One's vocabulary needs constant fertilizing or it will die.

EVELYN WAUGH (1903–66), British novelist. *The Diaries of Evelyn Waugh* (ed. by Michael Davie, 1976), entry for 25 Dec. 1962.

40 A new word is like a fresh seed sewn on the ground of the discussion.

LUDWIG WITTGENSTEIN (1889–1951), Austrian philosopher. *Culture and Value* (ed. by G. H. von Wright with Heikki Nyman, 1980), 1929 entry.

41 The word-coining genius, as if thought plunged into a sea of words and came up dripping.

VIRGINIA WOOLF (1882–1941), British novelist. *The Common Reader,* "Notes on an Elizabethan Play" (First Series, 1925), on the merits of Elizabethan drama.

42 Words are always getting conventionalized to some secondary meaning. It is one of the works of poetry to take the truants in custody and bring them back to their right senses.

W. B. YEATS (1865–1939), Irish poet, playwright. Letter, 3 Feb. 1889 (published in *Collected Letters,* vol 1, ed. by John Kelly, 1986). "Poets are the policemen of language," Yeats added, "they are always arresting those old reprobates the words."

See also Tolstoy on ACTION; Daumal on EXPERIENCE; LANGUAGE; Havel on LITERATURE AND SOCIETY; Wittgenstein on MEANING; Marceau on SILENCE; SPEECHES AND SPEECHMAKING.

WILLIAM WORDSWORTH

1 Just for a handful of silver he left us,
Just for a riband to stick in his coat—

. . .

We that had loved him so, followed him,
 honoured him,
Lived in his mild and magnificent eye,
Learned his great language, caught his clear
 accents,
Made him our pattern to live and to die!
Shakespeare was of us, Milton was for us,
Burns, Shelley, were with us—they watch from
 their graves!
He alone breaks from the van and the freemen,
—He alone sinks to the rear and the slaves!

ROBERT BROWNING (1812–89), English poet. *The Lost Leader,* st. 1.

2 To judge from a single conversation, he made the impression of a narrow and very English mind; of one who paid for his rare elevation by general tameness and conformity. Off his own beat, his opinions were of no value.

RALPH WALDO EMERSON (1803–82), U.S. essayist, poet, philosopher. *English Traits,* ch. 1 (1856). Emerson met Wordsworth on his first voyage to England in Aug. 1833.

3 For the sake of a few fine imaginative or domestic passages, are we to be bullied into a certain philosophy engendered in the whims of an egotist?

JOHN KEATS (1705–1821), English poet. Letter, 3 Feb. 1818 (published in *Letters of John Keats,* no. 44, ed. by Frederick Page, 1954).

4 Wordsworth went to the Lakes, but he was never a lake poet. He found in stones the sermons he had already hidden there.

OSCAR WILDE (1854–1900), Anglo-Irish playwright, author. Vivian, in "The Decay of Lying" (published in *Intentions,* 1891).

WORK

1 Something made greater by ourselves and in turn that makes us greater.

MAYA ANGELOU (b. 1928), U.S. author. Interview in *Black Scholar* (Jan.-Feb. 1977), defining work.

2 In order that people may be happy in their work, these three things are needed: They must be fit for it: they must not do too much of it: and they must have a sense of success in it—not a doubtful sense, such as needs some testimony of others for its confirmation, but a sure sense, or rather knowledge, that so much work has been done well, and fruitfully done, whatever the world may say or think about it.

W. H. AUDEN (1907–73), Anglo-American poet. *A Certain World,* "Work, Labor, and Play" (1970).

3 A tremendous number of people in America work very hard at something that bores them. Even a rich man thinks he has to go down to the office everyday. Not because he likes it but because he can't think of anything else to do.

W. H. AUDEN (1907–73), Anglo-American poet. *The Table Talk of W. H. Auden,* "November 16, 1946" (comp. by Alan Ansen, ed. by Nicholas Jenkins, 1990).

4 I am afraid that the pleasantness of an employment does not always evince its propriety.

JANE AUSTEN (1775–1817), English novelist. Elinor, in *Sense and Sensibility,* ch. 13 (1811).

5 It is not real work unless you would rather be doing something else.

J. M. BARRIE (1860–1937), British playwright. Rectorial address, 3 May 1922, St. Andrew's University, Scotland.

6 Anyone can do any amount of work, provided it isn't the work he is supposed to be doing.

ROBERT BENCHLEY (1889–1945), U.S. humorous writer. Quoted in: *The Algonquin Wits* (ed. by Robert E. Drennan, 1968). Benchley's own method is also quoted in the book: "I do most of my work sitting down. That's where I shine."

7 Whatsoever thy hand findeth to do, do it with thy might; for there is no work, nor device, nor knowledge, nor wisdom, in the grave whither thou goest.

BIBLE, HEBREW. *Ecclesiastes* 9:10.

8 After all, it is hard to master both life and work equally well. So if you are bound to fake one of them, it had better be life.

JOSEPH BRODSKY (b. 1940), Russian-born U.S. poet, critic.

Interview in *Writers at Work* (Eighth Series, ed. by George Plimpton, 1988).

9 Measure not the work
Until the day's out and the labour done,
Then bring your gauges.

ELIZABETH BARRETT BROWNING (1806–61), English poet. *Aurora Leigh*, bk. 5 (1857).

10 Poor workers! First they're cuckolded, and, as if that weren't enough, then they're beaten! Work's a curse, Saturno. I say to hell with the work you have to do to earn a living! That kind of work does us no honor; all it does is fill up the bellies of the pigs who exploit us. But the work you do because you like to do it, because you've heard the call, you've got a vocation—that's ennobling! We should all be able to work like that. Look at me, Saturno—I don't work. And I don't care if they hang me, I *won't* work! Yet I'm alive! I may live badly, but at least I don't have to work to do it!

LUIS BUÑUEL (1900–1983), Spanish filmmaker. Don Lope, in the film *Tristana* (1970), largely derived from the novel of the same name by the Spanish novelist and dramatist Galdós. But where Galdós criticized his character for laziness, Buñuel praises him.

11 Work with some men is as besetting a sin as idleness.

SAMUEL BUTLER (1835–1902), English author. *Samuel Butler's Notebooks* (1951).

12 A man perfects himself by working. Foul jungles are cleared
away, fair seed-fields rise instead, and stately cities; and withal
the man himself first ceases to be a jungle, and foul unwholesome
desert thereby. . . . The man is now a man.

THOMAS CARLYLE (1795–1881), Scottish essayist, historian. *Past and Present*, bk. 3, ch. 11 (1843).

13 Nowher so bisy a man as he ther nas,
And yet he semed bisier than he was.

GEOFFREY CHAUCER (1340–1400), English poet. *The Canterbury Tales*, General Prologue (c. 1387–1400), of the Sergeant of the Lawe.

14 Personally, I have nothing against work, particularly when performed, quietly and unobtrusively, by someone else. I just don't happen to think it's an appropriate subject for an "ethic."

BARBARA EHRENREICH (b. 1941), U.S. author, columnist. *The Worst Years of Our Lives*, "Goodbye To The Work Ethic" (1991; first published 1988).

15 We must hold a man amenable to reason for the choice of his daily craft or profession. It is not an excuse any longer for his deeds that they are the custom of his trade. What business has he with an evil trade?

RALPH WALDO EMERSON (1803–82), U.S. essayist, poet, philosopher. *Essays*, "Spiritual Laws" (First Series, 1841).

16 One of the saddest things is that the only thing that a man can do for eight hours a day, day after day, is work. You can't eat eight hours a day nor drink for eight hours a day nor make love for eight hours—all you can do for eight hours is work. Which is the reason why man makes himself and everybody else so miserable and unhappy.

WILLIAM FAULKNER (1897–1962), U.S. novelist. Interview in *Writers at Work* (First Series, ed. by Malcolm Cowley, 1958).

17 The idea that to make a man work you've got to hold gold in front of his eyes is a growth, not an axiom. We've done that for so long that we've forgotten there's any other way.

F. SCOTT FITZGERALD (1896–1940), U.S. author. Amory Blaine, in *This Side of Paradise*, bk. 2, ch. 5 (1920).

18 Clearly the most unfortunate people are those who must do the same thing over and over again, every minute, or perhaps twenty to the minute. They deserve the shortest hours and the highest pay.

JOHN KENNETH GALBRAITH (b. 1908), U.S. economist. *Made to Last*, ch. 4 (1964).

19 I have long been of the opinion that if work were such a splendid thing the rich would have kept more of it for themselves.

BRUCE GROCOTT (b. 1940), British Labour politician. Quoted in: *Observer* (London, 22 May 1988).

20 The highest reward that God gives us for good work is the ability to do better work.

ELBERT HUBBARD (1856–1915), U.S. author. *Selected Writings*, vol. 1, "Index" (1921).

21 Industrial man—a sentient reciprocating engine having a fluctuating output, coupled to an iron wheel revolving with uniform velocity. And then we wonder why this should be the golden age of revolution and mental derangement.

ALDOUS HUXLEY (1894–1963), British author. Bruno Rontini's notes, in *Time Must Have a Stop*, ch. 30 (1944).

22 I like work; it fascinates me. I can sit and look at it for hours. I love to keep it by me; the idea of getting rid of it nearly breaks my heart.

JEROME K. JEROME (1859–1927), British author. *Three Men in a Boat*, ch. 15 (1889).

23 It is wonderful when a calculation is made, how little the mind is actually employed in the discharge of any profession.

SAMUEL JOHNSON (1709–84), English author, lexicographer. Quoted in: James Boswell, *Life of Samuel Johnson*, 6 April 1775 (1791).

24 No longer diverted by other emotions, I work the way a cow grazes.

KÄTHE KOLLWITZ (1867–1945), German artist. *Diaries and Letters* (ed. by Hans Kollwitz, 1955), April 1910 entry.

25 Why should I let the toad *work*
Squat on my life?
Can't I use my wit as a pitchfork
And drive the brute off?

PHILIP LARKIN (1922–85), British poet. *Toads*, first verse.

26 You'll never succeed in idealizing hard work. Before you can dig mother earth you've got to take off your ideal jacket. The harder a man works, at brute labour, the thinner becomes his idealism, the darker his mind.

D. H. LAWRENCE (1885–1930), British author. *Studies in Classic American Literature*, ch. 8 (1924).

27 Work is life, you know, and without it, there's nothing but fear and insecurity.

> JOHN LENNON (1940–80), British rock musician. *Twenty-Four Hours*, 15 Dec. 1969, BBC-TV.

28 To work—to work! It is such infinite delight to know that we still have the best things to do.

> KATHERINE MANSFIELD (1888–1923), New Zealand-born British author. Letter, 7 Dec. 1916, to Bertrand Russell (published in *Collected Letters*, vol 1, ed. by Vincent O'Sullivan and Margaret Scott, 1984).

29 In communist society, where nobody has one exclusive sphere of activity but each can become accomplished in any branch he wishes, society regulates the general production and thus makes it possible for me to do one thing today and another tomorrow, to hunt in the morning, fish in the afternoon, rear cattle in the evening, criticize after dinner, just as I have a mind, without ever becoming hunter, fisherman, shepherd or critic.

> KARL MARX (1818–83) AND FRIEDRICH ENGELS (1820–95), German social philosophers, revolutionaries. *The German Ideology*, sct. 1 (first published 1845–46; repr. in *Karl Marx and Friedrich Engels: Collected Works*, vol. 5, 1976). This thesis represented Marx's attempt—later abandoned—to reconcile his conflicting doctrines of the abolition of the division of labor, and the necessity of highly developed forms of production.

30 Labor is work that leaves no trace behind it when it is finished, or if it does, as in the case of the tilled field, this product of human activity requires still more labor, incessant, tireless labor, to maintain its identity as a "work" of man.

> MARY MCCARTHY (1912–89), U.S. author, critic. "The Vita Activa," in *New Yorker* (18 Oct. 1958; repr. in *On the Contrary*, 1961).

31 Where the whole man is involved there is no work. Work begins with the division of labor.

> MARSHALL MCLUHAN (1911–80), Canadian communications theorist. *Understanding Media*, ch. 14 (1964).

32 Toil is man's allotment; toil of brain, or toil of hands, or a grief that's more than either, the grief and sin of idleness.

> HERMAN MELVILLE (1819–91), U.S. author. *Mardi: and a Voyage Thither*, ch. 63 (1849).

33 I suspect that American workers have come to lack a work ethic. They do not live by the sweat of their brow.

> KIICHI MIYAZAWA (b. 1919), Japanese politician, prime minister. *Daily Telegraph* (London, 5 Feb. 1992).

34 A man at work, making something which he feels wll exist because he is working at it and wills it, is exercising the energies of his mind and soul as well as of his body. Memory and imagination help him as he works. Not only his own thoughts, but the thoughts of the men of past ages guide his hands; and, as part of the human race, he creates. If we work thus we shall be men, and our days will be happy and eventful.

> WILLIAM MORRIS (1834–96), English artist, writer, printer. *Signs of Change*, "Useful Work *versus* Useless Toil" (1888).

35 Work! Labour the *aspergas me* of life; the one great sacrament of humanity from which all other things flow—security, leisure, joy, art, literature, even divinity itself.

> SEAN O'CASEY (1884–1964), Irish dramatist. *Rose and Crown*, "In New York Now," vol. 5 (1952).

36 Work expands so as to fill the time available for its completion. General recognition of this fact is shown in the proverbial phrase "It is the busiest man who has time to spare."

> C. NORTHCOTE PARKINSON (1909–93), British historian, political scientist. "Parkinson's Law," the opening words of *Parkinson's Law, or The Pursuit of Progress* (1958), though the axiom was first published in *Economist* (London, 19 Nov. 1955).

37 It's true hard work never killed anybody, but I figure, why take the chance?

> RONALD REAGAN (b. 1911), U.S. Republican politician, president. Speech, 22 April 1987, to the annual Gridiron Dinner, Washington, D.C.

38 If you have great talents, industry will improve them: if you have but moderate abilities, industry will supply their deficiency.

> SIR JOSHUA REYNOLDS (1723–92), English artist, critic. Speech, 11 Dec. 1769, to students of the Royal Academy, London.

39 Far and away the best prize that life offers is the chance to work hard at work worth doing.

> THEODORE ROOSEVELT (1858–1919), U.S. Republican (later Progressive) politician, president. Labor Day speech, 7 Sept. 1903, Syracuse, N.Y.

40 It is too difficult to think nobly when one thinks only of earning a living.

> JEAN-JACQUES ROUSSEAU (1712–78), Swiss-born French philosopher, political theorist. *Confessions*, bk. 2, ch. 9 (written 1766–70; published 1781–88).

41 Nothing makes a man so selfish as work.

> GEORGE BERNARD SHAW (1856–1950), Anglo-Irish playwright, critic. Brassbound, in *Captain Brassbound's Conversion*, act 3.

42 Perpetual devotion to what a man calls his business, is only to be sustained by perpetual neglect of many other things.

> ROBERT LOUIS STEVENSON (1850–94), Scottish novelist, essayist, poet. *Virginibus Puerisque*, "An Apology for Idlers" (1881).

43 The greatest analgesic, soporific, stimulant, tranquilizer, narcotic, and to some extent even antibiotic—in short, the closest thing to a genuine panacea—known to medical science is work.

> THOMAS SZASZ (b. 1920), U.S. psychiatrist. *The Second Sin*, "Medicine" (1973).

44 There is always the danger that we may just do the work for the sake of the work. This is where the respect and the love and the devotion come in—that we do it to God, to Christ, and that's why we try to do it as beautifully as possible.

> MOTHER TERESA (b. 1910), Albanian-born Roman Catholic missionary. *A Gift for God*, "Imitation of Christ" (1975).

45 The really efficient laborer will be found not to crowd his day with work, but will saunter to his task surrounded by a wide halo of ease and leisure.

HENRY DAVID THOREAU (1817–62), U.S. philosopher, author, naturalist. *Journals* (1906), entry for 31 March 1842. The thought also found its way into Thoreau, *A Week on the Concord and Merrimack Rivers*, "Sunday" (1849).

46   Intellectual "work" is misnamed; it is a pleasure, a dissipation, and is its own highest reward.

MARK TWAIN (1835–1910), U.S. author. *A Connecticut Yankee in King Arthur's Court*, ch. 28 (1889).

47   Let us be grateful to Adam, our benefactor. He cut us out of the "blessing" of idleness and won for us the "curse" of labor.

MARK TWAIN (1835–1910), U.S. author. *Following the Equator*, ch. 33, "Pudd'nhead Wilson's New Calendar" (1897).

48   A work is never completed except by some accident such as weariness, satisfaction, the need to deliver, or death: for, in relation to who or what is making it, it can only be one stage in a series of inner transformations.

PAUL VALÉRY (1871–1945), French poet, essayist. "Recollection" (published in *Collected Works*, vol. 1, 1972).

49   Work to survive, survive by consuming, survive to consume: the hellish cycle is complete.

RAOUL VANEIGEM (b. 1934), Belgian Situationist philosopher. *The Revolution of Everyday Life*, ch. 7, sct. 2 (1967; tr. 1983).

50   I suppose I have a really loose interpretation of "work," because I think that just being alive is so much work at something you don't always want to do. . . . The machinery is always going. Even when you sleep.

ANDY WARHOL (1928–1987), U.S. pop artist. *From A to B and Back Again*, ch. 6 (1975).

51   Work is the curse of the drinking classes.

OSCAR WILDE (1854–1900), Anglo-Irish playwright, author. Quoted in: Hesketh Pearson, *Life of Oscar Wilde*, ch. 12 (1946).

See also CAREERS; Franklin on THE GOLDEN RULE; THE OFFICE; Kollwitz on OLD AGE AND AGING; PROFESSIONS; Trollope on RETIREMENT; Voltaire on SELF-SUFFICIENCY; Ruskin on SLAVERY.

THE WORKING CLASS

1   The working-class . . . is now issuing from its hiding-place to assert an Englishman's heaven-born privilege of doing as he likes, and is beginning to perplex us by marching where it likes, meeting where it likes, bawling what it likes, breaking what it likes.

MATTHEW ARNOLD (1822–88), English poet, critic. *Culture and Anarchy*, ch. 3 (1869).

2   The history of all countries shows that the working class exclusively by its own effort is able to develop only trade-union consciousness.

VLADIMIR ILYICH LENIN (1870–1924), Russian revolutionary leader. *What Is to Be Done?*, ch. 2, sct. A (1902).

3   The worst fault of the working classes is telling their children they're not going to succeed, saying: "There is life, but it's not for you."

JOHN MORTIMER (b. 1923), British barrister, novelist. *Daily Mail* (London, 31 May 1988).

4   In every one of those little stucco boxes there's some poor bastard who's never free except when he's fast asleep and dreaming that he's got the boss down the bottom of a well and is bunging lumps of coal at him.

GEORGE ORWELL (1903–50), British author. *Coming up for Air*, pt. 1, ch. 2 (1939).

5   Admiration of the proletariat, like that of dams, power stations, and aeroplanes, is part of the ideology of the machine age.

BERTRAND RUSSELL (1872–1970), British philosopher, mathematician. *Unpopular Essays*, "The Superior Virtue of the Oppressed" (1950).

6   The same people who are murdered slowly in the mechanized slaughterhouses of work are also arguing, singing, drinking, dancing, making love, holding the streets, picking up weapons and inventing a new poetry.

RAOUL VANEIGEM (b. 1934), Belgian Situationist philosopher. *The Revolution of Everyday Life*, ch. 5 (1967; tr. 1983).

7   That's what being in the working class is all about—how to get out of it.

NEVILLE KENNETH WRAN (b. 1926), Australian barrister, politician. *Sydney Morning Herald* (19 June 1982)

See also Sutton on CLASS; Mussolini on INTERNATIONALISM; LABOR.

THE WORLD

1   We could say, then, that man is an instrument the world employs to renew its own image constantly.

ITALO CALVINO (1923–85), Italian author, critic. Saul Steinberg, *Still Life and Architecture*, Introduction (1982; repr. in *The Literature Machine*, 1987).

2   The best philosophical attitude to adopt towards the world is a union of the sarcasm of gaiety with the indulgence of contempt.

SÉBASTIEN-ROCH NICOLAS DE CHAMFORT (1741–94), French writer, wit. *Maximes et Pensées*, vol. 1, no. 31 (1796; tr. 1902).

3   We create the world in which we live; if that world becomes unfit for human life, it is because we tire of our responsibility.

CYRIL CONNOLLY (1903–74), British critic. *Enemies of Promise*, pt. 2, ch. 16 (1938).

4   The real world is not easy to live in. It is rough; it is slippery. Without the most clear-eyed adjustments we fall and get crushed. A man must stay sober: not always, but most of the time.

CLARENCE DAY (1874–1935), U.S. essayist. *The Crow's Nest*, "In His Baby Blue Ship" (1921).

5   The Sage of Toronto . . . spent several decades marveling at the numerous freedoms created by a "global village" instantly and effortlessly accessible to all. Villages, unlike towns, have always been ruled by conformism, isolation, petty surveillance, boredom and repetitive malicious gossip about the same families. Which is a precise enough description of the global spectacle's present vulgarity.

GUY DEBORD (b. 1931), French Situationist philosopher. *Com-*

ments on the *Society of the Spectacle,* ch. 12 (1988; tr. 1990), of Marshall McLuhan's notion of the "global village."

6   One may say the eternal mystery of the world is its comprehensibility.

ALBERT EINSTEIN (1879–1955), German-born U.S. physicist. Quoted in: Freeman Dyson, *Disturbing the Universe,* ch. 5 (1979).

7   Some say the world will end in fire,
Some say in ice.
From what I've tasted of desire
I hold with those who favor fire.
But if it had to perish twice,
I think I know enough of hate
To say that for destruction ice
Is also great
And would suffice.

ROBERT FROST (1874–1963), U.S. poet. *Fire and Ice.*

8   The world is a beautiful book, but of little use to him who cannot read it.

CARLO GOLDONI (1707–93), Italian dramatist. Lord Arthur, in *Pamela,* act 1, sc. 14 (1746).

9   The world is not black and white. More like black and grey.

GRAHAM GREENE (1904–91), British novelist. Quoted in: *Observer* (London, 2 Jan. 1983).

10   That cold accretion called the world, which, so terrible in the mass, is so unformidable, even pitiable, in its units.

THOMAS HARDY (1840–1928), English novelist, poet. *Tess of the D'Urbervilles,* ch. 13 (1891).

11   The world, that gray-bearded and wrinkled profligate, decrepit, without being venerable.

NATHANIEL HAWTHORNE (1804–64), U.S. author. *The House of the Seven Gables,* ch. 12 (1851).

12   If today there is a proper American "sphere of influence" it is this fragile sphere called earth upon which all men live and share a common fate—a sphere where our influence must be for peace and justice.

HUBERT H. HUMPHREY (1911–78), U.S. Democratic politician, vice president. Speech, 6 Jan. 1967, Buffalo, N.Y.

13   I have no other pictures of the world apart from those which express evanescence, and callousness, vanity and anger, emptiness, or hideous useless hate. Everything has merely confirmed what I had seen and understood in my childhood: futile and sordid fits of rage, cries suddenly blanketed by the silence, shadows swallowed up for ever by the night.

EUGèNE IONESCO (b. 1912), Rumanian-born French playwright. "Testimony: When I Write" (April 1958; repr. in *Notes and Counter-Notes,* pt. 2, 1962).

14   How can one take delight in the world unless one flees to it for refuge?

FRANZ KAFKA (1883–1924), German novelist, short-story writer. *The Collected Aphorisms,* no. 25 (Oct. 1917-Feb. 1918; published in *Shorter Works,* vol. 1, ed. and tr. by Malcolm Pasley, 1973).

15   Call the world if you please "the vale of soul-making." Then you will find out the use of the world.

JOHN KEATS (1795–1821), English poet. Letter, written 14 Feb.-3 May 1819, to his brother and sister-in-law, George and Georgiana Keats (published in *Letters of John Keats,* no. 123, ed. by Frederick Page, 1954).

16   The world is a prison. That's why solitary confinement is the best place in it.

KARL KRAUS (1874–1936), Austrian satirist. *Die Fackel,* no. 264/65 (Vienna, 18 Nov. 1908; repr. in Thomas Szasz, *Anti-Freud: Karl Kraus's Criticism of Psychoanalysis and Psychiatry,* ch. 8, 1976).

17   If we cannot accept the importance of the world, which considers itself important, if in the midst of that world our laughter finds no echo, we have but one choice: to take the world as a whole and make it the object of our game; to turn it into a toy.

MILAN KUNDERA (b. 1929), Czech author, critic. *Immortality,* pt. 7, ch. 5 (1991).

18   The world is . . . the natural setting of, and field for, all my thoughts and all my explicit perceptions. Truth does not "inhabit" only "the inner man," or more accurately, there is no inner man, man is in the world, and only in the world does he know himself.

MAURICE MERLEAU-PONTY (1907–61), French philosopher. *Phenomenology of Perception,* Preface (1945).

19   The world has *not* to be put in order: the world *is* order incarnate. It is for us to put ourselves in unison with this order.

HENRY MILLER (1891–1980), U.S. author. *Sexus,* ch. 9 (1949).

20   Perhaps when distant people on other planets pick up some wave-length of ours all they hear is a continuous scream.

IRIS MURDOCH (b. 1919), British novelist, philosopher. Alfred Ludens, in *The Message to the Planet,* pt. 6 (1989).

21   The world was not created once and for all time for each of us individually. There are added to it in the course of our life things of which we have never had any suspicion.

MARCEL PROUST (1871–1922), French novelist. *Remembrance of Things Past,* vol 11, "The Sweet Cheat Gone," ch. 1 (1925; tr. by Scott Monkrieff, 1930).

22   The world is a perpetual caricature of itself; at every moment it is the mockery and the contradiction of what it is pretending to be.

GEORGE SANTAYANA (1863–1952), U.S. philosopher, poet. *Soliloquies in England,* "Dickens" (1922).

23   A man's interest in the world is only the overflow from his interest in himself. When you are a child your vessel is not yet full; so you care for nothing but your own affairs. When you grow up, your vessel overflows; and you are a politician, a philosopher, or an explorer and adventurer. In old age the vessel dries up: there is no overflow: you are a child again.

GEORGE BERNARD SHAW (1856–1950), Anglo-Irish playwright, critic. Captain Shotover, in *Heartbreak House,* act 2.

24   Once kick the world, and the world and you will live together at a reasonably good understanding

JONATHAN SWIFT (1667–1745), Anglo-Irish satirist. *Letter of Advice to a Young Poet* (1 Dec. 1720).

25 This visible world is wonderfully to be delighted in, and highly to be esteemed, because it is the theatre of God's righteous Kingdom.

THOMAS TRAHERNE (1636–74), English clergyman, poet, mystic. *Centuries*, "Second Century," no. 97 (written c. 1672; first published 1908).

26 The world is a stage, but the play is badly cast.

OSCAR WILDE (1854–1900), Anglo-Irish playwright, author. *Lord Arthur Savile's Crime*, ch. 1 (1891).

27 The world is a funny paper read backwards. And that way it isn't so funny.

TENNESSEE WILLIAMS (1914–83), U.S. dramatist. Self-interview, in London *Observer* (7 April 1957).

28 The beauty of the world . . . has two edges, one of laughter, one of anguish, cutting the heart asunder.

VIRGINIA WOOLF (1882–1941), British novelist. *A Room Of One's Own*, ch. 1 (1929)

See also Wittgenstein on HISTORY; Melville on PHILOSOPHY; Butler on PUBLIC OPINION.

WORLD WAR I

1 It's raining my soul, it's raining, but it's raining dead eyes.

GUILLAUME APOLLINAIRE (1880–1918), Italian-born French poet, critic. *La Nuit d'avril 1915*, in *Calligrammes* (1918), on enemy fire.

2 The War was decided in the first twenty days of fighting, and all that happened afterwards consisted in battles which, however formidable and devastating, were but desperate and vain appeals against the decision of Fate.

SIR WINSTON CHURCHILL (1874–1965), British statesman, writer. Preface to E. L. Spears, *Liaison 1914* (1930).

3 The government will . . . go on in the highly democratic method of conscripting American manhood for European slaughter.

EMMA GOLDMAN (1869–1940), U.S. anarchist. "Address to the Jury," in *Mother Earth* (July 1917).

4 Trench stinks of shallow buried dead
Where Tom stands at the periscope,
Tired out. After nine months he's shed
All fear, all faith, all hate, all hope.

ROBERT GRAVES (1895–1985), British poet, novelist. *Through the Periscope* (1915; first published in *Recalling War*, 1988).

5 The lamps are going out all over Europe; we shall not see them lit again in our lifetime.

LORD GREY OF FALLODEN (1862–1933), British statesman. Remark, 3 Aug. 1914 (the eve of Britain's declaration of war against Germany), London. Quoted in: Grey, *Twenty-Five Years*, vol. 2, ch. 18 (1925).

6 Viewed as a drama, the war is somewhat disappointing.

D. W. GRIFFITHS (1874–1948), U.S. producer-director. Quoted in: Leslie Halliwell, *Halliwell's Filmgoer's Companion* (1984).

7 The war was a mirror; it reflected man's every virtue and every vice, and if you looked closely, like an artist at his drawings, it showed up both with unusual clarity.

GEORGE GROSZ (1893–1959), German artist. *A Small Yes and a Big No*, ch. 7 (1955; tr. 1982).

8 In the fall the war was always there but we did not go to it any more.

ERNEST HEMINGWAY (1899–1961), U.S. author. *Men without Women*, "In Another Country" (1927).

9 Their Name Liveth for Evermore

RUDYARD KIPLING (1865–1936), British author, poet. Inscription carved over lists of the dead in the Commonwealth war cemeteries, echoing *Ecclesiasticus* 44:14, "Their bodies are buried in peace; but their name liveth for evermore." Kipling, who had himself lost a son in the fighting, had been invited to devise suitable texts by the Imperial War Graves Commission.

10 In these loud times which boom with the horrible symphony of actions which produce reports and of reports which cause actions.

KARL KRAUS (1874–1936), Austrian satirist. "In These Great Times," speech, 19 Nov. 1914 (published in *Die Fackel*, Vienna, Dec. 1914; repr. in *In These Great Times: A Karl Kraus Reader*, ed. by Harry Zohn, 1976).

11 I can only see death and more death, till we are black and swollen with death.

D. H. LAWRENCE (1885–1930), British author. Letter, 2 June 1915 (published in *The Letters of D. H. Lawrence*, vol 2, ed. by George J. Zytaruk and James T. Boulton, 1981).

12 Then down came the lid—the day was lost, for art, at Sarajevo. World-politics stepped in, and a war was started which has not ended yet: a "war to end war." But it merely ended art. It did not end war.

WYNDHAM LEWIS (1882–1957), British author, painter. *Blasting and Bombardiering*, pt. 5, "Toward an Art-Less Society" (1937).

13 God grant we may not have a European war thrust upon us, and for such a stupid reason too, no I don't mean stupid, but to have to go to war on account of tiresome Servia beggars belief.

MARY (1867–1953), Wife of George V, Queen Consort of Great Britain. Letter, 28 July 1914, to her aunt, Princess Augusta, Grand-Duchess of Mecklenburg-Strelitz (Germany).

14 There died a myriad,
And of the best, among them,
For an old bitch gone in the teeth,
For a botched civilization.

EZRA POUND (1885–1972), U.S. poet, critic. *Hugh Selwyn Mauberly*.

15 We are fighting in the quarrel of civilization against barbarism, of liberty against tyranny. Germany has become a menace to the whole world. She is the most dangerous enemy of liberty now existing.

THEODORE ROOSEVELT (1858–1919), U.S. Republican (later Progressive) politician, president. Speech, April 1917, Oyster Bay, Long Island. Roosevelt added: "The man who does not think it was America's duty to fight for her own sake in view of the infamous conduct of Germany toward us stands on a level with a man who wouldn't think it necessary to fight in a private quarrel because his wife's face was slapped."

16 And all this madness, all this rage, all this flaming death of our civilization and our hopes, has been brought about because a set of official gentlemen, living luxurious lives, mostly stupid, and all without imagination or heart, have chosen that it should occur rather than that any one of them should suffer some infinitesimal rebuff to his country's pride.

> BERTAND RUSSELL (1872–1970), British philosopher, mathematician. Letter to *Nation* (London, 16 Aug. 1914; repr. in *The Autobiography of Bertrand Russell,* vol. 2, ch. 1, 1968). The letter was written 12 Aug. 1914, eight days after the outbreak of war.

17 As a lover of truth, the national propaganda of all the belligerent nations sickened me. As a lover of civilization, the return to barbarism appalled me.

> BERTAND RUSSELL (1872–1970), British philosopher, mathematician. *The Autobiography of Bertrand Russell,* vol. 2, ch. 1 (1968).

18 All of you young people who served in the war. You are a lost generation. . . . You have no respect for anything. You drink yourselves to death.

> GERTRUDE STEIN (1874–1946), U.S. author. Remark to Ernest Hemingway. Quoted in: Hemingway, *A Moveable Feast,* ch. 3 (1964).

19 When every autumn people said it could not last through the winter, and when every spring there was still no end in sight, only the hope that out of it all some good would accrue to mankind kept men and nations fighting. When at last it was over, the war had many diverse results and one dominant one transcending all others: disillusion.

> BARBARA TUCHMAN (1912–89), U.S. historian. *The Guns of August,* "Afterword" (1962).

20 Nowadays it is the fashion to emphasize the horrors of the last war. I didn't find it so horrible. There are just as horrible things happening all round us today, if only we had eyes to see them.

> LUDWIG WITTGENSTEIN (1889–1951), Austrian philosopher. Conversation in 1934 (published in *Personal Recollections,* ch. 6, ed. by Rush Rhees, 1981).

See also Russell on WAR; Geddes on WINNING.

WORLD WAR II

1 We had won. Pimps got out of their polished cars and walked the streets of San Francisco only a little uneasy at the unusual exercise. Gamblers, ignoring their sensitive fingers, shook hands with shoeshine boys. . . . Beauticians spoke to the shipyard workers, who in turn spoke to the easy ladies. . . . I thought if war did not include killing, I'd like to see one every year. Something like a festival.

> MAYA ANGELOU (b. 1928), U.S. author. *Gather Together in My Name,* vol. 2, Prologue (1974).

2 Gracious Lord, oh bomb the Germans.
Spare their women for Thy Sake,
And if that is not too easy
We will pardon Thy Mistake.
But gracious Lord, whate'er shall be,
Don't let anyone bomb me.

> JOHN BETJEMAN (1906–84), British poet. *In Westminster Abbey,* st. 2, in *Old Lights for New Chancels* (1940).

3 Germany collapsed as a result of having engaged in a struggle for empire with the concepts of provincial politics.

> ALBERT CAMUS (1913–60), French-Algerian philosopher, author. *The Rebel,* pt. 3, "State Terrorism and Irrational Terror" (1951; tr. 1953).

4 How horrible, fantastic, incredible it is that we should be digging trenches and trying on gas masks here because of a quarrel in a faraway country between people of whom we know nothing.

> NEVILLE CHAMBERLAIN (1869–1940), British Conservative politician, prime minister. Radio broadcast, 27 Sept. 1938, on Germany's annexation of the Sudetanland, Czechoslovakia.

5 This is no war for domination or imperial aggrandisement or material gain. . . . It is a war . . . to establish, on impregnable rocks, the rights of the individual and it is a war to establish and revive the stature of man.

> SIR WINSTON CHURCHILL (1874–1965), British statesman, writer. Speech, 3 Sept. 1939, to the House of Commons, on that day's declaration of war against Germany by Britain and France.

6 The worst thing about war was the sitting around and wondering what you were doing morally.

> PAUL FUSSELL (b. 1924), U.S. historian. *Times* (London, 28 Nov. 1991).

7 Whoever lights the torch of war in Europe can wish for nothing but chaos.

> ADOLF HITLER (1889–1945), German dictator. Speech, 21 May 1935, Reichstag, Berlin.

8 This war no longer bears the characteristics of former inter-European conflicts. It is one of those elemental conflicts which usher in a new millennium and which shake the world once in a thousand years.

> ADOLF HITLER (1889–1945), German dictator. Speech, 26 April 1942, to the Reichstag, Berlin.

9 Today we know that World War II began not in 1939 or 1941 but in the 1920's and 1930's when those who should have known better persuaded themselves that they were not their brother's keeper.

> HUBERT H. HUMPHREY (1911–78), U.S. Democratic politician, vice president. Speech, 11 Nov. 1965, Arlington Memorial Cemetery, Washington, D.C.

10 And while I am talking to you mothers and fathers, I give you one more assurance. I have said this before, but I shall say it again and again and again: Your boys are not going to be sent into any foreign wars.

> FRANKLIN D. ROOSEVELT (1882–1945), U.S. Democratic politician, president. Speech, 30 Oct. 1940, Boston, during election campaign for Roosevelt's third term as president.

11 If France is to be judged, judge her not by the effects of her defeat but by her readiness to sacrifice herself.

> ANTOINE DE SAINT-EXUPÉRY (1900–1944), French aviator, author. *Flight to Arras,* ch. 15 (1942).

12 O I know they make war because they want peace; they hate so that they may live; and they destroy the present to make the world safe for the future. When have they not done and said they did it for that?

> ELIZABETH SMART (1913–86), Canadian author, poet. *Necessary Secrets* (ed. by Alice Van Wart, 1991), entry for 18 Feb. 1941.

See also Weil on CIVILIZATION; James on GERMANY AND THE GERMANS.

WORLDLINESS

1 I have been in love, and in debt, and in drink,
This many and many a year.

> ALEXANDER BROME (1620–66), English poet. Opening lines of *The Mad Lover*.

2 He, in his developed manhood, stood,
A little sunburnt by the glare of life.

> ELIZABETH BARRETT BROWNING (1806–61), English Poet. *Aurora Leigh*, bk. 4 (1857), of Romney.

3 What should I have known or written had I been a quiet, mercantile politician or a lord in waiting? A man must travel, and turmoil, or there is no existence.

> LORD BYRON (1788–1824), English poet. Letter, 31 Aug. 1820, to poet Thomas Moore (published in *Byron's Letters and Journals*, vol. 7, ed. by Leslie A. Marchand, 1973–81).

4 I've been up the mountain and I had a choice. Should I come down? So I came down. God said, "Okay, you've been up on the mountain, now you go down. You're on your own, free. Check in later, but now you're on your own."

> BOB DYLAN (b. 1941), U.S. singer, songwriter. On his decision to return to live performances in 1975. Quoted in: Clinton Heylin, *Dylan: Behind the Shades*, ch. 22 (1991). Shortly after, Dylan embarked on the "Rolling Thunder Review."

5 The mark of the man of the world is absence of pretension. He does not make a speech; he takes a low business-tone, avoids all brag, is nobody, dresses plainly, promises not at all, performs much, speaks in monosyllables, hugs his fact. He calls his employment by its lowest name, and so takes from evil tongues their sharpest weapon. His conversation clings to the weather and the news, yet he allows himself to be surprised into thought, and the unlocking of his learning and philosophy.

> RALPH WALDO EMERSON (1803–82), U.S. essayist, poet, philosopher. *The Conduct of Life*, "Culture" (1860).

6 The world, as a rule, does not live on beaches and in country clubs.

> F. SCOTT FITZGERALD (1896–1940), U.S. author. Letter (undated) to his daughter Frances Scott Fitzgerald (first published in *The Crack-Up*, ed. by Edmund Wilson, 1945). Fitzgerald was referring to the life of a writer: "So much writing nowadays suffers both from lack of an attitude and from sheer lack of any material, save what is accumulated in a purely social life."

7 That observation which is called knowledge of the world will be found much more frequently to make men cunning than good.

> SAMUEL JOHNSON (1709–84), English author, lexicographer. *Rambler*, no. 4 (London, 31 March 1750; repr. in *Works of Samuel Johnson*, vol. 3, ed. by W. J. Bate and Albrecht B. Strauss, 1969)

See also Butler on INFALLIBILITY; La Fontaine on SELF-KNOWLEDGE.

WORSHIP

1 Worship is transcendent wonder.

> THOMAS CARLYLE (1795–1881), Scottish essayist, historian. *On Heroes and Hero-Worship*, lecture 1, "The Hero as Divinity" (1841).

2 When we really worship anything, we love not only its clearness but its obscurity. We exult in its very invisibility.

> G. K. CHESTERTON (1874–1936), British author. *All Things Considered*, "The Fallacy of Success" (1908).

3 Reverence is the highest quality of man's nature; and that individual, or nation, which has it slightly developed, is so far unfortunate. It is a strong spiritual instinct, and seeks to form channels for itself where none exists; thus Americans, in the dearth of other objects to worship, fall to worshiping themselves.

> LYDIA M. CHILD (1802–80), U.S. abolitionist, writer, editor. Letter, 26 May 1843 (published in *Letters from New York*, vol. 1, letter 18, 1843).

4 It is only when men begin to worship that they begin to grow.

> CALVIN COOLIDGE (1872–1933), U.S. Republican politician, president. Speech, 6 July 1922, Fredericksburg, Va.

5 I daresay anything can be made holy by being sincerely worshipped.

> IRIS MURDOCH (b. 1919), British novelist, philosopher. Maisie Tether, in *The Message to the Planet*, pt. 5 (1989).

See also PRAYER; RELIGION.

WORTH

1 If a thing is worth doing, it is worth doing badly.

> G. K. CHESTERTON (1874–1936), British author. *What's Wrong with the World*, pt. 4, ch. 14 (1910).

2 We'll never know the worth of water till the well go dry.

> SCOTTISH PROVERB (18th century). Collected in James Kelly, *Complete Collection of Scottish Proverbs*, no. 351 (1721). The proverb has antecedents going back to at least 1628.

3 Wealth, religion, military victory have more rhetorical than efficacious worth.

> GEORGE SANTAYANA (1863–1952), U.S. philosopher, poet. *The Life of Reason*, "Reason in Society," ch. 2 (1905–6).

4 The real price of everything, what everything really costs to the man who wants to acquire it, is the toil and trouble of acquiring it.

> ADAM SMITH (1723–90), Scottish economist. *The Wealth of Nations*, vol. 1, bk. 1, ch. 5 (1776).

5 The cost of a thing is the amount of what I will call life which is required to be exchanged for it, immediately or in the long run.

> HENRY DAVID THOREAU (1817–62), U.S. philosopher, author, naturalist. *Walden*, "Economy" (1854).

See also Baker on SOCIALISM; VALUE.

WRITERS

1   The writer has a grudge against society, which he documents with accounts of unsatisfying sex, unrealized ambition, unmitigated loneliness, and a sense of local and global distress. The square, overpopulation, the bourgeois, the bomb and the cocktail party are variously identified as sources of the grudge. There follows a little obscenity here, a dash of philosophy there, considerable whining overall, and a modern satirical novel is born.

RENATA ADLER (b. 1938), U.S. author, film critic. *Toward a Radical Middle*, "Salt into Old Scars" (1971; first published 1963).

2   Writers must fortify themselves with pride and egotism as best they can. The process is analogous to using sandbags and loose timbers to protect a house against flood. Writers are vulnerable creatures like anyone else. For what do they have in reality? Not sandbags, not timbers. Just a flimsy reputation and a name.

BRIAN ALDISS (b. 1925), British science fiction writer. *Bury My Heart at W. H. Smith's*, "Apéritif" (1990).

3   The hard necessity of bringing the judge on the bench down into the dock has been the peculiar responsibility of the writer in all ages of man.

NELSON ALGREN (1909–81), U.S. author. Preface added to his prose-poem *Chicago: City on the Make* (1961; original work published 1951).

4   Every writer hopes or boldly assumes that his life is in some sense exemplary, that the particular will turn out to be universal.

MARTIN AMIS (b. 1949), British novelist. *Observer* (London, 30 Aug. 1987).

5   No poet or novelist wishes he were the only one who ever lived, but most of them wish they were the only one alive, and quite a number fondly believe their wish has been granted.

W. H. AUDEN (1907–73), Anglo-American poet. *The Dyer's Hand*, pt. 1, "Writing" (1963).

6   Any writer, I suppose, feels that the world into which he was born is nothing less than a conspiracy against the cultivation of his talent.

JAMES BALDWIN (1924–87), U.S. author. *Notes of a Native Son*, "Autobiographical Notes" (1955).

7   The responsibility of a writer is to excavate the experience of the people who produced him.

JAMES BALDWIN (1924–87), U.S. author. *A Dialogue* (1973; with Nikki Giovanni), from a conversation in London, 4 Nov. 1971.

8   To endow the writer publicly with a good fleshly body, to reveal that he likes dry white wine and underdone steak, is to make even more miraculous for me, and of a more divine essence, the products of his art. Far from the details of his daily life bringing nearer to me the nature of his inspiration and making it clearer, it is the whole mystical singularity of his condition which the writer emphasizes by such confidences. For I cannot but ascribe to some superhumanity the existence of beings vast enough to wear blue pyjamas at the very moment when they manifest themselves as universal conscience.

ROLAND BARTHES (1915–80), French semiologist. *Mythologies*, "The Writer on Holiday" (1957; tr. 1972).

9   On the day when a young writer corrects his first proof-sheet he is as proud as a schoolboy who has just got his first dose of pox.

CHARLES BAUDELAIRE (1821–67), French poet. *My Heart Laid Bare* (written c. 1865; publ. in *Intimate Journals*, sct. 71, 1887; tr. by Christopher Isherwood 1930; rev. by Don Bachardy, 1989).

10   The free-lance writer is a man who is paid per piece or per word or perhaps.

ROBERT BENCHLEY (1889–1945), U.S. humorous writer. Quoted by James Thurber in: *Bermudian* (Nov. 1950).

11   I was an only child. I lost both my parents. By the time I was twenty I was bald. I'm homosexual. In the way of circumstances and background to transcend I had everything an artist could possibly want. It was practically a blueprint. I was programmed to be a novelist or a playwright. But I'm not.

ALAN BENNETT (b. 1934), British playwright. Leslie Halliwell, in *Prick up Your Ears: The Screenplay* (1987).

12   Essential characteristic of the really great novelist: a Christ-like, all-embracing compassion.

ARNOLD BENNETT (1867–1931), British novelist. *The Journals of Arnold Bennett* (1932), entry for 25 Oct. 1897.

13   A writer never reads his work. For him, it is the unreadable, a secret, and he cannot remain face to face with it. A secret, because he is separated from it.

MAURICE BLANCHOT (b. 1907), French literary theorist, author. "The Essential Solitude," in *The Space of Literature* (1955; repr. in *The Gaze of Orpheus*, ed. by P. Adams Sitney, 1981).

14   No one who cannot limit himself has ever been able to write.

NICOLAS BOILEAU-DESPRÉAUX (1636–1711), French poet, critic. *L'Art Poétique*, cto. 1 (1674).

15   Like all writers, he measured the achievements of others by what they had accomplished, asking of them that they measure him by what he envisaged or planned.

JORGE LUIS BORGES (1899–1986), Argentinian author. *Ficciones*, "The Secret Miracle" (1944; tr. 1962), of Jaromir Hladik.

16   For your born writer, nothing is so healing as the realization that he has come upon the right word.

CATHERINE DRINKER BOWEN (1897–1973), U.S. author. *Adventures of a Biographer*, ch. 11 (1946).

17   Every writing career starts as a personal quest for sainthood, for self-betterment. Sooner or later, and as a rule quite soon, a man discovers that his pen accomplishes a lot more than his soul.

JOSEPH BRODSKY (b. 1940), Russian-born U.S. poet, critic. *Less Than One: Selected Essays*, "The Power of the Elements" (1986; first published 1980).

18   But this I know; the writer who possesses the creative gift owns something of which he is not always master—something that at times strangely wills and works for itself. . . . If the result be attractive, the World will praise you, who little deserve praise; if it be repulsive, the same World will blame you, who almost as little deserve blame.

CHARLOTTE BRONTË (1816–55), English novelist. Emily Brontë, *Wuthering Heights*, Preface (1850).

19 Great writers are the saints for the godless.

ANITA BROOKNER (b. 1938), British novelist, art historian. *Novelists in Interview* (ed. by John Haffenden, 1985).

20 Without, or with, offence to friends or foes,
I sketch your world exactly as it goes.

LORD BYRON (1788–1824), English poet. *Don Juan*, cto. 8, st. 89

21 Nothing so fretful, so despicable as a Scribbler, see what *I* am, & what a parcel of Scoundrels I have brought about my ears, & what language I have been obliged to treat them with to deal with them in their own way;—all this comes of Authorship.

LORD BYRON (1788–1824), English poet. Letter, 2 Sept. 1811, to Byron's half-sister, Augusta Leigh (published in *Byron's Letters and Journals*, vol. 2, ed. by Leslie A. Marchand, 1973–81).

22 In general I do not draw well with literary men—not that I dislike them but I never know what to say to them after I have praised their last publication.

LORD BYRON (1788–1824), English poet. *Detached Thoughts*, no. 53 (1821–22; published in *Byron's Letters and Journals*, vol. 9, ed. by Leslie A. Marchand, 1979).

23 To note an artist's limitations is but to define his talent. A reporter can write equally well about everything that is presented to his view, but a creative writer can do his best only with what lies within the range and character of his deepest sympathies.

WILLA CATHER (1876–1947), U.S. author. *Not Under Forty*, "Miss Jewett" (1936).

24 Any man who can write a page of living prose adds something to our life, and the man who can, as I can, is surely the last to resent someone who can do it even better. An artist cannot deny art, nor would he want to. A lover cannot deny love.

RAYMOND CHANDLER (1888–1959), U.S. author. Letter, 25 May 1957, to Chandler's literary agent Helga Greene (published in *Raymond Chandler Speaking*, 1962).

25 The task of an American writer is not to describe the misgivings of a woman taken in adultery as she looks out of a window at the rain but to describe four hundred people under the lights reaching for a foul ball. This is ceremony.

JOHN CHEEVER (1912–82), U.S. author. *John Cheever: The Journals*, "The Sixties" (ed. by Robert Gottlieb, 1991), 1963 entry.

26 The writer who loses his self-doubt, who gives way as he grows old to a sudden euphoria, to prolixity, should stop writing immediately: the time has come for him to lay aside his pen.

COLETTE (1873–1954), French author. Speech on being elected to the Belgian Academy (published in *Earthly Paradise*, pt. 4, "Lady of Letters," ed. by Robert Phelps, 1966).

27 Justice to my readers compels me to admit that I write because I have nothing to do; justice to myself induces me to add that I will cease to write the moment I have nothing to say.

C. C. COLTON (1780–1832), English author, clergyman. *Lacon*, vol. 1, Preface (1820).

28 A great writer creates a world of his own and his readers are proud to live in it. A lesser writer may entice them in for a moment, but soon he will watch them filing out.

CYRIL CONNOLLY (1903–74), British critic. *Enemies of Promise*, pt. 1, ch. 1 (1938).

29 The more books we read, the clearer it becomes that the true function of a writer is to produce a masterpiece and that no other task is of any consequence.

CYRIL CONNOLLY (1903–74), British critic. *The Unquiet Grave*, pt. 1 (1944; rev. 1951).

30 When writers meet they are truculent, indifferent, or over-polite. Then comes the inevitable moment. A shows B that he has read something of B's. Will B show A? If not, then A hates B, if yes, then all is well. The only other way for writers to meet is to share a quick pee over a common lamp-post.

CYRIL CONNOLLY (1903–74), British critic. "The Journal of Cyril Connolly 1928–1937" (published in David Pryce-Jones, *Journal and Memoir*, 1983, p. 269).

31 In most cases a favorite writer is more with us in his book than he ever could have been in the flesh; since, being a writer, he is one who has studied and perfected this particular mode of personal incarnation, very likely to the detriment of any other. I should like as a matter of curiosity to see and hear for a moment the men whose works I admire; but I should hardly expect to find further intercourse particularly profitable.

CHARLES HORTON COOLEY (1864–1929), U.S. sociologist. *Human Nature and the Social Order*, ch. 3 (1902).

32 There are hardly half a dozen writers in England today who have not sold out to the enemy. Even when their good work has been a success, Mammon grips them and whispers: "More money for more work."

ALEISTER CROWLEY (1875–1947), British occultist. *The Confessions of Aleister Crowley*, ch. 65 (1929; rev. 1970).

33 Herman Melville was as separated from a civilized literature as the lost Atlantis was said to have been from the great peoples of the earth.

EDWARD DAHLBERG (1900–1977), U.S. author, critic. *Alms For Oblivion*, "Moby Dick: A Hamitic Dream" (1964).

34 What has a writer to be bombastic about? Whatever good a man may write is the consequence of accident, luck, or surprise, and nobody is more surprised than an honest writer when he makes a good phrase or says something truthful.

EDWARD DAHLBERG (1900–1977), U.S. author, critic. *Alms for Oblivion*, "No Love and No Thanks" (1964).

35 I think of an author as somebody who goes into the marketplace and puts down his rug and says, "I will tell you a story," and then he passes the hat.

ROBERTSON DAVIES (b. 1913), Canadian novelist, journalist. *The Enthusiasms of Robertson Actor*, "The Table Talk of Robertson Davies" (1990).

36 The writer's language is to some degree the product of his own action; he is both the historian and the agent of his own language.

PAUL DE MAN (1919–83), Belgian-born U.S. literary critic. *Blindness and Insight*, ch. 8 (1971).

37 Writers are always selling somebody out.

JOAN DIDION (b. 1934), U.S. essayist. *Slouching Towards Bethlehem*, Preface (1968).

38 An author who speaks about his own books is almost as bad as a mother who talks about her own children.

BENJAMIN DISRAELI (1804–81), English statesman, author. Speech, 19 Nov. 1873; at a banquet given by the city of Glasgow to Disraeli, on his inauguration as Lord Rector of Glasgow University.

39 Of the creative spirits that flourished in Concord, Massachusetts, during the middle of the nineteenth century, it might be said that Hawthorne loved men but felt estranged from them, Emerson loved ideas even more than men, and Thoreau loved himself.

LEON EDEL (b. 1907), U.S. biographer, critic. Opening sentence of "Henry D. Thoreau" (published in *University of Minnesota Pamphlets on American Writers*, no. 90, 1970).

40 There is no luck in literary reputation. They who make up the final verdict upon every book are not the partial and noisy readers of the hour when it appears; but a court as of angels, a public not to be bribed, not to be entreated, and not to be overawed, decides upon every man's title to fame.

RALPH WALDO EMERSON (1803–82), U.S. essayist, poet, philosopher. *Essays*, "Spiritual Laws" (First Series, 1841).

41 Talent alone cannot make a writer. There must be a man behind the book; a personality which, by birth and quality, is pledged to the doctrines there set forth, and which exists to see and state things so, and not otherwise.

RALPH WALDO EMERSON (1803–82), U.S. essayist, poet, philosopher. *Representative Men*, "Goethe" (1850).

42 Mr. Faulkner, of course, is interested in making your mind rather than your flesh creep.

CLIFTON FADIMAN (b. 1904), U.S. essayist. *New Yorker* (21 April 1934).

43 If a writer has to rob his mother, he will not hesitate; the "Ode on a Grecian Urn" is worth any number of old ladies.

WILLIAM FAULKNER (1897–1962), U.S. novelist. Interview in *Writers at Work* (First Series, ed. by Malcolm Cowley, 1958).

44 If I had not existed, someone else would have written me, Hemingway, Dostoevski, all of us.

WILLIAM FAULKNER (1897–1962), U.S. novelist. Interview in *Writers at Work* (First Series, ed. by Malcolm Cowley, 1958).

45 My idea is always to reach my generation. The wise writer . . . writes for the youth of his own generation, the critics of the next, and the schoolmasters of ever afterward.

F. SCOTT FITZGERALD (1896–1940), U.S. author. "Self-interview," in *New York Tribune* (7 May 1920; repr. in Matthew J. Bruccoli, *Some Sort of Epic Grandeur*, ch. 16, 1981). The interview was later used by Fitzgerald in *The Author's Apology*—a letter to the American Booksellers Convention, May 1920.

46 Mostly, we authors must repeat ourselves—that's the truth. We have two or three great moving experiences in our lives—experiences so great and moving that it doesn't seem at the time that anyone else has been so caught up and pounded and dazzled and astonished and beaten and broken and rescued and illuminated and rewarded and humbled in just that way ever before.

F. SCOTT FITZGERALD (1896–1940), U.S. author. "One Hundred False Starts," in *Saturday Evening Post* (4 March 1933; repr. in *Afternoon of an Author, A Selection of Uncollected Stories and Essays*, ed. by Arthur Mizener, 1958).

47 Writers aren't people exactly. Or, if they're any good, they're a whole *lot* of people trying so hard to be one person. It's like actors, who try so pathetically not to look in mirrors. Who lean *back*ward trying—only to see their faces in the reflecting chandeliers.

F. SCOTT FITZGERALD (1896–1940), U.S. author. Cecilia Brady, in *The Last Tycoon*, ch. 1 (1941).

48 Our work . . . is to present things that are as they are.

FREDERICK II (1194–1250), King of Sicily, Holy Roman Emperor. Prologue to Frederick's work on falconry, *De Arte Venandi cum Avibus* (1244–50).

49 The writer probably knows what he meant when he wrote a book, but he should immediately forget what he meant when he's written it.

WILLIAM GOLDING (1911–93), British author. *Novelists in Interview* (ed. by John Haffenden, 1985).

50 I don't regard Brecht as a man of iron-grey purpose and intellect, I think he is a theatrical whore of the first quality.

SIR PETER HALL (b. 1930), British theater director. Quoted in: *The Frank Muir Book*, "Theatre" (1976).

51 Whatever an author puts between the two covers of his book is public property; whatever of himself he does not put there is his private property, as much as if he had never written a word.

GAIL HAMILTON (1833–96), U.S. writer, humorist. *Country Living and Country Thinking*, Preface (1862).

52 If a nation loses its storytellers, it loses its childhood.

PETER HANDKE (b. 1942), Austrian author, playwright, poet. *Independent* (London, 9 June 1988).

53 The role of the writer is not simply to arrange Being according to his own lights; he must also serve as a medium to Being and remain open to its often unfathomable dictates. This is the only way the work can transcend its creator and radiate its meaning further than the author himself can see or perceive.

VÁCLAV HAVEL (b. 1936), Czech playwright, president. *Disturbing the Peace*, ch. 2 (1986; tr. 1990).

54 They're fancy talkers about themselves, writers. If I had to give young writers advice, I would say don't listen to writers talking about writing or themselves.

LILLIAN HELLMAN (1905–84), U.S. playwright. *New York Times* (21 Feb. 1960).

55 A serious writer is not to be confounded with a solemn writer. A serious writer may be a hawk or a buzzard or even a popinjay, but a solemn writer is always a bloody owl.

ERNEST HEMINGWAY (1899–1961), U.S. author. *Death in the Afternoon*, ch. 16 (1932).

56 Writing, at its best, is a lonely life. Organizations for writers palliate the writer's loneliness, but I doubt if they improve his writing. He grows in public stature as he sheds his loneliness and often his work deteriorates. For he does his work alone and if he is a good enough writer he must face eternity, or the lack of it, each day.

ERNEST HEMINGWAY (1899–1961), U.S. author. Address recorded for the Nobel Prize Committee, 10 Dec. 1954, accepting the Nobel Prize for literature (published in Carlos Baker, *Hemingway: the Writer as Artist*, ch. 13, 3rd ed., 1963).

57 The most essential gift for a good writer is a built-in, shock-proof, shit detector. This is the writer's radar and all great writers have had it.

ERNEST HEMINGWAY (1899–1961), U.S. author. Interview in *Paris Review* (Flushing, N.Y., Spring 1958; repr. in *Writers at Work*, Second Series, ed. by George Plimpton, 1963).

58 We are all apprentices in a craft where no one ever becomes a master.

ERNEST HEMINGWAY (1899–1961), U.S. author. *New York Journal-American* (11 July 1961).

59 I hold any writer sufficiently justified who is himself in love with his theme.

HENRY JAMES (1843–1916), U.S. author. *Italian Hours*, "Venice" (written 1882; published 1909).

60 He is outside of everything, and alien everywhere. He is an aesthetic solitary. His beautiful, light imagination is the wing that on the autumn evening just brushes the dusky window.

HENRY JAMES (1843–1916), U.S. author. *Anthology Library of the World's Best Literature*, vol 12, Introduction (1897), said of Nathaniel Hawthorne.

61 I know not, Madam, that you have a right, upon moral principles, to make your readers suffer so much.

SAMUEL JOHNSON (1709–84), English author, lexicographer. To Mrs. Thomas Sheridan, on publication of her novel, *Memoirs of Mrs. Sydney Biddulph*. Quoted in: James Boswell, *Life of Samuel Johnson*, 1763 (1791).

62 The greatest part of a writer's time is spent in reading, in order to write; a man will turn over half a library to make one book.

SAMUEL JOHNSON (1709–84), English author, lexicographer. Quoted in: James Boswell, *Life of Samuel Johnson*, 6 April 1775 (1791).

63 I'd rather be a lightning rod than a seismograph.

KEN KESEY (b. 1935), U.S. author. Quoted in: Tom Wolfe, *The Electric Kool-Aid Acid Test*, ch. 1 (1968).

64 I believe that it is my job not only to write books but to have them published. A book is like a child. You have to defend the life of a child.

GEORGE KONRÁD (b. 1933), Hungarian writer, politician. *Sunday Correspondent* (London, 15 April 1990).

65 I hate the actor and audience business. An author should be in among the crowd, kicking their shins or cheering them on to some mischief or merriment.

D. H. LAWRENCE (1885–1930), British author. Letter, 22 Jan. 1925 (published in *The Letters of D. H. Lawrence*, vol 5, ed. by James T. Boulton, 1987).

66 Nowadays three witty turns of phrase and a lie make a writer.

G. C. LICHTENBERG (1742–99), German physicist, philosopher. *Aphorisms*, "Notebook D," aph. 25 (written 1765–99; tr. by R. J. Hollingdale, 1990).

67 It's very hard to be a gentleman and a writer.

W. SOMERSET MAUGHAM (1874–1965), British author. Ashenden, in *Cakes and Ale*, ch. 11 (1930).

68 Give me a condor's quill! Give me Vesuvius' crater for an inkstand!

HERMAN MELVILLE (1819–91), U.S. author. *Moby-Dick*, ch. 104 (1851).

69 I was brought up in the great tradition of the late nineteenth century: that a writer never complains, never explains and never disdains.

JAMES A. MICHENER (b. 1907), U.S. novelist. Quoted in: *Observer* (London, 26 Nov. 1989).

70 A man writes to throw off the poison which he has accumulated because of his false way of life. He is trying to recapture his innocence, yet all he succeeds in doing (by writing) is to inoculate the world with a virus of his disillusionment. No man would set a word down on paper if he had the courage to live out what he believed in.

HENRY MILLER (1891–1980), U.S. author. *Sexus*, ch. 1 (1949).

71 The shelf life of the modern hardback writer is somewhere between the milk and the yoghurt.

JOHN MORTIMER (b. 1923), British barrister, novelist. Quoted in: *Sunday Times* (London, 27 Dec. 1987).

72 I'm the kind of writer that people think other people are reading.

V. S. NAIPAUL (b. 1932), Trinidad-born British writer. *Radio Times* (London, 24 March 1979).

73 For a creative writer possession of the "truth" is less important than emotional sincerity.

GEORGE ORWELL (1903–50), British author. *Inside the Whale and Other Essays*, "Inside the Whale" (1940).

74 He is a man of thirty-five, but looks fifty. He is bald, has varicose veins and wears spectacles, or would wear them if his only pair were not chronically lost. If things are normal with him, he will be suffering from malnutrition, but if he has recently had a lucky streak, he will be suffering from a hangover. At present it is half past eleven in the morning, and according to his schedule he should have started work two hours ago; but even if he had made any serious effort to start he would have been frustrated by the almost continuous ringing of the telephone bell, the yells of the baby, the rattle of an electric drill out in the street, and the heavy boots of his creditors clumping up the stairs. The most recent interruption was the arrival of the second post, which brought him two circulars and an income tax demand printed in red. Needless to say this person is a writer.

GEORGE ORWELL (1903–50), British author. "Confessions of a Book Reviewer" (1946; repr. in *The Collected Essays, Journalism and Letters of George Orwell*, vol. 4, ed. by Sonia Orwell and Ian Angus, 1968).

75 All writers are vain, selfish and lazy, and at the very bottom of their motives lies a mystery. Writing a book is a long, exhausting struggle, like a long bout of some painful illness. One would never undertake such a thing if one were not driven by some demon whom one can neither resist nor understand.

> GEORGE ORWELL (1903–50), British author. "Why I Write" (1947; repr. in *Collected Essays,* 1961).

76 One reason writers write is out of revenge. Life hurts; certain ideas and experiences hurt; one wants to clarify, to set out illuminations, to replay the old bad scenes and get the *Treppenworte* said—the words one didn't have the strength or ripeness to say when those words were necessary for one's dignity or survival.

> CYNTHIA OZICK (b. 1928), U.S. novelist, short-story writer. *Writers at Work* (Eighth Series, 1988). Later in the interview Ozick compared the writer to "a beast howling inside a coal-furnace, heaping the coals on itself to increase the fire."

77 Writers, you know, are the beggars of Western society.

> OCTAVIO PAZ (b. 1914), Mexican poet. Quoted in: *Independent on Sunday* (London, 30 Dec. 1990).

78 Why did I write? what sin to me unknown
Dipt me in ink, my parents', or my own?

> ALEXANDER POPE (1688–1744), English satirical poet. *Epistle to Dr. Arbuthnot.*

79 Good writers are those who keep the language efficient. That is to say, keep it accurate, keep it clear.

> EZRA POUND (1885–1972), U.S. poet, critic. *The ABC of Reading,* ch. 3 (1934).

80 Great writers arrive among us like new diseases—threatening, powerful, impatient for patients to pick up their virus, irresistible.

> CRAIG RAINE (b. 1944), British poet, critic. *Independent on Sunday* (London, 18 Nov. 1990).

81 Whores and writers, Mahound. We are the people you can't forgive.

> SALMAN RUSHDIE (b. 1948), Indian-born British author. The "famous satirist" Baal, in *The Satanic Verses,* "Return to Jahilia" (1988). Mahound, Prophet of Jahilia, replies, "Writers and whores. I see no difference."

82 I make no complaint. I am a writer. I do not accept my condition; I will strive to change it; but I inhabit it, I am trying to learn from it.

> SALMAN RUSHDIE (b. 1947), Indian-born British author. *Independent on Sunday* (London, 4 Feb. 1990).

83 You must not suppose, because I am a man of letters, that I never tried to earn an honest living.

> GEORGE BERNARD SHAW (1856–1950), Anglo-Irish playwright, critic. *The Irrational Knot,* Preface (1905).

84 I cringe when critics say I'm a master of the popular novel. What's an unpopular novel?

> IRWIN SHAW (b. 1913), U.S. author. *Observer* (London, 6 March 1983).

85 The writer is either a practising recluse or a delinquent, guilt-ridden one; or both. Usually both.

> SUSAN SONTAG (b. 1933), U.S. essayist. "When Writers Talk among Themselves," in *New York Times* (5 Jan. 1986).

86 O Grub Street! how do I bemoan thee,
Whose graceless children scorn to own thee!

. . . Yet *thou* hast greater cause to be
Ashamed of them, than they of thee.

> JONATHAN SWIFT (1667–1745), Anglo-Irish satirist. *On Poetry: A Rhapsody.* Samuel Johnson, in his *Dictionary* of 1755, included the definition "grubstreet," defining it as "Originally the name of a street in Moorfields in London, much inhabited by writers of small histories, dictionaries, and temporary poems, whence any mean production is called *grubstreet.*"

87 As a man has no right to kill one of his children if it is diseased or insane, so a man who has made the gradual and conscious expression of his personality in literature the aim of his life, has no right to suppress himself any carefully considered work which seemed good enough when it was written. Suppression, if it is deserved, will come rapidly enough from the same causes that suppress the unworthy members of a man's family.

> J. M. SYNGE (1871–1909), Irish poet, dramatist. Draft of a preface in "Notebook 16." Quoted in: *The Collected Works of J. M. Synge,* vol. 1, Introduction (1962). [Some punctuation has been added to facilitate understanding.].

88 Many writers who choose to be active in the world lose not virtue but time, and that stillness without which literature cannot be made.

> GORE VIDAL (b. 1925), U.S. novelist, critic. *Réalités* (Aug. 1966). "That is sad," Vidal added, "until one recalls how many bad books the world may yet be spared because of the busyness of writers."

89 Each writer is born with a repertory company in his head. Shakespeare has perhaps 20 players, and Tennessee Williams has about 5, and Samuel Beckett one—and maybe a clone of that one. I have 10 or so, and that's a lot. As you get older, you become more skillful at casting them.

> GORE VIDAL (b. 1925), U.S. novelist, critic. *Times Herald* (Dallas, 18 June 1978).

90 Most bad books get that way because their authors are engaged in trying to justify themselves. If a vain author is an alcoholic, then the most sympathetically portrayed character in his book will be an alcoholic. This sort of thing is very boring for outsiders.

> STEPHEN VIZINCZEY (b. 1933), Hungarian novelist, critic. "A Writer's Ten Commandments," in *Writers' Monthly* (London, July 1985; repr. in *Truth and Lies in Literature,* 1986).

91 In a sense the world dies every time a writer dies, because, if he is any good, he has been a wet nurse to humanity during his entire existence and has held earth close around him, like the little obstetrical toad that goes about with a cluster of eggs attached to his legs.

> E. B. WHITE (1899–1985), U.S. author, editor. "Doomsday," in *New Yorker* (17 Nov. 1945; repr. in *Writings from the New Yorker 1927–1976,* ed. by Rebecca M. Dale, 1991).

92 From the point of view of literature Mr. Kipling is a genius who drops his aspirates. From the point of view of life, he is a reporter who knows vulgarity better than any one has ever known it.

> OSCAR WILDE (1854–1900), Anglo-Irish playwright, author. Gilbert, in *The Critic as Artist,* pt. 2 (published in *Intentions,* 1891).

93 His style is chaos illumined by flashes of lightning. As a writer he has mastered everything except language.

OSCAR WILDE (1854–1900), Anglo-Irish playwright, author. Vivian, in "The Decay of Lying" (published in *Intentions*, 1891), of author George Meredith.

94 The future author is one who discovers that language, the exploration and manipulation of the resources of language, will serve him in winning through to his way.

THORNTON WILDER (1897–1975), U.S. novelist, dramatist. Interview in *Writers at Work* (First Series, ed. by Malcolm Cowley, 1958).

95 Every secret of a writer's soul, every experience of his life, every quality of his mind is written large in his works.

VIRGINIA WOOLF (1882–1941), British novelist. *Orlando*, ch. 4 (1928).

96 The creations of a great writer are little more than the moods and passions of his own heart, given surnames and Christian names, and sent to walk the earth.

W. B. YEATS (1865–1939), Irish poet, playwright. Letter to the editor of the *Daily Express* (Dublin, 27 Feb. 1895; published in *Collected Letters*, vol. 1, ed. by John Kelly, 1986).

See also Solotaroff on AGGRESSION; Dahlberg, Johnson on ART; Joyce on ARTISTS; Fitzgerald on BIOGRAPHY; Benjamin on BOOKS; THOMAS CARLYLE; Fitzgerald on CLICHES; Maugham on CRITICS; Hemingway on DICTIONARIES; Moore on EDITING; Chandler on ENGLAND AND THE ENGLISH; Conrad on EXAGGERATION; Auden on FAME; F. SCOTT FITZGERALD; Butler on GENIUS; ERNEST HEMINGWAY; HISTORIANS; Connolly on HOTELS; Updike on INTERVIEWS; HENRY JAMES; SAMUEL JOHNSON; JAMES JOYCE; D. H. LAWRENCE; Auden, Hemingway on LITERATURE AND SOCIETY; Don DeLillo on MADNESS; HENRY MILLER; Melville on OBSTINACY; Dryden, Proctor on PLAGIARISM; EDGAR ALLAN POE; POETS; Havel on THE PRESIDENT; MARCEL PROUST; Barstow on READING; WILLIAM SHAKESPEARE; Auden on SLAVERY; Updike on TASTE; Parker, Woolf on WOMEN AND THE ARTS; WRITING.

WRITING

1 Some writers confuse authenticity, which they ought always to aim at, with originality, which they should never bother about.

W. H. AUDEN (1907–73), Anglo-American poet. *The Dyer's Hand*, pt. 1, "Writing" (1962).

2 A word is a bud attempting to become a twig. How can one not dream while writing? It is the pen which dreams. The blank page gives the right to dream.

GASTON BACHELARD (1884–1962), French scientist, philosopher, literary theorist. *The Poetics of Reverie*, "Introduction," sct. 6 (1960; tr. 1969).

3 Who wants to become a writer? And why? Because it's the answer to everything. To "Why am I here?" To uselessness. It's the streaming reason for living. To note, to pin down, to build up, to create, to be astonished at nothing, to cherish the oddities, to let nothing go down the drain, to make something, to make a great flower out of life, even if it's a cactus.

ENID BAGNOLD (1889–1981), British novelist, playwright. *Autobiography*, ch. 3 (1969).

4 Work on good prose has three steps: a musical stage when it is composed, an architectonic one when it is built, and a textile one when it is woven.

WALTER BENJAMIN (1892–1940), German critic, philosopher. *One-Way Street*, "Caution: Steps" (1928; repr. in *One-Way Street and Other Writings*, 1978).

5 To write is to make oneself the echo of what cannot cease speaking—and since it cannot, in order to become its echo I have, in a way, to silence it. I bring to this incessant speech the decisiveness, the authority of my own silence.

MAURICE BLANCHOT (b. 1907), French literary theorist, author. *The Space of Literature*, ch. 1, "The Essential Solitude" (1955; tr. 1982).

6 Every writer "creates" his own precursors. His work modifies our conception of the past, as it will modify the future.

JORGE LUIS BORGES (1899–1986), Argentinian author. *Kafka and his Precursors* (1951; repr. in *Other Inquisitions*, 1960; tr. 1964).

7 The aim, if reached or not, makes great the life: Try to be Shakespeare, leave the rest to fate!

ROBERT BROWNING (1812–89), English poet. *Bishop Blougram's Apology*.

8 Writing is more than anything a compulsion, like some people wash their hands thirty times a day for fear of awful consequences if they do not. It pays a whole lot better than this type of compulsion, but it is no more heroic.

JULIE BURCHILL (b. 1960), British journalist, author. *Sex and Sensibility*, Introduction (1992).

9 The trouble began with Forster. After him it was considered ungentlemanly to write more than five or six novels.

ANTHONY BURGESS (b. 1917), British author, critic. *Guardian* (London, 24 Feb. 1989). Burgess has written more than twenty novels.

10 The only living works are those which have drained much of the author's own life into them.

SAMUEL BUTLER (1835–1902), English author. *Samuel Butler's Notebooks* (1951, p. 194).

11 To withdraw *myself* from *myself* . . . has ever been my sole, my entire, my sincere motive in scribbling at all.

LORD BYRON (1788–1824), English poet. *Byron's Letters and Journals*, vol 3 (ed. by Leslie A. Marchand, 1974), entry for 27 Nov. 1813. "The end of all scribblement is to amuse," Byron had written in another letter, 3 Oct. 1810.

12 If I don't write to empty my mind, I go mad. As to that regular, uninterrupted love of writing . . . I do not understand it. I feel it as a torture, which I must get rid of, but never as a pleasure. On the contrary, I think composition a great pain.

LORD BYRON (1788–1824), English poet. Letter, 2 Jan. 1821, to poet Thomas Moore (published in *Byron's Letters and Journals*, vol. 8, ed. by Leslie A. Marchand, 1973–81).

13 The process of writing has something infinite about it. Even though it is interrupted each night, it is one single notation.

ELIAS CANETTI (b. 1905), Austrian novelist, philosopher. *The Secret Heart Of The Clock: Notes, Aphorisms, Fragments 1973–1985*, "1973" (1991).

14 Writing is a dreadful Labour, yet not so dreadful as Idleness.

THOMAS CARLYLE (1795–1881), Scottish essayist, historian. *Two Notebooks of Thomas Carlyle* (1898, p. 136).

15   Writing ought either to be the manufacture of stories for which there is a market demand—a business as safe and commendable as making soap or breakfast foods—or it should be an art, which is always a search for something for which there is no market demand, something new and untried, where the values are intrinsic and have nothing to do with standardized values.

WILLA CATHER (1876–1947), U.S. author. *On Writing*, "On the Art of Fiction" (written 1920; published 1949).

16   Writing is to descend like a miner to the depths of the mine with a lamp on your forehead, a light whose dubious brightness falsifies everything, whose wick is in permanent danger of explosion, whose blinking illumination in the coal dust exhausts and corrodes your eyes.

BLAISE CENDRARS [FREDERIC SAUSER] (1887–1961), Swiss-born novelist, poet. *Le Lotissement du Ciel* (1949). Quoted in: Mary Anne Caws, *Selected Poems: Blaise Cendrars*, Introduction (1979).

17   There is something about the literary life that repels me, all this desperate building of castles on cobwebs, the long-drawn acrimonious struggle to make something important which we all know will be gone forever in a few years, the miasma of failure which is to me almost as offensive as the cheap gaudiness of popular success.

RAYMOND CHANDLER (1888–1959), U.S. author. Letter, 22 April 1949, to publisher Hamish Hamilton (published in *Raymond Chandler Speaking*, 1962).

18   Who often, but without success, have pray'd
For apt Alliteration's artful aid.

CHARLES CHURCHILL (1731–64), English clergyman, poet. *The Prophecy of Famine*.

19   If you describe things as better than they are, you are considered to be a romantic; if you describe things as worse than they are, you will be called a realist; and if you describe things exactly as they are, you will be thought of as a satirist.

QUENTIN CRISP (b. 1908), British author. *The Naked Civil Servant*, ch. 24 (1968).

20   Writing is conscience, scruple, and the farming of our ancestors.

EDWARD DAHLBERG (1900–1977), U.S. author, critic. *Alms for Oblivion*, "For Sale" (1964).

21   To write is a humiliation.

EDWARD DAHLBERG (1900–1977), U.S. author, critic. *The Carnal Myth*, Introduction (1968).

22   The ambivalence of writing is such that it can be considered both an act and an interpretive process that follows after an act with which it cannot coincide. As such, it both affirms and denies its own nature.

PAUL DE MAN (1919–83), Belgian-born U.S. literary critic. "Literary History and Literary Modernity," lecture, Sept. 1969 (repr. in *Blindness and Insight*, 1971; rev. 1983).

23   Writing is a socially acceptable form of schizophrenia.

E. L. DOCTOROW (b. 1931), U.S. novelist. Interview in *Writers at Work* (Eighth Series, ed. by George Plimpton, 1988).

24   Writing is turning one's worst moments into money.

J. P. DONLEAVY (b. 1926), Irish-American novelist. *Playboy* (Chicago, May 1979).

25   The first essential in writing about anything is that the writer should have no experience of the matter.

ISADORA DUNCAN (1878–1927), U.S. dancer. *My Life*, Introduction (1927).

26   I have the conviction that excessive literary production is a social offence.

GEORGE ELIOT (1819–80), English novelist. Letter, 11 Sept. 1871.

27   Writing a novel without being asked seems a bit like having a baby when you have nowhere to live.

LUCY ELLMAN (b. 1956), U.S. novelist. *Guardian* (London, 16 Jan. 1992).

28   A pathological business, writing, don't you think? Just look what a writer actually does: all that unnatural tense squatting and hunching, all those rituals: pathological!

HANS MAGNUS ENZENSBERGER (b. 1929), German poet, critic. Quoted in: *Guardian* (London, 30 Aug. 1990).

29   My own experience has been that the tools I need for my trade are paper, tobacco, food, and a little whisky.

WILLIAM FAULKNER (1897–1962), U.S. novelist. Interview in *Writers at Work* (First Series, ed. by Malcolm Cowley, 1958).

30   Only amateurs say that they write for their own amusement. Writing is not an amusing occupation. It is a combination of ditch-digging, mountain-climbing, treadmill and childbirth. Writing may be interesting, absorbing, exhilirating, racking, relieving. But amusing? Never!

EDNA FERBER (1887–1968), U.S. writer. *A Peculiar Treasure*, ch. 1 (1939).

31   Often I think writing is a sheer paring away of oneself leaving always something thinner, barer, more meager.

F. SCOTT FITZGERALD (1896–1940), U.S. author. Letter, 27 April 1940, to his daughter Frances Scott Fitzgerald (published in *The Letters of F. Scott Fitzgerald*, ed. by Andrew Turnbull, 1963).

32   All good writing is *swimming under water* and holding your breath.

F. SCOTT FITZGERALD (1896–1940), U.S. author. Letter (undated) to his daughter Frances Scott Fitzgerald (first published in *The Crack-Up*, ed. by Edmund Wilson, 1945).

33   Ultimately, literature is nothing but carpentry. With both you are working with reality, a material just as hard as wood.

GABRIEL GARCÍA MÁRQUEZ (b. 1928), Colombian author. Interview in *Writers at Work* (Sixth Series, ed. by George Plimpton, 1985).

34   It has always been my practice to cast a long paragraph in a single mould, to try it by my ear, to deposit it in my memory, but to suspend the action of the pen till I had given the last polish to my work.

EDWARD GIBBON (1737–94), English historian. *Memoirs of My*

Life (1796; published in Routledge, *Autobiography*, 1971, p. 103).

35 Prose is architecture, not interior decoration, and the Baroque is over.

ERNEST HEMINGWAY (1899–1961), U.S. author. *Death in the Afternoon*, ch. 16 (1932).

36 Do you remember how old Ford was always writing how Conrad suffered so when he wrote? How it was un metier de chien etc. Do you suffer when you write? I don't at all. Suffer like a bastard when don't write, or just before, and feel empty and fucked out afterwards. But never feel as good as while writing.

ERNEST HEMINGWAY (1899–1961), U.S. author. Letter, 14 Nov. 1945, to poet and critic Malcolm Cowley (published in *Selected Letters*, ed. by Carlos Baker, 1981), on the writers Ford Madox Ford and Joseph Conrad.

37 Composition is, for the most part, an effort of slow diligence and steady perseverance, to which the mind is dragged by necessity or resolution, and from which the attention is every moment starting to more delightful amusements.

SAMUEL JOHNSON (1709–84), English author, lexicographer. *Adventurer*, no. 138 (London, 2 March 1754; repr. in *The Works of Samuel Johnson*, vol. 2, ed. by W. J. Bate, John M. Bullitt and L. F. Powell, 1963).

38 In all pointed sentences, some degree of accuracy must be sacrificed to conciseness.

SAMUEL JOHNSON (1709–84), English author, lexicographer. "On the Bravery of the English Common Soldier," in *Works of Samuel Johnson, LL.D.*, vol. 10 (ed. by Sir John Hawkins, 1787).

39 One man is as good as another until he has written a book.

BENJAMIN JOWETT (1817–93), English scholar, essayist. Quoted in: *Life and Letters of Benjamin Jowett*, vol. 1, ch. 8 (ed. by Abbott and Campbell, 1897).

40 No pen, no ink, no table, no room, no time, no quiet, no inclination.

JAMES JOYCE (1882–1941), Irish author. Letter, 7 Dec. 1906, to Joyce's brother, written from Rome in a state of disillusion (published in *Letters of James Joyce*, vol. 2, 1966). See Joyce on ITALY AND THE ITALIANS.

41 This is something that I cannot get over—that a whole line could be written by half a man, that a work could be built on the quicksand of a character.

KARL KRAUS (1874–1936), Austrian satirist. *Nachts*, ch. 6 (1918).

42 Making a book is a craft, like making a clock; it needs more than native wit to be an author.

JEAN DE LA BRUYÈRE (1645–96), French writer, moralist. *Characters*, "Of Books," aph. 3 (1688).

43 It's hard enough to write a good drama, it's much harder to write a good comedy, and it's hardest of all to write a drama with comedy. Which is what life is.

JACK LEMMON (b. 1925), U.S. actor. *Independent* (London, 21 Feb. 1990).

44 The only phenomenon with which writing has always been concomitant is the creation of cities and empires, that is the integration of large numbers of indi-viduals into a political system, and their grading into castes or classes. .. It seems to have favored the exploitation of human beings rather than their enlightenment.

CLAUDE LÉVI-STRAUSS (b. 1908), French anthropologist. *Tristes Tropiques*, ch. 28 (1955).

45 As I take up my pen I feel myself so full, so equal to my subject, and see my book so clearly before me in embryo, I would almost like to try to say it all in a single word.

G. C. LICHTENBERG (1742–99), German physicist, philosopher. *Aphorisms*, "Notebook E," aph. 52 (written 1765–99; tr. by R. J. Hollingdale, 1990).

46 All books are either dreams or swords,
You can cut, or you can drug, with words.

AMY LOWELL (1874–1925), U.S. poet. *Sword Blades and Poppy Seed*, st. 3.

47 Writing books is the closest men ever come to childbearing.

NORMAN MAILER (b. 1923), U.S. author. "Mr. Mailer Interviews Himself" (first published in *New York Times Book Review*, 17 Sept. 1965; repr. in *Conversations with Norman Mailer*, ed. by J. Michael Lennon, 1988).

48 Habits in writing as in life are only useful if they are broken as soon as they cease to be advantageous.

W. SOMERSET MAUGHAM (1874–1965), British author. *The Summing Up*, ch. 48 (1938).

49 The need to express oneself in writing springs from a malajustment to life, or from an inner conflict which the adolescent (or the grown man) cannot resolve in action. Those to whom action comes as easily as breathing rarely feel the need to break loose from the real, to rise above, and describe it. . . . I do not mean that it is enough to be maladjusted to become a great writer, but writing is, for some, a method of resolving a conflict, provided they have the necessary talent.

ANDRÉ MAUROIS (1885–1967), French author, critic. *The Art of Writing*, "The Writer's Craft," sct. 1 (1960).

50 You enter a state of controlled passivity, you relax your grip and accept that even if your declared intention is to justify the ways of God to man, you might end up interesting your readers rather more in Satan.

IAN MCEWAN (b. 1938), British author. *A Move Abroad*, Preface (1989), on novel-writing.

51 You expect far too much of a first sentence. Think of it as analagous to a good country breakfast: what we want is something simple, but nourishing to the imagination. Hold the philosophy, hold the adjectives, just give us a plain subject and verb and perhaps a wholesome, nonfattening adverb or two.

LARRY MCMURTRY (b. 1936), U.S. screenwriter, novelist, essayist. Godwin, in *Some Can Whistle*, pt. 1, ch. 3 (1989).

52 I always write a good first line, but I have trouble in writing the others.

MOLIÈRE (1622–73), French dramatist. Mascarille, in *Les Précieuses Ridicules*, sc. 11.

53 Writing is like getting married. One should never commit oneself until one is amazed at one's luck.

IRIS MURDOCH (b. 1919), British novelist, philosopher. *The*

Black Prince, "Bradley Pearson's Foreword" (1973). The narrator is here discussing his own literary output: three short books in 40 years.

54　Style and Structure are the essence of a book; great ideas are hogwash.

VLADIMIR NABOKOV (1899–1977), Russian-born U.S. novelist, poet. Interview in *Writers at Work* (Fourth Series, ed. by George Plimpton, 1976).

55　The only way out is the way through, just as you cannot escape from death except by dying. Being unable to write, you must examine in writing this being unable, which becomes for the present—henceforth?—the subject to which you are condemned.

HOWARD NEMEROV (1920–91), U.S. poet, novelist, critic. *Journal of the Fictive Life,* "Reflexions of the Novelist Felix Ledger," sct. B (1965).

56　Good novels are not written by orthodoxy-sniffers, nor by people who are conscience-stricken about their own orthodoxy. Good novels are written by people who are not frightened.

GEORGE ORWELL (1903–50), British author. *Inside the Whale and Other Essays,* "Inside the Whale" (1940).

57　If you're going to write, don't pretend to write down. It's going to be the best you can do, and it's the fact that it's the best you can do that kills you.

DOROTHY PARKER (1893–1967), U.S. humorous writer. Interview in *Writers at Work* (First Series, ed. by Malcolm Cowley, 1958).

58　When we see a natural style we are quite amazed and delighted, because we expected to see an author and find a man.

BLAISE PASCAL (1623–62), French scientist, philosopher. *Pensées* (1670; no. 675 ed. by Krailsheimer, no. 29 ed. by Brunschvicg).

59　True ease in writing comes from art, not chance,
As those move easiest who have learned to dance.
'Tis not enough no harshness gives offence,
The sound must seem an echo to the sense.

ALEXANDER POPE (1688–1744), English satirical poet. *An Essay on Criticism.*

60　Good authors, too, who once knew better words
Now only use four-letter words
Writing prose . . .
Anything goes.

COLE PORTER (1893–1964), U.S. composer, lyricist. *Anything Goes* (1934).

61　Nothing written for pay is worth printing. ONLY what has been written AGAINST the market.

EZRA POUND (1885–1972), U.S. poet, critic. *Ezra Pound in Melbourne: Helix 13/14* (1983). Pound himself was largely freed from the necessity to earn a living thanks to his wife Dorothy Shakespear's private income.

62　I perceived that to express those impressions, to write that essential book, which is the only true one, a great writer does not, in the current meaning of the word, invent it, but, since it exists already in each one of us, interprets it. The duty and the task of a writer are those of an interpreter.

MARCEL PROUST (1871–1922), French novelist. *Remembrance of Things Past,* vol. 12, "Time Regained," ch. 3 (1927; tr. by Stephen Hudson, 1931).

63　Books choose their authors; the act of creation is not entirely a rational and conscious one.

SALMAN RUSHDIE (b. 1947), Indian-born British author. *Independent on Sunday* (London, 4 Feb. 1990).

64　It is necessary to write, if the days are not to slip emptily by. How else, indeed, to clap the net over the butterfly of the moment? for the moment passes, it is forgotten; the mood is gone; life itself is gone. That is where the writer scores over his fellows: he catches the changes of his mind on the hop. Growth is exciting; growth is dynamic and alarming. Growth of the soul, growth of the mind.

VITA SACKVILLE-WEST (1892–1962), British novelist, poet. *Twelve Days,* ch. 1 (1928).

65　Writing is a question of finding a certain rhythm. I compare it to the rhythms of jazz. Much of the time life is a sort of rhythmic progression of three characters. If one tells oneself that life is like that, one feels it less arbitrary.

FRANÇOISE SAGAN (b. 1935), French novelist, playwright. Interview in *Writers at Work* (First Series, ed. by Malcolm Cowley, 1958).

66　The trade of authorship is a violent, and indestructible obsession.

GEORGE SAND (1804–76), French novelist. Letter, 4 March 1831 (published in *The Letters of George Sand,* 1930).

67　Thus, with child to speak, and helpless in my throes,
Biting my truant pen, beating myself for spite:
Fool! said my muse to me, look in thy heart, and write.

SIR PHILIP SIDNEY (1554–86), English poet, diplomat, soldier. *Astrophel and Stella,* Sonnet 1.

68　Writing is not a profession, but a vocation of unhappiness.

GEORGES SIMENON (1903–85), French mystery writer. Interview in *Writers at Work* (First Series, ed. by Malcolm Cowley, 1958).

69　What I like in a good author isn't what he says, but what he whispers.

LOGAN PEARSALL SMITH (1865–1946), U.S. essayist, aphorist. *Afterthoughts,* "Art and Letters" (1931).

70　The best emotions to write out of are anger and fear or dread. . . . The least energizing emotion to write out of is admiration. It is very difficult to write out of because the basic feeling that goes with admiration is a passive contemplative mood.

SUSAN SONTAG (b. 1933), U.S. essayist. Taped conversation, 1980, in Victor Bockris, *With William Burroughs: A Report from the Bunker,* "On Writing" (1981).

71　The discipline of the written word punishes both stupidity and dishonesty.

JOHN STEINBECK (1902–68), U.S. author. "In Awe of Words" (first published in 75th Anniversary edition of *The Exonian,* Exeter University; repr. in *Writers at Work,* Fourth Series, ed. by George Plimpton, 1977).

72 What you're trying to do when you write is to crowd the reader out of his own space and occupy it with yours, in a good cause. You're trying to take over his sensibility and deliver an experience that moves from mere information.

ROBERT STONE (b. 1937), U.S. novelist. Interview in *Writers at Work* (Eighth Series, ed. by George Plimpton, 1988).

73 What an occupation! To sit and flay your fellow men and then offer their skins for sale and expect them to buy them.

J. AUGUST STRINDBERG (1849–1912), Swedish dramatist, novelist, poet. *The Cloister*, vol. 3 (tr. by Claud Field, 1898; repr. 1969, p. 118).

74 Let's face it, writing is hell.

WILLIAM STYRON (b. 1925), U.S. novelist. Interview in *Writers at Work* (First Series, ed. by Malcolm Cowley, 1958). Writing, Styron said in the same interview, is a "fine therapy for people who are perpetually scared of nameless threats . . . for jittery people."

75 A perfectly healthy sentence, it is true, is extremely rare. For the most part we miss the hue and fragrance of the thought; as if we could be satisfied with the dews of the morning or evening without their colors, or the heavens without their azure.

HENRY DAVID THOREAU (1817–62), U.S. philosopher, author, naturalist. *A Week on the Concord and Merrimack Rivers*, "Sunday" (1849).

76 When all things are equal, translucence in writing is more effective than transparency, just as glow is more revealing than glare.

JAMES THURBER (1894–1961), U.S. humorist, illustrator. Memo to *New Yorker* (1959; first published in *New York Times Book Review*, 4 Dec. 1988).

77 No doubt I shall go on writing, stumbling across tundras of unmeaning, planting words like bloody flags in my wake. Loose ends, things unrelated, shifts, nightmare journeys, cities arrived at and left, meetings, desertions, betrayals, all manner of unions, adulteries, triumphs, defeats . . . these are the facts.

ALEXANDER TROCCHI (1925–83), Italo-Scottish novelist, poet, translator. *Cain's Book* (1960; repr. 1973, p. 3).

78 Yes, it's hard to write, but it's harder not to.

CARL VAN DOREN (1885–1950), U.S. man of letters. In answer to a question put to him by Mary Margaret McBride. Quoted by James Thurber in: *Bermudian* (Nov. 1950).

79 Writing saved me from the sin and inconvenience of violence.

ALICE WALKER (b. 1944), U.S. author, critic. "*One* Child of One's Own," in *Ms.* (New York, Aug. 1979).

80 Every drop of ink in my pen ran cold.

HORACE WALPOLE (1717–97), English author. Letter, 3 July 1752 .

81 Once in seven years I burn all my sermons; for it is a shame if I cannot write better sermons now than I did seven years ago.

JOHN WESLEY (1703–91), English preacher, founder of Methodism. Reporting the words of "a good man," in journal entry, 1 Sept. 1778.

82 Writing is not like painting where you add. It is not what you put on the canvas that the reader sees. Writing is more like a sculpture where you remove, you eliminate in order to make the work visible. Even those pages you remove somehow remain.

ELIE WIESEL (b. 1928), Rumanian-born U.S. writer. Interview in *Writers at Work* (Eighth Series, ed. by George Plimpton, 1988).

83 We are nauseated by the sight of trivial personalities decomposing in the eternity of print.

VIRGINIA WOOLF (1882–1941), British novelist. *The Common Reader*, "The Modern Essay" (First Series, 1925).

84 I was in a queer mood, thinking myself very old: but now I am a woman again—as I always am when I write.

VIRGINIA WOOLF (1882–1941), British novelist. *The Diary of Virginia Woolf*, vol. 3 (ed. by Anne O. Bell, 1980), entry for 31 May 1929.

See also AUTOBIOGRAPHY; BIOGRAPHY; Lawrence on BOOKS; Yeats on CREATIVITY; EDITING; FICTION; Thoreau on INSPIRATION; Gibbon, Porter on LANGUAGE; Inge on LITERATURE; Hemingway on MODESTY; White on OBSCENITY; Mizner on PLAGIARISM; Pound on POETRY; RESEARCH; Hebrew Bible on SCHOLARS AND SCHOLARSHIP; Le Guin on TRANSLATION; WRITERS.

WRITING: SCRIPTS AND SCREEN PLAYS

1 The most ordinary word, when put into place, suddenly acquires brilliance. That is the brilliance with which your images must shine.

ROBERT BRESSON (b. 1907), French film director. *Notes on the Cinematographer*, "1950–1958: Exercises" (1975).

2 You sell a screenplay like you sell a car. If someone drives it off a cliff, that's it.

RITA MAE BROWN (b. 1944), U.S. feminist writer. *Newsweek* (New York, 19 Aug. 1985).

3 The challenge of screenwriting is to say much in little and then take half of that little out and still preserve an effect of leisure and natural movement.

RAYMOND CHANDLER (1888–1959), U.S. author. "Writers in Hollywood," in *Atlantic Monthly* (Boston, Nov. 1945).

4 The impulse to perfection cannot exist where the definition of perfection is the arbitrary decision of authority. That which is born in loneliness and from the heart cannot be defended against the judgment of a committee of sycophants. The volatile essences which make literature cannot survive the clichés of a long series of story conferences.

RAYMOND CHANDLER (1888–1959), U.S. author. "Writers in Hollywood," in *Atlantic Monthly* (Boston, Nov. 1945).

5 The wise screen writer is he who wears his second-best suit, artistically speaking, and doesn't take things too much to heart. He should have a touch of cynicism, but only a touch. The complete cynic is as useless to Hollywood as he is to himself. He should do the best he can without straining at it. He should be scrupulously honest about his work, but he should not expect scrupulous honesty in return. He won't get it. And when he has had enough, he should say goodbye with a smile, because for all he knows he may want to go back.

RAYMOND CHANDLER (1888–1959), U.S. author. Letter, 10

Nov. 1950, to publisher Hamish Hamilton (published in *Raymond Chandler Speaking*, 1962). Chandler was then working with Billy Wilder on the script of *Double Indemnity*.

6 Out of the thousand writers huffing and puffing through movieland there are scarcely fifty men and women of wit or talent. The rest of the fraternity is deadwood. Yet, in a curious way, there is not much difference between the product of a good writer and a bad one. They both have to toe the same mark.

BEN HECHT (1893–1964), U.S. journalist, author, screenwriter. *A Child of the Century*, bk. 5, "Money is the Root" (1954).

7 A good film script should be able to do completely without dialogue.

DAVID MAMET (b. 1947), U.S. playwright. *Independent* (London, 11 Nov. 1988).

8 In a novel a hero can lay ten girls and marry a virgin for a finish. In a movie this is not allowed. The hero, as well as the heroine, has to be a virgin. The villain can lay anybody he wants, have as much fun as he wants cheating and stealing, getting rich and whipping the servants. But you have to shoot him in the end.

HERBERT MANKIEWICZ (1897–1953), U.S. journalist, screenwriter. Advice to fellow screenwriter Ben Hecht on his arrival in Hollywood. Quoted in: Hecht, *A Child of the Century*, bk. 5, "Diavolo, Again—" (1954).

9 I could be just a writer very easily. I am not a writer. I am a *screen*writer, which is half a filmmaker. . . . But it is *not* an art form, because screenplays are not works of art. They are invitations to others to collaborate on a work of art.

PAUL SCHRADER (b. 1946), U.S. director, screenwriter. Quoted in: Ian Hamilton, *Writers in Hollywood 1915–1951*, Preface (1990).

See also HOLLYWOOD AND WRITERS.

YOUTH

1 I've never understood why people consider youth a time of freedom and joy. It's probably because they have forgotten their own.

MARGARET ATWOOD (b. 1939), Canadian novelist, poet, critic. The narrator, in "Hair Jewelry," in *Ms.* (New York, 1976; repr. in *Dancing Girls*, 1977).

2 Youth is not a question of years: one is young or old from birth.

NATALIE CLIFFORD BARNEY (1876–1972), U.S.-born French author. Quoted in: "Samples from Almost Illegible Notebooks," in *Adam*, no. 299 (1962).

3 I am not young enough to know everything.

J. M. BARRIE (1860–1937), British playwright. Ernest, in *The Admirable Crichton*, act 1.

4 Rejoice, O young man, in thy youth; and let thy heart cheer thee in the days of thy youth, and walk in the ways of thine heart, and in the sight of thine eyes: but know thou, that for all these things God will bring thee into judgment.

BIBLE, HEBREW. *Ecclesiastes* 11:9.

5 It is good for a man that he bear the yoke in his youth.

BIBLE, HEBREW. *Lamentations* 3:27.

6 Time misspent in youth is sometimes all the freedom one ever has.

ANITA BROOKNER (b. 1938), British novelist, art historian. Blanche Vernon, in *The Misalliance*, ch. 10 (1986).

7 Young men are apt to think think themselves wise enough, as drunken men are apt to think themselves sober enough.

LORD CHESTERFIELD (1694–1773), English statesman, man of letters. Letter, 15 Jan. 1753 (first published 1774; repr. in *The Letters of the Earl of Chesterfield to His Son*, vol 2, no. 297, ed. by Charles Strachey, 1901).

8 Youth [is] a period of missed opportunities.

CYRIL CONNOLLY (1903–74), British critic. "The Journal of Cyril Connolly 1928–1937," in David Pryce-Jones, *Journal and Memoir* (1983, p. 163).

9 I remember my youth and the feeling that will never come back any more—the feeling that I could last for ever, outlast the sea, the earth, and all men; the deceitful feeling that lures us on to joys, to perils, to love, to vain effort—to death; the triumphant conviction of strength, the heat of life in the handful of dust, the glow in the heart that with every year grows dim, grows cold, grows small, and expires—and expires, too soon, too soon—before life itself.

JOSEPH CONRAD (1857–1924), Polish-born English novelist. Marlow, in *Youth* (1902).

10 The young always have the same problem—how to rebel and conform at the same time. They have now solved this by defying their parents and copying one another.

QUENTIN CRISP (b. 1908), British author. *The Naked Civil Servant*, ch. 19 (1968).

11 The hatred of the youth culture for adult society is not a disinterested judgment but a terror-ridden refusal to be hooked into the, if you will, ecological chain of breathing, growing, and dying. It is the demand, in other words, to remain children.

MIDGE DECTER (b. 1927), U.S. author, editor, social critic. *The New Chastity and Other Arguments Against Women's Liberation*, ch. 1 (1972).

12 We live in an age when to be young and to be indifferent can be no longer synonymous. We must prepare for the coming hour. The claims of the Future are represented by suffering millions; and the Youth of a Nation are the trustees of Posterity.

BENJAMIN DISRAELI (1804–81), English statesman, author. *Sybil*, bk. 6, ch. 13 (1845).

13 After all, life hasn't much to offer except youth and I suppose for older people the love of youth in others.

F. SCOTT FITZGERALD (1896–1940), U.S. author. Letter, 10 June 1917, to his favorite cousin Cecilia, written when he was 20 (published in *The Letters of F. Scott Fitzgerald*, ed. by Andrew Turnbull, 1963).

14 Everybody's youth is a dream, a form of chemical madness.

F. SCOTT FITZGERALD (1896–1940), U.S. author. John, in *The*

Diamond as Big as the Ritz, ch. 11 (1922). Kismine replies, "How pleasant then to be insane!"

15 Man's own youth is the world's youth; at least he feels as if it were, and imagines that the earth's granite substance is something not yet hardened, and which he can mould into whatever shape he likes.

NATHANIEL HAWTHORNE (1804–64), U.S. author. *The House of the Seven Gables,* ch. 12 (1851).

16 Youth itself is a talent—a perishable talent.

ERIC HOFFER (1902–83), U.S. philosopher. *The Passionate State of Mind,* aph. 32 (1955).

17 Youth enters the world with very happy prejudices in her own favour. She imagines herself not only certain of accomplishing every adventure, but of obtaining those rewards which the accomplishment may deserve. She is not easily persuaded to believe that the force of merit can be resisted by obstinacy and avarice, or its lustre darkened by envy and malignity.

SAMUEL JOHNSON (1709–84), English author, lexicographer. *Rambler,* no. 127 (London, 4 June 1751; repr. in *Works of Samuel Johnson,* vol 4, ed. by W. J. Bate and Albrecht B. Strauss, 1969).

18 The wine of youth does not always clear with advancing years; sometimes it grows turbid.

CARL JUNG (1875–1961), Swiss psychiatrist. *The Stages of Life* (1930; repr. in *Collected Works,* vol. 8, para. 774, ed. by William McGuire, 1960).

19 Enjoy the Spring of Love and Youth,
To some good angel leave the rest;
For Time will teach thee soon the truth,
There are no birds in last year's nest!

HENRY WADSWORTH LONGFELLOW (1807–82), U.S. poet. *It Is Not Always May.*

20 The American ideal is youth—handsome, empty youth.

HENRY MILLER (1891–1980), U.S. author. *The Wisdom of the Heart,* "Raimu" (1947). "In America," Miller explained, "youth means simply athleticism, disrespect, gangsterism, or sickly idealism expressing itself through thinly disguised and badly digested social science theories acted out by idiots who are desperadoes at heart."

21 There is nothing can pay one for that invaluable ignorance which is the companion of youth, those sanguine groundless hopes, and that lively vanity which makes all the happiness of life.

LADY MARY WORTLEY MONTAGU (1689–1762), English society figure, letter writer. Letter, c. 6 Dec. 1712, to her husband (published in *Selected Letters,* ed. by Robert Halsband, 1970).

22 The pursuit of happiness, which American citizens are obliged to undertake, tends to involve them in trying to perpetuate the moods, tastes and aptitudes of youth.

MALCOLM MUGGERIDGE (1903–90), British broadcaster. *The Most of Malcolm Muggeridge,* "Women of America" (1966).

23 Youth does not require reasons for living, it only needs pretexts.

JOSÉ ORTEGA Y GASSET (1883–1955), Spanish essayist, philosopher. *The Revolt of the Masses,* ch. 14, sct. 3 (1930).

24 Youth has no age.

PABLO PICASSO (1881–1973), Spanish artist. *Arts de France,* no. 6 (Paris, 1946; tr. in Dore Ashton, *Picasso on Art,* 1972).

25 Well, youth is the period of assumed personalities and disguises. It is the time of the sincerely insincere.

V. S. PRITCHETT (b. 1900), British author, critic. *Midnight Oil,* ch. 8 (1971).

26 When the newspapers have got nothing else to talk about, they cut loose on the young. The young are always news. If they are up to something, that's news. If they aren't, that's news too.

KENNETH REXROTH (1905–82), U.S. poet, critic, translator. *Assays,* "The Students Take Over" (1961; repr. in *The Rexroth Reader,* ed. by Eric Mottram, 1972).

27 Idle youth, enslaved to everything; by being too sensitive I have wasted my life.

ARTHUR RIMBAUD (1854–91), French poet. *Song of the Highest Tower,* in *Collected Poems* (written 1872; ed. by Oliver Bernard, 1962).

28 He wears the rose
Of youth upon him.

WILLIAM SHAKESPEARE (1564–1616), English dramatist, poet. Mark Antony, in *Antony and Cleopatra,* act 3, sc. 13, speaking of Caesar.

29 Don't let young people tell you their aspirations; when they drop them they will drop you.

LOGAN PEARSALL SMITH (1865–1946), U.S. essayist, aphorist. *All Trivia,* "Last Words" (1933).

30 To be young is all there is in the world. The rest is nonsense—and cant. They talk so beautifully about work and having a family and a home (and I do, too, sometimes)—but it's all worry and head-aches and respectable poverty and forced gushing. . . . Telling people how nice it is, when, in reality, you would give all of your *last* thirty years for one of your *first* thirty. Old people are tremendous frauds.

WALLACE STEVENS (1879–1955), U.S. poet. Letter, 21 March 1907, to his future wife Elsie Moll (published in *Letters of Wallace Stevens,* ch. 5, ed. by Holly Stevens, 1967).

31 For God's sake give me the young man who has brains enough to make a fool of himself!

ROBERT LOUIS STEVENSON (1850–94), Scottish novelist, essayist, poet. *Virginibus Puerisque,* "Crabbed Age and Youth" (1881).

32 There is a period near the beginning of every man's life when he has little to cling to except his unmanageable dream, little to support him except good health, and nowhere to go but all over the place.

E. B. WHITE (1899–1985), U.S. author, editor. *Essays of E. B. White,* "The Years of Wonder" (1977; first published, 1961).

33 Youth! There is nothing like youth. The middle-aged are mortgaged to Life. The old are in Life's lumber-room. But youth is the Lord of Life. Youth has a kingdom waiting for it. Every one is born a king, and most people die in exile.

OSCAR WILDE (1854–1900), Anglo-Irish playwright, author. Lord Illingworth, in *A Woman of No Importance,* act 3.

34 Those whom the gods love grow young.

OSCAR WILDE (1854–1900), Anglo-Irish playwright, author. *A*

Few Maxims for the Instruction of the Over-Educated, in *Saturday Review* (London, 17 Nov. 1894).

See also ADOLESCENCE; CHILDHOOD; CHILDREN; Burgess on DELINQUENCY; Disraeli on GENIUS; Carlyle on STUDENTS.

YOUTH AND AGE

1 What Youth deemed crystal, Age finds out was dew.

ROBERT BROWNING (1812–89), English poet. *Jochanan Hakkadosh*, st. 101.

2 The arrogance of age must submit to be taught by youth.

EDMUND BURKE (1729–97), Irish philosopher, statesman. Letter, 29 July 1782, to author Fanny Burney.

3 If youth but knew; if age but could.

HENRI ESTIENNE (1531–98), French scholar, publisher. *Les Prémices*, Epigram 191 (1594).

4 So different are the colours of life, as we look forward to the future, or backward to the past; and so different the opinions and sentiments which this contrariety of appearance naturally produces, that the conversation of the old and young ends generally with contempt or pity on either side.

SAMUEL JOHNSON (1709–84), English author, lexicographer. *Rambler*, no. 69 (London, 13 Nov. 1750; repr. in *Works of Samuel Johnson*, vol 3, ed. by W. J. Bate and Albrecht B. Strauss, 1969).

5 A hundred things are done today in the divine name of Youth, that if they showed their true colours would be seen by rights to belong rather to old age.

WYNDHAM LEWIS (1882–1957), British author, painter. *The Art of Being Ruled*, "The Family and Feminism," ch. 6 (1926).

6 The child thinks of growing old as an almost obscene calamity, which for some mysterious reason will never happen to itself. All who have passed the age of thirty are joyless grotesques, endlessly fussing about things of no importance and staying alive without, so far as the child can see, having anything to live for. Only child life is real life.

GEORGE ORWELL (1903–50), British author. "Such, Such Were the Joys" (1947; repr. in *The Collected Essays, Journalism and Letters of George Orwell*, ed. by Sonia Orwell and Ian Angus, 1968).

7 Youth doesn't reason, it acts. The old man reasons and would like to make the others act in his place.

FRANCIS PICABIA (1878–1953), French painter, poet. *591* (Paris, 21 Jan. 1952; repr. in *Écrits*, vol 2, "1925–1932," ed. by Olivier Revault d'Allones and Dominique Bouissou, 1978).

8 Do you set down your name in the scroll of youth, that are written down old with all the characters of age?

WILLIAM SHAKESPEARE (1564–1616), English dramatist, poet. Lord Chief Justice, to Falstaff, in *Henry IV*, pt. 2, act 1, sc. 2.

9 A man loves the meat in his youth that he cannot endure in his age.

WILLIAM SHAKESPEARE (1564–1616), English dramatist, poet. Benedick, in *Much Ado About Nothing*, act 2, sc. 3.

10 The denunciation of the young is a necessary part of the hygiene of older people, and greatly assists the circulation of their blood.

LOGAN PEARSALL SMITH (1865–1946), U.S. essayist, aphorist. *All Trivia*, "Last Words" (1933).

11 Youth, large, lusty, loving—Youth, full of grace, force, fascination.
Do you know that Old Age may come after you with equal grace, force, fascination?

WALT WHITMAN (1819–92), U.S. poet. *Youth, Day, Old Age and Night*.

12 In America the young are always ready to give to those who are older than themselves the full benefits of their inexperience.

OSCAR WILDE (1854–1900), Anglo-Irish playwright, author. "The American Invasion," in *Court and Society Review* (London, 23 March 1887; repr. in *Aristotle at Afternoon Tea: The Rare Oscar Wilde*, 1991).

See also Santayana on EMOTION; Shaw, Smith on GENERATIONS; Bradbury on INNOCENCE; Thoreau on MIDDLE AGE.

YUPPIES

1 The Yuppies are not defectors from revolt, they are a new race, assured, amnestied, exculpated, moving with ease in the world of performance, mentally indifferent to any objective other than that of change and advertising.

JEAN BAUDRILLARD (b. 1929), French semiologist. *America*, "The End of US Power?" (1986; tr. 1988).

2 The media have just buried the last yuppie, a pathetic creature who had not heard the news that the great pendulum of public conciousness has just swung from Greed to Compassion and from Tex-Mex to meatballs.

BARBARA EHRENREICH (b. 1941), U.S. author, columnist. *The Worst Years of Our Lives*, "Goodbye To The Work Ethic" (1991; first published 1988).

3 You will belong to that minority which, according to current Washington doctrine, must be protected in its affluence lest its energy and initiative be impaired. Your position will be in contrast to that of the poor, to whom money, especially if it is from public sources, is held to be deeply damaging.

JOHN KENNETH GALBRAITH (b. 1908), U.S. economist. *Guardian* (London, 28 July 1989).

4 The yuppie idea of a future ain't my idea of a future. Your safe car, and home, and job, and all the time rushing between the three—let's make people feel they can grow up and have some education, some interest in life! That's what counts!

JOE STRUMMER (b. 1952), British rock musician. Interview in *Melody Maker* (London, 23 July 1988).

Z

1 Thou whoreson Z, thou unnecessary letter.

WILLIAM SHAKESPEARE (1564–1616), English dramatist, poet. Kent, to the "villainous" messenger Oswald, in *King Lear*, act 2, sc. 2.

ZOOS

1   The zoo cannot but disappoint. The public purpose of zoos is to offer visitors the opportunity of looking at animals. Yet nowhere in a zoo can a stranger encounter the look of an animal. At the most, the animal's gaze flickers and passes on. They look sideways. They look blindly beyond.

> JOHN BERGER (b. 1926), British author, critic. *About Looking,* "Why Look at Animals?" (1980).

2   A Robin Redbreast in a cage
Puts all Heaven in a Rage.

> WILLIAM BLAKE (1757–1827), English poet, painter, engraver. *Auguries of Innocence,* in *Poems from the Pickering Manuscript* (c. 1808; repr. in *Complete Writings,* ed. by Geoffrey Keynes, 1957).

3   human wandering through the zoo
what do your cousins think of you

> DON MARQUIS (1878–1937), U.S. humorist, journalist. *archy at the zoo,* in *archy and mehitabel* (1927).

INDEX OF SOURCES

See also Fromm on The CONSUMER SOCIETY; Nietzsche on PARADISE; Bible: New Testament on WEALTH.

HEDONISM

1 To a man of pleasure every moment appears to be lost, which partakes not of the vivacity of movement.

JOSEPH ADDISON (1672–1719), English essayist. *Interesting Anecdotes, Memoirs, Allegories, Essays, and Poetical Fragments,* "The Man of Pleasure" (1794).

2 A man hath no better thing under the sun, than to eat, and to drink, and to be merry.

BIBLE, HEBREW. *Ecclesiastes* 8:15.

3 A true voluptuary will never abandon his mind to the grossness of reality. It is by exalting the earthly, the material, the *physique* of our pleasures, by veiling these ideas, by forgetting them altogether, or, at least, never naming them hardly to one's self, that we alone can prevent them from disgusting.

LORD BYRON (1788–1824), English poet. *Byron's Letters and Journals,* vol. 3 (ed. by Leslie Marchand, 1974), entry for 13 Dec. 1813.

4 Let us have wine and women, mirth and laughter, Sermons and soda-water the day after.

LORD BYRON (1788–1824), English poet. *Don Juan,* cto. 2, st. 178.

5 Oh, how desperately bored, in spite of their grim determination to have a Good Time, the majority of pleasure-seekers really are!

ALDOUS HUXLEY (1894–1963), British author. *Do What You Will,* "Holy Face" (1929).

6 Life admits not of delays; when pleasure can be had, it is fit to catch it: every hour takes away part of the things that please us, and perhaps part of our disposition to be pleased.

SAMUEL JOHNSON (1709–84), English author, lexicographer. Letter, 1 Sept. 1777, to James Boswell. Quoted in: Boswell, *Life of Samuel Johnson* (1791).

7 Ah, make the most of what we yet may spend, Before we too into the Dust descend.

OMAR KHAYYÁM (11–12th century), Persian astronomer and poet. *The Rubáiyát of Omar Khayyám,* st. 23 (tr. by Edward FitzGerald; first ed., 1859).

8 Name me, if you can, a better feeling than the one you get when you've half a bottle of Chivas in the bag with a gram of coke up your nose and a teenage lovely pulling off her tube top in the next seat over while you're doing a hundred miles an hour in a suburban side street.

P. J. O'ROURKE (b. 1947), U.S. journalist. *Republican Party Reptile,* "How to Drive Fast On Drugs While Getting Your Wing Wang Squeezed and Not Spill Your Drink" (1987).

9 God forgive me, I do still see that my nature is not to be quite conquered, but will esteem pleasure above all things; though, yet in the middle of it, it hath reluctancy after my business, which is neglected by my fallowing my pleasure. However, music and women I cannot but give way to, whatever my business is.

SAMUEL PEPYS (1633–1703), English diarist. Diary entry, 9 March 1666.

10 It is only by enlarging the scope of one's tastes and one's fantasies, by sacrificing everything to pleasure, that that unfortunate individual called man, thrown despite himself into this sad world, can succeed in gathering a few roses among life's thorns.

MARQUIS DE SADE (1740–1814), French author. *Philosophy in the Bedroom,* "To Libertines" (1795).

11 I do not find fault with equality for drawing men into the pursuit of forbidden pleasures, but for absorbing them entirely in the search for the pleasures that are permitted.

ALEXIS DE TOCQUEVILLE (1805–59), French social philosopher. *Democracy in America,* vol. 2, ch. 32 (1840).

HELL

1 Hell is out of fashion—institutional hells at any rate. The populated infernos of the 20th century are more private affairs, the gaps between the bars are the sutures of one's own skull. . . . A valid hell is one from which there is a possibility of redemption, even if this is never achieved, the dungeons of an architecture of grace whose spires point to some kind of heaven. The institutional hells of the present century are reached with one-way tickets, marked Nagasaki and Buchenwald, worlds of terminal horror even more final than the grave.

J. G. BALLARD (b. 1930), British author. "Visions of Hell," in *New Worlds* (London, March 1966; repr. in *Re/Search,* no. 8/9, San Francisco, 1984), review of Wyndham Lewis, *The Human Age.*

2 Of all the inhabitants of the inferno, none but Lucifer knows that hell is hell, and the secret function of purgatory is to make of heaven an effective reality.

ARNOLD BENNETT (1867–1931), British novelist. *The Journals of Arnold Bennett* (1932), entry for 18 March 1897.

3 And what have you laymen made of hell? A kind of penal servitude for eternity, on the lines of your convict prisons on earth, to which you condemn in advance all the wretched felons your police have hunted from the beginning—"enemies of society," as you call them. You're kind enough to include the blasphemers and the profane. What proud or reasonable man could stomach such a notion of God's justice? And when you find that notion inconvenient it's easy enough for you to put it on one side. . . . Hell is not to love any more, madame. Not to love any more!

GEORGES BERNANOS (1888–1948), French novelist, political writer. The priest to Madame la Comtesse, in *The Diary of a Country Priest,* ch. 5 (1936).

4 Hell is paved with great granite blocks hewn from the hearts of those who said, "I can do no other."

HEYWOOD BROUN (1888–1939), U.S. journalist, novelist. Quoted in: *Wit's End* (ed. by Robert E. Drennan, 1968).

5 I cannot help thinking that the *menace* of Hell makes as many devils as the severe penal codes of inhuman humanity make villains.

LORD BYRON (1788–1824), English poet. *Detached Thoughts,*

no. 96 (1821–22; published in *Byron's Letters and Journals*, vol. 9, ed. by Leslie A Marchand, 1979).

6 Abandon all hope, you who enter here!

DANTE ALIGHIERI (1265–1321), Italian poet. Inscription at the entrance to Hell, in *The Divine Comedy*, "The Inferno," cto. 3.

7 There sighs, lamentations and loud wailings resounded through the starless air, so that at first it made me weep; strange tongues, horrible language, words of pain, tones of anger, voices loud and hoarse, and with these the sound of hands, made a tumult which is whirling through that air forever dark, and sand eddies in a whirlwind.

DANTE ALIGHIERI (1265–1321), Italian poet. *The Divine Comedy*, "The Inferno," cto. 3.

8 Hell is oneself,
Hell is alone, the other figures in it
Merely projections. There is nothing to escape
   from
And nothing to escape to. One is always alone.

T. S. ELIOT (1888–1965), Anglo-American poet, critic. Edward, in *The Cocktail Party*, act 1, sc. 3.

9 To be in a world which is a hell, to be *of* that world and neither to believe in or guess at anything *but* that world is not merely hell but the only possible damnation: the act of a man damning himself. It may be—I hope it is—redemption to guess and perhaps perceive that the universe, the hell which we see for all its beauty, vastness, majesty, is only part of a whole which is quite unimaginable.

WILLIAM GOLDING (1911–93), British author. Lecture, 11 April 1980, Hamburg, Germany (repr. in *A Moving Target*, "Belief and Creativity," 1982).

10 The safest road to hell is the gradual one—the gentle slope, soft underfoot, without sudden turnings, without milestones, without signposts.

C. S. LEWIS (1898–1963), British author. Screwtape, in *The Screwtape Letters*, letter 12 (1942).

11 Hell hath no limits, nor is circumscrib'd
In one self place; for where we are is Hell,
And where Hell is, there must we ever be.

CHRISTOPHER MARLOWE (1564–93), English dramatist, poet. Mephistopheles, in *The Tragical History of Dr. Faustus*, act 2, sc. 1.

12 It is an open question whether any behavior based on fear of eternal punishment can be regarded as ethical or should be regarded as merely cowardly.

MARGARET MEAD (1901–78), U.S. anthropologist. Quoted in: *Redbook* (New York, Feb. 1971).

13 I believe that I am in hell, therefore I am there.

ARTHUR RIMBAUD (1854–91), French poet. *Une Saison en Enfer*, "Nuit de l'Enfer" (1874; repr. in *Collected Poems*, ed. by Oliver Bernard, 1962).

14 For mortal men there is but one hell, and that is the folly and wickedness and spite of his fellows; but once his life is over, there's an end to it: his annihilation is final and entire, of him nothing survives.

MARQUIS DE SADE (1740–1814), French author. Mme Clair-

will, in *L'Histoire de Juliette, ou les Prospérités du Vice*, pt. 2 (1797).

15 Here there is no hope, and consequently no duty, no work, nothing to be gained by praying, nothing to be lost by doing what you like. Hell, in short, is a place where you have nothing to do but amuse yourself.

GEORGE BERNARD SHAW (1856–1950), Anglo-Irish playwright, critic. The Statue, in *Man and Superman*, act 3.

16 The gates of Hell are open night and day;
Smooth the descent, and easy is the way:
But, to return, and view the cheerful skies;
In this, the task and mighty labour lies.

VIRGIL (70–19 B.C.), Roman poet. Sibyl of Cumae to Aeneas, in *Aeneid*, bk. 6 (tr. by John Dryden).

17 When I go to hell, I mean to carry a bribe: for look you, good gifts evermore make way for the worst persons.

JOHN WEBSTER (1580–1625), English dramatist. *The Duchess of Malfi*, act 5, sc. 2.

See also DAMNATION; Shaw on INTENTIONS; Shelley on LONDON; Shaw on MUSIC; Sartre on OTHER PEOPLE; Weil on PARADISE.

ERNEST HEMINGWAY

1 Hemingway is terribly limited. His technique is good for short stories, for people who meet once in a bar very late at night, but do not enter into relations. But not for the novel.

W. H. AUDEN (1907–73), Anglo-American poet. *The Table Talk of W. H. Auden*, "November 16, 1946" (comp. by Alan Ansen, ed. by Nicholas Jenkins, 1990).

2 Hemingway was a prisoner of his style. No one can talk like the characters in Hemingway except the characters in Hemingway. His style in the wildest sense finally killed him.

WILLIAM BURROUGHS (b. 1914), U.S. author. *The Adding Machine*, "A Word to the Wise Guy" (1985).

3 He is the bully on the Left Bank, always ready to twist the milksop's arm.

CYRIL CONNOLLY (1903–74), British critic. Quoted in: *The Observer* (London, 24 May 1964).

4 Hemingway is great in that alone of living writers he has saturated his work with the memory of physical pleasure, with sunshine and salt water, with food, wine and making love and the remorse which is the shadow of that sun.

CYRIL CONNOLLY (1903–74), British critic. *The Unquiet Grave*, pt. 3 (1944; rev. 1951).

5 He is gentle, as all real men are gentle; without tenderness, a man is uninteresting.

MARLENE DIETRICH (1904–92), German-born U.S. film actor. Quoted in: A. E. Hotchner, *Papa Hemingway*, pt. 1, ch. 1 (1966 ed.).

6 I hear you were seen running through Portugal in used B.V.D.s', chewing ground glass and collecting material for a story about boule players; that you were publicity man for Lindbergh; that you have finished a novel a hundred thousand words long consisting entirely of the word "balls" used in new groupings; that you have been naturalized a Spaniard, dress always in a wine-skin with "zipper" vent and are engaged in bootlegging Spanish Fly between St. Sebastian and Biarritz where your agents sprinkle it on the floor of the Casino. I hope I have been misinformed but, alas!, it all has too true a ring.

> F. SCOTT FITZGERALD (1896–1940), U.S. author. Letter, Dec. 1927, to Ernest Hemingway (published in *The Letters of F. Scott Fitzgerald*, ed. by Andrew Turnbull, 1963).

7 I started out very quiet and I beat Mr. Turgenev. Then I trained hard and I beat Mr. de Maupassant. I've fought two draws with Mr. Stendhal, and I think I had an edge in the last one. But nobody's going to get me in any ring with Mr. Tolstoy unless I'm crazy or I keep getting better.

> ERNEST HEMINGWAY (1899–1961), U.S. author. *New Yorker* (13 May 1950).

8 He has a capacity for enjoyment so vast that he gives away great chunks to those about him, and never even misses them. . . . He can take you to a bicycle race and make it raise your hair.

> DOROTHY PARKER (1893–1967), U.S. humorous writer. *New Yorker* (30 Nov 1929)

See also Fitzgerald on F. SCOTT FITZGERALD.

HERESY

1 For my name and memory I leave to men's charitable speeches, and to foreign nations and the next ages.

> FRANCIS BACON (1561–1626), English philosopher, essayist, statesman. Last will, 19 Dec. 1625 (published in *Works*, vol. 3, ed. 1765).

2 It may be you fear more to deliver judgment upon me than I fear judgment.

> GIORDANO BRUNO (1548–1600), Italian philosopher. Quoted in: I. Frith, *Life of Giordano Bruno*, ch. 11 (1887), to the inquisitors who had condemned him to death.

3 The conscience of the world is so guilty that it always assumes that people who investigate heresies must be heretics; just as if a doctor who studies leprosy must be a leper. Indeed, it is only recently that science has been allowed to study anything without reproach.

> ALEISTER CROWLEY (1875–1947), British occultist. *The Confessions of Aleister Crowley*, ch. 17 (1929; rev. 1970).

4 A heresy can spring only from a system that is in full vigor.

> ERIC HOFFER (1902–83), U.S. philosopher. *The Ordeal of Change*, ch. 5 (1964).

5 The difference between heresy and prophecy is often one of sequence. Heresy often turns out to have been prophecy—when properly aged.

> HUBERT H. HUMPHREY (1911–78), U.S. Democratic politician, vice president. Speech, 23 April 1966, Washington, D.C.

6 I shall never be a heretic; I may err in dispute, but I do not wish to decide anything finally; on the other hand, I am not bound by the opinions of men.

> MARTIN LUTHER (1483–1546), German leader of the Protestant Reformation. Letter, 28 Aug. 1518.

7 A man may be a heretic in the truth; and if he believe things only because his pastor says so, or the assembly so determines, without knowing other reason, though his belief be true, yet the very truth he holds becomes his heresy.

> JOHN MILTON (1608–74), English poet. *Areopagitica: a Speech for the Liberty of Unlicensed Printing to the Parliament of England* (1644).

8 If the individual, or heretic, gets hold of some essential truth, or sees some error in the system being practised, he commits so many marginal errors himself that he is worn out before he can establish his point.

> EZRA POUND (1885–1972), U.S. poet, critic. Interview in *Writers at Work* (Second Series, ed. by George Plimpton, 1963). Pound was obliquely referring to his own experience, and his incarceration in an American mental institution for ten years following his arrest for treason in 1945.

See also DISSENT.

HERITAGE

1 Stands the Church clock at ten to three?
And is there honey still for tea?

> RUPERT BROOKE (1887–1915), British poet. *The Old Vicarage, Grantchester*.

2 I love art, and I love history, but it is living art and living history that I love. . . . It is in the interest of living art and living history that I oppose so-called restoration. What history can there be in a building bedaubed with ornament, which cannot at the best be anything but a hopeless and lifeless imitation of the hope and vigour of the earlier world?

> WILLIAM MORRIS (1834–96), English artist, writer, printer. "The History of Pattern-Designing," lecture, 1882 (repr. in *The Collected Works of William Morris*, vol. 22, 1910–15).

3 It is *impossible*, as impossible as to raise the dead, to restore anything that has ever been great or beautiful in architecture. That which I have . . . insisted upon as the life of the whole, that spirit which is given only by the hand and eye of the workman, can never be recalled.

> JOHN RUSKIN (1819–1900), English art critic, author. Quoted in: E. P. Thompson, *William Morris*, pt. 2, ch. 7 (1955).

HERMITS

1 And he was driven from men, and did eat grass as oxen, and his body was wet with the dew of heaven, till his hairs were grown like eagles' feathers, and his nails like birds' claws.

> BIBLE, HEBREW. *Daniel* 4:33.

2 To fly from, need not be to hate, mankind:
All are not fit with them to sir and toil,
Nor is it discontent to keep the mind
Deep in its fountain, lest it overboil.

LORD BYRON (1788–1824), English poet. *Childe Harold's Pilgrimage,* cto. 3, st. 69.

3   To retire to the monastery, or the woods, or the sea, is to escape from the sharp suggestions that spur on ambition.

CHARLES HORTON COOLEY (1864–1929), U.S. sociologist. *Human Nature and the Social Order,* ch. 6 (1902).

4   He travels the fastest who travels alone.

RUDYARD KIPLING (1865–1936), British author, poet. *The Winners.*

5   To live alone one must be an animal or a god—says Aristotle. There is yet a third case: one must be both—a *philosopher.*

FRIEDRICH NIETZSCHE (1844–1900), German philosopher. *Twilight of the Idols,* , "Maxims and Arrows," aph. 3 (1889).

6   The world forgetting, by the world forgot.

ALEXANDER POPE (1688–1744), English satirical poet. *Eloisa to Abelard.*

7   The outer world, from which we cower into our houses, seemed after all a gentle habitable place; and night after night a man's bed, it seemed, was laid and waiting for him in the fields, where God keeps an open house.

ROBERT LOUIS STEVENSON (1850–94), Scottish novelist, essayist, poet. *Travels With a Donkey,* "A Night Among the Pines" (1879).

8   I went to the woods because I wished to live deliberately, to front only the essential facts of life, and see if I could not learn what it had to teach, and not, when I came to die, discover that I had not lived. . . . I wanted to live deep and suck out all the marrow of life, to live so sturdily and Spartan-like as to put to rout all that was not life, to cut a broad swath and shave close, to drive life into a corner, and reduce it to its lowest terms.

HENRY DAVID THOREAU (1817–62), U.S. philosopher, author, naturalist. *Walden,* "Where I Lived, and What I Lived For" (1854).

9   Eagles commonly fly alone. They are crows, daws, and starlings that flock together.

JOHN WEBSTER (1580–1625), English dramatist. Ferdinand, in *The Duchess of Malfi,* act 5, sc. 2.

See also Cocteau on ASCETICISM, SOLITUDE.

HERO-WORSHIP

1   I have always been a friend to hero-worship; it is the only rational one, and has always been in use amongst civilized people—the worship of spirits is synonymous with barbarism—it is mere fetish. . . . There is something philosophic in the worship of the heroes of the human race.

GEORGE BORROW (1803–81), English author. An "elderly individual," in *Lavengro,* ch. 23 (1851).

2   If youth is the period of hero-worship, so also is it true that hero-worship, more than anything else, perhaps, gives one the sense of youth. To admire, to expand one's

self, to forget the rut, to have a sense of newness and life and hope, is to feel young at any time of life.

CHARLES HORTON COOLEY (1864–1929), U.S. sociologist. *Human Nature and the Social Order,* ch. 8 (1902).

3   There is probably an element of malice in the readiness to overestimate people: we are laying up for ourselves the pleasure of later cutting them down to size.

ERIC HOFFER (1902–83), U.S. philosopher. *Reflections on the Human Condition,* aph. 129 (1973).

4   So long as men worship the Caesars and Napoleons, Caesars and Napoleons will duly rise and make them miserable.

ALDOUS HUXLEY (1894–1963), British author. *Ends and Means,* ch. 8 (1937).

5   I do honour the very flea of his dog.

BEN JONSON (1573–1637), English dramatist, poet. Cob, in *Every Man in His Humour,* act 4, sc. 4.

6   Hero-worship is strongest where there is least regard for human freedom.

HERBERT SPENCER (1820–1903), English philosopher. *Social Statistics,* pt. 4, ch. 30, sct.6 (1850).

7   The Americans are certainly hero-worshippers, and always take their heroes from the criminal classes.

OSCAR WILDE (1854–1900), Anglo-Irish playwright, author. Letter, 19 April 1882.

See also Bangs on HEROES.

HEROES

1   You lived too long, we have supped full with heroes,
they waste their deaths on us.

C. D. ANDREWS (1913–92), British poet, scholar. *To a Pilot Lost in Aragón, in London Town,* no. 459 (March 1938).

2   Listen, my friend, there are two races of beings. The masses teeming and happy—common clay, if you like—eating, breeding, working, counting their pennies; people who just live; ordinary people; people you can't imagine dead. And then there are the others—the noble ones, the heroes. The ones you can quite well imagine lying shot, pale and tragic; one minute triumphant with a guard of honor, and the next being marched away between two gendarmes.

JEAN ANOUILH (1910–87), French playwright. Henri, in *Point of Departure,* act 2.

3   They wouldn't be heroes if they were infallible, in fact they wouldn't be heroes if they weren't miserable wretched dogs, the pariahs of the earth, besides which the only reason to build up an idol is to tear it down again.

LESTER BANGS (1948–82), U.S. rock journalist. *Creem* (London, March 1975).

4   What is a society without a heroic dimension?

JEAN BAUDRILLARD (b. 1929), French semiologist. *America,* "Utopia Achieved" (1986; tr. 1988).

5   In our world of big names, curiously, our true